2025
STANDARD POSTAGE STAMP CATALOGUE

ONE HUNDRED AND EIGHTY-FIRST EDITION IN SIX VOLUMES

Volume 4B

M

EDITOR-IN-CHIEF	Jay Bigalke
EDITOR-AT-LARGE	Donna Houseman
CONTRIBUTING EDITOR	Charles Snee
EDITOR EMERITUS	James E. Kloetzel
SENIOR EDITOR /NEW ISSUES AND VALUING	Martin J. Frankevicz
ASSOCIATE EDITOR	David Hartwig
CATALOGUE COORDINATOR	Eric Wiessinger
SENIOR GRAPHIC DESIGNER	Cinda McAlexander
SALES DIRECTOR	David Pistello
SALES DIRECTOR	Eric Roth
SALES DIRECTOR	Brenda Wyen
SALES REPRESENTATIVE	Julie Dahlstrom

Released July 2024
Includes New Stamp Listings through the May 2024 *Scott Stamp Monthly* Catalogue Update

Copyright© 2024 by

AMOS MEDIA

1660 Campbell Road, Suite A, Sidney, OH 45365
Publishers of *Linn's Stamp News*, *Scott Stamp Monthly*, *Coin World* and *Coin World Monthly*.

Scott catalog editorial team contact information
scottstamp.com | scottcatalogueeditorial@amosmedia.com

Scott catalog customer service contact information
amosadvantage.com | cuserv@amosmedia.com | 800-572-6885 | Monday-Thursday 9 a.m. to 5 p.m.; Friday 9 a.m. to noon, Eastern Standard Time

Table of contents

Common Design	3A
Acknowledgments	Vol. 4A, 3A
Letter from the editor	Vol. 4A, 4A
Information on philatelic societies	Vol. 4A, 5A
Expertizing services	Vol. 4A, 9A
Information on catalogue values, grade and condition	Vol. 4A, 10A
Grading illustrations	Vol. 4A, 11A
Gum chart	Vol. 4A, 13A
Understanding the listings	Vol. 4A, 14A
Catalogue listing policy	Vol. 4A, 16A
Special notices	Vol. 4A, 17A
Abbreviations	Vol. 4A, 17A
Basic stamp information	Vol. 4A, 19A
Terminology	Vol. 4A, 26A
Pronunciation symbols	Vol. 4A, 28A
The British Commonwealth of Nations	Vol. 4A, 50A
Colonies, former colonies, offices, territories controlled by parent states	Vol. 4A, 52A
Dies of British Colonial stamps referred to in the catalogue	Vol. 4A, 53A
British Colonial and Crown Agents watermarks	Vol. 4A, 54A
Countries of the World M	1
2025 Volume 4A-4B catalogue number additions, deletions and changes	729
Index and Identifier	**730**
Currency conversion	737
Index to advertisers	743
Dealer directory yellow pages	744

See the following volumes for other country listings:
Volume 1A: United States, United Nations, Abu Dhabi-Australia; Volume 1B: Austria-B
Volume 2A: C-Cur; Volume 2B: Cyp-F
Volume 3G: Volume 3B: H-I
Volume 4A: J-L
Volume 5A: N-Phil; Volume 5B: Pit-Sam
Volume 6A: San-Tete; Volume 6B: Thai-Z

Scott Catalogue Mission Statement

The Scott Catalogue Team exists to serve the recreational, educational and commercial hobby needs of stamp collectors and dealers.
We strive to set the industry standard for philatelic information and products by developing and providing goods that help collectors identify, value, organize and present their collections.
Quality customer service is, and will continue to be, our highest priority.
We aspire toward achieving total customer satisfaction.

Copyright Notice

The contents of this book are owned exclusively by Amos Media Co. and all rights thereto are reserved under the Pan American and Universal Copyright Conventions.

Copyright ©2024 by Amos Media Co., Sidney, Ohio. Printed in U.S.A.

COPYRIGHT NOTE
Permission is hereby given for the use of material in this book and covered by copyright if:
(a) The material is used in advertising matter, circulars or price lists for the purpose of offering stamps for sale or purchase at the prices listed therein; and
(b) Such use is incidental to the business of buying and selling stamps and is limited in scope and length, i.e., it does not cover a substantial portion of the total number of stamps issued by any country or of any special category of stamps of any country; and
(c) Such material is not used as part of any catalogue, stamp album or computerized or other system based upon the Scott catalogue numbers, or in any updated valuations of stamps not offered for sale or purchase; and
(d) Such use is not competitive with the business of the copyright owner; and
(e) Such use is for editorial purposes in publications in the form of articles or commentary, except for computer software or the serialization of books in such publications, for which separate written permission is required.
Any use of the material in this book which does not satisfy all the foregoing conditions is forbidden in any form unless permission in each instance is given in writing by the copyright owner.

Trademark Notice

The terms SCOTT, SCOTT'S, SCOTT CATALOGUE NUMBERING SYSTEM, SCOTT CATALOGUE NUMBER, SCOTT NUMBER and abbreviations thereof, are trademarks of Amos Media Co., used to identify its publications and its copyrighted system for identifying and classifying postage stamps for dealers and collectors. These trademarks are to be used only with the prior consent of Amos Media Co.

No part of this work may be reproduced in any form or by any means, electronic or mechanical, including photocopying, without permission in writing from Amos Media Co., P.O. Box 4129, Sidney, OH 45365-4129.

ISBN 978-0-89487-729-2

Library of Congress Card No. 2-3301

COMMON DESIGN TYPES

Pictured in this section are issues where one illustration has been used for a number of countries in the Catalogue. Not included in this section are overprinted stamps or those issues which are illustrated in each country. Because the location of Never Hinged breakpoints varies from country to country, some of the values in the listings below will be for unused stamps that were previously hinged.

EUROPA
Europa, 1956

The design symbolizing the cooperation among the six countries comprising the Coal and Steel Community is illustrated in each country.

Belgium	496-497
France	805-806
Germany	748-749
Italy	715-716
Luxembourg	318-320
Netherlands	368-369

Nos. 496-497 (2)	9.00	.50
Nos. 805-806 (2)	5.25	1.00
Nos. 748-749 (2)	7.40	1.10
Nos. 715-716 (2)	9.25	1.25
Nos. 318-320 (3)	65.50	42.00
Nos. 368-369 (2)	25.75	1.50
Set total (13) Stamps	122.15	47.35

Europa, 1958

"E" and Dove — CD1

European Postal Union at the service of European integration.

1958, Sept. 13

Belgium	527-528
France	889-890
Germany	790-791
Italy	750-751
Luxembourg	341-343
Netherlands	375-376
Saar	317-318

Nos. 527-528 (2)	3.75	.60
Nos. 889-890 (2)	1.65	.55
Nos. 790-791 (2)	2.95	.60
Nos. 750-751 (2)	1.05	.60
Nos. 341-343 (3)	1.35	.90
Nos. 375-376 (2)	1.25	.75
Nos. 317-318 (2)	1.05	2.30
Set total (15) Stamps	13.05	6.30

Europa, 1959

6-Link Enless Chain — CD2

1959, Sept. 19

Belgium	536-537
France	929-930
Germany	805-806
Italy	791-792
Luxembourg	354-355
Netherlands	379-380

Nos. 536-537 (2)	1.55	.60
Nos. 929-930 (2)	1.40	.80
Nos. 805-806 (2)	1.35	.60
Nos. 791-792 (2)	.80	.50
Nos. 354-355 (2)	2.65	1.00
Nos. 379-380 (2)	2.10	1.85
Set total (12) Stamps	9.85	5.35

Europa, 1960

19-Spoke Wheel — CD3

First anniversary of the establishment of C.E.P.T. (Conference Europeenne des Administrations des Postes et des Telecommunications.) The spokes symbolize the 19 founding members of the Conference.

1960, Sept.

Belgium	553-554
Denmark	379
Finland	376-377
France	970-971
Germany	818-820
Great Britain	377-378
Greece	688
Iceland	327-328
Ireland	175-176
Italy	809-810
Luxembourg	374-375
Netherlands	385-386
Norway	387
Portugal	866-867
Spain	941-942
Sweden	562-563
Switzerland	400-401
Turkey	1493-1494

Nos. 553-554 (2)	1.25	.55
No. 379 (1)	.55	.50
Nos. 376-377 (2)	1.80	1.40
Nos. 970-971 (2)	.50	.50
Nos. 818-820 (3)	1.90	1.35
Nos. 377-378 (2)	7.00	2.75
No. 688 (1)	4.25	1.75
Nos. 327-328 (2)	1.30	1.85
Nos. 175-176 (2)	13.25	16.00
Nos. 809-810 (2)	.50	.50
Nos. 374-375 (2)	1.00	.80
Nos. 385-386 (2)	2.00	2.00
No. 387 (1)	1.00	.80
Nos. 866-867 (2)	3.05	1.75
Nos. 941-942 (2)	1.50	.75
Nos. 562-563 (2)	1.05	.55
Nos. 400-401 (2)	1.75	.75
Nos. 1493-1494 (2)	2.10	1.35
Set total (34) Stamps	45.75	35.90

Europa, 1961

19 Doves Flying as One — CD4

The 19 doves represent the 19 members of the Conference of European Postal and Telecommunications Administrations C.E.P.T.

1961-62

Belgium	572-573
Cyprus	201-203
France	1005-1006
Germany	844-845
Great Britain	382-384
Greece	718-719
Iceland	340-341
Italy	845-846
Luxembourg	382-383
Netherlands	387-388
Spain	1010-1011
Switzerland	410-411
Turkey	1518-1520

Nos. 572-573 (2)	.75	.50
Nos. 201-203 (3)	.90	.75
Nos. 1005-1006 (2)	.50	.50
Nos. 844-845 (2)	.60	.75
Nos. 382-384 (3)	.75	.75
Nos. 718-719 (2)	.80	.50
Nos. 340-341 (2)	1.10	.50
Nos. 845-846 (2)	.50	.50
Nos. 382-383 (2)	.55	.55
Nos. 387-388 (2)	.50	.50
Nos. 1010-1011 (2)	.60	.50
Nos. 410-411 (2)	1.90	.60
Nos. 1518-1520 (3)	1.55	.90
Set total (29) Stamps	11.00	8.90

Europa, 1962

Young Tree with 19 Leaves — CD5

The 19 leaves represent the 19 original members of C.E.P.T.

1962-63

Belgium	582-583
Cyprus	219-221
France	1045-1046
Germany	852-853
Greece	739-740
Iceland	348-349
Ireland	184-185
Italy	860-861
Luxembourg	386-387
Netherlands	394-395
Norway	414-415
Switzerland	416-417
Turkey	1553-1555

Nos. 582-583 (2)	.65	.65
Nos. 219-221 (3)	21.35	6.75
Nos. 1045-1046 (2)	.60	.50
Nos. 852-853 (2)	.65	.50
Nos. 739-740 (2)	2.00	1.15
Nos. 348-349 (2)	.85	.85
Nos. 184-185 (2)	1.45	2.75
Nos. 860-861 (2)	1.00	.55
Nos. 386-387 (2)	.75	.55
Nos. 394-395 (2)	1.35	.90
Nos. 414-415 (2)	1.75	1.70
Nos. 416-417 (2)	1.65	1.00
Nos. 1553-1555 (3)	2.05	1.10
Set total (28) Stamps	36.10	19.20

Europa, 1963

Stylized Links, Symbolizing Unity — CD6

1963, Sept.

Belgium	598-599
Cyprus	229-231
Finland	419
France	1074-1075
Germany	867-868
Greece	768-769
Iceland	357-358
Ireland	188-189
Italy	880-881
Luxembourg	403-404
Netherlands	416-417
Norway	441-442
Switzerland	429
Turkey	1602-1603

Nos. 598-599 (2)	1.60	.55
Nos. 229-231 (3)	18.30	8.65
No. 419 (1)	1.25	.55
Nos. 1074-1075 (2)	.60	.50
Nos. 867-868 (2)	.50	.55
Nos. 768-769 (2)	4.65	1.65
Nos. 357-358 (2)	1.20	1.20
Nos. 188-189 (2)	2.75	3.25
Nos. 880-881 (2)	.50	.50
Nos. 403-404 (2)	.75	.55
Nos. 416-417 (2)	1.30	1.00
Nos. 441-442 (2)	2.60	2.40
No. 429 (1)	.90	.60
Nos. 1602-1603 (2)	1.20	.50
Set total (27) Stamps	38.10	22.45

Europa, 1964

Symbolic Daisy — CD7

5th anniversary of the establishment of C.E.P.T. The 22 petals of the flower symbolize the 22 members of the Conference.

1964, Sept.

Austria	738
Belgium	614-615
Cyprus	244-246
France	1109-1110
Germany	897-898
Greece	801-802
Iceland	367-368
Ireland	196-197
Italy	894-895
Luxembourg	411-412
Monaco	590-591
Netherlands	428-429
Norway	458
Portugal	931-933
Spain	1262-1263
Switzerland	438-439
Turkey	1628-1629

No. 738 (1)	1.10	.25
Nos. 614-615 (2)	1.40	.60
Nos. 244-246 (3)	10.95	5.00
Nos. 1109-1110 (2)	.50	.50
Nos. 897-898 (2)	.50	.50
Nos. 801-802 (2)	4.15	1.55
Nos. 367-368 (2)	1.40	1.15
Nos. 196-197 (2)	4.50	4.25
Nos. 894-895 (2)	.50	.50
Nos. 411-412 (2)	.75	.55
Nos. 590-591 (2)	2.50	.70
Nos. 428-429 (2)	.75	.60
No. 458 (1)	3.50	3.50
Nos. 931-933 (3)	10.00	2.00
Nos. 1262-1263 (2)	1.15	.80
Nos. 438-439 (2)	1.65	.50
Nos. 1628-1629 (2)	2.00	.80
Set total (34) Stamps	47.30	23.75

Europa, 1965

Leaves and "Fruit" — CD8

1965

Belgium	636-637
Cyprus	262-264
Finland	437
France	1131-1132
Germany	934-935
Greece	833-834
Iceland	375-376
Ireland	204-205
Italy	915-916
Luxembourg	432-433
Monaco	616-617
Netherlands	438-439
Norway	475-476
Portugal	958-960
Switzerland	469
Turkey	1665-1666

Nos. 636-637 (2)	.50	.50
Nos. 262-264 (3)	10.80	7.45
No. 437 (1)	1.25	.55
Nos. 1131-1132 (2)	.70	.55
Nos. 934-935 (2)	.50	.50
Nos. 833-834 (2)	2.25	1.15
Nos. 375-376 (2)	2.50	1.75
Nos. 204-205 (2)	5.75	4.60
Nos. 915-916 (2)	.50	.50
Nos. 432-433 (2)	.75	.55
Nos. 616-617 (2)	3.25	1.65
Nos. 438-439 (2)	.55	.50
Nos. 475-476 (2)	2.40	1.90
Nos. 958-960 (3)	16.00	2.75
No. 469 (1)	1.15	.50
Nos. 1665-1666 (2)	2.00	1.25
Set total (32) Stamps	50.85	26.65

Europa, 1966

Symbolic Sailboat — CD9

1966, Sept.

Andorra, French	172
Belgium	675-676
Cyprus	275-277
France	1163-1164
Germany	963-964
Greece	862-863
Iceland	384-385
Ireland	216-217
Italy	942-943
Liechtenstein	415
Luxembourg	440-441
Monaco	639-640
Netherlands	441-442
Norway	496-497
Portugal	980-982
Switzerland	477-478
Turkey	1718-1719

No. 172 (1)	3.00	3.00
Nos. 675-676 (2)	.80	.50
Nos. 275-277 (3)	3.10	3.25
Nos. 1163-1164 (2)	.55	.50
Nos. 963-964 (2)	.50	.55
Nos. 862-863 (2)	2.10	1.05
Nos. 384-385 (2)	4.50	3.50
Nos. 216-217 (2)	2.35	3.75
Nos. 942-943 (2)	.50	.50
No. 415 (1)	.40	.35
Nos. 440-441 (2)	.70	.55
Nos. 639-640 (2)	2.00	.65
Nos. 441-442 (2)	.85	.50
Nos. 496-497 (2)	2.35	2.15
Nos. 980-982 (3)	15.90	2.25
Nos. 477-478 (2)	1.40	.60
Nos. 1718-1719 (2)	3.35	1.75
Set total (34) Stamps	44.35	25.40

COMMON DESIGN TYPES

Europa, 1967

Cogwheels — CD10

1967

Andorra, French	174-175
Belgium	688-689
Cyprus	297-299
France	1178-1179
Germany	969-970
Greece	891-892
Iceland	389-390
Ireland	232-233
Italy	951-952
Liechtenstein	420
Luxembourg	449-450
Monaco	669-670
Netherlands	444-447
Norway	504-505
Portugal	994-996
Spain	1465-1466
Switzerland	482
Turkey	B120-B121

Nos. 174-175 (2)	10.75	6.25
Nos. 688-689 (2)	1.05	.55
Nos. 297-299 (3)	2.55	2.90
Nos. 1178-1179 (2)	.55	.50
Nos. 969-970 (2)	.55	.55
Nos. 891-892 (2)	3.05	.85
Nos. 389-390 (2)	3.00	2.00
Nos. 232-233 (2)	2.25	2.30
Nos. 951-952 (2)	.60	.50
No. 420 (1)	.45	.40
Nos. 449-450 (2)	1.00	.70
Nos. 669-670 (2)	2.75	.70
Nos. 444-447 (4)	2.70	2.05
Nos. 504-505 (2)	2.00	1.80
Nos. 994-996 (3)	16.10	1.85
Nos. 1465-1466 (2)	.50	.50
No. 482 (1)	.60	.30
Nos. B120-B121 (2)	2.50	2.00
Set total (38) Stamps	52.95	26.70

Europa, 1968

Golden Key with C.E.P.T. Emblem — CD11

1968

Andorra, French	182-183
Belgium	705-706
Cyprus	314-316
France	1209-1210
Germany	983-984
Greece	916-917
Iceland	395-396
Ireland	242-243
Italy	979-980
Liechtenstein	442
Luxembourg	466-467
Monaco	689-691
Netherlands	452-453
Portugal	1019-1021
San Marino	687
Spain	1526
Switzerland	488
Turkey	1775-1776

Nos. 182-183 (2)	16.50	10.00
Nos. 705-706 (2)	1.25	.50
Nos. 314-316 (3)	1.70	2.90
Nos. 1209-1210 (2)	.85	.55
Nos. 983-984 (2)	.50	.55
Nos. 916-917 (2)	3.10	1.45
Nos. 395-396 (2)	3.00	2.20
Nos. 242-243 (2)	2.50	1.70
Nos. 979-980 (2)	.50	.50
No. 442 (1)	.45	.40
Nos. 466-467 (2)	.80	.70
Nos. 689-691 (3)	5.40	.95
Nos. 452-453 (2)	1.05	.70
Nos. 1019-1021 (3)	15.90	2.10
No. 687 (1)	.55	.35
No. 1526 (1)	.25	.25
No. 488 (1)	.40	.25
Nos. 1775-1776 (2)	2.50	1.25
Set total (35) Stamps	57.20	27.30

Europa, 1969

"EUROPA" and "CEPT" — CD12

Tenth anniversary of C.E.P.T.

1969

Andorra, French	188-189
Austria	837
Belgium	718-719
Cyprus	326-328
Denmark	458
Finland	483
France	1245-1246
Germany	996-997
Great Britain	585
Greece	947-948
Iceland	406-407
Ireland	270-271
Italy	1000-1001
Liechtenstein	453
Luxembourg	475-476
Monaco	722-724
Netherlands	475-476
Norway	533-534
Portugal	1038-1040
San Marino	701-702
Spain	1567
Sweden	814-816
Switzerland	500-501
Turkey	1799-1800
Vatican	470-472
Yugoslavia	1003-1004

Nos. 188-189 (2)	18.50	12.00
No. 837 (1)	.55	.25
Nos. 718-719 (2)	.75	.50
Nos. 326-328 (3)	1.60	2.70
No. 458 (1)	.75	.75
No. 483 (1)	2.50	.60
Nos. 1245-1246 (2)	.55	.50
Nos. 996-997 (2)	.70	.50
No. 585 (1)	.25	.25
Nos. 947-948 (2)	4.00	1.25
Nos. 406-407 (2)	4.20	2.40
Nos. 270-271 (2)	2.00	2.00
Nos. 1000-1001 (2)	.50	.50
No. 453 (1)	.45	.45
Nos. 475-476 (2)	.95	.50
Nos. 722-724 (3)	10.50	2.00
Nos. 475-476 (2)	1.35	1.00
Nos. 533-534 (2)	2.20	1.95
Nos. 1038-1040 (3)	17.75	2.40
Nos. 701-702 (2)	.90	.90
No. 1567 (1)	.25	.25
Nos. 814-816 (3)	4.00	2.85
Nos. 500-501 (2)	1.85	1.00
Nos. 1799-1800 (2)	2.50	1.65
Nos. 470-472 (3)	.75	.75
Nos. 1003-1004 (2)	4.00	4.00
Set total (51) Stamps	84.30	43.90

Europa, 1970

Interwoven Threads — CD13

1970

Andorra, French	196-197
Belgium	741-742
Cyprus	340-342
France	1271-1272
Germany	1018-1019
Greece	985, 987
Iceland	420-421
Ireland	279-281
Italy	1013-1014
Liechtenstein	470
Luxembourg	489-490
Monaco	768-770
Netherlands	483-484
Portugal	1060-1062
San Marino	729-730
Spain	1607
Switzerland	515-516
Turkey	1848-1849
Yugoslavia	1024-1025

Nos. 196-197 (2)	20.00	8.50
Nos. 741-742 (2)	1.10	.55
Nos. 340-342 (3)	1.70	2.75
Nos. 1271-1272 (2)	.65	.50
Nos. 1018-1019 (2)	.60	.50
Nos. 985, 987 (2)	6.35	1.60
Nos. 420-421 (2)	6.00	4.00
Nos. 279-281 (3)	2.55	2.50
Nos. 1013-1014 (2)	.50	.50
No. 470 (1)	.45	.45
Nos. 489-490 (2)	.80	.55
Nos. 768-770 (3)	6.35	2.10
Nos. 483-484 (2)	1.30	1.15
Nos. 1060-1062 (3)	18.95	2.35
Nos. 729-730 (2)	.90	.55
No. 1607 (1)	.25	.25
Nos. 515-516 (2)	1.85	.70
Nos. 1848-1849 (2)	2.50	1.50
Nos. 1024-1025 (2)	.80	.80
Set total (40) Stamps	73.60	31.80

Europa, 1971

"Fraternity, Cooperation, Common Effort" — CD14

1971

Andorra, French	205-206
Belgium	803-804
Cyprus	365-367
Finland	504
France	1304
Germany	1064-1065
Greece	1029-1030
Iceland	429-430
Ireland	305-306
Italy	1038-1039
Liechtenstein	485
Luxembourg	500-501
Malta	425-427
Monaco	797-799
Netherlands	488-489
Portugal	1094-1096
San Marino	749-750
Spain	1675-1676
Switzerland	531-532
Turkey	1876-1877
Yugoslavia	1052-1053

Nos. 205-206 (2)	20.00	7.75
Nos. 803-804 (2)	1.30	.55
Nos. 365-367 (3)	1.80	2.75
No. 504 (1)	2.50	.50
No. 1304 (1)	.45	.40
Nos. 1064-1065 (2)	.60	.50
Nos. 1029-1030 (2)	4.00	1.80
Nos. 429-430 (2)	5.00	3.75
Nos. 305-306 (2)	2.45	1.50
Nos. 1038-1039 (2)	.65	.50
No. 485 (1)	.45	.45
Nos. 500-501 (2)	1.00	.65
Nos. 425-427 (3)	1.25	1.70
Nos. 797-799 (3)	15.00	2.80
Nos. 488-489 (2)	1.20	.95
Nos. 1094-1096 (3)	16.15	1.75
Nos. 749-750 (2)	.65	.55
Nos. 1675-1676 (2)	.75	.55
Nos. 531-532 (2)	1.85	.65
Nos. 1876-1877 (2)	2.50	1.25
Nos. 1052-1053 (2)	.50	.50
Set total (43) Stamps	80.05	31.80

Europa, 1972

Sparkles, Symbolic of Communications CD15

1972

Andorra, French	210-211
Andorra, Spanish	62
Belgium	825-826
Cyprus	380-382
Finland	512-513
France	1341
Germany	1089-1090
Greece	1049-1050
Iceland	439-440
Ireland	316-317
Italy	1065-1066
Liechtenstein	504
Luxembourg	512-513
Malta	450-453
Monaco	831-832
Netherlands	494-495
Portugal	1141-1143
San Marino	771-772
Spain	1718
Switzerland	544-545
Turkey	1907-1908
Yugoslavia	1100-1101

Nos. 210-211 (2)	21.00	7.00
No. 62 (1)	60.00	60.00
Nos. 825-826 (2)	.95	.55
Nos. 380-382 (3)	2.45	3.25
Nos. 512-513 (2)	4.00	1.00
No. 1341 (1)	.50	.35
Nos. 1089-1090 (2)	1.10	.50
Nos. 1049-1050 (2)	2.00	1.55
Nos. 439-440 (2)	2.90	2.65
Nos. 316-317 (2)	5.25	3.05
Nos. 1065-1066 (2)	.55	.50
No. 504 (1)	.45	.45
Nos. 512-513 (2)	.95	.65
Nos. 450-453 (4)	1.20	1.70
Nos. 831-832 (2)	5.00	1.40
Nos. 494-495 (2)	1.20	.90
Nos. 1141-1143 (3)	15.85	1.50
Nos. 771-772 (2)	.70	.50
No. 1718 (1)	.50	.40
Nos. 544-545 (2)	1.65	.60
Nos. 1907-1908 (2)	4.00	2.00
Nos. 1100-1101 (2)	1.20	1.20
Set total (44) Stamps	133.40	91.70

Europa, 1973

Post Horn and Arrows — CD16

1973

Andorra, French	219-220
Andorra, Spanish	76
Belgium	839-840
Cyprus	396-398
Finland	526
France	1367
Germany	1114-1115
Greece	1090-1092
Iceland	447-448
Ireland	329-330
Italy	1108-1109
Liechtenstein	528-529
Luxembourg	523-524
Malta	469-471
Monaco	866-867
Netherlands	504-505
Norway	604-605
Portugal	1170-1172
San Marino	802-803
Spain	1753
Switzerland	580-581
Turkey	1935-1936
Yugoslavia	1138-1139

Nos. 219-220 (2)	20.00	11.00
No. 76 (1)	1.25	.85
Nos. 839-840 (2)	1.00	.65
Nos. 396-398 (3)	1.80	2.40
No. 526 (1)	1.25	.55
No. 1367 (1)	1.25	.75
Nos. 1114-1115 (2)	.85	.50
Nos. 1090-1092 (3)	2.10	1.40
Nos. 447-448 (2)	6.65	3.35
Nos. 329-330 (2)	3.95	2.00
Nos. 1108-1109 (2)	.50	.50
Nos. 528-529 (2)	.60	.60
Nos. 523-524 (2)	.90	.75
Nos. 469-471 (3)	.90	1.05
Nos. 866-867 (2)	15.00	2.40
Nos. 504-505 (2)	1.20	.95
Nos. 604-605 (2)	4.00	1.80
Nos. 1170-1172 (3)	24.95	2.15
Nos. 802-803 (2)	1.00	.60
No. 1753 (1)	.35	.25
Nos. 580-581 (2)	1.55	.60
Nos. 1935-1936 (2)	4.15	2.25
Nos. 1138-1139 (2)	1.15	1.10
Set total (46) Stamps	96.35	38.45

Europa, 2000

CD17

2000

Albania	2621-2622
Andorra, French	522
Andorra, Spanish	262
Armenia	610-611
Austria	1814
Azerbaijan	698-699
Belarus	350
Belgium	1818
Bosnia & Herzegovina (Moslem)	358
Bosnia & Herzegovina (Serb)	111-112
Croatia	428-429
Cyprus	959
Czech Republic	3120
Denmark	1189
Estonia	394
Faroe Islands	376
Finland	1129
Aland Islands	166
France	2771
Georgia	228-229

COMMON DESIGN TYPES 5A

Country	Numbers
Germany	2086-2087
Gibraltar	837-840
Great Britain (Jersey)	935-936
Great Britain (Isle of Man)	883
Greece	1959
Greenland	363
Hungary	3699-3700
Iceland	910
Ireland	1230-1231
Italy	2349
Latvia	504
Liechtenstein	1178
Lithuania	668
Luxembourg	1035
Macedonia	187
Malta	1011-1012
Moldova	355
Monaco	2161-2162
Poland	3519
Portugal	2358
Portugal (Azores)	455
Portugal (Madeira)	208
Romania	4370
Russia	6589
San Marino	1480
Slovakia	355
Slovenia	424
Spain	3036
Sweden	2394
Switzerland	1074
Turkey	2762
Turkish Rep. of Northern Cyprus	500
Ukraine	379
Vatican City	1152

Nos. 2621-2622 (2)	9.50	9.50
No. 522 (1)	2.00	1.00
No. 262 (1)	1.75	.80
Nos. 610-611 (2)	4.75	4.75
No. 1814 (1)	1.25	1.25
Nos. 698-699 (2)	6.00	6.00
No. 350 (1)	1.75	1.75
No. 1818 (1)	1.40	.60
No. 358 (1)	4.75	4.75
Nos. 111-112 (2)	110.00	110.00
Nos. 428-429 (2)	6.25	6.25
No. 959 (1)	2.10	1.40
No. 3120 (1)	1.20	.40
No. 1189 (1)	3.50	2.25
No. 394 (1)	1.25	1.25
No. 376 (1)	2.40	2.40
No. 1129 (1)	2.00	.60
No. 166 (1)	1.10	1.20
No. 2771 (1)	1.25	.40
Nos. 228-229 (2)	9.00	9.00
Nos. 2086-2087 (2)	4.35	2.10
Nos. 837-840 (4)	4.20	5.30
Nos. 935-936 (2)	2.40	2.40
No. 883 (1)	1.75	1.75
No. 363 (1)	1.90	1.90
Nos. 3699-3700 (2)	4.50	3.00
No. 910 (1)	1.60	1.60
Nos. 1230-1231 (2)	2.60	2.60
No. 2349 (1)	1.50	.40
No. 504 (1)	5.00	2.40
No. 1178 (1)	2.25	1.75
No. 668 (1)	1.50	1.50
No. 1035 (1)	1.40	.85
No. 187 (1)	3.00	3.00
Nos. 1011-1012 (2)	2.75	4.35
No. 355 (1)	3.50	3.50
Nos. 2161-2162 (2)	2.80	1.40
No. 3519 (1)	1.25	.75
No. 2358 (1)	1.95	.65
No. 455 (1)	2.00	.50
No. 208 (1)	2.25	.50
No. 4370 (1)	2.50	1.25
No. 6589 (1)	4.00	.85
No. 1480 (1)	1.00	1.00
No. 355 (1)	1.60	.80
No. 424 (1)	3.25	3.25
No. 3036 (1)	1.00	.40
No. 2394 (1)	3.00	1.50
No. 1074 (1)	2.10	1.05
No. 2762 (1)	2.75	2.00
No. 500 (1)	2.50	2.50
No. 379 (1)	4.50	3.00
No. 1152 (1)	1.75	1.75
Set total (68) Stamps	257.60	227.10

The Gibraltar stamps are similar to the stamp illustrated, but none have the design shown above. All other sets listed above include at least one stamp with the design shown, but some include stamps with entirely different designs. Bulgaria Nos. 4131-4132, Guernsey Nos. 802-803 and Yugoslavia Nos. 2485-2486 are Europa stamps with completely different designs.

PORTUGAL & COLONIES
Vasco da Gama

Fleet Departing CD20
Fleet Arriving at Calicut CD21
Embarking at Rastello CD22
Muse of History CD23
San Gabriel, da Gama and Camoens CD24
Archangel Gabriel, the Patron Saint CD25
Flagship San Gabriel CD26
Vasco da Gama CD27

Fourth centenary of Vasco da Gama's discovery of the route to India.

1898

Azores		93-100
Macao		67-74
Madeira		37-44
Portugal		147-154
Port. Africa		1-8
Port. Congo		75-98
Port. India		189-196
St. Thomas & Prince Islands		170-193
Timor		45-52

Nos. 93-100 (8)	113.50	73.50
Nos. 67-74 (8)	250.25	170.25
Nos. 37-44 (8)	60.55	37.25
Nos. 147-154 (8)	249.05	84.90
Nos. 1-8 (8)	44.00	29.25
Nos. 75-98 (24)	78.50	64.65
Nos. 189-196 (8)	25.25	15.50
Nos. 170-193 (24)	60.40	44.75
Nos. 45-52 (8)	33.50	23.25
Set total (104) Stamps	915.00	543.30

Pombal
POSTAL TAX
POSTAL TAX DUES

Marquis de Pombal — CD28
Planning Reconstruction of Lisbon, 1755 — CD29
Pombal Monument, Lisbon — CD30

Sebastiao Jose de Carvalho e Mello, Marquis de Pombal (1699-1782), statesman, rebuilt Lisbon after earthquake of 1755. Tax was for the erection of Pombal monument. Obligatory on all mail on certain days throughout the year. Postal Tax Dues are inscribed "Multa."

1925

Angola	RA1-RA3, RAJ1-RAJ3
Azores	RA9-RA11, RAJ2-RAJ4
Cape Verde	RA1-RA3, RAJ1-RAJ3
Macao	RA1-RA3, RAJ1-RAJ3
Madeira	RA1-RA3, RAJ1-RAJ3
Mozambique	RA1-RA3, RAJ1-RAJ3
Nyassa	RA1-RA3, RAJ1-RAJ3
Portugal	RA11-RA13, RAJ2-RAJ4
Port. Guinea	RA1-RA3, RAJ1-RAJ3
Port. India	RA1-RA3, RAJ1-RAJ3
St. Thomas & Prince Islands	RA1-RA3, RAJ1-RAJ3
Timor	RA1-RA3, RAJ1-RAJ3

Nos. RA1-RA3, RAJ1-RAJ3 (6)	6.60	5.40
Nos. RA9-RA11, RAJ2-RAJ4 (6)	6.60	6.60
Nos. RA1-RA3, RAJ1-RAJ3 (6)	7.80	7.65
Nos. RA1-RA3, RAJ1-RAJ3 (6)	36.50	17.25
Nos. RA1-RA3, RAJ1-RAJ3 (6)	7.95	14.70
Nos. RA1-RA3, RAJ1-RAJ3 (6)	3.75	3.60
Nos. RA1-RA3, RAJ1-RAJ3 (6)	85.50	76.50
Nos. RA11-RA13, RAJ2-RAJ4 (6)	8.75	8.55
Nos. RA1-RA3, RAJ1-RAJ3 (6)	5.85	5.40
Nos. RA1-RA3, RAJ1-RAJ3 (6)	4.05	4.05
Nos. RA1-RA3, RAJ1-RAJ3 (6)	4.95	3.45
Nos. RA1-RA3, RAJ1-RAJ3 (6)	3.90	3.45
Set total (72) Stamps	182.20	156.60

Vasco da Gama CD34
Mousinho de Albuquerque CD35
Dam CD36
Prince Henry the Navigator CD37
Affonso de Albuquerque CD38
Plane over Globe CD39

1938-39

Angola	274-291, C1-C9
Cape Verde	234-251, C1-C9
Macao	289-305, C7-C15
Mozambique	270-287, C1-C9
Port. Guinea	233-250, C1-C9
Port. India	439-453, C1-C8
St. Thomas & Prince Islands	302-319, 323-340, C1-C18
Timor	223-239, C1-C9

Nos. 274-291,C1-C9 (27)	121.45	20.95
Nos. 234-251,C1-C9 (27)	122.40	38.30
Nos. 289-305,C7-C15 (26)	889.60	338.55
Nos. 270-287,C1-C9 (27)	95.71	15.95
Nos. 233-250,C1-C9 (27)	130.20	49.15
Nos. 439-453,C1-C8 (23)	98.15	34.70
Nos. 302-319,323-340,C1-C18 (54)	468.30	263.80
Nos. 223-239,C1-C9 (26)	213.85	104.90
Set total (237) Stamps	2,140.	866.30

Lady of Fatima

Our Lady of the Rosary, Fatima, Portugal — CD40

1948-49

Angola	315-318
Cape Verde	266
Macao	336
Mozambique	325-328
Port. Guinea	271
Port. India	480
St. Thomas & Prince Islands	351
Timor	254

Nos. 315-318 (4)	68.00	20.60
No. 266 (1)	8.50	9.00
No. 336 (1)	90.00	30.00
Nos. 325-328 (4)	73.25	27.50
No. 271 (1)	6.50	6.00
No. 480 (1)	4.50	4.75
No. 351 (1)	8.50	7.00
No. 254 (1)	6.00	12.50
Set total (14) Stamps	265.25	117.35

A souvenir sheet of 9 stamps was issued in 1951 to mark the extension of the 1950 Holy Year. The sheet contains: Angola No. 316, Cape Verde No. 266, Macao No. 336, Mozambique No. 325, Portuguese Guinea No. 271, Portuguese India Nos. 480, 485, St. Thomas & Prince Islands No. 351, Timor No. 254. The sheet also contains a portrait of Pope Pius XII and is inscribed "Encerramento do Ano Santo, Fatima 1951." It was sold for 11 escudos.

Holy Year

Church Bells and Dove CD41
Angel Holding Candelabra CD42

Holy Year, 1950.

1950-51

Angola	331-332
Cape Verde	268-269
Macao	339-340
Mozambique	330-331
Port. Guinea	273-274
Port. India	490-491, 496-503
St. Thomas & Prince Islands	353-354
Timor	258-259

Nos. 331-332 (2)	7.60	1.35
Nos. 268-269 (2)	7.35	4.75
Nos. 339-340 (2)	110.00	34.00
Nos. 330-331 (2)	3.00	1.60
Nos. 273-274 (2)	8.50	5.05
Nos. 490-491,496-503 (10)	14.50	7.30
Nos. 353-354 (2)	10.50	7.25
Nos. 258-259 (2)	8.75	5.00
Set total (24) Stamps	170.20	66.30

A souvenir sheet of 8 stamps was issued in 1951 to mark the extension of the Holy Year. The sheet contains: Angola No. 331, Cape Verde No. 269, Macao No. 340, Mozambique No. 331, Portuguese Guinea No. 275, Portuguese India No. 490, St. Thomas & Prince Islands No. 354, Timor No. 258, some with colors changed. The sheet contains doves and is inscribed 'Encerramento do Ano Santo, Fatima 1951.' It was sold for 17 escudos.

Holy Year Conclusion

Our Lady of Fatima — CD43

Conclusion of Holy Year. Sheets contain alternate vertical rows of stamps and labels bearing quotation from Pope Pius XII, different for each colony.

1951

Angola	357
Capo Verde	270
Macao	352
Mozambique	356
Port. Guinea	275
Port. India	506
St. Thomas & Prince Islands	355
Timor	270

No. 357 (1)	4.50	1.60
No. 270 (1)	1.75	1.25
No. 352 (1)	110.00	23.00
No. 356 (1)	3.25	1.75
No. 275 (1)	2.00	1.00
No. 506 (1)	2.50	1.60
No. 355 (1)	3.50	2.75
No. 270 (1)	3.75	2.75
Set total (8) Stamps	131.25	35.70

COMMON DESIGN TYPES

Medical Congress

CD44

First National Congress of Tropical Medicine, Lisbon, 1952. Each stamp has a different design.

1952

Angola	358
Cape Verde	287
Macao	364
Mozambique	359
Port. Guinea	276
Port. India	516
St. Thomas & Prince Islands	356
Timor	271

No. 358 (1)	1.35	.45
No. 287 (1)	.95	.75
No. 364 (1)	20.00	7.00
No. 359 (1)	1.90	.90
No. 276 (1)	.75	.65
No. 516 (1)	7.50	3.25
No. 356 (1)	.75	.30
No. 271 (1)	2.00	1.60
Set total (8) Stamps	35.20	14.90

Postage Due Stamps

CD45

1952

Angola	J37-J42
Cape Verde	J31-J36
Macao	J53-J58
Mozambique	J51-J56
Port. Guinea	J40-J45
Port. India	J47-J52
St. Thomas & Prince Islands	J52-J57
Timor	J31-J36

Nos. J37-J42 (6)	3.15	2.95
Nos. J31-J36 (6)	2.80	2.30
Nos. J53-J58 (6)	27.80	12.05
Nos. J51-J56 (6)	2.40	1.95
Nos. J40-J45 (6)	2.70	2.55
Nos. J47-J52 (6)	6.10	6.10
Nos. J52-J57 (6)	2.85	2.70
Nos. J31-J36 (6)	4.00	2.35
Set total (48) Stamps	51.80	32.95

Sao Paulo

Father Manuel da Nobrega and View of Sao Paulo — CD46

Founding of Sao Paulo, Brazil, 400th anniv.

1954

Angola	385
Cape Verde	297
Macao	382
Mozambique	395
Port. Guinea	291
Port. India	530
St. Thomas & Prince Islands	369
Timor	279

No. 385 (1)	.80	.30
No. 297 (1)	.95	.80
No. 382 (1)	30.00	6.00
No. 395 (1)	.75	.30
No. 291 (1)	.50	.35
No. 530 (1)	1.00	.55
No. 369 (1)	.70	.50
No. 279 (1)	2.00	1.40
Set total (8) Stamps	36.70	10.20

Tropical Medicine Congress

CD47

Sixth International Congress for Tropical Medicine and Malaria, Lisbon, Sept. 1958. Each stamp shows a different plant.

1958

Angola	409
Cape Verde	303
Macao	392
Mozambique	404
Port. Guinea	295
Port. India	569
St. Thomas & Prince Islands	371
Timor	289

No. 409 (1)	3.50	1.00
No. 392 (1)	13.00	6.00
No. 404 (1)	3.50	1.50
No. 295 (1)	4.50	2.00
No. 569 (1)	1.75	.75
No. 371 (1)	2.75	2.00
No. 289 (1)	5.50	4.25
Set total (7) Stamps	34.50	17.50

Sports

CD48

Each stamp shows a different sport.

1962

Angola	433-438
Cape Verde	320-325
Macao	394-399
Mozambique	424-429
Port. Guinea	299-304
St. Thomas & Prince Islands	374-379
Timor	313-318

Nos. 433-438 (6)	5.55	3.20
Nos. 320-325 (6)	16.05	7.40
Nos. 394-399 (6)	129.85	28.95
Nos. 424-429 (6)	6.55	2.45
Nos. 299-304 (6)	6.00	3.00
Nos. 374-379 (6)	6.80	3.20
Nos. 313-318 (6)	11.65	5.90
Set total (42) Stamps	182.45	54.10

Anti-Malaria

Anopheles Funestus and Malaria Eradication Symbol — CD49

World Health Organization drive to eradicate malaria.

1962

Angola	439
Cape Verde	326
Macao	400
Mozambique	430
Port. Guinea	305
St. Thomas & Prince Islands	380
Timor	319

No. 439 (1)	2.25	.90
No. 400 (1)	12.00	4.00
No. 430 (1)	2.00	.50
No. 305 (1)	1.50	.60
No. 380 (1)	2.25	1.25
No. 319 (1)	2.25	1.40
Set total (6) Stamps	22.25	8.65

Airline Anniversary

Map of Africa, Super Constellation and Jet Liner — CD50

Tenth anniversary of Transportes Aereos Portugueses (TAP).

1963

Angola	490
Cape Verde	327
Mozambique	434
Port. Guinea	318
St. Thomas & Prince Islands	381

No. 490 (1)	1.35	.35
No. 327 (1)	1.50	1.10
No. 434 (1)	.55	.25
No. 318 (1)	1.25	.60
No. 381 (1)	.80	.50
Set total (5) Stamps	5.45	2.80

National Overseas Bank

Antonio Teixeira de Sousa — CD51

Centenary of the National Overseas Bank of Portugal.

1964, May 16

Angola	509
Cape Verde	328
Port. Guinea	319
St. Thomas & Prince Islands	382
Timor	320

No. 509 (1)	.90	.45
No. 328 (1)	1.50	1.30
No. 319 (1)	.95	.60
No. 382 (1)	.95	.50
No. 320 (1)	1.50	1.30
Set total (5) Stamps	5.80	4.15

ITU

ITU Emblem and the Archangel Gabriel — CD52

International Communications Union, Cent.

1965, May 17

Angola	511
Cape Verde	329
Macao	402
Mozambique	464
Port. Guinea	320
St. Thomas & Prince Islands	383
Timor	321

No. 511 (1)	1.25	.65
No. 329 (1)	2.90	2.25
No. 402 (1)	9.00	3.00
No. 464 (1)	.65	.25
No. 320 (1)	2.50	1.00
No. 383 (1)	2.00	1.00
No. 321 (1)	2.20	1.40
Set total (7) Stamps	20.50	9.55

National Revolution

CD53

40th anniv. of the National Revolution. Different buildings on each stamp.

1966, May 28

Angola	525
Cape Verde	338
Macao	403
Mozambique	465
Port. Guinea	329
St. Thomas & Prince Islands	392
Timor	322

No. 525 (1)	.50	.25
No. 338 (1)	.85	.75
No. 403 (1)	9.00	3.75
No. 465 (1)	.65	.30
No. 329 (1)	.85	.65
No. 392 (1)	.80	.50
No. 322 (1)	2.40	1.40
Set total (7) Stamps	15.05	7.60

Navy Club

CD54

Centenary of Portugal's Navy Club. Each stamp has a different design.

1967, Jan. 31

Angola	527-528
Cape Verde	339-340
Macao	412-413
Mozambique	478-479
Port. Guinea	330-331
St. Thomas & Prince Islands	393-394
Timor	323-324

Nos. 527-528 (2)	2.35	1.20
Nos. 339-340 (2)	2.70	2.30
Nos. 412-413 (2)	18.00	4.70
Nos. 478-479 (2)	1.75	.65
Nos. 330-331 (2)	1.65	.90
Nos. 393-394 (2)	3.30	1.30
Nos. 323-324 (2)	4.25	2.40
Set total (14) Stamps	34.00	13.45

Admiral Coutinho

CD55

Centenary of the birth of Admiral Carlos Viegas Gago Coutinho (1869-1959), explorer and aviation pioneer. Each stamp has a different design.

1969, Feb. 17

Angola	547
Cape Verde	355
Macao	417
Mozambique	484
Port. Guinea	335
St. Thomas & Prince Islands	397
Timor	335

No. 547 (1)	.85	.35
No. 355 (1)	.60	.25
No. 417 (1)	7.50	2.25
No. 484 (1)	.30	.25
No. 335 (1)	.50	.25
No. 397 (1)	.70	.35
No. 335 (1)	2.50	1.40
Set total (7) Stamps	12.95	5.10

Administration Reform

Luiz Augusto Rebello da Silva — CD56

Centenary of the administration reforms of the overseas territories.

1969, Sept. 25

Angola	549
Cape Verde	357
Macao	419
Mozambique	491
Port. Guinea	337
St. Thomas & Prince Islands	399
Timor	338

No. 549 (1)	.30	.25
No. 357 (1)	.65	.40
No. 419 (1)	12.50	2.00
No. 491 (1)	.30	.25
No. 337 (1)	.35	.25
No. 399 (1)	.60	.45
No. 338 (1)	1.40	.70
Set total (7) Stamps	16.10	4.30

Marshal Carmona

CD57

Birth centenary of Marshal Antonio Oscar Carmona de Fragoso (1869-1951), President of Portugal. Each stamp has a different design.

1970, Nov. 15

Angola	563
Cape Verde	359
Macao	422
Mozambique	493
Port. Guinea	340
St. Thomas & Prince Islands	403
Timor	341

No. 563 (1)	.45	.25
No. 359 (1)	.70	.50
No. 422 (1)	5.00	1.75
No. 493 (1)	.40	.25
No. 340 (1)	.45	.25

COMMON DESIGN TYPES

No. 403 (1)		.90	.40
No. 341 (1)		1.00	.50
Set total (7) Stamps		8.90	3.90

Olympic Games

CD59

20th Olympic Games, Munich, Aug. 26-Sept. 11. Each stamp shows a different sport.

1972, June 20

Angola	569
Cape Verde	361
Macao	426
Mozambique	504
Port. Guinea	342
St. Thomas & Prince Islands	408
Timor	343

No. 569 (1)	.65	.25
No. 361 (1)	.85	.40
No. 426 (1)	2.50	1.50
No. 504 (1)	.30	.25
No. 342 (1)	.95	.25
No. 408 (1)	.60	.25
No. 343 (1)	1.60	.80
Set total (7) Stamps	7.45	3.70

Lisbon-Rio de Janeiro Flight

CD60

50th anniversary of the Lisbon to Rio de Janeiro flight by Arturo de Sacadura and Coutinho, March 30-June 5, 1922. Each stamp shows a different stage of the flight.

1972, Sept. 20

Angola	570
Cape Verde	362
Macao	427
Mozambique	505
Port. Guinea	343
St. Thomas & Prince Islands	409
Timor	344

No. 570 (1)	.35	.25
No. 362 (1)	.85	.40
No. 427 (1)	40.00	12.00
No. 505 (1)	.30	.25
No. 343 (1)	.35	.25
No. 409 (1)	.50	.25
No. 344 (1)	1.25	.90
Set total (7) Stamps	43.60	14.30

WMO Centenary

WMO Emblem — CD61

Centenary of international meterological cooperation.

1973, Dec. 15

Angola	571
Cape Verde	363
Macao	429
Mozambique	509
Port. Guinea	344
St. Thomas & Prince Islands	410
Timor	345

No. 571 (1)	.45	.25
No. 363 (1)	.85	.40
No. 429 (1)	15.00	2.50
No. 509 (1)	.40	.25
No. 344 (1)	.55	.40
No. 410 (1)	.80	.50
No. 345 (1)	3.75	2.75
Set total (7) Stamps	21.80	7.05

FRENCH COMMUNITY

Upper Volta can be found under Burkina Faso in Vol. 1
Madagascar can be found under Malagasy in Vol. 3

Colonial Exposition

People of French Empire — CD70

Women's Heads — CD71

France Showing Way to Civilization CD72

"Colonial Commerce" CD73

International Colonial Exposition, Paris.

1931

Cameroun	213-216
Chad	60-63
Dahomey	97-100
Fr. Guiana	152-155
Fr. Guinea	116-119
Fr. India	100-103
Fr. Polynesia	76-79
Fr. Sudan	102-105
Gabon	120-123
Guadeloupe	138-141
Indo-China	140-142
Ivory Coast	92-95
Madagascar	169-172
Martinique	129-132
Mauritania	65-68
Middle Congo	61-64
New Caledonia	176-179
Niger	73-76
Reunion	122-125
St. Pierre & Miquelon	132-135
Senegal	138-141
Somali Coast	135-138
Togo	254-257
Ubangi-Shari	82-85
Upper Volta	66-69
Wallis & Futuna Isls.	85-88

Nos. 213-216 (4)	23.00	18.25
Nos. 60-63 (4)	22.00	22.00
Nos. 97-100 (4)	26.00	26.00
Nos. 152-155 (4)	22.00	22.00
Nos. 116-119 (4)	19.75	19.75
Nos. 100-103 (4)	18.00	18.00
Nos. 76-79 (4)	30.00	30.00
Nos. 102-105 (4)	19.00	19.00
Nos. 120-123 (4)	17.50	17.50
Nos. 138-141 (4)	19.00	19.00
Nos. 140-142 (3)	12.00	11.50
Nos. 92-95 (4)	22.50	22.50
Nos. 169-172 (4)	9.25	0.50
Nos. 129-132 (4)	21.00	21.00
Nos. 65-68 (4)	22.00	22.00
Nos. 61-64 (4)	20.00	18.50
Nos. 176-179 (4)	24.00	24.00
Nos. 73-76 (4)	20.50	20.50
Nos. 122-125 (4)	22.00	22.00
Nos. 132-135 (4)	24.00	24.00
Nos. 138-141 (4)	20.00	20.00
Nos. 135-138 (4)	22.00	22.00
Nos. 254-257 (4)	22.00	22.00
Nos. 82-85 (4)	21.00	21.00
Nos. 66-69 (4)	19.00	19.00
Nos. 85-88 (4)	31.00	35.00
Set total (103) Stamps	548.50	543.00

Paris International Exposition
Colonial Arts Exposition

"Colonial Resources"
CD74   CD77

Overseas Commerce CD75

Exposition Building and Women CD76

"France and the Empire" — CD78

Cultural Treasures of the Colonies — CD79

Souvenir sheets contain one imperf. stamp.

1937

Cameroun	217-222A
Dahomey	101-107
Fr. Equatorial Africa	27-32, 73
Fr. Guiana	162-168
Fr. Guinea	120-126
Fr. India	104-110
Fr. Polynesia	117-123
Fr. Sudan	106-112
Guadeloupe	148-154
Indo-China	193-199
Inini	41
Ivory Coast	152-158
Kwangchowan	132
Madagascar	191-197
Martinique	179-185
Mauritania	69-75
New Caledonia	208-214
Niger	77-83
Reunion	167-173
St. Pierre & Miquelon	165-171
Senegal	172-178
Somali Coast	139-145
Togo	258-264
Wallis & Futuna Isls.	89

Nos. 217-222A (7)	18.80	20.30
Nos. 101-107 (7)	23.60	27.60
Nos. 27-32, 73 (7)	28.10	32.10
Nos. 162-168 (7)	22.50	24.50
Nos. 120-126 (7)	24.00	28.00
Nos. 104-110 (7)	21.15	36.50
Nos. 117-123 (7)	58.50	75.00
Nos. 106-112 (7)	23.60	27.60
Nos. 148-154 (7)	19.55	21.05
Nos. 193-199 (7)	17.70	19.70
No. 41 (1)	21.00	27.50
Nos. 152-158 (7)	22.20	26.20
No. 132 (1)	9.25	11.00
Nos. 191-197 (7)	19.25	21.75
Nos. 179-185 (7)	19.95	21.70
Nos. 69-75 (7)	20.50	24.50
Nos. 208-214 (7)	39.00	50.50
Nos. 73-83 (7)	40.60	45.10
Nos. 167-173 (7)	21.70	23.20
Nos. 165-171 (7)	49.60	64.00
Nos. 172-178 (7)	21.00	23.80
Nos. 139-145 (7)	25.60	32.60
Nos. 258-264 (7)	20.40	20.40
No. 89 (1)	19.00	37.50
Set total (154) Stamps	606.55	742.10

Curie

Pierre and Marie Curie — CD80

40th anniversary of the discovery of radium. The surtax was for the benefit of the Intl. Union for the Control of Cancer.

1938

Cameroun	B1
Cuba	B1-B2
Dahomey	B2
France	B76
Fr. Equatorial Africa	B1
Fr. Guiana	B3
Fr. Guinea	B2
Fr. India	B6
Fr. Polynesia	B5
Fr. Sudan	B1
Guadeloupe	B3
Indo-China	B14
Ivory Coast	B2
Madagascar	B2
Martinique	B2
Mauritania	B3
New Caledonia	B4
Niger	B1
Reunion	B4
St. Pierre & Miquelon	B3
Senegal	B3
Somali Coast	B2
Togo	B1

No. B1 (1)	10.00	10.00
Nos. B1-B2 (2)	12.00	3.35
No. B2 (1)	9.50	9.50
No. B76 (1)	21.00	12.50
No. B1 (1)	24.00	24.00
No. B3 (1)	13.50	13.50
No. B2 (1)	8.75	8.75
No. B6 (1)	10.00	10.00
No. B5 (1)	20.00	20.00
No. B1 (1)	12.50	12.50
No. B3 (1)	11.00	10.50
No. B14 (1)	12.00	12.00
No. B2 (1)	11.00	7.50
No. B2 (1)	11.00	11.00
No. B2 (1)	13.00	13.00
No. B3 (1)	7.75	7.75
No. B4 (1)	16.50	17.50
No. B1 (1)	16.50	16.50
No. B4 (1)	14.00	14.00
No. B3 (1)	21.00	22.50
No. B3 (1)	10.50	10.50
No. B2 (1)	7.75	7.75
No. B1 (1)	20.00	20.00
Set total (24) Stamps	313.25	294.60

Caillie

Rene Caillie and Map of Northwestern Africa — CD81

Death centenary of Rene Caillie (1799-1838), French explorer. All three denominations exist with colony name omitted.

1939

Dahomey	108-110
Fr. Guinea	161-163
Fr. Sudan	113-115
Ivory Coast	160-162
Mauritania	109-111
Niger	84-86
Senegal	188-190
Togo	265-267

Nos. 108-110 (3)	1.20	3.60
Nos. 161-163 (3)	1.20	3.20
Nos. 113-115 (3)	1.20	3.20
Nos. 160-162 (3)	1.05	2.55
Nos. 109-111 (3)	1.05	3.80
Nos. 84-86 (3)	2.35	2.35
Nos. 188-190 (3)	1.05	2.90
Nos. 265-267 (3)	1.05	3.30
Set total (24) Stamps	10.15	24.90

New York World's Fair

Natives and New York Skyline — CD82

1939

Cameroun	223-224
Dahomey	111-112
Fr. Equatorial Africa	78-79
Fr. Guiana	169-170
Fr. Guinea	164-165
Fr. India	111-112
Fr. Polynesia	124-125
Fr. Sudan	116-117
Guadeloupe	155-156
Indo-China	203-204
Inini	42-43
Ivory Coast	163-164
Kwangchowan	133-134
Madagascar	209-210
Martinique	186-187
Mauritania	112-113
New Caledonia	215-216
Niger	87-88
Reunion	174-175
St. Pierre & Miquelon	205-206
Senegal	191-192
Somali Coast	179-180
Togo	268-269
Wallis & Futuna Isls.	90-91

Nos. 223-224 (2)	2.80	2.40
Nos. 111-112 (2)	1.60	3.20
Nos. 78-79 (2)	1.60	3.20
Nos. 169-170 (2)	2.60	2.60
Nos. 164-165 (2)	1.60	3.20
Nos. 111-112 (2)	3.00	8.00
Nos. 124-125 (2)	4.80	4.80
Nos. 116-117 (2)	1.60	3.20
Nos. 155-156 (2)	2.50	2.50
Nos. 203-204 (2)	2.05	2.05
Nos. 42-43 (2)	7.50	9.00
Nos. 163-164 (2)	1.50	3.00
Nos. 133-134 (2)	2.50	2.50
Nos. 209-210 (2)	1.50	2.50

COMMON DESIGN TYPES

Nos. 186-187 (2)	2.35	2.35
Nos. 112-113 (2)	1.40	2.80
Nos. 215-216 (2)	3.35	3.35
Nos. 87-88 (2)	1.60	2.80
Nos. 174-175 (2)	2.80	2.80
Nos. 205-206 (2)	4.80	6.00
Nos. 191-192 (2)	1.40	2.80
Nos. 179-180 (2)	1.40	2.80
Nos. 268-269 (2)	1.40	2.80
Nos. 90-91 (2)	5.00	6.00
Set total (48) Stamps	62.65	86.65

French Revolution

Storming of the Bastille — CD83

French Revolution, 150th anniv. The surtax was for the defense of the colonies.

1939

Cameroun	B2-B6
Dahomey	B3-B7
Fr. Equatorial Africa	B4-B8, CB1
Fr. Guiana	B4-B8, CB1
Fr. Guinea	B3-B7
Fr. India	B7-B11
Fr. Polynesia	B6-B10, CB1
Fr. Sudan	B2-B6
Guadeloupe	B4-B8
Indo-China	B15-B19, CB1
Inini	B1-B5
Ivory Coast	B3-B7
Kwangchowan	B1-B5
Madagascar	B3-B7, CB1
Martinique	B3-B7
Mauritania	B4-B8
New Caledonia	B5-B9, CB1
Niger	B2-B6
Reunion	B5-B9, CB1
St. Pierre & Miquelon	B4-B8
Senegal	B4-B8, CB1
Somali Coast	B3-B7
Togo	B2-B6
Wallis & Futuna Isls.	B1-B5

Nos. B2-B6 (5)	60.00	60.00
Nos. B3-B7 (5)	47.50	47.50
Nos. B4-B8,CB1 (6)	120.00	120.00
Nos. B4-B8,CB1 (6)	79.50	79.50
Nos. B3-B7 (5)	47.50	47.50
Nos. B7-B11 (5)	28.75	32.50
Nos. B6-B10,CB1 (6)	122.50	122.50
Nos. B2-B6 (5)	50.00	50.00
Nos. B4-B8 (5)	50.00	50.00
Nos. B15-B19,CB1 (6)	85.00	85.00
Nos. B1-B5 (5)	80.00	100.00
Nos. B3-B7 (5)	43.75	43.75
Nos. B1-B5 (5)	46.25	46.25
Nos. B3-B7,CB1 (6)	65.50	65.50
Nos. B3-B7 (5)	52.50	52.50
Nos. B4-B8 (5)	42.50	42.50
Nos. B5-B9,CB1 (6)	101.50	101.50
Nos. B2-B6 (5)	60.00	60.00
Nos. B5-B9,CB1 (6)	87.50	87.50
Nos. B4-B8 (5)	67.50	72.50
Nos. B4-B8,CB1 (6)	56.50	56.50
Nos. B3-B7 (5)	45.00	45.00
Nos. B2-B6 (5)	42.50	42.50
Nos. B1-B5 (5)	80.00	110.00
Set total (128) Stamps	1,562.	1,621.

Plane over Coastal Area — CD85

All five denominations exist with colony name omitted.

1940

Dahomey	C1-C5
Fr. Guinea	C1-C5
Fr. Sudan	C1-C5
Ivory Coast	C1-C5
Mauritania	C1-C5
Niger	C1-C5
Senegal	C12-C16
Togo	C1-C5

Nos. C1-C5 (5)	4.00	4.00
Nos. C1-C5 (5)	4.00	4.00
Nos. C1-C5 (5)	4.00	4.00
Nos. C1-C5 (5)	3.80	3.80
Nos. C1-C5 (5)	3.50	3.50
Nos. C1-C5 (5)	3.50	3.50
Nos. C12-C16 (5)	3.50	3.50
Nos. C1-C5 (5)	3.15	3.15
Set total (40) Stamps	29.45	29.45

Defense of the Empire

Colonial Infantryman — CD86

1941

Cameroun	B13B
Dahomey	B13
Fr. Equatorial Africa	B8B
Fr. Guiana	B10
Fr. Guinea	B13
Fr. India	B13
Fr. Polynesia	B12
Fr. Sudan	B12
Guadeloupe	B10
Indo-China	B19B
Inini	B7
Ivory Coast	B13
Kwangchowan	B7
Madagascar	B9
Martinique	B9
Mauritania	B14
New Caledonia	B11
Niger	B12
Reunion	B11
St. Pierre & Miquelon	B8B
Senegal	B14
Somali Coast	B9
Togo	B10B
Wallis & Futuna Isls.	B7

No. B13B (1)	1.60	
No. B13 (1)	1.20	
No. B8B (1)	3.50	
No. B10 (1)	1.40	
No. B13 (1)	1.40	
No. B13 (1)	1.25	
No. B12 (1)	3.50	
No. B12 (1)	1.40	
No. B10 (1)	1.00	
No. B19B (1)	3.00	
No. B7 (1)	1.75	
No. B13 (1)	1.25	
No. B7 (1)	.85	
No. B9 (1)	1.50	
No. B9 (1)	1.40	
No. B14 (1)	.95	
No. B12 (1)	1.40	
No. B11 (1)	1.60	
No. B8B (1)	4.50	
No. B14 (1)	1.25	
No. B9 (1)	1.60	
No. B10B (1)	1.10	
No. B7 (1)	1.75	
Set total (23) Stamps	40.15	

Each of the CD86 stamps listed above is part of a set of three stamps. The designs of the other two stamps in the set vary from country to country. Only the values of the Common Design stamps are listed here.

Colonial Education Fund

CD86a

1942

Cameroun	CB3
Dahomey	CB4
Fr. Equatorial Africa	CB5
Fr. Guiana	CB4
Fr. Guinea	CB4
Fr. India	CB3
Fr. Polynesia	CB4
Fr. Sudan	CB4
Guadeloupe	CB3
Indo-China	CB5
Inini	CB4
Ivory Coast	CB4
Kwangchowan	CB4
Malagasy	CB4
Martinique	CB3
Mauritania	CB4
New Caledonia	CB4
Niger	CB4
Reunion	CB4
St. Pierre & Miquelon	CB3
Senegal	CB5
Somali Coast	CB3
Togo	CB3
Wallis & Futuna	CB3

No. CB3 (1)	1.10	
No. CB4 (1)	.80	5.50
No. CB5 (1)	.80	
No. CB4 (1)	1.10	
No. CB4 (1)	.40	5.50
No. CB3 (1)	.90	
No. CB4 (1)	2.00	
No. CB4 (1)	.40	5.50
No. CB3 (1)	1.10	
No. CB5 (1)	2.00	
No. CB3 (1)	1.25	
No. CB4 (1)	1.00	5.50
No. CB4 (1)	1.00	
No. CB5 (1)	.65	
No. CB3 (1)	1.00	
No. CB4 (1)	.80	
No. CB4 (1)	2.25	
No. CB4 (1)	.35	
No. CB4 (1)	.90	
No. CB3 (1)	7.00	
No. CB5 (1)	.80	6.50
No. CB3 (1)	.70	
No. CB3 (1)	.35	
No. CB3 (1)	2.00	
Set total (24) Stamps	30.65	28.50

Cross of Lorraine & Four-motor Plane — CD87

1941-5

Cameroun	C1-C7
Fr. Equatorial Africa	C17-C23
Fr. Guiana	C9-C10
Fr. India	C1-C6
Fr. Polynesia	C3-C9
Fr. West Africa	C1-C3
Guadeloupe	C1-C2
Madagascar	C37-C43
Martinique	C1-C2
New Caledonia	C7-C13
Reunion	C18-C24
St. Pierre & Miquelon	C1-C7
Somali Coast	C1-C7

Nos. C1-C7 (7)	6.30	6.30
Nos. C17-C23 (7)	10.40	6.35
Nos. C9-C10 (2)	3.80	3.10
Nos. C1-C6 (6)	9.30	15.00
Nos. C3-C9 (7)	13.75	10.00
Nos. C1-C3 (3)	9.50	3.90
Nos. C1-C2 (2)	3.75	2.50
Nos. C37-C43 (7)	5.60	3.80
Nos. C1-C2 (2)	3.00	1.60
Nos. C7-C13 (7)	8.85	7.30
Nos. C18-C24 (7)	7.05	5.00
Nos. C1-C7 (7)	11.60	9.40
Nos. C1-C7 (7)	13.95	11.10
Set total (71) Stamps	106.85	85.35

Somali Coast stamps are inscribed "Djibouti".

Transport Plane — CD88

Caravan and Plane — CD89

1942

Dahomey	C6-C13
Fr. Guinea	C6-C13
Fr. Sudan	C6-C13
Ivory Coast	C6-C13
Mauritania	C6-C13
Niger	C6-C13
Senegal	C17-C25
Togo	C6-C13

Nos. C6-C13 (8)	7.15	
Nos. C6-C13 (8)	5.75	
Nos. C6-C13 (8)	8.00	
Nos. C6-C13 (8)	11.15	
Nos. C6-C13 (8)	9.75	
Nos. C6-C13 (8)	6.20	
Nos. C17-C25 (9)	9.45	
Nos. C6-C13 (8)	6.75	
Set total (65) Stamps	64.20	

Red Cross

Marianne CD90

The surtax was for the French Red Cross and national relief.

1944

Cameroun	B28
Fr. Equatorial Africa	B38
Fr. Guiana	B12
Fr. India	B14
Fr. Polynesia	B13
Fr. West Africa	B1
Guadeloupe	B12
Madagascar	B15
Martinique	B11
New Caledonia	B13
Reunion	B15
St. Pierre & Miquelon	B13
Somali Coast	B13
Wallis & Futuna Isls.	B9

No. B28 (1)	2.00	1.60
No. B38 (1)	1.60	1.20
No. B12 (1)	1.75	1.25
No. B14 (1)	1.50	1.25
No. B13 (1)	2.00	1.60
No. B1 (1)	6.50	4.75
No. B12 (1)	1.40	1.00
No. B15 (1)	.90	.90
No. B11 (1)	1.20	1.20
No. B13 (1)	1.50	1.50
No. B15 (1)	1.60	1.10
No. B13 (1)	2.60	2.60
No. B13 (1)	1.75	2.00
No. B9 (1)	3.00	3.00
Set total (14) Stamps	29.30	24.95

Eboue

CD91

Felix Eboue, first French colonial administrator to proclaim resistance to Germany after French surrender in World War II.

1945

Cameroun	296-297
Fr. Equatorial Africa	156-157
Fr. Guiana	171-172
Fr. India	210-211
Fr. Polynesia	150-151
Fr. West Africa	15-16
Guadeloupe	187-188
Madagascar	259-260
Martinique	196-197
New Caledonia	274-275
Reunion	238-239
St. Pierre & Miquelon	322-323
Somali Coast	238-239

Nos. 296-297 (2)	2.40	1.95
Nos. 156-157 (2)	2.55	2.00
Nos. 171-172 (2)	2.45	2.00
Nos. 210-211 (2)	2.20	1.95
Nos. 150-151 (2)	3.60	2.85
Nos. 15-16 (2)	2.40	2.40
Nos. 187-188 (2)	2.05	1.60
Nos. 259-260 (2)	2.00	1.45
Nos. 196-197 (2)	2.05	1.55
Nos. 274-275 (2)	3.40	3.00
Nos. 238-239 (2)	2.40	2.00
Nos. 322-323 (2)	4.40	3.45
Nos. 238-239 (2)	2.45	2.10
Set total (26) Stamps	34.35	28.30

Victory

Victory CD92

European victory of the Allied Nations in World War II.

1946, May 8

Cameroun	C8
Fr. Equatorial Africa	C24
Fr. Guiana	C11
Fr. India	C7

COMMON DESIGN TYPES

9A

Fr. Polynesia	C10
Fr. West Africa	C4
Guadeloupe	C3
Indo-China	C19
Madagascar	C44
Martinique	C3
New Caledonia	C14
Reunion	C25
St. Pierre & Miquelon	C8
Somali Coast	C8
Wallis & Futuna Isls.	C1

No. C8 (1)	1.60	1.20
No. C24 (1)	1.60	1.25
No. C11 (1)	1.75	1.25
No. C7 (1)	1.00	4.00
No. C10 (1)	2.75	2.00
No. C4 (1)	1.60	1.20
No. C3 (1)	1.25	1.00
No. C19 (1)	1.00	.55
No. C44 (1)	1.00	.35
No. C3 (1)	1.30	1.00
No. C14 (1)	1.50	1.25
No. C25 (1)	1.10	.90
No. C8 (1)	2.10	2.10
No. C8 (1)	1.75	1.40
No. C1 (1)	2.25	1.90
Set total (15) Stamps	23.55	21.35

Chad to Rhine

Leclerc's Departure from Chad — CD93

Battle at Cufra Oasis — CD94

Tanks in Action, Mareth — CD95

Normandy Invasion — CD96

Entering Paris — CD97

Liberation of Strasbourg — CD98

"Chad to the Rhine" march, 1942-44, by Gen. Jacques Leclerc's column, later French 2nd Armored Division.

1946, June 6

Cameroun	C9-C14
Fr. Equatorial Africa	C25-C30
Fr. Guiana	C12-C17
Fr. India	C8-C13
Fr. Polynesia	C11-C16
Fr. West Africa	C5-C10
Guadeloupe	C4-C9
Indo-China	C20-C25
Madagascar	C45-C50
Martinique	C4-C9
New Caledonia	C15-C20
Reunion	C26-C31
St. Pierre & Miquelon	C9-C14
Somali Coast	C9-C14
Wallis & Futuna Isls.	C2-C7

Nos. C9-C14 (6)	12.05	9.70
Nos. C25-C30 (6)	14.70	10.80
Nos. C12-C17 (6)	12.65	10.35
Nos. C8-C13 (6)	12.80	15.00
Nos. C11-C16 (6)	17.55	13.40
Nos. C5-C10 (6)	16.05	11.95
Nos. C4-C9 (6)	12.00	9.60
Nos. C20-C25 (6)	6.40	6.40
Nos. C45-C50 (6)	10.30	8.40
Nos. C4-C9 (6)	8.85	7.30
Nos. C15-C20 (6)	13.40	11.90
Nos. C26-C31 (6)	10.25	6.55
Nos. C9-C14 (6)	17.30	14.35
Nos. C9-C14 (6)	18.10	12.65
Nos. C2-C7 (6)	13.75	10.45
Set total (90) Stamps	196.15	158.80

UPU

French Colonials, Globe and Plane — CD99

Universal Postal Union, 75th anniv.

1949, July 4

Cameroun	C29
Fr. Equatorial Africa	C34
Fr. India	C17
Fr. Polynesia	C20
Fr. West Africa	C15
Indo-China	C26
Madagascar	C55
New Caledonia	C24
St. Pierre & Miquelon	C18
Somali Coast	C18
Togo	C18
Wallis & Futuna Isls.	C10

No. C29 (1)	8.00	4.75
No. C34 (1)	16.00	12.00
No. C17 (1)	11.50	8.75
No. C20 (1)	20.00	15.00
No. C15 (1)	12.00	8.75
No. C26 (1)	4.75	4.00
No. C55 (1)	4.00	2.75
No. C24 (1)	7.50	5.00
No. C18 (1)	20.00	12.00
No. C18 (1)	14.00	10.50
No. C18 (1)	8.50	7.00
No. C10 (1)	11.00	8.25
Set total (12) Stamps	137.25	98.75

Tropical Medicine

Doctor Treating Infant — CD100

The surtax was for charitable work.

1950

Cameroun	B29
Fr. Equatorial Africa	B39
Fr. India	B15
Fr. Polynesia	B14
Fr. West Africa	B3
Madagascar	B17
New Caledonia	B14
St. Pierre & Miquelon	B14
Somali Coast	B14
Togo	B11

No. B29 (1)	7.25	5.50
No. B39 (1)	7.25	5.50
No. B15 (1)	6.00	4.00
No. B14 (1)	10.50	8.00
No. B3 (1)	9.50	7.25
No. B17 (1)	5.50	5.50
No. B14 (1)	6.75	5.25
No. B14 (1)	16.00	15.00
No. B14 (1)	7.75	6.25
No. B11 (1)	5.00	3.50
Set total (10) Stamps	81.50	65.75

Military Medal

Medal, Early Marine and Colonial Soldier — CD101

Centenary of the creation of the French Military Medal.

1952

Cameroun	322
Comoro Isls.	39
Fr. Equatorial Africa	186
Fr. India	233
Fr. Polynesia	179
Fr. West Africa	57
Madagascar	286
New Caledonia	295
St. Pierre & Miquelon	345
Somali Coast	267
Togo	327
Wallis & Futuna Isls.	149

No. 322 (1)	7.25	3.25
No. 39 (1)	45.00	37.50
No. 186 (1)	8.00	5.50
No. 233 (1)	5.50	7.00
No. 179 (1)	13.50	10.00
No. 57 (1)	8.75	6.50
No. 286 (1)	3.75	2.50
No. 295 (1)	6.50	6.00
No. 345 (1)	16.00	15.00
No. 267 (1)	9.00	8.00
No. 327 (1)	5.50	4.75
No. 149 (1)	7.25	7.25
Set total (12) Stamps	136.00	113.25

Liberation

Allied Landing, Victory Sign and Cross of Lorraine — CD102

Liberation of France, 10th anniv.

1954, June 6

Cameroun	C32
Comoro Isls.	C4
Fr. Equatorial Africa	C38
Fr. India	C18
Fr. Polynesia	C22
Fr. West Africa	C17
Madagascar	C57
New Caledonia	C25
St. Pierre & Miquelon	C19
Somali Coast	C19
Togo	C19
Wallis & Futuna Isls.	C11

No. C32 (1)	7.25	4.75
No. C4 (1)	32.50	19.00
No. C38 (1)	12.00	8.00
No. C18 (1)	11.00	8.00
No. C22 (1)	10.00	8.00
No. C17 (1)	12.00	5.50
No. C57 (1)	3.25	2.00
No. C25 (1)	7.50	5.00
No. C19 (1)	19.00	12.00
No. C19 (1)	10.50	8.50
No. C19 (1)	7.00	5.50
No. C11 (1)	11.00	8.25
Set total (12) Stamps	143.00	94.50

FIDES

Plowmen — CD103

Efforts of FIDES, the Economic and Social Development Fund for Overseas Possessions (Fonds d' Investissement pour le Developpement Economique et Social). Each stamp has a different design.

1956

Cameroun	326-329
Comoro Isls.	43
Fr. Equatorial Africa	189-192
Fr. Polynesia	181
Fr. West Africa	65-72
Madagascar	292-295
New Caledonia	303
St. Pierre & Miquelon	350
Somali Coast	268-269
Togo	331

Nos. 326-329 (4)	6.90	3.20
No. 43 (1)	2.25	1.60
Nos. 189-192 (4)	3.20	1.65
No. 181 (1)	4.00	2.00
Nos. 65-72 (8)	16.00	6.35
Nos. 292-295 (4)	2.25	1.20
No. 303 (1)	1.90	1.10
No. 350 (1)	6.00	4.00
Nos. 268-269 (2)	5.35	3.15
No. 331 (1)	4.25	2.10
Set total (27) Stamps	52.10	26.35

Flower

CD104

Each stamp shows a different flower.

1958-9

Cameroun	333
Comoro Isls.	45
Fr. Equatorial Africa	200-201
Fr. Polynesia	192
Fr. So. & Antarctic Terr.	11
Fr. West Africa	79-83
Madagascar	301-302
New Caledonia	304-305
St. Pierre & Miquelon	357
Somali Coast	270
Togo	348-349
Wallis & Futuna Isls.	152

No. 333 (1)	1.60	.80
No. 45 (1)	5.25	4.25
Nos. 200-201 (2)	3.60	1.60
No. 192 (1)	6.50	4.00
No. 11 (1)	8.75	7.50
Nos. 79-83 (5)	10.45	5.60
Nos. 301-302 (2)	1.60	.60
Nos. 304-305 (2)	8.00	3.00
No. 357 (1)	4.50	2.25
No. 270 (1)	4.25	1.40
Nos. 348-349 (2)	1.10	.50
No. 152 (1)	3.25	3.25
Set total (20) Stamps	58.85	34.75

Human Rights

Sun, Dove and U.N. Emblem — CD105

10th anniversary of the signing of the Universal Declaration of Human Rights.

1958

Comoro Isls.	44
Fr. Equatorial Africa	202
Fr. Polynesia	191
Fr. West Africa	85
Madagascar	300
New Caledonia	306
St. Pierre & Miquelon	356
Somali Coast	274
Wallis & Futuna Isls.	153

No. 44 (1)	9.00	9.00
No. 202 (1)	2.40	1.25
No. 191 (1)	13.00	8.75
No. 85 (1)	2.40	2.00
No. 300 (1)	.80	.40
No. 306 (1)	2.00	1.50
No. 356 (1)	3.50	2.50
No. 274 (1)	3.50	2.10
No. 153 (1)	4.50	4.50
Set total (9) Stamps	41.10	32.00

C.C.T.A.

CD106

Commission for Technical Cooperation in Africa south of the Sahara, 10th anniv.

1960

Cameroun	339
Cent. Africa	3
Chad	66
Congo, P.R.	90
Dahomey	138
Gabon	150
Ivory Coast	180
Madagascar	317
Mali	9
Mauritania	117
Niger	104
Upper Volta	89

No. 339 (1)	1.60	.75
No. 3 (1)	1.60	.75
No. 66 (1)	1.75	.50
No. 90 (1)	1.00	1.00
No. 138 (1)	.50	.25
No. 150 (1)	1.25	1.10
No. 180 (1)	1.10	.50
No. 317 (1)	.60	.30
No. 9 (1)	1.20	.50
No. 117 (1)	.75	.40
No. 104 (1)	.85	.45
No. 89 (1)	.65	.40
Set total (12) Stamps	12.85	6.90

COMMON DESIGN TYPES

Air Afrique, 1961

Modern and Ancient Africa, Map and Planes — CD107

Founding of Air Afrique (African Airlines).

1961-62

Cameroun	C37
Cent. Africa	C5
Chad	C7
Congo, P.R.	C5
Dahomey	C17
Gabon	C5
Ivory Coast	C18
Mauritania	C17
Niger	C22
Senegal	C31
Upper Volta	C4

No. C37 (1)	1.00	.50
No. C5 (1)	1.00	.65
No. C7 (1)	1.00	.25
No. C5 (1)	1.75	.90
No. C17 (1)	.80	.40
No. C5 (1)	11.00	6.00
No. C18 (1)	2.00	1.25
No. C17 (1)	2.40	1.25
No. C22 (1)	1.75	.90
No. C31 (1)	.80	.30
No. C4 (1)	3.50	1.75
Set total (11) Stamps	27.00	14.15

Anti-Malaria

CD108

World Health Organization drive to eradicate malaria.

1962, Apr. 7

Cameroun	B36
Cent. Africa	B1
Chad	B1
Comoro Isls.	B1
Congo, P.R.	B3
Dahomey	B15
Gabon	B4
Ivory Coast	B15
Madagascar	B19
Mali	B1
Mauritania	B16
Niger	B14
Senegal	B16
Somali Coast	B15
Upper Volta	B1

No. B36 (1)	1.00	.45
No. B1 (1)	1.40	1.40
No. B1 (1)	1.00	1.00
No. B1 (1)	3.50	3.50
No. B3 (1)	1.40	1.00
No. B15 (1)	.75	.75
No. B4 (1)	1.00	1.00
No. B15 (1)	1.25	1.25
No. B19 (1)	.75	.50
No. B1 (1)	1.25	.60
No. B16 (1)	.50	.50
No. B14 (1)	.75	.75
No. B16 (1)	1.10	.65
No. B15 (1)	7.00	7.00
No. B1 (1)	.75	.70
Set total (15) Stamps	23.40	20.55

Abidjan Games

CD109

Abidjan Games, Ivory Coast, Dec. 24-31, 1961. Each stamp shows a different sport.

1962

Cent. Africa	19-20, C6
Chad	83-84, C8
Congo, P.R.	103-104, C7
Gabon	163-164, C6
Niger	109-111
Upper Volta	103-105

Nos. 19-20,C6 (3)	4.15	2.85
Nos. 83-84,C8 (3)	5.80	1.55
Nos. 103-104,C7 (3)	3.85	1.80
Nos. 163-164,C6 (3)	5.00	3.00
Nos. 109-111 (3)	2.60	1.25
Nos. 103-105 (3)	2.80	1.75
Set total (18) Stamps	24.20	12.20

African and Malagasy Union

Flag of Union — CD110

First anniversary of the Union.

1962, Sept. 8

Cameroun	373
Cent. Africa	21
Chad	85
Congo, P.R.	105
Dahomey	155
Gabon	165
Ivory Coast	198
Madagascar	332
Mauritania	170
Niger	112
Senegal	211
Upper Volta	106

No. 373 (1)	2.00	.75
No. 21 (1)	1.25	.75
No. 85 (1)	1.25	.25
No. 105 (1)	1.50	.50
No. 155 (1)	1.25	.90
No. 165 (1)	1.60	1.25
No. 198 (1)	2.10	.75
No. 332 (1)	.80	.50
No. 170 (1)	.75	.50
No. 112 (1)	.80	.50
No. 211 (1)	.80	.50
No. 106 (1)	1.10	.75
Set total (12) Stamps	15.20	8.20

Telstar

Telstar and Globe Showing Andover and Pleumeur-Bodou — CD111

First television connection of the United States and Europe through the Telstar satellite, July 11-12, 1962.

1962-63

Andorra, French	154
Comoro Isls.	C7
Fr. Polynesia	C29
Fr. So. & Antarctic Terr.	C5
New Caledonia	C33
St. Pierre & Miquelon	C26
Somali Coast	C31
Wallis & Futuna Isls.	C17

No. 154 (1)	2.00	1.60
No. C7 (1)	4.50	2.75
No. C29 (1)	11.50	8.00
No. C5 (1)	29.00	21.00
No. C33 (1)	25.00	18.50
No. C26 (1)	7.25	4.50
No. C31 (1)	1.00	1.00
No. C17 (1)	3.75	3.75
Set total (8) Stamps	84.00	61.10

Freedom From Hunger

World Map and Wheat Emblem — CD112

U.N. Food and Agriculture Organization's "Freedom from Hunger" campaign.

1963, Mar. 21

Cameroun	B37-B38
Cent. Africa	B2
Chad	B2
Congo, P.R.	B4
Dahomey	B16
Gabon	B5
Ivory Coast	B16
Madagascar	B21
Mauritania	B17
Niger	B15
Senegal	B17
Upper Volta	B2

Nos. B37-B38 (2)	2.25	.75
No. B2 (1)	1.25	1.25
No. B2 (1)	1.10	.50
No. B4 (1)	1.40	1.00
No. B16 (1)	.80	.80
No. B5 (1)	1.00	1.00
No. B16 (1)	1.50	1.50
No. B21 (1)	.60	.45
No. B17 (1)	.60	.60
No. B15 (1)	.75	.75
No. B17 (1)	.80	.50
No. B2 (1)	.75	.70
Set total (13) Stamps	12.80	9.80

Red Cross Centenary

CD113

Centenary of the International Red Cross.

1963, Sept. 2

Comoro Isls.	55
Fr. Polynesia	205
New Caledonia	328
St. Pierre & Miquelon	367
Somali Coast	297
Wallis & Futuna Isls.	165

No. 55 (1)	7.50	6.00
No. 205 (1)	15.00	12.00
No. 328 (1)	8.00	6.75
No. 367 (1)	12.00	5.50
No. 297 (1)	6.25	6.25
No. 165 (1)	4.00	4.00
Set total (6) Stamps	52.75	40.50

African Postal Union, 1963

UAMPT Emblem, Radio Masts, Plane and Mail — CD114

Establishment of the African and Malagasy Posts and Telecommunications Union.

1963, Sept. 8

Cameroun	C47
Cent. Africa	C10
Chad	C9
Congo, P.R.	C13
Dahomey	C19
Gabon	C13
Ivory Coast	C25
Madagascar	C75
Mauritania	C22
Niger	C27
Rwanda	36
Senegal	C32
Upper Volta	C9

No. C47 (1)	2.25	1.00
No. C10 (1)	1.90	.90
No. C9 (1)	1.80	.60
No. C13 (1)	1.40	.75
No. C19 (1)	.75	.25
No. C13 (1)	1.90	.90
No. C25 (1)	2.50	1.50
No. C75 (1)	1.25	.80
No. C22 (1)	1.50	.60
No. C27 (1)	1.25	.60
No. 36 (1)	1.10	.75
No. C32 (1)	1.75	.50
No. C9 (1)	1.50	.75
Set total (13) Stamps	20.85	9.80

Air Afrique, 1963

Symbols of Flight CD115

First anniversary of Air Afrique and inauguration of DC-8 service.

1963, Nov. 19

Cameroun	C48
Chad	C10
Congo, P.R.	C14
Gabon	C18
Ivory Coast	C26
Mauritania	C26
Niger	C35
Senegal	C33

No. C48 (1)	1.25	.40
No. C10 (1)	1.80	.60
No. C14 (1)	1.60	.60
No. C18 (1)	1.25	.65
No. C26 (1)	1.00	.50
No. C26 (1)	.70	.25
No. C35 (1)	1.00	.55
No. C33 (1)	2.00	.65
Set total (8) Stamps	10.60	4.20

Europafrica

Europe and Africa Linked — CD116

Signing of an economic agreement between the European Economic Community and the African and Malagasy Union, Yaounde, Cameroun, July 20, 1963.

1963-64

Cameroun	402
Cent. Africa	C12
Chad	C11
Congo, P.R.	C16
Gabon	C19
Ivory Coast	217
Niger	C43
Upper Volta	C11

No. 402 (1)	2.25	.60
No. C12 (1)	2.50	1.75
No. C11 (1)	1.60	.50
No. C16 (1)	1.60	1.00
No. C19 (1)	1.25	.75
No. 217 (1)	1.10	.35
No. C43 (1)	.85	.50
No. C11 (1)	1.50	.80
Set total (8) Stamps	12.65	6.25

Human Rights

Scales of Justice and Globe — CD117

15th anniversary of the Universal Declaration of Human Rights.

1963, Dec. 10

Comoro Isls.	56
Fr. Polynesia	206
New Caledonia	329
St. Pierre & Miquelon	368
Somali Coast	300
Wallis & Futuna Isls.	166

No. 56 (1)	7.50	6.00
No. 205 (1)	15.00	12.00
No. 329 (1)	7.00	6.00
No. 368 (1)	7.00	3.50
No. 300 (1)	8.50	8.50
No. 166 (1)	7.00	7.00
Set total (6) Stamps	52.00	43.00

PHILATEC

Stamp Album, Champs Elysees Palace and Horses of Marly — CD118

Intl. Philatelic and Postal Techniques Exhibition, Paris, June 5-21, 1964.

1963-64

Comoro Isls.	60
France	1078
Fr. Polynesia	207
New Caledonia	341
St. Pierre & Miquelon	369
Somali Coast	301
Wallis & Futuna Isls.	167

No. 60 (1)	4.00	3.50
No. 1078 (1)	.25	.25
No. 206 (1)	15.00	10.00

COMMON DESIGN TYPES

No. 341 (1)	6.50	6.50
No. 369 (1)	11.00	8.00
No. 301 (1)	7.75	7.75
No. 167 (1)	3.00	3.00
Set total (7) Stamps	47.50	39.00

Cooperation

CD119

Cooperation between France and the French-speaking countries of Africa and Madagascar.

1964

Cameroun	409-410
Cent. Africa	39
Chad	103
Congo, P.R.	121
Dahomey	193
France	1111
Gabon	175
Ivory Coast	221
Madagascar	360
Mauritania	181
Niger	143
Senegal	236
Togo	495

Nos. 409-410 (2)	2.50	.50
No. 39 (1)	.90	.50
No. 103 (1)	1.00	.25
No. 121 (1)	.90	.35
No. 193 (1)	.80	.35
No. 1111 (1)	.25	.25
No. 175 (1)	.90	.60
No. 221 (1)	1.10	.35
No. 360 (1)	.60	.25
No. 181 (1)	.60	.35
No. 143 (1)	.80	.40
No. 236 (1)	1.60	.85
No. 495 (1)	.70	.25
Set total (14) Stamps	12.65	5.25

ITU

Telegraph, Syncom Satellite and ITU Emblem — CD120

Intl. Telecommunication Union, Cent.

1965, May 17

Comoro Isls.	C14
Fr. Polynesia	C33
Fr. So. & Antarctic Terr.	C8
New Caledonia	C40
New Hebrides	124-125
St. Pierre & Miquelon	C29
Somali Coast	C36
Wallis & Futuna Isls.	C20

No. C14 (1)	18.00	9.00
No. C33 (1)	80.00	52.50
No. C8 (1)	200.00	160.00
No. C40 (1)	10.00	8.00
Nos. 124-125 (2)	32.25	27.25
No. C29 (1)	24.00	11.50
No. C36 (1)	15.00	9.00
No. C20 (1)	16.00	16.00
Set total (9) Stamps	395.25	293.25

French Satellite A-1

Diamant Rocket and Launching Installation CD121

Launching of France's first satellite, Nov. 26, 1965.

1965-66

Comoro Isls.	C16a
France	1138a
Reunion	359a
Fr. Polynesia	C41a
Fr. So. & Antarctic Terr.	C10a
New Caledonia	C45a
St. Pierre & Miquelon	C31a
Somali Coast	C40a
Wallis & Futuna Isls.	C23a

No. C16a (1)	9.00	9.00
No. 1138a (1)	.65	.65
No. 359a (1)	3.50	3.00
No. C41a (1)	14.00	14.00
No. C10a (1)	29.00	24.00
No. C45a (1)	7.00	7.00
No. C31a (1)	14.50	14.50
No. C40a (1)	7.00	7.00
No. C23a (1)	8.50	8.50
Set total (9) Stamps	93.15	87.65

French Satellite D-1

D-1 Satellite in Orbit CD122

Launching of the D-1 satellite at Hammaguir, Algeria, Feb. 17, 1966.

1966

Comoro Isls.	C17
France	1148
Fr. Polynesia	C42
Fr. So. & Antarctic Terr.	C11
New Caledonia	C46
St. Pierre & Miquelon	C32
Somali Coast	C49
Wallis & Futuna Isls.	C24

No. C17 (1)	4.00	4.00
No. 1140 (1)	.25	.25
No. C42 (1)	7.00	4.75
No. C11 (1)	57.50	40.00
No. C46 (1)	2.25	2.00
No. C32 (1)	9.00	6.00
No. C49 (1)	4.25	2.75
No. C24 (1)	3.50	3.50
Set total (8) Stamps	87.75	63.25

Air Afrique, 1966

Planes and Air Afrique Emblem CD123

Introduction of DC-8F planes by Air Afrique.

1966

Cameroun	C79
Cent. Africa	C35
Chad	C26
Congo, P.R.	C42
Dahomey	C42
Gabon	C47
Ivory Coast	C32
Mauritania	C57
Niger	C63
Senegal	C47
Togo	C54
Upper Volta	C31

No. C79 (1)	.80	.25
No. C35 (1)	1.00	.50
No. C26 (1)	.85	.25
No. C42 (1)	1.00	.25
No. C42 (1)	.75	.25
No. C47 (1)	.90	.35
No. C32 (1)	1.00	.60
No. C57 (1)	.60	.30
No. C63 (1)	.70	.35
No. C47 (1)	.80	.30
No. C54 (1)	.80	.25
No. C31 (1)	.75	.50
Set total (12) Stamps	9.95	4.15

African Postal Union, 1967

Telecommunications Symbols and Map of Africa — CD124

Fifth anniversary of the establishment of the African and Malagasy Union of Posts and Telecommunications, UAMPT.

1967

Cameroun	C90
Cent. Africa	C46
Chad	C37
Congo, P.R.	C57
Dahomey	C61
Gabon	C58
Ivory Coast	C34
Madagascar	C85
Mauritania	C65
Niger	C75
Rwanda	C1-C3
Senegal	C60
Togo	C81
Upper Volta	C50

No. C90 (1)	2.40	.65
No. C46 (1)	2.25	.85
No. C37 (1)	2.00	.60
No. C57 (1)	1.60	.60
No. C61 (1)	1.75	.95
No. C58 (1)	2.00	.85
No. C34 (1)	3.50	1.50
No. C85 (1)	1.25	.60
No. C65 (1)	1.25	.60
No. C75 (1)	1.40	.60
Nos. C1-C3 (3)	2.05	1.25
No. C60 (1)	1.75	.50
No. C81 (1)	1.90	.30
No. C50 (1)	1.80	.70
Set total (16) Stamps	26.90	10.55

Monetary Union

Gold Token of the Ashantis, 17-18th Centuries — CD125

West African Monetary Union, 5th anniv.

1967, Nov. 4

Dahomey	244
Ivory Coast	259
Mauritania	238
Niger	204
Senegal	294
Togo	623
Upper Volta	181

No. 244 (1)	.65	.65
No. 259 (1)	.85	.40
No. 238 (1)	.45	.25
No. 204 (1)	.55	.25
No. 294 (1)	.60	.25
No. 623 (1)	.60	.25
No. 181 (1)	.65	.35
Set total (7) Stamps	4.35	2.40

WHO Anniversary

Sun, Flowers and WHO Emblem CD126

World Health Organization, 20th anniv.

1968, May 4

Afars & Issas	317
Comoro Isls.	73
Fr. Polynesia	241-242
Fr. So. & Antarctic Terr.	31
New Caledonia	367
St. Pierre & Miquelon	377
Wallis & Futuna Isls.	169

No. 317 (1)	3.00	3.00
No. 73 (1)	2.40	1.75
Nos. 241-242 (2)	22.00	12.75
No. 31 (1)	62.50	47.50
No. 367 (1)	4.00	2.25
No. 377 (1)	12.00	9.00
No. 169 (1)	5.75	5.75
Set total (8) Stamps	111.65	82.00

Human Rights Year

Human Rights Flame — CD127

1968, Aug. 10

Afars & Issas	322-323

Comoro Isls.	76
Fr. Polynesia	243-244
Fr. So. & Antarctic Terr.	32
New Caledonia	369
St. Pierre & Miquelon	382
Wallis & Futuna Isls.	170

Nos. 322-323 (2)	6.75	4.00
No. 76 (1)	3.25	3.25
Nos. 243-244 (2)	24.00	14.00
No. 32 (1)	55.00	47.50
No. 369 (1)	2.75	1.50
No. 382 (1)	8.00	5.50
No. 170 (1)	3.25	3.25
Set total (9) Stamps	103.00	79.00

2nd PHILEXAFRIQUE

CD128

Opening of PHILEXAFRIQUE, Abidjan, Feb. 14. Each stamp shows a local scene and stamp.

1969, Feb. 14

Cameroun	C118
Cent. Africa	C65
Chad	C48
Congo, P.R.	C77
Dahomey	C94
Gabon	C82
Ivory Coast	C38-C40
Madagascar	C92
Mali	C65
Mauritania	C80
Niger	C104
Senegal	C68
Togo	C104
Upper Volta	C62

No. C118 (1)	3.25	1.25
No. C65 (1)	1.75	1.75
No. C48 (1)	2.40	1.00
No. C77 (1)	2.00	1.75
No. C94 (1)	2.25	2.25
No. C82 (1)	2.00	2.00
Nos. C38-C40 (3)	14.50	14.50
No. C92 (1)	1.75	.85
No. C65 (1)	1.75	1.00
No. C80 (1)	1.90	.75
No. C104 (1)	3.00	1.90
No. C68 (1)	2.00	1.40
No. C104 (1)	2.25	.45
No. C62 (1)	4.00	3.25
Set total (16) Stamps	44.80	34.10

Concorde

Concorde in Flight — CD129

First flight of the prototype Concorde supersonic plane at Toulouse, Mar. 1, 1969.

1969

Afars & Issas	C56
Comoro Isls.	C29
France	C42
Fr. Polynesia	C50
Fr. So. & Antarctic Terr.	C18
New Caledonia	C63
St. Pierre & Miquelon	C40
Wallis & Futuna Isls.	C30

No. C56 (1)	26.00	16.00
No. C29 (1)	18.00	12.00
No. C42 (1)	.75	.35
No. C50 (1)	55.00	35.00
No. C18 (1)	55.00	37.50
No. C63 (1)	27.50	20.00
No. C40 (1)	32.50	11.00
No. C30 (1)	15.00	10.00
Set total (8) Stamps	229.75	141.85

Development Bank

Bank Emblem — CD130

African Development Bank, fifth anniv.

COMMON DESIGN TYPES

1969

Cameroun	499
Chad	217
Congo, P.R.	181-182
Ivory Coast	281
Mali	127-128
Mauritania	267
Niger	220
Senegal	317-318
Upper Volta	201

No. 499 (1)	.80	.25
No. 217 (1)	.90	.25
Nos. 181-182 (2)	1.00	.50
No. 281 (1)	.70	.40
Nos. 127-128 (2)	1.00	.50
No. 267 (1)	.60	.25
No. 220 (1)	.70	.30
Nos. 317-318 (2)	1.55	.50
No. 201 (1)	.65	.30
Set total (12) Stamps	7.90	3.25

ILO

ILO Headquarters, Geneva, and Emblem — CD131

Intl. Labor Organization, 50th anniv.

1969-70

Afars & Issas	337
Comoro Isls.	83
Fr. Polynesia	251-252
Fr. So. & Antarctic Terr.	35
New Caledonia	379
St. Pierre & Miquelon	396
Wallis & Futuna Isls.	172

No. 337 (1)	2.75	2.00
No. 83 (1)	1.25	.75
Nos. 251-252 (2)	24.00	12.50
No. 35 (1)	15.00	10.00
No. 379 (1)	2.25	1.10
No. 396 (1)	10.00	5.50
No. 172 (1)	2.75	2.75
Set total (8) Stamps	58.00	34.60

ASECNA

Map of Africa, Plane and Airport — CD132

10th anniversary of the Agency for the Security of Aerial Navigation in Africa and Madagascar (ASECNA, Agence pour la Securite de la Navigation Aerienne en Afrique et a Madagascar).

1969-70

Cameroun	500
Cent. Africa	119
Chad	222
Congo, P.R.	197
Dahomey	269
Gabon	260
Ivory Coast	287
Mali	130
Niger	221
Senegal	321
Upper Volta	204

No. 500 (1)	2.00	.60
No. 119 (1)	2.00	.80
No. 222 (1)	1.00	.25
No. 197 (1)	2.00	.40
No. 269 (1)	.90	.55
No. 260 (1)	1.75	.75
No. 287 (1)	.90	.40
No. 130 (1)	.90	.40
No. 221 (1)	1.40	.70
No. 321 (1)	1.60	.50
No. 204 (1)	1.75	1.00
Set total (11) Stamps	16.20	6.35

U.P.U. Headquarters

CD133

New Universal Postal Union headquarters, Bern, Switzerland.

1970

Afars & Issas	342
Algeria	443
Cameroun	503-504
Cent. Africa	125
Chad	225
Comoro Isls.	84
Congo, P.R.	216
Fr. Polynesia	261-262
Fr. So. & Antarctic Terr.	36
Gabon	258
Ivory Coast	295
Madagascar	444
Mali	134-135
Mauritania	283
New Caledonia	382
Niger	231-232
St. Pierre & Miquelon	397-398
Senegal	328-329
Tunisia	535
Wallis & Futuna Isls.	173

No. 342 (1)	2.50	1.40
No. 443 (1)	1.10	.40
Nos. 503-504 (2)	2.60	.55
No. 125 (1)	1.75	.70
No. 225 (1)	1.20	.25
No. 84 (1)	5.50	2.00
No. 216 (1)	1.00	.25
Nos. 261-262 (2)	20.00	10.00
No. 36 (1)	40.00	27.50
No. 258 (1)	.90	.55
No. 295 (1)	1.10	.50
No. 444 (1)	.55	.25
Nos. 134-135 (2)	1.05	.50
No. 283 (1)	.60	.30
No. 382 (1)	3.00	1.50
Nos. 231-232 (2)	1.50	.60
Nos. 397-398 (2)	34.00	16.25
Nos. 328-329 (2)	1.55	.55
No. 535 (1)	.60	.25
No. 173 (1)	3.25	3.25
Set total (26) Stamps	123.75	67.55

De Gaulle

CD134

First anniversary of the death of Charles de Gaulle, (1890-1970), President of France.

1971-72

Afars & Issas	356-357
Comoro Isls.	104-105
France	1325a
Fr. Polynesia	270-271
Fr. So. & Antarctic Terr.	52-53
New Caledonia	393-394
Reunion	380a
St. Pierre & Miquelon	417-418
Wallis & Futuna Isls.	177-178

Nos. 356-357 (2)	12.50	7.50
Nos. 104-105 (2)	9.00	5.75
No. 1325a (1)	3.00	2.50
Nos. 270-271 (2)	51.50	29.50
Nos. 52-53 (2)	40.00	29.50
Nos. 393-394 (2)	23.00	11.75
No. 380a (1)	9.25	8.00
Nos. 417-418 (2)	56.50	31.00
Nos. 177-178 (2)	20.00	16.25
Set total (16) Stamps	224.75	141.75

African Postal Union, 1971

UAMPT Building, Brazzaville, Congo — CD135

10th anniversary of the establishment of the African and Malagasy Posts and Telecommunications Union, UAMPT. Each stamp has a different native design.

1971, Nov. 13

Cameroun	C177
Cent. Africa	C89
Chad	C94
Congo, P.R.	C136
Dahomey	C146
Gabon	C120
Ivory Coast	C47
Mauritania	C113
Niger	C164
Rwanda	C8
Senegal	C105
Togo	C166
Upper Volta	C97

No. C177 (1)	2.00	.50
No. C89 (1)	2.25	.85
No. C94 (1)	1.50	.50
No. C136 (1)	1.60	.75
No. C146 (1)	1.75	.80
No. C120 (1)	1.75	.70
No. C47 (1)	2.00	1.00
No. C113 (1)	1.10	.65
No. C164 (1)	1.25	.60
No. C8 (1)	2.75	2.50
No. C105 (1)	1.60	.50
No. C166 (1)	1.25	.40
No. C97 (1)	1.50	.70
Set total (13) Stamps	22.30	10.45

West African Monetary Union

African Couple, City, Village and Commemorative Coin — CD136

West African Monetary Union, 10th anniv.

1972, Nov. 2

Dahomey	300
Ivory Coast	331
Mauritania	299
Niger	258
Senegal	374
Togo	825
Upper Volta	280

No. 300 (1)	.65	.25
No. 331 (1)	1.00	.50
No. 299 (1)	.75	.25
No. 258 (1)	.65	.30
No. 374 (1)	.50	.30
No. 825 (1)	.60	.25
No. 280 (1)	.60	.25
Set total (7) Stamps	4.75	2.10

African Postal Union, 1973

Telecommunications Symbols and Map of Africa — CD137

11th anniversary of the African and Malagasy Posts and Telecommunications Union (UAMPT).

1973, Sept. 12

Cameroun	574
Cent. Africa	194
Chad	294
Congo, P.R.	289
Dahomey	311
Gabon	320
Ivory Coast	361
Madagascar	500
Mauritania	304
Niger	287
Rwanda	540
Senegal	393
Togo	849
Upper Volta	297

No. 574 (1)	1.75	.40
No. 194 (1)	1.25	.75
No. 294 (1)	1.75	.40
No. 289 (1)	1.60	.50
No. 311 (1)	1.25	.55
No. 320 (1)	1.40	.75
No. 361 (1)	2.50	1.00
No. 500 (1)	1.10	.35
No. 304 (1)	1.10	.40
No. 287 (1)	.90	.60
No. 540 (1)	3.00	2.00
No. 393 (1)	1.60	.50
No. 849 (1)	1.00	.35
No. 297 (1)	1.25	.70
Set total (14) Stamps	21.45	9.25

Philexafrique II — Essen

CD138

CD139

Designs: Indigenous fauna, local and German stamps. Types CD138-CD139 printed horizontally and vertically se-tenant in sheets of 10 (2x5). Label between horizontal pairs alternately commemorates Philexafrique II, Libreville, Gabon, June 1978, and 2nd International Stamp Fair, Essen, Germany, Nov. 1-5.

1978-1979

Benin	C286a
Central Africa	C201a
Chad	C239a
Congo Republic	C246a
Djibouti	C122a
Gabon	C216a
Ivory Coast	C65a
Mali	C357a
Mauritania	C186a
Niger	C292a
Rwanda	C13a
Senegal	C147a
Togo	C364a

No. C286a (1)	9.00	8.50
No. C201a (1)	7.50	7.50
No. C239a (1)	7.50	4.00
No. C246a (1)	7.00	7.00
No. C122a (1)	6.50	6.50
No. C216a (1)	6.50	4.00
No. C65a (1)	9.00	9.00
No. C357a (1)	5.00	3.00
No. C186a (1)	5.50	5.00
No. C292a (1)	6.00	6.00
No. C13a (1)	4.00	4.00
No. C147a (1)	10.00	4.00
No. C364a (1)	3.00	1.50
Set total (13) Stamps	86.50	70.00

BRITISH COMMONWEALTH OF NATIONS

The listings follow established trade practices when these issues are offered as units by dealers. The Peace issue, for example, includes only one stamp from the Indian state of Hyderabad. The U.P.U. issue includes the Egypt set. Pairs are included for those varieties issued with bilingual designs se-tenant.

Silver Jubilee

Windsor Castle and King George V — CD301

Reign of King George V, 25th anniv.

1935

Antigua	77-80
Ascension	33-36
Bahamas	92-95
Barbados	186-189
Basutoland	11-14
Bechuanaland Protectorate	117-120
Bermuda	100-103
British Guiana	223-226
British Honduras	108-111
Cayman Islands	81-84
Ceylon	260-263
Cyprus	136-139
Dominica	90-93
Falkland Islands	77-80
Fiji	110-113
Gambia	125-128
Gibraltar	100-103
Gilbert & Ellice Islands	33-36
Gold Coast	108-111
Grenada	124-127
Hong Kong	147-150
Jamaica	109-112
Kenya, Uganda, Tanzania	42-45
Leeward Islands	96-99
Malta	184-187
Mauritius	204-207
Montserrat	85-88
Newfoundland	226-229
Nigeria	34-37
Northern Rhodesia	18-21

COMMON DESIGN TYPES 13A

Nyasaland Protectorate............47-50
St. Helena 111-114
St. Kitts-Nevis 72-75
St. Lucia 91-94
St. Vincent 134-137
Seychelles 118-121
Sierra Leone 166-169
Solomon Islands 60-63
Somaliland Protectorate 77-80
Straits Settlements 213-216
Swaziland 20-23
Trinidad & Tobago 43-46
Turks & Caicos Islands 71-74
Virgin Islands 69-72

The following have different designs but are included in the omnibus set:

Great Britain 226-229
Offices in Morocco (Sp. Curr.) 67-70
Offices in Morocco (Br. Curr.).......226-229
Offices in Morocco (Fr. Curr.) 422-425
Offices in Morocco (Tangier).....508-510
Australia 152-154
Canada 211-216
Cook Islands 98-100
India 142-148
Nauru 31-34
New Guinea 46-47
New Zealand 199-201
Niue 67-69
Papua 114-117
Samoa 163-165
South Africa 68-71
Southern Rhodesia 33-36
South-West Africa 121-124

Nos. 77-80 (4)	20.25	23.25
Nos. 33-36 (4)	58.50	127.50
Nos. 92-95 (4)	25.00	46.00
Nos. 186-189 (4)	30.00	50.30
Nos. 11-14 (4)	11.60	21.25
Nos. 117-120 (4)	15.75	36.00
Nos. 100-103 (4)	16.80	58.50
Nos. 223-226 (4)	22.35	35.50
Nos. 108-111 (1)	15.25	16.35
Nos. 81-84 (4)	21.60	24.50
Nos. 260-263 (4)	10.40	21.60
Nos. 136-139 (4)	39.75	34.40
Nos. 90-93 (4)	18.85	19.85
Nos. 77-80 (4)	55.00	14.75
Nos. 110-113 (4)	20.25	34.00
Nos. 125-128 (4)	13.05	25.25
Nos. 100-103 (4)	28.75	42.75
Nos. 33-36 (4)	36.80	67.00
Nos. 108-111 (4)	25.75	78.10
Nos. 124-127 (4)	16.70	40.60
Nos. 147-150 (4)	73.75	20.75
Nos. 109-112 (4)	24.20	50.50
Nos. 42-45 (4)	10.25	11.75
Nos. 96-99 (4)	35.75	49.60
Nos. 184-187 (4)	22.00	33.70
Nos. 204-207 (4)	44.60	58.25
Nos. 85-88 (4)	10.25	30.25
Nos. 226-229 (4)	17.50	12.05
Nos. 34-37 (4)	17.50	73.00
Nos. 18-21 (4)	17.00	15.00
Nos. 47-50 (4)	43.50	82.50
Nos. 111-114 (4)	31.15	36.70
Nos. 72-75 (4)	11.80	18.65
Nos. 91-94 (4)	16.00	20.80
Nos. 134-137 (4)	9.45	21.25
Nos. 118-121 (4)	15.75	40.00
Nos. 166-169 (4)	23.60	50.35
Nos. 60-63 (4)	29.00	38.00
Nos. 77-80 (4)	17.00	48.25
Nos. 213-216 (4)	15.00	25.10
Nos. 20-23 (4)	6.80	18.25
Nos. 43-46 (4)	18.60	37.50
Nos. 71-74 (1)	0.00	14.50
Nos. 69-72 (4)	25.00	55.25
Nos. 226-229 (4)	5.15	9.90
Nos. 67-70 (4)	13.60	30.70
Nos. 226-229 (4)	16.30	56.00
Nos. 422-425 (4)	9.35	3.95
Nos. 508-510 (3)	26.00	33.50
Nos. 152-154 (3)	49.50	45.35
Nos. 211-216 (6)	23.85	13.35
Nos. 98-100 (3)	9.65	12.00
Nos. 142-148 (7)	28.85	14.00
Nos. 31-34 (4)	12.35	13.15
Nos. 46-47 (2)	4.35	1.70
Nos. 199-201 (3)	23.00	28.50
Nos. 67-69 (3)	19.25	31.00
Nos. 114-117 (4)	9.20	17.50
Nos. 163-165 (3)	4.40	6.50
Nos. 68-71 (4)	57.50	153.00
Nos. 33-36 (4)	27.75	45.25
Nos. 121-124 (4)	13.00	36.10
Set total (245) Stamps	1,401.	2,231.

Coronation

Queen Elizabeth and King George VI — CD302

1937

Aden 13-15
Antigua 81-83
Ascension 37-39
Bahamas 97-99
Barbados 190-192
Basutoland 15-17
Bechuanaland Protectorate......121-123
Bermuda 115-117
British Guiana 227-229
British Honduras 112-114
Cayman Islands 97-99
Ceylon 275-277
Cyprus 140-142
Dominica 94-96
Falkland Islands 81-83
Fiji 114-116
Gambia 129-131
Gibraltar 104-106
Gilbert & Ellice Islands 37-39
Gold Coast 112-114
Grenada 128-130
Hong Kong 151-153
Jamaica 113-115
Kenya, Uganda, Tanzania 60-62
Leeward Islands 100-102
Malta 188-190
Mauritius 208-210
Montserrat 89-91
Newfoundland 230-232
Nigeria 50-52
Northern Rhodesia 22-24
Nyasaland Protectorate 51-53
St. Helena 115-117
St. Kitts-Nevis 76-78
St. Lucia 107-109
St. Vincent 130-140
Seychelles 122-124
Sierra Leone 170-172
Solomon Islands 64-66
Somaliland Protectorate 81-83
Straits Settlements 235-237
Swaziland 24-26
Trinidad & Tobago 47-49
Turks & Caicos Islands 75-77
Virgin Islands 73-75

The following have different designs but are included in the omnibus set:

Great Britain 234
Offices in Morocco (Sp. Curr.) 82
Offices in Morocco (Fr. Curr.) 439
Offices in Morocco (Tangier).....514
Canada 237
Cook Islands 109-111
Nauru 35-38
Newfoundland 233-243
New Guinea 48-51
New Zealand 223-225
Niue 70-72
Papua 118-121
South Africa 74-78
Southern Rhodesia 38-41
South-West Africa 125-132

Nos. 13-15 (3)	2.70	5.65
Nos. 81-83 (3)	1.85	8.00
Nos. 37-39 (3)	2.75	2.75
Nos. 97-99 (3)	1.05	3.45
Nos. 190-192 (3)	1.10	1.95
Nos. 15-17 (3)	1.15	3.00
Nos. 121-123 (3)	.95	3.35
Nos. 115-117 (3)	1.25	5.00
Nos. 227-229 (3)	1.50	3.05
Nos. 112-114 (3)	1.20	2.40
Nos. 97-99 (3)	1.10	2.70
Nos. 275-277 (3)	8.25	10.35
Nos. 140-142 (3)	3.75	6.50
Nos. 94-96 (3)	.85	2.40
Nos. 81-83 (3)	2.90	2.30
Nos. 114-116 (3)	1.35	5.75
Nos. 129-131 (3)	.95	3.95
Nos. 104-106 (3)	2.25	6.45
Nos. 37-39 (3)	.85	2.15
Nos. 112-114 (3)	3.10	10.00
Nos. 128-130 (3)	1.00	.85
Nos. 151-153 (3)	17.00	17.75
Nos. 113-115 (3)	1.25	1.25
Nos. 60-62 (3)	1.25	2.35
Nos. 100-102 (3)	1.55	4.00
Nos. 188-190 (3)	1.25	1.60
Nos. 208-210 (3)	1.75	3.50
Nos. 89-91 (3)	1.00	3.35
Nos. 230-232 (3)	7.00	2.80
Nos. 50-52 (3)	3.25	8.50
Nos. 22-24 (3)	.95	2.25
Nos. 51-53 (3)	1.05	1.30
Nos. 115-117 (3)	1.45	2.05
Nos. 76-78 (3)	.95	2.15
Nos. 107-109 (3)	1.05	2.05
Nos. 138-140 (3)	.80	4.75
Nos. 122-124 (3)	1.20	1.90
Nos. 170-172 (3)	1.95	5.65
Nos. 64-66 (3)	.90	2.00
Nos. 81-83 (3)	1.10	3.50
Nos. 235-237 (3)	3.25	1.60
Nos. 24-26 (3)	.75	2.70
Nos. 47-49 (3)	1.10	3.20
Nos. 75-77 (3)	1.25	.95
Nos. 73-75 (3)	2.20	6.90
No. 234 (1)	.30	.25
No. 82 (1)	.80	.60
No. 439 (1)	.50	.25
No. 514 (1)	1.25	.50
No. 237 (1)	.35	.25
Nos. 109-111 (3)	.85	.80
Nos. 35-38 (4)	1.25	5.50
Nos. 233-243 (11)	41.90	30.40
Nos. 48-51 (4)	1.40	7.90
Nos. 223-225 (3)	1.75	2.25
Nos. 70-72 (3)	.90	2.05
Nos. 118-121 (4)	1.60	5.25
Nos. 74-78 (5)	7.60	9.35
Nos. 38-41 (4)	3.55	15.50
Nos. 125-132 (8)	5.00	8.40
Set total (189) Stamps	166.10	268.90

Peace

King George VI and Parliament Buildings, London — CD303

Return to peace at the close of World War II.

1945-46

Aden 28-29
Antigua 96-97
Ascension 50-51
Bahamas 130-131
Barbados 207-208
Bermuda 131-132
British Guiana 242-243
British Honduras 127-128
Cayman Islands 112-113
Ceylon 293-294
Cyprus 156-157
Dominica 112-113
Falkland Islands 97-98
Falkland Islands Dep..........1L9-1L10
Fiji 137-138
Gambia 144-145
Gibraltar 119-120
Gilbert & Ellice Islands 52-53
Gold Coast 128-129
Grenada 143-144
Jamaica 136-137
Kenya, Uganda, Tanzania 90-91
Leeward Islands 116-117
Malta 206-207
Mauritius 223-224
Montserrat 104-105
Nigeria 71-72
Northern Rhodesia 46-47
Nyasaland Protectorate 82-83
Pitcairn Islands 9-10
St. Helena 128-129
St. Kitts-Nevis 91-92
St. Lucia 127-128
St. Vincent 152-153
Seychelles 149-150
Sierra Leone 186-187
Solomon Islands 80-81
Somaliland Protectorate 108-109
Trinidad & Tobago 62-63
Turks & Caicos Islands 80-81
Virgin Islands 88-89

The following have different designs but are included in the omnibus set:

Great Britain 264-265
Offices in Morocco (Tangier)....523-524
Aden
 Kathiri State of Seiyun 12-13
 Qu'aiti State of Shihr and Mukalla 12-13
Australia 200-202
Basutoland 29-31
Bechuanaland Protectorate......137-139
Burma 66-69
Cook Islands 127-130
Hong Kong 174-175
India 195-198
 Hyderabad 51-53
New Zealand 247-257
Niue 90-93
Pakistan-Bahawalpur O16
Samoa 191-194
South Africa 100-102
Southern Rhodesia 67-70
South-West Africa 153-155
Swaziland 38-40
Zanzibar 222-223

Nos. 28-29 (2)	.95	2.50
Nos. 96-97 (2)	.50	.80
Nos. 50-51 (2)	.80	2.00
Nos. 130-131 (2)	.50	1.40
Nos. 207-208 (2)	.50	1.10
Nos. 131-132 (2)	.55	.55
Nos. 242-243 (2)	1.05	1.40
Nos. 127-128 (2)	.50	.50
Nos. 112-113 (2)	.80	.50
Nos. 293-294 (2)	.60	2.10
Nos. 156-157 (2)	.90	.70
Nos. 112-113 (2)	.50	.50
Nos. 97-98 (2)	.90	1.35
Nos. 1L9-1L10 (2)	1.30	1.00
Nos. 137-138 (2)	.75	1.75
Nos. 144-145 (2)	.60	.95
Nos. 119-120 (2)	.75	1.00
Nos. 52-53 (2)	.50	1.10
Nos. 128-129 (2)	1.85	3.75
Nos. 143-144 (2)	.50	.95
Nos. 136-137 (2)	2.00	13.50
Nos. 90-91 (2)	.65	.85
Nos. 116-117 (2)	.50	1.50
Nos. 206-207 (2)	.65	2.00
Nos. 223-224 (2)	.50	1.05
Nos. 104-105 (2)	.50	.50
Nos. 71-72 (2)	.70	2.75
Nos. 46-47 (2)	1.25	2.00
Nos. 82-83 (2)	.55	.60
Nos. 9-10 (2)	1.40	.60
Nos. 128-129 (2)	.65	.70
Nos. 91-92 (2)	.50	.50
Nos. 127-128 (2)	.50	.60
Nos. 152-153 (2)	.50	.50
Nos. 149-150 (2)	.55	.50
Nos. 186-187 (2)	.50	.50
Nos. 80-81 (2)	.50	1.50
Nos. 108-109 (2)	.70	.50
Nos. 62-63 (2)	.75	1.85
Nos. 90-91 (2)	.50	.50
Nos. 88-89 (2)	.50	.50
Nos. 264-265 (2)	.50	.50
Nos. 523-524 (2)	2.00	2.55
Nos. 12-13 (2)	.50	.90
Nos. 12-13 (2)	.50	1.25
Nos. 200-202 (3)	1.60	1.25
Nos. 29-31 (3)	2.10	2.60
Nos. 137-139 (3)	2.05	4.75
Nos. 66-69 (4)	1.50	1.25
Nos. 127-130 (4)	2.00	1.85
Nos. 174-175 (2)	6.75	2.75
Nos. 195-198 (4)	5.60	5.50
Nos. 51-53 (3)	1.50	1.70
Nos. 247-257 (11)	3.35	3.65
Nos. 90-93 (4)	1.70	2.20
No. O16 (1)	15.00	10.00
Nos. 191-194 (4)	2.05	1.00
Nos. 100-102 (3)	1.00	3.25
Nos. 67-70 (4)	1.40	1.75
Nos. 153-155 (3)	1.85	3.25
Nos. 38-40 (3)	2.40	5.50
Nos. 222-223 (2)	.65	1.00
Set total (151) Stamps	86.15	118.15

Silver Wedding

King George VI and Queen Elizabeth
CD304 CD305

1948-49

Aden 30-31
 Kathiri State of Seiyun 14-15
 Qu'aiti State of Shihr and Mukalla 14-15
Antigua 98-99
Ascension 52-53
Bahamas 148-149
Barbados 210-211
Basutoland 39-40
Bechuanaland Protectorate......147-148
Bermuda 133-134
British Guiana 244-245
British Honduras 129-130
Cayman Islands 116-117
Cyprus 158-159
Dominica 114-115
Falkland Islands 99-100
Falkland Islands Dep..........1L11-1L12
Fiji 139-140
Gambia 146-147
Gibraltar 121-122
Gilbert & Ellice Islands 54-55
Gold Coast 142-143
Grenada 145-146
Hong Kong 178-179
Jamaica 138-139
Kenya, Uganda, Tanzania 92-93
Leeward Islands 118-119
Malaya
 Johore 128-129
 Kedah 55-56
 Kelantan 44-45
 Malacca 1-2
 Negri Sembilan 36-37

COMMON DESIGN TYPES

Pahang 44-45
Penang 1-2
Perak 99-100
Perlis 1-2
Selangor 74-75
Trengganu 47-48
Malta 223-224
Mauritius 229-230
Montserrat 106-107
Nigeria 73-74
North Borneo 238-239
Northern Rhodesia 48-49
Nyasaland Protectorate 85-86
Pitcairn Islands 11-12
St. Helena 130-131
St. Kitts-Nevis 93-94
St. Lucia 129-130
St. Vincent 154-155
Sarawak 174-175
Seychelles 151-152
Sierra Leone 188-189
Singapore 21-22
Solomon Islands 82-83
Somaliland Protectorate 110-111
Swaziland 48-49
Trinidad & Tobago 64-65
Turks & Caicos Islands 92-93
Virgin Islands 90-91
Zanzibar 224-225

The following have different designs but are included in the omnibus set:

Great Britain 267-268
 Offices in Morocco (Sp. Curr.) 93-94
 Offices in Morocco (Tangier) 525-526
Bahrain 62-63
Kuwait 82-83
Oman 25-26
South Africa 106
South-West Africa 159

Nos. 30-31 (2)	40.40	56.50
Nos. 14-15 (2)	17.85	16.00
Nos. 14-15 (2)	18.55	12.50
Nos. 98-99 (2)	13.55	15.75
Nos. 52-53 (2)	55.55	50.45
Nos. 148-149 (2)	45.25	40.30
Nos. 210-211 (2)	18.35	13.55
Nos. 39-40 (2)	52.80	55.25
Nos. 147-148 (2)	42.85	47.75
Nos. 133-134 (2)	47.75	55.25
Nos. 244-245 (2)	24.25	28.45
Nos. 129-130 (2)	25.25	53.20
Nos. 116-117 (2)	25.25	33.50
Nos. 158-159 (2)	58.50	78.00
Nos. 114-115 (2)	25.25	32.75
Nos. 99-100 (2)	112.10	76.10
Nos. 1L11-1L12 (2)	4.25	6.00
Nos. 139-140 (2)	18.20	11.50
Nos. 146-147 (2)	21.30	21.25
Nos. 121-122 (2)	61.00	78.00
Nos. 54-55 (2)	14.25	26.25
Nos. 142-143 (2)	35.25	48.20
Nos. 145-146 (2)	21.75	21.75
Nos. 178-179 (2)	329.00	106.75
Nos. 138-139 (2)	30.35	75.25
Nos. 92-93 (2)	51.00	68.00
Nos. 118-119 (2)	7.00	8.25
Nos. 128-129 (2)	29.25	53.25
Nos. 55-56 (2)	35.25	50.25
Nos. 44-45 (2)	35.75	62.75
Nos. 1-2 (2)	35.40	49.75
Nos. 36-37 (2)	28.10	38.20
Nos. 44-45 (2)	28.00	38.05
Nos. 1-2 (2)	40.50	37.80
Nos. 99-100 (2)	27.80	37.75
Nos. 1-2 (2)	33.50	58.00
Nos. 74-75 (2)	30.25	25.30
Nos. 47-48 (2)	32.75	61.75
Nos. 223-224 (2)	40.55	45.25
Nos. 229-230 (2)	19.25	45.25
Nos. 106-107 (2)	8.75	17.25
Nos. 73-74 (2)	17.85	22.80
Nos. 238-239 (2)	35.30	45.75
Nos. 48-49 (2)	100.30	90.25
Nos. 85-86 (2)	18.25	35.25
Nos. 11-12 (2)	44.50	54.00
Nos. 130-131 (2)	32.80	42.80
Nos. 93-94 (2)	13.25	10.50
Nos. 129-130 (2)	22.25	40.25
Nos. 154-155 (2)	27.75	30.25
Nos. 174-175 (2)	52.80	67.80
Nos. 151-152 (2)	16.25	48.25
Nos. 188-189 (2)	25.25	29.75
Nos. 21-22 (2)	116.00	45.40
Nos. 82-83 (2)	13.40	13.40
Nos. 110-111 (2)	8.40	8.75
Nos. 48-49 (2)	40.30	47.75
Nos. 64-65 (2)	31.80	50.25
Nos. 92-93 (2)	16.25	22.75
Nos. 90-91 (2)	16.25	22.25
Nos. 224-225 (2)	29.60	38.00
Nos. 267-268 (2)	30.40	25.25
Nos. 93-94 (2)	17.10	25.75
Nos. 525-526 (2)	22.90	32.75
Nos. 62-63 (2)	38.50	58.00
Nos. 82-83 (2)	69.50	45.50
Nos. 25-26 (2)	41.00	42.50

No. 106 (1)	.80	1.00
No. 159 (1)	1.10	.35
Set total (136) Stamps	2,542.	2,754.

U.P.U.

Mercury and Symbols of Communications CD306

Plane, Ship and Hemispheres CD307

Mercury Scattering Letters over Globe — CD308

U.P.U. Monument, Bern — CD309

Universal Postal Union, 75th anniversary.

1949

Aden 32-35
 Kathiri State of Seiyun 16-19
 Qu'aiti State of Shihr and Mukalla 16-19
Antigua 100-103
Ascension 57-60
Bahamas 150-153
Barbados 212-215
Basutoland 41-44
Bechuanaland Protectorate ..149-152
Bermuda 138-141
British Guiana 246-249
British Honduras 137-140
Brunei 79-82
Cayman Islands 118-121
Cyprus 160-163
Dominica 116-119
Falkland Islands 103-106
Falkland Islands Dep. 1L14-1L17
Fiji 141-144
Gambia 148-151
Gibraltar 123-126
Gilbert & Ellice Islands 56-59
Gold Coast 144-147
Grenada 147-150
Hong Kong 180-183
Jamaica 142-145
Kenya, Uganda, Tanzania 94-97
Leeward Islands 126-129
Malaya
 Johore 151-154
 Kedah 57-60
 Kelantan 46-49
 Malacca 18-21
 Negri Sembilan 59-62
 Pahang 46-49
 Penang 23-26
 Perak 101-104
 Perlis 3-6
 Selangor 76-79
 Trengganu 49-52
Malta 225-228
Mauritius 231-234
Montserrat 108-111
New Hebrides, British 62-65
New Hebrides, French 79-82
Nigeria 75-78
North Borneo 240-243
Northern Rhodesia 50-53
Nyasaland Protectorate 87-90
Pitcairn Islands 13-16
St. Helena 132-135
St. Kitts-Nevis 95-98
St. Lucia 131-134
St. Vincent 170-173
Sarawak 176-179
Seychelles 153-156
Sierra Leone 190-193
Singapore 23-26
Solomon Islands 84-87
Somaliland Protectorate 112-115
Southern Rhodesia 71-72
Swaziland 50-53
Tonga 87-90
Trinidad & Tobago 66-69
Turks & Caicos Islands 101-104
Virgin Islands 92-95
Zanzibar 226-229

The following have different designs but are included in the omnibus set:

Great Britain 276-279
 Offices in Morocco (Tangier) 546-549
Australia 223
Bahrain 68-71
Burma 116-121
Ceylon 304-306
Egypt 281-283
India 223-226
Kuwait 89-92
Oman 31-34
Pakistan-Bahawalpur 26-29, O25-O28
South Africa 109-111
South-West Africa 160-162

Nos. 32-35 (4)	5.85	8.45
Nos. 16-19 (4)	2.75	16.00
Nos. 16-19 (4)	2.60	8.00
Nos. 100-103 (4)	3.60	7.70
Nos. 57-60 (4)	11.10	9.00
Nos. 150-153 (4)	5.35	9.30
Nos. 212-215 (4)	4.40	14.85
Nos. 41-44 (4)	4.75	10.00
Nos. 149-152 (4)	3.35	7.25
Nos. 138-141 (4)	4.75	6.15
Nos. 246-249 (4)	2.75	4.20
Nos. 137-140 (4)	3.30	6.35
Nos. 79-82 (4)	9.50	8.45
Nos. 118-121 (4)	3.60	7.25
Nos. 160-163 (4)	4.60	10.70
Nos. 116-119 (4)	2.30	5.65
Nos. 103-106 (4)	14.00	17.10
Nos. 1L14-1L17 (4)	14.60	14.50
Nos. 141-144 (4)	3.35	15.75
Nos. 148-151 (4)	2.75	7.10
Nos. 123-126 (4)	5.90	8.75
Nos. 56-59 (4)	4.30	13.00
Nos. 144-147 (4)	2.55	10.35
Nos. 147-150 (4)	2.15	3.55
Nos. 180-183 (4)	66.75	19.95
Nos. 142-145 (4)	2.50	2.45
Nos. 94-97 (4)	2.90	4.00
Nos. 126-129 (4)	3.05	9.60
Nos. 151-154 (4)	4.70	8.90
Nos. 57-60 (4)	4.80	12.00
Nos. 46-49 (4)	4.25	12.65
Nos. 18-21 (4)	4.25	17.30
Nos. 59-62 (4)	3.50	10.75
Nos. 46-49 (4)	3.00	7.25
Nos. 23-26 (4)	5.10	11.75
Nos. 101-104 (4)	3.65	10.75
Nos. 3-6 (4)	3.95	14.25
Nos. 76-79 (4)	4.90	12.30
Nos. 49-52 (4)	5.55	12.25
Nos. 225-228 (4)	4.50	4.85
Nos. 231-234 (4)	3.70	7.05
Nos. 108-111 (4)	3.30	4.35
Nos. 62-65 (4)	1.60	4.25
Nos. 79-82 (4)	15.40	22.00
Nos. 75-78 (4)	2.80	9.25
Nos. 240-243 (4)	7.15	6.50
Nos. 50-53 (4)	5.00	6.50
Nos. 87-90 (4)	4.55	6.60
Nos. 13-16 (4)	15.05	14.25
Nos. 132-135 (4)	4.85	7.10
Nos. 95-98 (4)	4.35	5.55
Nos. 131-134 (4)	2.55	3.85
Nos. 170-173 (4)	2.20	5.05
Nos. 176-179 (4)	13.40	13.35
Nos. 153-156 (4)	3.00	5.15
Nos. 190-193 (4)	2.90	9.15
Nos. 23-26 (4)	19.00	13.70
Nos. 84-87 (4)	4.05	4.90
Nos. 112-115 (4)	3.95	9.95
Nos. 71-72 (4)	1.95	2.25
Nos. 50-53 (4)	2.80	4.65
Nos. 87-90 (4)	3.00	5.25
Nos. 66-69 (4)	3.55	6.80
Nos. 101-104 (4)	3.05	8.90
Nos. 92-95 (4)	2.60	5.90
Nos. 226-229 (4)	4.95	13.50
Nos. 276-279 (4)	1.35	1.00
Nos. 546-549 (4)	2.60	16.00
No. 223 (1)	.40	.40
Nos. 68-71 (4)	4.75	16.50
Nos. 116-121 (6)	7.30	5.35
Nos. 304-306 (3)	3.35	4.25
Nos. 281-283 (3)	5.75	2.70
Nos. 223-226 (4)	27.25	10.50
Nos. 89-92 (4)	6.10	10.25
Nos. 31-34 (4)	8.00	17.50
Nos. 26-29, O25-O28 (8)	2.40	44.00
Nos. 109-111 (3)	2.00	2.70
Nos. 160-162 (3)	3.00	5.50
Set total (313) Stamps	466.45	742.80

University

Arms of University College CD310

Alice, Princess of Athlone CD311

1948 opening of University College of the West Indies at Jamaica.

1951

Antigua 104-105
Barbados 228-229
British Guiana 250-251
British Honduras 141-142
Dominica 120-121
Grenada 164-165
Jamaica 146-147
Leeward Islands 130-131
Montserrat 112-113
St. Kitts-Nevis 105-106
St. Lucia 149-150
St. Vincent 174-175
Trinidad & Tobago 70-71
Virgin Islands 96-97

Nos. 104-105 (2)	1.35	3.75
Nos. 228-229 (2)	1.75	2.65
Nos. 250-251 (2)	1.10	1.25
Nos. 141-142 (2)	1.40	2.20
Nos. 120-121 (2)	1.40	1.75
Nos. 164-165 (2)	1.20	1.60
Nos. 146-147 (2)	1.05	.70
Nos. 130-131 (2)	1.35	4.00
Nos. 112-113 (2)	.85	2.00
Nos. 105-106 (2)	1.40	2.25
Nos. 149-150 (2)	1.40	1.50
Nos. 174-175 (2)	1.00	2.15
Nos. 70-71 (2)	1.00	4.20
Nos. 96-97 (2)	1.50	3.75
Set total (28) Stamps	17.75	33.75

Coronation

Queen Elizabeth II — CD312

1953

Aden 47
 Kathiri State of Seiyun 28
 Qu'aiti State of Shihr and Mukalla 28
Antigua 106
Ascension 61
Bahamas 157
Barbados 234
Basutoland 45
Bechuanaland Protectorate 153
Bermuda 142
British Guiana 252
British Honduras 143
Cayman Islands 150
Cyprus 167
Dominica 141
Falkland Islands 121
Falkland Islands Dependencies 1L18
Fiji 145
Gambia 152
Gibraltar 131
Gilbert & Ellice Islands 60
Gold Coast 160
Grenada 170
Hong Kong 184
Jamaica 153
Kenya, Uganda, Tanzania 101
Leeward Islands 132
Malaya
 Johore 155
 Kedah 82
 Kelantan 71
 Malacca 27
 Negri Sembilan 63
 Pahang 71
 Penang 27
 Perak 126
 Perlis 28
 Selangor 101
 Trengganu 74
Malta 241

COMMON DESIGN TYPES

15A

Mauritius	250
Montserrat	127
New Hebrides, British	77
Nigeria	79
North Borneo	260
Northern Rhodesia	60
Nyasaland Protectorate	96
Pitcairn Islands	19
St. Helena	139
St. Kitts-Nevis	119
St. Lucia	156
St. Vincent	185
Sarawak	196
Seychelles	172
Sierra Leone	194
Singapore	27
Solomon Islands	88
Somaliland Protectorate	127
Swaziland	54
Trinidad & Tobago	84
Tristan da Cunha	13
Turks & Caicos Islands	118
Virgin Islands	114

The following have different designs but are included in the omnibus set:

Great Britain	313-316
Offices in Morocco (Tangier)	579-582
Australia	259-261
Bahrain	92-95
Canada	330
Ceylon	317
Cook Islands	145-146
Kuwait	113-116
New Zealand	280-284
Niue	104-105
Oman	52-55
Samoa	214-215
South Africa	192
Southern Rhodesia	80
South-West Africa	244-248
Tokelau Islands	4

No. 47 (1)	1.25	1.25
No. 28 (1)	.75	1.50
No. 28 (1)	1.10	.60
No. 106 (1)	.40	.75
No. 61 (1)	1.25	2.75
No. 157 (1)	1.40	.75
No. 234 (1)	1.00	.25
No. 45 (1)	.50	.60
No. 153 (1)	.50	.35
No. 142 (1)	.85	.50
No. 252 (1)	.45	.25
No. 143 (1)	.60	.40
No. 150 (1)	.40	1.75
No. 167 (1)	2.75	.25
No. 141 (1)	.40	.40
No. 121 (1)	.90	1.50
No. 1L18 (1)	1.80	1.40
No. 145 (1)	1.00	.60
No. 152 (1)	.50	.50
No. 131 (1)	.80	2.20
No. 60 (1)	.65	2.25
No. 160 (1)	1.00	.25
No. 170 (1)	.30	.25
No. 184 (1)	3.00	.30
No. 153 (1)	.70	.25
No. 101 (1)	.40	.25
No. 132 (1)	1.00	2.25
No. 155 (1)	1.40	.30
No. 82 (1)	2.25	.60
No. 71 (1)	1.60	1.60
No. 27 (1)	1.10	1.50
No. 63 (1)	1.40	.65
No. 71 (1)	2.25	.25
No. 27 (1)	1.75	.30
No. 126 (1)	1.60	.25
No. 28 (1)	1.75	4.00
No. 101 (1)	1.75	.25
No. 74 (1)	1.60	1.00
No. 241 (1)	.75	.25
No. 250 (1)	1.10	.25
No. 127 (1)	.60	.45
No. 77 (1)	.75	.60
No. 79 (1)	.40	.25
No. 260 (1)	1.75	1.00
No. 60 (1)	.70	.25
No. 96 (1)	.75	.75
No. 19 (1)	2.00	3.50
No. 139 (1)	1.25	1.25
No. 119 (1)	.35	.25
No. 156 (1)	.70	.35
No. 185 (1)	.50	.50
No. 196 (1)	1.75	1.75
No. 172 (1)	.80	.80
No. 194 (1)	.40	.40
No. 27 (1)	2.50	.40
No. 88 (1)	1.00	1.00
No. 127 (1)	.40	.25
No. 54 (1)	.30	.25
No. 84 (1)	.30	.25
No. 13 (1)	1.00	1.75
No. 118 (1)	.40	1.10
No. 114 (1)	.40	1.00
Nos. 313-316 (4)	11.40	4.05
Nos. 579-582 (4)	10.90	5.30
Nos. 259-261 (3)	3.60	2.75
Nos. 92-95 (4)	15.25	12.75
No. 330	.30	.25
No. 317 (1)	1.40	.25
Nos. 145-146 (2)	2.65	2.65
Nos. 113-116 (4)	16.00	8.50
Nos. 280-284 (5)	3.30	4.55
Nos. 104-105 (2)	2.25	1.50
Nos. 52-55 (4)	14.25	6.50
Nos. 214-215 (2)	2.50	.80
No. 192 (1)	.45	.30
No. 80 (1)	7.25	7.25
Nos. 244-248 (5)	3.00	2.35
No. 4 (1)	2.75	2.75
Set total (106) Stamps	162.10	115.95

Separate designs for each country for the visit of Queen Elizabeth II and the Duke of Edinburgh.

Royal Visit 1953

1953

Aden	62
Australia	267-269
Bermuda	163
Ceylon	318
Fiji	146
Gibraltar	146
Jamaica	154
Kenya, Uganda, Tanzania	102
Malta	242
New Zealand	286-287

No. 62 (1)	.65	4.00
Nos. 267-269 (3)	2.75	2.05
No. 163 (1)	.50	.25
No. 318 (1)	1.00	.25
No. 146 (1)	.65	.35
No. 146 (1)	.75	.25
No. 154 (1)	.50	.25
No. 102 (1)	.50	.25
No. 242 (1)	.30	.25
Nos. 286-287 (2)	.50	.25
Set total (13) Stamps	8.10	8.40

West Indies Federation

Map of the Caribbean CD313

Federation of the West Indies, April 22, 1958.

1958

Antigua	122-124
Barbados	248-250
Dominica	161-163
Grenada	184-186
Jamaica	175-177
Montserrat	143-145
St. Kitts-Nevis	136-138
St. Lucia	170-172
St. Vincent	198-200
Trinidad & Tobago	86-88

Nos. 122-124 (3)	5.80	3.80
Nos. 248-250 (3)	1.60	2.90
Nos. 161-163 (3)	1.95	1.85
Nos. 184-186 (3)	1.50	1.20
Nos. 175-177 (3)	2.65	3.45
Nos. 143-145 (3)	2.35	1.35
Nos. 136-138 (3)	3.00	3.10
Nos. 170-172 (3)	2.05	2.80
Nos. 198-200 (3)	1.50	1.75
Nos. 86-88 (3)	2.40	2.35
Set total (30) Stamps	24.80	24.55

Freedom from Hunger

Protein Food — CD314

U.N. Food and Agricultural Organization's "Freedom from Hunger" campaign.

1963

Aden	65
Antigua	133
Ascension	89
Bahamas	180
Basutoland	83
Bechuanaland Protectorate	194
Bermuda	192
British Guiana	271
British Honduras	179
Brunei	100
Cayman Islands	168
Dominica	181
Falkland Islands	146
Fiji	198
Gambia	172
Gibraltar	161
Gilbert & Ellice Islands	76
Grenada	190
Hong Kong	218
Malta	291
Mauritius	270
Montserrat	150
New Hebrides, British	93
North Borneo	296
Pitcairn Islands	35
St. Helena	173
St. Lucia	179
St. Vincent	201
Sarawak	212
Seychelles	213
Solomon Islands	109
Swaziland	108
Tonga	127
Tristan da Cunha	68
Turks & Caicos Islands	138
Virgin Islands	140
Zanzibar	280

No. 65 (1)	1.50	1.75
No. 133 (1)	.35	.35
No. 89 (1)	1.00	.50
No. 180 (1)	.65	.65
No. 83 (1)	.50	.25
No. 194 (1)	.50	.50
No. 192 (1)	1.00	.50
No. 271 (1)	.45	.25
No. 179 (1)	.60	.25
No. 100 (1)	3.25	2.25
No. 168 (1)	.55	.30
No. 181 (1)	.30	.25
No. 146 (1)	10.50	2.50
No. 198 (1)	3.50	2.25
No. 172 (1)	.50	.25
No. 161 (1)	4.00	2.25
No. 76 (1)	1.40	.40
No. 190 (1)	.30	.25
No. 218 (1)	37.50	5.00
No. 291 (1)	1.40	2.20
No. 270 (1)	.45	.25
No. 150 (1)	.55	.35
No. 93 (1)	.60	.25
No. 296 (1)	1.90	.75
No. 35 (1)	3.50	1.50
No. 173 (1)	2.25	1.10
No. 179 (1)	.40	.40
No. 201 (1)	.90	.50
No. 212 (1)	1.60	1.00
No. 213 (1)	.85	.35
No. 109 (1)	3.00	.85
No. 108 (1)	.50	.50
No. 127 (1)	.60	.35
No. 68 (1)	.75	.35
No. 138 (1)	.30	.25
No. 140 (1)	.50	.50
No. 280 (1)	1.50	.80
Set total (37) Stamps	89.90	33.00

Red Cross Centenary

Red Cross and Elizabeth II — CD315

1963

Antigua	134-135
Ascension	90-91
Bahamas	183-184
Basutoland	84-85
Bechuanaland Protectorate	195-196
Bermuda	193-194
British Guiana	272-273
British Honduras	180-181
Cayman Islands	169-170
Dominica	182-183
Falkland Islands	147-148
Fiji	203-204
Gambia	173-174
Gibraltar	162-163
Gilbert & Ellice Islands	77-78
Grenada	191-192
Hong Kong	219-220
Jamaica	203-204
Malta	292-293
Mauritius	271-272
Montserrat	151-152
New Hebrides, British	94-95
Pitcairn Islands	36-37
St. Helena	174-175
St. Kitts-Nevis	143-144
St. Lucia	180-181
St. Vincent	202-203
Seychelles	214-215
Solomon Islands	110-111
South Arabia	1-2
Swaziland	109-110
Tonga	134-135
Tristan da Cunha	69-70
Turks & Caicos Islands	139-140
Virgin Islands	141-142

Nos. 134-135 (2)	1.00	2.00
Nos. 90-91 (2)	6.75	3.35
Nos. 183-184 (2)	2.30	2.80
Nos. 84-85 (2)	1.20	.90
Nos. 195-196 (2)	.95	.85
Nos. 193-194 (2)	3.00	2.80
Nos. 272-273 (2)	.85	.60
Nos. 180-181 (2)	1.00	2.50
Nos. 169-170 (2)	1.10	3.00
Nos. 182-183 (2)	.70	1.05
Nos. 147-148 (2)	18.00	5.50
Nos. 203-204 (2)	3.25	2.80
Nos. 173-174 (2)	.80	1.00
Nos. 162-163 (2)	6.25	5.40
Nos. 77-78 (2)	2.00	3.50
Nos. 191-192 (2)	.80	.50
Nos. 219-220 (2)	18.75	7.35
Nos. 203-204 (2)	.75	1.65
Nos. 292-293 (2)	1.95	5.25
Nos. 271-272 (2)	.85	.50
Nos. 151-152 (2)	1.00	.75
Nos. 94-95 (2)	1.00	.50
Nos. 36-37 (2)	2.50	4.00
Nos. 174-175 (2)	1.70	2.30
Nos. 143-144 (2)	.90	.90
Nos. 180-181 (2)	1.25	1.25
Nos. 202-203 (2)	.90	.90
Nos. 214-215 (2)	1.00	1.50
Nos. 110-111 (2)	1.25	1.15
Nos. 1-2 (2)	1.25	1.25
Nos. 109-110 (2)	1.10	1.10
Nos. 134-135 (2)	1.00	1.25
Nos. 69-70 (2)	1.15	.80
Nos. 139-140 (2)	.55	1.00
Nos. 141-142 (2)	.80	1.25
Set total (70) Stamps	89.60	73.20

Shakespeare

Shakespeare Memorial Theatre, Stratford-on-Avon CD316

400th anniversary of the birth of William Shakespeare.

1964

Antigua	151
Bahamas	201
Bechuanaland Protectorate	197
Cayman Islands	171
Dominica	184
Falkland Islands	149
Gambia	192
Gibraltar	164
Montserrat	153
St. Lucia	196
Turks & Caicos Islands	141
Virgin Islands	143

No. 151 (1)	.35	.25
No. 201 (1)	.60	.35
No. 197 (1)	.35	.35
No. 171 (1)	.35	.30
No. 184 (1)	.35	.35
No. 149 (1)	1.60	.50
No. 192 (1)	.35	.25
No. 164 (1)	.55	.25
No. 153 (1)	.35	.25
No. 196 (1)	.45	.25
No. 111 (1)	.00	.25
No. 140 (1)	.45	.45
Set total (12) Stamps	6.05	3.80

ITU

ITU Emblem CD317

Intl. Telecommunication Union, cent.

1965

Antigua	153-154
Ascension	92-93
Bahamas	219-220
Barbados	265-266
Basutoland	101-102
Bechuanaland Protectorate	202-203
Bermuda	196-197
British Guiana	293-294
British Honduras	187-188
Brunei	116-117
Cayman Islands	172-173
Dominica	185-186
Falkland Islands	154-155
Fiji	211-212
Gibraltar	167-168
Gilbert & Ellice Islands	87-88
Grenada	205-206
Hong Kong	221-222
Mauritius	291-292
Montserrat	157-158
New Hebrides, British	108-109

COMMON DESIGN TYPES

Pitcairn Islands...........................52-53
St. Helena................................180-181
St. Kitts-Nevis.........................163-164
St. Lucia..................................197-198
St. Vincent..............................224-225
Seychelles................................218-219
Solomon Islands......................126-127
Swaziland.................................115-116
Tristan da Cunha.......................85-86
Turks & Caicos Islands.........142-143
Virgin Islands.........................159-160

Nos. 153-154 (2)	1.45	1.35
Nos. 92-93 (2)	1.90	1.30
Nos. 219-220 (2)	1.35	1.50
Nos. 265-266 (2)	1.50	1.25
Nos. 101-102 (2)	.85	.65
Nos. 202-203 (2)	1.10	.75
Nos. 196-197 (2)	2.15	2.25
Nos. 293-294 (2)	.50	.50
Nos. 187-188 (2)	.75	.75
Nos. 116-117 (2)	1.75	1.75
Nos. 172-173 (2)	1.00	.85
Nos. 185-186 (2)	.55	.55
Nos. 154-155 (2)	6.75	3.15
Nos. 211-212 (2)	2.00	1.05
Nos. 167-168 (2)	6.40	5.95
Nos. 87-88 (2)	.85	.60
Nos. 205-206 (2)	.50	.50
Nos. 221-222 (2)	10.50	4.75
Nos. 291-292 (2)	1.10	.50
Nos. 157-158 (2)	1.05	1.15
Nos. 108-109 (2)	.65	.50
Nos. 52-53 (2)	1.65	1.90
Nos. 180-181 (2)	.80	.60
Nos. 163-164 (2)	.60	.60
Nos. 197-198 (2)	1.25	1.25
Nos. 224-225 (2)	.80	.90
Nos. 218-219 (2)	.75	.60
Nos. 126-127 (2)	.70	.55
Nos. 115-116 (2)	.70	.70
Nos. 85-86 (2)	1.00	.65
Nos. 142-143 (2)	.50	.50
Nos. 159-160 (2)	.85	.85
Set total (64) Stamps	54.25	40.70

Intl. Cooperation Year

ICY Emblem — CD318

1965

Antigua.....................................155-156
Ascension...................................94-95
Bahamas..................................222-223
Basutoland...............................103-104
Bechuanaland Protectorate....204-205
Bermuda..................................199-200
British Guiana.........................295-296
British Honduras....................189-190
Brunei.......................................118-119
Cayman Islands......................174-175
Dominica.................................187-188
Falkland Islands.....................156-157
Fiji..213-214
Gibraltar..................................169-170
Gilbert & Ellice Islands.........104-105
Grenada...................................207-208
Hong Kong.............................223-224
Mauritius.................................293-294
Montserrat...............................176-177
New Hebrides, British............110-111
New Hebrides, French...........126-127
Pitcairn Islands........................54-55
St. Helena................................182-183
St. Kitts-Nevis.........................165-166
St. Lucia..................................199-200
Seychelles................................220-221
Solomon Islands.....................143-144
South Arabia.............................17-18
Swaziland.................................117-118
Tristan da Cunha.......................87-88
Turks & Caicos Islands........144-145
Virgin Islands.........................161-162

Nos. 155-156 (2)	.55	.50
Nos. 94-95 (2)	1.30	1.40
Nos. 222-223 (2)	.65	1.90
Nos. 103-104 (2)	.75	.85
Nos. 204-205 (2)	.85	1.00
Nos. 199-200 (2)	2.05	1.25
Nos. 295-296 (2)	.55	.50
Nos. 189-190 (2)	.60	.55
Nos. 118-119 (2)	.85	.85
Nos. 174-175 (2)	1.00	.75
Nos. 187-188 (2)	.55	.55
Nos. 156-157 (2)	6.00	1.65
Nos. 213-214 (2)	1.95	1.25
Nos. 169-170 (2)	1.30	2.75
Nos. 104-105 (2)	.85	.60
Nos. 207-208 (2)	.50	.50
Nos. 223-224 (2)	11.00	3.50
Nos. 293-294 (2)	.65	.50
Nos. 176-177 (2)	.80	.65
Nos. 110-111 (2)	.50	.50
Nos. 126-127 (2)	12.00	12.00

Nos. 54-55 (2)	1.60	1.85
Nos. 182-183 (2)	.95	.50
Nos. 165-166 (2)	.80	.60
Nos. 199-200 (2)	.55	.55
Nos. 220-221 (2)	.80	.60
Nos. 143-144 (2)	.70	.60
Nos. 17-18 (2)	1.20	.50
Nos. 117-118 (2)	.75	.75
Nos. 87-88 (2)	1.05	.65
Nos. 144-145 (2)	.50	.50
Nos. 161-162 (2)	.65	.50
Set total (64) Stamps	54.80	41.60

Churchill Memorial

Winston Churchill and St. Paul's, London, During Air Attack — CD319

1966

Antigua.....................................157-160
Ascension...................................96-99
Bahamas..................................224-227
Barbados..................................281-284
Basutoland...............................105-108
Bechuanaland Protectorate....206-209
Bermuda..................................201-204
British Antarctic Territory........16-19
British Honduras....................191-194
Brunei.......................................120-123
Cayman Islands......................176-179
Dominica.................................189-192
Falkland Islands.....................158-161
Fiji..215-218
Gibraltar..................................171-174
Gilbert & Ellice Islands.........106-109
Grenada...................................209-212
Hong Kong.............................225-228
Mauritius.................................295-298
Montserrat...............................178-181
New Hebrides, British............112-115
New Hebrides, French...........128-131
Pitcairn Islands........................56-59
St. Helena................................184-187
St. Kitts-Nevis.........................167-170
St. Lucia..................................201-204
St. Vincent..............................241-244
Seychelles................................222-225
Solomon Islands.....................145-148
South Arabia.............................19-22
Swaziland.................................119-122
Tristan da Cunha.......................89-92
Turks & Caicos Islands........146-149
Virgin Islands.........................163-166

Nos. 157-160 (4)	3.05	3.05
Nos. 96-99 (4)	10.00	6.40
Nos. 224-227 (4)	2.30	3.20
Nos. 281-284 (4)	3.00	4.95
Nos. 105-108 (4)	2.80	3.25
Nos. 206-209 (4)	2.50	2.50
Nos. 201-204 (4)	4.00	4.75
Nos. 16-19 (4)	41.20	18.00
Nos. 191-194 (4)	2.45	1.30
Nos. 120-123 (4)	7.65	6.55
Nos. 176-179 (4)	3.10	3.65
Nos. 189-192 (4)	1.15	1.15
Nos. 158-161 (4)	12.75	9.55
Nos. 215-218 (4)	4.40	3.00
Nos. 171-174 (4)	4.75	5.30
Nos. 106-109 (4)	1.50	1.30
Nos. 209-212 (4)	1.10	1.10
Nos. 225-228 (4)	52.50	11.40
Nos. 295-298 (4)	3.70	3.75
Nos. 178-181 (4)	1.60	1.55
Nos. 112-115 (4)	2.30	1.00
Nos. 128-131 (4)	8.35	8.35
Nos. 56-59 (4)	4.45	6.10
Nos. 184-187 (4)	1.85	1.95
Nos. 167-170 (4)	1.50	1.70
Nos. 201-204 (4)	1.50	1.50
Nos. 241-244 (4)	1.50	1.75
Nos. 222-225 (4)	3.20	4.35
Nos. 145-148 (4)	1.50	1.60
Nos. 19-22 (4)	2.95	2.20
Nos. 119-122 (4)	1.70	2.55
Nos. 89-92 (4)	5.95	2.70
Nos. 146-149 (4)	1.60	1.75
Nos. 163-166 (4)	1.90	1.90
Set total (136) Stamps	205.75	135.10

Royal Visit, 1966

Queen Elizabeth II and Prince Philip — CD320

Caribbean visit, Feb. 4 - Mar. 6, 1966.

1966

Antigua.....................................161-162
Bahamas..................................228-229

Barbados..................................285-286
British Guiana.........................299-300
Cayman Islands......................180-181
Dominica.................................193-194
Grenada...................................213-214
Montserrat...............................182-183
St. Kitts-Nevis.........................171-172
St. Lucia..................................205-206
St. Vincent..............................245-246
Turks & Caicos Islands........150-151
Virgin Islands.........................167-168

Nos. 161-162 (2)	3.50	2.60
Nos. 228-229 (2)	3.05	3.05
Nos. 285-286 (2)	3.00	2.00
Nos. 299-300 (2)	2.35	.85
Nos. 180-181 (2)	3.45	1.80
Nos. 193-194 (2)	3.00	.60
Nos. 213-214 (2)	.80	.50
Nos. 182-183 (2)	2.00	1.00
Nos. 171-172 (2)	.90	.75
Nos. 205-206 (2)	1.50	1.35
Nos. 245-246 (2)	2.75	1.35
Nos. 150-151 (2)	1.00	.50
Nos. 167-168 (2)	1.75	1.75
Set total (26) Stamps	29.05	18.10

World Cup Soccer

Soccer Player and Jules Rimet Cup — CD321

World Cup Soccer Championship, Wembley, England, July 11-30.

1966

Antigua.....................................163-164
Ascension.................................100-101
Bahamas..................................245-246
Bermuda..................................205-206
Brunei.......................................124-125
Cayman Islands......................182-183
Dominica.................................195-196
Fiji..219-220
Gibraltar..................................175-176
Gilbert & Ellice Islands.........125-126
Grenada...................................230-231
New Hebrides, British............116-117
New Hebrides, French...........132-133
Pitcairn Islands........................60-61
St. Helena................................188-189
St. Kitts-Nevis.........................173-174
St. Lucia..................................207-208
Seychelles................................226-227
Solomon Islands.....................167-168
South Arabia.............................23-24
Tristan da Cunha.......................93-94

Nos. 163-164 (2)	.80	.85
Nos. 100-101 (2)	2.50	2.00
Nos. 245-246 (2)	.65	.65
Nos. 205-206 (2)	1.75	1.75
Nos. 124-125 (2)	1.30	1.25
Nos. 182-183 (2)	.75	.65
Nos. 195-196 (2)	1.20	.75
Nos. 219-220 (2)	1.70	.60
Nos. 175-176 (2)	2.00	3.55
Nos. 125-126 (2)	.70	.60
Nos. 230-231 (2)	.65	.95
Nos. 116-117 (2)	1.00	1.00
Nos. 132-133 (2)	7.00	7.00
Nos. 60-61 (2)	2.00	2.00
Nos. 188-189 (2)	1.25	.60
Nos. 173-174 (2)	.85	.80
Nos. 207-208 (2)	1.15	.90
Nos. 226-227 (2)	.85	.75
Nos. 167-168 (2)	1.10	1.10
Nos. 23-24 (2)	1.90	.55
Nos. 93-94 (2)	1.25	.80
Set total (42) Stamps	32.35	29.10

WHO Headquarters

World Health Organization Headquarters, Geneva — CD322

1966

Antigua.....................................165-166
Ascension.................................102-103
Bahamas..................................247-248
Brunei.......................................126-127
Cayman Islands......................184-185
Dominica.................................197-198
Fiji..224-225
Gibraltar..................................180-181
Gilbert & Ellice Islands.........127-128
Grenada...................................232-233
Hong Kong.............................229-230
Montserrat...............................184-185

New Hebrides, British............118-119
New Hebrides, French...........134-135
Pitcairn Islands........................62-63
St. Helena................................190-191
St. Kitts-Nevis.........................177-178
St. Lucia..................................209-210
St. Vincent..............................247-248
Seychelles................................228-229
Solomon Islands.....................169-170
South Arabia.............................25-26
Tristan da Cunha.......................99-100

Nos. 165-166 (2)	1.15	.55
Nos. 102-103 (2)	6.60	3.35
Nos. 247-248 (2)	.80	.80
Nos. 126-127 (2)	1.35	1.35
Nos. 184-185 (2)	2.25	1.20
Nos. 197-198 (2)	.75	.75
Nos. 224-225 (2)	4.70	3.30
Nos. 180-181 (2)	6.50	6.75
Nos. 127-128 (2)	.80	.70
Nos. 232-233 (2)	.85	.55
Nos. 229-230 (2)	11.25	2.30
Nos. 184-185 (2)	1.00	1.00
Nos. 118-119 (2)	.75	.50
Nos. 134-135 (2)	8.50	8.50
Nos. 62-63 (2)	5.50	7.00
Nos. 190-191 (2)	3.50	1.50
Nos. 177-178 (2)	.60	.60
Nos. 209-210 (2)	.80	.80
Nos. 247-248 (2)	1.15	1.05
Nos. 228-229 (2)	1.25	.65
Nos. 169-170 (2)	.95	.80
Nos. 25-26 (2)	2.10	.70
Nos. 99-100 (2)	1.90	1.25
Set total (46) Stamps	64.95	45.90

UNESCO Anniversary

"Education" CD323

"Science" (Wheat ears & flask enclosing globe). "Culture" (lyre & columns). 20th anniversary of the UNESCO.

1966-67

Antigua.....................................183-185
Ascension.................................108-110
Bahamas..................................249-251
Barbados..................................287-289
Bermuda..................................207-209
Brunei.......................................128-130
Cayman Islands......................186-188
Dominica.................................199-201
Gibraltar..................................183-185
Gilbert & Ellice Islands.........129-131
Grenada...................................234-236
Hong Kong.............................231-233
Mauritius.................................299-301
Montserrat...............................186-188
New Hebrides, British............120-122
New Hebrides, French...........136-138
Pitcairn Islands........................64-66
St. Helena................................192-194
St. Kitts-Nevis.........................179-181
St. Lucia..................................211-213
St. Vincent..............................249-251
Seychelles................................230-232
Solomon Islands.....................171-173
South Arabia.............................27-29
Swaziland.................................123-125
Tristan da Cunha.....................101-103
Turks & Caicos Islands........155-157
Virgin Islands.........................176-178

Nos. 183-185 (3)	1.90	2.50
Nos. 108-110 (3)	11.00	5.80
Nos. 249-251 (3)	2.35	2.35
Nos. 287-289 (3)	2.35	2.15
Nos. 207-209 (3)	3.80	3.90
Nos. 128-130 (3)	4.65	5.40
Nos. 186-188 (3)	2.50	1.50
Nos. 199-201 (3)	1.60	.75
Nos. 183-185 (3)	6.50	3.25
Nos. 129-131 (3)	2.50	2.45
Nos. 234-236 (3)	1.10	1.20
Nos. 231-233 (3)	49.50	24.00
Nos. 299-301 (3)	2.10	1.50
Nos. 186-188 (3)	2.40	2.40
Nos. 120-122 (3)	1.90	1.90
Nos. 136-138 (3)	7.75	7.75
Nos. 64-66 (3)	4.05	4.00
Nos. 192-194 (3)	5.25	3.65
Nos. 179-181 (3)	.90	.90
Nos. 211-213 (3)	1.15	1.15
Nos. 249-251 (3)	2.30	1.35
Nos. 230-232 (3)	2.40	2.40
Nos. 171-173 (3)	2.00	1.50
Nos. 27-29 (3)	5.50	5.50
Nos. 123-125 (3)	1.40	1.40
Nos. 101-103 (3)	2.00	1.40
Nos. 155-157 (3)	1.15	1.20
Nos. 176-178 (3)	1.40	1.30
Set total (84) Stamps	133.40	94.55

COMMON DESIGN TYPES

Silver Wedding, 1972

Queen Elizabeth II and Prince Philip
CD324

Designs: borders differ for each country.

1972

Anguilla	161-162
Antigua	295-296
Ascension	164-165
Bahamas	344-345
Bermuda	296-297
British Antarctic Territory	43-44
British Honduras	306-307
British Indian Ocean Territory	48-49
Brunei	186-187
Cayman Islands	304-305
Dominica	352-353
Falkland Islands	223-224
Fiji	328-329
Gibraltar	292-293
Gilbert & Ellice Islands	206-207
Grenada	466-467
Hong Kong	271-272
Montserrat	200-207
New Hebrides, British	169-170
New Hebrides, French	188-189
Pitcairn Islands	127-128
St. Helena	271-272
St. Kitts-Nevis	257-258
St. Lucia	328-329
St Vincent	344-345
Seychelles	309-310
Solomon Islands	248-249
South Georgia	35-36
Tristan da Cunha	178-179
Turks & Caicos Islands	257-258
Virgin Islands	241-242

Nos. 161-162 (2)	1.10	1.50
Nos. 295-296 (2)	.50	.50
Nos. 164-165 (2)	.70	.70
Nos. 344-345 (2)	.60	.60
Nos. 296-297 (2)	.50	.65
Nos. 43-44 (2)	6.50	5.65
Nos. 306-307 (2)	.80	.80
Nos. 48-49 (2)	2.00	1.00
Nos. 186-187 (2)	.70	.70
Nos. 304-305 (2)	.75	.75
Nos. 352-353 (2)	.65	.65
Nos. 223-224 (2)	1.00	1.15
Nos. 328-329 (2)	.70	.70
Nos. 292-293 (2)	.60	.50
Nos. 206-207 (2)	.50	.50
Nos. 466-467 (2)	.70	.70
Nos. 271-272 (2)	1.70	1.50
Nos. 286-287 (2)	.50	.50
Nos. 169-170 (2)	.50	.50
Nos. 188-189 (2)	1.25	1.25
Nos. 127-128 (2)	.90	.85
Nos. 271-272 (2)	.60	1.20
Nos. 257-258 (2)	.65	.65
Nos. 328-329 (2)	.75	.75
Nos. 344-345 (2)	.55	.55
Nos. 309-310 (2)	.90	.90
Nos. 248-249 (2)	.50	.50
Nos. 35-36 (2)	1.40	1.40
Nos. 178-179 (2)	.70	.70
Nos. 257-258 (2)	.60	.60
Nos. 241-242 (2)	.50	.50
Set total (62) Stamps	30.20	29.15

Princess Anne's Wedding

Princess Anne and Mark Phillips — CD325

Wedding of Princess Anne and Mark Phillips, Nov. 14, 1973.

1973

Anguilla	179-180
Ascension	177-178
Belize	325-326
Bermuda	302-303
British Antarctic Territory	60-61
Cayman Islands	320-321
Falkland Islands	225-226
Gibraltar	305-306
Gilbert & Ellice Islands	216-217
Hong Kong	289-290
Montserrat	300-301
Pitcairn Islands	135-136
St. Helena	277-278
St. Kitts-Nevis	274-275
St. Lucia	349-350
St. Vincent	358-359
St. Vincent Grenadines	1-2
Seychelles	311-312
Solomon Islands	259-260
South Georgia	37-38
Tristan da Cunha	189-190
Turks & Caicos Islands	286-287
Virgin Islands	260-261

Nos. 179-180 (2)	.55	.55
Nos. 177-178 (2)	.60	.60
Nos. 325-326 (2)	1.10	.50
Nos. 302-303 (2)	.50	.50
Nos. 60-61 (2)	1.10	1.10
Nos. 320-321 (2)	.50	.50
Nos. 225-226 (2)	.70	.60
Nos. 305-306 (2)	.60	.50
Nos. 216-217 (2)	.50	.50
Nos. 289-290 (2)	2.65	2.00
Nos. 300-301 (2)	.55	.55
Nos. 135-136 (2)	.70	.60
Nos. 277-278 (2)	.50	.50
Nos. 274-275 (2)	.50	.50
Nos. 349-350 (2)	.50	.50
Nos. 358-359 (2)	.50	.50
Nos. 1-2 (2)	.50	.50
Nos. 311-312 (2)	.65	.65
Nos. 259-260 (2)	.70	.70
Nos. 37-38 (2)	.75	.75
Nos. 189-190 (2)	.50	.50
Nos. 286-287 (2)	.50	.50
Nos. 260-261 (2)	.50	.50
Set total (46) Stamps	16.15	14.60

Elizabeth II Coronation Anniv.

CD326 CD327

CD328

Designs: Royal and local beasts in heraldic form and simulated stonework. Portrait of Elizabeth II by Peter Grugeon. 25th anniversary of coronation of Queen Elizabeth II.

1978

Ascension	229
Barbados	474
Belize	397
British Antarctic Territory	71
Cayman Islands	404
Christmas Island	87
Falkland Islands	275
Fiji	384
Gambia	380
Gilbert Islands	312
Mauritius	464
New Hebrides, British	258
New Hebrides, French	278
St. Helena	317
St. Kitts-Nevis	354
Samoa	472
Solomon Islands	000
South Georgia	51
Swaziland	302
Tristan da Cunha	238
Virgin Islands	337

No. 229 (1)	2.00	2.00
No. 474 (1)	1.35	1.35
No. 397 (1)	4.50	5.00
No. 71 (1)	6.00	6.00
No. 404 (1)	2.00	2.00
No. 87 (1)	3.50	4.00
No. 275 (1)	4.00	5.50
No. 384 (1)	1.75	1.75
No. 380 (1)	1.50	1.50
No. 312 (1)	1.25	1.25
No. 464 (1)	2.10	2.10
No. 258 (1)	1.75	1.75
No. 278 (1)	3.50	3.50
No. 317 (1)	1.75	1.75
No. 354 (1)	1.00	1.00
No. 472 (1)	2.10	2.10
No. 368 (1)	2.50	2.50
No. 51 (1)	3.00	3.00
No. 302 (1)	1.60	1.60
No. 238 (1)	1.50	1.50
No. 337 (1)	1.80	1.80
Set total (21) Stamps	50.45	52.95

Queen Mother Elizabeth's 80th Birthday

CD330

Designs: Photographs of Queen Mother Elizabeth. Falkland Islands issued in sheets of 50; others in sheets of 9.

1980

Ascension	261
Bermuda	401
Cayman Islands	443
Falkland Islands	305
Gambia	412
Gibraltar	393
Hong Kong	364
Pitcairn Islands	193
St. Helena	341
Samoa	532
Solomon Islands	426
Tristan da Cunha	277

No. 261 (1)	.40	.40
No. 401 (1)	.45	.75
No. 443 (1)	.40	.40
No. 305 (1)	.40	.40
No. 412 (1)	.40	.50
No. 393 (1)	.30	.25
No. 364 (1)	1.10	1.25
No. 193 (1)	.60	.60
No. 341 (1)	.50	.50
No. 532 (1)	.55	.55
No. 426 (1)	.50	.50
No. 277 (1)	.45	.45
Set total (12) Stamps	6.05	6.55

Royal Wedding, 1981

Prince Charles and Lady Diana — CD331

CD331a

Wedding of Charles, Prince of Wales, and Lady Diana Spencer, St. Paul's Cathedral, London, July 29, 1981.

1981

Antigua	623-627
Ascension	294-296
Barbados	547-549
Barbuda	497-501
Bermuda	412-414
Brunei	268-270
Cayman Islands	471-473
Dominica	701-705
Falkland Islands	324-326
Falkland Islands Dep.	1L59-1L61
Fiji	442-444
Gambia	426-428
Ghana	759-764
Grenada	1051-1055
Grenada Grenadines	440-443
Hong Kong	373-375
Jamaica	500-503
Lesotho	335-337
Maldive Islands	906-909
Mauritius	520-522
Norfolk Island	280-282
Pitcairn Islands	206-208
St. Helena	353-355
St. Lucia	543-549
Samoa	558-560
Sierra Leone	509-518
Solomon Islands	450-452
Swaziland	382-384
Tristan da Cunha	294-296
Turks & Caicos Islands	486-489
Caicos Island	8-11
Uganda	314-317
Vanuatu	308-310
Virgin Islands	406-408

Nos. 623-627 (5)	6.55	2.55
Nos. 294-296 (3)	1.00	1.00
Nos. 547-549 (3)	.90	.90
Nos. 497-501 (5)	10.95	10.95
Nos. 412-414 (3)	2.00	2.00
Nos. 268-270 (3)	2.15	4.50
Nos. 471-473 (3)	1.20	1.30
Nos. 701-705 (5)	8.35	2.35
Nos. 324-326 (3)	1.65	1.70
Nos. 1L59-1L61 (3)	1.45	1.45
Nos. 442-444 (3)	1.35	1.35
Nos. 426-428 (3)	.90	.80
Nos. 759-764 (6)	6.20	6.20
Nos. 1051-1055 (5)	9.85	1.85
Nos. 440-443 (4)	2.35	2.35
Nos. 373-375 (3)	3.10	2.85
Nos. 500-503 (4)	1.45	1.35
Nos. 335-337 (3)	.90	.90
Nos. 906-909 (4)	1.55	1.55
Nos. 520-522 (3)	2.15	2.15
Nos. 280-282 (3)	1.75	1.75
Nos. 206-208 (3)	1.20	1.10
Nos. 353-355 (3)	.85	.85
Nos. 543-549 (5)	7.00	7.00
Nos. 558-560 (3)	.85	.85
Nos. 509-518 (10)	15.50	15.50
Nos. 450-452 (3)	1.25	1.25
Nos. 382-384 (3)	1.30	1.25
Nos. 294-296 (3)	.90	.90
Nos. 486-489 (4)	2.20	2.20
Nos. 8-11 (4)	5.00	5.00
Nos. 314-317 (4)	3.10	3.00
Nos. 308-310 (3)	1.15	1.15
Nos. 406-408 (3)	1.10	1.10
Set total (131) Stamps	109.15	92.95

Princess Diana

CD332 CD333

Designs: Photographs and portrait of Princess Diana, wedding or honeymoon photographs, royal residences, arms of issuing country. Portrait photograph by Clive Friend. Souvenir sheet margins show family tree, various people related to the princess. 21st birthday of Princess Diana of Wales, July 1.

1982

Antigua	663-666
Ascension	313-316
Bahamas	510-513
Barbados	585-588
Barbuda	544-547
British Antarctic Territory	92-95
Cayman Islands	486-489
Dominica	773-776
Falkland Islands	348-351
Falkland Islands Dep.	1L72-1L75
Fiji	470-473
Gambia	447-450
Grenada	1101A-1105
Grenada Grenadines	485-491
Lesotho	372-375
Maldive Islands	952-955
Mauritius	548-551
Pitcairn Islands	213-216
St. Helena	372-375
St. Lucia	591-594
Sierra Leone	531-534
Solomon Islands	471-474
Swaziland	406-409
Tristan da Cunha	310-313
Turks and Caicos Islands	531-534
Virgin Islands	430-433

Nos. 663-666 (4)	8.25	7.35
Nos. 313-316 (4)	3.50	3.50
Nos. 510-513 (4)	6.00	3.85
Nos. 585-588 (4)	3.40	3.25
Nos. 544-547 (4)	9.75	7.70
Nos. 92-95 (4)	4.25	3.45
Nos. 486-489 (4)	4.75	2.70
Nos. 773-776 (4)	7.05	7.05
Nos. 348-351 (4)	2.95	2.95
Nos. 1L72-1L75 (4)	2.50	2.60
Nos. 470-473 (4)	3.25	2.95
Nos. 447-450 (4)	2.90	2.85
Nos. 1101A-1105 (7)	16.05	15.55
Nos. 485-491 (7)	17.65	17.65
Nos. 372-375 (4)	4.00	4.00
Nos. 952-955 (4)	5.50	3.90
Nos. 548-551 (4)	5.00	5.00
Nos. 213-216 (4)	1.90	1.85
Nos. 372-375 (4)	2.00	2.00
Nos. 591-594 (4)	8.70	8.70
Nos. 531-534 (4)	7.20	7.20
Nos. 471-474 (4)	2.90	2.90
Nos. 406-409 (4)	3.85	2.25

COMMON DESIGN TYPES

Nos. 310-313 (4)	3.65	1.45
Nos. 486-489 (4)	2.20	2.20
Nos. 430-433 (4)	3.00	3.00
Set total (110) Stamps	142.15	127.85

250th anniv. of first edition of Lloyd's List (shipping news publication) & of Lloyd's marine insurance.

CD335 — Bahamas 5c

Designs: First page of early edition of the list; historical ships, modern transportation or harbor scenes.

1984

Ascension	351-354
Bahamas	555-558
Barbados	627-630
Cayes of Belize	10-13
Cayman Islands	522-526
Falkland Islands	404-407
Fiji	509-512
Gambia	519-522
Mauritius	587-590
Nauru	280-283
St. Helena	412-415
Samoa	624-627
Seychelles	538-541
Solomon Islands	521-524
Vanuatu	368-371
Virgin Islands	466-469

Nos. 351-354 (4)	2.90	2.55
Nos. 555-558 (5)	4.15	2.95
Nos. 627-630 (4)	6.10	5.15
Nos. 10-13 (4)	4.85	4.85
Nos. 522-526 (5)	9.30	8.45
Nos. 404-407 (4)	3.50	3.65
Nos. 509-512 (4)	5.30	4.90
Nos. 519-522 (4)	4.20	4.30
Nos. 587-590 (4)	9.40	9.40
Nos. 280-283 (4)	2.40	2.35
Nos. 412-415 (4)	2.40	2.40
Nos. 624-627 (4)	2.55	2.35
Nos. 538-541 (4)	5.00	5.00
Nos. 521-524 (4)	4.65	3.95
Nos. 368-371 (4)	1.85	1.85
Nos. 466-469 (4)	4.25	4.25
Set total (65) Stamps	72.80	68.35

Queen Mother 85th Birthday

CD336 — Ascension Island 12p

Designs: Photographs tracing the life of the Queen Mother, Elizabeth. The high value in each set pictures the same photograph taken of the Queen Mother holding the infant Prince Henry.

1985

Ascension	372-376
Bahamas	580-584
Barbados	660-664
Bermuda	469-473
Falkland Islands	420-424
Falkland Islands Dep.	1L92-1L96
Fiji	531-535
Hong Kong	447-450
Jamaica	599-603
Mauritius	604-608
Norfolk Island	364-368
Pitcairn Islands	253-257
St. Helena	428-432
Samoa	649-653
Seychelles	567-571
Zil Elwannyen Sesel	101-105
Solomon Islands	543-547
Swaziland	476-480
Tristan da Cunha	372-376
Vanuatu	392-396

Nos. 372-376 (5)	4.65	4.65
Nos. 580-584 (5)	7.70	6.45
Nos. 660-664 (5)	8.00	6.70
Nos. 469-473 (5)	9.40	9.40
Nos. 420-424 (5)	7.35	6.65
Nos. 1L92-1L96 (5)	8.00	8.00
Nos. 531-535 (5)	6.15	6.15
Nos. 447-450 (4)	9.50	8.50
Nos. 599-603 (5)	6.15	7.00
Nos. 604-608 (5)	11.30	11.30
Nos. 364-368 (5)	5.00	5.00
Nos. 253-257 (5)	5.30	5.95
Nos. 428-432 (5)	5.25	5.25
Nos. 649-653 (5)	8.40	7.55
Nos. 567-571 (5)	8.70	8.70
Nos. 101-105 (5)	6.60	6.60
Nos. 543-547 (5)	3.95	3.95
Nos. 476-480 (5)	7.75	7.25
Nos. 372-376 (5)	5.40	5.40
Nos. 392-396 (5)	5.25	5.25
Set total (99) Stamps	139.80	135.70

Queen Elizabeth II, 60th Birthday

CD337 — Bahamas 10c

1986, April 21

Ascension	389-393
Bahamas	592-596
Barbados	675-679
Bermuda	499-503
Cayman Islands	555-559
Falkland Islands	441-445
Fiji	544-548
Hong Kong	465-469
Jamaica	620-624
Kiribati	470-474
Mauritius	629-633
Papua New Guinea	640-644
Pitcairn Islands	270-274
St. Helena	451-455
Samoa	670-674
Seychelles	592-596
Zil Elwannyen Sesel	114-118
Solomon Islands	562-566
South Georgia	101-105
Swaziland	490-494
Tristan da Cunha	388-392
Vanuatu	414-418
Zambia	343-347

Nos. 389-393 (5)	2.80	3.30
Nos. 592-596 (5)	2.75	3.70
Nos. 675-679 (5)	3.25	3.10
Nos. 499-503 (5)	4.65	5.15
Nos. 555-559 (5)	4.55	5.60
Nos. 441-445 (5)	3.95	4.95
Nos. 544-548 (5)	3.00	3.00
Nos. 465-469 (5)	8.75	6.75
Nos. 620-624 (5)	2.75	2.70
Nos. 470-474 (5)	2.25	2.10
Nos. 629-633 (5)	3.50	3.50
Nos. 640-644 (5)	4.10	4.10
Nos. 270-274 (5)	2.80	2.70
Nos. 451-455 (5)	2.50	3.05
Nos. 670-674 (5)	2.55	2.55
Nos. 592-596 (5)	2.70	2.70
Nos. 114-118 (5)	2.15	2.15
Nos. 562-566 (5)	2.90	2.90
Nos. 101-105 (5)	3.30	3.65
Nos. 490-494 (5)	2.15	2.15
Nos. 388-392 (5)	3.00	3.00
Nos. 414-418 (5)	3.10	3.10
Nos. 343-347 (5)	1.65	1.60
Set total (115) Stamps	75.10	77.50

Royal Wedding

Marriage of Prince Andrew and Sarah Ferguson — CD338

1986, July 23

Ascension	399-400
Bahamas	602-603
Barbados	687-688
Cayman Islands	560-561
Jamaica	629-630
Pitcairn Islands	275-276
St. Helena	460-461
St. Kitts	181-182
Seychelles	602-603
Zil Elwannyen Sesel	119-120
Solomon Islands	567-568
Tristan da Cunha	397-398
Zambia	348-349

Nos. 399-400 (2)	1.60	1.60
Nos. 602-603 (2)	2.75	2.75
Nos. 687-688 (2)	2.00	1.25
Nos. 560-561 (2)	1.70	2.35
Nos. 629-630 (2)	1.35	1.35
Nos. 275-276 (2)	2.40	2.40
Nos. 460-461 (2)	1.05	1.05
Nos. 181-182 (2)	1.50	2.25
Nos. 602-603 (2)	2.50	2.50
Nos. 119-120 (2)	2.30	2.30
Nos. 567-568 (2)	1.00	1.00
Nos. 397-398 (2)	1.40	1.40
Nos. 348-349 (2)	1.10	1.30
Set total (26) Stamps	22.65	23.50

Queen Elizabeth II, 60th Birthday

CD339 — Dominica 2c

Queen Elizabeth II & Prince Philip, 1947 Wedding Portrait — CD339

Designs: Photographs tracing the life of Queen Elizabeth II.

1986

Anguilla	674-677
Antigua	925-928
Barbuda	783-786
Dominica	950-953
Gambia	611-614
Grenada	1371-1374
Grenada Grenadines	749-752
Lesotho	531-534
Maldive Islands	1172-1175
Sierra Leone	760-763
Uganda	495-498

Nos. 674-677 (4)	8.00	8.00
Nos. 925-928 (4)	5.50	6.20
Nos. 783-786 (4)	23.15	23.15
Nos. 950-953 (4)	7.25	7.25
Nos. 611-614 (5)	8.25	7.90
Nos. 1371-1374 (4)	6.80	6.80
Nos. 749-752 (4)	6.75	6.75
Nos. 531-534 (4)	5.25	5.25
Nos. 1172-1175 (4)	6.25	6.25
Nos. 760-763 (4)	5.25	5.25
Nos. 495-498 (4)	8.50	8.50
Set total (44) Stamps	90.95	91.30

Royal Wedding, 1986

CD340 — Dominica 45c

Designs: Photographs of Prince Andrew and Sarah Ferguson during courtship, engagement and marriage.

1986

Antigua	939-942
Barbuda	809-812
Dominica	970-973
Gambia	635-638
Grenada	1385-1388
Grenada Grenadines	758-761
Lesotho	545-548
Maldive Islands	1181-1184
Sierra Leone	769-772
Uganda	510-513

Nos. 939-942 (4)	7.00	8.75
Nos. 809-812 (4)	14.55	14.55
Nos. 970-973 (4)	7.25	7.25
Nos. 635-638 (4)	7.80	7.80
Nos. 1385-1388 (4)	8.30	8.30
Nos. 758-761 (4)	9.00	9.00
Nos. 545-548 (4)	7.45	7.45
Nos. 1181-1184 (4)	8.45	8.45
Nos. 769-772 (4)	5.35	5.35
Nos. 510-513 (4)	9.25	10.00
Set total (40) Stamps	84.40	86.90

Lloyds of London, 300th Anniv.

CD341 — Bahamas 10c

Designs: 17th century aspects of Lloyds, representations of each country's individual connections with Lloyds and publicized disasters insured by the organization.

1986

Ascension	454-457
Bahamas	655-658
Barbados	731-734
Bermuda	541-544
Falkland Islands	481-484
Liberia	1101-1104
Malawi	534-537
Nevis	571-574
St. Helena	501-504
St. Lucia	923-926
Seychelles	649-652
Zil Elwannyen Sesel	146-149
Solomon Islands	627-630
South Georgia	131-134
Trinidad & Tobago	484-487
Tristan da Cunha	439-442
Vanuatu	485-488

Nos. 454-457 (4)	5.00	5.00
Nos. 655-658 (4)	8.90	4.95
Nos. 731-734 (4)	12.50	8.35
Nos. 541-544 (4)	8.00	6.60
Nos. 481-484 (4)	5.45	3.85
Nos. 1101-1104 (4)	4.25	4.25
Nos. 534-537 (4)	11.00	7.85
Nos. 571-574 (4)	8.35	8.35
Nos. 501-504 (4)	8.70	7.15
Nos. 923-926 (4)	8.80	8.80
Nos. 649-652 (4)	12.85	12.85
Nos. 146-149 (4)	11.25	11.25
Nos. 627-630 (4)	7.00	4.45
Nos. 131-134 (4)	6.30	3.70
Nos. 484-487 (4)	10.25	6.35
Nos. 439-442 (4)	7.60	7.60
Nos. 485-488 (4)	4.85	4.85
Set total (68) Stamps	141.05	116.20

Moon Landing, 20th Anniv.

CD342 — Nevis 15c

Designs: Equipment, crew photographs, spacecraft, official emblems and report profiles created for the Apollo Missions. Two stamps in each set are square in format rather than like the stamp shown; see individual country listings for more information.

1989

Ascension	468-472
Bahamas	674-678
Belize	916-920
Kiribati	517-521
Liberia	1125-1129
Nevis	586-590
St. Kitts	248-252
Samoa	760-764
Seychelles	676-680
Zil Elwannyen Sesel	154-158
Solomon Islands	643-647
Vanuatu	507-511

Nos. 468-472 (5)	9.40	8.60
Nos. 674-678 (5)	23.00	19.70
Nos. 916-920 (5)	29.25	21.60
Nos. 517-521 (5)	12.50	12.50
Nos. 1125-1129 (5)	8.50	8.50
Nos. 586-590 (5)	7.50	7.50
Nos. 248-252 (5)	8.00	8.25
Nos. 760-764 (5)	9.85	9.35
Nos. 676-680 (5)	16.05	16.05
Nos. 154-158 (5)	26.85	26.85
Nos. 643-647 (5)	9.00	6.75
Nos. 507-511 (5)	8.60	8.60
Set total (60) Stamps	168.50	154.20

Queen Mother, 90th Birthday

CD343 — British Indian Ocean Territory 24p

CD344 — British Indian Ocean Territory £1

Designs: Portraits of Queen Elizabeth, the Queen Mother. See individual country listings for more information.

1990

Ascension	491-492
Bahamas	698-699
Barbados	782-783
British Antarctic Territory	170-171
British Indian Ocean Territory	106-107

COMMON DESIGN TYPES

Cayman Islands	622-623
Falkland Islands	524-525
Kenya	527-528
Kiribati	555-556
Liberia	1145-1146
Pitcairn Islands	336-337
St. Helena	532-533
St. Lucia	969-970
Seychelles	710-711
Zil Elwannyen Sesel	171-172
Solomon Islands	671-672
South Georgia	143-144
Swaziland	565-566
Tristan da Cunha	480-481

Nos. 491-492 (2)	4.75	4.75
Nos. 698-699 (2)	5.25	5.25
Nos. 782-783 (2)	4.00	3.70
Nos. 170-171 (2)	6.00	6.00
Nos. 106-107 (2)	18.00	18.50
Nos. 622-623 (2)	4.00	5.50
Nos. 524-525 (2)	4.75	4.75
Nos. 527-528 (2)	6.05	6.05
Nos. 555-556 (2)	4.75	4.75
Nos. 1145-1146 (2)	3.25	3.25
Nos. 336-337 (2)	4.25	4.25
Nos. 532-533 (2)	5.25	5.25
Nos. 969-970 (2)	4.60	4.60
Nos. 710-711 (2)	6.60	6.60
Nos. 171-172 (2)	8.25	8.25
Nos. 671-672 (2)	5.00	5.30
Nos. 143-144 (2)	5.50	6.50
Nos. 565-566 (2)	4.10	4.10
Nos. 480-481 (2)	5.60	5.60
Set total (38) Stamps	109.95	112.95

Queen Elizabeth II, 65th Birthday, and Prince Philip, 70th Birthday

CD345 — CD346

Designs: Portraits of Queen Elizabeth II and Prince Philip differ for each country. Printed in sheets of 10 + 5 labels (3 different) between. Stamps alternate, producing 5 different triptychs.

1991

Ascension	506a
Bahamas	731a
Belize	970a
Bermuda	618a
Kiribati	572a
Mauritius	734a
Pitcairn Islands	349a
St. Helena	555a
St. Kitts	319a
Samoa	791a
Seychelles	724a
Zil Elwannyen Sesel	178a
Solomon Islands	689a
South Georgia	150a
Swaziland	587a
Vanuatu	541a

No. 506a (1)	3.50	3.75
No. 731a (1)	4.00	4.00
No. 970a (1)	4.25	4.25
No. 618a (1)	3.50	4.00
No. 572a (1)	4.00	4.00
No. 734a (1)	4.00	4.00
No. 349a (1)	3.25	3.25
No. 555a (1)	2.75	2.75
No. 319a (1)	3.00	3.00
No. 791a (1)	3.75	3.75
No. 724a (1)	5.00	5.00
No. 178a (1)	6.25	6.25
No. 689a (1)	3.75	3.75
No. 150a (1)	4.75	7.00
No. 587a (1)	4.00	4.00
No. 541a (1)	2.50	2.50
Set total (16) Stamps	62.25	65.25

Royal Family Birthday, Anniversary

CD347

Queen Elizabeth II, 65th birthday, Charles and Diana, 10th wedding anniversary: Various photographs of Queen Elizabeth II, Prince Philip, Prince Charles, Princess Diana and their sons William and Henry.

1991

Antigua	1446-1455
Barbuda	1229-1238
Dominica	1328-1337
Gambia	1080-1089
Grenada	2006-2015
Grenada Grenadines	1331-1340
Guyana	2440-2451
Lesotho	871-875
Maldive Islands	1533-1542
Nevis	666-675
St. Vincent	1485-1494
St. Vincent Grenadines	769-778
Sierra Leone	1387-1396
Turks & Caicos Islands	913-922
Uganda	918-927

Nos. 1446-1455 (10)	21.70	20.05
Nos. 1229-1238 (10)	125.00	119.50
Nos. 1328-1337 (10)	30.20	30.20
Nos. 1080-1089 (10)	24.65	24.40
Nos. 2006-2015 (10)	25.45	22.10
Nos. 1331-1340 (10)	23.85	23.35
Nos. 2440-2451 (12)	21.40	21.15
Nos. 871-875 (5)	13.55	13.55
Nos. 1533-1542 (10)	28.10	28.10
Nos. 666-675 (10)	23.65	23.65
Nos. 1485-1494 (10)	26.75	25.90
Nos. 769-778 (10)	25.40	25.40
Nos. 1387-1396 (10)	26.35	26.35
Nos. 913-922 (10)	27.50	25.30
Nos. 918-927 (10)	17.65	17.65
Set total (147) Stamps	461.20	446.65

Queen Elizabeth II's Accession to the Throne, 40th Anniv.

CD348

Various photographs of Queen Elizabeth II with local Scenes.

1992

Antigua	1513-1518
Barbuda	1306-1311
Dominica	1414-1419
Gambia	1172-1177
Grenada	2047-2052
Grenada Grenadines	1368-1373
Lesotho	881-885
Maldive Islands	1637-1642
Nevis	702-707
St. Vincent	1582-1587
St. Vincent Grenadines	829-834
Sierra Leone	1482-1487
Turks and Caicos Islands	978-987
Uganda	990-995
Virgin Islands	742-746

Nos. 1513-1518 (6)	15.00	15.10
Nos. 1306-1311 (6)	125.25	83.65
Nos. 1414-1419 (6)	12.50	12.50
Nos. 1172-1177 (6)	15.00	14.85
Nos. 2047-2052 (6)	15.95	15.95
Nos. 1368-1373 (6)	17.00	15.35
Nos. 881-885 (5)	11.90	11.90
Nos. 1637-1642 (6)	17.55	17.55
Nos. 702-707 (6)	13.55	13.55
Nos. 1582-1587 (6)	14.40	14.40
Nos. 829-834 (6)	19.65	19.65
Nos. 1482-1487 (6)	22.50	22.50
Nos. 913-922 (10)	27.50	25.30
Nos. 990-995 (6)	19.50	19.50
Nos. 742-746 (5)	15.50	15.50
Set total (92) Stamps	362.75	317.25

CD349

1992

Ascension	531-535
Bahamas	744-748
Bermuda	623-627
British Indian Ocean Territory	119-123
Cayman Islands	648-652
Falkland Islands	549-553
Gibraltar	605-609
Hong Kong	619-623
Kenya	563-567
Kiribati	582-586
Pitcairn Islands	362-366
St. Helena	570-574
St. Kitts	332-336
Samoa	805-809
Seychelles	734-738
Zil Elwannyen Sesel	183-187
Solomon Islands	708-712
South Georgia	157-161
Tristan da Cunha	508-512
Vanuatu	555-559
Zambia	561-565

Nos. 531-535 (5)	6.10	6.10
Nos. 744-748 (5)	6.90	4.70
Nos. 623-627 (5)	7.40	7.55
Nos. 119-123 (5)	22.75	19.25
Nos. 648-652 (5)	7.60	6.60
Nos. 549-553 (5)	5.95	5.90
Nos. 605-609 (5)	3.55	3.85
Nos. 619-623 (5)	5.10	5.25
Nos. 563-567 (5)	7.80	7.75
Nos. 582-586 (5)	3.85	3.85
Nos. 362-366 (5)	5.35	5.35
Nos. 570-574 (5)	5.70	5.70
Nos. 332-336 (5)	6.60	5.50
Nos. 805-809 (5)	7.85	5.90
Nos. 734-738 (5)	10.55	10.55
Nos. 183-187 (5)	9.40	9.40
Nos. 708-712 (5)	5.00	5.30
Nos. 157-161 (5)	5.60	5.90
Nos. 508-512 (5)	8.75	8.30
Nos. 555-559 (5)	3.10	3.10
Nos. 561-565 (5)	5.20	5.15
Set total (105) Stamps	150.10	140.95

Royal Air Force, 75th Anniversary

CD350

1993

Ascension	557-561
Bahamas	771-775
Barbados	842-846
Belize	1003-1008
Bermuda	648-651
British Indian Ocean Territory	136-140
Falkland Is.	573-577
Fiji	687-691
Montserrat	830-834
St. Kitts	351-355

Nos. 557-561 (5)	15.60	14.60
Nos. 771-775 (5)	24.65	21.45
Nos. 842-846 (5)	14.15	12.85
Nos. 1003-1008 (6)	21.15	16.50
Nos. 648-651 (4)	9.65	10.45
Nos. 136-140 (5)	16.10	16.10
Nos. 573-577 (5)	10.85	10.85
Nos. 687-691 (5)	17.75	17.40
Nos. 830-834 (5)	14.10	14.10
Nos. 351-355 (5)	22.80	23.55
Set total (50) Stamps	166.80	157.85

Royal Air Force, 80th Anniv.

Design CD350 Re-inscribed

1990

Ascension	697-701
Bahamas	807-811
British Indian Ocean Terr.	198-202
Cayman Islands	754-758
Fiji	814-818
Gibraltar	755-759
Samoa	957-961
Turks & Caicos Islands	1258-1265
Tuvalu	763-767
Virgin Islands	879-883

Nos. 697-701 (5)	16.10	16.10
Nos. 807-811 (5)	10.00	10.00
Nos. 136-140 (5)	16.10	16.10
Nos. 754-758 (5)	15.25	15.25
Nos. 814-818 (5)	14.00	12.75
Nos. 755-759 (5)	7.85	9.00
Nos. 957-961 (5)	15.70	14.90
Nos. 1258-1265 (2)	27.50	27.50
Nos. 763-767 (5)	7.75	7.75
Nos. 879-883 (5)	15.00	15.00
Set total (47) Stamps	148.85	147.00

End of World War II, 50th Anniv.

CD351

CD352

1995

Ascension	613-617
Bahamas	824-828
Barbados	891-895
Belize	1047-1050
British Indian Ocean Territory	163-167
Cayman Islands	704-708
Falkland Islands	634-638
Fiji	720-724
Kiribati	662-668
Liberia	1175-1179
Mauritius	803-805
St. Helena	646-654
St. Kitts	389-393
St. Lucia	1018-1022
Samoa	890-894
Solomon Islands	799-803
South Georgia	198-200
Tristan da Cunha	562-566

Nos. 613-617 (5)	21.50	21.50
Nos. 824-828 (5)	22.00	18.70
Nos. 891-895 (5)	14.20	11.90
Nos. 1047-1050 (4)	8.25	5.90
Nos. 163-167 (5)	16.25	16.25
Nos. 704-708 (5)	17.65	13.95
Nos. 634-638 (5)	18.65	17.15
Nos. 720-724 (5)	17.50	14.50
Nos. 662-668 (7)	12.55	12.55
Nos. 1175-1179 (5)	15.25	11.15
Nos. 803-805 (3)	7.50	7.50
Nos. 646-654 (9)	26.10	26.10
Nos. 389-393 (5)	16.40	16.40
Nos. 1018-1022 (5)	12.25	10.15
Nos. 890-894 (5)	15.25	14.50
Nos. 799-803 (5)	14.75	14.75
Nos. 198-200 (3)	14.50	15.50
Nos. 562-566 (5)	20.10	20.10
Set total (91) Stamps	290.65	268.55

UN, 50th Anniv.

CD353

1995

Bahamas	839-842
Barbados	901-904
Belize	1055-1058
Jamaica	847-851
Liberia	1187-1190
Mauritius	813-816
Pitcairn Islands	436-439
St. Kitts	398-401
St. Lucia	1023-1026
Samoa	900-903
Tristan da Cunha	568-571
Virgin Islands	807-810

Nos. 839-842 (4)	7.15	6.40
Nos. 901-904 (4)	7.00	5.75
Nos. 1055-1058 (4)	6.90	4.70
Nos. 847-851 (5)	5.40	5.45
Nos. 1187-1190 (4)	10.90	10.90
Nos. 813-816 (4)	4.55	4.55
Nos. 436-439 (4)	8.15	8.15
Nos. 398-401 (4)	6.15	7.15
Nos. 1023-1026 (4)	7.50	7.25
Nos. 900-903 (4)	9.35	8.20
Nos. 568-571 (4)	13.50	13.50
Nos. 807-810 (4)	7.45	7.45
Set total (49) Stamps	93.90	89.45

Queen Elizabeth, 70th Birthday

CD354

COMMON DESIGN TYPES

1996

Ascension	632-635
British Antarctic Territory	240-243
British Indian Ocean Territory	176-180
Falkland Islands	653-657
Pitcairn Islands	446-449
St. Helena	672-676
Samoa	912-916
Tokelau	223-227
Tristan da Cunha	576-579
Virgin Islands	824-828

Nos. 632-635 (4)	5.30	5.30
Nos. 240-243 (4)	9.45	8.15
Nos. 176-180 (5)	11.50	11.50
Nos. 653-657 (5)	13.55	11.20
Nos. 446-449 (4)	8.60	8.60
Nos. 672-676 (5)	12.45	12.70
Nos. 912-916 (5)	10.50	10.50
Nos. 223-227 (5)	10.50	10.50
Nos. 576-579 (4)	8.35	8.35
Nos. 824-828 (5)	11.30	11.30
Set total (46) Stamps	101.50	98.10

Diana, Princess of Wales (1961-97)

CD355

1998

Ascension	696
Bahamas	901A-902
Barbados	950
Belize	1091
Bermuda	753
Botswana	659-663
British Antarctic Territory	258
British Indian Ocean Terr.	197
Cayman Islands	752A-753
Falkland Islands	694
Fiji	819-820
Gibraltar	754
Kiribati	719A-720
Namibia	909
Niue	706
Norfolk Island	644-645
Papua New Guinea	937
Pitcairn Islands	487
St. Helena	711
St. Kitts	437A-438
Samoa	955A-956
Seychelles	802
Solomon Islands	866-867
South Georgia	220
Tokelau	252B-253
Tonga	980
Niuafo'ou	201
Tristan da Cunha	618
Tuvalu	762
Vanuatu	718A-719
Virgin Islands	878

No. 696 (1)	5.25	5.25
Nos. 901A-902 (2)	5.30	5.30
No. 950 (1)	6.25	6.25
No. 1091 (1)	10.00	10.00
No. 753 (1)	5.00	5.00
Nos. 659-663 (5)	8.25	8.80
No. 258 (1)	5.50	5.50
No. 197 (1)	5.50	5.50
Nos. 752A-753 (3)	7.40	7.40
No. 694 (1)	5.00	5.00
Nos. 819-820 (2)	5.25	5.25
No. 754 (1)	1.10	3.25
Nos. 719A-720 (2)	4.60	4.60
No. 909 (1)	1.75	1.75
No. 706 (1)	5.50	5.50
Nos. 644-645 (2)	5.60	5.60
No. 937 (1)	6.25	6.25
No. 487 (1)	4.75	4.75
No. 711 (1)	4.25	4.25
Nos. 437A-438 (2)	5.15	5.15
Nos. 955A-956 (2)	7.00	7.00
No. 802 (1)	6.25	6.25
Nos. 866-867 (2)	5.40	5.40
No. 220 (1)	4.50	5.00
Nos. 252B-253 (2)	6.00	6.00
No. 980 (1)	4.00	4.00
No. 201 (1)	6.50	6.50
No. 618 (1)	5.00	5.00
No. 878 (1)	3.50	3.50
No. 762 (1)	8.00	8.00
Nos. 718A-719 (2)	4.50	4.50
Set total (46) Stamps	168.30	171.50

Wedding of Prince Edward and Sophie Rhys-Jones

CD356

1999

Ascension	729-730
Cayman Islands	775-776
Falkland Islands	729-730
Pitcairn Islands	505-506
St. Helena	733-734
Samoa	971-972
Tristan da Cunha	636-637
Virgin Islands	908-909

Nos. 729-730 (2)	4.50	4.50
Nos. 775-776 (2)	4.95	4.95
Nos. 729-730 (2)	14.00	14.00
Nos. 505-506 (2)	7.00	7.00
Nos. 733-734 (2)	5.00	5.00
Nos. 971-972 (2)	5.00	5.00
Nos. 636-637 (2)	7.50	7.50
Nos. 908-909 (2)	7.50	7.50
Set total (16) Stamps	55.45	55.45

1st Manned Moon Landing, 30th Anniv.

CD357

1999

Ascension	731-735
Bahamas	942-946
Barbados	967-971
Bermuda	778
Cayman Islands	777-781
Fiji	853-857
Jamaica	889-893
Kiribati	746-750
Nauru	465-469
St. Kitts	460-464
Samoa	973-977
Solomon Islands	875-879
Tuvalu	800-804
Virgin Islands	910-914

Nos. 731-735 (5)	12.80	12.80
Nos. 942-946 (5)	14.10	14.10
Nos. 967-971 (5)	9.45	8.25
No. 778 (1)	9.00	9.00
Nos. 777-781 (5)	9.25	9.25
Nos. 853-857 (5)	9.25	8.45
Nos. 889-893 (5)	8.30	7.18
Nos. 746-750 (5)	8.60	8.60
Nos. 465-469 (5)	7.55	7.10
Nos. 460-464 (5)	11.35	11.65
Nos. 973-977 (5)	12.60	12.45
Nos. 875-879 (5)	7.50	7.50
Nos. 800-804 (5)	6.75	6.75
Nos. 910-914 (5)	11.75	11.75
Set total (66) Stamps	138.25	134.83

Queen Mother's Century

CD358

1999

Ascension	736-740
Bahamas	951-955
Cayman Islands	782-786
Falkland Islands	734-738
Fiji	858-862
Norfolk Island	688-692
St. Helena	740-744
Samoa	978-982
Solomon Islands	880-884
South Georgia	231-235
Tristan da Cunha	638-642
Tuvalu	805-809

Nos. 736-740 (5)	15.50	15.50
Nos. 951-955 (5)	13.75	12.65
Nos. 782-786 (5)	8.35	8.35
Nos. 734-738 (5)	30.00	28.25
Nos. 858-862 (5)	12.80	13.25
Nos. 688-692 (5)	9.50	9.50
Nos. 740-744 (5)	16.15	16.15
Nos. 978-982 (5)	12.50	12.10
Nos. 880-884 (5)	7.50	7.00
Nos. 231-235 (5)	29.75	30.00
Nos. 638-642 (5)	18.00	18.00
Nos. 805-809 (5)	7.00	7.00
Set total (60) Stamps	180.80	177.75

Prince William, 18th Birthday

CD359

2000

Ascension	755-759
Cayman Islands	797-801
Falkland Islands	762-766
Fiji	889-893
South Georgia	257-261
Tristan da Cunha	664-668
Virgin Islands	925-929

Nos. 755-759 (5)	15.50	15.50
Nos. 797-801 (5)	11.15	10.90
Nos. 762-766 (5)	24.60	22.50
Nos. 889-893 (5)	12.90	12.90
Nos. 257-261 (5)	29.00	28.75
Nos. 664-668 (5)	21.50	21.50
Nos. 925-929 (5)	14.50	14.50
Set total (35) Stamps	129.15	126.55

Reign of Queen Elizabeth II, 50th Anniv.

CD360

2002

Ascension	790-794
Bahamas	1033-1037
Barbados	1019-1023
Belize	1152-1156
Bermuda	822-826
British Antarctic Territory	307-311
British Indian Ocean Territory	239-243
Cayman Islands	844-848
Falkland Islands	804-808
Gibraltar	896-900
Jamaica	952-956
Nauru	491-495
Norfolk Island	758-762
Papua New Guinea	1019-1023
Pitcairn Islands	552
St. Helena	788-792
St. Lucia	1146-1150
Solomon Islands	931-935
South Georgia	274-278
Swaziland	706-710
Tokelau	302-306
Tonga	1059
Niuafo'ou	239
Tristan da Cunha	706-710
Virgin Islands	967-971

Nos. 790-794 (5)	14.10	14.10
Nos. 1033-1037 (5)	15.25	15.25
Nos. 1019-1023 (5)	12.90	12.90
Nos. 1152-1156 (5)	17.10	15.10
Nos. 822-826 (5)	18.00	18.00
Nos. 307-311 (5)	23.00	23.00
Nos. 239-243 (5)	19.40	19.40
Nos. 844-848 (5)	13.25	13.25
Nos. 804-808 (5)	23.00	22.00
Nos. 896-900 (5)	4.50	6.50
Nos. 952-956 (5)	16.65	16.65
Nos. 491-495 (5)	17.75	17.75
Nos. 758-762 (5)	15.90	15.90
Nos. 1019-1023 (5)	14.50	14.50
No. 552 (1)	8.50	8.50
Nos. 788-792 (5)	19.75	19.75
Nos. 1146-1150 (5)	12.25	12.25
Nos. 931-935 (5)	12.40	12.40
Nos. 274-278 (5)	28.00	28.50
Nos. 706-710 (5)	12.50	12.50
Nos. 302-306 (5)	14.50	14.50
No. 1059 (1)	8.00	8.00
No. 239 (1)	8.75	8.75
Nos. 706-710 (5)	18.50	18.50
Nos. 967-971 (5)	16.50	16.50
Set total (113) Stamps	384.95	384.45

Queen Mother Elizabeth (1900-2002)

CD361

2002

Ascension	799-801
Bahamas	1044-1046
Bermuda	834-836
British Antarctic Territory	312-314
British Indian Ocean Territory	245-247
Cayman Islands	857-861
Falkland Islands	812-816
Nauru	499-501
Pitcairn Islands	561-565
St. Helena	808-812
St. Lucia	1155-1159
Seychelles	830
Solomon Islands	945-947
South Georgia	281-285
Tokelau	312-314
Tristan da Cunha	715-717
Virgin Islands	979-983

Nos. 799-801 (3)	8.85	8.85
Nos. 1044-1046 (3)	9.10	9.10
Nos. 834-836 (3)	12.25	12.25
Nos. 312-314 (3)	18.75	18.75
Nos. 245-247 (3)	17.35	17.35
Nos. 857-861 (5)	15.00	15.00
Nos. 812-816 (5)	28.50	28.50
Nos. 499-501 (3)	14.00	14.00
Nos. 561-565 (5)	15.25	15.25
Nos. 808-812 (5)	12.00	12.00
Nos. 1155-1159 (5)	12.00	12.00
No. 830 (1)	6.50	6.50
Nos. 945-947 (3)	9.25	9.25
Nos. 281-285 (5)	19.50	19.50
Nos. 312-314 (3)	11.85	11.85
Nos. 715-717 (3)	16.25	16.25
Nos. 979-983 (5)	23.50	23.50
Set total (63) Stamps	249.90	249.90

Head of Queen Elizabeth II

CD362

2003

Ascension	822
Bermuda	865
British Antarctic Territory	322
British Indian Ocean Territory	261
Cayman Islands	878
Falkland Islands	828
St. Helena	820
South Georgia	294
Tristan da Cunha	731
Virgin Islands	1003

No. 822 (1)	12.50	12.50
No. 865 (1)	50.00	50.00
No. 322 (1)	9.50	9.50
No. 261 (1)	11.00	11.00
No. 878 (1)	14.00	14.00
No. 828 (1)	9.00	9.00
No. 820 (1)	9.00	9.00
No. 294 (1)	8.50	8.50
No. 731 (1)	10.00	10.00
No. 1003 (1)	10.00	10.00
Set total (10) Stamps	143.50	143.50

Coronation of Queen Elizabeth II, 50th Anniv.

CD363

2003

Ascension	823-825
Bahamas	1073-1075
Bermuda	866-868
British Antarctic Territory	323-325

British Indian Ocean Territory 262-264
Cayman Islands.........................879-881
Jamaica 970-972
Kiribati 825-827
Pitcairn Islands..........................577-581
St. Helena 821-823
St. Lucia 1171-1173
Tokelau 320-322
Tristan da Cunha......................732-734
Virgin Islands.........................1004-1006

Nos. 823-825 (3)	12.50	12.50
Nos. 1073-1075 (3)	13.00	13.00
Nos. 866-868 (2)	14.25	14.25
Nos. 323-325 (3)	23.00	23.00
Nos. 262-264 (3)	28.00	28.00
Nos. 879-881 (3)	19.25	19.25
Nos. 970-972 (3)	10.00	10.00
Nos. 825-827 (3)	13.00	13.00
Nos. 577-581 (5)	14.40	14.40
Nos. 821-823 (3)	7.25	7.25
Nos. 1171-1173 (3)	8.75	8.75
Nos. 320-322 (3)	17.25	17.25
Nos. 732-734 (3)	16.75	16.75
Nos. 1004-1006 (3)	25.00	25.00
Set total (43) Stamps	222.40	222.40

Prince William, 21st Birthday

CD364

2003

Ascension 826
British Indian Ocean Territory 265
Cayman Islands.........................882-884
Falkland Islands 829
South Georgia 295
Tokelau 323
Tristan da Cunha............................735
Virgin Islands..........................1007-1009

No. 826 (1)	7.25	7.25
No. 265 (1)	8.00	8.00
Nos. 882-884 (3)	6.95	6.95
No. 829 (1)	13.50	13.50
No. 295 (1)	8.50	8.50
No. 323 (1)	7.25	7.25
No. 735 (1)	6.00	6.00
Nos. 1007-1009 (3)	10.00	10.00
Set total (12) Stamps	67.45	67.45

Order your 2023 Scott & Minkus Foreign Supplements today!

SCOTT SPECIALTY SERIES

Item No.	Supplement Title	Available	Retail	AA
261AN23	Antigua***	October	$10.99	$9.34
642S023	Argentina	September	$24.99	$21.24
362AR23	Armenia	August	$20.99	$17.84
210S023	Australia	September	$28.99	$24.64
211S023	Australia Dependencies	September	$28.99	$24.64
300S023	Austria	May	$31.49	$26.77
362AZ23	Azerbaijan***	August	$24.99	$21.24
261BH23	Bahamas***	June	$15.99	$13.59
361S023	Baltic States (Estonia/Latvia/Lithuania)	August	$24.99	$21.24
362BL23	Belarus	August	$24.99	$21.24
303S023	Belgium	August	$28.99	$24.64
261BR23	Bermuda	June	$15.99	$13.59
643S023	Bolivia***	September	$15.99	$13.59
718S023	Bosnia & Herzegovina	May	$24.99	$21.24
644S023	Brazil	May	$24.99	$21.24
261BA23	British Antarctic Territory	July	$20.99	$17.84
270BI23	British Indian Ocean Territory***	May	$15.99	$13.59
240S023	Canada	May	$31.49	$26.77
245S023	Canada - Master Narratives	May	$35.49	$30.17
261CI23	Cayman Islands***	June	$15.99	$13.59
645S023	Chile***	September	$15.99	$13.59
646S023	Colombia	September	$15.99	$13.59
307S023	Czech Republic & Slovakia	August	$28.99	$24.64
345DM23	Denmark	June	$20.99	$17.84
648S023	Dominican Republic	September	$20.99	$17.84
261FI23	Falkland Islands and South Georgia	July	$20.99	$17.84
345FI23	Faroe Islands	June	$15.99	$13.59
345FN23	Finland/Aland	June	$28.99	$24.64
310S023	France	May	$41.99	$35.69
625S023	French Polynesia	August	$15.99	$13.59
626S023	French Southern & Antarctic Territory	August	$20.99	$17.84
362GR23	Georgia	August	$15.99	$13.59
315S323	Germany	May	$20.99	$17.84
203GB23	Gibraltar	May	$20.99	$17.84
200S023	Great Britain	May	$28.99	$34.64

SCOTT SPECIALTY SERIES (CONTINUED)

Item No.	Supplement Title	Available	Retail	AA
200M023	Great Britain Machins***	May	$13.99	$11.89
320S023	Greece	June	$28.99	$24.64
345GR23	Greenland	June	$20.99	$17.84
202GN23	Guernsey & Alderney	May	$28.99	$24.64
275HK23	Hong Kong	June	$28.99	$24.64
323S023	Hungary	August	$28.99	$24.64
345IC23	Iceland***	June	$13.99	$11.89
618S023	India	July	$27.49	$23.37
201S023	Ireland	June	$20.99	$17.84
202IM23	Isle of Man	May	$28.99	$24.64
500S023	Israel Singles	August	$17.99	$15.29
501S023	Israel Tab Singles	August	$17.99	$15.29
325S023	Italy	October	$20.99	$17.84
510S023	Japan	July	$54.99	$46.74
202JR23	Jersey	May	$28.99	$24.64
515S023	Korea	June	$20.99	$17.84
719S023	Kosovo	May	$20.99	$17.84
362KY23	Kyrgyzstan (includes Express)	August	$20.99	$17.84
619S023	Laos***	July	$12.99	$11.04
367S023	Liechtenstein	June	$15.99	$13.59
330S023	Luxembourg	August	$15.99	$13.59
620S023	Malaysia	July	$28.99	$24.64
203ML23	Malta	May	$20.99	$17.84
430S023	Mexico	September	$24.99	$21.24
362MD23	Moldova	August	$15.99	$13.59
333S023	Monaco & French Andorra	May	$24.99	$21.24
713S023	Namibia	October	$15.99	$13.59
621S023	Nepal	July	$15.99	$13.59
335S023	Netherlands	August	$49.99	$42.49
261NK23	Nevis and St. Kitts***	October	$13.99	$11.89
630S023	New Caledonia	August	$15.99	$13.59
220S023	New Zealand	September	$28.99	$24.64
221S023	New Zealand Dependencies	September	$54.99	$46.74
345NR23	Norway***	June	$14.99	$12.74
673S023	Pakistan***	July	$11.99	$10.19
520S023	People's Republic of China	July	$29.99	$25.49
530S023	People's Republic of China/Taiwan	July	$29.99	$25.49
338S023	Poland	August	$24.99	$21.24

SCOTT SPECIALTY SERIES (CONTINUED)

Item No.	Supplement Title	Available	Retail	AA
178S023	Pony Express - Narratives	March	$28.99	$24.64
340S023	Portugal/Azores/Maderia	September	$28.99	$24.64
360S023	Russia	September	$41.99	$35.69
328S023	San Marino	July	$15.99	$13.59
275SG23	Singapore	September	$28.99	$24.64
669S023	South Africa***	October	$20.99	$17.84
355S023	Spain & Spanish Andorra	July	$28.99	$24.64
622S023	Sri Lanka***	July	$24.99	$21.24
270SH23	St. Helena***	May	$13.99	$11.89
261SL23	St. Lucia***	October	$10.99	$9.34
607S023	St. Pierre & Miquelon	May	$17.99	$15.29
345SW23	Sweden	September	$20.99	$17.84
365S023	Switzerland	June	$20.99	$17.84
362TJ23	Tajikistan	August	$15.99	$13.59
540S023	Thailand	October	$20.99	$17.84
270TC23	Tristan da Cunha***	May	$15.99	$13.59
505S023	Turkey	August	$28.99	$24.64
362UK23	Ukraine	September	$24.99	$21.24
362UZ23	Uzbekistan	August	$20.99	$17.84
637S023	Vanuatu	August	$15.99	$13.59
375S023	Vatican City	July	$15.99	$13.59
261VI23	Virgin Islands***	October	$15.99	$13.59
638S023	Wallis & Futuna	August	$15.99	$13.59

2023 Minkus Supplements
MINKUS WORLDWIDE SERIES

Item No.	Supplement Title	Available	Retail	AA
MCA23	Canada	May	$39.99	$33.99
MFR23	France	May	$39.99	$33.99
MGM23	Germany	May	$20.99	$17.84
MBE123	Great Britain, Ireland (Br. Euro V.1)	June	$33.49	$28.47
MIS23	Israel Singles	August	$16.99	$14.44
MIST23	Israel Tab Singles	August	$16.99	$14.44
MSWZ23	Switzerland	June	$19.99	$16.99
MVA23	Vatican City	July	$15.99	$13.59

*** These supplements are on the schedule tentatively to be produced and there is a possibility they are postponed until the following year.

FREE SHIPPING FOR ORDERS OF $75 OR MORE!*
*Within the continental United States

AmosAdvantage.com | 1-800-572-6885

ORDERING INFORMATION: *AA prices apply to paid subscribers of Amos Media titles, or for orders placed online. Prices, terms and product availability subject to change.
SHIPPING & HANDLING: U.S.: Orders total $0-$10.00 charged $4.99 shipping. U.S. Order total $10.01-$74.99 charged $9.99 shipping. Orders totaling $75+ will ship FREE! Taxes will apply in CA, OH, & IL. Canada: 20% of order total. Minimum charge $19.99 Maximum charge $200.00. Foreign orders are shipped via FedEx Intl. or USPS and billed actual freight.

MACAO

MACAO
mə-'kau

LOCATION — Off the Chinese coast at the mouth of the Canton River
GOVT. — Special Administrative Area of China (PRC) (as of 12/20/99)
AREA — 8 sq. mi.
POP. — 649,000 (2020 est.)
CAPITAL — Macao

Formerly a Portuguese overseas territory. The territory includes the two small adjacent islands of Coloane and Taipa.

1000 Reis = 1 Milreis
78 Avos = 1 Rupee (1894)
100 Avos = 1 Pataca (1913)

Catalogue values for unused stamps in this country are for Never Hinged items, beginning with Scott 339 in the regular postage section, Scott C16 in the air post section, Scott J50 in the semi-postal section, and Scott RA11 in the postal tax section.

Watermarks

Wmk. 232 — Maltese Cross

Portuguese Crown — A1

Perf. 12½, 13½

1884-85 Typo. Unwmk.

1	A1	5r black	20.00	14.50
2	A1	10r orange	33.50	22.00
3	A1	10r green ('85)	32.00	19.50
4	A1	20r bister	43.00	36.50
5	A1	20r rose ('85)	57.50	36.50
6	A1	25r rose	30.00	11.25
7	A1	25r violet ('85)	40.00	24.00
8	A1	40r blue	180.00	72.50
9	A1	40r yellow ('85)	57.00	32.50
10	A1	50r green	267.50	120.00
11	A1	50r blue ('85)	64.00	40.00
12	A1	80r gray ('85)	215.00	60.00
13	A1	100r red lilac	80.00	39.00
a.		100r lilac	80.00	39.00
14	A1	200r orange	77.00	36.50
15	A1	300r chocolate	107.50	40.00
		Nos. 1-15 (15)	1,304.	604.75

All values exist both perf 12½ and 13½. The cheaper variety is listed above. For detailed listings, see the Scott Classic Specialized Catalogue of stamps and Covers.
The reprints of the 1885 issue are printed on smooth, white chalky paper, ungummed and on thin white paper with shiny white gum and clean-cut perforation 13½.
For surcharges see Nos. 16-28, 108-109.

No. 13a Surcharged in Black

1884 Without Gum Perf. 12½

16	A1	80r on 100r lilac	150.00	85.00
a.	Inverted surcharge		200.00	75.00
b.	Without accent on "e" of "reis"		170.00	100.00
c.	Perf. 13½		170.00	85.00
d.	As "b," perf. 13½		190.00	100.00

Nos. 6 and 10 Surcharged in Black, Blue or Red

b

1885 Without Gum

17	A1(b)	5r on 25r rose, perf. 12½ (Bk)	36.00	19.00
a.	With accent on "e" of "Reis"		55.00	21.00
b.	Double surcharge		225.00	190.00
c.	Inverted surcharge		475.00	325.00
d.	Perf. 13½		190.00	160.00
e.	As "d," inverted surcharge		300.00	225.00
18	A1(b)	10r on 25r rose (Bl)	70.00	37.50
a.	Accent on "e" of "Reis"		35.00	28.00
b.	Pair, one without surcharge		—	
19	A1(b)	10r on 50r grn, perf. 13½ (Bl)	700.00	400.00
a.	Perf. 12½		800.00	500.00
20	A1(b)	20r on 50r green, perf. 12½ (Bk)	70.00	27.50
a.	Double surcharge		160.00	400.00
b.	Accent on "e" of "Reis"		37.50	30.00
21	A1(b)	40r on 50r grn, perf. 12½ (R)	350.00	190.00
a.	Perf. 13½		400.00	180.00
		Nos. 17-21 (5)	1,226.	674.00

c

1885 Without Gum

22	A1(c)	5r on 25r rose (Bk)	55.00	37.50
a.	Original value not obliterated			
23	A1(c)	10r on 50r green (Bk)	55.00	37.50
a.	Inverted surcharge		175.00	
b.	Perf. 12½		65.00	37.50

Nos. 12, 13a and 14 Surcharged in Black

1887

24	A1	5r on 80r gray (Bk)	55.00	20.00
a.	"l" of "Reis" 4mm high		120.00	95.00
b.	Perf. 12½		130.00	95.00
25	A1	5r on 100r lilac	275.00	160.00
a.	Perf. 12½		225.00	95.00
26	A1	10r on 80r gray	95.00	37.50
a.	"R" 4mm high		170.00	150.00
b.	Double surcharge		350.00	
27	A1	10r on 200r orange	350.00	160.00
a.	"R" 4mm high, "e" without accent		425.00	180.00
b.	Perf. 12½		325.00	160.00
28	A1	20r on 80r gray	140.00	55.00
a.	"R" 4mm high		160.00	120.00
b.	Perf 12½		150.00	80.00
c.	"R" 4mm high, "e" without accent		190.00	100.00
		Nos. 24-28 (5)	915.00	432.50

The surcharges with larger "R" (4mm) have accent on "e." Smaller "R" is 3mm high.
Occasionally Nos. 24, 26 and 28 may be found with original gum. Values the same.

Coat of Arms — A6

Red Surcharge
Without Gum

1887, Oct. 20 Perf. 12½

32	A6	5r green & buff	15.00	11.00
a.	With labels, 5r on 10r		120.00	110.00
b.	With labels, 5r on 20r		140.00	110.00
c.	With labels, 5r on 40r		120.00	110.00
33	A6	10r green & buff	23.00	14.00
a.	With labels, 10r on 10r		140.00	130.00
b.	With labels, 10r on 60r		170.00	140.00
34	A6	40r green & buff	37.50	23.00
a.	With labels, 40r on 20r		225.00	170.00
b.	With labels, 40r on 10r		225.00	190.00
		Nos. 32-34 (3)	75.50	48.00

Nos. 32-34 were local provisionals, created by perforating contemporary revenue stamps to remove the old value inscriptions and then surcharging the central design portion. The unused portion of the design was normally removed prior to use. For simplicity's sake, we refer to these extraneous portions of the original revenue stamps as "labels."

The overprint exists only in unused condition with several other denominations of labels. The 5r exists with 30r labels. Value, $400. The 10r exists with 20r and 30r labels. Values, $350 and $425, respectively. The 40r exists with 30r labels. Value, $450.

King Luiz — A7

Typographed and Embossed
1888, Jan. Perf. 12½
Chalk-surfaced Paper

35	A7	5r black	29.50	7.00
36	A7	10r green	31.00	14.75
a.	Perf. 13½		145.00	83.00
37	A7	20r rose	50.00	22.50
a.	Double impression		300.00	225.00
38	A7	25r violet	57.50	22.50
39	A7	40r chocolate	57.50	26.75
a.	Perf. 13½		122.50	57.50
40	A7	50r blue	82.00	23.50
a.	Perf. 13½		70.00	46.50
b.	As "a," double impression		300.00	225.00
41	A7	80r gray	127.50	39.00
a.	Imperf., pair		—	
b.	Perf. 13½		67.50	39.00
42	A7	100r brown	72.50	39.00
a.	Perf. 13½		77.50	37.50
43	A7	200r gray lilac	147.50	77.50
a.	Perf. 13½		135.00	55.00
b.	As "a," double impression		300.00	
44	A7	300r orange	147.50	77.50
a.	Perf. 13½		135.00	55.00
		Nos. 35-44 (10)	802.50	360.00

Nos. 37-44 were issued without gum.
For surcharges and overprints see Nos. 45, 58-66B, 110-118, 164-170, 239, Timor Nos. P1-P3.

No. 43 Surcharged in Red

1892 Without Gum Perf. 13½

45	A7	30r on 200r gray lil	120.00	55.00
a.	Perf. 12½		110.00	50.00
b.	As "a," inverted surcharge		120.00	55.00

King Carlos — A9

1894, Nov. 15 Typo. Perf. 11½

46	A9	5r yellow	14.00	5.75
47	A9	10r redsh violet	14.00	5.75
48	A9	15r chocolate	20.75	8.00
49	A9	20r lavender	37.00	9.25
50	A9	25r green	54.00	18.50
51	A9	50r lt blue	58.00	34.00
a.	Perf. 13½		850.00	600.00
52	A9	75r carmine	105.00	47.50
53	A9	80r yellow green	57.50	37.00
54	A9	100r brown, buff	62.50	34.75
55	A9	150r carmine, rose	65.00	34.75
56	A9	200r dk blue, blue	85.00	52.50
57	A9	300r dk blue, sal	127.50	62.50
		Nos. 46-57 (12)	700.25	350.25

Nos. 49-57 were issued without gum, No. 49 with or without gum.
For surcharges and overprints see Nos. 119-130, 171-181, 183-186, 240-251, 257-258.

Stamps of 1888 Surcharged in Red, Green or Black

1894 Without Gum Perf. 12½

58	A7	1a on 5r black (R)	18.00	9.25
a.	Short "1"		17.00	7.75
b.	Inverted surcharge		140.00	150.00
c.	Double surcharge		320.00	275.00
d.	Surch. on back instead of face		200.00	170.00
59	A7	3a on 20r car (G)	19.00	9.25
a.	Inverted surcharge		140.00	140.00
60	A7	4a on 25r violet (Bk)	36.00	19.00
a.	Inverted surcharge		100.00	90.00
61	A7	6a on 40r choc (Bk)	37.50	14.50
a.	Perf. 13½		30.00	25.00
62	A7	8a on 50r blue (R)	75.00	37.00
a.	Double surch., one inverted		225.00	200.00
b.	Inverted surcharge		225.00	190.00
c.	Perf. 13½		130.00	86.00
d.	As #62, double surch.		180.00	160.00
63	A7	13a on 80r gray (Bk)	38.00	15.00
a.	Double surcharge		325.00	190.00
64	A7	16a on 100r brn (Bk)	75.00	37.50
a.	Perf. 13½		180.00	190.00
b.	As "a," inverted surcharge		200.00	150.00
c.	As "#64," inverted surcharge		325.00	190.00
65	A7	31a on 200r gray lil (Bk)	100.00	55.00
a.	Inverted surcharge		225.00	200.00
b.	Perf. 13½		95.00	55.00
66	A7	47a on 300r org (G)	110.00	55.00
a.	Double surcharge		225.00	170.00
		Nos. 58-66 (9)	508.50	251.50

The style of type used for the word "PROVISORIO" on Nos. 58 to 66 differs for each value.
A 2a on 10r green was unofficially surcharged and denounced by the authorities. Value, $500.

On No. 45

66B	A7	5a on 30r on 200r	300.00	150.00
c.	Perf. 13½		300.00	150.00

Common Design Types pictured following the introduction.

Vasco da Gama Issue
Common Design Types

1898, Apr. 1 Engr. Perf. 12½ to 16

67	CD20	½a blue green	12.50	9.25
68	CD21	1a red	12.50	9.25
69	CD22	2a red violet	15.00	9.75
70	CD23	4a yellow green	20.75	14.00
71	CD24	8a dark blue	34.50	20.00
72	CD25	12a violet brown	54.00	33.50
73	CD26	16a bister brown	47.00	33.50
74	CD27	24a bister	54.00	41.00
		Nos. 67-74 (8)	250.25	170.25

For overprints and surcharges see Nos. 187-194.

MACAO

King Carlos — A11

1898-1903 Typo. Perf. 11½
Name and Value in Black except #103

75	A11	½a gray	5.50	1.80
a.		Perf. 12½	28.00	15.00
b.		As #75, black ("MACAU" and denom.) inverted	150.00	140.00
76	A11	1a orange	5.50	1.80
a.		Perf. 12½	28.00	15.00
b.		As #76, black ("MACAU" and denom.) inverted	250.00	225.00
77	A11	2a yellow green	7.00	2.15
a.		Black ("MACAU" and denom.) inverted	200.00	170.00
78	A11	2a gray grn ('03)	8.00	3.75
a.		Black ("MACAU" and denom.) inverted	35.00	35.00
79	A11	2½a red brown	10.75	4.00
80	A11	3a gray violet	10.75	4.00
81	A11	3a slate ('03)	8.00	3.75
82	A11	4a sea green	13.25	9.50
83	A11	4a carmine ('03)	8.00	3.75
84	A11	5a gray brn ('00)	17.75	6.75
85	A11	5a pale yel brn ('03)	11.50	6.25
86	A11	6a red brn ('03)	13.25	6.25
87	A11	8a blue	16.25	6.75
88	A11	8a gray brn ('03)	19.00	9.50
89	A11	10a sl bl ('00)	17.75	6.75
90	A11	12a rose	22.00	14.75
91	A11	12a red lil ('03)	73.50	29.50
92	A11	13a violet	26.50	14.75
93	A11	13a gray lilac ('03)	29.50	15.25
94	A11	15a pale ol grn ('03)	132.50	41.00
95	A11	16a dk blue, bl	25.00	14.75
96	A11	18a org brn, pink ('03)	48.00	29.50
97	A11	20a brn, yelsh ('00)	55.00	19.75
98	A11	24a brown, buff	32.50	16.50
99	A11	31a red lilac	38.50	18.75
100	A11	31a red lil, pink ('03)	48.00	29.50
101	A11	47a dk blue, rose	62.50	27.00
102	A11	47a dull bl, straw ('03)	81.00	39.50
103	A11	78a blk & red, bl ('00)	103.00	34.00
		Nos. 75-103 (29)	949.75	420.75

Issued without gum: Nos. 76a, 77, 79-80, 82, 84, 89, 94, 97 and 103.

For surcharges and overprints see Nos. 104-107, 132-136, 141, 147-157D, 159-161, 182, 195-209, 253-255, 258A.

Nos. 92, 95, 98-99 Surcharged in Black

1900 Without Gum
104	A11	5a on 13a violet	21.00	7.25
105	A11	10a on 16a dk bl, bl	23.50	9.00
106	A11	15a on 24a brn, buff	26.00	12.75
107	A11	20a on 31a red lilac	39.50	21.00
		Nos. 104-107 (4)	110.00	50.00

Nos. 106-107 were issued with and without gum.

Regular Issues Surcharged

On Stamps of 1884-85
1902 Black Surcharge Perf. 11½
108	A1	6a on 10r orange	41.00	18.00
a.		Double surcharge	240.00	160.00
109	A1	6a on 10r green	28.00	11.00

On Stamps of 1888
Red Surcharge Perf. 12½
110	A7	6a on 5r black	12.00	7.00
a.		Inverted surcharge	170.00	95.00

Black Surcharge
111	A7	6a on 10r green	11.00	7.00
112	A7	6a on 40r choc	11.00	7.00
a.		Double surcharge	170.00	80.00
b.		Perf. 13½	41.00	18.00
113	A7	18a on 20r rose	27.00	10.50
a.		Double surcharge	135.00	75.00
b.		Inverted surcharge	225.00	110.00
114	A7	18a on 25r violet	275.00	75.00
115	A7	18a on 80r gray	300.00	120.00
a.		Double surcharge	375.00	275.00
116	A7	18a on 100r brown	65.00	40.00
a.		Perf. 13½	140.00	60.00
117	A7	18a on 200r gray lil	275.00	120.00
a.		Perf. 12½	225.00	95.00
118	A7	18a on 300r orange	49.00	23.00
a.		Perf. 11½	50.00	25.00

Issued without gum: Nos. 110-118.

Nos. 109 to 118 inclusive, except No. 111, have been reprinted. The reprints have white gum and clean-cut perforation 13½ and the colors are usually paler than those of the originals.

On Stamps of 1894
1902-10 Perf. 11½, 13½
119	A9	6a on 5r yellow	11.00	5.50
a.		Inverted surcharge	160.00	100.00
120	A9	6a on 10r red vio	32.00	11.00
121	A9	6a on 15r choc	26.00	11.00
122	A9	6a on 25r green	12.50	5.50
123	A9	6a on 80r yel grn	12.50	5.50
124	A9	6a on 100r brn, buff, perf 13½	21.00	8.75
		Perf. 11½	35.00	17.00
125	A9	6a on 200r bl, bl	14.00	5.50
a.		Vert. half used as 3a on cover ('10)		95.00
126	A9	18a on 20r lavender	32.00	13.50
127	A9	18a on 50r lt blue	35.00	13.50
a.		Perf. 11½	100.00	33.00
128	A9	18a on 75r carmine	33.00	13.50
129	A9	18a on 150r car, rose	33.00	14.50
130	A9	18a on 300r bl, sal	35.00	13.50

On Newspaper Stamp of 1893
Perf. 12½
131	N3	18a on 2½r brown	14.00	9.00
a.		Perf. 13½	33.00	17.00
b.		Perf. 11½	47.00	22.00
		Nos. 108-131 (24)	1,405.	568.75

Issued without gum: Nos. 122-130, 131b.

Stamps of 1898-1900 Overprinted in Black

1902 Perf. 11½
132	A11	2a yellow green	27.00	9.50
133	A11	4a sea green	48.75	16.50
134	A11	8a blue	28.50	11.50
135	A11	10a slate blue	31.50	13.25
136	A11	14a rose	90.00	39.50
		Nos. 132-136 (5)	225.75	90.25

Issued without gum: Nos. 133, 135.
Reprints of No. 133 have shiny white gum and clean-cut perforation 13½. Value $1.

No. 91 Surcharged

1905 Without Gum
141	A11	10a on 12a red lilac	50.00	25.00

For overprint see No. 182.

Nos. J1-J3 Overprinted

1910, Oct. Perf. 11½x12
144	D1	½a gray green	20.00	12.00
a.		Inverted overprint	65.00	40.00
b.		Double overprint	60.00	60.00
c.		Pair, one without ovpt.		
145	D1	1a yellow green	26.00	12.00
a.		Inverted overprint	65.00	40.00
146	D1	2a slate	43.00	14.00
a.		Inverted overprint	120.00	55.00
		Nos. 144-146 (3)	89.00	38.00

No. 144 issued without gum, Nos. 145-146 with and without gum.

Stamps of 1898-1903 Overprinted in Carmine or Green

Overprint 24½mm long. "A" has flattened top.

Lisbon Overprint
1911, Apr. 2 Perf. 11½
147	A11	½a gray	2.60	.95
a.		Inverted overprint	20.00	20.00
147B	A11	1a orange	2.50	.95
c.		Inverted overprint	20.00	20.00
148	A11	2a gray green	2.50	.95
a.		Inverted overprint	17.50	15.00
149	A11	3a slate	6.25	.95
a.		Inverted overprint	17.50	15.00
150	A11	4a carmine (G)	6.75	3.75
		4a pale yel brn (error)	60.00	42.50
a.		As No. 150, inverted overprint	57.50	57.50
151	A11	5a pale yel brn	6.75	4.95
152	A11	6a red brown	6.75	4.95
153	A11	8a gray brown	6.75	4.95
154	A11	10a slate blue	6.75	4.95
155	A11	13a gray lilac	12.50	5.50
a.		Inverted overprint	60.00	55.00
156	A11	16a dk blue, bl	12.50	5.50
a.		Inverted overprint	60.00	60.00
157	A11	18a org brn, pink	19.75	7.50
157A	A11	20a brown, straw	19.75	7.50
157B	A11	31a red lil, pink	29.75	9.85
157C	A11	47a dull bl, straw	49.50	12.95
157D	A11	78a blk & red, bl	83.50	19.00
		Nos. 147-157D (16)	274.85	95.15

Issued without gum: Nos. 151, 153-157D.

Coat of Arms — A14

Red Surcharge
1911 Perf. 11½x12
158	A14	1a on 5r brn & buff	38.00	16.00
a.		"1" omitted	120.00	80.00
b.		Inverted surcharge	130.00	70.00

Stamps of 1900-03 Surcharged

Diagonal Halves
Black Surcharge
1911 Without Gum Perf. 11½
159	A11	2a on half of 4a car	75.00	50.00
a.		"2" omitted	150.00	120.00
d.		Inverted surcharge	225.00	130.00
e.		Entire stamp	270.00	
		Double surcharge	125.00	
159C	A11	5a on half of 10a sl bl (#89)	1,100.	600.00
e.		Entire stamp	8,750.	4,500.

Red Surcharge
160	A11	5a on half of 10a sl bl (#89)	900.00	600.00
a.		Inverted surcharge	1,100.	800.00
b.		Entire stamp	11,000.	5,000.
161	A11	5a on half of 10a sl bl (#135)	225.00	190.00
a.		Inverted surcharge	500.00	300.00
b.		Entire stamp	475.00	

Nos. 159-161 normally were bisected by the government before being placed on sale.

A15

Laid or Wove Paper
1911 Perf. 12x11½
162	A15	1a black	750.00	525.00
a.		"Correio"	3,250.	—
163	A15	2a black	800.00	525.00
a.		"Correio"	3,250.	—

The vast majority of used stamps were not canceled.

Surcharged Stamps of 1902 Overprinted in Red or Green

Overprint 23mm long. "A" has pointed top.

Local Overprint

1913 Without Gum Perf. 11½
164	A1	6a on 10r grn (R)	70.00	15.00
a.		"REPUBLICA" double	500.00	105.00

Perf. 12½, 13½
165	A7	6a on 5r black (G)	26.00	13.00
166	A7	6a on 10r grn (R)	39.00	20.00
167	A7	6a on 40r choc (R)	19.00	8.50
a.		Perf. 13½	90.00	43.00
168	A7	18a on 20r car (G)	30.00	12.50
169	A7	18a on 100r brn (R)	130.00	60.00
a.		Perf. 13½	160.00	110.00
170	A7	18a on 300r org (R)	55.00	13.00
a.		Perf. 13½	70.00	28.00
		Nos. 164-170 (7)	369.00	142.00

1913 Without Gum Perf. 11½
171	A9	6a on 10r red vio (G)	50.00	34.00
172	A9	6a on 10r red vio (R)	450.00	42.50
173	A9	6a on 15r choc (R)	24.00	8.00
174	A9	6a on 25r green (R)	25.00	11.00
175	A9	6a on 80r yel grn (R)	24.00	9.00
176	A9	6a on 100r brn, buff (R), buff, perf. 13½ (R)	39.00	12.50
a.		Perf. 11½	41.00	15.00
177	A9	18a on 20r lav (R)	55.00	26.00
178	A9	18a on 50r lt bl (R)	29.00	9.00
a.		Perf. 13½	36.00	11.50
179	A9	18a on 75r car (G)	31.00	10.00
180	A9	18a on 150r car, rose (G)	32.50	12.00
181	A9	18a on 300r dk bl, sal (R)	55.00	21.00

On No. 141
182	A11	10a on 12a red lil	37.50	11.00
		Nos. 171-182 (12)	852.00	206.00

"Republica" overprint exists inverted on Nos. 171-181.

Stamps of Preceding Issue Surcharged

1913 Without Gum Perf. 11½
183	A9	2a on 18a on 20r (R)	20.00	7.00
184	A9	2a on 18a on 50r (R)	20.00	7.00
a.		Perf. 13½	20.00	8.50
185	A9	2a on 18a on 75r (G)	20.00	7.00
186	A9	2a on 18a on 10r (G)	20.00	7.00
			80.00	28.00
		Nos. 183-186 (4)		

"Republica" overprint exists inverted on Nos. 183-186. Value, each $20.

The 2a surcharge exists inverted or double on Nos. 183-186. For values, see Classic Specialized Catalogue.

Vasco da Gama Issue Overprinted or Surcharged

j k

187	CD20 (j)	½a blue green	15.00	8.25
188	CD21 (j)	1a red	16.50	8.25
189	CD22 (j)	2a red violet	16.50	8.25
a.		Double ovpt., one inverted	100.00	100.00
190	CD23 (j)	4a yellow grn	15.00	8.25
191	CD24 (j)	8a dk blue	20.25	12.00
192	CD25 (k)	10a on 12a vio brn	46.50	23.50
193	CD26 (j)	16a bister brn	28.00	13.25
194	CD27 (j)	24a bister	42.50	17.75
		Nos. 187-194 (8)	200.25	99.50

Stamps of 1898-1903 Overprinted in Red or Green

1913 Without Gum Perf. 11½
195	A11	4a carmine (G)	400.00	150.00
a.		Double overprint	800.00	400.00
b.		Inverted overprint	800.00	
196	A11	5a yellow brn	90.00	29.00
a.		Inverted overprint	100.00	40.00
197	A11	6a red brown	250.00	95.00
a.		Inverted overprint	475.00	
198	A11	8a gray brown	1,500.	600.00
b.		Inverted overprint	5,500.	1,500.

MACAO

198A	A11	10a dull blue	27,500.	—
199	A11	13a violet	250.00	85.00
a.		Inverted overprint	375.00	140.00
200	A11	13a gray lilac	150.00	50.00
a.		Inverted overprint	290.00	
201	A11	16a blue, bl	75.00	29.00
202	A11	18a org brn, pink	75.00	29.00
a.		Inverted overprint	95.00	
203	A11	20a brown, yelsh	90.00	36.00
204	A11	31a red lil, pink	90.00	42.50
a.		Inverted overprint	95.00	
205	A11	47a dull bl, straw	130.00	60.00

Only 28 examples of No. 198A were sold by the Post Office.

Stamps of 1911-13 Surcharged

On Stamps of 1911 With Lisbon "Republica"

1913

206	A11	½a on 5a yel brn (R)	30.00	8.00
a.		"½ Avo" inverted	100.00	62.50
207	A11	4a on 8a gray brn (R)	60.00	12.50
a.		"4 Avos" inverted	120.00	62.50

On Stamps of 1913 With Local "Republica"

208	A11	1a on 13a violet (R)	350.00	70.00
209	A11	1a on 13a gray lil (R)	28.00	11.00
a.		Srch. on #155 (error)	1,150.	900.00
		Nos. 206-209 (4)	468.00	101.50

Issued without gum: Nos. 207-209.

"Ceres" — A16

Name and Value in Black

1913   Chalky Paper   Perf. 15x14

210	A16	½a olive brown	2.60	1.50
211	A16	1a black	2.60	1.80
212	A16	2a blue green	2.60	1.80
213	A16	4a carmine	7.25	3.40
214	A16	5a lilac brown	7.25	5.50
215	A16	6a lt violet	7.25	5.50
216	A16	8a lilac brown	7.25	5.50
217	A16	10a deep blue	7.25	5.50
218	A16	12a yellow brn	10.50	5.50
219	A16	16a slate	21.00	12.00
220	A16	20a orange brn	19.25	12.00
221	A16	40a plum	19.75	11.50
222	A16	58a brown, grn	36.00	26.00
223	A16	76a brown, pink	70.00	29.50
224	A16	1p orange, sal	93.00	36.00
225	A16	3p green, sal	185.00	112.00
		Nos. 210-225 (16)	498.55	275.00

1919   Ordinary Paper   Perf. 15x14

226	A16	½a olive brown	11.00	5.50
a.		Inscriptions inverted	50.00	
227	A16	1a black	11.00	5.50
a.		Inscriptions inverted	50.00	
b.		Inscriptions double	50.00	
228	A16	2a blue green	27.00	14.00
a.		Inscriptions inverted	40.00	
229	A16	4a carmine	85.00	32.50
		Nos. 226-229 (4)	134.00	57.50

1922-24   Perf. 12x11½

230	A16	½a olive brown	3.25	1.45
231	A16	1a black	3.25	1.45
232	A16	1½a yel grn ('24)	2.75	1.85
233	A16	2a blue green	7.25	3.25
234	A16	3a org brn	9.50	4.00
235	A16	4a carmine	21.50	10.25
236	A16	4a lemon ('24)	13.75	6.50
237	A16	6a gray ('23)	48.00	26.50
238	A16	8a lilac brown	21.00	10.00
238A	A16	10a pale bl ('23)	26.50	10.75
238B	A16	12a yellow brown	28.75	11.75
238C	A16	14a lilac ('24)	40.75	16.00
238D	A16	16a slate	270.00	200.00
238E	A16	24a sl grn ('23)	24.00	15.25
238F	A16	32a org brn ('24)	39.00	18.50
238G	A16	56a dl rose ('24)	48.00	23.75
238H	A16	72a brown ('23)	57.00	28.00
238I	A16	1p org ('24)	190.00	41.00

Glazed Paper

238J	A16	3p pale turq ('24)	407.50	185.00
238K	A16	5p car rose ('24)	335.00	185.00
		Nos. 230-238K (20)	1,597.50	800.50

For surcharges see Nos. 256, 259-267.
Nos. 222-238K exist with the five-pointed stars on each side of "MACAU" in various positions. Position I, upright, pointing up. Position II, inverted, pointing down. Position III, star leaning to the right. Position IV, star leaning to the left. Nos. 210-229 are most common with both stars in position I. Other positions are worth more. Nos. 230-238K are most common with the left star in position III and the right star in position IV. Other positions are worth more.

Preceding Issues and No. P4 Overprinted in Carmine

On Stamps of 1902 With Lisbon "Republica"

Perf. 11½, 12, 12½, 13½, 11½x12

1915

239	A7	6a on 10r green	70.00	46.00
240	A9	6a on 5r yellow	19.00	8.50
241	A9	6a on 10r red vio	19.00	9.00
a.		Inverted surcharge	30.00	20.00
242	A9	6a on 15r choc	16.00	7.75
243	A9	6a on 25r green	17.00	9.00
244	A9	6a on 80r yel grn	19.00	9.00
245	A9	6a on 100r brn, buff	18.00	9.00
a.		Inverted surcharge	30.00	20.00
b.		Perf. 13½	18.00	9.00
246	A9	6a on 200r bl, bl	23.00	13.00
247	A9	18a on 20r lav	30.00	13.00
248	A9	18a on 50r lt bl	30.00	14.50
a.		Perf. 13½		
249	A9	18a on 75r car	30.00	14.50
250	A9	18a on 150r car, rose	45.00	22.50
251	A9	18a on 300r bl, sal	65.00	25.00

Perf. 12½

252	N3	18a on 2½a brn	29.00	13.50
a.		Perf. 13½	32.50	14.00

With Additional Overprint

253	A11	8a blue	27.00	15.00
254	A11	10a slate blue	26.00	14.00
a.		"Provisorio" double	110.00	

On Stamp of 1905

255	A11	10a on 12a red lil	29.00	15.00
a.		Inverted surcharge	35.00	22.00
		Nos. 239-255 (17)	510.00	258.25

Issued without gum: Nos. 243-251 and 255.

No. 217 Surcharged

Without Gum

1919-20   Perf. 15x14

256	A16	½a on 5a lilac brn	150.00	60.00
a.		"AVO" omitted	110.00	110.00

Nos. 243 and 244 Surcharged

257	A9	2a on 6a on 25r green	900.00	350.00
258	A9	2a on 6a on 80r yel grn	375.00	200.00

No. 152 Surcharged

258A	A11	2a on 6a red brown	375.00	150.00
		Nos. 256-258A (4)	1,800.	760.00

Issued without gum: Nos. 256-258A.

Stamps of 1913-24 Surcharged

1931-33   Perf. 12x11½

259	A16	1a on 24a slate grn ('33)	16.75	6.50
260	A16	2a on 32a org brn ('33)	16.75	6.50
261	A16	4a on 12a bis brn ('33)	16.75	6.50
262	A16	5a on 6a lt gray ('33)	90.00	56.50
264	A16	7a on 8a lil brn	27.00	8.00
265	A16	12a on 14a lilac	27.00	8.00
266	A16	15a on 16a dk gray ('33)	27.00	8.00
267	A16	20a on 56a dull rose ('33)	70.00	52.00

Chalky Paper
Perf. 15x14

263	A16	5a on 6a lt vio ('33)	33.00	17.75
		Nos. 259-267 (9)	324.25	169.75

"Portugal" and Vasco da Gama's Flagship "San Gabriel" — A17

Wmk. 232

1934, Feb. 1   Typo.   Perf. 11½

268	A17	½a bister	1.10	.60
269	A17	1a olive brown	1.10	.60
270	A17	2a blue green	1.90	.90
271	A17	3a violet	2.20	.90
272	A17	4a black	2.75	.90
273	A17	5a gray	2.75	1.05
274	A17	6a brown	2.75	1.05
275	A17	7a brt rose	4.00	1.40
276	A17	8a brt blue	4.00	1.40
277	A17	10a red orange	9.50	2.60
278	A17	12a dark blue	9.50	2.60
279	A17	14a olive green	9.50	2.60
280	A17	15a maroon	9.50	2.60
281	A17	20a orange	9.50	2.60
282	A17	30a apple green	18.00	4.90
283	A17	40a violet	18.00	4.90
284	A17	50a olive bister	28.00	8.50
285	A17	1p lt blue	94.00	26.00
286	A17	2p brown org	115.00	36.00
287	A17	3p emerald	185.00	59.00
288	A17	5p dark violet	285.00	89.00
		Nos. 268-288 (21)	813.05	250.10

See Nos. 316-323. For overprints and surcharges see Nos. 306-315, C1-C6, J43-J49.

Common Design Types

Perf. 13½x13

1938, Aug. 1   Engr.   Unwmk.
Name and Value in Black

289	CD34	1a gray green	1.70	.75
290	CD34	2a orange brown	1.95	1.20
291	CD34	3a dk vio brn	1.95	1.20
292	CD34	4a brt green	1.95	1.20
293	CD35	5a dk carmine	1.95	1.20
294	CD35	6a slate	2.50	3.00
295	CD35	8a rose violet	3.40	4.95
296	CD37	10a brt red vio	4.00	4.95
297	CD37	12a red	4.25	4.95
298	CD37	15a orange	4.25	4.95
299	CD36	20a blue	22.00	6.25
300	CD36	40a gray black	22.00	7.75
301	CD36	50a brown	22.00	7.75
302	CD38	1p brown car	71.00	22.00
303	CD38	3p olive green	115.00	38.50
304	CD38	3p blue violet	160.00	57.00
305	CD38	6p red brown	260.00	82.00
		Nos. 289-305 (17)	699.90	249.60

For surcharge see No. 315A.

Stamps of 1934 Surcharged in Black

a   b

1941   Wmk. 232   Perf. 11½x12

306	A17(a)	1a on 6a brown	12.00	8.00
307	A17(b)	2a on 6a brown	4.85	4.15
308	A17(b)	3a on 6a brown	4.85	4.15
309	A17(a)	5a on 7a brt rose	157.50	96.00
310	A17(b)	5a on 7a brt rose	22.50	11.50
311	A17(a)	5a on 8a brt blue	26.50	16.00
312	A17(b)	5a on 8a brt blue	15.75	11.50
313	A17(b)	8a on 30a apple grn	15.25	9.50
314	A17(b)	8a on 40a violet	15.25	9.50
315	A17(b)	8a on 50a ol bis	15.25	9.50
		Nos. 306-315 (10)	289.70	179.80

No. 294 Surcharged in Black

1941   Unwmk.   Perf. 13½x13

315A	CD35	3a on 6a slate	130.00	55.00

Counterfeits exist.

"Portugal" Type of 1934

1934 Issue   1942 Issue

The lines in the background are more widely spaced than on the original 1934 issue; also the 1942 issue has no imprint at Lower Right.

1942   Litho.   Rough Perf. 12
Thin Paper Without Gum

316	A17	1a olive brown	4.00	2.15
317	A17	2a blue green	4.00	2.15
318	A17	3a vio, perf. 11	40.00	14.00
a.		Perf. 12	31.00	13.75
319	A17	6a brown	31.50	12.25
a.		Perf. 11	45.00	25.00
b.		Perf. 11	49.00	27.00
320	A17	10a red orange	19.50	9.25
321	A17	20a orange	19.50	8.25
a.		Perf. 11	59.00	22.50
322	A17	30a apple green	23.50	12.25
323	A17	40a violet	47.00	16.25
		Nos. 316-323 (8)	189.00	75.55

Nos. 316-323 doesn't have imprint on lower right and lines in background are more widely spaced than on the original 1934 issue.

MACAO

Macao Dwelling — A18

Pagoda of Barra — A19

Designs: 2a, Mountain fort. 3a, View of Macao. 8a, Praia Grande Bay. 10a, Leal Senado Square. 20a, Sao Jeronimo Hill. 30a, Marginal Ave. 50a, Relief of Goddess Ma. 1p, Gate of Cerco. 3p, Post Office. 5p, Solidao Walk.

1948, Dec. 20   Litho.   Perf. 10½

324	A18	1a dk brn & org	1.75	.95
325	A19	2a rose brn & rose	1.30	.95
326	A18	3a brn vio & lil	3.00	1.50
327	A18	8a rose car & rose	2.25	2.00
328	A18	10a lil rose & rose	3.75	2.75
329	A18	20a dk blue & gray	4.75	3.50
330	A18	30a black & gray	12.00	6.00
331	A18	50a brn & pale bis	22.00	12.50
332	A19	1p emer & pale grn	102.50	31.00
333	A19	2p scarlet & rose	90.00	38.75
334	A19	3p dl grn & gray grn	102.50	41.00
335	A18	5p vio bl & gray	180.00	38.75
		Nos. 324-335 (12)	525.80	179.65
		Set, never hinged	1,500.	

See Nos. 341-347A.

Catalogue values for unused stamps in this section, from this point to the end of the section, are for Never Hinged items.

Lady of Fatima Issue
Common Design Type

1949, Feb. 1   Unwmk.   Perf. 14½

| 336 | CD40 | 8a scarlet | 90.00 | 30.00 |

Symbols of the UPU — A20

1949, Dec. 24   Litho.   Unwmk.

| 337 | A20 | 32a claret & rose | 200.00 | 50.00 |

75th anniv. of the formation of the UPU.

Holy Year Issue
Common Design Types

1950, July 26   Perf. 13x13½

| 339 | CD41 | 32a dk slate gray | 55.00 | 16.00 |
| 340 | CD42 | 50a carmine | 55.00 | 18.00 |

Scenic Types of 1948
Designs as before.

1950-51   Perf. 14

341	A18	1a violet & rose	8.25	1.75
342	A19	2a ol bis & yel	8.25	1.75
343	A18	3a org red & buff	12.75	2.15
344	A18	8a slate & gray	18.25	3.00
345	A18	10a red brn & org	22.00	6.50
346	A18	30a vio bl & bl	58.00	7.75
347	A18	50a ol grn & yel grn	84.00	8.75
347A	A19	1p dk org brn & org brn	157.50	43.50
		Nos. 341-347A (8)	369.00	75.15

A 1p ultra & vio, perf. 11, was not sold in Macao. Value $150.

Nos. 341-347 issued in 1951, the 1p in 1950.

Dragon — A21

1951   Perf. 11½x12

| 348 | A21 | 1a org yel, *lemon* | 5.50 | 2.20 |
| 349 | A21 | 2a dk grn, *blue* | 5.50 | 2.20 |

Shaded Background

350	A21	10a vio brn, *blue*	18.75	4.75
351	A21	10a brt pink, *blue*	17.75	4.75
		Nos. 348-351 (4)	47.50	13.90

Nos. 348-351 were isuued without gum.
For overprints see Nos. J50-J52.

Holy Year Extension Issue
Common Design Type

1951, Dec. 3   Litho.   Perf. 14

| 352 | CD43 | 60a mag & pink + label | 110.00 | 23.00 |

Stamp without label sells for much less.

Fernao Mendes Pinto — A22

Portraits: 2a and 10a, St. Francis Xavier. 3a and 50a, Jorge Alvares. 6a and 30a, Luis de Camoens.

1951, Aug. 27   Perf. 11½

Background Color

353	A22	1a steel bl & gray bl	1.25	.60
354	A22	2a dk brn & ol grn	1.80	.60
355	A22	3a deep grn & grn	2.30	1.20
356	A22	6a purple	8.00	1.55
357	A22	10a red brn & org	18.00	2.75
358	A22	20a brown car	29.50	5.85
359	A22	30a dk brn & ol grn	49.00	9.50
360	A22	50a red & orange	119.00	22.00
		Nos. 353-360 (8)	228.85	44.05

Sampan A23

Junk A24

Design: 5p, Junk.

1951, Nov. 1   Unwmk.

361	A23	1p vio bl & bl	74.00	5.45
362	A24	3p black & vio	255.00	25.00
363	A23	5p henna brown	315.00	54.50
		Nos. 361-363 (3)	644.00	84.95

Medical Congress Issue
Common Design Type

Design: Sao Rafael Hospital.

1952, June 16   Unwmk.   Perf. 13½

| 364 | CD44 | 6a black & purple | 20.00 | 7.00 |

St. Francis Xavier Issue

Statue of St. Francis Xavier — A25

16a, Arm of St. Francis. 40a, Tomb of St. Francis.

1952, Nov. 28   Litho.   Perf. 14

365	A25	3a blk, *grnsh gray*	6.75	1.60
366	A25	16a choc, *buff*	28.00	5.25
367	A25	40a blk, *blue*	40.00	9.25
		Nos. 365-367 (3)	74.75	16.10

400th anniv. of the death of St. Francis Xavier.

Statue of Virgin Mary — A26

1953, Apr. 28   Unwmk.   Perf. 13½

368	A26	8a choc & beige	8.25	2.00
369	A26	10a blue blk & tan	28.25	7.50
370	A26	50a ol grn & gray brn	48.00	11.25
		Nos. 368-370 (3)	84.50	20.75

Exhibition of Sacred Missionary Art, held at Lisbon in 1951.

Stamp of Portugal and Arms of Colonies — A27

1954, Mar. 9   Photo.   Perf. 13

| 371 | A27 | 10a multicolored | 23.00 | 5.50 |

Cent. of Portugal's first postage stamps.

Firecracker Flower — A28

Flowers: 3a, Forget-me-not. 5a, Dragon claw. 10a, Nunflower. 16a, Narcissus. 30a, Peach flower. 39a, Lotus flower. 1p, Chrysanthemum. 3p, Cherry blossoms. 5p, Tangerine blossoms.

1953, Sept. 22   Perf. 11½

Flowers in Natural Colors

372	A28	1a dark red	1.10	.60
373	A28	3a dark green	1.10	.60
374	A28	5a dark brown	1.45	.65
375	A28	10a dp grnsh blue	1.45	.65
376	A28	16a yellow brown	2.35	.80
377	A28	30a dk olive grn	5.50	1.65
378	A28	39a violet blue	6.00	1.65
379	A28	1p deep plum	13.75	1.95
380	A28	3p dark gray	26.75	4.25
381	A28	5p deep carmine	50.00	7.00
		Nos. 372-381 (10)	109.45	19.80

For surcharges see Nos. 443-444.

Sao Paulo Issue
Common Design Type

1954, Aug. 4   Litho.   Perf. 13½

| 382 | CD46 | 39a org, cream & blk | 30.00 | 6.00 |

Sao Paulo founding, 400th anniversary.
For surcharge see No. 445.

Map of Colony — A29

Inscriptions and design in brown, red, green, ultra & yellow (buff on 10a, 40a, 90a)

1956, May 10   Perf. 12½x13½

383	A29	1a pale green	1.15	.75
384	A29	3a pale gray	2.50	.95
385	A29	5a pale pink	3.45	1.40
386	A29	10a buff	7.50	1.70
387	A29	30a lt blue	14.25	2.35
388	A29	40a pale green	21.75	3.25
389	A29	90a pale gray	34.50	6.00
390	A29	1.50p pink	55.00	7.50
		Nos. 383-390 (8)	140.10	23.90

Exhibition Emblems and View — A30

1958, Nov. 8   Litho.   Perf. 14½

| 391 | A30 | 70a multicolored | 12.50 | 3.75 |

World's Fair, Brussels, Apr. 17-Oct. 19.

Tropical Medicine Congress Issue
Common Design Type

Design: Cinnamomum camphora.

1958, Nov. 15   Perf. 13½

| 392 | CD47 | 20a multicolored | 13.00 | 6.00 |

Armillary Sphere — A31

1960, June 25   Litho.   Perf. 13½

| 393 | A31 | 2p multicolored | 23.00 | 8.00 |

500th anniversary of the death of Prince Henry the Navigator.

Sports Issue
Common Design Type

Sports: 10a, Field hockey. 16a, Wrestling. 20a, Table tennis. 50a, Motorcycling. 1.20p, Relay race. 2.50p, Badminton.

1962, Feb. 9   Perf. 13½

Multicolored Design

394	CD48	10a blue & yel grn	3.60	.90
395	CD48	16a brt pink	4.25	1.80
396	CD48	20a orange	6.00	2.00
397	CD48	50a rose	11.00	2.50
398	CD48	1.20p blue & beige	43.50	5.75
399	CD48	2.50p gray & brown	61.50	16.00
		Nos. 394-399 (6)	129.85	28.95

Anti-Malaria Issue
Common Design Type

Design: Anopheles hyrcanus sinensis.

1962, Apr. 7   Litho.   Perf. 13½

| 400 | CD49 | 40a multicolored | 12.00 | 4.00 |

Bank Building — A32

1964, May 16   Unwmk.   Perf. 13½

| 401 | A32 | 20a multicolored | 19.00 | 4.00 |

Centenary of the National Overseas Bank of Portugal.

ITU Issue
Common Design Type

1965, May 17   Litho.   Perf. 14½

| 402 | CD52 | 10a pale grn & multi | 9.00 | 3.00 |

National Revolution Issue
Common Design Type

Design: 10a, Infante D. Henrique School and Count de S. Januario Hospital.

1966, May 28   Litho.   Perf. 11½

| 403 | CD53 | 10a multicolored | 9.00 | 3.75 |

Drummer, 1548 — A32a

Designs: 15a, Soldier with sword, 1548. 20a, Harquebusier, 1649. 40a, Infantry officer, 1783. 50a, Infantry soldier, 1783. 60a, Colonial infantry soldier (Indian), 1902. 1p, Colonial infantry soldier (Chinese), 1903. 3p, Colonial infantry soldier (Chinese) 1904.

1966, Aug. 8   Litho.   Perf. 13

404	A32a	10a multicolored	3.00	.75
405	A32a	15a multicolored	5.50	1.40
406	A32a	20a multicolored	6.50	1.40
407	A32a	40a multicolored	10.75	1.60
408	A32a	50a multicolored	12.50	2.75
409	A32a	60a multicolored	29.50	3.25
410	A32a	1p multicolored	37.00	5.50
411	A32a	3p multicolored	65.00	14.00
		Nos. 404-411 (8)	169.75	30.65

Navy Club Issue, 1967
Common Design Type

Designs: 10a, Capt. Oliveira E. Carmo and armed launch Vega. 20a, Capt. Silva Junior and frigate Dom Fernando.

1967, Jan. 31   Litho.   Perf. 13

| 412 | CD54 | 10a multicolored | 5.25 | 1.20 |
| 413 | CD54 | 20a multicolored | 12.75 | 3.50 |

MACAO

Arms of Pope Paul VI and Golden Rose — A33

1967, May 13		Perf. 12½x13
414	A33 50a multicolored	15.00 3.00

50th anniversary of the apparition of the Virgin Mary to three shepherd children at Fatima.

Cabral Issue

Cabral Monument, Lisbon — A34

Design: 70a, Cabral monument, Belmonte.

1968, Apr. 22	Litho.	Perf. 14
415	A34 20a multicolored	8.50 1.60
416	A34 70a multicolored	14.25 4.40

500th anniversary of the birth of Pedro Alvares Cabral, navigator who took possession of Brazil for Portugal.

Admiral Coutinho Issue
Common Design Type

Design: 20a, Adm. Coutinho with sextant, vert.

1969, Feb. 17	Litho.	Perf. 14
417	CD55 20a multicolored	7.50 2.25

Church of Our Lady of the Relics, Vidigueira — A35

Vasco da Gama Issue

1969, Aug. 29	Litho.	Perf. 14
418	A35 1p multicolored	22.50 3.00

Vasco da Gama (1469-1524), navigator.

Administration Reform Issue
Common Design Type

1969, Sept. 25	Litho.	Perf. 14
419	CD56 90a multicolored	12.50 2.00

Bishop D. Belchior Carneiro — A36

1969, Oct. 16	Litho.	Perf. 13
420	A36 50a multicolored	7.50 1.50

4th centenary of the founding of the Santa Casa da Misericordia in Macao.

King Manuel I Issue

Portal of Mother Church, Golega — A37

1969, Dec. 1	Litho.	Perf. 14
421	A37 30a multicolored	12.50 1.75

500th anniversary of the birth of King Manuel I.

Marshal Carmona Issue
Common Design Type

5a, Antonio Oscar Carmona in general's uniform.

1970, Nov. 15	Litho.	Perf. 14
422	CD57 5a multicolored	5.00 1.75

Dragon Mask — A38

1971, Sept. 30		Perf. 13½
423	A38 5a lt blue & multi	1.95 .90
424	A38 10a Lion mask	8.00 1.35

Lusiads Issue

Portuguese Delegation at Chinese Court — A39

1972, May 25	Litho.	Perf. 13
425	A39 20a citron & multi	25.00 8.00

4th centenary of publication of The Lusiads by Luiz Camoens.

Olympic Games Issue
Common Design Type

Design: Hockey and Olympic emblem.

1972, June 20		Perf. 14x13½
426	CD59 50a multicolored	2.50 1.50

Lisbon-Rio de Janeiro Flight Issue
Common Design Type

Design: "Santa Cruz" landing in Rio de Janeiro.

1972, Sept. 20	Litho.	Perf. 13½
427	CD60 5p multicolored	40.00 12.00

Pedro V Theater and Lyre — A42

1972, Dec. 25	Litho.	Perf. 13½
428	A42 2p multicolored	20.00 4.50

Centenary of Pedro V Theater, Macao.

WMO Centenary Issue
Common Design Type

1973, Dec. 15	Litho.	Perf. 13
429	CD61 20a blue grn & multi	15.00 2.50

Viscount St. Januario — A44

Design: 60a, Hospital, 1874 and 1974.

1974, Jan. 25	Litho.	Perf. 13½
430	A44 15a multicolored	2.00 .95
431	A44 60a multicolored	6.00 1.30

Viscount St. Januario Hospital, Macao, cent. For surcharge see No. 457.

George Chinnery, Self-portrait — A45

1974, Sept. 23	Litho.	Perf. 14
432	A45 30a multicolored	7.50 2.50

George Chinnery (1774-1852), English painter who lived in Macao.

Macao-Taipa Bridge — A46

Design: 2.20p, Different view of bridge.

1974, Oct. 7	Litho.	Perf. 14x13½
433	A46 20a multicolored	3.25 1.50
434	A46 2.20p multicolored	26.50 3.00

Inauguration of the Macao-Taipa Bridge. For surcharge see No. 446.

Man Raising Banner — A47

1975, Apr. 25		Perf. 12
435	A47 10a ocher & multi	5.00 3.00
436	A47 1p multicolored	22.50 6.95

Revolution of Apr. 25, 1974, 1st anniv.

Pou Chai Pagoda — A48

Design: 20p, Tin Hau Pagoda.

1976, Jan. 30	Litho.	Perf. 13½x13
437	A48 10p multicolored	20.00 6.50
438	A48 20p multicolored	44.50 11.00

A 1p stamp for the 400th anniv. of the Macao Diocese was prepared but not issued. Some stamps were sold in Lisbon. Value $150.

"The Law" A50

1978	Litho.	Perf. 13½
440	A50 5a blk, dk & lt blue	11.95 4.50
441	A50 2p blk, org brn & buff	250.00 20.00
442	A50 5p blk, ol & yel grn	90.00 20.00
	Nos. 440-442 (3)	351.95 44.50

Legislative Assembly, Aug. 9, 1976.

Nos. 376, 378, 382, 434 Surcharged

1979, Nov.		
443	A28 10a on 16a	13.50 6.00
444	A28 30a on 39a (#378)	16.75 6.00
445	CD46 30a on 39a (#382)	74.00 30.00
446	A46 2p on 2.20p	14.75 12.25
	Nos. 443-446 (4)	119.00 54.25

Luis do Camoens (1524-80), Poet — A51

1981, June	Litho.	Perf. 13½
447	A51 10a multicolored	1.70 1.45
448	A51 30a multicolored	3.25 1.60
449	A51 1p multicolored	7.50 4.75
450	A51 3p multicolored	11.50 7.00
	Nos. 447-450 (4)	23.95 14.80

Buddha, Macao Cathedral — A52

1981, Sept.		
451	A52 15a multicolored	.85 .60
452	A52 40a multicolored	1.30 .60
453	A52 50a multicolored	2.15 .75
454	A52 60a multicolored	3.25 1.15
455	A52 1p multicolored	4.15 1.50
456	A52 2.20p multicolored	10.25 2.15
	Nos. 451-456 (6)	21.95 6.75

Transcultural Psychiatry Symposium.

No. 431 Surcharged

1981	Litho.	Perf. 13½
457	A44 30a on 60a multi	10.75 2.05

Health Services Building — A53

Designs: Public Buildings and Monuments: 40a, Guia Lighthouse. 1p, Portas do Cerco. 2p, Luis de Camoes Museum. 10p, School Welfare Service Building.

1982, June 10	Litho.	Perf. 12x12½
458	A53 30a shown	.75 .40
459	A53 40a multicolored	.95 .40
460	A53 1p multicolored	1.85 .45
461	A53 2p multicolored	3.75 .80
462	A53 10p multicolored	16.25 5.50
	Nos. 458-462 (5)	23.55 7.55

See Nos. 472-476, 489-493.

Autumn Festivals — A54

Designs: Painted paper lanterns.

1982, Oct. 1		Perf. 12x11½
463	A54 40a multicolored	4.50 1.75
464	A54 1p multicolored	12.00 3.95
465	A54 2p multicolored	14.75 7.75
466	A54 5p multicolored	33.75 12.50
	Nos. 463-466 (4)	65.00 25.95

Geographical Position — A55

1982, Dec. 1	Litho.	Perf. 13
467	A55 50a Aerial view	15.00 2.60
468	A55 3p Map	50.00 10.50

World Communications Year — A56

No. 469, Telephone operators. No. 470, Mailman, mailbox. No. 471, Globe, satellites.

1983, Feb. 16		Perf. 13½
469	A56 60a multicolored	2.75 .70
470	A56 3p multicolored	6.00 3.95
471	A56 6p multicolored	11.25 6.75
	Nos. 469-471 (3)	20.00 11.40

Architecture Type of 1982

No. 472, Social Welfare Institute. No. 473, St. Joseph's Seminary. No. 474, St. Dominic's Church. No. 475, St. Paul's Church ruins. No. 476, Senate House.

1983, May 12	Litho.	Perf. 13
472	A53 40a multi	.50 .40
473	A53 80a multi	1.10 .65
474	A53 1.50p multi	1.85 1.20

MACAO

475	A53 2.50p multi	2.65	2.25
476	A53 7.50p multi	8.50	5.25
	Nos. 472-476 (5)	14.60	9.75

Medicinal Plants — A57

No. 477, Asclepias curassavica. No. 478, Acanthus ilicifolius. No. 479, Melastoma sanguineum. No. 480, Nelumbo nucifera. No. 481, Bombax malabaricum. No. 482, Hibiscus mutabilis.

1983, July 14 Litho. Perf. 13½x14
477	A57 20a multi	1.60	.85
478	A57 40a multi	2.40	.85
479	A57 60a multi	3.25	1.25
480	A57 70a multi	4.50	1.90
481	A57 1.50p multi	6.75	2.80
482	A57 2.50p multi	12.75	5.25
a.	Souvenir sheet of 6, #477-482	275.00	180.00
	Nos. 477-482 (6)	31.25	12.90

No. 482a sold for 6.50p.

16th Century Discoveries A58

1983, Nov. 15 Litho. Perf. 13½x14
483	4p multicolored	10.00	6.00
484	4p multicolored	10.00	6.00
a.	A58 Pair, #483-484	21.00	12.50

A60

1984, Jan. 25 Litho. Perf. 13½
485	A60 60a multicolored	12.00	8.00
a.	Booklet pane of 5	65.00	

New Year 1984 (Year of the Rat).
No. 485a has straight edges.
See Nos. 504, 522, 540, 560, 583, 611, 639, 662, 684, 718, 757, 804.

A61

Design of First Stamp Issue, 1884.

1984, Mar. 1 Litho. Perf. 12½
486	A61 40a orange & blk	2.00	.70
487	A61 3p gray & blk	5.00	2.00
488	A61 5p sepia & blk	10.75	4.25
a.	Souvenir sheet of 3, #486-488	50.00	40.00
	Nos. 486-488 (3)	17.75	7.45

Centenary of Macao postage stamps.

Architecture Type of 1982

No. 489, Holy House of Mercy. No. 490, St. Lawrence Church. No. 491, King Peter V Theater. No. 492, Palace of St. Sancha. No. 493, Moorish barracks.

1984, May 18 Litho. Perf. 13½
489	A53 20a multicolored	.50	.50
490	A53 60a multicolored	.90	.90
491	A53 90a multicolored	1.40	1.05
492	A53 3p multicolored	3.35	1.35
493	A53 15p multicolored	10.50	4.75
	Nos. 489-493 (5)	16.65	8.35

Birds, Ausipex '84 Emblem — A62

30a, Kingfishers. 40a, European jay. 50a, White eyes. 70a, Hoopoe. 2.50p, Peking nightingale. 6p, Wild duck.

1984, Sept. 21 Litho. Perf. 13
494	A62 30a multicolored	1.65	.65
495	A62 40a multicolored	1.75	.70
496	A62 50a multicolored	2.85	.90
497	A62 70a multicolored	4.75	1.20
498	A62 2.50p multicolored	9.50	3.15
499	A62 6p multicolored	17.50	5.00
	Nos. 494-499 (6)	38.00	11.40

Philakorea '84 Emblem, Fishing Boats — A63

1984, Oct. 22 Litho.
500	A63 20a Hok lou t'eng	1.50	.45
501	A63 60a Tai t'ong	2.60	1.15
502	A63 2p Tai mei chai	6.50	2.25
503	A63 5p Ch'at pong t'o	14.25	5.50
	Nos. 500-503 (4)	24.85	9.35

New Year Type of 1984

1985, Feb. 13 Litho. Perf. 13½
504	A60 1p Water buffalo	10.00	4.50
a.	Booklet pane of 5	45.00	

Intl. Youth Year — A65

1985, Apr. 19 Litho. Perf. 13½
505	A65 2.50p shown	7.50	1.35
506	A65 3p Clasped hands	9.75	3.15

Visit of President Eanes of Portugal — A66

1985, May 27 Litho.
507	A66 1.50p multicolored	6.25	3.00

Luis de Camoens Museum, 25th Anniv. — A67

Silk paintings by Chen Chi Yun. No. 508, Two travelers, hermit. No. 509, Traveling merchant. No. 510, Conversation in a garden. No. 511, Veranda of a house.

1985, June 27 Litho.
508	A67 2.50p multi	11.75	2.75
509	A67 2.50p multi	11.75	2.75
510	A67 2.50p multi	11.75	2.75
511	A67 2.50p multi	11.75	2.75
a.	Block or strip of 4, #508-511	50.00	50.00
	Nos. 508-511 (4)	47.00	11.00

Butterflies, World Tourism Assoc. Emblem — A68

No. 512, Euploea midamus. No. 513, Hebomoia glaucippe. No. 514, Lethe confusa. No. 515, Heliophorus epicles. No. 516, Euthalia phemius seitzi. No. 517, Troides helena.

1985, Sept. 27 Litho.
512	A68 30a multi	2.10	.40
513	A68 50a multi	2.50	.60
514	A68 70a multi	4.00	.65
515	A68 2p multi	5.50	1.65
516	A68 4p multi	11.75	2.90
517	A68 7.50p multi	16.00	5.75
a.	Sheet of 6, #512-517	275.00	140.00
	Nos. 512-517 (6)	41.85	11.95

World Tourism Day.

Cargo Boats — A69

Designs: 50a, Tou. 70a, Veng Seng Lei motor junk. 1p, Tong Heng Long No. 2 motor junk. 6p, Fong Vong San cargo ship.

1985, Oct. 25 Perf. 14
518	A69 50a multicolored	1.50	.45
519	A69 70a multicolored	4.00	.95
520	A69 1p multicolored	7.00	2.10
521	A69 6p multicolored	12.25	5.75
	Nos. 518-521 (4)	24.75	9.25

New Year Type of 1984

1986, Feb. 3 Perf. 13½
522	A60 1.50p Tiger	8.50	2.00
a.	Booklet pane of 5	45.00	

No. 522a has straight edges.

City of Macau, 400th Anniv. — A71

1986, Apr. 10 Litho. Perf. 13½
523	A71 2.20p multicolored	9.50	3.75

Musical Instruments — A72

1986, May 22
524	A72 20a Suo-na	5.75	1.60
525	A72 50a Sheng	6.50	2.25
526	A72 60a Er-hu	8.00	2.75
527	A72 70a Ruan	13.00	3.50
528	A72 5p Cheng	30.00	4.95
529	A72 8p Pi-pa	36.50	9.00
a.	Souvenir sheet of 6, #524-529	375.00	125.00
	Nos. 524-529 (6)	99.75	24.05

AMERIPEX '86.

Ferries — A73

1986, Aug. 28 Litho. Perf. 13
530	A73 10a Hydrofoil	1.00	.55
531	A73 40a Hovermarine	4.25	1.05
532	A73 3p Jetfoil	6.75	2.30
533	A73 7.5p High-speed ferry	15.00	5.00
	Nos. 530-533 (4)	27.00	8.90

Fortresses — A74

No. 534, Taipa. No. 535, Sao Paulo do Monte. No. 536, Our Lady of Guia. No. 537, Sao Francisco.

1986, Oct. 3 Litho. Perf. 12½
534	A74 2p multi	16.00	8.50
535	A74 2p multi	16.00	8.50
536	A74 2p multi	16.00	8.50
537	A74 2p multi	16.00	8.50
a.	Block or strip of 4, #534-537	100.00	70.00
	Nos. 534-537 (4)	64.00	34.00

Macao Security Forces, 10th anniv. No. 537a has continuous design.

A75

Dr. Sun Yat-sen A76

1986, Nov. 12 Litho. Perf. 12½
538	A75 70a multicolored	7.00	3.50

Souvenir Sheet
539	A76 1.30p shown	90.00	65.00

New Year Type of 1984

1987, Jan. 21 Perf. 13½
540	A60 1.50p Hare	9.50	2.25
a.	Booklet pane of 5	60.00	

No. 540a has straight edges.

Shek Wan Ceramic Figures in the Luis de Camoens Museum — A78

No. 541, Medicine man (4/1). No. 542, Choi San, god of good fortune (4/2). No. 543, Yi, sun god (4/3). No. 544, Chung Kuei, conqueror of demons (4/4).

1987, Apr. 10 Litho. Perf. 13½
541	A78 2.20p multi	10.25	6.50
542	A78 2.20p multi	10.25	6.50
543	A78 2.20p multi	10.25	6.50
544	A78 2.20p multi	10.25	6.50
a.	Block or strip of 4, #541-544	45.00	30.00
	Nos. 541-544 (4)	41.00	26.00

Dragon Boat Festival — A79

50a, Dragon boat race. 5p, Figurehead.

1987, May 29 Litho. Perf. 13½
545	A79 50a multi	4.75	1.25
546	A79 5p multi	13.25	4.25

Decorated Fans — A80

1987, July 29 Litho. Perf. 12½
547	A80 30a multicolored	7.00	1.90
548	A80 70a multi, diff.	14.25	3.25
549	A80 1p multi, diff.	33.50	5.50
550	A80 6p multi, diff.	45.00	12.25
a.	Souvenir sheet of 4, #547-550	500.00	250.00
	Nos. 547-550 (4)	99.75	22.90

Casino Gambling — A81

1987, Sept. 30 Perf. 13½
551	A81 20a Fan-tan	16.25	6.75
552	A81 40a Cussec	16.25	6.75
553	A81 4p Baccarat	16.25	6.75
554	A81 7p Roulette	16.25	6.75
	Nos. 551-554 (4)	65.00	27.00

MACAO

Traditional Transportation — A82

10a, Market wagon. 70a, Enclosed Sedan chair. 90a, Rickshaw. 10p, Tricycle rickshaw. 7.50p, Open Sedan chair.

1987, Nov. 18	Litho.		Perf. 13½	
555	A82	10a multi	1.35	.90
556	A82	70a multi	4.00	1.40
557	A82	90a multi	5.75	1.65
558	A82	10p multi	17.75	7.50
	Nos. 555-558 (4)		28.85	11.45

Souvenir Sheet

559	A82	7.50p Sedan chair, diff.	70.00	35.00

New Year Type of 1984

1988, Feb. 10	Litho.		Perf. 13½	
560	A60	2.50p Dragon	9.00	6.00
a.	Booklet pane of 5		60.00	

No. 560a has straight edges.

Wildlife Protection — A84

No. 561, Erinaceus europaeus. No. 562, Meles meles. No. 563, Lutra lutra. No. 564, Manis pentadactyla.

1988, Apr. 14	Litho.		Perf. 12½x12	
561	A84	3p multi	7.50	2.75
562	A84	3p multi	7.50	2.75
563	A84	3p multi	7.50	2.75
564	A84	3p multi	7.50	2.75
a.	Block or strip of 4, #561-564		50.00	22.00
	Nos. 561-564 (4)		30.00	11.00

World Health Organization, 40th Anniv. — A85

1988, June 1	Litho.		Perf. 13½	
565	A85	60a Breast-feeding	3.75	1.15
566	A85	80a Immunization	6.75	1.35
567	A85	2.40p Blood donation	10.50	4.25
	Nos. 565-567 (3)		21.00	6.75

Modes of Transportation — A86

20a, Bicycles. 50a, Vespa, Lambretta. 3.30p, 1907 Rover 20hp. 5p, 1912 Renault delivery truck. 7.50p, 1930s Sedan.

1988, July 15		Litho.	
568	A86	20a multi	1.45	.60
569	A86	50a multi	2.85	.90
570	A86	3.30p multi	7.50	2.20
571	A86	5p multi	13.00	4.75
	Nos. 568-571 (4)		24.80	8.45

Souvenir Sheet

572	A86	7.50p multi	90.00	45.00

1988 Summer Olympics, Seoul — A87

1988, Sept. 19		Litho.	
573	A87	40a Hurdles	2.15	.75
574	A87	60a Basketball	3.50	.90
575	A87	1p Soccer	6.00	1.85
576	A87	8p Table tennis	11.25	4.50
	Nos. 573-576 (4)		22.90	8.00

Souvenir Sheet

577	Sheet of 5, #573-576, 577a	100.00	90.00
a.	A87 5p Tae kwon do	40.00	

World Post Day — A88

1988, Oct. 10	Litho.		Perf. 14	
578	A88	13.40p Electronic mail	7.50	6.50
579	A88	40p Express mail	17.50	20.00

35th Macao Grand Prix — A89

1988, Nov. 24	Litho.		Perf. 12½	
580	A89	80a Sedan	2.10	.85
581	A89	2.80p Motorcycle	6.25	2.10
582	A89	7p Formula 3	16.75	4.50
a.	Souvenir sheet of 3, #580-582		125.00	95.00
	Nos. 580-582 (3)		25.10	7.45

New Year Type of 1984

1989, Jan. 20	Litho.		Perf. 13½	
583	A60	6p Snake	11.00	1.00
a.	Booklet pane of 5		60.00	

No. 583a has straight edges. Value for No. 583 is for stamp perfed on 4 sides.

Occupations — A91

1989, Mar. 1	Litho.		Perf. 12x12½	
584	A91	50a Water carrier	1.15	.35
585	A91	1p Tan-kya woman	2.25	.70
586	A91	4p Tin-tin (junk) man	4.50	2.50
587	A91	5p Tofu peddler	6.00	2.90
	Nos. 584-587 (4)		13.90	6.45

See Nos. 612-615, 640-643.

Watercolors by George Smirnoff in the Luis de Camoens Museum — A92

1989, Apr. 10	Litho.		Perf. 12½x12	
588	A92	2p multi (4-1)	3.25	1.25
589	A92	2p multi (4-2)	3.25	1.25
590	A92	2p multi (4-3)	3.25	1.25
591	A92	2p multi (4-4)	3.25	1.25
a.	Block or strip of 4, #588-591		15.00	5.50
	Nos. 588-591 (4)		13.00	5.00

Snakes — A93

No. 592, Naja naja. No. 593, Bungarus fasciatus. No. 594, Trimeresurus albolabris. No. 595, Elaphe radiata.

1989, July 7		Litho.	
592	A93	2.50p multicolored	4.25	1.75
593	A93	2.50p multicolored	4.25	1.75
594	A93	2.50p multicolored	4.25	1.75
595	A93	2.50p multicolored	4.25	1.75
a.	Block or strip of 4, #592-595		18.00	10.00
	Nos. 592-595 (4)		17.00	7.00

Traditional Games — A94

1989, July 31	Litho.		Perf. 13½	
596	A94	10a Talu	1.40	.60
597	A94	60a Triol	4.25	.75
598	A94	3.30p Chiquia	5.75	2.00
599	A94	5p Xadrez Chines	7.50	3.50
	Nos. 596-599 (4)		18.90	6.85

Airplanes — A95

50a, Over church. 70a, American over lighthouse. 2.80p, Over wharf. 4p, Over junk. 7.50p, Over harbor.

1989, Oct. 9		Litho.	
600	A95	50a multi	.75	.40
601	A95	70a multi	1.55	.55
602	A95	2.80p multi	2.40	1.25
603	A95	4p multi	4.25	2.05
	Nos. 600-603 (4)		8.95	4.25

Souvenir Sheet

604	A95	7.50p multi	45.00	27.50

No. 604 contains one 40x30mm stamp.

World Stamp Expo '89, Washington, DC — A96

1989, Nov. 17	Litho.		Perf. 12½	
605	A96	40a Malacca	.70	.30
606	A96	70a Thailand	1.35	.40
607	A96	90a India	2.00	.95
608	A96	2.50p Japan	3.25	1.30
609	A96	7.50p China	6.75	2.60
	Nos. 605-609 (5)		14.05	5.25

Souvenir Sheet

610	Sheet of 6, #605-609, 610a	75.00	50.00
a.	A96 3p Macao	22.50	17.50

Influence of the Portuguese in the Far East.

New Year Type of 1984

1990, Jan. 19	Litho.		Perf. 13½	
611	A60	4p Horse	5.75	2.25
a.	Booklet pane of 5		35.00	

No. 611a has straight edges. Value for No. 611 is for stamp perfed on 4 sides.

Occupations Type of 1989

30a, Long chau singer. 70a, Cobbler. 1.50p, Scribe. 7.50p, Net fisherman.

1990, Mar. 1	Litho.		Perf. 12x12½	
612	A91	30a multicolored	1.35	.85
613	A91	70a multicolored	2.60	1.50
614	A91	1.50p multicolored	4.15	1.05
615	A91	7.50p multicolored	12.00	4.60
	Nos. 612-615 (4)		20.00	8.90

Souvenir Sheet

Penny Black, 150th Anniv. — A99

1990, May 3		Litho.		Perf. 12
616	A99	10p multicolored	45.00	30.00

Stamp World London 90.

Lutianus Malabaricus — A100

No. 618, Epinephelus megachir. No. 619, Macropodus opercularis. No. 620, Ophiocephalus maculatus.

1990, June 8			Perf. 12x12½	
617	A100	2.40p shown	3.25	1.75
618	A100	2.40p multicolored	3.25	1.75
619	A100	2.40p multicolored	3.25	1.75
620	A100	2.40p multicolored	3.25	1.75
a.	Block or strip of 4, #617-620		16.00	8.00
	Nos. 617-620 (4)		13.00	7.00

Decorative Porcelain — A101

1990, Aug. 24	Litho.		Perf. 12½	
621	A101	3p shown	3.00	1.80
622	A101	3p Furniture	3.00	1.80
623	A101	3p Toys	3.00	1.80
624	A101	3p Artificial flowers	3.00	1.80
a.	Souvenir sheet of 4, #621-624		55.00	20.00
b.	Block or strip of 4, #621-624		15.00	8.00
	Nos. 621-624 (4)		12.00	7.20

Asian Games, Beijing — A102

1990, Sept. 22	Litho.		Perf. 13½	
625	A102	80a Cycling	1.00	.50
626	A102	1p Swimming	1.45	.65
627	A102	3p Judo	5.00	1.40
628	A102	4.20p Shooting	7.50	2.20
	Nos. 625-628 (4)		14.95	4.75

Souvenir Sheet

629	Sheet of 5, #625-628, 629a	65.00	40.00
a.	A102 6p Martial arts	20.00	20.00

Compass Roses from Portuguese Charts — A103

Charts by 16th century cartographers: Lazaro Luis, Diogo Homem, Fernao Vaz Dourado, and Luiz Teixeira.

1990, Oct. 9	Litho.		Perf. 13½	
630	A103	50a shown	1.20	.70
631	A103	1p multi, diff.	2.15	.65
632	A103	3.50p multi, diff.	5.25	1.65
633	A103	6.50p multi, diff.	10.25	2.65
	Nos. 630-633 (4)		18.85	5.45

Souvenir Sheet

634	A103	5p multi, diff.	75.00	40.00

Games with Animals — A104

1990, Nov. 15	Litho.		Perf. 14	
635	A104	20a Cricket fight	1.05	.45
636	A104	80a Bird fight	2.75	.80
637	A104	1p Greyhound race	3.85	1.10
638	A104	10p Horse race	11.25	3.35
	Nos. 635-638 (4)		18.90	5.70

New Year Type of 1984

1991, Feb. 8	Litho.		Perf. 13½	
639	A60	4.50p Ram	6.50	1.50
b.	Booklet pane of 5		37.50	

No. 639b has straight edges.

MACAO

Occupations Type of 1987

80a, Knife grinder. 1.70p, Flour puppet vender. 3.50p, Street barber. 4.20p, Fortune teller.

1991, Mar. 1			Perf. 14	
640	A91	80a multi	1.20	.60
641	A91	1.70p multi	2.25	.65
642	A91	3.50p multi	5.25	1.95
643	A91	4.20p multi	8.75	2.65
		Nos. 640-643 (4)	17.45	5.25

Shells — A106

No. 644, Murex pecten. No. 645, Harpa harpa. No. 646, Chicoreus rosarius. No. 647, Tonna zonata.

1991, Apr. 18		Litho.	Perf. 14	
644	A106	3p multi	4.15	2.00
645	A106	3p multi	4.15	2.00
646	A106	3p multi	4.15	2.00
647	A106	3p multi	4.15	2.00
a.		Strip of 4, #644-647	20.75	13.50
		Nos. 644-647 (4)	16.60	8.00

Chinese Opera — A107

Various performers in costume.

1991, June 5		Litho.	Perf. 13½	
648	A107	60a multicolored	1.90	.50
649	A107	80a multicolored	3.40	.55
650	A107	1p multicolored	4.90	1.15
651	A107	10p multicolored	14.75	3.75
		Nos. 648-651 (4)	24.95	5.95

Flowers — A108

Designs: 1.70p, Delonix regia. 3p, Ipomoea cairica. 3.50p, Jasminum mesnyi. 4.20p, Bauhinia variegata.

1991, Oct. 9		Litho.	Perf. 13½	
652	A108	1.70p multicolored	2.10	.60
653	A108	3p multicolored	3.00	1.20
654	A108	3.50p multicolored	5.30	1.65
655	A108	4.20p multicolored	6.00	3.00
a.		Souvenir sheet of 4, #652-655	80.00	40.00
		Nos. 652-655 (4)	16.40	6.45

Cultural Exchange — A109

Namban screen: No. 656, Unloading boat.

1991, Nov. 16		Litho.	Perf. 12	
656	A109	4.20p multicolored	3.75	1.50
657	A109	4.20p shown	3.75	1.50
a.		Souvenir sheet of 2, #656-657	42.50	25.00

Holiday Greetings — A110

1.70p, Lunar New Year. 3p, Santa Claus, Christmas. 3.50p, Old man. 4.20p, Girl at New Year party.

1991, Nov. 29		Litho.	Perf. 14½	
658	A110	1.70p multicolored	1.60	.60
659	A110	3p multicolored	2.75	.90
660	A110	3.50p multicolored	4.40	1.25
661	A110	4.20p multicolored	8.75	2.20
		Nos. 658-661 (4)	17.50	4.95

New Year Type of 1984

1992, Jan. 28		Litho.	Perf. 13½	
662	A60	4.50p Monkey	5.00	4.00
a.		Booklet pane of 5	30.00	

No. 662a has straight edges.

Paintings of Doors and Windows — A111

1992, Mar. 1		Litho.	Perf. 14	
663	A111	1.70p multicolored	1.30	.75
664	A111	3p multi, diff.	3.10	1.15
665	A111	3.50p multi, diff.	4.40	2.85
666	A111	4.20p multi, diff.	6.00	3.75
		Nos. 663-666 (4)	14.80	8.50

Mythological Chinese Gods — A112

No. 667, T'it Kuai Lei (4-1). No. 668, Chong Lei Kun (4-2). No. 669, Cheong Kuo Lou (4-3). No. 670, Loi Tong Pan (4-4).

1992, Apr. 3		Litho.	Perf. 14	
667	A112	3.50p multi	10.00	4.75
668	A112	3.50p multi	10.00	4.75
669	A112	3.50p multi	10.00	4.75
670	A112	3.50p multi	10.00	4.75
a.		Block or strip of 4, #667-670	42.50	22.50
		Nos. 667-670 (4)	40.00	19.00

See Nos. 689-692.

Lion Dance Costume — A113

Designs: 2.70p, Lion, diff. 6p, Dragon.

1992, May 22				
671	A113	1p multicolored	1.20	.55
672	A113	2.70p multicolored	2.00	.80
673	A113	6p multicolored	4.75	1.65
		Nos. 671-673 (3)	7.95	3.00

World Columbian Stamp Expo '92, Chicago.

1992 Summer Olympics, Barcelona — A114

1992, July 1		Litho.	Perf. 13	
674	A114	80a High jump	.85	.35
675	A114	4.20p Badminton	1.80	.90
676	A114	4.70p Roller hockey	2.50	1.30
677	A114	5p Yachting	3.90	1.70
a.		Souvenir sheet of 4, #674-677	27.50	16.00
		Nos. 674-677 (4)	9.05	4.25

Temples — A115

1992, Oct. 9			Perf. 14	
678	A115	1p Na Cha	1.25	.60
679	A115	1.50p Kun Iam	1.45	.85
680	A115	1.70p Hong Kon	2.30	1.40
681	A115	6.50p A Ma	5.00	3.00
		Nos. 678-681 (4)	10.00	5.85

See Nos. 685-688.

Portuguese-Chinese Friendship — A116

1992, Nov. 27		Litho.	Perf. 14	
682	A116	10p multicolored	4.50	2.50
a.		Souv. sheet, perf. 13½	22.50	20.00

Tung Sin Tong Charity Organization, Cent. — A117

1992, Nov. 27			Perf. 12x11½	
683	A117	1p multicolored	2.25	.70

New Year Type of 1984

1993, Jan. 18		Litho.	Perf. 13½	
684	A60	5p Rooster	5.00	1.50
a.		Booklet pane of 5	27.50	

No. 684a has straight edges.

Temple Type of 1992

1993, Mar. 1		Litho.	Perf. 14	
685	A115	50a T'am Kong	.45	.35
686	A115	2p T'in Hau	1.45	.50
687	A115	3.50p Lin Fong	2.20	1.00
688	A115	8p Pau Kong	2.90	2.15
		Nos. 685-688 (4)	7.00	4.00

Mythological Chinese Gods Type of 1992

Designs: No. 689, Lam Ch'oi Wo seated on crane in flight. No. 690, Ho Sin Ku, seated on peach flower. No. 691, Hon Seong Chi throwing peonies from basket. No. 692, Ch'ou Kuok K'ao seated on gold plate.

1993, Apr. 1		Litho.	Perf. 14	
689	A112	3.50p multi (4-1)	2.25	2.00
690	A112	3.50p multi (4-2)	2.25	2.00
691	A112	3.50p multi (4-3)	2.25	2.00
692	A112	3.50p multi (4-4)	2.25	2.00
a.		Block or strip of 4, #689-692	12.50	10.00
		Nos. 689-692 (4)	9.00	8.00

Chinese Wedding — A118

No. 693, Three children celebrating. No. 694, Bride. No. 695, Groom. No. 696, Woman with parasol, person being carried. 8p, Bride & groom.

1993, May 19			Perf. 14	
693	A118	3p multicolored	1.65	1.10
694	A118	3p multicolored	1.65	1.10
695	A118	3p multicolored	1.65	1.10
696	A118	3p multicolored	1.65	1.10
a.		Strip of 4, #693-696	7.50	7.50
		Nos. 693-696 (4)	6.60	4.40

Souvenir Sheet
Perf. 14½x14

697	A118	8p multicolored	17.50	15.00

No. 697 contains one 50x40mm stamp.

World Environment Day — A119

1993, June 5		Litho.	Perf. 14	
698	A119	1p multicolored	3.00	1.00

Birds — A120

No. 699, Falco peregrinus. No. 700, Aquila obrysaetos. No. 701, Asio otus. No. 702, Tyto alba.

1993, June 27				
699	A120	3p multicolored	1.60	1.10
700	A120	3p multicolored	1.60	1.10
701	A120	3p multicolored	1.60	1.10
702	A120	3p multicolored	1.60	1.10
a.		Block or strip of 4, #699-702	7.50	6.00
b.		Souvenir sheet of 4, #699-702	17.50	12.50
		Nos. 699-702 (4)	6.40	4.40

Union of Portuguese Speaking Capitals — A121

1993, July 30		Litho.	Perf. 13½	
703	A121	1.50p multicolored	1.50	.75

Portuguese Arrival in Japan, 450th Anniv. — A122

50a, Japanese using musket. 3p, Catholic priests. 3.50p, Exchanging items of trade.

1993, Sept. 22		Litho.	Perf. 12x11½	
704	A122	50a multicolored	.90	.35
705	A122	3p multicolored	2.25	.95
706	A122	3.50p multicolored	2.85	1.10
		Nos. 704-706 (3)	6.00	2.40

See Portugal Nos. 1964-1966.

Flowers — A123

Designs: 1p, Spathodea campanulata. 2p, Tithonia diversifolia. 3p, Rhodomyrtus tomentosa. 8p, Passiflora foetida.

1993, Oct. 9			Perf. 14½	
707	A123	1p multicolored	.75	.35
708	A123	2p multicolored	1.50	.60
709	A123	3p multicolored	1.75	.90
710	A123	8p multicolored	3.00	2.40
a.		Souvenir sheet of 4, #707-710	22.50	20.00
		Nos. 707-710 (4)	7.00	4.25

Portuguese Ships — A124

1993, Nov. 5		Litho.	Perf. 14	
711	A124	1p Caravel	.85	.55
712	A124	2p Round caravel	1.45	.45
713	A124	3.50p Nau	1.85	.75
714	A124	4.50p Galleon	2.80	1.75
a.		Souvenir sheet of 4, #711-714	11.50	10.00
		Nos. 711-714 (4)	6.95	3.50

Macao Grand Prix, 40th Anniv. — A125

1993, Nov. 16		Litho.	Perf. 13½	
715	A125	1.50p Stock car	1.15	.65
716	A125	2p Motorcycle	1.90	.85
717	A125	4.50p Formula 1 race car	2.90	2.00
		Nos. 715-717 (3)	5.95	3.50

MACAO

New Year Type of 1984
1994, Feb. 3   Litho.   *Perf. 13½*
718	A60	5p Dog	5.00	1.60
a.		Booklet pane of 5	27.50	

New Year 1994 (Year of the Dog). No. 718a has straight edges.

Prince Henry the Navigator (1394-1460) — A126

1994, Mar. 4   Litho.   *Perf. 12*
719	A126	3p multicolored	3.50	1.75

See Portugal No. 1987.

Scenes of Macao, by George Chinnery (1774-1852) A127

Designs: No. 720, Hut, natives. No. 721, S. Tiago Fortress. No. 722, Overview of Praia Grande. No. 723, S. Francisco Church.

1994, Mar. 21   *Perf. 14*
720	A127	3.50p multi (4-1)	1.85	1.25
721	A127	3.50p multi (4-2)	1.85	1.25
722	A127	3.50p multi (4-3)	1.85	1.25
723	A127	3.50p multi (4-4)	1.85	1.25
a.		Block or strip of 4, #720-723	8.00	5.50
b.		Souvenir sheet of 4, #720-723	17.50	12.50
		Nos. 720-723 (4)	7.40	5.00

Spring Festival of New Lunar Year — A128

Designs: 1p, Girl, woman shopping. 2p, Celebration. 3.50p, Couple preparing food at table. 4.50p, Old man making decorations.

1994, Apr. 6
724	A128	1p multicolored	.55	.35
725	A128	2p multicolored	1.10	.55
726	A128	3.50p multicolored	1.40	1.00
727	A128	4.50p multicolored	1.90	1.35
		Nos. 724-727 (4)	4.95	3.25

Mythological Chinese Gods — A129

Statuettes: No. 728, Happiness. No. 729, Prosperity. No. 730, Longevity.

1994, May 9   Litho.   *Perf. 12*
728	A129	3p multi (3-1)	3.25	2.00
729	A129	3p multi (3-2)	3.25	2.00
730	A129	3p multi (3-3)	3.25	2.00
a.		Strip of 3, #728-730	10.00	6.00
b.		Souvenir sheet of 3, #728-730	22.50	15.00
		Nos. 728-730 (3)	9.75	6.00

A130

1994 World Cup Soccer Championships, US: Various soccer players.

1994, June 1
731	A130	2p multicolored	1.20	.55
732	A130	3p multicolored	1.90	.80
733	A130	3.50p multicolored	2.15	1.00
734	A130	4.50p multicolored	2.75	1.65
a.		Souvenir sheet of 4, #731-734	14.00	12.50
		Nos. 731-734 (4)	8.00	4.00

A131

Traditional Chinese shops: 1p, Rice shop. 1.50p, Medicinal drink shop. 2p, Salt fish shop. 3.50p, Pharmacy.

1994, June 27   Litho.   *Perf. 12*
735	A131	1p multi	.75	.30
736	A131	1.50p multi	.85	.50
737	A131	2p multi	1.85	.80
738	A131	3.50p multi	2.50	1.15
		Nos. 735-738 (4)	5.95	2.75

Navigation Instruments — A132

1994, Sept. 13   Litho.   *Perf. 12*
739	A132	3p Astrolabe	2.25	1.25
740	A132	3.50p Quadrant	3.15	1.80
741	A132	4.50p Sextant	3.50	1.95
		Nos. 739-741 (3)	8.90	5.00

12th Asian Games, Hiroshima 1994 — A133

1994, Sept. 30   Litho.   *Perf. 12*
742	A133	1p Fencing	.80	.40
743	A133	2p Gymnastics	1.70	.60
744	A133	3p Water polo	2.50	.85
745	A133	3.50p Pole vault	3.00	1.40
		Nos. 742-745 (4)	8.00	3.25

Bridges — A134

1994, Oct. 8
746	A134	1p Nobre de Carvalho	.65	.50
747	A134	8p Friendship	3.50	1.90

Fortune Symbols — A135

Designs: 3p, Child, carp, water lily. 3.50p, Basket of peaches, child, bats. 4.50p, Flower, child playing mouth organ.

1994, Nov. 7   Litho.   *Perf. 12*
748	A135	3p multicolored	2.25	1.35
749	A135	3.50p multicolored	2.50	1.80
750	A135	4.50p multicolored	3.25	2.85
		Nos. 748-750 (3)	8.00	6.00

Religious Art — A136

Designs: 50a, Stained glass, angel's head. 1p, Stained glass, Holy Ghost. 1.50p, Silver sacrarium. 2p, Silver salver. 3p, Ivory sculpture, Escape to Egypt. 3.50p, Gold & silver chalice.

1994, Nov. 30
751	A136	50a multicolored	.35	.30
752	A136	1p multicolored	.60	.30
753	A136	1.50p multicolored	.90	.40
754	A136	2p multicolored	1.25	.55
755	A136	3p multicolored	1.60	.85
756	A136	3.50p multicolored	1.85	1.10
		Nos. 751-756 (6)	6.55	3.50

New Year Type of 1984
1995, Jan. 25   Litho.   *Perf. 13½*
757	A60	5.50p Boar	4.50	1.50
a.		Booklet pane of 5	27.50	

Tourism — A138

Scenes of Macao, by Lio Man Cheong: 50a, Walkway beside pond. 1p, Lighthouse. 1.50p, Temple. 2p, Buildings along coast. 2.50p, Columns, temple. 3p, Ruins on hill overlooking city. 3.50p, Bridge. 4p, Trees in park.

1995, Mar. 1   Litho.   *Perf. 12*
758	A138	50a multicolored	.40	.40
759	A138	1p multicolored	.70	.50
760	A138	1.50p multicolored	.95	.60
761	A138	2p multicolored	1.30	.85
762	A138	2.50p multicolored	1.45	1.00
763	A138	3p multicolored	1.60	1.30
764	A138	3.50p multicolored	2.00	1.45
765	A138	4p multicolored	2.60	1.85
		Nos. 758-765 (8)	11.00	7.95

World Day of the Consumer A139

1995, Mar. 15
766	A139	1p multicolored	2.00	.65

Asian Pangolin — A140

No. 767, Facing left (4-1). No. 768, Hanging by tail (4-2). No. 769, On tree limb (4-3). No. 770, On tree stump (4-4).

1995, Apr. 10
767	A140	1.50p multi	1.75	.70
768	A140	1.50p multi	1.75	.70
769	A140	1.50p multi	1.75	.70
770	A140	1.50p multi	1.75	.70
a.		Block or strip of 4, #767-770	7.50	6.50
		Nos. 767-770 (4)	7.00	2.80

World wildlife Fund. Issued in sheets of 16 stamps.

Legend of Buddhist Goddess Kun Iam — A141

No. 772, Seated atop dragon, holding flower. No. 773, Meditating. No. 774, Holding infant. 8p, Goddess with many faces, hands.

1995, May 5   Litho.   *Perf. 12*
771	A141	3p multicolored	3.25	1.40
772	A141	3p multicolored	3.25	1.40
773	A141	3p multicolored	3.25	1.40
774	A141	3p multicolored	3.25	1.40
a.		Block or strip of 4, #771-774	15.00	10.00
		Nos. 771-774 (4)	13.00	5.60

Souvenir Sheet
775	A141	8p multicolored	30.00	20.00

Senado Square — A142

Designs: No. 776, Street, bell tower. No. 777, Street, plaza, shops. No. 778, Fountain, plaza. No. 779, Plaza, buildings. 8p, Bell tower, building, horiz.

1995, June 24   Litho.   *Perf. 12*
776	A142	2p multicolored	1.60	.85
777	A142	2p multicolored	1.60	.85
778	A142	2p multicolored	1.60	.85
779	A142	2p multicolored	1.60	.85
a.		Strip of 4, #776-779	6.75	4.00
		Nos. 776-779 (4)	6.40	3.40

Souvenir Sheet
780	A142	8p multicolored	15.00	10.00

Temple Type of 1992
1995, July 17   Litho.   *Perf. 12*
781	A115	50a Kuan Tai	.65	.40
782	A115	1p Pak Tai	.90	.40
783	A115	1.50p Lin K'ai	1.30	.60
784	A115	3p Sek Kam Tong	2.40	1.30
785	A115	3.50p Fok Tak	2.75	1.50
		Nos. 781-785 (5)	8.00	4.20

Singapore '95 — A143

Birds: No. 786, Gurrulax canorus. No. 787, Serinus canarius. No. 788, Zosterops japonica. No. 789, Leiothrix lutea. 10p, Copsychus saularis.

1995, Sept. 1   Litho.   *Perf. 12*
786	A143	2.50p multicolored	1.80	1.05
787	A143	2.50p multicolored	1.80	1.05
788	A143	2.50p multicolored	1.80	1.05
789	A143	2.50p multicolored	1.80	1.05
a.		Strip of 4, #786-789	8.00	5.00
		Nos. 786-789 (4)	7.20	4.20

Souvenir Sheet
790	A143	10p multicolored	24.00	14.00

Intl. Music Festival — A144

1995, Oct. 9   Litho.   *Perf. 12*
791	A144	1p Pipa (6-1)	1.75	.45
792	A144	1p Erhu (6-2)	1.75	.45
793	A144	1p Gongo (6-3)	1.75	.45
794	A144	1p Sheng (6-4)	1.75	.45
795	A144	1p Xiao (6-5)	1.75	.45
796	A144	1p Tambor (6-6)	1.75	.45
a.		Block of 6, #791-796	12.00	4.00
		Nos. 791-796 (6)	10.50	2.70

Souvenir Sheet
797	A144	8p Musicians, horiz.	14.00	7.50

UN, 50th Anniv. — A145

1995, Oct. 24   Litho.   *Perf. 12*
798	A145	4.50p multicolored	2.25	1.50

Macao Intl. Airport — A146

Designs: 1p, Airplane above terminal. 1.50p, Boeing 747 on ground, terminal. 2p, Hangars, 747 with boarding ramp at door. 3p, Airplane, control tower. 8p, Boeing 747 over runway.

1995, Dec. 8   Litho.   *Perf. 12*
799	A146	1p multicolored	1.05	.45
800	A146	1.50p multicolored	1.55	.65
801	A146	2p multicolored	2.05	.85
802	A146	3p multicolored	2.60	1.30
		Nos. 799-802 (4)	7.25	3.25

Souvenir Sheet   *Perf. 12½*
803	A146	8p multicolored	20.00	12.00

No. 803 contains one 51x38mm stamp.

MACAO

New Year Type of 1984
Miniature Sheet of 12

Designs: a, like #485. b, like #504. c, like #522. d, like #540. e, like #560. f, like #583. g, like #611. h, like #639. i, like #662. j, like #684. k, like #718. l, like #757.

1995, Dec. 15   Litho.   Perf. 13½
804 A60 1.50p #a.-l. + label   27.50 12.50

New Year 1996 (Year of the Rat) — A147

1996, Feb. 12   Litho.   Perf. 12
805 A147 5p multicolored   3.75 2.50
Souvenir Sheet
806 A147 10p like No. 805   12.00 10.50

Traditional Chinese Bird Cages — A148

1996, Mar. 1   Litho.   Perf. 12
807 A148 1p multi (4-1)   .80 .35
808 A148 1.50p multi (4-2)   1.15 .45
809 A148 3p multi (4-3)   2.10 .80
810 A148 4.50p multi (4-4)   3.45 1.20
  Nos. 807-810 (4)   7.50 2.80
Souvenir Sheet
811 A148 10p purple & multi   17.50 11.00

Paintings, by Herculano Estorninho A149

Scenes of Macao: 50a, Boats. 1.50p, Street, buildings at night, vert. 3p, Fronts of buildings during day, vert. 5p, Townhouse complex. 10p, Entrance to building, vert.

1996, Apr. 1
812 A149 50a multi (4-1)   .60 .25
813 A149 1.50p multi (4-2)   1.30 .45
814 A149 3p multi (4-3)   2.15 .85
815 A149 5p multi (4-4)   3.75 1.40
  Nos. 812-815 (4)   7.80 2.95
Souvenir Sheet
816 A149 10p multi   10.00 6.50

Myths and Legends — A150

Designs: No. 817, Man holding staff, Tou Tei (3-1). No. 818, Man riding tiger, Choi San (3-2). No. 819, Man on top of fireplace, Chou Kuan (3-3).

1996, Apr. 30   Litho.   Perf. 12
817 A150 3.50p multi   1.85 1.50
818 A150 3.50p multi   1.85 1.50
819 A150 3.50p multi   1.85 1.50
  a. Strip of 3, #817-819   5.75 5.25
  b. Souvenir sheet of 3, #817-819   17.50 11.00
  Nos. 817-819 (3)   5.55 4.50

Traditional Chinese Tea Houses — A151

Designs: No. 820, Two men seated at table. No. 821, Cook holding steaming tray of food, woman, baby. No. 822, Woman holding up papers. No. 823, Waiter pouring tea, man seated. 8p, Food, serving bowl.

1996, May 17   Perf. 12
820 A151 2p multi (4-1)   2.00 .95
821 A151 2p multi (4-2)   2.00 .95
822 A151 2p multi (4-3)   2.00 .95
823 A151 2p multi (4-4)   2.00 .95
  a. Block of 4, #820-823   8.50 4.00
  Nos. 820-823 (4)   8.00 3.80
Souvenir Sheet
824 A151 8p multi   15.00 11.00

No. 823a is a continuous design. China '96 (No. 824).

Greetings Stamps — A152

Designs: 50a, Get well. 1.50p, Congratulations on new baby. 3p, Happy birthday. 4p, Marriage congratulations.

1996, June 14   Litho.   Perf. 12
825 A152 50a multi (4-1)   .60 .35
826 A152 1.50p multi (4-2)   .80 .50
827 A152 3p multi (4-3)   2.15 .85
828 A152 4p multi (4-4)   2.45 1.30
  Nos. 825-828 (4)   6.00 3.00

1996 Summer Olympic Games, Atlanta — A153

2p, Swimming (4-1). 3p, Soccer (4-2). 3.50p, Gymnastics (4-3). 4.50p, Sailboarding (4-4). 10p, Boxing.

1996, July 19
829 A153 2p multi   1.05 .65
830 A153 3p multi   1.70 1.00
831 A153 3.50p multi   1.90 1.10
832 A153 4.50p multi   2.30 1.50
  Nos. 829-832 (4)   6.95 4.25
Souvenir Sheet
833 A153 10p multi   11.00 7.00

Civil and Military Emblems — A154

No. 834, Bird looking left. No. 835, Dragon. No. 836, Bird looking right. No. 837, Leopard.

1996, Sept. 18
834 A154 2.50p bl & multi (4-1)   1.70 .80
835 A154 2.50p grn & multi (4-2)   1.70 .80
836 A154 2.50p grn & multi (4-3)   1.70 .80
837 A154 2.50p pur & multi (4-4)   1.70 .80
  a. Block or strip of 4, #834-837   7.00 3.40
  Nos. 834-837 (4)   6.80 3.20

See Nos. 947-951.

Fishing with Nets — A155

Boats, fish in sea: No. 838, Six small nets extended from mast of boat. No. 839, Modern trawler. No. 840, Junk trawling. No. 841, Sailboat with nets extended from both sides.

1996, Oct. 9   Litho.   Perf. 12
838 A155 3p multi (4-1)   1.70 .80
839 A155 3p multi (4-2)   1.70 .80
840 A155 3p multi (4-3)   1.70 .80
841 A155 3p multi (4-4)   1.70 .80
  a. Strip of 4, #838-841   7.00 3.40
  Nos. 838-841 (4)   6.80 3.20

Legislative Assembly, 20th Anniv. — A156

1996, Oct. 15   Litho.   Perf. 12x12½
842 A156 2.80p multicolored   2.25 1.40
Souvenir Sheet
843 A156 8p like No. 842   14.00 7.50

Paper Kites — A157

No. 844, Dragonfly (4-1). No. 845, Butterfly (4-2). No. 846, Owl in flight (4-3). No. 847, Standing owl (4-4). No. 848, Dragon.

1996, Oct. 21   Litho.   Perf. 12
844 A157 3.50p multi   2.45 1.00
845 A157 3.50p multi   2.45 1.00
846 A157 3.50p multi   2.45 1.00
847 A157 3.50p multi   2.45 1.00
  a. Strip or block of 4, #844-847   10.25 10.25
  Nos. 844-847 (4)   9.80 4.00
Souvenir Sheet   Perf. 12½
848 A157 8p multi   14.50 8.00

No. 848 contains one 51x38mm stamp.

Traditional Chinese Toys — A158

1996, Nov. 13   Litho.   Perf. 12
849 A158 50a shown   .65 .40
850 A158 1p Fish   1.55 1.05
851 A158 3p Doll   4.50 2.00
852 A158 4.50p Dragon   7.75 2.80
  Nos. 849-852 (4)   14.45 6.25

New Year 1997 (Year of the Ox) — A159

1997, Jan. 23   Litho.   Perf. 12
853 A159 5.50p multicolored   3.75 4.00
Souvenir Sheet
854 A159 10p multicolored   10.50 8.00

No. 854 is a continuous design.

Lucky Numbers — A160

2p, "2," Simplicity. 2.80p, "8," Prosperity. 3p, "3," Progress. 3.90p, "9," Longevity. 9p, Man outside house.

1997, Feb. 12   Litho.   Perf. 12
855 A160 2p multi   1.05 .55
856 A160 2.80p multi   1.30 .65
857 A160 3p multi   1.50 .70
858 A160 3.90p multi   2.05 1.10
  Nos. 855-858 (4)   5.90 3.00
Souvenir Sheet
859 A160 9p multi   7.75 6.00

Hong Kong '97 (No. 859).

Paintings of Macao, by Kwok Se — A161

2p, Junks. 3p, Fortress on side of mountain. 3.50p, Retreat house. 4.50p, Cerco Gate. 8p, Rooftop of building, horiz.

1997, Mar. 1   Litho.   Perf. 12
860 A161 2p multicolored   1.05 .40
861 A161 3p multicolored   1.80 .70
862 A161 3.50p multicolored   1.95 .85
863 A161 4.50p multicolored   2.70 1.25
  Nos. 860-863 (4)   7.50 3.20
Souvenir Sheet
864 A161 8p multicolored   8.75 8.00

A162

Boat People: 1p, Old woman seated. 1.50p, Woman wearing hat. 2.50p, Woman carrying baby. 5.50p, Man, boy.

1997, Mar. 26   Litho.   Perf. 12
865 A162 1p multicolored   .70 .35
866 A162 1.50p multicolored   .85 .45
867 A162 2.50p multicolored   1.30 .75
868 A162 5.50p multicolored   2.85 1.50
  a. Block or strip of 4, #865-868   6.00 3.75
  Nos. 865-868 (4)   5.70 3.05

Temple A-Ma — A163

No. 869, Steps leading to entrance. No. 870, People strolling past temple, one with umbrella. No. 871, People outside pagoda, pedicab. No. 872, Towers from temple, one emiting smoke. 8p, Boat.

1997, Apr. 29   Litho.   Perf. 12
869 A163 3.50p multicolored   1.00 .85
870 A163 3.50p multicolored   1.00 .85
871 A163 3.50p multicolored   1.00 .85
872 A163 3.50p multicolored   1.00 .85
  a. Strip of 4, #869-872   1.00 .85
  Nos. 869-872 (4)   4.00 3.40
Souvenir Sheet
873 A163 8p multicolored   4.50 4.00

Drunken Dragon Festival — A164

Stylized designs: 2p, Two men, one holding dragon. 3p, Man holding up dragon. 5p, Two men, one holding horn. 9p, Dragon, man, horiz.

1997, May 14
874 A164 2p multicolored   .60 .35
875 A164 3p multicolored   1.00 .55
876 A164 5p multicolored   1.60 1.10
  a. Strip of 3, #874-876   3.50 3.50
  Nos. 874-876 (3)   3.20 2.00
Souvenir Sheet
877 A164 9p multicolored   6.50 5.75

Father Luís Fróis, 400th Death Anniv. — A165

No. 879, Father Fróis, cathedral, vert.

1997, June 9   Litho.   Perf. 12
878 A165 2.50p multi (2-1)   .90 .75
879 A165 2.50p multi (2-2)   .90 .75

See Portugal Nos. 2165-2167.

MACAO

Legends and Myths — A166

Gods of Protection: No. 880, Wat Lot. No. 881, San Su. No. 882, Chon Keng. No. 883, Wat Chi Kong.
10p, Chon Keng and Wat Chi Kong.

1997, June 18	Litho.	Perf. 12
880 A166 2.50p multicolored	.90	.65
881 A166 2.50p multicolored	.90	.65
882 A166 2.50p multicolored	.90	.65
883 A166 2.50p multicolored	.90	.65
a. Strip or block of 4, #880-883	3.75	3.50
Nos. 880-883 (4)	3.60	2.60

Souvenir Sheet

| 884 A166 10p multicolored | 4.00 | 4.00 |

No. 884 contains one 40x40mm stamp.

Macao Red Cross, 77th Anniv. A167

1997, July 12		Perf. 12½
885 A167 1.50p multicolored	.70	.65

No. 885 is printed se-tenant with label.

Verandas — A168

Various architectural styles.
8p, Close up of veranda, vert.

1997, July 30	Litho.	Perf. 12
886 A168 50a multi (6-1)	.35	.30
887 A168 1p multi (6-2)	.35	.35
888 A168 1.50p multi (6-3)	.45	.45
889 A168 2p multi (6-4)	.55	.55
890 A168 2.50p multi (6-5)	.75	.75
891 A168 3p multi (6-6)	.85	.85
a. Block of 6, #886-891	3.50	3.50
Nos. 886-891 (6)	3.30	3.20

Souvenir Sheet

| 892 A168 8p multicolored | 5.00 | 4.50 |

Traditional Chinese Fans — A169

1997, Sept. 24	Litho.	Perf. 12
893 A169 50a Planta (4-1)	.40	.30
894 A169 1p Papel (4-2)	.40	.35
895 A169 3.50p Seda (4-3)	1.10	1.10
896 A169 4p Pluma (4-4)	1.40	1.40
a. Strip or block of 4, #893-896	3.50	3.25
Nos. 893-896 (4)	3.30	3.15

Souvenir Sheet

| 897 A169 9p Sandalo | 5.75 | 5.50 |

Fong Soi (Chinese Geomancy) — A170

Chinese principles of Yin and Yang related to the five elements of the ancient Zodiac.

1997, Oct. 9	Litho.	Perf. 12
898 A170 50a green & multi	.40	.30
899 A170 1p orange & multi	.40	.40
900 A170 1.50p brown & multi	.55	.50
901 A170 2p yellow & multi	.65	.60
902 A170 2.50p blue & multi	.75	.70
a. Strip of 5, #898-902	3.00	2.75
Nos. 898-902 (5)	2.75	2.50

Souvenir Sheet

| 903 A170 10p green & multi | 5.50 | 5.00 |

Martial Arts — A171

1997, Nov. 19		
904 A171 1.50p Kung Fu	.65	.45
905 A171 3.50p Judo	1.25	.95
906 A171 4p Karate	1.85	1.35
a. Strip of 3, #904-906	3.75	3.00
Nos. 904-906 (3)	3.75	2.75

New Year 1998 (Year of the Tiger) — A172

1998, Jan. 18	Litho.	Perf. 12
907 A172 5.50p multicolored	2.15	2.05

Souvenir Sheets

| 908 A172 10p multicolored | 4.75 | 4.50 |
| a. Ovptd. in sheet margin | 5.00 | 4.75 |

No. 908 is a continuous design.
No. 908a overprinted in Gold in Sheet Margin with "Amizade Luso-Chinesa / Festival de Macao" & Chinese Text.

Street Vendors — A173

Vendors at stands, carts: No. 909, 1p, Frying foods. 1.50p, Food products, eggs. 2p, Clothing items. 2.50p, Balloons. 3p, Flowers. 3.50p, Fruits and vegetables.
6p, Vendor at fruit and vegetable stand, diff.

1998, Feb. 13	Litho.	Perf. 12
909 A173 1p multi (6-1)	.40	.35
910 A173 1.50p multi (6-2)	.50	.45
911 A173 2p multi (6-3)	.65	.55
912 A173 2.50p multi (6-4)	.70	.75
913 A173 3p multi (6-5)	1.00	.95
914 A173 3.50p multi (6-6)	1.25	1.20
a. Block of 6, #909-914	4.75	4.50
Nos. 909-914 (6)	4.50	4.25

Souvenir Sheets

| 915 A173 6p multicolored | 3.00 | 2.75 |
| a. Ovptd. in sheet margin | 3.25 | 3.00 |

No. 915a overprinted in Gold in Sheet Margin with "Amizade Luso-Chinesa / Festival de Macao" & Chinese Text.

Traditional Gates — A174

Inscriptions: 50a, "Beco da Sé." 1p, "Pátio da Ilusão." 3.50p, "Travessa da galinhas." 4p, "Beco das Felicidades."
9p, "Seminário d S. José," vert.

1998, Mar. 1		
916 A174 50a multi (4-1)	.35	.30
917 A174 1p multi (4-2)	.45	.40
918 A174 3.50p multi (4-3)	1.60	1.50
919 A174 4p multi (4-4)	2.10	1.95
Nos. 916-919 (4)	4.50	4.15

Souvenir Sheets

| 920 A174 9p multicolored | 4.50 | 4.25 |
| a. Ovptd. in sheet margin | 4.75 | 4.50 |

No. 920a overprinted in Gold in Sheet Margin with "Amizade Luso-Chinesa / Festival de Macao" & Chinese Text.

Myths and Legends — A175

Gods of Ma Chou: No. 921, Holding baby. No. 922, Watching image appear in smoke. No. 923, With cherubs. No. 924, Hovering over junks.
10p, Face.

1998, Apr. 23	Litho.	Perf. 12
921 A175 4p multi (4-1)	1.50	1.25
922 A175 4p multi (4-2)	1.50	1.25
923 A175 4p multi (4-3)	1.50	1.25
924 A175 4p multi (4-4)	1.50	1.25
a. Strip of 4, #921-924	6.25	6.00
Nos. 921-924 (4)	6.00	5.00

Souvenir Sheets

| 925 A175 10p multicolored | 4.50 | 4.25 |
| a. Ovptd. in sheet margin | 4.75 | 4.50 |

No. 925a overprinted in Gold in Sheet Margin with "Amizade Luso-Chinesa / Festival de Macao" & Chinese Text.

Voyage to India by Vasco da Gama, 500th Anniv. — A176

Designs: 1p, Sailing ship. 1.50p, Vasco da Gama. 2p, Map, sailing ship.
8p, Compass rose.

1998, May 20	Litho.	Perf. 12
926 A176 1p multi (3-1)	.75	.45
927 A176 1.50p multi (3-2)	1.00	.55
928 A176 2p multi (3-3)	1.35	.85
a. Strip of 3, #926-928	3.40	2.00
Nos. 926-928 (3)	3.10	1.85

Souvenir Sheet

| 929 A176 8p multicolored | 7.50 | 6.50 |

Nos. 926-929 are inscribed "1598" instead of "1498," and were withdrawn after two days. For corrected version, see Nos. 943-946.

Oceans — A177

Stylized designs: 2.50p, Mermaid, shells, sailing ship, compass rose. 3p, Compass rose, fish, oil derrick.
9p, Sailing ship, seagull, fish, cloud, sun.

1998, May 22		
930 A177 2.50p multi (2-1)	1.05	.85
931 A177 3p multi (2-2)	1.20	1.00
a. Pair, #930-931	2.35	2.00

Souvenir Sheets

| 932 A177 9p multicolored | 4.00 | 3.50 |
| a. Ovptd. in sheet margin | 4.25 | 3.75 |

No. 932a overprinted in Gold in Sheet Margin with "Amizade Luso-Chinesa / Festival de Macao" & Chinese Text.

1998 World Cup Soccer Championships, France — A178

Various soccer plays.

1998, June 10	Litho.	Perf. 12
933 A178 3p multicolored	1.20	1.10
934 A178 3.50p multicolored	1.50	1.45
935 A178 4p multicolored	1.75	1.70
936 A178 4.50p multicolored	2.35	2.15
Nos. 933-936 (4)	6.80	6.40

Souvenir Sheets

| 937 A178 9p multicolored | 5.75 | 4.25 |
| a. Ovptd. in sheet margin | 6.50 | 5.00 |

No. 937a overprinted in Gold in Sheet Margin with "Amizade Luso-Chinesa / Festival de Macao" & Chinese Text.

Chinese Opera Masks — A179

1.50p, Lio, Seak Chong (4-1). 2p, Wat, Chi Kong (4-2). 3p, Kam, Chin Pao (4-3). 5p, Lei, Kwai (4-4).
8p, Masked player.

1998, July 28	Litho.	Perf. 12
938 A179 1.50p multi	.60	.40
939 A179 2p multi	.75	.55
940 A179 3p multi	1.00	.85
941 A179 5p multi	1.75	1.55
a. Strip or block of 4, #938-941	4.50	3.75
Nos. 938-941 (4)	4.10	3.35

Souvenir Sheets

| 942 A179 8p multi | 5.25 | 3.50 |
| a. Ovptd. in sheet margin | 8.75 | 6.00 |

No. 942a overprinted in Gold in Sheet Margin with "Amizade Luso-Chinesa / Festival de Macao" & Chinese Text.

Vasco da Gama Type of 1998 Inscribed "1498"

1998, Sept. 4	Litho.	Perf. 12
943 A176 1p like #926	.60	.30
944 A176 1.50p like #927	.95	.45
945 A176 2p like #928	1.20	.75
a. Strip of 3, #943-945	3.00	2.75
Nos. 943-945 (3)	2.75	1.50

Souvenir Sheets

| 946 A176 8p like #929 | 4.00 | 3.75 |
| a. Ovptd. in sheet margin | 7.50 | 7.00 |

Issued to correct the error on Nos. 926-929.
No. 946a overprinted in Gold in Sheet Margin with "Amizade Luso-Chinesa / Festival de Macao" & Chinese Text.

Civil and Military Emblems Type of 1996

Designs: 50a, Lion. 1p, Dragon. 1.50p, Bird looking right. 2p, Bird looking left.
9p, Bird flying.

1998, Sept. 9		
947 A154 50a multi (4-1)	.30	.25
948 A154 1p multi (4-2)	.60	.35
949 A154 1.50p multi (4-3)	.75	.45
950 A154 2p multi (4-4)	.95	.55
a. Strip or block of 4, #947-950	2.75	1.75
Nos. 947-950 (4)	2.60	1.60

Souvenir Sheets

| 951 A154 9p multicolored | 4.25 | 4.00 |
| a. Ovptd. in sheet margin | 4.75 | 4.50 |

No. 951a overprinted in Gold in Sheet Margin with "Amizade Luso-Chinesa / Festival de Macao" & Chinese Text.

Kun Iam Temple — A180

Scenes inside temple compound: No. 952, Buddha figure standing. No. 953, Entrance gate, man running, benches. No. 954, Entrance to building, people. No. 955, People, stream, pagoda, flowers.
10p, Table, chairs, top of incense burner.

1998, Oct. 9	Litho.	Perf. 12
952 A180 3.50p multicolored	1.35	1.00
953 A180 3.50p multicolored	1.35	1.00
954 A180 3.50p multicolored	1.35	1.00
955 A180 3.50p multicolored	1.35	1.00
a. Block of 4, #952-955	5.75	5.00
Nos. 952-955 (4)	5.40	4.00

Souvenir Sheets

| 956 A180 10p multicolored | 4.50 | 4.25 |
| a. Ovptd. in sheet margin | 5.50 | 5.25 |

No. 956a overprinted in Gold in Sheet Margin with "Amizade Luso-Chinesa / Festival de Macao" & Chinese Text.

Paintings of Macao, by Didier Rafael Bayle — A181

Designs: 2p, Street scene, buggy, vert. 3p, People standing outside of buildings. 3.50p, Building atop wall. 4.50p, Buildings, house along street, vert.
8p, Top of building.

MACAO

1998, Nov. 11 Litho. Perf. 12
957	A181	2p multi (4-1)	.50	.40
958	A181	3p multi (4-2)	.75	.60
959	A181	3.50p multi (4-3)	.90	.70
960	A181	4.50p multi (4-4)	1.10	.90
		Nos. 957-960 (4)	3.25	2.60

Souvenir Sheets
| 961 | A181 | 8p multicolored | 2.25 | 2.25 |
| a. | | Ovptd. in sheet margin | 2.50 | 2.50 |

No. 961a overprinted in Gold in Sheet Margin with "Amizade Luso-Chinesa / Festival de Macao" & Chinese Text.

Tiles — A182

Designs: 1p, Dragon. 1.50p, Sailing ship. 2.50p, Chinese junk. 5.50p, Peacock. 10p, Building, lighthouse.

1998, Dec. 8
962	A182	1p multi (4-1)	.45	.35
963	A182	1.50p multi (4-2)	.60	.50
964	A182	2.50p multi (4-3)	.95	.70
965	A182	5.50p multi (4-4)	1.80	1.50
a.		Block or strip of 4, #962-965	4.00	3.25
		Nos. 962-965 (4)	3.80	3.05

Souvenir Sheets
| 966 | A182 | 10p multicolored | 5.25 | 5.00 |
| a. | | Ovptd. in sheet margin | 5.50 | 5.25 |

No. 966a overprinted in Gold in Sheet Margin with "Amizade Luso-Chinesa / Festival de Macao" & Chinese Text.

New Year 1999 (Year of the Rabbit) — A183

1999, Feb. 8 Litho. Perf. 12
| 967 | A183 | 5.50p multicolored | 2.00 | 1.75 |

Souvenir Sheet
| 968 | A183 | 10p multicolored | 10.00 | 6.50 |
| a. | | Ovptd. in sheet margin | 10.00 | 6.50 |

No. 968 is a continuous design.
No. 968a overprinted in gold in sheet margin with "Amizade Luso-Chinesa / Transferencia da Soberania de / MACAU 1999 / Sichuan Chengdu," dates and Chinese text.

Characters from Novel, "Dream of the Red Mansion," by Cao Xueqin — A184

1999, Mar. 1 Litho. Perf. 12
969	A184	2p Bao Yu (6-1)	1.95	.60
970	A184	2p Dayiu (6-2)	1.95	.60
971	A184	2p Bao Chai (6-3)	1.95	.60
972	A184	2p Xi Feng (6-4)	1.95	.60
973	A184	2p San Jie (6-5)	1.95	.60
974	A184	2p Qing Wen (6-6)	1.95	.60
a.		Block of 6, #969-974	12.25	4.00
		Nos. 969-974 (6)	11.70	3.60

Souvenir Sheet
| 975 | A184 | 8p Bao Yu & Dayiu | 15.00 | 12.50 |
| a. | | Ovptd. in sheet margin | 15.00 | 12.50 |

No. 975a overprinted in gold in sheet margin with "Amizade Luso-Chinesa / Transferencia da Soberania de / MACAU 1999 / Sichuan Chengdu," dates and Chinese text.

Maritime Heritage — A185

1999, Mar. 19 Litho. Perf. 12
976	A185	1.50p Sailing ships	.95	.70
977	A185	2.50p Marine life	1.35	1.00
a.		Pair, #976-977	2.50	1.85

Souvenir Sheet
| 978 | A185 | 6p Whale, vert. | 2.75 | 2.35 |
| a. | | Ovptd. in sheet margin | 3.00 | 2.50 |

Australia '99, World Stamp Expo.

No. 978a overprinted in gold in sheet margin with "Amizade Luso-Chinesa / Transferencia da Soberania de / MACAU 1999 / Sichuan Chengdu," dates and Chinese text.

First Portugal-Macao Flight, 75th Anniv. — A186

Airplanes: No. 979, Breguet 16 Bn2, "Patria." No. 980, DH9.

1999, Apr. 19 Litho. Perf. 12
979	A186	3p multicolored	1.60	1.25
980	A186	3p multicolored	1.60	1.25
a.		Souvenir sheet, #979-980	3.85	3.60
b.		As "a," ovptd. in sheet margin	4.00	3.80

See Portugal Nos. 2289-2290.
No. 980a is a continuous design.
No. 980b overprinted in gold in sheet margin with "Amizade Luso-Chinesa / Transferencia da Soberania de / MACAU 1999 / Sichuan Chengdu," dates and Chinese text.

A187

Traditional Water Carrier: a, 1p, Woman carrying container (4-1). b, 1.50p, Filling container from pump (4-2). c, 2p, Drawing water from well (4-3). d, 2.50p, Filling containers from faucet (4-4).
7p, Woman carrying containers up stairs.

1999, Apr. 28 Perf. 12
Horiz. Strip or Block of 4
| 981 | A187 | #a.-d. | 2.00 | 1.75 |

Souvenir Sheet
| 982 | A187 | 7p multicolored | 3.85 | 3.40 |
| a. | | Ovptd. in sheet margin | 4.00 | 3.60 |

No. 981 was issued in sheets of 4 strips or blocks, each in a different order.
No. 982a overprinted in gold in sheet margin with "Amizade Luso-Chinesa / Transferencia de Soberania de / MACAU 1999 / China Shanghai," date and Chinese text.

A188

Telecommunications — No. 983: a, 50a, Sea-Me-We cable. b, 1p, Satellite dishes. c, 3.50p, Cellular phones. d, 4p, Television. e, 4.50p, Internet.
8p, Computer mouse.

1999, May 5 Litho. Perf. 12
| 983 | A188 | Strip of 5, #a.-e. | 5.75 | 4.75 |

Souvenir Sheet
| 984 | A188 | 8p multi | 4.25 | 3.85 |
| a. | | Ovptd. in sheet margin | 4.50 | 4.00 |

No. 984 has a holographic image. Soaking in water may affect hologram.
No. 984a is overprinted in gold in sheet margin with "Amizade Luso-Chinesa / Transferencia de Soberania de / MACAU 1999 / China Shanghai," date and Chinese text.

Modern Buildings, Construction A189

1p, Cultural Center. 1.50p, Museum of Macao. 2p, Maritime Museum. 2.50p, Maritime Terminal. 3p, University of Macao. 3.50p, Public Administration Building. 4.50p, World Trade Center. 5p, Coloane Go-kart Track. 8p, Bank of China. 12p, Ultramarine National Bank.

1999, June 2 Litho. Perf. 12
989	A189	1p multi	.50	.40
990	A189	1.50p multi	.60	.45
991	A189	2p multi	1.00	.75
992	A189	2.50p multi	1.35	.95
993	A189	3p multi	1.50	1.10
994	A189	3.50p multi, vert.	1.70	1.20
995	A189	4.50p multi, vert.	2.10	1.70
996	A189	5p multi, vert.	2.35	1.85
997	A189	8p multi, vert.	3.60	3.00
998	A189	12p multi, vert.	5.25	4.25
		Nos. 989-998 (10)	19.95	15.65

TAP SEAC Buildings — A190

No. 999 — Various buildings with denominations in: a, Greenish blue. b, Orange. c, Dull yellow. d, Blue green (blue door).
10p, Orange.

1999, June 24
| 999 | A190 | 1.50p Strip of 4, #a.-d. | 3.60 | 2.75 |

Souvenir Sheet
| 1000 | A190 | 10p multicolored | 4.90 | 4.65 |
| a. | | Ovptd. in sheet margin | 4.90 | 4.65 |

No. 1000a overprinted in gold in sheet margin with "Amizade Luso-Chinesa / Transferencia de Soberania de / MACAU 1999 / Guangdong Cantao," date and Chinese text.

Dim Sum — A191

No. 1001 — Table settings with: a, Brown teapot. b, Two food platters. c, Two bamboo steamers. d, Flowered teapot.
9p, Various platters.

1999, Aug. 21
| 1001 | A191 | 2.50p Strip of 4, #a.-d. | 4.00 | 3.75 |

Souvenir Sheet
| 1002 | A191 | 9p multicolored | 4.75 | 4.25 |
| a. | | Ovptd. in sheet margin | 4.50 | 4.00 |

China 1999 World Philatelic Exhibition (No. 1002).
No. 1002a overprinted in gold in sheet margin with "Amizade Luso-Chinesa / Transferencia de Soberania de / MACAU 1999 / Guangdong Cantao," date and Chinese text.

Modern Sculpture — A192

Various unidentified sculptures.

1999, Oct. 9 Litho. Perf. 12
Background Color
1003	A192	1p red violet	.70	.45
1004	A192	1.50p brown, vert.	.85	.60
1005	A192	2.50p gray brn, vert.	1.50	1.20
1006	A192	3.50p blue grn	1.80	1.55
		Nos. 1003-1006 (4)	4.85	3.80

Souvenir Sheet
| 1007 | A192 | 10p blue gray | 5.00 | 4.75 |
| a. | | Ovptd. in sheet margin | 5.00 | 4.75 |

No. 1007a overprinted in gold in sheet margin with "Amizade Luso-Chinesa / Transferencia de Soberania de / MACAU 1999 / Zhejiang Hangzhou," date and Chinese text.

Meeting of Portuguese and Chinese Cultures — A193

No. 1008: a, 1p, Ships. b, 1.50p, Building. c, 2p, Bridge. d, 3p, Fort.
10p, Fort, diff.

1999, Nov. 19 Litho. Perf. 12¼
| 1008 | A193 | Strip of 4, #a.-d. | 3.35 | 2.75 |

Souvenir Sheet
| 1009 | A193 | 10p multi | 4.90 | 4.70 |
| a. | | Ovptd. in sheet margin | 4.75 | 4.50 |

Perforations in corners of stamps on Nos. 1008-1009 are star-shaped.
No. 1009a overprinted in gold in sheet margin with "Amizade Luso-Chinesa / Transferencia de Soberania de / MACAU 1999 / Zhejiang Hangzhou," date and Chinese text.
See Portugal No. 2339.

Retrospective of Macao's Portuguese History — A194

No. 1010: a, 1p, Globe. b, 1.50p, Fort. c, 2p, Chinese, Portuguese people. d, 3.50p, Skyline, Nobre de Carvalho bridge.
9p, Arms.

1999, Dec. 19
| 1010 | A194 | Block or strip of 4, #a.-d. | 5.30 | 3.80 |

Souvenir Sheet
| 1011 | A194 | 9p multi | 4.90 | 4.50 |
| a. | | Ovptd. in sheet margin | 4.75 | 4.25 |

No. 1011a overprinted in gold in sheet margin with "Amizade Luso-Chinesa / Transferencia de Soberania de / MACAU 1999 / Macau," date and Chinese text.
Perforations in corners of stamps on Nos. 1010-1011 are star-shaped.
See Portugal No. 2340.

Special Administrative Region of People's Republic of China

Establishment of Special Administrative Region — A195

No. 1012: a, 1p, Temple, dragon. b, 1.50p, Friendship Bridge, dragon boats. c, 2p, Cathedral, Santa Claus, Christmas tree. d, 2.50p, Lighthouse, race cars. e, 3p, Building, dragons. f, 3.50p, Building, crowd.
8p, Flower.

1999, Dec. 20 Litho. Perf. 12
| 1012 | A195 | Block of 6, #a.-f. | 4.75 | 4.75 |

Souvenir Sheet
| 1013 | A195 | 8p multi | 6.00 | 6.00 |
| a. | | Ovptd. in sheet margin | 4.50 | 4.50 |

No. 1013a overprinted in gold in sheet margin with "Amizade Luso-Chinesa / Transferencia de Soberania de / MACAU 1999 / China — Macau," dte., "O futuro de Macau será melhor" and Chinese text.

Souvenir Sheet

Millennium — A196

2000, Jan. 1 Litho. Perf. 12¼
| 1014 | A196 | 8p multi | 3.75 | 3.75 |

Perforations in corners of stamp are star-shaped.

MACAO

New Year 2000 (Year of the Dragon) — A197

2000, Jan. 28   *Perf. 12¼*
1015 A197 5.50p multi   2.75   2.75
Souvenir Sheet
1016 A197 10p multi   20.00 20.00
Perforations in corners of stamps on Nos. 1015-1016 are star-shaped.

Historic Buildings — A198

2000, Mar. 1   Litho.   *Perf. 12¼*
1017   Strip of 4   3.25 3.25
   a. A198 1p green circles   .40 .40
   b. A198 1.50p pink circles   .65 .65
   c. A198 2p brown circles   .80 .80
   d. A198 3p blue circles   1.20 1.20
Souvenir Sheet
1018 A198 9p Brown circles   3.50 3.50
Perforations in corners of stamps are star-shaped.

Chinese Calligraphy — A199

No. 1019 — Characters: a, Rectangle with bisecting line. b, Rectangle with lines inside. c, 8 horizontal lines, 3 vertical lines. d, 3 spots to left of 6 touching lines.
8p, Characters shown on Nos. 1019a-1019d.

2000, Mar. 23
1019 A199   Block of 4   4.50 4.50
   a.-d. 3p any single   .95 .95
Souvenir Sheet
1020 A199 8p multi   3.25 3.25
Bangkok 2000 Stamp Exhibition (No. 1020). Perforations in corners of stamps are star-shaped.

Scenes From "A Journey to the West" A200

No. 1021: a, 1p, Monkey and tiger. b, 1.50p, Monkey on tree. c, 2p, Monkey and spear carrier. d, 2.50p, Spear carrier and dog. e, 3p, Man in robe. f, 3.50p, Monkey in palm of hand.
9p, Monkey with stick, horiz.

2000, May 5   Litho.   *Perf. 12¼*
1021 A200   Block of 6, #a-f   9.50 9.50
Souvenir Sheet
1022 A200 9p multi   14.00 14.00
Perforations in corners of stamps are star-shaped.

Board Games — A201

Designs: 1p, Chinese chess. 1.50p, Chess. 2p, Go. 2.50p, Parcheesi.

2000, June 8
1023-1026 A201   Set of 4   3.25 3.25
Souvenir Sheet
1027 A201 9p Chinese checkers   7.00 7.00
Perforations in corners of stamps are star-shaped.

Tea Rituals — A202

2000, July 7
1028   Horiz. strip of 4   4.75 4.75
   a. A202 2p Square table, 4 people   9.00 9.00
   b. A202 3p Round table, 5 people   .75 .60
   c. A202 3.50p Round table, 3 people   1.00 .90
   d. A202 4.50p Square table, 3 people   1.25 1.10
Souvenir Sheet
1029 A202 8p Woman pouring tea   3.25 3.25
Perforations in corners are star-shaped. World Stamp Expo 2000, Anaheim (No. 1029).

Tricycle Drivers A203

No. 1030: a, Driver pointing. b, Driver wearing yellow cap. c, Driver sitting on saddle. d, Driver with feet on saddle. e, Driver with crossed legs. f, Driver repairing tricycle.
8p, Driver standing next to tricycle, vert.

2000, Sept. 1   Granite Paper
1030 A203 2p Block of 6, #a-f   3.50 3.50
Souvenir Sheet
1031 A203 8p multi   3.25 3.25
Perforations in corners of stamps are star-shaped.

Sculpture Type of 1999 Inscribed "Macau, China"

Various unidentified sculptures with background colors of: 1p, Brown. 2p, Green, vert. 3p, Purple, vert. 4p, Purple.
10p, Gray blue.

2000, Oct. 9   Granite Paper
1032-1035 A192   Set of 4   3.25 3.25
Souvenir Sheet
1036 A192 10p multi   10.00 10.00
Perforations in corners of stamps are star-shaped.

Ceramics and Chinaware — A204

No. 1037: a, Style. b, Color. c, Form. d, Function. e, Design. f, Export.

2000, Oct. 31   Granite Paper
1037 A204 2.50p Sheet of 6, #a-f   9.50 9.50
Souvenir Sheet
1038 A204 8p Plate design   10.00 10.00
No. 1038 contains one 38mm diameter stamp. Perforations in corners of No. 1037 are star-shaped.

Jade Ornaments A205

Various ornaments. Colors of country name: 1.50p, Purple. 2p, Green, vert. 2.50p, Red, vert. 3p, Blue.
9p, Red, vert.

2000, Nov. 22   Granite Paper
1039-1042 A205   Set of 4   3.25 3.25
Souvenir Sheet
1043 A205 9p multi   7.50 7.50
Perforations in corners of stamps are star-shaped.

Special Administrative Region, 1st Anniv. — A206

No. 1044: a, 2p, Dancers, flags. b, 3p, Monument, dragon.

2000, Dec. 20   Litho.   *Perf. 12¼*
Granite Paper (#1044)
1044 A206   Horiz. pair, #a-b   2.25 2.25
Souvenir Sheet
Litho. & Embossed
Perf. 13½x13
1045 A206 18p Flags, monument   9.00 9.00
No. 1045 contains one 60x40mm stamp. Perforations in corners of No. 1044 are star-shaped.

New Year 2001 (Year of the Snake) — A207

2001, Jan. 18   Litho.   *Perf. 13x13¼*
1046 A207 5.50p multi   3.75 3.75
Souvenir Sheet
Granite Paper
1047 A207 10p multi   15.00 15.00

Seng-Yu Proverbs — A208

Designs: No. 1048, Sleeping on a woodpile and tasting gall (4-1). No. 1049, Watching over a stump waiting for a rabbit (4-2). No. 1050, The fox making use of the tiger's fierceness (4-3). No. 1051, Meng Mu moving house three times (4-4).
8p, Man and bell.

2001, Feb. 1   Photo.   *Perf. 11¾*
Granite Paper
1048 A208 2p multi   .65 .65
   a. Booklet pane of 1, plain paper   3.50
1049 A208 2p multi   .65 .65
   a. Booklet pane of 1, plain paper   3.50
1050 A208 2p multi   .65 .65
   a. Booklet pane of 1, plain paper   3.50
1051 A208 2p multi   .65 .65
   a. Booklet pane of 1, plain paper   3.50
   Booklet, #1048a-1051a   20.00
Nos. 1048-1051 (4)   2.60 2.60
Souvenir Sheet
1052 A208   5.25 5.25
Hong Kong 2001 Stamp Exhibition (No. 1052). Booklet containing Nos. 1048a-1051a sold for 35p.

Traditional Implements A209

Designs: 1p, Abacus. 2p, Plane. 3p, Iron. 4p, Balance scale.
8p, Abacus, plane, iron, balance scale.

2001, Mar. 1   Litho.   *Perf. 14½x14*
1053-1056 A209   Set of 4   3.50 3.50
Souvenir Sheet
1057 A209 8p multi   3.75 3.75

Religious Beliefs — A210

No. 1058: a, Buddha. b, People in prayer. c, Re-enactment of Christ carrying cross. d, People in procession.
8p, Symbols.

2001, Apr. 12   Litho.   *Perf. 14½x14*
1058   Strip or block of 4   3.00 3.00
   a. A210 1p multi   .30 .30
   b. A210 1.50p multi   .50 .45
   c. A210 2p multi   .70 .65
   d. A210 2.50p multi   .90 .85
Souvenir Sheet
Photo.
Perf.
1059 A210 8p multi   4.00 4.00
No. 1059 contains one 60mm diameter stamp.

Rescue Workers — A211

No. 1060: a, Fireman. b, Hazardous materials worker. c, Fireman, diff. d, Ambulance crew.
8p, Firemen, diff

2001, May 2   Litho.   *Perf. 14½x14*
1060   Horiz. strip of 4   4.00 4.00
   a. A211 1.50p multi   .55 .45
   b. A211 2.50p multi   .85 .80
   c. A211 3p multi   .95 .90
   d. A211 4p multi   1.30 1.25
Souvenir Sheet
Perf. 14x14½
1061 A211 8p multi   9.50 9.50
No. 1061 contains one 60x40mm stamp.

Internet and E-Commerce A212

Designs: 1.50p, Keys. 2p, Envelope with "@" symbol. 2.50p, Hand-held computer. 3p, Computer.
6p, Linked computers.

2001, June 30   Litho.   *Perf. 14½x14*
1062-1065 A212   Set of 4   3.50 3.50
Souvenir Sheet
1066 A212 6p multi   4.75 4.75

Emblem of 2008 Summer Olympics, Beijing — A213

2001, July 14   Photo.   *Perf. 13x13¼*
1067 A213 1p multi + label   1.00 .60
No. 1067 printed in sheets of 12 stamp + label pairs with one large central label. See People's Republic of China No. 3119, Hong Kong No. 940. No. 1067 with different label is from People's Republic of China No. 3119a.

MACAO

The Romance of Three Kingdoms — A214

Designs: a, Men praying (4-1). b, Man with spear (4-2). c, Men at outdoors table (4-3). d, Man on horseback (4-4).
7p, Man with sword, horiz.

2001, Aug. 1   Litho.   Perf. 14x14½
1068   A214   3p Block of 4, #a-d   5.00   5.00
Souvenir Sheet
Perf. 14½x14
1069   A214   7p multi   15.00   15.00

2001 Census — A215

Designs: 1p, Buildings, students, child health care. 1.50p, Buildings, street scene. 2.50p, Bridge, people.
6p, Buildings, students, child health care, street scene, bridge, people.

2001, Aug. 23   Litho.   Perf. 14x14½
1070-1072   A215   Set of 3   2.00   2.00
Souvenir Sheet
1073   A215   6p multi   4.00   4.00
No. 1073 contains one 89x39mm stamp.

Stores A216

No. 1074: a, 1.50p, Municipal market. b, 2.50p, Store with red window frames. c, 3.50p, Store, parked bicycles. d, 4.50p, Store, parked cars.
7p, Store tower and windows.

2001, Sept. 13   Perf. 14½x14
1074   A216   Block of 4, #a-d   4.25   4.25
Souvenir Sheet
Perf. 14x14½
1075   A216   7p multi   4.00   4.00

DNA A217

Fingerprint and: a, 1p, Guanine. b, 2p, Cytosine. c, 3p, Adenine. d, 4p, Thymine.
8p, Adenine, horiz.

2001, Oct. 9   Photo.   Perf. 14x13½
Granite Paper
1076   A217   Block of 4, #a-d   4.00   4.00
Souvenir Sheet
Perf. 13½x14
1077   A217   8p multi   6.00   6.00
No. 1077 contains one 44x29mm stamp.

Parks and Gardens A218

No. 1078: a, 1.50p, Comendador Ho Yin Garden. b, 2.50p, Mong Há Hill Municipal Park. c, 3p, City of Flowers Garden. 4.50p, Taipa Grande Nature Park.
8p, Art Garden.

2001, Nov. 30   Litho.   Perf. 13½x14
Granite Paper
1078   A218   Block of 4, #a-d   3.75   3.75
Souvenir Sheet
1079   A218   8p multi   4.75   4.75

I Ching — A219

A219a

No. 1080 — Position of broken bars in trigrams (pa kua): a, No broken bars. b, First and second. c, Second and third. d, Second. e, First and third. f, First. g, Third. h, First, second and third.

2001, Dec. 10   Photo.   Perf. 13
Granite Paper
1080   A219   2p Sheet of 8, #a-h   5.75   5.75
Souvenir Sheet
Perf. 13½x13¼
1081   A219a   8p shown   5.00   5.00
No. 1080 contains eight 39x34mm hexagonal stamps. See Nos. 1111, 1126, 1135, 1203, 1241, 1306, 1360.

New Year 2002 (Year of the Horse) — A220

Horse's head: 5.50p, With frame. 10p, With continuous design.

2002, Jan. 28   Litho.   Perf. 14½x14
1082   A220   5.50p multi   3.00   3.00
Souvenir Sheet
1083   A220   10p multi   12.50   12.50

Characters From Novel "Dream of the Red Mansion II," by Cao Xuequin — A221

No. 1084: a, Lao Lao (6/1). b, Jin Chuan (6/2). c, Zi Juan (6/3). d, Xiang Yun (6/4). e, Liu Lang (6/5). f, Miao Yu (6/6).
8d, Woman reading book.

2002, Mar. 1   Perf. 14x14½
1084   A221   2p Block of 6, #a-f   5.25   5.25
Souvenir Sheet
1085   A221   8p multi   37.50   37.50

Tou-tei Festival A222

No. 1086: a, 1.50p, Opera. b, 2.50p, Dinner in appreciation of the elderly. c, 3.50p, Burning of religious objects. d, 4.50p, Preparing roasted pork.
8p, People watching performance, vert.

2002, Mar. 15   Perf. 14½x14
1086   A222   Block of 4, #a-d   4.25   4.25
Souvenir Sheet
Perf. 14x14½
1087   A222   8p multi   15.00   15.00

Church of St. Paul, 400th Anniv. — A223

Various church statues: 1p, 3.50p. 8p, Statue in niche.

2002, Apr. 12   Perf. 14½x14
1088-1089   A223   Set of 2   3.00   3.00
Souvenir Sheet
Perf. 14x14½
1090   A223   8p multi   6.50   6.50
No. 1090 contains one 30x40mm stamp.

Participation of Chinese Team in 2002 World Cup Soccer Championships — A224

No. 1091: a, 1p, Goalie. b, 1.50p, Two players.

Perf. 12 Syncopated
2002, May 16   Photo.
1091   A224   Horiz. pair, #a-b   1.50   1.50
A souvenir sheet containing Nos. 1091a-1091b, People's Republic of China No. 3198 and Hong Kong Nos. 978a-978b exists. Value, $50.

Environmental Protection — A225

Designs: 1p, Conservation of maritime resources. 1.50p, Reforestation. 2p, Recycling. 2.50p, Protection of swamps. 3p, Reuse of resources. 3.50p, Municipal cleaning. 4p, Air purification. 4.50p, Health and hygiene. 8p, Quiet and comfort.

2002, June 5   Litho.   Perf. 13x13¼
1092-1100   A225   Set of 9   9.00   7.00

Zheng Guanying (1842-1921), Reformer and Author — A226

Zheng and: a, 1p, Another man. b, 2p, Harbor scene. c, 3p, Men at table. d, 3.50p, Chinese text.
6p, Zheng seated at table.

2002, July 24   Perf. 14
1101   A226   Strip or block of 4, #a-d   5.00   5.00
Souvenir Sheet
1102   A226   6p multi   11.00   11.00
No. 1102 contains one 40x60mm stamp.

Honesty and Equality — A227

Various buildings: 1p, 3.50p.

2002, Sept. 13   Litho.   Perf. 14½x14
1103-1104   A227   Set of 2   1.75   1.75

Macao Snack Food A228

No. 1105: a, 1p, Bolinhas de peixe (fish balls). b, 1.50p, Carne de vitela seca (dried veal). c, 2p, Bolo (cake). d, 2.50p, Sat Kei Ma. 7p, Pastry.

2002, Sept. 26   Litho.   Perf. 13¼x13
1105   A228   Block of 4, #a-d   3.25   3.25
Souvenir Sheet
1106   A228   7p multi   6.00   6.00

Portions of Nos. 1105-1106 were applied by a thermographic process, producing a raised, shiny effect. No. 1106 contains one 50x50mm diamond-shaped stamp.

MACAO

Filial Love A229

No. 1107: a, 1p, Farmer and elephant (O amor filial comove a Deus). b, 1.50p, Man and woman (Abanar a almofada e aquecer a manta). c, 2p, Man and bamboo plants (Chorar sobre o bambu fez crescer rebentos). d, 2.50p, Man and fish (Pescar para a mae deitado no gelo).
No. 1107E: f, Man with arms extended (Mal agasalhado mas tolerante com a madrasta). g, Man and woman (Saltaram carpas da nascente). h, Man with hat (Quem tem amor filial é também fiel). i, Man (Lealdade de pai, amor filial do filho).
7p, Man wearing deer's head (Dar leite de veado aos pais).

2002, Oct. 9   Litho.   *Perf. 14*
1107   A229   Block of 4, #a-d   4.25   4.25
1107E   Souvenir booklet   19.50
   f.-i.   A229 4.50p Any booklet pane of 1   3.75   3.75
Souvenir Sheet
Perf. 13½x13
1108   A229   7p multi   12.00   12.00

Particle Physics A230

No. 1109: a, Unified electroweak interaction theory developed by Steven Weinberg, Sheldon Lee Glashow and Abdus Salam. b, Discovery of W and Z subatomic particles by Carlo Rubbia, 1983. c, Higgs diagram, developed by Richard Feynman and Peter Higgs. d, CERN large electron positron collider, 1989. e, Classification of particles and prediction of quarks by Murray Gell-Mann and George Zweig. f, Unification theory of Albert Einstein.
8p, Detection of positive and negative W particles, CERN LEP, 1996.

2002, Nov. 22   *Perf. 14x14½*
1109   A230   1.50p Block of 6, #a-f   7.50   7.50
Souvenir Sheet
1110   A230   8p multi   11.50   11.50

I Ching Type of 2001 and

Peace Dance — A231

No. 1111 — Position of broken bars in trigrams (pa kua): a, Fourth. b, First, second and fourth. c, Second, third and fourth. d, Second and fourth. e, First, third and fourth. f, First and fourth. g, Third and fourth. h, First, second, third and fourth.

2002, Dec. 13   *Perf. 14*
Granite Paper
1111   A219   2p Sheet of 8, #a-h   15.00   15.00
Souvenir Sheet
Perf. 11¼x13½
1112   A231   8p multi   7.50   7.50
No. 1111 contains eight 39x34 hexagonal stamps. Stamps from No. 1111 have Roman numeral II below "I Ching" and "Pa Kua."

New Year 2003 (Year of the Ram) — A232

2003, Jan. 2   *Perf. 14½x14*
1113   A232   5.50p multi   3.00   3.00
Souvenir Sheet
1113A   A232   10p multi   12.50   12.50

Legend of Liang Shanbo and Zhu Yingtai — A233

No. 1114: a, People seated and reading. b, People on bridge. c, People, tea pot and cups. d, Man holding red paper.
9p, People with butterfly wings.

2003, Feb. 15   Litho.   *Perf. 13x13½*
1114   Horiz. strip of 4   4.25   4.25
   a.-d.   A233 3.50p Any single   .90   .90
Souvenir Sheet
1115   A233   9p multi   18.00   18.00
No. 1115 contains one 40x60mm stamp.

The Outlaws of the Marsh A234

No. 1116: a, Song Jiang. b, Lin Chong. c, Wu Song. d, Lu Zhishen. e, Wu Yong. f, Hua Rong.
8p, Heróis do Monte Liang Shan.

2003, Mar. 1   *Perf. 13½x14*
Granite Paper (#1116)
1116   A234   2p Block of 6, #a-f   5.25   5.25
Souvenir Sheet
Perf. 14x14½
1117   A234   8p multi   17.50   17.50

Basic Law of Macao, 10th Anniv. — A235

Designs: 1p, Building, doves, cover of book of laws. 4.50p, Children, doves, flags of Macao and People's Republic of China, law book.

2003, Mar. 31   *Perf. 14*
1118-1119   A235   Set of 2   3.25   3.25

Traditional Chinese Medicine — A236

No. 1120 — Various medicines: a, 1.50p. b, 2p. c, 3p. d, 3.50p.
8p, Man holding bowl of medicine, horiz.

2003, May 28
1120   A236   Block of 4, #a-d   5.25   5.25
Souvenir Sheet
1121   A236   8p multi   15.00   15.00

Historic Buildings on Taipa and Coloane Islands — A237

Various buildings.

2003, June 18
1122   Horiz. strip of 4   3.75   3.75
   a.   A237 1p multi   .40   .40
   b.   A237 1.50p multi   .65   .65
   c.   A237 2p multi   .80   .80
   d.   A237 3.50p multi   1.25   1.25
Souvenir Sheet
1123   A237   9p multi   7.50   7.50

Everyday Life in the Past — A238

No. 1124: a, Calligrapher at table. b, Puppet maker. c, Man with food cart. d, Washerwoman. e, Woman with decorative lanterns. f, Man carrying food tray above head, man with baskets. g, Photographer. h, Man in chicken costume playing horn.
8p, Barber.

2003, July 30   *Perf. 13½x13*
1124   Block of 8   7.50   7.50
   a.-h.   A238 1.50p Any single   .80   .80
Souvenir Sheet
Perf. 14x14½
1125   A238   8p multi   9.00   9.00

I Ching Type of 2001 and

Woman and Child A239

No. 1126 — Position of broken bars in trigrams (pa kua): a, Second. b, Second, fifth and sixth. c, Second, fourth and fifth. d, Second and fifth. e, Second, fourth and sixth. f, Second and sixth. g, Second and fourth. h, Second, fourth, fifth and sixth.

2003, Sept. 10   *Perf. 14*
Granite Paper
1126   A219   2p Sheet of 8, #a-h   8.50   8.50
Souvenir Sheet
Perf. 14x13½
1127   A239   8p multi   4.50   4.50
No. 1126 contains eight 39x34mm hexagonal stamps. Stamps from No. 1126 have Roman numeral III below text "Pa Kua" and "I Ching."

Launch of First Manned Chinese Spacecraft A240

No. 1128: a, 1p, Astronaut. b, 1.50p, Ship, Shenzhou spacecraft.

2003, Oct. 16   *Perf. 13x13½*
1128   A240   Pair, #a-b   1.75   1.75
A booklet containing No. 1128, People's Republic of China No. 3314 and Hong Kong No. 1062 exists. The booklet sold for a premium over face value. Value $12.50.

50th Grand Prix of Macao A241

No. 1129: a, 1p, Race car #5. b, 1.50p, Yellow race car #11. c, 2p, Red race car #11. d, 3p, Motorcycle #5. e, 3.50p, Race car #15. f, 4.50p, Race car #3.
12p, Race car and motorcycle.

Litho. & Embossed
2003, Oct. 29   *Perf. 14*
1129   A241   Sheet of 6, #a-f   9.00   9.00
Souvenir Sheet
Litho. With Hologram Applied
Perf.
1130   A241   12p multi   9.00   9.00
No. 1129 contains six 36x27mm stamps that have varnish applied to raised portions.

Macao Museum of Art A242

No. 1131 — Artwork depicting: a, 1p, Man in hooded cloak. b, 1.50p, Hill overlooking harbor. c, 2p, Ruins of St. Paul's Church. d, 2.50p, Two men.
7p, Waterfront buildings, boats in harbor.

2003, Dec. 1   Litho.   *Perf. 14½x14*
1131   A242   Block of 4 #a-d   3.00   3.00
Souvenir Sheet
1132   A242   7p multi   12.50   12.50
No. 1132 contains one 57x55mm stamp.

New Year 2004 (Year of the Monkey) — A243

2004, Jan. 8   *Perf. 14½x14*
1133   A243   5.50p shown   3.00   3.00
Souvenir Sheet
1134   A243   10p Monkey, diff.   7.75   7.75

I Ching Type of 2001 and

Man Chiseling Stone A244

No. 1135 — Position of broken bars in trigrams (pa kua): a, Second and third. b, Second, third, fifth and sixth. c, Second, third, fourth and fifth. d, Second, third and fifth. e, Second, third, fourth and sixth. f, Second, third and sixth. g, Second, third and fourth. h, Second, fourth, fifth and sixth.

2004, Mar. 1   *Perf. 14*
Granite Paper
1135   A219   2p Sheet of 8, #a-h   15.00   15.00
Souvenir Sheet
Perf. 14x13½
1136   A244   8p multi   16.00   16.00
No. 1135 contains eight 39x34mm hexagonal stamps. Stamps from No. 1135 have Roman numeral IV below text "Pa Kua" and "I Ching."

MACAO

Li Sao — A245

No. 1137: a, Orientaçao. b, Cultivo. c, Aconselhamento pela Irma. d, Transmissao de esperança pela fênix. e, Viagens e reflexoes. f, Local da vida eterna.
8p, Li Sao, horiz.

2004, May 28   *Perf. 13½x14*
Granite Paper
1137 A245 1.50p Block of 6, #a-f   5.00   5.00
Souvenir Sheet
Perf. 14x13½
1138 A245   8p multi   15.00 15.00

God of Guan Di — A246

2004, June 30   *Perf. 13½x14*
Granite Paper
1139   Horiz. strip of 4   4.25   4.25
  a. A246 1.50p shown   .45   .45
  b. A246 2.50p God, diff.   .85   .85
  c. A246 3.50p God, diff.   1.15   1.15
  d. A246 4.50p God, diff.   1.40   1.40
Souvenir Sheet
Perf. 14x13½
1140 A246   9p God, diff.   12.50 12.50
No. 1140 contains one 40x40mm stamp.

2004 Summer Olympics, Athens — A247

Designs: 1p, Woman runner. 1.50p, Long jump. 2p, Discus. 3.50p, Javelin.

2004, July 30   *Perf. 13¼*
Granite Paper
1141-1144 A247   Set of 4   3.50   3.50

Deng Xiaoping (1904-97), Chinese Leader — A248

Designs: 1p, Saluting. 1.50p, Wearing white shirt.
8p, As young man.

2004, Aug. 22   *Litho.*   *Perf. 13x13¼*
1145-1146 A248   Set of 2   1.60   1.60
Souvenir Sheet
Litho. & Embossed
Perf.
1147 A248   8p multi   9.00   9.00
No. 1147 contains one 40mm diameter stamp.

Intl. Fireworks Display Contest — A249

No. 1148 — Various landmarks and fireworks displays: a, 1p. b, 1.50p. c, 2p. d, 4.50p. 9p, Statue and fireworks, vert.

Litho. & Silk Screened
2004, Sept. 2   *Perf. 13¼*
Granite Paper
1148 A249   Block of 4, #a-d   5.00   5.00
Souvenir Sheet
Perf. 13x13¼
1149 A249   9p multi   37.50 37.50
No. 1149 contains one 40x60mm stamp.

People's Republic of China, 55th Anniv. — A250

No. 1150 — Buildings and: a, 1p, Flag of People's Republic of China. b, 1.50p, Flag of Macao. c, 2p, Arms of People's Republic of China. d, 3p, Arms of Macao.
7p, Buildings.

2004, Oct. 1   *Litho.*   *Perf. 13x13¼*
Granite Paper
1150 A250   Block of 4, #a-d   5.50   5.50
Souvenir Sheet
Perf. 13¼x13
1151 A250   7p multi   15.00 15.00
No. 1151 contains one 60x40mm stamp.

Cosmology — A251

No. 1152: a, 1p, Expansion and acceleration of the Universe. b, 1.50p, Cosmic radiation. c, 2p, Fluctuations of galaxies. d, 3.50p, What is the Universe?
8p, Big Bang Theory.

2004, Oct. 9   *Perf. 12¼*
1152 A251   Block or strip of 4, #a-d   2.75   2.75
Souvenir Sheet
1153 A251   8p multi   7.00   7.00

Macao Garrison of the People's Liberation Army — A252

No. 1154 — Flag and, in foreground: a, 1p, Soldier holding sword. b, 1p, Soldier in tank. c, 1.50p, Soldiers in car. d, 1.50p, Soldiers giving blood. e, 3.50p, Soldier at attention holding gun. f, 3.50p, Soldier with helmet and rifle with bayonet.
8p, Soldiers in car, vert.

2004, Dec. 1   *Perf. 13x13¼*
1154 A252   Block of 6, #a-f   7.50   7.50
Souvenir Sheet
1155 A252   8p multi   15.00 15.00
No. 1155 contains one 40x60mm stamp.

Establishment of Special Administrative District, 5th Anniv. — A253

Lotus flowers and various buildings.

2004, Dec. 20   *Litho.*   *Perf. 14½x14*
1156   Horiz. strip of 4   4.25   4.25
  a. A253 1.50p multi   .70   .70
  b. A253 2p multi   .85   .85
  c. A253 2.50p multi   1.00   1.00
  d. A253 3p multi   1.25   1.25
Souvenir Sheet
Litho. & Embossed
1157 A253   10p multi   7.00   7.00

Air Macau, 10th Anniv. — A254

2004, Dec. 28   *Litho.*   *Perf. 14*
1158 A254   8p multi   13.00 13.00

New Year 2005 (Year of the Rooster) — A255

2005, Jan. 13   *Litho.*   *Perf. 14½x14*
1159 A255   5.50p shown   3.50   3.50
Souvenir Sheet
1160 A255   10p Rooster, diff.   6.50   6.50

Everyday Life in the Past — A256

No. 1161: a, Cook (8/1). b, Man holding pole with hanging bottles (8/2). c, Man at work at small table (8/3). d, Textile worker (8/4). e, Man cutting coconuts (8/5). f, Cook at cart (8/6). g, Cook under lantern (8/7). h, Seamstress (8/8).
8p, Mailman on bicycle.

2005, Mar. 1   *Perf. 12¼*
1161   Block of 8   6.50   6.50
  a.-h. A256 1.50p Any single   .65   .65
Souvenir Sheet
1162 A256   8p multi   22.50 22.50

Sai Van Bridge — A257

Designs: 1p, Bridge. 3.50p, Bridge and approaches.
8p, Bridge tower, vert.

2005, Mar. 23   *Perf. 14*
1163-1164 A257   Set of 2   2.50   2.50
Souvenir Sheet
1165 A257   8p multi   22.50 22.50

Libraries — A258

2005, Apr. 15
1166   Horiz. strip of 4   6.50   6.50
  a. A258 1p Central Library   .60   .50
  b. A258 1.50p Sir Robert Ho Tung Library   .90   .60
  c. A258 2p Coloane Library   1.25   .75
  d. A258 3.50p Mong Há Library   2.00   1.00
Souvenir Sheet
1167 A258   8p Public Commercial Assoc. Library   15.00 15.00
No. 1167 contains one 60x40mm stamp.

Mothers and Offspring — A259

2005, May 8   *Perf. 14½x14*
1168   Horiz. strip of 4 + 4 alternating labels   6.00   6.00
  a. A259 1p Humans + label   .75   .75
  b. A259 1.50p Kangaroos + label   1.05   .90
  c. A259 2p Birds and nest + label   1.50   1.20
  d. A259 3.50p Ducks + label   2.70   2.40
Labels could be personalized, with sheets containing 5 strips and 20 labels selling for 60p.

The Romance of the Western Chamber — A260

No. 1169 — Inscriptions: a, Espreitando a Beldade à Luz da Lua (6/1). b, Ying Ying Ouvindo Música (6/2). c, O Amor e Ansiedade de Zhang Sheng (6/3). d, A Interrogaçao da Dama (6/4). e, Sonhando com Ying Ying na Pensao (6/5). f, A Uniao dos Amados (6/6).
8p, A Espera da Lua.

2005, June 10   *Perf. 13¼x14*
Granite Paper
1169 A260   2p Block of 6, #a-f   5.00   5.00
Souvenir Sheet
Perf. 14x13¼
1170 A260   8p multi   30.00 30.00

Voyages of Admiral Zheng He, 600th Anniv. — A261

No. 1171: a, Admiral Zheng He. b, Giraffe. c, Ship and map.
8p, Ships.

2005, June 28   *Litho.*   *Perf. 13x13½*
1171 A261   Horiz. strip of 3   3.25   3.25
  a.   1p multi   .70   .50
  b.-c.   1.50p Either single   .95   .75
Souvenir Sheet
Perf. 13¼
1172 A261   8p multi   3.50   3.50
No. 1172 contains one 50x30mm stamp.

UNESCO World Heritage Sites — A262

Various buildings in Historical Center of Macao World Heritage Site with background colors of: a, 1p, White. b, 1.50p, Red. c, 2p, Orange. d, 3.50p, Dark green.
8p, Green.

2005, July 16   *Perf. 14*
1173 A262   Block of 4, #a-d   5.00   5.00
Souvenir Sheet
1174 A262   8p multi   18.00 18.00

4th East Asian Games, Macao — A263

No. 1175 — Stylized athletes and: a, 1p, Olympic Swimming Pool of Macao. b, 1.50p, Nautical Center, Praia Grande. c, 2p, Tennis Academy. d, 2.50p, IPM Sports Pavilion. e, 3.50p, Macao Stadium. f, 4.50p, Tap Seac Sports Pavilion.
8p, Sports Arena.

MACAO

2005, Aug. 30 — Perf. 14x13¼
Granite Paper
1175 A263 Block of 6, #a-f 5.50 5.50
Souvenir Sheet
Perf.
1176 A263 8p multi 12.50 12.50

No. 1176 contains one 55x38mm oval stamp.

Macao Bank Notes, Cent. — A264

Designs: 1p, 1 pataca note. 1.50p, 5 pataca note. 3p, 10 pataca note. 4.50p, 50 pataca note.
8p, 100 pataca note.

2005, Sept. 2 — Perf. 13½x14
Granite Paper
1177-1180 A264 Set of 4 6.50 6.50
Souvenir Sheet
1181 A264 8p multi 40.00 40.00

Great Chinese Inventions — A265

No. 1182: a, 1p, Textile loom. b, 1.50p, Paper. c, 2p, Metal smelting. d, 4.50p, Calendar.
8p, Seismograph.

2005, Oct. 9 — Perf. 14x13½
Granite Paper
1182 A265 Block of 4, #a-d 10.00 10.00
Souvenir Sheet
1183 A265 8p multi 25.00 25.00

Chaos and Fractal Mathematics — A266

No. 1184: a, 1p, Hilbert's Curve. b, 1p, Tree Fractal. c, 1.50p, Sierpinski Triangle. d, 1.50p, Chaos Game. e, 2p, Von Koch Curve. f, 2p, Cantor Set.
8p, Julia Set.

2005, Nov. 16 — Perf. 14
1184 A266 Block of 6, #a-f 6.00 6.00
Souvenir Sheet
1185 A266 8p multi 8.00 8.00

New Year 2006 (Year of the Dog) — A267

2006, Jan. 9   Litho. — Perf. 13x13¼
1186 A267 5.50p multi 3.50 3.50
Souvenir Sheet
1187 A267 10p multi 21.00 21.00

Lanterns — A268

No. 1188 — Various lanterns: a, (4/1). b, (4/2). c, (4/3). d, (4/4).

2006, Feb. 12 — Perf. 13¼x13
1188 Horiz. strip of 4 3.60 3.60
a.-b. A268 1p Either single .60 .50
c.-d. A268 1.50p Either single .80 .60
Souvenir Sheet
Perf. 13x13¼
1189 A268 8p multi 12.50 12.50

Everyday Life in the Past — A269

No. 1190: a, Cook (8/1). b, Food vendor (8/2). c, Man holding scissors (8/3). d, Man with small round table (8/4). e, Cobbler (8/5). f, Man with pots (8/6). g, Man hammering pails (8/7). h, Man carrying goods suspended from stick (8/8).
8p. Man looking at kettle.

2006, Mar. 1 — Perf. 14
1190 Block of 8 6.00 6.00
a.-h. A269 1.50p Any single .70 .55
Souvenir Sheet
1191 A269 8p multi 12.50 12.50

Items from Communications Museum — A270

No. 1192: a, Rubber stamp (8/1). b, Scale (8/2). c, Mail box (8/3). d, Mail sorting boxes (8/4). e, Telephone (8/5). f, Telephone switching equipment (8/6). g, Radio (8/7). h, Submarine cable (8/8).
10p, Macao #1, horiz.

2006, May 18 — Perf. 13¼x14
Granite Paper
1192 A270 Block of 8 6.00 6.00
a.-h. 1.50p Any single .65 .65
Souvenir Sheet
1193 A270 10p multi 37.50 37.50

2006 World Cup Soccer Championships, Germany — A271

Various soccer players.

Litho. & Embossed
2006, June 9 — Perf. 13¼
1194 A271 Block of 4 3.75 3.75
a. 1.50p multi .40 .40
b. 2.50p multi .75 .75
c. 3.50p multi 1.00 1.00
d. 4p multi 1.25 1.25

Fans — A272

No. 1195 — Various pictures on fans: a, (5/1). b, (5/2). c, (5/3). d, (5/4). e, (5/5).
10p, Three children.

2006, June 28   Litho. — Perf. 14x13¼
Granite Paper
1195 Vert. strip of 5 5.75 5.75
a.-b. A272 1.50p Either single .60 .60
c.-d. A272 2.50p Either single .90 .90
e. A272 3.50p multi 1.25 1.25
Souvenir Sheet
1196 A272 10p multi 19.00 19.00

No. 1196 contains one 40x30mm stamp.

21st China Adolescents Invention Contest — A273

No. 1197: a, 1.50p, Models of molecules, laboratory equipment (4/1). b, 2p, Dish antenna, Earth, windmills (4/2). c, 2.50p, Gear, compass, pyramid and diagrams (4/3). d, 3.50p, Invention, computer keyboard and mouse (4/4).
10p, Atomic model, contest venue, vert.

2006, July 28 — Perf. 14
1197 A273 Block of 4, #a-d 7.50 7.50
Souvenir Sheet
1198 A273 10p multi 10.00 10.00

No. 1198 contains one 40x60mm stamp.

Street Scenes — A274

No. 1199: a, Rua de S. Domingos (4/1). b, Rua de Camilo Pessanha (4/2). c, Calcada de S. Francisco Xavier (4/3). d, Travessa da Paixao (4/4).
10p, Largo de Santo Agostinho.

2006, Sept. 13 — Perf. 13½x14
Granite Paper
1199 Block of 4 4.25 4.25
a.-b. A274 1.50p Either single .50 .50
c. A274 2.50p multi .90 .90
d. A274 3.50p multi 1.25 1.25
Souvenir Sheet
Perf. 14x13½
1200 A274 10p multi 10.00 10.00

University of Macao, 25th Anniv. — A275

No. 1201 — Inscriptions for Faculty of: a, Social Sciences and Humanities (5/1). b, Law (5/2). c, Science and Education (5/3). d, Science and Technology (5/4). e, Business Management (5/5).
10p, University emblem.

2006, Sept. 28 — Perf. 13x13½
1201 Horiz. strip of 5 4.30 4.30
a.-e. A275 1.50p Any single .75 .60
Souvenir Sheet
1202 A275 10p multi 30.00 30.00

I Ching Type of 2001 and Two Women A276

No. 1203 — Position of broken bars in trigrams (pa kua): a, Sixth. b, First, second and sixth. c, Second, third and sixth. d, Second and sixth. e, First, third and sixth. f, First and sixth. g, Third and sixth. h, First, second, third and sixth.

2006, Oct. 9 — Perf. 13
1203 A219 2p Sheet of 8, #a-h 12.50 12.50
Souvenir Sheet
1204 A276 10p shown 20.00 20.00

No. 1204 contains eight 39x34mm hexagonal stamps. Stamps from No. 1135 have Roman numeral "V" below text "Pa Kua" and "I Ching."

Jesuits — A277

Designs: No. 1205, 1.50p, Matteo Ricci (1552-1610), missionary, and red Chinese chop. No. 1206, 1.50p, St. Francis Xavier (1506-52), missionary, and cross. No. 1207, 3.50p, Allesandro Valignano (1539-1606), missionary, and capital. No. 1208, 3.50p, Melchior Carneiro (c. 1516-83), in red bishop's stole.
10p, St. Ignatius Loyola (1491-1556), founder of Society of Jesus.

2006, Nov. 30   Litho. — Perf. 13½x14
1205-1208 A277 Set of 4 2.75 2.75
Souvenir Sheet
Perf. 14x13½
1209 A277 10p multi 20.00 20.00

New Year 2007 (Year of the Pig) — A278

2007, Jan. 8   Litho. — Perf. 13x13¼
1210 A278 5.50p multi 3.75 3.75
Souvenir Sheet
1211 A278 10p multi 30.00 30.00

Shek Wan Ceramics A279

No. 1212: a, 1.50p, Lao Zi (4/1). b, 1.50p, Lu Yu (4/2). c, 1.50p, Philosopher (4/3). d, 2.50p, Luo Han Seated (4/4).
8p, Concubine After Bath.

2007, Feb. 3
1212 A279 Block of 4, #a-d 7.50 7.50
Souvenir Sheet
1213 A279 8p multi 12.50 12.50

Everyday Life in the Past — A280

No. 1214: a, Man carrying tray on head (8/1). b, Man pouring tea into bowls (8/2). c, Rickshaw (8/3). d, People around table looking into bowl (8/4). e, Seamstress (8/5). f, Shoemaker (8/6). g, Ceramics artists (8/7). h, Embroiderer at booth (8/8).
10p, Festival dragon.

2007, Mar. 1 — Perf. 14
1214 Block of 8 8.50 8.50
a.-h. A280 1.50p Any single .75 .75
Souvenir Sheet
1215 A280 10p multi 9.50 9.50

MACAO

Traditional Chinese Shops — A281

No. 1216: a, 1.50p, Seamstress's shop (4/1). b, 1.50p, Acupuncturist and herbalist (4/2). c, 2.50p, Print shop (4/3). d, 3.50p, Restaurant (4/4).
10p, Street scene with man carting sign from shop.

2007, May 8			Perf. 14½x14	
1216	A281	Block of 4, #a-d	7.50	7.50
Souvenir Sheet				
1217	A281	10p multi	22.50	22.50

Seng Yu Proverbs — A282

Designs: Nos. 1218, 1223a, 1.50p, The Foolish Old Man Moved a Mountain (pink frame, 4/1). Nos. 1219, 1223b, 1.50p, The Friendship Between Guan and Bao (blue green frame, 4/2). Nos. 1220, 1223c, 3.50p, Calling Black White (lilac frame, 4/3). Nos. 1221, 1223d, 3.50p, The Quarrel Between Snipe and Clam (orange frame, 4/4).
10p, Horses and riders before riderless horse pulling cart, horiz.

2007, June 1			Perf. 14	
1218-1221	A282	Set of 4	13.00	13.00
Souvenir Sheet				
1222	A282	10p multi	20.00	20.00

Self-Adhesive Booklet Stamps
Serpentine Die Cut 14

1223		Booklet pane, #1223a-1223d	17.00	17.00
		Complete booklet, 2 #1223	34.00	

No. 1222 contains one 60x40mm stamp.

A Journey to the West A283

No. 1224: a, 1.50p, King and entourage, sprite with stick on cloud (6/1). b, 1.50p, Sprite on cloud, woman dreaming of horned spirit (6/2). c, 2p, Man with foot pierced by spear tip, woman, sprite without stick on cloud (6/3). d, 2p, Sprite on cloud battling other sprites (6/4). e, 2.50p, Sprite with stick, sprite with rake, sprite with swords (6/5). f, 2.50p, Sprite with rake on cloud, spirit with eight hands, spider (6/6).
10p, Sprite and sun.

2007, June 18			Perf. 14	
1224	A283	Block of 6, #a-f	37.50	37.50
Souvenir Sheet				
1225	A283	10p multi	37.50	37.50

Scouting, Cent. — A284

Lord Robert Baden-Powell, Macao Scouting emblem, flag ceremony and: 1.50p, Scout with semaphore flags. 2p, Scouts saluting. 2.50p, Scouts setting up campfire. No. 1229, 3.50p, Scouts lashing sticks together. No. 1230, 3.50p, Scout giving directions to other Scout.
10p, Flag, cannon and buildings, vert.

2007, July 9			Perf. 13x13¼	
1226-1230	A284	Set of 5	7.50	7.50
Souvenir Sheet				
Perf. 13¼x13				
1231	A284	10p multi	12.50	12.50

Arrival of Robert Morrison (1782-1834), First Protestant Missionary in China, Bicent. — A285

Morrison and: 1.50p, Lilac panel. 3.50p, Yellow panel.

2007, Sept. 28	Litho.	Perf. 13x13¼	
1232-1233	A285	Set of 2	1.75 1.75

Souvenir Sheet

Mount Kangrinboqe, Tibet — A286

2007, Oct. 9			Perf. 14	
1234	A286	10p multi	12.50	12.50

Applications of the Golden Ratio — A287

No. 1235: a, 1.50p, Fibonacci sequence. b, 2p, Sunflower spirals. c, 2.50p, Penrose tiling. d, 3.50p, Nautilus shell.
10p, Phi and equation.

2007, Oct. 26			Perf. 13¼x13	
1235	A287	Block of 4, #a-d	5.00	5.00
Souvenir Sheet				
1236	A287	10p multi	12.50	12.50

Chinese Philosophers — A288

No. 1237 Chinese character and: a, 1.50p, Lao Tzu (Lao Zi). b, 2.50p, Chuang Tzu (Zhuang Zi). c, 3.50p, Confucius (Confúcio). d, 4p, Meng Tzu (Méncio).
10p, Lao Tzu, Chuang Tzu, Confucius, Meng Tzu.

Litho. & Embossed

2007, Nov. 30			Perf. 13x13¼	
1237	A288	Block of 4, #a-d	14.00	14.00
Souvenir Sheet			**Perf.**	
1238	A288	10p multi	17.50	17.50

No. 1238 contains one 42mm diameter stamp.

New Year 2008 (Year of the Rat) — A289

No. 1239: a, Metal sculpture of rat. b, Wood carving of rat. c, Watercolor painting of rat. d, Fireworks and laser light image of rat. e, Clay teapot depicting rat.
10p, Clay teapot depicting rat and 2008 Beijing Summer Olympics emblem.

Litho., Litho. & Embossed with Foil and Hologram Application (#1239e, 1240)

2008, Jan. 23			Perf. 14¼	
1239		Horiz. strip of 5	11.00	11.00
a.-d.	A289	1.50p Any single	1.50	1.50
e.	A289	5p multi	4.75	4.75
Souvenir Sheet				
1240	A289	10p multi	12.00	12.00

No. 1240 contains one 50x50mm diamond-shaped stamp.

I Ching Type of 2001 and

Man Steering Raft A290

No. 1241 — Position of broken bars in trigrams (pa kua): a, Fourth and sixth. b, First, second, fourth and sixth. c, Second, third, fourth and sixth. d, Second, fourth and sixth. e, First, third, fourth and sixth. f, First, fourth and sixth. g, Third, fourth and sixth. h, First, second, third, fourth and sixth.

2008, Mar. 1	Litho.	Perf. 14	
Granite Paper			
1241	A219	2p Sheet of 8, #a-h	15.00 15.00
Souvenir Sheet			
1242	A290	10p multi	20.00 20.00

No. 1241 contains eight 39x34mm hexagonal stamps. Stamps from No. 1241 have Roman numeral "VI" below text "Pa Kua" and "I Ching."

Olympic Torch Relay — A291

Designs: 1.50p, Man holding Olympic torch, Parthenon. 3.50p, Mascot holding Olympic torch, lotus flower.
10p, Olympic torch, doves, vert.

2008, May 3			Perf. 13x13¼	
1243-1244	A291	Set of 2	1.25	1.25
Souvenir Sheet			**Perf. 13**	
1245	A291	10p multi	3.50	3.50

No. 1245 contains one 40x70mm stamp.

Western Legends — A292

No. 1246: a, The Golden Apple. b, The Gordian Knot. c, The Trojan Horse. d, The Riddle of the Sphinx.
10p, Cupid and Psyche, horiz.

2008, June 2			Perf. 13¼x14	
Granite Paper				
1246		Horiz. strip of 4	10.00	10.00
a.	A292	1.50p multi	1.00	1.00
b.	A292	2.50p multi	2.00	2.00
c.	A292	3.50p multi	2.75	2.75
d.	A292	4.00p multi	3.25	3.25
Souvenir Sheet				
Perf. 14x13¼				
1247	A292	10p multi	22.50	22.50

Native Cuisine of Macao and Singapore — A293

No. 1248: a, Panqueca Indiana. b, Arroz de Frango à Hainan. c, Carne de Porco à Alentejana. d, Lombo de Bacalhau Braseado em Lascas. e, Laksa. f, Saté. g, Arroz Frito à Yangzhou. h, Frango Frito.
No. 1249, vert.: a, Arroz no Tacho de Porcelana. b, Caranguejo con Piri-piri.

2008, July 4			Perf. 13¼x14	
Granite Paper				
1248	A293	Block of 8	11.00	11.00
a.-d.		1.50p Any single	.75	.75
e.-h.		3.50p Any single	1.90	1.90
Souvenir Sheet				
1249		Sheet of 2	12.00	12.00
a.-b.	A293	5p Either single	5.50	5.50

See Singapore Nos. 1318-1320.

Historic Center of Macau UNESCO World Heritage Site — A294

Designs: 1.50p, Fortaleza do Monte. 2p, Largo do Lilau. 2.50p, Lou Kau House. 3p, Largo do Senado. 3.50p, Sam Kai Vui Kun. 4p, Igreja da Sé. 4.50p, Quartel dos Mouros. 5p, St. Anthony's Church.

2008, July 31	Litho.	Perf. 13x13½	
1250	A294	1.50p multi	.35 .35
1251	A294	2p multi	.50 .50
1252	A294	2.50p multi	.65 .65
1253	A294	3p multi	.75 .75
1254	A294	3.50p multi	.90 .90
1255	A294	4p multi	1.10 1.10
1256	A294	4.50p multi	1.25 1.25
1257	A294	5p multi	1.40 1.40
		Nos. 1250-1257 (8)	6.90 6.90

2008 Summer Olympics, Beijing — A295

Designs: 5p, National Aquatics Center. 10p, National Stadium.

2008, Aug. 8			Perf. 13x13½	
1258	A295	5p multi	1.75	1.75
Souvenir Sheet			**Perf. 13**	
1259	A295	10p multi	8.00	8.00

No. 1259 contains one 54x74mm irregular, six-sided stamp.

20th Macao Intl. Fireworks Display Contest — A296

No. 1260 — Fireworks displays over various sections of Macao: a, 1.50p. b, 2.50p. c, 3.50p. d, 5p.

2008, Oct. 1	Litho.	Perf. 14x13½	
Granite Paper			
1260	A296	Sheet of 4, #a-d	12.00 12.00
Souvenir Sheet			
1261	A296	10p shown	8.00 8.00

Celebration — A297

MACAO

No. 1262: a, 1.50p, "Celebration" in many languages. b, 3.50p, UPU emblem.

2008, Oct. 9   *Perf. 14*
1262 A297   Horiz. pair, #a-b   9.00   9.00

The images in the frames of Nos. 1262a-1262b could be personalized for an additional fee. The generic images are shown.

Souvenir Sheet

Lijiang, People's Republic of China — A298

2008, Nov. 7
1263 A298   10p multi   12.50   12.50

Traditional Handicrafts — A299

Designs: 1.50p, Ivory carving. 2p, Ceramic painting. 2.50p, Basket weaving. 3.50p, Wood carving. 10p, Beaded embroidery.

2008, Dec. 1   *Perf. 13x13¼*
1264-1267 A299   Set of 4   3.00   3.00

Souvenir Sheet
Perf. 13¼x13
1268 A299   10p multi   12.00   12.00

No. 1268 contains one 60x40mm stamp.

Louis Braille (1809-52), Educator of the Blind — A300

2009, Jan. 4   *Litho.*   *Perf. 13¼*
1269 A300   5p black   2.50   2.50

New Year 2009 (Year of the Buffalo) — A301

No. 1270: a, Metal sculpture of buffalo head. b, Wood carving of buffalo head. c, Watercolor drawing of buffalo head. d, Fireworks display of buffalo head. e, Clay teapot with buffalo design. 10p, Clay teapot with buffalo design, diff.

Litho. (1.50p), Litho. & Embossed With Foil Application (5p, 10p)

2009, Jan. 9   *Perf. 14¼*
1270   Horiz. strip of 5   35.00   35.00
  a.-d. A301 1.50p Any single   4.25   4.25
  e. A301 5p multi   16.00   16.00

Souvenir Sheet
1271 A301   10p multi   25.00   25.00

No. 1271 contains one 50x50mm diamond-shaped stamp.

Opening of Kun Iam Treasury — A302

No. 1272 — Crowd of worshipers and holders of incense sticks with red chop at: a, Top. b, Lower left. c, Lower right. d, Left. 10p, Woman praying, horiz.

2009, Feb. 20   *Litho.*   *Perf. 13¼x13*
1272   Horiz. strip of 4   6.00   6.00
  a. A302 1.50p multi   .75   .75
  b. A302 2.50p multi   1.20   1.20
  c. A302 3.50p multi   1.65   1.65
  d. A302 4p multi   1.85   1.85

Souvenir Sheet
Perf. 13x13¼
1273 A302   10p multi   20.00   20.00

Traditional Tools — A303

Designs: 1.50p, Sand basin for compacting firecrackers. 2.50p, Whetstone. 3.50p, Stone grain mill. 4p, Cake mold. 10p, All four tools.

2009, Mar. 1   *Perf. 14½x14*
1274-1277 A303   Set of 4   4.00   4.00

Souvenir Sheet
Perf. 14x14½
1278 A303   10p multi   12.00   12.00

No. 1278 contains one 60x40mm stamp.

Souvenir Sheet

Buddha, Longmen Cave — A304

2009, Apr. 8   *Perf. 14*
1279 A304   10p multi   27.50   27.50

China 2009 World Stamp Exhibition, Luoyang.

Labor Day — A305

"5," "1" and: 1.50p, Construction workers, Macao Tower. 5p, Haulers, ruins of St. Paul's Church. 10p, Men lifting diamond-shaped "5.1." box.

2009, May 1   *Perf. 13x13¼*
1280-1281 A305   Set of 2   2.25   2.25
Souvenir Sheet
1282 A305   10p multi   15.00   15.00

The Mantis Stalking the Cicada — A306

A Fond Dream on Nanke — A307

Songs of Chu on All Sides — A308

Give the Last Measure of Devotion — A309

Design: 10p, Marking the boat to find the sword, horiz.

2009, June 1   *Litho.*   *Perf. 14*
1283 A306   1.50p multi   1.30   1.30
1284 A307   1.50p multi   1.30   1.30
1285 A308   3.50p multi   3.20   3.20
1286 A309   3.50p multi   3.20   3.20
  Nos. 1283-1286 (4)   9.00   9.00
Souvenir Sheet
1287 A309   10p multi   11.00   11.00

Booklet Stamps
Self-Adhesive
Serpentine Die Cut 14
1288 A306   1.50p multi   1.50   1.50
1289 A307   1.50p multi   1.50   1.50
1290 A308   3.50p multi   3.00   3.00
1291 A309   3.50p multi   3.00   3.00
  a. Booklet pane of 8, 2 each #1288-1291   20.00
  Nos. 1288-1291 (4)   2.60   2.60

Seng Yu proverbs. No. 1287 contains one 60x40mm stamp.

People's Republic of China, 60th Anniv. — A310

No. 1292 — Lanterns and: a, 1.50p, Archway. b, 2.50p, Soldier in tank. c, 3.50p, Children exercising. d, 4p, Soldiers and flag of People's Republic of China. 10p, Archway, soldiers and flag of People's Republic of China, horiz.

2009, Oct. 1   *Litho.*   *Perf. 13¼x13*
1292 A310   Block of 4, #a-d   7.50   7.50
Souvenir Sheet
Photo.
Perf. 13
1293 A310   10p multi   15.00   15.00

No. 1293 contains one 60x40mm stamp.

Porcelain Plate Paintings by Sou Farong — A311

Designs: 1.50p, Bodhisattva Ksitigarbha. 5p, Bodhisattva Avalokitsavara.

2009, Oct. 9   *Litho.*   *Perf. 13x13¼*
1294-1295 A311   Set of 2   7.50   7.50

Pui Ching Middle School, 120th Anniv. — A312

No. 1296: a, 1.50p, Building and basketball court. b, 2p, Building, diff. c, 2.50d, Buildings. d, 3.50p, Bust and fireplace. 10p, Building and fountain.

2009, Nov. 29   *Litho.*   *Perf. 13½x14*
Granite Paper
1296 A312   Block or strip of 4, #a-d   9.50   9.50
Souvenir Sheet
1297 A312   10p multi   37.50   37.50

Macao Science Center — A313

No. 1298: a, 1.50p, Aerial view of entire complex. b, 2.50p, Exhibition Center and Planetarium. c, 3.50p, Ground-level view of entire complex. d, 4p, Ground-level view of Exhibition Center and Convention Center. 10p, Top of Exhibition Center.

2009, Dec. 19   *Perf. 13½x14*
Granite Paper
1298 A313   Block or strip of 4, #a-d   9.50   9.50
Souvenir Sheet
1299 A313   10p multi   22.00   22.00

People's Liberation Army Garrison in Macao, 10th Anniv. — A314

No. 1300: a, Soldiers with martial arts stances. b, Two women officers. c, Soldiers with gun. d, Soldiers and children with cannon. e, Soldiers and children planting tree. f, Soldiers repairing tank. 10p, Soldiers on parade, vert.

2009, Dec. 20   *Perf. 13x13¼*
1300   Block of 6   22.00   22.00
  a.-f. A314 1.50p Any single   3.00   3.00
Souvenir Sheet
Perf. 13x13½
1301 A314   10p multi   25.00   25.00

No. 1301 contains one 40x60mm stamp.

Return of Macao to China, 10th Anniv. — A315

No. 1302: a, Golden Lotus sculpture, flags of People's Republic of China and Macao. b, Senado Square and Macao Tower. c, Macao waterfront. 10p, Golden Lotus, gate, vert.

Perf. 13¼x13 Syncopated
2009, Dec. 20   *Photo.*
1302 A315   Horiz. strip of 3   6.50   6.50
  a.-c. 1.50p Any single   1.85   1.85
Souvenir Sheet
Perf. 13x13½
1303 A315   10p multi   26.00   26.00

No. 1303 contains one 40x60mm stamp. See People's Republic of China Nos. 3791-3793.

New Year 2010 (Year of the Tiger) — A316

No. 1304: a, Clay sculpture of tiger and cub. b, Fireworks display of tiger's head. c, Watercolor drawing of tiger. d, Wood carving of tiger. e, Metal sculpture of tiger. 10p, Metal sculpture of tiger, diff.

Litho. (1.50p), Litho. & Embossed with Hologram and Foil Application (5p, 10p)

2010, Jan. 2   *Perf. 14¼*
1304   Horiz. strip of 5   37.50   37.50
  a.-d. A316 1.50p Any single   4.25   4.25
  e. A316 5p multi   15.50   15.50
Souvenir Sheet
1305 A316   10p multi   9.00   9.00

No. 1305 contains one 50x50mm diamond-shaped stamp.

I Ching Type of 2001 and

Child With Toy — A317

No. 1306 — Position of broken bars in trigrams (pa kua): a, First and second. b, First, second, fifth and sixth. c, First, second, fourth and fifth. d, First, second and fifth. e, First, second, fourth and sixth. f, First, second and

MACAO

sixth. g, First, second and fourth. h, First, second, fourth, fifth and sixth.

2010, Mar. 1	Litho.	Perf. 13
Granite Paper		
1306 A219	2p Sheet of 8, #a-h	16.00 16.00

Souvenir Sheet
Perf. 13½
1307 A317 10p multi 16.00 16.00

No. 1306 contains eight 39x34 hexagonal stamps. Stamps from No. 1306 have Roman numeral "VII" below text "Pa Kua" and "I Ching."

Intl. Women's Day, Cent. — A318

No. 1308 — Women in various costumes: a, 1.50p. b, 2.50p. c, 3.50p. d, 4p. 10p, Three women, vert.

2010, Mar. 8		Perf. 13¼x14
Granite Paper		
1308 A318	Block of 4, #a-d	7.50 7.50

Souvenir Sheet
1309 A318 10p multi 13.00 13.00

No. 1309 contains one 40x60mm stamp.

Expo 2010, Shanghai — A319

Designs: 3.50p, Rabbits. 4p, Chinese lanterns. 10p, Rabbit and Chinese lanterns.

2010, May 1		Perf. 13¼x14
Granite Paper		
1310-1311 A319	Set of 2	1.75 1.75

Souvenir Sheet
1312 A319 10p multi 10.00 10.00

Macau Branch of Bank of China, 60th Anniv. A320

No. 1313 — Yellow ribbons forming "60," Bank of China emblem and: a, 1.50p, Street lamp, ruins of St. Paul's Church. b, 2.50p, Buildings. c, 3.50p, "10" from banknote, 1000-pataca banknote. d, 4p, Child, stylized people, people shaking hands. 10p, Buildings, lotus flower, Bank of China emblem.

2010, June 21		Perf. 13¼x14
Granite Paper		
1313 A320	Block of 4, #a-d	27.50 27.50

Souvenir Sheet
1314 A320 10p multi 35.00 35.00

No. 1314 contains one 60x40mm stamp.

Historic Center of Macao UNESCO World Heritage Site — A321

No. 1315 — Buildings near St. Augustine's Square: a, 1.50p, Dom Pedro V Theater. b, 2.50p, Sir Robert Ho Tung Library. c, 3.50p, St. Augustine's Church. d, 4p, Seminary and Church of St. Joseph. 10p, Building on Square.

2010, July 15		Perf. 14x13¼
Granite Paper		
1315 A321	Block of 4, #a-d	7.50 7.50

Souvenir Sheet
1316 A321 10p multi 7.50 7.50

Stained-Glass Windows — A322

Stained-glass window from St. Lawrence's Church, Macao: 5.50p, Detail. 10p, Entire window, horiz.

2010, Aug. 30		Perf. 13¼x13
Granite Paper		
1317 A322	5.50p multi	3.75 3.75

Souvenir Sheet
Perf. 13x13¼
1318 A322 10p multi 17.50 17.50

See Aland Islands Nos. 306-307.

Carvings of Religious Figures A323

No. 1319: a, 1.50p, Buddha. b, 2.50p, Na Tcha. c, 3.50p, Kun Iam. d, 4p, Tin Hau. 10p, The Eight Immortals, horiz.

2010, Sept. 7		Perf. 14
1319 A323	Block or strip of 4, #a-d	17.50 17.50

Souvenir Sheet
1320 A323 10p multi 25.00 25.00

No. 1320 contains one 60x30mm stamp.

Old Telephones — A324

No. 1321 — Various old telephones with background color of: a, 1.50p, Green. b, 2.50p, Pink. c, 3.50p, Yellow. d, 4p, Blue. 10p, Old telephone, horiz.

2010, Sept. 1	Litho.	Perf. 14
1321 A324	Block or strip of 4, #a-d	3.75 3.75

Souvenir Sheet
1322 A324 10d multi 15.00 15.00

No. 1322 contains one 60x40mm stamp.

Macao Food Festival, 10th Anniv. — A325

Designs: 1.50p, Wonton soup. 2.50p, Xiao Long Bao (steamed buns). 3.50p, Sushi. 4p, Pastel de nata (egg tart). 10p, Portuguese chicken.

2010, Nov. 5		Perf. 13¼x13
1323-1326 A325	Set of 4	6.00 6.00

Souvenir Sheet
1327 A325 10p multi 17.50 17.50

Traditional Clothing — A326

No. 1328: a, 1.50p, Man in Tang suit. b, 2.50p, Woman in qipao. c, 3.50p, Woman in blouse and long skirt. d, 4p, Man in tunic suit. 10p, Two women, horiz.

2010, Nov. 30		
1328 A326	Block of 4, #a-d	14.00 14.00

Souvenir Sheet
1329 A326 10p multi 56.00 56.00

No. 1329 contains one 60x40mm stamp.

Giant Pandas — A327

Panda, domed building and: 1.50p, Chapel of Our Lady of Penha. 5p, Ruins of St. Paul's Church. 10p, Two pandas, domed building, Ruins of St. Paul's Church.

2010, Dec. 18		Perf. 13¼x13
1330-1331 A327	Set of 2	10.00 10.00

Souvenir Sheet
Perf. 13x13¼
1332 A327 10p multi 15.00 15.00

No. 1332 contains one 40x60mm stamp.

New Year 2011 (Year of the Rabbit) — A328

No. 1333: a, Clay sculpture of rabbit. b, Fireworks and laser light image of rabbit. c, Watercolor painting of rabbit. d, Wood carving rabbit. e, Metal sculpture of rabbit. 10p, Metal sculpture of rabbit, diff.

Litho., Litho. & Embossed with Foil and Hologram Application (5p, 10p)

2011, Jan. 5		Perf. 13¼x13
1333	Horiz. strip of 5	4.75 4.75
a.-d.	A328 1.50p Any single	.60 .60
e.	A328 5p multi	1.90 1.90

Souvenir Sheet
Perf. 14¼
1334 A328 10p multi 7.75 7.75

No. 1334 contains one 50x50mm diamond-shaped stamp.

Ancient City of Fenghuang — A329

2011, Mar. 1	Litho.	Perf. 13x13¼
1335 A329	10p multi	15.00 15.00

Public Buildings — A330

Designs: 1.50p, Government Headquarters. 2.50p, Monetary Authority. 3.50p, Holy House of Mercy Hospice. 4p, Macao Foundation.

2011, Apr. 19		Perf. 14
1336-1339 A330	Set of 4	3.50 3.50

Cantonese Naamyam — A331

No. 1340 — Musician near: a, 1.50p, Building archway. b, 2.50p, Junk with sails up. c, 3.50p, Wall and awning. d, 4p, Harbor. 10p, Musician near wall.

2011, May 30		Perf. 13¼x13
1340 A331	Block of 4, #a-d	9.25 9.25

Souvenir Sheet
1341 A331 10p multi 21.00 21.00

Legend of the White Snake A332

No. 1342: a, 1.50p, Lady Bai Suzhen and Xu Xian meeting when traveling the lake (6/1). b, 1.50p, Revelation to Xu Xian that Lady Bai is a snake during Dragon Boat Festival (6/2). c, 2p, Lady Bai steals herb to save husband (6/3). d, 2p, Fight between dragon and white snake (6/4). e, 2.50p, Lady Bai captive in pagoda (6/5). f, 2.50p, Flooding of the Jinshan Temple (6/6). 10p, Lacy Bai with sword, horiz.

2011, July 28		Perf. 13¼x13
1342 A332	Block of 6, #a-f	7.50 7.50

Souvenir Sheet
Perf. 13¼
1343 A332 10p multi 8.50 8.50

No. 1343 contains one 60x30mm stamp.

Worldwide Fund for Nature, 50th Anniv. — A333

MACAO

No. 1344 — Birds: a, 1.50p, Pycnonotus sinensis. b, 2.50p, Streptopelia chinensis. c, 3.50p, Ixobrychus sinensis. d, 4.50p, Centropus sinensis.

2011, Sept. 11   Litho.   Perf. 14x13¼
Granite Paper

1344	A333	Block of 4, #a-d	7.50	7.50
e.		Souvenir sheet, #1344a-1344d	12.50	12.50

Famous Men A334

No. 1345: a, 1.50p, Lin Zexu (1785-1850), scholar. b, 2.50p, Ye Ting (1896-1946), military leader. c, 3.50p, Xian Xinghai (1905-45), composer. d, 4p, Ho Yin, industrialist and philanthropist.
10p, Lin Zexu, Ye Ting, Xian Xinghai and Ho Yin, vert.

2011, Oct. 9   Litho.   Perf. 14

1345	A334	Block or strip of 4, #a-d	7.50	7.50

Souvenir Sheet
Litho. With Foil Application

1346	A334	10p multi	12.50	12.50

No. 1346 contains one 40x60mm stamp.

25th Macao Intl. Music Festival A335

No. 1347 — Musical note, web and: a, 1.50p, Vertical ovals. b, 2.50p, Parabolas. c, 3.50p, Circles. d, 4p, Lines.
10p, Horizontal oval.

2011, Oct. 9   Perf. 14x13½
Granite Paper

1347	A335	Block or strip of 4, #a-d	13.50	13.50

Souvenir Sheet

1348	A335	10p multi	21.50	21.50

Chinese Revolution, Cent. — A336

No. 1349 — Flags and: a, 1.50p, Gao Jianfu (1879-1951), painter, Macao office of Chinese Revolutionary League. b, 2.50p, Huang Xing (1874-1916), revolutionary leader, Huanghuagang Mausoleum of 72 Martyrs. c, 3.50p, Xiong Bingkun (1885-1969), revolutionary leader, Uprising Gate. d, 4p, Dr. Sun Yat-sen (1866-1925), President of Republic of China, office of Provisional President.
10p, Flags, China #185.

2011, Oct. 10   Litho.   Perf. 13x13¼

1349	A336	Block or strip of 4, #a-d	5.50	5.50

Souvenir Sheet
Photo. Perf. 13¼x13

1350	A336	10p multi	6.00	6.00

No. 1350 contains one 60x40mm stamp.

Kiang Wu Hospital Charitable Association, 140th Anniv. — A337

Building and: 1.50p, Plaque. 2.50p, Statue of Dr. Sun Yat-sen. 3.50p, Crushing wheel. 4p, Magnetic resonance imaging machine.
10p, Statue of Dr. Sun Yat-sen, scenes from modern hospital.

2011, Oct. 28   Litho.   Perf. 14x13½
Granite Paper

1351-1354	A337	Set of 4	25.00	25.00

Souvenir Sheet

1355	A337	10p multi	85.00	85.00

No. 1355 contains one 40x40mm stamp.

New Year 2012 (Year of the Dragon) — A338

No. 1356: a, Metal sculpture of dragon. b, Wood carving of dragon. c, Fireworks display of dragon. d, Clay sculpture of dragon. e, Watercolor painting of dragon.
12p, Watercolor painting of dragon, diff.

Litho., Litho. & Embossed with Foil and Hologram Application (5p)
2012, Jan. 5   Perf. 14¼

1356		Horiz. strip of 5	8.25	8.25
a.-d.		A338 1.50p Any single	1.00	1.00
e.		A338 5p multi	2.50	2.50

Souvenir Sheet
Litho. & Embossed With Foil Application
Perf. 13¼

1357	A338	12p multi	7.75	7.75

No. 1357 contains one 50x50mm diamond-shaped stamp.

Smoke-Free Macao — A339

Macao skyline and: 1.50p, "2012" with "no smoking" symbol replacing zero. 5p, "No smoking" symbol.

2012, Jan. 31   Litho.   Perf. 14

1358-1359	A339	Set of 2	3.75	3.75

I Ching Type of 2001 and

Woman and Child A340

No. 1360 — Position of broken bars in trigrams (pa kua): a, First, second and third. b, First, second, third, fifth and sixth. c, First, second, third, fourth and fifth. d, First, second, third and fifth. e, First, second, third, fourth and sixth. f, First, second, third and sixth. g, First, second, third and fourth. h, First, second, third, fourth, fifth and sixth.

2012, Mar. 1   Perf. 14
Granite Paper

1360	A219	2p Sheet of 8, #a-h	4.00	4.00

Souvenir Sheet
Perf. 14x13¼

1361	A340	10p multi	6.00	6.00

No. 1360 contains eight 39x34mm hexagonal stamps. Stamps from No. 1360 have Roman numeral "VIII" below text "Pa Kuang 'I Ching.'"

Tai Fung Bank, 70th Anniv. — A341

Designs: 1.50p, Man, rectangular emblem with Portuguese and Chinese text. 2.50p, Building, emblem with Chinese characters. 3.50p, Building, round emblem with Portuguese and Chinese text. 4p, Emblem with serpents.

10p, 70th anniversary emblem.

2012, Mar. 28   Perf. 13x13¼
Granite Paper

1362-1365	A341	Set of 4	3.00	3.00

Souvenir Sheet
Perf. 13¼x13

1366	A341	10p multi	6.00	6.00

No. 1366 contains one 60x40mm stamp.

Historic Views of Fishing Harbor — A342

Various views of harbor, boats and structures.

2012, May 18   Perf. 13x13¼
Granite Paper

1367		Horiz. strip of 4	3.25	3.25
a.		A342 1.50p multi	.40	.40
b.		A342 2.50p multi	.65	.65
c.		A342 3.50p multi	.90	.90
d.		A342 4p multi	1.00	1.00

Souvenir Sheet
Perf. 13½x13

1368	A342	10p multi	3.50	3.50

No. 1368 contains one 60x40mm stamp.

Hou Kong Middle School, 80th Anniv. — A343

No. 1369: a, 1.50p, Students working on models of Chinese junks, students painting and writing Chinese characters. b, 2.50p, Students participating in sporting events. c, 3.50p, Students participating in performing arts. d, 4p, Teacher and student in classroom, student taking piano lesson, child holding artwork, children at play.
10p, Students parading on track with school emblem and banner, school band, vert.

2012, June 10   Perf. 13x13¼
Granite Paper

1369	A343	Block of 4, #a-d	6.00	6.00

Souvenir Sheet
Perf. 13½

1370	A343	10p multi	13.00	13.00

No. 1370 contains one 40x40mm stamp.

Tung Sin Tong Charitable Society, 120th Anniv. — A344

No. 1371: a, 1.50p, Woman playing piano, line of children. b, 2.50p, Students in classroom. c, 3.50p, Health care. d, 4p, People of various ages.
10p, Roof of building, fireworks.

2012, Aug. 8   Perf. 14x13¼
Granite Paper

1371	A344	Block of 4, #a-d	8.00	8.00

Souvenir Sheet

1372	A344	10p multi	22.00	22.00

Legend of the Cowherd and the Weaving Maid A345

No. 1373: a, 1.50p, Cowherd and cow, denomination at LR. b, 1.50p, Cowherd taking clothes of bathing maid, denomination at LL. c, 2p, Children playing with cow, cowherd watching maid weaving, denomination at LR. d, 2p, Maid being abducted, denomination at LL. e, 2.50p, Children and cowherd on knees at edge of sea, denomination at LR. f, 2.50p, Cowherd tossing water, old man and woman, denomination at LL.
10p, Cowherd, maid, children, birds, vert.

2012, Aug. 23   Perf. 14x13¼
Granite Paper

1373	A345	Block of 6, #a-f	4.25	4.25

Souvenir Sheet

1374	A345	10p multi	6.50	6.50

No. 1374 contains one 40x60mm stamp.

Safeguarding of Honesty and Transparency, 20th Anniv. — A346

20th anniversary emblem and: 2p, Buildings and bridge. 5p, Buildings.

2012, Sept. 20   Perf. 14x13¼
Granite Paper

1375-1376	A346	Set of 2	3.75	3.75

Paintings of Macao Scenes by Lok Cheong — A347

No. 1377: a, 1.50p, Temple, painting of boat on rock. b, 2.50p, Trees. c, 3.50p, People in park. d, 4p, People walking near large trees.
10p, Macao skyline, vert.

2012, Sept. 21   Perf. 13x13¼
Granite Paper

1377	A347	Block of 4, #a-d	3.00	3.00

Souvenir Sheet
Perf. 13½

1378	A347	10p multi	17.50	17.50

No. 1378 contains one 40x40mm stamp.

Henrique de Senna Fernandes (1923-2010), Writer — A348

2012, Oct. 9   Litho.   Perf. 14

1379	A348	5p multi	1.75	1.75

Scenes From *The Peony Pavilion* A349

No. 1380: a, 1.50p, Du Liniang falls asleep under tree (6/1). b, 1.50p, Du Liniang drawing

MACAO

(6/2). c, 2p, Lord of the Underworld and Du Liniang (6/3). d, 2p, Du Liniang and Liu Mengmei (6/4). e, 2.50p, Du Liniang and Liu Mengmei under tree (6/5). f, 2.50p, Wedding (6/6).
12p, Du Liniang and Liu Mengmei, diff.

2012, Nov. 30   **Perf. 13¼x13**
Granite Paper
1380 A349   Block of 6, #a-f   17.50 17.50
Souvenir Sheet
Perf. 13¼
1381 A349   12p multi   20.00 20.00
No. 1381 contains one 30x60mm stamp.

New Year 2013 (Year of the Snake) — A350

No. 1382: a, Metal sculpture of snake. b, Wood carving of snake. c, Fireworks display of snake. d, Clay sculpture of snake. e, Watercolor painting of snake.
12p, Watercolor painting of snake, diff.

Litho., Litho. & Embossed with Foil and Hologram Application (5p)
2013, Jan. 3   **Perf. 14¼**
1382   Horiz. strip of 5   12.00 12.00
   a.-d.   A350 1.50p Any single   1.45 1.45
   e.   A350 5p multi   3.50 3.50
Souvenir Sheet
Litho. & Embossed With Foil Application
1383 A350   12p multi   11.50 11.50
No. 1383 contains one 50x50mm diamond-shaped stamp.

Macao Chamber of Commerce, Cent. — A351

No. 1384 — Chamber of Commerce emblem and: a, 1.50p, Chamber of Commerce leader, building, abacus. b, 2.50p, Chamber of Commerce leader, documents, Chamber of Commerce members clapping. c, 3.50p, Chamber of Commerce leader, leaders shaking hands, Chamber of Commerce seal and embosser. d, 4p, Chamber of Commerce members casting ballots, building.
12p, Building.

2013, Jan. 23   **Litho.**   **Perf. 14x13½**
Granite Paper
1384 A351   Block of 4, #a-d   4.75 4.75
Souvenir Sheet
1385 A351   12p multi   17.50 17.50
No. 1385 contains one 40x40mm stamp.

Souvenir Sheet

Diaolou (Watchtower), Kaiping, People's Republic of China — A352

2013, Mar. 1   **Perf. 14x13¼**
Granite Paper
1386 A352   12p multi   4.50 4.50

Basic Law of Macao, 20th Anniv. — A353

Various people with denomination in: 1.50p, Green square. 5p, Red square.

2013, Mar. 31   **Perf. 14**
1387-1388 A353   Set of 2   1.75 1.75

First Macao Fire Brigade, 130th Anniv. A354

No. 1389: a, 1.50p, Manual pump wagon, c. 1877, Central Fire Station (4/1). b, 2.50p, 1955 Ladder truck, Taipa Fire Station (4/2). c, 3.50p, 2008 Aerial ladder truck, Areia Preta Fire Station (4/3). d, 4p, 2007 High Reach Extendable Turret Stinger, Fire Brigade Headquarters and Sai Van Lake Fire Station (4/4).
12p, 19th cent. horse-drawn steam pump, Fire Brigade Command Building, vert.

2013, Apr. 25   **Perf. 14x13¼**
Granite Paper
1389 A354   Block of 4, #a-d   7.50 7.50
Souvenir Sheet
1390 A354   12p multi   9.00 9.00
No. 1390 contains one 40x60mm stamp.

Items in Macao Museum A355

No. 1391: a, 1.50p, Nativity scene carved in mother-of-pearl (4/1). b, 2.50p, Painted stone sculpture of Madonna and Child (4/2). c, 3.50p, Elephant-shaped Kraak porcelain vessel (4/3). d, 4p, Bronze bell of St. Paul's Church (4/4).
12p, 16th cent. copperplate engraving of Macao, by Theodore de Bry, horiz.

2013, May 10   **Perf. 13¼x13**
1391 A355   Block of 4, #a-d   7.50 7.50
Souvenir Sheet
1392 A355   12p multi   10.00 10.00
No. 1392 contains one 60x40mm stamp.

Na Tcha, Child God of War A356

No. 1393 — Various depictions of Na Tcha with background color of: a, 2p, Pale orange (4/1). b, 2.50p, Blue black (4/2). c, 3.50p, Red (4/3). d, 4p, Dull blue (4/4).
12p, Na Tcha, orange background.

2013, June 25   **Perf. 13¼x13**
1393 A356   Block of 4, #a-d   9.00 9.00
Souvenir Sheet
1394 A356   12p multi   17.50 17.50

Scenes From The Romance of the Three Kingdoms — A357

No. 1395: a, 2p, Rescue of the young prince (4/1). b, 2.50p, Control of Yi Province (4/2). c, 3.50p, Drowning of the Seven Armies (4/3). d, 4p, Zhuge Liang prays to the stars (4/4).
12p, Unification of the Three Kingdoms under the Jin Dynasty, horiz.

2013, Sept. 13   **Litho.**   **Perf. 13¼x13**
Granite Paper
1395 A357   Block of 4, #a-d   12.50 12.50
Souvenir Sheet
Perf. 13x13¼
1396 A357   12p multi   30.00 30.00

Streets of Macao A358

No. 1397: a, 2p, Avenida de Almeida Ribiero (4/1). b, 2.50p, Calçada dos Quartéis (4/2). c, 3.50p, Calçada do Teatro (4/3). d, 4p, Beco do Lilau (4/4).
12p, Calçada da Igreja de Sao Lázaro, vert.

2013, Oct. 9   **Litho.**   **Perf. 14x13¼**
Granite Paper
1397 A358   Block of 4, #a-d   7.50 7.50
Souvenir Sheet
Perf. 13¼x14
1398 A358   12p multi   12.50 12.50

Christmas — A359

Designs: 3.50p, Church, statue of angel (2/1). 5p, Church, statue of angel, diff. (2/2).
12p, Statue of Madonna and Child.

2013, Oct. 21   **Litho.**   **Perf. 14x13¼**
Granite Paper
1399-1400 A359   Set of 2   2.25 2.25
Souvenir Sheet
1401 A359   12p multi   8.00 8.00

Chinese Calligraphy and Painting — A360

No. 1402: a, Yu Un, by Leong Chong Hin, Guan Wanli, Situ Qi, Chui Tak Kei and Lin Jin (potted plants, 6/1). b, Literary Meeting in Goi Meng House, by Gu Danming (fan, 6/2). c, Blessings of Autumn, by Huang Yunyu, Guan Wanli, U Kuan Wai, Zhou Paiyun, Zhao Wenfeng, Tam Van Iao, Kam Hang, Chan Chi Vai, Chui Tak Kei and Lin Jin (flowers, 6/3). d, Autumn, by Situ Qi, Chui Tak Kei and Huang Haoming (yellow and blue flowers, 6/4). e, Announcement of Spring, by Chui Tak Kei (bird in blossoming tree, 6/5). f, Heroic Kapok, by Chui Tak Kei (tree with red blossoms, 6/6).
12p, Sparrows and Red Leaves, by Deng Fen, Situ Qi and Lin Jin.

2013, Nov. 1   **Litho.**   **Perf. 13x13¼**
Granite Paper
1402 A360   2p Block of 6, #a-f   11.00 11.00
Souvenir Sheet
1403 A360   12p multi   25.00 25.00

60th Macao Grand Prix A361

No. 1404 — Race cars or motorcycles (#1404c) from: a, 1954 (6/1). b, 1963 (6/2). c, 1973 (6/3). d, 1983 (6/4). e, 1993 (6/5). f, 2003 (6/6).
12p, 2013 race car, older car.

2013, Nov. 8   **Litho.**   **Perf. 14x13¼**
Granite Paper
1404 A361   2p Block of 6, #a-f   6.00 6.00
Souvenir Sheet
Litho. With Foil Application
Perf.
1405 A361   12p multi   7.00 7.00
No. 1405 contains one 55x38mm oval stamp.

Trade and Cooperation Agreement Between Macao and the European Union, 20th Anniv. — A362

Flags of Macao and the European Union, "20" and various symbols with denomination color of: 1.50p, Green (2/1). 5p, Dark blue (2/2).

2013, Nov. 23   **Litho.**   **Perf. 14**
1406-1407 A362   Set of 2   1.75 1.75

New Year 2014 (Year of the Horse) — A363

No. 1408: a, Metal sculpture of horse (5/1). b, Watercolor painting of horse (5/2). c, Horse in fireworks (5/3). d, Clay figurine of horse (5/4). e, Wood carving of horse (5/5).
12p, Wood carving of horse, diff.

Litho., Litho. & Embossed With Foil Application (5p, 12p)
2014, Jan. 3   **Perf. 13¾**
Granite Paper
1408   Horiz. strip of 5   3.50 3.50
   a.-d.   A363 2p Any single   .50 .50
   e.   A363 5p multi   1.25 1.25
Souvenir Sheet
Perf. 14¼
1409 A363   12p multi   7.00 7.00
No. 1409 contains one 50x50mm diamond-shaped stamp.

Conde de Sao Januário General Hospital, 140th Anniv. — A364

Designs: 2p, Old hospital building (4/1). 2.50p, Modern hospital building (4/2). 3.50p, Accreditation emblem, surgeons (4/3). 4p, 140th anniversary emblem, doctors examining patient (4/4).
12p, Old and new hospital buildings, 140th anniversary emblem.

MACAO

2014, Jan. 6   Litho.   Perf. 13x13¼
Granite Paper
1410-1413 A364 Set of 4   6.00 6.00
Souvenir Sheet
Perf. 13¼x13
1414 A364 12p multi   7.00 7.00
No. 1414 contains one 60x40mm stamp.

Macao Post, 130th Anniv. A365

No. 1415: a, 2p, Macao Post Headquarters (4/1). b, 2.50p, Arch of post office (4/2). c, 3.50p, Museum of Communications (4/3). d, 4p, Emblems for postal services (4/4). 12p, Macao Post Headquarters (2/1). 50p, Tower and arches of Macao Post Headquarters (2/2), vert.

2014, Mar. 1   Litho.   Perf. 14x13¼
Granite Paper
1415 A365 Block or strip of 4, #a-d   6.00 6.00
Souvenir Sheets
Litho. With Foil Application
Perf. 13½x14
1416 A365 12p multi   7.50 7.50
Litho.
Perf. 13½
Silk-Faced Granite Paper
1417 A365 50p multi   60.00 60.00
No. 1416 contains one 40x40mm stamp.
No. 1417 contains one 30x60mm stamp.

Animal Protection — A366

No. 1418: a, 2p, Dog (4/1). b, 2.50p, Cat (4/2). c, 3.50p, Cat, diff. (4/3). d, 4p, Dog, diff. (4/4). 12p, Dog and chain-link fence.

2014, Apr. 28   Litho.   Perf. 14x13¼
Granite Paper
1418 A366 Block or strip of 4, #a-d   6.00 6.00
Souvenir Sheet
Perf. 13½x14
1419 A366 12p multi   8.50 8.50
No. 1419 contains one 60x40mm stamp.

Characters From *The Outlaws of the Marsh* — A367

No. 1420: a, Shi Jin, with tattooed back (6/1). b, Chai Jin, wearing purple robe (6/2). c, Yang Zhi, unsheathing sword (6/3). d, Chao Gai, holding spear (6/4). e, Ruan Xiaoqi, holding oar (6/5). f, Gongsun Sheng, holding leaf (6/6). 12p, Chao Gai and Chai Jin, horiz.

2014, June 26   Litho.   Perf. 13¼x13
Granite Paper
1420 A367 2p Block of 6, #a-f   11.00 11.00
Souvenir Sheet
Perf. 13x13¼
1421 A367 12p multi   10.00 10.00

New Campus of the University of Macao — A368

No. 1422 — Various buildings with stamps numbered: a, (4/1). b, (4/2). c, (4/3). d, (4/4). 12p, Building, diff.

2014, Sept. 5   Litho.   Perf. 13x13¼
Granite Paper
1422 A368 2p Block or strip of 4, #a-d 5.00 5.00
Souvenir Sheet
1423 A368 12p multi   17.50 17.50

Magic Squares A369

No. 1424: a, 2p, Magic word square (6/1). b, 3p, Bent diagonal square by Benjamin Franklin (6/2). c, 4p, Melancolia I magic square by Albrecht Dürer (6/3). d, 5p, Xuan Ji Tu Chinese palindromic square by Su Hui (6/4). e, 7p, Panmagic square by Lee Sallows (6/5). f, 9p, Magic square construction method by Simon de la Loubère (6/6). 12p, Magic square of dots on turtle shell, by Luo Shu, horiz.

2014, Oct. 9   Litho.   Perf. 13¼x13
Granite Paper
1424 A369 Sheet of 6, #a-f, + 3 labels 9.50 9.50
Souvenir Sheet
1425 A369 12p multi   7.50 7.50
No. 1425 contains one 60x40mm stamp.
See Nos. 1465-1466.

General Post Offices A370

No. 1426 — General Post Office in: a, Macao. b, Bangkok, Thailand.

2014, Nov. 1   Litho.   Perf. 13x13¼
Granite Paper
1426 A370 5.50p Horiz. pair, #a-b   4.50 4.50
See Thailand No. 2826.

Lin Zexu Memorial Museum A371

No. 1427 — Lin Zexu (1785-1850), Qing Dynasty official: a, Wearing robe depicting crane (4/1). b, With Opium War battle in background (4/2). c, Seated with Portuguese naval officer (4/3). d, Meeting Portuguese naval officer at harbor (4/4). 12p, Lin Zexu, diff.

2014, Nov. 5   Litho.   Perf. 13x13¼
Granite Paper
1427 A371 2p Block of 4, #a-d   9.00 9.00
Souvenir Sheet
Perf. 13¼x13
1428 A371 12p multi   10.00 10.00
No. 1428 contains one 60x40mm stamp.

Paintings of Macao by Kam Cheong Ling (1911-91) — A372

No. 1429 — Paintings depicting: a, 2p, Ships (4/1). b, 2p, Fountain and street scene (4/2). c, 3p, Market stalls near building (4/3). d, 5p, Gate near church (4/4). 12p, People on verandah.

2014, Nov. 12   Litho.   Perf. 13x13¼
Granite Paper
1429 A372 Block of 4, #a-d   3.00 3.00
Souvenir Sheet
Perf. 13½
1430 A372 12p multi   3.75 3.75
No. 1430 contains one 40x40mm stamp.

Macao Special Administrative Region, 15th Anniv. — A373

No. 1431: a, Clothing on mannequins in store, building, gears (4/1). b, Buildings, blue sky (4/2). c, Buildings, orange sky (4/3). d, Building and world map (4/4). 12p, Building with flags.

2014, Dec. 20   Litho.   Perf. 13x13¼
Granite Paper
1431 A373 2p Block of 4, #a-d   4.50 4.50
Souvenir Sheet
Perf. 13¼x13
1432 A373 12p multi   6.75 6.75
No. 1432 contains one 60x40mm stamp.

People's Liberation Army Garrison in Macao, 15th Anniv. — A374

No. 1433: a, Soldiers at flag ceremony (6/1). b, Soldier in camouflage uniform (6/2). c, Soldiers looking at sign (6/3). d, Soldier putting military helmet on child (6/4). e, Musicians (6/5). f, Soldier guiding shooter (6/6). 12p, Soldiers at attention in front of building.

2014, Dec. 20   Litho.   Perf. 13x13¼
1433 A374 2p Block of 6, #a-f   7.00 7.00
Souvenir Sheet
Perf. 13¼x13
1434 A374 12p multi   7.25 7.25
No. 1434 contains one 60x40mm stamp.

New Year 2015 (Year of the Goat) — A375

No. 1435: a, Metal sculpture of goat (5/1). b, Watercolor of goat (5/2). c, Goat in fireworks (5/3). d, Clay figurine of goat (5/4). e, Wood carving of goat (5/5). 12p, Wood carving of goat, diff.

Litho., Litho & Embossed With Foil Application (5p, 12p)
2015, Jan. 5   Perf. 13¾
Granite Paper (#1435)
1435   Horiz. strip of 5   3.25 3.25
a.-d. A375 2p Any single   .50   .50
e.   A375 5p multi   1.25 1.25
Souvenir Sheet
Perf. 14¼
1436 A375 12p multi   3.00 3.00
No. 1436 contains one 50x50mm diamond-shaped stamp.

Rotary International, 110th Anniv. — A376

Rotary International emblem and: 5.50p, Rotary International founder Paul Harris (1868-1947). 12p, People tending to child in wheelchair, vert.

2015, Feb. 16   Litho.   Perf. 13x13¼
Granite Paper
1437 A376 5.50p multi   1.40 1.40
Souvenir Sheet
1438 A376 12p multi   3.00 3.00
No. 1438 contains one 40x60mm stamp.

Crescent Lake, Dunhuang, People's Republic of China — A377

2015, Mar. 1   Litho.   Perf. 13x13¼
Granite Paper
1439 A377 12p multi   3.75 3.75

Intl. Association of Portuguese-Speaking Countries, 25th Anniv. — A378

2015, Apr. 27   Litho.   Perf. 13¼x13
Granite Paper
1440 A378 5.50p multi   1.40 1.40
See Angola No. , Brazil No. 3000, Cape Verde No. 1004, Guinea-Bissau No. , Mozambique No. , Portugal No. , St. Thomas & Prince Islands No. 2061, Timor No.

Wetlands Wildlife A379

No. 1441: a, 2p, Uca arcuata (4/1). b, 3p, Boleophthalmus pectinirostris (4/2). c, 4.50p, Microhyla ornata (4/3). d, 5.50p, Trimeresurus aurora (4/4). 12p, Platalea minor.

2015, May 5   Litho.   Perf. 14x13½
Granite Paper
1441 A379 Block or strip of 4, #a-d   3.75 3.75
Souvenir Sheet
1442 A379 12p multi   3.00 3.00

Xian Xinghai (1905-45), Composer A380

MACAO

Stamps dated: a, 2p, 1905 (4/1). b, 3p, 1934 (4/2). c, 4.50p, 1939 (4/3). d, 5.50p, 1945 (4/4).
12p, Xian Xinghai conducting.

2015, June 13   Litho.   Perf. 14x13½
Granite Paper
1443		Horiz. strip of 4	3.75	3.75
a.		A380 2p multi	.50	.50
b.		A380 3p multi	.75	.75
c.		A380 4.50p multi	1.10	1.10
d.		A380 5.50p multi	1.40	1.40

Souvenir Sheet
| 1444 | A380 | 12p multi | 3.00 | 3.00 |

Guia Lighthouse, 150th Anniv. — A381

Designs: 2p, Top of lighthouse (2/1). 5.50p, Doorway (2/2).
12p, Lighthouse and flag, vert.

2015, July 8   Litho.   Perf. 13x13¼
Granite Paper
| 1445-1446 | A381 | Set of 2 | 1.90 | 1.90 |

Souvenir Sheet   Perf. 13¼x13
| 1447 | A381 | 12p multi | 3.00 | 3.00 |

Historic Center of Macao's Designation as UNESCO World Heritage Site, 10th Anniv. — A382

No. 1448 — Various buildings, Macao residents and tourists: a, 2p (4/1). b, 3p (4/2). c, 4.50p (4/3). d, 5.50p (4/4).
12p, Tourists at food cart.

2015, July 15   Litho.   Perf. 14x13½
Granite Paper
| 1448 | A382 | Block or strip of 4, #a-d | 3.75 | 3.75 |

Souvenir Sheet
| 1449 | A382 | 12p multi | 3.00 | 3.00 |

Water and Life A383

No. 1450: a, 2p, Woman getting water from hydrant, leaf, technician monitoring computers (4/1). b, 3p, Fish, technician examining test tube of water (4/2). c, 4.50p, Fountain, water purification plant (4/3). d, 5.50p, Bowl of soup, glass of water, building near waterfront (4/4).
12p, Fountain near waterfront.

2015, July 31   Litho.   Perf. 14x13½
Granite Paper
| 1450 | A383 | Block of 4, #a-d | 3.75 | 3.75 |

Souvenir Sheet   Perf. 13½x14
| 1451 | A383 | 12p multi | 3.00 | 3.00 |

No. 1451 contains one 60x40mm stamp.

End of World War II, 70th Anniv. — A384

Designs: 2p, Soldier with rifle, Marco Polo Bridge, Beijing (2/1). 5.50p, Chinese soldiers, Great Wall of China (2/2).

2015, Sept. 3   Litho.   Perf. 14x13½
Granite Paper
| 1452-1453 | A384 | Set of 2 | 1.90 | 1.90 |

Old Streets and Alleys — A385

Designs: 2p, Rua da Sé (8/1). 2.50p, Rua dos Ervanários (8/2). 3p, Rua da Felicidade (8/3). 3.50p, Rua da Figueira (8/4). 4p, Rua de Eduardo Marques (8/5). 4.50p, Calçada do Embaixador (8/6). 5p, Rua da Erva (8/7). 5.50p, Calçada das Verdades (8/8).

2015, Sept. 22   Litho.   Perf. 13½x14
Granite Paper
| 1454-1461 | A385 | Set of 8 | 7.50 | 7.50 |

Festivities — A386

No. 1462: a, 2p, Lion dancers (2/1). b, 4.50p, Balloons (2/2).

2015, Oct. 9   Litho.   Perf. 13x13¼
Granite Paper
| 1462 | A386 | Horiz. pair, #a-b | 1.60 | 1.60 |

The images in the frames of Nos. 1462a-1462b could be personalized for an additional fee. The generic images are shown.

Scenes from *Jiu Ge*, Poem by Qu Yuan A387

No. 1463: a, The God and Goddess of River Xiang (6/1). b, The Lords of Fate - the Greater and Lesser (6/2). c, The Lord of the East (6/3). d, The Mountain Spirit (6/4). e, Hymn to the Fallen (6/5). f, Honoring the Spirits (6/6).
12p, Jiu Ge.

2015, Oct. 30   Litho.   Perf. 13½x14
Granite Paper
| 1463 | A387 | 2p Block of 6, #a-f | 3.00 | 3.00 |

Souvenir Sheet
| 1464 | A387 | 12p multi | 3.00 | 3.00 |

No. 1464 contains one 30x60mm stamp.

Magic Squares Type of 2014

No. 1465: a, 1p, Most Perfect magic square, by Emory McClintock and Kathleen Timpson Ollerenshaw (3/1). b, 6p, Patchwork magic square, by David M. Collison (3/2). c, 8p, Ixohoxi 88 magic square, by Inder Taneja (3/3).
12p, Method of Knight's Tour magic square, by Joseph S. Madachy, horiz.

2015, Nov. 12   Litho.   Perf. 13½x14
Granite Paper
| 1465 | A369 | Sheet of 3, #a-c, + 6 labels | 3.75 | 3.75 |

Souvenir Sheet
| 1466 | A369 | 12p multi | 3.00 | 3.00 |

No. 1466 contains one 60x40mm stamp.

Tai Chi Chuan A388

No. 1467 — Various body positions with denomination at: a, 2p, LL (4/1). b, 2p, LR (4/2). c, 3p, LL (4/3). d, 3p, LR (4/4).

2015, Nov. 30   Litho.   Perf. 13½x14
Granite Paper
| 1467 | A388 | Block of 4, #a-d | 2.50 | 2.50 |

Yellow River A389

Nos. 1468 and 1469: a, Headwaters (9/1). b, Winding River, Lanzhou (9/2). c, Ningxia Alluvial Plains (9/3). d, Vast Terrirory of Hetao (9/4). e, Hukou Golden Waterfall (9/5). f, Hukou Golden Waterfall and river running through Shanxi (9/6). g, Mountainous region of Luoyang (9/7). h, River running through Henan (9/8). i, Clear River reaching East China Sea (9/9).

Litho. With Foil Application
2015, Dec. 10   Perf. 13¼
Granite Paper
| 1468 | A389 | Sheet of 9 | 4.50 | 4.50 |
| a.-i. | | 2p Any single | .50 | .50 |

Litho.   Perf. 14x13½
1469	A389	Booklet pane of 9	6.25	—
a.-i.		2p Any single		.65
		Complete booklet, #1469	6.25	

Complete booklet sold for 25p

New Year 2016 (Year of the Monkey) — A390

No. 1470: a, Metal sculpture of monkey (5/1). b, Wood carving of monkey (5/2). c, Watercolor painting of monkey (5/3). d, Clay figurine of monkey (5/4). e, Monkey in fireworks (5/5).
12p, Monkey in fireworks, diff.

Litho., Litho. & Embossed With Foil Application (5.50p, 12p)
2016, Jan. 22   Perf. 13¾
Granite Paper
1470		Horiz. strip of 5	4.00	4.00
a.-b.		A390 2p Either single	.50	.50
c.-d.		A390 3p Either single	.75	.75
e.		A390 5.50p multi	1.40	1.40

Souvenir Sheet   Perf. 14¼
| 1471 | A390 | 12p multi | 3.00 | 3.00 |

No. 1471 contains one 50x50mm diamond-shaped stamp.

Structures at the Imperial Palace, Beijing — A391

No. 1472: a, 2p, Palace of Peace and Longevity (4/1). b, 3p, Gate of Divine Prowess (4/2). c, 4.50p, Hall of Radiating Justice (4/3). d, 5.50p Hall of Spring and Happiness (4/4).
12p, Hall of Supreme Harmony.

2016, Mar. 1   Litho.   Perf. 13x13¼
Granite Paper
| 1472 | A391 | Block or strip of 4, #a-d | 3.75 | 3.75 |

Souvenir Sheet   Perf. 13¼x13
| 1473 | A391 | 12p multi | 3.00 | 3.00 |

No. 1473 contains one 60x40mm stamp.

Macao Police Force, 325th Anniv. A392

No. 1474: a, 2p, Policeman and policewoman (4/1). b, 3p, Police officers with drawn weapons, police at flag ceremony (4/2). c, 4.50p, Policewoman checking identity card (4/3). d, 5.50p, Policeman on motorcycle, police officer on traffic duty (4/4).
12p, Police officers in various uniforms.

2016, Mar. 14   Litho.   Perf. 13x13¼
| 1474 | A392 | Block or strip of 4, #a-d | 3.75 | 3.75 |

Souvenir Sheet   Perf. 13¼x13
| 1475 | A392 | 12p multi | 3.00 | 3.00 |

No. 1475 contains one 60x40mm stamp.

Ballad of Mulan — A393

No. 1476: a, Mulan decides to replace her father in the army (4/1). b, Mulan becomes a heroine in war (4/2). c, Mulan refusing honors and returning home (4/3). d, Mulan reveals her identity as a woman (4/4).
12p, Mulan on horseback.

2016, Apr. 8   Litho.   Perf. 13¼x13½
Granite Paper
1476		Horiz. strip of 4	3.75	3.75
a.		A393 2p multi	.50	.50
b.		A393 3p multi	.75	.75
c.		A393 4.50p multi	1.10	1.10
d.		A393 5.50p multi	1.40	1.40

Souvenir Sheet   Perf. 13¼
| 1477 | A393 | 12p multi | 3.00 | 3.00 |

No. 1477 contains one 30x60mm stamp.

Paintings of Macao, by Chan Chi Vai A394

No. 1478 — Various paintings depicting: a, 2p, Octagon Pavilion (4/1). b, 3p, Skyline (4/2). c, 4.50p, Street view and Our Lady of Penha Church on hill (4/3). d, 5.50p, St. Lawrence's Church (4/4).
12p, Fishermen, boats and nets.

2016, Apr. 28   Litho.   Perf. 14x13½
Granite Paper
| 1478 | A394 | Block or strip of 4, #a-d | 3.75 | 3.75 |

Souvenir Sheet   Perf. 13½x14
| 1479 | A394 | 12p multi | 3.00 | 3.00 |

No. 1479 contains one 60x40mm stamp.

Items in Maritime Museum A395

No. 1480: a, 2p, Chu Tai Sin, protector god of fishermen (4/1). b, 3p, Octant (4/2). c, 4.50p, Tai To Junk (4/3). d, 5.50p, Black ship (4/4).
12p, Compass.

MACAO

2016, May 18 Litho. Perf. 13x13¼
Granite Paper
1480 A395 Block of 4, #a-d 3.75 3.75
Souvenir Sheet
Perf.
1481 A395 12p multi 3.00 3.00
No. 1481 contains one 38mm diameter stamp.

2016 Volleyball World Grand Prix Preliminary Matches, Macao — A396

No. 1482: a, 2p, Three women volleyball players. b, 5.50p, Two women volleyball players.
12p, Woman player and volleyball.

2016, June 17 Litho. Perf. 14x13½
Granite Paper
1482 A396 Horiz. pair, #a-b 1.90 1.90
Souvenir Sheet
Perf. 13½x14
1483 A396 12p multi 3.00 3.00
No. 1483 contains one 60x40mm stamp.

2016 Summer Olympics, Rio de Janeiro — A397

No. 1484: a, 2p, Runner. b, 3p, Gymnast. c, 4.50p, High jumper. d, 5.50p, Diver.

2016, July 29 Litho. Perf. 14x13½
Granite Paper
1484 A397 Block of 4, #a-d 3.50 3.50

Yangtze River A398

No. 1485: a, Geladaindong Snow Mountain, Tiger Leaping Gorge (9/1). b, Yuzhong Peninsula, Chaotian Gate and Dongsui Gate Yangtze River Bridge, Chongqing (9/2). c, Baidicheng Temple, Qutang Gorge, Wu Gorge, Xiling Gorge (9/3). d, Gezhouba Dam, Wuhan Yangtze River Bridge, Dongting Lake, Yueyang Tower (9/4). e, Lushan Mountain, Lushan Conference Site, Fairy Cave of Lushan, Lushan Hydroelectric Power Station (9/5). f, Huangshan Mountain, Lotus Peak (0/6). g, Nanjing Yangtze River Bridges, Purple Mountain Observatory (9/7). h, Plum Garden, Wuxi, Tiger Hill Pagoda, Langshan Mountain, Jiangyin Bridge (9/8). i, Bund, Pudong, Pudong International Airport, China Expo 2010 Pavilion, Nanpu Bridge, Sutong Bridge, Chongming Island, Shanghai (9/9).

2016, July 11 Litho. Perf. 14x13¼
Granite Paper
1485 A398 2p Sheet of 9, #a-i 4.50 4.50
j. Booklet pane of 9, #1485a-1485i 6.25 —
Complete booklet, #1485j 6.25
Complete booklet sold for 25p.

Paintings by Macao Artists A399

No. 1486: a, 2p, Nest-bound Birds, by Lok Cheong (6/1). b, 2p, Post Office, by Kwok Se (6/2). c, 2p, Meeting at the Later Year, by Ng Meng (6/3). d, 3p, Fishing Alone in the Willow Shade, by Kuan Man Le (6/4). e, 3p, The Lifestyle of Fishing Harbor, by Kam Cheong Ling (6/5). f, 3p, A Ma temple, by Tam Chi Sang (6/6).
12p, Sai Van Waterfront, by Lok Cheong, The Convent of the Precious Blood, by Kam Cheong Ling. Sailing Boats, by Kwok Se.

2016, Aug. 25 Litho. Perf. 13x13¼
1486 A399 Block of 6, #a-f 3.75 3.75
Souvenir Sheet
Perf. 13¼x13
1487 A399 12p multi 3.00 3.00
No. 1487 contains one 60x40mm stamp.

Ye Ting (1896-1946), General — A400

Ye Ting wearing: 2p, Suit and tie. 5.50p, Military uniform.
12p, Ye Ting seated on chair.

2016, Sept. 10 Litho. Perf. 13½x14
Granite Paper
1488-1489 A400 Set of 2 1.90 1.90
Souvenir Sheet
Perf. 14x13½
1490 A400 12p multi 3.00 3.00
No. 1490 contains one 40x40mm stamp.

Chinese Landscape Paintings — A401

No. 1491 — Various paintings by unattributed artists: a, 2p, (4/1). b, 3p, (4/2). c, 4.50p, (4/3). d, 5.50p, (4/4).
12p, Waterfall.

2016, Oct. 9 Litho. Perf. 13½
Granite Paper
1491 A401 Block or horiz. strip of 4, #a-d 3.75 3.75
Souvenir Sheet
Perf. 13¼x13
1492 A401 12p multi 3.00 3.00

Sun Yat-sen (1866-1925), President of the Republic of China — A402

No. 1493 — Sun Yat-sen: a, 2p, Wearing traditional Chinese clothing (4/1). b, 3p, Wearing suit and tie (4/2). c, 3.50p, With wife (4/3). d, 4.50p, Wearing military uniform (4/4).
12p, Sun Yat-sen and soldiers.

Perf. 13 Syncopated
2016, Nov. 12 Photo.
Granite Paper
1493 A402 Block or strip of 4, #a-d 3.25 3.25
Souvenir Sheet
Perf. 14 Syncopated
1494 A402 12p multi 3.00 3.00
No. 1494 contains one 60x40mm stamp.

50th Macao Motorcycle Grand Prix — A403

No. 1495 — Rider on: a, 2p, Motorcycle No. 28 (4/1). b, 3p, Motorcycle No. 4 (4/2). c, 4.50p, Motorcycle No. 5 (4/3). d, 5.50p, Motorcycle with Pepsi emblems (4/4).
12p, Rider on motorcycle No. 1.

Perf. 13x13¼ Syncopated
2016, Nov. 18 Litho.
Granite Paper
1495 A403 Block or strip of 4, #a-d 3.75 3.75
Souvenir Sheet
1496 A403 12p multi 3.00 3.00

Strange Tales of Liao Zhai, by Pu Songling (1640-1715) — A404

No. 1497 — Story scenes: a, Mural (8/1). b, Qing Feng (8/2). c, Judge Lu (8/3). d, Nie Xiaoqian (8/4). e, The Magnanimous Girl (8/5). f, Lian Xiang (8/6). g, Zhang Cheng (8/7). h, Exchange of Brides (8/8).
12p, Painted Skin, horiz.

2016, Dec. 1 Litho. Perf. 14¼
Granite Paper
1497 A404 Block of 8, #a-h 4.00 4.00
Souvenir Sheet
Perf. 14 Syncopated
1498 A404 12p multi 3.00 3.00
No. 1498 contains one 60x40mm stamp.

New Year 2017 (Year of the Rooster) — A405

No. 1499: a, Metal sculpture of rooster (5/1). b, Wood carving of rooster (5/2). c, Watercolor painting of rooster (5/3). d, Clay figurine of rooster (5/4). e, Rooster in fireworks (5/5).
12p, Rooster in fireworks, diff.

Litho., Litho. & Embossed With Foil Application (5.50p, 12p)
2017, Jan. 5 Perf. 14¼x14
Granite Paper
1499 Horiz. strip of 5 4.00 4.00
a.-b. A405 2p Either single .50 .50
c.-d. A405 3p Either single .75 .75
e. A405 5.50p multi 1.40 1.40
Souvenir Sheet
Perf. 14¼
1500 A405 12p multi 3.00 3.00
No. 1500 contains one 50x50mm diamond-shaped stamp.

Common Roots A406

No. 1501: a, 2p, Artisans at work (4/1). b, 3p, Parade (4/2). c, 4.50p, Angels, ruins of St. Paul's Church (4/3). d, 5.50p, Dancers (4/4).
12p, Ship.

Perf. 13x13¼ Syncopated
2017, Feb. 10 Litho.
Granite Paper
1501 A406 Block or strip of 4, #a-d 3.75 3.75
Souvenir Sheet
Perf. 14x13½
1502 A406 12p multi 3.00 3.00
No. 1502 contains one 40x40mm stamp.

Religious Figures — A407

No. 1503: a, 2p, Confucius. b, 3p, Siddhartha Gautama. c, 5p, Lao Tzu.

2017, Mar. 1 Litho. Perf. 14x13½
Granite Paper
1503 Horiz. strip of 3 2.50 2.50
a. A407 2p multi .50 .50
b. A407 3p multi .75 .75
c. A407 5p multi 1.25 1.25

Scenes From Chinese Opera "Farewell My Concubine" — A408

No. 1504: a, 2p, Emperor's military expedition. b, 3p, Clashes between Liu and Xiang. c, 4.50p, Concubine performs the Sword Dance. d, 5.50p, Emperor ends his life at Wujiang River.
12p, Ambush on all sides.

Perf. 13x13¼ Syncopated
2017, June 8 Litho.
Granite Paper
1504 A408 Block of 4, #a-d 3.75 3.75
Souvenir Sheet
Perf. 12 Syncopated
1505 A408 12p multi 3.00 3.00
No. 1505 contains one 60x40mm stamp.

Social Welfare Services A409

No. 1506 — Social Welfare Building, heart and: a, 2p, Mother and child. b, 3p, Family. c, 4.50p, Woman and elderly woman. d, 5.50p, Child assisting blind man.
12p, Hands in heart.

Perf. 13½x13¼ Syncopated
2017, July 3 Litho.
Granite Paper
1506 A409 Block of 4, #a-d 3.75 3.75
Souvenir Sheet
Perf. 14 Syncopated
1507 A409 12p multi 3.00 3.00
No. 1507 contains one 60x40mm stamp.

Chinese People's Liberation Army, 90th Anniv. — A410

MACAO

No. 1508: a, 2p, Soldiers and tank. b, 2p, Sailors and aircraft carrier. c, 2p, Pilot and airplanes. d, 3p, Army flag and missile launcher. e, 3p, Rocket and satellite. f, 3p, Military officers in vehicles in parade.
12p, Soldiers marching in parade.

Perf. 13x13¼ Syncopated
2017, Aug. 1   Litho.
Granite Paper
| 1508 | A410 | Block of 6, #a-f | 3.75 | 3.75 |

Souvenir Sheet
Perf. 12 Syncopated
| 1509 | A410 | 12p multi | 3.00 | 3.00 |

No. 1509 contains one 60x40mm stamp.

Tung Sin Tong, 125th Anniv. A411

No. 1510 — 125th anniversary emblem and: a, 2p, Children's services. b, 3p, Medical services. c, 4.50p, Social services. d, 5.50p, Elderly services.
12p, Medical and social services, horiz.

Perf. 13¼x13¾ Syncopated
2017, Aug. 8   Litho.
Granite Paper
| 1510 | A411 | Horiz. strip of 4, #a-d | 3.75 | 3.75 |

Souvenir Sheet
Perf. 12 Syncopated
| 1511 | A411 | 12p multi | 3.00 | 3.00 |

No. 1511 contains one 40x40mm stamp.

Camilo Pessanha (1867-1926), Poet — A412

Drawing of Pessanha: 2p, Seated. 5.50p, Holding poem and woman.
12p, Pessanha and head of woman.

Perf. 13¼x14 Syncopated
2017, Sept. 7   Litho.
Granite Paper
| 1512-1513 | A412 | Set of 2 | 1.90 | 1.90 |

Souvenir Sheet
| 1514 | A412 | 12p multi | 3.00 | 3.00 |

Lotus Flowers A413

No. 1515 — Various lotus flowers numbered: a, 2p, 4/1. b, 3p, 4/2. c, 4.50p, 4/3. d, 5.50p, 4/4.
12p, 1/1, vert.

2017, Oct. 9   Litho.   Perf. 13x13¼
Granite Paper
| 1515 | A413 | Block of 4, #a-d | 3.75 | 3.75 |

Souvenir Sheet
Perf. 13¼x13
| 1516 | A413 | 12p multi | 3.00 | 3.00 |

Furniture A414

No. 1517: a, 2p, Rosewood painting desk. b, 3p, Tai-Shi chair. c, 4.50p, Rosewood armchairs. d, 5.50p, Painted zitan screen.
12p, Rosewood canopy bed, vert.

Perf. 13x13½ Syncopated
2017, Nov. 10   Litho.
Granite Paper
| 1517 | A414 | Block of 4, #a-d | 3.75 | 3.75 |

Souvenir Sheet
Perf. 12 Syncopated
| 1518 | A414 | 12p multi | 3.00 | 3.00 |

No. 1518 contains one 40x60mm stamp.

Miniature Sheet

Seven Buddhas of the Past A415

No. 1519: a, 2p, Vipasyin (cerise frame, 7/1). b, 2p, Sikhin (light green frame, 7/2). c, 2p, Visvabhu (orange frame, 7/3). d, 3p, Krakucchanda (light blue frame 7/4). e, 3p, Kanakamuni (yellow orange frame, 7/5). f, 3p, Kasyapa (bright yellow green frame, 7/6). g, 4.50p, Sakyamuni (bright rose red frame, 7/7).

Perf. 12 Syncopated
2017, Nov. 21   Litho.
Granite Paper
| 1519 | A415 | Sheet of 7, #a-g | 4.75 | 4.75 |

Worldwide Fund for Nature (WWF) — A416

No. 1520 — Chinese white dolphin: a, 2p, One dolphin (4/1). b, 3p, Adult and juvenile (4/2). c, 4.50p, Adult and juvenile, diff. (4/3). d, 5.50p, One dolphin, diff. (4/4).

Perf. 13x13¼ Syncopated
2017, Dec. 1   Litho.
Granite Paper
| 1520 | A416 | Block of 4, #a-d | 3.75 | 3.75 |
| e. | | Souvenir sheet of 4, #1520a-1520d | 3.75 | 3.75 |

New Year 2018 (Year of the Dog) — A417

No. 1521: a, Metal sculpture of dog (5/1). b, Wood carving of dog (5/2). c, Watercolor painting of dog (5/3). d, Dog in fireworks (5/4). e, Dog-shaped clay teapot (5/5).
12p, Dog-shaped clay teapot, diff.

Litho., Litho. & Embossed With Foil Application (5.50p, 12p)
2018, Jan. 5   Perf. 14¼
1521		Horiz. strip of 5	4.00	4.00
a.-b.	A417	2p Either single	.50	.50
c.-d.	A417	3p Either single	.75	.75
e.	A417	5.50p multi	1.40	1.40

Souvenir Sheet
Granite Paper
| 1522 | A417 | 12p multi | 3.00 | 3.00 |

No. 1522 contains one 50x50mm diamond-shaped stamp.

Macao 2018 International Stamp Exhibition — A418

No. 1523: a, 2p, Paper-cutting vendor. b, 3p, Fish vendor. c, 5.50p, Baked goods vendor.
12p, Food vendor.

Perf. 13x13½ Syncopated
2018, Mar. 1   Litho.   Perf. 13½x13
Granite Paper
| 1523 | A418 | Horiz. strip of 3, #a-c | 2.60 | 2.60 |

Souvenir Sheet
| 1524 | A418 | 12p multi | 3.00 | 3.00 |

Salt Evaporation Ponds, Mangkang, People's Republic of China — A419

Perf. 13½ Syncopated
2018, Apr. 12   Litho.
| 1525 | A419 | 12p multi | 3.00 | 3.00 |

Fables and Fairy Tales A420

No. 1526: a, 2p, *The Happy Prince*, by Oscar Wilde. b, 3p, *Little Red Riding Hood*, by the Brothers Grimm. c, 4.50p, *The Emperor's New Clothes*, by Hans Christian Andersen. d, 5.50p, *The Boy Who Cried Wolf*, by Aesop.
12p, Swallow over castle.

Litho. With Foil Application
Perf. 13x13¼ Syncopated
2018, May 30   Granite Paper
| 1526 | A420 | Block of 4, #a-d | 3.75 | 3.75 |

Souvenir Sheet
| 1527 | A420 | 12p multi | 3.00 | 3.00 |

Joy A421

No. 1528: a, 2p, Fireworks. b, 4.50p, Chinese lanterns.

Perf. 13x13¼ Syncopated
2018, June 26   Litho.
Granite Paper
| 1528 | A421 | Horiz. pair, #a-b | 1.60 | 1.60 |

Chinese Documents — A422

No. 1529 — Various documents: a, 2p. b, 3p. c, 4.50p. d, 5.50p.
12p, Document, horiz.

Perf. 13¼x13 Syncopated
2018, July 6   Litho.
Granite Paper
| 1529 | A422 | Block of 4, #a-d | 3.75 | 3.75 |

Souvenir Sheet
Perf. 13x13½
| 1530 | A422 | 12p multi | 3.00 | 3.00 |

Tang Xianzu (1550-1616), Playwright — A423

No. 1531 — Various characters from Tang Xianzu works: a, 2p, (4/1). b, 3p, (4/2). c, 4.50p, (4/3). d, 5.50p, (4/4).
12p, Man near water.

Perf. 13x13½ Syncopated
2018, July 27   Litho.
Granite Paper
| 1531 | A423 | Block of 4, #a-d | 3.75 | 3.75 |

Souvenir Sheet
Perf. 12 Syncopated
| 1532 | A423 | 12p multi | 3.00 | 3.00 |

No. 1532 contains one 60x40mm stamp.

Macao Daily News, 60th Anniv. A424

No. 1533: a, 2p, Newspaper deliverer on bicycle (4/1). b, 3p, Newspaper, type slugs, man selecting type (4/2). c, 4.50p, Newspaper on printing press (4/3). d, 5.50p, Building and electronic newspaper (4/4).
12p, Building and newspaper printing plant.

Perf. 13x13½ Syncopated
2018, Aug. 15   Litho.
Granite Paper
| 1533 | A424 | Block of 4, #a-d | 3.75 | 3.75 |

Souvenir Sheet
Perf. 12 Syncopated
| 1534 | A424 | 12p multi | 3.00 | 3.00 |

No. 1534 contains one 60x40mm stamp.

Macao 2018 International Philatelic Exhibition — A425

No. 1535: a, 2p, Youths near barricade, string of firecrackers (4/1). b, 3p, Dragon dance (4/2). c, 4.50p, Dragon boat race (4/3). d, 5.50p, Cathedral of the Nativity of Our Lady (4/4).
12p, Building and fountain.

Perf. 13x13½ Syncopated
2018, Sept. 23   Litho.
Granite Paper
| 1535 | A425 | Block of 4, #a-d | 3.75 | 3.75 |

Souvenir Sheet
| 1536 | A425 | 12p multi | 3.00 | 3.00 |

Birds and Spring Flowers A426

MACAO

No. 1537 — Various paintings of birds and flowers: a, 2p, (4/1). b, 3p, (4/2). c, 4.50p, (4/3). d, 5.50p, (4/4).
12p, Birds and flowers, horiz.

2018, Oct. 9 Litho. Perf. 14¼x14½
| 1537 | A426 | Block of 4, #a-d | 3.75 | 3.75 |

Souvenir Sheet
Perf. 14¼x14 Syncopated
| 1538 | A426 | 12p multi | 3.00 | 3.00 |

No. 1538 contains one 60x40mm stamp.

Forum for Economic and Trade Cooperation Between China and Portuguese-Speaking Countries, 15th Anniv. — A427

Designs: 2p, Emblem and "15" (2/1). 5.50p, Emblem and map (2/2). 12p, Speech balloons and silhouette of Macao landmarks.

Perf. 13½x13 Syncopated
2018, Oct. 12   Litho.
Granite Paper
| 1539-1540 | A427 | Set of 2 | 1.90 | 1.90 |

Souvenir Sheet
| 1541 | A427 | 12p multi | 3.00 | 3.00 |

Opening of Hong Kong-Zhuhai-Macao Bridge — A428

No. 1542: a, Bridge (3/1). b, Artificial island and tunnel entrance (3/2). c, Road at tunnel entrance (3/3).
12p, Bridge pillar, vert.

Perf. 13 Syncopated
2018, Oct. 30   Photo.
1542		Horiz. strip of 3	2.75	2.75
a.	A428	2p multi	.50	.50
b.	A428	3p multi	.75	.75
c.	A428	5.50p multi	1.40	1.40
d.		Sheet of 9, Macao #1542a-1542c, Hong Kong #1970a-1970c, People's Republic of China #4584-4586	10.50	10.50

Souvenir Sheet
Perf. 14 Syncopated
| 1543 | A428 | 12p multi | 3.00 | 3.00 |

No. 1542d sold for 40p and $40 in Hong Kong, and is identical to Hong Kong No. 1970. See Hong Kong No. 1970.

65th Macao Grand Prix A429

No. 1544: a, 2p, Car No. 30 (6/1). b, 2p, Car No. 10 (6/2). c, 2p, Car No. 48 (6/3). d, 3p, Car No. 9 (6/4). e, 3p, Motorcycle No. 9 (6/5). f, 3p, Car No. 8 (6/6).

Perf. 13½x13 Syncopated
2018, Nov. 15   Litho.
Granite Paper
| 1544 | A429 | Block of 6, #a-f | 3.75 | 3.75 |

New Year 2019 (Year of the Pig) — A430

No. 1545: a, Metal sculpture of pig (5/1). b, Wood carving of pigs (5/2). c, Watercolor painting of pigs (5/3). d, Pig in fireworks (5/4). e, Pig-shaped clay teapots (5/5).
12p, Pig-shaped clay teapots, diff.

Litho., Litho. & Embossed With Foil Application (5.50p, 12p)
2019, Jan. 5   Perf. 13¾
Granite Paper
1545		Horiz. strip of 5	4.00	4.00
a.-b.	A430	2p Either single	.50	.50
c.-d.	A430	3p Either single	.75	.75
e.	A430	5.50p multi	1.40	1.40

Souvenir Sheet
Perf. 14¼
| 1546 | A430 | 12p multi | 3.00 | 3.00 |

No. 1546 contains one 50x50mm diamond-shaped stamp.

Macao Post and Telecommunications, 135th Anniv. — A431

Designs; 2p, Headquarters and postmark. 5.50p, Building and text. 50p, Headquarters.

2019, Mar. 1   Litho.   Perf. 13¼x13
Granite Paper
| 1547-1548 | A431 | Set of 2 | 1.90 | 1.90 |

Litho., Sheet Margin Litho. With Foil Application
Souvenir Sheet
| 1549 | A431 | 50p gold & multi | 12.50 | 12.50 |

Feast of Kun Iam A432

No. 1550 — Kun Iam with: a, 2p, Lotus flower. b, 5.50p, Willow branch.
12p, Kun Iam, horiz.

2019, Mar. 25   Litho.   Perf. 13x13¼
Granite Paper
| 1550 | A432 | Horiz. pair, #a-b | 1.90 | 1.90 |

Souvenir Sheet
Perf. 13¼x13
| 1551 | A432 | 12p gold & multi | 3.00 | 3.00 |

30th Macao Festival of Arts A433

No. 1552 — Various works of art: a, 2p. b, 3p. c, 4.50p. d, 5.50p.
12p, Bubbles in Motion.

Perf. 13½ Syncopated
2019, May 3   Litho.
| 1552 | A433 | Block of 4, #a-d | 3.75 | 3.75 |

Souvenir Sheet
Perf. 13¾x13½ Syncopated
| 1553 | A433 | 12p multi | 3.00 | 3.00 |

Holy House of Mercy, 450th Anniv. A434

No. 1554 — Inscriptions: a, 2p, Lar de Nossa Senhora de Misericórdia (House of Our Lady of Mercy). b, 3p, Creche (Nursery). c, 4.50p, Centro de Reabilitação de Cegos (Rehabilitation Center for the Blind). d, 5.50p, Albergue da Santa Casa da Misericordia (Holy House of Mercy Hostel).
12p, Bishop Belchior Carneiro (1516-83), founder.

2019, May 15   Litho.   Perf. 13¼x13
Granite Paper
| 1554 | A434 | Block or strip of 4, #a-d | 3.75 | 3.75 |

Souvenir Sheet
| 1555 | A434 | 12p multi | 3.00 | 3.00 |

Macao Lotus A435

No. 1556 — Various drawings of lotus: a, 2p, b, 3p. c, 5.50p.
12p, Lotus, diff.

2019, June 3   Litho.   Perf. 14¼
| 1556 | A435 | Horiz. strip of 3, #a-c | 2.60 | 2.60 |

Souvenir Sheet
Perf. 14
| 1557 | A435 | 12p multi | 3.00 | 3.00 |

No. 1557 contains one 40x40mm stamp.

Return to Common Roots A436

No. 1558: a, 2p, Rickshaw and pianist. b, 3p, Chinese woman and children, ship and temple. c, 4.50p, Chinese wedding ceremony. d, 5.50p, Western wedding ceremony.
12p, Religious procession.

Perf. 12 Syncopated
2019, July 26   Litho.
Granite Paper
| 1558 | A436 | Block of 4, #a-d | 3.75 | 3.75 |
| 1559 | A436 | 12p silver & multi | 3.00 | 3.00 |

No. 1559 contains one 40x40mm stamp.

30th Macao International Fireworks Display Contest — A437

No. 1560 — Various fireworks displays over Macao buildings: a, 2.50p. b, 4p. c, 4.50p. d, 6p.
12p, Fireworks display over building, horiz.

Perf. 13¼x14 Syncopated
2019, Aug. 30   Litho.
Granite Paper
| 1560 | A437 | Block or strip of 4, #a-d | 4.25 | 4.25 |

Souvenir Sheet
Perf. 12 Syncopated
| 1561 | A437 | 12p multi | 3.00 | 3.00 |

No. 1561 contains one 60x40mm stamp.

Court Buildings — A438

Designs; 2.50p, Court of Second and Last Instances. 4p, Base Criminal Court.
12p, Old Court Building.

Perf. 13½x13¼ Syncopated
2019, Sept. 13   Litho.
Granite Paper
| 1562-1563 | A438 | Set of 2 | 1.60 | 1.60 |

Souvenir Sheet
| 1564 | A438 | 12p multi | 3.00 | 3.00 |

Guandong-Hong Kong-Macao Greater Bay Area — A439

No. 1565 — View of: a, 2.50p, Guangzhou. b, 4p, Hong Kong. c, 4.50p, Macao. d, 6p, Shenzhen.
12p, Buildings in Macao and Hong Kong, map.

Perf. 13x13¼ Syncopated
2019, Sept. 26   Litho.
Granite Paper
| 1565 | A439 | Block or strip of 4, #a-d | 4.25 | 4.25 |

Souvenir Sheet
| 1566 | A439 | 12p multi | 3.00 | 3.00 |

People's Republic of China, 70th Anniv. A440

No. 1567: a, 2.50p, Lighthouse. b, 4p, Dancers and musicians. c, 4.50p, Bridge and ships. d, 6p, Space exploration.
12p, Bridge and satellite.

Perf. 14 Syncopated
2019, Oct. 1   Litho.
Granite Paper (#1567)
| 1567 | A440 | Block or strip of 4, #a-d | 4.25 | 4.25 |

Souvenir Sheet
Perf. 13¼x13½ Syncopated
| 1568 | A440 | 12p multi | 3.00 | 3.00 |

Mount Tai, People's Republic of China A441

No. 1569: a, 2.50p, Longevity Bridge. b, 4p, Jade Emperor Temple. c, 4.50p, Tiankuang Palace. d, 6p, Daguan Peak.
12p, Heavenly Southern Gate.

2019, Oct. 9   Litho.   Perf. 13¼
| 1569 | A441 | Block or strip of 4, #a-d | 4.25 | 4.25 |

Souvenir Sheet
| 1570 | A441 | 12p multi | 3.00 | 3.00 |

A booklet containing No. 1568, People's Republic of China No. 4666, and Hong Kong No. 2027 sold for 40p.

MACAO

Sheng Kung Hui Choi Kou School, Cent. — A442

No. 1571: a, 2.50p, Choi Ko Middle School emblem, classroom. b, 4p, Emblem, school children, school building. c, 6p, Emblem, school children.
12p, School building, emblem.

2019, Oct. 18 Litho. *Perf. 13¼*
Granite Paper

| 1571 | A442 | Horiz. strip of 3, #a-c | 3.25 | 3.25 |

Souvenir Sheet
Perf. 13x13½

| 1572 | A442 | 12p multi | 3.00 | 3.00 |

No. 1572 contains one 40x60mm stamp.

Scenic Spots — A443

Designs: 2.50p, Penha Hill. 3p, Nam Van Lake, Sai Van Lake and Macao Tower. 3.50p, Senado Square. 4p, Long Chao Kok. 4.50p, Coloane Fishing Village. 5p, Paixao Alley. 5.50p, Happiness Street. 6p, Hong Kong-Zhuhai-Macao Bridge.

Perf. 13 Syncopated
2019, Nov. 22 Litho.
Granite Paper

1573	A443	2.50p multi	.65	.65
1574	A443	3p multi	.75	.75
1575	A443	3.50p multi	.90	.90
1576	A443	4p multi	1.00	1.00
1577	A443	4.50p multi	1.10	1.10
1578	A443	5p multi	1.25	1.25
1579	A443	5.50p multi	1.40	1.40
1580	A443	6p multi	1.50	1.50
		Nos. 1573-1580 (8)	8.55	8.55

Opening of Taipa Line of Macao Light Rapid Transit — A444

Designs; 2.50p, Passengers and train at station. 4p, Passengers in train.
12p, Train.

2019, Dec. 10 Litho. *Perf. 13x13¼*
Granite Paper

| 1581-1582 | A444 | Set of 2 | 1.60 | 1.60 |

Souvenir Sheet

| 1583 | A444 | 12p multi | 3.00 | 3.00 |

No. 1583 contains one 60x30mm stamp.

Macao Special Administrative Region, 20th Anniv. — A445

No. 1584 — Part of 20th anniversary emblem: a, 2.50p. b, 4p. c, 4.50p. d, 6p.
12p, Lotus flower.

Perf. 13½x13¼ Syncopated
2019, Dec. 20 Litho.
Granite Paper

| 1584 | A445 | Block of 4, #a-d | 4.25 | 4.25 |

Souvenir Sheet
Perf. 13

| 1585 | A445 | 12p multi | 3.00 | 3.00 |

No. 1585 contains one 50x50mm diamond-shaped stamp.

Return of Macao to People's Republic of China, 20th Anniv. — A446

No. 1586: a, 2.50p, Flags of People's Republic of China and Macao, people, Lotus Flower sculpture (3-1). b, 2.50p, Dragon, dancers, buildings of Macao (3-2). c, 2.50p, Buildings and bridges of Macao (3-3).

Perf. 13¼x13 Syncopated
2019, Dec.20 Photo.

| 1586 | | Sheet of 6, #1586a-1586c, People's Republic of China #4692-4697 | 5.50 | 5.50 |
| a.-c. | A446 | 2.50p Any single | 1.40 | 1.40 |

No. 1586 sold for 22p.

People's Liberation Army Garrison in Macao, 20th Anniv. — A447

No. 1587: a, 2.50p, Soldiers marching. b, 2.50p, Soldiers disinfecting streets. c, 4p, Soldiers and flag of People's Republic of China. d, 4p, Soldiers studying map. e, 4.50p, Soldiers in hazardous material suits. f, Soldiers raising flags of People's Republic of China and Macao.
12p, Flag of People's Liberation Army, building, vert.

Perf. 13½x13 Syncopated
2019, Dec. 20 Litho.

| 1587 | A447 | Block of 6, #a-f | 5.50 | 5.50 |

Souvenir Sheet
Perf. 14 Syncopated

| 1588 | A447 | 12p multi | 3.00 | 3.00 |

New Year 2020 (Year of the Rat) A448

No. 1589 — Rats and various foods: a, 2.50p. b, 4p. c, 4.50p. d, 6p.
14p, Rats at dinner table.

Perf. 13x13¼ Syncopated
2020, Jan. 5 Litho.
Granite Paper

| 1589 | A448 | Block of 4, #a-d | 4.25 | 4.25 |

Souvenir Sheet
Perf. 12 Syncopated

| 1590 | A448 | 14p multi | 3.50 | 3.50 |

No. 1590 contains one 40x40mm stamp.

Macao Federation of Trade Unions, 70th Anniv. — A449

No. 1591: a, 2.50p, Child workers with wheelbarrow. b, 4p, Classroom, medical personnel examining patient. c, 4.50p, Medical technician, children at day care, festival dragon, Tai chi practitioners. d, 6p, People at work.
14p, Crowd of people in heart-shaped design.

Perf. 13½x13¼ Syncopated
2020, Jan. 20 Litho.
Granite Paper

| 1591 | A449 | Block of 4, #a-d | 4.25 | 4.25 |

Souvenir Sheet
Perf. 14 Syncopated

| 1592 | A449 | 14p multi | 3.50 | 3.50 |

No. 1592 contains one 60x40mm stamp.

Traditional Snack Foods — A450

No. 1593: a, 2.50p, Pudim de arroz doce (rice pudding). b, 4p, Bolachas com maltose (maltose crackers). c, 4.50p, Doce de barba de drâgon (dragon's beard candy). d, 6p, Castanhas assadas (roasted chestnuts).
14p, Doce de pintura artística (sugar painting).

Perf. 13½x13 Syncopated
2020, Mar. 1 Litho.

| 1593 | A450 | Block of 4, #a-d | 4.25 | 4.25 |

Souvenir Sheet

| 1594 | A450 | 14p multi | 3.50 | 3.50 |

Medicinal Plants — A451

No. 1595: a, 2.50p, Rhodomyrtus tomentosa. b, 4p, Desmos chinensis. c, 4.50p, Gardenia jasminoides. d, 6p, Schefflera heptaphylla.
14p, Chrysanthemum indicum.

Perf. 13x13¼ Syncopated
2020, Apr. 20 Litho.
Granite Paper

| 1595 | A451 | Block or strip of 4, #a-d | 4.25 | 4.25 |

Souvenir Sheet

| 1596 | A451 | 14p multi | 3.50 | 3.50 |

Women's General Association of Macao, 70th Anniv. — A452

Designs: 2.50p, Four seated women and infant. 4p, Woman and four children. 4.50p, Woman receiving diploma from man. 6p, Two women assisting elderly people.
14p, Three women, girl, 70th anniversary cake.

Perf. 13x13½ Syncopated
2020, May 21 Litho.
Granite Paper

| 1597-1600 | A452 | Set of 4 | 4.25 | 4.25 |

Souvenir Sheet
Perf. 12 Syncopated

| 1601 | A452 | 14p multi | 3.50 | 3.50 |

No. 1601 contains one 60x40mm stamp.

Macao Red Cross, Cent. — A453

Designs: 4.50p, Shown. 14p, "10," Chinese character, Red Cross volunteers.

Perf. 13x13½ Syncopated
2020, June 12 Litho.
Granite Paper

| 1602 | A453 | 4.50p gold & multi | 1.10 | 1.10 |

Souvenir Sheet
Perf. 12 Syncopated

| 1603 | A453 | 14p gold & multi | 3.50 | 3.50 |

No. 1603 contains one 40x40mm stamp.

COVID-19 Pandemic — A454

Designs: 2.50p, Health care worker wearing protective gear. 14p, Fingers making heart, horiz.

Perf. 13½x13¼ Syncopated
2020, June 24 Litho.

| 1604 | A454 | 2.50p multi | .65 | .65 |

Souvenir Sheet
Perf. 13 Syncopated

| 1605 | A454 | 14p multi | 3.50 | 3.50 |

Chinese Medicine A455

No. 1606: a, 2.50p, Terapeutica (medicinal herbs). b, 4p, Acupunctura (acupuncture). c, 4.50p, Ventosaterapia (cupping). d, 6p, Massagem Tuina (tui na massage).
14p, Diagnóstico (diagnosis of ailment).

Perf. 13½x13¼ Syncopated
2020, July 3 Litho.

| 1606 | A455 | Block of 4, #a-d | 4.25 | 4.25 |

Souvenir Sheet
Perf. 14 Syncopated

| 1607 | A455 | 14p multi | 3.50 | 3.50 |

No. 1607 conatins one 60x40mm stamp.

Luo Shen Fu (Ode to the Goddess of the Luo River), Poem by Cao Zhi (192-232) — A456

No. 1608 — Inscription: a, 2.50p, Encontro (meeting, 4/1). b, 4p, Afecto (affection, 4/2). c, 4.50p, Despedida (farewell, 4/3). d, 6p, Apego (attachment, 4/4) 14p, Luo Shen Fu, horiz.

Perf. 14 Syncopated
2020, Aug. 10 Litho.

| 1608 | A456 | Block or strip of 4, #a-d | 4.25 | 4.25 |

Souvenir Sheet

| 1609 | A456 | 14p multi | 3.50 | 3.50 |

No. 1609 contains one 60x40mm stamp.

MACAO

Chinese Educators' Association of Macao, Cent. — A457

No. 1610: a, 2.50p, Buildings, book, teacher and students. b, 4p, Parade float of the association, medals. c, 4.50p, Teacher in classroom with students, book. d, 6p, Student activities. 14p, Chinese characters, horiz.

Perf. 13¼x14 Syncopated
2020, Sept. 10 Litho.
Granite Paper
1610 A457 Block or strip of 4, #a-d   4.25   4.25
Souvenir Sheet
Perf. 12 Syncopated
1611 A457 14p multi   3.50   3.50
No. 1611 contains one 60x40mm stamp.

Scenes From Various Tang Dynasty Poems — A458

No. 1612 — Scene and poetry in Chinese characters with denomination of: a, 2.50p. b, 4p. c, 4.50p. d, 6p. 14p, Temple.

Perf. 12 Syncopated
2020, Sept. 28 Litho.
Granite Paper
1612 A458 Block of 4, #a-d   4.25   4.25
Souvenir Sheet
Perf. 12x11¾ Syncopated
1613 A458 14p multi   3.50   3.50
No. 1613 contains one 60x40mm stamp.

Protected Animals — A459

No. 1614: a, 2.50p, Amur leopard (leopardo de-amur). b, 4p, Humpback whale (baleia-jubarte). c, 4.50p, Hawksbill turtle (tartaruga-de-pente). d, 6p, Cross River gorilla (gorila-do-rio-cross). 14p, Javan rhinoceros and Vaquita.

Perf. 13½x13¼ Syncopated
2020, Oct. 9 Litho.
Granite Paper
1614 A459 Block of 4, #a-d   4.25   4.25
Souvenir Sheet
Perf. Syncopated
1615 A459 14p multi   3.50   3.50
No. 1615 contains one 55x38mm oval stamp.

Characters From Novels by Jin Yong (1924-2018) — A460

No. 1616 — Characters from *The Legend of the Condor Heroes* with denomination of: a, 2.50p, Guo Jing and Huang Rong. b, 4p, Mu Yi, Yang Kang and Mu Nianci. c, 4.50p, Huang Yaoshi and Ouyang Feng. d, 6p, Hong Qigong, Duan Zhixing, Wang Chongyang, and Zhou Botong. 14p, Characters from *The Book and the Sword.*

Perf. 13x13¼ Syncopated
2020, Oct. 30 Litho.
Granite Paper
1616 A460 Block or strip of 4, #a-d   4.25   4.25
Souvenir Sheet
Perf. 12x11¾ Syncopated
1617 A460 14p multi   3.50   3.50
No. 1617 contains one 60x40mm stamp.

Digital Electronics — A461

No. 1618: a, 2.50p, Truth table and logic diagram for "not" (nao) gate (40x30mm). b, 2.50p, Truth table and logic diagram for "and" (e) gate (40x30mm). c, 2.50p, Truth table and logic diagram for "or" (ou) gate (40x30mm). d, 4p, Electronic circuit and Venn diagrams for "not" (nao) gate (40x60mm). e, 4p, Electronic circuit and Venn diagrams for "and" (e) gate (40x60mm). f, 4p, Electronic circuit and Venn diagrams for "or" (ou) gate (40x60mm). 14p, Half-adder logic diagram, vert.

Perf. 12 Syncopated
2020, Nov. 30 Litho.
1618 A461 Sheet of 6, #a-f   5.00   5.00
Souvenir Sheet
Perf. 13¼x14 Syncopated
1619 A461 14p multi   3.50   3.50
No. 1619 contains one 30x40mm stamp.

Ludwig van Beethoven (1770-1827), Composer — A462

No. 1620: a, 2.50p, Silhouette of Beethoven, G clef, ear, ear horn, back of piano. b, 4p, Beethoven playing piano. 14p, Beethoven, hands and keyboard.

Perf. 14 Syncopated
2020, Dec. 16 Litho.
1620 A462 Horiz. pair, #a-b   1.75   1.75
Souvenir Sheet
1621 A462 14p multi   3.50   3.50

New Year 2021 (Year of the Ox) A463

No. 1622: a, 2.50p, Yellow cow and spring flowers. b, 4p, Dairy cow and vines. c, 4.50p, Wild ox and autumn leaves. d, 6p, Yak and pine tree. 14p, Ox, diff.

Perf. 13¼x14 Syncopated
2021, Jan. 5 Litho.
Granite Paper
1622 A463 Block of 4, #a-d   4.25   4.25
Souvenir Sheet
1623 A463 14p multi   3.50   3.50

Printing Bureau, 120th Anniv. A464

No. 1624: a, 2.50p, Old printing press. b, 4p, Modern pressroom equipment. 14p, Printed bulletin.

Perf. 13 Syncopated
2021, Feb. 22 Litho.
Granite Paper
1624 A464 Horiz. pair, #a-b   1.75   1.75
Souvenir Sheet
1625 A464 14p multi   3.50   3.50

Hukou Waterfall A465

Perf. 13 Syncopated
2021, Mar. 1 Litho.
1626 A465 14p multi   3.50   3.50

Libraries A466

No. 1627: a, 2.50p, Wong Ieng Kuan Library in Luis de Caomoes Garden. b, 4p, Patane Library. c, 4.50p, Taipa Library. d, 6p, Seac Pai Van Library. 14p, Senado Library.

Perf. 13½x13¼ Syncopated
2021, Apr. 23 Litho.
1627 A466 Block or strip of 4, #a-d   4.25   4.25
Souvenir Sheet
1628 A466 14p multi   3.50   3.50

Procession of Our Lady of Fatima — A467

No. 1629: a, 2.50p, Cross and women holding candles. b, 4p, Three children, statue of Our Lady of Fatima, rose. 14p, Procession on street in Macao, vert.

Perf. 13½x13¼ Syncopated
2021, May 13 Litho.
1629 A467 Horiz. pair, #a-b   1.60   1.60
Souvenir Sheet
Perf. 13¼x13½ Syncopated
1630 A467 14p multi   3.50   3.50

Buddha's Birthday Festival A468

No. 1631: a, 2.50p, Buddha seated on lotus petals. b, 4p, Buddha with hand raised. 14p, Buddha with hand raised, diff.

Perf. 14x13¾ Syncopated
2021, May 19 Litho.
1631 A468 Pair, #a-b   1.60   1.60
Souvenir Sheet
1632 A468 14p multi   3.50   3.50

Shops in Macao A469

No. 1633: a, 2.50p, Seng Kei Pak Chok Restaurant. b, 4p, Tong Iec Pak Fa Fui Food Store. c, 4.50p, Chee Lee Yuen Jewelry Store. d, 6p, Fong Kei Bakery. 14p, Items available at establishments depicted on Nos. 1633a-1633d.

Perf. 13x13¼ Syncopated
2021, June 11 Litho.
Granite Paper
1633 A469 Block or strip of 4, #a-d   4.25   4.25
Souvenir Sheet
1634 A469 14p multi   3.50   3.50

Chinese Communist Party, Cent. — A470

No. 1635: a, 2.50p, May Fourth Movement Monument, site of the First National Congress of the Communist Party of China. b, 4p, Red Boat of South Lake, May Thirteenth Movement Monument. c, 4.50p, Provisional Central Government Building, Nanchang Uprising Monument. d, 6p, Baota Mountain, Yan'an, bridge, Anti-Japanese Guerilla War Monument. 14p, Monument to the People's Heroes and Gate of Heavenly Peace.

Perf. 13x13¼ Syncopated
2021, July 1 Litho.
Granite Paper
1635 A470 Block of 4, #a-d   4.25   4.25
Souvenir Sheet
1636 A470 14p multi   3.50   3.50

Wushu Practitioners — A471

No. 1637: a, 2.50p, Constant training. b, 4p, Yi Jin Jing exercises. c, 4.50p, Lion dance. d, 6p, Choi Lei Fat fighters. 14p, Hands of Wushu practitioner.

MACAO

Perf. 13x13¼ Syncopated
2021, Sept. 13   Litho.
Granite Paper
1637 A471 Block or strip of 4, #a-d   4.25   4.25
Souvenir Sheet
Perf. 12 Syncopated
1638 A471 14p multi   3.50   3.50
No. 1638 contains one 40x40mm stamp.

Insects — A472

No. 1639: a, 2.50p, Chlorophorus macauensis. b, 4p, Mortonagrion hirosei. c, 4.50p, Toxorhynchites macaensis. d, 6p, Pyrocoelia analis.
14p, Leptanilla macauensis.

Perf. 13x13¼ Syncopated
2021, Oct. 9   Litho.
Granite Paper
1639 A472 Block or strip of 4, #a-d   4.25   4.25
Souvenir Sheet
1640 A472 14p multi   3.50   3.50

Kiang Wu Hospital Charitable Association, 150th Anniv. — A473

Designs: 2.50p, Kiang Wu Hospital. 4p, Students at Kiang Wu Nursing College. 4.50p, Kiang Peng School. 6p, Nurse taking patient's blood pressure, family.
14p, Kiang Wu Hospital, diff.

Perf. 13x13¼ Syncopated
2021, Oct. 28   Litho.
Granite Paper
1641-1644 A473 Set of 4   4.25   4.25
Souvenir Sheet
Perf. 12 Syncopated
1645 A473 14p multi   3.50   3.50
No. 1645 contains one 40x40mm stamp.

Unitary Police Service, 20th Anniv. A474

No. 1646: a, 2.50p, Three police officers responding to call. b, 4p, Police officers with diagram. c, 4.50p, Police in control room. d, 6p, Police officers, video surveillance system, Ruins of St. Paul's Church.
14p, Four police officers, Ruins of St. Paul's Church, vert.

Perf. 13x13¼ Syncopated
2021, Oct. 29   Litho.
Granite Paper
1646 A474 Block or strip of 4, #a-d   4.25   4.25
Souvenir Sheet
Perf. 12 Syncopated
1647 A474 14p multi   3.50   3.50
No. 1647 contains one 40x60mm stamp.

Macao Customs Service, 20th Anniv. A475

No. 1648: a, 2.50p, Customs officers at back of truck. b, 4p, Customs officer using electronic tablet. c, 4.50p, Customs officers on Customs Service ship. d, 6p, Customs officers in rescue boat rescuing man.
14p, Customs Service ship and rescue boat.

Perf. 13x13¼ Syncopated
2021, Nov. 1   Litho.
Granite Paper
1648 A475 Block or strip of 4, #a-d   4.25   4.25
Souvenir Sheet
1649 A475 14p multi   3.50   3.50

Macao Grand Prix Museum — A476

No. 1650: a, 2.50p, Unnumbered race car. b, 4p, Race car No. 1. c, 4.50p, Motorcycle No. 8. d, 6p, Race car No. 2.
14p, Trophy and race car No. 5.

Perf. 13x13¼ Syncopated
2021, Nov. 18   Litho.
Granite Paper
1650 A476 Block or strip of 4, #a-d   4.25   4.25
Souvenir Sheet
1651 A476 14p multi   3.50   3.50

40th Macao International Marathon — A477

Designs: 2.50p, Runners. 4p, Runners crossing finish line.
14p, Runners leaving bridge, horiz.

2021, Dec. 3   Litho.   Perf. 14
Granite Paper
1652 A477 2.50p multi   .65   .65
1653 A477 4p multi   1.00   1.00
Souvenir Sheet
Perf. 14 Syncopated
1654 A477 14p multi   3.50   3.50
No. 1654 contains one 60x40mm stamp.

New Year 2022 (Year of the Tiger) A478

No. 1655: a, 2.50p, Tiger cub and two adult tigers. b, 4p, Tiger facing right. c, 4.50p, Head of tiger. d, 6p, Tiger facing forward.
14p, Head of tiger, diff.

Perf. 13x13¼ Syncopated
2022, Jan. 5   Litho.
Granite Paper
1655 A478 Block of 4, #a-d   4.25   4.25
Souvenir Sheet
Perf. Syncopated
1656 A478 14p multi   3.50   3.50
No. 1656 contains one 38mm diameter stamp.

Red Cotton Tree Flowers A480

No. 1659 — Various paintings of flowers by Ieong Tai Meng: a, 2.50p. b, 4p.

14p, Flowers, diff.

Perf. 13¼x14 Syncopated
2022, Mar. 1   Litho.
Granite Paper
1659 A480 Pair, #a-b   1.60   1.60
Souvenir Sheet
Perf. 12 Syncopated
1660 A480 14p multi   3.50   3.50
No. 1660 contains one 40x40mm stamp.

Hui Neng (638-713), 6th Patriarch of Chan Buddhism A481

No. 1661 — Various depictions of Hui Neng and other people numbered: a, 5/1. b, 5/2. c, 5/3. d, 5/4. e, 5/5.
14p, Hui Neng, vert.

Perf. 13x13¼ Syncopated
2022, Mar. 10   Litho.
Granite Paper
1661   Horiz. strip of 5   6.25   6.25
   a.-b. A481 2.50p Either single   .60   .60
   c.-d. A481 4p Either single   1.00   1.00
   e. A481 6p multi   1.50   1.50
Souvenir Sheet
Perf. 12 Syncopated
1662 A481 14p multi   3.50   3.50
No. 1662 contains one 40x60mm stamp.

Nursery Service of the Women's General Association, 70th Anniv. — A482

Woman, stuffed animals and: 2.50p, Two children at flower garden. 4p, Two children wearing caps.
14p, Child on tricycle, photograph of opening of nursery.

Perf. 13½x13¼ Syncopated
2022, May 21   Litho.
Granite Paper
1663-1664 A482 Set of 2   1.60   1.60
Souvenir Sheet
1665 A482 14p multi   3.50   3.50

Signing of World Heritage Convention, 50th Anniv. — A483

No. 1656 — UNESCO World Heritage emblem and sketches of various buildings, with denominations of: a, 2.50p. b, 4p. c, 4.50p. d, 6p.
14p, Emblem and sketch of building, diff.

Perf. 12 Syncopated
2022, June 10   Litho.
Granite Paper
1666 A483 Block or strip of 4, #a-d   4.25   4.25
Souvenir Sheet
1667 A483 14p multi   3.50   3.50

Feast of Saint John — A484

Flowers and: 2.50p, Plate of food, glass of beer, building. 4p, Musicians.
14p, St. John the Baptist.

Perf. 14 Syncopated
2022, June 24   Litho.
Granite Paper
1668-1669 A484 Set of 2   1.60   1.60
Souvenir Sheet
1670 A484 14p multi   3.50   3.50

Macanese Cuisine — A485

No. 1671 — Dish of: a, 2.50p, Stir-fried meat. b, 4p, Pork stew. c, 4.50p, Meat stew. d, 6p, Braised and roasted pork.
14p, Almond and coconut cake.

Perf. 14 Syncopated
2022, July 20   Litho.
Granite Paper
1671 A485 Block or strip of 4, #a-d   4.25   4.25
Souvenir Sheet
1672 A485 14p multi   3.50   3.50

School Buildings — A486

Designs: No. 1673, 2.50p, Primary section of Matteo Ricci College (6/1). No. 1674, 2.50p, Macao Portuguese School (6/2). No. 1675, 4p, Chinese section of St. Rose of Lima Secondary School (6/3). No. 1676, 4p, Ling Nam School (6/4). No. 1677, 6p, Pui Tou School (6/5). No. 1678, 6p, Pui Ching Middle School (6/6).

Perf. 13½ Syncopated
2022, Sept. 9   Litho.
Granite Paper
1673-1678 A486 Set of 6   6.25   6.25

Banco Nacional Ultramarino, 120th Anniv. — A487

No. 1679 — Various watercraft and 120th anniv. emblem, with denomination and bank buildings in: a, 2.50p, Orange brown. b, 4p, Purple. c, 4.50p, Yellow green. d, 6p, Blue.
14p, Bank buildings in red and black.

Perf. 13x13¼ Syncopated
2022, Sept. 20   Litho.
Granite Paper
1679 A487 Block or strip of 4, #a-d   4.25   4.25
Souvenir Sheet
1680 A487 14p multi   3.50   3.50

Chapel of Our Lady of Penha, 400th Anniv. A488

No. 1681: a, 2.50p, Chapel. b, 4p, Statue of Our Lady of Lourdes.
14p, Chapel and grotto.

MACAO

Perf. 13¼x14 Syncopated
2022, Oct. 9   Litho.
Granite Paper
1681   A488   Pair, #a-b   1.60   1.60
Souvenir Sheet
Perf. 12 Syncopated
1682   A488   14p multi   3.50   3.50
No. 1682 contains one 40x60mm stamp.

Modern Buildings A489

No. 1683: a, 2.50p, Mong-Ha Sports Center (4/1). b, 4p, Marine and Water Bureau (4/2). c, 4.50p, Qingmao Port Building (4/3). d, 6p, Hengqin Port Building (4/4).
14p, Services Platform Complex for Commercial and Trade Cooperation Between China and Portuguese-speaking Countries.

Perf. 13⅛ Syncopated
2022, Oct. 28   Litho.
Granite Paper
1683   A489   Block or strip of 4, #a-d   4.25   4.25
Souvenir Sheet
1684   A489   14p multi   3.50   3.50

Transmac, 70th Anniv. — A490

Designs: 2.50p, Bus and buildings. 4p, Buses at terminal.
14p, Articulated bus and smaller-sized bus.

Perf. 13½ Syncopated
2022, Nov. 8   Litho.
Granite Paper
1685-1686   A490   Set of 2   1.60   1.60
Souvenir Sheet
1687   A490   14p multi   3.50   3.50

Poetry of the Song Dynasty A491

No. 1688: a, 2.50p, Like a Dream, by Li Qingzhao (1084-c. 1155) (4/1). b, 4p, Nanxiangzhi, by Xin Qiji (1140-1207) (4/2). c, 4.50p, Sand-sifting Waves, by Wang Anshi (1021-86) (4/3). d, 6p, Calming the Wind and Waves, by Su Shi (1037-1101) (4/4).
14p, Nian Nu Jiao - Reminiscing Olden Days at Chibi, by Su Shi.

Perf. 12 Syncopated
2022, Nov. 18   Litho.
Granite Paper
1688   A491   Block or strip of 4, #a-d   4.25   4.25
Souvenir Sheet
1689   A491   14p multi   3.50   3.50

Tung Sin Tong Charitable Society, 130th Anniv. — A492

No. 1690 — Tung Sin Tong members assisting others, with stamps numbered: a, 2.50p, (4/1). b, 4p, (4/2). c, 4.50p, (4/3). d, 6p, (4/4).
14p, Tung Sin tong member examining person's forearm.

Perf. 13x13¼ Syncopated
2022, Nov. 22   Litho.
Granite Paper
1690   A492   Block of 4, #a-d   4.25   4.25
Souvenir Sheet
Perf. 12 Syncopated
1691   A492   14p multi   3.50   3.50
No. 1691 contains one 40x40mm stamp.

The Eighteen Arhats — A493

No. 1692 — One of the 18 Arhats numbered at bottom: a, (18/1). b, (18/2). c, (18/3). d, (18/4). e, (18/5). f, (18/6). g, (18/7). h, (18/8). i, (18/9). j, (18/10). k, (18/11). l, (18/12). m, (18/13). n, (18/14). o, (18/15). p, (18/16). q, (18/17). r, (18/18).

Perf. 13¼x13¾ Syncopated
2022, Dec. 1   Litho.
1692   Sheet of 18   12.00
   a.-r.   A493 2.50p Any single   .65   .65

New Year 2023 (Year of the Rabbit) A494

No. 1693 — Flowers and rabbit: a, 2.50p, Crouching. b, 4p, Facing right. c, 4.50p, Facing forward. d, 6p, Facing left.
14p, Flower and rabbit, horiz.

Perf. 14 Syncopated
2023, Jan. 5   Litho.
Granite Paper
1693   A494   Block of 4, #a-d   4.25   4.25
Souvenir Sheet
1694   A494   14p multi   3.50   3.50
No. 1694 contains one 60x40mm diameter stamp.

Chamber of Commerce, 110th Anniv. — A495

No. 1695: a, 2.50p, People standing in storefront. b, 4p, People seated at table. c, 4.50p, Athletes with flag. d, 6p, People planting tree.
14p, Buildings and map.

Perf. 13x13½ Syncopated
2023, Mar. 1   Litho.
Granite Paper
1695   A495   Block or strip of 4, #a-d   4.25   4.25
Souvenir Sheet
Perf. 12x11¾ Syncopated
1696   A495   14p multi   3.50   3.50
No. 1695 contains one 60x40mm stamp.

Promulgation of the Basic Law of Macao, 30th Anniv. — A496

Designs; 2.50p, "30," copies of Basic Law, people. 4p, Lotus Flower sculpture, flowers, people holding flags and copy of Basic Law.

Perf. 13½x13¼ Syncopated
2023, Mar. 31   Litho.
Granite Paper
1697-1698   A496   Set of 2   1.60   1.60

Dragon — A497

Turtle — A498

Phoenix — A499

Pixiu — A500

Qilin — A501

Design: 14p, Dragon and Phoenix.

Perf. 13x13¼ Syncopated
2023, June 6   Litho.
Granite Paper
1699   Horiz strip of 5, #a-e   5.00   5.00
  a.   A497 2.50p multi   .65   .65
  b.   A498 2.50p multi   .65   .65
  c.   A499 4p multi   1.00   1.00
  d.   A500 4p multi   1.00   1.00
  e.   A501 6p multi   1.50   1.50
Souvenir Sheet
Perf. 12x11¾ Syncopated
1700   A501   14p multi   3.50   3.50
Auspicious animals of Ancient China. No. 1700 contains one 60x40mm stamp.

Lou Pan Temples A502

No. 1701: a, 2.50p, Entryway with door. b, 4p, Entryway with cornice.
14p, Statue.

Perf. 13¼x14 Syncopated
2023, July 28   Litho.
Granite Paper
1701   A502   Horiz. pair, #a-b   1.60   1.60
Souvenir Sheet
1702   A502   14p multi   3.50   3.50

St. Augustine's Square A503

Lilau Square A504

Ruins of St. Paul's Church A505

Cathedral Square A506

Design: 14p, Senado Square, horiz.

Perf. 14 Syncopated
2023, Sept. 1   Litho.
Granite Paper
1703   Strip or block of 4   4.25   4.25
  a.   A503 2.50p multi   .65   .65
  b.   A504 4p multi   1.00   1.00
  c.   A505 4.50p multi   1.10   1.10
  d.   A506 6p multi   1.50   1.50
Souvenir Sheet
Perf. 13½x13¼ Syncopated
1704   A506   14p multi   3.50   3.50
Tourist attractions.

Souvenir Sheet

Belt and Road Initiative, 10th Anniv. A507

Litho. With Foil Application
Perf. 13x12½ Syncopated
2023, Sept. 7
1705   A507   10p multi   2.50   2.50

Rejoicing A508

No. 1706: a, 2.50p, Chinese lanterns, people at Lotus Flower sculpture, people eating (2/1). b, 4p, Champagne flutes (2/2).

Perf. 13¼ Syncopated
2023, Oct. 9   Litho.
Granite Paper
1706   A508   Horiz. pair, #a-b   1.75   1.75

Henrique de Senna Fernandes (1923-2010), Writer — A509

Fernandes wearing: 2.50p, Black bowtie (2/1). 4p, White tie (2/2).
14p, Red striped tie, horiz.

Perf. 13 Syncopated
2023, Oct. 13   Litho.
Granite Paper
1707   A509   2.50p multi   .65   .65

MACAO

1708	A509	4p multi	1.00	1.00
		Souvenir Sheet		
1709	A509	14p multi	3.50	3.50

No. 1709 contains one 40x30mm stamp.

SEMI-POSTAL STAMPS

Orbis International, 30th Anniv. — SP1

No. B1: a, 1.50p+1p, Orbis airplane, surgeons. b, 5p+1p, Doctor administering eye examination, eye chart.

2012, Oct. 9   Litho.   Perf. 13x13¼
Granite Paper
| B1 | SP1 | Horiz. pair, #a-b | 2.25 | 2.25 |

AIR POST STAMPS

Stamps of 1934 Overprinted or Surcharged in Black

a   b

1936   Wmk. 232   Perf. 11½
C1	A17 (a)	2a blue green	6.00	3.25
C2	A17 (a)	3a violet	7.25	3.25
C3	A17 (b)	5a on 6a brown	7.25	3.25
C4	A17 (a)	7a brt rose	7.25	3.25
C5	A17 (a)	8a brt blue	19.50	8.50
C6	A17 (a)	15a maroon	47.50	19.75
		Nos. C1-C6 (6)	94.75	41.25

Common Design Type
Name and Value in Black

1938, Aug. 1   Engr.   Unwmk.
Perf. 13½x13
C7	CD39	1a scarlet	1.65	1.25
C8	CD39	2a purple	2.05	1.65
C9	CD39	3a orange	2.75	2.05
C10	CD39	5a ultra	6.00	3.15
C11	CD39	10a lilac brn	9.25	4.85
C12	CD39	20a dk green	16.25	7.50
C13	CD39	50a red brown	27.00	10.75
C14	CD39	70a rose car	41.75	17.75
C15	CD39	1p magenta	83.00	40.00
		Nos. C7-C15 (9)	189.70	88.95

No. C13 exists with overprint "Exposicao Internacional de Nova York, 1939-1940" and Trylon and Perisphere. Value $325.

Catalogue values for unused stamps in this section, from this point to the end of the section, are for never hinged items.

Plane over Bay of Grand Beach — AP1

1960, Dec. 11   Litho.   Perf. 14
C16	AP1	50a shown	4.85	.90
C17	AP1	76a Penha Chapel	9.75	2.85
C18	AP1	3p Macao	27.25	4.50
C19	AP1	5p Bairro de Mong Ha	34.00	4.50
C20	AP1	10p Penha and Bay	54.50	5.00
		Nos. C16-C20 (5)	130.35	17.75
		Set, hinged		37.50

No. C17 Surcharged

1979, Aug. 3   Litho.   Perf. 14
| C21 | AP1 | 70a on 76a multi | 40.00 | 7.50 |

POSTAGE DUE STAMPS

Numeral of Value — D1

Name and Value in Black
Perf. 11½x12

1904, July   Typo.   Unwmk.
J1	D1	½a gray green	3.25	1.50
a.		Name & value inverted	150.00	85.00
J2	D1	1a yellow grn	3.50	1.50
J3	D1	2a slate	3.50	1.50
J4	D1	4a pale brown	4.95	1.50
J5	D1	5a red orange	6.25	3.50
J6	D1	8a gray brown	7.40	3.50
J7	D1	12a red brown	10.50	5.00
J8	D1	20a dull blue	20.50	9.25
J9	D1	40a carmine	27.50	12.00
J10	D1	50a rose red	46.00	22.00
J11	D1	1p gray violet	92.00	35.00
		Nos. J1-J11 (11)	225.35	96.25

Issued without gum: Nos. J7-J11. Issued with or without gum: No. J4. Others issued with gum.

For overprints see Nos. 144-146, J12-J32.

Issue of 1904 Overprinted in Carmine or Green

Overprint 24½mm long. "A" has flattened top.

1911   Lisbon Overprint
J12	D1	½a gray green	2.00	1.30
J13	D1	1a yellow green	2.15	1.30
J14	D1	2a slate	2.50	1.40
J15	D1	4a pale brown	2.90	1.50
J16	D1	5a orange	3.25	1.60
J17	D1	8a gray brown	6.50	1.75
J18	D1	12a red brown	11.25	3.00
J19	D1	20a dull blue	15.00	4.25
J20	D1	40a carmine (G)	24.50	9.25
J21	D1	50a orange	39.00	14.00
J22	D1	1p gray violet	61.00	28.00
		Nos. J12-J22 (11)	170.05	67.35

Issued without gum: Nos. J19-J22.

Issue of 1904 Overprinted in Red or Green

Overprint 23mm long. "A" has pointed top.

1914   Local Overprint
J22A	D1	½a gray green	2,250.	1,000.
J23	D1	1a yellow green	5.25	3.50
J24	D1	2a slate	5.25	3.50
J25	D1	4a pale brown	6.00	3.75
J26	D1	5a orange	10.00	4.75
J27	D1	8a gray brown	10.00	4.75
J28	D1	12a red brown	11.75	5.50
J29	D1	20a dull blue	17.75	10.00
J30	D1	40a car (G)	28.50	14.00
a.		Double ovpt., red and green	150.00	40.00
J31	D1	50a orange	36.00	19.50
J32	D1	1p gray violet	60.00	23.50
		Nos. J23-J32 (10)	190.50	92.75

Issued without gum: Nos. J28, J30-J32.

D2

Name and Value in Black

1947   Typo.   Perf. 11½x12
J33	D2	1a red violet	3.50	3.50
J34	D2	2a purple	3.50	3.50
J35	D2	4a dark blue	3.50	3.75
J36	D2	5a chocolate	4.00	4.00
J37	D2	8a red violet	5.50	4.50
J38	D2	12a orange brown	9.00	4.50
J39	D2	20a yellow green	13.50	10.50
J40	D2	40a brt carmine	16.50	13.75
J41	D2	50a orange yellow	22.00	21.00
J42	D2	1p blue	27.00	25.00
		Nos. J33-J42 (10)	108.00	94.00
		Set, never hinged	275.00	

Stamps of 1934 Surcharged "PORTEADO" and New Values in Carmine

1949, May 1   Wmk. 232
J43	A17	1a on 4a brnsh blk	3.25	2.00
J44	A17	2a on 6a brown	3.25	2.00
J45	A17	4a on 8a brt blue	3.50	2.40
J46	A17	5a on 10a red org	3.50	2.85
J47	A17	8a on 12a dk blue	5.00	4.50
J48	A17	12a on 30a apple grn	8.25	6.00
J49	A17	20a on 40a violet	8.75	8.00
		Nos. J43-J49 (7)	35.50	27.75
		Set, never hinged	60.00	

Catalogue values for unused stamps in this section, from this point to the end of the section, are for Never Hinged items.

Nos. 348, 349 and 351 Overprinted or Surcharged in Black or Carmine

1951, June 6   Unwmk.
J50	A21	1a org yel, lem	2.15	1.75
J51	A21	2a dk grn, bl (C)	2.65	1.75
J52	A21	7a on 10a brt pink, bl	3.45	2.15
		Nos. J50-J52 (3)	8.25	5.65

Common Design Type

1952   Photo. & Typo.   Perf. 14
Numeral in Red; Frame Multicolored
J53	CD45	1a violet blue	1.60	.70
J54	CD45	3a chocolate	1.75	.70
J55	CD45	5a indigo	1.75	.85
J56	CD45	10a dark red	3.20	1.60
J57	CD45	30a indigo	6.00	2.45
J58	CD45	1p chocolate	13.50	5.75
		Nos. J53-J58 (6)	27.80	12.05

WAR TAX STAMPS

Victory — WT1

Overprinted in Black or Carmine

1919, Aug. 11   Unwmk.   Perf. 15x14
| MR1 | WT1 | 2a green | 12.00 | 7.50 |
| MR2 | WT1 | 11a green (C) | 49.00 | 28.00 |

Nos. MR1-MR2 were also for use in Timor. A 9a value was issued for revenue and telegram use. Value $30.

NEWSPAPER STAMPS

Nos. P1-P2   No. P3

Typographed and Embossed
1892-93   Unwmk.   Perf. 12½
Black Surcharge
Without Gum
P1	A7	2½r on 40r choc	14.50	5.75
a.		Inverted surcharge	95.00	95.00
b.		Perf. 13½		7.50
c.		As "b," inverted surcharge	110.00	90.00
P2	A7	2½r on 80r gray	18.00	11.00
a.		Inverted surcharge	110.00	100.00
b.		Double surcharge	105.00	92.50
c.		Perf. 13½	90.00	60.00
P3	A7	2½r on 10r grn ('93)	15.00	12.50
a.		Double surcharge		75.00
b.		Perf. 13½	15.00	16.00
c.		Inverted surcharge	75.00	
		Nos. P1-P3 (3)	47.50	29.25

N3   N4

1893-94   Typo.   Perf. 11½
P4	N3	2½r brown	18.00	12.50
a.		Perf. 12½	13.50	7.75
b.		Perf. 13½	15.00	9.25
P5	N4	½a on 2½r brn (Bk) ('94)	9.00	5.75
a.		Double surcharge	90.00	85.00
b.		Perf. 12½	22.50	18.00
c.		Perf. 13½		225.00

For surcharges see Nos. 131, 252.

POSTAL TAX STAMPS

Pombal Commemorative Issue
Common Design Types

1925, Nov. 3   Engr.   Unwmk.   Perf. 12½
RA1	CD28	2a red org & blk	5.50	2.60
RA2	CD29	2a red org & blk	7.00	2.60
RA3	CD30	2a red org & blk	7.50	2.75
		Nos. RA1-RA3 (3)	20.00	7.95

Symbolical of Charity — PT1

1930, Dec. 25   Litho.   Perf. 11
RA4	PT1	5a dk brown, yel	75.00	39.00
a.		Horiz. pair, imperf. vert.	500.00	
b.		Horiz. pair, imperf. between	425.00	

PT2

1945-47   Perf. 12
RA5	PT2	5a blk brn, yel	35.00	32.50
RA6	PT2	5a bl, bluish, perf 11x11½ ('47)	45.00	35.00
RA7	PT2	10a grn, citron	22.50	27.00
RA8	PT2	15a org, buff	22.50	23.50
RA9	PT2	20a rose red, sal	57.50	35.00
RA10	PT2	50a red vio, pnksh, perf 11x11½	60.00	46.50
		Nos. RA5-RA10 (6)	242.50	199.50

Perf. 11½
RA5a		5a blk brn, yel	90.00	54.00
RA7a		10a grn, citron	45.00	33.00
RA8a		15a org, buff	45.00	33.00
RA9a		20a rose red, sal	75.00	45.00

Perf. 10
| RA10a | | 50a red vio, pnksh | 300.00 | 180.00 |

Catalogue values for unused stamps in this section, from this point to the end of the section, are for Never Hinged items.

1953-56   Perf. 10½x11½
RA11	PT2	10a bl, pale grn ('56)	6.00	3.00
RA12	PT2	20a chocolate, yel	14.00	9.25
a.		Perf. 10	9.00	8.25
RA13	PT2	50a car, pale rose	25.50	16.50
		Nos. RA11-RA13 (3)	45.50	28.75

1958   Perf. 12x11½
| RA14 | PT2 | 1a gray grn, grnsh | 2.10 | 1.00 |
| RA15 | PT2 | 2a rose lilac, grysh | 2.55 | 1.40 |

MACAO — MACEDONIA

Type of 1945-47 Redrawn
Imprint: "Lito. Imp. Nac.-Macau"

1961-66			Perf. 11	
RA16	PT2	1a gray grn, *grnsh*	2.30	2.00
RA17	PT2	2a rose lil, *grysh*	2.30	2.00
RA18	PT2	10a bl, *pale grn* ('62)	2.30	2.00
RA19	PT2	20a brn, *yel* ('66)	3.00	3.25
		Nos. RA16-RA19 (4)	9.90	9.25

Nos. RA16-RA19 have accent added to "E" in "Assistencia."
Nos. RA4-RA19 were issued without gum.

Types of 1945-47 Redrawn and Surcharged

PT3

1976-79	Litho.		Perf. 11x11½	
RA19A	PT3	20a on 3p blk, *brn* ('78)	4.00	2.25
RA19B	PT3	20a on 5p brn, *yel*	27.50	19.00
RA20	PT3	20a on 1p yel grn, *cream* ('79)	5.50	4.00

Nos. RA19A-RA20 have no accent above "E," no imprint and were not issued without surcharge.

No. RA8 Surcharged

Methods and Perfs As Before

1981				
RA20A	PT2	10a on 15a #RA8	6.50	4.00

No. RA17 Surcharged

Methods and Perfs As Before

1981			Without Gum	
RA21	PT2	20a on 2a #RA17	5.00	3.00

POSTAL TAX DUE STAMPS

Pombal Commemorative Issue
Common Design Types

1925		Unwmk.	Perf. 12½	
RAJ1	CD28	4a red orange & blk	5.50	3.10
RAJ2	CD29	4a red orange & blk	5.50	3.10
RAJ3	CD30	4a red orange & blk	5.50	3.10
		Nos. RAJ1-RAJ3 (3)	16.50	9.30

MACEDONIA
,ma-sə-'dō-nē-ə

LOCATION — Central Balkans, bordered on the north by Serbia, to the east by Bulgaria, on the south by Greece and by Albania on the west.
GOVT. — Republic
AREA — 9,928 sq. mi.
POP. — 2,080,000 (2020 est.)
CAPITAL — Skopje

Formerly a constituent republic in the Socialist Federal Republic of Yugoslavia. Declared independence on Nov. 21, 1991.

100 Deni (de) = 1 Denar (d)

Catalogue values for all unused stamps in this country are for Never Hinged items.

Watermark
Wmk. 387

Bas Relief — A1

1992-93	Litho.		Perf. 13½x13	
1	A1	30d multicolored	.80	.45
			Perf. 10	
2	A1	40d multicolored	.65	.45

Issued: 30d, 9/8/92; 40d, 3/15/93.
For surcharges see Nos. 21, 42.

Christmas — A2

Frescoes: 100d, Nativity Scene, 16th cent. 500d, Virgin and Child, 1422.

1992, Dec. 10	Litho.		Perf. 13x13½	
3	A2	100d multicolored	1.10	1.10
4	A2	500d multicolored	2.50	2.50

Natl. Flag — A3

1993, Mar. 15			Perf. 13½x13	
5	A3	10d multicolored	.55	.35
6	A3	40d multicolored	1.50	1.10
7	A3	50d multicolored	1.75	1.35
		Nos. 5-7 (3)	3.80	2.80

For surcharges see Nos. 23, 40-41.

Fish — A4

Designs: 50d, 1000d, Rutilus macedonicus. 100d, 2000d, Salmothymus achridanus.

1993, Mar. 15			Perf. 10	
8	A4	50d multicolored	.35	.35
9	A4	100d multicolored	.45	.45
10	A4	1000d multicolored	3.20	3.25
11	A4	2000d multicolored	4.75	4.50
		Nos. 8-11 (4)	8.75	8.55

Easter — A5

1993, Apr. 16				
12	A5	300d multicolored	3.00	2.25

Trans-Balkan Telecommunications Network — A6

1993, May 6				
13	A6	500d multicolored	1.30	1.00

Admission to the UN, Apr. 8, 1993 — A7

1993, July 28				
14	A7	10d multicolored	1.40	1.10

Ilinden Uprising, 90th Anniv. — A8

1993, Aug. 2				
15	A8	10d multicolored	1.40	1.10

Souvenir Sheet
Imperf

| 16 | A8 | 30d multicolored | 4.00 | 4.00 |

A9

1993, Nov. 4				
17	A9	4d multicolored	.65	.65

Size: 85x67mm
Imperf

| 18 | A9 | 40d multicolored | 5.50 | 5.50 |

Macedonian Revolutionary Organization, cent.

Christmas — A10

1993, Dec. 31			Perf. 10	
19	A10	2d Nativity Scene	.75	.75
20	A10	20d Adoration of the Magi	3.25	3.25

Nos. 1, 5, RA1 Surcharged

1994, Apr. 2		Perfs., Etc. as Before		
21	A1	2d on 30d multi	.35	.35
22	PT1	8d on 2.50d multi	1.25	1.25
23	A3	15d on 10d multi	2.75	2.75
		Nos. 21-23 (3)	4.35	4.35

Size and location of surcharge varies.

Easter — A11

1994, Apr. 29	Litho.		Perf. 10	
24	A11	2d multicolored	.70	.45

Revolutionaries A12

Designs: 8d, Kosta Racin (1908-43), writer. 15d, Grigor Prlicev (1830-93), writer. 20d, Nikola Vapzarov (1909-42), poet. 50d, Goce Delchev (1872-1903), politician.

1994, May 23				
25	A12	8d multicolored	.70	.50
26	A12	15d multicolored	1.10	1.00
27	A12	20d multicolored	2.25	1.50
28	A12	50d multicolored	3.25	2.50
		Nos. 25-28 (4)	7.30	5.50

Intl. Year of the Family — A13

1994, June 21				
29	A13	2d multicolored	.70	.25

Liberation Day, 50th Anniv. — A14

Designs: 5d, St. Prohor Pcinski Monastery, up close. 50d, View of entire grounds.

1994, Aug. 2	Litho.		Perf. 10	
30	A14	5d multicolored	.60	.45

Size: 108x73mm
Imperf

| 31 | A14 | 50d multicolored | 4.00 | 3.25 |

Swimming Marathon, Ohrid Lake — A15

1994, Aug. 22				
32	A15	8d multicolored	.80	.60

Stamp Day — A16

1994, Sept. 12				
33	A16	2d multicolored	1.25	.85

MACEDONIA

Nova Makedonija, Mlad Boretz, & Makedonka Newspapers, 50th Anniv. — A17

1994, Sept. 13   Litho.   Perf. 10
34   A17   2d multicolored   1.25   .65

St. Kliment of Ohrid Library, 50th Anniv. — A18

Manuscripts: 2d, 15th cent. 10d, 13th cent.

1994, Sept. 29   Litho.   Perf. 10
35   A18   2d multi   .30   .30
36   A18   10d multi, vert.   1.60   1.40

Macedonian Radio, 50th Anniv. — A19

1994, Dec. 26   Litho.   Perf. 10
37   A19   2d multicolored   .75   .45

Wildlife Conservation A20

1994, Dec. 26   Litho.   Perf. 10
38   A20   5d Pinus peluse   .50   .50
39   A20   10d Lynx lynx martinoi   1.25   1.00

Nos. 2, 6 Surcharged in Black or Gold

a

b

Perfs., Etc. as Before

1995, Mar. 13   Litho.
40   A3(a)   2d on 40d #6   1.75   1.75
41   A3(b)   2d on 40d #6   1.00   1.00
42   A1(a)   5d on 40d #2 (G)   .75   .75
  Nos. 40-42 (3)   3.50   3.50

Easter — A21

1995, Apr. 23   Litho.   Perf. 10
43   A21   4d multicolored   .70   .45

End of World War II, 50th Anniv. — A22

1995, May 9   Litho.   Perf. 10
44   A22   2d multicolored   1.25   .90

Macedonian Red Cross, 50th Anniv. — A23

1995, May 20   Litho.   Perf. 10
45   A23   2d multicolored   1.30   .90

Wilhelm Röntgen (1845-1923), Discovery of the X-Ray, Cent. — A24

1995, May 20   Litho.   Perf. 10
46   A24   2d multicolored   1.50   .90

Vojdan Cernodrinski (1875-1951), Theater Festival, 50th Anniv. — A25

1995, June 8
47   A25   10d multicolored   1.30   .80

Death of Prince Marko Kraljevic, 600th Anniv. — A26

1995, June 22
48   A26   20d multicolored   2.10   1.40

Gorgi Puleski (1818-95), Writer — A27

1995, July 8
49   A27   2d multicolored   1.10   1.10

Writer's Festival, Struga — A28

1995, Aug. 23   Litho.   Perf. 10
50   A28   2d multicolored   1.40   1.10

Mosque of Tetovo — A29

1995, Oct. 4
51   A29   15d multicolored   1.40   1.10

Architecture — A30

1995, Oct. 4   Litho.   Perf. 10
52   A30   2d Malesevija   .30   .30
53   A30   20d Krakornica   2.00   1.10
  See Nos. 81-83 and design A63a.

Motion Pictures, Cent. — A31

Film strip of early movie and: No. 54, Auguste and Louis Lumiére. No. 55, Milton and Janaki Manaki, Macedonian cinematographers.

1995, Oct. 6   Perf. 10 on 3 Sides
54   10d multicolored   1.25   1.25
55   10d multicolored   1.25   1.25
  a.   A31 Pair, #54-55   4.00   4.00

UN, 50th Anniv. — A32

20d, Blocks, globe in nest. 50d, Blocks, sun.

1995, Oct. 24
56   A32   20d multicolored   1.60   1.10
57   A32   50d multicolored   3.50   2.25

Christmas — A33

1995, Dec. 13
58   A33   15d multicolored   1.50   1.10

Birds — A34

15d, Pelecanus crispus. 40d, Gypaetus barbatus.

1995, Dec. 14
59   A34   15d multicolored   2.00   1.25
60   A34   40d multicolored   4.00   2.50

Reform of Macedonian Language, 50th Anniv. — A35

1995, Dec. 18
61   A35   5d multicolored   .70   .50

St. Bogorodica Church, Ohrid, 700th Anniv. — A36

Designs: 8d, Detail of fresco, exterior view, St. Kliment of Ohrid (840-916). 50d, Portion of fresco inside church, #62.

1995, Dec. 19
62   A36   8d multicolored   .90   .90
  Size: 80x61mm
  Imperf
62A   A36   50d multicolored   60.00   60.00

Macedonia's Admission to UPU, 1st Anniv. — A37

10d, Post office, Skopje.

1995, Dec. 27
62B   A37   10d multicolored   1.00   1.00

Admission to Council of Europe (CE) and Organization for Security and Cooperation in Europe (OSCE) — A37a

1995, Dec. 27
62C   A37a   20d multicolored   2.75   2.75

Modern Olympic Games, Cent., 1996 Summer Olympic Games, Atlanta — A38

1996, May 20   Litho.   Perf. 10
63   A38   2d Kayak race   .60   .60
64   A38   8d Basketball, vert.   .80   .80
65   A38   15d Swimming   1.50   1.50
66   A38   20d Wrestling   2.50   2.50
67   A38   40d Boxing, vert.   4.00   4.00
68   A38   50d Running, vert   5.50   5.50
  Nos. 63-68 (6)   14.90   14.90

Intl. Decade to Fight Illegal Drugs — A39

1996, July 11   Litho.   Perf. 10
69   A39   20d multicolored   2.00   2.00

Children's Paintings — A40

1996, July 15
70   A40   2d Boy   .35   .35
71   A40   8d Girl   .90   .90

Peak of Czar Samuel of Bulgaria's Power, 1000th Anniv. — A41

1996, July 19
72   A41   40d multicolored   4.00   4.00

G. Petrov (1865-1921), Revolutionary — A42

1996, Aug. 2
73   A42   20d multicolored   2.00   2.00

Independence, 5th Anniv. — A43

1996, Sept. 8
74   A43   10d multicolored   1.00   1.00

MACEDONIA

Vera Ciriviri-Trena (1920-44), Freedom Fighter — A44

Mother Teresa (1910-97) — A45

1996, Nov. 22		Litho.	Perf. 13x13½
75	A44 20d multicolored	4.00	4.00
76	A45 40d multicolored	8.00	7.50

Europa.

Christmas — A46

Designs: No. 77, Tree, children caroling in snow. No. 78, Candle, nuts, apples.

1996, Dec. 14		Litho.	Perf. 10
77	A46 10d multicolored	.60	.60
78	A46 10d multicolored	.60	.60
a.	Pair, #77-78	2.00	2.00

Terra Cotta Tiles — A47

Nos. 79a, 80a, 4d, Daniel in lions den. Nos. 79b, 80b, 8d, Sts. Christopher & George. Nos. 79c, 80c, 20d, Joshua, Caleb. Nos. 79d, 80d, 50d, Unicorn.

1996, Dec. 19		Blocks of 4, #a.-d.
79	A47 bl grn & multi	7.50 7.50
80	A47 yel grn & multi	7.50 7.50

Traditional Architecture Type of 1995

1996

81	A30 2d House, Nistrovo	.25 .25
82	A30 8d House, Brodets	.80 .80
83	A30 10d House, Niviste	.90 .90
	Nos. 81-83 (3)	1.95 1.95

Issued: 8d, 12/20; 2d, 10d, 12/25. See Nos. 112-116.

Butterflies — A49

4d, Pseudochazara cingovskii. 40d, Colias balcanica.

1996, Dec. 21			
84	A49 4d multicolored	.30	.30
85	A49 40d multicolored	3.75	3.75

UNICEF, 50th Anniv. — A50

40d, UNESCO, 50th anniv.

1996, Dec. 31		Perf. 14½
86	A50 20d shown	2.25 2.25
87	A50 40d multicolored	4.25 4.25

Alpine Skiing Championships, 50th Anniv. — A51

1997, Feb. 7		Perf. 10
88	A51 20d multicolored	2.00 2.00

Alexander Graham Bell (1847-1922) — A52

1997, Mar. 12		
89	A52 40d multicolored	3.00 3.00

Ancient Roman Mosaics, Heraklia and Stobi — A53

1997, Mar. 26			Perf. 10
90	A53	2d Wild dog	.40 .40
91	A53	8d Bull	.65 .65
92	A53	20d Lion	1.60 1.60
93	A53	40d Leopard with prey	4.00 4.00
	Nos. 90-93 (4)		6.65 6.65

Size: 79x50mm

Imperf

94	A53 50d Deer, peacocks	7.00 7.00

No. 94 has simulated perforations within the design.

Cyrilic Alphabet, 1100th Anniv. — A54

Cyrillic inscriptions and: No. 95, Gold embossed plate. No. 96, St. Cyril (827-69), St. Methodius (825-84), promulgators of Cyrillic alphabet.

1997, May 2		Perf. 10
95	A54 10d multicolored	.75 .60
96	A54 10d multicolored	.75 .60
a.	Pair, #95-96	2.10 2.10

A55

Europa (Stories and Legends): 20d, Man kneeling down, another seated in background. 40d, Man, tree, bird dressed as man.

1997, June 6		Perf. 15x14
97	A55 20d multicolored	2.25 2.00
98	A55 40d multicolored	5.00 3.50

5th Natl. Ecology Day — A56

1997, June 5		Perf. 10
99	A56 15d multicolored	1.60 1.60

St. Naum — A57

1997, July 3		Perf. 10
100	A57 15d multicolored	1.60 1.60

Mushrooms A58

2d, Cantharellus cibarius. 15d, Boletus aereus. 27d, Amanita caesarea. 50d, Morchella conica.

1997, Nov. 7		Litho.	Perf. 10
101	A58 2d multicolored	.60	.60
102	A58 15d multicolored	1.25	1.25
103	A58 27d multicolored	2.00	2.00
104	A58 50d multicolored	3.50	3.50
	Nos. 101-104 (4)	7.35	7.35

Week of the Child — A59

1997, Oct. 11		
105	A59 27d multicolored	2.25 2.25

Minerals — A60

1997, Oct. 10		
106	A60 27d Stibnite	2.00 2.00
107	A60 40d Lorandite	3.50 3.50

Mahatma Gandhi (1869-1948) — A61

1998, Feb. 4		Litho.	Perf. 13½
108	A61 30d multicolored	2.50	2.50

Pythagoras (c. 570-c. 500 BC), Greek Philosopher, Mathematician A62

1998, Feb. 6		
109	A62 10d multicolored	1.40 1.40

1998 Winter Olympic Games, Nagano A63

Designs: 4d, Slalom skier. 30d, Cross country skiers.

1998, Feb. 7		
110	A63 4d multi + label	.45 .45
111	A63 30d multi + label	3.50 3.50

Nos. 110-111 were each printed with a se-tenant label.

Traditional Architecture — A63a

Location of home: 2d, Novo Selo. 4d, Jablanica. 16d, Kiselica. 20d, Konopnica. 30d, Ambar. 50d, Galicnik.

1998

112	A63a 2d multicolored	.30	.30
113	A63a 4d multicolored	.35	.35
113A	A63a 16d multicolored	.95	.95
114	A63a 20d multicolored	1.15	1.15
115	A63a 30d multicolored	1.75	1.75
116	A63a 50d multicolored	3.00	3.00
	Nos. 112-116 (6)	7.50	7.50

Issued: 2d, 4d, 30d, 2/9; 20d, 50d, 2/12; 16d, 6/10. See Nos. 146-148.

Painting, "Exodus," by Kole Manev — A64

1998, Feb. 11		
117	A64 30d multicolored	3.00 3.00

Exodus from Aegean Macedonia, 50th anniv.

Neolithic Artifacts — A65

Designs: 4d, Water flasks. 18d, Animal-shaped bowl. 30d, Woman figure. 60d, Bowl.

1998, Apr. 29		Litho.	Perf. 13½
118	A65 4d multicolored	.25	.25
119	A65 18d multicolored	.85	.85
120	A65 30d multicolored	1.25	1.25
121	A65 60d multicolored	3.25	3.25
	Nos. 118-121 (4)	5.60	5.60

1998 World Cup Soccer Championships, France — A66

4d, Looking down at soccer field, ball. 30d, Soccer field with world map in center.

1998, Apr. 30		
122	A66 4d multicolored	.30 .30
123	A66 30d multicolored	2.25 2.25

Natl. Festivals — A67

Europa: 30d, Dancers, Strumica. 40d, People wearing masks, Vevcani.

1998, May 5		Litho.	Perf. 13½
124	A67 20d multicolored	0.05	1.70
125	A67 40d multicolored	3.75	2.25

Carnival Cities Congress, Strumica — A68

1998, May 10		Litho.	Perf. 13½
126	A68 30d multicolored	2.25	2.25

MACEDONIA

World Ecology Day — A69

4d, Stylized flower. 30d, Smokestack uprooting tree.

1998, June 5 **Litho.** **Perf. 13½**
| 127 | A69 | 4d multicolored | .30 | .30 |
| 128 | A69 | 30d multicolored | 1.75 | 1.75 |

Dimitri Cupovski, 120th Birth Anniv. — A70

1998, June 30
| 129 | A70 | 16d multicolored | 1.10 | 1.10 |

Railroads in Macedonia, 125th Anniv. — A72

30d, Document, building, early steam locomotive, vert. 60d, Locomotive, 1873.

1998, Aug. 9 **Litho.** **Perf. 13½**
| 130 | A72 | 30d multicolored | 2.00 | 2.00 |
| 131 | A72 | 60d multicolored | 4.00 | 4.00 |

Fossil Skulls Found in Macedonia A73

Designs: 4d, Ursus spelaeus. 8d, Mesopithecus pentelici. 18d, Tragoceros. 30d, Aceratherium incisivum.

1998, Sept. 17
132	A73	4d multicolored	.30	.30
133	A73	8d multicolored	.50	.50
134	A73	18d multicolored	1.10	1.10
135	A73	30d multicolored	2.00	2.00
		Nos. 132-135 (4)	3.90	3.90

The Liturgy of St. John Chrysostom, Cent. — A74

Design: Atanas Badev, composer.

1998, Sept. 21
| 136 | A74 | 25d multicolored | 1.75 | 1.75 |

Children's Day — A75

1998, Oct. 5
| 137 | A75 | 30d multicolored | 2.10 | 2.10 |

Beetles — A76

4d, Cerambyx cerdo. 8d, Rosalia alpina. 20d, Oryctes nasicornis. 40d, Lucanus cervus.

1998, Oct. 20
138	A76	4d multicolored	.25	.25
139	A76	8d multicolored	.45	.45
140	A76	20d multicolored	1.10	1.10
141	A76	40d multicolored	2.25	2.25
		Nos. 138-141 (4)	4.05	4.05

A77

Christmas and New Year — A77a

1998, Nov. 20
| 142 | A77 | 4d multicolored | .25 | .25 |
| 143 | A77a | 30d multicolored | 2.00 | 2.00 |

Universal Declaration of Human Rights, 50th Anniv. — A78

1998, Dec. 10
| 144 | A78 | 30d multicolored | 2.00 | 2.00 |

Sharplaninec Dog — A79

1999, Jan. 20 **Litho.** **Perf. 13¼**
| 145 | A79 | 15d multi | 1.50 | 1.50 |

Architecture Type of 1998
"Republica Macedonia" in Cyrillic
Location of home: 1d, Bogomila. 4d, Svekani. 5d, Teovo.

1999 **Litho.** **Perf. 13¼**
146	A63a	1d multi	.30	.30
147	A63a	4d multi	.35	.35
148	A63a	5d multi	.35	.35
		Nos. 146-148 (3)	1.00	1.00

Issued: 4d, 2/1; 5d, 2/25; 1d, 11/5.

Icons — A80

Designs: 4d, 1535 Slepche Monastery Annunciation icon, Demir Hisar, by Dimitar Zograf. 8d, 1862 St. Nicholas Church icon, Ohrid. 18d, 1535 Slepche Monastery Madonna and Child icon, Demir Hisar. 30d, 1393-94 Zrze Monastery Jesus icon, Prilep. 50d, 1626 Lesnovo Monastery Jesus icon, Probishtip.

1999, Mar. 3 **Perf. 11¾**
149	A80	4d multi	.30	.30
150	A80	8d multi	.55	.55
151	A80	18d multi	1.25	1.25
152	A80	30d multi	1.90	1.90
		Nos. 149-152 (4)	4.00	4.00

Souvenir Sheet
| 153 | A80 | 50d multi | 3.25 | 3.25 |

Dimitar A. Pandilov (1899-1963), Painter — A81

1999, Mar. 14 **Perf. 13¼**
| 154 | A81 | 4d multi | .60 | .60 |

Telegraphy in Macedonia, Cent. — A82

1999, Apr. 22
| 155 | A82 | 4d multi | .60 | .60 |

Saints Cyril and Methodius University, Skopje, 50th Anniv. — A83

1999, Apr. 24
| 156 | A83 | 8d multi | .70 | .70 |

Issued in sheets of 8 + label.

Council of Europe, 50th Anniv. — A84

1999, May 5
| 157 | A84 | 30d multi | 2.50 | 2.25 |

Europa — A85

Natl. Parks: 30d, Pelister. 40d, Mavrovo.

1999, May 5
| 158 | A85 | 30d multi | 2.50 | 1.25 |
| 159 | A85 | 40d multi | 3.50 | 1.75 |

Ecology — A86

1999, June 5
| 160 | A86 | 30d multi | 2.00 | 2.00 |

Macedonian Leaders from the Middle Ages — A87

Designs: a, 30d, Strez (1204-14). b, 8d, Gorgi Voytech (1072-1073). c, 18d, Dobromir Hrs (1195-1203). d, 4d, Petar Deljan (1040-41).

1999, June 25
| 161 | A87 | Block of 4, #a.-d. | 4.00 | 4.00 |

Kuzman Sapkarev (1834-1909), Folklorist — A88

1999, Sept. 1 **Litho.** **Perf. 13¼**
| 162 | A88 | 4d multi | .60 | .60 |

Flowers — A89

Designs: 4d, Crocus scardicus. 8d, Astragalus mayeri. 18d, Campanula formanekiana. 30d, Viola kosaninii.

1999, Sept. 16
163	A89	4d multi	.30	.30
164	A89	8d multi	.55	.55
165	A89	18d multi	1.25	1.25
166	A89	30d multi	2.00	2.00
		Nos. 163-166 (4)	4.10	4.10

Children's Day — A90

1999, Oct. 4
| 167 | A90 | 30d multi | 1.90 | 1.90 |

UPU, 125th Anniv. — A91

1999, Oct. 9
| 168 | A91 | 5d Post horn, emblem | .30 | .30 |
| 169 | A91 | 30d Emblem, post horn | 2.00 | 2.00 |

Krste Petkov Misirkov (1875-1926), Writer — A92

1999, Nov. 18
| 170 | A92 | 5d multi | .60 | .60 |

Christmas — A93

1999, Nov. 24
| 171 | A93 | 30d multi | 1.75 | 1.75 |

New Year's Day — A94

1999, Nov. 24 **Perf. 13¼**
| 172 | A94 | 5d multi | .40 | .40 |

Slavic Presence in Macedonia, 1400th Anniv. — A95

1999, Oct. 27 **Litho.** **Perf. 13¼**
| 173 | A95 | 5d multi | .55 | .55 |

MACEDONIA

Christianity, 2000th Anniv. — A96

Icons and frescoes: 5d, Altar cross, St. Nikita Monastery, vert. 10d, Fresco of Holy Mother of God, St. Mark's Monastery. 15d, St. Clement of Ohrid, vert. 30d, Fresco of Apostle Paul St. Andrew's Monastery, vert. 50d, St. Sophia's Cathedral, Ohrid, vert.

2000, Jan. 19				
174-177	A96	Set of 4	3.25	3.25
		Souvenir Sheet		
178	A96	50d multi	2.75	2.75

No. 178 contains one 30x31mm stamp.

Millennium — A97

No. 179: a, 5d, "2000." b, 30d, Religious symbols.

2000, Feb. 16				
179	A97	Vert. pair, #a-b	2.25	2.25

Silver Jewelry — A98

Designs: 5d, Pin with icon, Ohrid, 19th cent. 10d, Bracelet, Bitola, 20th cent. 20d, Earrings, Ohrid, 18th cent. 30d, Brooch, Bitola, 19th-20th cent.

2000, Mar. 1	Litho.	Perf. 13¼		
180-183	A98	Set of 4	3.75	3.75

Macedonian Philatelic Society, 50th Anniv. — A99

2000, Mar. 19				
184	A99	5d multi	.55	.55

World Meteorological Organization, 50th Anniv. — A100

2000, Mar. 23	Litho.	Perf. 13¼		
185	A100	30d multi	1.75	1.75

Easter — A101

2000, Apr. 21	Litho.	Perf. 13¼		
186	A101	5d multi	.40	.40

Europa, 2000
Common Design Type

2000, May 9		Perf. 14		
187	CD17	30d multi	3.00	3.00

2000 Summer Olympics, Sydney — A102

Designs: 5d, Runners. 30d, Wrestlers.

2000, May 17		Perf. 13¼		
188-189	A102	Set of 2	2.40	2.40

Ecology — A103

2000, June 5	Litho.	Perf. 13¼		
190	A103	5d multi	.60	.60

Architecture Type of 1998

2000, July 28				
191	A63a	6d House, Zdunje	.65	.65

Printing Pioneers — A104

Designs: 6d, Theodosius Sinaitski. 30d, Johannes Gutenberg.

2000, July 28				
192-193	A104	Set of 2	2.25	2.25

Mother Teresa (1910-97) — A105

2000, Aug. 26				
194	A105	6d multi	.65	.65

Birds — A106

Designs: 6d, Egretta garzeta. 10d, Ardea cinerea. 20d, Ardea purpurea. 30d, Plegadis falcinellus.

2000, Sept. 14				
195-198	A106	Set of 4	4.00	4.00

Children's Week — A107

2000, Oct. 2		Perf. 13¼		
199	A107	6d multi	.55	.55

Duke Dimo Hadi Dimov (1875-1924) — A108

2000, Oct. 20				
200	A108	6d multi	.55	.55

Economics Faculty of Sts. Cyril & Methodius Univ., 50th Anniv. — A109

2000, Nov. 1				
201	A109	6d multi	.55	.55

Joachim Krchovski, 250th Anniv. of Birth — A110

2000, Nov. 8				
202	A110	6d multi	.90	.90

Christmas A111

2000, Nov. 22				
203	A111	30d multi	1.75	1.75

UN High Commissioner For Refugees, 50th Anniv. — A112

Designs: 6d, Handprints. 30d, Globe, hands.

2001, Jan. 10	Litho.	Perf. 13¼		
204-205	A112	Set of 2	2.10	2.10

Worldwide Fund for Nature (WWF) — A113

Imperial eagle: a, 6d, Facing right. b, 8d, With chick. c, 10d, In flight, and close-up of head. d, 30d, Close-up of head.

2001, Feb. 1	Litho.	Perf. 14		
206	A113	Block of 4, #a-d	3.25	3.25

Partenija Zografski (1818-1876) A114

2001, Feb. 6	Litho.	Perf. 13¼		
207	A114	6d multi	.50	.50

Native Costumes — A115

Designs: 6d, Dolmi Polog. 12d, Albanian. 18d, Reka. 30d, Skopska Crna Gora. 50d, Women, men in costumes, house, vegetables.

2001, Mar. 1		Perf. 13¼		
208-211	A115	Set of 4	3.75	3.75
		Souvenir Sheet		
		Imperf		
		Granite Paper		
212	A116	50d multi	3.00	3.00

Lazar Licenoski (1901-64), Painter — A117

2001, Mar. 23		Perf. 13¼		
213	A117	6d multi	.55	.55

National Archives, 50th Anniv. — A118

2001, Apr. 1				
214	A118	6d multi	.50	.50

Easter — A119

2001, Apr. 15				
215	A119	6d multi	.55	.55

Europa A120

No. 216, Boat on lake: a, 10d. b, 30d.

2001, May 16		Granite Paper		
216	A120	Horiz. pair, #a-b	3.00	3.00

Revolt Against Ottoman Rule, 125th Anniv. — A121

2001, May 20	Litho.	Perf. 13¼		
217	A121	6d multi	.55	.55

2nd Individual European Chess Championships A122

2001, June 1	Litho.	Perf. 13¼		
218	A122	36d multi	2.25	2.25
a.		Booklet pane of 4	13.00	
		Booklet, #218a	13.00	

Booklet sold for 145d.

Boats in Lake Dojran — A123

2001, June 5	Litho.	Perf. 13¼		
219	A123	6d multi	.55	.55

MACEDONIA

Architecture Type of 1998
Perf. 13¼
2001, June 25 Litho. Unwmk.
220 A63a 6d House, Mitrasinci .55 .55

Independence, 10th Anniv. — A124
2001, Sept. 8 Wmk. 387
221 A124 6d multi .55 .55

Trees — A125
Designs: 6d, Juniperus excelsa. 12d, Quercus macedonica. 24d, Arbutus andrachne. 36d, Quercus coccifera.
Perf. 13¼
2001, Sept. 12 Litho. Unwmk.
222-225 A125 Set of 4 4.50 4.50

Children's Day — A126
Perf. 13¼
2001, Oct. 1 Litho. Unwmk.
226 A126 6d multi .55 .55

Year of Dialogue Among Civilizations — A127
2001, Oct. 9 Granite Paper
227 A127 36d multi 2.10 2.10

Nature Museum, 75th Anniv. — A128
2001, Oct. 26
228 A128 6d multi .60 .60

Christmas — A129
2001, Nov. 22
229 A129 6d multi .55 .55

Nobel Prizes, Cent. — A130
2001, Dec. 10 Litho. *Perf. 13¼*
230 A130 36d multi 2.25 2.25

2002 Winter Olympics, Salt Lake City — A131
Designs: 6d, Skier. 36d, Skier, diff.
2002, Jan. 16 Litho. Perf. 14
231-232 A131 Set of 2 2.25 2.25

Ancient Coins — A132
Designs: 6d, King Lykkeios of Paeonia obol, 359-340 B.C. 12d, Alexander III tetradrachm. 24d, Kings of Macedon tetrobol, 185-165 B.C. 36d, Philip II of Macedon gold stater. 50d, Kings of Macedon coin.
2002, Mar. 1
233-236 A132 Set of 4 5.00 5.00
Souvenir Sheet
237 A132 50d multi 4.00 4.00

Petar Mazev (1927-93), Painter — A133
2002, Apr. 15
238 A133 6d multi .60 .60

Dimitar Kondovski (1927-93), Painter — A134
2002, Apr. 15
239 A134 6d multi .60 .60

Leonardo da Vinci (1452-1519) and Mona Lisa — A135
2002, Apr. 15
240 A135 36d multi 2.10 2.10

Easter — A136
2002, Apr. 24
241 A136 6d multi .60 .60

Europa — A137
Designs: 6d, Acrobat, bicycle on wire, seal. 36d, Ball on wire, bicycle.
2002, May 9
242-243 A137 Set of 2 3.00 3.00

2002 World Cup Soccer Championships, Japan and Korea — A138
2002, May 15
244 A138 6d multi 2.25 2.25

Environmental Protection A139
2002, June 5
245 A139 6d multi .55 .55

National Arms — A140
Background colors: 10d, Blue. 36d, Greenish blue.
2002, June 18
246-247 A140 Set of 2 2.75 2.75

Architecture A141
Buildings in: 36d, Krushevo. 50d, Bitola.
2002, June 26 *Perf. 13¼*
248-249 A141 Set of 2 4.50 4.50

A142
Designs: 6d, Metodija Andonov Cento (1902-57), 1st President of Antifascist Council for the Natl. Liberation of Macedonia.
2002, Aug. 18 Litho. *Perf. 13¼*
250 A142 6d multi .55 .55

Nikola Karev (1877-1905), President of Krushevo Republic, Aug. 1903 — A143
2002, Aug. 18
251 A143 18d multi 1.10 1.10

Fauna A144
No. 252: a, 6d, Perdix perdix. b, 12d, Sus scrofa. c, 24d, Rupicapra rupicapra. d, 36d, Alectoris graeca.
2002, Sept. 11 *Perf. 14*
252 A144 Block of 4, #a-d 4.50 4.50

Children's Day — A145
2002, Oct. 1
253 A145 6d multi .60 .60

Architecture Type of 1998
2002, Nov. 5 *Perf. 13¼*
254 A63a 3d House, Jachince .30 .30
255 A63a 9d House, Ratevo .55 .55

Christmas — A146
2002, Nov. 20
256 A146 9d multi .60 .60

Andreja Damjanov (1813-78), Builder of Churches — A147
2003, Jan. 21
257 A147 36d multi 2.00 2.00

Musical Instruments — A148
Designs: 9d, Gajda. 10d, Tambura. 20d, Kemene. 50d, Tapan.
2003, Feb. 19 Litho. *Perf. 13¼*
258-261 A148 Set of 4 5.50 5.50

Scouting In Macedonia, 50th Anniv. — A149
2003, Feb. 22
262 A149 9d multi .75 .75

Krste Petkov Misirkov Macedonian Language Institute, 50th Anniv. — A150
2003, Mar. 5
263 A150 9d multi .65 .65

Europa — A151
Poster art: No. 264, 36d, 1966 poster. No. 265, 36d, 1994 Intl. Triennial of Graphic Art poster.
2003, May 9 *Perf. 13¼x13½*
Granite Paper
264-265 A151 Set of 2 4.00 3.00

MACEDONIA

Ursus Arctos — A152

2003, June 5 — Perf. 13½x13¼
266 A152 9d multi .80 .80

Building, Skopje — A153

Building, Resen — A154

2003, June 16
267 A153 10d multi .60 .60
268 A154 20d multi 1.10 1.10

Macedonian Arms — A155

Designs: 9d, Latin lettering. 36d, Cyrillic lettering.

2003, June 23 — Perf. 13¼x13½
269-270 A155 Set of 2 3.00 3.00

World Youth Handball Championships A156

2003, July 30
271 A156 36d multi 2.25 2.25
Printed in sheets of 8 + label.

Ilinden Uprising, Cent. — A157

Uprising participants and: 9d, Seal. 36d, Memorial. 50d, Seal, diff.

2003, Aug. 2 — Perf. 13½x13¼
272-273 A157 Set of 2 2.60 2.60

Souvenir Sheet
274 A157 50d multi + label 2.75 2.75

Paintings — A158

Paintings by: 9d, Nikola Martinovski (1903-73). 36d, Vincent van Gogh (1853-90), horiz.

Perf. 13½x13¼, 13¼x13½
2003, Aug. 18
275-276 A158 Set of 2 2.50 2.50

Flowers — A159

Designs: 9d, Colchicum macedonicum. 20d, Viola allchariensis. 36d, Tulipa mariannae. 50d, Thymus oehmianus.

Perf. 13¼x13½
2003, Sept. 25 Litho.
277-280 A159 Set of 4 6.25 6.25

Writers — A160

Designs: No. 281, 9d, Jeronim de Rada (1814-1903). No. 282, 9d, Said Najdeni (1864-1903).

2003, Sept. 30 Perf. 13½x13¼
281-282 A160 Set of 2 1.10 1.10

Children's Day — A161

2003, Oct. 6 Perf. 13¼x13½
283 A161 9d multi .70 .70

Kresnensko Uprising, 125th Anniv. — A162

2003, Oct. 17 Perf. 13½x13¼
284 A162 9d multi .65 .65

Dimitar Vlahov (1878-1953), Politician — A163

2003, Nov. 8 Litho. Perf. 13½x13¼
285 A163 9d multi .65 .65

Christmas — A164

2003, Nov. 19
286 A164 9d multi .65 .65

Handicrafts — A165

Designs: 5d, Tassels. 9d, Pitcher. 10d, Kettle. 20d, Ornament.

2003-04 Litho. Perf. 13¼x13½
287 A165 3d multi .30 .30
288 A165 5d multi .35 .35
289 A165 9d multi .55 .55
290 A165 10d multi .65 .65
291 A165 12d multi .75 .75
292 A165 20d multi 1.25 1.25
Nos. 287-292 (6) 3.85 3.85
Issued: 9d, 12/16; 10d, 1/21/04; 5d, 20d, 6/4/04; 3d, 12d, 6/4/04.

Powered Flight, Cent. — A166

Perf. 13½x13¼
2003, Dec. 17 Litho.
293 A166 50d multi 2.40 2.40

Paintings Type of 2003

Designs: No. 294, 9d, Street and Buildings, by Tomo Vladimirski (1904-71), vert. No. 295, 9d, Street Scene, by Vangel Kodzoman (1904-94).

Perf. 13½x13¼, 13¼x13½
2004, Feb. 14
294-295 A158 Set of 2 1.25 1.25

Decorated Weapons — A167

Designs: 10d, Sword, 1806. 20d, Saber, 19th cent. 36d, Gun, 18th cent. 50d, Rifle, 18th cent.

2004, Mar. 10 Perf. 13¼x13½
Stamps + Labels
296-299 A167 Set of 4 6.50 6.50

Rugs — A168

Various rugs: 36d, 50d.

2004, Mar. 24
300-301 A168 Set of 2 5.00 5.00

Konstandin Kristoforidhi, Publisher of First Albanian Dictionary in Macedonia — A169

2004, Apr. 19
302 A169 36d multi 2.00 2.00

House, Kratovo — A170

2004, Apr. 23 Perf. 13½x13¼
303 A170 20d multi 1.40 1.40

Macedonian Intention to Enter European Union — A171

2004, May 4
304 A171 36d multi 2.10 2.10

Europa — A172

No. 305 — People at beach: a, Denomination at left. b, Denomination at right.

Perf. 13¼x13½
2004, May 7 Wmk. 387
305 A172 50d Horiz. pair, #a-b 4.00 4.00

Prespa Ecopark — A173

Perf. 13¼x13½
2004, June 5 Litho. Unwmk.
306 A173 36d multi 2.10 2.10

2004 Summer Olympics, Athens — A174

No. 307 — Map of Europe, Olympic rings with flags and 2004 Summer Olympics emblem at: a, Left. b, Right.

Perf. 13½x13¼
2004, June 16 Wmk. 387
307 A174 50d Horiz. pair, #a-b 4.50 4.50

Sami Frasheri (1850-1904), Writer — A175

Perf. 13½x13¼
2004, June 18 Litho. Unwmk.
308 A175 12d multi .85 .85

FIFA (Fédération Internationale de Football Association), Cent. — A176

2004, July 3
309 A176 100d multi 5.50 5.50

Marko Cepenkov (1829-1920), Writer — A177

2004, Sept. 1
310 A177 12d multi .85 .85

Vasil Glavinov (1869-1929), Politician — A178

2004, Sept. 1 Perf. 13¼x13½
311 A178 12d multi .85 .85

Birds — A179

Designs: 12d, Bombycilla garrulus. 24d, Lanius senator. 36d, Monticola saxatilis. 48d, Pyrrhula pyrrhula. 60d, Tichodroma muraria.

MACEDONIA

Perf. 13¼x13½
2004, Sept. 25 **Litho.**
312-315 A179 Set of 4   7.00 7.00
Souvenir Sheet
Imperf.
316 A179 60d multi   3.75 3.75
No. 316 contains one 27x36mm stamp.

Children's Day — A180

2004, Oct. 4 **Litho.** **Perf. 13½x13¼**
317 A180 12d multi   .90 .90

Information Technology Society Summit — A181

2004, Oct. 16
318 A181 36d multi   2.00 2.00

Aseman Gospel, 1000th Anniv. — A182

2004, Oct. 27 **Litho.** **Perf. 13½x13¼**
319 A182 12d multi   .90 .90

Marco Polo (1254-1324), Explorer — A183

2004, Nov. 10
320 A183 36d multi   2.00 2.00

Christmas — A184

2004, Nov. 24 **Perf. 13¼x13½**
321 A184 12d multi   .90 .90

Konstantin Miladinov (1830-62), Poet — A185

2005, Feb. 4 **Perf. 13½x13¼**
322 A185 36d multi   2.10 2.10

Illuminated Manuscripts — A186

Designs: 12d, Manuscript from 16th-17th cent. 24d, Manuscript from 16th cent.

2005, Mar. 9 **Perf. 13¼x13½**
323-324 A186 Set of 2   2.25 2.25

A187

Embroidery A188

2005, Mar. 23 **Perf. 13½x13¼**
325 A187 36d multi   2.25 2.25
326 A188 50d multi   2.75 2.75

Art — A189

Designs: 36d, Sculpture by Ivan Mestrovic. 50d, Painting by Paja Jovanovic, horiz.

Perf. 13½x13¼, 13¼x13½
2005, Apr. 6
327-328 A189 Set of 2   5.00 5.00

First Book in Albanian Language, 450th Anniv. — A190

2005, Apr. 27 **Perf. 13¼x13½**
329 A190 12d multi   .90 .90

Skanderbeg (1405-68), Albanian National Hero — A191

2005, Apr. 27
330 A191 36d multi   2.25 2.25

Europa A192

Designs: a, 36d, Wheat, bread. b, 60d, Peppers, plate of food.

2005, May 9 **Perf. 13½x13¼**
331 A192 Horiz. pair, #a-b   5.75 5.75

Vlachs' Day, Cent. — A193

2005, Apr. 27 **Litho.** **Perf. 13½x13¼**
332 A193 12d multi   .85 .85

Environmental Protection — A194

2005, June 4 **Perf. 13¼x13½**
333 A194 36d multi   2.40 2.40

Friezes — A195

Frieze from: 3d, 16th cent. 4d, 15th cent. 6d, 16th cent., diff. 8d, 1883-84. 12d, 16th cent., diff.

2005, June 8 **Litho.** **Perf. 13¼x13½**
334-338 A195 Set of 5   2.10 2.10

First Automobile in Macedonia, Cent. — A196

First Glider in Macedonia, 50th Anniv. — A197

Perf. 13½x13¼
2005, June 15 **Litho.**
339 A196 12d multi   .75 .75
340 A197 36d multi   2.25 2.25

Intl. Year of Physics — A198

2005, June 30
341 A198 60d multi   3.00 3.00

Fruit — A199

Designs: 12d, Malus Miller (apples). 24d, Prunus persica (peaches). 36d, Prunus avium (cherries). 48d, Prunus sp. (plums). 100d, Pyrus sp. (pears), vert.

2005, Sept. 14 **Litho.** **Wmk. 387**
342-345 A199 Set of 4   7.25 7.25
Souvenir Sheet
Perf. 13¼x13½
346 A199 100d multi   6.25 6.25

Smolar Waterfall — A200

Perf. 13¼x13½
2005, Sept. 28 **Unwmk.**
347 A200 24d multi   1.60 1.60

Hans Christian Andersen (1805-75), Author — A201

2005, Oct. 3 **Litho.** **Perf. 13½x13¼**
348 A201 12d multi   1.35 1.35

Kozjak Dam — A202

2005, Oct. 25
349 A202 12d multi   .85 .85

Brsjac Rebellion, 125th Anniv. — A203

2005, Oct. 28
350 A203 12d multi   .85 .85

Rila Congress, Cent. — A204

2005, Oct. 28 **Perf. 13¼x13½**
351 A204 12d multi   .85 .85

Europa Stamps, 50th Anniv. (in 2006) A205

Emblems and Europa stamps: Nos. 352a, 353a, 60d, #243. Nos. 352b, 353b, 170d, #158. Nos. 352c, 353c, 250d, #97. Nos. 352d, 353d, 350d, #76.

2005, Nov. 14 **Perf. 13½x13¼**
352 A205 Block of 4, #a-d   50.00 50.00
Souvenir Sheet
353 A205 Sheet of 4, #a-d   50.00 50.00
Stamp sizes: Nos. 352a-352d, 40x30mm; Nos. 353a-353d, 40x29mm.

Whitewater Kayaker — A206

2005, Nov. 23
354 A206 36d multi   2.00 2.00

Christmas — A207

2005, Nov. 23 **Perf. 13¼x13½**
355 A207 12d multi   .90 .90

Macedonia Post Emblem — A208

Perf. 13¼x13½
2005, Dec. 14 **Litho.**
356 A208 12d multi   .85 .85

2006 Winter Olympics, Turin — A209

Designs: 36d, Skiing. 60d, Ice hockey.

2006, Jan. 26
357-358 A209 Set of 2   5.75 5.75

MACEDONIA

Fresco and Matejce Monastery — A210

Isaac Celebi Mosque — A211

2006, Mar. 8
| 359 | A210 | 12d multi | .60 | .60 |
| 360 | A211 | 24d multi | 1.50 | 1.50 |

Léopold Sédar Senghor (1906-2001), First President of Senegal — A212

2006, Mar. 20   *Perf. 13½x13¼*
361   A212   36d multi   2.10   2.10

Handicrafts With Inlaid Mother-of-Pearl — A213

Designs: 12d, Wooden shoes. 24d, Decorative objects.

2006, Mar. 22   *Perf. 13¼x13½*
362-363   A213   Set of 2   2.10   2.10

Wood Carving by Makarie Negriev Frckovski — A214

Cupola of St. Peter's Basilica, Vatican City, 450th Anniv. — A215

2006, Apr. 5   *Perf. 13½x13¼*
| 364 | A214 | 12d multi | .60 | .60 |
| 365 | A215 | 36d multi | 1.90 | 1.90 |

Zivko Firfov (1906-84), Composer — A216

2006, Apr. 26   *Perf. 13¼x13½*
366   A216   24d multi   1.40   1.40

Wolfgang Amadeus Mozart (1756-91), Composer — A217

2006, Apr. 26
367   A217   60d multi   3.75   3.75

Europa — A218

Designs: 36d, Lettered balls. 60d, Lettered blocks.

2006, May 9   *Perf. 13½x13¼*
368-369   A218   Set of 2   5.25   5.25

Souvenir Sheet

Macedonian Europa Stamps, 10th Anniv. — A219

No. 370: a, Pope John Paul II (1920-2005). b, Mother Teresa (1910-97).

2006, May 9   *Perf. 13¼x13½*
370   A219   60d Sheet of 2, #a-b   5.00   5.00

Fight Against Desertification — A220

2006, June 5   *Litho.*   *Perf. 13½x13¼*
371   A220   12d multi   .90   .90

Grand Prix Racing, Cent. — A221

2006, June 14   *Litho.*
372   A221   36d multi   2.10   2.10

Nikola Tesla (1856-1943), Electrical Engineer — A222

2006, June 28   *Litho.*
373   A222   24d multi   1.75   1.75

Christopher Columbus (1451-1506), Explorer — A223

2006, June 28
374   A223   36d multi   1.50   1.50

Containers — A224

2006, Aug. 30   *Litho.*   *Perf. 12¾x13*
| 375 | A224 | 3d Carafe | .30 | .30 |
| 376 | A224 | 6d Pitcher, bowl | .50 | .50 |

Shells — A225

Designs: 12d, Ancylus scalariformis. 24d, Macedopyrgula pavlovici. 36d, Gyraulus trapezoides. 48d, Valvata hirsutecostata. 72d, Ochridopyrgula macedonica.

2006, Sept. 6   *Litho.*   *Perf. 13¼x13½*
377-380   A225   Set of 4   7.25   7.25

Souvenir Sheet
381   A225   72d multi   4.25   4.25

UNICEF, 60th Anniv. — A226

2006, Oct. 2   *Perf. 13½x13¼*
382   A226   12d multi   .85   .85

Lynx and Galicica Natl. Park — A227

2006, Oct. 2
383   A227   24d multi   1.50   1.50

World Senior Men's and Women's Bowling Championships — A228

2006, Oct. 20
384   A228   36d multi   2.00   2.00

Bishop Frang Bardhi (1606-43) — A229

Pres. Boris Trajkovski (1956-2004) — A230

Kemal Ataturk (1881-1938), Turkish Statesman — A231

Archbishop Dositheus, 100th Anniv. of Birth — A232

2006, Oct. 25   *Perf. 13¼x13½*
385	A229	12d multi	.60	.60
386	A230	12d multi	.60	.60
387	A231	24d multi	1.40	1.40
388	A232	24d multi	1.40	1.40
		Nos. 385-388 (4)	4.00	4.00

Christmas — A233

2006, Nov. 22   *Perf. 13½x13¼*
389   A233   12d multi   .85   .85

Metal Objects — A234

Designs: 4d, Handled container, Bitola, 19th cent. 5d, Wine flask, Skopje, 20th cent., vert. 10d, Bell, Skopje, 18th cent., vert. 12d, Lidded container, Prilep, 18th-19th cent., vert.

Perf. 13x12¾, 12¾x13
2006, Nov. 30
390	A234	4d multi	.30	.30
391	A234	5d multi	.30	.30
392	A234	10d multi	.65	.65
393	A234	12d multi	.80	.80
		Nos. 390-393 (4)	2.05	2.05

Kokino Megalithic Observatory — A235

Designs: 12d, Mold for amulet. 36d, Sunrise over observatory.

2007, Jan. 31   *Perf. 13¼x13½*
394-395   A235   Set of 2   2.50   2.50

Nos. 394-395 each were printed in sheets of 8 + label.

Monastery Anniversaries — A236

Designs: 12d, Slivnica Monastery, 400th anniv. 36d, St. Nikita Monastery, 700th anniv., vert.

Perf. 13½x13¼, 13¼x13½
2007, Jan. 31
396-397   A236   Set of 2   2.75   2.75

Handicrafts — A237

Designs: 12d, Tepelak, Kicevo, 18th-19th cent. 36d, Casket, Ohrid, 19th cent.

2007, Feb. 14   *Perf. 13½x13¼*
398-399   A237   Set of 2   2.50   2.50

Fish — A238

Designs: 12d, Cobitis vardarensis. 36d, Zingel balcanicus. 60d, Chondrostoma vardarense. No. 403, 100d, Barbus macedonicus.
No. 404, 100d, Leuciscus cephalus.

2007, Feb. 28
400-403   A238   Set of 4   10.00   10.00

Souvenir Sheet
404   A238   100d multi   5.00   5.00

Epos of Freedom, Mosaic by Borko Lazeski — A239

Head of a Woman, by Pablo Picasso — A240

2007, Mar. 14   *Perf. 13½x13¼*
405   A239   36d multi   2.00   2.00

Perf. 13¼x13½
406   A240   100d multi   6.00   6.00

Cubism, cent.

MACEDONIA

Intl. Francophone Day — A241

2007, Mar. 20   *Perf. 13½x13¼*
407 A241 12d multi   .70 .70

Cat — A242

2007, Apr. 9   *Perf. 13¼x13½*
408 A242 12d multi   .75 .75

Europa — A243

Macedonian Scouting emblem and: 60d, Scout camp. 100d, Scout, tent, vert.

Perf. 13½x13¼, 13¼x13½
2007, May 9   Litho.
409-410 A243 Set of 2   8.75 8.75

Souvenir Sheet

Europa — A243a

2007, May 9   Litho.   *Perf. 13½x13¼*
411 A243a 160d multi   37.50 37.50
Scouting, cent.

Discovery of St. Cyril's Grave, 150th Anniv. — A244

2007, May 23   *Perf. 13¼x13½*
412 A244 50d multi   2.50 2.50

Smokestacks and Clock — A245

2007, June 5   Litho.   *Perf. 13¼x13½*
413 A245 12d multi   .85 .85

Carl von Linné (1707-78), Botanist A246

Notes of Dmitri Mendeleev (1834-1907), Chemist A247

2007, June 20   *Perf. 13¼x13½*
414 A246 36d multi   1.90 1.90
   Perf. 13½x13¼
415 A247 36d multi   1.90 1.90

Euro-Atlantic Partnership Council Security Forum, Ohrid — A248

2007, June 28   *Perf. 13½x13¼*
416 A248 60d multi   2.75 2.75

Intl. Sailing Federation, Cent. — A249

2007, July 31   Litho.   *Perf. 13½x13¼*
417 A249 35d multi   2.00 2.00

Maminska River Waterfall — A250

Perf. 13¼x13½
2007, Sept. 19   Litho.
418 A250 12d multi   .85 .85

Mitrush Kuteli (1907-67), Writer A251

Fan S. Noli (1882-1965), Albanian Prime Minister A252

2007, Sept. 25
419 A251 12d multi   .80 .80
420 A252 12d multi   .80 .80

Children's Day — A253

2007, Oct. 1   Litho.   *Perf. 13½x13¼*
421 A253 12d multi   .80 .80

Launch of Sputnik 1, 50th Anniv. — A254

2007, Oct. 4   Litho.   *Perf. 13½x13¼*
422 A254 36d multi   2.00 2.00

Petre Prlicko (1905-95), Actor — A255

2007, Oct. 31   Litho.   *Perf. 13½x13¼*
423 A255 12d multi   .80 .80

Jordan Hadzi Konstantinov-Dzinot (1821-82), Educator — A256

2007, Oct. 31
424 A256 12d multi   .80 .80

Handbag — A257

2007, Nov. 9   Litho.   *Perf. 12¾x13*
425 A257 12d multi   .80 .80

Christmas A258

Perf. 13½x13¼
2007, Nov. 21   Litho.
426 A258 12d multi   .80 .80

Tose Proeski (1981-2007), Singer — A259

2007, Dec. 15   *Perf. 13¼x13½*
427 A259 12d multi   .80 .80

Earrings — A260

Designs: 12d, Earrings with pigeon design, 2nd cent. B.C. 24d, Earring with lion design, 4th cent. B.C., vert.

Perf. 13½x13¼, 13¼x13½
2008, Jan. 23   Litho.
428-429 A260 Set of 2   2.50 2.50

Launch of Explorer 1 Satellite, 50th Anniv. — A261

2008, Jan. 31   Litho.   *Perf. 13¼x13½*
430 A261 24d multi   1.60 1.60

High-speed Train — A262

2008, Feb. 27   *Perf. 13½x13¼*
431 A262 100d multi   6.50 6.50

Worldwide Fund for Nature (WWF) — A263

No. 432 — Upupa epops: a, 12d, In flight. b, 24d, Head. c, 48d, On branch, facing left with insect in beak. d, 60d, On branch, facing right.

Perf. 13½x13¼
2008, Mar. 28   Litho.
432 A263 Block of 4, #a-d   7.00 7.00

Bulldog — A264

2008, Apr. 16   Litho.   *Perf. 13¼x13½*
433 A264 30d multi   2.00 2.00

Europa A265

No. 434 — Envelopes over: a, 50d, Western Hemisphere, dark blue panel at top, country name in yellow. b, 100d, Asia, Eastern Europe and Africa, dark blue panel at top, country name in pink.
No. 435, 50d: a, As No. 434a, green panel at top. b, As No. 434b, green panel at top. c, As No. 434a, blue panel at top, country name in orange. d, As No. 434b, blue panel at top, country name in orange.

2008, May 7   Litho.   *Perf. 13½x13¼*
434 A265 Horiz. pair, #a-b   10.00 10.00
Miniature Sheet
435 A265 50d Sheet of 4, #a-d   20.00 20.00

No. 435 was sold with, but not attached to, a booklet cover.

Robert Schuman, Macedonian and European Union Flags — A266

Macedonian and European Union Flags, Eiffel Tower, Paris — A267

Macedonian and European Union Flags, Ljubljana, Slovenia — A268

Perf. 13¼x13½, 13½x13¼
2008, May 22
436 A266 36d multi   2.10 2.10
437 A267 50d multi   3.00 3.00
438 A268 50d multi   3.00 3.00
Nos. 436-438 (3)   8.10 8.10

Environmental Protection A269

2008, June 5   Litho.   *Perf. 13½x13¼*
439 A269 12d multi   .80 .80

Rudolf Diesel (1858-1918), Inventor — A270

2008, June 18   *Perf. 13¼x13½*
440 A270 30d multi   2.00 2.00

MACEDONIA

2008 Summer Olympics, Beijing — A271

Designs: 12d, Sailing. 18d, Rhythmic gymnastics. 20d, Tennis. 36d, Equestrian.

Perf. 13½x13¼
2008, June 25 Litho.
441-444 A271 Set of 4 5.50 5.50

Eqrem Cabej (1908-80), Linguist — A272

2008, Aug. 6 Litho. **Perf. 13½x13¼**
445 A272 12d multi .80 .80

14th Intl. Congress of Slavists, Ohrid — A273

2008, Sept. 10
446 A273 12d multi .80 .80

Flowers — A274

Designs: 1d, Helichrysum zivojinii. 12d, Pulsatilla halleri, horiz. 50d, Stachys iva, horiz. No. 450, 72d, Fritillaria macedonica. No. 451, 72d, Centaurea grbavacensis.

Perf. 13¼x13½, 13½x13¼
2008, Sept. 10
447-450 A274 Set of 4 6.50 6.50
Souvenir Sheet
451 A274 72d multi 3.75 3.75

Matka Cave — A275

2008, Sept. 24 **Perf. 13½x13¼**
452 A275 12d multi .80 .80

Children's Day — A276

2008, Oct. 6
453 A276 12d multi .80 .80

European Women's Handball Championships A277

2008, Oct. 15
454 A277 30d multi 1.60 1.60

Religious Song Lyrics by St. John Kukuzel (c. 1280-1360) — A278

2008, Oct. 22 Litho. **Perf. 13¼x13½**
455 A278 12d multi .80 .80

Giacomo Puccini (1858-1924), Opera Composer A279

2008, Oct. 22 **Perf. 13½x13¼**
456 A279 100d multi 5.25 5.25

Kosta Racin (1908-43), Poet — A280

2008, Nov. 5 **Perf. 13¼x13½**
457 A280 12d multi .80 .80

Albanian Language, Cent. — A281

Perf. 13¼x13½
2008, Nov. 14 Litho.
458 A281 12d multi .80 .80

Christmas A282

Perf. 13½x13¼
2008, Nov. 19 Litho.
459 A282 12d multi .70 .70

Cities A283 A284

Designs: No. 460, Bitola. No. 461, Ohrid. No. 462, Tetovo. No. 463, Skople. No. 464, Stip.

2008, Dec. 4 Litho. **Perf. 12¾x13**
Denomination Color
460 A283 12d blue .75 .75
461 A283 12d black .75 .75
462 A283 12d red .75 .75
463 A284 12d gray blue .75 .75
464 A284 12d gray green .75 .75
Nos. 460-464 (5) 3.75 3.75

See Nos. 484-485, 499, 500.

Lech Walesa and Solidarity Emblem — A285

2008, Dec. 8 **Perf. 13¼x13½**
465 A285 50d multi 3.00 3.00

Friendship between Macedonia and Poland. Printed in sheets of 8 + label.

Blacksmithing — A286

Designs: 10d, Blacksmiths and anvil. 20d, Horseshoe.

2009, Jan. 21
466-467 A286 Set of 2 1.90 1.90

Yuri Gagarin (1934-68). First Man in Space — A287

2009, Feb. 4 **Perf. 13½x13¼**
468 A287 50d multi 2.75 2.75

Printed in sheets of 8 + label.

Campaign Against Breast Cancer — A288

2009, Mar. 2 **Perf. 13¼x13½**
469 A288 15d multi .85 .85

Composers A289

Designs: 12d, Trajko Prokopiev (1909-79) and Todor Skalovski (1909-2004). 60d, George Friedrich Handel (1685-1759) and Joseph Haydn (1732-1809).

2009, Mar. 18 **Perf. 13½x13¼**
470-471 A289 Set of 2 3.50 3.50

No. 471 was printed in sheets of 8 + label.

Horses — A291

A290

2009, Apr. 15 Litho. **Perf. 13¼x13½**
Granite Paper
472 A290 20d multi 1.00 1.00
473 A291 50d multi 2.50 2.50

Europa — A292

Design: 50d, Hen, chicks, wolf, sheep, Pleiades and Venus. 100d, Cowherd, cows and Orion. 150d, Rooster and Moon, vert.

2009, May 6 Litho. **Perf. 13½x13¼**
474 A292 50d multi 3.75 3.75
475 A292 100d multi 7.00 7.00
Souvenir Sheet
Perf. 13x13½
476 A292 150d multi 19.00 19.00

Intl. Year of Astronomy.

Prague, Flags of Czech Republic and Macedonia A293

Pippi Longstocking, Flag of Macedonia A294

2009, May 9 Litho. **Perf. 13½x13¼**
477 A293 10d multi .55 .55
Perf. 13¼x13½
478 A294 60d multi 3.50 3.50

Macedonia in the European Union. No. 478 was printed in sheets of 8 + label.

Vrelo Cave — A295

2009, June 5 **Perf. 13½x13¼**
479 A295 12d multi .85 .85

Louis Braille (1809-52), Educator of the Blind — A296

Perf. 13½x13¼
2009, June 17 Litho.
480 A296 18d multi 1.00 1.00

Charles Darwin (1809-82), Naturalist — A297

2009, June 17
481 A297 18d multi 1.10 1.10

Boat and Compass Rose — A298

Boat's Bow — A299

2009, June 24 **Perf. 13½x13¼**
482 A298 18d multi 1.00 1.00
Perf. 13¼x13½
483 A299 18d multi 1.00 1.00

Cities Type of 2008

Designs: 16d, Strumica. 18d, Prilep.

MACEDONIA

2009		Perf. 12¾x13
	Denomination	Color
484 A283	16d brown	.90 .90
485 A283	18d blue	1.10 1.10

Issued: 16d, 8/7; 18d, 7/27.

Organized Soccer in Macedonia, Cent. — A300

2009, Aug. 12 — Perf. 13¼x13½
486 A300 18d multi — 1.10 1.10

Cyclist A301

Bicycle Pedal A302

2009, Sept. 2 Litho. Perf. 13¼x13½
487 A301 18d multi — 1.00 1.00
Perf. 13½x13¼
488 A302 18d multi — 1.00 1.00

Giro d'Italia bicycle race, cent.

Fauna — A303

Dr. Stankos Karaman (1889-1959), Zoologist, and Crustaceans — A304

Designs: 2d, Pelobates syriacus balcanicus. 3d, Salmo letnica. 6d, Austropotamobius torrentium macedonicus. 8d, Triturus macedonicus.

2009, Sept. 9 Litho. Perf. 13½x13¼
489-492 A303 Set of 4 — 1.40 1.40
Souvenir Sheet
Perf. 13¼x13½
493 A304 100d multi — 5.00 5.00

Dimitar Andonov Papradishki (1859-1954), Painter — A305

2009, Sept. 30 Perf. 13½x13¼
494 A305 16d multi — .95 .95

Elbasan Normal School and Pedagogical High School, 150th Anniv. — A306

2009, Oct. 14 Perf. 13¼x13½
495 A306 16d multi — .95 .95

Filip Shiroka (1859-1935), Poet A307

Krume Kepeski (1909-88), Linguist A308

Petre M. Andreevski (1934-2006), Writer — A309

2009, Nov. 4 Litho. Perf. 13¼x13½
496 A307 16d multi — .85 .85
497 A308 16d multi — .85 .85
Perf. 13½x13¼
498 A309 16d multi — .85 .85
Nos. 496-498 (3) — 2.55 2.55

Cities Type of 2008 and

Struga — A309a

Delchevo — A309b

Kumanovo — A309c

Resen — A309d

Designs: No. 499, Gostivar. No. 500, Kichevo.

2009, Nov. 11 Litho. Perf. 12¾x13
	Denomination	Color
499 A283	16d gray blue	.80 .80
500 A283	16d Prus blue	.80 .80
501 A309a	16d brown	.80 .80
502 A309b	16d brown	.80 .80
503 A309c	18d brown	.80 .80
504 A309d	18d black	.80 .80

Nos. 499-504 (6) — 4.80 4.80

Christmas — A310

Perf. 13¼x13½
2009, Nov. 18 Litho.
505 A310 16d multi — .85 .85

Helicopter A311

2010, Feb. 10 Perf. 13½x13¼
506 A311 50d multi — 2.75 2.75

2010 Winter Olympics, Vancouver — A312

Olympic rings, Vancouver Olympics emblem, inukshuk and: 50d, Ski jumper. 100d, Ice hockey goalie.

2010, Feb. 12 Perf. 13¼x13½
507-508 A312 Set of 2 — 6.00 6.00

Nos. 507-508 each were printed in sheets of 8 + label.

Souvenir Sheet

International Women's Day — A313

No. 509 — Flower with denomination in: a, UL. b, UR.

2010, Mar. 8
509 A313 18d Sheet of 2, #a-b — 2.00 2.00

St. Peter's Church, Golem Grad Island, 650th Anniv. — A314

Perf. 13½x13¼
2010, Mar. 25 Litho.
510 A314 18d multi — 1.00 1.00

A315

Parrots — A316

2010, Apr. 14 Perf. 13¼x13½
511 A315 20d multi — 1.25 1.25
Perf. 13½x13¼
512 A316 40d multi — 2.25 2.25

Europa — A317

2010, May 5
513 A317 100d multi — 8.00 8.00

Macedonian Chairmanship of the Council of Europe — A318

2010, May 8
514 A318 18d multi — 1.00 1.00

Macedonia in the European Union — A319

Buildings: 20d, European Parliament, Brussels. 50d, Main Post Office, Madrid.

2010, May 8
515-516 A319 Set of 2 — 4.00 4.00

Debar — A319a

Gevgelija — A319b

Kratovo — A319c

Veles — A319d

Krusevo — A319e

2010 Litho. Perf. 12¾x13
	Denomination	Color
517 A319a	16d brown	.35 .35
518 A319b	16d white	.35 .35
519 A319c	16d orange brown	.35 .35
520 A319d	18d olive brown	.90 .90
521 A319e	18d blue	.90 .90

Nos. 517-521 (5) — 2.85 2.85
Issued: No. 520, 5/8; others, 6/2.

Castanea Sativa — A320

2010, June 5 Litho. Perf. 13½x13¼
522 A320 20d multi — 1.10 1.10

Robert Schumann (1810-56), Composer A321

Frédéric Chopin (1810-49), Composer A322

2010, June 8 Perf. 13½x13¼
523 A321 50d multi — 3.00 3.00
Perf. 13¼x13½
524 A322 60d multi — 3.50 3.50

2010 World Cup Soccer Championships, South Africa — A323

Emblem and: 50d, Soccer ball in goal net. 100d, Soccer ball at midfield, vert. 150d, Soccer ball, map of South Africa.

Perf. 13½x13¼, 13¼x13½
2010, June 11
525-526 A323 Set of 2 — 8.00 8.00
Souvenir Sheet
527 A323 150d multi — 8.00 8.00

50th Ohrid Summer Festival — A324

2010, June 30 Perf. 13¼x13½
528 A324 18d multi — 1.00 1.00

MACEDONIA

Mother Teresa (1910-97), Humanitarian — A325

2010, Aug. 26   Litho.   *Perf. 13*
529 A325 60d multi   2.75 2.75
See Albania No. 2889, Kosovo No. 154.

Bayram Festival — A326

2010, Sept. 9   Litho.   *Perf. 13¼x13½*
530 A326 50d multi   2.10 2.10

Awarding of First Prize in Poetry Contest to "The Serdar," by Gligor Prlicev, 150th Anniv. — A327

2010, Sept. 10   *Perf. 13¼*
531 A327 100d multi   4.25 4.25

A328

Flora and Fauna — A329

Designs: 18d, Chara ohridana. 20d, Gocea ohridana. 44d, Surirella spiralis. 100d, Ochridaspongia rotunda.

Perf. 13¼x13½
2010, Sept. 10   Litho.
532 A328 18d multi   .85 .85
533 A329 20d multi   1.10 1.10
534 A328 44d multi   2.25 2.25
535 A329 100d multi   4.75 4.75
Nos. 532-535 (4)   8.95 8.95

Henri Dunant (1828-1910), Founder of Red Cross A330

Robert Koch (1843-1910), Bacteriologist A331

Jacques Cousteau (1910-97), Marine Conservationist A332

2010, Oct. 20   *Perf. 13¼x13½*
536 A330 10d multi   .50 .50
Perf. 13½x13¼
537 A331 20d multi   .95 .95
538 A332 20d multi   .95 .95
Nos. 536-538 (3)   2.40 2.40

St. Naum (c. 830-910) A333

Dimitar Miladinov (1810-62), Folklorist A334

2010, Nov. 5   *Perf. 13½x13¼*
539 A333 18d multi   .95 .95
Perf. 13¼x13½
540 A334 18d multi   .95 .95

First Multiparty Elections in Macedonia A335

2010, Nov. 11   *Perf. 13½x13¼*
541 A335 16d multi   .85 .85

Marin Barleti (c. 1450-c. 1512), Historian — A336

2010, Nov. 15   *Perf. 13¼x13½*
542 A336 20d multi   .95 .95

Jama, Sculpture by Dimo Todorovski (1910-83) A337

Painting by Dimce Koco (1910-93) A338

2010, Nov. 15   *Perf. 13½x13¼*
543 A337 50d multi   2.60 2.60
544 A338 50d multi   2.60 2.60

Christmas A339

2010, Nov. 22   Litho.
545 A339 16d multi   .85 .85

Kavadarci A340

Kriva Palanka A341

Negotin A342

Probistip A343

Kocani A344

Sveti Nikole A345

Radovici — A346

2010, Dec. 11   *Perf. 12¾x13*
Denomination Color
546 A340 16d aquamarine   .90 .90
547 A341 16d aquamarine   .90 .90
548 A342 16d purple   .90 .90
549 A343 16d black   .90 .90
550 A344 18d red   1.00 1.00
551 A345 18d black   1.00 1.00
Perf. 13x12¾
552 A346 18d red   1.00 1.00
Nos. 546-552 (7)   6.60 6.60

Coin From Reign of Constantine Dragas, c. 1371-95 — A347

2011, Feb. 28   *Perf. 13½x13¼*
553 A347 50d multi   2.50 2.50

First Man in Space, 50th Anniv. — A348

2011, Mar. 4   Litho.   *Perf. 13¼x13½*
554 A348 40d multi   13.00 13.00

Opening of Holocaust Memorial Center of the Jews From Macedonia, Skopje — A349

2011, Mar. 8   *Perf. 13½x13¼*
555 A349 100d multi   5.25 5.25

Macedonian Shepherd — A350

2011, Apr. 11   *Perf. 13¼x13¼*
556 A350 50d multi   2.75 2.75

Princess Diana (1961-97) — A351

2011, Apr. 12
557 A351 100d multi   5.50 5.50

Intl. Year of Chemistry A352

2011, Apr. 13   *Perf. 13½x13¼*
558 A352 60d multi   3.25 3.25

First Automobile, 125th Anniv. — A353

First Automobile in Skopje, Cent. — A354

2011, Apr. 15   *Perf. 13½x13¼*
559 A353 20d multi   1.10 1.10
Perf. 13¼x13½
560 A354 70d multi   3.50 3.50

Statue of James Watt (1736-1819), Engineer, and Diagram of His Steam Engine — A355

2011, Apr. 20   *Perf. 13½x13¼*
561 A355 60d multi   3.50 3.50

European Capitals — A356

Designs: No. 562, 40d, Warsaw, Poland. No. 563, 40d, Budapest, Hungary.

2011, May 4
562-563 A356 Set of 2   5.25 5.25

Europa — A357

Designs: 50d, Forest in autumn. No. 565, 100d, Forest in winter. No. 566, 100d, Forest in spring.

2011, May 5   *Perf. 13½x13¼*
564-565 A357 Set of 2   8.50 8.50
Souvenir Sheet
566 A357 100d multi   7.50 7.50
Intl. Year of Forests.

Albanian Language Newspaper, Shkupi, Cent. — A358

2011, June 10
567 A358 60d multi   3.25 3.25

Struga Poetry Evenings, 50th Anniv. — A359

2011, June 15
568 A359 40d multi   2.25 2.25

45

MACEDONIA

Souvenir Sheet

Iustinianus Primus Law Faculty, Saints Cyril and Methodius University, Skopje, 60th Anniv. — A360

2011, July 1
569 A360 100d multi   5.00 5.00

Vinica — A361

2011, July 27   Perf. 13x12¾
570 A361 10d multi   .65 .65

Bayram Festival — A362

                                Perf. 13½x13¼
2011, Aug. 30   Litho.
571 A362 50d multi   2.60 2.60

2011 European Basketball Championships, Lithuania A363

2011, Aug. 31   Perf. 13¼
572 A363 70d multi   3.50 3.50
Values are for stamps with surrounding selvage.

Independence, 20th Anniv. — A364

2011, Sept. 5   Perf. 13½x13¼
573 A364 20d multi   1.25 1.25

Ljubomir Belogaski (1912-94), Painter — A365

2011, Sept. 14
574 A365 20d multi   1.10 1.10

Franz Liszt (1811-86), Composer — A366

2011, Sept. 21   Perf. 13¼x13½
575 A366 50d black & silver   2.75 2.75

Ernest Hemingway (1899-1961), Writer — A367

2011, Oct. 11   Perf. 13½x13¼
576 A367 50d multi   2.75 2.75

Migjeni (Millos Gjergj Nikolla, 1911-38), Writer — A368

2011, Oct. 19
577 A368 20d multi   1.10 1.10

Angelarios (1911-86), Archbiship of Ohrid — A369

2011, Oct. 26   Perf. 13¼x13½
578 A369 40d multi   2.40 2.40

Buildings
A370   A371
Buildings in: 16d, Demir Hisar. 18d, Dojran.

2011, Nov.   Perf. 12¾x13
579 A370 16d multi   .85 .85
580 A371 18d multi   .95 .95

Worldwide Fund for Nature (WWF) — A372

No. 581 — Spermophilus citellus: a, 12d, Two adults and butterfly. b, 24d, Adult and three juveniles. c, 48d, Adult and juvenile. d, 60d, Six adults and den.

2011, Dec. 13   Perf. 13¼x13½
581 A372 Block of 4, #a-d   6.00 6.00

Butterflies A373

Designs: 12d, Parnassius apollo. 24d, Zerynthia polyxena. 48d, Parnassius mnemosyne. 60d, Elphinstonia penia.

2011, Dec. 19   Perf. 13½x13¼
582-585 A373 Set of 4   7.50 7.50

Christmas A374

2011, Dec. 20   Litho.
586 A374 18d multi   1.25 1.25

Gjerasim Qiriazi (1858-94), Founder of Protestant Church of Albania — A375

2011, Dec. 28
587 A375 20d multi   1.10 1.10

Tapestry — A376

2012, Feb. 20   Perf. 13¼x13½
588 A376 20d multi   1.10 1.10

Turtle — A377

2012, Apr. 3   Perf. 13½x13¼
589 A377 100d multi   5.00 5.00

Jets — A379

2012, Apr. 4
590 A378 40d multi   15.50 15.50
   a. With corrected spelling of
       country name (added Cyrillic "E")   2.60 2.60
591 A379 60d multi   3.00 3.00
Country name is misspelled on No. 590.

Invention of the Telegraph, 175th Anniv. — A380

2012, Apr. 5   Litho.
592 A380 100d multi   5.00 5.00

European Capitals — A381

Designs: 20d, Nicosia, Cyprus. 40d, Copenhagen, Denmark.

2012, Apr. 9   Perf. 13¼x13½
593-594 A381 Set of 2   27.50 27.50
593a   With corrected spelling of
        country name (added Cyrillic "E")   1.25 1.25
594a   With corrected spelling of
        country name (added Cyrillic "E")   2.40 2.40
Country name is misspelled on Nos. 593-594.

Europa — A382

Designs: 20d, Building and aerial view of city. No. 596, 100d, Equestrian statue. No. 597, 100d, Bridge, horiz.

2012, Apr. 13   Perf. 13¼x13½
595-596 A382 Set of 2   6.25 6.25
                Souvenir Sheet
                                Perf. 13½x13¼
597 A382 100d multi   6.50 6.50

Sinking of the Titanic, Cent. — A383

2012, Apr. 17
598 A383 100d multi   4.25 4.25

Introduction of Denar as Currency, 20th Anniv. — A384

2012, Apr. 26
599 A384 50d multi   2.75 2.75

Berovo A385   Valandovo A386

Makedonska Kamenica — A387

2012   Perf. 12¾x13
           Denomination Color
600 A385 2d gray   .30 .30
601 A386 16d blue   .80 .80
602 A387 18d rose   .90 .90
       Nos. 600-602 (3)   1.65 1.65
       Issued: 2d, 6/4; 16d, 18d, 6/6.

Zani i Maleve Orchestra, Cent. — A388

2012, June 12   Perf. 13½x13¼
603 A388 40d multi   2.25 2.25

2012 Summer Olympics, London — A389

Designs: 50d, Hurdles. 100d, Wrestling.

2012, June 24
604-605 A389 Set of 2   7.00 7.00

MACEDONIA

Bayram Festival — A390

2012, Aug. 19		Perf. 13¼x13½	
606	A390	50d multi	2.60 2.60

Premiere of Opera "Otello," by Giuseppe Verdi, 125th Anniv. — A391

2012, Sept. 11		Perf. 13½x13¼	
607	A391	40d multi	2.25 2.25

Bats — A392

Designs: 10d, Rhinolophus euryale. 20d, Rhinolophus ferrumequinum. 50d, Rhinolophus hipposideros. 100d, Miniopterus schreibersii.

2012, Sept. 18			
608-611	A392	Set of 4	7.25 7.25

Kole Nedelkovski (1912-41), Poet — A393

2012, Oct. 16			
612	A393	50d multi	2.50 2.50

Gabriel II (1912-92), Archbishop of Ohrid — A394

2012, Oct. 16		Perf. 13¼x13½	
613	A394	60d multi	2.75 2.75

Grimm's Fairy Tales, 200th Anniv. — A395

2012, Dec. 3	Litho.	Perf. 13½x13¼	
614	A395	20d multi	1.10 1.10

Christmas — A396

2012, Dec. 11		Perf. 13¼x13½	Litho.
615	A396	50d multi	2.25 2.25

Kitchenware A397

Designs: 40d, Lidded bowl and decorative pattern. 50d, Plate and decorative pattern.

2013, Feb. 27		Perf. 13½x13¼	
616-617	A397	Set of 2	4.50 4.50

Rabbit — A398

2013, Mar. 14		Perf. 13¼x13½	Litho.
618	A398	60d multi	3.25 3.25

Motorcycle — A399

2013, Mar. 21		Perf. 13¼x13½	Litho.
619	A399	50d multi	2.75 2.75

Invention of Pneumatic Tires by John Boyd Dunlop (1840-1921), 125th Anniv. — A400

2013, Apr. 3		Perf. 13½x13¼	
620	A400	40d multi	1.90 1.90

Vladimir Zworykin (1888-1982), Inventor, Diagram, and Television — A401

2013, Apr. 3	Litho.	Perf. 13½x13¼	
621	A401	50d multi	2.25 2.25

European Capitals — A402

Designs: 40d, Dublin, Ireland. 60d, Vilnius, Lithuania.

2013, Apr. 17	Litho.	Perf. 13½x13¼	
622-623	A402	Set of 2	5.00 5.00

Europa — A403

Designs: 40d, Postal van facing left. 60d, Postal van facing right. 100d, Postal truck and van.

2013, Apr. 22	Litho.	Perf. 13½x13¼	
624-625	A403	Set of 2	5.25 5.25

Souvenir Sheet
Perf. 13¾x13

626	A403	100d multi	5.25 5.25

Ali Riza Ulqinaku (1855-1913), Writer — A404

2013, June 10		Perf. 13¼x13½	Litho.
627	A404	16d multi	.85 .85

Rexhep Mitrovica (1887-1967), Prime Minister of Albania — A405

2013, June 10		Perf. 13½x13¼	Litho.
628	A405	18d multi	.90 .90

Mission of Saints Cyril and Methodius to Slavic Lands, 1150th Anniv. — A406

2013, June 24		Perf. 13½x13¼	Litho.
629	A406	40d multi	5.00 5.00

Building, Demir Kapija A407

Building, Makedonski Brod A408

2013	Litho.	Perf. 12¾x13	
630	A407	16d multi	.70 .70
631	A408	16d multi	.70 .70

Issued: No. 630, 7/5; No. 631, 7/18.

Skopje Earthquake, 50th Anniv. — A409

2013, July 26	Litho.	Perf. 13½x13¼	
632	A409	100d multi	4.00 4.00

Bayram Festival — A410

2013, July 30	Litho.	Perf. 13½x13¼	
633	A410	40d multi	1.75 1.75

Vasil Chekalarov (1874-1913), Bulgarian Revolution Leader — A411

2013, Sept. 10		Perf. 13¼x13½	Litho.
634	A411	16d multi	.75 .75

Gjurchin Kokaleski (1775-1863), Local Chieftain, Writer of First Macedonian Autobiography A412

2013, Sept. 10		Perf. 13½x13¼	Litho.
635	A412	18d multi	.85 .85

Ohrid-Debar Rebellion, Cent. — A413

2013, Sept. 19		Perf. 13¼x13½	Litho.
636	A413	60d multi	2.75 2.75

2013 Men's European Basketball Championships, Slovenia — A414

2013, Sept. 20	Litho.	Perf. 13¼	
637	A414	90d multi	3.75 3.75

Values are for stamps with surrounding selvage.

Diplomatic Relations Between Macedonia and People's Republic of China, 20th Anniv. — A415

2013, Oct. 15	Litho.	Perf. 13½x13¼	
638	A415	100d multi	4.50 4.50

Mushrooms — A416

No. 639: a, Boletus satanas, butterfly, ladybug. b, Myriostoma coliforme, butterfly, lizard. c, Caloscypha fulgens, insect. d, Terana caerulea, insect.

2013, Oct. 16	Litho.	Perf. 13¼x13½	
639		Horiz. strip of 4	8.25 8.25
a.	A416	10d multi	.45 .45
b.	A416	20d multi	.90 .90
c.	A416	50d multi	2.25 2.25
d.	A416	100d multi	4.50 4.50

Petre Bogdanov-Kocko (1913-88), Composer A417

2013, Nov. 13		Perf. 13½x13¼	Litho.
640	A417	20d multi	1.00 1.00

Richard Wagner (1883-83), Composer A418

2013, Nov. 13		Perf. 13½x13¼	Litho.
641	A418	40d multi	2.00 2.00

Christmas A419

2013, Dec. 11		Perf. 13½x13¼	Litho.
642	A419	40d multi	2.00 2.00

MACEDONIA

Vegetables — A420

2013, Dec. 28 Litho. Perf. 12¾x13
| 643 | A420 | 8d Tomatoes | .40 | .40 |
| 644 | A420 | 10d Eggplants | .50 | .50 |

Calculator A421

Shopping Cart A422

2014, Jan. 14 Litho. Perf. 12¾x13
| 645 | A421 | 8d multi | .40 | .40 |
| 646 | A422 | 8d multi | .40 | .40 |

Decorative Jewelry — A423

Various pieces from 19th-20th cent. from Bitola: 24d, 40d, vert.

Perf. 13½x13¼, 13¼x13½
2014, May 22 Litho.
| 647-648 | A423 | Set of 2 | 3.00 | 3.00 |

2014 Winter Olympics, Sochi, Russia — A424

Designs: 50d, Ice hockey. 100d, Ski jumping.

2014, May 23 Litho. Perf. 13¼
| 649-650 | A424 | Set of 2 | 7.00 | 7.00 |

Values are for stamps with surrounding selvage.

Michelangelo (1475-1564), Sculptor and Painter — A425

2014, May 27 Litho. Perf. 13½x13¼
| 651 | A425 | 144d multi | 6.50 | 6.50 |

Goldfish — A426

Designs: 21d, Goldfish in water. 60d, Goldfish and air bubbles.

2014, May 28 Litho. Perf. 13½x13¼
| 652-653 | A426 | Set of 2 | 4.75 | 4.75 |

Truck — A427

2014, May 29 Litho. Perf. 13½x13¼
| 654 | A427 | 50d multi | 2.25 | 2.25 |

No. 654 was printed in sheets of 8 + central label.

Galileo Galilei (1564-1642), Astronomer A428

2014, May 30 Litho. Perf. 13½x13¼
| 655 | A428 | 20d multi | 1.25 | 1.25 |

No. 655 was printed in sheets of 8 + central label.

George Stephenson (1781-1848), Railway Builder, and Rocket Locomotive A429

2014, May 30 Litho. Perf. 13½x13¼
| 656 | A429 | 40d multi | 1.75 | 1.75 |

No. 656 was printed in sheets of 8 + central label.

European Capitals — A430

Designs: 40d, Acropolis, Athens, Greece. 60d, Colosseum, Rome, Italy.

2014, June 3 Litho. Perf. 13½x13¼
| 657-658 | A430 | Set of 2 | 4.25 | 4.25 |

Nos. 657-658 were each printed in sheets of 8 + central label.

Europa — A431

Designs: 40d, Zurna. No. 660, 50d, Three-holed ocarina (light green background). No. 661, 50d: a, Tambura (gray green background). b, Two tamburas (pale pink background). c, Kemene and bow (pale orange background). d, Gajda (pale blue background). 60d, Drum.

2014, June 4 Litho. Perf. 13½x13¼
659-660	A431	Set of 2	4.00	4.00
661		Miniature Sheet	9.00	9.00
a.-d.	A431	50d Any single	2.25	2.25
		Souvenir Sheet		
662	A431	60d multi	2.75	2.75

No. 661 was sold with but unattached to a booklet cover.

Peoni Spelunking Club, 50th Anniv. — A432

2014, June 4 Litho. Perf. 13¼x13½
| 663 | A432 | 80d multi | 3.75 | 3.75 |

2014 World Cup Soccer Championships, Brazil — A433

Designs: 50d, Soccer ball and emblem. 100d, Soccer ball, emblem and Christ the Redeemer statue.

Perf. 13¼x13½
2014, June 12 Litho.
| 664-665 | A433 | Set of 2 | 7.25 | 7.25 |

Nos. 664-665 were each printed in sheets of 8 + central label.

Vegetables — A434

2014 Litho. Perf. 12¾
666	A434	6d Cabbage	.30	.30
667	A434	16d Beans	.70	.70
668	A434	18d Cauliflower	.80	.80
	Nos. 666-668 (3)		1.80	1.80

Issued: 6d, 7/2; 16d, 6/13; 18d, 6/20.
See Nos. 715-717, 735-737.

Bayram Festival — A435

Perf. 13½x13¼
2014, June 15 Litho.
| 669 | A435 | 40d multi | 1.75 | 1.75 |

Battle of Belasitsa (Kleidion), 1000th Anniv. — A436

Perf. 13½x13¼
2014, June 29 Litho.
| 670 | A436 | 50d multi | 2.25 | 2.25 |

Charlie Chaplin (1889-1977), Actor — A437

2015, Apr. 21 Litho. Perf. 13½x13¼
| 671 | A437 | 50d multi | 2.25 | 2.25 |

Dated 2014.

Vladimir Komarov (1927-67), Cosmonaut A438

2015, Apr. 21 Litho. Perf. 13½x13¼
| 672 | A438 | 50d multi | 2.25 | 2.25 |

Dated 2014.

Famous Men — A439

Designs: 16d, Tashko Karadza (1914-42), resistance leader. 18d, Ivan Tocko (1914-73), writer. 20d, Nexhat Agolli (1914-49), politician. 24d, Sterjo Spasse (1914-89), writer.

2015, Apr. 21 Litho. Perf. 13¼x13½
| 673-676 | A439 | Set of 4 | 3.25 | 3.25 |

Dated 2014.

Pigeons — A440

No. 677: a. Columba palumbus. b, Columba oenas. c, Columba livia. d, Columba livia forma domestica.

2015, Apr. 21 Litho. Perf. 13½x13¼
677		Vert. strip of 4	7.50	7.50
a.	A440	11d multi	.45	.45
b.	A440	20d multi	.80	.80
c.	A440	50d multi	2.10	2.10
d.	A440	100d multi	4.00	4.00

Dated 2014.

Christmas — A441

2015, Apr. 21 Litho. Perf. 13¼x13½
| 678 | A441 | 40d multi | 1.75 | 1.75 |

Dated 2014.

2015 Men's World Handball Championships, Qatar — A442

2015, Apr. 22 Litho. Perf. 13¼x13½
| 679 | A442 | 100d multi | 4.00 | 4.00 |

Serinus Canaria Domestica — A443

Designs: 31d, Serinus canaria domestica, one bird. 50d, Serinus canaria domestica, two birds.

2015, Apr. 23 Litho. Perf. 13¼x13½
| 680-681 | A443 | Set of 2 | 3.25 | 3.25 |

No. 680 has incorrect Latin name for bird depicted (Carduelis carduelis).

20th Century Ceramic Pitcher — A444

2015, Apr. 24 Litho. Perf. 13¼x13½
| 682 | A444 | 50d multi | 2.10 | 2.10 |

Battle of Gallipoli, Cent. — A445

2015, Apr. 27 Litho. Perf. 13½x13¼
| 683 | A445 | 70d multi | 3.00 | 3.00 |

Benjamin Franklin (1706-90) — A446

2015, Apr. 29 Litho. Perf. 13¼x13¼
| 684 | A446 | 60d multi | 2.50 | 2.50 |

MACEDONIA

Cat and Bicycle — A447
2015, Apr. 29 Litho. Perf. 13½x13¼
685 A447 100d multi 4.25 4.25

European Capitals — A448
Designs: 40d, Riga, Latvia. 60d, Luxembourg, Luxembourg.
2015, Apr. 29 Litho. Perf. 13½x13¼
686-687 A448 Set of 2 4.25 4.25
Nos. 686-687 were each printed in sheets of 8 + central label.

Europa — A449
Old toys: 50d, Yo-yo. 100d, Rocking horse. 150d, Spinning top.
2015, May 6 Litho. Perf. 13½x13¼
688-689 A449 6.00 6.00
Souvenir Sheet
690 A449 150d multi 6.00 6.00

Souvenir Sheet
2015 Eurovision Song Contest — A450
2015, May 7 Litho. Perf. 13½x13¼
691 A450 100d multi 4.00 4.00

Invention of the Saxophone, 175th Anniv. — A451
2015, May 8 Litho. Perf. 13¼x13½
692 A451 44d multi 1.90 1.90
No. 692 was printed in sheets of 8 + central label.

Pyotr I. Tchaikovsky (1840-93), Composer A452
2015, May 8 Litho. Perf. 13½x13¼
693 A452 100d multi 4.00 4.00
No. 693 was printed in sheets of 8 + central label.

Carrots — A453
2015, July 2 Litho. Perf. 12¾
694 A453 2d multi .35 .35

Bayram Festival — A454
2015, July 15 Litho. Perf. 13¼x13½
695 A454 40d multi 1.75 1.75

2015 European Basketball Championships A455
2015, Sept. 4 Litho. Perf. 13¼x13½
696 A455 50d multi 2.10 2.10
No. 696 was printed in sheets of 8 + central label.

Mirce Acev (1915-43), Resistance Leader A456

Ibrahim Temo (1865-1939), Politician A457

Jane Sandanski (1872-1915), Revolution Leader A458

Ali Pasha of Tepelena (1740-1822), Ruler of Albania A459

Arthur Miller (1915-2005), Playwright A460

Perf. 13¼x13½
2015, Sept. 17 Litho.
697 A456 16d multi .70 .70
698 A457 16d multi .70 .70
699 A458 18d multi .75 .75
Perf. 13½x13¼
700 A459 18d multi .75 .75
701 A460 20d multi .85 .85
Nos. 697-701 (5) 3.75 3.75

Flowers A461
2015, Oct. 14 Litho. Perf. 13¼x13½
702 A461 Block of 4, #a-d 7.25 7.25
No. 702: a, 11d, Thymus serpyllum. b, 20d, Calendula officinalis. c, 50d, Hypericum perforatum. d, 100d, Urtica dioica.

Christmas A462
2015, Dec. 8 Litho. Perf. 13½x13¼
703 A462 40d multi 1.75 1.75

Souvenir Sheet

Mountain Tourism A463
Perf. 13½x13¼
2016, Mar. 23 Litho.
704 A463 144d multi + label 6.00 6.00
See Kosovo No. 300.

St. Clement of Ohrid (c. 840-916) — A464
2016, Apr. 25 Litho. Perf. 13¼x13½
705 A464 18d multi .75 .75

Hamster — A465
2016, Apr. 26 Litho. Perf. 13½x13¼
706 A465 81d multi 3.25 3.25

Donatello (c. 1386-1466), Sculptor — A466
2016, Apr. 27 Litho. Perf. 13¼x13½
707 A466 40d multi 1.75 1.75

European Capitals — A467
Designs: 40d, Houses, Amsterdam, Netherlands. 60d, Bratislava Castle, Bratislava, Slovakia.
2016, Apr. 29 Litho. Perf. 13½x13¼
708-709 A467 Set of 2 4.25 4.25

A468

A469

A470

Europa A471
No. 712: a, Fishing boat on lake, bird in flight. b, Foliage near shore. c, Dock. d, Pelican.
2016, May 10 Litho. Perf. 13½x13¼
710 A468 50d multi 2.10 2.10
711 A469 100d multi 4.25 4.25
Miniature Sheet
712 A470 50d Sheet of 4, #a-d 0.00 0.00
Souvenir Sheet
Perf. 13¼x13½
713 A471 144d multi 5.75 5.75

Train — A472
2016, Apr. 28 Litho. Perf. 13½x13¼
714 A472 44d multi 1.75 1.75

Vegetables Type of 2014
2016, May 13 Litho. Perf. 12¾
715 A434 3d Garlic .35 .35
716 A434 6d Beets .35 .35
717 A434 13d Peppers .60 .60
Nos. 715-717 (3) 1.30 1.30

Bayram Festival — A473
2016, June 9 Litho. Perf. 13¼x13½
718 A473 44d multi 1.75 1.75

2016 European Soccer Championships France — A474
Perf. 13½x13¼
2016, June 10 Litho.
719 A474 101d multi 4.25 4.25

René Laennec (1781-1826), Inventor of Stethoscope A475
2016, July 12 Litho. Perf. 13½x13¼
720 A475 40d multi 1.60 1.60

MACEDONIA

Claude Elwood Shannon (1916-2001), Mathematician and Electrical Engineer — A476

2016, July 12 Litho. Perf. 13½x13¼
721 A476 50d multi   2.10 2.10

2016 Summer Olympics, Rio de Janeiro — A477

Designs: 40d, Wrestling. 60d, Judo. 50d, Macedonian Olympic emblem, vert.

2016, Aug. 5 Litho. Perf. 13½x13¼
722-723 A477 Set of 2   4.25 4.25
Souvenir Sheet
Perf. 13¼x13½
724 A477 50d multi   2.10 2.10

First Albanian Language School in Macedonia, 75th Anniv. — A478

2016, Sept. 7 Litho. Perf. 13½x13¼
725 A478 50d multi   2.10 2.10

Independence, 25th Anniv. — A479

2016, Sept. 8 Litho. Perf. 13¼x13½
726 A479 18d multi   .85 .85

Lorenc Antoni (1909-91), Composer — A480

Perf. 13¼x13½
2016, Sept. 12 Litho.
727 A480 20d multi   .85 .85

Antonio Vivaldi (1678-1741), Composer A481

Perf. 13½x13¼
2016, Sept. 12 Litho.
728 A481 40d multi   1.60 1.60

Walt Disney (1901-66), Animated Film Producer, and Film Characters A482

Perf. 13½x13¼
2016, Sept. 20 Litho.
729 A482 50d multi   2.10 2.10

Orce Nikolov (1916-42), Syndicalist Movement Leader — A483

Perf. 13¼x13½
2016, Sept. 20 Litho.
730 A483 18d multi   .75 .75

Tajar Zavalani (1903-66), Historian — A484

Perf. 13¼x13½
2016, Sept. 20 Litho.
731 A484 18d multi   .75 .75

Mammals — A485

No. 732: a, Meles meles. b, Vormela peregusna. c, Mustela nivalis. d, Lutra lutra.

2016, Oct. 20 Litho. Perf. 13½x13¼
732   Vert. strip of 4   8.00 8.00
a. A485 11d multi   .45 .45
b. A485 20d multi   .80 .80
c. A485 50d multi   2.25 2.25
d. A485 100d multi   4.50 4.50

Christmas — A486

2016, Nov. 7 Litho. Perf. 13½x13¼
733 A486 40d multi   1.60 1.60

Churches — A487

No. 734: a, 44d, Trinity Cathedral, St. Petersburg, Russia. b, 100d, Church of St. John the Theologian, Ohrid, Macedonia.

Perf. 13½x13¼
2016, Dec. 23 Litho.
734 A487 Horiz. pair, #a-b   5.50 5.50
See Russia No. 7796.

Vegetables Type of 2014
2016-17 Litho. **Perf. 12¾**
735 A434 18d Spinach   .65 .65
736 A434 18d Zucchinis   .65 .65
737 A434 18d Potatoes   .65 .65
    Nos. 735-737 (3)   1.95 1.95
Issued: No. 735, 11/16; No. 736, 3/15/17; No. 737, 3/22/17.

Mustafa Pasha Mosque, Skopje, 525th Anniv. — A488

2017, Apr. 27 Litho. Perf. 13½x13¼
738 A488 18d multi   .65 .65

2017 World Men's Handball Championships, France — A489

2017, Apr. 27 Litho. Perf. 13½x13¼
739 A489 86d multi   3.25 3.25

Iguana — A490

2017, Apr. 28 Litho. Perf. 13½x13¼
740 A490 144d multi   5.25 5.25

Edmond Halley (1656-1741), Astronomer, and Halley's Comet — A491

2017, May 3 Litho. Perf. 13½x13¼
741 A491 88d multi   3.25 3.25

17th Century Ship — A492

2017, May 4 Litho. Perf. 13¼x13½
742 A492 144d multi   5.25 5.25

European Capitals — A493

Designs: No. 743, 32d, Harbor of Valletta, Malta, and flag of Malta. No. 744, 32d, Big Ben, London, and flag of Great Britain, vert.

Perf. 13½x13¼, 13¼x13½
2017, May 5 Litho.
743-744 A493 Set of 2   2.40 2.40

Samuel's Fortress, Ohrid — A494

Skopje Fortress — A495

Skopje Fortress A496

2017, May 8 Litho. Perf. 13½x13¼
745 A494 73d multi   2.75 2.75
746 A495 73d multi   2.75 2.75
Souvenir Sheet
747 A496 144d multi   5.25 5.25
Europa.

Apis Mellifera Macedonica — A497

Bee and: 18d, Flower and honeycomb. 72d, Hive and flower.

2017, Jue 5 Litho. Perf. 13½x13¼
748-749 A497 Set of 2   3.50 3.50

Arasta Mosque, Skopje — A498

Perf. 13½x13¼
2017, June 23 Litho.
750 A498 18d multi   .70 .70
Bajram Festival.

Cvetan Dimov (1910-42), Communist Party Leader — A499

2017, July 6 Litho. Perf. 13¼x13½
751 A499 18d multi   .70 .70

Faik Konica (1875-1942), Writer and Albanian Ambassador to United States — A500

2017, July 6 Litho. Perf. 13¼x13½
752 A500 18d multi   .70 .70

Michael Faraday (1791-1867), Chemist and Physicist — A501

2017, July 6 Litho. Perf. 13¼x13½
753 A501 73d multi   3.00 3.00

Macedonian Army, 25th Anniv. — A502

Perf. 13½x13¼
2017, Aug. 18 Litho.
754 A502 18d multi   .70 .70

2017 European Men's Basketball Championships A503

Perf. 13½x13¼
2017, Aug. 31 Litho.
755 A503 86d multi   3.50 3.50

Muhammad Ali (1942-2016), Boxer — A504

Perf. 13¼x13½
2017, Sept. 12 Litho.
756 A504 86d multi   3.50 3.50

Arturo Toscanini (1867-1957), Conductor A505

MACEDONIA

Perf. 13½x13¼
2017, Sept. 21   Litho.
757   A505   72d multi   2.75   2.75

Auguste Rodin (1840-1917), Sculptor — A506

Perf. 13½x13¼
2017, Sept. 28   Litho.
758   A506   88d multi   3.50   3.50

Rare Disease Day — A507

2017, Oct. 4   Litho.   **Perf. 13½x13¼**
759   A507   48d multi   1.90   1.90

Macedonian Academy of Science and Arts, 50th Anniv. — A508

2017, Oct. 9   Litho.   **Perf. 13½x13¼**
760   A508   18d multi   .70   .70

Flora — A509

No. 761: a, Cannabis sativa. b, Gossypium hirsutum. c, Nicotianum tabacum. d, Papaver somniferum.

2017, Oct. 19   Litho.   **Perf. 13¼**
761   Horiz. strip of 4   7.00   7.00
   a.   A509   11d multi   .45   .45
   b.   A509   20d multi   .75   .75
   c.   A509   50d multi   1.90   1.90
   d.   A509   100d multi   3.75   3.75

Christmas — A510

Perf. 13¼x13½
2017, Nov. 22   Litho.
762   A510   18d multi   .70   .70

Declaration of the Ohrid Archbishopric as Autocephalous, 50th Anniv. — A511

Perf. 13½x13¼
2017, Dec. 12   Litho.
763   A511   18d multi   .70   .70

Matka Canyon — A512

Perf. 13½x13¼
2017, Dec. 19   Litho.
764   A512   48d multi   1.90   1.90
Tourism.

Kiro Gligorov (1917-2012), First President — A513

Perf. 13¼x13½
2017, Dec. 22   Litho.
765   A513   18d multi   .70   .70

Vegetables — A514

2017, Dec. 22   Litho.   **Perf. 12¾**
766   A514   18d Celeriac   .70   .70
767   A514   18d Butternut squash   .70   .70
768   A514   18d Radishes   .70   .70
769   A514   18d Red onions   .70   .70
   Nos. 766-769 (4)   2.80   2.80

Skanderbeg (1405-68), Albanian Leader of Rebellion Against Turks — A515

2018, Jan. 10   Litho.   **Perf. 13¼x13½**
770   A515   18d multi   .75   .75

2018 Winter Olympics, Pyeongchang, South Korea — A516

Designs: 72d, Figure skating. 73d, Luge.

2018, Feb. 6   Litho.   **Perf. 13½x13¼**
771-772   A516   Set of 2   5.75   5.75

Gold Funerary Mask — A517

2018, Feb. 8   Litho.   **Perf. 13½x13¼**
773   A517   48d multi   1.90   1.90

Sheep — A518

Designs: 72d, Ram. 86d, Flock of sheep.

2018, Mar. 7   Litho.   **Perf. 13½x13¼**
774-775   A518   Set of 2   6.50   6.50

Streptomycin, 75th Anniv. — A519

James Prescott Joule (1818-89), Physicist — A520

Perf. 13½x13¼
2018, Mar. 14   Litho.
776   A519   48d multi   2.00   2.00
777   A520   86d multi   3.50   3.50

Nicolaus Copernicus (1473-1543), Astronomer A521

Perf. 13½x13¼
2018, Mar. 28   Litho.
778   A521   73d multi   3.00   3.00
   Souvenir Sheet
779   A521   102d multi   4.25   4.25

Steam Train From Kicevo — A522

2018, Apr. 4   Litho.   **Perf. 13½x13¼**
780   A522   144d multi   5.75   5.75

European Capitals — A523

Designs: No. 781, 48d, Schönbrunn Palace, Vienna, Austria. No. 782, 48d, St. Nedelya Church, Sofia, Bulgaria.

2018, Apr. 25   Litho.   **Perf. 13½**
781-782   A523   Set of 2   3.75   3.75

A524

Europa A525

Designs: 73d, Babuna River Bridge, Veles. 80d, Stone bridge over Gradeska River, Mariovo.
No. 785: a, Gorenica Bridge, Debar. b, Babuna River Bridge, Veles, diff. c, Stone bridge over Gradeska River, Mariovo, diff. d, Elenski-Skok Bridge, Mogorche. 144d, Gorenica Bridge, Debar, vert.

2018, May 2   Litho.   **Perf. 13½**
783-784   A524   Set of 2   3.75   3.75
785   A525   50d Sheet of 4, #a-d   6.00   6.00
   Souvenir Sheet
   Perf. 13¼x13½
786   A524   144d multi   5.50   5.50

No. 785 was sold with, but unattached to, a booklet cover.

Bajram Festival — A526

2018, June 3   Litho.   **Perf. 13½**
787   A526   10d multi   .70   .70

2018 World Cup Soccer Championships, Russia — A527

Emblem and: 72d, Soccer ball. 88d, Goal netting.

2018, June 5   Litho.   **Perf. 13¼x13½**
788-789   A527   Set of 2   6.00   6.00

Koco Racin (1908-43), Poet — A528

Perf. 13¼x13½
2018, June 13   Litho.
790   A528   18d multi   .70   .70

Deportation of Jews From Macedonia, 75th Anniv. — A529

Perf. 13½x13¼
2018, Sept. 19   Litho.
791   A529   50d multi   1.90   1.90

Admission to Universal Postal Union, 25th Anniv. — A530

2018, Oct. 9   Litho.   **Perf. 13¼x13½**
792   A530   73d multi   2.75   2.75

Milan Firfov (1943-2012), Musician A531

Claude Debussy (1862-1918), Composer A532

2018, Oct. 17   Litho.   **Perf. 13¼x13½**
793   A531   48d multi   1.75   1.75
794   A532   80d multi   3.00   3.00

Jacopo Tintoretto (1518-94), Painter A533

Ibrahim Kodra (1918-2006), Painter A534

2018, Nov. 5   Litho.   **Perf. 13¼x13½**
795   A533   72d multi   2.75   2.75
796   A534   88d multi   3.25   3.25

Values for No. 795 are for stamps with surrounding selvage.

Miniature Sheet

Fish A535

No. 797: a, 11d, Squalius vardarensis. b, 20d, Alburnus macedonicus. c, 50d, Anguilla anguilla. d, 100d, Salmo letnica.

2018, Nov. 21   Litho.   **Perf. 14**
797   A535   Sheet of 4, #a-d   6.75   6.75

MACEDONIA

Christmas — A536

2018, Dec. 4	Litho.	Perf. 13½x13¼
798	A536	18d multi	.70	.70

2019 World Men's Handball Championships, Denmark and Germany — A537

2019, Jan. 10	Litho.	Perf. 13¼x13½
799	A537	72d multi	2.75	2.75

Terracotta Figurine of "Great Mother" — A538

2019, Feb. 4	Litho.	Perf. 13½x13¼
800	A538	50d multi	1.90	1.90

REPUBLIC OF NORTH MACEDONIA

Jashar Bej Shkupi (1860-1919), Politician — A539

Perf. 13½x13¼
2019, Mar. 19			Litho.
801	A539	50d multi	1.90	1.90

Following an agreement with Greece, the Republic of Macedonia changed its name to the Republic of North Macedonia on Feb. 12, 2019.

Rade Jovchevski Korchagin (1919-43), Partisan Leader — A540

Perf. 13¼x13½
2019, Mar. 19			Litho.
802	A540	50d multi	1.90	1.90

Napoleon Bonaparte (1769-1821), Emperor of the French — A541

Perf. 13½x13¼
2019, Mar. 19			Litho.
803	A541	144d multi	5.25	5.25

A542

Donkeys — A543

Perf. 13½x13¼
2019, Mar. 20			Litho.
804	A542	20d multi	.75	.75
805	A543	124d multi	4.50	4.50

André-Jacques Garnerin (1769-1823), Inventor of Parachute — A544

Perf. 13½x13¼
2019, Mar. 21			Litho.
806	A544	72d multi	2.75	2.75

Thermometer and Anders Celsius (1701-44), Physicist — A545

Perf. 13½x13¼
2019, Mar. 21			Litho.
807	A545	100d multi	3.75	3.75

Apollo 11 Space Flight, 50th Anniv. — A546

Perf. 13½x13¼
2019, Mar. 21			Litho.
808	A546	101d multi	3.75	3.75

North Atlantic Treaty Organization, 70th Anniv. — A547

2019, Apr. 4	Litho.	Perf. 13½x13¼
809	A547	70d multi	2.60	2.60

Horse-drawn Carriage — A548

2019, Apr. 4	Litho.	Perf. 13½x13¼
810	A548	100d multi	3.75	3.75

European Capitals — A549

Designs: No. 811, 48d, Harbor, Helsinki, Finland. No. 812, 48d, Palace of the Parliament, Bucharest, Romania.

2019, Apr. 25		Litho.	Perf. 13½x13¼
811-812	A549	Set of 2	3.50	3.50

Europa — A550

Birds: No. 813, 72d, Circus aeruginosus. No. 814, 72d, Circus pygargus. No. 815, horiz.: a, Falco biarmicus. b, Falco naumanni. c, Falco vespertinus. d, Falco peregrinus. 144d, Buteo rufinus.

Perf. 13¼x13½, 13½ (#815)
2019, May 2			Litho.
813-814	A550	Set of 2	5.25	5.25
815	A550	50d Sheet of 4, #a-d	7.25	7.25

Souvenir Sheet
| 816 | A550 | 144d multi | 5.25 | 5.25 |

No. 815 was sold with, but unattached to, a booklet cover.

U. S. Pres. Woodrow Wilson (1856-1924), and Newspaper Articles — A551

2019, May 6	Litho.	Perf. 13½x13¼
817	A551	30d multi	1.10	1.10

Signing of the Treaty of Versailles, cent.

Visit of Pope Francis to North Macedonia A552

2019, May 7	Litho.	Perf. 13½x13¼
818	A552	144d multi	5.25	5.25

Vegetables — A553

Designs: 1d, Broccoli. 2d, Peas. 3d, Fava beans. 5d, Cucumbers. 8d, Kohlrabi. 10d, Leeks.

2019, May 27		Litho.	Perf. 12¾x13
819	A553	1d multi	.25	.25
820	A553	2d multi	.25	.25
821	A553	3d multi	.25	.25
822	A553	5d multi	.25	.25
823	A553	8d multi	.30	.30
824	A553	10d multi	.40	.40
		Nos. 819-824 (6)	1.70	1.70

See Nos. 884-888.

Bajram Festival — A554

2019, June 3	Litho.	Perf. 13½x13¼
825	A554	50d multi	1.90	1.90

International Year of Indigenous Languages — A555

2019, June 5	Litho.	Perf. 13¼x13½
826	A555	30d multi	1.10	1.10

Alport Syndrome and Rare Disease Day — A556

Perf. 13½x13¼
2019, June 10			Litho.
827	A556	18d multi	.70	.70

Periodic Table of Elements, 150th Anniv. — A557

2019, Oct. 9	Litho.	Perf. 13½x13¼
828	A557	50d multi	1.90	1.90

University of Tetovo, 25th Anniv. — A558

2019, Oct. 9	Litho.	Perf. 13¼x13½
829	A558	50d multi	1.90	1.90

Liberation of Skopje, 75th Anniv. — A559

2019, Oct. 9	Litho.	Perf. 13½x13¼
830	A559	100d multi	3.75	3.75

2019 Drone Flying World Cup, Prilep — A560

2019, Oct. 10	Litho.	Perf. 13½x13¼
831	A560	72d multi	2.60	2.60

Macedonian Philharmonic Orchestra, 75th Anniv. — A561

2019, Oct. 17	Litho.	Perf. 13½x13¼
832	A561	44d multi	1.60	1.60

Antonio Stradivari (1644-1737), Crafter of Musical Instruments A562

2019, Oct. 17	Litho.	Perf. 13½x13¼
833	A562	100d multi	3.75	3.75

Nestor Aleksiev Mircevski (1873-1969), Wood Carver — A563

Perf. 13½x13¼
2019, Nov. 21			Litho.
834	A563	72d multi	2.60	2.60

Rembrandt van Rijn (1606-69), Painter — A564

Perf. 13½x13¼
2019, Nov. 21			Litho.
835	A564	101d multi	3.75	3.75

Flowers A565

No. 836: a, 10d, Gentiana lutea. b, 20d, Primula veris. c, 50d, Adonis vernalis. d, 101d, Allium ursinum.

Perf. 13½x13¼
2019, Nov. 28			Litho.
836	A565	Block of 4, #a-d	6.50	6.50

MACEDONIA

Christmas — A566

2019, Dec. 4 Litho. Perf. 13¼x13½
837 A566 50d multi 1.90 1.90

2020, Summer Olympics, Tokyo — A567

2020, Jan. 13 Litho. Perf. 13¼x13½
838 A567 144d multi 5.25 5.25

The 2020 Summer Olympics were postponed until 2021 because of the COVID-19 pandemic.

St. Jovan Bigorski Monastery, 1000th Anniv. — A568

2020, Jan. 13 Litho. Perf. 13½x13¼
839 A568 88d multi 3.25 3.25

Ludwig van Beethoven (1770-1827), Composer A569

Perf. 13½x13¼
2020, Feb. 10 Litho.
840 A569 144d multi 5.25 5.25

Gorgije Zografski (1871-1945), Painter — A570

Perf. 13¼x13½
2020, Feb. 10 Litho.
841 A570 18d multi .65 .65

Goat — A571

Perf. 13¼x13½
2020, Feb. 10 Litho.
842 A571 100d multi 3.75 3.75

Raphael (1483-1520), Painter — A572

Perf. 13½x13¼
2020, Feb. 10 Litho.
843 A572 101d multi 3.75 3.75

The painting on the stamp, Portrait of a Young Man, was printed by an imitator of Raphael.

Magnetic Field Theories of André-Marie Ampère (1775-1836), 200th Anniv. — A573

2020, Mar. 9 Litho. Perf. 13½x13¼
844 A573 72d multi 2.60 2.60

Cornelis Drebbel (1572-1633), and His Submarine A574

2020, Mar. 9 Litho. Perf. 13½x13¼
845 A574 100d multi 3.50 3.50

Souvenir Sheet

Space Stations A575

No. 846: a, Skylab, United States. b, Mir, Russia. c, Tiangong, People's Republic of China.

2020, Mar. 9 Litho. Perf. 13½x13¼
846 A575 72d Sheet of 3, #a-cd 7.75 7.75

Membership of North Macedonia in the North Atlantic Treaty Organization — A576

2020, Apr. 9 Litho. Perf. 13¼x13½
847 A576 30d multi 1.10 1.10

Tram Car — A577

2020, Apr. 13 Litho. Perf. 13½x13¼
848 A577 101d multi 3.75 3.75

Kenzo Tange (1913-2005), Architect, and His Plan to Rebuild Skopje After 1963 Earthquake A578

2020, May 5 Litho. Perf. 13½x13¼
849 A578 30d multi 1.10 1.10

Brandenburg Gate, Berlin — A579

2020, May 8 Litho. Perf. 13½x13¼
850 A579 72d multi 2.00 2.00

No. 850 was printed in sheets of 8 + central label.

A581

Ancient Postal Routes A582

2020, May 8 Litho. Perf. 13½x13¼
852 A581 144d multi 5.25 5.25

Souvenir Sheet

853 A582 144d multi 5.25 5.25

Europa.

Bajram Festival — A583

2020, May 22 Litho. Perf. 13¼x13½
854 A583 50d multi 1.90 1.90

Bridge and Lake Ohrid, Struga — A584

Cavern, Pelicans and Lake Prespa — A585

2020, June 8 Litho. Perf. 13½x13¼
855 A584 30d multi 1.10 1.10
856 A585 30d multi 1.10 1.10

Slavko Janovski (1920-2000), Writer — A586

2020, July 6 Litho. Perf. 13¼x13½
857 A586 18d multi .70 .70

Haki Stermilli (1895-1953), Writer — A587

2020, July 6 Litho. Perf. 13¼x13½
858 A587 18d multi .70 .70

Charles Bukowski (1920-94), Writer — A588

2020, July 6 Litho. Perf. 13¼x13½
859 A588 72d multi 2.75 2.75

Diplomatic Relations Between North Macedonia and the United States, 25th Anniv. — A589

Perf. 13½x13¼
2020, Dec. 19 Litho.
860 A589 144d multi 5.75 5.75

Parashqevi Qiriazi (1880-1970), Teacher and Participant at Congress of Manastir — A590

Perf. 13¼x13½
2020, Dec. 22 Litho.
861 A590 18d multi .70 .70

Radio Skopje, 75th Anniv. — A591

Perf. 13½x13¼
2020, Dec. 22 Litho.
862 A591 32d multi 1.30 1.30

Adoption of National Flag, 25th Anniv. — A592

Perf. 13½x13¼
2020, Dec. 22 Litho.
863 A592 32d multi 1.30 1.30

Marko Tsepenkov (1829-1920), Folklorist — A593

Perf. 13¼x13½
2020, Dec. 22 Litho.
864 A593 34d multi 1.40 1.40

Macedonian Alphabet, 75th Anniv. — A594

Perf. 13½x13¼
2020, Dec. 22 Litho.
865 A594 72d multi 3.00 3.00

Florence Nightingale (1820-1910), Nurse — A595

Perf. 13½x13¼
2020, Dec. 22 Litho.
866 A595 72d multi 3.00 3.00

St. John Paul II (1920-2005) and St. Teresa of Calcutta (1910-97) — A596

MACEDONIA

Perf. 13½x13¼
2020, Dec. 22 Litho.
867 A596 144d multi 5.75 5.75

Snakes — A597

No. 868: a, 10d, Eryx jaculus. b, 20d, Zamenis situla. c, 50d, Vipera ammodytes. d, 101d, Vipera berus.

Perf. 13½x13¼
2020, Dec. 22 Litho.
868 A597 Block of 4, #a-d 7.25 7.25

Christmas — A598

Perf. 13¼x13½
2020, Dec. 22 Litho.
869 A598 50d multi 2.00 2.00

Acid Beta-glucosidase Molecule of Gaucher's Disease and Emblem of International Gaucher Alliance — A599

Perf. 13½x13¼
2021, Feb. 18 Litho.
870 A599 25d multi 1.00 1.00

Mosaic Depicting Peacock, Stobi — A600

Perf. 13½x13¼
2021, Feb. 18 Litho.
871 A600 88d multi 3.50 3.50

Double-decker Bus — A601

Perf. 13½x13¼
2021, Feb. 18 Litho.
872 A601 144d multi 5.75 5.75

Mediterranean Water Buffalos — A602

Perf. 13½x13¼
2021, Mar. 18 Litho.
873 A602 25d multi .95 .95

Blazhe Koneski (1921-93), Writer and Linguist — A603

2021, Apr. 5 Litho. Perf. 13¼x13½
874 A603 72d multi 3.00 3.00

Discovery of Insulin, Cent. — A604

2021, Apr. 16 Litho. Perf. 13½x13¼
875 A604 73d multi 3.00 3.00

Masked Health Worker and COVID-19 Viruses — A605

2021, Apr. 16 Litho. Perf. 13½x13¼
876 A605 144d multi 5.75 5.75

European Capitals — A606

Designs: No. 877, 72d, Ljubljana Castle, Ljubljana, Slovenia. No. 878, 72d, St. Mark's Square, Zagreb, Croatia. No. 879, 72d, Alfama neighborhood, Lisbon, Portugal.

2021, Apr. 26 Litho. Perf. 13½x13¼
877-879 A606 Set of 3 8.50 8.50

Bajram Festival — A607

2021, May 11 Litho. Perf. 13½x13¼
880 A607 25d multi 1.00 1.00

Endangered Animals — A608

Designs: No. 881, Lynx lynx balcanicus. No. 882: a, Capreolus capreolus. b, Canis lupus. c, Ursus arctos. d, Cygnus olor. No. 883, Bubo bubo.

2021, May 11 Litho. Perf. 13½x13¼
881 A608 144d multi 5.75 5.75
882 A608 50d Sheet of 4, #a-d 8.00 8.00

Souvenir Sheet
883 A608 144d multi 5.75 5.75
Europa.

Vegetables Type of 2019
Designs: 1d, Okra. 7d, Lettuce. 18d, Brussels sprouts. 20d, Parsley. 25d, Arugula.

2021, June 1 Litho. Perf. 12¾x13
884 A553 1d multi .25 .25
885 A553 7d multi .30 .30
886 A553 18d multi .70 .70
887 A553 20d multi .80 .80
888 A553 25d multi 1.00 1.00
Nos. 884-888 (5) 3.05 3.05

2020 European Soccer Championships A609

2021, June 1 Litho. Perf. 13½x13¼
889 A609 181d multi 7.25 7.25

The 2020 European Soccer Championships were postponed until 2021 because of the COVID-19 pandemic.

Caravaggio (1571-1610), Painter — A610

Perf. 13½x13¼
2021, June 24 Litho.
890 A610 36d multi 1.40 1.40

Souvenir Sheet

Ohrid Framework Agreement, 20th Anniv. — A611

2021, Aug. 4 Litho. Imperf.
891 A611 72d multi 2.75 2.75

Independence, 30th Anniv. — A612

2021, Sept. 6 Litho. Imperf.
892 A612 72d multi 2.75 2.75

Naim Frasheri (1846-1900), Poet — A613

Kole Chashule (1921-2009), Writer — A614

Fyodor Dostoevsky (1821-81), Writer — A615

Perf. 13½x13¼
2021, Sept. 24 Litho.
893 A613 25d multi .95 .95
894 A614 25d multi .95 .95
895 A615 73d multi 2.75 2.75
Nos. 893-895 (3) 4.65 4.65

Philosophy Faculty of Saints Cyril and Methodius University of Skopje, 75th Anniv. — A616

2021, Oct. 8 Litho. Perf. 13¼x13½
896 A616 144d multi 5.50 5.50

Zlatno Slavejche Children's Music Festival, Skopje, 50th Anniv. — A617

2021, Oct. 14 Litho. Perf. 13¼
897 A617 25d multi .95 .95

Louis Armstrong (1901-71), Musician — A618

2021, Oct. 14 Litho. Perf. 13¼
898 A618 144d multi 5.50 5.50

Flowers A619

No. 899: a, 10d, Centaurea soskae. b, 20d, Laserpitium ochridanum. c, 50d, Sempervivum galicicum. d, 101d, Dianthus galicicae.

Perf. 13½x13¼
2021, Nov. 10 Litho.
899 A619 Block of 4, #a-d 6.75 6.75

Christmas — A620

2021, Dec. 6 Litho. Perf. 13½x13¼
900 A620 25d multi .95 .95

Bishop Theodosius of Skopje (1846-1926) A621

Mirka Ginova (1916-46), Executed Freedom Fighter A622

Gjergj Fishta (1871-1940), Poet — A623

Perf. 13¼x13½
2021, Dec. 20 Litho.
901 A621 25d multi .95 .95
902 A622 25d multi .95 .95
903 A623 25d multi .95 .95
Nos. 901-903 (3) 2.85 2.85

René Descartes (1596-1650), Mathematician and Philosopher A624

2021, Dec. 20 Litho. Perf. 13¼
904 A624 36d multi 1.40 1.40

Ship, Compass and Ferdinand Magellan (1480-1521), Explorer — A625

Perf. 13½x13¼
2021, Dec. 20 Litho.
905 A625 72d multi .95 .95
First circumnavigation of Earth, 500th anniv.

A626

2022 Winter Olympics, Beijing — A627

MACEDONIA

2022, Feb. 4	**Litho.**		**Perf. 13¼x13½**	
906	A626	72d multi	2.60	2.60
			Perf. 13½x13¼	
907	A627	72d multi	2.60	2.60

Skopje Aqueduct — A628

2022, Feb. 25	**Litho.**		**Perf. 13¼**	
908	A628	44d multi	1.60	1.60

Epidermolysis Bullosa Awareness A629

2022, Feb. 28		**Perf. 13½x13¼**		
			Litho.	
909	A629	36d multi	1.30	1.30

Aco Stefanovski (1922-85), Actor — A630

Ava Gardner (1922-90), Actress — A631

2022, Mar. 16	**Litho.**		**Perf. 13¼**	
910	A630	72d multi	2.60	2.60
911	A631	144d multi	5.25	5.25

1972 Chess Olympiad, Skopje, 50th Anniv. — A632

2022, Mar. 23	**Litho.**		**Perf. 13¼**	
912	A632	36d multi	1.30	1.30

Emil Zátopek (1922-2000), Three-time Gold Medalist at 1952 Summer Olympics — A633

2022, Mar. 23	**Litho.**		**Perf. 13¼**	
913	A633	72d multi	2.60	2.60

Danco Zografski (1920-77), Historian — A634

2022, Apr. 14	**Litho.**		**Perf. 13¼**	
914	A634	25d multi	.85	.85

Louis Pasteur (1822-95), Microbiologist A635

2022, Apr. 14	**Litho.**		**Perf. 13¼**	
915	A635	144d multi	5.00	5.00

Souvenir Sheet

Thomas Edison (1847-1931), Inventor — A636

2022, Apr. 28	**Litho.**		**Imperf.**	
916	A636	144d multi	5.00	5.00

Souvenir Sheet

Bajram Festival A637

2022, Apr. 28	**Litho.**		**Imperf.**	
917	A637	25d multi	.85	.85

Souvenir Sheet

Gotse Delchev (1872-1903), Leader of Internal Macedonian Revolutionary Organization — A638

2022, May 4	**Litho.**		**Imperf.**	
918	A638	25d multi	.85	.85

Landmarks of Paris, France — A639

Landmarks of Prague, Czech Republic — A640

2022, May 5	**Litho.**		**Perf. 13¼**	
919	A639	72d multi	2.50	2.50
920	A640	72d multi	2.50	2.50

The Lying Shepherd Boy — A641

Legend of Itar Pejo — A642

Legend of Labin and Dojrana A643

2022, May 10	**Litho.**		**Perf. 13¼**	
921	A641	144d multi	5.00	5.00
922	A642	144d multi	5.00	5.00

Souvenir Sheet

923	A643	72d multi	2.50	2.50

Europa.

Yane Sandanski (1872-1915), National Hero — A644

2022, May 10	**Litho.**		**Perf. 13¼**	
924	A644	25d multi	.90	.90

Small Montmartre of Bitola Children's Art Festival — A645

2022, May 23	**Litho.**		**Perf. 13¼**	
925	A645	25d multi	.90	.90

Piet Mondrian (1872-1944) Painter — A646

2022, June 15	**Litho.**		**Perf. 13¼**	
926	A646	144d multi	5.00	5.00

Army of the Republic of North Macedonia, 30th Anniv. — A647

2022, Aug. 18	**Litho.**		**Perf. 13¼**	
927	A647	30d multi	1.00	1.00

Vidoe Podgorec (1934-97), Writer — A648

Aleksander Stavre Drenova (1872-1947), Poet — A649

Alija Isakovic (1932-97), Writer — A650

Molière (1622-73), Playwright and Actor — A651

2022, Sept. 14	**Litho.**		**Perf. 13¼**	
928	A648	25d multi	.80	.80
929	A649	25d multi	.80	.80
930	A650	25d multi	.80	.80
931	A651	144d multi	4.75	4.75
	Nos. 928-931 (4)		7.15	7.15

Albanian Orthography Congress, 50th Anniv. — A652

2022, Sept. 27	**Litho.**		**Perf. 13¼**	
932	A652	25d multi	.80	.80

National Opera and Ballet, 75th Anniv. — A653

2022, Sept. 27	**Litho.**		**Perf. 13¼**	
933	A653	25d multi	.80	.80

Youth Cultural Centor, Skopje, 50th Anniv. — A654

2022, Sept. 27	**Litho.**		**Perf. 13¼**	
934	A654	50d multi	1.60	1.60

International Union of Railways, Cent. — A655

2022, Sept. 27	**Litho.**		**Perf. 13¼**	
935	A655	144d multi	4.75	4.75

Aleksandar Sarievski (1922-2002), Singer — A656

Johannes Brahms (1833-97), Composer A657

Franz Schubert (1797-1828), Composer A658

2022, Oct. 12	**Litho.**		**Perf. 13¼**	
936	A656	25d multi	.80	.80
937	A657	144d multi	4.75	4.75
938	A658	144d multi	4.75	4.75
	Nos. 936-938 (3)		10.30	10.30

Sciurus Niger — A659

Erinaceus Europaeus A660

MACEDONIA

Micromus Minutus — A661

Talpa Europaea — A662

2022, Nov. 2 Litho. Perf. 13¼
939 A659 10d multi .35 .35
940 A660 20d multi .70 .70
941 A661 50d multi 1.75 1.75
942 A662 101d multi 3.50 3.50
Nos. 939-942 (4) 6.30 6.30

2022 World Cup Soccer Championships, Qatar — A663

2022, Nov. 21 Litho. Perf. 13¼
943 A663 181d multi 6.25 6.25

Christmas — A664

2022, Dec. 6 Litho. Perf. 13¼
944 A664 25d multi .90 .90

Ichthyosis Awareness A665

2023, Feb. 28 Litho. Perf. 13¼
945 A665 36d multi 1.25 1.25

Church of St. Panteleimon, Nerezi — A666

2023, Feb. 28 Litho. Perf. 13¼
946 A666 111d multi 4.00 4.00

Blaise Pascal (1623-62), Mathematician A667

2023, Mar. 16 Litho. Perf. 13¼
947 A667 111d multi 4.00 4.00

100th Birthday of Meti Krliu, Politician A668

Vera Jocikj (1923-44), War Heroine A669

Gjorgi Kolozov (1948-2003), Actor — A670

Gustave Eiffel (1832-1923), Civil Engineer, and Eiffel Tower — A671

2023, Mar. 29 Litho. Perf. 13¼
948 A668 25d multi .90 .90
949 A669 25d multi .90 .90
950 A670 79d multi 2.75 2.75
951 A671 144d multi 5.00 5.00
Nos. 948-951 (4) 9.55 9.55

Bajram Festival — A672

2023, Apr. 19 Litho. Perf. 13¼
952 A672 30d multi 1.10 1.10

Buildings in Madrid, Spain A673

Buildings in Stockholm, Sweden A674

2023, May 4 Litho. Perf. 13¼
953 A673 79d multi 2.75 2.75
954 A674 79d multi 2.75 2.75

Interlocking Hands — A675

Handprint — A676

2023, May 10 Litho. Perf. 13¼
955 A675 100d multi 3.50 3.50
956 A676 144d multi 5.00 5.00
Europa.

24 Hours of Le Mans Automobile Race, Cent. — A677

2023, June 1 Litho. Perf. 13¼
957 A677 144d multi 5.00 5.00

1963 Skopje Earthquake, 60th Anniv. — A678

2023, July 26 Litho. Perf. 13¼
958 A678 36d multi 1.30 1.30

Luran Ahmeti (1974-2021), Actor — A679

2023, July 26 Litho. Perf. 13¼
959 A679 36d multi 1.30 1.30

Independence of Israel, 75th Anniv. — A680

2023, July 26 Litho. Perf. 13¼
960 A680 111d multi 4.00 4.00

Arben Xhaferi (1948-2012), Politician — A681

2023, Aug. 15 Litho. Perf. 13¼
961 A681 36d multi 1.25 1.25

Nikola Martinoski (1903-73), Painter — A682

2023, Sept. 20 Litho. Perf. 13¼
962 A682 79d multi 2.75 2.75

North Macedonian 2023 Chairmanship of Organization for Security and Cooperation in Europe — A683

2023, Sept. 20 Litho. Perf. 13¼
963 A683 100d multi 3.50 3.50

Pablo Picasso (1881-1973), Painter — A684

2023, Sept. 20 Litho. Perf. 13¼
964 A684 181d multi 6.25 6.25

Aco Shopov (1923-82), Poet A685

Lutvi Rusi (1923-81), Journalist A686

Hasan Prishtina (1873-1973), Prime Minister of Albania A687

Pablo Neruda (1904-73), 1971 Nobel Laureate in Literature A688

2023, Sept. 27 Litho. Perf. 13¼
965 A685 30d multi 1.10 1.10
966 A686 30d multi 1.10 1.10
967 A687 36d multi 1.25 1.25
968 A688 79d multi 2.75 2.75
Nos. 965-968 (4) 6.20 6.20

Vaska Ilieva (1923-2001), Folk Singer — A689

2023, Nov. 8 Litho. Perf. 13¼
969 A689 25d multi .90 .90

Enrico Caruso (1873-1921), Opera Singer — A690

2023, Nov. 8 Litho. Perf. 13¼
970 A690 72d multi 2.60 2.60

North Macedonian Postal Agency, 15th Anniv. — A691

2023, Nov. 16 Litho. Perf. 13¼
971 A691 36d multi 1.30 1.30

Flora — A692

Designs: 10d, Alchemilla peristerica. 20d, Sempervivum octopodes. 30d, Crocus pelistericus. 101d, Festuca pelisterica.

2023, Nov. 29 Litho. Perf. 13¼
972-975 A692 Set of 4 5.75 5.75

Parashqevi (1880-1970) and Sevasti Qiriazi (c. 1871-1949), Writers and Educators A693

2023, Nov. 29 Litho. Perf. 13¼
976 A693 36d multi 1.30 1.30

Christmas — A694

2023, Nov. 29 Litho. Perf. 13¼
977 A694 30d multi 1.10 1.10

POSTAL TAX STAMPS

Men Blowing Horns — PT1

1991, Dec. 30 Litho. Perf. 13½
RA1 PT1 2.50d multicolored 1.10 1.10
No. RA1 was required on mail Dec. 31, 1991-Sept. 8, 1992. For surcharge see No. 22.

MACEDONIA

Anti-Cancer Week — PT2

Designs: Nos. RA2, RA6, Emblems, inscriptions. Nos. RA3, RA7, Magnetic resonance imaging scanner. Nos. RA4, RA8, Overhead scanner, examination table. No. RA5, RA9c, Mammography imager. No. RA9, Ultra sound computer.

1992, Mar. 1		Litho.	Perf. 10	
RA2	PT2	5d multicolored	.70	.70
RA3	PT2	5d multicolored	.70	.70
RA4	PT2	5d multicolored	.70	.70
RA5	PT2	5d multicolored	.70	.70
a.	Block of 4, #RA2-RA5		4.00	4.00
RA6	PT2	5d multicolored	.30	.30
RA7	PT2	5d multicolored	.30	.30
RA8	PT2	5d multicolored	.30	.30
RA9	PT2	5d multicolored	.30	.30
a.	Block of 4, #RA6-RA9		1.50	1.50
b.	Souv. sheet of 3, #RA7-RA9, RA9c		25.00	25.00
c.	PT2 5d multicolored		.45	.45
	Nos. RA2-RA9 (8)		4.00	4.00

Inscription at right reads up on No. RA2 and down on No. RA6. Designs on Nos. RA7-RA8, RA9c are without red cross symbol.
Souvenir folders with perf. and imperf. sheets of RA9b sold for 40d. Value for both sheets in folder, $60.
Obligatory on mail Mar. 1-8.
See Nos. RA28-RA31.

Red Cross Week — PT3

Designs: RA10, Slogans. No. RA11, Airplanes dropping supplies. No. RA12, Aiding traffic accident victim. No. RA13, Evacuating casualties from building.

1992, May 8			Perf. 10	
RA10		10d multicolored	.25	.25
RA11		10d multicolored	.25	.25
RA12		10d multicolored	.25	.25
RA13		10d multicolored	.25	.25
a.	PT3 Block of 4, #RA10-RA13			

Nos. RA10-RA13 exist with silver-colored borders in perf. and imperf. miniature sheets that sold for 80d. Value for both sheets $9.
Obligatory on mail May 8-15.

PT4

Solidarity Week: No. RA14, Skopje earthquake. No. RA15, Woman holding girl. No. RA16, Mother carrying infant. No. RA17, Mother, children, airplane.
130d, Woman, child, airport control tower.

1992, June 1			Perf. 10	
RA14	PT4	20d multicolored	.25	.25
RA15	PT4	20d multicolored	.25	.25
RA16	PT4	20d multicolored	.25	.25
RA17	PT4	20d multicolored	.25	.25
a.	Block of 4		1.25	

Size: 74x97mm
Imperf

| RA18 | PT4 | 130d multicolored | 3.25 3.25 |

No. RA18 also exists with perf. vignette. Same value.
Obligatory on mail June 1-7.
See No. RA55.

PT5

Anti-Tuberculosis Week: No. RA20, Nurse, infant. No. RA21, Nurse giving oxygen to patient. No. RA22, Infant in bed.
200d, Child being treated by nurse.

1992, Sept. 14			Perf. 10	
RA19	PT5	20d multicolored	.25	.25
RA20	PT5	20d multicolored	.25	.25
RA21	PT5	20d multicolored	.25	.25
RA22	PT5	20d multicolored	.25	.25
a.	Block of 4, #RA19-RA22		1.25	1.25

Size: 74x97mm
Imperf

| RA23 | PT5 | 200d vermilion & multi | 3.00 3.00 |

No. RA23 exists with magenta inscriptions, and also with perf. vignette and either magenta or vermilion inscriptions. Obligatory on mail Sept. 14-21.

Red Cross Fund — PT6

1993, Feb. 1		Litho.	Perf. 10	
RA24	PT6	20d Shown	.30	.30
RA25	PT6	20d Marguerites	.30	.30
RA26	PT6	20d Carnations	.30	.30
RA27	PT6	20d Mixed bouquet	.30	.30
a.	Block of 4, #RA24-RA27		1.25	1.25

Nos. RA24-RA27 exist in perf. or imperf. miniature sheets with either gold or silver backgrounds and inscriptions, that sold for 500d each. Value for both sheets $12.
Obligatory on mail Feb. 1-28.

Cancer Therapy Type of 1992

Designs: No. RA28, Nuclear medicine caduceus, inscriptions. No. RA29, Radiographic equipment. No. RA30, Radiology machine. No. RA31, Scanner.

1993, Mar. 1		Litho.	Perf. 10	
RA28	PT2	20d multicolored	.30	.30
RA29	PT2	20d multicolored	.30	.30
RA30	PT2	20d multicolored	.30	.30
RA31	PT2	20d multicolored	.30	.30
a.	Block of 4, #RA28-RA31		1.25	1.25

Nos. RA28-RA31 exist in perf. & imperf. miniature sheets with gold background or inscription, that sold for 500d each. Value for both sheets $7.50.
Obligatory on mail Mar. 1-8.

Red Cross Week — PT7

No. RA32, Inscriptions. No. RA33, Man holding baby. No. RA34, Patient in wheelchair. No. RA35, Carrying stretcher.

1993, May 8			Perf. 10	
RA32	PT7	50d multicolored	.25	.25
RA33	PT7	50d multicolored	.25	.25
RA34	PT7	50d multicolored	.25	.25
RA35	PT7	50d multicolored	.25	.25
a.	Block of 4, #RA32-RA35		1.25	1.25

Perf. & imperf. miniature sheets of Nos. RA32-RA35 exist with yellow inscription tablets that sold for 700d each. Value for both sheets $7.50.
Obligatory on mail May 8-15.

| 1993, June 1 | | | Perf. 10 | |

No. RA36, Skopje earthquake. No. RA37, Unloading boxes. No. RA38, Labeling boxes. No. RA39, Boxes, fork lift.

RA36	PT7	50de multi	.25	.25
RA37	PT7	50de multi	.25	.25
RA38	PT7	50de multi	.25	.25
RA39	PT7	50de multi	.25	.25
a.	Block of 4, #RA36-RA39		1.25	1.25

Perf. & imperf. miniature sheets of Nos. RA36-RA39 exist with gold inscription tablets that sold for 7d each. Value for both sheets $5.
Obligatory on mail June 1-7.

| 1993, Sept. 14 | | | Perf. 10 |

Designs: Nos. RA40, Inscriptions. Nos. RA41, Children in meadow. Nos. RA42, Bee on flower. No. RA43, Goat behind rock.

RA40	PT7	50de black, gray & red	.25	.25
RA41	PT7	50de green & multi	.25	.25
RA42	PT7	50de green & multi	.25	.25
RA43	PT7	50de green & multi	.25	.25
a.	Block of 4, #RA40-RA43		1.25	1.25

Nos. RA41-RA43 exist in perf. & imperf. miniature sheets that sold for 15d each. Values for both sheets $3.50. Nos. RA40-RA43 exist with yellow omitted, resulting in blue stamps. Value of the blue set $4.25.
Obligatory on mail Sept. 14-21.
See Nos. RA52-RA54.

Anti-Cancer Week — PT8

No. RA44, Inscription, emblem. No. RA45, Lily. No. RA46, Mushroom. No. RA47, Swans.

1994, Mar. 1			Perf. 10	
RA44	PT8	1d multi	.25	.25
RA45	PT8	1d multi	.25	.25
RA46	PT8	1d multi	.25	.25
RA47	PT8	1d multi	.25	.25
a.	Block of 4, #RA44-RA47		1.40	1.40

Nos. RA44-RA47 without silver color exist in perf. & imperf. miniature sheets and sold for 20d each. Value for both sheets $7.
Obligatory on mail Mar. 1-8.

Red Cross Type of 1993 and PT9

1994, May 8		Litho.	Perf. 10	
RA51	PT9	1d shown	.25	.25
RA52	PT7	1d like #RA41	.25	.25
RA53	PT7	1d like #RA39	.25	.25
RA54	PT7	1d like #RA33	.25	.25
a.	Block of 4, #RA51-RA54		1.25	1.25

Nos. RA51-RA54 exist without denomination in perf. & imperf. miniature sheets and sold for 30d each. Value for both sheets $9.
Obligatory on mail May 8-15, 1994.

Skopje Earthquake Type of 1993

| 1994, June 1 | | | | |
| RA55 | PT4 | 1d like #RA14 | .75 | .75 |

Obligatory on mail June 1-7, 1994.

Red Cross Fund — PT10

No. RA57, Globe. No. RA58, AIDS awareness. No. RA59, Condoms.

1994, Dec. 1		Litho.	Perf. 10	
RA56	PT10	2d shown	.25	.25
RA57	PT10	2d multi	.25	.25
RA58	PT10	2d multi	.25	.25
RA59	PT10	2d multi	.25	.25
a.	Block of 4, #RA56-RA59		1.25	1.25

Size: 80x95mm
Imperf

| RA60 | PT10 | 40d like RA57 | 3.00 3.00 |

Country name and value omitted from vignette on No. RA60, which also exists with perf. vignette. Obligatory on mail Dec. 1-8.

Anti-Cancer Week — PT11

1995, Mar. 1				
RA61	PT11	1d shown	.25	.25
RA62	PT11	1d White lilies	.25	.25
RA63	PT11	1d Red lilies	.25	.25
RA64	PT11	1d Red roses	.25	.25
a.	Block of 4, Nos. RA61-RA64		1.25	1.25

Size: 97x74mm
Imperf

| RA65 | PT11 | 30d like #RA61, RA64 | 3.00 3.00 |

Blue inscriptions, country name, and value omitted from vignette on No. RA65, which also exists with perf. vignette. Obligatory on mail Mar. 1-8.

Red Cross Fund — PT12

Designs: No. RA66, Red Cross emblem. No. RA67, Red Cross volunteers holding clipboards. No. RA68, Young volunteers wearing white shirts. No. RA69, RA70, Red Cross, Red Crescent symbols, globe.

1995, May 8				
RA66	PT12	1d multicolored	.25	.25
RA67	PT12	1d multicolored	.25	.25
RA68	PT12	1d multicolored	.25	.25
RA69	PT12	1d blue & multi	.25	.25
a.	Strip of 4, Nos. RA70-RA73		1.25	1.25

Size: 68x85mm
Imperf

| RA70 | PT12 | 30d multicolored | 3.00 3.00 |

No. RA70 also exists with perf. vignette. Obligatory on mail May 8-15.

Solidarity Week — PT13

| 1995, June 1 | | | | |
| RA71 | PT13 | 1d shown | .50 | .50 |

Size: 85x70

| RA72 | PT13 | 30d like No. RA75 | 2.25 2.25 |

No. RA72 also exists with perf. vignette. Obligatory on mail June 1-7.

Robert Koch (1843-1910), Bacteriologist — PT14

| 1995, Sept. 14 | | Litho. | Perf. 10 | |
| RA73 | PT14 | 1d shown | .65 | .65 |

Size: 90x73mm
Imperf

| RA74 | PT14 | 30d like No. RA73 | 2.25 2.25 |

No. RA74 exists with perf. vignette. Obligatory on mail Sept. 14-21.

Children's Week — PT15

1995, Oct. 2		Litho.	Die Cut
		Self-Adhesive	
RA75	PT15	2d blue violet & red	1.00 1.00

Obligatory on mail 10/2-8.

PT16

MACEDONIA

1995, Nov. 1   Litho.   Perf. 10
RA76   PT16   1d multicolored   .50   .50
              Size: 90x72mm
              Imperf
RA77   PT16   30d like #RA76   2.60 2.60
   Red Cross, AIDS awareness.
   No. RA77 also exists with perf. vignette.
   Obligatory on mail Nov. 1-7.

Red Cross — PT17

1996, Mar. 1   Litho.   Perf. 10
RA78   PT17   1d multicolored   .60   .60
              Size: 98x76mm
              Imperf
RA79   PT17   30d like #RA78   2.25 2.25
   No. RA79 also exists with perf. vignette.
   Obligatory on mail Mar. 1-8.

PT18   Red Cross Week — PT19

Fundamental principles of Red Cross, Red Crescent Societies, inscriptions in: No. RA81, Macedonian. No. RA82, English. No. RA83, French. RA84, Spanish.

1996, May 8   Litho.   Perf. 10
RA80   PT18   1d multicolored   .25   .25
RA81   PT19   1d multicolored   .25   .25
RA82   PT19   1d multicolored   .25   .25
RA83   PT19   1d multicolored   .25   .25
RA84   PT19   1d multicolored   .25   .25
   a.   Strip of 5, #RA80-RA84   1.40 1.40
   Obligatory on mail May 8-15.

Red Cross, Solidarity Week — PT20

1996, June 1   Litho.   Perf. 10
RA86   PT20   1d multicolored   .50   .50
   No. RA86 exists without country name or denomination in perf. & imperf. miniature sheets and sold for 30d each. Value for both sheets $5.50. Obligatory on mail June 1-7, 1996.

Red Cross, Fight Tuberculosis Week — PT21

1996, Sept. 14   Litho.   Perf. 10
RA87   PT21   1d multicolored   .55   .55
              Size: 80x90mm
              Imperf
RA88   PT21   30d like #RA87   2.25 2.25
   No. RA88 also exists with perf. vignette.
   Obligatory on mail Sept. 14-21.

Red Cross, AIDS Awareness PT22

1996, Dec. 6
RA89   PT22   1d multicolored   .55   .55

              Size: 90x73mm
              Imperf
RA90   PT22   30d like #RA89   2.50 2.50
   No. RA90 also exists with perf. vignette.
   Obligatory on mail Dec. 1-7.

Red Cross, Cancer Week — PT23

1997, Apr. 1
RA91   PT23   1d Cross in pale org   .50   .50
   a.   Cross in red   1.10 1.10
   No. RA91 obligatory on mail Apr. 1-8.
   No. RA91a issued 5/8.

Red Cross — PT24

1997, May 8
RA92   PT24   1d multicolored   1.90 1.90
   Obligatory on mail May 8-15.

Children's Day — PT25

1997, June 1
RA93   PT25   1d Cross in deep vermilion .60   .60
   a.   Cross in red   .75   .75
   Obligatory on mail June 1-8.

Red Cross, Anti-Tuberculosis PT26

1997, Sept. 14
RA94   PT26   1d multicolored   1.00 1.00
   Obligatory on mail, Sept. 14-21.

Red Cross — PT27

1997, Dec. 1   Litho.   Perf. 10
RA95   PT27   1d multicolored   .75   .75
   Obligatory on mail Dec. 1-7.

Red Cross Fight Against Cancer — PT28

1998, Mar. 1   Perf. 13½
RA96   PT28   1d multicolored   .75   .75
   Obligatory on mail Mar. 1-8.

Red Cross, Humanity — PT29

1998, May 8
RA97   PT29   2d multicolored   .65   .65
   Obligatory on mail May 8-15.

Red Cross — PT30

1998, June 1   Litho.   Perf. 13½
RA98   PT30   2d multicolored   .65   .65
   Obligatory on mail June 1-7, 1998.

Fight Tuberculosis — PT31

1998, Sept. 14   Litho.   Perf. 13½
RA99   PT31   2d multicolored   .75   .75
   Obligatory on mail Sept. 14-21, 1998.

AIDS Awareness — PT32

1998, Dec. 1
RA100 PT32   2d multicolored   .75   .75
   Obligatory on mail Dec. 1-7, 1998.

Red Cross Fight Against Cancer — PT33

1999, Mar. 1   Litho.   Perf. 13¼
RA101 PT33   2d multi   .65   .65
   Obligatory on mail Mar. 1-7, 1999.

Red Cross — PT34

1999, May 8
RA102 PT34   2d multi   .65   .65
   Obligatory on mail May 8-15, 1999.

Red Cross, Solidarity Week — PT35

1999, June 1
RA103 PT35   2d multi   .65   .65
   Obligatory on mail June 1-7, 1999.

Fight Tuberculosis — PT36

1999, Sept. 14   Litho.   Perf. 13¼
RA104 PT36   2d multi   .65   .65
   Obligatory on mail Sept. 14-21.

AIDS Awareness PT37

1999, Dec. 1
RA105 PT37   2.50d multi   .75   .75
   Obligatory on mail Dec. 1-7.

Anti-Cancer Week — PT38

2000, Mar. 1   Litho.   Perf. 13¼
RA106 PT38   2.50d multi   .65   .65
   Obligatory on mail Mar. 1-8.

Red Cross — PT39

2000, May 8
RA107 PT39   2.50d multi   .65   .65
   Obligatory on mail May 8-15.

Red Cross — PT40

2000, June 1
RA108 PT40   2.50d multi   .65   .65
   Obligatory on mail June 1-7.

Red Cross — PT41

2000 Sept. 14   Litho.   Perf. 13¼
RA109 PT41   3d multi   .90   .90
   Obligatory on mail Sept. 14-21.

Fight Against AIDS — PT42

2000 Dec. 1
RA110 PT42   3d multi   1.00 1.00
   Obligatory on mail Dec. 1-7.

MACEDONIA

Fight Against Cancer — PT43

2001, Mar. 1   Litho.   Perf. 13¼
RA111 PT43 3d multi   .65   .65
Obligatory on mail Mar. 1-8.

Red Cross — PT44

2001, May 8
RA112 PT44 3d multi   .65   .65
Obligatory on mail May 8-15.

Red Cross Solidarity Week — PT45

2001, June 1
RA113 PT45 3d multi   .65   .65
Obligatory on mail June 1-7.

Fight Against Tuberculosis — PT46

2001, Sept. 14
RA114 PT46 3d multi   .65   .65
Obligatory on mail Sept. 14-21.

Campaign Against AIDS — PT47

2001, Dec. 1   Litho.   Perf. 13¼
RA115 PT47 3d multi   1.00   1.00
Obligatory on mail Dec. 1-7.

Campaign Against Cancer — PT48

2002, Mar. 1
RA116 PT48 3d multi   .80   .80
Obligatory on mail Mar. 1-8.

Red Cross Week — PT49

2002, May 8   Litho.   Perf. 13¼
RA117 PT49 3d multi   .65   .65
Obligatory on mail May 8-15.

Red Cross Solidarity Week — PT50

2002, June 1
RA118 PT50 3d multi   .65   .65
Obligatory on mail June 1-7.

Tuberculosis Prevention PT51

2002, Sept. 14
RA119 PT51 3d multi   1.00   1.00
Obligatory on mail Sept. 14-21.

Campaign Against AIDS — PT52

2002, Dec. 1
RA120 PT52 3d multi   .75   .75

Campaign Against Cancer — PT53

2003, Mar. 1   Litho.   Perf. 13¼
RA121 PT53 4d multi   .75   .75
Obligatory on mail Mar. 1-8.

Campaign Against AIDS — PT54

2003, May 8
RA122 PT54 4d multi   1.00   1.00
Obligatory on mail May 8-15.

Red Cross Solidarity — PT55

2003, June 1   Perf. 13¼x13½
RA123 PT55 4d multi   .65   .65
Obligatory on mail June 1-7.

Tuberculosis Prevention PT56

Perf. 13½x13¼
2003, Sept. 14   Litho.
RA124 PT56 4d multi   .65   .65
Obligatory on mail Sept. 14-21.

Campaign Against AIDS — PT57

2003, Dec. 1   Litho.   Perf. 13¼x13½
RA125 PT57 4d multi   1.00   1.00
Obligatory on mail Dec. 1-7.

Campaign Against Cancer — PT58

2004, Mar. 1
RA126 PT58 4d multi   .90   .90
Obligatory on mail Mar. 1-8.

Red Cross Week — PT59

2004, May 8
RA127 PT59 4d multi   .65   .65
Obligatory on mail May 8-15.

Red Cross Solidarity Week — PT60

2004, June 1   Litho.   Perf. 13¼x13½
RA128 PT60 6d multi   .65   .65
Obligatory on mail June 1-7.

Tuberculosis Week — PT61

2004, Sept. 14   Perf. 13½x13¼
RA129 PT61 6d multi   .65   .65
Obligatory on mail Sept. 14-21.

Campaign Against AIDS — PT62

2004, Dec. 1   Litho.   Perf. 13½x13¼
RA130 PT62 6d multi   1.00   1.00
Obligatory on mail Dec. 1-7.

Campaign Against Cancer — PT63

2005, Mar. 1   Perf. 13¼x13½
RA131 PT63 6d multi   1.00   1.00
Obligatory on mail Mar. 1-8.

Red Cross — PT64

2005, May 8   Litho.   Perf. 13½x13¼
RA132 PT64 6d multi   1.00   1.00
Obligatory on mail May 8-15.

Campaign Against Tuberculosis PT65

Perf. 13½x13¼
2005, Sept. 14   Litho.
RA133 PT65 6d multi   .65   .65
Obligatory on mail Sept. 14-21.

Campaign Against AIDS — PT66

2005, Dec. 1   Perf. 13¼x13½
RA134 PT66 6d multi   1.10   1.10
Obligatory on mail Dec. 1-7.

Campaign Against Breast Cancer — PT67

2006, Mar. 1   Litho.   Perf. 13¼x13½
RA135 PT67 6d multi   1.00   1.00
Obligatory on mail Mar. 1-7.

Red Cross Week — PT68

2006, May 18   Litho.   Perf. 13¼x13½
RA136 PT68 6d multi   .90   .90
Obligatory on mail May 8-15.

Campaign Against Tuberculosis PT69

2006, Sept. 14   Perf. 13½x13¼
RA137 PT69 6d multi   .90   .90
Obligatory on mail Sept. 14-21.

Campaign Against AIDS — PT70

2006, Dec. 1
RA138 PT70 6d multi   .90   .90
Obligatory on mail Dec. 1-7.

MACEDONIA

Campaign Against Cancer — PT71
2007, Mar. 1 Litho. Perf. 13¼x13½
RA139 PT71 6d multi .60 .60
Obligatory on mail Mar. 1-8.

Red Cross Week — PT72
2007, May 8
RA140 PT72 6d multi .75 .75
Obligatory on mail May 8-15.

Campaign Against Tuberculosis — PT73
2007, Sept. 14
RA141 PT73 6d multi .60 .60
Obligatory on mail Sept. 14-21.

Campaign Against AIDS — PT74
2007, Dec. 1 Perf. 13½x13¼
RA142 PT74 6d multi 1.00 1.00
Obligatory on mail Dec. 1-8.

Campaign Against Cancer — PT75
2008, Mar. 1 Litho. Perf. 13½x13¼
RA143 PT75 6d multi .90 .90
Obligatory on mail Mar. 1-8.

Red Cross Week — PT76
2008, May 8
RA144 PT76 6d multi .65 .65
Obligatory on mail May 8-15.

Campaign Against Tuberculosis — PT77
2008, Sept. 14 Perf. 13¼x13½
RA145 PT77 6d multi .65 .65
Obligatory on mail Sept. 14-21.

Campaign Against AIDS — PT78
2008, Dec. 1 Perf. 13½x13¼
RA146 PT78 6d multi 1.00 1.00
Obligatory on mail Dec. 1-8.

Campaign Against Cancer — PT79
2009, Mar. 1 Perf. 13¼x13½
RA147 PT79 6d multi .65 .65
Obligatory on mail Mar. 1-8.

Red Cross Week — PT80
2009, May 8 Perf. 13½x13¼
RA148 PT80 6d multi .65 .65
Obligatory on mail May 8-15.

Campaign Against Tuberculosis PT81
2009, Sept. 14
RA149 PT81 6d multi .90 .90
Obligatory on mail Sept. 14-21.

Campaign Against AIDS — PT82
2009, Dec. 1
RA150 PT82 8d multi 1.00 1.00
Obligatory on mail Dec. 1-7.

Campaign Against Cancer — PT83
2010, Mar. 1 Perf. 13¼x13½
Granite Paper
RA151 PT83 8d multi .90 .90
Obligatory on mail Mar. 1-7.

Red Cross Week — PT84
2010, May 8 Litho.
Granite Paper
RA152 PT84 8d multi .65 .65
Obligatory on mail May 8-15.

Campaign Against Tuberculosis PT85
2010, Sept. 14 Perf. 13½x13¼ Litho.
Granite Paper
RA153 PT85 8d multi .90 .90
Obligatory on mail Sept. 14-21.

Campaign Against AIDS — PT86
2010, Dec. 1 Perf. 13¼x13½
Granite Paper
RA154 PT86 8d multi 1.10 1.10
Obligatory on mail Dec. 1-7.

Campaign Against Cancer — PT87
2011, Mar. 1 Granite Paper
RA155 PT87 8d multi .85 .85
Obligatory on mail Mar. 1-8.

Red Cross Week — PT88
2011, May 8
RA156 PT88 8d multi .65 .65
Obligatory on mail May 8-15.

Campaign Against Tuberculosis — PT89
2011, Sept. 14
RA157 PT89 8d multi .90 .90
Obligatory on mail Sept. 14-21.

Campaign Against AIDS — PT90
2011, Dec. 1
RA158 PT90 8d multi 1.10 1.10
Obligatory on mail Dec. 1-7.

Campaign Against Cancer — PT91
2012, Mar. 1
RA159 PT91 8d multi .80 .80
Obligatory on mail Mar. 1-8.

Red Cross Week — PT92
2012, May 8
RA160 PT92 8d multi .75 .75
Obligatory on mail May 8-15.

Campaign Against Tuberculosis — PT93
2012, Sept. 14
RA161 PT93 8d multi .75 .75
Obligatory on mail Sept. 14-21.

Campaign Against AIDS — PT94
2012, Dec. 1 Litho. Perf. 13¼x13½
RA162 PT94 8d multi 1.00 1.00
Obligatory on mail Dec. 1-7.

Campaign Against Cancer — PT95
2013, Mar. 1 Litho. Perf. 13¼x13½
RA163 PT95 8d multi .80 .80
Obligatory on mail Mar. 1-8.

Red Cross Week — PT96
2013, May 8 Litho. Perf. 13¼x13½
RA164 PT96 8d multi .75 .75
Intl. Red Cross, 150th anniv. Obligatory on mail May 8-15.

Campaign Against Tuberculosis — PT97

MACEDONIA

Perf. 13¼x13½
2013, Sept. 14 Litho.
RA165 PT97 8d multi .75 .75
Obligatory on mail Sept. 14-21.

Campaign Against AIDS — PT98

2013, Dec. 1 Litho. *Perf. 13¼x13½*
RA166 PT98 8d multi 1.00 1.00
Obligatory on mail Dec. 1-7.

Campaign Against Cancer — PT99

2014, Mar. 1 Litho. *Perf. 13¼x13½*
RA167 PT99 8d multi .80 .80
Obligatory on mail Mar. 1-8.

Red Cross Week — PT100

2014, May 8 Litho. *Perf. 13¼x13½*
RA168 PT100 8d multi .75 .75
Obligatory on mail May 8-15.

Red Cross, 50th Anniv. — PT101

2015, May 8 Litho. *Perf. 13¼x13½*
RA169 PT101 8d multi .70 .70
Obligatory on mail May 8-15.

Campaign Against Tuberculosis — PT102

Perf. 13¼x13½
2015, Sept. 14 Litho.
RA170 PT102 9d multi .70 .70
Obligatory on mail Sept. 14-21.

Red Cross Week — PT103

2016, May 8 Litho. *Perf. 13¼x13½*
RA171 PT103 8d multi .70 .70
Obligatory on mail May 8-15.

Campaign Against Tuberculosis — PT104

Perf. 13¼x13½
2016, Sept. 14 Litho.
RA172 PT104 9d multi .35 .35
Obligatory on mail Sept. 14-21.

Campaign Against AIDS — PT105

2016, Dec. 1 Litho. *Perf. 13¼x13½*
RA173 PT105 9d multi .35 .35
Obligatory on mail Dec. 1-7.

Campaign Against Cancer — PT106

2017, Mar. 1 Litho. *Perf. 13¼x13½*
RA174 PT106 9d multi .30 .30
Obligatory on mail Mar. 1-8.

Red Cross Week — PT107

2017, May 8 Litho. *Perf. 13¼x13½*
RA175 PT107 9d multi .35 .35
Obligatory on mail May 8-15.

Campaign Against Tuberculosis — PT108

Perf. 13¼x13½
2017, Sept. 14 Litho.
RA176 PT108 9d multi — —
Obligatory on mail Sept. 14-21.

Campaign Against AIDS — PT109

2017, Dec. 1 Litho. *Perf. 13¼x13½*
RA177 PT109 9d multi .35 .35
Obligatory on mail Dec. 1-7.

Campaign Against Cancer — PT110

2018, Mar. 1 Litho. *Perf. 13¼x13½*
RA178 PT110 9d multi .35 .35
Obligatory on mail Mar. 1-8.

Red Cross Week — PT111

2018, May 8 Litho. *Perf. 13¼x13½*
RA179 PT111 9d multi .35 .35
Obligatory on mail May 8-15.

Campaign Against Tuberculosis — PT112

Perf. 13¼x13½
2018, Sept. 14 Litho.
RA180 PT112 9d multi .35 .35
Obligatory on mail Sept. 14-21.

Campaign Against AIDS — PT113

2018, Dec. 1 Litho. *Perf. 13¼x13½*
RA181 PT113 9d multi .35 .35
Obligatory on mail Dec. 1-7.

Campaign Against Tuberculosis PT114

Perf. 13¼x13½
2019, Sept. 14 Litho.
RA182 PT114 9d multi .35 .35
Obligatory on mail Sept. 14-21.

Red Cross Week — PT115

2021, May 8 Litho. *Perf. 13¼x13½*
RA183 PT115 8d multi .35 .35
Obligatory on mail May 8-15.

ISSUED UNDER GERMAN OCCUPATION

During World War II, Yugoslav Macedonia was annexed by Bulgaria. From April 1941 until Sept. 8, 1944, Bulgarian stamps were used in the region. On Sept. 8, 1944, Bulgaria signed an armistice with the Allies, and Macedonia was occupied by German forces. A puppet state was created, which collapsed upon the German withdrawal on Nov. 13.

> Catalogue values for all unused stamps in this section are for Never Hinged examples. Hinged stamps are worth approximately 60% of the values shown.

Bulgaria Nos 364//413 Overprinted in Black or Red (R)

Ovpt. I   Ovpt. II

Photo., Typo. (#N1, N2)
1944, Oct. 28   *Perf. 13*

Overprinted I
N1 A177 1 l on 10st red org (#364) 8.00 16.00
N2 A178 3 l on 15st blue (#365) (R) 8.00 16.00

Overprinted II
N3 A201 6 l on 10st dk blue (#398) (R) 9.50 26.00
N4 A201 9 l on 15st Prus blue (#399) (R) 9.50 26.00
N5 A201 9 l on 15st dk ol brn (#400) (R) 14.50 30.00
N6 A209 15 l on 4 l ol gray (#411) (R) 47.50 60.00
N7 A210 20 l on 7 l dp blue (#412) (R) 72.50 65.00
N8 A211 30 l on 14 l fawn (#413) 80.00 110.00
Nos. N1-N8 (8) 249.50 349.00

There are two types of both overprints, differing in the font of the "9" in the year date. Values for the more common types are given above.

MADAGASCAR

,mad-ə-'gas-kər

British Consular Mail

Postage stamps issued by the British Consulate in Madagascar were in use for a short period until the British relinquished all claims to this territory in favor of France in return for which France recognized Great Britain's claims in Zanzibar.

See Malagasy Republic for stamps inscribed "Madagascar."

12 Pence = 1 Shilling

British Consular Mail stamps of Madagascar were gummed only in one corner. Unused values are for stamps without gum. Examples having the original corner gum will command higher prices. Most used examples of these stamps have small faults and values are for stamps in this condition. Used stamps without faults are scarce and are worth more. Used stamps are valued with the commonly used crayon or pen cancellations.

"B C M" and Arms — A1

Handstamped "British Vice-Consulate"
Black Seal Handstamped

1884			Unwmk.	Typo.	Rouletted
1	A1	1p violet		550.	450.
b.	Seal omitted			10,000.	10,000.
2	A1	2p violet		375.	325.
3	A1	3p violet		425.	350.
4	A1	4p violet 1 oz.		6,000.	5,250.
a.	"1 oz." corrected to "4 oz." in mss.			1,000.	725.
b.	Seal omitted			10,000.	10,000.
5	A1	6p violet		500.	500.
6	A1	1sh violet		525.	475.
7	A1	1sh6p violet		525.	525.
8	A1	2sh violet		850.	900.
9	A1	1p on 1sh vio			
10	A1	4½p on 1sh vio			
11	A1	6p red		1,325.	825.

1886 Violet Seal Handstamped
| 12 | A1 | 4p violet | 1,800. | — |
| 13 | A1 | 6p violet | 2,750. | — |

Handstamped "British Consular Mail" as on A3
Black Seal Handstamped
| 14 | A1 | 4p violet | 1,850. | — |

Violet Seal Handstamped
| 15 | A1 | 4p violet | 7,500. | — |

The 1, 2, 3 and 4 pence are inscribed "POSTAL PACKET," the other values of the series are inscribed "LETTER."

"British Vice-Consulate" — A2

Three types of A2 and A3:
I — "POSTAGE" 29½mm. Periods after "POSTAGE" and value.
II — "POSTAGE" 29½mm. No periods.
III — "POSTAGE" 24½mm. Period after value.

1886 Violet Seal Handstamped
16	A2	1p rose, I	400.	—
a.	Type II		1,350.	
17	A2	1½p rose, I	1,500.	875.
a.	Type II		3,000.	
18	A2	2p rose, I	400.	—
19	A2	3p rose, I	575.	400.
a.	Type II		1,350.	
20	A2	4p rose, III	500.	—
21	A2	4½p rose, I	725.	350.
a.	Type II		2,250.	
22	A2	6p rose, II	1,700.	—
23	A2	8p rose, III	2,750.	1,900.
a.	Type III		700.	
24	A2	9p rose	1,350.	—
24A	A2	1sh rose, III	22,500.	—
24B	A2	1sh6p rose, III	12,500.	—
25	A2	2sh rose, III	6,500.	—

Black Seal Handstamped
Type I
26	A2	1p rose	145.	275.
27	A2	1½p rose	3,000.	1,300.
28	A2	2p rose	200.	—
29	A2	3p rose	4,000.	1,450.
30	A2	4½p rose	3,850.	575.
31	A2	8p rose	5,000.	3,150.
32	A2	9p rose	4,750.	2,900.
32A	A2	2sh rose, III	—	—

"British Consular Mail" — A3

1886 Violet Seal Handstamped
33	A3	1p rose, II	175.	—
34	A3	1½p rose, II	275.	—
35	A3	2p rose, II	325.	—
36	A3	3p rose, II	210.	—
37	A3	4p rose, III	475.	—
38	A3	4½p rose, III	225.	—
39	A3	6p rose, III	500.	—
40	A3	8p rose, III	1,450.	—
a.	Type I		1,750.	
41	A3	9p rose, I	475.	—
42	A3	1sh rose, III	1,750.	—
43	A3	1sh6p rose, III	1,750.	—
44	A3	2sh rose, III	1,750.	—

Black Seal Handstamped
45	A3	1p rose, I	135.	—
a.	Type II		135.	210.
46	A3	1½p rose, I	170.	300.
a.	Type II		145.	200.
47	A3	2p rose, I	190.	—
a.	Type II		150.	200.
48	A3	3p rose, I	170.	260.
a.	Type II		170.	210.
49	A3	4p rose, III	375.	—
50	A3	4½p rose, I	190.	240.
a.	Type II		160.	200.
51	A3	6p rose, II	170.	260.
52	A3	8p rose, II	200.	—
a.	Type III		2,250.	
53	A3	9p rose, I	225.	375.
54	A3	1sh rose, III	625.	—
55	A3	1sh6p rose, III	775.	—
56	A3	2sh rose, III	775.	—

Seal Omitted
45b	A3	1p rose, II	5,000.	—
46b	A3	1½p rose, II	5,250.	—
48b	A3	3p rose, II	8,000.	—
49a	A3	4p rose, III	6,250.	—
50b	A3	4½p rose, II	8,750.	—
51a	A3	6p rose, II	9,500.	—
52b	A3	8p rose, II	6,250.	—
53a	A3	9p rose, I	8,250.	—
54a	A3	1sh rose, III	8,500.	—
55a	A3	1sh6p rose, III	7,250.	—
56a	A3	2sh rose, III	8,500.	—

Some students of these issues doubt that the 1886 "seal omitted" varieties were regularly issued.

Red Seal Handstamped
| 57 | A3 | 3p rose, I | — | 20,000. |
| 58 | A3 | 4½p rose, I | — | 12,750. |

LOCAL STAMPS

BRITISH INLAND MAIL

During the Franco-Hova War of 1894-95, regular postal services in Madagascar were disrupted. To facilitate mail from British merchants and the British Vice-Consul, the Malagasy government approved the creation of a local postal service, British Inland Mail. This service carried correspondence to the port of Vatomandry, from which it was sent to Durban, Natal. Natal stamps were affixed to carry mail to final destinations. The service operated from Jan. 1, 1895, through Sept. 30, 1895.

L1

1895, Jan. 1 Rouletted in Black
Thick Laid Paper
| L1 | L1 | 4d black | 75.00 | 24.00 |

Black on Colored Wove Paper
L2	L1	1d blue gray	60.00	17.50
a.	Tete-beche pair	180.00	
L3	L1	6d pale yellow	65.00	17.50
a.	Tete-beche pair	195.00	52.50
L4	L1	8d salmon	65.00	17.50
a.	Tete-beche pair	195.00	52.50
L5	L1	1sh fawn	70.00	17.50
a.	Tete-beche pair	210.00	52.50
L6	L1	2sh bright rose	90.00	32.50
a.	Tete-beche pair	270.00	97.50
	Italic "2" at left	160.00	80.00
L7	L1	4sh gray	90.00	32.50
a.	Tete-beche pair	270.00	97.50
	Nos. L1-L7 (7)	515.00	159.00

Nos. L1-L7 were typeset by the London Missionary Society, Antananarivo. Nos. 2-7 exist on paper with papermaker's watermark.

Malagasy Runners — L2

1895, Mar. Typo. Perf. 12
L8	L2	2d blue, inscr. "VOAMENA"	16.00	67.50
a.	Horiz. pair, imperf. between	450.00	
b.	Vert. pair, imperf. between	800.00	
L9	L2	4d rose, inscr. "ROAVOAMENA"	16.00	67.50
a.	Horiz. pair, imperf. between	275.00	
b.	Vert. pair, imperf. between	325.00	
c.	Horiz. pair, imperf. vertically	300.00	
L10	L2	6d green, inscr. "SIKAJY"	16.00	85.00
a.	Horiz. pair, imperf. between	1,000.	
L11	L2	1sh deep blue, inscr. "KIROBO"	16.00	140.00
a.	Horiz. pair, imperf. between	600.00	
L12	L2	2sh chocolate, inscr. "LOSO"	40.00	190.00
a.	Horiz. pair, imperf. between	750.00	
b.	Vert. pair, imperf. between	1,000.	
L13	L2	4sh purple, inscr. "ARIARY"	70.00	275.00
a.	Horiz. pair, imperf. between	2,250.	
	Nos. L8-L13 (6)	174.00	825.00

Nos. 8-13 were printed by John Haddon & Co., London.

Eastern Auctions Ltd.

Every two months our Mail Auction features about 2000 individually described and profusely illustrated lots.

There is NO BUYER'S COMMISSION.

We make every effort to present material for every collecting interest and budget. Large lots and individual stamps from worldwide countries and areas are always offered. Contact us to receive a complimentary catalogue of our next Mail Sale.

P.O. Box 250 - Bathurst - New Brunswick - E2A 3Z2 - Canada
Tel: 1(506) 548-8986 - Fax: 1(506) 546-6627
email: contact@easternauctions.com
website: www.easternauctions.com

Toll Free in North America
1(800) 667-8267

MADEIRA

mə-'dir-ə

LOCATION — A group of islands in the Atlantic Ocean northwest of Africa
GOVT. — Part of the Republic of Portugal
AREA — 314 sq. mi.
POP. — 150,574 (1900)
CAPITAL — Funchal

These islands are considered an integral part of Portugal and since 1898 postage stamps of Portugal have been in use. See Portugal for issues also inscribed Madeira, starting in 1980.

1000 Reis = 1 Milreis
100 Centavos = 1 Escudo (1925)

It is recommended that the rare overprinted 1868-81 stamps be purchased accompanied by certificates of authenticity from competent experts.

Portugal 1866-70 King Luiz Stamps Overprinted in Black

On Portugal Nos. 19-23

1868, Jan. 1   **Unwmk.**   **Imperf.**

2	A14	20r bister	210.00	150.00
a.		Inverted overprint		
b.		Rouletted		
3	A14	50r green	210.00	150.00
4	A14	80r orange	225.00	155.00
a.		Double overprint		
5	A14	100r lilac	225.00	155.00
		Nos. 2-5 (4)	870.00	610.00

The 5r black does not exist as a genuinely imperforate original.
Reprints of 1885 are on stout white paper, ungummed. (Also, 5r, 10r and 25r values were overprinted.) Reprints of 1905 are on ordinary white paper with shiny gum and have a wide "D" and "R." Value, $30 each.

Lozenge Perf.

2c	A14	20r	—	—
3a	A14	50r	—	—
4b	A14	80r	—	—
5a	A14	100r	—	—

Portugal Nos. 25-33 Overprinted in Red or Black

1868-70   **Perf. 12½**

6	A14	5r black (R)	60.00	42.50
a.		Double overprint	140.00	
8	A14	10r yellow	102.50	82.50
9	A14	20r bictor	150.00	120.00
10	A14	25r rose	67.50	12.00
a.		Inverted overprint		
b.		Double overprint		82.50
11	A14	50r green	200.00	150.00
a.		Inverted overprint		82.50
12	A14	80r orange	190.00	150.00
13	A14	100r lilac	190.00	150.00
a.		Inverted overprint		
14	A14	120r blue	130.00	85.00
15	A14	240r violet ('70)	600.00	450.00
		Nos. 6-15 (9)	1,690.	1,242.

Two types of 5r differ in the position of the "5" at upper right.
The reprints are on stout white paper, ungummed, with rough perforation 13½, and on thin white paper with shiny white gum and clean-cut perforation 13½. The overprint has the wide "D" and "R" and the first reprints included the 5r with both black and red overprint. Value $30 each.

Portugal 1870-84 King Luiz Overprinted in Red or Black

On Portugal Nos. 34-51

1871-80   **Perf. 12½**

16	A15	5r black (R)	11.00	7.00
a.		Inverted overprint		
b.		Double overprint	90.00	60.00
c.		Perf. 14	97.50	60.00
d.		Ribbed paper	35.00	21.00
e.		Perf. 13½ ('76)	15.00	8.50
18	A15	10r yellow	35.00	22.50
a.		Perf. 13½ ('74)	37.50	13.00
19	A15	10r bl grn ('79)	150.00	120.00
a.		Perf. 13½	190.00	145.00
20	A15	10r yel grn ('80)	80.00	60.00
a.		Perf. 13½	85.00	62.50
21	A15	15r brn ('75)	21.00	12.00
a.		Perf. 13½ ('76)	62.50	42.50
22	A15	20r bister	34.00	22.50
a.		Perf. 13½ ('74)	45.00	28.00
23	A15	25r rose	13.50	5.00
a.		Inverted overprint	50.00	40.00
b.		Double overprint	72.50	67.50
e.		Perf. 13½ ('74)	15.00	5.50
24	A15	50r green ('72)	67.50	30.00
a.		Double overprint		
b.		Inverted overprint	200.00	190.00
c.		Ribbed paper	150.00	70.00
d.		Perf. 13½ ('74)	87.50	40.00
25	A15	50r blue ('80)	125.00	55.00
a.		Perf. 13½	87.50	50.00
26	A15	80r orange ('72)	90.00	70.00
a.		Perf. 13½ ('74)	130.00	95.00
27	A15	100r pale lil ('73)	90.00	50.00
a.		Perf. 14	180.00	85.00
b.		Perf. 13½	130.00	70.00
c.		Ribbed paper	225.00	
28	A15	120r blue	125.00	82.50
a.		Ribbed paper	300.00	190.00
b.		Double overprint	550.00	400.00
29	A15	150r blue ('76)	180.00	145.00
a.		Perf. 13½	200.00	160.00
30	A15	150r yel, perf. 13½ ('79)	350.00	260.00
31	A15	240r vio ('74)	800.00	550.00
a.		Ribbed paper	2,100.	1,400.
32	A15	300r vio, perf. 13½ ('76)	82.50	70.00
		Nos. 16-32 (16)	2,255.	1,562.

There are two types of the overprint, the second one having a broad "D."
The reprints have the same characteristics as those of the 1868-70 issues. Value, $30 each.

Portugal Nos. 52-54 Overprinted in Red or Black

King Luiz — A5

1880-81

33	A3	5r black	35.00	21.00
34	A4	25r pearl gray	35.00	21.00
a.		Inverted overprint	75.00	70.00
b.		Perf. 13½	35.00	24.50
35	A5	25r lilac, perf. 13½	50.00	27.00
a.		25r purple brown	42.50	27.00
b.		25r gray	42.50	27.00
c.		As "a", perf. 12½	35.00	14.00
d.		As "b", perf. 12½	35.00	14.00
		Nos. 33-35 (3)	120.00	69.00

Nos. 33, 34 and 35 have been reprinted on stout white paper, ungummed, and the last three on thin white paper with shiny white gum. The perforations are as previously described. Value, $27.50 each.

Common Design Types pictured following the introduction.

Vasco da Gama Issue
Common Design Types

1898, Apr. 1   **Engr.**   **Perf. 14-15**

37	CD20	2½r blue grn	2.40	1.25
38	CD21	5r red	2.40	1.25
39	CD22	10r red violet	3.75	1.50
40	CD23	25r yel green	3.00	1.25
41	CD24	50r dk blue	8.50	3.75
42	CD25	75r vio brown	11.50	7.25
43	CD26	100r bister brn	11.50	8.00
44	CD27	150r bister	17.50	13.00
		Nos. 37-44 (8)	60.55	37.25

Nos. 37-44 with "REPUBLICA" overprint and surcharges are listed as Portugal Nos. 199-206.

Ceres — A6

1928, May 1   **Engr.**   **Perf. 13½**
Value Typographed in Black

45	A6	3c deep violet	.60	.70
46	A6	4c orange	.60	.70
47	A6	5c light blue	.60	.70
48	A6	6c brown	.70	.80
49	A6	10c red	.70	.80
50	A6	15c yel green	.70	.80
51	A6	16c red brown	.70	.80
52	A6	25c violet rose	.70	.80
53	A6	32c blue grn	.70	.80
54	A6	40c yel brown	.70	.80
55	A6	50c slate	.70	.80
56	A6	64c Prus blue	.70	.80
57	A6	80c dk brown	.70	.80
58	A6	96c carmine rose	5.00	5.00
59	A6	1e black	.75	.85
a.		Value omitted	42.50	45.00
60	A6	1.20e light rose	.75	.85
61	A6	1.60e ultra	.75	.85
62	A6	2.40e yellow	2.10	2.25
63	A6	3.36e dull green	3.00	3.00
64	A6	4.50e brown red	3.00	3.00
65	A6	7e dark blue	6.00	7.00
		Nos. 45-65 (21)	30.15	32.90

It was obligatory to use these stamps in place of those in regular use on May 1, June 5, July 1 and Dec. 31, 1928, Jan. 1 and 31, May 1 and June 5, 1929. The amount obtained from this sale was donated to a fund for building a museum.
Less than very fine examples sell for much less.

NEWSPAPER STAMP

Portugal No. P1 Overprinted in Black

1876, July 1   **Unwmk.**   **Perf. 12½**

P1	N1	2½r olive green	10.00	5.75
a.		Inverted overprint	50.00	
b.		Perf. 13½	10.00	5.75

The reprints have the same papers, gum, perforations and overprint as the reprints of the regular issues.

POSTAL TAX STAMPS

Pombal Commemorative Issue
Common Design Types

1925   **Unwmk.**   **Engr.**   **Perf. 12½**

RA1	CD28	15c gray & black	1.25	1.40
RA2	CD29	15c gray & black	1.25	1.40
RA3	CD30	15c gray & black	1.25	1.40
		Nos. RA1-RA3 (3)	3.75	4.20

POSTAL TAX DUE STAMPS

Pombal Commemorative Issue
Common Design Types

1925   **Unwmk.**   **Perf. 12½**

RAJ1	CD28	30c gray & black	1.40	3.50
RAJ2	CD29	30c gray & black	1.40	3.50
RAJ3	CD30	30c gray & black	1.40	3.50
		Nos. RAJ1-RAJ3 (3)	4.20	10.50

MALAGASY REPUBLIC

‚mal-lə-ˈgə-sē

Madagascar (French)

Malagasy Democratic Republic

Republic of Madagascar

LOCATION — Large Island off the coast of southeastern Africa
GOVT. — Republic
AREA — 226,658 sq. mi.
POP. — 27,690,000 (2020 est.)
CAPITAL — Antananarivo

Madagascar became a French protectorate in 1885 and a French colony in 1896 following several years of dispute among France, Great Britain, and the native government. The colony administered the former protectorates of Anjouan, Grand Comoro, Mayotte, Diego-Suarez, Nossi-Be and Sainte-Marie de Madagascar. Previous issues of postage stamps are found under these individual headings. The Malagasy Republic succeeded the colony in 1958 and became the Democratic Republic of Malagasy in 1975. The official name was again changed in 1993 to Republic of Madagascar.
For British Consular Mail stamps of 1884-1886, see Madagascar.

100 Centimes = 1 Franc
100 Centimes = 1 Ariary (1976)

See France No. 2767 for stamp inscribed "Madagascar."

Catalogue values for unused stamps in this country are for Never Hinged items, beginning with Scott 241 in the regular postage section, Scott B15 in the semi-postal section, Scott C37 in the airpost section, and Scott J31 in the postage due section.

French Offices in Madagascar

The general issues of French Colonies were used in these offices in addition to the stamps listed here.

Stamps of French Colonies Surcharged in Black

Overprint Type "a"

1889   **Unwmk.**   **Perf. 14x13½**

1	A9	05c on 10c blk, lav	725.	220.
a.		Inverted surcharge	1,950.	1,300.
2	A9	05c on 25c blk, rose	725.	220.
a.		Inverted surcharge	1,950.	1,300.
b.		25c on 10c lav (error)	11,500.	10,000.
3	A9	25c on 40c red, straw	650.	200.
a.		Inverted surcharge	1,700.	1,300.

1891   Overprint Type "b"

4	A9	05c on 40c red, straw	235.00	100.00
5	A9	15c on 25c blk, rose	235.00	110.00
a.		Surcharge vertical	275.00	145.00

Overprint Type "c"

6	A9	5c on 10c blk, lav	275.00	125.00
a.		Double surcharge	1,000.	900.00
7	A9	5c on 25c blk, rose	275.00	125.00

See Senegal Nos. 4, 8 for similar surcharge on 20c, 30c.
Forgeries of Nos. 1-7 exist.

A4

WITHOUT GUM

1891   **Type-set**   **Imperf.**

8	A4	5c blk, green	165.00	32.50
9	A4	10c blk, lt bl	125.00	40.00
10	A4	15c ultra, pale bl	125.00	47.50
11	A4	25c brn, buff	30.00	22.50
12	A4	1fr blk, yellow	1,300.	300.00
13	A4	5fr vio & blk, lil	2,400.	1,275.

Stamps of France 1876-90, Overprinted in Red or Black

1895   **Perf. 14x13½**

14	A15	5c grn, grnsh (R)	22.50	11.00
15	A15	10c blk, lav (R)	50.00	32.50
16	A15	15c bl (R)	72.50	22.00
17	A15	25c blk, rose (R)	100.00	25.00
18	A15	40c red, straw (Bk)	95.00	45.00
19	A15	50c rose, rose (Bk)	110.00	55.00

MALAGASY REPUBLIC

20	A15	75c dp vio, *org* (R)	125.00	62.50	
21	A15	1fr brnz grn, *straw* (Bk)	135.00	72.50	
22	A15	5fr vio, *lav* (Bk)	220.00	100.00	
		Nos. 14-22 (9)	930.00	425.50	

Majunga Issue

1876-86 France Stamps Surcharged

1895
Manuscript Surcharge in Red

22A	A15	0,15c on 25c blk, *rose*		8,000.
22B	A15	0,15c on 1fr brnz grn, *straw*		6,000.

Handstamped in Black

22C	A15	15c on 25c blk, *rose*		12,750.
22D	A15	15c on 1fr brnz grn, *straw*		11,750.

On most of No. 22C and all of No. 22D the manuscript surcharge of Nos. 22A-22B was washed off. Three types of "15" were used for No. 22C.

Stamps of France, 1876-84, Surcharged

1896

23	A15	5c on 1c blk, *bl*	6,400.	2,500.
24	A15	15c on 2c brn, *buff*	2,600.	1,000.
25	A15	25c on 3c gray, *grysh*	3,400.	1,100.
26	A15	25c on 4c cl, *lav*	6,400.	1,950.
27	A15	25c on 40c red, *straw*	1,650.	875.

The oval of the 5c and 15c surcharges is smaller than that of the 25c, and it does not extend beyond the edges of the stamp as the 25c surcharge does.

Excellent counterfeits of the surcharges on Nos. 22A to 27 exist.

Issues of the Colony

Navigation and Commerce — A7

1896-1906		Typo.	Perf. 14x13½	
Colony Name in Blue or Carmine				
28	A7	1c blk, *lil bl*	3.50	1.10
29	A7	2c claret, *buff*	3.50	1.50
a.		Name in blue black	4.50	4.50
30	A7	4c claret, *lav*	3.50	1.80
31	A7	5c grn, *grnsh*	10.00	1.50
32	A7	5c yel grn ('01)	2.00	1.10
33	A7	10c blk, *lav*	10.00	2.25
34	A7	10c red ('00)	3.50	1.10
35	A7	15c blue, quadrille paper	14.00	1.50
36	A7	15c gray ('00)	2.50	1.50
37	A7	20c red, *grn*	7.25	2.25
38	A7	25c blk, *rose*	11.00	4.50
39	A7	25c blue ('00)	25.00	32.50
40	A7	30c brn, *bis*	10.00	3.75
41	A7	35c blk, *yel* ('06)	45.00	7.25
42	A7	40c red, *straw*	11.00	6.00
43	A7	50c car, *rose*	14.50	3.00
44	A7	50c brn, *az* ('00)	32.50	45.00
45	A7	75c dp vio, *org*	7.00	4.50
46	A7	1fr brnz grn, *straw*	14.50	3.75
a.		Name in blue ('99)	30.00	22.00
47	A7	5fr red lil, *lav* ('99)	37.50	32.50
		Nos. 28-47 (20)	267.75	158.35

Perf. 13½x14 stamps are counterfeits.

For surcharges see Nos. 48-55, 58-60, 115-118, 127-128.

Nos. 32, 43, 44 and 46, affixed to pressboard with animals printed on the back, were used as emergency currency in the Comoro Islands in 1920.

Surcharged in Black

1902

48	A7	05c on 50c car, *rose*	7.25	6.00
a.		Inverted surcharge	120.00	120.00
49	A7	10c on 5fr red lil, *lav*	25.00	22.00
a.		Inverted surcharge	125.00	125.00
50	A7	15c on 1fr ol grn, *straw*	9.50	8.75
a.		Inverted surcharge	120.00	120.00
b.		Double surcharge	400.00	400.00
		Nos. 48-50 (3)	41.75	36.75

Surcharged in Black

51	A7	0,01 on 2c claret, *buff*	11.50	11.50
a.		Inverted surcharge	72.50	72.50
b.		"00,1" instead of "0,01"	150.00	155.00
c.		As "b" inverted	210.00	—
d.		Comma omitted	210.00	210.00
e.		Name in blue black	11.50	11.50
52	A7	0,05 on 30c brn, *bis*	11.50	11.50
a.		Inverted surcharge	72.50	72.50
b.		"00,5" instead of "0,05"	100.00	100.00
c.		As "b" inverted	2,550.	—
d.		Comma omitted	210.00	210.00
53	A7	0,10 on 50c car, *rose*	9.50	9.50
a.		Inverted surcharge	72.50	72.50
b.		Comma omitted	210.00	210.00
54	A7	0,15 on 75c vio, *org*	7.25	7.25
a.		Inverted surcharge	72.50	72.50
b.		Comma omitted	210.00	210.00
55	A7	0,15 on 1fr ol grn, *straw*	14.50	14.50
a.		Inverted surcharge	110.00	110.00
b.		Comma omitted	275.00	275.00
		Nos. 51-55 (5)	54.25	54.25

Surcharged On Stamps of Diego-Suarez

56	A11	0,05 on 30c brn, *bis*	165.00	145.00
a.		"00,5" instead of "0,05"	1,350.	1,350.
b.		Inverted surcharge	1,450.	1,450.
57	A11	0,10 on 50c car, *rose*	5,000.	5,000.

Counterfeits of Nos. 56-57 exist with surcharge both normal and inverted.

Surcharged in Black

58	A7	0,01 on 2c claret, *buff*	11.50	11.50
a.		Inverted surcharge	72.50	72.50
b.		Comma omitted	210.00	210.00
59	A7	0,05 on 30c brn, *bis*	11.50	11.50
a.		Inverted surcharge	72.50	72.50
b.		Comma omitted	210.00	210.00
60	A7	0,10 on 50c car, *rose*	9.50	9.50
a.		Inverted surcharge	72.50	72.50
b.		Comma omitted	210.00	210.00
		Nos. 58-60 (3)	32.50	32.50

Surcharged On Stamps of Diego-Suarez

61	A11	0,05 on 30c brn, *bis*	165.00	145.00
a.		Inverted surcharge	1,450.	1,450.
62	A11	0,10 on 50c car, *rose*	5,000.	5,000.

BISECTS

During alleged stamp shortages at several Madagascar towns in 1904, it is claimed that bisects were used. After being affixed to letters, these bisects were handstamped "Affranchissement - exceptionnel - (faute de timbres)" and other inscriptions of similar import. The stamps bisected were 10c, 20c, 30c and 50c denominations of Madagascar type A7 and Diego-Suarez type A11. The editors believe these provisionals were unnecessary and speculative.

Zebu, Traveler's Tree and Lemur — A8

1903		Engr.	Perf. 11½	
63	A8	1c dk violet	1.00	1.00
a.		On bluish paper	7.00	6.00
64	A8	2c olive brn	1.00	1.00
65	A8	4c brown	1.25	1.25
66	A8	5c yellow grn	6.00	1.90
67	A8	10c red	11.00	1.25
68	A8	15c carmine	15.00	1.25
a.		On bluish paper	160.00	160.00
69	A8	20c orange	5.75	2.50
70	A8	25c dull blue	25.00	5.00
71	A8	30c pale red	40.00	14.00
72	A8	40c gray vio	27.50	5.50
73	A8	50c brown org	42.50	27.50
74	A8	75c orange yel	55.00	27.50
75	A8	1fr dp green	55.00	27.50
76	A8	2fr slate	75.00	30.00
77	A8	5fr gray black	87.50	90.00
		Nos. 63-77 (15)	448.50	237.15

Nos. 63-77 exist imperf. Value of set, $600.

For surcharges see Nos. 119-124, 129.

Transportation by Sedan Chair — A9

1908-28		Typo.	Perf. 13½x14	
79	A9	1c violet & ol	.25	.25
80	A9	2c red & ol	.25	.25
81	A9	4c ol brn & brn	.25	.25
82	A9	5c bl grn & ol	1.00	.30
83	A9	5c blk & rose ('22)	.30	.30
84	A9	10c rose & brown	1.00	.30
85	A9	10c bl grn & ol grn ('22)	.60	.40
86	A9	10c org brn & vio ('25)	.35	.35
87	A9	15c dl vio & rose ('16)	.35	.35
88	A9	15c dl grn & lt grn ('27)	.70	.70
89	A9	15c dk bl & rose red ('28)	1.60	1.00
90	A9	20c org & brn	.70	.45
91	A9	25c blue & blk	3.00	1.00
92	A9	25c vio & blk ('22)	.40	.30
93	A9	30c brown & blk	3.00	1.35
94	A9	30c rose red & brn ('22)	.65	.40
95	A9	30c grn & red vio ('25)	.65	.45
96	A9	30c dp grn & yel grn ('27)	1.35	1.00
97	A9	35c red & black	2.00	1.00
98	A9	40c vio brn & blk	1.35	.70
99	A9	45c bl grn & blk	1.00	.70
100	A9	45c red & ver ('25)	.35	.45
101	A9	45c gray lil & mag ('27)	1.25	1.00
102	A9	50c violet & blk	1.00	.70
103	A9	50c blue & blk ('22)	1.00	.65
104	A9	50c blk & org ('25)	1.00	.40
105	A9	60c vio, *pnksh* ('25)	.70	.70
106	A9	65c black & bl ('25)	1.00	.75
107	A9	75c rose red & blk	1.00	.70
108	A9	85c grn & ver ('25)	1.35	.85
109	A9	1fr brown & ol	1.00	.70
110	A9	1fr dull blue ('25)	1.25	1.00
111	A9	1fr rose & grn ('28)	5.75	4.50
112	A9	1.10fr bis & bl grn ('28)	2.00	2.00
113	A9	2fr blue & olive	4.00	1.60
114	A9	5fr vio & vio brn	12.50	5.50
		Nos. 79-114 (36)	55.90	33.30

75c violet on pinkish stamps of type A9 are No. 138 without surcharge.

For surcharges and overprints see Nos. 125-126, 130-146, 178-179, 212-214, B1.

Preceding Issues Surcharged in Black or Carmine

1912, Nov.			Perf. 14x13½	
115	A7	5c on 15c gray (C)	1.00	1.00
116	A7	5c on 20c red, *grn*	1.35	1.35
a.		Inverted surcharge	175.00	
117	A7	5c on 30c brn, *bis* (C)	1.40	1.40
118	A7	10c on 75c vio, *org*	10.00	14.00
a.		Double surcharge	310.00	
119	A8	5c on 2c ol brn (C)	1.00	1.00
120	A8	5c on 20c org	1.00	1.00
121	A8	5c on 30c pale red	1.75	1.75
122	A8	10c on 40c gray vio (C)	1.75	1.75
123	A8	10c on 50c brn org	3.50	4.50
124	A8	10c on 75c org yel	6.00	7.25
a.		Inverted surcharge	230.00	
		Nos. 115-124 (10)	28.75	35.00

Two spacings between the surcharged numerals are found on Nos. 115 to 118. For detailed listings, see the *Scott Classic Specialized Catalogue of Stamps and Covers*.

Stamps of Anjouan, Grand Comoro Island, Mayotte and Mohéli with similar surcharges were also available for use in Madagascar and the entire Comoro archipelago.

Preceding Issues Surcharged in Red or Black

g   h

1921			On Nos. 98 & 107	
125	A9 (g)	30c on 40c (R)	2.50	2.50
126	A9 (g)	60c on 75c	3.25	3.25
		On Nos. 45 & 47		
127	A7 (g)	60c on 75c (R)	12.50	12.50
a.		Inverted surcharge	220.00	220.00
128	A7 (h)	1fr on 5fr	1.10	1.10
		On No. 77		
129	A8 (h)	1fr on 5fr (R)	100.00	100.00
		Nos. 125-129 (5)	119.35	119.35

Stamps and Type of 1908-16 Surcharged in Black or Red

No. 130   No. 131

130	A9	1c on 15c dl vio & rose	.75	1.10
131	A9	25c on 35c red & blk	6.50	6.50
132	A9	25c on 35c red & blk (R)	32.50	32.50
133	A9	25c on 40c brn & blk	7.00	5.00
134	A9	25c on 45c grn & blk	4.50	4.50
		Nos. 130-134 (5)	51.25	49.60
		Nos. 125-134 (10)	170.60	168.95

Stamps and Type of 1908-28 Surcharged with New Value and Bars

1922-27				
135	A9	25c on 15c dl vio & rose	.35	.35
a.		Double surcharge	95.00	
136	A9	25c on 2fr bl & ol	.35	.50
137	A9	25c on 5fr vio & vio brn	.35	.35
138	A9	60c on 75c vio, *pnksh*	.60	.60
139	A9	65c on 75c rose red & blk	1.10	1.10
140	A9	85c on 45c bl grn & blk	1.90	1.45
141	A9	90c on 75c dl red & rose red	1.25	1.10
142	A9	1.25fr on 1fr lt bl (R)	.75	.50
143	A9	1.50fr on 1fr dp bl & dl bl	.75	.60
144	A9	3fr on 5fr grn & vio	2.50	1.45
145	A9	10fr on 5fr org & rose lil	10.00	6.00
146	A9	20fr on 5fr rose & sl bl	10.00	8.00
		Nos. 135-146 (12)	29.90	22.00

Years of issue: No. 138, 1922; Nos. 136, 137, 1924; Nos. 135, 139-140, 1925; No. 142, 1926; Nos. 141, 143-146, 1927.
See Nos. 178-179.

Sakalava Chief A10

Hova Woman A12

Hova with Oxen — A11

Bétsiléo Woman — A13

MALAGASY REPUBLIC

Perf. 13½x14, 14x13½

1930-44   Typo.

147	A11	1c dk bl & bl grn ('33)	.25	.25
148	A10	2c brn red & dk brn	.25	.25
149	A10	4c dk brn & vio	.25	.25
150	A11	5c lt grn & red	.25	.25
151	A12	10c dull org & grn	.35	.25
152	A13	15c red	.25	.25
153	A11	20c yel brn & dk bl	.35	.25
154	A12	25c vio & dk brn	.35	.25
155	A13	30c Prus blue	.80	.45
156	A10	40c grn & red	.80	.50
157	A13	45c dull violet	1.00	.55
158	A11	65c brn & vio	1.25	.90
159	A13	75c dk brown	.95	.65
160	A11	90c brn red & dk red	1.40	.90
161	A12	1fr yel brn & dk bl	2.00	1.25
162	A12	1fr dk red & car rose ('38)	1.25	1.00
163	A12	1.25fr dp bl & dk brn ('33)	1.60	1.25
164	A10	1.50fr dk & dp bl	5.50	1.50
165	A10	1.50fr brn & dk red ('38)	.75	.65
165A	A10	1.50fr dk red & brn ('44)	.65	.65
166	A11	1.75fr dk brn & dk red ('33)	4.25	2.00
167	A10	5fr vio & dk brn	1.25	1.00
168	A10	20fr yel brn & dk bl	2.00	2.00
		Nos. 147-168 (23)	27.75	17.25

Common Design Types pictured following the introduction.

Colonial Exposition Issue
Common Design Types

1931   Engr.   *Perf. 12½*
Name of Country in Black

169	CD70	40c deep green	1.75	1.25
170	CD71	50c violet	2.50	1.75
171	CD72	90c red orange	2.50	1.75
172	CD73	1.50fr dull blue	2.50	1.75
		Nos. 169-172 (4)	9.25	6.50

General Joseph Simon Galliéni — A14
Size: 21½x34½mm

1931   Engr.   *Perf. 14*

173	A14	1c ultra	.50	.45
174	A14	50c orange brn	1.40	.35
175	A14	2fr deep red	6.00	4.25
176	A14	3fr emerald	5.50	3.00
177	A14	10fr dp orange	4.00	3.00
		Nos. 173-177 (5)	17.40	11.05

Nos. 113 and 109 Surcharged

1932   *Perf. 13½x14*

178	A9	25c on 2fr bl & ol	.75	.60
179	A9	50c on 1fr brn & ol	.75	.60

No. 178 has numerals in thick block letters.
No. 136 has thin shaded numerals.

Galliéni Type of 1931

1936-40   Photo.   *Perf. 13½, 13x13½*
Size: 21x34mm

180	A14	3c sapphire ('40)	.30	.30
181	A14	45c brt green ('40)	.65	.65
182	A14	50c yellow brown	.30	.25
183	A14	60c brt red lil ('40)	.50	.35
184	A14	70c brt rose ('40)	.65	.45
185	A14	90c copper brn ('39)	.65	.65
186	A14	1.40fr org yel ('40)	1.00	.65
187	A14	1.60fr purple ('40)	1.00	.65
188	A14	2fr dk carmine	.50	.25
189	A14	3fr green	4.50	2.25
190	A14	3fr violet blk ('39)	1.00	1.00
		Nos. 180-190 (11)	11.05	7.45

Paris International Exposition Issue
Common Design Types

1937, Apr. 15   Engr.   *Perf. 13*

191	CD74	20c dp violet	1.60	1.60
192	CD75	30c dk green	1.60	1.60
193	CD76	40c car rose	1.60	1.60
194	CD77	50c dk brn & blk	1.25	1.25
195	CD78	90c red	1.60	1.60
196	CD79	1.50fr ultra	1.60	1.60
		Nos. 191-196 (6)	9.25	9.25

Colonial Arts Exhibition Issue
Common Design Type
Souvenir Sheet

1937   *Imperf.*

197	CD74	3fr orange red	10.00	12.50

Jean Laborde — A15

1938-40   *Perf. 13*

198	A15	35c green	.70	.35
199	A15	55c dp purple	.70	.35
200	A15	65c orange red	1.00	.35
201	A15	80c violet brn	.70	.35
202	A15	1fr rose car	1.00	.35
203	A15	1.25fr rose car ('39)	.65	.30
204	A15	1.75fr dk ultra	1.75	.75
205	A15	2.15fr yel brn	2.75	1.75
206	A15	2.25fr dk ultra ('39)	.65	.65
207	A15	2.50fr blk brn ('40)	.65	.65
208	A15	10fr dk green ('40)	1.25	1.25
		Nos. 198-208 (11)	11.80	7.10

New York World's Fair Issue
Common Design Type

1939, May 10   Engr.   *Perf. 12½x12*

209	CD82	1.25fr car lake	.75	1.25
210	CD82	2.25fr ultra	.75	1.25

Porters Carrying Man in Chair, and Marshal Petain — A15a

1941   Engr.   *Perf. 12x12½*

210A	A15a	1fr bister brn	.35	
210B	A15a	2.50fr blue	.35	

Nos. 210A-210B were issued by the Vichy government in France but were not placed on sale in Madagascar.
For overprints see Nos. B13-B14.

Type of 1930-44 Surcharged in Black with New Value

1942   *Perf. 14x13½*

211	A11	50c on 65c dk brn & mag	2.50	.75

French Explorers de Hell, Passot & Jehenne — A15h

1942   Engr.   *Perf. 13x13½*

211A	A15b	1.50fr blue & red brn	1.10	

Centenary of French colonies of Mayotte and Nossi Bé.
No. 211A was issued by the Vichy government in France, but was not placed on sale in Madagascar.

Nos. 143, 145-146 with Additional Overprint in Red or Black

1942   Unwmk.   *Perf. 14x13½*

212	A9	1.50fr on 1fr (R)	1.75	1.75
213	A9	10fr on 5fr (Bk)	10.00	10.00
214	A9	20fr on 5fr (R)	12.50	12.50

Stamps of 1930-40 Overprinted Like Nos. 212-214 in Black or Red or

215	A10	2c brn red & dk brn	2.25	2.25
216	A14	3c sapphire (R)	115.00	115.00
217	A13	15c deep red	12.00	12.00
218	A11	65c dk brn & mag	5.00	5.00
219	A14	70c brt rose	2.50	2.50
220	A15	80c violet brn	5.00	5.00
221	A14	1.40fr orange yel	2.50	2.50
222	A10	1.50fr dk bl & dp bl (R)	2.50	2.25
223	A10	1.50fr brn & dk red	5.00	5.00
224	A15	1.60fr purple	2.50	2.50
225	A15	2.25fr dk ultra (R)	5.00	5.00
226	A15	2.50fr black brn (R)	6.00	6.00
227	A15	10fr dk green	9.00	9.00
228	A10	20fr yel brn & dk bl (R)	725.00	750.00

Stamps of 1930-40 Surcharged in Black or Red

229	A11	5c on 1c dk bl & bl grn	1.25	1.25
230	A15	10c on 55c dp pur	1.75	1.75
231	A15	30c on 65c org red	1.75	1.75
232	A14	50c on 90c cop brn	1.25	1.25
233	A12	1fr on 1.25fr dp bl & dk brn	12.00	12.00
234	A15	1fr on 1.25fr rose car	12.50	12.50
235	A10	1.50fr on 1.75fr dk brn & dk red	1.25	1.25
236	A15	1.50fr on 1.75fr ultra (R)	1.25	1.25
237	A15	2fr on 2.15fr yel brn	1.75	1.75

No. 211 with additional Overprint Like Nos. 217-218 in Black

239	A11	50c on 65c dk brn & mag	2.25	2.25

New York World's Fair Stamp Overprinted Like Nos. 217-218 in Red
Perf. 12½x12

240	CD82	2.25fr ultra	5.00	5.00
		Nos. 212-227,229-240 (27)	240.50	240.25

Catalogue values for unused stamps in this section, from this point to the end of the section, are for Never Hinged items.

Traveler's Tree — A16

1943   Unwmk.   Photo.   *Perf. 14x14½*

241	A16	5c ol gray	.25	.25
242	A16	10c pale rose vio	.25	.25
243	A16	15c emerald	.25	.25
244	A16	30c dp orange	.25	.25
245	A16	40c slate bl	.25	.25
246	A16	80c dk red brn	.25	.25
247	A16	1fr dull blue	.30	.25
248	A16	1.50fr crim rose	.55	.40
249	A16	2fr dull yel	.55	.45
250	A16	2.50fr brt ultra	.55	.45
251	A16	4fr aqua & red	.70	.55
252	A16	5fr green & blk	.70	.55
253	A16	10fr sal pink & dk bl	1.00	.85
254	A16	20fr dl vio & brn	1.40	1.20
		Nos. 241-254 (14)	7.25	6.20

For surcharges see Nos. 255-256, 261-268.

Types of 1930-44 without "RF"
1943-44

254A	A11	20c yel brn & dk bl	.75	
254B	A14	60c lilac rose	1.10	
254C	A12	1fr dk red & car rose	1.90	
254D	A10	1.50fr brn & dk red	1.50	
254E	A10	5fr vio & dk brn	3.75	

On type A10, the two panels at the top of the frame have been reversed, with the value at the left and a blank (RF removed) panel at right.
Nos. 254A-254E were issued by the Vichy government in France, but were not placed on sale in Madagascar.

Nos. 241 and 242 Surcharged with New Values and Bars in Red or Blue

1944

255	A16	1.50fr on 5c (R)	1.25	.55
256	A16	1.50fr on 10c (Bl)	1.75	.85

Nos. 229 and 224 Surcharged with New Values and Bars in Red or Black
Perf. 14x13½, 14

257	A11	50c on 5c on 1c (R)	3.00	.70
258	A14	1.50fr on 1.60fr (Bk)	3.00	.95
		Nos. 255-258 (4)	9.00	3.05

Eboué Issue
Common Design Type

1945   Engr.   *Perf. 13*

259	CD91	2fr black	.75	.50
260	CD91	25fr Prus green	1.25	.95

Nos. 241, 243 and 250 Surcharged with New Values and Bars in Carmine or Black

1945   *Perf. 14x14½*

261	A16	50c on 5c ol gray (C)	.55	.45
262	A16	60c on 5c ol gray (C)	.70	.55
263	A16	70c on 5c ol gray (C)	1.00	.50
264	A16	1.20fr on 5c ol gray (C)	.85	.70
265	A16	2.40fr on 25c emer	.85	.70
266	A16	3fr on 25c emer	.85	.70
267	A16	4.50fr on 25c emer	1.25	1.00
268	A16	15fr on 2.50fr brt ultra (C)	1.25	1.00
		Nos. 261-268 (8)	7.30	5.60

Southern Dancer A17

Gen. J. S. Galliéni A20

Herd of Zebus — A18

Sakalava Man and Woman — A19

Betsimisaraka Mother and Child — A21

General Jacques C. R. A. Duchesne A22

Marshal Joseph J. C. Joffre A23

Perf. 13x13½, 13½x13

1946   Photo.   Unwmk.

269	A17	10c green	.25	.25
270	A17	30c orange	.25	.25
271	A17	40c brown ol	.25	.25
272	A17	25c violet brn	.25	.25
273	A18	60c dp ultra	.40	.25
274	A18	80c blue grn	.50	.25
275	A19	1fr brown	.90	.25
276	A19	1.20fr green	.40	.25

MALAGASY REPUBLIC

276A	A20	1.50fr dk red	.40	.25
277	A20	2fr slate blk	.40	.25
278	A20	3fr dp claret	.60	.25
278A	A21	3.60fr dk car rose	1.00	.65
279	A21	4fr dp ultra	.60	.25
280	A21	5fr red orange	.85	.25
281	A22	6fr dk grnsh bl	.60	.25
282	A22	10fr red brn	.85	.25
283	A23	15fr violet brn	1.20	.30
284	A23	20fr dk vio bl	1.60	.65
285	A23	25fr brown	2.40	1.00
		Nos. 269-285 (19)	13.20	6.35

Military Medal Issue
Common Design Type
Engraved and Typographed

1952, Dec. 1   Unwmk.   Perf. 13
286 CD101 15fr multicolored   3.75   2.50
Creation of the French Military Medal, cent.

Tropical Flowers — A24
Long-tailed Ground Roller — A25

1954   Engr.
287	A24	7.50fr ind & gray grn	1.50	.25
288	A25	8fr brown carmine	1.25	.35
289	A25	15fr dk grn & dp ultra	2.50	.35
		Nos. 287-289 (3)	5.25	.95

Colonel Lyautey and Royal Palace, Tananarive — A26

1954-55
| 290 | A26 | 10fr vio bl, ind & bl ('55) | 1.20 | .25 |
| 291 | A26 | 40fr dk sl bl & red brn | 1.75 | .35 |

FIDES Issue
Common Design Type
Designs: 3fr, Tractor and modern settlement. 5fr, Gallieni school. 10fr, Pangalanes Canal. 15fr, Irrigation project.

1956, Oct. 22   Engr.   Perf. 13x12½
292	CD103	3fr gray vio & vio brn	.40	.25
293	CD103	5fr org brn & dk vio brn	.40	.35
294	CD103	10fr indigo & lilac	.60	.35
295	CD103	15fr grn & bl grn	.85	.35
		Nos. 292-295 (4)	2.25	1.20

Coffee — A26a

1956, Oct. 22   Perf. 13
296 A26a 20r red brn & dk brn   .90   .25

Manioc A27
Vanilla A28

Design: 4fr, Cloves.

1957, Mar. 12   Unwmk.   Perf. 13
297	A27	2fr bl, grn & sepia	.35	.25
298	A28	4fr dp grn & red	.75	.25
299	A28	12fr dk vio, dl grn & sepia	.75	.35
		Nos. 297-299 (3)	1.85	.85

Malagasy Republic
Human Rights Issue
Common Design Type

1958, Dec. 10   Engr.   Perf. 13
300 CD105 10fr brn & dk bl   .80   .40
Universal Declaration of Human Rights, 10th anniversary.
"CF" stands for "Communauté française."

> **Imperforates**
> Most Malagasy stamps from 1958 onward exist imperforate in issued and trial colors, and also in small presentation sheets in issued colors.

Flower Issue
Common Design Type
Perf. 12½x12, 12x12½

1959, Jan. 31   Photo.
| 301 | CD104 | 6fr Datura, horiz. | .40 | .25 |
| 302 | CD104 | 25fr Poinsettia | 1.20 | .35 |

Flag and Assembly Building — A29
Flag and Map — A30

1959, Feb. 28   Engr.   Perf. 13
| 303 | A29 | 20fr brn vio, car & emer | .35 | .25 |
| 304 | A30 | 25fr gray, red & emer | .70 | .25 |
Proclamation of the Malagasy Republic.

French and Malagasy Flags and Map — A31

1959, Feb. 28
305 A31 60fr multi   1.60   .50
Issued to honor the French Community.

Chionaema Pauliani A32
Ylang-ylang A33

Designs: 30c, 40c, 50c, 3fr, Various butterflies. 5fr, Sisal. 8fr, Pepper. 10fr, Rice. 15fr, Cotton.

1960   Unwmk.   Perf. 13
306	A32	30c multicolored	.25	.25
307	A32	40c emer, sep & red brn	.25	.25
308	A32	50c vio brn, blk & stl bl	.25	.25
309	A32	1fr ind, red & dl pur	.25	.25
310	A32	3fr ol, vio blk & org	.25	.25
311	A32	5fr red, brn & emer	.35	.25
312	A33	6fr dk grn & brt yel	.40	.25
313	A32	8fr crim rose, emer & blk	.40	.25
314	A33	10fr dk grn, yel grn & lt brn	.80	.25
315	A32	15fr brown & grn	.80	.25
		Nos. 306-315 (10)	4.00	2.50

Family Planting Trees — A34

1960, Feb. 1   Engr.   Perf. 13
316 A34 20fr red brn, buff & grn   .90   .30
Issued for the "Week of the Tree," Feb. 1-7.

C.C.T.A. Issue
Common Design Type

1960, Feb. 22
317 CD106 25fr lt bl grn & plum   .60   .30

Pres. Philibert Tsiranana and Map — A36

1960, Mar. 25   Unwmk.   Perf. 13
318 A36 20fr green & brn   .35   .25

Athletes of Two Races — A37

1960   Engr.   Perf. 13
319 A37 25fr choc, org brn & ultra   .60   .30
First Games of the French Community, Apr. 13-18, at Tananarive.

Pres. Philibert Tsiranana — A38

1960, July 29   Unwmk.   Perf. 13
320 A38 20fr red, blk & brt grn   .35   .25
Issued to honor Pres. Tsiranana, "Father of Independence." For surcharge see No. B18.

Gray Lemur — A39

Designs: 4fr, Ruffed lemur, horiz. 12fr, Mongoose lemur.

1961, Dec. 9   Perf. 13
321	A39	2fr brn & grnsh bl	.25	.25
322	A39	4fr brn, grn & blk	.25	.25
323	A39	12fr grn & red brn	.55	.25
		Nos. 321-323,C67-C69 (6)	12.80	5.20

Pres. Tsiranana Bridge, Sofia River — A40

1962, Jan. 4   Unwmk.   Perf. 13
324 A40 25fr bright blue   1.00   .25

First Train Built at Tananarive — A41

1962, Feb. 1
325 A41 20fr dk grn   1.10   .30

UN and Malagasy Flags over Government Building, Tananarive — A42

1962, Mar. 14   Perf. 13
| 326 | A42 | 25fr multicolored | .45 | .25 |
| 327 | A42 | 85fr multicolored | 1.90 | .55 |
Malagasy Republic's admission to the UN. For surcharge see No. 409.

Ranomafana Village — A43

Designs: 30fr, Tritriva crater lake. 50fr, Foulpointe shore. 60fr, Fort Dauphin.

1962, May 7   Engr.   Perf. 13
328	A43	10fr sl grn, grnsh bl & cl	.25	.25
329	A43	30fr sl grn, cl & grnsh bl	.65	.25
330	A43	50fr ultra, cl & sl grn	.90	.30
331	A43	60fr cl, ultra & sl grn	1.10	.40
		Nos. 328-331,C70 (5)	4.65	1.80

African and Malgache Union Issue
Common Design Type

1962, Sept. 8   Photo.   Perf. 12½x12
332 CD110 30fr grn, bluish grn, red & gold   .80   .80
First anniversary of the African and Malgache Union.

Arms of Republic and UNESCO Emblem — A44

1962, Sept. 3   Unwmk.
333 A44 20fr rose, emer & blk   .60   .25
First Conference on Higher Education in Africa, Tananarive, Sept. 3-12.

Power Station — A45

Designs: 8fr, Atomic reactor and atom symbol, horiz. 10fr, Oil derrick. 15fr, Tanker, horiz.

Perf. 12x12½, 12½x12
1962, Oct. 18   Litho.
334	A45	5fr blue, yel & red	.25	.25
335	A45	8fr blue, red & yel	.30	.25
336	A45	10fr multicolored	.40	.25
337	A45	15fr bl, red brn & blk	.50	.25
		Nos. 334-337 (4)	1.45	1.00
Industrialization of Madagascar.

Factory and Globe — A46

1963, Jan. 7   Typo.   Perf. 14x13½
338 A46 25fr dp org & blk   .55   .25
International Fair at Tamatave.

MALAGASY REPUBLIC

Hertzian Cable, Tananarive-Fianarantsoa — A47

1963, Mar. 7 Photo. Perf. 12½x12
339 A47 20fr multi   .55 .25

Madagascar Blue Pigeon A48

Gastrorchis Humblotii A49

Birds: 2fr, Blue coua. 3fr, Red fody. 6fr, Madagascar pigmy kingfisher.
Orchids: 10fr, Eulophiella roempleriana. 12fr, Angraecum sesquipedale.

1963 Unwmk. Perf. 13
340 A48 1fr multi   .55 .30
341 A48 2fr multi   .55 .30
342 A48 3fr multi   .75 .30
343 A48 6fr multi   .75 .30
344 A49 8fr multi   .60 .30
345 A49 10fr multi .75 .45
346 A49 12fr multi .75 .50
Nos. 340-346,C72-C74 (10) 17.45 6.60

Arms — A50

Arms of: 1.50fr, Antsirabe. 5fr, Antalaha. 10fr, Tulear. 15fr, Majunga. 20fr, Fianarantsoa. 25fr, Tananarive. 50fr, Diégo-Suarez.
Imprint: "R. Louis del. So. Ge. Im."

1963-65 Litho. Perf. 13
Size: 23½x35½mm
347 A50 1.50fr multi ('64) .25 .25
348 A50 5fr multi ('65)   .25 .25
349 A50 10fr multi ('64)   .25 .25
350 A50 15fr multi ('64)   .35 .25
351 A50 20fr multi   .50 .25
352 A50 25fr multi   .55 .25
353 A50 50fr multi ('65)   1.25 .50
Nos. 347-353 (7) 3.40 2.00
See Nos. 388-390, 434-439.
For surcharge see No. 503.

Map and Centenary Emblem — A51

1963, Sept. 2 Perf. 12x12½
354 A51 30fr multi   1.00 .50
Centenary of the International Red Cross.

Globe and Hands Holding Torch — A52

1963, Dec. 10 Engr. Perf. 12½
355 A52 60fr ol, ocher & car   .85 .40
Universal Declaration of Human Rights, 15th anniv.

Scouts and Campfire — A53

1964, June 6 Engr. Perf. 13
356 A53 20fr dk red, org & car   .70 .30
40th anniv. of the Boy Scouts of Madagascar.

Europafrica Issue

Dove and Globe — A54

1964, July 20 Engr.
357 A54 45fr ol grn, brn red & blk 1.00 .35
First anniversary of economic agreement between the European Economic Community and the African and Malgache Union.

Carved Statue of Woman — A55

Malagasy Art: 30fr, Statue of sitting man.

1964, Oct. 20 Unwmk. Perf. 13
358 A55 6fr dk bl, brt bl & sepia .45 .25
359 A55 30fr dp grn, ol bis & dk brn .80 .30
Nos. 358-359,C79 (3) 3.00 1.45

Cooperation Issue
Common Design Type

1964, Nov. 7 Engr. Perf. 13
360 CD119 25fr blk, dk brn & org brn   .60 .25

University Emblem — A56

1964, Dec. 5 Litho. Perf. 13x12½
361 A56 65fr red, blk & grn   .60 .35
Founding of the University of Madagascar, Tannanarive. The inscription reads: "Foolish is he who does not do better than his father."

Jejy — A57

Valiha Player — A58

Musical instruments: 3fr, Kabosa (lute). 8fr, Hazolahy (sacred drum).

1965 Engr. Perf. 13
Size: 22x36mm
362 A57 3fr mag, vio bl & dk brn   .50 .25
363 A57 6fr emer, rose lil & dk brn .60 .25
364 A57 8fr brn, grn & blk   .90 .25
Photo. Perf. 12½x13
365 A58 25fr multi   1.75 .60
Nos. 362-365,C80 (5) 8.25 3.35

PTT Receiving Station, Foulpointe — A59

1965, May 8 Engr. Perf. 13
366 A59 20fr red org, dk grn & ocher   .50 .25
Issued for Stamp Day, 1965.

ITU Emblem, Old and New Telecommunication Equipment — A60

1965, May 17
367 A60 50fr ultra, red & grn   1.00 .40
ITU, centenary.

Jean Joseph Rabearivelo — A61

1965, June 22 Photo. Perf. 13x12½
368 A61 40fr dk brn & org   .60 .30
Issued to honor the poet Jean Joseph Rabearivelo, pen name of Joseph Casimir, (1901-37).

Pres. Philibert Tsiranana — A62

1965, Oct. 18 Perf. 13x12½
369 A62 20fr multi   .25 .25
  a. Souv. sheet of 4   1.00 1.00
370 A62 25fr multi   .40 .25
  a. Souv. sheet of 4   2.00 2.00
55th birthday of President Philibert Tsiranana.

Mail Coach — A63

History of the Post: 3fr, Early automobile. 4fr, Litter. 10fr, Mail runner, vert. 12fr, Mail boat. 25fr, Oxcart. 30fr, Old railroad mail car. 65fr, Hydrofoil.

1965-66 Engr. Perf. 13
371 A63 3fr vio, dp bis & sky bl ('66)   .40 .25
372 A63 4fr ultra, grn & dk brn ('66)   .35 .25
373 A63 10fr multi   .35 .25
374 A63 12fr multi   .40 .25
375 A63 20fr bis, grn & red brn   .90 .30
376 A63 25fr sl grn, dk brn & org   .85 .30
377 A63 30fr pck bl, red & sep ('66)   2.50 .50
378 A63 65fr vio, brn & Prus bl ('66)   2.00 .50
Nos. 371-378 (8) 7.75 2.60

Leper's Crippled Hands — A64

1966, Jan. 30
379 A64 20fr dk grn, dk brn & red   .70 .30
Issued for the 13th World Leprosy Day.

Couple Planting Trees — A65

1966, Feb. 21
380 A65 20fr dk brn, pur & bl grn   .60 .25
Reforestation as a national duty.

Tiger Beetle — A66

Insects: 6fr, Mantis. 12fr, Long-horned beetle. 45fr, Weevil.

1966 Photo. Perf. 12½x12
Insects in Natural Colors
381 A66 1fr brick red   .95 .25
382 A66 6fr rose claret   1.25 .25
383 A66 12fr Prus blue   2.40 .40
384 A66 45fr lt yel grn   3.25 .75
Nos. 381-384 (4) 7.85 1.65

Stamp of 1903 — A67

1966, May 8 Engr. Perf. 13
385 A67 25fr red & sepia   .80 .30
Issued for Stamp Day 1966.

Betsileo Dancers — A68

1966, June 13 Photo. Perf. 12½x13
Size: 36x23mm
386 A68 5fr multi   .55 .25
See No. C83.

Symbolic Tree and Emblems A69

1966, June 26
387 A69 25fr multi   .60 .25
Conference of the Organisation Commune Africaine et Malgache (OCAM), Tananarive.
No. 387 dated "JUIN 1966," original date "Janvier 1966" obliterated with bar. Exists without overprint "JUIN 1966" and bar. Value $100.

Arms Type of 1963-65
Imprint: "S. Gauthier So. Ge. Im."
20fr, Mananjary. 30fr, Nossi-Bé. 90fr, Antsohihy.

1966-68 Litho. Perf. 13
Size: 23½x35½mm
388 A50 20fr multi ('67)   .40 .25
389 A50 30fr multi   .45 .25
390 A50 90fr multi ('68) 1.50 .40
Nos. 388-390 (3) 2.35 .90
For surcharge see No. 503.

Singers and Map of Madagascar — A70

MALAGASY REPUBLIC

1966, Oct. 14   Engr.   *Perf. 13*
392   A70   20fr red brn, grn & dk car rose   .60   .25
Issued in honor of the National Anthem.

UNESCO Emblem — A71

1966, Nov. 4
393   A71   30fr red, yel & slate   .60   .25
UNESCO, 20th anniv.

Lions Emblem — A72

1967, Jan. 14   Photo.   *Perf. 13x12½*
394   A72   30fr multi   .60   .30
50th anniversary of Lions International.

Rice Harvest — A73

1967, Jan. 27   *Perf. 12½x13*
395   A73   20fr multi   .60   .25
FAO International Rice Year.

Adventist Temple, Tanambao-Tamatave — A74

Designs: 5fr, Catholic Cathedral, Tananarive, vert. 10fr, Mosque, Tamatave.

1967, Feb. 20   Engr.   *Perf. 13*
396   A74   3fr lt ultra, grn & bis   .25   .25
397   A74   5fr brt rose lil, grn & vio   .25   .25
398   A74   10fr dp bl, brn & grn   .30   .25
   Nos. 396-398 (3)   .80   .75

Norbert Raharisoa at Piano — A75

1967, Mar. 23   Photo.   *Perf. 12½x12*
399   A75   40fr citron & multi   .70   .25
Norbert Raharisoa (1914-1963), composer.

Jean Raoult Flying Blériot Plane, 1911 — A76

45fr, Georges Bougault and hydroplane, 1926.

1967, Apr. 28   Engr.   *Perf. 13*
Size: 35½x22mm
400   A76   5fr gray bl, brn & grn   .80   .30
401   A76   45fr brn, stl bl & blk   1.60   .60
   Nos. 400-401,C84 (3)   11.40   4.90
History of aviation in Madagascar.

Ministry of Equipment and Communications A77

1967, May 8   Engr.   *Perf. 13*
402   A77   20fr ocher, ultra & grn   .60   .25
Issued for Stamp Day, 1967.

Lutheran Church, Tananarive, Madagascar Map — A78

1967, Sept. 24   Photo.   *Perf. 12x12½*
403   A78   20fr multi   .70   .25
Lutheran Church in Madagascar, cent.

Map of Madagascar and Emblems — A79

1967, Oct. 16   Engr.   *Perf. 13*
404   A79   90fr red brn, bl & dk red   1.10   .40
Hydrological Decade (UNESCO), 1965-74.

Dance of the Bilo Sakalavas — A80

Design: 30fr, Atandroy dancers.

1967, Nov. 25   Photo.   *Perf. 13x12½*
Size: 22x36mm
405   A80   2fr lt grn & multi   .30   .25
406   A80   30fr multi   .60   .25
   Nos. 405-406,C86-C87 (4)   6.90   2.50

Woman's Face, Scales and UN Emblem — A81

1967, Dec. 16   *Perf. 12½x13*
407   A81   50fr emer, dk bl & brn   .70   .30
UN Commission on the Status of Women.

Human Rights Flame — A82

1968, Mar. 16   Litho.   *Perf. 13x12½*
408   A82   50fr blk, ver & grn   .70   .30
International Human Rights Year.

No. 327 Surcharged with New Value and 3 Bars

1968, June 4   Engr.   *Perf. 13*
409   A42   20fr on 85fr multi   .70   .40

"Industry" — A83

Designs: 20fr, "Agriculture" (mother and child carrying fruit and grain, and cattle), vert.

40fr, "Communications and Investments," (train, highway, factory and buildings).

1968, July 15
410   A83   10fr rose car, grn & dk pur   .25   .25
411   A83   20fr dp car, grn & blk   .30   .25
412   A83   40fr brn, vio & sl bl   .60   .25
   Nos. 410-412 (3)   1.15   .75
Completion of Five-year Plan, 1964-68.

Church, Translated Bible, Cross and Map of Madagascar A84

1968, Aug. 18   Photo.   *Perf. 12½x12*
413   A84   20fr multi   .55   .25
Sesquicentennial of Christianity in Madagascar.

Isotry-Fitiavana Protestant Church — A85

12fr, Catholic Cathedral, Fianarantsoa. 50fr, Aga Khan Mosque, Tananarive.

1968, Sept. 10   Engr.   *Perf. 13*
414   A85   4fr red brn, brt grn & dk brn   .25   .25
415   A85   12fr plum, bl & hn brn   .30   .25
416   A85   50fr brt grn, bl & indigo   .60   .25
   Nos. 414-416 (3)   1.15   .75

President and Mrs. Tsiranana — A86

1968, Oct. 14   Photo.   *Perf. 12½x12*
417   A86   20fr car, org & blk   .30   .25
418   A86   30fr car, grnsh bl & blk   .50   .25
   a. Souv. sheet of 4, 2 each #417-418   1.50   1.00
10th anniv. of the Republic.

Madagascar Map and Cornucopia with Coins — A87

1968, Nov. 3   Photo.   *Perf. 12½x12*
419   A87   20fr multi   .60   .25
50th anniversary of the Malagasy Savings Bank.

Striving Mankind — A88

1968, Dec. 3   Photo.   *Perf. 12½x12*
420   A88   15fr ultra, yel & crim   .30   .25
421   A88   45fr vio bl & multi   .55   .25
Completion of Five-Year Plan, 1964-68.

Queen Adelaide Receiving Malagasy Delegation, London, 1836 — A89

1969, Mar. 29   Photo.   *Perf. 12x12½*
422   A89   250fr multi   4.75   2.50
Malagasy delegation London visit, 1836-37.

Cogwheels, Wrench and ILO Emblem — A90

1969, Apr. 11   *Perf. 12½x12*
423   A90   20fr grn & multi   .50   .25
ILO, 50th anniv.

Telecommunications and Postal Building, Tananarive — A91

1969, May 8   Engr.   *Perf. 13*
424   A91   30fr bl, brt grn & car lake   .60   .25
Issued for Stamp Day 1969.

Steering Wheel, Map, Automobiles — A92

1969, June 1   Photo.   *Perf. 12*
425   A92   65fr multi   1.00   .30
Automobile Club of Madagascar, 20th anniv.

Pres. Philibert Tsiranana — A93

1969, June 26   Photo.   *Perf. 12x12½*
426   A93   20fr multi   .60   .25
10th anniversary of the inauguration of Pres. Philibert Tsiranana.

Banana Plants — A94

1969, July 7   Engr.   *Perf. 13*
427   A94   5fr shown   .65   .25
428   A94   15fr Lichi tree   1.25   .25

Runners — A95

1969, Sept. 9   Engr.   *Perf. 13*
429   A95   15fr yel grn, brn & red   .55   .25
Issued to commemorate the 19th Olympic Games, Mexico City, Oct. 12-27, 1968.

MALAGASY REPUBLIC

Malagasy House, Highlands — A96

Malagasy Houses: No. 430, Betsileo house, Highlands. No. 431, Tsimihety house, West Coast, horiz. 60fr, Malagasy house, Highlands.

1969-70	Engr.	Perf. 13
430 A96 20fr bl, ol & ver	.25	.25
431 A96 20fr sl, brt grn & red	.25	.25
432 A96 40fr blk, bl & dk red	.45	.25
433 A96 60fr vio bl, dp grn & brn	.75	.30
Nos. 430-433 (4)	1.70	1.05

Issued: 40fr, 60fr, 11/25/69; others, 11/25/70.

Arms Type of 1963-65

1fr, Maintirano. 10fr, Ambalavao. No. 436, Morondava. No. 437, Ambatondrazaka. No. 438, Fenerive-Est. 80fr, Tamatave.

1970-72	Photo.	Perf. 13
434 A50 1fr multi	.30	.25
435 A50 10fr multi ('72)	.60	.26
436 A50 25fr multi ('71)	.75	.25
437 A50 25fr multi ('71)	.75	.25
438 A50 25fr multi ('72)	1.10	.25
439 A50 80fr pink & multi	1.75	.30
Nos. 434-439 (6)	5.15	1.55

The 10fr, 80fr are dated "1970." No. 437 is dated "1971." Nos. 434, 438 are dated "1972." Sizes: Nos. 434, 436, 22x37mm; others, 25½x36mm.
Imprints: "S. Gauthier" on Nos. 434, 438; "S. Gauthier Delrieu" on others.

Carnelian — A97

Semi-precious Stones: 12fr, Yellow calcite. 15fr, Quartz. 20fr, Ammonite.

Perf. 12x12½ (5, 20fr), 13 (12, 15fr)		
1970-71		Photo.
440 A97 5fr brn, dl rose & yel	4.25	1.00
441 A97 12fr multi ('71)	4.75	1.00
442 A97 15fr multi ('71)	6.25	1.50
443 A97 20fr grn & multi	17.50	2.00
Nos. 440-443 (4)	32.75	5.50

UPU Headquarters Issue
Common Design Type

1970, May 20	Engr.	Perf. 13
444 CD133 20fr lil rose, brn & ultra	.55	.25

UN Emblem and Symbols of Justice — A98

1970, June 26	Engr.	Perf. 13
445 A98 50fr blk, ultra & org	.70	.30

25th anniversary of the United Nations.

Fruits of Madagascar A99

1970, Aug. 18	Photo.	Perf. 13
446 A99 20fr multi	1.00	.25

Volute Delessertiana A100

Shells: 10fr, Murex tribulus. 20fr, Spondylus.

1970, Sept. 9	Photo.	Perf. 13
447 A100 5fr Prus bl & multi	.80	.25
448 A100 10fr vio & multi	.95	.25
449 A100 20fr multi	2.40	.30
Nos. 447-449 (3)	4.15	.80

Aye-aye A101

1970, Oct. 7	Photo.	Perf. 12½
450 A101 20fr multi	2.00	.35

Intl. Conference for Nature Conservation, Tananarive, Oct. 7-10.

Pres. Tsiranana — A102

1970, Dec. 30	Photo.	Perf. 12½
451 A102 30fr grn & lt brn	.60	.25

60th birthday of Pres. Philibert Tsiranana.

Tropical Soap Factory, Tananarive A103

Designs: 15fr, Comina chromium smelting plant, Andriamena. 50fr, Textile mill, Majunga.

1971, Apr. 14	Photo.	Perf. 12½x12
452 A103 5fr multi	.30	.25
	Engr.	Perf. 13
453 A103 15fr vio bl, blk & ocher	.35	.25
	Photo.	Perf. 13
454 A103 50fr multi	.65	.25
Nos. 452-454 (3)	1.30	.75

Economic development.

Globe, Agriculture, Industry, Science — A104

1971, Apr. 22	Photo.	Perf. 12½x12
455 A104 5fr multi	.30	.25

Extraordinary meeting of the Council of the C.E.E.-E.A.M.A. (Communauté Economique Européen-Etats Africains et Malgache Associés).

Mobile Rural Post Office — A105

1971, May 8		Perf. 13
456 A105 25fr multi	.60	.25

Stamp Day.

Gen. Charles de Gaulle — A106

1971, June 26	Engr.	Perf. 13
457 A106 30fr ultra, blk & rose	1.00	.35

In memory of Charles de Gaulle (1890-1970), President of France.
For surcharge see No. B24.

Madagascar Hilton, Tananarive — A107

Design: 25fr, Hotel Palm Beach, Nossi-Bé.

1971, July 23	Photo.	
458 A107 25fr multi	.50	.25
	Engr.	
459 A107 65fr vio bl, brn & lt grn	.85	.30

Trees and Post Horn — A108

1971, Aug. 6	Photo.	Perf. 12½x12
460 A108 3fr red, yel & grn	.50	.25

Forest preservation campaign.

House, South West Madagascar A109

10fr, House from Southern Madagascar.

1971, Nov. 25		Perf. 13x12½
461 A109 5fr lt bl & multi	.25	.25
462 A109 10fr lt bl & multi	.35	.25

Children Playing, and Cattle — A110

1971, Dec. 11	Litho.	Perf. 13
463 A110 50fr grn & multi	1.10	.30

UNICEF, 25th anniv.

Cable-laying Railroad Car, PTT Emblem — A111

1972, Apr. 8	Engr.	Perf. 13
464 A111 45fr slate grn, red & choc	2.00	.40

Coaxial cable connection between Tananarive and Tamatave.

Philibert Tsiranana Radar Station A112

1972, Apr. 8	Photo.	Perf. 13½
465 A112 85fr bl & multi	1.00	.40

A113

Voters and Pres. Tsiranana.

1972, May 1		Perf. 12½x13
466 A113 25fr yel & multi	.55	.35

Presidential election, Jan. 30, 1972.

Stamp Day — A114

1972, May 30	Photo.	Perf. 12x12½
467 A114 10fr Mail delivery	.60	.25

Emblem and Stamps of Madagascar — A115

Stamps shown are #352, 410, 429, 449.

1972, June 26		Perf. 13
468 A115 25fr org & multi	.50	.25
469 A115 40fr org & multi	.60	.30
470 A115 100fr org & multi	1.50	.50
a. Souv. sheet of 3, #468-470	3.50	3.50
Nos. 468-470 (3)	2.60	1.05

2nd Malgache Philatelic Exhibition, Tananarive, June 26-July 9.

Andapa-Sambava Road and Monument A116

1972, July 6		Perf. 12½x12
471 A116 50fr multi	.60	.30

Opening of the Andapa-Sambava road.

Diesel Locomotive A117

1972, July 6	Engr.	Perf. 13
472 A117 100fr multicolored	4.00	.50

Razafindrahety College — A118

1972, Aug. 6		
473 A118 10fr choc, bl & red brn	.45	.25

Razafindrahety College, Tananarive, sesqui.

Volleyball — A119

1972, Aug. 6	Typo.	Perf. 12½x13
474 A119 12fr orange, blk & brn	.60	.25

African volleyball championship.

MALAGASY REPUBLIC

Oil Refinery, Tamatave — A120

1972, Sept. 18   Engr.   Perf. 13
475 A120 2fr bl, bister & slate grn   .50   .25

Ravoahangy Andrianavalona Hospital — A121

1972, Oct. 14   Photo.   Perf. 13x12½
476 A121 6fr multi   .45   .25

Plowing — A122

1972, Nov. 15   Photo.   Perf. 13½x14
477 A122 25fr gold & multi   .70   .30

Betsimisaraka Costume — A123

Design: 15fr, Merina costume.

1972, Dec. 30   Photo.   Perf. 13x12½
478 A123 10fr blue & multi   .35   .25
479 A123 15fr brown & multi   .65   .25

Farmer and Produce — A124

1973, Feb. 6   Photo.   Perf. 13
480 A124 25fr lt blue & multi   .60   .25

10th anniversary of the Malagasy Committee of "Freedom from Hunger Campaign." For surcharge see No. 499.

Volva Volva — A125

Shells: 10fr, Lambis chiragra. 15fr, 40fr, Harpa major. 25fr, Like 3fr.

1973, Apr. 5   Litho.   Perf. 13
481 A125 3fr olive & multi   .25   .25
482 A125 10fr blue grn & multi   .45   .25
483 A125 15fr brt blue & multi   .70   .25
484 A125 25fr lt blue & multi   1.10   .30
485 A125 40fr multicolored   1.40   .30
486 A125 50fr red lilac & multi   2.10   .40
    Nos. 481-486 (6)   6.00 1.75

Tsimandoa Mail Carrier — A126

1973, May 13   Engr.   Perf. 13
487 A126 50fr ind, ocher & sl grn   .75   .30
Stamp Day 1973.

Builders and Map of Africa — A127

1973, May 25   Photo.   Perf. 13
488 A127 25fr multicolored   .60   .25
Organization for African Unity, 10th anniversary.

Campani Chameleon A128

Various Chameleons: 5fr, 40fr, Male nasutus. 10fr, 85fr, Female nasutus. 60fr, Like 1fr.

1973, June 15   Photo.   Perf. 13x12½
489 A128 1fr dp car & multi   .30   .25
490 A128 5fr brown & multi   .30   .25
491 A128 10fr green & multi   .45   .25
492 A128 40fr red lilac & multi   1.20   .25
493 A128 60fr dk blue & multi   1.75   .40
494 A128 85fr brown & multi   2.50   .60
    Nos. 489-494 (6)   6.50 2.00

Lady's Slipper — A129

Orchids: 25fr, 40fr, Pitcher plant.

1973, Aug. 6   Photo.   Perf. 12½
495 A129 10fr multicolored   .55   .25
496 A129 25fr rose & multi   .75   .30
497 A129 40fr lt blue & multi   1.75   .35
498 A129 100fr multicolored   3.75   .70
    Nos. 495-498 (4)   6.80 1.60

No. 480 Surcharged with New Value, 2 Bars, and Overprinted in Ultramarine

"SECHERESSE/SOLIDARITE AFRICAINE"

1973, Aug. 16   Perf. 13
499 A124 100fr on 25fr multi   1.40   .50
African solidarity in drought emergency.

African Postal Union Issue
Common Design Type

1973, Sept. 12   Engr.   Perf. 13
500 CD137 100fr vio, red & slate grn   1.10   .35

Greater Dwarf Lemur — A131

Design: 25fr, Weasel lemur, vert.

1973, Oct. 9   Engr.   Perf. 13
501 A131 5fr brt green & multi   .75   .30
502 A131 25fr ocher & multi   1.75   .60
    Nos. 501-502, C117-C118 (4)   9.50 3.20
Lemurs of Madagascar.

No. 389 Surcharged

1974, Feb. 9   Litho.   Perf. 13
503 A50 25fr on 30fr multi   .50   .25

Scouts Helping to Raise Cattle — A132

Design: 15fr, Scouts building house; African Scout emblem.

1974, Feb. 14   Engr.   Perf. 13
504 A132 4fr blue, slate & emer   .25   .25
505 A132 15fr chocolate & multi   .30   .25
    Nos. 504-505, C122-C123 (4)   4.55 1.85
Malagasy Boy Scouts.

Mother with Children and Clinic — A133

1974, May 24   Photo.   Perf. 13
506 A133 25fr multicolored   .45   .25
World Population Year.

Rainibetsimisaraka A134

1974, July 26   Photo.   Perf. 13
507 A134 25fr multicolored   .65   .30
In memory of Rainibetsimisaraka, independence leader.

Marble Blocks — A135

Design: 25fr, Marble quarry.

1974, Sept. 27   Photo.   Perf. 13
508 A135 4fr multicolored   .80   .25
509 A135 25fr multicolored   2.10   .45
Malagasy marble.

Europafrica Issue

Links, White and Black Faces, Map of Europe and Africa — A136

1974, Oct. 17   Engr.   Perf. 13
510 A136 150fr dk brown & org   1.75   .60

Grain and Hand — A137

1974, Oct. 29
511 A137 80fr light blue & ocher   1.00   .35
World Committee against Hunger.

Tuléar Dog — A138

Design: 100fr, Hunting dog.

1974, Nov. 26   Photo.   Perf. 13x13½
512 A138 50fr multicolored   2.50   .50
513 A138 100fr multicolored   3.50   .90

Malagasy Citizens — A139

1974, Dec. 9   Perf. 13½x13
514 A139 5fr blue grn & multi   .25   .25
515 A139 10fr multicolored   .25   .25
516 A139 20fr yellow grn & multi   .35   .25
517 A139 60fr orange & multi   .90   .25
    Nos. 514-517 (4)   1.75 1.00
Introduction of "Fokonolona" community organization.

Symbols of Development A140

1974, Dec. 16   Photo.   Perf. 13x13½
518 A140 25fr ultra & multi   .30   .25
519 A140 35fr blue grn & multi   .50   .25
National Council for Development.

Woman, Rose, Dove and Emblem — A141

1975, Jan. 21   Engr.   Perf. 13
520 A141 100fr brn, emer & org   1.10   .40
International Women's Year 1975.

Col. Richard Ratsimandrava A142

1975, Apr. 25   Photo.   Perf. 13
521 A142 15fr brown & salmon   .25   .25
522 A142 25fr black, bl & brn   .35   .25
523 A142 100fr blk, lt grn & brn   1.25   .30
    Nos. 521-523 (3)   1.85   .80
Ratsimandrava (1933-1975), head of state.

Sofia Bridge — A143

1975, May 29   Litho.   Perf. 12½
524 A143 45fr multicolored   .80   .30

MALAGASY REPUBLIC

Count de Grasse and "Randolph" — A144

Design: 50fr, Marquis de Lafayette, "Lexington" and HMS "Edward."

1975, June 30	Litho.	Perf. 11		
525	A144	40fr multicolored	.50	.25
526	A144	50fr multicolored	.65	.30
	Nos. 525-526,C137-C139 (5)		7.15	2.10

American Bicentennial.
For overprints see Nos. 564-565, C164-C167.

Euphorbia Viguieri — A145

Tropical Plants: 25fr, Hibiscus. 30fr, Plumieria rubra acutifolia. 40fr, Pachypodium rosulatum.

1975, Aug. 4	Photo.	Perf. 12½		
527	A145	15fr lemon & multi	.25	.25
528	A145	25fr black & multi	.45	.25
529	A145	30fr orange & multi	.60	.30
530	A145	40fr dk red & multi	1.00	.30
	Nos. 527-530,C141 (5)		4.20	2.00

Brown, White, Yellow and Black Hands Holding Globe — A146

1975, Aug. 26	Litho.	Perf. 12		
531	A146	50fr multicolored	.70	.25

Namibia Day (independence for South-West Africa.)

Woodpecker A147

1975, Sept. 16	Litho.	Perf. 14x13½		
532	A147	25fr shown	.55	.25
533	A147	40fr Rabbit	.85	.25
534	A147	50fr Frog	1.10	.30
535	A147	75fr Tortoise	1.60	.45
	Nos. 532-535,C145 (5)		6.00	1.70

International Exposition, Okinawa.

Lily Waterfall — A148

Design: 40fr, Lily Waterfall, different view.

1975, Sept. 17	Litho.	Perf. 12½		
536	A148	25fr multicolored	.50	.25
537	A148	40fr multicolored	.65	.25

4-man Bob Sled — A149

100fr, Ski jump. 140fr, Speed skating.

1975, Nov. 19	Litho.	Perf. 14		
538	A149	75fr multicolored	.60	.25
539	A149	100fr multicolored	1.00	.30
540	A149	140fr multicolored	1.50	.40
	Nos. 538-540,C149-C150 (5)		7.75	2.15

12th Winter Olympic games, Innsbruck, 1976.
For overprints see Nos. 561-563, C161-C163.

Pirogue — A150

Designs: 45fr, Boutre (Arabian coastal vessel).

1975, Nov. 20	Photo.	Perf. 12½		
541	A150	8fr multicolored	.50	.25
542	A150	45fr ultra & multi	1.75	.40

Canadian Canoe and Kayak A151

Design: 50fr, Sprint and Hurdles.

1976, Jan. 21	Litho.	Perf. 14x13½		
543	A151	40fr multicolored	.45	.25
544	A151	50fr multicolored	.55	.25
	Nos. 543-544,C153-C155 (5)		6.65	2.30

21st Summer Olympic games, Montreal.
For overprints see Nos. 571-572, C168-C171.

Count Zeppelin and LZ-127 over Fujiyama, Japan — A152

Designs (Count Zeppelin and LZ-127 over): 50fr, Rio. 75fr, NYC. 100fr, Sphinx.

1976, Mar. 3		Perf. 11		
545	A152	40fr multicolored	.40	.25
546	A152	50fr multicolored	.50	.25
547	A152	75fr multicolored	1.00	.30
548	A152	100fr multicolored	1.20	.35
	Nos. 545-548,C158-C159 (6)		9.35	2.65

75th anniversary of the Zeppelin.

Worker, Globe, Eye Chart and Eye — A153

1976, Apr. 7	Photo.	Perf. 12½		
549	A153	100fr multicolored	1.40	.50

World Health Day: "Foresight prevents blindness."

Aragonite — A154

50fr, Petrified wood. 150fr, Celestite.

1976, May 7	Photo.	Perf. 12½		
550	A154	25fr blue & multi	1.40	.50
551	A154	50fr blue grn & multi	3.50	1.00
552	A154	150fr orange & multi	10.50	2.00
	Nos. 550-552 (3)		15.40	3.50

Alexander Graham Bell and First Telephone A155

50fr, Telephone lines, 1911. 100fr, Central office, 1895. 200fr, Cable ship, 1925. 300fr, Radio telephone. 500fr, Intelsat 4 satellite and globe.

1976, May 13	Litho.	Perf. 14		
553	A155	25fr multicolored	.25	.25
554	A155	50fr multicolored	.45	.25
555	A155	100fr multicolored	.75	.30
556	A155	200fr multicolored	1.50	.45
557	A155	300fr multicolored	2.40	.50
	Nos. 553-557 (5)		5.35	1.75

Souvenir Sheet

| 558 | A155 | 500fr multicolored | 4.25 | 1.40 |

Cent. of 1st telephone call by Alexander Graham Bell, Mar. 10, 1876.

Children with Books — A156

Design: 25fr, Children with books, vert.

1976, May 25	Litho.			
559	A156	10fr multicolored	.25	.25
560	A156	25fr multicolored	.50	.25

Books for children.

Nos. 538-540 Overprinted

a. VAINQUEUR ALLEMAGNE FEDERALE
b. VAINQUEUR KARL SCHNABL AUTRICHE
c. VAINQUEUR SHEILA YOUNG ETATS-UNIS

1976, June 17				
561	A149 (a)	75fr multi	.60	.30
562	A149 (b)	100fr multi	1.00	.30
563	A149 (c)	140fr multi	1.50	.60
	Nos. 561-563,C161-C162 (5)		6.80	2.75

12th Winter Olympic games winners.

Nos. 525-526 Overprinted "4 Juillet / 1776-1976"

1976, July 4				
564	A144	40fr multicolored	.45	.30
565	A144	50fr multicolored	.60	.40
	Nos. 564-565,C164-C166 (5)		6.80	2.50

American Bicentennial

Graph of Projected Landing Spots on Mars A157

Viking project to Mars: 100fr, Viking probe in flight. 200fr, Viking probe on Mars. 300fr, Viking probe over projected landing spot. 500fr, Viking probe approaching Mars.

1976, July 17	Litho.	Perf. 14		
566	A157	75fr multicolored	.45	.25
567	A157	100fr multicolored	.75	.30
568	A157	200fr multicolored	1.50	.40
569	A157	300fr multicolored	2.25	.60
	Nos. 566-569 (4)		4.95	1.55

Souvenir Sheet

| 570 | A157 | 500fr multicolored | 4.50 | 1.00 |

Nos. 543-544 Overprinted

a. A. ROGOV / V. DIBA
b. H. CRAWFORD / J. SCHALLER

1977, Jan.				
571	A151 (a)	40fr multi	.45	.25
572	A151 (b)	50fr multi	.60	.30
	Nos. 571-572,C168-C170 (5)		6.80	2.40

21st Summer Olympic games winners.

Rainandriamampandry — A158

Portrait: No. 574, Rabezavana.

1976-77	Litho.	Perf. 12x12½		
573	A158	25fr multicolored	.75	.25
574	A158	25fr multicolored	.25	.25

Rainandriamampandry was Malagasy Foreign Minister who signed treaties in 1896.
Issued: No. 573, 10/15; No. 574, 3/29/77.

"Indian Ocean - Zone of Peace." — A159

Design: 60fr, Globe with Africa and Indian Ocean, doves, vert. 160fr, Doves, Indian Ocean on Globe.

		Perf. 12½x12, 12x12½		
1976, Nov. 18				
575	A159	60fr multicolored	.60	.25
576	A159	160fr shown	1.40	.50

Coat of Arms — A160

1976, Dec. 30	Litho.	Perf. 12		
577	A160	25fr multicolored	.40	.25

Democratic Republic of Malagasy, 1st anniv.

Lt. Albert Randriamaromanana — A161

Portrait: No. 578, Avana Ramanantoanina.

1977, Mar. 29				
578	A161	25fr multicolored	.30	.25
579	A161	25fr multicolored	.30	.25

National Mausoleum A162

1977, Mar. 29		Perf. 12½x12		
580	A162	100fr multicolored	1.25	.40

MALAGASY REPUBLIC

Family — A163

1977, Apr. 7   Perf. 12x12½
581 A163 5fr org yel & multi   .40   .25
World Health Day: Immunization protects the children.

Tananarive Medical School A164

1977, June 30   Litho.   Perf. 12½x12
582 A164 250fr multicolored   2.10   .80
80th anniversary of Tananarive Medical School.

Mail Bus — A165

1977, Aug. 18   Litho.   Perf. 12½x12
583 A165 35fr multicolored   .50   .25
Rural mail delivery.

Telegraph Operator A166

1977, Sept. 13   Litho.   Perf. 12½x12
584 A166 15fr multicolored   .50   .25
Telegraph service Tananarive-Tamatave, 90th anniv.

Malagasy Art — A167

1977, Sept. 29   Perf. 12x12½
585 A167 10fr multicolored   .50   .25
Malagasy Academy, 75th anniversary.

Lenin and Russian Flag A168

1977, Nov. 7   Litho.   Perf. 12½x12
586 A168 25fr multicolored   2.60   .35
60th anniversary of Russian October Revolution.

Raoul Follereau, Map of Malagasy — A169

1978, Jan. 28   Litho.   Perf. 12x12½
587 A169 5fr multicolored   1.75   .30
25th anniversary of Leprosy Day.

Antenna, ITU Emblem — A170

1978, May 17   Litho.   Perf. 12x12½
588 A170 20fr multicolored   .50   .25
10th World Telecommunications Day.

Black and White Men Breaking Chains of Africa — A171

1978, June 22   Photo.   Perf. 12½x12
589 A171 60fr multicolored   .75   .25
Anti-Apartheid Year.

Boy and Girl, Arch: Pen, Gun and Hoe — A172

1978, July 28   Litho.   Perf. 12½x12
590 A172 125fr multicolored   1.25   .40
Youth, the pillar of revolution.

Farm Workers, Factory, Tractor — A173

1978, Aug. 24
591 A173 25fr multicolored   .50   .25
Socialist cooperation.

Women — A174

1979, Mar. 8   Litho.   Perf. 12½x12
592 A174 40fr multicolored   .50   .25
Women, supporters of the revolution.

Children Bringing Gifts — A175

1979, June 1   Litho.   Perf. 12x12½
593 A175 10fr multicolored   .50   .25
International Year of the Child.

Lemur Macaco — A176

Fauna: 25fr, Lemur catta, vert. 1000fr, Foussa.

     Perf. 12½x12, 12x12½
1979, July 6   Litho.
594 A176 25fr multi   .60   .25
595 A176 125fr multi   2.25   .35
596 A176 1000fr multi   8.25   1.50
Nos. 594-596,C172-C173 (5)   12.75   2.60

Jean Verdi Salomon — A177

1979, July 25   Perf. 12x12½
597 A177 25fr multicolored   .50   .25
Jean Verdi Salomon (1913-1978), poet.

Talapetraka (Medicinal Plant) — A178

1979, Sept. 27   Litho.   Perf. 12½
598 A178 25fr multicolored   .75   .25

Map of Magagascar, Dish Antenna — A179

1979, Oct. 12
599 A179 25fr multicolored   .50   .25

Stamp Day 1979 — A180

1979, Nov. 9
600 A180 500fr multicolored   4.50   1.40

Jet, Map of Africa — A181

1979, Dec. 12   Perf. 12½
601 A181 50fr multicolored   .75   .25
ASECNA (Air Safety Board), 20th anniversary.

Lenin Addressing Workers in the Winter Palace — A182

1980, Apr. 22   Litho.   Perf. 12x12½
602 A182 25fr multicolored   .70   .25
Lenin's 110th birth anniversary.

Bus and Road in Madagascar Colors — A183

1980, June 15   Litho.   Perf. 12x12½
603 A183 30fr multicolored   .50   .25
Socialist Revolution, 5th anniversary.

Flag and Map under Sun — A184

1980, June 26   Perf. 12½x12
604 A184 75fr multicolored   .75   .25
Independence, 20th anniversary.

Armed Forces Day — A185

1980, Aug.   Litho.   Perf. 12½x12
605 A185 50fr multicolored   .60   .25

Dr. Joseph Raseta (1886-1979) A186

1980, Oct. 15   Litho.   Perf. 12x12½
606 A186 30fr multicolored   .50   .25

Anatirova Temple Centenary A187

1980, Nov. 27   Litho.   Perf. 12½x12
607 A187 30fr multicolored   .50   .25

Hurdles, Olympic Torch, Moscow '80 Emblem A188

1980, Dec. 29
608 A188 30fr shown   .45   .25
609 A188 75fr Boxing   .85   .30
Nos. 608-609,C175-C176 (4)   6.95   2.75
22nd Summer Olympic Games, Moscow, July 19-Aug. 3.

Democratic Republic of Madagascar, 5th Anniversary A189

1980, Dec. 30   Perf. 12x12½
610 A189 30fr multicolored   .50   .25

MALAGASY REPUBLIC

Downhill Skiing — A190

1981, Jan. 26   Litho.   Perf. 12½x12
611 A190 175fr multicolored   1.60   .60
13th Winter Olympic Games, Lake Placid, Feb. 12-24, 1980.

Angraecum Leonis — A191

80fr, Angraecum ramosum. 170fr, Angraecum sesquipedale.

1981, Mar. 23   Litho.   Perf. 11½
612 A191   5fr shown   .40   .25
613 A191 80fr multicolored   1.40   .30
614 A191 170fr multicolored   2.25   .65
   Nos. 612-614 (3)   4.05 1.20
For surcharge, see No. 1474B.

Intl. Year of the Disabled — A192

1981, June 12   Litho.   Perf. 12
615 A192 25fr Student at desk   .35   .25
616 A192 80fr Carpenter   .75   .30

A193

1981, July 10   Litho.   Perf. 12½x12
617 A193 15fr multicolored   .25   .25
618 A193 45fr multicolored   .55   .25
13th World Telecommunications Day.

Neil Armstrong on Moon (Apollo 11) — A194

Space Anniversaries: 30fr, Valentina Tereshkova. 90fr, Yuri Gagarin.

1981, July 23   Perf. 11½
619 A194 30fr multicolored   .30   .25
620 A194 80fr shown   .80   .25
621 A194 90fr multicolored   .90   .25
   Nos. 619-621 (3)   2.00   .75

Brother Raphael Louis Rafiringa (1854-1919) — A195

1981, Aug. 10   Litho.   Perf. 12
622 A195 30fr multi   .50   .25

World Literacy Day — A196

1981, Sept. 8
623 A196 30fr multi   .50   .25

World Food Day — A197

1981, Oct. 16   Litho.   Perf. 12x12½
624 A197 200fr multi   1.90   .60
See No. 635.

Oaths of Magistracy Renewal A198

1981, Oct. 30   Perf. 12½x12
625 A198 30fr blk & lil rose .50   .25

Dove, by Pablo Picasso (1881-1973) A199

1981, Nov. 18   Photo.   Perf. 11½x12
626 A199 80fr multi   1.00   .30

20th Anniv. of UPU Membership A200

Design: Nos. C76, C77, emblem.

1981, Nov. 19   Litho.   Perf. 12
627 A200   5fr multi   .25   .25
628 A200 30fr multi   .45   .25

TB Bacillus Centenary A201

1982, June 21   Litho.   Perf. 12
629 A201 30fr multi   .60   .25

Jeannette Mpihira (1903-1981), Actress and Singer — A202

1982, June 24   Perf. 12½
630 A202 30fr multi   .50   .25

Haliaeetus Vociferoides (Ankoay) A203

25fr, Vanga curvirostris, horiz. 30fr, Leptosomus discolor, horiz.

1982, July
631 A203 25fr multi   1.10   .25
632 A203 30fr multi   1.40   .25
633 A203 200fr shown   4.75   .70
   Nos. 631-633 (3)   7.25 1.20

Pierre Louis Boiteau (1911-1980), Educator — A204

1982, Sept. 13
634 A204 30fr multi   .50   .25

World Food Day Type of 1981
1982, Oct. 16   Perf. 12x12½
635 A197 80fr multi   .75   .25
No. 635 is overprinted "EFA POLO ARIARY" on the text.

25th Anniv. of Launching of Sputnik I — A205

10fr, Sputnik I. 80fr, Yuri Gagarin, Vostok I. 100fr, Soyuz-Salyut.

1982, Oct. 4   Litho.   Perf. 12
636 A205 10fr multicolored   .25   .25
637 A205 80fr multicolored   .65   .25
638 A205 100fr multicolored   .85   .30
   Nos. 636-638 (3)   1.75   .80

1982 World Cup — A206

Designs: Various soccer players.

1982, Oct. 14   Perf. 12x12½
639 A206 30fr multi   .30   .25
640 A206 40fr multi   .40   .25
641 A206 80fr multi   .80   .25
   Nos. 639-641 (3)   1.50   .75

Souvenir Sheet
Perf. 11½x12½
642 A206 450fr multi   3.75 1.60

Scene at a Bar, by Edouard Manet (1832-1883) A207

30fr, Lady in a White Dress. 170fr, Portrait of Mallarme. 400fr, The Fifer, vert.

1982, Nov. 25   Perf. 12½x12
643 A207   5fr shown   .55   .25
644 A207 30fr multicolored   .75   .30
645 A207 170fr multicolored   3.50   .70
   Nos. 643-645 (3)   4.80 1.25

Souvenir Sheet
Perf. 11½x12½
646 A207 400fr multi   8.00 2.00
For surcharge, see No. 1475B.

Local Fish — A208

5fr, Lutianus sebae. 20fr, Istiophorus platypterus. 30fr, Pterois volitans. 50fr, Thunnus albacares. 200fr, Epinephelus fasciatus. 450fr, Latimeria chalumnae.

1982, Dec. 14   Perf. 11½
647 A208   5fr multi   .30   .25
648 A208 20fr multi   .30   .25
649 A208 30fr multi   .55   .25
650 A208 50fr multi   1.00   .25
651 A208 200fr multi   3.00   .60
   Nos. 647-651 (5)   5.15 1.60

Souvenir Sheet
Perf. 12½x12½
652 A208 450fr multi   5.00 2.00
No. 652 contains one stamp 38x26mm.

Fort Mahavelona Ruins A209

30fr, Ramena Beach. 400fr, Flowering jacaranda trees.

1982, Dec. 22   Perf. 12½x12
653 A209 10fr shown   .25   .25
654 A209 30fr multicolored   .25   .25
655 A209 400fr multicolored   3.00 1.00
   Nos. 653-655 (3)   3.50 1.50

60th Anniv. of USSR A210

1982, Dec. 29
656 A210 10fr Tractors   .25   .25
657 A210 15fr Pylon   .25   .25
658 A210 30fr Kremlin, Lenin .25   .25
659 A210 150fr Arms   1.25   .50
   Nos. 656-659 (4)   2.00 1.25

World Communications Year — A211

80fr, Stylized figures holding wheel.

1983, May 17   Litho.   Perf. 12
660 A211 30fr multi   .30   .25
661 A211 80fr multi   .65   .30

Organization of African Unity, 20th Anniv. — A212

1983, May 25   Litho.   Perf. 12
662 A212 30fr multi   .50   .25

MALAGASY REPUBLIC

Henri Douzon, Lawyer and Patriot — A213

1983, June 27	Litho.		Perf. 12
663	A213	30fr multi	.50 .25

Souvenir Sheet

Manned Flight Bicentenary — A214

500fr, Montgolfiere balloon.

1983, July 20	Litho.		Perf. 12
664	A214	500fr multicolored	5.00 2.00

Souvenir Sheet

Raphael, 500th Birth Anniv. A215

500fr, The Madonna Connestable.

1983, Aug. 10	Litho.		Perf. 12
665	A215	500fr multi	5.00 2.00

Lemur A216

Various lemurs: No. 666, Daubentonia madagascariensis. No. 667, Microcebus murinus. No. 668, Lemur variegatus, vert. No. 669, Propithecus verreauxi, vert. No. 670, Indri indri. No. 671, Perodicticus potto, vert.

Perf. 12½x12, 12x12½

1983, Dec. 6			Litho.
666	A216	30fr multicolored	.55 .25
667	A216	30fr multicolored	.55 .25
668	A216	30fr multicolored	.55 .25
669	A216	30fr multicolored	.55 .25
670	A216	200fr multicolored	3.50 .80
		Nos. 666-670 (5)	5.70 1.80

Souvenir Sheet

| 671 | A216 | 500fr multi | 6.50 2.00 |

1984 Winter Olympics — A217

1984, Jan. 20	Litho.		Perf. 11½
672	A217	20fr Ski jumping	.25 .25
673	A217	30fr Speed skating	.25 .25
674	A217	30fr Downhill skiing	.25 .25
675	A217	30fr Hockey	.25 .25
676	A217	200fr Figure skating	2.00 .60
		Nos. 672-676 (5)	3.00 1.60

Souvenir Sheet

| 677 | A217 | 500fr Cross-country skiing | 4.50 2.00 |

No. 677 contains one stamp 48x32mm.

Vintage Cars A218

1984, Jan. 27			Perf. 12½x12
678	A218	15fr Renault, 1907	.25 .25
679	A218	30fr Benz, 1896	.30 .25
680	A218	30fr Baker, 1901	.30 .25
681	A218	30fr Blake, 1901	.30 .25
682	A218	200fr FIAL, 1908	2.40 .60
		Nos. 678-682 (5)	3.55 1.60

Souvenir Sheet
Perf. 12½x11½

| 683 | A218 | 450fr Russo-Baltique, 1909 | 4.50 2.00 |

Pastor Ravelojaona (1879-1956), Encyclopedist — A219

1984, Feb. 14			Perf. 12x12½
684	A219	30fr multi	.50 .25

See No. 704.

Madonna and Child, by Correggio (1489-1534) A220

Various Correggio paintings.

1984, May 5	Litho.		Perf. 12x12½
685	A220	5fr multi	.25 .25
686	A220	20fr multi	.25 .25
687	A220	30fr multi	.35 .25
688	A220	80fr multi	.75 .30
689	A220	200fr multi	2.10 .60
		Nos. 685-689 (5)	3.70 1.65

Souvenir Sheet

| 690 | A220 | 400fr multi | 5.50 2.00 |

World Chess Federation, 60th Anniv. — A221

No. 691, Paris landmarks. No. 692, Wilhelm Steinitz. No. 693, Champion, cup. No. 694, Vera Menchik. No. 695, Champion, cup, diff. No. 696, Children playing chess.

1984, July 27			
691	A221	5fr multi	.25 .25
692	A221	20fr multi	.35 .25
693	A221	30fr multi	.55 .25
694	A221	30fr multi	.55 .25
695	A221	215fr multi	3.25 .80
		Nos. 691-695 (5)	4.95 1.80

Souvenir Sheet

| 696 | A221 | 400fr multi | 6.00 2.00 |

1984 Summer Olympics — A222

1984, Aug. 10			
697	A222	100fr Soccer	1.00 .35

Butterflies — A223

No. 698, Eudaphaenura splendens. No. 699, Othreis boseae. No. 700, Pharmacophagus antenor. No. 701, Acraea hova. No. 702, Epicausis smithii. 400fr, Papilio delandii.

1984, Aug. 30	Litho.		Perf. 11½
698	A223	15fr multicolored	.60 .25
699	A223	50fr multicolored	1.25 .25
700	A223	50fr multicolored	1.25 .25
701	A223	50fr multicolored	1.25 .25
702	A223	200fr multicolored	4.50 .65
		Nos. 698-702 (5)	8.85 1.65

Miniature Sheet
Perf. 11½x12½

| 703 | A223 | 400fr multicolored | 5.50 2.00 |

No. 703 contains one stamp 37x52mm.

Famous People Type

Jean Ralaimongo (1884-1944).

1984, Oct. 4			Perf. 12x12½
704	A219	50fr Portrait	.60 .25

Children's Rights — A225

50fr, Youths in school bag.

1984, Nov. 20	Litho.		Perf. 12½x12
705	A225	50fr multicolored	.50 .25

Malagasy Orchids — A226

20fr, Disa incarnata. 235fr, Eulophiella roempleriana. 400fr, Gastrorchis tuberculosa.

1984, Nov. 20	Litho.		Perf. 12
706	A226	20fr multi	.30 .25
707	A226	235fr multi	3.25 .70
		Nos. 706-707,C180-C182 (5)	6.55 1.70

Miniature Sheet
Perf. 12x12½

| 708 | A226 | 400fr multi | 7.50 2.00 |

No. 708 contains one stamp 30x42mm.

Cotton Seminar, UN Trade and Development Conference — A227

100fr, UN emblem, cotton bolls.

1984, Dec. 15	Litho.		Perf. 13x12½
709	A227	100fr multicolored	1.00 .30

Malagasy Language Bible, 150th Anniv. — A228

1985, Feb. 11	Litho.		Perf. 12½x12
710	A228	50fr multi	.50 .25

1985 Agricultural Census — A229

50fr, Census taker, farmer.

1985, Feb. 21	Litho.		Perf. 12x12½
711	A229	50fr multicolored	.50 .25

Allied Defeat of Nazi Germany, 40th Anniv. A230

20fr, Russian flag-raising, Berlin, 1945. 50fr, Normandie-Niemen squadron shooting down German fighter planes. No. 714, Soviet Victory Parade, Red Square, Moscow. No. 715, Victorious French troops marching through Arc de Triomphe, vert.

1985			Perf. 12½x12, 12x12½
712	A230	20fr multi	.30 .25
713	A230	50fr multi	.30 .35
714	A230	100fr multi	.90 .35
715	A230	100fr multi	3.00 .70
		Nos. 712-715 (4)	4.50 1.65

Issue dates: Nos. 712-714, 5/9; No. 715, Oct.

Cats and Dogs — A231

Designs: No. 716, Siamese. No. 717, Bichon. No. 718, Abyssinian, vert. No. 719, Cocker spaniel, vert. No. 720, Poodle. No. 721, Kitten.

1985, Apr. 25	Perf. 12x12½, 12x12½
716	A231	20fr multicolored	.30 .25
717	A231	20fr multicolored	.30 .25
718	A231	20fr multicolored	.75 .25
719	A231	100fr multicolored	1.40 .35
720	A231	235fr multicolored	3.50 .80
		Nos. 716-720 (5)	6.25 1.90

Souvenir Sheet

| 721 | A231 | 400fr multicolored | 6.00 2.00 |

No. 721 contains one stamp 42x30mm, perf. 12½x12.

Gymnastic Event, Natl. Stadium, Atananarivo A232

1985, July 9			Perf. 12½x12
722	A232	50fr multi	.45 .25

Natl. Socialist Revolution, 10th anniv.

Commemorative Medal, Memorial Stele — A233

1985, July 9			
723	A233	50fr multi	1.25 .25

Independence, 25th anniv.

MALAGASY REPUBLIC

Intl. Youth Year — A234

1985, Sept. 18   *Perf. 12*
724 A234 100fr Emblem, map   1.00 .35

Natl. Red Cross, 70th Anniv. — A235

1985, Oct. 3   *Perf. 12x12½*
725 A235 50fr multi   .90 .25

Indira Gandhi — A236

1985, Oct. 31   *Perf. 13½*
726 A236 100fr multi   1.25 .35

22nd World Youth and Student's Festival, Moscow — A237

1985, Nov.   *Perf. 12*
727 A237 50fr multi   .50 .25

Rouen Cathedral at Night, by Monet — A238

Impressionist paintings: No. 729, View of Sea at Sainte-Marie, by van Gogh, horiz. 45fr, Young Woman in Black, by Renoir. 50fr, The Red Vineyard at Arles, by van Gogh, horiz. 100fr, Boulevard des Capucines in Paris, by Monet, horiz. 400fr, In the Garden, by Renoir.

1985, Oct. 25   *Litho.*   *Perf. 12*
728 A238 20fr multi   .50 .25
729 A238 20fr multi   .50 .25
730 A238 45fr multi   .90 .25
731 A238 50fr multi   1.10 .25
732 A238 100fr multi   2.40 .50
Nos. 728-732 (5)   5.40 1.50

Souvenir Sheet
Perf. 12x12½
733 A238 400fr multi   6.00 2.75
No. 733 contains one 30x42mm stamp.

UN, 40th Aniv. — A239

1985, Oct. 31   *Perf. 12*
734 A239 100fr multi   1.00 .30

Orchids — A240

No. 735, Aeranthes grandiflora, vert. No. 736, Angraecum magdalanae. No. 737, Aerangis stylosa, vert. No. 738, Angraecum eburneum longicalcar, vert. No. 739, Angraecum sesquipedale, vert. No. 740, Angraecum aburneum superbum, vert.

1985, Nov. 8
735 A240 20fr multi   1.00 .25
736 A240 45fr multi   1.50 .25
737 A240 50fr multi   1.75 .30
738 A240 100fr multi   3.25 .50
739 A240 100fr multi   3.25 .50
Nos. 735-739 (5)   10.75 1.80

Souvenir Sheet
Perf. 12x12½
740 A240 400fr multi   8.00 2.50
No. 740 contains one 30x42mm stamp.

INTERCOSMOS A241

Cosmonauts, rockets, satellites, probes and natl. flags of: No. 741, USSR, Czechoslovakia. No. 742, Soyuz-Apollo emblem. No. 743, USSR, India. No. 744, USSR, Cuba. No. 745, USSR, France. No. 746, Halley's Comet, probe.

1985, Nov.   *Perf. 12x12½*
741 A241 20fr multicolored   .25 .25
742 A241 20fr multicolored   .25 .25
743 A241 50fr multicolored   .55 .25
744 A241 100fr multicolored   1.00 .30
745 A241 200fr multicolored   1.90 .65
Nos. 741-745 (5)   3.95 1.70

Souvenir Sheet
746 A241 400fr multicolored   5.50 1.75
No. 746 contains one stamp 42x30mm.

Democratic Republic, 10th Anniv. — A242

1985, Dec. 30   *Litho.*   *Perf. 12½x12*
747 A242 50fr Industrial symbols   .45 .25

Natl. Insurance and Securities Co. (ARO), 10th Anniv. — A243

1986, Jan. 20   *Perf. 12x12½*
748 A243 50fr dk brn, yel org & gray brn   .45 .25

Paintings in the Tretyakov Gallery, Moscow A244

Designs: 20fr, Still-life with Flowers and Fruit, 1839, by I. Chroutzky. No. 760, Portrait of Alexander Pushkin, 1827, by O. Kiprenski, vert. No. 751, Portrait of an Unknown Woman, 1883, by I. Kramskoi. No. 752, The Crows Have Returned, 1872, by A. Sakrassov, vert. 100fr, March, 1895, by I. Levitan. 450fr, Portrait of Pavel Tretyakov, 1883, by I. Repin, vert.

Perf. 12½x12, 12x12½
1986, Apr. 26   *Litho.*
749 A244 20fr multi   .25 .25
750 A244 50fr multi   .80 .25
751 A244 50fr multi   .80 .25
752 A244 50fr multi   .80 .25
753 A244 100fr multi   2.25 .40
Nos. 749-753 (5)   4.90 1.40

Souvenir Sheet
754 A244 450fr multi   4.50 2.00

1986 World Cup Soccer Championships, Mexico — A245

1986, May 31   *Perf. 13½*
755 A245 150fr multi   1.40 .45

Paintings in Russian Museums A246

No. 756, David and Urie, by Rembrandt, vert. No. 757, Danae, by Rembrandt. No. 758, Portrait of the Nurse of the Infant Isabella, by Rubens, vert. No. 759, The Alliance of Earth and Water, by Rubens, vert. No. 760, Portrait of an Old Man in Red, by Rembrandt. No. 761, The Holy Family, by Raphael.

Perf. 12x12½, 12½x12
1986, Mar. 24   *Litho.*
756 A246 20fr multi   .25 .25
757 A246 50fr multi   .70 .25
758 A246 50fr multi   .70 .25
759 A246 50fr multi   .70 .25
760 A246 50fr multi   .75 .25
Nos. 756-760 (5)   3.10 1.25

Souvenir Sheet
Perf. 11½x12½
761 A246 450fr multi   3.50 2.50

UN Child Survival Campaign — A247

1986, June 1   *Litho.*   *Perf. 12x12½*
762 A247 60fr multi   .80 .25

A248

1986, July 17
763 A248 10fr Sable   .25 .25
764 A248 10fr Chaus   .25 .25
765 A248 60fr Serval   .70 .25
766 A248 60fr Caracal   .70 .25
767 A248 60fr Bengal   .70 .25
Nos. 763-767 (5)   2.60 1.25

Souvenir Sheet
Perf. 12½x12
768 A249 450fr Golden   4.75 2.00

Wildcats A249

Intl. Peace Year — A249a

1986, Sept. 12   *Perf. 12*
769 A249a 60fr shown   .55 .25
770 A249a 150fr multicolored   1.25 .40

World Post Day — A250

1986, Oct. 9   *Litho.*   *Perf. 13x12½*
771 A250 60fr multi   .60 .25
772 A250 150fr multi   1.40 .40
No. 772 is airmail.

A251

Birds A252

No. 773, Xenopirostris daimi, vert. No. 774, Falculea palliata. No. 775, Coua gigas. No. 776, Coua cristata. No. 777, Cianolanius madagascariensis, vert.
450fr, Bubulcus ibis ibis.

Perf. 12x12½, 12½x12
1986, Dec. 23   *Litho.*
773 A251 60fr multicolored   .80 .25
774 A251 60fr multicolored   .80 .25
775 A251 60fr multicolored   .80 .25
776 A251 60fr multicolored   .80 .25
777 A251 60fr multicolored   .80 .25
Nos. 773-777 (5)   4.00 1.25

Souvenir Sheet
778 A252 450fr multi   6.00 2.00

Endangered Species — A254

No. 779, Lophotibis cristata, vert. No. 780, Coracopsis nigra. No. 781, Crocodylus niloticus. No. 782, Geochelone yniphora.
450fr, Centropus toulou, vert.

Perf. 12x12½, 12½x12
1987, Mar. 13   *Litho.*
779 A253 60fr multicolored   .90 .25
780 A253 60fr multicolored   .90 .25
781 A254 60fr multicolored   .90 .25
782 A254 60fr multicolored   .90 .25
Nos. 779-782 (4)   3.60 1.00

Souvenir Sheet
783 A253 450fr multicolored   5.50 2.00

MALAGASY REPUBLIC

Anti-Colonial Revolt, 40th Anniv. — A255

1987, Mar. 29			Perf. 12	
784	A255	60fr multicolored	.50	.25
785	A256	60fr multicolored	.50	.25

1st Games of Indian Ocean Towns — A257

1987, Apr. 15			Perf. 13½	
786	A257	60fr multicolored	.55	.25
787	A257	150fr multicolored	1.25	.40

Le Sarimanok A258

1987, Apr. 15				
788	A258	60fr Port side	.60	.25
789	A258	150fr Starboard side	1.40	.40

African and Madagascar Coffee Organization, 25th Anniv. — A259

1987, Apr. 24		Litho.	Perf. 12	
790	A259	60fr Coffee plant	.60	.25
791	A259	150fr Map	1.50	.40

Halley's Comet A260

Space probes: 60fr, Giotto, ESA. 150fr, Vega 1, Russia. 250fr, Vega 2, Russia. 350fr, Planet-A1, Japan. 400fr, Planet-A2, Japan. 450fr, ICE, US. 600fr, Halley, Giotto.

1987, May 13			Perf. 13½	
792	A260	60fr multi	.40	.25
793	A260	150fr multi	.90	.25
794	A260	250fr multi	1.75	.40
795	A260	350fr multi	2.50	.60
796	A260	400fr multi	2.75	.65
797	A260	450fr multi	3.25	.70
	Nos. 792-797 (6)		11.55	2.85

Souvenir Sheet

| 798 | A260 | 600fr multi | 4.50 | 1.00 |

Litho. & Embossed 'Gold Foil' Stamps
These stamps generally are of a different design format than the rest of the issue. Since there is a commemorative inscription tying them to the issue a separate illustration is not being shown.

1988 Calgary Winter Olympics — A261

Men's Downhill A262

No. 799, Biathlon. No. 801, Luge. No. 802, Speed skating. No. 803, Hockey. No. 804, Pairs figure skating. No. 804A, Speed skating. No. 805A, Slalom skiing.

1987, May 13				
799	A261	60fr multi	.40	.25
800	A261	150fr shown	.90	.25
801	A261	250fr multi	1.75	.40
802	A261	350fr multi	2.50	.60
803	A261	400fr multi	2.75	.65
804	A261	450fr multi	3.25	.70
	Nos. 799-804 (6)		11.55	2.85

Litho. & Embossed

| 804A | A261 | 1500fr multi | 10.00 | |

Souvenir Sheets
Litho.

| 805 | A262 | 600fr shown | 4.75 | 1.25 |

Litho. & Embossed

| 805A | A262 | 1500fr multi | 7.50 | |

No. 804A exists in souvenir sheet of 1. Value, $40.

Jean-Joseph Rabearivelo (d. 1937), Poet — A263

1987, June 22			Perf. 13½	
806	A263	60fr multi	.50	.25

1992 Summer Olympics, Barcelona A264

Athletes, emblem and art or architecture: 60fr, Equestrian, and the Harlequin, by Picasso. 150fr, Weight lifting, church. 250fr, Hurdles, Canaletas Fountain. 350fr, High jump, amusement park. 400fr, Men's gymnastics, abbey. 450fr, Rhythmic gymnastics, Arc de Triomphe. 600fr, Equestrian, Columbus monument.

1987, Oct. 7		Litho.	Perf. 13½	
807	A264	60fr multi	.25	.25
808	A264	150fr multi	.80	.25
809	A264	250fr multi	1.40	.40
810	A264	350fr multi	2.00	.60
811	A264	400fr multi	2.25	.65
812	A264	450fr multi	2.50	.70
	Nos. 807-812 (6)		9.20	2.85

Souvenir Sheet

| 813 | A264 | 600fr multi | 3.75 | 1.25 |

Nos. 811-813 are airmail.

A265

Discovery of America, 500th Anniv. (in 1992) — A266

Anniv. emblem and: 60fr, Bartolomeu Dias (c. 1450-1500), Portuguese navigator, departure from De Palos, 1492. 150fr, Henry the Navigator (1394-1460), prince of Portugal, Samana Cay. 250fr, A. De Marchena landing, 1492. 350fr, Paolo Toscanelli dal Pozzo (1397-1482), Italian physician and cosmographer, La Navidad Fort. 400fr, Queen Isabella I, Barcelona, 1493. 450fr, Christopher Columbus, the Nina. 600fr, Landing in New World, 1492.

1987, Sept. 24		Litho.	Perf. 13½	
814	A265	60fr multi	.30	.25
815	A265	150fr multi	.80	.30
816	A265	250fr multi	1.25	.55
817	A265	350fr multi	1.90	.85
818	A265	400fr multi	2.25	1.00
819	A265	450fr multi	2.50	1.10
	Nos. 814-819 (6)		9.00	4.05

Souvenir Sheet

| 820 | A266 | 600fr multi | 4.00 | 1.50 |

A267

1987, July 27			Perf. 12½x12	
821	A267	60fr multicolored	.50	.25

Natl. telecommunications research laboratory.

A268

1987, Aug. 14				
822	A268	60fr lt blue, blk & brt ultra	.50	.25

Rafaravavy Rasalama (d. 1837), Christian martyr.

Antananarivo-Tamatave Telegraph Link, Cent. — A269

1987, Sept. 15			Perf. 12x12½	
823	A269	60fr multicolored	.50	.25

Pasteur Institute, Paris, Cent. — A270

1987, Oct. 26			Perf. 13½	
824	A270	250fr multicolored	1.25	.50

City of Berlin, 750th Anniv. — A271

Design: Anniv. emblem, television tower and the Interhotel in East Berlin.

1987, Oct. 18		Litho.	Perf. 12½x12	
825	A271	150fr multicolored	.50	.30

Schools Festival — A272

1987, Oct. 23			Perf. 12x12½	
826	A272	60fr multicolored	.50	.25

Paintings in the Pushkin Museum, Moscow A273

Designs: 10fr, After the Shipwreck (1847), by Eugene Delacroix (1798-1863). No. 828, Still-life with Swan (c. 1620), by Frans Snyders (1579-1647). No. 829, Jupiter and Callisto (1744), by Francois Boucher (1703-1770), vert. No. 830, Chalet in the Mountains (1874), by Jean Desire Gustav Courbet (1819-1877). 150fr, At the Market (1564), by Joachim Bueckelaer. 1000fr, Minerva (1560), by Paolo Veronese (1528-1588), vert.

Perf. 12½x12, 12x12½

1987, Nov. 10				
827	A273	10fr multi	.55	.25
828	A273	60fr multi	.70	.25
829	A273	60fr multi	.70	.25
830	A273	60fr multi	.70	.25
831	A273	150fr multi	1.40	.25
	Nos. 827-831 (5)		4.05	1.25

Souvenir Sheet

| 832 | A273 | 1000fr multi | 7.00 | 2.75 |

Pan-African Telecommunications Union, 10th Anniv. — A274

1987, Dec. 28			Perf. 13x12½	
833	A274	250fr multicolored	.60	.45

Intl. Year of Shelter for the Homeless A275

250fr, Family in shelter, rain, vert.

1988, Feb. 15		Litho.	Perf. 12	
834	A275	80fr shown	.25	.25
835	A275	250fr multicolored	.60	.25

Fauna — A276

Designs: 60fr, Hapalemur simus. 150fr, Propithecus diadema diadema. 250fr, Indri indri. 350fr, Varecia variegata variegata. 550fr, Madagascar young heron. No. 841, Nossi-Be chameleon. No. 842, Uratelornis (bird).

1988, Apr. 18		Litho.	Perf. 13½	
836	A276	60fr multicolored	1.75	.75
837	A276	150fr multicolored	2.25	.75
838	A276	250fr multicolored	3.25	1.00
839	A276	350fr multicolored	5.00	1.25
840	A276	550fr multicolored	1.50	.60
841	A276	1000fr multicolored	3.50	1.60
	Nos. 836-841 (6)		17.25	5.95

Souvenir Sheet

| 842 | A276 | 1500fr multicolored | 6.50 | 6.50 |

Conservation and service organization emblems: World Wildlife Fund (60fr, 150fr, 250fr and 350fr); Rotary Intl. (550fr and No. 842); and Scouting trefoil (No. 841). Nos. 838-

MALAGASY REPUBLIC

839 denominations are black outlined in white, not black text on gray boxes like Nos. 836-837. Nos. 840-841 exist in souvenir sheet of 2. For overprints see Nos. 1134, 1154.

October Revolution, Russia, 70th Anniv. — A277

No. 843, Lenin. No. 844, Revolutionaries. No. 845, Lenin, revolutionaries.

1988, Mar. 7	Litho.	Perf. 12x12½		
843	A277	60fr multi	.60	.25
844	A277	60fr multi	.60	.25
845	A277	150fr multi	1.25	.25
	Nos. 843-845 (3)		2.45	.75

1988 Winter Olympics, Calgary — A278

No. 846, Pairs figure skating. No. 847, Slalom. No. 848, Speed skating. No. 849, Cross-country skiing. No. 850, Ice hockey. No. 851, Ski jumping.

1988, May 11		Perf. 11½		
846	A278	20fr multicolored	.25	.25
847	A278	60fr multicolored	.25	.25
848	A278	60fr multicolored	.25	.25
849	A278	100fr multicolored	.30	.25
850	A278	250fr multicolored	.70	.30
	Nos. 846-850 (5)		1.75	1.30
Souvenir Sheet				
851	A278	800fr multicolored	2.50	1.75

Discovery of Radium by Pierre and Marie Curie, 90th Anniv. — A279

1988, July 14	Litho.	Perf. 12		
852	A279	150fr blk & rose lil	.50	.25

OAU, 25th Anniv. — A280

1988, May 25	Litho.	Perf. 13		
853	A280	80fr multi	.50	.25

Natl. Telecommunications and Posts Institute, 20th Anniv — A281

1988, June 22		Perf. 13½		
854	A281	80fr multi	.50	.25

Saint-Michel College, Cent. — A282

1988, July 9				
855	A282	250fr multi	.55	.30

Alma-Ata Declaration, 10th Anniv. — A283

1988, Aug. 11	Litho.	Perf. 12		
856	A283	60fr multi	.50	.25

WHO, 40th Anniv. — A284

1988, Aug. 11				
857	A284	150fr multi	.50	.25

Tsimbazaza Botanical and Zoological Park, 150th Anniv. A285

20fr, Lemur habitat. 80fr, Lemur and young. 1000fr, Lemur and mato.

	Perf. 12x12½, 12½x12			
1988, Aug. 22				
858	A285	20fr multi	.25	.25
859	A285	80fr multi	.45	.25
860	A285	250fr shown	1.10	.40
	Nos. 858-860 (3)		1.80	.90
Souvenir Sheet				
861	A285	1000fr multi	3.50	2.25
	Size of No. 859: 25x37mm.			

Boy Scouts Studying Birds and Butterflies — A286

Designs: 80fr, Upupa epops maginata, Coua caerulea and scout photographing bird. 250fr, Chrysiridia croesus and comparing butterfly to a sketch. 270fr, Nelicurvius nelicourvi, Foudia omissa and constructing bird feeder. 350fr, Papilio dardanuo and studying butterflies with magnifying glass. 550fr, Coua critata and tagging bird. No. 867, Argema mittrei and writing observations. No. 868, Merops superciliosus and recording bird calls. No. 868A, Euchloron megaera. No. 868B, Rhynchee.

1988, Sept. 29				
862	A286	80fr multi	.25	.25
863	A286	250fr multi	.55	.30
864	A286	270fr multi	.60	.30
865	A286	350fr multi	.80	.40
866	A286	550fr multi	1.25	.60
867	A286	1500fr multi	3.75	1.60
	Nos. 862-867 (6)		7.00	3.45
Souvenir Sheet				
868	A286	1500fr multi	3.50	2.25
Litho. & Embossed				
Perf. 13½				
868A	A286	5000fr gold & multi		8.00
Souvenir Sheet				
868B	A286	5000fr gold & multi		8.00

No. 868 contains one stamp 36x51mm. Nos. 868A-868B dated 1989. Nos. 868A-868B exist imperf.

Composers and Entertainers A287

Designs: 80fr, German-made clavier and Carl Philipp Emanuel Bach (1714-1788), organist and composer. 250fr, Piano and Franz Peter Schubert (1797-1828), Austrian composer. 270fr, Scene from opera Carmen, 1875, and Georges Bizet (1838-1875), French composer. 350fr, Scene from opera Pelleas et Melisande, 1902, and Claude Debussy (1862-1918), French composer. 550fr, George Gershwin (1898-1937), American composer. No. 874, Elvis Presley (1935-1977), American entertainer. No. 875, Rimsky-Korsakov (1844-1908), Russian composer, and Le Coq d'Or from the opera of the same name.

1988, Oct. 28	Perf. 12x12½, 12½x12			
869	A287	80fr multi	.25	.25
870	A287	250fr multi	.55	.30
871	A287	270fr multi	.60	.30
872	A287	350fr multi	.80	.40
873	A287	550fr multi	1.25	.60
874	A287	1500fr multi	3.50	1.60
	Nos. 869-874 (6)		6.95	3.45
Souvenir Sheet				
875	A287	1500fr multi	3.25	3.25

For overprints see Nos. 1135-1136.

Intl. Fund for Agricultural Development (IFAD), 10th Anniv. — A288

1988, Sept. 4	Litho.	Perf. 12		
876	A288	250fr multi	.50	.25

School Feast — A289

1988, Nov. 22				
877	A289	80fr multi	.50	.25

A290

Paintings: 20fr, The Squadron of the Sea, Black Feodossia, by Ivan Aivazovski, vert. No. 879, Seascape with Sailing Ships, by Simon de Vlieger, vert. No. 880, The Ship Lesnoie, by N. Semenov, vert. 100fr, The Merchantman, Orel, by N. Golitsine. 250fr, Naval Exercises, by Adam Silo, vert. 550fr, On the River, by Abraham Beerstraten.

1988, Dec. 5	Perf. 12x12½, 12½x12			
878	A290	20fr multi	.25	.25
879	A290	80fr multi	.30	.25
880	A290	80fr multi	.30	.25
881	A290	100fr shown	.40	.25
882	A290	250fr multi	.90	.25
	Nos. 878-882 (5)		2.15	1.25
Souvenir Sheet				
Perf. 11½x12½				
883	A291	550fr shown	2.00	1.00

World Wildlife Fund — A292

Insect species in danger of extinction: 20fr, Tragocephala crassicornis. 80fr, Polybothris symptuosa-gema. 250fr, Euchroea auripigmenta. 350fr, Stellognata maculata.

1988, Dec. 13		Perf. 12		
884	A292	20fr multi	1.00	—
885	A292	80fr multi	6.50	—
886	A292	250fr multi	22.50	—
887	A292	350fr multi	30.00	—
	Nos. 884-887 (4)		60.00	—

Intl. Red Cross and Red Crescent Organizations, 125th Annivs. — A293

80fr, Globe, stretcher-bearers, vert. 250fr, Emblems, Dunant.

1988, Dec. 27	Litho.	Perf. 12		
888	A293	80fr multicolored	.25	.25
889	A293	250fr multicolored	.55	.30

UN Declaration of Human Rights, 40th Anniv. (in 1988) — A294

1989, Jan. 10				
890	A294	80fr shown	.25	.25
891	A294	250fr Hands, "4" and "0"	.60	.30
	Dated 1988.			

Transportation — A295

Designs: 80fr, 1909 Mercedes-Benz Blitzen Benz. 250fr, Micheline ZM 517 Tsikirity, Tananarive-Moramanga line. 270fr, Bugatti Coupe Binder 41. 350fr, Electric locomotive 1020-DES OBB, Germany. 1500fr, Souleze Autorail 701 DU GFN, Madagascar No. 897, 1913 Opel race car. No. 898, Bugatti Presidential Autorail locomotive and Bugatti Type 57 Atalante automobile.

1989, Jan. 24		Perf. 13½		
892	A295	80fr multi	.25	.25
893	A295	250fr multi	.40	.25
894	A295	270fr multi	.50	.25
895	A295	350fr multi	.60	.35
896	A295	1500fr multi	2.50	1.00
897	A295	2500fr multi	3.50	2.00
	Nos. 892-897 (6)		7.75	4.10
Souvenir Sheet				
898	A295	2500fr multi	5.00	3.50

Nos. 893-897 exist imperf. Value, set $13.

Dinosaurs A296

20fr, Tyrannosaurus. 80fr, Stegosaurus. 250fr, Arsinoitherium. 450fr, Triceratops. 600fr, Sauralophus, vert.

1989, Feb. 1	Litho.	Perf. 12½x12		
899	A296	20fr multicolored	.25	.25
900	A296	80fr multicolored	1.10	.25
901	A296	250fr multicolored	3.25	.50
902	A296	450fr multicolored	4.50	1.00
	Nos. 899-902 (4)		9.10	2.00

MALAGASY REPUBLIC

Souvenir Sheet
Perf. 11½x12½
903 A296 600fr multicolored 2.75 1.25

Women as the Subject of Paintings — A297

Designs: 20fr, *Tahitian Pastorales*, by Gauguin. No 905, *Portrait of a Young Woman*, by Titian, vert. No. 906, *Portrait of a Little Girl*, by Jean-Baptiste Greuze (1725-1805), vert. 100fr, *Woman in Black*, by Renoir, vert. 250fr, *Lacemaker*, by Vassili Tropinine, vert. 550fr, *The Annunciation*, by Cima Da Conegliano (c. 1459-1517), vert.

1989, Feb. 10		Perf. 12½x12, 12x12½
904 A297	20fr multi	.25 .25
905 A297	80fr multi	.25 .25
906 A297	80fr multi	.25 .25
907 A297	100fr multi	.35 .25
908 A297	250fr multi	.75 .30
Nos. 904-908 (5)		1.85 1.30

Souvenir Sheet
Perf. 11½x12½
909 A297 550fr multi 1.60 1.00

Orchids — A298

No. 910, *Sobennikoffia robusta*, vert. No. 911, *Grammangis fallax*. No. 912, *Cymbidiella humblotii*, vert. No. 913, *Angraecum sororium*, vert. No. 914, *Oenia oncidiiflora*, vert. 1000fr, *Aerangis curnowiana*.

1989, Feb. 28	Litho.	Perf. 12
910 A298	5fr multicolored	.30 .30
911 A298	10fr multicolored	.30 .25
912 A298	80fr multicolored	.60 .25
913 A298	80fr multicolored	.60 .25
914 A298	250fr multicolored	1.60 .35
Nos. 910-914 (5)		3.40 1.35

Souvenir Sheet
915 A298 1000fr multi 3.00 2.00

Jawaharlal Nehru (1889-1964), 1st Prime Minister of Independent India — A299

1989, Mar. 7	Litho.	Perf. 13
916 A299	250fr multi	.50 .35

Ornamental Mineral Industry — A300

1989, Apr. 12	Litho.	Perf. 13½
917 A300	80fr Rose quartz	.30 .25
918 A300	250fr Petrified wood	.90 .30

Views of Antananarivo A301

Designs: 5fr, Mahamasina Sports Complex, Ampefiloha Quarter. 20fr, Andravoahangy and Anjanahary Quarters. No. 921, Zoma Market and Faravohitra Quarter. No. 922, Andohan'Analakely Quarter and March 29th monument. 250fr, Independence Avenue and Jean Ralaimongo monument. 550fr, Queen's Palace and Andohalo School on Lake Anosy.

1989, Mar. 31	Litho.	Perf. 13½
919 A301	5fr multi	.25 .25
920 A301	20fr multi	.25 .25
921 A301	80fr multi	.25 .25
922 A301	80fr multi	.25 .25
923 A301	250fr multi	.50 .25
924 A301	550fr multi	.90 .35
Nos. 919-924 (6)		2.40 1.60

Visit of Pope John Paul II — A302

1989, Apr. 28		Perf. 12x12½
925 A302	80fr shown	.30 .25
926 A302	250fr Pope, map	1.00 .25

French Revolution, Bicent. — A303

250fr, Storming of the Bastille.

1989, July 7	Litho.	Perf. 12½
927 A303	250fr multicolored	.60 .25

Phobos Space Program for the Exploration of Mars — A304

1989, Aug. 29	Litho.	Perf. 12½x12
928 A304	20fr Mars 1	.25 .25
929 A304	80fr Mars 3	.25 .25
930 A304	80fr Zond 2	.25 .25
931 A304	250fr Mariner 9	.55 .25
932 A304	270fr Viking 2	.65 .30
Nos. 928-932 (5)		1.95 1.30

Souvenir Sheet
933 A304 550fr Phobos .... 1.50 .60

PHILEXFRANCE '89 and French Revolution, Bicent. — A305

Exhibition emblems, key people and scenes from the revolution: 250fr, Honore-Gabriel Riqueti (1749-1791), Count of Mirabeau, at the meeting of Estates-General, June 23, 1789. 350fr, Camille Desmoulins (1760-1794), call to arms, July 12, 1789. 1000fr, Lafayette (1757-1834), women's march on Versailles, Oct. 5, 1789. 1500fr, King tried by the National Convention, Dec. 26, 1792. 2500fr, Charlotte Corday (1768-1793), assassination of Marat, July 13, 1793. 3000fr, Bertrand Barere de Vieuzac, Robespierre, Jean-Marie Collot D'Herbois, Lazare Nicolas Carnot, George Jacques Danton, Georges Auguste Couthon, Pierre-Louis Prieur, Antoine Saint-Just and Marc Guillaume Vadier, Committee of Public Safety, July, 1793. No. 939A, Family saying farewell to Louis XVI. No. 939B, Danton and the Club of the Cordeliers.

1989, July 14	Litho.	Perf. 13½
934 A305	250fr multicolored	.35 .25
935 A305	350fr multicolored	.50 .25
936 A305	1000fr multicolored	1.20 .65
937 A305	1500fr multicolored	2.00 1.00
938 A305	2500fr multicolored	3.50 1.60
Nos. 934-938 (5)		7.55 3.75

Souvenir Sheet
939 A305 3000fr multicolored 4.00 4.00

Litho. & Embossed
939A A305 5000fr gold & multi 6.00

Souvenir Sheet
939B A305 5000fr gold & multi 6.00

Nos. 939A-939B exist imperf.
For overprints see Nos. 1161-1165, 1166A-1166B.

French Revolution, Bicent. A306

Paintings and sculpture: 5fr, *Liberty Guiding the People*, by Eugene Delacroix. 80fr, "La Marseillaise" from *Departure of the Volunteers in 1792*, high relief on the Arc de Triomphe, 1833-35, by Francois Rude. 250fr, *The Tennis Court Oath*, by David.

1989, Oct. 25		Perf. 12½x12
940 A306	5fr multicolored	.25 .25
941 A306	80fr multicolored	.45 .25
942 A306	250fr multicolored	.90 .25
Nos. 940-942 (3)		1.60 .75

No. 942 is airmail.

Rene Cassin (1887-1976), Nobel Peace Prize Winner and Institute Founder — A307

1989, Nov. 21		Perf. 12
943 A307	250fr multicolored	.50 .25

Intl. Law Institute of the French-Speaking Nations, 25th anniv.

Hapalemur aureus — A308

1989, Dec. 5	Litho.	Perf. 12
944 A308	250fr multicolored	1.00 .35

A309 A309a

Various athletes, cup and: 350fr, Cavour Monument, Turin. 1000fr, Christopher Columbus Monument, Genoa, 1903. 1500fr, Michelangelo's *David*. 2500fr, *Abduction of Proserpina*, by Bernini, Rome. 3000fr, Statue of Leonardo da Vinci, 1903. 5000fr, Castel Nuovo, Naples.

1989, Dec. 12	Litho.	Perf. 13½
945 A309	350fr multicolored	.45 .25
946 A309	1000fr multicolored	1.20 .65
947 A309	1500fr multicolored	2.00 1.00
948 A309	2500fr multicolored	3.00 1.60
Nos. 945-948 (4)		6.65 3.50

Souvenir Sheet
949 A309 3000fr multicolored 3.50 2.00

Litho. & Embossed
949A A309a 5000fr gold & multi 8.00

1990 World Cup Soccer Championships, Italy.
For overprints see Nos. 1137-1140.

A310

1989, Oct. 7	Litho.	Perf. 13½
950 A310	80fr Long jump	.25 .25
951 A310	250fr Pole vault	.35 .25
952 A310	550fr Hurdles	.80 .42
953 A310	1500fr Cycling	2.25 1.10
954 A310	2000fr Baseball	3.00 1.45
955 A310	2500fr Tennis	3.75 1.75
Nos. 950-955 (6)		10.40 5.20

Souvenir Sheet
956 A310 3000fr Soccer 4.50 2.10

1992 Summer Olympics, Barcelona.

Scenic Views and Artifacts — A311

No. 957, Queen Isalo Rock. No. 958, Sakalava pipe. No. 959, Sakalava combs. No. 960, Lowry Is., Diego Suarez Bay.

1990, May 29	Size: 47x33mm (#958, 960)
957 A311	70fr multi	.25 .25
958 A311	70fr multi	.25 .25
959 A311	150fr multi	.30 .25
960 A311	150fr multi	.30 .25
Nos. 957-960 (4)		1.10 1.00

Fish — A312

5fr, *Heniochus acuminatus*. 20fr, *Simenhelys dofleinl*. 80fr, *Rhinobatos percellens*. 250fr, *Epinephelus fasciatus*. 320fr, *Sphyrna zygaena*. 550fr, *Latimeria chalumnae*.

1990, Apr. 26	Litho.	Perf. 12
961 A312	5fr multicolored	.25 .25
962 A312	20fr multicolored	.25 .25
963 A312	80fr multicolored	.25 .25
964 A312	250fr multicolored	1.00 .25
965 A312	320fr multicolored	1.40 .35
Nos. 961-965 (5)		3.15 1.35

Souvenir Sheet
966 A312 550fr multicolored 3.50 1.50

Nos. 962-963 vert. Nos. 961-966 inscribed 1989.

Moon Landing, 20th Anniv. — A314

Designs: 80fr, Voyager 2, Neptune. 250fr, Hydro 2000 flying boat. 550fr, NOAA satellite. 1500fr, Magellan probe, Venus. 2000fr, Concorde. 2500fr, Armstrong, Aldrin, Collins, lunar module. 3000fr, Apollo 11 astronauts, first step on moon.

1990, June 19	Litho.	Perf. 13½
967 A314	80fr multicolored	.25 .25
968 A314	250fr multicolored	.25 .25
969 A314	550fr multicolored	.65 .40
970 A314	1500fr multicolored	1.75 .85
971 A314	2000fr multicolored	2.40 1.00
972 A314	2500fr multicolored	2.90 1.25
Nos. 967-972 (6)		8.20 4.00

Souvenir Sheet
973 A314 3000fr multicolored 3.50 2.00

For overprint see No. 1304.
Nos. 967-972 exist in souvenir sheets of 1, and se-tenant in a sheet of 6.

1992 Winter Olympics, Albertville — A315

MALAGASY REPUBLIC

350fr, Bobsled. 1000fr, Speed skating. 1500fr, Nordic skiing. 2500fr, Super giant slalom. No. 978, Giant slalom. No. 978A, Pairs figure skating. No. 978B, Ice hockey.

1990, July 17
974	A315	350fr multi	.50	.25
975	A315	1000fr multi	1.50	.75
976	A315	1500fr multi	2.25	1.10
977	A315	2500fr multi	3.75	1.90
		Nos. 974-977 (4)	8.00	4.00

Souvenir Sheet
978	A315	3000fr multi	4.50	2.25

Litho. & Embossed
978A	A315	5000fr multi	8.00

Souvenir Sheet
978B	A315	5000fr multi	8.00

Nos. 978A-978B exist imperf.
For overprints see Nos. 1141-1145.

A316

1990, June 19   Litho.   Perf. 12
979	A316	250fr blk, ultra & bl	.50	.25

Intl. Maritime Organization, 30th anniv.

African Development Bank, 25th Anniv. — A317

1990, June 19
980	A317	80fr multicolored	.50	.25

Campaign Against Polio — A318

1990, June 28
981	A318	150fr multicolored	.50	.25

Independence, 30th Anniv. — A319

1990, Aug. 22
982	A319	100fr multicolored	.50	.25

3rd Indian Ocean Games — A320

1990, Aug. 24   Perf. 12½x12
983	A320	100fr yellow & multi	.35	.25
984	A320	350fr lil rose & multi	.65	.30

A322

1990, Oct. 19   Litho.   Perf. 12
986	A322	350fr multicolored	.75	.30

Ho Chi Minh (1890-1969), Vietnamese leader.

Lemurs — A323

No. 987, Avahi laniger. No. 988, Lemur fulvus sanfordi. No. 989, Lemur fulvus albifrons. No. 990, Lemur fulvus collaris. No. 991, Lepulemur ruficaudatus. No. 992, Lemur fulvus fulvus.

1990, Nov. 23   Litho.   Perf. 11½
987	A323	10fr multi	.25	.25
988	A323	20fr multi	.35	.25
989	A323	20fr multi	.35	.25
990	A323	100fr multi	.80	.25
991	A323	100fr multi	.80	.25
		Nos. 987-991 (5)	2.55	1.25

Souvenir Sheet
992	A323	350fr multi	3.00	.50

Shells — A324

40fr, Tridacna squamosa. 50fr, Terebra demidiata, Terebra subulata.

1990, Dec. 21   Perf. 12½
993	A324	40fr multicolored	.80	.25
994	A324	50fr multicolored	.80	.25

Anniversaries and Events — A325

100fr, Charles de Gaulle, liberation of Paris, 1944. 350fr, Galileo probe orbiting Jupiter. 800fr, Apollo 11 crew & Columbia command module, 1st Moon landing, 1969. 900fr, De Gaulle, 1942. 1250fr, Concorde jet, TGV high-speed train. 2500fr, De Gaulle as head of provisional government, 1944. 3000fr, Apollo 11 crew, Eagle lunar module. No. 1001A, De Gaulle with Roosevelt & Churchill. No. 1001B, Charles de Gaulle.

1990, Dec. 28   Litho.   Perf. 13½
995	A325	100fr multi	.25	.25
996	A325	350fr multi	.60	.30
997	A325	800fr multi	1.40	.70
998	A325	900fr multi	1.60	.90
999	A325	1250fr multi	2.25	1.10
1000	A325	2500fr multi	4.50	2.25
		Nos. 995-1000 (6)	10.60	5.40

Souvenir Sheet
1001	A325	3000fr multi	4.00	2.00

Litho. & Embossed
1001A	A325	5000fr gold & multi	7.50

Souvenir Sheet
1001B	A325	5000fr gold & multi	7.50

Nos. 995-1000, 1001A exist in souvenir sheets of 1. A souvenir sheet containing Nos. 996-997 exists.

Mushrooms — A325b

Designs: 25fr, Boletus edulis. 100fr, Suillus luteus. 350fr, Amanita muscaria. 450fr, Boletus calopus. 680fr, Boletus erythropus. 800fr, Leccinum scabrum. 900fr, Leccinum testaceoscabrum. 1500fr, Lycoperdon perlatum.

1990, Dec. 28   Litho.   Perf. 12
1001C	A325b	25fr multi	.25	.25
1001D	A325b	100fr multi	.40	.25
1001E	A325b	350fr multi	.85	.25
1001F	A325b	450fr multi	1.25	.30
1001G	A325b	680fr multi	1.75	.45
1001H	A325b	800fr multi	1.90	.50
1001I	A325b	900fr multi	2.10	.60

Imperf   Size: 71x91mm
1001J	A325b	1500fr multi	4.50	4.50
		Nos. 1001C-1001J (8)	13.00	7.10

For surcharges, see Nos. 1478A, 1479.

Intl. Literacy Year — A326

20fr, Book, guiding hands, vert. 100fr, Open Book, hand holding pencil.

1990, Dec. 30   Perf. 12
1002	A326	20fr multi	.25	.25
1003	A326	100fr multi	.25	.25

Dogs — A326a

Designs: 30fr, Greyhound. 50fr, Japanese spaniel. 140fr, Toy terrier. 350fr, Chow. 500fr, Miniature pinscher. 800fr, Afghan. 1140fr, Papillon. 1500fr, Shih tzu.

1991, Mar. 20   Litho.   Perf. 12
1003A	A326a	30fr multi	.25	.25
1003B	A326a	50fr multi	.25	.25
1003C	A326a	140fr multi	.60	.25
1003D	A326a	350fr multi	.90	.25
1003E	A326a	500fr multi	1.25	.30
1003F	A326a	800fr multi	2.10	.50
1003G	A326a	1140fr multi	3.00	.75

Imperf   Size: 70x90mm
1003H	A326a	350fr multi	4.00	1.40
		Nos. 1003A-1003H (8)	12.35	3.95

Nos. 1003D-1003H are airmail.

Democratic Republic of Madagascar, 15th Anniv. (in 1990) — A327

1991, Apr. 8   Litho.   Perf. 12
1004	A327	100fr multicolored	.25	.25

Dated 1990.

Trees — A328

140fr, Adansonia fony. 500fr, Didierea madagascariensis.

1991, June 20   Litho.   Perf. 13½
1005	A328	140fr multi	.55	.25
1006	A328	500fr multi	1.25	.40

Scouts, Insects and Mushrooms — A329

Insects: 140fr, Helictopleurus splendidicollis. 640fr, Cocles contemplator. 1140fr, Euchroea oberthurii.

Mushrooms: 500fr, Russula radicans. 1025fr, Russula singeri. 3500fr, Lactariopsis pandani.

4500fr, Euchroea spinnasuta fairmaire and Russula aureotacta.

1991, Aug. 2   Litho.   Perf. 13½
1007	A329	140fr multicolored	.35	.25
1008	A329	500fr multicolored	.90	.30
1009	A329	640fr multicolored	1.00	.40
1010	A329	1025fr multicolored	1.75	.65
1011	A329	1140fr multicolored	2.10	.70
1012	A329	3500fr multicolored	5.25	2.25
		Nos. 1007-1012 (6)	11.35	4.55

Souvenir Sheet
1013	A329	4500fr multicolored	7.00	5.75

Nos. 1007-1012 exist in souvenir sheets of 1.
For overprints see Nos. 1149-1156.

Discovery of America, 500th Anniv. — A330

Designs: 15fr, Ship, 9th cent.. 65fr, Clipper ship, 1878. 140fr, Golden Hind. 500fr, Galley, 18th cent. 640fr, Galleon Ostrust, 1721, vert. 800fr, Caravel Amsterdam, 1539, vert. 1025fr, Santa Maria, 1492. 1500fr, Map.

1991, Sept. 10   Litho.   Perf. 12
1014	A330	15fr multicolored	.25	.25
1015	A330	65fr multicolored	.25	.25
1016	A330	140fr multicolored	.55	.25
1017	A330	500fr multicolored	1.25	.30
1018	A330	640fr multicolored	1.50	.40
1019	A330	800fr multicolored	1.60	.50
1020	A330	1025fr multicolored	1.75	.65

Size: 90x70mm
1021	A330	1500fr multicolored	3.50	1.50
		Nos. 1014-1021 (8)	10.65	4.10

No. 1021 contains one 40x27mm perf. 12 label in center of stamp picturing ships and Columbus.
For surcharge see No. 1480.

Domesticated Animals — A331

Designs: 140fr, Dog. 500fr, Arabian horse. 640fr, House cats. 1025fr, Himalayan cats. 1140fr, Draft horse. 5000fr, German shepherd. 10,000fr, Horse, cat & dog.

1991, Sept. 27   Litho.   Perf. 13½
1022	A331	140fr multicolored	.25	.25
1023	A331	500fr multicolored	.90	.30
1024	A331	640fr multicolored	1.00	.40
1025	A331	1025fr multicolored	1.75	.65
1026	A331	1140fr multicolored	2.25	.70
1027	A331	5000fr multicolored	7.25	3.25
		Nos. 1022-1027 (6)	13.40	5.55

Souvenir Sheet
1028	A331	10,000fr multicolored	13.00	6.50

Nos. 1022-1028 exist imperf. and in souvenir sheets of 1.

MALAGASY REPUBLIC

Birds A332

Designs: 40fr, Hirundo rustica. 55fr, Circus melanoluecos, vert. 60fr, Cuculas canorus, vert. 140fr, Threskiornis aethiopicus. 210fr, Porphyrio poliocephalus. 500fr, Coracias garrulus. 2000fr, Oriolus oriolus. 1500fr, Upupa epops.

Perf. 12½x12, 12x12½
1991, Dec. 10   Litho.

1029	A332	40fr multicolored	.25	.25
1030	A332	55fr multicolored	.25	.25
1031	A332	60fr multicolored	.25	.25
1032	A332	140fr multicolored	.45	.25
1033	A332	210fr multicolored	.70	.25
1034	A332	500fr multicolored	1.00	.35
1035	A332	2000fr multicolored	3.00	1.10

Size: 70x90mm
Imperf

1036	A332	1500fr multicolored	3.00	1.40
	Nos. 1029-1036 (8)		8.90	4.10

1992 Winter Olympics, Albertville — A333

5fr, Cross-country skiing. 15fr, Biathlon. 60fr, Ice hockey. 140fr, Downhill skiing. 640fr, Figure skating. 1000fr, Ski jumping. 1140fr, Speed skating. 1500fr, Three hockey players.

1991, Dec. 30   Litho.   Perf. 12x12½

1037	A333	5fr multi	.25	.25
1038	A333	15fr multi	.25	.25
1039	A333	60fr multi	.25	.25
1040	A333	140fr multi	.45	.25
1041	A333	640fr multi	1.25	.40
1042	A333	1000fr multi	1.60	.70
1043	A333	1140fr multi	2.00	.75

Imperf
Size: 90x70mm

1044	A333	1500fr multi	3.00	1.40
	Nos. 1037-1044 (8)		9.05	4.25

For surcharge see No. 1482.

Paul Minault College, 90th Anniv. — A333a

1991   Litho.   Perf. 13½
| 1044A | A333a | 140fr multicolored | .65 | .30 |

Space Program — A334

Designs: 140fr, Astronauts repairing space telescope. 500fr, Soho solar observation probe. 640fr, Topex-Poseidon, observing oceans. 1025fr, Hipparcos probe, Galaxy 3C75. 1140fr, Voyager II surveying Neptune. 5000fr, Adeos, ETS VI, earth observation and communications satellites. 7500fr, Crew of Apollo 11.

1992, Apr. 22   Perf. 13½
1045	A334	140fr multi	.25	.25
1046	A334	500fr multi	.70	.30
1047	A334	640fr multi	.90	.40
1048	A334	1025fr multi	1.40	.65
1049	A334	1140fr multi	1.60	.70

1050	A334	5000fr multi	6.75	3.25
a.	Souvenir sheet of 6, #1045-1050		19.00	19.00
	Nos. 1045-1050 (6)		11.60	5.55

Souvenir Sheet
| 1051 | A334 | 7500fr multi | 12.00 | 9.75 |

Nos. 1045-1050 exist in souvenir sheets of one.

Entertainers A335

100fr, Ryuichi Sakamoto. 350fr, John Lennon. 800fr, Bruce Lee. 900fr, Sammy Davis, Jr. 1250fr, John Wayne. 2500fr, James Dean. 3000fr, Clark Gable y Vivien Leigh.

1992, Apr. 29
1052	A335	100fr multi	.25	.25
1053	A335	350fr multi	.60	.25
1054	A335	800fr multi	1.50	.50
1055	A335	900fr multi	1.75	.60
1056	A335	1250fr multi	1.90	.80
1057	A335	2500fr multi	3.50	1.60
	Nos. 1052-1057 (6)		9.50	4.00

Souvenir Sheet
| 1058 | A335 | 3000fr multi | 5.25 | 2.00 |

Nos. 1052-1057 exist in souvenir sheets of one.

Fight Against AIDS — A336

1992, July 29   Litho.   Perf. 12
| 1059 | A336 | 140fr lil rose & black | .40 | .25 |

Dated 1991.

Reforestation A337

1992, July 29   Litho.   Perf. 12
| 1060 | A337 | 140fr black & green | .30 | .25 |

Dated 1991.

1990 Sports Festival — A338

1992, Aug. 20
| 1061 | A338 | 140fr multicolored | .35 | .25 |

Dated 1991.

Meteorology in Madagascar, Cent. — A339

1992, Nov. 10   Litho.   Perf. 12x12½
| 1062 | A339 | 140fr multicolored | .40 | .25 |

Fruit A341

10fr, Litchis. 50fr, Oranges. 60fr, Apples. 140fr, Peaches. 555fr, Bananas. 800fr, Avocados, vert. 1400fr, Mangoes, vert. 1600fr, Mixed fruit.

Perf. 12½x12, 12x12½
1992, May 27   Litho.
1064	A341	10fr multi	.30	.25
1065	A341	50fr multi	.30	.25
1066	A341	60fr multi	.35	.25
1067	A341	140fr multi	.50	.25
1068	A341	555fr multi	1.25	.45
1069	A341	800fr multi	1.75	.60
1070	A341	1400fr multi	3.00	1.25

Size: 89x70mm
Imperf
| 1071 | A341 | 1600fr multi | 3.25 | 1.40 |
| | Nos. 1064-1071 (8) | | 10.70 | 4.70 |

For surcharges, see Nos. 1477, 1479B, 1486.

1992 Summer Olympics, Barcelona — A342

65fr, Women's gymnastics. 70fr, High jump. 120fr, Archery. 140fr, Cycling. 675fr, Weight lifting. 720fr, Boxing. 1200fr, Canoeing. 1600fr, Volleyball. 5000fr, Judo.

1992, June 30   Perf. 11½
1072	A342	65fr multi	.25	.25
1073	A342	70fr multi	.25	.25
1074	A342	120fr multi	.25	.25
1075	A342	140fr multi	.30	.25
1076	A342	675fr multi	1.10	.45
1077	A342	720fr multi	1.10	.50
1078	A342	1200fr multi	1.75	.75

Imperf
Size: 90x70mm
| 1078A | A342 | 1600fr multi | 3.00 | 1.40 |
| | Nos. 1072-1078A (8) | | 8.00 | 4.10 |

Litho. & Embossed
Perf. 13½
| 1079 | A342 | 5000fr multi | 8.00 | |

For surcharge, see No. 1473A.

Butterflies A344

Designs: 15fr, Eusemia bisma. 35fr, Argema mittrei, vert. 65fr, Alcidis aurora. 140fr, Agarista agricola. 600fr, Trogonoptera croesus. 850fr, Trogonodtera priamus. 1300fr, Pereute leucodrosime. 1500fr, Chrysirridia madagaskariensis.

Perf. 12½x12, 12x12½
1992, June 24   Litho.
1080	A344	15fr multicolored	.25	.25
1081	A344	35fr multicolored	.25	.25
1082	A344	65fr multicolored	.45	.25
1083	A344	140fr multicolored	.70	.25
1084	A344	600fr multicolored	1.50	.45
1085	A344	850fr multicolored	2.00	.60
1086	A344	1300fr multicolored	2.50	.85

Imperf
Size: 70x90mm
| 1087 | A344 | 1500fr multicolored | 4.75 | 1.50 |
| | Nos. 1080-1087 (8) | | 12.40 | 4.40 |

For surcharge, see No. 1485.

Anniversaries and Events — A345

Designs: 500fr, Jean-Henri Dunant, delivery of Red Cross supplies. 640fr, Charles de Gaulle, battle of Bir Hacheim. 1025fr, Brandenburg Gate, people on Berlin wall. 1500fr, Village health clinic, Rotary, Lions emblems. 3000fr, Konrad Adenauer. 3500fr, Dirigible LZ4, hanger on Lake Constance, Ferdinand von Zeppelin. 7500fr, Wolfgang Amadeus Mozart at piano, palace, cathedral in Salzburg.

1992, Dec. 8   Litho.   Perf. 13½
1088	A345	500fr multicolored	.70	.30
1089	A345	640fr multicolored	.90	.45
1090	A345	1025fr multicolored	1.50	.75
1091	A345	1500fr multicolored	2.00	1.00
1092	A345	3000fr multicolored	4.25	2.00
1093	A345	3500fr multicolored	5.00	2.50
	Nos. 1088-1093 (6)		14.35	7.00

Souvenir Sheet
| 1094 | A345 | 7500fr multicolored | 10.00 | 5.00 |

Intl. Red Cross (No. 1088). Battle of Bir Hacheim, 50th anniv. (No. 1089). Brandenburg Gate, bicent. and destruction of Berlin Wall, 3rd anniv. (No. 1090). Konrad Adenauer, 25th death anniv. (No. 1092). Ferdinand von Zeppelin, 75th death anniv. (No. 1093). Mozart, death bicent. (in 1991), (No. 1094).
For overprint see No. 1146.

1994 World Cup Soccer Championships, U.S. — A346

Soccer players, Georgia landmarks: 140fr, Ficklin Home, Macon. 640fr, Herndon Home, Atlanta. 1025fr, Cultural Center, Augusta. 5000fr, Old Governor's Mansion, Milledgeville. 7500fr, Player, stars, stripes.

1992, Dec. 15   Litho.   Perf. 13½
1095	A346	140fr multicolored	.25	.25
1096	A346	640fr multicolored	.90	.45
1097	A346	1025fr multicolored	1.40	.75
1098	A346	5000fr multicolored	7.00	3.50
	Nos. 1095-1098 (4)		9.55	4.95

Souvenir Sheet
| 1099 | A346 | 7500fr multicolored | 10.25 | 5.25 |

Miniature Sheet

Inventors and Inventions — A347

No. 1100: a, Gutenberg (1394?-1468), printing press. b, Newton (1642-1727), telescope. c, John Dalton (1766-1844), atomic theory. d, Louis-Jacques-Mande Daguerre (1789-1851), photographic equipment. e, Faraday (1791-1867), electric motor. f, Orville (1871-1948), Wilbur Wright (1867-1912), motor-powered airplane. g, Bell (1847-1922), telephone. h, Edison (1847-1931), phonograph. i, Benz (1844-1929), motor-driven vehicle. j, Charles Parsons (1854-1931), steam turbine. k, Diesel (1858-1913), Diesel engine. l, Marconi, radio. m, Auguste-Marie-Louis Lumiere (1862-1954), Louis-Jean Lumiere (1864-1948), motion pictures. n, Oberth (1894-1989), rocketry. o, John W. Mauchly (1907-1980), John P. Eckert, electronic computer. p, Arthur Schawlow, laser.

1993, Apr. 27
| 1100 | A347 | 500fr Sheet of 16, #a.-p. | 11.00 | 5.50 |

Dated 1990.

MALAGASY REPUBLIC

Transportation — A348

No. 1101 — Race cars: a, 20fr, 1956 Bugatti. b, 20fr, 1968 Ferrari. c, 140fr, 1962 Lotus MK25. d, 140fr, 1970 Matra. e, 1250fr, 1963 Porsche. f, 1250fr, 1980 Ligier JS11. g, 3000fr, 1967 Honda. h, 3000fr, 1992 B192 Benetton.

No. 1102 — Locomotives: a, 20fr, C62, Japan, 1948. b, 20fr, SZD, USSR, 1975. c, 140fr, MU A1A-A1A, Norway, 1954. d, 140fr, Series 26 2-D-2, Africa, 1982. e, 1250fr, Amtrak Metroliner, US, 1967. f, 1250fr, VIA, Canada, 1982. g, 3000fr, Diesel, Union Pacific RR, US, 1969. h, 3000fr, Atlantic, TGV, France, 1990.

1993, Mar. 23
| 1101 | A348 | Block of 8, #a.-h. | 12.00 | 6.00 |
| 1102 | A348 | Block of 8, #a.-h. | 12.00 | 6.00 |

Dated 1990.

Wildlife A349

No. 1103 — Birds: a, 45fr, Coua verreauxi. b, 45fr, Asio helvola hova. c, 60fr, Coua cristata. d, 60fr, Euryceros prevostii. e, 140fr, Coua gigas. f, 140fr, Foudia madagascariensis. g, 3000fr, Falculea palliata. h, 3000fr, Eutriorchis astur.

No. 1104 — Butterflies: a, 45fr, Chrysiridia madagascariensis. b, 45fr, Hypolimnas misippus. c, 60fr, Charaxes antamboulou. d, 60fr, Papilio antenor. e, 140fr, Hypolimnas dexithea. f, 140fr, Charaxes andranodorus. g, 3000fr, Euxanthe madagascariensis. h, 3000fr, Papilio grosesmithi.

1993, May 27
| 1103 | A349 | Block of 8, #a.-h. | 8.75 | 4.25 |
| 1104 | A349 | Block of 8, #a.-h. | 8.75 | 4.25 |

Dated 1991.

Intl. Conference on Nutrition, Rome — A350

1992, Nov. 3
| 1105 | A350 | 500fr multicolored | 1.00 | .40 |

Automobiles A351

1993, Jan. 28   Litho.   Perf. 12
1106	A351	20fr BMW	.25	.25
1107	A351	40fr Toyota	.25	.25
1108	A351	60fr Cadillac	.25	.25
1109	A351	65fr Volvo	.25	.25
1110	A351	140fr Mercedes Benz	.25	.25
1111	A351	640fr Ford	1.00	.50
1112	A351	3000fr Honda	5.00	2.50

Size: 90x70mm
Imperf
| 1113 | A351 | 2000fr Renault | 3.00 | 1.50 |
| | | Nos. 1106-1113 (8) | 10.25 | 5.75 |

Birds — A352

Designs: 50fr, Anodorhynchus hyacinthinus. 60fr, Nymphicus hollandicus. 140fr, Melopsittacus undulatus. 500fr, Aratinga jandaya. 675fr, Melopsittacus undulatus, diff. 800fr, Cyanoramphus novaezelandiae. 1750fr, Nestor notabilis. 2000fr, Ara militaris.

1993, Feb. 24
1114	A352	50fr multicolored	.40	.25
1115	A352	60fr multicolored	.40	.25
1116	A352	140fr multicolored	.50	.25
1117	A352	500fr multicolored	1.75	.45
1118	A352	675fr multicolored	2.50	.65
1119	A352	800fr multicolored	2.75	.70
1120	A352	1750fr multicolored	6.00	1.50

Size: 71x91mm
Imperf
| 1121 | A352 | 2000fr multicolored | 5.00 | 2.00 |
| | | Nos. 1114-1121 (8) | 19.30 | 6.05 |

For surcharges, see Nos. 1473B, 1479C, 1488.

Mollusks — A353

40fr, Turbo marmoratus. 60fr, Mitra mitra. 65fr, Argonauta argo. 140fr, Conus textile. 500fr, Aplysia depilans. 675fr, Harpa amouretta. 2500fr, Cypraea tigris. 2000fr, Architectonica maxima.

1993, Feb. 3
1122	A353	40fr multi	.25	.25
1123	A353	60fr multi	.25	.25
1124	A353	65fr multi	.25	.25
1125	A353	140fr multi	.30	.25
1126	A353	500fr multi	1.10	.45
1127	A353	675fr multi	1.50	.70
1128	A353	2500fr multi	4.50	2.25

Size: 70x90mm
Imperf
| 1129 | A353 | 2000fr multi | 5.00 | 1.75 |
| | | Nos. 1122-1129 (8) | 13.15 | 6.15 |

For surcharge, see No. 1478.

Boat, Barges, Pangalanes Canal — A354

1993, Jan. 29   Litho.   Perf. 12
| 1130 | A354 | 140fr multicolored | .40 | .25 |

Miniature Sheet

Ships — A355

No. 1131: a, 5fr, Egyptian ship. b, 5fr, Mediterranean galley. c, 5fr, Great Western, England, 1837. d, 5fr, Mississippi River sidewheeler, US, 1850. e, 15fr, Bireme, Phoenicia. f, 15fr, Viking long ship. g, 15fr, Clermont, US, 1806. h, 15fr, Pourquoi-pas, France, 1936. i, 140fr, Santa Maria, Spain, 1492. j, 140fr, HMS Victory, England, 1765. k, 140fr, Fact motor yacht, Monaco. l, 140fr, Bremen, Germany, 1950. m, 10,000fr, Sovereign of the Seas, England, 1637. n, 10,000fr, Cutty Sark, England, 1869. o, 10,000fr, Savannah, US, 1959. p, 10,000fr, Condor, Australia.

1993, Apr. 6   Litho.   Perf. 13½
| 1131 | A355 | Sheet of 16, #a.-p. | 50.00 | 25.00 |

Miniature Sheet

Nobel Prize Winners in Physics, Chemistry and Medicine — A356

No. 1132: a, Albert Einstein, Niels Bohr. b, Wolfgang Pauli, Max Born. c, Joseph Thomson, Johannes Stark. d, Otto Hahn, Hideki Yukawa. e, Owen Richardson, William Shockley. f, Albert Michelson, Charles Townes. g, Wilhelm Wien, Lev Landau. h, Karl Braun, Sir Edward Appleton. i, Percy Bridgman, Nikolai Semenov. j, Sir William Ramsay, Glenn Seaborg. k, Otto Wallach, Hermann Staudinger. l, Richard Synge, Alex Theorell. m, Thomas Morgan, Hermann Muller. n, Allvar Gullstrand, Willem Einthoven. o, Sir Charles Sherrington, Otto Loewi. p, Jules Bordet, Sir Alexander Fleming.

1993, Mar. 11
| 1132 | A356 | 500fr Sheet of 16, #a.-p. | 11.00 | 5.50 |

Alex misspelled on No. 1132l.

Miniature Sheet

Lemurs A357

No. 1133: a, 60fr, Hapalemur simus. b, 150fr, Propithecus diadema. c, 250fr Indri indri. d, 350fr, Varecia variegata.

1992, Oct. 9   Litho.   Perf. 13½
| 1133 | A357 | Sheet of 4, #a.-d. | 5.50 | 2.00 |

World Post Day.

No. 840 Ovptd. in Silver

1993, Sept. 28   Litho.   Perf. 13½
| 1134 | A276 | 550fr multicolored | 3.75 | 1.90 |

Exists in souvenir sheet of 1.

No. 874 Ovptd. in Silver Overprint includes Guitar and reads "THE ELVIS'S GUITAR / 15th ANNIVERSARY OF HIS DEATH / 1977-1992" in English or French

1993, Sept. 28
1135	A287	1500fr English ovpt.	2.50	1.10
1136	A287	1500fr French ovpt.	2.50	1.10
	a.	Pair, #1135-1136	5.00	2.25

No. 1135 exists in souvenir sheet of 1.

Nos. 945-948 Ovptd. in Gold

Nos. 974-978 Ovptd. in Gold

1993, Sept. 28
1137	A309	350fr multicolored	.50	.30
1138	A309	1000fr multicolored	1.50	.75
1139	A309	1500fr multicolored	2.25	1.25
1140	A309	2500fr multicolored	3.75	1.90
		Nos. 1137-1140 (4)	8.00	4.20

1993, Sept. 28
1141	A315	350fr multicolored	.50	.25
1142	A315	1000fr multicolored	1.50	.75
1143	A315	1500fr multicolored	2.25	1.10
1144	A315	2500fr multicolored	3.75	1.90
		Nos. 1141-1144 (4)	8.00	4.00

Souvenir Sheet
| 1145 | A315 | 3000fr multicolored | 4.75 | 2.50 |

No. 1088 Overprinted in Red

1993, Sept. 28
| 1146 | A345 | 500fr multicolored | 3.50 | 1.75 |

Exists in souvenir sheet of 1, overprinted in red or green.

Miniature Sheet

Commercial Airlines A358

No. 1147: a, 10fr, Lufthansa, Germany. b, 10fr, Air France. c, 10fr, Air Canada. d, 10fr, ANA, Japan. e, 60fr, British Airways. f, 60fr, DO-X, Germany. g, 60fr, Shinmeiwa, Japan. h, 60fr, Royal Jordanian. i, 640fr, Alitalia, Italy. j, 640fr, Hydro 2000, France-Europe. k, 640fr, Boeing 314 Clipper, US. l, 640fr, Air Madagascar. m, 5000fr, Emirates Airlines, United Arab Emirates n, 5000fr, Scandinavian Airways. o, 5000fr, KLM, Netherlands. p, 5000fr, Air Caledonia.

1993, Nov. 22   Litho.   Perf. 13½
| 1147 | A358 | Sheet of 16, #a.-p. | 30.00 | 15.00 |

Dated 1990.

Miniature Sheet

Painters A359

No. 1148: a, 50fr, Leonardo Da Vinci. b, 50fr, Titian. c, 50fr, Hembrandt. d, 50fr, J.M.W. Turner (1775-1851). e, 640fr, Michelangelo. f, 640fr, Rubens. g, 640fr, Goya. h, 640fr, Delacroix (1798-1863). i, 1000fr, Monet. j, 1000fr, Gauguin. k, 1000fr, Toulouse Lautrec (1864-1901). l, 1000fr, Dali (1904-89). m, 2500fr, Renoir. n, 2500fr, Van Gogh. o, 2500fr, Picasso. p, 2500fr, Andy Warhol.

1993, May 10
| 1148 | A359 | Sheet of 16, #a.-p. | 22.50 | 11.50 |

The local currency on Nos. 1148m-1148p is obliterated by a black overprint.

Nos. 1007-1013 Ovptd. in Gold

MALAGASY REPUBLIC

No. 841 Ovptd. in Metallic Green

1993, Sept. 28 Litho. Perf. 13½
1149	A329	140fr multicolored	.25	.25
1150	A329	500fr multicolored	.65	.30
1151	A329	640fr multicolored	.90	.40
1152	A329	1025fr multicolored	1.25	.60
1153	A329	1140fr multicolored	1.50	.75
1154	A276	1500fr multicolored	2.00	1.00
1155	A329	3500fr multicolored	4.50	2.25
		Nos. 1149-1155 (7)	11.05	5.55

Souvenir Sheet
1156	A329	4500fr multicolored	6.00 3.00

Fauna — A360

No. 1157 — Dogs: a, 40fr, Golden retriever. b, 140fr, Fox terrier. c, 40fr, Coton de tulear. d, 140fr, Langhaar.
No. 1158 — Cats: a, 40fr, Birman. b, 140fr, Egyptian. c, 40fr, European creme. d, 140fr, Rex du Devon.
No. 1159 — Reptiles: a, 1000fr, Phelsuma madagascariensis. b, 2000fr, Cameleon de parson. c, 1000fr, Laticauda laticaudata. d, 2000fr, Testudo radiata.
No. 1160 — Beetles: a, 1000fr, Euchroea spininasuta. b, 2000fr, Orthophagus minnulus klug. c, 1000fr, Helictopleurus radicollis. d, 2000fr, Euchroea coelestis.

1993, Dec. 7 Litho. Perf. 13½
1157	A360	Block of 4, #a.-d.	.50	.25
1158	A360	Block of 4, #a.-d.	.50	.25
1159	A360	Block of 4, #a.-d.	8.00	4.00
1160	A360	Block of 4, #a.-d.	8.00	4.00
e.		Sheet of 16, #1157-1160	18.00	8.50

Dated 1991.

Nos. 934-938 Ovptd. in Metallic Blue
Nos. 939-939B Ovptd. in Metallic Red Lilac

1993, Sept. 28
1161	A305	250fr multicolored	.35	.25
1162	A305	350fr multicolored	.50	.25
1163	A305	1000fr multicolored	1.50	.75
1164	A305	1500fr multicolored	2.25	1.10
1165	A305	2500fr multicolored	3.75	1.90
		Nos. 1161-1165 (5)	8.35	4.25

Souvenir Sheet
1166	A305	3000fr multi	4.50

Litho. & Embossed
Perf. 13½
1166A	A305	5000fr gold & multi	8.00

Souvenir Sheet
1166B	A305	5000fr gold & multi	8.00

Nos. 1161-1165 exist in souvenir sheets of 1, and in a sheet containing Nos. 1161-1165 plus label.
A number has been reserved for an additional value in this set.

Marine Life — A361

No. 1167 — Shells: a, 15fr, Chicoreus torrefactus. b, 15fr, Fasciolaria filamentosa. c, 30fr, Stellaria solaris. d, 30fr, Harpa ventricosa lamarck.
No. 1168 — Crustaceans: a, 1250fr, Panulirus. b, 1250fr, Stenopus hispidus. c, 1500fr, Pagure. d, 1500fr, Bernard l'hermite.
No. 1169 — Fish: a, 15fr, Pigopytes diacanthus. b, 15fr, Coelacanth latimeria chalumnae. c, 30fr, Ostracion cyanurus. d, 30fr, Coris gaimardi. e, 1250fr, Balistapus undulatus. f, 1250fr, Forcipiger longirostris. g, 1500fr, Adioryx diadema. h, 1500fr, Pterois lunulata.

1993, Nov. 26 Perf. 13½
1167	A361	Block of 4, #a.-d.	.25	.25
1168	A361	Block of 4, #a.-d.	7.25	3.50
1169	A361	Block of 8, #a.-h.	7.25	3.50
i.		Sheet of 16, #1167-1169	16.50	7.50

Dated "1991."

Flora — A362

No. 1170 — Orchids: a, 45fr, Oceonia oncidiflora. b, 60fr, Cymbidella rhodochica. c, 140fr, Vanilla planifolia. d, 3000fr, Phaius humblotii.
No. 1171 — Fruits: a, 45fr, Artocarpus altilis. b, 60fr, Eugenia malaceensis. c, 140fr, Jambosa domestica. d, 3000fr, Papaya.
No. 1172 — Mushrooms: a, 45fr, Russula annulata. b, 60fr, Lactarius claricolor. c, 140fr, Russula tuberculosa. d, 3000fr, Russula fistulosa.
No. 1173 — Vegetables: a, 45fr, Sweet potatoes. b, 60fr, Yams. c, 140fr, Avocados. d, 3000fr, Mangoes.

1993, Dec. 15 Litho. Perf. 13
1170	A362	Strip of 4, #a.-d.	4.25	2.25
1171	A362	Strip of 4, #a.-d.	4.25	2.25
1172	A362	Strip of 4, #a.-d.	4.25	2.25
1173	A362	Strip of 4, #a.-d.	4.25	2.25
e.		Sheet of 16, #1170-1173	18.00	9.00

1994 Winter Olympics, Lillehammer A362a

Designs: 140fr, Biathlon. 1250fr, Ice hockey. 2000fr, Figure skating. 2500fr, Slalom skiing. 5000fr, Downhill skiing. No. 1173K, Ski jumping. No. 1173L, Speed skating.

1994, Jan. 19 Litho. Perf. 13
1173F-1173I	A362a	Set of 4	18.50	9.25

Souvenir Sheet
1173J	A362a	5000fr multi	7.25 3.50

Litho. & Embossed
1173K	A362a	10,000fr gold & multi	13.00

Souvenir Sheet
1173L	A362a	10,000fr gold & multi	13.00

No. 1173K exists in a souvenir sheet of 1.
For overprints see Nos. 1288A-1288E.

1996 Summer Olympics, Atlanta A362b

Scene in Atlanta, event: 640fr, 1892 Windsor Hotel Americus, dressage. 1000fr, Covington Courthouse, women's shot put. 1500fr, Carolton Community Activities Center, table tennis. 3000fr, Newman Historic Commercial Court Square, soccer.
7500fr, Relay race runner. No. 1173R, Pole vault, vert. No. 1173S, Hurdles, vert.

1994, Jan. 19
1173M-1173P	A362b	Set of 4	19.50	9.50

Souvenir Sheet
1173Q	A362b	7500fr multi	27.00 13.50

Litho. & Embossed
1173R	A362b	5000fr gold & multi	7.50

Souvenir Sheet
1173S	A362b	5000fr gold & multi	8.00

Prehistoric Animals — A363

Designs: 35fr, Dinornis maximus, vert. 40fr, Ceratosaurus, vert. 140fr, Mosasavrus, vert. 525fr, Protoceratops. 640fr, Styvacosaurus. 755fr, Smilodon. 1800fr, Uintatherium. 2000fr, Tusks of mammuthus, trees, vert.

1995, Feb. 23 Litho. Perf. 12
1174-1180	A363	Set of 7	4.50	4.50

Souvenir Sheet
1181	A363	2000fr multicolored	3.50 1.50

For surcharge see No. 1474A.

Wild Animals — A364

Designs: 10fr, Panthera pardus. 30fr, Martes. 60fr, Vulpes vulpes. 120fr, Canis lupus. 140fr (No. 1186), Fennecus zerda. 140fr (No. 1187), Panthera leo. 3500fr, Uncia uncia.
2000fr, Panthera onca.

1995, Mar. 21
1182-1188	A364	Set of 7	5.00	5.00

Souvenir Sheet
1189	A364	2000fr multicolored	3.50 3.50

D-Day Landings, Normandy, 50th Anniv. — A365

No. 1190: a, 3000fr, American troops, flamethrower. b, 1500fr, Coming ashore. c, 3000fr, Explosion, German commander pointing.
No. 1191 — Liberation of Paris, 50th anniv.: a, 3000fr, Notre Dame, resistance fighters, crowd. b, 1500fr, Arch de Triomphe, woman cheering. c, 3000fr, Eiffel Tower, parade, French troops.

1994 Perf. 13½
1190	A365	Strip of 3, #a.-c.	6.75	3.50
1191	A365	Strip of 3, #a.-c.	6.75	3.50

Nos. 1190b, 1191b are 30x47mm. Nos. 1190-1191 are continuous design.

Aquarium Fish — A366

Designs: 10fr, Pomacanthus imperator. 30fr, Betta splendens. 45fr, Trichogaster leeri. 95fr, Labrus bimaculatus. No. 1196, 140fr, Synodontis nigreventris. No. 1197, 140fr, Cichlasoma biocellatum. 3500fr, Fudulus heteroclitus.
2000fr, Carassius auratus, vert.

1994, June 28 Litho. Perf. 12½x12
1192-1198	A366	Set of 7	5.75	5.75

Souvenir Sheet
Perf. 12x12½
1199	A366	2000fr multicolored	3.25 3.25

Modern Locomotives A367

Designs: 5fr, Superviem Odoriko. 15fr, Morrison Knudsen Corporation. 140fr, ER-200. 265fr, General Motors. 300fr, New Jersey Transit. 575fr, Siemens Inter-City Express. 2500fr, Sweden's Fast Train.
2000fr, Alstham T60.

1993, Nov. 10 Perf. 12
1200-1206	A367	Set of 7	5.00	4.50

Souvenir Sheet
1207	A367	2000fr multicolored	3.25 1.50

For surcharge, see No. 1475A, 1477A.

Cathedrals — A368

Cathedral, location: 10fr, Antwerp, Belgium. 100fr, Cologne, Germany. 120fr, Antsirabe, Masdagascar. 140fr, Kremlin, Moscow. 525fr, Notre Dame, Paris. 605fr, Toledo, Spain. 2500fr, St. Stephens, Vienna.
2000fr, Westminster Abbey, London.

1995, Feb. 14 Perf. 12x12½
1208-1214	A368	Set of 7	4.50	4.50

Souvenir Sheet
1215	A368	2000fr multicolored	2.75 2.75

Dated 1994.
No. 1215 is inscribed with country name only in the sheet margin.
For surcharge, see No. 1472B.

Insects — A369

Designs: 20fr, Necrophorus tomentosus. 60fr, Dynastes tityus. 140fr, Megaloxantha bicolor. 605fr, Calosoma sycophanta. 720fr, Chrysochroa mirabilis. 1000fr, Crioceris asparaqi. 1500fr, Cetonia aurata. 2000fr, Goliathus goliathus.

1994, Feb. 2 Perf. 12
1216-1222	A369	Set of 7	5.50	5.50

Size: 85x58mm
Imperf
1223	A369	2000fr multicolored	2.25 1.25

For surcharge, see No. 1478B.

Miniature Sheet

PHILAKOREA '94 — A370

MALAGASY REPUBLIC

No. 1224: a, 100fr, John Lennon, Ella Fitzgerald. b, 140fr, Marilyn Monroe, Elvis Presley. c, 550fr, U.S. Pres. Bill Clinton, Louis Armstrong.

1995, Feb. 23   **Perf. 12**
1224 A370 Sheet of 2 each, #a.-c. + 3 labels   4.75   2.25

Ancient Art & Architecture A371

Designs: No. 1225, 350fr, Statue of Augustus, vert. No. 1226, 350fr, Statue, Land Surveyor, vert. No. 1227, 350fr, Painting, "Child of Thera," vert. No. 1228, 350fr, Sarcophagous, Cerveteri and Wife, vert. No. 1229, 350fr, Statue, Athena of Fidia, vert. No. 1230, 405fr, Colosseum, Rome. No. 1231, 405fr, Mask of Agamemnon, vert. No. 1232, 405fr, Forum of Caesar. No. 1233, 405fr, She-Wolf suckling Romulus & Remus. No. 1234, 405fr, Parthenon, Athens. No. 1235, 525fr, Carthaginian mask, vert. No. 1236, 525fr, Bust of Emperor Tiberius, vert. No. 1237, 525fr, Statue of Alexander the Great, vert. No. 1238, 525fr, Detail, Taormina Theater, vert. No. 1239, 525fr, Denarius of Caesar. No. 1240, 605fr, Forum, Pompeii, vert. No. 1241, 605fr, Bronze statue, Riace, vert. No. 1242, 605fr, Venus de Milo, vert. No. 1243, 605fr, Bronze statue, Archer, vert. No. 1244, 605fr, Pont Du Gard Aqueduct, Nimes.

1994   Litho.   **Perf. 13½**
1225-1244 A071 Set of 20   0.50   0.25

Elvis Presley (1935-77) A371a

Design: No. 1244B, "The King," "Presley," Elvis wearing black.

Litho. & Embossed
1994, June 8   **Perf. 13½**
1244A A371a 10,000fr gold & multi   12.00
Souvenir Sheet
1244B A371a 10,000fr gold & multi   12.00
Exists in sheets of 4.

The Stuff of Heroes, by Philip Kaufman — A372

No. 1245: a, 140fr, Astronaut. b, 140fr, Astronaut up close, walking. c, 5000fr, Spacecraft, astronaut.

1994
1245 A372 Strip of 3, #a.-c.   3.75   1.90
Motion pictures, cent. No. 1245 is a continuous design and exists in souvenir sheet of 1 with scenes from the film "Blade Runner."
No. 1245c is 60x47mm.

Intl. Olympic Committee, Cent. — A373

No. 1246: a, 2500fr, Flag. b, 2500fr, Olympic flame. c, 3500fr, Pierre de Coubertin.

1994
1246 A373 Strip of 3, #a.-c.   5.75   2.75
No. 1246 is a continuous design and exists in souvenir sheet of 1. No. 1246c is 60x47mm.

ILO, 75th Anniv. A374

1994   Litho.   **Perf. 13½**
1247 A374 140fr multicolored   .25   .25

A374a

Designs: 30fr, Mahafaly jewelry. 60fr, Sakalava fork and spoon. 140fr, Antandroy jewelry. 430fr, Sakalava jewelry. 580fr, Antaimoro Ambalavao paper. 1250fr Sakalava jewelry, diff. 1500fr, Inlaid cabinet. 2000fr, Ampanihy tapestry.

1995, Feb. 2   Litho.   **Perf. 11¼**
1247A A374a 30fr multi
1247B A374a 60fr multi
1247C A374a 140fr multi
1247D A374a 430fr multi
1247E A374a 580fr multi
1247F A374a 1250fr multi
1247G A374a 1500fr multi
Souvenir Sheet
Imperf
1247H A374a 2000fr multi

For surcharges, see Nos. 1472, 1477B, 1484.

Modern Ships — A375

Ships: 45fr, Russian car ferry. 50fr, Australian cargo. 100fr, Japanese cruise. 140fr, US cruise. 300fr, English hovercraft. 350fr, Danish cargo. 3000fr, Korean container ship. 2000fr, Finnish car ferry, vert.

1994   Litho.   **Perf. 12**
1248-1254 A375 Set of 7   4.50   4.50
Souvenir Sheet
1255 A375 2000fr multicolored   3.25   3.25

1994 World Cup Soccer Championships, U.S. — A375a

Player at: No. 1255A, Left. No. 1255B, Right.

Litho. & Embossed
1994, Aug. 24   **Perf. 13½**
1255A A375a 10,000fr gold & multi   12.00
Souvenir Sheet
1255B A375a 10,000fr gold & multi   12.00

Sports — A377

5fr, Hurdles. 140fr, Boxing. 525fr, Gymnastics. 550fr, Weight lifting. 640fr, Swimming. 720fr, Equestrian. 1500fr, Soccer. 2000fr, Running, horiz.

1995, Apr. 4   Litho.   **Perf. 12**
1264-1270 A377 Set of 7   5.00   2.50
Souvenir Sheet
1271 A377 2000fr multicolored   3.25   1.25

A378

Orchids: 50fr, Paphiopedilum siamense. 65fr, Cypripedium calceolus. 70fr, Ophrys oestrifera. 140fr, Cephalanthera rubra. 300fr, Cypripedium macranthon. 640fr, Calanthe vestita. 2500fr, Cypripedium guttatum. 2000fr, Oncidium tigrinum.

1993, Nov. 10   Litho.   **Perf. 12**
1272-1278 A378 Set of 7   6.00   2.50
Size: 90x70mm
Imperf
1279 A378 2000fr multicolored   3.25   1.25

Sharks — A379

Designs: 10fr, Galeocerdo cuvieri. 45fr, Pristiophorus japonicus. 140fr, Rhincodon typus. 270fr, Sphyrna zygaena. 600fr, Carcharhinus longimanus. 1200fr, Stegostoma tigrinum. 1500fr, Scapanorhynchus owstoni. 2000fr, Galeorhinus zyopterus.

1993, Sept. 22   **Perf. 12**
1280-1286 A379 Set of 7   5.00   2.50
Size: 70x90mm
Imperf
1287 A379 2000fr multicolored   3.25   1.25

Archaea Workmani — A380

1994   **Perf. 15**
1288 A380 500fr multicolored   1.00   .75

Nos. 1173F-1173J Ovptd. With Names of Winners in Silver or Gold

Overprinted in silver: 140fr, "M. DEDARD / CANADA." 1250fr, "MEDAILLE D'OR / SUEDE." 2000fr, "O. BAYUL / UKRAINE." 2500fr, "M. WASMEIER / ALLEMAGNE." 5000fr,
Overprinted in gold: 5000fr, "D. COMPAGNONI / ITALIE."

1994, Aug. 30   Litho.   **Perf. 13**
1288A-1288D A362a Set of 4   18.50   9.25
Souvenir Sheet
1288E A362a 5000fr multi   7.25   3.50

Marilyn Monroe (1926-62), Elvis Presley (1935-77) — A381

Scenes from films: No. 1289, 100fr, Gentlemen Prefer Blondes. No. 1290, 100fr, Clambake, Roustabout, Viva Las Vegas. 550fr, Some Like it Hot. 1250fr, Girls, Girls, Girls, King Creole. 5000fr, Niagara. 10,000fr, Double Trouble, Kid Gallahad, Speedway.

1995, Aug. 15   Litho.   **Perf. 13½**
1289-1294 A381 Set of 6   12.50   12.50
Nos. 1289-1294 exist in souvenir sheets of 1.

Motion Pictures, Cent. — A382

Actor, film: No. 1295, 140fr, James Dean, Rebel Without a Cause. No. 1296, 140fr, Burt Lancaster, Vera Cruz. 5000fr, Elvis Presley, Speedway. 10,000fr, Marilyn Monroe, How to Marry a Millionaire.

1995, Aug. 16   Litho.   **Perf. 13½**
1295-1298 A382 Set of 4   11.00   11.00
a. Miniature sheet of 4, #1295-1298   17.50   17.50
Nos. 1295-1298 exist in souvenir sheets of 1.

Locusts — A383

Designs: No. 1299, Assylidae, natural enemy of the locust. No. 1300, Locust eating corn, vert. No. 1301, Gathering locusts for consumption.

1995, Sept. 26   Litho.   **Perf. 13½**
1299 A383 140fr multicolored   .90   .25
1300 A383 140fr multicolored   .90   .25
1301 A383 140fr multicolored   .90   .25
Nos. 1299-1301 (3)   2.70   .75

Malagasyan Bible, 160th Anniv. — A384

1995, June 21   Litho.   **Perf. 15**
1302 A384 140fr multicolored   .25   .25

World Post Day — A385

1995, Oct. 9   **Perf. 13½**
1303 A385 500fr multicolored   .80   .35

Nos. 967-972 Ovptd. in Silver

1996, Jan. 21   Litho.   **Perf. 13½**
1304 A314 2000fr on No. 971   3.50   1.75
1304A A314 Sheet of 6, #b-g, 1304

No. 1304 exists in souvenir sheet of 1, overprinted in gold or silver. No. 1304A exists with gold overprint.

MALAGASY REPUBLIC

Death of Charles de Gaulle, 25th Anniv. — A386

No. 1305: a, 100fr, World War I battle. b, 100fr, As President of France. c, 100fr, Brazzaville, 1940. d, 500fr, Pierre Brossolette, Churchill, De Gaulle. e, 500fr, Young woman. f, 500fr, Yak 9T, Gen. Leclerc. g, 1500fr, Liberation of Paris. h, 1500fr, De Gaulle as younger man. i, 1500fr, Jean Moulin, Free French barricade in Paris. j, 7500fr, Writing Tourbillon de L'Histoire, Colombey Les Deux Eglises. k, 7500fr, Giving speech as older diplomat. l, 7500fr, Doves, French flag, older De Gaulle standing on hilltop.

1996, Apr. 28   Litho.   Perf. 13½
1305 A386 Sheet of 12, #a.-l.   21.50 10.75
See design A390.

Famous People — A387

Designs: 1500fr, Wilhelm Steinitz (1836-1900), American chess master. 1750fr, Emmanuel Lasker (1868-1941), German chess master. 2000fr, Enzo Ferrari (1898-1988), automobile designer. 2500fr, Thomas Stafford, American astronaut, A.A. Leonov, Russian cosmonaut. 3000fr, Jerry Garcia (d. 1995), musician. 3500fr, Ayrton Senna (1960-94), race car driver. 5000fr, Paul-Emile Victor (1907-95), polar explorer. 7500fr, Paul Harris (1868-1947), founder of Rotary Intl.

1996, Feb. 20
1306-1313 A387 Set of 8   20.00 10.00
Nos. 1306-1313 exist in souvenir sheets of 1.

UN and UNICEF, 50th Anniv. — A388

Designs: No. 1314, 140fr, Hand holding shaft of grain, UN emblem. No. 1315, 140fr, UN building, flags, map, woman feeding child. No. 1316, 140fr, Child holding plate of food, child holding UNICEF emblem. 7500fr, Two children, UNICEF emblem.

1996, Aug. 30
1314-1317 A388 Set of 4   5.25 2.50
Nos. 1314-1317 exist in souvenir sheets of 1.

Jade A389

No. 1318: a, 175fr, People on mountain. b, Carving of insect, leaves. c, Chops on a chain. d, Insect in stone.

1996, Apr. 20   Litho.   Perf. 13½
1318 A389 Sheet of 4, #a.-d.   2.50 1.25

A390

No. 1319: Bruce Lee (1940-73), various portraits.
No. 1320: John Lennon (1940-80), various portraits.
No. 1321: Locomotives: a, Train going left. b, Train going right. c, ICE Train, Germany. d, Eurostar.
No. 1322: Louis Pasteur (1822-95), various portraits.
No. 1323: Francois Mitterrand (1916-96), various portraits.
No. 1324: Intl. Space Station: a, Shuttle Atlantis, MIR Space Station. b, MIR. c, Intl. Space Station. d, Shuttle, Alpha section of station.

Sheets of 4, #a.-d.

1996   Litho.   Perf. 13½
1319 A390 500fr multicolored   2.25 1.10
1320 A390 1500fr multicolored 3.75 1.90
1321 A390 1500fr multicolored 3.75 1.90
1322 A390 1750fr multicolored 4.25 2.10
1323 A390 2000fr multicolored 5.00 2.50
1324 A390 2500fr multicolored 6.25 3.00

Post Day A396

Various local post offices: a, 500fr. b, 1000fr. c, 3500fr. d, 5000fr.

1996, Oct. 16   Litho.   Perf. 13½
1325 A396 Sheet of 4, #a.-d.   6.25 3.00

United Nations Program for International Drug Control — A396a

Perf. 11¾x11½
1996, Oct. 23   Photo.
1325E A396a 140fr multi   —

Sports Cars A397

No. 1326: a, Mercedes W196 driven by Juan Manuel Fangio. b, Porsche 911 Carrera. c, Porsche 917-30. d, Mercedes 600 SEC.

1996
1326 A397 3000fr Sheet of 4, #a.-d.   7.50 3.75

1996 Olympic Games, Atlanta

Perf. 11¾x11½
1996, Dec. 27   Litho. Granite Paper
1326E A397a 140fr Judo
1326F A397a 140fr Tennis

UN, 50th Anniv. — A398

140fr, Private sector promotion. 500fr, Lemur, tortoise. 1025fr, Doctor and family. 1500fr, Grain stalks.

1995, Oct. 24   Litho.   Perf. 11½x11¾
1327 A398 140fr multi
1328 A398 500fr multi   — 5.00
1329 A398 1025fr multi   — —
1330 A398 1500fr multi   — —

For surcharge see No. 1490A.

1998 Winter Olympics, Nagano — A399

Designs: 160fr, Ice hockey. 350fr, Pairs figure skating. 5000fr, Biathlon. 7500fr, Freestyle skiing. 12,500fr, Speed skating.

1997   Litho.   Perf. 13½
1331-1334 A399 Set of 4   6.75 3.50

Souvenir Sheet
1335 A399 12,500fr multicolored   6.50 3.25
No. 1335 contains one 42x60mm stamp.

1998 World Cup Soccer Championships, France — A400

Various soccer plays: 300fr, 1350fr, 3000fr, 10,000fr.

1997
1336-1339 A400 Set of 4   7.75 4.00

Souvenir Sheet
1340 A400 12,500fr Player, ball   6.50 3.25
No. 1340 contains one 42x60mm stamp.

Greenpeace, 25th Anniv. — A401

Views of Rainbow Warrior I: 1500fr, At anchor. 3000fr, Under sail. 3500fr, Going left, small raft. 5000fr, Going forward at full speed. 12,500fr, Under sail, vert.

1996, Apr. 16   Litho.   Perf. 13½
1341-1344 A401 Set of 4   5.50 2.75

Souvenir Sheet
1345 A401 12,500fr multicolored   5.50 2.75

Dinosaurs — A402

No. 1346: a, Herrerasaurus, archaeopteryx. b, Segnosaurus, dimorphodon. c, Sauropelta, proavis.
No. 1347: a, Eudimorphodon, eustreptospondylus. b, Triceratops, rhamphorychus. c, Pteranodon, segnosaurus.
12,500fr, Tenontosaurus, deinonychus, vert.

1998, Feb. 25
1346 A402 1350fr Sheet of 3, #a.-c.   2.25 1.10
1347 A402 5000fr Sheet of 3, #a.-c.   8.00 4.00

Souvenir Sheet
1348 A402 12,500fr multicolored   6.50 3.25
Dated 1997.

Meteorites and Minerals — A403

No. 1349 — Meteorites: a, Iron, found in Chile. b, Iron, found in Alvord, Iowa. c, Silicate in lunar meteorite, found in Antarctica.
No. 1350 — Minerals: a, Agate, dioptase. b, Malachite, garnet. c, Chrysolile, wulfenite.
12,500fr, Mars meteorite, found in Antarctica.

1998, Feb. 25
1349 A403 3000fr Sheet of 3, #a.-c.   5.00 2.50
1350 A403 7500fr Sheet of 3, #a.-c.   12.00 6.00

Souvenir Sheet
1351 A403 12,500fr multicolored   6.50 3.25
Dated 1997.

World Post Day — A404

1997, Oct. 21   Litho.   Perf. 13½
1352 A404 300fr multicolored   5.50 2.75

Radio Nederland in Madagascar, 25th Anniv. — A404a

Perf. 11¾x11½
1997, Sept. 18   Litho. Granite Paper
1352A A404a 500fr multi   — —

Third Francophone Games — A404b

Background colors: 300fr, Light blue. 1850fr, Beige.

1997, Oct. 9   Litho.   Perf. 11½x11¾ Granite Paper
1352B-1352C A404b Set of 2   1.75 1.75

For surcharge, see No. 1490.

Diana, Princess of Wales (1961-97) — A405

MALAGASY REPUBLIC

No. 1353 — Diana wearing: a, High-collared white dress. b, Halter-style dress. c, Choker necklace, purple dress. d, Wide-brimmed hat. e, Jeweled choker necklace. f, White dress, no necklace. g, Black dress. h, White dress, pearls. i, Red dress.
No. 1354 — Portraits of Diana: a, Wearing jeweled necklace. b, With Pope John Paul II. c, Wearing beaded jacket. d, With Nelson Mandela. e, With man from India. f, With Emperor Akihito. g, Holding infant. h, Receiving flowers from child. i, Visiting sick child.
No. 1355, 12,500fr, With Mother Teresa (in margin). No. 1356, 12,500fr, With Princess Grace (in margin). No. 1357, 12,500fr, With land mine victim. No. 1358, 12,500fr, Rose-colored dress, hat.

1998, Feb. 18   Litho.   Perf. 13½
| 1353 | A405 | 1350fr Sheet of 9, #a.-i. | 6.50 | 3.25 |
| 1354 | A405 | 1750fr Sheet of 9, #a.-i. | 8.50 | 4.25 |

Souvenir Sheets
| 1355-1358 | A405 | Set of 4 | 27.00 | 14.00 |

Nos. 1355-1358 each contain one 42x60mm stamp.

Pasteur Institute of Madagascar, Cent. — A405a

1998   Litho.   Perf. 11¾x11½
| 1358A | A405a | 500fr multi | — | — |
| 1358B | A405a | 2500fr multi | — | — |

An additional stamp was issued in this set. The editors would like to examine it.

1998 World Cup Soccer Championships, France — A406

No. 1359 — Group A: a, Brazil. b, Scotland. c, Morocco. d, Norway.
No. 1360 — Group B: a, Italy. b, Chile. c, Cameroun. d, Austria.
No. 1361 — Group C: a, France. b, South Africa. c, Saudi Arabia. d, Denmark.
No. 1362 — Group D: a, Spain. b, Nigeria. c, Paraguay. d, Bulgaria.
No. 1363 — Group E: a, Netherlands. b, Belgium. c, South Korea. d, Mexico.
No. 1364 — Group F: a, Germany. b, US. c, Yugoslavia. d, Iran.
No. 1365 — Group G: a, Romania. b, Colombia. c, England. d, Tunisia.
No. 1366 — Group H: a, Argentina. b, Japan. c, Jamaica. d, Croatia.

1998, July 10   Litho.   Perf. 13½
Sheets of 4, #a.-d.
1359	A406	1350fr multi	2.75	1.40
1360	A406	1500fr multi	3.00	1.50
1361	A406	1700fr multi	3.50	1.75
1362	A406	2000fr multi	4.00	2.00
1363	A406	2500fr multi	5.00	2.50
1364	A406	3000fr multi	6.00	3.00
1365	A406	3500fr multi	7.00	3.50
1366	A406	5000fr multi	10.00	5.00

Sheets exist without Group A-Group H inscriptions. Stamps on these sheets have different denominations, and some design details differ. These sheets were allegedly on sale for a brief time before withdrawal.

Antsirabe Military Academy, 30th Anniv. — A406a

1998   Litho.   Perf. 11½x11¾
| 1366E | A406a | 500fr multi | — | — |
| 1366F | A406a | 2500fr multi | — | — |

Insects, Butterflies, Mushrooms, Minerals — A407

No. 1367 — Insects: a, Batocera wallacei, heliocopris antenor. b, Carabus auratus, calosome.
No. 1368 — Butterflies: a, Catopsilia thauruma. b, Iphiclides podalirius.
No. 1369 — Mushrooms: a, Hygrocybe punicea. b, Lepista nuda.
No. 1370 — Insects: a, Euchroma gigantea, goliathus goliathus. b, Pyrrbocor apterus, Acroninus longimanus.
No. 1371 — Butterflies: a, Hypolimnas dexithea. b, Colotis zoe.
No. 1372 — Mushrooms: a, Boletus edulis bull. b, Hygrophorus hypotheium.
No. 1373 — Minerals: a, Vanadinite. b, Carnotite.
No. 1374, 12,500fr, Papilio dardanus. No. 1375, 12,500fr, Albatrellus ovinus.

1998   Litho.   Perf. 13½
Sheets of 2, #a.-b.
1367	A407	1350fr multi	1.60	.70
1368	A407	2500fr multi	3.00	1.25
1369	A407	3000fr multi	3.50	1.50
1370	A407	3500fr multi	4.00	1.75
1371	A407	5000fr multi	5.75	2.50
1372	A407	7500fr multi	8.25	3.75
1373	A407	10,000fr multi	11.00	5.00

Souvenir Sheets
| 1374-1375 | A407 | Set of 2 | 14.00 | 6.50 |

Nos. 1374-1375 each contain one 36x42mm stamp.

Personalities — A408

Designs: No. 1376, Andrianary Ratianarivo (1895-1949). No. 1377, Odeam Rakoto (1922-73). No. 1378, Fredy Rajaofera (1902-68).

1997, Aug. 21
| 1376-1378 | A408 | 140fr Set of 3 | .45 | .25 |

The Titanic A409

No. 1379 — Faces of the Titanic: a, 1300fr, J. Pierpont Morgan, owner, White Star Line. b, 1300fr, J. Bruce Ismay, director, White Star Line. c, 1300fr, Lord James Pirrie, builder, Harland & Wolff. d, 1300fr, Alexander Carlisle, designer, Harland & Wolff. e, 1300fr, Edward John Smith, Captain of Titanic. f, 1750fr, Arthur Rostron, Captain of Carpathia.
No. 1380 — Rescue: a, 1350fr, Women and children first. b, 1350fr, Lifeboats lowered. c, 1350fr, Lifeboats called back. d, 1350fr, Captain Smith hands child to safety. e, 1700fr, Few saved from water. f, 1700fr, Reaching Carpathia.
No. 1381, vert. — Various pictures of ship taken from period postcards: a, 300fr. b, 5000fr. c, 5000fr. d, 7500fr.
No. 1382 — Interior of ship: a, 800fr, Grand staircase. b, 800fr, Reception area. c, 850fr, Restaurant. d, 850fr, Stateroom. e, 1300fr, Turkish baths. f, 10,000fr, Swimming pool.
No. 1383 — Building the ship: a, 1450fr, Drafting room, 1907-08. b, 2050fr, Hull constructed, 1909-11. c, 5000fr, Launch, May 31, 1911. d, 7500fr, Fitting out, 1911-12.
No. 1384 — The aftermath: a, 300fr, "The Sun" post lastest bulletins. b, 450fr, Paperboys on street. c, 1050fr, Hearses, coffins at dock. d, 5000fr, Wallace Hartley, "The Last Tune." e, 10,000fr, Engineers Monument, 1914.

1998, Sept. 10   Litho.   Perf. 13½
1379	A409	Sheet of 6, #a.-f.	3.50	1.50
1380	A409	Sheet of 6, #a.-f.	3.75	1.60
1381	A409	Sheet of 4, #a.-d.	6.25	2.50
1382	A409	Sheet of 6, #a.-f.	6.50	2.75
1383	A409	Sheet of 4, #a.-d.	7.00	3.00
1384	A409	Sheet of 5, #a.-e.	7.25	3.25

No. 1381 contains four 37½x49mm stamps. No. 1382 contains six 49x38mm stamps. No. 1384, five 28x35mm stamps.

Famous Disasters at Sea A410

No. 1385: a, 160fr, Sinking of the Titanic, 1912. b, 160fr, Torpedoing of the Lusitania, 1915. c, 1350fr, Burning of the Atlantique, 1933. d, 1350fr, Burning of the Normandie, 1942. e, 1350fr, Wilhelm Gustloff being torpedoed, 1945. f, 1350fr, Sinking of the Andrea Doria, 1956. g, 3500fr, Burning of the Queen Elizabeth, 1972. h, 3500fr, Sinking of the Amoco Cadiz, 1978. i, 3500fr, Sinking of the Estonia, 1994.
No. 1386, Various scenes of Titanic disaster.

1998, Nov. 6   Litho.   Perf. 13½
| 1385 | A410 | Sheet of 9, #a.-i. | 7.75 | 3.75 |

Souvenir Sheet
| 1386 | A410 | 12,500fr multicolored | 6.25 | 3.00 |

No. 1386 contains one 120x51mm stamp.

Trains, Sports Cars, Airplanes A411

No. 1387 — Trains: a, Steam locomotive, 477.043, China. b, Kruckenberg Zeppelin Train, Germany. c, Mountain 498, China. d, Gottardo tram, Switzerland. e, TGV 001, France. f, ET-403, Germany. g, Le Shuttle, France. h, Shinkansen, Japan. i, TGV Alexander Dumas, France.
No. 1388 — Sports cars: a, Opel Kapitan, Germany. b, Volkswagen Beetle, Germany. c, Fiat Topolino, Italy. d, Facel Delahaye, France-England. e, Bristol Series 407, England. f, Alfa Romeo 2500, Italy. g, Chrysler Viper GTS, US. h, McLaren F1, England. i, Mercedes Brabus SLK, Germany.
No. 1389 — Airplanes: a, Aerospatiale STS 2000, France. b, Piggyback Space Shuttle, US. c, Hermes Rocket, France, Germany, Italy. d, Northrop B-35, US. e, Airbus A310, A321, A340. Europe. f, Armstrong Whitworth A.W52, Great Britain. g, Concorde, UK, France, going right. h, Tupolev, Russia. i, Concorde, France, UK, going left.

1998, Nov. 6
1387	A411	1700fr Sheet of 9, #a.-i.	7.50	3.75
1388	A411	2000fr Sheet of 9, #a.-i.	9.00	4.50
1389	A411	3000fr Sheet of 9, #a.-i.	13.50	6.75

Balloons A412

No. 1390: a, 300fr, "Pilatre de Rozier," Montgolfier, 1783. b, 300fr, Charles and Robert, 1783. c, 300fr, Blanchard and Jeffries, 1785. d, 350fr, "Pilatre de Rozier," 1785. e, 350fr, "Testu-Brissy," 1798. f, 350fr, "Atlantic," 1858. g, 5000fr, "Small World," 1959. h, 5000fr, "Strato-lab High 5", 1961. i, 5000fr, "Double Eagle II", 1978.
10,000fr, Auguste Piccard (1884-1962), balloon.

1998, Nov. 6
| 1390 | A412 | Sheet of 9, #a.-i. | 8.50 | 4.25 |

Souvenir Sheet
| 1391 | A412 | 10,000fr multicolored | 5.00 | 2.50 |

No. 1391 contains one 42x51mm stamp.

Butterflies and Moths — A413

No. 1392: a, 1950fr, Citrus swallowtail. b, 1950fr, Mocker swallowtail. c, 1950fr, Striped policeman. d, 1950fr, Golden piper. e, 1950fr, Painted lady. f, 1950fr, Monarch. g, 250fr, Gold-banded forester. h, 250fr, Madagascan sunset moth. i, 250fr, Palla butterfly. j, 250fr, Blue pansy. k, 250fr, Common grass blue. l, 250fr, Crimson tip.
1800fr, Cabbage butterfly, vert. No. 1394, Broad-bordered grass yellow. 2250fr, Figtree blue. 3500fr, African migrant, vert.

1999, Mar. 24
| 1392 | A413 | Sheet of 12, #a.-l. | 7.50 | 3.50 |

Souvenir Sheets
1393	A413	1800fr multicolored	1.25	.55
1394	A413	1950fr multicolored	1.40	.60
1395	A413	2250fr multicolored	1.50	.65
1396	A413	3500fr multicolored	2.50	1.00

Birds — A414

No. 1397: a, 250fr, Madagascar blue pigeon. b, 250fr, White-tailed tropicbird. c, 1350fr, Madagascan red fody. d, 1350fr, Crested drongo. e, 250fr, Namaqua dove. f, 250fr, Helmet bird. g, 1350fr, Blue-crowned roller. h, 1350fr, Red-eyed roller. i, 250fr, Coral-billed nuthatch. j, 250fr, Wattled false sunbird. k, 1350fr, Short-legged ground roller. l, 1350fr, Pied crow.
No. 1398, 4000fr, Barn owl. No. 1399, 4000fr, Goliath heron.
No. 1400, 7200fr, Marsh harrier hawk, horiz. No. 1401, 7200fr, Vasa parrot, horiz.

1999, Feb. 17   Litho.   Perf. 13½
| 1397 | A414 | Sheet of 12, #a.-l. | 4.75 | 1.75 |

Souvenir Sheets
| 1398-1399 | A414 | Set of 2 | 4.25 | 1.50 |
| 1400-1401 | A414 | Set of 2 | 7.75 | 2.75 |

New Year 1999 (Year of the Rabbit) A415

No. 1402 — Stylized rabbits: a, Facing right. b, Looking right over shoulder. c, Looking left over shoulder. d, Facing left.
10,000fr, Facing forward.

1999, Apr. 7   Litho.   Perf. 14
| 1402 | A415 | 1500fr Sheet of 4, #a.-d. | 3.00 | 1.25 |

Souvenir Sheet
| 1403 | A415 | 10,000fr multi | 4.75 | 3.75 |

MALAGASY REPUBLIC

Grain and Map — A415a

1999-2000 Litho. Perf. 13½
1403A	A415a	450fr brn & multi	—	—
1403B	A415a	900fr red & multi	—	—
f.		Dated "2000"	—	
1403C	A415a	900fr green & multi	—	—
1403D	A415a	1500fr (300a) blue & multi	—	—
1403E	A415a	5600fr multi	—	—

Nos. 1403D and 1403E are airmail. Denomination is at bottom on No. 1403A. On No. 1403D, the denomination is at the bottom with large capital and lower case letters. Nos. 1403A and 1403C are dated "2000."

For surcharge, see No. 1617.

Lizards A416

World Wildlife Fund: a, 1700fr, Chamaeleo minor (on branch). b, 2400fr, Phelsuma standingi. c, 300fr, Chamaeleo balteatus. d, 2050fr, Chamaeleo minor (on rock). e, 2050fr, as "d," inscribed "Urplatus fimbriatus."

1999, Apr. 7
1404	A416	Block of 4, #a.-d.	8.75	8.75
f.		Block of 4, #1404a-1404c, 1404e	5.25	5.25

Issued in sheets of 16 stamps.
Issued: No. 1404e, 7/23.

Fauna — A417

Designs: No. 1405, 1950fr, Toucan. No. 1406, 1950fr, Hummingbird. No. 1407, 1950fr, Dendrobates pumilis. No. 1408, 1950fr, Jaguar, vert. No. 1409, 1950fr, Dendrobate (frog). No. 1410, 1950fr, Pangolin.
No. 1411: a, Three-toed sloth (d). b, Chameleon (e). c, Loris (f). d, Tree frog. e, Tarsier. f, Civet (i). g, Cicada. h, Callicore butterfly. i, Python (f).
No. 1412: a, Flying fox (bat). b, Galago (a, d, e). c, Squirrel monkey (f). d, Red kingfisher e, Blue parrot (h). f, Heliconide butterfly. g, Oranutan (d). h, Tamarin. i, Ocelot (h).
No. 1413, 10,000fr, Tiger. No. 1414, 10,000fr, Leopard.

1999, Apr. 7
1405-1410	A417	Set of 6	4.50	4.50
1411	A417	2250fr Sheet of 9, #a.-i.	7.50	7.50
1412	A417	2450fr Sheet of 9, #a.-i.	7.75	7.75

Souvenir Sheets
| 1413-1414 | A417 | Set of 2 | 7.50 | 7.50 |

Film Stars A418

No. 1414A: b, Antonio Banderas. c, Glenn Close. d, Harrison Ford. e, Pamela Anderson. f, Tom Hanks. g, Michelle Pfeiffer. h, Leonardo Di Caprio. i, Sharon Stone. j, Tom Cruise.
No. 1415: a, Catherine Deneuve. b, Gérard Depardieu. c, John-Paul Belmondo. d, John Reno. e, Johnny Hallyday. f, Christopher Lambert. g, Jean Gabin. h, Alain Delon. i, Brigitte Bardot.

1999 Litho. Perf. 13½
1414A	A418	2500fr Sheet of 9, #b.-j.	12.00	12.00
1415	A418	3500fr Sheet of 9, #a.-i.	11.50	11.50

Fauna — A419

No. 1416: a, Rotary International emblem and Hapalemur gris, satellite. b, Rotary International emblem and Lemur vari, satellite. c, Rotary International emblem and Hanka. d, Scouting emblem, comet ,and Sifaka de verreaux. e, Scouting emblem, comet, and Euplere de goudot. f, Scouting emblem, comet, and Potamochere. g, Lions International emblem and Rousette geante, satellite. h, Lions International emblem, Lampira, comet. i, Lions International emblem, Maki catta, satellite.
No. 1416J — Butterfly and : k, Gibbon lar. l, Macaque rhesus. m, Maki macaco. n, Gélada. o, Maki brun. p, Nasique. q, Maki vari. r, Mandrill. s, Hapalémur gris.

1999 Sheets of 9 + 3 Labels
1416	A419	2500fr Sheet of 9, #a.-i., + 3 labels	10.00	10.00
1416J	A419	3500fr Sheet of 9, #k.-s., + 3 labels	14.00	14.00

Intl. Year of the Ocean — A420

Designs: No. 1417, Scarus gibbus. No, 1418, Gramma loreto. No. 1419, Arusetta asfur. No. 1420, Daseyllus trimaculatus.
No. 1421: a, Hyporhamphus unifasciatus. b, Delphinus delphis. c, Cetorhinus maximus. d, Manta birostris. e, Chactodon capistratus. f, Microspathodon chysurus.
No. 1422: a, Coryphaena hippurus. b, Diodon holacanthus. c, Aequorea aequorea. d, Sphyraena barracuda. e, Octopus vulgaris. f, Acanthurus bahianus. g, Gymnothorax moringa. h, Limulus polyphemus. i, Pristis pictinata.
No. 1423: a, 1350fr, Balistoides niger. b, 1350fr, Isiophorus platypterus. c, 2750fr, Carcharhinus limbatus. d, 2750fr, Carcharodon carcharias. e, 1350fr, Zanclus cornutus. f, 1350fr, Mermaid's face. g, 2750fr, Gramma loreto. h, 2750fr, Rhinecanthus aculeatus. i, 1350fr, Lactoria cornuta. j, 1350fr, Hippocampus kuda. k, 2750fr, Pygoplites diancanthus. l, 2750fr, Epinephelus lanceolatus. m, 1350fr, Echinaster sepositus. n, 1350fr, Ocypede quadrata. o, 2750fr, Amphiprion clarkii. p, 2750fr, Cyphoma gibbosum.
No. 1424, 7200fr, Odontaspis taurus, vert. No. 1425, 7200fr, Stenalla plagiodon.

1999, June 10 Perf. 14
| 1417-1420 | A420 | 550fr Set of 4 | 1.75 | 1.75 |

Sheets of 6, 9 or 16
1421	A420	550fr Sheet of 6, #a.-f.	1.60	1.60
1422	A420	3500fr Sheet of 9, #a.-i.	15.00	15.00
1423	A420	Sheet of 16, #a.-p.	15.00	15.00

Souvenir Sheets
| 1424-1425 | A420 | Set of 2 | 7.25 | 7.25 |

No. 1423a-1423p are each 33x52mm. Dated 1998.

Trains A421

No. 1426, 4000fr: a, Danish State Railways, 1950-59. b, France, 1963. c, East Germany, 1980. d, Finnish State Railways, 1950. e, Canada, 1949. f, West Germany, 1952.
No. 1427, 4000fr: a, Light Branch 4-4-0 locomotive, Ireland, 1948. b, 4-8-0 locomotive, Argentina, 1949. c, 2-8-0 locomotive, US, 1943. d, Gold rush steam engine, US, 1870. e, Royal Blue, US, 1870-80. f, Queensland Railways, Australia, 1952.
No. 1428, 4000fr: a, 0-4-0 Lightning, England, 1829. b, Grampton, Namur, Belgium, 1848. c, Lion, England, 1838. d, Borsig, Germany, 1841. e, Baldwin "Eight-coupled" locomotive, US, 1846. f, Crampton, England, 1848.
No. 1429, 10,000fr, Diesel multiple-unit express train, Japan. No. 1430, 10,000fr, 4-8-0 steam locomotive, US, 19th cent.

1999, June 22 Sheets of 6, #a-f
| 1426-1428 | A421 | Set of 3 | 27.00 | 27.00 |

Souvenir Sheets
| 1429-1430 | A421 | Set of 2 | 7.50 | 7.50 |

Nos. 1429-1430 each contain one 76x50mm stamp. No. 1426c is incorrectly inscribed with date, "1930."

A422 / Dinosaurs — A423

Designs: 500fr each — No. 1431, Stenonychosaurus, vert. No. 1432, Iguanodon, vert. No. 1433, Staurikosaurus, vert. No. 1434, Plateosaurus, vert.
500fr each — No. 1435, Antrodemus. No. 1436, Corythosaurus, vert. No. 1437, Stegosaurus, vert. No. 1438, Lambeosaurus, vert. No. 1439, Hypsilophodon, vert.
No. 1440: a, Psittacosaurus. b, Allosaurus. c, Stegosaurus. d, Hypsilophodon. e, Triceratops. f, Camptosaurus. g, Compsognathus. h, Carnotaurus.
No. 1441, vert: a, Brachiosaurus. b, Tyrannosaurus. c, Plateosaurus. d, Hadrosaurus. e, Triceratops. f, Iguanodon.
No. 1442, 12,500fr, Styracosaurus. No. 1443, 12,500fr, Brachiosaurus, vert. No. 1444, 12,500fr, Tyrannosaurus rex, vert.

1999, July 6 Litho. Perf. 14
1431-1434	A422	Set of 4	1.10	1.10
1435-1439	A423	Set of 5	1.40	1.40
1440	A422	1850fr Sheet of 8, #a.-h.	5.50	5.50
1441	A422	1950fr Sheet of 6, #a.-f.	4.50	4.50

Souvenir Sheets
| 1442-1444 | A422 | Set of 3 | 13.50 | 13.50 |

Nos. 1431-1439 dated 1998. Numbers have been reserved for additional values in this set.

Princess Diana — A424

1999, Aug. 10 Litho. Perf. 13½
| 1446 | A424 | 1950fr multicolored | 1.00 | 1.00 |

Issued in sheets of six stamps. Compare with Type A434.

Picasso Paintings — A425

Designs: 2750fr, Bacchanalia, 1955. 7200fr, Picador, 1971, vert. 7500fr, Seated Nude, 1906-07, vert.
12,500fr, The Two Saltimbanques, 1901, vert.

1999, Aug. 10 Litho. Perf. 13x13¼
| 1447-1449 | A425 | Set of 3 | 6.75 | 6.75 |

Souvenir Sheet
| 1450 | A425 | 12,500fr multi | 4.75 | 4.75 |

Dated 1998.

Mahatma Gandhi — A426

Perf. 13½x13¼
1999, Aug. 10 Litho.
| 1451 | A426 | 2250fr Profile | 1.25 | 1.25 |

Souvenir Sheet
| 1452 | A426 | 12,500fr Gandhi shirtless | 4.75 | 4.75 |

No. 1451 issued in sheets of four stamps. Dated 1998.

Indian Ocean Commission, 15th Anniv. — A427

1999 Litho. Perf. 13¼
| 1453 | A427 | 500fr multicolored | .60 | .60 |

Fire Fighting Apparatus — A429

No. 1456, 2500fr: a, Pumper Boat "Dauphin," Africa. b, 60T Pumper, US. c, Fire train, Switzerland.
No. 1457, 2500fr: a, Gillois amphibian engine, Germany. b, Ford FMC pumper. c, Cherry picker pumper, Iraq.

1999 Sheets of 3, #a-c
| 1456-1457 | A429 | Set of 2 | 7.00 | 7.00 |

Trains A430

No. 1458, 3500fr: a, Pen-y-Darren, England. b, Pennsylvania Railroad locomotive. c, Norfolk and Western locomotive.
No. 1459, 3500fr: a, TGV Postal, France. b, TGV, Sweden. c, Magnetic train "Europa."

1999 Sheets of 3, #a-c
| 1458-1459 | A430 | Set of 2 | 9.50 | 9.50 |

Airplanes A431

No. 1460, 5000fr: a, Short-Mayo Composite. b, Boeing 747. c, Concorde, Air France poster.
No. 1461, 5000fr: a, Concorde, KLM poster. b, 1931 Curtiss F9C. c, Macchi-Castoldi MC72.

1999 Sheets of 3, #a-c
| 1460-1461 | A431 | Set of 2 | 13.00 | 13.00 |

Space Achievements — A432

No. 1462, 7500fr: a, Viking. b, Voyager. c, Apollo 11.

MALAGASY REPUBLIC

No. 1463, 7500fr: a, Dog Laika. b, Yuri Gagarin, Vostok spacecraft. c, Mir space station.

1999   Sheets of 3, #a-c
1462-1463 A432 Set of 2   20.00   20.00

Boy Scouts A433

Scouts, No. 1464: a, Bandaging thigh. b, Splinting arm. c, Making sling. d, Pulling tape from roll.
No. 1464E: f, Oeniella polystachys. g, Cynorkis lowiana. h, Oeceoclades saundersiana. i, Cynorkis purpurascens.
No. 1465: a, Upupa epops. b, Nettapus auritus. c, Leptosomus discolor. d, Brachypteracias squamigera.
No. 1465E: f, Euchraca spinnasuta. g, Cricket. h, Scorpion. i, Euchroea nigrostellata.
No. 1466: a, Charaxes antamboulou. b, Hypolimnas misippus. c, Papilio demodocus. d, Papilio antenor.
No. 1467: a, Eucalyptoboletus. b, Cantharellus congolencis. c, Gomphus. d, Russula.
No. 1468: a, Jasper. b, Granite. c, Rhodonite. d, Morganite.
No. 1469: a, Soccer. b, Chess. c, Table tennis. d, Cycling.

1999   Litho.   Perf. 13¼
Sheets of 4, #a.-d.

1404	A433	1350fr multi	2.25	2.75
1464E	A433	1500fr multi	3.00	3.00
1465	A433	1950fr multi	4.00	4.00
1465E	A433	2000fr multi	4.00	4.00
1466	A433	2500fr multi	4.75	4.75
1467	A433	3000fr multi	5.50	5.50
1468	A433	5000fr multi	8.75	8.75
1469	A433	7500fr multi	13.50	13.50
Nos. 1464-1469 (8)			45.75	46.25

No. B27 Handstamp Surcharged in Violet

Printing Methods and Perfs as before

1999 (?)
1471   SP7   60fr on 350fr+20fr on 250fr+20fr

Various Stamps Surcharged

No. 1472   No. 1472B
No. 1473A   No. 1473B
No. 1474A   No. 1474B
No. 1475   No. 1475A
No. 1476A   No. 1476B
No. 1477
No. 1478   No. 1478B
No. 1485
No. 1487
No. 1488
No. 1489

Printing Methods and Perfs as Before

1998-2000 (?)

1472	A374a	300fr on 430fr #1247D	—	
1472A	A360	300fr on 605fr #1219	—	
1472B	A368	300fr on 605fr #1213	—	
1473A	A342	300fr on 675fr #1076	—	
1473B	A352	300fr on 675fr #1118	—	
1474	A342	300fr on 720fr #1077	—	
1474A	A363	300fr on 755fr #1179	—	
1474B	A191	400fr on 170fr #614	—	
1475	A221	400fr on 215fr #695	—	
1475A	A367	400fr on 265fr #1203	—	
1475B	A207	500fr on 170fr #645	—	
1476A	A363	500fr on 525fr #1177	—	
1476B	A368	500fr on 525fr #1212	—	
1477	A341	500fr on 555fr #1068	—	
1477A	A367	500fr on 575fr #1205	—	
1477B	A374a	500fr on 580fr #1247E	—	
1478	A353	500fr on 675fr #1127	—	
1478A	A325b	500fr on 680fr #1001G	—	
1478B	A369	500fr on 720fr #1220	—	
1479	A325b	500fr on 800fr #1001H	—	
1479B	A341	500fr on 800fr #1069	—	
1479C	A352	500fr on 800fr #1119	—	
1480	A330	500fr on 1025fr #1020	—	
1482	A333	500fr on 1140fr #1043	—	
1483	A379	500fr on 1200fr #1285	—	
1484	A374a	500fr on 1250fr #1247F	—	
1485	A344	500fr on 1300fr #1086	—	
1486	A341	500fr on 1400fr #1070	—	
1487	A379	500fr on 1500fr #1285	—	
1488	A352	500fr on 1750fr #1120	—	
1489	A363	500fr on 1800fr #1180	—	
1490	A404b	500fr on 1850fr #1352C	—	
1490A	A398	1500fr on 1025fr #1329	—	

No. 1484 has a silver surcharge.
Shifted, inverted and double overprints exist.
At least 5 additional surcharges have been reported. The editors would like to examine them.

20th Century Celebrities — A434

No. 1491: a, Princess Diana. b, Kwame Nkrumah. c, Gen. Georgy Zhukov. d, Samora Machel. e, Gen. Moshe Dayan. f, Mahatma Gandhi. g, Jacqueline Kennedy. h, Gen. John Pershing.

1999   Litho.   Perf. 13½
1491   A434   1950fr Sheet of 8, #a.-h.   7.25   7.25

Famous People — A435

Designs: No. 1492, 900fr, Razafindrakotohasina Rahantavololona. No. 1493, 900fr, Gen. Gabriel Ramanantsoa. No. 1494, 900fr, Rasalama. No. 1495, 900fr, Dr. Ralivao Ramiaramañana. No. 1496, 900fr, Jerôme-Henri Cardinal Rakotomalala. No. 1497, 900fr, Rakotovao Razakaboana.

2000, Jan. 12   Litho.   Perf. 14
1492-1497   A435   Set of 6   3.00   3.00

UPU, 125th Anniv. A436

UPU emblem, postmen of various eras and: 1000fr, Mailbox. 1200fr, Postmen, space shuttle, airplane, cargo. 1800fr, Cable-laying ships. 3200fr, 19th century diligence, modern mail truck. 3500fr, balloon, Apollo 15 astronaut. 5000fr, Stentor satellite, Claude Chappe's semaphore. 5600fr, Micheline ZM 517, Autorail Bouleze 701. 7500fr, Old and modern mail trains.

1999   Litho.   Perf. 13¼
1498-1505 A436 Set of 8   13.00   13.00
Nos. 1498-1505 exist in souvenir sheets of 1.

The Incredible Hulk — A437

No. 1506: a, Hulk with gray skin, wearing white shirt. b, Head of Hulk, red background. c, Hulk with fist raised, blue background. d, Hulk with red violet pants, lilac background. e, Hulk with ripped shirt, orange background. f, Hulk wearing sunglasses. g, Hulk shirtless, orange and red background. h, Hulk holding shirt, red violet and orange background. i, Hulk, multicolored striped background.
12,500fr, Hulk, yellow and orange background.

1999, Apr. 29   Litho.   Perf. 13¼
1506   A437   1800fr Sheet of 9, #a-i   7.00   7.00

Souvenir Sheet
1507   A437   12,500fr multi   6.00   6.00
No. 1507 contains one 36x42mm stamp.

Silver Surfer A438

No. 1509: a, Silver Surfer at left, dark blue green background. b, Head of Silver Surfer, red brown background. c, Silver Surfer at right, black background with large star. d, Silver Surfer on surfboard, purple background. e, Head of Silver Surfer, green background. f, Silver Surfer carrying surfboard, purple background. g, Silver Surfer, Earth and outer space in background. h, Silver Surfer, multicolored striped background. i, Silver Surfer on surfboard, outer space background with red and blue spots.
12,500fr, Silver Surfer, diff.

1999, Apr. 29
1508   A438   1800fr Sheet of 9, #a-i   7.00   7.00

Souvenir Sheet
1509   A438   12,500fr multi   6.00   6.00
No. 1509 contains one 36x42mm stamp.

MALAGASY REPUBLIC

Spiderman — A439

No. 1510: a, Peter Parker turning into Spiderman. b, Spiderman with fist at upper right. c, Spiderman crouching. d, Spiderman holding silk at top. e, Head of Spiderman. f, Spiderman with rays around head. g, Spiderman with arms together, on silk. h, Spiderman with two strands of silk. i, Spiderman with large black spider on front of costume, and netting under arms.
12,500fr, Spiderman with arms raised.

1999, Apr. 29
1510 A439 3200fr Sheet of 9, #a-i 11.50 11.50

Souvenir Sheet
1511 A439 12,500fr multi 6.00 6.00

No. 1511 contains one 30x42mm stamp.

Garfield A440

No. 1512: a, Garfield sitting. b, Garfield looking between legs. c, Garfield holding teddy bear. d, Garfield climbing wall. e, Garfield sticking out tongue. f, Garfield with legs crossed. g, Garfield asleep. h, Garfield standing. i, Odie.

1999, Apr. 29
1512 A440 3200fr Sheet of 9, #a-i 11.50 11.50

Miniature Sheets

Trains A441

No. 1513, 800fr: a, Locomotive PK 102 on Brickaville to Fonavana line. b, Locomotive in Diego-Suarez region, 1904. c, 030T locomotive, 1922. d, BBB Alsthom Diesel-electric, 1937.
No. 1514, 1500fr: a, Locomotive 42104, 1906. b, Decauville 60 gauge locomotive. c, Mallet 020+020T locomotive, 1916. d, Garratt No. 101 locomotive, 1925.
No. 1515, 2000fr: a, Billard ZM 111 rail car, 1938. b, BB AD16 locomotive. c, Brissoneau Diesel-electric rail car, 1958. d, BBB 2nd Series 106-112, 1958.
No. 1516, 3500fr: a, Train at Fianarantsoa Station. b, AD 12 Alsthom locomotive. c, Mallet 131+131 St. Leonard. d, Micheline ZM 514.
No. 1517, 4000fr: a, Decauville 0.20 gauge 1m locomotive. b, BB235 Diesel. c, Baldwin 031 T locomotive. d, BBB Alsthom Diesel locomotive, 1935.
No. 1518, 4400fr: a, Decauville 60 gauge Montagne d'Ambre locomotive. b, Brissoneau & Lotz Diesel, 1938. c, Mallet 120+020 T locomotive, 1902. d, Corpet-Louvet locomotive.
No. 1519, 5200fr: a, Adiz BB229 locomotive. b, 030T Weidnecht locomotive, 1901. c, Jung locomotive, 1922. d, Billard rail car, 1934.

No. 1520, 10,000fr: a, Mallet 020+020 locomotive, 1925. b, Decauville 030 locomotive, 1907. c, Garratt 130+031 locomotive, 1925. d, Nosy Be 030N1, 1868.

2000, July 21 Perf. 13¼
Sheets of 4, #a-d
1513-1520 A441 Set of 8 45.00 45.00

Miniature Sheets

2000 Summer Olympics, Sydney — A442

No. 1521, 500fr: a, Soccer. b, Handball. c, Judo. d, Kayaking.
No. 1522, 1350fr: a, Cycling. b, Swimming. c, Boxing. d, Fencing.
No. 1523, 2500fr: a, Basketball. b, Cycling, diff. c, Equestrian. d, Running.
No. 1524, 3200fr: a, Weight lifting. b, Javelin. c, Equestrian, diff. d, Yachting.
No. 1525, 5000fr: a, Shot put. b, Women's gymnastics. c, Men's tennis. d, High jump.
No. 1526, 7500fr: a, Diving. b, Wrestling. c, Table tennis. d, Pole vault.
12,500fr, Kayaking and equestrian, horiz.

2000, Aug. 2 Litho.
Sheets of 4, #a-d
1521-1526 A442 Set of 6 25.00 25.00

Souvenir Sheet
1527 A442 12,500fr multi 4.00 4.00

No. 1527 contains one 57x51mm stamp and exists imperf.

Space Achievements — A443

Launches of: No. 1528, 1500fr, Gemini 1. No. 1529, 1500fr, Saturn 1. No. 1530, 1500fr, Apollo 6. No. 1531, 1500fr, Mercury-Redstone 3. No. 1532, 1500fr, Mariner 4. No. 1533, 1500fr, Titan IIIC. No. 1534, 1500fr, Discovery. No. 1535, 1500fr, Soyuz 19.
No. 1536, 3500fr — Spacecraft: a, Cassini-Huygens. b, Exosat. c, ICE. d, Solar Mesosphere Explorer. e, Mir Space Station. f, Observer.
No. 1537, 3500fr — Spacecraft: a, Mars 1. b, Solar Max. c, Venera 4. d, Skylab. e, Space Shuttle Challenger. f, Mars 3.
No. 1538, 4400fr — Spacecraft: a, Ranger 1. b, Mariner 4. c, Gemini 9. d, Gemini 2. e, Apollo 15. f, Gemini 12.
No. 1539, 5000fr — Spacecraft: a, Agena. b, Syncom 1. c, Olympus 1. d, FLT Satcom. e, Skynet 4B. f, COBE.
No. 1540, 6800fr, horiz.: a, Skylab. b, Agena c, Agena 2. d, X-36. e, Space Shuttle. f, Dale Gardner spacewalking.
No. 1541, 6800fr, horiz.: a, Hermes prototype. b, Pioneeer 10. c, Venture Star. d, Viking. e, Spacecraft landing on Mars. f, Mars Rover.
No. 1542, 10,000fr, Apollo 1 mission patch. No. 1543, 10,000fr, Apollo 9 mission patch. No. 1544, 10,000fr, Apollo 11 mission patch. No. 1545, 10,000fr, Apollo-Soyuz mission patch. No. 1546, 10,000fr, Columbia Space Shuttle mission patch. No. 1547, 12,500fr, Gemini 4 mission patch. No. 1548, 12,500fr, Gemini 12 mission patch. No. 1549, 12,500fr, Gemini 9 mission patch, horiz. No. 1550, 12,700fr, Huygens Probe approaching Titan. No. 1551, 12,700fr, Space Shuttle at Space Station, horiz.

Perf. 14, 14¾ (#1540-1541, 1550-1551)
2000, Sept. 22
1528-1535 A443 Set of 8 3.75 3.75
Sheets of 6, #a-f
1536-1541 A443 Set of 6 55.00 55.00
Souvenir Sheets
1542-1551 A443 Set of 10 35.00 35.00

Solar Eclipse — A444

2001, June 21 Perf. 13x13¼
1552 A444 5600fr multi — —

Dialogue Among Civilizations A445

2001, Oct. 12 Perf. 13½x13¼
1553 A445 3500fr multi 2.50 2.50

Miniature Sheets

Flora and Fauna A446

No. 1554, 250fr — Turtles: a, Tortue geante des Seychelles. b, Tortue luth. c, Tortue panthere. d, Caouanne. e, Cistude d'Europe. f, Chelonee.
No. 1555, 400fr — Fish: a, Astronotus ocellatus. b, Cyphotilapia frontosa. c, Bothriolepis. d, Pseudanthias tuka. e, Cleidopus gloriamaris. f, Ablabys taenionotus.
No. 1556, 500fr — Owls: a, Grand duc de Virginie. b, Chouette cheveche Brahmans. c, Grand duc du cap. d, Grand duc d'Afrique. e, Hibou moyen duc. f, Petit duc Choliba.
No. 1557, 1500fr, vert. — Turtles: a, Tortue à cou cache d'Afrique. b, Tortue à dos diamante. c, Tortue d'Hermann. d, Tortue Grecque. e, Tortue caret. f, Geochelone denticulata.
No. 1558, 2500fr, vert. — Parrots: a, Ara militaire. b, Ara vert. c, Ara macao. d, Ara hyacinthe. e, Perroquet de Meyer. f, Ara ararauna.
No. 1559, 3400fr, vert. — Bears and pandas: a, Ours lippu. b, Ours noir. c, Ours polaire. d, Petit panda. e, Ours des cocotiers. f, Ours à collier.
No. 1560, 3500fr — Insects and spiders: a, Xylocopa violacea. b, Triatoma infestans. c, Myrmecia gulosa. d, Mantis religiosa. e, Atrax robustus. f, Euglosse.
No. 1561, 4000fr, vert. — Primates: a, Ouistiti mignon. b, Tamarin lion d'ore. c, Singe de nuit. d, Magot. e, Vervet. f, Ouakari.
No. 1562, 4200fr — Flowers: a, Stapelia wilmaniae. b, Centaurea montana. c, Pagonia suffruticosa. d, Acanthosicyos horrida. e, Erimophila colorhabdos. f, Amaryllis belladonna.
No. 1563, 4400fr — Orchids: a, Cattleya amethystoglossa. b, Vanda coerulea. c, Orchis robusta. d, Orchis papilionacea. e, Orchis fragrans. f, Orchis italica.

Perf. 13½x13¼, 13¼x13½
2001, Oct. 25
Sheets of 6, #a-f
1554-1563 A446 Set of 10 47.50 47.50

The following items inscribed "Repoblikan'i Madigaskara" have been declared "illegal" by Madagascar postal officials:
Sheets of nine 2000fr stamps: Motorbikes; Concorde; Elephants; Birds (2 different).
Sheets of nine stamps: Dinosaurs.
Sheet of six 5600fr stamps: Mars Exploration.
Sheets of four 5600fr stamps: Chess; Prehistoric horses; Mushrooms and eagles; Mushrooms and cats; Mushrooms and butterflies; Mushrooms and owls (2 different).
Sheet of three 5600fr stamps: Nude females (3 different).
Sheet of four 5000fr stamps: Monet paintings.
Souvenir sheets of one 1750fr stamp: Marilyn Monroe (8 different).
Souvenir sheets of two 7500fr stamps: Marilyn Monroe.
Souvenir sheet of one 12,500fr stamp: J. Baptiste Simeon Chardin.
Souvenir sheets of one: Actors Robert De Niro, Robert Redford and Leonardo DiCaprio; Actress Michelle Pfeiffer; Concorde (2 different); Fire fighting (4 different).

Famous Men — A447

Designs: No. 1564, 1500fr, Rakoto Frah (1925-2001), flutist. No. 1565, 1500fr, Albert Rakoto Ratsimamanga (1907-2001), ambassador.

2002, Oct. 9 Litho. Perf. 13x12¾
1564-1565 A447 Set of 2 2.75 2.75

Primates — A448

Design: 1000fr, Verreaux's sifaka (propheteque de Verreauxi). 2500fr, Lemur catta.

2002, Oct. 9 Litho. Perf. 13x12¾
1566 A448 1000fr multi
1567 A448 2500fr multi 1.75 1.75

Furcifer Pardalis — A448a

2002, Oct. 9 Litho. Perf. 12¾x13
1568 A448a 3000fr multi

Flora — A449

Designs: 100fr, Chorisia ventricosa. 350fr, Eichhornia crassipes, vert. 400fr, Didieraceae. 500fr, Palm tree, Nosy Iranja, vert. 900fr, Ravinala, vert. 4400fr, Takhtajania perrieri. 6800fr, Ravinala, diff., vert.

Perf. 12¾x13, 13x12¾
2002, Oct. 9 Litho.
1569-1575 A449 Set of 7 12.50 12.50

For surcharge, see No. 1621.

MALAGASY REPUBLIC

Diplomatic Relations Between Madagascar and People's Republic of China, 30th Anniv. — A450

2002, Nov. 6   Perf. 12
1576   A450   2500fr multi   1.90   1.90

5 Iraimbilanja = 1 Ariary

Establishment of Japan International Cooperation Agency Bureau in Madagascar — A451

2003, Dec. 4   Litho.   Perf. 13¼x13¼
1577   A451   300a multi   2.25   2.25

The ariary officially replaced the franc on Aug. 1, 2003.

Indri Indri — A452

Denomination color: 500a, Bister. 3000a, White.

2003, Dec. 4   Litho.   Perf. 13¼x13
1578   A452   500a multi   1.75   1.75
1579   A452   3000a multi   —   —

First Catholic Church in Madagascar — A453

House, Falafa — A454

House in High Plateaus — A455

Pirate Cemetery, Ste. Marie — A456

2003, Dec. 4   Litho.   Perf. 13¼x13½
1580   A453   800a multi   2.50   2.50
1581   A454   900a multi   3.00   3.00
1582   A455   1100a multi   3.50   3.50
1583   A456   2000a multi   6.25   6.25
   Nos. 1580-1583 (4)   15.25   15.25

Indian Ocean Commission, 20th Anniv. — A457

2003, Dec. 4   Litho.   Perf. 13¼x13
1584   A457   1200a multi   —

Flowers — A458

Designs: 20a, Xyloolaena perrieri. 100a, Megistostegium microphyllum. 120a, Tambourissa, horiz. 200a, Leptolaena diospyroidea. 300a, Ochna greveanum. 1500a, Schizolaena tampoketsana.

   Perf. 13¼x13, 13x13¼
2003, Dec. 4
1585   A458   20a multi   —   —
1586   A458   100a multi   —   —
1587   A458   120a multi   —   —
1588   A458   200a multi   —   —
1589   A458   300a multi   —   —
1590   A458   1500a multi   —   —

World Health Day — A459

2004, Oct. 9   Litho.   Perf. 13½x13
1591   A459   300a multi   1.75   1.75

Isalo Wolf Rock Formation — A460

Nosy Mitsio — A461

Fort Dauphin — A462

Tamatave A463

Dancers at Rova of Ambohimanga A464

Red Tsingy, Irodo A465

Lemur and Ostriches A466

   Perf. 13¼x13, 13x13¼
2004, Nov. 15   Litho.
1592   A460   400a multi   1.25   .50
1593   A461   600a multi   .60
1594   A462   1000a multi   2.75   1.00
1595   A463   1200a multi   1.25
1596   A464   2000a multi   5.25   1.50
1597   A465   5000a multi   13.00   3.25
1598   A466   10,000a multi   30.00   6.00

Royalty — A467

Designs: 20a, Ranavalona I, 1828-61. 80a, Ranavalona III, 1883-96. 100a, Radama I, 1810-28. 200a, Radama II, 1861-63. 500a, Rasoherina, 1863-68. 800a, Andrianampoinimerina, 1787-1810. 1500a, Ranavalona II, 1863-83.

2004, Nov. 15   Litho.   Perf. 13¼x13
1599-1605   A467   Set of 7   15.00   15.00

For surcharge, see No. 1618.

Rotary International, Cent. — A468

2005, Feb. 23   Perf. 13x13¼
1606   A468   2100a multi   2.60   2.60

Medical Cooperation Between Madagascar and People's Republic of China, 30th Anniv. — A469

No. 1607 — Medical workers, patients and Chinese and Madagascar: a, 1500a, Flags. b, 2300a, Arms.

2005, Dec. 8   Perf. 12
1607   A469   Pair, #a-b   3.50   3.50

Miniature Sheet

Orchids A470

No. 1608, 1500a: a, Aerangis cryptodon. b, Aeranthes grandiflora. c, Aeranthes henrici. d, Aeranthes peyrotii. e, Oeccoclades spathulitera. f, Angraecum sesquipedale. g, Cynorchis elata. h, Angraecum viguieri. i, Gastrochis humblotii. j, Gastrochis lutea. k, Gastrochis pulcher. l, Jumellea sagittata. m, Microcoelia gilpinae. n, Angraecum praestans.

2005, Dec. 29   Perf. 13¼x13
1608   A470   Sheet of 14, #a-n,   + 2 labels   19.50   19.50

Campaign Against AIDS — A471

2006, Feb. 10
1609   A471   300a multi   .40   .40

Mpitandrina Rainimamonjisoa (1805-82) — A472

2006, Mar. 1
1610   A472   300a blk & lt blue   .40   .40

Madagascar Philatelists Association, 20th Anniv. (in 2004) — A473

2006, Mar. 1
1611   A473   300a multi   .40   .40

Léopold Sédar Senghor (1906-2001), First President of Senegal — A474

2006, Mar. 20
1612   A474   2000a multi   2.00   2.00

Seventh Indian Ocean Islands Games — A475

2007, June 22   Litho.   Perf. 13
1613   A475   300a multi   .40   .40

Ile Sainte Marie Whale Festival — A476

Designs: 1100a, Two whales. 3000a, Whale and two fish, vert.

   Perf. 13x13¼, 13¼x13
2007, Aug. 2   Litho.
1614-1615   A476   Set of 2   8.50   8.50

Régis Rajemisa-Raolison (1913-90), Linguist, Founder of Havatsa Upem — A477

2008, May 15   Litho.   Perf. 13
1616   A477   300a red & black   .40   .40

No. 1403E Surcharged

MALAGASY REPUBLIC

No. 1600 Surcharged

Methods and Perfs As Before
2008, Sept. 29
1617 A415a 300a on 5600fr
 #1403E 1.10 1.10
1618 A467 300a on 80a #1600 1.10 1.10
 No. 1617 is airmail.

Postman Delivering Mail — A478
2008, Oct. 21   Litho.   Perf. 13¼x13
1619 A478 100a multi .25 .25

"Post For All" — A479
2009, Oct. 9   Litho.   Perf. 13x13¼
1620 A479 300a multi

Madagascar postal authorities have declared as "illegal" the following stamps inscribed "Madagascar" having the following themes: 90th anniversary of the Chinese Communist Party (from 1999), International Year of Astronomy (from 2009), Pierre Fredy, Baron de Coubertin (from 2012), Richard Wagner (from 2013), 200th anniversary of the Romanov Dynasty (from 2013), and Year of the Monkey (from 2016).

No. 1573 Surcharged

Method and Perf. As Before
2010, May 14
1621 A449 300a on 900fr #1573 .55 .55

Military Forces, 50th Anniv. — A480
Perf. 13¼x13½
2010, June 26   Litho.
1622 A480 300a multi .65 .65

Flowers — A481
Designs: 100a, Physena sessiliflora. 200a, Pentachlaena latifolia. 300a, Rhopalocarpus similis. 500a, Asteropeia amblyocarpa, vert.

2011, Feb. 16   Perf. 13½
1623 A481 100a multi — —
1624 A481 200a multi — —
1625 A481 300a multi — —
1626 A481 500a multi — —
 Dated 2010.

Antananarivo City Hall — A482

Jean Laborde Blast Furnace — A483

Red Cirque of Mahajanga — A484

2013, Jan. 30   Litho.   Perf. 13½
1627 A482 300a multi 1.25 1.25
1628 A483 1600a multi 4.25 4.25
1629 A484 1900a multi 5.25 5.25
 Nos. 1627-1629 (3) 10.75 10.75

Landscapes A485

Designs: Nos. 1630, 1636a, 1500a, Bridge, Tsingy de Bemaraha National Park, Malagasy Republic. Nos. 1632, 1636c, 2500a, Royal Palace, Antananarivo. Nos. 1633, 1636d, 3000a, Heilongjiang, People's Republic of China. No. 1636b, 2100a, Avenue of the Baobabs, Malagasy Republic. No. 1636e, 4000a, Three Gorges, Yellow River, People's Republic of China. No. 1636f, 4200a, Nüwa Palace, People's Republic of China. No. 1634, 4000a, Three Gorges, Yellow River, People's Republic of China. No. 1635, 4200a, Nüwa Palace, People's Republic of China.

2014, May 12   Litho.   Perf. 12
1630 A485 1500a multi — —
1632 A485 2500a multi — —
1633 A485 3000a multi — —
1634 A485 4000a multi — —
1635 A485 4200a multi — —

Litho. With Plastic Lenticular Lens Affixed
1636 A485 Sheet of 6, #a-f — —

One additional item was issued in this set. The editors would like to examine any examples.

Green Turtle — A486
2014, Oct. 9   Litho.   Perf. 13x13¼
1637 A486 1500a multi 1.10 1.10
 See Comoro Islands No., France No. 4695, French Southern & Antarctic Territories No. 511, Mauritius No. 1144, Seychelles No. 904.

Mammals — A487
Designs: 2000a, Hequ horse. 5000a, Zebu. 6000a, Giant pandas. 10,000a, Propithecus coquereli.

2014, July 21   Litho.   Perf. 12
1638 A487 2000a multi — —
1639 A487 5000a multi — —
1640 A487 6000a multi — —
1641 A487 10,000a multi — —
 a. Souvenir sheet of 4, #1638-1641 — —

Beatification of St. John Paul II — A488
2015, May 4   Litho.   Perf. 13¼
1642 A488 2000a multi — —

Nosy Antafana — A489
2015, May 22   Litho.   Perf. 13¼
1643 A489 100a multi — —

Flora and Fauna — A490
Designs: 1500a, Hildegardia ankaranensis. 1600a, Ouratea obtusifolia. 5000a, Propithecus candidus, vert.

2015, June 15   Litho.   Perf. 13¼
1644-1646 A490 Set of 3 — —

16th Francophonie Summit, Antananarivo A491
2016, Nov. 21   Litho.   Perf. 11¼x12
1647 A491 500a multi — —

Nelson Mandela (1918-2013), President of South Africa — A492
2016   Litho.   Perf. 13½x13¾
1648 A492 3500a multi — —

15th World Conference of Grand Masonic Lodges, Antananarivo A493
2017, May 25   Litho.   Perf. 13
1649 A493 10,000a multi — —
 a. Souvenir sheet of 1 + 3 labels — —

Miniature Sheet

A494

Regional Arms and Emblems A495

No. 1651: a, Itasy Region. b, Diana Region. c, Bongolava Region. d, Betsiboka Region. e, Anosy Region. f, Analamanga Region. g, Vatovavy-Fitovinany Region. h, Haute-Matsiatra Region. i, Vakinankaratra Region. j, Sava Region. k, Menabe Region. l, Amoron'i Mania Region.
No. 1652: a, Melaky Region. b, Atsinanana Region. c, Atsimo-Atsinanana Region. d, Atsimo-Andrefana Region. e, Boeny Region. f, Ihorombe Region. g, Analanjirofo Region. h, Androy Region. i, Alaotro-Mangoro Region. j, Sofia Region.

Perf. 13¼; 13¼x13¾ (#1652)
2016   Litho.
1651 A494 500a Sheet of 12, #a-l — —
1652 A495 500a Sheet of 10, #a-j — —

Rotary International District 920 Inner Wheel, 25th Anniv. — A496
2018, Apr. 28   Litho.   Perf. 13x12¾
1653 A496 500a multi — —
 a. Souvenir sheet of 1 — —

SEMI-POSTAL STAMPS

No. 84 Surcharged in Red

1915, Feb.   Unwmk.   Perf. 13½x14
B1 A9 10c + 5c rose & brn 1.50 1.50

Curie Issue
Common Design Type
1938, Oct. 24   Perf. 13
B2 CD80 1.75fr + 50c brt ultra 11.00 11.00

French Revolution Issue
Common Design Type
Name and Value Typographed in Black
1939, July 5   Photo.
B3 CD83 45c + 25c grn 9.50 9.50
B4 CD83 70c + 30c brn 9.50 9.50
B5 CD83 90c + 35c red org 9.50 9.50
B6 CD83 1.25fr + 1fr rose pink 9.50 9.50
B7 CD83 2.25fr + 2fr blue 9.50 9.50
 Nos. B3-B7 (5) 47.50 47.50

MALAGASY REPUBLIC

Common Design Type and

Malgache Sharpshooter SP1

Tank Corpsman SP2

1941		Photo.		Perf. 13½
B8	SP1	1fr + 1fr red		1.50
B9	CD86	1.50fr + 3fr maroon		1.50
B10	SP2	2.50fr + 1fr blue		1.75
		Nos. B8-B10 (3)		4.75

Nos. B8-B10 were issued by the Vichy government in France, but were not placed on sale in Madagascar.

Nos. 162, 190 Surcharged "SECOURS +50c NATIONAL"

1942			
B11	A12	1fr + 50c dk red & car rose	.40
B12	A14	3fr + 50c olive black	.40

Nos. B11-B12 were issued by the Vichy government in France, but were not placed on sale in Madagascar.

Petain Type of 1941 Surcharged in Black or Blue (Bl)

1944	Engr.	Perf. 12½x12
B13	50c + 1.50fr on 2.50fr deep blue (Bl)	.80
B14	+ 2.50fr on 1fr bister brown	.80

Colonial Development Fund. Nos. B13-B14 were issued by the Vichy government in France, but were not placed on sale in Madagascar.

Catalogue values for unused stamps in this section, from this point to the end of the section, are for Never Hinged items.

Red Cross Issue
Common Design Type

1944	Unwmk.	Perf. 14½x14
B15	CD90 5fr + 20fr dk grn	.90 .90

The surtax was for the French Red Cross and national relief.

Gen. J. S. Galliéni and Malagasy Plowing — SP3

1946, Nov.	Engr.	Perf. 13
B16	SP3 10fr + 5fr dk vio brn	.40 .40

50th anniv. of Madagascar's as a French Colony.

Tropical Medicine Issue
Common Design Type

1950, May 15		
B17	CD100 10fr + 2fr dk Prus grn & brn vio	5.50 5.50

The surtax was for charitable work.

Malagasy Republic
No. 320 Surcharged in Ultramarine with New Value and: "FETES DE L'INDEPENDANCE"

1960, July 29	Engr.	Perf. 13
B18	A38 20fr + 10fr red, blk & brt grn	.60 .35

Anti-Malaria Issue
Common Design Type

1962, Apr. 7		Perf. 12½x12
B19	CD108 25fr + 5fr yel grn	.75 .50

Post Office, Tamatave — SP4

1962, May 8	Engr.	Perf. 13
B20	SP4 25fr + 5fr sl grn, bl & lt red brn	.70 .35

Issued for Stamp Day, 1962.

Freedom from Hunger Issue
Common Design Type

1963, Mar. 21		Perf. 13
B21	CD112 25fr + 5fr red org, plum & brn	.60 .45

FAO "Freedom from Hunger" campaign.

Type of 1962
20fr+5fr, Central Parcel P. O., Tananarive.

1963, May 8		Engr.
B22	SP4 20fr + 5fr bl grn & red brn	.60 .35

Issued for Stamp Day, 1963.

Postal Savings and Checking Accounts Building, Tananarive — SP5

1964, May 8	Unwmk.	Perf. 13
B23	SP5 25fr + 5fr bl, bis & dk grn	.80 .50

Issued for Stamp Day, 1964.

No. 457 Surcharged in Violet Blue

1972, June 26	Engr.	Perf. 13
B24	A106 30fr + 20fr multi	.90 .50

Charles de Gaulle memorial.

SP6

1989, June 15		Litho.
B25	SP6 80fr + 20fr Torch bearer	.50 .25

Village games.

SP7

1990, Aug. 7	Litho.	Perf. 12
B26	SP7 100fr+20fr on 80fr+20fr	.45 .25
B27	SP7 350fr+20fr on 250fr+20fr	.80 .35

3rd Indian Ocean Games. Nos. B26-B27 were not issued without surcharge. For surcharge see No. 1471.

AIR POST STAMPS

Airplane and Map of Madagascar — AP1

Perf. 13x13½

1935-41		Photo.	Unwmk.
C1	AP1	50c yellow green	.65 .45
C2	AP1	90c yel grn ('41)	.35
C3	AP1	1.25fr claret	.50 .50
C4	AP1	1.50fr bright blue	.50 .50
C5	AP1	1.60fr br blue ('41)	.35 .35
C6	AP1	1.75fr orange	9.50 3.75
C7	AP1	2fr Prus blue	.90 .45
C8	AP1	3fr dp org ('41)	.35 .35
C9	AP1	3.65fr ol blk ('38)	1.25 .60
C10	AP1	3.90fr turq grn ('41)	.70 .70
C11	AP1	4fr rose	45.00 3.25
C12	AP1	4.50fr black	27.50 2.50
C13	AP1	5.50fr ol blk ('41)	.70 .70
C14	AP1	6fr rose lil ('41)	.70 .70
C15	AP1	6.90fr dl vio ('41)	.70 .70
C16	AP1	8fr rose lilac	1.50 .90
C17	AP1	8.50fr green	1.50 1.10
C18	AP1	9fr ol grn ('41)	.70 .70
C19	AP1	12fr violet brown	1.00 .65
C20	AP1	12.50fr dull violet	2.40 1.00
C21	AP1	15fr org yel ('41)	1.00 12.00
C22	AP1	16fr olive green	1.90 1.25
C23	AP1	20fr dark brown	3.50 1.40
C24	AP1	50fr brt ultra ('38)	6.50 4.50
		Nos. C1,C3-C24 (23)	109.30 39.00

According to some authorities the 90c was not placed on sale in Madagascar.

Airplane and Map of Madagascar — AP1a

Type of 1935-41 without "RF"
1942-44
Map in Red, Tablet & Value in Blue (except #C25)

C25	AP1a	50c yel grn	.25
C25A	AP1a	90c yel grn	.55
C25B	AP1a	1.25fr claret	.30
C25C	AP1a	1.50fr brt black	.50
C25D	AP1a	2fr Prus blue	.50
C25E	AP1a	3.65fr ol blk	.65
C25F	AP1a	4fr rose	.65
C25G	AP1a	4.50fr black	.50
C25H	AP1a	5fr red brown	.90
C25I	AP1a	8fr rose lilac	.90
C25J	AP1a	8.50fr green	.90
C25K	AP1a	10fr green	.65
C25L	AP1a	12.50fr dull violet	.70
C25M	AP1a	16fr ol grn	.70
C25N	AP1a	20fr dk brn	1.25
C25O	AP1a	50fr brt ultra	1.75
		Nos. C25-C25O (16)	11.65

Nos. C25-C25O were issued by the Vichy government in France, but were not placed on sale in Madagascar.

Airplane Over Farm AP1b

1942-44	Engr.	Perf. 13
C26	AP1b 100fr red brown	.65

No. C26 was issued by the Vichy government in France, but was not placed on sale in Madagascar.

Air Post Stamps of 1935-38 Overprinted in Black

1942			Perf. 13x13½
C27	AP1	1.50fr brt bl & red	6.50 6.50
C28	AP1	1.75fr org & red	92.50 92.50
C29	AP1	8fr rose lil & red	2.10 2.10
C30	AP1	12fr vio brn & red	4.00 4.00
C31	AP1	12.50fr dl vio & red	2.50 2.50
C32	AP1	16fr ol grn & red	6.50 6.50
C33	AP1	50fr brt ultra & red	4.00 4.00

Nos. C3, C9, C17 Surcharged in Black

C34	AP1	1fr on 1.25fr	4.75 4.75
C35	AP1	3fr on 3.65fr	1.25 1.25
C36	AP1	8fr on 8.50fr	1.40 1.40
		Nos. C27-C36 (10)	125.50 125.50

Catalogue values for unused stamps in this section, from this point to the end of the section, are for Never Hinged items.

Common Design Type

1943		Photo.	Perf. 14½x14
C37	CD87	1fr dk orange	.25 .25
C38	CD87	1.50fr brt red	.25 .25
C39	CD87	5fr brown red	.40 .35
C40	CD87	10fr black	.40 .35
C41	CD87	25fr ultra	.90 .55
C42	CD87	50fr dk green	1.40 .80
C43	CD87	100fr plum	2.00 1.25
		Nos. C37-C43 (7)	5.60 3.80

Victory Issue
Common Design Type
Perf. 12½

1946, May 8	Unwmk.	Engr.
C44	CD92 8fr brown red	1.00 .35

European victory of the Allied Nations in World War II.

Chad to Rhine Issue
Common Design Types

1946, June 6		
C45	CD93 5fr brt blue	1.50 1.25
C46	CD94 10fr dk car rose	1.60 1.25
C47	CD95 15fr gray grn	1.60 1.25
C48	CD96 20fr brown olive	1.75 1.40
C49	CD97 25fr dk violet	1.75 1.50
C50	CD98 50fr brown org	2.10 1.75
	Nos. C45-C50 (6)	10.30 8.40

Tamatave AP2

Allegory of Air Mail — AP3

Plane over Map of Madagascar — AP4

MALAGASY REPUBLIC

Perf. 13½x12½, 12½x13½

1946 Photo. Unwmk.
C51	AP2	50fr bl vio & car	1.50	.50
C52	AP3	100fr brn & car	4.00	.90
C53	AP4	200fr bl grn & brn	7.50	2.00
		Nos. C51-C53 (3)	13.00	3.40

No. C52 Overprinted in Carmine

1948, Oct. 26 Perf. 12½x13½
C54 AP3 100fr brn & car 45.00 65.00

Issued to publicize the French claim to Antarctic Adelie Land, discovered by Jules S. C. Dumont d'Urville in 1840.

UPU Issue
Common Design Type

1949, July 4 Engr. Perf. 13
C55 CD99 25fr multi 4.00 2.75

Scene Near Bemananga AP5

1952, June 30 Unwmk. Perf. 13
C56 AP5 500fr brn, blk brn & dk grn 25.00 6.50

Liberation Issue
Common Design Type

1954, June 6
C57 CD102 15fr vio & vio brn 3.25 2.00

Pachypodes AP6

Designs: 100fr, Antsirabé viaduct, grey-headed gull. 200fr, Ring-tailed lemurs.

1954, Sept. 20
C58	AP6	50fr dk bl grn & dk grn	3.50	.70
C59	AP6	100fr dp ultra, blk & choc	5.75	1.40
C60	AP6	200fr dk grn & sep	19.00	4.50
		Nos. C58-C60 (3)	28.25	6.60

Malagasy Republic

Sugar Cane Harvest AP7

Charaxes Antamboulou — AP8

Designs: 40fr, Tobacco field. 100fr, Chrysiridia Madagascariensis. 200fr, Argema mittrel, vert. 500fr, Mandrare bridge.

1960 Unwmk. Engr. Perf. 13
C61	AP7	30fr grn, vio brn & pale brn	2.00	.25
C62	AP7	40fr Prus grn & ol gray	2.00	.25
C63	AP8	50fr multi	3.50	.35
C64	AP8	100fr sl grn, emer & org	5.00	.50
C65	AP8	200fr pur & yel	7.50	1.40
C66	AP7	500fr Prus grn, bis & ultra	12.00	2.50
		Nos. C61-C66 (6)	32.00	5.25

Diademed Sifakas AP9

Lemurs: 85fr, Indri. 250fr, Verreaux's sifaka.

1961, Dec. 9 Unwmk. Perf. 13
C67	AP9	65fr slate grn & red brn	1.50	.70
C68	AP9	85fr olive, blk & brn	3.75	1.00
C69	AP9	250fr Prus grn, blk & mar	6.50	2.75
		Nos. C67-C69 (3)	11.75	4.45

For surcharge see No. C90.

Plane over Nossi-Bé — AP10

1962, May 7 Engr. Perf. 13
C70 AP10 100fr red brn, bl & dk grn 1.75 .60
 a. Souv. sheet of 5, #328-331, C70 5.00 1.50

1st Malagasy Philatelic Exhibition, Tananarive, May 5-13.

Turbojet Airliner, Emblem AP11

1963, Apr. 18 Unwmk. Perf. 13
C71 AP11 500fr dk bl, red & grn 8.00 3.25

Madagascar commercial aviation.

Helmet Bird AP12

Birds: 100fr, Pitta-like ground roller. 200fr, Crested wood ibis.

1963, Aug. 12 Photo. Perf. 13x12½
C72	AP12	40fr multi	1.75	.65
C73	AP12	100fr multi	4.00	1.25
C74	AP12	200fr multi	7.00	2.25
		Nos. C72-C74 (3)	12.75	4.15

African Postal Union Issue
Common Design Type

1963, Sept. 8 Perf. 12½
C75 CD114 85fr grn, ocher & red 1.25 .80

Map of Madagascar, Jet Plane and UPU Emblem — AP13

1963, Nov. 2 Engr. Perf. 13
| C76 | AP13 | 45fr dk car, grnsh bl & ultra | .65 | .25 |
| C77 | AP13 | 85fr dk car, vio & bl | 1.10 | .50 |

Malagasy Republic's admission to the UPU, Nov. 2, 1961.

Meteorological Center, Tananarive and Tiros Satellite — AP14

1964, Mar. 23 Unwmk.
C78 AP14 90fr org brn, ultra & grn 1.50 .90

UN 4th World Meteorological Day, Mar. 23.

Zebu, Wood Sculpture — AP15

1964, Oct. 20 Engr. Perf. 13
C79 AP15 100fr lil rose, dk vio & brn 1.75 .90

Musical Instrument Type of Regular Issue
200fr, Lokanga bara (stringed instrument).

1965, Feb. 16 Unwmk. Perf. 13
Size: 26x47mm
C80 A57 200fr grn, org & choc 4.50 2.00

Nurse Weighing Infant, and ICY Emblem AP16

Design: 100fr, Small boy and girl, child care scenes and ICY emblem.

1965, Sept. 20 Engr. Perf. 13
| C81 | AP16 | 50fr multi | .55 | .25 |
| C82 | AP16 | 100fr multi | 1.10 | .55 |

International Cooperation Year.

Dance Type of Regular Issue
250fr, Dance of a young girl, Sakalava, vert.

1966, June 13 Photo. Perf. 13
Size: 27x49mm
C83 A68 250fr multi 4.75 2.00

Aviation Type of Regular Issue
Design: 500fr, Dagnaux and his Bréguet biplane, 1927.

1967, Apr. 28 Engr. Perf. 13
Size: 48x27mm
C84 A76 500fr Prus bl, blk & brn 9.00 4.00

No. C84 for the 40th anniv. of the 1st Majunga-Tananarive flight.

African Postal Union Issue, 1967
Common Design Type

1967, Sept. 9 Engr. Perf. 13
C85 CD124 100fr ol bis, red brn & brt pink 1.25 .60

Dancer Type of Regular Issue
Designs: 100fr, Tourbillon dance, horiz. 200fr, Male dancer from the South.

1967-68 Photo. Perf. 11½
Size: 38x23mm
C86 A80 100fr multi ('68) 2.00 .60
Perf. 13
Size: 27x48mm
C87 A80 200fr multi 4.00 1.40

Issue dates: 100fr, Nov. 25; 200fr, Nov. 25.

WHO Emblem, Bull's Head Totem and Palm Fan — AP17

1968, Apr. 7 Photo. Perf. 12½x13
C88 AP17 200fr bl, yel brn & red 2.00 .90

WHO, 20th anniv.; Intl. Congress of Medical Science, Apr. 2-12.

Tananarive-Ivato International Airport.— AP18

1968, May 8 Engr. Perf. 13
C89 AP18 500fr lt red brn, dl bl & dl grn 6.75 3.00

Issued for Stamp Day.

No. C68 Surcharged in Vermilion with New Value and 2 Bars

1968, June 24 Engr. Perf. 13
C90 AP9 20fr on 85fr multi .75 .25

PHILEXAFRIQUE Issue

Lady Sealing Letter, by Jean Baptiste Santerre — AP19

1968, Dec. 30 Photo. Perf. 12½x12
C91 AP19 100fr lilac & multi, with label 3.25 .70

Issued to publicize PHILEXAFRIQUE Philatelic Exhibition in Abidjan, Feb. 14-23. Printed with alternating lilac label.

2nd PHILEXAFRIQUE Issue
Common Design Type

Design: 50fr, Madagascar No. 274, map of Madagascar and Malagasy emblem.

1969, Feb. 14 Engr. Perf. 13
C92 CD128 50fr gray, brn red & sl grn 1.75 .85

Sunset over Madagascar Highlands, by Henri Ratovo AP20

Painting: 100fr, On the Seashore of the East Coast of Madagascar, by Alfred Razafinjohany.

1969, Nov. 5 Photo. Perf. 12x12½
| C93 | AP20 | 100fr brn & multi | 1.50 | .65 |
| C94 | AP20 | 150fr multi | 3.00 | 1.25 |

MALAGASY REPUBLIC

Lunar Landing Module and Man on the Moon — AP21

1970, July 20   **Engr.**   **Perf. 13**
C95   AP21   75fr ultra, dk gray & sl grn   1.25   .40

1st anniv. of man's 1st landing on the moon.

Boeing 737 — AP22

1970, Dec. 18   **Engr.**   **Perf. 13**
C96   AP22   200fr bl, red brn & grn   3.00   .90

Jean Ralaimongo (1884-1944) — AP23

Portraits: 40fr, René Rakotobe (1918-71). 65fr, Albert Sylla (1909-67). 100fr, Joseph Ravoahangy Andrianavalona (1893-1970).

1971-72   **Photo.**   **Perf. 12½; 13 (40fr)**
C97   AP23   25fr red brn, org & blk   .40   .25
C98   AP23   40fr dp cl, ocher & blk   .60   .25
C99   AP23   65fr grn, lt grn & blk   .50   .25
C100   AP23   100fr vio bl, lt bl & blk   1.25   .35
Nos. C97-C100 (4)   2.75   1.10

Famous Malagasy men.
Issued: No. C98, 7/25/72; others, 10/14/71.

African Postal Union Issue

"Mpisikidy" by G. Rakotovao and UAMPT Building, Brazzaville, Congo — AP24

1971, Nov. 13   **Photo.**   **Perf. 13x13½**
C105   AP24   100fr bl & multi   1.25   .45

10th anniv. of African and Malagasy Posts and Telecommunications Union (UAMPT).

Running Olympic Village — AP25

Design: 200fr, Judo, Olympic Stadium.

1972, Sept. 11   **Photo.**   **Perf. 13½**
C106   AP25   100fr multi   1.40   .60
C107   AP25   200fr multi   2.50   .85

20th Olympic Games, Munich, 8/26-9/11.

Mohair Goat — AP26

1972, Nov. 15
C108   AP26   250fr multi   5.00   1.60

Adoration of the Kings, by Andrea Mantegna AP27

Christmas: 85fr, Virgin and Child, Florentine School, 15th century, vert.

1972, Dec. 15   **Photo.**   **Perf. 13**
C109   AP27   85fr gold & multi   1.00   .45
C110   AP27   150fr gold & multi   2.25   .70

Landing Module, Astronauts and Lunar Rover — AP28

1973, Jan. 25   **Engr.**   **Perf. 13**
C111   AP28   300fr dp cl, gray & brn   4.00   1.40

Apollo 17 moon mission, Dec. 7-19, 1972.

The Burial of Christ, by Grunewald AP29

Easter: 200fr, Resurrection, by Mattias Grunewald, vert. Both paintings from panels of Issenheim altar.

1973, Mar. 22   **Photo.**   **Perf. 13**
C112   AP29   100fr gold & multi   1.25   .45
C113   AP29   200fr gold & multi   2.75   .70

Early Excursion Car — AP30

Design: 150fr, Early steam locomotive.

1973, July 25   **Photo.**   **Perf. 13x12½**
C114   AP30   100fr multi   1.50   .70
C115   AP30   150fr multi   2.25   1.00

WMO Emblem, Radar, Map of Madagascar, Hurricane — AP31

1973, Sept. 3   **Engr.**   **Perf. 13**
C116   AP31   100fr blk, ultra & org   1.50   .50

Cent. of intl. meteorological cooperation.

Lemur Type of Regular Issue

Designs: 150fr, Lepilemur mustelinus, vert. 200fr, Cheirogaleus major.

1973, Oct. 9   **Engr.**   **Perf. 13**
C117   A131   150fr multi   2.75   .90
C118   A131   200fr multi   4.25   1.40

Pres. John F. Kennedy, US Flag — AP32

1973, Nov. 22   **Photo.**   **Perf. 13**
C119   AP32   300fr multi   3.00   1.40

10th anniv. of the death of John F. Kennedy.

Soccer AP33

1973, Dec. 20   **Engr.**   **Perf. 13**
C120   AP33   500fr lil rose, dk brn & org brn   5.50   2.00

World Soccer Cup, Munich, 1974.
For overprint see No. C130.

Copernicus, Ranger and Heliocentric System AP34

1974, Jan. 22
C121   AP34   250fr multi   4.00   1.10

500th anniversary of the birth of Nicolaus Copernicus (1473-1543), Polish astronomer.

Scout Type of Regular Issue

Designs (African Scout Emblem and): 100fr, Scouts bringing sick people to Red Cross tent, horiz. 300fr, Scouts fishing and fish, horiz.

1974, Feb. 14   **Engr.**   **Perf. 13**
C122   A132   100fr multi   1.00   .35
C123   A132   300fr multi   3.00   1.00

Camellia, Hummingbird, Table Tennis Player — AP35

100fr, Girl player, flower and bird design.

1974, Mar. 19   **Engr.**   **Perf. 13**
C124   AP35   50fr bl & multi   1.00   .30
C125   AP35   100fr multi   1.75   .60

Table Tennis Tournament, Peking.

Autorail Micheline AP36

Malagasy Locomotives: 85fr, Track inspection trolley. 200fr, Garratt (steam).

1974, June 7   **Engr.**   **Perf. 13**
C126   AP36   50fr multi   .75   .35
C127   AP36   85fr multi   1.25   .45
C128   AP36   200fr multi   3.00   .95
Nos. C126-C128 (3)   5.00   1.75

Letters and UPU Emblem AP37

1974, July 9   **Engr.**   **Perf. 13**
C129   AP37   250fr multi   3.50   1.10

Centenary of Universal Postal Union.
For overprint see No. C133.

No. C120 Overprinted: "R.F.A. 2 / HOLLANDE 1"

1974, Aug. 20   **Engr.**   **Perf. 13**
C130   AP33   500fr multi   5.00   2.00

World Cup Soccer Championship, 1974, victory of German Federal Republic.

Link-up in Space, Globe, Emblem AP38

250fr, Link-up, globe and emblem, diff.

1974, Sept. 12
C131   AP38   150fr org, bl & slate grn   1.25   .65
C132   AP38   250fr bl, brn & slate grn   2.75   .90

Russo-American space cooperation
For overprints see Nos. C142-C143.

No. C129 Overprinted

1974, Oct. 9   **Engr.**   **Perf. 13**
C133   AP37   250fr multi   2.00   .70

100 years of international collaboration.

Adoration of the Kings, by J. L. David — AP39

Christmas: 300fr, Virgin of the Cherries and Child, by Quentin Massys.

1974, Dec. 20   **Photo.**   **Perf. 13**
C134   AP39   200fr gold & multi   2.25   .60
C135   AP39   300fr gold & multi   3.50   1.10

UN Emblem and Globe AP40

1975, June 24   **Litho.**   **Perf. 12½**
C136   AP40   300fr grn, bl & blk   3.00   .90

United Nations Charter, 30th anniversary.

American Bicentennial Type, 1975

Designs: 100fr, Count d'Estaing and "Languedoc." 200fr, John Paul Jones, "Bonhomme Richard" and "Serapis." 300fr, Benjamin Franklin, "Millern" and "Montgomery." 500fr, George Washington and "Hanna."

93

MALAGASY REPUBLIC

1975, June 30 **Litho.** *Perf. 11*
C137 A144 100fr multi 1.00 .30
C138 A144 200fr multi 2.00 .50
C139 A144 300fr multi 3.00 .75
  Nos. C137-C139 (3) 6.00 1.55
Souvenir Sheet
C140 A144 500fr multi 7.00 1.50
  For overprints see Nos. C164-C167.

Flower Type of 1975
Design: 85fr, Turraea sericea.

1975, Aug. 4 **Photo.** *Perf. 12½*
C141 A145 85fr dp grn, yel & org 1.90 .90

Nos. C131-C132 Overprinted

1975, Aug. 5 **Engr.** *Perf. 13*
C142 AP38 150fr multi 1.25 .45
C143 AP38 250fr multi 2.40 .75
Apollo Soyuz link-up in space, July 17, 1975.

Bas-relief and Stupas AP41

1975, Aug. 10 **Engr.** *Perf. 13*
C144 AP41 50fr bl, car & bister 1.40 .35
UNESCO campaign to save Borobudur Temple, Java.

Exposition Type, 1975
1975, Sept. 16 **Litho.** *Perf. 14x13½*
C145 A147 125fr Deer 1.90 .45
Souvenir Sheet
C146 A147 300fr Jay 4.75 1.00

Hurdling and Olympic Rings AP42

1975, Oct. 9 **Litho.** *Perf. 12½*
C147 AP42 75fr multi .90 .30
C148 AP42 200fr multi 2.10 .70
Pre-Olympic Year 1975.

12th Winter Olympics Type, 1975
Designs: 200fr, Cross-country skiing. 245fr, Down-hill skiing. 450fr, Figure skating, pairs.

1975, Nov. 19 *Perf. 14*
C149 A149 200fr multi 2.25 .55
C150 A149 245fr multi 2.40 .65
Souvenir Sheet
C151 A149 450fr multi 3.75 1.40
For overprints see Nos. C161-C163.

Landing Module, Apollo 14 Emblem — AP43

1976, Jan. 18 **Engr.** *Perf. 13*
C152 AP43 150fr red, grn & ind 1.50 .50
Apollo 14 moon landing, 5th anniversary. For overprint see No. C157.

21st Summer Olympics Type, 1976
Designs: 100fr, Shot-put and long jump. 200fr, Gymnastics, horse and balance bar. 300fr, Diving, 3-meter and platform. 500fr, Swimming, free-style and breast stroke.

1976, Jan. 21 **Litho.** *Perf. 13½*
C153 A151 100fr multi 1.00 .30
C154 A151 200fr multi 1.90 .60
C155 A151 300fr multi 2.75 .90
  Nos. C153-C155 (3) 5.65 1.80
Souvenir Sheet
C156 A151 500fr multi 4.50 1.40
For overprints see Nos. C168-C171.

No. C152 Overprinted: "5e Anniversaire / de la mission / APOLLO XIV"

1976, Feb. 5 **Engr.** *Perf. 13*
C157 AP43 150fr red, grn & indigo 1.75 .70
Apollo 14 moon landing, 5th anniversary.

Zeppelin Type of 1976
Designs (Count Zeppelin and LZ-127 over): 200fr, Brandenburg Gate, Berlin 300fr, Parliament, London. 450fr, St. Peter's Cathedral, Rome.

1976, Mar. 3 **Litho.** *Perf. 11*
C158 A152 200fr multi 2.50 .60
C159 A152 300fr multi 3.75 .90
Souvenir Sheet
C160 A152 450fr multi 5.50 1.40

Nos. C149-C151 Overprinted

(a)

(b)

(c)

1976, June 17
C161 A149 (a) 200fr multi 1.60 .60
C162 A149 (b) 245fr multi 2.10 .80
Souvenir Sheet
C163 A149 (c) 450fr multi 4.50 2.75
12th Winter Olympic games winners.

Nos. C137-C140 Overprinted in Black

1976, July 4
C164 A144 100fr multi 1.00 .30
C165 A144 200fr multi 2.00 .60
C166 A144 300fr multi 2.75 .90
  Nos. C164-C166 (3) 5.75 1.80
Souvenir Sheet
C167 A144 500fr multi 4.00 2.75
American Bicentennial.

Nos. C153-C156 Overprinted

(a)

(b)

(c)

(d)

1977, Jan.
C168 A151 (a) 100fr multi 1.00 .30
C169 A151 (b) 200fr multi 2.00 .65
C170 A151 (c) 300fr multi 2.75 .90
  Nos. C168-C170 (3) 5.75 1.85
Souvenir Sheet
C171 A151 (d) 500fr multi 4.50 2.75
21st Summer Olympic Games winners.

Fauna Type of 1979
1979, July 6
C172 A176 20fr Tortoises .45 .25
C173 A176 95fr Macaco lemurs 1.20 .25

International Palestinian Solidarity Day — AP44

1979, Nov. 29 **Litho.** *Perf. 12x12½*
C174 AP44 60fr multi .60 .25

Olympic Type of 1980
1980, Dec. 29 **Litho.** *Perf. 12½x12*
C175 A188 250fr Judo 1.90 .70
C176 A188 500fr Swimming 3.75 1.50

Stamp Day — AP45

1981, Dec. 17 **Litho.** *Perf. 12x12½*
C177 AP45 90fr multi .75 .25

20th Anniv. of Pan-African Women's Org. — AP46

1982, Aug. 6 **Litho.** *Perf. 12*
C178 AP46 80fr dk brn & lt brn .70 .25

Hydroelectric Plant, Andekaleka — AP47

1982, Sept. 13 *Perf. 12½x12*
C179 AP47 80fr multi .70 .25

Orchid Type of 1984
No. C180, Eulophiella elisabethae, horiz. No. C181, Grammangis ellisii, horiz. No. C182, Grammangis spectabilis.

1984, Nov. 20 **Litho.** *Perf. 12*
C180 A226 50fr multi 1.00 .25
C181 A226 50fr multi 1.00 .25
C182 A226 50fr multi 1.00 .25
  Nos. C180-C182 (3) 3.00 .75

Solar Princess, by Sadiou Diouf — AP48

1984, Dec. 22 **Litho.** *Perf. 12*
C183 AP48 100fr multi .90 .25
Intl. Civil Aviation Org., 40th anniv.

Halley's Comet — AP49

1986, Apr. 5 **Litho.** *Perf. 12½x13*
C184 AP49 150fr multi 1.25 .50

Admission of Madagascar into the UPU, 25th Anniv. — AP50

1986, Dec. 23 **Litho.** *Perf. 11½*
C185 AP50 150fr multi 1.25 .40

Air Madagascar, 25th Anniv. — AP51

1987, June 17 **Litho.** *Perf. 12x12½*
C186 AP51 60fr Piper Aztec .55 .25
C187 AP51 60fr Twin Otter .55 .25
C188 AP51 150fr Boeing 747 1.10 .30
  Nos. C186-C188 (3) 2.20 .80

Socialist Revolution, 15th Anniv. — AP52

1990, June 16 **Litho.** *Perf. 13½*
C189 AP52 100fr Map .25 .25
C190 AP52 350fr Architecture .60 .30

MALAGASY REPUBLIC

Madagascan Bible Society, 25th Anniv. — AP53

1990, Sept. 17   **Perf. 12½**
C191 AP53 25fr lt bl & multi .25 .25
C192 AP53 100fr lt bl, blk & grn, vert. .30 .25

Stamp Day AP54

1990, Oct. 9   **Litho.**   **Perf. 13x12½**
C193 AP54 350fr multicolored 1.25 .30

World Environment Day — AP55

1992, June 5   **Litho.**   **Perf. 12½**
C194 AP55 140fr multicolored .50 .25

World Post Day — AP56

1992, Oct. 9   **Litho.**   **Perf. 13½**
C195 AP56 500fr multicolored .80 .35

Girl Guides, 50th Anniv. — AP57

1993, Aug.   **Litho.**   **Perf. 11½**
C196 AP57 140fr multicolored .50 .25

AP58

1993, Nov. 20   **Litho.**   **Perf. 12**
C197 AP58 500fr multicolored .90 .40
African Industrialization Day.

Zone A Conference — AP59

1994   **Litho.**   **Perf. 11½x11, 11x11½**
C198 AP59 140fr shown .25 .25
C199 AP59 500fr Logo, vert. .70 .40

Madagascar Hilton, 25th Anniv. — AP60

1995, Oct. 8   **Litho.**   **Perf. 13½**
C200 AP60 500fr black, blue & bister .80 .60

ACCT, 25th Anniv. — AP60a

1996, Aug. 9   **Litho.**   **Perf. 14¾x15**
C200A AP60a 500fr multi .70 .45

FAO, 50th Anniv. — AP60b

Designs: 140fr, Map, FAO emblem, grains. 500fr, FAO emblem, map, grains, diff.

1995, Aug. 16   **Litho.**   **Perf. 15**
C200B AP60b 140fr multi
C200C AP60b 500fr multi
Set of 2 130.00 130.00

UN Industrial Development Organization, 30th Anniv. — AP60c

   Perf. 11¾x11½
1996, June 17   **Litho.**
Granite Paper
C200D AP60c 140fr multi .25 .25

Souvenir Sheet

Zheng He, Chinese Navigator — AP61

1998   **Litho.**   **Perf. 13½**
C201 AP61 5700fr multicolored 3.00 1.50

AIR POST SEMI-POSTAL STAMPS

French Revolution Issue
Common Design Type
Unwmk.
1939, July 5   **Photo.**   **Perf. 13**
Name and Value in Orange
CB1 CD83 4.50fr + 4fr brn blk 18.00 18.00

"Maternity" Statue at Tannarive City Hall — SPAP1

Manankavaly Free Milk Station — SPAP2

Mother & Children SPAP3

1942, June 22   **Engr.**   **Perf. 13**
CB2 SPAP1 1.50fr + 3.50fr lt grn .65
CB3 SPAP2 2fr + 6fr yel brn .65
CB4 SPAP3 3fr + 9fr car red .65
Nos. CB2-CB4 (3) 1.95
Native children's welfare fund.
Nos. CB2-CB4 were issued by the Vichy government in France, but were not placed on sale in Madagascar.

Colonial Education Fund
Common Design Type
1942, June 22
CB5 CD86a 1.20fr + 1.80fr blue & red .65
No. CB5 was issued by the Vichy government in France, but was not placed on sale in Madagascar.

POSTAGE DUE STAMPS

Postage Due Stamps and Types of French Colonies Overprinted in Red or Blue

1896   **Unwmk.**   **Imperf.**
J1 D1 5c blue (R) 12.00 9.50
J2 D1 10c brown (R) 11.00 8.00
J3 D1 20c yellow (Bl) 10.00 8.00
J4 D1 30c rose red (Bl) 11.00 8.00
J5 D1 40c lilac (R) 80.00 50.00
J6 D1 50c gray vio (Bl) 18.00 9.00
J7 D1 1fr dk grn (R) 80.00 65.00
Nos. J1-J7 (7) 222.00 157.50

Governor's Palace — D2

1908-24   **Typo.**   **Perf. 13½x14**
J8 D2 2c vio brn .25 .25
J9 D2 4c violet .25 .25
J10 D2 5c green .25 .25
J11 D2 10c deep rose .25 .25
J12 D2 20c olive green .40 .40
J13 D2 40c brn, straw .45 .45
J14 D2 50c brn, bl .60 .60
J15 D2 60c orange ('24) .60 .60
J16 D2 1fr dark blue 1.10 1.10
Nos. J8-J16 (9) 4.15 4.15

Type of 1908 Issue Surcharged

1924-27
J17 D2 60c on 1fr org 1.90 1.90

Surcharged

J18 D2 2fr on 1fr lil rose ('27) .90 .90
J19 D2 3fr on 1fr ultra ('27) .90 .90

Postage Due Stamps of 1908-27 Ovptd. or Srchd. in Black

1943   **Perf. 13½x14**
J20 D2 10c dp rose .95 .95
J21 D2 20c olive grn .95 .95
J22 D2 30c on 5c green .95 .95
J23 D2 40c brn, straw 1.00 1.00
J24 D2 50c brn, blue 1.40 1.40
J25 D2 60c orange .95 .95
J26 D2 1fr dark blue .95 .95
J27 D2 1fr on 2c vio brn 4.50 4.50
J28 D2 2fr on 1fr lil rose 1.10 1.10
J29 D2 2fr on 4c vio 2.10 2.10
J30 D2 3fr on 1fr ultra 1.25 1.25
Nos. J20-J30 (11) 16.10 16.10

Catalogue values for unused stamps in this section, from this point to the end of the section, are for Never Hinged items.

D3

1947   **Photo.**   **Perf. 13**
J31 D3 10c dk violet .25 .25
J32 D3 30c brown .25 .25
J33 D3 50c dk bl grn .25 .25
J34 D3 1fr dp orange .25 .25
J35 D3 2fr red violet .45 .45
J36 D3 3fr red brown .45 .45
J37 D3 4fr blue .50 .50
J38 D3 5fr henna brown .55 .55
J39 D3 10fr slate green .70 .70
J40 D3 20fr vio blue 1.75 1.75
Nos. J31-J40 (10) 5.40 5.40

Malagasy Republic

Independence Monument — D4

Engraved; Denomination Typographed
1962, May 7   **Unwmk.**   **Perf. 13**
J41 D4 1fr brt green .25 .25
J42 D4 2fr copper brn .25 .25
J43 D4 3fr brt violet .25 .25
J44 D4 4fr slate .25 .25
J45 D4 5fr red .25 .25
J46 D4 10fr yellow grn .25 .25
J47 D4 20fr dull claret .25 .25
J48 D4 40fr blue .55 .55
J49 D4 50fr rose red .85 .85
J50 D4 100fr black 1.60 1.60
Nos. J41-J50 (10) 4.75 4.75

MALAWI

mə-'lä-wē

LOCATION — Southeast Africa
GOVT. — Republic in British Commonwealth
AREA — 36,100 sq. mi.
POP. — 19,130,000 (2020 est.)
CAPITAL — Lilongwe

The British Protectorate of Nyasaland became the independent state of Malawi on July 6, 1964, and a republic on July 6, 1966.

12 Pence = 1 Shilling
20 Shillings = 1 Pound
100 Tambalas = 1 Kwacha (1970)

Catalogue values for all unused stamps in this country are for Never Hinged items.

Watermark

Wmk. 357 — Multiple Cockerel

Dr. H. Kamuzu Banda and Independence Monument — A1

Prime Minister Banda and: 6p, Sun rising from lake. 1sh3p, National flag. 2sh6p, Coat of Arms.

1964, July 6   Unwmk.   Perf. 14½   Photo.

1	A1	3p dk gray & lt ol green	.25	.50
2	A1	6p car rose, red, gold & bl	.25	.25
3	A1	1sh3p dull vio, blk, red & grn	.30	.25
4	A1	2sh6p multicolored	.25	.75
a.		Blue omitted	2,750.	
		Nos. 1-4 (4)	1.30	1.75

Malawi's independence, July 6, 1964.

Mother and Child — A2

Designs: 1p, Chambo fish. 2p, Zebu bull. 3p, Peanuts. 4p, Fishermen in boat. 6p, Harvesting tea. 9p, Tung nut, flower and leaves. 1sh, Lumber and tropical pine branch. 1sh3p, Tobacco drying and Turkish tobacco plant. 2sh6p, Cotton industry. 5sh, Monkey Bay, Lake Nyasa. 10sh, Afzelia tree (pod mahogany). £1, Nyala antelope, vert.

1964, July 6   Size: 23x19mm

5	A2	½p lilac	.25	.50
6	A2	1p green & black	.25	.25
7	A2	2p red brown	.30	.25
8	A2	3p pale brn, brn red & grn	.30	.25
9	A2	4p org yel & indigo	.95	.25

Size: 41½x25, 25x41½mm

10	A2	6p bl, vio bl & brt yel grn	.80	.25
11	A2	9p grn, yel & brn	.50	.25
12	A2	1sh yel, brn & dk green	.35	.25
13	A2	1sh3p red brn & olive	.65	.45
14	A2	2sh6p blue & brown	1.40	1.10
15	A2	5sh multicolored	1.25	3.25
16	A2	10sh org brn, grn & gray	2.25	2.25
17	A2	£1 yel & dk brn	7.50	6.00
		Nos. 5-17 (13)	16.75	15.50

See Nos. 26, 41-51. For surcharges see Nos. 27-28.

Star of Bethlehem over World — A3

1964, Dec. 1   Photo.   Perf. 14½

18	A3	3p brt green & gold	.25	.25
19	A3	6p lilac rose & gold	.25	.25
20	A3	1sh3p lilac & gold	.25	.25
21	A3	2sh6p ultra & gold	.25	.30
a.		Souvenir sheet of 4	1.50	1.50
		Nos. 18-21 (4)	1.00	1.05

Christmas. No. 21a contains Nos. 18-21 with simulated perforations.

Sixpence, Shilling, Florin and Half-Crown Coins — A4

1965, Mar. 1   Unwmk.   Perf. 13x13½
Coins in Silver and Black

22	A4	3p green	.25	.25
23	A4	9p rose	.25	.25
a.		Silver omitted	—	
24	A4	1sh6p rose violet	.25	.25
25	A4	3sh dark blue	.30	.75
a.		Souvenir sheet of 4	1.60	1.60
		Nos. 22-25 (4)	1.05	1.50

First coinage of Malawi. No. 25a contains Nos. 22-25 with simulated perforations. Sold for 6sh.

Type of 1964 Redrawn
1965, June 1   Photo.   Perf. 14½

26	A2	5sh "Monkey Bay-Lake Malawi"	6.00	1.25

Nos. 13-14 Surcharged with New Value and Two Bars
1965, June 14

27	A2	1sh6p on 1sh3p	.50	.25
28	A2	3sh on 2sh6p	.35	.25

John Chilembwe, Rebels and Church at Mbwombwe — A5

1965, Aug. 20   Photo.   Perf. 14½

29	A5	3p yel grn & purple	.25	.25
30	A5	9p red org & olive	.25	.25
31	A5	1sh6p dk & red brn	.25	.25
32	A5	3sh dull bl & green	.25	.25
a.		Souvenir sheet of 4, #29-32	7.00	7.00
		Nos. 29-32 (4)	1.00	1.00

50th anniversary of the revolution of Jan. 23, 1915, led by John Chilembwe (1871-1915), missionary.

Microscope and Open Book — A6

1965, Oct. 6   Perf. 14

33	A6	3p emer & slate	.25	.25
34	A6	9p brt rose & slate	.25	.25
35	A6	1sh6p purple & slate	.25	.25
36	A6	3sh ultra & slate	.25	.30
a.		Souvenir sheet of 4, #33-36	4.75	4.75
		Nos. 33-36 (4)	1.00	1.05

Opening of the University of Malawi in temporary quarters in Chichiri secondary school, Blantyre. The University will be located in Zomba.

African Danaine — A7

Designs: Various butterflies.

1966, Feb. 15   Perf. 13x13½   Unwmk.

37	A7	4p multicolored	1.25	.25
38	A7	9p multicolored	2.00	.25
39	A7	1sh6p lil, blk & blue	2.25	.45
40	A7	3sh blue, dk brn & bis	3.50	6.75
a.		Souvenir sheet of 4, #37-40	22.50	22.50
		Nos. 37-40 (4)	9.00	7.70

See No. 51.

Type of 1964

Designs: ½p, Mother & Child. 1p, Chambo fish. 2p, Zebu bull. 3p, Peanuts. 6p, Harvesting tea. 9p, Tung nut, flower and leaves. 1sh, Lumber and tropical pine branch. 1sh6p, Curing tobacco and Burley tobacco plant. 5sh, Monkey Bay, Lake Nyasa. 10sh, Afzelia tree (pod mahogany). £2, Cyrestis camillus sublineatus (butterfly).

Wmk. 357
1966-67   Photo.   Perf. 14½
Size: 23x19mm

41	A2	½p lilac	.25	.25
42	A2	1p green & black	.25	.25
43	A2	2p red brown ('67)	.25	.25
44	A2	3p multi ('67)	.25	.25

Size: 41½x25mm

45	A2	6p blue, vio bl & brt yel grn ('67)	2.00	.80
46	A2	9p grn, yel & brn ('67)	2.25	.25
47	A2	1sh yel, brn & dk green	.30	.25
48	A2	1sh6p choc & emer	.50	.25
49	A2	5sh multi ('67)	7.00	2.75
50	A2	10sh org brn, grn & gray ('67)	17.50	19.00
51	A7	£2 dl vio, yel & blk	27.50	26.00
		Nos. 41-51 (11)	58.05	50.30

British Central Africa Stamp 1891 — A8

1966, May 4   Perf. 14½

54	A8	4p yel grn & sl blue	.25	.25
55	A8	9p dull rose & sl blue	.25	.25
56	A8	1sh6p lil & slate blue	.25	.25
57	A8	3sh blue & slate blue	.25	.50
a.		Souvenir sheet of 4, #54-57	6.00	6.00
		Nos. 54-57 (4)	1.00	1.25

Postal service, 75th anniv.

President Kamuzu Banda — A9

Perf. 14x14½
1966, July 6   Wmk. 357

58	A9	4p green, sil & brn	.25	.25
59	A9	9p magenta, sil & brn	.25	.25
60	A9	1sh6p violet, sil & brn	.25	.25
61	A9	3sh blue, sil & brn	.25	.25
a.		Souvenir sheet of 4, #58-61	2.50	2.50
		Nos. 58-61 (4)	1.00	1.00

Republic Day, July 6, 1966; 2nd anniv. of Independence.

Star over Bethlehem — A10

1966, Oct. 12   Photo.   Perf. 14½x14

63	A10	4p dp green & gold	.25	.25
64	A10	9p plum & gold	.25	.25
65	A10	1sh6p orange & gold	.25	.25
66	A10	3sh deep blue & gold	.25	.50
		Nos. 63-66 (4)	1.00	1.25

Christmas.

Ilala I, 1875 — A11

Steamers on Lake Malawi: 9p, Dove, 1892. 1sh6p, Chauncey Maples, 1901. 3sh, Guendolen, 1899.

1967, Jan. 4   Perf. 14½x14

67	A11	4p emer, blk & yel	.45	.25
a.		Yellow omitted	750.00	
68	A11	9p car rose, blk & yel	.50	.35
69	A11	1sh6p lt vio, blk & red	.75	.60
70	A11	3sh ultra, blk & red	1.50	1.75
		Nos. 67-70 (4)	3.20	2.95

Pseudotropheus Auratus — A12

Fish of Lake Malawi: 9p, Labeotropheus trewavasae. 1sh6p, Pseudotropheus zebra. 3sh, Pseudotropheus tropheops.

1967, May 3   Photo.   Perf. 12½x12

71	A12	4p green & multi	.65	.25
72	A12	9p ocher & multi	.80	.25
73	A12	1sh6p multicolored	1.00	.25
74	A12	3sh ultra & multi	1.60	1.75
		Nos. 71-74 (4)	4.05	2.50

Nos. 73 and 74 exist imperf. Value, pairs, each, $400.

Rising Sun and Cogwheel — A13

Perf. 13½x13
1967, July 5   Litho.   Unwmk.

75	A13	4p black & brt grn	.25	.25
76	A13	9p black & car rose	.25	.25
77	A13	1sh6p black & brt pur	.25	.25
78	A13	3sh black & brt ultra	.25	.25
a.		Souvenir sheet of 4, #75-78	1.10	1.10
		Nos. 75-78 (4)	1.00	1.00

Malawi industrial development.

Nativity — A14

Perf. 14x14½
1967, Oct. 12   Photo.   Wmk. 357

79	A14	4p vio blue & green	.25	.25
80	A14	9p vio blue & red	.25	.25
81	A14	1sh6p vio blue & yel	.25	.25
82	A14	3sh bright blue	.25	.25
a.		Souvenir sheet of 4, #79-82, perf. 14x13½	1.25	1.25
		Nos. 79-82 (4)	1.00	1.00

Christmas.

Calotropis Procera — A15

Wild Flowers: 9p, Borreria dibrachiata. 1sh6p, Hibiscus rhodanthus. 3sh, Bidens pinnatipartita.

1968, Apr. 24   Litho.   Perf. 13½x13

83	A15	4p green & multi	.30	.25
84	A15	9p pale grn & multi	.30	.25
85	A15	1sh6p lt green & multi	.30	.25
86	A15	3sh brt blue & multi	.30	.80
a.		Souvenir sheet of 4, #83-86	3.00	3.00
		Nos. 83-86 (4)	1.20	1.55

Thistle No. 1, 1902 — A16

Locomotives: 9p, G-class steam engine, 1954. 1sh6p, "Zambesi" diesel locomotive No. 202, 1963. 3sh, Diesel rail car No. 1, 1955.

MALAWI

1968, July 24 Photo. Perf. 14x14½
87	A16	4p gray grn & multi	.25	.25
88	A16	9p red & multi	.55	.50
89	A16	1sh6p cream & multi	.90	.80
90	A16	3sh lt ultra & multi	1.25	2.50
a.	Souv. sheet of 4, #87-90, perf. 14		5.00	5.00
	Nos. 87-90 (4)		2.95	4.05

Nativity, by Piero della Francesca — A17

Paintings: 9p, Adoration of the Shepherds, by Murillo. 1sh6p, Adoration of the Shepherds, by Guido Reni. 3sh, Nativity with God the Father and the Holy Ghost, by Giovanni Batista Pittoni.

1968, Nov. 6 Photo. Wmk. 357
91	A17	4p black & multi	.25	.25
92	A17	9p multicolored	.25	.25
93	A17	1sh6p multicolored	.25	.25
94	A17	3sh blue & multi	.25	.25
a.	Souvenir sheet of 4, #91-94, perf. 14x13½		.70	.70
	Nos. 91-94 (4)		1.00	1.00

Christmas.

Scarlet-chested Sunbird — A18

Nyasa Lovebird — A19

Birds: 2p, Violet-backed starling. 3p, White-browed robin-chat. 4p, Red-billed firefinch. 9p, Yellow bishop. 1sh, Southern carmine bee-eater. 1sh6p, Grayheaded bush shrike. 2sh, Paradise whydah. 3sh, African paradise flycatcher. 5sh, Bateleur. 10sh, Saddlebill. £1, Purple heron. £2, Livingstone's lorie.

1968, Nov. 13 Perf. 14½
Size: 23x19, 19x23mm
95	A18	1p multicolored	.25	.25
96	A18	2p multicolored	.25	.25
97	A18	3p multicolored	.25	.25
98	A18	4p multicolored	.35	.35
99	A19	6p multicolored	1.50	.25
100	A19	9p multicolored	1.00	.60

Perf. 14
Size: 42x25, 25x42mm
101	A18	1sh multicolored	.90	.25
102	A18	1sh6p multicolored	3.75	7.00
103	A19	2sh multicolored	6.50	7.00
104	A19	3sh multicolored	5.50	4.00
105	A19	5sh multicolored	4.25	4.00
106	A19	10sh multicolored	5.25	7.00
107	A19	£1 multicolored	7.50	16.00
109	A18	£2 multicolored	37.50	42.50
	Nos. 95-109 (14)		74.75	89.70

No. 104 was surcharged "00t Special United Kingdom Delivery Service" in 5 lines and issued Feb. 8, 1971, during the British postal strike. The 30t was to pay a private postal service. Values: unused 50c, used $2.25.

See Nos. 136-137. For overprint see No. 131.

ILO Emblem — A20

Photo., Gold Impressed (Emblem)
Perf. 14x14½
1969, Feb. 5 Wmk. 357
110	A20	4p deep green	.25	.25
111	A20	9p dk rose brown	.25	.25
112	A20	1sh6p dark gray	.25	.25
113	A20	3sh dark blue	.25	.25
a.	Souvenir sheet of 4, #110-113		1.60	1.60
	Nos. 110-113 (4)		1.00	1.00

ILO, 50th anniversary.

White Fringed Ground Orchid — A21

Malawi Orchids: 9p, Red ground orchid. 1sh6p, Leopard tree orchid. 3sh, Blue ground orchid.

1969, July 9 Litho. Perf. 13½
114	A21	4p gray & multi	.30	.30
115	A21	9p gray & multi	.55	.55
116	A21	1sh6p gray & multi	.75	.75
117	A21	3sh gray & multi	1.60	1.60
a.	Souvenir sheet of 4, #114-117		3.00	3.00
	Nos. 114-117 (4)		3.20	3.20

African Development Bank Emblem — A22

1969, Sept. 10 Perf. 14
118	A22	4p multicolored	.25	.25
119	A22	9p multicolored	.25	.25
120	A22	1sh6p multicolored	.25	.25
121	A22	3sh multicolored	.25	.25
a.	Souvenir sheet of 4, #118-121		.90	.90
	Nos. 118-121 (4)		1.00	1.00

African Development Bank, 5th anniv.

"Peace on Earth" — A23

1060, Nov. 5 Photo. Perf. 14x14½
122	A23	2p citron & blk	.25	.25
123	A23	4p Prus blue & blk	.25	.25
124	A23	9p scarlet & blk	.25	.25
125	A23	1sh6p purple & blk	.25	.25
126	A23	3sh ultra & blk	.25	.25
a.	Souvenir sheet of 5, #122-126		1.25	1.25
	Nos. 122-126 (5)		1.25	1.25

Christmas.

Bean Blister Beetle — A24

Insects: 4p, Elegant grasshopper. 1sh6p, Pumpkin ladybird. 3sh, Praying mantis.

1970, Feb. 4 Litho. Perf. 14x14½
127	A24	4p multicolored	.30	.25
128	A24	9p multicolored	.30	.25
129	A24	1sh6p multicolored	.55	.50
130	A24	3sh multicolored	1.00	1.00
a.	Souvenir sheet of 4, #127-130		3.00	3.00
	Nos. 127-130 (4)		2.15	2.00

No. 102 Overprinted in Black

Rand Easter Show MALAWI 1970

1970, Mar. 18 Photo. Perf. 14
| 131 | A18 | 1sh6p multicolored | .80 | 2.00 |

75th Anniversary Rand Easter Show, Johannesburg, South Africa, Mar. 24-Apr. 6.

Runner — A25

1970, June 3 Litho. Perf. 13
132	A25	4p green & dk blue	.25	.25
133	A25	9p rose & dk bl	.25	.25
134	A25	1sh6p dull yel & blue	.25	.25

135	A25	3sh blue & dk blue	.25	.25
a.	Souvenir sheet of 4, #132-135		1.00	1.00
	Nos. 132-135 (4)		1.00	1.00

9th Commonwealth Games, Edinburgh, Scotland, July 16-25.

Dual Currency Issue
Bird Type of 1968 with Denominations in Tambalas

Designs: 10t/1sh, Southern carmine bee-eater. 20t/2sh, Paradise whydah.

1970, Sept. 2 Photo. Perf. 14½
Size: 42x25mm
| 136 | A18 | 10t/1sh multicolored | 1.75 | .35 |
| 137 | A18 | 20t/2sh multicolored | 2.50 | 2.50 |

Aegocera Trimenii — A26

Moths of Malawi: 9p, Epiphora bauhiniae. 1sh6p, Parasa karschi. 3sh, Teracotona euprepia.

Perf. 11x11½
1970, Sept. 30 Wmk. 357
138	A26	4p multicolored	.35	.35
139	A26	9p multicolored	.50	.50
140	A26	1sh6p lt vio & multi	.85	.85
141	A26	3sh multicolored	1.90	1.90
a.	Souvenir sheet of 4, #138-141		6.50	6.50
	Nos. 138-141 (4)		3.60	3.60

Mother and Child — A27

1970, Nov. 4 Litho. Perf. 14½
142	A27	2p black & yel	.25	.25
143	A27	4p black & emer	.25	.25
144	A27	9p black & dp org	.25	.25
145	A27	1sh6p black & red lil	.25	.25
146	A27	3sh black & ultra	.25	.25
a.	Souv. sheet of 5, #142-146 + label		1.40	1.40
	Nos. 142-146 (5)		1.25	1.25

Christmas.

Decimal Currency

Greater Kudu A28

Eland A29

Antelopes: 2t, Nyala. 3t, Reedbuck. 5t, Puku. 8t, Impala. 15t, Klipspringer. 20t, Livingstone's suni. 30t, Roan antelope. 50t, Waterbuck. 1k, Bushbuck. 2k, Red duiker. 4k, Gray bush duiker.

Perf. 13½x14 (A28), 14x14½ (A29)
1971, Feb. 15 Litho. Wmk. 357
148	A28	1t dull vio & multi	.25	.25
a.	Perf. 14½x14, coil		.55	.40
b.	Perf. 14 ('74)		.45	1.50
149	A28	2t dp yel & multi	.25	.25
150	A28	3t ap grn & multi	.25	.25
a.	Perf. 14 ('74)		.65	1.25
151	A28	5t multicolored	.35	1.00
a.	Perf. 14 ('74)		.65	1.75
152	A28	8t org red & multi	.35	.75
153	A29	10t green & multi	.50	.35
154	A29	15t brt pur & multi	1.25	.40
155	A29	20t bl gray & multi	1.50	.90
156	A29	30t dull blue & multi	9.00	1.50
157	A29	50t multicolored	1.25	.75
158	A29	1k multicolored	3.00	1.00
159	A29	2k gray & multi	4.25	3.00
160	A29	4k multicolored	21.00	22.50
	Nos. 148-160 (13)		43.20	32.90

Decimal Coins — A30

1971, Feb. 15 Perf. 14½
161	A30	3t multicolored	.25	.25
162	A30	8t dull red & multi	.25	.25
163	A30	15t purple & multi	.25	.25
164	A30	30t brt blue & multi	.30	.30
a.	Souvenir sheet of 4, #161-164		1.60	1.60
	Nos. 161-164 (4)		1.05	1.05

Introduction of decimal currency and coinage.

Engravings by Albrecht Dürer — A31

Design: Nos. 165, 167, 169, 171, Christ on the Cross. Nos. 166, 168, 170, 172, The Resurrection.

1971, Apr. 7 Litho. Perf. 14x13½
165	3t emerald & black	.25	.25
166	3t emerald & black	.25	.25
a.	A31 Pair, #165-166	.30	.30
167	8t orange & black	.25	.25
168	8t orange & black	.25	.25
a.	A31 Pair, #167-168	.30	.30
169	15t red lilac & black	.25	.25
170	15t red lilac & black	.25	.25
a.	A31 Pair, #169-170	.50	.50
171	30t blue & black	.25	.25
172	30t blue & black	.25	.25
a.	Souv. sheet of 4, #165, 167, 169, 171	2.25	2.25
a.	Souv. sheet of 4, #166, 168, 170, 172	1.75	1.75
b.	A31 Pair, #171-172	.65	.65
	Nos. 165-172 (8)	2.00	2.00

Easter. Printed checkerwise in sheets of 25.

Holarrhena Febrifuga — A32

Flowering Shrubs and Trees: 8t, Brachystegia spiciformis. 15t, Securidaca longepedunculata. 30t, Pterocarpus rotundifolius.

1971, July 14 Litho. Wmk. 357
173	A32	3t gray & multi	.25	.25
174	A32	8t gray & multi	.25	.25
175	A32	15t gray & multi	.35	.30
176	A32	30t gray & multi	.50	.50
a.	Souvenir sheet of 4, #173-176		2.50	2.50
	Nos. 173-176 (4)		1.35	1.30

Drum Major — A33

1971, Oct. 5 Perf. 14x14½
| 177 | A33 | 30t lt blue & multi | .90 | .90 |

50th anniversary of Malawi Police Force.

Madonna and Child, by William Dyce — A34

Paintings of Holy Family by: 8t, Martin Schongauer. 15t, Raphael. 30t, Bronzino.

1971, Nov. 10 Perf. 14½
178	A34	3t green & multi	.25	.25
179	A34	8t carmine & multi	.25	.25
180	A34	15t dp claret & multi	.30	.30

MALAWI

181	A34	30t dull blue & multi	.60	.60
a.		Souvenir sheet of 4, #178-181	2.00	2.00
		Nos. 178-181 (4)	1.40	1.40

Christmas.

Vickers Viscount — A35

Airplanes: 8t, Hawker Siddeley 748. 15t, Britten Norman Islander. 30t, B.A.C. One Eleven.

1972, Feb. 9   Litho.   Perf. 13½x14

182	A35	3t brt grn, blk & red	.30	.25
183	A35	8t red org & black	.50	.25
184	A35	15t dp rose lil, red & black	.80	.75
185	A35	30t vio blue & multi	1.40	1.40
a.		Souvenir sheet of 4, #182-185	10.00	10.00
		Nos. 182-185 (4)	3.00	2.65

Publicity for Air Malawi.

Figures, Chencherere Hill — A36

Rock Paintings: 8t, Lizard and cat, Chencherere Hill. 15t, Symbols, Diwa Hill. 30t, Sun behind rain, Mikolongwe Hill.

1972, May 10   Perf. 13½

186	A36	3t black & yel grn	.30	.25
187	A36	8t black & dp car	.35	.25
188	A36	15t black, vio & car	.55	.45
189	A36	30t black, blue & yel	1.25	1.25
a.		Souv. sheet of 4, #186-189, perf. 15	4.50	4.50
		Nos. 186-189 (4)	2.45	2.20

Athlete and Olympic Rings — A37

1972, Aug. 9   Perf. 14x14½

190	A37	3t gray, black & green	.25	.25
191	A37	8t gray, black & scar	.25	.25
192	A37	15t gray, black & lilac	.25	.25
193	A37	30t gray, black & blue	.40	.40
a.		Souvenir sheet of 4, #190-193	2.10	2.10
		Nos. 190-193 (4)	1.15	1.15

20th Olympic Games, Munich, 8/26-9/10.

Malawi Coat of Arms — A38

1972, Oct. 20   Litho.   Perf. 13½x14

| 194 | A38 | 15t blue & multi | .65 | .65 |

18th Commonwealth Parliamentary Conference, Malawi, Oct. 1972.

Adoration of the Kings, by Orcagna — A39

Paintings of the Florentine School: 8t, Madonna and Child Enthroned, anonymous. 15t, Madonna and Child with Sts. Bonaventura and Louis of Toulouse, by Carlo Crivelli. 30t, Madonna and Child with St. Anne, by Jean de Bruges.

Perf. 14½x14

1972, Nov. 8   Wmk. 357

195	A39	3t lt olive & multi	.25	.25
196	A39	8t carmine & multi	.25	.25
197	A39	15t purple & multi	.25	.25
198	A39	30t blue & multi	.50	.50
a.		Souvenir sheet of 4, #195-198	1.50	1.50
		Nos. 195-198 (4)	1.25	1.25

Christmas.

Charaxes Bohemani — A40

8t, Uranothauma crawshayi. 15t, Charaxes acuminatus. No. 202, "Euphaedra zaddachi". No. 203, Amauris ansorgei.

1973   Perf. 13½x14

199	A40	3t shown	.65	.25
200	A40	8t multicolored	1.00	.25
201	A40	15t multicolored	1.20	.25
202	A40	30t multicolored	5.75	7.00
a.		Souvenir sheet of 4, #199-202	16.00	16.00
203	A40	30t multicolored	6.00	7.00
		Nos. 199-203 (5)	14.60	14.90

Issued: Nos. 199-202, 2/7; No. 203, 4/5.

Dr. Livingstone and Map of West Africa — A41

Livingstone Choosing Site for Mission — A42

1973   Litho.   Perf. 13½x14

204	A41	3t apple grn & multi	.25	.25
205	A41	8t red orange & multi	.25	.25
206	A41	15t multicolored	.25	.25
207	A41	30t blue & multi	.45	.45
a.		Souvenir sheet of 4, #204-207	1.75	1.75
208	A42	50t black & multi	.50	.50
a.		Souvenir sheet of 1	1.40	1.40
		Nos. 204-208 (5)	1.70	1.70

Dr. David Livingstone (1813-73), medical missionary and explorer.

Issued: Nos. 204-207, 207a, 5/1; No. 208, 208a, 12/12.

Thumb Dulcitone (Kalimba) — A43

African Musical Instruments: 8t, Hand zither (bangwe; vert.). 15t, Hand drum (ng'oma; vert.). 30t, One-stringed fiddle (kaligo).

1973, Aug. 8   Wmk. 357   Perf. 14

209	A43	3t brt green & multi	.25	.25
210	A43	8t red & multi	.25	.25
211	A43	15t violet & multi	.25	.25
212	A43	30t blue & multi	.25	.25
a.		Souvenir sheet of 4, #209-212	3.25	3.25
		Nos. 209-212 (4)	1.00	1.00

The Three Kings — A44

1973, Nov. 8   Perf. 13½x14

213	A44	3t blue & multi	.25	.25
214	A44	8t ver & multi	.25	.25
215	A44	15t multicolored	.25	.25
216	A44	30t orange & multi	.25	.25
a.		Souvenir sheet of 4, #213-216	1.25	1.25
		Nos. 213-216 (4)	1.00	1.00

Christmas.

Largemouth Black Bass — A45

Designs: Game fish.

1974, Feb. 20   Litho.   Perf. 14x14½

217	A45	3t shown	.40	.25
218	A45	8t Rainbow trout	.45	.30
219	A45	15t Lake salmon	1.00	.75
220	A45	30t Triggerfish	2.00	2.00
a.		Souvenir sheet of 4, #217-220	5.25	5.25
		Nos. 217-220 (4)	3.85	3.30

30th anniv. of Angling Society of Malawi.

UPU Emblem, Map of Africa with Malawi — A46

1974, Apr. 24   Perf. 13½

221	A46	3t green & bister	.25	.25
222	A46	8t ver & bister	.25	.25
223	A46	15t lilac & bister	.25	.25
224	A46	30t gray & bister	.35	.35
a.		Souvenir sheet of 4, #221-224	1.60	1.60
		Nos. 221-224 (4)	1.10	1.10

Centenary of Universal Postal Union.

Capital Hill, Lilongwe and Pres. Kamuzu Banda — A47

1974, July 3   Litho.   Perf. 14

225	A47	3t emerald & multi	.25	.25
226	A47	8t red & multi	.25	.25
227	A47	15t lilac & multi	.25	.25
228	A47	30t vio blue & multi	.25	.25
a.		Souvenir sheet of 4, #225-228	1.00	1.00
		Nos. 225-228 (4)	1.00	1.00

10th anniversary of independence.

Madonna of the Meadow, by Giovanni Bellini — A48

Paintings: 8t, Holy Family, by Jacob Jordaens. 15t, Nativity, by Peter F. de Grebber. 30t, Adoration of the Shepherds, by Lorenzo di Credi.

1974, Dec. 4   Litho.   Perf. 13½x14

229	A48	3t dk green & multi	.25	.25
230	A48	8t multicolored	.25	.25
231	A48	15t purple & multi	.25	.25
232	A48	30t dk blue & multi	.25	.25
a.		Souvenir sheet of 4, #229-232	1.00	1.00
		Nos. 229-232 (4)	1.00	1.00

Christmas.

African Snipe A49

Double-banded Sandgrouse A50

Birds: 3t, Blue quail. 5t, Red-necked francolin. 8t, Harlequin quail. 10t, Spurwing goose. 15t, Denham's bustard. 20t, Knob-billed duck. 30t, Helmeted guinea fowl. 50t, Pigmy goose. 1k, Garganey. 2k, White-faced tree duck. 4k, Green pigeon.

Wmk. 357

1975, Feb. 19   Litho.   Perf. 14

Size: 17x21, 21x17mm

233	A49	1t multicolored	.35	2.00
234	A50	2t multicolored	.50	2.00
235	A49	3t multicolored	1.90	1.60
236	A49	5t multicolored	4.50	1.50
237	A50	8t multicolored	6.00	1.25

Perf. 14½

Size: 25x41, 41x25mm

238	A49	10t multicolored	5.50	.60
239	A49	15t multicolored	4.50	4.50
240	A49	20t multicolored	1.50	2.00
241	A49	30t multicolored	1.90	.80
242	A49	50t multicolored	3.00	2.00
243	A50	1k multicolored	5.00	7.50
244	A49	2k multicolored	12.00	13.00
245	A50	4k multicolored	24.00	16.00
		Nos. 233-245 (13)	70.65	54.75

See Nos. 270-279. For overprints see Nos. 263, 294.

Malawi Coat of Arms — A51

Coil Stamps

1975-84   Perf. 14½x14

246	A51	1t dark violet blue	.80	.40
247	A51	5t red ('84)	2.25	2.25

"Mpasa" — A52

Designs: Lake Malawi ships.

1975, Mar. 12   Wmk. 357   Perf. 13½

251	A52	3t shown	.35	.30
252	A52	8t "Ilala II"	.55	.45
253	A52	15t "Chauncy Maples"	1.00	1.00
254	A52	30t "Nkwazi"	2.25	2.25
a.		Souvenir sheet of 4, #251-254, perf. 14½	4.50	4.50
		Nos. 251-254 (4)	4.15	4.00

Habenaria Splendens — A53

Orchids of Malawi: 10t, Eulophia cucullata. 20t, Disa welwitschii. 40t, Angraecum conchiferum.

1975, June 6   Litho.   Perf. 14½

255	A53	3t lt green & multi	.55	.25
256	A53	10t red org & multi	.65	.25
257	A53	20t dull vio & multi	1.00	.40
258	A53	40t multicolored	2.25	2.25
a.		Souvenir sheet of 4, #255-258	11.00	11.00
		Nos. 255-258 (4)	4.45	3.15

Bush Baby — A54

1975, Sept. 3   Litho.   Perf. 14

259	A54	3t shown	.25	.25
260	A54	10t Leopard	.40	.30
261	A54	20t Roan antelope	.80	.80
262	A54	40t Burchell's zebra	2.00	2.00
a.		Souvenir sheet of 4, #259-262	6.50	6.50
		Nos. 259-262 (4)	3.45	3.35

Animals of Malawi.

No. 242 Overprinted in Black

1975, Dec. 9   Litho.   Perf. 14½

| 263 | A50 | 50t multicolored | 1.75 | 2.25 |

10th African, Caribbean and Pacific Ministerial Conference.

MALAWI

Adoration of the Kings, French — A55

Christmas: 10t, Nativity, 16th century, Spanish. 20t, Nativity, by Pierre Raymond, 16th century. 40t, Angel Appearing to the Shepherds, 14th century, English.

1975, Dec. 12		Perf. 13x13½		
264	A55	3t multicolored	.25	.25
265	A55	10t multicolored	.25	.25
266	A55	20t purple & multi	.25	.25
267	A55	40t blue & multi	.25	.25
a.		Souv. sheet of 4, #264-267, perf. 14	2.60	2.60
		Nos. 264-267 (4)	1.00	1.00

Bird Types of 1975

1975	Litho.	Unwmk.	Perf. 14	
		Size: 21x17mm		
270	A50	3t multicolored	5.00	3.50
		Perf. 14½		
		Size: 25x41mm		
273	A49	10t multicolored	3.00	3.75
274	A49	15t multicolored	3.00	4.25
279	A49	2k multicolored	8.00	15.00
		Nos. 270-279 (4)	19.00	26.50

For overprint see No. 293.

Alexander Graham Bell — A56

		Perf. 14x14½		
1976, Mar. 24		Litho.	Wmk. 357	
281	A56	3t green & black	.25	.25
282	A56	10t dp lilac rose & blk	.25	.25
283	A56	20t brt purple & blk	.25	.25
284	A56	40t brt blue & blk	.50	.50
a.		Souvenir sheet of 4, #281-284	2.25	2.25
		Nos. 281-284 (4)	1.25	1.25

Centenary of first telephone call by Alexander Graham Bell, Mar. 10, 1876.

President Kamuzu Banda — A57

1976, July 1		Photo.	Perf. 13	
285	A57	3t brt green & multi	.25	.25
286	A57	10t multicolored	.25	.25
287	A57	20t violet & multi	.25	.25
288	A57	40t dull blue & multi	.55	.55
a.		Souvenir sheet of 4, #285-288	1.75	1.75
		Nos. 285-288 (4)	1.30	1.30

10th anniversary of the Republic.

Bagnall Diesel No. 100 — A58

Diesel Locomotives: 10t, Shire class No. 503. 20t, Nippon Sharyo No. 301. 40t, Hunslet No. 110.

1976, Oct. 1		Litho.	Perf. 14½	
289	A58	3t emerald & multi	.50	.30
290	A58	10t red & multi	1.00	.40
291	A58	20t lilac & multi	1.75	1.75
292	A58	40t blue & multi	3.00	3.00
a.		Souvenir sheet of 4, #289-292	7.00	7.00
		Nos. 289-292 (4)	6.25	5.45

Malawi Railways.

Nos. 274 and 241 Overprinted

1976, Oct. 22		Litho.	Unwmk.	
293	A49	15t multicolored	2.75	1.40
		Wmk. 357		
294	A49	30t multicolored	3.25	3.25

Blantyre Mission centenary.

Christ Child on Straw Bed — A59

1976, Dec. 6		Wmk. 357	Perf. 14	
295	A59	3t green & multi	.25	.25
296	A59	10t magenta & multi	.25	.25
297	A59	20t purple & multi	.25	.25
298	A59	40t dk blue & multi	.25	.25
a.		Souvenir sheet of 4, #295-298	2.25	2.25
		Nos. 295-298 (4)	1.00	1.00

Christmas.

Ebony Ancestor Figures — A60

Handicrafts: 10t, Ebony elephant, horiz. 20t, Ebony rhinoceros, horiz. 40t, Wooden antelope.

1977, Apr. 1		Litho.	Wmk. 357	
299	A60	4t yellow & multi	.25	.25
300	A60	10t black & multi	.25	.25
301	A60	20t ocher & multi	.25	.25
302	A60	40t ver & multi	.25	.25
a.		Souvenir sheet of 4, #299-302	2.25	2.25
		Nos. 299-302 (4)	1.00	1.00

Chileka Airport, Blantyre, and VC10 — A61

Transportation in Malawi: 10t, Leyland bus on Blantyre-Lilongwe Road. 20t, Ilala II on Lake Malawi. 40t, Freight train of Blantyre-Nacala line on overpass.

1977, July 12		Litho.	Perf. 14½	
303	A61	4t multicolored	.45	.25
304	A61	10t multicolored	.45	.40
305	A61	20t multicolored	1.10	.95
306	A61	40t multicolored	1.75	3.25
a.		Souvenir sheet of 4, #303-306	4.25	4.25
		Nos. 303-306 (4)	3.75	4.85

Pseudotropheus Johanni — A62

Lake Malawi Fish: 10t, Pseudotropheus livingstoni. 20t, Pseudotropheus zebra. 40t, Genyochromis mento.

Wmk. 357, Unwmkd.

1977, Oct. 4		Litho.	Perf. 13½x14	
307	A62	4t multicolored	.40	.25
308	A62	10t multicolored	.60	.30
309	A62	20t multicolored	1.40	.60
310	A62	40t multicolored	1.60	1.50
a.		Souvenir sheet of 4, #307-310	5.00	5.00
		Nos. 307-310 (4)	4.00	2.65

No. 309 with watermark is scarce. Value, $100. Values about the same for Nos. 307-308, 310 and 310a with or without watermark.

Virgin and Child, by Bergognone — A63

Virgin and Child: 10t, with God the Father and Angels, by Ambrogio Bergognone. 20t, detail from Bottigella altarpiece, by Vincenzo Foppa. 40t, with the fountain, by Jan Van Eyck.

		Perf. 14x13½		
1977, Nov. 21			Unwmk.	
311	A63	4t multicolored	.25	.25
312	A63	10t red & multi	.25	.25
313	A63	20t lilac & multi	.25	.25
314	A63	40t vio blue & multi	.40	.40
a.		Souvenir sheet of 4, #311-314	3.25	3.25
		Nos. 311-314 (4)	1.15	1.15

Christmas.

Entry into Jerusalem, by Giotto — A64

Giotto Paintings: 10t, Crucifixion. 20t, Descent from the Cross. 40t, Jesus Appearing to Mary.

1978, Mar. 1		Litho.	Perf. 12x12½	
315	A64	4t multicolored	.25	.25
316	A64	10t multicolored	.25	.25
317	A64	20t multicolored	.30	.25
318	A64	40t multicolored	.60	.60
a.		Souvenir sheet of 4, #315-318	2.50	2.50
		Nos. 315-318 (4)	1.40	1.35

Easter.

Lions, Wildlife Fund Emblem — A65

Animals and Wildlife Fund Emblem: 4t, Nyala, vert. 20t, Burchell's zebras. 40t, Reedbuck, vert.

1978, June 1		Unwmk.	Perf. 13x13½	
319	A65	4t multicolored	4.00	1.00
320	A65	10t multicolored	10.00	2.00
321	A65	20t multicolored	17.50	3.00
322	A65	40t multicolored	25.00	10.00
a.		Souvenir sheet of 4, #319-322, perf. 13½	100.00	75.00
		Nos. 319-322 (4)	56.50	16.00

Malamulo Seventh Day Adventist Church — A66

Virgin and Child and: 10t, Likoma Cathedral. 20t, St. Michael's and All Angel's, Blantyre. 40t, Zomba Catholic Cathedral.

1978, Nov. 15		Wmk. 357	Perf. 14	
323	A66	4t multicolored	.25	.25
324	A66	10t multicolored	.25	.25
325	A66	20t multicolored	.25	.25
326	A66	40t multicolored	.40	.40
a.		Souvenir sheet of 4, #323-326	1.25	1.25
		Nos. 323-326 (4)	1.15	1.15

Christmas.

Vanilla Polylepis — A67

Orchids of Malawi: 2t, Cirrhopetalum umbellatum. 5t, Calanthe natalensis. 7t, Ansellia gigantea. 8t, Tridactyle bicaudata. 10t, Acampe pachyglossa. 15t, Eulophia quartiniana. 20t, Cyrtorchis arcuata. 30t, Eulophia tricristata. 50t, Disa hamatopetala. 75t, Cynorchis glandulosa. 1k, Aerangis kotschyana. 1.50k, Polystachya dendrobiiflora. 2k, Disa ornithantha. 4k, Cytorchis praetermissa.

1979, Jan. 2		Litho.	Perf. 13½	
327	A67	1t multicolored	.60	.30
328	A67	2t multicolored	.60	.30
329	A67	5t multicolored	.60	.30
330	A67	7t multicolored	.60	.50
331	A67	8t multicolored	.60	.30
332	A67	10t multicolored	.60	.30
333	A67	15t multicolored	.60	.40
334	A67	20t multicolored	.70	.55
335	A67	30t multicolored	1.50	.40
336	A67	50t multicolored	1.25	.60
337	A67	75t multicolored	2.50	4.00
338	A67	1k multicolored	2.25	1.75
339	A67	1.50k multicolored	3.00	4.75
340	A67	2k multicolored	4.00	2.75
341	A67	4k multicolored	9.00	8.50
		Nos. 327-341 (15)	28.40	25.70

Brachystegia Spiciformis — A68

Trees: 10t, Widdringtonia nodiflora. 20t, Sandalwood. 40t, African mahogany.

1979, Jan. 21			Perf. 14x13½	
342	A68	5t multicolored	.30	.25
343	A68	10t multicolored	.35	.35
344	A68	20t multicolored	.60	.50
345	A68	40t multicolored	.75	2.25
a.		Souvenir sheet of 4, #342-345	3.00	3.00
		Nos. 342-345 (4)	2.00	3.35

National Tree Planting Day.

Railroad Bridge — A69

Designs: 10t, Station and train. 20t, 40t, Train passing through man-made pass, diff.

1979, Feb. 17		Litho.	Perf. 14½	
346	A69	5t multicolored	.30	.25
347	A69	10t multicolored	.50	.25
348	A69	20t multicolored	.80	.75
349	A69	40t multicolored	1.40	2.00
a.		Souvenir sheet of 4, #346-349	5.75	5.75
		Nos. 346-349 (4)	3.00	3.35

Inauguration of Salima-Lilongwe Railroad.

Malawi Boy and IYC Emblem A70

Designs: Malawi children and IYC emblem.

1979, July 10		Wmk. 357	Perf. 14	
350	A70	5t multicolored	.25	.25
351	A70	10t multicolored	.25	.25
352	A70	20t multicolored	.35	.30
353	A70	40t multicolored	.55	.55
		Nos. 350-353 (4)	1.40	1.35

International Year of the Child.

Malawi No. 1 — A71

Stamps of Malawi: 10t, #2. 20t, #3. 40t, #4.

1979, Sept. 17		Litho.	Perf. 13½x14	
354	A71	5t multicolored	.25	.25
355	A71	10t multicolored	.25	.25
356	A71	20t multicolored	.25	.25
357	A71	40t multicolored	.25	.25
a.		Souvenir sheet of 4, #354-357	1.25	1.25
		Nos. 354-357 (4)	1.00	1.00

Sir Rowland Hill (1795-1879), originator of penny postage.

MALAWI

Christmas A72

Designs: Landscapes.

1979, Nov. 15 Litho. Perf. 13½x14
358	A72	5t multicolored	.25 .25
359	A72	10t multicolored	.25 .25
360	A72	20t multicolored	.25 .25
361	A72	40t multicolored	.50 2.00
		Nos. 358-361 (4)	1.25 2.75

Limbe Rotary Club Emblem — A73

Malawi Rotary Club Emblems: 10t, Blantyre. 20t, Lilongwe. 40t, Rotary Intl.

1980, Feb. 23 Litho. Perf. 13½
362	A73	5t multicolored	.25 .25
363	A73	10t multicolored	.25 .25
364	A73	20t multicolored	.25 .25
365	A73	40t multicolored	.60 2.00
a.		Souvenir sheet of 4, #362-365	2.50 2.50
		Nos. 362-365 (4)	1.35 2.75

Rotary International, 75th anniversary.

Mangochi District Post Office, 1976, London 1980 Emblem — A74

London 1980 Emblem and: 10t, New Blantyre sorting office, 1979. 20t, Mail transfer hut, Walala. 1k, Nyasaland Post Office, Chiromo, 1891.

1980, May 6 Wmk. 357 Perf. 14½
366	A74	5t blue green & blk	.25 .25
367	A74	10t red & black	.25 .25
368	A74	20t dp violet & black	.25 .25
369	A74	1k dk blue & black	.40 .40
a.		Souvenir sheet of 4, #366-369	2.00 2.00
		Nos. 366-369 (4)	1.15 1.15

London 1980 International Stamp Exhibition, May 6-14.

Agate Nodule — A75

1980, Aug. 20 Litho. Perf. 13½
370	A75	5t shown	1.00 .25
371	A75	10t Sunstone	1.25 .25
372	A75	20t Smoky Quartz	2.50 .60
373	A75	1k Kyanite crystal	5.50 7.50
		Nos. 370-373 (4)	10.25 8.60

Elephants Drinking (Christmas) — A76

1980, Nov. 10 Litho. Perf. 13
374	A76	5t shown	.50 .45
375	A76	10t Flowers	.45 .35
376	A76	20t Train	1.10 .90
377	A76	1k Bird	1.75 2.10
		Nos. 374-377 (4)	3.80 3.80

Livingstone's Suni — A77

10t, Blue duikers. 20t, African buffalo. 1k, Lichtenstein's hartebeests.

1981, Feb. 4 Litho. Perf. 14½
378	A77	7t shown	.25 .25
379	A77	10t multicolored	.30 .25
380	A77	20t multicolored	.50 .40
381	A77	1k multicolored	1.75 1.75
		Nos. 378-381 (4)	2.80 2.65

Standard A Earth Station — A78

10t, Blantyre International Gateway Exchange. 20t, Standard B Earth Station. 1k, Satellite and earth.

1981, Apr. 24 Litho. Perf. 14½
382	A78	7t shown	.25 .25
383	A78	10t multicolored	.25 .25
384	A78	20t multicolored	.30 .25
385	A78	40t multicolored	1.50 1.90
a.		Souvenir sheet of 4, #382-385	2.75 2.75
		Nos. 382-385 (4)	2.30 2.65

International communications.

World Food Day — A79

1981, Sept. 11 Litho. Perf. 14
386	A79	7t Corn	.25 .25
387	A79	10t Rice	.25 .25
388	A79	20t Finger millet	.50 .25
389	A79	1k Wheat	1.40 1.40
		Nos. 386-389 (4)	2.40 2.15

Holy Family, by Lippi — A80

Christmas: 7t, Adoration of the Shepherds, by Murillo, vert. 20t, Adoration of the Shepherds, by Louis Le Nain. 1k, Virgin and Child, St. John the Baptist and Angel, by Paolo Morando, vert.

Perf. 13½x13, 13x13½

1981, Nov. 26 Litho.
390	A80	7t multicolored	.25 .25
391	A80	10t multicolored	.30 .25
392	A80	20t multicolored	.60 .55
393	A80	1k multicolored	1.50 1.50
		Nos. 390-393 (4)	2.65 2.55

Wildlife in Natl. Parks — A81

1982, Mar. 15 Litho. Perf. 14½x14
394	A81	7t Impalas	.25 .25
395	A81	10t Lions	.45 .25
396	A81	20t Kudus	.75 .25
397	A81	1k Flamingos	3.00 3.00
		Nos. 394-397 (4)	4.45 3.75

Kamuzu Academy A82

Designs: Academy views.

1982, July 1 Litho. Perf. 14½
398	A82	7t multicolored	.25 .25
399	A82	20t multicolored	.30 .25
400	A82	30t multicolored	.45 .40
401	A82	1k multicolored	1.50 1.50
		Nos. 398-401 (4)	2.50 2.40

1982 World Cup — A83

1982, Sept. Perf. 14x14½
402	A83	7t Players	1.10 1.00
403	A83	20t World Cup	2.00 2.00
404	A83	30t Stadium	2.50 2.50
		Nos. 402-404 (3)	5.60 5.50

Souvenir Sheet
405	A83	1k Emblem on field	2.50 2.50

Remembrance Day — A84

Designs: War Memorials.

1982, Nov. 5 Perf. 14½
406	A84	7t Blantyre	.25 .25
407	A84	20t Zomba	.25 .25
408	A84	30t Chichiri, badges	.30 .25
409	A84	1k Lilongwe	1.00 1.50
		Nos. 406-409 (4)	1.80 2.30

Commonwealth Day — A85

7t, Kwacha Intl. Conf. Ctr. 20t, Tea picking, Mulanje. 30t, Map. 1k, Pres. Banda, flag.

1983, Mar. 14 Wmk. 357 Perf. 14
410	A85	7t multicolored	.25 .25
411	A85	20t multicolored	.25 .25
412	A85	30t multicolored	.30 .25
413	A85	1k multicolored	.65 1.00
		Nos. 410-413 (4)	1.45 1.75

The Miraculous Draught of Fishes, by Raphael (1483-1517) A86

Designs: 7t, 20t, 30t, Details. 1k, Entire painting. 7t, 20t vert.

1983, Apr. 4 Litho. Wmk. 357
414	A86	7t multicolored	.40 .30
415	A86	20t multicolored	1.00 1.00
416	A86	30t multicolored	1.40 1.40
		Nos. 414-416 (3)	2.80 2.70

Souvenir Sheet
417	A86	1k multicolored	3.00 3.00

Fish Eagles — A87

Designs: a, Lakeside sentinel. b, Gull-like, far-carrying call. c, Diving on its fish prey. d, Prey captured. e, Feeding on its catch. Nos. 418a-418e in continuous design.

1983, July 11 Wmk. 357 Perf. 14½
418		Strip of 5	17.50 17.50
a.-e.	A87	30t multicolored	2.00 2.00

Manned Flight Bicentenary A88

Kamuzu Intl. Airport.

1983, Aug. 31 Litho. Perf. 14
419	A88	7t multicolored	.25 .25
420	A88	20t multi, diff.	.45 .35
421	A88	30t multi, diff.	.60 .60
422	A88	1k multi, diff.	1.75 1.75
a.		Souvenir sheet of 4, #419-422	3.50 3.50
		Nos. 419-422 (4)	3.05 2.95

Christmas — A89

Local flowers: 7t, Clerodendrium myricoides. 20t, Gloriosa superba. 30t, Gladiolus laxiflorus. 1k, Aframomum angustifolium.

1983, Nov. 1 Wmk. 357 Perf. 14
423	A89	7t multicolored	.60 .35
424	A89	20t multicolored	1.40 1.00
425	A89	30t multicolored	1.75 1.40
426	A89	1k multicolored	4.75 4.75
		Nos. 423-426 (4)	8.50 7.50

Aquarium Species, Lake Malawi — A90

Designs: 1t, Melanochromis auratus. 2t, Haplochromis compressiceps. 5t, Labeotropheus fuelleborni. 7t, Pseudotropheus lombardoi. 8t, Gold pseudotropheus zebra. 10t, Trematocranus jacobfreibergi. 15t, Melanochromis crabro. 20t, Marbled pseudotropheus. 30t, Labidochromis caeruleus. 40t, Haplochromis venustus. 50t, Aulonacara of Thumbi. 75t, Melanochromis vermivorus. 1k, Pseudotropheus zebra. 2k, Trematocranus spp. 4k, Aulonacara of Mbenje.

Perf. 14½x14

1984, Feb. 2 Wmk. 373
Inscribed "1984" below design
427	A90	1t multicolored	.45 1.00
428	A90	2t multicolored	.45 1.00
429	A90	5t multicolored	.45 1.00
430	A90	7t multicolored	.45 .40
431	A90	8t multicolored	.45 .40
432	A90	10t multicolored	.45 .30
433	A90	15t multicolored	.45 .30
434	A90	20t multicolored	.55 .30
435	A90	30t multicolored	.65 .50
436	A90	40t multicolored	1.10 .65
437	A90	50t multicolored	2.75 2.50
438	A90	75t multicolored	4.00 4.00
439	A90	1k multicolored	4.50 4.50
440	A90	2k multicolored	6.50 6.50
441	A90	4k multicolored	9.25 9.25
		Nos. 427-441 (15)	32.45 32.60

Inscribed "1986" below design
1986
427a	A90	1t multicolored	1.75 1.00
430a	A90	7t multicolored	1.75 .40
431a	A90	8t multicolored	1.75 .30
432a	A90	10t multicolored	1.75 .30
433a	A90	15t multicolored	1.75 .30
434a	A90	20t multicolored	2.25 .30
435a	A90	30t multicolored	2.50 .50
436a	A90	40t multicolored	4.50 .65
		Nos. 427a-436a (8)	18.00 3.85

Nyika Red Hare — A91

1984, Feb. 2 Wmk. 357 Perf. 14
442	A91	7t shown	.70 .25
443	A91	20t Sun squirrel	1.25 .45
444	A91	30t Hedgehog	1.75 1.00
445	A91	1k Genet	2.50 3.75
		Nos. 442-445 (4)	6.20 5.45

1984 Summer Olympics — A92

MALAWI

1984, June 1   Litho.   Perf. 14
446	A92	7t Running	.25	.25
447	A92	20t Boxing	.60	.30
448	A92	30t Bicycling	.90	.90
449	A92	1k Long jump	1.60	1.60
a.		Souvenir sheet of 4, #446-449	4.50	4.50
		Nos. 446-449 (4)	3.35	3.05

Local Butterflies — A93

7t, Euphaedra neophron. 20t, Papilio dardanus. 30t, Antanartia schaeneia. 1k, Spindasis.

1984, Aug. 1   Photo.   Perf. 11½
Granite Paper
450	A93	7t multicolored	1.75	.35
451	A93	20t multicolored	3.50	.50
452	A93	30t multicolored	4.50	1.25
453	A93	1k multicolored	7.75	8.00
		Nos. 450-453 (4)	17.50	10.10

Christmas — A94

Virgin and Child Paintings.

Wmk. 357
1984, Oct. 15   Litho.   Perf. 14½
454	A94	7t Duccio	.75	.30
455	A94	20t Raphael	2.00	.40
456	A94	30t Lippi	2.50	1.25
457	A94	1k Wilton diptych	5.25	7.50
		Nos. 454-457 (4)	10.50	9.15

Fungi — A94a

7t, Leucopaxillus gracillimus. 20t, Limacella guttata. 30t, Termitomyces eurhizles. 1k, Xerulina asprata.

1985, Jan. 23   Perf. 14½x14
458	A94a	7t multi	1.50	.45
459	A94a	20t multi	3.75	.55
460	A94a	30t multi	4.25	1.50
461	A94a	1k multi	8.50	8.50
		Nos. 458-461 (4)	18.00	11.00

Southern African Development Coordination Conference A95

1985, Apr. 1   Litho.   Perf. 14
462	A95	7t Forestry	1.25	.35
463	A95	15t Communications	2.00	.40
464	A95	20t Transportation	4.50	1.50
465	A95	1k Fishing	7.25	7.25
		Nos. 462-465 (4)	15.00	9.50

Ships on Lake Malawi — A96

1985, June 3   Perf. 13½x13
466	A96	7t Ufulu	1.00	.40
467	A96	15t Chauncy Maples	2.25	.40
468	A96	20t Mtendere	3.00	1.00
469	A96	1k Ilala	5.75	5.75
a.		Souvenir sheet of 4, #466-469, perf. 13x12	13.00	13.00
		Nos. 466-469 (4)	12.00	7.55

Audubon Birth Bicent. — A97

7t, Stierling's woodpecker. 15t, Lesser seed-cracker. 20t, Gunning's akalat. 1k, Boehm's bee-eater.

1985, Aug. 1   Litho.   Perf. 14
470	A97	7t multicolored	1.50	.50
471	A97	15t multicolored	2.75	.50
472	A97	20t multicolored	3.00	1.00
473	A97	1k multicolored	5.25	5.25
a.		Souvenir sheet of 4, #470-473	15.00	15.00
		Nos. 470-473 (4)	12.50	7.25

Christmas — A98

Paintings: 7t, The Virgin of Humility, by Jaime Serra. 15t, Adoration of the Magi, by Stefano da Zevio. 20t, Madonna and Child, by Gerard van Honthorst. 1k, Virgin of Zbraslav, by a Master of Vissi Brod.

Perf. 11½x12
1985, Oct. 14   Unwmk.
474	A98	7t multicolored	.45	.30
475	A98	15t multicolored	1.10	.35
476	A98	20t multicolored	1.50	.55
477	A98	1k multicolored	3.75	4.75
		Nos. 474-477 (4)	6.80	5.95

Halley's Comet — A99

8t, Earth, comet and Giotto trajectories. 15t, Comet over Earth. 20t, Over Malawi. 1k, Giotto probe.

1986, Feb. 10   Wmk. 357   Perf. 14½
478	A99	8t multi	1.00	.35
479	A99	15t multi	1.10	.35
480	A99	20t multi	1.75	.45
481	A99	1k multi	3.25	5.50
		Nos. 478-481 (4)	7.10	6.65

1986 World Cup Soccer Championships, Mexico — A100

Various soccer plays.

Perf. 12x11½
1986, May 26   Unwmk.
Granite Paper
482	A100	8t multicolored	1.00	.30
483	A100	15t multicolored	1.50	.65
484	A100	20t multicolored	2.00	.65
485	A100	1k multicolored	5.00	5.50
a.		Souvenir sheet of 4, #482-485	14.00	14.00
		Nos. 482-485 (4)	9.50	7.00

Natl. Independence, 20th Anniv. — A101

1986, June 30   Litho.   Perf. 14
486	A101	8t Pres. Banda	2.25	2.25
487	A101	15t Natl. flag	1.25	.25
488	A101	20t Natl. crest	1.40	.35
489	A101	1k Natl. airline	4.75	5.25
		Nos. 486-489 (4)	9.65	8.10

Christmas — A102

Paintings: 8t, Virgin and Child, by Botticelli (1445-1510). 15t, Adoration of the Shepherds, by Guido Reni (1575-1642). 20t, Madonna of the Veil, by Carlo Dolci (1616-86). 1k, Adoration of the Magi, by Jean Bourdichon.

1986, Dec. 15   Litho.   Perf. 11½
490	A102	8t multicolored	.75	.25
491	A102	15t multicolored	1.25	.25
492	A102	20t multicolored	2.00	.50
493	A102	1k multicolored	5.25	8.00
		Nos. 490-493 (4)	9.25	9.00

World Wildlife Fund — A103

Bugeranus carunculatus.

1987, Jan. 30   Wmk. 357   Perf. 14½
494	A103	8t Wattled crane	2.75	.45
495	A103	15t Two cranes	4.00	.60
496	A103	20t Nesting	4.75	.90
497	A103	75t Crane in water	8.75	8.75
		Nos. 494-497 (4)	20.25	10.70

1988, Oct.   Wmk. 373
494a	A103	8t	7.75	1.75
495a	A103	15t	11.00	3.25
496a	A103	20t	12.00	3.75
497a	A103	75t	16.50	15.00
		Nos. 494a-497a (4)	47.25	23.75

British Steam Locomotives A104

10t, Shamrock No. 2, 1902. 25t, D Class No. 8, 1914. 30t, Thistle No. 1, 1902. 1k, Kitson No. 6, 1903.

1987, May 25   Litho.   Perf. 14x13½
498	A104	10t multi	3.25	.45
499	A104	25t multi	4.50	.60
500	A104	30t multi	5.00	1.00
501	A104	1k multi	9.00	9.00
		Nos. 498-501 (4)	21.75	11.05

Hippopotamus — A105

10t, Feeding. 25t, Swimming, roaring. 30t, Mother and young swimming. 1k, At rest, egret.

1987, Aug. 24   Photo.   Perf. 12½
Granite Paper
502	A105	10t multi	2.00	.35
503	A105	25t multi	3.75	.50
504	A105	30t multi	3.75	.85
505	A105	1k multi	9.50	8.75
a.		Souvenir sheet of 4, #502-505	19.00	19.00
		Nos. 502-505 (4)	19.00	10.45

Wild Flowers — A106

10t, Stathmostelma spectabile. 25t, Pentanisia schweinfurthii. 30t, Chironia krebsii. 1k, Ochna macrocalyx.

1987, Oct. 19   Litho.   Perf. 14   Unwmk.
506	A106	10t multicolored	1.25	.25
507	A106	25t multicolored	2.50	.35
508	A106	30t multicolored	3.00	.70
509	A106	1k multicolored	5.00	5.00
		Nos. 506-509 (4)	11.75	6.30

Locally Carved and Staunton Chessmen — A107

1988, Feb. 8   Wmk. 384   Perf. 14½
510	A107	15t Knights	2.00	.30
511	A107	35t Bishops	3.00	.90
512	A107	50t Rooks	3.50	1.75
513	A107	2k Queens	8.25	8.25
		Nos. 510-513 (4)	16.75	11.20

1988 Summer Olympics, Seoul — A108

1988, June 13   Unwmk.   Perf. 14
514	A108	15t High jump	.60	.25
515	A108	35t Javelin	.90	.40
516	A108	50t Women's tennis	1.25	.70
517	A108	2k Shot put	2.50	2.50
a.		Souvenir sheet of 4, #514-517	6.50	6.50
		Nos. 514-517 (4)	5.25	3.85

Birds — A109

Designs: 1t, Eastern fores scrub-warbler. 2t, Yellow-throated warbler. 5t, Moustached green tinkerbird. 7t, Waller's chestnut-wing starling. 8t, Oriole finch. 10t, No. 533A, Starred robin. 15t, Bar-tailed trogon. 20t, Green twinspot. 30t, Gray cuckoo shrike. 40t, Black-fronted bush shrike. 50t, White-tailed crested flycatcher. 75t, Green barbet. 1k, Cinnamon dove. 2k, Silvery-cheeked hornbill. 4k, Crowned eagle. No. 533, Red and blue sunbird.

Perf. 11½x12, 15x14½ (#533)
1988-94   Photo.
Granite Paper (1t-4k)
518	A109	1t multicolored	.75	1.00
519	A109	2t multicolored	.75	1.00
520	A109	5t multicolored	.75	1.00
521	A109	7t multicolored	.75	1.00
522	A109	8t multicolored	.75	1.00
523	A109	10t multicolored	2.25	.25
524	A109	15t multicolored	.75	.75
525	A109	20t multicolored	.75	.25
526	A109	30t multicolored	.75	.25
527	A109	40t multicolored	.80	.40
528	A109	50t multicolored	1.90	.90
529	A109	75t multicolored	1.00	1.00
530	A109	1k multicolored	1.10	1.10
531	A109	2k multicolored	2.00	2.00
532	A109	4k multicolored	3.75	3.75
533	A109	10k multicolored	16.00	12.00
533A	A109	10k multicolored	13.00	5.00
		Nos. 518-533A (17)	47.80	33.75

Issue dates: 10k, Oct. 3, No. 533A, 1994; others, July 25.

For surcharges, see Nos. 840-841, 842-845, 851-853.

Common Design Types pictured following the introduction.

Lloyds of London, 300th Anniv.
Common Design Type

15t, Royal Exchange, 1844. 35t, Opening of the Nkula Falls hydroelectric power station, horiz. 50t, Air Malawi passenger jet, horiz. 2k, Cruise ship Queen Elizabeth (Seawise University) on fire, Hong Kong, 1972.

MALAWI

Wmk. 373

1988, Oct. 24	Litho.	Perf. 14	
534 CD341 15t multicolored		.50	.30
535 CD341 35t multicolored		1.00	.50
536 CD341 50t multicolored		3.25	.80
537 CD341 2k multicolored		6.25	6.25
Nos. 534-537 (4)		11.00	7.85

Christmas — A110

Paintings: 15t, Madonna in the Church, by Jan Van Eyck (d. 1441). 35t, Virgin, Infant Jesus and St. Anne, by Leonardo da Vinci. 50t, Virgin and Angels, by Cimabue (c. 1240-1302). 2k, Virgin and Child, by Alesso Baldovinetti (c. 1425-1499).

1988, Nov. 28	Unwmk.	Perf. 14	
538 A110 15t multicolored		.90	.30
539 A110 35t multicolored		1.60	.40
540 A110 50t multicolored		2.00	.90
541 A110 2k multicolored		4.75	4.75
Nos. 538-541 (4)		9.25	6.35

Angling Soc. of Malawi, 50th Anniv. — A111

1989, Apr. 11			
542 A111 15t Tsungwa		1.10	.25
543 A111 35t Mpasa		2.00	.40
544 A111 50t Yellow fish		2.75	1.75
545 A111 2k Tiger fish		7.25	7.25
Nos. 542-545 (4)		13.10	9.65

Natl. Independence, 25th Anniv. — A112

15t, Independence Arch. 35t, Grain silos. 50t, Capital Hill. 2k, Reserve Bank Headquarters.

1989, June 26			
546 A112 15t multi		1.10	.30
547 A112 35t multi		2.50	.50
548 A112 50t multi		3.50	1.75
549 A112 2k multi		8.25	8.25
Nos. 546-549 (4)		15.35	10.80

African Development Bank, 25th Anniv. — A113

15t, Blantyre Digital Telex Exchange. 40t, Dzalanyama steer. 50t, Mikolongwe heifer. 2k, Zebu bull.

1989, Oct. 30			
550 A113 15t multi		1.25	.30
551 A113 40t multi		2.25	.50
552 A113 50t multi		2.75	1.75
553 A113 2k multi		7.25	7.25
Nos. 550-553 (4)		13.50	9.80

Cooperation with the UN, 25th Anniv. — A114

40t, House, diff. 50t, Thatched dwelling, house. 2k, Tea Plantation.

1989, Dec. 1		Perf. 14	
554 A114 15t shown		1.25	.30
555 A114 40t multi		2.25	.45
556 A114 50t multi		3.00	1.75
557 A114 2k multi		6.50	6.50
Nos. 554-557 (4)		13.00	9.00

Rural Housing Program.

Christmas A115

Designs: 15t, St. Michael and All Angels Church. 40t, Limbe Cathedral. 50t, Nkhoma CCAP Church. 2k, Likoma Is. Cathedral.

1989, Dec. 15			
558 A115 15t multicolored		1.25	.30
559 A115 40t multicolored		2.25	.45
560 A115 50t multicolored		3.00	1.75
561 A115 2k multicolored		6.50	6.50
Nos. 558-561 (4)		13.00	9.00

Classic Cars — A116

15t, Ford Sedan, 1915. 40t, Two-seater Ford, 1915. 50t, Ford, 1915. 2k, Chevrolet Luxury Bus, 1930.

		Perf. 14x13½	
1990, Apr. 2	Litho.	Unwmk.	
562 A116 15t multi		1.50	.40
563 A116 40t multi		2.75	1.00
564 A116 50t multi		3.50	2.00
565 A116 2k multi		8.75	8.75
a. Souvenir sheet of 4, #562-565, perf. 13x12		25.00	25.00
Nos. 562-565 (4)		16.50	12.15

World Cup Soccer Championships, Italy — A117

40t, Two players. 50t, Shot on goal. 2k, World Cup Trophy.

1990, June 14	Litho.	Perf. 14	
566 A117 15t shown		1.25	.30
567 A117 40t multicolored		2.75	.75
568 A117 50t multicolored		3.50	2.00
569 A117 2k multicolored		8.50	8.50
a. Souvenir sheet of 4, #566-569		17.00	17.00
Nos. 566-569 (4)		16.00	11.55

SADCC, 10th Anniv. — A118

1990, Aug. 24	Litho.	Perf. 14	
570 A118 15t Map		1.10	.40
571 A118 40t Chambo		2.00	.55
572 A118 50t Cedar trees		6.25	2.00
573 A118 2k Nyala		7.75	7.75
a. Souvenir sheet of 4, #570-573		16.00	16.00
Nos. 570-573 (4)		17.10	10.70

Christmas — A119

Paintings by Raphael: 15t, Virgin and Child. 40t, The Transfiguration, detail. 50t, St. Catherine of Alexandrie. 2k, The Transfiguration.

1990, Nov. 26		Perf. 13½x14	
574 A119 15t multicolored		1.25	.40
575 A119 40t multicolored		2.50	.60
576 A119 50t multicolored		3.50	2.00
577 A119 2k multicolored		8.75	8.75
a. Souvenir sheet of 4, #574-577, perf. 12x13		17.00	17.00
Nos. 574-577 (4)		16.00	11.75

Orchids — A120

15t, Aerangis kotschyana. 40t, Angraecum eburneum. 50t, Aerangis luteo alba. 2k, Cyrtorchis arcuata.

1990, Dec. 7			
578 A120 15t multi		1.75	.40
579 A120 40t multi		3.50	1.00
580 A120 50t multi		3.75	2.00
581 A120 2k multi		11.50	11.50
a. Souvenir sheet of 4, #578-581, perf. 12x13		21.00	21.00
Nos. 578-581 (4)		20.50	14.90

Wild Animals — A121

1991, Apr. 23	Litho.	Perf. 14x13½	
582 A121 20t Buffalo		1.50	.40
583 A121 60t Cheetah		3.50	1.50
584 A121 75t Greater kudu		3.50	1.50
585 A121 2k Black rhinoceros		13.00	10.00
a. Souvenir sheet of 4, #582-585, perf. 13x12		22.00	22.00
Nos. 582-585 (4)		21.50	13.40

Malawi Postal Services, Cent. — A122

20t, Chiromo Post Office, 1891. 60t, Mail exchange hut, Walala. 75t, Mangochi Post Office. 2k, Standard A Earth station, 1981.

1991, July 2		Perf. 14x13½	
586 A122 20t multicolored		1.75	.40
587 A122 60t multicolored		2.50	1.00
588 A122 75t multicolored		2.75	1.25
589 A122 2k multicolored		9.00	7.50
a. Souvenir sheet of 4, #586-589, perf. 13x12		17.00	17.00
Nos. 586-589 (4)		16.00	10.15

Insects — A123

20t, Red locust. 60t, Weevil. 75t, Cotton stainer bug. 2k, Pollen beetle.

1991, Sept. 21		Perf. 13½x14	
590 A123 20t multi		1.75	.40
591 A123 60t multi		3.50	1.50
592 A123 75t multi		3.50	1.75
593 A123 2k multi		8.75	7.50
Nos. 590-593 (4)		17.50	11.15

Christmas — A124

20t, Christ Child in manger. 60t, Adoration of the Magi. 75t, Nativity. 2k, Virgin and Child.

1991, Nov. 26	Litho.	Perf. 13½x14	
594 A124 20t multi		.90	.35
595 A124 60t multi		2.75	.60
596 A124 75t multi		3.25	1.00
597 A124 2k multi		7.50	7.50
Nos. 594-597 (4)		14.40	9.45

Birds A125

Designs: a, Red bishop. b, Lesser striped swallow. c, Long-crested eagle. d, Lilac-breasted roller. e, African paradise flycatcher. f, White-fronted bee-eater. g, White-winged black tern. h, Brown-backed fire-finch. i, White-browed robin-chat. j, African fish eagle. k, Malachite kingfisher. l, Cabani's masked weaver. m, African barn owl. n, Yellow-bellied sunbird. o, Lesser flamingo. p, Crowned crane. q, African pitta. r, African darter. s, White-faced tree duck. t, African pied wagtail.

1992, Apr. 7	Litho.	Perf. 14	
598 A125 75t Sheet of 20, #a.-t.		60.00	60.00

1992 Summer Olympics, Barcelona A126

1992, July 28	Litho.	Perf. 13½	
600 A126 20t Long jump		1.40	.35
601 A126 60t High jump		2.00	.80
602 A126 75t Javelin		2.50	1.10
603 A126 2k Running		4.75	4.75
a. Souvenir sheet of 4, #600-603		12.50	12.50
Nos. 600-603 (4)		10.65	7.00

Christmas — A127

Details from paintings: 20t, Angel from The Annunciation, by Philippe de Champaigne. 75t, Virgin and Child, by Bernardino Luini. 95t, Virgin and Child, by Sassoferrato. 2k, Mary from The Annunciation, by Champaigne.

1992, Nov. 9	Litho.	Perf. 14	
604 A127 20t multicolored		.80	.25
605 A127 75t multicolored		1.90	.50
606 A127 95t multicolored		2.40	.80
607 A127 2k multicolored		5.50	5.50
Nos. 604-607 (4)		10.60	7.05

Intl. Space Year — A128

Designs: 20t, Voyager II, Saturn. 75t, Center of a galaxy. 95t, Kanjedza II ground station. 2k, Communication satellite.

1992, Dec. 7	Litho.	Perf. 13½	
608 A128 20t multicolored		1.00	.35
609 A128 75t multicolored		2.25	.85
610 A128 95t multicolored		2.50	1.00
611 A128 2k multicolored		5.50	5.00
Nos. 608-611 (4)		11.25	7.20

Fruit — A129

20t, Strychnos spinosa. 75t, Adansonia digitata. 95t, Ximenia caffra. 2k, Uapaca kirkiana.

1993, Mar. 21	Litho.	Perf. 13½x14	
612 A129 20t multi		1.00	.30
613 A129 75t multi		2.50	1.00
614 A129 95t multi		2.75	1.10
615 A129 2k multi		4.75	4.75
Nos. 612-615 (4)		11.00	7.15

MALAWI

Butterflies — A130

20t, Apaturopsis cleocharis. 75t, Euryphura achlys. 95t, Cooksonia aliciae. 2k, Charaxes protoclea azota.

1993, June 28	Litho.	Perf. 13		
616	A130	20t multi	1.25	.40
617	A130	75t multi	2.75	1.00
618	A130	95t multi	3.25	1.60
619	A130	2k multi	4.75	4.50
	Nos. 616-619 (4)		12.00	7.50

A131

Dinosaurs — A132

Designs: No. 623a, Tyrannosaurus Rex. b, Dilophosaurus. c, Brachiosaurus. d, Gallimimus. e, Triceratops. f, Velociraptor.

1993, Dec. 30	Litho.	Perf. 13		
620	A131	20t Kentrosaurus	1.10	.75
621	A131	75t Stegosaurus	2.50	2.25
622	A131	95t Sauropod	3.00	2.50
	Nos. 620-622 (3)		6.60	5.50

Miniature Sheet

| 623 | A132 | 2k Sheet of 6, #a.-f. | 20.00 | 20.00 |

Christmas — A133

20t, Holy family. 75t, Shepherds. 95t, Wise men. 2k, Adoration of the magi.

1993, Nov. 30	Photo.	Perf. 11½		
	Granite Paper			
624	A133	20t multi	.45	.45
625	A133	75t multi	.55	.45
626	A133	95t multi	.70	.70
627	A133	2k multi	2.00	2.00
	Nos. 624-627 (4)		3.70	3.60

Fish of Lake Malawi — A134

Designs: 20t, Pseudotropheus socolofi. 75t, Melanochromis auratus. 95t, Pseudotropheus lombardoi. 1k, Labeotropheus trewavasae. 2k, Pseudotropheus zebra. 4k, Pseudotropheus elongatus.

1994, Mar. 21	Litho.	Perf. 14x15		
628	A134	20t multicolored	.45	.35
629	A134	75t multicolored	1.10	.45
630	A134	95t multicolored	1.25	.55
631	A134	1k multi	1.25	.90
632	A134	2k multicolored	2.50	2.25
633	A134	4k multicolored	4.25	4.00
	Nos. 628-633 (6)		10.80	8.50

Ships of Lake Malawi — A135

1994, Oct. 19	Litho.	Perf. 13x13½		
634	A135	20t Ilala	.70	.55
635	A135	75t MV Ufulu	1.10	.55
636	A135	95t The Pioneer	1.40	.65
637	A135	2k Dove	2.25	2.25
	Nos. 634-637 (4)		5.45	4.00

Souvenir Sheet

| 638 | A135 | 5k Monteith | 8.50 | 8.50 |

Christmas A136

Details or entire paintings: 20t, Virgin and Child, by Durer, vert. 75t, Magi Present Gifts to Infant Jesus, Franco-Flemish Book of Hours, vert. 95t, The Nativity, by Fra Filippo Lippi. 2k, Nativity with Magi, by Rogier van der Weyden.

1994, Nov. 30	Litho.	Perf. 14½		
639	A136	20t multicolored	.55	.55
640	A136	75t multicolored	.65	.55
641	A136	95t multicolored	.80	.55
642	A136	2k multicolored	2.40	2.75
	Nos. 639-642 (4)		4.40	4.40

Pres. Bakili Muluzi — A137

1995, Apr. 10	Litho.	Perf. 11½x12		
643	A137	40t red & multi	.45	.45
644	A137	1.40k green & multi	.45	.45
645	A137	1.80k blue & multi	.55	.55
646	A137	2k brn org & multi	.80	.80
	Nos. 643-646 (4)		2.25	2.25

Establishment of COMESA (Common Market for Eastern & Southern African States).

Christmas A138

40t, Pre-schoolers. 1.40k, Dispensing medicine. 1.80k, Water supply. 2k, Voluntary return.

1995, Nov. 13	Litho.	Perf. 11½		
	Granite Paper			
647	A138	40t multi	.70	.70
648	A138	1.40k multi	.70	.70
649	A138	1.80k multi	.90	.90
650	A138	2k multi	1.25	1.25
	Nos. 647-650 (4)		3.55	3.55

Butterflies A139

1996, Dec. 5	Photo.	Perf. 11½		
	Granite Paper			
651	A139	60t Precis tugela	.60	.60
652	A139	3k Papilo pelodorus	1.40	.75
653	A139	4k Acrea acrita	1.50	.90
654	A139	10k Malantis leda	3.25	3.00
	Nos. 651-654 (4)		6.75	5.25

For surcharges, see Nos. 848, 850.

Christmas — A140

Designs: 10t, Instructor, children raising hands. 20t, Children enacting nativity scene. 30t, Children standing with hands clasped. 60t, Mother and child.

1996, Dec. 12		Granite Paper		
655	A140	10t multicolored	.90	.90
656	A140	20t multicolored	.90	.90
657	A140	30t multicolored	1.00	.90
658	A140	60t multicolored	2.00	1.75
	Nos. 655-658 (4)		4.80	4.45

UN, 50th Anniv. — A141

40t, Telecommunications & training. 1.40k, Clean water is essential for health. 1.80k, Protecting the environment, Mt. Mulanje. 2k, Food security.

1995, Oct. 30	Litho.	Perf. 11½		
659	A141	40t multicolored	.90	.90
660	A141	1.40k multicolored	.90	.90
661	A141	1.80k multicolored	1.10	1.10
662	A141	2k multicolored	1.10	1.10
a.	Souvenir sheet, #659-662		4.50	4.50
	Nos. 659-662 (4)		4.00	4.00

Paul Harris (1868-1947), Founder of Rotary, Intl. — A142

Rotary, Intl. emblem and: 60t, Map of Malawi. 3k, Eagle. 1.40k, Leopard.

1997, Oct. 6	Litho.	Perf. 11½		
663	A142	60t multicolored	.65	.65
664	A142	3k multicolored	1.10	1.10
665	A142	4.40k multicolored	1.60	1.60
666	A142	5k shown	1.75	1.75
	Nos. 663-666 (4)		5.10	5.10

UNICEF, 50th Anniv. — A143

Designs: 60t, Care and protection. 3k, Education. 4.40k, Nutrition. 5k, Immunization.

1997, Oct. 31	Litho.	Perf. 11¾x11½		
667	A143	60t multi	.90	.90
668	A143	3k multi	.90	.90
669	A143	4.40k multi	1.50	1.50
670	A143	5k multi	1.90	1.90
	Nos. 667-670 (4)		5.20	5.20

A144

Christmas: 60t, Holy Night, by Carlo Maratta. 3k, The Nativity, by Bernardino Luini. 4.40k, Adoration of the Magi, by Luini. 5k, Holy Family.

1997, Dec. 15		Perf. 11¾		
671	A144	60t multi	1.00	1.00
672	A144	3k multi	1.00	1.00
673	A144	4.40k multi	1.60	1.60
674	A144	5k multi	2.10	2.10
	Nos. 671-674 (4)		5.70	5.70

A145

Diana, Princess of Wales (1961-97): Various portraits.

1998, Nov. 30	Litho.	Perf. 14½		
675	A145	60t multicolored	.40	.40
676	A145	6k multicolored	.50	.50
677	A145	7k multicolored	.55	.55
678	A145	8k multicolored	.65	.65
a.	Souvenir sheet, Nos. 675-678		2.50	2.50
	Nos. 675-678 (4)		2.10	2.10

Tourism — A146

60t, Tattooed Rock, Mwalawamphini, Cape Maclear, vert. 6k, War Memorial Tower, Zomba, vert. 7k, Mtengatenga Postal hut, Walala. 8k, Original P.I.M. Church, Chiradzulu.

1998, Dec. 2	Litho.	Perf. 13		
679	A146	60t multicolored	.60	.60
680	A146	6k multicolored	.70	.70
681	A146	7k multicolored	.90	.90
682	A146	8k multicolored	1.10	1.10
	Nos. 679-682 (4)		3.30	3.30

Universal Declaration of Human Rights, 50th Anniv. — A147

Basic rights: 60t, Voting. 6k, Education. 7k, Equal justice. 8k, Owning property.

1998, Dec. 10				
683	A147	60t multicolored	.60	.60
684	A147	6k multicolored	.70	.70
685	A147	7k multicolored	.90	.90
686	A147	8k multicolored	1.10	1.10
	Nos. 683-686 (4)		3.30	3.30

Christmas — A148

Design: Madonna and Child.

1998, Dec. 15	Photo.	Perf. 11¾		
	Granite Paper			
687	A148	60t multi	15.00	15.00
688	A148	6k multi	15.00	15.00
689	A148	7k Angel	15.00	15.00
690	A148	8k multi	15.00	15.00

Christmas — A149

60t, Madonna & Child. 6k, Nativity. 7k, Adoration of the Magi. 8k, Flight into Egypt.

1999, Dec. 13	Photo.	Perf. 11¾		
691	A149	60t multi	1.00	1.00
692	A149	6k multi	1.00	1.00
693	A149	7k multi	1.20	1.20
694	A149	8k multi	1.50	1.50
	Nos. 691-694 (4)		4.70	4.70

Southern African Development Community A150

60t, Map of Africa. 6k, Malambe fruit juice bottles. 7k, Fishing resources research boat R/V Ndunduma. 8k, Locomotive.

	Perf. 13¼x13½, 13½x13¼			
2000, Feb. 22	Litho.			
695	A150	60t multi, vert.	.75	.75
696	A150	6k multi, vert.	.75	.75
697	A150	7k multi	1.00	1.00
698	A150	8k multi	1.25	1.25
	Nos. 695-698 (4)		3.75	3.75

MALAWI

Modern British Commonwealth, 50th Anniv. — A151

African musical instruments: 60t, Ng'oma. 6k, Kaligo. 7k, Kalimba. 8k, Chisekese.

2000, Feb. 22			Perf. 13¼x13½	
699	A151	60t multi	.75	.75
700	A151	6k multi	.75	.75
701	A151	7k multi	1.00	1.00
702	A151	8k multi	1.25	1.25
		Nos. 699-702 (4)	3.75	3.75

Christmas — A152

Designs: 5k, Madonna and Child. 18k, Nativity. 20k, Madonna and Child, diff.

2000, Dec. 12	Photo.	Perf. 11¾	
703-705	A152	Set of 3	3.25 3.25

Butterflies — A153

Designs: 1k, Euxanthe wakefieldi. 2k, Psuedacraea boisdurali. 4k, Catacroptera cloanthe. 5k, Myrina silenus ficedula. 10k, Cymothoe zombana. 20k, Charaxes castor. 50k, Charaxes pythoduras ventersi. 100k, Iolaus lalos.

2002 ?		Litho.	Perf. 14½x13¾	
706	A153	1k multi	.40	.40
707	A153	2k multi	.40	.40
708	A153	4k multi	.40	.40
709	A153	5k multi	.40	.40
710	A153	10k multi	.40	.40
711	A153	20k multi	.95	.95
712	A153	50k multi	3.00	3.00
713	A153	100k multi	5.50	5.50
		Nos. 706-713 (8)	11.45	11.45

For surcharges, see Nos. 846, 849, 855, 921.

Worldwide Fund for Nature (WWF) — A154

Kobus vardonii: a, Male. b, Two males butting heads. c, Male and female. d, Herd.

		Perf. 13¼x13½	
2003, Nov. 10		Litho.	
714	Strip of 4	8.00	8.00
a.-d.	A154 50k Any single	1.00	1.00
e.	Souvenir sheet, 2 #714	16.00	16.00

Butterflies, Birds, Orchids and Mushrooms — A155

No. 715, 50k — Butterflies: a, Bebearia octogramma. b, Charaxes nobilis. c, Cymothoe beckeri. d, Salamis anteva. e, Charaxes xiphares. f, Bebearia arcadius Fabricius.
No. 716, 50k, vert. — Birds: a, Upupa epops. b, Psittacus erithacus. c, Terathopus ecaudatus. d, Polemaetus bellicosus. e, Agapornis personatus. f, Scotopelia peli.
No. 717, 50k, vert. — Orchids: a, Angraecum eburneum. b, Ancistrochilus rothschildianus. c, Angraecum infundibulare. d, Ansellia africana. e, Disa veitchii. f, Angraecum compactum.
No. 718, 50k — Mushrooms: a, Pleurotus ostreatus. b, Macrolepiota procera. c, Amanita vaginata. d, Cantharellus tubaeformis. e, Hydnum repandum. f, Trametes versicolor.
No. 719, 180k, Carterocephalus palaemon. No. 720, 180k, Ardea cinerea. No. 721, 180k, Aerangis kotschyana. No. 722, 180k, Auricularia auricula, vert.

	Perf. 13¼x13½, 13½x13¼	
2003, Nov. 10		
	Sheets of 6, #a-f	
715-718	A155 Set of 4	45.00 45.00
	Souvenir Sheets	
719-722	A155 Set of 4	26.00 26.00

Tour de France Bicycle Race, Cent. (in 2003) — A156

No. 723: a, Joop Zoetemelk, 1980. b, Bernard Hinault, 1981. c, Hinault, 1982. d, Laurent Fignon, 1983. 180k, Miguel Indurain, 1991-95.

2004, Feb. 6		Perf. 13¼	
723	A156 75k Sheet of 4, #a-d	6.75	6.75
	Souvenir Sheet		
724	A156 180k multi	4.75	4.75

Powered Flight, Cent. (in 2003) — A157

No. 725: a, Vickers Vimy. b, D.H. 9A. c, Messerschmidt Bf. d, Mitsubishi A6M3. 180k, Fiat CR-2.

2004, Feb. 6		Perf. 14	
725	A157 75k Sheet of 4, #a-d	6.00	6.00
	Souvenir Sheet		
726	A157 180k multi	4.00	4.00

General Motors Automobiles — A158

No. 727, 75k — Cadillacs: a, 1959 Eldorado. b, 1962 Series 62. c, 1961 Sedan De Ville. d, 1930 V-16.
No. 728, 75k — Corvettes: a, 1965 convertible. b, 1965 Stingray. c, 1979. d, 1998.
No. 729, 180k, 1954 Cadillac Eldorado. No. 730, 180k, 1998 Corvette, diff.

2004, Feb. 6	Litho.	Perf. 14	
	Sheets of 4, #a-d		
727-728	A158 Set of 2	12.00	12.00
	Souvenir Sheets		
729-730	A158 Set of 2	8.25	8.25

The following items inscribed "Malawi" have been declared "illegal" by Malawi postal officials:
Souvenir sheets of three 80k stamps depicting Birds of prey; cats; locomotives; Ferrari Formula 1 cars.

A sheetlet of eight hexagonal 15k depicting the national birds of South African Postal Operators Association (SAPOA) countries was produced in limited quantities.

Rotary International, Cent. — A159

No. 731: a, 25k, Boys in classroom. b, 55k, Boy in wheelchair. c, 60k, Doctor examining patient. d, 65k, Nurse monitoring baby in incubator.

2005, July 25	Litho.	Perf. 13¼	
731	A159 Sheet of 4, #a-d	7.00	7.00

Butterflies — A161

Design: 5k, Myrina silenus ficedula. 10k, Cymothoe zombana. 20k, Charaxes castor. 40k, Papilio pelodorus. 50k, Charaxes pythoduras ventersi, 65k, Papilio pelodorus, 75k, Acrita acrita. 100k, Iolaus lalos. 105k, Acrea acrita. 110k, Euxanthe wakefieldi. 115k, Pseudacraea boisdurali.

2007		Litho.	Perf. 13¼x12¾	
733	A161	5k multi	.25	.25
734	A161	10k multi	.40	.40
735	A161	20k multi	.70	.70
736	A161	40k multi	1.25	1.25
736A	A161	50k multi	1.50	1.50
737	A161	65k multi	1.60	1.60
738	A161	75k multi	2.00	2.00
739	A161	100k multi	2.25	2.25
740	A161	105k multi	2.25	2.25
741	A161	110k multi	2.75	2.75
742	A161	115k multi	3.00	3.00
		Nos. 733-742 (11)	17.95	17.95

Compare with Type A153. For surcharges, see Nos. 847, 854, 911-914, 922, 923.

Stop Child Abuse — A162

2008, Nov. 19	Litho.	Perf. 13x13¼	
744	A162 40k multi	2.50	2.50

Endangered Animals — A163

No. 745: a, Black rhinoceros. b, Sable antelope. c, Zebra. d, African buffalo. 325k, Roan antelope.

2009, Sept. 30		Perf. 11½x12	
745	A163 65k Sheet of 4, #a-d	7.00	7.00

	Souvenir Sheet		
	Perf. 11½x11¼		
746	A163 325k multi	7.00	7.00

Hippopotamus Amphibius — A164

No. 747 — Hippopotamus: a, Head, facing right. b, Reclining. c, Standing. d, Pair in water.
325k, Hippopotamus, vert.

2009, Sept. 30		Perf. 11½x12	
747	A164 105k Sheet of 4, #a-d	7.25	7.25

	Souvenir Sheet		
	Perf. 11¼x11½		
748	A164 325k multi	5.75	5.75

A165

Wildlife — A166

No. 749: a, Lion. b, Elephant shrew. c, Black-backed jackal. d, Reedbuck. e, African elephant. f, Warthog.
325k, Leopard.

2009, Sept. 30		Perf. 11½x11¼	
749	A165 110k Sheet of 6, #a-f	11.50	11.50

| | Souvenir Sheet | | |
| 750 | A166 325k multi | 5.75 | 5.75 |

Worldwide Fund for Nature (WWF) — A167

No. 751 — Lilian's loverbirds: a, Six birds on branches. b, Seven birds in flight. c, Two birds on branch, four in flight. d, Birds on ground and in flight.

2009, Sept. 30		Perf. 13¼	
751	Strip of 4	10.00	10.00
a.-d.	A167 115k Any single	2.00	2.00
e.	Sheet of 8, 2 each #751a-751d	20.00	20.00

MALAWI

Numerous items inscribed "Malawi" have been declared illegal by Malawi postal officials, incuding items with dates of 2007 and 2008 having topics of:

Rugby World Cup, Nelson Mandela, Mahatma Gandhi, Dalai Lama, and Pope John Paul II, Coral, Horses, Minerals, Birds, Bees, Exotic fish, Owls, Dinosaurs, Minerals and Scouts, Space, Automobiles, Mushrooms, Internet and Basketball stars.

Malawi postal officials have also declared "illegal" many other items with dates from 2005-2012 having a variety of topics.

Miniature Sheet

National Animals — A168

No. 752: a, Nyala (Malawi). b, Nyala (Zimbabwe). c, Burchell's zebra (Botswana). d, Oryx (Namibia). e, Buffalo (Zambia).

Litho. With Foil Application
2010, July 7   Perf. 13¾
752 A168 55k Sheet of 5, #a-e   25.00 25.00

See Botswana No. 838, Namibia Nos. 1141-1142, Zambia Nos. 1097-1101, Zimbabwe Nos. 1064-1068.

Miniature Sheet

2010 World Cup Soccer Championships, South Africa — A169

No. 753 — Soccer players, ball, 2010 World Cup mascot and flag of: a, Namibia. b, South Africa. c, Zimbabwe. d, Malawi. e, Swaziland. f, Botswana. g, Mauritius. h, Lesotho. i, Zambia.

2010, Dec. 20   Litho.   Perf. 13¾
753 A169 105k Sheet of 9, #a-i   25.00 25.00

See Botswana Nos. 896-905, Lesotho No. , Mauritius No. 1086, Namibia No. 1188, South Africa No. 1403, Swaziland Nos. 794-803, Zambia Nos. 1115-1118, and Zimbabwe Nos. 1112-1121.

A single sheetlet of 9 omnibus issues exist containing a gold-faced stamp of the 753 design. See footnote under Namibia 1188.

For surcharges, see Nos. 915-917.

Christmas A170

Various creche figures with bottom panel color of: No. 754, 65k, Red. No. 755, 65k, Blue violet. No. 756, 65k, Claret. No. 757, 65k, Green.

2010, Dec. 20   Perf. 13x13¼
754-757 A170 Set of 4   5.00 5.00

Partnership Between Malawi and European Union, 35th Anniv. (in 2010) — A171

Flags of Malawi and European Union and: No. 758, 65k, Partnership projects. No. 759, 65k, Family, 35th anniversary emblem, vert.

2011, Jan. 18   Perf. 14
758-759 A171 Set of 2   6.00 6.00
759a   Souvenir sheet of 2, #758-759   6.00 6.00

Big Game Animals — A172

Designs: 80k, Buffalo. 100k, Leopard. 135k, Black rhinoceros. 140k, Elephant. 145k, Lion.

2011, Nov. 3   Perf. 14x13¼
760-764 A172 Set of 5   11.00 11.00
764a   Souvenir sheet of 5, #760-764   11.00 11.00

Christmas — A173

Designs: 80k, Angels proclaiming Gospel to shepherds. 100k, Shepherds lauding Jesus. 135k, Wise men following the star. 140k, Wise men giving Jesus gifts. 145k, Simeon blessing baby Jesus.

2011, Dec. 16   Perf. 13¼x14
765-769 A173 Set of 5   22.50 22.50
769a   Souvenir sheet of 5, #765-769   22.50 22.50

Pan-African Tsetse and Trypasonomiasis Eradication Campaign A174

Stamps with white frames: No. 770, 65k. Man, tsetse fly, zebu, map of Malawi, campaign emblem. No. 771, 105k, Campaign emblem. No. 772, 110k, Tsetse flies, map of Malawi, campaign emblem. No. 773, 115k, Tsetse fly, map of Malawi, campaign emblem. No. 774: a, 65k, Like No. 770, dull brown frame. b, 105k, Like No. 771, orange frame. c, 110k, Like No. 772, blue frame. d, 115k, Like No. 770, brown violet frame.

2012, Jan. 25   Perf. 14
770 770 A174   Cet of 4   11.00 11.00
Souvenir Sheet
774 A174   Sheet of 4, #a-d   11.00 11.00

Campaign Against AIDS — A175

Inscriptions: 80k, Stop AIDS keep the promise (red AIDS ribbon, map of Malawi). 100k, Male involvement (man and woman wearing AIDS ribbons). 135k, HTC (man, woman and doctor). 140k, Stop AIDS keep the promise (man and woman wearing AIDS ribbons). 145k, PMTCT (pregnant woman and nurse).

2012, Sept. 5   Perf. 13¼x12¾
775-779 A175 Set of 5   10.00 10.00

One hundred sheetlets of five stamps inscribed "Standard Postage" were created and given to bulk purchasers of Nos. 775-779. The sheet margin is inscribed "Not For Sale" and the individual stamps on the sheet were not valid for postage.

Dances — A176

Designs: 165k, Vimbuza. 260k, Uyeni. 270k, Tchopa. 280k, Masewe. 290k, Gule wa Mkulu.

2012, July   Litho.   Perf. 14
780-784 A176 Set of 5   10.50 10.50
784a   Souvenir sheet of 5, #780-784   10.50 10.50

Lake Malawi — A177

Designs: 100k, MV Mtendere. 265k, Sunrise on Lake Malawi. 420k, Otter Point, Cape Maclear. 430k, Sunset on Lake Malawi. 450k, Fish eagle poised for a kill. 480k, Kayakers on Lake Malawi. 500k, Satellite map of Lake Malawi. 840k, Cichlids in Lake Malawi. 860k, Fish eagle catching fish. 900k, Lizard Island.

2014, Apr. 25   Litho.   Perf. 14½x14
785-794 A177 Set of 10   30.00 30.00
794a   Souvenir sheet of 10, #785-794   30.00 30.00

Independence, 50th Anniv. — A178

Flag and: 330k, Independence Ark. 520k, Hastings Kamuzu Banda, first president. 560k, Corn silos. 600k, Parliament. 670k, Zebras.

2014, Oct. 21   Litho.   Perf. 13x13½
795 A178 330k multi   2.10 2.10
  a.   Booklet pane of 1   2.10
796 A178 520k multi   3.25 3.25
  a.   Booklet pane of 1   3.25
797 A178 560k multi   3.50 3.50
  a.   Booklet pane of 1   3.50
798 A178 600k multi   3.75 3.75
  a.   Booklet pane of 1   3.75
799 A178 670k multi   4.25 4.25
  a.   Booklet pane of 1   4.25
   Complete booklet, #795a, 796a, 797a, 798a, 799a   17.00
  b.   Souvenir sheet of 5, #795-799   17.00 17.00
   Nos. 795-799 (5)   16.85 16.85

For surcharges, see Nos. 918, 920.

Christmas A179

Designs: 330k, Christmas tree, candles, bells, street lights. 520k, Christmas tree, gifts. 560k, Christmas tree with star, snow in background. 600k, Undecorated Christmas tree. 670k, Christmast tree with star, tree branches in background.

2014   Litho.   Perf. 14½x14
800-804 A179 Set of 5   11.00 11.00
804a   Souvenir sheet of 5, #800-804   11.00 11.00

For surcharge, see No. 919.

Fish A180

No. 805: a, 100k, Kampango catfish. b, 200k, Four cichlids. c, 200k, Three striped cichlids. d, 400k, Butter fish. e, 500k, Mud fish. f, 700k, Chambo. g, 730k, Copadichromis chrysonotus. h, 870k, Mpasa.

No. 806: a, One cichlid facing backwards. b, Yellow cichlid facing left.

No. 807, 350k, Sanjika. No. 808, 350k, Blue Malawi cichlid. No. 809, 350k, Tilapia. No. 810, 730k, Metriaclima callainos.

2016, Apr. 6   Litho.   Perf. 13x13¼
805 A180   Sheet of 8, #a-h   11.00 11.00
Souvenir Sheets
806 A180 350k Sheet of 2, #a-b   2.10 2.10
807-810 A180   Set of 4   5.25 5.25

A181

Birds A182

No. 811: a, 200k, White dove sparrow. b, 400k, Emerald cuckoo. c, 500k, Yellow-bellied sunbird. d, 700k, Klaas's cuckoo. e, 730k, Blue waxbill. f, 870k, Bee-eater.

No. 812, 350k, Collared sunbird. No. 813, 350k, Bee-eater, diff. No. 814, 350k, African yellow white-eye. No. 815, 350k, Bohm's bee-eater. No. 816, 350k, White dove sparrow, diff. No. 817, 350k, Klaas's cuckoo. No. 818, 350k, Yellow-bellied sunbird.

2016, May 27   Litho.   Perf. 13x13¼
811 A181   Sheet of 6, #a-f   9.75 9.75
Souvenir Sheets
     Perf. 13¼x13
812-818 A182   Set of 7   7.00 7.00

Wild Fruits A183

No. 819: a, 200k, Ximenia caffra. b, 400k, Strychnos spinosa. c, 500k, Azanza garckeana. d, 700k, Flacourtia indica. e, 730k, Ziziphus mauritiana. f, 870k, Vitex doniana.

No. 820, 350k, Maboque fruta (Strychnos spinosa). No. 821, 350k, Vitex doniana, diff. No. 822, 350k, Baobab fruit. No. 823, 350k, Indian jujubes. No. 824, 350k, Flacourtia indica, diff. No. 825, 350k, Masukus.

2016, July 6   Litho.   Perf. 13x13¼
819 A183   Sheet of 6, #a-f   9.50 9.50
Souvenir Sheets
820-825 A183   Set of 6   6.00 6.00

Endangered Animals — A184

No. 826: a, 100k, Syncerus caffer. b, 200k, Hippopotami. c, 400k, Rhinoceroses. d, 700k, Eyes of Panthera pardus. e, 700k, Head of

MALAWI

Panthera pardus. f, 730k, Loxodonta africana. g, 870k, Panthera leo.
No. 827, 350k, Syncerus caffer, diff. No. 828, 350k, Hippopotamus. No. 829, 350k, Rhinoceros. No. 830, 350k, Eyes of Panthera pardus. No. 831, 350k, Loxodonta africana, diff. No. 832, 350k, Head of Panthera leo. No. 833, 350k, Zebras.

2016, Aug. 6   Litho.   Perf. 13x13¼
| 826 | A184 | Sheet of 7, #a-g | 10.50 | 10.50 |

Souvenir Sheets
| 827-833 | A184 | Set of 7 | 6.75 | 6.75 |

Herbs A185

No. 834: a, 100k, Hibiscus sabdariffa. b, 200k, Neem tree. c, 400k, Bird's eye chilis. d, 500k, Bidens pilosa. e, 500k, Aloe vera. f, 730k, Artemisia annua. g, 870k, Amaranthus.
No. 835, 350k, Bidens pilosa, diff. No. 836, 350k, Silver artemisia. No. 837, 350k, Moringa. No. 838, 350k, Bird's eye chilis, diff. No. 839, 730k, Amaranthus, diff.

2016, Oct. 9   Litho.   Perf. 13x13¼
| 834 | A185 | Sheet of 7, #a-g | 9.25 | 9.25 |

Souvenir Sheets
| 835-839 | A185 | Set of 5 | 6.00 | 6.00 |

Nos. 521, 529 Surcharged

Methods, Paper and Perfs. As Before
2016, Nov. 7
| 840 | A109 | 520k on 7t #521 | 1.50 | 1.50 |
| 841 | A109 | 815k on 75t #529 | 2.25 | 2.25 |

Nos. 526, 528, 530, 531 Surcharged Like No. 840
Methods, Paper and Perfs As Before
2017, July 1
842	A109	600k on 30t #526	1.75	1.75
843	A109	600k on 1k #530	1.75	1.75
844	A109	600k on 2k #531	1.75	1.75
845	A109	900k on 50t #528	2.50	2.50
		Nos. 842-845 (4)	7.75	7.75

Nos. 653, 654, 706, 707 and 737 Surcharged

No. 846   No. 848

2018, Feb. 6   Litho.
846	A153	600k on 1k #706	4.00	4.00
847	A161	900k on 65k #737	4.00	4.00
848	A139	1150k on 4k #653	4.00	4.00
849	A153	1200k on 2k #707	4.00	4.00
850	A139	2000k on 10k #654	4.00	4.00
		Nos. 846-850 (5)	20.00	20.00

Nos. 522, 525, 527, 706, 737 Surcharged in Red Like No. 846
Methods, Paper and Perfs. As Before
2018
851	A109	600k on 8t #522	1.75	1.75
852	A109	600k on 20t #525	1.75	1.75
853	A109	900k on 40t #527	2.50	2.50
854	A161	900k on 65k #737	2.50	2.50
855	A153	1280k on 1k #706	3.50	3.50
		Nos. 851-855 (5)	12.00	12.00

Birds A186

No. 856: a, Crow. b, Wagtail. c, Fish eagle. d, Flycatcher. e, Hamerkop. f, Kingfisher.
No. 857, 450k, Unidentified bird (Archilochus colubris). No. 858, 450k, Fish eagle. No. 859, 450k, Hamerkop. No. 860, 450k, Kingfisher. No. 861, 450k, Marsh harrier. No. 862, 450k, Egret.

2018, June 4   Litho.   Perf. 14x13¼
| 856 | A186 | 700k Sheet of 6, #a-f | | 12.00 | 12.00 |

Souvenir Sheets   Perf. 13¾
| 857-862 | A186 | Set of 6 | 7.50 | 7.50 |

Nos. 857-862 each contain one 35x35mm stamp.

Mushrooms — A188

No. 863: Various unnamed mushrooms, as shown.
No. 864, 450k, Branched oyster mushrooms. No. 865, 450k, Portabella mushrooms. No. 866, 450k, Psathyrella cap mushrooms. No. 867, 450k, Pleurotus ostreatus. No. 868, 450k, Amanita calyptoderma. No. 869, 450k, Chanterelles.

2018, Aug.   Litho.   Perf. 14x13¼
| 863 | A187 | 700k Sheet of 6, #a-f | | 11.50 | 11.50 |

Souvenir Sheets   Perf. 13¾
| 864-869 | A188 | Set of 6 | 7.50 | 7.50 |

A189

A190

Translocation of Elephants — A195

No. 870: a, Arrival of helicopter. b, Ropes wrapped around tusks of raised elephant. c, Man pulling on tusk. d, Men pushing standing elephant. e, Elephant with bound feet hanging from crane. f, Men standing behind elephant on ground.

2018, Oct. 2   Litho.   Perf. 14x13¼
| 870 | A189 | 700k Sheet of 6, #a-f | | 11.50 | 11.50 |

Souvenir Sheets   Perf. 13¾
871	A190	450k multi	1.25	1.25
872	A191	450k multi	1.25	1.25
873	A192	450k multi	1.25	1.25
874	A193	450k multi	1.25	1.25
875	A194	450k multi	1.25	1.25
876	A195	450k multi	1.25	1.25
		Nos. 871-876 (6)	7.50	7.50

Nos. 870-876 are dated 2017.

Vultures A197

No. 877: a, Lappet-faced vulture. b, White-rumped vulture. c, Cinereous vulture. d, White-backed vulture. e, Ruppell's vulture. f, Griffon vulture.

No. 878, 450k, Lappet-faced vulture, diff. No. 879, 450k, White-rumped vulture, diff. No. 880, 450k, Cinereous vulture, diff. No. 881, 450k, White-backed vulture, diff. No. 882, 450k, Hooded vulture.

2018, Dec. 3   Litho.   Perf. 14x13¼
| 877 | A196 | 700k Sheet of 6, #a-f | | 11.50 | 11.50 |

Souvenir Sheets   Perf. 13¾
| 878-882 | A197 | Set of 5 | 6.25 | 6.25 |

Wildlife A199

No. 883: a, Chipembere (rhinoceros). b, Mkango (lions). c, Kambuku (leopard). d, Njati (buffalo). e, Njobvu (elephants). f, Mvuwu (hippopotamus).
No. 884, 450k, Rhinoceros, diff. No. 885, 450k, Lion, diff. No. 886, 450k, Leopard, diff. No. 887, 450k, Buffalo, diff. No. 888, 450k, Elephant, diff. No. 889, 450k, Hippopotamus, diff.

2018 ?   Litho.   Perf. 14x13¼
| 883 | A198 | 700k Sheet of 6, #a-f | | 11.00 | 11.00 |

Souvenir Sheets   Perf. 13¾
| 884-889 | A199 | Set of 6 | 7.00 | 7.00 |

Insects A201

No. 890: a, Mavu (hornet). b, Ladybug. c, Gulugufe (butterfly). d, Chiswamphika (preying mantis). e, Chiwala (grasshopper). f, Njuchi (bee).
No. 891, 450k, Hornet, diff. No. 892, 450k, Grasshopper, diff. No. 893, 450k, Bee, diff. No. 894, 450k, Nyerere (ant). No. 895, 450k, Ngumbi (termites). No. 896, 450k, Nunkhadala (locust).

2019, Feb. 5   Litho.   Perf. 14x13¼
| 890 | A200 | 700k Sheet of 6, #a-f | | 11.50 | 11.50 |

Souvenir Sheets   Perf. 13¾
| 891-896 | A201 | Set of 6 | 7.50 | 7.50 |

Nos. 890-896 are dated 2018.

MALAWI — MALAYA

MALAWI (continued)

Gemstones — A203

No. 897: a, Smoky quartz. b, Sunstones. c, Rubies. d, Iolite. e, Kynite. f, Fire quartz cluster.
No. 898, 450k, Sunstones, diff. No. 899, 450k, Kynite, diff. No. 900, 450k, Aquamarine. No. 901, 450k, Emeralds. No. 902, 450k, Prairie agates. No. 903, 450k, Sapphires.

2019, Aug. 8   Litho.   Perf. 14x13¼
897 A202 700k Sheet of 6, #a-f   11.50   11.50

Souvenir Sheets
Perf. 13¾
898-903 A203 Set of 6   7.50   7.50
Nos. 897-903 are dated 2018.

A204

Domesticated Birds — A205

No. 904: a, Chinziri (quail). b, Nkhanga (helmeted guineafowl). c, Nkhuku tembo (turkey). d, Nkhunda (pigeon). e, Bakha (duck). f, Tambala (rooster).
No. 905, 450k, Quail, diff. No. 906, 450k, Helmeted guineafowl, diff. No. 907, 450k, Turkey, diff. No. 908, 450k, Pigeons, diff. No. 909, 450k, Duck, diff. No. 910, 450k, Rooster, diff.

2019, Oct. 8   Litho.   Perf. 14x13¼
904 A204 700k Sheet of 6, #a-f   11.50   11.50

Souvenir Sheets
Perf. 13¾
905-910 A205 Set of 6   7.50   7.50
Nos. 904-910 are dated 2018.

Nos. 741-742 Surcharged
Small Font Surcharges
No. 911   No. 912

Large Font Surcharges
No. 913   No. 914

Methods and Perfs. As Before
2020
Small Font Surcharges
911 A161 600k on 110k #741   1.60   1.60
912 A161 900k on 115k #742   2.40   2.40
Large Font Surcharges
913 A161 600k on 110k #741   1.60   1.60
914 A161 900k on 115k #742   2.40   2.40
Nos. 911-914 (4)   8.00   8.00

No. 753 Surcharged in Black, Blue and Black, and Red and Black

Typical Surcharge (Position of New Denomination Varies on Stamps in Sheet)

Nos. 915-917 — Soccer players, ball, 2010 World Cup mascot and flag of: a, Namibia. b, South Africa. c, Zimbabwe. d, Malawi. e, Swaziland. f, Botswana. g, Mauritius. h, Lesotho. i, Zambia.

Methods and Perfs. As Before
2021
915 A169 Sheet of 9 (Bk)   —   —
   a.-i. 600k on 105k Any single   —   —
916 A169 Sheet of 9 (Bl & Bk)   —   —
   a.-i. 900k on 105k Any single   —   —
917 A169 Sheet of 9 (R & Bk)   —   —
   a.-i. 1280k on 105k Any single   —   —

Nos. 797, 799, 802 Srchd.

Methods and Perfs. As Before
2021, Dec. 15
918 A178 600k on 560k #797   1.50   1.50
919 A179 900k on 560k #802   2.25   2.25
920 A178 1280k on 670k #799   3.25   3.25
Nos. 918-920 (3)   7.00   7.00

Nos. 707, 740 Surcharged

Methods and Perfs. As Before
2022, June
921 A153 600k on 2k #707   —   —
922 A161 900k on 105k #740   —   —
New denomination is at upper left on No. 922.

No. 740 Surcharged With New Denomination at Upper Right

Methods and Perfs. As Before
2022
923 A161 900k on 105k #740   —   —

POSTAGE DUE STAMPS

D1

Wmk. 357
1967, Sept. 1   Litho.   Perf. 11½
J1 D1 1p deep lilac rose   .30   4.50
J2 D1 2p sepia   .30   4.50
J3 D1 4p lilac   .30   5.00
J4 D1 6p dark blue   .40   5.50
J5 D1 8p emerald   .55   6.00
J6 D1 1sh black   .65   6.00
Nos. J1-J6 (6)   2.50   31.50

Values in Decimal Currency
1971, Feb. 15   Size: 18x23mm
J7 D1 2t sepia   .35   4.25
J8 D1 4t lilac   .50   4.25
J9 D1 6t dark blue   .80   4.50
J10 D1 8t green   1.10   4.50
J11 D1 10t black   1.40   4.50
Nos. J7-J11 (5)   4.15   22.00

Type of 1971 Redrawn
1975   Wmk. 357   Perf. 14
Size: 17x21mm
J12 D1 2t brown   1.75   5.00
No. J12 has accent mark over "W."

1977-78   Litho.   Unwmk.   Perf. 14
Size: 18x21mm
J13 D1 2t sepia   9.00   4.50
J14 D1 4t rose lilac   9.00   4.50
J15 D1 8t brt green ('78)   4.00   4.50
J16 D1 10t black   9.00   5.25
Nos. J13-J16 (4)   31.00   18.75

1982   Wmk. 357, Sideways
J13a D1 2t   .60   4.00
J14a D1 4t   .60   4.00
J16a D1 10t   .60   4.00
Nos. J13a-J16a (3)   1.80   12.00

1989   Litho.   Unwmk.   Perf. 15x14
Size: 18x20½mm
J13b D1 2t   3.75   5.50
J14b D1 4t   3.75   5.50
J15a D1 8t   3.75   5.50
J16b D1 10t   3.75   5.50
Nos. J13b-J16b (4)   15.00   22.00

MALAYA
mə-ˈlā-ə

Federated Malay States

LOCATION — Malay peninsula
GOVT. — British Protectorate
AREA — 27,585 sq. mi.
CAPITAL — Kuala Lumpur

The Federated Malay States consisted of the sultanates of Negri Sembilan, Pahang, Perak and Selangor.
Stamps of the Federated Malay States replaced those of the individual states and were used until 1935, when individual issues were resumed.

100 Cents = 1 Dollar

Catalogue values for unused stamps in this country are for Never Hinged items, beginning with Scott 80 in the regular postage section, Scott J20 in the postage due section, Scott 128 in Johore, Scott 55 in Kedah, Scott 44 in Kelantan, Scott 1 in Malacca, Scott 36 in Negri Sembilan, Scott 44 in Pahang, Scott 1 in Penang, Scott 99 in Perak, Scott 1 in Perlis, Scott 74 in Selangor, and Scott 47 in Trengganu.

Watermarks

Wmk. 47 — Multiple Rosettes   Wmk. 71 — Rosette

Wmk. 338 — PTM Multiple

(PTM stands for Persekutuan Tanah Melayu, or Federation of Malaya.)

Stamps of Straits Settlements overprinted "BMA MALAYA" are listed in Straits Settlements.

Stamps and Type of Negri Sembilan Overprinted in Black

FEDERATED MALAY STATES

1900   Wmk. 2   Perf. 14
1 A2 1c lilac & green   3.50   12.00
2 A2 2c lilac & brown   35.00   75.00
3 A2 3c lilac & black   3.00   7.00
4 A2 5c lilac & olive   80.00   195.00
5 A2 10c lilac & org   16.00   55.00
6 A2 20c green & olive   97.50   120.00
7 A2 25c grn & car rose   260.00   400.00
8 A2 50c green & black   105.00   160.00
Nos. 1-8 (8)   600.00   1,024.

Overprinted on Perak Nos. 51, 53, 57-58, 60-61
1900
9 A9 5c lilac & olive   27.50   75.00
10 A9 10c lilac & org   40.00   75.00

Wmk. 1
11 A10 $1 green & lt grn   210.00   275.00
12 A10 $2 green & car rose   175.00   325.00
13 A10 $5 green & ultra   525.00   750.00
   Revenue cancel   75.00
13A A10 $25 green & org   15,500.
   Revenue cancel   275.00
Nos. 9-13 (5)   977.50   1,500.
No. 10 with bar omitted is an essay.

Elephants and Howdah — A3

1900   Typo.
14 A3 $1 green & lt green   200.   200.
15 A3 $2 grn & car rose   190.   210.
16 A3 $5 green & ultra   475.   500.
   Revenue cancel   25.
17 A3 $25 grn & orange   5,000.   1,950.
   Revenue cancel   125.
Nos. 14-17 (4)   5,865.   2,860.
High values with revenue cancellations are plentiful and inexpensive.

Tiger — A4

Stamps of type A4 are watermarked sideways.

1901   Wmk. 2
18a A4 1c green & gray   6.00   1.25
19b A4 3c brn & gray brn   13.50   .25
20a A4 4c carmine & gray   12.50   9.25
21 A4 5c scar & grn, yel   3.00   3.75
22a A4 8c ultra & gray   26.00   9.50
23a A4 10c violet & gray   90.00   17.50
24 A4 20c black & gray vio   26.00   17.50
25b A4 50c brn org & gray brn   115.00   110.00
Nos. 18a-25b (8)   284.50   118.00

1904-10   Wmk. 3
26a A4 1c grn & gray brown   50.00   .85
27 A4 3c brown & gray   77.50   1.60
28 A4 4c rose & black   8.50   1.00
29 A4 5c scar & grn, yel   12.00   3.25
30c A4 8c ultra & gray brn ('07)   11.00   6.25
31c A4 10c claret & black   42.50   .75

107

MALAYA — Federation of Malaya

32	A4	20c blk & gray vio ('05)	24.00	1.50
33b	A4	50c orange & gray ('06)	72.50	18.00

The 1c and 4c are on ordinary paper, the other values on both ordinary and chalky papers. The least expensive varieties are shown. For comprehensive listing, see Scott Classic Specialized Catalogue.

Chalky Paper

34	A3	$1 green & lt green ('07)	110.00	57.50
35	A3	$2 green & car rose ('06)	125.00	140.00
36	A3	$5 grn & ultra ('06)	325.00	160.00
		Revenue cancellation		25.00
37	A3	$25 grn & org ('10)	2,200.	825.00
		Revenue cancellation		75.00
		Nos. 26a-37 (12)	3,058.	1,216.

High values with revenue cancellations are plentiful and inexpensive.

1906-22 Ordinary Paper

Two dies for Nos. 38 and 44:
I — Thick line under "Malay."
II — Thin line under "Malay."

38	A4	1c dull grn, die II	16.00	.25
b.		Die I	27.50	.55
39	A4	1c brown ('19)	3.00	1.25
40	A4	2c green ('19)	2.50	.55
41	A4	3c brown	10.50	.25
42	A4	3c carmine ('09)	5.00	.25
43	A4	3c dp gray ('19)	2.50	.25
44	A4	4c scar, die II	2.25	.25
b.		Die I ('19)	3.75	5.50
45	A4	6c orange ('19)	3.25	4.00
46	A4	8c ultra ('09)	16.00	1.40
47	A4	10c ultra ('19)	9.00	2.25
48	A4	35c red, yellow	7.50	17.50
		Nos. 38-48 (11)	77.50	28.20

1922-32 Wmk. 4 Ordinary Paper

49	A4	1c brown ('22)	2.25	4.75
50	A4	1c black ('23)	.85	.25
51	A4	2c dk brown ('25)	14.00	15.00
52	A4	2c green ('26)	3.00	.25
53	A4	3c dp gray ('23)	2.50	7.50
54	A4	3c green ('24)	2.75	2.00
55	A4	3c brown ('27)	5.00	.50
56	A4	4c scar (II) ('23)	4.00	.60
57	A4	4c orange ('26)	1.50	.25
c.		Unwatermarked	425.00	300.00
58	A4	5c vio, yel ('22)	1.25	.25
59	A4	5c dk brown ('32)	3.50	.25
60	A4	6c orange ('22)	1.00	.55
61	A4	6c scarlet ('26)	1.50	.25
62	A4	10c ultra ('23)	1.75	8.50
63	A4	10c ultra & blk ('23)	2.50	.80
64	A4	10c vio, yel, chalky paper ('31)	4.00	.55
65	A4	12c ultra ('22)	1.75	.25

Chalky Paper

66	A4	20c blk & vio ('23)	5.00	2.75
a.		Ordinary paper	72.50	5.25
67	A4	25c red vio & ol vio ('29)	3.50	3.00
68	A4	30c yel & dl vio ('29)	4.00	5.00
69	A4	35c red, yel, ordinary paper ('28)	6.00	27.50
70	A4	35c dk vio & car ('31)	17.00	15.00
71	A4	50c org & blk ('24)	17.00	20.00
72	A4	50c blk, bl grn ('31)	5.50	2.50
73	A3	$1 gray grn & yel grn ('26)	24.00	100.00
a.		$1 green & blue green	24.00	60.00
74	A3	$2 grn & car ('26)	42.50	95.00
75	A3	$5 grn & ultra ('25)	210.00	280.00
76	A3	$25 grn & org ('28)	2,250.	2,500.
		Revenue cancel		175.00
		Nos. 49-75 (27)	387.60	593.25

1931-34

77	A4	$1 red & blk, blue	15.00	5.25
78	A4	$2 car & green, yel ('34)	6.50	50.00
79	A4	$5 car & green, emer ('34)	350.00	280.00
		Nos. 77-79 (3)	371.50	335.25

FEDERATION OF MALAYA

GOVT. — Sovereign state in British Commonwealth of Nations
AREA — 50,700 sq. mi.
POP. — 7,139,000 (est. 1961)
CAPITAL — Kuala Lumpur

The Federation comprised the nine states of Johore, Pahang, Negri Sembilan, Selangor, Perak, Kedah, Perlis, Kelantan and Trengganu and the settlements of Penang and Malacca.

Malaya joined the Federation of Malaysia in 1963.

100 Sen (Cents) = 1 Dollar (1957)

Catalogue values for unused stamps in this section are for Never Hinged items.

The Peace Issue of 1946 8c stamp inscribed "MALAYAN UNION" was not issued.

Rubber Tapping — A5
Map of Federation — A6

Designs: 12c, Federation coat of arms. 25c, Tin dredge and flag.

Perf. 13x12½, 12½
Engr., Litho.

1957, May 5			Wmk. 314	
80	A5	6c blue, red & yel	1.00	.30
a.		Yellow omitted	85.00	
81	A5	12c car & multi	1.75	1.10
82	A5	25c multicolored	3.75	.40
83	A6	30c dp claret & red org	1.50	.30
		Nos. 80-83 (4)	8.00	2.10

Chief Minister Tunku Abdul Rahman and People of Various Races — A7

Perf. 12½

1957, Aug. 31		Wmk. 4	Engr.	
84	A7	10c brown	.80	.35

Independence Day, Aug. 31.

United Nations Emblem — A8

Design: 30c, UN emblem, vert.

Perf. 13½, 12½

1958, Mar. 5			Wmk. 314	
85	A8	12c rose red	.45	1.00
86	A8	30c plum	.65	1.00

Conf. of the Economic Commission for Asia and the Far East (ECAFE), Kuala Lumpur, Mar. 5-15.

Merdeka Stadium and Flag — A9
Tuanku Abdul Rahman, Paramount Ruler of Malaya — A10

Perf. 13½x14½, 14½x13½

1958, Aug. 31		Photo.	Wmk. 314	
87	A9	10c multicolored	.30	.30
88	A10	30c multicolored	.60	.90

1st anniv. of the Independence of the Federation of Malaya.

A11
Torch of Freedom and Broken Chain — A12

Perf. 12½x13, 13x12½

1958, Dec. 10		Litho.	Wmk. 314	
89	A11	10c multicolored	.25	.25

Photo.

| 90 | A12 | 30c green | .70 | .70 |

10th anniv. of the signing of the Universal Declaration of Human Rights.

Mace and People — A13

Perf. 12½x13½

1959, Sept. 12		Photo.	Unwmk.	
91	A13	4c rose red	.30	.30
92	A13	10c violet	.30	.30
93	A13	25c yellow green	.60	.40
		Nos. 91-93 (3)	1.20	1.00

1st Federal Parliament of Malaya, inauguration.

WRY Emblem — A14

Design: 30c, Similar to 12c, vert.

Perf. 13½, 13

1960, Apr. 7		Engr.	Wmk. 314	
94	A14	12c lilac	.30	.80
95	A14	30c dark green	.30	.30

World Refugee Year, 7/1/59-6/30/60.

Rubber Tree Seedling on Map of Malaya — A15

Perf. 13x13½

1960, Sept. 19		Litho.	Unwmk.	
96	A15	6s red brn, grn & blk	.25	1.25
97	A15	30s ultra, yel grn & blk	.60	.75

15th meeting of the Intl. Rubber Study Group and the Natural Rubber Research Conference, Kuala Lumpur, Sept. 26-Oct. 1.

Tuanku Syed Putra — A16

Perf. 13½x14½

1961, Jan. 4		Photo.	Wmk. 314	
98	A16	10s blue & black	.30	.30

Installation of Tuanku Syed Putra of Perlis as Paramount Ruler (Yang di-Pertuan Agong).

Colombo Plan Emblem — A17

1961, Oct. 30		Unwmk.	Perf. 13½	
99	A17	12s rose pink & black	.55	3.25
100	A17	25s brt yellow & black	1.10	2.00
101	A17	30s brt blue & black	.90	1.00
		Nos. 99-101 (3)	2.55	6.25

13th meeting of the Consultative Committee for Technical Co-operation in South and South East Asia, Kuala Lumpur, Oct. 30-Nov. 18.

Malaria Eradication Emblem — A18

Wmk. PTM Multiple (338)

1962, Apr. 7			Perf. 14x14½	
102	A18	25s orange brown	.35	.60
103	A18	30s dull violet	.35	.30
104	A18	50s ultramarine	.60	.80
		Nos. 102-104 (3)	1.30	1.70

WHO drive to eradicate malaria.

Palmyra Leaf — A19

1962, July 21		Photo.	Perf. 13½	
105	A19	10s violet & gldn brown	.35	.35
106	A19	20s bluish grn & gldn brn	1.00	1.25
107	A19	50s car rose & gldn brn	2.25	2.25
		Nos. 105-107 (3)	3.60	3.85

National Language Month. Watermark inverted on alternating stamps.

Children and their Future Shadows — A20

1962, Oct. 1		Wmk. 338	Perf. 13½	
108	A20	10s bright rose lilac	.25	.25
109	A20	25s ocher	.70	1.25
110	A20	30s bright green	3.00	.25
		Nos. 108-110 (3)	3.95	1.75

Free primary education introduced Jan. 1962.

Forms of Food Production and Ears of Wheat — A21

1963, Mar. 21		Unwmk.	Perf. 11½	
		Granite Paper		
111	A21	25s lt ol grn & lil rose	3.00	4.00
112	A21	30s dk car & lil rose	3.25	1.75
113	A21	50s ultra & lil rose	3.25	4.00
		Nos. 111-113 (3)	9.50	9.75

FAO "Freedom from Hunger" campaign.

Cameron Highlands Dam and Pylon — A22

1963, June 26		Wmk. 338	Perf. 14	
114	A22	20s purple & brt green	.80	.25
115	A22	30s ultra & brt green	1.25	1.50

Opening of the Cameron Highlands hydroelectric plant.

Check listings for individual states for additional stamps inscribed "Malaya."

MALAYA — Federation of Malaya — Johore

POSTAGE DUE STAMPS

1924-26 Typo. Wmk. 4 Perf. 14½x14
J1	D1	1c violet	4.75	50.00
J2	D1	2c black	2.25	12.00
J3	D1	4c green ('26)	3.25	8.00
J4	D1	8c red	6.00	47.50
J5	D1	10c orange	10.00	17.50
J6	D1	12c ultramarine	10.00	27.50
		Nos. J1-J6 (6)	36.25	162.50

1936-38 Perf. 14½x14
J7	D2	1c dk violet ('38)	17.50	1.10
J8	D2	4c yellow green	40.00	1.40
J9	D2	8c scarlet	20.00	5.00
J10	D2	10c yel orange	25.00	.50
J11	D2	12c blue violet	40.00	16.00
J12	D2	50c black ('38)	30.00	5.50
		Nos. J7-J12 (6)	172.50	29.50

Nos. J7-J12 were also used in Straits Settlements.
For overprints see Nos. NJ1-NJ20, Malacca Nos. NJ1-NJ6.

1945-49
J13	D2	1c reddish violet	5.00	2.25
J14	D2	3c yel green	10.00	3.00
J15	D2	5c org scarlet	6.00	2.00
J16	D2	8c yel org ('49)	13.00	16.00
J17	D2	9c yel orange	40.00	50.00
J18	D2	15c blue vio	110.00	30.00
J19	D2	20c dk blue ('48)	10.00	6.50
		Nos. J13-J19 (7)	194.00	109.75

For surcharge see No. J34.

Catalogue values for unused stamps in this section, from this point to the end of the section, are for Never Hinged items.

1951-54 Wmk. 4 Perf. 14
J20	D2	1c dull violet ('52)	.70	1.75
J21	D2	2c dk gray ('53)	1.25	2.25
J22	D2	3c green ('52)	37.50	20.00
J23	D2	4c dk brown ('53)	.70	7.00
J24	D2	5c vermilion	50.00	13.00
J25	D2	8c yel orange	2.50	10.00
J26	D2	12c magenta ('54)	1.25	6.50
J27	D2	20c deep blue	10.00	6.75
		Nos. J20-J27 (8)	103.90	67.25

Nos. J13-J27 were used throughout the Federation and in Singapore, later in Malaysia.

1957-63 Ordinary Paper Perf. 12½
J21a	D2	2c ('60)	4.50	24.00
b.		2c, chalky paper ('62)	1.75	16.00
c.		Vert. pair, imperf. horiz.		22,500.
J23a	D2	4c ('60)	3.50	25.00
b.		4c, chalky paper ('62)	1.00	20.00
J26a	D2	12c, chalky paper ('62)	5.00	32.50
J27a	D2	20c	8.00	25.00
b.		20c, chalky paper ('62)	12.50	50.00
		Nos. J21a-J27a (4)	21.00	100.50

1965 Wmk. 314 Perf. 12
J28	D2	1c plum	1.50	16.00
J29	D2	2c bluish black	1.10	22.50
J30	D2	4c brown	1.75	16.00
J31	D2	8c yel orange	2.50	22.50
J32	D2	12c magenta	6.50	40.00
J33	D2	20c dark blue	10.00	50.00
		Nos. J28-J33 (6)	23.35	167.00

Nos. J28-J33 were used in Malaysia.

1964, Apr. 14 Perf. 12½
J28a	D2	1c	.50	19.00
J29a	D2	2c	1.75	16.00
J30a	D2	4c	1.00	16.00
J32a	D2	12c	2.25	22.50
J33a	D2	20c	3.00	37.50
		Nos. J28a-J33a (5)	8.50	111.00

No. J16 Surcharged "10 cents"

1965, Jan. Wmk. 4
J34	D2	10c on 8c yel orange	.60	3.00

OCCUPATION STAMPS

Issued Under Japanese Occupation

Malayan Fruit and Fronds — OS1
Tin Dredging — OS2
Monument to Japanese War Dead — OS3

1943 Unwmk. Litho. Perf. 12½
N30	OS1	2c emerald	1.00	.25
a.		Rouletted	2.25	2.25
b.		Imperf., pair	6.50	6.50
N31	OS2	4c rose red	3.00	.25
a.		Rouletted	2.25	2.25
b.		Imperf., pair	6.50	6.50
N32	OS3	8c dull blue	.50	.25
		Nos. N30-N32 (3)	4.50	.75

Malayan Plowman — OS4

1943, Sept. 1
N33	OS4	8c violet	11.00	3.50
N34	OS4	15c carmine red	8.00	3.50

Publicity for Postal Savings which had reached a $10,000,000 total in Malaya.

Rubber Tapping OS5
Seaside Houses OS6
Japanese Shrine, Singapore OS7
Sago Palms OS8
Johore Bahru and Strait of Johore OS9
Malay Mosque, Kuala Lumpur OS10

1943, Oct. 1
N35	OS5	1c gray green	1.75	.70
N36	OS5	3c olive gray	1.00	.25
N37	OS6	10c red brown	1.25	.25
N38	OS7	15c violet	1.75	5.00
N39	OS8	30c olive green	1.50	.50
N40	OS9	50c blue	5.00	5.00
N41	OS10	70c dull blue	32.50	16.00
		Nos. N35-N41 (7)	44.75	27.70

Rice Planting and Map of Malaysia — OS11

1944, Feb. 15
N42	OS11	8c carmine	17.50	4.00
N43	OS11	15c violet	5.00	4.00

Issued on the anniversary of the fall of Singapore to commemorate the "Birth of New Malaya".

OCCUPATION POSTAGE DUE STAMPS

Stamps and Type of Postage Due Stamps of 1936-38 Handstamped in Black, Red or Brown

No. NJ7

1942 Wmk. 4 Perf. 14½x14
NJ1	D2	1c violet	14.00	35.00
a.		Brown overprint	190.00	225.00
b.		Red overprint	200.00	250.00
NJ2	D2	3c yellow green	87.50	97.50
a.		Red overprint	450.00	475.00
NJ3	D2	4c yellow green	95.00	60.00
		On cover, from		1,250.
a.		Brown overprint	220.00	250.00
b.		Red overprint	67.50	60.00
NJ4	D2	8c red	190.00	150.00
a.		Brown overprint	375.00	375.00
b.		Red overprint	275.00	175.00
NJ5	D2	10c yellow orange	40.00	65.00
a.		Brown overprint	110.00	140.00
b.		Red overprint	475.00	475.00
NJ6	D2	12c blue violet	27.50	60.00
a.		Red overprint	475.00	460.00
NJ7	D2	50c black	82.50	125.00
a.		Red overprint	750.00	825.00
		Nos. NJ1-NJ7 (7)	536.50	592.50

Overprinted in Black

1942
NJ8	D2	1c violet	3.50	11.00
NJ9	D2	3c yel green	27.50	35.00
NJ10	D2	4c yel green	25.00	12.50
NJ11	D2	8c red	37.50	35.00
NJ12	D2	10c yel orange	2.00	17.50
NJ13	D2	12c blue violet	2.00	50.00
		Nos. NJ8-NJ13 (6)	97.50	161.00

The 9c and 15c with this overprint were not regularly issued.

Postage Due Stamps of 1936-45 Overprinted

1943
NJ14	D2	1c reddish vio	2.25	6.00
NJ15	D2	3c yel green	2.25	5.00
NJ15A	D2	4c yel green	70.00	52.50
NJ16	D2	5c scarlet	1.50	5.00
NJ17	D2	9c yel orange	.90	8.50
NJ18	D2	10c yel orange	2.25	9.00
NJ19	D2	12c magenta	2.25	25.00
NJ20	D2	15c blue violet	2.25	10.00
		On cover, from		
		Nos. NJ14-NJ20 (8)	83.65	121.00

No. NJ15A is said to have been extensively forged.

ISSUED UNDER THAI OCCUPATION

For use in Kedah, Kelantan, Perlis and Trengganu

War Memorial — OS1

1943, Dec. Unwmk. Litho. Perf. 12½
2N1	OS1	1c pale yellow	35.00	37.50
2N2	OS1	2c buff	14.00	24.00
a.		Imperf., pair	1,000.	
2N3	OS1	3c pale green	20.00	45.00
		Imperf., pair		
2N4	OS1	4c dull lilac	15.00	32.50
2N5	OS1	8c rose	15.00	24.00
2N6	OS1	15c lt blue	42.50	65.00
		Nos. 2N1-2N6 (6)	148.50	235.50

Perf. 12½x11
2N2b	OS1	2c buff	20.00	24.00
2N3b	OS1	3c pale green	30.00	45.00
2N4b	OS1	4c dull lilac	20.00	37.50
2N5b	OS1	8c rose	20.00	24.00
2N6b	OS1	15c lt blue	45.00	72.50
		Nos. 2N2b-2N6b (5)	135.00	203.00

These stamps, in cent denominations, were for use only in the four Malayan states ceded to Thailand by the Japanese. The states reverted to British rule in September 1945. Stamps denominated 5c and 10c were prepared but not issued.

JOHORE

jə-ˈhōr

LOCATION — At the extreme south of the Malay Peninsula. Linked to Singapore by a causeway.
AREA — 7,330 sq. mi.
POP. — 1,009,649 (1960)
CAPITAL — Johore Bahru

Stamps of the Straits Settlements Overprinted in Black

Overprinted

1876 Wmk. 1 Perf. 14
1	A2	2c brown	21,500.	7,000.
b.		Double overprint		

Overprinted

Overprint 13 to 14mm Wide
1884-86 Wmk. 2
1A	A2	2c rose	225.00	225.00
c.		Double overprint	1,100.	

No. 2d

Without Period
Overprint 16¾x2mm ("H" & "E" wide)
2	A2	2c rose	3,200.	800.
a.		Double overprint		2,500.

Overprinted

Overprint 11x2½mm
3	A2	2c rose ('86)	130.00	140.00

MALAYA — Johore

Overprinted

Overprint 17½x2¾mm

4	A2	2c rose ('85)	9,000. —

Overprinted

Overprint 12½ to 15x2¾mm

5	A2	2c rose	25.00 22.50

Overprinted

Overprint 9x2½mm

7	A2	2c rose ('86)	80.00 65.00
a.	Double overprint		850.00

Overprinted

Overprint 9x3mm

8	A2	2c rose ('86)	72.50 67.50

Overprinted

Overprint 14 to 15x3mm

9	A2	2c rose	25.00 12.50

Tall "J" 3½mm high

10	A2	2c rose	300.00 200.00

Overprinted

1888

11	A2	2c rose	225.00 75.00
b.	Double overprint		950.00

Overprinted

Overprint 12½ to 13x2½mm

1890-91

12	A2	2c rose	27.50 27.00

Overprint 12x2¾mm

13	A2	2c rose ('91)	10,500.

Surcharged in Black

1891

14	A3(a)	2c on 24c green	47.50 62.50
15	A3(b)	2c on 24c green	150.00 160.00
16	A3(c)	2c on 24c green	30.00 45.00
a.	"CENST"		1,000. 525.00
17	A3(d)	2c on 24c green	140.00 150.00
	Nos. 14-17 (4)		367.50 417.50

Sultan Abubakar — A5

1891-94 Typo. Unwmk.

18	A5	1c lilac & vio ('94)	1.00 .60
19	A5	2c lilac & yellow	.75 1.75
20	A5	3c lil & car rose ('94)	.75 .60
21	A5	4c lilac & black	3.25 22.50
22	A5	5c lilac & green	8.50 22.50
23	A5	6c lilac & blue	9.50 22.50
24	A5	$1 green & car rose	90.00 190.00
	Nos. 18-24 (7)		113.75 260.45

For surcharges and overprints see Nos. 26-36.

Stamps of 1892-94 Surcharged in Black

1894

26	A5	3c on 4c lilac & blk	3.00 .65
a.	No period after "Cents"		125.00 85.00
27	A5	3c on 5c lilac & grn	2.40 4.25
a.	No period after "Cents"		275.00 175.00
28	A5	3c on 6c lilac & bl	4.00 7.50
a.	No period after "Cents"		210.00 240.00
29	A5	3c on $1 grn & car	14.50 85.00
a.	No period after "Cents"		500.00 900.00
	Nos. 26-29 (4)		23.90 97.40

Coronation of Sultan Ibrahim
Stamps of 1892-94 Overprinted

Overprinted "KEMAHKOTAAN"

1896

30	A5	1c lilac & violet	.60 1.25
31	A5	2c lilac & yellow	.60 1.25
32	A5	3c lilac & car rose	.65 1.25
33	A5	4c lilac & black	1.00 3.00
34	A5	5c lilac & green	6.00 8.00
35	A5	6c lilac & blue	4.00 7.00
36	A5	$1 green & car rose	70.00 135.00
	Nos. 30-36 (7)		82.85 156.75

Overprinted "KETAHKOTAAN"

30a	A5	1c	5.00 6.00
31a	A5	2c	6.50 8.50
32a	A5	3c	14.50 20.00
33a	A5	4c	3.50 21.00
34a	A5	5c	4.25 8.50
35a	A5	6c	9.00 20.00
36a	A5	$1	42.50 190.00
	Nos. 30a-36a (7)		85.25 274.00

Sultan Ibrahim — A7

1896-99 Typo. Wmk. 71

37	A7	1c green	1.00 3.50
38	A7	2c green & blue	.60 1.40
39	A7	3c green & vio	6.00 3.75
40	A7	4c grn & car rose	1.25 3.75
41	A7	4c yel & red ('99)	1.75 2.50
42	A7	5c green & brn	2.40 5.00
43	A7	6c green & yel	2.40 7.50
44	A7	10c green & black	8.50 55.00
45	A7	25c green & vio	10.00 50.00
46	A7	50c grn & car rose	19.00 52.50
47	A7	$1 lilac & green	37.50 85.00
48	A7	$2 lilac & car rose	55.00 100.00
49	A7	$3 lilac & blue	50.00 140.00
50	A7	$4 lilac & brn	52.50 100.00
51	A7	$5 lilac & orange	100.00 150.00
	Nos. 37-51 (15)		347.90 759.90

On Nos. 44-46 the numerals are on white tablets. Numerals of Nos. 48-51 are on tablets of solid color.

Stamps of 1896-1926 with revenue cancellations sell for a fraction of those used postally.

For surcharges see Nos. 52-58.

Nos. 40-41 Surcharged in Black

1903

52	A7	3c on 4c yel & red	.80 1.25
a.	Without bars		4.00 27.50

53	A7	10c on 4c grn & car rose	3.00 14.50
a.	Without bars		27.50 85.00

Bars on Nos. 52-53 were handruled with pen and ink.

Surcharged

54	A7	50c on $3 lilac & blue	35.00 87.50

Surcharged

55	A7	$1 on $2 lil & car rose	75.00 140.00
a.	Inverted "e" in "one"		2,000.

Surcharged

1904

56	A7	10c on 4c yel & red	25.00 42.50
a.	Double surcharge		8,750.
57	A7	10c on 4c grn & car rose	10.50 72.50
58	A7	50c on $5 lil & org	80.00 175.00
	Nos. 56-58 (3)		115.50 290.00

Sultan Ibrahim — A8

The 10c, 21c, 25c, 50c, and $10 to $500 denominations of type A8 show the numerals on white tablets. The numerals of the 8c, 30c, 40c, and $2 to $5 denominations are shown on tablets of solid colors.

1904-10 Typo. Wmk. 71
Ordinary Paper

59	A8	1c violet & green	2.00 .40
a.	Chalky paper ('09)		18.00 12.50
60	A8	2c vio & brn org	3.00 4.25
a.	Chalky paper ('10)		20.00 22.50
61	A8	3c violet & black	5.00 .60
62	A8	4c violet & red	9.25 4.50
63	A8	5c violet & ol grn	2.50 3.00
64	A8	8c violet & blue	4.25 17.50
65	A8	10c violet & black	52.50 11.50
a.	Chalky paper ('10)		120.00 82.50
66	A8	25c violet & green	8.50 42.50
67	A8	50c violet & red	47.50 17.50
68	A8	$1 green & vio	19.00 72.50
69	A8	$2 green & car	32.50 62.50
70	A8	$3 green & blue	45.00 87.50
71	A8	$4 green & brn	45.00 125.00
72	A8	$5 green & org	65.00 100.00
73	A8	$10 green & blk	125.00 210.00
74	A8	$50 green & blue	425.00 575.00
75	A8	$100 green & scar	625.00 1,000.
	Revenue cancel		60.00
	Nos. 59-73 (15)		466.00 759.25

Nos. 74 and 75 were theoretically available for postage but were mostly used for revenue purposes.

For surcharge see No. 86.

1912-19 Wmk. 47 Chalky Paper

76	A8	1c violet & green	1.25 .25
77	A8	2c violet & orange	6.00 1.00
78	A8	3c violet & black	10.00 .70
79	A8	4c violet & red	30.00 1.00
80	A8	5c violet & ol grn	10.00 2.75
81	A8	8c violet & blue	4.50 14.00
82	A8	10c violet & black	60.00 3.00
83	A8	25c violet & green	27.50 55.00
84	A8	50c violet & red ('19)	77.50 145.00
85	A8	$1 green & vio ('18)	120.00 125.00
	Nos. 76-85 (10)		346.75 347.70

No. 64 Surcharged

1912 Wmk. 71

86	A8	3c on 8c vio & blue	15.00 11.50
a.	"T" of "CENTS" omitted		1,750.

1918-20 Typo. Wmk. 3
Chalky Paper

87	A8	2c violet & orange	1.00 7.75
88	A8	2c vio & grn ('19)	1.00 5.50
89	A8	4c violet & red	1.75 .70
90	A8	5c vio & ol grn ('20)	2.00 15.00
91	A8	10c violet & blue	2.00 1.75
92	A8	21c vio & org ('19)	3.00 3.25
93	A8	25c vio & grn ('20)	9.00 45.00
94	A8	50c vio & red ('19)	25.00 67.50
95	A8	$1 grn & red vio	15.00 77.50
96	A8	$2 green & scar	27.50 67.50
97	A8	$3 green & blue	75.00 145.00
98	A8	$4 green & brn	90.00 210.00
99	A8	$5 green & org	145.00 240.00
100	A8	$10 green & blk	450.00 625.00
	Nos. 87-100 (14)		847.25 1,511.
	Set, ovptd. "SPECIMEN"		750.00

1921-40 Wmk. 4

101	A8	1c violet & black	.30 .25
102	A8	2c vio & brn ('24)	1.25 4.25
103	A8	2c grn & dk grn ('28)	.75 .40
104	A8	3c green ('25)	2.25 6.25
105	A8	3c dull vio & brn ('28)	1.40 1.50
106	A8	4c vio & red	2.50 .25
107	A8	5c vio & ol grn	.50 .25
108	A8	6c vio & red brn	.50 .50
109	A8	10c vio & blue	20.00 37.50
110	A8	10c vio & green ('22)	.50 .25
111	A8	12c vio & blue	1.25 1.60
111A	A8	12c ultra ('40)	57.50 4.00
112	A8	21c dull vio & org ('28)	2.75 3.50
113	A8	25c vio & green	5.50 1.25
114	A8	30c dull vio & grn ('36)	9.50 15.00
115	A8	40c dull vio & brn ('36)	10.50 15.00
116	A8	50c violet & red	3.75 1.60
117	A8	$1 grn & red vio	3.75 4.25
118	A8	$2 grn & red	10.00 5.00
119	A8	$3 grn & blue	85.00 105.00
120	A8	$4 grn & brn ('26)	110.00 190.00
121	A8	$5 grn & org	67.50 52.50
122	A8	$10 grn & blk	325.00 450.00
123	A8	$50 grn & ultra	1,450.
	Revenue cancel		110.00
124	A8	$100 grn & red	2,000.
	Revenue cancel		160.00
125	A8	$500 ultra & org brn ('26)	23,000.
	Revenue cancel		325.00
	Nos. 101-122 (23)		721.95 897.10

Nos. 123, 124 and 125 were available for postage but were probably used only fiscally.

Sultan Ibrahim, Sultana — A9

1935, May 15 Engr. Perf. 12½

126	A9	8c grn & vio	6.75 3.50
	Never hinged		10.00

Sultan Ibrahim — A10

1940, Feb. Perf. 13½

127	A10	8c blue & blk	26.00 1.35
	Never hinged		40.00

Catalogue values for unused stamps in this section, from this point to the end of the section, are for Never Hinged items.

Silver Wedding Issue
Common Design Types
Inscribed: "Malaya Johore"

Perf. 14x14½

1948, Dec. 1 Wmk. 4 Photo.

128	CD304	10c purple	.25 .75

Perf. 11½x11
Engr.; Name Typo.

129	CD305	$5 green	29.00 52.50

Common Design Types
Pictured following the introduction.

MALAYA — Johore — Kedah

Sultan Ibrahim — A11

1949-55 Wmk. 4 Typo. Perf. 18
130	A11	1c black	.75	.25
131	A11	2c orange	.40	.30
132	A11	3c green	2.50	1.10
133	A11	4c chocolate	2.00	.25
134	A11	5c rose vio ('52)	3.00	.30
135	A11	6c gray	2.00	.25
a.		Wmk. 4a (error)	3,250.	2,150.
136	A11	8c rose red	5.50	1.40
137	A11	8c green ('52)	10.00	2.25
138	A11	10c plum	1.50	.25
a.		Imperf., pair	5,000.	
139	A11	12c rose red ('52)	11.00	9.00
140	A11	15c ultra	5.00	.45
141	A11	20c dk grn & blk	3.75	1.25
142	A11	20c ultra ('52)	2.00	.30
143	A11	25c org & rose lil	4.00	.25
144	A11	30c plum & rose red ('55)	3.25	2.75
145	A11	35c dk vio & rose red ('52)	12.00	2.25
146	A11	40c dk vio & rose red	8.50	18.00
147	A11	50c ultra & blk	5.50	.30
148	A11	$1 vio brn & ultra	13.00	2.50
149	A11	$2 rose red & emer	32.50	13.50
150	A11	$5 choc & emer	52.50	17.50
		Nos. 130-150 (21)	180.65	74.40

UPU Issue
Common Design Types
Inscribed: "Malaya-Johore"
Engr.; Name Typo. on 15c, 25c

1949, Oct. 10 Perf. 13½, 11x11½
151	CD306	10c rose violet	.00	.40
152	CD307	15c indigo	2.00	1.25
153	CD308	25c orange	.80	3.50
154	CD309	50c slate	1.60	3.75
		Nos. 151-154 (4)	4.70	8.90

Coronation Issue
Common Design Type

1953, June 2 Engr. Perf. 13½x13
| 155 | CD312 | 10c magenta & black | 1.40 | .30 |

Sultan Ibrahim — A12

1955, Nov. 1 Wmk. 4 Perf. 14
| 156 | A12 | 10c carmine lake | .35 | .35 |

Sultan Ibrahim's Diamond Jubilee.

Sultan Ismail and Johore State Crest Seal — A13

1960, Feb. 10 Unwmk. Photo.
Granite Paper Perf. 11½
| 157 | A13 | 10c multicolored | .35 | .35 |

Coronation of Sultan Ismail.

Types of Kedah 1957 with Portrait of Sultan Ismail
1960 Wmk. 314 Engr. Perf. 13
158	A8	1c black	.25	.50
159	A8	2c red orange	.25	1.25
160	A8	4c dark brown	.25	.25
161	A8	5c dk car rose	.25	.25
162	A8	8c dark green	2.25	3.50
163	A7	10c violet brown	.35	.25
164	A7	20c blue	2.25	1.00
165	A7	50c ultra & black	.60	.30
166	A8	$1 plum & ultra	4.50	6.00
167	A8	$2 red & green	15.00	22.50
168	A8	$5 ol, grn & brn	35.00	42.50
		Nos. 158-168 (11)	60.95	78.30

Starting in 1965, issues of Johore are listed with Malaysia.

POSTAGE DUE STAMPS

D1

1938, Jan. 1 Typo. Wmk. 4 Perf. 12½
J1	D1	1c rose red	22.50	50.00
J2	D1	4c green	45.00	45.00
J3	D1	8c dull yellow	50.00	160.00
J4	D1	10c bister brown	50.00	57.50
J5	D1	12c rose violet	60.00	140.00
		Nos. J1-J5 (5)	227.50	452.50

OCCUPATION POSTAGE DUE STAMPS

Issued under Japanese Occupation

Johore Nos. J1-J5 Overprinted in Black, Brown or Red

1942 Wmk. 4 Perf. 12½
NJ1	D1	1c rose red	52.50	85.00
NJ2	D1	4c green	82.50	95.00
NJ3	D1	8c dull yellow	145.00	150.00
NJ4	D1	10c bister brown	52.50	72.50
NJ5	D1	12c rose violet	105.00	115.00
		Nos. NJ1-NJ5 (5)	437.50	517.50

Johore Nos. J1-J5 Overprinted in Black

1943
NJ6	D1	1c rose red	10.00	35.00
NJ7	D1	4c green	8.00	40.00
NJ8	D1	8c dull yellow	10.00	42.50
NJ9	D1	10c bister brown	9.50	50.00
NJ10	D1	12c rose violet	11.00	70.00
		Nos. NJ6-NJ10 (5)	48.50	237.50

Nos. NJ6-NJ10 exist with second character sideways. See Scott Classic Specialized catalogue for listings.

KEDAH

ˈke-də

LOCATION — On the west coast of the Malay Peninsula.
AREA — 3,660 sq. mi.
POP. — 752,706 (1960)
CAPITAL — Alor Star

Sheaf of Rice A1

Native Plowing A2

Council Chamber — A3

1912-21 Engr. Wmk. 3 Perf. 14
1	A1	1c green & indigo	.70	.30
2	A1	1c brown ('19)	.75	.60
3	A1	2c green ('19)	.60	.35
4	A1	3c car & black	5.00	.35
5	A1	3c dk violet ('19)	.75	4.00
6	A1	4c slate & car	12.00	.30
7	A1	4c scarlet ('19)	2.75	3.50
8	A1	5c org brown & grn	2.75	3.50
9	A1	8c ultra & blk	4.25	4.00
10	A2	10c black brn & bl	2.75	1.25
11	A2	20c yel grn & blk	12.50	5.00
12	A2	21c red vio & vio ('19)	6.25	70.00
13	A2	25c red vio & bl ('21)	2.10	37.50
14	A2	30c car & black	3.50	12.00
15	A2	40c lilac & blk	4.00	22.50
16	A2	50c dull bl & brn	10.00	14.00
17	A2	$1 scar & blk, yel	17.50	24.00
18	A3	$2 dk brn & dk grn	25.00	95.00
19	A3	$3 dk bl & blk, bl	135.00	190.00
20	A3	$5 car & black	135.00	200.00
		Nos. 1-20 (20)	385.90	685.65

There are two types of No. 7, one printed from separate plates for frame and center, the other printed from a single plate.
Overprints are listed after No. 45.

Stamps of 1912 Surcharged

1919
21	A3	50c on $2 dk brn & dk grn	80.00	90.00
a.		"C" of ovpt. inserted by hand	1,450.	1,650.
22	A3	$1 on $3 dk bl & blk, blue	22.50	110.00

1921-36 Wmk. 4

Two types of 1c:
I — The 1's have rounded corners, small top serif. Small letters "c".
II — The 1's have square-cut corners, large top serif. Large letters "c".

Two types of 2c:
I — The 2's have oval drops. Letters "c" are fairly thick and rounded.
II — The 2's have round drops. Letters "c" thin and slightly larger.

23	A1	1c brown	1.50	.25
24	A1	1c blk (I) ('22)	1.00	.25
a.		1c black (II) ('39)	170.00	5.00
25	A1	2c green (I)	1.50	.25
a.		2c green (II) ('40)	350.00	8.00
26	A1	3c dk violet	1.00	.80
27	A1	3c green ('22)	2.75	1.00
28	A1	4c carmine	7.50	.25
29	A1	4c dull vio ('26)	1.50	.25
30	A1	5c yellow ('22)	3.00	.25
31	A1	6c scarlet ('26)	2.50	.80
32	A1	8c gray ('36)	22.50	.75
33	A2	10c blk brn & bl	3.25	1.00
34	A2	12c dk ultra & blk ('26)	10.00	5.00
35	A2	20c green & blk	8.00	3.00
36	A2	21c red vio & vio	3.25	17.50
37	A2	25c red vio & bl	3.25	9.00
38	A2	30c red & blk ('22)	4.00	11.00
39	A2	35c claret ('26)	22.50	45.00
40	A2	40c red vio & blk	8.00	65.00
41	A2	50c dp blue & brn	4.75	27.50
42	A3	$1 scar & blk, yel ('24)	80.00	85.00
43	A3	$2 brn & green	17.50	125.00
44	A3	$3 dk bl & blk, bl	80.00	110.00
45	A3	$5 car & black	115.00	200.00
		Nos. 23-45 (23)	404.25	708.35

For overprints see Nos. N1-N6.

Stamps of 1912-21 Overprinted in Black: "MALAYA-BORNEO EXHIBITION." in Three Lines

1922 Wmk. 3
3A	A1	2c green	5.00	27.50
12A	A1	21c red vio & vio	45.00	95.00
13A	A2	25c red vio & blue	47.50	110.00
b.		Inverted overprint	1,625.	
16A	A2	50c dull blue & brn	50.00	125.00

Wmk. 4
23A	A1	1c brown	7.50	30.00
26A	A1	3c dark violet	5.50	50.00
29A	A1	4c carmine	6.00	25.00
33A	A2	10c blk brn & blue	14.50	50.00
		Nos. 3A-33A (8)	181.00	512.50

Industrial fair at Singapore, Mar. 31-Apr. 15, 1922.
On Nos. 12a, 13a and 16a, "BORNEO" exists both 14mm and 15mm wide.

Sultan of Kedah, Sir Abdul Hamid Halim Shah — A4

1937, July Wmk. 4 Perf. 12½
46	A4	10c sepia & ultra	4.00	2.25
47	A4	12c gray vio & blk	42.50	5.50
48	A4	25c brn vio & ultra	10.00	5.50
49	A4	30c dp grn & grn	10.00	11.50
50	A4	40c brn vio & blk	5.00	16.00
51	A4	50c dp blue & sepia	10.00	5.50
52	A4	$1 dk green & blk	4.00	11.00
53	A4	$2 dk brn & yel grn	90.00	85.00
54	A4	$5 dp car & black	27.50	170.00
		Nos. 46-54 (9)	203.00	312.25
		Set, never hinged	315.00	

For overprints see Nos. N7-N15.

Catalogue values for unused stamps in this section, from this point to the end of the section, are for Never Hinged items.

Silver Wedding Issue
Common Design Types
Inscribed: "Malaya Kedah"

1948, Dec. 1 Photo. Perf. 14x14½
| 55 | CD304 | 10c purple | .25 | .25 |

Perf. 11½x11
Engraved; Name Typographed
| 56 | CD305 | $5 rose car | 35.00 | 50.00 |

UPU Issue
Common Design Types
Inscribed: "Malaya-Kedah"
Engr.; Name Typo. on 15c, 25c

1949, Oct. 10 Perf. 13½, 11x11½
57	CD306	10c rose violet	.25	1.25
58	CD307	15c indigo	2.25	1.75
59	CD308	25c orange	.80	3.25
60	CD309	50c slate	1.50	6.00
		Nos. 57-60 (4)	4.80	12.00

Sheaf of Rice A5

Sultan Tungku Badlishah A6

1950-55 Wmk. 4 Typo. Perf. 18
61	A5	1c black	.70	.30
62	A5	2c orange	.50	.25
63	A5	3c green	2.00	1.00
64	A5	4c chocolate	.75	.25
65	A5	5c rose vio ('52)	5.50	3.00
66	A5	6c gray	.70	.25
67	A5	8c rose red	3.75	3.00
68	A5	8c green ('52)	5.50	3.00
69	A5	10c plum	.70	.25
70	A5	12c rose red ('52)	5.50	3.00
71	A5	15c ultramarine	5.00	.70
72	A5	20c dk grn & blk	5.00	3.00
73	A5	20c ultra ('52)	2.50	.35
74	A6	25c org & rose lilac	1.50	.50
75	A6	30c plum & rose red ('55)	6.00	1.50
76	A6	35c dk vio & rose red ('52)	6.25	2.00
77	A6	40c dk vio & rose red	7.50	10.00
78	A6	50c ultra & black	6.00	.35
79	A6	$1 vio brown & ultra	7.00	8.00
80	A6	$2 rose red & emer	30.00	45.00
81	A6	$5 choc & emerald	67.50	90.00
		Nos. 61-81 (21)	169.85	177.70

Coronation Issue
Common Design Type

1953, June 2 Engr. Perf. 13½x13
| 82 | CD312 | 10c magenta & black | 2.25 | .60 |

Fishing Craft — A7

Weaving and Sultan — A8

Portrait of Sultan Tungku Badlishah and: 1c, Copra. 2c, Pineapples. 4c, Rice field. 5c, Mosque. 8c, East Coast Railway. 10c, Tiger. 50c, Aborigines with blowpipes. $1, Government offices. $2, Bersilat.

Perf. 13x12½, 12½x13
1957 Engr. Wmk. 314
83	A8	1c black	.35	.60
84	A8	2c red orange	.50	1.75
85	A8	4c dark brown	1.00	1.00
86	A8	5c dk car rose	.35	.75
87	A8	8c dark green	3.00	10.00
88	A7	10c chocolate	1.00	.50
89	A7	20c blue	3.50	3.25

MALAYA — Kedah — Kelantan

Perf. 12½, 13½ ($1)

90	A7	50c ultra & black	3.25	4.25
91	A8	$1 plum & ultra	9.00	15.00
92	A8	$2 red & green	32.50	45.00
		Revenue cancel		.20
93	A8	$5 ol grn & brown	55.00	47.50
		Revenue cancel		.35
		Nos. 83-93 (11)	108.80	129.60

See Nos. 95-105.

Sultan Abdul Halim — A9

Perf. 14x14½

1959, Feb. 20 Photo. Wmk. 314

94	A9	10c ultra, red & yellow	.80	.30

Installation of the Sultan of Kedah, Abdul Halim.

Types of 1957

Designs as before with portrait of Sultan Abdul Halim.

Perf. 13x12½, 12½x13, 13½

1959-62 Engr. Wmk. 314

95	A8	1c black	.25	.85
96	A8	2c red orange	.25	2.00
97	A8	4c dark brown	.25	.85
98	A8	5c dk car rose	.25	.30
99	A8	8c dark green	4.00	4.00
100	A7	10c chocolate	1.00	.30
101	A7	20c blue	1.00	1.00
102	A7	50c ultra & blk, perf. 12½x13 ('60)	.35	1.75
a.		Perf. 12½	.35	.60
103	A8	$1 plum & ultra	2.50	3.00
104	A8	$2 red & green	15.00	22.50
105	A8	$5 ol grn & brn, perf. 13x12½ ('62)	35.00	19.00
a.		Perf. 12½	20.00	22.50
		Nos. 95-105 (11)	59.85	55.55

Starting in 1965, issues of Kedah are listed with Malaysia.

OCCUPATION STAMPS

Issued Under Japanese Occupation

Stamps of Kedah 1922-36, Overprinted in Red or Black

1942, May 13 Wmk. 4 Perf. 14

N1	A1	1c black (R)	9.50	15.00
N2	A1	2c green (R)	35.00	35.00
N3	A1	4c dull violet (R)	9.50	4.00
N4	A1	5c yellow (R)	7.50	7.50
a.		Black overprint	300.00	325.00
N5	A1	6c scarlet (Bk)	6.50	25.00
N6	A1	8c gray (R)	7.50	5.00

Nos. 46 to 54 Overprinted in Red

Perf. 12½

N7	A4	10c sepia & ultra	18.00	20.00
N8	A4	12c gray vio & blk	42.50	60.00
N9	A4	25c brn vio & ultra	18.00	27.50
a.		Black overprint	450.00	350.00
N10	A4	30c dp car & yel grn	60.00	85.00
N11	A4	40c brn vio & blk	50.00	50.00
N12	A4	50c dp blue & sep	50.00	50.00
N13	A4	$1 dk grn & blk	175.00	160.00
a.		Inverted overprint	875.00	1,000.
N14	A4	$2 dk brn & yel green	225.00	190.00
N15	A4	$5 dp car & blk	100.00	125.00
a.		Black overprint	1,750.	1,400.
		Nos. N1-N15 (15)	814.00	859.00

KELANTAN

kə-ˈlan-ˌtan

LOCATION — On the eastern coast of the Malay Peninsula.
AREA — 5,750 sq. mi.
POP. — 545,620 (1960)

CAPITAL — Kota Bharu

Symbols of Government — A1

1911-15 Typo. Wmk. 3 Perf. 14

Ordinary Paper

1	A1	1c gray green	8.00	1.25
a.		1c green	7.25	.35
2	A1	3c rose red	5.00	.25
3	A1	4c black & red	1.90	.25
4	A1	5c grn & red, yel	12.00	1.25
5	A1	8c ultramarine	6.25	1.25
6	A1	10c black & violet	35.00	.90

Chalky Paper

7	A1	30c violet & red	12.50	3.00
8	A1	50c black & org	10.00	3.00
9	A1	$1 green & emer	55.00	45.00
10	A1	$1 grn & brn ('15)	75.00	2.40
11	A1	$2 grn & car rose	1.90	3.75
12	A1	$5 green & ultra	4.75	4.00
13	A1	$25 green & org	55.00	110.00
		Nos. 1-13 (13)	282.30	176.30

For overprints see listings after No. 26. For surcharges see Nos. N20-N22.

1921-28 Wmk. 4

Ordinary Paper

14	A1	1c green	5.00	.75
15	A1	1c black ('23)	1.00	.60
16	A1	2c brown	7.50	4.75
17	A1	2c green ('26)	5.50	.60
18	A1	3c brown ('27)	5.00	1.50
19	A1	4c black & red	3.50	.25
20	A1	5c grn & red, yel	1.75	.25
21	A1	6c claret	3.50	2.00
22	A1	6c rose red ('28)	5.00	5.00
23	A1	10c black & violet	3.00	.25

Chalky Paper

24	A1	30c dull vio & red ('26)	5.00	6.00
25	A1	50c black & orange	7.25	52.50
26	A1	$1 green & brown	35.00	90.00
		Nos. 14-26 (13)	88.00	164.45

Stamps of 1911-21 Overprinted in Black in Three Lines

1922 Wmk. 3

3A	A1	4c black & red	7.00	50.00
4A	A1	5c green & red, yel	7.50	50.00
7A	A1	30c violet & red	8.00	80.00
8A	A1	50c black & orange	11.00	90.00
10A	A1	$1 green & brown	35.00	125.00
11A	A1	$2 green & car rose	95.00	275.00
12A	A1	$5 green & ultra	275.00	525.00

Wmk. 4

14A	A1	1c green	4.00	55.00
23A	A1	10c black & violet	7.50	75.00
		Nos. 3A-23A (9)	450.00	1,325.

Industrial fair at Singapore. Mar. 31-Apr. 15, 1922.

Sultan Ismail — A2

Size: 21½x30mm

1928-33 Engr. Perf. 12

27	A2	$1 ultramarine	17.50	85.00

Perf. 14

28	A2	$1 blue ('33)	75.00	47.50

Sultan Ismail — A2a

Size: 22½x34½mm

1937-40 Perf. 12

29	A2a	1c yel & ol green	1.75	.65
30	A2a	2c deep green	5.50	.25
31	A2a	4c brick red	5.50	1.00
32	A2a	5c red brown	3.00	.25
33	A2a	6c car lake	16.00	12.50
34	A2a	8c gray green	3.00	.25
35	A2a	10c dark violet	22.50	3.50
36	A2a	12c deep blue	5.50	8.50
37	A2a	25c vio & red org	6.00	4.75
38	A2a	30c scar & dk vio	40.00	27.50
39	A2a	40c blue grn & org	7.00	45.00
40	A2a	50c org & ol grn	55.00	10.00
41	A2a	$1 dp grn & dk violet	40.00	16.00
42	A2a	$2 red & red brn ('40)	250.00	275.00
43	A2a	$5 rose lake & org ('40)	550.00	950.00
		Nos. 29-43 (15)	1,011.	1,355.
		Set, never hinged		1,525.

For overprints see Nos. N1-N19.

> Catalogue values for unused stamps in this section, from this point to the end of the section, are for Never Hinged items.

Common Design Types pictured following the introduction.

Silver Wedding Issue
Common Design Types
Inscribed: "Malaya Kelantan"

Perf. 14x14½

1948, Dec. 1 Wmk. 4 Photo.

44	CD304	10c purple	.75	2.75

Perf. 11½x11
Engraved; Name Typographed

45	CD305	$5 rose car	35.00	60.00

UPU Issue
Common Design Types
Inscribed: "Malaya-Kelantan"

Engr.; Name Typog. on 15c, 25c
1949, Oct. 10 Perf. 13½, 11x11½

46	CD306	10c rose violet	.40	.40
47	CD307	15c indigo	2.25	2.75
48	CD308	25c orange	.60	6.50
49	CD309	50c slate	1.00	3.00
		Nos. 46-49 (4)	4.25	12.65

Sultan Ibrahim — A3

Perf. 18
1951, July 11 Wmk. 4 Typo.

50	A3	1c black	.50	.40
51	A3	2c orange	1.20	.40
52	A3	3c green	6.75	1.75
53	A3	4c chocolate	2.00	.30
54	A3	6c gray	.80	.30
55	A3	8c rose red	6.00	4.50
56	A3	10c plum	.75	.30
57	A3	15c ultramarine	9.00	.80
58	A3	20c dk green & blk	7.50	15.00
59	A3	25c orange & plum	2.25	.80
60	A3	40c vio brn & rose red	17.50	27.50
61	A3	50c dp ultra & blk	8.00	.60
62	A3	$1 vio brown & ultra	10.00	16.50
63	A3	$2 rose red & emer	47.50	70.00
64	A3	$5 choc & emer	72.50	82.50

1952-55

65	A3	5c rose violet	1.50	.50
66	A3	8c green	7.50	2.25
67	A3	12c rose red	7.50	4.00
68	A3	20c ultramarine	2.00	.25
69	A3	30c plum & rose red ('55)	1.60	6.50
70	A3	35c dk vio & rose red	2.50	1.75
		Nos. 50-70 (21)	214.85	236.90

Compare with Pahang A8, Perak A16, Selangor A15, Trengganu A5.

Coronation Issue
Common Design Type

1953, June 2 Engr. Perf. 13½x13

71	CD312	10c magenta & black	1.60	1.60

Aborigines with Blowpipes A4

Government Offices and Sultan A5

Portrait of Sultan Ibrahim and: 1c, Copra. 2c, Pineapples. 4c, Rice field. 5c, Mosque. 8c, East Coast Railway. 10c, Tiger. 20c, Fishing craft. 50c, Aborigines with blowpipes. $1, Government Offices and Sultan. $2, Bersilat. $5, Weaving.

Perf. 13x12½, 12½x13, 13½ ($1)

1957-63 Engr. Wmk. 314

72	A5	1c black	.25	.45
73	A5	2c red orange	.90	1.50
74	A5	4c dark brown	.45	.25
75	A5	5c dk car rose	.45	.25
76	A5	8c dark green	2.25	3.25
77	A4	10c chocolate	3.00	.25
78	A4	20c blue	2.50	.45
79	A4	50c ultra & blk ('60)	1.00	.60
a.		Perf 12½	1.00	1.25
80	A5	$1 plum & ultra	8.00	2.00
81	A5	$2 red & grn ('63)	15.00	32.50
a.		Perf. 12½	19.00	9.00
82	A5	$5 ol grn & brn ('63)	27.50	37.50
a.		Perf. 12½	24.00	14.00
		Nos. 72-82 (11)	61.30	79.00

Sultan Yahya Petra — A6

1961, July 17 Photo. Perf. 14½x14

83	A6	10s multicolored	.55	1.00

Installation of Sultan Yahya Petra.

Types of 1957 with Portrait of Sultan Yahya Petra

Designs as before.

Perf. 13x12½, 12½x13

1961-62 Engr. Wmk. 338

84	A5	1c black	.25	2.75
85	A5	2c red orange	.60	3.00
86	A5	4c dark brown	1.75	2.00
87	A5	5c dk car rose	1.75	.60
88	A5	8c dark green	14.00	15.00
89	A4	10c violet brown ('61)	1.75	.40
90	A4	20c blue	10.00	2.50
		Nos. 84-90 (7)	30.10	26.25

Starting in 1965, issues of Kelantan are listed with Malaysia.

OCCUPATION STAMPS

Issued Under Japanese Occupation

Kelantan No. 35 Handstamped in Black

1942 Wmk. 4 Perf. 12

N1	A2a	10c dark violet	400.00	500.00

Some authorities believe No. N1 was not regularly issued.

Kelantan Nos. 29-40 Surcharged in Black or Red and Handstamped with Oval Seal "a" in Red

Sunakawa-a   Handa-b

MALAYA — Kelantan — Malacca — Negri Sembilan

1942

N2	1c on 50c org & ol green	225.00	150.00
a.	With "b" seal	160.00	200.00
N3	2c on 40c bl grn & org	300.00	200.00
a.	With "b" seal	160.00	200.00
N4	5c on 12c dp bl (R)	200.00	200.00
N5	8c on 5c red brn (R)	175.00	100.00
a.	With "b" seal (R)	110.00	175.00
N6	10c on 6c car lake	475.00	500.00
a.	With "b" seal	120.00	200.00
N7	12c on 8c gray grn (R)	60.00	140.00
N8	30c on 4c brick red	2,500.	2,250.
N9	40c on 2c dp grn (R)	70.00	100.00
N10	50c on 1c yel & ol green	1,800.	1,500.

Kelantan Nos. 29-40, 19-20, 22 Surcharged in Black or Red and Handstamped with Oval Seal "b" in Red

N10A	1c on 50c org & ol grn	350.00	200.00
N11	2c on 40c bl grn & org	900.00	350.00
N11A	4c on 30c scar & dark vio	2,500.	1,400.
N12	5c on 12c dp bl (R)	350.00	200.00
N13	6c on 25c vio & red org	375.00	200.00
N14	8c on 5c red brn (R)	500.00	150.00
N15	10c on 6c car lake	100.00	125.00
N16	12c on 8c gray grn (R)	225.00	375.00
a.	Seal omitted	70.00	120.00
N17	25c on 10c dk vio	1,600.	1,500.
N17A	30c on 4c brick red	2,500.	2,250.
N18	40c on 2c dp grn (R)	70.00	100.00
N19	50c on 1c yel & ol green	1,800.	1,500.

Perf. 14

N20	$1 on 50c blk & red (R)	60.00	85.00
N21	$2 on 5c grn & red, yel	60.00	85.00
N22	$5 on 6c rose red	60.00	85.00

Examples of Nos. N2-N22 without handstamped seal are from the remainder stocks sent to Singapore after Kelantan was ceded to Thailand. Some authorities believe stamps without seals were used before June 1942.

ISSUED UNDER THAI OCCUPATION

1943, Nov. 15 — Perf. 11

2N1	OS1	1c violet & black	240.00	375.00
2N2	OS1	2c violet & black	300.00	300.00
2N3	OS1	4c violet & black	300.00	375.00
2N4	OS1	8c violet & black	300.00	300.00
2N5	O31	10c violet & black	450.00	550.00
	Nos. 2N1-2N5 (5)		1,590.	1,900.

Stamps with centers in red are revenues.

MALACCA

mə-'la-kə

Melaka

LOCATION — On the west coast of the Malay peninsula.
AREA — 640 sq. mi.
POP. — 318,110 (1960)
CAPITAL — Malacca

Catalogue values for unused stamps in this section are for Never Hinged items.

Common Design Types pictured following the introduction.

Silver Wedding Issue
Common Design Types
Inscribed: "Malaya Malacca"
Perf. 14x14½

1948, Dec. 1 — Wmk. 4 — Photo.

1	CD304	10c purple	.40	2.25

Engraved; Name Typographed
Perf. 11½x11

2	CD305	$5 lt brown	35.00	47.50

Type of Straits Settlements, 1937-41, Inscribed "Malacca"
Perf. 18

1949, Mar. 1 — Wmk. 4 — Typo.

3	A29	1c black	.40	.85
4	A29	2c orange	1.00	.60
5	A29	3c green	.40	2.25
6	A29	4c chocolate	.40	.25
7	A29	6c gray	.90	1.10
8	A29	8c rose red	.90	7.50
9	A29	10c plum	.40	.25
10	A29	15c ultramarine	3.50	.85
11	A29	20c dk green & blk	.60	7.00
12	A29	25c org & rose lil	.60	.85
13	A29	40c dk vio & rose red	1.50	13.00
14	A29	50c ultra & black	1.50	1.50
15	A29	$1 vio brn & ultra	15.00	26.00
16	A29	$2 rose red & emer	27.50	27.50
17	A29	$5 choc & emer	60.00	50.00
	Nos. 3-17 (15)		114.60	139.50

See Nos. 22-26.

UPU Issue
Common Design Types
Inscribed: "Malaya-Malacca"
Engr.; Name Typo. on 15c, 25c
Perf. 13½, 11x11½

1949, Oct. 10 — Wmk. 4

18	CD306	10c rose violet	.35	.55
19	CD307	15c indigo	2.40	2.75
20	CD308	25c orange	.50	8.50
21	CD309	50c slate	1.00	5.50
	Nos. 18-21 (4)		4.25	17.30

Type of Straits Settlements, 1937-41, Inscribed "Malacca"

1952, Sept. 1 — Wmk. 4 — Perf. 18

22	A29	5c rose violet	1.25	1.75
23	A29	8c green	6.00	5.25
24	A29	12c rose red	6.00	9.50
25	A29	20c ultramarine	7.50	3.00
26	A29	35c dk vio & rose red	6.00	3.75
	Nos. 22-26 (5)		26.75	23.25

Coronation Issue
Common Design Type

1953, June 2 — Engr. — Perf. 13½x13

27	CD312	10c magenta & black	1.10	1.50

Queen Elizabeth II — A1

1954-55 — Wmk. 4 — Typo. — Perf. 18

29	A1	1c black	.25	.75
30	A1	2c orange	.40	1.25
31	A1	4c chocolate	1.50	.25
32	A1	5c rose violet	.40	2.75
33	A1	6c gray	.25	.40
34	A1	8c green	.55	3.00
35	A1	10c plum	2.00	.25
36	A1	12c rose red	.40	3.25
37	A1	20c ultramarine	.25	1.25
38	A1	25c orange & plum	.25	1.75
39	A1	30c plum & rose red ('55)	.25	.40
40	A1	35c vio brn & rose red	.25	1.50
41	A1	50c ultra & black	4.00	2.75
42	A1	$1 vio brn & ultra	7.50	12.00
43	A1	$2 rose red & grn	29.00	45.00
44	A1	$5 choc & emerald	29.00	45.00
	Nos. 29-44 (16)		76.25	124.05

Types of Kedah with Portrait of Queen Elizabeth II
Perf. 13x12½, 12½x13

1957 — Engr. — Wmk. 314

45	A8	1c black	.25	.55
46	A8	2c red orange	.25	.55
47	A8	4c dark brown	.50	.25
48	A8	5c dark car rose	.50	.25
49	A8	8c dark green	2.25	3.00
50	A7	10c chocolate	.45	.25
51	A7	20c blue	2.50	1.00

Perf. 12½, 13½ ($1)

52	A7	50c ultra & black	1.00	1.00
53	A8	$1 plum & ultra	6.00	4.75
54	A8	$2 red & green	20.00	27.50
55	A8	$5 olive grn & brn	22.50	47.50
	Nos. 45-55 (11)		56.20	86.60

Types of Kedah, 1957, With Melaka Tree and Mouse Deer Replacing Portrait of Queen Elizabeth II
Perf. 13x12½, 12½x13, 13½ ($1)

1960, Mar. 15 — Engr. — Wmk. 314

56	A8	1c black	.25	.50
57	A8	2c red orange	.25	.70
58	A8	4c dark brown	.25	.25
59	A8	5c dark car rose	.25	.25
60	A8	8c dark green	3.50	3.75
61	A7	10c violet brown	.45	.25
62	A7	20c blue	2.25	1.00
63	A7	50c ultra & black	1.25	1.00
64	A8	$1 plum & ultra	5.00	3.25
65	A8	$2 red & green	7.50	15.00
66	A8	$5 ol grn & brn	14.00	17.50
	Nos. 56-66 (11)		34.95	43.45

Starting in 1965, issues of Malacca (Melaka) are listed with Malaysia.

OCCUPATION STAMPS

Issued Under Japanese Occupation
Stamps of Straits Settlements, 1937-41 Handstamped in Carmine

The handstamp covers four stamps. Values are for single stamps. Blocks of four showing complete handstamp sell for six times the price of singles.

1942 — Wmk. 4 — Perf. 14

N1	A29	1c black	125.00	90.00
N2	A29	2c brown orange	75.00	75.00
N3	A29	3c green	80.00	90.00
N4	A29	5c brown	175.00	175.00
N5	A29	8c gray	300.00	150.00
N6	A29	10c dull violet	125.00	125.00
N7	A29	12c ultramarine	140.00	140.00
N8	A29	15c ultramarine	100.00	125.00
N9	A29	30c org & vio		3,500.
N10	A29	40c dk vio & rose red	700.00	700.00
N11	A29	50c blk, *emerald*	1,100.	1,100.
N12	A29	$1 red & blk, *bl*	1,350.	1,250.
N13	A29	$2 rose red & gray grn		3,500.
N14	A29	$5 grn & red, *grn*	3,500.	—

Some authorities believe Nos. N9, N13, and N14 were not regularly issued.

OCCUPATION POSTAGE DUE STAMPS

Malaya Postage Due Stamps and Type of 1936-38, Handstamped Like Nos. N1-N14 in Carmine

1942 — Wmk. 4 — Perf. 14½x14

NJ1	D2	1c violet	250.00	225.00
NJ2	D2	4c yel green	275.00	275.00
NJ3	D2	8c red	3,500.	2,250.
NJ4	D2	10c yel orange	550.00	525.00
NJ5	D2	12c blue violet	800.00	725.00
NJ6	D2	50c black	3,000.	2,000.
	Nos. NJ1-NJ6 (6)		8,375.	6,000.

Pricing note above No. N1 also applies to Nos. NJ1-NJ6.

NEGRI SEMBILAN

'ne-grē səm-'bē-lən

LOCATION — South of Selangor on the west coast of the Malay Peninsula, bordering on Pahang on the east and Johore on the south.
AREA — 2,580 sq. mi.
POP. — 401,742 (1960)
CAPITAL — Seremban

Stamps of the Straits Settlements Overprinted in Black

1891 — Wmk. 2 — Perf. 14
Overprint 14½ to 15mm Wide

1	A2	2c rose	3.50	16.50

Tiger — A1

1891-94 — Typo.

2	A1	1c green ('93)	4.00	1.25
3	A1	2c rose	4.00	15.00
4	A1	5c blue ('94)	35.00	47.50
	Nos. 2-4 (3)		43.00	63.75

Tiger Head — A2

1895-99

5	A2	1c lilac & green	25.00	11.50
6	A2	2c lilac & brown	42.50	140.00
7	A2	3c lilac & car rose	18.00	3.00
8	A2	5c lilac & olive	16.00	16.00
9	A2	8c lilac & blue	35.00	22.50
10	A2	10c lilac & orange	32.50	17.00
11	A2	15c green & vio	50.00	90.00
12	A2	20c grn & ol ('99)	80.00	45.00
13	A2	25c grn & car rose	85.00	110.00
14	A2	50c green & black	90.00	80.00
	Nos. 5-14 (10)		473.00	535.00

For surcharges see Nos. 15-16, 19-20; Federated Malay States Nos. 1-8.

Stamps of 1891-99 Surcharged

1899 — Blue-green Surcharge

15	A2	4c on 8c lil & blue	13.50	5.00
a.	Double surcharge	3,000.	2,500.
b.	Pair, one without surcharge	10,000.	5,750.
c.	Double surcharge, 1 green, 1 red	1,000.	1,100.

Black Surcharge

16	A2	4c on 8c lil & blue	1,400.	*1,500.*

Surcharge on No. 16 is thinner and sharper than on No. 15.

Same Surcharge and Bar in Black

17	A1	4c on 1c green	3.50	25.00
18	A1	4c on 5c blue	1.50	17.00
19	A2	4c on 3c lil & car rose	6.00	27.50
a.	Double surcharge	2,750.	1,200.
b.	Pair, one without surcharge	15,000.	7,000.
c.	Bar omitted	1,000.	800.00
g.	Inverted surcharge	2,500.	1,650.

Bar at bottom on Nos. 17-18, at top on No. 19.

No. 11 Surcharged in Black

1900

20	A2	1c on 15c grn & vio	125.00	350.00
a.	Inverted period	500.00	1,350.

Arms of Negri Sembilan — A4

1935-41 — Typo. — Wmk. 4

21	A4	1c black ('36)	1.40	.25
22	A4	2c dp green ('36)	1.40	.25
22A	A4	2c brown org ('41)	4.00	75.00
22B	A4	3c green ('41)	40.00	11.00
23	A4	4c brown orange	2.00	.25
24	A4	5c chocolate	2.00	.25
25	A4	6c rose red	17.50	2.75

113

MALAYA — Negri Sembilan — Pahang

25A	A4	6c gray ('41)	5.00	140.00
26	A4	8c gray	2.00	.40
27	A4	10c dull vio ('36)	1.40	.25
28	A4	12c ultra ('36)	3.25	.75
28A	A4	15c ultra ('41)	11.00	75.00
29	A4	25c rose red & dull vio ('36)	2.00	1.00
30	A4	30c org & dull vio ('36)	3.50	2.50
31	A4	40c dull vio & car	3.50	3.00
32	A4	50c blk, *emer* ('36)	6.50	2.25
33	A4	$1 red & blk, *bl* ('36)	5.00	7.00
34	A4	$2 rose red & grn ('36)	60.00	22.50
35	A4	$5 brn red & grn, *emer* ('36)	40.00	135.00
		Nos. 21-35 (19)	211.45	479.40
		Set, never hinged	375.00	

For overprints see Nos. N1-N31.

Catalogue values for unused stamps in this section, from this point to the end of the section, are for Never Hinged items.

Common Design Types pictured following the introduction.

Silver Wedding Issue
Common Design Types
Inscribed: "Malaya Negri Sembilan"
1948, Dec. 1   Photo.   Perf. 14x14½
| 36 | CD304 | 10c purple | .60 | .70 |

Perf. 11½x11
Engraved; Name Typographed
| 37 | CD305 | $5 green | 27.50 | 37.50 |

Arms of Negri Sembilan — A5

1949-55   Wmk. 4   Typo.   Perf. 18
38	A5	1c black	1.25	.25
39	A5	2c orange	1.00	.25
40	A5	3c green	.60	.45
41	A5	4c chocolate	.30	.25
42	A5	5c rose violet	1.00	.45
43	A5	6c gray	2.25	.25
44	A5	8c rose red	.80	.95
45	A5	8c green	5.50	2.25
46	A5	10c plum	.40	.25
47	A5	12c rose red	5.50	3.25
48	A5	15c ultramarine	4.25	.45
49	A5	20c dk green & blk	2.25	2.00
50	A5	20c ultramarine	2.00	.35
51	A5	25c org & rose lilac	1.00	.35
52	A5	30c plum & rose red ('55)	2.00	2.75
53	A5	35c dk vio & rose red	1.50	3.75
54	A5	40c dk vio & rose red	4.75	6.00
55	A5	50c ultra & black	5.00	.45
56	A5	$1 vio brn & ultra	6.00	2.25
57	A5	$2 rose red & emer	18.00	27.50
58	A5	$5 choc & emerald	60.00	75.00
		Nos. 38-58 (21)	125.35	129.45

UPU Issue
Common Design Types
Inscribed: "Malaya-Negri Sembilan"
Engr.; Name Typo. on 15c, 25c
1949, Oct. 10   Perf. 13½, 11x11½
59	CD306	10c rose violet	.25	.25
60	CD307	15c indigo	1.40	3.50
61	CD308	25c orange	.75	3.00
62	CD309	50c slate	1.10	4.00
		Nos. 59-62 (4)	3.50	10.75

Coronation Issue
Common Design Type
1953, June 2   Engr.   Perf. 13½x13
| 63 | CD312 | 10c magenta & black | 1.40 | .65 |

Types of Kedah with Arms of Negri Sembilan
Perf. 13x12½, 12½x13, 13½ ($1)
1957-63   Engr.   Wmk. 314
64	A8	1c black	.25	.25
65	A8	2c red orange	.25	.25
66	A8	4c dark brown	.25	.25
67	A8	5c dk car rose	.25	.25
68	A8	8c dark green	2.00	1.60
69	A7	10c chocolate	2.00	.25
70	A7	20c blue	1.00	.25
71	A7	50c ultra & blk ('60)	.60	.25
a.		Perf. 12½	1.75	1.50
72	A8	$1 plum & ultra	4.50	2.25
73	A8	$2 red & grn ('63)	20.00	32.50
a.		Perf. 12½	15.00	20.00
74	A8	$5 ol grn & brn ('62)	27.50	25.00
a.		Perf. 12½	20.00	26.00
		Nos. 64-74 (11)	58.60	63.10

Negri Sembilan State Crest and Tuanku Munawir — A6

1961, Apr. 17   Unwmk.   Perf. 14x13
| 75 | A6 | 10s blue & multi | .45 | .70 |

Installation of Tuanku Munawir as ruler (Yang di-Pertuan Besar) of Negri Sembilan. Starting in 1965, issues of Negri (Negeri) Sembilan are listed with Malaysia.

OCCUPATION STAMPS
Issued under Japanese Occupation

Stamps and Type of Negri Sembilan, 1935-41, Handstamped in Red, Black, Brown or Violet

1942   Wmk. 4   Perf. 14
N1	A4	1c black	25.00	16.00
N2	A4	2c brown org	16.00	17.50
N3	A4	3c green	21.00	21.00
N4	A4	5c chocolate	29.00	27.50
N5	A4	6c rose red	600.00	600.00
N6	A4	6c gray	150.00	150.00
N7	A4	8c gray	87.50	87.50
N8	A4	8c rose red	55.00	47.50
N9	A4	10c dark violet	110.00	110.00
N10	A4	12c ultramarine	900.00	900.00
N11	A4	15c ultramarine	20.00	11.00
N12	A4	25c rose red & dk vio	35.00	40.00
N13	A4	30c org & dk vio	175.00	190.00
N14	A4	40c dk vio & car	750.00	750.00
N15	A4	$1 red & blk, *bl*	140.00	140.00
N16	A4	$5 brn red & grn, *emerald*	325.00	350.00

The 8c rose red is not known to have been issued without overprint.
Some authorities believe Nos. N5 and N7 were not regularly issued.

Stamps of Negri Sembilan, 1935-41, Overprinted in Black

N17	A4	1c black	6.00	4.00
a.		Inverted overprint	20.00	27.50
b.		Dbl. ovpt., one invtd.	52.50	67.50
N18	A4	2c brown orange	8.00	5.50
N19	A4	3c green	12.00	2.50
N20	A4	5c chocolate	3.00	3.00
N21	A4	6c gray	6.50	6.50
a.		Inverted overprint		1,000.
N22	A4	8c rose red	8.00	5.50
N23	A4	10c dk violet	5.50	5.50
N24	A4	15c ultramarine	17.50	4.75
N25	A4	25c rose red & dk vio	6.00	6.75
N26	A4	30c org & dk vio	6.00	6.00
N27	A4	$1 red & blk, *bl*	140.00	175.00
		Nos. N17-N27 (11)	218.50	225.00

The 8c rose red is not known to have been issued without overprint.

Negri Sembilan, Nos. 21, 24 and 29, Overprinted or Surcharged in Black

a

b

c

1943
N28	A4	1c black	2.25	1.90
a.		Inverted overprint	42.50	42.50
N29	A4	2c on 5c choc	2.00	1.40
N30	A4	6c on 5c choc	2.25	1.40
a.		"6 cts." inverted	350.00	400.00

| N31 | A4 | 25c rose red & dk violet | 4.00 | 4.50 |
| | | Nos. N28-N31 (4) | 10.50 | 9.20 |

The Japanese characters read: "Japanese Postal Service."

PAHANG
pə-ˈhaŋ

LOCATION — On the east coast of the Malay Peninsula, bordering Johore on the south, Parak and Selangor on the west, and Trengganu on the north.
AREA — 13,820 sq. mi.
POP. — 338,210 (1960)
CAPITAL — Kuala Lipis

Stamps of the Straits Settlements Overprinted in Black

Overprinted

Overprint 16x2¾mm

1889   Wmk. 2   Perf. 14
1	A2	2c rose	165.00	60.00
2	A3	8c orange	1,800.	2,000.
3	A7	10c slate	225.00	300.00

Overprinted

Overprint 12½x2mm

| 4 | A2 | 2c rose | 15.00 | 15.00 |

Overprinted

1890   Overprint 15x2½mm
| 5 | A2 | 2c rose | 12,750. | 3,250. |

Overprinted

Overprint 16x2¾mm
| 6 | A2 | 2c rose | 135.00 | 16.00 |

Surcharged in Black

a. "Two" italic. "CENTS" larger and bold. (Row 6)

b. "Two" upright. "CENTS" larger and bold. (Rows 7-9)

c. "Two" italic. "CENTS" smaller and thinner. (Rows 1-5)

d. "Two" upright. "CENTS" smaller and thinner. (Row 10)

1891
7	A3 (a)	2c on 24c green	1,200.	1,300.
8	A3 (b)	2c on 24c green	450.00	475.00
9	A3 (c)	2c on 24c green	275.00	325.00
10	A3 (d)	2c on 24c green	1,250.	1,300.
		Nos. 7-10 (4)	3,175.	3,400.

A5

1892-95   Typo.
11	A5	1c green	5.00	4.00
12	A5	2c rose	5.50	4.00
13	A5	5c blue	12.50	47.50
		Nos. 11-13 (3)	23.00	55.50

For surcharges see Nos. 21-22.

A6

1895-99
14	A6	3c lilac & car rose	10.75	3.75
14A	A6	4c lil & car rose ('99)	20.00	19.50
15	A6	5c lilac & olive	55.00	25.00
		Nos. 14-15 (3)	85.75	48.25

For surcharge see No. 28.

Stamps of Perak, 1895-99, Overprinted Pahang.

1898-99
16	A9	10c lilac & orange	27.50	32.50
17	A9	25c green & car rose	95.00	190.00
18	A9	50c green & black	500.00	575.00
18A	A9	50c lilac & black	300.00	425.00

Overprinted Pahang.

Wmk. 1
19	A10	$1 green & lt grn	425.	700.
20	A10	$5 green & ultra	1,700.	3,250.
		Nos. 16-20 (6)	3,048.	5,173.

No. 13 Cut in Half Diagonally & Srchd. in Red & Initials "JFO" in ms.

1897, Aug. 2   Wmk. 2
Red Surcharge
21	A5	2c on half of 5c blue	1,750.	450.
a.		Black surcharge	10,750.	3,500.
22	A5	3c on half of 5c blue	1,750.	450.
a.		Black surcharge	10,750.	3,500.
d.		Se-tenant pair, #21, 22	5,500.	1,200.

Perak No. 52 Surcharged Pahang Four cents

1898
| 25 | A9 | 4c on 8c lilac & blue | 4.50 | 6.50 |
| b. | | Inverted surcharge | 3,250. | 1,500. |

Surcharged on pieces of White Paper Pahang Five cents

1898   Without Gum   Imperf.
| 26 | | 4c black | | 5,250. |
| 27 | | 5c black | | 3,250. |

MALAYA — Pahang — Penang

Pahang No. 15 Surcharged *Four cents.*

1899
Perf. 14
28	A6	4c on 5c lilac & olive	25.00	75.00

Sultan Abu Bakar — A7

1935-41 Typo. Wmk. 4 Perf. 14
29	A7	1c black ('36)	.25	.25
30	A7	2c dp green ('36)	1.40	.25
30A	A7	3c green ('41)	10.00	19.00
31	A7	4c brown orange	.70	.25
32	A7	5c chocolate	.70	.25
33	A7	6c rose red ('36)	12.00	3.50
34	A7	8c gray	2.00	.25
34A	A7	8c rose red ('41)	3.00	60.00
35	A7	10c dk violet ('36)	1.75	.25
36	A7	12c ultra ('36)	2.10	2.00
36A	A7	15c ultra ('41)	14.00	65.00
37	A7	25c rose red & pale vio ('36)	3.00	1.50
38	A7	30c org & dk vio ('36)	1.50	1.25
39	A7	40c dk vio & car	1.25	2.40
40	A7	50c black, emer ('36)	2.50	2.00
41	A7	$1 red & blk, blue ('36)	2.50	8.00
42	A7	$2 rose red & green ('36)	15.00	50.00
43	A7	$5 brn red & grn, emer ('36)	6.00	87.50
		Nos. 29-43 (18)	79.65	303.65

The 3c was printed on both ordinary and chalky paper; the 15c only on chalky paper; other values only on chalky paper.

Values for Nos. 34A used and 36A used are for stamps with legible postmarks dated in 1941.

A 2c brown orange and 6c gray, type A7, exist, but are not known to have been regularly issued.

For overprints see Nos. N1-N21.

> Catalogue values for unused stamps in this section, from this point to the end of the section, are for Never Hinged items.

Common Design Types pictured following the introduction.

Silver Wedding Issue
Common Design Types
Inscribed: "Malaya Pahang"
Perf. 14x14½

1948, Dec. 1		Photo.	Wmk. 4	
44	CD304	10c purple	.50	.55

UPU Issue
Common Design Types
Inscribed: "Malaya-Pahang"
Perf. 11½x11

Engraved; Name Typographed

| 45 | CD305 | $5 green | 27.50 | 37.50 |

UPU Issue
Common Design Types
Inscribed: "Malaya-Pahang"
Engr.; Name Typo. on 15c, 25c

1949, Oct. 10		Perf. 13½, 11x11½		
46	CD306	10c rose violet	.30	.25
47	CD307	15c indigo	1.10	1.50
48	CD308	25c orange	.60	2.50
49	CD309	50c slate	1.00	3.00
		Nos. 46-49 (4)	3.00	7.25

Sultan Abu Bakar — A8

Perf. 18
1950, June 1		Wmk. 4	Typo.	
50	A8	1c black	.30	.30
51	A8	2c orange	.30	.30
52	A8	3c green	.30	.80
53	A8	4c chocolate	2.25	.35
54	A8	6c gray	.50	.35
55	A8	8c rose red	.50	2.00
56	A8	10c plum	.30	.35
57	A8	15c ultramarine	.75	.35
58	A8	20c dk green & blk	1.00	3.00
59	A8	25c org & rose lilac	.50	.30
60	A8	40c dk vio & rose red	2.25	8.50
61	A8	50c dp ultra & black	1.50	.35
62	A8	$1 vio brn & ultra	3.50	3.50
63	A8	$2 rose red & emer	16.00	30.00
64	A8	$5 choc & emer	65.00	90.00

1952-55
65	A8	5c rose violet	.50	.70
66	A8	8c green	1.25	1.10
67	A8	12c rose red	1.50	1.25
68	A8	20c ultramarine	2.50	.30
69	A8	30c plum & rose red ('55)	2.75	.50
70	A8	35c dk vio & rose red	1.00	.35
		Nos. 50-70 (21)	104.45	144.60

Coronation Issue
Common Design Type

1953, June 2		Engr.	Perf. 13½x13	
71	CD312	10c magenta & black	2.25	.25

Types of Kedah with Portrait of Sultan Abu Bakar
Perf. 13x12½, 12½x13, 13½ ($1)

1957-62		Engr.	Wmk. 314	
72	A8	1c black	.25	.25
73	A8	2c red orange	.25	.25
74	A8	4c dark brown	.25	.25
75	A8	5c dark car rose	.25	.25
76	A8	8c dark green	2.25	2.25
77	A7	10c chocolate	1.25	.25
78	A7	20c blue	2.75	.25
79	A7	50c ultra & blk ('60)	1.00	.25
a.		Perf. 12½	.60	1.00
80	A8	$1 plum & ultra	10.00	2.75
81	A8	$2 red & green ('62)	9.00	22.50
a.		Perf. 12½	7.50	11.00
82	A8	$5 ol grn & brn ('60)	15.00	24.00
a.		Perf. 12½	14.00	17.50
		Nos. 72-82 (11)	42.25	53.25

Starting in 1965, issues of Pahang are listed with Malaysia.

OCCUPATION STAMPS

Issued under Japanese Occupation

Stamps of Pahang, 1935-41, Handstamped in Black, Red, Brown or Violet

1942		Wmk. 4	Perf. 14	
N1	A7	1c black	60.00	55.00
N1A	A7	3c green	625.00	350.00
N2	A7	5c chocolate	22.50	14.50
N3	A7	8c rose red	30.00	9.00
N3A	A7	8c gray	1,650.	1,100.
N4	A7	10c dk violet	575.00	225.00
N5	A7	12c ultramarine	3,000.	2,900.
N6	A7	15c ultramarine	190.00	130.00
N7	A7	25c rose red & pale vio	29.00	30.00
N8	A7	30c org & dk vio	22.50	35.00
N9	A7	40c dk vio & car	32.50	40.00
N10	A7	50c blk, emerald	1,875.	1,900.
N11	A7	$1 red & blk, bl	350.00	350.00
N12	A7	$5 brown red & grn, emer	875.00	1,000.

Stamps of Pahang, 1935-41, Overprinted in Black

N13	A7	1c black	3.50	5.00
N14	A7	5c chocolate	2.00	2.00
N15	A7	8c rose red	40.00	3.75
N16	A7	10c violet brown	20.00	11.00
N17	A7	12c ultramarine	4.75	27.50
N18	A7	25c rose red & pale vio	9.50	42.50
N19	A7	30c org & dk vio	4.00	20.00
		Nos. N13-N19 (7)	83.75	111.75

Pahang No. 32 Overprinted and Surcharged in Black

e †

1943
| N20 | A7(e) | 6c on 5c chocolate | 2.00 | 2.00 |
| N21 | A7(f) | 6c on 5c chocolate | 2.50 | 3.00 |

The Japanese characters read: "Japanese Postal Service."

PENANG

pə-naŋ

LOCATION — An island off the west coast of the Malay Peninsula, plus a coastal strip called Province Wellesley.
AREA — 400 sq. mi.
POP. — 616,254 (1960)
CAPITAL — Georgetown

> Catalogue values for unused stamps in this section are for Never Hinged items.

Common Design Types pictured following the introduction.

Silver Wedding Issue
Common Design Types
Inscribed: "Malaya Penang"
Perf. 14x14½

1948, Dec. 1		Wmk. 4	Photo.	
1	CD304	10c purple	.50	.30

Perf. 11½x11

Engraved; Name Typographed

| 2 | CD305 | $5 lt brown | 40.00 | 37.50 |

Type of Straits Settlements, 1937-41, Inscribed "Penang"

1949-52			Perf. 18	
3	A29	1c black	1.50	.30
4	A29	2c orange	1.50	.30
5	A29	3c green	.60	1.25
6	A29	4c chocolate	.50	.25
7	A29	5c rose vio ('52)	4.25	4.00
8	A29	6c gray	1.50	.30
9	A29	8c rose red	1.25	5.00
10	A29	8c green ('52)	4.00	3.00
11	A29	10c plum	.50	.25
12	A29	12c rose red ('52)	4.50	9.00
13	A29	15c ultramarine	2.00	.40
14	A29	20c dk grn & blk	2.75	1.50
15	A29	20c ultra ('52)	3.25	1.50
16	A29	25c org & rose lilac	3.00	1.25
17	A29	35c dk vio & rose red ('52)	3.25	1.50
18	A29	40c dk vio & rose red	4.25	15.00
19	A29	50c ultra & black	5.50	.30
20	A29	$1 vio brn & ultra	20.00	3.00
21	A29	$2 rose red & emer	26.00	2.50
22	A29	$5 choc & emer	52.50	3.75
		Nos. 3-22 (20)	142.60	54.35

UPU Issue
Common Design Types
Inscribed: "Malaya-Penang"
Engr.; Name Typo. on 15c, 25c

1949, Oct. 10		Perf. 13½, 11x11½		
23	CD306	10c rose violet	.25	.25
24	CD307	15c indigo	2.50	3.75
25	CD308	25c orange	.60	3.75
26	CD309	50c slate	1.75	4.00
		Nos. 23-26 (4)	5.10	11.75

Coronation Issue
Common Design Type

1953, June 2		Engr.	Perf. 13½x13	
27	CD312	10c magenta & black	1.75	.30

Type of Malacca, 1954

1954-55		Wmk. 4	Typo.	Perf. 18
29	A1	1c black	.25	.85
30	A1	2c orange	.60	.10
31	A1	4c chocolate	1.25	.25
32	A1	5c rose violet	2.25	4.25
33	A1	6c gray	.25	1.00
34	A1	8c green	.30	4.00
35	A1	10c plum	.25	.25
36	A1	12c rose red	.35	4.00
37	A1	20c ultra	.60	.25
38	A1	25c orange & plum	.40	.25
39	A1	30c plum & rose red ('55)	.40	.25
40	A1	35c vio brn & rose red	.80	.95
41	A1	50c ultra & black	.65	.25
42	A1	$1 vio brn & ultra	2.75	.25
43	A1	$2 rose red & grn	15.00	4.25
44	A1	$5 choc & emerald	47.50	4.25
		Nos. 29-44 (16)	73.60	25.80

Types of Kedah with Portrait of Queen Elizabeth II
Perf. 13x12½, 12½x13

1957		Engr.	Wmk. 314	
45	A8	1c black	.30	1.50
46	A8	2c red orange	.30	1.25
47	A8	4c dark brown	.25	.25
48	A8	5c dk car rose	.30	.50
49	A8	8c dark green	2.50	2.75
50	A7	10c chocolate	.40	.25
51	A7	20c blue	1.00	.60

Perf. 12½, 13½ ($1)

52	A7	50c ultra & black	1.75	.85
53	A8	$1 plum & ultra	8.50	1.00
54	A8	$2 red & green	22.50	18.00
55	A8	$5 ol green & brown	27.50	15.00
		Nos. 45-55 (11)	65.35	41.95

Types of Kedah, 1957 with Penang State Crest and Areca-nut Palm Replacing Portrait of Elizabeth II
Perf. 13x12½, 12½x13, 13½ ($1)

1960, Mar. 15		Engr.	Wmk. 314	
56	A8	1c black	.25	1.75
57	A8	2c red orange	.25	1.75
58	A8	4c dark brown	.25	.25
59	A8	5c dk car rose	.25	.25
60	A8	8c dark green	3.00	5.25
61	A7	10c violet brown	.35	.25
62	A7	20c blue	.55	.25
63	A7	50c ultra & black	.35	.25
64	A8	$1 plum & ultra	7.50	1.90
65	A8	$2 red & green	8.00	7.25
		Revenue cancel		.20
66	A8	$5 ol green & brown	14.00	9.50
		Nos. 56-66 (11)	34.75	28.65

Starting in 1965, issues of Penang (Pulau Pinang) are listed with Malaysia.

OCCUPATION STAMPS

Issued under Japanese Occupation

Stamps of Straits Settlements, 1937-41, Overprinted in Red or Black

1942		Wmk. 4	Perf. 14	
N1	A29	1c black (R)	10.00	4.00
a.		Inverted overprint	725.00	725.00
b.		Double overprint	350.00	350.00
N2	A29	2c brown orange	12.00	5.25
a.		Inverted overprint	180.00	
b.		Double overprint	675.00	
N3	A29	3c green (R)	10.00	10.00
a.		Double overprint, one inverted	475.00	
N4	A29	5c brown (R)	4.75	10.00
a.		Double overprint	675.00	525.00
b.		"N PPON" for "NIPPON"	220.00	
N5	A29	8c gray (R)	3.00	1.60
a.		Double overprint	625.00	
b.		"N PPON" for "NIPPON"	75.00	70.00
N6	A29	10c dull vio (R)	2.00	2.50
a.		Double overprint	500.00	500.00
b.		Double overprint, one inverted	450.00	450.00
N7	A29	12c ultra (H)	5.75	25.00
a.		Double overprint	500.00	
b.		Double overprint, one inverted	750.00	725.00
c.		"N PPON" for "NIPPON"	575.00	
N8	A29	15c ultra (R)	2.00	5.00
a.		Inverted overprint	450.00	450.00
b.		Double overprint	675.00	675.00
c.		"N PPON" for "NIPPON"	120.00	150.00
N9	A29	40c dk vio & rose red	9.00	25.00
N10	A29	50c black, emer	5.25	42.50
N11	A29	$1 red & blk, bl	14.00	55.00
a.		Inverted overprint	1,400.	
N12	A29	$2 rose red & green	70.00	120.00
N13	A29	$5 grn & red, grn	900.00	950.00
		Nos. N1-N13 (13)	1,048.	1,256.

Stamps of Straits Settlements Handstamped Okugawa Seal in Red

1942		Wmk. 4	Perf. 14	
N14	A29	1c black	14.00	18.00
N15	A29	2c brown orange	27.50	30.00
N16	A29	3c green	23.00	30.00
N17	A29	5c brown	35.00	42.50
N18	A29	8c gray	42.50	55.00
N19	A29	10c dull violet	57.50	60.00
N20	A29	12c ultramarine	55.00	60.00
N21	A29	15c ultramarine	65.00	65.00
N22	A29	40c dk vio & rose red	125.00	130.00
N23	A29	50c blk, emerald	230.00	260.00
N24	A29	$1 red & blk, bl	325.00	350.00

MALAYA — Penang — Perak

N25	A29	$2 rose red & gray grn	1,000.	850.00
N26	A29	$5 grn & red, grn	3,500.	1,800.
		Nos. N14-N26 (13)	5,500.	3,751.

Uchibori Seal Handstamped in Red

N14a	A29	1c	215.00	180.00
N15a	A29	2c	215.00	150.00
N16a	A29	3c	130.00	130.00
N17a	A29	5c	3,750.	3,750.
N18a	A29	8c	130.00	130.00
N19a	A29	10c	240.00	240.00
N20a	A29	12c	150.00	165.00
N21a	A29	15c	170.00	175.00
		Nos. N14a-N21a (8)	5,000.	4,920.

PERAK

ˈper-ə-ˌak

LOCATION — On the west coast of the Malay Peninsula.
AREA — 7,980 sq. mi.
POP. — 1,327,120 (1960)
CAPITAL — Taiping

Straits Settlements No. 10 Handstamped in Black

1878 Wmk. 1 Perf. 14

1	A2	2c brown	2,250.	2,300.

Overprinted

Overprint 17x3½mm Wide
1880-81

2	A2	2c brown	50.00	90.00

Overprinted

Overprint 12 to 13½mm wide

3	A2	2c brown ('81)	200.00	200.00

Same Overprint on Straits Settlements Nos. 40, 41a
1883 Wmk. 2

4	A2	2c brown	26.50	90.00
a.		Double overprint	750.00	
5	A2	2c rose	50.00	70.00
c.		Double overprint	775.00	

Overprinted

Overprint 14 to 15½mm Wide

6	A2	2c rose	5.50	4.00
a.		Inverted overprint	475.00	600.00
b.		Double overprint	700.00	700.00

For surcharge, see No. 19E.

Overprinted

Overprint 12¾ to 14mm Wide
1886-90

7	A2	2c rose	2.50	8.00
a.		"FERAK" corrected by pen	450.00	650.00

Overprinted

Overprint 10x1¾mm

8	A2	2c rose	30.00	62.50

1891

Overprint 13mm long

9	A2	2c bright rose		3,900.

Overprinted

Overprint 12-12½x2¾mm

10	A2	2c rose	15.50	57.50
a.		Double overprint	1,650.	

Overprinted

Overprint 10½-10¾x2½mm

11	A2	2c rose	225.00	230.00

Overprinted

Overprint 13x2¾mm

11A	A2	2c rose		3,750.

Straits Settlements Nos. 11, 41a, 42 Surcharged in Black or Blue

q, r, s, t

12	A2(q)	2c on 4c rose, as #3 ('83)	750.00	350.00
13	A2(t)	1c on 2c rose	350.00	150.00
a.		Without period after "CENT" ('90)	—	300.00
14	A2(r)	1c on 2c rose	75.00	92.50
a.		Without period after "PERAK"	850.00	850.00
b.		Double surcharge	1,250.	
15	A2(s)	1c on 2c rose (Bl)	75.00	85.00
15A	A2(s)	1c on 2c rose (Bk)	2,150.	1,600.

In type "r" PERAK is 11½ to 14mm wide.

Surcharged in Black

16	A2	1c on 2c rose	210.00	210.00
a.		Double surcharge	2,000.	2,000.

Surcharged

18	A2	1c on 2c rose	3,250.	3,500.
b.		Double surcharge, one inverted		

Surcharged

18A	A2	1c on 2c rose	1,750.	1,000.

Surcharged

19	A2	1c on 2c rose	4.25	20.00
a.		Double surcharge, one inverted		
b.		Inverted surcharge		3,750.
c.		"One" inverted		
d.		Double surcharge		1,400.

No. 6 surcharged in Italic Serifed Capital Letters

1886

19E	A2	1c on 2c rose	4,750.	3,750.

Straits Settlements No. 41a Surcharged

u, v, w, x, y, z, h

1889-90

20	A2(u)	1c on 2c rose	4.00	10.00
a.		Italic Roman "K" in "PE-RAK"	37.50	57.50
b.		Double surcharge	1,400.	
21	A2(v)	1c on 2c rose	800.00	975.00
23	A2(w)	1c on 2c rose	27.50	55.00
a.		"PREAK"	900.00	1,100.
24	A2(x)	1c on 2c rose	150.00	175.00
25	A2(y)	1c on 2c rose	17.50	27.50
26	A2(z)	1c on 2c rose	18.00	27.50
27	A2(h)	1c on 2c rose	37.50	57.50

Straits Settlements Nos. 41a, 48, 54 Surcharged in Black

a, b, c, d, e, f, g

1891 Wmk. 2

28	A2(a)	1c on 2c rose	2.75	15.00
a.		Bar omitted	215.00	
29	A2(a)	1c on 6c violet	110.00	42.50
30	A3(b)	2c on 24c grn	32.50	16.50
31	A2(c)	1c on 2c rose	9.75	52.50
a.		Bar omitted	1,000.	
32	A2(d)	1c on 2c rose	2.75	20.00
a.		Bar omitted	450.00	
33	A2(d)	1c on 6c violet	110.00	95.00
34	A3(d)	2c on 24c grn	85.00	42.50
35	A2(e)	1c on 2c rose	9.75	50.00
a.		Bar omitted	1,000.	
36	A2(e)	1c on 6c violet	210.00	210.00
37	A3(e)	2c on 24c grn	140.00	80.00
38	A2(f)	1c on 6c violet	210.00	200.00
39	A3(f)	2c on 24c grn	140.00	95.00
40	A2(g)	1c on 6c violet	210.00	200.00
41	A3(g)	2c on 24c grn	140.00	95.00
		Nos. 28-41 (14)	1,363.	1,214.

A7

1892-95 Typo. Perf. 14

42	A7	1c green	2.40	.45
43	A7	2c rose	1.80	.45
44	A7	2c orange ('95)	1.10	9.50
45	A7	5c blue	3.50	8.00
		Nos. 42-45 (4)	8.80	18.40

For overprint see No. O10.

Type of 1892 Surcharged in Black

1895

46	A7	3c on 5c rose	4.25	5.50

A9, A10

1895-99 Wmk. 2 Perf. 14

47	A9	1c lilac & green	3.25	.60
48	A9	2c lilac & brown	3.50	.60
49	A9	3c lil & car rose	4.50	.60
50	A9	4c lil & car rose ('99)	20.00	7.50
51	A9	5c lilac & olive	12.00	.80
52	A9	8c lilac & blue	50.00	.75
53	A9	10c lilac & orange	17.00	.65
54	A9	25c grn & car rose ('96)	225.00	14.00
55	A9	50c lilac & black	52.50	52.50
56	A9	50c grn & blk ('99)	240.00	190.00

Wmk. 1

57	A10	$1 green & lt grn	325.00	225.00
58	A10	$2 grn & car rose ('96)	450.00	375.00
59	A10	$3 grn & ol ('96)	650.00	575.00
60	A10	$5 green & ultra	675.00	625.00
61	A10	$25 grn & org ('96)	11,000.	4,500.
		Nos. 47-57 (11)	952.75	493.00

For surcharges and overprint see Nos. 62-68, O11, Malaya Nos. 9-13A.

Stamps of 1895-99 Surcharged in Black

i, k, m, n

1900 Wmk. 2

62	A9(i)	1c on 2c lil & brn	1.00	2.75
63	A9(k)	1c on 4c lil & car rose	1.00	17.50
a.		Double surcharge	1,350.	
64	A9(i)	1c on 5c lil & ol	3.25	22.50
65	A9(i)	3c on 8c lil & blue	13.50	19.00
a.		No period after "Cent"	225.00	325.00
b.		Double surcharge	550.00	625.00

MALAYA — Perak — Perlis

66	A9(i)	3c on 50c grn & blk	6.00	12.50
a.		No period after "Cent"	150.00	240.00

Wmk. 1

67	A10(m)	3c on $1 grn & lt grn	60.00	160.00
a.		Double surcharge	1,650.	
b.		A10(n) Thin "t" in "Cent".	325.00	550.00
c.		As "b," double surcharge	3,000.	
68	A10(m)	3c on $2 grn & car rose	52.50	90.00
		Nos. 62-68 (7)	137.25	324.25

Sultan Iskandar — A14

1935-37   Typo.   Wmk. 4
Chalky Paper

69	A14	1c black ('36)	3.50	.25
70	A14	2c dp green ('36)	3.50	.25
71	A14	4c brown orange	3.50	.25
72	A14	5c chocolate	.80	.25
73	A14	6c rose red ('37)	12.50	6.50
74	A14	8c gray	1.00	.25
75	A14	10c dk vio ('36)	1.00	.25
76	A14	12c ultra ('36)	4.75	1.00
77	A14	25c rose red & pale vio ('36)	3.50	1.00
78	A14	30c org & dark vio ('36)	5.00	1.50
79	A14	40c dk vio & car	8.00	8.00
80	A14	50c blk, emer ('36)	10.00	1.75
81	A14	$1 red & blk, bl ('36)	3.00	1.40
82	A14	$2 rose red & grn ('36)	45.00	8.00
83	A14	$5 brn red & grn, emer ('36)	175.00	37.50
		Nos. 69-83 (15)	280.05	68.15
		Set, never hinged	200.00	

Sultan Iskandar — A15

1938-41

84	A15	1c black ('39)	7.00	.25
85	A15	2c dp green ('39)	4.50	.25
85A	A15	2c brn org, thin, striated paper ('41)	1.75	25.00
85B	A15	3c green ('41)	1.50	18.00
a.		Ordinary paper	5.50	10.50
86	A15	4c brn org ('39)	20.00	.25
87	A15	5c choc ('39)	3.50	.25
88	A15	6c rose red ('39)	14.00	.25
89	A15	8c gray	16.00	.25
89A	A15	8c rose red, thin, striated paper ('41)	.55	95.00
90	A15	10c dk violet	18.00	.25
91	A15	12c ultra, ordinary paper	13.00	2.00
91A	A15	15c ultra ('41)	2.25	20.00
92	A15	25c rose red & pale vio ('39)	27.50	4.00
93	A15	30c org & dk vio, chalky paper	5.00	3.00
94	A15	40c dk vio & rose red	27.50	3.00
95	A15	50c blk, emerald	17.50	1.25
96	A15	$1 red & blk, bl ('40)	75.00	32.50
97	A15	$2 rose red & grn ('40)	100.00	85.00
98	A15	$5 red, emer ('40)	160.00	525.00
		Nos. 84-98 (18)	514.55	815.50
		Set, never hinged	1,325.	

For overprints see Nos. N1-N40.

Catalogue values for unused stamps in this section, from this point to the end of the section, are for Never Hinged items.

Common Design Types pictured following the introduction.

Silver Wedding Issue
Common Design Types
Inscribed: "Malaya Perak"

1948, Dec. 1   Photo.   Perf. 14x14½

99	CD304	10c purple	.30	.25

Engraved; Name Typographed
Perf. 11½x11

100	CD305	$5 green	27.50	37.50

UPU Issue
Common Design Types
Inscribed: "Malaya-Perak"
Engr.; Name Typo. on 15c, 25c
Perf. 13½, 11x11½

1949, Oct. 10   Wmk. 4

101	CD306	10c rose violet	.25	.25
102	CD307	15c indigo	1.50	2.00
103	CD308	25c orange	.40	5.00
104	CD309	50c slate	1.50	3.50
		Nos. 101-104 (4)	3.65	10.75

Sultan Yussuf Izuddin Shah — A16

1950, Aug. 17   Typo.   Perf. 18

105	A16	1c black	.25	.40
106	A16	2c orange	.25	.40
107	A16	3c green	3.00	1.40
108	A16	4c chocolate	.75	.40
109	A16	6c gray	.40	.40
110	A16	8c rose red	1.60	2.25
111	A16	10c plum	.25	.40
112	A16	15c ultramarine	1.10	.50
113	A16	20c dk grn & blk	1.60	.75
114	A16	25c org & plum	.90	.30
115	A16	40c vio brn & rose red	5.00	7.00
116	A16	50c dp ultra & blk	5.00	.30
117	A16	$1 vio brn & ultra	7.00	1.10
118	A16	$2 rose red & emer	17.00	7.50
119	A16	$5 choc & emerald	42.50	22.50

1952-55

120	A16	5c rose violet	.50	2.00
121	A16	8c green	1.40	1.25
122	A16	12c rose red	1.40	5.00
123	A16	20c ultramarine	1.10	.30
124	A16	30c plum & rose red ('55)	2.25	.30
125	A16	35c dk vio & rose red	1.40	.40
		Nos. 105-125 (21)	94.65	54.85

Coronation Issue
Common Design Type

1953   Engr.   Perf. 13½x13

126	CD312	10c magenta & black	1.60	.25

Types of Kedah with Portrait of Sultan Yussuf Izuddin Shah
Perf. 13x12½, 12½x13, 13½ ($1)

1957-61   Engr.   Wmk. 314

127	A8	1c black	.25	.30
128	A8	2c red orange	.45	1.00
129	A8	4c dark brown	.25	.25
130	A8	5c dk car rose	.25	.25
131	A8	8c dark green	2.50	4.00
132	A7	10c chocolate	2.25	.25
133	A7	20c blue	2.25	.25
134	A7	50c ultra & blk ('60)	.45	.25
a.		Perf. 12½	.60	1.00
135	A8	$1 plum & ultra	7.50	.50
136	A8	$2 red & grn ('61)	7.00	4.25
a.		Perf. 12½	5.00	5.00
137	A8	$5 org & brn ('60)	14.00	9.00
a.		Perf. 12½	15.00	13.00
		Nos. 127-137 (11)	37.15	20.30

Starting with 1963, issues of Perak are listed with Malaysia.

OFFICIAL STAMPS

Stamps and Types of Straits Settlements Overprinted in Black

1890   Wmk. 1   Perf. 14

O1	A3	12c blue	325.00	400.00
O2	A3	24c green	775.00	900.00

Wmk. 2

O3	A2	2c rose	10.00	10.00
a.		No period after "S"	100.00	125.00
b.		Double overprint	1,100.	1,100.
O4	A2	4c brown	37.50	40.00
a.		No period after "S"	210.00	275.00
O5	A2	6c violet	45.00	60.00
O6	A3	8c orange	55.00	67.50
O7	A7	10c slate	80.00	80.00
O8	A3	12c vio brown	275.00	350.00
O9	A3	24c green	225.00	240.00

P.G.S. stands for Perak Government Service.

Perak No. 45 Overprinted Service.

1894

O10	A7	5c blue	140.00	1.25
a.		Inverted overprint	1,750.	525.00

Same Overprint on No. 51

1897

O11	A9	5c lilac & olive	3.50	.60
a.		Double overprint	750.00	450.00

OCCUPATION STAMPS

Issued under Japanese Occupation

Stamps of Perak, 1938-41, Handstamped in Black, Red, Brown or Violet

1942   Wmk. 4   Perf. 14

N1	A15	1c black	75.00	50.00
N2	A15	2c brn orange	40.00	21.00
N3	A15	3c green	35.00	37.50
N4	A15	5c chocolate	12.50	11.00
N5	A15	8c gray	125.00	65.00
N6	A15	8c rose red	50.00	50.00
N7	A15	10c dk violet	27.50	27.50
N8	A15	12c ultramarine	300.00	275.00
N9	A15	15c ultramarine	25.00	35.00
N10	A15	25c rose red & pale vio	27.50	30.00
N11	A15	30c org & dk vio	35.00	40.00
N12	A15	40c dk vio & rose red	900.00	425.00
N13	A15	50c blk, emer	60.00	60.00
N14	A15	$1 red & blk, bl	675.00	450.00
N15	A15	$2 rose red & grn	5,750.	6,000.
N16	A15	$5 red, emer	650.00	

Some authorities claim No. N6 was not regularly issued. This overprint also exists on No. 85.

Stamps of Perak, 1938-41, Overprinted in Black

N16A	A15	1c black	150.00	
N17	A15	2c brn org	4.50	4.50
a.		Inverted overprint	75.00	75.00
N18	A15	3c green	1.50	1.60
a.		Inverted overprint	27.50	30.00
N18B	A15	5c chocolate	135.00	
N19	A15	8c rose red	1.50	.55
a.		Inverted overprint	4.50	10.00
b.		Dbl. ovpt., one invtd.	250.00	275.00
c.		Pair, one without ovpt.	500.00	
N20	A15	10c dk violet	22.50	9.50
N21	A15	15c ultramarine	16.00	6.00
N21A	A15	30c org & dk vio	140.00	
N22	A15	50c blk, emer	4.00	8.00
N23	A15	$1 red & blk, bl	625.00	675.00
N24	A15	$5 red, emerald	100.00	100.00
a.		Inverted overprint	350.00	425.00

Some authorities claim Nos. N16A, N18B and N21A were not regularly issued.

Overprinted on Perak No. 87 and Surcharged in Black "2 Cents"

N25	A15	2c on 5c chocolate	2.00	5.00

Perak Nos. 84 and 89A Overprinted in Black

N26	A15	1c black	7.00	11.00
a.		Inverted overprint	20.00	47.50
N27	A15	8c rose red	12.50	3.75
a.		Inverted overprint	13.50	27.50

Overprinted on Perak No. 87 and Surcharged in Black "2 Cents"

N28	A15	2c on 5c chocolate	2.75	6.50
a.		Inverted overprint	17.50	50.00
b.		As "a," "2 Cents" omitted	52.50	75.00

Stamps of Perak, 1938-41, Overprinted or Surcharged in Black

No. N31

No. N32

1943

N29	A15	1c black	1.25	1.75
N30	A15	2c brn orange	35.00	35.00
N31	A15	2c on 5c choc	1.00	1.00
a.		"2 Cents" inverted	35.00	40.00
b.		Entire surcharge inverted	40.00	45.00
N32	A15	2c on 5c choc	1.40	1.40
a.		Vertical characters invtd.	35.00	40.00
b.		Entire surcharge inverted	35.00	40.00
N33	A15	3c green	37.50	37.50
N34	A15	5c chocolate	1.00	1.00
a.		Inverted overprint	50.00	60.00
N35	A15	8c gray	35.00	35.00
N36	A15	8c rose red	1.25	3.50
a.		Inverted overprint	35.00	40.00
N37	A15	10c dk violet	1.25	1.50
N38	A15	30c org & dk vio	5.50	5.50
N39	A15	50c blk, emerald	90.00	175.00
N40	A15	$5 red, emerald	5.50	32.50
		Nos. N29-N40 (12)	215.65	335.15

No. N34 was also used in the Shan States of Burma. The Japanese characters read: "Japanese Postal Service."

Some authorities claim Nos. N30, N33 and N35 were not regularly issued.

PERLIS

'per-ləs

LOCATION — On the west coast of the Malay peninsula, adjoining Siam and Kedah.
AREA — 310 sq. mi.
POP. — 97,645 (1960)
CAPITAL — Kangar

Catalogue values for unused stamps in this section are for Never Hinged items.

Common Design Types pictured following the introduction.

Silver Wedding Issue
Common Design Types
Inscribed: "Malaya Perlis"
Perf. 14x14½

1948, Dec. 1   Photo.   Wmk. 4

1	CD304	10c purple	1.00	3.00

Engraved; Name Typographed
Perf. 11½x11

2	CD305	$5 lt brown	32.50	55.00

UPU Issue
Common Design Types
Inscribed: "Malaya-Perlis"
Engr.; Name Typo. on 15c, 25c

1949, Oct. 10   Perf. 13½, 11x11½

3	CD306	10c rose violet	.40	2.00
4	CD307	15c indigo	1.40	4.50
5	CD308	25c orange	.65	3.50
6	CD309	50c slate	1.50	4.25
		Nos. 3-6 (4)	3.95	14.25

Raja Syed Putra — A1

Perf. 18

1951, Mar. 26   Wmk. 4   Typo.

7	A1	1c black	.25	1.00
8	A1	2c orange	.75	.70
9	A1	3c green	1.75	5.25
10	A1	4c chocolate	1.75	1.50
11	A1	6c gray	1.50	2.50
12	A1	8c rose red	3.75	7.50
13	A1	10c plum	1.25	.50
14	A1	15c ultramarine	5.00	8.50
15	A1	20c dk green & blk	4.50	11.50
16	A1	25c org & rose lilac	2.25	3.75
17	A1	40c dk vio & rose red	5.00	29.00
18	A1	50c ultra & black	4.75	7.00
19	A1	$1 vio brn & ultra	10.00	27.50
20	A1	$2 rose red & emer	20.00	60.00
21	A1	$5 choc & emerald	70.00	125.00

1952-55

22	A1	5c rose violet	.75	3.75
23	A1	8c green	2.75	4.50
24	A1	12c rose red	2.00	6.25
25	A1	20c ultramarine	1.25	1.75

117

MALAYA — Perlis — Selangor

26	A1	30c plum & rose red ('55)	2.75	15.00
27	A1	35c dk vio & rose red	3.00	8.50
		Nos. 7-27 (21)	145.00	330.95

Coronation Issue
Common Design Type

1953, June 2   Engr.   Perf. 13½x13

28	CD312	10c magenta & black	1.75	4.00

Types of Kedah with Portrait of Raja Syed Putra

Perf. 13x12½, 12½x13, 12½ ($2, $5), 13½ ($1)

1957-62   Engr.   Wmk. 314

29	A8	1c black	.25	.40
30	A8	2c red orange	.25	.40
31	A8	4c dark brown	.25	.25
32	A8	5c dk car rose	.25	.25
33	A8	8c dark green	2.50	2.25
34	A7	10c chocolate	1.50	3.00
35	A7	20c blue	3.50	5.00
36	A7	50c ultra & blk ('62)	3.50	4.75
a.		Perf. 12½	1.50	4.00
37	A8	$1 plum & ultra	10.00	14.00
38	A8	$2 red & green	10.00	10.00
39	A8	$5 ol green & brown	15.00	13.00
		Nos. 29-39 (11)	47.00	53.30

Starting in 1965, issues of Perlis are listed with Malaysia.

SELANGOR

sə-'laŋ-ər

LOCATION — South of Perak on the west coast of the Malay Peninsula.
AREA — 3,160 sq. mi.
POP. — 1,012,891 (1960)
CAPITAL — Kuala Lumpur

Stamps of the Straits Settlements Overprinted

Handstamped in Black or Red

1878   Wmk. 1   Perf. 14

1	A2	2c brown (Bk)	—	

Wmk. 2   Perf.

2	A2	2c brown (R)	600.00	

The authenticity of Nos. 1-2 is questioned.

Overprinted in Black

1882

3	A2	2c brown	—	3,300.

Overprinted

Overprint 16 to 16¾mm Wide

1881   Wmk. 1

5	A2	2c brown	140.00	140.00
a.		Double overprint		

Overprint 16 to 17mm Wide

1882-83   Wmk. 2
"S" wide, all other letters narrow

6	A2	2c brown	200.00	160.00
7	A2	2c rose	160.00	125.00

Overprinted

Overprint 14¼x3mm

8	A2	2c rose	11.50	24.00
a.		Double overprint	975.00	850.00

Overprinted

Overprint 14½ to 15½mm Wide

1886-89

9	A2	2c rose	42.50	55.00

Overprinted

Overprint 16½x1¾mm

9A	A2	2c rose	67.50	72.50
b.		Double overprint		1,000.

Overprinted

Overprint 15½ to 17mm Wide
With Period

10	A2	2c rose	140.00	90.00

Without Period

11	A2	2c rose	14.50	3.25

Same Overprint, but Vertically

12	A2	2c rose	22.50	37.50

Overprinted

12A	A2	2c rose	150.00	3.75

Overprinted

Overprint 17mm Wide

13	A2	2c rose	1,700.	1,850.

Overprinted

14	A2	2c rose	400.00	175.00

Overprinted Vertically

1889

15	A2	2c rose	725.00	40.00

Overprinted Vertically

Overprint 19 to 20¾mm Wide

16	A2	2c rose	325.00	95.00

Similar Overprint, but Diagonally

17	A2			3,000.

Overprinted Vertically

18	A2		90.00	6.75

Same Overprint Horizontally

18A	A2	2c rose		4,500.

Surcharged in Black

1891

19	A3 (a)	2c on 24c green	40.00	75.00
20	A3 (b)	2c on 24c green	225.00	275.00
21	A3 (c)	2c on 24c green	225.00	250.00
22	A3 (d)	2c on 24c green	125.00	150.00
23	A3 (e)	2c on 24c green	225.00	275.00
		Nos. 19-23 (5)	840.00	1,025.

No. 22a occurred in the first printing in one position (R. 8/3) in the sheet.

1891-95   Typo.   Wmk. 2

24	A6	1c green	1.75	.30
25	A6	2c rose	4.00	1.25
26	A6	2c orange ('95)	3.00	1.00
27	A6	5c blue	27.50	5.25
		Nos. 24-27 (4)	36.25	7.80

Type of 1891 Surcharged

1894

28	A6	3c on 5c rose	5.00	.70

1895-99   Wmk. 2   Perf. 14

29	A8	3c lilac & rose	7.00	.35
30	A8	5c lilac & olive	8.50	.35
31	A8	8c lilac & blue	55.00	8.50
32	A8	10c lilac & orange	13.50	2.50
33	A8	25c grn & car rose	90.00	60.00
34	A8	50c lilac & black	80.00	29.00
35	A8	50c green & black	475.00	140.00

Wmk. 1

36	A9	$1 green & lt grn	65.00	150.00
37	A9	$2 grn & car rose	250.00	300.00
38	A9	$3 green & olive	600.00	500.00
39	A9	$5 green & ultra	300.00	400.00
40	A9	$10 grn & brn vio	800.00	1,000.
41	A9	$25 green & org	4,000.	4,000.
		Nos. 29-39, Ovpt. "SPECIMEN"		450.00

High values with revenue cancellations are plentiful and inexpensive.

Surcharged in Black

1900   Wmk. 2

42	A8	1c on 5c lilac & olive	75.00	125.00
43	A8	1c on 50c grn & blk	3.50	29.00
a.		Surcharge reading "cent One cent."		3,500.
44	A8	3c on 50c grn & blk	6.00	26.00
		Nos. 42-44 (3)	84.50	180.00

Mosque at Klang — A12
Sultan Sulaiman — A13

1935-41   Typo.   Wmk. 4   Perf. 14

45	A12	1c black ('36)	.30	.25
46	A12	2c dp green ('36)	.55	.25
46A	A12	2c org brn ('41)	2.25	1.25
46B	A12	3c green ('41)	1.25	8.00
47	A12	4c orange brown	.30	.25
48	A12	5c chocolate	.70	.25
49	A12	6c rose red ('37)	4.00	.25
50	A12	8c gray	.35	.25
51	A12	10c dk violet ('36)	.35	.25
52	A12	12c ultra ('36)	.90	.25
52A	A12	15c ultra ('41)	7.00	35.00
53	A12	25c rose red & pale vio ('36)	.60	.80
54	A12	30c org & dk vio ('36)	.60	1.10
55	A12	40c dk vio & car	1.50	1.25
56	A12	50c blk, emer ('36)	1.00	.50
57	A13	$1 red & black, blue ('36)	6.00	1.10
58	A13	$2 rose red & green ('36)	17.50	9.50
59	A13	$5 brn red & grn, emer ('36)	55.00	30.00
		Nos. 45-59 (18)	100.15	90.50
		Set, never hinged		170.00

Nos. 46A-46B were printed on both ordinary and chalky paper; 15c only on ordinary paper; other values only on chalky paper.
An 8c rose red was prepared but not issued.
For overprints see Nos. N1-N15, N18A-N24, N26-N39.

Sultan Hisam-ud-Din Alam Shah — A14

1941

72	A14	$1 red & blk, blue	11.50	7.00
73	A14	$2 car & green	30.00	40.00
		Set, never hinged		70.00

A $5 stamp of type A14, issued during the Japanese occupation with different overprints (Nos. N18, N25A, N42), also exists without overprint. The unoverprinted stamp was not issued. Value $125.
For overprints see Nos. N16-N17, N24A, N25, N40-N41.

Catalogue values for unused stamps in this section, from this point to the end of the section, are for Never Hinged items.

Common Design Types pictured following the introduction.

Silver Wedding Issue
Common Design Types
Inscribed: "Malaya Selangor"

Perf. 14x14½

1948, Dec. 1   Photo.   Wmk. 4

74	CD304	10c purple	.25	.30

Perf. 11½x11

Engraved; Name Typographed

75	CD305	$5 green	30.00	25.00

UPU Issue
Common Design Types
Inscribed: "Malaya-Selangor"

Engr.; Name Typo. on Nos. 77 & 78

1949, Oct. 10   Perf. 13½, 11x11½

76	CD306	10c rose violet	.40	.30
77	CD307	15c indigo	2.50	2.50
78	CD308	25c orange	.50	4.50
79	CD309	50c slate	1.50	5.00
		Nos. 76-79 (4)	4.90	12.30

Sultan Hisam-ud-Din Alam Shah — A15

1949, Sept. 12   Typo.   Perf. 18

80	A15	1c black	.25	.60
81	A15	2c orange	.30	1.50
82	A15	3c green	4.00	2.00
83	A15	4c chocolate	.50	.35

MALAYA — Selangor — Sungei Ujong

84	A15	6c gray	.35	.35
85	A15	8c rose red	2.00	1.25
86	A15	10c plum	.25	.25
87	A15	15c ultramarine	8.00	.35
88	A15	20c dk grn & black	5.00	.50
89	A15	25c orange & rose lil	2.00	.35
90	A15	40c dk vio & rose red	11.00	8.00
91	A15	50c ultra & black	3.50	.35
92	A15	$1 vio brn & ultra	4.00	.60
93	A15	$2 rose red & emer	15.00	1.10
94	A15	$5 choc & emerald	55.00	3.00

1952-55

95	A15	5c rose violet	1.00	2.75
96	A15	8c green	1.00	1.75
97	A15	12c rose red	1.25	3.50
98	A15	20c ultramarine	1.25	.35
99	A15	30c plum & rose red ('55)	2.25	2.25
100	A15	35c dk vio & rose red	1.50	1.50
		Nos. 80-100 (21)	119.40	32.65

Coronation Issue
Common Design Type

1953, June 2 Engr. Perf. 13½x13

101	CD312	10c magenta & black	1.75	.25

A16

Sultan Hisam-ud-Din Alam Shah — A17

Designs as in Kelantan, 1957.

Perf. 13x12½, 12½x13, 13½ ($1)

1957-60 Engr. Wmk. 314

102	A17	1c black	.25	2.50
103	A17	2c red orange	.50	1.00
104	A17	4c dark brown	.25	.25
105	A17	5c dark car rose	.25	.25
106	A17	8c dark green	3.00	4.00
107	A16	10c chocolate	2.50	.25
108	A16	20c blue	3.25	.25
109	A16	50c ultra & blk ('60)	1.00	.25
a.		Perf. 12½	.40	.25
110	A17	$1 plum & ultra	4.50	.25
a.		Perf. 12½	4.00	3.00
112	A17	$5 ol grn & brn ('60)	12.00	2.40
a.		Perf. 12½	12.00	3.00
		Nos. 102-112 (11)	33.00	14.40

See Nos. 114-120.

Sultan Salahuddin Abdul Aziz Shah — A18

1961, June 28 Photo. Perf. 14½x14

113	A18	10s multicolored	.30	.25

Sultan Salahuddin Abdul Aziz Shah, Installation.

Types of 1957 with Portrait of Sultan Salahuddin Abdul Aziz Shah
Designs as before.

Perf. 13x12½, 12½x13

1961-62 Engr. Wmk. 338

114	A17	1c black	.40	2.75
115	A17	2c red orange	.40	3.00
116	A17	4c dark brown	1.00	.25
117	A17	5c dark car rose	1.00	.25
118	A17	8c dark green	4.75	6.00
119	A16	10c vio brown ('61)	.90	.25
120	A16	20c blue	8.00	1.50
		Nos. 114-120 (7)	16.45	14.00

Starting in 1965, issues of Selangor are listed with Malaysia.

OCCUPATION STAMPS
Issued under Japanese Occupation

Stamps of Selangor 1935-41 Handstamped Vertically or Horizontally in Black, Red, Brown or Violet

1942, Apr. 3 Wmk. 4 Perf. 14

N1	A12	1c black	15.00	21.00
N2	A12	2c deep green	2,300.	1,500.
N3	A12	2c orange brown	55.00	55.00
N4	A12	3c green	35.00	17.00
N5	A12	5c chocolate	10.00	10.00
N6	A12	6c rose red	200.00	200.00
N7	A12	8c gray	27.50	27.50
N8	A12	10c dark violet	22.50	27.50
N9	A12	12c ultramarine	47.50	47.50
N10	A12	15c ultramarine	17.00	20.00
N11	A12	25c rose red & pale vio	80.00	95.00
N12	A12	30c org & dk vio	15.00	20.00
N13	A12	40c dk vio & car	100.00	140.00
N14	A12	50c blk, emerald	40.00	47.50
N15	A13	$5 brn red & grn, emer	275.00	275.00

Some authorities believe No. N15 was not issued regularly.

Handstamped Vertically on Stamps and Type of Selangor 1941 in Black or Red

N16	A14	$1 red & blk, bl	67.50	80.00
N17	A14	$2 car & green	80.00	110.00
N18	A14	$5 brn red & grn, emer	110.00	110.00

Stamps and Type of Selangor, 1935-41, Overprinted in Black

1942, May

N10A	A12	1c black	110.00	110.00
N19	A12	3c green	1.00	1.00
N19A	A12	5c chocolate	110.00	110.00
N20	A12	10c dark violet	35.00	35.00
N21	A12	12c ultramarine	2.75	5.00
N22	A12	15c ultramarine	5.50	4.00
N23	A12	30c org & dk vio	35.00	35.00
N24	A12	40c dk vio & car	4.00	4.00
N24A	A14	$1 red & blk, bl	35.00	35.00
N25	A14	$2 car & green	24.00	30.00
N25A	A14	$5 red & grn, emer	55.00	55.00
		Nos. N18A-N25A (11)	417.25	424.00

Overprint is horizontal on $1, $2, $5.
On Nos. N18A and N19 the overprint is known reading up, instead of down.
Some authorities claim Nos. N18A, N19A, N20, N23, N24A and N25A were not regularly issued.

Selangor No. 46B Overprinted in Black

1942, Dec.

N26	A12	3c green	400.00	400.00

Stamps and Type of Selangor, 1935-41, Ovptd. or Srchd. in Black or Red

i k

l m

1943

N27	A12(i)	1c black	1.40	1.40
N28	A12(k)	1c black (R)	.90	.90
N29	A12(l)	2c on 5c choc (R)	.90	.90
N30	A12(i)	3c green	1.00	1.00
N31	A12(l)	3c on 5c choc	.65	1.00
N32	A12(k)	5c choc (R)	.65	1.00
N33	A12(l)	6c on 5c choc	.25	.90
N34	A12(m)	6c on 5c choc	.25	1.00
N35	A12(i)	12c ultra	1.40	1.60
N36	A12(i)	15c ultra	6.75	10.00
N37	A12(k)	15c ultra	13.50	13.50
N38	A12(m)	$1 on 10c dk vio	.50	1.40
N39	A12(m)	$1.50 on 30c org & dk vio	.50	1.40
N40	A14(i)	$1 red & blk, blue	6.75	8.50
N41	A14(i)	$2 car & grn	24.00	24.00
N42	A14(i)	$5 brn red & grn, emer	50.00	55.00
		Nos. N27-N42 (16)	109.40	123.50

The "i" overprint is vertical on Nos. N40-N42 and is also found reading in the opposite direction on Nos. N30, N35 and N36.
The overprint reads: "Japanese Postal Service."

Singapore is listed following Sierra Leone.

SUNGEI UJONG

ˈsuŋ ü-juŋ,

Formerly a nonfederated native state on the Malay Peninsula, which in 1895 was consolidated with the Federated State of Negri Sembilan.

Stamps of the Straits Settlements Overprinted in Black

Overprinted

1878 Wmk. 1 Perf. 14

2	A2	2c brown	4,400.	4,600.

Overprinted

4	A2	2c brown		435.00
5	A2	4c rose	1,950.	1,950.

No. 5 is no longer recognized by some experts.

Overprinted

1882-83 Wmk. 2

6	A2	2c brown		350.00
7	A2	4c rose	5,500.	6,000.

This overprint on the 2c brown, wmk. 1, is probably a trial printing.

Overprinted

11	A2	2c brown	300.00	375.00

Overprinted

1881-84

14	A2	2c brown	1,675.	750.00
15	A2	2c rose	140.00	140.00
a.		"Ujong" printed sideways		
b.		"Sungei" printed twice		
16	A2	4c brown	275.00	400.00
17	A3	8c orange	2,000.	1,600.
18	A7	10c slate	675.00	575.00

Overprinted

19	A2	2c brown	60.00	175.00

Overprinted

1885-90 Without Period

20	A2	2c rose	55.00	70.00

With Period

21	A2	2c rose	115.00	80.00
a.		"UNJOG"	5,500.	3,900.

Overprinted

22	A2	2c rose	90.00	100.00
a.		Double overprint	775.00	875.00

Overprinted

23	A2	2c rose	115.00	135.00

Overprinted

24	A2	2c rose	27.50	47.50
a.		Double overprint		

Overprinted

25	A2	2c rose	100.00	115.00

Overprinted

26	A2	2c rose	160.00	160.00
c.		Double overprint		

Overprinted

Overprint 14-16x3mm

26A	A2	2c rose	15.00	17.00

Overprinted

26B	A2	2c rose	50.00	27.50

Stamp of 1883-91 Surcharged

a b

c d

1891

27	A3 (a)	2c on 24c green	260.	260.
28	A3 (b)	2c on 24c green	1,100.	1,100.
29	A3 (c)	2c on 24c green	440.	500.
30	A3 (d)	2c on 24c green	1,100.	1,100.
		Nos. 27-30 (4)	2,900.	2,960.

On Nos. 27-28, SUNGEI is 14 ½mm, UJONG 12¾x2 ½mm.

A3

119

MALAYA — Sungei Ujong — Trengganu

Sungei Ujong

1891-94   Typo.   Perf. 14
31	A3	2c rose	40.00	32.50
32	A3	2c orange ('94)	2.25	5.00
33	A3	5c blue ('93)	10.00	7.50
		Nos. 31-33 (3)	52.25	45.00

Type of 1891 Surcharged in Black

1894
34	A3	1c on 5c green	1.25	.90
35	A3	3c on 5c rose	3.00	8.50

A4

1895
36	A4	3c lilac & car rose	25.00	8.00

Stamps of Sungei Ujong were superseded by those of Negri Sembilan in 1895.

TRENGGANU

treŋ-ˈgä-ˌnü

LOCATION — On the eastern coast of the Malay Peninsula.
AREA — 5,050 sq. mi.
POP. — 302,171 (1960)
CAPITAL — Kuala Trengganu

Sultan Zenalabidin
A1   A2

1910-19   Typo.   Wmk. 3   Perf. 14
Ordinary Paper
1a	A1	1c blue green	2.10	1.25
2	A1	2c red vio & brn ('15)	1.25	1.10
3	A1	3c rose red	2.75	2.75
4	A1	4c brn orange	4.25	7.00
5	A1	4c grn & org brn ('15)	2.50	5.75
6	A1	4c scarlet ('19)	1.50	2.50
7	A1	5c gray	1.75	7.00
8	A1	5c choc & gray ('15)	3.00	2.40
9	A1	8c ultramarine	1.75	16.00
10	A1	10c red & grn, yel ('15)	1.75	2.75
11a	A1	10c violet, pale yel	3.75	16.00
12	A1	20c red vio & vio	4.25	9.00
13	A1	25c dl vio & grn ('15)	13.00	47.50
14	A1	30c blk & dl vio ('15)	13.50	67.50
15	A1	50c blk & sep, grn	5.75	17.50
16	A1	$1 red & blk, blue	22.50	27.50
17	A1	$3 red & grn, grn ('15)	235.00	600.00
18	A2	$5 lil & blue grn	255.00	850.00
19	A2	$25 green & car	1,800.	2,750.
		Revenue Cancel		300.00
		Nos. 1a-19 (19)	2,375.	4,334.

On No. 19 the numerals and Arabic inscriptions at top, left and right are in color on a colorless background.
Overprints are listed after No. 41. For surcharges see Nos. B1-B4.

Sultan Badaru'l-alam
A3   A4

1921-38   Wmk. 4   Perf. 14
Chalky Paper
20	A3	1c black ('25)	2.75	1.75
21	A3	2c deep green	2.10	3.00
22	A3	3c dp grn ('25)	1.00	1.15
23	A3	3c lt brn ('38)	42.50	20.00
24	A3	4c rose red	4.25	1.80
25	A3	5c choc & gray	3.25	7.25
26	A3	5c vio, yel ('25)	2.75	1.80
27	A3	6c orange ('24)	7.50	1.00
28	A3	8c gray ('38)	47.50	8.75
29	A3	10c ultramarine	3.50	1.50
30	A3	12c ultra ('25)	7.00	6.75
31	A3	20c org & dl vio	4.00	2.00
32	A3	25c dk vio & grn	4.75	4.00
33	A3	30c blk & dl vio	5.50	4.00
34	A3	35c red, yel ('25)	8.00	9.00
35	A3	50c car & green	11.50	4.75
36	A3	$1 ultra & vio, bl ('29)	13.50	5.50
37	A3	$3 red & green, emer ('25)	80.00	215.00
38	A4	$5 red & grn, yel ('38)	500.00	3,500.
39	A4	$25 blue & lil	1,250.	3,500.
40	A4	$50 org & green	3,000.	4,750.
41	A4	$100 red & green	8,750.	10,500.
		Nos. 20-37 (18)	253.35	298.40

On Nos. 39 to 41 the numerals and Arabic inscriptions at top, left and right are in color on a colorless background.
A 2c orange, 6c gray, 8c rose red and 15c ultramarine, type A3, exist, but are not known to have been regularly issued.
For surcharges and overprints see Nos. 45-46, N1-N60.

Stamps of 1910-21 Overprinted in Black

1922, Mar.   Wmk. 3
8A	A1	5c chocolate & gray	5.00	47.50
10A	A1	10c red & green, yel	5.00	47.50
12A	A1	20c red vio & violet	8.50	47.50
13A	A1	25c dull vio & green	4.75	47.50
14A	A1	30c black & dull vio	5.25	47.50
15A	A1	50c blk & sepia, grn	9.50	47.50
16A	A1	$1 red & blk, blue	18.00	95.00
17A	A1	$3 red & grn, green	250.00	550.00
18A	A2	$5 lil & blue green	400.00	725.00

Wmk. 4
21A	A3	2c deep green	7.50	47.50
24A	A3	4c rose red	7.75	47.50
		Nos. 8A-24A (11)	721.25	1,750.

Industrial fair at Singapore, Mar. 31-Apr. 15.

1921   Wmk. 3   Chalky Paper
42	A3	$1 ultra & vio, bl	18.00	35.00
43	A3	$3 red & grn, emer	140.00	255.00
44	A4	$5 red & green, yel	155.00	425.00
		Nos. 42-44 (3)	313.00	715.00

Types of 1921-25 Surcharged in Black

1941, May 1   Wmk. 4   Perf. 13½x14
45	A3	2c on 5c magenta, yel	6.00	6.00
46	A3	8c on 10c lt ultra	9.50	8.50

For overprints see Nos. N30-N33, N46-N47, N59-N60.

Catalogue values for unused stamps in this section, from this point to the end of the section, are for Never Hinged items.

Common Design Types pictured following the introduction.

Silver Wedding Issue
Common Design Types
Inscribed: "Malaya Trengganu"

1948, Dec. 1   Photo.   Perf. 14x14½
47	CD304	10c purple	.25	1.75

Engraved; Name Typographed   Perf. 11½x11
48	CD305	$5 rose car	32.50	60.00

UPU Issue
Common Design Types
Inscribed: "Malaya-Trengganu"
Engr.; Name Typo. on 15c, 25c
Perf. 13½, 11x11½

1949, Oct. 10   Wmk. 4
49	CD306	10c rose violet	.65	.75
50	CD307	15c indigo	1.75	4.00
51	CD308	25c orange	1.25	4.00
52	CD309	50c slate	1.90	3.50
		Nos. 49-52 (4)	5.55	12.25

Sultan Ismail Nasiruddin Shah—A5

1949, Dec. 27   Typo.   Perf. 18
53	A5	1c black	1.00	.75
		Lightly hinged	.50	
54	A5	2c orange	1.25	.75
		Lightly hinged	.65	
55	A5	3c green	6.50	7.00
		Lightly hinged	3.25	
56	A5	4c chocolate	.60	.55
		Lightly hinged	.30	
57	A5	6c gray	2.25	1.10
		Lightly hinged	2.50	
58	A5	8c rose red	1.45	4.25
		Lightly hinged	1.00	
59	A5	10c plum	.60	.45
		Lightly hinged	.30	
60	A5	15c ultramarine	9.50	1.00
		Lightly hinged	4.75	
61	A5	20c dk grn & black	9.50	4.00
		Lightly hinged	4.75	
62	A5	25c org & rose lilac	2.75	2.25
		Lightly hinged	2.25	
63	A5	40c dk vio & rose red	14.00	27.50
		Lightly hinged	7.00	
64	A5	50c dp ultra & black	2.75	2.25
		Lightly hinged	1.50	
65	A5	$1 vio brn & ultra	6.50	17.50
		Lightly hinged	3.25	
66	A5	$2 rose red & emer	42.50	45.00
		Lightly hinged	30.00	
67	A5	$5 choc & emerald	80.00	67.50
		Lightly hinged	55.00	

1952-55
68	A5	5c rose violet	.45	1.75
69	A5	8c green	1.45	1.75
70	A5	12c rose red	1.45	3.75
71	A5	20c ultramarine	1.60	.75
72	A5	30c plum & rose red ('55)	1.90	5.50
73	A5	35c dk vio & rose red	2.50	3.50
		Nos. 53-73 (21)	190.50	198.85

Coronation Issue
Common Design Type

1953, June 2   Engr.   Perf. 13½x13
74	CD312	10c magenta & blk	1.50	1.00

Types of Kedah with Portrait of Sultan Ismail
Perf. 13x12½, 12½x13, 13½ ($1), 12½ ($2)

1957-63   Engr.   Wmk. 314
75	A8	1c black	.30	.50
76	A8	2c red orange	1.00	.50
77	A8	4c dark brown	.30	.50
78	A8	5c dark car rose	.30	.50
79	A8	8c dark green	9.00	.50
80	A7	10c chocolate	.40	.50
81	A7	20c blue	.85	.60
82	A7	50c blue & blk	.40	2.40
	a.	Perf. 12½	.50	2.25
83	A8	$1 plum & ultra	9.50	9.50
84	A8	$2 red & green	18.00	12.00
85	A5	$5 ol grn & brn, perf. 12½	27.50	25.00
	a.	Perf. 13x12½	32.50	30.00
		Nos. 75-85 (11)	67.55	52.50

Issued: 20c, No. 85, 6/26/57; 2c, 50c, $1, 7/25/57; 10c, 8/4/57; 1c, 4c, 5c, 8c, $2, 8/21/57; No. 82a, 5/17/60; No. 85a, 8/13/63.
Starting in 1965, issues of Trengganu are listed with Malaysia.

SEMI-POSTAL STAMPS

Nos. 3, 4 and 9 Surcharged

1917, Oct.   Wmk. 3   Perf. 14
B1	A1	3c + 2c rose red	1.50	10.00
	a.	"CSOSS"	90.00	225.00
	b.	Comma after "2c"	9.50	45.00
	c.	Pair, one without surcharge	4,750.	4,250.
B2	A1	4c + 2c brn org	2.25	19.00
	a.	"CSOSS"	250.00	400.00
	b.	Comma after "2c"	17.50	67.50
B3	A1	8c + 2c ultra	3.50	37.50
	a.	"CSOSS"	160.00	400.00
	b.	Comma after "2c"	8.50	87.50
		Nos. B1-B3 (3)	7.25	66.50

Same Surcharge on No. 5

1918
B4	A1	4c + 2c grn & org brn	4.25	50.00
	a.	Pair, one without surcharge	5,000.	

POSTAGE DUE STAMPS

D1

Perf. 14
1937, Aug. 10   Typo.   Wmk. 4
J1	D1	1c rose red	8.00	62.50
J2	D1	4c green	9.00	67.50
J3	D1	8c lemon	47.50	375.00
J4	D1	10c light brown	120.00	110.00
		Nos. J1-J4 (4)	184.50	615.00
		Set, never hinged	290.00	

For overprints see Nos. NJ1-NJ4.

OCCUPATION STAMPS

Issued under Japanese Occupation

No. N6   No. N17A

Stamps of Trengganu, 1921-38, Handstamped in Black or Brown

1942   Wmk. 4   Perf. 14
N1	A3	1c black	110.00	110.00
N2	A3	2c deep green	175.00	250.00
N3	A3	3c lt brown	140.00	110.00
N4	A3	4c rose red	250.00	175.00
N5	A3	5c violet, yel	17.50	19.00
N6	A3	6c orange	13.50	25.00
N7	A3	8c gray	17.50	25.00
N8	A3	10c ultra	37.50	45.00
N9	A3	12c ultra	15.00	47.50
N10	A3	20c org & dl vio	15.00	50.00
N11	A3	25c dk vio & grn	13.50	52.50
N12	A3	30c blk & dl vio	17.50	47.50
N13	A3	35c red, yel	37.50	62.50
N14	A3	50c car & grn	125.00	95.00
N15	A3	$1 ultra & vio, blue	5,750.	5,750.
N16	A3	$3 red & grn, emerald	125.00	130.00
N17	A4	$5 red & grn, yellow	300.00	425.00
N17A	A4	$25 blue & lil	2,150.	
N17B	A4	$50 org & grn	20,000.	
N17C	A4	$100 red & grn	2,450.	

Handstamped in Red
N18	A3	1c black	275.00	225.00
N19	A3	2c dp green	260.00	275.00
N20	A3	5c violet, yel	40.00	20.00
N21	A3	6c orange	475.00	20.00
N22	A3	8c gray	275.00	225.00
N23	A3	10c ultra	425.00	275.00
N24	A3	12c ultra	55.00	62.50
N25	A3	20c org & dl vio	35.00	35.00
N26	A3	25c dk vio & grn	40.00	40.00
N27	A3	30c blk & dl vio	45.00	45.00
N28	A3	35c red, yellow	40.00	20.00
N29	A3	$3 red & grn, emerald	100.00	40.00
N29A	A3	$25 blue & lil	10,000.	500.00

Handstamped on Nos. 45 and 46 in Black or Red
N30	A3	2c on 5c (Bk)	75.00	75.00
N31	A3	2c on 5c (R)	75.00	75.00
N32	A3	8c on 10c (Bk)	20.00	45.00
N33	A3	8c on 10c (R)	30.00	40.00

Stamps of Trengganu, 1921-38, Overprinted in Black

1942
N34	A3	1c black	15.00	17.00
N35	A3	2c deep green	100.00	140.00
N36	A3	3c light brown	16.00	29.00
N37	A3	4c rose red	15.00	20.00
N38	A3	5c violet, yel	10.00	20.00
N39	A3	6c orange	10.00	17.00
N40	A3	8c gray	67.50	70.00
N41	A3	12c ultramarine	10.00	13.50
N42	A3	20c org & dl vio	13.50	25.00
N43	A3	25c dk vio & grn	13.50	17.00

MALAYA — Trengganu — MALAYSIA

N44	A3	30c blk & dl vio	13.50	20.00
N45	A3	$3 red & grn, *emer*	100.00	140.00

Overprinted on Nos. 45 and 46 in Black

N46	A3	2c on 5c mag, *yel*	13.50	17.00
N47	A3	8c on 10c lt ultra	11.50	20.00
		Nos. N34-N47 (14)	409.00	515.50

Stamps of Trengganu, 1921-38, Overprinted in Black

1943

N48	A3	1c black	13.50	19.00
N49	A3	2c deep green	13.50	27.50
N50	A3	5c violet, *yel*	11.50	27.50
N51	A3	6c orange	15.00	27.50
N52	A3	8c gray	95.00	67.50
N53	A3	10c ultramarine	100.00	175.00
N54	A3	12c ultramarine	19.00	35.00
N55	A3	20c org & dl vio	20.00	35.00
N56	A3	25c dl vio & grn	19.00	35.00
N57	A3	30c blk & dl vio	20.00	35.00
N58	A3	35c red, *yellow*	20.00	40.00

Overprinted on Nos. 45 and 46 in Black

N59	A3	2c on 5c mag, *yel*	11.00	35.00
N60	A3	8c on 10c lt ultra	27.50	25.00
		Nos. N48-N60 (13)	385.00	584.00

The Japanese characters read: "Japanese Postal Service."

OCCUPATION POSTAGE DUE STAMPS

Trengganu Nos. J1-J4 Handstamped in Black or Brown

1942   Wmk. 4   Perf. 14

NJ1	D1	1c rose red	67.50	95.00
NJ2	D1	4c green	125.00	125.00
NJ3	D1	8c lemon	25.00	67.50
NJ4	D1	10c light brown	25.00	50.00
		Nos. NJ1-NJ4 (4)	242.50	337.50

The handstamp reads: "Seal of Post Office of Malayan Military Department."

MALAYSIA

mə-'lā-zhē-ə

LOCATION — Malay peninsula and northwestern Borneo
GOVT. — Federation within the British Commonwealth
AREA — 127,317 sq. mi.
POP. — 32,370,000 (2020 est.)
CAPITAL — Putrajaya (administrative); Kuala Lumpur (financial)

The Federation of Malaysia was formed Sept. 16, 1963, by a merger of the former Federation of Malaya, Singapore, Sarawak, and North Borneo (renamed Sabah), totaling 14 states. Singapore withdrew in 1965.

Sabah and Sarawak, having different rates from mainland Malaysia, continued to issue their own stamps after joining the federation. The system of individual state issues was extended to Perak in Oct. 1963, and to the 10 other members in Nov. 1965.

100 Cents (Sen) = 1 Dollar (Ringgit)

Catalogue values for all unused stamps in this country are for Never Hinged items.

Watermarks

Wmk. 233 — "Harrison & Sons, London" in Script

Wmk. 338 — PTM Multiple

Wmk. 378 — Multiple POS in Octagonal Frame

Wmk. 380 — "POST OFFICE"

Wmk. 388 — Multiple "SPM"

Map of Malaysia and 14-point Star — A1

Wmk. PTM Multiple (338)
1963, Sept. 16   Photo.   Perf. 14

1	A1	10s violet & yellow	1.60	.25
	a.	Yellow omitted	525.00	
2	A1	12s green & yellow	1.50	.60
3	A1	50s dk red brown & yel	1.50	.25
		Nos. 1-3 (3)	4.60	1.10

Formation of the Federation of Malaysia.

Orchids — A2

1963, Oct. 3   Unwmk.   Perf. 13x14

4	A2	6s red & multi	1.25	1.25
5	A2	25s black & multi	1.50	.75

4th World Orchid Conf., Singapore, Oct. 8-11.

Parliament and Commonwealth Parliamentary Association Emblem — A4

1963, Nov. 4   Perf. 13½

7	A4	20s dk car rose & gold	.90	.40
8	A4	30s dk green & gold	1.00	.25

9th Commonwealth Parliamentary Assoc. Conf.

Globe, Torch, Snake and Hands — A5

1964, Oct. 10   Photo.   Perf. 14x13

9	A5	25s Prus grn, red & blk	.25	.25
10	A5	30s lt violet, red & blk	.25	.25
11	A5	50s dull yellow, red & blk	.35	.25
		Nos. 9-11 (3)	.85	.75

Eleanor Roosevelt, 1884-1962.

ITU Emblem and Radar Tower — A6

1965, May 17   Photo.   Perf. 11½   Granite Paper

12	A6	2c violet, blk & org	.70	1.75
13	A6	25c brown, blk & org	2.00	.60
14	A6	50c emerald, blk & brn	2.50	.30
		Nos. 12-14 (3)	5.20	2.65

Cent. of the ITU.

National Mosque, Kuala Lumpur — A7

1965, Aug. 27   Wmk. 338   Perf. 14½

15	A7	6c dark car rose	.25	.25
16	A7	15c dark red brown	.25	.25
17	A7	20c Prussian green	.35	.30
		Nos. 15-17 (3)	.85	.80

Natl. Mosque at Kuala Lumpur, opening.

Control Tower and Airport — A8

1965, Aug. 30   Perf. 14½x14

18	A8	15c blue, blk & grn	.35	.25
	a.	Green omitted	40.00	
19	A8	30c brt pink, blk & grn	.75	.30

Intl. Airport at Kuala Lumpur, opening.

Crested Wood Partridge — A9

1965, Sept. 9   Photo.   Perf. 14½

20	A9	25c orange & multi	.65	.25
21	A9	30c tan & multi	.75	.25
	a.	Blue omitted	375.00	
	b.	Yellow omitted	550.00	
22	A9	50c rose & multi	1.40	.25
	a.	Yellow omitted	300.00	
	b.	Imperf. pair	200.00	
	c.	Scarlet omitted	120.00	
23	A9	75c yel grn & multi	1.40	.25
24	A9	$1 ultra & multi	1.75	.25
25	A9	$2 maroon & multi	7.00	.35
	a.	Imperf. pair	200.00	
26	A9	$5 dk grn & multi	16.00	2.00
27	A9	$10 brt red & multi	40.00	7.00
	a.	Imperf. pair	275.00	
		Nos. 20-27 (8)	68.95	10.60

Birds: 30c, Fairy bluebird. 50c, Blacknaped oriole. 75c, Rhinoceros hornbill. $1, Zebra dove. $2, Argus pheasant. $5, Indian paradise flycatcher. $10, Banded pitta.

Soccer and Sepak Raga (Ball Game) — A10

1965, Dec. 14   Unwmk.   Perf. 13

28	A10	25c shown	.35	1.10
29	A10	30c Runner	.40	.25
30	A10	50c Diver	.55	.30
		Nos. 28-30 (3)	1.30	1.65

3rd South East Asia Peninsular Games, Kuala Lumpur, Dec. 14-21.

National Monument, Kuala Lumpur — A11

1966, Feb. 8   Wmk. 338   Perf. 13½

31	A11	10c yellow & multi	.25	.25
	a.	Blue omitted	225.00	
32	A11	20c ultra & multi	1.25	.45

The National Monument by US sculptor Felix W. de Weldon commemorates the struggle of the people of Malaysia for peace and for freedom from communism.

Tuanku Ismail Nasiruddin — A12

1966, Apr. 11   Unwmk.   Perf. 13½

33	A12	15c yellow & black	.25	.25
34	A12	50c blue & black	.35	.35

Installation of Tuanku Ismail Nasiruddin of Trengganu as Paramount Ruler (Yang di-Pertuan Agong).

Penang Free School — A13

Design: 50c, like 20c with Malayan inscription and school crest added.

Perf. 13x12½
1966, Oct. 21   Photo.   Wmk. 338

35	A13	20c multicolored	.40	.30
36	A13	50c multicolored	1.15	.40

Penang Free School, 150th anniversary.

Mechanized Plowing and Palms — A14

No. 38, Rural health nurse, mother and child, dispensary. No. 39, Communication: train, plane, ship, cars and radio tower. No. 40, School children. No. 41, Dam and rice fields.

1966, Dec. 1   Unwmk.   Perf. 13

37	A14	15c bister brn & multi	.35	.25
38	A14	15c blue & multi	.35	.25
39	A14	15c crimson & multi	2.00	.30
40	A14	15c ol green & multi	.35	.25
41	A14	15c yellow & multi	.35	.25
		Nos. 37-41 (5)	3.40	1.30

Malaysia's First Development Plan.

Maps Showing International and South East Asia Telephone Links — A15

1967, Mar. 30   Photo.   Perf. 13

42	A15	30c multicolored	1.00	.50
43	A15	75c multicolored	3.75	4.25

Completion of the Hong Kong-Malaysia link of the South East Asia Commonwealth Cable, SEACOM.

Hibiscus and Rulers of Independent Malaysia — A16

1967, Aug. 31   Wmk. 338   Perf. 14

44	A16	15c yellow & multi	.30	.25
45	A16	50c blue & multi	1.25	.80

10th anniversary of independence.

MALAYSIA

Arms of Sarawak and Council Mace — A17

1967, Sept. 8   **Photo.**
46 A17 15c yel green & multi   .25   .25
47 A17 50c multicolored   .35   .50
Representative Council of Sarawak, cent.

Straits Settlements No. 13 and Malaysia No. 20 — A18

30c, Straits Settlements #15, Malaysia #21. 50c, Straits Settlements #17, Malaysia #22.

1967, Dec. 2   **Unwmk.**   **Perf. 11½**
48 A18 25c brt blue & multi   1.25   2.50
   a. Horiz. tête-bêche pair   3.50   7.50
49 A18 30c dull green & multi   1.50   2.25
   a. Horiz. tête-bêche pair   4.25   6.50
50 A18 50c yellow & multi   2.25   3.00
   a. Horiz. tête-bêche pair   6.50   8.00
   Nos. 48-50 (3)   5.00   7.75

Cent. of the Malaysian (Straits Settlements) postage stamps.

Tapped Rubber Tree and Molecular Unit — A20

Tapped Rubber Tree and: 30c, Rubber packed for shipment. 50c, Rubber tires for Vickers VC 10 plane.

Wmk. 338
1968, Aug. 29   **Perf. 12**
53 A20 25c brick red, blk & org   .30   .25
54 A20 30c yellow, black & org   .40   .30
55 A20 50c ultra, black & org   .50   .30
   Nos. 53-55 (3)   1.20   .85
Natural Rubber Conference, Kuala Lumpur.

Olympic Rings, Mexican Hat and Cloth — A21

75c, Olympic rings & Malaysian batik cloth.

1968, Oct. 12   **Wmk. 338**   **Perf. 12**
56 A21 30c rose red & multi   .30   .25
57 A21 75c ocher & multi   .60   .35
19th Olympic Games, Mexico City, 10/12-27.

Tunku Abdul Rahman Putra Al-Haj — A22

Various portraits of Prime Minister Tunku Abdul Rahman Putra Al-Haj with woven pandanus patterns as background. 50c is horiz.

Perf. 13½
1969, Feb. 8   **Photo.**   **Unwmk.**
58 A22 15c gold & multi   .35   .25
59 A22 20c gold & multi   .55   1.25
60 A22 50c gold & multi   .65   .30
   Nos. 58-60 (3)   1.55   1.80
Issued for Solidarity Week, 1969.

Malaysian Girl Holding Sheaves of Rice — A23

1969, Dec. 8   **Wmk. 338**   **Perf. 13½**
61 A23 15c silver & multi   .30   .25
62 A23 75c gold & multi   1.10   1.40
International Rice Year.

Kuantan Radar Station — A24

Intelsat III Orbiting Earth — A25

Perf. 14x13
1970, Apr. 6   **Photo.**   **Unwmk.**
63 A24 15c multicolored   .80   .25
   a. Tête-bêche pair   2.00   3.00
64 A25 30c multicolored   1.25   2.25
65 A25 30c gold & multi   1.40   2.25
   Nos. 63-65 (3)   3.45   4.75

Satellite Communications Earth Station at Kuantan, Pahang, Malaysia.
No. 63 was printed tete beche (50 pairs) in sheet of 100 (10x10).

Blue-branded King Crow — A26

Butterflies: 30c, Saturn. 50c, Common Nawab. 75c, Great Mormon. $1, Orange albatross. $2, Raja Brooke's birdwing. $5, Centaur oakblue. $10, Royal Assyrian.

1970, Aug. 31   **Litho.**   **Perf. 13x13½**
66 A26 25c multicolored   1.00   .25
67 A26 30c multicolored   1.50   .25
68 A26 50c multicolored   1.75   .25
69 A26 75c multicolored   2.00   .25
70 A26 $1 multicolored   2.75   .25
71 A26 $2 multicolored   3.50   .25
72 A26 $5 multicolored   5.25   2.25
73 A26 $10 multicolored   14.00   4.00
   Nos. 66-73 (8)   31.75   7.75

ILO Emblem — A27

1970, Sept. 7   **Perf. 14½x13½**
74 A27 30c gray & blue   .25   .25
75 A27 75c rose & blue   .30   .30
50th anniv. of the ILO.

UN Emblem and Doves — A28

Designs: 25c, Doves in elliptical arrangement. 30c, Doves arranged diagonally.

1970, Oct. 24   **Litho.**   **Perf. 13x12½**
76 A28 25c lt brown, blk & yel   .35   .30
77 A28 30c lt blue, yel & black   .35   .30
78 A28 50c lt ol green & black   .40   .55
   Nos. 76-78 (3)   1.10   1.15
25th anniversary of the United Nations.

Sultan Abdul Halim — A29

Perf. 14½x14
1971, Feb. 20   **Photo.**   **Unwmk.**
79 A29 10c yellow, blk & gold   .40   .35
80 A29 15c purple, blk & gold   .40   .35
81 A29 50c blue, blk & gold   .65   1.50
   Nos. 79-81 (3)   1.45   2.20
Installation of Sultan Abdul Halim of Kedah as Paramount Ruler.

Bank Building and Crescent — A30

1971, May 15   **Photo.**   **Perf. 14**
82 A30 25c silver & black   2.00   1.50
83 A30 50c gold & brown   3.50   1.25

Opening of Main office of the Negara Malaysia Bank. Nos. 82-83 have circular perforations around vignette set within a white square of paper, perf. on 4 sides.

Malaysian Parliament — A31

Malaysian Parliament, Kuala Lumpur — A32

1971, Sept. 13   **Litho.**   **Perf. 13½**
84 A31 25c multicolored   1.50   .50
Perf. 12½x13
85 A32 75c multicolored   3.50   1.75
17th Commonwealth Parliamentary Conference, Kuala Lumpur.

Malaysian Festival — A33

1971, Sept. 18   **Perf. 14½**
86 A33 Strip of 3   6.25   5.50
   a. 30c Dancing couple   1.75   .75
   b. 30c Dragon   1.75   .75
   c. 30c Flags and stage horse   1.75   .75

Visit ASEAN (Association of South East Asian Nations) Year.

Elephant and Tiger — A34

Children's Drawings: No. 88, Cat and kittens. No. 89, Sun, flower and chick. No. 90, Monkey, elephant and lion in jungle. No. 91, Butterfly and flowers.

1971, Oct. 2   **Perf. 12½**
Size: 35x28mm
87 A34 15c pale yellow & multi   2.50   .60
88 A34 15c pale yellow & multi   2.50   .60
Size: 21x28mm
89 A34 15c pale yellow & multi   2.50   .60
Size: 35x28mm
90 A34 15c pale yellow & multi   2.50   .60
91 A34 15c pale yellow & multi   2.50   .60
   a. Strip of 5, #87-91   14.00   13.00
25th anniv. of UNICEF.

Track and Field — A35

30c, Sepak Raga (a ball game). 50c, Hockey.

1971, Dec. 11   **Perf. 14½**
92 A35 25c orange & multi   1.00   .40
93 A35 30c violet & multi   1.25   .50
94 A35 50c green & multi   1.50   .95
   Nos. 92-94 (3)   3.75   1.85
6th South East Asia Peninsular Games. Kuala Lumpur, Dec. 11-18.

South East Asian Tourist Attractions — A36

Designs include stylized map.

1972, Jan. 31   **Litho.**   **Perf. 14½**
95 A36 Strip of 3   8.50   8.50
   a. 30c Flag at left   2.00   1.00
   b. 30c High rise building   2.00   1.00
   c. 30c Horse & rider   2.00   1.00

Pacific Area Tourist Assoc. Conference.

Secretariat Building — A37

50c, Kuala Lumpur Secretariat Building by night.

1972, Feb. 1   **Perf. 14½x14**
96 A37 25c lt blue & multi   1.10   1.25
97 A37 50c black & multi   2.75   1.25
Achievement of city status by Kuala Lumpur.

Social Security Emblem — A38

1973, July 2   **Litho.**   **Perf. 14½x13½**
98 A38 10c orange & multi   .25   .25
99 A38 15c yellow & multi   .25   .25
100 A38 50c gray & multi   .50   1.40
   Nos. 98-100 (3)   1.00   1.90
Introduction of Social Security System.

WHO Emblem — A39

Design: 30c, WHO emblem, horiz.

1973, Aug. 1   **Perf. 13x12½, 12½x13**
101 A39 30c yellow & multi   .60   .25
102 A39 75c blue & multi   1.30   2.50
25th anniv. of World Health Org.

Flag of Malaysia, Fireworks, Hibiscus — A40

MALAYSIA

1973, Aug. 31   Litho.   Perf. 14½
103	A40	10c olive & multi	.50	.30
104	A40	15c brown & multi	.55	.30
105	A40	50c gray & multi	2.10	1.60
		Nos. 103-105 (3)	3.15	2.20

10th anniversary of independence.

INTERPOL and Malaysian Police Emblems — A41

Design: 75c, "50" with INTERPOL and Malaysian police emblems.

1973, Sept. 15   Perf. 12½
| 106 | A41 | 25c brown org & multi | 1.00 | .45 |
| 107 | A41 | 75c deep violet & multi | 2.50 | 2.00 |

50th anniv. of the Intl. Criminal Police Organization (INTERPOL).

MAS Emblem and Plane — A42

1973, Oct. 1   Litho.   Perf. 14½
108	A42	15c green & multi	.25	.25
109	A42	30c blue & multi	.60	.55
110	A42	50c brown & multi	1.40	1.60
		Nos. 108-110 (3)	2.25	2.40

Inauguration of Malaysian Airline System.

View of Kuala Lumpur — A43

1974, Feb. 1   Litho.   Perf. 12½x13
| 111 | A43 | 25c multicolored | .80 | .75 |
| 112 | A43 | 50c multicolored | 1.60 | 1.75 |

Establishment of Kuala Lumpur as a Federal Territory.

Development Bank Emblem and Projects — A44

1974, Apr. 25   Litho.   Perf. 13½
| 113 | A44 | 30c gray & multi | .55 | .45 |
| 114 | A44 | 75c bister & multi | .90 | 1.75 |

7th annual meeting of the Board of Governors of the Asian Development Bank.

Map of Malaysia and Scout Emblem — A45

Scout Saluting, Malaysian and Scout Flags — A46

Design: 50c, Malaysian Scout emblem.

Perf. 14x13½, 13x13½ (15c)
1974, Aug. 1   Litho.
115	A45	10c multicolored	.55	.30
116	A46	15c multicolored	.90	.25
117	A45	50c multicolored	2.50	2.75
		Nos. 115-117 (3)	3.95	3.90

Malaysian Boy Scout Jamboree.

Power Installations, NEB Emblem — A47

National Electricity Board Building — A48

Perf. 14x14½, 13½x14½
1974, Sept. 1   Litho.
| 118 | A48 | 30c multicolored | .65 | .45 |
| 119 | A48 | 75c multicolored | 1.10 | 2.25 |

National Electricity Board, 25th anniversary.

"100," UPU and P.O. Emblems — A49

1974, Oct. 9   Litho.   Perf. 14½x13½
120	A49	25c olive, red & yel	.35	.35
121	A49	30c blue, red & yel	.35	.35
122	A49	75c ocher, red & yel	.75	1.60
		Nos. 120-122 (3)	1.45	2.30

Centenary of Universal Postal Union.

Gravel Pump Tin Mine — A50

Designs: 20c, Open cast mine. 50c, Silver tin ingot and tin dredge.

1974, Oct. 31   Litho.   Perf. 14
123	A50	15c silver & multi	1.50	.30
124	A50	20c silver & multi	2.25	2.00
125	A50	50c silver & multi	5.50	5.00
		Nos. 123-125 (3)	9.25	7.30

4th World Tin Conference, Kuala Lumpur.

Hockey, Cup and Emblem — A51

1975, Mar. 1   Litho.   Perf. 14
| 126 | A51 | 30c yellow & multi | 1.25 | .50 |
| 127 | A51 | 75c blue & multi | 2.75 | 2.00 |

Third World Cup Hockey Tournament, Kuala Lumpur, Mar. 1-15.

Trade Union Emblem and Workers — A52

1975, May 1   Litho.   Perf. 14x14½
128	A52	20c orange & multi	.25	.25
129	A52	25c lt green & multi	.35	.25
130	A52	30c ultra & multi	.50	.50
		Nos. 128-130 (3)	1.10	1.00

Malaysian Trade Union Cong., 25th anniv.

National Women's Organization Emblem and Heads — A53

1975, Aug. 25   Litho.   Perf. 14
131	A53	10c emerald & multi	.45	.30
132	A53	15c lilac rose & multi	.45	.30
133	A53	50c blue & multi	1.40	2.00
		Nos. 131-133 (3)	2.30	2.60

International Women's Year.

Ubudiah Mosque, Perak — A54

b, Zahir Mosque, Kedah. c, National Mosque, Kuala Lumpur. d, Sultan Abu Bakar Mosque, Johore. e, Kuching State Mosque, Sarawak.

1975, Sept. 22   Litho.   Perf. 14½x14
| 134 | | Strip of 5 | 14.50 | 9.50 |
| a.-e. | A54 | 15c single stamp | 2.40 | .40 |

Koran reading competition 1975, Malaysia.

Rubber Plantation and Emblem — A55

Designs: 30c, "50" in form of latex cup and tire with emblem. 75c, Six test tubes showing various aspects of natural rubber.

1975, Oct. 22   Litho.   Perf. 14x14½
135	A55	10c gold & multi	.45	.30
136	A55	30c gold & multi	1.25	.60
137	A55	75c gold & multi	3.00	2.00
		Nos. 135-137 (3)	4.70	2.90

Rubber Research Institute of Malaysia, 50th anniversary.

Butterflies — A55a

No. 137A, Hebomoia glauclppe aturia. No. 137B, Precis orithya wallacei.

Coil Stamps

1976, Feb. 6   Perf. 14
| 137A | A55a | 10c multicolored | 3.50 | 7.00 |
| 137B | A55a | 15c multicolored | 3.50 | 7.00 |

Scrub Typhus — A56

Designs: 25c, Malaria (microscope, blood cells, slides). $1, Beri-beri (grain and men).

1976, Feb. 6   Litho.   Perf. 14
138	A56	20c red orange & multi	.70	.30
139	A56	25c ultra & multi	.85	.30
140	A56	$1 yellow & multi	1.60	2.25
		Nos. 138-140 (3)	3.15	2.85

Institute for Medical Research, Kuala Lumpur, 75th anniversary.

Sultan Jahya Petra — A57

Perf. 14½x13½
1976, Feb. 28   Photo.
141	A57	10c yel, black & bis	.35	.25
142	A57	15c lilac, black & bis	.30	.25
143	A57	50c blue, black & bis	2.75	2.25
		Nos. 141-143 (3)	3.40	2.75

Installation of Sultan Jahya Petra of Kelantan as Paramount Ruler (Yang di-Pertuan Agong).

Council and Administrative Buildings — A58

1976, Aug. 17   Litho.   Perf. 12½
144	A58	15c orange & black	.45	.25
145	A58	20c brt red lilac & black	.55	.35
146	A58	50c blue & black	1.00	1.25
		Nos. 144-146 (3)	2.00	1.85

Opening of the State Council Complex and Administrative Building, Sarawak.

Provident Fund Building — A59

Provident Fund Emblems — A60

50c, Provident Fund Building at night.

Perf. 13½x14½, 14½ (A60)
1976, Oct. 18   Litho.
147	A59	10c blue & multi	.50	.35
148	A60	25c gray & multi	.45	.60
149	A59	50c violet & multi	.65	1.25
		Nos. 147-149 (3)	1.60	2.20

Employees' Provident Fund, 25th anniv.

Rehabilitation of the Blind — A61

75c, Blind man casting large shadow.

1976, Nov. 20   Perf. 13½x14½
| 150 | A61 | 10c multicolored | .50 | .30 |
| 151 | A61 | 75c multicolored | 1.50 | 2.25 |

25th anniv. of the Malaysian Assoc. for the Blind.

Abdul Razak and Crowd — A62

Designs: b, Abdul Razak in cap and gown at lectern. c, Abdul Razak pointing to new roads and bridges on map. d, New constitution. e, Abdul Razak addressing Association of Southeast Asian Countries.

1977, Jan. 14   Photo.   Perf. 14x14½
| 152 | | Strip of 5 | 8.00 | 8.00 |
| a.-e. | A62 | 15c single stamp | 1.00 | .35 |

Prime Minister Tun Haji Abdul Razak bi Dato Hussein (1922-1976).

FELDA Housing Development — A63

Design: 30c, View of oil palm settlement area and FELDA emblem.

1977, July 7   Litho.   Perf. 13½x14½
| 153 | A63 | 15c multicolored | .55 | .30 |
| 154 | A63 | 30c multicolored | .90 | 1.75 |

Federal Land Development Authority (FELDA), 21st anniversary.

ASEAN, 10th Anniv. — A64

75c, Flags of ASEAN members: Malaysia, Philippines, Singapore, Thailand and Indonesia.

1977, Aug. 8   Litho.   Perf. 13½x14½
| 155 | A64 | 10c multicolored | .50 | .25 |
| 156 | A64 | 75c multicolored | 1.00 | .90 |

SEA Games Emblems — A65

Designs: 20c, Ball, symbolic of 9 participating nations. 75c, Running.

MALAYSIA

Perf. 13½x14½
1977, Nov. 19   **Litho.**
157 A65 10c multicolored .30 .25
158 A65 30c multicolored .30 .25
159 A65 75c multicolored .75 1.60
   Nos. 157-159 (3) 1.35 2.10
9th South East Asia Games, Kuala Lumpur.

Bank Emblem — A66

1978, Mar. 15   **Litho.**   **Perf. 14**
160 A66 30c multicolored .40 .25
161 A66 75c multicolored .80 .80
2nd annual meeting of Islamic Development Bank Governors, Kuala Lumpur, Mar. 1978.

Government Building — A67

Designs: Views of Shah Alam.

1978, Dec. 7   **Litho.**   **Perf. 13½x14½**
162 A67 10c multicolored .25 .25
163 A67 30c multicolored .30 .25
164 A67 75c multicolored .85 1.75
   Nos. 162-164 (3) 1.40 2.25
Inauguration of Shah Alam as state capital of Selangor.

Mobile Post Office in Village — A68

Designs: 25c, General Post Office, Kuala Lumpur. 50c, Motorcyclist, rural mail delivery.

1978, July 10   **Perf. 13**
165 A68 10c multicolored 1.00 .40
166 A68 25c multicolored 1.10 1.75
167 A68 50c multicolored 1.40 2.75
   Nos. 165-167 (3) 3.50 4.90
4th Conf. of Commonwealth Postal Administrators.

Jamboree Emblem A69

Bees and Honeycomb A70

1978, July 26   **Litho.**   **Perf. 13½**
168 A69 15c multicolored 1.00 .30
169 A70 $1 multicolored 3.75 3.00
4th Boy Scout Jamboree, Sarawak.

Globe, Crest and WHO Emblem — A71

1978, Sept. 30   **Perf. 13½x14½**
170 A71 15c blue, red & black .45 .35
171 A71 30c green, red & black .65 .45
172 A71 50c pink, red & black 1.00 .80
   Nos. 170-172 (3) 2.10 1.60
Global eradication of smallpox.

Dome of the Rock — A72

1978, Aug. 21   **Litho.**   **Perf. 12½**
173 A72 15c red & multi 1.00 .35
174 A72 30c blue & multi 2.50 2.50
For Palestinian fighters and their families.

Tiger — A73

Designs: 40c, Cobego. 50c, Chevrotain. 75c, Pangolin. $1, Leatherback turtle. $2, Tapir. $5, Gaur. $10, Orangutan, vert.

Perf. 15x14½, 14½x15
1979, Jan. 4   **Litho.**   **Wmk. 378**
175 A73 30c multicolored .50 .25
176 A73 40c multicolored .55 .25
177 A73 50c multicolored .90 .25
178 A73 75c multicolored 1.00 .25
179 A73 $1 multicolored 1.25 .25
180 A73 $2 multicolored 2.00 .75
181 A73 $5 multicolored 5.75 2.00
182 A73 $10 multicolored 10.00 3.00
   Nos. 175-182 (8) 21.95 7.00

1983-87   **Unwmk.**
175a A73 30c ('84) 1.40 .70
176a A73 40c ('84) 1.50 .55
177a A73 50c ('84) 1.90 .55
178a A73 75c ('87) 11.00 8.50
179a A73 $1 5.25 .55
180a A73 $2 7.00 .85
181a A73 $5 ('85) 20.00 7.00
182a A73 $10 ('86) 32.50 10.50
   Nos. 175a-182a (8) 80.55 29.20

Central Bank of Malaysia — A74

10c, Central Bank of Malaysia & emblem.

Perf. 13½
1979, Jan. 26   **Litho.**   **Unwmk.**
183 A74 10c multicolored, horiz. .30 .30
184 A74 75c multicolored 1.10 1.40
Central Bank of Malaysia, 20th anniv.

Year of the Child Emblem — A75

Intl. Year of the Child: 15c, Children of the world, globe and ICY emblem. $1, Children at play, ICY emblem.

1979, Feb. 24   **Perf. 14**
185 A75 10c multicolored .50 .25
186 A75 15c multicolored .40 .25
187 A75 $1 multicolored 3.25 3.50
   Nos. 185-187 (3) 4.15 4.00

Symbolic Rubber Plant — A76

Designs: 10c, Symbolic palm. 75c, Symbolic rubber products.

1978, Nov. 28   **Litho.**   **Perf. 13**
188 A76 10c brt green & gold .25 .25
189 A76 20c multicolored .45 .25
190 A76 75c brt green & gold .60 .90
   Nos. 188-190 (3) 1.30 1.40
Centenary of rubber production (in 1977).

Rafflesia Hasseltii — A77

Flowers: 2c, Pterocarpus indicus. 5c, Lagerstroemia speciosa. 10c, Durio zibethinus. 15c, Hibiscus. 20c, Rhododendron scortechinii. 25c, Phaeomeria speciosa.

Perf. 15x14½
1979, Apr. 30   **Wmk. 378**
191 A77 1c multicolored .25 .25
192 A77 2c multicolored .25 .25
193 A77 5c multicolored .25 .25
   a. Unwmkd. ('84)
194 A77 10c multicolored .25 .25
   a. White flowers, unwmkd. ('84) .25 .25
195 A77 15c multicolored .25 .25
   a. 15c yel & multi, unwmkd. ('83) .25 .25
196 A77 20c multicolored .30 .25
   a. 20c greenish & multi, unwmkd. ('83) .25 .25
197 A77 25c multicolored .35 .25
   a. Unwmkd. ('85) 5.00
   Nos. 191-197 (7) 1.90 1.75

Temengor Hydroelectric Dam — A78

Designs: 25c, 50c, Dam and river, diff.

Perf. 13½x14½
1979, Sept. 19   **Litho.**   **Unwmk.**
198 A78 15c multicolored .30 .30
199 A78 25c multicolored .70 .50
200 A78 50c multicolored 1.00 1.25
   Nos. 198-200 (3) 2.00 2.05

"TELECOM 79" — A79

Telecom Emblem and: 15c, Telephone receiver and globes. 50c, Modes of communication.

1979, Sept. 20   **Perf. 13½**
Size: 34x25mm
201 A79 10c multicolored .35 .50
202 A79 15c multicolored .25 .25

Perf. 14
Size: 39x28mm
203 A79 50c multicolored .85 2.25
   Nos. 201-203 (3) 1.45 3.00
3rd World Telecommunications Exhibition, Geneva, Sept. 20-26.

Haji Ahmad Shah — A80

1980, July 10   **Litho.**   **Perf. 14½**
204 A80 10c multicolored .25 .40
205 A80 15c multicolored .25 .25
206 A80 50c multicolored .70 2.00
   Nos. 204-206 (3) 1.20 2.65
Installation of Sultan Haji Ahmad Shah of Pahang as Paramount Ruler (Yang di-Pertuan Agong).

Pahang-Sarawak Cable — A81

Designs: 15c, Dial with views of Kuantan and Kuching. 50c, Telephone and maps.

1980, Aug. 31   **Litho.**   **Perf. 13½**
207 A81 10c shown .25 .35
208 A81 15c multicolored .25 .25
209 A81 50c multicolored .35 1.75
   Nos. 207-209 (3) .85 2.35

National University of Malaysia, 10th Anniversary — A82

15c, Jalan Pantai Baru campus. 75c, Great Hall & Tun Haji Abdul Razak (1st chancellor).

1980, Sept. 2   **Litho.**   **Perf. 13½**
210 A82 10c shown .25 .25
211 A82 25c multicolored .25 .25
212 A82 75c multicolored .50 2.75
   Nos. 210-212 (3) 1.00 3.25

Hegira (Pilgrimage Year) — A83

1980, Nov. 9
213 A83 15c multicolored .30 .25
214 A83 50c multicolored .45 1.25

International Year of the Disabled — A84

10c, Child learning to walk. 15c, Seamstress. 75c, Athlete.

1981, Feb. 14   **Litho.**   **Perf. 13½**
215 A84 10c multicolored .50 .25
216 A84 15c multicolored .55 .25
217 A84 75c multicolored 1.50 3.25
   Nos. 215-217 (3) 2.55 3.75

Sultan Mahmud of Trengganu — A85

1981, Mar. 21   **Litho.**   **Perf. 14½**
218 A85 10c multicolored .25 .25
219 A85 15c multicolored .25 .25
220 A85 50c multicolored .90 .30
   Nos. 218-220 (3) 1.40 .80

Industrial Training Seminar — A86

Designs: Various workers.

1981, May 2   **Litho.**   **Perf. 13½**
221 A86 10c multicolored .35 .25
222 A86 15c multicolored .25 .25
223 A86 30c multicolored .35 .25
224 A86 75c multicolored .60 2.00
   Nos. 221-224 (4) 1.55 2.75

World Energy Conference, 25th anniv. — A87

10c, "25". 15c, Sources of Energy. 75c, Non-renewable energy.

1981, June 17   **Litho.**   **Perf. 13½**
225 A87 10c multicolored .40 .30
226 A87 15c multicolored .35 .30
227 A87 75c multicolored 1.75 3.25
   Nos. 225-227 (3) 2.50 3.85

Centenary of Sabah — A88

15c, Views, 1881 and 1981. 80c, Traditional and modern farming.

1981, Aug. 31   **Litho.**   **Perf. 12**
228 A88 15c multicolored .60 .30
229 A88 80c multicolored 3.00 4.00

Rain Tree — A89

50c, Simber tree, vert. 80c, Borneo camphor-wood, vert.

MALAYSIA

1981, Dec. 16   Litho.   *Perf. 14*
230 A89 15c shown .50 .25
231 A89 50c multicolored 1.50 1.25
232 A89 80c multicolored 3.00 4.00
    Nos. 230-232 (3) 5.00 5.50

Scouting Year and Jamboree, Apr. 9-16 — A90

1982, Apr. 10   Litho.   *Perf. 13½x13*
233 A90 15c Jamboree emblem .40 .30
234 A90 50c Flag, emblem 1.00 .75
235 A90 80c Emblems, knot 1.75 4.00
    Nos. 233-235 (3) 3.15 5.05

15th Anniv. of Assoc. of South East Asian Nations (ASEAN) — A91

1982, Aug. 8   Litho.   *Perf. 14*
236 A91 15c Meeting Center .40 .25
237 A91 $1 Flags 1.75 3.00

Dome of the Rock, Jerusalem — A92

1982, Aug. 21   *Perf. 13½*
238 A92 15c multicolored 1.50 .35
239 A92 $1 multicolored 4.50 5.25

For the freedom of Palestine.

25th Anniv. of Independence A93

10c, Kuala Lumpur. 15c, Independence celebration. 50c, Parade. 80c, Independence ceremony.

1982, Aug. 31   Litho.   *Perf. 14*
240 A93 10c multicolored .25 .25
241 A93 15c multicolored .25 .25
242 A93 50c multicolored .40 .40
243 A93 80c multicolored .70 2.50
  a. Souvenir sheet of 4, #240-243 15.00 15.00
  b. Souvenir sheet of 4, #240-243 10.00 10.00
    Nos. 240-243 (4) 1.60 3.40

No. 243a has a narrow silver frame around the center vignette of the 10c value. This frame was removed for the second printing, No. 243b.

Traditional Games — A94

1982, Oct. 30   *Perf. 13½*
244 A94 10c Shadow play 1.00 .95
245 A94 15c Cross top 1.00 .35
246 A94 75c Kite flying 2.75 4.25
    Nos. 244-246 (3) 4.75 4.95

Handicrafts A95

1982, Nov. 26   Litho.   *Perf. 13x13½*
247 A95 10c Sabah hats .40 .45
248 A95 15c Gold-threaded cloth .40 .45
249 A95 75c Sarawak pottery 1.90 3.25
    Nos. 247-249 (3) 2.70 4.15

Commonwealth Day — A96

15c, Flag. 20c, Seri Paduka Baginda. 40c, Oil palm refinery. $1, Globe.

1983, Mar. 14   Litho.   *Perf. 14*
250 A96 15c multicolored .30 .25
251 A96 20c multicolored .30 .25
252 A96 40c multicolored .45 .40
253 A96 $1 multicolored .70 2.25
    Nos. 250-253 (4) 1.75 3.15

First Shipment of Natural Gas, Bintulu, Sarawak — A97

15c, Bintulu Port Authority emblem. 20c, LNG Tanker Tenaga Satu. $1, Gas plant.

1983, Jan. 22   Litho.   *Perf. 12*
254 A97 15c multi 1.10 .35
  a. Perf. 13½ 30.00 10.00
255 A97 20c multi 1.40 1.00
  a. Perf. 13½ 35.00 3.50
256 A97 $1 multi 4.50 6.25
  a. Perf. 13½ 60.00 12.50
    Nos. 254-256 (3) 7.00 7.60
    Nos. 254a-256a (3) 125.00 19.25

Freshwater Fish — A98

No. 257a, Tilapia nilotica. No. 257b, Cyprinus carpio. No. 258a, Puntius gonionotus. No. 258b, Ctenopharyngodon idellus.

1983, June 15   *Perf. 12x12½*
257 Pair 4.00 3.00
  a. A98 20c multicolored 1.00 .35
  b. A98 20c multicolored 1.00 .35
  c. As #257, perf. 13½x14 11.00 11.00
258 Pair 5.00 2.50
  a. A98 40c multicolored 1.50 .40
  b. A98 40c multicolored 1.50 .40
  c. As #258, perf. 13½x14 11.50 11.50

Opening of East-West Highway A99

15c, Lower Sungei Pergau Bridge. 20c, Sungei Perak Reservoir Bridge. $1, Map.

1983, July 1   *Perf. 14x13½*
259 A99 15c multicolored .75 .25
260 A99 20c multicolored 1.00 .60
261 A99 $1 multicolored 4.50 6.25
    Nos. 259-261 (3) 6.25 7.10

Armed Forces, 50th Anniv. A100

Designs: 15c, Royal Malaysian Aircraft. 20c, Navy vessel firing missile. 40c, Battle at Pasir Panjang. 80c, Trooping of the Royal colors.

1983, Sept. 16   Litho.   *Perf. 13½*
262 A100 15c multicolored 1.25 .25
263 A100 20c multicolored 1.50 .45
264 A100 40c multicolored 2.25 2.25
265 A100 80c multicolored 4.00 4.75
  a. Souvenir sheet of 4, #262-265 12.00 12.00
    Nos. 262-265 (4) 8.00 7.70

Helmeted Hornbill — A101

20c, Wrinkled Hornbill. 50c, White crested Hornbill. $1, Rhinoceros Hornbill.

1983, Oct. 26   Litho.   *Perf. 13½*
266 A101 15c shown 1.00 .25
267 A101 20c multicolored 1.25 .50
268 A101 50c multicolored 2.50 2.50
269 A101 $1 multicolored 3.75 5.00
    Nos. 266-269 (4) 8.50 8.25

25th Anniv. of Begara Bank — A102

Branch offices.

1984, Jan. 26   Litho.   *Perf. 13½x14*
270 A102 20c Ipoh 1.00 .35
271 A102 $1 Alor Setar 2.00 3.25

10th Anniv. of Federal Territory — A103

Views of Kuala Lumpur. 20c, 40c vert.

Perf. 14x13½, 13½x14
1984, Feb. 1   Litho.
272 A103 20c multicolored 1.00 .50
273 A103 40c multicolored 1.40 1.25
274 A103 80c multicolored 4.00 6.00
    Nos. 272-274 (3) 6.40 7.75

Labuan Federal Territory — A104

20c, Development symbols, map, arms. $1, Flag, map.

1984, Apr. 16   Litho.   *Perf. 13½x14*
275 A104 20c multicolored 1.50 .40
276 A104 $1 multicolored 4.75 5.25

Traditional Weapons — A105

No. 277, Keris Semenanjung. No. 278, Keris Pekakak. No. 279, Keris Jawa. No. 280, Tumbuk Lada.

1984, May 30   *Perf. 13x14*
277 A105 40c multicolored 1.00 1.00
278 A105 40c multicolored 1.00 1.00
279 A105 40c multicolored 1.00 1.00
280 A105 40c multicolored 1.00 1.00
  a. Block of 4, #277-280 5.00 5.00

Asia-Pacific Broadcasting Union, 20th Anniv. — A106

1984, June 23   *Perf. 14x14½*
281 A106 20c Map, waves 1.50 .40
282 A106 $1 "20" 2.50 4.25

Kuala Lumpur Post Office Opening — A107

15c, Facsimile transmission. 20c, Building. $1, Mail bag conveyor.

1984, Oct. 29   *Perf. 12x11½*
283 A107 15c multicolored .80 .35
284 A107 20c multicolored .80 .35
285 A107 $1 multicolored 2.00 4.00
    Nos. 283-285 (3) 3.60 4.70

Installation of Sultan of Johore as 8th Paramount Ruler of Malaysia A108

Sultan Mahmood, Arms A109

1984, Nov. 15   Litho.   *Perf. 12*
286 A108 15c multicolored 1.00 .40
287 A108 20c multicolored 1.00 .35
288 A109 40c multicolored 1.25 .90
289 A109 80c multicolored 2.25 4.25
    Nos. 286-289 (4) 5.50 5.90

Malaysian Hibiscus — A110

10c, White hibiscus. 20c, Red hibiscus. 40c, Pink hibiscus. $1, Orange hibiscus.

1984, Dec. 12   Litho.   *Perf. 13½*
290 A110 10c multi 1.00 .40
291 A110 20c multi 1.00 .35
292 A110 40c multi 2.00 2.00
293 A110 $1 multi 3.25 5.00
    Nos. 290-293 (4) 7.25 7.75

Parliament, 25th Anniv. — A111

20c, Badge, vert. $1, Parliament, Kuala Lumpur.

Perf. 13½x14, 14x13½
1985, Mar. 30   Litho.
294 A111 20c multi .80 .30
295 A111 $1 multi 1.75 3.00

Protected Wildlife — A112

10c, Prionodon linsang. 40c, Nycticebus coucang, vert. $1, Petaurista elegans, vert.

1985, Apr. 25   *Perf. 14*
296 A112 10c multicolored 1.50 .55
297 A112 40c multicolored 1.75 1.25
298 A112 $1 multicolored 4.50 6.00
    Nos. 296-298 (3) 7.75 7.80

Intl. Youth Year — A113

20c, Youth solidarity. $1, Participation in natl. development.

1985, May 15   *Perf. 13*
299 A113 20c multicolored 1.10 .40
300 A113 $1 multicolored 4.00 5.00

Malaya Railways Centenary — A114

Locomotives: 15c, Steam engine, 1885. 20c, Diesel-electric, 1957. $1, Diesel, 1963. 80c, Train leaving Kuala Lumpur Station, 1938.

1985, June 1   *Perf. 13*
301 A114 15c multicolored 2.00 .50
302 A114 20c multicolored 2.10 .50
303 A114 $1 multicolored 5.25 6.25
    Nos. 301-303 (3) 9.35 7.25

MALAYSIA

Souvenir Sheet
Perf. 14x13
304 A114 80c multi 10.00 11.00

No. 304 contains one stamp 48x32mm.

Proton Saga — A115

1985, July 9   *Perf. 14*
305 A115 20c multicolored ...... 1.25 .30
306 A115 40c multicolored ...... 1.75 .80
307 A115 $1 multicolored 3.75 5.75
    Nos. 305-307 (3) 6.75 6.85

Inauguration of natl. automotive industry.

Sultan Salahuddin Abdul Aziz, Selangor Coat of Arms — A116

1985, Sept. 5   *Perf. 13*
308 A116 15c multicolored ...... .70 .60
309 A116 20c multicolored ...... .80 .60
310 A116 $1 multicolored 3.75 6.00
    Nos. 308-310 (3) 5.25 7.20

25th anniv. of coronation.

Penang Bridge Opening — A117

1985, Sept. 15   *Litho.*   *Perf. 13½x13*
311 A117 20c shown ...... 1.40 .45
312 A117 40c Bridge, map ...... 2.75 .75

Size: 44x28mm
Perf. 12½
313 A117 $1 Map 4.00 5.25
    Nos. 311-313 (3) 8.15 6.45

Natl. Oil Industry A118

15c, Offshore rig, vert. 20c, 1st refinery. $1, Map of oil and gas fields.

1985, Nov. 4   *Perf. 12½*
314 A118 15c multi ...... 1.40 .45
315 A118 20c multi ...... 1.40 .45
316 A118 $1 multi 5.00 5.25
    Nos. 314-316 (3) 7.80 6.15

Coronation of Paduka Seri, Sultan of Perak — A119

1985, Dec. 9   *Perf. 14*
317 A119 15c lt blue & multi ...... .55 .40
318 A119 20c lilac & multi ...... .80 .40
319 A119 $1 gold & multi 3.75 6.00
    Nos. 317-319 (3) 5.10 6.80

Birds — A120

No. 320, Lophura ignita, vert. No. 321, Pavo malacense, vert. No. 322, Lophura bulweri. No. 323, Argusianus argus.

Wmk. 388
1986, Mar. 11   *Litho.*   *Perf. 13¼*
320 A120 20c multicolored ...... 2.50 .40
  a. Perf. 12 ...... 4.75 1.25
321 A120 20c multicolored ...... 2.50 .40
  a. Pair, #320-321 ...... 5.00 1.50
  b. Perf. 12 ...... 7.50 2.00
  c. Pair, #320a, 321b 12.50 8.25
322 A120 40c multicolored ...... 4.00 .50
  a. Perf. 12 ...... 8.25 1.50

323 A120 40c multicolored ...... 5.00 .50
  a. Pair, #322-323 ...... 9.00 1.90
  b. Perf. 12 ...... 7.25 1.50
  c. Pair, #322a, 323b 15.50 11.50
    Nos. 320-323 (4) 14.00 1.80

PATA '86, Pacific Area Travel Assoc. Conference, Persidangan — A121

No. 324: a, Two women dancing. b, Woman in red. c, Man and woman.
No. 325: a, Woman in gold. b, Woman holding fan. c, Woman in violet.

Perf. 15x14½
1986, Apr. 14   *Litho.*   *Unwmk.*
324   Strip of 3 ...... 3.00 3.25
  a.-c. A121 20c any single ...... .75 1.00
325   Strip of 3 ...... 4.00 4.00
  a.-c. A121 40c any single 1.00 1.25

Malaysia Games A122

Games Emblem A123

Flags — A124

Wmk. 388
1986, Apr. 14   *Litho.*   *Perf. 12*
326 A122 20c multicolored ...... 1.60 .50
327 A123 40c multicolored 4.50 2.00
328 A124 $1 multicolored 6.00 6.50
    Nos. 326-328 (3) 12.10 9.00

Nephelium Lappaceum A125

Averrhoa Carambola A126

No. 330, Ananas comosus. No. 331, Durio zibethinus. No. 332, Garcinia mangostana. No. 332C, Musa sapientum. No. 334, Musa sapientum. No. 335, Mangifera odorata. No. 336, Carica papaya.

Litho. (#329-332), Photo. (#333-336)
Perf. 12 (#329-332)
1986-2000   *Wmk. 388*
329 A125 40c shown ...... .40 .25
  a. Perf. 13½x14 ...... .75
330 A125 50c multi ...... .60 .25
  a. Perf. 13½x14 ...... .75
331 A125 80c multi ...... .95 .35
  a. Perf. 13½x14 ...... 1.25
332 A125 $1 multi ...... 1.00 .35
  a. Perf. 13½x14 ...... 1.25

Perf. 13½x14
332B A126 $2 multi ('99) ...... 3.50 .90
332C A126 $5 multi ('00) 6.00 2.25
332D A126 $10 multi ('02) 10.00 4.00

Perf. 13½
Wmk. 233
333 A126 $2 shown ...... 2.00 .65
334 A126 $5 multi 4.00 1.10
335 A126 $10 multi 6.75 3.75
336 A126 $20 multi 12.00 5.50
    Nos. 329-336 (9) 33.70 14.45

No. 332C issued 2000; balance of set issued 6/5/86.
Compare with Nos. 766A-766H.

Natl. Assoc. for the Prevention of Drug Abuse, 10th Anniv. — A127

1986, June 26   *Wmk. 388*   *Perf. 13*
337 A127 20c Skull ...... .85 .45
338 A127 40c Dove ...... 1.40 .65
339 A127 $1 Addict, vert. 4.25 3.50
    Nos. 337-339 (3) 6.50 4.60

Malaysian Airlines Kuala Lumpur-Los Angeles Inaugural Flight — A128

20c, Flight routes map. 40c, MAS emblem, new route. $1, Emblem, stops.

1986, July 31   *Perf. 14x13½*
340 A128 20c multi ...... 2.00 .50
341 A128 40c multi ...... 2.50 .70
342 A128 $1 multi 5.50 4.00
    Nos. 340-342 (3) 10.00 5.20

Industrial Productivity — A129

20c, Construction, vert. 40c, Industry. $1, Automobile factory.

1986, Nov. 3   *Litho.*   *Perf. 14*
343 A129 20c multi ...... .75 .40
344 A129 40c multi 1.60 1.00
345 A129 $1 multi 4.75 5.75
    Nos. 343-345 (3) 7.10 7.15

Historic Buildings — A130

15c, Istana Lama Seri Menanti, Negri Sembilan. 20c, Istana Kenangan, Perak. 40c, Bangunan Stadthuys, Malacca. $1, Istana Kuching, Sarawak.

1986, Dec. 20   *Perf. 13*
346 A130 15c multicolored ...... .90 .30
347 A130 20c multicolored ...... .90 .30
348 A130 40c multicolored ...... 2.00 .70
349 A130 $1 multicolored 3.00 4.50
    Nos. 346-349 (4) 6.80 5.80

See design A146.

Folk Music Instruments A131

1987, Mar. 7   *Litho.*   *Perf. 12*
350 A131 15c Sompotan ...... 1.00 .65
351 A131 20c Sapih ...... 1.00 .65
352 A131 50c Serunai, vert. ...... 2.40 .
353 A131 80c Rebab, vert. 4.00 2.25
    Nos. 350-353 (4) 8.40 4.20

Intl. Year of Shelter for the Homeless A132

20c, Model village. $1, Symbols of family, shelter.

1987, Apr. 6   *Litho.*   *Perf. 12*
354 A132 20c multi ...... .75 .30
355 A132 $1 multi 3.75 1.50

UN Anti-Drug Campaign and Congress, Vienna — A133

No. 356, Health boy, family, rainbow. No. 357, Holding drugs. No. 358, Child warding off drugs. No. 359, Drugs, damaged body in capsule.

1987, June 8   *Litho.*   *Perf. 13½x13*
356   20c multi ...... .75 .75
357   20c multi ...... .75 .75
  a. A133 Pair, #356-357 ...... 3.00 3.00
358   40c multi ...... 1.75 .75
359   40c multi ...... 1.75 .75
  a. A133 Pair, #358-359 ...... 7.00 3.00
    Nos. 356-359 (4) 5.00 3.00

Nos. 357a, 359a have continuous designs.

Kenyir Hydroelectric Power Station Inauguration A134

1987, July 13   *Perf. 12*
360 A134 20c Power facility, dam ...... 1.60 .40
361 A134 $1 Side view 3.50 1.75

33rd Commonwealth Parliamentary Conference — A135

20c, Maces, parliament. $1, Parliament, maces, diff.

1987, Sept. 1   *Litho.*   *Perf. 12*
362 A135 20c multi ...... .55 .25
363 A135 $1 multi 1.50 1.10

Transportation and Communications Decade in Asia and the Pacific (1985-94) — A136

Designs: 15c, Satellites, Earth, satellite dish. 20c, Car, diesel train, Kuala Lumpur Station. 40c, MISC container ship. $1, Malaysia Airlines jet, Kuala Lumpur Airport.

1987, Oct. 26   *Perf. 13½x13*
364 A136 15c multicolored ...... 1.25 .60
365 A136 20c multicolored ...... 1.25 .70
366 A136 40c multicolored 2.25 1.25
367 A136 $1 multicolored 4.25 6.00
    Nos. 364-367 (4) 9.00 8.55

Protected Wildcats — A137

1987, Nov. 14
368 A137 15c Felis temminckii ...... 2.50 .50
369 A137 20c Felis planiceps ...... 3.00 .75
370 A137 40c Felis marmorata 4.00 1.75
371 A137 $1 Neofelis nebulosa 8.00 7.50
    Nos. 368-371 (4) 17.50 10.50

ASEAN, 20th Anniv. — A138

1987, Dec. 14   *Litho.*   *Perf. 13*
372 A138 20c "20," flags ...... .35 .25
373 A138 $1 Flags, Earth 1.60 1.50

Opening of Sultan Salahuddin Abdul Aziz Shah Mosque, Selangor — A139

Dome, minarets and: 15c, Arches. 20c, Sultan Abdul Aziz Shah, Selangor crest. $1, Interior, vert.

MALAYSIA

1988, Mar. 11   **Litho.**   *Perf. 12*
374	A139	15c multicolored	.50	.35
375	A139	20c multicolored	.50	.35
376	A139	$1 multicolored	1.40	2.25
		Nos. 374-376 (3)	2.40	2.95

Opening of Sultan Ismail Power Station, Trengganu — A140

1988, Apr. 4   *Perf. 13*
| 377 | A140 | 20c shown | .40 | .30 |
| 378 | A140 | $1 Station, diff. | 2.00 | 1.25 |

Wildlife Protection A141

Birds: No. 379, Hypothymis azurea. No. 380, Dicaeum cruentatum. No. 381, Aethopyga siparaja. No. 382, Cymbirhynchus macr-orhynchos.

1988, June 30   **Litho.**   *Perf. 13*
379		20c multicolored	.70	.70
380		20c multicolored	.70	.70
a.		Pair, #379-380	3.75	3.75
381		50c multicolored	1.40	1.40
382		50c multicolored	1.40	1.40
a.	A141	Pair, #381-382	6.50	6.50
		Nos. 379-382 (4)	4.20	4.20

A142

Independence of Sabah and Sarawak, 25th Anniv. — A143

1988, Aug. 31   **Litho.**   *Perf. 13x13½*
383	A142	20c Sabah	.65	.70
384	A142	20c Sarawak	.65	.70
a.		Pair, #383-384	1.40	1.50
385	A143	$1 State and natl. symbols	2.25	3.25
		Nos. 383-385 (3)	3.55	4.65

Nudibranchs — A144

Marine Life A145

No. 386: a, Glossodoris atromarginata. b, Phyllidia ocellata. c, Chromodoris annae. d, Flabellina macassarana. e, Fryeria ruppelli. No. 387, Pomacanthus annularis.

1988, Dec. 17   **Litho.**   *Perf. 12*
| 386 | | Strip of 5 | 6.00 | 6.00 |
| a.-e. | | A144 20c any single | .75 | .25 |

Souvenir Sheet
Perf. 14
| 387 | A145 | $1 multicolored | 5.25 | 5.25 |

No. 387 contains one stamp 50x40mm.

Historic Buildings, Malacca — A146

No. 388, Perisytiharan Kemerdekaan Memorial. No. 389, Istana Kesultanan. $1, Porta da Santiago.

Perf. 13½x13, 13x13½
1989, Apr. 15   **Litho.**
388	A146	20c multicolored	.50	.35
389	A146	20c multicolored	.50	.35
390	A146	$1 multicolored, vert.	1.90	1.50
		Nos. 388-390 (3)	2.90	2.20

See design A130.

Crustaceans — A147

No. 391, Tetralia nigrolineata. No. 392, Neopetrolisthes maculatus. No. 393, Periclimenes holthuisi. No. 394, Synalpheus neomeris.

Wmk. 388
1989, June 29   **Litho.**   *Perf. 12*
391	A147	20c multicolored	.50	.50
392	A147	20c multicolored	.50	.50
a.		Pair, #391-392	1.60	1.60
393	A147	40c multicolored	.90	.90
394	A147	40c multicolored	.90	.90
a.		Pair, #393-394	2.75	2.75
		Nos. 391-394 (4)	2.80	2.80

7th Natl. Scout Jamboree — A148

10c, Map, badges. 20c, Scout salute, natl. flag. 80c, Camping out.

1989, July 26   *Perf. 13½x13, 13x13½*
395	A148	10c multicolored	.50	.45
396	A148	20c multicolored	.50	.45
397	A148	80c multicolored	2.50	3.00
		Nos. 395-397 (3)	3.50	3.90

Nos. 395-396 vert.

15th SEA Games, Kuala Lumpur — A149

Designs: 10c, Cycling, horiz. 20c, Track events, horiz. 50c, Swimming. $1, Torchbearer, stadium and flags.

Perf. 13½x13, 13x13½
1989, Aug. 20   **Litho.**   **Wmk. 388**
398	A149	10c multicolored	.40	.60
399	A149	20c multicolored	.40	.50
400	A149	50c multicolored	1.25	.80
401	A149	$1 multicolored	2.10	3.50
		Nos. 398-401 (4)	4.15	5.40

Installation of Sultan Azlan as Supreme Ruler — A150

1989, Sept. 18   *Perf. 13x13½*
402	A150	20c multicolored	.35	.25
403	A150	40c multicolored	.60	.30
404	A150	$1 multicolored	1.40	2.25
		Nos. 402-404 (3)	2.35	2.80

Commonwealth Heads of Government Meeting — A151

1989, Oct. 18   *Perf. 13½x13, 13x13½*
405	A151	20c Conference center	.40	.30
406	A151	50c Folk dancers, vert.	.80	.60
407	A151	$1 Map, flag	1.60	2.50
		Nos. 405-407 (3)	2.80	3.40

Malaysia Airlines Inaugural Non-stop Flight to London, Dec. 2 — A152

No. 408, Passenger jet, Malaysian clock tower, Big Ben. No. 409, Passenger jet, Malaysian skyscraper, Westminster Palace. $1, Map, passenger jet.

1989, Dec. 2   **Wmk. 388**   *Perf. 13*
408	A152	20c shown	2.00	2.00
409	A152	20c multicolored	2.00	2.00
a.		Pair, #408-409	4.50	4.50
410	A152	$1 multicolored	5.50	5.50
		Nos. 408-410 (3)	9.50	9.50

National Park, 50th Anniv. — A153

1989, Dec. 28   *Perf. 13x13½*
| 411 | A153 | 20c Map, sloth | 1.50 | .40 |
| 412 | A153 | $1 Crested arguses | 4.00 | 4.00 |

Visit Malaysia.

Visit Malaysia Year — A154

20c, Map. 50c, Drummers. $1, Yachts, scuba divers.

1990, Jan. 11   *Perf. 12*
413	A154	20c multicolored	.60	.50
414	A154	50c multicolored	1.40	1.10
415	A154	$1 multicolored	2.25	3.25
		Nos. 413-415 (3)	4.25	4.85

Wildflowers — A155

15c, Dillenia suffruticosa. 20c, Mimosa pudica. 50c, Ipomoea carnea. $1, Nymphaea pubescens.

1990, Mar. 12
416	A155	15c multicolored	.30	.30
417	A155	20c multicolored	.30	.30
418	A155	50c multicolored	.80	.80
419	A155	$1 multicolored	1.20	2.25
		Nos. 416-419 (4)	2.60	3.65

Kuala Lumpur — A156

Wmk. 388
1990, May 14   **Litho.**   *Perf. 12*
420	A156	20c Flag, rainbow, vert.	.40	.40
421	A156	40c shown	.70	.50
422	A156	$1 Cityscape	1.50	2.75
		Nos. 420-422 (3)	2.60	3.65

South-South Consultation and Cooperation Conference A157

1990, June 1   *Perf. 13*
| 423 | A157 | 20c shown | .45 | .35 |
| 424 | A157 | 80c Emblem | 1.75 | 2.25 |

Alor Setar, 250th Anniv. — A158

40c, Musicians, vert. $1, Government bldg., vert.

1990, June 2   *Perf. 12*
425	A158	20c shown	.40	.30
426	A158	40c multicolored	.70	.35
427	A158	$1 multicolored	1.50	3.00
		Nos. 425-427 (3)	2.60	3.65

Intl. Literacy Year — A159

20c, Letters, sign language. 40c, People reading. $1, Globe, pen nib, vert.

1990, Sept. 8   *Perf. 12*
428	A159	20c multicolored	.45	.35
a.		Perf. 13	17.50	
429	A159	40c multicolored	.85	.40
430	A159	$1 multicolored	1.75	2.50
		Nos. 428-430 (3)	3.05	3.20

Turtles — A160

15c, Dermochelys coriacea. 20c, Chelonia mydas. 40c, Eretmochelys imbricata. $1, Lepidochelys olivacea.

1990, Nov. 17
431	A160	15c multicolored	1.25	.30
432	A160	20c multicolored	1.25	.30
433	A160	40c multicolored	1.50	.65
434	A160	$1 multicolored	3.25	3.75
		Nos. 431-434 (4)	7.25	5.00

MARA (Council of Indigenous People), 25th Anniv. — A161

1991, Apr. 25
435	A161	20c Construction	.30	.30
436	A161	40c Education	.50	.35
437	A161	$1 Banking & industry	.70	2.00
		Nos. 435-437 (3)	1.50	2.65

Wasps — A162

Designs: 15c, Eustenogaster calyptodoma. 20c, Vespa affinis indonensis. 50c, Sceliphron javanum. $1, Ampulex compressa.

1991, July 29
438	A162	15c multicolored	.35	.30
439	A162	20c multicolored	.35	.30
440	A162	50c multicolored	.75	.40
441	A162	$1 multicolored	1.75	1.75
a.		Souvenir sheet of 4, #438-441, perf. 14½x14	5.00	5.00
		Nos. 438-441 (4)	3.20	2.75

Prime Ministers A163

No. 442, Tunku Abdul Rahman Putra Al-Haj (1903-90). No. 443, Tun Hussein Onn (1922-90). No. 444, Tun Abdul Razak Hussein (1922-76).

1991, Aug. 30
442	A163	$1 multicolored	.90	1.00
443	A163	$1 multicolored	.90	1.00
444	A163	$1 multicolored	.90	1.00
		Nos. 442-444 (3)	2.70	3.00

127

MALAYSIA

Historic Buildings A164

Designs: 15c, Istana Maziah, Trengganu. 20c, Istana Besar, Johore. 40c, Istana Bandar, Kuala Langat, Selangor. $1, Istana Jahar, Kelantan.

1991, Nov. 7
445	A164	15c multicolored	.35	.30
446	A164	20c multicolored	.35	.30
447	A164	40c multicolored	.55	.40
448	A164	$1 multicolored	1.40	2.25
	Nos. 445-448 (4)		2.65	3.25

Sarawak Museum, Cent. — A165

Museum buildings, fabric pattern and: 30c, Brass lamp. $1, Vase.

1991, Dec. 21
| 449 | A165 | 30c multicolored | .40 | .30 |
| 450 | A165 | $1 multicolored | 1.40 | 2.00 |

Malaysian Postal Service — A166

Designs: No. 451a, Postman on bicycle. b, Postman on motorcycle. c, Mail truck. d, Mail truck, diff., oil tank. e, Globe, airplane.

1992, Jan. 1
| 451 | A166 | 30c Strip of 5, #a.-e. | 3.50 | 3.50 |

Malaysian Tropical Forests — A167

Designs: 20c, Hill Dipterocarp Forest, Dyera costulata. 50c, Mangrove Swamp Forest, Rhizophora apiculata. $1, Lowland Dipterocarp Forest, Neobalanocarpus heimii.

1992, Mar. 23
452	A167	20c multicolored	.35	.35
453	A167	50c multicolored	.80	.50
454	A167	$1 multicolored	1.10	2.25
	Nos. 452-454 (3)		2.25	3.10

Installation of Yang di-Pertuan Besar of Negri Sembilan, Silver Jubilee — A168

1992, Apr. 18
| 455 | A168 | 30c Portrait, arms | .35 | .25 |
| 456 | A168 | $1 Building | 1.25 | 2.00 |

1992 Thomas Cup Champions in Badminton — A169

1992, July 25   **Perf. 12**
| 457 | A169 | $1 Cup, flag | .90 | 1.20 |
| 458 | A169 | $1 Players | .90 | 1.20 |

Souvenir Sheet
| 459 | A169 | $2 multicolored | 2.50 | 2.50 |

No. 459 contains one 75x28mm stamp.

ASEAN, 25th Anniv. — A170

1992, Aug. 8
460	A170	30c shown	.55	.40
461	A170	50c Flora	1.00	.60
462	A170	$1 Architecture	1.60	2.00
	Nos. 460-462 (3)		3.15	3.00

Postage Stamps in Malaysia, 125th Anniv. — A171

No. 463, Straits Settlements #1, Malaya #84. No. 464, Straits Settlements #2, Malaysia #2. No. 465, Straits Settlements #11, Malaysia #421. No. 466, Straits Settlements #14, Malaysia #467. No. 467, Flag, simulated stamp.

1992, Sept. 1
463	A171	30c multicolored	.60	.25
464	A171	30c multicolored	.60	.25
a.		Pair #463-464	1.75	1.75
465	A171	50c multicolored	1.00	.25
466	A171	50c multicolored	1.00	.25
a.		Pair #465-466	2.25	2.25
	Nos. 463-466 (4)		3.20	1.00

Souvenir Sheet
| 467 | A171 | $2 multicolored | 2.50 | 2.50 |

Kuala Lumpur '92.

Coral A174

No. 471: a, Acropora. b, Dendronephthya. c, Dendrophyllia. d, Sinularia. e, Melithaea. No. 472, Subergorgia.

1992, Dec. 21
| 471 | A173 | 30c Strip of 5, #a.-e. | 4.50 | 4.50 |

Souvenir Sheet
| 472 | A174 | $2 multicolored | 4.50 | 5.00 |

16th Asian-Pacific Dental Congress — A175

Children from various countries: No. 473, 4 girls. No. 474, 4 girls, 1 holding koala. Dentists, flags of: No. 475, Japan, Malaysia, South Korea. No. 476, New Zealand, Thailand, People's Republic of China, Indonesia.

1993, Apr. 24
473	A175	30c multicolored	.60	.60
474	A175	30c multicolored	.60	.60
a.		Pair, #473-474	1.50	1.50
475	A175	50c multicolored	.90	.90
476	A175	$1 multicolored	1.75	1.75
a.		Pair, #475-476	3.50	3.50
	Nos. 473-476 (4)		3.85	3.85

30c, Fairway, vert. 50c, Old, new club houses, vert. $1, Sand trap.

1993, June 24
477	A176	30c multicolored	.80	.55
478	A176	50c multicolored	1.50	.70
479	A176	$1 multicolored	2.40	3.00
	Nos. 477-479 (3)		4.70	4.25

Royal Selangor Golf Club, cent.

Wildflowers — A177

20c, Alpinia rafflesiana. 30c, Achasma megalocheilos. 50c, Zingiber spectabile. $1, Costus speciosus.

1993, Aug. 2
480	A177	20c multicolored	.65	.50
481	A177	30c multicolored	.65	.50
482	A177	50c multicolored	1.75	.65
483	A177	$1 multicolored	2.25	3.00
	Nos. 480-483 (4)		5.30	4.65

14th Commonwealth Forestry Conference A178

30c, Globe, forest. 50c, Hand holding trees. $1, Trees under dome, vert.

1993, Sept. 13
484	A178	30c multicolored	.75	.50
485	A178	50c multicolored	1.40	.60
486	A178	$1 multicolored	1.90	2.25
	Nos. 484-486 (3)		4.05	3.35

Nos. 484-486 with Bangkok '93 Emblem Added
Wmk. 388

1993, Oct. 1   **Litho.**   **Perf. 12**
486A	A178	30c multicolored	4.50	4.00
486B	A178	50c multicolored	5.50	5.00
486C	A178	$1 multicolored	10.00	8.50
	Nos. 486A-486C (3)		20.00	17.50

Kingfishers — A179

1993, Oct. 23
487		30c Halcyon smyrnensis	1.00	1.00
488		30c Alcedo meninting	1.00	1.00
a.	A179	Pair, #487-488	2.50	2.50
489		50c Halcyon concreta	1.60	1.60
490		50c Ceyx erithacus	1.60	1.60
a.	A179	Pair, #489-490	4.00	4.00
	Nos. 487-490 (4)		5.20	5.20

30c, SME MD3-160 airplane. 50c, Eagle X-TS airplane. $1, Patrol boat KD Kasturi. $2, Map of Malaysia.

1993, Dec. 7
491	A180	30c multicolored	.60	.40
492	A180	50c multicolored	1.25	.70
493	A180	$1 multicolored	1.75	2.25
	Nos. 491-493 (3)		3.60	3.35

Souvenir Sheet
| 494 | A180 | $2 multicolored | 3.00 | 3.00 |

Langkawi Intl. Maritime and Aerospace Exhibition (LIMA '93).

Visit Malaysia Year — A181

1994, Jan. 1
495	A181	20c Jeriau Waterfalls	.40	.40
496	A181	30c Flowers	.50	.45
497	A181	50c Marine life	1.00	.60
498	A181	$1 Wildlife	1.50	2.00
	Nos. 495-498 (4)		3.40	3.45

See Nos. 527A-527D.

Kuala Lumpur Natl. Planetarium A182

Designs: 30c, Exterior. 50c, Interior displays. $1, Theater auditorium.

1994, Feb. 7
499	A182	30c multicolored	.50	.40
500	A182	50c multicolored	.90	.65
501	A182	$1 multicolored	1.75	2.25
	Nos. 499-501 (3)		3.15	3.30

Orchids — A183

Designs: 20c, Spathoglottis aurea. 30c, Paphiopedilum barbatum. 50c, Bulbophyllum lobbii. $1, Aerides odorata. $2, Grammatophyllum speciosum.

1994, Feb. 17
502	A183	20c multicolored	.55	.35
503	A183	30c multicolored	.55	.40
504	A183	50c multicolored	.90	.70
505	A183	$1 multicolored	1.60	2.25
	Nos. 502-505 (4)		3.60	3.70

Souvenir Sheet
| 506 | A183 | $2 multicolored | 3.75 | 3.75 |

Hong Kong '94 (No. 506).

World Islamic Civilization Festival '94 — A184

1994, June 17
507	A184	20c Decorative bowl	.35	.30
508	A184	30c Celestial sphere	.40	.30
509	A184	50c Dinar coins	.55	.55
510	A184	$1 Decorative tile	1.10	1.25
	Nos. 507-510 (4)		2.40	2.40

See Nos. 528-531.

Veterinary Services, Cent. — A185

1994, July 26
511	A185	30c shown	.60	.40
512	A185	50c Meat processing	.80	.60
513	A185	$1 Cattle, laboratory	1.60	2.00
	Nos. 511-513 (3)		3.00	3.00

Electrification, Cent. — A186

1994, Sept. 3
514	A186	30c Laying cable	.55	.40
515	A186	30c Lighted city	.55	.40
a.		Pair, #514-515	1.40	1.40
516	A186	$1 Futuristic city	1.40	1.75
	Nos. 514-516 (3)		2.50	2.55

North-South Expressway A187

1994, Sept. 8
517	A187	30c shown	.40	.30
518	A187	50c Interchange	.55	.55
519	A187	$1 Bridge	1.25	1.60
	Nos. 517-519 (3)		2.20	2.35

MALAYSIA

A188

1994, Sept. 22
520	A188	30c pink & multi		.45	.30
521	A188	50c yellow & multi		.60	.40
522	A188	$1 green & multi		1.10	1.60
		Nos. 520-522 (3)		2.15	2.30

Installation of 10th Yang Di-Pertuan Agong (Head of State).

A189

1994, Oct. 29   Wmk. 388   Litho.   Perf. 14
523	A189	$1 shown		1.25	1.25
524	A189	$1 Mascot		1.25	1.25
a.		Pair, #523-524 + label		2.75	3.25

1998 Commonwealth Games, Kuala Lumpur.

Official Opening of Natl. Library Building — A190

1994, Dec. 16
525	A190	30c Library building		.45	.35
526	A190	50c Computer terminal		.60	.45
527	A190	$1 Manuscript		1.25	1.00
		Nos. 525-527 (3)		2.30	1.80

Nos. 495-498 with Added Inscription

1994, Nov. 8   Wmk. 388   Litho.   Perf. 12
527A	A181	20c multicolored		.75	.85
527B	A181	30c multicolored		1.25	.95
527C	A181	50c multicolored		1.75	1.50
527D	A181	$1 multicolored		3.00	2.75
		Nos. 527A-527D (4)		6.75	6.05

Nos. 507-510 with Added Inscription

1994, Aug. 16   Wmk. 388   Litho.   Perf. 12
528	A184	20c multicolored		1.40	1.40
529	A184	30c multicolored		1.10	1.10
530	A184	50c multicolored		2.75	2.75
531	A184	$1 multicolored		5.50	5.50
		Nos. 528-531 (4)		10.75	10.75

A191

1994, Nov. 10   Unwmk.   Perf. 14½
532	A191	30c shown		.65	.35
533	A191	$1 Building complex		1.30	1.50

Memorial to Tunku Abdul Rahman Putra Al-Haj (1903-1990), former Prime Minister.

Fungi — A192

1995, Jan. 18   Perf. 14½x14
534	A192	20c Bracket fungus		.45	.30
535	A192	30c Cup fungus		.50	.30
536	A192	50c Veil fungus		.80	.40
537	A192	$1 Coral fungus		1.75	2.75
		Nos. 534-537 (4)		3.50	3.75

Neofelis Nebulosa — A193

1995, Apr. 18   Wmk. 373   Perf. 13½
538	A193	20c shown		.35	.30
539	A193	30c With young		.55	.40
540	A193	50c With mouth open		.90	.75
541	A193	$1 Lying on rock		1.75	2.00
a.		Strip of 4, #538-541		5.00	5.00

Nos. 538-541 were issued in sheets of 16 stamps.

World Wildlife Fund.

Marine Life — A194

1995, Apr. 10   Wmk. 388   Perf. 12
Booklet Stamps
542	A194	20c Feather stars		.90	.90
543	A194	20c Sea fans		.90	.90
a.		Pair, #542-543		2.00	2.00
b.		Booklet pane, 5 each #542-543		9.75	9.75
		Complete booklet, #543b		10.00	
544	A194	30c Soft coral		1.20	1.20
545	A194	30c Cup coral		1.20	1.20
a.		Pair, #544-545		2.60	2.60
b.		Booklet pane, 5 each #544-545		13.00	13.00
		Complete booklet, #543b		14.00	
		Nos. 542-545 (4)		4.20	4.20

X-Ray, Cent. — A195

No. 546, Early machine x-raying hand. No. 547, CAT scan machine. $1, Chest x-ray.

1995, May 29
546	A195	30c multicolored		.55	.70
547	A195	50c multicolored		.55	.70
a.		Pair, #546-547		1.25	1.60
548	A195	$1 multicolored		1.50	1.75
		Nos. 546-548 (3)		2.60	3.15

1998 Commonwealth Games, Kuala Lumpur — A196

Various sporting events: No. 549, Badminton, cricket, shooting, tennis, weight lifting, hurdles, field hockey. No. 550, Cycling, lawn bowling, boxing, basketball, rugby, gymnastics.

Wmk. 388
1995, Sept. 10   Litho.   Perf. 14
549	A196	$1 multicolored		2.25	2.25
550	A196	$1 multicolored		2.25	2.25
a.		Pair, #549-550 + label		5.00	5.00

Traditional Weapons — A197

1995, Sept. 1   Litho.   Perf. 14
551	A197	20c Jemblah		.30	.25
552	A197	30c Keris panjang		.30	.25
553	A197	50c Kerambit		.45	.35
554	A197	$1 Keris sundang		.90	1.50
		Nos. 551-554 (4)		1.95	2.35

Souvenir Sheet
555	A197	$2 Lading terus		3.50	3.50

Singapore '95.

UN, 50th Anniv. — A198

1995, Oct. 24   Perf. 13½
556	A198	30c shown		.40	.30
557	A198	$1 UN emblem		1.10	1.25

Intl. Assoc. of Travel Agents (IATA), 50th Anniv. A199

Jet, globe and: No. 558, Historic buildings. No. 559, Sydney Opera House, Great Wall of China. No. 560, Eiffel Tower, Tower Bridge. No. 561, Hollywood Walk of Fame, Latin American pyramid.

1995, Oct. 30   Perf. 14
558		30c multicolored		.65	.65
559		30c multicolored		.65	.65
a.		A199 Pair, #558-559		1.75	1.75
560		50c multicolored		.90	.90
561		50c multicolored		.90	.90
a.		A199 Pair, #560-561		2.25	2.25
		Nos. 558-561 (4)		3.10	3.10

Turtles — A200

No. 562, Chelonia mydas. No. 563, Dermochelys coriacea.

Perf. 14x14½
1995, Sept. 26   Litho.   Wmk. 388
Booklet Stamps
562	A200	30c multi		2.00	1.25
563	A200	30c multi		2.00	1.25
a.		Booklet pane, 5 each #562-563		22.00	16.00
		Complete booklet, #563a		24.00	

Proton Cars, 10th Anniv. — A201

No. 564, 1985 Saga 1.5. No. 565, 1992 Iswara 1.5 aeroback. No. 566, 1992, Iswara 1.5 sedan. No. 567, 1993 Wira 1.6 sedan. No. 568, 1993 Wira 1.6 aeroback. No. 569, 1994 Rally. No. 570, 1994 Satria 1.0. No. 571, 1995 Perdana 2.0. No. 572, 1995 Wira 1.6 aeroback. No. 573, 1995 Wira 1.8 sedan.

1995, Dec.   Litho.   Perf. 14
Booklet Stamps
564	A201	30c multicolored		1.00	1.00
565	A201	30c multicolored		1.00	1.00
566	A201	30c multicolored		1.00	1.00
567	A201	30c multicolored		1.00	1.00
568	A201	30c multicolored		1.00	1.00
569	A201	30c multicolored		1.00	1.00
570	A201	30c multicolored		1.00	1.00
571	A201	30c multicolored		1.00	1.00
572	A201	30c multicolored		1.00	1.00
573	A201	30c multicolored		1.00	1.00
a.		Booklet pane, Nos. 564-573		10.00	10.00
		Complete booklet, No. 573a		10.00	

A202

Malaysia East Asia Satellite: 30c, Ariane 4 being launched. 50c, Satellite in Earth orbit over East Asia. $1, Satellite Control Center, Langkawai.
$5, Satellite entering orbit, horiz.

1996, Jan. 13   Perf. 13½
574	A202	30c multicolored		.40	.30
575	A202	50c multicolored		.60	.50
576	A202	$1 multicolored		1.10	1.60
		Nos. 574-576 (3)		2.10	2.40

Souvenir Sheet
Perf. 14
577	A202	$5 multicolored		7.25	7.25

No. 577 contains a holographic image. Soaking in water may affect the hologram.

Pitcher Plants — A203

No. 578, Nepenthes sanguinea. No. 579, Nepenthes macfarlanei. No. 580, Nepenthes rajah. No. 581, Nepenthes lowii.

Perf. 13½, 14½x14 (#580-581)
1996, Apr. 16   Litho.   Wmk. 388
578	A203	30c multicolored		.30	.30
579	A203	30c multicolored		.30	.30
a.		Pair, Nos. 578-579		.75	.90
580	A203	50c multicolored		.45	.40
581	A203	50c multicolored		.45	.40
a.		Pair, Nos. 580-581		1.20	1.40
		Nos. 578-581 (4)		1.50	1.40

Birds of Prey — A204

Designs: 20c, Haliastur indus. 30c, Spilornis cheela. 50c, Haliaeetus leucogaster. $1, Spizaetus cirrhatus.
$2, Spizaetus alboniger, vert.

Wmk. 388
1996, May 18   Litho.   Perf. 14
582	A204	20c multicolored		.40	.40
583	A204	30c multicolored		.45	.45
584	A204	50c multicolored		.65	.65
585	A204	$1 multicolored		1.50	2.00
		Nos. 582-585 (4)		3.00	3.50

Souvenir Sheet
586	A204	$2 multicolored		4.50	4.50

CHINA '96 (No. 586).

Intl. Day Against Drug Abuse and Illicit Drug Trafficking — A205

Designs: No. 587, Family, drugs burning. No. 588, Various sporting activities, marajuana plants. $1, Family, rainbow.

Wmk. 388
1996, June 26   Litho.   Perf. 14
587	A205	30c multicolored		.40	.30
588	A205	30c multicolored		.40	.30
a.		Pair, #587-588		1.00	1.25
589	A205	$1 multicolored		1.75	1.75
		Nos. 587-589 (3)		2.55	2.35

Butterflies — A206

No. 590, Graphium sarpedon. No. 591, Melanocyma faunula. No. 592, Delias hyparete. No. 593, Trogonoptera brookiana. No. 594, Terinos terpander.

1996, Sept. 27   Litho.   Perf. 14½x14
Booklet Stamps
590	A206	30c multicolored		1.75	1.25
591	A206	30c multicolored		1.75	1.25
592	A206	30c multicolored		1.75	1.25
593	A206	30c multicolored		1.75	1.25

MALAYSIA

594	A206	30c multicolored	1.75	1.25
a.		Pane of 10, 2 each #590-594	17.50	17.50
		Nos. 590-594 (5)	8.75	6.25

Kuala Lumpur Tower — A207

30c, Artist's impression. 50c, Tower head diagram. $1, Tower head, city at night. $2, Kuala Lumpur Tower, vert.

Perf. 13½
1996, Oct. 1   Litho.   Unwmk.

595	A207	30c multicolored	.35	.25
596	A207	50c multicolored	.50	.30
597	A207	$1 multicolored	1.10	1.40
		Nos. 595-597 (3)	1.95	1.95

Souvenir Sheet

598	A207	$2 multicolored	2.50	2.50
a.		With added inscription in sheet margin	2.50	2.50

No. 598a inscribed with TAIPEI '96 emblem, issued 10/16/96.

14th Conference of Confederation of Asian and Pacific Accountants A208

1996, Oct. 7   Perf. 13½x14

599	A208	30c CAPA logo	.50	.40
600	A208	$1 Globe	1.10	1.25

Natl. Science Center — A209

30c, Model of molecular structure. 50c, Model of atom, Science Center. $1, Natl. Science Center.

Unwmk.
1996, Nov. 29   Litho.   Perf. 14

601	A209	30c multicolored	.45	.35
602	A209	50c multicolored	.60	.40
603	A209	$1 multicolored	1.10	1.25
		Nos. 601-603 (3)	2.15	2.00

Souvenir Sheet

Stamp Week — A210

Wildlife: a, 20c, Nycticebus coucang. b, 30c, Calloscurius prevostii. c, 50c, Attacus atlas. d, $1, Hylobates lar. e, $1, Buceros rhinoceros. f, $2, Hemigalus derbyanus.

1996, Dec. 2

604	A210	Sheet of 6, #a.-f.	4.25	4.25

No. 604d is 30x60mm. Nos. 605e-605f are 60x30mm.

Birds — A211

Designs: 20c, Muscicapella hodgsoni. 30c, Leiothrix argentauris. 50c, Dicaeum celibicum. $1, Aethopyga mystacalis.

Perf. 13½x14
1997, Jan. 4   Litho.   Unwmk.

605	A211	20c multicolored	.35	.35
606	A211	30c multicolored	.45	.35
607	A211	50c multicolored	.65	.40
608	A211	$1 multicolored	1.40	1.60
		Nos. 605-608 (4)	2.85	2.70

16th Commonwealth Games, Kuala Lumpur '98 — A212

1996, Dec. 21   Perf. 12

609	A212	30c Running	.45	.25
610	A212	30c Hurdles	.45	.25
a.		Pair, #609-610	1.10	.90
611	A212	50c High jump	.75	.35
612	A212	50c Javelin	.75	.35
a.		Pair, #611-612	1.75	1.50
		Nos. 609-612 (4)	2.40	1.20

Intl. Cricket Cup Champions — A213

1997, Mar. 24   Litho.   Perf. 14

613	A213	30c shown	.35	.35
614	A213	50c Batsman	.50	.50
615	A213	$1 Wicket keeper	1.25	1.50
		Nos. 613-615 (3)	2.10	2.35

Aviation in Malaysia, 50th Anniv. — A214

Designs: 30c, Jet, world map. 50c, Jet approaching Kuala Lumpur. $1, Airplane tailfins of four Malaysian airlines.

Perf. 14, 13½ (#617)
1997, Apr. 2   Wmk. 388

616	A214	30c multicolored	.55	.40
617	A214	50c multicolored	.95	.75
618	A214	$1 multicolored	2.00	2.25
a.		Perf. 13½	4.00	2.00
		Nos. 616-618 (3)	3.50	3.40

A215

Light Rail Transit System: No. 620, Two trains, one on bridge, Kuala Lumpur skyline.

Perf. 14x14½
1997, Mar. 1   Litho.   Unwmk.
Booklet Stamps

619	A215	30c shown	1.60	.80
620	A215	30c multicolored	1.60	.80
a.		Booklet pane, 5 each #619-620	16.00	16.00
		Complete booklet, #620a	16.00	

Highland Flowers — A216

No. 621, Schima wallichi. No. 622, Aeschynanthus longicalyx. No. 623, Aeschynanthus speciosa. No. 624, Phyllagathis tuberculata. No. 625, Didymocarpus quinquevulnerus.

Booklet Stamps
1997, May 7   Perf. 14½x14

621	A216	30c multicolored	.70	.70
622	A216	30c multicolored	.70	.70
623	A216	30c multicolored	.70	.70
624	A216	30c multicolored	.70	.70
625	A216	30c multicolored	.70	.70
a.		Booklet pane, 2 each #621-625	7.50	7.50
		Complete booklet, #625a	8.00	
		Nos. 621-625 (5)	3.50	3.50

Ruler's Council, Cent. — A217

Unwmk.
1997, July 31   Litho.   Perf. 14

626	A217	30c Photo, 1897	.35	.30
627	A217	50c Emblem, arms	.55	.40
628	A217	$1 Emblem	.90	1.40
		Nos. 626-628 (3)	1.80	2.10

ASEAN, 30th Anniv. — A218

50c, "30," emblem. $1, Emblem, color bars.

1997, Aug. 8   Wmk. 388   Perf. 13½

629	A218	30c shown	.65	.40
630	A218	50c multicolored	.85	.50
631	A218	$1 multicolored	1.50	1.75
		Nos. 629-631 (3)	3.00	2.65

A219

Coral: 20c, Tubastrea. 30c, Melithaea. 50c, Aulostomus chinensis. $1, Symphillia.

1997, Aug. 23   Unwmk.   Perf. 14½

632	A219	20c multicolored	.30	.30
633	A219	30c multicolored	.30	.30
634	A219	50c multicolored	.40	.35
635	A219	$1 multicolored	1.10	1.25
		Nos. 632-635 (4)	2.10	2.20

A220

1997, Aug. 25   Perf. 13x13½
Booklet Stamps

636	A220	30c Career women	.70	.40
637	A220	30c Family	.70	.40
a.		Booklet pane, 5 each #636-637	7.00	7.00
		Complete booklet, #637a	7.00	

20th Intl. Conf. of Pan-Pacific and Southeast Asia Women's Assoc., Kuala Lumpur.

9th World Youth Soccer Championships A221

30c, Mascot. 50c, Soccer ball, players, flag. $1, Map of Malaysia, silhouettes of players, soccer ball.

Perf. 13½x13
1997, June 16   Unwmk.

638	A221	30c multicolored	.30	.30
639	A221	50c multicolored	.45	.40

Perf. 13x12½

640	A221	$1 multicolored	1.00	1.40
		Nos. 638-640 (3)	1.75	2.10

Souvenir Sheet

Chelonia Mydas A222

1997, Aug. 23   Litho.   Perf. 14½

641	A222	$2 multicolored	3.00	3.25

Year of the Coral Reef.

7th Summit Level of the Group of 15 — A223

$1, Emblem, natl. flags of member nations.

Perf. 12, 13½ (#643)
1997, Nov. 3   Litho.   Unwmk.

642	A223	30c shown	.30	.30
643	A223	$1 multicolored	1.25	1.25

Stamp Week — A224

Protected wildlife: a, 20c, Tomistoma schlegelli. b, 30c, Tarsius bancanus, vert. c, 50c, Cervus unicolor, vert. d, $2, Rollulus rouloul. e, $2, Scleropages formosus.

1997, Dec. 1   Perf. 14½

644	A224	Sheet of 5, #a.-e.	3.25	3.25

Philately in Malaysia, 50th Anniv. A225

Malpex '97: a, 20c, Straits Settlements #7. b, 30c, #605-608. c, 50c, #604. d, $1, Early cover from Straits Settlements.

1997, Sept. 9   Perf. 12½

645	A225	Sheet of 4, #a.-d.	3.25	3.25
e.		Ovptd. in sheet margin in gold	2.00	2.00

No. 645e is inscribed in sheet margin with INDEPEX '97 exhibition emblem.

Rare Fruit — A226

20c, Bouea macrophylla. 30c, Sandoricum koetjape. 50c, Nephelium ramboutan-ake. $1, Garcinia atroviridis.

1998, Jan. 10   Perf. 13½

646	A226	20c multicolored	.25	.25
647	A226	30c multicolored	.30	.30
648	A226	50c multicolored	.40	.30
649	A226	$1 multicolored	.75	1.25
		Nos. 646-649 (4)	1.70	2.10

MALAYSIA

Kuala Lumpur '98 Games — A227

1998, Feb. 23			Perf. 12	
650	A227	30c Field hockey	.60	.60
651	A227	30c Women's netball	.60	.60
a.		Pair, #650-651 + label	1.40	1.40
652	A227	50c Cricket	.85	.85
653	A227	50c Rugby	.85	.85
a.		Pair, #652-653 + label	1.90	1.90
		Nos. 650-653 (4)	2.90	2.90

Kuala Lumpur '98 Games A228

Stadiums for the venues: a, 1r, Utama Bukit Jalil. b, 50c, Tertutup. c, 30c, Hoki. d, 20c, Renang Complex.

Wmk. 388

1998, Feb. 23	Litho.	Perf. 13½	
654	A228	Sheet of 4, #a.-d.	2.50 2.50

Early Coins — A229

Coin's region, date: 20c, Trengganu, 1793-1808. 30c, Kedah, 1661-87. 50c, Johore, 1597-1615. $1, Kelantan, 1400-1780.

Wmk. 388

1998, Apr. 11		Litho.	Perf. 13½	
655	A229	20c multicolored	.30	.30
a.		Perf. 14¼	3.00	.25
656	A229	30c multicolored	.40	.30
657	A229	50c multicolored	.45	.30
a.		Perf. 14¼	4.25	.35
658	A229	$1 multicolored	.70	1.10
		Nos. 655-658 (4)	1.85	2.00

Kuala Lumpur International Airport — A230

Designs: 30c, Tower, tramway, airplanes. 50c, Tower, airplanes at terminal. $1, Tower, airplane in air, airport below. $2, Tower, globe overhead.

1998, June 27			Perf. 12	
659	A230	30c multicolored	.35	.30
a.		Perf. 12½	5.00	
660	A230	50c multicolored	.65	.30
661	A230	$1 multicolored	1.00	1.75
a.		Perf. 12½	6.00	3.75
		Nos. 659-661 (3)	2.00	2.35

Souvenir Sheet
Perf. 14

662	A230	$2 multicolored	2.50 2.75

No. 662 contains one 26x36mm stamp.

Malaysian Red Crescent Society, 50th Anniv. — A231

30c, Rescue boat. $1, Mobile rescue unit.

1998, May 8			Perf. 13½	
663	A231	30c multicolored	.45	.40
a.		Perf. 14¼	2.75	2.75
664	A231	$1 multicolored	1.25	.60
a.		Perf. 14¼	2.75	2.75

Watermark on No. 664a is inverted. No. 664a also exists with watermark upright. Value $10.

Medicinal Plants — A234

20c, Solanum torvum. 30c, Tinospora crispa. 50c, Jatropha podagrica. $1, Hibiscus rosa-sinensis.

Wmk. 388

1998, July 18	Litho.	Perf. 13¾	
671	A234	20c multicolored	.25 .25
672	A234	30c multicolored	.30 .30

Perf. 14¼

673	A234	50c multicolored	.40 .30
674	A234	$1 multicolored	.60 1.25
		Nos. 671-674 (4)	1.55 2.10

1998 Commonwealth Games, Kuala Lumpur — A235

a, 20c, Weight lifting. b, 20c, Badminton. c, 30c, Field hockey goalie. d, 30c, Field hockey. e, 20c, Netball. f, 20c, Shooting. g, 30c, Cycling. h, 30c, Lawn bowling. i, 50c, Gymnastics. j, 50c, Cricket. k, $1, Swimming. l, $1, Squash. m, 50c, Rugby. n, 50c, Running. o, $1, Boxing. p, $1, Bowling.

Perf. 14½x15

1998, Sept. 11	Litho.	Wmk. 388	
675	A235	Sheet of 16, #a.-p.	7.00 7.50

Modernization of Rail Transport — A236

Designs: 30c, Putra-LRT, 1998. 50c, Star-LRT, 1996. $1, KTM Commuter, 1995.

1998, Oct. 3			Perf. 13¾, 14¼	
676	A236	30c multicolored	.30	.30
a.		Perf. 14¼	3.25	
677	A236	50c multicolored	.55	.35
a.		Perf. 14¼	1.25	.30
678	A236	$1 multicolored (Perf. 14¼)	1.10	1.25
		Nos. 676-678 (3)	1.95	1.90

1998 APEC (Asia-Pacific Economic Cooperation) Conference A237

Design: $1, Petronas Towers, people working with computers, office workers.

1990, Nov. 14			Perf. 13½	
679	A237	30c shown	2.25	.35
a.		Perf. 14½	.70	.35
680	A237	$1 multicolored	.85	1.10
a.		Perf. 14½	3.75	3.75

Insects — A238

Designs: a, 20c, Xylotrupes gideon, vert. b, 30c, Pomponia imperatoria, vert. c, 50c, Phyllium pulchrifolium, vert. d, $2, Hymenopus coronatus. e, $2, Macrolyristes corporalis.

Wmk. 388

1998, Nov. 28	Litho.	Perf. 12½	
681	A238	Sheet of 5, #a.-e.	3.25 3.75

Stamp Week. Nos. 681a-681c are each 30x40mm.

Gold Medal Winners at 16th Commonwealth Games — A238a

No. 681F: h, 30c, Air rifle. i, 30c, 48kg boxing. j, 30c, 50km walk. k, 30c, 69kg clean and jerk weight lifting. l, 50c, Men's doubles, bowling. m, 50c, Men's singles, bowling. n, 50c, Men's doubles, badminton. o, 50c, Men's singles, badminton. p, $1, Rhythmic gymnastics (64x26mm).
$2, Team photograph.

Perf. 13¾x14

1998, Dec. 12	Litho.	Wmk. 388	
681F	A238a	Sheet of 9, #h.-p., + 2 labels	10.00 10.00

Souvenir Sheet

| 681G | A238a | $2 multi | 4.25 4.25 |

No. 681G contains one 128x80mm stamp.

Intl. Year for Older Persons — A239

No. 683, World map, people, diff.

Wmk. 388

1999, Jan. 28	Litho.	Perf. 14	
682	A239	$1 shown	.85 1.00
683	A239	$1 multicolored	.85 1.00

Fruit — A240

Designs: 20c, Syzygium malaccense. 30c, Garcinia prainiana. 50c, Mangifera caesia. $1, Salacca glabrescens.

1999, Feb. 27			Perf. 12	
684	A240	20c multicolored	.25	.25
685	A240	30c multicolored	.30	.25
686	A240	50c multicolored	.40	.30
687	A240	$1 multicolored	.70	1.00
a.		Strip of 4, #684-687	1.75	1.75
		Nos. 684-687 (4)	1.65	1.80

Domestic Cats — A241

Designs: 30c, Kucing Malaysia. 50c, Siamese. $1, Abyssinian.
No. 691: a, British shorthair. b, Scottish fold.
No. 692: a, Birman. b, Persian.

1999, Apr. 1		Litho.	Perf. 12	
688	A241	30c multicolored	.35	.30
689	A241	50c multicolored	.55	.30
690	A241	$1 multicolored	.80	1.00
		Nos. 688-690 (3)	1.70	1.60

Sheets of 2

| 691 | A241 | $1 #a.-b. | 1.30 1.30 |
| 692 | A241 | $1 #a.-b. | 1.30 1.30 |

Protected Mammals — A242

Wmk. 388

1999, May 28		Litho.	Perf. 12	
693	A242	20c Rhinoceros	.35	.45
694	A242	30c Panther	.25	.25
695	A242	50c Bear	.40	.55
696	A242	1r Elephant	.80	1.10
697	A242	2r Orangutan	1.50	1.75
a.		Strip of 5, #693-697	3.75	3.75
b.		Souvenir sheet, #697	2.25	2.25

Nos. 693-697 were issued in sheet containing 4 each. No. 697b is a continuous design.

Intl. Congress on AIDS in Asia and the Pacific, Kuala Lumpur — A244

Perf. 14, 13½ (#700, 701)

1999, June 19	Litho.	Wmk. 388	
699	A244	30c shown	.35 .35
700	A244	50c Emblems, hearts	.50 .40
701	A244	1r Emblem as heart	.90 1.25
		Nos. 699-701 (3)	1.75 2.00

P. Ramlee (1929-73), Actor, Director — A245

Designs: 20c, Wearing chain around neck. 30c, Wearing bow tie. 50c, Holding gun. No. 705, Behind camera.
No. 706: a, Wearing cap. b, With hands in air. c, Holding microphone. d, Wearing army uniform.
No. 707, Wearing patterned hat. No. 708, Wearing plaid shirt.

Perf. 13½x13¾

1999, July 24	Litho.	Wmk. 388	
702	A245	20c multicolored	.40 .40
703	A245	30c multicolored	.50 .40
704	A245	50c multicolored	.75 .50
705	A245	$1 multicolored	1.30 1.50
a.		Perf. 14¼	1.10 1.30
		Nos. 702-705 (4)	2.95 2.80

Strip of 4

| 706 | A245 | 30c #a.-d. | 3.50 3.50 |

Souvenir Sheets
Perf. 14¼

| 707 | A245 | $1 multicolored | 10.00 10.00 |
| 708 | A245 | $1 multicolored | 10.00 10.00 |

No. 706 printed in sheets of 16 stamps.

Water Plants and Fish — A246

No. 709, Monochoria hastata. No. 710, Trichopsis vittatus. No. 711, Limnocharis flava. No. 712, Betta imbellis. No. 713, Nymphaea pubescens. No. 714, Trichogaster trichopterus. No. 715, Ipomea aquatica. No. 716, Helostoma temmincki. No. 717, Eichhornia crassipes. No. 718, Sphaerichthys osphronemoides.

Perf. 13¾x14

1999, July 31	Litho.	Wmk. 388	
709	A246	10c multi	.30 .30
710	A246	10c multi	.30 .30
a.		Pair, #709-710	.75 .75
711	A246	15c multi	.30 .30
712	A246	15c multi	.30 .30
a.		Pair, #711-712	.75 .75
713	A246	25c multi	.30 .30
714	A246	25c multi	.30 .30
a.		Pair, #713-714	.85 .85
715	A246	50c multi	.45 .45
716	A246	50c multi	.45 .45
a.		Pair, #715-716	1.25 1.25
717	A246	50c multi	.45 .45
718	A246	50c multi	.45 .45
a.		Pair, #717-718	1.25 1.25
b.		Block of 10 with bottom row of perforations perf 14½	4.50 4.50
		Nos. 709-718 (10)	3.60 3.60

Trees — A247

MALAYSIA

Designs: No. 719, Dryobalanops aromatica. No. 720, Alstonia angustiloba. No. 721, Fagraea fragrans. No. 722, Lagerstroemia floribunda. No. 723, Elateriospermum tapos.

Perf. 14x13½
1999, Aug. 14   Litho.   Wmk. 388

719	A247	30c multicolored	.60	.60
720	A247	30c multicolored	.60	.60
721	A247	30c multicolored	.60	.60
722	A247	30c multicolored	.60	.60
723	A247	30c multicolored	.60	.60
a.		Strip of 5, #719-723	3.00	3.00
		Complete bklt., 4 ea #719-723	12.00	

Petronas Towers — A248

Designs: 30c, Daytime view. 50c, Architectural drawing. $1, Nighttime view. $5, Hologram.

Perf. 14x14¼
1999, Aug. 30   Litho.   Unwmk.

724	A248	30c multicolored	.35	.30
725	A248	50c multicolored	.45	.40
726	A248	$1 multicolored	.90	1.10
		Nos. 724-726 (3)	1.70	1.80

Souvenir Sheet
Perf. 14½x14¼

727	A248	$5 multicolored	5.00	5.00

No. 727 contains one 30x50mm stamp with a holographic image. Soaking in water may affect hologram. No. 727 exists imperf.

Taiping, 125th Anniv. — A249

Designs: 20c, Rickshaw, Peace Hotel. 30c, Automobile, building. 50c, Train, train station. $1, Airplanes, airport building. $2, Building, horse-drawn carriage.

Unwmk.
1999, Sept. 1   Litho.   Perf. 12

728	A249	20c multi	.45	.45
729	A249	30c multi	.45	.45
730	A249	50c multi	.55	.45
731	A249	$1 multi	1.10	1.50
		Nos. 728-731 (4)	2.55	2.85

Souvenir Sheet

732	A249	$2 multi	5.00	5.00

Tenaga Nasional, 50th Anniv. — A250

Designs: 30c, Power station at night. 50c, High tension wire towers, control room. No. 735, Kuala Lumpur at night.
No. 736, Van, vert. No. 737, High tension wire towers, vert.

Perf. 14¼x14½
1999, Sept. 9   Litho.   Unwmk.

733	A250	30c multicolored	.40	.30
734	A250	50c multicolored	.55	.35
735	A250	$1 multicolored	1.05	1.50
		Nos. 733-735 (3)	2.00	2.15

Souvenir Sheets
Perf. 13½x13¾

736	A250	$1 multicolored	1.00	1.25
737	A250	$1 multicolored	1.00	1.25

National Theater — A251

Various performers and views of building.

1999   Litho.   Wmk. 388   Perf. 12¼
Panel Colors

738	A251	30c red	.35	.30
739	A251	50c green	.45	.40
740	A251	$1 violet	.80	1.10
		Nos. 738-740 (3)	1.60	1.80

Installation of 11th Yang Di-Pertuan Agong (Head of State) — A252

Tuanku Salehuddin Abdul Aziz Shah ibni al-Marhum Hisamuddin Alam Shah and: 30c, Flag. 50c, Old building. $1, Modern building.
No. 744: a, Purple background. b, Yellow background. c, Blue background.

Perf. 13¾x13½
1999, Sept. 23   Litho.   Wmk. 388

741	A252	30c multicolored	.30	.25

Perf. 14¼

742	A252	50c multicolored	.40	.30
743	A252	$1 multicolored	.80	1.00

Perf. 14x13¾

744	A252	30c Strip of 3, #a.-c.	2.00	2.40
		Nos. 741-744 (4)	3.50	3.95

Size of Nos. 744a-744c: 24x30mm.

21st World Road Congress A253

Unwmk.
1999, Oct. 3   Litho.   Perf. 12

745	A253	30c Entrance ramp	.30	.30
746	A253	50c Bridge	.45	.35
747	A253	$1 Interchange	.90	1.10
		Nos. 745-747 (3)	1.65	1.75

A254

1999 Malaysia Grand Prix A255

Racing helmets and: 20c, Canopy over track's stands. 30c, Stands. 50c, Car on track. $1, side view of car.
No. 752: a, 20c, Stands b, 30c, Race control building. c, 50c, Pits. d, $1, Track.

Unwmk.
1999, Oct. 16   Litho.   Perf. 12

748	A254	20c multi	.40	.35
749	A254	30c multi	.40	.35
750	A254	50c multi	.50	.45
751	A254	$1 multi	.90	1.10
		Nos. 748-751 (4)	2.20	2.25

Perf. 12½

752	A255	Strip or block of 4, #a.-d.	2.50	2.75

No. 752 printed in sheets of 16 stamps.

UPU, 125th Anniv. — A256

Designs: 20c, Computer, envelopes. 30c, Globe, stamps. 50c, World map, airplane. $1, Malaysian Post Office emblem.

Perf. 13¾x13½
1999, Dec. 18   Litho.   Wmk. 388

753	A256	20c multi	.40	.40
754	A256	30c multi	.40	.40

Perf. 14¼

755	A256	50c multi	.50	.50
756	A256	$1 multi	.90	1.30
		Nos. 753-756 (4)	2.20	2.60

Sultan of Pahang, 25th Anniv. of Reign — A257

Sultan and: a, Flowers. b, Butterfly, flower, highway. c, Divers, beach. d, Automobile plant. e, Palace.

Wmk. 388
1999, Oct. 23   Litho.   Perf. 14¼

757	A257	30c Strip of 5, #a.-e.	2.50	2.50

Malaysia '99 World Cup Golf Tournament — A258

20c, World Cup. 30c, Ball on tee. 50c, Fairway and green. $1, Clubhouse and flag.

Perf. 14x13¾ Syncopated
1999, Nov. 18

758	A258	20c multi	.40	.40
759	A258	30c multi	.40	.40
760	A258	50c multi	.45	.45
761	A258	$1 multi	.90	1.25
a.		Sheet, 5 each #758-761	10.00	10.00
		Nos. 758-761 (4)	2.15	2.50

Flowers — A259

No. 762: a, Strelitzia augusta. b, Heliconia rostrata. c, Heliconia psittacorum (yellow petals). d, Heliconia stricta. e, Musa violescens. f, Strelitzia reginae. g, Heliconia colgantea. h, Heliconia psittacorum (pink and blue petals). i, Heliconia latispatha. j, Phaoemeria speciosa.

1999, Nov. 29   Wmk. 388   Perf. 12¼

762	A259	30c Block or strip of 10, #a.-j.	5.00	5.00
k.		Sheet, 2 blocks #762	10.00	10.00

Millennium — A260

Stamp number in parentheses.
No. 763: a, Vine, bird (1). b, Pottery, waterfall (2). c, Frog, forest (3). d, People and machine, cultivated land (4). e, Fish, boat and lighthouse (5). f, Chevrotain, house (6). g, Elephant, forest (7). h, Dagger, ship (8). i, Clock tower, archway (9). j, Boat with sail, palm trees (10).
No. 764: a, Man with musical instrument, native people (11). b, Lantern and nautilus shell, native people (12). c, Doctor and patient, native people (13). d, Badminton player, native people (14). e, Dancer, native women (15). f, Motorcycle, automobile and highway (16). g, Butterfly, race car, airplane and tower (17). h, Train, satellite and city buildings (18). i, Computer operator, mosque (19). j, Truck, ship (20).
No. 765, $1, Sailing ship, horiz. No. 766, $1, Airplane, horiz.

1999-2000   Perf. 12¾x12½

763	A260	30c Block of 10, #a.-j.	5.50	5.00
k.		Sheet of 2 #763	11.00	11.00
764	A260	30c Block or strip of 10, #a.-j.	5.50	5.00
k.		Sheet, 2 #764 blocks	11.00	11.00

Perf. 12½x12¾
Wmk. 388

765-766	A260	Set of 2	5.50	5.50

Issued: No. 763, 12/31/99; No. 764, 1/1/00. No. 765, 12/31/99; No. 766, 1/1/00.

Fruit Type of 1986 Redrawn With "Sen" Instead of "C" and "RM" Instead of "$"

Perf. 13¾x14
2002-04   Litho.   Wmk. 388

766A	A125	40sen Like #329	6.00	6.00
766B	A125	50sen Like #330	6.00	6.00
766D	A125	1r Like #332 ('04)	—	—
766E	A126	2r Like #333 ('04)	—	—
766G	A126	10r Like #335	6.00	6.00
766H	A126	20r Like #336	6.00	6.00

New Year 2000 (Year of the Dragon) A261

No. 767 — Artifacts depicting dragons from: a, New stone age. b, 100 B.C. c, 800. d, 200 B.C. e, 700.
No. 768 — Fish: a, Osteoglossum bicirrhosum. b, Scleropages leichardti. c, Scleropages formosus (Prussian blue background). d, Osteoglossum ferreirai. e, Scleropages formosus (bister background).
No. 768G, Dragon on boat prow (square orientation). No. 768H, Dragon in parade (square orientation).

Wmk. 388
2000, Jan. 6   Litho.   Perf. 13¼

767	A261	30c Strip of 5, #a.-e.	2.25	2.25
f.		Sheet, 4 #767	9.00	9.00
768	A261	30c Strip of 5, #a.-e.	2.25	2.25
f.		Sheet, 4 #768	9.00	9.00

Souvenir Sheets

768G	A261	$1 multi	1.50	1.50
768H	A261	$1 multi	1.50	1.50

Dawei 2000 World Team Table Tennis Championships A262

30c, Paddles, globe. 50c, Tiger mascot playing table tennis. No. 771, Paddles, ball.
No. 772: a, Mascot, table and net. b, Paddles and table.

2000, Feb. 19   Perf. 13½

769	A262	30c multi	.35	.35
770	A262	50c multi	.35	.35
771	A262	$1 multi	.85	.95
		Nos. 769-771 (3)	1.55	1.65

Souvenir Sheet
Perf. 14¼

772	A262	$1 Sheet, #a.-b.	1.75	1.75

Souvenir Sheets

Millennium — A263

No. 773, Man, sailboat.
No. 774: a, Mt. Everest climbers with Malaysian flag. b, People with backpacks. c, Parachutist, people with flag, automobile.

2000, Feb. 26   Wmk. 388   Perf. 12

773	A263	50c Sheet of 1	.80	.80
774	A263	50c Sheet of 3, #a.-c.	2.50	2.50

2nd Global Knowledge Conference — A264

No. 775: a, Finger pointing. b, Eye, globe.
No. 776: a, Head facing right. b, Head facing left.

MALAYSIA

2000, Mar. 7   *Perf. 13½*
775   A264   30c Pair, a.-b., + central label   .90   .90
Perf. 14x14¼
776   A264   50c Pair, a.-b., + central label   1.30   1.30

Islamic Arts Museum, Kuala Lumpur — A265

20c, Inverted dome. 30c, Main dome. No. 778A, Like No. 778 but with central design element entirely in gold. 50c, Ottoman panel. $1, Art of the mosque.

Perf. 13¾x13½ Syncopated
2000, Apr. 6   Wmk. 388
777   A265   20c multi   .40   .40
778   A265   30c multi   .40   .40
778A   A265   30c multi   .40   .40
779   A265   50c multi   .50   .40
780   A265 $1 multi   1.00   1.40
    Nos. 777-780 (5)   2.70   3.00

Boats A266

No. 781: a, Perahu Buatan Barat. b, Perahu Payang (red and blue). c, Perahu Burung. d, Perahu Payang (red, white and green).

Perf. 14x13½
2000, Apr. 15   Litho.   Wmk. 388
781   A266   Block of 4   2.00   2.00
  a.-d.   30c Any single   .30   .30
  e.   Booklet pane, 5 each #a-d   10.50
   Complete booklet, #781e   10.50

Unit Trust Investment Week — A267

30c, Emblem, women with flags. 50c, People, Kuala Lumpur skyline. $1, People, globe.

Perf. 13½x13¾
2000, Apr. 20   Litho.   Unwmk.
782   A267   30c multi   .45   .45
783   A267   50c multi   .60   .45
784   A267 $1 multi   1.10   1.40
   Nos. 782-784 (3)   2.15   2.30

Thomas and Uber Cup Badminton Championships A268

No. 785: a, Male player. b, Flags, Thomas Cup (with handles). c, Mascot. d, Flags, Uber Cup. e, Female player.
$1, Thomas Cup, vert.

Perf. 12½x12¾
2000, May 11   Wmk. 388
785   Horiz. strip of 5   2.00   2.00
  a.-e.   A268 30c Any single   .30   .30
Souvenir Sheet
Perf. 12¾x12½x12x12½
786   A268 $1 multi   2.00   2.25
No. 785 printed in sheets of 10 strips and ten labels.

Children's Games — A269

No. 787: a, Hopscotch. b, Tarik Upih. c, Kite flying. d, Marbles. e, Hoops and sticks.

2000, June 24   *Perf. 13½x13¾*
787   Horiz. strip of 5   3.75   3.75
  a.-e.   A269 30c Any single   .50   .50
  f.   Miniature sheet, 4 #787   16.50   16.00

Islamic Conference of Foreign Ministers, 27th Session — A270

No. 788: a, Red globe, electronic circuitry. b, Blue globe, Islamic design. c, Emblem, flower, butterfly. d, Green globe, Islamic design, diff. e, Purple globe, pens.

2000, June 26   *Perf. 13¾x13½*
788   Horiz. strip of 5   2.00   2.00
  a.-e.   A270 30c Any single   .25   .25

National Census — A271

No. 789: a, Family, map. b, Family in house, appliances. c, People on pie chart. d, Map, diplomas, mortarboard, workers. e, Male and female symbols.

2000, July 5   *Perf. 14¼*
789   Horiz. strip of 5   2.25   2.25
  a.-e.   A271 30c Any single   .25   .25

Birds — A272

Designs: 20c, Polyplectron inopinatum. 30c, Rheinardia ocellata. 50c, Argisianus argus. $1, Lophura erythropthalma. $2, Rheinardia ocellata, diff.

2000, July 22   *Perf. 13x13¼*
790   A272   20c multi   .55   .55
791   A272   30c multi   .55   .55
  a.   Sheet of 20   20.00
792   A272   50c multi   .70   .55
793   A272 $1 multi   1.50   1.50
   Nos. 790-793 (4)   3.30   3.15
Souvenir Sheet
Perf. 13¾x14
794   A272 $2 multi   3.00   3.00
No. 794 contains one 32x27mm stamp.

Intl. Union of Forestry Research World Congress — A274

No. 795: a, Shorea macrophylla. b, Dyera costulata. c, Alstonia angustiloba. d, Hopea odorata. e, Adenanthera pavonina.

No. 796 — Trees, 10c: a, Fagraea fragrans. b, Dryobalanops aromatica. c, Terminalia catappa. d, Samanea saman. e, Dracontomelon dao.
No. 797 — Leaves, 15c: a, Heritiera javanica. b, Johannesteijsmannia altifrons. c, Macaranga gigantea. d, Licuala grandis. e, Endospermum diadenum.
No. 798 — Tree barks, 25c: a, Pterocymbium javanicum. b, Dryobalanops aromatica. c, Dipterocarpus costulatus. d, Shorea leprosula. e, Ochanostachys amentacea.
No. 799 — Fauna, 50c: a, Muscicapa indigo. b, Nycticebus coucang. c, Felis marmorata. d, Cyprinus carpio. e, Trimeresurus wagleri.
Illustration A274 reduced.

             Wmk. 388
2000, Aug. 7   Litho.   *Perf. 12*
795   Horiz. strip of 5   3.75   3.75
  a.-e.   A273 30c Any single   .70   .70
  f.   Sheet of 4 each #a-e   15.00   15.00
Sheets of 5, #a-e, + label
796-799   A274   Set of 4   8.00   8.00

Medical Research Institute, Cent. — A275

Designs: 30c, Institute in 1901, Brugia malayi, Beri-beri. 50c, Institute in 1953, Clostridium bifermentans malaysia, Anophelese campestris. $1, Institute in 1976, chromatograph of DNA sequence, Eurycoma longifolia.

Perf. 13¾x13½, 14¼ (50c, $1, $2)
2000, Aug. 24   Unwmk.
800-802   A275   Set of 3   2.25   1.25
Souvenir Sheet
Wmk. 388
803   A275 $2 Molecular model   2.40   2.40

Protected Mammals — A276

Designs: 20c, Cynogale bennettii (mouth open). No. 805, 30c, Cynogale bennettii (mouth closed). 50c, Arctictis binturong. $1, Arctictis binturong, diff.
No. 808: a, Hemigalus hosei. b, Paradoxurus hermaphroditus. c, Paguma larvata. d, Viverra tangalunga. e, Arctogalidia trivirgata.
No. 809: a, Hemigalus derbyanus. b, Prionodon linsang.

2000, Aug. 26   Wmk. 388   *Perf. 13¼*
804-807   A276   Set of 4   1.10   .55
808   Horiz. strip of 5   1.50   1.50
  a.-e.   A276 30c Any single   .25   .25
Souvenir Sheet
809   A276 $1 Sheet of 2, #a-b   2.75   2.75

Rural and Industrial Development Authority, Trust Council for Indigenous People, 50th Anniv. — A277

Designs: 30c, Gear wheels. 50c, Compass, stethoscope. $1, Computer mouse and diskette.

2000, Sept. 14   *Perf. 14¼*
810-812   A277   Set of 3   2.25   2.25
  810a   Sheet of 20   2.50   2.50

Children's Games — A278

No. 813, 20c: a, Gasing. b, Baling tin.
No. 814, 30c: a, Letup-letup. b, Sepak raga.

Perf. 14¼, 13¾x13½ (#814)
2000, Sept. 16
Horiz. Pairs, #a-b
813-814   A278   Set of 2   2.10   1.25

World Heart Day — A279

No. 815: a, People walking, cyclist. b, People jumping rope, playing with hula hoop and ball. c, Boy flying kite, children playing soccer. d, People exercising. e, Man gardening.

2000, Sept. 24   *Perf. 12¼*
815   Horiz. strip of 5   2.10   1.25
  a.-e.   A279 30c Any single   .25   .25

Rhododendrons — A280

No. 816: a, Brookeanum. b, Jasminiflorum. c, Scortechinii. d, Pauciflorum.
No. 817: a, Crassifloium. b, Longiflorum. c, Javanicum. d, Variolosum. e, Acuminatum. f, Praetervisum. g, Himantodes. h, Maxwellii. i, Erocoides. j, Fallacinum.
$1, Malayanum.

2000, Oct. 9
816   A280   30c Block of 4, #a-d   1.40   .80
817   A280   30c Block of 10, #a-j   3.00   1.50
Souvenir Sheet
818   A280 $1 multi   1.60   1.60

Dragonflies and Damselflies — A282

No. 819: a, Vestalis gracilis. b, Crocothemis s. servilia male. c, Trithemis aurora. d, Pseudothemis jorina. e, Diplacodes nebulosa. f, Crocothemis s. servilia female. g, Neurobasis c. chinensis male. h, Burmagomphus divaricatus. i, Ictinogomphus d. melanops. j, Orthetrum testaceum. k, Trithemis festiva. l, Drachythemis contaminata. m, Neurobasis c. chinensis female. n, Neurothemis fluctuans. o, Acisoma panorpoides. p, Orthetrum s. sabina. q, Rhyothemis p. phyllis. r, Rhyothemis obsolescens. s, Neurothemis t. tulia. t, Lathrecista a. asiatica. u, Aethriamanta gracilis. v, Diplacodes trivialis. w, Neurothemis fulvia. x, Rhyothemis triangularis. y, Orthetrum glaucum.
No. 820: a, Neurobasis c. chinensis. b, Aristocypha fenestrella (with blue sky). c, Vestalis gracilis. d, Nannophya pymaea. e, Aristocypha fenestrella (no sky). f, Rhyothemis p. phyllis. g, Crocothemis s. servilia. h, Euphaea ochracea male. i, Euphaea ochracea female. j, Ceriagrion cerinorubellum.

2000, Nov. 25   *Perf. 14¼x13¾ Sync.*
819   A281   Sheet of 25   11.50   11.50
  a.-y.   (30c) Any single   .30   .30

MALAYSIA

Booklet Stamps
Perf. 13½x14 Syncopated
820	Block of 10	5.25	5.25
a.-j.	A282 30c Any single	.30	.30
k.	Booklet pane, 2 #820	10.50	
	Booklet, #820k	10.50	

Quails and Partridges — A283

Designs: 30c, Coturnix chinensis. 50c, Arborophila campbelli. $1, Turnix suscitator.
No. 824: a, Arborophila charltonii. b, Haematortyx sanguiniceps.

Wmk. 388, Unwmkd. (#822-823)
Perf. 13¾x13½, 14¼ (30c)
2001, Jan. 22   Litho.
821-823	A283	Set of 3	3.50	3.50

Souvenir Sheet
Perf. 14¼x14¼x13¾x14¼
824	A283	$2 Sheet of 2, #a-b	4.75	4.75

Creation of Putrajaya Federal Territory — A284

Designs: 30c, Perdana Putra Building (Prime Minister's office building). $1, Perdana Putra Building, highway, government office buildings.

Perf. 13¾x13½, 14¼ ($1)
2001, Feb. 1   Litho.   Wmk. 388
825-826	A284	Set of 2	3.25	1.60

Sabah and Sarawak Beads A285

No. 827: a, Pinakol. b, Mareik Empang. c, Glass beads. d, Orot.

Wmk. 388
2001, Feb. 17   Litho.   Perf. 13¾
827	A285	30c Block of 4, #a-d	2.40	1.25

Flowers — A286

Designs: 30c, Cananga odorata. 50c, Mimusops elengi. $1, Mesua ferrea. $2, Michelia champaca.

2001, Mar. 27   Perf. 13¾, 14¼ ($1)
828-830	A286	Set of 3	3.25	1.60

Souvenir Sheet
Perf. 13¾x14¼x13¾x13¾
831	A286	$2 multi	3.25	3.25

Cultural Items A287

No. 832, 30c: a, Sireh Junjung. b, Penggendong Anak.
No. 833, 50c: a, Jebak Puyuh. b, Bekas Bara.

2001, June 11   Perf. 13¾
Horiz. pairs, #a-b
832-833	A287	Set of 2	2.75	1.25

Automobiles A288

No. 834: a, 1995 Perodua Kancil. b, 1995 Proton Tiara. c, 1995 Perodua Rusa. d, 1997 Proton Putra. e, 1999 Inokom Permas. f, 1999 Perodua Kembara. g, 2000 Proton GTi. h, 2000 TD2000. i, 2000 Perodua Kenari. j, 2000 Proton Waja.

2001, July 9
834	Block of 10	6.25	2.75
a.-j.	A288 30c Any single	.30	.30
	Booklet, #834	6.25	

Bantams — A289

Designs: 30c, Ayam Serama. 50c, Ayam Kapan. $1, Ayam Serama and chicks. $3, Ayam Hutan, horiz.

Perf. 12¾x12½, 12 (50c)
2001, Aug. 1
835-837	A289	Set of 3	2.75	1.25

Souvenir Sheet
Perf. 12½
838	A289	$3 multi	5.25	5.25
a.	As #838, with PhilaNippon '01 Emblem in margin	—	—

No. 838 contains one 45x35mm stamp.

21st South East Asia Games — A290

Designs: 20c, Diving. 30c, Gymnastics. 50c, Bowling. $1, Weight lifting. $2, Cycling. $5, Running.

2001, Sept. 8   Perf. 13½x13¾
839-843	A290	Set of 5	4.75	2.25

Souvenir Sheet
844	A290	$5 multi	6.75	6.75

2001 World Dental Federation Congress — A291

2001, Sept. 27   Perf. 14¼
845	A291	$1 multi	2.10	1.00

Employees' Provident Fund, 50th Anniv. — A292

Designs: 30c, Headquarters. 50c, Bar graph. $1, Emblem, man and woman.

Perf. 14¼, 13¾x13½ ($1)
2001, Oct. 1
846-848	A292	Set of 3	2.75	1.25

Forestry Dept., Cent. — A293

Designs: 30c, Satellite, map, trees. 50c, Trees, leaf. $1, Seedlings and forest.

2001, Nov. 10   Perf. 14¼
849-851	A293	Set of 3	2.75	2.00

Stamp Week — A294

Marine life: 20c, Tridacna gigas. 30c, Hippocampus sp. 50c, Oreaster occidentalis. $1, Cassis cornuta. $3, Dugong dugon.

2001, Nov. 10   Perf. 13¾x13½
852-855	A294	Set of 4	3.00	1.75

Souvenir Sheet
Perf. 14¼
856	A294	$3 multi	3.25	3.25

No. 856 exists imperf. with a slightly larger, numbered margin. Value $5.

2002 KL Field Hockey World Cup — A295

Designs: 30c, Player with ball. 50c, Goaltender. $1, Player with ball, diff. $3, Player, stadium playing field.

Perf. 13½x13¾
2002, Jan. 2   Wmk. 388
857-859	A295	Set of 3	3.00	1.75

Souvenir Sheet
Perf. 12¾x12½x12x12½
860	A295	$3 multi	3.25	3.25

No. 860 exists imperf. with a numbered margin.

Flowers — A296

Designs: 30c, Couroupita guianensis. No. 862, $1, Camellia nitidissima. No. 863, $1, Couroupita guianensis, diff. No. 864: a, Schima brevifolia, horiz. b, Schima brevifolia.

2002, Feb. 5   Wmk. 380   Perf. 12¾
861-863	A296	Set of 3	2.75	1.40

Souvenir Sheet
864	A296	$2 Sheet of 2, #a-b	3.25	3.25

See People's Republic of China No. 3180.

Snakes — A297

Designs: No. 865, 30c, Gonyophis margaritatus. No. 866, 30c, Python reticulatus. 50c, Bungarus candidus. $1, Maticora bivirgata.
No. 869: a, Ophiophagus hannah (brown). b, Ophiophagus hannah (black and white striped).

2002, Mar. 5   Wmk. 388   Perf. 14¼
865-868	A297	Set of 4	3.75	1.75

Souvenir Sheet
Perf. 13¼
869	A297	$2 Sheet of 2, #a-b	4.00	4.00

Nos. 865-868 were each printed in sheets of 20 + 5 labels. No. 869 exists imperf. Value $5.

Express Rail Link — A298

Designs: 30c, Kuala Lumpur Central Station.

No. 871: a, Train and station. b, Train, airplane and control tower.
No. 872: a, Train with red violet stripe, train with red stripe. b, Yellow and blue train, train with blue, orange and red stripes.
$2, Train with red violet stripe.

2002, Apr. 13   Wmk. 388   Perf. 12
870	A298	30c multi	1.00	1.00
871	A298	50c Horiz. pair, #a-b	2.75	1.25

Souvenir Sheets
Perf. 12½x12¾
872	A298	$1 Sheet of 2, #a-b	2.75	2.75

Perf. 12½x12¾x12½x12
873	A298	$2 multi	2.75	2.75

17th World Orchid Congress — A299

No. 874: a, Paraphalenopsis labukensis. b, Renanthera bella.
50c, Paphiopedilum sanderianum.
No. 876: a, Coelogyne pandurata. b, Phalaenopsis amabilis.
$5, Cleisocentron merrillianum.

2002, Apr. 24   Wmk. 380   Perf. 12¾
874	A299	30c Horiz. pair, #a-b	1.40	.80
875	A299	50c multi	1.10	.80
876	A299	$1 Horiz. pair, #a-b	3.50	1.25
	Nos. 874-876 (3)		6.00	2.85

Souvenir Sheet
Perf. 13
Unwmk.
877	A299	$5 multi	7.00	7.00

No. 877 contains one 45x40mm stamp and exists imperf.

Installation of 12th Yang Di-Pertuan Agong — A300

Yang Di-Pertuan Agongs — A301

Background colors: 30c, Green. 50c, Red violet. $1, Yellow.
No. 881 — Ordinal number of Yang Di-Pertuan Agong: a, 1st. b, 2nd. c, 3rd. d, 4th. e, 5th. f, 6th. g, 7th. h, 8th. i, 9th. j, 10th. k, 11th. l, 12th.

2002, Apr. 25   Wmk. 380   Perf. 12¾
878-880	A300	Set of 3	3.50	3.50

Miniature Sheet
881	A301	$1 Sheet of 12, #a-l	5.25	5.25

Aquatic Plants — A302

Designs: 30c, Cryptocoryne purpurea. 50c, Barclaya kunstleri.
No. 884: a, Neptunia oleracea. b, Monochoria hastata.
No. 885: a, $1, Eichhornia crassipes, vert. b, $2, Nymphaea pubescens.

Perf. 12, 12½x12¾ (#884)
2002, May 11   Wmk. 388
882	A302	30c multi	.60	.60
883	A302	50c multi	1.00	.60
884	A302	$1 Horiz. pair, #a-b	3.50	3.25
	Nos. 882-884 (3)		5.10	4.45

MALAYSIA

Souvenir Sheet
Perf. 12¾x12½x12x12½, 12 (#885b)
885 A302 Sheet of 2, #a-b 7.00 7.00

Tropical Birds — A303

No. 886, 30c: a, Dryocopus javensis. b, Oriolus chinensis.
No. 887, $1: a, Anthreptes rhodolaema. b, Irena puella.
$5, Dicaeum trigonostigma.

2002, June 27   *Perf. 12¾x12½*
Horiz. Pairs, #a-b
886-887 A303 Set of 2 6.00 3.00
Souvenir Sheet
Perf. 12¾x12½x12x12½
888 A303 $5 multi 7.75 7.75
No. 888 contains one 60x40mm stamp.
See Singapore Nos. 1014-1017.

Islands and Beaches — A304

No. 889, 30c: a, Pulau Sibu, Johore. b, Pulau Perhentian, Trengganu.
No. 890, 50c: a, Pulau Manukan, Sabah. b, Pulau Tioman, Pahang.
No. 891, $1: a, Pulau Singa Besar, Kedah. b, Pulau Pangkor, Perak.
No. 892: a, Batu Ferringhi, Penang. b, Port Dickson, Negri Sembilan.

      Wmk. 380
2002, July 31   Litho.   *Pert. 12¾*
Horiz. Pairs, #a-b
889-891 A304 Set of 3 6.50 3.25
Souvenir Sheet
892 A304 $1 Sheet of 2, #a-b 4.25 2.00

Malaysian Unity — A305

No. 893: a, Musicians. b, Children at play.
50c, Seven people (80x29mm).
$2, People pulling rope.

      Wmk. 380
2002, Aug. 24   Litho.   *Perf. 12¾*
893 A305 30c Horiz. pair, #a-b 1.40 .80
894 A305 50c multi 1.00 .80
Souvenir Sheet
895 A305 $2 multi 3.00 1.50

Zainal Abidin bin Ahmad (1895-1973), Academic — A306

Abidin bin Ahmad: 00c, And blackboard.
No. 897: a, And typewriter. b, And building.
$1, In library, vert.

      Perf. 13½x13¼
2002, Sept. 17   **Wmk. 388**
896 A306 30c multi .75 .75
897 A306 50c Horiz. pair, #a-b 2.00 1.40
Souvenir Sheet
Perf. 13¼x13½
898 A306 $1 multi 2.75 1.40

Clothing — A307

Designs: No. 899, 30c, Green blouse. No. 900, 30c, Red blouse. No. 901, 50c, Yellow blouse. No. 902, 50c, Red blouse, diff.
$2, Blouse and skirt.

   Perf. 12¾ (30c), 12¾x13¼ (50c)
2002, Nov. 2
899-902 A307 Set of 4 3.50 1.60
Souvenir Sheet
903 A307 $2 multi 3.50 1.60
No. 903 contains one 35x70mm stamp.

Sultan Idris University, 80th Anniv. — A308

Designs: 30c, Suluh Budiman Building.
No. 905: a, Tadahan Selatan. b, Chancellory Building.

2002, Nov. 29   *Perf. 12x12x13½x12*
904 A308 30c multi .70 .70
  a. Perf. 12 .30 .30
    Perf. 12
905 A308 50c Horiz. pair, #a-b 2.60 1.10
  c. As "a", perf. 12x13½x12 .40 .25
  d. As "b", perf. 12x12x10½x12 .40 .25
  e. Pair, #905c-905d .85 .40
  f. As "a", perf. 13½ — —
  g. As "b", perf. 13½ — —

Wild and Tame Animals — A309

No. 906, 30c: a, Felis bengalensis. b, Felis catus.
No. 907, $1: a, Cacatua sulphurea. b, Ketupa ketupu.
No. 908, $1: a, Ratufa affinis. b, Oryctolagus cuniculus.
No. 909, $1, horiz.: a, Carassius auratus. b, Diodon liturosus.

2002, Dec. 17   *Perf. 12½*
Horiz. pairs, #a-b
906-907 A309 Set of 2 5.50 2.75
Souvenir Sheets of 2, #a-b
Perf. 13½x12x13¼x13½, 13½x13½x12x13¼ (#909)
908-909 A309 Set of 2 6.50 3.25
Stamp Week.

Endangered Animals — A310

Southorn cerow: 30c, Head.
No. 911: a, Serow laying down. b, Serow walking.

2003, Jan. 25   *Perf. 12¾x12½*
910 A310 30c multi .75 .75
911 A310 50c Horiz. pair, #a-b 2.25 1.00

13th Conference of Heads of State or Government of Non-Aligned Countries — A311

No. 912, 30c — Malaysian flag, world map, conference emblem and: a, Doves, years of previous conferences (1961-1979). b, Hands, years of conferences (1983-2003).
No. 913, 50c — Globe, conference emblem and: a, Map of Malaysia. b, Dove, "2003," Malaysian flag.

2003, Feb. 6   *Perf. 12½x12¾*
Horiz. pairs, #a-b
912-913 A311 Set of 2 3.00 1.50

Roses — A312

Designs: No. 914, Pink Rosa hybrida. No. 915, Red Rosa hybrida.
No. 916: a, Yellow Rosa hybrida. b, Floribunda.
No. 917: a, 1r, Floribunda miniature (29x40mm). b, 2r, Rosa centifolia (29x81mm).

      Wmk. 380
2003, Feb. 22   Litho.   *Perf. 13¾*
914 A312 30c shown .60 .50
915 A312 30c multi .60 .50
916 A312 50c Horiz. pair, #a-b 1.75 1.00
  Nos. 914-916 (3) 2.95 2.00
Souvenir Sheet
Perf. 12¾
917 A312 Sheet of 2, #a-b 3.25 1.60
Nos. 914-917 are impregnated with a rose scent.

Tunku Abdul Rahman Putra Al-Haj (1903-90), Prime Minister — A313

Designs: 30c, Wearing brown hat. 50c, Wearing suit and tie.
No. 920: a, Wearing dark robe. b, Wearing light robe.
No. 921, With arm raised.

      Perf. 12¾x12½
2003, Mar. 4   **Wmk. 388**
918 A313 30c multi .50 .50
919 A313 50c multi .60 .50
920 A313 $1 Horiz. pair, #a-b 2.75 1.40
  Nos. 918-920 (3) 3.85 2.40
Souvenir Sheet
Perf. 13½
921 A313 $1 multi 2.50 1.25

Fighting Fish — A314

Designs: 30c, Red and blue Betta splendens. No. 923, Yellow Betta splendens.
No. 924: a, Blue Betta splendens. b, Red Betta splendens.
No. 925: a, Betta imbellis. b, Betta coccina.

   Perf. 12½x12¾, 13½x13¼ (#923)
2003, Apr. 20
922 A314 30c multi .65 .55
923 A314 50c multi .80 .55
924 A314 $1 Horiz. pair, #a-b 3.50 1.75
  Nos. 922-924 (3) 4.95 2.85
Souvenir Sheet
Perf. 13½x13¾ Syncopated
925 A314 50c Sheet of 2, #a-b 3.00 1.40
No. 925 contains two 33x28mm stamps.

Clock Towers — A315

Designs: No. 926, 30c, Malacca, 1050. No. 927, 30c, Penang, 1897. No. 928, 30c, Sungai Petani, 1936. No. 929, 30c, Teluk Intan, 1885. No. 930, 30c, Sarawak State Council Monument, 1967.
No. 931: a, Sultan Abdul Samad Building, 1897. b, Taiping Clock Tower, Perak, 1881.

2003, May 24   *Perf. 12¾x12½*
926-930 A315 Set of 5 2.75 1.25
  930a Booklet pane, 2 each #926-930 6.00
  Complete booklet, #930a 6.00

Souvenir Sheet
Perf. 12x12½x12¾x12½
931 A315 $1 Sheet of 2, #a-b 2.75 1.50

Beaches and Islands — A316

No. 932, 30c: a, Beach, Ligitan Island, Sabah. b, Map of Ligitan Island.
No. 933, 50c: a, Beach, Sipadan Island, Sabah. b, Map of Sipadan Island.
No. 934, vert.: a, Aerial view of Sipadan Island. b, Map of Ligitan Island.

Litho. (#932a-934a), Litho. & Embossed (#932b-934b)
2003, June 28   **Wmk. 380**   *Perf. 13¼*
Horiz. Pairs, #a-b
932-933 A316 Set of 2 2.75 1.25
Souvenir Sheet
Perf. 12¾
934 A316 50c Sheet of 2, #a-b 2.75 1.25

Independence, 46th Anniv. — A317

Designs: 30c, Flag and clock tower. No. 936, $1, Flag (59x40mm).
No. 937, Tunku Abdul Rahman Putra in motorcade, horiz.

2003, Aug. 19   Litho.   *Perf. 12¾*
935-936 A317 Set of 2 2.75 1.25
Souvenir Sheet
937 A317 $1 black 2.75 1.25
No. 937 contains one 59x40mm stamp.

Motorcycles and Scooters Made in Malaysia — A318

Designs: 30c, Modenas Jaguh 175.
No. 939: a, Modenas Kriss 2. b, Modenas Kriss SG.
No. 940: a, Modenas Karisma 125. b, Modenas Kriss 1.
No. 941, $1: a, Comel Turbulence RG125. b, Comel Cyclone GP150.
No. 942, $1: a, MZ 125SM. b, MZ Perintis 1205 Classic.
No. 943, $1: a, Caviga Momos 125R. b, Nitro NE150 Windstar.
No. 944, $1: a, Demak Adventurer. b, Demak Beetle.

2003, Aug. 27   *Perf. 12¾*
938 A318 30c multi .75 .75
939 A318 50c Horiz. pair, #a-b 2.00 .85
940 A318 50c Horiz. pair, #a-b 2.00 .85
  Nos. 938-940 (3) 4.75 2.45
Souvenir Sheets of 2, #a-b
941-944 A318 Set of 4 8.25 4.00
See Nos. 950-952.

10th Islamic Summit Conference — A319

No. 945, 30c: a, Putrajaya Convention Center. b, Arabic text.
No. 946, 50c: a, Mosque at left, field of flag. b, Mosque at right, flag stripes.

2003, Oct. 3   *Perf. 12¾*
Horiz. Pairs, #a-b
945-946 A319 Set of 2 3.00 1.50

MALAYSIA

50th World Children's Day — A320

Designs: 20c, World map, children in ring.
No. 948: a, Family, house, car, flag. b, Children with kite, graduate, man at computer, rocket, airplane.
No. 949: a, Text. b, Book, school, flag, kite, rainbow, soccer ball, automobile and flower.

2003, Oct. 11   Perf. 13½x13¼   **Wmk. 388**
947 A320   20c multi   .75   .75
   a.   Perf. 12½x12¾   .30   .30

Perf. 12
948 A320   30c Horiz. pair, #a-b   1.75   1.10
   c.   As "a," perf. 12½x12¾   .35   .35
   d.   As "b," perf. 12½x12¾   .35   .35
949 A320   30c Horiz. pair, #a-b   1.75   1.10
   c.   As "a," perf. 12½x12¾   .35   .35
   d.   As "b" perf. 12½x12¾   .35   .35
   e.   Booklet pane 2 each #947a, 948c, 948d, 949c, 949d   2.75
     Complete booklet, #949e   2.75

Nos. 938-940 with Bangkok 2003 Emblem Added at Upper Right

Wmk. 380
2003, Oct. 4   Litho.   **Perf. 12¾**
950 A318   30c Like #938   .70   .50
951 A318   50c Like #939, horiz. pair, #a-b   1.75   .85
952 A318   50c Like #940, horiz. pair, #a-b   1.75   .85
   Nos. 950-952 (3)   4.20   2.20

Monkeys — A321

Designs: No. 953, Red leaf monkey, tail above branch. No. 954, Red leaf monkey, tail below branch.
No. 955: a, Proboscis monkey sitting on branch. b, Proboscis monkey reaching for branch.

2003, Dec. 16
953 A321   30c multi   .60   .60
954 A321   30c multi   .60   .60
955 A321   50c Horiz. pair, #a-b   1.75   1.75
   Nos. 953-955 (3)   2.95   2.95

Lighthouses — A322

Designs: No. 956, 30c, Muka Head Lighthouse. No. 957, 30c, One Fathom Bank Lighthouse. No. 958, 30c, Althingsburg Lighthouse. No. 959, 30c, Pulau Undan Lighthouse. $1, Tanjung Tuan Lighthouse.

Perf. 12¾x12½
2004, Jan. 31   **Wmk. 388**
956-959 A322   Set of 4   3.00   1.40

Souvenir Sheet
Perf. 13½
960 A322 $1 multi   3.00   1.40

Convention on Biological Diversity — A323

Designs; 30c, Flora and fauna. No. 962, 50c, DNA molecule, leaf, laboratory equipment, model showing human organs. No. 963, 50c, Convention emblem, world map.

2004, Feb. 9   **Wmk. 380**   **Perf. 12¾**
961-963 A323   Set of 3   3.00   1.50

Commonwealth Tourism Ministers' Meeting — A324

Emblem and: 30c, World map, city skyline, golf ball. 50c, World map, rocky shoreline. $1, Malaysian tourist attractions, vert.

2004, Mar. 19
964-966 A324   Set of 3   3.25   1.60

National Service Program — A325

Designs: 30c, Emblem. 50c, Emblem, people on ropes. $1, Emblem, people with flag. $2, Emblem, man saluting.

2004, May 22   **Wmk. 380**   **Perf. 12¾**
967-969 A325   Set of 3   3.25   1.60

Souvenir Sheet
Perf. 13½
Wmk. 388
970 A325 $2 multi   3.25   1.60

Malaysia - People's Republic of China Diplomatic Relations, 30th Anniv. — A326

No. 971, 30c: a, Malaysian flag, ship. b, Chinese flag, ship.
No. 972, $1: a, Ship, handshake. b, Flags, ship, world map.
$2, Malaysian and Chinese buildings, horiz.

Perf. 12¾x12½
2004, May 31   **Wmk. 388**
     Horiz. pairs, #a-b
971-972 A326   Set of 2   3.25   1.60

Souvenir Sheet
973 A326 $2 multi   2.75   1.40
   a.   World Stamp Championship emblem added in margin in blue and black   2.75   1.40

No. 973 contains one 60x40mm stamp.
No. 973a issued 8/28.

Mammals — A327

No. 974, 30c: a, Bos javanicus. b, Bos gaurus.
No. 975, $1: a, Panthera tigris. b, Elephas maximusp.
$2, Tapirus indicus, vert.

Perf. 13½x13¼
2004, June 14   **Wmk. 388**
     Horiz. pairs, #a-b
974-975 A327   Set of 2   5.00   2.50

Souvenir Sheet
Perf. 12¾
Wmk. 380
976 A327 $2 multi   3.00   1.50
     See Nos. 1041-1045.

Multimedia Super Corridor — A328

Emblem and: 30c, MSC Building, flags. 50c, Globe, Petronas Towers, binary code. $1, Hand with identity card, people using computers, butterfly, cross-section of brain. $2, Map of Multimedia Super Corridor, vert.

     Horizontal Pairs
2004, July 11   **Wmk. 380**   **Perf. 12¾**
977-979 A328   Set of 3   1.75   .85

Souvenir Sheet
Perf. 12¾x12½
Wmk. 388
980 A328 $2 multi   2.50   1.25

Ports — A329

No. 981: a, Johore. b, Kota Kinabalu.
No. 982: a, Kuantan. b, Penang.
$1, Bintulu. $2, Northport.

12, 13½ (#983)
2004, July 24   **Wmk. 388**
981 A329   30c Horiz. pair, #a-b   1.20   .80
982 A329   50c Horiz. pair, #a-b   1.75   .75
983 A329 $1 multi   1.75   1.75
   Nos. 981-983 (3)   4.70   4.30

Souvenir Sheet
984 A329 $2 multi   2.75   1.40

Transportation A330

Designs: 30c, Trishaw. 50c, Rickshaw. $1, Padi horse.
$2, Bullock cart, vert.

Perf. 12, 13½x13¼ (1r)
2004, Aug. 18   Litho.   **Wmk. 388**
985-987 A330   Set of 3   2.10   1.00

Souvenir Sheet
Perf. 14
988 A330 $2 multi   2.75   1.40
   a.   Kuala Lumpur Stamp Show emblem in sheet margin   2.75   1.40

No. 988 contains one 40x50mm stamp and exists imperf.
No. 988a issued 9/3/04.

Matang Mangroves, Perak, Cent. — A331

No. 989, 30c: a, Monkey on mangrove tree root. b, Insect on plant.
No. 990, $1: a, Boat, shells. b, Birds, tree.
$2, Young trees.

2004, Oct. 4   **Wmk. 380**   **Perf. 12¾**
     Horiz. pairs, #a-b
989-990 A331   Set of 2   4.00   2.00

Souvenir Sheet
991 A331 $2 multi   2.25   1.10

Marine Life — A332

Designs: 30c, Humpback whale. 50c, Octopus. $1, Bottlenose dolphin.
$2, Thornback ray.

Wmk. 380
2004, Oct. 9   Litho.   **Perf. 12¾**
992-994 A332   Set of 3   2.75   1.40

Souvenir Sheet
995 A332 $2 multi   2.25   1.10
   a.   Stamp Week emblem in sheet margin   2.25   1.10

Medicinal Plants — A333

Designs: 30c, Eurycoma longifolia. 50c, Labisia pumila.
No. 998: a, Pithecellobium bubalinum benth. b, Alleurites moluccana.
$2, Ficus deltoidea jack.

Wmk. 380
2004, Dec. 11   Litho.   **Perf. 12¾**
996 A333   30c multi   .40   .25
997 A333   50c multi   .60   .30
998 A333 $1 Horiz. pair, #a-b   2.10   1.00
   Nos. 996-998 (3)   3.10   1.55

Souvenir Sheet
999 A333 $2 multi   2.50   1.25

Rare Rhododendrons A334

Designs: No. 1000, 30c, Rhododendron nervulosum. No. 1001, 30c, Rhododendron stenophyllum. 50c, Rhododendron rugosum. $1, Rhododendron stapfianum.
$2, Rhododendron lowii, horiz.

2005, Jan. 11   **Wmk. 380**   **Perf. 12¾**
1000-1003 A334   Set of 4   3.50   1.75

Souvenir Sheet
1004 A334 $2 multi   2.50   1.25

Fifth Minister's Forum on Infrastructure Development in the Asia-Pacific Region, Kuala Lumpur — A335

Emblems and: 30c, Kuala Lumpur skyline. 50c, Train and buildings. $1, Train station and airplane.

2005, Jan. 24   **Wmk. 388**   **Perf. 12**
1005-1007 A335   Set of 3   3.00   1.50

Birds — A336

Designs: 30c, Crested honey buzzard. 50c, Purple heron. $1, Lesser crested tern.
$2, Dunlin.

2005, Feb. 3   **Wmk. 388**   **Perf. 13½**
1008-1010 A336   Set of 3   3.00   1.50

Souvenir Sheet
1011 A336 $2 multi   3.00   1.50
   a.   Like #1011, with Pacific Explorer World Stamp Expo emblem in margin   3.00   1.50

No. 1011a issued 4/21.

Proton Gen-2 Automobile A337

2005, Feb. 7   **Wmk. 388**   **Perf. 13½**
     Color of Automobile
1012 A337   30c beige   .40   .25
   a.   Perf. 12   .40   .25
   b.   Booklet pane, 10 #1012a   4.00
     Complete booklet, #1012b   4.00
1013 A337   50c bright blue   .60   .30
1014 A337 $1 red   1.75   .85
   Nos. 1012-1014 (3)   2.75   1.40

Souvenir Sheet
1015 A337 $2 dark blue, vert.   2.00   1.00

MALAYSIA

Dances — A338

Designs: 30c, Bharata Natyam and Kathak. 50c, Kipas and Payaung. $1, Zapin and Asyik. $2, Datun Julud and Sumazau.

	2005, Apr. 9	Wmk. 388	Perf. 12	
1016	A338	30c multi	.35	.25
a.		Perf. 13½	.35	.25
1017	A338	50c multi	.50	.25
1018	A338	$1 multi	1.00	.50
	Nos. 1016-1018 (3)		1.85	1.00

Souvenir Sheet
Perf. 13½

1019	A338	$2 multi	2.25	1.10

Songkets — A339

Designs: 30c, Pucuk Rebung Gigi Yu. 50c, Bunga Bertabur Pecah Lapan. No. 1022: a, Pucuk Rebung Gigi Yu dan Bunga Kayoban. b, Teluk Berantai Bunga Pecah Empat. $2, Potong Wajik Bertabur.

Perf. 12¾x12½

	2005, Apr. 29		Wmk. 388	
1020	A339	30c multi	.30	.25
1021	A339	50c multi	.50	.25
1022	A339	$1 Horiz. pair, #a-b	1.60	.80
	Nos. 1020-1022 (3)		2.40	1.30

Souvenir Sheet

1023	A339	$2 multi	2.00	1.00

Birds — A340

Designs: 20c, Spotted dove. 30c, Ochraceous bulbul. 40c, Long-tailed parakeet. 50c, White-rumped shama. 75c, Olive-backed sunbird. $1, Green-winged pigeon. $2, Banded pitta. $5, Imperial pigeon.

	2005, May 14		Perf. 13½x14	
1024	A340	20c multi	.35	.25
1025	A340	30c multi	.40	.25
1026	A340	40c multi	.50	.25
1027	A340	50c multi	.60	.30
1028	A340	75c multi	.80	.40
1029	A340	$1 multi	.90	.45
1030	A340	$2 multi	1.75	.85
1031	A340	$5 multi	3.25	1.60
	Nos. 1024-1031 (8)		8.55	4.35

University of Malaysia, Cent. — A341

Designs: 30c, Dewan Tunku Canselor. 50c, Perpustakaan. No. 1034, Pusat Perubatan. No. 1035: a, Rimba Ilmu. b, Koleksi Muzium Seni Asia.

	2005, June 9	Wmk. 388	Perf. 12	
1032	A341	30c multi	.30	.25
b.		Perf. 13½	.30	.25
	Booklet pane, 10 #1032a	3.00		
	Complete booklet, #1032b	3.00		
1033	A341	50c multi	.50	.25

Perf. 13½

1034	A341	$1 multi	.90	.45
	Nos. 1032-1034 (3)		1.70	.95

Souvenir Sheet
Perf. 12½

1035	A341	$1 Sheet of 2, #a-b	1.60	.80

Malaysia — China Relations, 600th Anniv. — A342

Designs: No. 1036, 30c, Chinese chop. No. 1037, 30c, Ship. 50c, Malaysian and Chinese men talking. $1, Decorated plate. $2, Ornament and coin.

Perf. 12¾x12½

	2005, July 21	Litho.	Wmk. 388	
1036-1039	A342	Set of 4	1.75	.85

Souvenir Sheet

1040	A342	$2 multi	1.50	.75

Mammals Type of 2004

Endangered mammals: No. 1041, 30c, Malay weasel. No. 1042, 30c, Yellow-throated marten. 50c, Hairy-nosed otter. $1, Large spotted civet. $2, Long-tailed porcupine, vert.

Perf. 13½, 12 (50c, $1)

	2005, July 27			
1041-1044	A327	Set of 4	2.50	1.25
1042a		Perf. 12	.40	.25

Souvenir Sheet
Perf. 12¾x12½

1045	A327	$2 multi	2.00	1.00
a.		As #1045, with Taipei 2005 emblem in sheet margin	2.00	1.00

No. 1045a issued 8/19.

Water Transport — A343

Designs: 30c, Perahu kotak. 50c, Sampan. $1, Rakit buluh. $2, Perahu batang, vert.

	2005, Aug. 9		Perf. 13½	
1046-1048	A343	Set of 3	1.75	.85

Souvenir Sheet
Perf. 14x13½

1049	A343	$2 multi	2.00	1.00

No. 1049 contains one 40x55mm stamp.

Malay College, Kuala Kangsar, Cent. — A344

Designs: 30c, School building. No. 1051, 50c, Tree. No. 1052, 50c, Prep school. No. 1053, vert.: a, Sultan Idris Murchidul 'Adzam Shah. b, Sultan Alaiddin Sulaiman Shah. c, Yam Tuan Tuanku Muhamad Shah. d, Sultan Ahmad Al-Mu'adzam Shah.

	2005, Aug. 30		Perf. 13½	
1050-1052	A344	Set of 3	1.50	.75

Souvenir Sheet
Perf. 12x11¾

1053	A344	50c Sheet of 4, #a-d	1.60	.80

No. 1053 contains four 22x61mm stamps.

Reptiles — A345

Designs: No. 1054, 30c, Varanus rudicollis. No. 1055, 30c, Varanus dumerilii. 50c, Gonocephalus grandis. $1, Crocodylus porosus. $2, Varanus salvator, vert.

	2005, Sept. 28		Perf. 13½	
1054-1057	A345	Set of 4	2.50	1.25

Souvenir Sheet
Perf. 14x13½

1058	A345	$2 multi	1.75	.85

No. 1058 contains one 40x50mm stamp.

Kites — A346

Designs: 30c, Wau Jala Budi. 50c, Wau Bulan. $1, Wau Kucing. $2, Wau Merak.

	2005, Oct. 10		Perf. 13½, 12 ($1)	
1059-1061	A346	Set of 3	2.00	1.00
1060a		Perf. 12	.40	.25

Souvenir Sheet

1062	A346	$2 multi	1.60	.80

Batik — A347

Designs: 30c, Binaan Asasi. 50c, Pesona Sutera. $1, Malaysia Bersatu. $2, Penyatuan.

	2005, Dec. 2		Perf. 12¾x12½	
1063-1065	A347	Set of 3	1.40	.70

Souvenir Sheet

1066	A347	$2 multi	1.40	.70

11th ASEAN Summit, Kuala Lumpur — A348

Emblem and: 30c, Flags of participating nations. 50c, Motto. $1, Aerial view of Kuala Lumpur.

	2005, Dec. 12		Perf. 12½x12¾	
1067-1069	A348	Set of 3	1.40	.70

Islands and Marine Life — A349

Designs: No. 1070, 30c, Erica Reef, Nudibranch. No. 1071, 30c, Mariveles Reef, Sea cucumber. No. 1072, $1, Swallow Island, Sea star. No. 1073, $1, Investigator Reef, bivalve. $2, Erica Reef, Mariveles Reef, Swallow Island, Investigator Reef, and Ubi Reef.

	2005, Dec. 22	Perf. 12½x12¾, 13½ ($1)		
1070-1073	A349	Set of 4	2.00	1.00

Souvenir Sheet
Perf. 14

1074	A349	$2 multi	2.25	1.10

No. 1074 contains one 50x40mm stamp.

Ducks — A350

Designs: 30c, Anas crecca. No. 1076, 30c, Cairina scutulata. No. 1077, 50c, Anas acuta. No. 1078, 50c, Anas clypeata. $2, Phalacrocorax carbo.

	2006, Jan. 26	Litho.	Wmk. 388	
1075-1078	A350	Set of 4	2.50	1.25
1076a		Perf. 12	.40	.25

Souvenir Sheet

1079	A350	$2 multi	2.75	1.40

Negara Audit Institute, Cent. — A351

Designs: 30c, Building. No. 1081, 50c, Documents. No. 1082, 50c, Emblems.

	2006, Feb. 14		Perf. 12½x12¾	
1080-1082	A351	Set of 3	1.25	.60

Fruits — A352

Designs: 30c, Artocarpus sericicarpus. 50c, Phyllanthus acidus. No. 1085, $1, Garcinia hombroniana. No. 1086, $1: a, Lepisanthes alata. b, Baccaurea polyneura.

Perf. 13¾x13½ Syncopated

	2006, Mar. 28			
1083-1085	A352	Set of 3	1.60	.80

Souvenir Sheet
Perf. 13¾ Syncopated

1086	A352	$1 Sheet of 2, #a-b	1.60	.80

Mountains — A353

No. 1087, 30c: a, Mt. Kinabalu and orchid. b, Gunung Ledang (Mt. Ophir) and flower. No. 1088, 50c: a, Mt. Jerai and orchid. b, Mt. Mulu. $2, Mt. Tahan.

Litho. & Embossed
Perf. 13½x13¼

	2006, Apr. 26		Wmk. 388	
	Horiz. Pairs, #a-b			
1087-1088	A353	Set of 2	2.50	1.25

Souvenir Sheet
Perf. 14
Litho.

1088C	A353	$2 multi	1.60	.80

No. 1088C contains one 50x40mm stamp.

Fish — A354

Designs: 30c, Leptobarbus hoevenii. No. 1090, 50c, Hampala macrolepidota. No. 1091, 50c, Pangasius sp. $1, Probarbus jullieni. $5, Clarias batrachus, Mystus nemurus.

	2006, May 25	Litho.	Wmk. 388	
1089-1092	A354	Set of 4	2.50	1.25

Souvenir Sheet
Litho. With Hologram Applied
Perf. 13¼

1093	A354	$5 multi	3.50	1.75

No. 1093 contains one 70x33mm stamp.

A355

Designs: No. 1094, 50c, Emblem and leaf. No. 1095, 50c, Anniversary emblem and people reading. $1, Emblem, books and electronic devices.

	2006, June 22		Perf. 12½x12¾	
1094-1096	A355	Set of 3	1.90	.95

Dewan Bahasa Dan Pustaka (Malay Language Governing Board), 50th Anniv.

MALAYSIA

Federal Land Development Authority, 50th Anniv. — A356

Designs: 30c, Palm plantation, fruit. 50c, Buildings. $1, Globe and buildings.

2006, July 7	Litho.	Perf. 12½x12¾
1097-1099 A356	Set of 3	1.75 .85

Sultan Azlan Shah Gallery — A357

Designs: 30c, Gallery emblem, sword and sheath. 50c, Gallery building. $1, Gallery emblem, headdress.

2006, July 18		Perf. 12
1100-1102 A357	Set of 3	1.75 .85

Festivals — A358

Designs: 30c, Eid al-Fitr. 50c, Tahun Baru Cina (Chinese New Year). No. 1105, $1, Deepavali. No. 1106, $1, vert.: a, Tadau Kaamatan. b, Pesta Gawai.

2006, Aug. 15		Perf. 12
1103-1105 A358	Set of 3	1.75 .85

Souvenir Sheet
Perf. 12½

| 1106 A358 | $1 Sheet of 2, #a-b | 1.60 .80 |

Men's and Women's Traditional Costumes — A359

Designs: No. 1107, 50c, Malaysian (blue green background). No. 1108, 50c, Indian (orange background). No. 1109, 50c, Chinese (red background). No. 1110, $1, vert.: a, Iban (blue background). b, Kadazan (tan background).

2006, Aug. 29		Perf. 12¾x12½
1107-1109 A359	Set of 3	1.75 .85

Souvenir Sheet
Perf. 13¼x13½

| 1110 A359 | $1 Sheet of 2, #a-b | 2.00 1.00 |

Semi-aquatic Animals — A360

Designs: 30c, Periophthalmodon schlosseri. 50c, Pagurus bernhardus. No. 1113, $1, Cuora amboinensis. No. 1114, $1, vert.: a, Polypedates leucomystax. b, Varanus salvator. c, Cynogale bennettii. d, Xenochrophis trianguligera.

Perf. 13½x13¼

2006, Oct. 9	Litho.	Wmk. 388
1111-1113 A360	Set of 3	2.00 1.00

Souvenir Sheet
Perf. 13¾x14¼ Syncopated

| 1114 A360 | $1 Sheet of 4, #a-d | 2.75 1.40 |

Stamp Week. No. 1114 contains four 29x34mm stamps.

18th Intl. Federation of Gynecology and Obstetrics Congress — A361

"FIGO" and: 30c, Woman and tree leaves. No. 1116, 50c, Map, woman's torso. No. 1117, 50c, Map, fetus.

2006, Nov. 6		Perf. 12½x12¾
1115-1117 A361	Set of 3	1.75 .85

2006 Far East & South Pacific Games for the Disabled, Kuala Lumpur — A362

Designs: 30c, Wheelchair racing. 50c, Swimming. $1, Wheelchair tennis. $2, Wheelchair basketball.

2006, Nov. 25		Perf. 12¾x12½
1118-1120 A362	Set of 3	2.00 1.00

Souvenir Sheet
Perf. 13½

| 1121 A362 | $2 multi | 2.50 1.25 |

ASEAN Dialogue with People's Republic of China, 15th Anniv. — A363

Designs: 30c, ASEAN emblem, Chinese flag, map with flags. 50c, Great Wall of China, flasks, port, highway, ASEAN emblem and Chinese flag. $1, Bow with ASEAN emblem and Chinese flag.

Perf. 12, 13½x13¼ ($1)

2006, Nov. 30	Set of 3	2.00 2.00
1122-1124 A363		

25th General Assembly of World Veterans Federation, Kuala Lumpur — A364

Emblem and: 30c, Map. 50c, "25," Kuala Lumpur buildings. $1, Malaysian flag, sculpture of soldiers.

Perf. 13½x13¼, 12 (50c)

2006, Dec. 4	Litho.	Wmk. 388
1125 A364	30c multi	.40 .25
1126 A364	50c multi	.60 .30
1127 A364	$1 multi	1.10 .55
a.	Perf. 12	1.10 .55
	Nos. 1125-1127 (3)	2.10 1.10

South Pole Expedition A365

Designs: 30c, Mountains, sled, tent. 50c, Man on skis pulling sled. $1, Man on skis pulling sled with parasail.

2006, Dec. 28		Perf. 13½x13¼
1128-1130 A365	Set of 3	2.50 1.25

Marine Life — A373

Designs: No. 1139, Leaf scorpionfish. No. 1140, Orange-striped triggerfish. No. 1141: a, Chambered nautilus. b, Spotted boxfish.

Perf. 13½x13¼

2007, Feb. 6	Litho.	Wmk. 388
1139 A373	50c multi	.70 .35
a.	Perf. 12	.70 .35
1140 A373	50c multi	.70 .35
a.	Perf. 12	.70 .35

Souvenir Sheet

| 1141 A373 | $1 Sheet of 2, #a-b | 2.25 1.10 |

Dated 2006. See Brunei Nos. 588-590.

Tourism A374

No. 1142: a, Hornbill, forest and flower. b, Diver and coral reef.
No. 1143: a, Buildings. b, Handicrafts.
No. 1144: a, Woman with red dress, with arms raised. b, Woman with red dress holding fan. c, Woman with blue dress. d, Woman with black dress. e, Woman with red and black dress with geometric patterns. f, Satay, Ketupat dan Aie Sirap. g, Yee Sang. h, Banana leaf rice dan Teh Tarik. i, Hinava. j, Manok Pansuh.
$2, Flag and buildings, vert.

2007, Mar. 19		Perf. 13½x13¼
1142 A374	30c Horiz. pair, #a-b	.75 .35

Perf. 12

| 1143 A374 | 50c Horiz. pair, #a-b | 1.50 .75 |

Booklet Stamps
Perf. 13½x13¼

| 1144 A374 | 30c Booklet pane of 10, #a-j | 3.00 1.50 |
| | Compete booklet, #1144 | 3.00 |

Souvenir Sheet
Perf. 13¼x13½

| 1145 A374 | $2 multi | 2.00 1.00 |

No. 1145 contains one 30x50mm stamp.

Installation of 13th Yang Di-Pertuan Agong — A375

13th Yang Di-Pertuan Agong and background colors of: 30c, Yellow. 50c, Green. $1, Purple.

2007, Apr. 26		Perf. 12½
1146-1148 A375	Set of 3	2.00 1.00

Amphibians A376

Designs: 30c, Pedostibes hosii. No. 1150, 50c, Megophrys nasuta. No. 1151, 50c, Nyctixalus pictus. $1, Rana laterimaculata.

2007, May 3		Perf. 12
1149-1151 A376	Set of 3	2.00 1.00

Souvenir Sheet
Perf. 13¼

| 1152 A376 | $1 multi | 1.40 .70 |

No. 1152 contains one 35x33mm stamp.

Airplanes — A377

Designs: 30c, Shorts SC-7 Skyvan. No. 1154, 50c, GAF N22 Nomad. No. 1155, 50c, De Havilland Canada DHC 7-110. No. 1156: a, Airspeed Consul. b, Douglas DC-3.

2007, May 24		Perf. 12
1153-1155 A377	Set of 3	1.60 .80

Souvenir Sheet
Perf. 13½x13¼

| 1156 A377 | $1 Sheet of 2, #a-b | 1.75 .85 |

Clock Towers — A378

Designs: 30c, J. W. W. Birch Clock Tower, 1917. 50c, Atkinson Clock Tower, 1905. $1, Alor Setar Clock Tower, 1912.

Perf. 13¼x14x13¼x13½

2007, June 6		
1157-1159 A378	Set of 3	2.00 1.00

Children's Folk Tales — A379

Designs: Nos. 1160a, 1161a, Bawang Putah Bawang Merah. Nos. 1160b, 1161b, Badang. Nos. 1160c, 1162a, Sang Kancil Dengan Buaya. Nos. 1160d, 1162b, Sang Kancil Menolong Kerbau. No. 1160e, Mat Jenin. $5, Si Tanggang.

Perf. 13½x13¼

2007, June 26	Litho.	Wmk. 388
1160	Horiz. strip of 5	2.00 2.00
a.-e.	A379 30c Any single	.40 .30
f.	Booklet pane, 2 each #1160a-1160e	4.00 —
	Complete booklet, #1160f	4.00
1161	Horiz. pair	1.25 .60
a.-b.	A379 50c Any single	.60 .30
1162	Horiz. pair	1.25 .60
a.-b.	A379 50c Any single	.60 .30

Souvenir Sheet
Litho. With Foil Application
Perf. 14

| 1163 A379 | $5 multi | 4.00 2.00 |

No. 1163 contains one 50x38mm stamp.

Insects A380

No. 1164, 30c: a, Fulgora pyrorhyncha. b, Dysdercus cingulatus.
No. 1165, 50c: a, Valanga nigricornis. b, Rhaphipodus hopei.
$5, Antheraea helferi, horiz.

2007, July 7		Perf. 12¾x12½
		Horiz. Pairs, #a-b
1164-1165 A380	Set of 2	1.75 .85

Souvenir Sheet
Perf. 14

| 1166 A380 | $5 multi | 4.00 2.00 |

No. 1166 contains one 50x38mm stamp.

Police Force, 200th Anniv. — A381

Designs: 30c, Police and building. No. 1168, 50c, Police near jeep and in river, policeman wearing shorts. No. 1169, 50c, Police officers, cars, motorcycles, building and computer operator.

2007, July 24		Perf. 13½x13¼
1167-1169 A381	Set of 3	1.75 .85

Association of South East Asian Nations (ASEAN), 40th Anniv. — A382

MALAYSIA

No. 1170: a, Secretariat Building, Bandar Seri Begawan, Brunei. b, National Museum of Cambodia. c, Fatahillah Museum, Jakarta, Indonesia. d, Typical house, Laos. e, Malayan Railway Headquarters Building, Kuala Lumpur. f, Yangon Post Office, Myanmar (Burma). g, Malacañang Palace, Philippines. h, National Museum of Singapore. i, Vimanmek Mansion, Bangkok, Thailand. j, Presidential Palace, Hanoi, Viet Nam.

2007, Aug. 8 — Perf. 13¾x14¼
1170 Block of 10 5.00 5.00
a.-j. A382 50c Any single .50 .50

See Brunei No. 607, Burma No. 370, Cambodia No. 2339, Indonesia Nos. 2120-2121, Laos Nos. 1717-1718, Philippines Nos. 3103-3105, Singapore No. 1265, Thailand No. 2315, Viet Nam Nos. 3302-3311.

Malaysian Independence, 50th Anniv. — A383

No. 1171 — Anniversary emblem, flag and: a, Dato' Onn Jaafar. b, Tunku Abdul Rahman Putra Al-Haj. c, Tun Abdul Razak. d, Tun Tan Cheng Lock. e, Tun V. T. Sambanthan.

No. 1172 — Anniversary emblem and: a, Tunku Abdul Rahman Putra Al-Haj, buildings, people, flag, statue. b, Petronas Twin Towers, government building, automobile and bridge.

No. 1173: a, Tunku Abdul Rahman Putra Al-Haj signing declaration of independence and anniversary emblem. b, Anniversary emblem. $5, Flag.

2007, Aug. 31 — Perf. 13½x13¼
1171 Horiz. strip of 5 2.00 2.00
a.-e. A383 30c any single .40 .40
1172 Horiz. pair .80 .80
a.-b. A383 30c any single .40 .40
1173 Horiz. pair 1.00 1.00
a.-b. A383 50c any single .50 .50

Souvenir Sheet
Perf. 13¼
1174 A383 $5 multi 4.00 2.00

No. 1174 contains one 70x33mm stamp and has foil application in margin.

Petronas Twin Towers, Kuala Lumpur, 2007 Recipient of Aga Khan Award for Architecture — A384

2007, Sept. 4 — Perf. 13¼x13½
1175 A384 50c multi 3.00 1.50

National and State Arms — A385

No. 1176: a, Malaysia. b, Kedah. c, Negri Sembilan. d, Pahang. e, Kelantan. f, Johore. g, Perak. h, Perlis. i, Selangor. j, Trengganu. k, Sarawak. l, Penang. m, Sabah. n, Malacca.

2007, Sept. 25 — Perf. 13¾x14
1176 Block of 14 5.75 4.25
a.-n. A385 50c Any single .40 .30

Vegetables — A386

Designs: No. 1177, 50c, Solanum ferox. No. 1178, 50c, Etlingera elatior. No. 1179, 50c, Momordica charantia.
No. 1180: a, Luffa aegyptiaca. b, Psophocarpus tetragonolobus. c, Sesbania grandiflora. d, Solanum torvum.

Perf. 13¾x13½ Syncopated
2007, Nov. 26
1177-1179 A386 Set of 3 1.40 .70

Souvenir Sheet
Perf. 13¾x14 Syncopated
1180 A386 $1 Sheet of 4, #a-d 2.75 1.40

Kuala Lumpur Equestrian Grand Prix — A387

Horses: 30c, Oldenburger. No. 1182, 50c, Dutch Warmblood. No. 1183, 50c, Hanoverian.

2007, Dec. 13 — Perf. 13½
1181-1183 A387 Set of 3 1.50 .75

Bridges — A388

Designs: 30c, Merdeka Bridge, Kedah. No. 1185, 50c, Kota Bridge, Selangor. No. 1186, 50c, Victoria Bridge, Perak. $1, Sungai Segamat Bridge, Johore.

2008, Feb. 28 — Perf. 13¾x13¼ Litho. Wmk. 388
1184-1187 A388 Set of 4 2.00 1.00

Nocturnal Animals — A389

Designs: No. 1188, 30c, Mydaus javanensis. No. 1189, 30c, Echinosorex gymnurus. 50c, Catopuma temminckii. $1, Pteropus vampyrus.
No. 1192: a, $2, Tarsius bancanus (30x40mm). b, $3, Nycticebus coucang (60x40mm).

2008, Mar. 13 — Perf. 13½x13¼
1188-1191 A389 Set of 4 1.75 .85

Souvenir Sheet
Perf. 12¾x12½
1192 A389 Sheet of 2, #a-b 3.75 1.75
c. As #1192, imperf. 3.75 1.75

Butterflies A390

No. 1193: a, Smaller wood nymph. b, Malaysian lacewing.
50c, Malay red harlequin. $1, Glorious begum.
No. 1195A, Common rose. No. 1195B, Blue glassy tiger. No. 1195C, Green dragontail.
$5, Five-bar swordtail.

2008, Apr. 24 — Perf. 13½x13¼
1193 A390 30c Horiz. pair, #a-b .40 .30
d. As #1193, perf. 12 .40 .30
e. As #1193a, perf. 12 .40 .30
f. As #1193b, perf. 12 .40 .30
1194 A390 50c multi .40 .30
1195 A390 $1 multi .65 .40
Nos. 1193-1195 (3) 1.45 1.00

Booklet Stamps
1195A A390 30c multi .40 .25
1195B A390 30c multi .40 .25
1195C A390 30c multi .40 .25
d. Booklet pane, 2 each #1193a-1193b, 1195A-1195C 3.00 —
Complete booklet, #1195Cd 3.00
Nos. 1195A-1195C (3) 1.20 .75

Souvenir Sheet
Perf. 14
1196 A390 $5 multi 3.75 1.75

No. 1196 contains one 50x38mm stamp and has die cut slits in the sheet margin.

St. John Ambulance in Malaysia, Cent. — A391

Centenary emblem and: 30c, Emergency ambulance service. 50c, First aid. $1, Cardiopulmonary resuscitation.

2008, May 22 — Perf. 13½x13¼
1197-1199 A391 Set of 3 2.75 1.40

Cultural Items A393

2008, June 10 — Perf. 13½x13¼
1200 A392 30c Batu Giling .30 .25
1201 A392 50c Supu .45 .45
Perf. 13¼x13¾
1202 A393 50c Kukur Kelapa .45 .45
Nos. 1200-1202 (3) 1.20 1.15

Intl. Dragon Boat Federation Club Crew World Championships A394

Designs: 30c, Boats 6 and 3. 50c, Boats 5 and 2. $1, Boats 4 and 1. $2, Boat 5.

2008, Aug. 1 — Perf. 13½x13¼ Litho. Wmk. 388
1203-1205 A394 Set of 3 1.75 .85

Souvenir Sheet
1206 A394 $2 multi 1.60 .80
a. Imperf. 1.60 .80

No. 1206 contains one 80x30mm stamp.

Malaysian Scouting Association, Cent. — A395

Centenary emblem, scouting emblems and: 30c, Scouts reading map, Lord Robert Baden-Powell. No. 1208, 50c, Scouts' water activities. No. 1209, 50c, Scouts on monkey bridge.

2008, Aug. 14 — Perf. 13½x13¼
1207-1209 A395 Set of 3 1.50 .75

Art — A396

Designs: 30c, Semangat Ledang, by Syed Ahmad Jamal. 50c, Musim Buah, by Chuah Thean Teng, vert. $1, Pago-pago, by Latiff Mohidin.

2008, Aug. 28 — Perf. 12½x12¾
1210 A396 30c multi .35 .25
Perf. 12¾x12½
1211 A396 50c multi .60 .30
Size:35x35mm
Perf. 13¼
1212 A396 $1 multi .80 .50
Nos. 1210-1212 (3) 1.75 1.05

Miniature Sheet

Royal Headgear — A397

No. 1213 — Headgear for: a, Leaders of Eight states and Yang Di-Pertuan Agong. b, Yang Di-Pertuan Agong. c, Sultan of Kedah. d, Yang Di-Pertuan Agong of Negri Sembilan. e, Sultan of Pahang. f, Sultan of Kelantan. g, Sultan of Perak. h, Raja of Perlis. i, Sultan of Selangor. j, Sultan of Trengganu.

2008, Sept. 16 — Perf. 13¾x14
1213 A397 50c Sheet of 10, #a-j 5.50 2.75

Flowers A398

No. 1214, 30c: a, Goniothalamus tapis. b, Gloriosa superba.
No. 1215, 50c: a, Quisqualis indica. b, Michelia figo.
$5, Epiphyllum oxypetalum, vert.

Wmk. 388
2008, Oct. 9 — Litho. Perf. 13½
Horiz. Pairs, #a-b
1214-1215 A398 Set of 2 2.25 1.10

Souvenir Sheet
Perf. 14
1216 A398 $5 multi 3.75 1.90

No. 1216 contains one 39x50mm stamp.

National Space Program — A399

Designs: 30c, Soyuz-TMA II rocket on launch pad. No. 1218, 50c, Malaysian astronaut. No. 1219, 50c, Intl. Space Station.
No. 1220: a, Rocket lifting off from launch pad. b, Rocket above Earth.

2008, Oct. 21 — Perf. 13¼x13¾
1217-1219 A399 Set of 3 1.60 .80

Souvenir Sheet
1220 A399 $1 Sheet of 2, #a-b 1.75 .85

Shells — A400

Designs: No. 1221, 30c, Burnt murex. No. 1222, 30c, Horned helmet. No. 1223, 50c, Triton's trumpet. No. 1224, 50c, Frog shell. $2, Venus comb murex.

2008, Nov. 11 — Perf. 11¾
1221-1224 A400 Set of 4 2.00 1.00

Souvenir Sheet
Perf. 12¾x12½
1224A A400 $2 multi 2.00 1.00
b. Imperf. 2.00 1.00

No. 1224A contains one 60x40mm stamp.

The Kampung Boy, Cartoons by Lat — A401

Designs: Nos. 1225a, 1226a, The Kampung Boy (29x33mm). Nos. 1225b, 1226b, Permainan Anak Kampung (58x33mm). Nos. 1225c, 1226c, Guru Sekolah Yang Garang (58x33mm). Nos. 1225d, 1226d, Town Boy (29x33mm). No. 1225e, Kampung Boy drawing picture (29x33mm).

MALAYSIA

$5, Malaysian daily life (60x40mm).

Perf. 13¾x14 Syncopated
2008, Dec. 1
1225		Horiz. strip of 5	1.50	1.50
a.-e.		A401 30c Any single	.30	.30
		Complete booklet, 2 #1225	3.00	
1226		Horiz. strip of 4	2.25	2.25
a.-d.		A401 50c Any single	.30	.30

Souvenir Sheet
Perf. 12¾x12½
1227	A401	$5 silver & blk	3.75	1.90

Schools — A402

Designs: No. 1228, 50c, SMK Convent Bukit Nanas, Kuala Lumpur. No. 1229, 50c, SMK St. Thomas, Kuching, Sarawak. No. 1230, 50c, SMK Victoria (Victoria Institution), Kuala Lumpur. No. 1231, 50c, SM All Saints, Kota Kinabalu, Sabah.

2008, Dec. 16   **Perf. 13½x13¼**
1228-1231	A402	Set of 4	2.25	1.10

Birds — A403

Designs: 30c, Polyplectron malacense. No. 1233, 50c, Mycteria cinerea. No. 1234, 50c, Myiophonus robinsoni.
$5, Aceros subruficollis.

Perf. 13½x13¼
2009, Jan. 21   **Litho.**   **Wmk. 388**
1232-1234	A403	Set of 3	2.00	1.00

Souvenir Sheet
Perf. 12
Litho. & Embossed
1235	A403	$5 multi	4.00	2.00
a.		With China 2009 World Stamp Exhibition emblem in sheet margin	4.00	2.00

Nos. 1235 and 1235a each contain one 45x35mm stamp.

Traditional Wedding Costumes — A404

No. 1236: a, Bajau. b, Orang Ulu. c, Indian. d, Chinese. e, Malayan.
No. 1237: a, Malayan, diff. b, Chinese, diff. c, Indian, diff. d, Orang Ulu, diff. e, Bajau, diff.

Perf. 13¼x13½
2009, Mar. 23   **Litho.**
1236		Horiz. strip of 5	1.50	1.50
a.-e.		A404 30c Any single	.30	.30
		Complete booklet, 2 each #1236a-1236e	3.00	
1237		Horiz. strip of 5	2.50	2.50
a.-e.		A404 50c Any single	.50	.50

UNESCO World Heritage Sites — A405

No. 1238, 50c: a, Taman Negara Mulu, Sarawak, and tarsier. b, Taman Kinabalu, Sabah, and bird.
No. 1239, 50c: a, Town Square, Banda Hilir, Malacca, and door. b, Old City Hall, George Town, Penang, and windows.
No. 1240, 50c: a, Building, Banda Hilir, Malacca. b, Lenticular cloud over Taman Kinabalu, Sabah. c, Buildings, George Town, Penang. d, Cave, Taman Negara Mulu.

2009, Apr. 9   **Perf. 13½x13¼**
Horiz. Pairs, #a-b
1238-1239	A405	Set of 2	1.25	.60

Perf. 14x13½
1240	A405	50c Sheet of 4, #a-d	1.25	.60

No. 1240 contains four 60x25mm stamps.

Engineering Projects of the Past and Present — A406

No. 1241, 30c — Transportation and port: a, Past. b, Present.
No. 1242, 30c — Telecommunication and power: a, Past. b, Present.
No. 1243, 50c — Road, bridge and dam: a, Past. b, Present.

Perf. 12½x12¾
2009, Apr. 20   **Wmk. 388**
Horiz. Pairs, #a-b
1241-1243	A406	Set of 3	2.50	1.25

Palm Trees — A407

Designs: No. 1244, 50c, Licuala grandis. No. 1245, 50c, Caryota mitis. No. 1246, 50c, Livistona saribus.
$3, Livistona endauensis and Johannesteijsmannia altifrons.

2009, May 19   **Unwmk.**   **Perf. 13¼**
1244-1246	A407	Set of 3	1.50	.75

Souvenir Sheet
Perf. 12
1247	A407	$3 multi	2.25	1.10

No. 1247 contains one 70x50mm L-shaped stamp.

Nature Conservation A408

Inscriptions: 30c, Clean Water. No. 1249, 50c, Go Green. No. 1250, 50c, Fresh Air.

Perf. 13¾x13½
2009, June 18   **Unwmk.**
1248-1250	A408	Set of 3	1.75	.85

Miniature Sheet

Traditional Houses — A409

No. 1251 Inscriptions: a, Rumah Traditional Melayu, Selangor. b, Rumah Dusun Lotud, Sabah. c, Rumah Kutai, Perak. d, Rumah Tiang 12, Kelantan. e, Rumah Panjang Iban, Sarawak. f, Rumah Orang Semai, Pahang. g, Rumah Limas, Johor. h, Rumah Panjang, Kedah. i, Rumah Limas Bungkus, Terengganu. j, Rumah Adat Minangkabau, Negeri Sembilan. k, Rumah Serambi Gajah Menyusu, Pulau Pinang. l, Rumah Bumbung Panjang, Perlis. m, Rumah Melayu Melaka, Melaka. n, Rumah Laut Bajau, Sabah. o, Rumah Serambi, Pahang. p, Rumah Ketua Bidayuh, Sarawak.

Perf. 12½x12¾
2009, July 9   **Wmk. 388**
1251	A409	50c Sheet of 16, #a-p	6.00	3.00

Tubers — A410

Designs: No. 1252, 30c, Manihot esculenta crantz. No. 1253, 30c, Ipomoea batatas. No. 1254, 50c, Dioscorea alata. No. 1255, 50c, Pachyrrhizus erosus.
$3, Colocasia esculenta.

Perf. 13¼
2009, July 23   **Litho.**   **Unwmk.**
1252-1255	A410	Set of 4	1.50	.75

Souvenir Sheet
Perf. 13¼ Syncopated
1256	A410	$3 multi	2.25	1.10

No. 1256 contains one 45x45mm stamp.

"One Malaysia" Campaign — A411

"1" and: Nos. 1257, 1260, Map of Malaysia. Nos. 1258, 1261, People in ring around Malaysian flag in heart. Nos. 1259, 1262, Lightbulb, seven people. No. 1263, Computer, Kuala Lumpur skyline, gauge, dish antenna, microscope, man at chart, woman with clipboard. No. 1264, Flower, people, gavel, building, traditional hat.
$5, Eight people around "1."

Perf. 13¾x14 Syncopated
2009, Aug. 31   **Wmk. 388**
1257	A411	30c multi	.40	.30
1258	A411	30c multi	.40	.30
1259	A411	30c multi	.40	.30
		Nos. 1257-1259 (3)	1.20	.90

Booklet Stamps
Perf. 13¾x13½ Syncopated
1260	A411	30c multi	.40	.30
1261	A411	30c multi	.40	.30
1262	A411	30c multi	.40	.30
1263	A411	30c multi	.40	.30
1264	A411	30c multi	.40	.30
a.		Booklet pane of 10, 2 each #1260-1264	4.00	—
		Complete booklet, #1264a	4.00	
		Nos. 1260-1264 (5)	2.00	1.50

Souvenir Sheet
Perf. 13¼x13½
1265	A411	$5 multi	3.75	1.90

No. 1265 contains one 30x40mm stamp that has a clear holographic coating.

First Malaysian Submarine A412

Submarine, flag of Malaysia and Navy crest with denomination at: 30c, LR. No. 1267, 50c, UR. No. 1268, 50c, LR.

2009, Sept. 3   **Perf. 13½x13¼**
1266-1268	A412	Set of 3	1.50	.75

Energy Efficient Buildings — A413

Designs: 30c, Green Energy Office Building, Bangi. 50c, Low Energy Office Building, Putrajaya. $1, Diamond Building, Putrajaya.

2009, Sept. 9   **Perf. 13¼x13½**
1269-1271	A413	Set of 3	1.75	.85
1270a		Perf. 14	.40	.40
1271a		Perf. 14	.75	.35

Declaration of the Rights of the Child, 20th Anniv. — A414

No. 1272: a, Girl with pinwheel. b, Boy drinking. c, Boy carrying backpack. d, Girl under umbrella.

2009, Oct. 9   **Litho.**   **Perf. 13½**
1272	A414	30c Block of 4, #a-d	1.50	.75

Litho. & Embossed
1273	A414	$1 shown	1.00	.50

Arachnids A415

Designs: No. 1274, 30c, Curved spiny spider. No. 1275, 30c, Fighting spider. 50c, St. Andrew's cross spider. $1, Golden orb-web spider.
$5, Black scorpion.

Perf. 13¾x13½
2009, Dec. 7   **Litho.**   **Wmk. 388**
1274-1277	A415	Set of 4	2.00	1.00

Souvenir Sheet
Litho. & Embossed
Perf. 13¾x13
1278	A415	$5 multi	3.00	1.50

No. 1278 contains one 64x32mm hexagonal stamp.

Malaysian Currency — A416

No. 1279, 50c — 1990 10 sen coin (orange ring): a, Obverse (with date). b, Reverse.
No. 1280, 50c — 1990 20 sen coin (green ring): a, Obverse (with date). b, Reverse.
No. 1281, 50c — 1990 50 sen coin (blue ring): a, Obverse (with date). b, Reverse.
$5, 50 ringgit banknote, horiz.

Perf. 13¼
2010, Jan. 18   **Litho.**   **Unwmk.**
Vertical Pairs, #a-b
1279-1281	A416	Set of 3	1.75	.85

Souvenir Sheet
Litho. With Foil Application
Perf. 14x13½
1282	A416	$5 multi	3.00	1.50

No. 1282 contains one 50x40mm stamp.

A416a

Flag in "1" — A416b

MALAYSIA

2010 Litho. Wmk. 388 Perf. 13¾
Stamp and Label Separated By Perforations
1282A A416a 30c multi + label 13.50 13.50

Stamp and Label Not Separated By Perforations
Perf. 14¼
1282B A416b 30c multi 18.00 18.00
1282C A416b 60c multi 24.00 24.00
Nos. 1282A-1282C (3) 55.50 55.50

Issued: No. 1282A, 2/4; No. 1282B, May. Labels could be personalized. No. 1282A was issued in sheets of 20 + 20 labels that sold for $6. No. 1282B was issued in sheets of 20 that sold for $19. No. 1282C was issued in sheets of 10 that sold for $19.

New Year 2010 (Year of the Tiger) — A417

No. 1283: a, Korean tiger. b, Malayan tiger.

Perf. 13½x14
2010, Feb. 23 Litho. Wmk. 388
1283 A417 50c Horiz. pair, #a-b .60 .30

Ferns — A418

No. 1284: a, Helminthostachys zeylanica. b, Stenochlaena palustris. c, Platycerium coronarium. d, Dicraopteris linearis. e, Diplazium esculentum.
$3, Asplenium nidus, Matonia pectinata, Dipteris conjugata, horiz.

Perf. 13¼x13½
2010, Mar. 10 Litho. Wmk. 388
1284 Horiz. strip of 5 1.50 .75
a.-e. A418 50c Any single .30 .25

Souvenir Sheet
Perf. 14
1285 A418 $3 multi 1.90 .95

No. 1285 contains one 100x45mm stamp.

A419

Local Markets A420

No. 1286: 30c: a, Woman with vegetables at Kelantan market. b, Kelantan market.
No. 1287, 50c: a, Fruit at market, Sabah. b, Handicrafts at market, Sabah.
No. 1288 — Market in Sarawak: a, $1, Woman and vegetables. b, $2, Woman and man with potted plants.
No. 1289 — Market in Kedah: a, $1, Man looking at textiles, pile of baskets. b, $2, Man and woman shopping.

2010, Mar. 23 Perf. 13¼
Horiz. Pairs, #a-b
1286-1287 A419 Set of 2 1.00 .50

Souvenir Sheets
Perf. 13¼x13½
Sheets of 2, #a-b
1288-1289 A420 Set of 2 3.75 1.90

Medical Excellence in Malaysia — A421

Designs: 30c, Limbal stem cell deficiency. 50c, Premaxilla retractor. $1, Arm transplant.

2010, Apr. 26 Perf. 13¼
1290-1292 A421 Set of 3 1.25 .60

Fireflies — A422

Designs: No. 1293, 30c, Pteroptyx bearni. No. 1294, 30c, Pteroptyx valida. No. 1295, 50c, Lychnuris sp. No. 1296, 50c, Diaphanes sp.
$5, Pteroptyx tener.

2010, May 10 Litho. Perf. 12¼
1293-1296 A422 Set of 4 1.00 .50

Souvenir Sheet
Litho. With Hologram
Perf. 12¾x12½
1297 A422 $5 multi 3.00 1.50

No. 1297 contains one 60x40mm stamp.

Malaysian Railways — A423

No. 1298: a, Commuter train. b, ETS train. 50c, Blue Tiger. $1, 56 Class train.
No. 1301, 20 Class train. No. 1302, Commuter and ETS trains. No. 1303, Blue Tiger. No. 1304, 56 Class train. No. 1305, FMSR Class T train.
$3, FMSR Class T train, vert.

2010, June 22 Litho. Perf. 12
1298 A423 30c Horiz. pair, #a-b .40 .25

Size: 70x25mm
1299 A423 50c multi .35 .25
1300 A423 $1 multi .65 .30
Nos. 1298-1300 (3) 1.40 .80

Booklet Stamps
1301 A423 30c multi .25 .25
1302 A423 30c multi .25 .25
1303 A423 30c multi .25 .25
1304 A423 30c multi .25 .25
1305 A423 30c multi .25 .25
a. Vert. strip of 5, #1301-1305 1.00 1.00
b. Booklet pane of 10, 2 each #1301-1305 2.00
Complete booklet, #1305b 2.00

Souvenir Sheet
Perf. 13½
1306 A423 $3 multi 1.90 .95
a. As #1306, with Bangkok 2010 emblem in margin 1.90 .95
b. As #1306, with PhilaNippon '11 emblem in margin 2.00 1.00

No. 1306 contains one 30x50mm stamp.

Flowers — A424

Designs: 30c, Nelumbium nelumbo. 50c, Hydrangea macrophylla. 60c, Bougainvillea. 70c, Hippeastrum reticulatum. 80c, Hibiscus rosa-sinensis. 90c, Ipomoea indica. $1, Canna orientalis. $2, Allamanda cathartica.

2010, July 1 Perf. 14x13¾
1307 A424 30c multi .25 .25
1308 A424 50c multi .30 .25
1309 A424 60c multi .40 .25
1310 A424 70c multi .45 .25
1311 A424 80c multi .50 .25
1312 A424 90c multi .55 .30
1313 A424 $1 multi .65 .30
1314 A424 $2 multi 1.25 .60
Nos. 1307-1314 (8) 4.35 2.45

Threatened Habitats — A425

Habitats: 60c, Forest. 70c, Marine. 80c, River.

Perf. 13¾x14 Syncopated
2010, July 15
1315-1317 A425 Set of 3 1.40 .70

Grand Knight of Valor Award — A426

Grand Knight of Valor Award and: 60c, Soldiers, tank. 70c, People, Kuala Lumpur skyline. 80c, Soldiers, building.

2010, July 30 Perf. 12¾x12½
1318-1320 A426 Set of 3 1.40 .70

Miniature Sheets

A427

Traditional Festive Food — A428

Nos. 1321 and 1322 — Various foods of people of: a, Malaysia, text at top. b, Malaysia, text at bottom. c, China, text at top. d, China, text at bottom. e, India, text at top. f, India, text at bottom. g, Sabah, text at top. h, Sabah, text at bottom. i, Sarawak, text at top. j, Sarawak, text at bottom. Foods on Nos. 1321 and 1322 are different.
No. 1323: a, Chinese foods. b, Indian foods. c, Malaysian foods.

2010, Aug. 10 Perf. 13¼
1321 A427 Sheet of 10 5.25 2.60
a.-j. 60c Any single .50 .25

Booklet Stamps
1322 A427 Booklet pane of 10 4.00 —
a.-j. 60c Any single .40 .25

Souvenir Sheet
1323 A428 Sheet of 3 2.00 1.00
a.-c. $1 Any single .65 .30

Life of Aboriginal People A429

Designs: 60c. Women holding ketuk buluh (musical instruments). 70c, Man shooting with blowpipe. 80c, Man carving figures.

2010, Sept. 27 Wmk. 388
1324-1326 A429 Set of 3 1.40 .70

Old Post Offices — A430

No. 1327: a, Jalan Kelang Lama Post Office, Kuala Lumpur. b, Layang-Layang Post Office. c, Jalan Raja Post Office. d, Temangan Post Office. e, Merlimau Post Office. f, Seremban General Post Office. g, Fraser Hill (Bukit Fraser) Post Office. h, Kuala Kangsar Post Office. i, Kaki Bukit Post Office. j, Jalan Bagan Luar Post Office. k, Kudat Post Office. l, Kuching General Post Office. m, Kajang Post Office. n, Kuala Terengganu Post Office. o, Kuala Lumpur General Post Office, flag of Federal Territory. p, Johor Bahru General Post Office, flag of Johore. q, Sungai Petani Post Office, flag of Kedah. r, Rantau Panjang Post Office, flag of Kelantan. s, Alor Gajah Post Office, flag of Malacca. t, Bandar Baru Serting Post Office, flag of Negri Sembilan. u, Ringlet Post Office, flag of Pahang. v, Tronoh Post Office, flag of Perak. w, Kangar Post Office, flag of Perlis. x, Bukit Mertajam Post Office, flag of Penang. y, Kota Kinabalu General Post Office, flag of Sabah. z, Sarikei Post Office, flag of Sarawak. aa, Bukit Rotan Post Office, flag of Selangor. ab, Jerteh Post Office, flag of Trengganu.

Perf. 13¾x13½ Syncopated
2010, Oct. 9
1327 Sheet of 28 11.00 11.00
a.-ab. A430 60c Any single .35 .25

"Malaysia is Number 1" — A431

Handcrafted products, "Malaysia is Number 1" emblem and: No. 1328, 30c, Computer mouse, satellite dish. No. 1329, 30c, Astronaut and spaceship. No. 1330, 50c, Buildings. No. 1331, 50c, Robot.

2010, Nov. 10 Perf. 13¼x13½
1328-1331 A431 Set of 4 1.10 .55

Children's Games — A432

No. 1332, 60c: a, Batu Seremban. b, Congkak.
No. 1333, 60c: a, Galah Panjang. b, Kondakondi.
No. 1334, 60c: a, Perang-perang. b, Telefon Tin.
$5, Main Bayang-bayang.

Litho. With Glitter Affixed
Perf. 13¾x14¼
2010, Dec. 13 Unwmk.
Self-Adhesive
Horiz. Pairs, #a-b
1332-1334 A432 Set of 3 2.40 1.25

Souvenir Sheet
Die Cut Perf. 13½x13¼
1335 A432 $5 multi 3.25 1.60

No. 1335 contains one 75x50mm stamp.

Pets — A433

Child and: 60c, Rabbit. 80c, Cat. $1, Dog.
No. 1339, $5, Rabbit. No. 1340, $5, Rabbit, with Indipex 2011 emblem.

2011 Litho. Wmk. 388 Perf. 13¼
1336-1338 A433 Set of 3 1.60 .80

Souvenir Sheets
1339 A433 $5 multi 3.25 1.60
1340 A433 $5 multi 3.50 1.75

Issued: Nos. 1336-1339, 1/18; No. 1340, 2/18. Indipex 2011 World Philatelic Exhibition (No. 1340).

MALAYSIA

Highlands Tourism — A434

Designs: 50c, Funicular railroad, Bukit Bendera. 60c, Tea picker, Cameron Highlands. 90c, Cable car and station, Mat Cincang Mountain, Langkawi. $1, Cabbage patch, Kundasang.

2011, Feb. 21		Perf. 13½x13¼
1341-1344	A434 Set of 4	2.00 1.00

Malaysia, Winners of 2010 Suzuki Cup — A435

Designs: No. 1345, 60c, Medal and emblem of Malaysian soccer team. No. 1346, 60c, Suzuki Cup and tournament emblem, vert. (30x50mm).

Perf. 13¼, 13¼x13½ (#1346)

2011, Feb. 28			
1345-1346	A435	Set of 2	.80 .40

Spices — A436

Designs: No. 1347, 60c, Cinnamon. 90c, Star anise. $1, Cardamom.

No. 1350, 60c: a, Fennel seed, text at top. b, Fennel seed, text at bottom. c, Turmeric, text at top. d, Turmeric, text at bottom. e, Chili peppers, text at top. f, Chili peppers, text at bottom. g, Coriander, text at top. h, Coriander, text at bottom. i, White pepper, text at top. j, White pepper, text at bottom.

No. 1351: a, $1, Various spice on stone, spice crushing roller. b, $2, Various spices on stone.

2011, Mar. 28			Perf. 13¼
1347-1349	A436	Set of 3	1.75 .85
1350		Booklet pane of 10	4.00 —
a.-j.	A436 60c Any single		.40 .25
l.	Complete booklet, #1350		4.00

Souvenir Sheet
Perf. 14x13¼

| 1351 | A436 | Sheet of 2, #a-b | 2.00 1.00 |

No. 1351 contains two 50x60mm stamps.

National Heritage Artifacts — A437

No. 1352: a, Malay belt buckle. b, Gold coin showing deer. c, Sireh set (betel containers) of Sultan Abdul Samad of Selangor. d, Gold coin of Sultan Muzaffar Shah of Johore. e, Arch of sitting Buddha.

No. 1353: a, Royal Trengganu tobacco box. b, Gold Coin of Sultan Alau'uddin Riayat Shah. c, Dong S'on bell. d, Gold coin of Sultan Zainal Abidin II of Trengganu. e, Statue of Avalokitesvara.

2011, Apr. 11		Perf. 12½x12¾
1352	Horiz. strip of 5	2.00 1.00
a.-e.	A437 60c Any single	.40 .25
1353	Horiz. strip of 5	2.00 1.00
a.-e.	A437 60c Any single	.40 .25

Personalized Stamps — A438

No. 1354: a, Bunga Raya. b, Durian. c, Handicraft. d, Wau Bulan.

2011, Apr. 28		Perf. 13¾x14
1354	Block of 4	1.40 .70
a.-b.	A438 35c Either single	.25 .25
c.-d.	A438 65c Either single	.45 .25

No. 1354 printed in sheets containing two blocks of 4. The right halves of Nos. 1354a and 1354c and the left halves of Nos. 1354b and 1354d could be personalized. Images showing silver handicrafts are generic images. Compare with No. B1.

Virtues — A439

No. 1355 — Inscriptions in black: a, Love. b, Hardworking. c, Courteous. d, Mutual respect. e, Independent. f, Awareness. g, Kind hearted. h, Thankful ("Thank you" in green in 7 different languages). i, Living in harmony. j, Integrity.

2011, June 13		Perf. 12¾x12½
1355	Block of 10	4.00 2.00
a.-j.	A439 60c Any single	.40 .25
k.	As "h," "Thank you" in green in 8 different languages	.40 .25
l.	Block of 10, #1355a-1355g, 1355i-1355k	4.00 2.00

Issued: Nos. 1355k, 1355l, 7/18.

Aviation in Malaysia, Cent. — A440

Designs: 60c, Early monoplane. 80c, Airport control tower, passenger airplane and fuel truck. $1, Airport terminal, jets.

2011, July 7	Litho.	Wmk. 388
1356-1358	A440 Set of 3	1.60 .80

Miniature Sheet

Royal Palaces — A441

No. 1359 — Palace, arms and map of: a, Kuala Lumpur. b, Negri Sembilan. c, Selangor. d, Perlis. e, Trengganu. f, Kedah. g, Kelantan. h, Pahang. i, Johore. k, Perak.

2011, July 18		Perf. 14½x14¼
1359	A441 Sheet of 10	7.00 3.50
a.-j.	$1 Any single	.70 .35

Miniature Sheet

Friendship Between Indonesia and Malaysia — A442

No. 1360: a, National Monument, Malaysia. b, Proclamation Monument, Indonesia. c, 1959 Malaya and North Borneo $1 banknote. d, 1945 5-sen Indonesia banknote. e, Malaya #84. f, Indonesia #1LM1. g, Gallus gallus. h, Gallus varius.

2011, Aug. 8		Perf. 12½x12¾
1360	A442 Sheet of 8	5.00 2.40
a.-h.	90c Any single	.60 .30

See Indonesia Nos. 2284-2285.

Art — A443

Designs: 60c, Datuk Bajau Horseman, North Borneo, by Mohd Hoessein Enas, 1963. 90c, Ayam Jantan, sculpture by Anthony Lau, 1963, horiz. $1, Flag, by Nik Zainal Abidin Nik Salleh, 1970, horiz.

Perf. 12¾x12½, 12½x12¾

2011, Sept. 19		
1361-1363	A443 Set of 3	1.60 .80

Mailboxes — A444

No. 1364 — Mailbox, building and postal service emblem with inscription at bottom: a, Bukit Bendera, Pulau Pinang. b, Bukit Fraser, Pahang. c, Melaka Bandaraya Bersejarah. d, Seremban, Negeri Sembilan. e, Pejabat Pos Besar, Kuala Lumpur.

Litho. & Embossed
Perf. 13½x14

2011, Oct. 10		Wmk. 388
1364	Horiz. strip of 5	3.25 1.60
a.-e.	A444 $1 Any single	.65 .30

Mailboxes A445

Mailbox, buildings and inscription at LL: No. 1365, Bukit Bendera, Pulau Pinang. No. 1366, Bukit Fraser, Pahang. No. 1367, Melaka Bandaraya Bersejarah. No. 1368, Seremban, Negeri Sembilan. No. 1369, Pejabat Pos Besar, Kuala Lumpur.

Serpentine Die Cut 13x12¾

2011, Oct. 10	Litho.	Unwmk.

Booklet Stamps Self-Adhesive

1365	A445 60c multi	.40 .25
1366	A445 60c multi	.40 .25
1367	A445 60c multi	.40 .25
1368	A445 60c multi	.40 .25
1369	A445 60c multi	.40 .25
a.	Booklet pane of 10, 2 each #1365-1369	4.00
	Nos. 1365-1369 (5)	2.00 1.25

Tunnel Construction A446

No. 1370, 60c: a, Tunneling through. b, TBM after breakthrough.
No. 1371, 60c: a, Tunnel breakthrough. b, Construction gantry.
No. 1372, 60c: a, Road tunnel. b, Schematic cross-section.
No. 1373, vert.: a, Vignettes of Nos. 1370a, 1371a, 1371b. b, Vignettes of Nos. 1370b, 1372a, 1372b.

Perf. 13¼x14¼ Syncopated

2011, Nov. 21	Litho.	Unwmk.

Vert. Pairs, #a-b

| 1370-1372 | A446 Set of 3 | 2.40 1.25 |

Souvenir Sheet
Self-Adhesive
Litho. With Three-Dimensional Plastic Affixed
Serpentine Die Cut 12x12¾

1373	A446 Sheet of 2	3.25 1.60
a.	$2 multi	1.25 .60
b.	$3 multi	2.00 1.00

No. 1373 contains two 35x40mm stamps.

Regalia A447

Designs: 60c, Crown (Gandik diraja). 80c, Belt buckle (Pending diraja). 90c, Throne (Singgahsana).

Wmk. 388

2011, Dec. 12	Litho.	Perf. 14
1374-1376	A447 Set of 3	1.50 .75

Women Creating Textiles — A448

No. 1377: a, Cindai. b, Songket. c, Pua Kumbu. d, Ci Xiu. e, Rangkit.

Wmk. 388

2012, Jan. 12	Litho.	Perf. 12
1377	Horiz. strip of 5	2.00 1.00
a.-e.	A448 60c Any single	.40 .25

Souvenir Sheets
Variable Perfs. 13½-14

| 1378 | A449 $3 multi | 2.00 1.00 |
| a. | With Indonesia 2012 World Stamp Championships emblem in sheet margin, perf. 13½ | 2.00 1.00 |

Litho. With Foil Application

| 1379 | A449 $5 gold & multi | 3.50 1.75 |
| a. | With Indonesia 2012 World Stamp Championships emblem in sheet margin, variable perfs. 13¼-13½ | 3.50 1.75 |

Yes to Life, No to Drugs Campaign — A450

No. 1380: a, Family. b, Children at play.

Perf. 13¾x13

2012, Feb. 27	Litho.	Wmk. 388
1380	A450 60c Horiz. pair, #a-b	.80 .40
1381	A450 $1 shown	.70 .35

Malaysian Antarctic Research Program — A451

MALAYSIA

Design: 60c, Map of Antarctica, flag of Malaysia, scientist, emblem.
No. 1383: a, World map, emblem. b, Penguins, bacteria, scientist, emblem (70x35mm).

2012, Mar. 8   Wmk. 388   Perf. 13¼
| 1382 | A451 | 60c multi | .40 | .25 |
| 1383 | A451 | 90c Horiz. pair, #a-b | 1.25 | .60 |

Marine Life — A452

Designs: No. 1384, Red-spotted coral crab. No. 1385, Leopard moray eel. No. 1386, Mandarinfish. No. 1387, Blue sea star. $5, Green sea turtle, Robust ghostpipefish, Thorny seahorse.

2012, Mar. 21   Perf. 12
1384	A452	60c multi	.40	.25
1385	A452	60c multi	.40	.25
	a.	Perf. 13½	.40	.25
1386	A452	60c multi	.40	.25
	a.	Perf. 13½	.40	.25
1387	A452	60c multi	.40	.25
	a.	Perf. 13½	.40	.25
	Nos. 1384-1387 (4)		1.60	1.00

Souvenir Sheet   Perf. 12½
| 1388 | A452 | $5 multi | 3.25 | 1.60 |

No. 1388 contains one 90x35mm stamp.

Installation of 14th Yang Di-Pertuan Agong — A453

Designs: 60c, 14th Yang Di-Pertuan Agong, yellow green frame. 80c, 14th Yang Di-Pertuan Agong and wife, horiz. $1, 14th Yang Di-Pertuan Agong, red frame.
No. 1392: a, Malaysia #79. b, 14th Yang Di-Pertuan Agong, gold frame.

Wmk. 388
2012, Apr. 11   Litho.   Perf. 14
| 1389-1391 | A453 | Set of 3 | 1.60 | .80 |

Souvenir Sheet   Litho. With Foil Application
1392		Sheet of 2	3.25	1.60
	a.	A453 $2 multi	1.25	.60
	b.	A453 $3 multi	2.00	1.00
	c.	As #1392, with added emblem in gold in sheet margin	3.25	1.60

Issued: No. 1392c, 1/1/13. No. 1392c has added emblem similar to a circular cancel inscribed "100 Tahun Setem Kedah & 125 Tahun Perkhidmatan Pos Di Kedah" and "Pameran Setem."

Aromatic Plants — A454

Designs: 60c, Polygonum minus. $1, Mentha piperita.
a, $5, Kaffir lime, vert.

Perf. 14¾x14 Syncopated
2012, May 24   Litho.
| 1393-1394 | A454 | Set of 2 | 1.00 | .50 |

Souvenir Sheet   Perf. 14x14¾ Syncopated
| 1395 | A454 | $5 multi | 3.25 | 1.60 |

No. 1395 is impregnated with a lime scent.

2012 World Gas Conference, Kuala Lumpur — A455

Inscriptions: No. 1396, 60c, Securing Gas Supply. No. 1397, 60c, Enhancing Gas Demand. No. 1398, 60c, A Sustainable Future. No. 1399, 60c, Foundation For Growth.

2012, June 4   Wmk. 388   Perf. 12½
| 1396-1399 | A455 | Set of 4 | 1.50 | .75 |

Miniature Sheet

Yang Di-Pertuan Agongs — A456

No. 1400 — Photograph and Roman numeral of Yang Di-Pertuan Agong: a, XI. b, XII. c, XIII. d, X. e, I. f, IX. g, II. h, VIII. i, III. j, VII. k, VI. l, V. m, IV. n, XIV. Nos. 1400a-1400m are 35x35mm, No. 1400n is 70x70mm.

Litho. With Foil Application
2012, June 21   Wmk. 388   Perf. 13¼
1400	A456	Sheet of 14 + 2 labels	12.00	6.00
	a.-m.	$1 Any single	.65	.30
	n.	$5 multi	3.25	1.60

Traditional Occupations — A457

No. 1401: a, Tukang seni kertas (artist decorating lanterns). b, Tukang tilik (men with bird and cage).
No. 1402: a, Penjaja satay (satay griller). b, Penjaja nasi kandar (man carrying pot and baskets).
No. 1403: a, Penjaja lemang (woman stirring pot). b, Penjaja manisan (confection vender with bicycle). c, Tukang ubat tradisional (food vendor on mat). d, Penjaja pasembor (juice vendor on bicycle). e, Tukang dobi (laundry men).

2012, June 21   Litho.   Wmk. 388
1401	A457	Horiz. pair	1.00	.50
	a.-b.	80c Either single	.50	.25
1402	A457	Horiz. pair	1.30	.65
	a.-b.	$1 Either single	.65	.30

Booklet Stamps
1403	A457	Horiz. strip of 5	2.00	1.25
	a.-e.	60c Any single	.40	.25
	f.	Booklet pane of 10, 2 each #1403a-1403e	4.00	
		Complete booklet, #1403f	4.00	

Coins — A458

Designs: No. 1404, 60c, Obverse of 5-cent coin (lilac background). No. 1405, 60c, Reverse of 5-cent coin (no numeral on coin, lilac background). No. 1406, 60c, Obverse of 10-cent coin (light blue background). No. 1407, 60c, Reverse of 10-cent coin (no numeral on coin, light blue background). No. 1408, 60c, Obverse of 20-cent coin (light green background). No. 1409, 60c, Reverse of 20-cent coin (no numeral on coin, light green background). No. 1410, 60c, Obverse of 50-cent coin (pink background). No. 1411, 60c, Reverse of 50-cent coin (no numeral on coin, pink background).

Litho. & Embossed With Foil Application
2012, July 16   Unwmk.   Perf. 14
| 1404-1411 | A458 | Set of 8 | 3.25 | 1.60 |

Banknotes — A459

No. 1412: a, 1-ringgit banknote. b, 50-ringgit banknote. c, 20-ringgit banknote.
No. 1413: a, 100-ringgit banknote. b, 5-ringgit banknote. d, 10-ringgit banknote.

Litho. With Foil Application   Perf. 14x13¼
2012, July 10   Unwmk.
1412	A459	Sheet of 3	9.75	5.00
	a.-c.	$5 Any single	3.25	1.60
1413	A459	Sheet of 3	9.75	5.00
	a.-c.	$5 Any single	3.25	1.60

National Unity — A460

Inscriptions below "Perpaduan": No. 1414, 60c, Bahasa. No. 1415, 60c, Gotong-Royong. No. 1416, 60c, Sukan. No. 1417, 60c, Tarian.

Perf. 13¼x13½
2012, Aug. 30   Litho.   Wmk. 388
| 1414-1417 | A460 | Set of 4 | 1.60 | .80 |

British Royalty — A461

Designs: No. 1418, $1.50, Malaya Selangor #101 No. 1419, $1.50, Duke and Duchess of Cambridge.
No. 1420: a, Like No. 1418. b, Like No. 1419.

2012, Sept. 13   Perf. 14
| 1418-1419 | A461 | Set of 2 | 2.00 | 1.00 |

Souvenir Sheet
1420		Sheet of 2	3.25	1.60
	a.-b.	A461 $2.50 Either single	1.60	.80
	c.	As No. 1420, with Thailand 2013 World Stamp Exhibition emblem in sheet margin	3.25	1.60

Reign of Queen Elizabeth II, 60th anniv. (Nos. 1418, 1420a), Wedding of Prince William and Catherine Middleton (Nos. 1419, 1420b).
Issued: No. 1420c, 8/2/13.

Festivals — A462

Inscriptions: No. 1421, 60c, Hari Raya Aidiladha (Eid ul-Adha). No. 1422, 60c, Perayaan Kuih Bulan (Chinese mid-autumn festival). No. 1423, 60c, Pesta Kaul (Kaul Festival). No. 1424, 60c, Regatta Lepa. No. 1425, 60c, Thaipusam.

Malacca, 750th Anniv. — A463

Litho. With Foil Application   Perf. 13½x14
2012, Sept. 27   Unwmk.
| 1421-1425 | A462 | Set of 5 | 2.00 | 1.00 |

Anniversary emblem and: 50c, Tokong Cheng Hoon Teng (Cheng Hoon Teng Temple). 90c, Masjid Kampong Hulu (Kampong Hulu Mosque).
750c, Muzium Yang Di-Pertua Negeri Malaka (Malacca Governor's Museum).

Wmk. 388
2012, Oct. 7   Litho.   Perf. 12
| 1426-1427 | A463 | Set of 2 | .95 | .45 |

Souvenir Sheet   Litho. With Foil Application   Perf. 13¼
| 1428 | A463 | 750c multi | 5.00 | 2.50 |

No. 1428 contains one 70x35mm stamp. See No. 1496.

World Post Day — A464

Malaysian Postal Service and Universal Postal Union emblems: 60c, Postman with bicycle, 1950. 80c, Postman on scooter, 1970. No. 1431, $1, Postman on scooter, 1990. No. 1432: a, $1, Postman holding scooter, emblems. b, $2, Five postmen (90x35mm).

Perf. 12½, 12½x12½x12x12½ (#1432b)
2012, Oct. 22   Litho.
| 1429-1431 | A464 | Set of 3 | 1.00 | .50 |

Souvenir Sheet
1432		Sheet of 2	2.00	1.00
	a.	A464 $1 multi	.65	.30
	b.	A464 $2 multi	1.30	.65

Greetings Stamps — A466

No. 1433 — Inscription: a, Flora & Fauna / Malaysia. b, Bendera Malaysia / Malaysian Flag. c, Batik / Malaysia. d, Latarlangit Malaysia / Malaysian Skyline.
No. 1434 — Inscription: a, Bendera Malaysia / Malaysian Flag (flag in circle). b, Perayaan / Celebration. c, Tulus Ikhlas / Yours Sincerely. d, Salam / Greetings.

Perf. 10½x10¼
2012, Nov. 5   Wmk. 388
1433	A465	Block or vert. strip of 4	1.60	.80
	a.-d.	60c Any single	.40	.25
1434	A466	Block or vert. strip of 4	1.60	.80
	a.-d.	60c Any single	.40	.25

Children's Hobbies — A467

No. 1435, 60c: a, Girl baking cookies. b, Girl collecting stamps.
No. 1436, 60c: a, Boy playing soccer. b, Robot fishing.
No. 1437, 60c: a, Boy playing drums. b, Boy with camera.
$5, Children reading letters.

MALAYSIA

Perf. 13½x13¼
2012, Nov. 19 Litho. Unwmk.
Horiz. Pairs, #a-b
1435-1437 A467 Set of 3 2.40 1.25
Souvenir Sheet
Litho. With Foil Application
Perf. 12
Wmk. 388
1438 A467 $5 multi 3.25 1.60
No. 1438 contains one 70x45mm stamp.

Postal History of Kedah — A468

Designs: No. 1439, 90c, Malaya-Kedah #1. No. 1440, 90c, Malaya-Kedah #16. No. 1441, 90c, Malaya-Kedah #20.
$3, Kedah cancel on postal card from Siam, vert.

Perf. 14 Syncopated
2012, Dec. 20 Litho. Wmk. 388
1439-1441 A468 Set of 3 1.75 .90
Souvenir Sheet
Perf. 14¼
1442 A468 $3 multi 2.00 1.00
Postage stamps of Kedah, 100th anniv. No. 1442 contains one 28x38mm stamp.

Woodpeckers — A469

Designs: 60c, Banded woodpecker. 80c, Common flameback woodpecker. $1, Lesser yellownape woodpecker.
$5, White-bellied woodpecker, horiz.

2013, Jan. 13 Perf. 13¼x13½
1443-1445 A469 Set of 3 1.60 .80
Souvenir Sheet
Perf. 13¾x13½
1446 A469 $5 multi 3.25 1.60
No. 1446 contains one 64x48mm stamp.

Exotic Pets — A470

Designs: 60c, African pygmy hedgehog. 80c, Green iguana. $1, Sugar glider.
$3, $5, Royal python.

Perf. 13¼x13½
2013, Feb. 5 Litho. Wmk. 388
1447-1449 A470 Set of 3 1.60 .80
1447a   Perf. 12   .40 .25
Souvenir Sheets
1450 A470 $3 multi 2.00 1.00
Litho. With Foil Application
1451 A470 $5 multi 3.25 1.60
Nos. 1450-1451 each contain one 30x50mm stamp.

National Unity — A471

No. 1452, 60c — Map of Malaysia, "1" and various people with inscription: a, Semangat Kasih Sayang. b, Semangat Keprihatinan.
No. 1453, 60c — Map of Malaysia, "1" and various people with inscription: a, Semangat Kerjasama. b, Semangat Kemasyarakatan.

Wmk. 388
2013, Mar. 26 Litho. Perf. 13¼
Horiz. Pairs, #a-b
1452-1453 A471 Set of 2 1.60 .80

Lighthouses A472

Designs: 50c, Pulau Rimau Lighthouse, Penang. No. 1455, 60c, Fort Cornwallis Lighthouse, Penang. No. 1456, 60c, Pulau Angsa Lighthouse, Selangor.
$5, One Fathom Bank Lighthouse, Selangor, vert.

Perf. 13½x13¼
2013, Apr. 30 Litho. Unwmk.
Granite Paper
1454-1456 A472 Set of 3 1.25 .60
Souvenir Sheet
Perf. 13¼x13½
1457 A472 $5 multi 3.25 1.60

Miniature Sheets

Malaysian Forests — A473

No. 1458 — Royal Belum Forest: a, Gould's frogmouth. b, Helmeted hornbill. c, Rafflesia azlanii. d, Trevesia burckii. e, Trilobite larvae.
No. 1459 — Maliau Basin Forest: a, Borneo pygmy elephant (30x40mm). b, Maliau Waterfall (50x40mm). c, Nepenthes veitchii (30x40mm). d, Dead leaf mantis (30x40mm). e, Violin beetle (30x40mm).
No. 1460 — Taman Negara Forest: a, Asian bearcat (30x40mm). b, Berkoh Cascade (30x40mm). c, Heteropoda davidbowie (30x40mm). d, Malayan peacock pheasant (50x40mm). e, Bioluminescent mushrooms (30x40mm).

Serpentine Die Cut 12¾
2013, May 13 Litho. Unwmk.
Self-Adhesive
1458 A473 Sheet of 5 3.25
a.-e. $1 Any single   .65 .30
1459 A473 Sheet of 5 3.25
a.-e. $1 Any single   .65 .30
1460 A473 Sheet of 5 3.25
a.-e. $1 Any single   .65 .30
Nos. 1458-1460 (3) 9.75

Marine Life A474

No. 1461, 60c: a, Sea anemone. b, Soft coral.
No. 1462, 60c: a, Feather stars. b, Sea pen.
$5, Table coral.

Perf. 13½x13¼
2013, June 28 Litho. Unwmk.
Horiz. Pairs, #a-b
1461-1462 A474 Set of 2 1.50 .75
Souvenir Sheet
1463 A474 $5 multi 3.25 1.60
No. 1463 contains one 75x26mm stamp.

Salad Ingredients — A475

No. 1464, 60c: a, Centella asiatica. b, Parkia speciosa.
No. 1465, 60c: a, Psophocarpus tetragonolobus. b, Annacardium occidentale.

Wmk. 388
2013, July 25 Litho. Perf. 13¼
Vert. Pairs, #a-b
1464-1465 A475 Set of 2 1.50 .75

Third Tri-Nation Stamp Exhibition — A476

Exhibition emblem, buildings and flags of Malaysia, Singapore and Thailand with: 90c, Flat flags. $2, Flags blowing in wind.
$3, Exhibition emblem, Hibiscus rosa-sinensis, Vanda Miss Joaquim, Cassia fistula.

Unwmk.
2013, Aug. 23 Litho. Perf. 14
1466-1467 A476 Set of 2 1.75 .90
Souvenir Sheet
Self-Adhesive
Die Cut Perf. 12
1468 A476 $3 multi 1.90 .95
No. 1468 contains one 54x38mm triangular stamp.

Museums A477

No. 1469: a, Chimney Museum, Labuan. b, Sungai Lembing Museum, Pahang. c, Adat Museum (Tradition Museum), Jelebu, Negri Sembilan. d, Tekstil Negara Museum (Natl. Textile Museum), Kuala Lumpur.
No. 1470: a, Perak Museum, Taiping, Perak. b, Negara Museum (Natl. Museum), Kuala Lumpur. c, Lembah Bujang Archaeological Museum, Kedah. d, Galeria Perdana, Langkawi, Kedah. e, Kota Kayang Museum, Perlis. f, Labuan Museum, Labuan.

Perf. 14x14¼ Syncopated
2013, Aug. 31 Litho. Unwmk.
1469   Horiz. strip of 4 1.60 .80
a.-d. A477 60c Any single .40 .25
1470   Block of 6 2.40 1.25
a.-f. A477 60c Any single .40 .25
The right part of Nos. 1469a-1469d and 1470a-1470f has a rectangle of thermochromic ink, which, when warmed, reveals an item from the museum shown. See Nos. 1494-1495 for stamps dated "2014" without thermochromic ink.

Formation of the Federation of Malaysia, 50th Anniv. A478

Perf. 13½x13¼
2013, Sept. 16 Litho. Wmk. 388
1471 A478 60c multi .40 .25

A479

A480

Art by Disabled Children A481

Litho. & Thermography
2013, Oct. 22 Unwmk. Perf. 13¼
Granite Paper
1472 A479 60c multi .40 .25
1473 A480 60c multi .40 .25
1474 A480 60c multi .40 .25
Nos. 1472-1474 (3) 1.20 .75

Fruit — A482

Designs: 60c, Passiflora edulis. 80c, Annona squamosa. $1.20, Cynometra cauliflora.

Perf. 13¼x13½
2013, Oct. 28 Litho. Wmk. 388
1475-1477 A482 Set of 3 1.60 .80

RHB Bank, Cent. A483

No. 1478: a, First bank branch building, Old Market Square, Kuala Lumpur. b, First automatic teller machine. c, Launch of Kwong Yik Bank Headquarters. d, RHB Bank Headquarters.

Litho. With Foil Application
2013, Nov. 23 Unwmk. Perf. 14¼
Granite Paper
1478 A483 60c Block of 4, #a-d 1.50 .75

Baba-Nyonya (Peranakan Chinese) Heritage — A484

No. 1479, 60c: a, Nyonyaware. b, Nyonya beaded slippers.
No. 1480, 80c: a, Malacca Peranakan townhouse. b, Baba and Nyonya wedding attire.
$5, Nyonya Kebaya embroidery.

Unwmk.
2013, Nov. 29 Litho. Perf. 14
Horiz. Pairs, #a-b
1479-1480 A484 Set of 2 1.75 .85
Souvenir Sheet
1481 A484 $5 multi 3.25 1.60
No. 1481 contains one 50x60mm stamp with laser-cut holes in the vignette.

Endangered Cats — A485

MALAYSIA

No. 1482: a, Panthera pardus with spotted fur. b, Panthera pardus with black fur.
No. 1483, Neofelis nebulosa. No. 1484, Neofelis diardi.
$3, Panthera tigris jacksoni, vert.

Perf. 13½x13¼
2013, Dec. 23   Litho.   Wmk. 388
1482		Horiz. pair	.80	.40
a.-b.	A485	60c Either single	.40	.25
1483	A485	80c multi	.50	.25
1484	A485	80c multi	.50	.25
		Nos. 1482-1484 (3)	1.80	.90

Souvenir Sheet
Perf. 13¼x13½
1485	A485	$3 multi	1.90	.95
a.		As No. 1485, with Four Nations Stamp Show emblem in sheet margin	1.90	.95

Issued: No. 1485a, 5/27/14.

New Year 2014 (Year of the Horse) A486

No. 1486, 50c — Inscription: a, Sukan Polo. b, Unit Berkuda DBKL.
No. 1487, 80c — Inscription: a, Unit Berkuda PSP PDRM. b, Unit Berkuda Kor Armor Diraja.
$3, Horse and rider, white background. $5, Horse and rider, gold background.

Perf. 13x13¼
2014, Jan. 27   Litho.   Unwmk.
Horiz. Pairs, #a-b
1486-1487	A486	Set of 2	1.60	.80

Souvenir Sheets
1488-1489	A486	Set of 2	4.75	2.40

Roses — A487

Designs: 60c, White hybrid tea roses. 70c, Yellow Grandiflora roses. $1.20, Pink English roses.
$5, Hybrid tea roses.

Unwmk.
2014, Feb. 14   Litho.   Perf. 13
1490-1492	A487	Set of 3	1.60	.80

Souvenir Sheet
Perf.
1493	A487	$5 multi	3.25	1.60

No. 1493 contains one 52x50mm heart-shaped stamp and is impregnated with a rose scent.

Museums Type of 2013 Without Thermochromic Ink

No. 1494: a, Chimney Museum, Labuan. b, Sungai Lembing Museum, Pahang. c, Adat Museum (Tradition Museum), Jelebu, Negri Sembilan. d, Tekstil Negara Museum (Natl. Textile Museum), Kuala Lumpur.
No. 1495: a, Perak Museum, Taiping, Perak. b, Negara Museum (Natl. Museum), Kuala Lumpur. c, Lembah Bujang Archaeological Museum, Kedah. d, Galeria Perdana, Langkawi, Kedah. e, Kota Kayang Museum, Perlis. f, Labuan Museum, Labuan.

Perf. 14¼ Syncopated
2014, Mar. 13   Litho.   Unwmk.
Dated "2014"
1494		Horiz. strip of 4	1.60	.80
a.-d.	A477	50c Any single	.40	.25
1495		Block of 6	2.40	1.25
a.-f.	A477	60c Any single	.40	.25

Nos. 1494a-1494d and 1495a-1495f lack the thermographic ink present on Nos. 1469a-1469d and 1470a-1470f that covers an item from the museum. Stamps with thermographic ink are dated "2013" only.

No. 1427 Redrawn With Added Emblem
Wmk. 388
2014, May 24   Litho.   Perf. 12
1496	A463	90c multi	.55	.30

The emblem added to No. 1496 is inscribed "Melaka and Jogja City of Museums 2014" and is to the right of the flag emblem on No. 1427.

Opening of World Scout Bureau, Kuala Lumpur A488

Scouting trefoil and: 30c, Display at World Scout Bureau. 50c, Malaysian scouting emblem, trefoil made of Scouts. 60c, Malaysian scouting emblem, buildings.

Perf. 13½x13¼
2014, June 18   Litho.   Wmk. 388
1497-1499	A488	Set of 3	.90	.45

Opening of Kuala Lumpur International Airport 2 — A489

Inscriptions: No. 1500, 80c, Main Terminal Building. No. 1501, 80c, Skybridge. No. 1502, 80c, Departure Hall. No. 1503, 80c, Gateway@klia2.
$5, Aerial view of airport.

Perf. 14¼x14
2014, June 24   Litho.   Unwmk.
1500-1503	A489	Set of 4	2.00	1.00

Souvenir Sheet
1504	A489	$5 multi	3.25	1.60

Fruit — A490

Designs: 60c, Artocarpus heterophyllus. 80c, Durio zibethinus. $1.20, Cucumis melo. $1.40, Averrhoa carambola.

Wmk. 388
2014, July 17   Litho.   Perf. 13¼
1505-1508	A490	Set of 4	2.50	1.25

Independence, 57th Anniv. — A491

Perf. 13½x13¼
2014, Aug. 31   Litho.   Wmk. 388
1509	A491	60c multi	.40	.25

Local Foods of Malaysia and Hong Kong — A492

Flower and: No. 1510, $1.40, Nasi lemak. No. 1511, $1.40, Satay. No. 1512, $1.40, Egg waffle. No. 1513, $1.40, Poon choi.

Unwmk.
2014, Oct. 19   Litho.   Perf. 14
1510-1513	A492	Set of 4	3.50	1.75
1513a		Souvenir sheet of 4, #1510-1513	6.50	1.75

See Hong Kong Nos. 1683-1686.

Folk Tales A493

No. 1514, 60c: a, Tun Kudu. b, Tun Fatimah.
No. 1515, 60c: a, Mahsuri. b, Merong Maha Wangsa.
No. 1516, 60c: a, Hang Tuah. b, Tun Teja.

Perf. 13½x13¼
2014, Oct. 27   Litho.   Wmk. 388
Horiz. Pairs, #a-b
1514-1516	A493	Set of 3	2.25	1.10

Souvenir Sheet

2014 World Youth Stamp Exhibition, Kuala Lumpur — A494

Litho. With Foil Application
2014, Nov. 5   Wmk. 388   Perf. 14
1517	A494	$5 multi	3.00	1.50

2014 World Youth Stamp Exhibition, Kuala Lumpur — A501

No. 1518: a, $1, India #6 on cover, two India #5 on cover (40x60mm). b, $2, Three India #2, two India #4 on cover (40x30mm).
No. 1519: a, $2, Pongo pygmaeus. b, $3, Panthera tigris jacksoni.
No. 1520: a, $2, Hibiscus rosa-sinensis (30x50mm). b, $3, Rafflesia arnoldii (60x570mm).
No. 1521, India #7, two India #6 on cover. No. 1522, Sultan Abdul Samad Building, Kuala Lumpur. No. 1523, Mak Yong dancer. No. 1524, The Princess of Gunung Ledang.

Litho., Litho. with Foil Application (#1520, 1524)
Perf. 13½, 14 (#1520b)
2014, Dec. 1   Wmk. 388
1518	A495	Sheet of 2, #a-b	1.75	.85
1519	A496	Sheet of 2, #a-b	3.00	1.50
1520	A497	Sheet of 2, #a-b	3.00	1.50

Souvenir Sheets
1521	A498	$3 multi	1.75	.85
1522	A499	$5 multi	3.00	1.50
1523	A500	$5 multi	3.00	1.50
1524	A501	$5 multi	3.00	1.50
		Nos. 1518-1524 (7)	18.50	9.20

Sultan Abdul Halim Mu'adzam Bridge, Penang — A502

Bridge: No. 1525, $1.20, At night. No. 1526, $1.20, In daylight.

Perf. 13¼x13½
2014, Dec. 31   Litho.   Wmk. 388
1525-1526	A502	Set of 2	1.40	.70

Medicinal Plants — A503

Designs: 60c, Orthosiphon stamineus. 70c, Hibiscus sabdariffa. 80c, Andrographis paniculata. $3, Clinacanthus nutans.

Perf. 13¼x13½
2015, Jan. 20   Litho.   Wmk. 388
1527-1529	A503	Set of 3	1.25	.60

Souvenir Sheet
Perf. 14
1530	A503	$3 multi	1.75	.85

No. 1530 contains one 40x50mm stamp.

Malaysian Chairmanship of ASEAN — A504

Emblem, flags of ASEAN countries and and: 60c, Handshake, people. 80c, Upraised hands. $1.20, Stylized hand holding plant.

Perf. 13¼x13½
2015, Jan. 27   Litho.   Wmk. 388
1531	A504	60c multi	.35	.25
a.		Perf. 13¼x14	.35	.25
1532	A504	80c multi	.45	.25
a.		Perf. 13¼x14	.45	.25
1533	A504	$1.20 multi	.70	.35
a.		Perf. 13¼x14	.70	.35
		Nos. 1531-1533 (3)	1.50	.85

145

MALAYSIA

Farm Animals — A505

Designs: 60c, Anser cygnoides. 80c, Bubalus bubalis. $1.20, Gallus domesticus. $3, Capra aegagrus hircus, denomination at UR, vert.
$15, Like $3, denomination at LR, vert.

Perf. 13x13¼
2015, Feb. 16 Litho. Unwmk.
1534-1536 A505 Set of 3 1.50 .75
Souvenir Sheets
Perf. 14¼x14½
1537 A505 $3 multi 1.75 .85
Self-Adhesive On Wood Veneer
Die Cut Perf. 6¾
1538 A505 $15 brown & red 8.25 4.25
No. 1537 contains one 48x66mm stamp.
No. 1538 contains one 45x60mm stamp.

International Cooperative Project on Giant Panda Conservation — A506

Flags of Malaysia and People's Republic of China and panda named: No. 1539, 70c, Liang Liang. No. 1540, 70c, Xing Xing.
No. 1541: a, Liang Liang, diff. b, Xing Xing, diff.

Perf. 13¼x13
2015, Feb. 25 Litho. Unwmk.
1539-1540 A506 Set of 2 .80 .40
Souvenir Sheet
On Flocked Granite Paper With Ripples
Perf. 13½x13¼
1541 A506 $4 Sheet of 2, #a-b 4.50 2.25
No. 1541 contains two 28x45mm stamps.

Endangered Marine Life — A507

Designs: 60c, Anoxypristis cuspidata. 80c, Balaenoptera musculus. $1.40, Orcinus orca. $5, Megaptera novaeangliae.

Perf. 13½x13¼
2015, Apr. 13 Litho. Unwmk.
1542-1544 A507 Set of 3 1.60 .80
Litho. With Foil Application
Souvenir Sheet
Perf. 14¼
1545 A507 $5 multi 3.00 1.50
No. 1545 contains one 45x38mm octagonal stamp.

Souvenir Sheet

Penny Black, 175th Anniv. A508

Wmk. 388
2015, Apr. 30 Litho. Perf. 14
1546 A508 $3 multi 1.75 .85

International Telecommunication Union, 150th Anniv. — A509

150th anniv. emblem and: 60c, Telephones. 70c, Television, radio, microphone and antenna. 80c, Satellite, satellite dish, cell phone, map of Asia and Australia.

Wmk. 388
2015, May 17 Litho. Perf. 13¼
1547-1549 A509 Set of 3 1.25 .60

Marine Life — A510

Designs: No. 1550, 60c, Phyllorhiza punctata. No. 1551, 60c, Hypselodoris bullockii. No. 1552, $1.20, Trapezia areolata. No. 1553, $1.20, Hymenocera picta.

Perf. 13¼x13½
2015, June 8 Litho. Unwmk.
1550-1553 A510 Set of 4 1.90 .95
See Thailand Nos. 2857-2860.

Birds — A511

Designs: 60c, Nycticorax nycticorax. 70c, Butorides striatus. 80c, Ardea cinerea, horiz. $5, Ixobrychus cinnamomeus, horiz.

Perf. 13¼x13½, 13½x13¼
2015, June 25 Litho. Unwmk.
1554-1556 A511 Set of 3 1.10 .55
Souvenir Sheet
Perf. 14¼
1557 A511 $5 multi 2.75 1.40
No. 1557 contains one 50x40mm stamp.

Pearls — A512

Designs: 60c, Circle South Sea pearls. 70c, Baroque South Sea pearls. 80c, Drop South Sea pearls.
$5, Round South Sea pearl.

Perf. 14x14¼
2015, July 29 Litho. Unwmk.
1558-1560 A512 Set of 3 1.10 .55
Souvenir Sheet
Litho. & Embossed With Foil Application
Perf.
1561 A512 $5 multi 2.60 1.25
No. 1561 contains one 38mm diameter stamp.

Flags and Emblem of Association of Southeast Asian Nations — A513

Wmk. 388
2015, Aug. 8 Litho. Perf. 13¼
1562 A513 50c multi .25 .25
See Brunei No. 656, Burma Nos. 417-418, Cambodia No. 2428, Indonesia No. 2428,

Laos No. 1906, Philippines No. 3619, Singapore No. 1742, Thailand No. 2875, Viet Nam No. 3529.

Mosques — A514

Designs: 70c, Zahir Mosque, Alor Setar, Kedah. 80c, Kota Kinabalu City Mosque. $1, National Mosque.

Perf. 13½x13¼
2015, Aug. 27 Litho. Unwmk.
1563-1565 A514 Set of 3 1.25 .60

Malaysia Day A515

No. 1566, 60c: a, Musicians and dancers (60x25mm). b, Emblem (30x25mm).
No. 1567, 70c: a, Malaysians at play (60x25mm). b, People holding Malaysian flag (30x25mm).
$3, Heart, people holding flagpole bearing Malaysian flag.

Perf. 14x13½
2015, Sept. 15 Litho. Wmk. 388
Horiz. pairs, #a-b
1566-1567 A515 Set of 2 1.25 .60
Souvenir Sheet
Perf. 13¼x14
1568 A515 $3 multi 1.40 .70
No. 1568 contains one 70x45mm stamp.

World Post Day — A516

Wmk. 388
2015, Oct. 9 Litho. Perf. 13¼
1569 A516 60c multi .30 .25

Stamp Week — A517

Wmk. 388
2015, Oct. 27 Litho. Perf. 13¼
1570 A517 60c multi .30 .25

Islands — A518

No. 1571: a, Pulau Tenggol, Trengganu. b, Pulau Tinggi, Johore.
No. 1572: a, Pulau Sembilang, Pahang. b, Pulau Satang, Sarawak.
$3, Pulau Mataking, Sabah.

Unwmk.
2015, Nov. 17 Litho. Perf. 14
1571 A518 Horiz. pair .70 .35
a.-b. 70c Either single .35 .25
1572 A518 Horiz. pair .80 .40
a.-b. 80c Either single .40 .25
Souvenir Sheet
1573 A518 $3 multi 1.40 .70

Four Nations Stamp Exhibition, Malacca — A519

Traditional clothing of men and women from: No. 1574, 60c, Malaysia. No. 1575, 60c, Singapore. No. 1576, 60c, Indonesia. No. 1577, 60c, Thailand.

$3, Show emblem, men and women from Malaysia, Singapore, Indonesia and Thailand.

Perf. 14x13¾
2015, Dec. 4 Litho. Wmk. 388
1574-1577 A519 Set of 4 1.10 .55
Souvenir Sheet
Imperf
1578 A519 $3 multi 1.40 .70
No. 1578 contains one 80x80mm diamond-shaped stamp.

Locomotives — A520

Designs: 60c, Hitachi Diesel hydraulic locomotive. 70c, Railbus. 80c, Diesel multiple unit. $5, Vulcan steam locomotive, vert.

Unwmk.
2015, Dec. 28 Litho. Perf. 13
1579-1581 A520 Set of 3 1.00 .50
Souvenir Sheet
Perf. 14x13¾ Syncopated
1582 A520 $5 multi 2.40 1.25
a. As No. 1582, with Thailand 2016 Intl. Stamp Exhibition emblem added in sheet margin 2.50 1.25
No. 1582 contains one 40x55mm stamp.

Primates — A521

Designs: 60c, Macaque. 70c, Silvered leaf monkeys. 80c, White-handed gibbons. No. 1586: a, One Agile gibbon. b, Three Agile gibbons.
$3, Agile gibbon.

Perf. 13¼, 13¼x13½ (#1586)
2016, Jan. 26 Litho. Unwmk.
1583-1585 A521 Set of 3 1.00 .50
Souvenir Sheets
1586 A521 $3 Sheet of 2, #a-b 3.00 1.50
1587 A521 $3 multi 1.50 .75

Traditional Dances — A522

Dance: No. 1588, 60c, Cempaka Sari. No. 1589, 60c, Reben. No. 1590, 60c, Odissi. No. 1591, 60c, Magunatip. No. 1592, 60c, Rejang Be'uh.

Perf. 13½x14
2016, Feb. 3 Litho. Wmk. 388
1588-1592 A522 Set of 5 1.50 .75

Flowers — A523

No. 1593 — Bread flowers: a, No insects on flower. b, Insects on flowers.

MALAYSIA

No. 1594 — Yellow saracas: a, Butterfly on flower at UR. b, Butterfly on flower at left.
No. 1595 — Cannonball flowers: a, Bee at right. b, Bee at left.
$5, Cape jasmine, vert.

Perf. 14¼x14
2016, Mar. 7 Litho. Unwmk.
1593 A523 70c Vert. pair, #a-b .75 .40
1594 A523 80c Vert. pair, #a-b .85 .40
1595 A523 80c Vert. pair, #a-b .85 .40
Nos. 1593-1595 (3) 2.45 1.20

Souvenir Sheet
Perf. 14¼
1596 A523 $5 multi 2.60 1.40

No. 1596 contains one 40x70mm stamp and is impregnated with a jasmine scent..

Writers — A524

Designs: No. 1597, 80c, Arena Wati (1925-2009). No. 1598, 80c, Tongkat Warrant (1929-2001). No. 1599, 80c, Keris Mas (1922-92).

Perf. 13½
2016, Apr. 29 Litho. Unwmk.
1597-1599 A524 Set of 3 1.25 .60

River Watercraft A525

Designs: 70c, Longboat. 80c, Express boat. 90c, Ferry boat.
$3, Raft, vert.

Perf. 14x13½
2016, May 26 Litho. Unwmk.
1600-1602 A525 Set of 3 1.25 .60

Souvenir Sheet
1603 A525 $3 multi 1.50 .75

No. 1603 contains one 40x60mm stamp.

Tamil Calligraphy A526
Chinese Calligraphy A527
Arabic Calligraphy — A528

Design: $5, Tamil, Chinese and Arabic calligraphy, horiz.

Unwmk.
2016, June 28 Litho. Perf. 14
1604 A526 70c multi .35 .25
1605 A527 80c multi .40 .25
1606 A528 90c multi .45 .25
Nos. 1604-1606 (3) 1.20 .75

Souvenir Sheet
Perf. 14x14¼
1607 A528 $5 multi 2.50 1.25

No. 1607 contains one 60x45mm stamp.

Flag and Tourist Attractions of Kedah — A529

Flag and Tourist Attractions of Kelantan — A530

No. 1608: a, Muzium Padi (Rice Museum), Menara Alor Setar (Alor Setar Tower). b, Lembah Bujang, Candi Bendang Dalam.
No. 1609: a, Kampung Kraftangan dan Muzium Kraf (Craft Museum), Songket. b, Wau Bulan (moon kite).
No. 1610, vert.: a, Flag of Kedah, Pulau Langkawi. b, Flag of Kelantan, Pantai Bisikan Bayu (beach), Perahu Kolek (Kolek boat).

Perf. 14x13¼
2016, July 27 Litho. Unwmk.
1608 A529 80c Horiz. pair, #a-b .80 .40
1609 A530 80c Horiz. pair, #a-b .80 .40

Souvenir Sheet
Perf. 13¼x14
1610 A530 $2 Sheet of 2, #a-b 2.00 1.00

No. 1610 contains two 30x50mm stamps.

Flora and Fauna A532

A531

Designs: $2, Giant panda Nuan Nuan.
No. 1612: a, 30c, Tragulus kanchil. b, 50c, Meliponula ferruginea. c, 50c, Piper sarmentosum. d, 60c, Polyplectron malacense. e, 60c, Rana erythraea. f, 70c, Amyda cartilaginea. g, 80c, Tor tambroides.

Perf. 13¼x14
2016, Aug. 23 Litho. Unwmk.
Souvenir Sheet
1611 A531 $2 multi 1.00 .50
  a. Imperf. 1.00 .50

Miniature Sheet
Self-Adhesive
Die Cut Perf. 12
1612 A532 Sheet of 7, #a-g 2.00 1.00

Battles — A533

Designs: No. 1613, 80c, Kota Malawati, Selangor. No. 1614, 60c, Kota Mat Salleh, Sabah. No. 1615, 80c, Kota Libau Rentap, Sarawak. No. 1616, 80c, Bukit Kepong, Johore.
$3, Kota Bharu, Kelantan, vert.

Perf. 14x13¼
2016, Sept. 15 Litho. Unwmk.
1613-1616 A533 Set of 4 1.40 .70

Souvenir Sheet
Perf. 13¼x14
1617 A533 $3 multi 1.50 .75

No. 1617 contains one 40x50mm stamp.

International Stamps — A534

Inscriptions: 10c, Festivals. 20c, Local fruits. 50c, Wildlife. $1, Unity. $2, Places of worship. $5, Our nation. $10, Flora. $20, Handicrafts.

Perf. 14x13¾
2016, Oct. 1 Litho. Wmk. 388
1618 A534 10c multi .25 .25
1619 A534 20c multi .25 .25
1620 A534 50c multi .25 .25
1621 A534 $1 multi .50 .25
1622 A534 $2 multi 1.00 .50
1623 A534 $5 multi 2.40 1.25
1624 A534 $10 multi 5.00 2.50
1625 A534 $20 multi 9.75 5.00
Nos. 1618-1625 (8) 19.40 10.25

Postal Workers — A535

Postal worker: 60c, On horse. 70c, In boat. 80c, On bicycle.
$3, Postal worker at table, vert.

Unwmk.
2016, Oct. 9 Litho. Perf. 14
1626-1628 A535 Set of 3 1.00 .50

Souvenir Sheet
1629 A535 $3 multi 1.50 .75

Penang Free School, 200th Anniv. — A536

A536a

Crest and various views of school: 70c, 80c, 90c.
$5, Crest and ribbon.

Unwmk.
2016, Oct. 21 Litho. Perf. 14
1630-1632 A536 Set of 3 1.25 .60

Souvenir Sheet
Litho. With Foil Application
Perf. 14¼x14
1633 A536a $5 gold & multi 2.40 1.25

No. 1633 contains one 50x50mm stamp.

Houses of Worship — A537

Designs: No. 1634, 60c, Tokong Tong Perak. No. 1635, 60c, Gurdwara Sahib Shapha, Kuala Lumpur. No. 1636, 60c, Kuil Sri Kandaswamy, Kuala Lumpur. No. 1637, 60c, St. Francis Xavier Church, Malacca. No. 1638, 60c, Masjid Kapitan Keling, Penang

Perf. 13¼
2016, Nov. 21 Litho. Unwmk.
1634-1638 A537 Set of 5 1.40 .70

Girl Guides Association of Malaysia, Cent. — A538

Designs: No. 1639, 85c, Girl Guides and badges. No. 1640, 85c, Girl Guides camping. No. 1641, 85c, Girl Guide, salute and knot.

Perf. 13¼x13½
2016, Dec. 9 Litho. Unwmk.
1639-1641 A538 Set of 3 1.25 .60

End of Term of 14th Yang di-Pertuan Agong — A539

Sultan Abdul Halim of Kedah: 85c With people and building. 95c, Reviewing soldiers. $1.05, With attendants, reviewing soldiers.
$3, Sultan Abdul Halim in automobile, vert.

Perf. 13¾x13½
2016, Dec. 14 Litho. Wmk. 388
1642-1644 A539 Set of 3 1.25 .65

Souvenir Sheet
Perf. 13½x13¼
1645 A539 $3 multi 1.40 .70

No. 1645 contains one 40x60mm stamp.

Gold Medalists at 2016 Paralympics, Rio de Janeiro A540

Perf. 14¼x14
2016, Dec. 20 Litho. Unwmk.
1646 A540 95c multi .45 .25

New Year 2017 (Year of the Rooster) — A541

Designs: 85c, Two roosters. 95c, Rooster, hen and chicks. $1.05, Two roosters, diff.
$3, $8, Rooster and Chinese inscription, vert.

Perf. 14¼x14
2017, Jan. 10 Litho. Unwmk.
1647-1649 A541 Set of 3 1.40 .70

Souvenir Sheets
Perf. 14¼
1650 A541 $3 multi 1.40 .70
1651 A541 $8 multi 3.75 1.90

Nos. 1650-1651 each contain one 38x45 octagonal stamp.

Chinese Food — A542

Various Chinese foods: 85c, 95c, $1.05.
$5, Chinese foods, diff.

Unwmk.
2017, Jan. 24 Litho. Perf. 14
1652-1654 A542 Set of 3 1.40 .70

Souvenir Sheet
Perf.
1655 A542 $5 multi 2.25 1.10

No. 1655 contains one 38mm diameter stamp.

Chung Ling High School, George Town, Cent. — A543

Emblem and various school buildings: 85c, 95c, $1.05.
$5, School building and emblem, vert.

MALAYSIA

2017, Feb. 9		Unwmk. Litho.		Perf. 14
1656-1658	A543	Set of 3	1.40	.70

Souvenir Sheet
Litho. & Embossed

| 1659 | A543 | $5 multi | 2.25 | 1.10 |

No. 1658 contains one 45x60mm stamp.

Orchids — A544

Designs: 60c, Rhynchostylis retusa. 70c, Phalaenopsis violacea. 80c, Vanda helvola. 90c, Paphiopedilum lowii. $1, Arachnis flos-aeris. $1.10, Papilionanthe hookeriana.

		Perf. 14x13¾		
2017, Feb. 21		Litho.		Wmk. 388
1660	A544	60c multi	.30	.25
1661	A544	70c multi	.35	.25
1662	A544	80c multi	.35	.25
1663	A544	90c multi	.40	.25
1664	A544	$1 multi	.45	.25
1665	A544	$1.10 multi	.50	.25
		Nos. 1660-1665 (6)	2.35	1.50

Souvenir Sheet
Imperf

1666	A544	Sheet of 6	3.25	1.60
a.	A544	60c Like #1660	.40	.25
b.	A544	70c Like #1661	.45	.25
c.	A544	80c Like #1662	.50	.25
d.	A544	90c Like #1663	.55	.25
e.	A544	$1 Like #1664	.65	.30
f.	A544	$1.10 Like #1665	.70	.35

No. 1666 sold for $7. Nos. 1666a-1666f each have at least one side abutting the brown frame around the six stamps.

Kadazandusun and Dayak Foods — A545

Various Kadazanusun and Dayak foods: 60c, Tuak, Lihing, Kek Lapis, Tapai Pulut, Kuih Jala. 80c, Ambuyat and Linut. 90c, Manuk Pansuh, Hinava and Umai. $5, Kadazanusun and Dayak foods, diff.

		Unwmk.		
2017, Mar. 16		Litho.		Perf. 14
1667-1669	A545	Set of 3	1.10	.55

Souvenir Sheet
Perf.

| 1670 | A545 | $5 multi | 2.25 | 1.10 |

No. 1670 contains one 38mm diameter stamp.

Eid Al-Fitr Greetings — A546

Deepavali Greetings — A547

Chinese New Year Greetings — A548

Festival Greetings — A549

		Perf. 14x13¼		
2017, Mar. 28		Litho.		Unwmk.
1671	A546	80c multi	.40	.25
1672	A547	80c multi	.40	.25
1673	A548	80c multi	.40	.25
		Nos. 1671-1673 (3)	1.20	.75

Souvenir Sheet
Perf. 13¼x13¾

| 1674 | A549 | $5 multi | 2.25 | 1.10 |

Installation of Sultan Muhammad V of Kelantan as 15th Yang di-Pertuan Agong — A550

Designs: 60s, Sultan. $5, Sultan and microphone.

		Perf. 13¼x13½		
2017, Apr. 24		Litho.		Wmk. 388
1675	A550	60c multi	.30	.25
a.		Imperf.	.30	.25

Souvenir Sheet
Perf. 13½x13¼

| 1676 | A550 | $5 multi | 2.40 | 1.25 |

No. 1676 contains one 40x60mm stamp.

Palm Oil Industry, Cent. — A551

Centenary emblem and: 60c, World map, palms, palm kernels and palm oil products. 80c, Tractor and harvester in plantation. $1, Harvester and ox-drawn cart. $3, Palm fruit and kernels.

		Perf. 13½x13¼		
2017, May 18		Litho.		Wmk. 388
1677-1679	A551	Set of 3	1.10	.55

Souvenir Sheet
Perf. 14

| 1680 | A551 | $3 multi | 1.40 | .70 |

No. 1680 contains one 50x40mm stamp.

Malaysian Foods — A552

Designs: 60c, Kek Raya Kepala Meja, Kuih Pelita, Agar-agar. 80c, Ketupat and Sate. 90c, Lemang, Ketupat Palas, Rendang, Serunding. $5, Malaysian foods, diff.

		Perf. 13¼x14		
2017, June 6		Litho.		Unwmk.
1681-1683	A552	Set of 3	1.10	.55

Souvenir Sheet
Perf.

| 1684 | A552 | $5 multi | 2.40 | 1.25 |

No. 1684 contains one 38mm diameter stamp.

A553

Batik A554

Batik A555

No. 1685: a, Block batik tools. b, Finished block batik fabric.
No. 1686: a, Canting batik tool. b, Finished canting batik fabric.
No. 1687: a, Tied fabrics. b, Finished tie and dye batik fabric.
No. 1688: a, Metal block. b, Wood block.

		Unwmk.		
2017, June 20		Litho.		Perf. 14
1685	A553	60c Horiz. pair, #a-b	.60	.30
1686	A554	60c Horiz. pair, #a-b	.60	.30
1687	A555	60c Horiz. pair, #a-b	.60	.30
		Nos. 1685-1687 (3)	1.80	.90

Souvenir Sheet
Litho. & Embossed With Foil Application
Perf. 14x14¼

| 1688 | A555 | $3 Sheet of 2, #a-b | 3.00 | 1.50 |

Nos. 1685-1687 were each printed in sheets containing 10 pairs and 5 central labels. No. 1688 contains two 35x35mm stamps.

Mass Transit A556

No. 1689: a, Bus. b, Train.
80c, Bus. b, Train in station. 90c, Trains and passengers on train station platform. $5, Front of train.

		Perf. 14¼		
2017, July 17		Litho.		Unwmk.
1689	A556	60c Horiz. pair, #a-b	.60	.30
1690	A556	80c multi	.40	.25
1691	A556	90c multi	.45	.25
		Nos. 1689-1691 (3)	1.45	.80

Souvenir Sheet
Litho. & Embossed
Perf. 14½x14¾

| 1692 | A556 | $5 multi | 2.50 | 1.25 |

No. 1689 was printed in sheet containing 10 pairs + 5 central labels. Nos. 1690-1691 were each printed in sheets containing 20 stamps + 5 labels. No. 1692 contains one 37x37mm stamp.

Association of Southeast Asian Nations, 50th Anniv. — A557

Designs: 60c, Hibiscus rosa-sinensis. $3, Hibiscus rosa-sinensis, vert.

		Perf. 14x14¼		
2017, Aug. 8		Litho.		Unwmk.
1693	A557	60c multi	.30	.25

Souvenir Sheet

| 1694 | A557 | $3 multi | 1.50 | .75 |

No. 1694 contains one 35x70mm stamp.

2017 Southeast Asian Games, Kuala Lumpur — A558

Designs: No. 1695, 60c, Emblem. No. 1696, 60c, Mascot carrying torch. No. 1697, 60c, Mascot playing badminton. No. 1698, 60c, Mascot in uniform.

		Perf. 13¼x14		
2017, Aug. 19		Litho.		Unwmk.
1695-1698	A558	Set of 4	1.25	.60

Straits Settlements Postage Stamps, 150th Anniv. — A559

Designs: 60c, Straits Settlements #1, 2 and 3. 80c, Straits Settlements #4, 5 and 6. 90c, Straits Settlements #7, 8 and 9. $5, Watermark illustration 1 and Straits Settlements #10, 14 and 18.

2017		Litho. Unwmk.	Perf. 14½x14	
1699-1701	A559	Set of 3	1.25	.60

Souvenir Sheet
Perf. 14x14½

| 1702 | A559 | $5 multi | 2.25 | 1.10 |

Issued: Nos. 1699-1701, 9/1; No. 1702, 12/4. No. 1702 contains one 40x50mm stamp.

Miniature Sheet

Malaysian Yang Di-Pertuan Agongs — A560

No. 1703 — Picture of Yang Di-Pertuan Agong and Roman numeral: a, $1, I (30x50mm). b, $1, II (30x50mm). c, $1, III (30x50mm). d, $1, IV (30x50mm). e, $1, V (30x50mm). f, $1, VI, (30x50mm). g, $1, VII (30x50mm). h, $1, VIII (30x50mm). i, $1, IX (30x50mm). j, $1, X (30x50mm). k, $1, XI (30x50mm). l, $1, XII (30x50mm). m, $1, XIII (30x50mm). n, $1, XIV (30x50mm). o, $5, XV (30x64mm).

Litho., Litho. With Foil Application (#1703o)
Perf. 14¼x14½

2017, Sept. 9				Unwmk.
1703	A560	Sheet of 15, #a-o, + 2 labels	9.00	4.50

"My Country" — A561

Negaraku emblem and: No. 1704, 50c, Five people and Malaysian flag. No. 1705, 50c, Malaysian flag, men, women and soldiers. No. 1706, 60c, Five people and Malaysian flag, diff. No. 1707, 60c, Bicyclists with Malaysian flags riding in street.
$3 and $6, Negaraku emblem and map of Malaysia.

		Perf. 14x13¼		
2017, Sept. 14		Litho.		Unwmk.
1704-1707	A561	Set of 4	1.10	.55

Souvenir Sheets

| 1708 | A561 | $3 multi | 1.50 | .75 |

Litho. & Silk-Screened

| 1709 | A561 | $6 multi | 3.00 | 1.50 |

Nos. 1708-1709 each contain one 40x40mm stamp.

MALAYSIA

149

World Post Day — A562

No. 1710, 50c — Inscription in arc: a, Write. b, Repeat.
No. 1711, 50c — Inscription in arc: a, Send. b, Receive.

	Perf. 14¼x14		
2017, Oct. 9	Litho.		Unwmk.
	Vert. Pairs, #a-b		
1710-1711	A562	Set of 2	.95 .50

Indian Foods — A563

Designs: 60c, Vadai, Muruku, Paal Kova and Payasam. 80c, Thosai and Idhli. 90c, Nasi Daun Pisang.
$5, Indian foods, diff.

	Perf. 13¼x13½		
2017, Oct. 17	Litho.		Unwmk.
1712-1714	A563	Set of 3	1.10 .55
	Souvenir Sheet		
	Perf.		
1715	A563	$5 multi	2.40 1.25

No. 1715 contains one 38mm diameter stamp.

Visit to Malaysia of Prince Charles and Duchess of Cornwall — A564

Designs: No. 1716, $1, Prince Charles. No. 1717, $1, Duchess of Cornwall.
$6, Prince Charles and Duchess of Cornwall, horiz.

	Wmk. 388		
2017, Nov. 3	Litho.		Perf. 14
1716-1717	A564	Set of 2	.90 .45
	Souvenir Sheet		
	Perf. 13¼x13½		
1718	A564	$6 multi	2.75 1.40

No. 1718 contains one 60x50mm stamp.

Sarawak State Legislative Assembly, 150th Anniv. — A565

	Perf. 14¼x14		
2017, Nov. 8	Litho.		Unwmk.
1719	A565	60c multi	.30 .25

No. 1719 was printed in sheets of 10 + 5 central labels.

A566

A567

Tourist Destinations — A568

No. 1720 — Flag of Trengganu and: a, Crystal Mosque, Trengganu State Museum, Maziah Palace. b, Lake Tenyir, Redang Island, turtle and reef.
No. 1721 — Flag of Pahang and: a, Abu Bakar Palace, Fraser's Hill, Sungai Lembing Mines. b, National Elephant Conservation Center, Mossy Forest, Tioman Island.
No. 1722 — Flag of Perak and: a, Leaning Tower of Teluk Intan, Ubudiah Mosque, Perak Royal Museum. b, Taiping Zoo, Royal Belum State Park, Pangkor Island.

	Perf. 14x13¼		
2017, Nov. 21	Litho.		Unwmk.
1720	A566	60c Vert. pair, #a-b	.55 .30
1721	A567	60c Vert. pair, #a-b	.55 .30
1722	A568	60c Vert. pair, #a-b	.55 .30
		Nos. 1720-1722 (3)	1.65 .90

Nos. 1720-1722 were each printed in sheets containing 10 pairs + 5 central labels.

Legoland Malaysia Theme Park — A569

Inscriptions: No. 1723, 60c, Water Activities. No. 1724, 60c, Quality Time. No. 1725, 60c, Sightseeing. No. 1726, 60c, Recreation. No. 1727, 60c, Picnic Time. No. 1728, 60c, Extreme Activities.

	Perf. 14x13¼		
2017, Dec. 4	Litho.		Unwmk.
1723-1728	A569	Set of 6	1.90 .95

Working Dogs — A570

Designs: No. 1729, 60c, Belgian shepherd protection dogs. No. 1730, 60c, Golden retriever guide dogs. No. 1731, 60c, Border collie search and rescue dogs.
No. 1732: a, $2, Labrador retriever drug detection dog. b, $3, German shepherd police dog.

	Perf. 13½x13¼		
2018, Jan. 18	Litho.		Unwmk.
1729-1731	A570	Set of 3	.95 .45
	Souvenir Sheet		
1732	A570	Sheet of 2, #a-b	2.60 1.40

Fish — A571

Designs: No. 1733, 60c, Mahseers. No. 1734, 60c, Pearl gouramis. No. 1735, 60c, Harlequin rasboras.
$5, Golden arowanas.

	Perf. 14x13½		
2018, Jan. 30	Litho.		Unwmk.
1733-1735	A571	Set of 3	.95 .45
	Souvenir Sheet		
	Litho. With Foil Application		
	Perf. 13¾x13¼		
1736	A571	$5 multi	2.60 1.40

No. 1736 contains one 55x36mm stamp.

Rivers A572

Designs: 60c, Pahang River. 80c, Kinabatangan River.
$8, Rajang River.

	Perf. 13¼		
2018, Feb. 27	Litho.		Unwmk.
1737-1738	A572	Set of 2	.75 .35
	Souvenir Sheet		
1739	A572	$8 multi	4.25 2.10

No. 1739 contains one 160x30mm stamp.

Yu Hua Kajang School, Cent. — A573

Designs: No. 1740, 60c, School with "1934" date above arch. No. 1741, 60c, School with "1990" date on pediment. No. 1742, 60c, School and flags.
$5, School crest, vert.

	Perf. 14x13½		
2018, Mar. 3	Litho.		Unwmk.
1740-1742	A573	Set of 3	.95 .45
	Souvenir Sheet		
	Perf.		
1743	A573	$5 multi	2.60 1.40

No. 1743 contains one 58x63mm stamp.

Electric Train Service A574

Designs: No. 1744, 60c, Class 91 train. No. 1745, 60c, Class 92 train. 80c, Class 93 train.
$5, Class 93 train and route map.

2018	Litho.	Unwmk.	Perf. 14
1744-1746	A574	Set of 3	1.10 .55
1746a		Horiz. strip of 3, #1744-1746	1.10 .55
	Souvenir Sheet		
	Perf. 13½		
1747	A574	$6 multi	3.25 1.60
1747A	A574	$6 As #1747, with Thailand 2018 emblem added on stamp	3.00 1.50

Issued: No. 1744-1747, 3/20; No. 1747A, 11/28. Nos. 1747, 1747A each contain one 55x40mm stamp.

Musical Instruments — A575

Designs: No. 1748, 60c, Sitar. No. 1749, 60c, Pipa. No. 1750, 80c, Sape. No. 1751, 80c, Sundatang.
$5, Musicians playing various instruments, horiz.

	Perf. 13½		
2018, Apr. 10	Litho.		Unwmk.
1748-1751	A575	Set of 4	1.40 .70
	Souvenir Sheet		
	Perf. 14½x14		
1752	A575	$5 multi	2.60 1.40

No. 1752 contains one 75x56mm stamp.

Citrus Fruits — A576

Designs: No. 1753, 60c, Citrus aurantifolia. No. 1754, 60c, Citrus hystrix. No. 1755, 60c, Citrus microcarpa.
$6, Citrus grandis.

	Perf. 13¼		
2018, Apr. 24	Litho.		Unwmk.
1753-1755	A576	Set of 3	.95 .45
	Souvenir Sheet		
	Perf.		
1756	A576	$6 multi	3.00 1.50

No. 1756 contains one 38mm diameter stamp.

Medicinal Plants — A577

Designs: 60c, Dogfruit. 80c, Freshwater mangrove. $1, Butter fruit.
$3, Bitter beans.

	Perf. 13¼		
2018, May 17	Litho.		Unwmk.
1757-1759	A577	Set of 3	1.25 .60
	Souvenir Sheet		
	Perf. 13¼x13		
1760	A577	$3 multi	1.50 .75

No. 1760 contains one 40x73mm stamp.

Sabah Tourist Attractions — A578

Designs: 60c, Sabah Tourism Board Heritage Building, Kota Kinabalu City Mosque, North Borneo Railway, Tun Mustapha Tower. 80c, Mount Kinabalu, Orangutan, Bornean bristlehead, Sipadan Island.
$3, Map of Sabah, Bukit Trig, Keningau Oath Stone, Nepenthes x trusmadiensis, Sabah Handicraft Center, cinnamon stick.

	Perf. 13¼		
2018, June 5	Litho.		Unwmk.
1761-1762	A578	Set of 2	.70 .35
	Souvenir Sheet		
	Perf. 12		
1763	A578	$3 multi	1.50 .75

No. 1763 contains one 50x50mm stamp.

Bridges A579

Designs: No. 1764, 60c, Abdul Jalil Bridge, Kuala Kangsar, Perak. No. 1765, 60c, Tamparuli Bridge, Tamparuli, Sabah. No. 1766, 80c, Seri Wawasan Bridge, Putrajaya. No. 1767, 80c, Darul Hana Bridge, Kuching, Sarawak.

	Perf. 14x14¼		
2018, June 28	Litho.		Unwmk.
1764-1767	A579	Set of 4	1.40 .70

Opening of Telegraph Museum, Taiping — A580

Designs: No. 1768, 60c, Transmitter key and Morse code. No. 1769, 60c, Receiver and

MALAYSIA

Morse code. No. 1770, 60c, Gutta percha, grinder stone and submarine cable.
$3, Museum (Post and Telegraph Office of 1885), Taiping.

Perf. 13x13¼ Syncopated
2018, July 16 Litho. Unwmk.
1768-1770 A580 Set of 3 .90 .45
Souvenir Sheet
Perf. 14x14¼
1771 A580 $3 multi 1.50 .75
No. 1771 contains one 80x42mm stamp.

Historical Museums — A581

Designs: No. 1772, 60c, National Museu, Kuala Lumpur, and mural of Hang Tuah. No. 1773, 60c, Perak Museum, Taiping, and first train coach. No. 1774, 60c, Sarawak Museum, Kuching, and burial huts.
$6.50, Malacca History and Ethnography Museum, Malacca City, statue of Admiral Cheng Ho, Queen Victoria Fountain.

Perf. 13½x13¼
2018, July 23 Litho. Unwmk.
1772-1774 A581 Set of 3 .90 .45
Souvenir Sheet
Perf. 13½
1775 A581 $6.50 multi + label 3.25 1.60
No. 1775 contains one 71x40mm stamp.

Blowpipes — A582

Blowpipes: No. 1776, 60c, Orang Asli hunter. No. 1777, 60c, Dayak hunter. No. 1778, 60c, Murut hunter.
$3, Dayak hunter with blowpipe, monkey, horiz.

Perf. 13½x14
2018, Aug. 14 Litho. Unwmk.
1776-1778 A582 Set of 3 .90 .45
Souvenir Sheet
Perf. 14x14¼
1779 A582 $3 multi 1.50 .75
No. 1779 contains one 80x42mm stamp.

National Day — A583

Outlines of people and: No. 1780, 60c, Malaysian flag. No. 1781, 60c, Malaysian flag and buildings.
$5, Malaysian flag and National Day emblem.

Perf. 13½x13
2018, Aug. 31 Litho. Unwmk.
1780-1781 A583 Set of 2 .60 .30
Souvenir Sheet
Perf.
1782 A583 $5 multi 2.40 1.25
No. 1782 contains one 53x51mm heart-shaped stamp.

Malaysia Day — A584

Half of *Merdeka*, painting by Syed Thajudeen: No. 1783, 60c, Left half (pale yellow frame at left). No. 1784, 60c, Right half (pale yellow frame at right).
$5, *Negaraku*, painting by Thajudeen.

Perf. 13¼
2018, Sept. 16 Litho. Unwmk.
1783-1784 A584 Set of 2 .60 .30
Souvenir Sheet
Perf. 14½x14¼
1785 A584 $5 multi 2.40 1.25
No. 1785 contains one 62x72mm stamp.

World Post Day — A585

Crowd and mailman on: 60c, Bicycle. 80c, Motorcycle.
$3, Crowd and mailmen on bicycle and motorcycle.

Perf. 13¼
2018, Oct. 9 Litho. Unwmk.
1786-1787 A585 Set of 2 .70 .35
Size: 100x70mm
Imperf
1788 A585 $3 multi 1.50 .75

A586
A587
A588

Jit Sin High School, Bukit Mertajam, Penang, Cent. — A589

Perf. 13x13¼
2018, Oct. 25 Litho. Unwmk.
1789 A586 60c multi .30 .25
1790 A587 60c multi .30 .25
1791 A588 60c multi .30 .25
Nos. 1789-1791 (3) .90 .75
Souvenir Sheet
Litho. & Embossed
Perf. 13
1792 A589 $8 multi 4.00 2.00

Leisure Activities — A590

Inscriptions: No. 1793, 60c, Bermain layang-layang (kite flying). No. 1794, 60c, Bermain alat muzik (playing musical instruments). No. 1795, 60c, Memancing (fishing). No. 1796, 60c, Mengumpul setem (stamp collecting). No. 1797, 60c, Merekacipta (inventing).

Perf. 13¼x13½
2018, Nov. 12 Litho. Unwmk.
1793-1797 A590 Set of 5 1.50 .75

A591

Festivals A592

Designs: No. 1798, 60c, Hari Raya Aidilfitri (Eid al-Fitr). No. 1799, 60c, Pesta Gawai (Gawai Festival). No. 1800, 60c, Tadau Kaamatan (Kaamatan Festival). No. 1801, 60c, Deepavali (Diwali). No. 1802, 60c, Tahun Baharu Cina (Chinese New Year).
$5, Celebrants of Chinese New Year, Kaamatan Festival, Gawai Festival, Eid al-Fitr, and Diwali in building, horiz.

Unwmk.
2019, Jan. 15 Litho. **Perf. 13**
1798-1802 A591 Set of 5 1.50 .75
Litho. With Glitter Affixed
Imperf
1803 A592 $5 multi 2.50 1.25

Exotic Foods — A593

Designs: No. 1804, 60c, Acaudina Salad and Beronok sea cucumber. No. 1805, 60c, Fried grasshoppers and Valanga grasshoppers. No. 1806, 60c, Porcupine rendang and steak, Malayan porcupine.
$3, Horseshoe crab egg salad.

2019, Feb. 19 Litho. **Perf. 13½**
1804-1806 A593 Set of 3 .90 .45
Souvenir Sheet
Perf. 14½
1807 A593 $3 multi 2.50 1.25
No. 1807 contains one 38x38mm stamp.

Flag and Tourist Attractions of Malacca — A594

Flag and Tourist Attractions of Sarawak — A595

No. 1808: a, Demang Abdul Ghani Gallery, Merlimau. b, Bedchamber, pillar and lidded pot.
No. 1809: a, Alu-Alu dancer. b, Sarawak Cultural Village, loom and fabric, urn.
No. 1810: a, Malacca River Cruise, Maritime Museum, Malacca City, flag of Malacca. b, Sarawak River Cruise, Sarawak Astana, Kuching, flag of Sarawak.

2019, Mar. 15 Litho. **Perf. 13¼**
1808 A594 60c Horiz. pair, #a-b .60 .30
1809 A595 60c Horiz. pair, #a-b .60 .30
Souvenir Sheet
Perf. 12
1810 A595 $3 Sheet of 2, #a-b 2.00 1.00
No. 1810 contains two 35x50mm stamps.

Honeybees — A596

Designs: No. 1811, 60c, Apis andreniformis. No. 1812, 60c, Apis cerana. No. 1813, 60c, Apis dorsata.
No. 1814 — Heterotrigona itama: a, On honeycomb. b, On flower.

2019, Apr. 9 Litho. **Perf. 14**
1811-1813 A596 Set of 3 .90 .45
Souvenir Sheet
1814 A596 $2 Sheet of 2, #a-b 2.00 1.00

Houses of Worship — A597

Designs: No. 1815, 80c, Sultan Ismail Petra Silver Jubilee Mosque, Rantau Panjang (1/5). No. 1816, 80c, Hong San Si Temple, Kuching (2/5). No. 1817, 80c, Sri Kathirvel Murugan Maha Parasakthi Patchai Amman Temple, Taiping (3/5). No. 1818, 80c, St. George's Church, George Town, Penang (4/5). No. 1819, 80c, Gurdwara Sahib (Sikh Temple), Labuan (5/5).

2019, May 11 Litho. **Perf. 13¼**
1815-1819 A597 Set of 5 1.90 .95

Sour Fruits — A598

Designs: No. 1820, 60c, Eleiodoxa conferta. No. 1821, 60c, Mangifera pajang. No. 1822, 60c, Garcinia xanthochymus.
$3, Tamarindus indica, horiz.

2019, June 19 Litho. **Perf. 14**
1820-1822 A598 Set of 3 .90 .45
Souvenir Sheet
Perf. 14¼
1823 A598 $3 multi 1.50 .75
No. 1823 contains one 45x38mm octagonal stamp.

Souvenir Sheet

Sarawak No. 1 A599

2019, July 18 Litho. **Perf. 13¼x13½**
1824 A599 $5 multi 2.40 1.25
Sarawak postage stamps, 150th anniv.

MALAYSIA

Wildlife Conservation — A600

Designs: No. 1825, 60c, Malayan sun bears. No. 1826, 60c, Pangolins. No. 1827, 60c, Asian elephants. No. 1828, $5, Sumatran rhinoceroses. No. 1829, $5, Malayan tigers.

2019, July 28 Litho. Perf. 13¾x13½
1825-1827 A600 Set of 3 .90 .45

Souvenir Sheets
Perf. 14½x14
1828-1829 A600 Set of 2 5.00 2.50

Nos. 1828-1829 each contain one 50x30mm stamp.

Installation of Sultan Abdullah of Pahang as 16th Yang Di-Pertuan Agong — A601

Designs: 60c, Sultan Abdullah. 80c, Sultan Abdullah and his wife, Tunku Azizah Aminah Maimunah. $1, Sultan Abdullah, diff. $5, Sultan Abdullah, diff.

2019, July 30 Litho. Perf. 14x14½
1830-1832 A601 Set of 3 1.25 .60

Souvenir Sheet
1833 A601 $5 multi 2.40 1.25

No. 1833 contains one 40x70mm stamp.

Traditional Costumes — A602

ASEAN Post emblem and: 60c, Woman and man in traditional costumes. $5, Women and men in traditional costumes, horiz.

2019, Aug. 8 Litho. Perf. 14x14½
1834 A602 60c multi .30 .25

Souvenir Sheet
Perf. 14
1835 A602 $5 multi 2.40 1.25

No. 1835 contains one 80x60mm stamp.

Caves — A603

Designs: No. 1836, 60c, Tempurung Cave, Perak, Malayan racerunner. No. 1837, 60c, Gomantong Caves, Sabah, Black-nest swiftlet. No. 1838, 60c, Kelam Cave, Perlis, Cave centipede. $5, Niah Painted Cave, Sarawak.

2019, Aug. 22 Litho. Perf. 14
1836-1838 A603 Set of 3 .85 .45

Souvenir Sheet
Perf. 14¼x14
1839 A603 $5 multi 2.40 1.25

No. 1839 contains one 70x25mm stamp.
No. 1839 has laser cut out of cave entrance.

Malaysia Day — A604

Foods: 60c, Teh Tarik, Puding Kelapa, Krim Gula Apong, Bubur Cha-cha. 80c, Kuih Cincin, Kuih Ketayap, Apam Balik, Kek Lapis. $1, Roti Canai, Hinava, Mi Kolok, Nasi Lemak Bungkus. $5, Air Batu Campur, vert.

2019, Sept. 16 Litho. Perf. 13
1840-1842 A604 Set of 3 1.25 .60

Souvenir Sheet
Perf. 13½
1843 A604 $5 multi 2.40 1.25

No. 1843 contains one 30x50mm stamp.

World Post Day — A605

Mail box at: 50c, Mount Kinabalu. 80c, Tanjung Piai (southernmost point in mainland Asia).

2019, Oct. 9 Litho. Perf. 14
1844-1845 A605 Set of 2 .65 .30

Crafts — A606

Designs: 60c, Carved wood souvenir box. 80c, Ceramic vase from Sarawak. $1, Woven bamboo containers. $5, Necklace.

2019, Dec. 4 Litho. Perf. 13¼x13½
1846-1848 A606 Set of 3 1.25 .60

Souvenir Sheet
Litho. & Embossed
Perf. 14¼x14
1849 A606 $5 multi 2.50 1.25

No. 1849 contains one 46x90mm stamp.

Jawi Calligraphy — A607
Tamil Calligraphy — A608
Chinese Calligraphy — A609
Jawi, Tamil and Chinese Calligraphy — A610

2020, Feb. 6 Litho. Perf. 13¼x13½
1850 A607 60c multi .30 .25
1851 A608 80c multi .40 .25
1852 A609 $1 multi .50 .25
Nos. 1850-1852 (3) 1.20 .75

Souvenir Sheet
Perf. 14¼x14
1853 A610 $3 multi 1.50 .75

Marine Life — A611

Designs: $1.30, Hawksbill turtle. $1.40, Humpback dolphin. $1.50, Whale shark. $1.70, Small giant clam. $1.90, Dugong. $5, Hawksbill turtle, diff.

Perf. 13½x13¼
2020, June 18 Litho. Unwmk.
1854 A611 $1.30 multi .60 .30
1855 A611 $1.40 multi .65 .35
1856 A611 $1.50 multi .70 .35
1857 A611 $1.70 multi .80 .40
1858 A611 $1.90 multi .90 .45
Nos. 1854-1858 (5) 3.65 1.85

Souvenir Sheet
Perf.
1859 A611 $5 multi 2.40 1.25

No. 1859 contains one 38mm diameter stamp.

Wild Flowers — A612

Designs: 60c, Melastoma malabathricum. $1.30, Asystasia gangetica. $1.50, Tridax procumbens. $5, Dillenia suffruticosa.

Perf. 13½x14
2020, July 9 Litho. Unwmk.
1860-1862 A612 Set of 3 1.60 .80

Souvenir Sheet
Perf. 14
1863 A612 $5 multi 2.40 1.25

No. 1863 contains one 40x35mm hexagonal stamp.

Proclamation of National Principles, 50th Anniv. — A614

No. 1864 — Principle in Malay, (emblem with background color of): a, Belief in God (green). b, Loyalty to king and country (yellow). c, Supremacy of the Constitution (blue). d, Rule of law (pink). e, Courtesy and morality (orange). $5, Emblem and map of Malaysia.

Perf. 13¼x13½
2020, Aug. 18 Litho. Unwmk.
1864 Horiz. strip of 5 1.50 .75
a.-e. A613 60c Any single .30 .25

Souvenir Sheet
Litho. With Foil Application
Perf. 14¼
1865 A614 $5 gold & multi 2.40 1.25

Putrajaya as Seat of the Federal Government, 25th Anniv. — A615

No. 1866: a, Jambatan Seri Gemilang (Seri Gemilang Bridge). b, Masjid Tuanku Mizan Zainal Abidin (Tuanku Mizan Zainal Abidin Mosque). c, Perdana Putra (Office of the Prime Minister). d, Perbadanan Putrajaya (Putrajaya Corporation Building). e, Istana Kehakiman (Palace of Justice).

Wmk. 388
2020, Aug. 28 Litho. Perf. 13½
1866 Horiz. strip of 5 3.25 1.50
a.-e. A615 $1.30 Any single .65 .30

Declaration of the Formation of Malaysia in Kuala Lumpur — A616
Declaration of the Formation of Malaysia in Kuching — A617
Declaration of the Formation of Malaysia in Jesselton — A618

Wmk. 388
2020, Sept. 16 Litho. Perf. 14
1867 Horiz. strip of 3 2.00 .90
a. A616 $1.30 multi .65 .30
b. A617 $1.30 multi .65 .30
c. A618 $1.30 multi .65 .30

World Post Day — A619

No. 1868: a, Mobile Post Office. b, Customer at self-service postal machine. c, Woman removing mail from open post office box.

Perf. 13½x13¼
2020, Nov. 5 Litho. Wmk. 388
1868 Horiz. strip of 3 2.00 .90
a.-c. A619 $1.30 Any single .65 .30

Shorea Faguetiana Flower and Tree — A620

Design: $8, Tallest angiosperm (Shorea faguetiana) in the world, Sabah, vert.

Wmk. 388
2020, Dec. 29 Litho. Perf. 13¾
1869 A620 90c multi .45 .25

Souvenir Sheet
Litho. & Embossed
Perf. 13x13¾
1870 A620 $8 multi 4.00 2.00
a. As #1870, with The Malaysia Book of Records emblem overprinted in sheet margin in gold 3.75 1.90

Issued: No. 1870a, 9/5/22. No. 1870 contains one 35x180mm stamp.

MALAYSIA

Constitution of Johore, 125th Anniv. — A621

No. 1871: a, Sultan Sir Abu Bakar (1833-95), cover of 1895 Constitution, and seal. b, Page from 1895 Constitution. $5, Constitutions of 1895, 1961 and 2008, horiz.

Perf. 14¼
		2020, Dec. 31 Litho. Unwmk.		
1871	A621	$1 Horiz. pair, #a-b	1.00	.50

Souvenir Sheet
| 1872 | A621 | $5 sil & multi | 2.50 | 1.25 |

No. 1872 contains one 70x38mm stamp. Though Nos. 1871-1872 have a first day of issue cancel of Dec. 31, 2020, the stamps were not put on sale until Jan. 27, 2021.

Malaysian Cattle Breeds — A622

No. 1873: a, Kedah-Kelantan cow. b, Nelore cow. c, Brahman cow. d, Bali cow. $5, Unnamed cow breed, horiz.

Perf. 14¼
		2021, Mar. 18 Litho. Unwmk.		
1873		Horiz. strip of 4	2.60	1.25
a.-d.	A622	$1.30 Any single	.65	.30

Souvenir Sheet
Litho. & Embossed With Foil Application
Perf. 14x14¼
| 1874 | A622 | $5 gold & multi | 2.40 | 1.25 |

No. 1874 contains one 60x45mm stamp.

Radio Television Malaysia, 75th Anniv. — A623

No. 1875: a, Radio and radio waves. b, Black-and-white television and test pattern. c, Color television and color pattern. d, Smartphone and Wifi icon.

Perf. 13½
		2021, Mar. 18 Litho. Unwmk.		
1875		Horiz. strip of 4	2.60	1.25
a.-d.	A623	$1.30 Any single	.65	.30

Islands A624

Designs: 70c, Rawa Island, Johore. 80c, Lang Tengah Island, Trengganu. $1.90, Lakei Island, Sarawak. $5, Bohey Dulang Island, Sabah.

Perf. 14¼
		2021, Aug. 5 Litho. Unwmk.		
1876-1878	A624	Set of 3	1.75	.85

Souvenir Sheet
Perf. 13¼x13½
| 1879 | A624 | $5 multi | 2.40 | 1.25 |

No. 1879 contains one 60x40mm stamp.

Durian Cultivars — A625

No. 1880: a, Durio zibethinus Buluh Bawah D160. b, Durio zibethinus Duri Hitam D200. c, Durio zibethinus Durian Kampung Premium. d, Durio graveolens Durian Dalit. $5, Durio zibethinus Raja Kunyit D197, horiz.

Perf. 13¼x13½
		2021, Aug. 19 Litho. Unwmk.		
1880		Horiz. strip of 4	1.25	.60
a.-d.	A625	60c Any single	.30	.25

Souvenir Sheet
Perf. 14½
| 1881 | A625 | $5 multi | 2.40 | 1.25 |

No. 1881 contains one 45x38mm octagonal stamp. For stamp with additional inscription, see No. 1906A.

Campaign Against COVID-19 — A626

No. 1882: a, Policeman. b, Doctor. c, Soldier. d, Nurse.

Perf. 13¼x14
		2021, Sept. 9 Litho. Unwmk.		
1882		Horiz. strip of 4	3.00	1.40
a.-d.	A626	$1.50 Any single	.75	.35

World Post Day A627

No. 1883: a, Postman on bicycle, mail recipient. b, Mail recipient, airplane, postman on motorcycle.

Perf. 13½
		2021, Oct. 9 Litho. Unwmk.		
1883	A627	$1.30 Horiz. pair, #a-b	1.25	.65

Tales of Hang Tuah — A628
Terengganu Inscribed Stone — A629
Letters of Sultam Abdul Hamid Halim Shah — A630

Perf. 14x13¼
		2021, Nov. 14 Litho. Unwmk.		
1884	A628	60c multi	.30	.30
1885	A629	90c multi	.45	.30
1886	A630	$1.30 multi	.60	.30
		Nos. 1884-1886 (3)	1.35	.90

Malaysia Cup Soccer Tournament, Cent. — A631

No. 1887 — Trophy from: a, 1921. b, 2021.

Perf. 14¼x13¾
		2021, Dec. 27 Litho. Unwmk.		
1887	A631	$1.90 Horiz. pair, #a-b	1.90	.95

A632

Edible Flowers A633

Designs: 60c, Bunga betik (papaya flower) and boiled papaya flowers. $1.30, Bunga telang (Asian pigeonwings) and pressed rice cakes. $5, Bunga kantan (torch ginger) and bamboo chicken.

Perf. 14x14¼
		2021, Dec. 31 Litho. Unwmk.		
1888-1889	A632	Set of 2	.95	.45

Souvenir Sheet
Perf. 13¼x13½
| 1890 | A633 | $5 multi | 2.40 | 1.25 |

For stamp with added inscription, see No. 1906B.

Traditional Cooking — A634

No. 1891: a, Kuih akok. b, Kuih bakar.
No. 1892: a, Kuih kapit. b, Kuih jala. $5, Kuih bahulu.

Unwmk.
		2022, Feb. 15 Litho. Perf. 14		
1891	A634	30c Horiz. pair, #a-b	.30	.30
1892	A634	$1.50 Horiz. pair, #a-b	1.50	.75

Souvenir Sheet
Perf. 13½x13¼
| 1893 | A634 | $5 multi | 2.40 | 1.25 |

No. 1893 contains one 28x64mm stamp.

Endangered Animals — A635

Designs: No. 1894, 50c, Stump-tailed macaques. No. 1895, 50c, Spiny terrapins. No. 1896, 80c, Small-clawed otters. No. 1897, 80c, Banded broadbills. $5, Malayan tigers.

Perf. 13½x13¼
		2022, Mar. 17 Litho.		
1894-1897	A635	Set of 4	1.25	.60

Souvenir Sheet
Perf. 14¼
| 1898 | A635 | $5 multi | 2.40 | 1.25 |

No. 1898 contains one 45x38mm octagonal stamp.

Waterfalls, Flora and Fauna — A636

Designs: 50c, Lata Kinjang Waterfall, Perak, and Neolissochilus hexagonolepis. 60c, Tawai Waterfall, Sabah, and Nepenthes rafflesiana. 90c, Kubah Waterfall, Sarawak, and Rhacophorus pardalis.

		2022, May 12 Litho. Perf. 14		
1899-1901	A636	Set of 3	.95	.45

Traditional Boats A637

Designs: 30c, Iban Community boat, Sarawak. $1.50, Bajau Community boat, Sabah. $5, Kolek barat, Kelantan.

		2022, June 29 Litho. Perf. 14¼		
1902-1903	A637	Set of 2	.85	.40

Souvenir Sheet
| 1904 | A637 | $5 multi | 2.25 | 1.10 |

For stamp with added inscription, see No. 1906.

City Status of Kuala Lumpur, 50th Anniv. — A638

		2022, July 7 Litho. Perf. 13¾x14¼		
1905	A638	$1.50 multi	.70	.35

Boats Type of 2022 With Added Inscription for Indonesia 2022 Philatelic Exhibition at Lower Left
		2022, Aug. 4 Litho. Perf. 14¼		
1906	A637	$1.50 Like #1903	.70	.35

Durians Type of 2021 With Added Inscription for MAHA 2022 Agricultural Exhibition
Souvenir Sheet
		2022, Aug. 4 Litho. Perf. 14½		
1906A	A625	$5 Like #1881	2.25	1.10

Edible Flowers Type of 2021 With Added Inscription for MAHA 2022 Agricultural Exhibition
Souvenir Sheet
		2022, Aug. 4 Litho. Perf. 13¼x13½		
1906B	A633	$5 Like #1890	2.25	1.10

Men's Headdresses — A639

Designs: No. 1907, 70c, Tanjak. No. 1908, 70c, Tempok. No. 1909, 80c, Lavung Tepo/Dok. No. 1910, 80c, Siga. $5, Ketapu.

MALAYSIA — Johore

2022, Aug. 10 — Litho. — Perf. 13¼x13½
1907-1910	A639	Set of 4	1.40	.70

Souvenir Sheet
Perf. 14x14½
1911	A639	$5 multi	2.25	1.10

No. 1911 contains one 40x48mm stamp.

Kebayas — A640

Inscription: 50c, Kebaya Sulam. $1.30, Kebaya Pendek. $5, Kebaya Labuh.

2022, Oct. 27 — Litho. — Perf. 14
1912-1913	A640	Set of 2	.80	.40

Souvenir Sheet
Perf. 13½x13¼
1914	A640	$5 multi	2.10	1.10

No. 1914 contains one 31x64mm stamp.

Recycling — A641

2022, Nov. 2 — Litho. — Perf. 13¾x14¼
1915	A641	$1.50 multi	.70	.35

Sultan Idris Education University, Cent. — A642

Perf. 13½x13¼
2022, Nov. 30 — Litho.
1916	A642	$1.30 multi	.60	.30

Leisure Activities A643

Designs: 30c, People riding bicycles. 60c, People gardening. 90c, Coin collecting. $5, People camping.

2022, Dec. 10 — Litho. — Perf. 14¼x14
1917-1919	A643	Set of 3	.85	.45

Souvenir Sheet
Perf. 14¼
1920	A643	$5 multi	2.25	1.10

No. 1920 contains one 48x48mm stamp.

University Administrators — A644

Designs: 30c, Diraja Ungku Aziz (1922-2020), economist.. $1, Mohamed Rashdan bin Hj. Baba (1935-2020), agronomist. $1.30, Khoo Kay Kim (1937-2019), historian.

2022, Dec. 20 — Litho. — Perf. 13¼x13
1921-1923	A644	Set of 3	1.25	.60

Animals — A645

Designs: 30c, Betta splendens. 50c, Felis catus. $1.30, Melopsittacus undulatus. $5, Oryctolagus cuniculus, horiz.

2023, Feb. 23 — Litho. — Perf. 14
1924-1926	A645	Set of 3	.95	.45

Souvenir Sheet
Perf. 14¼
1927	A645	$5 multi	2.25	1.10

No. 1927 contains one 45x38mm octagonal stamp.

Coins A646

Obverse and reverse of coins from: No. 1928a, Malacca, 1445-59. No. 1928b, Kedah, 1710-73. $1.50, Johore, 1718-22. $5, Kelantan, 1400.

2023, Apr. 15 — Litho. — Perf. 14¼x14
1928	A646	50c Horiz. pair, #a-b	.45	.30
1929	A646	$1.50 multi	.70	.35

Litho. & Embossed With Foil Application
Souvenir Sheet
1930	A646	$5 multi	2.25	1.10

No. 1930 contains one 50x30mm stamp.

Research Institutes — A647

Designs: 30c, Forest Research Institute of Malaysia. 70c, Institute of Medical Research. $1.30, Malaysia Palm Oil Board.

2023, May 18 — Litho. — Perf. 13¼x13¾
1931-1933	A647	Set of 3	1.00	.50

Mountains — A648

Designs: 60c, Mt. Korbu. $1.30, Mt. Kinabalu.

2023, June 27 — Litho. — Perf. 14¼x14
1934-1935	A648	Set of 2	.85	.40

Oldest Neobalanocarpus Heimii Tree in Malaysia — A649

No. 1936: a, Trunk and canopy. b, Base, leaves, blossoms and seeds

2023, July 27 — Litho. — Perf. 14
1936	A649	$1.50 Horiz. pair, #a-b	1.40	.70

SEMI-POSTAL STAMPS

Typhoon Haiyan Disaster Relief Fund SP1

No. B1: a, Bunga Raya. b, Durian. c, Handicraft. d, Wau Bulan.

Perf. 13¾x14
2013, Nov. 14 — Litho. — Wmk. 388
B1	Sheet of 8, #B1a, B1b, B1e, B1f, 2 each #B1c, B1d		6.25	6.25
a.-b.	SP1 35c+65c Either single		.75	.75
c.-d.	SP1 65c+35c Either single		.75	.75
e.	As "a", perf. 13¾x14x14¼x14		.75	.75
f.	As "b", perf. 13¾x14x14¼x14		.75	.75

No. B1 sold for $10.

POSTAGE DUE STAMPS

Until 1966 Malaysia used postage due stamps of the Malayan Postal Union. See listings under Malaya.

D1

Wmk. 338 Upright
1966, Aug. 15 — Litho. — Perf. 14½x14
J1	D1	1c pink	.25	4.00
J2	D1	2c slate	.60	2.25
J3	D1	4c lt yellow green	1.00	8.00
J4	D1	8c bright green	2.10	14.00
J5	D1	10c ultramarine	1.50	2.25
J6	D1	12c purple	1.10	4.00
J7	D1	20c brown	1.75	4.00
J8	D1	50c olive bister	3.50	7.00
		Nos. J1-J8 (8)	11.80	45.50

Wmk. 338 Sideways
1972, May 23
J4a	D1	8c bright green	7.75	22.50
J5a	D1	10c ultramarine	7.75	15.00
J7a	D1	20c brown	10.50	15.00
J8a	D1	50c olive bister	11.50	20.00
		Nos. J4a-J8a (4)	37.50	72.50

1980-86 — Litho. — Unwmk.
J9	D1	2c slate	.35	3.00
J10	D1	8c bright green	.60	6.00
J11	D1	10c blue	.60	2.75
J11A	D1	12c maroon ('86)	14.00	18.00
J12	D1	20c brown	.80	3.25
J13	D1	50c olive bister	1.25	3.75
		Nos. J9-J13 (6)	17.60	36.75

D2

1986, Sept. 15 — Litho. — Perf. 12x11½
J14	D2	5c brt rose & lil rose	.25	1.10
J15	D2	10c blk, gray, org & tan	.25	1.10
J16	D2	20c deep org & yel org	.40	.65
J17	D2	50c blue grn & lt bl grn	.60	.90
J18	D2	$1 brt blue & lt ultra	1.10	2.00
		Nos. J14-J18 (5)	2.60	5.15

JOHORE

Vanda Hookeriana and Sultan Ismail — A14

Orchids: 2c, Arundina graminifolia. 5c, Paphiopedilum niveum. 6c, Spathoglottis plicata. 10c, Arachnis flosaeris. 15c, Rhyncostylis retusa. 20c, Phalaenopsis violacea.

Wmk. 338
1965, Nov. 15 — Photo. — Perf. 14½
Flowers in Natural Colors
169	A14	1c blk & lt grnsh bl	.25	.25
a.	Black omitted		375.00	
b.	Watermark sideways ('70)		1.60	6.00
170	A14	2c black, red & gray	.25	.80
171	A14	5c black & Prus bl	.25	.25
a.	Yellow omitted		110.00	
172	A14	6c black & lt lil	.40	.25
173	A14	10c black & lt ultra	.40	.25
a.	Watermark sideways ('70)		3.00	2.50
174	A14	15c blk, lil rose & grn	1.50	.35
175	A14	20c black & brown	1.50	.65
a.	Purple omitted		300.00	
		Nos. 169-175 (7)	4.55	2.80

Malayan Jezebel and Sultan Ismail — A15

Butterflies: 2c, Black-veined tiger. 5c, Clipper. 6c, Lime butterfly. 10c, Great orange tip. 15c, Blue pansy. 20c, Wanderer.

Perf. 13½x13
1971, Feb. 1 — Litho. — Unwmk.
176	A15	1c multicolored	.50	1.75
177	A15	2c multicolored	1.40	2.50
178	A15	5c multicolored	1.75	.40
179	A15	6c multicolored	1.75	2.50
180	A15	10c multicolored	1.75	.55
181	A15	15c multicolored	1.75	.50
182	A15	20c multicolored	1.75	1.00
		Nos. 176-182 (7)	10.65	9.20

1977 — Photo.
176a	A15	1c	3.00	3.50
177a	A15	2c	3.00	5.25
178a	A15	5c	3.00	.70
180a	A15	10c	4.50	.35
181a	A15	15c	9.25	.35
182a	A15	20c	11.50	1.00
		Nos. 176a-182a (6)	34.25	11.15

Differentiating the lithograph and photogravure printings of the Butterflies issues:

Denominations and inscriptions have straight edges on the lithographed printings and broken edges on the photogravure printings.

Background colors and portrait show prominent screen dots on the lithographed stamps, but these features appear almost solid on the photogravure stamps except under high magnification.

Rafflesia Hasseltii and Sultan Ismail — A16

Flowers: 2c, Pterocarpus indicus. 5c, Lagerstroemia speciosa. 10c, Durio zibethinus. 15c, Hibiscus. 20c, Rhododendron scortechinii. 25c, Phaeomeria speciosa.

Wmk. 378
1979, Apr. 30 — Litho. — Perf. 14½
183	A16	1c multicolored	.25	.75
184	A16	2c multicolored	.25	.75
185	A16	5c multicolored	.25	.50
186	A16	10c multicolored	.25	.25
187	A16	15c multicolored	.25	.25
188	A16	20c multicolored	.25	.25
189	A16	25c multicolored	.40	3.00
		Nos. 183-189 (7)	1.90	3.00

1984 — "Johor" in round type
185a	A16	5c	1.10	1.40
186a	A16	10c	1.10	1.40
187a	A16	15c	.75	.25
188a	A16	20c	1.25	.55
		Nos. 185a-188a (4)	4.20	3.60

Agriculture, State Arms and Sultan Mahmood Iskandar Al-Haj, Regent — A19

Wmk. 388
1986, Oct. 25 — Litho. — Perf. 12
190	A19	1c Coffea liberica	.35	.35
191	A19	2c Cocos nucifera	.35	.35
192	A19	5c Theobroma cacao	.35	.35
193	A19	10c Piper nigrum	.35	.35
194	A19	15c Hevea brasiliensis	.35	.35

MALAYSIA — Johore — Kedah — Kelantan

195	A19	20c Elaeis guineensis	.35	.35
196	A19	30c Oryza sativa	.50	.50
		Nos. 190-196 (7)	2.60	2.60

1994-99?

192a	A19	5c Perf. 14	3.25	.25
192b	A19	5c Perf. 15x14½ ('95)	1.75	
192c	A19	5c Perf. 14x14½ ('98)	19.00	
193a	A19	10c Perf. 14	3.25	.25
193b	A19	10c Perf. 14x14½ ('96)	4.25	.25
193c	A19	10c Perf. 15x14½ ('99)	14.00	
194	A19	20c Perf. 14	2.00	.25
195b	A19	20c Perf. 15x14½	1.60	
195c	A19	20c Perf. 14x14½ ('96)	14.50	.40
196a	A19	30c Perf. 14	3.25	.25
196b	A19	30c Perf. 15x14½	13.50	1.00
196c	A19	30c Perf. 14x14½	3.75	

Agriculture and State Arms Type of 1986 Redrawn With Denominations in "Sen"
Perf. 14x13¾

2002 Litho. Wmk. 388

196D	A19	30sen Oryza sativa	—	—
e.		Perf. 15x14½	—	

Flowers, Arms and Sultan Mahmood Iskandar Ibni Al-Marhum Sultan Ismail — A20

Designs: 5c, Nelumbium nelumbo. 10c, Hydrangea macrophylla. 20c, Hippeastrum reticulatum. 30c, Bougainvillea. 40c, Ipomoea indica. 50c, Hibiscus rosa-sinensis.

Perf. 14¾x14½

2007, Dec. 31 Litho. Wmk. 388

197	A20	5c multi	.35	.25
a.		Perf. 14x13¾	.35	.25
198	A20	10c multi	.35	.25
a.		Perf. 14x13¾	.35	

Perf. 14x13¾

199	A20	20c multi	.35	.25
200	A20	30c multi	.35	.25
201	A20	40c multi	.35	.25
202	A20	50c multi	.45	.25
a.		Souvenir sheet of 6, #197a, 198a, 199-202	2.25	1.10
		Nos. 197-202 (6)	2.20	1.50

Coronation of Sultan Ibrahim — A21

Various photographs of Sultan Ibrahim in uniform: 60c, 80c, $1.
$5. Sultan Ismail and Raja Zarith Sofiah.

Unwmk.

2015, Mar. 23 Litho. *Perf. 13*

203-205	A21	Set of 3	1.40	.70

Souvenir Sheet

206	A21	$5 multi	2.75	1.40

Flowers, Arms and Sultan Ibrahim — A22

Designs: 10c, Nelumbium nelumbo. 20c, Hydrangea macrophylla. 30c, Hippeastrum reticulatum. 40c, Bougainvillea. 50c, Ipomoea indica. 60c, Hibiscus rosa-sinensis.

Perf. 14x13¾

2016, Feb. 25 Litho. Wmk. 388

207	A22	10c multi	.25	.25
208	A22	20c multi	.25	.25
209	A22	30c multi	.25	.25
210	A22	40c multi	.25	.25
211	A22	50c multi	.25	.25
212	A22	60c multi	.30	.25
a.		Souvenir sheet of 6, #207-212	1.10	.55
		Nos. 207-212 (6)	1.55	1.50

Miniature Sheet

Wild Orchids, Arms of Johore and Sultan Ibrahim A23

No. 213: a, 5c, Bulbophyllum virescens. b, 10c, Corybas carinatus. c, 20c, Vanilla griffithii. d, 30c, Phaius subtrilobus. e, 40c, Dendrobium macrophyllum var. ternatense. f, 50c, Anoectochilus reinwardtii.

Perf. 13½x13

2018, Dec. 4 Litho. Unwmk.

213	A23	Sheet of 6, #a-f	.75	.35

KEDAH

Orchid Type of Johore, 1965, with Portrait of Sultan Abdul Halim
Wmk. 338

1965, Nov. 15 Photo. *Perf. 14½*
Flowers in Natural Colors

106	A14	1c blk & lt grnsh bl	.30	1.25
a.		Black omitted	250.00	
b.		Watermark sideways ('70)	2.50	5.25
107	A14	2c black, red & gray	.30	1.50
108	A14	5c black & Prus bl	.30	.30
109	A14	6c black & lt lil	.30	.30
110	A14	10c black & lt ultra	.50	.30
a.		Watermark sideways ('70)	1.50	4.00
111	A14	15c blk, lil rose & grn	1.75	.30
112	A14	20c black & brown	2.00	.90
		Nos. 106-112 (7)	5.45	5.05

Butterfly Type of Johore, 1971, with Portrait of Sultan Abdul Halim
Perf. 13½x13

1971, Feb. 1 Litho. Unwmk.

113	A15	1c multicolored	.35	1.50
114	A15	2c multicolored	.45	1.50
115	A15	5c multicolored	1.10	.30
116	A15	6c multicolored	1.10	1.75
117	A15	10c multicolored	1.10	.30
118	A15	15c multicolored	1.10	.30
119	A15	20c multicolored	1.40	.60
		Nos. 113-119 (7)	6.60	6.25

1977 Photo. Same Designs

114a	A15	2c	22.50	17.00
115a	A15	5c	5.00	1.25
117a	A15	10c	11.00	.75
118a	A15	15c	3.50	.50
119a	A15	20c	5.00	2.25
		Nos. 114a-119a (5)	47.00	21.75

For differentiating the lithograph and photogravure printings of the Butterflies issues, see notes after Johore No. 182a.

Flower Type of Johore, 1979, with Portrait of Sultan Abdul Halim
Wmk. 378

1979, Apr. 30 Litho. *Perf. 14½*

120	A16	1c multicolored	.25	.80
121	A16	2c multicolored	.25	.80
122	A16	5c multicolored	.25	.50
123	A16	10c multicolored	.25	.25
a.		Unwmkd. ('85)	22.00	3.25
124	A16	15c multicolored	.25	.25
a.		Unwmkd. ('84)	1.00	1.00
125	A16	20c multicolored	.35	.25
a.		Pale yellow flowers ('84)	.35	.25
126	A16	25c multicolored	.40	.25
		Nos. 120-126 (7)	2.00	3.10

25th Anniv. of Installation of Sultan Abdul Halim — A10

20c, Portrait, vert. 40c, View from Mt. Gunung Jerai. 50c, Rice fields, Mt. Gunung Jerai.

1983, July 15 Litho. *Perf. 13½*

127	A10	20c multi	1.10	.35
128	A10	40c multi	2.25	2.25
129	A10	50c multi	3.00	4.75
		Nos. 127-129 (3)	6.35	7.35

Agriculture and State Arms Type of Johore with Sultan Abdul Halim
Wmk. 388

1986, Oct. 25 Litho. *Perf. 12*

130	A19	1c multicolored	.30	.30
131	A19	2c multicolored	.30	.30
132	A19	5c multicolored	.30	.30
133	A19	10c multicolored	.30	.30
134	A19	15c multicolored	.30	.30
135	A19	20c multicolored	.30	.30
136	A19	30c multicolored	.30	.30
		Nos. 130-136 (7)	2.10	2.10

1986?

132a	A19	5c Perf. 15x14½	4.25	.40
132b	A19	5c Perf. 14	1.25	
133a	A19	10c Perf. 14	3.00	.30
133b	A19	10c Perf. 14x13¾, unwmk.	8.50	
135a	A19	20c Perf. 14	1.00	.25
135b	A19	20c Perf. 15x14½	—	—
135c	A19	20c Perf. 14x14½	—	—
136a	A19	30c Perf. 14x14½	2.25	.25
136b	A19	30c Perf. 14x13½	3.00	.25
136c	A19	30c Perf. 15x14½	3.00	.25
136d	A19	30c Perf. 14	—	

Agriculture and State Arms Type of Johore of 1986 With Sultan Abdul Halim Redrawn With Denomination in "Sen"

2003 ? Litho. Wmk. 388 *Perf. 14*

136E	A19	30sen multi	—	

Flowers and Arms Type of Johore of 2007 With Portrait of Sultan Abdul Halim
Perf. 14x13¾

2007, Dec. 31 Litho. Wmk. 388

137	A20	5c multi	.30	.25
138	A20	10c multi	.30	.25
139	A20	20c multi	.30	.25
140	A20	30c multi	.30	.25
141	A20	40c multi	.50	.25
142	A20	50c multi	.65	.30
a.		Souvenir sheet of 6, #137-142	2.25	1.10
		Nos. 137-142 (6)	2.40	1.55

Reign of Sultan Abdul Halim, 50th Anniv. — A11

Sultan and: 30c, Buildings, farm field. 50c, Buildings. $1, Buildings and anniversary emblem.

Perf. 13½x13¼x12x13¼

2008, July 15

143-145	A11	Set of 3	1.10	1.10

Installation of Sultan Sallehuddin — A15

Perf. 14x14¼

2018, Oct. 22 Litho. Unwmk.

146	A12	60c multi	.30	.25
147	A13	60c multi	.30	.25
148	A14	60c multi	.30	.25
		Nos. 146-148 (3)	.90	.75

Souvenir Sheet

149	A15	$5 multi	2.40	1.25

Miniature Sheet

Wild Orchids, Arms of Kedah and Sultan Sallehuddin — A16

No. 150: a, 5c, Bulbophyllum virescens. b, 10c, Corybas carinatus. c, 20c, Vanilla griffithii. d, 30c, Phaius subtrilobus. e, 40c, Dendrobium macrophyllum var. ternatense. f, 50c, Anoectochilus reinwardtii.

Perf. 13½x13

2018, Dec. 4 Litho. Unwmk.

150	A16	Sheet of 6, #a-f	.75	.35

KELANTAN

Orchid Type of Johore, 1965, with Portrait of Sultan Yahya Petra
Wmk. 338

1965, Nov. 15 Photo. *Perf. 14½*
Flowers in Natural Colors

91	A14	1c blk & lt grnsh bl	.35	1.10
a.		Watermark sideways ('70)	1.40	7.50
92	A14	2c black, red & gray	.25	1.50
93	A14	5c black & Prus bl	.25	.25
94	A14	6c black & lt lil	.80	2.00
95	A14	10c black & lt ultra	.40	.25
a.		Watermark sideways ('70)	4.25	4.75
96	A14	15c blk, lil rose & grn	1.75	.25
97	A14	20c black & brown	1.75	1.50
		Nos. 91-97 (7)	5.55	6.85

Butterfly Type of Johore, 1971, with Portrait of Sultan Yahya Petra
Perf. 13½x13

1971, Feb. 1 Litho. Unwmk.

98	A15	1c multicolored	.30	2.00
99	A15	2c multicolored	.30	2.00
100	A15	5c multicolored	1.25	.50
101	A15	6c multicolored	1.25	2.25
102	A15	10c multicolored	1.40	.25
103	A15	15c multicolored	2.00	.25
104	A15	20c multicolored	2.50	1.25
		Nos. 98-104 (7)	9.00	8.50

1977 Photo.

98a	A15	1c	1.25	4.25
100a	A15	5c	7.75	3.50
102a	A15	10c	8.50	3.00
103a	A15	15c	16.00	1.10
		Nos. 98a-103a (4)	33.50	11.85

For differentiating the lithograph and photogravure printings of the Butterflies issues, see notes after Johore No. 182a.

Flower Type of Johore, 1979, with Portrait of Sultan Yahya Petra
Wmk. 378

1979, Apr. 30 Litho. *Perf. 14½*

105	A16	1c multicolored	.25	.90
106	A16	2c multicolored	.25	.90
107	A16	5c multicolored	.25	.70
a.		Unwmkd. ('86)	.75	1.25
108	A16	10c multicolored	.25	.25
a.		White flowers ('84)	.30	.25
109	A16	15c multicolored	.25	.25
110	A16	20c multicolored	.25	.25
a.		Pale yellow flowers ('84)	.35	.25
111	A16	25c multicolored	.45	.55
		Nos. 105-111 (7)	1.95	3.80

Sultan Tengku Ismail Petra, Installation — A7

MALAYSIA — Kelantan — Malacca — Negri Sembilan

Kelantan (continued)

1980, Mar. 30   Litho.   *Perf. 14½*

112	A7	10c multicolored	.35	.65
113	A7	15c multicolored	.50	.35
114	A7	50c multicolored	1.25	2.50
		Nos. 112-114 (3)	2.10	3.50

Agriculture and State Arms Type of Johore with Sultan Ismail Petra
Wmk. 388

1986, Oct. 25   Litho.   *Perf. 12*

115	A19	1c multicolored	.30	.30
116	A19	2c multicolored	.30	.30
117	A19	5c multicolored	.30	.30
118	A19	10c multicolored	.30	.30
119	A19	15c multicolored	.30	.30
120	A19	20c multicolored	.30	.30
121	A19	30c multicolored	.30	.30
		Nos. 115-121 (7)	2.10	2.10

1986?

116a	A19	2c Perf. 15x14½	3.00	.50
117a	A19	5c Perf. 14		
118a	A19	10c Perf. 14	3.00	.50
120a	A19	20c Perf. 14	3.25	.50
121a	A19	30c Perf. 14	1.00	.25
121b	A19	30c Perf. 14x14½		

Reign of Sultan Tengku Ismail Petra, 25th Anniv. — A8

Sultan and various buildings: 30c, 50c, $1.

Perf. 13½, 12 (50c)

2004, Feb. 29   Litho.   Wmk. 388

122-124   A8   Set of 3   .95   .45

Flowers and Arms Type of Johore of 2007 With Portrait of Sultan Ismail Petra

Perf. 14x13¾

2007, Dec. 31   Litho.   Wmk. 388

125	A20	5c multi	.30	.25
126	A20	10c multi	.30	.25
127	A20	20c multi	.30	.25
128	A20	30c multi	.35	.25
129	A20	40c multi	.50	.25
130	A20	50c multi	.65	.30
a.	Souvenir sheet of 6, #125-130		2.25	1.10
	Nos. 125-130 (6)		2.40	1.55

Flowers, Arms and Sultan Muhammad V — A9

Designs: 10c, Nelumbium nelumbo. 20c, Hydrangea macrophylla. 30c, Hippeastrum reticulatum. 40c, Bougainvillea. 50c, Ipomoea indica. 60c, Hibiscus rosa-sinensis.

Perf. 14x13¾

2018, Feb. 13   Litho.   Wmk. 388

131	A9	10c multi	.25	.25
132	A9	20c multi	.25	.25
133	A9	30c multi	.25	.25
134	A9	40c multi	.25	.25
135	A9	50c multi	.25	.25
136	A9	60c multi	.30	.25
a.	Souvenir sheet of 6, #131-136, imperf.		1.10	.55
	Nos. 131-136 (6)		1.55	1.50

Miniature Sheet

Wild Orchids, Arms of Kelantan and Sultan Muhammad V — A10

No. 137: a, 5c, Bulbophyllum virescens. b, 10c, Corybas carinatus. c, 20c, Vanilla griffithii. d, 30c, Phaius subtrilobus. e, 40c, Dendrobium macrophyllum var. ternatense. f, 50c, Anoectochilus reinwardtii.

Perf. 13½x13

2018, Dec. 4   Litho.   Unwmk.

137   A10   Sheet of 6, #a-f   .75   .35

MALACCA
(Melaka)

Orchid Type of Johore, 1965, with State Crest
Wmk. 338

1965, Nov. 15   Photo.   *Perf. 14½*
Flowers in Natural Colors

67	A14	1c blk & lt grnsh blue	.25	1.50
a.	Watermark sideways ('70)		1.50	7.50
68	A14	2c blk, red & gray	.25	1.25
69	A14	5c black & Prus bl	.25	.25
70	A14	6c black & lt lilac	.40	.90
71	A14	10c black & lt ultra	.30	.25
a.	Watermark sideways ('70)		6.25	7.00
72	A14	15c blk, lil rose & grn	1.75	.30
73	A14	20c black & brown	2.50	.95
	Nos. 67-73 (7)		5.70	5.40

Butterfly Type of Johore, 1971, with State Crest

Perf. 13½x13

1971, Feb. 1   Litho.   Unwmk.

74	A15	1c multicolored	.60	2.00
75	A15	2c multicolored	1.00	2.00
76	A15	5c multicolored	1.50	.90
77	A15	6c multicolored	1.50	2.75
78	A15	10c multicolored	1.50	.65
79	A15	15c multicolored	2.75	.60
80	A15	20c multicolored	2.75	2.25
	Nos. 74-80 (7)		11.60	11.15

1977   Photo.

74a	A15	1c	6.00	9.00
76a	A15	5c	2.75	2.25
78a	A15	10c	7.00	2.25
79a	A15	15c	17.50	.75
80a	A15	20c	6.50	4.25
	Nos. 74a-80a (5)		39.75	18.50

For differentiating the lithograph and photogravure printings of the Butterflies issues, see notes after Johore No. 182a.

Flower Type of Johore, 1979, with State Crest
Wmk. 378

1979, Apr. 30   Litho.   *Perf. 14½*

81	A16	1c multicolored	.25	1.10
82	A16	2c multicolored	.25	1.10
83	A16	5c multicolored	.25	.90
84	A16	10c multicolored	.25	.30
85	A16	15c multicolored	.25	.25
86	A16	20c multicolored	.35	.25
87	A16	25c multicolored	.45	.70
	Nos. 81-87 (7)		2.05	4.60

1983-86   Unwmk.

84a	A16	10c ('85)	1.25	2.75
85a	A16	15c ('86)	.65	.50
86a	A16	20c	.65	1.10
	Nos. 84a-86a (3)		2.55	

Agriculture and State Arms Type of Johore
Wmk. 388

1986, Oct. 25   Litho.   *Perf. 12*

88	A19	1c multicolored	.30	.30
89	A19	2c multicolored	.30	.30
90	A19	5c multicolored	.30	.30
91	A19	10c multicolored	.30	.30
92	A19	15c multicolored	.30	.30
93	A19	20c multicolored	.30	.30
94	A19	30c multicolored	.40	.30
	Nos. 88-94 (7)		2.20	2.10

1986?   Litho.

90a	A19	5c Perf. 14	1.25	.25
91a	A19	10c Perf. 14x13¾	1.00	.25
91b	A19	10c Perf. 15x14½	1.75	.25
93a	A19	20c Perf. 14	1.00	.25
94a	A19	30c Perf. 14	4.50	.25
94b	A19	30c Perf. 15x14½	6.25	.35
94c	A19	30c Perf. 14x14½		

Flowers and Arms Type of Johore of 2007

Perf. 14x13¾, 14¾x14½ (20c)

2007, Dec. 31   Litho.   Wmk. 388

95	A20	5c multi	.25	.25
96	A20	10c multi	.25	.25
97	A20	20c multi	.25	.25
a.	Perf. 14x13¾		.25	.25
98	A20	30c multi	.40	.25
99	A20	40c multi	.50	.30
100	A20	50c multi	.65	.35
a.	Souvenir sheet of 6, #95, 96, 97a, 98-100		2.25	1.10
	Nos. 95-100 (6)		2.30	1.65

Miniature Sheet

Wild Orchids and Arms of Malacca A2

No. 101: a, 5c, Bulbophyllum virescens. b, 10c, Corybas carinatus. c, 20c, Vanilla griffithii. d, 30c, Phaius subtrilobus. e, 40c, Dendrobium macrophyllum var. ternatense. f, 50c, Anoectochilus reinwardtii.

Perf. 13½x13

2018, Dec. 4   Litho.   Unwmk.

101   A2   Sheet of 6, #a-f   .75   .35

NEGRI SEMBILAN
(Negeri Sembilan)

Orchid Type of Johore, 1965, with State Crest
Wmk. 338

1965, Nov. 15   Photo.   *Perf. 14½*
Flowers in Natural Colors

76	A14	1c blk & lt grnsh blue	.25	1.50
a.	Watermark sideways ('70)		3.25	6.00
77	A14	2c black, red & gray	.25	1.50
78	A14	5c black & Prus blue	.50	.25
79	A14	6c black & lt lilac	.50	.60
80	A14	10c black & lt ultra	.50	.25
81	A14	15c blk, lil rose & grn	1.50	.25
82	A14	20c black & brown	1.50	.90
	Nos. 76-82 (7)		4.50	5.25

Tuanku Ja'afar and Crest of Negri Sembilan — A7

1968, Apr. 8   Photo.   *Perf. 13½*

83	A7	15c brt blue & multi	.25	.60
84	A7	50c yellow & multi	.40	1.25

Installation of Tuanku Ja'afar ibni Al-Marhum as ruler (Yang di-Pertuan Besar) of Negri Sembilan.

Butterfly Type of Johore, 1971, with State Crest

Perf. 13½x13

1971, Feb. 1   Litho.   Unwmk.

85	A15	1c multicolored	.40	1.75
86	A15	2c multicolored	.60	1.75
87	A15	5c multicolored	.90	.30
88	A15	6c multicolored	1.00	1.75
89	A15	10c multicolored	1.25	.30
90	A15	15c multicolored	2.00	.30
91	A15	20c multicolored	2.00	.45
	Nos. 85-91 (7)		8.15	6.60

1977   Photo.

86a	A15	2c	2.25	4.50
87a	A15	5c	2.25	1.50
89a	A15	10c	11.00	1.25
90a	A15	15c	17.50	.50
91a	A15	20c	5.50	2.00
	Nos. 86a-91a (5)		38.50	9.75

For differentiating the lithograph and photogravure printings of the Butterflies issues, see notes after Johore No. 182a.

Flower Type of Johore, 1979, with State Crest
Wmk. 378

1979, Apr. 30   Litho.   *Perf. 14½*

92	A16	1c multicolored	.25	1.10
93	A16	2c multicolored	.25	1.10
94	A16	5c multicolored	.25	.30
a.	Unwmkd. ('85)		1.00	1.60
95	A16	10c multicolored	.25	.25
a.	White flowers ('84)		.25	.25
96	A16	15c multicolored	.35	.25
a.	Unwmkd. ('84)		.75	.75
97	A16	20c multicolored	.35	.25
a.	Pale yellow flowers ('84)		.35	.25
98	A16	25c multicolored	.45	.25
	Nos. 92-98 (7)		2.15	3.50

Agriculture and State Arms Type of Johore
Wmk. 388

1986, Oct. 25   Litho.   *Perf. 12*

99	A19	1c multicolored	.30	.30
100	A19	2c multicolored	.30	.30
101	A19	5c multicolored	.30	.30
102	A19	10c multicolored	.30	.30
103	A19	15c multicolored	.30	.30
104	A19	20c multicolored	.40	.30
105	A19	30c multicolored	.30	.30
	Nos. 99-105 (7)		2.20	2.10

1986?   Litho.

101a	A19	5c Perf. 14	1.25	.25
101b	A19	5c Perf. 15x14½		.25
102a	A19	10c Perf. 14	1.00	.25
102b	A19	10c Perf. 14x13¼	8.25	.35
104a	A19	20c Perf. 14	2.50	.25
104b	A19	20c Perf. 15x14½		
104c	A19	20c Perf. 14		
105a	A19	30c Perf. 14	3.50	.25
105b	A19	30c Perf. 14x14½	5.25	.25

Royal Heritage of Negri Sembilan — A8

Designs: 30c, Eight long keris. 50c, Audience Hall. $1, Tuanku Ja'afar Ibni Al-Marhum Tuanku Abdul Rahman, ruler of Negri Sembilan. $2, Tuanku Ja'afar and wife.

Perf. 12¾x12½

2007, Aug. 2   Litho.   Wmk. 388

106-108   A8   Set of 3   1.10   .55

Souvenir Sheet

109   A8 $2 multi   1.25   .60

Flowers and Arms Type of Johore of 2007 With Portrait of Tuanku Jaafar Ibni Al-Marhum Tuanku Abdul Rahman

Perf. 14x13¾, 14¾x14½ (30c)

2007, Dec. 31   Litho.   Wmk. 388

110	A20	5c multi	.25	.25
111	A20	10c multi	.25	.25
112	A20	20c multi	.25	.25
113	A20	30c multi	.40	.25
114	A20	40c multi	.50	.30
a.	Perf. 14¾x14½		.50	.30
115	A20	50c multi	.65	.35
a.	Perf. 14¾x14½		.65	.40
	Nos. 110-115 (6)		2.30	1.65

Installation of Tuanku Muhriz Ibni Al-Marhum Tuanku Munawir — A9

Tuanku Muhriz: 30c, Wearing white headdress. 50c, Wearing black hat. $1, With wife, Tuanku Aishah Rohani, horiz. (58x34mm)

Perf. 13¾x14 Syncopated

2009, Oct. 26   Litho.   Wmk. 388

116-118   A9   Set of 3   1.10   .55

Flowers and Arms Type of Johore of 2007 with Portrait of Tuanku Muhriz Ibni Al-Marhum Tuanku Munawir

Designs as before.

Perf. 14x13¾

2009, Nov. 24   Litho.   Wmk. 388

119	Sheet of 6		.95	.45
a.	A20 5c multi		.25	.25
b.	A20 10c multi		.25	.25
c.	A20 20c multi		.25	.25
d.	A20 30c multi		.25	.25
e.	A20 40c multi		.25	.25
f.	A20 50c multi		.30	.25

Tuanku Muhriz's headdress extends well to the left of his ear on Nos. 119a-119f, much less that seen in illustration A9. The headdress of Tuanku Jaafar on Nos. 110-115 does not extend to the left past his ear.

Miniature Sheet

Wild Orchids, Arms of Negri Sembilan, and Yang di-Pertuan Besar Tuanku Muhriz ibni Al-Marhum Tuanku Munawir — A10

MALAYSIA — Negri Sembilan — Pahang — Penang — Perak

No. 120: a, 5c, Bulbophyllum virescens. b, 10c, Corybas carinatus. c, 20c, Vanilla griffithii. d, 30c, Phaius subtilobus. e, 40c, Dendrobium macrophyllum var. ternatense. f, 50c, Anoectochilus reinwardtii.

Perf. 13½x13

2018, Dec. 4		Litho.		Unwmk.	
120	A10	Sheet of 6, #a-f		.75	.35

PAHANG

Orchid Type of Johore, 1965, with Portrait of Sultan Abu Bakar

Wmk. 338

1965, Nov. 15		Photo.		Perf. 14½	
Flowers in Natural Colors					
83	A14	1c blk & lt grnsh bl		.25	1.10
a.		Watermark sideways ('70)		2.25	6.50
84	A14	2c black, red & gray		.25	1.10
a.		Unwmkd. ('85)			
85	A14	5c black & Prus bl		.35	.25
86	A14	6c black & lt lil		.40	1.10
87	A14	10c black & lt ultra		.30	.25
a.		Watermark sideways ('70)		1.50	3.25
88	A14	15c blk, lil rose & grn		1.25	.25
89	A14	20c black & brown		1.75	.40
		Nos. 83-89 (7)		4.55	4.45

Butterfly Type of Johore, 1971, Portrait of Sultan Abu Bakar

Perf. 13½x13

1971, Feb. 1		Litho.		Unwmk.	
90	A15	1c multicolored		.30	1.50
91	A15	2c multicolored		.40	1.75
92	A15	5c multicolored		.80	.40
93	A15	6c multicolored		1.25	2.00
94	A15	10c multicolored		1.25	.30
95	A15	15c multicolored		2.00	.30
96	A15	20c multicolored		2.25	.45
		Nos. 90-96 (7)		8.25	6.70

In 1973 booklet panes of 4 of the 5c, 10c, 15c were made from sheets.

Sultan Haji Ahmad Shah — A9

1975, May 8		Litho.		Perf. 14x14½	
97	A9	10c lilac, gold & black		.45	1.10
98	A9	15c yellow, green & black		.80	.25
99	A9	50c ultra, dk blue & black		2.00	4.00
		Nos. 97-99 (3)		3.25	5.40

Installation of Sultan Haji Ahmad Shah as ruler of Pahang.

Black-veined Tiger and Sultan Haji Ahmad Shah — A18

1977-78					
100	A18	2c multi ('78)		65.00	60.00
101	A18	5c multicolored		.85	1.10
102	A18	10c multi ('78)		1.25	.85
103	A18	15c multi ('78)		1.75	1.00
104	A18	20c multi ('78)		4.50	2.50
		Nos. 100-104 (5)		73.35	65.45

Flower Type of Johore, 1979, with Portrait of Sultan Haji Ahmad Shah

Wmk. 378

1979, Apr. 30		Litho.		Perf. 14½	
105	A16	1c multicolored		.25	.90
106	A16	2c multicolored		.25	.90
107	A16	5c multicolored		.25	.25
a.		5c brt rose pink & yel flowers ('84)		.25	.25
108	A16	10c multicolored		.25	.25
a.		Unwmkd. ('85)		1.25	1.50
109	A16	15c multicolored		.25	.25
110	A16	20c multicolored		.30	.25
a.		Unwmkd. ('84)		1.00	.30
111	A16	25c multicolored		.45	.40
		Nos. 105-111 (7)		2.00	3.20

Agriculture and State Arms Type of Johore with Sultan Haji Ahmad Shah

Wmk. 388

1986, Oct. 25		Litho.		Perf. 12	
112	A19	1c multicolored		.30	.30
113	A19	2c multicolored		.30	.30
114	A19	5c multicolored		.30	.30
115	A19	10c multicolored		.30	.30
116	A19	15c multicolored		.30	.30
117	A19	20c multicolored		.30	.30
118	A19	30c multicolored		.45	.30
		Nos. 112-118 (7)		2.25	2.15

1986?					
112a	A19	1c Perf. 13½x14		6.50	.35
114a	A19	5c Perf. 14x13¾			
115a	A19	10c Perf. 15x14½		8.50	.50
115b	A19	10c Perf. 14x13½		1.75	.40
117a	A19	20c Perf. 14		1.00	.25
117b	A19	20c Perf. 15x14½			
118a	A19	30c Perf. 14		3.00	.25
118b	A19	30c Perf. 15x14½		6.50	.50

Agriculture and State Arms Type of Johore of 1986 with Sultan Haji Ahmad Shah Redrawn With Denomination in "Sen"

2002 ?		Litho.	Wmk. 388	Perf. 14	
118C	A19	30sen multi			—

Flowers and Arms Type of Johore of 2007 With Portrait of Sultan Haji Ahmad Shah

Perf. 14x13¾

2007, Dec. 31		Litho.		Wmk. 388	
119	A20	5c multi		.25	.25
120	A20	10c multi		.25	.25
121	A20	20c multi		.25	.25
122	A20	30c multi		.40	.25
123	A20	40c multi		.50	.25
124	A20	50c multi		.65	.35
a.		Souvenir sheet of 6, #119-124		2.25	1.10
		Nos. 119-124 (6)		2.30	1.60

Pahang Royalty and Regalia — A19

Regalia and: 60c, Sultan Haji Ahmad Shah, Sultana Hajjah Kalson. 80c, Sultan in uniform. $1, Sultan in robe.

2010, Oct. 24		Litho.		Perf. 14	
125-127	A19	Set of 3		1.60	.80

Reign of Sultan Haji Ahmad Shah, 40th Anniv. — A20

Wmk. 388

2014, Dec. 23		Litho.		Perf. 14	
128	A20	60c multi		.35	.25

Miniature Sheet

Wild Orchids, Arms of Pahang, and Sultan Haji Ahmad Shah — A21

No. 129: a, 5c, Bulbophyllum virescens. b, 10c, Corybas carinatus. c, 20c, Vanilla griffithii. d, 30c, Phaius subtilobus. e, 40c, Dendrobium macrophyllum var. ternatense. f, 50c, Anoectochilus reinwardtii.

Perf. 13½x13

2018, Dec. 4		Litho.		Unwmk.	
129	A21	Sheet of 6, #a-f		.75	.35

PENANG
(Pulau Pinang)

Orchid Type of Johore, 1965, with State Crest

Wmk. 338

1965, Nov. 15		Photo.		Perf. 14½	
Orchids in Natural Colors					
67	A14	1c black & lt grnsh bl		.25	1.10
a.		Watermark sideways ('70)		1.75	5.50
68	A14	2c black, red & gray		.25	1.10
69	A14	5c black & Prus blue		.40	.25
a.		Prussian blue omitted		750.00	
b.		Yellow omitted		75.00	
70	A14	6c black & lt lilac		.50	1.10
71	A14	10c black & lt ultra		.30	.25
a.		Watermark sideways ('70)		7.25	3.75
72	A14	15c black, lil rose & grn		1.10	.25
73	A14	20c black & brown		1.60	.40
		Nos. 67-73 (7)		4.40	4.45

Butterfly Type of Johore, 1971, with State Crest

Perf. 13½x13

1971, Feb. 1		Litho.		Unwmk.	
74	A15	1c multicolored		.40	1.75
75	A15	2c multicolored		.60	1.75
76	A15	5c multicolored		1.25	.30
77	A15	6c multicolored		1.25	1.75
78	A15	10c multicolored		1.40	.25
79	A15	15c multicolored		1.50	.25
80	A15	20c multicolored		1.75	.50
		Nos. 74-80 (7)		8.15	6.55

1977				Photo.	
74a	A15	1c		6.00	7.00
76a	A15	5c		3.50	.50
78a	A15	10c		6.00	.50
79a	A15	15c		18.00	.50
80a	A15	20c		8.25	.90
		Nos. 74a-80a (5)		41.75	9.40

For differentiating the lithograph and photogravure printings of the Butterflies issues, see notes after Johore No. 182a.

Flower Type of Johore, 1979, with State Crest

Wmk. 378

1979, Apr. 30		Litho.		Perf. 14½	
81	A16	1c multicolored		.25	.90
82	A16	2c multicolored		.25	.90
83	A16	5c multicolored		.25	.30
84	A16	10c multicolored		.25	.25
85	A16	15c multicolored		.25	.25
86	A16	20c multicolored		.30	.25
87	A16	25c multicolored		.40	.25
		Nos. 81-87 (7)		1.95	3.10

1984-85				Unwmk.	
83a	A16	5c		.40	.40
84a	A16	10c ('85)		5.75	2.25
85a	A16	15c		.65	.35
86a	A16	20c		.90	.35

The State arms are larger on Nos. 83a-86a.

Agriculture and State Arms Type of Johore

Wmk. 388

1986, Oct. 25		Litho.		Perf. 12	
88	A19	1c multicolored		.30	.30
89	A19	2c multicolored		.30	.30
90	A19	5c multicolored		.30	.30
91	A19	10c multicolored		.30	.30
92	A19	15c multicolored		.30	.30
93	A19	20c multicolored		.30	.30
94	A19	30c multicolored		.30	.30
		Nos. 88-94 (7)		2.10	2.10

1986?					
90a	A19	5c Perf. 14x13¾		2.50	.25
90b	A19	5c Perf. 15x14½		2.50	.25
91a	A19	10c Perf. 14		1.00	.25
91b	A19	10c Perf. 14x14½		3.00	.25
91c	A19	10c Perf. 15x14½		2.50	.25
93a	A19	20c Perf. 14		1.00	.25
93b	A19	20c Perf. 14x14½		4.00	.25
93c	A19	20c Perf. 15x14½		4.00	.25
94a	A19	30c Perf. 14		1.00	.25
94b	A19	30c Perf. 14x14½		2.50	.25
94c	A19	30c Perf. 15x14½		2.50	.25

Agriculture and State Arms Type of Johore of 1986 Redrawn With Denomination in "Sen"

2003 ?		Litho.	Wmk. 388	Perf. 14	
94D	A19	30sen multi			—
e.		Perf. 15x14½			

Flowers and Arms Type of Johore of 2007

Perf. 14x13¾

2007, Dec. 31		Litho.		Wmk. 388	
95	A20	5c multi		.25	.25
96	A20	10c multi		.25	.25
97	A20	20c multi		.25	.25
98	A20	30c multi		.40	.25
99	A20	40c multi		.50	.30
100	A20	50c multi		.65	.35
a.		Souvenir sheet of 6, #95-100		2.25	1.10
		Nos. 95-100 (6)		2.30	1.65

Miniature Sheet

Wild Orchids and Arms of Penang A1

No. 101: a, 5c, Bulbophyllum virescens. b, 10c, Corybas carinatus. c, 20c, Vanilla griffithii. d, 30c, Phaius subtilobus. e, 40c, Dendrobium macrophyllum var. ternatense. f, 50c, Anoectochilus reinwardtii.

Perf. 13½x13

2018, Dec. 4		Litho.		Unwmk.	
101	A1	Sheet of 6, #a-f		.75	.35

PERAK

Sultan Idris Shah — A17

Wmk. 338

1963, Oct. 26		Photo.		Perf. 14	
138	A17	10c yel, blk, blue & brn		.35	.25

Installation of Idris Shah as Sultan of Perak.

Orchid Type of Johore, 1965, with Portrait of Sultan Idris Shah

1965, Nov. 15		Wmk. 338		Perf. 14½	
Flowers in Natural Colors					
139	A14	1c blk & lt grnsh bl		.25	.40
a.		Watermark sideways ('70)		2.50	6.50
140	A14	2c black, red & gray		.25	.60
141	A14	5c black & Prus blue		.30	.25
a.		Yellow omitted		80.00	
142	A14	6c black & lt lilac		.30	.30
143	A14	10c black & lt ultra		.30	.25
a.		Watermark sideways ('70)		7.50	3.75
144	A14	15c blk, lil rose & grn		.80	.25
a.		Lilac rose omitted		900.00	
145	A14	20c black & brown		1.25	.25
		Nos. 139-145 (7)		3.45	2.30

Butterfly Type of Johore, 1971, with Portrait of Sultan Idris Shah

Perf. 13½x13

1971, Feb. 1		Litho.		Unwmk.	
146	A15	1c multicolored		.35	1.75
147	A15	2c multicolored		.90	1.75
148	A15	5c multicolored		1.10	.25
149	A15	6c multicolored		1.10	1.75
150	A15	10c multicolored		1.25	.25
151	A15	15c multicolored		1.25	.35
152	A15	20c multicolored		1.75	.35
		Nos. 146-152 (7)		7.70	6.45

In 1973 booklet panes of 4 of the 5c, 10c, 15c were made from sheets.

1977				Photo.	
146a	A15	1c		1.75	3.50
148b	A15	5c		4.00	.65
150b	A15	10c		3.25	.75
151b	A15	15c		11.00	.50
152a	A15	20c		4.50	1.40
		Nos. 146a-152a (5)		24.50	6.80

For differentiating the lithograph and photogravure printings of the Butterflies issues, see notes after Johore No. 182a.

Flower Type of Johore, 1979, with Portrait of Sultan Idris Shah

Wmk. 378

1979, Apr. 30		Litho.		Perf. 14½	
153	A16	1c multicolored		.25	.75
154	A16	2c multicolored		.25	.75
155	A16	5c multicolored		.25	.25
a.		Brt rose pink & yel flowers ('84)		.25	.25
156	A16	10c multicolored		.25	.25
a.		White flowers ('84)		.25	.25
157	A16	15c multicolored		.30	.25
a.		Unwmkd. ('85)		1.00	.25
158	A16	20c multicolored		.35	.25
a.		Unwmkd. ('84)		.90	.40
159	A16	25c multicolored		.45	.25
		Nos. 153-159 (7)		2.10	2.75

MALAYSIA — Perak — Perlis — Sabah

Perak (continued)

Agriculture and State Arms Type of Johore with Tun Azlan Shah, Raja
Wmk. 388

1986, Oct. 25		Litho.		Perf. 12	
160	A19	1c multicolored		.25	.25
161	A19	2c multicolored		.25	.30
162	A19	5c multicolored		.25	.25
163	A19	10c multicolored		.25	.25
164	A19	15c multicolored		.25	.25
165	A19	20c multicolored		.25	.25
166	A19	30c multicolored		.35	.25
		Nos. 160-166 (7)		1.85	1.80

1986?

161a	A19	2c Perf. 14x14½	3.00	.30
162a	A19	5c Perf. 14	3.00	.25
162b	A19	5c Perf. 15x14½	4.00	.25
163a	A19	10c Perf. 14x13¼	1.00	.25
164a	A19	20c Perf. 14	4.00	.35
165a	A19	20c Perf. 14¾x14½	2.75	.45
166a	A19	30c Perf. 14x14½	3.50	.35
166b	A19	30c Perf. 15x14½	7.50	1.00
166c	A19	30c Perf. 14x13½	6.00	.35
166d	A19	30c Perf. 14	—	—

Flowers and Arms Type of Johore of 2007 With Portrait of Sultan Azlan Shah
Perf. 14x13¾

2007, Dec. 31		Litho.		Wmk. 388	
167	A20	5c multi		.25	.25
168	A20	10c multi		.25	.25
169	A20	20c multi		.25	.25
170	A20	30c multi		.40	.25
171	A20	40c multi		.50	.30
172	A20	50c multi		.65	.35
a.	Souvenir sheet of 6, #167-172		2.25	1.10
	Nos. 167-172 (6)		2.30	1.65

Reign of Sultan Azlan Shah, 25th Anniv. — A18

Sultan and: 30c, Sultana Tuanku Bainun. 50c, Mosque. $1, Sultana, diff.

Perf. 13½x13¼

2009, Feb. 3		Litho.		Wmk. 388	
173-175	A18	Set of 3		1.00	.50

Installation of Sultan Nazrin Muizzuddin Shah — A19

Designs: 60s, Sultan Nazrin. 80s, Sultan Nazrin and Raja Zara. $1.20, Sultan Nazrin, diff. $5, Sultan Nazrin and Raja Zara, diff.

Perf. 13¼x13½

2015, May 6		Litho.		Unwmk.	
176-178	A19	Set of 3		1.50	.75
		Souvenir Sheet			
179	A19	$5 multi		3.00	1.50

No. 179 contains one 42x70mm stamp.

Flowers, Arms and Sultan Nazrin Muizzuddin Shah — A20

Designs: 10c, Nelumbium nelumbo. 20c, Hydrangea macrophylla. 30c, Hippeastrum reticulatum. 40c, Bougainvillea. 50c, Ipomoea indica. 60c, Hibiscus rosa-sinensis.

Perf. 14x13¾

2016, Mar. 21		Litho.		Wmk. 388	
180	A20	10c multi		.25	.25
181	A20	20c multi		.25	.25
182	A20	30c multi		.25	.25
183	A20	40c multi		.25	.25
184	A20	50c multi		.25	.25
185	A20	60c multi		.30	.25
a.	Souvenir sheet of 6, #180-185, imperf.		1.10	.55
	Nos. 180-185 (6)		1.55	1.50

Miniature Sheet

Wild Orchids, Arms of Perak, and Sultan Nazrin Muizzuddin Shah — A21

No. 186: a, 5c, Bulbophyllum virescens. b, 10c, Corybas carinatus. c, 20c, Vanilla griffithii. d, 30c, Phaius subtrilobus. e, 40c, Dendrobium macrophyllum var. ternatense. f, 50c, Anoectochilus reinwardtii.

Perf. 13½x13

2018, Dec. 4		Litho.		Unwmk.	
186	A21	Sheet of 6, #a-f		.75	.35

PERLIS

Orchid Type of Johore, 1965, with Portrait of Regent Yang Teramat Mulia
Wmk. 338

1965, Nov. 15		Photo.		Perf. 14½	
		Flowers in Natural Colors			
40	A14	1c black & lt grnsh bl		.30	.90
41	A14	2c black, red & gray		.35	1.25
42	A14	5c black & Prus blue		.30	.30
43	A14	6c black & lt lilac		.60	1.25
44	A14	10c black & ultra		.85	.35
45	A14	15c blk, lil rose & grn		1.25	.50
46	A14	20c black & brown		1.25	1.60
		Nos. 40-46 (7)		4.90	6.15

Butterfly Type of Johore, 1971, with Portrait of Sultan Syed Putra
Perf. 13½x13

1971, Feb. 1		Litho.		Unwmk.	
47	A15	1c multicolored		.25	1.10
48	A15	2c multicolored		.30	1.75
49	A15	5c multicolored		1.10	1.10
50	A15	6c multicolored		1.25	2.75
51	A15	10c multicolored		1.75	1.10
52	A15	15c multicolored		1.75	.50
53	A15	20c multicolored		1.75	2.25
		Nos. 47-53 (7)		8.15	10.55

In 1973 booklet panes of 4 of the 5c, 10c, 15c were made from sheets.

1977 Photo.

51b	A15	10c	190.00	9.50
52b	A15	15c	5.50	2.75
53a	A15	20c	175.00	32.50
		Nos. 51b-53a (3)	370.50	44.75

For differentiating the lithograph and photogravure printings of the Butterflies issues, see notes after Johore No. 182a.

Sultan Syed Putra — A2

1971, Mar. 28		Litho.		Perf. 13½x13	
54	A2	10c silver, yel & black		.30	2.00
55	A2	15c silver, blue & blk		.35	.65
56	A2	50c silver, lt vio & blk		.90	4.00
		Nos. 54-56 (3)		1.55	6.65

25th anniversary of the installation of Syed Putra as Raja of Perlis. Sold throughout Malaysia on Mar. 28, then only in Perlis.

Flower Type of Johore, 1979, with Portrait of Sultan Syed Putra
Wmk. 378

1979, Apr. 30		Litho.		Perf. 14½	
57	A16	1c multicolored		.25	.90
58	A16	2c multicolored		.25	.90
59	A16	5c multicolored		.25	.90
60	A16	10c multicolored		.25	.25
61	A16	15c multicolored		.25	.25
62	A16	20c multicolored		.30	.25
a.	Unwmk. ('85)		1.75	1.75
63	A16	25c multicolored		.45	.75
		Nos. 57-63 (7)		2.00	4.20

Agriculture and State Arms Type of Johore with Tuanku Syed Putra, Raja
Wmk. 388

1986, Oct. 25		Litho.		Perf. 12	
64	A19	1c multicolored		.30	.45
65	A19	2c multicolored		.30	.45
66	A19	5c multicolored		.30	.30
67	A19	10c multicolored		.30	.30
68	A19	15c multicolored		.30	.30
69	A19	20c multicolored		.30	.30
70	A19	30c multicolored		.40	.30
		Nos. 64-70 (7)		2.20	2.40

1986?

67a	A19	10c Perf. 15x14½	4.25	.45
70a	A19	30c Perf. 14	5.25	.25
70b	A19	30c Perf. 15x14½	14.50	

Reign of Tuanku Syed Putra Jamalullail, Raja of Perlis, 50th Anniv. — A3

30c, Industry and produce. $1, Palace.

Wmk. 388

1995, Dec. 4		Litho.		Perf. 14	
71	A3	30c green & multi		.80	.80
72	A3	$1 blue & multi		2.40	2.40

Installation of Raja Tuanku Syed Sirajuddin Putra Jamalullail — A4

Denomination color: 30c, Blue. 50c, Green. $1, Purple.
$2, Raja and wife, horiz.

Perf. 13½x13¾

2001, May 7		Litho.		Wmk. 388	
73-75	A4	Set of 3		.95	.45
		Souvenir Sheet			
		Perf. 14¼x13½x13¾x13½			
76	A4	$2 multi		1.10	1.10

Flowers and Arms Type of Johore of 2007 With Portrait of Raja Tuanku Syed Sirajuddin Putra Jamalullail
Perf. 14x13¾

2007, Dec. 31		Litho.		Wmk. 388	
77	A20	5c multi		.25	.25
78	A20	10c multi		.25	.25
79	A20	20c multi		.25	.25
80	A20	30c multi		.40	.25
81	A20	40c multi		.50	.30
82	A20	50c multi		.65	.35
a.	Souvenir sheet of 6, #77-82		2.25	1.10
	Nos. 77-82 (6)		2.30	1.65

Miniature Sheet

Wild Orchids, Arms of Perlis, and Raja Tuanku Syed Sirajuddin Putra Jamalullail — A5

No. 83: a, 5c, Bulophyllum virescens. b, 10c, Corybas carinatus. c, 20c, Vanilla griffithii. d, 30c, Phaius subtrilobus. e, 40c, Dendrobium macrophyllum var. ternatense. f, 50c, Anoectochilus reinwardtii.

Perf. 13½x13

2018, Dec. 4		Litho.		Unwmk.	
83	A5	Sheet of 6, #a-f		.75	.35

SABAH

North Borneo Nos. 280-295 Overprinted

On 1c-75c   On $1-$10

Perf. 13x12½, 12½x13

1964, July 1		Engr.		Wmk. 314	
1	A92	1c lt red brn & grn		.25	.35
2	A92	4c orange & olive		.25	.45
3	A92	5c violet & sepia		.25	.35
4	A92	6c bluish grn & sl		1.10	.35
5	A92	10c rose red & lt grn		2.00	.35
6	A92	12c dull green & brn		.25	.35
7	A92	20c ultra & blue grn		4.25	.35
8	A92	25c rose red & gray		.90	.80
9	A92	30c gray ol & sepia		.40	.30
10	A92	35c redsh brn & stl bl		.40	.30
11	A92	50c brn org & blue grn		.40	.30
12	A92	75c red vio & sl blue		3.75	.90
13	A93	$1 yel green & brn		9.50	1.75
14	A93	$2 slate & brown		15.00	3.00
15	A93	$5 brown vio & grn		17.00	13.00
16	A93	$10 blue & carmine		17.00	29.00
		Nos. 1-16 (16)		72.70	51.90

Orchid Type of Johore, 1965, with State Crest
Wmk. 338

1965, Nov. 15		Photo.		Perf. 14½	
		Flowers in Natural Colors			
17	A14	1c black & lt grnsh bl		.30	1.10
18	A14	2c black, red & gray		.30	1.50
19	A14	5c black & Prus bl		.45	.30
20	A14	6c black & lt lilac		.45	1.25
21	A14	10c black & lt ultra		.40	.25
a.	Watermark sideways ('70)		5.50	5.50
22	A14	15c black, lil rose & grn		2.00	.30
23	A14	20c black & brown		3.00	.70
		Nos. 17-23 (7)		6.90	5.35

Butterfly Type of Johore, 1971, with State Crest
Perf. 13½x13

1971, Feb. 1		Litho.		Unwmk.	
24	A15	1c multicolored		.60	2.25
25	A15	2c multicolored		.70	2.25
26	A15	5c multicolored		.70	.40
27	A15	6c multicolored		.90	1.75
28	A15	10c multicolored		1.00	.25
29	A15	15c multicolored		1.25	.25
30	A15	20c multicolored		1.30	1.10
		Nos. 24-30 (7)		6.45	8.25

In 1973 booklet panes of 4 of the 5c, 10c, 15c were made from sheets.

1977 Photo.

24a	A15	1c	1.75	4.25
25a	A15	2c	1.75	4.25
26b	A15	5c	10.00	2.25
28b	A15	10c	2.00	1.00
29b	A15	15c	2.50	.30
30a	A15	20c	225.00	10.00
		Nos. 24a-29b (5)	18.00	12.05

For differentiating the lithograph and photogravure printings of the Butterflies issues, see notes after Johore No. 182a.

Flower Type of Johore, 1979, with State Crest
Wmk. 378

1979, Apr. 30		Litho.		Perf. 14½	
32	A16	1c multicolored		.35	1.50
33	A16	2c multicolored		.35	1.50
34	A16	5c multicolored		.35	.45
35	A16	10c multicolored		.35	.35
36	A16	15c multicolored		.50	.35
37	A16	20c multicolored		.60	.35
38	A16	25c multicolored		.75	.35
		Nos. 32-38 (7)		3.25	4.85

1983-85 Unwmk.

35a	A16	10c ('85)	5.50	7.25
36a	A16	15c	2.75	.90
37a	A16	20c	17.00	1.75

Agriculture and State Arms Type of Johore
Wmk. 388

1986, Oct. 25		Litho.		Perf. 12	
39	A19	1c multicolored		.30	.30
40	A19	2c multicolored		.30	.25
41	A19	5c multicolored		.25	.25
42	A19	10c multicolored		.30	.25
43	A19	15c multicolored		.30	.25

MALAYSIA — Sabah — Sarawak — Selangor — Trengganu

44	A19	20c multicolored	.30	.25
45	A19	30c multicolored	.35	.25
		Nos. 39-45 (7)	2.15	1.80

1986?

40a	A19	2c Perf. 15x14½	3.25	.35
42a	A19	10c Perf. 14x13¾		
45a	A19	30c Perf. 14	1.00	.25
45b	A19	30c Perf. 15x14½	4.75	.30

Flowers and Arms Type of Johore of 2007

Perf. 14x13¾

2007, Dec. 31   Litho.   Wmk. 388

46	A20	5c multi	.25	.25
47	A20	10c multi	.25	.25
48	A20	20c multi	.25	.25
49	A20	30c multi	.40	.25
50	A20	40c multi	.50	.30
51	A20	50c multi	.65	.35
a.		Souvenir sheet of 6, #46-51	2.25	1.10
		Nos. 46-51 (6)	2.30	1.65

Miniature Sheet

Wild Orchids and Arms of Sabah — A1

No. 52: a, 5c, Bulbophyllum virescens. b, 10c, Corybas carinatus. c, 20c, Vanilla griffithii. d, 30c, Phaius subtrilobus. e, 40c, Dendrobium macrophyllum var. ternatense. f, 50c, Anoectochilus reinwardtii.

Perf. 13½x13

2018, Dec. 4   Litho.   Unwmk.

| 52 | A1 | Sheet of 6, #a-f | .75 | .35 |

SARAWAK

Types of Sarawak of 1955-57

Perf. 11x11½, 11½x11

1964-65   Engr.   Wmk. 314

215	A23	1c green	.25	1.00
216	A23	2c red orange	1.00	13.50
217	A24	6c green blue	7.00	5.25
218	A24	10c dark green	2.25	1.40
219	A24	12c purple	3.75	12.00
220	A24	15c ultra	1.50	17.50
221	A24	20c brown & olive	1.00	2.00
222	A24	25c brt grn & brn	4.25	6.00
		Nos. 215-222 (8)	21.00	58.65

Issued: 20c, 6/9/64; 2c, 15c, 8/17/65; others, 9/9/64.

Orchid Type of Johore (Malaysia), 1965, with State Crest

Wmk. 338

1965, Nov. 15   Photo.   Perf. 14½

Flowers in Natural Colors

228	A14	1c black & lt grnsh bl	.25	1.25
229	A14	2c black, red & gray	.30	2.50
230	A14	5c black & Prus blue	1.50	.30
231	A14	6c black & lt lilac	.90	2.25
232	A14	10c black & lt ultra	1.25	.25
233	A14	15c blk, lil rose & grn	1.75	.25
234	A14	20c black & brown	2.50	.55
		Nos. 228-234 (7)	8.45	7.30

Clipper and State Crest — A26

1c, Delias ninus. 2c, Danaus melanippus. 5c, Parthenos sylvia. 6c, Papilio demoleus. 10c, Hebomnia glauceppe. 15c, Precis orithya. 20c, Valeria valeria.

Perf. 13½x13

1971, Feb. 1   Litho.   Unwmk.

235	A26	1c multicolored	.85	2.25
236	A26	2c multicolored	.95	2.25
237	A26	5c multicolored	2.00	.25
a.		Booklet pane of 4 ('73)	9.00	
238	A26	6c multicolored	2.00	3.00
239	A26	10c multicolored	2.00	.25
a.		Booklet pane of 4 ('73)	9.00	
240	A26	15c multicolored	3.00	.25
a.		Booklet pane of 4 ('73)	13.00	
241	A26	20c multicolored	3.00	1.50
		Nos. 235-241 (7)	13.80	9.75

Clipper and New State Crest — A27

Changed Colors, Designs as Before

1977-78   Photo.   Unwmk.

242	A27	1c multi ('78)	8.50	15.00
243	A27	2c multi ('78)	20.00	16.00
244	A27	5c multicolored	2.50	2.00
245	A27	10c multicolored	1.50	.80
246	A27	15c multicolored	3.00	.30
247	A27	20c multi ('78)	7.00	5.75
		Nos. 242-247 (6)	42.50	39.85

Flower Type of Johore, 1979, with State Crest

1979, Apr. 30   Wmk. 47   Perf. 14½

248	A16	1c multicolored	.25	.40
249	A16	2c multicolored	.25	.40
250	A16	5c multicolored	.25	.50
251	A16	10c multicolored	.30	.25
252	A16	15c multicolored	.30	.25
253	A16	20c multicolored	.60	.25
254	A16	25c multicolored	.90	.70
		Nos. 248-254 (7)	2.85	2.75

1983-86   Unwmk.

250a	A16	5c ('86)	1.00	1.25
251a	A16	10c ('85)	1.00	1.10
253a	A16	20c	1.00	1.10
		Nos. 250a-253a (3)	3.00	3.45

Agriculture and State Arms Type of Johore With Shield Divided into 3 Parts of Different Colors

Designs like Johore Nos. 190-196.

Wmk. 388

1986, Oct. 25   Litho.   Perf. 12

255	A19	1c multicolored	.25	.25
256	A19	2c multicolored	.25	.25
257	A19	5c multicolored	.30	.25
258	A19	10c multicolored	.40	.25
259	A19	15c multicolored	.55	.25
260	A19	20c multicolored	.55	.25
261	A19	30c multicolored	1.00	.25
		Nos. 255-261 (7)	3.30	1.75

Agricultural Items and Arms With Yellow Shield Divided by Diagonal Bands of Black and Red — A28

Designs like Johore Nos. 190-196.

1986-96   Litho.   Wmk. 388   Perf. 12

262	A28	1c multicolored	.25	.25
263	A28	2c multicolored	.25	.25
a.		Perf. 15x14½	3.00	
264	A28	5c multicolored	.25	.25
a.		Perf 14 ('96)	.90	.25
265	A28	10c multicolored	.25	.25
a.		Perf. 14 ('95)	2.00	
b.		Perf. 15x14½ ('95)	2.00	
c.		Perf. 14x14½ ('96)	4.50	.35
266	A28	15c multicolored	.25	.25
267	A28	20c multicolored	.30	.25
268	A28	30c multicolored	.40	.25
a.		Perf. 14 ('94)	1.75	.25
b.		Perf. 15x14½ ('94)	4.00	.35
c.		Perf. 14x14½ ('94)	4.25	.45
		Nos. 262-268 (7)	1.95	1.75

Flowers and Sarawak Arms — A29

Designs like Johore Nos. 207-212.

Perf. 14x13¾

2007, Dec. 31   Litho.   Wmk. 388

269	A29	5c multi	.25	.25
270	A29	10c multi	.30	.25
271	A29	20c multi	.35	.25
272	A29	30c multi	.50	.25
273	A29	40c multi	.60	.30
274	A29	50c multi	.75	.35
a.		Souvenir sheet of 6, #269-274	3.00	2.50
		Nos. 269-274 (6)	2.75	1.65

Miniature Sheet

Wild Orchids and Arms of Sarawak — A30

No. 275: a, 5c, Bulbophyllum virescens. b, 10c, Corybas carinatus. c, 20c, Vanilla griffithii. d, 30c, Phaius subtrilobus. e, 40c, Dendrobium macrophyllum var. ternatense. f, 50c, Anoectochilus reinwardtii.

Perf. 13½x13

2018, Dec. 4   Litho.   Unwmk.

| 275 | A30 | Sheet of 6, #a-f | .75 | .35 |

SELANGOR

Orchid Type of Johore, 1965, with Portrait of Sultan Salahuddin Abdul Aziz Shah

Wmk. 338

1965, Nov. 15   Photo.   Perf. 14½

Flowers in Natural Colors

121	A14	1c blk & lt grnsh bl	.25	.25
a.		Watermark sideways ('70)	1.60	7.25
122	A14	2c black, red & gray	.30	1.50
a.		Rose carmine omitted		
123	A14	5c black & Prus blue	.35	.25
124	A14	6c black & lt lilac	.35	.25
125	A14	10c black & lt ultra	.35	.25
a.		Watermark sideways ('70)	5.25	1.75
126	A14	15c blk, lil rose & grn	1.25	.25
127	A14	20c black & brown	2.25	.25
a.		Watermark sideways ('70)	9.25	9.50
		Nos. 121-127 (7)	5.10	3.00

Butterfly Type of Johore, 1971, with Portrait of Sultan Salahuddin Abdul Aziz Shah

Perf. 13½x13

1971, Feb. 1   Litho.   Unwmk.

128	A15	1c multicolored	.65	1.75
129	A15	2c multicolored	1.25	1.75
130	A15	5c multicolored	1.25	.30
131	A15	6c multicolored	1.25	1.75
132	A15	10c multicolored	1.60	.30
133	A15	15c multicolored	1.25	.30
134	A15	20c multicolored	1.25	.40
		Nos. 128-134 (7)	8.50	6.55

In 1973 booklet panes of 4 of the 5c, 10c, 15c were made from sheets.

1977   Photo.

128a	A15	1c	.80	4.25
130b	A15	5c	3.75	1.50
132b	A15	10c	7.75	1.50
133b	A15	15c	9.00	.40
134a	A15	20c	4.50	1.25
		Nos. 128a-134a (5)	25.80	8.90

For differentiating the lithograph and photogravure printings of the Butterflies issues, see notes after Johore No. 182a.

Flower Type of Johore, 1979, with Portrait of Sultan Salahuddin Abdul Aziz Shah

Wmk. 378

1979, Apr. 30   Litho.   Perf. 14½

135	A16	1c multicolored	.25	.90
136	A16	2c multicolored	.25	.90
137	A16	5c multicolored	.25	.25
a.		brt rose pink & yel flowers ('84)	.65	.80
138	A16	10c multicolored	.25	.25
a.		Unwmkd. ('85)	.85	1.00
139	A16	15c multicolored	.25	.25
a.		Unwmkd. ('84)	.85	.85
140	A16	20c multicolored	.30	.25
a.		pale yellow flowers ('84)	1.00	.50
141	A16	25c multicolored	.40	.25
		Nos. 135-141 (7)	1.95	3.05

Agriculture and State Arms Type of Johore with Sultan Salahuddin Abdul Aziz Shah

Wmk. 388

1986, Oct. 25   Litho.   Perf. 12

142	A19	1c multicolored	.30	.30
143	A19	2c multicolored	.30	.30
144	A19	5c multicolored	.30	.25
145	A19	10c multicolored	.30	.25
146	A19	15c multicolored	.30	.25
147	A19	20c multicolored	.30	.25
148	A19	30c multicolored	.35	.25
		Nos. 142-148 (7)	2.15	1.85

1986?

144a	A19	5c Perf. 14x14½	13.00	
144b	A19	5c Perf. 15x14½	4.25	.25
144c	A19	5c Perf. 14x13½	.90	.25
145a	A19	10c Perf. 14	3.25	.25
145b	A19	10c Perf. 15x14½	1.50	.25
145c	A19	10c Perf. 14x14½		—
147a	A19	20c Perf. 14	1.00	.25
147b	A19	20c Perf. 14x14½		
147c	A19	20c Perf. 15x14½		
148a	A19	30c Perf. 14	1.00	.25
148b	A19	30c Perf. 14x14½	8.50	.25
148c	A19	30c Perf. 15x14½	5.00	.25

Agriculture and State Arms Type of Johore of 1986 with Sultan Salahuddin Abdul Aziz Shah Redrawn with Denomination in "Sen"

2003 ?   Litho.   Wmk. 388   Perf. 14

148D	A19	30sen multi		—
e.		Perf. 15x14½		—

Coronation of Sultan Sharafuddin Idris Shah — A19

Designs: 30c, Wearing yellow hat. 50c, Wearing naval uniform. 1r, Wearing crown.

Perf. 12 (30c), 12¾x12½

2003, Mar. 8   Litho.   Wmk. 388

| 149-151 | A19 | Set of 3 | .95 | .45 |

Flowers and Arms Type of Johore of 2007 With Portrait of Sultan Sharafuddin Idris Shah

Perf. 14¾x14½

2007, Dec. 31   Litho.   Wmk. 388

152	A20	5c multi	.25	.25
a.		Perf. 14x13¾	.25	.25
153	A20	10c multi	.25	.25
a.		Perf. 14x13¾	.25	.25

Perf. 14x13¾

154	A20	20c multi	.25	.25
155	A20	30c multi	.40	.25
156	A20	40c multi	.50	.30
157	A20	50c multi	.65	.35
a.		Souvenir sheet of 6, #152a, 153a, 154-157	2.25	1.10
		Nos. 152-157 (6)	2.30	1.65

Miniature Sheet

Wild Orchids, Arms of Selangor, and Sultan Sharafuddin Idris Shah — A20

No. 158: a, 5c, Bulbophyllum virescens. b, 10c, Corybas carinatus. c, 20c, Vanilla griffithii. d, 30c, Phaius subtrilobus. e, 40c, Dendrobium macrophyllum var. ternatense. f, 50c, Anoectochilus reinwardtii.

Perf. 13½x13

2018, Dec. 4   Litho.   Unwmk.

| 158 | A20 | Sheet of 6, #a-f | .75 | .35 |

TRENGGANU

Orchid Type of Johore, 1965, with Portrait of Sultan Ismail

Wmk. 338

1965, Nov. 15   Photo.   Perf. 14½

Flowers in Natural Colors

86	A14	1c black & lt grnsh bl	.25	1.75
87	A14	2c black, red & gray	.30	1.75
88	A14	5c black & Prus blue	.35	.60
89	A14	6c black & lt lilac	.40	1.75
90	A14	10c black & lt ultra	.35	.25
91	A14	15c blk, lil rose & grn	1.40	.25
92	A14	20c black & brown	1.50	1.25
		Nos. 86-92 (7)	4.55	7.60

MALAYSIA — Trengganu — Wilayah Persekutuan — MALDIVE ISLANDS 159

Tuanku Ismail Nasiruddin — A6

Perf. 14½x13½
1970, Dec. 16		Photo.		Unwmk.
93	A6	10c multicolored	.90	2.25
94	A6	15c brt yellow multi	.70	1.10
95	A6	50c dp plum & multi	1.10	2.75
		Nos. 93-95 (3)	2.70	6.10

Installation of Tuanku Ismail Nasiruddin Shah as Sultan of Trengganu, 25th anniv.

Butterfly Type of Johore, 1971, with Portrait of Sultan Ismail Nasiruddin

Perf. 13½x13
1971, Feb. 1		Litho.		Unwmk.
96	A15	1c multicolored	.35	2.25
97	A15	2c multicolored	.70	2.25
98	A15	5c multicolored	.90	1.10
99	A15	6c multicolored	1.50	2.50
100	A15	10c multicolored	1.75	.60
101	A15	15c multicolored	2.25	.30
102	A15	20c multicolored	2.25	2.00
		Nos. 96-102 (7)	9.70	11.00

In 1970 booklet panes of 4 of the 5c, 10c, 15c were made from sheets.

1977				Photo.
98b	A15	5c	24.00	9.50
100b	A15	10c	8.25	3.75
101b	A15	15c	5.25	1.50
		Nos. 98b-101b (3)	37.50	14.75

For differentiating the lithograph and photogravure printings of the Butterflies issues, see notes after Johore No. 182a.

Flower Type of Johore, 1979, with Portrait of Sultan Ismail Nasiruddin

Wmk. 378
1979, Apr. 30		Litho.		Perf. 14½
103	A16	1c multicolored	.25	1.10
104	A16	2c multicolored	.25	1.10
105	A16	5c multicolored	.25	.50
106	A16	10c multicolored	.25	.25
107	A16	15c multicolored	.30	.25
108	A16	20c multicolored	.35	.25
109	A16	25c multicolored	.45	.40
		Nos. 103-109 (7)	2.10	3.85

1983-86				Unwmk.
106a	A16	10c ('86)	13.50	4.25
107a	A16	15c ('85)	.90	1.25
108a	A16	20c	3.00	3.25
109a	A16	25c Pale salmon flowers	.90	1.10
		Nos. 106a-109a (4)	18.30	

The portrait and State arms are smaller.

Agriculture and State Arms Type of Johore with Sultan Mahmud Al Marhum

Wmk. 388
1986, Oct. 25		Litho.		Perf. 12
110	A19	1c multicolored	.30	.30
111	A19	2c multicolored	.30	.30
112	A19	5c multicolored	.30	.30
113	A19	10c multicolored	.30	.30
114	A19	15c multicolored	.30	.30
115	A19	20c multicolored	.30	.30
116	A19	30c multicolored	.40	.30
		Nos. 110-116 (7)	2.20	2.10

1986?				
110a	A19	1c Perf. 13½x14	4.25	.35
112a	A19	5c Perf. 14		
113a	A19	10c Perf. 14		
115a	A19	20c Perf. 14	7.25	.25
116a	A19	30c Perf. 14	7.25	.30
116b	A19	30c Perf. 14½x14½		

Installation of HRH Sultan Mizan Zainal Abidin — A7

Sultan Abidin and: 30c, Istana Maziah. 50c, Istana Maziah, 1903. $1, Masjid Tengku Tengah Zaharah.

Wmk. 388
1999, Mar. 4		Litho.		Perf. 14¼
117	A7	30c multicolored	.50	.25

Perf. 14½
| 118 | A7 | 50c multicolored | .75 | .50 |

Perf. 13¾
| 119 | A7 | $1 multicolored | 1.40 | 2.50 |
| | | Nos. 117-119 (3) | 2.65 | 3.25 |

Flowers and Arms Type of 2007 With Portrait of Sultan Mizan Zainal Abidin

Perf. 14x13¾
2007, Dec. 31		Litho.		Wmk. 388
120	A20	5c multi	.25	.25
121	A20	10c multi	.25	.25
122	A20	20c multi	.25	.25
123	A20	30c multi	.40	.25
124	A20	40c multi	.50	.30
125	A20	50c multi	.65	.35
a.		Souvenir sheet of 6, #120-125	2.25	1.10
		Nos. 121-125 (5)	2.05	1.40

Miniature Sheet

Wild Orchids, Arms of Trengganu, and Sultan Mizan Zainal Abidin — A8

No. 126: a, 5c, Bulbophyllum virescens. b, 10c, Corybas carinatus. c, 20c, Vanilla griffithii. d, 30c, Phaius subtrilobus. e, 40c, Dendrobium macrophyllum var. ternatense. f, 50c, Anoectochilus reinwardtii.

Perf. 13½x13
2018, Dec. 4		Litho.		Unwmk.
126	A8	Sheet of 6, #a-f	.75	.35

WILAYAH PERSEKUTUAN

Agriculture and State Arms Type of Johore

Wmk. 388
1986, Oct. 25		Litho.		Perf. 12
1	A19	1c multicolored	.25	.25
2	A19	2c multicolored	.25	.25
3	A19	5c multicolored	.25	.25
4	A19	10c multicolored	.25	.25
5	A19	15c multicolored	.25	.25
6	A19	20c multicolored	.25	.25
7	A19	30c multicolored	.40	.25
		Nos. 1-7 (7)	1.90	1.75

1986?				
3a	A19	5c Perf. 14	3.00	
3b	A19	5c Perf. 15x14½	7.50	
4a	A19	10c Perf. 14	3.00	
4b	A19	10c Perf. 14	7.50	
4c	A19	10c Perf. 14¾x14½		
6a	A19	20c Perf. 14	1.00	
6b	A19	20c Perf. 15x14½		
7a	A19	30c Perf. 14	1.00	
7b	A19	30c Perf. 15x14½	4.00	
7c	A19	30c Perf. 14x14½		

Agriculture and State Arms Type of Johore of 1986 Redrawn With "Sen" Instead of "C"

Designs as before

Perf. 14x13¾
2002 ?		Litho.		Wmk. 388
10	A19	5sen multi		—

Perf. 14x14¾
| 11 | A19 | 10sen multi | | — |

Perf. 14x13¾
| 13 | A19 | 20sen multi | | — |

Perf. 15x14½
| 14 | A19 | 30sen multi | | — |

Additional stamps were released in this set and also for other states. The editors would like to examine any examples.

2002 ?		Litho.		Wmk. 388
11a	A19	10sen Perf. 14x13¾	—	
11b	A19	10sen Perf. 15x14½	—	
13a	A19	20sen Perf. 14x14¾	—	
13b	A19	20sen Perf. 15x14½	—	
14a	A19	30sen Perf. 14x13¾	—	
14b	A19	30sen Perf. 14x14½	—	

Flowers and Arms Type of Johore of 2007

Perf. 14x13¾
2007, Dec. 31		Litho.		Wmk. 388
15	A20	5c multi	.25	.25
a.		Perf. 14¾x14½	.25	.25
16	A20	10c multi	.25	.25
a.		With microprinting to right of flower ('21 ?)		
17	A20	20c multi	.25	.25
a.		With microprinting to right of flower ('21 ?)		
18	A20	30c multi	.40	.25
a.		With microprinting to right of flower ('21 ?)		
19	A20	40c multi	.50	.30
a.		With microprinting to right of flower ('21 ?)		
20	A20	50c multi	.65	.35
a.		Souvenir sheet of 6, #15-20	2.25	1.10
b.		With microprinting to right of flower ('21 ?)		
		Nos. 15-20 (6)	2.30	1.65

Miniature Sheet

Wild Orchids and Arms of Wilayah Persekutuan — A1

No. 21: a, 5c, Bulbophyllum virescens. b, 10c, Corybas carinatus. c, 20c, Vanilla griffithii. d, 30c, Phaius subtrilobus. e, 40c, Dendrobium macrophyllum var. ternatense. f, 50c, Anoectochilus reinwardtii.

Perf. 13½x13
2018, Dec. 4		Litho.		Unwmk.
21	A1	Sheet of 6, #a-f	.75	.35

MALDIVE ISLANDS

'mol-,div 'i-lənds

LOCATION — A group of 2,000 islands in the Indian Ocean about 400 miles southwest of Ceylon.
GOVT. — Republic
AREA — 115 sq. mi.
POP. — 541,000 (2020 est.)
CAPITAL — Male

Maldive Islands was a British Protectorate, first as a dependency of Ceylon, then from 1948 as an independent sultanate, except for a year (1953) as a republic. The islands became completely independent on July 26, 1965, and became a republic again on November 11, 1968.

100 Cents = 1 Rupee
100 Larees = 1 Rufiyaa (1951)

Catalogue values for unused stamps in this country are for Never Hinged items, beginning with Scott 20.

Watermarks

Wmk. 47 — Multiple Rosette

Wmk. 233 — "Harrison & Sons, London" in Script

Stamps of Ceylon, 1904-05, Overprinted

1906, Sept. 9		Wmk. 3		Perf. 14
1	A36	2c orange brown	17.50	35.00
2	A37	3c green	28.00	40.00
3	A37	4c yellow & blue	40.00	62.50
4	A38	5c dull lilac	4.00	4.50
5	A40	15c ultramarine	80.00	125.00
6	A40	25c bister	90.00	160.00
		Nos. 1-6 (6)	259.50	427.00

Minaret of Juma Mosque, near Male — A1

1909		Engr.		Wmk. 47
7	A1	2c orange brown	2.25	4.50
a.		Perf 13½x14	2.50	.90
8	A1	3c green	.50	.70
9	A1	5c red violet	.50	.35
10	A1	10c carmine	7.50	.80
		Nos. 7-10 (4)	10.75	6.35

Type of 1909 Issue Redrawn

Perf. 14½x14
1933		Photo.		Wmk. 233
11	A1	2c gray	2.00	1.90
12	A1	3c yellow brown	.55	2.00
13	A1	5c brown lake	42.50	7.50
14	A1	6c brown red	1.10	4.25
15	A1	10c green	.65	.40
16	A1	15c gray black	6.50	21.00
17	A1	25c red brown	6.50	21.00
18	A1	50c red violet	6.50	26.00
19	A1	1r blue black	11.00	21.00
		Nos. 11-19 (9)	77.30	105.05

On the 6c, 15c, 25c and 50c, the right hand panel carries only the word "CENTS."

Nos. 11-19 exist with watermark vert. and horiz. The 5c with vert. watermark sells for twice the price of the horiz. watermark.

Catalogue values for unused stamps in this section, from this point to the end of the section, are for Never Hinged items.

Palm Tree and Seascape — A2

1950, Dec. 24		Engr.		Unwmk. Perf. 13
20	A2	2 l olive green	4.50	5.50
21	A2	3 l deep blue	17.00	3.00
22	A2	5 l dp blue green	17.00	3.00
23	A2	6 l red brown	1.25	1.75
24	A2	10 l red	1.25	1.00
25	A2	15 l orange	1.25	1.00
26	A2	25 l rose violet	1.25	4.00
27	A2	50 l violet blue	1.50	6.00
28	A2	1r dark brown	14.00	40.00
		Nos. 20-28 (9)	59.00	65.25

Maldive Fish — A3

1952				
29	A3	3 l shown	1.75	.75
30	A3	5 l Urns	.90	2.00

Harbor of Male — A4
Fort and Governor's Palace — A5

Perf. 13½ (A4), 11½x11 (A5)
1950		Engr.		Unwmk.
31	A4	2 l lilac	.25	.25
32	A4	3 l gray green	.25	.25
33	A4	5 l reddish brown	.25	.25
34	A4	6 l blue violet	.25	.25
35	A4	10 l light green	.25	.25
36	A4	15 l brown	.25	.25
37	A4	25 l rose red	.25	.25
38	A4	50 l orange	.25	.25
39	A5	1r light green	.40	.30
40	A5	5r ultramarine	1.00	.65
41	A5	10r magenta	2.10	1.25
		Nos. 31-41 (11)	5.50	4.20

Bicyclists and Olympic Emblem — A6

Design: 25 l, 50 l, 1r, Basketball, vert.

MALDIVE ISLANDS

Perf. 11½x11, 11x11½
1960, Aug. 20   Engr.
42	A6	2 l rose violet & green	.25	.25
43	A6	3 l grnsh gray & plum	.25	.25
44	A6	5 l vio brn & dk blue	.25	.25
45	A6	10 l brt green & brn	.25	.25
46	A6	15 l brown & blue	.25	.25
47	A6	25 l rose red & olive	.25	.25
48	A6	50 l orange & dk vio	.25	.25
49	A6	1r brt green & plum	.40	.75
		Nos. 42-49 (8)	2.15	2.60

17th Olympic Games, Rome, 8/25-9/11.

World Refugee Year Emblem — A7

1960, Oct. 15   Perf. 11½x11
50	A7	2 l orange, vio & grn	.25	.25
51	A7	3 l green, brn & red	.25	.25
52	A7	5 l sepia, grn & red	.25	.25
53	A7	10 l dull pur, grn & red	.25	.25
54	A7	15 l gray grn, pur & red	.25	.25
55	A7	25 l redsh brn, ultra & ol	.25	.25
56	A7	50 l rose, olive & blue	.25	.25
57	A7	1r gray, car rose & vio	.35	.50
		Nos. 50-57 (8)	2.10	2.25

WRY, July 1, 1959-June 30, 1960.

Tomb of Sultan — A8

Designs: 3 l, Custom house. 5 l, Cowry shells. 6 l, Old royal palace. 10 l, Road to Minaret, Juma Mosque, Male. 15 l, Council house. 25 l, Government secretariat. 50 l, Prime minister's office. 1r, Tomb and sailboats. 5r, Tomb by the sea. 10r, Port.

1960, Oct. 15   Perf. 11½x11
Various Frames
58	A8	2 l lilac	.25	.25
59	A8	3 l green	.25	.25
60	A8	5 l brown orange	3.50	3.50
61	A8	6 l bright blue	.25	.25
62	A8	10 l carmine rose	.25	.25
63	A8	15 l sepia	.25	.25
64	A8	25 l dull violet	.25	.25
65	A8	50 l slate	.25	.25
66	A8	1r orange	.25	.25
67	A8	5r dark blue	8.00	.55
68	A8	10r dull green	12.50	2.10
		Nos. 58-68 (11)	26.00	8.15

Stamps in 25r, 50r and 100r denominations were also issued, but primarily for revenue purposes. Value for the three stamps, $350.

Coconuts A9

Map of Male Showing Population Distribution A10

Perf. 14x14½, 14½x14
1961, Apr. 20   Photo.   Unwmk.
Coconuts in Ocher
69	A9	2 l green	.25	.25
70	A9	3 l ultramarine	.25	.25
71	A9	5 l lilac rose	.25	.25
72	A9	10 l red orange	.25	.25
73	A9	15 l black	.25	.25
74	A10	25 l multicolored	.25	.25
75	A10	50 l multicolored	.25	.25
76	A10	1r multicolored	.50	.70
		Nos. 69-76 (8)	2.25	2.45

Pigeon and 5c Stamp of 1906 — A11

Designs: 10 l, 15 l, 20 l, Post horn and 3c stamp of 1906. 25 l, 50 l, 1r, Laurel branch and 2c stamp of 1906.

1961, Sept. 9   Perf. 14½x14
77	A11	2 l violet blue & mar	.25	.25
78	A11	3 l violet blue & mar	.25	.25
79	A11	5 l violet blue & mar	.25	.25
80	A11	6 l violet blue & mar	.25	.25
81	A11	10 l maroon & green	.25	.25
82	A11	15 l maroon & green	.25	.25
83	A11	20 l maroon & green	.25	.25
84	A11	25 l green, mar & blk	.25	.25
85	A11	50 l green, mar & blk	.25	.25
86	A11	1r green, mar & blk	.35	.35
a.		Souvenir sheet of 4	2.40	3.00
		Nos. 77-86 (10)	2.60	2.60

55th anniv. of the 1st postage stamps of the Maldive Islands.
No. 86a contains 4 No. 86, with simulated perforations.

Malaria Eradication Emblem — A12

1962, Apr. 7   Engr.   Perf. 13½x13
87	A12	2 l orange brown	.25	.25
88	A12	3 l green	.25	.25
89	A12	5 l blue	.25	.25
90	A12	10 l vermilion	.25	.25
91	A12	15 l black	.25	.25
92	A12	25 l dark blue	.25	.25
93	A12	50 l green	.25	.35
94	A12	1r purple	.35	.45
		Nos. 87-94 (8)	2.10	2.30

WHO drive to eradicate malaria.

Children and Map of Far East and Americas — A13

UNICEF, 15th Anniv.: 25 l, 50 l, 1r, 5r, Children and Map of Africa, Europe and Asia.

Perf. 14½x14
1962, Sept. 9   Photo.   Unwmk.
Children in Multicolor
95	A13	2 l sepia	.25	.25
96	A13	6 l violet	.25	.25
97	A13	10 l dark green	.25	.25
98	A13	15 l ultramarine	.25	.25
99	A13	25 l blue	.25	.25
100	A13	50 l bright green	.25	.25
101	A13	1r rose claret	.25	.25
102	A13	5r emerald	.50	.90
		Nos. 95-102 (8)	2.25	2.65

Sultan Mohamed Farid Didi — A14

1962, Nov. 29   Perf. 14x14½
Portrait in Orange Brown and Sepia
103	A14	3 l bluish green	.25	.25
104	A14	5 l slate	.25	.25
105	A14	10 l blue	.35	.35
106	A14	20 l olive	.35	.35
107	A14	50 l dk carmine rose	.35	.35
108	A14	1r dark purple	.45	.45
		Nos. 103-108 (6)	2.00	2.00

9th anniv. of the enthronement of Sultan Mohamed Farid Didi.

Regal Angelfish, Sultan's Crest and Skin Diver A15

Tropical Fish: 10 l, 25 l, Moorish idol. 50 l, Diadem squirrelfish. 1r, Surgeonfish. 5r, Orange butterflyfish.

1963, Feb. 2   Perf. 13½
109	A15	2 l multicolored	.25	.25
110	A15	3 l multicolored	.25	.25
111	A15	5 l multicolored	.25	.25
112	A15	10 l multicolored	.35	.35
113	A15	25 l multicolored	.75	.75
114	A15	50 l multicolored	1.25	.70
115	A15	1r multicolored	1.50	.75
116	A15	5r multicolored	6.00	6.00
		Nos. 109-116 (8)	10.60	9.30

Fish in Net — A16

Design: 5 l, 10 l, 50 l, Wheat emblem and hand holding rice, vert.

1963, Mar. 21   Photo.   Perf. 12
117	A16	2 l green & lt brown	.35	.35
118	A16	5 l dull rose & lt brn	.55	.55
119	A16	7 l grnsh blue & lt brn	.75	.75
120	A16	10 l blue & lt brown	.85	.85
121	A16	25 l brn red & lt brn	2.75	2.75
122	A16	50 l violet & lt brown	4.00	4.00
123	A16	1r rose cl & lt brn	6.50	6.50
		Nos. 117-123 (7)	15.75	15.75

FAO "Freedom from Hunger" campaign.

Centenary Emblem — A17

1963, Oct.   Unwmk.   Perf. 14x14½
124	A17	2 l dull purple & red	.25	.25
125	A17	15 l slate green & red	.90	.90
126	A17	50 l brown & red	1.60	1.60
127	A17	1r dk blue & red	2.25	1.75
128	A17	4r dk ol grn & red	4.50	4.50
		Nos. 124-128 (5)	9.50	9.00

Centenary of the International Red Cross.

Scout Emblem and Knot — A18

1963, Dec. 7   Unwmk.   Perf. 13½
129	A18	2 l purple & dp green	.25	.25
130	A18	3 l brown & dp green	.25	.25
131	A18	25 l dk blue & dp green	.25	.25
132	A18	1r dp car & dp grn	.50	.50
		Nos. 129-132 (4)	1.25	1.25

11th Boy Scout Jamboree, Marathon, Aug. 1963. Printed in sheets of 12 (3x4) with ornamental borders and inscriptions.

Mosque at Male — A19

Wmk. 314
1964, Aug. 10   Engr.   Perf. 11½
133	A19	2 l rose violet	.25	.25
134	A19	3 l green	.25	.25
135	A19	10 l carmine rose	.25	.25
136	A19	40 l black brown	.30	.30
137	A19	60 l blue	.45	.45
138	A19	85 l orange brown	.60	.60
		Nos. 133-138 (6)	2.10	2.10

Conversion of the Maldive Islanders to Mohammedanism in 1733 (1153 by Islamic calendar).

Shot Put and Maldive Arms — A20

15 l, 25 l, 50 l, 1r, Runner, Maldive arms.

Perf. 14x13½
1964, Oct. 6   Litho.   Wmk. 314
139	A20	2 l grnsh bl & dull vio	.25	.25
140	A20	3 l red brn & maroon	.25	.25
141	A20	5 l dk green & gray	.25	.25
142	A20	10 l plum & indigo	.25	.25
143	A20	15 l bis brn & dk brn	.30	.30
144	A20	25 l dk bl & bluish blk	.55	.40
145	A20	50 l olive & black	.85	.45
146	A20	1r gray & dk purple	1.25	.75
a.		Souvenir sheet of 3	2.50	4.00
		Nos. 139-146 (8)	3.95	2.90

18th Olympic Games, Tokyo, Oct. 10-25.
No. 146a contains 3 imperf. stamps similar to Nos. 144-146.

General Electric Observation Communication Satellite — A21

Perf. 14½
1965, July 1   Photo.   Unwmk.
147	A21	5 l dark blue	.25	.25
148	A21	10 l brown	.25	.25
149	A21	25 l green	.50	.50
150	A21	1r magenta	1.00	1.00
		Nos. 147-150 (4)	2.00	2.00

Quiet Sun Year, 1964-65. Printed in sheets of 9 (3x3) with ornamental borders and inscriptions.

Queen Nefertari Holding Sistrum and Papyrus — A22

Designs: 3 l, 10 l, 25 l, 1r, Ramses II.

1965, Sept. 1   Litho.   Wmk. 314
151	A22	2 l dull bl grn & mar	.25	.25
152	A22	3 l lake & green	.25	.25
153	A22	5 l green & lake	.25	.25
154	A22	10 l dk blue & ocher	.30	.25
155	A22	15 l redsh brn & ind	.55	.25
156	A22	25 l dull lil & indigo	.80	.25
157	A22	50 l green & brown	1.00	.40
158	A22	1r brown & green	1.40	.50
		Nos. 151-158 (8)	4.80	2.40

UNESCO world campaign to save historic monuments in Nubia.

John F. Kennedy and Doves — A23

Design: 1r, 2r, President Kennedy and hands holding olive branches.

1965, Oct. 1   Photo.   Unwmk.   Perf. 12
159	A23	2 l slate & brt pink	.25	.25
160	A23	5 l brown & brt pink	.25	.25
161	A23	25 l blue blk & brt pink	.25	.25
162	A23	1r red lil, yel & grn	.25	.25
163	A23	2r sl green, yel & grn	.45	.45
a.		Souvenir sheet of 4	2.75	3.25
		Nos. 159-163 (5)	1.45	1.45

No. 163a contains 4 imperf. stamps similar to No. 163.

UN Flag — A24

1965, Nov. 24   Photo.   Perf. 12
Flag in Aquamarine
164	A24	3 l red brown	.25	.25
165	A24	10 l violet	.30	.25
166	A24	1r dark olive brown	.90	.35
		Nos. 164-166 (3)	1.45	.85

20th anniversary of the United Nations.

MALDIVE ISLANDS

ICY Emblem — A25

1965, Dec. 20   Photo.   Perf. 12

167	A25	5 l bister & dk brn	.25	.25
168	A25	15 l dull vio & dk brn	.35	.25
169	A25	50 l olive & dk brn	.75	.25
170	A25	1r orange & dk brn	1.40	1.40
171	A25	2r blue & dk brn	1.75	3.50
a.		Souvenir sheet of 3	6.50	6.50
		Nos. 167-171 (5)	4.50	5.70

Intl. Cooperation Year. No. 171a contains three imperf. stamps with simulated perforations similar to Nos. 169-171.

Sea Shells — A26

A27

Coat of Arms and: 2 l, 10 l, 30 l, No. 181, Conus alicus and cymatium maldiviensis (shells). 5 l, 10r, Conus litteratus and distorsia reticulata (shells). 7 l, No. 182, 2r, India-rubber vine flowers. 15 l, 50 l, 5r, Crab plover and gull. 3 l, 20 l, 1.50r, Reinwardtia trigynia.

1966, June 1   Unwmk.   Perf. 12

172	A26	2 l multicolored	.25	1.10
173	A27	3 l multicolored	.25	1.10
174	A26	5 l multicolored	.25	.25
175	A27	7 l multicolored	.25	.25
176	A26	10 l multicolored	.85	.25
177	A27	15 l multicolored	3.25	.30
178	A27	20 l multicolored	.70	.30
179	A26	30 l multicolored	2.40	.35
180	A26	50 l multicolored	5.25	.50
181	A26	1r multicolored	3.50	.60
182	A27	1r multicolored	3.50	.60
183	A27	1.50r multicolored	3.25	3.25
184	A27	2r multicolored	4.50	3.75
185	A26	5r multicolored	20.00	15.00
186	A26	10r multicolored	20.00	20.00
		Nos. 172-186 (15)	68.20	47.60

Flag — A28

1966, July 26   Perf. 14x14½

187	A28	10 l grnsh blue, red & grn	3.25	.65
188	A28	1r ocher, brn, red & grn	7.00	1.50

1st anniv. of full independence from Great Britain.

Luna 9 on Moon A29

Designs: 25 l, 1r, 5r, Gemini 6 and 7, rendezvous in space. 2r, Gemini spaceship as seen from second Gemini spaceship.

1966, Nov. 1   Litho.   Perf. 15x14

189	A29	10 l gray bl, lt brn & ultra	.25	.25
190	A29	25 l car rose & green	.30	.25
191	A29	50 l green & dp org	.55	.25
192	A29	1r org brn & grnsh bl	.90	.40
193	A29	2r violet & green	1.20	.60
194	A29	5r Prus blue & pink	1.75	1.60
a.		Souvenir sheet of 3	6.75	6.25
		Nos. 189-194 (6)	4.95	3.35

Rendezvous in space of Gemini 6 and 7 (US), Dec. 4, 1965, and the soft landing on Moon by Luna 9 (USSR), Feb. 3, 1966. No. 194a contains 3 imperf. stamps similar to Nos. 192-194 with simulated perforations.

UNESCO Emblem, Owl and Book — A30

20th anniv. of UNESCO: 3 l, 1r, Microscope, globe and communication waves. 5 l, 5r, Palette, violin and mask.

1966, Nov. 15   Litho.   Perf. 15x14

195	A30	2 l green & multi	.40	.40
196	A30	3 l lt violet & multi	.40	.40
197	A30	5 l orange & multi	.75	.40
198	A30	50 l rose & multi	7.00	.75
199	A30	1r citron & multi	8.00	1.25
200	A30	5r multicolored	22.00	20.00
		Nos. 195-200 (6)	38.55	23.20

Winston Churchill and Coffin on Gun Carriage A31

10 l, 25 l, 1r, Churchill and catafalque.

1967, Jan. 1   Perf. 14½x13½

201	A31	2 l ol grn, red & dk blue	.40	.45
202	A31	10 l Prus grn, red & dk blue	2.75	.35
203	A31	15 l grn, red & dk bl	3.50	.35
204	A31	25 l vio, red & dk bl	5.00	.40
205	A31	1r brn, red & dk bl	13.00	1.25
206	A31	2.50r brn lake, red & dk blue	30.00	17.50
		Nos. 201-206 (6)	54.65	20.30

Sir Winston Spencer Churchill (1874-1965), statesman and World War II leader.

Soccer and Jules Rimet Cup — A32

Designs: 3 l, 5 l, 25 l, 50 l, 1r, Various scenes from soccer and Jules Rimet Cup. 2r, British flag, Games' emblem and Big Ben Tower, London.

1967, Mar. 22   Photo.   Perf. 14x13½   Unwmk.

207	A32	2 l ver & multi	.35	.55
208	A32	3 l olive & multi	.35	.55
209	A32	5 l brt purple & multi	.35	.55
210	A32	25 l brt green & multi	1.25	.35
211	A32	50 l orange & multi	1.90	.35
212	A32	1r brt blue & multi	3.25	.75
213	A32	2r brown & multi	5.75	3.75
a.		Souvenir sheet of 3	13.50	12.50
		Nos. 207-213 (7)	13.20	6.85

England's victory in the World Soccer Cup Championship. No. 213a contains 3 imperf. stamps similar to Nos. 211-213.

Clown Butterflyfish A33

Tropical Fish: 3 l, 1r, Four-saddled puffer. 5 l, Indo-Pacific blue trunkfish. 6 l, Striped triggerfish. 50 l, 2r, Blue angelfish.

1967, May 1   Photo.   Perf. 14

214	A33	2 l brt violet & multi	.30	.45
215	A33	3 l emerald & multi	.30	.45
216	A33	5 l org brn & multi	.30	.25
217	A33	6 l brt blue & multi	.30	.25
218	A33	50 l olive & multi	3.50	.40
219	A33	1r rose red & multi	6.50	.80
220	A33	2r orange & multi	12.00	9.00
		Nos. 214-220 (7)	23.20	11.60

Plane at Hulule Airport A34

Designs: 5 l, 15 l, 50 l, 10r, Plane over administration building, Hulule Airport.

1967, July 26   Perf. 14x13½

221	A34	2 l citron & lil	.25	.40
222	A34	5 l violet & green	.45	.25
223	A34	10 l lt green & lilac	.55	.25
224	A34	15 l yel bister & grn	.90	.25
225	A34	30 l sky blue & vio bl	1.60	.25
226	A34	50 l brt pink & brn	2.25	.30
227	A34	5r org & vio blue	5.50	5.00
228	A34	10r lt ultra & dp brn	7.25	8.50
		Nos. 221-228 (8)	18.75	15.20

For overprints see Nos. 235-242.
Higher denominations, primarily for revenue use, also were issued.

Man and Music Pavilion and EXPO '67 Emblem A35

Designs: 5 l, 50 l, 2r, Man and his Community Pavilion and EXPO '67 emblem.

Perf. 14x13½

1967, Oct. 1   Photo.   Unwmk.

EXPO '67 Emblem in Gold

229	A35	2 l ol gray, ol & brt rose	.25	.25
230	A35	5 l ultra, grnsh blue & brn	.25	.25
231	A35	10 l brn red, lt grn & red org	.25	.25
232	A35	50 l brn, grnsh blue & org	.45	.25
233	A35	1r vio, grn & rose lil	.85	.45
234	A35	2r dk grn, emer & red brn	1.75	1.10
a.		Souvenir sheet of 2	5.25	5.25
		Nos. 229-234 (6)	3.80	2.55

EXPO '67 Intl. Exhibition, Montreal, Apr. 28-Oct. 27. No. 234a contains 2 imperf. stamps similar to Nos. 233-234 with simulated perforations.

Nos. 221-228 Overprinted in Gold: "International Tourist Year 1967"

1967, Dec. 1   Photo.   Perf. 14x13½

235	A34	2 l citron & lilac	.30	.35
236	A34	5 l violet & green	.30	.30
237	A34	10 l lt green & lilac	.30	.30
238	A34	15 l yel bister & grn	.30	.30
239	A34	30 l sky blue & vio bl	.35	.30
240	A34	50 l brt pink & brn	.65	.35
241	A34	5r org & vio blue	4.00	4.00
242	A34	10r lt ultra & dp brn	5.50	5.50
		Nos. 235-242 (8)	11.70	11.40

The overprint is in 3 lines on the 2 l, 10 l, 30 l, 5r; one line on the 5 l, 15 l, 50 l, 10r.

Lord Baden-Powell, Wolf Cubs, Campfire and Flag Signals — A36

Boy Scouts: 3 l, 1r, Lord Baden-Powell, Boy Scout saluting and drummer.

1968, Jan. 1   Litho.   Perf. 14x14½

243	A36	2 l yel, brown & green	.25	.25
244	A36	3 l lt bl, ultra & rose car	.25	.25
245	A36	25 l dp org, red brn & vio blue	1.60	.40
246	A36	1r yel grn, grn & red brn	3.50	1.60
		Nos. 243-246 (4)	5.60	2.50

Sheets of 12 (4x3) with decorative border.
For overprints see Nos. 278-281.

French Satellites D-1 and A-1 A37

3 l, 25 l, Luna 10, USSR. 7 l, 1r, Orbiter & Mariner, US. 10 l, 2r, Edward White, Virgil Grissom & Roger Chaffee, US. 5r, Astronaut V. M. Komarov, USSR.

1968, Jan. 27   Photo.   Perf. 14

247	A37	2 l dp ultra & brt pink	.25	.25
248	A37	3 l dk ol bis & vio	.25	.25
249	A37	7 l rose car & ol	.30	.25
250	A37	10 l blk, gray & dk bl	.30	.25
251	A37	25 l purple & brt grn	.30	.25
252	A37	50 l brown org & blue	.50	.25
253	A37	1r dk sl grn & vio brn	1.10	.35
254	A37	2r blk, bl & dk brn	1.75	1.00
a.		Souvenir sheet of 2	5.25	5.75
255	A37	5r blk, tan & lil rose	4.25	2.50
		Nos. 247-255 (9)	9.00	5.30

International achievements in space and to honor American and Russian astronauts, who gave their lives during space explorations in 1967. No. 254a contains 2 imperf. stamps similar to Nos. 253-254.

Shot Put — A38

Design: 6 l, 15 l, 2.50r, Discus.

1968, Feb. 1   Litho.   Perf. 11½

256	A38	2 l emerald & multi	.25	.25
257	A38	6 l dull yel & multi	.25	.25
258	A38	10 l multicolored	.25	.25
259	A38	15 l orange & multi	.25	.25
260	A38	1r blue & multi	.60	.30
261	A38	2.50r rose & multi	1.40	1.40
		Nos. 256-261 (6)	3.00	2.70

19th Olympic Games, Mexico City, 10/12-27.

View of the Lagoon Near Venice, by Richard P. Bonington A39

Seascapes: 1r, Ulysses Deriding Polyphemus (detail), by Joseph M. W. Turner. 2r, Sailboat at Argenteuil, by Claude Monet. 5r, Fishing Boats at Saintes-Maries, by Vincent Van Gogh.

1968, Apr. 1   Photo.   Perf. 14

262	A39	50 l ultra & multi	1.10	.30
263	A39	1r dk green & multi	1.60	.40
264	A39	2r multicolored	2.75	1.75
265	A39	5r multicolored	7.50	4.50
		Nos. 262-265 (4)	12.95	6.95

Montgolfier Balloon, 1783, and Zeppelin LZ-130, 1928 — A40

History of Aviation: 3 l, 1r, Douglas DC-3, 1033, and Boeing 707, 1958. 5 l, 50 l, Lilienthal's glider, 1892, and Wright brothers' plane, 1905. 7 l, 2r, British-French Concorde and Supersonic Boeing 733, 1968.

1968, June 1   Photo.   Perf. 14x13

266	A40	2 l yel grn, ultra & bis brn	.25	.35
267	A40	3 l org brn, grnsh bl & lil	.25	.35
268	A40	5 l grnsh bl, sl grn & lilac	.30	.25
269	A40	7 l org, dl & ultra	1.10	.50
270	A40	10 l rose lil, bl & brn	.65	.25
271	A40	50 l ol, sl grn & mag	2.10	.35
272	A40	1r ver, blue & emer	3.50	.75
273	A40	2r ultra, ol & brn vio	17.50	11.00
		Nos. 266-273 (8)	25.65	13.85

Issued in sheets of 12.

WHO Headquarters, Geneva — A41

MALDIVE ISLANDS

1968, July 15 Litho. *Perf. 14½x13*
274	A41	10 l	grnsh bl, bl grn & vio	1.00	.25
275	A41	25 l	org, ocher & grn	1.50	.25
276	A41	1r	emer, brt grn & brown	4.00	.70
277	A41	2r	rose lil, dp rose lil & dk blue	6.50	4.75
		Nos. 274-277 (4)		13.00	5.95

20th anniv. of WHO.

Nos. 243-246 Overprinted "International / Boy Scout Jamboree, / Farragut Park, Idaho, / U.S.A. / August 1-9, 1967"

1968, Aug. 1 *Perf. 14x14½*
278	A36	2 l	multicolored	.25	.45
279	A36	3 l	multicolored	.25	.45
280	A36	25 l	multicolored	1.50	.85
281	A36	1r	multicolored	4.50	1.90
		Nos. 278-281 (4)		6.50	3.25

1st anniv. of the Intl. Boy Scout Jamboree in Farragut State Park, ID.

Marine Snail Shells — A42

2 l, 50 l, Common curlew & redshank. 1r, Angel wings (clam shell) & marine snail shell.

1968, Sept. 24 Photo. *Perf. 14x13*
282	A42	2 l	ultra & multi	.45	.70
283	A42	10 l	brown & multi	1.10	.35
284	A42	25 l	multicolored	1.60	.30
285	A42	50 l	multicolored	8.25	1.25
286	A42	1r	multicolored	4.00	1.25
287	A42	2r	multicolored	5.00	6.00
		Nos. 282-287 (6)		20.40	9.80

Discus — A43

50 l, Runner. 1r, Bicycling. 2r, Basketball.

1968, Oct. 12 *Perf. 14*
288	A43	10 l	ultra & multi	.30	.35
289	A43	50 l	multicolored	.55	.35
290	A43	1r	plum & multi	3.00	.60
291	A43	2r	violet & multi	3.50	2.25
		Nos. 288-291 (4)		7.35	3.55

19th Olympic Games, Mexico City, 10/12-27.
For overprints see Nos. 302-303.

Republic

Dhow — A44

Republic Day: 1r, Coat of arms, map and flag of Maldive Islands.

Perf. 14x14½
1968, Nov. 11 Unwmk.
| 292 | A44 | 10 l | yel grn, ultra & dk brn | 1.50 | .35 |
| 293 | A44 | 1r | ultra, red & emerald | 3.50 | 1.10 |

The Thinker, by Auguste Rodin — A45

Rodin Sculptures and UNESCO Emblem: 10 l, Hands. 1.50r, Sister and Brother. 2.50r, The Prodigal Son.

1969, Apr. 10 Photo. *Perf. 13½*
294	A45	6 l	emerald & multi	.40	.40
295	A45	10 l	multicolored	.45	.45
296	A45	1.50r	brt blue & multi	2.00	2.00

297	A45	2.50r	multicolored	2.75	2.75
a.		Souvenir sheet of 2		8.50	8.50
		Nos. 294-297 (4)		5.60	5.60

Intl. Human Rights Year and honoring UNESCO.
No. 297a contains 2 imperf. stamps similar to Nos. 296-297.

Astronaut Gathering Rock Samples on Moon — A46

Designs: 6 l, Lunar landing module. 1.50r, Astronaut on steps of module. 2.50r, Astronaut with television camera.

1969, Sept. 25 Litho. *Perf. 14*
298	A46	6 l	multicolored	.45	.25
299	A46	10 l	multicolored	.45	.25
300	A46	1.50r	multicolored	1.75	1.40
301	A46	2.50r	multicolored	2.50	2.25
a.		Souvenir sheet of 4		3.75	3.75
		Nos. 298-301 (4)		5.15	4.15

Man's 1st moon landing. See note after US No. C76.
Exist imperf.
No. 301a contains stamps similar to Nos. 298-301, with designs transposed on 10 l and 2.50r. Simulated perfs.
For overprints see Nos. 343-345.

Nos. 289-290 Overprinted: "REPUBLIC OF MALDIVES" and Commemorative Inscriptions

Designs: 50 l, overprinted "Gold Medal Winner / Mohamed Gammoudi / 5000m. run / Tunisia." 1r, overprinted "Gold Medal Winner / P. Trentin—Cycling / France."

1969, Dec. 10 Photo. *Perf. 14*
| 302 | A43 | 50 l | multicolored | .50 | .60 |
| 303 | A43 | 1r | multicolored | 1.25 | 1.10 |

Columbia Daumon Victoria, 1899 — A47

Automobiles (pre-1908): 5 l, 50 l, Duryea Phaeton, 1902. 7 l, 1r, Packard S.24, 1906. 10 l, 2r, Autocar Runabout, 1907. 25 l, like 2 l.

1970, Feb. 1 Litho. *Perf. 12*
304	A47	2 l	multicolored	.25	.25
305	A47	5 l	brt pink & multi	.25	.25
306	A47	7 l	ultra & multi	.30	.25
307	A47	10 l	ver & multi	.35	.25
308	A47	25 l	ocher & multi	.90	.30
309	A47	50 l	olive & multi	1.75	.40
310	A47	1r	orange & multi	3.00	.70
311	A47	2r	multicolored	4.00	4.50
a.		Souvenir sheet of 2, #310-311, perf. 11½		6.50	6.50
		Nos. 304-311 (8)		10.80	6.90

Exist imperf.

Orange Butterflyfish — A48

Fish: 5 l, Spotted triggerfish. 25 l, Spotfin turkeyfish. 50 l, Forceps fish. 1r, Imperial angelfish. 2r, Regal angelfish.

1970, Mar. 1 Litho. *Perf. 10½*
312	A48	2 l	multicolored	.35	.60
313	A48	5 l	orange & multi	.55	.60
314	A48	25 l	emerald & multi	1.40	.60
315	A48	50 l	brt pink & multi	2.10	.95
316	A48	1r	lt vio bl & multi	2.75	1.40
317	A48	2r	olive & multi	4.50	4.00
		Nos. 312-317 (6)		11.65	8.15

UN Headquarters, New York and UN Emblem — A49

25th anniv. of the UN: 10 l, Surgeons, nurse and WHO emblem. 25 l, Student, performer, musician and UNESCO emblem. 50 l, Children reading and playing, and UNICEF emblem. 1r, Lamb, cock, fish, grain and FAO emblem. 2r, Miner and ILO emblem.

1970, June 26 Litho. *Perf. 13½*
318	A49	2 l	multicolored	.25	.25
319	A49	10 l	multicolored	.75	.25
320	A49	25 l	multicolored	1.60	.25
321	A49	50 l	multicolored	1.90	.30
322	A49	1r	multicolored	2.25	.75
323	A49	2r	multicolored	4.50	2.00
		Nos. 318-323 (6)		11.25	3.80

IMCO Emblem, Buoy and Ship — A50

Design: 1r, Lighthouse and ship.

1970, July 26 Litho. *Perf. 13½*
| 324 | A50 | 50 l | multicolored | .60 | .35 |
| 325 | A50 | 1r | multicolored | 4.00 | .90 |

10th anniv. of the Intergovernmental Maritime Consultative Organization (IMCO).

EXPO Emblem and Australian Pavilion — A51

EXPO Emblem and: 3 l, West German pavilion. 10 l, US pavilion. 25 l, British pavilion. 50 l, Russian pavilion. 1r, Japanese pavilion.

1970, Aug. 1 *Perf. 13½x14*
326	A51	2 l	green & multi	.25	.25
327	A51	3 l	violet & multi	.25	.25
328	A51	10 l	brown & multi	.50	.25
329	A51	25 l	multicolored	.95	.25
330	A51	50 l	claret & multi	1.25	.35
331	A51	1r	ultra & multi	1.90	.70
		Nos. 326-331 (6)		5.10	2.05

EXPO '70 International Exhibition, Osaka, Japan, Mar. 15-Sept. 13, 1970.

Guitar Player, by Watteau — A52

Paintings: 7 l, Guitar Player in Spanish Costume, by Edouard Manet. 50 l, Guitar-playing Clown, by Antoine Watteau. 1r, Mandolin Player and Singers, by Lorenzo Costa (inscribed Ercole Roberti). 2.50r, Guitar Player and Lady, by Watteau. 5r, Mandolin Player, by Frans Hals.

1970, Aug. 1 Litho. *Perf. 14*
332	A52	3 l	gray & multi	.25	.25
333	A52	7 l	yellow & multi	.25	.25
334	A52	50 l	multicolored	.45	.45
335	A52	1r	multicolored	.85	.85
336	A52	2.50r	multicolored	2.10	2.10
337	A52	5r	multicolored	3.50	3.50
a.		Souvenir sheet of 2		8.00	8.00
		Nos. 332-337 (6)		7.40	7.40

No. 337a contains 2 stamps similar to Nos. 336-337 but rouletted 13 and printed se-tenant.

Education Year Emblem and Adult Education — A53

Education Year Emblem and: 10 l, Teacher training. 25 l, Geography class. 50 l, Classroom. 1r, Instruction by television.

1970, Sept. 7 Litho. *Perf. 14*
338	A53	5 l	multicolored	.45	.25
339	A53	10 l	multicolored	.45	.25
340	A53	25 l	multicolored	.75	.25
341	A53	50 l	multicolored	1.00	.40
342	A53	1r	multicolored	2.50	.80
		Nos. 338-342 (5)		5.15	1.95

Issued for International Education Year.

Nos. 299-301 Overprinted in Silver: "Philympia / London 1970"

1970, Sept. 18
343	A46	10 l	multicolored	.30	.30
344	A46	1.50r	multicolored	.85	.85
345	A46	2.50r	multicolored	1.25	1.25
		Nos. 343-345 (3)		2.40	2.40

Issued to commemorate Philympia 1970, London Philatelic Exhibition, Sept. 18-26.
This overprint was also applied to No. 301a. Value $9.

Soccer Play, Rimet Cup — A54

Various Soccer Scenes, and Rimet Cup.

1970 Litho. *Perf. 13½*
346	A54	3 l	emerald & multi	.25	.25
347	A54	6 l	rose lilac & multi	.30	.25
348	A54	7 l	dp orange & multi	.30	.25
349	A54	25 l	blue & multi	1.00	.25
350	A54	1r	olive & multi	3.50	1.00
		Nos. 346-350 (5)		5.35	2.00

Jules Rimet 9th World Soccer Championships, Mexico City, May 30-June 21.

Boy Holding UNICEF Flag — A55

UNICEF, 25th. Anniv.: 10 l, 2r, Girl holding balloon with UNICEF emblem.

1971, Apr. 1 Litho. *Perf. 12*
351	A55	5 l	pink & multi	.25	.25
352	A55	10 l	lt blue & multi	.25	.25
353	A55	1r	yellow & multi	1.75	.70
354	A55	2r	pale lilac & multi	3.00	2.00
		Nos. 351-354 (4)		5.25	3.20

Astronauts Swigert, Lovell and Haise — A56

Safe return of Apollo 13: 20 l, Spacecraft and landing module. 1r, Capsule and boat in Pacific Ocean.

1971, Apr. 27 *Perf. 14*
355	A56	5 l	dull purple & multi	.25	.25
356	A56	20 l	multicolored	.50	.25
357	A56	1r	brt blue & multi	1.10	.70
		Nos. 355-357 (3)		1.85	1.20

MALDIVE ISLANDS

Flowers Symbolizing Races and World — A57

1971, May 3
358	A57	10 l multicolored	.30	.30
359	A57	25 l gray & multi	.35	.30

Intl. year against racial discrimination.

Mother and Child, by Auguste Renoir — A58

Mother and Child Paintings by: 7 l, Rembrandt. 10 l, Titian. 20 l, Degas. 25 l, Berthe Morisot. 1r, Rubens. 3r, Renoir.

1971, Sept. Litho. Perf. 12
360	A58	5 l multicolored	.25	.25
361	A58	7 l multicolored	.25	.25
362	A58	10 l multicolored	.35	.25
363	A58	20 l multicolored	.90	.25
364	A58	25 l multicolored	1.00	.25
365	A58	1r multicolored	3.00	.70
366	A58	3r multicolored	5.50	4.00
	Nos. 360-366 (7)		11.25	5.95

Capt. Alan B. Shepard, Jr. — A59

10 l, Maj. Stuart A. Roosa. 1.50r, Com. Edgar D. Mitchell. 5r, Apollo 14 shoulder patch.

1971, Nov. 11 Photo. Perf. 12½
367	A59	6 l dp grn & multi	.40	.30
368	A59	10 l claret & multi	.50	.30
369	A59	1.50r ultra & multi	3.50	3.25
370	A59	5r multicolored	10.00	7.50
	Nos. 367-370 (4)		14.40	11.35

Apollo 14 US moon landing mission, 1/31-2/9.

Ballerina, by Degas — A60

Paintings: 10 l, Dancing Couple, by Auguste Renoir. 2r, Spanish Dancer, by Edouard Manet. 5r, Ballerinas, by Degas. 10r, Moulin Rouge, by Henri Toulouse-Lautrec.

1971, Nov. 19 Litho. Perf. 14
371	A60	5 l plum & multi	.25	.25
372	A60	10 l green & multi	.25	.25
373	A60	2r org brn & multi	2.50	2.10
374	A60	5r dk blue & multi	4.25	3.50
375	A60	10r multicolored	6.50	6.00
	Nos. 371-375 (5)		13.75	11.60

Nos. 371-375 Overprinted Vertically: "ROYAL VISIT 1972"

1972, Mar. 13 Litho. Perf. 14
376	A60	5 l plum & multi	.25	.25
377	A60	10 l green & multi	.25	.25
378	A60	2r org brn & multi	3.75	3.00
379	A60	5r dk blue & multi	6.75	6.75
380	A60	10r multicolored	7.50	7.50
	Nos. 376-380 (5)		18.50	17.75

Visit of Elizabeth II and Prince Philip.

Book Year Emblem — A61

1972, May 1 Perf. 13x13½
381	A61	25 l orange & multi	.30	.25
382	A61	5r multicolored	1.90	1.75

International Book Year.

National Costume of Scotland — A62

National Costumes: 15 l, Netherlands. 25 l, Norway. 50 l, Hungary. 1r, Austria. 2r, Spain.

1972, May 15 Perf. 12
383	A62	10 l gray & multi	.60	.25
384	A62	15 l lt brown & multi	.70	.25
385	A62	25 l multicolored	1.00	.25
386	A62	50 l lt brown & multi	2.00	.45
387	A62	1r gray & multi	2.50	.75
388	A62	2r lt olive & multi	4.50	3.00
	Nos. 383-388 (6)		11.30	4.95

Stegosaurus A63

Designs: Prehistoric reptiles.

1972, May 31 Perf. 14
389	A63	2 l shown	.25	.50
390	A63	7 l Edaphosaurus	.25	.45
391	A63	25 l Diplodocus	.45	.45
392	A63	50 l Triceratops	1.00	.75
393	A63	2r Pteranodon	3.75	2.00
394	A63	5r Tyrannosaurus	15.00	9.50
	Nos. 389-394 (6)		20.70	13.65

Set exists imperf.
A souvenir sheet has two stamps similar to Nos. 393-394 with simulated perforations. It was not regularly issued. Value, $50.

Sapporo '72 Emblem, Cross Country Skiing — A64

1972, June Litho. Perf. 14
395	A64	3 l shown	.25	.25
396	A64	6 l Bobsledding	.25	.25
397	A64	15 l Speed skating	.25	.25
398	A64	50 l Ski jump	.90	.40
399	A64	1r Figure skating	1.50	.50
400	A64	2.50r Ice hockey	5.00	3.00
	Nos. 395-400 (6)		8.15	4.65

11th Winter Olympic Games, Sapporo, Japan, Feb. 3-13.
Exists imperf. Value, set $15.

Boy Scout Saluting — A65

Scout: 15 l, with signal flags. 50 l, Bugler. 1r, Drummer.

1972, Aug. 1
401	A65	10 l Prus grn & multi	.55	.25
402	A65	15 l dk red & multi	.80	.25
403	A65	50 l dp grn & multi	2.60	1.10
404	A65	1r purple & multi	4.00	1.75
	Nos. 401-404 (4)		7.95	3.35

13th International Boy Scout Jamboree, Asagiri Plain, Japan, Aug. 2-11, 1971.
Exists imperf. Value, set $17.50.

Olympic Emblems, Bicycling — A66

1972, Oct. Litho. Perf. 14½x14
405	A66	5 l shown	.25	.25
406	A66	10 l Running	.25	.25
407	A66	25 l Wrestling	.25	.25
408	A66	50 l Hurdles, women's	.30	.30
409	A66	2r Boxing	1.25	1.10
410	A66	5r Volleyball	3.50	3.00
	Nos. 405-410 (6)		5.80	5.15

Souvenir Sheet
Perf. 15

411	Sheet of 2		5.00	5.00
a.	A66 3r like 50 l		2.00	2.00
b.	A66 4r like 10 l		2.50	2.50

20th Olympic Games, Munich, 8/26-9/11.
Nos. 405-410 exist imperf. Value, set $15.
For overprints see Nos. 417-410.

Globe, Environment Emblem — A67

1972, Nov. 15 Litho. Perf. 14½
412	A67	2 l violet & multi	.25	.25
413	A67	3 l brown & multi	.25	.25
414	A67	15 l blue & multi	.30	.30
415	A67	50 l red & multi	.70	.60
416	A67	2.50r green & multi	2.75	2.50
	Nos. 412-416 (5)		4.25	3.90

UN Conference on Human Environment, Stockholm, June 5-16.
Nos. 412-416 exist imperf.

No. 409 Overprinted   No. 410 Overprinted

No. 411a Overprinted   No. 411b Overprinted

1973, Feb. Litho. Perf. 14½x14
417	A66(a)	2r multicolored	3.00	1.75
418	A66(b)	5r multicolored	4.50	3.00

Souvenir Sheet
419	Sheet of 2		7.50	7.50
a.	A66(c) 3r multicolored		2.75	2.75
b.	A66(d) 4r multicolored		3.00	3.00

Gold medal winners in 20th Olympic Games: Viatschesiav Lemechev, USSR, middleweight boxing; Japanese team, volleyball; Annelie Ehrhardt, Germany, 100m. hurdles; Frank Shorter, US, marathon.
No. 419 exists imperf. Value, $20.

Flowers, by Vincent Van Gogh — A68

Paintings of flowers by: 2 l, 3 l, 1r, 5r, Auguste Renoir (each different). 50 l, 2r, Ambrosius Bosschaert. 3r, Van Gogh.

1973, Feb. Perf. 13½
420	A68	1 l blue & multi	.25	.25
421	A68	2 l tan & multi	.25	.25
422	A68	3 l lilac & multi	.30	.25
423	A68	50 l ultra & multi	.45	.25
424	A68	1r emerald & multi	1.10	.45
425	A68	5r magenta & multi	2.50	4.75
	Nos. 420-425 (6)		4.85	6.20

Souvenir Sheet
Perf. 15

426	Sheet of 2		7.50	7.50
a.	A68 2r black & multi		2.00	2.25
b.	A68 3r black & multi		2.50	2.75

Nos. 420-426 exist imperf.

Scouts Treating Injured Lamb — A69

Designs: 2 l, 1r, Lifesaving. 3 l, 5r, Agricultural training. 4 l, 2r, Carpentry. 5 l, Leapfrog.

1973, Aug. Litho. Perf. 14½
427	A69	1 l black & multi	.25	.25
428	A69	2 l black & multi	.25	.25
429	A69	3 l black & multi	.25	.25
430	A69	4 l black & multi	.25	.25
431	A69	5 l black & multi	.25	.25
432	A69	1r black & multi	2.10	.60
433	A69	2r black & multi	4.00	3.75
434	A69	3r black & multi	5.00	5.00
	Nos. 427-434 (8)		12.35	10.60

Souvenir Sheet
435	A69 5r black & multi		8.00	8.00

24th Boy Scout World Conference (1st in Africa), Nairobi, Kenya, July 16-21.
Exist imperf. Values: set, $25; souvenir sheet, $35.
For overprints see Nos. 571-574.

Herschel's Marlin — A70

Fish and Ships: 2 l, 4r, Skipjack tuna. 3 l, Bluefin tuna. 5 l, 2.50r, Dolphinfish. 60 l, 75 l, Red snapper. 1.50r, Yellow crescent tail. 3r, Plectropoma maculatum. 5r, Like 1 l. 10r, Spanish mackerel.

1973, Aug. Perf. 14½
Size: 38½x24mm
436	A70	1 l lt green & multi	.25	.25
437	A70	2 l dull org & multi	.25	.25
438	A70	3 l brt red & multi	.25	.25
439	A70	5 l multicolored	.25	.25

Size: 28x22mm
440	A70	60 l yellow & multi	.30	.30
441	A70	75 l purple & multi	.75	.40

Size: 38½x24mm
442	A70	1.50r violet & multi	1.00	.75
443	A70	2.50r blue & multi	1.75	1.50
444	A70	3r multicolored	2.00	2.00
445	A70	10r orange & multi	6.00	5.00
	Nos. 436-445 (10)		12.80	10.95

Souvenir Sheet
Perf. 15

446	Sheet of 2		17.50	17.50
a.	A70 4r carmine & multi		5.50	5.50
b.	A70 5r bright green & multi		6.50	6.50

Nos. 436-445 exist imperf.

MALDIVE ISLANDS

Goldenfronted Leafbird — A71

2 l, 3r, Fruit bat. 3 l, 50 l, Indian starred tortoise. 4 l, 5r, Kallima inachus (butterfly).

1973, Oct.			Litho.	Perf. 14½
447	A71	1 l brt pink & multi	.25	.25
448	A71	2 l brt blue & multi	.25	.25
449	A71	3 l ver & multi	.25	.25
450	A71	4 l citron & multi	.25	.25
451	A71	50 l emerald & multi	.40	.40
452	A71	2r lt violet & multi	3.25	3.25
453	A71	3r multicolored	4.50	3.00
		Nos. 447-453 (7)	9.15	7.65

Souvenir Sheet

| 454 | A71 | 5r yellow & multi | 17.50 | 17.50 |

Lantana Camara — A72

Native Flowers: 2 l, Nerium oleander. 3 l, 2r, Rosa polyantha. 4 l, Hibiscus manihot. 5 l, Bougainvillea glabra. 10 l, 3r, Plumera alba. 50 l, Poinsettia pulcherrima. 5r, Ononis natrix.

1973, Dec. 19			Litho.	Perf. 14
455	A72	1 l ultra & multi	.25	.25
456	A72	2 l dp orange & multi	.25	.25
457	A72	3 l emerald & multi	.25	.25
458	A72	4 l blue grn & multi	.25	.25
459	A72	5 l lemon & multi	.25	.25
460	A72	10 l lilac & multi	.25	.25
461	A72	50 l yel grn & multi	.25	.25
462	A72	5r red & multi	2.75	2.75
		Nos. 455-462 (8)	4.50	4.50

Souvenir Sheet

463		Sheet of 2	4.50	4.50
a.		A72 2r lilac & multi	1.25	1.50
b.		A72 3r blue & multi	2.00	2.25

Tiros Weather Satellite — A73

Designs: 2 l, 10r, Nimbus satellite. 3 l, 3r, Nomad weather ("weater") station. 4 l, A.P.T. instant weather picture (radar). 5 l, Richard's electrical wind speed recorder. 2r, like 1 l.

1974, Jan. 10				Perf. 14½
464	A73	1 l olive & multi	.25	.25
465	A73	2 l multicolored	.25	.25
466	A73	3 l brt blue & multi	.25	.25
467	A73	4 l ocher & multi	.25	.25
468	A73	5 l ocher & multi	.25	.25
469	A73	2r ultra & multi	2.50	2.25
470	A73	3r orange & multi	3.25	2.75
		Nos. 464-470 (7)	7.00	6.25

Souvenir Sheet

| 471 | A73 | 10r lilac & multi | 8.00 | 8.00 |

World Meteorological Cooperation, cent.

Apollo Spacecraft, John F. Kennedy — A74

Designs: 2 l, 3r, Mercury spacecraft and John Glenn. 3 l, Vostok 1 and Yuri Gagarin. 4 l, Vostok 6 and Valentina Tereshkova. 5 l, Soyuz 11 and Salyut spacecrafts. 2r, Skylab. 10r, Like 1 l.

1974, Feb. 1			Litho.	Perf. 14½
472	A74	1 l multicolored	.25	.25
473	A74	2 l multicolored	.25	.25
474	A74	3 l multicolored	.25	.25
475	A74	4 l multicolored	.25	.25
476	A74	5 l multicolored	.25	.25
477	A74	2r multicolored	3.00	2.75
478	A74	3r multicolored	3.75	3.25
		Nos. 472-478 (7)	8.00	7.25

Souvenir Sheet

| 479 | A74 | 10r multicolored | 12.00 | 12.00 |

Space explorations of US and USSR. Exist imperf. Values: set, $20; souvenir sheet, $70.

Skylab and Copernicus A75

Copernicus, Various Portraits and: 2 l, 1.50r, Futuristic orbiting station. 3 l, 5r, Futuristic flight station. 4 l, Mariner 2 on flight to Venus. 5 l, Mariner 4 on flight to Mars. 25 l, like 1 l. 10r, Copernicus Orbiting Observatory.

1974, Apr. 10			Litho.	Perf. 14½
480	A75	1 l multicolored	.25	.25
481	A75	2 l multicolored	.25	.25
482	A75	3 l multicolored	.25	.25
483	A75	4 l multicolored	.25	.25
484	A75	5 l multicolored	.25	.25
485	A75	25 l multicolored	.60	.60
486	A75	1.50r multicolored	2.25	2.00
487	A75	5r multicolored	5.75	5.25
		Nos. 480-487 (8)	9.85	9.10

Souvenir Sheet

| 488 | A75 | 10r multicolored | 15.00 | 15.00 |

Exist imperf. Values: set, $17.50; souvenir sheet, $50.

"Motherhood," by Picasso — A76

Picasso Paintings: 2 l, Harlequin and his Companion. 3 l, Pierrot Sitting. 20 l, 2r, Three Musicians. 75 l, L'Aficionada. 3r, 5r, Still life.

1974, May				Perf. 14
489	A76	1 l multicolored	.25	.25
490	A76	2 l multicolored	.25	.25
491	A76	3 l multicolored	.25	.25
492	A76	20 l multicolored	.35	.30
493	A76	75 l multicolored	.50	.30
494	A76	5r multicolored	4.75	3.50
		Nos. 489-494 (6)	6.35	4.85

Souvenir Sheet

495		Sheet of 2	7.50	7.50
a.		A76 2r multicolored	2.10	2.10
b.		A76 3r multicolored	3.25	3.25

Pablo Picasso (1881-1973), painter.

UPU Emblem, Old and New Trains — A77

UPU Emblem and: 2 l, 2.50r, Old and new ships. 3 l, Zeppelin and jet. 1.50r, Mail coach and truck. 4r, 5r, Like 1 l.

1974, May			Litho.	Perf. 14½, 13½
496	A77	1 l lt green & multi	.25	.25
497	A77	2 l yellow & multi	.25	.25
498	A77	3 l rose & multi	.25	.25
499	A77	1.50r yel green & multi	.75	.75
500	A77	2.50r blue & multi	1.25	1.25
501	A77	5r ocher & multi	3.50	3.50
		Nos. 496-501 (6)	6.25	6.25

Souvenir Sheet

| 502 | A77 | 4r ver & multi | 5.50 | 5.50 |

UPU cent. Exist imperf. Values: set, $10; souvenir sheet, $22.50.
Nos. 496-501 were printed in sheets of 50, perf. 14½, and also in sheets of 5 plus label, perf. 13½. The label shows UPU emblem, post horn, globe and carrier pigeon. Value, set of 6 sheets, $30.

Capricorn — A78

Designs: Zodiac signs and constellations.

1974, July 3				
503	A78	1 l shown	.25	.25
504	A78	2 l Aquarius	.25	.25
505	A78	3 l Pisces	.25	.25
506	A78	4 l Aries	.25	.25
507	A78	5 l Taurus	.25	.25
508	A78	6 l Gemini	.25	.25
509	A78	7 l Cancer	.25	.25
510	A78	10 l Leo	.30	.30
511	A78	15 l Virgo	.30	.30
512	A78	20 l Libra	.30	.30
513	A78	25 l Scorpio	.30	.30
514	A78	5r Sagittarius	8.50	8.50
		Nos. 503-514 (12)	11.45	11.45

Souvenir Sheet

| 515 | A78 | 10r Sun | 22.50 | 22.50 |

Stamp size of 10r: 50x37mm.

Soccer and Games' Emblem — A79

Various soccer scenes & games' emblem.

1974, July 31			Litho.	Perf. 14½
516	A79	1 l brown & multi	.25	.25
517	A79	2 l green & multi	.25	.25
518	A79	3 l ultra & multi	.25	.25
519	A79	4 l red & multi	.25	.25
520	A79	75 l lt blue & multi	.45	.40
521	A79	4r olive & multi	2.00	2.00
522	A79	5r lilac & multi	4.00	2.00
		Nos. 516-522 (7)	7.45	5.40

Souvenir Sheet

| 523 | A79 | 10r rose & multi | 8.00 | 8.00 |

World Cup Soccer Championship, Munich, June 13-July 7. Exist imperf. Values: set, $14; souvenir sheet, $12.

Churchill and WWII Plane — A80

Churchill: 2 l, As pilot. 3 l, First Lord of the Admiralty and battleship. 4 l, 10r, Aircraft carrier. 5 l, RAF fighters. 60 l, Anti-aircraft unit. 75 l, Tank. 5r, Seaplane.

1974, Nov. 30			Litho.	
524	A80	1 l multicolored	.25	.25
525	A80	2 l multicolored	.25	.25
526	A80	3 l multicolored	.25	.25
527	A80	4 l multicolored	.25	.25
528	A80	5 l multicolored	.25	.25
529	A80	60 l multicolored	2.40	1.25
530	A80	75 l multicolored	3.00	1.25
531	A80	5r multicolored	11.00	11.00
		Nos. 524-531 (8)	17.65	14.75

Souvenir Sheet

| 532 | A80 | 10r multicolored | 17.50 | 17.50 |

Sir Winston Churchill (1874-1965). Exist imperf. Values: set, $17.50; souvenir sheet, $20.

Cassis Nana A81 / Cypraea Diliculum A82

2 l, Murex triremus. 3 l, Harpa major. 4 l, Lambis chiragra. 5 l, Conus pennaceus. 75 l, Clanculus pharaonis. 5r, Chicoreus ramosus.

1975, Jan. 25			Perf. 14½, 14 (A82)	
533	A81	1 l shown	.25	.25
534	A81	2 l multicolored	.25	.25
535	A81	3 l multicolored	.25	.25
536	A81	4 l multicolored	.30	.25
537	A81	5 l multicolored	.35	.30
538	A82	60 l shown	2.25	2.25
539	A82	75 l multicolored	2.75	2.75
540	A81	5r multicolored	7.50	7.50
		Nos. 533-540 (8)	13.90	13.80

Souvenir Sheet
Perf. 13½

541		Sheet of 2	12.50	12.50
a.		A81 2r like 3 l	3.75	3.75
b.		A81 3r like 2 l	4.75	4.75

Sea shells, including cowries.

Throne A83 / Eid-Miskith Mosque A84

Designs: 10 l, Ornamental candlesticks (dullisa). 25 l, Tree-shaped lamp. 60 l, Royal umbrellas. 3r, Tomb of Al-Hafiz Abu-al Barakath al-Barubari.

1975, Feb. 22			Litho.	Perf. 14
542	A83	1 l multicolored	.25	.25
543	A83	10 l multicolored	.25	.25
544	A83	25 l multicolored	.25	.25
545	A83	60 l multicolored	.25	.25
546	A84	75 l multicolored	.35	.25
547	A84	3r multicolored	1.40	1.25
		Nos. 542-547 (6)	2.75	2.50

Historic relics and monuments.

Tropical Fruit — A85

1975, Mar.			Litho.	Perf. 14½
548	A85	2 l Guava	.25	.25
549	A85	4 l Maldive mulberry	.25	.25
550	A85	5 l Mountain apples	.25	.25
551	A85	10 l Bananas	.25	.25
552	A85	20 l Mangoes	.25	.25
553	A85	50 l Papaya	.70	.60
554	A85	1r Pomegranates	1.20	.65
555	A85	5r Coconut	6.00	5.50
		Nos. 548-555 (8)	9.15	8.00

Souvenir Sheet
Perf. 13½

556		Sheet of 2	10.00	10.00
a.		A85 2r like 10 l	2.75	3.25
b.		A85 3r like 2 l	3.25	3.75

Phyllangia — A86

Corals, sea urchins and starfish: 2 l, Madrepora oculata. 3 l, Acropora gravida. 4 l, Stylotella. 5 l, Acropora cervicornis. 60 l, Strongylocentrotus pupuratus. 75 l, Pisaster ochraceus. 5r, Marthasterias glacialis.

1975, June 6			Litho.	Perf. 14½
557	A86	1 l shown	.25	.25
558	A86	2 l multicolored	.25	.25
559	A86	3 l multicolored	.25	.25
560	A86	4 l multicolored	.25	.25
561	A86	5 l multicolored	.25	.25
562	A86	60 l multicolored	.60	.25
563	A86	75 l multicolored	.90	.25
564	A86	5r multicolored	4.25	3.00
		Nos. 557-564 (8)	7.00	4.75

Souvenir Sheet
Imperf

| 565 | A86 | 4r like 1 l | 11.00 | 11.00 |

"10," Clock Tower and Customs House — A87

"10" and: 5 l, Government offices. 7 l, North Eastern waterfront, Male. 15 l, Mosque and Minaret. 10r, Sultan Park and Museum.

MALDIVE ISLANDS

1975, July 26		Litho.	Perf. 14½
566	A87	4 l salmon & multi	.25 .25
567	A87	5 l lt blue & multi	.25 .25
568	A87	7 l bister & multi	.25 .25
569	A87	15 l lilac & multi	.25 .25
570	A87	10r lt green & multi	3.25 6.00
		Nos. 566-570 (5)	4.25 7.00

10th anniversary of independence.

Nos. 432-435 Overprinted

Overprint reads: "14th Boy Scout Jamboree / July 29-Aug. 7, 1975"

1975, July 26		Litho.	Perf. 14½
571	A69	1r multicolored	.55 .55
572	A69	2r multicolored	1.40 .90
573	A69	3r multicolored	2.25 1.75
		Nos. 571-573 (3)	4.20 3.20

Souvenir Sheet
| 574 | A69 | | 7.50 7.50 |

Nordjamb 75, 14th World Boy Scout Jamboree, Lillehammer, Norway, July 29-Aug. 7.

Madura-Prau Bedang — A88

Sailing ships, except 5r: 2 l, Ganges patile. 3 l, Indian palla, vert. 4 l, "Odhi", vert. 5 l, Maldivian schooner. 25 l, Cutty Sark. 1r, 10r, Maldivian baggala, vert. 5r, Freighter Maldive Courage.

1975, July 26			Perf. 14½
575	A88	1 l multicolored	.25 .25
576	A88	2 l multicolored	.25 .25
577	A88	3 l multicolored	.25 .25
578	A88	4 l multicolored	.25 .25
579	A88	5 l multicolored	.25 .25
580	A88	25 l multicolored	.65 .30
581	A88	1r multicolored	1.00 .60
582	A88	5r multicolored	3.00 3.00
		Nos. 575-582 (8)	5.90 5.15

Souvenir Sheet
Perf. 13½
| 583 | A88 | 10r multicolored | 10.00 10.00 |

Butterflies — A89

1 l, Brahmaea Wallichii. 2 l, Teoinopalpus imperialis. 3 l, Cethosia biblis. 4 l, Hestia jasonia. 5 l, Apatura. 25 l, Kallima horsfieldi. 1.50r, Hebomoia leucippe. 5r, Papilio memnon.

1975, Sept. 7		Litho.	Perf. 14½
584	A89	1 l shown	.25 .25
585	A89	2 l multicolored	.25 .25
586	A89	3 l multicolored	.25 .25
587	A89	4 l multicolored	.25 .25
588	A89	5 l multicolored	.25 .25
589	A89	25 l multicolored	.65 .40
590	A89	1.50r multicolored	2.75 2.75
591	A89	5r multicolored	8.50 7.00
		Nos. 584-591 (8)	13.15 11.40

Souvenir Sheet
Perf. 13½
| 592 | A89 | 10r like 25 l | 20.00 20.00 |

Dying Slave by Michelangelo — A90

Works by Michelangelo: 2 l, 4 l, 1r, 5r, paintings from Sistine Chapel. 3 l, Apollo. 5 l, Bacchus. 2r, 10r, David.

1975, Oct. 9		Litho.	Perf. 14½
593	A90	1 l blue & multi	.25 .25
594	A90	2 l multicolored	.25 .25
595	A90	3 l red & multi	.25 .25
596	A90	4 l multicolored	.25 .25
597	A90	5 l emerald & multi	.25 .25
598	A90	1r multicolored	1.00 1.00
599	A90	2r red & multi	1.75 1.75
600	A90	5r multicolored	3.50 3.50
		Nos. 593-600 (8)	7.50 7.50

Souvenir Sheet
Perf. 13½
| 601 | A90 | 10r multicolored | 6.50 6.50 |

Michelangelo Buonarotti (1475-1564), Italian sculptor, painter and architect.

Cup and Vase — A91

Designs: 4 l, Boxes. 50 l, Vase with lid. 75 l, Bowls with covers. 1r, Worker finishing vases.

1975, Dec.		Litho.	Perf. 14
602	A91	2 l ultra & multi	.25 .25
603	A91	4 l rose & multi	.25 .25
604	A91	50 l multicolored	.25 .25
605	A91	75 l blue & multi	.35 .35
606	A91	1r multicolored	.65 .45
		Nos. 602-606 (5)	1.75 1.55

Maldivian lacquer ware.

Map of Islands and Atolls — A92

Designs: 5 l, Yacht at anchor. 7 l, Sailboats. 15 l, Deep-sea divers and corals. 3r, Hulule Airport. 10r, Cruising yachts.

1975, Dec. 25		Litho.	Perf. 14
607	A92	4 l multicolored	.25 .25
608	A92	5 l multicolored	.25 .25
609	A92	7 l multicolored	.25 .25
610	A92	15 l multicolored	.30 .25
611	A92	3r multicolored	2.25 2.25
612	A92	10r multicolored	6.50 6.50
		Nos. 607-612 (6)	9.80 9.75

Tourist publicity.

Cross-country Skiing — A93

Winter Olympic Games' Emblem and: 2 l, Speed skating. 3 l, Figure skating, pair. 4 l, Bobsled. 5 l, Ski jump. 25 l, Figure skating, woman. 1.15r, Slalom. 4r, Ice hockey. 10r, Skiing.

1976, Jan. 10		Litho.	Perf. 14½
613	A93	1 l multicolored	.25 .25
614	A93	2 l multicolored	.25 .25
615	A93	3 l multicolored	.25 .25
616	A93	4 l multicolored	.25 .25
617	A93	5 l multicolored	.25 .25
618	A93	25 l multicolored	.25 .25
619	A93	1.15r multicolored	.90 .90
620	A93	4r multicolored	1.50 1.50
		Nos. 613-620 (8)	3.90 3.90

Souvenir Sheet
Perf. 13½
| 621 | A93 | 10r multicolored | 7.00 7.00 |

12th Winter Olympic Games, Innsbruck, Austria, Feb. 4-15. Exist imperf. Values: set, $7; souvenir sheet, $14.

Gen. Burgoyne, by Joshua Reynolds — A94

Paintings: 2 l, John Hancock, by John S. Copley. 3 l, Death of Gen. Montgomery, by John Trumbull, horiz. 4 l, Paul Revere, by Copley. 5 l, Battle of Bunker Hill, by Trumbull, horiz. 2r, Crossing of the Delaware, by Thomas Sully, horiz. 3r, Samuel Adams, by Copley. 5r, Surrender of Cornwallis, by Trumbull, horiz.

10r, Washington at Dorchester Heights, by Gilbert Stuart.

1976, Feb. 15			Perf. 14½
622	A94	1 l multicolored	.25 .25
623	A94	2 l multicolored	.25 .25
624	A94	3 l multicolored	.25 .25
625	A94	4 l multicolored	.25 .25
626	A94	5 l multicolored	.25 .25
627	A94	2r multicolored	2.00 2.00
628	A94	3r multicolored	2.25 2.25
629	A94	5r multicolored	2.50 2.50
		Nos. 622-629 (8)	8.00 8.00

Souvenir Sheet
Perf. 13½
| 630 | A94 | 10r multicolored | 15.00 15.00 |

American Bicentennial. Nos. 622-629 exist imperf, same value as perf. For overprints see Nos. 639-642.

Thomas Alva Edison — A95

Designs: 2 l, Alexander Graham Bell and his telephone. 3 l, Telephones of 1919, 1937 and 1972. 10 l, Cable tunnel. 20 l, Equalizer circuit assembly. 1r, Ships laying underwater cable. 10r, Intelsat IV-A over earth station.
4r, Telephones of 1876, 1890 and 1879 Edison telephone.

1976, Mar. 10		Litho.	Perf. 14½
631	A95	1 l multicolored	.25 .25
632	A95	2 l multicolored	.25 .25
633	A95	3 l multicolored	.25 .25
634	A95	10 l multicolored	.25 .25
635	A95	20 l multicolored	.25 .25
636	A95	1r multicolored	.65 .65
637	A95	10r multicolored	5.50 5.50
		Nos. 631-637 (7)	7.40 7.40

Souvenir Sheet
Perf. 13½
| 638 | A95 | 4r multicolored | 7.50 7.50 |

Centenary of first telephone call by Alexander Graham Bell, Mar. 10, 1876. Exist imperf. Values: set, $14; souvenir sheet, $15.

Nos. 627-630 Overprinted in Silver or Black

Overprint reads MAY 29TH-JUNE 6TH "INTERPHIL" 1976

1976, May 29		Litho.	Perf. 14½
639	A94	2r multicolored (S)	1.50 1.50
640	A94	3r multicolored (S)	2.00 2.00
641	A94	5r multicolored (B)	2.50 2.50
		Nos. 639-641 (3)	6.00 6.00

Souvenir Sheet
Perf. 13½
| 642 | A94 | 10r multicolored (S) | 10.00 10.00 |

Interphil 76 Intl. Philatelic Exhibition, Philadelphia, Pa., May 29-June 6. Overprint on 3r and 10r vertical. Same overprint in one horizontal silver line in margin of No. 642.

Wrestling — A96

Olympic Rings and: 2 l, Shot put. 3 l, Hurdles. 4 l, Hockey. 5 l, Women running. 6 l, Javelin. 1.50r, Discus. 5r, Volleyball. 10r, Hammer throw.

1976, June 1			Perf. 14½
643	A96	1 l multicolored	.25 .25
644	A96	2 l multicolored	.25 .25
645	A96	3 l salmon & multi	.25 .25
646	A96	4 l multicolored	.25 .25
647	A96	5 l pink & multi	.25 .25
648	A96	6 l multicolored	.25 .25
649	A96	1.50r bister & multi	1.25 1.25
650	A96	5r lilac & multi	3.00 4.25
		Nos. 643-650 (8)	5.75 7.00

Souvenir Sheet
Perf. 13½
| 651 | A96 | 10r lemon & multi | 7.50 7.50 |

21st Olympic Games, Montreal, Canada, July 17-Aug. 1.

Bonavist Beans — A97

Designs: 4 l, 20 l, Beans. 10 l, Eggplant. 50 l, Cucumber. 75 l, 2r, Snake gourd. 1r, Balsam pear.

1976-77		Litho.	Perf. 14
652	A97	2 l green & multi	.25 .25
653	A97	4 l lt blue & multi	.55 .55
654	A97	10 l ocher & multi	.55 .55
655	A97	20 l blue & multi ('77)	.55 .55
656	A97	50 l multicolored	.70 .70
657	A97	75 l bister & multi	.90 .90
658	A97	1r lilac & multi	1.30 1.30
659	A97	2r bis & multi ('77)	2.40 2.40
		Nos. 652-659 (8)	7.20 7.20

1976 stamps issued July 26.

Viking I and Mars — A98

Design: 20r, Landing craft on Mars.

1976, Dec. 2		Litho.	Perf. 14
660	A98	5r multicolored	2.00 2.00

Souvenir Sheet
| 661 | A98 | 20r multicolored | 10.00 10.00 |

Viking I US Mars Mission.

Coronation Ceremony A99

Designs: 2 l, Elizabeth II and Prince Philip. 3 l, Queen, Prince Philip, Princes Edward and Andrew. 1.15r, Queen in procession. 3r, State coach. 4r, Queen, Prince Philip, Princess Anne and Prince Charles.
10r, Queen and Prince Charles.

1977, Feb. 6			Perf. 14x13½, 12
662	A99	1 l multicolored	.40 .40
663	A99	2 l multicolored	.40 .40
664	A99	3 l multicolored	.40 .40
665	A99	1.15r multicolored	.60 .60
666	A99	3r multicolored	1.25 1.50
667	A99	4r multicolored	1.25 1.60
		Nos. 662-667 (6)	4.30 4.90

Souvenir Sheet
| 668 | A99 | 10r multicolored | 5.00 5.00 |

25th anniv. of the reign of Elizabeth II. Nos. 662-667 were printed in sheets of 40 (4x10), perf. 14x13½, and sheets of 5 plus label, perf. 12, in changed colors.
Nos. 662-668 exist imperf. Value, set $12.50.

Beethoven in Bonn, 1785 — A100

Designs: 2 l, Moonlight Sonata and portrait, 1801. 3 l, Goethe and Beethoven, Teplitz, 1811. 4 l, Beethoven, 1815, and his string instruments. 5 l, Beethoven House, Heiligenstadt, 1817. 25 l, Composer's hands, gold medal. 2r, Missa Solemnis, portrait, 1823. 5r, Portrait, 1825, hearing aids.
4r, Piano, room where Beethoven died, death mask.

1977, Mar. 26		Litho.	Perf. 14
669	A100	1 l multicolored	.25 .25
670	A100	2 l multicolored	.25 .25
671	A100	3 l multicolored	.35 .35
672	A100	4 l multicolored	.35 .35
673	A100	5 l multicolored	.35 .35
674	A100	25 l multicolored	1.50 .25

MALDIVE ISLANDS

675	A100	2r multicolored	4.00	3.50
676	A100	5r multicolored	6.50	6.50
		Nos. 669-676 (8)	13.55	11.80

Souvenir Sheet

677	A100	4r multicolored	8.50	8.50

Ludwig van Beethoven (1770-1827), composer, 150th death anniversary.

Electronic Tree and ITU Emblem — A101

90 l, Central Telegraph Office, Maldives. 10 l, Parabolic antenna, satellite communications earth station.
5r, Intelsat IV over map.

1977, May 17   Litho.   Perf. 14

678	A101	10 l multicolored	.25	.25
679	A101	90 l multicolored	.50	.50
680	A101	10r multicolored	3.50	3.50
		Nos. 678-680 (3)	4.25	4.25

Souvenir Sheet

681	A101	5r multicolored	4.50	4.50

Inauguration of Satellite Earth Station and for World Telecommunications Day.

Portrait by Gainsborough — A102

Paintings: 2 l, 5 l, 10r, Rubens. 3 l, 95 l, 4 l, 1r, Gainsborough.
5r, Titian.

1977, May 20

682	A102	1 l multicolored	.25	.25
683	A102	2 l multicolored	.25	.25
684	A102	3 l multicolored	.25	.25
685	A102	4 l multicolored	.25	.25
686	A102	5 l multicolored	.25	.25
687	A102	95 l multicolored	.80	.60
688	A102	1r multicolored	.80	.65
689	A102	10r multicolored	4.00	6.00
		Nos. 682-689 (8)	6.85	8.50

Souvenir Sheet

690	A102	5r multicolored	4.00	4.00

Birth annivs. of Thomas Gainsborough; Peter Paul Rubens; Titian.

Lesser Frigate Birds — A103

Birds: 2 l, Crab plovers. 3 l, Long-tailed tropic bird. 4 l, Wedge-tailed shearwater. 5 l, Gray heron. 20 l, White tern. 95 l, Cattle egret. 1.25r, Blacknaped terns. 5r, Pheasant coucals.
10r, Striated herons.

1977, July 26   Litho.   Perf. 14½

691	A103	1 l multicolored	.25	.25
692	A103	2 l multicolored	.25	.25
693	A103	3 l multicolored	.25	.25
694	A103	4 l multicolored	.25	.25
695	A103	5 l multicolored	.25	.25
696	A103	20 l multicolored	.90	.90
697	A103	95 l multicolored	2.25	1.60
698	A103	1.25r multicolored	2.50	2.50
699	A103	5r multicolored	6.50	6.50
		Nos. 691-699 (9)	13.40	12.15

Souvenir Sheet

700	A103	10r multicolored	25.00	25.00

Charles A. Lindbergh — A104

Designs: 2 l, Lindbergh and Spirit of St. Louis. 3 l, Mohawk plane, horiz. 4 l, Lebaudy l airship, 1902, horiz. 5 l, Count Ferdinand von Zeppelin, and Zeppelin in Pernambuco. 1r, Los Angeles, U. S. Navy airship, 1924, horiz. 3r, Henry Ford and Lindbergh, 1942. 10r, Vickers airship, 1917.
5r, Spirit of St. Louis, Statue of Liberty and Eiffel Tower, horiz. 7.50r, German naval airship over battleship, horiz.

Perf. 13x13½, 13½x13

1977, Oct. 31   Litho.

701	A104	1 l multicolored	.25	.25
702	A104	2 l multicolored	.25	.25
703	A104	3 l multicolored	.25	.25
704	A104	4 l multicolored	.25	.25
705	A104	5 l multicolored	.25	.25
706	A104	1r multicolored	.60	.30
707	A104	3r multicolored	1.40	1.60
708	A104	10r multicolored	3.25	5.25
		Nos. 701-708 (8)	6.50	8.40

Souvenir Sheet

709		Sheet of 2	12.50	12.50
a.	A104	5r multicolored	3.75	3.75
b.	A104	7.50r multicolored	4.75	4.75

Charles A. Lindbergh's solo transatlantic flight from New York to Paris, 50th anniv., and 75th anniv. of first navigable airship.

Boat Building — A105

Maldivian Occupations: 15 l, High sea fishing. 20 l, Cadjan weaving. 90 l, Mat weaving. 2r, Lacemaking, vert.

1977, Dec. 12

710	A105	6 l multicolored	.85	.85
711	A105	15 l multicolored	1.50	1.50
712	A105	20 l multicolored	1.75	1.75
713	A105	90 l multicolored	4.00	4.00
714	A105	2r multicolored	5.50	5.00
		Nos. 710-714 (5)	13.60	13.10

Rheumatic Heart — A106

X-Ray Pictures: 50 l, Shoulder. 2r, Hand. 3r, Knee.

1978, Feb. 9   Perf. 14

715	A106	1 l multicolored	.25	.25
716	A106	50 l multicolored	.40	.40
717	A106	2r multicolored	.75	.75
718	A106	3r multicolored	.85	.85
		Nos. 715-718 (4)	2.25	2.10

World Rheumatism Year.

Otto Lilienthal's Glider, 1890 — A107

Designs: 2 l, Chanute's glider, 1896. 3 l, Wright brothers testing glider, 1900. 4 l, A. V. Roe's plane with paper-covered wings, 1908. 5 l, Wilbur Wright showing his plane to King Alfonso of Spain, 1909. 10 l, Roe's second biplane. 20 l, Alexander Graham Bell and Wright brothers in Washington D.C., 1910. 95 l, Clifton Hadley's triplane, 1910. 5r, British B.E.2 planes, Upavon Field, 1914.
10r, Wilbur Wright flying first motorized plane, 1903.

1978, Feb. 27   Litho.   Perf. 13x13½

719	A107	1 l multicolored	.25	.35
720	A107	2 l multicolored	.25	.35
721	A107	3 l multicolored	.25	.35
722	A107	4 l multicolored	.25	.35
723	A107	5 l multicolored	.25	.35
724	A107	10 l multicolored	.80	.40
725	A107	20 l multicolored	2.00	.40
726	A107	95 l multicolored	5.00	2.25
727	A107	5r multicolored	11.50	11.50
		Nos. 719-727 (9)	20.55	16.30

Souvenir Sheet

Perf. 14

728	A107	10r multicolored	12.50	12.50

75th anniversary of first motorized airplane.

Edward Jenner, Vaccination Discoverer — A108

Designs: 15 l, Foundling Hospital, London, where children were first inoculated, 1743, horiz. 50 l, Newgate Prison, London, where first experiments were carried out, 1721.

1978, Mar. 15   Perf. 14

729	A108	15 l multicolored	.65	.30
730	A108	50 l multicolored	1.50	.65
731	A108	2r multicolored	2.75	2.75
		Nos. 729-731 (3)	4.90	3.70

World eradication of smallpox.

TV with Maldives Broadcasting Symbol — A109

Designs: 25 l, Circuit pattern. 1.50r, Station control panel, horiz.

1978, Mar. 29

732	A109	15 l multicolored	.55	.55
733	A109	25 l multicolored	.80	.80
734	A109	1.50r multicolored	2.25	2.25
		Nos. 732-734 (3)	3.60	3.60

Inauguration of Maldive Islands television.

Sailing Ship — A110

Ships: 1 l, Phoenician. 2 l, Two-master. 5 l, Freighter Maldive Trader. 1r, Trading schooner. 1.25r, 4r, Sailing boat. 3r, Barque Bangala. (1 l, 2 l, 5 l, 1.25r, 4r, horiz.)

1978, Apr. 27   Litho.   Perf. 14½

735	A110	1 l multicolored	.25	.25
736	A110	2 l multicolored	.25	.25
737	A110	3 l multicolored	.25	.25
738	A110	5 l multicolored	.25	.25
739	A110	1r multicolored	.50	.50
740	A110	1.25r multicolored	1.00	1.00
741	A110	3r multicolored	1.50	1.50
742	A110	4r multicolored	1.75	1.75
a.		Souvenir sheet of 2	3.25	3.25
		Nos. 735-742 (8)	5.75	5.75

No. 742a contains No. 742 and a 1r stamp in the design of No. 736.

The Ampulla — A111

Designs: 2 l, Scepter with dove. 3 l, Orb with cross. 1.15r, St. Edward's crown. 2r, Scepter with cross. 5r, Queen Elizabeth II.
10r, Anointing spoon.

1978, May 15   Perf. 14

743	A111	1 l multicolored	.25	.25
744	A111	2 l multicolored	.25	.25
745	A111	3 l multicolored	.25	.25
746	A111	1.15r multicolored	.25	.25
747	A111	2r multicolored	.30	.30
748	A111	5r multicolored	.60	.60
		Nos. 743-748 (6)	1.90	1.90

Souvenir Sheet

749	A111	10r multicolored	2.00	2.00

Coronation of Elizabeth II, 25th anniv.
Nos. 743-748 were printed in sheets of 40 and in sheets of 3 + label, in changed colors. Labels show coronation regalia.

Capt. James Cook — A112

Designs: 2 l, Kamehameha I statue, Honolulu. 3 l, "Endeavour" and boat. 25 l, Capt. Cook and route of his 3rd voyage. 75 l, "Discovery" and "Resolution," map of Hawaiian Islands, horiz. 1.50r, Capt. Cook's first meeting with Hawaiians, horiz. 10r, Capt. Cook's death, horiz.
5r, "Endeavour."

1978, July 15   Litho.   Perf. 14½

750	A112	1 l multicolored	.25	.25
751	A112	2 l multicolored	.25	.25
752	A112	3 l multicolored	.25	.25
753	A112	25 l multicolored	.50	.35
754	A112	75 l multicolored	1.25	1.25
755	A112	1.50r multicolored	1.75	1.75
756	A112	10r multicolored	6.50	6.50
		Nos. 750-756 (7)	10.75	10.60

Souvenir Sheet

757	A112	5r multicolored	14.00	14.00

Schizophrys Aspera — A113

Maldivian Crabs and Lobster: 2 l, Atergatis floridus. 3 l, Percnon planissimum. 90 l, Portunus granulatus. 1r, Carpilius maculatus. No. 763, Huenia proteus. 25r, Etisus laevimanus. No. 765, Panulirus longipes, vert.

1978, Aug. 30   Litho.   Perf. 14

758	A113	1 l multicolored	.25	.25
759	A113	2 l multicolored	.25	.25
760	A113	3 l multicolored	.25	.25
761	A113	90 l multicolored	.60	.40
762	A113	1r multicolored	.60	.40
763	A113	3r multicolored	1.00	1.00
764	A113	25r multicolored	5.50	5.50
		Nos. 758-764 (7)	8.45	8.05

Souvenir Sheet

765	A113	2r multicolored	2.75	2.75

Four Apostles, by Dürer — A114

Paintings by Albrecht Dürer (1471-1528): 20 l, Self-portrait, age 27. 55 l, Virgin and Child with Pear. 1r, Rhinoceros, horiz. 1.80r, Hare. 3r, The Great Piece of Turf.
10r, Columbine.

1978, Oct. 28   Litho.   Perf. 14

766	A114	10 l multicolored	.25	.25
767	A114	20 l multicolored	.25	.25
768	A114	55 l multicolored	.25	.25
769	A114	1r multicolored	.30	.30
770	A114	1.80r multicolored	.60	.60
771	A114	3r multicolored	.90	.90
		Nos. 766-771 (6)	2.55	2.55

Souvenir Sheet

772	A114	10r multicolored	4.00	4.00

Palms and Fishing Boat — A115

Designs: 5 l, Montessori School. 10 l, TV tower and ITU emblem, vert. 25 l, Island with beach. 50 l, Boeing 737 over island. 95 l, Walk along the beach. 1.25r, Fishing boat at dawn. 2r, Presidential residence. 5r, Afeefuddin Mosque.
3r, Fishermen preparing nets.

1978, Nov. 11   Litho.   Perf. 14½

773	A115	1 l multicolored	.25	.25
774	A115	5 l multicolored	.25	.25
775	A115	10 l multicolored	.25	.25
776	A115	25 l multicolored	.25	.25
777	A115	50 l multicolored	.25	.25
778	A115	95 l multicolored	.30	.25

MALDIVE ISLANDS

779	A115	1.25r multicolored	.50	.50
780	A115	2r multicolored	.65	1.10
781	A115	5r multicolored	1.25	2.25
		Nos. 773-781 (9)	3.95	5.35

Souvenir Sheet

782	A115	3r multicolored	2.50	2.50

10th anniversary of Republic.

Human Rights Emblem — A116

1978, Dec. 10   *Perf. 14*

783	A116	30 l multicolored	.25	.25
784	A116	90 l multicolored	.40	.50
785	A116	1.80r multicolored	.65	1.00
		Nos. 783-785 (3)	1.30	1.75

Universal Declaration of Human Rights, 30th anniversary.

Rare Spotted Cowrie — A117

Sea Shells: 2 l, Imperial cone. 3 l, Green turban. 10 l, Giant spider conch. 1r, Leucodon cowrie. 1.80r, Fig cone. 3r, Glory of the sea. 5r, Top vase.

1979, Jan.   *Litho.*   *Perf. 14*

786	A117	1 l multicolored	.25	.25
787	A117	2 l multicolored	.25	.25
788	A117	3 l multicolored	.25	.25
789	A117	10 l multicolored	.45	.25
790	A117	1r multicolored	2.00	.40
791	A117	1.80r multicolored	3.00	2.50
792	A117	3r multicolored	4.50	3.75
		Nos. 786-792 (7)	10.70	7.65

Souvenir Sheet

793	A117	5r multicolored	14.00	14.00

Dellman Delivering Mail — A118

Designs: 2 l, Royal mail coach, 1840, horiz. 3 l, First London letter box, 1855. 1.55r, Great Britain No. 1 and post horn. 5r, Maldive Islands No. 5 and carrier pigeon. 10r, Rowland Hill.

1979, Feb. 28   *Litho.*   *Perf. 14*

794	A118	1 l multicolored	.25	.25
795	A118	2 l multicolored	.25	.25
796	A118	3 l multicolored	.25	.25
797	A118	1.55r multicolored	.45	.45
798	A118	5r multicolored	.80	.80
		Nos. 794-798 (5)	2.00	2.00

Souvenir Sheet

799	A118	10r multicolored	2.00	2.00

Sir Rowland Hill (1795-1879), originator of penny postage.

Nos. 794-798 were also each issued in sheetlets of 5 stamps and 1 label, perf. 12 with changed colors. Values: set, $1.50; set of sheetlets, $9.

For overprints see Nos. 853-855.

Girl with Teddy Bear — A119

IYC Emblem, Boy and: 1.25r, Model boat. 2r, Rocket launcher. 3r, Blimp. 5r, Train.

1979, May 10   *Litho.*   *Perf. 14*

800	A119	5 l multicolored	.25	.25
801	A119	1.25r multicolored	.40	.40
802	A119	2r multicolored	.50	.50
803	A119	3r multicolored	.65	.65
		Nos. 800-803 (4)	1.80	1.80

Souvenir Sheet

804	A119	5r multicolored	1.25	1.25

International Year of the Child.

White Feathers, by Matisse — A120

Paintings by Henri Matisse (1869-1954): 25 l, Joy of Life. 30 l, Eggplants. 1.50r, Harmony in Red. 5r, Still-life. 4r, Water Pitcher.

1979, Aug. 20   *Litho.*   *Perf. 14*

805	A120	20 l multicolored	.25	.25
806	A120	25 l multicolored	.25	.25
807	A120	30 l multicolored	.25	.25
808	A120	1.50r multicolored	.45	.45
809	A120	5r multicolored	.75	.75
		Nos. 805-809 (5)	1.95	1.95

Souvenir Sheet

810	A120	4r multicolored	4.00	4.00

Sari and Mosque — A121

National Costumes: 75 l, Sashed apron dress. Male Harbor. 90 l, Serape with necklace, radar station. 95 l, Flowered dress, mosque and minaret.

1979, Aug. 22   *Litho.*   *Perf. 14*

811	A121	50 l multicolored	.25	.25
812	A121	75 l multicolored	.25	.25
813	A121	90 l multicolored	.30	.30
814	A121	95 l multicolored	.35	.35
		Nos. 811-814 (4)	1.15	1.15

Maldive Wildflowers — A122

1 l, Gloriosa Superba. 3 l, Hibiscus. 50 l, Barringtonia asiatica. 1r, Abutilon indicum. 5r, Guettarda speciosa. 4r, Pandanus odoratissimus.

1979, Oct. 29   *Litho.*   *Perf. 14*

815	A122	1 l shown	.25	.25
816	A122	3 l multicolored	.25	.25
817	A122	50 l multicolored	.25	.25
818	A122	1r multicolored	.40	.40
819	A122	5r multicolored	1.00	1.00
		Nos. 815-819 (5)	2.15	2.15

Souvenir Sheet

820	A122	4r multicolored	1.75	1.75

Handicraft Exhibition A123

10 l, Jar and cup. 1.30r, Tortoise-shell jewelry. 2r, Wooden boxes. 5r, Bracelets, necklace.

1979, Nov. 11

821	A123	5 l shown	.25	.25
822	A123	10 l multicolored	.25	.25
823	A123	1.30r multicolored	.45	.45
824	A123	2r multicolored	.60	.60
		Nos. 821-824 (4)	1.55	1.55

Souvenir Sheet

825	A123	5r multicolored	1.25	1.25

Postal Scenes — A123a

1 l, Goofy delivering package. 2 l, Mickey at mailbox. 3 l, Goofy buried in letters. 4 l, Minnie Mouse, Pluto. 5 l, Mickey Mouse on skates. 10 l, Donald Duck at mailbox. 15 l, Chip and Dale carrying letter. 1.50r, Donald Duck on unicycle. 5r, Donald Duck wheeling crate. 4r, Pluto at mailbox.

1979, Dec.   *Litho.*   *Perf. 11*

826	A123a	1 l multicolored	.25	.25
827	A123a	2 l multicolored	.25	.25
828	A123a	3 l multicolored	.25	.25
829	A123a	4 l multicolored	.25	.25
830	A123a	5 l multicolored	.25	.25
831	A123a	10 l multicolored	.25	.25
832	A123a	15 l multicolored	.25	.25
833	A123a	1.50r multicolored	.75	.75
834	A123a	5r multicolored	2.25	2.25
		Nos. 826-834 (9)	4.75	4.75

Souvenir Sheet

835	A123a	4r multicolored	5.50	5.50

National Day — A124

Designs: 5 l, Post Ramadan dancing. 15 l, Festival of Eeduu. 95 l, Sultan's ceremonial band. 2r, Music festival. 5r, Sword dance.

1980, Jan. 19   *Litho.*   *Perf. 14*

836	A124	5 l multicolored	.25	.25
837	A124	15 l multicolored	.25	.25
838	A124	95 l multicolored	.35	.35
839	A124	2r multicolored	.60	.60
		Nos. 836-839 (4)	1.45	1.45

Souvenir Sheet

840	A124	5r multicolored	2.00	2.00

Leatherback Turtle — A125

1980, Feb. 17   *Litho.*   *Perf. 14*

841	A125	1 l shown	.25	.25
842	A125	2 l Flatback turtle	.25	.25
843	A125	5 l Hawksbill turtle	.25	.25
844	A125	10 l Loggerhead turtle	.25	.25
845	A125	75 l Olive ridley	.50	.50
846	A125	10r Atlantic ridley	3.00	3.00
		Nos. 841-846 (6)	4.50	4.50

Souvenir Sheet

847	A125	4r Green turtle	2.00	2.00

Paul Harris in Rotary Emblem — A126

1980, Mar.   *Litho.*   *Perf. 14*

848	A126	75 l shown	.45	.45
849	A126	90 l Family	.50	.50
850	A126	1r Grain	.50	.50
851	A126	10r Caduceus	2.75	2.75
		Nos. 848-851 (4)	4.20	4.20

Souvenir Sheet

852	A126	5r Anniversary emblem	1.75	1.75

Rotary International, 75th anniversary.

Nos. 797-799 Overprinted "LONDON 1980"

1980, May 6   *Litho.*   *Perf. 14*

853	A118	1.55r multicolored	2.00	1.75
854	A118	5r multicolored	4.00	4.00

Souvenir Sheet

855	A118	10r multicolored	7.00	7.00

London 1980 International Stamp Exhibition, May 6-14. Sheet margin overprinted "Earls Court—London 6-14 May 1980."

Swimming, Moscow '80 Emblem — A127

1980, June 4   *Litho.*   *Perf. 14*

856	A127	10 l shown	.25	.25
857	A127	50 l Sprinting	.25	.25
858	A127	3r Shot put	.75	.75
859	A127	4r High jump	1.00	1.00
		Nos. 856-859 (4)	2.25	2.25

Souvenir Sheet

860	A127	5r Weight lifting	1.25	1.25

22nd Summer Olympic Games, Moscow, July 19-Aug. 3.

White-tailed Tropic Bird — A128

95 l, Sooty tern. 1r, Brown noddy. 1.55r, European curlew. 2r, Wilson's petrel. 4r, Caspian tern. 5r, Red-footed & brown boobies.

1980, July 10   *Litho.*   *Perf. 14*

861	A128	75 l shown	.30	.25
862	A128	95 l multi	.30	.30
863	A128	1.55r multi	.40	.30
864	A128	1.55r multi	.55	.55
865	A128	2r multi	.65	.65
866	A128	4r multi	1.20	1.20
		Nos. 861-866 (6)	3.40	3.25

Souvenir Sheet

867	A128	5r multi	8.00	8.00

Seal of Sultan Ibrahim II (1720-1750) A129

Sultans' Seals: 2 l, Mohamed Imadudeen II (1704-1720). 5 l, Mohamed Bin Haji Ali (1692-1701). 1r, Kuda Mohamed Rasgefaanu (1687-1691). 2r, Ibrahim Iskander I (1648-1687). 3r, Ibrahim Iskander, second seal.

1980, July 26

868	A129	1 l violet brn & blk	.25	.25
869	A129	2 l violet brn & blk	.25	.25
870	A129	5 l violet brn & blk	.25	.25
871	A129	1r violet brn & blk	.40	.40
872	A129	2r violet brn & blk	.50	.50
		Nos. 868-872 (5)	1.65	1.65

Souvenir Sheet

873	A129	3r violet brn & blk	.85	.85

Queen Mother Elizabeth, 80th Birthday — A130

1980, Sept. 29   *Perf. 14*

874	A130	4r multicolored	1.25	1.25

Souvenir Sheet   *Perf. 12*

875	A130	5r multicolored	1.60	1.60

Munnaaru Tower — A131

10 l, Hukuru Miskiiy Mosque. 30 l, Medhuziyaaraiy Shrine. 55 l, Koran verses on wooden tablets. 90 l, Mother teaching son. 2r, Map and arms of Maldives.

167

MALDIVE ISLANDS

1980, Nov. 9	Litho.		Perf. 15
876 A131	5 l shown	.25	.25
877 A131	10 l multicolored	.25	.25
878 A131	30 l multicolored	.25	.25
879 A131	55 l multicolored	.30	.30
880 A131	90 l multicolored	.45	.45
Nos. 876-880 (5)		1.50	1.50

Souvenir Sheet

| 881 A131 | 2r multicolored | .80 | 1.00 |

Hegira (Pilgrimage Year).

Malaria Eradication Control — A132

1980, Nov. 30			Perf. 14
882 A132	15 l shown	.30	.30
883 A132	25 l Balanced diet	.30	.30
884 A132	1.50r Oral hygiene	1.00	1.00
885 A132	5r Clinic visit	3.25	3.25
Nos. 882-885 (4)		4.85	4.85

Souvenir Sheet

| 886 A132 | 4r like #885 | 1.50 | 1.50 |

World Health Day. No. 886 shows design of No. 885 in changed colors.

The Cheshire Cat — A133

Designs: Scenes from Walt Disney's Alice in Wonderland. 5r, vert.

1980, Dec. 22			Perf. 11
887 A133	1 l multicolored	.25	.25
888 A133	2 l multicolored	.25	.25
889 A133	3 l multicolored	.25	.25
890 A133	4 l multicolored	.25	.25
891 A133	5 l multicolored	.25	.25
892 A133	10 l multicolored	.25	.25
893 A133	15 l multicolored	.25	.25
894 A133	2.50r multicolored	2.25	2.25
895 A133	4r multicolored	2.50	2.50
Nos. 887-895 (9)		6.50	6.50

Souvenir Sheet

| 896 A133 | 5r multicolored | 5.00 | 5.00 |

Ridley Turtle — A134

1980, Dec. 29	Litho.		Perf. 14
897 A134	90 l multicolored	2.25	.60
898 A134	1.25r Angel flake fish	2.75	1.25
899 A134	2r Spiny lobster	3.25	1.75
Nos. 897-899 (3)		8.25	3.60

Souvenir Sheet

| 900 A134 | 4r Fish | 3.50 | 3.50 |

Tomb of Ghaazee Muhammad Thakurufaan A135

National Day (Furniture and Palace of Muhammad Thakurufaan): 20 l, Hanging lamp, 16th century, vert. 30 l, Chair, vert. 95 l, Utheem Palace. 10r, Couch, vert.

1981, Jan. 7			Perf. 15
901 A135	10 l multicolored	.25	.25
902 A135	20 l multicolored	.25	.25
903 A135	30 l multicolored	.25	.25
904 A135	95 l multicolored	.60	.30
905 A135	10r multicolored	2.75	2.75
Nos. 901-905 (5)		4.10	3.80

Common Design Types pictured following the introduction.

Royal Wedding Issue
Common Design Type

1r, Couple. 2r, Buckingham Palace. 5r, Charles. 10r, Royal state coach.

1981, June 22	Litho.		Perf. 14
906 CD331a	1r multi	.25	.25
907 CD331a	2r multi	.25	.25
908 CD331a	5r multi	.30	.30
Nos. 906-908 (3)		.80	.80

Souvenir Sheet

| 909 CD331 | 10r multi | .75 | .75 |

Nos. 906-908 also printed in sheets of 5 plus label, perf. 12, in changed colors. Value, set $1.

Majlis Chamber, 1932 — A136

50th Anniv. of Citizens' Majlis (Grievance Rights); 1r, Sultan Muhammed Shamsuddin III (instituted system, 1932), vert. 4r, Constitution, 1932.

1981, June 27			Perf. 15
910 A136	95 l multicolored	.30	.30
911 A136	1r multicolored	.35	.35

Souvenir Sheet

| 912 A136 | 4r multicolored | 2.50 | 2.50 |

Self-portrait with Palette, by Picasso (1881-1973) — A137

Child Holding a Dove A138

1981, Aug. 26	Litho.		Perf. 14
913 A137	5 l shown	.25	.25
914 A137	10 l Woman in Blue	.25	.25
915 A137	25 l Boy with a Pipe	.30	.25
916 A137	30 l Card Player	.30	.25
917 A137	90 l Sailor	.40	.40
918 A137	3r Self-portrait	.80	.80
919 A137	5r Harlequin	1.00	1.00

Imperf

| 920 A138 | 10r shown | 2.75 | 2.75 |
| Nos. 913-920 (8) | | 6.05 | 5.95 |

No. 5 on Airmail Cover — A139

1981, Sept. 9	Litho.		Perf. 14
921 A139	25 l multicolored	.25	.25
922 A139	75 l multicolored	.25	.25
923 A139	5r multicolored	.70	1.00
Nos. 921-923 (3)		1.20	1.50

Postal service, 75th anniv.

Hulule Intl. Airport Opening — A140

5 l, Jet taking off. 20 l, Passengers leaving jet. 1.80r, Refueling. 5r, Terminal.

1981, Nov. 11			
924 A140	5 l multicolored	.25	.25
925 A140	20 l multicolored	.25	.25
926 A140	1.80r multicolored	1.00	1.00
927 A140	4r shown	1.20	2.00
Nos. 924-927 (4)		2.70	3.50

Souvenir Sheet

| 928 A140 | 5r multicolored | 2.50 | 2.50 |

Intl. Year of the Disabled — A141

2 l, Homer. 5 l, Cervantes. 1r, Beethoven. 5r, Van Gogh. 4r, Helen Keller, Anne Sullivan.

1981, Nov. 18	Litho.		Perf. 14½
929 A141	2 l multi	.25	.25
930 A141	5 l multi	.25	.25
931 A141	1r multi	2.00	2.00
932 A141	5r multi	3.50	4.25
Nos. 929-932 (4)		6.00	6.75

Souvenir Sheet

| 933 A141 | 4r multi | 3.50 | 3.50 |

Decade for Women — A142

1981, Nov. 25			Perf. 14
934 A142	20 l Preparing fish	.25	.25
935 A142	90 l 16th cent. woman	.25	.25
936 A142	1r Tending yam crop	.30	.30
937 A142	2r Making coir rope	.55	.55
Nos. 934-937 (4)		1.35	1.35

Fishermen's Day — A143

5 l, Collecting bait. 15 l, Fishing boats. 90 l, Fisherman holding catch. 1.30r, Sorting fish. 3r, Loading fish for export.

1981, Dec. 10			
938 A143	5 l multi	.45	.25
939 A143	15 l multi	.85	.25
940 A143	90 l multi	1.50	.60
941 A143	1.30r multi	2.10	1.00
Nos. 938-941 (4)		4.90	2.10

Souvenir Sheet

| 942 A143 | 3r multi | 1.75 | 1.75 |

World Food Day — A144

1981, Dec. 30	Litho.		Perf. 14
943 A144	10 l Breadfruit	.35	.25
944 A144	25 l Hen, chicks	.80	.25
945 A144	30 l Corn	.80	.25
946 A144	75 l Skipjack tuna	2.25	.45
947 A144	1r Pumpkins	2.75	.60
948 A144	2r Coconuts	3.25	2.25
Nos. 943-948 (6)		10.20	4.05

Souvenir Sheet

| 949 A144 | 5r Eggplants | 2.50 | 2.50 |

50th Anniv. of Walt Disney's Pluto (1980) — A145

4r, Scene from Chain Gang, 1930. 6r, The Pointer, 1939.

1982, Mar. 29	Litho.		Perf. 13½x14
950 A145	4r multi	2.25	2.25

Souvenir Sheet

| 951 A145 | 6r multi | 3.25 | 3.25 |

Princess Diana Issue
Common Design Type

1982, July 15	Litho.		Perf. 14½x14
952 CD332	95 l Balmoral	.50	.25
953 CD332	3r Honeymoon	1.25	.65
954 CD332	5r Diana	1.75	1.00
Nos. 952-954 (3)		3.50	1.90

Souvenir Sheet

| 955 CD332 | 8r Diana, diff. | 2.00 | 2.00 |

Nos. 952-954 also issued in sheetlets of 5 plus label. Nos. 952-955 and the sheetlets of 5 eixst imperf. Value: 952-954, $9.
For overprints and surcharges see Nos. 966-969, 1050, 1052, 1054, 1056.

Scouting Year — A146

1982, Aug. 9	Litho.		Perf. 14
956 A146	1.30r Saluting	.40	.40
957 A146	1.80r Fire building	.50	.50
958 A146	4r Lifesaving	1.10	1.10
959 A146	5r Map reading	1.50	1.50
Nos. 956-959 (4)		3.50	3.50

Souvenir Sheet

| 960 A146 | 10r Flag, emblem | 2.50 | 2.50 |

1982 World Cup — A147

Various soccer players.

1982, Oct. 4	Litho.		Perf. 14
961 A147	90 l multicolored	1.25	.60
962 A147	1.50r multicolored	1.75	1.10
963 A147	3r multicolored	2.50	1.75
964 A147	5r multicolored	2.75	2.50
Nos. 961-964 (4)		8.25	5.95

Souvenir Sheet

| 965 A147 | 10r multicolored | 4.50 | 4.50 |

Nos. 952-955 Overprinted: "ROYAL BABY/21.6.82"

1982, Oct. 18			Perf. 14½x14
966 CD332	95 l multicolored	.50	.50
967 CD332	3r multicolored	.75	.75
968 CD332	5r multicolored	1.00	1.00
Nos. 966-968 (3)		2.25	2.25

Souvenir Sheet

| 969 CD332 | 8r multicolored | 3.50 | 3.50 |

Birth of Prince William of Wales, June 21. Nos. 966-968 also issued in sheetlets of 5 + label. Nos. 966-969 and the sheetlets of 5 exists imperf. Value: 966-968, $7.50
For surcharges see Nos. 1051, 1053, 1055, 1057.

TB Bacillus Cent. — A148

5 l, Koch isolating bacillus. 15 l, Slide, microscope. 95 l, Koch, 1905. 3r, Koch, book illus. plates. 5r, Koch in lab.

1982, Nov. 22			Perf. 14½
970 A148	5 l multi	.25	.25
971 A148	15 l multi	.25	.25
972 A148	95 l multi	.55	.45
973 A148	3r multi	1.00	1.00
Nos. 970-973 (4)		2.05	1.95

Souvenir Sheet

| 974 A148 | 5r multi | 1.25 | 1.25 |

MALDIVE ISLANDS

Natl. Education — A149

Designs: 90 l, Basic education scheme, 1980-85. 95 l, Formal primary education. 1.30r, Teacher training. 2.50r, Educational materials production. 6r, Thanna typewriter.

1982, Nov. 15

975	A149	90 l multicolored	.25	.25
976	A149	95 l multicolored	.25	.25
977	A149	1.30r multicolored	.25	.25
978	A149	2.50r multicolored	.45	.45
		Nos. 975-978 (4)	1.20	1.20

Souvenir Sheet

979	A149	6r multicolored	1.25	1.25

Manned Flight Bicentenary — A150

90 l, Blohm & Voss Ha-139. 1.45r, Macchi Castoldi MC-72. 4r, Boeing F4B-3. 5r, Le France. 10r, Nadar's Le Geant.

1983, July 28 Litho. Perf. 14

980	A150	90 l multi	2.25	.75
981	A150	1.45r multi	2.75	1.75
982	A150	4r multi	4.50	3.25
983	A150	5r multi	4.60	3.60
		Nos. 980-983 (4)	14.00	9.25

Souvenir Sheet

984	A150	10r multi	3.25	3.25

For overprints see Nos. 1020-1022.

Roughtooth Dolphin — A151

40 l, Indopacific humpback dolphin. 4r, Finless porpoise. 6r, Pygmy sperm whale. 5r, Striped dolphins.

1983, Sept. 6 Litho. Perf. 14

985	A151	30 l shown	.75	.75
986	A151	40 l multi	.75	.75
987	A151	4r multi	4.00	4.00
988	A151	6r multi	9.50	9.50
		Nos. 985-988 (4)	15.00	15.00

Souvenir Sheet

989	A151	5r multi	5.50	5.50

Classic Cars — A152

5 l, Curved Dash Oldsmobile, 1902. 30 l, Aston Martin Tourer, 1932. 40 l, Lamborghini Miura, 1966. 1r, Mercedes-Benz 300sl, 1954. 1.45r, Stutz Bearcat, 1913. 5r, Lotus Elite, 1958. 10r, Grand Prix Sunbeam, 1924.

1983, Aug. 15 Litho. Perf. 14½x15

990	A152	5 l multi	.25	.25
991	A152	30 l multi	.60	.40
992	A152	40 l multi	.60	.45
993	A152	1r multi	1.00	.75
994	A152	1.45r multi	1.25	1.25
995	A152	5r multi	2.00	2.00
		Nos. 990-995 (6)	5.70	5.10

Souvenir Sheet

996	A152	10r multi	6.50	6.50

World Communications Year — A153

50 l, Dish antenna. 1r, Mail transport. 2r, Ship-to-shore communications. 10r, Land-air communications. 20r, Telephone calls.

1983, Oct. 9   Perf. 14

997	A153	50 l multicolored	.30	.30
998	A153	1r multicolored	.60	.60
999	A153	2r multicolored	1.10	1.10
1000	A153	10r multicolored	5.50	5.50
		Nos. 997-1000 (4)	7.50	7.50

Souvenir Sheet

1001	A153	20r multicolored	4.50	4.50

Raphael, 500th Birth Anniv. — A154

90 l, La Donna Gravida. 3r, Jeanne of Aragon. 4r, The Woman with the Unicorn. 6r, La Muta. 10r, The Knights Dream.

1983, Oct. 25 Litho. Perf. 13½x14

1002	A154	90 l multi	.45	.45
1003	A154	3r multi	1.00	1.00
1004	A154	4r multi	1.50	1.50
1005	A154	6r multi	2.00	2.00
		Nos. 1002-1005 (4)	4.95	4.95

Souvenir Sheet

1006	A154	10r multi	3.00	3.00

Intl. Palestinian Solidarity Day — A155

Various refugees, mosque.

1983, Nov. 29 Litho. Perf. 14

1007	A155	4r multicolored	1.75	1.75
1008	A155	5r multicolored	2.25	2.25
1009	A155	6r multicolored	2.75	2.75
		Nos. 1007-1009 (3)	6.75	6.75

Natl. Development Programs — A156

7 l, Education. 10 l, Health care. 5r, Food production. 6r, Fishing industry. 10r, Inter-atoll transportation.

1983, Dec. 10 Litho. Perf. 13½x14

1010	A156	7 l multi	.25	.25
1011	A156	10 l multi	.50	.25
1012	A156	5r multi	1.50	1.25
1013	A156	6r multi	2.25	1.50
		Nos. 1010-1013 (1)	1.60	3.25

Souvenir Sheet

1014	A156	10r multi	2.25	2.25

1984, Feb.   Perf. 14

1015	A157	50 l Baseball	.25	.25
1016	A157	1.55r Swimming	.70	.70
1017	A157	3r Judo	1.25	1.25
1018	A157	4r Shot put	1.75	1.75
		Nos. 1015-1018 (4)	3.95	3.95

Souvenir Sheet

1019	A157	10r Handball	2.75	2.75

23rd Olympic Games, Los Angeles, 7/28-8/12
For overprints see Nos. 1090-1094.

Nos. 982-984 Overprinted

Overprint reads "19th UPU/CONGRESS HAMBURG"

1984   Litho.   Perf. 14

1020	A150	4r multicolored	1.75	1.40
1021	A150	5r multicolored	1.75	1.60

Souvenir Sheet

1022	A150	10r multicolored	2.75	2.75

Tourism — A158

7 l, Island resorts. 15 l, Cruising. 20 l, Snorkeling. 2r, Wind surfing. 4r, Scuba diving. 6r, Night fishing. 8r, Big game fishing. 10r, Nature (turtle).

1984, Sept. 21 Litho. Perf. 14½

1023	A158	7 l multi	.45	.45
1024	A158	15 l multi	.45	.45
1025	A158	20 l multi	.45	.45
1026	A158	2r multi	1.10	1.10
1027	A158	4r multi	2.25	2.25
1028	A158	6r multi	3.50	3.50
1029	A158	8r multi	4.50	4.50
1030	A158	10r multi	5.50	5.50
		Nos. 1023-1030 (8)	18.20	18.20

50th Anniv. of Donald Duck — A160

Scenes from various cartoons and movies.

1984, Nov. Litho. Perf. 14

1040	A160	3 l multi	.25	.25
1041	A160	4 l multi	.25	.25
1042	A160	5 l multi	.25	.25
1043	A160	10 l multi	.25	.25
1044	A160	15 l multi	.25	.25
1045	A160	25 l multi	.25	.25
1045A	A160	5r multi, perf. 12x12½	2.25	2.25
1046	A160	8r multi	2.50	2.50
1047	A160	10r multi	3.00	3.00
		Nos. 1040-1047 (9)	9.25	9.25

Souvenir Sheets

1048	A160	15r multi	5.00	5.00
1049	A160	15r multi	5.00	5.00

Nos. 952-955, 966-969 Surcharged

1984, July Litho. Perf. 14½x14

1050	CD332	1.45r on 95 l #952	2.50	2.00
1051	CD332	1.45r on 95 l #966	2.50	2.00
1052	CD332	1.45r on 3r #953	2.50	2.00
1053	CD332	1.45r on 3r #967	2.50	2.00
1054	CD332	1.45r on 5r #954	2.50	2.00
1055	CD332	1.45r on 5r #968	2.50	2.00
		Nos. 1050-1055 (6)	15.00	12.00

Souvenir Sheet

1056	CD332	1.45r on 8r #955	2.50	2.00
1057	CD332	1.45r on 8r #969	2.50	2.00

Namibia Day — A161

1984, Aug. 26   Perf. 15

1058	A161	6r Breaking chain	1.25	1.25
1059	A161	8r Family, rising sun	1.25	1.25

Souvenir Sheet

1060	A161	10r Map, sun	2.25	2.25

Ausipex '84 — A162

5r, Frangipani. 10r, Cooktown orchid. 15r, Sun orchids.

1984, Sept. 21

1061	A162	5r multi	2.25	1.75
1062	A162	10r multi	4.75	3.75

Souvenir Sheet

1063	A162	15r multi	10.00	10.00

150th Birth Anniv. of Edgar Degas — A163

75 l, Portrait of Edmond Duranty. 2r, Portrait of James Tissot. 5r, Portrait of Achille Degas. 10r, Lady with Chrysanthemums. 15r, Self-Portrait.

1984, Oct. Litho. Perf. 14

1064	A163	75 l multi	.25	.25
1065	A163	2r multi	.50	.50
1066	A163	5r multi	1.00	1.00
1067	A163	10r multi	1.75	1.75
		Nos. 1064-1067 (4)	3.50	3.50

Souvenir Sheet

1068	A163	15r multi	3.50	3.50

Opening of Islamic Center — A164

2r, Mosque. 5r, Mosque, minaret, vert.

1984, Nov. 11 Litho. Perf. 15

1069	A164	2r multi	.50	.50
1070	A164	5r multi	1.10	1.10

40th Anniv., International Civil Aviation Organization — A165

7 l, Boeing 737. 4r, Lockheed L-1011. 6r, McDonnell Douglas DC-10. 8r, Lockheed L-1011. 15r, Shorts SC7 Skyvan.

1984, Nov. 19 Litho. Perf. 14

1071	A165	7 l multi	.35	.35
1072	A165	4r multi	2.40	2.00
1073	A165	6r multi	3.25	3.25
1074	A165	8r multi	4.00	4.00
		Nos. 1071-1074 (4)	10.00	9.60

Souvenir Sheet

1075	A165	15r multi	4.00	4.00

450th Anniv. of the Death of Correggio — A166

5r, Detail from The Day. 10r, Detail from The Night. 15r, Portrait of a Man.

1984, Dec. 10 Litho. Perf. 14

1076	A166	5r multi	1.00	1.00
1077	A166	10r multi	1.60	1.60

Souvenir Sheet

1078	A166	15r multi	3.75	3.75

John J. Audubon — A167

Illustrations from Audubon's Birds of America: 3r, Flesh-footed shearwater, vert. 3.50r, Little grebe. 4r, Great cormorant, vert. 4.50r, White-faced storm petrel. 15r, Red-necked phalarope.

1985, Mar. 9 Litho. Perf. 14

1079	A167	3r multi	1.75	.80
1080	A167	3.50r multi	2.00	.90
1081	A167	4r multi	2.00	1.00
1082	A167	4.50r multi	2.00	1.10
		Nos. 1079-1082 (4)	7.75	3.80

Souvenir Sheet

1083	A167	15r multi	5.00	5.00

See Nos. 1195-1204.

MALDIVE ISLANDS

Natl. Security Services — A168

15 l, Drill. 20 l, Combat training. 1r, Fire fighting. 2r, Coast guard. No. 1088, Parade, vert. No. 1089, Badge, cannon.

1985, June 6   Litho.   Perf. 14

1084	A168	15 l multi	.50	.25
1085	A168	20 l multi	.50	.25
1086	A168	1r multi	2.00	.40
1087	A168	2r multi	2.50	.90
1088	A168	10r multi	3.25	3.25
		Nos. 1084-1088 (5)	8.75	5.05

Souvenir Sheet

| 1089 | A168 | 10r multi | 2.75 | 2.75 |

Nos. 1015-1019 Overprinted

Overprint includes Country or "Gold Medalist," Winner and Nation in 3 Lines

50 l, Japan. 1.55r, Theresa Andrews. 3r, Frank Wieneke. 4r, Claudia Loch. 10r, US.

1985, July 17

1090	A157	50 l multi	.30	.25
1091	A157	1.55r multi	.55	.55
1092	A157	3r multi	1.10	1.10
1093	A157	4r multi	1.25	1.25
		Nos. 1090-1093 (4)	3.20	3.15

Souvenir Sheet

| 1094 | A157 | 10r multi | 2.00 | 2.00 |

Queen Mother, 85th Birthday — A169

1r, Wearing tiara. 4r, At Middlesex Hospital, horiz. 7r, Wearing fur stole. 15r, With Prince of Wales.

1985-86   Perf. 14, 12 (1r, 4r, 10r)

1095	A169	1r multi	.45	.45
1096	A169	3r like 1r	.55	.55
1097	A169	4r multi	.65	.65
1098	A169	5r like 4r	.90	.90
1099	A169	7r multi	1.10	1.10
1100	A169	10r like 7r	1.75	1.75
		Nos. 1095-1100 (6)	5.40	5.40

Souvenir Sheet

| 1101 | A169 | 15r multi | 3.50 | 3.50 |

Issued: 1r, 4r, 10r, 1/4/86; 3r, 5r, 7r, 15r, 8/20/85. Nos. 1095, 1097, 1100 printed in sheets of 5 + label.

Johann Sebastian Bach, Composer — A170

Portrait, Invention No. 1 in C Major and: 15 l, Lira da Braccio. 2r, Tenor oboe. 4r, Serpent. 10r, Table organ.

1985, Sept. 3   Perf. 14

1102	A170	15 l multi	.25	.25
1103	A170	2r multi	.65	.65
1104	A170	4r multi	.90	.90
1105	A170	10r multi	1.75	1.75
		Nos. 1102-1105 (4)	3.55	3.55

Souvenir Sheet

| 1106 | A170 | 15r Portrait | 3.25 | 3.25 |

Ships — A171

3 l, Masodi. 5 l, Naalu Baththeli. 10 l, Addu Odi. 2.60r, Masdhoni, 2nd generation. 2.70r, Masdhoni. 3r, Baththeli Dhoni. 5r, Inter 1. 10r, Yacht Dhoni.

1985, Sept. 23

1107	A171	3 l multi	.25	.25
1108	A171	5 l multi	.25	.25
1109	A171	10 l multi	.25	.25
1110	A171	2.60r multi	1.75	1.75
1111	A171	2.70r multi	1.75	1.75
1112	A171	3r multi	2.00	1.75
1113	A171	5r multi	3.00	3.00
1114	A171	10r multi	4.50	4.50
		Nos. 1107-1114 (8)	13.75	13.50

For surcharge, see No. 1493B.

World Tourism Org., 10th Anniv. — A172

1985, Oct. 2

1115	A172	6r Wind surfing	2.50	2.50
1116	A172	8r Scuba diving	3.00	3.00

Souvenir Sheet

| 1117 | A172 | 15r Kuda Hithi Resort | 5.00 | 5.00 |

Maldives Admission to UN, 20th Anniv. — A173

15r, Flags, UN building.

1985, Oct. 24

1118	A173	20 l shown	.25	.25
1119	A173	15r multi	2.75	2.75

UN 40th Anniv., Intl. Peace Year — A174

15 l, UN Building. 2r, IPY emblem. 4r, Security Council. 10r, Lion, lamb. 15r, UN Building, diff.

1985, Oct. 24   Litho.   Perf. 14

1120	A174	15 l multi	.25	.25
1121	A174	2r multi	.65	.65
1122	A174	4r multi	.90	.90
1123	A174	10r multi	1.25	1.25
		Nos. 1120-1123 (4)	3.05	3.05

Souvenir Sheet

| 1124 | A174 | 15r multi | 2.50 | 2.50 |

Nos. 1120-1121, 1123-1124, vert.

Intl. Youth Year — A175

90 l, Culture. 6r, Games. 10r, Community service, vert. 15r, Youth camp, vert.

1985, Nov. 20   Perf. 15

1125	A175	90 l multi	.35	.35
1126	A175	6r multi	1.00	1.00
1127	A175	10r multi	1.25	1.25
		Nos. 1125-1127 (3)	2.60	2.60

Souvenir Sheet

| 1128 | A175 | 15r multi | 2.50 | 2.50 |

Summit Nations Flags, Dedication by Pres. Maumoon A176

1985, Dec. 8   Perf. 14

| 1129 | A176 | 3r multicolored | 2.25 | 2.25 |

South Asian Regional Cooperation, SARC, 1st Summit, Dec. 7-8, 1985.

Tuna — A177

1985, Dec. 10

1130	A177	25 l Frigate	.45	.45
1131	A177	75 l Little tuna	.75	.75
1132	A177	3r Dogtooth	2.00	1.00
1133	A177	5r Yellowfin	2.25	1.25
		Nos. 1130-1133 (4)	5.45	3.45

Souvenir Sheet

| 1134 | A177 | 15r Skipjack | 4.50 | 4.50 |

Fisherman's Day.

Mark Twain, American Novelist — A178

Disney characters and Twain quotes.

1985, Dec. 21

1135	A178	2 l multicolored	.25	.25
1136	A178	3 l multicolored	.25	.25
1137	A178	4 l multicolored	.25	.25
1138	A178	20 l multicolored	.25	.25
1139	A178	4r multicolored	1.25	1.25
1140	A178	13r multicolored	1.75	1.75
		Nos. 1135-1140 (6)	4.00	4.00

Souvenir Sheet

| 1141 | A178 | 15r multicolored | 6.50 | 6.50 |

Intl. Youth Year. 4r issued in sheet of 8.

The Brothers Grimm A179

Disney characters in Doctor Knowall.

1985, Dec. 21

1142	A179	1 l multicolored	.25	.25
1143	A179	5 l multicolored	.25	.25
1144	A179	10 l multicolored	.25	.25
1145	A179	15 l multicolored	.25	.25
1146	A179	3r multicolored	1.00	1.00
1147	A179	14r multicolored	5.00	5.00
		Nos. 1142-1147 (6)	7.00	7.00

Souvenir Sheet

| 1148 | A179 | 15r multicolored | 6.50 | 6.50 |

3r issued in sheets of 8.

World Disarmament Day — A180

1986, Feb. 10   Perf. 14½x14

1149	A180	1.50r shown	—	—
1150	A180	10r Dove		

Halley's Comet — A181

Designs: 20 l, NASA space telescope. 1.50r, Giotto space probe. 2r, Plant-A probe, Japan. 4r, Edmond Halley, Stonehenge. 5r, Vega probe, USSR. 15r, Comet over Male.

1986, Apr. 29

1151	A181	20 l multicolored	.50	.50
1152	A181	1.50r multicolored	1.25	1.25
1153	A181	2r multicolored	1.25	1.25
1154	A181	4r multicolored	2.00	2.00
1155	A181	5r multicolored	2.00	2.00
		Nos. 1151-1155 (5)	7.00	7.00

Souvenir Sheet

| 1156 | A181 | 15r multicolored | 6.50 | 6.50 |

See Nos. 1210-1215.

Statue of Liberty, Cent. — A182

Detail of statue and: 50 l, Walter Gropius (1883-1969), architect. 70 l, John Lennon (1940-1980), musician. 1r, George Balanchine (1904-1983), choreographer. 10r, Franz Werfel (1890-1945), writer.

1986, May 5

1157	A182	50 l multicolored	.40	.40
1158	A182	70 l multicolored	1.90	1.25
1159	A182	1r multicolored	2.00	1.25
1160	A182	10r multicolored	4.00	4.00
		Nos. 1157-1160 (4)	8.30	6.90

Souvenir Sheet

| 1161 | A182 | 15r multicolored | 7.50 | 7.50 |

AMERIPEX '86 — A183

US stamps and Disney portrayals of American legends: 3 l, #1317, Johnny Appleseed. 4 l, #1122, Paul Bunyan. 5 l, #1381, Casey at the Bat. 10 l, #. 1548, Tales of Sleepy Hollow. 15 l, #922, John Henry. 20 l, #1061, Windwagon Smith. 13r, #1409, Mike Fink. 14r, #993, Casey Jones.

No. 1170, Remember the Alamo, #1330. No. 1171, Pocahontas, #328-330.

1986, May 22   Perf. 11

1162	A183	3 l multicolored	.25	.25
1163	A183	4 l multicolored	.25	.25
1164	A183	5 l multicolored	.25	.25
1165	A183	10 l multicolored	.25	.25
1166	A183	15 l multicolored	.25	.25
1167	A183	20 l multicolored	.25	.25
1168	A183	13r multicolored	7.00	7.00
1169	A183	14r multicolored	8.00	8.00
		Nos. 1162-1169 (8)	16.50	16.50

Souvenir Sheets   Perf. 14

1170	A183	15r multicolored	6.50	6.50
1171	A183	15r multicolored	6.50	6.50

Queen Elizabeth II, 60th Birthday

Common Design Type

1r, Girl Guides' rally, 1938. 2r, Canada visit, 1985. 12r, At Sandringham, 1970. 15r, Royal Lodge, 1940.

1986, May 29   Perf. 14

1172	CD339	1r multicolored	.25	.25
1173	CD339	2r multicolored	.50	.50
1174	CD339	12r multicolored	2.00	2.00
		Nos. 1172-1174 (3)	2.75	2.75

Souvenir Sheet

| 1175 | CD339 | 15r multicolored | 3.50 | 3.50 |

For overprints see Nos. 1288-1291.

1986 World Cup Soccer Championships, Mexico — A184

Various soccer plays.

1986, June 18   Litho.   Perf. 14

1176	A184	15 l multicolored	.75	.30
1177	A184	2r multicolored	2.50	1.75
1178	A184	4r multicolored	4.00	3.50
1179	A184	10r multicolored	7.50	7.50
		Nos. 1176-1179 (4)	14.75	13.05

Souvenir Sheet

| 1180 | A184 | 15r multicolored | 5.50 | 5.50 |

For overprints see Nos. 1205-1209.

MALDIVE ISLANDS

Royal Wedding Issue, 1986
Common Design Type
Designs: 10 l, Prince Andrew and Sarah Ferguson. 2r, Andrew. 12r, Andrew on ship's deck in uniform.
15r, Couple, diff.

1986, July 23
1181	CD340	10 l multi	.25	.25
1182	CD340	2r multi	.70	.70
1183	CD340	12r multi	3.00	3.00
	Nos. 1181-1183 (3)		3.95	3.95

Souvenir Sheet
1184	CD340	15r multi	4.50	4.50

Marine Life — A185

Designs: 50 l, Sea fan, moorish idol. 90 l, Regal angelfish. 1r, Anemone fish. 2r, Stinging coral, tiger cowrie. 3r, Emperor angelfish, staghorn coral. 4r, Black-naped tern. 5r, Fiddler crab, staghorn coral. 10r, Hawksbill turtle. No. 1193, Trumpet fish. No. 1194, Long-nosed butterflyfish.

1986, Sept 22   Litho.   Perf. 15
1185	A185	50 l multicolored	1.50	.40
1186	A185	90 l multicolored	2.00	.55
1187	A185	1r multicolored	2.00	.55
1188	A185	2r multicolored	2.50	1.50
1189	A185	3r multicolored	2.50	2.00
1190	A185	4r multicolored	2.75	2.75
1191	A185	5r multicolored	2.50	2.50
1192	A185	10r multicolored	3.00	3.00
	Nos. 1185-1192 (8)		18.75	13.25

Souvenir Sheets
1193	A185	15r multicolored	6.00	6.00
1194	A185	15r multicolored	6.00	6.00

Nos. 1185-1187 and 1189 show the World Wildlife Fund emblem.

Audubon Type of 1985
Birds: 3 l, Little blue heron. 4 l, White-tailed kite, vert. 5 l, Greater shearwater. 10 l, Magnificent frigatebird, vert. 15 l, Eared grebe, vert. 20 l, Common merganser, vert. 13r, Great-footed hawk. 14r, Greater prairie chicken.
No. 1203, White-fronted goose. No. 1204, Northern fulmar, vert.

1986, Oct. 9   Litho.   Perf. 14
1195	A167	3 l multicolored	.40	.40
1196	A167	4 l multicolored	.40	.40
1197	A167	5 l multicolored	.40	.40
1198	A167	10 l multicolored	.45	.45
1199	A167	15 l multicolored	.90	.90
1200	A167	20 l multicolored	.95	.95
1201	A167	13r multicolored	5.75	5.75
1202	A167	14r multicolored	5.75	5.75
	Nos. 1195-1202 (8)		15.00	15.00

Souvenir Sheets
1203	A167	15r multicolored	11.00	11.00
1204	A167	15r multicolored	11.00	11.00

Nos. 1197, 1199-1201 printed se-tenant with labels picturing a horned puffin, gray kingbird, downy woodpecker and water pipit, respectively.

Nos. 1176-1180 Overprinted in Gold
Overprint reads "WINNERS / Argentina 3 / W. Germany 2"

1986, Oct. 25
1205	A184	15 l multicolored	.40	.30
1206	A184	2r multicolored	1.25	1.10
1207	A184	4r multicolored	2.00	2.00
1208	A184	10r multicolored	2.75	2.75
	Nos. 1205-1208 (4)		6.40	6.15

Souvenir Sheet
1209	A184	15r multicolored	3.75	3.75

Nos. 1151-1156 Overprinted with Halley's Comet Symbol in Silver

1986, Oct. 30
1210	A181	20 l multicolored	.65	.40
1211	A181	1.50r multicolored	1.25	1.25
1212	A181	1.50r multicolored	1.50	1.50
1213	A181	4r multicolored	2.00	2.00
1214	A181	5r multicolored	2.00	2.00
	Nos. 1210-1214 (5)		7.40	7.15

Souvenir Sheet
1215	A181	15r multicolored	6.00	6.00

UNESCO, 40th Anniv. — A186

1986, Nov. 4   Perf. 15
1216	A186	1r Aviation	.75	.30
1217	A186	2r Boat-building	.90	.90
1218	A186	3r Education	1.00	1.00
1219	A186	5r Research	1.50	1.50
	Nos. 1216-1219 (4)		4.15	3.70

Souvenir Sheet
1220	A186	15r Ocean exploration	2.75	2.75

Mushrooms A187

Designs: 15 l, Hypholoma fasciculare. 50 l, Kuehneromyces mutabilis, vert. 1r, Amanita muscaria, vert. 2r, Agaricus campestris. 3r, Amanita pantherina, vert. 4r, Coprinus comatus vert. 5r, Pholiota spectabilis. 10r, Pluteus cervinus.
No. 1229, Armillaria mellea. No. 1230, Stropharia aeruginosa.

1986, Dec. 31   Litho.   Perf. 15
1221	A187	15 l multicolored	.75	.25
1222	A187	50 l multicolored	1.60	.45
1223	A187	1r multicolored	1.75	.60
1224	A187	2r multicolored	2.00	1.50
1225	A187	3r multicolored	2.00	1.75
1226	A187	4r multicolored	2.00	2.00
1227	A187	5r multicolored	2.00	2.00
1228	A187	10r multicolored	3.00	3.00
	Nos. 1221-1228 (8)		15.10	11.55

Souvenir Sheets
1229	A187	15r multicolored	6.50	6.50
1230	A187	15r multicolored	6.50	6.50

Flowers — A188

1987, Jan. 29   Litho.   Perf. 15
1231	A188	10 l Ixora	.25	.25
1232	A188	20 l Frangipani	.25	.25
1233	A188	50 l Crinum	.65	.65
1235	A188	2r Pink rose	.90	.90
1236	A188	4r Flamboyant	1.75	1.75
1238	A188	10r Ground orchid	4.75	4.75
	Nos. 1231-1238 (6)		8.15	8.15

Souvenir Sheet
1239	A188	15r Gardenia	2.75	2.75
1240	A188	15r Oleander	2.75	2.75

Girl Guides, 75th Anniv. (in 1985) — A189

1987, Apr. 4   Litho.   Perf. 15
1241	A189	15 l Nature study	.25	.25
1242	A189	2r Guides, rabbits	.65	.65
1243	A189	4r Bird-watching	2.10	2.10
1244	A189	12r Lady Baden-Powell, flag	2.40	2.40
	Nos. 1241-1244 (4)		5.40	5.40

Souvenir Sheet
1245	A189	15r Sailing	2.50	2.50

Indigenous Trees and Plants — A190

50 l, Thespesia populnea, vert. 1r, Cocos nucifera, vert. 2r, Calophyllum mophyllum, vert. 3r, Xyanthosoma indica. 5r, Ipomoea batatas. 7r, Artocarpus altilis, vert.
15r, Cocos nucifera, diff., vert.

1987, Apr. 22   Litho.   Perf. 14
1246	A190	50 l multi	.25	.25
1247	A190	1r multi	.25	.25
1248	A190	2r multi	.40	.40
1249	A190	3r multi	.60	.60
1250	A190	5r multi	1.00	1.00
1251	A190	7r multi	1.25	1.25
	Nos. 1246-1251 (6)		3.75	3.75

Souvenir Sheet
1252	A190	15r multi	2.75	2.75

A191

15 l, Intrepid, 1970. 1r, France II, 1974. 2r, Gretel, 1962. 12r, Volunteer, 1887.
15r, Defender Vs. Valkyrie III, 1895.

1987, May 4   Litho.   Perf. 15
1253	A191	15 l multi	.25	.25
1254	A191	1r multi	.25	.25
1255	A191	2r multi	.40	.40
1256	A191	12r multi	2.25	2.25
	Nos. 1253-1256 (4)		3.15	3.15

Souvenir Sheet
1257	A192	15r multi	2.75	2.75

America's Cup — A192

Butterflies — A193

15 l, Precis octavia. 20 l, Pachliopta hector. 50 l, Teinopalpus imperialis. 1r, Kallima horsfieldi. 2r, Cethosia biblis. 4r, Hestia jasonia. 7r, Papilio memnon. 10r, Meneris tulbaghia.
No. 1266, Acraea violae acraeinae. No. 1267, Hebomoia leucipe.

1987, Dec. 16   Litho.   Perf. 15
1258	A193	15 l multi	.50	.50
1259	A193	20 l multi	.50	.50
1260	A193	50 l multi	.75	.40
1261	A193	1r multi	1.00	.45
1262	A193	2r multi	1.50	1.25
1263	A193	4r multi	2.25	2.25
1264	A193	7r multi	2.75	2.75
1265	A193	10r multi	3.25	3.25
	Nos. 1258-1265 (8)		12.50	11.35

Souvenir Sheets
1266	A193	15r multi	4.50	4.50
1267	A193	15r multi	4.50	4.50

Scientists — A194

Designs: 1.50r, Sir Isaac Newton using prism to demonstrate his Theory of Light, horiz. 3r, Euclid (c. 300 B.C.), mathematician. 4r, Gregor Johann Mendel (1822-1884), botanist; father of genetics. 5r, Galileo, 1st man to observe 4 moons of Jupiter, horiz.
15r, Apollo spacecraft orbiting the moon.

1988, Jan. 10   Perf. 14
1268	A194	1.50r multicolored	1.25	1.00
1269	A194	3r multicolored	1.75	1.75
1270	A194	4r multicolored	1.75	1.75
1271	A194	5r multicolored	3.00	3.00
	Nos. 1268-1271 (4)		7.75	7.50

Souvenir Sheet
1272	A194	15r multi	5.75	5.75

Disney Characters, Space Exploration A195

3 l, Weather satellite. 4 l, Navigation satellite. 5 l, Communication satellite. 10 l, Moon rover. 20 l, Space shuttle. 13r, Space docking. 14r, Voyager 2.
No. 1280, 1st Man on Moon. No. 1281, Space station colony.

1988, Feb. 15
1273	A195	3 l multi	.25	.25
1274	A195	4 l multi	.25	.25
1275	A195	5 l multi	.25	.25
1276	A195	10 l multi	.25	.25
1277	A195	20 l multi	.25	.25
1278	A195	13r multi	5.00	5.00
1279	A195	14r multi	5.00	5.00
	Nos. 1273-1279 (7)		11.25	11.25

Souvenir Sheets
1280	A195	15r multi	6.25	6.25
1281	A195	15r multi	6.25	6.25

Nos. 1276-1278 and 1281 vert.

WHO, 40th Anniv. — A196

1988, Apr. 7   Litho.   Perf. 14
1282	A196	2r Immunization	.45	.45
1283	A196	4r Clean water	.80	.80

For overprints see Nos. 1307-1308.

World Environment Day — A197

1988, May 9   Perf. 15
1284	A197	15 l Save water	.25	.25
1285	A197	75 l Protect the reef	.25	.25
1286	A197	2r Conserve nature	.85	.85
	Nos. 1284-1286 (3)		1.35	1.35

Souvenir Sheet
1287	A197	15r Banyan tree, vert.	4.00	4.00

Nos. 1172-1175 Overprinted in Gold
Overprint reads "40th WEDDING ANNIVERSARY/ H.M. QUEEN ELIZABETH II/ H.R.H. THE DUKE OF EDINBURGH"

1988, July 7   Litho.   Perf. 14
1288	CD339	1r multicolored	.50	.25
1289	CD339	2r multicolored	.75	.55
1290	CD339	12r multicolored	3.00	3.00
	Nos. 1288-1290 (3)		4.25	3.80

Souvenir Sheet
1291	CD339	15r multicolored	4.50	4.50

Transportation and Communication Decade for Asia and the Pacific — A198

Globe and: 2r, Postal communications. 3r, Earth satellite telecommunications technology. 5r, Space telecommunications technology. 10r, Automobile, aircraft and ship.

1988, May 31   Litho.   Perf. 14
1292	A198	2r multicolored	1.25	1.25
1293	A198	3r multicolored	1.75	1.75
1294	A198	5r multicolored	2.75	2.75
1295	A198	10r multicolored	5.50	5.50
	Nos. 1292-1295 (4)		11.25	11.25

For overprints, see Nos. 1344-1345.

MALDIVE ISLANDS

1988 Summer Olympics, Seoul — A199

15 l, Discus. 2r, 100-Meter sprint. 4r, Gymnastics, horiz. 12r, Steeplechase, horiz. 20r, Tennis, horiz.

1988, July 16
1296	A199	15 l multi	.25	.25
1297	A199	2r multi	.40	.40
1298	A199	4r multi	.75	.75
1299	A199	12r multi	2.25	2.25
	Nos. 1296-1299 (4)		3.65	3.65

Souvenir Sheet
1300	A199	20r multi	4.25	4.25

For overprints see Nos. 1311-1315.

Intl. Year of Shelter for the Homeless — A200

1988, July 20
1301	A200	50 l Medical clinic	.35	.35
1302	A200	3r Prefab housing	1.10	1.10

Souvenir Sheet
1303	A200	15r Construction site	2.00	2.00

Intl. Fund for Agricultural Development (IFAD), 10th Anniv. — A201

7r, Breadfruit. 10r, Mango, vert. 15r, Coconut palm, yellowtail tuna.

1988, July 30
1304	A201	7r multi	1.00	1.00
1305	A201	10r multi	1.50	1.50

Souvenir Sheet
1306	A201	15r multi	2.75	2.75

Nos. 1282-1283 Ovptd.

1988, Dec. 1   Litho.   Perf. 14
1307	A196	2r multicolored	.35	.35
1308	A196	4r multicolored	.65	.65

Intl. Day for the Fight Against Aids.

John F. Kennedy (1917-1963), 35th US President — A202

Space achievements: a, Apollo launch. b, 1st Man on the Moon. c, Earth and astronaut driving moon rover. d, Space module and Kennedy.
15r, Kennedy addressing the nation.

1989, Feb. 19
1309	A202	Strip of 4	9.00	9.00
a.-d.		5r any single	2.00	2.00

Souvenir Sheet
1310	A202	15r multicolored	4.00	4.00

No. 1296 Overprinted

No. 1297 Overprinted

No. 1298 Overprinted

No. 1299 Overprinted

No. 1300 Overprinted

1989, Apr. 29   Litho.   Perf. 14
1311	A199	15 l multicolored	.25	.25
1312	A199	2r multicolored	.65	.65
1313	A199	4r multicolored	1.40	1.40
1314	A199	12r multicolored	4.00	4.00
	Nos. 1311-1314 (4)		6.30	6.30

Souvenir Sheet
1315	A199	20r multi	6.50	6.50

Paintings by Titian (b. 1489) — A203

Designs: 15 l, Portrait of Benedetto Varchi, c. 1540. 1r, Portrait of a Young Man in a Fur, 1515. 2r, King Francis I of France, 1538. 5r, Portrait of Pietro Aretino, 1545. 15r, The Bravo, c. 1520. 20r, The Concert, 1512.
No. 1322, An Allegory of Prudence, c. 1565. No. 1323, Portrait of Francesco Maria Della Rovere.

1989, May 15   Litho.   Perf. 13½x14
1316	A203	15 l multicolored	.25	.25
1317	A203	1r multicolored	.25	.25
1318	A203	2r multicolored	.50	.50
1319	A203	5r multicolored	1.25	1.25
1320	A203	15r multicolored	4.00	4.00
1321	A203	20r multicolored	4.00	4.00
	Nos. 1316-1321 (6)		10.25	10.25

Souvenir Sheets
1322	A203	20r multicolored	4.25	4.25
1323	A203	20r multicolored	4.25	4.25

"Thirty-six Views of Mt. Fuji" — A204

Prints by Hokusai (1760-1849): 15 l, Fuji from Hodogaya. 50 l, Fuji from Lake Kawaguchi. 1r, Fuji from Owari. 2r, Fuji from Tsukudajima in Edo. 4r, Fuji from a Teahouse at Yoshida. 6r, Fuji from Tagonoura. 10r, Fuji from Mishima-goe. 12r, Fuji from the Sumida River in Edo.
No. 1332, Fuji from Fukagawa in Edo. No. 1333, Fuji from Inume Pass.

1989   Perf. 14
1324	A204	15 l multicolored	.25	.25
1325	A204	50 l multicolored	.25	.25
1326	A204	1r multicolored	.25	.25
1327	A204	2r multicolored	.50	.40
1328	A204	4r multicolored	.80	.80
1329	A204	6r multicolored	1.00	1.00
1330	A204	10r multicolored	2.25	2.25
1331	A204	12r multicolored	2.25	2.25
	Nos. 1324-1331 (8)		7.55	7.45

Souvenir Sheets
1332	A204	18r multicolored	4.25	4.25
1333	A204	18r multicolored	4.25	4.25

Hirohito (1901-1989) and enthronement of Akihito as emperor of Japan.
Issue dates: No. 1332, 10/16, others, 9/2.

Tropical Fish — A205

Designs: 20 l, Clown triggerfish. 50 l, Blue surgeonfish. 1r, Bluestripe snapper. 2r, Oriental sweetlips. 3r, Wrasse. 8r, Treadfin butterflyfish. 10r, Bicolor parrotfish. 12r, Saber squirrelfish.
No. 1342, Butterfly perch. No. 1343, Semicircle angelfish.

1989, Oct. 16   Litho.   Perf. 14
1334	A205	20 l multicolored	.25	.25
1335	A205	50 l multicolored	.40	.25
1336	A205	1r multicolored	.50	.30
1337	A205	2r multicolored	.70	.70
1338	A205	3r multicolored	.90	.90
1339	A205	8r multicolored	1.60	1.60
1340	A205	10r multicolored	2.00	2.00
1341	A205	12r multicolored	2.00	2.00
	Nos. 1334-1341 (8)		8.35	8.00

Souvenir Sheet
1342	A205	15r multicolored	6.50	6.50
1343	A205	15r multicolored	6.50	6.50

Nos. 1293-1294 Overprinted in Silver

1989, July 5   Litho.   Perf. 14
1344	A198	3r multicolored	1.25	1.25
1345	A198	5r multicolored	2.25	2.25

World Stamp Expo '89 Emblem, Disney Characters and Japanese Automobiles A206

Designs: 15 l, 1907 Takuri Type 3. 50 l, 1917 Mitsubishi Model A. 1r, 1935 Datsun Roadstar. 2r, 1940 Mazda. 4r, 1959 Nissan Bluebird 310. 6r, 1958 Subaru 360. 10r, 1966 Honda 5800. 12r, 1966 Daihatsu Fellow.
No. 1354, 1981 Isuzu Trooper II. No. 1355, 1985 Toyota Supra.

1989, Nov. 17   Litho.   Perf. 14x13½
1346	A206	15 l multicolored	.25	.25
1347	A206	50 l multicolored	.40	.30
1348	A206	1r multicolored	.70	.50
1349	A206	2r multicolored	1.00	.75
1350	A206	4r multicolored	1.50	1.25
1351	A206	6r multicolored	1.75	1.75
1352	A206	10r multicolored	3.25	3.25
1353	A206	12r multicolored	3.75	3.75
	Nos. 1346-1353 (8)		12.60	11.80

Souvenir Sheets
1354	A206	20r multicolored	5.50	5.50
1355	A206	20r multicolored	5.50	5.50

The Marine Corps War Memorial, Arlington, VA — A207

1989, Nov. 17   Litho.   Perf. 14
1356	A207	8r multicolored	2.75	2.75

World Stamp Expo '89.

1st Moon Landing, 20th Anniv. — A208

Designs: 1r, *Eagle* lunar module. 2r, Aldrin setting up solar wind experiment. 6r, Seismic experiment. 10r, Nixon, astronauts.
18r, Armstrong descending ladder.

1989, Nov. 24   Perf. 14
1357	A208	1r multicolored	.30	.30
1358	A208	2r multicolored	.50	.50
1359	A208	6r multicolored	1.25	1.25
1360	A208	10r multicolored	2.00	2.00
	Nos. 1357-1360 (4)		4.05	4.05

Souvenir Sheet
1361	A208	18r multicolored	7.50	7.50

Railway Pioneers — A209

Designs: 10 l, Sir William Cornelius Van Horne (1843-1915), chairman of Canadian Pacific Railway, map and locomotive, 1894. 25 l, Matthew Murray, built rack locomotives for Middleton Colliery. 50 l, Louis Favre (1826-1879), built the St. Gotthard (spiral) Tunnel, 1881. 2r, George Stephenson (1781-1848), locomotive, 1825. 6r, Richard Trevithick (1771-1833), builder of 1st rail locomotive, 1804. 8r, George Nagelmackers, Orient Express dining car, 1869. 10r, William Jessop, Surrey horse-drawn cart on rails, 1770. 12r, Isambard Kingdom Brunel (1806-1859), chief engineer of Great Western Railway, introduced standard gauge, 1830's.
No. 1370, George Pullman (1831-1897), *Pioneer* passenger car. No. 1371, Rudolf Diesel (1858-1913), inventor of the diesel engine, 1892, and diesel train.

1989, Dec. 26   Litho.   Perf. 14
1362	A209	10 l multicolored	.25	.25
1363	A209	25 l multicolored	.35	.25
1364	A209	50 l multicolored	.40	.25
1365	A209	2r multicolored	.75	.55
1366	A209	6r multicolored	1.50	1.50
1367	A209	8r multicolored	1.75	1.75
1368	A209	10r multicolored	2.50	2.50
1369	A209	12r multicolored	3.00	3.00
	Nos. 1362-1369 (8)		10.50	10.05

Souvenir Sheets
1370	A209	18r multicolored	5.00	5.00
1371	A209	18r multicolored	5.00	5.00

Anniversaries and Events (in 1989) — A210

Designs: 20 l, Flag of India, Jawaharlal Nehru, Mahatma Gandhi. 50 l, Syringe, opium poppies, vert. 1r, William Shakespeare, birthplace, Stratford-on-Avon. 2r, Flag of France, storming of the Bastille, Paris, 1789, vert. 3r, Concorde jet, flags of France, Britain. 8r, George Washington, Mount Vernon estate,

MALDIVE ISLANDS

Virginia. 10r, Capt. William Bligh, the *Bounty*. 12r, Ships in port.
No. 1380, 1st Televised baseball game, 1939, vert. No. 1381, Franz von Taxis (1458-1517), vert.

1990, Feb. 15		Litho.	Perf. 14	
1372	A210	20 l multicolored	.25	.25
1373	A210	50 l multicolored	.25	.25
1374	A210	1r multicolored	.60	.60
1375	A210	2r multicolored	1.10	1.10
1376	A210	3r multicolored	1.75	1.75
1377	A210	8r multicolored	5.50	5.50
1378	A210	10r multicolored	7.00	7.00
1379	A210	12r multicolored	8.50	8.50
		Nos. 1372-1379 (8)	24.95	24.95

Souvenir Sheets

1380	A210	18r multicolored	7.00	7.00
1381	A210	18r multicolored	7.00	7.00

Birth cent. of Nehru (20 l); SAARC Year for Combatting Drug Abuse (50 l); 425th birth anniv. of Shakespeare (1r); French Revolution, bicent. (2r); first test flight of the Concorde supersonic jet, 20th anniv. (3r); American presidency, bicent. (8r); Mutiny on the *Bounty*, bicent. (10r); Hamburg, 800th anniv. (12r); 1st televised baseball game, 50th anniv. (No. 1380); and European postal communications, 500th anniv. (No. 1381).

Johann von Taxis was the first postmaster of Thurn & Taxis in 1489, not Franz, who is credited on No. 1381.

Natl. Independence, 25th Anniv. — A211

Designs: 20 l, Bodu Thakurufaanu Memorial Center, Utheemu. 25 l, Islamic Center, Male. 50 l, Natl. flag, UN, Islamic Conf., Commonwealth and SAARC emblems. 2r, Muleeaage, Male. 5r, Natl. Security Service, Maldives. 10r, Natl. crest, emblem of the Citizens' Majlis (parliament).

1990, Jan. 1		Litho.	Perf. 14	
1382	A211	20 l multicolored	.25	.25
1383	A211	25 l multicolored	.25	.25
1384	A211	50 l multicolored	.25	.25
1385	A211	2r multicolored	.30	.30
1386	A211	5r multicolored	.90	.90
		Nos. 1382-1386 (5)	1.95	1.95

Souvenir Sheet

1387	A211	10r multicolored	4.25	4.25

French Revolution, Bicent. (in 1989) — A212

Paintings: 15 l, *Louis XVI in Coronation Robes*, by Duplessis. 50 l, *Monsieur Lavoisier and His Wife*, by David. 1r, *Madame Pastoret*, by David. 2r, *Oath of Lafayette at the Festival of Federation*, by David. 4r, *Madame Trudaine*, by David. 6r, *Chenard Celebrating the Liberation of Savoy*, by Boilly. 10r, *An Officer Swears Allegiance to the Constitution*, artist unknown. 12r, *Self-portrait*, by David.
No. 1396, *The Tennis Court Oath, June 20, 1789*, by David, horiz. No. 1397, *Jean-Jacques Rousseau and the Symbols of the Revolution*, by Jeaurat.

1990, Jan. 11		Litho.	Perf. 14	
1388	A212	15 l multicolored	.25	.25
1389	A212	50 l multicolored	.45	.25
1390	A212	1r multicolored	.65	.35
1391	A212	2r multicolored	1.00	.70
1392	A212	4r multicolored	1.75	1.50
1393	A212	6r multicolored	2.40	2.40
1394	A212	10r multicolored	4.00	4.00
1395	A212	12r multicolored	4.00	4.00
		Nos. 1388-1395 (8)	14.50	13.45

Souvenir Sheets

1396	A212	20r multicolored	6.50	6.50
1397	A212	20r multicolored	6.50	6.50

Stamp World London '90 — A213

Walt Disney characters demonstrating sports popular in Britain: 15 l, Rugby. 50 l, Curling. 1r, Polo. 2r, Soccer. 4r, Cricket. 6r, Horse racing, Ascot. 10r, Tennis. 12r, Lawn bowling.
No. 1406, Fox hunting. No. 1407, Golf, St. Andrews, Scotland.

1990		Litho.	Perf. 14x13½	
1398	A213	15 l multicolored	.30	.25
1399	A213	50 l multicolored	.45	.25
1400	A213	1r multicolored	.65	.40
1401	A213	2r multicolored	.90	.75
1402	A213	4r multicolored	1.75	1.50
1403	A213	6r multicolored	2.25	2.00
1404	A213	10r multicolored	3.50	3.50
1405	A213	12r multicolored	3.50	3.50
		Nos. 1398-1405 (8)	13.30	12.15

Souvenir Sheets

1406	A213	20r multicolored	7.50	7.50
1407	A213	20r multicolored	7.50	7.50

Penny Black, 150th Anniv. — A214

1990, May 3		Litho.	Perf. 15x14	
1408	A214	8r Silhouettes	2.25	2.25
1409	A214	12r Silhouettes, diff.	2.50	2.50

Souvenir Sheet

1410	A214	18r Penny Black	5.00	5.00

Queen Mother 90th Birthday
A215   A216

No. 1413, As Lady Bowes-Lyon, diff.
No. 1414, On Wedding Day, diff.

1990, July 8			Perf. 14	
1411	A215	6r shown	1.00	1.00
1412	A216	6r shown	1.00	1.00
1413	A215	6r multi	1.00	1.00
		Nos. 1411-1413 (3)	3.00	3.00

Souvenir Sheet

1414	A216	18r multi	3.00	3.00

Nos. 1411-1413 printed in sheets of 9.

A217
A218
A219

Islamic Heritage Year — A220

1990, July 22		Litho.	Perf. 14	
1415	A217	1r blue & black	.35	.35
1416	A218	1r blue & black	.35	.35
1417	A218	1r Building, diff.	.35	.35
1418	A219	2r blue & black	.45	.45
1419	A220	2r blue & black	.45	.45
1420	A219	2r Building, diff.	.45	.45
	a.	Block of 6, #1415-1420	2.50	2.50

Great Crested Tern — A221

Design: 25 l, Great Crested Tern. 50 l, Koel. 1r, White tern. 3.50r, Cinnamon bittern. 6r, Sooty tern. 8r, Audubon's shearwater. 12r, Brown noddy. 15r, Lesser frigatebird.
No. 1429, White-tailed tropicbird. No. 1430, Grey heron.

1990, Aug. 9		Litho.	Perf. 14	
1421	A221	25 l multicolored	.25	.25
1422	A221	50 l multicolored	.25	.25
1423	A221	1r multicolored	.35	.35
1424	A221	3.50r multicolored	.90	.90
1425	A221	6r multicolored	1.40	1.40
1426	A221	8r multicolored	1.60	1.60
1427	A221	12r multicolored	2.50	2.50
1428	A221	15r multicolored	2.75	2.75
		Nos. 1421-1428 (8)	10.00	10.00

Souvenir Sheets

1429	A221	18r multicolored	4.50	4.50
1430	A221	18r multicolored	4.50	4.50

World War II Milestones A222

Designs: 15 l, US Marines repulse Japanese invasion of Wake Island, Dec. 11, 1941. 25 l, Gen. Stilwell begins offensive in Burma, Mar. 4, 1944. 50 l, US begins offensive in Normandy, July 3, 1944. 1r, US forces secure Saipan, July 9, 1944. 2.50r, D-Day, June 6, 1944. 3.50r, Allied forces land in Norway, Apr. 14, 1940. 4r, Adm. Mountbatten named Chief of Combined Operations, Mar. 18, 1942. 6r, Gen. MacArthur accepts Japanese surrender, Sept. 2, 1945. 10r, Potsdam Conference, July 16, 1945. 12r, Allied invade Sicily, July 10, 1943. 18r, Atlantic convoys.

1990, Aug. 9		Litho.	Perf. 14	
1431	A222	15 l multicolored	.25	.25
1432	A222	25 l multicolored	.30	.25
1433	A222	50 l multicolored	.40	.25
1434	A222	1r multicolored	.55	.40
1435	A222	2.50r multicolored	.90	.80
1436	A222	3.50r multicolored	1.10	1.10
1437	A222	4r multicolored	1.40	1.40
1438	A222	6r multicolored	2.75	2.75
1439	A222	10r multicolored	2.75	2.75
1440	A222	12r multicolored	3.00	3.00
		Nos. 1431-1440 (10)	13.40	12.95

Souvenir Sheet

1441	A222	18r multicolored	5.50	5.50

5th SAARC Summit A224

Designs: 75 l, Satellite communications. 3.50r, Flags. 20r, Map.

1990, Nov. 21		Litho.	Perf. 14	
1442	A223	75 l multicolored	.30	.30
1443	A223	3.50r multicolored	1.75	1.50

Souvenir Sheet

1444	A224	20r multicolored	5.50	5.50

Flowers — A225

Designs: 20l, Spathoglottis plicata. 75 l, Hippeastrum puniceum. 2r, Tecoma stans. 3.50r, Catharanthus roseus. 10r, Ixora coccinea. 12r,

Clitoria ternatea. 15r, Caesalpinia pulcherrima.
No. 1452, Rosa sp. No. 1453, Plumeria obtusa. No. 1454, Jasminum grandiflorum. No. 1455, Hibiscus tiliaceous.

1990, Dec. 9		Litho.	Perf. 14	
1445	A225	20 l multicolored	.25	.25
1446	A225	75 l multicolored	.25	.25
1447	A225	2r multicolored	.65	.65
1448	A225	3.50r multicolored	1.10	1.10
1449	A225	10r multicolored	3.25	3.25
1450	A225	12r multicolored	4.00	4.00
1451	A225	15r multicolored	4.75	4.75
		Nos. 1445-1451 (7)	14.25	14.25

Souvenir Sheets

1452	A225	20r multicolored	3.50	3.50
1453	A225	20r multicolored	3.50	3.50
1454	A225	20r multicolored	3.50	3.50
1455	A225	20r multicolored	3.50	3.50

Expo '90, Intl. Garden and Greenery Exposition, Osaka, Japan.
2r, 3.50r, 10r, 12r are horiz.

Bonsai — A226

Designs: 20 l, Winged Euonymus. 50 l, Japanese black pine. 1r, Japanese five needle pine. 3.50r, Flowering quince. 5r, Chinese elm. 8r, Japanese persimmon. 10r, Japanese wisteria. 12r, Satsuki azalea.
No. 1464, Sargent juniper. No. 1465, Trident maple.

1990-91

1456	A226	20 l multicolored	.25	.25
1457	A226	50 l multicolored	.25	.25
1458	A226	1r multicolored	.30	.30
1459	A226	3.50r multicolored	1.25	1.25
1460	A226	5r multicolored	1.50	1.50
1461	A226	8r multicolored	2.50	2.50
1462	A226	10r multicolored	3.00	3.00
1463	A226	12r multicolored	3.75	3.75
		Nos. 1456-1463 (8)	12.80	12.80

Souvenir Sheets

1464	A226	20r multicolored	6.00	6.00
1465	A226	20r multicolored	6.00	6.00

Expo '90, Intl. Garden and Greenery Exposition, Osaka, Japan.
Issued: 50 l, 1r, 8r, 10r, No. 1464, 12/9/90; 20 l, 3.50r, 5r, 12r, No. 1465, 1/29/91.

Aesop's Fables A227

Walt Disney characters: 15 l, Tortoise and the Hare. 50 l, Town Mouse and Country Mouse. 1r, Fox and the Crow. 3.50r, Travellers and the Bear. 4r, Fox and the Lion. 6r, Mice and the Cat. 10r, Fox and the Goat. 12r, Dog in the Manger.
No. 1474, Miller, his Son and the Ass, vert. No. 1475, Miser's Gold, vert.

1990, Dec. 11		Litho.	Perf. 14	
1466	A227	15 l multicolored	.25	.25
1467	A227	50 l multicolored	.25	.25
1468	A227	1r multicolored	.35	.35
1469	A227	3.50r multicolored	1.25	1.25
1470	A227	4r multicolored	1.50	1.50
1471	A227	6r multicolored	2.00	2.00
1472	A227	10r multicolored	3.50	3.50
1473	A227	12r multicolored	4.00	4.00
		Nos. 1466-1473 (8)	13.10	13.10

Souvenir Sheets

1474	A227	20r multicolored	6.50	6.50
1475	A227	20r multicolored	6.50	6.50

Intl. Literacy Year.

A228

MALDIVE ISLANDS

Steam Locomotives: 20 l, "31" Class, East African Railways. 50 l, Mikado, Sudan Railways. 1r, Beyer-Garratt GM Class, South African Railways. 3r, "7th" Class, Rhodesia Railways. 5r, Central Pacific 229. 8r, Reading 415. 10r, Porter Narrow-guage. 12r, Great Northern 515.

No. 1484, American Standard 315. No. 1485, East African Railways 5950.

1990, Dec. 15

1476	A228	20 l multicolored	.25	.25
1477	A228	50 l multicolored	.25	.25
1478	A228	1r multicolored	.40	.40
1479	A228	3r multicolored	1.25	1.25
1480	A228	5r multicolored	2.00	2.00
1481	A228	8r multicolored	3.25	3.25
1482	A228	10r multicolored	4.00	4.00
1483	A228	12r multicolored	4.75	4.75
		Nos. 1476-1483 (8)	16.15	16.15

Souvenir Sheets

1484	A228	20r multicolored	8.25	8.25
1485	A228	20r multicolored	8.25	8.25

A229

Various players from participating countries: 1r, Holland. 2.50r, England. 3.50r, Argentina. 5r, Brazil. 7r, Italy. 10r, Russia. 15r, West Germany.

No. 1490, Austria. No. 1491, South Korea. No. 1492, Italy (dk blue shirt). No. 1493, Argentina (blue & white shirt).

1990, Dec. 27

1486	A229	1r multicolored	.40	.40
1487	A229	2.50r multicolored	1.00	1.00
1487A	A229	3.50r multicolored	1.60	1.60
1488	A229	5r multicolored	2.10	2.10
1488A	A229	7r multicolored	2.75	2.75
1489	A229	10r multicolored	4.25	4.25
1489A	A229	15r multicolored	6.25	6.25
		Nos. 1486-1489A (7)	18.35	18.35

Souvenir Sheets

1490	A229	18r multicolored	4.50	4.50
1491	A229	18r multicolored	4.50	4.50
1492	A229	20r multicolored	4.50	4.50
1493	A229	20r multicolored	4.50	4.50

World Cup Soccer Championships, Italy.

Nos. 1110 and 1111 Surcharged

No. 1493B

Methods and Perfs As Before

1990

1493A	A171	3.50r on 2.60r #1110	—	—
1493B	A171	3.50r on 2.70r #1111	—	—

Peter Paul Rubens (1577-1640), Painter — A230

Entire works or details from paintings by Rubens: 20 l, Summer. 50 l, Landscape with Rainbow. 1r, Wreckage of Aeneas. 2.50r, Chateau de Steen. 3.50r, Landscape with Herd of Cows. 7r, Ruins of Palantine. 10r, Landscape with Peasants and Cows. 12r, Wagon Fording a Stream.

No. 1502, Landscape with a Sunset. No. 1503, Peasants with Cattle by a Stream in a Woody Landscape. No. 1504, Shepherd with his Flock in a Wooded Landscape. No. 1505, Stuck Wagon.

1991, Feb. 7   Litho.   Perf. 14x13½

1494	A230	20 l multicolored	.25	.25
1495	A230	50 l multicolored	.25	.25
1496	A230	1r multicolored	.35	.35
1497	A230	2.50r multicolored	.80	.80
1498	A230	3.50r multicolored	1.10	1.10
1499	A230	7r multicolored	2.10	2.10
1500	A230	10r multicolored	3.25	3.25
1501	A230	12r multicolored	3.75	3.75
		Nos. 1494-1501 (8)	11.85	11.85

Souvenir Sheets

1502-1505	A230	20r each	4.75	4.75

First Marathon Run, 490 B.C. — A231

Events and anniversaries (in 1990): 1r, Anthony Fokker (1890-1939), aircraft builder. 3.50r, Launch of first commercial satellite, 25th anniv. 7r, East, West German foreign ministers sign re-unification documents, Oct. 3, 1990, horiz. 8r, Magna Carta, 775th anniv. 10r, Dwight D. Eisenhower. 12r, Winston Churchill. 15r, Pres. Reagan destroying Berlin Wall, horiz.

No. 1514, Brandenburg Gate, horiz. No. 1515, Battle of Britain, 50th anniv., horiz.

1991, Mar. 11   Perf. 14

1506	A231	50 l multicolored	.45	.25
1507	A231	1r multicolored	1.00	.45
1508	A231	3.50r multicolored	1.50	1.50
1509	A231	7r multicolored	1.75	1.75
1510	A231	8r multicolored	2.50	2.50
1511	A231	10r multicolored	2.25	2.25
1512	A231	12r multicolored	5.00	4.00
1513	A231	15r multicolored	3.00	3.00
		Nos. 1506-1513 (8)	17.45	15.70

Souvenir Sheets

1514	A231	20r multicolored	7.00	7.00
1515	A231	20r multicolored	7.00	7.00

Global Warming — A232

1991, Apr. 10

1516	A232	3.50r Dhoni	2.00	1.25
1517	A232	7r Freighter	3.50	3.50

Year of the Girl Child — A233

1991, Apr. 14

1518	A233	7r multicolored	2.25	2.25

Year of the Child — A234

Children's drawings: 3.50r, Beach scene. 5r, City scene. 10r, Visualizing fruit. 25r, Scuba diver.

1991, May 10

1519	A234	3.50r multicolored	1.25	1.25
1520	A234	5r multicolored	1.90	1.90
1521	A234	10r multicolored	3.75	3.75
1522	A234	25r multicolored	8.50	8.50
		Nos. 1519-1522 (4)	15.40	15.40

Paintings by Vincent Van Gogh — A235

Designs: 15 l, Japanese Vase with Roses and Anemones, vert. 20 l, Still Life: Red Poppies and Daisies, vert. 2r, Vincent's Bedroom in Arles. 3.50r, The Mulberry Tree. 7r, Blossoming Chestnut Branches. 10r, Morning: Peasant Couple Going to Work. 12r, Still Life: Pink Roses. 15r, Child with Orange, vert.

No. 1531, Courtyard of the Hospital at Arles. No. 1532, Houses in Auvers, vert.

1991, June 6   Litho.   Perf. 13½

1523	A235	15 l multicolored	.30	.30
1524	A235	20 l multicolored	.30	.30
1525	A235	2r multicolored	.75	.75
1526	A235	3.50r multicolored	1.40	1.40
1527	A235	7r multicolored	2.75	2.75
1528	A235	10r multicolored	4.00	4.00
1529	A235	12r multicolored	4.50	4.50
1530	A235	15r multicolored	5.75	5.75
		Nos. 1523-1530 (8)	19.75	19.75

Sizes: 100x75mm, 75x100mm

Imperf

1531	A235	25r multicolored	7.00	7.00
1532	A235	25r multicolored	7.00	7.00

Royal Family Birthday, Anniversary Common Design Type

1r, 3.50r, 7r, 15r, No. 1542, Charles and Diana, 10th wedding anniversary. 2r, 5r, 8r, 12r, Queen Elizabeth II, 65th birthday. No. 1541, Elizabeth, Philip. No. 1542, Charles, Diana, sons.

1991, July 4   Litho.   Perf. 14

1533	CD347	1r multi	.30	.30
1534	CD347	2r multi	.60	.60
1535	CD347	3.50r multi	1.10	1.10
1536	CD347	5r multi	1.50	1.50
1537	CD347	7r multi	2.10	2.10
1538	CD347	8r multi	2.50	2.50
1539	CD347	12r multi	3.75	3.75
1540	CD347	15r multi	4.25	4.25
		Nos. 1533-1540 (8)	16.10	16.10

Souvenir Sheets

1541	CD347	25r multi	5.75	5.75
1542	CD347	25r multi	6.25	6.25

Hummel Figurines — A236

Designs: 10 l, No. 1552a, Child painting. 25 l, No. 1552b, Boy reading at table. 50 l, No. 1552c, Boy with back pack. 2r, No. 1551a, School Girl. 3.50r, No. 1551b, The Bookworm (boy sitting and reading). 8r, No. 1551c, Little Brother's Lesson. 10r, No. 1551d, School Girls. 25r, No. 1552d, Three school boys.

1991, July 25   Litho.   Perf. 14

1543	A236	10 l multicolored	.25	.25
1544	A236	25 l multicolored	.25	.25
1545	A236	50 l multicolored	.30	.25
1546	A236	2r multicolored	.60	.60
1547	A236	3.50r multicolored	1.00	1.00
1548	A236	8r multicolored	2.25	2.25
1549	A236	10r multicolored	2.25	2.25
1550	A236	25r multicolored	4.75	4.75
		Nos. 1543-1550 (8)	11.65	11.60

Souvenir Sheets

1551	A236	5r Sheet of 4, #a.-d.	3.50	3.50
1552	A236	8r Sheet of 4, #a.-d.	5.50	5.50

Japanese Steam Locomotives A237

1991, Aug. 25   Litho.   Perf. 14

1553	A237	15 l C 57, vert.	.50	.25
1554	A237	25 l Series 6250	.75	.30
1555	A237	1r D 51, vert.	1.25	.40
1556	A237	3.50r Series 8620	2.00	1.25
1557	A237	5r Class 10	2.25	1.75
1558	A237	7r C 61, vert.	2.50	2.50
1559	A237	10r Series 9600	2.50	2.50
1560	A237	12r D 52	2.75	2.75
		Nos. 1553-1560 (8)	14.50	11.70

Souvenir Sheets

1561	A237	20r Class 1080	4.00	4.00
1562	A237	20r C 56	4.00	4.00

Phila Nippon '91.

Butterflies A238

10 l, Blue salamis. 25 l, Mountain beauty. 50 l, Lucerne blue. 2r, Monarch. 3.50r, Common rose. 5r, Black witch. 8r, Oriental swallowtail. 10r, Gaudy commodore.

No. 1571, Pearl crescent. No. 1572, Friar.

1991, Dec. 2   Litho.   Perf. 14

1563	A238	10 l multi	.40	.40
1564	A238	25 l multi	.55	.55
1565	A238	50 l multi	.75	.75
1566	A238	2r multi	1.25	1.25
1567	A238	3.50r multi	1.75	1.75
1568	A238	5r multi	2.00	2.00
1569	A238	8r multi	2.50	2.50
1570	A238	12r multi	2.50	2.50
		Nos. 1563-1570 (8)	11.70	11.70

Souvenir Sheets

1571	A238	20r multi	5.00	5.00
1572	A238	20r multi	5.00	5.00

No. 1570 inscribed "guady."

Japanese Space Program A239

Designs: 15 l, H-11 Launch Vehicle. 20 l, H-II Orbiting plane. 2r, Geosynchronous satellite 5. 3.50r, Marine observation satellite-1. 7r, Communications satellite 3. 10r, Broadcasting satellite-2. 12r, H-1 Launch Vehicle, vert. 15r, Space flier unit, space shuttle.

No. 1581, Katsura tracking and data acquisition station. No. 1582, M-3S II Launch vehicle, vert.

1991, Dec. 11

1573	A239	15 l multicolored	.50	.30
1574	A239	20 l multicolored	.50	.30
1575	A239	2r multicolored	1.25	.75
1576	A239	3.50r multicolored	1.60	1.40
1577	A239	7r multicolored	2.40	2.40
1578	A239	10r multicolored	2.75	2.75
1579	A239	12r multicolored	3.00	3.00
1580	A239	15r multicolored	3.00	3.00
		Nos. 1573-1580 (8)	15.00	13.90

Souvenir Sheets

1581	A239	20r multicolored	6.50	6.50
1582	A239	20r multicolored	6.50	6.50

Miniature Sheet

World War II Leaders of the Pacific Theater — A240

a, Franklin D. Roosevelt. b, Douglas MacArthur. c, Chester Nimitz. d, Jonathan Wainwright. e, Ernest King. f, Claire Chennault. g, William Halsey. h, Marc Mitscher. i, James Doolittle. j, Raymond Spruance.

1991, Dec. 30   Litho.   Perf. 14½x15

1583	A240	3.50r Sheet of 10, #a.-j.	16.00	16.00

Grand Prix Race Cars — A241

Designs: 20 l, Williams FW-07. 50 l, Brabham BT50 BMW Turbo. 1r, Williams FW-11 Honda. 3.50r, Ferrari 312 T3. 5r, Lotus Honda 99T. 7r, Benetton Ford B188. 10r, Tyrrell P34 Six-wheeler. 21r, Renault RE-30B Turbo.

No. 1592, Ferrari F189. No. 1593, Brabham BT50 BMW Turbo, diff.

1991, Dec. 28   Litho.   Perf. 14

1584	A241	20 l multicolored	.25	.25
1585	A241	50 l multicolored	.45	.30
1586	A241	1r multicolored	.60	.40
1587	A241	3.50r multicolored	1.25	1.25
1588	A241	5r multicolored	1.75	1.75
1589	A241	7r multicolored	2.00	2.00
1590	A241	10r multicolored	2.25	2.25
1591	A241	21r multicolored	4.00	4.00
		Nos. 1584-1591 (8)	12.55	12.20

Souvenir Sheets

1592	A241	25r multicolored	7.75	7.75
1593	A241	25r multicolored	7.75	7.75

MALDIVE ISLANDS

Miniature Sheet

Enzo Ferrari (1898-1988) — A242

Ferrari Race cars: a, 1957 Testa Rossa. b, 1966 275GTB. c, 1951 "Aspirarta." d, Testarossa. f, 1958 Dino 246. g, 1952 Type 375. h, Mansell's Formula One. i, 1975 312T.

1991, Dec. 28
| 1594 | A242 | 5r Sheet of 9, #a.-i. | 16.00 | 16.00 |

17th World Scout Jamboree — A243

Designs: 10r, Scouts diving on reef. 11r, Hand making scout sign, emblem, vert. 18r, Lord Robert Baden-Powell, vert. 20r, Czechoslovakian scout (local) stamp, vert.

1991, Dec. 30
| 1595 | A243 | 10r multicolored | 2.50 | 2.50 |
| 1596 | A243 | 11r multicolored | 2.50 | 2.50 |

Souvenir Sheets
| 1597 | A243 | 18r multicolored | 3.00 | 3.00 |
| 1598 | A243 | 20r multicolored | 3.00 | 3.00 |

Wolfgang Amadeus Mozart, Death Bicent — A244

Portrait of Mozart and: 50 l, Schwarzenberg Palace. 1r, Spa at Baden. 2r, Royal Palace, Berlin. 5r, Viennese Masonic seal. 7r, St. Marx. No. 1604, Josephsplatz, Vienna. No. 1605, Bust of Mozart, vert.

1991, Dec. 30
1599	A244	50 l multicolored	.25	.25
1600	A244	1r multicolored	.25	.25
1601	A244	2r multicolored	.55	.55
1602	A244	5r multicolored	1.25	1.25
1603	A244	7r multicolored	1.75	1.75
1604	A244	20r multicolored	5.00	5.00
		Nos. 1599-1604 (6)	9.05	9.05

Souvenir Sheet
| 1605 | A244 | 20r multicolored | 4.00 | 4.00 |

Brandenburg Gate, Bicent. — A245

Designs: 20 l, Flag. 1.75 l, Man embracing child, Berlin wall. 4r, Soldiers behind barricade, demonstrator. 15r, World War I Iron Cross. No. 1610, Helmet. No. 1611, 1939 helmet. No. 1612, Studded helmet.

1991, Dec. 30
1606	A245	20 l multicolored	.25	.25
1607	A245	1.75r multicolored	.45	.45
1608	A245	4r multicolored	1.00	1.00
1609	A245	15r multicolored	3.25	3.25
		Nos. 1606-1609 (4)	4.95	4.95

Souvenir Sheets
1610	A245	18r multicolored	3.50	3.50
1611	A245	18r multicolored	3.50	3.50
1612	A245	18r multicolored	3.50	3.50

Anniversaries and Events — A246

Designs: No. 1613, Otto Lilienthal, glider No. 16. No. 1614, "D-Day," Normandy 1944, Charles de Gaulle. 7r, Front of locomotive, vert. 8r, Kurt Schwitters, artist and Landesmuseum. 9r, Map, man in Swiss costume. 10r, Charles de Gaulle in Madagascar, 1958. 12r, Steam locomotive. 15r, Portrait of Charles de Gaulle, vert. 20r, Locomotive and coal car.

1991, Dec. 30   Litho.   Perf. 14
1613	A246	6r multicolored	2.25	2.25
1614	A246	6r multicolored	1.75	1.75
1615	A246	7r multicolored	2.00	2.00
1616	A246	8r multicolored	2.25	2.25
1617	A246	9r multicolored	2.50	2.50
1618	A246	10r multicolored	2.75	2.75
1619	A246	12r multicolored	3.25	3.25
		Nos. 1613-1619 (7)	16.75	16.75

Souvenir Sheets
| 1620 | A246 | 15r multicolored | 3.50 | 3.50 |
| 1621 | A246 | 20r multicolored | 4.00 | 4.00 |

First glider flight, cent. (No. 1613). Charles de Gaulle, birth cent. in 1990 (Nos. 1614, 1618, & 1620). Trans-Siberian Railway, cent. (Nos. 1615, 1619 & 1621). Hanover, 750th anniv. (#1616). Swiss Confederation, 700th anniv. (No. 1617).

No. 1621 contains one 58x43mm stamp.

Birds — A247

Designs: 10 l, Numenius phaeopus. 25 l, Egretta alba. 50 l, Ardea cinerea. 2r, Phalacrocorax aristotelis. 3.50r, Sterna dougallii. 5r, Tringa nebularia. 6.50r+50 l, Neophron percnopterus. 8r, Upupa epops. 10r, Elanus caeruleus. 25r, Eudocimus ruber. 30r, Falco peregrinus. 40r, Milvus migrans. 50r, Pluvialis squatarola.

Perf. 14½, 13 (6.50r+50 l, 30r, 40r)

1992-94
1624	A247	10 l multi	.30	.30
1625	A247	25 l multi	.30	.30
1626	A247	50 l multi	.30	.30
1627	A247	2r multi	.70	.70
1628	A247	3.50r multi	1.25	1.25
1629	A247	5r multi	1.75	1.75
1630	A247	6.50r +50 l multi	2.00	2.00
1631	A247	8r multi	2.75	2.75
1632	A247	10r multi	3.50	3.50
1633	A247	25r multi	5.50	5.50
1634	A247	30r multi	7.00	7.00
1635	A247	40r multi	10.00	10.00
1636	A247	50r multi	12.50	12.50
		Nos. 1624-1636 (13)	47.85	47.85

Issued: 10 l, 25 l, 50 l, 2r, 3.50r, 5r, 8r, 10r, 25r, 2/17/92; 6.50r+50 l, 30r, 11/93; 40r, 1994(?).

See No. 2323.

Queen Elizabeth II's Accession to the Throne, 40th Anniv.
Common Design Type

No. 1641, Queen, palm trees. No. 1642, Queen, boat.

1992, Feb. 6   Perf. 14
1637	CD348	1r multicolored	.30	.30
1638	CD348	3.50r multicolored	1.00	1.00
1639	CD348	7r multicolored	2.00	2.00
1640	CD348	10r multicolored	2.75	2.75
		Nos. 1637-1640 (4)	6.05	6.05

Souvenir Sheets
| 1641 | CD348 | 18r multicolored | 5.75 | 5.75 |
| 1642 | CD348 | 18r multicolored | 5.75 | 5.75 |

This set differs from the common design in that the Queen's portrait and local view are separated by a curved line rather than with a cypher outline.

Disney Characters on World Tour — A248

Designs: 25 l, Mickey on Flying Carpet Airways. 50 l, Goofy at Big Ben, London. 1r, Mickey in Holland. 2r, Pluto eating pasta, Italy. 3r, Mickey, Donald do sombero stomp in Mexico. 3.50r, Mickey, Goofy, and Donald form Miki Tiki, Polynesia. 5r, Goofy's Alpine antics, Austria. 7r, Mickey Maus, Germany. 10r, Donald as Samurai Duck. 12r, Mickey in Russia. 15r, Mickey's Oom-pah Band in Germany. No. 1654, Mickey, globe. No. 1655, Donald in Ireland chasing leprechaun with pot of gold at end of rainbow, horiz. No. 1655A, Pluto, kangaroo with joey, Australia.

1992, Feb. 4   Perf. 13x13½
1643	A248	25 l multi	.25	.25
1644	A248	50 l multi	.25	.25
1645	A248	1r multi	.35	.35
1646	A248	2r multi	.65	.65
1647	A248	3r multi	.90	.90
1648	A248	3.50r multi	.90	.90
1649	A248	5r multi	1.25	1.25
1650	A248	7r multi	1.50	1.50
1651	A248	10r multi	2.00	2.00
1652	A248	12r multi	2.50	2.50
1653	A248	15r multi	2.50	2.50
		Nos. 1643-1653 (11)	13.05	13.05

Souvenir Sheets
1654	A248	25r multi	5.00	5.00
1655	A248	25r multi	4.00	4.00
1655A	A248	25r multi	4.00	4.00

While the rest of the set has the same issue date as Nos. 1644-1645, 1647, 1653-1654, their dollar value was lower when they were released.

Fish — A249

Designs: 7 l, Blue surgeonfish. 20 l, Bigeye. 50 l, Yellowfin tuna. 1r, two-spot red snapper. 3.50r, Sabre squirrelfish. 5r, Picasso triggerfish. 8r, Bennet's butterflyfish. 10r, Parrotfish. 12r, Grouper. 15r, Skpjack tuna. No. 1666, Clownfish. No. 1667, Sweetlips. No. 1667A, Treadfin butterflyfish. No. 1667B, Clown triggerfish.

1992, Mar. 23   Litho.   Perf. 14
1656	A249	7 l multicolored	.30	.30
1657	A249	20 l multicolored	.30	.30
1658	A249	50 l multicolored	.30	.30
1659	A249	1r multicolored	.30	.30
1660	A249	3.50r multicolored	1.00	1.00
1661	A249	5r multicolored	1.40	1.40
1662	A249	8r multicolored	2.25	2.25
1663	A249	10r multicolored	2.50	2.50
1664	A249	12r multicolored	3.00	3.00
1665	A249	15r multicolored	3.50	3.50
		Nos. 1656-1665 (10)	14.85	14.85

Souvenir Sheets
1666	A249	20r multicolored	3.25	3.25
1667	A249	20r multicolored	3.25	3.25
1667A	A249	20r multicolored	3.25	3.25
1667B	A249	20r multicolored	3.25	3.25

World Columbian Stamp Expo '92, Chicago — A250

Walt Disney characters in Chicago; 1r, Mickey as Indian with Jean Baptiste Pointe du Sable, founder of Chicago. 3.50r, Donald at old Chicago post office, 1831. 7r, Donald in old Fort Dearborn. 15r, Goofy, mastodon at Museum of Science and Industry. 25r, Minnie and Mickey at Ferris wheel midway, Columbian Exposition, 1893, horiz.

1992, Apr. 15   Perf. 13½x14
1668	A250	1r multicolored	.30	.30
1669	A250	3.50r multicolored	1.10	1.10
1670	A250	7r multicolored	2.10	2.10
1671	A250	15r multicolored	4.25	4.25
		Nos. 1668-1671 (4)	7.75	7.75

Souvenir Sheet
Perf. 14x13½
| 1672 | A250 | 25r multicolored | 5.50 | 5.50 |

No. 1671 identifies Field Museum as Museum of Science and Industry.

Granada '92 — A251

Disney characters in old Alhambra, Granada: 2r, Minnie in Court of Lions. 5r, Goofy bathing in Lions Fountain. 8r, Mickey walking near Gate of Justice. 12r, Donald Duck serenading Daisy in Vermilion Towers. No. 1682, Goofy and Mickey outside Towers of the Alhambra.

1992, Apr. 15   Perf. 13½x14
1678	A251	2r multicolored	.90	.60
1679	A251	5r multicolored	1.75	1.75
1680	A251	8r multicolored	2.25	2.25
1681	A251	12r multicolored	2.75	2.75
		Nos. 1678-1681 (4)	7.65	7.35

Souvenir Sheet
| 1682 | A251 | 25r multicolored | 5.50 | 5.50 |

Flowers of the United States — A252

Flowers of the World — A253

1992, Apr. 26   Litho.   Perf. 14½
1688	A252	25 l U.S.	.25	.25
1689	A252	50 l Australia	.25	.25
1690	A252	2r England	.70	.70
1691	A252	3.50r Brazil	1.25	1.25
1692	A252	5r Holland	1.75	1.75
1693	A252	8r France	2.75	2.75
1694	A252	10r Japan	3.25	3.25
1695	A252	15r Africa	4.75	4.75
		Nos. 1688-1695 (8)	14.95	14.95

Souvenir Sheets
Perf. 14
| 1696 | A253 | 25r org, yel & red vio flowers | 5.00 | 5.00 |
| 1696A | A253 | 25r red, pink & yel flowers | 5.00 | 5.00 |

No. 1696 contains one 57x43mm stamp. No. 1696A contains one 57x34mm stamp.

Natl. Security Service, Cent. — A254

3.50r, Coast Guard. 5r, Infantry. 10r, Aakootey. 15r, Fire department. 20r, Sultan in procession.

1992, Apr. 21   Perf. 14
1697	A254	3.50r multi	1.25	1.25
1698	A254	5r multi	2.25	2.25
1699	A254	10r multi	4.75	4.75
1700	A254	15r multi	7.00	7.00
		Nos. 1697-1700 (4)	15.25	15.25

Souvenir Sheet
| 1701 | A254 | 20r multi | 7.00 | 7.00 |

A255

Mushrooms: 10 l, Laetiporus sulphureus. 25 l, Coprinus atramentarius. 50 l, Gandoderma lucidum. 3.50r, Russula aurata. 5r, Polyporus umbellatus. 8r, Suillus grevillei. 10r, Clavaria zollingeri. No. 1709, Boletus edulis. No. 1710, Trametes cinnabarina. No. 1711, Marasmius oreades.

1992, May 14   Litho.   Perf. 14
1702	A255	10 l multicolored	.25	.25
1703	A255	25 l multicolored	.25	.25
1704	A255	50 l multicolored	.25	.25
1705	A255	3.50r multicolored	1.00	1.00
1706	A255	5r multicolored	1.25	1.25
1707	A255	8r multicolored	2.25	2.25
1708	A255	10r multicolored	2.50	2.50
1709	A255	25r multicolored	6.50	6.50
		Nos. 1702-1709 (8)	14.25	14.25

MALDIVE ISLANDS

Souvenir Sheets
1710	A255	25r multicolored	6.75	6.75
1711	A255	25r multicolored	6.75	6.75

A256

10 l, Hurdles. 1r, Boxing. 3.50r, Women's running. 5r, Discus. 7r, Basketball. 10r, Race walking. 12r, Rhythmic gymnastics. 20r, Fencing.
No. 1720, Olympic flame. No. 1721, Olympic rings, flags.

1992, June 1
1712	A256	10 l multi	.25	.25
1713	A256	1r multi	.25	.25
1714	A256	3.50r multi	.90	.90
1715	A256	5r multi	1.25	1.25
1716	A256	7r multi	1.75	1.75
1717	A256	10r multi	2.50	2.50
1718	A256	12r multi	3.00	3.00
1719	A256	20r multi	5.00	5.00

Nos. 1712-1719 (8) 14.90 14.90

Souvenir Sheets
1720	A256	25r multi	5.00	5.00
1721	A256	25r multi	5.00	5.00

1992 Summer Olympics, Barcelona.

A256a

1992 Winter Olympics, Albertville: 5r, Two-man bobsled. 8r, Free-style ski jump. 10r, Women's cross-country skiing.
No. 1725, Women's slalom skiing, horiz. No. 1726, Men's figure skating.

1992, June 1 **Litho.** **Perf. 14**
1722	A256a	5r multicolored	1.00	1.00
1723	A256a	8r multicolored	1.60	1.60
1724	A256a	10r multicolored	2.00	2.00

Nos. 1722-1724 (3) 4.60 4.60

Souvenir Sheets
1725	A256a	25r multicolored	4.75	4.75
1726	A256a	25r multicolored	4.75	4.75

Dinosaurs — A257

Designs: 5 l, Deinonychus. 10 l, Styracosaurus. 25 l, Mamenchisaurus. 50 l, Stenonychosaurus. 1r, Parasaurolophus. 1.25r, Scelidosaurus. 1.75r, Tyrannosaurus. 2r, Stegosaurus. 3.50r, Iguanodon. 4r, Anatosaurus. 5r, Monoclonius. 7r, Tenontosaurus. 8r, Brachiosaurus. 10r, Euoplocephalus. 25r, Triceratops. 50r, Apatosaurus.
No. 1743, Iguanodon, allosaurus. No. 1744, Hadrosaur. No. 1745, Tyrannosaurus, triceratops. No. 1746, Brachiosaurus, iguanodons.

1992, Sept. 15 **Litho.** **Perf. 14**
1727	A257	5 l multicolored	.25	.25
1728	A257	10 l multicolored	.25	.25
1729	A257	25 l multicolored	.25	.25
1730	A257	50 l multicolored	.25	.25
1731	A257	1r multicolored	.25	.25
1732	A257	1.25r multicolored	.30	.30
1733	A257	1.75r multicolored	.40	.40
1734	A257	2r multicolored	.45	.45
1735	A257	3.50r multicolored	.80	.80
1736	A257	4r multicolored	.90	.90
1737	A257	5r multicolored	1.10	1.10
1738	A257	7r multicolored	1.60	1.60
1739	A257	8r multicolored	1.90	1.90
1740	A257	10r multicolored	2.25	2.25
1741	A257	25r multicolored	5.75	5.75
1742	A257	50r multicolored	11.50	11.50

Nos. 1727-1742 (16) 28.20 28.20

Souvenir Sheets
1743	A257	25r multicolored	5.00	5.00
1744	A257	25r multicolored	5.00	5.00
1745	A257	25r multicolored	5.00	5.00
1746	A257	25r multicolored	5.00	5.00

Genoa '92.

1992 Summer Olympics, Barcelona A258

10 l, Pole vault, vert.. 25 l, Pommel horse. 50 l, Shot put, vert. 1r, Horizontal bar. 2r, Triple jump. 3.50r, Table tennis, vert. 7r, Wrestling. 9r, Baseball, vert. 12r, Swimming. 25r, Decathlon (high jump).

1992, June 1 **Litho.** **Perf. 14**
1747	A258	10 l multicolored	.25	.25
1748	A258	25 l multicolored	.25	.25
1749	A258	50 l multicolored	.25	.25
1750	A258	1r multicolored	.25	.25
1751	A258	2r multicolored	.50	.50
1752	A258	3.50r multicolored	.90	.90
1753	A258	7r multicolored	1.90	1.90
1754	A258	9r multicolored	2.10	2.10
1755	A258	25r multicolored	3.00	3.00

Nos. 1747-1755 (9) 9.40 9.40

Souvenir Sheet
1756	A258	25r multicolored	9.00	9.00

Souvenir Sheets

Mysteries of the Universe — A259

No. 1757, Loch Ness monster. No. 1758, Explosion of the Hindenburg. No. 1759, Crystal skulls. No. 1760, Black holes. No. 1761, UFO over Washington State. No. 1762, UFO near Columbus, Ohio. No. 1763, Explosion at Chernobyl, 1986. No. 1764, Crop circles of Great Britain. No. 1765, Ghosts of English castles and mansions. No. 1766, Drawings of Plain of Nasca, Peru, vert. No. 1767, Stonehenge, England, vert. No. 1768, Bust of Plato, the disappearance of Atlantis. No. 1769, Footprint of Yeti (abominable snowman), vert. No. 1770, Pyramids of Giza. No. 1771, Bermuda Triangle, vert. No. 1772, The Mary Celeste, vert.

1992, Oct. 28
1757-1772	A259	25r Set of 16	105.00	105.00

1994 World Cup Soccer Championships, US — A260

Players of 1990 German team: 10 l, Jurgen Klinsmann. 25 l, Pierre Littbarski. 50 l, Lothar Matthaus. 1r, Rudi Voller. 2r, Thomas Hassler. 3.50r, Thomas Berthold. 4r, Jurgen Kohler. 5r, Berti Vogts, trainer. 6r, Bodo Illgner. 7r, Klaus Augenthaler. 8r, Franz Beckenbauer, coach. 10r, Andreas Brehme. 12r, Guido Buchwald.
No. 1786, Team members, horiz. No. 1787, Unidentified player in action, horiz.

1992, Aug. 10 **Litho.** **Perf. 14**
1773	A260	10 l multicolored	.25	.25
1774	A260	25 l multicolored	.25	.25
1775	A260	50 l multicolored	.25	.25
1776	A260	1r multicolored	.25	.25
1777	A260	2r multicolored	.60	.60
1778	A260	3.50r multicolored	1.00	1.00
1779	A260	4r multicolored	1.10	1.10
1780	A260	5r multicolored	1.50	1.50
1781	A260	6r multicolored	1.75	1.75
1782	A260	7r multicolored	2.00	2.00
1783	A260	8r multicolored	2.25	2.25
1784	A260	10r multicolored	3.00	3.00
1785	A260	12r multicolored	3.50	3.50

Nos. 1773-1785 (13) 17.70 17.70

Souvenir Sheets
1786	A260	35r multicolored	6.50	6.50
1787	A260	35r multicolored	6.50	6.50

Souvenir Sheet

New York Public Library A261

1992, Oct. 28 **Litho.** **Perf. 14**
1788	A261	20r multicolored	7.50	7.50

Postage Stamp Mega Event '92, New York City.

Walt Disney's Goofy, 60th Anniv. A262

Scenes from Disney cartoon films: 10 l, Father's Weekend, 1953. 50 l, Symphony Hour, 1942. 75 l, Frank Duck Brings 'Em Back Alive, 1946. 1r, Crazy with the Heat, 1947. 2r, The Big Wash, 1948. 3.50r, How to Ride a Horse, 1950. 5r, Two Gun Goofy, 1952. 8r, Saludos Amigos, 1943, vert. 10r, How to Be a Detective, 1952. 12r, For Whom the Bulls Toil, 1953. 15r, Double Dribble, 1946, vert.
No. 1801, Mickey and the Beanstalk, 1947. No. 1802, Double Dribble, 1946, vert., diff. No. 1803, The Goofy Success Story, 1955.

Perf. 14x13½, 13½x14
1992, Dec. 7 **Litho.**
1789	A262	10 l multicolored	.25	.25
1791	A262	50 l multicolored	.25	.25
1792	A262	75 l multicolored	.25	.25
1793	A262	1r multicolored	.25	.25
1794	A262	2r multicolored	.50	.50
1795	A262	3.50r multicolored	.90	.90
1796	A262	5r multicolored	1.25	1.25
1797	A262	8r multicolored	2.00	2.00
1798	A262	10r multicolored	2.25	2.25
1799	A262	12r multicolored	2.75	2.75
1800	A262	15r multicolored	3.50	3.50

Nos. 1789-1800 (11) 14.15 14.15

Souvenir Sheets
1801	A262	20r multicolored	4.25	4.25
1802	A262	20r multicolored	4.25	4.25
1803	A262	20r multicolored	4.25	4.25

A number has been reserved for an additional value in this set.

A263

Anniversaries and Events — A264

Designs: 1r, Zeppelin on bombing raid over London during World War I. No. 1805, German, French flags, Konrad Adenauer, Charles de Gaulle. No. 1806, Radio telescope. No. 1807, Columbus studying globe. No. 1808, Indian rhinoceros. 7r, WHO, ICN, and FAO emblems. 8r, Green sea turtle. No. 1811, Lion's Intl. emblem and Melvin Jones, founder. No. 1812, Yacht America, first America's Cup winner, 1851. 12r, Columbus claiming San Salvador for Spain. No. 1814, Voyager 1 approaching Saturn. No. 1815, NATO flag, airplanes, Adenauer. No. 1816, Graf Zeppelin over New York City.
No. 1817, Landsat satellite. No. 1818, Count Zeppelin. No. 1819, Santa Maria. No. 1820, Konrad Adenauer. No. 1821, Zubin Mehta, music director, NY Philharmonic, vert. No. 1822, Scarlet macaw. No. 1823, Friedrich Schmiedl (b. 1902), rocket mail pioneer.

1992-93 **Litho.** **Perf. 14**
1804	A263	1r multicolored	.30	.30
1805	A263	3.50r multicolored	.90	.90
1806	A263	3.50r multicolored	.70	.70
1807	A263	6r multicolored	1.50	1.50
1808	A263	6r multicolored	1.25	1.25
1809	A263	7r multicolored	1.40	1.40
1810	A263	8r multicolored	1.60	1.60
1811	A263	10r multicolored	1.75	1.75
1812	A263	10r multicolored	1.75	1.75
1813	A263	12r multicolored	2.75	2.75
1814	A263	15r multicolored	2.75	2.75
1815	A263	15r multicolored	3.75	3.75
1816	A263	20r multicolored	5.50	5.50

Nos. 1804-1816 (13) 25.90 25.90

Souvenir Sheets
1817	A263	20r multicolored	6.00	6.00
1818	A263	20r multicolored	6.25	6.25
1819	A263	20r multicolored	6.25	6.25
1820	A263	20r multicolored	6.00	6.00
1821	A264	20r multicolored	6.75	6.75
1822	A263	20r multicolored	6.00	4.60
1823	A263	20r multicolored	6.50	6.50

Nos. 1817-1823 (7) 43.75 42.35

Count Zeppelin, 75th anniv. of death (Nos. 1804, 1816, 1818). Konrad Adenauer, 25th anniv. of death (Nos. 1805, 1815, 1820). Intl. Space Year (Nos. 1806, 1814, 1817). Columbus' discovery of America, 500th anniversary (Nos. 1807, 1813, 1819). Earth Summit, Rio de Janeiro (Nos. 1808, 1810, 1822). Intl. Conference on Nutrition, Rome (No. 1809). Lions Intl., 75th anniversary (No. 1811). America's Cup yacht race (No. 1812). New York Philharmonic, 150th anniv. (No. 1821).
No. 1823 contains one 27x35mm stamp.
Issue dates: Nos. 1805, 1808, 1810, 1815, 1820, 1822, Jan. 1993. Others, Nov. 1992.

Miniature Sheet

Western Films A265

Actors and film: No. 1824a, Jimmy Stewart and Marlene Dietrich, Destry Rides Again, 1939. b, Gary Cooper, The Westerner, 1940. c, Henry Fonda, My Darling Clementine, 1940. d, Alan Ladd, Shane, 1953. e, Kirk Douglas and Burt Lancaster, Gunfight at the O.K. Coral, 1957. f, Steve McQueen, The Magnificent Seven, 1960. g, Robert Redford and Paul Newman, Butch Cassidy & The Sundance Kid, 1969. h, Jack Nicholson and Randy Quaid, The Missouri Breaks, 1976.
No. 1825, Clint Eastwood, Pale Rider. No. 1826, John Wayne, The Searchers, 1956.

1992-93 **Litho.** **Perf. 13½x14**
1824	A265	5r Sheet of 8, #a.-h.	11.00	11.00

Souvenir Sheets
1825	A265	20r multicolored	5.25	5.25
1826	A265	20r multicolored	5.25	5.25

Issued: Nos. 1824-1825, 1992; No. 1826, 1/1993.

Miniature Sheet

Opening of Euro Disney Resort, Paris A266

Disney characters in paintings by French impressionists — No. 1827: a, Minnie on theater balcony. b, Goofy playing cards. c, Mickey and Minnie walking by outdoor cafe. d, Mickey fishing. e, Goofy dancing to music of harp player. f, Mickey and Minnie in boat. g, Minnie on dance floor. h, Mickey strolling through country. i, Minnie standing behind Polynesian woman.

1992, Dec. **Perf. 14x13½**
1827	A266	5r Sheet of 9, #a.-	15.00	15.00

Souvenir Sheets
1828	A266	20r Goofy	3.75	3.75
1829	A266	20r Minnie	3.75	3.75
1830	A266	20r Mickey	3.75	3.75

Perf. 13½x14
1831	A266	20r Donald Duck, vert.	3.75	3.75

MALDIVE ISLANDS

SAARC Year of the Environment — A267

Designs: 25 l, Waterfall, drought area. 50 l, Clean, polluted beaches. 5r, Clean, polluted ocean. 10r, Clean island with vegetation, island polluted with trees dying.

1992, Dec. 30   Litho.   **Perf. 14**
1832	A267	25 l multicolored	.25	.25
1833	A267	50 l multicolored	.25	.25
1834	A267	5r multicolored	.90	.90
1835	A267	10r multicolored	1.75	1.75
	Nos. 1832-1835 (4)		3.15	3.15

Elvis Presley (1935-1977) — A268

a, Portrait. b, With guitar. c, With microphone.

1993, Jan. 7
1836	A268	3.50r Strip of 3, #a.-c.	2.75	2.75

A set of 4 stamps commemorating South Asia Tourism year, formerly listed as Nos. 1837-1840, were prepared but not issued.

Miniature Sheets

Madame Seriziat — A270

Louvre Museum, Bicent.
Details or entire paintings, by Jacques-Louis David (1748-1825):
No. 1841: b, Pierre Seriziat. c, Madame de Verninac. d, Madame Recamier. e, Self-portrait. f, General Bonaparte. g-h, The Lictors Returning to Brutus the Bodies of his Sons (left, right).
Paintings by Jean-Baptiste-Camillo Corot (1706-1875)
No. 1842: a, Self-portrait. b, The Woman in Blue. c, The Study. b, The Jeweled Woman. d, Young Girl in her Dressing Room. e, Haydee. f, Chartres Cathedral. g, The Belfry at Douai. h, The Bridge at Mantes.
Paintings by Jean-Honore Fragonard (1732-1806):
No. 1843: a, The Study. b, Denis Diderot. c, Marie-Madeleine Guimard. d, The Inspiration. e, Tivoli Cascades. f, The Music Lesson. g, The Bolt. h, Blindman's Buff.
No. 1844, The Gardens of the Villa D'Este, Tivoli, by Jean-Baptiste-Camille Corot, horiz.
No. 1845, Young Tiger Playing with its Mother, by Delacroix.

1993, Jan. 7   Litho.   **Perf. 12**
Sheets of 8
1841	A270	8r #a.-h. + label	11.00	11.00
1842	A270	8r #a.-h. + label	11.00	11.00
1843	A270	8r #a.-h. + label	11.00	11.00

Souvenir Sheets
Perf. 14½
1844	A270	20r multicolored	6.00	6.00
1845	A270	20r multicolored	6.00	6.00

Nos. 1844-1845 contains one 80x55mm stamp.

Miniature Sheet

Coronation of Queen Elizabeth II, 40th Anniv. — A271

Designs: a, 3.50r, Official coronation photograph. b, 5r, St. Edward's crown. c, 10r, Dignitaries viewing ceremony. d, 10r, Queen, Prince Philip examining banknote.

1993, June 2   **Perf. 13½x14**
1846	A271	Sheet, 2 ea #a.-d.	13.00	13.00

A number has been reserved for an additional value in this set.

Shells — A272

Designs: 7 l, Precious wentletrap. 15 l, Purple sea snail. 50 l, Arabian cowrie. 3.50r, Major harp. 4r, Royal paper bubble. 5r, Sieve cowrie. 6r, Episcopal miter. 7r, Camp pitarvenus. 8r, Eyed auger. 10r, Onyx cowrie. 12r, Map cowrie. 20r, Caltrop murex.
No. 1856, Scorpion spider conch. No. 1857, Black striped triton. No. 1857A, Bull's-mouth helmet.

1993, July 15   Litho.   **Perf. 14**
1848	A272	7 l multicolored	.30	.30
1849	A272	15 l multicolored	.30	.30
1850	A272	50 l multicolored	.30	.30
1850A	A272	3.50r multicolored	1.00	1.00
1850B	A272	4r multicolored	1.10	1.10
1851	A272	5r multicolored	1.40	1.40
1852	A272	6r multicolored	1.75	1.75
1852A	A272	7r multicolored	1.90	1.90
1853	A272	8r multicolored	2.25	2.25
1854	A272	10r multicolored	2.75	2.75
1854A	A272	12r multicolored	3.25	3.25
1855	A272	20r multicolored	5.75	5.75
	Nos. 1848-1855 (12)		22.05	22.05

Souvenir Sheets
1856	A272	25r multicolored	8.00	8.00
1857	A272	25r multicolored	8.00	8.00
1857A	A272	25r multicolored	8.00	8.00

Endangered Animals — A273

7 l, Sifaka lemur. 10 l, Snow leopard. 15 l, Numbat. 25 l, Gorilla. 2r, Koalas. 3.50r, Cheetah. 5r, Yellow-footed rock wallaby. 7r, Orangutan. 8r, Black lemur. 10r, Black rhinoceros. 15r, Humpback whale. 20r, Mauritius parakeet.
No. 1866, Asian elephant. No. 1867, Tiger. No. 1867A, Giant panda.

1993, July 20   Litho.   **Perf. 14**
1857B	A273	7 l multicolored	.30	.30
1858	A273	10 l multicolored	.30	.30
1859	A273	15 l multicolored	.30	.30
1859A	A273	25 l multicolored	.30	.30
1860	A273	2r multicolored	.65	.65
1860A	A273	3.50r multicolored	1.10	1.40
1861	A273	5r multicolored	1.50	1.50
1862	A273	7r multicolored	2.10	2.10
1863	A273	8r multicolored	2.40	2.40
1864	A273	10r multicolored	3.00	3.00
1865	A273	15r multicolored	4.25	4.25
1865A	A273	20r multicolored	5.50	5.50
	Nos. 1857B-1865A (12)		21.70	22.00

Souvenir Sheets
1866	A273	25r multicolored	8.00	8.00
1867	A273	25r multicolored	8.00	8.00
1867A	A273	25r multicolored	8.00	8.00

Miniature Sheets

Fish — A274

No. 1868: b, Black pyramid butterflyfish. c, Bird wrasse. d, Checkerboard wrasse. e, Blue face angelfish. f, Bannerfish. g, Threadfin butterflyfish. h, Picasso triggerfish. i, Pennantfish. j, Grouper. k, Black back butterflyfish. l, Redfin triggerfish. m, Redfin butterflyfish.
No. 1868A: n, Yellow goatfish. o, Emperor angelfish. p, Madagascar butterflyfish. q, Empress angelfish. r, Longnose butterfly. s, Racoon butterflyfish. t, Harlequin filefish. u, Wedgetailed triggerfish. v, Clark's anemonefish. w, Clown triggerfish. x, Zebra lionfish. y, Maldive clownfish.
No. 1869, Goldbelly anemone, vert. No. 1869A, Klein's butterflyfish, vert.

1993, June 30   **Perf. 14x13½**
Sheets of 12
1868	A274	3.50r #b.-m.	10.00	10.00
1868A	A274	3.50r #n.-y.	10.00	10.00

Souvenir Sheets
Perf. 12x13
1869	A274	25r multicolored	6.00	6.00
1869A	A274	25r multicolored	6.00	6.00

Miniature Sheets

Birds — A275

No. 1870: a, Pallid harrier. b, Cattle egret. c, Koel (b). d, Tree pipit. e, Short-ear owl. f, European kestrel. g, Yellow wagtail. h, Common heron. i, Black bittern. j, Common snipe. k, Little egret. l, Little stint.
No. 1871: a, Gull-billed tern. b, Long-tailed tropicbird (a). c, Frigate bird. d, Wilson's petrel. e, White tern. f, Brown booby. g, Marsh harrier. h, Common noddy. i, Little heron. j, Turnstone. k, Curlew. l, Crab plover.
No. 1872, Caspian tern, horiz. No. 1873, Audubon's shearwater, horiz.

1993, July 5   **Perf. 13½x14**
1870	A275	3.50r Sheet of 12, #a.-l.	9.50	9.50
1871	A275	3.50r Sheet of 12, #a.-l.	9.50	9.50

Souvenir Sheet
Perf. 13x12
1872	A275	25r multicolored	6.00	6.00
1873	A275	25r multicolored	6.00	6.00

No. 1871 is horiz.

Year of Productivity — A276 / A277

1993, July 25   **Perf. 14**
1874	A276	7r multicolored	1.40	1.40
1875	A277	10r multicolored	2.10	2.10

A278

Picasso (1881-1973): 3.50r, Still Life with Pitcher and Apples, 1919. 5r, Bowls and Jug, 1908. 10r, Bowls of Fruit and Loaves, 1908. 20r, Green Still Life, 1914, horiz.

1993, Oct. 11   Litho.   **Perf. 14**
1876	A278	3.50r multicolored	.80	.80
1877	A278	5r multicolored	1.10	1.10
1878	A278	10r multicolored	2.25	2.25
	Nos. 1876-1878 (3)		4.15	4.15

Souvenir Sheet
1879	A278	20r multicolored	5.00	5.00

A279

Copernicus (1473-1543): 3.50r, Early astronomical instrument. 15r, Astronaut wearing Manned Maneuvering Unit. 20r, Copernicus.

1993, Oct. 11
1880	A279	3.50r multicolored	.90	.90
1881	A279	15r multicolored	4.00	4.00

Souvenir Sheet
1882	A279	20r multicolored	5.00	5.00

Royal Wedding of Crown Prince Naruhito, Princess Masako — A280

3.50r, Crown Prince Naruhito. 10r, Princess Masako, horiz. 25r, Princess Masako.

1993, Oct. 11
1883	A280	3.50r multicolored	.65	.65
1884	A280	10r multicolored	2.00	2.00

Souvenir Sheet
1885	A280	25r multicolored	6.00	6.00

1994 Winter Olympics, Lillehammer, Norway — A281

8r, Marina Kiehl, gold medalist, women's downhill, 1988. 15r, Vegard Ulvang, gold medalist, cross-country skiing, 1992.
25r, Soviet ice hockey goalie, 1980.

1993, Oct. 11
1886	A281	8r multicolored	1.75	1.75
1887	A281	15r multicolored	3.50	3.50

Souvenir Sheet
1888	A281	25r multicolored	6.00	6.00

MALDIVE ISLANDS

Polska '93 — A282

Fine arts: 3.50r, Zolte Roze, by Menasze Seidenbeutel, 1932. 5r, Cracow Historical Museum. 8r, Apples and Curtain, by Waclaw Borowski.
25r, Seascape, by Roman Sielski, 1931, horiz.

1993, Oct. 11   Litho.   *Perf. 14*

1889	A282	3.50r multicolored	.85 .85
1890	A282	5r multicolored	1.10 1.10
1891	A282	8r multicolored	1.90 1.90
	Nos. 1889-1891 (3)		3.85 3.85

Souvenir Sheet

| 1892 | A282 | 25r multicolored | 5.00 5.00 |

Butterflies A283

7 l, Commander. 20 l, Blue tiger. 25 l, Centaur oakblue. 50 l, Common banded peacock. 5r, Glad-eye bushbrown. 6.50r + 50 l, Common tree nymph. 7r, Lemon emigrant. 10r, Blue pansy. 12r, Painted lady. 15r, Blue mormon. 18r, Tamil yeoman. 20r, Crimson rose.
No. 1905, Common imperial, vert. No. 1906, Great orange tip, vert. No. 1907, Black prince, vert.

1993, Oct. 25

1893	A283	7 l multi	.25 .25
1894	A283	20 l multi	.25 .25
1895	A283	25 l multi	.25 .25
1896	A283	50 l multi	.25 .25
1897	A283	5r multi	1.40 1.40
1898	A283	6.50 l + 50 l multi	2.00 2.00
1899	A283	7r multi	2.00 2.00
1900	A283	10r multi	2.75 2.75
1901	A283	12r multi	3.50 3.50
1902	A283	15r multi	4.25 4.25
1903	A283	18r multi	5.00 5.00
1904	A283	20r multi	5.50 5.50
	Nos. 1893-1904 (12)		27.40 27.40

Souvenir Sheets

1905	A283	25r multi	7.50 7.50
1906	A283	25r multi	7.50 7.50
1907	A283	25r multi	7.50 7.50

Aviation Anniversaries A284

Designs: 3.50r, Zeppelin on bombing raid caught in British search lights, vert. 5r, Homing pigeon. 10r, Dr. Hugo Eckener, vert. 15r, Airmail service medal, Jim Edgerton's Jenny, mail truck. 20r, USS Macon approaching mooring mast, vert.
Each 25r: No. 1913, Blanchard's balloon, 1793, vert. No. 1914, Santos-Dumont's flight around Eiffel Tower, 1901, vert.

1993, Nov. 22   Litho.   *Perf. 14*

| 1908-1912 | A284 | Set of 5 | 14.00 14.00 |

Souvenir Sheets

| 1913-1914 | A284 | Set of 2 | 9.50 9.50 |

Dr. Hugo Eckener, 125th birth anniv. (3.50r, 10r, 20r, No. 1913).

Miniature Sheets

First Ford Engine, First Benz Four-Wheeled Car, Cent. — A285

No. 1915: a, 1915 Model T (b, d-e). b, Henry Ford (e). c, Drawing of 1st Ford engine (b, e-f). d, 1993 Ford Probe GT (e). e, 1947 Ford Sportsman, front (f). f, As "f," rear (e). g, 1915 Ford advertisement (j). h, 1955 Ford Thunderbird (g, i). i, Ford emblem (f, h). j, 1958 Edsel Citation. k, 1941 Ford half-ton pickup. l, Model T.
No. 1916: a, 1937 Daimler-Benz Straight 8 (b). b, Karl Benz (e). c, Mercedes-Benz advertisement (f). d, 1929 Mercedes 38-250SS (e). e, 1893 Benz Viktoria (f, h). f, Mercedes star emblem (i). g, WWI Mercedes engine. h, 1957 Mercedes-Benz 300SL Gullwing (g). i, 1993 Mercedes Benz SL coupe/roadster (h). j, 1906 Benz 4-cylinder car (k). k, Early Benz advertisement. l, Benz Viktoria, 1893.
No. 1917, 1933 Ford Model Y. No. 1918, 1955 Mercedes 300S.

1993, Nov. 22

| 1915 | A285 | 3.50r Sheet of 12, #a.-l. | 12.00 12.00 |
| 1916 | A285 | 3.50r Sheet of 12, #a.-l. | 12.00 12.00 |

Souvenir Sheets

| 1917 | A285 | 25r multi | 6.00 6.00 |
| 1918 | A285 | 25r multi | 6.00 6.00 |

Peter and the Wolf — A286

Characters and scenes from Disney animated film: 7 l, Ivan, Sonia, Sasha and Peter track the Wolf. 15 l, Grandpa forbids Peter to go. 20 l, Peter sets off for the first time. 25 l, Yascha, Vladimir and Mischa arrive. 50 l, Sasha is on the lookout. 1r, The Wolf frightens everyone.
No. 1925: Part 1 — a, Peter dreams of hunting a real Wolf. b, Peter sneaks out when grandpa dozes off. c, Peter treks off to hunt the Wolf. d, Sasha joins Peter. e, Sonia joins the hunt too. f, Peter stops Ivan from teasing Sasha. g, Ivan warns Peter of the Wolf. h, Ivan, Peter and Sasha seek safety in a tree. i, The Wolf is vicious when pursued.
No. 1926: Part 2 — a, The Wolf comes upon Sonia, stunned senseless. b, Sasha attacks the Wolf. c, The Wolf is about to eat poor Sasha. d, Peter fires his popgun at the Wolf. e, The Wolf chases Sonia. f, Ivan catches the Wolf by the tail. g, Peter and Ivan string up the Wolf. h, Sasha enlists help from three hunters. i, Ivan and Peter turn the Wolf upside down.

1993, Dec. 20

| 1919-1924 | A286 | Set of 6 | 1.00 1.00 |

Miniature Sheets of 9

| 1925 | A286 | 3.50r #a.-i. | 7.50 7.50 |
| 1926 | A286 | 3.50r #a.-i. | 7.50 7.50 |

Souvenir Sheets

| 1927 | A286 | 25r Sonia | 5.00 5.00 |
| 1928 | A286 | 25r Ivan | 5.00 5.00 |

Fine Art — A287

Paintings by Rembrandt: 50 l, Girl with a Broom. No. 1931, 3.50r, Young Girl at half-open Door. 5r, The Prophetess Hannah (Rembrandt's Mother). 7r, Woman with a Pink Flower. 12r, Lucretia. No. 1939, 15r, Lady with an Ostich Feather Fan.
Paintings by Matisse: 2r, Girl with Tulips (Jeanne Vaderin). No. 1932, 3.50r. Portrait of Greta Moll. 6.50r, The Idol. 9r, Mme. Matisse in Japanese Robe. 10r, Portrait of MMe Matisse (The Green Line). No. 1940, 15r, The Woman with the Hat.
Each 25r: No. 1941, Married Couple with 3 Children (A Family Group), by Rembrandt, horiz. No. 1942, The Painter's Family, by Matisse. No. 1942A: The Music Makers, by Rembrandt.

1994, Jan. 11   Litho.   *Perf. 13*

| 1929-1940 | A287 | Set of 12 | 21.00 21.00 |

Souvenir Sheets

| 1941-1942A | A287 | Set of 3 | 21.00 21.00 |

No. 1942A issued Feb. 2.

1994 World Cup Soccer US — A288

Players, country: 7 l, Windischmann, US; Giannini, Italy. 20 l, Carnevale, Gascoigne. 25 l, Platt & teammates, England. 3.50r, Koeman, Holland; Klinsmann, Germany. 5r, Quinn, Ireland; Maldini, Italy. 7r, Lineker, England. 15r, Hassan, Egypt; Moran, Ireland. 18r, Canniggia, Argentina.
Each 25r: No. 1951, Conejo, Costa Rica; Mozer, Brazil, horiz. No. 1952, Armstrong & Balboa, US; Ogris, Austria.

1994, Jan. 11   *Perf. 14*

| 1943-1950 | A288 | Set of 8 | 13.00 13.00 |

Souvenir Sheets

| 1951-1952 | A288 | Set of 2 | 12.50 12.50 |

A289

Hong Kong '94 A290

Stamps, Moon-Lantern Festival, Hong Kong: No. 1953, Hong Kong #416, girls, lanterns. No. 1954, Lanterns, #660.
No. 1955 — Cloisonne Enamel, Qing Dynasty: a, Vase. b, Flower holder. c, Elephant with vase on back. d, Pot (Tibetan-style lama's milk-tea pot. e, Fo-dog. f, Pot with swing handle.

1994, Feb. 18   Litho.   *Perf. 14*

1953	A289	4r multicolored	.80 .80
1954	A289	4r multicolored	.80 .80
a.	Pair, #1953-1954		1.60 1.60

Miniature Sheet

| 1955 | A290 | 2r Sheet of 6, #a.-f. | 6.75 6.75 |

Nos. 1953-1954 issued in sheets of 5 pairs. No. 1954a is a continuous design.
New Year 1994 (Year of the Dog) (No. 1955e).

Sierra Club, Cent. — A290a

Various animals, each 6.50r:
Nos. 1956: a.-b., Prairie dog. c.-e. Woodland caribou. f, Galapagos penguin.
No. 1957, vert: a, Humpback whale. b.-c., Ocelot. d, Snow monkey. e, Prairie dog. f, Golden lion tamarin.
No. 1958: a.-b., Golden lion tamarin. c.-d., Humpback whale. e, Bengal tiger. f, Ocelot. g.-h., Snow monkey.
No. 1959, vert: a.-b., Galapagos penguin. c.-d., Bengal tiger. e.-g., Philippine tarsier. h, Sierra Club centennial emblem.

1994, May 20   Litho.   *Perf. 14*

Miniature Sheets of 6, #a-f

| 1956-1957 | A290a | Set of 2 | 20.00 20.00 |

Miniature Sheets of 8, #a-h

| 1958-1959 | A290a | Set of 2 | 24.00 24.00 |

Dome of the Rock, Jerusalem — A291

1994, June 10   *Perf. 13½*

| 1960 | A291 | 8r multicolored | 1.60 1.60 |

A292

Designs: 25 l, Elasmosaurus. 50 l, Dilophosaurus. 1r, Avimimus. 5r, Chasmosaurus. 8r, Edmontonia. 10r, Anatosaurus. 15r, Velociraptor. 20r, Spinosaurus.
No. 1969, each 3r: a, Dimorphodon. b, Megalosaurus. c, Kuehneosaurus. d, Dryosaurus. e, Kentrosaurus. f, Barapasaurus (c). g, Tenontosaurus. h, Elaphrosaurus (i). i, Maiasaura. j, Huayangosaurus. k, Rutiodon. l, Pianitzkysaurus.
No. 1970, each 3r: a, Quetzalcoatlus. b, Daspletosaurus. c, Pleurocoelus. d, Baryonyx. e, Pentaceratops. f, Kritosaurus. g, Microvenator (h). h, Nodosaurus. i, Montanaceratops. j, Dromiceiomimus. k, Dryptosaurus. l, Parkosaurus.
Each 25r: No. 1971, Gallimimus. No. 1972, Plateosaurus, vert.

1994, June 20   *Perf. 14*

| 1961-1968 | A292 | Set of 8 | 17.00 17.00 |

Miniature Sheets of 12, #a-l

| 1969-1970 | A292 | Set of 2 | 20.00 20.00 |

Souvenir Sheets

| 1971-1972 | A292 | Set of 2 | 10.00 10.00 |

Nos. 1969-1970 are continuous design.

Locomotives — A293

Designs: 25 l, 2-6-6-0 Mallet, Indonesia, horiz. 50 l, C62, Japan, horiz. 1r, D51, Japan. 5r, 4-6-0 Steam, India. 8r, Class 485 electric, Japan, horiz. 10r, Class WP Pacific, India. 15r, "People" class RM 4-6-2, China. 20r, C57, Japan, horiz.
No. 1981: a, W Class 0-6-2, India. b, C53 Class, Indonesia. c, C-10, Japan. d, Hanomag 4-8-0, India. e, Hakari bullet train, Japan. f, C-55, Japan.
Each 25r: No. 1982, 4-4-0, Indonesia. No. 1983, Series 8620, Japan.

1994, July 4

| 1973-1980 | A293 | Set of 8 | 12.00 12.00 |

Miniature Sheet of 6

| 1981 | A293 | 6.50r +50 l, #a.-f. | 8.00 8.00 |

Souvenir Sheets

| 1982-1983 | A293 | Set of 2 | 11.00 11.00 |

Domestic Cats — A294

Designs: 7 l, Japanese bobtail, horiz. 20 l, Siamese. 25 l, Persian longhair, horiz. 50 l, Somali. 3.50r, Oriental shorthair, horiz. 5r, Burmese, horiz. 7r, Bombay, horiz. 10r, Turkish van. 12r, Javanese. 15r, Singapura, horiz. 18r, Turkish angora. 20r, Egyptian mau.
Each 25r: No. 1996, Birman. No. 1997, Korat. No. 1998, Abyssinian.

1994, July 11

| 1984-1995 | A294 | Set of 12 | 20.00 20.00 |

Souvenir Sheets

| 1996-1998 | A294 | Set of 3 | 16.50 16.50 |

MALDIVE ISLANDS

Miniature Sheets of 6

1994 World Cup Soccer Championships, US — A295

No. 1999: a, 10 l, Franco Baresi, Italy, Stuart McCall, Scotland. b, 25 l, McCarthy, Great Britain, Lineker, Ireland. c, 50 l, J. Helt, Denmark, R. Gordillo, Spain. d, 5r, Martin Vasquez, Spain, Enzo Scifo, Belgium. e, 10r, Emblem. f, 12r, Tomas Brolin, Sweden, Gordon Durie, Scotland.
No. 2000, vert.: a, Bebeto, Brazil. b, Lothar Matthaus, Great Britain. c, Diego Maradona, Argentina. d, Stephane Chapuisat, Switzerland. e, George Hagi, Romania. f, Carlos Valderrama, Colombia.
No. 2001, Hossam Hassan, 2nd Egyptian player.

1994, Aug. 4	Litho.	Perf. 14
1999 A295	Sheet of 6, #a.-f.	5.50 5.50
2000 A295	6.50r Sheet of 6, #a.-f.	7.50 7.50

Souvenir Sheet

| 2001 A295 | 10r multicolored | 4.00 4.00 |

D-Day, 50th Anniv. — A296

Designs: 2r, Amphibious DUKW approaches Utah Beach. 4r, Landing craft tank, Sword Beach. 18r, Landing craft infantry damaged at Omaha Beach.
No. 2006, Canadian commandos, Juno Beach.

1994, Aug. 8		
2003-2005 A296	Set of 3	4.50 4.50

Souvenir Sheet

| 2006 A296 | 25r multicolored | 5.75 5.75 |

A297

Intl. Olympic Committee, Cent. — A298

Designs: 7r, Linford Christie, Great Britain, track 1988. 12r, Koji Gushiken, Japan, gymnastics, 1984.
25r, George Hackl, Germany, single luge, 1994.

1994, Aug. 8		
2007 A297	7r multicolored	1.25 1.25
2008 A297	12r multicolored	2.25 2.25

Souvenir Sheet

| 2009 A298 | 25r multicolored | 5.50 5.50 |

A299

PHILAKOREA '94 — A300

Designs: 50 l, Suwan Folk Village duck pond. 3.50r, Youngduson Park. 20r, Ploughing, Hahoe Village, Andong region.
Ceramics, Choson & Koryo Dynasties: No. 2013a, Pear-shaped bottle. b, Vase. c, Vase with repaired lip. d, Labed vase, stoneware. e, Vase, celadon-glazed. f, Vase, unglazed stone. g, Ritual water sprinkler. h, Celadon-glazed vase.
25r, Hunting (detail from eight-panel screen, Choson Dynasty), vert.

1994, Aug. 8	Perf. 14, 13½ (#2013)	
2010-2012 A299	Set of 3	5.25 5.25

Miniature Sheet of 8

| 2013 A300 | 3r #a -h | 5.25 5.25 |

Souvenir Sheet

| 2014 A299 | 25r multicolored | 5.50 5.50 |

First Manned Moon Landing, 25th Anniv. — A301

No. 2015, each 5r: a, Apollo 11 crew. b, Apollo 11 patch, signatures of crew. c, "Buzz" Aldrin, lunar module, Eagle. d, Apollo 12 crew. e, Apollo 12 patch, signatures of crew. f, Alan Bean transporting ALSEP.
No. 2016, each 5r: a, Apollo 16 crew. b, Apollo 16 patch, signatures of crew. c, John Young gives a "Navy salute." d, Apollo 17 crew. e, Apollo 17 patch, signatures of crew. f, Night launch of Apollo 17.
25r, Launch at Baikonur.

1994, Aug. 8		Perf. 14
	Miniature Sheets of 6, #a-f	
2015-2016 A301	Set of 2	14.00 14.00

Souvenir Sheet

| 2017 A301 | 25r multicolored | 5.50 5.50 |

UN Development Plan — A302

1r, Woman, baby, undernourished man, city on island. 8r, Island native, case worker, island, ship.

1994	Litho.	Perf. 14
2018 A302	1r multicolored	.25 .25
2019 A302	8r multicolored	2.00 2.00

Miniature Sheet of 12

Space Exploration — A304

No. 2020: a, Voyager 2. b, Sputnik. c, Apollo-Soyuz. d, Apollo 10 descent. e, Apollo 11 mission insignia. f, Hubble space telescope. g, Buzz Aldrin. h, RCA lunar cam. i, Lunar rover. j, Jim Irwin. k, Apollo 12 lunar module. l, Lunar soil extraction.
Each 25r: No. 2021, David Scott in open hatch of Apollo 9 command module. No. 2022, Alan Shepard, Jr. waving salute from moon, Apollo 14, horiz.

1994, Aug. 8	Litho.	Perf. 14
2020 A304	5r #a.-l.	17.50 17.50

Souvenir Sheets

| 2021-2022 A304 | Set of 2 | 14.00 14.00 |

Aminiya School, 50th Anniv. — A305

15 l, Discipline. 50 l, Arts. 1r, Emblem, hand holding book, vert. 8r, Girls carrying books, vert. 10r, Sports. 11r, Girls cheering, vert. 13r, Science.

1994, Nov. 28		
2023-2029 A305	Set of 7	8.75 8.75

ICAO, 50th Anniv. — A306

Designs: 50 l, Boeing 747. 1r, De Havilland Comet 4. 2r, Male Intl. Airport, Maldives. 3r, Lockheed 1649 Super Star. 8r, European Airbus. 10r, Dornier Do228.
25r, Concorde.

1994, Dec. 31		
2030-2035 A306	Set of 6	8.50 8.50

Souvenir Sheet

| 2036 A306 | 25r multicolored | 5.75 5.75 |

Miniature Sheets of 9

Water Birds — A307

Designs: No. 2037a, Northern pintail (b, d). b, Comb duck (c). c, Ruddy duck. d, Garganey (a, e, g, h). e, Lesser whistling duck (b, c, f). f, Green winged teal. g, Fulvous whistling duck. h, Northern shoveler (e). i, Cotton pygmy goose (h).
No. 2038, vert.: a, Pochard (b). b, Mallard (c, e, f). c, Wigeon. d, Northern shoveler (e, g). e, Northern pintail (h). f, Garganey (e, i). g, Tufted duck. h, Ferruginous duck (i). i, Red-crested pochard.
Each 25r: No. 2039, Cotton pygmy goose, vert. No. 2040, Garganey, diff.

1995, Feb. 27	Litho.	Perf. 14
2037 A307	5r #a -i	8.25 8.25
2038 A307	6.50r + 50 l #a.-i.	11.50 11.50

Souvenir Sheets

| 2039-2040 A307 | Set of 2 | 11.00 11.00 |

Monuments of the World — A308

Designs: 7 l, Taj Mahal. 10 l, Washington Monument. 15 l, Mt. Rushmore Memorial. 25 l, Arc de Triomphe, vert. 50 l, Sphinx, vert. 5r, El Castillo Monument of the Toltec, Chichen Itza, Yucatan, Mexico. 8r, Toltec monument, Tula, Mexico, vert. 12r, Victory Column, Berlin, vert.
Each 25r: No. 2049, Moai statues, Easter Island. No. 2050, Stonehenge.

1995, Feb. 28		
2041-2048 A308	Set of 8	6.00 6.00

Souvenir Sheets

| 2049-2050 A308 | Set of 2 | 9.00 9.00 |

No. 2049 contains one 43x57mm stamp, No. 2050 one 85x28mm stamp.

Donald Duck, 60th Birthday (in 1994) A309

Scenes from "Donald and the Wheel:" 3 l, Racing chariot. 4 l, Standing on log. 5 l, Operating steam locomotive. 10 l, Looking at cave drawing, vert. 20 l, Sitting in "junked" car, vert. 25 l, Listening to phonograph. 5r, Climbing on mammoth. 20r, Pushing old car.
Disney Duck family orchestra, vert., each 5r: No. 2059a, Donald Duck, saxophone. b, Moby Duck, violin. c, Feathry Duck, banjo. d, Daisy Duck, harp. e, Gladstone Gander, clarinet. f, Dewey, Louie, Huey, oboe. g, Gus Goose, flute. h, Ludwig von Drake, trombone.
Donald Duck family portraits, vert., each 5r: No. 2060a, Daisy. b, Donald. c, Grandma. d, Gus Goose. e, Gyro Gearloose, f, Huey, Dewey, Louie. g, Ludwig von Drake. h, Scrooge McDuck.
Each 25r: No. 2061, Dixieland band, vert. No. 2062, Donald conducting symphony orchestra. No. 2063, Donald being photographed, vert. No. 2064, Huey, Dewey, Louie in family portrait.

1995, Mar. 22	Perf. 13½x13, 13x13½	Litho.
2051-2058 A309	Set of 8	6.50 6.50
	Miniature Sheets of 8, #a-h	
2059-2060 A309	Set of 2	17.00 17.00

Souvenir Sheets

| 2061-2064 A309 | Set of 4 | 18.00 18.00 |

Eid Greetings — A310

1r, Mosque. 1r, Rose. 8r, Hibiscus. 10r, Orchids.

1995, May 1	Litho.	Perf. 14
2065-2068 A310	Set of 4	4.25 4.25

Whales, Dolphins, & Porpoises A311

Nos. 2069-2072: 1r, Killer whale. 2r, Bottlenose dolphin. 8r, Humpback whale. 10r, Common dolphin.
No. 2073, each 3r: a, Hourglass dolphin. b, Bottlenose dolphin. c, Dusky dolphin. d, Spectacled porpoise. e, Fraser's dolphin. f, Commerson's dolphin. g, Spinner dolphin. h, Dalls dolphin. i, Spotted dolphin. j, Indus river dolphin. k, Hector's dolphin. l, Amazon river dolphin.
No. 2074, each 3r: a, Right whale (d). b, Killer whale (a). c, Humpback whale (f). d, Beluga. e, Narwhale. f, Blue whale (e, g). g, Bowhead whale (h, k). h, Fin whale (d, e, g). i, Pilot whale. j, Grey whale. k, Sperm whale (l). l, Goosebeaked whale.
Each 25r: No. 2075, Hourglass dolphin. No. 2076, Sperm whale.

1995, May 16		
2069-2072 A311	Set of 4	4.00 4.00
	Miniature Sheets of 12, #a-l	
2073-2074 A311	Set of 2	15.50 15.50

Souvenir Sheets

| 2075-2076 A311 | Set of 2 | 12.00 12.00 |

Singapore '95.

UN, 50th Anniv. — A311a

Designs: 30 l, Emblem, security of small states. 8r, Women in development. 11r, Peace

MALDIVE ISLANDS

keeping, peace making operations. 13r, Disarmament.

1995, July 6   Litho.   Perf. 14
2076A-2076D   A311a   Set of 4   5.75   5.75

UN, 50th Anniv. — A312

No. 2077: a, 6.50r+50 l, Child, dove flying left. b, 8r, Earth from space. c, 10r, Child, Dove flying right.
25r, UN emblem, dove.

1995, July 6   Litho.   Perf. 14
2077   A312   Strip of 3, #a.-c.   4.50   4.50
Souvenir Sheet
2078   A312   25r multicolored   4.50   4.50

No. 2077 is a continuous design.

FAO, 50th Anniv. — A312a

7r, Food for all. 8r, Dolphin-friendly fishing.

1995   Litho.   Perf. 14
2078A   A312a   7r multi   1.25   1.25
2078B   A312a   8r multi   1.40   1.40

FAO, 50th Anniv. — A313

No. 2079: a, 6.50r+50 l, Child eating. b, 8r, FAO emblem. c, 10r, Mother, child.
25r, Food emblem, child, horiz.

1995, July 6
2079   A313   Strip of 3, #a.-c.   6.00   6.00
Souvenir Sheet
2080   A313   25r multicolored   6.00   6.00

1995 Boy Scout Jamboree, Holland — A314

No. 2081: a, 10r, Natl. flag, scouts, tents. b, 12r, Scout cooking. c, 15r, Scouts sitting before tents.
25r, Scout playing flute, camp at night, vert.

1995, July 6
2081   A314   Strip of 3, #a.-c.   6.75   6.75
Souvenir Sheet
2082   A314   25r multicolored   4.50   4.50

No. 2081 is a continuous design.

Queen Mother, 95th Birthday A315

No. 2083: a, Drawing. b, Blue print dress, pearls. c, Formal portrait. d, Blue outfit.
25r, Pale violet hat, violet & blue dress.

1995, July 6   Perf. 13½x14
2083   A315   5r Block or strip of 4, #a.-d.   4.00   4.00
Souvenir Sheet
2084   A315   25r multicolored   5.75   5.75

No. 2083 was issued in sheets of 2. Sheets of Nos. 2083-2084 exist overprinted in margin with black frame and text "In Memoriam 1900-2002."

Natl. Library, 50th Anniv. — A316

Designs: 2r, Boys seated at library table. 8r, Two people standing, two at table.
10r, Library entrance.

1995, July 12   Perf. 14
2085   A316   2r multicolored   .30   .30
2086   A316   8r multicolored   1.25   1.25
Size: 100x70mm
Imperf
2087   A316   10r multicolored   1.60   1.60

Miniature Sheets of 6 or 8

End of World War II, 50th Anniv. — A317

No. 2088: a, 203mm Red Army howitzer. b, Ruins of Hitler's residence, Berchtesgaden. c, Operation Manna, Allies drop food to starving Dutch. d, Soviet IL-1 fighter. e, Inmates, British troops burn last hut at Belsen. f, Last V1 Buzz Bomb launched against London. g, US 3rd Armored Division passes through ruins of Cologne. h, Gutted Reichstag, May 7, 1946.
No. 2089: a, Grumman F6F-3 Hellcat. b, F4-U1 attacking with rockets. c, Douglas Dauntless. d, Guadalcanal, Aug. 7, 1942. e, US Marines in Alligator landing craft. f, US Infantry landing craft.
Each 25r: No. 2090, Allied soldiers with smiling faces. No. 2091, Corsair fighters.

1995, July 6   Litho.   Perf. 14
2088   A317   5r #a.-h. + label   7.25   7.25
2089   A317   6.50r +50 l #a.-f. + label   9.00   9.00
Souvenir Sheets
2090-2091   A317   Set of 2   10.00   10.00

Turtles — A318

Hawksbill turtle: No. 2092a, Crawling. b, Two in water. c, One crawling out of water. d, Swimming.
No. 2093: a, Spur-thighed tortoise. b, Aldabra turtle. c, Loggerhead turtle. d, Olive ridley. e, Leatherback turtle. f, Green turtle. g, Atlantic ridley. h, Hawsbill turtle.
25r, Chelonia mydas.

1995, Aug. 22
2092   A318   10r Strip of 4, #a.-d.   10.00   10.00
Miniature Sheet of 8
2093   A318   3r #a.-h.   10.00   10.00
Souvenir Sheet
2094   A318   25r multicolored   13.00   13.00

World Wildlife Fund (No. 2092). No. 2092 was printed in sheets of 12 stamps.

Fourth World Conference on Women, Beijing — A318a

Designs: 30 l, Woman at computer. 1r, Woman high jumping. 8r, Women dancing. 11r, Woman pilot.

1995, Aug. 24   Litho.   Perf. 12¼
2094A-2094D   A318a   Set of 4   —

Miniature Sheets

Singapore '95 — A319

Mushrooms, butterflies, each 2r: No. 2095a, Russula aurata, papilio demodocus. b, Kallimoides rumia, lepista saeva. c, Lapista nuda, hypolimnas salmacis. d, Precis octavia, boletus subtomentosus.
No. 2096: a, 5r, Gyroporus castaneus, hypolimnas salmacis. b, 8r, Papilio dardanus, Gomphidius glutinosus. c, 10r, Russula olivacea, precis octavia. d, 12r, Prepona praeneste, boletus edulis.
Each 25r: No. 2097, Hypolimnas salmacis, boletus rhodoxanthus, vert. No. 2098, Amanita muscaria, kallimoides rumia, vert.

1995, Oct. 18   Litho.   Perf. 14
2095   A319   Sheet of 4, #a.-d.   2.00   2.00
2096   A319   Sheet of 4, #a.-d.   10.00   10.00
Souvenir Sheets
2097-2098   A319   Set of 2   10.00   10.00

Flowers — A320

Designs: 1r, Ballade tulip. 3r, White mallow. 5r, Regale trumpet lily. 7r, Lilactime dahlia. 8r, Blue ideal iris. 10r, Red crown imperial.
No. 2105, a, Dendrobium waipahu beauty. b, Brassocattleya Jean Murray "Allan Christenson." c, Cymbidium Fort George "Lewes." d, Paphiopedilum malipoense. e, Cycnoches chlorochilon. f, Rhyncholaelia digbgana. g, Lycaste deppei. h, Masdevallia constricta. i, Paphiopedilum Clair de Lune "Edgard Van Belle."
Each 25r: No. 2106, Psychopsis krameriana. No. 2107, Cockleshell orchid.

1995, Dec. 4   Litho.   Perf. 14
2099-2104   A320   Set of 6   7.25   7.25
Miniature Sheet
2105   A320   5r Sheet of 9, #a.-i.   9.25   9.25
Souvenir Sheets
2106-2107   A320   Set of 2   9.00   9.00

Miniature Sheet

Elvis Presley (1935-77) — A321

Various portraits.

1995, Dec. 8   Perf. 13½x14
2108   A321   5r Sheet of 9, #a.-i.   8.00   8.00
Souvenir Sheet
Perf. 14x13½
2109   A321   25r multi, horiz.   4.50   4.50

Miniature Sheets

John Lennon (1940-80), Entertainer — A322

No. 2110, Various portraits.
No. 2111: a, 10r, As young man. b, 8r, Younger man with glasses. c, 3r, With beard. d, 2r, Older picture without beard.
No. 2112, Standing at microphone.

1995, Dec. 8
2110   A322   5r Sheet of 6, #a.-f.   9.00   9.00
2111   A322   Sheet of 4, #a.-d.   7.00   7.00
Souvenir Sheet
2112   A322   25r multicolored   7.25   7.25

Nobel Prize Fund Established, Cent. — A323

Recipients: No. 2113, each 5r: a, Bernardo A. Houssay, medicine, 1947. b, Paul H. Müller, medicine, 1948. c, Walter R. Hess, medicine, 1949. d, Sir MacFarlane Burnet, medicine, 1960. e, Baruch S. Blumberg, medicine, 1976. f, Daniel Nathans, medicine, 1978. g, Glenn T. Seaborg, chemistry, 1951. h, Ilya Prigogine, chemistry, 1977. i, Kenichi Fukui, chemistry, 1981.
No. 2114, each 5r: a, Johannes Van Der Waals, physics, 1910. b, Charles Édouard Guillaume, physics, 1920. c, Sir James Chadwick, physics, 1935. d, Willem Einthoven, medicine, 1924. e, Henrik Dam, medicine, 1943. f, Sir Alexander Fleming, medicine, 1945. g, Hermann J. Muller, medicine, 1946. h, Rodney R. Porter, medicine, 1972. i, Werner Arber, medicine, 1978.
No. 2115, each 5r: a, Dag Hammarskjold, peace, 1961. b, Alva R. Myrdal, peace, 1982. c, Archbishop Desmond M. Tutu, peace, 1984. d, Rudolf C. Eucken, literature, 1908. e, Aleksandr Solzhenitsyn, literature, 1970. f, Gabriel Garcia Márquez, literature, 1982. g, Chen N. Yang, physics, 1957. h, Karl A. Müller, physics, 1987. i, Melvin Schwartz, physics, 1988.
No. 2116, each 5r: a, Niels Bohr, physics, 1922. b, Ben R. Mottelson, physics, 1975. c, Patrick White, literature, 1973. d, Elias Canetti, literature, 1981. e, Theodor Kocher, medicine, 1909. f, August Krogh, medicine, 1920. g, William P. Murphy, medicine, 1934. h, John H. Northrop, chemistry, 1946. i, Luis F. Leloir, chemistry, 1970.
No. 2117, each 5r: a, Carl Spitteler, literature, 1919. b, Henri Bergson, literature, 1927. c, Johannes V. Jensen, literature, 1944. d, Antoine-Henri Becquerel, physics, 1903. e, Sir William H. Bragg, physics, 1915. f, Sir William L. Bragg, physics, 1915. g, Fredrik Bajer, peace, 1908. h, Léon Bourgeois, peace, 1920. i, Karl Branting, peace, 1921.
No. 2118, each 5r: a, Robert A. Millikan, physics, 1923. b, Louis V. de Broglie, physics, 1929. c, Ernest Walton, physics, 1951. d, Richard Willstätter, chemistry, 1915. e, Lars Onsager, chemistry, 1968. f, Gerhard Herzberg, chemistry, 1971. g, William B. Yeats, literature, 1923. h, George B. Shaw, literature, 1925. i, Eugene O'Neill, literature, 1936.
Each 25r: No. 2119, Eisaku Sato, peace, 1974. No. 2120, Robert Koch, medicine, 1905. No. 2121, Otto Wallach, chemistry, 1910. No.

MALDIVE ISLANDS

2122, Konrad Bloch, medicine, 1964. No. 2123, Samuel Beckett, literature, 1969. No. 2124, Hideki Yukawa, physics, 1949.

1995, Dec. 28   Litho.   Perf. 14
Miniature Sheets of 9, #a-i
2113-2118   A323   Set of 6   48.00   48.00
Souvenir Sheets
2119-2124   A323   Set of 6   24.00   24.00

1996 Summer Olympics, Atlanta — A324

Designs: 1r, Rhythmic gymnastics, Tokyo, 1964. 3r, Archery, Moscow, 1980. 5r, Diving, Stockholm, 1912. 7r, High jump, London, 1948. 10r, Track and field, Berlin, 1936. 12r, Hurdles, Amsterdam 1928.
No. 2131: a, Montreal 1976. b, Decathlon. c, Olympic pin, Moscow, 1980. d, Fencing. e, Olympic medal. f, Equestrian. g, Sydney, 2000. h, Track and field. i, Seoul, 1988.
Each 25r: No. 2132, Olympic torch, vert. No. 2133, Olympic flame, vert.

1996, Jan. 25   Litho.   Perf. 14
2125-2130   A324   Set of 6   7.75   7.75
Miniature Sheet
2131   A324   5r Sheet of 9, #a.-i.   9.00   9.00
Souvenir Sheets
2132-2133   A324   Set of 2   10.50   10.50

Paintings from Metropolitan Museum of Art — A325

No. 2134, each 4r: a, Self-portrait, by Degas. b, Andromache & Astyanax, by Prud'hon. c, René Grenier, by Toulouse-Lautrec. d, The Banks of the Biévre Near Bicetre, by Rousseau. e, The Repast of the Lion, by Rousseau. f, Portrait Yves Gobillard-Morisot, by Degas. g, Sunflowers, by Van Gogh. h, The Singer in Green, by Degas.
No. 2135, each 4r: a, Still Life, by Fantin-Latour. b, Portrait of a Lady in Gray, by Degas. c, Apples & Grapes, by Monet. d, The Englishman, by Toulouse-Lautrec. e, Cypresses, by Van Gogh. f, Flowers in Chinese Vase, by Redon. g, The Gardener, by Seurat. h, Large Sunflowers I, by Nolde.
By Manet: No. 2136, each 4r: a, The Spanish Singer. b, Young Man in Costume of Majo. c, Mademoiselle Victorine. d, Boating. e, Peonies. f, Woman with a Parrot. g, George Moore. h, The Monet Family in Their Garden.
No. 2137, each 4r7: a, Goldfish, by Matisse. b, Spanish Woman: Harmony in Blue, by Matisse. c, Nasturtiums & the "Dance" II, by Matisse. d, The House Behind Trees, by Braque. e, Máda Primavesi, by Klimt. f, Head of a Woman, by Picasso. g, Woman in White, by Picasso. h, Harlequin, by Picasso.
Each 25r: No. 2138, Northeaster, by Homer. No. 2139, The Fortune Teller, by Georges de la Tour. No. 2140, Santi (Sanzio), Ritratto di Andrea Navagero E Agostino Beazzano, by Raphael. No. 2141, Portrait of a Woman, by Rubens.

1996, Apr. 22   Litho.   Perf. 13½x14
Sheets of 8, #a-h + label
2134-2137   A325   Set of 4   55.00   55.00
Souvenir Sheets
Perf. 14
2138-2141   A325   Set of 4   22.50   22.50
Nos. 2138-2141 each contain one 85x57mm stamp.
Nos. 2140-2141 are not in the Metropolitan Museum.
Nos. 2134-2141 exist imperf. Value, set $100.

Disney Characters Visit China A326

No. 2142, each 2r: a, Mickey at the Great Wall. b, Pluto's encounter in the Temple Garden. c, Minnie saves the pandas. d, Mickey sails with the junks. e, Goofy at the grottoes. f, Donald, Daisy at the marble boat.
No. 2143, each 2r: a, Traditional fishing with Donald, Goofy. d, Mickey, Minnie in dragon boat. e, Donald at Peking Opera. f, Mickey, Minnie, in Chinese Garden.
No. 2144, vert: a, Mickey, Minnie snowballing at ice pagoda. b, Donald, Mickey fly Chinese kites. c, Goofy plays anyiwu. d, Mickey, Goofy, origami. e, Donald, Mickey in dragon dance.
No. 2145, 5r, Mickey viewing Guilin. No. 2146, 7r, Mickey, Minnie at Moon Festival. No. 2147, 8r, Donald enjoying traditional Chinese food.

1996, May 10   Perf. 14x13½, 13½x14
Sheets of 6, #a-f
2142-2143   A326   Set of 2   11.50   11.50
Sheet of 5, #a-e
2144   A326   3r #a.-e. + label   6.00   6.00
Souvenir Sheets
2145   A326   5r multicolored   2.00   2.00
2146   A326   7r multicolored   2.50   2.50
2147   A326   8r multicolored   3.00   3.00
CHINA '96, 9th Asian Intl. Philatelic Exhibition.

1996 Summer Olympic Games, Atlanta — A327

Gold medalists: 1r, Stella Walsh, 100-meters, 1932. 3r, Emil Zatopek, 10,000-meters, 1952, vert. 10r, Olga Fikotova, discus throw, 1956. 12r, Joan Benoit, women's marathon, 1984.
No. 2152: a, Ethel Catherwood, high jump, 1928. b, Mildred "Babe" Didrikson, javelin, 1932. c, Francina (Fanny) Blankers-Koen, hurdles, 1948. d, Tamara Press, shot put, 1960. e, Lia Manoliu, discus, 1968. f, Роза Мота, women's marathon, 1988.
Gold medalists in weight lifting, vert: No. 2153a, Yanko Rusev, lightweight, 1980. b, Peter Baczako, middle heavyweight, 1980. c, Leonid Taranenko, heavyweight, 1980. d, Aleksandr Kurlovich, heavyweight, 1988. e, Assen Zlatev, middleweight, 1980. f, Zeng Guoqiang, flyweight, 1984. g, Yurik Vardanyan, heavyweight, 1980. h, Sultan Rakhmanov, super heavyweight, 1980. i, Vassily Alexeev, super heavyweight, 1972.
Each 25r: No. 2154, Irena Szewinska, gold medal winner, 400-meters, 1976. No. 2155, Naim Suleymanoglu, gold medal winner, weight lifting, 1988, vert.

1996, May 27   Litho.   Perf. 14
2148-2151   A327   Set of 4   5.75   5.75
Miniature Sheets
2152   A327   5r Sheet of 6, #a.-f.   6.50   6.50
2153   A327   5r Sheet of 9, #a.-i.   9.50   9.50
Souvenir Sheets
2154-2155   A327   Set of 2   11.00   11.00
Olymphilex '96 (No. 2155).

Queen Elizabeth II, 70th Birthday — A329

Designs: a, Portrait. b, As younger woman wearing hat, pearls. c, Younger picture seated at desk.
25r, On balcony with Queen Mother.

1996, June 21   Litho.   Perf. 13½x14
2164   A329   8r Strip of 3, #a.-c.   5.50   5.50
Souvenir Sheet
2165   A329   25r multicolored   6.25   6.25
No. 2164 was issued in sheets of 9 stamps.

UNICEF, 50th Anniv. — A330

Designs: 5r (No. 2166), 7r (No. 2167), 7r (No. 2167A), girl, blue margin, 10r (No. 2168), Girls of different races.
25r, Baby girl.

1996, July 10   Perf. 14
2166-2168   A330   Set of 4   4.50   4.50
Souvenir Sheet
2169   A330   25r multicolored   4.50   4.50

Butterflies — A331

No. 2170, vert: a, Cymothoe cocccinata. b, Morpho rhetenor. c, Callicore lidwina (b, d). d, Heliconius erato.
No. 2171: a, Epiphora albida. b, Satyrus dryas. c, Satyrus lena. d, Papilio tynderaeus. e, Urota Suraka. f, Satyrus nercis.
No. 2172, vert: a, Spicebush swallowtail. b, Giant swallowtail. c, Lime swallowtail caterpillar (b). d, Painted beauty (c). e, Monarch caterpillar. f, Monarch (e, g). g, Monarch caterpillar & pupa. h, Harris' checkerspot.
Each 25r: No. 2173, Heliconius cydno, vert. No. 2174, Zebra, vert.

1996, July 10
2170   A331   7r Strip of 4, #a.-d.   5.25   5.25
2171   A331   7r Sheet of 6, #a.-f.   8.00   8.00
2172   A331   7r Sheet of 8, #a.-h.   11.00   11.00
Souvenir Sheets
2173-2174   A331   Set of 2   11.00   11.00
No. 2170 was issued in sheets of 8 stamps.

Space Exploration — A332

Designs: No. 2175a, Sputnik I, 1957. b, Apollo 11 Command Module returns to earth, 1969. c, Skylab, 1973. d, Edward White, 1st US astronaut to walk in space, 1965. e, Mariner 9, 1st artificial satellite of Mars, 1971. f, Apollo and Soviet Soyuz dock together, 1975.
25r, Apollo 8 being launched, 1968, vert.

1996, July 10   Perf. 14
2175   A332   6r Sheet of 6, #a.-f.   6.50   6.50
Souvenir Sheet
2176   A332   25r multicolored   5.25   5.25

Trains — A333

No. 2177, each 3r: a, Electric container train, Germany. b, John Blenkinsop's rack locomotive. c, DB Diesel electric, West Germany. d, Timothy Hackworth's "Royal George," 1827. e, Robert Stephenson (1803-59). f, Trevithick's "New Castle" locomotive. g, Trevithick's locomotive No. 5, 1826. h, Passenger shuttle, English Channel Tunnel.
No. 2178, each 3r: a, Southern Pacific's "Daylight," San Francisco, US, 1952. b, Timothy Hackworth's "Sans Pareil." c, Chicago & North Western, US. d, Richard Trevithick's "Pen-Y-Darran" locomotive. e, Isambard Kingdom Brunel (1806-59). f, Great Western engine of 1838. g, Passenger train, Canada. h, Mohawk & Hudson Railroad "Experiment," 1832. i, "The ICE," Germany.
No. 2179, each 3r: a, F4 OPH Diesel locomotives, US. b, Stephenson's "Experiment." c, Indian Pacific Intercontinental, Australia. d, George Stephenson's engine, 1815. e, George Stephenson (1781-1848). f, Stephenson's "Rocket," 1829. g, British Rail 125 HST. h, First rail passenger coach, "Experiment," 1825. i, TOFAC, US.
Each 25r: No. 2180, Tom Thumb, 1830. No. 2181, The DeWitt Clinton, 1831. No. 2182, The General, 1855.

1996, Sept. 2   Litho.   Perf. 14
Sheets of 9, #a-i
2177-2179   A333   Set of 3   24.00   24.00
Souvenir Sheets
2180-2182   A333   Set of 3   16.00   16.00

Fauna — A334

Endangered animals:
No. 2183, each 5r: a, Shoebill stork. b, Red-billed hornbill. c, Hippopotamus. d, Gorilla. e, Lion. f, Gray-crowned crane.
No. 2184, each 5r: a, Giant panda. b, Indian elephant. c, Arrow poison frog. d, Mandrill. e, Snow leopard. f, California condor.
Wildlife:
No. 2185, vert, each 5r: a, Yellow baboon. b, Zebra duiker. c, Yellow-backed duiker. d, Pygmy hippopotamus. e, Large-spotted genet. f, African spoonbill. g, White-faced whistling duck. h, Helmeted gunieafowl.
No. 2186, vert, each 5r: a, Bongo. b, Bushback. c, Namaqua dove. d, Hoopoe. e, African fish eagle. f, Egyptian goose. g, Saddle-billed stork. h, Blue-breasted kingfisher.
Each 25r: No. 2187, Tiger, vert. No. 2188, Leopard.

1996, Sept. 9   Sheet of 6
2183-2184   A334   Set of 2   20.00   20.00
Sheet of 8
2185-2186   A334   Set of 2   26.50   26.50
Souvenir Sheets
2187-2188   A334   Set of 2   12.00   12.00

Motion Pictures, Cent. A335

Progressive scenes from "Pluto and the Flypaper," each 4r:" Nos. 2189a-2189h, Scenes 1-8. No. 2191a-2191i, Scenes 9-17.
Progressive scenes from "Mickey Mouse in The Little Whirlwind, each 4r:" Nos. 2190a-2190h, Scenes 1-8. Nos. 2192a-2192i, Scenes 9-17.
Each 25r: No. 2193, Scene from "Pluto and the Flypaper." No. 2194, Scene from "Mickey Mouse in The Little Whirlwind."

1996, Dec. 2   Litho.   Perf. 13½x14
Sheets of 8, #a-h, + Label
2189-2190   A335   Set of 2   25.00   25.00
Sheets of 9, #a-i
2191-2192   A335   Set of 2   27.50   27.50
Souvenir Sheets
2193-2194   A335   Set of 2   18.50   18.50

Fauna — A336

Designs: a, Saguinus oedipus. b, Bison bonasus. c, Panthera tigris. d, Tetrao urogallus. e, Ailuropoda melanoleuca. f, Trogonoptera brookiana. g, Castor canadensis. h, Lelopelma hamiltoni. i, Trichechus manatus latirostris.
25r, Pan troglodytes.

1996   Litho.   Perf. 14
2195   A336   7r Sheet of 9, #a.-i.   12.50   12.50
Souvenir Sheet
2196   A336   25r multicolored   5.00   5.00

Turtle Preservation — A336a

1996 ?   Litho.   Perf. 12¾
2196A   Horiz. strip of 3   —   —
  b.   A336a 1r Turtle's head   —   —
  c.   A336a 7r Turtle's plastron   —   —
  d.   A336a 8r Two turtles   —   —

MALDIVE ISLANDS

Hong Kong '97 — A337

Chinese motifs inside letters: No. 2197a, "H." b, "O." c, "N." d, "G" (birds). e, "K." f, "O," diff. g, "N." h, "G" (junk). 25r, "Hong Kong."

	1997, Feb. 12		Litho.	Perf. 14
2197	A337	5r Sheet of 8, #a.-h.	8.50	8.50

Souvenir Sheet

2198	A337	25r multicolored	5.25	5.25

No. 2198 contains one 77x39mm stamp.

Birds — A338

a, Gymnogyps californianus. b, Larus audouinii. c, Fratercula artica. d, Pharomachrus mocinno. e, Amazona vittata. f, Paradisaea minor. g, Nipponia nippon. h, Falco punctatus. i, Strigops habroptilus. 25r, Campephilus principalis.

1997, Feb. 12				
2199	A338	5r Sheet of 9, #a.-i.	10.50	10.50

Souvenir Sheet

| 2200 | A338 | 25r multicolored | 6.25 | 6.25 |

Eagles A339 A340

Designs: 1r, Crowned solitary eagle. 2r, African hawk eagle, horiz. 3r, Lesser spotted eagle. 5r, Steller's sea eagle. 8r, Spanish imperial eagle, horiz. 10r, Harpy eagle. 12r, Crested serpent eagle, horiz.

Bald eagles: No. 2208: a, Wings upward in flight. b, Looking backward on limb. c, Up close, head left. d, Up close, head right. e, On limb. f, In flight.

No. 2209, American bald eagle, horiz. No. 2210, Bald eagle.

1997, Mar. 20			Litho.	Perf. 14
2201-2207	A339	Set of 7	8.00	8.00
2208	A340	5r Sheet of 6, #a.-f.	6.00	6.00

Souvenir Sheets

| 2209 | A339 | 25r multicolored | 4.75 | 4.75 |
| 2210 | A340 | 25r multicolored | 4.75 | 4.75 |

Automobiles A341

No. 2211, each 5r: a, 1911 Blitzer Benz, Germany. b, 1917 Datsun, Japan. c, 1929 Auburn 8-120, US. d, 1996 Mercedes-Benz C280, Germany. e, Suzuki UR-1, Japan. f, Chrysler Atlantic, US.

No. 2212, each 5r: a, 1961 Mercedes-Benz 190SL, Germany. b, 1916 Kwaishinha DAT, Japan. c, 20/25 Rolls-Royce Roadster, England. d, 1997 Mercedes-Benz SLK, Germany. e, 1996 Toyota Camry, Japan. f, 1959 Jaguar MK2, England.

Each 25r: No. 2213, 1939 VW built by Dr. Porsche. No. 2214, Mazda RX-01.

1997, Mar. 27			Sheets of 6, #a-f
2211-2212	A341	Set of 2	11.50 11.50

Souvenir Sheets

| 2213-2214 | A341 | Set of 2 | 9.50 9.50 |

1998 Winter Olympics, Nagano — A342

Medalists: 2r, Ye Qiaobo, 1992 speed skating. 3r, Leonhard Stock, 1980 downhill. 8r, Bjorn Daehlie, 1992 cross-country skiing. 12r, Wolfgang Hoppe, 1984 bobsledding.

No. 2219: a, Herma Von Szabo-Planck, 1924 figure skating. b, Katarina Witt, 1988 figure skating. c, Natalia Bestemianova, Andrei Bukin, 1988 ice dancing. d, Jayne Torvill, Christopher Dean, 1984 ice dancing.

Each 25r: No. 2220, Sonja Henie, 1924 figure skating. No. 2221, Andree Joly, Pierre Brunet, 1932 figure skating.

1997, Mar. 13			Litho.	Perf. 14
2215-2218	A342	Set of 4	5.25	5.25
2219	A342	5r Block of 4, #a.-d.	4.25	4.25

Souvenir Sheets

| 2220-2221 | A342 | Set of 2 | 11.00 | 11.00 |

No. 2219 was issued in sheets of 8 stamps.

Ships — A343

Designs: 1r, SS Patris II, 1926, Greece. 2r, MV Infanta Beatriz, 1928, Spain. 8r, SS Stavangerjord, 1918, Norway. 12r, MV Baloeran, 1929, Holland.

No. 2226, each 3r: a, SS Vasilefs Constantinos, 1914, Greece. b, SS Cunene, 1911, Portugal. c, MV Selandia, 1912, Denmark. d, SS President Harding, 1921, US. e, MV Ulster Monarch, 1929, Great Britain. f, SS Matsonia, 1913, US. g, SS France, 1911, France. h, SS Campania, 1893, Great Britain. i, SS Klipfontein, 1922, Holland.

No. 2227, each 3r: a, MV Eridan, 1929, France. b, SS Mount Clinton, 1921, US. c, SS Infanta Isabel, 1912, Spain. d, SS Suwa Maru, 1914, Japan. e, SS Yorkshire, 1920, Great Britain. f, MV Highland Chieftan, 1929, Great Britain. g, MV Sardinia, 1920, Norway. h, SS San Guglielmo, 1911, Italy. i, SS Avila, 1927, Great Britain.

Each 25r: No. 2228, SS Mauritania, 1907, Great Britain. No. 2229, SS United States, 1952, US. No. 2230, SS Queen Mary, 1930, Great Britain. No. 2231, Royal Yacht Brittania sailing into Hong Kong harbor.

1997, Apr. 1				
2222-2225	A343	Set of 4	6.00	6.00
		Sheets of 9, #a-i		
2226-2227	A343	Set of 2	12.50	12.50

Souvenir Sheets

| 2228-2231 | A343 | Set of 4 | 22.00 | 22.00 |

No. 2231 contains one 57x42mm stamp.

UNESCO, 50th Anniv. — A344

1r, Prayer wheels, Lhasa, vert. 2r, Roman ruins, Temple of Diana, Portugal. 3r, Cathedral of Santa Maria Hildesheim, Germany. 7r, Monument of Nubia at Abu Simbel, Egypt, vert. 8r, Entrance to Port of Mandraki, Rhodes, Greece. 10r, Nature Reserve of Scandola, France. 12r, Temple on the Lake, China.

No. 2232, vert, each 5r: a, Virunga Natl. Park, Zaire. b, Valley of Mai Nature Reserve, Seychelles. c, Kandy, Sri Lanka. d, Taj Mahal, India. e, Istanbul, Turkey. f, Sana'a, Yemen. g, Blenheim Palace, Oxfordshire, England. h, Grand Canyon Natl. Park, US.

No. 2233, vert, each 5r: a, Gondar, Ethiopia. b, Bwindi Natl. Park, Uganda. c, Bemaraha Nature Reserve, Madagascar. d, Buddhist ruins of Takht-i-Bahi, Pakistan. e, Anuradhapura, Sri Lanka. f, Cairo, Egypt. g, Ruins at Petra, Jordan. h, Natl. Park of Ujung Kulon, Indonesia.

Sites in China, vert: No. 2234, each 5r: a-f, Mount Taishan. g-h, Terracotta warriors.

Sites in Japan: No. 2235, each 8r: a-e, Horyu-Ji.

No. 2236, each 8r: a, Monastery of Agios Stefanos Meteora, Greece. b, Taj Mahal, India. c, Cistercian Abbey of Fontenay, France. d, Yakushima, Japan. e, Cloisters of the Convent, San Gonzalo, Portugal.

No. 2237, each 8r: a, Olympic Natl. Park, US. b, Nahanni Waterfalls, Canada. c, Los Glaciares Natl. Park, Argentina. d, Bonfin Salvador Church, Brazil. e, Convent of the Companions of Jesus, Morelia, Mexico.

Each 25r: No. 2238, Temple, Chengde, China. No. 2239, Serengeti Natl. Park, Tanzania. No. 2240, Anuradhapura, Sri Lanka. No. 2241, Monument to Fatehpur Sikri, India.

1997, Apr. 7				
2231A-2231G	A344	Set of 7	5.75	5.75
		Sheets of 8, #a-h, + Label		
2232-2234	A344	Set of 3	22.00	22.00
		Sheets of 5, #a-e, + Label		
2235-2237	A344	Set of 3	22.00	22.00

Souvenir Sheets

| 2238-2241 | A344 | Set of 4 | 18.00 | 18.00 |

Queen Elizabeth II, Prince Philip, 50th Wedding Anniv. — A345

No. 2242: a, Queen. b, Royal Arms. c, Queen, Prince seated on thrones. d, Queen, Prince holding baby. e, Buckingham Palace. f, Prince. 25r, Queen wearing crown.

1997, June 12			Litho.	Perf. 14
2242	A345	5r Sheet of 6, #a.-f.	7.75	7.75

Souvenir Sheet

| 2243 | A345 | 25r multicolored | 5.50 | 5.50 |

Paintings by Hiroshige (1797-1858) A346

No. 2244: a, Dawn at Kanda Myojin Shrine. b, Kiyomizu Hall & Shinobazu Pond at Ueno. c, Ueno Yamashita. d, Moon Pine, Ueno. e, Flower Pavilion, Dango Slope, Sendagi. f, Shitaya Hirokoji.

Each 25r: No. 2245, Seido and Kanda River from Shohei Bridge. No. 2246, Hilltop View, Yushima Tenjin Shrine.

1997, June 12				Perf. 13½x14
2244	A346	8r Sheet of 6, #a.-f.	8.50	8.50

Souvenir Sheets

| 2245-2246 | A346 | Set of 2 | 9.00 | 9.00 |

Heinrich von Stephan (1831-97) — A347

a, Early mail messenger, India. b, Von Stephan, UPU emblem. c, Autogiro, Washington DC.

1997, June 12				Perf. 14
2247	A347	2r Sheet of 3, #a.-c.	3.25	3.25

PACIFIC 97.
A number has been reserved for a souvenir sheet with this set.

A348

3r, South Asian Assoc. for Regional Cooperation (SAARC) Summit. 5r,

1997, May 12			Litho.	Perf. 13
2249	A348	3r shown	.60	.60
2250	A348	5r Flags, "SAARC"	1.10	1.10

A349

Birds: 30 l, Anous stolidus. 1r, Spectacled owl. 2r, Buffy fish owl. 3r, Peregrine falcon. 5r, Golden eagle. 8r, Bateleur. No. 2257, 10r, Crested caracara. No. 2258, 10r, Childonias hybrida. 15r, Sula sula.

No. 2260: a, Rueppell's parrot. b, Blue-headed parrot. c, St. Vincent parrot. d, Gray parrot. e, Masked lovebird. f, Sun parakeet.

Each 25r: No. 2261, Secretary bird. No. 2262, Bald eagle.

1997				Perf. 14
2251-2259	A349	Set of 9	9.75	9.75
2260	A349	7r Sheet of 6, #a.-f.	8.25	8.25

Souvenir Sheets

| 2261-2262 | A349 | Set of 2 | 11.50 | 11.50 |

A350

Flowers: 1r, Canarina eminii. 2r, Delphinium macrocentron. 3r, Leucadendron discolor. 5r, Nymphaea caerulea. 7r, Rosa multiflora. 8r, Bulbophyllum barbigerum. 12r, Hibiscus vitifolius.

No. 2270, horiz: a, Acacia seyal. b, Gloriosa superba. c, Gnidia subcordata. d, Platycelphium voense. e, Aspilia mossambicensis. f, Adenium obesum.

Each 25r: No. 2271, Aerangis rhodosticta, horiz. No. 2272, Dichrostachys cinerea, horiz.

1997, June 24			Litho.	Perf. 14½x14
2263-2269	A350	Set of 7	7.50	7.50
				Perf. 14x14½
2270	A350	8r Sheet of 6, #a.-f.	12.00	12.00

Souvenir Sheets

| 2271-2272 | A350 | Set of 2 | 18.00 | 18.00 |

No. 2267 is 16x20mm. See No. 2543. For surcharge, see No. 2543A.

A351

Dinosaurs — A352

5r, Archaeopteryx. 8r, Mosasaurus. 12r, Deinonychus. 15r, Triceratops.

No. 2277, each 7r: a, Diplodocus (b, c, d, e, f). b, Tyrannosaurus rex (c, e, f). c, Pteranodon. d, Montanaceratops. e, Dromaeosaurus (d). f, Oviraptor (e).

No. 2278, each 7r: a, Euoplocephalus. b, Compsognathus. c, Herrerasaurus. d, Styracosaurus. e, Baryonyx. f, Lesothosaurus.

No. 2279, each 7r: a, Triceratops. b, Pachycephalosaurus. c, Iguanodon. d, Tyrannosaurus. e, Corythosaurus. f, Stegosaurus.

No. 2280, each 7r: a, Troodon (d). b, Brachosaurus (c). c, Saltasaurus (a, b, d, e, f). d, Oviraptor. e, Parasaurolophus (f). f, Psittacosaurus.

MALDIVE ISLANDS

No. 2281, Tyrannosaurus rex. No. 2282, Archaeopteryx.

1997, Nov. 20   Litho.   *Perf. 14*
2273-2276 A351 Set of 4   7.25   7.25
Sheets of 6, #a-f
2277 A351 7r #a.-f.   7.50   7.50
2278-2280 A352 Set of 3   22.50   22.50
Souvenir Sheets
2281 A351 25r multicolored   11.50   11.50
2282 A352 25r multicolored   11.50   11.50

1998 World Cup Soccer Championships, France — A353

Past winners: 1r, Brazil, 1994. 2r, West Germany, 1954. 3r, Argentina, 1986. 7r, Argentina, 1978. 8r, England, 1966. 10r, Brazil, 1970.
Various scenes from 1966 finals, England v. West Germany, each 3r: Nos. 2289a-2289h.
Italian tournament winners, each 3r: No. 2290: a, Paulo Rossi, Italy, 1982. b, Zoff & Gentile, Italy, 1982. c, Angelo Schiavio, Italy. d, 1934 team. e, 1934 team entering stadium. f, 1982 team. g, San Paolo Stadium, Italy. h, 1938 team.
Brazilian teams, players, each 3r: No. 2291: a, 1958 team pictue. b, Luis Bellini, 1958. c, 1962 team. d, Carlos Alberto, 1970. e, Mauro, 1962. f, 1970 team. g, Dunga, 1994. h, 1994 team.
Each 25r: No. 2292, Klinsmann, Germany. No. 2293, Ronaldo, Brazil, vert. No. 2294, Schmeichel, Denmark, vert.

Perf. 14x13½, 13½x14
1997, Dec. 10   Litho.
2283-2288 A353 Set of 6   5.75   5.75
Sheets of 8 + Label
2289-2291 A353 Set of 3   13.50   13.50
Souvenir Sheets
2292-2294 A353 Set of 3   15.50   15.50

Diana, Princess of Wales (1961-97) — A354

Various portraits, color of sheet margin, each 7r: No. 2295, Pale pink. No. 2296, Pale yellow. No. 2297, Pale blue.
Each 25r: No. 2298, Diana on ski lift. No. 2299, In polka dot dress. No. 2300, Wearing lei.

1998, Feb. 9   Litho.   *Perf. 13½*
Sheets of 6, #a-f
2295-2297 A354 Set of 3   20.00   20.00
Souvenir Sheets
2298-2300 A354 Set of 3   13.50   13.50

John F. Kennedy (1917-63) — A355

Various portraits.

1998   Litho.   *Perf. 13½x14*
2301 A355 5r Sheet of 9, #a.-i.   8.50   8.50

Nelson Mandela, Pres. of South Africa — A356

1998   *Perf. 14*
2302 A356 4r multicolored   1.60   1.60

Classic Airplanes A357

No. 2303: a, Yakovlev Yak 18. b, Beechcraft Bonanza. c, Piper Cub. d, Tupolev Tu-95. e, Lockheed C-130 Hercules. f, Piper PA-28 Cherokee. g, Mikoyan-Gurevich MiG-21. h, Pilatus PC-6 Turbo Porter. i, Antonov An-2.
25r, KC-135E.

1998
2303 A357 5r Sheet of 9, #a.-i.   8.50   8.50
Souvenir Sheet
2304 A357 25r multicolored   4.50   4.50
No. 2304 contains one 85x28mm stamp.

Cats — A358

Designs, vert: 5r, White American shorthair. 8r, Sphinx. 10r, Tabby American shorthair. 12r, Scottish fold.
No. 2309, each 7r: a, American curl, Maine coon (d). b, Maine coon (a, d, e). c, Siberian (f). d, Somali. e, European Burmese (d). f, Nebelung.
No. 2310, each 7r: a, Bicolor British shorthair (b). b, Manx. c, Tabby American shorthair (b, e, f). d, Silver tabby Persian (e). e, Oriental white. f, Norwegian forest cat (e).
Each 30r: No. 2311, Snowshoe, vert. No. 2312, Norwegian forest cat, vert.

1998, June 1   Litho.   *Perf. 14*
2305-2308 A358 Set of 4   6.00   6.00
Sheets of 6, #a-f
2309-2310 A358 Set of 2   14.00   14.00
Souvenir Sheets
2311-2312 A358 Set of 2   11.00   11.00

Airplanes A359

Designs: 2r, Boeing 737 HS. 7r, Boeing 727. 8r, Boeing 747, 1970. 10r, Boeing 737.
No. 2317, each 5r: a, FSW Fighter. b, V-Jet II. c, Pilatus PC-12. d, Citation Exel. e, Stutz Bearcat (stamp actually shows Pitts S-2S Special). f, Cessna T-37 (R) g, Peregrine business jet. h, Beech Baron 58.
No. 2318, each 5r: a, CL-215. b, P-3 Orion. c, Yak 54. d, Cessna float plane. e, CL-215 Amphibian. f, CL-215 SAR Amphibian. g, Twin Otter. h, Rockwell Quail.
Each 25r: No. 2319, Falcon Jet. No. 2320, Beechcraft Model 18.

1998, Aug. 10   Litho.   *Perf. 14*
2313-2316 A359 Set of 4   4.75   4.75
Sheets of 8, #a-h
2317-2318 A359 Set of 2   14.50   14.50
Souvenir Sheets
2319-2320 A359 Set of 2   10.00   10.00

The Titanic — A360

No. 2321: a, Capt. Edward J. Smith's cap. b, Deck chair. c, Fifth Officer Harold Lowe's coat button. d, Lifeboat. e, Steering wheel. f, Lifejacket.
25r, Newpaper picture of the Titanic at sea.

1998, Sept. 27   Litho.   *Perf. 14*
2321 A360 7r Sheet of 6, #a.-f.   8.75   8.75
Souvenir Sheet
2322 A360 25r multicolored   5.25   5.25

Bird Type of 1992
1998, Oct. 26   Litho.   *Perf. 14½*
2323 A247 100r Anas clypeata   14.00   14.00

IFAD, 20th Anniv. — A361

Designs: 1r, Papaya tree. 5r, Fruits. 7r, Fishermen on boat. 8r, Coconut tree. 10r, Vegetables.

1998, Nov. 30   Litho.   *Perf. 14*
2324-2328 A361 Set of 5   5.50   5.50

Ferrari Automobiles — A361a

No. 2028A: c, 250 TR. d, 1957 250 GT TDF. e, 250 GT.
25r, 365 GTC 2+2.

1998, Dec. 15   Litho.   *Perf. 14*
2328A A361a 10r Sheet of 3, #c-e   5.25   5.25
Souvenir Sheet
Perf. 13¾x14¼
2328B A361a 25r multi   4.25   4.25
No. 2328A contains three 39x25mm stamps.

1998 World Scout Jamboree, Chile — A362

a, Robert Baden-Powell inspecting Scouts, Amesbury, c. 1909. b, Lord, Lady Baden-Powell, children, South Africa Tour, 1927. c, Robert Baden-Powell pins merit badges on Chicago Scouts, 1926.

1998, Dec. 15
2329 A362 12r Sheet of 3, #a.-c.   6.75   6.75

Diana, Princess of Wales (1961-97) — A363

No. 2330: a, Inscription panel at left. b, Panel at right.

1998, Dec. 15   *Perf. 14½x14*
2330 A363 10r Horiz. pair, #a-b   3.75   3.75
Size: 95x56mm
Litho. & Embossed
Die Cut Perf. 7½
2331 A364 50r shown
2332 A364 50r Rose, Diana
No. 2330 was issued in sheets of 3 pairs.

Fish — A365

Designs: No. 2333, 50 l, Threadfin butterfly fish. No. 2334, 50 l, Queen angelfish. 1r, Oriental sweetlips. No. 2336, 7r, Bandit angelfish. No. 2337, 7r, Achilles tang. 8r, Red-headed butterfly fish. 50r, Blue striped butterfly fish.
No. 2340: a, Mandarinfish. b, Copperbanded butterfly fish. c, Harlequin tuskfish. d, Yellow tailed demoiselle. e, Wimplefish. f, Red emperor snapper. g, Clown triggerfish. h, Common clown. i, Regal tang.
No. 2341: a, Emperor angelfish. b, Common squirrelfish. c, Lemonpeel angelfish. d, Powderblue surgeon. e, Moorish idol. f, Bicolor cherub. g, Scribbled angelfish. h, Two-banded anemonefish. i, Yellow tang.
Each 25r: No. 2342, Porkfish. No. 2343, Long-nosed butterfly fish.

1998, Dec. 10   Litho.   *Perf. 14*
2333-2339 A365 Set of 7   13.50   13.50
2340 A365 3r Sheet of 9, #a.-i.   4.75   4.75
2341 A365 7r Sheet of 9, #a.-i.   8.25   8.25
Souvenir Sheets
2342-2343 A365 Set of 2   9.00   9.00

Intl. Year of the Ocean — A366

Marine life: No. 2344, Skipjack tuna.
No. 2345: a, 25 l, Triton. b, 50 l, Napoleon wrasse. c, 1r, Whale shark. d, 3r, Gray reef shark. e, 7r, Blue whale.
No. 2346: a, Harp seal. b, Killer whale. c, Sea otter. d, Beluga. e, Narwhal. f, Walrus. g, Sea lion. h, Humpback salmon. i, Emperor penguin.
No. 2347: a, Ocean sunfish. b, Opalescent squid. c, Electric eel. d, Corded neptune.
Each 25r: No. 2348, Horseshoe crab. No. 2349, Blue whale. No. 2350, Triton, diff.

1999, Apr. 1   Litho.   *Perf. 14*
2344 A366 7r multicolored   1.25   1.25
Sheets of 6, 9, 4
2345 A366 #a.-e. + 1 #2344   3.50   3.50
2346 A366 5r #a.-i.   8.00   8.00
2347 A366 8r #a.-d.   5.75   5.75
Souvenir Sheets
2348-2350 A366 Set of 3   13.50   13.50
No. 2344 was issued in sheets of 6.
No. 2350 incorrectly inscribed Coral Reef.

MALDIVE ISLANDS

Mickey Mouse, 70th Anniv. (in 1998) — A367

No. 2351, each 5r: Various pictures of Mickey Mouse.
No. 2352, each 5r: Various pictures of Minnie Mouse.
No. 2353, each 7r: Various pictures of Donald Duck.
No. 2354, each 7r: Various pictures of Daisy Duck.
No. 2355, each 7r: Various pictures of Goofy.
No. 2356, each 7r: Various pictures of Pluto.
Each 25r: No. 2357, Minnie sipping drink. No. 2358, Minnie looking backward. No. 2359, Mickey grabbing Donald's hand, horiz. No. 2360, Minnie wearing pearls. No. 2361, Mickey with hand on head. No. 2362, Mickey after throwing ball.

Perf. 13½x14, 14x13½ (#2359)
1999, May 27   Litho.
2351-2352	A367	Set of 2	12.00	12.00
2353-2356	A367	Set of 4	30.00	30.00

Souvenir Sheets
2357-2362	A367	Set of 6	25.00	25.00

Stamp in No. 2358 is printed se-tenant with label.
Sheets similar to Nos. 2351-2352 with "5Rs" denomination and Nos. 2353-2356 with "25Rs" exist. Value, set of 6 sheets, $195.

Butterflies — A368

50 l, Great orange tip. 1r, Large green aporandria. 2r, Common mormon. 3r, African migrant. 5r, Common pierrot. 10r, Giant redeye.
No. 2369, vert, each 7r: a, Common red flash. b, Burmese lascar. c, Common peirrot. d, Baron. e, Leaf blue. f, Great orange tip.
No. 2370, vert, each 7r: a, Crimson tip. b, Tawny rajah. c, Leafwing butterfly. d, Great egg-fly. e, Blue admiral. f, African migrant.
Each 25r: No. 2371, Crimson tip. No. 2372, Large oak blue.

1999, June 8   Litho.   Perf. 14
2363-2368	A368	Set of 6	3.75	3.75

Sheets of 6, #a-f
2369-2370	A368	Set of 2	15.00	15.00

Souvenir Sheets
2371-2372	A368	Set of 2	10.00	10.00

Dinosaurs — A369

Designs: 1r, Scelidosaurus. 3r, Yansudaurus. 5r, Ornitholestes. 8r, Astrodon.
No. 2377, vert, each 7r: a, Anchisaurus. b, Pterenodon. c, Barosaurus. d, Iguanodon. e, Archaeopteryx. f, Ceratosaurus.
No. 2378, each 7r: a, Stegosaurus. b, Corythosaurus. c, Celiosaurus. d, Avimimus. e, Styracosaurus. f, Massospondylus.
No. 2379, vert, each 7r: a, Dimorphodon. b, Rhamphorhynchus. c, Allosaurus. d, Leaellynasaura. e, Troodon. f, Syntarsus.
Each 25r: No. 2380, Brachiosaurus. No. 2381, Megalosaurus.

1999, June 22
2373-2376	A369	Set of 4	3.25	3.25

Sheets of 6, #a-f
2377-2379	A369	Set of 3	24.50	24.50

Souvenir Sheets
2380-2381	A369	Set of 2	10.00	10.00

Marine Environment Wildlife — A370

30 l, Broderip's cowrie. 1r, Fairy tern. 3r, Darker Maldivian green heron. 7r, Blackflag sandperch. 8r, Coral hind. 10r, Olive ridley turtle.
No. 2388, each 5r: a, Brown booby. b, Red-tailed tropicbird. c, Sooty tern. d, Striped dolphin. e, Long-snouted spinner dolphin. f, Crab plover. g, Hawksbill turtle. h, Indo-Pacific sergeant. i, Yellowfin tuna.
No. 2389, each 5r: a, Manta ray. b, Green turtle. c, Pan-tropical spotted dolphin. d, Moorish idols. e, Threadfin anthias. f, Goldbar wrasse. g, Palette surgeonfish. h, Three spot angelfish. i, Oriental sweetlips.
Each 25r: No. 2390, Cinnamon bittern. No. 2391, Blue-faced angelfish.

1999, Oct. 26   Litho.   Perf. 14
2382-2387	A370	Set of 6	6.00	6.00

Sheets of 9, #a-i
2388-2389	A370	Set of 2	16.50	16.50

Souvenir Sheets
2390-2391	A370	Set of 2	9.50	9.50

Trains — A371

Designs: 50 l, 2-2-2 locomotive, Egypt. 1r, Le Shuttle, France. 2r, 4-4-0 Gowan & Marx, US. 3r, TGV, France. 5r, Ae 6/6 electric locomotive, Switzerland. 8r, Stephenson's Long-boilered 2-4-0 locomotive, Great Britain. 10r, The Philadelphia, Austria. 15r. E class, Great Britain.
No. 2400, each 7r: a, Stephenson's Long-boilered 2-4-0 locomotive, diff. b, 4-2-2 Cornwall, Great Britain. c, First locomotive, Germany. d, Great Western, Great Britain. e, Standard Stephenson 2-4-0, France. f, 2-2-2 Meteor, Great Britain.
No. 2401, each 7r: a, Type 4 class 4t, Great Britain. b, 1500 horsepower Diesel-electric locomotive, Malaysia. c, Co-Co 7000 Class, France. d, Diesel-hydraulic passenger locomotive, Thailand. e, Diesel-hydraulic locomotive, Burma. f, Hikari, Japan.
No. 2402, 25r, 2-2-2, Passenger locomotive, France. No. 2403, 25r, King Arthur class, Great Britain.

1999, Oct. 26
2392-2399	A371	Set of 8	7.50	7.50

Sheets of 6, #a-f
2400-2401	A371	Set of 2	14.50	14.50

Souvenir Sheets
2402-2403	A371	Set of 2	10.00	10.00

A372

Queen Mother (b. 1900) — A373

No. 2404: a, With King George VI, 1936. b, In 1941. c, In 1960. d, In 1981. 25r, At Order of the Garter Service.

Gold Frames
1999, Dec. 1   Litho.   Perf. 14
2404	A372	7r Sheet of 4, #a.-d., + label	6.00	6.00

Souvenir Sheet
Perf. 13¾
2405	A372	25r multi	6.00	6.00

Litho. & Embossed
Die Cut Perf. 8¾
Without Gum
2406	A373	50r gold & multi		

No. 2405 contains one 38x51mm stamp.
See Nos. 2605-2606.

Hokusai Paintings — A374

No. 2407, each 7r: a, A Coastal view. b, Bath House by a Lake. c, Drawings (horse). d, Drawings (two birds). e, Evening Cool at Ryogoku. f, Girls Boating.
No. 2408, each 7r: a, Haunted House. b, Juniso Shrine at Yotsuya. c, Drawings (one bird). d, Drawings (two people). e, Lover in the Snow. f, Mountain Tea House.
Each 25r: No. 2409, Girls Gathering Spring Herbs, vert. No. 2410, Scene in the Yoshiwara, vert.

1999, Dec. 23   Perf. 13¾
Sheets of 6, #a.-f.
2407-2408	A374	Set of 2	17.00	17.00

Souvenir Sheets
2409-2410	A374	Set of 2	10.00	10.00

IBRA '99, Nuremberg — A375

Trains (as described): 12r, Drache, 1848. 15r, Der Adler, 1833.

1999, Dec. 23   Perf. 14x14½
2411-2412	A375	Set of 2	6.00	6.00

The illustrations of the two stamps were switched.

Souvenir Sheets

PhilexFrance '99 — A376

Trains: No. 2413, Standard Stephenson 2-4-0, 1837. No. 2414, Long-boilered Stephenson, 1841.

1999, Dec. 23   Perf. 13¾
2413-2414	A376	25r each	8.00	8.00

Rights of the Child — A377

No. 2415: a, Black denomination in UL. b, White denomination in UL. c, Black denomination in UR.
25r, Peter Ustinov, UNICEF goodwill ambassador.

1999, Dec. 23   Perf. 14
2415	A377	10r Sheet of 3, #a.-c.	6.25	6.25

Souvenir Sheet
2416	A377	25r multi	4.50	4.50

Mars Colony of the Future — A378

No. 2417, each 5r: a, Phobos and Deimos. b, Improved Hubble Telescope. c, Passenger shuttle. d, Skyscrapers. e, Taxi cab. f, Landing facilities. g, Vegetation. h, Walking on Mars. i, Mars rover.
No. 2418, each 5r: a, Russian Phobos 25. b, Earth and moon. c, Space shuttle. d, Lighthouse. e, Excursion space liner. f, Inner-city shuttle. g, Viking lander. h, Air and water purification plants. i, Life in a Mars city.
Each 25r: No. 2419, Mars, vert. No. 2420, Astronaut, vert.

2000, Jan. 24   Litho.   Perf. 14
Sheets of 9, #a.-i.
2417-2418	A378	Set of 2	18.00	18.00

Souvenir Sheets
2419-2420	A378	Set of 2	10.00	10.00

Millennium — A379

Highlights of 1750-1800: a, American Declaration of Independence, 1776. b, Hot air balloon flight by Montgolfier brothers, 1783. c, French Revolution begins with storming of the Bastille, 1789. d, James Watt patents steam engine, 1769. e, Wolfgang Amadeus Mozart born, 1756. f, Ts'ao Hsueh-ch'in publishes "Dream of the Red Chamber," 1791. g, Napoleon conquers Egypt, 1798. h, Catherine the Great becomes Empress of Russia, 1762. i, Joseph Priestley discovers oxygen, 1774. j, Benjamin Franklin publishes studies on electricity, 1751. k, Edward Jenner develops vaccination against smallpox, 1796. l, French and Indian War, 1754. m, Jean Honoré Fragonard paints "The Swing," c. 1766. n, Ludwig van Beethoven born, 1770. o, Louis marries Marie Antoinette, 1770. p, Capt. James Cook explores in South Pacific, discovers east coast of Australia, 1770 (60x40mm). q, Luigi Galvani experiments with electricity on nerves and muscles, c. 1780.

2000, Feb. 1   Perf. 12¾x12½
2421	A379	3r Sheet of 17, #a.-q., + label	10.00	10.00

Destination 2000 Tourism Campaign — A380

Designs: a, Yellow flowers. b, School of fish. c, Airplane, boat prow. d, White flowers. e, Lionfish. f, Windsurfers.

2000, Feb. 1   Perf. 13¾
2422	A380	7r Sheet of 6, #a.-f.	9.00	9.00

Solar Eclipse, Aug. 11, 1999 — A381

MALDIVE ISLANDS

No. 2423 (Sky background), each 7r: a, First contact. b, Second contact. c, Totality. d, Third contact. e, Fourth contact. f, Observatory.
No. 2424 (Outer space background), each 7r: a, First contact. b, Second contact. c, Totality. d, Third contact. e, Fourth contact. f, Solar and heliospheric observatory.

2000, Mar. 8   Litho.   Perf. 14
Sheets of 6, #a.-f.
2423-2424 A381 Set of 2   14.50 14.50

Butterflies — A382

No. 2425, each 5r: a, Red lacewing. b, Large oak blue. c, Yellow coster. d, Great orange tip. e, Common pierrot. f, Cruiser. g, Hedge blue. h, Great egg-fly. i, Common tiger.
No. 2426, each 5r: a, Common wall. b, Kohi-noor. c, Indian red admiral. d, Tawny rajah. e, Blue triangle. f, Orange albatross. g, Common rose swallowtail. h, Jeweled nawab. i, Striped blue crow.
Each 25r: No. 2427, Large tree nymph. No. 2428, Blue pansy.

2000, Apr. 10   Litho.   Perf. 13¼x13½
Sheets of 9, #a-i
2425-2426 A382 Set of 2   18.00 18.00
Souvenir Sheets
2427-2428 A382 Set of 2   10.00 10.00

Paintings of Anthony Van Dyck A383

No. 2429, each 5r: a, Martin Rijckaert. b, Frano Snydoro. o, Quentin Simono. d, Lucas van Uffel, 1622. e, Nicolaes Rockox. f, Nicholas Lanier.
No. 2430, each 5r: a, Inigo Jones. b, Lucas van Uffel, (actually detail from John, Count of Nassau-Sieger and his Family) c. 1622-25. c, Margaretha de Vos, Wife of Frans Snyders. d, Peter Breughel the Younger. e, Cornelis van der Geest. f, Francois Langlois as a Savoyard.
No. 2431, each 5r: a, Portrait of a Family. b, Earl and Countess of Denby and Their Daughter. c, Family Portrait. d, A Genoese Nobleman with his Children. e, Thomas Howard, Earl of Arundel, and His Grandson. f, The Woman in Gold (Battonia Balbi with her Children).
Each 25r: No. 2432, John, Count of Nassau-Siegen, and His Family. No. 2433, The Lomellini Family. No. 2434, Lucas and Cornelis de Wael. No. 2435, The Painter Jan de Wael and His Wife Gertrude de Jode. No. 2436, Sir Kenelm and Lady Digby with Their Two Eldest Sons. No. 2437, Sir Philip Herbert, 4th Earl of Pembroke, and His Family.

2000, May 1   Perf. 13¾
Sheets of 6, #a-f
2429-2431 A383 Set of 3   42.50 42.50
Souvenir Sheets
2432-2437 A383 Set of 6   20.00 20.00

Trains — A384

Designs: 5r, Shinkansen, Japan. 8r, Super Azusa, Japan. No. 2440, 10r, Spacia, Japan. 15r, Nozomi, Japan.
No. 2442, each 10r: a, 1909 Shanghai-Nanking Railway 4-6-2. b, 1910 Shanghai-Nanking Railway 4-2-2. c, 1914 Manchurian Railway 4-6-2. d, 1934 Chinese National Railway Hankow Line 4-8-4. e, 1949 Chinese National Railway 2-8-2. f, 1949 Chinese National Railway 2-10-0.
No. 2443, each 10r: a, 1856 East Indian Railway "Fawn" 2-2-2. b, 1893 East Indian Railway 4-4-0. c, 1909 Bengal-Nagpur Railway 4-2-2. d, 11924 Great Peninsular Railway 4-6-0. e, 1932 North Western Railway 4-6-2. f, 1949 Indian National Railway 4-6-2.
Each 25r: No. 2444, Chinese National Railways Class JS 2-8-2. No. 2445, Indian National Railway Class WP 4-6-2.

2000, June 8   Litho.   Perf. 14
2438-2441 A384 Set of 4   6.50 6.50
Sheets of 6, #a-f
2442-2443 A384 Set of 2   20.00 20.00
Souvenir Sheets
2444-2445 A384 Set of 2   10.00 10.00

The Stamp Show 2000, London (Nos. 2442-2445). Nos. 2444-2445 each contain one 57x42mm stamp.

Millennium A385

Designs: 10 l, Republic Monument. 30 l, Bodu Thakurufaanu Memorial Center. 1r, Health services. No. 2449, 7r, Hukuru Miskily. No. 2450, 7r, Male Intl. Airport. 10r, Educational development.
No. 2452, 25r, People's Majlis. No. 2453, 25r, Economic development. No. 2454, 25r, Islamic Center.

2000, Aug. 31   Litho.   Perf. 14
2446-2451 A385 Set of 6   6.25 6.25
Souvenir Sheets
Perf. 13¼
2452-2454 A385 Set of 3   13.50 13.50

Souvenir Sheets

First Public Railways, 175th Anniv. — A386

No. 2455: a, Locomotion No. 1, George Stephenson. b, William Hedley's Puffing Billy.

2000, Sept. 13   Perf. 14
2455 A386 10r Sheet of 2, #a-b   4.75 4.75

2000 Summer Olympics, Sydney — A387

No. 2456: a, Suzanne Lenglen. b, Fencing. c, Olympic Stadium, Tokyo, and Japanese flag. d, Ancient Greek long jumper.

2000, Sept. 13
2456 A387 10r Sheet of 4, #a-d   7.75 7.75

First Zeppelin Flight, Cent. A388

No. 2457, horiz.: a, Graf Zeppelin. b, Graf Zeppelin II. c, LZ-9.

2000, Sept. 13   Perf. 14
2457 A388 13r Sheet of 3, #a-c   7.00 7.00
Souvenir Sheet
Perf. 13¾
2458 A388 25r LZ-88   6.25 6.25

No. 2457 contains three 39x25mm stamps.

Apollo-Soyuz Mission, 25th Anniv. — A389

No. 2459, vert.: a, Apollo 18 and Soyuz 19. b, Soyuz 19. c, Apollo 18.

2000, Sept. 13   Perf. 14
2459 A389 13r Sheet of 3, #a-c   6.75 6.75
Souvenir Sheet
2460 A380 25r Soyuz 19   5.50 5.50

Orchids — A390

Designs: 50 l, Dendrobium crepidatum. 1r, Eulophia guineensis. 2.50r, Cymbidium finlaysonianum. 3.50r, Paphiopedilum druryi.
No. 2465, 10r: a, Aerides odorata. b, Dendrobium chrysotoxum. c, Dendrobium anosmum. d, Calypso bulbosa. e, Paphiopedilum fairrieanum. f, Cynorkis fastigiata.
No. 2466, 10r: a, Angraecum gormiryanum. b, Phalaenopsis amabilis. c, Thrixspermum cantipeda. d, Phaius tankervilleae. e, Rhynchostylis gigantea. f, Papilionanthe teres.
No. 2467, 25r, Cymbidium dayanum. No. 2468, 25r, Spathoglottis plicata.

2000, Sept. 13
2461-2464 A390 Set of 4   1.25 1.25
Sheets of 6, #a-f
2465-2466 A390 Set of 2   22.00 22.00
Souvenir Sheets
2467-2468 A390 Set of 2   10.00 10.00

Birds — A391

Designs: 15 l, White tern. 25 l, Brown booby. 30 l, White-collared kingfisher, vert. 1r, Black-winged stilt, vert.
No. 2473, 10r: a, Great frigatebird. b, Common noddy. c, Common tern. d, Sula sula. e, Sooty tern. f, Phaeton leturus.
No. 2474, 10r, vert.: a, White-collared kingfisher. b, Island thrush. c, Red-tailed tropicbird. d, Peregrine falcon. e, Night heron. f, Great egret.
No. 2475, 13r: a, Ringed plover. b, Turnstone. c, Thicknee. d, Black-bellied plover. e, Crab plover. f, Curlew.
No. 2476, 25r, Great cormorant, vert. No. 2477, 25r, Cattle egret, vert.

2000, Sept. 13   Perf. 13¾
2469-2472 A391 Set of 4   2.50 2.50
Sheets of 6, #a-f
2473-2475 A391 Set of 3   32.50 32.50
Souvenir Sheets
2476-2477 A391 Set of 2   10.00 10.00

Motorcycles — A392

No. 2478, 7r: a, 1907 Matchless. b, 1966 Manch 4 1200 TTS. c, 1957 Lambretta LD-150. d, 1990 Yamaha XJP 1200. e, 1885 Daimler. f, 1950-60 John Player Norton.
No. 2479, 7r: a, 1969 Honda CB 750. b, 1913 Harley-Davidson. c, 1925 Bohmerland. d, 1910 American Indian. e, 1993 Triumph Trophy 1200. f, 1928, Moto Guzzi 500S.
No. 2480, 25r, 1960 Electra Glide. No. 2481, 25r, 1950 Harley-Davidson.

2000, Oct. 30   Perf. 13¼x13½
Sheets of 6, #a-f
2478-2479 A392 Set of 2   17.00 17.00
Souvenir Sheets
2480-2481 A392 Set of 2   10.00 10.00

A393

Marine Life A394

No. 2482: a, Longnosed filefish. b, Hawaiian squirrelfish. c, Freckled hawkfish. d, McCosker's flasher wrasse. e, Pygoplites diacanthus. f, Paraeentzopyge venusta.
No. 2483, 5r: a, Chaetodon lunula. b, Stethojulis albovittata. c, Green turtle. d, Jobfish. e, Damsel fish. f, Chaetodon meyeri. g, Cirrhilabrus exquisitus. h, Anemonefish.
No. 2484, 5r: a, Coris aygula. b, Snapper. c, Sea bass. d, Chaetodon bennetti. e, Pelagic snapper. f, Cardinalfish. g, Thalassoma hardwicke. h, Surgeonfish.
No. 2485, 5r: a, Grouper. b, Pygoplites diacanthus. c, Forcipiger flavissimus. d, Goatfish. e, Trumpet fish. f, Anthias. g, Centropyge bispinosus. h, Sweetlips.
No. 2486, 25r, H. aberrans. No. 2487, 25r, Angelfish. No. 2488, 25r, Moray eel. No. 2489, 25r, Spiny buttonfish.

2000, Nov. 15   Litho.   Perf. 14
2482 A393 5r Sheet of 6, #a-f   5.50 5.50
Sheets of 8, #a-h
2483-2485 A394 Set of 3   21.00 21.00
Souvenir Sheets
2486 A393 25r multi   4.25 4.25
2487-2489 A394 Set of 3   13.00 13.00

Flowers A395

No. 2490, 5r: a, Corn lily. b, Clivia. c, Red hot poker. d, Crown of thorns. e, Cape daisy. f, Geranium.
No. 2491, 5r, horiz.: a, Fringed hibiscus. b, Erica vestita. c, Bird-of-paradise. d, Peacock orchid. e, Mesembryanthemums. f, African violets.

MALDIVE ISLANDS

No. 2492, 25r, Gladiolus. No. 2493, 25r, Calla lily, horiz.

2000, Nov. 15
Sheets of 6, #a-f
2490-2491 A395 Set of 2 14.00 14.00
Souvenir Sheets
2492-2493 A395 Set of 2 10.00 10.00

Airplanes, Automobiles and Trains — A396

Designs: 2.50r, Papyrus, vert. 3r, Hiawatha. 12r, Supermarine SGB. 13r, MLX01.
No. 2498, 5r: a, Thrust SSC. b, Curtiss R3C-2. c, Rocket. d, BB-9004. e, Mallard. f, TGV.
No. 2499, 5r: a, Lockheed XP-80. b, Mikoyan MiG-23. c, Tempest. d, Bluebird. e, Blue Flame. f, Thrust 2.
No. 2500, 25r, Bell X-1. No. 2501, 25r, Lockheed SR-71 Blackbird, vert.

2000, Nov. 29
2494-2497 A396 Set of 4 5.25 5.25
Sheets of 6, #a-f
2498-2499 A396 Set of 2 10.00 10.00
Souvenir Sheets
2500-2501 A396 Set of 2 8.50 8.50

Paintings from the Prado A397

No. 2502, 7r: a, The Nobleman with the Golden Chain, by Tintoretto. b, Triumphal Arch, by Domenichino. c, Don Garcia de Medici, by Bronzino. d, Micer Marsilio from Micer Marsilio and His Wife, by Lorenzo Lotto. e, La Infanta Maria Antoinetta Fernanda, by Jacopo Amigoni. f, Wife from Micer Marsilio and his Wife.
No. 2503, 7r: a, Two women with headdresses. b, Woman in red. c, Men. d, The Duke of Lerma on Horseback, by Rubens. e, The Death of Seneca, by the Workshop of Rubens. f, Marie de Medici by Rubens. a-c from Achilles Amongst the Daughters of Lycomedes, by Peter Paul Rubens and Anthony Van Dyck.
No. 2504, 7r: a, Self-portrait, by Albrecht Dürer. b, A Woman and Her Daughter, by Adriaen van Cronenburgh. c, Portrait of a man, by Dürer. d, Woman and children. e, Artemisia, by Rembrandt. f, The Artist. d, f from The Artist and His Family, by Jacob Jordaens.
No. 2505, 7r: a, The Painter Andrea Sacchi, by Carlo Maratta. b, Two men. c, Charles Cecil Roberts, by Pompeo Girolamo Batoni. d, Francesco Albani, by Sacchi. e, Three men. f, William Hamilton, by Batoni. b, e from The Turkish Ambassador to the Court of Naples, by Giuseppe Bonito.
No. 2506, 7r: a, The Marquesa of Villafranca, by Francisco de Goya. b, Maria Ruthven, by Van Dyck. c, Cardinal-Infante Ferdinand, by Van Dyck. d, Frederik Hendrik, Prince of Orange, by Van Dyck. e, Van Dyck from Self-portrait with Endymion Porter. f, Porter from Self-portrait with Endymion Porter.
No. 2507, 7r: a, Philip V, by Hyacinthe Rigaud. b, Louis XIV, by Rigaud. c, Don Luis, Prince of Asturias, by Michel-Ange Houasse. d, Duke Carlo Emanuele II of Savoy with His Wife and Son, by Charles Dauphin. e, Kitchen Maid by Charles-François Hutin. f, Hurdygurdy Player, by Georges de La Tour.
No. 2508, 25r, Elizabeth of Valois, by Sofonisba Anguisciola. No. 2509, 25r, Camilla Gonzaga, Countess of San Segundo with Her Three Children, by Parmigianino. No. 2510, 25r, The Turkish Ambassador to the Court of Naples. No. 2511, 25r, Duke Carlo Emanuele of Savoy with His Wife and Son. No. 2512, 25r, The Artist and His Family, horiz. No. 2513, 25r, The Devotion of Rudolf I, by Rubens and Jan Wildens, horiz.

Perf. 12x12¼, 12¼x12
2000, Nov. 29
Sheets of 6, #a-f
2502-2507 A397 Set of 6 42.50 42.50
Souvenir Sheets
2508-2513 A397 Set of 6 26.00 26.00
España 2000 Intl. Philatelic Exhibition.

Porsche Automobiles — A398

No. 2514, 12r: a, 1966 911S. b, 1988 959. c, 1995 993 Carrera.
No. 2515, 12r: a, 1963 356 SC. b, 1975 911 Turbo. c, Unidentified.

2000, Nov. 30 **Litho.** **Perf. 14**
Sheets of 3, #a-c
2514-2515 A398 Set of 2 12.50 12.50
Souvenir Sheet
2516 A398 25r 2000 Boxter 4.25 4.25
No. 2516 contains one 56x42mm stamp.

Mushrooms — A399

Designs: 30 l, Cortinarius collinitus. 50 l, Russula ochroleuca. 2r, Lepiota acutesquamosa. 3r, Hebeloma radicosum. 13r, Amanita echinocephala. 15r, Collybia iocephala.
No. 2523, 7r: a, Tricholoma aurantium. b, Pholiota spectabilis. c, Russula caerulea. d, Amanita phalloides. e, Mycena strobilinoides. f, Boletus satanas.
No. 2524, 7r: a, Amanita muscaria. b, Mycena lilacifolia. c, Coprinus comatus. d, Morchella crassipes. e, Russula nigricans. f, Lepiota procera.
No. 2525, 25r, Tricholoma aurantium, diff. No. 2526, 25r, Lepiota procera, diff.

2001, Jan. 2
2517-2522 A399 Set of 6 5.75 5.75
Sheets of 6, #a-f
2523-2524 A399 Set of 2 14.50 14.50
Souvenir Sheets
2525-2526 A399 Set of 2 8.50 8.50

Battle of Britain, 60th Anniv. A400

No. 2527, 5r: a, German commanders look across the English Channel. b, The armorers make ready. c, The German attack begins. d, Germany bombs the British coast. e, Germany bombs British cities. f, Luftwaffe sets St. Paul's Cathedral ablaze. g, Aerial dogfight. h, A British Spitfire is shot down.
No. 2528, 5r: a, Leaders of Great Britain. b, British pilots prepare to confront the Luftwaffe. c, RAF planes take off. d, British aircraft meet the enemy. e, Luftwaffe meets tough resistance. f, Dogfight above English Channel. g, German planes fall short of their objective. h, Many German planes are shot down.
No. 2529, 25r, Hawker Hurricane. No. 2530, 25r, Messerschmitt ME 109.

2001, Jan. 2 **Perf. 14**
Sheets of 8, #a-h
2527-2528 A400 Set of 2 14.50 14.50
Souvenir Sheets
2529-2530 A400 Set of 2 8.50 8.50

Rijksmuseum, Amsterdam, Bicent. (in 2000) — A401

No. 2531, 7r: a, Donkey's head and rider from Donkey Riding on the Beach, by Isaac Lazarus Israels. b, The Paternal Admonition, by Gerard Terborch, the Younger. c, The Sick Woman, by Jan Havicksz Steen. d, Girls with red hats from Donkey Riding on the Beach. e, Pompeius Occo, by Dirck Jacobsz. f, Woman With a Child in a Pantry, by Pieter de Hooch.
No. 2532, 7r: a, The Holy Kinship, by Geertgen tot Sint Jans. b, Sir Thomas Gresham, by Anthonis Mor. c, Self-portrait as St. Paul, by Rembrandt. d, Cleopatra's Banquet, by Gerard Lairesse. e, Still Life With Flowers in a Glass, by Jan Brueghel, the Elder. f, Portrait of a Man, Possibly Nicolaes Hasselaer, by Frans Hals.
No. 2533, 7r: a, Rembrandt's Mother, by Gerard Dou. b, Portrait of a Girl Dressed in Blue, by Jan Cornelisz Verspronck. c, Old Woman at Prayer, by Nicolaes Maes. d, Feeding the Hungry from The Seven Works of Charity, by the Master of Alkmaar. e, The Threatened Swan, by Jan Asselyn. f, The Daydreamer, by Maes.
No. 2534, 7r: a, Woman seated in doorway, from The Little Street, by Jan Vermeer. b, Two women from The Love Letter, by Vermeer. c, Woman in Blue Reading a Letter, by Vermeer. d, Woman and pillar from The Love Letter. e, The Milkmaid, by Vermeer. f, Arched doorway, from The Little Street.
No. 2535, 25r, Johannes Wtenbogaert, by Rembrandt. No. 2536, 25r, The Staalmeesters (The Syndics), by Rembrandt. No. 2537, 25r, The Night Watch, by Rembrandt. No. 2538, 25r, Shipwreck on a Rocky Coast, by Wijnandus Johannes Joseph Nuyen, horiz.

2001, Jan. 15 **Perf. 13¾**
Sheets of 6, #a-f
2531-2534 A401 Set of 4 30.00 30.00
Souvenir Sheets
2535-2538 A401 Set of 4 17.00 17.00

Ill-fated Ships A402

No. 2539, 5r: a, Milton Iatrides, 1970. b, Cyclops, 1918. c, Marine Sulphur Queen, 1963. d, Rosalie, 1840. e, Mary Celeste, 1872. f, Atlanta, 1880.
No. 2540, 5r: a, Windfall, 1962. b, Kobenhavn, 1928. c, Pearl, 1874. d, HMS Bulwark, 1914. e, Patriot, 1812. f, Lusitania, 1915.
No. 2541, 25r, La Boussole and L'Astrolabe, 1789. No. 2542, 25r, Titanic, 1912.

2001, Feb. 12 **Perf. 14**
Sheets of 6, #a-f
2539-2540 A402 Set of 2 10.00 10.00
Souvenir Sheets
2541-2542 A402 Set of 2 8.50 8.50

Flower Type of 1997
2001, Mar. 1 **Perf. 14¾x14**
Size: 16x20mm
2543 A350 10r Like #2267 1.75 1.75

No. 2267 Surcharged

Method and Perf. As Before
2001, Mar. 1
2543A A350 10r on 7r #2267 —

Islam in Maldive Islands, 848th Anniv. A403

No. 2544: a, Dharumavantha Rasgefaanu Mosque. b, Plaque of Hukurumiskiiy. c, Learning the Holy Koran. d, Institute of Islamic Studies. e, Center for the Holy Koran. f, Islamic Center.
25r, Medhu Ziyaarath.

2001, July 9 **Litho.** **Perf. 13¾**
2544 A403 10r Sheet of 6, #a-f 10.00 10.00
Souvenir Sheet
2545 A403 25r multi 4.25 4.25

Fish — A404

Designs: No. 2546, 10r, Pterois miles. No. 2547, 10r, Pomacanthus imperator.

2001, July 16 **Perf. 14x14¾**
2546-2547 A404 Set of 2 3.50 3.50

Pontiac Trans-Am Automobiles — A405

No. 2548, 12r: a, 1970. b, 1989. c, 1994.
No. 2549, 12r: a, 1976. b, 1988. c, 1988 Coupe.

2001 **Perf. 14**
Sheets of 3, #a-c
2548-2549 A405 Set of 2 12.50 12.50
Souvenir Sheet
Perf. 14¼
2550 A405 25r 1999 4.25 4.25
Nos. 2548-2549 each contain three 42x28mm stamps.

Automobiles A406

Designs: 1r, 1930 Pierce-Arrow. 2r, 1938 Mercedes-Benz 540K. 8r, 1934 Duesenberg J. 10r, 1931 Bugatti Royale.
No. 2555, 7r: a, 1931 Auburn convertible sedan. b, 1931 Mercedes SSKL. c, 1929 Packard roadster. d, 1940 Chevrolet. e, 1915 Mercer. f, 1941 Packard sedan.
No. 2556, 7r: a, 1932 Chevrolet roadster. b, 1929 Cadillac Fleetwood roadster. c, 1928 Bentley Speed Six. d, 1930 Cadillac Fleetwood. e, 1936 Ford convertible. f, 1929 Hudson Phaeton.
No. 2557, 25r, 1930 Cord Brougham. No. 2558, 25r, 1931 Rolls-Royce P-1.

2001 **Perf. 14**
2551-2554 A406 Set of 4 3.50 3.50
Sheets of 6, #a-f
2555-2556 A406 Set of 2 14.50 14.50
Souvenir Sheets
2557-2558 A406 Set of 2 8.50 8.50

MALDIVE ISLANDS

KITAGAWA UTAMARO

Phila Nippon '01, Japan — A407

No. 2559, 7r (28x42mm) — Prints of women by Utamaro: a, Reed Blind. b, Model Young Women Woven in Mist. b, Woman with Parasol. c, High-ranked Courtesan, Five Shades of Ink in the Northern Quarter. d, Comparison of Beauties of the Southern Quarter. e, The Barber.
No. 2560, 7r — Actors by Shunsho Katsukawa: a, Danjuro Ichikawa V (black kimono, 28x85mm). b, Danjuro Ichikawa V (arm raised, 28x85mm). b, Danjuro Ichikawa V (arms crossed on chest, 28x85mm). d, Danjuro Ichikawa V (wrapped in kimono, 28x85mm). e, Tomoeman Otani I and Mitsugaro Bando I (56x85mm).
No. 2561, 25r, The Courtesan Hinazuru of the House Called Keizetsuro, by Utamaro. No. 2562, 25r, Jomyo Tsutsui and the Priest Ichirai on the Uji Bridge, by Kiyomasu Torii.

2001, July 18	Litho.		Perf. 14
Sheets of 5, #a-e			
2559-2560	A407	Set of 2	12.00 12.00
Souvenir Sheets			
		Perf. 13¾	
2561-2562	A407	Set of 2	8.50 8.50

Giuseppe Verdi (1813-1901), Opera Composer — A408

No. 2563: a, Alfred Piccaver. b, Rigoletto costume, Heinrich. c, Rigoletto costume, Cologne. d, Cornell MacNeil.
25r, Matteo Manuguerra.

2001, Aug. 26			Perf. 14
2563	A408	10r Sheet of 4, #a-d	6.75 6.75
Souvenir Sheet			
2564	A408	25r multi	4.25 4.25

Mao Zedong (1893-1976) — A409

No. 2565: a, Red background. b, Blue background. c, Gray background.
25r, Wearing cap.

2001, Aug. 26			Perf. 13¾
2565	A409	15r Sheet of 3, #a-c	7.75 7.75
Souvenir Sheet			
2566	A409	25r multi	4.25 4.25

Queen Victoria (1819-1901) — A410

No. 2567: a, Earring at right. b, Earring at left. c, As old woman. d, In black dress.
25r, With hand on chin.

2001, Aug. 26			Perf. 14
2567	A410	10r Sheet of 4, #a-d	6.75 6.75
Souvenir Sheet			
2568	A410	25r multi	4.25 4.25

Queen Elizabeth II, 75th Birthday — A411

No. 2569: a, Without hat. b, Wearing large crown. c, Wearing tiara. d, Wearing red uniform. e, Wearing black cape and hat. f, Wearing tan hat.
25r, Wearing crown, diff.

2001, Aug. 26			
2569	A411	7r Sheet of 6, #a-f	7.25 7.25
Souvenir Sheet			
2570	A411	25r multi	4.25 4.25

Nobel Prizes, Cent. — A412

No. 2571 — Economics laureates: a, Simon Kuznets, 1971. b, Wassily Leontief, 1973. c, Lawrence R. Klein, 1980. d, Friedrich A. von Hayek, 1974. e, Leonid V. Kantorovich, 1975.
No. 2572, 7r — Peace laureates: a, Ernesto T. Moneta, 1907. b, Albert J. Luthuli, 1960. c, Henri Dunant, 1901. d, Charles Albert Gobat, 1902. e, Sean MacBride, 1974. f, Elie Ducommun, 1902.
No. 2573, 7r — Peace laureates: a, Adolfo Pérez Esquivel, 1980. b, Mikhail S. Gorbachev, 1990. c, Betty Williams, 1976. d, Alfonso Garcia Robles, 1982. e, Paul D'Estournelles de Constant, 1909. f, Louis Renault, 1907.
No. 2574, 25r, Trygve Haavelmo, Economics, 1989. No. 2575, 25r, Vicente Aleixandre, Literature, 1977. No. 2576, 25r, Octavio Paz, Literature, 1990.

2001, Sept. 29	Litho.		Perf. 14
2571	A412	7r Sheet of 5, #a-e	6.00 6.00
Sheets of 6, #a-f			
2572-2573	A412	Set of 2	14.50 14.50
Souvenir Sheets			
2574-2576	A412	Set of 3	13.00 13.00

Mercedes-Benz Automobiles, Cent. — A413

Designs: 2.50r, 1939 W165 Grand Prix. 5r, 1928 460 Nürburg Sport Roadster. 8r, 1928 Boattail Speedster. 15r, 1909 Blitzen Benz.

No. 2581, 7r: a, 1927 680S. b, 1934 150. c, 1936 540K Roadster. d, 1933 770 Grosser Mercedes. e, 1958 220SE. f, 1990 500SL.
No. 2582, 7r: a, 1933 290. b, 1927 Model S. c, 1953 300SL Coupe. d, 1911 Benz Victoria. e, 1968 280SL. f, 1937 W125 Grand Prix.
No. 2583, 25r, 1931 370S. No. 2584, 25r, 1955 300SLR.

2001, Oct. 30	Litho.		Perf. 14
2577-2580	A413	Set of 4	5.25 5.25
Sheets of 6, #a-f			
2581-2582	A413	Set of 2	14.50 14.50
Souvenir Sheets			
2583-2584	A413	Set of 2	8.50 8.50

2002 World Cup Soccer Championships, Japan and Korea — A414

World Cup Trophy and: 1r, Eusebio, Portugal, Portuguese flag. 3r, Johan Cruyff, Netherlands, Netherlands flag. 7r, French player and flag. 10r, Japanese player and flag. 12r, Seoul World Cup Stadium, horiz. 15r, 1930 World Cup poster.
25r, Gerd Müller's winning goal for West Germany, 1974, vert.

2001, Nov. 28			
2585-2590	A414	Set of 6	8.25 8.25
Souvenir Sheet			
2591	A414	25r multi	4.25 4.25

No. 2591 contains one 42x56mm stamp.

Princess Diana (1961-97) — A415

No. 2592: a, Pink rose. b, White rose. c, Yellow rose. d, Beige rose.
25r, Wearing pearl necklace.

2001, Dec. 26			
2592	A415	10r Sheet of 4, #a-d	6.75 6.75
Souvenir Sheet			
2593	A415	25r multi	4.25 4.25

New Year 2002 (Year of the Horse) — A416

No. 2594 — Paintings by Xu Beihong: a, Running Horse (painting 45mm tall). b, Standing Horse. c, Running Horse (painting 49mm tall). d, Horse (painting 44mm tall). e, Horse (painting 48mm tall).
15r, Horse, horiz.

2001, Dec. 26			Perf. 14
2594	A416	5r Sheet of 5, #a-e	5.50 5.50
Souvenir Sheet			
		Perf. 14x14½	
2595	A416	15r multi	2.60 2.60

No. 2594 contains five 31x63mm stamps.

Pres. John F. Kennedy — A417

No. 2596, 5r: a, At Dexter, 1927. b, At Harvard, 1935. c, In Navy, 1943. d, At wedding, 1953. e, With brother Robert, 1956. f, At Presidential inauguration, 1961.
No. 2597, 5r: a, With Nikita Khrushchev, 1961. b, With Harold Macmillan. c, With Charles de Gaulle, 1961. d, With Jawaharlal Nehru, 1962. e, With Konrad Adenauer, 1963. f, With Dr. Martin Luther King, Jr., 1963.
No. 2598, 25r, Portrait. No. 2599, 25r, With wife, 1961.

2001, Dec. 26			Perf. 14
Sheets of 6, #a-f			
2596-2597	A417	Set of 2	13.00 13.00
Souvenir Sheets			
2598-2599	A417	Set of 2	8.50 8.50

Moths — A418

No. 2600, 7r: a, Cymothoe lucasi. b, Milionia grandis. c, Ornithoptera eroesus. d, Hyantis hodeva. e, Ammobiota festiva. f, Blue salamis.
No. 2601, 7r: a, Zygaena occitanica. b, Campyloes desgodinsi. c, Bhutanitis thaidina. d, Six-tailed helicopsis. e, Parnassius charltonius. f, Acraea ecucogiap.
No. 2602: a, Papilio dardanus. b, Baomisa hieroglyphica. c, Troides prattorum. d, Funonia rhadama.
No. 2603, 25r, Hypolera cassotis. No. 2604, 25r, Euphydryas maturna, vert.

2001, Dec. 26			Litho.
Sheets of 6, #a-f			
2600-2601	A418	Set of 2	14.50 14.50
2602	A418	10r Sheet of 4, #a-d	6.75 6.75
Souvenir Sheets			
2603-2604	A418	Set of 2	8.50 8.50

Queen Mother Type of 1999 Redrawn

No. 2605: a, With King George VI, 1936. b, In 1941. c, In 1960. d, In 1981.
25r, At Order of the Garter Service.

2001, Dec.			Perf. 14
Yellow Orange Frames			
2605	A372	7r Sheet of 4, #a-d, + label	4.75 4.75
Souvenir Sheet			
		Perf. 13¾	
2606	A372	25r multi	4.25 4.25

Queen Mother's 101st birthday. No. 2606 contains one 38x51mm stamp slightly darker than that found on No. 2405. Sheet margins of Nos. 2605-2606 lack embossing and gold arms and frames found on Nos. 2404-2405.

MALDIVE ISLANDS

Reign of Queen Elizabeth II, 50th Anniv. — A419

No. 2607: a, With Princess Margaret. b, Wearing white hat. c, Wearing tiara. d, Holding flowers. 25r, At coronation.

2002, Feb. 6		Litho.	Perf. 14¼	
2607	A419	10r Sheet of 4, #a-d	7.75	7.75

Souvenir Sheet

| 2608 | A419 | 25r multi | | 4.25 | 4.25 |

Cats — A420

Designs: 3r, Havana brown. 5r, American wirehair. 8r, Norwegian forest cat. 10r, Seal point Siamese.
No. 2613, 7r: a, British blue. b, Red mackerel Manx. c, Scottish fold. d, Somali. e, Balinese. f, Exotic shorthair.
No. 2614, 7r, horiz.: a, Persian. b, Exotic shorthair, diff. c, Ragdoll. d, Manx. e, Tonkinese. f, Scottish fold, diff. 25r, Blue mackerel tabby Cornish rex.

2002, Apr. 8			Perf. 14	
2609-2612	A420	Set of 4	4.75	4.75

Sheets of 6, #a-f

| 2613-2614 | A420 | Set of 2 | 14.50 | 14.50 |

Souvenir Sheet

| 2615 | A420 | 25r multi | 4.25 | 4.25 |

Birds — A421

Designs: 1r, Swinhoe's snipe. 2r, Oriental honey buzzard. 3r, Asian koel. No. 2619, 5r, Red-throated pipet. No. 2620, 7r, Short-eared owl. 10r, Eurasian spoonbill. 12r, Pied wheatear. 15r, Oriental pratincole.
No. 2624, 5r: a, Lesser noddy. b, Roseate tern. c, Frigate minor. d, Saunder's tern. e, White-bellied storm petrel. f, Red-footed booby.
No. 2625, 5r: a, Cattle egret. b, Barn swallow. c, Osprey. d, Little heron. e, Ruddy turnstone. f, Sooty tern.
No. 2626, 7r: a, Rose-ringed parakeet. b, Common swift. c, Lesser kestrel. d, Golden oriole. e, Asian paradise flycatcher. f, Indian roller.
No. 2627, 7r: a, Pallid harrier. b, Gray heron. c, Blue-tailed bee-eater. d, White-breasted water hen. e, Cotton pygmy goose. f, Maldivian pond heron.
No. 2628, 25r, White-tailed tropicbird. No. 2629, 25r, Greater flamingo. No. 2630, 25r, Cinnamon bittern. No. 2631, 25r, White tern.

2002, Apr. 8				
2616-2623	A421	Set of 8	10.00	10.00

Sheets of 6, #a-f

| 2624-2627 | A421 | Set of 4 | 27.50 | 27.50 |

Souvenir Sheets

| 2628-2631 | A421 | Set of 4 | 17.00 | 17.00 |

Prehistoric Animals — A422

No. 2632, 7r: a, Sivatherium. b, Flat-headed peccary. c, Shasta ground sloth. d, Harlan's ground sloth. e, European woolly rhinoceros. f, Dwarf pronghorn.
No. 2633, 7r: a, Macrauchenia. b, Gyptodon. c, Nesodon. d, Imperial tapir. e, Short-faced bear. f, Mammoth.
No. 2634, 25r, Saber-toothed cat. No. 2635, 25r, Woolly mammoth, vert.

2002, May 21		Sheets of 6, #a-f	
2632-2633	A422	Set of 2	15.00 15.00

Souvenir Sheets

| 2634-2635 | A422 | Set of 2 | 8.50 8.50 |

2002 Winter Olympics, Salt Lake City — A423

Designs: No. 2636, 12r, Freestyle skiing. No. 2637, 12r, Downhill skiing.

2002, July 11	Litho.	Perf. 13½x13¼
2636-2637	A423	Set of 2	4.50 4.50
a.	Souvenir sheet, #2636-2637	4.50 4.50

Intl. Year of Mountains — A424

No. 2638: a, Mt. Ama Dablam, Nepal. b, Mt. Clements, US. c, Mt. Artesonraju, Peru. d, Mt. Cholatse, Nepal. 25r, Balloon and Mt. Jefferson, US.

2002, July 11		Perf. 14
2638	A424	15r Sheet of 4, #a-d	10.50 10.50

Souvenir Sheet

| 2639 | A424 | 25r multi | 4.25 4.25 |

20th World Scout Jamboree, Thailand — A425

No. 2640, vert.: a, Temple. b, Thailand Scout. c, Merit badges. 25r, Mountain climbing merit badge.

2002, July 11

| 2640 | A425 | 15r Sheet of 3, #a-c | 7.75 7.75 |

Souvenir Sheet

| 2641 | A425 | 25r multi | 4.25 4.25 |

World Customs Organization, 50th Anniv. — A426

2002, Aug. 12		Perf. 13¾
2642	A426	50r multi	8.50 8.50

Elvis Presley (1935-77) — A427

2002, Oct. 7

| 2643 | A427 | 5r multi | 1.25 1.25 |

Printed in sheets of 9.

Flowers and Butterflies — A428

No. 2644, 7r — Flowers: a, Morning glory. b, Wedding bell anemone. c, Barrett Browning narcissus. d, Persian jewel nigella. e, Whirligig pink osteospermum. f, Brown lasso iris.
No. 2645, 7r — Orchids: a, Laelia gouldiana. b, Cattleya Louise Georgiana. c, Laeliocattleya Christopher Gubler. d, Miltoniopsis Bert Field Crimson Glow. e, Lemboglossum bictoniense. f, Derosara Divine Victor.
No. 2646, 7r — Butterflies: a, Morpho menelus. b, Small postman. c, Hewitson's blue hairstreak. d, Green swallowtail. e, Cairns birdwing. f, Queen.
No. 2647, 25r, Little pink beauty aster. No. 2648, 25r, Angraecum veitchii, vert. No. 2649, 25r, Cymothoe lurida butterfly.

2002, Nov. 4	Litho.	Perf. 14
Sheets of 6, #a-f		
2644-2646	A428	Set of 3	22.50 22.50

Souvenir Sheets

| 2647-2649 | A428 | Set of 3 | 12.00 12.00 |

2002 World Cup Soccer Championships, Japan and Korea — A429

No. 2650, 7r: a, Torsten Frings sliding. b, Roberto Carlos. c, Frings kicking. d, Ronaldo pointing. e, Oliver Neuville. f, Ronaldo with ball.
No. 2651, 7r: a, Eul Yong Lee, Alpay Ozalan. b, Myung Bo Hong, Hakan Sukur. c, Emre Belozoglu, Chong Gug Song. d, Ergun Penbe, Chong Gug Song. e, Ergun Penbe, Ki Hyeon Seol. f, Chong Gug Song, Hakan Unsal.
No. 2652, 15r: a, Cafu and Neuville. b, Hands holding World Cup.
No. 2653, 15r: a, Dietmar Hamann. b, Cafu holding World Cup.

No. 2654, 15r: a, Ilhan Mansiz. b, Young Pyo Lee.
No. 2655, 15r: a, Hakan Sukur. b, Sang Chul Yoo.

2002, Nov. 12		Perf. 13½
Sheets of 6, #a-f		
2650-2651	A429	Set of 2	13.50 13.50

Souvenir Sheets of 2, #a-b

| 2652-2655 | A429 | Set of 4 | 19.00 19.00 |

Teddy Bears, Cent. A430

No. 2656: a, Hairdresser. b, Construction worker. c, Gardener. d, Chef.
No. 2657, 12r: a, Mother. b, Sister and brother. c, Father.
No. 2658, 12r: a, Nurse. b, Doctor. c, Dentist.
No. 2659, 30r, Soccer player. No. 2660, 30r, Golfer. No. 2661, 30r, Snow boarder.

2002, Nov. 18		Perf. 14
2656	A430	8r Sheet of 4, #a-d	5.00 5.00

Sheets of 3, #a-c

| 2657-2658 | A430 | Set of 2 | 11.50 11.50 |

Souvenir Sheets

| 2659-2661 | A430 | Set of 3 | 14.00 14.00 |

First Non-Stop Solo Transatlantic Flight, 75th Anniv. — A430a

No. 2661A, 12r — Various photos of Charles Lindbergh and Spirit of St. Louis: c, Blue. d, Brown. e, Gray. f, Red violet.
No. 2661B, 12r: g, Donald Hall, designer of Spirit of St. Louis. h, Charles Lindbergh. i, Lindbergh, Spirit of St. Louis (Lindbergh distorted). j, Lindbergh, Hall and President Mahoney of Ryan Aircraft.

2002, Dec. 2	Litho.	Perf. 14
2661A	A430a	12r Sheet of 4, #c-f	7.50 7.50
2661B	A430a	12r Sheet of 4, #g-j	7.50 7.50

Princess Diana (1961-97)
A431   A432

2002, Dec. 2

| 2662 | A431 | 12r multi | 1.90 1.90 |
| 2663 | A432 | 12r multi | 1.90 1.90 |

Nos. 2662-2663 were each printed in sheets of 4.

MALDIVE ISLANDS

Pres. John F. Kennedy (1917-63) — A432a

No. 2663A: b, With father Joseph P., and brother Joseph, Jr. c, At age 11. d, Inspecting Boston waterfront, 1951. e, As Navy Ensign, 1941. f, With sister Kathleen in London, 1939. g, With Eleanor Roosevelt, 1951.

2002, Dec. 2		Litho.		Perf. 14	
2663A	A432a	7r Sheet of 6, #b-g		7.25	7.25

Pres. Ronald Reagan — A433

Designs: No. 2664, Green background. No. 2665, Blue background.
No. 2666: a, Wearing brown suit. b, Wearing black suit with red tie.

2002, Dec. 2					
2664	A433	12r multi		1.90	1.90
2665	A433	12r multi		1.90	1.90
a.		Horiz. pair, #2664-2665		4.00	4.00
2666	A433	12r Horiz. pair, #a-b		4.00	4.00
		Nos. 2664-2666 (3)		7.80	7.80

Nos. 2664-2665 were printed in sheets containing two of each stamp. No. 2666 was printed in sheets containing two pairs.

Amphilex 2002 Intl. Stamp Exhibition, Amsterdam — A434

No. 2667, 7r — Life of Queen Mother Juliana and Prince Bernhard: a, Wedding, 1937. b, Birth of Princess Beatrix, 1938. c, Exile in Canada, 1940-45. d, Installation of Juliana as queen, 1948. e, Zeeland flood, 1953. f, Royal couple.
No. 2668, 7r — Portraits depicting Queen Beatrix by: a, Pauline Hille. b, John Klinkenberg. c, Beatrice Filius. d, Will Kellermann. e, Graswinckel. f, Marjolijn Spreeuwenberg.

Sheets of 6, #a-f

2002, Dec. 8				Perf. 14	
2667-2668	A434	Set of 2		13.50	13.50

Fish A435 **Birds and Sharks A436**

Designs: 10 l, Flame basslet. 15 l, Teardrop butterflyfish. 20 l, Hamburg damselfish. 25 l, Bridled tern. 50 l, Blue-lined surgeonfish. 1r, Common tern. 2r, Common noddy. No. 2676, Yellow-breasted wrasse. No. 2677, Blue shark. 4r, Harlequin filefish. 5r, Orangespine unicornfish. 10r, Emperor angelfish. 12r, Bullseye. 20r, Scalloped hammerhead shark.

Perf. 14 (A435), 10¾x13 (25 l, 1r, 2r), 13¼x14 (#2677, 20r)

2002, Dec. 24					
2669	A435	10 l multi		.25	.25
2670	A435	15 l multi		.25	.25
2671	A435	20 l multi		.25	.25
2672	A435	25 l multi		.25	.25
2673	A435	50 l multi		.25	.25
2674	A436	1r multi		.25	.25
2675	A436	2r multi		.30	.30
2676	A435	2.50r multi		.40	.40
2677	A435	2.50r multi		.40	.40
2678	A435	4r multi		.60	.60
2679	A435	5r multi		.75	.75
2680	A435	10r multi		1.50	1.50
2681	A435	12r multi		1.90	1.90
2682	A436	20r multi		3.00	3.00
		Nos. 2669-2682 (14)		10.35	10.35

Tourism, 30th Anniv. A437

No. 2683: a, Atolls. b, Sand spit. c, Surfer. d, Underwater scene.

2002, Dec. 25				Perf. 13½	
2683	A437	12r Sheet of 4, #a-d		7.50	7.50

Popeye A438

No. 2684, vert: a, Diving. b, Surfing. c, Sailboarding. d, Baseball. e, Hurdles. f, Tennis.
25r, Volleyball.

2003, Jan. 27				Perf. 14	
2684	A438	7r Sheet of 6, #a-f		6.50	6.50
Souvenir Sheet					
2685	A438	25r multi		4.00	4.00

National Museum, 50th Anniv. — A439

Various museum items: 3r, 3.50r, 6.50r, 22r.

2003, Jan. 31				Litho.	
2686-2689	A439	Set of 4		5.50	5.50

UNICEF — A440

Designs: 2.50r, Father and child. 5r, Mother kissing child. 20r, Child learning to walk.

2003, Jan. 31				Perf. 15x14	
2690-2692	A440	Set of 3		4.50	4.50

Shells — A441

Designs: No. 2693, 10r, Sundial shell. No. 2694, 10r, Cardita clam. No. 2695, 10r, Corn shell. No. 2696, 10r, Cowrie shell.

2003, Mar. 25				Litho.	Perf. 13¼
2693-2696	A441	Set of 4		7.00	7.00

Astronauts Killed in Space Shuttle Columbia Accident — A442

No. 2697: a, Mission Specialist 1 David M. Brown. b, Commander Rick D. Husband. c, Mission Specialist 4 Laurel Blair Salton Clark. d, Mission Specialist 4 Kalpana Chawla. e, Payload Commander Michael P. Anderson. f, Pilot William C. McCool. g, Payload Specialist 4 Ilan Ramon.

2003, Apr. 7				Perf. 13½x13¼	
2697	A442	7r Sheet of 7, #a-g		7.75	7.75

Coronation of Queen Elizabeth II, 50th Anniv. — A443

No. 2698: a, Wearing hat. b, Wearing crown. c, Wearing tiara.
25r, Wearing tiara, diff.

2003, May 26				Perf. 14	
2698	A443	15r Sheet of 3, #a-c		6.00	6.00
Souvenir Sheet					
2699	A443	25r multi		4.00	4.00

Prince William, 21st Birthday A444

No. 2700: a, As toddler. b, Wearing red and blue tie. c, Wearing tie with blue squares.
25r, As toddler, wearing cap.

2003, May 26					
2700	A444	15r Sheet of 3, #a-c		6.00	6.00
Souvenir Sheet					
2701	A444	25r multi		4.00	4.00

Paintings by Albrecht Dürer (1471-1528) A445

Designs: 3r, Drummer and Piper from wing of the Jabach Altarpiece. 5r, Portrait of a Young Man. 7r, Wire-drawing Mill, horiz. 10r, Innsbruck from the North, horiz.
No. 2706: a, Portrait of Jacob Muffel. b, Portrait of Hieronymus Holzschuher. c, Portrait of Johannes Kleberger. d, Self-portrait.

25r, The Weiden Mill, horiz.

2003, June 17				Perf. 14¼	
2702-2705	A445	Set of 4		4.50	4.50
2706	A445	12r Sheet of 4, #a-d		6.50	6.50
Souvenir Sheet					
2707	A445	25r multi		4.00	4.00

Japanese Art — A446

Designs: 2r, Detail from The Actor Sojuro Nakamura as Mitsukuni, by Yoshitaki Utagawa. 5r, Detail from The Actor Sojuro Nakamura as Mitsukuni, by Yoshitaki Utagawa, diff. 7r, The Ghost of Koheiji Kohada, by Hokuei Shunkosai. 15r, Ariwara no Narihira as Seigen, by Kunisada Utagawa.
No. 2712: a, The Ghost of Mitsumune Shikibunojo, by Kunisada Utagawa. b, Fuwa Bansakui, by Yoshitoshi Tsukioka. c, The Lantern Ghost of Oiwa, by Shunkosai. d, The Greedy Hag, by Tsukioka.
25r, The Spirit of Sogoro Sakura Haunting Koszuke Hotta.

2003, June 17					
2708-2711	A446	Set of 4		4.75	4.75
2712	A446	10r Sheet of 4, #a-d		5.25	5.25
Souvenir Sheet					
2713	A446	25r multi		4.00	4.00

Paintings by Joan Miró (1893-1983) A447

Designs: 3r, Untitled painting, 1934. 5r, Hirondelle Amour. 10r, Two Women. 15r, Women Listening to Music.
No. 2718: a, Woman and Birds. b, Nocturne. c, Morning Star. d, The Escape Ladder.
No. 2719, 25r, Rhythmic Personages, vert. No. 2720, 25r, Women Encircled by the Flight of a Bird, vert.

2003, June 17				Perf. 14¼	
2714-2717	A447	Set of 4		5.25	5.25
2718	A447	12r Sheet of 4, #a-d		6.50	6.50
Size: 83x104mm					
Imperf					
2719-2720	A447	Set of 2		7.00	7.00

Tour de France Bicycle Race, Cent. A448

No. 2721, 10r: a, Maurice Garin, 1903. b, Henri Cornet, 1904. c, Louis Trousselier, 1905. d, René Pottier, 1906.
No. 2722, 10r: a, Lucien Petit-Breton on Bicycle, 1907. b, Head of Petit-Breton, 1907. c, François Faber, 1909. d, Octave Lapize, 1910.
No. 2723, 10r: a, Eddy Merckx, 1974. b, Bernard Thévenet, 1975. c, Lucien Van Impe, 1976. d, Thévenet, 1977.
No. 2724, 25r, Bernard Hinault, 1979. No. 2725, 25r, Henri Desgranges. No. 2726, 25r, Le Réveil Matin Cafe, Montgeron, France.

2003, July 3				Perf. 13¼	
Sheets of 4, #a-d					
2721-2723	A448	Set of 3		17.50	17.50
Souvenir Sheets					
2724-2726	A448	Set of 3		10.00	10.00

189

MALDIVE ISLANDS

Powered Flight, Cent. A449

No. 2727, 10r — Alberto Santos-Dumont's: a, Airship No. 1. b, Airship No. 4. c, Airship with 14bis airplane. d, Airship No. 16.
No. 2728, 10r: a, Santos Dumont with Demoiselle airplane. b, Demoiselle airplane. c, Voisin-Farman No. 1 biplane. d, Gold Bug, built by Glenn Curtiss.
No. 2729, 25r, Santos-Dumont's Airship No. 6. No. 2730, 25r, Santos-Dumont's 14bis Airplane.

2003, July 14   **Perf. 14**
Sheets of 4, #a-d
2727-2728 A449 Set of 2   12.50 12.50
Souvenir Sheets
2729-2730 A449 Set of 2   8.00 8.00

Paintings of Paul Klee (1879-1940) — A450

No. 2731, horiz.: a, Near Taormina, Scirocco. b, Small Town Among the Rocks. c, Still Life with Props. d, North Room.
25r, Dame Demon.

2003, Dec. 4   **Perf. 13½**
2731 A450 10r Sheet of 4, #a-d   6.25 6.25
Souvenir Sheet
2732 A450 25r multi   4.00 4.00

Maumoon Abdul Gayoom, 25th Anniv. as President — A451

Litho. & Embossed
2003   **Die Cut Perf. 8**
Without Gum
2733 A451 200r gold & multi   32.50 32.50

Norman Rockwell (1894-1978) A452

No. 2734 — Four Seasons Calendar: Man and Boy, 1948: a, Winter (ice skating). b, Spring (resting amidst flowers). c, Summer (fishing). d, Autumn (raking leaves).
25r, Illustration for Hallmark Cards, 1937.

2003, Dec. 4   **Litho.**   **Perf. 13¼**
2734 A452 10r Sheet of 4, #a-d   6.25 6.25
Imperf
2735 A452 25r shown   4.00 4.00
No. 2734 contains four 38x50mm stamps.

Intl. Year of Fresh Water A453

No. 2736: a, Ari Atoll. b, Fresh water for all. c, Desalination plant, Malé.
25r, Community rain water tank.

2003, Dec. 22   **Perf. 14**
2736 A453 15r Sheet of 3, #a-c   6.00 6.00
Souvenir Sheet
2737 A453 25r multi   4.00 4.00

Fish — A454

Designs: 1r, Clown triggerfish. 7r, Sixspot grouper. 10r, Long-nosed butterflyfish. 15r, Longfin bannerfish.
No. 2742: a, Goldtail demoiselle. b, Queen coris. c, Eight-banded butterflyfish. d, Meyer's butterflyfish. e, Exquisite butterflyfish. f, Yellowstripe snapper. g, Yellowback anthias. h, Black-spotted moray. i, Clown anemonefish.
No. 2743: a, Bluestreak cleaner wrasse. b, Threeband demoiselle. c, Palette surgeonfish. d, Emperor snapper. e, Bicolor angelfish. f, Picasso triggerfish.
25r, Chevron butterflyfish.

2003, Dec. 22
2738-2741 A454 Set of 4   5.25 5.25
2742 A454 4r Sheet of 9, #a-i   5.75 5.75
2743 A454 7r Sheet of 6, #a-f   6.75 6.75
Souvenir Sheet
2744 A454 25r multi   4.00 4.00
Nos. 2738-2741 were each printed in sheets of four.

Butterflies — A455

Designs: 3r, Yamfly. 5r, Striped blue crow. 8r, Indian red admiral. 15r, Great eggfly.
No. 2749, horiz.: a, Blue triangle. b, Monarch. c, Broad-bordered grass yellow. d, Red lacewing. e, African migrant. f, Plain tiger.
25r, Beak butterfly.

2003, Dec. 22
2745-2748 A455 Set of 4   5.25 5.25
2749 A455 7r Sheet of 6, #a-f   7.25 7.25
Souvenir Sheet
2750 A455 25r multi   4.25 4.25

Birds — A456

Designs: 15 l, Great frigatebird. 20 l, Ruddy turnstone. 25 l, Hoopoe. 1r, Cattle egret.
No. 2755: a, Red-billed tropicbird. b, Red-footed booby. c, Common tern. d, Caspian tern. e, Common curlew. f, Black-bellied plover.
25r, Gray heron.

2003, Dec. 22
2751-2754 A456 Set of 4   6.50 6.50
2755 A456 7r Sheet of 6, #a-f   7.25 7.25
Souvenir Sheet
2756 A456 25r multi   4.25 4.25

Paintings by Pablo Picasso (1881-1973) — A457

No. 2757: a, Portrait of Jaime Sabartés, 1901. b, Portrait of the Artist's Wife (Olga), 1923. c, Portrait of Olga, 1923. d, Portrait of Jaime Sabartés, 1904.
30r, The Tragedy, 1903.

2003, Dec. 4   **Litho.**   **Perf. 13¼**
2757 A457 10r Sheet of 4, #a-d   6.25 6.25
Imperf
2758 A457 30r multi   4.75 4.75
No. 2757 contains four 37x50mm stamps.

Flowers — A458

Designs: 30 l, Coelogyne asperata. 75 l, Calanthe rosea. 2r, Eria javanica. 10r, Spathoglottis affinis.
No. 2763, horiz.: a, Bird of paradise. b, Flamingo flower. c, Red ginger. d, Cooktown orchid. e, Vanda tricolor. f, Chinese hibiscus.
25r, Morning glory.

2003, Dec. 22   **Perf. 14**
2759-2762 A458 Set of 4   2.50 2.50
2763 A458 7r Sheet of 6, #a-f   6.75 6.75
Souvenir Sheet
2764 A458 25r multi   4.00 4.00

FIFA (Fédération Internationale de Football Association) Cent. — A459

World Cup winning teams: No. 2765, 5r, Germany, 1974. No. 2766, 5r, Argentina, 1978. No. 2767, 5r, Italy, 1982. No. 2768, 5r, Argentina, 1986. No. 2769, 5r, Germany, 1990. No. 2770, 5r, Brazil, 1994. No. 2771, 5r, France, 1998. No. 2772, 5r, Brazil, 2002.

2004, Mar. 8   **Perf. 13½**
2765-2772 A459 Set of 8   7.00 7.00

Paintings by Gao Jian-fu (1879-1951) — A460

No. 2773: a, Landscape. b, Moon Night. c, Fox. d, Spider web. e, Woman with mirror. f, Man sitting on ground.

No. 2774: a, Eagle. b, Sunset.

2004, Mar. 8   **Perf. 13¼**
2773 A460 7r Sheet of 6, #a-f   5.75 5.75
2774 A460 12r Sheet of 2, #a-b   3.25 3.25
2004 Hong Kong Stamp Expo.

Cessation of Concorde Flights — A461

No. 2775: a, F-BVFD, Rio de Janeiro. b, F-BVFC, New York. c, F-BTSD, Honolulu. d, F-BTSD, Lisbon. e, F-BVFA, Washington. f, F-BVFD, Dakar, Senegal. g, G-BOAC, Singapore. h, G-BOAA, Sydney. i, G-BOAD, Hong Kong. j, G-BOAD, Amsterdam. k, G-BOAE, Tokyo. l, G-BOAF, Madrid.
No. 2776, 25r, 214 G-BOAG, Museum of Flight, Seattle. No. 2777, 25r, 214 G-BOAG, horizon. No. 2778, 25r, 204 G-BOAC, British flag.

2004, Mar. 8   **Perf. 13¼x13½**
2775 A461 1r Sheet of 12, #a-l   1.60 1.60
Souvenir Sheets
2776-2778 A461 Set of 3   10.00 10.00

Paintings in the Hermitage, St. Petersburg, Russia — A462

Designs: 1r, Self-portrait, by Anthony van Dyck. 3r, Self-portrait, by Michael Sweerts. 7r, Anna Dalkeith, Countess of Morton, by van Dyck. 12r, Lady Anna Kirk, by van Dyck.
No. 2783: a, Portrait of Prince Alexander Kurakin, by Marie-Louise-Elisabeth Vigée-Lebrun. b, Portrait of a Lady in Waiting to the Infanta Isabella, by Peter Paul Rubens. c, Portrait of a Lady in Blue, by Thomas Gainsborough. d, The Actor Pierre Jéliotte in the Role of Apollo, by Louis Tocqué.
No. 2784, 25r, The Stolen Kiss, by Jean-Honoré Fragonard, horiz. No. 2785, 25r, A Scene from Corneille's Tragedy "La Comte d'Essex," by Nicolas Lancret, horiz.

2004, Mar. 29   **Perf. 14¼**
2779-2782 A462 Set of 4   4.00 4.00
2783 A462 10r Sheet of 4, #a-d   5.25 5.25
Souvenir Sheets
2784-2785 A462 Set of 2   6.75 6.75

D-Day, 60th Anniv. A463

No. 2786, 6r: a, Gen. Dwight Eisenhower. b, Field Marshal Guenther von Kluge. c, Air Marshal Sir Trafford Leigh-Mallory. d, Field Marshal Walter Model. e, Field Marshal Gerd von Rundstedt. f, Sir Arthur Tedder.

MALDIVE ISLANDS

No. 2787, 6r: a, Maj. Gen. Clarence Huebner. b, Brig. Gen. Anthony McAuliffe. c, Maj. Gen. Leonard Gerow. d, Gen. Adolf Galland. e, Brig. Gen. W. M. Hoge. f, Maj. Gen. Sir Percy Hobart.
No. 2788, 6r: a, Rear Admiral Kirk. b, Field Marshal Erwin Rommel. c, Gen. George Marshall. d, Gen. Jan Smuts. e, Gen. Lt. Gunther Blumentritt. f, Maj. Gen. J. Lawton Collins.
No. 2789, 6r: a, Winston Churchill. b, Adm. Sir Bertram Ramsay. c, Gen. Lt. Dietrich Kraiss. d, Maj. Gen. Richard Gale. e, Gen. George Patton. f, Maj. Gen. Maxwell Taylor.
No. 2790, 6r, horiz.: a, Lt. Gen. Omar Bradley. b, Rear Admiral Hall. c, Maj. Gen. Huebner. d, Adm. Karl Dönitz. e, Rear Admiral Wilkes. f, Capt. Chauncey Camp.
No. 2791, 30r, Gen. Henry Arnold. No. 2792, 30r, Rear Adm. Donald Moon. No. 2793, 30r, Lt. Gen. Sir Frederick Morgan. No. 2794, 30r, Gen. Sir Bernard Montgomery. No. 2795, 30r, Rear Adm. Carlton Bryant, horiz.

Perf. 13½x13¼, 13¼x13½
2004, May 19   Sheets of 6, #a-f
2786-2790   A463   Set of 5   28.00 28.00
Souvenir Sheets
2791-2795   A463   Set of 5   24.00 24.00

Paintings by Paul Cézanne (1839-1906) — A464

No. 2796, horiz.: a, Still Life with Peppermint Bottle and Blue Rug. b, House in Provence. c, Le Château Noir. d, Basket of Apples.
25r, Boy in a Red Waistcoat Leaning on his Elbow.

2004, July 6   Perf. 13¼
2796   A464   10r Sheet of 4, #a-d   6.25 6.25
Imperf
2797   A464   25r multi   4.00 4.00
No. 2796 contains four 50x37mm stamps.

Paintings by Henri Rousseau (1844-1910) — A465

No. 2798, horiz.: a, Nègre Attaqué par un Jaguar. b, Paysage Exotique. c, La Cascade. d, Le Repas du Lion. 25r, Le Rêve.

2004, July 6   Perf. 13¼
2798   A465   10r Sheet of 4, #a-d   6.25 6.25
Imperf
2799   A465   25r multi   4.00 4.00
No. 2798 contains four 50x37mm stamps.

Paintings by Henri Matisse (1869-1954) — A466

No. 2800, horiz.: a, Conversation. b, Still Life with a Blue Tablecloth. c, Seville Still Life II. d, Woman Before an Aquarium.
25r, Interior at Nice.

2004, July 6   Perf. 13¼
2800   A466   10r Sheet of 4, #a-d   6.25 6.25
Imperf
2801   A466   25r multi   4.00 4.00
No. 2800 contains four 50x37mm stamps.

Steam Locomotives, 200th Anniv. — A467

No. 2802, 12r: a, Planet Class 2-2-0. b, American 4-4-0. c, Newmar. d, Class 500 4-6-0.
No. 2803, 12r: a, Firefly Class 2-2-2. b, French "Single." c, Medoc Class 2-4-0. d, German 4-4-0.
No. 2804, 12r: a, Adler 2-2-2. b, Beuth 2-2-2. c, Northumbrian 0-2-2. d, Class 4-6-2.
No. 2805, 12r: a, Woodburning Beyer Garratt 4-8-2+2-8-4. b, Double headed train over Kaaiman River, Africa. c, Garratt 4-8-2+2-8-4. d, Class 15 Garratt.
No. 2806, 12r: a, East African Railways Garratt. b, Rhodesian Railways 12th Class. c, Class 2-6-2. d, Class 19D 4-8-2.
No. 2807, 12r: a, Evening Star. b, Britannia. c, The George Stephenson. d, Sudan Railways 310 2-8-2.
No. 2808, 30r, Claud Hamilton Class 4-4-0. No. 2809, 30r, Class P8 4-6-0. No. 2810, 30r, Vauxhall 2-2-0. No. 2811, 30r, American, diff. No. 2812, 30r, The Lord Nelson. No. 2813, 30r, Flying Scotsman.

2004, July 6   Perf. 13¼x13½
Sheets of 4, #a-d
2802-2807   A467   Set of 6   15.00 15.00
Souvenir Sheets
2808-2813   A467   Set of 6   28.00 28.00

Jules Verne (1828-1905), Writer — A468

No. 2814, 12r: a, Archipelago on Fire. b, Clovis Dardentor. c, The Golden Volcano. d, Le Superbe Orénoque.
No. 2815, 12r — Michael Strogoff, Courier of the Czar: a, People (pink background). b, People in grass (green background). c, People (blue background). d, Animal and head in grass (green background).
No. 2816, 12r — Family Without a Name: a, Woman. b, Soldier. c, Crowd. d, Soldiers and Indian with guns.
No. 2817, 12r — César Cascabel: a, Men pushing train car (blue green background). b, Man (brown background). c, Crevasse (blue green background). d, Crowd and sign (pink background).
No. 2818, 12r — The Lighthouse at the End of the World: a, Men on ship. b, Man with arm extended. c, Rocks. d, Fisherman with hat.
No. 2819, 25r, The Survivors of the Chancellor. No. 2820, 25r, Keraban the Inflexible. No. 2821, 25r, Family Without a Name, diff. No. 2822, 25r, César Cascabel, diff. No. 2823, 25r, The Lighthouse at the End of the World, diff.

2004, July 29   Perf. 13¼x13½
Sheets of 4, #a-d
2814-2818   A468   Set of 5   37.00 37.00
Souvenir Sheets
2819-2823   A468   Set of 5   19.00 19.00

Marilyn Monroe — A469

2004, Aug. 16   Perf. 13½x13¼
2824   A469   7r multi   1.25 1.25
Printed in sheets of 6.

George Herman "Babe" Ruth (1895-1948), Baseball Player — A470

No. 2826: a, Swinging bat. b, Wearing cap, striped uniform. c, Holding two bats. d, Profile of Ruth.

2004
2825   A470   3r shown   .55 .55
2826   A470   10r Sheet of 4, #a-d   6.25 6.25
No. 2825 printed in sheets of 16. World Series, 100th anniv.

Paintings by Salvador Dalí (1904-89) — A471

No. 2827: a, The Endless Enigma. b, The Persistence of Memory. c, Soft Construction with Boiled Beans — Premonition of Civil War. d, Still Life — Fast Moving.
25r, Figure on the Rocks.

2004, July 6   Litho.   Perf. 13½
2827   A471   10r Sheet of 4, #a-d   6.25 6.25
Imperf
2828   A471   25r multi   4.00 4.00
No. 2827 contains four 50x37mm stamps.

2004 Summer Olympics, Athens — A472

Designs: 2r, Gold medal, 1904 St. Louis Olympics. 5r, Krater depicting Olympic athletes. 7r, Count Jean de Beaumont, Intl. Olympic Committee member. 12r, Pommel horse, horiz.

2004, Sept. 30   Perf. 14¼
2829-2832   A472   Set of 4   4.25 4.25

Sharks A473

No. 2833: a, Silvertip shark. b, Silky shark. c, Great white shark. d, Gray reef shark.
$25, Starry smoothhound shark.

2004, Nov. 4
2833   A473   10r Sheet of 4, #a-d   6.25 6.25
Souvenir Sheet
2834   A473   25r multi   4.00 4.00

Starfish — A474

Designs: No. 2835, 10r, Fromia monilis (green background). No. 2836, 10r, Linckia laevigata. No. 2837, 10r, Nardoa novaecalidoniae. No. 2838, 10r, Fromia monilis (red background).

2004, Nov. 4   Perf. 15x14
2835-2838   A474   Set of 4   6.25 6.25

Worldwide Fund for Nature (WWF) — A475

No. 2839 — Eurypegasus draconis and: a, Country name at LL, denomination at LR. b, Country name at UL, denomination at LR, dark background. c, Country name at LR, denomination at UL. d, Country name at UL, denomination at LR, light background.

2004, Dec. 15   Litho.   Perf. 14
2839   A475   7r Block of 4, #a-d   4.50 4.50
  e.   Miniature sheet, 2 each #2839a-2839d   9.00 9.00

Butterflies — A476

No. 2840, horiz.: a, Red lacewing. b, Amesia sanguiflua. c, Pericallia galactina. d, Limenitis dudu subsp.
25r, Lime butterfly.

2004, Dec. 15
2840   A476   10r Sheet of 4, #a-d   6.25 6.25
Souvenir Sheet
2841   A476   25r multi   4.00 4.00

Dolphins — A477

No. 2842: a, Striped dolphin. b, Amazon River dolphin. c, Bottlenose dolphin. d, Spinner dolphin.
25r, Long-snouted spinner dolphin.

MALDIVE ISLANDS

2004, Dec. 15   Litho.   Perf. 14
2842   A477   10r Sheet of 4, #a-d   6.25   6.25
Souvenir Sheet
2843   A477   25r multi   4.00   4.00

Reptiles and Amphibians — A478

No. 2844, horiz.: a, Eyelash pit viper. b, Basilisk lizard. c, Calico snake. d, Maki frog. 25r, Naja melanoleuca.

2004, Dec. 15
2844   A478   10r Sheet of 4, #a-d   6.25   6.25
Souvenir Sheet
2845   A478   25r multi   4.00   4.00

Mushrooms — A479

No. 2846, horiz.: a, Parrot mushroom. b, Hygrocybe miniata. c, Aleuria aurantia. d, Thaxterogaster porphyreum. 25r, Galerina autumnalis.

2004, Dec. 15
2846   A479   10r Sheet of 4, #a-d   6.25   6.25
Souvenir Sheet
2847   A479   25r multi   4.00   4.00

Prehistoric Animals — A480

No. 2848, 10r: a, Macroplata. b, Ichthyosaurus. c, Shonisaurus. d, Archelon.
No. 2849, 10r, vert.: a, Albertosaurus. b, Iguanodon. c, Deinonychus, name at right. d, Baryonyx.
No. 2850, 10r, vert.: a, Deinonychus, name at left. b, Styracosaurus. c, Ornitholestes. d, Euoplocephalus.
No. 2851, 10r, vert.: a, Pterodactylus. b, Cearadactylus. c, Pterosaur. d, Sordes.
No. 2852, 25r, Muraeonosaurus. No. 2853, 25r, Styracosaurus, diff. No. 2854, 25r, Leptoceratops. No. 2855, 25r, Archaeopteryx.

2004, Dec. 15   Perf. 14
Sheets of 4, #a-d
2848-2851   A480   Set of 4   25.00   25.00
Souvenir Sheets
2852-2855   A480   Set of 4   16.00   16.00

Souvenir Sheet

Deng Xiaoping (1904-97), Chinese Leader — A481

2005, Jan. 26
2856   A481   25r multi   4.00   4.00

2004 European Soccer Championships, Portugal — A482

No. 2857, vert.: a, Jupp Derwall. b, René Vandereycke. c, Horst Hrubesch. d, Stadio Olimpico.
25r, 1980 Germany team.

2005, Jan. 26   Perf. 14
2857   A482   12r Sheet of 4, #a-d   7.50   7.50
Souvenir Sheet
2858   A482   25r multi   4.00   4.00
No. 2857 contains four 28x42mm stamps.

Rotary International, Cent. — A483

No. 2859 — Chicago skyline: a, Part of Sears Tower at R. b, Sears Tower at L. c, CNA Tower (red brick building) at L.
25r, Telecommunications tower.

2005, July 12   Litho.   Perf. 12¾
2859   A483   15r Sheet of 3, #a-c   7.00   7.00
Souvenir Sheet
2860   A483   25r multi   4.00   4.00

Hans Christian Andersen (1805-75), Author — A484

No. 2861: a, Statue of Andersen wearing hat. b, Photograph of Andersen. c, Statue of Andersen without hat.
25r, Little Mermaid Statue, Copenhagen.

2005, Sept. 20
2861   A484   15r Sheet of 3, #a-c   7.00   7.00
Souvenir Sheet
2862   A484   25r multi   4.00   4.00

World Cup Soccer Championships, 75th Anniv. — A485

No. 2863: a, Oscar. b, Karl-Heinz Rummenigge. c, Oliver Kahn.
25r, Karlheinz Forster.

2005, Sept. 20   Perf. 13¼
2863   A485   15r Sheet of 3, #a-c   7.00   7.00
Souvenir Sheet
Perf. 12¼x12
2864   A485   25r multi   4.00   4.00

Battle of Trafalgar, Bicent. A486

No. 2865, vert.: a, Admiral Cuthbert Collingwood. b, Napoleon Bonaparte. c, Admiral Horatio Nelson. d, Capt. Thomas Masterman Hardy.
25r, Ships at battle.

2005, Sept. 20   Perf. 12¾
2865   A486   10r Sheet of 4, #a-d   7.00   7.00
Souvenir Sheet
2866   A486   25r multi   4.25   4.25

Albert Einstein (1879-1955), Physicist — A487

No. 2867, horiz. — Portraits of Einstein in: a, Red brown (denomination at R). b, Pink & blue (denomination at L). c, Green & pink (denomination at R). d, Brown (denomination at L).
25r, Einstein, diff.

2005, Sept. 20
2867   A487   15r Sheet of 4, #a-d   6.25   6.25
Souvenir Sheet
2868   A487   25r multi   4.00   4.00

Elvis Presley (1935-77) — A488

No. 2869, 7r — Photographs of Presley from: a, 1956 (sepia). b, 1957. c, 1958. d, 1964. e, 1967. f, 1968.
No. 2870, 7r — Photographs of Presley from: a, 1956 (black and white). b, 1960. c, 1962. d, 1969. e, 1973. f, 1975.

2005, Nov. 15   Perf. 13¾x13¼
Sheets of 6, #a-f
2869-2870   A488   Set of 2   13.00   13.00

Elvis Presley (1935-77) — A489

Litho. & Embossed
2006, Jan. 17   Die Cut Perf 7½
Without Gum
2871   A489   85r gold & multi   13.50   13.50

Miniature Sheets

Children's Drawings — A490

No. 2872, 10r — Sea Life: a, Bubbles, by Raquel Bobolia. b, Bubble Fish, by Sarah Bowen. c, Lipfish, by Elsa Fleisher. d, Flounder, by Erica Malchowski.
No. 2873, 10r — Birds: a, Purple Bird, by Anna Badger. b, Parrots, by Nick Abrams. c, Pretty Bird, by Jessie Abrams. d, Royal Parrot, by Ashley Mondfrans.
No. 2874, 10r — Flowers: a, Orange Sunflower, by Brett Walker. b, Red Flower, by Jessica Shutt. c, Flower Pot, by Nick Abrams. d, Blue Flower Vase, by Trevor Nielsen.

2006, Jan. 24   Litho.   Perf. 13¼
Sheets of 4, #a-d
2872-2874   A490   Set of 3   19.00   19.00

Skates and Rays — A491

Designs: 20 l, Himantura uamak. 1r, Manta birostris. 2r, Taeniura lymma. 20r, Aetobatus narinari.

2006, Feb. 27   Perf. 13¾x14¼
2875-2878   A491   Set of 4   4.00   4.00

Souvenir Sheet

South Asian Association for Regional Cooperation, 20th Anniv. — A492

2006, Mar. 9   Perf. 13¼
2879   A492   25r multi   4.00   4.00

2006 Winter Olympics, Turin — A493

Designs: 7r, Norway #B52. 8r, Poster for 1952 Oslo Winter Olympics, vert. 10r, Poster for 1936 Garmisch-Partenkirchen Winter Olympics, vert. 12r, Germany #B79, vert.

2006, May 9   Perf. 14¼
2880-2883   A493   Set of 4   5.75   5.75

MALDIVE ISLANDS

Miniature Sheet

Marilyn Monroe (1926-62), Actress — A527

No. 2973: a, Face. b, In car. c, Wearing patterned blouse, in room. d, With hand near chin.

2009, Oct. 21			**Perf. 12½x12¾**	
2973	A527	16r Sheet of 4, #a-d	10.00	10.00

Whales — A528

Designs: 10 l, Beluga whale. No. 2975, 12r, Hector's beaked whale. 16r, Beaked whale. 18r, Baird's beaked whale.
No. 2978, 12r, horiz.: a, Dwarf sperm whale. b, Pygmy sperm whale. c, Baird's beaked whale, diff. d, Sperm whale. e, Shepherd's beaked whale. f, Cuvier's beaked whale.

2009, Oct. 21			**Perf. 12½**	
2974-2977	A528	Set of 4	7.25	7.25
2978	A528	12r Sheet of 6, #a-f	11.50	11.50

Butterflies — A529

Designs: 10 l, Crimson rose. 16r, Common Mormon. 18r, Common jay. 20r, Common tiger.
No. 2983, horiz.: a, Small salmon Arab. b, Lemon pansy. c, Tamil yeoman. d, Dark blue tiger.
No. 2984: a, Common jezebel. b, Common gull.

2009, Oct. 21			**Perf. 12½**	
2979-2982	A529	Set of 4	8.50	8.50
		Perf. 12		
2983	A529	12r Sheet of 4, #a-d	7.50	7.50
		Souvenir Sheet		
2984	A529	15r Sheet of 2, #a-b	4.75	4.75

Chinese Aviation, Cent. A530

No. 2985 — Airplanes: a, Y-5. b, Y-7. c, Y-8. d, Y-12.
25r, MA60.

2009, Nov. 12	**Litho.**		**Perf. 14¼**	
2985	A530	9r Sheet of 4, #a-d	5.75	5.75
		Souvenir Sheet		
2986	A530	25r multi	4.00	4.00

Aeropex 2009, Beijing. No. 2985 contains four 42x28mm stamps.

Worldwide Fund for Nature (WWF) — A531

No. 2987 — Melon-headed whale: a, Pod of whales underwater. b, Pod of whales at surface, swimming right. c, Whale. d, Pod of whales at surface, swimming left.

2009, Nov. 18			**Perf. 13¼**	
2987		Block or strip of 4	5.00	5.00
a.-d.		A531 8r Any single	1.25	1.25
e.		Sheet of 8, 2 each #2987a-2987d	10.00	10.00

First Man on the Moon, 40th Anniv. A532

No. 2988, vert.: a, Apollo 11 Command and Service Modules. b, Apollo 11 Command, Service and Lunar Modules. c, Neil Armstrong. d, Apollo 11 Lunar Module.
30r, Crew of Apollo 11.

2009, July 20	**Litho.**		**Perf. 13¼**	
2988	A532	12r Sheet of 4, #a-d	7.50	7.50
		Souvenir Sheet		
2989	A532	30r multi	4.75	4.75

Intl. Year of Astronomy.

Miniature Sheets

Mushrooms — A533

Mushrooms — A534

No. 2990: a, Copelandia bispora. b, Copelandia cyanescens. c, Psilocybe semilanceata. d, Volvariella volvacea.
No. 2991: Various unnamed mushrooms.

2009, Nov. 18			**Perf. 11½**	
2990	A533	8r Sheet of 4, #a-d	5.00	5.00
2991	A534	8r Sheet of 6, #a-f	7.50	7.50

Flowers A535

No. 2992: a, Nelumbo nucifera. b, Rosa bracteata. c, Freycinetia cumingiata. d, Thespesia lampas. e, Plumeria champa. f, Plumeria cubensis.
No. 2993: a, Lagerstroemia speciosa. b, Plumeria alba.
No. 2994: a, Plumeria rubra. b, Hibiscus tiliaceus.

2009, Dec. 9				
2992	A535	10r Sheet of 6, #a-f	9.50	9.50
		Souvenir Sheets		
2993	A535	15r Sheet of 2, #a-b	4.75	4.75
2994	A535	15r Sheet of 2, #a-b	4.75	4.75

Souvenir Sheet

New Year 2010 (Year of the Tiger) A536

No. 2995: a, Chinese characters. b, Tiger.

2010, Jan. 4	**Litho.**		**Perf. 12**	
2995	A536	25r Sheet of 2, #a-b	8.00	8.00

Shells — A537

Designs: 10 l, Conus abbas. 12r, Conus amadis. 16r, Conus bengalensis. 18r, Pinctada margaritifera.
No. 3000: a, Harpa costata. b, Phalium fimbria. c, Zoila friendii friendii. d, Cyprae leucodon tenuidon.

2010, June 22			**Perf. 11¼x11½**	
2996-2999	A537	Set of 4	7.25	7.25
		Perf. 12x11½		
3000	A537	15r Sheet of 4, #a-d	9.50	9.50

Miniature Sheets

Election of Pres. John F. Kennedy, 50th Anniv. A538

No. 3001, 15r: a, Pres. Kennedy at lectern. b, Pulitzer Prize medal. c, Civil Rights Act of 1964. d, Peace Corps emblem.
No. 3002, 15r: a, Vice-president Lyndon B. Johnson. b, Pres. Kennedy. c, Brochures for 1960 presidential election. d, Campaign placard.

2010, June 22			**Perf. 13¼**	
		Sheets of 4, #a-d		
3001-3002	A538	Set of 2	19.00	19.00

Girl Guides, Cent. A539

No. 3003, horiz.: a, Three Girl Guides. b, Two Girl Guides, "100." c, Girl Guide climbing rock. d, Two Girl Guides jumping.
30r, Brownie.

2010, June 22			**Perf. 13x13¼**	
3003	A539	16r Sheet of 4, #a-d	10.00	10.00
		Souvenir Sheet		
		Perf. 13¼x13		
3004	A539	30r multi	4.75	4.75

Reptiles A540

No. 3005: a, Olive ridley turtle. b, Blood sucker lizard. c, Indian wolf snake. d, Green turtle.
No. 3006: a, Common house gecko. b, Loggerhead turtle.

2010, June 22			**Perf. 11½**	
3005	A540	15r Sheet of 4, #a-d	9.50	9.50
		Souvenir Sheet		
		Perf. 11½x12		
3006	A540	15r Sheet of 2, #a-b	4.75	4.75

Birds A541

No. 3007, horiz.: a, White-tailed tropicbird. b, Common tern. c, Bar-tailed godwit. d, Crab plover. e, Whimbrel. f, Black-winged stilt.
30r, Asian koel.

2010, June 22			**Perf. 11½x12**	
3007	A541	8r Sheet of 6, #a-f	7.50	7.50
		Souvenir Sheet		
		Perf. 11¼x11½		
3008	A541	30r multi	4.75	4.75

Souvenir Sheets

A542

A543

A544

Elvis Presley (1935-77) A545

2010, June 22			**Perf. 13½**	
3009	A542	25r multi	4.00	4.00
3010	A543	25r multi	4.00	4.00
3011	A544	25r multi	4.00	4.00
3012	A545	25r multi	4.00	4.00
		Nos. 3009-3012 (4)	16.00	16.00

MALDIVE ISLANDS

Muhammad Ali's Boxing Gold Medal in 1960 Summer Olympics, 50th Anniv. — A596

No. 3013 — Ali: a, Black-and-white photo. b, Sepia photo.
No. 3014 — Silhouette of Ali and photo of Ali: a, Wearing gold medal, country name at top. b, Throwing punch, country name at top. c, As "b," country name at bottom. d, As "a," country name at bottom.

		2010, June 22	**Litho.**	**Perf. 12x11½**	
3013	A596	15r Vert. pair, #a-b		4.75	4.75
3014	A596	15r Sheet of 4, #a-d		9.50	9.50

Souvenir Sheet

Girl Guides, Cent. A597

No. 3015: a, Girl Guides emblem and centenary text. b, Maldives Girl Guides 50th anniversary emblem.

		2010, June 22		**Perf. 11¾x12¼**	
3015	A597	12r Sheet of 2, #a-b		3.75	3.75

Winning Artwork in Children's Prevention of Child Abuse Stamp Design Contest — A598

No. 3016 — Art by: a, 10 l, Aishath Shamha Nizam. b, 20 l, Shaulaan Shafeeq. c, 95 l, Sameen Moosa. d, 5r, Zaha Mohamed Ziyad.
No. 3017, vert. — Art by: a, 25 l, Emau Ahmed Saleem. b, 50 l, Rishwan Naseem. c, 1r, Ahmed Nafiu. d, 2r, Sam'aan Abdul Raheem. e, 3r, Ummu Haanee Hussain. f, 4r, Fathimath Shaufa Easa. g, 6r, Hussain Hazim. h, 7r, Fathimath Afaaf Bushree.

		2010, June 22		**Perf. 13¼**	
3016	A598	Sheet of 4, #a-d		1.00	1.00
3017	A598	Sheet of 8, #a-h		3.75	3.75

Miniature Sheet

Chinese Zodiac Animals A599

No. 3018: a, Rat. b, Ox. c, Tiger. d, Rabbit. e, Dragon. f, Snake. g, Horse. h, Ram. i, Monkey. j, Rooster. k, Dog. l, Pig.

2010, Jan. 4

3018	A599	3r Sheet of 12, #a-l		5.75	5.75

Souvenir Sheet

New Year 2010 (Year of the Rabbit) A600

		2010, June 22		**Perf. 12**	
3019	A600	19r Sheet of 2		6.00	6.00
a.		Single stamp		3.00	3.00

Diplomatic Relations Between the Maldive Islands and People's Republic of China, 40th Anniv. — A601

No. 3020: a, Dhoni. b, Treasure boat of Admiral Zheng He. c, Lacquerware. d, Hornless dragon vase. e, Hawksbill turtle. f, Chinese sturgeon.

		2012	**Litho.**	**Perf. 12**	
3020	A601	40r Block of 6, #a-f		31.00	31.00
g.		Souvenir sheet of 6, #3020a-3020f		31.00	31.00

Worldwide Fund for Nature (WWF) — A602

Amaurornis phoenicurus: Nos. 3021a, 3022d, Single bird in flight. Nos. 3021b, 3022a, Single bird at water's edge. Nos. 3021c, 3022b, Two birds. Nos. 3021d, 3022c, Adult bird and chicks.
70r, Amaurornis phoenicurus and flower.

2013, Sept. 30 Litho. Perf. 13x13¼
Stamp Size: 40x30mm

3021		Horiz. strip of 4	12.00	12.00
a.-d.		Any single	3.00	3.00
e.		Souvenir sheet of 8, 2 each #3021a-3021d, + central label	24.00	24.00

Miniature Sheet
Stamp Size: 47x37mm
Perf. 13¼

3022	A602	22r Sheet of 4, #a-d	12.00	12.00

Souvenir Sheet

3023	A602	70r multi	9.25	9.25

Wildlife of the Indian Ocean A603

No. 3024, 20r — Seals: a, Arctocephalus pusillus. b, Arctocephalus forsteri. c, Neophoca cinerea. d, Arctocephalus tropicalis.
No. 3025, 20r — Dugong dugon: a, Three dugongs facing right. b, One dugong facing left. c, One dugong facing right. d, Three dugongs facing left.
No. 3026, 20r — Whales: a, Caperea marginata. b, Indopacetus pacificus. c, Balaenoptera edeni. d, Balaenoptera physalus.
No. 3027, 20r — Starfish: a, Fromia indica, Pentaceraster cumingi. b, Astropecten aranciacus, Asterias rubens. c, Protoreaster linckii, Choriaster granulatus. d, Two Protoreaster nodosus.
No. 3028, 22r — Dolphins: a, Tursiops truncatus above water, facing right. b, Tursiops truncatus above water, facing left. c, Tursiops truncatus underwater, facing right. d, Tursiops aduncus.
No. 3029, 22r — Birds: a, Sula leucogaster. b, Fregata ariel. c, Sula sula. d, Puffinus carneipes.
No. 3030, 22r — Fish: a, Nemateleotris decora. b, Forcipiger flavissimus. c, Odonus niger. d, Oxycirrhites typus.
No. 3031, 22r — Shells: a, Phalium areola. b, Cypraea cribraria. c, Conus vexillum. d, Strombus sinuatus.
No. 3032, 22r — Turtles: a, Caretta caretta. b, Dermochelys coriacea. c, Eretmochelys imbricata. d, Chelonia mydas.
No. 3033, 60r, Neophoca cinerea, diff. No. 3034, 60r, Dugong dugon facing left, diff. No. 3035, 60r, Balaenoptera musculus. No. 3036, 60r, Iconaster longimanus, Fromia monilis. No. 3037, 70r, Tursiops truncatus, diff. No. 3038, 70r, Pelecanus onocrotalus. No. 3039, 70r, Chaetodon auriga. No. 3040, 70r, Melo aethiopicus. No. 3041, 70r, Dermochelys coriacea, diff.

2013, Sept. 30 Litho. Perf. 13¼
Sheets of 4, #a-d

3024-3032	A603	Set of 9	100.00	100.00

Souvenir Sheets

3033-3041	A603	Set of 9	77.50	77.50

Fauna and Flora A604

No. 3042, 20r — Fruit bats: a, Pteropus giganteus ariel, bat in flight at left. b, Pteropus giganteus ariel, bat hanging at left. c, Pteropus hypomelanus maris, bat hanging at left. d, Pteropus hypomelanus maris, bat flying at left.
No. 3043, 20r — Protected marine species: a, Rhincodon typus. b, Chelonia mydas. c, Charonia variegata. d, Cheilinus undulatus.
No. 3044, 20r — Water birds: a, Pelecanus onocrotalus. b, Gallinago stenura. c, Anous stolida. d, Anas clypeata.
No. 3045, 20r — Lizards: a, Hemidactylus frenatus, climbing. b, Calotes versicolor, facing left. c, Calotes versicolor, facing right. d, Hemidactylus frenatus, with eggs.
No. 3046, 20r — Crocdylus porosus: a, Crocodile at left with head turning right, crocodile at right with open mouth. b, Crocodile at left with head turning right and with mouth open, crocodile at right facing forward. c, Crocodile at left with head turning left, crocodile at right with mouth open. d, Crocodiles at left and right facing forward.
No. 3047, 22r — Orchids: a, Orchis mascula. b, Cattleya coccinea. c, Dendrobium crumenatum. d, Phalaenopsis cultivar.
No. 3048, 22r — Asio flammeus: a, Owl at left flying to left. b, Owl at left flying to right. c, Owl at left flying to right, vine in background. d, Owl at left flying over water to left.
No. 3049, 22r — Birds of prey: a, Asio flammeus, bird at left on branch. b, Falco subbuteo. c, Buteo buteo. d, Circus aeruginosus.
No. 3050, 22r — Tropical butterflies: a, Sasakia charonda. b, Graphium sarpedon luctatius. c, Evenus regalis. d, Godyris duilia.
No. 3051, 22r — Fish: a, Chaetodon benetti. b, Manata birostris. c, Carcharhinus amblyrhynchos. d, Zanclus cornutus.
No. 3052, 60r, Pteropus giganteus ariel, diff. No. 3053, 60r, Myrichthys colubrinus. No. 3054, 60r, Philomachus pugnax. No. 3055, 60r, Calotes versicolor, diff. No. 3056, 70r, Crocodylus porosus, diff. No. 3057, 70r, Orchis mascula, diff. No. 3058, 70r, Asio flammeus, diff. No. 3059, 70r, Pandion haliaetus. No. 3060, 70r, Vindula dejone erotella. No. 3061, 70r, Juvenile Pomacanthus imperator.

2013, Oct. 25 Litho. Perf. 13¼
Sheets of 4, #a-d

3042-3051	A604	Set of 10	110.00	110.00

Souvenir Sheets

3052-3061	A604	Set of 10	85.00	85.00

Mohandas K. Gandhi (1869-1948), Indian Independence Leader — A605

No. 3062 — Gandhi and: a, Lotus flower. b, Salt marchers, Indian flag. c, Women, Indian flag. d, Peacock.
70r, Gandhi, Jawaharlal Nehru, tiger, vert.

Litho. With Three-Dimensional Plastic Affixed

2013, Nov. 18 Perf. 13¼

3062	A605	22r Sheet of 4, #a-d	11.50	11.50

Souvenir Sheet

3063	A605	70r multi	9.25	9.25

No. 3063 contains one 51x66mm stamp.

Famous People A606

No. 3064, 20r — Marilyn Monroe (1926-62), actress: a, With skirt rising at right. b, With hand touching hair at right. c, In chair at right. d, Holding open umbrella at right.
No. 3065, 20r — Pierre de Coubertin (1863-1937), founder of modern Olympics, and: a, Swimmer. b, Runner. c, Cyclist. d, Fencers.
No. 3066, 20r — Brazilian 2013 Confederations Cup soccer players: a, Marcelo. b, Fred. c, Hulk. d, David Luiz.
No. 3067, 20r — Bobby Fischer (1943-2008), chess player, and: a, King and rook. b, Pawn and knight. c, King and pawn. d, Queen.
No. 3068, 20r — Birth of Prince George of Cambridge: a, Duchess of Cambridge holding Prince George at left, Duke and Duchess of Cambridge with Prince George at right. b, Duke and Duchess of Cambridge with Prince George at left, Prince Charles and Princess Diana with Prince William at right. c, Duke and Duchess of Cambridge with Prince George at left, Prince George at right. d, Duke of Cambridge holding Prince George at left, Duke and Duchess of Cambridge with Prince George at right.
No. 3069, 22r — Valentina Tereshkova, first woman in space: a, With Yuri Gagarin (1934-68), cosmonaut. b, And Vostok 6. c, With medical technician, at right. d, Holding pen, at right.
No. 3070, 22r — 95th birthday of Nelson Mandela (1918-2013), President of South Africa: a, Mandela and Dalai Lama. b, Mandela and Pope John Paul II (1920-2005). c, Mandela and Kofi Annan. d, Mandela and Princess Diana (1961-97).
No. 3071, 22r — Elvis Presley (1935-77): a, Holding microphone at right. b, Without hat at left, playing guitar at right. c, Wearing hat at left, playing guitar at right. d, Holding guitar at right.
No. 3072, 22r — Paintings by Pablo Picasso (1881-1973): a, Bottle of Vieux Marc, Glass, Guitar and Newspaper, 1913. b, Study for a Head Crying, 1937, Jacqueline with Crossed Hands, 1954. c, A Boy with a Pipe, 1905, Two Acrobats with a Dog, 1905. d, Houses on the Hill Horta de Ebro, 1909.
No. 3073, 60r, Monroe, vert. No. 3074, 60r, Coubertin and Olympic torch, vert. No. 3075, 60r, Neymar, vert. No. 3076, 60r, Fischer examining chess board, vert. No. 3077, 60r, Duke and Duchess of Cambridge with Prince George, vert. No. 3078, 70r, Tereshkova and Vostok 6 rocket, vert. No. 3079, 70r, Mandela, vert. No. 3080, 70r, Presley, vert. No. 3081, 70r, Head of a Woman, by Picasso, vert.

2013, Nov. 18 Litho. Perf. 13¼
Sheets of 4, #a-d

3064-3072	A606	Set of 9	100.00	100.00

Souvenir Sheets

3073-3081	A606	Set of 9	75.00	75.00

Brasiliana 2013 Intl. Philatelic Exhibition (Nos. 3066, 3075). Nos. 3073-3081 each contain one 51x66 mm stamp.

MALDIVE ISLANDS

Transportation and Space — A607

No. 3082, 20r — Yuri Gagarin (1934-68), cosmonaut, and: a, Vostok 1 capsule in space. b, Vostok 1 capsule and booster in space. c, Vostok 1 rocket and emblem. d, Vostok 1 capsule on Earth.
No. 3083, 20r — Steam trains: a, Jenny Lind. b, Thompson L1 Class. c, GWR Iron Duke Class. d, Eureka.
No. 3084, 20r — Rescue boats: a, Koos van Messel KNRM, Netherlands. b, RS 103 Dagfinn Paust, Norway. c, AMF Pauanui, New Zealand. d, Autonomous Rescue and Recovery Craft in North Sea.
No. 3085, 20r — History of the automobile: a, 1955 Abarth A Coupe Boano. b, 1950 Volkswagen Beetle. c, 1927 Mercedes-Benz 600 Cabriolet. d, 1953 Fiat BV Demon Rouge.
No. 3086, 20r — Formula 1 race cars: a, McLaren-Mercedes MP4-24. b, Force India VJM06. c, Williams FW35. d, Ferrari F60.
No. 3087, 20r — Concorde: a, Air France Concorde. b, Braniff Concorde. c, Aerospatiale BAC Concorde. d, Singapore Airlines Concorde.
No. 3088, 22r — Fire engines: a, 1970 Seagraves pumper. b, 1000 LTI ALF 75 Quint. c, 1950 Dennis F7. d, 2001 E-One 75-foot Quint.
No. 3089, 22r — Seaplanes: a, Short S-25 Sandringham 4. b, De Havilland Canada DHC-2 Beaver. c, Republic RC-3 Seabee. d, Grumman HU-16B Albatross.
No. 3090, 22r — High-speed trains: a, Frecciarossa 1000. b, Javelin. c, Acela Express. d, HSR-350x.
No. 3091, 22r — Space tourism: a, SpaceShipOne. b, EADS Astrium. c, Armadillo Aerospace. d, XCOR Aerospace.
No. 3092, 60r, Gagarin and Vostok 1, diff. No. 3093, 60r, Best Friend of Charleston. No. 3094, 60r, SK Hermann Marwede, Germany. No. 3095, 60r, 1886 Benz Patent Motorwagen. No. 3096, 60r, Renault R28 race car. No. 3097, 70r, British Airways Concorde. No. 3098, 70r, 1987 Sutphen 100-foot Platform Quint fire engine. No. 3099, 70r, Rans S-7 Courier. No. 3100, 70r, Eurostar. No. 3101, 70r, SpaceX Dragon.

2013, Dec. 2   Litho.   Perf. 13¼
Sheets of 4, #a-d
3082-3091 A607 Set of 10   110.00 110.00
Souvenir Sheets
3092-3101 A607 Set of 10   85.00   85.00

Famous People A608

No. 3102, 20r — Race car and Ayrton Senna (1960-94), driver: a, With hand on chin, wearing red racing suit with shoulder patch. b, Hands not visible, wearing red racing suit, no shoulder patch visible. c, Hands not visible, wearing racing suit, no shoulder patch visible. d, With hand on chin, wearing white shirt.
No. 3103, 20r — Giacomo Puccini (1858-1924), composer, and scene from opera: a, Madame Butterfly. b, Tosca. c, Turandot. d, Turandot (Sarasota Opera production).
No. 3104, 20r — Nelson Mandela (1918-2013), President of South Africa: a, Behind microphone. b, With Dalai Lama. c, With Fidel Castro. d, Behind lectern.
No. 3105, 20r — Charles Lindbergh (1902-74), aviator: a, Lindbergh and airplane facing left. b, Nose of airplane, airplane over ocean. c, Airplane, map of Lindbergh's transatlantic flight. d, Lindbergh and nose of The Spirit of St. Louis.
No. 3106, 20r — Paintings by Salvador Dalí (1904-89): a, Swans Reflecting Elephants, 1937. b, The Persistence of Memory, 1931. c, The Enigma of My Desire, 1929. d, Weaning of Furniture Nutrition, 1934.
No. 3107, 20r — Bette Davis (1908-89), actress: a, On telephone at right. b, Wearing green dress at right. c, Wearing dress with shoulder straps at right. d, Wearing white dress and flower garland in hair at right.
No. 3108, 22r — Frida Kahlo (1907-54), painter, and: a, Roots, 1943. b, The Wounded Deer, 1946. c, The Dream (The Bed), 1940. d, My Dress Hangs There, 1933.
No. 3109, 22r — Marie Curie (1867-1934), chemist: a, Alone in laboratory at left. b, Radiation warning sign and atom at left. c, Molecular diagrams at left. d, With husband, Pierre, in laboratory at left.
No. 3110, 22r — Christoph Willibald Gluck (1714-87), composer, and: a, Echo and Narcissus; painting by John William Waterhouse. b, Harp. c, Violin. d, The Death of Alcestis, painting by Pierre Peyron.
No. 3111, 22r — Charlie Chaplin (1889-1977), actor, and: a, Paulette Goddard, in scene from Modern Times, 1936. b, Billy Armstrong, in scene from His New Job, 1915. c, Baby, in scene from The Great Dictator, 1940. d, Martha Raye, in scene from Monsieur Verdoux, 1947.
No. 3112, 60r, Senna and race car, diff. No. 3113, 60r, Puccini and poster for Madame Butterfly. No. 3114, 60r, Mandela, diff. No. 3115, 60r, Lindbergh and airplane, diff. No. 3116, 60r, Sleep, painting by Dalí, 1937. No. 3117, 70r, Davis, diff. No. 3118, 70r, The Love Embrace of the Universe, the Earth (Mexico), Myself, Diego and Señor Xolotl, painting by Kahlo, 1949. No. 3119, 70r, Curie, diff. No. 3120, 70r, Gluck and title page of libretto of Iphigénie en Tauride. No. 3121, 70r, Chaplin and Virginia Cherrill, in scene from City Lights, 1931.

2014, Feb. 20   Litho.   Perf. 13¼
Sheets of 4, #a-d
3102-3111 A608 Set of 10   110.00 110.00
Souvenir Sheets
3112-3121 A608 Set of 10   85.00   85.00

Impressionist Paintings — A609

No. 3122, 20r — Paintings by Mary Cassatt: a, At the Theater. b, Portrait of Alexander J. Cassatt and His Son Robert Kelso Cassatt. c, Mother and Child. d, The Banjo Lesson.
No. 3123, 20r — Paintings by Edgar Degas: a, The Cafe Concert (The Song of the Dog). b, The Ballet Class. c, The Belleli Family. d, Edmondo and Therese Morbilli.
No. 3124, 20r — Paintings by Edouard Manet: a, Railway. b, Argenteuil. c, Tarring the Boat. d, The Rest, Portrait of Berthe Morisot.
No. 3125, 20r — Paintings by Berthe Morisot: a, Eugene Manet with His Daughter at Bougival. b, Paule Gobillard Painting. c, Dahlias. d, The Mother and Sister of the Artist.
No. 3126, 20r — Paintings by Camille Pissarro: a, L'Hermitage à Pontoise. b, Apple Picking. c, The Effect of Snow at Montfoucault. d, Coteau de l'Hermitage, Pontoise.
No. 3127, 22r — Paintings by Paul Cezanne: a, The Card Players. b, Maison Maria with a View of Chateau Noir. c, Still Life, Drapery, Pitcher and Fruit Bowl. d, Lady in Blue.
No. 3128, 22r — Paintings by Armand Guillaumin: a, Madame Guillaumin Reading. b, Cottages in a Landscape. c, Windmills in Holland. d, Vase of Chrysanthemums
No. 3129, 22r — Paintings by Claude Monet: a, The Beach at Etretat. b, Springtime. c, Camille Monet and a Child in the Artist's Garden at Argenteuil. d, Entrance to the Port at Trouville.
No. 3130, 22r — Paintings by Pierre-Auguste Renoir: a, The Clearing. b, Dance in the Country. c, The Seine at Asnieres (The Skiff). d, Still Life with a Pomegranate.
No. 3131, 22r — Paintings by American Impressionists: a, Portrait of Miss Dora Wheeler, by William Merritt Chase. b, Morning Light, by Childe Hassam. c, The House in Giverny, by Frederick Carl Frieseke. d, Fireside Dreams, by Julian Alden Weir.
No. 3132, 60r, Children Playing on the Beach, by Cassatt. No. 3133, 60r, Orchestra of the Opera, by Degas. No. 3134, 60r, The Grand Canal of Venice (Blue Venice), by Manet. No. 3135, 60r, Peasant Girl Among Tulips, by Morisot. No. 3136, 60r, White Frost (Woman Breaking Wood), by Pissarro. No. 3137, 70r, The Seine at Bercy, by Cézanne. No. 3138, 70r, Moulin Boucharon, Crozant, by Guillaumin. No. 3139, 70r, The boardwalk on the Beach at Trouville, by Monet. No. 3140, 70r, Two Sisters (On the Terrace), by Renoir. No. 3141, 70r, Gloucester Harbor Sun, by Willard Metcalf.

2014, Mar. 5   Litho.   Perf. 13¼
Sheets of 4, #a-d
3122-3131 A609 Set of 10   110.00 110.00
Souvenir Sheets
3132-3141 A609 Set of 10   85.00   85.00

Fauna of the Indian Ocean Area A610

No. 3142, 20r — Sharks: a, Alopias vulpinus. b, Galeocerdo cuvier. c, Carcharhinus limbatus. d, Squalus acanthias.
No. 3143, 20r — Octopi: a, Octopus cyanea. b, Octopus vulgaris. c, Octopus ornatus. d, Octopus kaurna.
No. 3144, 20r — Crustaceans: a, Carpilius convexus. b, Lysmata amboinensis. c, Panulirus ornatus. d, Hoplophrys oatesi.
No. 3145, 20r — Frogs: a, Mantidactylus madecassus. b, Sooglossus thomasseti. c, Litoria maini. d, Dyscophus antongilii.
No. 3146, 20r — Reptiles: a, Calotes versicolor. b, Varanus komodoensis. c, Lycodon aulicus. d, Dermochelys coriacea.
No. 3147, 22r — Owls: a, Phodilus badius. b, Otrix leptogrammica. c, Aegolius funereus. d, Bubo zeylonensis.
No. 3148, 22r — Birds of prey: a, Asio flammeus. b, Circus macrourus. c, Pernis ptilorhynchus. d, Falco amurensis.
No. 3149, 22r — Butterflies: a, Euploea mulciber. b, Papilio clytia. c, Danaus genutia. d, Graphium agamemnon.
No. 3150, 22r — Deep water creatures: a, Serpula. b, Anoplogaster cornuta. c, Argyropelecus hemigymnus. d, Bathynomus giganteus.
No. 3151, 22r — Jellyfish: a, Atolla wyvillei. b, Chironex fleckeri. c, Carybdea sivickisi. d, Mastigias papua.
No. 3152, 60r, Isurus oxyrinchus. No. 3153, 60r, Octopus kaurma, diff. No. 3154, 60r, Periclimenes imperator. No. 3155, 60r, Mantella expectata. No. 3156, 60r, Caretta caretta. No. 3157, 70r, Tyto alba. No. 3158, 70r, Falco naumanni. No. 3159, 70r, Chrysiridia rhipheus. No. 3160, 70r, Chaunacidae. No. 3161, 70r, Chrysaora quinquecirrha.

2014, Apr. 1   Litho.   Perf. 13¼
Sheets of 4, #a-d
3142-3151 A610 Set of 10   110.00 110.00
Souvenir Sheets
3152-3161 A610 Set of 10   85.00   85.00

Painting by He Xiangning (1878-1972) — A611

2014, May 7   Litho.   Perf. 13¼
3162 A611 22r multi   3.00   3.00
No. 3162 was printed in sheets of 4.

Miniature Sheet
E. Marinella Necktie Company, Naples, Cent. — A612

No. 3163: a, Storefront, vert. b, 100th anniv. emblem, vert. c, Painting of Naples. d, 100th anniv. emblem, signature of E. Marinella, denomination in olive brown. e, 100th anniv. emblem, signature of E. Marinella, denomination in dull yellow.

Perf. 13¼x13 (vert. stamps), 13x13¼
2014, May 7   Litho.
3163 A612 20r Sheet of 5, #a-e   13.00 13.00

A613

No. 3164, 20r — Marriage of Joe DiMaggio and Marilyn Monroe, 60th anniv.: a, DiMaggio swinging bat at left, Monroe at right. b, Couple at left, DiMaggio at right. c, Monroe at left, DiMaggio at right. d, DiMaggio at left, Monroe holding bat at right.
No. 3165, 20r — Red List of endangered animals, 50th anniv.: a, Spizaetus bartelsi. b, Leontopithecus rosalia. c, Hippocampus capensis. d, Capra falconeri.
No. 3166, 20r — Channel Tunnel, 20th anniv.: a, Eurostar Class 373. b, British Rail Class 92. c, ICE 3 M. d, Eurotunnel Class 9.
No. 3167, 20r — Paintings by Wassily Kandinsky (1866-1944): a, Color Study: Squares with Concentric Circles. b, Black Frame. c, The Last Judgment. d, Improvisation 19.
No. 3168, 20r — Start of World War I, cent.: a, Emperor Wilhelm II of Germany (1859-1941). Mark I tank. b, Two Fokker E.III airplanes. c, Soldier wearing gas mask, map. d, Marshal Joseph Joffre (1852-1931), trench-digging machine.
No. 3169, 22r — Battle of the Bulge, 70th anniv.: a, American flag, soldiers in trench. b, Airplane above German tanks. c, Soldier watching comrades march through snow. d, Soldiers and tanks.
No. 3170, 22r — Paintings by Henri Matisse (1869-1954): a, Still Life with Apples on a Pink Tablecloth. b, Dishes and Fruit. c, Small Odalisque in Purple Robe. d, Still Life with Sleeper.
No. 3171, 22r — Renault automobiles: a, 1931 Renault Primaquatre KZ 6. b, 2013 Renault Twizy RS F1 Concept. c, 2014 Renault KWID Concept. d, 1961 Renault Alpine A110.
No. 3172, 22r — Elvis Presley (1935-77), 60th Anniv. of First Single: a, Holding guitar. b, Blue Moon of Kentucky cover at right. c, 45rpm record at right. d, Elvis 75: Good Rockin' Tonight image at right.
No. 3173, 60r, Monroe and DiMaggio, diff. No. 3174, 60r, Abronia graminea. No. 3175, 60r, Two Eurostar Class 373 trains. No. 3176,

MALDIVE ISLANDS

60r, Composition IV, by Kandinsky. No. 3177, 60r, Soldier wearing goggles and face mask, Joseph Gallieni (1849-1916), military governor of Paris. No. 3178, 70r, Gen. Dwight D. Eisenhower (1890-1969), map of battle. No. 3179, 70r, Lemons and Saxifrages, by Matisse. No. 3180, 70r, 1922 Renault NN Torpedo. No. 3181, 70r, Presley and his first 45rpm record.

2014, May 7 Litho. Perf. 13¼
Sheets of 4, #a-d

| 3164-3172 | A613 | Set of 9 | 97.50 | 97.50 |

Souvenir Sheets

| 3173-3181 | A613 | Set of 9 | 75.00 | 75.00 |

Souvenir Sheets

A614

2014 World Cup Soccer Championships, Brazil — A615

No. 3182 — Various soccer players and: a, Emblem at UL. b, Mascot at UR. c, "2014 FIFA World Cup Brazil" at LL.
No. 3183 — Various soccer players and: a, Soccer field and Maldive Islands flag at UL. b, Emblem of Soccer Association of Maldives at UR. c, Soccer field and whistle at LL.

2014, July 3 Litho. Perf. 12¾x13¼

| 3182 | A614 | 15r Sheet of 3, #a-c, + 9 labels | 6.00 | 6.00 |
| 3183 | A615 | 15r Sheet of 3, #a-c, + 9 labels | 6.00 | 6.00 |

Chess and Sports A616

No. 3184, 20r — Chess players: a, Garry Kasparov. b, Viswanathan Anand. c, Vladimir Kramnik. d, Levon Aronian.
No. 3185, 20r — Cricket players: a, Ian Botham. b, Sachin Tendulkar. c, Sir Vivian Richards. d, Kapil Dev.
No. 3186, 20r — Judokas: a, Ilias Iliadis. b, Udo Quellmalz. c, Ole Bischof. d, Kosei Inoue.
No. 3187, 20r — 2014 Winter Olympics, Sochi, Russia: a, Figure skating. b, Ski jumping. c, Luge. d, Ice hockey.
No. 3188, 20r — Rally racing: a, Citroen DS3 WRC. b, Mitsubishi Lancer Evolution VII. c, Citroen C4 WRC. d, Subaru Impreza.
No. 3189, 22r — Golfers: a, Greg Norman. b, Jack Nicklaus. c, Vijay Singh. d, Phil Mickelson.
No. 3190, 22r — Table tennis players: a, Jan-Ove Waldner. b, Liu Guoliang. c, Zhang Jike. d, Deng Yaping.
No. 3191, 22r — Horse racing: a, Three horses running right. b, Two steeplechase horses. c, Four horses running left. d, Three steeplechase horses.
No. 3192, 22r — First heavyweight championship of Muhammad Ali, 50th anniv.: a, Full color image of Ali at left, black-and-white image of Ali and opponent at UR, denomination at UL. b, Ali and opponent, denomination at UR. c, Ali and opponent, denomination at UL. d, Full color image of Ali at right, dimmed color image of Ali and opponent at left, denomination at UR.

No. 3193, 60r, Magnus Carlsen. No. 3194, 60r, Sir Donald Bradman (1908-2001). No. 3195, 60r, Teddy Riner. No. 3196, 60r, Cross-country skiing. No. 3197, 60r, Ford Focus RS. No. 3198, 70r, Tiger Woods. No. 3199, 70r, Li Xianxia. No. 3200, 70r, Race horses and starting gate. No. 3201, 70r, Ali, referee, knocked-out opponent.

2014, July 3 Litho. Perf. 13¼
Sheets of 4, #a-d

| 3184-3192 | A616 | Set of 9 | 100.00 | 100.00 |

Souvenir Sheets

| 3193-3201 | A616 | Set of 9 | 75.00 | 75.00 |

Paintings by Flemish Artists A617

No. 3202, 20r — Paintings by Peter Paul Rubens (1577-1640): a, Samson and Delilah. b, Drunken Silenus. c, The Entombment. d, Satyr and Girl.
No. 3203, 20r — Paintings by Quentin Matsys (1466-1530): a, Madonna and Child with the Lamb. b, Portrait of a Woman. c, Portrait of Erasmus of Rotterdam. d, Ill-matched Lovers.
No. 3204, 20r — Paintings by Dieric Bouts (1410-75): a, Mater Dolorosa. b, Lamentation. c, The Meeting of Abraham and Melchizedek. d, The Execution of the Innocent Man.
No. 3205, 20r — Paintings by Pieter Brueghel, the Elder (1525-69) and the Younger (1564-1638): a, Parable of the Blind, by the Elder. b, The Adoration of the Magi, by the Younger. c, The Spring, by the Younger. d, The Fight Between Carnival and Lent, by the Elder.
No. 3206, 22r — Paintings by Rogier van der Weyden (1400-64): a, Group of Men. b, Portrait of a Lady. c, Saints Margaret and Apollonia. d, The Magdalene Reading.
No. 3207, 22r — Paintings by Jan van Eyck (1385-1441): a, St. Jerome. b, The Soldiers of Christ. c, The Ince Hall Madonna. d, Stigmatization of St. Francis.
No. 3208, 22r — Paintings by Sir Anthony van Dyck (1599-1641): a, Crowning with Thorns. b, Blessed Joseph Hermann. c, Rubens Mourning His Wife. d, Portrait of the Three Eldest Children of Charles I.
No. 3209, 22r — Paintings by Frans Hals, the Elder (1582-1666): a, Fisher Boy. b, Shrovetide Revelers. c, Officers and Sergeants of the St. Hadrian Civic Guard. d, Fisher Girl.
No. 3210, 22r — Paintings by Hans Memling (1430-94): a, Mystic Marriage of St. Catherine. b, Virgin and Child Enthroned with Two Angels. c, Annunciation. d, The Nativity (left wing of triptych of the Adoration of the Magi).
No. 3211, 60r, Night Scene, by Rubens. No. 3212, 60r, The Moneylender and His Wife, by Matsys. No. 3213, 60r, Adoration of the Magi (middle panel of The Pearl of Brabant triptych), by Bouts. No. 3214, 60r, Hunters in the Snow, by Brueghel the Elder. No. 3215, 70r, Virgin and Child by van der Weyden. No. 3216, 70r, The Arnolfini Wedding, by van Eyck. No. 3217, 70r, Saint Rosalie Interceding for the Plague-stricken of Palermo, by van Dyck. No. 3218, 70r, Young Man with a Skull, by Hals. No. 3219, 70r, Christ Surrounded by Musician Angels, by Memling.

2014, July 3 Litho. Perf. 13¼
Sheets of 4, #a-d

| 3202-3210 | A617 | Set of 9 | 100.00 | 100.00 |

Souvenir Sheets

| 3211-3219 | A617 | Set of 9 | 77.50 | 77.50 |

A618

No. 3220, 20r — Cassini Mission to Saturn, 10th anniv.: a, Cassini-Huygens probe and Saturn, antenna at left. b, Solar system. c, Cassini-Huygens probe above Saturn. d, Cassini-Huygens probe, antenna at right.
No. 3221, 20r — Galileo Galilei (1564-1642), astronomer, with: a, Telescope, sun and planets. b, Cardinals, telescope, planets. c, Assistants, balance, satellite, planets. d, Hubble Space Telescope.
No. 3222, 20r — Awarding of Nobel Peace Prize to Dr. Martin Luther King, Jr., 50th anniv.: a, King and microphones. b, King and Pres. John F. Kennedy. c, King holding Nobel medal. d, King with hands together.
No. 3223, 20r — Hermitage Museum, St. Petersburg, Russia, 250th anniv.: a, Card Game, by Theodor Rombouts. b, Cleopatra's Feast, by Jacob Jordaens. c, Lesson of Singing, by Jan Josef Horemans II. d, Continence of Scipio, by Pompeo Batoni.
No. 3224, 20r — German players at 2014 World Cup Soccer Championships, Brazil: a, Mario Götze. b, Manuel Neuer. c, Thomas Müller. d, Miroslav Klose.
No. 3225, 22r — Circumnavigation of Graf Zeppelin, 85th anniv.: a, U.S. Capitol, LZ-127 Graf Zeppelin. b, Ferdinand von Zeppelin, New York City. c, Hugo Eckener and LZ-127 Graf Zeppelin. d, LZ-127 Graf Zeppelin and mountain.
No. 3226, 22r — King Felipe VI of Spain and: a, Crowd and flagbearer. b, Picture of King as child. c, Queen Letizia and crowd at palace. d, Parents, King Juan Carlos and Queen Sofia.
No. 3227, 22r — Deng Xiaoping (1904-97), Paramount leader of People's Republic of China, and: a, Mao Zedong (1893-1976), chairman of Chinese Communist Party. b, Baling River Bridge, dove, flag of People's Republic of China. c, CRH380A, statue of Mao Zedong, flag of People's Republic of China. d, Chinese buildings.
No. 3228, 22r — Third Intl. Conference on Small Island Developing States: a, Woman wearing headdress. b, Red Cross worker feeding infant. c, Two children. d, Samoan prime minister Tuilaepa Lupesoliai Sailele Malielegaoi, solar panels, wind generators.
No. 3229, 22r — 17th Asian Games, Incheon, South Korea: a, Boxing, Northeast Asia Trade Tower, Incheon. b, Weight lifting, Incheon buildings. c, Cycling, Incheon Munhak Stadium. d, Sailboarding, Incheon Bridge.
No. 3230, 60r, Cassini-Huygens probe, Saturn, diff. No. 3231, 60r, Galileo looking through telescope, space probe. No. 3232, 60r, King, Nobel medal, diff. No. 3233, 60r, Jephthah's Daughter, by Pieter van Lint. No. 3234, 60r, Klose, diff. No. 3235, 70r, LZ-127 Graf Zeppelin. No. 3236, 70r, King Felipe VI of Spain, flag of Spain, Royal Palace, Madrid. No. 3237, 70r, Deng Xiaoping, rocket, Great Wall of China. No. 3238, 70r, Chinese diplomat Wu Hongbo, beach scene, smokestacks, polar bear. No. 3239, 70r, Stylized archer, gymnast, tennis player.

Litho., Litho. With Foil Application (#3224, 3234)
2014, Oct. 7 Perf. 13¼
Sheets of 4, #a-d

| 3220-3229 | A618 | Set of 10 | 110.00 | 110.00 |

Souvenir Sheets

| 3230-3239 | A618 | Set of 10 | 85.00 | 85.00 |

A619

No. 3240, 20r — Cats: a, Siberian cat. b, Head of Abyssinian cat. c, Abyssinian cat. d, Sphynx.
No. 3241, 20r — Dolphins: a, Stenella frontalis. b, Delphinus delphis. c, Cephalorhynchus hectori. d, Lagenorhynchus obliquidens.
No. 3242, 20r — Butterflies: a, Lycaena virgaureae. b, Polygonia interrogationis. c, Heliconius cydno. d, Morpho peleides.
No. 3243, 20r — Turtles: a, Chelonoidis nigra. b, Chelonia mydas, Latin name at LR. c, Podocnemis expansa. d, Chelonia mydas, Latin name at UR.
No. 3244, 20r — Mushrooms: a, Cantharellus cibarius. b, Kuehneromyces mutabilis. c, Macrolepiota procera. d, Boletus badius.
No. 3245, 20r — Dogs: a, Nova Scotia duck tolling retriever. b, Belgian shepherd jumping. c, Belgian shepherd running. d, Boxer.
No. 3246, 22r — Dinosaurs: a, Tylosaurus, Pteranodon. b, Cryolophosaurus. c, Tyrannosaurus rex. d, Kentrosaurus.

No. 3247, 22r — Orchids: a, Brassolaeliocattleya "Taiwan Queen." b, Paphiopedilum cultivar. c, Encyclia cultivar. d, Phalaenopsis cultivar.
No. 3248, 22r — Minerals: a, Turquoise. b, Desert rose. c, Marcasite. d, Elbaite.
No. 3249, 22r — Lighthouses: a, Peggy's Cove Lighthouse, Nova Scotia, Canada. b, Ploumanac'h Lighthouse, France. c, Hornby Lighthouse, Australia. d, Brant Point Lighthouse, Massachusetts.
No. 3250, 60r, British shorthair cat. No. 3251, 60r, Lagenorhynchus obliquidens, diff. No. 3252, 60r, Aporia crataegi. No. 3253, 60r, Chelonia mydas, diff. No. 3254, 60r, Boletus edulis. No. 3255, 70r, Russian wolfhounds. No. 3256, 70r, Nanotyrannus. No. 3257, 70r, Paphiopedilum callosum. No. 3258, 70r, Copper sulphate. No. 3259, 70r, Portland Head Lighthouse, Maine.

2014, Oct. 14 Litho. Perf. 13¼
Sheets of 4, #a-d

| 3240-3249 | A619 | Set of 10 | 110.00 | 110.00 |

Souvenir Sheets

| 3250-3259 | A619 | Set of 10 | 85.00 | 85.00 |

Nos. 3247 and 3257 are impregnated with an orchid scent.

Birds A620

No. 3260, 20r — Pelecanus onocrotalus (pelican): a, With green fish entering mouth. b, With fish in mouth, wings spread. c, Two birds. d, With orange fish entering mouth.
No. 3261, 20r — Songbirds: a, Anthus trivialis. b, Acridotheres tristis, Cethosia biblis butterfly. c, Corvus splendens, Parantica aglea. d, Motacilla cinerea.
No. 3262, 20r — Pigeons and fruit: a, Columba livia, Mangifera indica. b, Columba livia, Cocos nucifera. c, Streptopelia orientalis, Passiflora edulis. d, Streptopelia turtur, Musa acuminata.
No. 3263, 20r — Water birds and corals: a, Fulica atra, Dendrophyllia sp. b, Gallinula chloropus, Plerogyra sinuosa. c, Amaurornis phoenicurus, Acropora robusta. d, Gallicrex cinerea, Trachyphyllia geoffroyi.
No. 3264, 20r — Wading birds and insects: a, Ardea cinerea, Delias eucharis. b, Ardeola grayii, Enallagma maldivensis. c, Phalacrocorax fuscicollis, Anoplolepis gracilipes. d, Platalea leucorodia, Glyphodes bivitralis.
No. 3265, 22r — Birds of prey: a, Falco subbuteo. b, Falco amurensis. c, Falco tinnunculus. d, Falco naumanni.
No. 3266, 22r — Seabirds and shells: a, Calonectris leucomelas, Melo aethiopica. b, Oceanites oceanicus, Acrosterigma dupuchensis. c, Puffinus lherminieri, Casmaria ponderosa ponderosa. d, Puffinus pacificus, Harpa major.
No. 3267, 22r — Bee-eaters and orchids: a, Merops apiaster, Cattleya labiata. b, Merops apiaster, Vanda tricolor. c, Merops apiaster, Cymbidium dayanum. d, Merops apiaster, Vanda denisoniana.
No. 3268, 22r — Owls and mushrooms: a, Asio flammeus, Lactarius indigo. b, Asio flammeus, Ganoderma lucidum. c, Asio flammeus, Coprinopsis atramentaria. d, Asio flammeus, Leucocoprinus birnbaumii.
No. 3269, 22r — Terns and lighthouses: a, Sterna dougallii, Pemaquid Lighthouse, Maine. b, Sterna hirundo, Portland Head Lighthouse, Maine. c, Hydroprogne, caspia, Cape Neddick Lighthouse, Maine. d, Onychoprion fuscata, Cloch Lighthouse, Scotland.
No. 3270, 60r, Pelecanus onocrotalus, diff. No. 3271, 60r, Passer domesticus. No. 3272, 60r, Streptopelia orientalis, Carica papaya. No. 3273, 60r, Gallinula chloropus, Acropora sp. No. 3274, 60r, Bulbulcus ibis, Darna furva. No. 3275, 70r, Circus pygargus. No. 3276, 70r, Bulweria bulwerii, Tridacna gigas. No. 3277, 70r, Merops apiaster, Cymbidium hybrid. No. 3278, 70r, Asio flammeus, Psilocybe aztecorum. No. 3279, 70r, Hydroprogne caspia, Heceta Head Lighthouse, Oregon.

2014, Dec. 15 Litho. Perf. 13¼
Sheets of 4, #a-d

| 3260-3269 | A620 | Set of 10 | 110.00 | 110.00 |

Souvenir Sheets

| 3270-3279 | A620 | Set of 10 | 85.00 | 85.00 |

MALDIVE ISLANDS

History of Transportation — A621

No. 3280, 20r — Sled dogs: a, Two dogs, sled and driver. b, Nine dogs, sled and driver. c, Eight dogs, sled and driver. d, Four dogs.
No. 3281, 20r — Pioneers of aviation: a, 1907 Cornu helicopter. b, 1906 Santos-Dumont 14-bis. c, 1903 Wright Flyer. d, 1892-97 Adler Avion III.
No. 3282, 20r — Motorcycles: a, 1894 Hildebrand & Wolfmüller, Germany. b, 1920, Lea Francis 500cc, United Kingdom. c, 1950 Indian Chief Blackhawk, United States. d, 2014 Johammer 31 electric, Austria.
No. 3283, 20r — Special transporation: a, Volvo V70 police cars. b, Chevrolet Tahoe fire trucks. c, Canadian Coast Guard patrol boat Private Robertson V.C. d, Canadair CL-215 firefighting plane.
No. 3284, 20r — Electric transportation: a, BMW i8. b, Tesla Model S. c, R1 tram. d, Honda Orees.
No. 3285, 22r — Horse-drawn transportation: a, Darouche. b, Culky. c, Ctagecoach. d, Hearse.
No. 3286, 22r — Ships: a, Viking drekkar, 9th cent. b, Fleet of Christopher Columbus, 1492. c, RMS Titanic, 1912. d, HMS Helsingborg, 2003.
No. 3287, 22r — Submarines: a, Type VIIC U-boat. b, Yury Dolgorukiy. c, HMAS Sheean. d, Type XXVIIB U-boat.
No. 3288, 22r — Trains and their inventors: a, Puffing Devil, Richard Trevithick (1771-1833). b, Planet type locomotive, Robert Stephenson (1803-59). c, The Rocket, George Stephenson (1781-1848). d, Seguin locomotive, Marc Seguin (1786-1875).
No. 3289, 22r — Spaceships: a, Virgin Galactic's SpaceShip Two. b, Space Shuttle Enterprise. c, Orion spacecraft. d, Space Shuttle Columbia.
No. 3290, 60r, Sled dog team, sled and driver. No. 3291, 60r, Santos-Dumont No. 9 airship, 1903. No. 3292, 60r, 1912 Zenith Gradua 770 motorcycle, United Kingdom. No. 3293, 60r, Dodge Magnum police car. No. 3294, 60r, Hyundai Aebulle Concept motorcycle. No. 3295, 70r, Barouche, diff. No. 3296, 70r, MS Majesty of the Seas, 1992. No. 3297, 70r, Oscar II Class submarine. No. 3298, 70r, The Rocket, George Stephenson, diff. No. 3299, 70r, Rosetta spacecraft.

2015, Jan. 13   Litho.   Perf. 13¼
Sheets of 4, #a-d

| 3280-3289 | A621 | Set of 10 | 110.00 | 110.00 |

Souvenir Sheets

| 3290-3299 | A621 | Set of 10 | 85.00 | 85.00 |

No. 3300, 20r — Pyotr Ilyich Tchaikovsky (1840-93), composer: a, Tchaikovsky, Volha Haiko in *Swan Lake*. b, Miyako Yoshida and Ed Watson in *Ondine*. c, Eleonora Abbagnato and Mathias Heymann in *Sleeping Beauty*. d, Tchaikovsky, Artem Ovcharenko in *The Nutcracker*.
No. 3301, 20r — Scenes from D-Day, 70th anniv., and: a, Gen. Dwight D. Eisenhower (1890-1969). b, Gen. Bernard Montgomery (1887-1976). c, Gen. Omar Bradley (1892-1981). d, Admiral Bertram Ramsay (1883-1945).
No. 3302, 20r — 2014 Nobel laureates: a, Isamu Akasaki, Physics. b, Eric Betzig, Chemistry. c, Malala Yousafzai, Peace. d, Edvard Moser, Physiology or Medicine.
No. 3303, 20r — New Year 2015 (Year of the Goat): a, Two white goats. b, Two brown goats. c, One white goat, head of black and white goat. d, Two white goats with collar.
No. 3304, 22r — Albert Einstein (1879-1955), physicist: a, Einstein and mushroom cloud. b, Gravity Probe B and black hole. c, Gravity Probe B. d, Einstein and warped space-time.
No. 3305, 22r — Sophia Loren, actress: a, Wearing red blouse at left. b, Adjusting man's flower on lapel at left. c, With towel on head at left. d, With arms crossed at left.
No. 3306, 22r — John Lennon (1940-80), rock musician, with: a, Wife, Yoko Ono. b, Yellow Submarine. c, Other members of the Beatles, on beach. d, Other members of the Beatles, in costumes.
No. 3307, 22r — Tiger Woods, golfer: a, Wearing white cap. b, Wearing black sweater and red shirt at left. c, Wearing gray shirt. d, Wearing red shirt and black cap at left.
No. 3308, 22r — Scenes from Liberation of Paris, 70th anniv., and: a, Gen. Charles de Gaulle (1890-1970). b, Jacques Chaban-Delmas (1915-2000), politician. c, Georges Bidault (1899-1983), politician. d, Major Gen. Raymond O. Barton (1889-1963).
No. 3309, 22r — Mars Orbiter Mission Mangalyaan, and: a, Mylswamy Annadurai, rocket launch. b, Mars and stars. c, Mars. d, M.V. Kotwal, flight path.
No. 3310, 60r, Eisenhower, diff. No. 3311, 60r, 2014 Nobel laureate William Moerner (Chemistry), Patrick Modiano (Literature), Hiroshi Amano (Physics), Yousafzai, John O'Keefe (Physiology or Medicine). No. 3312, 60r, Two goats, diff. No. 3313, 70r, Einstein and Gravity Probe B. No. 3314, 70r, Loren, diff. No. 3315, 70r, Lennon and Yoko Ono, diff. No. 3316, 70r, Woods, diff. No. 3317, 70r, De Gaulle, diff. No. 3318, 70r, Mangalyaan and surface of Mars.

2015, Jan. 13   Litho.   Perf. 13¼
Sheets of 4, #a-d

| 3300-3309 | A622 | Set of 10 | 110.00 | 110.00 |

Souvenir Sheets

| 3310-3318 | A622 | Set of 9 | 80.00 | 80.00 |

Dated 2014.

Fauna of the Indian Subcontinent — A623

No. 3319, 20r — Panthera uncia: a, Snow leopard facing right. b, Snow leopard facing left. c, Adult and juvenile snow leopards. d, Snow leopard and head of snow leopard.
No. 3320, 20r — Dolphins: a, One Tursiops aduncus. b, Two Tursiops aduncus. c, Stenella coeruleoalba. d, Steno bredanensis.
No. 3321, 20r — Parrots: a, Loriculus vernalis. b, Psittacula columboides. c, Psittacula derbiana. d, Psittacula eupatria.
No. 3322, 20r — Owls: a, Otus bakkamoena. b, Athene brama. c, Ketupa flavipes. d, Bubo bengalensis.
No. 3323, 20r — Fish: a, Gnathanodon speciosus. b, Gomphosus varius. c, Ostorhinchus dispar. d, Coris gaimard.
No. 3324, 22r — Monkeys. a, Macaca silenus. b, Hoolock hoolock. c, Trachypithecus geei. d, Presbytis entellus.
No. 3325, 22r — Panthera tigrio tigris: a, On rocks, facing right. b, Walking left. c, Walking right. d, Drinking.
No. 3326, 22r — Elephas maximus: a, Two elephants. b, Elephant facing right. c, Head of elephant facing right. d, Head of elephant facing left.
No. 3327, 22r — Butterflies: a, Pachliopta hector. b, Troides minos. c, Papilio clytia. d, Papilio polymnestor.
No. 3328, 22r — Turtles: a, Lepidochelys olivacea. b, Eretmochelys imbricata. c, Chelonia mydas. d, Lissemys punctata.
No. 3329, 60r, Two Panthera uncia leaping. No. 3330, 60r, Delphinus capensis. No. 3331, 60r, Psittacula cyanocephala. No. 3332, 60r, Bubo bengalensis, diff. No. 3333, 60r, Cephalopholis argus. No. 3334, 70r, Macaca radiata. No. 3335, 70r, Panthera tigris tigris, diff. No. 3336, 70r, Elephas maximus, diff. No. 3337, 70r, Papilio agestor. No. 3338, 70r, Pangshura tecta.

2015, Jan. 28   Litho.   Perf. 13¼
Sheets of 4, #a-d

| 3319-3328 | A623 | Set of 10 | 110.00 | 110.00 |

Souvenir Sheets

| 3329-3338 | A623 | Set of 10 | 85.00 | 85.00 |

Paintings A624

No. 3339, 20r — Paintings by Paul Gauguin (1848-1903): a, Self-portrait with Manao tu Papau. b, Tahitian Landscape. c, Still Life with Teapot and Fruit. d, Christ in the Garden of Olives.
No. 3340, 20r — Paintings by Robert Antoine Pinchon (1886-1943): a, Seine in Rouen at Sunset. b, The English Bridge, Sunset. c, Poppy Garden. d, Boats, Fécamp.
No. 3341, 20r — Paintings by Henri Rousseau (1844-1910): a, Myself: Portrait-Landscape. b, Exotic Landscape. c, The Football Players. d, The Muse Inspiring the Poet.
No. 3342, 20r — Paintings by Paul Signac (1863-1935): a, Sunday. b, Women at the Well. c, Capo di Noli. d, Grand Canal (Venice).
No. 3343, 20r — Paintings by Henri de Toulouse-Lautrec (1864-1901): a, Self-portrait in Front of a Mirror. b, A Box at the Theater. c, The Englishman at the Moulin Rouge. d, Aristide Bruant in His Cabaret.
No. 3344, 22r — Paintings by Emile Bernard (1868-1941): a, Self-portrait with a Vase of Flowers. b, Buckwheat Harvesters at Pont-Aven. c, Yellow Tree. d, Breton Peasants.
No. 3345, 22r — Paintings by Paul Cézanne (1839-1906): a, Self-portrait with Palette. b, Still Life with Compotier. c, Still Life, Flowers in a Vase. d, The House with the Cracked Walls.
No. 3346, 22r — Paintings by Georges Lemmen (1865-1916): a, Self-portrait. b, Carnival: The Carousel. c, View of the Thames. d, Still Life with Fan.
No. 3347, 22r — Paintings by Odilon Redon (1840-1916): a, Self-portrait. b, Lady of the Flowers. c, The Buddha. d, Butterflies.
No. 3348, 22r — Paintings by Vincent van Gogh (1853-90): a, Self-portrait with Gray Felt Hat. b, Café Terrace at Night. c, Sunflowers. d, Wheatfield with Crows.
No. 3349, 60r, The Siesta, by Gauguin, horiz. No. 3350, 60r, The Buckot, by Pinchon, horiz. No. 3351, 60r, The Sleeping Gypsy, by Rousseau, horiz. No. 3352, 60r, The Port of Saint-Tropez, by Signac, horiz. No. 3353, 60r, Divan Japonais, by Toulouse-Lautrec, horiz. No. 3354, 70r, Breton Women with Parasols, by Bernard, horiz. No. 3355, 70r, Mont Sainte-Victoire, by Cézanne, horiz. No. 3356, 70r, Beach at Heist, by Lemmen, horiz. No. 3357, 70r, Ophelia Among the Flowers, by Redon, horiz. No. 3358, 70r, The Starry Night, by van Gogh, horiz.

2015, Jan. 28   Litho.   Perf. 13¼
Sheets of 4, #a-d

| 3339-3348 | A624 | Set of 10 | 110.00 | 110.00 |

Souvenir Sheets

| 3349-3358 | A624 | Set of 10 | 85.00 | 85.00 |

Nos. 3349-3358 each contain one 66x45mm stamp.

Resorts — A625

Designs: No. 3359, 15r, Kuredu Resort. No. 3360, 15r, Komandoo Island Resort and Spa. No. 3361, 15r, Vilamendhoo Island Resort and Spa. No. 3362, 15r, Meeru Island Resort and Spa. No. 3363, 15r, Veligandu Island Resort and Spa.

2015, Feb. 1   Litho.   Perf. 13¼

| 3359-3363 | A625 | Set of 5 | 9.75 | 9.75 |

Souvenir Sheet

Visit to Maldive Islands of Xi Jinping, President of People's Republic of China — A626

2015, Apr. 15   Litho.   Perf. 13¼x12¾
On Silk-Faced Paper

| 3364 | A626 | 88r multi | 11.50 | 11.50 |

A627

No. 3365, 20r — Ingrid Bergman (1915-82), actress: a, With hand on shoulder. b, With Academy Award. c, With hair parted in the middle. d, Wearing dp turquoise blue robe.
No. 3366, 20r — Elvis Presley (1935-77): a, With large microphone. b, Holding microphone. c, Playing guitar. d, With guitar in background.
No. 3367, 20r — 85th birthday of Edwin "Buzz" Aldrin, astronaut: a, Aldrin with camera. b, Aldrin with Apollo 11 Lunar Module. c, Aldrin with Apollo 11 Command and Lunar Modules. d, Aldrin with rocket launch.
No. 3368, 20r — Nelson Mandela (1918-2013), President of South Africa: a, With globe and dove. b, With Nobel medal, South African flag. c, With Nobel Medal, South African flag, hand touching chin. d, Holding dove.
No. 3369, 20r — End of World War II, 70th anniv. a, Soldiers and flag of Great Britain. b, Soldiers and flag of Germany. c, Soldiers and flag of Soviet Union. d, Soldiers and flag of United States.
No. 3370, 22r — Ludwig van Beethoven (1770-1827), composer: a, With score and neck of stringed instrument. b, Holding papers, harpsichord in background. c, Holding papers, keyboard in background. d, With score at lower left.
No. 3371, 22r — Boris Pasternak (1890-1960), writer: a, With Nobel medal and papers. b, With pen tip. c, With quill and ink well. d, With Nobel medal.
No. 3372, 22r — Frank Sinatra (1915-98), singer: a, Wearing hat. b, Holding Academy Award. c, Holding microphone. d, With Hollywood Walk of Fame star.
No. 3373, 22r — Chess players: a, Viswanathan Anand, flag of India. b, Sergey Karjakin, flag of Russia. c, Vladimir Kramnik, flag of Russia. d, Shakhriyar Mamedyarov, flag of Azerbaijan.
No. 3374, 22r — Battle of Waterloo, 200th anniv. a, Battle of Waterloo, by Aleksandr Yurievich Averyanov. b, Portrait of Gebhard Leberecht von Blücher, by George Dawe. c, Napoleon at Waterloo, by Thomas Jones Barker. d, Battle of Waterloo, by William Holmes Sullivan.
No. 3375, 60r, Bergman and scene from *Casablanca*, horiz. No. 3376, 60r, Presley, horiz. No. 3377, 60r, Aldrin, horiz. No. 3378, 60r, Mandela, horiz. No. 3379, 60r, World War II soldiers, horiz. No. 3380, 70r, Beethoven, horiz. No. 3381, 70r, Pasternak and his characters, horiz. No. 3382, 70r, Sinatra, horiz. No. 3383, 70r, Magnus Carlsen, chess player, horiz. No. 3384, 70r, Wellington at Waterloo, by Robert Alexander Hillingford, horiz.

2015, Apr. 15   Litho.   Perf. 13¼
Sheets of 4, #a-d

| 3365-3374 | A627 | Set of 10 | 110.00 | 110.00 |

Souvenir Sheets

| 3375-3384 | A627 | Set of 10 | 85.00 | 85.00 |

Nos. 3375-3384 each contain one 60x40mm stamp.

MALDIVE ISLANDS

Sports
A628

No. 3385, 20r — Cycling: a, Cyclist with yellow and green, shirt, orange helmet. b, Cyclist with blue and orange shirt, blue helmet, dark blue bicycle. c, Cyclist with violet and blue shirt, light blue helmet, red bicycle. d, Cyclist with green and yellow shirt, blue helmet.

No. 3386, 20r — Cricket: a, Batsman with red and blue shirt, ball at right. b, Batsman with red and blue shirt, ball at left. c, Batsman with green and yellow shirt. d, Batsman and wicket-keeper.

No. 3387, 20r — Formula 1 race cars: a, Orange red car. b, Orange yellow car. c, Blue and yellow car. d, Red and orange car.

No. 3388, 20r — Tennis: a, Player with violet and green shirt. b, Player with green and light green shirt. c, Player with light blue shirt. d, Female player.

No. 3389, 20r — Baseball: a, Catcher with mask off. b, Batter swinging. c, Batter about to swing. d, Catcher with mask on.

No. 3390, 22r — Water sports: a, Slalom canoeing. b, Sailing. c, Surfing. d, Jet skiing.

No. 3391, 22r — Table tennis: a, Player with carmine red and orange shirt. b, Player with olive green and dark blue shirt. c, Player with green and yellow shirt. d, Player with orange brown and blue shirt.

No. 3392, 22r — Rugby: a, Player with red and light blue shirt tackling player with green and violet shirt. b, One player. c, Player with green and violet shirt tackling player with light blue shirt. d, Three players.

No. 3393, 22r — Golf: a, Female golfer. b, Golfer with orange cap. c, Golfer with green cap. d, Golfer with light blue cap.

No. 3394, 22r — Soccer: a, Player with violet and orange shirt. b, Player with red and beige shirt. c, Player with yellow and red shirt. d, Player with green and yellow shirt.

No. 3395, 60r, Cycling, diff. No. 3396, 60r, Cricket, diff. No. 3397, 60r, Formula 1 race car, diff. No. 3398, 60r, Tennis, diff. No. 3399, 60r, Baseball, diff. No. 3400, 70r, Kayaking. No. 3401, 70r, Table tennis, diff. No. 3402, 70r, Rugby, diff. No. 3403, 70r, Golf, diff. No. 3404, 70r, Soccer, diff.

2015, Apr. 22   Litho.   Perf. 13¼
Sheets of 4, #a-d
3385-3394 A628 Set of 10 110.00 110.00
Souvenir Sheets
3395-3404 A628 Set of 10 85.00 85.00

Flora and Fauna
A629

No. 3405, 20r — Ailuropoda melanoleuca: a, Panda on rock. b, Panda eating. c, Panda standing. d, Men examining juvenile panda.

No. 3406, 20r — Cats: a, Selkirk Rex. b, Maine Coon. c, Ragdoll. d, Sphynx.

No. 3407, 20r — Dogs: a, Boxer. b, Labrador retrievers. c, Huskies. d, German shepherds.

No. 3408, 20r — Kingfishers: a, Alcedo websteri. b, Actenoides lindsayi. c, Halcyon smyrnensis. d, Actenoides concretus.

No. 3409, 20r — Orchids and butterflies: a, Zygopetalum sp., Aglais io. b, Phalaenopsis sp., Papilio ulysses. c, Cymbidium sp., Protographium marcellus. d, Vanda sp., Polygonia interrogationis.

No. 3410, 22r — Orcinus orca: a, Three killer whales underwater. b, Killer whale facing left. c, Killer whale facing right. d, Killer whale underwater.

No. 3411, 22r — Eagles: a, Haliaeetus leucocephalus. b, Terathopius ecaudatus. c, Ictinaetus malaiensis. d, Aquila heliaca.

No. 3412, 22r — Owls and mushrooms: a, Bubo virginianus, Leccinum aurantiacum. b, Pulsatrix perspicillata, Cantharellus cibarius. c, Strix varia, Amanita muscaria. d, Asio flammeus, Boletus edulis.

No. 3413, 22r — Shells: a, Epitonium scalare. b, Melongena corona. c, Acanthocardia tuberculata. d, Pinctada radiata.

No. 3414, 22r — Dinosaurs and minerals: a, Preondactylus buffarinii, Wulfenite. b, Elasmosaurus platyurus, Barite. c, Stegosaurus armatus, Fluorite. d, Carnotaurus sastrei, Tanzanite.

No. 3415, 60r, Adult and juvenile Ailuropoda melanoleuca. No. 3416, 60r, Devon Rex cat. No. 3417, 60r, Rottweiler. No. 3418, 60r, Ceryle rudis. No. 3419, 60r, Epidendrum sp., Ornithoptera goliath. No. 3420, 70r, Orcinus orca, diff. No. 3421, 70r, Aquila chrysaetos. No. 3422, 70r, Tyto alba, Laetiporus sulphureus. No. 3423, 70r, Charonia variegata. No. 3424, 70r, Velociraptor mongoliensis, Calcite.

2015, May 25   Litho.   Perf. 13¼
Sheets of 4, #a-d
3405-3414 A629 Set of 10 110.00 110.00
Souvenir Sheets
3415-3424 A629 Set of 10 85.00 85.00

A630

No. 3425, 20r — New Horizons space probe: a, Pluto at left, probe at right. b, Atlas V rocket, probe and Pluto. c, Atlas V rocket, Haliaeetus leucocephala. d, Probe at left, Pluto at right.

No. 3426, 20r — Wright Brothers airplanes: a, Early Wright Model B. b, Wright Model HS. c, Wright Model L. d, Orville Wright piloting Model R.

No. 3427, 20r — Porsche 912, 50th anniv.: a, 1969 Porsche 912 Targa. b, 1969 Porsche 912. c, 1966 Porsche 912 coupe. d, 1968 Porsche 912 Targa.

No. 3428, 20r — Jacques-Yves Cousteau (1910-97), conservationist and film maker and: a, Chelonia mydas. b, Pomacanthus imperator. c, Carcharias taurus. d, Dendronephthya hemprichi.

No. 3429, 20r — Members of 1914-17 Endurance Antarctic expedition: a, Thomas Crean (1877-1938). b, Perce Blackborow (1896-1949), and cat. c, James Wordie (1889-1962). d, Frank Hurley (1885-1962).

No. 3430, 22r — Vasco da Gama (c. 1460-1524), explorer: a, 1498 arrival in Calicut. b, And his ship. c, Statue of da Gama, Goa, India, and St. Francis Church, Kochi, India. d, And Vasco da Gama Bridge, Lisbon.

No. 3431, 22r — High-speed trains: a, Talgo 350. b, Siemens Velaro RUS EVS2. c, E5 Series Shinkansen Hayabusa. d, ETR 500 Frecciarossa.

No. 3432, 22r — Louis Pasteur (1822-95), microbiologist, and: a, Dogue de Bordeaux. b, French bulldog. c, Entlebucher mountain dog. d, Redbone coonhound.

No. 3433, 22r — World War I, cent.: a, Australian soldiers. b, British machine gun crew at Battle of the Somme, 1916. c, Battle of Kajmakcalan, 1916. d, The Last Message, by Fortunino Matania (1881-1963).

No. 3434, 22r — Astronauts and cosmonauts: a, Alan B. Shepard, Jr. (1923-98), and Mercury capsule. b, Neil Armstrong (1930-2012) and Apollo 11 Lunar and Command modules. c, Valentina Tereshkova and Vostok 6. d, Alexeyi Leonov and Voskhod 2.

No. 3435, 60r, New Horizons space probe and Pluto, diff. No. 3436, 60r, 1905 Wright Flyer III. No. 3437, 60r, Porsche 912 Targa police car. No. 3438, 60r, Cousteau and Oceanographic Museum, Monaco. No. 3439, 60r, Endurance and Sir Ernest Shackleton (1874-1922), Antarctic explorer. No. 3440, 70r, Da Gama and ship, diff. No. 3441, 70r, Japanese L0 series Maglev train. No. 3442, 70r, Pasteur and Labrador retriever. No. 3443, 70r, The Second Battle of Ypres, by Richard Jack (1866-1952). No. 3444, 70r, Yuri Gagarin (1934-68) and Vostok 1.

2015, July 1   Litho.   Perf. 13¼
Sheets of 4, #a-d
3425-3434 A630 Set of 10 110.00 110.00
Souvenir Sheets
3435-3444 A630 Set of 10 85.00 85.00

2015 MonacoPhil Philatelic Exhibition. Monte Carlo (Nos. 3428, 3438).

A631   A632

A633   A634

A635

Independence, 50th Anniv. — A636

2015, July 26   Litho.   Perf. 13¼
3445 A631 10r multi   1.40 1.40
3446 A632 10r multi   1.40 1.40
3447 A633 15r multi   2.00 2.00
3448 A634 15r multi   2.00 2.00
3449 A635 25r multi   3.25 3.25
3450 A636 25r multi   3.25 3.25
   Nos. 3445-3450 (6)   13.30 13.30

Wildlife Conservation and Rehabilitation — A637

No. 3451, 20r — Ursus arctos: a, Bear standing, looking to left. b, Bear on large rock, looking to right. c, Bear on small rock, looking to right, mountain peak to right of face. d, Bear sitting on haunches.

No. 3452, 20r — Ailuropoda melanoleuca: a, Panda sitting on haunches with bamboo in mouth. b, Panda standing. c, Head of panda eating bamboo. d, Panda on stump.

No. 3453, 20r — Colobus monkeys: a, Head of Colobus angolensis. b, Procolobus kirkii. c, Adult and juvenile Colobus angolensis. d, Colobus guereza.

No. 3454, 20r — Elephants: a, Two Elephas maximus maximus. b, Three Elephas maximus indicus. c, Adult and juvenile Elephas maximus indicus. d, Elephas maximus sumatranus.

No. 3455, 20r — Dolphins: a, Stenella longirostris. b, Lagenodelphis hosei. c, Stenella coeruleoalba. d, Stenella attenuata.

No. 3456, 22r — Pumas and Jaguars: a, Adult and juvenile Puma concolor. b, One Panthera onca. c, Adult and juvenile Panthera onca. d, Puma concolor in tree.

No. 3457, 22r — Arctocephalus pusillus: a, One seal. b, Two seals, head of rear seal at left. c, Two seals, head of rear seal at right. d, Two seals, head of rear seal at right, head of front seal with nose near banner.

No. 3458, 22r — Spheniscus demersus: a, Two adults, one with wings extended, and hatchling in nest. b, Two adults and egg. c, Two adults. d, Two adults and large chick in nest.

No. 3459, 22r — Carcharodon carcharias: a, Two sharks, tail of lower shark touching circle at LR. b, One shark, nose below "I" and "V." c, One shark, nose below "E" and "S." d, Two sharks facing left.

No. 3460, 22r — Sea turtles: a, Lepidochelys kempii. b, Lepidochelys olivacea. c, Caretta caretta. d, Chelonia mydas.

No. 3461, 60r, Ursus arctos, diff. No. 3462, 60r, Ailuropoda melanoleuca, diff. No. 3463, 60r, Adult and juvenile Colobus angolensis, diff. No. 3464, 60r, Adult and juvenile Elephas maximus indicus, diff. No. 3465, 60r, Tursiops aduncus. No. 3466, 70r, Panthera onca, diff. No. 3467, 70r, Arctocephalus pusillus, diff. No. 3468, 70r, Two Spheniscus demersus, diff. No. 3469, 70r, Carcharodon carcharias, diff. No. 3470, 70r, Eretmochelys imbricata.

2015, Aug. 10   Litho.   Perf. 13¼
Sheets of 4, #a-d
3451-3460 A637 Set of 10 110.00 110.00
Souvenir Sheets
3461-3470 A637 Set of 10 85.00 85.00

Art
A638

No. 3471, 20r — Baroque era paintings: a, Boys Eating Grapes and Melon, by Bartolomé Esteban Murillo (1617-82). b, Boy Bitten by a Lizard, by Caravaggio (1571-1610). c, The Artist and His First Wife, Isabella Brant, in the Honeysuckle Bower, by Peter Paul Rubens (1577-1640). d, Charles I in Three Positions, by Anthony van Dyck (1599-1641).

No. 3472, 20r — Dutch Golden Age paintings: a, Girl with a Pearl Earring, by Johannes Vermeer (1632-75). b, Prayer Without End, by Nicolaes Maes (1634-93). c, The Lute Player, by Frans Hals (c. 1582-1666). d, The Prodigal Son in the Tavern, by Rembrandt (1606-69).

No. 3473, 20r — Impressionist paintings: a, Dancer Tilting, by Edgar Degas (1834-1917). b, Hide and Seek, by Berthe Morisot (1841-95). c, Woman with a Parasol, Facing Left, by Claude Monet (1840-1926). d, A Bar at the Folies-Bergère, by Edouard Manet (1832-83).

No. 3474, 20r — Post-impressionist paintings: a, Three Sunflowers in a Vase, by Vincent van Gogh (1853-90). b, Portrait of Félix Fénéon, by Paul Signac (1863-1935). c, Parau Api (Two Women of Tahiti), by Paul Gauguin (1848-1903). d, Mont Sainte-Victoire, by Paul Cézanne (1839-1906).

No. 3475, 20r — Cubist paintings: a, Champs de Mars: The Red Tower, by Robert Delaunay (1885-1941). b, Portrait of Two Women, by Diego Rivera (1886-1957). c, Portrait of Art Dealer Ambroise Vollard, by Pablo Picasso (1881-1973). d, Woman with Phlox, by Albert Gleizes (1881-1953).

No. 3476, 22r — Renaissance paintings: a, Mona Lisa, by Leonardo da Vinci (1452-1519). b, Madonna and Child (Salting Madonna), by Antonello da Messina (c. 1430-79). c, Saint Catherine of Alexandria, by Raphael (1483-1520). d, Self-portrait, by Albrecht Dürer (1471-1528).

No. 3477, 22r — Romantic era paintings: a, Two Men Contemplating the Moon, by Caspar David Friedrich (1774-1840). b, Revolt of Cairo, 21 October 1798, by Anne-Louis Girondet (1767-1824). c, Witches' Sabbath, by Francisco Goya (1746-1828). d, Lion Hunt, by Eugène Delacroix (1798-1863).

No. 3478, 22r — Realist paintings: a, Ivan the Terrible and His Son Ivan on November 16, 1581, by Ilya Repin (1844-1930). b, The Stone Breakers, by Gustave Courbet (1819-77). c, Man with a Hoe, by Jean-François Millet (1814-75). d, Landscape with a Clump of Trees, by Theéodore Rousseau (1812-67).

No. 3479, 22r — Symbolist paintings: a, Muse on Pegasus, by Odilon Redon (1840-1916). b, Music I, by Gustav Klimt (1862-1918). c, Fairy Tale II, by Mikalojus Konstantinas Ciurlionis (1875-1911). d, Hope, by George Frederic Watts (1817-1904).

No. 3480, 22r — Surrealist paintings: a, The Temptation of St. Anthony, by Salvador Dalí (1853-90). b, The Angel of the Home, by Max Ernst (1891-19765). c, The Son of Man, by René Magritte (1898-1967). d, The Song of Love, by Giorgio di Chirico (1888-1978).

No. 3481, 60r, The Cheat with the Ace of Diamonds, by Georges de la Tour (1593-1652), horiz. No. 3482, 60r, The Night Watch, by Rembrandt, horiz. No. 3483, 60r, Luncheon of the Boating Party, by Pierre-Auguste Renoir (1841-1919), horiz. No. 3484, 60r, Salon de Rue des Moulins, by Henri de Toulouse-Lautrec (1864-1901), horiz. No. 3485, 60r, Mandolin, Fruit Bowl and Plaster Arm, by Picasso, horiz. No. 3486, 70r, The Story of Nastagio degli Onesti: The Banquet in the Pine Forest, by Sandro Botticelli (c. 1445-1510), horiz. No. 3487, 70r, The Burial of the Sardine, by Goya, horiz. No. 3488, 70r, Young Ladies on the Banks of the Seine, by Courbet, horiz. No. 3489, 70r, The Dance of Life, by Edvard Munch (1863-1944), horiz. No. 3490, 70r, The Accommodations of Desire, by Dalí, horiz.

2015, Aug. 25   Litho.   Perf. 13¼
Sheets of 4, #a-d
3471-3480 A638 Set of 10 110.00 110.00
Souvenir Sheets
3481-3490 A638 Set of 10 85.00 85.00

MALDIVE ISLANDS

A639

No. 3491, 20r — George Frideric Handel (1685-1759), composer, and: a, Handel on Royal Barge with King George I, by Edouard Hamman. b, Ball. c, Handel playing harpsichord. d, Musicians.
No. 3492, 20r — Queen Elizabeth II, longest-reigning British monarch: a, With young Prince Charles and Princess Anne. b, With father, King George VI. c, In the Arctic, 1970. d, With Mother Teresa.
No. 3493, 20r — Birth of Princess Charlotte of Cambridge: a, Princes Charlotte with parents Duke and Duchess of Cambridge, royal estate. b, Princess Charlotte with father and brother, Prince George. c, Princess Charlotte with parents, framed proclamation. d, Princess Charlotte with parents, forest.
No. 3494, 20r — Nelson Mandela (1918-2013), President of South Africa, with: a, Pelé, Rhodochrosite. b, Dalai Lama, Poldervaartite and Bultfonteinite. c, Desmond Tutu, Hausmannite. d, South African coat of arms, Inesite.
No. 3495, 20r — International Year of Light: a, Prince Andrew. b, Optical demonstration of Ibn al-Haytham, physicist. c, James Clerk Maxwell, physicist. d, John Michael Dudley, physicist.
No. 3496, 22r — Penny Black, 175th anniv.: a, Sir Rowland Hill (1795-1879), postal reformer, and house he lived in. b, Hill and 1820 mail coach. c, Statue of Hill, Imperial Airways mail plane, Penny Black. d, Hill and 1969 Moon Landing cover, rocket launch.
No. 3497, 22r — Pony Express: a, William Hepburn Russell (1812-72), Pony Express executive, Simpson Springs, Utah station. b, Alexander Majors (1814-1900), Pony Express executive, Pony Express rider on horse. c, William B. Waddell (1807-72), Pony Express executive, Pony Express station. d, Richard Erastus Egan (1842-1918), Pony Express rider, Pony Express cover.
No. 3498, 22r — Marilyn Monroe (1926-62), actress: a, Holding umbrella. b, In Andy Warhol print. c, On Bus Stop movie poster. d, With Hollywood sign in background.
No. 3499, 22r — Mother Teresa (1910-97): a, Holding child. b, With Pope John Paul II. c, With high school named after her. d, With Pres. Ronald Reagan.
No. 3500, 22r — Scouting in the Maldive Islands: a, Pres. Maumoon Abdul Gayoom and injured Boy Scout who prevented assassination attempt against Gayoom. b, Lord Robert Baden-Powell and fish. c, Baden-Powell and Scout holding turtle. d, Gayoom shaking hands with Boy Scout in crowd.
No. 3501, 60r, Handel and musical score. No. 3502, 60r, Queen Elizabeth II in coach. No. 3503, 60r, Princess Charlotte and her parents, church. No. 3504, 60r, Mandela, South African coat of arms, Poldervaartite and Bultfonteinite. No. 3505, 60r, Sun, hands holding light bulb. No. 3506, 70r, Penny Black, Queen Victoria as child. No. 3507, 70r, Johnny Fry (1840-63), Pony Express rider. No. 3508, 70r, Monroe and city skyline. No. 3509, 70r, Mother Teresa, young woman. No. 3510, 70r, Fish, Scouts jumping into water from boat.

2015, Sept. 15   Litho.   Perf. 13¼
Sheets of 4, #a-d
3491-3500 A639   Set of 10   110.00 110.00
Souvenir Sheets
3501-3510 A639   Set of 10   85.00   85.00

Baa Atoll UNESCO Biosphere Reserve — A640

No. 3511: a, 5 l, Whale shark. b, 10 l, Lesser frigatebird. c, 25 l, Manta ray. d, 50 l, Lacquer work of Thulhaadhoo Island.

2015, Dec. 2   Litho.   Perf. 13¼
3511 A640   Booklet pane of 4, #a-d   .25   .25
    Complete booklet, #3511   .25   .25

Birds and Fish A641

No. 3512, 20r — Birds of prey: a, Asio flammeus. b, Buteo buteo. c, Circus aeruginosus. d, Falco peregrinus.
No. 3513, 20r — Ducks: a, Aythya fuligula. b, Anas crecca. c, Anas querquedula. d, Dendrocygna javanica.
No. 3514, 20r — Fish: a, Zebrasoma scopas. b, Pseudanthias evansi. c, Lutjanus sebae, Chaetodon interruptus. d, Aetobatus narinari.
No. 3515, 20r — Fish: a, Forcipiger flavissimus, Rhinecanthus aculeatus. b, Paracheilinus mccoskeri, Kentrocapros rosapinto. c, Macropharyngodon bipartitus, Cheilodipterus quinquelineatus. d, Epibulus insidiator.
No. 3516, 20r — Fish: a, Oxymonacanthus longirostris. b, Paracheilinus mccoskeri, Nemateleotris decora, Lactoria fornasini. c, Thalassoma amblycephalum, Antennarius maculatus. d, Lutjanus kasmira.
No. 3517, 22r — Sea birds: a, Fregata minor. b, Sula sula. c, Phaethon lepturus. d, Oceanites oceanicus.
No. 3518, 22r — Terns: a, Gelochelidon nilotica. b, Sterna dougallii. c, Onychoprion fuscatus. d, Thalasseus bergii.
No. 3519, 22r — Wading birds: a, Nycticorax nycticorax. b, Philomachus pugnax. c, Gallinago gallinago. d, Himantopus himantopus.
No. 3520, 22r — Fish: a, Chlorurus sordidus, Anampses lineatus, Taeniura lymma. b, Dendrochirus biocellatus, Cirrhilabrus rubrisquamis. c, Ostracion meleagris, Oxycirrhites typus. d, Taeniura lymma, Anampses lineatus, Arothron meleagris.
No. 3521, 22r — Sharks: a, Rhinocodon typus. b, Carcharhinus limbatus, country name in white. c, Carcharhinus longimanus. d, Carcharhinus limbatus, country name in dark blue.
No. 3522, 60r, Asio flammeus, diff. No. 3523, 60r, Anas clypeata. No. 3524, 60r, Amphiprion nigripes. No. 3525, 60r, Cheilodipterus quinquelineatus, Coris cuvieri. No. 3526, 60r, Sphyraena barracuda. No. 3527, 70r, Larus canus. No. 3528, 70r, Onychoprion anaethetus. No. 3529, 70r, Nycticorax nycticorax, diff. No. 3530, 70r, Gorgasia maculata, Chlorurus sordidus. No. 3531, 70r, Isurus oxyrinchus.

2015, Dec. 9   Litho.   Perf. 13¼
Sheets of 4, #a-d
3512-3521 A641   Set of 10   110.00 110.00
Souvenir Sheets
3522-3531 A641   Set of 10   85.00   85.00

A642

No. 3532, 20r — Princess Diana (1961-97): a, Wearing wedding dress at left. b, As child wearing red blouse at left. c, With Prince Charles. d, Holding child.
No. 3533, 20r — Pres. Abraham Lincoln (1809-65). a, At left, Lincoln, Union generals and tent at right. b, At right, four Union soldiers at left. c, At left, three Confederate soldiers at right. d, At right, Union soldiers and flag bearer at left.
No. 3534, 20r — Niccolò Paganini (1782-1840), composer: a, Playing violin at left. b, Playing violin at right. c, Playing violin in front of building at right. d, Playing guitar.
No. 3535, 20r — Athletes at 2015 World Track and Field Championships, Beijing: a, Vivian Cheruiyot and flag of Kenya. b, Ashton Eaton and U.S. flag. c, Jessica Ennis-Hill, flag of Great Britain. d, Derek Drouin, flag of Canada.
No. 3536, 20r — Concorde: a, British Airways Concorde taking off. b, British Airways Concorde in flight. c, Air France Concorde in flight. d, British Airways Concorde on ground.
No. 3537, 22r — First spacewalk, 50th anniv.: a, Edward H. White II (1930-67) at left. Earth at right. b, Alexey Leonov at right. c, Leonov at left. d, White at left, rocket launch at right.
No. 3538, 22r — World War II bombing of Dresden, 70th anniv.: a, Sir Arthur Harris (1892-1984). b, Medic treating bombing victim. c, Child holding stuffed animal. d, Airplane over Dresden.
No. 3539, 22r — 65th birthday of Narendra Modi, Prime Minister of India: a, Modi and Mother Teresa (1910-97). b, Modi and Indian buildings. c, Modi and flag of India. d, Modi and Mahatma Gandhi (1869-1948).
No. 3540, 22r — 2016 European Soccer Championships: a, Senes Erzik, Bacary Sagna. b, Moussa Sissoko. c, Yohan Cabaye. d, Laurent Koscielny, Angel María Villar.
No. 3541, 22r — Rotary International in Sri Lanka and the Maldive Islands: a, Nutrition project for children under 5 years old. b, Polio eradication. c, Mother and child health camps. d, Mathematics lab.
No. 3542, 60r, Princess Diana, and her children, Princes Henry and William. No. 3543, 60r, Lincoln, eagle and U.S. flag. No. 3544, 60r, Paganini playing violin, diff. No. 3545, 60r, Usain Bolt, flag of Jamaica. No. 3546, 60r, British Airways Concorde in flight, diff. No. 3547, 70r, Leonov, diff. No. 3548, 70r, Airplanes over Dresden. No. 3549, 70r, Modi and Pres. Barack Obama, flags of India and U.S. No. 3550, 70r, Michel Platini, Blaise Matuidi. No. 3551, 70r, George Jesuthasan, Rotary International district governor for Sri Lanka and the Maldive Islands, flags of Maldive Islands and Sri Lanka.

2015, Dec. 16   Litho.   Perf. 13¼
Sheets of 4, #a-d
3532-3541 A642   Set of 10   110.00 110.00
Souvenir Sheets
3542-3551 A642   Set of 10   85.00   85.00

Worldwide Fund for Nature (WWF) — A643

No. 3552 — Bolbometopon muricatum: a, Blue green fish facing right, yellow fish at LL. b, Blue green fish facing left. c, Blue green fish facing right, red vegetation at LL. d, Blue green fish facing left.
70r, Two Bolbometopon muricatum.

2016, Jan. 18   Litho.   Perf. 13¼
3552 A643   22r Sheet of 4, #a-d   12.00   12.00
Souvenir Sheet
3553 A643   70r multi   9.50   9.50

A644

No. 3554, 20r — Discovery of liquid salty water on Mars: a, Technician preparing HIRISE camera in laboratory. b, John Grunsfeld, astronaut. c, Mars, future astronaut on Mars, ocean wave. d, Mars Reconnaisance orbiter and Mars Curiosity rover.
No. 3555, 20r — Apollo space missions: a, Walter Schirra, Jr. (1923-2007), Apollo 7. b, Edwin "Buzz" Aldrin, Apollo 11. c, Jim Lovell, Apollo 13. d, Apollo 17 astronaut and lunar rover.
No. 3556, 20r — Seaplanes: a, 8Q TMV. b, 8Q-MBA. c, 8Q TMG. d, 8Q-TMF.
No. 3557, 20r — Tall ships: a, Christian Radich, Norway. b, Dar Mlodziezy, Poland. c, Georg Stage, Denmark. d, Belem, France.
No. 3558, 20r — 2015 Nobel laureates: a, Physiology or Medicine laureates, William C. Campbell, Youyou Tu, and Satoshi Omura. b, Chemistry laureates Tomas Lindahl, Paul Modrich, and Aziz Sancar. c, Economic Sciences laureate Angus Deaton. d, Physics laureates, Takaaki Kajita and Arthur B. McDonald.
No. 3559, 22r — British trains: a, BR Class 42 Warship. b, BR Class 396 Pendolino. c, Class 91 GEC Bo-Bo Mainline electric locomotive. d, InterCity 125 BR Class 43.
No. 3560, 22r — Fire engines: a, Scania P380. b, Mercedes-Benz Atego 1628. c, Excalibur Volvo FL6. d, U.S. Air Force Oshkosh fire truck 9.
No. 3561, 22r — Lighthouses: a, Portland Bill Lighthouse, United Kingdom. b, Tourlitis Lighthouse, Greece. c, Castle Hill Lighthouse, Rhode Island. d, Inner Range Lighthouse, Ontario, Canada.
No. 3562, 22r — Maldivian Red Crescent: a, Ambulance medics treating man. b, Health and social care. c, First aid training. d, Dengue prevention.
No. 3563, 60r, Atlas V rocket launch, Mars Reconnaisance orbiter. No. 3564, 60r, Schirra, diff. No. 3565, 60r, Seaplane 8Q TMH. No. 3566, 60r, STS Sedov, Russia. No. 3567, 60r, Svetlana Alexievich, 2015 Nobel laureate in Literature. No. 3568, 70r, BR standard class 7 700013 Oliver Cromwell. No. 3569, 70r, 1998 Pierce Lance II pumper. No. 3570, 70r, Marblehead Lighthouse, Ohio. No. 3571, 70r, Maldivian Red Cross emergency preparedness and response.

2016, Jan. 18   Litho.   Perf. 13¼
Sheets of 4, #a-d
3554-3562 A644   Set of 9   100.00 100.00
Souvenir Sheets
Perf. 13¼x13
3563-3571 A644   Set of 9   77.50   77.50

Nos. 3563-3571 each contain one 60x40mm stamp.

Souvenir Sheets

50th Anniversary of Independence Celebrations — A645

No. 3572, 10r — Releasing of Minivan 50 commemorative stamp issue: a, Official release of Minivan 50 stamp. b, Minivan 50 commemorative stamp issue.
No. 3573, 10r — Launching of Minivan 50 commemorative note: a, Minivan 50 commemorative note. b, Launching of Minivan 50 commemorative note.
No. 3574, 10r — Representing the replica of Kalhuohfummi: a, Replica of Kalhuohfummi. b, Presenting "Hungaanu Dhooni" of Kalhuohfummi to H.E.P.
No. 3575, 10r — Opening of Izzudheen Faalan: a, Honoring the model of Izzudheen Faalan to the President. b, Izzudheen Faalan.
No. 3576, 10r — Events on National Stadium: a, H. E. President and senior officials observing the events. b, Skydiver landing to National Stadium.
No. 3577, 10r — Sixth Regional 3R Forum in Asia and the Pacific: a, Opening ceremony of 3R Forum. b, Presenting of a curved sculpture.
No. 3578, 10r — Design of China-Maldives Friendship Bridge: a, Aerial view of model of Male-Hulhule Bridge. b, Land view of model of Male-Hulhule Bridge.
No. 3579, 10r — New phase of Hulhumale development: a, Hulhumale phase 1 and 2. b, Hulhumale phase 2 greening programs.
No. 3580, 10r — Display of cultural and development phases: a, Presenting of cultural life of Maldives. b, Float presented by MACL.
No. 3581, 10r — Reopening of Jumhooree Maidhaan: a, President greets the gathering. b, Fayvaaru Jumhooree Maidhaan.
No. 3582, 10r — Opening of Hulhudhaan Bageecha: a, Opening ceremony of Hulhudhaan Bageecha (plaque presentation). b, Opening ceremony of Hulhudhaan Bageecha (crowd).

2016, Jan. 27   Litho.   Perf. 13¼
Sheets of 2, #a-b
3572-3582 A645   Set of 11   30.00   30.00

MALDIVE ISLANDS

Paintings A646

No. 3583, 20r — Paintings by Francisco Goya (1746-1828): a, Hannibal the Conqueror. b, The Milkmaid of Bordeaux. c, Powder Factory in the Sierra. d, Manuel Godoy, Duke of Alcudia, "Prince of Peace."

No. 3584, 20r — Paintings by Eugène Boudin (1824-98): a, Unloading the Newfoundland Fishing Boat. b, Sailboats near Trouville. c, Cattle Market at Daoulas, Brittany. d, Beach Scene.

No. 3585, 20r — Paintings by Gustave Caillebotte (1848-94): a, The Europe Bridge. b, The Gardeners. c, Young Man Playing the Piano. d, Skiffs on the Yerres.

No. 3586, 20r — Paintings by Pablo Picasso (1881-1973): a, Interior with Girl Drawing. b, Still Life with Stone. c, Breakfast. d, Young Girl Throwing a Rock.

No. 3587, 20r — Paintings by Salvador Dalí (1904-89): a, Swans Reflecting Elephants. b, Tristan and Isolde. c, Atavism at Twilight. d, Metamorphosis of Narcissus.

No. 3588, 22r — Paintings by Peter Paul Rubens (1577-1640): a, Rubens and Helene Fourment in the Garden. b, Tiger Hunt. c, Landscape with Milkmaids and Cattle. d, The Four Evangelists.

No. 3589, 22r — Paintings by Diego Velazquez (1599-1660): a, Joseph's Tunic. b, Las Meninas. c, The Fable of Arachne. d, The Triumph of Bacchus.

No. 3590, 22r — Paintings by Johannes Vermeer (1632-75): a, The Astronomer. b, The Music Lesson. c, The Guitar Player. d, The Allegory of Painting.

No. 3591, 22r — Paintings by Pierre-Auguste Renoir (1841-1919): a, Dance at Le Moulin de la Galette. b, Mount Sainte Victoire. c, Portrait of Charles and Georges Durand-Ruel. d, The Seine at Asnieres.

No. 3592, 22r — Paintings by Vincent van Gogh (1853-90): a, Landscape with Plowed Fields. b, Starry Night Over the Rhône. c, The Night Café. d, The Yellow House.

No. 3593, 60r, Self-portrait with Spectacles, by Goya, vert. No. 3594, 60r, Le Havre, Commerce Basin, by Boudin, vert. No. 3595, 60r, Young Man at His Window, by Caillebotte, vert. No. 3596, 60r, The Absinthe Drinker, by Picasso, vert. No. 3597, 60r, Atavistic Vestiges after the Rain, by Dalí, vert. No. 3598, 70r, The Honeysuckle Bower, by Rubens, vert. No. 3599, 70r, Self-portrait, by Velazquez, vert. No. 3600, 70r, Girl with a Pearl Earring, by Vermeer, vert. No. 3601, 70r, Self-portrait, by Renoir, vert. No. 3602, 70r, Self-portrait, by van Gogh, vert.

2016, May 16 Litho. Perf. 13¼
Sheets of 4, #a-d
3583-3592 A646 Set of 10 110.00 110.00
Souvenir Sheets
3593-3602 A646 Set of 10 85.00 85.00

Nos. 3593-3602 each contain one 34x45mm stamp.

Flora, Fauna and Mushrooms — A647

No. 3603, 20r — Big cats: a, Panthera tigris tigris. b, Puma concolor couguar. c, Acinonyx jubatus raineyii. d, Panthera onca centralis.

No. 3604, 20r — Dogs: a, Afghan hound. b, Alaskan malamute. c, Icelandic sheepdog. d, Neapolitan mastiff.

No. 3605, 20r — Dolphins: a, Stenella frontalis. b, Delphinus delphis. c, Cephalorhynchus commersonii. d, Stenella coeruleoalba.

No. 3606, 20r — Butterflies and orchids: a, Papilio maraho, Cattleya coccinea. b, Rhetus periander, Cattleya purpurata. c, Papilio crino, Mormodes cogniauxii. d, Heliconius sapho, Disa uniflora.

No. 3607, 20r — Dinosaurs: a, Achelousaurus. b, Afrovenator. c, Nipponosaurus sachalinensis. d, Pyroraptor olympius.

No. 3608, 22r — Ursus maritimus: a, Sitting, head facing forward. b, Standing. c, Sitting, head facing left. d, Head of bear.

No. 3609, 22r — Owls and mushrooms: a, Strix nebulosa, Agaricus campestris. b, Athene noctua, Morchella esculenta. c, Tyto alba, Cortinarius caperatus. d, Asio otus, Armillaria mellea.

No. 3610, 22r — Shells: a, Harpulina arausiaca. b, Murex pecten. c, Ranularia schumacher. d, Drupa ricinus.

No. 3611, 22r — Turtles: a, Emydoidea blandingii. b, Rhinoclemmys pulcherrima. c, Chrysemys picta. d, Clemmys guttata.

No. 3612, 60r, Panthera leo leo. No. 3613, 60r, German shepherd. No. 3614, 60r, Inia geoffrensis. No. 3615, 60r, Battus philenor, Odontoglossum hallii. No. 3616, 60r, Stegosaurus. No. 3617, 70r, Adult and juvenile Ursus maritimus. No. 3618, 70r, Sceloglaux albifacies, Hygrophoropsis aurantiaca. No. 3619, 70r, Aporrhais pesgallinae. No. 3620, 70r, Eretmochelys imbricata.

2016, May 23 Litho. Perf. 13¾
Sheets of 4, #a-d
3603-3611 A647 Set of 9 100.00 100.00
Souvenir Sheets
3612-3620 A647 Set of 9 75.00 75.00

New Year 2016 (Year of the Monkey) A648

No. 3621 — Monkey in tree with end of tail: a, At right. b, At top. c, Not visible. d, At bottom.
70r, Head of monkey.

2016, May 23 Litho. Perf. 13¼
3621 A648 22r Sheet of 4, #a-d 11.50 11.50
Souvenir Sheet
3622 A648 70r multi 9.25 9.25

A649

No. 3623, 20r — Freddie Mercury (1946-91), rock musician: a, Two images of Mercury, British flag in background. b, Two images of Mercury, lights in background. c, Mercury in yellow jacket. d, Mercury in black jacket.

No. 3624, 20r — Marilyn Monroe (1926-62), actress: a, Looking in mirror at right. b, As Valentine Cowgirl and Miss Cheesecake. c, Holding mandolin at left. d, With face partially covered with red scarf.

No. 3625, 20r — Princess Diana (1961-97): a, With son, Prince William. b, Holding Pakistani child at hospital. c, With Queen Elizabeth II. d, With husband, Prince Charles, and two sons, Princes William and Harry.

No. 3626, 20r — Louis Blériot (1872-1936): a, In cockpit of airplane. b, Standing to right of airplane. c, Standing to left of airplane. d, Head of Blériot, airplane in flight.

No. 3627, 20r — Yuri Gagarin (1934-68), first man in space: a, Earth and Vostok 1 rocket. b, Gagarin seated, wearing space suit. c, Gagarin wearing military uniform, rocket launch. d, Statue of Gagarin, Vostok 1 in space.

No. 3628, 22r — Lord Robert Baden-Powell (1857-1941), founder of Scouting movement: a, Pinning award on Scout. b, With coat of arms. c, With wife, Olave (1889-1977). d, With Scouts saluting.

No. 3629, 22r — Scenes from Operas by Wolfgang Amadeus Mozart (1756-91), composer: a, The Pretend Garden-Maid (two characters). b, The Impresario. c, Apollo et Hyacinthus. d, The Pretend Garden-Maid (four characters).

No. 3630, 22r — Queen Elizabeth II: a, In coronation coach, 1953. b, With family. c, With British Royal Guard. d, Waving in Throne Room.

No. 3631, 22r — Attack on Pearl Harbor, 75th anniv.: a, Mitsubishi A6M Zeros flying to left. b, Zeros flying to right. c, Zero, USS Nevada Type 91 torpedo. d, U.S. forces fighting attack.

No. 3632, 22r — 2016 Summer Olympics, Rio de Janeiro: a, Weight lifting. b, Diving. c, Track cycling. d, Fencing.

No. 3633, 60r, Mercury, diff. No. 3634, 60r, Monroe in Gentlemen Prefer Blondes. No. 3635, 60r, Princess Diana and family of Prince William. No. 3636, 60r, Blériot, diff. No. 3637, 60r, Gagarin, diff. No. 3638, 70r, Baden-Powell and Scouting flag. No. 3639, 70r, Scene from Apollo et Hyacinthus, diff. No. 3640, 70r, Queen Elizabeth II and Buckingham Palace. No. 3641, 70r, Zeros attacking Pearl Harbor, diff. No. 3642, 70r, Freestyle wrestling, winner's stand and trophy.

2016, May 23 Litho. Perf. 13¼
Sheets of 4, #a-d
3623-3632 A649 Set of 10 110.00 110.00
Souvenir Sheets
3633-3642 A649 Set of 10 85.00 85.00

Personalized Stamps — A650

2016, June 13 Litho. Perf. 13x13¼
English Country Name in Red, Maldivian Country Name in Deep Greenish Blue, Denomination in Bright Blue
3643 A650 10r multi 1.40 1.40

English Country Name in Black, Maldivian Country Name in Red, Denomination in Orange
3644 A650 10r multi 1.40 1.40

English Country Name in Bright Blue, Maldivian Country Name in Bright Blue, Denomination in Purple
3645 A650 10r multi 1.40 1.40

English Country Name in Dark Blue, Maldivian Country Name in Dark Blue, Denomination in Black Thinner, Sharper Letters
3646 A650 10r multi 1.40 1.40
Nos. 3643-3646 (4) 5.60 5.60

English Country Name in Dark Blue, Maldivian Country Name in Dark Blue, Denomination in Black Thicker, Less Sharp Letters And Photographs of Atolls

3647	A650	10r Alifu Alifu	1.40	1.40
a.		Souvenir sheet of 1, perf. 13¼	1.40	1.40
3648	A650	10r Alifu Dhaalu	1.40	1.40
a.		Souvenir sheet of 1, perf. 13¼	1.40	1.40
3649	A650	10r Baa	1.40	1.40
a.		Souvenir sheet of 1, perf. 13¼	1.40	1.40
3650	A650	10r Dhaalu	1.40	1.40
a.		Souvenir sheet of 1, perf. 13¼	1.40	1.40
3651	A650	10r Faafu	1.40	1.40
a.		Souvenir sheet of 1, perf. 13¼	1.40	1.40
3652	A650	10r Gaafu Alifu	1.40	1.40
a.		Souvenir sheet of 1, perf. 13¼	1.40	1.40
3653	A650	10r Gaafu Dhaalu	1.40	1.40
a.		Souvenir sheet of 1, perf. 13¼	1.40	1.40
3654	A650	10r Gnaviyani	1.40	1.40
a.		Souvenir sheet of 1, perf. 13¼	1.40	1.40
3655	A650	10r Haa Alifu	1.40	1.40
a.		Souvenir sheet of 1, perf. 13¼	1.40	1.40
3656	A650	10r Haa Dhaalu	1.40	1.40
a.		Souvenir sheet of 1, perf. 13¼	1.40	1.40
3657	A650	10r Kaafu	1.40	1.40
a.		Souvenir sheet of 1, perf. 13¼	1.40	1.40
3658	A650	10r Laamu	1.40	1.40
a.		Souvenir sheet of 1, perf. 13¼	1.40	1.40
3659	A650	10r Lhaviyani	1.40	1.40
a.		Souvenir sheet of 1, perf. 13¼	1.40	1.40
3660	A650	10r Meemu	1.40	1.40
a.		Souvenir sheet of 1, perf. 13¼	1.40	1.40
3661	A650	10r Noonu	1.40	1.40
a.		Souvenir sheet of 1, perf. 13¼	1.40	1.40
3662	A650	10r Raa	1.40	1.40
a.		Souvenir sheet of 1, perf. 13¼	1.40	1.40
3663	A650	10r Seenu	1.40	1.40
a.		Souvenir sheet of 1, perf. 13¼	1.40	1.40
3664	A650	10r Shaviyani	1.40	1.40
a.		Souvenir sheet of 1, perf. 13¼	1.40	1.40
3665	A650	10r Thaa	1.40	1.40
a.		Souvenir sheet of 1, perf. 13¼	1.40	1.40
3666	A650	10r Vaavu	1.40	1.40
a.		Souvenir sheet of 1, perf. 13¼	1.40	1.40
		Nos. 3647-3666 (20)	28.00	28.00

Stamps with photographs of atolls were only printed on the stamps with thicker letters.

Sports and Chess A651

No. 3667, 20r — 50th birthday of Wasim Akram, cricket player: a, With cricket bowling trophy. b, And Gaddafi Stadium, Lahore, Pakistan. c, And National Cricket Stadium, Karachi, Pakistan. d, Bowling and batting.

No. 3668, 20r — 75th birthday of Pete Rose, baseball player: a, Holding batting helmet. b, On ground, touching base. c, Batting and with raised fist. d, Batting, stadium in background.

No. 3669, 20r — Ice hockey players: a, Skater approaching goaltender. b, Aerial view of face-off. c, Ice level view of face-off. d, Goaltender, defenseman and two offensive players.

No. 3670, 20r — Chess masters: a, Fabiano Caruana. b, Hikaru Nakamura. c, Viswanathan Anand. d, Anish Giri.

No. 3671, 22r — Alfredo Di Stéfano (1926-2014), soccer player: a, Kicking ball and celebrating goal. b, With trophies. c, Holding soccer ball. d, Bicycle kicking ball.

No. 3672, 22r — Judokas: a, Tagir Khaybulaev. b, Judoka in blue robe with hand near LL corner. c, Both judokas with heads on mat. d, Mansur Isaev.

No. 3673, 22r — Rugby players: a, Alun-Wyn Jones. b, David Pocock. c, Michael Hooper. d, Greig Laidlaw.

No. 3674, 22r — 2018 World Cup Soccer Championships, Russia: a, Vasili Berezutski and World Cup trophy. b, Dmitri Kombarov and Spartak Stadium, Moscow. c, Roman Eremenko and Mordovia Arena, Saransk. d, World Cup trophy and white, blue and red streamer.

No. 3675, 22r — 2016 Winter Olympics, Sochi, Russia: a, Matthias Mayer. b, Russian four-man bobsled team. c, Tatiana Volosozhar and Maxim Trankov. d, Joss Christensen.

No. 3676, 60r, Akram, diff. No. 3677. 60r, Rose, diff. No. 3678. 60r, Skater approaching goaltender, diff. No. 3679, 60r, Chess masters Magnus Carlsen and Vladimir Kramnik. No. 3680, 70r, Di Stéfano, diff. No. 3681, 70r, Judoka Arsen Galstyan. No. 3682, 70r, Rugby player Dan Carter. No. 3683, 70r, Hands holding World Cup trophy. No. 3684, 70r, Viktor Ahn, speed skater.

2016, July 4 Litho. Perf. 13¼
Sheets of 4, #a-d
3667-3675 A651 Set of 9 100.00 100.00
Souvenir Sheets
3676-3684 A651 Set of 9 77.50 77.50

2016 U.S. Presidential Election — A652

No. 3685: a, Candidates Donald Trump and Hillary Clinton. b, Trump. c, Statue of Liberty. d, Pres. Bill Clinton and wife, Hillary. 60r, Pres. Barack Obama, vert.

2016, July 4 Litho. Perf. 12½x12¾
3685 A652 20r Sheet of 4, #a-d 10.50 10.50

MALDIVE ISLANDS

Souvenir Sheet
Perf. 12

3686 A652 60r multi 8.00 8.00

2016 World Stamp Show, New York. No. 3686 contains one 49x63mm stamp.

Fauna — A653

No. 3687, 20r — Bears: a, Ursus thibetanus. b, Helarctos malayanus. c, Melursus ursinus. d, Ursus maritimus.

No. 3688, 20r — Cats: a, American Curl. b, Siamese. c, Singapura. d, Sphynx.

No. 3689, 20r — Birds of prey: a, Buteo buteo. b, Pandion haliaetus. c, Falco subbuteo. d, Circus macrourus.

No. 3690, 20r — Butterflies and minerals: a, Phoebis philea and orpiment. b, Zeuxidia amethystus and heterosite. c, Rothschildia aurota and agate. d, Morpho didius and labradorite.

No. 3691, 20r — Endangered species: a, Ara glaucogularis. b, Ailuropoda melanoleuca. c, Tapirus indicus. d, Pongo abelii.

No. 3692, 20r — Ailuropoda melanoleuca: a, Eating bamboo. b, With chin on paw. c, In water. d, Two pandas.

No. 3693, 20r — Wolves: a, Canis lupus arctos. b, Canis rufus. c, Canis lupus signatus. d, Canis lupus tundrarum.

No. 3694, 20r — Fish: a, Pseudanthias squamipinnis. b, Balistoides conspicillum. c, Rhinecanthus aculeatus. d, Balistoides viridescens.

No. 3695, 22r — Monitor lizards: a, Varanus bengalensis. b, Varanus beccarii. c, Varanus acanthurus. d, Varanus komodoensis.

No. 3696, 22r — Rare animals: a, Prolemur simus. b, Macroscelidea. c, Rhinopithecus avunculus. d, Lasiorhinus krefftii.

No. 3697, 60r, Tremarctos ornatus. No. 3698, 60r, Egyptian Mau cat. No. 3699, 60r, Circus aeruginosus. No. 3700, 60r, Marpesia berania and Böttinger marble. No. 3701, 60r, Cheilinus undulatus. No. 3702, 70r, Ailuropoda melanoleuca, diff. No. 3703, 70r, Canis lupus beothucus. No. 3704, 70r, Pygoplites diacanthus. No. 3705, 70r, Varanus salvadorii. No. 3706, 70r, Panthera uncia.

2016, July 20 Litho. Perf. 13¼
Sheets of 4, #a-d

3687-3696 A653 Set of 10 110.00 110.00

Souvenir Sheets

3697-3706 A653 Set of 10 85.00 85.00

A654

No. 3707, 20r — Royal Mail, 500th anniv.: a, Illustration of Post Office by Augustus Pudin, Sr. and Thomas Rowlandson. b, Mr. Bean in pillar box. c, Great Britain #1 (Penny Black). d, 1936 Austin 7 Type AVH Royal Mail van.

No. 3708, 20r — High-speed trains: a, CRH3. b, FLIRT. c, TGV. d, ICE.

No. 3709, 20r — Fire engines: a, Buffalo, Fire Engine 1. b, 1961 International-Bruco pumper. c, 1968 Ford C/Pierce 54-foot Squirt. d, 2004 Spartan Evolution.

No. 3710, 20r — Rescue vehicles: a, Westland WS-61 Sea King helicopter. b, AgustaWestland AW139 helicopter. c, Tamar-class lifeboat. d, NATO Submarine rescue system.

No. 3711, 20r — Christopher Columbus (1451-1506), explorer: a, Monument to Columbus and Queen Isabella, Madrid. b, The Niña. c, The Pinta. d, Columbus and compass rose.

No. 3712, 20r — Charles Darwin (1809-82), naturalist, and: a, Diplodocus. b, Aquilops. c, Diceratops. d, Microraptor.

No. 3713, 22r — Thomas Edison (1847-1931), inventor: a, Holding test tube. b, With phonograph. c, With factory. d, Holding lightbulb.

No. 3714, 22r — Albert Einstein (1879-1955), physicist, and: a, Lightbulb. b, Diagram of object affected by bending of space-time. c, Gear. d, Pipe.

No. 3715, 22r — Valentina Tereshkova, first woman in space: a, Wearing space helmet, head at left. b, In training. c, With Nikita Khrushchev. d, Wearing space helmet, head at right.

No. 3716, 60r, Portrait of Brian Tuke, first master of British posts, by Hans Holbein. No. 3717, 60r, British InterCity 125 train. No. 3718, 60r, 1967 ZIL 131 fire engine. No. 3719, 60r, Westland WS-61 Sea King helicopter, diff. No. 3720, 70r, Columbus and the Santa Maria. No. 3721, 70r, Darwin and Tyrannosaurus rex. No. 3722, 70r, Edison pouring liquids. No. 3723, 70r, Einstein, diff. No. 3724, 70r, Tereshkova and Vostok 6.

2016, Sept. 8 Litho. Perf. 13¼
Sheets of 4, #a-d

3707-3715 A654 Set of 9 100.00 100.00

Souvenir Sheets

3716-3724 A654 Set of 9 80.00 80.00

Souvenir Sheet

Maharaja Agrasen, Legendary King of Agroha — A655

2016, Sept. 8 Litho. Perf.
3725 A655 70r multi 9.25 9.25

A656

No. 3726, 20r — Prince (1958-2016), rock musician: a, On motorcycle. b, Behind microphone. c, With guitar. d, Close-up of face.

No. 3727, 20r — International Year of Pulses: a, José Graziano da Silva, Director General of Food and Agricultural Organization of the United Nations. b, Bowl of beans. c, Spoon with peas. d, Indian school children celebrating International Year of Pulses.

No. 3728, 20r — International Covenant on Civil and Political Rights, 50th anniv.: a, Dr. Martin Luther King, Jr. (1929-68), Malcolm X (1925-65), U.S. civil rights leaders, Edmund Pettus Bridge, Selma, Alabama, and U.S. flag. b, Nelson Mandela (1818-2013), President of South Africa, and barbed wire. c, Mahatma Gandhi (1869-1948), Indian independence leader, and lotus flower. d, Malala Yousafzai, recipient of 2014 Nobel Peace Prize, and flag of Pakistan.

No. 3729, 20r — Musee d'Orsay, Paris, 50th anniv.: a, Noon: Rest from Work, by Vincent van Gogh. b, Arearea, by Paul Gauguin. c, The Dance Class, by Edgar Degas. d, Dance at the Moulin de la Galette, by Pierre-Auguste Renoir.

No. 3730, 20r — Princess Charlotte of Cambridge, 1st birthday: a, With great-grandmother, Queen Elizabeth II. b, With brother, Prince George. c, Pushing cart with blocks. d, On chair, rocking horse in background.

No. 3731, 22r — Wedding of Prince Rainier III of Monaco and Grace Kelly, 60th anniv.: a, Couple with Prince at left, Monaco shoreline in background. b, Couple with Prince at right, Monaco skyline in background. c, Couple with Prince at left, Monte Carlo Casino in background. d, Couple, Prince at left, Prince's Palace in background.

No. 3732, 20r — Concorde in commercial air service, 40th anniv.: a, Queen Elizabeth II, Prince Philip, sheikhs and Concorde G-BOAE. b, Concorde G-BOAB. c, Pope John Paul II (1920-2005) leaving Concorde in Zambia. d, Paul and Linda McCartney with their children and Concorde G-BOAD.

No. 3733, 22r — Battle of Gallipoli, cent.: a, Soldier behind sandbags, soldiers at ladder. b, German General Otto Liman von Sanders (1855-1929) and German soldiers in trench. c, British General Ian Standish Monteith Hamilton (1853-1947). d, Four soldiers.

No. 3734, 22r — Battle of Moscow, 75th anniv.: a, Soldiers and Soviet General Georgy Zhukov (1896-1974). b, Soldiers in winter. c, Soldiers in damaged building. d, Soldiers and German Field Marshal Fedor von Bock (1880-1945).

No. 3735, 22r — Sergei Prokofiev (1891-1953), composer: a, With scene from movie *Ivan the Terrible*. b, At piano. c, With scene from his ballet *Romeo and Juliet*. d, With wolf and David Bowie (1947-2016), rock musician and narrator of *Peter and the Wolf*.

No. 3736, 60r, Prince holding guitar. No. 3737, 60r, Hand sorting beans, seedling. No. 3738, 60r, 14th Dalai Lama, recipient of 1989 Nobel Peace Prize. No. 3739, 60r, Sculpture, Hercules the Archer, by Antoine Bourdelle, and Portrait of Victor Laloux (1850-1937), architect. No. 3740, 60r, Princess Charlotte and her parents, the Duke and Duchess of Cambridge. No. 3741, 70r, Princess Grace and Prince Rainier III, diff. No. 3742, 70r, Concorde taking off. No. 3743, 70r, Soldiers at Battle of Gallipoli, diff. No. 3744, 70r, Soldiers at Battle of Moscow, diff. No. 3745, 70r, Prokofiev and scene from movie *Alexander Nevsky*.

2016, Sept. 8 Litho. Perf. 13¼
Sheets of 4, #a-d

3726-3735 A656 Set of 10 110.00 110.00

Souvenir Sheets

3736-3745 A656 Set of 10 87.50 87.50

Art — A657

No. 3746, 20r — Islamic art: a, Sad'i and the Youth of Kashgar, by Kamal ud-Din Behzad. b, Decorative panel from the mausoleum of Tuman Aka. c, Shah Abbas II of Persia and the Mughal Ambassador. d, Scene of Bahram Gur killing wolf from the Great Mongol Shahnameh.

No. 3747, 20r — Renaissance art: a, The Meeting of Leo I and Attila the Hun, by Raphael. b, The Birth of Venus, by Sandro Botticelli. c, The Last Judgment, by Michelangelo. d, The Rape of Europa, by Titian.

No. 3748, 20r — Rococo art: a, Declaration of Love, by Jean François de Troy. b, The Musical Contest, by Jean-Honoré Fragonard. c, The Shepherdess, by Fragonard. d, The Love Lesson, by Antoine Watteau.

No. 3749, 20r — Post-impressionist art: a, Irises, by Vincent van Gogh. b, The Contonary of Independence, by Henri Rousseau. c, At the Moulin-Rouge, by Henri de Toulouse-Lautrec. d, Still Life with a Curtain, by Paul Cézanne.

No. 3750, 20r — Surrealist art: a, Golconda, by René Magritte. b, Person Throwing a Stone at a Bird, by Joan Miró. c, The Red Tower, by Giorgio di Chirico. d, The Temptation of Saint Anthony, by Max Ernst.

No. 3751, 22r — Ancient Egyptian art: a, Queen Nefertiti playing a game. b, Bennu bird from an Egyptian papyrus. c, Marsh hunting scene from Nebamun tomb. d, Chariot scene from tomb of Tutankhamun.

No. 3752, 22r — Baroque art: a, Tancred and Erminia, by Nicolas Poussin. b, King Solomon, by Peter Paul Rubens. c, The Abduction of Europa, by Rembrandt. d, Supper at Emmaus, by Caravaggio.

No. 3753, 22r — Dutch Golden Age art: a, Still Life, by Willem Claeszoon Heda. b, Winter Landscape with Skaters, by Hendrick Avercamp. c, A Country House on the Vliet near Delft, by Jan van der Heyden. d, Beware of Luxury, by Jan Havickszoon Steen.

No. 3754, 22r — Impressionist art: a, Argenteuil, by Claude Monet. b, Hay Harvest at Eragny, by Camille Pissarro. c, Boating, by Edouard Manet. d, At the Races, by Edgar Degas.

No. 3755, 22r — Cubist art: a, Cubist Landscape, by Albert Gleizes. b, Fantômas, by Juan Gris. c, Mandolin and Guitar, by Pablo Picasso. d, The City, by Fernand Léger.

No. 3756, 60r, Scene from the Khamsa of Nizami manuscript, vert. No. 3757, 60r, Mona Lisa, by Leonardo da Vinci, vert. No. 3758, 60r, The Breakfast, by François Boucher, vert. No. 3759, 60r, Nafea faa ipoipo (When Will You Marry?), by Paul Gauguin, vert. No. 3760, 60r, Apparatus and Hand, by Salvador Dalí, vert. No. 3761, 70r, Wall painting of Nefertari, vert. No. 3762, 70r, David and Goliath, by Orazio Gentileschi, vert. No. 3763, 70r, The Milkmaid, by Johannes Vermeer, vert. No. 3764, 70r, Woman with a Pearl Necklace in a Loge, by Mary Cassatt, vert. No. 3765, 70r, Man with a Pipe, by Jean Metzinger, vert.

2016, Sept. 8 Litho. Perf. 13¼
Sheets of 4, #a-d

3746-3755 A657 Set of 10 110.00 110.00

Souvenir Sheets

3756-3765 A657 Set of 10 87.50 87.50

Nos. 3756-3765 each contain one 33x45mm stamp.

Miniature Sheets

Islands — A658

Underwater Life — A659

Tourist Attractions — A660

No. 3766: a, Palm tree and beach. b, Island in distance (no clouds). c, Island and boat. d, People, chaise lounges and umbrellas on beach. e, Airplane near small island. f, Aerial view of small island. g, Palm trees in garden. h, Bent palm tree on sand island. i, Aerial view of small group of islands. j, Island in distance (with clouds).

No. 3767: a, Divers and whale shark. b, Fish and coral reef. c, Fish and sea anemone. d, Underside of ray. e, Fish and turtle. f, Moray eel and coral. g, Coral reef. h, Dolphins. I, Spotted eagle ray. j, Octopus.

No. 3768: a, Inscriptions: a, Islamic Center. b, Convention Centre. c, Jumhooree Maidhan. d, National Museum. e, Hukuru Miskiy. f, Hulhudhaan Bageecha. g, Tsunami Bina. h, Utheemu Ganduvaru. i, Rasfannu Beach. j, Izzudheen Faalan.

2016, Oct. 17 Litho. Perf. 13¼

3766 A658 5r Sheet of 10, #a-j 6.75 6.75
3767 A659 5r Sheet of 10, #a-j 6.75 6.75
3768 A660 5r Sheet of 10, #a-j 6.75 6.75
  Nos. 3766-3768 (3) 20.25 20.25

Nos. 3766-3768 were also printed with a vertical column of 5 labels between the two vertical columns of stamps.

Wildlife — A661

Designs: No. 3769, 15r, Crow. No. 3770, 15r, Whale shark. No. 3771, 15r, Hermit crab.

2016, Oct. 17 Litho. Perf. 13x13¼
3769-3771 A661 Set of 3 6.00 6.00

MALDIVE ISLANDS

Marine Life — A662

No. 3772, 20r — Dolphins: a, Stenella longirostris. b, Stenella coeruleoalba. c, Tursiops truncatus. d, Lagenorhynchus obscurus.
No. 3773, 20r — Manta rays: a, Manta alfredi. b, Manta birostris and Manta alfredi, ray showing underside at left. c, Manta birostris. d, Manta birostris and Manta alfredi, ray showing underside at right.
No. 3774, 20r — Moray eels: a, Siderea grisea. b, Gymnothorax undulatus. c, Gymnothorax favagineus. d, Gymnothorax breedeni.
No. 3775, 20r — Butterflyfish: a, Chaetodon kleinii. b, Chaetodon ephippium. c, Chaetodon collare. d, Chaetodon citrinellus.
No. 3776, 20r — Corals: a, Platygyra daedalea. b, Tubastraea coccinea. c, Acropora cervicornis. d, Capnella thyrsoidea.
No. 3777, 22r — Whales: a, Physeter macrocephalus. b, Globicephala macrorhynchus. c, Balaenoptera brydei. d, Kogia sima.
No. 3778, 22r — Sharks: a, Carcharhinus longimanus facing left. b, Sphyrna mokarran. c, Galeocerdo cuvier. d, Carcharhinus longimanus facing right.
No. 3779, 22r — Triggerfish: a, Rhinecanthus rectangulus. b, Balistapus undulatus. c, Xanthichthys auromarginatus. d, Balistoides conspicillum.
No. 3780, 22r — Tunas: a, Thunnus maccoyii. b, Thunnus thynnus. c, Katsuwonus pelamis. d, Thunnus albacares.
No. 3781, 22r — Turtles: a, Dermochelys coriacea. b, Graptemys barbouri. c, Clemmys guttata. d, Caretta caretta.
No. 3782, 60r, Lagenodelphis hosei. No. 3783, 60r, Manta alfredi, diff. No. 3784, 60r, Gymnothorax javanicus. No. 3785, 60r, Chaetodon mitratus. No. 3786, 60r, Annella mollis. No. 3787, 70r, Balaenoptera musculus. No. 3788, 70r, Galeocerdo cuvier, diff. No. 3789, 70r, Rhinecanthus aculeatus. No. 3790, 70r, Thunnus alalunga. No. 3791, 70r, Chelus fimbriata.

2016, Nov. 17   Litho.   Perf. 13¼
Sheets of 4, #a-d
3772-3781 A662   Set of 10   110.00   110.00
Souvenir Sheets
3782-3791   Set of 10   85.00   85.00
Nos. 3782-3791 each contain one 48x33mm stamp.

Handicrafts — A663

No. 3792: a, Lacquer work vase. b, Raabandhi. c, Dhoani. d, Lacquer work container with lid.

2016, Dec. 26   Litho.   Perf. 13¼
3792 A663 15r Sheet of 4, #a-d   8.00   8.00

Fishermen's Day — A664

No. 3793: a, Bait fish about to be chummed. b, Bait in the net. c, Net fishing. d, Pole and line fishing.

2016, Dec. 26   Litho.   Perf. 13¼
3793 A664 15r Sheet of 4, #a-d   8.00   8.00

Dory — A665

Marlin — A666

Nemo — A667

Bailey — A668

Hank — A669

Destiny — A670

2016, Dec. 28   Litho.   Die Cut
Self-Adhesive
3794   Block of 6   16.50
 a. A665 20r multi   2.75   2.75
 b. A666 20r multi   2.75   2.75
 c. A667 20r multi   2.75   2.75
 d. A668 20r multi   2.75   2.75
 e. A669 20r multi   2.75   2.75
 f. A670 20r multi   2.75   2.75

Characters from animated movie Finding Dory.

A671

No. 3795, 20r — Commercial service of the Concorde, 40th anniv.: a, Two Concordes and airplane stairway truck. b, Concorde in flight with wheels partially deployed. c, Two Concordes in flight. d, Front view of Concorde.
No. 3796, 20r — William Boeing (1881-1956), aircraft manufacturer, and: a, Jet over New York City. b, Seaplane over city. c, Biplane with wheels. d, Biplane and jet.
No. 3797, 20r — Boston Light, 300th anniv.: a, Lighthouse and sailboat. b, Lighthouse and lamp. c, Lighthouse and fog signal cannon. d, Lighthouse and map of Boston Harbor.
No. 3798, 20r — Great Fire of London, 350th anniv.: a, Ye Deluge fire tanker. b, Drawing of firefighers using early pump fire engine to battle fire. c, St. Paul's Cathedral during Great Fire of London. d, Barrel with pumping mechanism, leather bucket.
No. 3799, 20r — 2016 Summer Paralympics, Rio de Janeiro: a, Athletics. b, Goalball. c, Weight lifting. d, Long jumper.
No. 3800, 22r — Bob Dylan, 2016 Nobel Literature laureate: a, Dylan wearing hat and Dylan playing guitar. b, Two images, "Bob Dylan" in white at left. c, Two images, "Bob Dylan" in white at right. d, Dylan wearing hat playing guitar.
No. 3801, 22r — Canonization of St. Teresa of Calcutta (1910-97): a, With other nuns and sick man. b, Holding baby. c, With three children. d, Spooning food into bowl.
No. 3802, 22r — Muhammad Ali (1942-2016), boxer: a, Fighting opponent. b, Shadow boxing. c, With punching bag. d, Stretching legs.
No. 3803, 22r — Spaceflight records: a, Yuri Gagarin (1934-68), first man in space, and Vostok 1. b, Alan B. Shepard, Jr. (1923-98), first American in space, and Freedom 7. c, Juno spacecraft, fastest man-made object. d, Bruce McCandless II (1937-2017) achieving first untethered space walk.
No. 3804, 22r — Battle of Verdun, cent.: a, Soldiers and trucks. b, Soldier in foreground aiming gun to left, soldiers and barbed wire in background. c, Soldier in foreground aiming gun to right. d, Soldiers firing machine gun.
No. 3805, 60r, Two Concordes in flight, diff. No. 3806, 60r, Boeing, Frederick Brant Rentschler (1887-1956), aircraft engine designer, and seaplane. No. 3807, 60r, Boston Light, diff. No. 3808, 60r, Hand-held squirt and water tank on wheels. No. 3809, 60r, Wheelchair rugby. No. 3810, 70r, Dylan singing. No. 3811, 70r, St. Teresa of Calcutta listening to man. No. 3812, 70r, Ali fighting Floyd Patterson (1935-2006). No. 3813, 70r, New Horizons, first spacecraft to explore Pluto. No. 3814, 70r, Nieuport airplane from Battle of Verdun.

2016, Dec. 28   Litho.   Perf. 13¼
Sheets of 4, #a-d
3795-3804 A671 Set of 10   110.00   110.00
Souvenir Sheets
3805-3814 A671 Set of 10   87.50   87.50

New Year 2017 (Year of the Rooster) A673

No. 3815 — Paintings of roosters by Qi Baishi (1863-1957): a, Large rooster facing left looking at ground. b, Small rooster facing left. c, Rooster and chicks. d, Large rooster facing left with head upright.
No. 3816, Rooster above Chinese text, by Qi Baishi.

2016, Dec. 28   Litho.   Perf. 13¼
3815 A672 22r Sheet of 4, #a-d   11.50   11.50
Souvenir Sheets
3816 A672 70r multi   9.25   9.25
3817 A673 70r multi   9.25   9.25

Flora, Fauna and Mushrooms — A674

No. 3818, 20r — Dugong dugon: a, Two facing left. b, One facing right. c, One facing left. d, Two facing right.
No. 3819, 20r — Doves: a, Treron phoenicoptera. b, Alectroenas sganzini. c, Streptopelia orientalis. d, Alectroenas pulcherrimus.
No. 3820, 20r — Moths and butterflies: a, Utetheisa pulchella. b, Delias eucharis. c, Racotis boarmiaria. d, Tirumala septentrionis.
No. 3821, 20r — Crabs and lobsters: a, Gecarcoidea natalis. b, Panulirus versicolor. c, Calcinus elegans. d, Birgus latro.
No. 3822, 20r — Flowers and trees: a, Plumeria apiculata. b, Ipomoea quamoclit. c, Jasminum sambac. d, Hibiscus tiliaceus.
No. 3823, 22r — Bats: a, Megaderma spasma. b, Pteropus giganteus. c, Leptonycteris yerbabuenae. d, Antrozous pallidus.
No. 3824, 22r — Ducks: a, Dendrocygna javanica. b, Aythya fuligula. c, Spatula querquedula. d, Spatula clypeata.
No. 3825, 22r — Owls and mushrooms: a, Bubo blakistoni, Morchella esculenta. b, Athene cunicularia, Psilocybe zapotecorum. c, Bubo africanus, Amanit phalloides. d, Bubo virginianus, Armillaria ostoyae.
No. 3826, 22r — Lizards: a, Calotes versicolor on leaf. b, Hemidactylus frenatus facing right. c, Hemidactylus frenatus facing left. d, Calotes versicolor on branch.
No. 3827, 22r — Spiders: a, Plexippus paykulli. b, Thomisus pugilis. c, Zosis geniculatus. d, Argiope anasuja.
No. 3828, 60r, Dugong dugon facing left, diff. No. 3829, 60r, Chalcophaps indica. No. 3830, 60r, Hydrillodes lentalis. No. 3831, 60r, Panulirus cygnus. No. 3832, 60r, Hibiscus rosa-sinensis. No. 3833, 70r, Rhinolophus ferrumequinum. No. 3834, 70r, Aythya nyroca. No. 3835, 70r, Strix nebulosa, Agaricus bitorquis. No. 3836, 70r, Calotes versicolor, diff. No. 3837, 70r, Thelacantha brevispina.

2017, Mar. 16   Litho.   Perf. 13¼
Sheets of 4, #a-d
3818-3827 A674 Set of 10   110.00   110.00
Souvenir Sheets
3828-3837 A674 Set of 10   85.00   85.00
Nos. 3828-3837 each contain one 48x33mm stamp.

A675

No. 3838, 20r — Sled dogs: a, Greenland dog. b, Samoyed. c, Alaskan malamute. d, Canadian Eskimo dog.
No. 3839, 20r — Horse and horse-drawn: a, Barouche. b, Stagecoach. c, Sulky. d, Hearse.
No. 3840, 20r — Steam trains: a, South Australian Railways 520 Class 4-8-4 No. 523. b, Pacific Steam Club locomotive 231 G 558. c, Union Pacific 844. d, London North Eastern Railway Class A4 4468 Mallard.
No. 3841, 20r — Motorcycles: a, Triumph TR6 Trophy. b, Harley-Davidson Model KH 888 CC flathead. c, MV Agusta Brutale 800. d, Moto Guzzi California 1400.
No. 3842, 20r — 2016 Nobel laureates: a, Chemistry laureate Jean-Pierre Sauvage. b, Physiology or Medicine laureate Yoshinori

MALDIVE ISLANDS

Ohsumi. c, Peace laureate Juan Manuel Santos. d, Economics laureate Bengt Holmström.

No. 3843, 22r — Automobiles, 130th anniv.: a, Benz Patent Motor Car. b, Carl Benz (1844-1929), automotive engineer, and Mercedes-Benz Cla. c, Mercedes-Simplex 60 HP Speedster Tribute. d, Mercedes-Benz F125 concept car.

No. 3844, 22r — Fire fighting vehicles: a, SPM fire truck. b, Cadillac Sedan fire car. c, Morris Magirus Tower Ladder fire engine. d, Lac Saint-François, Quebec, HME fire truck.

No. 3845, 22r — Special transport: a, Russian Army quad vehicle. b, Truck carrying wind turbine blade. c, Dragon Dream airship. d, Sikorsky CH-54 Tarhe helicopter.

No. 3846, 22r — First flight of the Hindenburg, 80th anniv.: a, Hindenburg disaster. b, Hindenburg airship and Paul von Hindenburg (1847-1934), President of Germany. c, Ernst A. Lehmann (1886-1937), Zeppelin captain. d, Cameramen filming Hindenburg disaster.

No. 3847, 22r — Shenzhou 11 linkup with Tiangong 2: a, Astronaut Jing Haipeng. b, Two astronauts return to Earth. c, Xi Jinping, President of People's Republic of China. d, Astronaut Chen Dong.

No. 3848, 60r, Siberian huskies. No. 3849, 60r, Horse and barouche, diff. No. 3850, 60r, West Country Class No. 34007 Wadebridge locomotive. No. 3851, 60r, BMW S1000RR motorcycle. No. 3852, 60r, Physics Nobel laureate David J. Thouless. No. 3853, 70r, Benz and business partner Max Rose in automobile. No. 3854, 70r, Rosenbauer Panther fire truck. No. 3855, 70r, Thomas Pesquet, astronaut, Soyuz TM-31 and International Space Station. No. 3856, 70r, Paul von Hindenburg and Hindenburg airship, diff. No. 3857, Jing Haipeng, diff.

2017, Mar. 16   Litho.   Perf. 13¼
Sheets of 4, #a-d

3838-3847 A675 Set of 10   110.00 110.00

Souvenir Sheets

3848-3857 A675 Set of 10   85.00 85.00

A676

No. 3858, 20r — Ludwig van Beethoven (1770-1827), composer, and: a, Horse-drawn carriage. b, Signature and city skyline. c, Performance in front of women. d, Performance in front of men.

No. 3859, 20r — Charlie Chaplin (1889-1977), film actor, in scene from: a, Sunnyside, 1919. b, The Circus, 1928. c, The Gold Rush, 1925. d, The Adventurer, 1917.

No. 3860, 20r — Ferdinand von Zeppelin (1838-1917), airship inventor: a, Zeppelin, automobile, women, airship. b, Zeppelin and airship. c, Zeppelin LZ-127 and Riparia riparia. d, Zeppelin LZ-127.

No. 3861, 20r — Valentina Tereshkova, first woman in space, and: a, Vostok 6 in orbit. b, Neil Armstrong (1930-2012), first man on Moon. c, Window of Vostok 6. d, Women's World Award, Valentina Tereshkova Cultural and Educational Center, Yaroslavl, Russia.

No. 3862, 20r — Paintings by Ivan Aivazovsky (1817-1900): a, The Tempest, 1851, and Self-portrait, 1874. b, View of Constantinople and the Bosporus, 1856. c, Evening in Cairo, 1870. d, Brig Mercury Attacked by Two Turkish Ships, 1892.

No. 3863, 22r — Battle of Stalingrad, 75th anniv.: a, Friedrich Paulus (1890-1957), German general. b, Ruins of Stalingrad. c, Soviet Army soldiers. d, Georgy Zhukov (1896-1974), Soviet general.

No. 3864, 22r — Princess Diana (1961-97), with: a, Young Prince Harry. b, Young Prince William. c, Prince Harry as adult and child. d, Prince William as adult and child.

No. 3865, 22r — Disappearance of Amelia Earhart, 80th anniv.: a, Earhart (1897-1937) receiving medal from Pres. Herbert Hoover (1874-1964). b, Earhart's Lockheed Vega 5b. c, Earhart and Avro 594 Avian III. d, Earhart and Lockheed Model 10 Electra.

No. 3866, 22r — Pres. John F. Kennedy (1917-63), with: a, Marilyn Monroe (1926-62), actress. b, PT-109, and medals. c, White House and wife, Jacqueline (1929-94). d, Presidential seal and Apollo 11 astronaut on Moon.

No. 3867, 22r — Painting details by Gustav Klimt (1862-1918): a, The Tree of Life, 1905. b, Portrait of Adele Bloch-Bauer I, 1907. c, Judith and the Head of Holofernes, 1901. d, Fulfillment, 1905-09.

No. 3868, 60r, Beethoven and signature. No. 3869, 60r, Chaplin in Limelight, 1952. No. 3870, 60r, Zeppelin and airships. No. 3871, 60r, Tereshkova and medal. No. 3872, 60r, The Ninth Wave, 1850, by Aivazovsky. No. 3873, 70r, Soviet soldiers crossing Volga River in Battle of Stalingrad. No. 3874, 70r, Princess Diana in wedding dress. No. 3875, 70r, Earhart in airplane cockpit. No. 3876, 70r, Pres. Kennedy giving last speech. No. 3877, 70r, The Kiss, by Klimt.

2017, Mar. 23   Litho.   Perf. 13¼
Sheets of 4, #a-d

3858-3867 A676 Set of 10   110.00 110.00

Souvenir Sheets

3868-3877 A676 Set of 10   85.00 85.00

Birds and Prehistoric Animals — A677

No. 3878, 20r — Owls: a, Strix varia. b, Ptilopsis leucotis. c, Tyto novaehollandiae melvillensis. d, Tyto alba.

No. 3879, 20r — Hornbills: a, Aceros undulatus. b, Rhinoplax vigil. c, Buceros rhinoceros. d, Bucorvus leadbeateri.

No. 3880, 20r — Indigobirds: a, Vidua funerea. b, Vidua camerunensis. c, Vidua wilsoni. d, Vidua chalybeata.

No. 3881, 20r — Sea birds: a, Pelecanus occidentalis. b, Morus bassanus. c, Fratercula arctica. d, Eudyptes chrysocome.

No. 3882, 20r — Flying dinosaurs: a, Dimorphodon macronyx. b, Pteranodon longiceps. c, Dsungaripterus weii. d, Nemicolopterus crypticus.

No. 3883, 22r — Parrots: a, Eolophus roseicapilla. b, Orthopsittica manilatus. c, Lophochroa leadbeateri. d, Cacatua galerita.

No. 3884, 22r — Birds of prey: a, Falco tinnunculus. b, Sarcoramphus papa. c, Milvus milvus. d, Falco subbuteo.

No. 3885, 22r — Kingfishers: a, Alcedo cristata. b, Ceryle rudis. c, Halcyon senegalensis. d, Alcedo atthis.

No. 3886, 22r — Dinosaurs: a, Parasaurolophus walkeri. b, Sinornithosaurus millenii. c, Dryosaurus altus. d, Dilophosaurus wetherilli.

No. 3887, 22r — Prehistoric water animals: a, Mesosaurus. b, Archelon. c, Cryptoclidus. d, Dunkleosteus terrelli.

No. 3888, 60r, Bubo scandiacus. No. 3889, 60r, Aceros cassidix. No. 3890, 60r, Vidua wilsoni, diff. No. 3891, 60r, Spheniscus demersus. No. 3892, 60r, Pterodactylus antiquus. No. 3893, 70r, Trichoglossus ornatus. No. 3894, 70r, Elanus leucurus. No. 3895, 70r, Corythornis cristatus. No. 3896, 70r, Chasmosaurus russelli. No. 3897, 70r, Elasmosaurus platyurus.

2017, May 17   Litho.   Perf. 13¼
Sheets of 4, #a-d

3878-3887 A677 Set of 10   110.00 110.00

Souvenir Sheets

3888-3897 A677 Set of 10   85.00 85.00

Paintings A678

No. 3898, 20r — Paintings by Berthe Morisot (1841-95): a, Hanging the Laundry Out to Dry, 1875. b, The Artist's Daughter Julie with Her Nanny, 1884. c, Eugène Manet on the Isle of Wight, 1875. d, The Basket Chair, 1882.

No. 3899, 20r — Paintings by Claude Monet (1840-1926): a, Woman with a Parasol, 1875. b, Impression, Sunrise, 1872. c, In the Garden, 1895. d, Agapanthus, 1914-26.

No. 3900, 20r — Paintings by Henri Matisse (1869-1954): a, Self-portrait, 1918. b, The Conversation, 1908-12. c, Harmony in Red (The Red Room), 1908. d, The Goldfish, 1912.

No. 3901, 20r — Paintings by Paul Signac (1863-1935): a, Evening Calm, Concarneau, Opus 220 (Allegro Maestoso), 1891. b, Place des Lices, St. Tropez, 1893. c, Golfe-Juan, 1896. d, The Port of Saint-Tropez, 1901-02.

No. 3902, 20r — Paintings by Ivan Aivazovsky (1817-1900): a, Portrait of Count Mikhail Loris-Melikov, 1888. b, View of Leander's Tower in Constantinople, 1848. c, Brig Mercury Attacked by Two Turkish Ships, 1892. d, Battle of Cesme at Night, 1848.

No. 3903, 22r — Paintings by Mary Cassatt (1844-1926): a, The Boating Party, 1893-94. b, Mother and Child, 1890. c, Lilacs in a Window, 1879. d, Children in the Garden (the Nurse), 1878.

No. 3904, 22r — Paintings by Vincent van Gogh (1853-90): a, Self-portrait with Bandaged Ear and Pipe, 1889. b, Sunflowers, 1887. c, Shoes, 1888. d, The Sower (after Millet), 1888.

No. 3905, 22r — Paintings by Alfred Sisley (1839-99): a, Bridge at Hampton Court, 1874. b, Small Meadows in Spring, c. 1881. c, Rest Along the Stream, Edge of the Wood, 1878. d, A Path at Les Sablons, 1883.

No. 3906, 22r — Paintings by Edouard Manet (1832-83): a, Boating, 1874. b, The Balcony, 1868-69. c, Music in the Tuileries, 1862. d, The Grand Canal of Venice (Blue Venice), 1875.

No. 3907, 22r — Paintings by Georges-Pierre Seurat (1859-91): a, Farm Women at Work, 1882-83. b, The Channel of Gravelines, Petit Fort Philippe, 1890. c, Le Bec du Hoc, Grandcamp, 1885. d, Gray Weather, Grande Jatte, 1886-88.

No. 3908, 60r — Paintings: a, The Cradle, by Morisot, 1872. No. 3909, 60r, Bridge Over a Pond of Water Lilies, by Monet, 1899. No. 3910, 60r, The Dream, by Matisse, 1940. No. 3911, 60r, Capo di Noli, by Signac, 1898. No. 3912, 60r, Golden Horn, by Aivazovsky, 1872. No. 3913, 70r, Young Girl at a Window, by Cassatt, 1883-84. No. 3914, 70r, Still Life: Vase With Fifteen Sunflowers, by van Gogh, 1889 (incorrect title on stamp). No. 3915, 70r, Bridge at Villeneuve-la-Garenne, by Sisley, 1872. No. 3916, 70r, Madame Manet, by Manet, 1880. No. 3917, 70r, The Circus, by Seurat, 1890-91.

2017, May 17   Litho.   Perf. 13¼
Sheets of 4, #a-d

3898-3907 A678 Set of 10   110.00 110.00

Souvenir Sheets

3908-3917 A678 Set of 10   85.00 85.00

A679

No. 3918, 20r — Andy Murray, tennis player: a, Wearing green shirt. b, Wearing orange shirt. c, Wearing white cap. d, With raised fist.

No. 3919, 20r — Table tennis players and flag of: a, Xu Xin, People's Republic of China. b, Dmitrij Ovtcharov, Germany. c, Fan Zhendong, People's Republic of China. d, Ma Long, People's Republic of China.

No. 3920, 20r — Chess players: a, Fabiano Caruana. b, Wesley So. c, Vladimir Kramnik. d, Maxime Vachier-Lagrave.

No. 3921, 22r — John Glenn (1921-2016), astronaut, and: a, Grumman F9F-2 Panther. b, F-86F nicknamed "MiG Mad Marine." c, Mercury space capsule. d, Space Shuttle Discovery.

No. 3922, 22r — Sir Vivian Richards, cricket player: a, Wearing red cap at left. b, Wearing black cap at left. c, Wearing no cap at left. d, Wearing red cap at left and holding cricket bat like a rifle.

No. 3923, 22r — Rugby players: a, Nine players. b, Ball carrier diving over attempted tackle. c, Tackler grabbing points of ball carrier. d, Three players.

No. 3924, 22r — Ice hockey players: a, Alexander Ovechkin. b, Bobby Orr. c, Sidney Crosby. d, Jaromir Jágr.

No. 3925, 22r — Pres. Franklin D. Roosevelt (1882-1945), with: a, Flag and Great Seal of the United States. b, His wife, Eleanor (1884-1962), and dog, Fala. c, Sir Winston Churchill (1874-1965), British Prime Minister. d, Flag of the United Nations.

No. 3926, 60r, Murray playing tennis. No. 3927, 60r, Ding Ning, flag of People's Republic of China. No. 3928, 60r, Magnus Carlsen playng chess. No. 3929, 60r, Glenn and NASA Distinguished Service medal. No. 3930, 70r, Richards, diff. No. 3931, 70r, Rugby scrum.

No. 3932, 70r, Wayne Gretzky playing ice hockey. No. 3933, Pres. Roosevelt at His Desk in the Oval Office, by Commander Edward M. Murray.

2017, May 17   Litho.   Perf. 13¼
Sheets of 4, #a-d

3918-3925 A679 Set of 8   87.50 87.50

Souvenir Sheets

3926-3933 A679 Set of 8   67.50 67.50

New Year 2018 (Year of the Dog) A680

No. 3934 — Pekingese dog with: a, Temple at UR. b, Temple at UL, ball at LR, c, Ball at LL, temple at UR. d, Temple at UL.

60r, Face of Pekingese dog, horiz.

Litho. With Foil Application
2017, May 17   Perf. 13¼

3934 A680 20r Sheet of 4, #a-d   10.50 10.50

Souvenir Sheet

3935 A680 60r multi   7.75 7.75

No. 3935 contains one 100x51mm stamp.

Science and Exploration — A681

No. 3936, 20r — Sir Alexander Fleming (1881-1955), microbiologist: a, Mycena haematopus. b, Fleming and microscope. c, Fleming and Penicillum conidia. d, Amanita muscaria.

No. 3937, 20r — Sir Ernest H. Shackleton (1874-1922), polar explorer: a, Shackleton and members of Trans-Antarctic Expedition. b, Shackleton and sled dog. c, Four members of Trans-Antarctic Expedition. d, Shackleton's ship, Endurance, sinking.

No. 3938, 20r — Jacques-Yves Cousteau (1910-97), oceanographer: a, SP-350 Denise. b, Cousteau in scuba gear. c, Cousteau holding boat rail. d, Anorep I submarine.

No. 3939, 20r — Alexander Graham Bell (1847-1922), inventor, and: a, 1876 telephone transmitter. b, 1881 metal detector. c, 1880 photophone of Bell and his assistant Charles Tainter. d, 1886-87 gramophone of Bell and Tainter.

No. 3940, 20r — Alfred Nobel (1833-96), inventor: a, Nobel medal and sticks of dynamite. b, Nobel and stick of dynamite. c, Nobel and model of nitroglycerin molecule. d, Explosion and stick of dynamite.

No. 3941, 20r — Space exploration: a, Apollo 15 astronaut James Irwin and Lunar Rover on Moon. b, Cassini-Huygens probe. c, Voyager 1. d, Spitzer Space Telescope.

No. 3942, 22r — Dmitri Mendeleev (1834-1907), chemist: a, Mendeleev and Periodic Table of Elements. b, Mendeleev and Russia #1906 and #3607. c, Mendeleev and students. d, Statue of Mendeleev and his home in St. Petersburg, Russia.

No. 3943, 22r — Wilbur Wright (1867-1912), co-inventor of airplane: a, Wright, commemorative medal, Wright Flyer II. b, Wright and woman in Wright Flyer. c, Wright Flyer II facing left. d, Wright Flyer facing right.

No. 3944, 22r — Ferdinand von Zeppelin (1838-1917), airship manufacturer: a, Zeppelin and airship in flight. b, Birds and LZ-130 Graf Zeppelin in flight. c, LZ-130 Graf Zeppelin over Egypt. d, Crewman on bridge of the Graf Zeppelin.

No. 3945, 22r — First Ferrari automobile, 90th anniv.: a, Driver in Ferrari 125 S facing right. b, Driver in Ferrari 125 S facing left. c, Driver in Ferrari 125 S with car number 128. d, Ferrari 125 S and manufacturer, Enzo Ferrari (1898-1988).

No. 3946, 60r, Fleming and Penicillum conidia, diff. No. 3947, 60r, Shackleton and Antarctica as seen from space. No. 3948, 60r, Cousteau and his ship, Calypso. No. 3949, 60r, Bell and 1875 telephone. No. 3950, 60r, Nobel and match lighting fuse on stick of dynamite. No. 3951, 60r, Spirit and Opportunity rovers on Mars. No. 3952, 70r, Mendeleev and Nobel medal he did not win. No. 3953, 70r, Wright and his brother Orville on Wright Flyer.

MALDIVE ISLANDS

No. 3954, 70r, Zeppelin and Graf Zeppelin in flight. No. 3955, 70r, Ferrari and Ferrari 125 S, diff.

2017, June 14　Litho.　Perf. 13¼
Sheets of 4, #a-d
3936-3945　A681　Set of 10　110.00　110.00
Souvenir Sheets
3946-3955　A681　Set of 10　85.00　85.00

Paintings
A682

No. 3956, 20r — Paintings of dogs: a, Laerte, the Greyhound, by Berthe Morisot (1841-95). b, Quail Hunting, by John Henry Dolph (1835-1903). c, Hunting Dogs with Dead Hare, by Gustave Courbet (1819-77). d, Itzcuintli Dog with Me, by Frida Kahlo (1907-54).

No. 3957, 20r — Paintings of birds of prey: a, Hawk Attacking Partridges and a Rabbit, by Jean-Baptiste Oudry (1686-1755). b, An Eagle, Swallow, Snipe and Finch in Flight, by Melchior d'Hondecoeter (1636-95). c, Eagles and Serpents Attacking Foxes, by Jan van Kessel the Elder (1626-79). d, Washington's Eagle, by John James Audubon (1785-1851).

No. 3958, 20r — Paintings of lighthouses: a, The Tower of Collioure in Moonrise, by Henri-Jean Guillaume Martin (1860-1943). b, Lighthouse Groix, by Paul Signac (1863-1935). c, The Lighthouse, by Charles Hoguet (1821-70). d, The Lighthouse at Two Lights, by Edward Hopper (1882-1967).

No. 3959, 20r — Paintings of trains: a, Train in the Snow, by Claude Monet (1840-1926). b, Speeding Train, by Ivo Pannaggi (1901-81). c, Super Power Steam Engine, by Arkady Alexandrovich Rylov (1870-1939). d, Compartment C Car, by Hopper.

No. 3960, 20r — Paintings of tall ships: a, Battle of Chios on 24 June, 1770, by Ivan Aivazovsky (1817-1900). b, The Capture of the Royal Prince, by William van de Velde II (1633-1707). c, Connecticut Shore Winter, by John Henry Twachtman (1853-1902). d, Cale d'Embarquement sur la Meuse à Rotterdam, by Eugène Boudin (1824-98).

No. 3961, 22r — Paintings of cats: a, Puss Napping, by George Baxter (1804-67). b, Early Irish Indian, by Louis Wain (1860-1939). c, Julie Manet with Cat, by Pierre-Auguste Renoir (1841-1919). d, Churning Butter, by Jean-François Millet (1814-75).

No. 3962, 22r — Paintings of horses: a, The Start of the Race of the Riderless Horses, by Horace Vernet (1789-1863). b, Arab Saddling His Horse, by Eugène Delacroix (1798-1863). c, Napoleon Crossing the Alps, by Jacques-Louis David (1748-1825). d, The Tower of Blue Horses, by Franz Marc (1880-1916).

No. 3963, 22r — Paintings of owls: a, Snowy Owl, by Audubon. b, An Owl's Lunch, by George William Sartorius (1759-1828). c, Bird Concert with Owl, by d'Hondecoeter. d, Mottled Owl, by Audubon.

No. 3964, 22r — Paintings of flowers: a, Flowers in a Vase, by Renoir. b, Flowers in a Crystal Vase, by Edouard Manet (1832-83). c, Irises, by Vincent van Gogh (1853-90). d, Orchids and Hummingbird, by Martin Johnson Heade (1819-1904).

No. 3965, 22r — Paintings of mushrooms: a, Gnome House, by Fritz Baumgarten (1883-1966). b, Illustration from *The Country Diary of and Edwardian Lady*, by Edith Blackwell Holden (1871-1920). c, Mushrooms, by William Aiken Walker (1839-1921). d, Ex Libris, by Gustaaf van de Wall Perné (1877-1911).

No. 3966, 60r, Tama, the Japanese Dog, by Manet. No. 3967, 60r, Peregrine Falcon, by Audubon. No. 3968, 60r, Highland Light, by Charles Webster Hawthorne (1872-1930). No. 3969, 60r, Bridges Across the Seine at Asnieres, by van Gogh. No. 3970, 60r, The Battle of Navarino, by Aivazovsky. No. 3971, 70r, Gabrielle Arnault as a Child, by Louis-Léopold Boilly (1761-1845). No. 3972, 70r, A Lion Attacking a Horse, by George Stubbs (1724-1806). No. 3973, 70r, The Little Owl, by Albrecht Dürer (1471-1528). No. 3974, 70r, Vase with Viscaria, by van Gogh. No. 3975, 70r, Three Red Mushrooms, by Arlo Zonneveld (1905-41).

2017, June 21　Litho.　Perf. 13¼
Sheets of 4, #a-d
3956-3965　A682　Set of 10　110.00　110.00
Souvenir Sheets
3966-3975　A682　Set of 10　85.00　85.00

Miniature Sheet

Bandung 2017 World Stamp
Exhibition, Bandung,
Indonesia — A683

No. 3976 — Colors of Siamese fighting fish: a, Dark blue and red. b, Light blue and orange. c, Red, blue and orange. d, Red.

2017, Sept. 12　Litho.　Perf. 13¼
3976　A683　22r Sheet of 4, #a-d　　11.50　11.50

Souvenir Sheet

Ursus
Arctos
Catching
Fish
A684

2017, Sept. 12　Litho.　Perf. 13¼
3977　A684　70r multi　9.00　9.00

A685

No. 3978, 20r — Ludwig van Beethoven (1770-1827), composer: a, With musical score on scroll. b, Holding pen, organ in background. c, With women and piano. d, Holding musical score.

No. 3979, 20r — 35th birthday of Prince William of Wales: a, With son, Prince George. b, Wearing military uniforms. c, With wife and children. d, As infant, with mother, Princess Diana.

No. 3980, 20r — Launch of dog, Laika, into space, 60th anniv.: a, Laika confined in space capsule. b, Laika being weighed by technician, Sputnik 2. c, Equipment strapped on Laika, Sputnik 2. d, Statue of Laika, Moscow, solar system.

No. 3981, 20r — Launch of Sputnik 1, 60th anniv.: a, Sputnik 1 in orbit. b, Sputnik designer Sergei Korolev (1907-66). c, Korolev, cosmonaut spacewalking. d, Launch of Sputnik 1.

No. 3982, 20r — Formula 1 race cars: a, Mercedes AMG F1 W05 and driver, Lewis Hamilton. b, Red Bull RB1. c, Mercedes F1 W05. d, Ferrari F14T.

No. 3983, 22r — Charlie Chaplin (1889-1977), movie actor, in scene from: a, Modern Times, 1936. b, Monsieur Verdoux, 1947. c, The Circus, 1928. d, City Lights, 1931.

No. 3984, 22r — Mother Teresa (St. Teresa of Calcutta, 1910-97), humanitarian: a, With arms raised. b, With candle. c, With hands clasped. d, Holding child.

No. 3985, 22r — Battle of Stalingrad, 75th anniv.: a, Statue of playing children after air strikes. b, Two soldiers and train. c, Four soldiers. d, The Motherland Calls statue and Monument to Heroes of the Battle of Stalingrad.

No. 3986, 22r — Bats: a, Barbastella barbastellus. b, Pipistrellus pygmaeus. c, Plecotus auritus. d, Acerodon jubatus.

No. 3987, 60r, Beethoven, diff. No. 3988, 60r, Princes Charles and William, Princess Diana. No. 3989, 60r, Laika in space. No. 3990, 60r, Sputnik 1 over map of world. No. 3991, 60r, Sauber C36 Ferrari. No. 3992, 70r, Chaplin in Shoulder Arms, 1918. No. 3993, 70r, Mother Teresa holding infant. No. 3994, 70r, Boats involved in Battle of Stalingrad. No. 3995, 70r, Pipistrellus pygmaeus, diff.

2017, Sept. 12　Litho.　Perf. 13¼
Sheets of 4, #a-d
3978-3986　A685　Set of 9　97.50　97.50
Souvenir Sheets
3987-3995　A685　Set of 9　75.00　75.00

Birdpex 2018 Philatelic Exhibition,
Mondorf-les-Bains,
Luxembourg — A686

No. 3996: a, Ardea melanocephala. b, Falco amurensis. c, Psittacula krameri. d, Haliastur indus.
60r, Ardea alba.

2017, Sept. 26　Litho.　Perf. 13¼
3996　A686　20r Sheet of 4, #a-d　10.50　10.50
Souvenir Sheet
3997　A686　60r multi　7.75　7.75

A687

No. 3998, 20r — Pandas: a, Ailurus fulgens facing right. b, Adult and juvenile Ailuropoda melanoleuca. c, Adult Ailuropoda melanoleuca. d, Ailurus fulgens facing forward.

No. 3999, 20r — Dolphins: a, Stenella frontalis. b, Cephalorhynchus commersonii. c, Cephalorhynchus hectori. d, Sousa teuszii.

No. 4000, 20r — Bees: a, Bombus lapidarius. b, Amegilla cingulata. c, Agapostemon texanus. d, Thyreus nitidulus.

No. 4001, 20r — Turtles: a, Macrochelys temminckii. b, Eretmochelys imbricata. c, Deirochelys reticulatia. d, Actinemys marmorata.

No. 4002, 20r — Mushrooms: a, Callistoporium luteo-olivaceum. b, Gyromitra esculenta. c, Craterellus cornucopioides. d, Imleria badia.

No. 4003, 22r — Butterflies and moths: a, Argynnis childreni. b, Automeris io. c, Saturnia pavonia. d, Eunica monima.

No. 4004, 22r — Fish: a, Pomacanthus annularis. b, Amphiprion nigripes. c, Oxycirrhites typus. d, Chelmon rostratus.

No. 4005, 22r — Shells and minerals: a, Morula uva, Aquamarine. b, Arcinella cornuta, Amethyst. c, Angeria sphaerula, Diopside. d, Opeatostoma pseudodon, Rhodochrosite.

No. 4006, 22r — Orchids: a, Pomacanthus annularis (incorrect name). b, Amphiprion nigripes (incorrect name). c, Oxycirrhites typus (incorrect name). d, Chelmon rostratus (incorrect name)

No. 4007, 20r, Adult and juvenile Ailuropoda melanoleuca, diff. No. 4008, 60r, Delphinus delphis. No. 4009, 60r, Bombus bohemicus. No. 4010, 60r, Clemmys guttata. No. 4011, 60r, Ganoderma lucidum. No. 4012, 70r, Polygonia interrogationis. No. 4013, 70r, Pterois antennata. No. 4014, 70r, Strombus gigas, Wulfenite. No. 4015, 70r, Chloraea magellanica.

2017, Sept. 26　Litho.　Perf. 13¼
Sheets of 4, #a-d
3998-4006　A687　Set of 9　97.50　97.50
Souvenir Sheet
4007-4015　A687　Set of 9　70.00　70.00

Space Exploration and
Astronomy — A688

No. 4016, 20r — International Space Station: a, Zvezda Service Module. b, Space Shuttle docked at International Space Station. c, International Space Station. d, Cupola.

No. 4017, 20r — Sergei Korolev (1907-66), spacecraft designer, and Yuri Gagarin (1934-68), first man in space: a, Korolev. b, Gagarin wearing space suit. c, Gagarin in Vostok capsule. d, Statue depicting Gagarin and Korolev.

No. 4018, 20r — Famous spacecraft: a, SpaceShipTwo. b, SpaceShipTwo with mother ship. c, Space Shuttle Discovery and Boeing 747 Shuttle Carrier. d, Soyuz-TMA.

No. 4019, 20r — Meteorities: a, Tamentit meteorite found in 1864. b, Esquel meteorite found in 1951. c, 1924 Johnstown, Colorado meteorite. d, Taza iron meteorite found in 2001.

No. 4020, 22r — China's first x-ray astronomical satellite: a, Satellite and planets. b, Chinasat-9A satellite setup. c, China launches its first x-ray space telescope. d, Satellite with panels extended.

No. 4021, 22r — Cassini probe of Saturn: a, Cassini near sixth-largest moon of Saturn, Enceladus. b, Cassini and rings of Saturn. c, Cassini. d, Saturn's moon, Tethys.

No. 4022, 22r — Space tourism: a, Virgin Galactic's SpaceShipTwo. b, XCOR Lynx. c, SpaceX Dragon and Falcon 9 rocket launcher. d, Blue Origin's New Shepard rocket.

No. 4023, 60r, International Space Station, diff. No. 4024, 60r, Korolev, diff. No. 4025, 60r, Apollo 17. No. 4026, 60r, Chondrite H5 meteorite. No. 4027, 70r, China's frist x-ray astronomical telescope, diff. No. 4028, 70r, Cassini burning in Saturn's atmosphere. No. 4029, 70r, Dennis Anthony Tito, first space tourist.

2018, Mar. 15　Litho.　Perf. 13¼
Sheets of 4, #a-d
4016-4022　A688　Set of 7　75.00　75.00
Souvenir Sheets
4023-4029　A688　Set of 7　57.50　57.50

Nos. 4023-4029 each contain one 41x41mm stamp.

A689

No. 4030, 20r — Princess Grace of Monaco (1929-82), and: a, Her signature and strip of film. b, Strip of film. c, Clapboard and automobile. d, Her coat of arms.

No. 4031, 20r — Princess Charlotte of Cambridge, second birthday: a, Princess Charlotte with mother, Duchess of Cambridge. b, Princess Charlotte with father, Prince William. c, Princess Charlotte with brother, Prince George. d, Princess Charlotte with mother and flowers.

No. 4032, 20r — Nelson Mandela (1918-2013), President of South Africa, with: a, 1910-2000 South Africa coat of arms. b, 14th Dalai Lama. c, Wife, Winnie (1936-2018). d, Statue depicting him in Parliament Square, London.

No. 4033, 20r — 2017 Nobel Laureates: a, Chemistry laureate Jacques Dubochet. b, Physiology or Medicine laureate Michael Rosbash. c, Physics laureate, Rainer Weiss. d, Physics laureate Barry Barish.

No. 4034, 22r — 70th wedding anniversary of Queen Elizabeth II and Prince Philip: a, Queen Elizabeth II. b, Queen Elizabeth II and her family. c, Queen Elizabeth II and Prince Philip. d, Queen Elizabeth II, Princes Philip and Charles at castle.

No. 4035, 22r — Sir Robert Baden-Powell (1857-1941), founder of Scouting movement: a, With merit badge and map of Africa. b, Wearing military uniform. c, Wearing Indian headdress. d, With wife, Olave (1889-1977).

No. 4036, 22r — Rotary International emblem and Paul P. Harris (1868-1947), founder of Rotary International: a, With person with water bucket. b, With other Rotarians. c, With children using crutches. d, Showing book to children.

MALDIVE ISLANDS

No. 4037, 22r — 2017 World Women's Chess Championship participants: a, Tan Zhongyi. b, Anna Muzychuk. c, Harika Dronavalli. d, Alexandria Kosteniuk.
No. 4038, 60r, Princess Grace, diff. No. 4039, 60r, Princess Charlotte holding flower. No. 4040, 60r, Mandela, giraffes and dancers. No. 4041, 60r, 2017 Nobel Chemistry laureate Richard Henderson. No. 4042, 70r, Queen Elizabeth II and Prince Philip, diff. No. 4043, 70r, Baden-Powell and Warner Goodyear, leader of Mafeking Cadets. No. 4044, 70r, Harris and child holding shovel. No. 4045, 70r, Tan Zhongyi and Muzychuk.

2018, Mar. 15   Litho.   Perf. 13¼
Sheets of 4, #a-d

| 4030-4037 | A689 | Set of 8 | 87.50 | 87.50 |

Souvenir Sheets

| 4038-4045 | A689 | Set of 8 | 67.50 | 67.50 |

Nos. 4038-4045 each contain one 41x41mm stamp.

A690

No. 4046, 20r — Concorde: a, Two airplanes flying to right. b, One airplane ascending. c, Two airplanes flying to left. d, One airplane descending.
No. 4047, 20r — Table tennis players wearing: a, Red shirt, paddle at shoulder height. b, Blue shirt, paddle behind net. c, Red shirt, paddle above head. d, Blue shirt, paddle at head height.
No. 4048, 20r — Special transport: a, 2005 Harley-Davidson FLHTPI Electra Glide motorcycle, 2009 Cadillac limousine. b, B-377-SG Super Guppy airplane, 1949 Volkswagen Type 1 Beetle. c, 2010 Fire Fighter II boat. d, 1956 Bell UH-1 Iroquois helicopter, 1940 Dodge WC-54 truck.
No. 4049, 20r — Dutch Golden Age paintings and their painters: a, The Dismissal of Hagar, by Gabriel Metsu (1629-67). b, Girl Reading a Letter at an Open Window, by Johannes Vermeer (1632-75). c, Beware of Luxury, by Jan Steen (c. 1626-79). d, Meebeeck Cruywagen Family, by Jacob van Loo (1614-70).
No. 4050, 20r — Post-impressionist paintings and their painters: a, Tahitian Landscape, by Paul Gauguin (1848-1903). b, Three Sunflowers in a Vase, by Vincent van Gogh (1853-90). c, Dining Room in the Country, by Pierre Bonnard (1867-1947). d, Mont Sainte-Victoire Seen from Bellevue, by Paul Cézanne (1839-1906).
No. 4051, 20r — Tigers: a, Panthera tigris tigris. b, Panthera tigris sumatrae. c, Head of Panthera tigris altaica. d, Panthera tigris altaica.
No. 4052, 20r — Sled dogs: a, Alaskan malamute. b, Alakan husky leaping. c, Two Siberian huskies running. d, Heads of two Siberian huskies.
No. 4053, 20r — Owls: a, Strix aluco. b, Asio flammeus. c, Bubo scandiacus. d, Megascops asio.
No. 4054, 22r — Birds of paradise: a, Diphyllodes respublica. b, Paradisaea rudolphi. c, Cicinnurus regius. d, Paradisaea apoda.
No. 4055, 22r — Manta birostris with: a, Tail at UR. b, Tail at LL. c, Tail at UL. d, Tail at LR.
No. 4056, 22r — Sharks: a, Rhizoprionodon terranovae, Carcharodon carcharias. b, Squatina californica. c, Sphyrna lewini, Squalus acanthias, Atelomycterus marmoratus. d, Etmopterus perryi, Pristiophorus japonicus.
No. 4057, 22r — Snakes: a, Dendroaspis polylepis. b, Causus rhombeatus. c, Notechis scutatus. d, Agkistrodon contortrix.
No. 4058, 22r — Japanese trains: a, E6 Series Shinkansen. b, KiHa201 Series. c, E653 Series. d, JNR Class D51.
No. 4059, 22r — Submarines: a, German midget submarine Seehund. b, U.S. midget submarine SS X-1. c, Soviet submarine Project 941. d, U.S. submarine USS Greeneville.
No. 4060, 22r — Professional golfers: a, Jordan Spieth, U.S. b, Rory McIlroy, Northern Ireland. c, Justin Rose, England. d, Hideki Matsuyama, Japan.
No. 4061, 60r, Concorde, diff. No. 4062, 60r, Table tennis player, diff. No. 4063, 60r, 2007 BAE Herti unmanned aerial vehicle, 2011 Bugatti Veyron. No. 4064, 60r, The Anatomy Lesson of Dr. Nicolaes Tulp, by Rembrandt van Rijn (1606-69). No. 4065, 60r, Wheat Field with Cypresses, by van Gogh. No. 4066, 60r, Panthera tigris jacksoni. No. 4067, 60r, Two Alaskan malamutes. No. 4068, 60r, Aegolius acadicus. No. 4069, 70r, Ptiloris victoriae. No. 4070, 70r, Manta birostris, diff. No. 4071, 70r, Carcharhinus longimanus, Naucrates ductor. No. 4072, 70r, Ophiophagus hannah. No. 4073, 70r, N700 Series Shinkansen. No. 4074, 70r, French submarine Terrible and French Pres. Emmanuel Macron. No. 4075, 70r, Golfer Dustin Johnson, U.S.

2018, Mar. 15   Litho.   Perf. 13¼
Sheets of 4, #a-d

| 4046-4060 | A690 | Set of 15 | 160.00 | 160.00 |

Souvenir Sheets

| 4061-4075 | A690 | Set of 15 | 125.00 | 125.00 |

A691

No. 4076, 20r — Ursus maritimus: a, Testing thin ice. b, Swimming underwaer, head at left. c, Swimming underwater, head at right. d, Adult and cubs.
No. 4077, 20r — Water birds: a, Anseranas semipalmata. b, Phoenicopterus chilensis. c, Pelecanus occidentalis. d, Branta canadensis.
No. 4078, 20r — Indian Oceran wildlife: a, Chelonia mydas. b, Duttaphrynus melanostictus. c, Octopus vulgaris. d, Rhinocodon typus.
No. 4079, 20r — Endangered species: a, Hippopotamus amphibius. b, Lycaon pictus. c, Dendrolagus ursinus. d, Diceros bicrornis.
No. 4080, 20r — Lighthouses: a, Saint Theodoroi Lighthouse, Greece. b, La Vieille Lighthouse, France. c, Cleveland Harbor West Pierhead Lighthouse, U.S. d, Toledo Harbor Lighthouse, U.S.
No. 4081, 20r — Fire engines: a, APSB-6.0-40-10 armored firefighting vehicle. b, Barkas B1000 fire truck. c, 1941 Horch 853 Sport Cabriolet. d, 1946 Dodge fire engine.
No. 4082, 20r — Realist paintings and their artists: a, Harvesters Resting (Ruth and Boaz), by Jean-François Millet (1814-75). b, Eugene Onegin and Vladimir Lensky's Duel, by Ilya Repin (1844-1930). c, Poachers in the Snow, by Gustave Courbet (1819-77). d, Max Schmitt in a Single Scull, by Thomas Eakins (1844-1916).
No. 4083, 20r — Professional tennis players: a, Andy Murray. b, Roger Federer. c, Alexander Zverev. d, Dominic Thiem.
No. 4084, 22r — Tropical fish: a, Holacanthus clarionensis. b, Melanotaenia boesemani. c, Centropyge interruptus. d, Liopropoma carmabi.
No. 4085, 22r — Dinosaurs: a, Plateosaurus engelhardti. b, Acrocanthosaurus atokensis. c, Troodon formosus. d, Corythosaurus casuarius.
No. 4086, 22r — Mohandas K. Gandhi (1869-1948), Indian nationalist leader, and: a, "God is truth." b, Taj Mahal. c, Bull. d, Lotus flower.
No. 4087, 22r — Engagement of Prince Harry and Meghan Markle. a, Couple, Markle at left. b, Markle. c, Prince Harry. d, Couple, Markle at right.
No. 4088, 22r — Dirigibles, with inscription: a, Lockheed Martin's hybrid airship SkyTug. b, Lockheed Martin's hybrid airship (in flight). c, Lockheed Martin's hybrid airship (on ground). d, High-Tech Airships — NASA's Next Challenge.
No. 4089, 22r — Chinese high-speed trains: a, CRH1A. b, CRH6 EMU. c, CRH5F. d, CRH5G.
No. 4090, 22r — Professional ice hockey players: a, Sidney Crosby. b, Andrei Markov. c, Connor McDavid. d, Braden Holtby.
No. 4091, 60r, Ursus maritimus and cubs, diff. No. 4092, 60r, Cygnus cygnus. No. 4093, 60r, Crocodylus porosus. No. 4094, 60r, Eretmochelys imbricata. No. 4095, 60r, Aniva Lighthouse, Russia. No. 4096, 60r, Kamaz 43253 fire truck. No. 4097, 60r, Harmony in Blue and Silver Trouville, by James Abbott McNeill Whistler (1834-1903). No. 4098, 60r, Tennis player Rafael Nadal. No. 4099, 70r, Astronotus ocellatus. No. 4100, 70r, Edmontonia rugosidens. No. 4101, 70r, Gandhi, diff. No. 4102, 70r, Prince Harry and Meghan Markle, diff. No. 4103, 70r, Lockheed Martin P-791 dirigible. No. 4104, 70r, Bombardier Zefiro 250. No. 4105, 70r, Ice hockey player Alex Ovechkin.

2018, May 10   Litho.   Perf. 13¼
Sheets of 4, #a-d

| 4076-4090 | A691 | Set of 15 | 160.00 | 160.00 |

Souvenir Sheets

| 4091-4105 | A691 | Set of 15 | 125.00 | 125.00 |

A692

No. 4106, 20r — Roald Amundsen (1872-1928), polar explorer: a, Looking forward. b, Looking right. c, With Ursus maritimus, Marie. d, With Dornier Wal seaplane.
No. 4107, 20r — Lamborghini Company 55th anniv.: a, Feruccio Lamborghini (1916-93), Lamborghini Countach LP 400 S. b, Roman Colosseum, Lamborghini Veneno. c, Lamborghini Diablo. d, Lamborghini, bull, and Lamborghini Aventador LP700-4.
No. 4108, 20r — Military planes: a, General Dynamics F-16 Fighting Falcon. b, Dassault Mirage 2000. c, McDonnell Douglas F/A-18 Hornet. d, British Aerospace Sea Harrier FA2.
No. 4109, 20r — Pigeons: a, Columba thomensis. b, Columba albitorques. c, Columba livia. d, Columba leucomela.
No. 4110, 20r — Birds of prey: a, Sagittarius serpentarius. b, Sarcoramphus papa. c, Hieraaetus pennatus. d, Pandion haliaetus.
No. 4111, 20r — Fishing birds: a, Anhinga anhinga. b, Fratercula arctica. c, Dutorides striata javanica. d, Egretta caerulea.
No. 4112, 20r — Turtles: a, Apalone spinifera. b, Trionyx ferox. c, Rafetus euphraticus. d, Pelodiscus sinensis.
No. 4113, 20r — Mushrooms: a, Russula paludosa. b, Cantharellus cibarius. c, Cortinarius violaceus. d, Lycoperdon echinatum.
No. 4114, 22r — Butterflies: a, Araschnia levana. b, Danaus genutia. c, Leptidea sinapis. d, Philaethria dido.
No. 4115, 22r — Minerals: a, Anglesite, Morocco. b, Celestine, Madagascar. c, Euclase, Zimbabwe. d, Spessartine, China.
No. 4116, 22r — Antonio Vivaldi (1678-1741), composer: a, Hands and musical score. b, Vivaldi and violin. c, Vivaldi playing violin. d, Orphan girls plyaing violins at the Ospedale della Pieta, Venice.
No. 4117, 22r — Audrey Hepburn (1929-93), actress: a, Wearing blue dress. b, With poodles. c, Sitting. d, Holding umbrella.
No. 4118, 22r — Works of Ivan Shishkin (1832-98), painter: a, "In the Wild North," 1891. b, "Rye," 1878. c, "Beach," date unknown. d, "Little House in Dusseldorf," 1856.
No. 4119, 22r — Orville Wright (1871-1948), aviation pioneer: a, Wright Flyer and tugboat. b, Wilbur Wright (1867-1912), aviation pioneer and wings of Wright Flyer. c, Orville Wright and Wright Flyer. d, Wright Flyer and Statue of Liberty.
No. 4120, 22r — Steam trains: a, GWR No. 6023 King Edward II. b, NZR KA 942. c, 35028 Clan Line. d, Parrot 477.043.
No. 4121, 60r, Amundsen, diff. No. 4122, 60r, Lamborghini Urraco P250. No. 4123, 60r, Sukhoi Su-34. No. 4124, 60r, Columba leuconota. No. 4125, 60r, Vultur gryphus. No. 4126, 60r, Pelecanus occidentalis. No. 4127, 60r, Apalone ferox. No. 4128, 60r, Verpa bohemica. No. 4129, 70r, Papilio glaucus. No. 4130, 70r, Aquamarine (beryl), Sri Lanka. No. 4131, 70r, Four Seasons, by Vivaldi (violin, snowflake, acorns, sunflower). No. 4132, 70r, Hepburn with her Hollywood Walk of Fame star. No. 4133, 70r, Shishkin. No. 4134, 70r, Orville Wright and Wright Flyer, diff. No. 4135, 70r, Southern Pacific 4449.

2018, May 17   Litho.   Perf. 13½
Sheets of 4, #a-d

| 4106-4120 | A692 | Set of 15 | 160.00 | 160.00 |

Souvenir Sheets

| 4121-4135 | A692 | Set of 15 | 125.00 | 125.00 |

Marine Scenes — A693

Designs: No. 4136, 15r, Sweet lips. No. 4137, 15r, Turtle. No. 4138, 15r, Manta ray. No. 4139, 15r, Diver facing forward. No. 4140, 15r, Whale shark. No. 4141, 15r, Diver with orange fish. No. 4142, 15r, Underwater beauty (fish and coral). No. 4143, 15r, Humphead Wrasse. No. 4144, 100r, Hermit Crab, vert.

2018, May 25   Litho.   Perf. 13x13¼

| 4136-4144 | A693 | Set of 9 | 28.00 | 28.00 |

A694

No. 4145, 20r — Pandas: a, Ailurus fulgens looking right. b, Ailuropoda melanoleuca hanging on branch. c, Ailurus melanoleuca standing on log. d, Ailuropoda fulgens curled up.
No. 4146, 20r — Cats: a, Persian. b, Devon Rex. c, Selkirk Rex. d, Exotic Shorthair.
No. 4147, 20r — Sea snakes: a, Hydrophis platurus. b, Aipysurus laevis. c, Laticauda colubrina. d, Kerilia jerdonii.
No. 4148, 20r — Orchids: a, Orchis purpurea. b, Oncidium sphacelatum. c, Coelogyne cristata. d, Epidendrum radicans.
No. 4149, 20r — Leo Tolstoy (1828-1910), writer, with: a, Book. b, Maxim Gorky (1868-1936), writer. c, Anton Chekhov (1860-1904), playwright. d, Inkwell and quill pen.
No. 4150, 20r — Paintings by Gustav Klimt (1862-1918): a, "Hygieia" (detail), 1900-07. b, "Fir Forest I," 1901. c, "Fruit Trees" (detail), 1901. d, "The Black Feather Hat," 1910.
No. 4151, 20r — Dr. Martin Luther King Jr. (1928-68), civil rights leader: a, Statue of King in Kelly Ingram Park, Birmingham, Alabama. b, King looking left. c, King and birth home in Atlanta, Georgia. d, King at March on Washington.
No. 4152, 20r — International Isle of Man TT Race: a, Conor Cummins, Padgetts Honda Racing team. b, James Hillier, Quattro Plant Kawasaki team. c, Nicky Hayden, Ducati MotoGP Team. d, Gary Johnson, BMW Motorrad Motorsport.
No. 4153, 22r — Dolphins: a, Orcaella brevirostris. b, Tursiops truncatus. c, Pseudorca crassidens. d, Delphinus delphis.
No. 4154, 22r — Flightless birds: a, Aptenodytes forsteri. b, Struthio camelus. c, Apteryx rowi. d, Eudyptes schlegeli.
No. 4155, 22r — Fish: a, Lutjanus kasmira. b, Balistoides conspicillum. c, Chaetodon ephippium. d, Gramma loreto.
No. 4156, 22r — John F. Kennedy (1917-63), 35th U.S. President: a, In boat. b, With rocket. c, In rifle scope. d, With wife, Jacqueline (1929-94).
No. 4157, 22r — Ford automobiles: a, Ford Galaxie. b, 1949 Ford sedan. c, Ford Capri Mk2. d, Ford Falcon XM Sedan.
No. 4158, 22r — Tall ships: a, Amerigo Vespucci. b, Simon Bolivar. c, HMS Bounty. d, Picton Castle.
No. 4159, 22r — Chess players: a, Peter Svidler. b, Fabiano Caruana. c, Vladimir Kramnik. d, Hikaru Nakamura.
No. 4160, 60r, Ailurus fulgens. No. 4161, 60r, Turkish Angora cat. No. 4162, 60r, Hydrophis platurus. No. 4163, 60r, Miltonia cuneate. No. 4164, 60r, Tolstoy, diff. No. 4165, 60r, "Portrait of Adele Bloch-Bauer II" (detail), by Klimt, 1912. No. 4166, 60r, King and U.S. flag. No. 4167, 60r, Guy Martin, Team Suzuki. No. 4168, 70r, Lipotes vexillifer. No. 4169, 70r, Porphyrio hochstetteri. No. 4170, 70r, Oxyurl rnites typus. No. 4171, 70r, Pres. Kennedy, U. S. flag, White House. No. 4172, 70r, Ford Model B. No. 4173, 70r, Lord Nelson. No. 4174, 70r, Magnus Carlsen.

2018, June 7   Litho.   Perf. 13½
Sheets of 4, #a-d

| 4145-4159 | A694 | Set of 15 | 160.00 | 160.00 |

Souvenir Sheets

| 4160-4174 | A694 | Set of 15 | 125.00 | 125.00 |

MALI

'mä-lē

(Federation of Mali)

LOCATION — West Africa
GOVT. — Republic within French Community
AREA — 482,077 sq. mi.
POP. — 20,250,000 (2020 est.)
CAPITAL — Dakar and Bamako

The Federation of Mali, founded Jan. 17, 1959, consisted of the Republic of Senegal and the French Sudan. It broke up in June, 1960. See Senegal.

100 Centimes = 1 Franc

Catalogue values for all unused stamps in this country are for Never Hinged items.

Flag and Map of Mali — A1

1959, Nov. 7   Unwmk.   Engr.   Perf. 13
| 1 | A1 | 25fr grn, car & dp claret | 1.00 | .50 |

Founding of the Federation of Mali.

Imperforates
Most Mali stamps exist imperforate in issued and trial colors, and also in small presentation sheets in issued colors.

Parrotfish — A2

Fish: 10fr, Triggerfish. 15fr, Psetta. 20fr, Blepharis crinitus. 25fr, Butterflyfish. 30fr, Surgeonfish. 85fr, Dentex.

1960, Mar. 5
Fish in Natural Colors
2	A2	5fr olive	.40	.25
3	A2	10fr brt grnsh blue	.40	.25
4	A2	15fr dark blue	.45	.25
5	A2	20fr gray green	.65	.35
6	A2	25fr slate green	1.10	.55
7	A2	30fr dark blue	1.50	.90
8	A2	85fr dark green	3.50	2.00
		Nos. 2-8 (7)	8.00	4.55

For overprints see Nos. 10-12.

Common Design Types
pictured following the introduction.

C.C.T.A. Issue
Common Design Type
1960, May 21   Perf. 13
| 9 | CD106 | 25fr lt vio & mag | 1.20 | .50 |

REPUBLIC OF MALI

GOVT. — Republic
AREA — 463,500 sq. mi.
POP. — 10,429,124 (1999 est.)
CAPITAL — Bamako

The Republic of Mali, formerly the French Sudan, proclaimed its independence on June 20, 1960, when the Federation of Mali ceased to exist.

Nos. 5-6 and 8 Ovptd.

1961, Jan. 15   Unwmk.   Engr.   Perf. 13
Fish in Natural Colors
10	A2	20fr gray green	1.25	.65
11	A2	25fr slate green	2.00	.65
12	A2	85fr dark green	3.25	1.60
		Nos. 10-12 (3)	6.50	2.90

Pres. Mamadou Konate — A3

Design: 25fr, Pres. Modibo Keita.

1961, Mar. 18
| 13 | A3 | 20fr green & black | .30 | .25 |
| 14 | A3 | 25fr maroon & black | .45 | .25 |

For miniature sheet see No. C11a.

Reading Class, Bullock Team and Factory — A4

1961, Sept. 22   Unwmk.   Perf. 13
| 15 | A4 | 25fr multi | .75 | .40 |

First anniversary of Independence.

Shepherd and Sheep — A5

Designs: 1fr, 10fr, 40fr, Cattle. 2fr, 15fr, 50fr, Mali Arts Museum. 3fr, 20fr, 60fr, Plowing. 4fr, 25fr, 85fr, Harvester.

1961, Dec. 24   Unwmk.   Engr.   Perf. 13
16	A5	50c car rose, blk & dk grn	.25	.25
17	A5	1fr grn, bl & bister	.25	.25
18	A5	2fr ultra, grn & org red	.25	.25
19	A5	3fr bl, grn & brn	.25	.25
20	A5	4fr bl grn, indigo & bis	.25	.25
21	A5	5fr bl, olive & maroon	.25	.25
22	A5	10fr ol blk, bl & sepia	.25	.25
23	A5	15fr ultra, grn & bis brn	.25	.25
24	A5	20fr bl, grn & org red	.35	.25
25	A5	25fr dk bl & yel grn	.45	.25
26	A5	30fr vio, grn & dk brn	.60	.30
27	A5	40fr sl grn, bl & org red	1.10	.30
28	A5	50fr ultra, grn & rose car	.55	.30
29	A5	60fr blue, green & brown	1.25	.30
30	A5	85fr bl, bis & dk red brn	1.90	.45
		Nos. 16-30 (15)	8.20	4.15

King Mohammed V of Morocco and Map of Africa — A6

1962, Jan. 4   Photo.   Perf. 12
| 31 | A6 | 25fr multicolored | .30 | .25 |
| 32 | A6 | 50fr multicolored | .55 | .25 |

1st anniv. of the conference of African heads of state at Casablanca.

Patrice Lumumba — A7

1962, Feb. 12   Unwmk.   Perf. 12
| 33 | A7 | 25fr choc & brn org | .35 | .25 |
| 34 | A7 | 100fr choc & emerald | 1.00 | .45 |

Issued in memory of Patrice Lumumba, Premier of the Congo (Democratic) Republic.

Pegasus and UPU Monument, Bern — A8

1962, Apr. 21   Perf. 12½x12
| 35 | A8 | 85fr red brn, yel & brt grn | 1.50 | .75 |

1st anniv. of Mali's admission to the UPU.

Map of Africa and Post Horn — A8a

1962, Apr. 23   Perf. 13½x13
| 36 | A8a | 25fr dk red brn & dp grn | .35 | .25 |
| 37 | A8a | 85fr dp green & org | 1.10 | .40 |

Establishment of African Postal Union.

Sansanding Dam — A9

Cotton Plant — A10

1962, Oct. 27   Photo.   Perf. 12
| 38 | A9 | 25fr gray, ultra & grn | .35 | .25 |
| 39 | A10 | 45fr multicolored | 1.25 | .40 |

Telstar, Earth and Television Set — A10a

1962, Nov. 24   Engr.   Perf. 13
| 40 | A10a | 45fr dk car, vio & brn | 1.00 | .45 |
| 41 | A10a | 55fr green, vio & ol | 1.20 | .55 |

1st television connection of the US and Europe through the Telstar satellite, 7/11-12.

Bull, Chemical Equipment, Chicks — A11

1963, Feb. 23   Unwmk.   Perf. 13
| 42 | A11 | 25fr red brn & grnsh bl | .50 | .25 |

Sotuba Zootechnical Institute. See No. C15.

Tractor — A12

1963, Mar. 21   Engr.
| 43 | A12 | 25fr vio bl, dk brn & blk | .55 | .25 |
| 44 | A12 | 45fr bl grn, red brn & grn | 1.00 | .30 |

FAO "Freedom from Hunger" campaign.

High Altitude Balloon and WMO Emblem — A13

1963, June 12   Photo.   Perf. 12½
Green Emblem; Yellow and Black Balloon
45	A13	25fr ultra	.35	.25
46	A13	45fr carmine rose	.70	.25
47	A13	60fr red brown	.90	.45
		Nos. 45-47 (3)	1.95	1.05

Studies of the atmosphere.

Winners, 800-meter Race — A14

20fr, Acrobatic dancers. 85fr, Soccer.

1963, Aug. 10   Unwmk.   Perf. 12
48	A14	5fr multi	.25	.25
49	A14	10fr multi	.25	.25
50	A14	20fr multi, horiz.	.60	.25
51	A14	85fr multi, horiz.	1.75	.75
		Nos. 48-51 (4)	2.85	1.50

Issued to publicize Youth Week.

Centenary Emblem — A15

1963, Sept. 1   Perf. 13½x13
Emblem in Gray, Yellow and Red
52	A15	5fr lt ol grn & blk	.25	.25
53	A15	10fr yellow & blk	.35	.25
54	A15	85fr red & blk	1.30	.75
		Nos. 52-54 (3)	1.90	1.25

Centenary of the International Red Cross.

Kaempferia Aethiopica — A16

Tropical plants: 70fr, Bombax costatum. 100fr, Adenium Honghel.

1963, Dec. 23   Unwmk.   Perf. 13
55	A16	30fr multicolored	.55	.25
56	A16	70fr multicolored	1.40	.45
57	A16	100fr multicolored	3.50	.60
		Nos. 55-57 (3)	5.45	1.30

Plane Spraying, Locust and Village — A17

Designs (each inscribed "O.ICMA."): 5fr, Head of locust and map of Africa, vert. 10fr, Locust in flight over map of Mali, vert.

1964, June 15   Engr.   Perf. 13
58	A17	5fr org brn, dl cl & grn	.35	.25
59	A17	10fr org brn, ol & bl grn	.75	.30
60	A17	20fr bis, org brn & yel grn	1.25	.50
		Nos. 58-60 (3)	2.35	1.05

Anti-locust campaign.

Soccer Player and Tokyo Stadium A18

Designs (stadium in background): 10fr, Boxer, vert. 15fr, Runner, vert. 85fr, Hurdler.

1964, June 27   Unwmk.
61	A18	5fr red, brt grn & dk pur	.25	.25
62	A18	10fr blk, dl bl & org brn	.30	.25
63	A18	15fr violet & dk red	.45	.25

MALI — Republic of Mali

64	A18 85fr vio, dk brn & sl grn	2.10	1.25
a.	Min. sheet of 4, #61-64	4.00	3.00
	Nos. 61-64 (4)	3.10	2.00

18th Olympic Games, Tokyo, Oct. 10-25.

IQSY Emblem and Eclipse of Sun — A19

1964, July 27 — Engr. — Perf. 13

65	A19 45fr multicolored	.90	.40

International Quiet Sun Year, 1964-65.

Map of Viet Nam — A20

1964, Nov. 2 — Photo. — Perf. 12x12½

66	A20 30fr multicolored	.60	.25

Issued to publicize the solidarity of the workers of Mali and those of South Viet Nam.

Defassa Waterbuck — A21

Designs: 5fr, Cape buffalo, horiz. 10fr, Scimitar-horned oryx. 30fr, Leopard, horiz. 90fr, Giraffe.

1965, Apr. 5 — Engr.

67	A21 1fr choc, brt bl & grn	.25	.25
68	A21 5fr grn, ocher & choc	.25	.25
69	A21 10fr grn, brt pink & bis brn	.45	.25
70	A21 30fr dk red, grn & choc	.90	.35
71	A21 90fr bis brn, sl & yel grn	2.25	.75
	Nos. 67-71 (5)	4.10	1.85

Abraham Lincoln — A22

1965, Apr. 15 — Photo. — Perf. 13x12½

72	A22 45fr black & multi	.75	.50
73	A22 55fr dp green & multi	.85	.60

Centenary of the death of Lincoln.

Denis Compressed Air Transmitter — A23

Designs: 30fr, Hughes telegraph system, horiz. 50fr, Lescurre heliograph.

1965, May 17 — Engr. — Perf. 13

74	A23 20fr orange, blk & bl	.35	.25
75	A23 30fr org, ocher & sl grn	.60	.30
76	A23 50fr org, dk brn & sl grn	1.10	.50
	Nos. 74-76 (3)	2.05	1.05

Centenary of the ITU.

Mother and infants — A24

Designs: 5fr, Mobile X-ray Unit and Lungs. 25fr, Examination of patient at Marchoux Institute and slide. 45fr, Biology laboratory.

1965, July 5 — Unwmk. — Perf. 13

77	A24 5fr lake, red & vio	.25	.25
78	A24 10fr brn ol, red & sl grn	.30	.25
79	A24 25fr dk brn, red & grn	.50	.50
80	A24 45fr dk brn, red & sl grn	1.00	.50
	Nos. 77-80 (4)	2.05	1.25

Issued to publicize the Health Service.

Swimmer — A25

1965, July 19 — Engr.

81	A25 5fr shown	.25	.25
82	A25 15fr Judo	.80	.30

1st African Games, Brazzaville, July 18-25.

Globe, Vase, Quill, Trumpet — A26

55fr, Mask, palette and microphones. 90fr, Dancers, mask and printed cloth.

1966, Apr. 4 — Engr. — Perf. 13

83	A26 30fr black, red & ocher	.45	.25
84	A26 55fr car rose, emer & blk	.90	.30
85	A26 90fr ultra, org & dk brn	1.25	.45
	Nos. 83-85 (3)	2.60	1.00

International Negro Arts Festival, Dakar, Senegal, Apr. 1-24.

WHO Headquarters, Geneva — A27

1966, May 3 — Photo. — Perf. 12½x13

86	A27 30fr org yel, bl & ol grn	.60	.25
87	A27 45fr org yel, bl & dl red	.75	.30

Inauguration of the WHO Headquarters.

Fishermen with Nets — A28

River Fishing: 4fr, 60fr, Group fishing with large net. 20fr, 85fr, Commercial fishing boats.

1966, May 30 — Engr. — Perf. 13

88	A28 3fr ultra & brn	.25	.25
89	A28 4fr Prus bl & org brn	.25	.25
90	A28 20fr dk brn, ultra & grn	.45	.25
91	A28 ultr dk brn, bl & dk grn	.60	.25
92	A28 60fr mag, brn & brt grn	.90	.30
93	A28 85fr dk pur, dl bl & grn	1.25	.60
	Nos. 88-93 (6)	3.70	1.90

Initiation of Pioneers — A29

Design: 25fr, Dance and Pioneer emblem.

1966, July 25 — Engr. — Perf. 13

94	A29 5fr multicolored	.25	.25
95	A29 25fr multicolored	.75	.25

Issued to honor the pioneers of Mali.

Inoculation of Zebu — A30

1967, Jan. 16 — Photo. — Perf. 12½x13

96	A30 10fr dp grn, yel grn & brn	.30	.25
97	A30 30fr Prus bl, bl & brn	.90	.30

Campaign against cattle plague.

View of Timbuktu and Tourist Year Emblem — A31

1967, May 15 — Engr. — Perf. 13

98	A31 25fr Prus bl, red lil & org	.60	.25

International Tourist Year, 1967.

Ugada Grandicollis A32

Insects: 5fr, Chelorrhina polyphemus, vert. 50fr, Phymateus cinctus.

1967, Aug. 14 — Engr. — Perf. 13

99	A32 5fr brt bl, sl grn & brn	.60	.25
100	A32 15fr sl grn, dk brn & red	1.00	.35
101	A32 50fr grn, dk brn & dp org	2.75	.75
	Nos. 99-101 (3)	4.35	1.35

Teacher and Adult Class — A33

1967, Sept. 8 — Photo. — Perf. 12½x13

102	A33 50fr black, grn & car	.85	.25

International Literacy Day, Sept. 8.

Europafrica Issue

Birds, New Buildings and Map — A34

1967, Sept. 18 — Perf. 12½x12

103	A34 45fr multicolored	1.00	.35

Lions Emblem and Crocodile — A35

1967, Oct. 16 — Photo. — Perf. 13x12½

104	A35 90fr yellow & multi	1.40	.75

50th anniversary of Lions International.

Water Cycle and UNESCO Emblem — A36

1967, Nov. 15 — Photo. — Perf. 13

105	A36 25fr multicolored	.60	.25

Hydrological Decade (UNESCO), 1965-74.

WHO Emblem — A37

1968, Apr. 8 — Engr. — Perf. 13

106	A37 90fr sl grn, dk car rose & bl	1.20	.40

20th anniv. of the World Health Organization.

Linked Hearts and People — A38

1968, Apr. 28 — Engr. — Perf. 13

107	A38 50fr sl grn, red & vio bl	.65	.25

International Day of Sister Communities.

Books, Student, Chart, and Map of Africa — A39

1968, Aug. 12 — Engr. — Perf. 13

108	A39 100fr carmine, ol & blk	1.00	.40

10th anniv. of the Intl. Assoc. for the Development of Libraries and Archives in Africa.

Michaux bicycle, 1861 — A40

Designs: 2fr, Draisienne, 1809. 5fr, De Dion-Douton automobile, 1804, horiz. 45fr, Panhard & Levassor automobile, 1914, horiz.

1968, Aug. 12

109	A40 2fr grn, olive & mag	.35	.25
110	A40 5fr lemon, indigo & red	.65	.25
111	A40 10fr brt grn, indigo & brn	1.10	.25
112	A40 45fr ocher, gray grn & blk	2.00	.30
	Nos. 109-112,C60-C61 (6)	7.70	2.05

Tourist Emblem with Map of Africa and Dove — A41

1969, May 12 — Photo. — Perf. 12½x13

113	A41 50fr lt ultra, grn & red	.60	.25

Year of African Tourism.

ILO Emblem and "OIT" — A42

1969, May 12 — Engr. — Perf. 13

114	A42 50fr vio, slate grn & brt bl	.45	.25
115	A42 60fr slate, red & ol brn	.75	.25

Intl. Labor Organization, 50th anniv.

Panhard, 1897, and Citroen 24, 1969 — A43

30fr, Citroen, 1923, Citroen DS 21, 1969.

1969, May 30 — Engr. — Perf. 13

116	A43 25fr blk, maroon & lemon	1.00	.25
117	A43 30fr blk, brt grn & dk grn	1.25	.25
	Nos. 116-117,C71-C72 (4)	6.10	1.45

MALI — Republic of Mali

Play Blocks — A44

Toys: 10fr, Mule on wheels. 15fr, Ducks. 20fr, Racing car and track.

1969		**Photo.**	**Perf.**	**12½x13**
118	A44	5fr red, gray & yel	.25	.25
119	A44	10fr red, yel & olive	.25	.25
120	A44	15fr red, salmon & yel grn	.30	.25
121	A44	20fr red, indigo & org	.35	.25
		Nos. 118-121 (4)	1.15	1.00

Intl. Toy Fair in Nuremberg, Germany.

Ram — A45

1969, Aug. 18		**Engr.**		**Perf. 13**
122	A45	1fr shown	.25	.25
123	A45	2fr Goat	.25	.25
124	A45	10fr Donkey	.30	.25
125	A45	35fr Horse	.90	.30
126	A45	90fr Dromedaries	1.40	.50
		Nos. 122-126 (5)	3.10	1.55

Development Bank Issue
Common Design Type

1969, Sept. 10				
127	CD130	50fr brt lil, grn & ocher	.35	.25
128	CD130	90fr ol brn, grn & ocher	.65	.25

Boy Being Vaccinated — A46

1969, Nov. 10		**Engr.**		**Perf. 13**
129	A46	50fr brn, indigo & brt grn	.75	.25

Campaign against smallbox and measles.

ASECNA Issue
Common Design Type

1969, Dec. 12		**Engr.**		**Perf. 13**
130	CD132	100fr dark slate green	.90	.40

African and Japanese Women — A47

150fr, Flags and maps of Mali and Japan.

1970, Apr. 13		**Engr.**		**Perf. 13**
131	A47	100fr brown, bl & ocher	.90	.40
132	A47	150fr dk red, yel grn & org	1.25	.50

Issued to publicize EXPO '70 International Exhibition, Osaka, Japan, Mar. 15-Sept. 13.

Satellite Telecommunications, Map of Africa and ITU Emblem — A48

1970, May 17		**Engr.**		**Perf. 13**
133	A48	90fr car rose & brn	.90	.40

World Telecommunications Day.

UPU Headquarters Issue
Common Design Type

1970, May 20		**Engr.**		**Perf. 13**
134	CD133	50fr dk red, bl grn & ol	.45	.25
135	CD133	60fr red lil, ultra & red brn	.60	.25

Post Office, Bamako — A49

Public Buildings: 40fr, Chamber of Commerce, Bamako. 60fr, Public Works Ministry, Bamako. 80fr, City Hall, Segou.

1970, Nov. 23		**Engr.**		**Perf. 13**
136	A49	30fr brn, brt grn & olive	.35	.25
137	A49	40fr brn, sl grn & dp claret	.45	.25
138	A49	60fr brn red, sl grn & gray	.60	.30
139	A49	80fr brn, brt grn & emer	.85	.40
		Nos. 136-139 (4)	2.25	1.20

Gallet 030T, 1882 — A50

Old Steam Locomotives: 40fr, Felou 030T, 1882. 50fr, Bechevel 230T, 1882. 80fr, Type 231, 1930. 100fr, Type 141, 1930.

1970, Dec. 14		**Engr.**		**Perf. 13**
140	A50	20fr brt grn, dk car & blk	1.75	.55
141	A50	40fr blk, dk grn & ocher	2.25	.65
142	A50	50fr bis brn, bl grn & blk	3.00	.90
143	A50	80fr car rose, blk & bl grn	4.25	1.10
144	A50	100fr ocher, bl grn & blk	7.00	1.75
		Nos. 140-144 (5)	18.25	4.95

Scout Sounding Retreat — A51

Boy Scouts: 5fr, Crossing river, horiz. 100fr, Canoeing, horiz.

		Perf. 13x12½, 12½x13		
1970, Dec. 28				**Litho.**
145	A51	5fr multicolored	.25	.25
146	A51	30fr multicolored	.50	.25
147	A51	100fr multicolored	1.25	.40
		Nos. 145-147 (3)	2.00	.90

Bambara Mask, San — A52

Designs: 25fr, Dogon mask, Bandiagara. 50fr, Kanaga ideogram. 80fr, Bambara ideogram.

1971, Jan. 25		**Photo.**		**Perf. 12x12½**
148	A52	20fr orange & multi	.25	.25
149	A52	25fr brt green & multi	.35	.25
150	A52	50fr dk purple & multi	.60	.25
151	A52	80fr blue & multi	.90	.25
		Nos. 148-151 (4)	2.10	1.00

Boy, Medical and Scientific Symbols — A53

1971, Mar. 22		**Engr.**		**Perf. 13**
152	A53	100fr dp car, ocher & grn	1.20	.50

B.C.G. inoculation (Bacillus-Calmette-Guerin) against tuberculosis, 50th anniv.

Boy Scouts, Mt. Fuji, Japanese Print — A54

1971, Apr. 19				
153	A54	80fr lt ultra, dp plum & brt grn	.75	.30

13th Boy Scout World Jamboree, Asagiri Plain, Japan, Aug. 2-10.

UNICEF Emblem, Hands and Rose — A55

60fr, UNICEF emblem, women & children, vert.

1971, May 24		**Engr.**		**Perf. 13**
154	A55	50fr brn org, car & dk brn	.45	.25
155	A55	60fr vio bl, grn & red brn	.60	.25

25th anniv. of UNICEF.

Mali Farmer — A56

Costumes of Mali: 10fr, Mali farm woman. 15fr, Tuareg. 60fr, Embroidered robe, Grand Boubou. 80fr, Ceremonial robe, woman.

1971, June 14		**Photo.**		**Perf. 13**
156	A56	5fr gray & multi	.25	.25
157	A56	10fr vio bl & multi	.30	.25
158	A56	15fr yellow & multi	.35	.25
159	A56	60fr gray & multi	.60	.25
160	A56	80fr tan & multi	.85	.30
		Nos. 156-160 (5)	2.35	1.30

Map of Africa with Communications Network — A57

1971, Aug. 16		**Photo.**		**Perf. 13**
161	A57	50fr bl, vio bl & org	.50	.25

Pan-African telecommunications system.

Hibiscus — A58

Flowers: 50fr, Poinsettia. 60fr, Adenium obesum. 80fr, Dogbane. 100fr, Satanocrater berhautii.

1971, Oct. 4		**Litho.**		**Perf. 14x13½**
162	A58	20fr multicolored	.45	.25
163	A58	50fr multicolored	.90	.30
164	A58	60fr multicolored	1.20	.35
165	A58	80fr multicolored	1.50	.45
166	A58	100fr multicolored	2.00	.55
		Nos. 162-166 (5)	6.05	1.90

For surcharge see No. 204.

Mother, Child and Bird (Sculpture) — A59

1971, Dec. 27		**Engr.**		**Perf. 13x12½**
167	A59	70fr mag, sepia & bl grn	.75	.30

Natl. Institute of Social Security, 15th anniv.

ITU Emblem — A60

1972, May 17		**Photo.**		**Perf. 13x13½**
168	A60	70fr blue, maroon & blk	.75	.25

4th World Telecommunications Day.

Clay Funerary Statuette — A61

Mali Art: 40fr, Female torso, wood. 50fr, Masked figure, painted stone. 100fr, Animals and men, wrought iron.

1972, May 29				**Perf. 12½x13**
169	A61	30fr org red & multi	.30	.25
170	A61	40fr yellow & multi	.45	.25
171	A61	50fr red & multi	.60	.25
172	A61	100fr lt green & multi	1.20	.40
		Nos. 169-172 (4)	2.55	1.15

Morse and Telegraph — A62

1972, June 5		**Engr.**		**Perf. 13**
173	A62	80fr red, emer & choc	.75	.35

Centenary of the death of Samuel F. B. Morse (1791-1872), inventor of the telegraph.

Weather Balloon over Africa — A63

1972, July 10		**Photo.**		**Perf. 12½x13**
174	A63	130fr multicolored	1.50	.60

12th World Meteorology Day.

Folk Dances — A64

10fr, Sarakolé Dance, Kayes. 20fr, LaGomba, Bamako. 50fr, Hunters' dance, Bougouni. 70fr, Koré Duga, Ségou. 80fr, Kanaga, Sanga. 120fr, Targui, Timbuktu.

1972, Aug. 21		**Photo.**		**Perf. 13**
175	A64	10fr shown	.30	.25
176	A64	20fr multi	.45	.25
177	A64	50fr multi	.60	.25
178	A64	70fr multi	.75	.30
179	A64	80fr multi	.95	.35
180	A64	120fr multi	1.40	.45
		Nos. 175-180 (6)	4.45	1.85

People, Book, Pencil — A65

1972, Sept. 8		**Typo.**		**Perf. 12½x13**
181	A65	80fr black & yel grn	.75	.25

World Literacy Day, Sept. 8.

MALI — Republic of Mali

"Edison Classique," Mali Instruments — A66

1972, Sept. 18   Engr.   *Perf. 13*
182   A66   100fr multicolored   1.00   .40
First Anthology of Music of Mali.

Aries A67

Signs of the Zodiac: No. 184, Taurus. No. 185, Gemini. No. 186, Cancer. No. 187, Leo. No. 188, Virgo. No. 189, Libra. No. 190, Scorpio. No. 191, Sagittarius. No. 192, Capricorn. No. 193, Aquarius. No. 194, Pisces.

1972, Oct. 23   Engr.   *Perf. 11*
183   A67   15fr lilac & bis brn   .25   .25
184   A67   15fr bister brn & blk   .25   .25
  a.   Pair #183-184   .50   .40
185   A67   35fr maroon & indigo   .55   .25
186   A67   35fr emerald & mar   .55   .25
  a.   Pair, #185-186   1.25   .40
187   A67   40fr blue & red brn   .60   .25
188   A67   40fr dk pur & red brn   .60   .25
  a.   Pair, #187-188   1.40   .40
189   A67   45fr dk blue & mar   .65   .30
190   A67   45fr maroon & brt grn   .65   .30
  a.   Pair, #189-190   1.50   .60
191   A67   65fr dk violet & ind   .90   .35
192   A67   65fr dk vio & gray ol   .90   .35
  a.   Pair, #191-192   2.00   .70
193   A67   90fr brt pink & ind   1.40   .60
194   A67   90fr brt pink & grn   1.40   .60
  a.   Pair, #193-194   3.00   1.25
   Nos. 183-194 (12)   8.70   4.00

Arrival of First Locomotive in Bamako, 1906 — A68

Designs (Locomotives): 30fr, Thies-Bamako, 1920. 60fr, Thies-Bamako, 1927. 120fr, Two Alsthom BB, 1947.

1972, Dec. 11   Engr.   *Perf. 13*
195   A68   10fr ind, brn & sl grn   1.90   .60
196   A68   30fr sl grn, ind & brn   3.75   1.25
197   A68   60fr sl grn, ind & brn   5.50   1.75
198   A68   120fr sl grn & choc   7.50   2.50
   Nos. 195-198 (4)   18.65   6.10

2nd African Games, Lagos, Nigeria, Jan. 7-18 — A69

1973, Jan. 15   Photo.   *Perf. 12½*
199   A69   70fr High jump   .50   .25
200   A69   270fr Discus   1.25   .60
201   A69   280fr Soccer   1.40   .85
   Nos. 199-201 (3)   3.15   1.70

INTERPOL Emblem and Headquarters A70

1973, Feb. 28   Photo.   *Perf. 13*
202   A70   80fr multi   .90   .25
50th anniversary of International Criminal Police Organization (INTERPOL).

Blind Man and Disabled Boy — A71

1973, Apr. 24   Engr.   *Perf. 12½x13*
203   A71   70fr dk car, brick red & blk   .60   .25
Help for the handicapped.

No. 166 Surcharged with New Value, 2 Bars, and Overprinted

Overprint reads "SECHERESSE / SOLIDARITE AFRICAINE".

1973, Aug. 16   Litho.   *Perf. 13½*
204   A58   200fr on 100fr multi   1.75   .75
African solidarity in drought emergency.

Cora — A72

Musical Instruments: 10fr, Balafon, horiz. 15fr, Djembe. 20fr, Guitar. 25fr, N'Djarka. 30fr, M'Bolon. 35fr, Dozo N'Goni. 40fr, N'Tamani.

Perf. 12½x13, 13x12½

1973, Dec. 10   Engr.
205   A72   5fr mar, dk grn & brn   .30   .25
206   A72   10fr bl & choc   .35   .25
207   A72   15fr brn, dk red & yel   .45   .25
208   A72   20fr mar & brn ol   .55   .25
209   A72   25fr org, yel & blk   .60   .25
210   A72   30fr vio bl & blk   .65   .25
211   A72   35fr dk red & brn   .75   .35
212   A72   40fr dk red & choc   .85   .35
   Nos. 205-212 (8)   4.50   2.20

Farmer with Newspaper, Corn — A73

1974, Mar. 11   Engr.   *Perf. 12½x13*
213   A73   70fr multi   .60   .25
"Kibaru," rural newspaper, 2nd anniv.

Soccer, Goalkeeper, Symbolic Globe and Net — A74

200fr, Games' emblem, soccer and ball.

1974, May 6   Engr.   *Perf. 13*
214   A74   270fr multi   1.10   .60
215   A74   280fr multi   1.90   .90
World Cup Soccer Championships, Munich, June 13-July 7. For surcharges see Nos. 219-220.

Old and New Ships, UPU Emblem — A75

90fr, Old and new planes, UPU emblem. 270fr, Old and new trains, UPU emblem.

1974, June 2   Engr.   *Perf. 12½x13*
216   A75   80fr brn & multir   .45   .25
217   A75   90fr ultra & multi   .65   .35
218   A75   270fr lt grn & multi   1.90   .85
   Nos. 216-218 (3)   3.00   1.45
Centenary of Universal Postal Union. For surcharges see Nos. 229-230.

Nos. 214-215 Surcharged and Overprinted in Black or Red

Overprint reads "R.F.A. 2 / HOLLANDE 1".

1974, Aug. 28   Engr.   *Perf. 13*
219   A74   300fr on 270fr multi   2.10   1.00
220   A74   330fr on 280fr multi (R)   2.40   1.10
World Cup Soccer Championship, 1974, victory of German Federal Republic.

Artisans of Mali — A76

1974, Sept. 16   Photo.   *Perf. 12½x13*
221   A76   50fr Weaver   .45   .25
222   A76   60fr Potter   .55   .25
223   A76   70fr Smiths   .60   .25
224   A76   80fr Sculptor   .70   .30
   Nos. 221-224 (4)   2.30   1.05

Niger River near Gao — A77

Landscapes: 20fr, The Hand of Fatma (rock formation), vert. 40fr, Gouina Waterfall. 70fr, Dogon houses, vert.

Perf. 13x12½, 12½x13

1974, Sept. 23
225   A77   10fr multi   .25   .25
226   A77   20fr multi   .25   .25
227   A77   40fr multi   .45   .25
228   A77   70fr multi   .65   .30
   Nos. 225-228 (4)   1.60   1.05

Nos. 216 and 218 Surcharged and Overprinted in Black or Red

Overprint reads "9 OCTOBRE 1974".

1974, Oct. 9   Engr.   *Perf. 13*
229   A75   250fr on 80fr multi   1.60   .80
230   A75   300fr on 270fr multi (R)   2.10   1.00
UPU Day.

Mao Tse-tung, Flags, Great Wall — A78

1974, Oct. 21   Engr.   *Perf. 13*
231   A78   100fr multi   2.75   .65
People's Republic of China, 25th anniv.

Artisans and Lions Emblem A79

100fr, View of Samanko and Lions emblem.

1975, Feb. 3   Photo.   *Perf. 13*
232   A79   90fr red & multi   .80   .25
233   A79   100fr blue & multi   1.00   .30
5th anniv. of lepers' rehabilitation village, Samanko, sponsored by Lions Intl. For surcharges see Nos. 303-304.

Fish — A80

Designs: 60fr, Tetrodon Fahaka. 70fr, Malopterurus electricus. 80fr, Citharinus latus. 90fr, Hydrocyon forskali. 110fr, Lates niloticus.

1975, May 12   Engr.   *Perf. 13*
234   A80   60fr shown   1.10   .30
235   A80   70fr multicolored   1.25   .35
236   A80   80fr multicolored   1.50   .40
237   A80   90fr multicolored   1.75   .45
238   A80   110fr multicolored   2.25   .50
   Nos. 234-238 (5)   7.85   2.00
See Nos. 256-260.

Woman and IWY Emblem — A81

1975, June 9   Engr.   *Perf. 13*
239   A81   150fr red & grn   1.00   .35
International Women's Year 1975.

Morris "Oxford," 1913 — A82

Automobiles: 130fr, Franklin "E," 1907. 190fr, Daimler, 1900. 230fr, Panhard & Levassor, 1895.

1975, June 16
240   A82   90fr blk, ol & lil   .70   .30
241   A82   130fr vio bl, gray & red   1.10   .40
242   A82   190fr bl, grn & indigo   1.60   .55
243   A82   230fr red, ultra & brn ol   1.80   .55
   Nos. 240-243 (4)   5.20   1.80

Carthaginian Tristater, 500 B.C. — A83

Ancient Coins: 170fr, Decadrachma, Syracuse, 413 B.C. 190fr, Acanthe tetradrachma, 400 B.C. 260fr, Didrachma, Eritrea, 480-445 B.C.

1975, Oct. 13   Engr.   *Perf. 13*
244   A83   130fr bl, cl & blk   .70   .25
245   A83   170fr emer, brn & blk   1.00   .50
246   A83   190fr grn, red & blk   1.40   .70
247   A83   260fr dp bl, org & blk   2.00   1.00
   Nos. 244-247 (4)   5.10   2.45

UN Emblem and "ONU" A84

1975, Nov. 10   Engr.   *Perf. 13*
248   A84   200fr emer & brt bl   1.10   .45
30th anniversary of UN.

A. G. Bell, Waves, Satellite, Telephone — A85

1976, Mar. 8   Litho.   *Perf. 12x12½*
249   A85   180fr brn, ultra & ocher   1.10   .40
Centenary of first telephone call by Alexander Graham Bell, Mar. 10, 1876.

MALI — Republic of Mali

Chameleon — A86

1976, Mar. 31 Litho. Perf. 12½
250	A86	20fr shown	.35	.25
251	A86	30fr Lizard	.50	.25
252	A86	40fr Tortoise	.70	.25
253	A86	90fr Python	1.60	.50
254	A86	120fr Crocodile	2.00	.60
		Nos. 250-254 (5)	5.15	1.85

Konrad Adenauer and Cologne Cathedral — A87

1976, Apr. 26 Engr. Perf. 13
255	A87	180fr mag & dk brn	1.20	.50

Konrad Adenauer (1876-1967), German Chancellor.

Fish Type of 1975

100fr, Heterotis niloticus. 120fr, Synodontis budgetti. 130fr, Heterobranchus bidorsalis. 150fr, Tilapia monodi. 220fr, Alestes macrolepidotus.

1976, June 28 Engr. Perf. 13
256	A80	100fr multi	.75	.25
257	A80	120fr multi	1.00	.25
258	A80	130fr multi	1.10	.30
259	A80	150fr multi	1.20	.40
260	A80	220fr multi	1.75	.50
		Nos. 256-260 (5)	5.80	1.70

Page from Children's Book — A88

1976, July 19
261	A88	130fr red & multi	.75	.35

Books for children.

"Le Roi de l'Air" — A89

1976, July 26 Litho. Perf. 12½x13
262	A89	120fr multi	1.25	.45

First lottery, sponsored by L'Essor newspaper.

"Do not overload scaffold" — A90

1976, Aug. 16 Litho. Perf. 13
263	A90	120fr multi	.60	.25

National Insurance Institute, 20th anniv.

Letters, UPU and UN Emblems — A91

1976, Oct. 4 Engr. Perf. 13
264	A91	120fr lil, org & grn	.75	.35

UN Postal Administration, 25th anniv.

Moto-Guzzi 254, Italy — A92

Motorcycles: 120fr, BMW 900, Germany. 130fr, Honda-Egli, Japan. 140fr, Motobecane LT-3, France.

1976, Oct. 18 Engr. Perf. 13
265	A92	90fr multi	1.00	.25
266	A92	120fr multi	1.25	.30
267	A92	130fr multi	1.25	.40
268	A92	140fr multi	1.50	.40
		Nos. 265-268 (4)	5.00	1.35

Fishing Boat, Muscat — A93

180fr, Coaster, Cochin China. 190fr, Fireboat, Dunkirk, 1878. 200fr, Nile river boat.

1976, Dec. 6 Engr. Perf. 13
269	A93	160fr multi	.80	.30
270	A93	180fr multi	.90	.30
271	A93	190fr multi	1.00	.35
272	A93	200fr multi	1.00	.45
		Nos. 269-272 (4)	3.70	1.40

Indigo Finch — A94

Birds: 25fr, Yellow-breasted barbet. 30fr, Vitelline masked weaver. 40fr, Bee-eater. 50fr, Senegal parrot.

1977, Apr. 18 Photo. Perf. 13
273	A94	15fr multi	.50	.25
274	A94	25fr multi	.90	.25
275	A94	30fr multi	1.10	.25
276	A94	40fr multi	1.40	.30
277	A94	50fr multi	1.80	.35
		Nos. 273-277 (5)	5.70	1.40

See Nos. 298-302.

Braille Statue, Script and Reading Hands — A95

1977, Apr. 25 Engr. Perf. 13
278	A95	200fr multi	1.25	.55

Louis Braille (1809-1852), inventor of the reading and writing system for the blind.

Electronic Tree, ITU Emblem — A96

1977, May 17 Photo.
279	A96	120fr dk brn & org	.50	.25

World Telecommunications Day.

Dragonfly — A97

Insects: 10fr, Praying mantis. 20fr, Tropical wasp. 35fr, Cockchafer. 60fr, Flying stag beetle.

1977, June 15 Photo. Perf. 13x12½
280	A97	5fr multi	.35	.25
281	A97	10fr multi	.50	.25
282	A97	20fr multi	.60	.25
283	A97	35fr multi	1.00	.25
284	A97	60fr multi	1.25	.30
		Nos. 280-284 (5)	3.70	1.30

Knight and Rook — A98

Chess Pieces: 130fr, Bishop and pawn, vert. 300fr, Queen and King.

1977, June 27 Engr. Perf. 13
285	A98	120fr multi	1.50	.45
286	A98	130fr multi	1.60	.55
287	A98	300fr multi	3.50	1.25
		Nos. 285-287 (3)	6.60	2.25

Europafrica Issue

Symbolic Ship, White and Brown Persons — A99

1977, July 18 Litho. Perf. 13
288	A99	400fr multi	2.00	.80

Horse, by Leonardo da Vinci — A100

Drawings by Leonardo da Vinci: 300fr, Head of Young Woman. 500fr, Self-portrait.

1977, Sept. 5 Engr. Perf. 13
289	A100	200fr dk brn & blk	1.25	.65
290	A100	300fr dk brn & ol	1.75	.65
291	A100	500fr dk brn & red	2.40	1.10
		Nos. 289-291 (3)	5.40	2.40

Hotel de l'Amitié, Bamako — A101

1977, Oct. 15 Litho. Perf. 13x12½
292	A101	120fr multi	.60	.25

Opening of the Hotel de l'Amitié, Oct. 15.

Dome of the Rock Jerusalem — A102

1977, Oct. 17 Perf. 12½
293	A102	120fr multi	.55	.25
294	A102	180fr multi	.85	.40

Palestinian fighters and their families.

Black Man, Chains and UN Emblem — A103

130fr, Statue of Liberty, people & UN emblem. 180fr, Black children & horse behind fence.

1978, Mar. 13 Engr. Perf. 13
295	A103	120fr multi	.55	.25
296	A103	130fr multi	.60	.25
297	A103	180fr multi	.90	.25
		Nos. 295-297 (3)	2.05	.85

International Year against Apartheid.

Bird Type of 1977

Birds: 20fr, Granatina bengala. 30fr, Lagonosticta vinacea. 50fr, Lagonosticta. 70fr, Turtle dove. 80fr, Buffalo weaver.

1978, Apr. 10 Litho. Perf. 13
298	A94	20fr multi	.65	.25
299	A94	30fr multi	.90	.25
300	A94	50fr multi	1.10	.30
301	A94	70fr multi	1.50	.40
302	A94	80fr multi	2.00	.50
		Nos. 298-302 (5)	6.15	1.70

Nos. 232-233 Surcharged with New Value, Bar and Overprinted

Overprint reads "XXe ANNIVERSAIRE DU LIONS CLUB DE BAMAKO 1958-1978".

1978, May 8 Photo.
303	A79	120fr on 90fr multi	.70	.25
304	A79	130fr on 100fr multi	.80	.25

20th anniversary of Bamako Lions Club.

Wall and Desert A105

1978, May 18 Litho. Perf. 13
306	A105	200fr multi	1.00	.40

Hammamet Conference for reclamation of the desert.

Mahatma Gandhi and Roses — A106

1978, May 29 Engr.
307	A106	140fr blk, brn & red	1.50	.30

Mohandas K. Gandhi (1869-1948), Hindu spiritual leader.

Dermestes A107

Insects: 25fr, Ground beetle. 90fr, Cricket. 120fr, Ladybird. 140fr, Goliath beetle.

1978, June 12 Photo. Perf. 13
308	A107	15fr multi	.55	.25
309	A107	25fr multi	.70	.25
310	A107	90fr multi	1.20	.25
311	A107	120fr multi	1.20	.30
312	A107	140fr multi	1.50	.35
		Nos. 308-312 (5)	5.15	1.40

Bridge A108

MALI — Republic of Mali

Design: 100fr, Dominoes, vert.

1978, June 26   Engr.
- 313 A108 100fr multi   .75   .25
- 314 A108 130fr multi   1.00   .30

Aristotle — A109

1978, Oct. 16   Engr.   Perf. 13
- 315 A109 200fr multi   1.20   .35

Aristotle (384-322 B.C.), Greek philosopher.

Human Rights and UN Emblems A110

1978, Dec. 11   Engr.   Perf. 13
- 316 A110 180fr red, bl & brn   1.25   .25

Universal Declaration of Human Rights, 30th anniversary.

Manatoo — A111

Endangered Wildlife: 120fr, Chimpanzee. 130fr, Damaliscus antelope. 180fr, Oryx. 200fr, Derby's eland.

1979, Apr. 23   Litho.   Perf. 12½
- 317 A111 100fr multi   .75   .25
- 318 A111 120fr multi   .90   .25
- 319 A111 130fr multi   1.00   .25
- 320 A111 180fr multi   1.40   .35
- 321 A111 200fr multi   1.50   .35
- Nos. 317-321 (5)   5.55   1.45

Boy Praying and IYC Emblem A112

IYC emblem and: 200fr, Girl and Boy Scout holding bird. 300fr, IYC emblem, boys with calf.

1979, May 7   Engr.   Perf. 13
- 322 A112 120fr multi   .60   .25
- 323 A112 200fr multi   .90   .35
- 324 A112 300fr multi   1.50   .50
- Nos. 322-324 (3)   3.00   1.10

International Year of the Child.

Judo and Notre Dame, Paris A113

1979, May 14   Engr.   Perf. 13
- 325 A113 200fr multi   1.40   .45

World Judo Championship, Paris.

Telecommunica-tions A114

1979, May 17   Litho.
- 326 A114 120fr multi   .60   .25

11th Telecommunications Day.

Wood Carving — A115

Sculptures from National Museum: 120fr, Ancestral figures. 130fr, Animal heads, and kneeling woman.

1979, May 18   Perf. 13x12½
- 327 A115 90fr multi   .45   .25
- 328 A115 120fr multi   .60   .25
- 329 A115 130fr multi   .75   .30
- Nos. 327-329 (3)   1.80   .80

International Museums Day.

Rowland Hill and Mali No. 15 — A116

130fr, Zeppelin & Saxony #1. 180fr, Concorde & France #3. 200fr, Stagecoach & US #2. 300fr, UPU emblem & Penny Black.

1979, May 21   Engr.   Perf. 13
- 330 A116 120fr multi   .55   .25
- 331 A116 130fr multi   .55   .25
- 332 A116 180fr multi   .75   .30
- 333 A116 200fr multi   .85   .30
- 334 A116 300fr multi   1.50   .55
- Nos. 330-334 (5)   4.20   1.65

Sir Rowland Hill (1795-1879), originator of penny postage.

Cora Players — A117

1979, June 4   Litho.   Perf. 13
- 335 A117 200fr multi   1.50   .50

Adenium Obesum and Sankore Mosque A118

Design: 300fr, Satellite, mounted messenger, globe and letter, vert.

1979, June 8   Photo.
- 336 A118 120fr multi   1.50   .75

    Engr.
- 337 A118 300fr multi   2.60   1.60

Philexafrique II, Libreville, Gabon, June 8-17. Nos. 336, 337 printed in sheets of 10 and 5 labels showing exhibition emblem.

Map of Mali — A119

Design: 300fr, Men planting trees.

1979, June 18   Litho.   Perf. 13x12½
- 338 A119 200fr multi   1.00   .40
- 339 A119 300fr multi   1.60   .70

Operation Green Sahel.

Lemons — A120

1979, June 25   Perf. 12½x13
- 340 A120 10fr shown   .25   .25
- 341 A120 60fr Pineapple   .45   .25
- 342 A120 100fr Papayas   .75   .25
- 343 A120 120fr Soursops   .85   .25
- 344 A120 130fr Mangoes   1.00   .25
- Nos. 340-344 (5)   3.30   1.25

Sigmund Freud — A121

1979, Sept. 17   Engr.   Perf. 13
- 345 A121 300fr vio bl & sepia   1.50   .60

Sigmund Freud (1856-1939), founder of psychoanalysis.

Timbuktu, Man and Camel — A122

Design: 130fr, Caillié, Map of Sahara.

1979, Sept. 27   Perf. 13x12½
- 346 A122 120fr multi   .75   .30
- 347 A122 130fr multi   .85   .35

René Caillié (1799-1838), French explorer, 180th birth anniversary.

Eurema Brigitta A123

120fr, Papilio pylades. 130fr, Melanitis leda satyridae. 180fr, Gonimbrasia belina occidentalis. 200fr, Bunaea alcinoe.

1979, Oct. 15   Litho.   Perf. 13
- 348 A123 100fr shown   1.10   .25
- 349 A123 120fr multi   1.25   .30
- 350 A123 130fr multi   1.40   .35
- 351 A123 180fr multi   2.00   .45
- 352 A123 200fr multi   2.25   .50
- Nos. 348-352 (5)   8.00   1.85

Greyhound A124

Designs: Dogs.

1979, Nov. 12   Litho.   Perf. 12½
- 353 A124 20fr multi   .65   .25
- 354 A124 50fr multi   .80   .25
- 355 A124 70fr multi   .95   .25
- 356 A124 80fr multi   1.20   .25
- 357 A124 90fr multi   1.40   .30
- Nos. 353-357 (5)   5.00   1.30

Wild Donkey — A125

1980, Feb. 4   Litho.   Perf. 13x13½
- 358 A125 90fr shown   .80   .25
- 359 A125 120fr Addax   1.00   .25
- 360 A125 130fr Cheetahs   1.15   .30
- 361 A125 140fr Mouflon   1.25   .35
- 362 A125 180fr Buffalo   1.80   .35
- Nos. 358-362 (5)   6.00   1.50

Photovoltaic Cell Pumping Station, Koni — A126

Solar Energy Utilization: 100fr, Sun shields, Dire. 120fr, Solar stove, Bamako. 130fr, Heliodynamic solar energy generating station, Dire.

1980, Mar. 10   Litho.   Perf. 13
- 363 A126 90fr multi   .45   .25
- 364 A126 100fr multi   .55   .25
- 365 A126 120fr multi   .60   .25
- 366 A126 130fr multi   .75   .25
- Nos. 363-366 (4)   2.35   1.00

For surcharge see No. 511.

Horse Breeding, Mopti — A127

1980, Mar. 17
- 367 A127 100fr shown   .80   .25
- 368 A127 120fr Nioro   .90   .25
- 369 A127 130fr Koro   1.00   .25
- 370 A127 180fr Coastal zone   1.25   .30
- 371 A127 200fr Banamba   1.25   .55
- Nos. 367-371 (5)   5.20   1.60

Alexander Fleming (Discoverer of Penicillin) — A128

1980, May 5   Engr.   Perf. 13
- 372 A128 200fr multi   1.25   .50

Avicenna and Medical Instruments A129

Design: 180fr, Avicenna as teacher (12th century manuscript illustration)

1980, May 12   Perf. 13x12½
- 373 A129 120fr multi   .65   .25
- 374 A129 180fr multi   .85   .35

Avicenna (980-1037), Arab physician and philosopher, 1000th birth anniversary.

Pilgrim at Mecca — A130

130fr, Praying hands, stars, Mecca. 180fr, Pilgrims, camels, horiz.

1980, May 26   Litho.   Perf. 13
- 375 A130 120fr shown   .55   .25
- 376 A130 130fr multi   .55   .25
- 377 A130 180fr multi   .80   .25
- Nos. 375-377 (3)   1.90   .80

Hegira, 1500th Anniversary.

MALI — Republic of Mali

Guavas — A131

1980, June 9
378	A131	90fr shown	.55	.25
379	A131	120fr Cashews	.60	.25
380	A131	130fr Oranges	.70	.25
381	A131	140fr Bananas	.90	.25
382	A131	180fr Grapefruit	1.00	.30
		Nos. 378-382 (5)	3.75	1.30

League of Nations, 60th Anniversary A132

1980, June 23   Engr.   Perf. 13
383	A132	200fr multi	.75	.30

Festival Emblem, Mask, Xylophone A133

1980, July 5   Litho.   Perf. 12½
384	A133	120fr multi	.60	.25

6th Biennial Arts and Cultural Festival, Bamako, July 5-15.

Sun Rising over Map of Africa — A134

1980, July 7   Engr.   Perf. 13
385	A134	300fr multi	1.10	.45

Afro-Asian Bandung Conference, 25th anniversary.

Market Place, Conference Emblem — A135

120fr, View of Mali, vert.

1980, Sept. 15   Litho.   Perf. 13
386	A135	120fr multi	.55	.25
387	A135	180fr shown	.85	.30

World Tourism Conf., Manila, Sept. 27.

Hydro-electric Dam and Power Station — A136

20th Anniversary of Independence: 120fr, Pres. Traore, flag of Mali, National Assembly building. 130fr, Independence monument, Bamako, Political Party badge, vert.

1980, Sept. 15   Perf. 13x12½
388	A136	100fr multi	.45	.25
389	A136	120fr multi	.60	.25
390	A136	130fr multi	.75	.30
		Nos. 388-390 (3)	1.80	.80

Utetheisa Pulchella — A137

60fr, Mylothis chloris pieridae. 70fr, Hypolimnas mishippus. 80fr, Papilio demodocus.

1980, Oct. 6   Perf. 13½
391	A137	50fr shown	.85	.25
392	A137	60fr multi	1.05	.25
393	A137	70fr multi	1.25	.30
394	A137	80fr multi	1.40	.35
		Nos. 391-394,C402 (5)	8.30	2.15

Fight Against Cigarette Smoking A138

1980, Oct. 13   Litho.   Perf. 12½x12
395	A138	200fr multi	1.10	.45

European-African Economic Convention — A139

1980, Oct. 20   Perf. 12½
396	A139	300fr multi	1.90	.60

Agricultural Map of West Africa — A140

West African Economic Council, 5th anniversary (Economic Maps): 120fr, Transportation. 130fr, Industry. 140fr, Communications.

1980, Nov. 5   Perf. 13½x13
397	A140	100fr multi	.50	.25
398	A140	120fr multi	.55	.25
399	A140	130fr multi	.65	.25
400	A140	140fr multi	.70	.30
		Nos. 397-400 (4)	2.40	1.05

African Postal Union, 5th Anniv. — A141

1980, Dec. 24   Photo.   Perf. 13½
401	A141	130fr multi	.75	.30

Senufo Fertility Statue — A142

Designs: Fertility statues.

1981, Jan. 12   Litho.   Perf. 13
402	A142	60fr Nomo dogon	.30	.25
403	A142	70fr shown	.40	.25
404	A142	90fr Bamanan	.55	.25
405	A142	100fr Spirit	.60	.25
406	A142	120fr Dogon	.95	.25
		Nos. 402-406 (5)	2.80	1.25

Mambi Sidibe — A143

Philosophers: 130fr, Amadou Hampate.

1981, Feb. 16   Perf. 12½x13
407	A143	120fr shown	.60	.25
408	A143	130fr multi	.60	.25

Hegira (Pilgrimage Year) — A144

1981, Feb. 23   Perf. 13
409	A144	120fr multi	.55	.25
410	A144	180fr multi	1.00	.35

Cattle Breeds — A145

Designs: 20fr, Kaarta zebu. 30fr, Peul du Macina zebu. 40fr, Maure zebu. 80fr, Touareg zebu. 100fr, N'Dama cow.

1981, Mar. 9   Perf. 12½
411	A145	20fr multi	.50	.25
412	A145	30fr multi	.65	.25
413	A145	40fr multi	.80	.25
414	A145	80fr multi	1.20	.25
415	A145	100fr multi	1.25	.30
		Nos. 411-415 (5)	4.40	1.30

See Nos. 433-437.

Flowers — A146

Designs: 50fr, Crinum de Moore. 100fr, Double Rose Hibiscus. 120fr, Pervenche. 130fr, Frangipani. 180fr, Orgueil de Chine.

1981, Mar. 16
416	A146	50fr multi	.30	.25
417	A146	100fr multi	.65	.25
418	A146	120fr multi	.80	.25
419	A146	130fr multi	1.00	.25
420	A146	180fr multi	1.25	.45
		Nos. 416-420 (5)	4.00	1.45

See Nos. 442-446.

Wrench Operated by Artificial Hand — A147

Perf. 13x12½, 12x13

1981, May 4   Engr.
421	A147	100fr Heads, vert.	.55	.25
422	A147	120fr shown	.60	.25

Intl. Year of the Disabled.

13th World Telecommunications Day — A148

1981, May 17   Litho.   Perf. 13x12½
423	A148	130fr multi	.75	.25

Pierre Curie, Lab Equipment A149

1981, May 25   Engr.
424	A149	180fr multi	1.25	.50

Curie (1859-1906), discoverer of radium.

Scouts at Water Hole A150

1981, June 8   Litho.   Perf. 13
425	A150	110fr multi	1.25	.30
426	A150	160fr Sending signals	1.75	.45
427	A150	300fr Salute, vert.	3.00	.70
		Nos. 425-427 (3)	6.00	1.45

Souvenir Sheet
428	A150	500fr Lord Baden-Powell	6.00	4.00

4th African Scouting Conf., Abidjan, June.

Nos. 425-428 Overprinted in Red in 2 or 3 Lines

Overprint reads "DAKAR 8 AOUT 1981/28e CONFÉRENCE MONDIALE DU SCOUTISME".

1981, June 29
429	A150	110fr multi	1.10	.30
430	A150	160fr multi	1.50	.45
431	A150	300fr multi	3.00	.70
		Nos. 429-431 (3)	5.60	1.45

Souvenir Sheet
432	A150	500fr multi	6.50	4.00

28th World Scouting Conf., Dakar, Aug. 8.

Various Goats — A150a

1981, Sept. 14   Litho.   Perf. 13x13½
433	A150a	10fr Maure	.25	.25
434	A150a	25fr Peul	.30	.25
435	A150a	140fr Sahel	1.10	.25
436	A150a	180fr Tuareg	1.40	.30
437	A150a	200fr Djallonke	1.60	.35
		Nos. 433-437 (5)	4.65	1.40

World UPU Day — A151

1981, Oct. 9   Engr.   Perf. 13
438	A151	400fr multi	2.25	.70

World Food Day — A152

1981, Oct. 16
439	A152	200fr multi	1.10	.40

Europafrica Economic Convention A153

1981, Nov. 23   Engr.   Perf. 13
440	A153	700fr multi	3.00	1.05

MALI — Republic of Mali

60th Anniv. of Tuberculosis Inoculation — A154

1981, Dec. 7   Perf. 13x12½
441 A154 200fr multi   1.10   .45

Flower Type of 1981

1982, Jan. 18   Litho.   Perf. 13
442 A146 170fr White water lilies   .85   .25
443 A146 180fr Red kapok bush   .90   .25
444 A146 200fr Purple mimosa   1.10   .30
445 A146 220fr Pobego lilies   1.10   .40
446 A146 270fr Satan's chalices   1.40   .50
     Nos. 442-446 (5)   5.35   1.70

Ceremonial Mask — A155

Designs: Various masks.

1982, Feb. 22   Litho.   Perf. 12½
447 A155 5fr multi   .25   .25
448 A155 35fr multi   .25   .25
449 A155 180fr multi   .90   .30
450 A155 200fr multi   1.00   .35
451 A155 250fr multi   1.20   .35
     Nos. 447-451 (5)   3.60   1.50

25th Anniv. of Sputnik I Flight — A156

1982, Mar. 29   Litho.   Perf. 13
452 A156 270fr multi   1.40   .50

Fight Against Polio — A157

1982, May 3
453 A157 180fr multi   .90   .35

Lions Intl. and Day of the Blind — A158

1982, May 10   Engr.
454 A158 260fr multi   1.40   .30

"Good Friends" Hairstyle — A159

Designs: Various hairstyles.

1982, May 24   Litho.
455 A159 140fr multi   .45   .25
456 A159 150fr multi   .60   .25
457 A159 160fr multi   .75   .30
458 A159 180fr multi   1.10   .35
459 A159 270fr multi   1.75   .60
     Nos. 455-459 (5)   4.65   1.75

Zebu — A160

Designs: Various breeds of zebu.

1982, July 5   Perf. 12½
460 A160 10fr multi   .30   .25
461 A160 60fr multi   .60   .25
462 A160 110fr multi   .90   .25
463 A160 140fr multi   1.40   .35
464 A160 200fr multi   1.50   .40
     Nos. 460-464 (5)   4.70   1.50

Wind Surfing (New Olympic Class) — A161

Designs: Various wind surfers.

1982, Nov. 22   Litho.   Perf. 12½x13
465 A161 200fr multi   .90   .35
466 A161 270fr multi   1.25   .50
467 A161 300fr multi   1.40   .60
     Nos. 465-467 (3)   3.55   1.45

Pres. John F. Kennedy — A162

800fr, Martin Luther King.

1983, Apr. 4   Engr.   Perf. 13
468 A162 800fr brown & red   3.25   1.25
469 A162 800fr brn, blue & pur   3.25   1.25

Oua Traditional Hairstyle — A163

1983, Apr. 25   Litho.
470 A163 180fr shown   1.00   .25
471 A163 200fr Nation   1.10   .25
472 A163 270fr Rond point   1.40   .35
473 A163 300fr Naamu-Naamu   1.50   .40
474 A163 500fr Bamba-Bamba   2.60   .70
     Nos. 470-474 (5)   7.60   1.95

World Communications Year — A164

1983, May 17   Litho.   Perf. 13
475 A164 180fr multi   1.00   .40

Bicent. of Lavoisier's Water Analysis — A165

1983, May 27   Engr.   Perf. 13
476 A165 300fr multi   1.40   .50

Musicians — A166

200fr, Banzoumana Sissoko. 300fr, Batourou Sekou Kouyate.

1983, June 13   Litho.   Perf. 13x13½
477 A166 200fr multi   .90   .25
478 A166 300fr multi   1.20   .35

Nicephore Niepce, Photography Pioneer, (1765-1833) — A167

400fr, Portrait, early camera.

1983, July 4   Engr.   Perf. 13
479 A167 400fr multi   1.75   .45

2nd Pan African Youth Festival — A168

Palestinian Solidarity — A169

1983, Aug. 22   Litho.   Perf. 12½
480 A168 240fr multi   1.10   .30
481 A169 270fr multi   1.20   .40

14th World UPU Day — A170

1983, Oct. 10   Engr.   Perf. 12½
482 A170 240fr multi   1.25   .35

For surcharge see No. 500.

Sahel Goat — A171

1984, Jan. 30   Litho.   Perf. 13
483 A171 20fr shown   .25   .25
484 A171 30fr Billy goat   .35   .25
485 A171 50fr Billy goat, diff.   .65   .25
486 A171 240fr Kaarta goat   1.60   .30
487 A171 350fr Southern goats   2.25   .45
     Nos. 483-487 (5)   5.10   1.50

For surcharges see Nos. 497-499, 501-502.

Rural Development — A172

5fr, Crop disease prevention. 90fr, Carpenters, horiz. 100fr, Tapestry weaving, horiz. 135fr, Metal workers, horiz.

1984, June 1   Litho.   Perf. 13
488 A172 5fr multi   .25   .25
489 A172 90fr multi   .75   .25
490 A172 100fr multi   .75   .30
491 A172 135fr multi   1.00   .45
     Nos. 488-491 (4)   2.75   1.25

Fragrant Trees — A173

515fr, Borassus flabelifer. 1225fr, Vitelaria paradoxa.

1984, June 1
492 A173 515fr multi   4.00   1.90
493 A173 1225fr multi   9.50   4.25

For surcharge see No. 583.

UN Infant Survival Campaign — A174

1984, June 12   Engr.
494 A174 120fr Child, hearts   1.10   .40
495 A174 135fr Children   1.25   .45

1984 UPU Congress — A175

135fr, Anchor, UPU emblem, view of Hamburg.

1984, June 18
496 A175 135fr multicolored   1.25   .40

Nos. 482-487 Surcharged

1984
497 A171 10fr on 20fr #483   .25   .25
498 A171 15fr on 30fr #484   .25   .25
499 A171 25fr on 50fr #485   .40   .25
500 A170 120fr on 240fr #482   1.50   .30
501 A171 120fr on 240fr #486   1.60   .30
502 A171 175fr on 350fr #487   2.25   .50
     Nos. 497-502 (6)   6.25   1.85

West African Economic Community, CEAO, 10th Anniv. — A176

1984, Oct. 22   Litho.   Perf. 13½
503 A176 350fr multi   2.75   1.50

For surcharge see No. 588.

Prehistoric Animals — A177

10fr, Dimetrodon. 25fr, Iguanodon, vert. 30fr, Archaeopteryx, vert.

1984, Nov. 5   Litho.   Perf. 12½
504 A177 10fr multi   .25   .25
505 A177 25fr multi   .40   .25
506 A177 30fr multi   .50   .25
507 A177 120fr Like 10fr   2.00   .40
508 A177 175fr Like 25fr   3.00   .60
509 A177 350fr Like 30fr   5.50   1.50
510 A177 470fr Triceratops   7.50   2.50
     Nos. 504-510 (7)   19.15   5.75

For surcharges see Nos. 579, 593.

MALI — Republic of Mali

No. 366 Overprinted "Aide au Sahel 84" and Surcharged

1984		Litho.		Perf. 13
511	A126	470fr on 130fr	3.75	2.25

Issued to publicize drought relief efforts.

Mali Horses — A178

90fr, Modern horse. 135fr, Horse from Beledougou. 190fr, Horse from Nara. 530fr, Horse from Trait.

1985, Jan. 21		Litho.		Perf. 13½
512	A178	90fr multi	.90	.35
513	A178	135fr multi	1.20	.45
514	A178	190fr multi	1.75	.70
515	A178	530fr multi	5.00	1.90
		Nos. 512-515 (4)	8.85	3.40

For surcharges see Nos. 586, 591.

Fungi — A179

120fr, Clitocybe nebularis. 200fr, Lepiota cortinarius. 485fr, Agavicus semotus. 525fr, Lepiota procera.

1985, Jan. 28		Litho.		Perf. 12½
516	A179	120fr multi	1.40	.90
517	A179	200fr multi	2.10	1.00
518	A179	485fr multi	5.25	1.75
519	A179	525fr multi	5.50	1.75
		Nos. 516-519 (4)	14.25	5.40

For surcharges see Nos. 589-590.

Health A180

Designs: 120fr, 32nd World Leprosy Day, Emile Marchoux (1862-1943), Marchoux Institute, 150th anniv. 135fr, Lions Intl., Samanko Convalescence Village, 15th anniv. 470fr, Anti-polio campaign, research facility, victim.

1985, Feb. 18		Litho.		Perf. 13
520	A180	120fr multi	.90	.40
521	A180	135fr multi	1.10	.45
522	A180	470fr multi	3.25	1.75
		Nos. 520-522 (3)	5.25	2.60

For surcharges see Nos. 580, 584. No. 522 is airmail.

Cultural and Technical Cooperation Agency, 15th Anniv. — A181

1985, Mar. 20				
523	A181	540fr brn & brt bl grn	4.50	1.75

Intl. Youth Year — A182

Youth activities: 120fr, Natl. Pioneers Movement emblem. 190fr, Agricultural production. 500fr, Sports.

1985, May 13			Perf. 12½x13
524	A182	120fr multi	1.00 .45
525	A182	190fr multi	1.75 .70
526	A182	500fr multi	4.50 1.75
		Nos. 524-526 (3)	7.25 2.90

For surcharge see No. 587.

PHILEXAFRICA '85, Lome, Togo — A183

No. 527, Education, telecommunications. No. 528, Road, dam, computers.

1985, June 24			Perf. 13
527	A183	250fr multi	2.25 1.50
528	A183	250fr multi	2.25 1.50
a.	Pair, #527-528 + label		5.50 4.50
	Nos. 527-528, C517-C518 (4)		8.50 5.50

Nos. 527-528 show the UPU emblem.

Cats — A184

1986, Feb. 15		Litho.	Perf. 13½
529	A184	150fr Gray	1.50 .55
530	A184	200fr White	2.25 .85
531	A184	300fr Tabby	3.00 1.10
		Nos. 529-531 (3)	6.75 2.50

For surcharge see No. 582.

Fight Against Apartheid — A185

120fr, Map, broken chain.

1986, Feb. 24			Perf. 13
532	A185	100fr shown	1.00 .35
533	A185	120fr multi	1.10 .45

Telecommunications and Agriculture — A186

1986, May 17		Litho.	Perf. 13
534	A186	200fr multi	1.50 .70

1986 World Cup Soccer Championships, Mexico — A187

Various soccer plays.

1986, May 24		Litho.	Perf. 12½
535	A187	160fr multi	1.20 .50
536	A187	225fr multi	2.00 .75
		Souvenir Sheet	
537	A187	500fr multi	3.75 2.75

For overprints surcharges see No. 539-541, 585.

James Watt (1736-1819), Inventor, and Steam Engine — A188

1986, May 26			Perf. 12½x12
538	A188	110fr multi	1.10 .40

For surcharge see No. 581.

Nos. 535-537 Ovptd. "ARGENTINE 3 / R.F.A. 2" in Red

1986, July 30		Litho.	Perf. 12½
539	A187	160fr multi	1.50 .70
540	A187	225fr multi	2.25 .90
		Souvenir Sheet	
541	A187	500fr multi	4.50 3.00

World Wildlife Fund A189

Derby's Eland, Taurotragus derbianus.

1986, Aug. 11		Litho.	Perf. 13
542	A189	5fr Adult head	1.20 .25
543	A189	20fr Adult in brush	2.25 .25
544	A189	25fr Adult walking	2.25 .25
545	A189	200fr Calf suckling	17.50 3.50
		Nos. 542-545 (4)	23.20 4.25

Henry Ford (1863-1947), Auto Manufacturer, Inventor of Mass Production — A190

150fr, Model A, 1903. 200fr, Model T, 1923. 225fr, Thunderbird, 1968. 300fr, Lincoln Continental, 1963.

1987, Feb. 16		Litho.	Perf. 13
546	A190	150fr multi	1.40 .50
547	A190	200fr multi	2.00 1.00
548	A190	225fr multi	2.25 1.10
549	A190	300fr multi	2.25 1.25
		Nos. 546-549 (4)	7.90 3.85

Bees — A191

100fr, Apis florea, Asia. 150fr, Apis dorsata, Asia. 175fr, Apis adansonii, Africa. 200fr, Apis mellifica, worldwide.

1987, May 11		Litho.	Perf. 13½
550	A191	100fr multi	1.10 .55
551	A191	150fr multi	1.40 .65
552	A191	175fr multi	1.75 .85
553	A191	200fr multi	2.10 1.00
		Nos. 550-553 (4)	6.35 3.05

Lions Club Activities A192

1988, Jan. 13		Litho.	Perf. 12½
554	A192	200fr multi	1.50 .85

World Health Organization, 40th Anniv. — A193

1988, Feb. 22		Litho.	Perf. 12½x12
555	A193	150fr multi	1.25 .55

For surcharge see No. 557.

John F. Kennedy (1917-1963), 35th US President — A194

1988, June 6		Litho.	Perf. 13
556	A194	640fr multi	5.25 2.50

For surcharge see No. 592.

No. 555 Surcharged in Dark Red

1988, June 13			Perf. 12½x12
557	A193	300fr on 150fr multi	2.60 1.60

Mali Mission Hospital in Mopti and World Medicine organization.

Organization of African Unity, 25th Anniv. — A194a

1988, June 27		Litho.	Perf. 12½
558	A194a	400fr multi	3.00 1.75

Universal Immunization Campaign A195

30fr, Inoculating woman. 50fr, Emblem, needles, diff. 175fr, Inoculating boy.

1989, May 2		Litho.	Perf. 13½
559	A195	20fr shown	.25 .25
560	A195	30fr multi	.30 .25
561	A195	50fr multi	.45 .25
562	A195	175fr multi	1.50 .80
		Nos. 559-562 (4)	2.50 1.55

Intl. Law Institute of the French-Speaking Nations — A196

1989, May 15			Perf. 12½
563	A196	150fr multi	1.40 .70
564	A196	200fr multi	1.75 .90

MALI — Republic of Mali

World Post Day — A197

1989, Oct. 9   Litho.   Perf. 13
565   A197   625fr multicolored   5.50   2.50
For surcharge see No. 594.

Visit of Pope John Paul II — A198

1990, Jan. 28   Litho.   Perf. 13x12½
566   A198   200fr multicolored   2.00   .75

Multinational Postal School, 20th Anniv. — A199

1990, May 31   Litho.   Perf. 12½
567   A199   150fr multicolored   1.40   .65

Independence, 30th Anniv. — A200

1990, Sept. 20   Litho.   Perf. 13x12½
568   A200   400fr multicolored   3.75   1.90

Intl. Literacy Year — A201

1990, Sept. 24   Litho.   Perf. 13½
569   A201   150fr grn & multi   1.25   .65
570   A201   200fr org & multi   2.00   .90

A202

Lions Intl. Water Project, 5th anniv. No. 572, Rotary Club fight against polio, 30th anniv.

1991, Feb. 25   Litho.   Perf. 13x12½
571   A202   200fr multicolored   2.00   1.00
572   A202   200fr multicolored   2.00   1.00

Tribal Dances of Mali — A203

1991, Apr. 29   Litho.   Perf. 12½
573   A203   50fr Takamba   .50   .30
574   A203   100fr Mandiani   .90   .60
575   A203   150fr Kono   1.40   .90
576   A203   200fr Songho   1.90   1.10
    Nos. 573-576 (4)   4.70   2.90

A204

1991, Dec. 2   Litho.   Perf. 12½
577   A204   200fr multicolored   2.00   1.00
Central Fund for Economic Cooperation, 50th anniv.

A205

1992, Mar. 26   Litho.   Perf. 12½
578   A205   150fr multicolored   1.40   .75
National Women's Movement.

Stamps of 1984-89 Srchd. in Black or Black & Silver

1992, June   Litho.   Perfs. as Before
579   A177   25fr on 470fr #510   —   —
580   A180   25fr on 470fr #522   —   —
581   A188   30fr on 110fr #538   —   —
582   A184   50fr on 300fr #531   —   —
583   A173   50fr on 1225fr #493   —   —
584   A180   150fr on 135fr #521 (Bk & S)   —   —
585   A187   150fr on 160fr #535   —   —
586   A178   150fr on 190fr #514   —   —
587   A182   150fr on 190fr #525   —   —
588   A176   150fr on 350fr #503   —   —
589   A179   150fr on 485fr #518   —   —
590   A179   150fr on 525fr #519   —   —
591   A178   150fr on 530fr #515   —   —
592   A194   200fr on 640fr #556   —   —
593   A177   240fr on 350fr #509   —   —
594   A197   240fr on 625fr #565   —   —

No. 580 is airmail. Size and location of surcharge varies. No. 585 also overprinted "Euro '92."

New Constitution, 1st Anniv. — A205a

1993, Jan. 12   Litho.   Perf. 11½x12
594A   A205a   150fr multi   25.00
594B   A205a   225fr multi   35.00

Martyr's Day, 2nd Anniv. — A206

1993, Mar. 26   Litho.   Perf. 11½
595   A206   150fr blue & multi   30.00   30.00
596   A206   160fr yellow & multi   30.00   30.00

Rotary Intl. and World Health Organization (WHO) — A206a

Designs: 150fr, Polio victims, Rotary emblem. 200fr, WHO emblem, pregnant woman receiving vaccination.

1993, Apr. 16   Litho.   Perf. 14
596A   A206a   150fr multi   25.00
596B   A206a   200fr multi   35.00

Lions Club in Mali, 35th Anniv. — A207

1993, Dec. 20   Litho.   Perf. 14½
597   A207   200fr blue & multi   30.00   30.00
598   A207   225fr red & multi   30.00   30.00

Monument, Liberty Place — A207a

1993, Dec. 20   Photo.   Perf. 11¾ Granite Paper
598A   A207a   20fr multi   —   —
598B   A207a   25fr multi   —   —
598C   A207a   50fr multi   —   —
598D   A207a   100fr multi   —   —
598E   A207a   110fr multi   —   —
598F   A207a   150fr multi   —   —
598G   A207a   200fr multi   —   —
598H   A207a   225fr multi   —   —
598I   A207a   240fr multi   —   —
598J   A207a   260fr multi   —   —
    Nos. 598A-598J (10)   125.00

1994 Winter Olympics, Lillehammer A208

150fr, Pairs figure skating. 200fr, Giant slalom. 225fr, Ski jumping. 750fr, Speed skating. 2000fr, Downhill skiing.

1994, Feb. 12   Litho.   Perf. 13
599   A208   150fr multi   .90   .50
600   A208   200fr multi   1.25   .75
601   A208   225fr multi   1.75   1.00
602   A208   750fr multi   3.00   1.75
    Nos. 599-602 (4)   6.90   4.00

Souvenir Sheet
603   A208   2000fr multi   8.00   8.00

No. 603 contains one 36x36mm stamp.
For overprints see Nos. 671-676.

1994 World Cup Soccer Championships, US — A209

Designs: 200fr, Juan Schiaffino, Uruguay. 240fr, Diego Maradona, Argentina. 260fr, Paolo Rossi, Italy. 1000fr, Franz Bookenbauor, Germany. 2000fr, Just Fontaine, France.

1994, Mar. 15   Litho.   Perf. 13
604   A209   200fr multicolored   .90   .90
605   A209   240fr multicolored   1.40   .80
606   A209   260fr multicolored   1.60   .90
607   A209   1000fr multicolored   5.00   2.75
    Nos. 604-607 (4)   8.90   5.35

Souvenir Sheet
608   A209   2000fr multicolored   8.00   8.00

For overprints see Nos. 677-681.

Dinosaurs — A210

a, 5fr, Scaphonyx. b, 10fr, Cynognathus. c, 15fr, Lesothosaurus. d, 20fr, Scutellosaurus. e, 25fr, Ceratosaurus. f, 30fr, Dilophosaurus. g, 40fr, Dryosaurus. h, 50fr, Heterodontosaurus. i, 60fr, Anatosaurus. j, 70fr, Saurornithoides. k, 80fr, Avimimus. l, 90fr, Saltasaurus. m, 300fr, Dromaeosaurus. n, 400fr, Tsintaosaurus. o, 600fr, Velociraptor. p, 700fr, Ouranosaurus.
2000fr, Daspletosaurus, iguanodon.

1994, Mar. 28
609   A210   Sheet of 16, #a.-p.   13.00   10.00

Souvenir Sheet
610   A210   2000fr multi   10.00   10.00

Insects — A211

Designs: 40fr, Sternuera castanea, vert. 50fr, Eudicella gralli. 100fr, Homoderus mellyi, vert. 200fr, Kraussaria angulifera.

1994, Mar. 30   Litho.   Perf. 13
611   A211   40fr multicolored   .40   .25
612   A211   50fr multicolored   .70   .35
613   A211   100fr multicolored   1.10   .60
614   A211   200fr multicolored   2.00   1.00
    Nos. 611-614 (4)   4.20   2.20

Vaccination Campaign Against Measles — A212

1994, Apr. 7   Litho.   Perf. 13½
615   A212   150fr black & green   .90   .50
616   A212   200fr black & blue   1.60   .90

Birds — A213

25fr, Pigeons. 30fr, Turkeys. 150fr, Crowned cranes, vert. 200fr, Chickens, vert.

1994, Apr. 25
617   A213   25fr multi   .30   .25
618   A213   30fr multi   .30   .25
619   A213   150fr multi   1.40   .70
620   A213   200fr multi   1.50   .80
    Nos. 617-620 (4)   3.50   2.00

Intl. Year of the Family — A213a

1994, May 2
620A   A213a   220fr multicolored   1.25   .60

MALI — Republic of Mali

Jazz Musicians — A214

200fr, Ella Fitzgerald. 225fr, Lionel Hampton. 240fr, Sarah Vaughan. 300fr, Count Basie. 400fr, Duke Ellington. 600fr, Miles Davis. 1500fr, Louis Armstrong.

1994, May 23	Litho.		Perf. 13	
621	A214	200fr multi	.80	.60
622	A214	225fr multi	1.00	.80
623	A214	240fr multi	1.25	.95
624	A214	300fr multi	1.75	1.40
625	A214	400fr multi	2.25	1.75
626	A214	600fr multi	3.00	2.25
		Nos. 621-626 (6)	10.05	7.75

Souvenir Sheet

627	A214	1500fr multi	8.00	8.00

No. 627 contains one 45x45mm stamp.

Ancient Art A215

Nos. 628-647: 15fr, Venus of Brassempouy, vert. 25fr, Petroglyphs, Tanum, vert. 45fr, Prehistoric cave drawings, vert. 50fr, Cave paintings, Lascaux. 55fr, Tomb of Amonherkhopeshef, vert. 65fr, God Anubis and the pharaoh. 75fr, Sphinx. 85fr, Bust of Nefertiti, vert. 95fr, Statue of Shibum, vert. 100fr, Standard of Ur. 130fr, Mesopotamian bull's head harp, vert. 135fr, Mesopotamian scroll. 140fr, Assyrian dignitary, vert. 180fr, Enameled horse, Babylon. 190fr, Assyrian carving of hunters, vert. 200fr, Mona Lisa of Nimrud, vert. 225fr, Carthaginian coin. 250fr, Phoenician sphinx, vert. 275fr, Persian archer, vert. 280fr, Ceramic and glass mask, vert.

1994, Aug. 24	Litho.		Perf. 13½	
628-647	A215	Set of 20	15.00	15.00

D-Day Landings, Normandy, 50th Anniv. — A216

Villiers-Bocage, June 12: No. 648a, Explosion, men being killed. b, Tank firing. c, Tank, men with weapons.
Beaumont-Sur-Sarthe, June 6: No. 649a, Explosion, airplanes. b, British airplanes, tanks. c, German tanks, soldier firing machine gun.
Utah Beach, June 6: No. 650a, Explosion, bow of landing craft. b, Stern of landing craft, soldiers. c, Landing craft filled with troops.
Aerial battle: No. 651a, British planes dropping bombs. b, British, German planes. c, British, German planes, explosion.
Sainte-Mere-Eglise, June 5: No. 652a, German troops firing on paratroopers. b, Church tower. c, Paratroopers, German troops.

1994, June 6			Strips of 3	
648	A216	200fr #a.-c.	3.25	2.00
649	A216	300fr #a.-c.	4.00	2.50
650	A216	300fr #a.-c.	4.00	2.50
651	A216	400fr #a.-c.	5.25	3.50
652	A216	400fr #a.-c.	5.25	3.50
		Nos. 648-652 (5)	21.75	14.00

Nos. 648-652 are each continuous designs. Nos. 648b, 649b, 650b, 651b, 652b are each 30x47mm.

Orchids, Vegetables, & Mushrooms — A217

Orchids: 25fr, Disa kewensis. 50fr, Angraecum eburneum. 100fr, Ansellia africana. Vegetables: 140fr, Sorghum. 150fr, Onions. 190fr, Corn. Mushrooms: 200fr, Lepiota (clitocybe) nebularis. 225fr, Macrolepiota (lepiota) procera. 500fr, Lepiota aspera.

1994, Sept. 12				
653	A217	25fr multicolored	.25	.25
654	A217	50fr multicolored	.35	.25
655	A217	100fr multicolored	.65	.35
a.		Souvenir sheet of 3, #653-655	11.00	7.50
656	A217	140fr multicolored	.70	.40
657	A217	150fr multicolored	.80	.45
658	A217	190fr multicolored	1.00	.45
a.		Souvenir sheet of 3, #656-658	11.00	7.50
659	A217	200fr multicolored	1.10	.75
660	A217	225fr multicolored	1.25	.75
661	A217	500fr multicolored	2.75	1.50
a.		Souvenir sheet of 3, #659-661	11.00	7.50
		Nos. 653-661 (9)	8.85	5.20

Moths, Butterflies & Insects — A218

Designs: 20fr, Polyptychus roseus. 30fr, Elymniopsis bammakoo. 40fr, Deilephila nerii. 150fr, Utetheisa pulchella. 180fr, Charaxes jasius. 200fr, Mylothris chloris.
Insects: 225fr, Goliath beetle. 240fr, Locust. 350fr, Praying mantis.

1994, Sept. 12				
662	A218	20fr multicolored	.25	.25
663	A218	30fr multicolored	.25	.25
664	A218	40fr multicolored	.25	.25
665	A218	150fr multicolored	.90	.50
666	A218	180fr multicolored	1.00	.55
667	A218	200fr multicolored	1.00	.60
a.		Souv. sheet of 6, #662-667	22.50	12.50
668	A218	225fr multicolored	1.10	.65
669	A218	240fr multicolored	1.25	.70
670	A218	350fr multicolored	1.60	.90
a.		Souv. sheet of 3, #668-670	11.00	6.50
		Nos. 662-670 (9)	7.60	4.65

Nos. 599-603 Ovptd. in Silver or Gold with Name of Olympic Medalist, Country

Overprints in silver: No. 671a, "Y. GORDEYEVA / S. GRINKOV / RUSSIE." No. 671b, "O. GRISHCHUK / Y. PLATOV / RUSSIE." No. 672a, "D. COMPAGNONI / ITALIE." No. 672b, "M. WASMEIER / ALLEMAGNE." No. 673a, "E. BREDESEN /NORVEGE." No. 673b, "J. WEISSFLOG / ALLEMAGNE." No. 674a, "B. BLAIR, U.S.A." No. 674b, "J.O. KOSS / NORVEGE."
Overprint in gold: No. 675, "L. KJUS / NORVEGE." No. 676, "P. WIBERG / SUEDE."

1994, Sept. 12	Litho.		Perf. 13	
671	A208	150fr Pair, #a.-b.	1.75	1.00
672	A208	200fr Pair, #a.-b.	2.75	1.50
673	A208	225fr Pair, #a.-b.	3.50	2.00
674	A208	750fr Pair, #a.-b.	10.00	5.50
		Nos. 671-674 (4)	18.00	10.00

Souvenir Sheet

675	A208	2000fr multicolored	8.00	6.00
676	A208	2000fr multicolored	8.00	6.00

Nos. 604-608 Ovptd. in Metallic Red

1994, Sept. 15	Litho.		Perf. 13	
677	A209	200fr multicolored	.90	.50
678	A209	240fr multicolored	1.25	.70
679	A209	260fr multicolored	1.40	.80
680	A209	1000fr multicolored	5.25	3.00
		Nos. 677-680 (4)	8.80	5.00

Souvenir Sheet

| 681 | A209 | 2000fr multicolored | 8.00 | 6.00 |

Intl. Olympic Committee, Cent. — A218a

1994, June 23	Litho.		Perf. 13½	
681A	A218a	150fr multicolored	1.10	.60
681B	A218a	200fr multicolored	1.60	.90

Exist in imperf souvenir sheets of 1.

Intl. Olympic Committee, Cent. A219

Pierre de Coubertin and: 225fr, Woman carrying flame, vert. 240fr, Olympic rings, vert. 300fr, Torch bearer. 500fr, Gold medal of Olympic rings.
600fr, Flame, statue of flag bearer.

1994, June 23			Perf. 13½	
682	A219	225fr multicolored	.90	.55
683	A219	240fr multicolored	1.00	.65
684	A219	300fr multicolored	1.60	1.00
685	A219	500fr multicolored	2.75	1.75
		Nos. 682-685 (4)	6.25	3.95

Souvenir Sheet

| 686 | A219 | 600fr multicolored | 3.50 | 2.25 |

Anniversaries & Events — A220

Designs: 150fr, Ernst Julius Opik, Galileo probe, impact of comet on Jupiter. 200fr, Clyde Tombaugh, probe moving toward Pluto. 500fr, Intl. Red Cross, Henri Dunant. 650fr, Crew of Apollo 11, 1st manned moon landing. 700fr, Lions Intl., Rotary Intl. 800fr, Gary Kasparov chess champion.

1995, Apr. 10	Litho.		Perf. 13½	
687	A220	150fr multicolored	.50	.30
688	A220	200fr multicolored	.80	.45
689	A220	500fr multicolored	2.25	1.25
690	A220	650fr multicolored	2.50	1.50
691	A220	700fr multicolored	2.75	1.75
692	A220	800fr multicolored	3.25	1.90
		Nos. 687-692 (6)	12.05	7.15

Nos. 687-692 exist in souvenir sheets of 1.

Motion Picture, Cent. — A221

Movie star, movie: 100fr, Kirk Douglas, Spartacus. 150fr, Elizabeth Taylor, Cleopatra. 200fr, Clint Eastwood, Sierra Torrid. 250fr, Marilyn Monroe, The River of No Return. 500fr, Arnold Schwarzenegger, Conan the Barbarian. 1000fr, Elvis Presley, Loving You. 1500fr, Charlton Heston, The Ten Commandments.

1994, May 23	Litho.		Perf. 13½	
693-698	A221	Set of 6	16.00	8.75

Souvenir Sheet

| 699 | A221 | 1500fr multicolored | 8.25 | 5.00 |

No. 695 is airmail.

Fight Against AIDS — A222

Designs: 150fr, Woman, man holding condoms. 225fr, Nurse with AIDS patient, researcher looking into microscope.

1994, June 30				
700	A222	150fr multicolored	1.10	.60
701	A222	225fr multicolored	1.60	.90

Tourism — A223

Designs: 150fr, Traditional buildings, statue, vert. 200fr, Sphinx, pyramids, ruins.

1994, Dec. 5				
702	A223	150fr multicolored	1.10	.60
703	A223	200fr multicolored	1.60	.90

1996 Summer Olympics, Atlanta A224

Designs: 25fr, Reiner Klimke, dressage. 50fr, Kristin Otto, swimming. 100fr, Hans-Gunther Winkler, equestrian. 150fr, Birgit Fischer-Schmidt, kayak. 200fr, Nicole Uphoff, dressage, vert. 225fr, Renate Stecher, track, vert. 230fr, Michael Gross, swimming. 250fr, Karin Janz, gymnastics. 550fr, Anja Fichtel, fencing, vert. 700fr, Heide Rosendahl-Ecker, track, vert.

1995, Mar. 27				
704-713	A224	Set of 10	12.50	8.00

Dated 1994.

Rotary Intl., 90th Anniv. — A225

1000fr, Paul Harris, logo. 1500fr, 1905, 1995 Logos.

1995, Oct. 18	Litho.		Perf. 14	
714	A225	1000fr multi	6.50	4.00

Souvenir Sheet

| 715 | A225 | 1500fr multi | 8.00 | 5.00 |

Miniature Sheets

Birds, Butterflies — A226

No. 716: a, Campephilus imperialis. b, Momotus momota. c, Ramphastos sulfuratus. d, Halcyon malimbica. e, Trochilus polytmus. f, Cardinalis cardinalis. g, Pharomachrus mocinno. h, Aratinga solstitialis. i, Amazona arausiaca. j, Eudocimus ruber. k, Carduelis cucullatus. l, Anodorhynchus hyacinthinus. m, Passerina leclancherii. n, Pipra mentalis. o, Rupicola rupicola. p, Sicalis flaveola.
No. 717: a, Capito niger. b, Chloroceryle amazona. c, Tersina virdis. d, Momotus momota. e, Campephilus menaloleucos. f, Leistes militaris. g, Sarcoramphus papa. h, Pilherodius pileatus. i, Tityra cayana. j, Tangara chilinsis. k, Amazona ochrocephala. l, Saltator maximus. m, Paroaria dominicana. n, Egretta tricolor. o, Piaya melanogaster. p, Thamnophilus doliatus.
No. 718: a, Paradise whydah (g). b, Red-necked francolin. c, Whale-headed stork (i). d, Ruff (j). e, Marabou stork (k). f, White pelican. g, Western curlew. h, Scarlet ibis. i, Great crested crebe. j, White spoonbill. k, African jacana. l, African pygmy goose.
No. 719: a, Ruby-throated hummingbird. b, Grape shoemaker, blue morpho butterflies. c, Northern hobby. d, Cuvier toucan (g). e, Black-

MALI — Republic of Mali

necked red cotinga (h). f, Green-winged macaws (i). g, Flamingo (j). h, Malachite kingfisher. i, Bushy-crested hornbill (l). j, Purple swamphen (k). k, Striped body (j, l). l, Painted lady butterfly.
Each 1000fr: No. 720, Topaza pella. No. 721, Sporophila lineola.

1995, Oct. 20   Litho.   Perf. 14
Sheets of 16 & 12
716	A226	50fr #a.-p.	6.50	4.00
717	A226	100fr #a.-p.	11.00	6.75
718	A226	150fr #a.-l.	12.00	7.25
719	A226	200fr #a.-l.	16.00	9.25
Nos. 716-719 (4)			45.50	27.25

Souvenir Sheets
| 720-721 | A226 | Set of 2 | 12.00 | 7.50 |

John Lennon (1940-80) — A227

1995   Litho.   Perf. 14
| 722 | A227 | 150fr multicolored | 1.25 | .70 |

No. 722 was issued in sheets of 16.

Miniature Sheets

Motion Pictures, Cent. — A228

Western actors: No. 723: a, Justus D. Barnes (misidentified as George Barnes). b, William S. Hart. c, Tom Mix. d, Wallace Beery. e, Gary Cooper. f, John Wayne.
Actresses and their directors: No. 724: a, Marlene Dietrich, Josef Von Sternberg. b, Jean Harlow, George Cukor. c, Mary Astor, John Huston (Houston on stamp). d, Ingrid Bergman, Alfred Hitchcock. e, Claudette Colbert, Cecil B. DeMille. f, Marilyn Monroe, Billy Wilder.
Musicals and their stars: No. 725: a, Singin' in the Rain, Gene Kelly. b, The Bandwagon, Anne Miller, Ray Bolger. c, Cabaret, Liza Minnelli, Joel Grey. d, The Sound of Music, Julie Andrews. e, Top Hat, Ginger Rogers, Fred Astaire. f, Saturday Night Fever, John Travolta.
Each 1000fr: No. 726, Robert Redford as the Sundance Kid. No. 727, Liv Ullman, actress, Ingmar Bergman, director. No. 728, Judy Garland in the Wizard of Oz.

1995, Dec. 8   Litho.   Perf. 13½x14
Sheets of 6
723	A228	150fr #a.-f.	5.25	3.50
724	A228	200fr #a.-f.	7.25	4.50
725	A228	240fr #a.-f.	9.00	5.50
Nos. 723-725 (3)			21.50	13.50

Souvenir Sheets
| 726-728 | A228 | Set of 3 | 16.00 | 10.00 |

Nos. 723-728 have various styles of lettering.

Miniature Sheet

Stars of Rock and Roll — A229

No. 729: a, Connie Francis. b, The Ronettes. c, Janis Joplin. d, Debbie Harry of Blondie. e, Cyndi Lauper. f, Carly Simon. No. 730, Bette Midler.

1995, Dec. 8
| 729 | A229 | 225fr Sheet of 6, #a.-f. | 8.00 | 5.00 |

Souvenir Sheet
| 730 | A229 | 1000fr multicolored | 5.25 | 3.50 |

Traditional Cooking Utensils — A230

5fr, Canaris, vert. 50fr, Mortier, calebasse, vert. 150fr, Fourneau. 200fr, Vans, vert. 500fr, Vans.

1995, Nov. 20   Litho.   Perf. 14
| 731-734 | A230 | Set of 4 | 2.75 | 1.75 |

Souvenir Sheet
| 735 | A230 | 500fr multicolored | 3.00 | 2.00 |

18th World Scout Jamboree, Holland — A231

Scout examining butterfly or mushroom: 150fr, Saturnia pyri. 225fr, Gonepteryx rhamni. 240fr, Myrina silenus. 500fr, Clitocybe nebularis. 650fr, Agaricus semotus. 725fr, Lepiota procera. 1500fr, Morpho cypris.

1995, Aug. 1   Litho.   Perf. 13½
| 736-741 | A231 | Set of 6 | 11.50 | 5.75 |

Souvenir Sheet
| 742 | A231 | 1500fr multicolored | 9.25 | 5.00 |

Nos. 736-741 exist in souvenir sheets of 1.

UN, 50th Anniv. — A232

Designs: 20fr, 170fr, UN emblem, scales of justice, doves, vert. 225fr, 240fr, Doves, UN emblem, four men of different races.

1995, Oct. 24   Litho.   Perf. 13
743	A232	20fr light blue & multi	.25	.25
744	A232	170fr light grn & multi	.80	.60
745	A232	225fr light pur & multi	1.10	.70
746	A232	240fr light org & multi	1.25	.95
Nos. 743-746 (4)			3.40	2.50

Ayrton Senna (1960-94), F-1 Race Car Driver — A233

1000fr, Jerry Garcia (1942-95), entertainer.

1995   Perf. 13½
| 747 | A233 | 500fr multicolored | 2.25 | 1.25 |
| 748 | A233 | 1000fr multicolored | 4.50 | 2.50 |

Nos. 747-748 exist in souvenir sheets of one.

A234

150fr, Charles de Gaulle. 200fr, De Gaulle, liberation of Paris. 240fr, Enzo Ferrari. 650fr, 1945-49 Greenland Expeditions of Paul Emile Victor. 725fr, Paul Harris. 740fr, Michael Schumacher.

1995
749	A234	150fr multicolored	.70	.35
750	A234	200fr multicolored	.90	.50
751	A234	240fr multicolored	1.10	.60
752	A234	650fr multicolored	3.00	1.75
753	A234	725fr multicolored	3.25	1.80
754	A234	740fr multicolored	3.50	1.90
Nos. 749-754 (6)			12.45	6.90

Nos. 749-754 exist in souvenir sheets of 1.

A235

Designs: 150fr, Second election party emblems, horiz. 200fr, Pres. Alpha Oumar Konare. 225fr, First election party emblems, horiz. 240fr, Natl. flag, map, party representations.

1995   Litho.   Perf. 13½
755	A235	150fr multicolored	.65	.35
756	A235	200fr multicolored	.80	.45
757	A235	225fr multicolored	.90	.50
758	A235	240fr multicolored	.95	.55
Nos. 755-758 (4)			3.30	1.85

Second Presidential elections.

A236

Economic Community of West African States (ECOWAS): 150fr, Regional integration, horiz. 200fr, Cooperation. 220fr, Prospect of creating one currency, horiz. 225fr, Peace and security, horiz.

1995
759	A236	150fr multicolored	.70	.35
760	A236	200fr multicolored	.90	.45
761	A236	220fr multicolored	1.00	.50
762	A236	225fr multicolored	1.00	.50
Nos. 759-762 (4)			3.60	1.80

Mushrooms — A237

Genus Russula: No. 763: a, Emetica. b, Laurocerasi. c, Rosacea. d, Occidentalis. e, Fragilis. f, Mariae. g, Eeruginea. h, Compacta.
Genus Bolotuo: No. 764: a, Follouo. b, Elagans. c, Castaneus. d, Edulls. e, Aereus. f, Granulatus. g, Cavipes. h, Badius.
Genus Lactarius: No. 765: a, Deliciosus. b, Luculentus. c, Pseudomucidus. d, Scrobiculatus. e, Deceptivus. f, Indigo. g, Peckii. h, Lignyotus.
Genus Amanita: No. 766a, Caesarea. b, Muscaria. c, Solitaria. d, Verna. e, Malleata. f, Phalloides. g, Citrina. h, Pantherina.
Each 1000fr: No. 767, Coprinus atramentarius. No. 768, Panaeolus subbalteatus.

1996, Mar. 15   Litho.   Perf. 14
763	A237	25fr Sheet of 8, #a.-h.	1.60	.95
764	A237	150fr Sheet of 8, #a.-h.	9.00	5.50
765	A237	200fr Sheet of 8, #a.-h.	12.00	7.25
766	A237	225fr Sheet of 8, #a.-h.	14.00	8.25

Souvenir Sheets
| 767-768 | A237 | Set of 2 | 14.00 | 9.00 |

Sites in Beijing — A238

No. 769: a, Bridge, Gateway to Hall of Supreme Harmony. b, Temple of Heaven. c, Great Wall. d, Hall of Supreme Harmony. e, Courtyard, Gate of Heavenly Purity. f, Younghe Gong Temple. g, Lang Ru Ting, Bridge of Seventeen Arches. h, Meridian Gate (Wu Men). i, Corner Tower.
Each 500fr: No. 770, Pagoda, vert. No. 771, Li Peng.

1996, May 13
| 769 | A238 | 100fr Sheet of 9, #a.-i. | 7.50 | 4.75 |

Souvenir Sheets
| 770-771 | A238 | Set of 2 | 7.00 | 4.75 |

No. 771 contains one 47x72mm stamp. CHINA '96 (Nos. 769, 771).

Trains — A239

Historic: No. 772: a, "Novelty," 1829. b, Premiere class Liverpool & Manchester Line, 1830. c, William Norris, 1843. d, Trevithick, 1000. e, Robert Stephenson "Rocket," 1829. f, "Puffing Billy," William Hedley, 1813.
No. 773: a, Subway Train, London. b, San Francisco cable car. c, Japanese monorail. d, Pantograph car, Stockholm. e, Double-decker tram, Hong Kong. f, Sacre-Coeur Cog Train, Montmartre, France.
No. 774: a, Docklands Light Railway, London. b, British Railway's high-speed diesel train. c, Japanese Bullet Train. d, Germany Inter-City Electric high speed train. e, French TGV high-speed electric train. f, German "Wuppertal" monorail.
Trains of China: No. 775: a, RM Class Pacific. b, Manchurian steam engine. c, SY Class 2-8-2, Tangshan. d, SL Class 4-6-2 Pacific. e, Chengtu-Kunming steam. f, Lanchow passenger train.
Each 500fr: No. 776, Rheingold Express, 1925. No. 777, Matterhorn cable car, vert. No. 778, Superchief, best long-distance diesel, US. No. 779, Shanghai-Nanking Railway.

1996, July 29
772	A239	180fr Sheet of 6, #a.-f.	8.00	5.00
773	A239	250fr Sheet of 6, #a.-f.	12.00	7.00
774	A239	310fr Sheet of 6, #a.-f.	14.00	8.50
775	A239	320fr Sheet of 6, #a.-f.	15.00	9.00

Souvenir Sheets
| 776-779 | A239 | Set of 4 | 13.00 | 10.00 |

Nos. 776-779 each contain one 57x43mm stamp.

Express Mail Service, 10th Anniv. — A240

Designs: 30fr, Man with package, vert. 40fr, Bird holding package, letter, vert. 90fr, World map, woman with letter holding telephone receiver. 320fr, 320fr, Mail van, hands holding letters, map.

1996, Sept. 1   Litho.   Perf. 14
780	A240	30fr multicolored	.25	.25
781	A240	40fr multicolored	.30	.25
782	A240	90fr multicolored	.55	.30
783	A240	320fr multicolored	1.75	1.00
Nos. 780-783 (4)			2.85	1.80

Queen Elizabeth II, 70th Birthday — A241

Designs: a, Portrait. b, Wearing blue & red hat. c, Portrait as young woman.
1000fr, Portrait as young girl.

MALI — Republic of Mali

1996, Sept. 9   **Perf. 13½x14**
784 A241 370fr Strip of 3, #a.-c.   4.75   2.50
Souvenir Sheet
785 A241 1000fr multicolored   4.75   2.50
No. 784 was issued in sheets of 9 stamps.

Nanking Bridge — A242

1996   **Litho.**   **Perf. 13½**
786 A242 270fr multicolored   2.50   1.25

Mosques — A243

1996
787 A243 250fr Djenne   3.50   2.25
788 A243 310fr Sankore   4.50   2.75

Pandas, Dogs, and Cats — A244

Panda, vert: No. 789: a, Climbing on branch. b, On bare limb. c, Closer view. d, Lying in branch with leaves.
Dogs, cats: No. 790: a, Azawakh. b, Basenji. c, Javanais. d, Abyssin.

1996
789 A244 150fr Sheet of 4, #a.-d.   3.25   1.75
790 A244 310fr Sheet of 4, #a.-d.   6.00   3.50
Nos. 789a-789d are 39x42mm.

Marilyn Monroe (1926-62) — A245

Various portraits.

1996
791 A245 320fr Sheet of 9, #a.-i.   14.00   8.00
Souvenir Sheet
792 A245 2000fr multicolored   9.50   5.50
No. 792 contains one 42x60mm stamp.

Entertainers — A246

No. 793: a, Frank Sinatra. b, Johnny Mathis. c, Dean Martin. d, Bing Crosby. e, Sammy Davis, Jr. f, Elvis Presley. g, Paul Anka. h, Tony Bennett. i, Nat "King" Cole.
No. 794, Various portraits of John Lennon.

1996   **Sheets of 9**
793 A246 250fr #a.-i.   10.00   5.50
794 A246 310fr #a.-i.   12.50   7.00

U.S. Space Shuttle, Challenger — A247

Designs: a, Halley's Comet, Andromeda Galaxy. b, Mars. c, Challenger, Saturn. d, Moon, Jupiter.
1000fr, Shuttle Challenger.

1996, Oct. 14   **Perf. 14**
795 A247 320fr Sheet of 4, #a.-d.   5.75   3.50
Souvenir Sheet
796 A247 1000fr multicolored   5.25   3.50
No. 796 contains one 85x29mm stamp.

Mickey's ABC's — A248

Disney characters in various scenes with:
No. 797: a, "MICKEY." b, "A." c, "B." d, "C." e, "D." f, "E." g, "F." h, "G." i, "H."
No. 798: a, "I." b, "J." c, "K." d, "L." e, "M." f, "N." g, "O." h, "P." i, "Q."
No. 799: a, "R." b, "S." c, "T." d, "U." e, "V." f, "W." g, "X." h, "Y." i, "Z."
Each 1000fr: No. 800, Mouse child holding "DE MICKEY" sign, horiz. No. 801, Mouse children with various letters.

1996, Oct. 15   **Litho.**   **Perf. 13½x14**
797 A248 50fr Sheet of 9, #a.-i.   2.25   1.50
798 A248 100fr Sheet of 9, #a.-i.   4.50   2.75
799 A248 200fr Sheet of 9, #a.-i.   9.00   5.50
Souvenir Sheets
800-801 A248 Set of 2   10.50   6.75

Sites in Beijing — A249

No. 802, Hall of Supreme Harmony. No. 803, Great Wall. No. 804, Hall of Prayers for Good Harvests, Temple of Heaven.

1996   **Perf. 13½**
802 A249 180fr multicolored   1.75   1.00
803 A249 180fr multicolored   1.75   1.00
804 A249 180fr multicolored   1.75   1.00
Nos. 802-804 (3)   5.25   3.00

Cotton Production — A250

Designs: 20fr, Cotton plant, vert. 25fr, People working in cotton fields. 50fr, Holding plant, vert. 310fr, Dumping cotton into cart.

1996   **Perf. 13½**
805 A250 20fr multicolored   .25   .25
806 A250 25fr multicolored   .25   .25
807 A250 50fr multicolored   .25   .25
808 A250 310fr multicolored   1.40   .70
Nos. 805-808 (4)   2.15   1.45

Birds and Snakes — A251

a, Crowned eagle in flight. b, Tufted eagle. c, Python. d, Gabon viper.
Songbirds: No. 810: a, Choucador splendide. b, Astrid ondulé. c, Martin chasseur. d, Coucou didric.
Butterfies: No. 811a, Salamis parhassus. b, Charaxes bohemani. c, Coeliades forestan. d, Mimacrea marshalli.

1996
809 A251 180fr Sheet of 4, #a.-d.   3.25   1.90
810 A251 250fr Sheet of 4, #a.-d.   4.50   2.75
811 A251 320fr Sheet of 4, #a.-d.   5.75   3.50

Third World — A252

Design: 250fr, Hot air balloon in flight.

1996
812 A252 180fr shown   2.50   1.40
813 A252 250fr multicolored   3.00   1.75

A253

1996
814 A253 180fr green & multi   1.00   .50
815 A253 250fr bister & multi   1.50   .75
Death of Abdoul Karim Camara (Cabral), 16th anniv.

A254

Dogs: No. 816, Airedale terrier. No. 817, Briard. No. 818, Schnauzer. No. 819, Chow chow.
Cats: No. 820, Turkish van. NO. 821, Sphynx. No. 822, Korat. No. 823, American curl.
Dogs, horiz.: No. 824: a, Basset hound. b, Dachshund. c, Brittany spaniel. d, Saint Bernard. e, Bernese mountain. f, Irish setter. g, Gordon setter. h, Poodle. i, Pointer.
Cats, horiz: No. 825: a, Scottish fold. b, Javanese. c, Norwegian forest. d, American shorthair. e, Turkish angora. f, British shorthair. g, Egyptian mau. h, Maine coon. i, Burmese.
Each 1000fr: No. 826, Newfoundland. No. 827, Flame point Himalayan Persian.

1997, Jan. 10   **Litho.**   **Perf. 14**
816-819 A254 100fr Set of 4   2.50   1.25
820-823 A254 150fr Set of 4   3.25   1.10
824 A254 150fr Sheet of 9, #a.-i.   7.50   3.75
825 A254 180fr Sheet of 9, #a.-i.   8.50   4.25
Souvenir Sheets
826-827 A254 Set of 2   11.00   6.75

Environmental Protection — A255

Fauna: No. 828: a, Dolphin. b, Okapi. c, Rhea. d, Black rhinocrhinoceros. e, Malayan tapir. f, Galapagos tortoise. g, Walrus. h, Gray wolf. i, Giraffe.
1000fr, Koala.

1997, Feb. 3
828 A255 250fr Sheet of 9, #a.-i.   11.50   8.50
Souvenir Sheet
829 A255 1000fr multicolored   5.00   3.75

Ships — A256

Warships: No. 830: a, Bellerophon, England, 1867. b, Chen Yuan, China 1882. c, Hiei, Japan, 1877. d, Kaiser, Austria, 1862. e, King Wilhelm, Germany, 1869. f, Re D'Italia, Italy, 1864.
Paddle steamers: No. 831: a, Arctic, US, 1849. b, Washington, France, 1847. c, Esploratore, Italy, 1863. d, Fuad, Turkey, 1864. e, Hope, Confederate States of America, 1864. f, Britannia, England, 1840.
Each 1000fr: No. 832, Arabia, England, 1851. No. 833, Northumberland, England, 1867.

1996, Dec. 20   **Litho.**   **Perf. 14**
830 A256 250fr Sheet of 6, #a.-f.   4.50   3.50
831 A256 320fr Sheet of 6, #a.-f.   8.50   4.25
Souvenir Sheets
832-833 A256 Set of 2   10.00   7.25

MALI — Republic of Mali

Wildlife — A257

Designs: a, Hippotragus niger. b, Damaliscus hunter. c, G. demidovii. d, Chimpanzee.

1996		Litho.		Perf. 13½
834	A257	250fr Sheet of 4, #a.-d.	5.00	2.50

UNESCO, 50th anniv.

Red Cross — A258

Dogs: a, Rottweiler. b, Newfoundland. c, German shepherd. d, Bobtail (English sheepdog).

1996				
835	A258	250fr Sheet of 4, #a.-d.	4.25	2.10

African Education Year — A259

100fr, Student with book, map, vert. 150fr, Classroom. 180fr, Families watching video program on farming techniques. 250fr, African people being educated, map, vert.

1996, Apr. 4			Perf. 14	
836	A259	100fr multicolored	.45	.45
837	A259	150fr multicolored	.65	.65
838	A259	180fr multicolored	.80	.80
839	A259	250fr multicolored	1.10	1.10
		Nos. 836-839 (4)	3.00	3.00

Nos. 836-839 were not available until March 1997.

Folk Dances — A260

1996			Perf. 13½	
840	A260	150fr Dounouba	.65	.65
841	A260	170fr Gomba	.75	.75
842	A260	225fr Sandia	1.40	1.40
843	A260	230fr Sabar	1.50	1.50
		Nos. 840-843 (4)	4.30	4.30

Service Organizations — A261

No. 844: a, Man carrying bags. b, Man drinking water. c, Child holding bowl of food. d, Mother feeding infant.
No. 845: a, Girl with food. b, Man holding rice bowl. c, Woman holding bowl of food. d, Child opening box of food.

1996				
844	A261	500fr Sheet of 4, #a.-d.	8.50	4.25
845	A261	650fr Sheet of 4, #a.-d.	11.50	5.75

79th Lions Intl. Convention (No. 844). 91st Rotary Intl. Convention (No. 845).

City of Canton, 2210th Anniv. — A262

Designs: a, Statue of goats. b, Seal. c, Boat. d, Fruits, tea pot. e, Buildings. f, Dragon.

1996				
846	A262	50fr Sheet of 6, #a.-f.	1.40	.80

FAO, 50th Anniv. — A264

Space satellite, fauna: a, MOP.2, grasshopper. b, Meteosat P.2, lion. c, Envisat, dolphins. d, Radar satellite, whale.

1996		Litho.		Perf. 13½
847	A264	310fr Sheet of 4, #a.-d.	5.00	2.50

Artifacts from Natl. Museum — A265

1996				
848	A265	5fr Kara	.25	.25
849	A265	10fr Hambe	.25	.25
850	A265	180fr Pinge	.80	.45
851	A265	250fr Merenkun	1.10	.60
		Nos. 848-851 (4)	2.40	1.55

Nos. 848-851 exist in souvenir sheets of 1.

1998 Winter Olympics, Nagano — A266

250fr, Speed skating. 310fr, Slalom skiing. 750fr, Figure skating. 900fr, Hockey. 2000fr, Downhill skiing.

1996				
852	A266	250fr multicolored	1.25	.65
853	A266	310fr multicolored	1.50	.85
854	A266	750fr multicolored	3.50	1.90
855	A266	900fr multicolored	4.00	2.25
		Nos. 852-855 (4)	10.25	5.65
		Souvenir Sheet		
856	A266	2000fr multicolored	10.00	5.50

Fauna, Mushrooms — A267

a, Ploceus ocularis. b, Hemiolaus coecolus. c, Hebeloma radicosum. d, Sparassus dufouri simon.

1996				
857	A267	750fr Sheet of 4, #a.-d.	13.00	7.25

New Year 1997 (Year of the Ox) — A268

No. 859, Black porcelain ox.

1997				
858	A268	500fr brown	2.25	1.25
		Size: 53x35mm		
859	A268	500fr multi	2.25	1.25

Nos. 858-859 exist in souvenir sheets of 1.

Butterflies — A269

No. 860, Black-lined eggar. No. 861, Common opae. No. 862, Veined tiger. No. 863, The basker.
No. 864: a, Natal barred blue. b, Common grass blue. c, Fire grid. d, Mocker swallowtail. e, Azure hairstreak. f, Mother-of-pearl butterfly. g, Boisduval's false asraea. h, Pirate butterfly. i, African moon moth.
No. 865, vert.: a, Striped policeman. b, Mountain sandman. c, Brown-veined white. d, Bowker's widow. e, Foxy charaxes. f, Pirate. g, African clouded yellow. h, Garden inspector.
Each 1000fr: No. 866, Plain tiger. No. 867, Beautiful tiger. No. 868, African clouded yellow, vert. No. 869, Zebra white, vert.

1997, Jan. 27			Perf. 14	
860-863	A269	180fr Set of 4	3.50	2.00
864	A269	150fr Sheet of 9, #a.-i.	6.25	3.50
865	A259	210fr Sheet of 8, #a.-h.	9.50	5.25
		Souvenir Sheets		
866-869	A269	Set of 4	24.00	14.00

Disney Characters — A270

Greetings stamps: 25fr, Goofy, Bon Voyage. 50fr, Mickey, Happy New Year. 100fr, Goofy, Happy Birthday. 150fr, Donald writing. 180fr, Minnie writing. 250fr, Mickey, Minnie, anniversary. 310fr, Mickey, Minnie going on vacation. 320fr, Mickey, Minnie kissing.
Each 1500fr: No. 878, Daisy Duck, horiz. No. 879, Huey, Dewey, Louie throwing school books in air, horiz.

1997, Mar. 1			Perf. 13½x14	
870-877	A270	Set of 8	7.00	4.00
		Souvenir Sheets		
878-879	A270	Set of 2	12.50	8.25

Bridges — A271

1997		Litho.		Perf. 14
880	A271	100fr Mahina	.50	.25
881	A271	150fr Selingue Dam	.80	.45
882	A271	180fr King Fahd	1.00	.55
883	A271	250fr Martyrs	1.50	.85
		Nos. 880-883 (4)	3.80	2.10

Dated 1996.

1998 World Cup Soccer Championships, France — A272

Various action scenes.

1997			Perf. 13½	
884	A272	180fr multicolored	1.00	.55
885	A272	250fr multicolored	1.25	.65
886	A272	320fr multicolored	1.50	.85
887	A272	1060fr multicolored	4.50	2.50
		Nos. 884-887 (4)	8.25	4.55
		Souvenir Sheet		
888	A272	2000fr multicolored	9.00	4.75

Dated 1996. No. 888 contains one 36x42mm stamp.

Formula I Race Car Drivers — A273

Designs: a, Michael Schumacher. b, Damon Hill. c, Jacques Villeneuve. d, Gerhard Berger.

1996		Litho.		Perf. 13½
889	A273	650fr Sheet of 4, #a.-d.	13.00	6.00

John F. Kennedy (1917-63) — A274

Various portraits.

1997				
890	A274	390fr Sheet of 9, #a.-i.	17.50	8.75

221

MALI — Republic of Mali

John Lennon (1940-80) — A275

Various portraits.

1997
891 A275 250fr Sheet of 9, #a.-i.   11.50 5.25

Deng Xiaoping (1904-97), Chinese Leader — A276

Designs: a, As young man. b, Without hat. c, With hat. d, As middle-aged man. 250fr, Being kissed by child.

1997   **Perf. 13½**
892 A276 250fr Sheet of 4, #a.-d. 5.50 2.50

Souvenir Sheet
Perf. 13x13½
893 A276 250fr multicolored   5.00 2.25

No. 893 contains 69x50mm stamp.

Elvis Presley, 20th Death Anniv. — A277

No. 894, Various portraits. No. 895, Portrait, Elvis on motorcycle.

1997   **Litho.**   **Perf. 13½**
894 A277 310fr Sheet of 9, #a.-i.   13.00 7.00

Souvenir Sheet
895 A277 2000fr multicolored   10.00 5.50

No. 895 contains one 42x51mm stamp.

Marine Life — A278

No. 896: a, Chaetodon auriga. b, Balistoides conspicillum. c, Forcipiger longirostris. d, Chelmon rostratus. e, Plectorhinchus diagrammus. f, Stegastes leucosticus. g, Chaetodon kleinii. h, Synchiropus splendidus. i, Platax orbicularis.
No. 897: a, Amphiprion percula. b, Holacanthus ciliaris. c, Chaetodon reticulatus. d, Pomacanthus imperator. e, Heniochus acuminatus. f, Lienardella fasciata. g, Zanclus cornutus. h, Scarus guacamaia. i, Lutjanus sebae.
No. 898: a, Tursiops truncatus. b, Phaethon lepturus. c, Istiophorus platypterus. d, Sphyrna zygaena. e, Reinhardtius hippoglossoides. f, Manta birostris. g, Thunnus albacares. h, Himantolophus groenlandicus. i, Tridacna gigas.
No. 899: a, Cypselurus heterurus. b, Sailboat. c, Delphinus delphis. d, Cacharodon carcharias. e, Orcinus orca (b, f). f, Salmo salar. g, Conger conger. h, Pomatomus saltatrix. i, Sphyraena barracuda.
Each 1000r: No. 900, Balaenoptera musculus. No. 901, Megaptera novaengliae, vert.

1997, Mar. 2 **Litho.** **Perf. 14**
896 A278 150fr Sheet of 9, #a.-i.   7.50 7.50
897 A278 180fr Sheet of 9, #a.-i.   8.00 8.00
898 A278 250fr Sheet of 9, #a.-i. 12.00 12.00
899 A278 310fr Sheet of 9, #a.-i. 15.00 15.00

Souvenir Sheets
900-901 A278 Set of 2   10.00 10.00

Transportation — A279

Cyclists: No. 902: a, Rudolph Lewis, 1912. b, Jacques Anquetil, 4-time Tour de France winner. c, Miguel Indurain, hour record holder.
Sailing ships: No. 903: a, Lightning, by Donald McKay, 1856. b, Olivier de Kersauson, winner of Jules Verne trophy. c, Lockheed Sea Shadow, US.
Motorcycles, cyclists: No. 904: a, Coventry Eagle-Jap 998cm3. b, Michael Doohan, Honda 500 NSRV4. c, Harley-Davidson, Heritage Softail classic FLSTC.
Airships: No. 905: a, "Gifford," steam-powered dirigible, 1852. b, Count Ferdinand von Zeppelin, Zeppelin NT LZ N07. c, Nobile N1, "Norge," 1926.
Trains: No. 906: a, Locomotive G 4/5 2-8-0, Switzerland. b, W.V. Siemens, ICE train, Germany. c, Maglev HSST-5, Japan.
Race cars: No. 907: a, 1949 Ferrari Type 166/MM. b, Michael Schumacher, F1 310B Ferrari. c, Ferrari F50.
Sled dogs: No. 908: a, Eskimo. b, Alaskan malamute. c, Siberian husky.
Aircraft: No. 909: a, Wright Brothers' first flight at Kitty Hawk. b, Andre Turcat, Concorde. c, X34 space vehicle.

1997   **Litho.**   **Perf. 13½**
902 A279 180fr Strip of 3, #a.-c.   2.50 1.25
903 A279 250fr Strip of 3, #a.-c.   3.25 1.75
904 A279 320fr Strip of 3, #a.-c.   4.25 2.50
905 A279 370fr Strip of 3, #a.-c.   4.75 2.75
906 A279 460fr Strip of 3, #a.-c.   6.00 3.00
907 A279 490fr Strip of 3, #a.-c.   6.75 3.50
908 A279 530fr Strip of 3, #a.-c.   7.50 3.75
909 A279 750fr Strip of 3, #a.-c. 10.00 5.00

Movie Stars — A281

Designs: a, John Wayne. b, Frank Sinatra. c, Rita Hayworth. d, Sammy Davis, Jr. e, Marilyn Monroe. f, Eddie Murphy. g, Elizabeth Taylor. h, James Dean. i, Robert Mitchum.

1997
910 A281 320fr Sheet of 9, #a.-i.   13.00 6.50

A282

A283

Diana, Princess of Wales (1961-97) — A284

Designs: No. 911, Various close-up portraits. No. 912, Pictures of various times in Diana's life.
Each 1500fr: No. 913, In pink dress with Pres. Clinton (in margin). No. 914, Wearing strapless evening dress. No. 915, Wearing hat and veil. No. 916, In blue dress with Nelson Mandela (in margin).

1997   **Litho.**   **Perf. 13½**
911 A282 250fr Sheet of 9, #a.-i. 10.00 5.00
912 A283 370fr Sheet of 9, #a.-i. 15.00 7.50

Souvenir Sheets
913-916 A284 Set of 4   24.00 14.50

Mars Pathfinder — A285

No. 917 — Dr. Cheick M. Diarra with: a, blue & multi background. b, green & multi background. c, Part of Mars in background. d, violet black & multi background.
No. 917E: f, Like #917a. g, Like #917b. h, Like #917c, i, Like #917d.

1997
917   A285 180fr Sheet of 4, #a.-d.   4.50 2.50
917E A285 320fr Sheet of 4, #f-i   6.75 3.50

Crested Porcupine — A286

World Wildlife Fund: a, Two adults. b, One adult crawling right. c, Mother with young. d, Adult with quills raised.

1998
918 A286 250fr Block of 4, #a.-d.   6.75 3.00

Churches — A287

5fr, Kita Basilica. 10fr, San Cathedral. 150fr, Bamako Cathedral. 370fr, Mandiakuy Church.

1997   **Litho.**   **Perf. 13½**
919 A287   5fr multi   .25   .25
920 A287   10fr multi   .25   .25
921 A287 150fr multi   .70   .35
922 A287 370fr multi 2.00   .85
     Nos. 919-922 (4)   3.20 1.70

Pieces from Natl. Museum — A288

20fr, Bamanan. 25fr, Dogon couple. 250fr, Tasmasheq. 310fr, Oil lamp, Boo.

1997
923 A288   20fr multicolored   .25   .25
924 A288   25fr multicolored   .25   .25
925 A288 250fr multicolored   1.40   .60
926 A288 310fr multicolored   1.75   .75
     Nos. 923-926 (4)   3.65 1.85

Cotton Industry — A289

30fr, Spools of threads. 50fr, Clothing. 180fr, Towels. 320fr, Textile production.

1997
927 A289   30fr multi   .25   .25
928 A289   50fr multi   .25   .25
929 A289 180fr multi   1.25   .50
930 A289 320fr multi   1.75   .75
     Nos. 927-930 (4)   3.50 1.75

"Star Wars" Motion Pictures — A290

Various scenes from: No. 931, "The Return of the Jedi." No. 932, "Star Wars." No. 933: "The Empire Strikes Back."

1997   **Litho.**   **Perf. 13½**
                   Sheets of 9
931 A290 180fr #a.-i.   7.50 7.50
932 A290 310fr #a.-i. 12.00 12.00
933 A290 320fr #a.-i. 13.00 13.00

MALI — Republic of Mali

Wild Animals — A291

Lions Intl. — No. 934: a, Lion. b, Cheetah standing. c, Cheetah lying down. d, Leopard. Rotary Intl. — No. 935: a, Giraffe. b, Addax. c, Kob. d, Okapi.

1997
934	A291	310fr Sheet of 4, #a.-d.	5.50	2.75
935	A291	320fr Sheet of 4, #a.-d.	6.75	3.50

Mars Pathfinder — A292

Insignia and various scenes of Pathfinder mission.

1997
936	A292	370fr Sheet of 9, #a.-i.	16.00	8.00

Cats — A293

No. 937: a, Sphynx. b, Siberian brown tabby. c, Somali creme. d, Java cream point. 1500fr, Chartreux.

1997   Litho.   Perf. 13½
937	A293	530fr Sheet of 4, #a.-d.	10.00	5.00

Souvenir Sheet
938	A293	1500fr multicolored	7.00	3.50

No. 938 contains one 36x42mm stamp.

Scouts and Birds — A294

1997   Color of Bird
939	A294	180fr yellow & black	1.00	.50
940	A294	490fr black & white	3.00	1.50
941	A294	530fr gray & yel org	3.25	1.60
		Nos. 939-941 (3)	7.25	3.00

Souvenir Sheets
942	A294	Sheet of 3, #a.-c. + 3 labels	10.00	5.00
943	A294	1500fr multicolored	7.00	7.00

No. 942 sold for 2200fr. Nos. 942a-942c have the same designs and denominations as Nos. 939-941 but have continuous background showing portion of scouting emblem. No. 943 contains 42x50mm stamp.

1997

Various mushrooms, scout: 250fr, Frying mushrooms. 320fr, Grilling mushrooms. 1060fr, Gathering mushrooms, placing in bag.

944	A294	250fr multicolored	1.40	.70
945	A294	320fr multicolored	1.75	.85
946	A294	1060fr multicolored	5.50	2.75
		Nos. 944-946 (3)	8.65	4.30

Souvenir Sheet
947	A294	Sheet of 3, #a.-c. + 3 labels	11.00	5.50

No. 947 sold for 2600fr. Nos. 947a-947c have the same designs and denominations as Nos. 944-946 but have continuous background showing portion of scouting emblem. A number has been reserved for an additional souvenir sheet with this set.

1998

Various minerals, scout: 150fr, Looking at minerals with magnifying glass. 750fr, Reading book. 900fr, Using chisel.

949	A294	150fr multicolored	.75	.40
950	A294	750fr multicolored	4.25	2.25
951	A294	900fr multicolored	5.00	2.50
		Nos. 949-951 (3)	10.00	5.15

Souvenir Sheet
952	A294	Sheet of 3, #a.-c. + 3 labels	12.00	6.00

No. 952 sold for 2800fr. Nos. 952a-952c have the same designs and denominations as Nos. 949-951 but have continuous background showing portion of scouting emblem.

1998   Litho.   Perf. 13½

Various butterflies, scout: 310fr, Photographing butterfly. 430fr, Using book to identify butterfly. 460fr, Holding and looking at butterfly.

954	A294	310fr multicolored	1.60	.80
955	A294	430fr multicolored	2.00	1.30
956	A294	460fr multicolored	3.00	1.50
		Nos. 954-956 (3)	6.60	3.60

Souvenir Sheet
957	A294	Sheet of 3, #a.-c. + 3 labels	10.00	5.00

No. 957 sold for 2200fr. Nos. 957a-957c have the same designs and denominations as Nos. 954-956 but have continuous background showing portion of scouting emblem. A number has been reserved for an additional souvenir sheet with this set.

Flame of Peace, Timbuktu — A295

1997
959	A295	180fr yellow & multi	3.00	1.50
960	A295	250fr dull red & multi	4.00	2.00

Dated 1996.

Pan-African Postal Union, 18th anniv. — A296

1998
961	A296	250fr Addax	1.60	.80

Local Views — A297

5fr, Mosque, Mopti. 10fr, Fertility doll, Mopti. 15fr, Fishermen. 20fr, Woman carrying bowls on head, Macina. 25fr, Friendship Hotel. 30fr, Sikasso I bill. 40fr, Camel caravan, Azalai. 50fr, Women's hair style, Kayes. 60fr, Old Dogon man. 70fr, Shepherd. 80fr, Playing musical instrument, Wassoulou. 90fr, Crest, Ciwara Bamanan.

1998
962	A297	5fr multi	.25	.25
963	A297	10fr multi, vert.	.25	.25
964	A297	15fr multi	.25	.25
965	A297	20fr multi, vert.	.25	.25
966	A297	25fr multi, vert.	.30	.30
967	A297	30fr multi, vert.	.30	.30
968	A297	40fr multi, vert.	.30	.30
969	A297	50fr multi, vert.	.30	.30
970	A297	60fr multi, vert.	.40	.40
971	A297	70fr multi, vert.	.40	.40
972	A297	80fr multi, vert.	.40	.40
973	A297	90fr multi, vert.	.40	.40
		Nos. 962-973 (12)	3.80	3.80

Travels of Pope John Paul II — A298

No. 974: a, Looking at book with Fidel Castro, Cuba. b, Walking with Castro, Cuba. c, With girl, Castro, Cuba. d, With boy, Nigeria. e, With three nuns, Cuba. f, Reading inscription on monument, Cuba. g, Holding crucifix, blessing child, Nigeria. h, Standing before monument, Nigeria. i, Giving blessing, people in traditional costumes, Nigeria.

Nos. 975a, 975c, 975d, 975e, 975f, 975g, 975i: Various portraits of Mother Teresa with Pope John Paul II. No. 975b, Pope John Paul II. No. 975h, Mother Teresa.

1998   Litho.   Perf. 13½
Sheets of 9
974	A298	310fr #a.-i.	12.00	6.00
975	A298	320fr #a.-i.	12.00	6.00

Animal Type of 1997

Dogs — No. 976: a, Dachshund. b, Persian hound. c, Chihuahua. d, Pug. 1500fr, Dalmatian.

1998   Litho.   Perf. 13½
976	A293	390fr Sheet of 4, #a.-d.	6.50	3.25

Souvenir Sheet
977	A293	1500fr multicolored	7.00	3.50

No. 977 contains one 36x42mm stamp.

Entertainers — A299

No. 978, Various portraits of James Dean. No. 979, opera singers: a, Placido Domingo. b, Luciano Pavarotti. c, Jose Carreras. d, Andrea Bocelli. e, Maria Callas. f, Jose Van Dam. g, Renata Tebaldi. h, Montserrat Caballe. i, Kiri Te Kanawa.

No. 980, actresses: a, Audrey Hepburn. b, Greta Garbo. c, Elizabeth Taylor. d, Grace Kelly. e, Jean Harlow. f, Ava Gardner. g, Lana Turner. h, Marilyn Monroe. i, Vivien Leigh.

1998   Litho.   Perf. 13½
Sheets of 9
978	A299	250fr #a.-i.	10.00	5.00
979	A299	310fr #a.-i.	14.00	7.00
980	A299	320fr #a.-i.	14.00	7.00

Chess Masters — A300

Portraits: a, Adolf Anderssen, 1818-79. b, Wilhelm Steinitz, 1836-1900. c, Emmanuel Lasker, 1868-1941. d, Alexandre Alekhine, 1892-1946. e, Tigran Petrosian, 1929-84. f, Boris Spassky, 1937. g, Bobby Fischer, 1943-2008. h, Garry Kasparov, 1963. i, Anatoli Karpov, 1951.

1998
981	A300	370fr Sheet of 9, #a.-i.	16.00	8.00

Eric Tabarly (1931-98), French Sailor — A301

Designs: a, Portrait. b, Tabarly at helm, yachts Pen Duick, Pen Duick VI. c, Tabarly, Charles de Gaulle.

1998
982	A301	390fr Sheet of 3, #a.-c.	5.00	2.50

No. 982b is 60x50mm.

France, 1998 World Cup Soccer Champions — A302

No. 983: a, Laurent Blanc. b, Lilian Thuram. c, David Trezeguet.
No. 984: a, Marcel Desailly. b, Fabien Barthez. c, Christian Karembeu.
No. 985: a, Didier Deschamps. b, Emmanuel Petit. c, Bixente Lizarazu.
No. 986: a, Youri Djorkaeff. b, Zinedine Zidane. c, Aime Jacquet.
2000fr, Team picture.

1998   Litho.   Perf. 13½
Sheets of 3
983	A302	250fr #a.-c.	4.50	2.25
984	A302	370fr #a.-c.	6.00	3.00
985	A302	390fr #a.-c.	6.75	3.50
986	A302	750fr #a.-c.	11.50	5.75

Souvenir Sheet
987	A302	2000fr multicolored	11.00	11.00

No. 987 contains one 57x51mm stamp.

Jacques-Yves Cousteau (1910-97), Underwater Explorer, Environmentalist — A303

No. 988: a, Cousteau, ship Calypso. b, Divers, underwater submersibles. c, Diver looking into submarine habitat, man playing chess.
No. 989: a, Portrait, Cousteau with Pres. John F. Kennedy. b, Divers retrieving amphora. c, Hard hat diver, Cousteau wearing early aqualung.

MALI — Republic of Mali

1998			Sheets of 3
988	A303	460fr #a.-c.	7.25 3.75
989	A303	490fr #a.-c.	8.25 4.25

Nos. 988b, 989b are each 60x51mm.

History of Chess — A304

Chess pieces, boards — No. 990: a, India, 18th cent. b, Italy, 1700. c, Siam, 18th cent. d, France, 1880. e, Austria, 1872. f, Germany, 1925. g, Yugoslavia, 20th cent. h, China, 20th cent. i, Russia, 20th cent.

No. 991, Albert V of Bavaria playing chess with his wife, Anne of Austria. No. 992, Arabian chess. No. 993, Japanese chess. No. 994, Nefertari, Ramses II playing chess.

1998	Litho.		Perf. 13½
990	A304	370fr Sheet of 9, #a.-i.	16.00 8.00

Souvenir Sheets

991-994	A304	1500fr each	8.00 4.00

Nos. 991-994 each contain one 57x51mm stamp.

Pope John Paul II — A305

No. 995: Various portraits of John Paul II portrayed with events, popes depicting papal history.

Pope John Paul II, famous cathedrals —No. 996: a, Chartres. b, Santiago de Compostela. c, St. Sophie, Novgorod, Russia. d, St. Peter's Basilica, Vatican City. e, Our Lady of Peace Basilica, Yamoussoukro, Ivory Coast. f, Milan.

Pope John Paul II, famous cathedrals —No. 997: a, Sacred Family, Barcelona. b, Saint Sophie, Kiev. c, Notre Dame, Lausanne. d, Cathedral of Mexico. e, Cathedral of Cologne. f, Burgos Cathedral.

1998	Litho.		Perf. 13½
		Sheets of 6 or 9	
995	A305	250fr #a.-i.	9.00 4.50
996	A305	370fr #a.-f.	8.00 4.00
997	A305	750fr #a.-f.	17.50 8.75

Granaries A306

1998	Litho.		Perf. 13½
998	A306	25fr Sénoufo, vert.	.25 .25
999	A306	180fr Sarakolé	.80 .40
1000	A306	310fr Minianka, vert.	1.60 .80
1001	A306	320fr Boo, vert.	1.60 .80
		Nos. 998-1001 (4)	4.25 2.35

Trees — A307

100fr, Tamarindus indica. 150fr, Adansonia digitata. 180fr, Acacia senegal. 310fr, Parkia biglobosa.

1998			
1002	A307	100fr multicolored	.60 .30
1003	A307	150fr multicolored	.80 .40
1004	A307	180fr multicolored	.90 .45
1005	A307	310fr multicolored	1.60 .80
		Nos. 1002-1005 (4)	3.90 1.95

National Museum Pieces — A308

1998			
1006	A308	50fr Bamanan	.25 .25
1007	A308	150fr Dogon	.65 .35
1008	A308	250fr Bamanan, diff.	1.25 .65
1009	A308	320fr Minianka	1.60 .80
		Nos. 1006-1009 (4)	3.75 2.05

Ants — A309

150fr, Solenopsis geminata. 180fr, Camponotus pennsylvanicus. 250fr, Monorium minimum. 310fr, Lasius niger.

1998			
1010	A309	150fr multi	.60 .30
1011	A309	180fr multi, vert.	.80 .40
1012	A309	250fr multi	1.25 .60
1013	A309	310fr multi	1.50 .75
		Nos. 1010-1013 (4)	4.15 2.05

Baladji Cisse (1924-77), Boxer — A309a

150fr, Cisse boxing. 250fr, In green jacket.

1999, May 12	Litho.		Perf. 13½
1013A	A309a	150fr multi	— —
1013B	A309a	250fr multi	— —

World Teachers' Day — A310

Various views of teachers working.

1999	Litho.		Perf. 13½
1014	A310	150fr multi, vert.	.70 .35
1015	A310	250fr multi, vert.	1.25 .65
1016	A310	370fr multi, vert.	1.75 .80
1017	A310	390fr multi	1.90 .95
		Nos. 1014-1017 (4)	5.60 2.75

Fight Against Poverty — A311

150fr, Agriculture. 180fr, Labor projects. 750fr, Food, vert. 1000fr, Potable water.

1999	Litho.		Perf. 13¼
1018	A311	150fr multi	.80 .40
1019	A311	180fr multi	1.00 .50
1020	A311	750fr multi	3.75 1.80
1021	A311	1000fr multi	4.75 2.50
		Nos. 1018-1021 (4)	10.30 5.20

UPU, 125th Anniv. — A312

UPU emblem and: 150fr, Airplane, train, boat. 250fr, Stick figures with letters. 310fr, Eagles, antelopes with letters. 320fr, Eagle with letter on mud structure, vert.

1999			
1022	A312	150fr multi	.70 .35
1023	A312	250fr multi	1.25 .65
1024	A312	310fr multi	1.50 .75
1025	A312	320fr multi	1.60 .80
		Nos. 1022-1025 (4)	5.05 2.55

Flora and Fauna — A313

No. 1026 — Reptiles: a, Pseudonaja textilis. b, Litoria chloris. c, Imantodes inornata. d, Pyton arboricole. e, Pachydactylus bibroni. f, Trimeresurus wagleri.

No. 1027 — Orchids: a, Epidendrum ellipticum. b, Oncidium macranthum. c, Miltoniopsis roezlii. d, Oncidium barbatum. e, Miltonia warscewiczii. f, Lockhartia oerstedii.

No. 1028 — Birds: a, Amandava subflava. b, Ploceus bojeri. c, Lagonosticta senegala. d, Uraeginthus bengalus. e, Monticola saxatilis. f, Saxicola torquata.

No. 1028G — Birds: h, Tyto alba. i, Pernis apivorus. j, Bubo africanus. k, Gypaetus barbatus meridionalis. l, Strix aluco. m, Milvus migrans.

No. 1029 — Butterflies: a, Cymothoe hypatha. b, Cymothoe sangaris. c, Top view, Charaxes fournierae. d, Male Catopsilia thauruma. e, Bottom view, Charaxes fournierae. f, Female Catopsilia thauruma.

No. 1030 — Mushrooms: a, Amanita muscaria. b, Amanita spissa. c, Helvella acetabulum. d, Pleurotus ostreatus. e, Phallus duplicatus. f, Cortinarius salor.

1999			Sheets of 6
1026	A313	350fr #a.-f.	10.00 5.00
1027	A313	390fr #a.-f.	11.00 5.50
1028	A313	430fr #a.-f.	12.00 6.00
1028G	A313	460fr #h-m	14.00 7.00
1029	A313	490fr #a.-f.	15.00 7.50
1030	A313	530fr #a.-f.	16.00 8.00
		Nos. 1026-1030 (6)	78.00 39.00

Rocks, Dinosaurs and Volcanoes — A314

No. 1031 — Dinosaurs and rocks: a, Edmontonia, Ensisheim meteorite. b, Iguanodon, Saint-Mesmin meteorite. c, Allosaurus, Pallasite meteorite. d, Troodon, Lunar meteorite. e, Lesothosaurus, rock from Bouvant. f, Carnotaurus, Axtell meteorite. g, Deinonychus, Orgueil meteorite. h, Dilophosaurus, rock from Douar Mghila. i, Psittacosaurus, L'Aigle meteorite.

No. 1032 — Volcanic eruptions and rocks: a, Popocatepetl, 1519, Peekskill meteorite. b, Santorin, 1645, Tamentit meteorite. c, Mt. Pelee, 1902, Ouallen meteorite. d, Herculaneum during Vesuvius eruption, 79, Chinguetti meteorite. e, Krakatoa, 1883, Pultush meteorite. f, Soufriere, 1979, rock from Sienne. g, Mt. St. Helens, 1980, Allende meteorite. h, Kilauea, 1984, Parnallee meteorite. i, Mt. Etna, 1986, Tamentit meteorite.

1500fr, Pompeii during Vesuvius eruption, 79.

1999	Sheets of 9		Perf. 13¼
1031	A314	250fr #a.-i.	11.00 5.50
1032	A314	310fr #a.-i.	15.00 7.50

Souvenir Sheet
Perf. 13½

1033	A314	1500fr multi	7.50 3.75

No. 1033 contains one 39x56mm stamp.

Space — A315

No. 1034: a, Hubble Space Telescope. b, Venera 12. c, Space shuttle. d, Ariane 5.

No. 1035: a, Apollo-Soyuz mission. b, Carl Sagan, Viking 1. c, Voyager 1. d, Giotto probe, Edmond Halley.

No. 1036: a, Frank Borman, Apollo 8. b, Neil Armstrong, Apollo 11. c, Luna 16 and Lunokhod 2. d, Surveyor 1.

No. 1037: a, Konstantin Tsiolkovsky. b, Robert H. Goddard. c, Hermann Oberth. d, Theodor von Kármán.

No. 1038: a, Laika, Sputnik 2. b, Yuri Gagarin, Vostok 1. c, Edward White, Gemini 4. d, John Glenn, Friendship 7.

No. 1039: a, Apollo 15 Lunar Rover. b, Pioneer 10. c, Skylab. d, Mariner 10.

1999	Sheets of 4		Perf. 13¼
1034	A315	250fr #a.-d.	5.50 2.75
1035	A315	310fr #a.-d.	6.00 3.00
1036	A315	320fr #a-d	6.50 3.25
1037	A315	500fr #a-d	11.00 5.50
1038	A315	750fr #a-d	15.00 7.50
1039	A315	900fr #a-d	18.00 9.00
		Nos. 1034-1039 (6)	62.00 31.00

The Malian government declared that sheets of 9 stamps containing 100, 150, 200, 250, 300, 350, 400, 450 and 500fr stamps with the following topics are "illegal": Trains, Chess, Prehistoric Animals, Ferdinand Magellan, Christopher Columbus, Mushrooms, Computers, Wolves, Minerals, International Red Cross, Composers, Horses, and Wild Animals (tiger, lion, eagle, etc.)

I Love Lucy A318

No. 1045: a, Lucy showing Fred open handcuffs. b, Lucy touching reclining Ricky while handcuffed. c, Fred watching Ricky glare at Lucy. d, Handcuffed Lucy and Ricky trying to go in opposite directions. e, Handcuffed Lucy and Ricky seated. f, Lucy and Ricky handcuffed on bed. g, Lucy trying to get off bed while handcuffed to Ricky. h, Handcuffed Ricky with hand between legs. i, Ricky with arm draped over Lucy.

No. 1046, 1000fr, Fred examining handcuffs on Lucy and Ricky. No. 1047, 1000fr, Lucy and Ricky looking down.

1999, May 20	Litho.		Perf. 13¼
1045	A318	320fr Sheet of 9, #a-i	16.00 16.00

Souvenir Sheets

1046-1047	A318	Set of 2	12.00 12.00

MALI — Republic of Mali

Garfield the Cat — A319

No. 1048: a, With eyes half shut, pink background. b, With eyes open, pink background. c, Touching chin. d, With eyes open and open mouth. e, Showing tongue. f, With eyes open, showing teeth. g, With eyes open, blue background. h, With eyes half shut, blue background. i, Odie.
1000fr, As mailman.

1999, May 20 Litho. Perf. 13¼

| 1048 | A319 | 250fr Sheet of 9, #a-i | 12.50 | 6.25 |

Souvenir Sheet

| 1049 | A319 | 1000fr multi | 5.50 | 2.75 |

No. 1049 contains one 36x42mm stamp.

Miniature Sheet

Millennium

No. 1050: a, Balloonists viewing Halley's Comet, 1910. b, Sinking of the Titanic, 1912. c, San Francisco Earthquake, 1906. d, Eruption of Mount Pelee, 1902.
No. 1051: a, Jules Verne, Scene from "20,000 Leagues Under the Sea," 1905. b, Commander William R. Anderson, USS Nautilus, map of Arctic region showing underwater voyage across North Pole, 1958. c, Discovery of tomb of King Tutankhamun, 1922. d, Transatlantic flight of Charles A. Lindbergh, 1927.
No. 1052: a, Marilyn Monroe (1926-62), actress. b, The Beatles, 1962. c, Neil Armstrong, first man on the Moon, 1969. d, Elvis Presley (1935-77).
No. 1053: a, Mohandas Gandhi, Independence of India, 1947. b, Jean Monnet (1888-1979), map of Europe, euro symbol, 1951 meeting of European Coal and Steel Community. c, Pres. John F. Kennedy (1917-63). d, First heart transplant by Dr. Christiaan Barnard, 1967.
No. 1054: a, Albert Einstein (1879-1955), Nobel Physics laureate, 1921. b, Nelson Mandela (1918-2013), Nobel Peace laureate, 1993. c, Sir Alexander Fleming discovers penicillin, 1928. d, Luc Montagnier discovers AIDS virus, 1982.
No. 1055: a, North polar expedition of Robert Peary, 1909. b, South polar expedition of Roald Amundsen, 1911. c, Sputnik 1, 1957. d, Yuri Gagarin, first man in space, 1961.
No. 1056: a, Mother Teresa holding Nobel diploma, dove. b, Princess Diana, rose, dove. c, Pope John Paul II. d, Fall of the Berlin Wall, doves.
No. 1057: a, Chales de Gaulle becomes President of France, 1958. b, André Turcat test pilots Concorde, 1969. c, Pelé and Brazilian team win World Cup, 1958. d, Zinedine Zidane and French team win World Cup, 1998.

1999, July 2 Litho. Perf. 13¼

1050	A320	250fr Sheet of 4, #a-d	—	—
1051	A320	310fr Sheet of 4, #a-d	—	—
1052	A320	320fr Sheet of 4, #a-d	—	—
1053	A320	390fr Sheet of 4, #a-d	—	—
1054	A320	430fr Sheet of 4, #a-d	—	—
1055	A320	460fr Sheet of 4, #a-d	—	—
1056	A320	490fr Sheet of 4, #a-d	—	—
1057	A320	530fr Sheet of 4, #a-d	—	—

Flags of the World — A321

No. 1058: a, Myanmar. b, Namibia. c, Nepal. d, Niger. e, Nigeria. f, Norway. g, Uganda. h, Pakistan. i, Netherlands. j, Peru. k, Philippines. l, Poland. m, New Zealand. n, Portugal. o, North Korea. p, Romania.
No. 1059: a, Russia. b, Rwanda. c, Singapore. d, Slovakia. e, Sudan. f, Sri Lanka. g, Sweden. h, Switzerland. i, Syria. j, Tanzania. k, Czech Republic. l, Thailand. m, Somalia. n, Tunisia. o, Turkey. p, Ukraine.
No. 1060: a, Finland. b, France. c, Great Britain. d, Greece. e, Guinea. f, Hungary. g, India. h, Indonesia. i, Iran. j, Iraq. k, Ireland. l, Iceland. m, Israel. n, Italy. o, Libya. p, Japan.
No. 1061: a, Cambodia. b, Cameroun. c, Canada. d, Chile. e, People's Republic of China. f, Colombia. g, Democratic Republic of the Congo. h, South Korea. i, Ivory Coast. j, Croatia. k, Cuba. l, Denmark. m, Egypt. n, United Arab Emirates. o, Spain. p, Ethiopia.
No. 1062: a, Afghanistan. b, South Africa. c, Albania. d, Algeria. e, Germany. f, United States. g, Angola. h, Saudi Arabia. i, Argentina. j, Australia. k, Austria. l, Bangladesh. m, Belgium. n, Bolivia. o, Brazil. p, Bulgaria.
No. 1063: a, Jordan. b, Kenya. c, Kuwait. d, Laos. e, Lebanon. f, Lithuania. g, Luxembourg. h, Madagascar. i, Malaysia. j, Mali. k, Viet Nam. l, Morocco. m, Mauritius. n, Mexico. o, Monaco. p, Mongolia.
No. 1064: a, Venezuela. b, Yemen. c, Uruguay. d, Zambia.

1999, Aug. 2 Litho. Perf. 13¼

1058	A321	20fr Sheet of 16, #a-p	—	—
1059	A321	25fr Sheet of 16, #a-p	—	—
1060	A321	50fr Sheet of 16, #a-p	—	—
1061	A321	100fr Sheet of 16, #a-p	5.00	2.50
q.		Cameroun, flag with green star		
r.		Sheet of 16, #1061a, 1061c-1061q	—	—
1062	A321	100fr Sheet of 16, #a-p	—	—
1063	A321	100fr Sheet of 16, #a-p	—	—
1064	A321	100fr Sheet of 4, #a-d	—	—

No. 1061b has a Cameroun flag with a yellow star.

Sikasso Cathedral — A322

No. 1065: a, Photograph. b, Drawing.

1999, Dec. 25 Litho. Perf. 13¼

| 1065 | A322 | 150fr Horiz. pair, #a-b | 1.75 | .85 |

Christianity, 2000th Anniv. — A323

No. 1066, 100fr: a, St. Louis. b, Construction of Amiens Cathedral, 13th cent. c, Joan of Arc. d, Pope John Paul II.
No. 1067, 180fr: a, Jesus Christ. b, Persecution of Christians by Nero. c, St. Peter. d, Charlemagne.

1999, Dec. 25 Sheets of 4, #a-d

| 1066-1067 | A323 | Set of 2 | 6.00 | 3.00 |

Religious Paintings — A324

No. 1068, 250fr: a, Heller Madonna, by Albrecht Dürer. b, Virgin and Child, by Dürer. c, Madonna with Sts. Francis and Liberale, by Giorgione. d, Virgin and Child, by Giorgione.
No. 1069, 310fr: a, Virgin and Child, by Fra Filippo Lippi. b, Virgin and Child with Two Angels, by Lippi. c, Virgin and Sleeping Child, by Andrea Mantegna. d, Madonna of Victory, by Mantegna.
No. 1070, 320fr: a, Virgin and Child, by Hugo van der Goes. b, Virgin and Child and landscape, by van der Goes. c, Madonna and Child with St. Peter and a Martyred Saint, by Paolo Veronese. d, Adoration of the Magi, by Veronese.
No. 1071, 370fr: a, Madonna and Child Between St. Peter and St. Sebastian, by Giovanni Bellini. b, Madonna and Child with Cherubim, by Bellini. c, Madonna and Child with Two Angels, by Sandro Botticelli. d, Bardi Madonna, by Botticelli.
No. 1072, 390fr: a, Rest During the Flight to Egypt, with the Virgin, by Corregio. b, The Night, by Corregio. c, Senigallia Madonna, by Piero della Francesca. d, Virgin and Child and Four Angels, by della Francesca.
No. 1073, 750fr: a, Virgin and Child (rectangular), by Quentin Massys. b, Virgin and Child (curved top) by Massys. c, Madonna and Saint Sixtus, by Raphael. d, Madonna of the Duke of Alba, by Raphael.

1999, Dec. 25 Sheets of 4, #a-d

| 1068-1073 | A324 | Set of 6 | 50.00 | 25.00 |

2000 Summer Olympics, Sydney — A325

No. 1074, 150fr — Equestrian events: a, Show jumping. b, Military jumping. c, Dressage, horse facing left. d, Dressage, horse facing right.
No. 1075, 460fr — Tennis: a, Woman with green trim on dress. b, Man with red trim on shirt. c, Woman, diff. d, Man, diff.
No. 1076, 530fr — Table tennis: a, Green and red shirt and shorts. b, White shirt, red shorts. c, White and red shirt, black shorts. d, Yellow and green shirt, black shorts.
No. 1077, 750fr — Basketball: a, Red and yellow uniform. b, Green uniform. c, White and red uniform. d, Yellow and green uniform.
1000fr, Hurdler, horse and rider, horiz.

2000, June 30 Sheets of 4, #a-d

| 1074-1077 | A325 | Set of 4 | 57.50 | 30.00 |

Souvenir Sheet

| 1078 | A325 | 1000fr multi | 7.50 | 3.75 |

No. 1078 contains one 57x85mm stamp.

2002 World Cup Soccer Championships, Japan and Korea — A326

No. 1079, 150fr: a, Pedro Cea. b, Schiavo. c, Luigi Colaussi. d, Juan Schiaffino.
No. 1080, 250fr: a, Fritz Walter. b, Pelé. c, Amarildo. d, Bobby Moore.
No. 1081, 320fr: a, Jairzinho. b, Franz Beckenbauer. c, Mario Kempes. d, Paolo Rossi.
No. 1082, 750fr: a, Diego Maradona. b, Jurgen Klinsmann. c, Romario. d, Zinedine Zidane.

2000, June 30 Sheets of 4, #a-d

| 1079-1082 | A326 | Set of 4 | 42.50 | 22.50 |

Fauna, Mushrooms and Prehistoric Animals — A327

No. 1083, 150fr — Birds: a, Ganga de Liechtenstein. b, Guepier à gorge blanche. c, Moineau domestique. d, Euplecte de feu. e, Irrisor namaquois. f, Pique-boeuf à bec jaune.
No. 1084, 180fr — Dogs: a, Dalmatian. b, Hungarian Kuvasz. c, Swedish shepherd. d, Ibiza dog. e, Golden retriever. f, Dachshund.
No. 1085, 250fr — Cats: a, White cat with orange eyes. b, Somali. c, Himalayan blue tortie point. d, Korat. e, Bombay. f, La Perm.
No. 1086, 310fr — Butterflies: a, Paralethe dendrophilis. b, Papilio ophidicephalus. c, Kallima jacksoni. d, Hypolimnas antevorta. e, Papilio nobilis. f, Euxanthe wakefieldi.
No. 1087, 320fr — Butterflies: a, Euxanthe eurinome. b, Euryphura chalcis. c, Dira mintha. d, Euphaedra zaddachi. e, Euphaedra neophron. f, Euxanthe tiberius.
No. 1088, 370fr — Mushrooms: a, Volvariella acystidiata. b, Leucopricus birnbaumii. c, Cystoderma elegans. d, Leucoprinus elaidis. e, Leucoprinus discoideus. f, Leucoagaricus carminescens.
No. 1089, 370fr — Birds: a, Pririt du cap. b, Petit duc scops. c, Ouette d'Egypte. d, Rollier d'Europe. e, Promerops du cap. f, Sauteur du cap.
No. 1090, 390fr — Mushrooms: a, Volvariella parvispora. b, Volvariella surrecta. c, Lentinus similis. d, Leucoagaricus holosericeus. e, Leucoagaricus pepinus. f, Agrocybe elegantior.
No. 1091, 460fr — Prehistoric animals: a, Psittacosaurus. b, Phororhacos. c, Coelophysis. d, Saurornithoides. e, Acanthopholis. f, Varannosaurus.
No. 1092, 490fr — Prehistoric animals: a, Dromiceiomimus. b, Placodus. c, Ceratosaurus. d, Heterodontosaurus. e, Diatryma. f, Ouranosaurus.

2000, Sept. 25 Sheets of 6, #a-f

| 1083-1092 | A327 | Set of 10 | 145.00 | 75.00 |

Campaign Against Malaria — A328

Designs: No. 1093, 150fr, Doctor, mother and child. No. 1094, 150fr, Man with briefcase, man with crutch, syringe. No. 1095, 150fr, Doctor, syringe. 430fr, Mother, child, syringe, quinine tablets.

2000

| 1093-1096 | A328 | Set of 4 | 4.00 | 2.00 |

Intl. Volunteers Year (in 2001) — A329

2000

| 1097 | A329 | 250fr multi | 1.00 | .50 |

Independence, 40th Anniv. — A330

Designs: 20fr, Provincial map. 375fr, Flag-raising ceremony, front and back of 50-franc banknote, vert.

MALI — Republic of Mali

2001		Litho.	Perf. 13
1099	A330	20fr multi	— —
1100	A330	375fr multi	— —

An additional stamp was issued in this set. The editors would like to examine it.

Senegal River Regional Organization A331

2001		Litho.	Perf. 12¾
1101	A331	30fr multi, dated "2004"	— —
1102	A331	100fr multi	— —
a.		Dated "2003"	— —
1103	A331	5000fr multi, dated "2002"	— —

A332 A333

Perf. 13¼ (A332), 13x12¾ (A333)

2002, Jan. 19			Litho.
1104	A332	195fr multi	—
1105	A333	255fr multi	—
1106	A332	385fr multi	—
1107	A333	395fr multi	—
1108	A332	565fr multi	—
1109	A332	975fr multi	—

23rd African Cup Soccer Tournament. Dated "2001."

Bobo Mask A334
Dogon Mask A335
Sénoufo Sanctuary Door A336
Bamanan Fertility Statue A337

2001-04		Litho.	Perf. 12¾
1110	A334	5fr multi	— —
1111	A335	10fr multi	— —
a.		Dated "2004"	— —
1112	A336	25fr multi	— —
a.		Dated "2004"	— —
1113	A334	40fr multi	— —
1114	A335	75fr multi	— —
a.		Dated "2004"	— —
1114B	A336	75fr multi	— —
1115	A334	195fr multi	— —
1116	A335	195fr multi	1.00 .50
a.		Dated "2005"	— —
1117	A334	235fr multi	— —
1118	A335	255fr multi	— —
1119	A337	255fr multi	1.40 .70
1120	A335	325fr multi	— —
1121	A336	385fr multi	— —
1122	A336	400fr multi	— —
1123	A337	500fr multi	— —
1124	A337	1000fr multi	— —

Issued: Nos. 1115, 1117, 1118, 1120, 1121-1123, 2001; Nos. 1110, 1111-1114, 2002. Nos. 1116, 1119, 2003. No. 1114B, 1124, 2004.

A338

AIDS Prevention — A339

2002, Jan. 10		Litho.	Perf. 12¾
1125	A338	195fr multi	— —
1127	A338	225fr multi	— —
1128	A339	225fr multi	— —
1129	A338	385fr multi	— —
1130	A339	385fr multi	— —

An additional stamp was issued in this set. The editors would like to examine any example of it.

Songhoi Woman's Hairstyle A340
Peulh Woman A341

Badiangara Cliffs — A342

Perf. 12¾, 13x12¾ (#1131)

2003, Mar. 7			Litho.
1131	A340	50fr multi	.25 .25
a.		Dated "2004"	—
1132	A341	385fr multi	2.25 2.25
a.		Dated "2004"	—
1133	A342	485fr multi	2.75 2.75

Balaphone Festival — A343

2003, Mar. 7		Litho.	Perf. 12¾
1134	A343	565fr multi	3.50 3.50

Men Drinking Tea in Desert — A344

2005, Aug. 18		Litho.	Perf. 12¾
1135	A344	10fr multi	—

See No. 1147.

Djenné Fair — A345

2005, Aug. 18		Litho.	Perf. 12¾
1136	A345	20fr multi	.50 .50

Map of Africa, Water Drop, Lions International Emblem — A346

2005, Aug. 18		Litho.	Perf. 12¾
1137	A346	465fr multi	4.50 4.50

World Summit on the Information Society, Tunis — A347

2005, Aug. 18		Litho.	Perf. 12¾x13
1138	A347	195fr multi	—
1139	A347	255fr multi	—
1140	A347	385fr multi	—

23rd Summit of Heads of State of Africa and France
A348 A349

2005, Aug. 18		Litho.	Perf. 13x12¾
1141	A348	195fr multi	—
1142	A349	195fr multi	—
1143	A348	255fr multi	—
1144	A349	255fr multi	—
1145	A348	385fr multi	—
1146	A349	385fr multi	—

Men Drinking Tea in Desert Type of 2005

2007		Litho.	Perf. 12¾
1147	A344	20fr multi	—

World AIDS Day — A349a

2008, Dec. 1		Litho.	Perf. 13
1148	A349a	195fr multi	—

Mother Nursing Baby — A350

2009, July 20		Litho.	Perf. 13x12¾
			Panel Color
1149	A350	195fr red	—
1150	A350	485fr green	—

Independence, 50th Anniv. — A351

50th anniversary emblem with: 5fr, Pale yellow background, orange yellow top panel, green bottom panel. 10fr, White background, orange yellow top panel, red bottom panel. 20fr, White background, orange yellow top and bottom panels. 25fr, Pale yellow background, green top panel, red bottom panel. 40fr, Light blue background, red top panel, orange yellow bottom panel. 100fr, Light blue background, red top panel, green bottom panel. 195fr, White background, red top and bottom panels. 565fr, White background, green top and bottom panels.

2010, Jan. 27		Litho.	Perf. 13
1151-1158	A351	Set of 8	11.50 11.50

Independence, 50th Anniv. — A352

Denomination color: 195fr, Green. 485fr, Red.

2010, Jan. 27		Litho.	Perf. 13
1159-1160	A352	Set of 2	8.00 8.00

Serval — A355

2014, Jan. 11		Litho.	Perf. 13¼
1163	A355	200fr multi	—
1164	A355	300fr multi	—
1165	A355	400fr multi	—
1166	A355	500fr multi	—
1167	A355	1000fr multi	—

Economic Community of West African States, 40th Anniv. — A356

2015, Dec. 17		Litho.	Perf. 13¼
1168	A356	400fr multi	—

Timbuktu Manuscripts A357

2015		Litho.	Perf. 13¼
1169	A357	100fr multi	—
1172	A357	500fr multi	—
1175	A357	1500fr multi	—

At least four additional stamps were issued in this set. The editors would like to examine any examples.

Malian postal officials have declared that souvenir sheets containing stamps commemorating the campaign against COVID-19 are illegal.

SEMI-POSTAL STAMPS

Anti-Malaria Issue
Common Design Type
Perf. 12½x12

1962, Apr. 7		Engr.	Unwmk.
B1	CD108	25fr + 5fr pale vio bl	1.25 .60

Algerian Family — SP1

1962, Dec. 24		Photo.	Perf. 12x12½
B2	SP1	25fr + 5fr multi	.70 .30

Issued for the national campaign to show the solidarity of the peoples of Mali and Algeria.

MALI — Republic of Mali

AIR POST STAMPS

Federation

Composite View of St. Louis, Senegal — AP1

1959, Dec. 11   **Unwmk.**   **Perf. 13**
C1   AP1   85fr multi   2.10   1.00

Founding of St. Louis, Senegal, tercentenary, and opening of the 6th meeting of the executive council of the French Community.

Birds — AP2

100fr, Amethyst starling. 200fr, Bateleur eagle, horiz. 500fr, Barbary shrike.

Perf. 12½x13, 13x12½
1960, Feb. 13   **Photo.**
C2   AP2   100fr multi   3.00   1.50
C3   AP2   200fr multi   7.00   2.50
C4   AP2   500fr multi   20.00   11.50
    Nos. C2-C4 (3)   30.00   15.50

Republic
Nos. C2-C4 Overprinted or Surcharged

1960, Dec. 18
C5   AP2   100fr multi   4.50   1.75
C6   AP2   200fr multi   6.75   3.00
C7   AP2   300fr on 500fr multi   10.00   6.00
C8   AP2   500fr multi   16.50   9.00
    Nos. C5-C8 (4)   37.75   19.75

Pres. Modibo Keita — AP3

Designs: 200fr, Mamadou Konate.

1961, Mar. 18   **Engr.**   **Perf. 13**
C9   AP3   200fr claret & gray brn   3.00   .95
C10   AP3   300fr grn & blk   4.50   1.25

Flag, Map, UN Emblem — AP4

1961, Mar. 18
C11   AP4   100fr multicolored   1.75   .75
   a.   Min. sheet of 3, #13, 14, C11   2.75   2.75

Proclamation of independence and admission to UN.

Sankore Mosque, Timbuktu — AP5

200fr, View of Timbuktu. 500fr, Bamako & arms.

1961, Apr. 15   **Unwmk.**   **Perf. 13**
C12   AP5   100fr Prus bl, red brn & gray   2.25   .60
C13   AP5   200fr grn, brn & red   4.50   1.75
C14   AP5   500fr red brn, Prus bl & dk grn   11.00   3.25
    Nos. C12-C14 (3)   17.75   5.60

Inauguration of Timbuktu airport and Air Mali.

Bull, Chemical Equipment and Chicks — AP6

1963, Feb. 23   **Engr.**
C15   AP6   200fr bis, mar & grnsh bl   4.25   1.50

Sotuba Zootechnical Institute.

Air Ambulance — AP7

Designs: 55fr, National Line plane loading. 100fr, Intl. Line Vickers Viscount in flight.

1963, Nov. 2   **Unwmk.**   **Perf. 13**
C16   AP7   25fr dk bl, emer & red brn   .35   .25
C17   AP7   55fr bis, bl & red brn   1.00   .35
C18   AP7   100fr dk bl, red brn & yel grn   1.75   .70
    Nos. C16-C18 (3)   3.10   1.30

Issued to publicize Air Mali.

Crowned Crane and Giant Tortoise — AP8

1963, Nov. 23   **Unwmk.**   **Perf. 13**
C19   AP8   25fr sepia, org & ver   1.25   .60
C20   AP8   200fr multi   5.25   2.25

Animal protection.

UN Emblem, Flag, Doves — AP9

1963, Dec. 10   **Engr.**
C21   AP9   50fr lt grn, yel & red   1.20   .50

15th anniversary of the Universal Declaration of Human Rights.

Cleopatra and Ptolemy at Kôm Ombo — AP10

1964, Mar. 9   **Unwmk.**   **Perf. 12**
C22   AP10   25fr dp claret & bister   .75   .35
C23   AP10   55fr dp claret & lt ol grn   1.50   .75

UNESCO world campaign to save historic monuments in Nubia.

Pres. John F. Kennedy — AP11

1964, Oct. 26   **Photo.**   **Perf. 12½**
C24   AP11   100fr sl, red brn & blk   2.25   1.25
   a.   Souv. sheet of 4   7.50   6.00

Touracos — AP12

200fr, Abyssinian ground hornbills, vert. 300fr, Egyptian vultures, vert. 500fr, Goliath herons.

1965, Feb. 15   **Engr.**   **Perf. 13**
C25   AP12   100fr grn, dk bl & red   2.25   .90
C26   AP12   200fr blk, red & brt bl   7.00   1.40
C27   AP12   300fr blk, sl grn & yel   10.50   2.50
C28   AP12   500fr sl grn, dk brn & claret   16.00   4.00
    Nos. C25-C28 (4)   35.75   8.80

UN Headquarters, New York, and ICY Emblem — AP13

1965, Mar. 15   **Unwmk.**   **Perf. 13**
C29   AP13   55fr bis, dk bl & vio brn   1.10   .40

International Cooperation Year.

Pope John XXIII — AP14

Perf. 12½x13
1965, Sept. 14   **Photo.**   **Unwmk.**
C30   AP14   100fr multi   2.10   1.00

Winston Churchill — AP15

1965, Oct. 11   **Engr.**   **Perf. 13**
C31   AP15   100fr brn & indigo   2.10   1.00

Dr. Albert Schweitzer and Sick Child — AP16

1965, Dec. 20   **Photo.**   **Perf. 12½**
C32   AP16   100fr multi   2.25   1.00
   a.   Souv. sheet of 4   9.00   9.00

Major Edward H. White and Gemini 4 — AP17

No. C34, Lt. Col. Alexei A. Leonov. 300fr, Gordon Cooper, Charles Conrad, Alexei Leonov & Pavel Belyayev, Parthenon, Athens, & vase, vert.

1966, Jan. 10
C33   AP17   100fr vio, yel, lt bl & blk   1.50   1.00
C34   AP17   100fr bl, red, yel & blk   1.50   1.00
C35   AP17   300fr multi   4.50   2.50
    Nos. C33-C35 (3)   7.50   4.50

Achievements in space research and 16th Intl. Astronautical Congress, Athens, Sept. 12-18, 1965.

Papal Arms and UN Emblem — AP18

1966, July 11   **Engr.**   **Perf. 13**
C36   AP18   200fr brt bl, grnsh bl & grn   3.00   1.50

Visit of Pope Paul VI to the UN, NYC, Oct. 4, 1965.

People and UNESCO Emblem — AP19

1966, Sept. 5   **Engr.**   **Perf. 13**
C37   AP19   100fr dk car rose, sl grn & ultra   2.10   1.25

20th anniv. of UNESCO.

Soccer Players, Ball, Globe, and Jules Rimet Cup — AP20

1966, Oct. 31   **Photo.**   **Perf. 13**
C38   AP20   100fr multi   2.25   1.25

8th International Soccer Championship Games, Wembley, England, July 11-30.

Crab and Mt. Fuji — AP21

1966, Nov. 30   **Photo.**   **Perf. 13**
C39   AP21   100fr multi   1.75   .75

9th Intl. Anticancer Cong., Tokyo, Oct. 23-29.

UNICEF Emblem and Children — AP22

MALI — Republic of Mali

1966, Dec. 10   Engr.
C40 AP22 45fr dp bl, bis brn & red lil   .90   .40
20th anniv. of UNICEF.

Land Cruisers in Hoggar Mountain Pass — AP23

1967, Mar. 20   Engr.   Perf. 13
C41 AP23 200fr multi   5.25   2.25
"Black Cruise 1924," which crossed Africa from Beni-Abbes, Algeria to the Indian Ocean and on to Tananarive, Madagascar, Oct. 28, 1924-June 26, 1925.

Diamant Rocket and Francesco de Lana's 1650 Flying Boat — AP24

Designs: 100fr, A-1 satellite and rocket launching adapted from Jules Verne. 200fr, D-1 satellite and bird-borne flying machine from 'The Man in the Moone'.

1967, Apr. 17   Engr.   Perf. 13
C42 AP24 50fr brt bl, pur & grn   .75   .25
C43 AP24 100fr dk Prus bl, dk car & lil   1.50   .50
C44 AP24 200fr sl bl, ol & pur   3.00   1.00
    Nos. C42-C44 (3)   5.25   1.75
Honoring French achievements in space.

Amelia Earhart and Map of Mali AP25

1967, May 29   Photo.   Perf. 13
C45 AP25 500fr bl & multi   8.00   3.00
Amelia Earhart's stop at Gao, West Africa, 30th anniv.

Paul as Harlequin, by Picasso — AP26

Picasso Paintings: 50fr, Bird Cage. 250fr, The Flutes of Pan.

1967, June 16   Perf. 12½
C46 AP26 50fr multi   1.00   .40
C47 AP26 100fr multi   2.10   .75
C48 AP26 250fr multi   4.50   1.60
    Nos. C46-C48 (3)   7.60   2.75
See Nos. C56, C58, C82.

Jamboree Emblem, Scout Knots and Badges — AP27

Design: 100fr, Scout with portable radio transmitter, tents and Jamboree badge.

1967, July 10   Engr.   Perf. 13
C49 AP27 70fr dk car, emer & bl grn   .90   .25
C50 AP27 100fr dk car lake, sl grn & blk   1.25   .30
   a. Strip of 2, #C49-C50 + label   3.00   1.75
12th Boy Scout World Jamboree, Farragut State Park, Idaho, Aug. 1-9.

Head of Horse, by Toulouse-Lautrec — AP28

300fr, Cob-drawn gig, by Toulouse-Lautrec.

Perf. 12x12½, 12½x12
1967, Dec. 11   Photo.
C51 AP28 100fr multi   2.50   1.00
C52 AP28 300fr multi, vert.   6.00   2.00
See Nos. C66-C67.

Grenoble — AP29

Design: 150fr, Bobsled course on Huez Alp.

1968, Jan. 8   Engr.   Perf. 13
C53 AP29 50fr bl, yel brn & grn   .75   .25
C54 AP29 150fr brn, vio bl & stl bl   1.90   .75
10th Winter Olympic Games, Grenoble, France, Feb. 6-18.

Painting Type of 1967 and

Roses and Anemones, by Van Gogh — AP30

Paintings: 150fr, Peonies in Vase, by Edouard Manet. 300fr, Bouquet, by Delarcroix. 500fr, Daisies in Vase, by Jean François Millet, horiz.

Perf. 13, 12½x12, 12x12½
1968, June 24   Photo.
C55 AP30 50fr multi   .75   .50
C56 AP26 150fr grn & multi   1.90   .65
C57 AP30 300fr grn & multi   3.75   1.40
C58 AP26 500fr car & multi   5.50   2.00
    Nos. C55-C58 (4)   11.90   4.55

Martin Luther King, Jr. — AP31

1968, July 22   Perf. 12½
C59 AP31 100fr rose lil, sal pink & blk   1.20   .40

Bicycle Type of Regular Issue
Designs: 50fr, Bicyclette, 1918. 100fr, Mercedes Benz, 1927, horiz.

1968, Aug. 12   Engr.   Perf. 13
C60 A40 50fr gray, dk grn & brick red   1.10   .30
C61 A40 100fr lemon, indigo & car   2.50   .70

Long Jumper and Satellite — AP32

100fr, Soccer goalkeeper and satellite.

1968, Nov. 25   Photo.   Perf. 12½
C62 AP32 100fr multi, horiz.   1.00   .60
C63 AP32 150fr multi   2.00   .80
19th Olympic Games, Mexico City, 10/12-27.

PHILEXAFRIQUE Issue

Editorial Department, by François Marius Granet — AP33

1968, Dec. 23   Photo.   Perf. 12½x12
C64 AP33 200fr multi   3.00   1.75
Issued to publicize PHILEXAFRIQUE Philatelic Exhibition in Abidjan, Feb. 14-23. Printed with alternating light green label.
See Nos. C85-C87, C110-C112, C205-C207, C216-C217.

2nd PHILEXAFRIQUE Issue
Common Design Type
100fr, French Sudan #64, sculpture.

1969, Feb. 14   Engr.   Perf. 13
C65 CD128 100fr pur & multi   1.75   1.00

Painting Type of 1967
Paintings: 150fr, Napoleon as First Consul, by Antoine Jean Gros, vert. 250fr, Bivouac at Austerlitz, by Louis François Lejeune.

Perf. 12½x12, 12x12½
1969, Feb. 25   Photo.
C66 AP28 150fr multi   3.00   1.25
C67 AP28 250fr multi   4.50   1.75
Napoleon Bonaparte (1769-1821).

Montgolfier's Balloon — AP34

Designs: 150fr, Ferber 5, experimental biplane. 300fr, Concorde.

1969, Mar. 10   Photo.   Perf. 13
C68 AP34 50fr multi   .60   .30
C69 AP34 150fr multi   1.90   .60
C70 AP34 300fr multi   3.75   1.40
   a. Strip of 3, #C68-C70   7.50   4.50
1st flight of the prototype Concorde plane at Toulouse, France, Mar. 1, 1969.
For overprints see Nos. C78-C80.

Auto Type of Regular Issue
55fr, Renault, 1898, Renault 16, 1969. 90fr, Peugeot, 1893, Peugeot 404, 1969.

1969, May 30   Engr.   Perf. 13
C71 A43 55fr rose car, blk & brt pink   1.60   .35
C72 A43 90fr blk, dp car & indigo   2.25   .60

Ronald Clarke, Australia, 10,000-meter Run, 1965 — AP35

World Records: 90fr, Yanis Lusis, USSR, Javelin, 1968. 120fr, Yoshinobu Miyake, Japan, weight lifting, 1967. 140fr, Randy Matson, US, shot put, 1968. 150fr, Kipchoge Keino, Kenya, 3,000-meter run, 1965.

1969, June 23   Engr.   Perf. 13
C73 AP35 60fr bl & ol brn   .35   .25
C74 AP35 90fr car rose & red brn   .55   .30
C75 AP35 120fr emer & gray ol   .80   .45
C76 AP35 140fr gray & brn   .85   .50
C77 AP35 150fr red org & blk   1.00   .60
    Nos. C73-C77 (5)   3.55   2.10
Issued to honor sports world records.

Nos. C68-C70 Overprinted in Red
Overprint includes Lunar Landing Module and "L'HOMME SUR LA LUNE / JUILLET 1969 / APOLLO 11".

1969, July 25   Photo.   Perf. 13
C78 AP34 50fr multi   .90   .60
C79 AP34 150fr multi   2.25   1.25
C80 AP34 300fr multi   3.50   2.00
   a. Strip of 3, #C78-C80   9.00   4.50
Man's 1st landing on moon, July 20, 1969. US astronauts Neil A. Armstrong and Col. Edwin E. Aldrin, Jr., with Lieut. Col. Michael Collins piloting Apollo 11.

Apollo 8, Moon and Earth — AP35a

Embossed on Gold Foil
1969, July 24   Die-cut perf 10½
C81 AP35a 2000fr gold   20.00   20.00
US Apollo 8 mission, the 1st men in orbit around the moon, Dec. 21-27, 1968.

Painting Type of 1967
500fr, Mona Lisa, by Leonardo da Vinci.

1969, Oct. 20   Photo.   Perf. 12½
C82 AP26 500fr multi   5.50   3.25

Mahatma Gandhi — AP36

1969, Nov. 24   Engr.   Perf. 13
C83 AP36 150fr brt bl, ol brn & red brn   3.00   .70

Map of West Africa, Post Horns and Lightning Bolts — AP37

1970, Feb. 23   Photo.   Perf. 12½
C84 AP37 100fr multi   .85   .40
11th anniversary of the West African Postal Union (CAPTEAO).

Painting Type of 1968
Paintings: 100fr, Madonna and Child, from Rogier van der Weyden school. 150fr, Nativity, by the master of Flemalle. 250fr, Madonna and Child with St. John, from the Dutch School.

1970, Mar. 2
C85 AP33 100fr multi   .85   .40
C86 AP33 150fr multi   1.25   .80
C87 AP33 250fr multi   2.75   1.40
    Nos. C85-C87 (3)   4.85   2.60

MALI — Republic of Mali

Roosevelt — AP38

1970, Mar. 30 Photo. *Perf. 12½*
C88 AP38 500fr red, lt ultra & blk 3.75 2.50
Pres. Franklin D. Roosevelt (1882-1945).

Lenin — AP39

1970, Apr. 22
C89 AP39 300fr pink, grn & blk 3.00 1.25

Jules Verne and Firing of Moon Rockets AP40

150fr, Jules Verne, rockets, landing modules & moon. 300fr, Jules Verne & splashdown.

1970, May 4
C90 AP40 50fr multi .80 .30
C91 AP40 150fr multi 2.00 .80
C92 AP40 300fr multi 3.50 1.60
  Nos. C90-C92 (3) 6.30 2.70

Nos. C90-C92 Overprinted in Red or Blue
Overprint reads "APOLLO XIII / EPOPEE SPATIALE / 11-17 AVRIL 1970".

1970, June Photo. *Perf. 12½*
C93 AP40 50fr multi (Bl) .50 .25
C94 AP40 150fr multi (R) 1.50 .80
C95 AP40 300fr multi (Bl) 3.00 1.60
  Nos. C93-C95 (3) 5.00 2.65
Flight and safe return of Apollo 13, Apr. 11-13, 1970.

Intelsat III AP41

Telecommunications Through Space: 200fr, Molniya I satellite. 300fr, Radar. 500fr, "Project Symphony" (various satellites).

1970, July 13 Engr. *Perf. 13*
C96 AP41 100fr gray, brt bl & org .70 .40
C97 AP41 200fr bl, gray & red lil 1.40 .55
C98 AP41 300fr org, dk brn & gray 2.25 1.60
C99 AP41 500fr dk brn, sl & grnsh bl 0.50 2.60
  Nos. C96-C99 (4) 7.85 5.05
For surcharges see Nos. C108-C109.

Auguste and Louis Lumière, Jean Harlow and Marilyn Monroe — AP42

1970, July 27 Photo. *Perf. 12½x12*
C100 AP42 250fr multi 4.50 2.00
Issued to honor Auguste Lumière (1862-1954), and his brother Louis Jean Lumière (1864-1948), inventors of the Lumière process

of color photography and of a motion picture camera.

Soccer AP43

1970, Sept. 7 Engr. *Perf. 13*
C101 AP43 80fr bl, dp car & brn ol .75 .30
C102 AP43 200fr dp car, bl grn & ol brn 2.00 .80
9th World Soccer Championships for the Jules Rimet Cup, Mexico City, May 30-June 21, 1970.

Rotary Emblem, Map of Mali and Ceremonial Antelope Heads — AP44

1970, Sept. 21 Photo. *Perf. 12½*
C103 AP44 200fr multi 2.25 1.25
Issued to honor Rotary International.

Men Holding UN Emblem, and Doves — AP45

1970, Oct. 5 Engr. *Perf. 13*
C104 AP45 100fr dk pur, red brn & dk bl .90 .50
25th anniversary of the United Nations.

Koran Page, Baghdad, 11th Century — AP46

Moslem Art: 200fr, Tree, and lion killing deer, mosaic, Jordan, c. 730, horiz. 250fr, Scribe, miniature, Baghdad, 1287.

1970, Oct. 26 Photo. *Perf. 12½x12*
C105 AP46 50fr multi .75 .30
C106 AP46 200fr multi 1.50 .65
C107 AP46 250fr multi 2.25 .95
  Nos. C105-C107 (3) 4.50 1.90

Nos. C97-C98 Surcharged and Overprinted
Overprint reads "LUNA 16 / PREMIERS PRELEVEMENTS AUTOMATIQUES / SUR LA LUNE / SEPTEMBRE 1970".

1970, Nov. 9 Engr. *Perf. 13*
C108 AP41 150fr on 200fr multi 1.00 .65
C109 AP41 250fr on 300fr multi 1.75 .95
Unmanned moon probe of the Russian space ship Luna 16, Sept. 12-24.

Painting Type of 1968
100fr, Nativity, Antwerp School, c. 1530. 250fr, Adoration of the Shepherds, by Hans Memling. 300fr, Adoration of the Kings, Flemish School, 17th cent.

1970, Dec. 1 Photo. *Perf. 12½x12*
C110 AP33 100fr brown & multi .80 .40
C111 AP33 250fr brown & multi 1.75 .95
C112 AP33 300fr brown & multi 2.50 1.25
  Nos. C110-C112 (3) 5.05 2.60
Christmas 1970.

Gamal Abdel Nasser — AP47
Embossed on Gold Foil

1970, Nov. 25 *Perf. 12½*
C113 AP47 1000fr gold 9.00 9.00
In memory of Gamal Abdel Nasser (1918-1970), President of Egypt.

Charles de Gaulle — AP48
Embossed on Gold Foil

1971, Feb. 8 *Die-cut Perf. 10*
C114 AP48 2000fr gold, red & dp ultra 60.00 60.00
In memory of Gen. Charles de Gaulle (1890-1970), President of France.

Alfred Nobel — AP49

1971, Feb. 22 Engr. *Perf. 13*
C115 AP49 300fr multi 3.00 1.00
Alfred Nobel (1833-1896), inventor of dynamite, sponsor of Nobel Prize.

Tennis, Davis Cup — AP50

Designs: 150fr, Derby at Epsom, horiz. 200fr, Racing yacht, America's Cup.

1971, Mar. 8
C116 AP50 100fr bl, lil & slate 1.40 .60
C117 AP50 150fr brn, brt grn & ol 2.00 .90
C118 AP50 200fr brt bl, ol & brn 2.75 1.25
  Nos. C116-C118 (3) 6.15 2.75

The Arabian Nights AP51

Designs: 180fr, Ali Baba and the 40 Thieves. 200fr, Aladdin's Lamp.

1971, Apr. 5 Photo. *Perf. 13*
C119 AP51 120fr gold & multi 1.50 .60
C120 AP51 180fr gold & multi 2.00 .90
C121 AP51 200fr gold & multi 2.50 1.00
  Nos. C119-C121 (3) 6.00 2.50

Olympic Rings and Sports AP52

1971, June 28 Photo. *Perf. 12½*
C122 AP52 80fr ultra, yel grn & brt mag .75 .30
Pre-Olympic Year.

Mariner 4 — AP53

Design: 300fr, Venera 5 in space.

1971, Sept. 13 Engr. *Perf. 13*
C123 AP53 200fr multi 1.40 .70
C124 AP53 300fr multi 2.10 .95
Space explorations of US Mariner 4 (200fr); and USSR Venera 5 (300fr).

Santa Maria, 1492 AP54

Famous Ships: 150fr, Mayflower, 1620. 200fr, Potemkin, 1905. 250fr, Normandie, 1935.

1971, Sept. 27
C125 AP54 100fr brn, bluish grn & pur 1.00 .40
C126 AP54 150fr sl grn, brn & pur 1.60 .70
C127 AP54 200fr car, bl & dk ol 2.10 .80
C128 AP54 250fr blk, bl & red 2.75 1.00
  Nos. C125-C128 (4) 7.45 2.90

Symbols of Justice and Maps AP55

1971, Oct. 18
C129 AP55 160fr mar, ocher & dk brn 1.20 .50
25th anniversary of the International Court of Justice in The Hague, Netherlands.

Statue of Zeus, by Phidias — AP56

The Seven Wonders of the Ancient World: 80fr, Cheops Pyramid and Sphinx. 100fr, Temple of Artemis, Ephesus, horiz. 130fr, Lighthouse at Alexandria. 150fr, Hanging Gardens of Babylon, horiz. 270fr, Mausoleum of Halicarnassus. 280fr, Colossus of Rhodes.

1971, Dec. 13
C130 AP56 70fr ind, dk red & pink .60 .25
C131 AP56 80fr brn, bl & blk .75 .25
C132 AP56 100fr org, ind & pur .90 .30
C133 AP56 130fr rose lil, bl & grnsh bl 1.10 .40
C134 AP56 150fr brn, brt grn & bl 1.25 .50
C135 AP56 270fr sl, brn & plum 2.10 .70
C136 AP56 280fr sl lil & ol 2.25 .80
  Nos. C130-C136 (7) 8.95 3.20

MALI — Republic of Mali

Nat "King" Cole — AP57

Famous American Black Musicians: 150fr, Erroll Garner. 270fr, Louis Armstrong.

1971, Dec. 6   Photo.   Perf. 13x12½
C137 AP57 130fr blk, brn & yel   2.25   .40
C138 AP57 150fr bl & yel   2.60   .50
C139 AP57 270fr blk, rose car & yel   4.25   .70
      Nos. C137-C139 (3)   9.10 1.60

Slalom and Japanese Child — AP58

200fr, Ice hockey & character from Noh play.

1972, Jan. 10   Engr.   Perf. 13
C140 AP58 150fr multicolored   1.10   .50
C141 AP58 200fr multicolored   1.50   .70
   a. Souv. sheet of 2, #C140-C141   3.00 3.00

11th Winter Olympic Games, Sapporo, Japan, Feb. 3-13.

Santa Maria della Salute, by Ippolito Caffi AP59

Paintings of Venice, by Ippolito Caffi: 270fr, Rialto Bridge. 280fr, St. Mark's Square, vert.

1972, Feb. 21   Photo.   Perf. 13
C142 AP59 130fr gold & multi   1.00   .45
C143 AP59 270fr gold & multi   1.50   .70
C144 AP59 280fr gold & multi   1.75   .75
      Nos. C142-C144 (3)   4.25 1.90

UNESCO campaign to save Venice.

Hands of 4 Races Holding Scout Flag — AP60

1972, Mar. 27   Engr.   Perf. 13
C145 AP60 200fr dk red, ocher & ol gray   1.75   .60

World Boy Scout Seminar, Cotonou, Dahomey, March, 1972.

"Your Heart is your Health" AP61

1972, Apr. 7   Engr.   Perf. 13
C146 AP61 150fr brt bl & red   1.50   .50

World Health Day.

Soccer Player and Frauenkirche, Munich — AP62

Designs (Sport and Munich Landmarks): 150fr, Judo and TV Tower, vert. 200fr, Steeplechase and Propylaeum, vert. 300fr, Runner and Church of the Theatines.

1972, Apr. 17
C147 AP62 50fr ocher, dk bl & grn   .40   .25
C148 AP62 150fr dk bl, ocher & grn   1.00   .45
C149 AP62 200fr dk bl & ocher   1.10   .60
C150 AP62 300fr dk bl, grn & ocher   1.75   .75
   a. Min. sheet of 4, #C147-C150   4.50 4.50
      Nos. C147-C150 (4)   4.25 2.05

20th Olympic Games, Munich, 8/26-9/10. For overprints see Nos. C165-C166, C168.

Apollo 15, Lunar Rover, Landing Module AP63

Design: 250fr, Cugnot's steam wagon and Montgolfier's Balloon.

1972, Apr. 27
C151 AP63 150fr multicolored   1.50   .80
C152 AP63 250fr multicolored   3.00 1.50

Development of transportation.

Cinderella AP64

Fairy Tales: 80fr, Puss in Boots. 150fr, Sleeping Beauty.

1972, June 19   Engr.   Perf. 13x12½
C153 AP64 70fr multicolored   1.10   .30
C154 AP64 80fr multicolored   1.25   .35
C155 AP64 150fr multicolored   2.00   .60
      Nos. C153-C155 (3)   4.35 1.25

Charles Perrault (1628-1703), French writer.

Astronauts and Lunar Rover on Moon AP65

1972, July 24   Engr.   Perf. 13
C156 AP65 500fr multicolored   3.00 1.40

US Apollo 16 moon mission, Apr. 15-27.

Book Year Emblem AP66

1972, Aug. 7   Litho.   Perf. 12½
C157 AP66 80fr bl, gold & grn   1.50   .60

International Book Year 1972.

Bamako Rotary Emblem with Crocodiles — AP67

1972, Oct. 9   Engr.   Perf. 13
C158 AP67 170fr dk brn, red & ultra   1.50   .60

10th anniv. of the Bamako Rotary Club.

Hurdler, Olympic Rings, Melbourne Cathedral, Kangaroo AP68

Designs (Olympic Rings and): 70fr, Boxing, Helsinki Railroad Station, arms of Finland, vert. 140fr, Running, Colosseum, Roman wolf. 150fr, Weight lifting, Tokyo stadium, phoenix, vert. 170fr, Swimming, University Library, Mexico City; Aztec sculpture. 210fr, Javelin, Munich Stadium, Arms of Munich. Stamps inscribed with name of gold medal winner of event shown.

1972, Nov. 13   Engr.   Perf. 13
C159 AP68 70fr red, ocher & ind   .40   .25
C160 AP68 90fr red brn, bl & sl   .45   .25
C161 AP68 140fr brn, brt grn & ol gray .75   .30
C162 AP68 150fr dk car, emer & gray ol .85   .35
C163 AP68 170fr red lil, brn & Prus bl 1.00   .40
C164 AP68 210fr ultra, emer & brick red 1.10   .50
      Nos. C159-C164 (6)   4.55 2.05

Retrospective of Olympic Games 1952-1972. For overprint see No. C167.

Nos. C148-C150, C164 Overprinted
   a. JUDO / RUSKA / 2 MEDAILLES D'OR
   b. STEEPLE / KEINO / MEDAILLE D'OR
   c. MEDAILLE D'OR / 90m. 48
   d. 100m.-200m. / BORZOV / 2 MEDAILLES D'OR

1972, Nov. 27   Engr.   Perf. 13
C165 AP62 150fr multi (a)   .90   .40
C166 AP62 200fr multi (b)   1.20   .50
C167 AP68 210fr multi (c)   1.40   .55
C168 AP62 300fr multi (d)   1.90   .70
      Nos. C165-C168 (4)   5.40 2.15

Gold medal winners in 20th Olympic Games: Wim Ruska, Netherlands, heavyweight judo (No. C165); Kipchoge Keino, Kenya, 3000m. steeplechase (No. C166); Klaus Wolfermann, Germany, javelin (No. C167); Valery Borzov, USSR, 100m., 200m. race (No. C168).

Emperor Haile Selassie — AP69

1972, Dec. 26   Photo.   Perf. 12½
C169 AP69 70fr grn & multi   .60   .25

80th birthday of Emperor Haile Selassie of Ethiopia.

Plane, Balloon, Route Timbuktu to Bamako AP70

300fr, Balloon, jet & route Timbuktu to Bamako.

1972, Dec. 29   Perf. 13½
C170 AP70 200fr multi   1.10   .50
C171 AP70 300fr bl & multi   1.90   .80

First postal balloon flight in Mali.

Bishop of 14th Century European Chess Set — AP71

Design: 200fr, Knight (elephant), from 18th century Indian set.

1973, Feb. 19   Engr.   Perf. 13
C172 AP71 100fr dk car, bl & ind   1.50   .60
C173 AP71 200fr blk, red & brn   3.00 1.25

World Chess Championship, Reykjavik, Iceland, July-Sept., 1972.

Postal Union Emblem, Letter and Dove — AP72

1973, Mar. 9   Photo.   Perf. 11½x11
C174 AP72 70fr bl, blk & org   .60   .25

10th anniv. (in 1971) of African Postal Union. This stamp was to be issued Dec. 8, 1971. It was offered by the agency on Mar. 9, 1973. Copies were sold in Mali as early as July or August, 1972.

No. C20, Collector's Hand and Philatelic Background — AP73

1973, Mar. 12   Engr.   Perf. 13
C175 AP73 70fr multi   1.50   .50

Stamp Day, 1973.

Astronauts and Lunar Rover on Moon — AP74

1973, Mar. 26
C176 AP74 250fr bl, indigo & bis   2.25 1.00

Souvenir Sheet
C177 AP74 350fr choc, vio bl & ultra   2.50 1.60

Apollo 17 US moon mission, 12/7-19/72.

Nicolaus Copernicus AP75

1973, Apr. 9   Engr.   Perf. 13
C178 AP75 300fr brt bl & mag   2.75 1.25

500th anniversary of the birth of Nicolaus Copernicus (1473-1543), Polish astronomer.

Dr. Armauer G. Hansen and Leprosy Bacillus AP76

1973, May 7   Engr.   Perf. 13
C179 AP76 200fr blk, yel grn & red   1.90   .85

Centenary of the discovery of the Hansen bacillus, the cause of leprosy.

Bentley and Alfa Romeo, 1930 AP77

Designs: 100fr, Jaguar and Talbot, 1953. 200fr, Matra and Porsche, 1972.

MALI — Republic of Mali

1973, May 21   Engr.   Perf. 13
C180 AP77 50fr bl, org & grn .45 .25
C181 AP77 100fr grn, ultra & car .80 .30
C182 AP77 200fr ind, grn & car 2.00 .60
Nos. C180-C182 (3) 3.25 1.15

50th anniversary of the 24-hour automobile race at Le Mans, France.

Camp Fire, Fleur-de-Lis — AP78

Designs (Fleur-de-Lis and): 70fr, Scouts saluting flag, vert. 80fr, Scouts with flags. 130fr, Lord Baden-Powell, vert. 270fr, Round dance and map of Africa.

1973, June 4
C183 AP78 50fr dk red, ultra & choc .35 .25
C184 AP78 70fr sl grn, dk brn & red .50 .25
C185 AP78 80fr mag, sl grn & ol .55 .25
C186 AP78 130fr brn, ultra & sl grn .90 .40
C187 AP78 270fr mag, gray & vio bl 1.75 .60
Nos. C183-C187 (5) 4.05 1.75

Mali Boy and Girl Scouts and International Scouts Congress.
For surcharges see Nos. C222-C223.

Swimming, US and "Africa" Flags — AP79

80fr, Discus, javelin, vert. 330fr, Runners.

1973, July 30   Engr.   Perf. 13
C188 AP79 70fr red, sl grn & bl .45 .25
C189 AP79 80fr vio bl, dk ol & red .55 .25
C190 AP79 330fr red & vio bl 2.10 .80
Nos. C188-C190 (3) 3.10 1.30

First African-United States sports meet.

Head and City Hall, Brussels — AP80

1973, Sept. 17   Engr.   Perf. 13
C191 AP80 70fr brt ultra, ol & vio .60 .25

Africa Weeks, Brussels, Sept. 15-30, 1973.

Perseus, by Benvenuto Cellini — AP81

Famous Sculptures: 150fr, Pietà, by Michelangelo. 250fr, Victory of Samothrace, Greek 1st century B.C.

1973, Sept. 24
C192 AP81 100fr dk car & sl grn .90 .30
C193 AP81 150fr dk car & dp cl 1.40 .50
C194 AP81 250fr dk car & dk ol 2.25 .80
Nos. C192-C194 (3) 4.55 1.60

Stephenson's Rocket and Buddicom Engine — AP82

Locomotives: 150fr, Union Pacific, 1890, and Santa Fe, 1940. 200fr, Mistral and Tokaido, 1970.

1973, Oct. 8   Engr.   Perf. 13
C195 AP82 100fr brn, bl & blk 1.00 .40
C196 AP82 150fr red, brt ultra & dk car 1.40 .70
C197 AP82 200fr ocher, bl & ind 2.10 .90
Nos. C195-C197 (3) 4.50 2.00

Apollo XI on Moon — AP83

75fr, Landing capsule, Apollo XIII. 100fr, Astronauts & equipment on moon, Apollo XIV. 280fr, Rover, landing module & astronauts on moon, Apollo XV. 300fr, Lift-off from moon, Apollo XVII.

1973, Oct. 25
C198 AP83 50fr vio, org & sl grn .30 .25
C199 AP83 75fr slate, red & bl .45 .25
C200 AP83 100fr slate, bl & ol brn .60 .30
C201 AP83 280fr vio bl, red & sl grn 1.50 .55
C202 AP83 300fr slate, red & sl grn 1.60 .80
Nos. C198-C202 (5) 4.45 2.15

Apollo US moon missions.
For surcharges see Nos. C224-C225.

Pablo Picasso — AP84

1973, Nov. 7   Litho.   Perf. 12½
C203 AP84 500fr multi 4.25 2.00

Pablo Picasso (1881-1973), painter.

John F. Kennedy — AP85

1973, Nov. 12
C204 AP85 500fr gold, brt rose lil & blk 3.50 1.75

Painting Type of 1968

100fr, Annunciation, by Vittore Carpaccio, horiz. 200fr, Virgin of St. Simon, by Federico Barocci. 250fr, Flight into Egypt, by Andrea Solario.

Perf. 13x12½, 12½x12, 12½x13
1973, Nov. 30   Litho.
C205 AP33 100fr blk & multi .75 .25
C206 AP33 200fr blk & multi 1.25 .60
C207 AP33 250fr blk & multi 1.75 .80
Nos. C205-C207 (3) 3.75 1.65

Christmas 1973.

Soccer Player and Ball — AP86

250fr, Goalkeeper & ball. 500fr, Frauenkirche, Munich, Arms of Munich & soccer ball, horiz.

1973, Dec. 3   Engr.   Perf. 13
C208 AP86 150fr emer, ol brn & red 1.10 .50
C209 AP86 250fr emer, vio bl & ol brn 1.90 .70

Souvenir Sheet
C210 AP86 500fr bl & multi 4.00 4.00

World Soccer Cup, Munich.

Musicians, Mosaic from Pompeii — AP87

Designs (Mosaics from Pompeii): 250fr, Alexander the Great in battle, vert. 350fr, Bacchants, vert.

1974, Jan. 21   Engr.   Perf. 13
C211 AP87 150fr sl bl, ol & rose 1.10 .30
C212 AP87 250fr mag, ol & ocher 1.50 .50
C213 AP87 350fr ol, dp brn & ocher 1.90 .70
Nos. C211-C213 (3) 4.50 1.50

Winston Churchill — AP88

1974, Mar. 18   Engr.   Perf. 13
C214 AP88 500fr black 3.00 1.25

Chess Game — AP89

1974, Mar. 25   Engr.   Perf. 13
C215 AP89 250fr multi 4.50 1.75

21st Chess Olympic Games, Nice 1974.

Painting Type of 1968
Paintings: 400fr, Crucifixion, Alsatian School, c. 1380, vert. 500fr, Burial of Christ, by Titian.

Perf. 12½x13, 13x12½
1974, Apr. 12   Photo.
C216 AP33 400fr multi 2.10 .90
C217 AP33 500fr multi 2.90 1.25

Easter 1974.

Lenin — AP90

1974, Apr. 22   Engr.   Perf. 13
C218 AP90 150fr vio bl & lake 2.00 .60

50th anniversary of the death of Lenin.

Women's Steeplechase — AP91

1974, May 20   Engr.   Perf. 13
C219 AP91 130fr bl, lil & brn 1.60 .60

World Horsewomen's Championship, La Baule, France, June 30-July 7.

Skylab Docking in Space — AP92

250fr, Skylab over globe with Africa.

1974, July 1   Engr.   Perf. 13
C220 AP92 200fr bl, sl & org 1.10 .50
C221 AP92 250fr lil, sl & org 1.90 .70

Skylab's flight over Africa, 1974.

Nos. C184-C185 Surcharged in Violet Blue

(a)   (b)

1974, July 8   Engr.   Perf. 13
C222 AP78 130fr on 70fr (a) 1.20 .50
C223 AP78 170fr on 80fr (b) 1.50 .60

11th Pan-Arab Jamboree and Pan-Arab Congress, Batrun, Lebanon, Aug. 1974.

Nos. C200-C201 Surcharged in Red

(c)

(d)

1974, July 15
C224 AP83 130fr on 100fr (c) .75 .40
C225 AP83 300fr on 280fr (d) 2.25 1.25

First manned moon landing, July 20, 1969, and first step on moon, July 21, 1969.

1906 and 1939 Locomotives AP93

Locomotives: 120fr, Baldwin, 1870, and Pacific, 1920. 210fr, Al., 1925, and Buddicom, 1847. 330fr, Hudson, 1938, and La Gironde, 1839.

1974, Oct. 7   Engr.   Perf. 13
C226 AP93 90fr dk car & multi .90 .40
C227 AP93 120fr ocher & multi 1.30 .50
C228 AP93 210fr org & multi 2.00 .70
C229 AP93 330fr grn & multi 3.00 1.10
Nos. C226-C229 (4) 7.20 2.70

MALI — Republic of Mali

Skier, Winter Sports and Olympic Rings — AP94

1974, Oct. 7
C230 AP94 300fr multi ... 2.10 .80

Holy Family, by Hans Memling — AP95

310fr, Virgin & Child, Bourgogne School. 400fr, Adoration of the Kings, by Martin Schongauer.

1974, Nov. 4   Photo.   Perf. 12½
C231 AP95 290fr multi ... 1.60 .60
C232 AP95 310fr multi ... 1.90 .70
C233 AP95 400fr multi ... 2.50 1.10
Nos. C231-C233 (3) ... 6.00 2.40

Christmas 1974.
See Nos. C238-C240, C267-C269.

Raoul Follereau — AP96

1974, Nov. 18   Engr.   Perf. 13
C234 AP96 200fr brt bl ... 2.25 .85

Raoul Follereau (1903-1977), apostle to the lepers and educator of the blind. See No. C468.

Europafrica Issue

Train, Jet, Cogwheel, Grain, Maps of Africa and Europe AP97

1974, Dec. 27   Engr.   Perf. 13
C235 AP97 100fr brn, grn & indigo ... .75 .30
C236 AP97 110fr ocher, vio bl & pur ... 1.00 .40

Painting Type of 1974

Designs: 200fr, Christ at Emmaus, by Phillipe de Champaigne, horiz. 300fr, Christ at Emmaus, by Paolo Veronese, horiz. 500fr, Christ in Majesty, Limoges, 13th century.

     Perf. 13x12½, 12½x13
1975, Mar. 24   Litho.
C238 AP95 200fr multi ... 1.60 .50
C239 AP95 300fr multi ... 1.90 .70
C240 AP95 500fr multi ... 2.50 1.25
Nos. C238-C240 (3) ... 6.00 2.45

Easter 1975.

"Voyage to the Center of the Earth" AP99

Jules Verne's Stories: 170fr, "From Earth to Moon" and Verne's portrait. 190fr, "20,000 Leagues under the Sea." 220fr, "A Floating City."

1975, Apr. 7   Engr.   Perf. 13
C241 AP99 100fr multi ... .60 .25
C242 AP99 170fr multi ... 1.00 .45
C243 AP99 190fr multi ... 1.10 .50
C244 AP99 220fr multi ... 1.40 .55
Nos. C241-C244 (4) ... 4.10 1.75

Dawn, by Michelangelo AP100

Design: 500fr, Moses, by Michelangelo.

1975, Apr. 28   Photo.   Perf. 13
C245 AP100 400fr multi ... 2.25 .90
C246 AP100 500fr multi ... 3.00 1.25

Michelangelo Buonarroti (1475-1564), Italian sculptor, painter and architect.

Astronaut on Moon — AP101

Designs: 300fr, Constellations Virgo and Capricorn. 370fr, Statue of Liberty, Kremlin, Soyuz and Apollo spacecraft.

1975, May 19   Engr.   Perf. 13
C247 AP101 290fr multi ... 1.10 .60
C248 AP101 300fr multi ... 1.10 .60
C249 AP101 370fr multi ... 1.90 .90
Nos. C247-C249 (3) ... 4.10 2.10

Soviet-American space cooperation.
For overprints see Nos. C264-C266.

Boy Scout, Globe, Nordjamb 75 Emblem — AP103

150fr, Boy Scout giving Scout sign. 290fr, Scouts around campfire.

1975, June 23   Engr.   Perf. 13
C251 AP103 100fr clar, brn & bl ... .60 .25
C252 AP103 150fr red, brn & grn ... .90 .30
C253 AP103 290fr bl, grn & clar ... 1.60 .65
Nos. C251-C253 (3) ... 3.10 1.20

Nordjamb 75, 14th Boy Scout Jamboree, Lillehammer, Norway, July 29-Aug. 7.

Battle Scene and Marquis de Lafayette AP104

300fr, Battle scene & George Washington. 370fr, Battle of Chesapeake Bay & Count de Grasse.

1975, July 7   Engr.   Perf. 13
C254 AP104 290fr lt bl & indigo ... 1.50 .60
C255 AP104 300fr lt bl & indigo ... 1.50 .60
C256 AP104 370fr lt bl & indigo ... 2.25 .90
    a. Strip of 3, #C254-C256 ... 6.00 3.50

Bicentenary of the American Revolution.
No. C256a has continuous design.

Schweitzer, Bach and Score — AP105

Designs: No. C257, Albert Einstein (1879-1955), theoretical physicist. No. No. C258, André-Marie Ampère (1775-1836), French physicist. 100fr, Clément Ader (1841-1925), French aviation pioneer. No. C260, Dr. Albert Schweitzer (1875-1965), Medical missionary and musician. No. C261, Sir Alexander Fleming (1881-1955), British bacteriologist, discoverer of penicillin.

1975   Engr.   Perf. 13
C257 AP105 90fr multi ... .90 .40
C258 AP105 90fr pur, org & bister ... .90 .40
C259 AP105 100fr bl, red & lilac ... .90 .40
C260 AP105 150fr grn, bl & dk grn ... 1.10 .60
C261 AP105 150fr lil, bl & brick red ... 1.10 .45
Nos. C257-C261 (5) ... 4.90 2.25

Issued: No. C257, 5/26; No. C258, 9/23; 100fr, 12/8; No. C260, 1/14; No. C261, 7/21.
For surcharge see No. C358.

Olympic Rings and Globe AP106

400fr, Montreal Olympic Games' emblem.

1975, Oct.
C262 AP106 350fr pur & bl ... 1.90 .75
C263 AP106 400fr blue ... 2.25 .85

Pre-Olympic Year 1975.

Nos. C247-C249 Overprinted:
"ARRIMAGE / 17 Juil. 1975"

1975, Oct. 20   Engr.   Perf. 13
C264 AP101 290fr multi ... 1.60 .60
C265 AP101 300fr multi ... 1.75 .65
C266 AP101 370fr multi ... 2.50 1.00
Nos. C264-C266 (3) ... 5.85 2.25

Apollo-Soyuz link-up in space, July 17, 1975.

Painting Type of 1974

Designs: 290fr, Visitation, by Ghirlandaio. 300fr, Nativity, Fra Filippo Lippi school. 370fr, Adoration of the Kings, by Velazquez.

1975, Nov. 24   Litho.   Perf. 12½x13
C267 AP95 290fr multi ... 1.50 .60
C268 AP95 300fr multi ... 1.75 .70
C269 AP95 370fr multi ... 2.40 1.10
Nos. C267-C269 (3) ... 5.65 2.40

Christmas 1975.

Concorde AP107

1976, Jan. 12   Litho.   Perf. 13
C270 AP107 500fr multi ... 3.75 1.50

Concorde supersonic jet, first commercial flight, Jan. 21, 1976.
For overprint see No. C315.

AP108

1976, Feb. 16   Litho.   Perf. 13
C271 AP108 120fr Figure skating ... .60 .25
C272 AP108 420fr Ski jump ... 2.00 .70
C273 AP108 430fr Slalom ... 2.00 .80
Nos. C271-C273 (3) ... 4.60 1.65

12th Winter Olympic Games, Innsbruck, Austria, Feb. 4-15.

AP109

Eye examination, WHO emblem.

1976, Apr. 5   Litho.   Perf. 12½
C274 AP109 130fr multi ... .75 .25

World Health Day: "Foresight prevents blindness."

Space Ship with Solar Batteries AP110

Design: 300fr, Astronaut working on orbital space station, vert.

1976, May 10   Engr.   Perf. 13
C275 AP110 300fr org, dk & lt bl ... 1.50 .60
C276 AP110 400fr mag, dk bl & org ... 2.25 .90

Futuristic space achievements.

American Eagle, Flag and Liberty Bell AP111

Designs: 400fr, Revolutionary War naval battle and American eagle. 440fr, Indians on horseback and American eagle, vert.

1976, May 24   Litho.   Perf. 12½
C277 AP111 100fr multi ... .60 .25
C278 AP111 400fr multi ... 2.25 .75
C279 AP111 440fr multi ... 2.40 .80
Nos. C277-C279 (3) ... 5.25 1.80

American Bicentennial. Nos. C278-C279 also for Interphil 76, International Philatelic Exhibition, Philadelphia, Pa, May 29-June 6.

Running AP112

Designs (Olympic Rings and): 250fr, Swimming. 300fr, Field ball. 440fr, Soccer.

1976, June 7   Engr.   Perf. 13
C280 AP112 200fr red brn & blk ... .90 .30
C281 AP112 250fr multi ... 1.25 .40
C282 AP112 300fr multi ... 1.75 .50
C283 AP112 440fr multi ... 2.25 .75
Nos. C280-C283 (4) ... 6.15 1.95

21st Olympic Games, Montreal, Canada, July 17-Aug. 1.

Cub Scout and Leader — AP113

Designs: 180fr, Scouts tending sick animal, horiz. 200fr, Night hike.

1976, June 14   Engr.   Perf. 13
C284 AP113 140fr ultra & red brn ... .75 .35
C285 AP113 180fr dk brn & multi ... 1.10 .45
C286 AP113 200fr brn org & vio bl ... 1.20 .50
Nos. C284-C286 (3) ... 3.05 1.30

First African Boy Scout Jamboree, Nigeria.

MALI — Republic of Mali

Mohenjo-Daro, Bull from Wall Relief — AP114

Design: 500fr, Man's head, animals, wall and UNESCO emblem.

1976, Sept. 6	Engr.		Perf. 13
C287	AP114	400fr blk, bl & pur	1.90 .60
C288	AP114	500fr dk red, bl & grn	2.60 1.10

UNESCO campaign to save Mohenjo-Daro excavations.

Europafrica Issue

Freighter, Plane, Map of Europe and Africa — AP115

1976, Sept. 20			
C289	AP115	200fr vio brn & bl	1.50 .70

Nativity, by Taddeo Gaddi — AP116

Paintings: 300fr, Adoration of the Kings, by Hans Memling. 320fr, Nativity, by Carlo Crivelli.

1976, Nov. 8	Litho.		Perf. 13x12½
C290	AP116	280fr multi	1.50 .50
C291	AP116	300fr multi	1.80 .60
C292	AP116	320fr multi	1.75 .75
	Nos. C290-C292 (3)		5.05 1.85

Christmas 1976.

Viking Flying to Mars — AP117

1000fr, Viking landing craft on Mars.

1976, Dec. 8	Engr.		Perf. 13
C293	AP117	500fr red, brn & bl	2.25 1.25
C294	AP117	1000fr multi	3.75 1.75
a.	Miniature sheet of 2		7.50 3.50

Operation Viking, US Mars mission, No. C294a contains 2 stamps similar to Nos. C293-C294 in changed colors.

Pres. Giscard d'Estaing, Village and Bambara Antelope — AP118

1977, Feb. 13	Photo.		Perf. 13
C295	AP118	430fr multi	2.75 .90

Visit of Pres. Valéry Giscard d'Estaing of France, Feb. 13-15.

Elizabeth II and Prince Philip — AP119

Designs: 200fr, Charles de Gaulle, vert. 250fr, Queen Wilhelmina, vert. 300fr, King Baudouin and Queen Fabiola. 480fr, Coronation of Queen Elizabeth II, vert.

1977, Mar. 21	Litho.		Perf. 12
C296	AP119	180fr multi	.90 .45
C297	AP119	200fr multi	1.00 .45
C298	AP119	250fr multi	1.25 .55
C299	AP119	300fr multi	1.50 .65
C300	AP119	480fr multi	2.40 1.00
	Nos. C296-C300 (5)		7.05 3.10

Personalities involved in de-colonization.

Newton, Rocket and Apple — AP120

1977, May 7	Engr.		Perf. 13
C301	AP120	400fr grn, brn & red	2.50 .90

Isaac Newton (1643-1727), natural philosopher and mathematician, 250th death anniversary.

Charles Lindbergh and Spirit of St. Louis — AP121

430fr, Spirit of St. Louis flying over clouds.

1977, Apr. 4	Litho.		Perf. 12
C302	AP121	420fr org & pur	2.25 .80
C303	AP121	430fr multi	2.25 .80

Charles A. Lindbergh's solo transatlantic flight from New York to Paris, 50th anniversary.

Sassenage Castle, Grenoble — AP122

1977, May 21	Litho.		Perf. 12½
C304	AP122	300fr multi	1.50 .60

Intl. French Language Council, 10th anniv.

Zeppelin No. 1, 1900 — AP123

Designs: 130fr, Graf Zeppelin, 1924. 350fr, Hindenburg aflame at Lakehurst, NJ, 1937. 500fr, Ferdinand von Zeppelin and Graf Zeppelin.

1977, May 30	Engr.		Perf. 13
C305	AP123	120fr multi	.60 .25
C306	AP123	130fr multi	.75 .25
C307	AP123	350fr multi	2.00 .65
C308	AP123	500fr multi	2.75 .75
	Nos. C305-C308 (4)		6.10 1.90

History of the Zeppelin.

Martin Luther King, American and Swedish Flags — AP124

Design: 600fr, Henri Dunant, Red Cross, Swiss and Swedish flags.

1977, July 4	Engr.		Perf. 13
C309	AP124	600fr multi	2.00 .70
C310	AP124	700fr multi	2.50 .75

Nobel Peace Prize recipients.

Soccer — AP125

Designs: 200fr, 3 soccer players, vert. 420fr, 3 soccer players.

1977, Oct. 3	Engr.		Perf. 13
C311	AP125	180fr multi	.60 .30
C312	AP125	200fr multi	.75 .35
C313	AP125	420fr multi	1.60 .70
	Nos. C311-C313 (3)		2.95 1.40

World Soccer Cup Elimination Games.

Mao Tse-tung and COMATEX Hall, Bamako — AP126

1977, Nov. 7	Engr.		Perf. 13
C314	AP126	300fr dull red	3.75 .90

Chairman Mao Tse-tung (1893-1976).

No. C270 Overprinted in Violet Blue: "PARIS NEW-YORK 22.11.77"

1977, Nov. 22	Litho.		Perf. 13
C315	AP107	500fr multi	9.00 5.50

Concorde, first commercial transatlantic flight, Paris to New York.

Virgin and Child, by Rubens — AP127

Rubens Paintings: 400fr, Adoration of the Kings. 600fr, Detail from Adoration of the Kings, horiz.

1977, Dec. 5	Perf. 12½x12, 12x12½		
C316	AP127	400fr gold & multi	1.40 .60
C317	AP127	500fr gold & multi	1.75 .80
C318	AP127	600fr gold & multi	2.40 1.00
	Nos. C316-C318 (3)		5.55 2.40

Christmas 1977, and 400th birth anniversary of Peter Paul Rubens (1577-1640).

Battle of the Amazons, by Rubens — AP128

Rubens Paintings: 300fr, Return from the fields. 500fr, Hercules fighting the Nemean Lion, vert.

	Perf. 12x12½, 12½x12		
1978, Jan. 16			Litho.
C319	AP128	200fr multi	.85 .30
C320	AP128	300fr multi	1.25 .50
C321	AP128	500fr multi	2.10 .80
	Nos. C319-C321 (3)		4.20 1.60

Peter Paul Rubens, 400th birth anniversary.

Schubert Composing "Winterreise" — AP129

Design: 300fr, Schubert and score, vert.

1978, Feb. 13			
C322	AP129	300fr multi	1.25 .50
C323	AP129	420fr multi	2.00 .70

Franz Schubert (1797-1828), Austrian composer.

Capt. Cook Receiving Hawaiian Delegation — AP130

Design: 300fr, Cook landing on Hawaii. Designs after sketches by John Weber.

1978, Feb. 27	Engr.		Perf. 13
C324	AP130	200fr multi	1.10 .40
C325	AP130	300fr multi	1.90 .55

Capt. James Cook (1728-1779), bicentenary of his arrival in Hawaii.

Soccer — AP131

250fr, One player. 300fr, Two players, horiz.

1978, Mar. 20			
C326	AP131	150fr multi	1.10 .30
C327	AP131	250fr multi	1.75 .50
a.	"REPUBLIQUE"		3.00 .90
C328	AP131	300fr multi	2.25 .60
a.	Min. sheet of 3, #C326-C328 + label		6.00 4.00
b.	As "a," #C326, C327a, C328		9.00 6.00
	Nos. C326-C328 (3)		5.10 1.40

World Soccer Cup Championships, Argentina, 1978, June 1-25.
Nos. C327 and C328a were issued in July to correct the spelling error.
For overprints see Nos. C338-C340.

Jesus with Crown of Thorns, by Dürer — AP132

430fr, Resurrection, by Albrecht Dürer.

1978, Mar. 28			
C329	AP132	420fr multi	2.50 .60
C330	AP132	430fr multi	2.75 .60

Easter 1978. See Nos. C359-C361.

Citroen, C3-Trefle, 1922 — AP133

Citroen Cars: 130fr, Croisiere Noire, 1924, tractor. 180fr, B14G, 1927. 200fr, "11" Tractor Avant, 1934.

1978, Apr. 24	Engr.		Perf. 13
C331	AP133	120fr multi	1.00 .25
C332	AP133	130fr multi	1.10 .25
C333	AP133	180fr multi	1.40 .40
C334	AP133	200fr multi	1.50 .45
	Nos. C331-C334 (4)		5.00 1.35

Andre Citroen (1878-1935), automobile designer and manufacturer.

UPU Emblem, World Map, Country Names — AP133a

MALI — Republic of Mali

Design: 130fr, UPU emblem, globe and names of member countries.

1978, May 15
C334A AP133a 120fr multi .70 .25
C335 AP133a 130fr red, grn & emer .85 .25

Centenary of Congress of Paris where General Postal Union became the Universal Postal Union.

Europafrica Issue

Zebra, Miniature by Mansur, Jehangir School, 1620 — AP134

Design: 100fr, Ostrich Incubating Eggs, Syrian Manuscript, 14th Century.

1978, July 24   Litho.   Perf. 13x12½
C336 AP134 100fr multi 1.50 .60
C337 AP134 110fr multi 1.50 .60

Nos. C326-C328a Overprinted in Black

(a) (b) (c)

1978, Aug. 7   Engr.   Perf. 13
C338 AP131 (a) 150fr multi .85 .35
C339 AP131 (b) 250fr multi 1.25 .50
C340 AP131 (c) 300fr multi 1.50 .60
 a. Souvenir sheet of 3 5.00 2.50
 Nos. C338-C340 (3) 3.60 1.45

Winners, World Soccer Cup Championship, Argentina. Overprints on No. C340a are green including label overprint: FINALE / ARGENTINA 3 HOLLANDE 1.

Elizabeth II in Coronation Robes — AP135

Design: 500fr, Coronation coach.

1978, Sept. 18   Litho.   Perf. 12½x12
C341 AP135 500fr multi 1.60 .65
C342 AP135 1000fr multi 3.25 1.50

Coronation of Queen Elizabeth II, 25th anniv.

US No. C3a and Douglas DC-3 — AP136

History of Aviation: 100fr, Belgium No. 252 and Stampe SV-4. 120fr, France No. C48 and Ader's plane No. 3. 130fr, Germany No. C2 and Junker Ju-52. 320fr, Japan No. C25 and Mitsubishi A-6M "Zero."

1978, Oct. 16   Engr.   Perf. 13
C343 AP136 80fr multi .35 .25
C344 AP136 100fr multi .45 .25
C345 AP136 120fr multi .55 .25
C346 AP136 130fr multi .60 .25
C347 AP136 320fr multi 1.50 .55
 Nos. C343-C347 (5) 3.45 1.55

Annunciation, by Dürer — AP137

Etchings by Dürer: 430fr, Virgin and Child. 500fr, Adoration of the Kings.

1978, Nov. 6
C348 AP137 420fr blk & rose car 1.40 .50
C349 AP137 430fr ol grn & brn 1.50 .60
C350 AP137 500fr blk & red 2.00 .70
 Nos. C348-C350 (3) 4.90 1.80

Christmas 1978 and 450th death anniversary of Albrecht Dürer (1471-1528), German painter.

Rocket and Trajectory Around Moon AP138

Design: 300fr, Spaceship circling moon.

1978, Nov. 20   Engr.   Perf. 13
C351 AP138 200fr multi 1.25 .60
C352 AP138 300fr multi 1.25 .70
 a. Pair, #C351-C352 + label 3.00 2.00

10th anniversary of 1st flight around moon.

Ader's Plane and Concorde AP139

Designs: 130fr, Wright Flyer A and Concorde. 200fr, Spirit of St. Louis and Concorde.

1979, Jan. 25   Litho.   Perf. 13
C353 AP139 120fr multi .60 .25
C354 AP139 130fr multi .75 .30
C355 AP139 200fr multi 1.40 .55
 Nos. C353-C355 (3) 2.75 1.10

1st supersonic commercial flight, 3rd anniv. For surcharges see Nos. C529-C531.

Philexafrique II-Essen Issue
Common Design Types

Designs: No. C356, Dromedary and Mali No. C26. No. C357, Bird and Lubeck No. 1.

1979, Jan. 29   Litho.   Perf. 13x12½
C356 CD138 200fr multi 2.25 1.00
C357 CD139 200fr multi 2.25 1.00
 a. Pair, #C356-C357 + label 5.00 3.00

No. C257 Surcharged

1979, Mar. 26   Engr.   Perf. 13
C358 AP105 130fr on 90fr multi 1.25 .50

Albert Einstein (1879-1955).

Easter Type of 1978

Dürer Etchings: 400fr, Jesus Carrying Cross. 430fr, Crucified Christ. 480fr, Pietà.

1979, Apr. 9
C359 AP132 400fr bl & blk 1.90 .70
C360 AP132 430fr red & blk 2.10 .75
C361 AP132 480fr ultra & blk 2.40 .85
 Nos. C359-C361 (3) 6.40 2.30

Easter 1979.

Basketball and Cathedral, Moscow — AP140

430fr, Soccer and St. Basil's Cathedral.

1979, Apr. 17   Litho.   Perf. 13
C362 AP140 420fr multi 1.75 .80
C363 AP140 430fr multi 1.75 .80

Pre-Olympic Year.

Mali #C92, Apollo Spacecraft AP141

Design: 500fr, Mali No. C176, lift-off.

1979, Oct. 22   Litho.   Perf. 12½x13
C364 AP141 430fr multi 1.75 .70
C365 AP141 500fr multi 2.00 .80

Apollo 11 moon landing, 10th anniversary.

Capt. Cook, Ship, Kerguelen Island AP142

Design: 480fr, Capt. Cook, Ship, Hawaii.

1979, Oct. 29   Perf. 13x12½
C366 AP142 300fr multi 1.40 .60
C367 AP142 480fr multi 2.00 .85

Capt. James Cook (1728-1779).

David Janowski (1868-1927), Chess Pieces — AP143

Chess Pieces and Grand Masters: 140fr, Alexander Alekhine (1892-1946). 200fr, W. Schlage. 300fr, Effim D. Bogoljubow (1889-1952).

1979, Nov. 30   Engr.   Perf. 13
C368 AP143 100fr red & brn .85 .25
C369 AP143 140fr multi 1.20 .25
C370 AP143 200fr multi 1.60 .40
C371 AP143 300fr multi 2.50 .55
 Nos. C368-C371 (4) 6.15 1.45

For overprints see Nos. C441-C442.

Adoration of the Kings, by Dürer — AP144

Christmas 1979: 400fr, 500fr, Adoration of the Kings by Dürer, diff.

1979, Dec. 10   Perf. 13x13½
C372 AP144 300fr brn org & brn 1.40 .50
C373 AP144 400fr bl & brn 1.90 .70
C374 AP144 500fr dk grn & brn 2.40 .90
 Nos. C372-C374 (3) 5.70 2.10

Jet, Map of Africa — AP145

1979, Dec. 27   Litho.   Perf. 12½
C375 AP145 120fr multi .75 .30

ASECNA (Air Safety Board), 20th anniv.

Train, Globe, Rotary Emblem — AP146

Rotary Intl., 75th Anniv.: 250fr, Jet. 430fr, Bamako Club emblem, meeting hall.

1980, Jan. 28   Litho.   Perf. 12½
C376 AP146 220fr multi 1.10 .40
C377 AP146 250fr multi 1.10 .40
C378 AP146 430fr multi 2.00 .70
 Nos. C376-C378 (3) 4.20 1.50

Speed Skating, Lake Placid '80 Emblem, Snowflake — AP147

1980, Feb. 11   Perf. 13
C379 AP147 200fr shown .90 .25
C380 AP147 300fr Ski jump 1.25 .50
 a. Souvenir sheet of 2 3.00 2.00

13th Winter Olympic Games, Lake Placid, NY, Feb. 12-24. No. C380a contains Nos. C379-C380 in changed colors.

Stephenson's Rocket, Mali No. 196 — AP148

Liverpool-Manchester Railroad, 150th Anniversary: 300fr, Stephenson's Rocket, Mali No. 142.

1980, Feb. 25   Engr.
C381 AP148 200fr multi 1.00 .25
C382 AP148 300fr multi 1.50 .50

Equestrian, Moscow '80 Emblem AP149

1980, Mar. 10   Engr.   Perf. 13
C383 AP149 200fr shown .85 .30
C384 AP149 300fr Yachting 1.20 .50
C385 AP149 400fr Soccer 1.90 .70
 a. Souvenir sheet of 3, #C383-C385 4.50 4.50
 Nos. C383-C385 (3) 3.95 1.50

22nd Summer Olympic Games, Moscow, July 19-Aug. 3. For overprints see Nos. C399-C401.

MALI — Republic of Mali

Jesus Carrying Cross, by Maurice Denis — AP150

Easter: 500fr, Jesus before Pilate, by Dürer.

1980, Mar. 31
C386	AP150 480fr brn & org red	2.25	.80
C387	AP150 500fr org red & brn	2.25	.80

Kepler, Copernicus and Solar System Diagram AP151

200fr, Kepler & diagram of earth's orbit.

1980, Apr. 7   Engr.   *Perf. 13*
C388	AP151 200fr multi, vert.	1.00	.30
C389	AP151 300fr multi	1.50	.50

Discovery of Pluto, 50th Anniversary AP152

1980, Apr. 21
C390	AP152 420fr multi	1.75	.75

Lunokhod I, Russian Flag AP153

Design: 500fr, Apollo and Soyuz spacecraft, flags of US and Russia.

1980, Apr. 28
C391	AP153 480fr multi	1.90	.70
C392	AP153 500fr multi	1.90	.70

Lunokhod I, 10th anniversary; Apollo-Soyuz space test program, 5th anniversary.

Rochambeau, French Fleet Landing at Newport, R.I. — AP154

French Cooperation in American Revolution: 430fr, Rochambeau and George Washington, eagle.

1980, June 16   Engr.   *Perf. 13*
C393	AP154 420fr multi	1.90	.75
C394	AP154 430fr multi	1.90	.75

Jet Flying Around Earth AP155

Designs: No. C396, Ship, people, attack. No. C397, Astronaut on moon. No. C398, Space craft, scientists, moon. Nos. C395-C396 from "Around the World in 80 Days;" Nos. C397-C398 from "From Earth to Moon."

1980, June 30   Engr.   *Perf. 11*
C395	AP155 100fr multi + label	.80	.25
C396	AP155 100fr multi + label	.80	.25
C397	AP155 150fr multi + label	1.10	.30
C398	AP155 150fr multi + label	1.10	.30
	Nos. C395-C398 (4)	3.80	1.10

Jules Verne (1828-1905), French science fiction writer. Nos. C395-C398 each printed se-tenant with label showing various space scenes.

Nos. C383-C385a Overprinted in Black
200fr — CONCOURS COMPLET/ INDIVIDUEL/ROMAN (It.)/ BLINOV (Urss) /SALNIKOV (Urss)
300fr — FINN/RECHARDT (Fin.)/ MAYR-HOFER (Autr.)/ BALACHOV (Urss)
400fr — TCHECOSLOVAQUIE/ ALLEMAGNE DE L'EST/URSS

1980, Sept. 8   Engr.   *Perf. 13*
C399	AP149 200fr multi	.85	.30
C400	AP149 300fr multi	1.25	.50
C401	AP149 400fr multi	1.90	.75
a.	Souvenir sheet of 3	4.25	4.25
	Nos. C399-C401 (3)	4.00	1.55

Butterfly Type of 1980
1980, Oct. 6   Litho.   *Perf. 13x12½*
Size: 48x36mm
C402	A137 420fr *Denaus chrysippus*	3.75	1.00

Charles De Gaulle, Map and Colors of France — AP156

1980, Nov. 9   Litho.   *Perf. 13½x13*
C403	AP156 420fr shown	3.00	.90
C404	AP156 430fr De Gaulle, cross	3.00	.90

Charles De Gaulle, 10th anniv. of death.

Mali No. 140, Amtrak Train AP157

Mali Stamps and Trains: 120fr, No. 195, Tokaido, Japan, vert. 200fr, No. 144, Rembrandt, Germany. 480fr, No. 143, TGV-001 France, vert.

1980, Nov. 17   Engr.   *Perf. 13*
C405	AP157 120fr multi	.60	.25
C406	AP157 130fr multi	.70	.25
C407	AP157 200fr multi	1.00	.40
C408	AP157 480fr multi	2.40	.90
	Nos. C405-C408 (4)	4.70	1.80

For overprint see No. C425.

Holy Family, by Lorenzo Lotto AP158

Christmas 1980 (Paintings): 400fr, Flight to Egypt, by Rembrandt, vert. 500fr, Christmas Night, by Gauguin.

1980, Dec. 1   Litho.   *Perf. 13x12½*
C409	AP158 300fr multi	1.40	.55
C410	AP158 400fr multi	1.75	.70
C411	AP158 500fr multi	2.10	.80
	Nos. C409-C411 (3)	5.25	2.05

Self-portrait, by Picasso — AP159

1981, Jan. 26   Litho.   *Perf. 12½x13*
C412	AP159 1000fr multi	5.50	2.00

Pablo Picasso (1881-1973).

Soccer Players — AP160

Designs: Soccer players.

1981, Feb. 28   *Perf. 13*
C413	AP160 100fr multi	.55	.25
C414	AP160 200fr multi	1.00	.35
C415	AP160 300fr multi	1.50	.50
	Nos. C413-C415 (3)	3.05	1.10

Souvenir Sheet
C416	AP160 600fr multi	3.25	1.75

World Cup Soccer preliminary games.

Mozart and Instruments AP161

225th Birth Anniversary of Wolfgang Amadeus Mozart: 430fr, Mozart and instruments, diff.

1981, Mar. 30   Litho.   *Perf. 13*
C417	AP161 420fr multi	2.00	.70
C418	AP161 430fr multi	2.00	.70

Jesus Falls on the Way to Calvary, by Raphael AP162

Easter 1981: 600fr, Ecce Homo, by Rembrandt.

1981, Apr. 6   *Perf. 12½x13*
C419	AP162 500fr multi	2.10	.80
C420	AP162 600fr multi	2.50	.90

Alan B. Shepard AP163

Exploration of Saturn AP164

Space Anniversaries. No. C422, Yuri Gagarin's flight, 1961. 430fr, Uranus discovery bicentennial, horiz.

1981, Apr. 21   Litho.   *Perf. 13*
C421	AP163 200fr multi	.90	.30
C422	AP163 200fr multi	.90	.30
C423	AP164 380fr multi	1.60	.55
C424	AP163 430fr multi	1.75	.65
	Nos. C421-C424 (4)	5.15	1.80

No. C408 Overprinted
Overprint reads "26 fevrier 1981 Record du monde de/vitesse-380 km/h."

1981, June 15   Engr.
C425	AP157 480fr multi	2.75	.90

New railroad speed record.

US No. 233, Columbus and His Fleet AP165

475th Death Anniversary of Christopher Columbus (Santa Maria and): 200fr, Spain No. 418, vert. 260fr, Spain No. 421, vert. 300fr, US No. 232.

1981, June 22
C426	AP165 180fr multi	.90	.30
C427	AP165 200fr multi	1.00	.35
C428	AP165 260fr multi	1.50	.55
C429	AP165 300fr multi	1.75	.65
	Nos. C426-C429 (4)	5.15	1.85

Columbia Space Shuttle AP166

Designs: Space shuttle.

1981, July 6   Litho.   *Perf. 13*
C430	AP166 200fr multi	.90	.30
C431	AP166 500fr multi	2.25	.90
C432	AP166 600fr multi	2.75	1.00
	Nos. C430-C432 (3)	5.90	2.20

Souvenir Sheet   *Perf. 12*
C433	AP166 700fr multi	4.00	2.00

For overprint see No. C440.

Harlequin on Horseback AP167

Picasso Birth Cent.: 750fr, Child Holding a Dove.

1981, July 15   *Perf. 12½x13*
C434	AP167 600fr multi	3.50	1.00
C435	AP167 750fr multi	4.00	1.10

Prince Charles and Lady Diana, St. Paul's Cathedral AP168

1981, July 20   *Perf. 12½*
C436	AP168 500fr shown	1.75	.70
C437	AP168 700fr Couple, coach	2.50	1.00

Royal wedding.

Christmas 1981 AP169

Designs: Virgin and Child paintings.

1981, Nov. 9   Litho.   *Perf. 12½x13*
C438	AP169 500fr Grunewald	2.25	.70
C439	AP169 700fr Correggio	3.00	1.00

See Nos. C451-C452, C464-C466, C475-C477, C488-C489, C511.

MALI — Republic of Mali

No. C433 Overprinted In Blue
Overprint reads "JOE ENGLE / RICHARD TRULY / 2 eme VOL SPATIAL".

1981, Nov. 12	Litho.		Perf. 12	
C440	AP166	700fr multi	4.00	1.50

Nos. C369, C371 Overprinted with Winners' Names and Dates

1981, Dec.	Engr.		Perf. 13	
C441	AP143	140fr multi	1.00	.35
C442	AP143	300fr multi	2.25	.60

Lewis Carroll (1832-1908) AP170

Designs: Scenes from Alice in Wonderland.

1982, Jan. 30	Litho.		Perf. 12½	
C443	AP170	110fr multi	2.50	.60
C444	AP170	130fr multi	2.50	.80
C445	AP170	140fr multi	2.50	1.00
	Nos. C443-C445 (3)		7.50	2.40

AP171

Portrait, by Gilbert Stuart.

1982, Feb. 8			Perf. 13	
C446	AP171	700fr multi	3.00	1.10

George Washington's Birth, 250th anniv. Incorrectly inscribed "Stuart Gilbert."

AP172

1982 World Cup: Various soccer players.

1982, Mar. 15	Litho.		Perf. 13	
C447	AP172	220fr multi	.90	.30
C448	AP172	420fr multi	1.60	.50
C449	AP172	500fr multi	1.75	.75
	Nos. C447-C449 (3)		4.25	1.55

Souvenir Sheet
Perf. 12½

C450	AP172	680fr multi	3.75	2.00

For overprints see Nos. C458-C461.

Art Type of 1981
Paintings: 680fr, Transfiguration, by Fra Angelico. 1000fr, Pieta, by Bellini, horiz.

Perf. 12½x13, 13x12½

1982, Apr. 19			Litho.	
C451	AP169	680fr multi	2.50	1.75
C452	AP169	1000fr multi	3.25	1.75

Mali No. O30, France No. 1985 AP174

1982, June 1			Perf. 13	
C453	AP174	180fr shown	1.00	.25
C454	AP174	200fr No. C356	1.25	.35
a.	Pair, #C453-C454 + label		2.75	1.40

PHILEXFRANCE '82 Intl. Stamp Exhibition, Paris, June 11-21.

Fire Engine, France, 1850 AP175

Designs: French fire engines.

1982, June 14				
C455	AP175	180fr shown	1.00	.25
C456	AP175	200fr 1921	1.00	.30
C457	AP175	270fr 1982	1.50	.45
	Nos. C455-C457 (3)		3.50	1.00

Nos. C447-C450 Overprinted with Finalists' and Scores in Brown, Black, Blue or Red

1982, Aug. 16	Litho.		Perf. 13	
C458	AP172	220fr multi (Brn)	1.10	.25
C459	AP172	420fr multi	1.50	.55
C460	AP172	500fr multi (Bl)	1.90	.75
	Nos. C458-C460 (3)		4.50	1.55

Souvenir Sheet
Perf. 12½

C461	AP172	680fr multi (R)	3.00	1.75

Italy's victory in 1982 World Cup.

Scouting Year AP176

300fr, Tent, Baden-Powell. 500fr, Salute, emblem.

1982			Perf. 12½	
C462	AP176	300fr multi	1.10	.35
C463	AP176	500fr multi	1.90	.80

Art Type of 1981
Boy with Cherries, by Edouard Manet (1832-83).

1982, Oct. 28	Litho.		Perf. 12½x13	
C464	AP169	680fr multi	3.75	1.25

Art Type of 1981
Madonna and Child Paintings.

1982, Nov. 10				
C465	AP169	500fr Titian	1.90	.75
C466	AP169	1000fr Bellini	3.75	1.75

Johann von Goethe (1749-1832), Poet — AP179

1982, Dec. 13	Engr.		Perf. 13	
C467	AP179	500fr multi	2.75	.85

Follereau Type of 1974

1983, Jan. 24				
C468	AP96	200fr dk brn	1.10	.35

Vostok VI, 20th Anniv. — AP180

400fr, Valentina Tereshkova.

1983, Feb. 14	Litho.		Perf. 12½	
C469	AP180	400fr multi	1.75	.60

Manned Flight, 200th Anniv. — AP181

500fr, Eagle transatlantic balloon. 700fr, Montgolfiere.

1983, Feb. 28			Perf. 13	
C470	AP181	500fr multi	2.50	.75
C471	AP181	700fr multi	3.50	1.10

Pre-Olympic Year AP182

1983, Mar. 14	Litho.		Perf. 13	
C472	AP182	180fr Soccer	.75	.25
C473	AP182	270fr Hurdles	1.10	.45
C474	AP182	300fr Wind surfing	1.50	.55
	Nos. C472-C474 (3)		3.35	1.25

Art Type of 1981
Raphael paintings.

1983, Mar. 28			Perf. 12½x13	
C475	AP169	400fr Transfiguration	1.60	.60
C476	AP169	600fr Deposition	2.40	.85

Art Type of 1981
Design: Family of Acrobats with Monkey, by Picasso (1881-1973).

1983, Apr. 30	Litho.		Perf. 12½x13	
C477	AP169	680fr multi	3.25	1.25

Lions Intl. AP185

1983, May 9			Perf. 12½	
C478		Pair	12.00	6.50
a.	AP185	700fr shown	3.00	1.10
b.	AP185	700fr Rotary Intl.	3.00	1.10

Challenger Spacecraft — AP186

1983, July 29	Litho.		Perf. 13	
C479	AP186	1000fr multi	3.75	1.25

Printed se-tenant with orange red label showing astronaut Sally Ride.

Paris-Dakar Auto Race AP187

240fr, Mercedes, 1914. 270fr, SSK, 1929. 500fr, W196, 1954. 1000fr, Mercedes van.

1983, Sept. 5	Litho.		Perf. 12½	
C480	AP187	240fr multi	1.20	.35
C481	AP187	270fr multi	1.40	.45
C482	AP187	500fr multi	2.75	.75
	Nos. C480-C482 (3)		5.35	1.55

Souvenir Sheet

C483	AP187	1000fr multi	6.50	2.00

For surcharge see No. C506.

Chess Game — AP188

300fr, Pawn, bishop. 420fr, Knight, castle. 500fr, King, Queen. 700fr, Various chess pieces.

1983, Oct. 24	Engr.		Perf. 13	
C484	AP188	300fr multi	2.00	.40
C485	AP188	420fr multi	2.40	.70
C486	AP188	500fr multi	3.25	.80
	Nos. C484-C486 (3)		7.65	1.90

Souvenir Sheet

C487	AP188	700fr multi	5.00	1.75

Art Type of 1981
Raphael Paintings: 700fr, Canigiani Madonna. 800fr, Madonna with Lamb.

1983, Nov. 7	Litho.		Perf. 12½x13	
C488	AP169	700fr multi	2.50	.90
C489	AP169	800fr multi	3.00	1.00

Portrait of Leopold Zborowski, by Amedeo Modigliani (1884-1920) AP190

1984, Feb. 13	Litho.		Perf. 12½x13	
C490	AP190	700fr multi	4.00	1.25

Abraham Lincoln — AP191

1984, Feb. 27			Perf. 12½	
C491	AP191	400fr Henri Dunant	1.60	.50
C492	AP191	540fr shown	2.00	.60

Duke Ellington — AP192

1984, Mar. 12			Perf. 13½x13	
C493	AP192	470fr Sidney Bechet	3.50	.90
C494	AP192	500fr shown	4.25	.90

Glider AP193

1984, Mar. 26				
C495	AP193	270fr shown	1.40	.35
C496	AP193	350fr Hang glider	1.60	.55

1984 Summer Olympics AP194

1984, Apr. 9			Perf. 13	
C497	AP194	265fr Weight lifting	1.40	.35
C498	AP194	440fr Equestrian	2.10	.55
C499	AP194	500fr Hurdles	2.50	.60

MALI — Republic of Mali

Souvenir Sheet
Perf. 12½
C500 AP194 700fr Yachting   4.50 1.75
For surcharges see Nos. C507-C510.

Easter 1984 — AP195

Paintings; 940fr, Crucifixion, by Rubens, vert. 970fr, Resurrection, by Mantegna.

1984, Apr. 24   *Engr.*
C501 AP195 940fr multi   5.25 1.25
C502 AP195 970fr multi   5.25 1.25

Gottlieb Daimler Birth Sesquicentenary — AP196

350fr, Mercedes Simplex. 470fr, Mercedes-Benz 370-S. 485fr, 500-SEC.

1984, June 1   *Engr.*   *Perf. 13*
C503 AP196 350fr multi   3.00 1.00
C504 AP196 470fr multi   4.25 1.25
C505 AP196 485fr multi   4.25 1.25
 Nos. C503-C505 (3)   11.50 3.50

No. C480 Overprinted and Surcharged

1984   *Litho.*   *Perf. 12½*
C506 AP187 120fr on 240fr
  #C400   1.40 .40

Nos. C497-C500 Overprinted and Surcharged

1984, Oct.   *Litho.*   *Perf. 13*
C507 AP194 135fr on 265fr   .90 .50
C508 AP194 220fr on 440fr   1.50 1.00
C509 AP194 250fr on 500fr   2.10 1.25
 Nos. C507-C509 (3)   4.50 2.75

Souvenir Sheet
C510 AP194 350fr on 700fr   4.50 3.00

Overprints refer to the winners of the events depicted.

Art Type of 1981
Painting: Virgin and Child, by Lorenzo Lotto.

1984, Nov. 20   *Litho.*   *Perf. 12½x13*
C511 AP169 500fr multi   4.25 2.00

Audubon Birth Bicentenary AP198

1985, Apr. 15   *Litho.*   *Perf. 13*
C512 AP198 180fr Kingfisher   1.40 .70
C513 AP198 300fr Bustard, vert.   2.50 1.25
C514 AP198 470fr Ostrich, vert.   4.25 2.00
C515 AP198 540fr Buzzard   5.25 2.10
 Nos. C512-C515 (4)   13.40 6.05

For surcharge see No. C560, C562, C567.

ASECNA Airlines, 25th Anniv. AP199

1985, June 10   *Perf. 12½*
C516 AP199 700fr multi   5.25 2.50

For surcharge see No. C559.

PHILEXAFRICA Type of 1985
No. C517, Boy Scouts, lion. No. C518, Satellite communications.

1985, June 24   *Perf. 13*
C517 A183 200fr multi   2.00 1.25
C518 A183 200fr multi   2.00 1.25
 a. Pair, #C517-C518 + label   5.75 3.00

Halley's Comet AP200

1986, Mar. 24   *Litho.*   *Perf. 12½*
C519 AP200 300fr multi   2.50 1.10

For surcharge see No. C558.

Statue of Liberty, Cent. AP201

1986, Apr. 7   *Perf. 13*
C520 AP201 600fr multi   5.25 2.25

Gottlieb Daimler Motorcycle AP202

1986, Apr. 14
C521 AP202 400fr multi   3.00 1.40

1st Internal combustion automotive engine, cent.

Paul Robeson (1898-1976), American Actor, Singer — AP203

500fr, Portrait, Show Boat.

1986, May 10
C522 AP203 500fr multi   5.00 1.75

Karl Eberth (1835-1926), Bacteriologist, and Typhoid Bacilli — AP204

1986, June 7   *Litho.*   *Perf. 12x12½*
C523 AP204 550fr multi   4.50 2.50

World Chess Championships AP205

1986, June 16   *Perf. 12½*
C524 AP205 400fr Chessmen   3.25 1.40
C525 AP205 500fr Knight   5.00 1.75

Disappearance of Jean Mermoz, 50th Anniv. — AP206

Mermoz and: 150fr, Latecoere-300 seaplane. 600fr, Cams 53 Oiseau Tango, seaplane. 625fr, Flight map, Le Comte de La Vaulx aircraft.

1986, Aug. 18   *Litho.*   *Perf. 13*
C526 AP206 150fr multi   1.50 .50
C527 AP206 600fr multi   4.50 1.75
C528 AP206 625fr multi   4.50 2.00
 Nos. C526-C528 (3)   10.50 4.25

Nos. C353-C355 Surcharged New Value and Overprinted

Overprint reads "1986-10e Anniversaire du 1er Vol/Commercial Supersonique".

1986, Sept. 29
C529 AP139 175fr on 120fr   1.50 .60
C530 AP139 225fr on 130fr   1.75 .80
C531 AP139 300fr on 200fr   2.75 1.00
 Nos. C529-C531 (3)   6.00 2.40

Hansen, Leprosy Bacillus, Follereau and Lepers AP207

1987, Jan. 26   *Litho.*   *Perf. 13*
C532 AP207 500fr multi   4.25 1.60

Gerhard Hansen (1841-1912), Norwegian physician who discovered the leprosy bacillus (1869); Raoul Follereau (1903-1977), philanthropist.

Konrad Adenauer (1876-1967), West German Chancellor — AP208

1987, Mar. 9   *Litho.*   *Perf. 13*
C533 AP208 625fr org, buff & blk   5.75 2.25

Pre-Olympics Year — AP209

Buddha and: 400fr, Runners. 500fr, Soccer players.

1987, Apr. 6   *Engr.*
C534 AP209 400fr blk & red brn   3.50 1.40
C535 AP209 500fr lil rose, ol grn
   & ol   4.50 1.75

25th Summer Olympics, Seoul, 1988.

Al Jolson in The Jazz Singer — AP210

1987, Apr. 20
C536 AP210 550fr dk red brn &
   car rose   7.00 2.25

Sound films, 60th anniv.

Albert John Luthuli (1899-1967), 1960 Nobel Peace Prize Winner — AP211

1987, May 26   *Engr.*   *Perf. 13*
C537 AP211 400fr multi   3.25 1.10

Service Organizations AP212

1987, June 8   *Litho.*   *Perf. 13*
C538 AP212 500fr Rotary Int'l.   4.00 1.60
C539 AP212 500fr Lions Int'l.   4.00 1.60

Coubertin, Ancient Greek Runners, Contemporary Athletes — AP213

400fr, 5-ring emblem, stadium.

1988, Feb. 14   *Litho.*   *Perf. 13*
C540 AP213 240fr shown   2.00 .80
C541 AP213 400fr multi   3.50 1.40

125th birth anniv. of Baron Pierre de Coubertin (1863-1937), French educator and sportsman who promulgated revival of the Olympic Games; 1988 Summer Olympics, Seoul.

For surcharge see No. C565

Harlequin, by Pablo Picasso (1881-1973) AP214

1988, Apr. 4   *Litho.*   *Perf. 13*
C542 AP214 600fr multi   5.50 2.00

For surcharge see No. C563.

1st Scheduled Transatlantic Flight of the Concorde (London-New York), 15th Anniv. — AP215

1988, May 2   *Perf. 13*
C543 AP215 500fr multi   4.50 2.00

Home Improvement for a Verdant Mali — AP216

10fr, Furnace, tree, field.

1989, Feb. 6   *Litho.*   *Perf. 12½*
C544 AP216 5fr shown   .25 .25
C545 AP216 10fr multi   .25 .25
C546 AP216 25fr like 5fr   .30 .25
C547 AP216 100fr like 10fr   1.00 .45
 Nos. C544-C547 (4)   1.80 1.20

MALI — Republic of Mali — MALTA

1st Man on the Moon, 20th Anniv. — AP217

1989, Mar. 13 Engr. Perf. 13
C548	AP217	300fr multi.	2.50	1.00
C549	AP217	500fr multi, vert.	4.25	1.60

For surcharges see Nos. C561, C564.

French Revolution, Bicent. — AP218

400fr, Women's march on Versailles. 600fr, Storming of the Bastille.

1989, July 3 Engr. Perf. 13
C550	AP218	400fr multi	4.00	1.40
C551	AP218	600fr multi	5.50	1.90

For surcharges see Nos. C566, C568.

World Cup Soccer Championships, Italy — AP219

1990, June 4 Litho. Perf. 13
C552	AP219	200fr multi	1.90	.70
C553	AP219	225fr multi, diff.	2.10	.80

Souvenir Sheet
C554	AP219	500fr like #C552	4.75	2.50

No. C552-C554 Overprinted in Red

1990, Aug. 13
C555	AP219	200fr on #C552	1.90	.85
C556	AP219	225fr on #C553	2.10	.85

Souvenir Sheet
C557	AP219	500fr on #C554	4.75	2.75

Nos. C512-C513, C515-C516, C519, C541-C542, C548-C551 Surcharged Like Nos. 579-594

1992, June Printing Methods as Before Perfs. as Before
C558	AP200	20fr on 300fr	—
C559	AP199	20fr on 700fr	—
C560	AP198	30fr on 180fr	20.00
C561	AP217	30fr on 500fr	—
C562	AP198	100fr on 540fr	20.00
C563	AP214	100fr on 600fr	—
C564	AP217	150fr on 300fr	—
C565	AP213	150fr on 400fr	—
C566	AP218	150fr on 400fr	—
C567	AP198	200fr on 300fr	20.00
C568	AP218	240fr on 600fr	—

Nos. C558-C568 (11) 60.00

Size and location of surcharge varies. No. C565 also overprinted "BARCELONE 92."

POSTAGE DUE STAMPS

Bambara Headpiece — D1

Perf. 14x13½

1961, Mar. 18 Engr. Unwmk.
J1	D1	1fr black	.25	.25
J2	D1	2fr bright ultra	.25	.25
J3	D1	5fr red lilac	.30	.25
J4	D1	10fr orange	.50	.25
J5	D1	20fr bright green	.75	.25
J6	D1	25fr red brown	.95	.30

Nos. J1-J6 (6) 3.00 1.55

Polyptychus Roseus — D2

No. J8, Deilephila Nerii. No. J9, Gynanisa maja. No. J10, Bunaea alcinoe. No. J11, Teracolus eris. No. J12, Colotis antevippe. No. J13, Charaxes epijasius. No. J14, Manatha microcera. No. J15, Hypokopelates otraeda. No. J16, Lipaphnaeus leonina. No. J17, Gonimbrasia hecate. No. J18, Lobounaea christyi. No. J19, Hypolimnas misippus. No. J20, Catopsilia florella.

1964, June 1 Photo. Perf. 11
Butterflies and Moths in Natural Colors
J7		1fr olive green	.30	.25
J8		1fr org & brn	.30	.25
a.	D2 Pair, #J7-J8		.60	.25
J9		2fr emer & brn	.40	.25
J10		2fr emer & brn	.40	.25
a.	D2 Pair, #J9-J10		.80	.25
J11		3fr rose lil & brn	.40	.25
J12		3fr rose lil & brn	.40	.25
a.	D2 Pair, #J11-J12		.80	.25
J13		5fr blk & rose	.40	.25
J14		5fr green	.40	.25
a.	D2 Pair, #J13-J14		.80	.25
J15		10fr yel, org & blk	.85	.35
J16		10fr blue	.85	.35
a.	D2 Pair, #J15-J16		1.75	.70
J17		20fr lt bl & brn	1.60	.70
J18		20fr lt bl & brn	1.60	.70
a.	D2 Pair, #J17-J18		3.25	1.40
J19		25fr grn & yel	2.25	1.00
J20		25fr dp grn & blk	2.25	1.00
a.	D2 Pair, #J19-J20		4.50	2.00

Nos. J7-J20 (14) 12.40 6.10

Nos. J7-J20 Surcharged

1984 Photo. Perf. 11
J21		5fr on 1fr #J7	.30	.25
J22		5fr on 1fr #J8	.30	.25
a.	D2 Pair, #J21-J22		.60	.25
J23		10fr on 2fr #J9	.30	.25
J24		10fr on 2fr #J10	.30	.25
a.	D2 Pair, #J23-J24		.60	.25
J25		15fr on 3fr #J11	.30	.25
J26		15fr on 3fr #J12	.30	.25
a.	D2 Pair, #J25-J26		.60	.25
J27		25fr on 5fr #J13	.40	.25
J28		25fr on 5fr #J14	.40	.25
a.	D2 Pair, #J27-J28		.80	.25
J29		50fr on 10fr #J15	.70	.30
J30		50fr on 10fr #J16	.70	.30
a.	D2 Pair, #J29-J30		1.40	.60
J31		100fr on 20fr #J17	1.60	.70
J32		100fr on 20fr #J18	1.60	.70
a.	D2 Pair, #J31-J32		3.25	1.40
J33		125fr on 25fr #J19	2.00	.85
J34		125fr on 25fr #J20	2.00	.85
a.	Pair, #J33-J34		4.00	1.70

Nos. J21-J34 (14) 11.20 5.70

OFFICIAL STAMPS

Dogon Mask — O1

Perf. 14x13½

1961, Mar. 18 Engr. Unwmk.
O1	O1	1fr gray	.30	.25
O2	O1	2fr red orange	.30	.25
O3	O1	3fr black	.30	.25
O4	O1	5fr light blue	.30	.25
O5	O1	10fr bister brown	.35	.25
O6	O1	25fr brt ultra	.75	.25
O7	O1	30fr car rose	.90	.25
O8	O1	50fr Prus green	1.00	.25
O9	O1	85fr red brown	1.50	.65
O10	O1	100fr emerald	1.50	.65
O11	O1	200fr red lilac	3.75	1.25

Nos. O1-O11 (11) 10.95 4.55

Mali Coat of Arms — O2

National Colors and Arms in Multicolor, Background in Light Green

1964, June 1 Photo. Perf. 12½
O12	O2	1fr green	.30	.25
O13	O2	2fr light vio	.30	.25
O14	O2	3fr gray	.30	.25
O15	O2	5fr lilac rose	.30	.25
O16	O2	10fr bright blue	.30	.25
O17	O2	25fr ocher	.35	.25
O18	O2	30fr dark green	.50	.25
O19	O2	50fr orange	.75	.25
O20	O2	85fr dark brown	.80	.60
O21	O2	100fr red	1.00	.60
O22	O2	200fr dk vio bl	1.80	.75

Nos. O12-O22 (11) 6.70 3.95

City Coats of Arms — O3

1981, Sept. Photo. Perf. 12½x13
O23	O3	5fr Gao	.30	.25
O24	O3	15fr Timbuktu	.35	.25
O25	O3	50fr Mopti	.45	.25
O26	O3	180fr Segou	1.00	.25
O27	O3	200fr Sikasso	1.25	.35
O28	O3	680fr Koulikoro	3.25	.90
O29	O3	700fr Kayes	3.75	1.10
O30	O3	1000fr Bamako	5.00	1.40

Nos. O23-O30 (8) 15.35 4.75

Nos. O23-O30 Surcharged

1984 Photo. Perf. 12½x13
O31	O3	15fr on 5fr	.30	.25
O32	O3	50fr on 15fr	.55	.25
O33	O3	120fr on 50fr	.95	.25
O34	O3	295fr on 180fr	2.50	.60
O35	O3	470fr on 200fr	3.50	.85
O36	O3	515fr on 680fr	3.75	1.00
O37	O3	845fr on 700fr	6.00	1.75
O38	O3	1225fr on 1000fr	10.00	2.25

Nos. O31-O38 (8) 27.55 7.20

MALTA
ˈmȯl-tə

LOCATION — A group of islands in the Mediterranean Sea off the coast of Sicily
GOVT. — Republic within the British Commonwealth
AREA — 122 sq. mi.
POP. — 442,000 (2020 est.)
CAPITAL — Valletta

The former colony includes the islands of Malta, Gozo, and Comino. It became a republic Dec. 13, 1974.

4 Farthings = 1 Penny
12 Pence = 1 Shilling
20 Shillings = 1 Pound
10 Mils = 1 Cent (1972)
100 Cents = 1 Pound (1972)
100 Cents = 1 Euro (2008)

> Catalogue values for unused stamps in this country are for Never Hinged items, beginning with Scott 206 in the regular postage section, Scott B1 in the semipostal section, Scott C2 in the air post section, and Scott J21 in the postage due section.

Watermark

Wmk. 354 — Maltese Cross, Multiple

Values for unused stamps are for examples with original gum as defined in the catalogue introduction. Very fine examples of Nos. 1-7 will have perforations touching the frameline on one or more sides due to the narrow spacing of the stamps on the plate. Stamps with perfs clear of the frameline are scarce and will command higher prices.

Queen Victoria — A1

1860-61 Unwmk. Typo. Perf. 14
1	A1	½p buff ('63)	900.00	425.00
2	A1	½p buff, bluish	1,400.	700.00
a.	Imperf. (single)		12,000.	

1863-80 Wmk. 1
3	A1	½p yellow buff ('75)	90.00	70.00
a.	½p brown orange ('67)		130.00	80.00
b.	½p orange yellow ('80)		450.00	120.00
c.	½p orange yellow ('80)		300.00	130.00
4	A1	½p golden yel (aniline) ('74)	350.00	400.00

1865 Perf. 12½
5	A1	½p buff	175.00	120.00
a.	½p yellow buff		425.00	190.00

1878 Perf. 14x12½
6	A1	½p buff	210.00	110.00
a.	Perf. 12½x14			

No. 6a unused is believed to be unique and is housed in the Royal Collection in London. It has a small fault.

1882 Wmk. 2 Perf. 14
7	A1	½p reddish orange ('84)	21.00	57.50

A2 A3

MALTA

Queen Victoria — A4

1885, Jan. 1
8	A1	½p green	6.00	.60
9	A2	1p car rose	14.50	.40
a.		1p rose	100.00	30.00
10	A3	2p gray	13.00	2.75
11	A4	2½p ultramarine	55.00	1.25
a.		2½p bright ultramarine	55.00	1.25
b.		2½p dull blue	70.00	3.25
12	A3	4p brown	13.00	3.50
a.		Imperf., pair	6,000.	6,000.
13	A3	1sh violet	60.00	14.00
		Nos. 8-13 (6)	161.50	22.50

For surcharge see No. 20.

Queen Victoria within Maltese Cross — A5

1886 — Wmk. 1
14	A5	5sh rose	125.00	95.00

Gozo Fishing Boat — A6

Ancient Galley — A7

1899, Feb. 4 — Engr. — Wmk. 2
15	A6	4½p black brown	28.00	17.50
16	A7	5p brown red	50.00	21.00

See Nos. 42-45.

"Malta" — A8

St. Paul after Shipwreck — A9

1899 — Wmk. 1
17	A8	2sh6p olive gray	47.50	17.50
18	A9	10sh blue black	110.00	75.00

See No. 64. For overprint see No. 85.

Valletta Harbor — A10

1901, Jan. 1 — Wmk. 2
19	A10	1f red brown	1.75	.55

See Nos. 28-29.

No. 11 Surcharged in Black **One Penny**

1902, July 4
20	A4	1p on 2½p dull blue	1.75	2.25
a.		"Pnney"	35.00	65.00
b.		Double surcharge	17,500.	4,500.

King Edward VII — A12

1903-04 — Typo.
21	A12	½p dark green	11.00	1.00
22	A12	1p car & black	17.50	.50
23	A12	2p gray & red vio	32.50	7.00
24	A12	2½p ultra & brn vio	35.00	5.25
25	A12	3p red vio & gray	2.25	.60
26	A12	4p brown & blk ('04)	30.00	21.00
27	A12	1sh violet & gray	32.50	9.50
		Nos. 21-27 (7)	160.75	44.85

1904-11 — Wmk. 3
28	A10	1f red brown ('05)	10.00	2.75
29	A10	1f dk brown ('10)	10.00	.25
30	A12	½p green	6.00	.35
31	A12	1p car & blk ('05)	27.50	.25
32	A12	1p carmine ('07)	4.00	.25
33	A12	2p gray & red vio ('05)	17.50	4.00
34	A12	2p gray ('11)	6.00	6.50
35	A12	2½p ultra & brn vio	40.00	.70
36	A12	2½p ultra ('11)	6.50	4.50
37	A12	4p brn & blk ('06)	13.00	9.00
38	A12	4p scar & blk, yel ('11)	4.75	5.50
39	A12	1sh violet & gray	57.50	2.40
40	A12	1sh blk, grn ('11)	8.75	4.50
41	A12	5sh scar & grn, yel ('11)	75.00	87.50

Engr.
42	A6	4½p black brn ('05)	45.00	9.00
43	A6	4½p orange ('11)	5.25	5.00
44	A7	5p red ('04)	45.00	9.00
45	A7	5p ol green ('10)	5.25	4.50
		Nos. 28-45 (18)	387.00	155.95

A13

A15

King George V — A16

1914-21 — Ordinary Paper — Typo.
49	A13	¼p brown	1.90	.25
50	A13	½p green	3.75	.35
51	A13	1p scarlet ('15)	3.25	.45
a.		1p carmine ('14)	1.75	.25
52	A13	2p gray ('15)	16.00	8.25
53	A13	2½p ultramarine	2.75	.70

Chalky Paper
54	A15	3p vio, yel	3.00	22.00
58	A13	6p dull vio & red vio	13.00	23.00
59	A15	1sh black, green	14.00	30.00
a.		1sh black, bl grn, bl back	22.50	35.00
b.		1sh black, emerald ('21)	10.00	50.00
c.		As "b," olive back	45.00	97.50
60	A16	2sh ultra & dl vio, bl	57.50	40.00
61	A16	5sh scar & grn, yel	105.00	115.00

Surface-colored Paper
62	A15	1sh blk, grn ('14)	17.50	50.00
		Nos. 49-54,58-62 (11)	237.65	290.00

See Nos. 66-68, 70-72. For overprints see Nos. 77-82, 84.

Valletta Harbor — A17

1915 — Ordinary Paper — Engr.
63	A17	4p black	17.50	7.75

St. Paul — A18

1919
64	A8	2sh6p olive green	82.50	95.00
65	A18	10sh black	3,500.	4,750.
		Revenue cancel		100.00

For overprint see No. 83.

George V — A19

1921-22 — Typo. — Wmk. 4
Ordinary Paper
66	A13	¼p brown	6.50	45.00
67	A13	½p green	7.00	37.50
68	A13	1p rose red	7.75	3.00
69	A19	2p gray	11.00	2.00
70	A13	2½p ultramarine	7.75	52.50

Chalky Paper
71	A13	6p dull vio & red vio	37.50	90.00
72	A16	2sh ultra & dull vio, bl	75.00	240.00

Engr. — Ordinary Paper
73	A18	10sh black	400.00	850.00
		Nos. 66-73 (8)	552.50	1,320.

For overprints and surcharge see Nos. 86-93, 97.

Stamps of 1914-19 Overprinted in Red or Black

1922 — Ordinary Paper — Wmk. 3
Overprint 21mm
77	A13	½p green	2.50	4.00
78	A13	2½p ultra	20.00	50.00

Chalky Paper
79	A15	3p violet, yel	5.00	30.00
80	A13	6p dull lil & red vio	7.50	40.00
81	A15	1sh black, emer	7.50	30.00

Overprint 28mm
82	A16	2sh ultra & dull vio, bl (R)	275.00	525.00

Ordinary Paper
83	A8	2sh6p olive grn	35.00	60.00

Chalky Paper
84	A16	5sh scar & grn, yel	65.00	110.00
		Nos. 77-84 (8)	417.50	849.00

Wmk. 1 — Ordinary Paper
85	A9	10sh blue black (R)	250.00	400.00

Same Overprint on Stamps of 1921

1922 — Wmk. 4
Ordinary Paper — Overprint 21mm
86	A13	¼p brown	.35	1.10
87	A13	½p green	5.50	16.00
88	A13	1p rose red	1.10	.25
89	A19	2p gray	5.50	.55
90	A13	2½p ultramarine	1.25	2.25

Chalky Paper
91	A13	6p dull vio & red vio	27.50	60.00

Overprint 28mm
92	A16	2sh ultra & dull vio, bl (R)	55.00	100.00

Ordinary Paper
93	A18	10sh black (R)	160.00	275.00
		Nos. 86-93 (8)	256.20	455.15

No. 69 Surcharged — One Farthing

1922, Apr. 15
97	A19	1f on 2p gray	.60	.60

"Malta" — A20

Britannia and Malta — A21

1922-26 — Chalky Paper — Typo.
98	A20	¼p brown	3.00	.70
99	A20	½p green	3.00	.25
100	A20	1p buff & plum	6.50	.25
101	A20	1p violet ('24)	4.75	.90
102	A20	1½p org brn ('23)	6.00	.25
103	A20	2p ol brn & turq	3.50	1.40
104	A20	2½p ultra ('26)	6.00	20.00
105	A20	3p ultramarine	6.50	3.25
a.		3p blue	9.50	3.75
106	A20	3p blk, yel ('26)	5.25	27.50
107	A20	4p yel & ultra	3.25	6.00
108	A20	6p ol grn & vio	7.00	5.00
109	A21	1sh ol brn & blue	15.00	4.75
110	A21	2sh ultra & ol brn	15.00	24.00
111	A21	2sh6p blk & red vio	14.50	17.50
112	A21	5sh ultra & org	24.00	55.00
113	A21	10sh ol brn & gray	70.00	175.00

Engr. — Ordinary Paper
114	A20	£1 rose car & blk ('25)	125.00	500.00
a.		£1 car red & blk ('22)	165.00	375.00
		Nos. 98-114 (17)	318.25	841.75

Type A20 stamps and have watermark sideways. No. 114 has watermark upright.
For overprints and surcharges see Nos. 115-129.

No. 105 Surcharged — Two pence halfpenny

1925, Dec.
115	A20	2½p on 3p ultramarine	2.00	7.50

Stamps of 1922-26 Overprinted — POSTAGE

1926
116	A20	¼p brown	1.75	8.25
117	A20	½p green	.80	.25
118	A20	1p violet	1.10	.25
119	A20	1½p orange brown	1.40	.70
120	A20	2p ol brn & turq	.85	2.25
121	A20	2½p ultramarine	1.40	2.25
122	A20	3p black, yel	.85	1.10
a.		Inverted overprint	200.00	550.00
123	A20	4p yel & ultra	27.50	42.50
124	A20	6p ol grn & vio	3.25	8.25
125	A21	1sh ol brn & bl	6.25	25.00
126	A21	2sh ultra & ol brown	60.00	160.00
127	A21	2sh6p blk & red vio	20.00	55.00
128	A21	5sh ultra & org	11.00	55.00
129	A21	10sh ol brn & gray	8.50	24.00
		Nos. 116-129 (14)	144.65	384.80

George V — A22

Valletta Harbor — A23

St. Publius — A24

Notabile (Mdina) — A25

Gozo Fishing Boat — A26

Statue of Neptune — A27

Ruins at Mnaidra — A28

St. Paul — A29

1926-27 — Typo. — Perf. 14½x14
131	A22	¼p brown	.90	.25
132	A22	½p green	.70	.25
133	A22	1p red	3.50	1.60

239

MALTA

134	A22	1½p orange brn	2.25	.25
135	A22	2p gray	5.25	18.00
136	A22	2½p blue	4.50	3.00
137	A22	3p dark violet	5.00	6.00
138	A22	4p org red & blk	3.75	20.00
139	A22	4½p yel buff & vio	4.00	7.50
140	A22	6p red & violet	5.00	9.00

Engr. Perf. 12½
Inscribed: "Postage"

141	A23	1sh black	7.50	12.00
142	A24	1sh6p green & blk	9.00	24.00
143	A25	2sh dp vio & blk	9.50	30.00
144	A26	2sh6p ver & black	23.00	60.00
145	A27	3sh blue & blk	23.00	50.00
146	A28	5sh grn & blk	26.00	82.50
147	A29	10sh car & blk	70.00	120.00
		Nos. 131-147 (17)	202.85	444.35

See Nos. 167-183. For overprints see Nos. 148-166.

Stamps and Type of 1926-27 Overprinted in Black

1928 — **Perf. 14½x14**

148	A22	¼p brown	1.75	.25
149	A22	½p green	1.75	.25
150	A22	1p red	2.00	3.75
151	A22	1p orange brown	5.25	.25
152	A22	1½p yel brown	2.75	1.00
153	A22	1½p red	5.00	.25
154	A22	2p gray	5.00	10.50
155	A22	2½p blue	2.25	.25
156	A22	3p dark violet	2.25	1.00
157	A22	4p org red & blk	2.25	2.00
158	A22	4½p yel & violet	2.50	1.10
159	A22	6p red & violet	2.50	1.75

Overprinted in Red

Perf. 12½

160	A23	1sh black	6.25	3.00
161	A24	1sh6p green & blk	14.50	12.00
162	A25	2sh dp vio & blk	30.00	75.00
163	A26	2sh6p ver & black	20.00	26.00
164	A27	3sh ultra & blk	25.00	35.00
165	A28	5sh yel grn & blk	42.50	75.00
166	A29	10sh car rose & black	75.00	110.00
		Nos. 148-166 (19)	248.50	358.35

Issued: Nos. 151, 153, Dec. 5; others, Oct. 1.

Types of 1926-27 Issue
Inscribed: "Postage & Revenue"

1930, Oct. 20 **Typo.** **Perf. 14½x14**

167	A22	¼p brown	.70	.25
168	A22	½p green	.70	.25
169	A22	1p yel brown	.70	.25
170	A22	1½p red	.80	.25
171	A22	2p gray	1.40	.60
172	A22	2½p blue	2.25	.25
173	A22	3p dark violet	1.75	.25
174	A22	4p org red & blk	1.40	7.50
175	A22	4½p yel & violet	3.75	1.40
176	A22	6p red & violet	3.25	2.50

Engr. Perf. 12½

177	A23	1sh black	11.00	25.00
178	A24	1sh6p green & blk	9.75	32.50
179	A25	2sh dp vio & blk	16.00	30.00
180	A26	2sh6p ver & black	20.00	65.00
181	A27	3sh ultra & blk	55.00	65.00
182	A28	5sh yel grn & blk	60.00	80.00
183	A29	10sh car rose & blk	120.00	200.00
		Nos. 167-183 (17)	308.45	511.00

Common Design Types pictured following the introduction.

Silver Jubilee Issue
Common Design Type

1935, May 6 **Perf. 11x12**

184	CD301	½p green & blk	.50	.70
185	CD301	2½p ultra & brn	2.00	4.00
186	CD301	6p ol grn & lt bl	5.50	6.50
187	CD301	1sh brn vio & ind	14.00	22.50
		Nos. 184-187 (4)	22.00	33.70
		Set, never hinged	40.00	

Coronation Issue
Common Design Type

1937, May 12 **Wmk. 4** **Perf. 13½x14**

188	CD302	½p deep green	.25	.25
189	CD302	1½p carmine	.50	.60
190	CD302	2½p bright ultra	.50	.75
		Nos. 188-190 (3)	1.25	1.60
		Set, never hinged	2.25	

Valletta Harbor — A30

Fort St. Angelo — A31

Verdala Palace — A32

Neolithic Ruins — A33

Victoria and Citadel, Gozo — A34

De l'Isle Adam Entering Mdina A35

St. John's Co-Cathedral A36

Mnaidra Temple A37

Statue of Antonio Manoel de Vilhena A38

Woman in Faldetta A39

St. Publius A40

Mdina Cathedral A41

Statue of Neptune A42

Palace Square — A43

St. Paul — A44

1938-43 **Wmk. 4** **Perf. 12½**

191	A30	1f brown	.25	.35
192	A31	½p green	2.75	.30
192A	A31	½p chnt ('43)	.35	.30
193	A32	1p chestnut	4.25	.35
193A	A32	1p grn ('43)	.40	.25
194	A33	1½p rose red	2.25	.30
194A	A33	1½p dk gray ('43)	.25	.25
195	A34	2p dark gray	2.25	1.75
195A	A34	2p rose red ('43)	.35	.25
196	A35	2½p blue	4.50	1.00
196A	A35	2½p violet ('43)	.40	.25
197	A36	3p violet	3.00	.80
197A	A36	3p blue ('43)	.30	.25
198	A37	4½p ocher & ol green	.30	.30
199	A38	6p rose red & ol green	1.75	.30
200	A39	1sh black	1.75	.55
201	A40	1sh6p sage grn & black	5.00	4.00
202	A41	2sh dk bl & lt grn	3.25	7.50
203	A42	2sh6p rose red & black	5.50	6.00
204	A43	5sh bl grn & blk	3.50	9.00
205	A44	10sh dp rose & blk	11.50	11.50
		Nos. 191-205 (21)	53.85	45.80
		Set, never hinged	75.00	

See No. 236a. For overprints see Nos. 208-222.

Catalogue values for unused stamps in this section, from this point to the end of the section, are for Never Hinged items.

Peace Issue
Common Design Type
Inscribed: "Malta" and Crosses

1946, Dec. 3 **Engr.** **Perf. 13½x14** **Wmk. 4**

206	CD303	1p bright green	.25	.25
207	CD303	3p dark ultra	.40	1.75

Stamps of 1938-43 Overprinted in Black or Carmine

a

1948, Nov. 25 **Perf. 12½**

208	A30	1f brown	.30	.25
209	A31	½p chestnut	.30	.25
210	A32	1p green	.30	.25
211	A33	1½p dk gray (C)	1.25	.25
212	A34	2p rose red	1.25	.25
213	A35	2½p violet (C)	.80	.25
214	A36	3p blue (C)	3.00	.25
215	A37	4½p ocher & ol grn	2.75	1.00
216	A38	6p rose red & ol green	3.25	.30
217	A39	1sh black	3.75	.45
218	A40	1sh6p sage grn & blk	2.50	.50
219	A41	2sh dk bl & lt grn (C)	6.00	2.50
220	A42	2sh6p rose red & blk	14.00	2.50
221	A43	5sh bl grn & blk (C)	26.00	3.50
222	A44	10sh dp rose & blk	26.00	25.00
		Nos. 208-222 (15)	91.45	37.50

The overprint is smaller on No. 208. It reads from lower left to upper right on Nos. 209 and 221.

See Nos. 235-240.

Silver Wedding Issue
Common Design Types
Inscribed: "Malta" and Crosses

1949, Jan. 4 **Photo.** **Perf. 14x14½**

223	CD304	1p dark green	.55	.25

Perf. 11½x11
Engr.

224	CD305	£1 dark blue	40.00	45.00

UPU Issue
Common Design Types
Inscribed: "Malta" and Crosses
Perf. 13½, 11x11½

1949, Oct. 10 **Engr.** **Wmk. 4**

225	CD306	2½p violet	.30	.25
226	CD307	3p indigo	3.00	1.10
227	CD308	6p dp carmine	.60	1.00
228	CD309	1sh slate	.60	2.50
		Nos. 225-228 (4)	4.50	4.85

Princess Elizabeth — A45

1950, Dec. 1 **Engr.** **Perf. 12x11½**

229	A45	1p emerald	.25	.25
230	A45	3p bright blue	.25	.25
231	A45	1sh gray black	.90	2.00
		Nos. 229-231 (3)	1.40	2.50

Visit of Princess Elizabeth.

Madonna and Child — A46

1951, July 12

232	A46	1p green	.25	.25
233	A46	3p purple	.55	.25
234	A46	1sh slate black	1.60	1.40
		Nos. 232-234 (3)	2.40	1.90

700th anniv. of the presentation of the scapular to St. Simon Stock.

Types of 1938-43 Overprinted Type "a" in Red or Black

1953, Jan. 8 **Wmk. 4** **Perf. 12½**

235	A32	1p gray (R)	.85	.25
236	A33	1½p green	.40	.25
a.		Overprint omitted	18,000.	
237	A34	2p ocher	.35	.25
238	A35	2½p rose red	.85	1.65
239	A36	3p violet (R)	.55	.25
240	A37	4½p ultra & ol grn (R)	.55	1.00
		Nos. 235-240 (6)	3.55	3.65

Coronation Issue
Common Design Type
Inscribed: "Malta" and Crosses

1953, June 3 **Engr.** **Perf. 13½x13**

241	CD312	1½p dk green black	.75	.25

Type of 1938-43 with Portrait of Queen Elizabeth II Inscribed: "Royal Visit 1954."

1954, May 3 **Perf. 12½**

242	A36	3p violet	.30	.25

Visit of Elizabeth II and the Duke of Edinburgh, 1954.

Central Altarpiece, Collegiate Parish Church, Cospicua — A47

Perf. 14½x13½

1954, Sept. 8 **Photo.** **Wmk. 4**

243	A47	1½p bright green	.30	.25
244	A47	3p ultramarine	.30	.25
245	A47	1sh gray black	.30	.25
		Nos. 243-245 (3)	.90	.75

Cent. of the promulgation of the Dogma of the Immaculate Conception.

Monument of the Great Siege, 1565 — A48

Auberge de Castille — A49

Designs: ½p, Wignacourt Aqueduct Horse-trough. 1p, Victory Church. 1½p, War Memorial. 2p, Mosta Dome. 3p, King's Scroll. 4½p, Roosevelt's Scroll. 6p, Neolithic Temples at Tarxien. 8p, Vedette. 1sh, Mdina Gate. 1sh6p, Les Gavroches. 2sh, Monument of Christ the King. 2sh6p, Monument of Nicolas Cottoner. 5sh, Raymond Perellos Monument. 10sh, St. Paul. £1, Baptism of Christ.

1956-57 **Engr.** **Perf. 11½**

246	A48	¼p violet	.30	.30
247	A48	½p yel orange	.50	.30
248	A48	1p black	1.15	.30
249	A48	1½p brt green	.35	.30
250	A48	2p brown	2.30	.30
251	A48	2½p orange brown	2.00	.45
252	A48	3p rose red	1.45	.30
253	A48	4½p blue	2.50	.95
254	A49	6p slate blue	.75	.30
255	A48	8p olive bister	3.75	1.25
256	A48	1sh purple	1.25	.40
257	A48	1sh6p Prus green	13.75	.50
258	A48	2sh olive green	12.50	3.75

MALTA

		Perf. 13½x13		
259	A48	2sh6p cop brown	9.75	3.25
260	A48	5sh emerald	15.50	3.75
261	A48	10sh dk carmine	38.75	18.00
262	A48	£1 yel brn ('57)	38.75	37.00
		Nos. 246-262 (17)	145.30	71.40

See Nos. 296-297.

First George Cross Issue

Symbol of Malta's War Effort — A50

Searchlights over Malta — A51

Design: 1sh, Bombed houses.

1957, Apr. 15   Perf. 14x14½, 14½x14   Photo.

Cross in Silver

263	A50	1½p green	.30	.25
264	A51	3p bright red	.30	.25
265	A50	1sh dark red brown	.30	.25
		Nos. 263-265 (3)	.90	.75

Award of the George Cross to Malta for its war effort.
See Nos. 269-274.

Symbols of Architecture — A52

Designs: 3p, Symbols of Industry, vert. 1sh, Symbols of electronics and chemistry and Technical School, Paola.

1958, Feb. 15   Perf. 14½x14, 14x14½   Wmk. 314

266	A52	1½p dp green & blk	.30	.25
267	A52	3p rose red, blk & gray	.30	.25
268	A52	1sh gray, blk & lilac	.30	.25
		Nos. 266-268 (3)	.90	.75

Technical education on Malta.

Second George Cross Issue
Types of 1957

1½p, Bombed-out family & searchlights. 3p, Convoy entering harbor. 1sh, Searchlight battery.

1958, Apr. 15   Perf. 14½x14, 14x14½

Cross in Silver

269	A51	1½p black & brt green	.30	.25
270	A50	3p black & vermilion	.30	.25
271	A51	1sh black & brt lilac	.30	.25
		Nos. 269-271 (3)	.90	.75

Third George Cross Issue
Types of 1957

Designs: 1½p, Air Raid Precautions Organization helping wounded. 3p, Allegory of Malta. 1sh, Mother and child during air raid.

1959, Apr. 15   Perf. 14x14½, 14½x14

272	A50	1½p gold, green & black	.80	.25
273	A51	3p gold, lilac & black	.80	.25
274	A50	1sh gold, gray & black	2.20	1.90
		Nos. 272-274 (3)	3.80	2.40

St. Paul's Shipwreck, Painting in St. Paul's Church, Valletta — A53

Statue of St. Paul, St. Paul's Grotto, Rabat — A54

Designs: 3p, Consecration of St. Publius. 6p, St. Paul leaving Malta; painting, St. Paul's Church, Valletta. 1sh, Angel holding tablet with quotations from Acts of the Apostles. 2sh6p, St. Paul and St. Paul's Bay islets.

1960, Feb. 9   Wmk. 314   Photo.   Perf. 13

275	A53	1½p bister, brt bl & gold	.30	.25
a.		Gold dates & crosses omitted	82.50	120.00
276	A53	3p lt blue, red lil & gold	.30	.25
277	A53	6p car, gray & gold	.30	.25

    Perf. 14x14½

278	A54	8p black & gold	.40	.65
279	A54	1sh brt cl & gold	.35	.25
280	A54	2sh6p brt grnsh bl & gold	1.10	3.25
a.		Gold omitted	2,400.	825.00
		Nos. 275-280 (6)	2.75	4.90

19th centenary of St. Paul's shipwreck on Malta.

Stamp of 1860 — A55

1960, Dec. 1   Perf. 13x13½   Engr.   Wmk. 314

281	A55	1½p multi	.30	.25
282	A55	3p multi	.35	.25
283	A55	6p multi	1.10	1.10
		Nos. 281-283 (3)	1.75	1.60

Centenary of Malta's first postage stamp.

Fourth George Cross Issue

George Cross — A56

Background designs: 3p, Sun and water. 1sh, Maltese crosses.

1961, Apr. 15   Photo.   Perf. 14½x14

284	A56	1½p gray, bister & buff	.30	.25
285	A56	3p ol gray, lt & dk grnsh blue	.30	.25
286	A56	1sh ol green, vio & lil	1.55	2.75
		Nos. 284-286 (3)	2.15	3.25

19th anniv. of the award of the George Cross to Malta.

Madonna Damascena — A57

Designs: 3p, Great Siege Monument by Antonio Sciortino. 6p, Grand Master La Valette (1557-1568). 1sh, Assault on Fort Elmo (old map).

1962, Sept. 7   Perf. 12½x12   Wmk. 314

287	A57	2p ultramarine	.30	.25
288	A57	3p dark red	.30	.25
289	A57	6p olive green	.30	.25
290	A57	1sh rose lake	.30	.40
		Nos. 287-290 (4)	1.20	1.15

Great Siege of 1565 in which the knights of the Order of St. John and the Maltese Christians defeated the Turks.

Freedom from Hunger Issue
Common Design Type

1963, June 4   Perf. 14x14½
291	CD314	1sh6p sepia	1.40	2.20

Red Cross Centenary Issue
Common Design Type

1963, Sept. 2   Litho.   Perf. 13
292	CD315	2p black & red	.30	.25
293	CD315	1sh6p ultra & red	1.65	5.00

Type of 1956
Designs as before.

1963-64   Engr.   Perf. 11½
296	A48	1p black	.55	.35
297	A48	2p brown ('64)	1.35	4.50

David Bruce and Themistocles Zammit — A58

1sh6p, Goat and laboratory equipment.

1964, Apr. 14   Photo.   Wmk. 314
298	A58	2p dl grn, blk & brn	.30	.25
a.		Black omitted	500.00	
299	A58	1sh6p rose lake & blk	.85	1.10

Anti-Brucellosis (Malta fever) Congress of the UN FAO, Valletta, June 8-13.

Nicola Cottoner Attending Sick Man and Congress Emblem — A59

6p, Statue of St. Luke & St. Luke's Hospital. 1sh6p, Sacra Infermeria, Valletta.

1964, Sept. 5   Perf. 13½x14   Wmk. 354
300	A59	2p multicolored	.30	.25
301	A59	6p multicolored	.55	.25
302	A59	1sh6p multicolored	1.20	2.10
		Nos. 300-302 (3)	2.05	2.60

1st European Cong. of Catholic Physicians, Malta, Sept. 6-10.

Independent State

Dove, Maltese Cross and British Crown — A60

Dove, Maltese Cross and: 3p, 1sh6p, Pope's tiara. 6p, 2sh6p, UN Emblem.

1964, Sept. 21   Perf. 14½x13½   Photo.

Gold and
303	A60	2p ol brn & red	.30	.25
304	A60	3p dk red brn & red	.30	.25
305	A60	6p sl blue & red	.45	.25
306	A60	1sh ultra & red	.55	.25
307	A60	1sh6p bl blk & red	1.40	.80
308	A60	2sh6p vio bl & red	1.60	3.75
		Nos. 303-308 (6)	4.60	5.55

Malta's independence.

Nativity — A61

Perf. 13x13½
1964, Nov. 3   Wmk. 354
309	A61	2p magenta & gold	.30	.25
310	A61	4p ultra & gold	.30	.25
311	A61	8p dp green & gold	.45	.45
		Nos. 309-311 (3)	1.05	.95

Cippus, Phoenician and Greek Inscriptions — A62

British Arms, Armory, Valletta — A63

Designs (History of Malta): ½p, Neolithic (sculpture of sleeping woman). 1½p, Roman (sculpture). 2p, Proto-Christian (lamp, Roman temple, Chrismon). 2½p, Saracen (tomb, 12th cent.). 3p, Siculo Norman (arch, Palazzo Gatto-Murina, Notabile). 4p, Knights of Malta (lamp base, cross, and armor of knights). 4½p, Maltese navy (16th cent. galleons). 5p, Fortifications. 6p, French occupation (Cathedral of Notabile, cap, fasces). 10p, Naval Arsenal.
1sh, Maltese Corps of the British Army (insignia). 1sh3p, International Eucharistic Congress, 1910 (angels adoring Eucharist and map of Malta). 1sh6p, Self Government, 1921 (Knights of Malta Hall, present assembly seat). 2sh, Civic Council, Gozo (Statue of Livia, Gozo City Hall). 2sh6p, State of Malta (seated woman and George Cross). 3sh, Independence (doves, UN emblem, British crown, and Pope's tiara).
5sh, "HAFMED," (headquarters and insigne of Allied Forces, Mediterranean). 10sh, Map of Mediterranean. £1, Catholicism (Sts. Paul, Publius and Agatha).

Perf. 14x14½, 14½ (A63)
1965-70   Photo.   Wmk. 354

312	A62	½p violet & yel	.30	.25
a.		½p double	11.00	
b.		½p double, one inverted		2,500.
c.		½p omitted	92.50	
313	A62	1p multi	.30	.25
a.		Booklet pane of 6 ('70)	.85	
314	A62	1½p multi	.30	.25
315	A62	2p multi	.30	.25
a.		Gold omitted	28.50	
b.		Booklet pane of 6 ('70)	1.10	
c.		Imperf. pair	300.00	
316	A62	2½p multi	1.10	.25
a.		Gold ("SARACENIC") omitted	120.00	
317	A62	3p multi	.30	.25
a.		Imperf., pair	325.00	
b.		Gold (windows) omitted	110.00	
c.		Pair, value omitted on one	1,200.	
d.		Silver ("MALTA") omitted	28.50	
e.		Silver ("MALTA") double	440.00	
318	A62	4p multi	1.10	.25
a.		Black (arms shading) omitted	77.50	
b.		Silver ("KNIGHTS OF MALTA") omitted	50.00	
c.		Silver ("MALTA") omitted	130.00	
d.		Imperf. pair	190.00	
319	A62	4½p multi	1.10	.75
a.		Silver ("MALTA") omitted	2,100.	
319A	A62	5p multi ('70)	.30	.25
b.		Booklet pane of 6 ('71)	1.75	
320	A62	6p multi	.30	.25
a.		Black omitted	120.00	
b.		Silver ("MALTA") omitted	50.00	
321	A63	8p multi	.55	.25
321A	A63	10p multi ('70)	.55	1.10
322	A63	1sh multi	.30	.25
323	A63	1sh3p multi	2.25	1.00
a.		Imperf. pair	440.00	
324	A63	1sh6p multi	.65	.25
a.		Queen's head omitted	400.00	
325	A63	2sh multi	.75	.25
326	A63	2sh6p multi	.75	.55
327	A63	3sh multi	1.10	.85
a.		Gold date (1964) omitted	250.00	
328	A63	5sh multi	3.75	1.10
329	A63	10sh multi	2.25	5.50
a.		Gold center emblem omitted	500.00	
330	A63	£1 multi	2.20	6.00
a.		Pink (shading on figures) omitted	35.00	
		Nos. 312-330 (21)	20.50	20.70

Issued: 5p, 10p, 8/1/70; others 1/7/65.
For surcharges see Nos. 447-449, 521.

241

MALTA

Dante, by Raphael — A64

1965, July 7		Unwmk.	Perf. 14	
331	A64	2p dark blue	.30	.25
332	A64	6p olive green	.30	.25
333	A64	2sh chocolate	.55	1.10
		Nos. 331-333 (3)	1.15	1.60

700th birth anniv. of Dante Alighieri.

Turkish Encampment and Fort St. Michael A65

Blockading Turkish Armada A66

Designs: 3p, Knights and Turks in battle. 8p, Arrival of relief force. 1sh, Trophy, arms of Grandmaster Jean de La Valette. 1sh6p, Allegory of Victory, mural by Calabrese from St. John's Co-Cathedral. 2sh6p, Great Siege victory medal; Jean de La Valette on obverse, David slaying Goliath on reverse.

		Perf. 14½x14, 13		
1965, Sept. 1		Photo.	Wmk. 354	
334	A65	2p multicolored	.30	.25
a.		Flag (red) omitted	475.00	
335	A65	3p multicolored	.30	.25
336	A66	6p multicolored	.30	.25
a.		Black omitted	475.00	
b.		Gold omitted	475.00	
337	A65	8p multicolored	.60	.75
a.		Gold (flag & dates) omitted	200.00	
338	A66	1sh multicolored	.30	.25
339	A65	1sh6p multicolored	.70	.30
340	A65	2sh6p multicolored	1.35	2.50
		Nos. 334-340 (7)	3.85	4.55

Great Siege (Turks against Malta), 4th cent.

The Three Wise Men — A67

		Perf. 11x11½		
1965, Oct. 7		Photo.	Wmk. 354	
341	A67	1p dk purple & red	.30	.25
342	A67	4p dk pur & blue	.30	.30
343	A67	1sh3p dk pur & dp mag	.30	.30
		Nos. 341-343 (3)	.90	.85

Winston Churchill, Map and Cross of Malta — A68

Winston Churchill: 3p, 1sh6p, Warships in Valletta Harbor and George Cross.

1966, Jan. 24		Perf. 14½x14		
344	A68	2p blk, gold & red	.30	.25
345	A68	3p dk grn, gold & blk	.30	.25
a.		Gold omitted	400.00	
346	A68	1sh dp cl, gold & red	.50	.25
a.		Gold omitted	185.00	
347	A68	1sh6p dk bl, gold & vio	.60	1.50
		Nos. 344-347 (4)	1.70	2.25

Grand Master Jean Parisot de la Valette — A69

3p, Pope St. Pius V. 6p, Map of Valletta. 1sh, Francesco Laparelli, Italian architect. 2sh6p, Girolamo Cassar, Maltese architect.

1966, Mar. 28		Unwmk.	Perf. 12	
348	A69	2p gold & multi	.30	.25
349	A69	3p gold & multi	.30	.25
a.		Gold omitted	925.00	
350	A69	6p gold & multi	.30	.25
351	A69	1sh gold & multi	.30	.25
352	A69	2sh6p gold & multi	.50	.65
		Nos. 348-352 (5)	1.70	1.65

400th anniversary of Valletta.

Kennedy — A70

		Perf. 15x14		
1966, May 28		Photo.	Wmk. 354	
353	A70	3p ol gray, blk & gold	.30	.25
a.		Gold omitted	325.00	
354	A70	1sh6p dull bl, blk & gold	.30	.25

President John F. Kennedy (1917-1963).

Trade Fair — A71

1966, June 16		Perf. 13x13½		
355	A71	2p multicolored	.30	.25
356	A71	8p gray & multi	.30	1.20
357	A71	2sh6p tan & multi	.30	1.20
		Nos. 355-357 (3)	.90	2.65

The 10th Malta Trade Fair.

Nativity — A72

1966, Oct. 7		Photo.	Wmk. 354	
358	A72	1p multicolored	.30	.25
359	A72	4p multicolored	.30	.25
360	A72	1sh3p multicolored	.30	.25
		Nos. 358-360 (3)	.90	.75

George Cross — A73

1967, Mar. 1		Perf. 14½x14		
361	A73	2p multicolored	.30	.25
362	A73	4p multicolored	.30	.25
363	A73	3sh slate & multi	.30	.45
		Nos. 361-363 (3)	.90	.95

25th anniv. of the award of the George Cross to Malta and Gozo for the war effort.

Crucifixion of St. Peter — A74

Keys, Tiara, Bible, Cross and Sword — A75

Design: 3sh, Beheading of St. Paul.

		Perf. 14½, 13½x14		
1967, June 28		Photo.	Wmk. 354	
364	A74	2p black & brn orange	.30	.25
365	A73	8p blk, gold & lt ol grn	.30	.25
366	A74	3sh black & brt blue	.30	.25
		Nos. 364-366 (3)	.90	.75

1900th anniv. of the martyrdom of the Apostles Peter and Paul.

St. Catherine of Siena by Melchior Gafá — A76

Sculptures by Gafá: 4p, St. Thomas from Villanova. 1sh6p, Christ's baptism. 2sh6p, St. John the Baptist.

1967, Aug. 1			Perf. 13½	
367	A76	2p blk, gold, buff & ultra	.30	.25
368	A76	4p gold, buff, blk & grn	.30	.25
369	A76	1sh6p gold, buff, blk & org brown	.30	.25
370	A76	2sh6p blk, gold, buff & dp car	.30	.25
		Nos. 367-370 (4)	1.20	1.00

Melchior Gafá (1635-67), Maltese sculptor.

Ruins of Megalithic Temples, Tarxien — A77

Designs: 6p, Facade of Palazzo Falzon, Notabile. 1sh, Facade of Old Parish Church, Birkirkara. 3sh, Entrance to Auberge de Castille.

1967, Sept. 12		Photo.	Perf. 14½	
371	A77	2p gold, Prus bl & blk	.30	.25
372	A77	6p org brn, blk, gray & gold	.30	.25
373	A77	1sh gold, ol, ind & blk	.30	.25
374	A77	3sh dk car, rose, blk, gray & gold	.30	.25
		Nos. 371-374 (4)	1.20	1.00

Issued to publicize the 15th Congress of the History of Architecture, Malta, Sept. 12-16.

Nativity A78

Design: 1sh4p, Angels facing left.

1967, Oct. 20			Perf. 13½x14	
375		1p slate, gold & red	.30	.25
a.		Red omitted (stars)	135.00	
376		8p slate, gold & red	.30	.25
377		1sh4p slate, gold & red	.30	.25
a.		A78 Triptych, #375-377	.50	.65
		Nos. 375-377 (3)	.90	.75

Sheets of Nos. 375-377 were arranged in 2 ways: sheets containing 60 stamps of the same denomination arranged tête bêche, and sheets containing 20 triptychs.

Arms of Malta A80

Designs: 4p, Queen Elizabeth II in the robes of the Order of St. Michael and St. George, vert. 3sh, Queen and map of Malta.

		Perf. 14½x14, 14x14½		
1967, Nov. 13		Photo.	Wmk. 354	
378	A80	2p slate & multi	.30	.25
a.		Grey-brown omitted	165.00	
379	A80	4p dp claret, blk & gold	.30	.25
380	A80	3sh black & gold	.30	.30
		Nos. 378-380 (3)	.90	.80

Visit of Queen Elizabeth II, Nov. 14-17.

Human Rights Flame and People — A81

1968, May 2		Photo.	Perf. 14½	
		Size: 40x19mm		
381	A81	2p sepia, dp car, blk & gold	.30	.25

		Perf. 12x12½		
		Size: 24x24mm		
382	A81	6p gray, dk blue, blk & gold	.30	.25
		Perf. 14½		
		Size: 40x19mm		
383	A81	2sh gray, grnsh blue, blk & gold	.30	.25
		Nos. 381-383 (3)	.90	.75

International Human Rights Year.

Fair Emblem — A82

		Perf. 14x14½		
1968, June 1		Photo.	Wmk. 354	
384	A82	4p black & multi	.30	.25
385	A82	8p Prus blue & multi	.30	.25
386	A82	3sh dp claret & multi	.30	.25
		Nos. 384-386 (3)	.90	.75

12th Malta Intl. Trade Fair, July 1-15.

La Valette in Battle Dress A83

La Valette's Tomb, Church of St. John, Valletta A84

Designs: 1p, Arms of Order of St. John of Jerusalem and La Valette's arms, horiz. 2sh6p, Putti bearing shield with date of La Valette's death, and map of Malta.

		Perf. 13x14, 14x13		
1968, Aug. 1		Photo.	Wmk. 354	
387	A83	1p black & multi	.30	.25
388	A83	8p dull blue & multi	.30	.25
389	A84	1sh6p blue grn & multi	.30	.25
390	A83	2sh6p dp claret & multi	.30	.25
		Nos. 387-390 (4)	1.20	1.00

400th anniv. of the death of Grand Master Jean de La Valette (1494-1568).

Star of Bethlehem, Shepherds and Angel — A85

8p, Nativity. 1sh4p, The Three Wise Men.

		Perf. 14½x14		
1968, Oct. 3			Wmk. 354	
391	A85	1p multicolored	.30	.25
392	A85	8p gray & multi	.30	.25
393	A85	1sh4p tan & multi	.30	.25
		Nos. 391-393 (3)	.90	.75

Christmas. Printed in sheets of 60 with alternate rows inverted.

"Agriculture" — A86

1sh, Greek medal and FAO emblem. 2sh6p, Woman symbolizing soil care.

1968, Oct. 21		Photo.	Perf. 12½x12	
394	A86	4p ultra & multi	.30	.25
395	A86	1sh gray & multi	.30	.25
396	A86	2sh6p multicolored	.30	.25
		Nos. 394-396 (3)	.90	.75

6th Regional Congress for Europe of the FAO, Malta, Oct. 28-31.

MALTA

Mahatma Gandhi — A87

Perf. 12x12½
1969, Mar. 24   Photo.   Wmk. 354
397 A87 1sh6p gold, blk & sepia .75 .25

Birth cent. of Mohandas K. Gandhi (1869-1948), leader in India's struggle for independence.

ILO Emblem — A88

1969, May 26   Perf. 13½x14½
398 A88 2p indigo, blue grn & gold .30 .25
399 A88 6p brn blk, red brn & gold .30 .25

50th anniv. of the ILO.

Sea Bed, UN Emblem and Dove — A89

Designs: 2p, Robert Samut, bar of music and coat of arms. 10p, Map of Malta and homing birds. 2sh, Grand Master Pinto and arms of Malta University.

1969, July 26   Photo.   Perf. 13½
400 A89 2p vio blk, blk, gold & red .30 .25
401 A89 5p gray, Prus blue, gold & blk .30 .25
402 A89 10p olive, blk & gold .30 .25
403 A89 2sh dk olive, blk, red & gold .30 .25
Nos. 400-403 (4) 1.20 1.00

Cent. of the birth of Robert Samut, composer of Natl. Anthem (2p); UN resolution on peaceful uses of the sea bed (5p); convention of Maltese emigrants (10p), Aug. 3-16; bicent. of the founding of Malta University (2sh).

June 17, 1919, Uprising Monument A90

"Tourism" A91

Designs: 5p, Maltese flag and 5 doves, horiz. 1sh6p, Dove and emblems of Malta, UN and Council of Europe. 2sh6p, Dove and symbols of trade and industry.

Perf. 13x12½
1969, Sept. 20   Photo.   Wmk. 354
404 A90 2p blk, gray, buff & gold .30 .25
405 A91 5p gray, blk, red & gold .30 .25
406 A91 10p gold, Prus blue, gray & blk .30 .25
407 A91 1sh6p gold, olive & multi .30 .45
408 A91 2sh6p gold, brn ol, gray & blk .30 .55
Nos. 404-408 (5) 1.50 1.75

Fifth anniversary of independence.

St. John the Baptist in Robe of Knight of Malta — A92

Mortar and Jars from Infirmary — A93

Designs: 1p, The Beheading of St. John By Caravaggio. 5p, Interior of St. John's Co-Cathedral. 6p, Allegory depicting functions of the Order. 8p, St. Jerome, by Caravaggio. 1sh6p, St. Gerard Receiving Godfrey de Bouillon, 1093, by Antoine de Favray. 2sh, Sacred vestments.

Perf. 14x13 (1p, 8p); 13½x14 (2p, 6p, 1sh6p); 13½ (5p) 12x12½ (10p, 2sh)
1970, Mar. 21   Photo.   Wmk. 354
409 A92 1p black & multi .30 .25
410 A92 2p black & multi .30 .25
411 A92 5p black & multi .30 .25
412 A92 6p black & multi .30 .25
413 A92 8p black & multi .30 .50
414 A92 10p black & multi .30 .25
415 A92 1sh6p black & multi .30 .40
416 A93 2sh black & multi .30 .55
Nos. 409-416 (8) 2.40 2.70

13th Council of Europe Art Exhibition in honor of the Order of St. John in Malta, Apr. 2-July 1.
Sizes: 1p, 8p, 54x38mm; 2p, 6p, 44x30mm; 5p, 37x37mm; 10p, 2sh, 60x19mm; 1sh6p, 44x33mm.

EXPO '70 Emblem A94

1970, May 29   Perf. 15
417 A94 2p gold & multi .30 .25
418 A94 5p gold & multi .30 .25
419 A94 3sh gold & multi .30 .25
Nos. 417-419 (3) .90 .75

Issued to publicize EXPO '70 International Exhibition, Osaka, Japan, Mar. 15-Sept. 13.

UN Emblem, Dove, Scales and Symbolic Figure — A95

Perf. 14x14½
1970, Sept. 30   Litho.   Wmk. 354
420 A95 2p brown & multi .30 .25
421 A95 5p purple & multi .30 .25
422 A95 2sh6p vio blue & multi .30 .25
Nos. 420-422 (3) .90 .75

25th anniversary of the United Nations.

Books and Quill — A96

Dun Karm, Books and Pens — A97

Perf. 13x14
1971, Mar. 20   Litho.   Wmk. 354
423 A96 1sh6p multicolored .30 .25
424 A97 2sh black & multi .30 .25

No. 423 issued in memory of Canon Gian Pietro Francesco Agius Sultana (De Soldanis; 1712-1770), historian and writer; No. 424 for the centenary of the birth of Mgr. Karm Psaila (Dun Karm, 1871-1961), Maltese poet.

Europa Issue, 1971
Common Design Type

1971, May 3   Perf. 13½x14½
Size: 32x22mm
425 CD14 2p olive, org & blk .30 .25
426 CD14 5p ver, org & black .30 .25
427 CD14 1sh6p gray, org & blk .65 1.20
Nos. 425-427 (3) 1.25 1.70

St. Joseph, by Giuseppe Cali — A98

Design: 5p, 1sh6p, Statue of Our Lady of Victory. 10p, Like 2p.

Perf. 13x13½
1971, July 24   Litho.   Wmk. 354
428 A98 2p dk blue & multi .30 .25
429 A98 5p gray & multi .30 .25
430 A98 10p multicolored .30 .25
431 A98 1sh6p multicolored .30 .45
Nos. 428-431 (4) 1.20 1.20

Centenary (in 1970) of the proclamation of St. Joseph as patron of the Universal Church (2p, 10p), and 50th anniversary of the coronation of the statue of Our Lady of Victory in Senglea, Malta.

Blue Rock Thrush — A99

Design: 2p, 1sh6p, Thistle, vert.

Perf. 14x14½, 14½x14
1971, Sept. 18
432 A99 2p multicolored .30 .25
433 A99 5p bister & multi .30 .25
434 A99 10p orange & multi .30 .45
435 A99 1sh6p bister & multi .40 .60
Nos. 432-435 (4) 1.30 1.55

Heart and WHO Emblem — A100

1972, Mar. 20   Perf. 14
436 A100 2p yel grn & multi .30 .25
437 A100 10p lilac & multi .30 .25
438 A100 2sh6p lt blue & multi .45 .90
Nos. 436-438 (3) 1.05 1.40

World Health Day, Apr. 7.

Coin Showing Mnara (Lampstand) — A101

Decimal Currency Coins: 2m, Maltese Cross. 3m, Bee and honeycomb. 1c, George Cross. 2c, Penthesilea. 5c, Altar, Megalithic Period. 10c, Grandmaster's Barge, 18th century. 50c, Great Siege Monument, by Antonio Sciortino.

Perf. 14 (16x21mm), 2m, 3m, 2c;
Perf. 14½x14 (21x26mm), 5m, 1c, 5c
1972, May 16
439 A101 2m rose red & multi .30 .25
440 A101 3m pink & multi .30 .25
441 A101 5m lilac & multi .30 .25
442 A101 1c multicolored .30 .25
443 A101 2c orange & multi .30 .25
444 A101 5c multicolored .30 .25

Perf. 13½
Size: 27x35mm
445 A101 10c yellow & multi .30 .25
446 A101 50c multicolored .85 1.10
Nos. 439-446 (8) 2.95 2.85

Coins to mark introduction of decimal currency.

Nos. 319A, 321 and 323 Surcharged with New Value and 2 Bars
Perf. 14x14½, 14½
1972, Sept. 30   Photo.   Wmk. 354
447 A62 1c3m on 5p multi .30 .25
448 A63 3c on 8p multi .30 .25
449 A63 5c on 1sh3p multi .30 .25
Nos. 447-449 (3) .90 .75

Europa Issue 1972

Sparkles, Symbolic of Communications — CD15

1972, Nov. 11   Litho.   Perf. 13x13½
450 CD15 1c3m yellow & multi .30 .25
451 CD15 3c multicolored .30 .25
452 CD15 5c pink & multi .30 .40
453 CD15 7c5m multicolored .30 .80
Nos. 450-453 (4) 1.20 1.70

Issued in sheets of 10 plus 2 labels (4x3). Labels are in top row.

Archaeology — A103

1973, Mar. 31   Litho.   Perf. 13½
Size: 22x24mm
454 A103 2m shown .30 .25
455 A103 4m History (knights) .30 .25
456 A103 5m Folklore .30 .25
457 A103 8m Industry .30 .25
458 A103 1c Fishing .30 .25
459 A103 1c3m Pottery .30 .25
460 A103 2c Agriculture .30 .25
461 A103 3c Sport .30 .25
462 A103 4c Marina .30 .25
463 A103 5c Fiesta .30 .25
464 A103 7c5m Regatta .30 .25
465 A103 10c Charity (St. Martin) .30 .25
466 A103 50c Education 2.20 .50
467 A103 £1 Religion 3.00 2.25

Perf. 13½x14
Size: 32x27mm
468 A103 £2 Arms of Malta 11.00 11.00
Nos. 454-468 (15) 19.80 16.75

Europa Issue 1973
Common Design Type

1973, June 2   Perf. 14
Size: 36½x19½mm
469 CD16 3c multicolored .30 .25
470 CD16 5c multicolored .30 .25
471 CD16 7c5m dk bl & multi .30 .55
Nos. 469-471 (3) .90 1.05

Woman with Grain, FAO Emblem — A104

7c5m, Mother and child, WHO emblem. 10c, Two heads, Human Rights flame.

1973, Oct. 6   Unwmk.   Perf. 13½
472 A104 1c3m yel grn, blk & gold .30 .25
473 A104 7c5m ultra, blk & gold .30 .45
474 A104 10c claret, blk & gold .30 .55
Nos. 472-474 (3) .90 1.25

World Food Program, 10th anniv.; WHO, 25th anniv.; Universal Declaration of Human Rights, 25th anniv.

Girolamo Cassar, Architect — A105

3c, Giuseppe Barth, opthalmologist. 5c, Nicolo' Isouard, composer. 7c5m, John Borg, botanist. 10c, Antonio Sciortino, sculptor.

1974, Jan. 12   Litho.   Perf. 14
475 A105 1c3m slate grn & gold .30 .25
476 A105 3c indigo & gold .30 .25
477 A105 5c olive gray & gold .30 .25
478 A105 7c5m slate blue & gold .30 .30
479 A105 10c brn vio & gold .30 .45
Nos. 475-479 (5) 1.50 1.50

Prominent Maltese.

Statue of Goddess, 3rd Millenium B.C. — A106

Europa (CEPT Emblem and): 3c, Carved door, Cathedral, Mdina, 11th cent, vert. 5c, Silver monstrance, 1689. 7c5m, "Vettina" (statue of nude woman), by Antonio Sciortino (1879-1947), vert.

MALTA

1974, July 13   *Perf. 13½x14, 14x13½*
480	A106	1c3m gray blue, blk & gold	.30	.25
481	A106	3c ol brn, blk & gold	.30	.25
482	A106	5c lilac, blk & gold	.30	.40
483	A106	7c5m dull grn, blk & gold	.40	.55
		Nos. 480-483 (4)	1.30	1.45

Heinrich von Stephan, Coach and Train, UPU Emblem — A107

UPU Emblem, von Stephan and: 5c, Paddle steamer and ocean liner. 7c5m, Balloon and jet. 50c, UPU Congress Building, Lausanne, and UPU Headquarters, Bern.

Wmk. 354
1974, Sept.   *Litho.*   *Perf. 13½*
484	A107	1c3m multicolored	.30	.25
485	A107	5c multicolored	.30	.25
486	A107	7c5m multicolored	.40	.25
487	A107	50c multicolored	1.10	.85
a.		Souvenir sheet of 4, #484-487	4.50	5.00
		Nos. 484-487 (4)	2.10	1.60

Centenary of Universal Postal Union.

President, Prime Minister, Minister of Justice at Microphone A108

1c3m, President, Prime Minister, Speaker at Swearing-in ceremony. 5c, Flag of Malta.

1975, Mar. 31   *Perf. 14*
488	A108	1c3m red & multi	.30	.25
489	A108	5c gray, red & black	.30	.25
490	A108	25c red & multi	.60	.85
		Nos. 488-490 (3)	1.20	1.35

Proclamation of the Republic, Dec. 13, 1974.

IWY Emblem, Mother and Child — A109

Designs: 3c, 20c, Secretary (woman in public life), IWY emblem. 5c, Like 1c3m.

Wmk. 354
1975, May 30   *Litho.*   *Perf. 13*
491	A109	1c3m violet & gold	.30	.25
492	A109	3c blue gray & gold	.30	.25
493	A109	5c olive & gold	.30	.25
494	A109	20c red brown & gold	.65	1.90
		Nos. 491-494 (4)	1.55	2.65

International Women's Year.

Allegory of Malta, by Francesco de Mura — A110

Europa: 15c, Judith and Holofernes, by Valentin de Boulogne.

1975, July 15   *Litho.*   *Perf. 14*
| 495 | A110 | 5c multicolored | .35 | .25 |
| 496 | A110 | 15c multicolored | .55 | .55 |

Floor Plan of Ggantija Complex, 3000 B.C. A111

Designs: 3c, View of Mdina. 5c, Typical Maltese town. 25c, Fort St. Angelo.

1975, Sept. 16   *Perf. 14*
497	A111	1c3m black & org	.30	.25
498	A111	3c org, pur & black	.30	.25
499	A111	5c gray, black & org	.30	.65
500	A111	25c org, tan & black	1.00	2.25
		Nos. 497-500 (4)	1.90	3.00

European Architectural Heritage Year.

"Right to Work" — A112

Designs: 5c, Protection of the Environment (Landscape). 25c, Maltese flags.

1975, Dec. 12   *Litho.*   *Wmk. 354*
501	A112	1c3m multicolored	.30	.25
502	A112	5c multicolored	.30	.25
503	A112	25c multicolored	.70	1.20
		Nos. 501-503 (3)	1.30	1.70

First anniversary of Malta Republic.

Republic Coat of Arms — A113

Perf. 13½x14
1976, Jan. 28   *Litho.*   *Wmk. 354*
| 504 | A113 | £2 black & multi | 7.50 | 6.75 |

Feast of Sts. Peter and Paul — A114

Designs: 1c3m, "Festa" (flags and fireworks), vert. 7c5m, Carnival. 10c, Good Friday (Christ carrying cross), vert.

1976, Feb. 26   *Litho.*   *Perf. 14*
505	A114	1c3m multicolored	.30	.25
506	A114	5c multicolored	.30	.25
507	A114	7c5m multicolored	.35	.60
508	A114	10c multicolored	.55	1.10
		Nos. 505-508 (4)	1.50	2.20

Maltese folk festivals.

Water Polo, Olympic Rings — A115

Olympic Rings and: 5c, Yachting. 30c, Running.

1976, Apr. 28   *Litho.*   *Perf. 13½x14*
509	A115	1c7m sl green & red	.30	.25
510	A115	5c dp blue & red	.30	.25
511	A115	30c sepia & red	.55	1.10
		Nos. 509-511 (3)	1.15	1.60

21st Olympic Games, Montreal, Canada, July 17-Aug. 1.

Europa — A116

1976, July 8   *Litho.*   *Wmk. 354*
| 512 | A116 | 7c Lace-making | .30 | .25 |
| 513 | A116 | 15c Stone carving | .30 | .50 |

Grandmaster Nicola Cotoner, Founder A117

5c, Dissected arm & hand. 7c, Dr. Fra Giuseppe Zammit, 1st professor. 11c, School & balustrade.

1976, Sept. 14   *Litho.*   *Perf. 13½*
514	A117	2c multicolored	.30	.25
515	A117	5c multicolored	.30	.25
516	A117	7c multicolored	.30	.25
517	A117	11c multicolored	.35	.65
		Nos. 514-517 (4)	1.25	1.40

School of Anatomy and Surgery, Valletta, 300th anniversary.

Armor of Grand Master Jean de La Valette — A118

Suits of Armor: 7c, Grand Master Aloph de Wignacourt. 11c, Grand Commander Jean Jacques de Verdelin.

1977, Jan. 20   *Litho.*   *Wmk. 354*
518	A118	2c green & multi	.30	.25
519	A118	7c brown & multi	.30	.25
520	A118	11c ultra & multi	.30	.45
		Nos. 518-520 (3)	.90	.95

No. 318 Surcharged with New Value and Bar
1977, Mar. 24   *Photo.*   *Perf. 14x14½*
| 521 | A62 | 1c7m on 4p multi | .30 | .25 |

Annunciation, Tapestry after Rubens A119

Crucifixion A120

Tapestries after Designs by Rubens: 7c, The Four Evangelists. 11c, Nativity. 20c, Adoration of the Kings.
Flemish tapestries commissioned for St. John's Co-Cathedral, Valletta.

Wmk. 354
1977, Mar. 30   *Litho.*   *Perf. 14*
522	A119	2c multicolored	.30	.25
523	A119	7c multicolored	.30	.25
524	A120	11c multicolored	.40	.45
525	A120	20c multicolored	.60	.75

1978, Jan. 26
Flemish Tapestries: 2c, Jesus' Entry into Jerusalem, by unknown painter. 7c, Last Supper, by Nicholas Poussin. 11c, Crucifixion, by Rubens. 25c, Resurrection, by Rubens.
526	A120	2c multicolored	.30	.25
527	A120	7c multicolored	.30	.25
528	A120	11c multicolored	.30	.25
529	A120	25c multicolored	.60	.55

1979, Jan. 24
Tapestries after Designs by Rubens (Triumph of): 2c, Catholic Church. 7c, Charity. 11c, Faith. 25c, Truth.
530	A119	2c multicolored	.30	.25
531	A119	7c multicolored	.30	.25
532	A119	11c multicolored	.30	.25
533	A119	25c multicolored	.70	.90
		Nos. 522-533 (12)	4.70	4.65

Consecration of St. John's Co-Cathedral, Valletta, 400th anniv. (Nos. 522-533). Peter Paul Rubens (1577-1640; Nos. 522-525). See Nos. 567-569.

Malta Map, Telecommunication A121

Designs: 1c, 6c, Map of Italy, Sicily, Malta and North Africa, telecommunication tower and waves, vert. 17c, like 8c.

Perf. 14x13½, 13½x14
1977, May 17   *Litho.*   *Wmk. 354*
535	A121	1c green, red & blk	.30	.25
536	A121	6c multicolored	.30	.25
537	A121	8c multicolored	.30	.25
538	A121	17c purple, red & blk	.65	.45
		Nos. 535-538 (4)	1.55	1.20

World Telecommunication Day.

View of Ta' L-Isperanza A122

Europa: 20c, Harbor, Is-Salini.

1977, July   *Litho.*   *Perf. 13½*
| 539 | A122 | 7c multicolored | .35 | .25 |
| 540 | A122 | 20c multicolored | .40 | .55 |

Issued in sheets of 10.

Help Given Handicapped Worker — A123

7c, Stonemason & shipbuilder. 20c, Mother holding dead son, & Service to the Republic order, horiz. Sculptures from Workers' Monument.

1977, Oct. 12   *Litho.*   *Wmk. 354*
541	A123	2c red brown & brn	.30	.25
542	A123	7c brown & dk brn	.30	.25
543	A123	20c multicolored	.45	.65
		Nos. 541-543 (3)	1.05	1.15

Tribute to Maltese workers.

Lady on Horseback and Soldier, by Dürer — A124

Dürer Engravings: 8c, Bagpiper. 17c, Madonna with Long-tailed Monkey.

1978, Mar. 7   *Perf. 14*
544	A124	1c7m dk blue, blk & red	.30	.25
545	A124	8c gray, blk & red	.30	.25
546	A124	17c dk grn, blk & red	.45	.45
		Nos. 544-546 (3)	1.05	.95

Albrecht Dürer (1471-1528), German painter and engraver.

Grand Master Nicola Cotoner Monument — A125

Europa: 25c, Grand Master Ramon Perellos monument, by Giusepe Mazzuoli. The monument on 7c is believed to be the work of Giovanni Batista Foggini.

1978, Apr. 26   *Perf. 14x13½*
| 547 | A125 | 7c multicolored | .30 | .25 |
| 548 | A125 | 25c multicolored | .40 | .45 |

Goalkeeper — A126

Argentina '78 Emblem and: 11c, 15c, different soccer scenes.

Perf. 14x13½
1978, June 6   *Litho.*   *Wmk. 354*
549	A126	2c multicolored	.30	.25
550	A126	11c multicolored	.30	.25
551	A126	15c multicolored	.30	.40
a.		Souvenir sheet of 3, #549-551	1.75	2.75
		Nos. 549-551 (3)	.90	.90

11th World Cup Soccer Championship, Argentina, June 1-25.

MALTA

Fishing Boat — A127

Designs: 5c, 17c Changing of colors. 7c, 20c, British soldier and oranges. 8c, like 2c.

1979, Mar. 31			Perf. 14	
552	A127	2c claret & multi	.30	.25
553	A127	5c claret & multi	.30	.25
554	A127	7c claret & multi	.30	.25
555	A127	8c dk blue & multi	.30	.30
556	A127	17c dk blue & multi	.45	.45
557	A127	20c dk blue & multi	.45	.45
		Nos. 552-557 (6)	2.10	1.95

End of military agreement between Malta and Great Britain.

Maltese Speronara and AirMalta Fuselage — A128

Europa: 25c, Coastal watch tower and radio link tower.

1979, May 9				
558	A128	7c multicolored	.30	.25
559	A128	25c multicolored	.45	.45

Children and Globe — A129

Designs: 7c, Children flying kites. 11c, Children in a circle holding hands.

1979, June 13			Perf. 14x13½, 14	
		Size: 20x38mm		
560	A129	2c multicolored	.30	.25
		Size: 27x33mm		
561	A129	7c multicolored	.30	.25
562	A129	11c multicolored	.30	.40
		Nos. 560-562 (3)	.90	.90

International Year of the Child.

Loggerhead Turtle — A130

Marine Life: 2c, Gibbula nivosa. 7c, Dolphinfish. 25c, Noble pen shell.

1979, Oct. 10		Litho.	Perf. 13½	
563	A130	2c multicolored	.30	.25
564	A130	5c multicolored	.30	.25
565	A130	7c multicolored	.30	.25
566	A130	25c multicolored	.75	1.00
		Nos. 563-566 (4)	1.65	1.75

Tapestry Types of 1977-79

Tapestries after Designs by Rubens: 2c, The Institution of Corpus Domini. 8c, The Destruction of Idolatry. 50c, Portrait of Grand Master Perellos, vert.

1980, Jan. 30		Wmk. 354	Perf. 14	
567	A120	2c multicolored	.30	.25
568	A120	8c multicolored	.30	.35
		Souvenir Sheet		
569	A119	50c multicolored	1.50	1.75

Victoria Citadel, Gozo — A131

Monument Restoration (UNESCO Emblem and): 2c5m, Hal Saflieni Catacombs, Paola, 2500 B.C., vert. 6c, Vilhena Palace, Mdina, 18th century, vert. 12c, St. Elmo Fort, Valletta, 16th century.

1980, Feb. 15				
570	A131	2c5m multicolored	.30	.25
571	A131	6c multicolored	.30	.25
572	A131	8c multicolored	.30	.45
573	A131	12c multicolored	.35	.65
		Nos. 570-573 (4)	1.25	1.60

Don Gorg Preca (1880-1962), Founder of Soc. of Christian Doctrine — A132

1980, Apr. 12		Litho.	Perf. 14x13½	
574	A132	2c5m gray violet	.30	.25

Ruzar Briffa (1906-1963), Poet, by Vincent Apap — A133

Europa (Vincent Apap Sculpture): 30c, Mikiel Anton Vassalli (1764-1829), freedom fighter and scholar.

1980, Apr. 29			Perf. 13½x14	
575	A133	8c slate grn & dp bis	.30	.25
576	A133	30c brown red & olive	.50	.55

Chess Pieces — A134

Designs: Chess pieces. 30c, vert.

1980, Nov.		Litho.	Perf. 14	
577	A134	2c5m multicolored	.30	.25
578	A134	8c multicolored	.35	.30
579	A134	30c multicolored	.60	.95
		Nos. 577-579 (3)	1.25	1.50

Chess Olympiad, Valletta, Nov. 20-Dec. 8.

Barn Owl — A135

1981, Jan. 20		Wmk. 354	Perf. 13½	
580	A135	3c shown	.30	.25
581	A135	8c Sardinian warbler	.40	.35
582	A135	12c Woodchat shrike	.50	.45
583	A135	23c Stormy petrel	.80	1.25
		Nos. 580-583 (4)	2.00	2.30

Europa Issue

Climbing the Gostra (Greasy Pole) — A136

1981, Apr. 28		Litho.	Perf. 14	
584	A136	8c Horse race	.30	.25
585	A136	30c shown	.45	.55

25th Intl. Fair of Malta, Naxxar, July 1-15 — A137

1981, June 12			Perf. 13½	
586	A137	4c multicolored	.30	.25
587	A137	25c multicolored	.55	.55

Disabled Artist — A138

1981, July 17		Litho.	Perf. 13½	
588	A138	3c shown	.30	.25
589	A138	35c Boy on crutches	.65	.55

Intl. Year of the Disabled.

World Food Day — A139

1981, Oct. 16		Litho.	Perf. 14	
590	A139	8c multicolored	.30	.25
591	A139	23c multicolored	.45	.45

Men Hauling Building Stone — A140

1981, Oct. 31		Wmk. 354	Perf. 14	
592	A140	5m shown	.30	.25
593	A140	1c Growing cotton	.30	.25
594	A140	2c Ship building	.40	.25
595	A140	3c Minting coins	.30	.25
596	A140	5c Artistic achievements	.30	.25
597	A140	6c Fishing	.70	.25
598	A140	7c Farming	.30	.75
599	A140	8c Quarrying	.70	.35
600	A140	10c Grape pressing	.30	.35
601	A140	12c Ship repairing	1.25	1.35
602	A140	15c Energy	.55	.90
603	A140	20c Communications	.60	.70
604	A140	25c Factories	.80	1.25
605	A140	50c Water drilling	2.15	2.25
606	A140	£1 Sea transport	3.50	4.75
607	A140	£3 Air transport	8.00	13.50
		Nos. 592-607 (16)	20.45	27.65

Shipbuilding and Repairing, Tarznar Shipyards — A141

1982, Jan. 29		Litho.	Perf. 13½x14	
608	A141	3c Assembly sheds	.30	.25
609	A141	8c Ships in dry dock	.30	.25
610	A141	13c Tanker	.45	.40
611	A141	27c Tanker, diff.	.90	.85
		Nos. 608-611 (4)	1.95	1.75

Man and Home for the Elderly A142

1982, Mar. 16		Litho.	Perf. 14	
612	A142	8c shown	.30	.25
613	A142	30c Woman, hospital	.85	.85

Europa Issue

Redemption of the Islands, 1428 — A143

30c, Declaration of Rights, 1802.

1982, Apr. 29		Litho.	Perf. 14	
614	A143	8c shown	.45	.25
615	A143	30c multicolored	.75	.75

1982 World Cup — A144

Designs: Various soccer players.

1982, June 11		Litho.	Perf. 14	
616	A144	3c multicolored	.30	.25
617	A144	12c multicolored	.50	.60
618	A144	15c multicolored	.55	.75
a.		Souvenir sheet of 3, #616-618	2.75	5.00
		Nos. 616-618 (3)	1.35	1.60

Brigantine A145

1982, Nov. 13			Litho.	
619	A145	3c shown	.30	.25
619A	A145	8c Tartana	.35	.30
619B	A145	12c Xebec	.45	.35
619C	A145	20c Speronara	.80	.60
		Nos. 619-619C (4)	1.90	1.50

See Nos. 637-640, 670-673, 686-689, 703-706.

Malta Railway Centenary A146

3c, Manning Wardle, 1883. 13c, Black Hawthorn, 1884. 27c, Beyer Peacock, 1895.

1983, Jan. 21		Wmk. 354	Perf. 14	
620	A146	3c multicolored	.30	.25
621	A146	13c multicolored	.65	.75
622	A146	27c multicolored	1.40	2.40
		Nos. 620-622 (3)	2.35	3.40

Commonwealth Day — A147

1983, Mar. 14				
623	A147	8c Map	.30	.40
624	A147	12c Transportation	.30	.50
625	A147	15c Beach, vert.	.35	.55
626	A147	23c Industry, vert.	.50	1.20
		Nos. 623-626 (4)	1.45	2.65

Europa Issue

Megalithic Temples, Ggantija A148

1983, May 5		Wmk. 354	Litho.	Perf. 14
627	A148	8c shown	.45	.35
628	A148	30c Fort St. Angelo	.55	1.10

World Communications Year — A149

1983, July 14		Litho.	Wmk. 354	Perf. 13½x14
629	A149	3c Dish antennas	.30	.25
630	A149	7c Ships	.30	.25
631	A149	13c Trucks	.55	.50
632	A149	20c Games emblem	.90	1.40
		Nos. 629-632 (4)	2.05	2.40

25th anniv. of Intl. Maritime Org. (7c); 30th anniv. of Customs Cooperation Council (10c); 9th Mediterranean Games, Casablanca, 9/3-17 (20c).

Monsignor Giuseppe De Piro (1877-1933), Founder of Missionary Society of St. Paul — A150

1983, Sept. 1		Litho.	Perf. 14	
633	A150	3c multicolored	.30	.25

40th Anniv. of General Workers' Union — A151

1983, Oct. 5		Litho.	Perf. 14x13½	
634	A151	3c Founding rally	.30	.25
635	A151	8c Family, workers	.30	.40
636	A151	27c Headquarters	1.05	1.40
		Nos. 634-636 (3)	1.65	2.05

MALTA

Ships Type of 1982

1983, Nov. 17 Litho. *Perf. 14x13½*
637 A145 2c Strangier, 1813 .30 .35
638 A145 12c Tigre 1839 .75 .90
639 A145 13c La Speranza, 1844 .80 1.00
640 A145 20c Wignacourt 1844 1.15 2.75
Nos. 637-640 (4) 3.00 5.00

Europa (1959-1984) A152

1984, Apr. 27 Wmk. 354 *Perf. 14*
641 A152 8c multicolored .35 .35
642 A152 30c multicolored .55 .55

Police Force, 170th Anniv. — A153

3c, Officer, 1880. 8c, Mounted policeman. 11c, Officer on motorcycle. 25c, Traffic duty, firemen.

1984, June 14 Litho. *Perf. 14x13½*
643 A153 3c multi .70 .55
644 A153 8c multi 1.25 1.00
645 A153 11c multi 1.50 1.20
646 A153 25c multi 2.25 1.75
Nos. 643-646 (4) 5.70 4.50

1984 Summer Olympics — A154

1984, July 26 Litho. *Perf. 13½x14*
647 A154 7c Running .30 .35
648 A154 12c Gymnastics .55 .75
649 A154 23c Swimming .95 1.25
Nos. 647-649 (3) 1.80 2.35

10th Anniv. of Republic — A155

1984, Dec. 12 Litho. Wmk. 354
650 A155 3c Dove on map .30 .30
651 A155 8c Fortress .65 .45
652 A155 30c Hands 2.10 2.75
Nos. 650-652 (3) 3.05 3.45

Malta Post Office Cent. — A156

1985, Jan. 2 Litho. *Perf. 14*
653 A156 3c No. 8 .40 .25
654 A156 8c No. 9 .65 .50
655 A156 12c No. 11 .90 1.55
656 A156 20c No. 12 1.40 1.90
a. Souvenir sheet of 4, #653-656 4.00 3.50
Nos. 653-656 (4) 3.35 4.20

International Youth Year — A157

13c, Three youths, vert. 27c, Female holding flame.

1985, Mar. 7 *Perf. 14x13½, 13½x14*
657 A157 2c shown .30 .25
658 A157 13c multi .70 .70
659 A157 27c multi 1.25 1.25
Nos. 657-659 (3) 2.25 2.20

European Music Year — A158

Europa: 8c, Nicolo Baldacchino (1895-1971), tenor. 30c, Francesco Azopardi (1748-1809), composer.

1985, Apr. 25 Litho. *Perf. 14*
660 A158 8c multicolored 1.10 .55
661 A158 30c multicolored 1.40 2.75

Guzeppi Bajada and Manwel Attard, Martyrs — A159

7c, Karmnu Abela, Wenzu Dyer. 35c, June 7 Uprising Memorial Monument, vert.

1985, June 7 *Perf. 14x14½, 14½x14*
662 A159 3c multicolored .30 .30
663 A159 7c multicolored .55 .55
664 A159 35c multicolored 1.60 1.60
Nos. 662-664 (3) 2.45 2.45

June 7 Uprising, 66th anniv.

UN, 40th Anniv. — A160

1985, July 26 *Perf. 13½x14*
665 A160 4c Stylized birds .25 .25
666 A160 11c Arrows .60 1.00
667 A160 31c Human figures 1.60 3.00
Nos. 665-667 (3) 2.45 4.25

Famous Men — A161

Portraits: 8c, George Mitrovich (1794-1885), politician and author, novel frontispiece, The Cause of the People of Malta Now Before Parliament. 12c, Pietru Caxaru (1438-1485), scholar, manuscript.

1985, Oct. 3 *Perf. 14*
668 A161 8c multicolored .85 .40
669 A161 12c multicolored 1.00 1.55

Ships Type of 1982

3c, Scotia paddle steamer, 1844. 7c, Tagliaferro, 1882. 15c, Gleneagles, 1885. 23c, L'Isle Adam, 1886.

1985, Nov. 27
670 A145 3c multi .60 .25
671 A145 7c multi .90 .55
672 A145 15c multi 1.20 1.75
673 A145 23c multi 2.10 2.50
Nos. 670-673 (4) 4.80 5.05

Intl. Peace Year — A162

8c, John XXIII Peace Laboratory. 11c, Unity. 27c, Peaceful coexistence.

Perf. 14x14½, 13½x14 (#675)
1986, Jan. 28 Litho. Wmk. 354
674 A162 8c multi 1.15 .35
675 A162 11c multi 1.35 1.35
676 A162 27c multi 2.25 4.00
Nos. 674-676 (3) 4.75 5.70
Size of No. 675: 43x27mm.

Europa Issue

Butterflies — A163

35c, Earth, air, fire and water.

1986, Apr. 3 *Perf. 14½x14*
677 A163 8c shown .75 .55
678 A163 35c multi 1.10 1.65

1986 World Cup Soccer Championships, Mexico — A164

3c, Heading the ball. 7c, Goalie catching ball. 23c, Dribbling.

1986, May 30 Wmk. 354 *Perf. 14*
679 A164 3c multi .55 .25
680 A164 7c multi 1.10 .55
681 A164 23c multi 2.85 4.75
a. Souvenir sheet of 3, #679-681 7.00 5.00
Nos. 679-681 (3) 4.50 5.55

Philanthropists A165

Designs: 2c, Fra Diegu (1831-1902). 3c, Adelaide Cini (1838-1885). 8c, Alfonso Maria Galea (1861-1941). 27c, Vincenzo Bugeja (1820-1890).

1986, Aug. 28 *Perf. 14½x14*
682 A165 2c multicolored .40 .25
683 A165 3c multicolored .45 .25
684 A165 8c multicolored .80 .40
685 A165 27c multicolored 2.25 4.00
Nos. 682-685 (4) 3.90 4.90

Ships Type of 1982

1986, Nov. 19 Wmk. 354 *Perf. 14*
686 A145 7c San Paul 1.35 .55
687 A145 10c Knight of Malta 1.65 1.10
688 A145 12c Valetta City 1.90 2.20
689 A145 20c Saver 3.00 3.25
Nos. 686-689 (4) 7.90 7.10

Malta Ornithological Society, 25th Anniv. — A166

3c, Erithacus rubecula. 8c, Falco peregrinus. 13c, Upupa epops. 23c, Calonectris diomedea.

1987, Jan. 26 Litho. *Perf. 14*
690 A166 3c multi 1.00 .55
691 A166 8c multi 2.00 1.00
692 A166 13c multi 2.75 3.75
693 A166 23c multi 3.25 5.50
Nos. 690-693 (4) 9.00 10.80

Nos. 691-692 vert.

Europa Issue

Limestone Buildings — A167

8c, Aquasun Lido. 35c, St. Joseph's Church, Manikata.

1987, Apr. 15 Litho. *Perf. 14½x14*
694 A167 8c multi .45 .55
695 A167 35c multi .65 1.90

Military Uniforms — A168

Uniforms of the Order of St. John of Jerusalem (1530-1798): 3c, Soldier, 16th cent. 7c, Officer, 16th cent. 10c, Flag bearer, 18th cent. 27c, General of the galleys, 18th cent.

1987, June 10 Wmk. 354 *Perf. 14*
696 A168 3c multi .80 .70
697 A168 7c multi 1.70 1.45
698 A168 10c multi 1.85 1.60
699 A168 27c multi 3.75 3.25
Nos. 696-699 (4) 8.10 7.00

See Nos. 723-726, 739-742, 764-767, 774-777.

European Environment Year — A169

Anniversaries and events: 8c, Esperanto movement, cent. 23s, Intl. Year of Shelter for the Homeless.

Perf. 14½x14
1987, Aug. 18 Wmk. 354
700 A169 5c shown 1.25 .50
701 A169 8c multicolored 2.00 .60
702 A169 23c multicolored 3.00 3.00
Nos. 700-702 (3) 6.25 4.10

Ships Type of 1982

1987, Oct. 16 Litho. *Perf. 14*
703 A145 7c Medina, 1969 .85 .75
704 A145 11c Rabat, 1974 2.40 2.20
705 A145 13c Ghawdex, 1979 2.75 2.50
706 A145 20c Pinto, 1987 3.50 3.00
Nos. 703-706 (4) 9.50 8.45

A170

Designs: 8c, Dr. Arvid Pardo, representative to UN from Malta who proposed the resolution. 12c, UN emblem.

Wmk. 354
1987, Dec. 18 Litho. *Perf. 14½*
707 A170 8c multicolored .90 .65
708 A170 12c multicolored 1.40 2.65

Souvenir Sheet
Perf. 13x13½
709 Sheet of 2 3.25 5.00
a. A170 8c multicolored 1.10 1.65
b. A170 12c multicolored 1.75 2.65

UN resolution for peaceful use of marine resources, 20th anniv. Nos. 709a-709b printed in a continuous design.

MALTA

Nazju Falzon (1813-1865), Clergyman — A171

Famous men: 3c, Monsignor Sidor Formosa (1851-1931), benefactor of the poor. 4c, Sir Luigi Preziosi (1888-1965), opthalmologist who developed an operation for the treatment of glaucoma. 10c, Father Anastasju Cuschieri (1876-1962), theologian, poet. 25c, Monsignor Pietru Pawl Saydon (1895-1971), translator, commentator on scripture.

Perf. 14½x14
1988, Jan. 23   Wmk. 354
710	A171	2c shown	.35	.35
711	A171	3c multicolored	.35	.35
712	A171	4c multicolored	.60	.60
713	A171	10c multicolored	.80	.80
714	A171	25c multicolored	2.00	2.00
		Nos. 710-714 (5)	4.10	4.10

Anniversaries and Events — A172

10c, Statue of youth and St. John Bosco in the chapel at St. Patrick's School, Sliema. 12c, Assumption of Our Lady, main altarpiece at Ta' Pinu Sanctuary, Gozo, completed in 1619 by Amodeo Bartolomeo Perugino. 14c, Christ the King monument at the Mall, Floriana, by Antonio Sciortino (1879-1947).

1988, Mar. 5   Litho.   Perf. 14
715	A172	10c multicolored	1.00	1.00
716	A172	12c multicolored	1.25	1.25
717	A172	14c multicolored	1.50	1.50
		Nos. 715-717 (3)	3.75	3.75

St. John Bosco (1815-88), educator (10c); Marian Year (12c); Intl. Eucharistic Congress, Malta, Apr. 24-28, 1913, 75th anniv. (14c).

Land, Sea and Air Transportation — A173

Europa (Transport and communication): 35c, Telecommunications.

1988, Apr. 0   Perf. 14
718	A173	10c multicolored	.85	.55
719	A173	35c multicolored	1.00	1.65

Intl. Anniversaries and Events — A174

Globe picturing hemispheres and: 4c, Red Cross, Red Crescent emblems. 18c, Symbolic design dividing world into north and south regions. 19c, Caduceus, EKG readout.

1988, May 25   Litho.   Perf. 14
720	A174	4c multicolored	.50	.35
721	A174	18c multicolored	1.25	1.65
722	A174	19c multicolored	1.25	1.65
		Nos. 720-722 (3)	3.00	3.65

Intl. Red Cross and Red Crescent Organizations, 125th anniv. (4c); European Public Campaign on North-South Interdependence and Solidarity (18c); WHO, 40th anniv. (19c).

Military Uniforms Type of 1987
Designs: 3c, Light Infantry private, 1800. 4c, Coast Artillery gunner, 1802. 10c, 1st Maltese Provincial Battalion field officer, 1805. 25c, Royal Malta Regiment subaltern, 1809.

1988, July 23   Litho.   Wmk. 354
723	A168	3c multicolored	.40	.25
724	A168	4c multicolored	.45	.30
725	A168	10c multicolored	1.45	1.30
726	A168	25c multicolored	2.90	4.50
		Nos. 723-726 (4)	5.20	6.35

A175

Perf. 14x13½
1988, Sept. 17   Wmk. 354
727	A175	4c Running	.30	.30
728	A175	10c Women's diving	.70	.70
729	A175	35c Basketball	2.00	2.00
		Nos. 727-729 (3)	3.00	3.00

1988 Summer Olympics, Seoul.

A176

1989, Jan. 28   Litho.   Perf. 13½
730	A176	2c Commonwealth	.30	.25
731	A176	3c Council of Europe	.30	.25
732	A170	4c United Nations	.30	.30
733	A176	10c Labor	.60	.70
734	A176	12c Justice	.65	.75

Size: 41x32mm
Perf. 14
735	A176	25c Liberty	1.40	1.90
		Nos. 730-735 (6)	3.55	4.15

Natl. independence, 25th anniv.

New Natl. Emblem A177

1989, Mar. 25   Perf. 14
736	A177	£1 multicolored	4.00	2.75

Children's Toys — A178

Europa.

1989, May 8
737	A178	10c Kite	.55	.55
738	A178	35c Dolls	1.00	1.65

Military Uniforms Type of 1987
3c, Officer of the Maltese Veterans, 1815. 4c, Subaltern of the Royal Malta Fencibles, 1839. 10c, Militia private, 1856. 25c, Royal Malta Fencibles Artillery colonel, 1875.

1989, June 24   Litho.   Wmk. 354
739	A168	3c multicolored	.45	.45
740	A168	4c multicolored	.50	.50
741	A168	10c multicolored	1.50	1.50
742	A168	25c multicolored	2.75	2.75
		Nos. 739-742 (4)	5.20	5.20

Anniversaries and Events — A179

1989, Oct. 17   Litho.   Wmk. 354
743	A179	3c multicolored	.30	.30
744	A179	4c multi, diff.	.30	.30
745	A179	10c multi, diff.	.65	.85
746	A179	14c multi, diff.	.80	1.10
747	A179	25c multi, diff.	1.30	2.75
		Nos. 743-747 (5)	3.35	5.30

UN Declaration on Social Progress and Development, 20th anniv. (3c); signing of the European Social Charter by Malta (4c); Council of Europe, 40th anniv. (10c); Natl. Teachers' Union, 70th anniv. (14c); assembly of the Knights of the Sovereign Military Order of Malta (25c).

Pres. Bush, Map and Gen.-Sec. Gorbachev A180

1989, Dec. 2   Litho.   Wmk. 354
748	A180	10c chalky blue, org & brn	1.40	1.40

US-Soviet summit, Malta, Dec. 2-3.

Europa 1990 — A181

Post offices: 10c, Auberge d'Italie, Valletta, 1574, vert. 35c, Branch P.O., Zebbug, 1987.

1990, Feb. 9
749	A181	10c multicolored	.55	.55
750	A181	35c multicolored	1.40	1.65

Anniversaries & Events — A182

1990, Apr. 7
751	A182	3c multi, vert.	.30	.25
752	A182	4c shown	.40	.25
753	A182	19c multicolored	1.60	1.80
754	A182	20c multi, vert.	1.60	1.80
		Nos. 751-754 (4)	3.90	4.10

UNESCO World Literacy Year (3c); subjection of Malta to Count Roger the Norman and subsequent rulers of Sicily, 900th anniv. (4c); 25th anniv. of Malta's membership in the ITU (19c); and 20th Congress of the Union of European Soccer Associations, Malta (20c).

British Poets and Novelists A183

4c, Samuel Taylor Coleridge. 10c, Lord Byron. 12c, Sir Walter Scott. 25c, William Makepeace Thackeray.

1990, May 3   Perf. 13½
755	A183	4c multi	.35	.35
756	A183	10c multi	.85	.85
757	A183	12c multi	1.15	1.15
758	A183	25c multi	2.00	2.00
		Nos. 755-758 (4)	4.35	4.35

Visit of Pope John Paul II, May 25-27 — A184

1990, May 25   Perf. 14
759	A184	4c St. Paul	.55	1.60
760	A184	25c Pope John Paul II	1.25	1.90
a.	Pair, #759-760		1.65	3.50

World Cup Soccer Championships, Italy — A185

Soccer ball &: 5c, flags. 10c, hands & goal net.

1990, June 8   Wmk. 354
761	A185	5c multicolored	.35	.30
762	A185	10c multicolored	.60	.90
763	A185	14c multicolored	.95	1.65
a.	Souvenir sheet of 3, #761-763		3.00	4.75
		Nos. 761-763 (3)	1.90	2.85

Military Uniforms Type of 1987
Designs: 3c, Captain, Royal Malta Militia, 1889. 4c, Field Officer, Royal Malta Artillery, 1905. 10c, Laborer, Malta Labor Corps, 1915. 25c, Lieutenant, King's Own Malta Regiment of Militia, 1918.

1990, Aug. 25   Perf. 14
764	A168	3c multicolored	.60	.25
765	A168	4c multicolored	1.00	.45
766	A168	10c multicolored	2.40	1.45
767	A168	25c multicolored	4.75	6.25
		Nos. 764-767 (4)	8.75	8.40

Maltese Philatelic Society, 25th Anniv. — A186

1991, Mar. 6   Litho.   Wmk. 354
768	A186	10c multicolored	.65	.75

Europa — A187

10c, Eurostar. 35c, Ariane 4, space plane.

1991, Mar. 16
769	A187	10c multi	.55	.55
770	A187	35c multi	.75	1.40

St. Ignatius of Loyola (1491-1556), Founder of Jesuit Order — A188

Designs: 4c, Marie Therese Pisani (1806-1865), Benedictine Nun, vert. 30c, St. John of the Cross (1542-1591), Christian mystic.

1991, Apr. 29   Litho.   Perf. 14
771	A188	3c multicolored	.30	.25
772	A188	4c multicolored	.30	.30
773	A188	30c multicolored	1.65	2.25
		Nos. 771-773 (3)	2.25	2.80

Military Uniforms Type of 1987
Colors Officers: 3c, Royal Malta Fencibles, 1860. 10c, Royal Malta Regiment of Militia, 1903. 19c, King's Own Malta Regiment, 1968. 25c, Armed Forces of Malta, 1991.

Wmk. 354
1991, Sept. 23   Litho.   Perf. 14
774	A168	3c multicolored	.45	.35
775	A168	10c multicolored	1.00	.75
776	A168	19c multicolored	2.00	1.50
777	A168	25c multicolored	2.65	2.00
		Nos. 774-777 (4)	6.10	4.60

Union Haddiema Maghqudin, 25th Anniv. — A189

1991, Sept. 23   Perf. 14x13½
778	A189	4c multicolored	.35	.35

Birds of Prey — A190

No. 779, Pernis apivorus. No. 780, Circus aeruginosus. No. 781, Falco eleonorae. No. 782, Falco naumanni.

1991, Oct. 3   Perf. 14
779	A190	4c multi	2.25	1.80
780	A190	4c multi	2.25	1.80
781	A190	10c multi	2.25	1.80
782	A190	10c multi	2.25	1.80
a.	Strip of 4, #779-782		9.00	7.50
		Nos. 779-782 (4)	9.00	7.20

World Wildlife Fund.

MALTA

Tourism — A191

Designs: 1c, Ta' Hagrat neolithic temples, Mgarr. 2c, Cottoner Gate. 3c, St. Michael's Bastion, Valletta. 4c, Spinola Palace, St. Julian's. 5c, Old church, Birkirkara. 10c, Wind surfing, Mellieha Bay. 12c, Boat anchored at Wied iz-Zurrieq. 14c, Mgarr Harbor, Gozo. 20c, Yacht Marina. 50c, Gozo Channel. £1, Statue of Arab Horses, by Sciortino. £2, Independence Monument, by Bonnici, vert.

1991, Dec. 9			Perf. 13½	
783	A191	1c multicolored	.35	.40
784	A191	2c multicolored	.45	.30
785	A191	3c multicolored	.45	.30
786	A191	4c multicolored	.50	.25
787	A191	5c multicolored	.55	.25
788	A191	10c multicolored	1.05	.25
789	A191	12c multicolored	1.25	.35
790	A191	14c multicolored	1.55	.40
791	A191	20c multicolored	2.15	.55
792	A191	50c multicolored	3.75	1.50
793	A191	£1 multicolored	6.25	2.75
794	A191	£2 multicolored	11.75	7.25
		Nos. 783-794 (12)	30.05	14.55

Malta Intl. Airport — A192

1992, Feb. 8			Perf. 14	
795	A192	4c shown	.85	.40
796	A192	10c Flags, airport	1.40	.75

Discovery of America, 500th Anniv. — A193

1992, Feb. 20			Perf. 14x14½	
797	A193	10c Columbus' fleet	.80	.60
798	A193	35c Columbus, map	1.65	1.90

Europa.

George Cross, 1942 — A194

George Cross and: 4c, Royal Malta Artillery. 10c, Siege Bell. 50c, Santa Maria convoy entering Grand Harbor.

1992, Apr. 15			Perf. 14	
799	A194	4c multicolored	.90	.25
800	A194	10c multicolored	1.35	.80
801	A194	50c multicolored	6.25	6.25
		Nos. 799-801 (3)	8.50	7.30

1992 Summer Olympics, Barcelona A195

1992, June 24				
802	A195	3c Runners	.50	.25
803	A195	10c High jump	.70	.65
804	A195	30c Swimmer	1.80	3.50
		Nos. 802-804 (3)	3.00	4.40

Historic Buildings A196

Designs: 3c, Church of the Flight of the Holy Family into Egypt, vert. 4c, St. John's Co-Cathedral. 19c, Church of the Madonna del Pilar, vert. 25c, Auberge de Provence.

1992, July 5				
805	A196	3c blk, gray & buff	.40	.25
806	A196	4c blk, salmon & buff	.40	.25
807	A196	19c blk, green & buff	2.00	3.25
808	A196	25c blk, pink & buff	2.25	3.25
		Nos. 805-808 (4)	5.05	7.00

University of Malta, 400th Anniv. — A197

4c, Early building, vert. 30c, Modern complex.

1992, Nov. 11				
809	A197	4c multi	.80	.25
810	A197	30c multi	2.75	4.75

Lions Intl., 75th Anniv. — A198

4c, We serve. 50c, Sight first campaign.

1993, Feb. 4				
811	A198	4c multi	.55	.25
812	A198	50c multi	3.00	3.25

Europa — A199

Contemporary paintings by: 10c, Pawl Carbonaro, vert. 35c, Alfred Chircop.

1993, Apr. 7				
813	A199	10c multicolored	.80	.55
814	A199	35c multicolored	1.60	2.25

5th Games of Small States of Europe — A200

1993, May 4			Perf. 13½x14	
815	A200	3c Torchbearer	.30	.25
816	A200	4c Cycling	1.60	.25
817	A200	10c Tennis	1.10	.80
818	A200	35c Sailing	1.80	3.15
a.		Souvenir sheet of 4, #815-818	5.00	6.00
		Nos. 815-818 (4)	4.80	4.45

Boy Scouts and Girl Guides of Malta — A201

3c, Leader bandaging girl. 4c, Bronze Cross. 10c, Scout at camp fire. 35c, Scout recieving Bronze Cross.

1993, July 21			Perf. 14	
819	A201	3c multi	.45	.25
820	A201	4c multi	.45	.25
821	A201	10c multi	1.00	.80
822	A201	35c multi	2.50	3.50
		Nos. 819-822 (4)	4.40	4.80

Girl Guides in Malta, 70th anniv. (No. 819). Award of Bronze Cross for Gallantry to Boy Scouts of Malta, 50th anniv. (Nos. 820-822).

A202

1993, Sept. 23			Perf. 14½x14	
823	A202	5c Papilio machaon	.40	.25
824	A202	35c Vanessa atalanta	1.90	2.50

A203

1993, Oct. 5			Perf. 13½	
825	A203	4c multicolored	.40	.45

General Worker's Union, 50th anniv.

Souvenir Sheet

Local Councils — A204

Designs showing various local coats of arms with denominations at: a, UL. b, UR. c, LL. d, LR.

1993, Nov. 20			Perf. 14½	
826	A204	Sheet of 4	1.65	2.45
a.-d.		5c any single	.35	.50

Dental Assoc. of Malta, 50th Anniv. — A205

Design: 44c, Dental instrument, teeth.

1994, Feb. 12				
827	A205	5c multicolored	.40	.35
828	A205	44c multicolored	2.20	2.75

Europa — A206

Designs: 14c, Sir Themistocles Zammit (1864-1935), discoverer of micro-organism causing undulant fever. 30c, Marble candelabrum, 2nd cent. B.C., Natl. Museum of Archaeology, Valletta.

1994, Mar. 29			Perf. 14	
829	A206	14c multicolored	.75	.35
830	A206	30c multicolored	1.75	2.25

Anniversaries and Events — A207

1994, May 10				
831	A207	5c shown	.30	.25
832	A207	9c Crosses	.55	.45
833	A207	14c Farm animals	.80	.70
834	A207	20c Factory worker	1.15	1.45
835	A207	25c Cathedral, vert.	1.25	1.60
		Nos. 831-835 (5)	4.05	4.45

Intl. Year of the Family (No. 831). Malta Red Cross Society, 3rd anniv. (No. 832). Agrarian Society, 150th anniv. (No. 833). ILO, 75th anniv. (No. 834). St. Paul's Anglican Cathedral, 150th anniv. (No. 835).

1994 World Cup Soccer Championships, U.S. — A208

1994, June 9				
836	A208	5c shown	.30	.25
837	A208	14c Ball, net, map	.60	.70
838	A208	30c Ball, field, map	1.60	3.75
a.		Souvenir sheet of 3, #836-838	4.25	5.50
		Nos. 836-838 (3)	2.50	4.70

Aviation Anniversaries & Events — A209

Aircraft, related objects: 5c, Trophy, map, Twin Comanche. 14c, Airshow emblem, Phantom jet, demonstration team in silhouette, Alouette helicopter, flag. 20c, Emblem, Avro York, old terminal building, DeHavilland Dove. 25c, Emblem, DeHavilland Comet, new terminal, Airbus 320.

1994, July 2				
839	A209	5c multicolored	.45	.25
840	A209	14c multicolored	1.60	.90
841	A209	20c multicolored	1.70	1.80
842	A209	25c multicolored	1.70	2.00
		Nos. 839-842 (4)	5.45	4.95

Intl. Air Rally of Malta, 25th anniv. (No. 839). Malta Intl. Airshow (No. 840). ICAO, 50th anniv. (Nos. 841-842).

First Manned Moon Landing, 25th Anniv. — A210

1994, July 20				
843	A210	14c multicolored	1.20	1.40

Christmas A211

No. 845, Angel in pink. No. 846, Madonna & child. No. 847, Angel in green.

1994, Oct. 26				
844	A211	5c shown	.30	.25
		Size: 28x40mm		
845	A211	9c +2c multi	.45	.60
846	A211	14c +3c multi	.70	1.10
847	A211	20c +3c multi	1.10	2.25
		Nos. 844-847 (4)	2.55	4.20

Antique Maltese Silver — A212

Designs: 5c, Ewer, Vilhena period. 14c, Balsamina, Pinto period. 20c, Coffee pot, Pinto period. 25c, Sugar box, Pinto period.

			Wmk. 354	
1994, Dec. 12			**Litho.**	**Perf. 14**
848	A212	5c multicolored	.45	.25
849	A212	14c multicolored	1.00	.70
850	A212	20c multicolored	1.35	1.80
851	A212	25c multicolored	1.60	2.50
		Nos. 848-851 (4)	4.40	5.25

Anniversaries & Events — A213

1995, Feb. 27				
852	A213	2c multicolored	.30	.25
853	A213	5c multicolored	.30	.25
854	A213	14c multicolored	.45	.55

MALTA

855	A213	20c multicolored	1.10	1.25
856	A213	25c multicolored	1.35	1.55
		Nos. 852-856 (5)	3.50	3.85

Natl. Assoc. of Pensioners, 25th anniv. (No. 852). Natl. Youth Council of Malta, 10th anniv. (No. 853). 4th World Conf. on Women, Beijing (No. 854). Malta Memorial District Nursing Assoc., 50th anniv. (No. 855). Louis Pasteur (1822-95) (No. 856).

Peace & Freedom — A214

1995, Mar. 29

857	A214	14c multicolored	1.10	.60
858	A214	30c multicolored	1.65	2.75

Europa: 14c, Hand with olive twig, rainbow, vert. 30c, Doves.

50th Anniversaries — A215

Designs: 5c, End of World War II, ships, planes. 14c, Formation of UN, people joining hands. 35c, FAO, hands holding bowl of wheat, FAO emblem.

1995, Apr. 21

859	A215	5c multicolored	.30	.25
860	A215	14c multicolored	.50	.55
861	A215	35c multi, vert.	1.45	2.00
		Nos. 859-861 (3)	2.25	2.80

Telecommunications & Electricity — A216

2c, Light bulb. 5c, Cable, binary numbers. 9c, Satellite dish. 14c, Sun's rays, trees. 20c, Telephone, satellite.

1995, June 15

862	A216	2c multi	.30	.25
863	A216	5c multi	.30	.25
864	A216	9c multi	.30	.45
865	A216	14c multi	.45	.60
866	A216	20c multi	.90	1.35
		Nos. 862-866 (5)	2.25	2.90

European Nature Conservation Year — A217

1995, July 24

867	A217	5c Ruins, Gírna	.70	.25
868	A217	14c Podarcis filfolensis	2.00	.70
869	A217	44c Pina halepensis	3.15	2.70
		Nos. 867-869 (3)	5.85	3.65

Antique Clocks — A218

Designs: 1c, Pinto's turret clock. 5c, Michelangelo Sapiano, long case & smaller clock. 14c, Arlogg tal-lira (case) clock. 25c, Maltese sundials.

1995, Oct. 5

870	A218	1c multicolored	.30	.55
871	A218	5c multicolored	.40	.25
872	A218	14c multicolored	1.35	.70
873	A218	25c multicolored	2.25	3.15
		Nos. 870-873 (4)	4.30	4.65

Christmas — A219

Designs: 5c, Christmas Eve children's procession. 5c+2c, Children carrying manger. 14c+3c, Boy carrying manger, boy with lamp. 25c+3c, Boy with lamp, balcony.

Wmk. 354
1995, Nov. 15   Litho.   Perf. 14

874	A219	5c multi	.30	.25

Size: 26x32mm

875	A219	5c +2c multi	.30	.45
876	A219	14c +3c multi	.90	1.15
877	A219	25c +3c multi	1.55	2.50
		Nos. 874-877 (4)	3.05	4.35

Surtax for child welfare organizations.

Child and Youth Welfare Organizations — A220

Silhouettes of youth, children, and: 5c, Maltese cross, Palace of the President. 14c, Fr. Nazzareno Camilleri, St. Patricks' School. 20c, St. Maria of St. Euphrasia Pelletier, convent building. 25c, Globe, children looking at pool.

1996, Feb. 29

878	A220	5c multicolored	.30	.25
879	A220	14c multicolored	.45	.45
880	A220	20c multicolored	.70	1.00
881	A220	25c multicolored	.85	1.45
		Nos. 878-881 (4)	2.30	3.15

President's Award, 35th anniv. (No. 878). Fr. Camilleri, 90th death anniv. (No. 879). St. Maria, death bicent. (No. 880). UNICEF, 50th anniv. (No. 881).

Prehistoric Art — A221

Sculptures, pottery from 5000-2500BC: 5c, People, animals. 14c, Two people seated, one with missing head. 20c, Venus figure, vert. 35c, Pitcher, vert.

1996, Mar. 29

882	A221	5c multicolored	.30	.25
883	A221	14c multicolored	.55	.60
884	A221	20c multicolored	.70	.90
885	A221	35c multicolored	1.35	2.70
		Nos. 882-885 (4)	2.90	4.45

Famous Women — A222

Europa: 14c, Mabel Strickland (1899-1988). 30c, Inez Soler (1910-1974).

1996, Apr. 24

886	A222	14c multicolored	.75	.60
887	A222	30c multicolored	2.00	2.20

Anniversaries and Events — A223

Designs: No. 888, UN, decade against drug abuse. No. 889, Malta Federation of Industry, 50th anniv. 14c, Self-government, 75th anniv. 44c, Guglielmo Marconi, radio, cent.

1996, June 5

888	A223	5c multicolored	.30	.25
889	A223	5c multicolored	.30	.25
890	A223	14c multicolored	.55	.55
891	A223	44c multicolored	1.35	2.25
		Nos. 888-891 (4)	2.50	3.30

1996 Summer Olympic Games, Atlanta — A224

1996, July 10

892	A224	2c Judo	.30	.25
893	A224	5c Running	.30	.25
894	A224	14c Swimming	.65	.70
895	A224	25c Shooting	1.00	1.45
		Nos. 892-895 (4)	2.25	2.65

Paintings, by or of Giuseppe Calì — A225

Designs: 5c, Boy cutting wheat. 14c, Dog. 20c, Woman with hoe standing on hillside, vert. 25c, Portrait of Calì, by Dingli, vert.

1996, Aug. 22

896	A225	5c multicolored	.30	.25
897	A225	14c multicolored	.60	.60
898	A225	20c multicolored	.80	1.00
899	A225	25c multicolored	.90	1.15
		Nos. 896-899 (4)	2.60	3.00

Buses — A226

2c, Tal-Gallarija "Diamond Star" No. 1990. 5c, Stewart "Tom Mix" No. 434. 14c, Diamond T "Verdala" No. 1764. 30c, Front control No. 3495.

Wmk. 354
1996, Sept. 26   Litho.   Perf. 14

900	A226	2c multicolored	.35	.25
901	A226	5c multicolored	.65	.25
902	A226	14c multicolored	1.25	.90
903	A226	30c multicolored	1.80	2.50
		Nos. 900-903 (4)	4.05	3.90

Christmas — A227

Stained glass windows: 5c+2c, Madonna and Child. 14c+3c, Angel flying right. 25c+3c, Angel flying left.

1996, Nov. 7

904	A227	5c shown	.30	.25

Size: 26x31mm

905	A227	5c +2c multi	.35	.55
906	A227	14c +3c multi	.70	1.25
907	A227	25c +3c multi	1.10	2.25
		Nos. 904-907 (4)	2.45	4.30

City Bicentennials — A228

1997, Feb. 20

908	A228	6c Hompesch	.30	.25
909	A228	16c Ferdinand	.65	.65
910	A228	26c Beland	1.00	1.10
a.		Souvenir Sheet of 3, #908-910	5.00	5.00
		Nos. 908-910 (3)	1.95	2.00

Treasures of Malta — A229

2c, Suggetta. 6c, Suggetta, diff. 16c, Sedan chair, vert. 27c, Sedan chair, diff., vert.

1997, Apr. 11

911	A229	2c multi	.30	.25
912	A229	6c multi	.30	.25
913	A229	16c multi	.65	.65
914	A229	27c multi	1.00	1.00
		Nos. 911-914 (4)	2.25	2.15

A230

Europa (Stories and Legends): 16c, Man carrying door, figure in front of house (Gahan). 35c, Woman kneeling in prayer, knight on white horse (St. Dimitri).

1997, May 5

915	A230	16c multicolored	1.10	.85
916	A230	35c multicolored	1.90	2.75

A231

Antonio Sciortino (1879-1947), sculptor.

1997, July 10

917	A231	1c multicolored	.30	.25
918	A231	16c multicolored	.70	.60

Gozo Cathedral, 300th Anniv. — A232

1997, July 10

919	A232	6c multi	.35	.35
920	A232	11c multi, diff.	.55	.45

Joseph Calleia (1897-1975), Actor — A233

1997, July 10

921	A233	6c multicolored	.35	.35
922	A233	22c multi, diff.	.90	.90

Pioneers of Education — A234

Designs: 6c, Dr. Albert V. Laferla (1887-1943). 16c, Sister Emilie de Vialar (1797-1856). 19c, Msgr. Paolo Pullicino (1815-90). 26c, Msgr. Tommaso Gargallo (c. 1544-1614).

Wmk. 354
1997, Sept. 24   Litho.   Perf. 14

923	A234	6c multicolored	.30	.30
924	A234	16c multicolored	.70	.70
925	A234	19c multicolored	.85	.85
926	A234	26c multicolored	.95	.95
		Nos. 923-926 (4)	2.80	2.80

MALTA

Christmas — A235

Designs: 6c, Nativity. 6c+2c, Madonna and Child, vert. 16c+3c, Joseph with donkey, vert. 26c+3c, Shepherd, sheep, vert.

1997, Nov. 12
927	A235	6c multi	.35	.35
928	A235	6c +2c multi	.40	.40
929	A235	16c +3c multi	.90	.90
930	A235	26c +3c multi	1.35	1.30
		Nos. 927-930 (4)	3.00	2.95

Victoria Lines, Cent. — A236

Designs: 2c, Fort, soldiers in front of wall. 16c, Soldiers with cannon, fort.

1997, Dec. 5
931	A236	2c multicolored	.30	.25
932	A236	16c multicolored	1.00	.70

Self-government, 50th Anniv. — A237

Designs: 6c, Man looking at paper, group of people. 37c, People in line waiting to vote.

1997, Dec. 5
933	A237	6c multicolored	.30	.25
934	A237	37c multicolored	1.65	2.25

Treasures of Malta — A238

Designs: No. 935, Vest. No. 936, Portrait of a Woman, by Antoine de Favray (1706-98). No. 937, Portrait of Woman Holding Girl, by de Favray. No. 938, Early woman's costume. 26c, Valletta, city of culture.

1998, Feb. 26
935	A238	6c multicolored	.40	.40
936	A238	6c multicolored	.40	.40
937	A238	16c multicolored	.85	.85
938	A238	16c multicolored	.85	.85
		Nos. 935-938 (4)	2.50	2.50

Souvenir Sheet
Perf. 13x13½
939	A238	26c multicolored	1.90	1.75

No. 939 contains one 39x48mm stamp.

French Occupation of Malta, Bicent. — A239

Designs: No. 940, Ferdinand von Hompesch, commander of Knights of St. John. No. 941, French fleet, map. No. 942, French coming ashore. No. 943, Napoleon Bonaparte.

Wmk. 239
1998, Mar. 28   Litho.   Perf. 14
940	A239	6c multicolored	.55	.75
941	A239	6c multicolored	.55	.75
a.		Pair, #940-941	1.25	1.75
942	A239	16c multicolored	.85	1.20
943	A239	16c multicolored	.85	1.20
a.		Pair, #942-943	2.30	3.30
		Nos. 940-943 (4)	2.80	3.90

National Festivals — A240

Europa: 16c, 35c, Various boats at annual regatta.

Wmk. 354
1998, Apr. 22   Litho.   Perf. 14
944	A240	16c multicolored	.55	.60
945	A240	35c multicolored	1.10	2.50

Intl. Year of the Ocean — A241

Designs: 2c, Diver, dolphin, vert. 6c, Diver, hand holding sea urchin, vert. 16c, Diver, Jacques Cousteau (1910-97), deep sea explorer. 27c, Two divers.

Wmk. 354
1998, May 27   Litho.   Perf. 14
946	A241	2c multicolored	.30	.30
947	A241	6c multicolored	.40	.30
948	A241	16c multicolored	1.05	1.25
949	A241	27c multicolored	1.30	1.50
		Nos. 946-949 (4)	3.05	3.35

1998 World Cup Soccer Championship, France — A242

Various soccer plays, flags from participating teams.

1998, June 10
950	A242	6c multicolored	.45	.45
951	A242	16c multicolored	.90	.90
952	A242	22c multicolored	1.65	1.65
a.		Souvenir sheet, #950-952	3.75	3.50
		Nos. 950-952 (3)	3.00	3.00

Anniversaries and Events — A243

1c, Intl. Maritime Organization, 50th anniv. 6c, Symbolic people, emblem, Universal Declaration of Human Rights. 11c, Cogs in wheels, Assoc. of General Retailers & Traders, 50th anniv. 19c, Roman god Mercury, Malta Chamber of Commerce, 150th anniv. 26c, Stylized planes, Air Malta, 25th anniv.

Wmk. 354
1998, Sept. 17   Litho.   Perf. 14
953	A243	1c multicolored	.30	.35
954	A243	6c multicolored	.45	.30
955	A243	11c multicolored	.75	.45
956	A243	19c multicolored	.95	1.55
957	A243	26c multicolored	1.25	2.75
		Nos. 953-957 (5)	3.70	5.40

Christmas — A244

Paintings by Mattia Preti (1613-99): 6c, Rest on the Flight to Egypt. 6c+2c, Virgin and Child with Saints Anthony the Abbot and John the Baptist. 16c+3c, Virgin and Child with Saints Raphael, Nicholas and Gregory. 26c+3c, Virgin and Child with Saints John the Baptist and Nicholas.

Wmk. 354
1998, Nov. 19   Litho.   Perf. 14
958	A244	6c multicolored	.35	.50
959	A244	6c +2c multi	.50	.70
960	A244	16c +3c multi	1.35	1.90
961	A244	26c +3c multi	1.70	2.40
		Nos. 958-961 (4)	3.90	5.50

Knights Hospitaller, Order of St. John of Jerusalem, 900th Anniv. — A245

2c, Fort St. Angelo. 6c, Grandmaster L'Isle Adam, vert. 16c, Grandmaster La Valette, vert. 27c, Auberge de Castille.

Wmk. 354
1999, Feb. 26   Litho.   Perf. 14
962	A245	2c multicolored	.30	.25
963	A245	6c multicolored	.45	.40
964	A245	16c multicolored	1.05	.95
965	A245	27c multicolored	1.90	1.75
		Nos. 962-965 (4)	3.70	3.35

Council of Europe, 50th Anniv. A246

Designs: 6c, European Parliament in session. 16c, Human Rights Building.

1999, Apr. 6
966	A246	6c multicolored	.65	.30
967	A246	16c multicolored	1.10	1.40

Nature Reserves A247

Europa: 16c, Charadrius dubius, Ghadira Nature Reserve. 35c, Alcedo atthis, Simar Nature Reserve.

Unwmk.
1999, Apr. 6   Litho.   Perf. 14
968	A247	16c multicolored	1.40	.60
969	A247	35c multicolored	1.65	2.20

UPU, 125th Anniv. — A248

UPU emblem and: a, 6c, Sailing ship, Valletta Bastions, Marsamxett Harbor. b, 16c, IBRA '99 emblem, Nuremberg, Germany. c, 22c, Philexfrance emblem, Eiffel Tower, Paris. d, 27c, Beijing '99 emblem, Beijing. e, 37c, Australia '99 emblem, Melbourne.

1999, June 2   Perf. 13¾x14
970	A248	Strip of 5, #a.-e.	8.00	9.75

Tourism A249

Sun shining and: 6c, Man, woman in boat, vert. 16c, Man taking picture of family posed with Knight of Malta, vert. 22c, Man basking in sun while frying egg on stomach. 27c, Girl with flowers, man pushing woman in horse-drawn carriage. 37c, Cave man among ruins pulling luggage, reading travel guide.

Perf. 14x13¾, 13¾x14
1999, June 16
971	A249	6c multicolored	.80	.25
972	A249	16c multicolored	1.15	.60
973	A249	22c multicolored	1.20	1.10
974	A249	27c multicolored	1.30	1.05
975	A249	37c multicolored	1.60	2.60
		Nos. 971-975 (5)	6.05	5.60

Marine Life — A250

No. 976: a, Pelagia noctiluca (jellyfish). b, Thalassoma pavo (fish with green stripes). c, Sepia officinalis (squid.) d, Sphaerechinus granularis (sea urchin). e, Epinephelus guaza (large fish). f, Diplodus vulgaris (fish with black stripes). g, Astroides calycularis (corals). h, Maia squinado (crab). i, Coris julis (fish with orange stripes). j, Octopus vulgaris (octopus). k, Charonia variegata (shell). l, Sparisoma cretense (red, green and blue fish). m, Hippocampus ramulosus (seahorse). n, Dardanus arrosor (hermit crab). o, Muraena helena (moray eel). p, Echinaster sepositus (starfish).

Perf. 13¾
1999, Aug. 25   Litho.   Unwmk.
976		Sheet of 16	11.00	14.50
a.-p.	A250	6c Any single	.75	.80

Animal names are on sheet margin only.

Uprising Against France, 200th Anniv. — A251

No. 977, Father Mikiel Scerri. No. 978, Sculpture. No. 979, French Gen. Belgrand de Vaubois. No. 980, British Capt. Alexander Ball.

1999, Oct. 6   Litho.   Perf. 14
977	A251	6c multicolored	.60	.70
978	A251	6c multicolored	.60	.70
a.		Pair, #977-978	1.65	1.90
979	A251	16c multicolored	1.05	1.40
980	A251	16c multicolored	1.05	1.40
a.		Pair, #979-980	2.75	3.75
		Nos. 977-980 (4)	3.30	4.20

Crowning of Painting of Our Lady of Mellieha, Cent. A252

6c, Crowned Madonna, vert.

1999, Oct. 6
981	A252	35c shown	1.55	1.90

Souvenir Sheet
982	A252	6c multicolored	.95	1.05

Flowers — A253

Designs: 2c, Pancratium maritimum. 4c, Iris pseudopumila. 6c, Narcissus tazetta. 16c, Crocus longiflorus. 25c, Ornithogalum arabicum. 46c, Tulipa sylvestris.

1999, Oct. 20   Litho.   Perf. 13¾
983	A253	2c multi	.30	.35
984	A253	4c multi	.30	.40
985	A253	6c multi	.30	.30
986	A253	16c multi	.70	.60
987	A253	25c multi	1.20	.95
988	A253	46c multi	2.50	1.90
		Nos. 983-988 (6)	5.30	4.50

See Nos. 1022-1027, 1061-1066, 1102-1107, 1139-1140, 1213-1214.

Christmas — A254

6c, Madonna & Child. 6c+3c, Carolers. 16c+3c, Santa Claus. 26c+3c, Tree, ornament.

1999, Nov. 27
989	A254	6c multi	.60	.80
990	A254	6c + 3c multi	.75	1.00
991	A254	16c + 3c multi	1.50	1.95
992	A254	26c + 3c multi	2.00	2.60
		Nos. 989-992 (4)	4.85	6.35

MALTA

Republic of Malta, 25th Anniv. — A255

6c, Legislative meeting room. 11c, Chambers of House of Representatives. 16c, Central Bank of Malta. 19c, Flags, aerial view of Valletta. 26c, Computer, airplane, port facilities.

1999, Dec. 10		Litho.	Perf. 14	
993	A255	6c multi	.40	.35
994	A255	11c multi	.60	.50
995	A255	16c multi	.80	.70
996	A255	19c multi	1.10	.95
997	A255	26c multi	1.40	1.20
		Nos. 993-997 (5)	4.30	3.70

Greetings — A256

Designs: 3c, Gift, roses. 6c, Roses, letter, picture frame. 16c, Heart, tulips. 20c, Clock, champagne bottle, glass. 22c, Roses, wedding rings.

Unwmk.

2000, Feb. 9		Litho.	Perf. 14	
998	A256	3c multi	.35	.25
999	A256	6c multi	.50	.40
1000	A256	16c multi	.95	.75
1001	A256	20c multi	1.00	.85
1002	A256	22c multi	1.30	1.05
		Nos. 998-1002 (5)	4.10	3.30

Malta in the 20th Century — A257

Designs: 6c, Cruise ship, small boat. 16c, Festival, musicians. 22c, Family walking, view of harbor. 27c, Farm family, Victoria Citadel, Gozo.

2000, Mar. 7			Perf. 13¾x14	
1003	A257	6c multi	.50	.50
1004	A257	16c multi	1.00	1.00
1005	A257	22c multi	1.25	1.25
1006	A257	27c multi	1.75	1.75
		Nos. 1003-1006 (4)	4.50	4.50

Sports — A258

Designs: 6c, Soccer players, trophy. 16c, Swimmer, sailboats. 26c, Judo, shooting, runners. 37c, Soccer players.

2000, Mar. 28			Perf. 14	
1007	A258	6c multi	.45	.30
1008	A258	16c multi	.80	.60
1009	A258	26c multi	1.20	1.20
1010	A258	37c multi	1.40	2.30
		Nos. 1007-1010 (1)	3.85	4.40

Malta Soccer Assoc., cent. (6c); 2000 Summer Olympics, Sydney (16c, 26c); European Soccer Championships (37c).

Europa, 2000 Common Design Type

2000, May 9			Perf. 14	
		Color of Large "E"		
1011	CD17	16c green	.85	.70
1012	CD17	46c blue	1.90	3.65

Air Transportation, Cent. — A259

No. 1013, D. H. 66 Hercules, 1928. No. 1014, Zeppelin LZ-127, 1933. No. 1015, Douglas DC-3 Dakota, 1949. No. 1016, Airbus A320.

2000, July 28				
1013	A259	6c multi	.50	.80
1014	A259	6c multi	.50	.80
a.		Pair, #1013-1014	1.40	2.30
1015	A259	16c multi	.95	1.50
1016	A259	16c multi	.95	1.50
a.		Pair, #1015-1016	2.75	4.25
b.		Souvenir sheet, #1013-1016	3.85	6.00
		Nos. 1013-1016 (4)	2.90	4.60

Fireworks A260

Denominations: 2c, 6c, 16c, 20c, 50c.

2000, July 19		Litho.	Perf. 13¾x14	
1017-1021	A260	Set of 5	3.85	6.00

Flower Type of 1999

Designs: 1c, Helichrysum melitense. 3c, Cistus creticus. 10c, Rosa sempervirens. 12c, Cynara cardunculus. 20c, Anacamptis pyramidalis. £2, Adonis microcarpa.

2000, Sept. 13		Litho.	Perf. 13¾	
1022	A253	1c multi	.30	.25
1023	A253	3c multi	.30	.55
1024	A253	10c multi	.45	.40
1025	A253	12c multi	.55	.50
1026	A253	20c multi	1.10	.80
1027	A253	£2 multi	8.75	5.50
		Nos. 1022-1027 (6)	11.45	8.00

Stampin' the Future Children's Stamp Design Contest Winners — A261

Artwork by: No. 1028, Bettina Paris. No. 1029, Roxana Caruana. No. 1030, Jean Paul Zammit. No. 1031, Chiara Borg.

2000, Oct. 18			Perf. 14x13¾	
1028-1031	A261	6c Set of 4	2.20	2.65

See also Nos. 1250, B85.

Christmas A262

Designs: 6c, Children, Holy Family. 6c+3c, Magi. 16c+3c, Christmas tree, Santa Claus, family. 26c, Christmas tree, church, family.

2000, Nov. 18		Litho.	Perf. 14	
1032-1035	A262	Set of 4	5.25	6.50
1035a		Souv. sheet, #1032-1035	5.25	7.00

Size of No. 1033: 23x27mm.

Carnival A263

Various scenes and cartoon mascots at LL with: 6c, Horn. 11c, Guitar, vert. 16c, Drum, vert. 19c, Tambourine, vert. 27c, Flute.

No. 1041 a, 12c, Clowns (black and white photo), mascot with tambourine, b, 37c, Clowns (color photo), mascot with drum.

Perf. 13¾x14, 14x13¾

2001, Feb. 23			Litho.	
1036-1040	A263	Set of 5	4.75	4.75

Souvenir Sheet Perf. 13¾

| 1041 | A263 | Sheet of 2, #a-b | 2.50 | 3.85 |

No. 1041 contains two 34x34mm stamps.

Lighthouses — A264

Designs: 6c, Sant'lermu. 16c, Gurdan. 22c, Delimara.

2001, Mar. 21			Perf. 14x13¾	
1042-1044	A264	Set of 3	3.60	3.30

Paintings by Edward Caruana Dingli — A265

Denominations: 2c, 4c, 6c, 10c, 26c.

2001, Apr. 18				
1045-1049	A265	Set of 5	3.00	4.25

Visit of Pope John Paul II — A266

Designs: 6c, Nazju Falzon, Gorg Preca, and Adeodata Pisani, Maltese beatified by Pope. 16c, Pope, statue. 75c, Falzon, Preca, Pisani and Pope.

2001, May 4			Perf. 14	
1050-1051	A266	Set of 2	2.25	1.90

Souvenir Sheet

| 1052 | A266 | 75c multi | 5.50 | 6.00 |

Europa — A267

Designs: 16c, Discoglossus pictus. 46c, Sympetrum fonscolombii.

2001, May 23		Litho.	Perf. 14x14¼	
1053-1054	A267	Set of 2	2.75	2.75

Birds A268

No. 1055: a, Larus cachinnans. b, Falco tinnunculus. c, Oriolus oriolus. d, Fringilla coelebs. e, Monticola solitarius. f, Merops apiaster. g, Hirundo rustica. h, Passer hispaniolensis. i, Sylvia conspicillata. j, Streptopelia turtur. k, Anas acuta. l, Ixobrychus minutus. m, Scolopax rusticola. n, Asio flammeus. o, Vanellus vanellus. p, Gallinula chloropus.

2001, June 22		Litho.	Perf. 13¾	
1055	A268	6c Sheet of 16, #a-p	15.50	15.50

Musical Instruments — A269

Designs: 1c, Whistle flute. 3c, Reed pipe. 14c, Maltese bagpipe. 20c, Friction drum. 25c, Frame drum.

2001, Aug. 22		Litho.	Perf. 13¾	
1056-1060	A269	Set of 5	3.25	4.25

Flower Type of 1999

Designs: 5c, Papaver rhoeas. 11c, Silene colorata. 19c, Anthemis arvensis. 27c, Borago officinalis. 50c, Chrysanthemum coronarium. £1, Malva sylvestris.

2001, Sept. 19				
1061-1066	A253	Set of 6	14.00	10.00

See No. 1269A.

Dogs — A270

Designs: 6c, Kelb tal-Fenek. 16c, Kelb tal-Kacca. 19c, Maltese. 35c, Kelb tal-But.

2001, Oct. 20		Litho.	Perf. 14	
1067-1070	A270	Set of 4	6.50	6.00

Worldwide Fund for Nature (WWF) — A271

Seahorses: No. 1071, 6c, Hippocampus guttulatus. No. 1072, 6c, Hippocampus hippocampus. No. 1073, 16c, Hippocampus guttulatus, diff. No. 1074, 16c, Hippocampus hippocampus, diff.

2002		Litho.	Perf. 14¼x14	
1071-1074	A271	Set of 4	3.00	5.00

Antique Furniture A272

Designs: 2c, Credenza. 4c, Bureau, vert. 11c, Table, vert. 26c, Armoire, vert. 60c, Credenza, diff.

2002, Mar. 27		Litho.	Perf. 14	
1075-1079	A272	Set of 5	5.25	7.00

Europa — A273

2002, May 9		Litho.	Perf. 14	
1080	A273	16c multi	1.40	1.10

Butterflies and Moths — A274

No. 1081: a, Hyles sammuii. b, Utetheisa pulchella. c, Ophiusa tirhaca. d, Phragmatobia fulginosa melitensis. e, Vanessa cardui. f, Polyommatus icarus. g, Gonepteryx cleopatra. h, Vanessa atalanta. i, Eucrostes indigenata. j, Macroglossum stellatarum. k, Lasiocampa quercus. l, Catoeala elocata. m, Maniola jurtina hyperhispulla. n, Pieris brassicae. o, Papilio machaon melitensis. p, Danaus chrysippus.

MALTA

2002, June — Perf. 13¾
1081 A274 6c Sheet of 16, #a-p   9.25 12.00

Maltese Cuisine — A275
Designs: 7c, Kusksu bil-ful. 12c, Qaqocc mimli. 16c, Lampuki. 27c, Qaghqa tal-kavatelli. 75c, Stuffat tal-fenek.

2002, Aug. 13 Litho. Perf. 14
1082-1085 A275 Set of 4   3.30 4.25
Souvenir Sheet
1086 A275 75c multi   4.50 6.00

Succulent Plants — A276
Designs: 1c, Yavia cryptocarpa. 7c, Aztekium hintonii, vert. 28c, Pseudolithos migiurtinus. 37c, Pierrebraunia brauniorum. 76c, Euphorbia turbiniformis.

2002, Sept. 25
1087-1091 A276 Set of 5   6.50 8.75

Famous Men — A277
Designs: 3c, Adrian Dingli (1817-1900), legislator. 7c, Oreste Kirkop (1923-98), opera singer. 15c, Father Athanasius Kircher (1602-80), vulcanologist. 35c, Father Saverio Cassar (1746-1805), Gozo Uprising leader. 50c, Emmanuele Vitale (1759-1802), commander in uprising against the French.

2002, Oct. 18 Litho. Perf. 14
1092-1096 A277 Set of 5   6.50 7.75

Christmas A278
Designs: 7c, Mary and Joseph in donkey cart. 16c, Angels, Magi, Holy Family in bus. 22c, Shepherds in field, Holy family on boat. 37c, Shepherds in field, Holy family in horse-drawn carriage. 75c, Angel, Magi, Holy Family and animals on galley.

2002, Nov. 20
1097-1101 A278 Set of 5   9.00 8.75

Flower Type of 1999
Designs: 7c, Vitex agnus-castus. 22c, Spartium junceum. 28c, Crataegus azalorus. 37c, Cercis siliquastrum. 45c, Myrtus communis. 76c, Pistacia lentiscus.

2003, Jan. 30 Perf. 13¾
1102 A253 7c multi   .55 .70
1103 A253 22c multi   1.90 1.85
1104 A253 28c multi   1.90 1.65
1105 A253 37c multi   2.50 1.60
1106 A253 45c multi   2.50 1.90
1107 A253 76c multi   5.50 3.25
  Nos. 1102-1107 (6)   14.85 10.95

Automobiles A279
Designs: 2c, 1965 Vanden Plas Princess. 7c, 1948 Allard "M" Type. 10c, 1904 Cadillac Model B. 26c, 1936 Fiat Cinquecento Model A Topolino. 35c, 1965 Ford Anglia Super.

2003, Feb. 26 Litho. Perf. 14
1108-1112 A279 Set of 5   4.50 5.75

Military Architecture A280
Designs: 1c, Fort St. Elmo. 4c, Rinella Battery. 11c, Fort St. Angelo. 16c, Reserve Post R15. 44c, Fort Tigné.

2003, Mar. 21 Litho. Perf. 14
1113-1117 A280 Set of 5   4.50 5.00

Martyrdom of St. George, 1700th Anniv. — A281
Various paintings depicting St. George: 3c, 7c, 14c, 19c, 27c.

2003, Apr. 23
1118-1122 A281 Set of 5   3.75 4.50

Europa — A282
Poster art: 16c, Cisk Beer. 46c, 1939 Carnival.

2003, May 9
1123-1124 A282 Set of 2   2.75 2.00

Games of Small European States — A283
Designs: 25c, Track and field. 50c, Shooting. 75c, Volleyball. £3, Swimming.

2003, May 21 Litho. Perf. 14x14¼
1125-1128 A283 Set of 4   20.00 22.00

Coronation of Queen Elizabeth II, 50th Anniv. — A284
Queen Elizabeth II: 12c, With woman. 15c, Seated in limousine. 22c, With Prince Philip, reading book. 60c, With Prince Philip, receiving book from man. £1, Queen and crowd of people.

2003, June 3
1129-1132 A284 Set of 4   4.50 4.50
Souvenir Sheet
1133 A284 £1 multi   6.00 8.25

Souvenir Sheet
Valletta Bastions A285

2003, July 1 Litho. Perf. 14x13¾
1134 A285 £1.50 multi + 4 labels   6.75 7.75
Elton John concert, July 6, 2003.

Shells A286
No. 1135: a, Chlamys pesfelis. b, Gyroscala lamellosa. c, Phalium granulatum. d, Fusiturris similis. e, Luria lurida. f, Bolinus brandaris. g, Charonia tritonis variegata. h, Clanculus corallinus. i, Fusinus syracusanus. j, Pinna nobilis. k, Acanthocardia tuberculata. l, Aporrhais pespelicani. m, Haliotis tuberculata lamellosa. n, Tonna galea. o, Spondylus gaederopus. p, Mitra zonata.

2003, Aug. 20 Litho. Perf. 13¾
1135 A286 7c Sheet of 16, #a-p   7.75 11.00

Sailboats A287
Designs: 8c, Malta-Syracuse Race. 22c, Middle Sea Race, vert. 35c, Royal Malta Yacht Club, vert.

2003, Sept. 30 Litho. Perf. 14
1136-1138 A287 Set of 3   4.00 4.50

Flower Type of 1999
Designs: 7c, Vitex agnus-castus. 16c, Crocus longiflorus.

Booklet Stamps
Size: 23x23mm

Serpentine Die Cut 12½ on 2 or 3 Sides
2003, Oct. 22 Self-Adhesive
1139 A253 7c multi   .75 .65
  a. Booklet pane of 12   7.75
1140 A253 16c multi   1.65 1.90
  a. Booklet pane of 6   8.75

Windmills A288
Designs: 11c, Is-Sur ta'San Mikiel, Valletta. 27c, Ta'Kola, Xaghra, vert. 45c, Tax-Xarolla, Zurrieq, vert.

2003, Oct. 29 Perf. 14
1141-1143 A288 Set of 3   5.50 6.00

Christmas — A289
Designs: 7c, The Annunciation, vert. 16c, Holy Family, vert. 22c, Adoration of the Magi. 50c, Adoration of the Magi.

2003, Nov. 12
1144-1147 A289 Set of 4   5.75 6.00

Letter Boxes — A290
Boxes from era of: 1c, Queen Victoria. 16c, King Edward VII. 22c, King George V, King George VI. 37c, Queen Elizabeth II. 76c, Independent Malta (Malta Post).

2004, Mar. 12
1148-1152 A290 Set of 5   11.00 11.00

Cats — A291
Various cats with denominations and country name in: 7c, Golden brown. 27c, Dark brown. 28c, Lilac. 50c, Red brown. 60c, Green.

2004, Mar. 26 Perf. 13¾
1153-1157 A291 Set of 5   11.00 11.00

Souvenir Sheet

Salesians in Malta, Cent. — A292

2004, Apr. 7 Perf. 14
1158 A292 75c multi   3.85 4.50

Fauna A293
No. 1159: a, Pipistrellus pygmaeus. b, Myotis blythi punicus. c, Mustela nivalis. d, Atelerix algirus fallax. e, Chamaeleo chamaeleon. f, Crocidura sicula. g, Chalcides ocellatus. h, Podarcis filfolensis filfolensis. i, Tarentola mauritanica. j, Hemidactylus turcicus. k, Elaphe situla. l, Coluber viridiflavus. m, Delphinus delphis. n, Stenella coeruleoalba. o, Monachus monachus. p, Chelonia mydas.

2004, Apr. 21 Perf. 13¾
1159 A293 16c Sheet of 16, #a-p   14.50 16.50

Admission to European Union — A294
Stars, map of Europe and: 16c, Flags of newly-admitted countries. 28c, Officials signing treaty.

2004, May 1 Perf. 14
1160-1161 A294 Set of 2   2.75 2.75

Europa A295
Designs: 16c, Youths jumping into water. 51c, People at archaeological site.

2004, May 19 Perf. 13¾x14
1162-1163 A295 Set of 2   4.00 4.00

Wayside Chapels A296
Designs: 3c, Lunzjata-Hal Milliere, Zurrieq. 7c, San Basilju, Mqabba. 39c, San Cir, Rabat.

MALTA

48c, Santa Lucija, Mtarfa. 66c, Ta' Santa Marija, Kemmuna.

2004, June 16	Litho.	Perf. 14
1164-1168 A296	Set of 5	10.00 11.00

Trams — A297

Designs: 19c, Side view of tram. 37c, Tram and conductor (22x40mm). 50c, Ticket (22x40mm). 75c, Tram and archway.

Perf. 13¾, 14 (37c, 50c)
2004, July 14
1169-1172 A297 Set of 4 11.00 11.50

2004 Summer Olympics, Athens — A298

Designs: 11c, Discus thrower. 16c, Doric column, olive wreath. 76c, Javelin thrower.

Perf. 14¼
2004, Aug. 13 Litho. Unwmk.
1173-1175 A298 Set of 3 7.00 7.50

Religious Festivals A299

Designs: 5c, Ascension Day. 15c, St. Gregory's Day. 27c, Pilgrimage on First Sunday in Lent. 51c, St. Martin's Day, vert. £1, Feast of Sts. Peter and Paul, vert.

Perf. 14x14¼, 14¼x14
2004, Sept. 15 Wmk. 354
1176-1180 A299 Set of 5 13.50 13.50

Works of Art — A300

Designs: 2c, Church of St. Mary, Attard. 20c, Mdina Cathedral organ, music by Benignon Zerafa, vert. 57c, Statue of St. Agatha, vert. 62c, Books, illustration for poem "The Turkish Galleon," by Gian Antonio Vassallo, vert. 72c, Icon of St. Paul, vert.

Perf. 14x14¼, 14¼x14
2004, Oct. 13 Litho. Wmk. 354
1181-1184 A300 Set of 4 10.00 12.00

Souvenir Sheet

| 1185 A300 72c multi | 3.85 6.00 |

Christmas A301

Various effigies of Infant Jesus: 7c, 16c, 22c, 50c. Nos. 1187-1189 vert.

Perf. 14x14¼, 14¼x14
2004, Nov. 10 Litho. Wmk. 354
1186-1189 A301 Set of 4 6.50 6.50

Historic Maps — A302

Designs: 1c, Map of Malta by Abbé Jean Quintin, 1536. 12c, Map of Malta by Antonio Lafreri, 1551. 37c, Fresco map of Malta, by Matteo Perez d'Aleccio, 1565. £1.02, Map of Gozo, Comino, Cominotto and Marfa Peninsula, by Fr. Luigi Bartolo, 1745.

Wmk. 354
2005, Jan. 19 Litho. Perf. 14
1190-1193 A302 Set of 4 10.00 11.00

Rotary International, Cent. — A303

Rotary emblem and: 27c, Dar il-Kaptan Home, Mtarfa, woman, man. 76c, Map of Malta.

Perf. 14x14¼
2005, Feb. 23 Litho. Wmk. 354
1194-1195 A303 Set of 2 5.00 7.75

Hans Christian Andersen (1805-75), Author A304

Paper Cutting by Andersen, Scissors A305

Designs: 60c, Pen, inkwell, illustration of duckling, manuscript handwritten by Andersen. 75c, Andersen's drawing of Casino dell'Orlogio, Rome, and boots.

Perf. 14x13¾
2005, Mar. 3 Litho. Wmk. 354
1196 A304 7c gray & black .40 .50
1197 A305 22c blue & black 1.00 1.25
1198 A305 60c multi 2.90 3.50
1199 A305 75c multi 3.50 4.25
Nos. 1196-1199 (4) 7.80 9.50

See Denmark Nos. 1323-1326.

Pope John Paul II (1920-2005) — A306

2005, Apr. 15 Perf. 14
1200 A306 51c multi 4.00 4.00

Miniature Sheet

Insects A307

No. 1201: a, Coccinella septempunctata. b, Chrysoperla carnea. c, Apis mellifera. d, Crocothermis erythraea. e, Anax imperator. f, Lampyris pallida. g, Henosepilachna elaterii. h, Forficula decipiens. i, Mantis religiosa. j, Eumenes lunulatus. k, Cerambyx cerdo. l, Gryllus bimaculatus. m, Xylocopa violacea. n, Cicada orni. o, Acrida ungarica. p, Oryctes nasicornis.

2005, Apr. 20 Perf. 14¼
1201 A307 16c Sheet of 16, #a-p 17.50 17.50

Europa — A308

Designs: 16c, Stuffed peppers, zucchini and eggplant. 51c, Fried rabbit in wine and garlic.

2005, May 9 Perf. 14¼x14
1202-1203 A308 Set of 2 4.00 4.75

Paintings Depicting St. Catherine A309

Designs: No. 1204, 28c, The Beheading of St. Catherine, by unknown artist. No. 1205, 28c, The Martyrdom of St. Catherine, by Mattia Preti, vert. No. 1206, 45c, St. Catherine Disputing the Philosophers, by Francesco Zahra. No. 1207, 45c, Mystic Marriage, by Sahra, vert.

Perf. 14x14¼, 14¼x14
2005, June 15 Litho. Wmk. 354
1204-1207 A309 Set of 4 6.50 8.25

Famous People — A310

Designs: 3c, Monsignor Michael Azzopardi (1910-87), religious educator. 19c, Egidio Lapira (1897-1970), dental surgeon. 20c, Petition of Guzeppi Callus (1505-61), doctor executed for taxation opposition. 46c, Hand and quill pen of Geronimo Matteo Abos (1715-60), composer. 76c, Gio Francesco Abela (1592-1655), historian, ambassador.

Wmk. 354
2005, July 13 Litho. Perf. 14¼
1208-1212 A310 Set of 5 7.25 9.00

Flower Type of 1999 Redrawn

Design: 7c, Vitex agnus-castus. 16c, Crocus longiflorus.

2005 Litho. Perf. 14¼
1213 A253 7c multi + label .50 .25
1214 A253 16c multi + label .90 .60

Nos. 1213-1214 have "2005" year date and "Printex Ltd" inscription at lower right. Additionally, No. 1213 has wider distance between denomination and country name than No. 1102, and No. 1214 has denomination and country name in a different font than No. 986. Nos. 1213-1214 were issued in sheets of 10 stamps and 10 labels. Labels could be personalized for an additional fee.

Horses and Mules at Work — A311

Designs: 11c, Horse-drawn hearse. 15c, Mule pulling plow. 62c, Mule at grindstone. 66c, Horse pulling cart.

Perf. 14x14¼
2005, Aug. 19 Litho. Wmk. 354
1215-1218 A311 Set of 4 8.00 10.00

End of World War II, 60th Anniv. — A312

Scenes from Battle of Malta: 2c, Civilians on food line. 5c, Royal Navy ships under attack. 25c, Anti-aircraft gunners. 51c, Aviators and planes. £1, Tanker "Ohio."

2005, Sept. 23
1219-1223 A312 Set of 5 15.00 14.50

Christmas A313

Mosaics of paintings by Envin Cremona from National Sanctuary of Our Lady of Ta' Pinu, Gozo: 7c, Nativity. 16c, Annunciation, vert. 22c, Adoration of the Magi. 50c, Flight into Egypt (68x27mm).

Perf. 14¼, 13¾x14 (50c)
2005, Oct. 12 Litho. Wmk. 354
1224-1227 A313 Set of 4 6.75 7.50

Souvenir Sheets

Commonwealth Heads of Governments Meeting — A314

Flags of Malta, British Commonwealth and: 14c, Commonwealth Heads of Government flag. 28c, Doves. 37c, Maltese cross. 75c, People.

Perf. 14x14¼
2005, Nov. 23 Litho. Wmk. 354
1228-1231 A314 Set of 4 8.00 8.00

Souvenir Sheet

Europa Stamps, 50th Anniv. A315

No. 1232: a, 5c, #677. b, 13c, #628. c, 23c, #540. d, 24c, #738.

2006, Jan. 3 Perf. 13¾x14
1232 A315 Sheet of 4, #a-d 3.25 5.00

Ceramics — A316

Designs: 7c, Neolithic terra-cotta female figurine. 16c, Roman terra-cotta head. 28c, Terra-cotta oil lamp holder. 37c, Sicilian maiolica plate. 60c, Stylized figure in traditional Maltese costume, by Ianni Bonnici.

Wmk. 354
2006, Feb. 25 Litho. Perf. 14¼
1233-1237 A316 Set of 5 8.00 9.25

Miniature Sheet

Pets A317

MALTA

No. 1238: a, Shetland pony. b, Chihuahua. c, Goldfish. d, Siamese cat. e, Siamese fighting fish. f, Ferret. g, Canary. h, Turtle. i, Chinchilla. j, Parakeet. k, Rabbit. l, Zebra finch. m, Pointer. n, Pigeon. o, Guinea pig. p, House cat.

Wmk. 354
2006, Mar. 14   **Litho.**   **Perf. 14¼**
1238   A317   Sheet of 16   15.50   16.50
   a.-h.   7c Any single   .95   1.00
   i.-p.   22c Any single   .95   1.00

Traditional Holy Week Celebrations — A318

Designs: 7c, Men carrying crosses. 15c, Men carrying crucifixion scene. 22c, Float. 27c, Men pulling statue of Jesus. 82c, Decorated altar.

2006, Apr. 12   **Perf. 14¼x14**
1239-1243   A318   Set of 5   8.50   8.50

Europa — A319

Designs: 16c, Shown. 51c, Stick figures, diff. (28x41mm).

Perf. 14¼, 14¼x14 (51c)
2006, May 9
1244-1245   A319   Set of 2   3.50   4.00

2006 World Cup Soccer Championships, Germany — A320

Designs: 7c, Bobby Charlton. 16c, Pelé. 27c, Franz Beckenbauer. 76c, Dino Zoff.

2006, June 2   **Perf. 14¼x14**
1246-1249   A320   Set of 4   5.00   6.00
   1249a   Souvenir sheet, #1246-1249   5.50   5.50

Stampin' The Future Type of 2000 Souvenir Sheet

2006, June 5   **Perf. 14**
1250   A261   £1.50 Like #1028   7.00   7.00

Ten percent of the sale went to the Rainforest Foundation.

Naval Vessels — A321

Designs: 8c, Gran Carraca di Rodi. 29c, Guillaume Tell (HMS Malta). 51c, USS Constitution. 76c, HMS Dreadnought. £1, Slava and USS Belknap.

Wmk. 354
2006, Aug. 18   **Litho.**   **Perf. 14¼**
1251-1255   A321   Set of 5   16.50   17.50

Greetings — A322

Inscriptions: 8c, Happy Birthday. 16c, Happy Anniversary. 27c, Congratulations. 37c, Best Wishes.

2006, Sept. 18
1256-1259   A322   Set of 4   4.25   4.50

Castles and Towers — A323

Designs: 7c, Wignacourt Tower. 16c, Verdala Castle. 27c, San Lucjan Tower. 37c, Kemmuna Tower. £1, Selmun Castle.

Perf. 14x14¼
2006, Sept. 29   **Litho.**   **Wmk. 354**
1260-1264   A323   Set of 5   12.00   12.00

Christmas A324

Designs: 8c, Paolino Vassallo (1856-1923), composer of "Inno per Natale," Nativity. 16c, Carmelo Pace (1906-93), composer of "They Heard the Angels," Magi on camels. 22c, Paul Nani (1906-86), composer of "Maltese Christmas," angels. 27c, Carlo Diacono (1876-1942), composer of "Notte di Natale," shepherds and angel. 50c, Wolfgang Amadeus Mozart (1756-91), composer of "Alma Dei Creatoris."

2006, Nov. 6   **Perf. 14¼**
1265-1268   A324   Set of 4   4.50   4.25

Souvenir Sheet
Perf. 13¾
1269   A324   50c multi   3.50   3.75

No. 1269 contains one 40x30mm stamp.

Flower Type of 1999 Redrawn
2006   **Litho.**   **Wmk. 354**   **Perf. 14¼**
1269A   A253   1c Like #1022   .45   .55

No. 1269A has a "2006" year date and "Printex Ltd." inscription at lower right. Additionally, the country name has a different font than No. 1022, with the lines in the lettering being of equal thickness throughout the letter on No. 1269A. Other differences in the vignette exist.

Due to the scheduled conversion to the euro on Jan. 1, 2008, Nos. 1270-1274 and all stamps issued in 2007 will show denominations in pounds and the not-yet-circulating euros.

Crafts — A325

Designs: 8c, Wrought iron window guard, blacksmith and anvil. 16c, Glass ornamental objects, glassblower. 22c, Filigree pendant, silversmith. 37c, Pottery, potter. 60c, Reed baskets, basket maker.

2006, Dec. 29   **Perf. 14¼**
1270-1274   A325   Set of 5   8.75   8.50

Sculptures from 3000-2500 B.C. — A326

Designs: 15c, Human head. 29c, Animals, horiz. 60c, Spirals, horiz. £1.50, Headless nude female.

Wmk. 354
2007, Feb. 28   **Litho.**   **Perf. 14¼**
1275-1278   A326   Set of 4   13.75   15.50

Miniature Sheet

Fruit A327

No. 1279: a, Opuntia ficus-indica (prickly pears). b, Viris vinifera (grapes). c, Eriobotrya japonica (loquats). d, Morus nigra (black mulberries). e, Ficus carica (figs). f, Citrus limonum (lemons). g, Pyrus communis (pear). h, Prunus persica (peaches). i, Punica granatum (pomegranates). j, Prunus salicina (plums). k, Citrullus vulgaris (watermelons). l, Citrus sinensis (orange). m, Olea europaea (olives). n, Lycopersicon esculentum (tomatoes). o, Malus domestica (apples). p, Cucumis melo (cantaloupe).

2007, Apr. 16
1279   A327   8c Sheet of 16, #a-p   9.50   9.50

Balconies — A328

Designs: 8c, Wrought iron balcony. 22c, Stone balcony. 27c, Balustraded balcony, National Library. 29c, Closed wooden balcony. 46c, Art Deco balcony by Silvio Mercieca. 51c, Ornamented balcony, Hostel de Verdelin, Valletta, horiz.

Wmk. 354
2007, Apr. 28   **Litho.**   **Perf. 14¼**
1280-1284   A328   Set of 5   8.50   8.50

Souvenir Sheet
Perf. 13¾
1285   A328   51c multi   3.25   4.25

No. 1285 contains one 37x28mm stamp.

Europa — A329

Emblems of Scout Association of Malta, Scouting Centenary and: 16c, Lord Robert Baden-Powell. 51c, Maltese scouts at 1957 Jamboree.

2007, May 9   **Perf. 14¼**
1286-1287   A329   Set of 2   4.50   5.00

Canonization of St. George Preca (1880-1962) — A330

Background color: 8c, Blue. £1, Orange.

Wmk. 354
2007, May 28   **Litho.**   **Perf. 14¼**
1288-1289   A330   Set of 2   6.00   8.25

Toys — A331

Photographs of children and: 2c, Rocking horse, tricycle, car. 3c, Baby carriage, drums and tops. 16c, Boats, beach pails and shovel. 22c, Dolls. 50c, Truck, motorcycle and race car.

2007, July 11   **Perf. 14¼x14**
1290-1294   A331   Set of 5   5.50   6.50

Paintings by Caravaggio A332

Designs: 5c, St. Jerome. 29c, The Beheading of St. John the Baptist (48x40mm). £2, The Beheading of St. John the Baptist, vert.

2007, July 20   **Perf. 14¼**
1295-1296   A332   Set of 2   3.25   3.00

Souvenir Sheet
1297   A332   £2 multi   13.25   16.00

Arrival of Caravaggio on Malta, 400th anniv. No. 1297 with an overprint in gold in the sheet margin marking the 400th anniv. of the death of Caravaggio was a limited edtition.

Motorcycles A333

Designs: 1c, 1954 Royal Enfield. 16c, 1941 Matchless G3/L. 27c, 1903 Minerva. 50c, 1965 Triumph Speed Twin.

Perf. 14x14¼
2007, Sept. 12   **Litho.**   **Wmk. 354**
1298-1301   A333   Set of 4   7.50   7.50

Greetings Stamps — A334

2007, Sept. 28   **Perf. 14¼**
1302   A334   8c Hearts   .55   .55
   a.   Sheet of 5 + 5 labels   13.50   13.50
1303   A334   8c Stars   .55   .55
   a.   Sheet of 5 + 5 labels   13.50   13.50
1304   A334   8c Roses   .55   .55
   a.   Sheet of 5 + 5 labels   13.50   13.50
1305   A334   8c Balloons   .55   .55
   a.   Sheet of 5 + 5 labels   13.50   13.50
1306   A334   8c Champagne flutes   .55   .55
   a.   Sheet of 5 + 5 labels   13.50   13.50
1307   A334   8c Teddy bears   .55   .55
   a.   Sheet of 5 + 5 labels   13.50   13.50
   Nos. 1302-1307 (6)   3.30   3.30

Labels on Nos. 1302a-1307a were personalizable, with full sheets each selling for £2, with a minimum purchase of two sheets of any stamp.

Paintings by John Martin Borg — A335

Designs: 11c, Mdina Skyline. 16c, Qrendi. 37c, Vittoriosa Waterfront. 46c, Mgarr Harbor, Gozo. 76c, Xlendi Bay, Gozo.

2007, Oct. 1   **Perf. 14¼**
1308-1312   A335   Set of 5   13.75   14.50

Fruit Type of 2007
Souvenir Sheet
2007, Oct. 18
1313   A327   75c Like #1279m   4.75   6.00

National Tree Planting Weekend. An unspecified portion of the proceeds of the sale went to the 34U Campaign.

MALTA

Bands — A336

Various bands: 4c, 15c, 21c, 22c, £1.

2007, Nov. 13
1314-1318 A336 Set of 5 12.00 12.00

Christmas — A337

Maltese arms and nave paintings in St. Andrew's Church, Luqa, by Giuseppe Cali: 8c, Madonna and Child. 16c, Holy Family with Women and Young Girl. 21c, Infant Jesus and Young Girl.

2007, Nov. 20
1319-1321 A337 Set of 3 4.00 4.00

See Vatican City Nos. 1370-1372.

Youth Soccer Association, 25th Anniv. — A338

Society of Christian Doctrine Museum, Cent. — A339

Religious Figures — A340

Treaty of Rome, 50th Anniv. A341

Designs: 16c, Monsignor Frangisk Bonnici (1852-1905), founder of St. Joseph Institute, Hamrun. 43c, Father Manwel Magri (1851-1907), ethnographer and archaeologist. 86c, Carolina Cauchi (1824-1907), founder of Dominican Sisters of Malta.

Wmk. 354
2007, Dec. 1 **Litho.** **Perf. 14¼**
1322 A338 4m multi .30 .25
1323 A339 9c multi .60 .60
1324 A340 16c multi 1.10 1.10
1325 A340 43c multi 3.00 3.00
1326 A340 86c multi 6.00 6.00
Nos. 1322-1326 (5) 11.00 10.95

Souvenir Sheet
Perf. 13¾
1327 A341 76c multi 5.00 6.75

No. 1327 contains one 40x30mm stamp.

Souvenir Sheet

Obverse and Reverse of Maltese Pound Coin A342

Wmk. 354
2007, Dec. 31 **Litho.** **Perf. 14¼**
1328 A342 £1 multi 5.50 5.50

Last day of use of pound currency.

100 Cents = 1 Euro
Souvenir Sheet

Introduction of Euro Currency — A343

No. 1329: a, Statue of Aphrodite, map of Cyprus. b, Sleeping Lady statue.

Wmk. 354
2008, Jan. 1 **Litho.** **Perf. 14¼**
1329 A343 €1 Sheet of 2, #a-b 3.75 4.75

See Cyprus No. 1088.

Souvenir Sheet

Obverse and Reverse of Maltese Euro Coin A344

2008, Jan. 1
1330 A344 €1 multi 5.50 6.75

Door Knockers — A345

Various door knockers with background color of: 26c, Blue. 51c, Red. 63c, Brown. €1.77, Green.

2008, Mar. 5 **Perf. 14¼x14**
1331-1334 A345 Set of 4 10.50 10.50

2008 Summer Olympics, Beijing — A346

Designs: 5c, Shooting. 12c, Swimming. €1.57, Running.

2008, Mar. 7 **Perf. 14x14¼**
1335-1337 A346 Set of 3 5.50 7.25

Europa A347

Mail room, postman with bicycle in: 37c, Sepia. €1.19, Black.

Wmk. 354
2008, May 9 **Litho.** **Perf. 14¼**
1338-1339 A347 Set of 2 5.50 5.50

Birth of St. Paul, 2000th Anniv. — A348

Statues depicting St. Paul from: 19c, Conversion of St. Paul Church, Safi. 68c, St. Paul's Shipwreck Church, Munxar. €1.08, St. Paul's Shipwreck Church, Rabat. €3, St. Paul's Shipwreck Church, Valletta.

2008, June 28
1340-1342 A348 Set of 3 7.00 7.00

Souvenir Sheet
1343 A348 €3 multi 7.50 7.50

Intl. Year of Planet Earth — A349

Emblem and: 7c, Sand dune. 86c, Tree in field. €1, Earth. €1.77, Sea coast.

Wmk. 354
2008, Aug. 11 **Litho.** **Perf. 14¼**
1344-1347 A349 Set of 4 12.00 12.00

Cruise Liners — A350

Designs: 63c, MSC Musica. €1.16, M.S. Voyager of the Seas. €1.40, M. S. Westerdam. €3, RMS Queen Elizabeth 2.

Perf. 14x14¼
2008, Nov. 18 **Litho.** **Wmk. 354**
1348-1351 A350 Set of 4 17.50 17.50

Christmas A351

Paintings: 19c, Madonna and Child with the Infant St. John the Baptist, by Francesco Trevisani. 26c, Nativity, by Master Alberto. 37c, Virgin and Child with the Infant St. John the Baptist, by Carlo Maratta.

2008, Nov. 27 **Perf. 14¼**
1352-1354 A351 Set of 3 3.25 2.75

Mushrooms — A352

Designs: 5c, Laetiorus sulphureus. 12c, Montagnea arenaria. 19c, Pleurotus eryngii. 26c, Inonotus indicus. €1.57, Suillus collinitus.

Wmk. 354
2009, Mar. 27 **Litho.** **Perf. 14¼**
1355-1359 A352 Set of 5 7.00 7.00

Postal Transportation A353

Designs: 9c, Airplane. 35c, Motorcycles. €2.50, Bicycles. €3, Mail boat to Gozo.

2009, Apr. 28
1360-1363 A353 Set of 4 15.00 15.00

Introduction of Euro Currency, 10th Anniv. — A354

Wmk. 354
2009, Apr. 30 **Litho.** **Perf. 14¼**
1364 A354 €2 multi 6.00 7.50

Europa — A355

Designs: 37c, Galileo Galilei, Sketch of Moon by Galileo, Lunar Module. €1.19, Telescope of William Lassell, M42 nebula.

2009, May 9 **Perf. 14¼x14**
1365 A355 37c multi 1.65 1.20
  a. Booklet pane of 5 8.25 —
    Complete booklet, #1365a 10.00
1366 A355 €1.19 multi 3.25 4.75

Intl. Year of Astronomy.

13th Games of the Small States of Europe, Cyprus — A356

Designs: 10c, Sailing. 19c, Judo. 37c, Shooting. 67c, Swimming. €1.77, Running.

2009, June 1 **Perf. 14x14¼**
1367-1371 A356 Set of 5 10.00 11.50

Cruise Liners Type of 2008

Designs: 37c, MS Seabourn Pride. 68c, MS Brilliance of the Seas. 91c, Costa Magica and Costa Atlantica. €2, MS MSC Splendida.

2009, July 15
1372-1375 A350 Set of 4 11.00 11.00

Scenic Views — A357

Designs: 2c, Mediterranean coast. 7c, Watchtower. 37c, Salt pans, Qbajjar, Gozo. €1.02, Ggantija Templo ruins.

Perf. 14¼x14
2009, Sept. 16 **Litho.** **Wmk. 354**
1376-1379 A357 Set of 4 4.50 5.00

Christmas — A358

Designs: 19c, Mater Admirabilis, in the manner of Botticelli by unknown artist. 37c, Madonna and Child, by Corrado Giaquinto. 63c, Madonna and Child, by Follower of Simone Cantarini.

Perf. 14¼x14
2009, Nov. 30 **Litho.** **Wmk. 354**
1380-1382 A358 Set of 3 4.25 4.50

History of Malta — A359

Inscriptions: 1c, Pleistocene Period. 2c, Early Temple Period. 5c, Late Temple Period. 7c, Bronze Period. 9c, Phoenician & Punic Period, vert. 10c, Roman Period. 19c, Byzantine Period, vert. 26c, Arab Period. 37c, Norman & Hohenstaufen Period, vert. 50c, Angevin & Aragaonese, vert. 51c, Knights of St. John. 63c, French Period. 68c, British Period, vert. 86c, Independence, vert. €1, Republic,

MALTA

vert. €1.08, E.U. Accession, vert. €5, Coat of arms, vert.

2009, Dec. 29   Perf. 14x14¼, 14¼x14

1383	A359	1c multi	.30	.30
1384	A359	2c multi	.30	.30
1385	A359	5c multi	.30	.30
1386	A359	7c multi	.30	.30
1387	A359	9c multi	.45	.45
1388	A359	10c multi	.45	.45
1389	A359	19c multi	.70	.35
1390	A359	26c multi	1.00	.65
1391	A359	37c multi	1.40	.85
1392	A359	50c multi	1.90	1.90
1393	A359	51c multi	1.90	1.90
1394	A359	58c multi	1.90	1.90
1395	A359	68c multi	2.25	2.25
1396	A359	86c multi	3.25	3.25
1397	A359	€1 multi	3.75	3.75
1398	A359	€1.08 multi	3.75	3.75
1399	A359	€5 multi	17.50	18.75

    a. Souvenir sheet, #1383-1399   42.50   42.50
    Nos. 1383-1399 (17)   41.40   41.40
    See Nos. 1443-1444.

Miniature Sheet

100-Ton Guns of Malta and Gibraltar — A360

No. 1400 — 100-ton gun from: a, Fort Rinella, Malta, 2010. b, Fort Rinella, 1882. c, Napier of Magdala Battery, Gibraltar, 1880. d, Napier of Magdala Battery, 2010.

    Wmk. 354
2010, Feb. 19   Perf. 13¾
1400   A360   75c Sheet of 4, #a-d   7.75   10.00

See Gibraltar No. 1221.

Balloons — A361

Islands — A362

Mortarboard and Diploma — A363

Wedding — A364

Champagne Bottle, Bucket and Flutes — A365

Clock Tower and Fireworks — A366

Hand Holding Trophy — A367

Map of Malta — A368

    Wmk. 354
2010, Mar. 17   Litho.   Perf. 14¼

1401	A361	19c multi	.65	.65
1402	A362	19c multi	.65	.65
1403	A363	19c multi	.65	.65
1404	A364	19c multi	.65	.65
1405	A365	19c multi	.65	.65
1406	A366	19c multi	.65	.65
1407	A367	19c multi	.65	.65
1408	A368	37c multi	1.25	1.25

    Nos. 1401-1408 (8)   5.80   5.80

Souvenir Sheet

Visit of Pope Benedict XVI to Malta — A369

2010, Mar. 17
1409   A369   €3 multi   10.00   10.00

Europa — A370

Characters from children's books: 37c, Puttinu u Toninu, by Dr. Philip Farrugia Randon. €1.19, Meta I-Milied Ma Glex (When Christmas Didn't Come), by Clare Azzopardi.

2010, May 4
1410-1411	A370	Set of 2	5.50	6.00
1411a		Booklet pane of 5 #1411	8.25	—
		Complete booklet, #1411a	10.00	

2010 World Cup Soccer Championships, South Africa — A371

Designs: 63c, Flags, map of Africa. €2.50, Mascot, flag and map of South Africa.

    Wmk. 354
2010, June 11   Litho.   Perf. 14¼
1412-1413	A371	Set of 2	8.50	10.00
1413a		Souvenir sheet, #1412-1413	8.50	10.00

Intl. Year of Biodiversity — A372

Designs: 19c, Maltese wall lizard. 68c, Storm petrel, vert. 86c, Maltese pyramidal orchid, vert. €1.40, Freshwater crab.

    Perf. 14x14¼, 14¼x14
2010, Sept. 23   Litho.   Wmk. 354
1414-1417   A372   Set of 4   10.00   10.00

Coastline Features — A373

Designs: 37c, Azure Window, Gozo. 51c, Blue Grotto, Zurrieq, vert. 67c, Ta' Cenc Cliffs, Gozo, vert. €1.16, Filfla.

    Perf. 14x14¼, 14¼x14
2010, Oct. 19   Litho.   Wmk. 354
1418-1421   A373   Set of 4   9.25   9.75

Christmas — A374

Designs: 19c, The Adoration of the Magi, by the Studio of Valerio Castello. 37c, The Flight Into Egypt, attributed to Filippo Paladini. 63c, Madonna di Maggio, by Pierre Guillemin, vert.

    Perf. 14x14¼, 14¼x14
2010, Nov. 9   Litho.   Wmk. 354
1422-1424   A374   Set of 3   4.50   4.75

Compare with type A358.

Souvenir Sheet

First Malta Stamp, 150th Anniv. — A375

2010, Dec. 1   Perf. 14¼x14
1425   A375   €2.80 multi   9.50   9.50

Maltese Landscape Paintings by Edward Said — A376

Designs: 19c, Valletta. 37c, Manoel Island. €1.57, Cittadella.

    Perf. 14x14¼
2011, Mar. 9   Litho.   Wmk. 354
1426-1428   A376   Set of 3   6.00   6.00

Miniature Sheet

Worldwide Fund for Nature (WWF), 50th Anniv. — A377

Various depictions of Chimaera monstrosa: a, 51c. b, 63c. c, 67c. d, 97c.

2011, Apr. 29   Perf. 13¾
1429   A377   Sheet of 4, #a-d   9.50   9.50

Europa — A378

Forest and: 37c, Butterfly and building. €1.19, Building.

2011, May 9   Perf. 14¼x14
1430-1431   A378   Set of 2   5.50   5.75

Intl. Year of Forests.

Miniature Sheets

Buses — A379

No. 1432: a, Reo bus on B'Kara route. b, Dodge T110L bus on Zabbar route. c, Leyland Comet bus on Zurrieq route. d, Ford V8 bus on Zebbug-Siggiewi route. e, Bedford SLD bus on Gudja-Ghaxaq route. f, Maltese Chassis Gozo Mail Bus. g, Federal Bus on Kalafrana route. h, Dodge T110L bus on Siggiewi route. i, Indiana bus on Rabat route. j, Austin CXD bus on Zetjun route.
No. 1433: a, Ford V8 bus on Sliema route. b, Commer Q4 bus on Lija route. c, Fordson BB bus on Mosta-Naxxar route. d, Thornycroft Sturdy ZE bus on Mellieha route. e, Bedford QL bus on Cospicua route. f, Magirus Deutz bus for all routes. g, Commer Q4 bus on Naxxar route. h, Bedford SB8 bus on Gozo route. i, Thames ET7 bus on B'Kara-St. Julians route. j, Bedford QL private hire bus.

2011, July 2   Perf. 14x14¼
1432	A379	20c Sheet of 10, #a-j	16.50	16.50
1433	A379	69c Sheet of 10, #a-j	35.00	35.00

Boats — A380

Designs: 26c, Ferry M.V. Ta'Pinu. 37c, Ferry M.V. Jean De La Vallete. 67c, Patrol boat P23. 91c, Tugboat M.V. Spinola.

    Perf. 14x14¼
2011, Aug. 10   Litho.   Wmk. 354
1434-1437   A380   Set of 4   7.50   7.50

Souvenir Sheet

Fishing Boat at Mgarr — A381

2011, Sept. 15   Perf. 13¾
1438   A381   €2.07 multi   6.50   6.50

See Iceland No. 1245.

Christmas — A382

Paintings: 20c, The Holy Family in an Interior, by Follower of Marcello Venusti. 37c, The Madonna and Child with Infant St. John the Baptist, by the Tuscan School. 63c, The Rest on the Flight to Egypt, attributed to Circle of Pieter van Mol.

2011, Nov. 15   Wmk. 354   Perf. 14¼
1439-1441   A382   Set of 3   3.75   3.75

MALTA

Souvenir Sheet

Malta No. 114 A383

2011, Dec. 2
1442 A383 €4.16 multi 12.50 13.50
Malta Senate and Legislative Assembly, 90th anniv.

History of Malta Type of 2009
Inscriptions: 20c, Byzantine Period, vert. 69c, British Period, vert.

Perf. 14¼x14
2012, Mar. 7 Litho. Wmk. 354
1443 A359 20c multi .75 .45
1444 A359 69c multi 2.20 2.20

Paintings of Maltese Sites — A384

Designs: 20c, Marsalforn, by H. M. Bateman. 26c, Qala, by Bateman. 37c, Ghajnsielem, by Bateman, vert. 67c, Inquisitor's Palace, by Edward Lear. 97c, Gran Fontana, by Lear.

Wmk. 354
2012, Mar. 23 Litho. **Perf. 14¼**
1445-1449 A384 Set of 5 7.50 7.50

Wedding Rings — A385

Mortarboard and Diploma A386

Christmas Ornaments A387

Comino Shoreline A388

Auberge de Castille, Painting by Charles Frederick de Brocktorff A389

St. John's Co-cathedral, Valletta — A390

Trophy — A391

Champagne Bottle and Flutes — A392

2012, Apr. 3
1450 A385 37c multi 1.20 1.40
1451 A386 37c multi 1.20 1.40
1452 A387 37c multi 1.20 1.40
1453 A388 37c multi 1.20 1.40
1454 A389 37c multi 1.20 1.40
1455 A390 37c multi 1.20 1.40
1456 A391 37c multi 1.20 1.40
1457 A392 37c multi 1.20 1.40
Nos. 1450-1457 (8) 9.60 11.20

Souvenir Sheet

Awarding of George Cross to Malta, 70th Anniv. A393

2012, Apr. 14
1458 A393 €4.16 multi 10.50 14.50

Europa A394

No. 1459 — Grand Harbour: a, 37c. b, €1.19.

2012, May 9
1459 A394 Horiz. pair, #a-b 5.25 5.25

Souvenir Sheet

2012 Summer Olympics, London — A395

No. 1460 — 2012 Olympic Games: a, 37c, Emblem. b, €2.11, Mascot.

2012, July 27
1460 A395 Sheet of 2, #a-b 6.25 6.25

Ships Involved in Operation Pedestal A396

No. 1461: a, S.S. Almeria Lykes. b, H.M.S. Amazon. c, H.M.S. Antelope. d, H.M.S. Ashanti. e, H.M.S. Badsworth. f, H.M.S. Bicester. g, H.M.S. Bramham. h, M.V. Brisbane Star.
No. 1462: a, R.F.A. Brown Ranger. b, H.M.S. Cairo. c, H.M.S. Charybdis. d, M.V. Clan Ferguson. e, H.M.S. Coltsfoot. f, H.M.S. Derwent. g, M.V. Deucalion. h, R.F.A. Dingledale.
No. 1463: a, M.V. Dorset. b, H.M.S. Eagle. c, M.V. Empire Hope. d, H.M.S. Eskimo. e, H.M.S. Foresight. f, H.M.S. Furious. g, H.M.S. Fury. h, H.M.S. Geranium.
No. 1464: a, M.V. Glenorchy. b, H.M.S. Hebe. c, H.M.S. Hythe. d, H.M.S. Icarus. e, H.M.S. Indomitable. f, H.M.S. Intrepid. g, H.M.S. Ithuriel. h, H.M.S. Jaunty.
No. 1465: a, H.M.S. Jonquil. b, H.M.S. Kenya. c, H.M.S. Keppel. d, H.M.S. Laforey. e, H.M.S. Ledbury. f, H.M.S. Lightning. g, H.M.S. Lookout. h, H.M.S. Malcolm.
No. 1466: a, H.M.S. Manchester. b, H.M.S. Matchless. c, M.V. Melbourne Star. d, H.M.S. Nelson. e, H.M.S. Nigeria. f, S.S. Ohio. g, H.M.S. Pathfinder. h, H.M.S. Penn.
No. 1467: a, H.M.S. Phoebe. b, M.V. Port Chalmers. c, H.M.S. Quentin. d, M.V. Rochester Castle. e, H.M.S. Rodney. f, H.M.S. Rye. g, H.M.S. Salvonia. h, S.S. Santa Elisa.
No. 1468: a, H.M.S. Sirius. b, H.M.S. Somali. c, H.M.S. Speedy. d, H.M.S. Spirea. e, H.M.S. Tartar. f, H.M.S. Una. g, H.M.S. Utmost. h, H.M.S. Vansittart.
No. 1469: a, H.M.S. Venomous. b, H.M.S. Victorious. c, H.M.S. Vidette. d, S.S. Waimarama. e, M.V. Wairangi. f, H.M.S. Westcott. g, H.M.S. Wilton. h, H.M.S. Wishart.
No. 1470: a, H.M.S. Wolverine. b, H.M.S. Wrestler. c, H.M.S. Zetland. d, H.M.S. P.34. e, H.M.S. P.42. f, H.M.S. P.44. g, H.M.S. P.46. h, M.L. 321.
No. 1471: a, M.L. 126. b, M.L. 134. c, M.L. 135. d, M.L. 168. e, H.M.S. P.211. f, H.M.S. P.222. g, M.L. 459. h, M.L. 462.

2012, Aug. 10
1461 Sheet of 8, #a-h,
 + 2 labels 12.00 12.00
 a.-h. A396 26c Any single 1.40 1.40
1462 Sheet of 8, #a-h,
 + 2 labels 12.00 12.00
 a.-h. A396 26c Any single 1.40 1.40
1463 Sheet of 8, #a-h,
 + 2 labels 12.00 12.00
 a.-h. A396 26c Any single 1.40 1.40
1464 Sheet of 8, #a-h,
 + 2 labels 12.00 12.00
 a.-h. A396 26c Any single 1.40 1.40
1465 Sheet of 8, #a-h,
 + 2 labels 12.00 12.00
 a.-h. A396 26c Any single 1.40 1.40
1466 Sheet of 8, #a-h,
 + 2 labels 12.00 12.00
 a.-h. A396 26c Any single 1.40 1.40
1467 Sheet of 8, #a-h,
 + 2 labels 12.00 12.00
 a.-h. A396 26c Any single 1.40 1.40
1468 Sheet of 8, #a-h,
 + 2 labels 12.00 12.00
 a.-h. A396 26c Any single 1.40 1.40
1469 Sheet of 8, #a-h,
 + 2 labels 12.00 12.00
 a.-h. A396 26c Any single 1.40 1.40
1470 Sheet of 8, #a-h,
 + 2 labels 12.00 12.00
 a.-h. A396 26c Any single 1.40 1.40
1471 Sheet of 8, #a-h,
 + 2 labels 12.00 12.00
 a.-h. A396 26c Any single 1.40 1.40
Nos. 1461-1471 (11) 132.00 132.00

Operation Pedestal, 70th anniv.

Historic Gates — A397

Designs: 20c, Notre Dame Gate, Zabbar. 37c, Couvre Port Gate, Victoria, vert. 67c, Lunzjata Valley Gate, Victoria, vert. 69c, Fort Chambray Gate, Ghajnsielem.

2012, Sept. 26
1472-1475 A397 Set of 4 5.50 5.75

Christmas — A398

Paintings: 20c, The Adoration of the Magi, by German Follower of Peter Paul Rubens. 37c, The Holy Family, by the Circle of Denys Calvaert. 63c, Holy Family, by the Dutch School.

2012, Oct. 31
1476-1478 A398 Set of 3 3.50 3.50

Souvenir Sheet

Blessed Gerard, by Antoine Favray — A399

2013, Feb. 15
1479 A399 €2.47 multi 8.00 8.50
Papal Bull of Pope Paschal II to Blessed Gerard concerning Hospital of St. John of Jerusalem, 900th anniv.

Souvenir Sheet

Paintings of Mattia Preti (1613-99) — A400

No. 1480: a, 97c, The Baptism of Christ (35x35mm). b, €1.87, Self-portrait (31x44mm).

2013, Feb. 23
1480 A400 Sheet of 2, #a-b 9.00 9.50

Fountains — A401

Designs: 6c, Vilhena Fountain, Floriana. 32c, Triton Fountain, Floriana, horiz. €2.62, Spinola Fountain, Valletta.

Perf. 14¼x14, 14x14¼
2013, Mar. 27 Wmk. 354
1481-1483 A401 Set of 3 8.50 8.50

Europa — A402

Postal vehicles: 37c, Ford Transit Mark 1 van. €1.19, Lambretta three-wheeled van.

2013, May 9 **Perf. 14x13½**
1484-1485 A402 Set of 2 5.00 5.00

European Maritime Day — A403

Ocean liners: 26c, Riviera. 51c, Costa Deliziosa. 97c, MS Ryndam.

2013, May 20 **Perf. 14x14¼**
1486-1488 A403 Set of 3 5.50 5.75

Mammals A404

Designs: 37c, Wild rabbit. €2.25, Maltese ox.

2013, June 20
1489-1490 A404 Set of 2 10.25 10.25

Souvenir Sheet

Grand Harbor, Malta A405

2013, Aug. 20 **Perf. 13½x13¾**
1491 A405 €4.51 multi 14.50 15.50
See Curaçao No. 137.

MALTA

Buses — A406

Designs: 6c, Park Royal-Commer airport bus, 1940s. 10c, Thornycroft bus on Valletta-St. Julian's Route, c. 1903. 37c, Victoria Hire Service bus, c. 1925. 52c, Bedford SB Royal Armed Forces bus, 1950s. €1.16, Thames ET6 police bus, 1970s. €2.25, Magirus-Deutz O3500 bus.

2013, Aug. 27		Perf. 14x14¼	
1492-1497	A406	Set of 6	21.00 20.00

Souvenir Sheet

International Red Cross, 150th Anniv. — A407

Wmk. 354
2013, Oct. 29	Litho.	Perf. 13¼	
1498	A407	€4.57 multi	13.50 14.00

Christmas — A408

Details from creche scene from Jesus of Nazareth Institute, Zejtun: 26c, 37c, 63c.
No. 1502 — Entire creche scene showing: a, Combined designs of 37c and 63c stamps. b, Design of 26c stamp and other creche figures.

Perf. 13¾x14
2013, Nov. 18	Litho.	Wmk. 354	
1499-1501	A408	Set of 3	3.50 3.50

Souvenir Sheet
| 1502 | A408 | €1 Sheet of 2, #a-b | 6.50 7.00 |

No. 1502 contains two 76x20mm stamps.

Fountains — A409

Fountain at: 42c, Floriana. 59c, San Anton Gardens, Attard, horiz. €1.25, Kercem.

Wmk. 354
2014, Jan. 3	Litho.	Perf. 14¼	
1503-1505	A409	Set of 3	6.50 7.00

Halls of the Knights Hospitaller, Acre, Israel and Valletta, Malta — A410

Wmk. 354
2014, Jan. 28	Litho.	Perf. 13¾	
1506	A410	51c multi	1.75 1.75

See Israel No. 2000.

Watercraft A411

Designs: No. 1507, 26c, Police boat at Valletta. No. 1508, 26c, Police boat at Sliema Ferries. No. 1509, €1.55, HMS Alexander. No. 1510, €1.55, HMS London.

Wmk. 354
2014, Mar. 18	Litho.	Perf. 14	
1507-1510	A411	Set of 4	17.50 17.50

Malta Police Force, 200th anniv. (Nos. 1507-1508); End of Military Facilities Agreement, 35th anniv. (Nos. 1509-1510).

Souvenir Sheet

Canonization of Popes John XXIII and John Paul II — A412

No. 1511: a, 26c, Pope John XXIII (1881-1963). b, €1.85, Pope John Paul II (1920-2005).

Wmk. 354
2014, Apr. 26	Litho.	Perf. 14¼	
1511	A412	Sheet of 2, #a-b	7.00 7.50

Admission to the European Union, 10th Anniv. — A413

Wmk. 354
2014, Apr. 30	Litho.	Perf. 14¼	
1512	A413	59c multi	2.20 2.20

Europa — A414

Details from painting by Girolamo Gianni: 59c, Man playing Maltese bagpipe. €2.19, Man playing drum.

Wmk. 354
2014, May 9	Litho.	Perf. 13½	
1513-1514	A414	Set of 2	8.50 8.50

Souvenir Sheet

National Anniversaries — A415

No. 1515: a, 59c, #308 redrawn with "50th Anniversary 1964-2014" added (27x33mm). b, €3, #489 redrawn with "40th Anniversary 1974-2014" added (44x31mm).

Perf. 14, 14x14¼ (No. 1515c)
2014, May 15	Litho.	Wmk. 354	
1515	A415	Sheet of 2, #a-b	10.75 11.00

Souvenir Sheet

2014 World Cup Soccer Championships, Brazil — A416

No. 1516: a, 59c, Emblem. b, €1.55, Mascot.

Wmk. 354
2014, June 12	Litho.	Perf. 14¼	
1516	A416	Sheet of 2, #a-b	6.00 6.50

Flowers — A417

Designs: 26c, Gladiolus italicus. 59c, Verbascum sinuatum. €1.16, Orchis conica.

Perf. 14x13¾
2014, June 27		Wmk. 354	
1517-1519	A417	Set of 3	6.00 6.00

See Nos. 1532-1534, 1555-1557, 1583-1585.

Euromed Postal Emblem and Mediterranean Sea — A418

Wmk. 354
2014, July 9	Litho.	Perf. 13¾	
1520	A418	€1.85 multi	5.25 6.00

Grand Masters of the Sovereign Military Order of Malta — A419

No. 1521: a, Philippe de Villiers de L'Isle-Adam. b, Pierino del Ponte. c, Didier de Saint-Jaille. d, Jean de Homedes. e, Claude de la Sengle. f, Jean de la Valette-Parisot. g, Pierre de Monte. h, Jean L'Evesque de la Cassière.
No. 1522: a, Hugues Loubenx de Verdala. b, Martin Garzez. c, Alof de Wignacourt. d, Luis Mendes de Vasconcellos. e, Antoine de Paule. f, Jean-Paul de Lascaris-Castellar. g, Martín de Redín. h, Annet de Clermont-Gessant. i, Raphael Cotoner. j, Nicolas Cotoner.
No. 1523: a, Gregorio Carafa. b, Adrien de Wignacourt. c, Ramon Perellos y Roccaful. d, Marc'Antonio Zondadari. e, Antonio Manoel de Vilhena. f, Raymond Despuig. g, Manuel Pinto de Fonseca. h, Francisco Ximenes de Texada. i, Emmanuel de Rohan-Polduc. j, Ferdinand von Hompesch zu Bolheim.

Wmk. 354
2014, Sept. 30	Litho.	Perf. 14¼	
1521	Sheet of 8 + 2 labels		6.50 7.75
a.-h.	A419 26c Any single		.75 .85
1522	Sheet of 10		7.75 8.75
a.-j.	A419 26c Any single		.75 .85
1523	Sheet of 10		7.75 8.75
a.-j.	A419 26c Any single		.75 .85
	Nos. 1521-1523 (3)		22.00 25.25

World War I, Cent. — A420

Poppy and: 10c, Bighi Hospital. 59c, Floriana Hospital. €2, HMHS Rewa.

Perf. 14x14¼
2014, Nov. 7		Wmk. 354	
1524-1526	A420	Set of 3	7.50 8.00

Christmas — A421

Actors in live Nativity scene in Ghajnsielem depicting: 26c, Holy Family. 59c, Adoration of the Magi, horiz. 63c, Shepherds, horiz. €1.16, Holy Family, diff.

Perf. 14¼x14, 14x14¼
2014, Nov. 17	Litho.	Wmk. 354	
1527-1530	A421	Set of 4	6.50 6.25

Malta and Yalta Conferences, 70th Anniv. — A422

No. 1531: a, Franklin D. Roosevelt and Winston Churchill meeting in Malta. b, Montgomery House, Floriana, Malta. c, Churchill, Roosevelt, Joseph Stalin and other officials at Yalta Conference.

Wmk. 354
2015, Feb. 4	Litho.	Perf. 14¼	
1531	Horiz. strip of 3		7.50 8.25
a.-c.	A422 €1 Any single		2.50 2.75

Flowers Type of 2014

Designs: 26c, Tragopogon hybridus. 59c, Anemone coronaria. €1.16, Arisarum vulgare.

Perf. 14x13¾
2015, Feb. 14	Litho.	Wmk. 354	
1532-1534	A417	Set of 3	4.50 4.25

Aqueducts A423

Designs: 42c, Fleur-de-lys Aqueduct. €1.55, Wignacourt Water Tower, Floriana, vert.

Wmk. 354
2015, Apr. 21	Litho.	Perf. 14¼	
1535-1536	A423	Set of 2	5.00 5.25

Souvenir Sheet

Gallipoli Campaign, Cent. — A424

Wmk. 354
2015, Apr. 25	Litho.	Perf. 13¾	
1537	A424	€3.59 multi	8.25 8.75

Penny Black, 175th Anniv. — A425

Wmk. 354
2015, May 2	Litho.	Perf. 13¾	
1538	A425	€1.21 multi	8.25 8.75

No. 1538 was printed in sheets of 3.

Europa — A426

Children playing with: 59c, Cart. €2.19, Hoop.

Wmk. 354
2015, May 9	Litho.	Perf. 13¾	
1539-1540	A426	Set of 2	6.25 6.25

MALTA

Culture in Malta — A427

Designs: 26c, Feast of St. George, Victoria. 59c, Regatta, Grand Harbor. €1.16, Easter procession, Zebbug.

	Wmk. 354		
2015, June 16	Litho.		Perf. 14¼
1541-1543 A427	Set of 3	4.50	4.25

Firilla — A428

	Wmk. 354		
2015, July 9	Litho.		Perf. 13¾
1544 A428	€3.59 multi	8.25	8.25

Ex-Voto Paintings A429

Painting from: 51c, 1835. 82c, 1839. €1, 1843.

	Wmk. 354		
2015, July 29	Litho.		Perf. 14¼
1545-1547 A429	Set of 3	5.25	5.25

St. John Bosco (1815-88) — A430

	Perf. 14¼x14		
2015, Aug. 14	Litho.		Wmk. 354
1548 A430	€2 multi	4.50	4.50

Souvenir Sheet

The Allegory of the Triumph of the Order, by Mattia Preti A431

	Wmk. 354		
2015, Sept. 7	Litho.		Perf. 13¼
1549 A431	€4.25 multi	10.00	10.50

Great Siege of Malta, 450th anniv.

Souvenir Sheet

United Nations, 70th Anniv. A432

	Wmk. 354		
2015, Oct. 24	Litho.		Perf. 14¼
1550 A432	€3.51 multi	7.75	7.75

Christmas — A433

Woodcuts by Albrecht Dürer: 26c, The Flight into Egypt. 59c, The Nativity of the Lord. 63c, The Adoration of the Magi.

	Wmk. 354		
2015, Nov. 14	Litho.		Perf. 14¼
1551-1553 A433	Set of 3	3.50	2.75

Souvenir Sheet

Commonwealth Heads of Government Meeting, Malta — A434

	Wmk. 354		
2015, Nov. 27	Litho.		Perf. 14¼
1554 A434	€3 multi	6.50	7.00

Flowers Type of 2014

Designs: 26c, Asphodelus aestivus. 59c, Anacamptis pyramidalis. €1.16, Ophrys melitensis.

	Perf. 14x13¾		
2016, Jan. 22			Wmk. 354
1555-1557 A117	Set of 3	4.50	4.25

Souvenir Sheet

Valletta, 450th Anniv. A435

	Wmk. 354		
2016, Mar. 28	Litho.		Perf. 14¼
1558 A435	€4.25 multi	10.00	10.50

Miniature Sheet

Worldwide Fund for Nature (WWF) — A436

No. 1559 — Shearwater: a, Flying right. b, Flying left. c, One on water. d, Four on water.

	Wmk. 354		
2016, Apr. 15	Litho.		Perf. 14¼
1559 A436	Sheet of 4	7.00	7.00
a.-d.	75c Any single	1.75	1.75

Europa — A437, A438

	Wmk. 354		
2016, May 9	Litho.		Perf. 14¼
1560 A437	59c multi	1.40	.85
1561 A438	€2.19 multi	5.00	5.50

Think Green Issue.

Paintings by Nicholas P. Krasnoff (1869-1947) — A439

Designs: No. 1562, €1, View from Vittoriosa Gate, Malta. No. 1563, €1, Dulber Palace, Crimea.

	Wmk. 354		
2016, May 24	Litho.		Perf. 14¼
1562-1563 A439	Set of 2	5.00	5.50

See Russia No. 7725.

Woman in Traditional Costume, Citadella, Gozo in Spring — A440

Woman on Ghajn Tuffieha Beach in Summer — A441

Woman and Verdala Palace in Autumn A442

Woman and Ghar-id-Dud in Winter A443

	2016, June 21	Litho.	Perf. 14¼
1564 A440	26c multi	.60	.55
1565 A441	51c multi	1.25	1.15
1566 A442	59c multi	1.40	1.30
1567 A443	€2 multi	4.50	4.15
Nos. 1564-1567 (4)		7.75	7.15

Coryphaena Hippurus A444

	Wmk. 354		
2016, July 9	Litho.		Perf. 14¼
1568 A444	€3.59 multi	8.25	8.75

2016 Summer Olympics, Rio de Janeiro A445

Designs: 42c, Shooting. 62c, Swimming. 90c, Weight lifting. €1.55, Relay race.

	Wmk. 354		
2016, Aug. 5	Litho.		Perf. 14¼
1569-1572 A445	Set of 4	8.00	8.00

Dominic Mintoff (1916-2012), Prime Minister — A446

	Wmk. 354		
2016, Aug. 6	Litho.		Perf. 14¼
1573 A446	€3 multi	6.75	6.75

Souvenir Sheet

HMS Hastings in Valletta Grand Harbor, by Charles von Brocktorff — A447

	Wmk. 354		
2016, Sept. 15	Litho.		Perf. 13¼
1574 A447	€3.59 multi	8.00	8.00

Balcony Corbels — A448

Various corbels with panel color of: 26c, Green. €1, Purple. €1.16, Red.

	Wmk. 354		
2016, Oct. 15	Litho.		Perf. 14¼
1575-1577 A448	Set of 3	5.50	5.50

Souvenir Sheet

Fortifications in Malta and San Marino — A449

No. 1578: a, 59c, Citadella, Gozo, Malta. b, €3, First Tower, San Marino.

	Wmk. 354		
2016, Oct. 18	Litho.		Perf. 13¾
1578 A449	Sheet of 2, #a-b	8.75	8.75

See San Marino No. 1975.

Christmas — A450

Designs: 26c, Nativity. 59c, Star of Bethlehem over manger. 63c, Adoration of the Magi.

	Wmk. 354		
2016, Nov. 18	Litho.		Perf. 13¾
1579-1581 A450	Set of 3	3.50	3.25

MALTA

Souvenir Sheet

Maltese Presidency of the Council of the European Union — A451

	Perf. 14¼x14		
2017, Jan. 12	Litho.		Wmk. 354
1582 A451	€3.59 multi	8.75	8.75

Flowers Type of 2014

Designs: 26c, Orchis collina. 42c, Ophrys lutea. €1.25, Serapias parviflora.

		Perf. 14x13¾	
2017, Feb. 24	Litho.		
1583-1585 A417	Set of 3	4.75	4.50

Balcony Corbels — A452

Various corbels with color of panel at bottom: 51c, Green. €1.32, Purple. €1.55, Red.

	Perf. 14¼x14		
2017, Mar. 30	Litho.		Wmk. 354
1586-1588 A452	Set of 3	8.50	8.50

Europa — A453

Designs: 59c, St. Agatha Tower. €2.19, Gourgion Tower.

	Perf. 14x14¼		
2017, May 19	Litho.		Wmk. 354
1589-1590 A453	Set of 2	7.00	7.00

Postal Uniforms — A454

Malta Post mascot wearing uniform from: 26c, 2017. 59c, Early 2000s. €1, 1980s. €2, Early 1900s.

			Wmk. 354
2017, May 31	Litho.		Perf. 14¼
1591-1594 A454	Set of 4	9.75	9.75

Traditional Handicrafts A455

Designs: 26c, Boat builder. 59c, Maker of bamboo fish traps. €1, Weaver. €3.51, Carriage decorator.

	Perf. 14x14¼		
2017, June 28	Litho.		Wmk. 354
1595-1598 A455	Set of 4	13.25	13.25

Tetraclinis Articulata A456

Sandarac trees with church at: 10c, Right. €3.63, Left.

	Perf. 14x14¼		
2017, July 10	Litho.		Wmk. 354
1599-1600 A456	Set of 2	9.75	10.00

Souvenir Sheet

Siege Bell War Memorial, Valletta — A457

	Perf. 14¼x14		
2017, Aug. 10	Litho.		Wmk. 354
1601 A457	€3 multi	8.75	8.75

Operation Pedestal, 75th anniv.

Miniature Sheet

Statues of the Virgin Mary A458

No. 1602 — Statues of the Virgin Mary from churches in: a, Attard. b, Dingli. c, Ghaxaq. d, Gudja. e, Mgarr. f, Mosta. g, Mqabba. h, Qrendi. i, Victoria, Gozo. j, Zebbug, Gozo.

	Perf. 14¼x14		
2017, Aug. 14	Litho.		Wmk. 354
1602 A458	26c Sheet of 10, #a-j	7.75	8.25

Feast of the Assumption.

Sculptures by Melchiorre Gafa' (1636-67) — A459

Designs: 20c, St. Rose of Lima. 42c, St. Catherine of Siena. 51c, The Annunciation. €1, Adoration of the Shepherds. €1.16, Nativity.

	Perf. 14¼x14		
2017, Sept. 4	Litho.		Wmk. 354
1603-1607 A459	Set of 5	8.25	7.75

Ships — A460

Models of: 63c, 18th cent. third rate ship of the line. €1.85, Sant'Anna carrack. €3.59, Third rate ship of the line, diff.

	Perf. 14x14¼		
2017, Sept. 29	Litho.		Wmk. 354
1608-1610 A460	Set of 3	15.50	16.00

Christmas — A461

Figurines of Infant Jesus from: 26c, Church of the Nativity of the Virgin Mary, Naxxar. 51c, Church of the Immaculate Conception, Cospicua. 59c, Basilica of Saints Peter and Paul, Nadur. 63c, Sanctuary of Our Lady of Grace, Zabbar.

	Perf. 14¼x14		
2017, Nov. 17	Litho.		Wmk. 354
1611-1614 A461	Set of 4	5.25	4.50

Miniature Sheets

A462

A463

A464

Traditional Floor Tile Patterns — A465

No. 1615: a, "M" in country name over brownish black arc. b, "M" in country name touching white circle at center of tile block. c, "M" in country name over dull claret embellishment outside of brown frame. d, "M" in country name over yellow brown and brownish black arc.

No. 1616: a, Year date entirely over brown red curve, curve of "P" in "Post" over brown red curve. b, Point of "7" in year date over yellow brown curve. c, Year date entirely over brown red curve with "Post" entirely over white area. d, Foot of "2" in year date and "Post" over white area.

No. 1617: a, Heavy gray shading below green line at right near right arm of cross and below lower right cross point, little gray shading above green line at left near left arm of cross, little gray shading at lower left corner, heavy gray shading at lower right corner. b, Little gray shading below green line at right near right arm of cross and below lower right cross point, heavy gray shading above green line at left near left arm of cross, heavy gray shading at lower left and right corners. c, Little gray shading below green line at right near right arm of cross and below lower right cross point, little gray shading above green line at left near left arm of cross, heavy gray shading along lower left horizontal perforations and lower right vertical perforations. d, Little gray shading below green line at right near right arm of cross and below lower right cross point, heavy gray shading above green line at left near perforations but little shading near left cross point, heavy gray shading along lower left vertical perforations and very dark gray shading along lower right vertical perforations.

No. 1618: a, Little gray shading in white triangle at upper right. b, Heavy gray shading in white triangle at upper left. c, Little gray shading in white triangle at upper left. d, Heavy gray shading in white triangle at upper right.

			Wmk. 354
2017, Dec. 12	Litho.		Perf. 14¼
1615 A462	25c Sheet of 4, #a-d	3.25	3.25
1616 A463	29c Sheet of 4, #a-d	3.50	3.50
1617 A464	59c Sheet of 4, #a-d	6.50	6.50
1618 A465	75c Sheet of 4, #a-d	11.00	11.00
Nos. 1615-1618 (4)		24.25	24.25

Traditional Costumes — A466

Designs: 26c, Man's farming wear. 59c, Man's farming wear with horga. €1.16, Hooded winter overcoat.

			Wmk. 354
2018, Feb. 9	Litho.		Perf. 14¼
1619-1621 A466	Set of 3	4.75	4.50

Ships — A467

Models of: 26c, Galley. 42c, Half galley, 1742. €1, Brigantine.

			Wmk. 354
2018, Mar. 23	Litho.		Perf. 14¼
1622-1624 A467	Set of 3	3.75	3.50

Europa — A468

Designs: 59c, Grand Harbour Breakwater Bridge. €2.19, Madliena Bridge.

			Wmk. 354
2018, May 3	Litho.		Perf. 14
1625-1626 A468	Set of 2	6.50	6.50
1625a	Sheet of 5 + label	6.50	6.50

No. 1625a was sold with, but unattached to, a booklet cover.

Valletta, 2018 European Capital of Culture — A469

Designs: 26c, Statues and stairway. 63c, Buildings, horiz. €2, Grand Master Jean Parisot de Valette and buildings, horiz.

			Wmk. 354
2018, May 22	Litho.		Perf. 14
1627-1629 A469	Set of 3	6.00	6.50

Souvenir Sheet

2018 World Cup Soccer Championships, Russia — A470

MALTA

2018, June 14 Wmk. 354 Litho. Perf. 14
1630 A470 €3 multi 7.00 7.00

Doors of House, Mdina — A471

Townhouse Doors and Windows — A472

2018, July 9 Wmk. 354 Litho. Perf. 14
1631 A471 20c multi .50 .35
1632 A472 90c multi 2.10 2.10

Gen. Dwight D. Eisenhower and Field Marshal Bernard Montgomery A473

British Officers at Planning Table A474

Gen. Eisenhower, Governor of Malta Lord Gort, Air Chief Marshal Sir Arthur Tedder — A475

2018, July 10 Wmk. 354 Litho. Perf. 14¼
1633 Horiz. strip of 3 6.50 7.75
 a. A473 €1 multi 2.25 2.65
 b. A474 €1 multi 2.25 2.65
 c. A475 €1 multi 2.25 2.65

Operation Husky (Invasion of Sicily), 75th anniv.

Church of St. John the Baptist, Gozo — A476

Ghajn Tuffieha Bay — A477

Gozo Aqueduct A478

Dwejra Bay — A479

2018, July 27 Wmk. 354 Litho. Perf. 14
1634 A476 26c multi .55 .55
1635 A477 42c multi .90 .90
1636 A478 59c multi 1.30 1.30
1637 A479 €1.25 multi 2.75 2.75
 Nos. 1634-1637 (4) 5.50 5.50

Religious Statues A480

Miniature Sheet

No. 1638 — Statue of: a, St. Paul, Valletta. b, Saints Peter and Paul, Nadur. c, Immaculate Conception, Hamrun. d, Our Lady of Mount Carmel, Mdina. e, St. Gaetan, Hamrun. f, St. Dominic, Valletta. g, St. Julian, St. Julian's h, St. Catherine, Zurrieq. i, Nativity of the Blessed Virgin, Senglea. j, Our Lady of Consolation, Gudja.

2018, Aug. 14 Wmk. 354 Litho. Perf. 14
1638 A480 26c Sheet of 10, #a-j 6.75 7.75

Miniature Sheet

Dogs A481

No. 1639: a, German pointer. b, Labrador retriever. c, French bulldog. d, Irish setter. e, Chow chow. f, Boxer. g, Golden retriever. h, Pharaoh's hound. i, Cavalier King Charles spaniel. j, Scottish terriers. k, Maltese dog. l, Border collie. m, Pug. n, Yorkshire terrier. o, Bernese Mountain dog. p, Chihuahua.

2018, Oct. 23 Wmk. 354 Litho. Perf. 14¼
1639 A481 59c Sheet of 16, #a-p 22.00 26.50

See No. 1690.

Souvenir Sheet

St. Pio of Pietrelcina (1887-1968) — A482

2018, Sept. 22 Wmk. 354 Litho. Perf. 14
1640 A482 €3 multi 7.00 7.50

Christmas — A483

Creche figurines depicting Jesus from: 26c, St. Helen's Basilica, Birkirkara. 59c, St. Catherine's Parish Church, Zejtun. 63c, Basilica of the Nativity of Our Lady, Xaghra, Gozo.

2018, Nov. 16 Wmk. 354 Litho. Perf. 14
1641-1643 A483 Set of 3 3.00 3.25

Diplomatic Relations Between Malta and Kyrgyzstan, 25th Anniv. — A484

No. 1644 — UNESCO World Heritage Sites: a, City of Valletta, Malta. b, Burana Tower, Kyrgyzstan.

2018, Nov. 23 Perf. 13¾x14 Wmk. 354
1644 A484 €1.16 Vert. pair, #a-b 5.25 6.00

See Kyrgyz Express Post Nos. 97-98.

Ships — A485

Models of: 26c, Felucca Dorada. €5, Gondola of Adrien de Wignacourt.

2019, Feb. 21 Perf. 14x14¼ Wmk. 354
1645-1646 A485 Set of 2 12.00 13.00

Council of Europe, 70th Anniv. — A486

Designs: 63c, "70" to left of Council of Europe emblem. €2, Council of Europe Building and "70" above years and Council of Europe emblem, vert.

2019, May 4 Wmk. 354 Litho. Perf. 14
1647-1648 A486 Set of 2 6.00 7.00

Europa — A487

Monticola solitarius: 59c, Facing right. €2, Facing left, vert.

2019, May 9 Wmk. 354 Litho. Perf. 14
1649-1650 A487 Set of 2 6.00 7.00
 1649a Sheet of 5 #1649 + label 6.75 6.75

No. 1649a was sold with, but unattached to, a booklet cover.

June 7, 1919 Riots Against Submission to British Rule, Cent. — A488

2019, June 6 Wmk. 354 Litho. Perf. 14
1651 A488 €5.59 multi 12.50 13.75

Female Map Plotters of World War II — A489

Designs: 28c, Woman and soldier. 48c, Soldier and three women, horiz. €2.28, Two women near map, horiz.

2019, June 10 Wmk. 354 Litho. Perf. 14
1652-1654 A489 Set of 3 6.25 6.75

Traditional Costumes — A490

Euromed Postal emblem and: 28c, Woman's skirt, blouse and scarf. 51c, Black faldetta. €1.25, Man's jacket and pants.

2019, July 9 Wmk. 354 Litho. Perf. 14¼
1655-1657 A490 Set of 3 5.00 5.75

Souvenir Sheet

First Man on the Moon, 50th Anniv. A491

Perf. 13½x13¼
2019, July 20 Litho. Wmk. 354
1658 A491 €2.28 multi 5.25 5.75

A492

A493

A494

Houses — A495

2019, July 30 Wmk. 354 Litho. Perf. 14¼
1659 A492 10c multi .25 .25
1660 A493 59c multi 1.40 1.40
1661 A494 63c multi 1.40 1.40
1662 A495 €1 multi 2.25 2.25
 Nos. 1659-1662 (4) 5.30 5.30

Miniature Sheet

Religious Statues A496

No. 1663 — Statue of: a, St. Publius, Floriana. b, St. Philip, Zebbug. c, St. Catherine, Zejtun. d, St. John the Baptist, Xewkija. e, St. Andrew, Luqa. f, The Annunciation, Balzan. q, St. Venera, Santa Venera. h, Our Lady of Pompei, Marsaxlokk. i, St. Lawrence, Birgu. j, Our Lady of Grace, Zabbar.

2019, Aug. 14 Wmk. 354 Litho. Perf. 14
1663 A496 28c Sheet of 10, #a-j 7.75 8.25

Express Mail Service, 20th Anniv. — A497

Perf. 14x14¼
2019, Sept. 10 Litho. Wmk. 354
1664 A497 €2 multi 4.75 5.25

MALTA

Entertainers — A498

Designs: No, 1665, 28c, Laurie Bellizzi (1922-93). No. 1666, 28c, Johnny Catania (1925-91). No. 1667, 28c, Charles Clews (1919-2009). No. 1668, 28c, Nosi Ghirlando (1908-64). No. 1669, 28c, Johnny Navarro (1912-97). No. 1670, 28c, Armando Urso (1918-76).

	Wmk. 354		
2019, Sept. 27	Litho.		Perf. 14¼
1665-1670 A498	Set of 6	3.50	3.15

Miniature Sheet

Mohandas K. Gandhi (1869-1948), Indian Nationalist Leader — A499

No. 1671 — Gandhi: a, Photograph, with hands together. b, Drawing. c, Photograph, kneeling wearing robe. d, Photograph, holding string of flowers.

	Wmk. 354		
2019, Oct. 2	Litho.		Perf. 14
1671 A499 59c Sheet of 4, #a-d		6.50	6.00

Palaces A500

No. 1672: a, Verdala Palace, Malta. b, Mogosoaia Palace, Romania.

	Wmk. 354		
2019, Oct. 14	Litho.		Perf. 14
1672 A500 50c Pair, #a-b		2.50	3.25

Joint Issue between Malta and Romania. No. 1672 was printed in sheets containing 5 pairs + 2 labels. See Romania Nos. 6332-6333.

Apiculture — A505

A501, A502, A503, A504, A505

	Wmk. 354		
2019, Nov. 22	Litho.		Perf. 14¼
1673	Horiz. strip of 5	4.50	5.00
a.	A501 30c multi	.70	.60
b.	A502 30c multi	.70	.60
c.	A503 30c multi	.70	.60
d.	A504 30c multi	.70	.60
e.	A505 30c multi	.70	.60

Christmas — A506

Creche figurines depicting infant Jesus from various churches: 28c, 59c, 63c.

	Wmk. 354		
2019, Nov. 29	Litho.		Perf. 14
1674-1676 A506	Set of 3	3.00	3.00

Front of Villa Francia, Lija — A507
House, Mdina — A508
Villa Gourgion, Hal Lija — A509
Rear of Villa Francia, Lija — A510

	Perf. 14¼x14		
2020, Feb. 14	Litho.		Wmk. 354
1677 A507 20c multi		.45	.45
1678 A508 30c multi		.65	.65
1679 A509 59c multi		1.40	1.40
1680 A510 €2 multi		4.50	4.50
Nos. 1677-1680 (4)		7.00	7.00

Miniature Sheets

Statues of St. Joseph A511

No. 1681, 30c — Statue location: a, Birkirkara. b, Kalkara. c, Manikata. d, Msida. e, Qala. f, Rabat. g, Xaghra. h, Birgu. i, Basilica of Birkirkara. j, Bormla.

No. 1682, 30c — Statue location: a, Ghajnsielem. b, Ghaxaq. c, Hamrun. d, Kirkop. e, Mosta. f, Qormi. g, Valletta. h, Zebbug. i, Zejtun. j, Zurrieq.

	Perf. 14¼x14		
2020, Mar. 18	Litho.		Wmk. 354
Sheets of 10, #a-j			
1681-1682 A511	Set of 2	15.00	15.00

Mediterranean Postal Routes Between Malta and Italy — A512

Franz von Taxis (1459-1517), European Postal Service Operator — A513

	Perf. 14¼x14		
2020, May 9	Litho.		Wmk. 354
1683 A512 59c multi		1.40	1.40
	Perf. 14x14¼		
1684 A513 €2 multi		4.50	4.50

Europa.

Woman Wearing Ghonnella A514
Corpus Christi Procession in Valletta A515

	Perf. 14x14¼		
2020, June 8	Litho.		Wmk. 354
1685 A514 30c multi		.70	.60
1686 A515 50c multi		1.20	1.50

Paintings by Edward Caruana Dingli (1876-1950).

Snack Foods — A516

Designs: 30c, Rustic biscuits. 59c, Biscuit rings with sesame seeds. €1.25, Coconut lamingtons.

	Perf. 14¼x14		
2020, July 9	Litho.		Wmk. 354
1687-1689 A516	Set of 3	5.00	5.00

Dogs Type of 2018
Miniature Sheet

No. 1690: a, West Highland white terrier. b, Cocker spaniel. c, Great Dane. d, Kelb talkacca. e, British bulldog. f, Weimaraner. g, Shar pei. h, English setter. i, Poodle. j, Beagle. k, Basset hound. l, Siberian husky. m, American Staffordshire terrier. n, Smooth fox terrier. o, German shepherd. p, Rottweiler.

	Wmk. 354		
2020, Sept. 24	Litho.		Perf. 14¼
1690 A481 51c Sheet of 16, #a-p		20.00	24.00

Souvenir Sheet

St. John Paul II (1920-2005) — A517

	Wmk. 354		
2020, Oct. 22	Litho.		Perf. 14¼
1691 A517 €3 multi		7.00	7.00

Viticulture — A518

No. 1692: a, Vineyard in Malta, grapes. b, Vineyard in Slovakia, wine bottle.

	Wmk. 354		
2020, Oct. 24	Litho.		Perf. 14¼
1692 A518 59c Pair, #a-b		3.50	3.50

Printed in sheets containing 5 each Nos. 1692a-1692b + 2 labels. See Slovakia No. 860.

Christmas A519

Various details from "The Nativity," fresco in Christ the Savior Parish Church, Lija, by Giuseppe Cali (1846-1930): 30c, 59c, 63c.

	Perf. 14x14¼		
2020, Nov. 24	Litho.		Wmk. 354
1693-1695 A519	Set of 3	3.75	3.75

Souvenir Sheet

Ludwig van Beethoven (1770-1827), Composer — A520

	Perf. 13½x13		
2020, Dec. 17	Litho.		Wmk. 354
1696 A520 €2.30 multi		5.75	5.75

A521, A522

Paintings of Health Care Workers in the COVID-19 Pandemic — A523

	Perf. 14¼x14		
2021, Jan. 29	Litho.		Wmk. 354
1697 A521 30c multi		.75	.75
1698	Vert. pair	1.50	1.50
a.	A522 30c multi	.75	.75
b.	A523 30c multi	.75	.75

Souvenir Sheets

Act Now Climate Action Campaign — A524

Designs: 50c, Man placing bottle in recycling bin. €1.25, Man carrying reusable shopping bag. €2, Bicyclist.

	Wmk. 354		
2021, Mar. 18	Litho.		Perf. 14¼
1699-1701 A524	Set of 3	9.00	9.00

Souvenir Sheet

Napoleon Bonaparte (1769-1821), Emperor of France — A525

MALTA

Perf. 13½x13¼
2021, May 5 Litho. Wmk. 354
1702 A525 €5 multi 11.50 11.50

Endangered Animals — A526

Designs: 59c, Mediterranean chameleon. €2, Painted frog.

Perf. 14x14¼
2021, May 12 Litho. Wmk. 354
1703 A526 59c multi 1.50 1.50
a. Sheet of 5 + label 6.75 6.75
1704 A526 €2 multi 5.00 5.00

Europa. Nos. 1703-1704 were each printed in sheets of 11 + label. No. 1703a was sold with, but unattached to, a booklet cover.

Historical Maps of Malta — A527

Various maps: 20c, 50c, 63c, €1.25.

Wmk. 354
2021, May 28 Perf. 13¾
1705-1708 A527 Set of 4 6.50 6.50

Prince Philip (1921-2021) — A528

Designs: 30c, Queen Elizabeth II and Prince Philip. €1, Prince Philip standing in automobile and saluting, horiz. €2, Queen Elizabeth II, Prince Philip and others near Villa Gruadamangia railing, horiz.

Perf. 14¼x14, 14x14¼
2021, June 10 Litho. Wmk. 354
1709-1711 A528 Set of 3 7.00 7.00

19th Century Gold and Pearl Jewelry — A529

Designs: 10c, Earrings. 30c, Maltese cross pendant. €2.50, Seed pearl brooch.

Wmk. 354
2021, July 12 Litho. Perf. 14¼
1712-1714 A529 Set of 3 6.00 6.00

2020 Summer Olympics, Tokyo — A530

Athlete: 59c, Jumping. €1.35, Running. €2.80, Hurdling.

Wmk. 354
2021, July 23 Litho. Perf. 14¼
1715-1717 A530 Set of 3 10.00 10.00

The 2020 Summer Olympics were postponed until 2021 because of the COVID-19 pandemic.

Miniature Sheet
Religious Statues A531

No. 1718 — Statue of: a, St. Dominic, Brgu. b, Visitation of Our Lady, Gharb. c, St. Bartholomew, Gharghur. d, Virgin Mary, Naxxar. e, Christ the King, Paola. f, St. George, Qormi. g, St. Paul, Rabat. h, St. Nicholas, Siggiewi. i, Stella Maris, Sliema. j, Our Lady of Mount Carmel, Valletta.

Perf. 14¼x14
2021, Aug. 25 Litho. Wmk. 354
1718 A531 30c Sheet of 10, #a-j 7.25 7.25

Ford Thames Bus — A532

Bedford OB Bus — A533

Ford Thames Bus — A534

Perf. 14x14¼
2021, Oct. 7 Litho. Wmk. 354
1719 A532 30c multi .70 .70
1720 A533 50c multi 1.25 1.25
1721 A534 86c multi 2.00 2.00
Nos. 1719-1721 (3) 3.95 3.95

Souvenir Sheet
Malta No. 83 A535

Perf. 14¼x14
2021, Nov. 1 Litho. Wmk. 354
1722 A535 €5.50 multi 13.00 13.00
Malta Senate and Legislative Assembly, cent.

Christmas — A536

Designs: 30c, Sheep and shepherds. 59c, Nativity. 63c, Magi following Star of Bethlehem.

Wmk. 354
2021, Nov. 15 Litho. Perf. 14¼
1723-1725 A536 Set of 3 3.50 3.50

Bedford OB Bus — A537

1953 Ford Thames Bus — A538

1939 REO Speedwagon Bus — A539

1953 Ford Thames Bus — A540

Perf. 14x14¼
2022, Feb. 12 Litho. Wmk. 354
1726 A537 30c multi .70 .70
1727 A538 51c multi 1.25 1.25
1728 A539 59c multi 1.30 1.30
1729 A540 €1 multi 2.25 2.25
Nos. 1726-1729 (4) 5.50 5.50

Souvenir Sheet
Visit to Malta of Pope Francis A541

Perf. 14¼x14
2022, Apr. 2 Litho. Wmk. 354
1700 A541 €5 multi 11.00 11.00

Europa — A542

Myths and legends: 59c, The Legend of Calypso. €2, The Legend of Speranza Cave.

Perf. 14¼x14
2022, May 9 Litho. Wmk. 354
1731 A542 59c multi 1.25 1.25
a. Souvenir sheet of 5 7.50
1732 A542 €2 multi 4.25 4.25

No. 1731a sold for €3.48, folded in a booklet cover to which it was unattached.

Souvenir Sheet
Queen Elizabeth II Waving During 1954 Royal Visit to Malta A543

Wmk. 354
2022, June 2 Litho. Perf. 13¾
1733 A543 €5 multi 11.00 11.00

Reign of Queen Elizabeth II (1952-2022), 70th anniv.

Malta Meteorological Office, Cent. — A544

Designs: 7c, Crescent moon and rain clouds. 37c, Leaves, full moon and rain cloud. €1.25, Crescent moon and rain clouds, diff.

Wmk. 354
2022, July 1 Litho. Perf. 14¼
1734-1736 A544 Set of 3 3.50 3.50

Phoenician Shipwreck Site, Xlendi, Gozo — A545

Citadel, Victoria, Gozo — A546

Perf. 14x14¼
2022, July 11 Litho. Wmk. 354
1737 A545 20c multi .40 .40
1738 A546 €5.50 multi 11.50 11.50

Miniature Sheet
Religious Statues A547

No. 1739 — Statue of: a, The Immaculate Conception, Bormla. b, The Immaculate Heart of Mary, Burmarrad. c, Our Lady of the Holy Rosary, Gudja. d, Our Lady of Loreto, Ghajnsielem. e, Our Lady of Perpetual Succor, Ta' Kercem. f, St. Leonard Abbot, Kirkop. g, The Transfiguration of Our Lord, Lija. h, The Holy Trinity, Marsa. i, Our Lady of Mount Carmel, Zurrieq. j, The Annunciation of Our Lady, Tarxien.

Perf. 14¼x14
2022, Aug. 12 Litho. Wmk. 354
1739 A547 37c Sheet of 10, #a-j 8.00 8.00

Souvenir Sheet
St. Teresa of Calcutta (1910-97) — A548

Perf. 14x14¼
2022, Sept. 5 Litho. Wmk. 354
1740 A548 €3 multi 6.50 6.50

Bottled Beverages — A549

Bottle of: 37c, Kinnie (soft drink). 57c, Medina (Gellewza wine). €1.40, Bajtra (prickly pear liqueur). €2, San Blas (beer).

Perf. 14¼x14
2022, Sept. 13 Litho. Wmk. 354
1741-1744 A549 Set of 4 8.50 8.50

Souvenir Sheet
Queen Elizabeth II (1926-2022) and Prince Philip (1921-2021) at Villa Guardamangia, Malta — A550

Perf. 14¼x14
2022, Sept. 19 Litho. Wmk. 354
1745 A550 €5 multi 13.50 13.50

MALTA

Malta Comic Convention, 10th Anniv. — A551

Emblem of Malta Comic Convention and comic art depicting: 5c, Swordsman, dragon at Hagar Qim Temple. €1.70, Superhero at Fort St. Angelo. €2.50, Man and woman fishing.

Wmk. 354
2022, Oct. 29   Litho.   **Perf. 14¼**
1746-1748   A551   Set of 3   10.00   10.00

Christmas — A552

Designs: 37c, Santa Claus reading list. €1.40, Elf removing letters from pillar box. No. 1751: a, Elf painting train. b, Elf sewing doll.

Wmk. 354
2022, Nov. 29   Litho.   **Perf. 14¼**
Stamps With White Frames
1749-1750   A552   Set of 2   6.50   6.50
Souvenir Sheet
Stamps Without White Frames
1751   A552   €1 Sheet of 2, #a-b   3.25   3.25

Souvenir Sheet

Christmas — A553

No. 1752 — Terracotta sculptures by Joseph Scerri depicting: a, Shepherds and lamb. b, Holy Family. c, Magi.

Wmk. 354
2022, Dec. 16   Litho.   **Perf. 14¼**
1752   A553   €1 Sheet of 3, #a-c   6.50   6.50

Souvenir Sheet

First Performance of National Anthem of Malta, Cent. — A554

No. 1753: a, Carmelo Psaila (1871-1961), priest and anthem's lyricist. b, Robert Samut (1869-1934), doctor and anthem's composer.

Wmk. 354
2022, Dec. 27   Litho.   **Perf. 14¼**
1753   A554   €3 Sheet of 2, #a-b   13.00   13.00

Illustration From Id-Denfil A555
Illustration From Il-Gojjin A556

Perf. 14¼x14
2023, Feb. 17   Litho.   **Wmk. 354**
1754   A555   37c multi   1.65   1.65
1755   A556   €3 multi   6.50   6.50
Children's textbooks.

Miniature Sheet

Malta Railway A557

No. 1756: a, Map of Malta Railway. b, Birkirkara Railway Station. c, Hamrun Railway Station. d, Museum Railway Station in Mtarfa. e, Valletta Railway Terminus.

Perf. 13¾x14
2023, Apr. 25   Litho.   **Wmk. 354**
1756   A557   €1.50 Sheet of 5, #a-e   16.50   16.50

Europa — A558

Wmk. 354
2023, May 9   Litho.   **Perf. 14¼**
1757   A558   €1.50 multi   3.25   3.25
   a.   Booklet pane of 5   16.50
No. 1757a was sold folded in a booklet cover to which it was unattached.

Souvenir Sheet

2023 Games of the Small States of Europe, Valletta A559

Wmk. 354
2023, May 29   Litho.   **Perf. 14¼**
1758   A559   €5 multi   11.00   11.00

Souvenir Sheets

Malta International Fireworks Festival — A560

Various fireworks displays: €1.70, €2.50.

Wmk. 354
2023, July 10   Litho.   **Perf. 14¼**
1759-1760   A560   Set of 2   9.25   9.25

Marine Life — A561

Designs: 1c, Porbeagle shark. 10c, Spinetail devil ray. 20c, Sperm whale. 50c, Atlantic bluefin tuna. €2.50, Swordfish.

Perf. 14x14¼
2023, July 28   Litho.   **Wmk. 354**
1761-1765   A561   Set of 5   7.25   7.25

Traditional Marketplaces A562

Designs: €1.50, Vendor and customers at outdoor fruit and vegetable market, Victoria, Gozo. €1.80, Worker at fish market, Marsaxlokk, vert.

Perf. 14x14¼, 14¼x14
2023, Aug. 8   Litho.   **Wmk. 354**
1766-1767   A562   Set of 2   7.25   7.25

Paintings by Francesco Zahra (1710-73) — A563

Paintings: 38c, The Virgin Mary. 58c, Self-portrait. €2.88, St. John the Evangelist. €3, The Martyrdom of St. George, horiz.

Perf. 14¼x14
2023, Aug. 19   Litho.   **Wmk. 354**
1768-1770   A563   Set of 3   8.25   8.25

Souvenir Sheet
Perf. 13¾
1771   A563   €3 multi   6.50   6.50
No. 1771 contains one 41x31mm stamp.

Miniature Sheet

Religious Statues A564

No. 1772 — Statue of: a, St. Martin of Tours, Bahrija. b, St. Helen, Birkirkara. c, Our Lady of the Lilies, Mqabba. d, St. Paul, Munxar, Gozo. e, Our Lady of Fatima, Pietà. f, Our Lady of Lourdes, Qrendi. g, St. Lucia, Ghawdex. h, Our Lady of the Sacred Heart, Sliema. i, St. Augustine, Valletta. j, Nativity of the Blessed Virgin, Ghawdex.

Perf. 14¼x14
2022, Aug. 31   Litho.   **Wmk. 354**
1772   A564   38c Sheet of 10, #a-j   8.25   8.25

Souvenir Sheet

Fort Manoel, 300th Anniv. A565

Wmk. 354
2023, Sept. 14   Litho.   **Perf. 13¾**
1773   A565   €3 multi   6.50   6.50

Malta Comic Convention — A566

Emblem of Malta Comic Convention and comic art depicting: 10c, Marine Man in flight, Valletta skyline. 38c, Woman wearing faldetta in Mdina. €1.50, Superhero holding flag of Malta, Valletta skyline.

Perf. 14¼x14
2023, Oct. 25   Litho.   **Wmk. 354**
1774-1776   A566   Set of 3   4.25   4.25

Christmas — A567

Star of Bethlehem and: 38c, Madonna and Child. €1.50, Angel. €2, Wreath.

Perf. 14¼x14
2023, Nov. 21   Litho.   **Wmk. 354**
1777-1779   A567   Set of 3   8.25   8.25

SEMI-POSTAL STAMPS

All semi-postal issues are for Christmas.

Catalogue values for unused stamps in this section are for Never Hinged items.

Two Peasants with Tambourine and Bagpipe — SP1

Star of Bethlehem and: 5p+1p, Angels with Trumpet and Harp, Star of Bethlehem and Mdina Cathedral. 1sh6p+3p, Choir boys singing Christmas carols.
The background of the 3 stamps together shows the Cathedral of Mdina, Malta, and surrounding countryside.

Wmk. 354
1969, Nov. 8   Litho.   **Perf. 12½**
B1   SP1   1p +1p multi   .30   .25
   a.   Gold omitted   200.00
B2   SP1   5p +1p multi   .30   .25
B3   SP1   1sh6p +3p multi   .30   .45
   a.   Triptych, #B1-B3   .40   .85
     Nos. B1-B3 (3)   .90   .95
Nos. B1-B3 were printed each in sheets of 60, and in sheets containing 20 triptychs.

Christmas Eve Procession — SP2

10p+2p, Nativity & Cathedral. 1sh6p+3p, Adoration of the Shepherds & Mdina Cathedral.

1970, Nov. 7   Photo.   **Perf. 14x13½**
B4   SP2   1p + ½p multi   .30   .25
B5   SP2   10p +2p multi   .30   .25
B6   SP2   1sh6p +3p multi   .30   .45
     Nos. B4-B6 (3)   .90   .95
Surtax for child welfare organizations.

Angel SP3

No. B8, Madonna & Child. No. B9, Shepherd.

1971, Nov. 8   **Perf. 14**
B7   SP3   1p + ½p multi   .25   .25
B8   SP3   10p +2p multi   .25   .25
B9   SP3   1sh6p +3p multi   .25   .40
   a.   Souv. sheet, #B7-B9, perf. 15   .85   2.75
     Nos. B7-B9 (3)   .75   .90

MALTA

1972, Dec. Litho. Perf. 13½

Designs: 3c+1c, Angel playing tambourine. 7c5m+1c5m, Angel singing.

B10	SP3	8m +2m dk gray & gold	.30	.25
B11	SP3	3c +1c dk purple & gold	.30	.45
B12	SP3	7c5m +1c5m slate & gold	.30	.55
a.		Souvenir sheet of 3, #B10-B12	2.00	3.75
		Nos. B10-B12 (3)	.90	1.25

1973, Nov. 10 Litho. Perf. 13½

8m+2m, Singers, organ pipes. 3c+1c, Virgin & Child with star. 7c5m+1c5m, Star, candles, buildings, tambourine.

B13	SP3	8m +2m multi	.30	.25
B14	SP3	3c +1c multi	.30	.65
B15	SP3	7c5m +1c5m multi	.50	1.65
a.		Souvenir sheet of 3, #B13-B15	5.75	8.25
		Nos. B13-B15 (3)	1.10	2.55
		Nos. B7-B15 (9)	2.75	4.70

Star and Holy Family — SP4

Designs: 3c+1c, Star and two shepherds. 5c+1c, Star and three shepherds. 7c5m+1c5m, Star and Three Kings.

1974, Nov. 22 Litho. Perf. 14

B16	SP4	8m +2m multi	.30	.25
B17	SP4	3c +1c multi	.30	.25
B18	SP4	5c +1c multi	.30	.40
B19	SP4	7c5m +1c5m multi	.30	.50
		Nos. B16-B19 (4)	1.20	1.40

Nativity, by Maestro Alberto SP5

8m+2m, Shepherds. 7c5m+1c5m, Three Kings.

1975, Nov. 4 Perf. 13½
Size: 24x23mm (#B20, B22); 49x23mm (#B21)

B20	SP5	8m +2m multi	.30	.25
B21	SP5	3c +1c multi	.45	.55
B22	SP5	7c5m +1c5m multi	.50	.85
a.		Triptych, #B20-B22	1.10	1.90
		Nos. B20-B22 (3)	1.25	1.65

Printed singly and as triptychs. Surtax for child welfare.

SP6

Madonna and Saints, by Domenico di Michelino — SP7

Details of Painting: 5c+1c, Virgin & Child. 7c5m+1c5m, St. Christopher & Bishop.

1976, Nov. 23 Litho. Perf. 13½

B23	SP6	1c +5m multi	.30	.25
B24	SP6	5c +1c multi	.30	.45
B25	SP6	7c +1c5m multi	.30	.45

Perf. 13½x14

B26	SP7	10c +2c multi	.30	.65
		Nos. B23-B26 (4)	1.20	1.80

Nativity — SP8

Crèche Figurines: 1c+5m, Annunciation to the Shepherds. 11c+1c5m, Shepherds.

Perf. 13½x14
1977, Nov. 16 Wmk. 354

B27	SP8	1c +5m multi	.30	.40
B28	SP8	7c +1c multi	.30	.45
B29	SP8	11c +1c5m multi	.30	.45
a.		Triptych, #B27-B29	.75	1.60
		Nos. B27-B29 (3)	.90	1.30

Nos. B27-B29 printed singly and as triptychs. No. B29a is not a continuous picture. Surtax was for child welfare.

Christmas Decorations, People and Church — SP9

Designs: 5c+1c, Decorations and angels. 7c+1c5m, Decorations and carolers. 11c+3c, Combined designs of Nos. B30-B32.

1978, Nov. 9 Litho. Perf. 14
Size: 24x30mm

B30	SP9	1c +5m multi	.30	.25
B31	SP9	5c +1c multi	.30	.25
B32	SP9	7c +1c5m multi	.30	.35

Perf. 13½
Size: 58x22½mm

B33	SP9	11c +3c multi	1.00	.45
		Nos. B30-B33 (4)	1.90	1.30

Nativity, by Giuseppe Cali — SP10

Designs (Cali Paintings): 5c+1c, 11c+3c, Flight into Egypt. 7c+1c5m, Nativity.

1979, Nov. 14 Litho. Perf. 14x13½

B34	SP10	1c +5m multi	.30	.25
B35	SP10	5c +1c multi	.30	.25
B36	SP10	7c +1c5m multi	.30	.25
B37	SP10	11c +3c multi	.35	.50
		Nos. B34-B37 (4)	1.25	1.25

Nativity, by Anton Inglott (1915-1945) SP11

Details of Painting: 2c+5m, Annunciation. 6c+1c, Angel. 8c+2c, Holy Family.

1980, Oct. 7 Litho. Perf. 14x13½
Size: 20x47mm

B38	SP11	2c +5m multi	.30	.25
B39	SP11	6c +1c multi	.30	.25
B40	SP11	8c +1c5m multi	.30	.40

Perf. 14½x14
Size: 47x39mm

B41	SP11	12c +3c shown	.30	.75
		Nos. B38-B41 (4)	1.20	1.65

SP12

1981, Nov. 18 Wmk. 354 Perf. 14

B42	SP12	2c +1c Children, vert.	.30	.25
B43	SP12	8c +2c Procession	.35	.25
B44	SP12	20c +3c Service, vert.	.55	1.20
		Nos. B42-B44 (3)	1.20	1.70

SP13

Three Kings Following Star: 2c+1c, Star. 8c+2c, Three Kings. 20c+3c, Entire design.

1982, Oct. 8 Litho. Perf. 13½

B45	SP13	2c +1c multi	.30	.25
B46	SP13	8c +2c multi	.45	.65

Perf. 14
Size: 45x36mm

B47	SP13	20c +3c multi	.85	1.40
		Nos. B45-B47 (3)	1.60	2.30

SP14

Illuminated Manuscripts, Book of Hours, 15th Cent.: 2c+1c, Annunciation. 8c+2c, Nativity. 20c+3c, Three Kings bearing gifts. Surtax was for child welfare.

1983, Sept. 6 Litho. Perf. 14

B48	SP14	2c +1c multi	.30	.25
B49	SP14	8c +2c multi	.75	.60
B50	SP14	20c +3c multi	1.40	1.65
		Nos. B48-B50 (3)	2.45	2.50

SP15

Paintings by Peter-Paul Caruana, Church of Our Lady of Porto Salvo, Valletta, 1850: 2c+1c, Visitation, vert. 8c+2c, Epiphany. 20c+3c, Jesus Among the Doctors.

1984, Oct. 5 Litho. Perf. 14

B51	SP15	2c +1c multi	.50	.70
B52	SP15	8c +2c multi	.90	1.55
B53	SP15	20c +3c multi	1.95	2.75
		Nos. B51-B53 (3)	3.35	5.00

SP16

No. B54, Adoration of the Magi. B55, Nativity. No. B56, Trumpeter Angels.

1985, Oct. 10 Litho. Perf. 14

B54	SP16	2c +1c multi	.40	.40
B55	SP16	8c +2c multi	.90	.90
B56	SP16	20c +3c multi	2.00	2.00
		Nos. B54-B56 (3)	3.30	3.30

Surtax for child welfare organizations.

SP17

Paintings by Giuseppe D'Arena (1633-1719): No. B57, The Nativity. No. B58, The Nativity, detail, vert. No. B59, The Epiphany.

1986, Oct. 10 Wmk. 354 Perf. 14½

B57	SP17	2c +1c multi	1.10	.85
B58	SP17	8c +2c multi	2.25	2.25
B59	SP17	20c +3c multi	2.75	3.25
		Nos. B57-B59 (3)	6.10	6.35

Surtax for child welfare organizations.

SP18

Illuminated text from choral books of the Veneranda Assemblea of St. John's Conventual Church, Valletta: No. B60, Mary's Visit to Elizabeth. No. B61, Nativity. No. B62, Adoration of the Magi.

1987, Nov. 6 Litho. Perf. 14

B60	SP18	2c +1c multi	.50	.70
B61	SP18	8c +2c multi	1.75	1.90
B62	SP18	20c +3c multi	3.25	3.25
		Nos. B60-B62 (3)	5.50	5.85

Surtax for child welfare organizations and the handicapped.

SP19

1988, Nov. 5 Litho. Perf. 14½x14

B63	SP19	3c +1c Shepherd	.35	.30
B64	SP19	10c +2c Nativity	.90	.75
B65	SP19	25c +3c Magi	1.75	2.00
		Nos. B63-B65 (3)	3.00	3.05

Surtax for child welfare organizations and the handicapped.

SP20

Various angels from frescoes by Mattia Preti in the vault of St. John's Co-Cathedral, Valletta, 1666.

1989, Nov. 11 Perf. 14

B66	SP20	3c +1c multi	.50	.45
B67	SP20	10c +2c multi	1.25	1.10
B68	SP20	20c +3c multi	2.00	3.25
		Nos. B66-B68 (3)	3.75	4.80

Surtax for child welfare organizations and the handicapped.

SP21

Creche figures — No. B69, Carrying water. No. B70, Nativity. No. B71, Shepherd. No. B70 measures 41x27mm.

1990, Nov. 10

B69	SP21	3c +1c multi	.30	.50
B70	SP21	10c +2c multi	.85	1.25
B71	SP21	25c +3c multi	1.60	2.00
		Nos. B69-B71 (3)	2.75	4.25

Surtax for child welfare organizations.

SP22

No. B72, Wise men. No. B73, Mary, Joseph, Jesus. No. B74, Shepherds.

1991, Nov. 6

B72	SP22	3c +1c multi	.60	.55
B73	SP22	10c +2c multi	1.10	1.50
B74	SP22	25c +3c multi	2.25	3.50
		Nos. B72-B74 (3)	3.95	5.55

Surtax for child welfare organizations.

SP23

MALTA — MANCHUKUO

Paintings from dome spandrels of Mosta Parish Church by Giuseppe Cali (1846-1930): 3c+1c, Nativity scene. 10c+2c, Adoration of the Magi. 25c+3c, Christ among the Elders in the Temple.

1992, Oct. 22
B75	SP23	3c +1c multi	.80	.55
B76	SP23	10c +2c multi	1.90	2.15
B77	SP23	25c +3c multi	2.25	5.25
		Nos. B75-B77 (3)	4.95	7.95

Surtax for child welfare organizations.

SP24

Designs: 3c+1c, Christ Child in manger. 10c+2c, Christmas tree. 25c+3c, Star.

1993, Nov. 20
B78	SP24	3c +1c multi	.30	.30
B79	SP24	10c +2c multi	.75	.90
B80	SP24	25c +3c multi	1.45	1.60
		Nos. B78-B80 (3)	2.50	2.80

Beginning with No. 845, semi-postal stamps are included with the postage portion of the set.

Christmas — SP25

Children's art: 6c+2c, Man with net chasing star. 15c+2c, People, Christmas tree. 16c+2c, People hugging. 19c+3c, Woman with shopping bags.

2001, Nov. 29 Litho. Perf. 14
B81-B84	SP25	Set of 4	4.75 6.25

Stampin' the Future Type of 2000
Souvenir Sheet
Wmk. 354

2006, Dec. 22 Litho. Perf. 14
B85	A261	£1.50 + (16c) Like #1029	8.75 9.25

Surtax was for the Valletta YMCA.

AIR POST STAMPS

No. 140 Overprinted

Perf. 14½x14
1928, Apr. 1 Typo. Wmk. 4
C1	A22	6p red & violet	2.00 1.25
		Never hinged	4.50

Catalogue values for unused stamps in this section, from this point to the end of the section, are for Never Hinged items.

Jet over Valletta — AP1

Designs: 3c, 5c, 20c, 35c, Winged emblem. 7c5m, 25c, like 4c.
Wmk. 354

1974, Mar. Litho. Perf. 13½
Cross Emblem in Red and Blue
C2	AP1	3c ol brown & gold	.30	.25
C3	AP1	4c dk blue & gold	.30	.25
C4	AP1	5c dk vio bl & gold	.30	.25
C5	AP1	7c5m sl green & gold	.30	.25
C6	AP1	20c vio brn & gold	.30	.45
C7	AP1	25c slate & gold	.30	.45
C8	AP1	35c brown & gold	.40	.85
		Nos. C2-C8 (7)	2.20	2.75

Jet and Megalithic Temple — AP2

Designs: 7c, 20c, Air Malta Boeing 720B approaching Malta. 11c, 75c, Jumbo jet landing at Luqa Airport. 17c, like 5c.

1978, Oct. 3 Litho. Perf. 13½
C9	AP2	5c multicolored	.30	.30
C10	AP2	7c multicolored	.35	.35
C11	AP2	11c multicolored	.40	.40
C12	AP2	17c multicolored	.50	.50
C13	AP2	20c multicolored	.75	.75
C14	AP2	75c multicolored	1.75	2.40
		Nos. C9-C14 (6)	4.05	4.70

Boeing 737, 1984 — AP3

8c, Boeing 720B, 1974. 16c, Vickers Vanguard, 1964. 23c, Vickers Viscount, 1958. 27c, Douglas DC3 Dakota, 1948. 38c, AW Atlanta, 1936. 75c, Dornier Wal, 1929.

1984, Jan. 26 Wmk. 354 Perf. 14
C15	AP3	7c shown	.30	.25
C16	AP3	8c multi	.30	.25
C17	AP3	16c multi	.30	.25
C18	AP3	23c multi	.35	.25
C19	AP3	27c multi	.40	.35
C20	AP3	38c multi	.65	.55
C21	AP3	75c multi	.80	.70
		Nos. C15-C21 (7)	3.10	2.60

POSTAGE DUE STAMPS

D1

1925 Typeset Unwmk. Imperf.
J1	D1	½p black, *white*	1.25	8.00
J2	D1	1p black, *white*	3.00	3.50
J3	D1	1½p black, *white*	2.75	3.50
J4	D1	2p black, *white*	12.00	21.00
J5	D1	2½p black, *white*	2.50	2.50
	a.	"2" of "½" omitted	1,000.	1,400.
J6	D1	3p black, *gray*	8.50	15.00
J7	D1	4p black, *orange*	4.50	8.50
J8	D1	6p black, *orange*	4.50	22.50
J9	D1	1sh black, *orange*	6.00	25.00
J10	D1	1sh6p black, *orange*	16.00	62.50
		Nos. J1-J10 (10)	61.00	172.00
		Set, never hinged	130.00	

These stamps were typeset in groups of 42. In each sheet there were four impressions of a group, two of them being inverted and making tete-beche pairs. Value set of tete-beche pairs $175.

Forged examples of No. J5a are known.

Maltese Cross — D2

Wmk. 4 Sideways
1925 Typo. Perf. 12
J11	D2	½p blue green	1.40	.70
J12	D2	1p violet	1.40	.50
J13	D2	1½p yellow brown	1.75	1.00
J14	D2	2p gray	8.50	1.25
J15	D2	2½p orange	2.25	1.25
J16	D2	3p dark blue	4.50	1.25
J17	D2	4p olive green	12.00	16.00
J18	D2	6p claret	3.50	4.75
J19	D2	1sh gray black	7.50	14.00
J20	D2	1sh6p deep rose	9.00	42.50
		Nos. J11-J20 (10)	51.80	83.20
		Set, never hinged	85.00	

In 1953-57 six values (½p-2p, 3p, 4p) were reissued on chalky paper in slightly different colors. Value, $14.

Catalogue values for unused stamps in this section, from this point to the end of the section, are for Never Hinged items.

1966 Wmk. 314 Perf. 12
J21	D2	2p sepia	8.75	26.00

Wmk. 354 Sideways
1968 Perf. 12½
J22	D2	½p green	.40	2.25
J23	D2	1p rose violet	.35	1.65
J24	D2	1½p bister brn	.40	3.50
J25	D2	2p brown black	.95	.75
J26	D2	2½p orange	.65	.75
J27	D2	3p Prus blue	.60	.60
J28	D2	4p olive	1.10	.90
J29	D2	6p purple	.80	1.90
J30	D2	1sh black	.95	1.65
J31	D2	1sh6p rose car	3.00	8.25
		Nos. J22-J31 (10)	9.20	22.20

1967, Nov. 9 Perf. 12
J22a	D2	½p	4.50	10.00
J23a	D2	1p	4.50	10.00
J25a	D2	2p	7.00	10.00
J28a	D2	4p	45.00	120.00
		Nos. J22a-J28a (4)	61.00	150.00

Numeral — D3

Perf. 13x13½
1973, Apr. 28 Litho. Wmk. 354
J32	D3	2m brown	.30	.25
J33	D3	3m brown orange	.30	.25
J34	D3	5m carmine	.30	.25
J35	D3	1c deep green	.30	.25
J36	D3	2c black	.35	.30
J37	D3	3c olive	.35	.30
J38	D3	5c violet blue	.55	.50
J39	D3	10c deep magenta	.75	.90
		Nos. J32-J39 (8)	3.20	3.00

Scroll — D4

Wmk. 354
1993, Jan. 4 Litho. Perf. 14
J40	D4	1c brt pink & lt pink	.30	.30
J41	D4	2c brt blue & lt blue	.30	.35
J42	D4	5c brt grn & lt grn	.30	.40
J43	D4	10c org yel & brt yel	.50	.50
		Nos. J40-J43 (4)	1.40	1.55

WAR TAX STAMPS

Nos. 50, 25 Overprinted

1918 Wmk. 3 Perf. 14
MR1	A13	½p green	2.25	.30

Wmk. 2
MR2	A12	3p red violet & gray	3.00	15.00

MANCHUKUO
ˈman-ˈchü-ˈkwō

LOCATION — Covering Manchuria, or China's three northeastern provinces — Fengtien, Kirin and Heilungkiang — plus Jehol province.
GOVT. — Independent state under Japanese influence
AREA — 503,013 sq. mi. (estimated)
POP. — 43,233,954 (1940 est.)
CAPITAL — Hsinking (Changchun)

Manchukuo was formed in 1932 with the assistance of Japan. In 1934 Henry Pu-yi, Chief Executive, was enthroned as Emperor Kang Teh. In 1945, when Japan surrendered to the Allies, the terms included the return of Manchukuo to China. The puppet state was dissolved.

100 Fen = 1 Yuan

Watermarks

Wmk. 141 — Horizontal Zigzag Lines

Wmk. 239 — Curved Wavy Lines

Wmk. 242 — Characters

Pagoda at Liaoyang
A1

Chief Executive Henry Pu-yi
A2

Five characters in top label.
Inscription reads "Manchu State Postal Administration."

Lithographed
Perf. 13x13½
1932, July 26 Unwmk.
White Paper
1	A1	½f gray brown	2.00	1.00
2	A1	1f dull red	2.25	1.50
3	A1	1½f lilac	7.00	7.00
4	A1	2f slate	7.00	7.50
5	A1	3f dull brown	9.50	9.50
6	A1	4f olive brown	3.50	.70
7	A1	5f green	5.00	1.50
8	A1	6f rose	12.00	5.50
9	A1	7f gray	5.00	3.00
10	A1	8f ocher	20.00	16.00
11	A1	10f orange	7.50	1.50
12	A2	13f dull brown	16.00	10.00
13	A2	15f rose	22.50	5.00
14	A2	16f turquoise grn	32.50	13.00
15	A2	20f gray brown	12.00	4.00
16	A2	30f orange	13.50	5.00
17	A2	50f olive green	27.50	5.00
18	A2	1y violet	45.00	17.50
		Nos. 1-18 (18)	249.75	114.20
		Set, never hinged	300.00	

A local provisional overprint of a horizontal line of four characters in red or black, reading "Chinese Postal Administration," was applied to Nos. 1-18 by followers of Gen. Su Ping-wen, who rebelled against the Manchukuo government in September, 1932. Many counterfeits exist.

See Nos. 23-31. For surcharges see Nos. 36, 59-61.

See note on local handstamps at end of the Manchukuo listings.

Flags, Map and Wreath
A3

Old State Council Building
A4

MANCHUKUO

1933, Mar. 1   **Perf. 12½**
19	A3	1f orange	8.00	5.50
20	A4	2f dull green	20.00	16.00
21	A3	4f light red	7.00	5.50
22	A4	10f deep blue	40.00	37.50
		Nos. 19-22 (4)	75.00	64.50
		Set, never hinged	110.00	

1st anniv. of the establishing of the State. Nos. 19-22 were printed in sheets of 100 with a special printing in sheets of 20.

Type of 1932
Perf. 13x13½
1934, Feb.   **Engr.**   **Wmk. 239**
Granite Paper

23	A1	½f dark brown	4.50	2.50
24	A1	1f red brown	5.00	1.25
25	A1	1½f dark violet	8.00	5.00
26	A1	2f slate	10.00	3.50
27	A1	3f brown	5.00	1.10
28	A1	4f olive brown	40.00	7.50
29	A1	10f deep orange	18.00	3.00
30	A2	15f rose	900.00	325.00
31	A2	1y violet	60.00	17.50
		Nos. 23-31 (9)	1,051.	366.35

For surcharge see No. 60.

Emperor's Palace A5
Phoenix A6

1934, Mar. 1   **Perf. 12½**
32	A5	1½f orange brown	7.00	5.50
33	A6	3f carmine	6.50	4.50
34	A5	6f green	20.00	12.50
35	A6	10f dark blue	32.50	20.00
		Nos. 32-35 (4)	66.00	42.50
		Set, never hinged	100.00	

Enthronement of Emperor Kang Teh. Nos. 32-35 were printed in sheets of 100, with a special printing in sheets of 20.

No. 6 Surcharged in Black

Perf. 13x13½
1934   **Unwmk.**   **White Paper**
36	A1	1f on 4f olive grn	7.00	5.00
		Never hinged	12.00	
a.		Brown surcharge	47.50	47.50
b.		Upper left character of surcharge omitted		
c.		Inverted surcharge	1,000.	1,000.

Pagoda at Liaoyang A7
Emperor Kang Teh A8

Six characters in top label instead of five as in 1902-04 issues. Inscription reads "Manchu Empire Postal Administration."

Perf. 13x13½
1934-36   **Wmk. 239**   **Engr.**
Granite Paper

37	A7	½f brown	.80	.60
38	A7	1f red brown	1.10	.60
39	A7	1½f dk violet	1.50	1.00
a.		Booklet pane of 6	200.00	
41	A7	3f brown ('35)	.90	.70
a.		Booklet pane of 6	200.00	
42	A7	5f dk blue ('35)	14.00	4.00
43	A7	5f gray ('36)	6.00	4.00
44	A7	6f rose ('35)	5.00	1.75
45	A7	7f dk gray ('36)	4.00	2.25
47	A7	9f red orange ('35)	3.75	1.75
50	A8	15f ver ('35)	4.00	1.75
51	A8	18f Prus grn ('35)	32.50	8.00
52	A8	20f dk brown ('35)	6.50	2.00
53	A8	30f orange brn ('35)	7.00	2.00
54	A8	50f ol grn ('35)	20.00	8.25
55	A8	1y dk violet ('35)	30.00	9.00
a.		1y violet	32.50	10.00
		Nos. 37-55 (15)	125.05	42.65
		Set, never hinged	155.00	

4f and 8f, type A7, were prepared but not issued. Values $45 and $15, respectively.

1935   **Wmk. 242**   **Perf. 13x13½**
57	A7	10f deep blue	13.00	2.50
58	A8	13f light brown	16.00	8.00
		Set, never hinged	42.00	

No. 6 Surcharged in Black
1935   **White Paper**   **Unwmk.**
59	A1	3f on 4f ol brn	70.00	60.00
		Never hinged	100.00	

No. 28 Surcharged in Black

1935   **Granite Paper**   **Wmk. 239**
60	A1	3f on 4f olive brn	10.00	6.00
		Never hinged	17.50	

Similar Surcharge on No. 14
1935   **White Paper**   **Unwmk.**
61	A2	3f on 16f turq grn	18.00	12.00
		Never hinged	24.00	
		Nos. 59-61 (3)	98.00	78.00

Orchid Crest of Manchukuo A9

Sacred White Mountains and Black Waters A10

No. 62

No. 63

1935, Jan. 1   **Engr.**   **Wmk. 141**
Granite Paper
62	A9	2f green	6.50	3.50
63	A10	4f dull ol grn	3.25	2.50
64	A9	8f ocher	4.75	3.75
65	A10	12f brown red	16.00	20.00
		Nos. 62-65 (4)	30.50	29.75
		Set, never hinged	44.00	

Nos. 62-65 exist imperforate.

No. 66

No. 70

1935   **Wmk. 242**
66	A9	2f yellow green	6.00	2.00
68	A9	8f ocher	8.00	8.00
70	A10	12f brown red	15.00	20.00
		Nos. 66-70 (3)	29.00	30.00
		Set, never hinged	40.00	

Nos. 62-70 issued primarily to pay postage to China, but valid for any postal use. See Nos. 75-78, 113, 115, 158. For surcharges see Nos. 101, 103-104, 106-109, People's Republic of China No. 2L19.

Mt. Fuji — A11
Phoenix — A12

Perf. 11, 12½ and Compound
1935, Apr. 1   **Engr.**   **Wmk. 242**
71	A11	1½f dull green	3.75	3.00
72	A12	3f orange	4.00	3.75
a.		3f red orange	7.50	6.00
73	A11	6f dk carmine	8.00	7.00
		Horiz. pair, imperf. btwn.	1,200.	
a.		Perf. 11x12½	50.00	40.00
74	A12	10f dark blue	10.00	8.50
a.		Perf. 12½x11	85.00	60.00
b.		Perf. 12½	30.00	27.50
		Nos. 71-74 (4)	25.75	22.25
		Set, never hinged	35.00	

Visit of the Emperor of Manchukuo to Tokyo.

Orchid Crest — A13

No. 75

No. 78

Unbroken lines of shading in the background of Nos. 76 and 78. Shading has been removed from right and left of the mountains. Nearly all lines have been removed from the lake. There are numerous other alterations in the design.

Types of A9 & A10 Redrawn

1936   **Litho.**   **Perf. 13x13½**   **Wmk. 242**
75	A13	2f lt green	1.50	1.00
76	A13	4f olive green	4.50	2.50
77	A13	8f ocher	5.00	2.50
78	A10	12f orange brn	47.50	32.50
		Nos. 75-78 (4)	58.50	38.50
		Set, never hinged	80.00	

Issued primarily to pay postage to China, but valid for any postal use. See No. 112. For surcharges see Nos. 102-106.

Wild Goose over Sea of Japan — A14

Communications Building at Hsinking — A15

Perf. 12x12½, 12½x12
1936, Jan. 26   **Wmk. 242**
79	A14	1½f black brown	4.50	3.00
80	A15	3f rose lilac	4.50	3.00
81	A14	6f carmine rose	9.00	8.00
82	A15	10f blue	14.00	10.00
		Nos. 79-82 (4)	32.00	24.00
		Set, never hinged	50.00	

Postal convention with Japan.

New State Council Building A16
Carting Soybeans A17

North Mausoleum at Mukden A18
Summer Palace at Chengteh A19

1936-37   **Wmk. 242**   **Perf. 13x13½**
83	A16	½f brown	.75	.60
84	A16	1f red brown	.75	.50
85	A16	1½f violet	7.00	5.00
a.		Booklet pane of 6	150.00	
86	A17	2f lt green ('37)	1.00	.50
a.		Booklet pane of 6	65.00	
87	A16	3f chocolate	1.25	.75
a.		Booklet pane of 6	375.00	
88	A18	4f lt ol grn ('37)	1.25	.75
a.		Booklet pane of 6	60.00	
89	A16	5f gray black	30.00	12.00
90	A17	6f carmine	1.25	.50
91	A18	7f brown blk	1.75	1.00
92	A18	9f red orange	2.25	1.25
93	A19	10f blue	2.50	.60
94	A18	12f dp orange ('37)	2.25	.60
95	A18	13f brown	42.50	37.50
96	A18	15f carmine	3.75	1.00

MANCHUKUO

97	A17	20f dk brown	2.25	.90
98	A19	30f chestnut brn	2.25	.90
99	A17	50f olive green	2.75	1.25
100	A19	1y violet	6.00	1.75
		Nos. 83–100 (18)	111.50	67.25
		Set, never hinged	160.00	

Nos. 83, 84, 86, 88 and 93 are known imperforate but were not regularly issued.

See Nos. 159-163. For overprints see Nos. 140-141, 148-151. For surcharges see People's Republic of China Nos. 2L1-2L2, 2L11-2L18, 2L20-2L37, 2L40-2L52.

1937 — Surcharged on No. 66

| 101 | A9 (a) | 2½f on 2f | 4.00 | 3.50 |

Surcharged on Nos. 75, 76 and 78

102	A13 (a)	2½f on 2f	4.50	3.50
103	A10 (b)	5f on 4f	5.50	4.50
104	A10 (c)	13f on 12f	14.00	12.00

Surcharged in Black on Nos. 75, 76 and 70

Space between bottom characters of surcharge 4½mm

105	A13 (d)	2½f on 2f	3.25	3.00
a.		Inverted surcharge	700.00	850.00
b.		Vert. pair, one without surch.	200.00	
106	A10 (b)	5f on 4f	4.50	4.00
107	A10 (c)	13f on 12f	13.50	12.50

Surcharged on No. 70

Space between characters 6½mm

| 108 | A10 (c) | 13f on 12f | 225.00 | 200.00 |

Same Surcharge on No. 63

Space between characters 4½mm — Wmk. 141

109	A10 (b)	5f on 4f	8.25	7.00
		Nos. 101-109 (9)	282.50	250.00
		Set, never hinged	390.00	

Nos. 101-109 were issued primarily to pay postage to China, but were valid for any postal use.

Rising Sun over Manchurian Plain — A20

Composite Picture of Manchurian City — A21

Perf. 12½

1937, Mar. 1   Litho.   Unwmk.

110	A20	1½f carmine rose	5.00	4.50
111	A21	3f blue green	4.00	3.50
		Set, never hinged	12.00	

5th anniv. of the founding of the State of Manchukuo.

Types of 1936
Perf. 13x13½   Engr.

1937   Wmk. 242

112	A13	2½f dk violet	1.25	1.00
113	A10	5f black	.65	.65
115	A10	13f dk red brown	2.25	1.00
		Nos. 112-115 (3)	4.15	2.65
		Set, never hinged	7.00	

Issued primarily to pay postage to China, but were valid for any postal use.

Pouter Pigeon A22

National Flag and Buildings A23

Perf. 12x12½

1937, Sept. 16   Unwmk.

116	A22	2f dark violet	3.25	2.50
117	A23	4f rose carmine	3.50	2.50
118	A20	10f dark green	6.75	5.00
119	A23	20f dark blue	9.00	7.00
		Nos. 116-119 (4)	22.50	17.00
		Set, never hinged	29.00	

Completion of the national capital, Hsinking, under the first Five-Year Construction Plan.

Map A24

Dept. of Justice Building A27

Japanese Residents' Association Building — A25

Postal Administration Building — A26

Perf. 12x12½, 13, 12½x13, 13x13½, 13½x13

1937, Dec. 1   Litho.   Unwmk.

121	A24	2f dark carmine	2.00	1.75
122	A25	4f green	3.50	2.50
123	A25	8f orange	6.00	5.00
124	A26	10f blue	6.50	5.00
125	A27	12f lt violet	7.50	7.50
126	A26	20f lilac brown	11.00	8.00
		Nos. 121-126 (6)	36.50	29.75
		Set, never hinged	48.00	

Issued in commemoration of the abolition of extraterritorial rights within Manchukuo.
Perf varieties exist on Nos. 122-126, lowest value listed, others about 25-35% higher.

New Year Greetings — A28

1937, Dec. 15   Engr.   Perf. 12x12½

127	A28	2f dk blue & red	3.00	2.00
		Never hinged	4.00	
a.		Double impression of border	17.50	

Issued to pay postage on New Year's greeting cards.

Map and Cross — A29

Wmk. 242

1938, Oct. 15   Litho.   Perf. 13

128	A29	2f lake & scarlet	2.00	1.50
129	A29	4f slate grn & scar	2.00	1.50
		Set, never hinged	6.00	

Founding of the Red Cross Soc. in Manchukuo.

Network of State Railroads in Manchukuo A30

Express Train "Asia" A31

1939, Oct. 21

130	A30	2f dk org, blk & dp bl	2.50	1.75
131	A31	4f dp blue & indigo	2.50	1.75
		Set, never hinged	7.00	

Attainment of 10,000 kilometers in the railway mileage in Manchuria.

Stork Flying above Mast of Imperial Flagship — A32

1940   Photo.   Unwmk.

132	A32	2f brt red violet	2.00	1.50
133	A32	4f brt green	2.00	1.50
		Set, never hinged	6.00	

Second visit of Emperor Kang Teh to Emperor Hirohito of Japan.

Census Taker and Map of Manchukuo A33

Census Form A34

1940, Sept. 10   Litho.   Wmk. 242

134	A33	2f vio brn & org	1.50	1.50
135	A34	4f black & green	1.50	1.50
a.		Double impression of green	100.00	
		Set, never hinged	4.00	

National census starting Oct. 1.

Message of Congratulation from Premier Chang Ching-hui A35

Dragon Dance A36

1940, Sept. 18   Engr.   Perf. 13x13½

| 136 | A35 | 2f carmine | 1.25 | 1.25 |

Perf. 13½x13

137	A36	4f indigo	1.25	1.25
a.		Imperf., pair	1,000.	
		Set, never hinged	3.50	

2600th anniversary of the birth of the Japanese Empire.

Soldier — A37

Perf. 13x13½

1941, May 25   Photo.   Unwmk.

138	A37	2f deep carmine	1.25	1.25
139	A37	4f bright ultra	1.25	1.25
		Set, never hinged	3.50	

Conscription Law, effective June 1, 1941.

Nos. 86 and 88 Overprinted in Red or Blue

Perf. 13x13½

1942, Feb. 16   Wmk. 242

140	A17	2f lt green (R)	1.25	1.25
141	A18	4f lt olive grn (Bl)	1.25	1.25
		Set, never hinged	3.50	

"Return of Singapore to East Asia, 9th year of Kang Teh."

Kengoku Shrine A38

Map of Manchukuo A39

Flag of Manchukuo — A40

Perf. 12x12½, 12½x12

1942, Mar. 1   Engr.

142	A38	2f carmine	.90	.90
143	A38	4f lilac	1.00	.90
144	A39	10f red, yel	2.25	2.25
145	A40	20f indigo, yel	3.00	3.00
		Nos. 142-145 (4)	7.15	7.05
		Set, never hinged	10.00	

"10th anniv. of Manchukuo, Mar. 1, 1942."

Allegory of National Harmony A41

Women of Five Races, Dancing A42

1942, Sept. 15

146	A41	3f orange	1.25	1.25
147	A42	6f light green	1.25	2.00
		Set, never hinged	3.50	

"10th anniv. of the founding of Manchukuo, Sept. 15, 1942."

Nos. 87 and 90 Overprinted in Green or Blue

1942, Dec. 8   Perf. 13x13½

148	A16	3f chocolate (G)	1.00	1.00
149	A17	6f carmine (Bl)	1.00	1.00
		Set, never hinged	3.00	

1st anniv. of the "Greater East Asia War." The overprint reads "Asiatic Prosperity Began This Day December 8, 1941."

Nos. 87 and 90 Overprinted in Red or Blue

1943, May 1

150	A16	3f chocolate (R)	1.00	1.00
151	A17	6f carmine (Bl)	1.00	1.00
		Set, never hinged	3.00	

Proclamation of the labor service law.

Red Cross Nurse Carrying Stretcher — A43

1943, Oct. 1   Photo.

| 152 | A43 | 6f green | 1.25 | 1.25 |
| | | Never hinged | 2.00 | |

5th anniv. of the founding of the Red Cross Society of Manchukuo, Oct. 1, 1938.

MANCHUKUO — MARIANA ISLANDS — MARIENWERDER

Smelting Furnace — A44

1943, Dec. 8		Unwmk.	Perf. 13
153	A44 6f red brown	1.25	1.25
	Never hinged		1.75

2nd anniv. of the "Greater East Asia War."

Chinese Characters A45

Japanese Characters A46

Perf. 13x13½
1944		Wmk. 242	Litho.
154	A45 10f rose	.80	1.25
a.	Imperf., vert. pair #154, 155	17.50	
	Vert. pair #154, 155	2.25	2.50
155	A46 10f rose	.80	5.00
156	A45 40f gray green	3.75	4.00
a.	Imperf., vert. pair #156, 157	60.00	
b.	40f with 10f vignette, perf.	300.00	400.00
c.	40f with 10f vignette, imperf.	450.00	
d.	Vert. pair #156, 157	8.00	14.00
157	A46 40f gray green	3.75	4.00
	Nos. 154-157 (4)	9.10	14.25
	Set, never hinged	13.50	

"Japan's Progress Is Manchukuo's Progress." Issued as propaganda for the close relationship of Japan and Manchukuo.
Frames of the 10f vignettes have rounded corners, those of the 40f vignettes have indented corners.

Types of 1935 and 1936-37
1944-45			Litho.
158	A10 5f gray black	1.25	2.75
a.	Imperf., pair	12.00	
159	A17 6f crimson rose	3.75	5.00
160	A19 10f light blue	6.50	8.00
161	A17 20f brown	2.50	4.00
162	A19 30f buff ('45)	2.75	4.00
163	A19 1y dull lilac	3.00	3.75
	Nos. 158-163 (6)	19.75	27.50
	Set, never hinged	29.00	

For surcharges see People's Republic of China Nos. 2L1, 2L14, 2L19, 2L24, 2L27, 2L30-2L31, 2L35, 2L37, 2L49, 2L52.

"One Heart, One Soul" — A47

1945, May 2			
164	A47 10f red	1.25	3.50
	Never hinged	2.50	
a.	Imperf., pair	12.00	25.00

Emperor's edict of May 2, 1935, 10th anniv.

AIR POST STAMPS

Sheep Grazing AP1

Railroad Bridge AP2

Wmk. Characters (242)
1936-37		Engr.	Perf. 13x13½
	Granite Paper		
C1	AP1 18f green	16.00	18.00
C2	AP1 19f blue green ('37)	6.00	7.00
C3	AP2 38f blue	17.50	17.50
C4	AP2 39f deep blue ('37)	3.00	4.25
	Nos. C1-C4 (4)	42.50	46.75
	Set, never hinged	54.00	

With the end of World War II and the collapse of Manchukuo, the Northeastern Provinces reverted to China. In many Manchurian towns and cities, the Manchukuo stamps were locally handstamped in ideograms: "Republic of China," "China Postal Service" or "Temporary Use for China." A typical example is shown above. Many of these local issues also were surcharged.

MARIANA ISLANDS

ˌmar-ē-ˈa-nə ˈī-ləndz

LOCATION — A group of 14 islands in the West Pacific Ocean, about 1500 miles east of the Philippines.
GOVT. — Possession of Spain, then of Germany
AREA — 246 sq. mi.
POP. — 59,000 (2020 est.)
CAPITAL — Saipan

Until 1899 this group belonged to Spain but in that year all except Guam were ceded to Germany.

100 Centavos = 1 Peso
100 Pfennig = 1 Mark (1899)

Values for unused stamps are for examples with original gum as defined in the catalogue introduction. Very fine examples of Nos. 1-6 will have perforations touching or just cutting into the design. Stamps with perfs clear on all sides and well centered are rare and sell for substantially more.

Issued under Spanish Dominion

Philippines Stamps Hstmpd. Vert. in Blackish Violet Reading Up or Down

1899, Sept.		Unwmk.	Perf. 14
1	A39 2c dark blue green	800.	350.
2	A39 3c dark brown	500.	275.
3	A39 5c car rose	800.	275.
4	A39 6c dark blue	5,000.	2,500.
5	A39 8c gray brown	500.	175.
6	A39 15c dull ol grn	1,700.	900.

Overprint forgeries of Nos. 1-6 exist.
No. 4 was issued in a quantity of 50 stamps.

Issued under German Dominion

Values for Nos. 11-16 are for postally used examples in the correct period of use. Favor cancellations exist and are valued at 25 percent to 50 percent of the values shown here if used during the correct period. Expertization is recommended.

Stamps of Germany, 1889-90, Overprinted in Black at 56 degree Angle

1900, May		Unwmk.	Perf. 13½x14½
11	A9 3pf dark brown	11.50	27.50
12	A9 5pf green	15.00	29.00
13	A10 10pf carmine	19.00	40.00
14	A10 20pf ultra	22.50	115.00
15	A10 25pf orange	60.00	145.00
b.	Inverted overprint	2,100.	
16	A10 50pf red brn	60.00	210.00
	Nos. 11-16 (6)	188.00	566.50

Forged cancellations exist on Nos. 11-16, 17-29.

Stamps of Germany, 1889-90, Overprinted in Black at 48 degree Angle

1899, Nov. 18			
11a	A9 3pf light brown	1,800.	1,800.
12a	A9 5pf green	2,250.	1,500.
13a	A10 10pf carmine	165.00	180.00
14a	A10 20pf ultra	165.00	180.00
15a	A10 25pf orange	2,400.	2,400.
16a	A10 50pf red brown	2,400.	2,250.

Kaiser's Yacht "Hohenzollern"
A4 **A5**

1901, Jan.		Typo.	Perf. 14
17	A4 3pf brown	1.00	1.50
18	A4 5pf green	1.00	1.65
19	A4 10pf carmine	1.00	3.75
20	A4 20pf ultra	1.10	6.50
21	A4 25pf org & blk, yel	1.50	11.50
22	A4 30pf org & blk, sal	1.50	12.00
23	A4 40pf lake & blk	1.50	12.00
24	A4 50pf pur & blk, sal	1.75	13.50
25	A4 80pf lake & blk, rose	2.25	22.50

Engr.
Perf. 14½x14

26	A5 1m carmine	4.00	65.00
27	A5 2m blue	5.50	92.50
28	A5 3m blk vio	7.50	120.00
29	A5 5m slate & car	140.00	450.00
	Nos. 17-29 (13)	169.60	812.40

Wmk. Lozenges (125)

1916-19		Typo.	Perf. 14
30	A4 3pf brown ('19)		1.00

Engr.
Perf. 14½x14

| 31 | A5 5m slate & carmine, 25x17 holes | | 30.00 |

Nos. 30 and 31 were never placed in use.

MARIENWERDER

mä-ˈrē-ən-ˌve̩ə̯rd-ər

LOCATION — Northeastern Germany, bordering on Poland
GOVT. — A district of West Prussia

By the Versailles Treaty the greater portion of West Prussia was ceded to Poland but the district of Marienwerder was allowed a plebiscite which was held in 1920 and resulted in favor of Germany.

100 Pfennig = 1 Mark

Plebiscite Issues

Symbolical of Allied Supervision of the Plebiscite — A1

1920		Unwmk. Litho.	Perf. 11½
1	A1 5pf green	.65	1.90
2	A1 10pf rose red	.65	1.60
3	A1 15pf gray	.65	2.10
4	A1 20pf brn org	.65	1.60
5	A1 25pf deep blue	.65	2.10
6	A1 30pf orange	.90	2.10
7	A1 40pf brown	.65	2.50
8	A1 50pf violet	.65	1.90
9	A1 60pf red brown	4.00	3.00
10	A1 75pf chocolate	.90	1.90
11	A1 1m brn & grn	.65	1.60
12	A1 2m dk vio	2.00	3.75
13	A1 3m red	4.75	5.50
14	A1 5m blue & rose	27.50	16.00
	Nos. 1-14 (14)	45.25	47.55
	Set, never hinged	130.00	

These stamps occasionally show parts of two papermakers' watermarks, consisting of the letters "O. B. M." with two stars before and after, or "P. & C. M."
Nos. 1-14 exist imperf.; value for set, $700. Nearly all exist part perf.

Stamps of Germany, 1905-19, Overprinted

1920		Wmk. 125	Perf. 14, 14½
24	A16 5pf green	16.00	21.00
a.	Inverted overprint	125.00	
	Never hinged	210.00	
b.	Double overprint, one inverted	450.00	750.00
	Never hinged	750.00	
26	A16 20pf bl vio	6.00	20.00
a.	Inverted overprint	62.50	135.00
	Never hinged	125.00	
b.	Double overprint	85.00	
	Never hinged	150.00	
28	A16 50pf vio & blk, buff	375.00	800.00
29	A16 75pf grn & blk	6.00	6.00
a.	Inverted overprint	62.50	135.00
	Never hinged	125.00	
30	A16 80pf lake & blk, rose	75.00	125.00
31	A17 1m car rose	85.00	125.00
a.	Inverted overprint	425.00	
	Never hinged	850.00	
	Nos. 24-31 (6)	563.00	1,097.
	Set, never hinged	1,200.	

Trial impressions were made in red, green and lilac, and with 2½mm instead of 3mm space between the lines of the overprint. These were printed on the 75pf and 80pf. The 1 mark was overprinted with the same words in 3 lines of large sans-serif capitals. All these are essays. Some were passed through the post, apparently with speculative intent.

Stamps of Germany, 1905-18, Surcharged

32	A22 1m on 2pf gray	25.00	37.50
33	A22 2m on 2½pf gray	12.00	16.00
a.	Inverted surcharge	50.00	125.00
	Never hinged	125.00	
34	A16 3m on 3pf brown	12.00	13.50
a.	Double surcharge	50.00	125.00
b.	Inverted surcharge	50.00	120.00
	Never hinged	100.00	
35	A22 5m on 7½pf org	12.00	13.50
a.	Inverted surcharge	50.00	125.00
	Never hinged	100.00	
b.	Double surcharge	50.00	120.00
	Never hinged	100.00	
	Nos. 32-35 (4)	61.00	80.50
	Set, never hinged	220.00	

There are two types of the letters "M," "C," "i" and "e" and of the numerals "2" and "5" in these surcharges.
Counterfeits exist of Nos. 24-35.

Stamps of Germany, 1920, Overprinted

1920, July			Perf. 15x14½
36	A17 1m red	2.50	3.50
37	A17 1.25m green	3.25	4.25
38	A17 1.50m yellow brown	4.25	4.75
39	A21 2.50m lilac rose	2.50	4.25
	Nos. 36-39 (4)	12.50	16.75
	Set, never hinged	32.50	

A2

1920		Unwmk.	Perf. 11½
40	A2 5pf green	3.25	1.60
41	A2 10pf rose red	3.25	1.60
42	A2 15pf gray	11.00	11.00
43	A2 20pf brn org	2.10	1.60
44	A2 25pf dp bl	11.00	14.50
45	A2 30pf orange	2.10	1.25
46	A2 40pf brown	2.10	1.25
47	A2 50pf violet	1.60	1.60
48	A2 60pf red brn	5.25	4.50
49	A2 75pf chocolate	5.25	4.25
50	A2 1m brn & grn	2.10	1.25
51	A2 2m dk vio	2.10	1.25
52	A2 3m light red	2.10	1.60
53	A2 5m blue & rose	3.25	2.25
	Nos. 40-53 (14)	56.45	49.75
	Set, never hinged	135.00	

269

MARSHALL ISLANDS

ˈmär-shəl ˈī-ləndz

LOCATION — Two chains of islands in the West Pacific Ocean, about 2,500 miles southeast of Tokyo
GOVT. — Republic
AREA — 70 sq. mi.
POP. — 65,507 (1999 est.)
CAPITAL — Dalap-Uliga-Darrit

The Marshall Islands were German possession from 1885 to 1914. Seized by Japan in 1914, the islands were taken by the US in WW II and became part of the US Trust Territory of the Pacific in 1947. By agreement with the USPS, the islands began issuing their own stamps in 1984, with the USPS continuing to carry the mail to and from the islands.

On Oct. 21, 1986 Marshall Islands became a Federation as a Sovereign State in Compact of Free Association with the US.

100 Pfennig = 1 Mark
100 Cents = 1 Dollar

> Catalogue values for unused stamps in this country are for Never Hinged items, beginning with Scott 31 in the regular postage section, and Scott C1 in the airpost section.

Watermark

Wmk. 125 — Lozenges

Issued under German Dominion

A1   A2

Stamps of Germany Overprinted "Marschall-Inseln" in Black

1897		Unwmk.		Perf. 13½x14½	
1	A1	3pf dark brown		130.00	625.00
a.		3pf light yellowish brn		3,500.	2,000.
2	A1	5pf green		110.00	500.00
3	A1	10pf carmine		45.00	140.00
4	A2	20pf ultra		45.00	140.00
5	A2	25pf orange		130.00	800.00
6	A2	50pf red brown		130.00	800.00
		Nos. 1-6 (6)		590.00	3,005.

Nos. 5 and 6 were not placed in use, but canceled stamps exist.

A small quantity of the 3pf, 5pf, 10pf and 20pf were issued at Jaluit. These have yellowish, dull gum. Later overprintings of Nos. 1-6 were sold only at Berlin, and have white, smooth, shiny gum. No. 1a belongs to the Jaluit issue. For detailed listings, see the *Scott Specialized Catalogue of Stamps and Covers.*

Forged cancellations are found on almost all Marshall Islands stamps.

Overprinted "Marschall-Inseln"

A1a   A2a

1899-1900					
7	A1a	3pf dk brn ('00)		4.25	5.00
a.		3pf light brown		265.00	675.00
8	A1a	5pf green		11.00	14.00
9	A2a	10pf car ('00)		12.00	14.00
a.		Half used as 5pf on postcard			8,000.
10	A2a	20pf ultra ('00)		15.00	22.50
11	A2a	25pf orange		17.50	37.50
12	A2a	50pf red brown		27.50	42.50
a.		Half used as 25pf on cover			35,000.
		Nos. 7-12 (6)		87.25	135.50

Values for Nos. 9a and 12a are for properly used items, addressed and sent to Germany.

Kaiser's Yacht "Hohenzollern"
A3   A4

1901		Unwmk.	Typo.	Perf. 14	
13	A3	3pf brown		.60	1.50
14	A3	5pf green		.60	1.50
15	A3	10pf carmine		.60	4.25
16	A3	20pf ultra		.85	8.50
17	A3	25pf org & blk, *yel*		.90	14.50
18	A3	30pf org & blk, *sal*		.90	14.50
19	A3	40pf lake & blk		.90	14.50
20	A3	50pf pur & blk, *sal*		1.50	21.00
21	A3	80pf lake & blk, *rose*		3.00	32.50

Perf. 14½x14

22	A4	1m carmine	4.50	75.00
23	A4	2m blue	6.00	110.00
24	A4	3m blk vio	9.00	180.00
25	A4	5m slate & car	150.00	450.00
		Nos. 13-25 (13)	179.35	927.75

Wmk. Lozenges (125)

1916		Typo.	Perf. 14	
26	A3	3pf brown		.75

Engr. Perf. 14½x14

27	A4	5m slate & carmine, 25x17 holes		35.00

Nos. 26 and 27 were never placed in use.

The stamps of Marshall Islands overprinted "G. R. I." and new values in British currency were all used in New Britain and are listed among the issues for that country.

Two unauthorized issues appeared in 1979. The 1st, a set of five for the "Establishment of Government, May 1, 1979," consists of 8c, 15c, 21c, 31c and 75c labels. The 75c is about the size of a postcard. The 2nd, a set of four se-tenant blocks of four 10c labels for the Intl. Year of the Child. This set also exists imperf. and with specimen overprints.

> Catalogue values for unused stamps in this section, from this point to the end of the section, are for Never Hinged items.

Inauguration of Postal Service
A5

No. 31, Outrigger canoe. No. 32, Fishnet. No. 33, Navigational stick chart. No. 34, Islet.

1984, May 2		Litho.	Perf. 14x13½	
31	A5	20c multicolored	.50	.50
32	A5	20c multicolored	.50	.50
33	A5	20c multicolored	.50	.50
34	A5	20c multicolored	.50	.50
a.		Block of 4, #31-34	2.00	2.00

Mili Atoll, Astrolabe — A6

Maps and Navigational Instruments: 3c, Likiep, Azimuth compass. 5c, Ebon, 16th cent. compass. 10c, Jaluit, anchor buoys. 13c, Ailinginae, Nocturnal. 14c, Wotho Atoll, navigational stick chart. 20c, Kwajalein and Ebeye, stick chart. 22c, Eniwetok, 18th cent. lodestone storage case. 28c, Ailinglaplap, printed compass. 30c, Majuro, navigational stickchart. 33c, Namu, stick chart. 37c, Rongelap, quadrant. 39c, Taka, map compass, 16th cent. sea chart. 44c, Ujelang, chronograph. 50c,

Maloelap and Aur, nocturlabe. $1, Arno, 16th cent. sector compass.

1984-85		Litho.	Perf. 15x14	
35	A6	1c shown	.25	.25
36	A6	3c multicolored	.25	.25
37	A6	5c multicolored	.25	.25
38	A6	10c multicolored	.25	.25
39	A6	13c multicolored	.25	.25
a.		Booklet pane of 10	8.00	
40	A6	14c multicolored	.30	.30
a.		Booklet pane of 10	7.50	—
41	A6	20c multicolored	.40	.40
a.		Booklet pane of 10	10.00	—
b.		Bklt. pane, 5 each 13c, 20c	9.25	—
42	A6	22c multicolored	.45	.45
a.		Booklet pane of 10	9.50	—
b.		Bklt. pane, 5 each 14c, 22c	8.50	—
43	A6	28c multicolored	.55	.55
44	A6	30c multicolored	.60	.60
45	A6	33c multicolored	.65	.65
46	A6	37c multicolored	.75	.75
47	A6	39c multicolored	.80	.80
48	A6	44c multicolored	.90	.90
49	A6	50c multicolored	1.00	1.00
49A	A6	$1 multicolored	2.00	2.00
		Nos. 35-49A (16)	9.65	9.65

Issued: 1c, 3c, 5c, 10c, 30c, $1, 6/12; 13c, 20c, 28c, 37c, 12/19/84; 14c, 22c, 33c, 39c, 44c, 50c, 6/5/85.

See Nos. 107-109.

No. 7 — A7

1984, June 19		Perf. 14½x15	
50	A7	40c shown	.60	.60
51	A7	40c No. 13	.60	.60
52	A7	40c No. 4	.60	.60
53	A7	40c No. 25	.60	.60
a.		Block of 4, #50-53	2.40	2.40

Philatelic Salon, 19th UPU Congress, Hamburg, June 19-26.

Ausipex '84 A8

Dolphins.

1984, Sept. 5		Litho.	Perf. 14	
54	A8	20c Common	.40	.40
55	A8	20c Risso's	.40	.40
56	A8	20c Spotter	.40	.40
57	A8	20c Bottlenose	.40	.40
a.		Block of 4, #54-57	1.60	1.60

Christmas — A9

1984, Nov. 7		Litho.	Perf. 14	
58	A9	Strip of 4	2.25	2.25
a.-d.		20c any single	.40	.40
e.		Sheet of 16	9.00	

Sheet background shows text from Marshallese New Testament, giving each stamp a different background.

Marshall Islands Constitution, 5th Anniv. — A10

1984, Dec. 19		Litho.	Perf. 14	
59	A10	20c Traditional chief	.40	.40
60	A10	20c Amata Kabua	.40	.40
61	A10	20c Chester Nimitz	.40	.40
62	A10	20c Trygve Lie	.40	.40
a.		Block of 4, #59-62	1.60	1.60

Audubon Bicentenary A11

1985, Feb. 15		Litho.	Perf. 14	
63	A11	22c Forked-tailed Petrel	.60	.60
64	A11	22c Pectoral Sandpiper	.60	.60
a.		Pair, #63-64	1.20	1.20
		Nos. 63-64,C1-C2 (4)	3.00	3.00

Sea Shells — A12

No. 65, Cymatium lotorium. No. 66, Chicoreus cornucervi. No. 67, Strombus aurisdanae. No. 68, Turbo marmoratus. No. 69, Chicoreus palmarosae.

1985, Apr. 17		Litho.	Perf. 14	
65	A12	22c multicolored	.45	.45
66	A12	22c multicolored	.45	.45
67	A12	22c multicolored	.45	.45
68	A12	22c multicolored	.45	.45
69	A12	22c multicolored	.45	.45
a.		Strip of 5, #65-69	2.25	2.25

See Nos. 119-123, 152-156, 216-220.

Decade for Women — A13

1985, June 5		Litho.	Perf. 14	
70	A13	22c Native drum	.40	.40
71	A13	22c Palm branches	.40	.40
72	A13	22c Pounding stone	.40	.40
73	A13	22c Ak bird	.40	.40
a.		Block of 4, #70-73	1.65	1.65

Reef and Lagoon Fish — A14

No. 74, Acanthurus dussumieri. No. 75, Adioryx caudimaculatus. No. 76, Ostracion meleacaris. No. 77, Chaetodon ephippium.

1985, July 15		Litho.	Perf. 14	
74	A14	22c multicolored	.45	.45
75	A14	22c multicolored	.45	.45
76	A14	22c multicolored	.45	.45
77	A14	22c multicolored	.45	.45
a.		Block of 4, #74-77	1.80	1.80

Intl. Youth Year — A15

IYY and Alele Nautical Museum emblems and: No. 78, Marshallese youths and Peace Corps volunteers playing basketball. No. 79, Legend teller reciting local history, girl listening to recording. No. 80, Islander explaining navigational stick charts. No. 81, Jabwa stick dance.

1985, Aug. 31		Litho.	Perf. 14	
78	A15	22c multicolored	.45	.45
79	A15	22c multicolored	.45	.45
80	A15	22c multicolored	.45	.45
81	A15	22c multicolored	.45	.45
a.		Block of 4, #78-81	1.80	1.80

1856 American Board of Commissions Stock Certificate for Foreign Missions — A16

Missionary ship Morning Star I: 22c, Launch, Jothan Stetson Shipyard, Chelsea, MA, Aug. 7, 1857. 33c, First voyage, Honolulu to the Marshalls, 1857. 44c, Marshall islanders pulling Morning Star I into Ebon Lagoon, 1857.

1985, Oct. 21		Litho.	Perf. 14	
82	A16	14c multicolored	.25	.25
83	A16	22c multicolored	.45	.45
84	A16	33c multicolored	.65	.65
85	A16	44c multicolored	.90	.90
		Nos. 82-85 (4)	2.25	2.25

Christmas.

MARSHALL ISLANDS

US Space Shuttle, Astro Telescope, Halley's Comet — A17

Comet tail and research spacecraft: No. 87, Planet A Space Probe, Japan. No. 88, Giotto spacecraft, European Space Agency. No. 89, INTERCOSMOS Project Vega spacecraft, Russia, France, etc. No. 90, US naval tracking ship, NASA observational aircraft, cameo portrait of Edmond Halley (1656-1742), astronomer. Se-tenant in continuous design.

1985, Nov. 21
86	A17	22c multicolored	1.00	1.00
87	A17	22c multicolored	1.00	1.00
88	A17	22c multicolored	1.00	1.00
89	A17	22c multicolored	1.00	1.00
90	A17	22c multicolored	1.00	1.00
a.		Strip of 5, #86-90	5.00	5.00

Medicinal Plants — A18

1985, Dec. 31   Litho.   Perf. 14
91	A18	22c Sida fallax	.45	.45
92	A18	22c Scaevola frutescens	.45	.45
93	A18	22c Guettarda speciosa	.45	.45
94	A18	22c Cassytha filiformis	.45	.45
a.		Block of 4, #91-94	1.90	1.90

Maps Type of 1984

$2, Wotje and Erikub, terrestrial globe, 1571. $5, Bikini, Stick chart. $10, Stick chart of the atolls.

1986-87   Perf. 15x14, 14 ($10)
107	A6	$2 multicolored	4.50	4.50
108	A6	$5 multicolored	9.50	9.50

Size: 31x31mm
109	A6	$10 multicolored	16.00	16.00
		Nos. 107-109 (3)	30.00	30.00

Issued: $2, $5, 3/7/86; $10, 3/31/87.

Marine Invertebrates A19

1986, Mar. 31   Litho.   Perf. 14½x14
110	A19	14c Triton's trumpet	1.50	1.50
111	A19	14c Giant clam	1.50	1.50
112	A19	14c Small giant clam	1.50	1.50
113	A19	14c Coconut crab	1.50	1.50
a.		Block of 4, #110-113	6.00	6.00

Souvenir Sheet

AMERIPEX '86, Chicago, May 22-June 1 — A20

Design: $1, Douglas C-54 Globester.

1986, May 22   Litho.   Perf. 14
114	A20	$1 multicolored	2.75	2.75

1st Around-the-world scheduled flight, 40th anniv. No. 114 has multicolored margin continuing the design and picturing US Air Transport Command Base, Kwajalein Atoll and souvenir card.

See Nos. C3-C6.

Operation Crossroads, Atomic Bomb Tests, 40th Anniv. — A21

Designs: No. 115, King Juda, Bikinians sailing tibinal canoe. No. 116, USS Sumner, amphibious DUKW, advance landing. No. 117, Evacuating Bikinians. No. 118, Land reclamation, 1986.

1986, July 1   Litho.   Perf. 14
115	A21	22c multicolored	.45	.45
116	A21	22c multicolored	.45	.45
117	A21	22c multicolored	.45	.45
118	A21	22c multicolored	.45	.45
a.		Block of 4, #115-118	1.90	1.90

See No. C7.

Seashells Type of 1985

No. 119, Ramose murex. No. 120, Orange spider. No. 121, Red-mouth frog shell. No. 122, Laciniate conch. No. 123, Giant frog shell.

1986, Aug. 1   Litho.   Perf. 14
119	A12	22c multicolored	.45	.45
120	A12	22c multicolored	.45	.45
121	A12	22c multicolored	.45	.45
122	A12	22c multicolored	.45	.45
123	A12	22c multicolored	.45	.45
a.		Strip of 5, #119-123	2.25	2.25

Game Fish — A22

1986, Sept. 10   Litho.
124	A22	22c Blue marlin	.40	.40
125	A22	22c Wahoo	.40	.40
126	A22	22c Dolphin fish	.40	.40
127	A22	22c Yellowfin tuna	.40	.40
a.		Block of 4, #124-127	1.60	1.60

Christmas, Intl. Peace Year — A23

1986, Oct. 28   Litho.   Perf. 14
128	A23	22c United Nations UR	.60	.60
129	A23	22c United Nations UL	.60	.60
130	A23	22c United Nations LR	.60	.60
131	A23	22c United Nations LL	.60	.60
a.		Block of 4, #128-131	2.50	2.50

See No. C8.

US Whaling Ships — A24

No. 132, James Arnold, 1854. No. 133, General Scott, 1859. No. 134, Charles W. Morgan, 1865. No. 135, Lucretia, 1884.

1987, Feb. 20   Litho.   Perf. 14
132	A24	22c multicolored	.50	.50
133	A24	22c multicolored	.50	.50
134	A24	22c multicolored	.50	.50
135	A24	22c multicolored	.50	.50
a.		Block of 4, #132-135	2.00	2.00

Historic and Military Flights — A25

Designs: No. 136, Charles Lindbergh commemorative medal, Spirit of St. Louis crossing the Atlantic, 1927. No. 137, Lindbergh flying in the Battle of the Marshalls, 1944. No. 138, William Bridgeman flying in the Battle of Kwajalein, 1944. No. 139, Bridgeman testing the Douglas Skyrocket, 1951. No. 140, John Glenn flying in the Battle of the Marshalls. No. 141, Glenn, the first American to orbit the Earth, 1962.

1987, Mar. 12   Litho.   Perf. 14½
136	A25	33c multicolored	.70	.70
137	A25	33c multicolored	.70	.70
a.		Pair, #136-137	1.40	1.40
138	A25	39c multicolored	.75	.75
139	A25	39c multicolored	.75	.75
a.		Pair, #138-139	1.50	1.50
140	A25	44c multicolored	.80	.80
141	A25	44c multicolored	.80	.80
a.		Pair, #140-141	1.60	1.60
		Nos. 136-141 (6)	4.50	4.50

Souvenir Sheet

CAPEX '87 — A26

1987, June 15   Litho.   Perf. 14
142	A26	$1 Map of flight	2.50	2.50

Amelia Earhart (1897-1937), American aviator who died during attempted round-the-world flight, 50th anniv. No. 142 has multicolored margin picturing Earhart's flight pattern from Calcutta, India, to the crash site near Barre Is., Marshall Is.

US Constitution Bicentennial A27

Excerpts from the Marshall Islands and US Constitutions: No. 143, We,... Marshall. No. 144, National seals. No. 145, We,... United States. No. 146, All we have.... No. 147, Flags. No. 148, to establish.... No. 149, With this Constitution.... No. 150, Stick chart, Liberty Bell. No. 151, to promote....

1987, July 16   Litho.   Perf. 14
143	A27	14c multicolored	.30	.30
144	A27	14c multicolored	.30	.30
145	A27	14c multicolored	.30	.30
a.		Triptych, #143-145	1.00	1.00
146	A27	22c multicolored	.40	.40
147	A27	22c multicolored	.40	.40
148	A27	22c multicolored	.40	.40
a.		Triptych, #146-148	1.25	1.25
149	A27	44c multicolored	.80	.80
150	A27	44c multicolored	.80	.80
151	A27	44c multicolored	.80	.80
a.		Triptych, #149-151	2.50	2.50
		Nos. 143-151 (9)	4.50	4.50

Triptychs printed in continuous designs.

Seashells Type of 1985

No. 152, Magnificent cone. No. 153, Partridge tun. No. 154, Scorpion spider conch. No. 155, Hairy triton. No. 156, Chiragra spider conch.

1987, Sept. 1   Litho.   Perf. 14
152	A12	22c multicolored	.40	.40
153	A12	22c multicolored	.40	.40
154	A12	22c multicolored	.40	.40
155	A12	22c multicolored	.40	.40
156	A12	22c multicolored	.40	.40
a.		Strip of 5, #152-156	2.00	2.00

Copra Industry — A28

1987, Dec. 10   Litho.   Perf. 14
157	A28	44c Planting coconut	.65	.65
158	A28	44c Making copra	.65	.65
159	A28	44c Bottling coconut oil	.65	.65
a.		Triptych, #157-159	2.00	2.00

Contest-winning crayon drawings by Amram Enox; design contest sponsored by the Tobular Copra Processing Co.

Biblical Verses — A29

1987, Dec. 10
160	A29	14c Matthew 2:1	.25	.25
161	A29	22c Luke 2:14	.40	.40
162	A29	33c Psalms 33:3	.60	.60
163	A29	44c Psalms 150:5	.75	.75
		Nos. 160-163 (4)	2.00	2.00

Christmas.

Marine Birds — A30

1988, Jan. 27
164	A30	44c Pacific reef herons	.75	.75
165	A30	44c Bar-tailed godwit	.75	.75
166	A30	44c Masked booby	.75	.75
167	A30	44c Northern shoveler	.75	.75
a.		Block of 4, #164-167	3.00	3.00

Fish — A31

Designs: 1c, Damselfish. 3c, Blackface butterflyfish. 14c, Hawkfish. 15c, Balloonfish. 17c, Trunk fish. 22c, Lyretail wrasse. 25c, Parrotfish. 33c, White-spotted boxfish. 36c, Spotted boxfish. 39c, Surgeonfish. 44c, Long-snouted butterflyfish. 45c, Trumpetfish. 56c, Sharp-nosed puffer. $1, Seahorse. $2, Ghost pipefish. $5, Big-spotted triggerfish. $10, Blue jack.

Perf. 14½x14, 14 (#187)

1988-89   Litho.
168	A31	1c multicolored	.25	.25
169	A31	3c multicolored	.25	.25
170	A31	14c multicolored	.25	.25
a.		Booklet pane of 10	3.75	—
171	A31	15c multicolored	.25	.25
a.		Booklet pane of 10	4.50	—
172	A31	17c multicolored	.30	.30
173	A31	22c multicolored	.35	.35
a.		Booklet pane of 10	5.00	—
b.		Bklt. pane, 5 each 14c, 22c	5.00	—
174	A31	25c multicolored	.35	.35
a.		Booklet pane of 10	7.25	—
b.		Bklt. pane, 5 each 15c, 25c	7.25	—
175	A31	33c multicolored	.60	.60
176	A31	36c multicolored	.65	.65
177	A31	39c multicolored	.75	.75
178	A31	44c multicolored	.80	.80
179	A31	45c multicolored	.80	.80
180	A31	56c multicolored	1.00	1.00
181	A31	$1 multicolored	1.90	1.90
182	A31	$2 multicolored	3.50	3.50

MARSHALL ISLANDS MICRONESIA AND PALAU

A Topical Paradise!

- Birds • Ships • Fish
- WWII • US Hist • Space

FREE PRICE LIST

Sets, Singles, Souvenir Sheets, Miniature Sheets, Booklets, Complete Year Sets

Marshalls 1984 - 2022
Micronesia 1984 - 2015
Palau 1983 - 2020

Marshall Islands WWII 1989-1995

Complete Set of 100
WWII Issues $165.80
With Tabs $207.25
Full Sheets $1250.00
Imperf Set of 99 $3,750.00
(Sc 266-W16 does not exist Imperf)

For the Topical Specialist:
1989-2006 Marshalls Press Sheets Archives Price List. Most Issues also Imperf. Available as full sheets, singles, pairs and blocks with gutters

Henry Gitner Philatelists, Inc.
P.O. Box 3077-S, Middletown, NY 10940
Tel: 845-343-5151 Fax: 845-343-0068
PayPal Toll Free: 1-800-947-8267
E-mail: hgitner@hgitner.com

PHILATELY - THE QUIET EXCITEMENT!

MARSHALL ISLANDS

183	A31	$5 multicolored	8.00	8.00
184	A31	$10 multi ('89)	16.00	16.00
		Nos. 168-184 (17)	36.00	36.00

Issued: Nos. 170a, 173a, 173b, 3/31/88; 15c, 25c, 36c, 45c, 7/19/; Nos. 171a, 174a, 174b, 12/15; $10, 3/31/89; others, 3/17/88.

1988 Summer Olympics, Seoul — A33

Athletes in motion: 15c, Javelin thrower. 25c, Runner.

1988, June 30   Litho.   Perf. 14

| 188 | A32 | 15c Strip of 5, #a-e | 1.65 | 1.65 |
| 189 | A33 | 25c Strip of 5, #a-e | 2.25 | 2.25 |

Souvenir Sheet

Pacific Voyages of Robert Louis Stevenson — A34

Stick chart of the Marshalls and: a, *Casco* sailing through the Golden Gate. b, At the Needles of Ua-Pu, Marquesas. c, *Equator* departing from Honolulu and Kaiulani, an Hawaiian princess. d, Chief's canoe, Majuro Lagoon. e, Bronze medallion, 1887, by Augustus St. Gaudens in the Tate Gallery, London. f, Outrigger canoe and S.S. *Janet Nicoll* in Majuro Lagoon. g, View of Apemama, Gilbert Is. h, Samoan outrigger canoe, Apia Harbor. i, Stevenson riding horse Jack at his estate, Vailima, Samoa.

1988, July 19   Litho.   Perf. 14

| 190 | A34 | Sheet of 9 | 6.25 | 4.50 |
| a.-i. | | 25c any single | .50 | .50 |

Robert Louis Stevenson (1850-1894), Scottish novelist, poet and essayist.

Colonial Ships and Flags — A35

Designs: No. 191, Galleon *Santa Maria de La Victoria*, 1526, and Spanish "Ragged Cross" ensign in use from 1516 to 1785. No. 192, Transport ships *Charlotte* and *Scarborough*, 1788, and British red ensign, 1707-1800. No. 193, Schooner *Flying Fish*, sloop-of-war *Peacock*, 1841, and U.S. flag, 1837-1845. No. 194, Steamer *Planet*, 1909, and German flag, 1867-1919.

1988, Sept. 2   Litho.   Perf. 14

191	A35	25c multicolored	.50	.50
192	A35	25c multicolored	.50	.50
193	A35	25c multicolored	.50	.50
194	A35	25c multicolored	.50	.50
a.		Block of 4, #191-194	2.00	2.00

Christmas — A36

No. 195, Santa Claus riding in sleigh. No. 196, Reindeer, hut and palm trees. No. 197, Reindeer and palm trees. No. 198, Reindeer, palm tree, fish. No. 199, Reindeer and outrigger canoe.

1988, Nov. 7   Litho.   Perf. 14

195	A36	25c multicolored	.50	.50
196	A36	25c multicolored	.50	.50
197	A36	25c multicolored	.50	.50
198	A36	25c multicolored	.50	.50
199	A36	25c multicolored	.50	.50
a.		Strip of 5, #195-199	2.50	2.50

No. 199a has a continuous design.

Tribute to John F. Kennedy — A37

No. 200, Nuclear threat diminished. No. 201, Signing the Test Ban Treaty. No. 202, Portrait. No. 203, US-USSR Hotline. No. 204, Peace Corps enactment.

1988, Nov. 22   Litho.   Perf. 14

200	A37	25c multicolored	.55	.55
201	A37	25c multicolored	.55	.55
202	A37	25c multicolored	.55	.55
203	A37	25c multicolored	.55	.55
204	A37	25c multicolored	.55	.55
a.		Strip of 5, #200-204	2.75	2.75

No. 204a has a continuous design.

US Space Shuttle Program and Kwajalein — A38

No. 205, Launch of *Prime* from Vandenberg Air Force Base downrange to the Kwajalein Missile Range. No. 206, *Prime* X023A/SV-5D lifting body reentering atmosphere. No. 207, Parachute landing and craft recovery off Kwajalein Is. No. 208, Shuttle over island.

1988, Dec. 23   Litho.   Perf. 14

205		25c multicolored	.50	.50
206		25c multicolored	.50	.50
207		25c multicolored	.50	.50
208		25c multicolored	.50	.50
a.		A38 Strip of 4, #205-208	2.00	2.00

NASA 30th anniv. and 25th anniv. of the Project PRIME wind tunnel tests. See No. C21.

Links to Japan — A39

Designs: No. 209, Typhoon Monument, Majuro, 1918. No. 210, Seaplane base and railway depot, Djarrej Islet, c. 1940. No. 211, Fishing boats. No. 212, Japanese honeymooners scuba diving, 1988.

1989, Jan. 19   Litho.   Perf. 14

209	A39	45c multicolored	.75	.75
210	A39	45c multicolored	.75	.75
211	A39	45c multicolored	.75	.75
212	A39	45c multicolored	.75	.75
a.		Block of 4, #209-212	3.00	3.00

Links to Alaska — A40

Paintings by Claire Fejes: No. 213, Island Woman. No. 214, Kotzebue, Alaska. No. 215, Marshallese Madonna.

1989, Mar. 31   Litho.   Perf. 14

213	A40	45c multi	.85	.85
214	A40	45c multi	.85	.85
215	A40	45c multi	.85	.85
a.		Strip of 3, #213-215	2.55	2.55

Printed in sheets of 9.

Seashells Type of 1985

No. 216, Pontifical miter. No. 217, Tapestry turban. No. 218, Flame-mouthed helmet. No. 219, Prickly Pacific drupe. No. 220, Blood-mouthed conch.

1989, May 15   Litho.   Perf. 14

216	A12	25c multi	.50	.50
217	A12	25c multi	.50	.50
218	A12	25c multi	.50	.50
219	A12	25c multi	.50	.50
220	A12	25c multi	.50	.50
a.		Strip of 5, #216-220	2.50	2.50

Souvenir Sheet

In Praise of Sovereigns, 1940, by Sanko Inoue — A41

1989, May 15   Litho.   Perf. 14

| 221 | A41 | $1 multicolored | 2.00 | 2.00 |

Hirohito (1901-89) and enthronement of Akihito as emperor of Japan.

Migrant Birds — A42

No. 222, Wandering tattler. No. 223, Ruddy turnstone. No. 224, Pacific golden plover. No. 225, Sanderling.

1989, June 27   Litho.   Perf. 14

222	A42	45c multi	.85	.85
223	A42	45c multi	.85	.85
224	A42	45c multi	.85	.85
225	A42	45c multi	.85	.85
a.		Block of 4, #222-225	3.40	3.40

Postal History — A43

PHILEXFRANCE '89 — A44

Designs: No. 226, Missionary ship *Morning Star V*, 1905, and Marshall Isls. #15 canceled. No. 227, Marshall Isls. #15-16 on registered letter, 1906. No. 228, *Prinz Eitel Friedrich*, 1914, and German sea post cancel. No. 229, Cruiser squadron led by SMS *Scharnhorst*, 1914, and German sea post cancel. No. 230: a, SMS *Bussard* and German sea post cancel and Germany #32. b, US Type A924 and Marshall Isls. #34a on FDC. c, LST 119 FPO, 1944, US Navy cancel and pair of US #853. d, Mail boat, 1936, cancel and Japan #222. e, Majuro PO f, Marshall Isls. cancel, 1951, and four US #803. No. 231, Germany #32 and Marshall Isls. cancel, 1889.

1989, July 7

226	A43	45c multicolored	.80	.80
227	A43	45c multicolored	.80	.80
228	A43	45c multicolored	.80	.80
229	A43	45c multicolored	.80	.80
a.		Block of 4, #226-229	3.25	3.25

Souvenir Sheets

230		Sheet of 6	10.00	10.00
a.-f.		A44 25c any single	1.50	1.50
231	A44	$1 multicolored	10.00	10.00

Nos. 230b and 230e are printed in a continuous design.

1st Moon Landing, 20th Anniv. — A45

Apollo 11: No. 232, Liftoff. No. 233, Neil Armstrong. No. 234, Lunar module *Eagle*. No. 235, Michael Collins. No. 236, Raising the American flag on the Moon. No. 237, Buzz Aldrin. $1, 1st step on the Moon and "We came in peace for all mankind."

1989, Aug. 1   Litho.   Perf. 13½

Booklet Stamps

232	A45	25c multicolored	1.25	1.25
233	A45	25c multicolored	1.25	1.25
234	A45	25c multicolored	1.25	1.25
235	A45	25c multicolored	1.25	1.25
236	A45	25c multicolored	1.25	1.25
237	A45	25c multicolored	1.25	1.25

Size: 75x32mm

238	A45	$1 multicolored	7.00	5.00
a.		Booklet pane of 7, #232-238	15.00	
		Nos. 232-238 (7)	14.50	12.50

Decorative inscribed selvage separates No. 238 from Nos. 232-237 and surrounds it like a souvenir sheet margin. Selvage around Nos. 232-237 is plain.

World War II

Anniversaries and events, 1939: No. 239, Invasion of Poland. No. 240, Sinking of HMS *Royal Oak*. No. 241, Invasion of Finland.
Battle of the River Plate: No. 242, HMS *Exeter*,. No. 243, HMS *Ajax*,. No. 244, Admiral Graf *Spee*,. No. 245, HMNZS *Achilles*,.

1989   Litho.   Perf. 13½

239	A46	25c W1 (1-1)	.60	.45
240	A46	45c W2 (1-1)	1.00	.75
241	A46	45c W3 (1-1)	1.00	.75
242	A46	45c W4 (4-1)	.80	.75
243	A46	45c W4 (4-2)	.80	.75
244	A46	45c W4 (4-3)	.80	.75
245	A46	45c W4 (4-4)	.80	.75
a.		Block of 4, #242-245	3.25	3.00

Issued: No. 239, 9/1; No. 240, 10/13; No. 241, 11/30; No. 245a, 12/13.

1940 — No. 246, Invasion of Denmark. No. 247, Invasion of Norway. No. 248, Katyn Forest Massacre. No. 249, Bombing of Rotterdam. No. 250, Invasion of Belgium. No. 251, Winston Churchill becomes prime minister of England. No. 252, Evacuation of the British Expeditionary Force at Dunkirk. No. 253, Evacuation at Dunkirk. No. 254, Occupation of Paris.

1990

246	A46	25c W5 (2-1)	.60	.50
247	A46	25c W5 (2-2)	.60	.50
a.		Pair, #246-247	1.25	1.00
248	A47	25c W6 (1-1)	.50	.50
249	A46	25c W8 (2-1)	.50	.50
250	A46	25c W8 (2-2)	.50	.50
a.		Pair, #249-250	1.00	1.00
251	A46	45c W7 (1-1)	1.00	.90
252	A46	45c W9 (2-1)	1.00	.90
253	A46	45c W9 (2-2)	1.00	.90
a.		Pair, #252-253	2.00	1.80
254	A47	45c W10 (1-1)	1.00	.90

Issued: No. 247a, 4/9; No. 248, 4/16; Nos. 249-251, 5/10; Nos. 252-253, 6/4; No. 254, 6/14.

1990

No. 255, Battle of Mers-el-Kebir, 1940. No. 256, Battles for the Burma Road, 1940-45.
US Destroyers for British bases: No. 257, HMS Georgetown (ex-USS Maddox). No. 258, HMS Banff (ex-USCGC Saranac). No. 259, HMS Buxton (ex-USS Edwards). No. 260, HMS Rockingham (ex-USS Swasey).
Battle of Britain: No. 261, Supermarine Spitfire Mark IA. No. 262, Hawker Hurricane Mark I. No. 263, Messerschmitt Bf109E. No. 264, Junkers JU87B-2. No. 265, Tripartite Pact Signed 1940.

255	A46	25c W11 (1-1)	.60	.50
256	A46	25c W12 (1-1)	.60	.50
257	A46	45c W13 (4-1)	1.00	.90
258	A46	45c W13 (4-2)	1.00	.90
259	A46	45c W13 (4-3)	1.00	.90
260	A46	45c W13 (4-4)	1.00	.90
a.		Block of 4, #257-260	4.00	4.00

MARSHALL ISLANDS

261	A46 45c W14 (4-1)		1.00	.90
262	A46 45c W14 (4-2)		1.00	.90
263	A46 45c W14 (4-3)		1.00	.90
264	A46 45c W14 (4-4)		1.00	.90
a.	Block of 4, #261-264		4.00	3.60
265	A46 45c W15		1.10	.90

Issued: No. 255, 7/3; No. 256, 7/18; No. 260a, 9/9; No. 264a, 9/15; No. 265, 9/27.

1990-91

Designs: No. 266, Roosevelt elected to third term, 1940. Battle of Taranto: No. 267, HMS Illustrious. No. 268, Fairey Swordfish. No. 269, RM Andrea Doria. No. 270, RM Conte di Cavour.

Roosevelt's Four Freedoms Speech: No. 271, Freedom of Speech. No. 272, Freedom from Want. No. 273, Freedom of Worship. No. 274, Freedom From Fear. No. 275, Battle of Beda Fomm, Feb. 5-7, 1941.

Germany Invades the Balkans: No. 276, Invasion of Greece. No. 277, Invasion of Yugoslavia.

Sinking of the Bismarck: No. 278, HMS Prince of Wales. No. 279, HMS Hood. No. 280, Bismarck. No. 281, Fairey Swordfish. No. 282, German Invasion of Russia, 1941.

266	A47 25c W16		.60	.50
267	A46 25c W17 (4-1)		.60	.50
268	A46 25c W17 (4-2)		.60	.50
269	A46 25c W17 (4-3)		.60	.50
270	A46 25c W17 (4-4)		.60	.50
a.	Block of 4, #266-270		2.50	2.00
271	A46 30c W18 (4-1)		.65	.60
272	A46 30c W18 (4-2)		.65	.60
273	A46 30c W18 (4-3)		.65	.60
274	A46 30c W18 (4-4)		.65	.60
a.	Block of 4, #271-274		2.60	2.40
275	A40 30c Tanks, W19		.60	.60
276	A47 29c W20 (2-1)		.60	.60
277	A47 29c W20 (2-2)		.60	.60
a.	Pair, #276-277		1.25	1.25
278	A40 50c W21 (4-1)		1.00	1.00
279	A46 50c W21 (4-2)		1.00	1.00
280	A46 50c W21 (4-3)		1.00	1.00
281	A46 50c W21 (4-4)		1.00	1.00
a.	Block of 4, #278-281		4.00	4.00
282	A46 30c Tanks, W22		.60	.60

Issued: No. 266, 11/5/90; No. 270a, 11/11/90; No. 274a, 1/6/91; No. 275, 2/5/91; No. 277a, 4/6/91; No. 281a, 5/27/91; No. 282, 6/22/91.

1991

1941 — Declaration of the Atlantic Charter: No. 283, Pres. Roosevelt and USS Augusta. No. 284, Churchill and HMS Prince of Wales. No. 285, Siege of Moscow.

Sinking of USS Reuben James: No. 286, Reuben James hit by torpedo. No. 287, German U-562 submarine.

Japanese attack on Pearl Harbor: No. 288, American warplanes. No. 289, Japanese warplanes. No. 290, USS Arizona. No. 291, Japanese aircraft carrier Akagi.

283	A47 29c W23 (2-1)		.60	.60
284	A47 29c W23 (2-2)		.60	.60
a.	Pair, #283-284		1.25	1.25
285	A46 29c W24		.60	.60
286	A46 30c W25 (2-1)		.60	.60
287	A46 30c W25 (2-2)		.60	.60
a.	Pair, #286-287		1.25	1.25
288	A47 50c W26 (4-1)		1.00	1.00
a.	Revised inscription		4.75	1.00
289	A47 50c W26 (4-2)		1.00	1.00
290	A47 50c W26 (4-3)		1.00	1.00
291	A47 50c W26 (4-4)		1.00	1.00
a.	Block of 4, #288-291		4.00	4.00
b.	Block of 4, #288a, 289-291		8.50	4.00

Inscriptions read "Peal" on No. 288 and "Pearl" on No. 288a.

Issued: No. 284a, 8/14; No. 285, 10/2; No. 287a, 10/31; No. 291a, 12/7.

1991-92

1941-42: No. 292, Japanese capture Guam. No. 293, Fall of Singapore.

First combat of the Flying Tigers: No. 294, Curtiss Tomahawk. No. 295, Mitsubishi Ki-21 on fire.

No. 296, Fall of Wake Island.

No. 297, Roosevelt and Churchill at Arcadia Conference. No. 298, Japanese tank entering Manila. No. 299, Japanese take Rabaul. No. 300, Battle of the Java Sea. No. 301, Rangoon falls to Japanese. No. 302, Japanese land on New Guinea. No. 303, MacArthur evacuated from Corregidor. No. 304, Raid on Saint-Nazaire. No. 305, Surrender of Bataan / Death March. No. 306, Doolittle Raid on Tokyo. No. 307, Fall of Corregidor.

292	A47 29c W27		.60	.60
293	A46 29c W28		.60	.60
294	A46 50c W29 (2-1)		1.00	1.00
295	A46 50c W29 (2-2)		1.00	1.00
a.	Pair, #294-295		2.00	2.00
296	A46 29c W30		.60	.60
297	A47 29c W31		.60	.60
298	A46 50c W32		1.00	1.00
299	A47 29c W33		.60	.60
300	A46 29c W34		.60	.60
301	A47 50c W35		1.00	1.00
302	A46 29c W36		.60	.60
303	A46 29c W37		.60	.60
304	A46 29c W38		.60	.60
305	A47 29c W39		.60	.60
306	A47 50c W40		1.00	1.00
307	A46 29c W41		.60	.60

Issued: Nos. 292-293, 12/10/91; No. 295a, 12/20/91; No. 296, 12/23/91; No. 297, 1/1/92; No. 298, 1/2/92; No. 299, 1/23/92; No. 300, 2/15/92; Nos. 301-302, 3/8/92; No. 303, 3/11/92; No. 304, 3/27/92; No. 305, 4/9/92; No. 306, 4/18/92; No. 307, 5/6/92.

1992

1942 — Battle of the Coral Sea: No. 308, USS Lexington. No. 309, Japanese Mitsubishi A6M2 Zeros. No. 310, Douglas SBD Dauntless dive bombers. No. 311, Japanese carrier Shoho.

Battle of Midway: No. 312, Japanese aircraft carrier Akagi. No. 313, U.S. Douglas SBD Dauntless dive bombers. No. 314, USS Yorktown. No. 315, Nakajima B5N2 Kate torpedo planes.

No. 316, Village of Lidice destroyed. No. 317, Fall of Sevastopol.

Convoy PQ17 destroyed: No. 318, British merchant ship in convoy. No. 319, German U-boats.

No. 320, Marines land on Guadalcanal. No. 323, Battle of Stalingrad. No. 324, Battle of Eastern Solomons.

No. 321, Battle of Savo Island. No. 322, Dieppe Raid. No. 325, Battle of Cape Esperance. No. 326, Battle of El Alamein.

Battle of Barents Sea: No. 327, HMS Sheffield. No. 328, Admiral Hipper.

308	A46 50c W42 (4-1)		1.00	1.00
a.	Revised inscription		2.00	1.00
309	A46 50c W42 (4-2)		1.00	1.00
a.	Revised inscription		2.00	1.00
310	A46 50c W42 (4-3)		1.00	1.00
a.	Revised inscription		2.00	1.00
311	A46 50c W42 (4-4)		1.00	1.00
a.	Block of 4, #308-311		4.00	4.00
b.	Revised inscription		2.00	1.00
c.	Block of 4, #308a-310a, 311b		8.50	4.00
312	A46 50c W43 (4-1)		1.00	1.00
313	A46 50c W43 (4-3)		1.00	1.00
314	A46 50c W43 (4-2)		1.00	1.00
315	A46 50c W43 (4-4)		1.00	1.00
a.	Block of 4, #312-315		4.00	4.00
316	A46 29c W44		.60	.60
317	A47 29c W45		.60	.60
318	A47 29c W46 (2-1)		.60	.60
319	A46 29c W46 (2-2)		.60	.60
a.	Pair, #318-319		1.25	1.25
320	A46 29c W47		.60	.60
321	A47 29c W48		.60	.60
322	A46 29c W49		.60	.60
323	A47 50c W50		1.25	1.00
324	A47 50c W51		.60	.60
325	A46 50c W52		1.25	1.00
326	A46 29c W53		.60	.60
327	A46 29c W54 (2-1)		.60	.60
328	A46 29c W54 (2-2)		.60	.60
a.	Pair, #327-328		1.25	1.25

Inscription reads "U.S.S. Lexington/Grumman F4F-3 Wildcat" on No. 308a, "Japanese Aichi D3A1 Vals/Nakajima B5N2 Kate" on No. 309a, "U.S. Douglas TBD-1 Devastators" on No. 310a, "Japanese Carrier Shoho/Mitsubishi A6M2 Zeros" on No. 311b.

Issued: No. 311a, 5/8/92; No. 315a, 6/4; No. 316, 6/9/92; No. 317, 7/4; No. 319a, 7/5; No. 320, 8/7; No. 321, 8/9; No. 322-323, 8/19; No. 324, 8/24; No. 325, 10/11; No. 326, 10/23; No. 328a, 12/31.

Vertical pairs, Nos. 312-313 and Nos. 314-315 have continuous designs.

No. 310 incorrectly identifies Douglas TBD torpedo bombers.

1993 Litho. Perf. 13½

1943 — No. 329, Casablanca Conf. No. 330, Liberation of Kharkov.

Battle of Bismarck Sea: No. 331, Japanese A6M Zeroes, destroyer Arashio. No. 332, U.S. P38 Lightnings, Australian Beaufighter. No. 333, Japanese destroyer Shirayuki. No. 334, U.S. A-20 Havoc, B-25 Mitchell.

No. 335, Interception of Admiral Yamamoto. Battle of Kursk: No. 336, German Tiger I. No. 337, Soviet T-34.

329	A40 29c W55		.65	.60
330	A46 29c W56		.65	.60
331	A46 50c W57 (4-1)		1.00	1.00
332	A46 50c W57 (4-2)		1.00	1.00
333	A46 50c W57 (4-3)		1.00	1.00
334	A46 50c W57 (4-4)		1.00	1.00
a.	Block of 4, #331-334		4.00	4.00
335	A46 50c W58		1.00	1.00
336	A46 29c W59 (2-1)		.85	.60
337	A46 29c W59 (2-2)		.85	.60
a.	Pair, #336-337		1.70	1.20
	Nos. 239-337 (99)		78.50	74.05

Issued: No. 329, 1/14; No. 330, 2/16; No. 334a, 3/3; No. 335, 4/18; No. 337a, 7/5.

See Nos. 467-524, 562-563.

Christmas — A57

Angels playing musical instruments.

1989, Oct. 25 Perf. 13½

341	A57 25c Horn		.80	.80
342	A57 25c Singing carol		.80	.80
343	A57 25c Lute		.80	.80
344	A57 25c Lyre		.80	.80
a.	Block of 4, #341-344		3.25	3.25

Miniature Sheet

Milestones in Space Exploration — A58

Designs: a, Robert Goddard and 1st liquid fuel rocket launch, 1926. b, *Sputnik*, 1st manmade satellite, 1957. c, 1st American satellite, 1958. d, Yuri Gagarin, 1st man in space, 1961. e, John Glenn, 1st American to orbit Earth, 1962. f, Valentina Tereshkova, 1st woman in space, 1963. g, Aleksei Leonov, 1st space walk, 1965. h, Edward White, 1st American to walk in space, 1965. i, Gemini-Titan 6A, 1st rendezvous in space, 1965. j, 1st Soft landing on the Moon, 1966. k, Gemini 8, 1st docking in space, 1966. l, 1st probe of Venus, 1967. m, Apollo 8, 1st manned orbit of the Moon, 1968. n, Apollo 11, 1st man on the Moon, 1969. o, Soyuz 11, 1st space station crew, 1971. p, Apollo 15, 1st manned lunar vehicle, 1971. q, *Skylab 2*, 1st American manned space station, 1973. r, 1st Flyby of Jupiter, 1973. s, Apollo-Soyuz, 1st joint space flight, 1975. t, 1st Landing on Mars, 1976. u, 1st flyby of Saturn, 1979. v, *Columbia*, 1st space shuttle flight, 1981. w, 1st probe beyond the solar system, 1983. x, 1st untethered space walk, 1984. y, Launch of space shuttle *Discovery*, 1988.

1989, Nov. 24 Litho. Perf. 13½

345	A58 Sheet of 25		25.00	25.00
a.-y.	25c any single		.90	.90

No. 345 contains World Stamp Expo '89 emblem on selvage.

Birds

A59 A59a

Designs: 1c, Black noddy. 5c, Red-tailed tropic bird. 10c, Sanderling. 12c, Black-naped tern. 15c, Wandering tattler. 20c, Bristle-thighed curlew. 23c, Northern shoveler. 25c, Brown noddy. 27c, Sooty tern. 29c, Wedge-tailed shearwater. 30c, Northern pintail. 35c, Pacific golden plover. 36c, Red footed booby. 40c, White tern. 50c, Great frigate bird. 52c, Great crested tern. 65c, Lesser sand plover. 75c, Little tern. $1, Pacific reef heron. $2, Masked booby.

1990-92 Litho. Perf. 13½

346	A59 1c multicolored		.25	.25
347	A59 5c multicolored		.25	.25
348	A59 10c multicolored		.25	.25
349	A59 12c multicolored		.25	.25
350	A59 15c multicolored		.30	.30
351	A59 20c multicolored		.40	.40
352	A59 23c multicolored		.45	.45
353	A59 25c multicolored		.50	.50
354	A59 27c multicolored		.55	.55
355	A59 29c multicolored		.60	.60
356	A59a 29c multicolored		.60	.60
357	A59 30c multicolored		.60	.60
358	A59 35c multicolored		.70	.70
359	A59 36c multicolored		.75	.75
360	A59 40c multicolored		.80	.80
361	A59 50c multicolored		1.00	1.00
a.	Min. sheet of 4 (#347, 350, 353, 361)		2.25	2.00
362	A59 52c multicolored		1.00	1.00
363	A59 65c multicolored		1.25	1.25
364	A59 75c multicolored		1.50	1.50
365	A59 $1 multicolored		2.00	2.00
365A	A59 $2 multicolored		4.00	4.00
	Nos. 346-365A (21)		18.00	18.00

No. 361a for ESSEN '90, Germany Apr. 19-22.

Issued: 5c, 15c, 25c, 50c, 3/8; 30c, 36c, 40c, $1, 10/11; No. 361a, 4/19; No. 355, 20c, 52c, 2/22/91; 27c, 3/8/91; 1c, 12c, 35c, $2, 11/6/91; No. 356, 2/3/92; 10c, 23c, 65c, 75c, 4/24/92.

See Nos. 430-433.

Children's Games — A60

1990, Mar. 15

366	A60 25c Lodidean		.80	.75
367	A60 25c Lejonjon		.80	.75
368	A60 25c Etobobo		.80	.75
369	A60 25c Didmakol		.80	.75
a.	Block of 4, #366-369		3.25	3.00

Penny Black, 150th Anniv. — A61

Designs: No. 370, Penny Black, 1840. No. 371, Essay by James Chalmers. No. 372, Essay by Robert Sievier. No. 373, Essay by Charles Whiting. No. 374, Essay by George Dickinson. No. 375, Medal engraved by William Wyon to celebrate Queen Victoria's first visit to London. $1, Engraver Charles Heath, engraving for master die.

1990, Apr. 6 Booklet Stamps

370	A61 25c multicolored		1.00	1.00
371	A61 25c multicolored		1.00	1.00
372	A61 25c multicolored		1.00	1.00
373	A61 25c multicolored		1.00	1.00
374	A61 25c multicolored		1.00	1.00
375	A61 25c multicolored		1.00	1.00

Size: 73x31mm

376	A61 $1 multicolored		4.00	4.00
a.	Booklet pane of 7, #370-376		10.00	—
	Nos. 370-376 (7)		10.00	10.00

Decorative inscribed selvage picturing part of a Penny Black proof sheet separates No. 376 from Nos. 370-375 in pane and surrounds it like a souvenir sheet margin. Selvage around Nos. 370-375 is plain.

Endangered Wildlife — A62

Sea Turtles: No. 377, Pacific green turtle hatchlings entering ocean. No. 378, Pacific great turtle under water. No. 379, Hawksbill hatchling, eggs. No. 380, Hawksbill turtle in water.

1990, May 3

377	25c multicolored		.80	.75
378	25c multicolored		.80	.75
379	25c multicolored		.80	.75
380	25c multicolored		.80	.75
a.	A62 Block of 4, #377-380		3.25	3.00

A63

MARSHALL ISLANDS

Design: 25c, Stick Chart, Canoe and Flag of the Republic of the Marshall Islands.

1990, Sept. 28   *Perf. 11x10½*
381 A63 25c multicolored   .95   .60

See No. 615, US No. 2507, Micronesia Nos. 124-126.

German Reunification — A64

1990, Oct. 3   *Perf. 13½*
382 A64 45c multicolored   1.25 1.00

Christmas — A65

1990, Oct. 25   *Litho.*   *Perf. 13½*
383 A65 25c multi   .75 .75
384 A65 25c multi   .75 .75
385 A65 25c multi   .75 .75
386 A65 25c multi   .75 .75
  a. Block of 4, #383-386   3.00 3.00

No. 383, Canoe, stick chart. No. 384, Missionary preaching. No. 385, Sailors dancing. No. 386, Youths dancing.

Breadfruit — A66

1990, Dec. 15   *Litho.*   *Perf. 12x12½*
387 A66 25c Harvesting   .75 .75
388 A66 25c Peeling, slicing   .75 .75
389 A66 25c Preserving   .75 .75
390 A66 25c Kneading dough   .75 .75
  a. Block of 4, #387-390   3.00 3.00

US Space Shuttle Flights, 10th Anniv. — A67

No. 391, 747 ferry. No. 392, Orbital release of LDEF. No. 393, Lift-off. No. 394, Landing.

1991, Apr. 12   *Litho.*   *Perf. 13½*
391 50c multi   .90 .90
392 50c multi   .90 .90
393 50c multi   .90 .90
394 50c multi   .90 .90
  a. A67 Block of 4, #391-394   3.75 3.75

Flowers — A68

No. 395, Ixora carolinensis. No. 396, Clerodendrum inerme. No. 397, Messerschmidia argentea. No. 398, Vigna marina.

1991, June 10   *Litho.*   *Perf. 13½*
395 A68 52c multi   1.10 1.00
396 A68 52c multi   1.10 1.00
397 A68 52c multi   1.10 1.00
398 A68 52c multi   1.10 1.00
  a. Miniature sheet of 4, #395-398   4.75 4.00
  b. Block of 4, #395-398, without inscription   4.50 4.00

Phila Nippon '91 (No. 398a). Stamps from miniature sheets inscribed C53A.

Operation Desert Storm — A69

1991, July 4   *Litho.*   *Perf. 13½*
399 A69 29c multicolored   .80 .60

Birds — A70

No. 400, Red-footed booby. No. 401, Great frigate bird (7-2). No. 402, Brown booby. No. 403, White tern. No. 404, Great frigate bird (7-5). No. 405, Black noddy. No. 406, White-tailed tropic bird.

1991, July 16   **Booklet Stamps**
400 A70 29c multi   1.25 .60
401 A70 29c multi   1.25 .60
402 A70 29c multi   1.25 .60
403 A70 29c multi   1.25 .60
404 A70 29c multi   1.25 .60
405 A70 29c multi   1.25 .60

Size: 75x33mm
406 A70 $1 multi   6.50 2.00
  a. Booklet pane of 7, #400-406   14.00 —
  Nos. 400-406 (7)   14.00 5.60

Decorative selvage separates No. 406 from Nos. 400-405 and surrounds it like a souvenir sheet margin.

Aircraft of Air Marshall Islands — A71

No. 407, Dornier 228. No. 408, Douglas DC-8. No. 409, Hawker Siddeley 748. No. 410, Saab 2000.

1991, Sept. 10   *Litho.*   *Perf. 13½*
407 A71 12c multi   .25 .25
408 A71 29c multi   .65 .50
409 A71 50c multi   1.10 .85
410 A71 50c multi   1.10 .85
  Nos. 407-410 (4)   3.10 2.45

Admission to United Nations — A72

1991, Sept. 24   *Litho.*   *Perf. 11x10½*
411 A72 29c multicolored   .70 .65

Christmas — A73

1991, Oct. 25   *Litho.*   *Perf. 13½*
412 A73 30c multicolored   .75 .75

Peace Corps in Marshall Islands, 25th Anniv. — A74

1991, Nov. 26   *Litho.*   *Perf. 11x10½*
413 A74 29c multicolored   .75 .60

Ships — A75

No. 414, Bulk cargo carrier, Emlain. No. 415, Tanker, CSK Valiant. No. 416, Patrol boat, Ionmeto. No. 417, Freighter, Micro Pilot.

1992, Feb. 15   *Litho.*   *Perf. 11x10½*
414 A75 29c multicolored   .80 .45
415 A75 29c multicolored   .80 .45
416 A75 29c multicolored   .80 .45
417 A75 29c multicolored   .80 .45
  a. Strip of 4, #414-417   3.25 2.00

Voyages of Discovery — A76

Designs: No. 418, Traditional tipnol. No. 419, Reconstructed Santa Maria. No. 420, Constellation Argo Navis. No. 421, Marshallese sailor, tipnol. No. 422, Columbus, Santa Maria. No. 423, Astronaunt, Argo Navis. $1, Columbus, sailor, and astronaunt.

1992, May 23   *Litho.*   *Perf. 13½*
Booklet Stamps
418 A76 50c multicolored   1.00 1.00
419 A76 50c multicolored   1.00 1.00
420 A76 50c multicolored   1.00 1.00
421 A76 50c multicolored   1.00 1.00
422 A76 50c multicolored   1.00 1.00
423 A76 50c multicolored   1.00 1.00

Size: 75x32mm
424 A76 $1 multicolored   4.00 2.00
  a. Booklet pane of 7, #418-424   10.00 —

Decorative selvage separates No. 424 from Nos. 418-423 and surrounds it like a souvenir sheet margin. See No. 1124.

Traditional Handicrafts — A77

1992, Sept. 9   *Litho.*   *Perf. 13½*
425 A77 29c Basket weaving   .60 .60
426 A77 29c Canoe models   .60 .60
427 A77 29c Wood carving   .60 .60
428 A77 29c Fan making   .60 .60
  a. Strip of 4, #425-428   2.40 2.40

Christmas — A78

1992, Oct. 29   *Litho.*   *Perf. 11x10½*
429 A78 29c multicolored   .70 .60

Bird Type of 1990

9c, Whimbrel. 22c, Greater scaup. 28c, Sharp-tailed sandpiper. 45c, Common teal.

1992, Nov. 10   *Litho.*   *Perf. 13½*
430 A59 9c multi   .25 .25
431 A59 22c multi   .45 .45
432 A59 28c multi   .55 .55
433 A59 45c multi   .90 .90
  Nos. 430-433 (4)   2.15 2.15

Reef Life — A79

1993, May 26   *Litho.*   *Perf. 13½*
434 A79 50c Butterflyfish   1.40 1.00
435 A79 50c Soldierfish   1.40 1.00
436 A79 50c Damselfish   1.40 1.00
437 A79 50c Filefish   1.40 1.00
438 A79 50c Hawkfish   1.40 1.00
439 A79 50c Surgeonfish   1.40 1.00

Size: 75x33mm
440 A79 $1 Parrotfish   5.50 2.00
  a. Booklet pane of 7, #434-440   13.00 —
  Nos. 434-440 (7)   13.90 8.00

Decorative selvage separates No. 440 from Nos. 434-439 and surrounds it like a souvenir sheet margin. See No. 1103.

Ships — A80

Marshallese Sailing Vessels — A81

Designs: 10c, Spanish galleon San Jeronimo. 14c, USCG Fisheries Patrol vessel Cape Corwin. 15c, British merchant ship Britannia. 19c, Island transport Micro Palm. 20c, Dutch ship Eendracht. 23c, Frigate HMS Cornwallis. 24c, U.S. naval schooner Dolphin. 29c, Missionary packet Morning Star. 30c, Russian brig Rurick. 32c, Spanish sailing ship Santa Maria de la Vittoria. 35c, German warship SMS Nautilus. 40c, British brig Nautilus. 45c, Japanese warships Nagara, Isuzu. 46c, Trading schooner Equator. 50c, Aircraft carrier USS Lexington CV-16. 52c, HMS Serpent. 55c, Whaling ship Potomac. 60c, Coast Guard cutter Assateague. 75c, British transport Scarborough. 78c, Whaler Charles W. Morgan. 95c, US steam vessel Tanager. $1, Walap, Eniwetok. $1, Barkentine hospital ship Tole Mour. $2, Walap, Jaluit. $2.90, Marshall Islands fishing vessels. $3, Schooner Victoria. $5, Tipnol, Ailuk. $10, Racing canoes.

Perf. 11x10½ (A80), 13½ (A81)
1993-95   *Litho.*
441 A80 10c multicolored   .25 .25
442 A80 14c multicolored   .30 .30
443 A80 15c multicolored   .30 .30
444 A80 19c multicolored   .40 .40
445 A80 20c multicolored   .40 .40
446 A80 23c multicolored   .45 .45
447 A80 24c multicolored   .50 .50
448 A80 29c multicolored   .60 .60
449 A80 30c multicolored   .60 .60
450 A80 32c multicolored   .65 .65
451 A80 35c multicolored   .70 .70
452 A80 40c multicolored   .80 .80
453 A80 45c multicolored   .90 .90
454 A80 46c multicolored   .95 .95
455 A80 50c multicolored   1.00 1.00
456 A80 52c multicolored   1.10 1.10
457 A80 55c multicolored   1.10 1.10
458 A80 60c multicolored   1.25 1.25
459 A80 75c multicolored   1.50 1.50
460 A80 78c multicolored   1.65 1.65
461 A80 95c multicolored   1.90 1.90
462 A80 $1 multicolored   2.00 2.00
463 A81 $1 multicolored   2.00 2.00
464 A81 $2 multicolored   4.00 4.00
465 A80 $2.90 multicolored   5.75 5.75
466 A80 $3 multicolored   6.00 6.00
466A A81 $5 multicolored   10.00 10.00
466B A81 $10 multicolored   20.00 20.00
  Nos. 441-466B (28)   67.05 67.05

Souvenir Sheet
Stamp Size: 46x26mm
466C A81 Sheet of 4, #d.-g.   3.75 3.50

No. 466C contains 15c, 23c, 52c and 75c stamps. Inscription reads "Hong Kong '94 Stamp Exhibition" in Chinese on Nos. 466Cd, 466Cg, and in English on Nos. 466Ce-466Cf. Issued: 15c, 24c, 29c, 50c, 6/24/93; 19c, 23c, 52c, 75c, 10/14/93; No. 463, 5/29/93; $2, 8/26. 10c, 30c, 35c, $2.90, 4/19/94; $5, 3/15/94; $10, 8/18/94; 20c, 40c, 45c, 55c, 9/23/94; No. 466C, 2/18/94; 14c, 46c, 95c, No. 462, 9/25/95; 32c, 60c, 78c, $3, 5/5/95. See No. 605.

World War II Type of 1989

1943 — Invasion of Sicily: No. 467, Gen. George S. Patton, Jr. No. 468, Gen. Bernard L. Montgomery. No. 469, Americans landing at at Licata. No. 470, British landing south of Syracuse.
Allied bomber raids on Schweinfurt: No. 471, B-17F Flying Fortresses and Bf-109 fighter. No. 472, Liberation of Smolensk. No. 473, Landings at Bougainville. No. 474, Invasion of Tarawa, 1943. No. 475, Teheran Conference, 1943.
Battle of North Cape: No. 476, HMS Duke of York. No. 477, Scharnhorst.
1944 — \No. 478, Gen. Dwight D. Eisenhower, SHAEF Commander. No. 479, Invasion of Anzio. No. 480, Siege of Leningrad lifted. No. 481, U.S. liberates Marshall Islands. #482, Japanese defeated at Truk. No. 483, Big Week, US bombing of Germany.

1993-94   *Litho.*   *Perf. 13½*
467 A46 52c W60 (4-1)   1.10 1.10
468 A46 52c W60 (4-2)   1.10 1.10
469 A46 52c W60 (4-3)   1.10 1.10
470 A46 52c W60 (4-4)   1.10 1.10
  a. Block of 4, #467-470   4.50 4.50
471 A46 50c W61   1.00 1.00
472 A47 29c W62   .60 .60
473 A46 29c W63   .60 .60
474 A46 50c W64   1.00 1.00
475 A47 52c W65   1.10 1.10
476 A46 29c W66 (2-1)   .60 .60
477 A46 29c W66 (2-2)   .60 .60
  a. Pair, #476-477   1.25 1.25
478 A46 29c W67   .60 .60
479 A46 50c W68   1.00 1.00
480 A46 52c W69   1.10 1.10

MARSHALL ISLANDS

481	A46	29c W70		.60	.60
482	A47	29c W71		.60	.60
483	A46	52c W72		1.10	1.10
	Nos. 467-483 (17)			14.90	14.90

Issued: Nos. 467-470, 7/10/93; No. 471, 8/17/93; No. 472, 9/25/93; No. 473, 11/1/93; No. 474, 11/20/93; No. 475, 12/1/93; Nos. 476-477, 12/26/93; No. 478, 1/16/94; No. 479, 1/22/94; No. 480, 1/27/94; No. 481, 2/4/94; No. 482, 2/17/94; No. 483, 2/20/94.

1994 Litho. Perf. 13½

1944 — No. 484, Lt. Gen. Mark Clark, Rome falls to the Allies.

D-Day-Allied landings in Normandy: No. 485, Horsa gliders. No. 486, U.S. P-51B Mustangs, British Hurricanes. No. 487, German gun defenses. No. 488, Allied amphibious landing.

No. 489, V-1 flying bombs strike England. No. 490, U.S. Marines land on Saipan.

First Battle of the Philippine Sea: No. 491, Grumman F6F-3 Hellcat.

No. 492, U.S. liberates Guam. No. 493, Warsaw uprising. No. 494, Liberation of Paris. No. 495, U.S. Marines land on Peliliu. No. 496, MacArthur returns to the Philippines. No. 497, Battle of Leyte Gulf.

German battleship Tirpitz sunk: No. 498, Avro Lancaster. No. 499, Tirpitz.

Battle of the Bulge: No. 500, Infantry. No. 501, Armor. No. 502, Aviation. No. 503, Lt. Col. Creighton W. Abrams, Brig. Gen. Anthony C. McAuliffe.

484	A47	50c W73		1.00	1.00
485	A46	75c W74 (4-1)		1.60	1.50
a.		Revised inscription		3.25	1.50
486	A46	75c W74 (4-2)		1.60	1.50
a.		Revised inscription		3.25	1.50
487	A46	75c W74 (4-3)		1.60	1.50
a.		Revised inscription		3.25	1.50
488	A46	75c W74 (4-4)		1.60	1.50
a.		Block of 4, #485-488		6.50	6.00
b.		Block of 4, #485a-487a, 488		12.00	6.00
489	A46	50c W75		1.00	1.00
490	A46	29c W76		.60	.60
491	A46	50c W77		1.00	1.00
492	A46	29c W78		.60	.60
493	A46	50c W79		1.00	1.00
494	A46	50c W80		1.00	1.00
495	A46	29c W81		.60	.60
496	A46	52c W82		1.00	1.00
497	A46	52c multicolored		1.00	1.00
498	A46	50c W84 (2-1)		1.00	1.00
499	A46	50c W84 (2-2)		1.00	1.00
a.		Pair, #498-499		2.00	2.00
500	A47	50c W85 (4-1)		1.00	1.00
501	A47	50c W85 (4-2)		1.00	1.00
502	A47	50c W85 (4-3)		1.00	1.00
503	A47	50c W85 (4-4)		1.00	1.00
a.		Block of 4, #500-503		5.00	4.00
	Nos. 484-503 (20)			21.20	20.80

Inscription reads "Horsa Gliders, Parachute Troops" on #485a, "British Typhoon-1B, U.S. P51B Mustangs" on #486a, "German Gun Defenses, Pointe du Hoc" on #487a.

Issued: No. 484, 6/4; No. 485-488, 6/6; No. 489, 6/13; No. 490, 6/15; No. 491, 6/19; No. 492, 7/21; No. 493, 8/1; 494, 8/25; No. 495, 9/15; No. 496, 10/20; No. 497, 10/24; Nos. 498-499, 11/12; Nos. 500-503, 12/16.

V-E Day — A81a

1995 Litho. Perf. 13½

1945 — No. 504, Stalin, Churchill, Roosevelt, Yalta Conference. No. 505, Meissen porcelain, bombing of Dresden, 1945. No. 506, Iwo Jima invaded by US Marines.

No. 507, Remagen Bridge taken by US forces.

No. 508, Okinawa invaded by US forces. No. 509, Death of Franklin D. Roosevelt. No. 510, US/USSR troops meet at Elbe River. No. 511, Russian troops capture Berlin. No. 512, Allies liberate concentration camps.

V-E Day: No. 513, German surrender, Rheims. No. 514, Times Square, New York. No. 515, Victory Parade, Moscow. No. 516, Buckingham Palace, London.

UN Charter signed: No. 517, 563, U.S. Pres. Harry S Truman, Veteran's Memorial Hall, San Francisco.

No. 518, Potsdam Conference Convenes. No. 519, Churchill resigns. No. 520, B-29 Enola Gay drops atomic bomb on Hiroshima.

V-J Day: No. 521, Mt. Fuji, ships in Tokyo Bay. No. 522, USS Missouri. No. 523, Adm. Nimitz signs surrender document. No. 524, Japanese delegation.

504	A47	32c W86		.65	.65
505	A47	55c W87		1.10	1.10
506	A47	$1 W88		2.25	2.00
507	A47	32c W89		.65	.65
508	A47	55c W90		1.10	1.10
509	A46	50c W91		1.00	1.00
510	A46	32c W92		.65	.65
511	A46	60c W93		1.25	1.25
512	A46	55c W94		1.10	1.10
513		75c W95 (4-1)		1.60	1.50
514		75c W95 (4-2)		1.60	1.50
515		75c W95 (4-3)		1.60	1.50
516		75c W95 (4-4)		1.60	1.50
a.		A81a Block of 4, #513-516		6.50	6.00
517	A46	32c W96		.65	.65
518	A46	55c W97		1.10	1.10
519	A47	60c W98		1.25	1.25
520	A46	$1 W99		2.25	2.00
521		75c W100 (4-1)		1.75	1.50
522		75c W100 (4-2)		1.75	1.50
523		75c W100 (4-3)		1.75	1.50
524		75c W100 (4-4)		1.75	1.50
a.		A81a Block of 4, #521-524		7.25	6.00
	Nos. 504-524 (21)			28.40	26.50

Issued: No. 504, 2/4/95; No. 505, 2/13/95; No. 506, 2/19/95; No. 507, 3/7/95; No. 508, 4/1/95; No. 509, 4/12/95; No. 516a, 5/8/95; No. 517, 6/26/95; No. 518, 7/7/95; No. 519, 7/26/95; No. 520, 8/6/95; No. 524a, 9/2/95.

Compare A81a stamps with A243.

Souvenir Sheets

No. 562a, like #303. No. 562b, like #496.

1994-95 Imperf.

562		Sheet of 2	2.00	2.00
a.-b.	A46 50c any single		1.00	1.00
563	A46	$1 like #517	2.00	2.00

No. 563 contains one 80x50mm stamp with UN 50th anniv. emblem.

Issued: No. 562, 10/20/94; No. 563, 6/26/95.

Nos. 525-561, 564-566 are unassigned.

Dedication of Capitol Building Complex — A82

Designs: No. 567, Capitol building. No. 568, Nitijela (parliament) building. No. 569, Natl. seal, vert. No. 570, Flag over complex, vert.

1993, Aug. 11 Litho. Perf. 11x10½

567	A82	29c multi (4-1)	.50	.50
568	A82	29c multi (4-2)	.50	.50

Perf. 10½x11

569	A82	29c multi (4-3)	.50	.50
570	A82	29c multi (4-4)	.50	.50
	Nos. 567-570 (4)		2.00	2.00

Souvenir Sheet

Christening of Mobil Super Tanker Eagle — A83

1993, Aug. 25 Perf. 13½

571	A83	50c multicolored	.85	.85

Marshallese Life in 1800's A84

No. 572, Woman, breadfruit (4-1). No. 573, Canoes, warrior (4-2). No. 574, Young chief (4-3). No. 575, Drummer, dancers (4-4).

1993, Sept. 15 Litho. Perf. 13½

572	A84	29c multi	.60	.60
573	A84	29c multi	.60	.60
574	A84	29c multi	.60	.60
575	A84	29c multi	.60	.60
a.		Block of 4, #572-575	2.40	2.40

Christmas — A85

1993, Oct. 25 Litho. Perf. 13½

576	A85	29c multicolored	.60	.60

Souvenir Sheet

Constitution, 15th Anniv. — A86

1994, May 1 Litho. Perf. 13½

577	A86	$2.90 multicolored	4.50	4.50

Souvenir Sheet

Marshall Islands Postal Service, 10th Anniv. A87

1994, May 2

578	A87	29c multicolored	.60	.60

1994 World Cup Soccer Championships, U.S. — A88

Design: No. 580, Soccer players, diff.

1994, June 17 Litho. Perf. 13½

579	A88	50c red & multi (2-1)	1.60	1.00
580	A88	50c blue & multi (2-2)	1.60	1.00
a.		Pair, #579-580	3.25	2.00

No. 580a has a continuous design.

Miniature Sheet

Solar System — A89

Mythological characters, symbols: a, Solar system. b, Sun. c, Moon. d, Mercury. e, Venus. f, Earth. g, Mars. h, Jupiter. i, Saturn. j, Uranus. k, Neptune. l, Pluto.

1994, July 20 Litho. Perf. 13½

582	A89	50c Sheet of 12, #a.-l.	12.00	12.00

First Manned Moon Landing, 25th Anniv. — A90

Designs: No. 583, First step onto Moon's surface. No. 584, Planting US flag on Moon. No. 585, Astronaut's salute to America, flag. No. 586, Astronaut stepping onto Moon, John F. Kennedy.

1994, July 20

583	A90	75c multi (4-1)	1.10	1.10
584	A90	75c multi (4-2)	1.10	1.10
585	A90	75c multi (4-3)	1.10	1.10
586	A90	75c multi (4-4)	1.10	1.10
a.		Block of 4, #583-586	4.50	4.50
b.		Souvenir sheet of 4, #583-586	4.50	4.50

Souvenir Sheet

Butterflies — A91

1994, Aug. 16 Litho. Perf. 13½

587	A91	Sheet of 3	3.75	3.75
a.		29c Meadow argus	.60	.60
b.		52c Brown awl	1.10	1.10
c.		$1 Great eggfly	2.00	2.00

PHILAKOREA '94.

Christmas — A92

1994, Oct. 28 Litho. Perf. 13½

588	A92	29c multicolored	.60	.60

Souvenir Sheet

New Year 1995 (Year of the Boar) A93

1995, Jan. 2 Litho. Perf. 13½

589	A93	50c multicolored	1.00	1.00

Marine Life A94

Designs: a, Meyer's butterflyfish, achilles tang, scuba diver. b, Scuba diver, moorish idols (a, d). c, Pacific green turtle, fairy basslets. d, Fairy basslets, emperor angelfish, orange-fin anemonefish.

1995, Mar. 20 Litho. Perf. 13½

590	A94	Block of 4	4.50	4.50
a.-d.		55c Any single	1.10	1.10

See Nos. 614, 644.

John F. Kennedy (1917-63), 35th Pres. of US — A95

Designs: a, PT-109. b, Taking presidential oath. c, Peace Corps volunteers. d, US aircraft, naval vessels, Cuban Missile Crisis. e, Signing Nuclear Test Ban Treaty. f, Eternal flame, Arlington Natl. Cemetery.

1995, May 29 Litho. Perf. 13½

591		Strip of 6	5.25	5.25
a.-f.	A95 55c Any single		1.00	1.00

275

MARSHALL ISLANDS

Marilyn Monroe (1926-1962), Actress — A96

Various portraits with background color: a, red. b, green. c, orange. d, violet.

1995, June 1   Litho.   *Perf. 13½*
592 A96 75c Block of 4, #a.-d.   5.75   5.75

No. 592 was issued in sheets of three blocks.

Cats — A97

Designs: a, Siamese, exotic shorthair. b, American shorthair, Persian. c, Maine coon, Burmese. d, Abyssinian, Himalayan.

1995, July 5   Litho.   *Perf. 13½*
593   Block of 4   2.50   2.50
   a.-d. A97 32c Any single   .60   .60

Mir-Space Shuttle Docking & Apollo-Soyuz Link-Up — A98

a, Space station Mir. b, Space shuttle Atlantis. c, Apollo command module. d, Soyuz spacecraft.

1995, June 29   Litho.   *Perf. 13½*
594 A98 75c Block of 4, #a.-d.   4.75   4.75

Nos. 594 is a continuous design.

Pacific Game Fish — A99

a, Pacific sailfish. b, Albacore. c, Wahoo. d, Pacific blue marlin. e, Yellowfin tuna. f, Giant trevally. g, Dolphin fish. h, Mako shark.

1995, Aug. 21   Litho.   *Perf. 13½*
595   Block of 8   11.00   11.00
   a.-h. A99 60c Any single   1.35   1.35

Island Legends A100

Designs: a, Inedel's Magic Kite. b, Lijebake Rescues Her Granddaughter. c, Jebro's Mother Invents the Sail. d, Limajnon Escapes to the Moon.

1995, Aug. 25   Litho.   *Perf. 13½*
596 A100 Block of 4 + 4 labels   2.50   2.50
   a.-d.   32c Any single   .60   .60

See Nos. 612, 643.

Miniature Sheet

Singapore '95 World Stamp Exhibition — A101

Orchids: a, Paphiopedilum armeniacum. b, Masdevallia veitchiana. c, Cattleya francis. d, Cattleya x guatemalensis.

1995, Sept. 1   Litho.   *Perf. 13½*
597 A101 32c Sheet of 4, #a.-d.   2.25   2.25

Souvenir Sheet

Intl. Stamp & Coin Expo, Beijing '95 A102

1995, Sept. 12
598 A102 50c Suzhou Gardens   .85   .85

Christmas — A103

1995, Oct. 31   Litho.   *Perf. 13½*
599 A103 32c multicolored   .55   .55

Miniature Sheet

Jet Fighter Planes — A104

a, Me 262-1a Schwalbe. b, Meteor F.MK8. c, F-80 Shooting Star. d, F-86 Sabre. e, F9F-2 Panther. f, MiG-15. g, F-100 Super Sabre. h, F-102A Delta Dagger. i, F-104 Starfighter. j, MiG-21 MT. k, F8U Crusader. l, F-105 Thunderbird. m, Saab J35 Draken. n, Fiat G91Y. o, F-4 Phantom II. p, Saab JA37 Viggen. q, Mirage F1C. r, F-14 Tomcat. s, F-15 Eagle. t, F-16 Fighting Falcon. u, Tornado F.MK3. v, Sukhoi Su-27UB. w, Mirage 2000C. x, Sea Harrier FRS.MK1. y, F-117 Nighthawk.

1995, Nov. 10
600 A104 32c Sheet of 25, #a.-y.   16.00   16.00

No. 600 was sold in uncut sheets of 6 panes.

See Nos. 617, 641, 666, 708, 728.

Yitzhak Rabin (1922-95), Israeli Prime Minister — A105

1995, Nov. 10   Litho.   *Perf. 14*
601 A105 32c multicolored   .55   .55

No. 601 was issued in sheets of 8.

Souvenir Sheet

New Year 1996 (Year of the Rat) A106

1996, Jan. 5   Litho.   *Perf. 13½*
602 A106 50c multicolored   .85   .85

Native Birds — A107

Designs: a, Blue-gray noddy. b, Gray-backed tern. c, Masked booby. d, Black-footed albatross.

1996, Feb. 26   Litho.   *Perf. 13½*
603   Block of 4   2.50   2.50
   a.-d. A107 32c Any single   .60   .60

Wild Cats — A108

a, Cheetah. b, Tiger. c, Lion. d, Jaguar.

1996, Mar. 8   Litho.   *Perf. 13½*
604   Block of 4   3.75   3.75
   a.-d. A108 55c Any single   .90   .90

Sailing Ship Type of 1993
Miniature Sheet

Designs: a, like #443. b, like #447. c, like #448. d, like #455. e, like #444. f, like #446. g, like #456. h, like #459. i, like #441. j, like #449. k, like #451. l, like #465. m, Malmel outrigger sailing canoe. n, like #445. o, like #452. p, like #453. q, like #457. r, like #450. s, like #458. t, like #460. u, like #466. v, like #442. w, like #454. x, like #459A. y, like #462.

1996, Apr. 18   Litho.   *Perf. 11x10½*
605 A80 32c Sheet of 25, #a.-y.   16.00   16.00

Olympic Games, Cent. — A109

First Olympic stamps, Greece: a, #119. b, #124. c, #123. d, #125.

1996, Apr. 27   Litho.   *Perf. 12*
606   Block of 4   4.00   4.00
   a.-d. A109 60c Any single   .95   .95

Issued in sheets of 4. A small number were were overprinted in gold in the margin for Olymphilex '96.

Miniature Sheet

History of the Marshall Islands — A110

a, Undersea eruptions form island bases. b, Coral reefs grow. c, Storms bring birds & seeds. d, Early human inhabitants arrive. e, Seen by Spanish explorers, 1527. f, Capt. John Marshall, RN, charts islands, 1788. g, Islands become German protectorate, 1885. h, Japan seizes islands, 1914. i, US troops liberate islands, 1944. j, Bikiniatoll evacuated for nuclear testing, 1946. k, Islands become UN Trust Territory, 1947. l, Independence, 1986.

1996, May 2   Litho.   *Perf. 13x12*
607 A110 55c Sheet of 12,
   #a.-l.   10.50   10.50

Elvis Presley's First #1 Hit, "Heartbreak Hotel," 40th Anniv. — A111

1996, May 5   *Perf. 10½x11*
608 A111 32c multicolored   .65   .65

Issued in sheets of 20.

Souvenir Sheet

China '96, 9th Asian Intl. Philatelic Exhibition — A112

Design: The Palance Museum, Shenyang.

1996, May 17   *Perf. 13½*
609 A112 50c multicolored   1.00   1.00

James Dean (1931-55), Actor — A113

1996, June 1   Litho.   *Perf. 10½x11*
610 A113 32c multicolored   .65   .65

No. 610 was issued in sheets of 20.

First Ford Automobile, Cent. — A114

Designs: a, 1896 Quadricycle. b, 1903 Model A Roadster. c, 1909 Model T Touring Car. d, 1929 Model A Station Wagon. e, 1955 Thunderbird. f, 1964 ½ Mustang convertible. g, 1995 Explorer. h, 1996 Taurus.

1996, June 4   Litho.   *Perf. 13½*
611   Sheet of 8   6.00   6.00
   a.-h. A114 60c Any single   .75   .75

MARSHALL ISLANDS

Island Legends Type of 1995

Designs: a, Kijeek An Letao. b, Mennin Jobwodda. c, Wa Kone, Waan Letao. d, Kouj.

1996, July 19
612	Block of 4 + 4 labels	2.25	2.25
a.-d.	A100 32c Any single	.55	.55

Steam Locomotives — A115

Designs: a, Pennsylvania K4, U.S. b, "Big Boy," US. c, Mallard, Great Britain. d, RENFE Class 242, Spain. e, DB Class 01, Germany. f, FS Group 691, Italy. g, "Royal Hudson," Canada. h, Evening Star, Great Britain. i, SAR 520 Class, Australia. j, SNCF 232.U1, France. k, QJ "Advance Forward," China. l, C62 "Swallow," Japan.

1996, Aug. 23   Litho.   *Perf. 13½*
613	Sheet of 12	11.00	11.00
a.-i.	A115 55c Any single	.90	.90

Marine Life Type of 1995

Designs: a, like #590a. b, like #590b. c, like #590c. d, like #590d.

1996, Oct. 21   Litho.   *Perf. 13½*
614	Block of 4	1.75	1.75
a.-d.	A94 32c Any single	.40	.40

Taipei '96, 10th Asian Intl. Philatelic Exhibition. Nos. 614a-614b have Chinese inscription. Nos. 614c-614d English.

Stick Chart, Canoe and Flag of the Republic Type of 1990

1996, Oct. 21   *Perf. 11x10½*
615	A63 $3 like No. 381	6.00	6.00

No. 615 inscribed "Free Association United States of America."

Angels from "Madonna and Child with Four Saints," by Rosso Fiorentino — A116

1996, Oct. 31   Litho.   *Perf. 13½*
616	A116 32c multicolored	.55	.55

Christmas.

Legendary Planes Type of 1995

Biplanes: a, JN-3 Jenny. b, SPAD XIII. c, Albatros D.III. d, DH-4 Llberty. e, Fokker Dr.1. f, F-1 Camel. g, Martin MB-2. h, MB-3A Tommy. i, Curtiss TS-1. j, P-1 Hawk. k, Boeing PW-9. l, Douglas 0-2H. m, LB-5 Pirate. n, 02U-1 Corsair. o, F8C Heldiver. p, Boeing F4B-4. q, J6B Gorfaloon. r, Martin DM. s, TT 1 Tiffi. t, O.П. 02 Cricket. u, Polikarpov I-15 Gull. v, Mk.1 Swordfish. w, Aichi D1A2. x, Grumman F3F. y, SOC-3 Seagull.

1996, Nov. 1
617	A104 32c Sheet of 25, #a.-y.	16.00	16.00

Native Crafts — A117

Designs: a, Fan making. b, Canoe models. c, Carving. d, Basketmaking.

1996, Nov. 7   Litho.   *Perf. 11x10½*
618	Block of 4	1.60	1.60
a.-d.	A117 32c Any single	.40	.40

See Nos. 629-630.

Souvenir Sheet

New Year 1997 (Year of the Ox) — A118

1997, Jan. 7   Litho.   *Perf. 13x13½*
619	A118 60c multicolored	1.25	1.25

Amata Kabua (1928-96), President of Marshall Islands — A119

1997, Jan. 27   Litho.   *Perf. 13½*
620	A119 32c multicolored	.65	.65
621	A119 60c multicolored	1.25	1.25

No. 621 has vertical inscriptions in English.

Elvis Presley (1935-77) — A120

Designs: a, "Rocking 50's." b, "Soaring 60's." c, "Sensational 70's."

1997, Jan. 8   Litho.   *Perf. 13½*
622	A120 32c Strip of 3, #a.-c.	2.00	2.00

Hong Kong '97 — A121

Hong Kong at sunrise, ships: No. 623: a, Walap. b, Junk.
Hong Kong at night, ships: No. 624: a, Canoe. b, Junk, diff.

1997, Feb. 12   *Perf. 12*
623	Sheet of 2 + 3 labels	1.25	1.25
a.-b.	A121 32c Any single	.60	.60
624	Sheet of 2 + 3 labels	1.25	1.25
a.-b.	A121 32c Any single	.60	.60

Christianity in Marshall Islands, 140th Anniv. — A122

Apostles: No. 625: a, Andrew. b, Matthew. c, Philip. d, Simon. e, Thaddeus. f, Thomas. g, Bartholomew. h, John. i, James the Lesser. j, James the Greater. k, Paul. l, Peter.
$3, The Last Supper, by Peter Paul Rubens.

1997, Mar. 28   *Perf. 13½*
625	Sheet of 12	14.50	14.50
a.-i.	A122 60c Any single	1.20	1.20

Souvenir Sheet
Perf. 13x13½
626	A122 $3 multicolored	6.00	6.00

No. 626 contains one 80x50mm stamp.

First Decade of 20th Century — A123

Designs: a, Family of immigrants. b, Dowager Empress, Boxers, China. c, Photography for every man. d, Dr. Walter Reed, mosquito. e, Sigmund Freud. f, Marconi, wireless transmitter. g, Enrico Caruso, phonograph. h, Wright Brothers, Flyer. i, Einstein. j, HMS Dreadnought. k, San Francisco earthquake, 1906. l, Gandhi, non-violent protestors. m, Picasso. n, Dawn of the automobile age. o, Man, camels, oil derrick amid sand dunes.

1997, Apr. 15   Litho.   *Perf. 13½*
627	Sheet of 15	18.00	18.00
a.-o.	A123 60c Any single	1.10	1.10

See Nos. 646, 654, 657, 679, 702, 711, 723, 726 and 730.

Deng Xiaoping (1904-97), Chinese Leader — A124

1997, Apr. 21
628	A124 60c multicolored	1.25	1.25

Crafts Type of 1996

Designs: Nos. 629a, 630a, Fan making. Nos. 629b, 630b, Canoe models. Nos. 629c, 630c, Wood carving. Nos. 629d, 630d, Basket making.

1997, May 29   Litho.   *Perf. 11x10½*
Self-Adhesive
629	Block of 4	2.50	2.50
a.-d.	A117 32c Any single	.60	.60

Serpentine Die Cut Perf. 11
Self-Adhesive
630	Strip of 4	2.50	2.50
a.-d.	A117 32c Any single	.60	.60

No. 629 was issued in sheets of 20 stamps. No. 630 was issued in sheets of 16 stamps. Die cutting does not extend through backing paper on No. 630.

Marshall Islands Stamps, Cent., US Stamps, 150th Anniv. — A126

1997, May 29   Litho.   *Perf. 13½*
Booklet Stamps
631	A126 50c No. 1	1.00	1.00
632	A126 50c No. 2	1.00	1.00
633	A126 50c No. 3	1.00	1.00
634	A126 50c No. 4	1.00	1.00
635	A126 50c No. 5	1.00	1.00
636	A126 50c No. 6	1.00	1.00
a.	Booklet pane, #631-636	6.00	

Size: 75x32mm
637	A126 $1 US Nos. 1 & 2	2.00	2.00
a.	Booklet pane of 1	2.00	
	Complete booklet, #636a, #637a	8.00	

PACIFIC 97.

Bristle-thighed Curlew — A127

World Wildlife Fund: a, Walking right. b, On tree branch. c, Standing with mouth open. d, In flight.

1997, June 6
638	Block or strip of 4	4.00	4.00
a.-d.	A127 16c Any single	1.00	1.00

Souvenir Sheet

Bank of China, Hong Kong — A128

1997, July 1   Litho.   *Perf. 13½*
639	A128 50c multicolored	1.00	1.00

Canoes — A129

Designs: a, Pacific Arts Festival canoe, Walap of Enewetak. b, Large Voyaging canoe, Walap of Jaluit. c. Racing canoe. d, Sailing canoe, Tipnol of Ailuk.

1997, July 10   Litho.   *Perf. 13½*
640	Block or strip of 4	2.50	2.50
a.-d.	A129 32c Any single	.60	.60

See No. 1111.

Legendary Aircraft Type of 1995

Designs: a, C-54 Skymaster. b, B-36 Peacemaker. c, F-86 Sabre. d, B-47 Stratojet. e, C-124 Globemaster II. f, C-121 Constellation. g, B-52 Stratofortress. h, F-100 Super Sabre. i, F-104 Starfighter. j, C-130 Hercules. k, F-105 Thunderchief. l, KC-135 Stratotanker. m, B-58 Hustler. n, F-4 Phantom II. o, T-38 Talon. p, C-141 Star Lifter. q, F-111 Aardvark. r, SR-71 "Blackbird." s, C-5 Galaxy. t, A-10 Thunderbolt II. u, F-15 Eagle. v, F-16 Fighting Falcon. w, F-117 Nighthawk. x, B-2 Spirit. y, C-17 Globemaster III.

1997, July 19,
641	A104 32c Sheet of 25, #a.-y.	16.00	16.00

USS Constitution, Bicent. — A130

1997, July 21
642	A130 32c multicolored	.65	.65

Island Legends Type of 1995

Designs: a, The Largo Pool of Mojit. b, The Beautiful Woman of Kwajalein. c, Sharks and Lowakalle Reef. d, The Demon of Adrie.

1997, Aug. 15   Litho.   *Perf. 13½*
643	Block of 4 +4 labels	2.50	2.50
a.-	A100 32c Any single		
d.		.60	.60

Marine Life Type of 1995

Designs: a, Watanabe's angelfish, gray reef shark. b, Raccoon butterflyfish. c, Flame angelfish. d, Square-spot fairy basslets.

1997, Aug. 21
644	Block of 4	4.75	4.75
a.-	A94 60c Any single		
d.		1.10	1.10

Diana, Princess of Wales (1961-97) — A131

Various portraits, background color: a, violet. b, blue. c, yellow orange.

MARSHALL ISLANDS

1997, Sept. 30   Litho.   Perf. 13½
645   Strip of 3   3.75 3.75
a.-c. A131 60c Any single   1.25 1.25
No. 645 printed in sheets with two vertical strips flanking three horizontal strips.

Events of the 20th Century Type
1910-19: a, Women mobilize for equal rights. b, Ernest Rutherford, model of atom. c, Sun Yat-sen. d, Sinking of the Titanic. e, Igor Stravinsky, The Rite of Spring. f, Ford begins assembly line production of autos. g, Archduke Franz Ferdinand, wife Sophie. h, German U-boat sinks Lusitania. i, Soldiers in trenches at Battle of Verdun. j, Patrick Pearse proclaims Irish Republic. k, Jews praying at Wailing Wall. l, Cruiser Aurora. m, Baron Manfred von Richthofen. n, German revolutionary troops, 1918. o, Negotiators write Treaty of Versailles.

1997, Oct. 15   Litho.   Perf. 13½
646   Sheet of 15   18.00 18.00
a.-o. A123 60c Any single   1.20 1.20

Christmas — A132

Cherubs from Sistine Madonna, by Raphael: No. 647, With hand under chin. No. 648, With arms folded under chin.

1997, Oct. 25
647   A132 32c multicolored   .60   .60
648   A132 32c multicolored   .60   .60
a.   Pair, #647-648   1.25 1.25

US State-Named Warships — A133

Designs: a.-z., aa.-ax.: USS Alabama-USS Wyoming in alphabetical order. USS Honolulu shown for Hawaii.

1997, Nov. 1
649   Sheet of 50   20.00 20.00
a.-ax. A133 20c Any single   .40   .40

Souvenir Sheet

Shanghai 97, Intl. Stamp and Coin Expo — A134

Treasure ship, Ming Dynasty.

1997, Nov. 19   Litho.   Perf. 13x13½
650   A134 50c multicolored   1.00 1.00

Souvenir Sheet

New Year 1998 (Year of the Tiger) A135

1998, Jan. 2   Litho.   Perf. 13x13½
651   A135 60c multicolored   1.25 1.25

Elvis Presley's 1968 Television Special — A136

Scenes from special: a, shown. b, Red background. c, Elvis in white suit.

1998, Jan. 8   Perf. 13½
652   Strip of 3   1.75 1.75
a.-c. A136 32c Any single   .55   .55

Sea Shells — A137

a, Chicoreus brunneus. b, Cypraea aurantium. c, Lambis chiragra. d, Tridanca squamosa.

1998, Feb. 13   Litho.   Perf. 13½
653   Strip of 4   2.50 2.50
a.-d. A137 32c Any single   .60   .60
Latin name on No. 653d is spelled incorrectly. See No. 1110.

Events of the 20th Century Type
1920-29: a, Radio broadcasting reaches the world. b, Quest for peace lurches forward. c, Architects reshape the world. d, Funerary mask of King Tutankhamen. e, USSR emerges as a Communist State. f, Nations emerge from Ottoman Empire, Kemal Ataturk. g, Arrival of the Jazz Age. h, Age of the rocket launched, Robert Goddard. i, Talkies arrive at the movie theater. j, Scourge of Fascism arrives. k, Man's universe expands. l, Penicillin launches antibiotic revolution. m, First glimmers of television. n, Aviation shrinks the world, Graf Zeppelin. o, World suffers economic depression.

1998, Mar. 16   Litho.   Perf. 13½
654   Sheet of 15   18.00 18.00
a.-o. A123 60c Any single   1.20 1.20

Canoes of the Pacific A138

a, Pahi Sailing canoe, Tuamotu Archipelago. b, Maori war canoe, New Zealand. c, Wa'a Kaukahi fishing canoe, Hawaii. d, Amatasi sailing canoe, Samoa. e, Ndrua sailing canoe, Fiji. f, Tongiaki voyaging canoe, Tonga. g, Tipairua traveling canoe, Tahiti. h, Walap sailing canoe, Marshall Islands.

1998, May 21   Litho.   Perf. 13½
655   A138 32c Sheet of 8, #a.-h.   5.00 5.00
See Nos. 690-698.

Berlin Airlift, 50th Anniv. A139

Designs: a, Douglas C-54/R4D-5. b, Avro York. c, Watching the flights of freedom. d, Berliners welcoming supplies.

1998, June 26   Litho.   Perf. 13½
656   A139 60c Block of 4, #a.-d.   4.75 4.75

Events of the 20th Century Type
1930-39: a, Economic depression engulfs the world. b, Scientists split the atom. c, Stalin's terror reigns in Soviet Union. d, Fascism becomes rampant. e, Engineers harness nature (Dneproges Dam). f, Streamlined design symbolizes bright future. g, Passengers travel airways in comfort. h, Artists protest the scourges of war. i, Media create indelible memories. j, Japanese agression arouses world opinion. k, Era of appeasement. l, Inventions pave way to future. m, Persecution of Jews portends holocaust. n, World War II begins in Europe. o, Movies cheer audiences.

1998, July 15
657   Sheet of 15   17.50 17.50
a.-o. A123 60c Any single   1.10 1.10

Czar Nicholas II — A140

No. 658, Coronation Czar Nicholas II, 1896. No. 659, Russo-Japanese War and the Cruiser Varyag, 1904-05. No. 660, Czar's Manifesto, 1905. No. 661, Peasant sower, Rasputin, 1905. No. 662, Czar with soldiers at the front, 1915. No. 663, Ipateva House, Ekaterinburg, 1917. $3, Family portrait.

1998, July 17   Perf. 13½
Booklet Stamps
658   A140 60c multicolored   1.25 1.25
659   A140 60c multicolored   1.25 1.25
660   A140 60c multicolored   1.25 1.25
661   A140 60c multicolored   1.25 1.25
662   A140 60c multicolored   1.25 1.25
663   A140 60c multicolored   1.25 1.25

Size: 60x54mm
Perf. 13½ at Top
664   A140 $3 multicolored   6.00 6.00
a.   Booklet pane, #658-664   13.50
       Complete booklet, #664a   13.50

George Herman "Babe" Ruth (1895-1948) — A141

1998, Aug. 16   Litho.   Perf. 13½
665   A141 32c multicolored   .65   .65

Legendary Aircraft Type of 1995
US Navy aircraft: a, NC-4. b, PBY-5 Catalina. c, TBD Devastator. d, SB2U Vindicator. e, F4F Wildcat. f, OS2U Kingfisher. g, SBD Dauntless. h, F4U Corsair. i, SB2C Helldiver. j, PV-Ventura. k, TBM Avenger. l, F6F Hellcat. m, PB4Y-2 Privateer. n, A-1J Skyraider. o, F2H Banshee. p, F9F-2B Panther. q, P5M Marlin. r, F-8 Crusader. s, F-4 Phantom II. t, A-6 Intruder. u, P-3 Orion. v, A-7 Corsair II. w, A-4 Skyhawk. x, S-3 Viking. y, F/A-18 Hornet.

1998, Aug. 28
666   A104 32c Sheet of 25, #a.-y.   16.00 16.00

Chevrolet Automobiles A142

Designs: a, 1912 Classic Six. b, 1931 Sports Roadster. c, 1941 Special Deluxe. d, 1955 Cameo Carrier Fleetside. e, 1957 Corvette. f, 1957 Bel Air. g, 1967 Camaro. h, 1970 Chevelle SS 454.

1998, Sept. 1
667   Sheet of 8   9.50 9.50
a.-h. A142 60c Any single   1.15 1.15

Marshallese Language and Alphabet — A143

Letter, example of Marshallese word beginning with letter: a, "A", Amata Kabua, first president. b, "A", Aj, to weave. c, "B", butterfly. d, "D", beautiful lady. e, "E", fish. f, "I", Rainbow. g, "J", mat. h, "K", house of government. i, "L", stars. j, "L", Tropicbird. k, "M", breadfruit. l, "M", Arrowroot plant. m, "N", Coconut tree. n, "N", Ocean wave. o, "N", shark tooth. p, "O", Fish net. q, "O", Tattoo. r, "O", Lionfish. s, "P", Visitor's hut. t, "R", Whale. u, "T", outrigger canoe. v, "U", Fire. w, "U", Dorsal fin of whale. x, "W", Woven sail.

1998, Sept. 14
668   Sheet of 24   16.00 16.00
a.-x. A143 33c Any single   .65   .65

New Buildings in Marshall Islands A144

a, Trust Company of the Marshall Islands, 1998. b, Embassy of the People's Republic of China, 1996. c, Outrigger Marshall Islands Resort, 1996.

1998, Oct. 12
669   Strip of 3   2.00 2.00
a.-c. A144 33c Any single   .65   .65

Christmas — A145

1998, Oct. 26
670   A145 32c Midnight angel   .65   .65

John Glenn's Return to Space — A146

No. 671, Friendship 7 launch, 1962. No. 672, Glenn in spacesuit, 1962. No. 673, Mercury capsule in space, 1962. No. 674, Shuttle Discovery Launch, 1998. No. 675, Astronaut and US Senator Glenn, 1998. No. 676, Shuttle Discovery in space, 1998.
$3, US #1193, astrological drawings.

1998, Oct. 29   Booklet Stamps
671   A146 60c multicolored   1.25 1.25
672   A146 60c multicolored   1.25 1.25
673   A146 60c multicolored   1.25 1.25
674   A146 60c multicolored   1.25 1.25
675   A146 60c multicolored   1.25 1.25
676   A146 60c multicolored   1.25 1.25

Size: 75x32mm
677   A146 $3 multicolored   6.00 6.00
a.   Booklet pane, #671-677   13.50
       Complete booklet, #677a   13.50

Souvenir Sheet

Antonov An-124 Delivering Drought Relief Supplies — A147

1998, Nov. 3   Litho.   Perf. 13½
678   A147 $3.20 multicolored   6.50 6.50

Events of the 20th Century Type
1940-49: a, Aviation assumes strategic importance. b, State of war becomes global. c, Missiles announce new age of warfare. d, Music raises spirits. e, Determined peoples fight for survival. f, The Holocaust. g, Mankind faces Atomic Age. h, War's end brings hope. i, Computer age dawns. j, Nations unite for peace. k, World demands justice from war criminals. l, A time for rebuilding. m, Transistor opens door to miniaturization. n, World divided by cold war. o, New China is proclaimed.

1998, Nov. 16   Litho.   Perf. 13½
679   Sheet of 15   17.50 17.50
a.-o. A123 60c Any single   1.15 1.15

Warships A148

MARSHALL ISLANDS

Designs: a, Trireme Galley. b, Trireme Romano. c, Viking Longship. d, Ming Treasure ship. e, The Mary Rose. f, Nuestra Señora del Rosario. g, Korean Turtle ship. h, Brederode. i, Galera Veneziana. j, Santisima Trinidad. k, Ville de Paris. l, HMS Victory. m, Bonhomme Richard. n, USS Constellation. o, USS Hartford. p, Fijian Ndrua. q, HMS Dreadnought. r, HMAS Australia. s, HMS Dorsetshire. t, Graf Spee. u, Yamato. v, USS Tautog. w, Bismarck. x, USS Hornet. y, USS Missouri.

1998, Dec. 1
680 A148 33c Sheet of 25,
　　　　#a.-y.　　16.00 16.00

Souvenir Sheet

New Year 1999 (Year of the Rabbit) A149

1999, Jan. 2   Litho.   Perf. 13x13½
681 A149 60c multicolored   1.25 1.25

Birds — A150

1c, Lesser golden plover. 3c, Siberian tattler. 20c, Brown noddy. 22c, Common fairy tern. 33c, Micronesian pigeon. 55c, Long-tailed cuckoo. $1, Christmas shearwater. $10, Eurasian tree sparrow.

1999, Jan. 9   Perf. 13½
682 A150   1c multicolored   .25   .25
683 A150   3c multicolored   .25   .25
684 A150 20c multicolored   .40   .40
685 A150 22c multicolored   .45   .45
686 A150 33c multicolored   .65   .65
687 A150 55c multicolored   1.10 1.10
688 A150 $1 multicolored   2.00 2.00
689 A150 $10 multicolored 15.00 15.00
　　Nos. 682-689 (8)   20.10 20.10
　　See Nos. 714-721.

Canoes of the Pacific Type

Designs: a, like #655a. b, like #655b. c, like #655c. d, like #655f. e, like #655e. f, like #655d. g, like #655g. h, like #655h.

1999, Jan. 25   Litho.   Perf. 13½
690 A138 33c Sheet of 8, #a.-h. 5.25 5.25

Self-Adhesive
Size: 40x25mm
Perf. 11x10½
691 A138 33c like #690a   .65 .65
692 A138 33c like #690b   .65 .65
693 A138 33c like #690c   .65 .65
694 A138 33c like #690d   .65 .65
695 A138 33c like #690e   .65 .65
696 A138 33c like #690f   .65 .65
697 A138 33c like #690g   .65 .65
698 A138 33c like #690h   .65 .65
　a. Block of 10, #691-697, 2 #698 6.50
　　Issued in sheets of 20.

Great American Indian Chiefs — A151

Designs: a, Tecumseh. b, Powhatan. c, Hiawatha. d, Dull knife. e, Sequoyah. f, Sitting Bull. g, Cochise. h, Red Cloud. i, Geronimo. j, Chief Joseph. k, Pontiac. l, Crazy Horse.

1999, Feb. 1   Perf. 13½
699 Sheet of 12   14.50 14.50
　a.-l. A151 60c Any single 1.15 1.15

National Flag — A152

1999, Feb. 5   Perf. 14
700 A152 33c multicolored   .65   .65

Flowers of the Pacific — A153

Designs: a, Plumeria. b, Vanda. c, Ilima. d, Tiare. e, White ginger. f, Hibiscus.

1999, Feb. 18   Perf. 13½
701 Block of 6   4.00 4.00
　a.-f. A153 33c Any single .65   .65

Events of the 20th Century Type

1950-59: a, World enters age of television. b, Cold war battles erupt. c, Vaccines conquer scourge of polio. d, U.S., USSR engage in arms race. e, Science begins to unravel genetic code. f, Conquests reach unconquered heights. g, Pageantry reassures commonwealth. h, Rock 'n' roll reshapes music beat. i, Suns sets on Colonial Empires. j, World condemns racial discrimination. k, Unrest challenges Communism's march. l, Vision of European Union takes form. m, Space race opens space age. n, Jets shrink time and distance. o, Microchip presages computer revolution.

1999, Mar. 15
702 Sheet of 15   18.00 18.00
　a.-o. A123 60c Any single 1.20 1.20

Souvenir Sheet

HMAS Australia A154

1999, Mar. 19
703 A154 $1.20 multicolored 2.50 2.50
　Australia '99, World Stamp Expo.

Elvis Presley — A155

1999, Apr. 6   Litho.   Perf. 13½
704 A155 33c multicolored   .65   .65

IBRA '99 World Stamp Exhibition, Nuremberg, Germany — A156

Designs: a, #25. b, #24. c, #23. d, #22.

1999, Apr. 27   Litho.   Perf. 13½
705 Sheet of 4   4.75 4.75
　a.-d. A156 60c Any single 1.15 1.15

Marshall Islands Constitution, 20th Anniv. A157

Design: 33c, Constitution Committee.

1999, May 1   Litho.   Perf. 13½
706 A157 33c multicolored   .65   .65

Marshall Islands Postal Service, 15th Anniv. A158

Portions of No. 607 and, clockwise: a, #572, 644, 689, 597d (b). b, #668c, 595c, 655h, 597a. c, #381, 570, 574, 668d. d, #597b, 643b, 621.

1999, May 2
707 A158 33c Block of 4, #a.-d. 2.50 2.50

Legendary Aircraft Type of 1995

a, Martin B-10B. b, Northrop A-17A Nomad. c, Douglas B-18 Bolo. d, Boeing B-17F Flying Fortress. e, Douglas A-20 Havoc. f, North American B-25B Mitchell. g, Consolidated B-24D Liberator. h, North American P-51B Mustang. i, Martin B-26 Marauder. j, Douglas A-26B Invader. k, Bell P-59 Airacomet. l, Boeing KC-97 Stratofreighter. m, Douglas A-1J Skyraider. n, Lockheed P2V-7 Neptune. o, North American B-45 Tornado. p, Boeing B-50 Superfortress. q, North American AJ-2 Savage. r, Grumman F9F Cougar. s, Douglas A-3 Skywarrior. t, Martin B-57E Canberra. u, Douglas EB-66 Destroyer. v, Grumman E-2A Hawkeye. w, Northrop F-5E Tiger II. x, McDonnell Douglas AV-8B Harrier II. y, Rockwell B-1B Lancer.

1999, June 1
708 A104 33c Sheet of 25,
　　　　#a.-y. 16.00 16.00

Souvenir Sheet

PhilexFrance 99 — A159

Design: $1, Astronaut, lunar rover.

1999, July 2   Litho.   Perf. 13½
709 A159 $1 multicolored   2.00 2.00

Souvenir Sheet

Tanker Alrehab A160

1999, July 15   Litho.   Perf. 13x13½
710 A160 60c multi   1.25 1.25

Events of the 20th Century Type

1960-69: a, Invention of the laser. b, Pill revolutionizes family planning. c, Gagarin becomes the Columbus of the cosmos. d, Communism advertizes failures. e, Planet Earth endangered. f, Superpowers totter on precipice of war. g, Spirit of ecumenism renews Christianity. h, Railways achieve record speeds. i, Cultural Revolution stuns China. j, Arab-Israeli War unsettles Middle East. k, Organ transplants repair human body. l, America engulfed in Vietnam War. m, Political assassinations shock world. n, Supersonic travel becomes a reality. o, Mankind leaps from Earth to Moon.

1999, July 15   Perf. 13½
711 Sheet of 15   18.00 18.00
　a.-o. A123 60c Any single 1.20 1.20

First Manned Moon Landing, 30th Anniv. A161

Designs: a, Saluting astronaut, Earth. b, Flag. c, Astronaut.

1999, July 20
712 A161 33c Sheet of 3, #a.-c. 2.00 2.00

Ships A162

Designs: a, Galleon Los Reyes, Spain, 1568. b, Frigate Dolphin, Great Britain, 1767. c, Bark Scarborough, Great Britain, 1788. d, Brig Rurick, Russia, 1817.

1999, Aug. 26
713 A162 33c Block of 4, #a.-d. 2.75 2.75
　　See No. 1112.

Bird Type of 1999

Designs: 5c, Black-tailed godwit. 40c, Franklin's gull. 45c, Rufous-necked stint. 75c, Kermadec petrel. $1.20, Purple-capped fruit dove. $2, Mongolian plover. $3.20, Cattle egret. $5, Dunlin.

1999, Sept. 16   Litho.   Perf. 13½
714 A150   5c multi   .25   .25
715 A150 40c multi   .80   .80
716 A150 45c multi   .90   .90
717 A150 75c multi   1.50 1.50
718 A150 $1.20 multi   2.40 2.40
719 A150 $2 multi   4.00 4.00
720 A150 $3.20 multi   6.50 6.50
721 A150 $5 multi   10.00 10.00
　　Nos. 714-721 (8)   26.35 26.35

Christmas — A163

1999, Oct. 26   Litho.   Perf. 13½
722 A163 33c multi   .65   .65

Events of the 20th Century Type

1970-79: a, Jumbo jets enter transatlantic service. b, China advances on world stage. c, Terrorists range the world. d, Space stations orbit earth. e, Oil crisis strangles world. f, China unearths underground army. g, Reign of death devastates Cambodia. h, Superpowers proclaim era of détente. i, America celebrates bicentennial. j, Personal computers reach markets. k, Diagnostic tools revolutionize medicine. l, Automobiles transport millions. m, Prospect of peace in Middle East. n, Compact disc revolutionizes recording. o, Islam's prophets resurgent.

1999, Nov. 15
723 Sheet of 15   18.00 18.00
　a.-o. A123 60c Any single 1.20 1.20

Millennium — A164

Earth and inscriptions: No. 724, "December 31, 1999." No. 725, "January 1, 2000."

1999, Dec. 31   Litho.   Perf. 13½
724 33c multi   .65   .65
725 33c multi   .65   .65
　a. A164 Pair, #724-725   1.30 1.30

Events of the 20th Century Type

1980-89: a, People unite in freedom's quest. b, Mankind confronts new diseases. c, Royal romance captivates the world. d, Information age begins. e, Armed conflicts upset peace. f, Cell phone revolutionizes communication. g, Every man a movie maker. h, Space exploration makes headlines. i, Disaster alerts public to nuclear risks. j, Perestroika signals change. k, Technology of war advances. l, Terrorism claims innocent victims. m, World's oceans

MARSHALL ISLANDS

endangered. n, Eys of the world on Tiananmen. o, Events signal "end of history."

2000, Jan. 15
726 Sheet of 15 18.00 18.00
a.-o. A123 60c Any single 1.20 1.20

Souvenir Sheet

New Year 2000 (Year of the Dragon) A165

2000, Jan. 20 Perf. 13x13½
727 A165 60c multi 1.25 1.25

Legendary Aircraft Type of 1995

Designs: a, P-26 Peashooter. b, N2S-1 Kaydet. c, P-35A. d, P-36A Hawk. e, P-40B Warhawk. f, P-38 Lightning. g, P-39D Airacobra. h, C-46 Commando. i, P-47D Thunderbolt. j, P-61B Black Widow. k, B-29 Superfortress. l, F7F-3N Tigercat. m, F8F-2 Bearcat. n, F-82, Twin Mustang. o, F-84G Thunderjet. p, FJ-1 Fury. q, C-119C Flying Boxcar. r, F3D-2 Skynight. s, F-89D Scorpion. t, F-94B Starfire. u, F4D Skyray. v, F3H-2 Demon. w, RF-101A/C Voodoo. x, U-2F Dragon Lady. y, OV-10 Bronco.

2000, Feb. 10 Perf. 13½
728 A104 33c Sheet of 25, #a.-y. 16.00 16.00

Roses — A166

Rose varieties: a, Masquerade. b, Tuscany Superb. c, Frau Dagmar Hastrup. d, Ivory Fashion. e, Charles De Mills. f, Peace.

2000, Feb. 23
729 Block of 6 4.00 4.00
a.-f. A166 33c Any single .65 .65

Events of the 20th Century Type

1990-99: a, Free markets and trade reshape world economy. b, Coalition expels Iraq from Kuwait. c, South Africans freed from apartheid. d, WWW revolutionizes information superhighway. e, Era of Soviet power ends. f, A lasting peace in Middle East is promised. g, Engineering triumphs alter landscape. h, Ethnic conflicts stun world. i, Athletes celebrate peaceful world competition. j, Scientists probe secrets of life. k, Hong Kong and Macao return to China. l, Space exploration captivates millions. m, World mourns global heroines. n, Architecture shows confidence in the future. o, World population soars to new record.

2000, Mar. 15 Litho. Perf. 13½
730 Sheet of 15 18.00 18.00
a.-o. A123 60c Any single 1.20 1.20

Pandas A167

a, Adult seated. b, Adult, seated, facing away, & cub. c, Adult holding cub. d, Two adults. e, Adult climbing. f, Adult & cub seated.

2000, Mar. 31 Perf. 11¾
731 A167 33c Block of 6, #a-f 4.00 4.00

American Presidents — A168

No. 732: a, 1c, George Washington. b, 2c, John Adams. c, 3c, Thomas Jefferson. d, 4c, James Madison. e, 5c, James Monroe. f, 6c, John Quincy Adams.
No. 733: a, 7c, Andrew Jackson. b, 8c, Martin Van Buren. c, 9c, William Henry Harrison. d, 10c, John Tyler. e, 11c, James K. Polk. f, 12c, Zachary Taylor.
No. 734: a, 13c, Millard Fillmore. b, 14c, Franklin Pierce. c, 15c, James Buchanan. d, 16c, Abraham Lincoln. e, 17c, Andrew Johnson. f, 18c, Ulysses S. Grant.
No. 735: a, 19c, Rutherford B. Hayes. b, 20c, James A. Garfield. c, 21c, Chester A. Arthur. d, 22c, Grover Cleveland. e, 23c, Benjamin Harrison. f, 24c, White House.
No. 736: a, 25c, William McKinley. b, 26c, Theodore Roosevelt. c, 27c, William H. Taft. d, 28c, Woodrow Wilson. e, 29c, Warren G. Harding. f, 30c, Calvin Coolidge.
No. 737: a, 31c, Herbert C. Hoover. b, 32c, Franklin D. Roosevelt. c, 33c, Harry S Truman. d, 34c, Dwight D. Eisenhower. e, 35c, John F. Kennedy. f, 36c, Lyndon B. Johnson.
No. 738: a, 37c, Richard M. Nixon. b, 38c, Gerald R. Ford. c, 39c, James E. Carter. d, 40c, Ronald W. Reagan. e, 41c, George H. W. Bush. f, 42c, William J. Clinton.

2000, Apr. 18 Perf. 13½
732 A168 Sheet of 6, #a-f .45 .45
733 A168 Sheet of 6, #a-f 1.25 1.25
734 A168 Sheet of 6, #a-f 1.90 1.90
735 A168 Sheet of 6, #a-f 2.60 2.60
736 A168 Sheet of 6, #a-f 3.25 3.25
737 A168 Sheet of 6, #a-f 4.00 4.00
738 A168 Sheet of 6, #a-f 4.75 4.75
Nos. 732-738 (7) 18.20 18.20

First Zeppelin Flight, Cent. A169

Designs: a, Original Zeppelin, 1900. b, Graf Zeppelin I, 1928. c, Hindenburg, 1936. d, Graf Zeppelin II, 1937.

2000, May 11 Perf. 13½
739 A169 33c Block of 4, #a-d 2.75 2.75

Sir Winston Churchill A170

No. 740, War correspondent in South Africa, 1899-1900. No. 741, Engagement and marriage to Clementine Hozier, 1908. No. 742, Young statesman, 1900-14. No. 743, Writer and academic, 1898-1960. No. 744, First Lord of the Admiralty, 1939-40. No. 745, Prime Minister, 1940-45. $1, Appointed knight, Nobel Prize for Literature, 1946-65.

2000, June 16 Litho. Perf. 13½
Booklet Stamps
740 A170 60c multi 1.25 1.25
741 A170 60c multi 1.25 1.25
742 A170 60c multi 1.25 1.25
743 A170 60c multi 1.25 1.25
744 A170 60c multi 1.25 1.25
745 A170 60c multi 1.25 1.25
Size: 87x67mm
Perf. 13½ at Top
746 A170 $1 multi 2.00 2.00
a. Booklet pane, #740-746 9.50
   Booklet, #746a 9.50

US Military, 225th Anniv. — A171

No. 747: a, Army. b, Navy. c, Marines.

2000, June 22 Perf. 13½
747 Horiz. strip of 3 2.00 2.00
a.-c. A171 33c Any single .65 .65

National Government — A172

No. 748: a, National seal. b, Nitijela, horiz. c, National flag. d, Capitol buildijng, horiz.

2000, July 4 Litho. Perf. 13½
748 A172 33c Block of 4, #a-d 2.75 2.75

Ships A173

No. 749: a, Half Moon. b, La Grande Hermine. c, Golden Hind. d, Mathew. e, Victoria. f, Sao Gabriel.

2000, July 20
749 A173 60c Block of 6, #a-f 7.25 7.25

Queen Mother, 100th Birthday A174

No. 750: a, As child. b, As young wife. c, As Queen. d, As Queen Mother.

2000, Aug. 4
750 A174 60c Block of 4, #a-d 5.00 5.00
Compare with No. 810.

Reef Life A175

No. 751: a, Green sea turtle. b, Blue-girdled angelfish. c, Clown triggerfish. d, Harlequin tuskfish. e, Lined butterflyfish. f, White-bonnet anemonefish. g, Longnose filefish. h, Emperor angelfish.

2000, Aug. 24
751 A175 Sheet of 8 5.50 5.50
a.-h. 33c Any single .65 .65

Butterflies — A176

No. 752: a, Holly blue. b, Swallowtail. c, Clouded yellow. d, Small tortoiseshell. e, Nettle tree. f, Long-tailed blue. g, Cranberry blue. h, Small heath. i, Pontic blue. j, Lapland fritillary k, Large blue. l, Monarch.

2000, Sept. 14 Perf. 11¾
752 A176 60c Sheet of 12, #a-l 14.50 14.50
See also Nos. 776, 798, 821, 876.

Reunification of Germany, 10th Anniv. — A177

2000, Oct. 3 Perf. 13½
753 A177 33c multi .65 .65

Submarines — A178

No. 754: a, USS S-44, 1925. b, USS Gato, 1941. c, USS Wyoming, 1996. d, USS Cheyenne, 1997.

2000, Oct. 12
754 A178 33c Block of 4, #a.-d. 2.75 2.75

Christmas — A179

2000, Oct. 26 Perf. 10¼x11¼
755 A179 33c multi .65 .65

MARSHALL ISLANDS

Sun Yat-sen A180

No. 756: a, As youth in Cuiheng village, 1866. b, As student in Honolulu and Hong Kong, 1879. c, As President of Tong Meng Hui, 1905. d, Revolution, 1911. e, President of the Republic of China, 1912. f, Principles of Democracy. g, Sun Yat-sen Memorial, Nanjing and Great Wall of China (87x62mm).

2000, Nov. 12   **Litho.**   **Perf. 13½**
756	A180	Booklet pane of 7	9.50	
a.-f.		60c Any single	1.25	1.25
g.		$1 multi, perf. 13½ at top	2.00	2.00
		Booklet, #756	9.50	

Souvenir Sheet

New Year 2001 (Year of the Snake) A181

2001, Jan. 2   **Litho.**   **Perf. 13x13¾**
| 757 | A181 | 80c multi | 1.60 | 1.60 |

Flowers of the Month A182

2001		Stamp + label	Perf. 11¾	
758	A182	34c Carnations	.70	.70
759	A182	34c Violets	.70	.70
760	A182	34c Jonquil	.70	.70
761	A182	34c Sweet pea	.70	.70
762	A182	34c Lily of the valley	.70	.70
763	A182	34c Rose	.70	.70
764	A182	34c Larkspur	.70	.70
765	A182	34c Poppy	.70	.70
766	A182	34c Aster	.70	.70
767	A182	34c Marigold	.70	.70
768	A182	34c Chrysanthemum	.70	.70
769	A182	34c Poinsettia	.70	.70
		Nos. 758-769 (12)	8.40	8.40

Issued: No. 758, 1/5; No. 759, 2/1; No. 760, 3/1; No. 761, 4/3; No. 762, 5/1; No. 763, 6/1; No. 764, 7/3; No. 765, 8/1; No. 766, 9/5; No. 767, 10/1; No. 768, 11/1; No. 769, 12/1.

Sailing Canoes — A183

Walaps of: $5, Jaluit. $10, Eniwetok.

2001, Jan. 19   **Engr.**   **Perf. 12¼**
770	A183	$5 green	10.00	10.00
771	A183	$10 blue	20.00	20.00

Famous People — A184

Designs: 34c, Pres. Amata Kabua. 55c, Robert Reimers, entrepreneur. 80c, Leonard Hacker, S. J., humanitarian. $1, Dwight Heine, educator.

2001, Jan. 22   **Litho.**   **Perf. 10¼x11¼**
772	A184	34c multi	.70	.70
773	A184	55c multi	1.10	1.10
774	A184	80c multi	1.60	1.60
775	A184	$1 multi	2.00	2.00
		Nos. 772-775 (4)	5.40	5.40

See Nos. 784, 817-819.

Butterflies Type of 2000

No. 776: a, Red admiral. b, Moroccan orange tip. c, Silver-studded blue. d, Marbled white. e, False Apollo. f, Ringlet. g, Map. h, Fenton's wood white. i, Grecian copper. j, Pale Arctic clouded yellow. k, Great banded greyling. l, Cardinal.

2001, Feb. 22   **Perf. 11¾**
| 776 | A176 | 80c Sheet of 12, #a-l | 20.00 | 20.00 |

Fairy Tales — A185

No. 777: a, Tom Thumb. b, Three Little Pigs. c, Gulliver's Travels. d, Cinderella. e, Gallant John. f, Ugly Duckling. g, Fisher and the Goldfish.

2001, Mar. 22   **Litho.**   **Perf. 13½**
777		Vert. strip of 7	5.00	5.00
a.-g.	A185	34c Any single	.70	.70

Watercraft Racing — A186

No. 778: a, Canoeing. b, Windsurfing. c, Cruising yachts. d, Sailing dinghy.

2001, Apr. 6
| 778 | A186 | 34c Block of 4, #a-d | 2.75 | 2.75 |

Manned Spaceflight, 40th Anniv. — A187

No. 779: a, Yuri A. Gagarin. b, Alan B. Shepard, Jr. c, Virgil I. Grissom. d, Gherman S. Titov.

2001, Apr. 12
779		Block of 4 + 4 labels	6.50	6.50
a.-d.	A187	80c Any single	1.60	1.60

Stamp Day — A188

2001, May 2
780	A188	34c multi	.70	.70
a.		Tete-beche pair	1.40	1.40

Achievements in Space — A189

No. 781: a, First U.S. astronaut in orbit, 1962. b, First space walk, 1965. c, First man on the Moon, 1969. d, First space shuttle, 1977.

2001, May 15
| 781 | A189 | 80c Block of 4, #a-d | 6.50 | 6.50 |

Marine Life — A190

No. 782: a, Longnose butterflyfish, star puffer, starfish. b, Nautilus. c, Raccoon butterflyfish. d, Porkfish, grouper.

2001, June 7
| 782 | A190 | 34c Block of 4, #a-d | 2.75 | 2.75 |

Sports A191

No. 783: a, Basketball. b, Bowling. c, Table tennis. d, Kayaking.

2001, June 26   **Perf. 11¾**
| 783 | A191 | 34c Block of 4, #a-d | 2.75 | 2.75 |

Famous People Type of 2001

Design: 57c, Atlan Anien, legislator.

2001, July 9   **Perf. 10¼x11¼**
| 784 | A184 | 57c multi | 1.10 | 1.10 |

Zodiac Signs A192

No. 785: a, Aries. b, Taurus. c, Gemini. d, Cancer. e, Leo. f, Virgo. g, Libra. h, Scorpio. i, Sagittarius. j, Capricorn. k, Aquarius. l, Pisces.

2001, July 17   **Perf. 11¾**
| 785 | A192 | 34c Sheet of 12, #a-l | 8.25 | 8.25 |

Phila Nippon '01 A193

No. 786: a, Black Cat, by Tan Axi. b, Brown Cat, by Tan Axi. c, Cliffs, by Wang Xinhai. d, Boat and Bridge, by Li Yan. e, Rooster, by Wang Xinlan. f, Great Wall, by Liu Zhong. g, Crane, by Wang Lynn. h, Baboon With Basket, by Wang Yani. i, Baboon in Tree, by Wang Yani. j, Umbrella, by Sun Yuan. k, Baboon With Fruit, by Wang Yani. l, Baboon on Ox, by Wang Yani.

2001, Aug. 1   **Litho.**   **Perf. 11¾**
| 786 | A193 | 80c Sheet of 12, #a-l | 20.00 | 20.00 |

US Naval Heroes in WWII Pacific Theater A194

No. 787: a, Adm. Raymond A. Spruance. b, Adm. Arleigh A. Burke. c, Adm. Ernest A. King. d, Adm. Richmond K. Turner. e, Adm. Marc A. Mitscher. f, Adm. Chester W. Nimitz. g, Lt. Edward H. O'Hare. h, Adm. William F. Halsey, Jr. i, The Sullivan Brothers.

2001, Aug. 24   **Perf. 13½**
| 787 | A194 | 80c Sheet of 9, #a-i | 14.50 | 14.50 |

Classic Cars A195

No. 788: a, 1916 Stutz Bearcat. b, 1909 Stanley Steamer. c, 1934 Citroen 7CV. d, 1910 Rolls-Royce Silver Ghost. e, 1927 Daimler. f, 1935 Hispano-Suiza Type 68V-12. g, 1928 Lancia Lambda V4. h, 1927 Volvo OV4.

2001, Sept. 11
| 788 | A195 | 34c Block of 8, #a-h | 5.50 | 5.50 |

See also Nos. 796, 809, 823, 828, 865.

Remembrance of Victims of Sept. 11, 2001 Terrorist Attacks — A196

No. 789: a, U.S. flag, "Blessed are those..." b, Statue of Liberty, "United we stand..." c, U.S. flag, "An attack on freedom..." d, U.S. flag, "In the great struggle..." e, Statue of Freedom, "We go forward..." f, U.S. flag, "In the face of terrorism..." g, American people (75x32mm).

2001, Oct. 11   **Litho.**   **Perf. 13½**
789		Booklet pane of 7	6.25	—
a.-f.	A196	34c Any single	.70	.70
g.		A196 $1 multi	2.00	2.00
		Booklet, #789	6.25	

Christmas — A197

MARSHALL ISLANDS

No. 790: a, Angel on high. b, Adoration of the Magi. c, Nativity scene. d, Adoration of the shepherds.

2001, Oct. 26
790 Strip of 4   2.80 2.80
 a.-d. A197 34c Any single   .70 .70

Airplanes A198

No. 791: a, Supermarine Sea Eagle. b, Gloster Sea Gladiator. c, DHC-6 Twin Otter. d, Shorts 330. e, Sandringham Flying Boat. f, De Havilland DHC-7. g, Beech Duke B60. h, Fokker Friendship F27. i, Consolidated B-24J Liberator. j, Vickers 953C Merchantman.

Perf. 11¼x10¼
2001, Nov. 13   Litho.
791 A198 80c Block of 10, #a-j   16.00 16.00

Souvenir Sheet

New Year 2002 (Year of the Horse) A199

2002, Jan. 2   *Perf. 13x13½*
792 A199 80c multi   1.60 1.60

Shells A200

No. 793: a, Frilled dogwinkle. b, Reticulated cowrie-helmet. c, New England neptune. d, Calico scallop. e, Lightning whelk. f, Hawkwing conch.

2002, Jan. 22   *Perf. 11¾*
793 A200 34c Block of 6, #a-f   4.25 4.25

Souvenir Sheet

Reign of Queen Elizabeth II, 50th Anniv. A201

2002, Feb. 6   Litho.   *Perf. 13x13½*
794 A201 80c multi   1.60 1.60

United We Stand — A202

2002, Feb. 11   *Perf. 13½*
795 A202 34c multi   .70 .70

Classic Cars Type of 2001

No. 796: a, 1909 Le Zebre. b, 1886 Hammel. c, 1902 Wolseley. d, 1899 Eysink. e, 1903 Dansk. f, 1907 Spyker. g, 1913 Fiat Model Zero. h, 1902 Weber.

2002, Feb. 26
796 A195 34c Block of 8, #a-h   5.50 5.50

Corals A203

No. 797: a, Mixed. b, Chalice. c, Elkhorn. d, Finger.

2002, Mar. 13
797 A203 34c Block of 4, #a-d   2.75 2.75

Butterflies Type of 2000

No. 798: a, Grayling. b, Eastern festoon. c, Speckled wood. d, Cranberry fritillary. e, Bath white. f, Meadow brown. g, Two-tailed pasha. h, Scarce swallowtail. i, Dusky grizzled skipper. j, Provençal short-tailed blue. k, Dryal. l, Comma.

2002, Mar. 25   *Perf. 11¾*
798 A176 80c Sheet of 12, #a-l   20.00 20.00

Horses in Art A204

No. 799: a, Horses, by Giorgio de Chirico. b, Tartar Envoys Give Horse to Qianlong, by Father Giuseppe Castiglione. c, Gathering Seaweed, by Anton Mauve. d, Mares and Foals, by George Stubbs. e, A Mare and Her Foal in a Spring Meadow, by Wilson Hepple. f, Horse with Child and a Dog, by Natale Attanasio. g, The Horse, by Waterhouse Hawkins. h, Attendants and a Horse, by Edgar Degas. i, Mares and Foals in a Landscape, by Stubbs. j, The Horse, by Guglielmo Ciardi. k, Little Blue Horse, by Franz Marc. l, Sketch for the Set of "Fire Bird," by Pavel Kuznetsov. 80c, Emperor Qianlong Leaving for his Summer Residence, by Castiglione.

2002, Apr. 15   Litho.   *Perf. 13½*
799 A204 34c Sheet of 12, #a-l   8.25 8.25

Souvenir Sheet
Perf. 13x13½
800 A204 80c multi   1.60 1.60

No. 800 contains one 80x50mm stamp.

Miniature Sheet

Russian Fairy Tale, "The Frog Princess" A205

No. 801: a, Ivan and his brothers shoot arrows. b, First brother finds a wife. c, Second brother finds a wife. d, Ivan and his Frog Princess. e, Ivan presents shirt to the king. f, Ivan presents bread to the king. g, Princess arrives at the ball. h, Princess dances for the king. i, Princess says goodbye to ivan. j, Ivan and the little hut. k, Ivan and the Princess reunited. l, Ivan and the Princess on a magic carpet.

2002, Apr. 26   Litho.   *Perf. 12½x12¼*
801 A205 37c Sheet of 12, #a-l   9.00 9.00

Carousel Figures A206

No. 802: a, Armored horse and rabbit. b, Zebra and camel. c, Horse, reindeer and angel. d, Horse, frog and tiger.

2002, May 13   Litho.   *Perf. 13½*
802 A206 80c Block of 4, #a-d   6.50 6.50

Birds A207

No. 803: a, Lesser golden plover. b, Siberian tattler. c, Brown noddy. d, Common fairy tern. e, Micronesian pigeon. f, Long-tailed cuckoo. g, Christmas shearwater. h, Eurasian tree sparrow. i, Black-tailed godwit. j, Franklin's gull. k, Rufous-necked stint. l, Kermadec petrel. m, Purple-capped fruit dove. n, Mongolian plover. o, Cattle egret. p, Dunlin.

2002, May 29
803 A207 37c Sheet of 16, #a-p   12.00 12.00

Benjamin Franklin (1706-90) — A208

No. 804: a, Inventor. b, Scholar.

2002, June 10   Litho.   *Perf. 13½*
804 A208 80c Horiz. pair, #a-b   3.25 3.25

Sea Turtles A209

No. 805: a, Loggerhead. b, Leatherback. c, Hawksbill. d, Green.

2002, June 25
805 A209 37c Block of 4, #a-d   3.00 3.00

Intl. Federation of Stamp Dealers' Associations, 50th Anniv. — A210

No. 806: a, Stamp collector. b, First day of issue. c, Father and daughter collectors. d, Young collector. e, Sharing Dad's stamp collection. f, The new generation.

2002, July 2
806 A210 80c Block of 6, #a-f   9.75 9.75

US Navy Ships A211

No. 807: a, USS Hartford. b, Bon Homme Richard. c, Prince de Neufchatel. d, USS Ohio. e, USS Onkahye. f, USS Oneida.

2002, July 18
807 A211 37c Block of 6, #a-f   4.50 4.50

See No. 827.

Insects and Spiders A212

No. 808: a, Black widow spider. b, Elderberry longhorn. c, Ladybug. d, Yellow garden spider. e, Dogbane beetle. f, Flower fly. g, Assassin bug. h, Ebony jewelwing. i, Velvet ant. j, Monarch caterpillar. k, Monarch butterfly. l, Eastern Hercules beetle. m, Bombardier beetle. n, Dung beetle. o, Spotted water beetle. p, True katydid. q, Spiny-back spider. r, Periodical cicada. s, Scorpionfly. t, Jumping spider.

2002, Aug. 2   Litho.   *Perf. 13½*
808 A212 23c Sheet of 20, #a-t   9.25 9.25

Classic Cars Type of 2001

No. 809: a, 1934 Hotchkiss. b, 1909 De Dion Bouton. c, 1922 Renault. d, 1927 Amilcar Surbaisse. e, 1943 Austin. f, 1913 Peugeot Bebe. g, 1927 O.M. Type 665 Superba. h, 1922 Elizalde Tipo 20C.

2002, Aug. 15
809 A195 80c Block of 8, #a-h   13.00 13.00

MARSHALL ISLANDS

Queen Mother Type of 2000 Redrawn
No. 810: a, As child. b, As young wife. c, As Queen. d, As Queen Mother.

2002, Aug. 30
810 A174 80c Block of 4, #a-d 6.50 6.50
Queen Mother Elizabeth (1900-2002).

Souvenir Sheet
Regal Princess A213

2002, Sept. 10 Perf. 13¼x13¾
811 A213 80c multi 1.60 1.60

World War I Heroes A214

No. 812: a, Adm. William S. Sims. b, Gen. William E. Mitchell. c, Cpl. Freddie Stowers. d, Maj. Gen. Smedley D. Butler. e, Capt. Edward V. Rickenbacker. f, Sgt. Alvin C. York. g, Maj. Gen. John A. Lejeune. h, Gen. John J. Pershing.

2002, Sept. 23 Perf. 13½
812 A214 80c Block of 8, #a-h 13.00 13.00

Christmas — A215

Snowman cookies with denomination in: a, Green. b, Red.

2002, Oct. 26 Litho. Perf. 13½
813 A215 37c Horiz. pair, #a-b 1.50 1.50

Souvenir Sheet
New Year 2003 (Year of the Ram) A216

2003, Jan. 2 Litho. Perf. 13x13¾
814 A216 80c multi 1.60 1.60

UN Membership, 12th Anniv. — A217

2003, Jan. 29 Perf. 11¼x10¼
815 A217 60c multi 1.25 1.25

Folktales A218

No. 816: a, Inedel's Magic Kite. b, Lijebake Rescues Her Granddaughter. c, Jebro's Mother Invents the Sail. d, Limajnon Escapes to the Moon.

2003, Jan. 29 Perf. 13½
816 A218 50c Block of 4, #a-d, + 4 labels 4.00 4.00

Famous People Type of 2001
Designs: 37c, Oscar deBrum (1929-2002), first Chief Secretary. $3.85, Senator Tipne Philippo (1933-2000). $13.65, Senator Henchi Balos (1946-2000).

Perf. 10¼x11¼
2003, Mar. 25 Litho.
817 A184 37c multi .75 .75
818 A184 $3.85 multi 7.75 7.75
819 A184 $13.65 multi 25.00 25.00
Nos. 817-819 (3) 33.50 33.50

The denomination of No. 819 was printed in a thermographic ink that changes color when warmed.

Marshallese Culture — A219

No. 820: a, Lagajimi, c. 1870s, by Franz Hernsheim (21x38mm). b, Old-style house with attic-like roof space (46x38mm). c, Tidal lake on Jabwor (46x38mm). d, Kabua, c. 1870s, by Hernsheim (21x38mm). e, Children in mat dresses (21x38mm). f, Jaluit pass, c. 1870s, by Hernsheim (46x38mm). g, Traditional Canoe, c. 1870s, by Hernsheim (46x38mm). h, Man in fishing attire (21x38mm).

2003, Mar. 25 Perf. 13½
820 A219 37c Block of 8, #a-h 6.00 6.00
See No. 824.

Butterflies Type of 2000
No. 821: a, False grayling. b, Green hairstreak. c, Purple-shot copper. d, Black-veined white. e, Arctic grayling. f, Greek clouded yellow. g, American painted lady. h, Wall brown. i, Polar fritillary. j, Mountain clouded yellow. k, Camberwell beauty. l, Large white.

2003, May 2 Litho. Perf. 11¾
821 A176 80c Sheet of 12, #a-l 20.00 20.00

Powered Flight, Cent. A220

No. 822: a, 1903 Wright Flyer. b, Curtiss JN-3 "Jenny." c, Douglas World Cruiser. d, "Spirit of St. Louis." e, Lockheed Vega. f, Boeing 314 Clipper. g, Douglas C-47 Skytrain. h, Boeing B-50 Superfortress. i, Antonov An-225 Mriya. j, B-2 Spirit.

2003, June 10 Perf. 13½
822 A220 37c Block of 10, #a-j 7.50 7.50

Classic Cars Type of 2001
No. 823: a, 1927 Alfa Romeo RLSS. b, 1912 Austro-Daimler Prince Henry. c, 1920 Mors 14/20 HP Tourer. d, 1926 AC Tourer. e, 1903 Scania, 1897 Vabis. f, 1914 Graf und Stift. g, 1919 Pic-Pic. h, 1911 Hispano-Suiza-Alfonso XIII.

2003, July 10 Litho. Perf. 13½
823 A195 37c Block of 8, #a-h 6.00 6.00

Marshallese Culture Type of 2003
No. 824: a, Kabua's Daughter on Pandanus, c. 1906, by Augustin Krämer (21x38mm). b, Traditional walap (46x38mm). c, Jabwor, Jaluit Atoll (46x38mm). d, Traditional and Modern Dress, by Augustin Erdland (21x38mm). e, Nemedj, c. 1905, by Krämer (21x38mm). f, Typhoon of 1905, by Josef Schmidlin (46x38mm). g, Marshallese Kor Kor, c. 1905, by Richard Deeken (46x38mm). h, Marshallese Grandfather, by Erdland (21x38mm).

2003, Aug. 7 Perf. 13½x13¼
824 A219 37c Block of 8, #a-h 6.00 6.00

Christmas Ornaments — A221

No. 825: a, Snowman. b, Jack-in-the-box. c, Toy soldier. d, Reindeer.

2003, Oct. 24 Perf. 13½
825 A221 37c Block of 4, #a-d 3.00 3.00

Souvenir Sheet
New Year 2004 (Year of the Monkey) A222

2004, Jan. 4 Litho. Perf. 13x13¾
826 A222 $1 multi 2.00 2.00

Ship Type of 2002
No. 827: a, Bonhomme Richard. b, HMS Resolution, denomination at UR. c, HMS Resolution, denomination at UL.

2004, Feb. 14 Perf. 13½
827 A211 37c Horiz. strip of 3, #a-c 2.25 2.25

Classic Cars Type of 2001
No. 828: a, 1906 Wolseley-Siddeley. b, 1901 Mors. c, 1908 Hutton. d, 1907 Metallurgique. e, 1902 Benz. f, 1900 Cudell. g, 1906 Peugeot. h, Mercedes 60.

2004, Mar. 15 Perf. 13½
828 A195 37c Block of 8, #a-h 6.00 6.00

Greetings — A223

No. 829: a, Thank you! b, Congratulations. c, Happy birthday. d, Best wishes. e, Get well soon. f, Love you, Dad. g, Love you, Mom. h, Best wishes, Get well soon, Love you, Mom, Congratulations, Love you, Dad, Happy birthday, Thank you.

2004, Apr. 15 Litho. Perf. 13½
829 A223 37c Sheet of 8, #a-h 6.00 6.00

Marshall Islands Postal Service, 20th Anniv. A224

Messenger and canoe with background colors of: 37c, Prussian blue. 60c, Brown. $2.30, Purple.

2004, May 2
830-832 A224 Set of 3 6.75 6.75

No. 832 printed in sheets of 8 stamps + 8 adjacent certified mail etiquettes. Value is for set with No. 832 with attached etiquette.

Lewis and Clark Expedition, Bicent. A225

No. 833 — Inscriptions: a, The saga begins. b, Westward bound. c, Endless bison.

2004, May 14
833 Horiz. strip of 3 2.25 2.25
 a.-c. A225 37c Any single .75 .75
See Nos. 840, 845, 855, 867, 871, 885.

D-Day, 60th Anniv. A226

No. 834: a, Horsa gliders and parachute troops. b, British Typhoon 1B and US P-51B Mustangs. c, German defenses and Pointe du Hoc. d, Allied amphibious landing.

2004, June 6 Litho. Perf. 13½
834 A226 37c Block of 4, #a-d 3.00 3.00

Marine Life A227

No. 835: a, Chambered nautilus, map cowrie, fish, coral, trumpet triton (2-1). b, Marlin spike, fish, coral, turban shell, Toulerei's cowrie (2-2).

2004, July 1
835 A227 37c Horiz. pair, #a-b 1.50 1.50

Pres. Ronald Reagan (1911-2004) — A228

2004, July 4
836 A228 60c multi 1.25 1.25

First Manned Moon Landing, 35th Anniv. A229

No. 837: a, Astronaut floating in space (4-1). b, Astronaut in space (4-2). c, Astronaut floating in orbit (4-3). d, Astronaut and Jupiter (4-4).

2004, July 20
837 A229 37c Block of 4, #a-d 3.00 3.00

MARSHALL ISLANDS

Festival of Arts — A230

No. 838: a, Woman showing fan making. b, Woman making baskets. c, Men carving. d, Children making canoe models. e, White ginger. f, Vanda. g, Tiare. h, Hibiscus. i, Breadfruit. j, Tattooed warrior. k, Young chiefs. l, Drummers and dancers.

2004, July 22
838 A230 37c Sheet of 12, #a-l   9.00 9.00

Aircraft — A231

No. 839: a, 1903 Wright Flyer. b, Blériot XI. c, Curtiss Golden Flyer. d, Curtiss Flying Boat. e, Deperdussin Racer. f, Sikorsky Il'ya Muromets. g, Fokker E1. h, Junkers J1. i, S.E. 5A. j, Handley Page O/400. k, Fokker D VII. l, Junkers F13. m, Lockheed Vega. n, M-130 Pan Am Clipper. o, Messerschmitt BF 109. p, Spitfire. q, Junkers Ju-88. r, A6M Zero. s, Ilyushin Il-2. t, Heinkel He-178. u, C-47 Skytrain. v, Piper Cub. w, Avro Lancaster. x, B-17F Flying Fortress. y, Messerschmitt Me-262. z, B-29 Superfortress. aa, P-51 Mustang. ab, Yak-9. ac, Bell Model 47 helicopter. ad, Bell X-1. ae, Beechcraft Bonanza. af, AN-225 Mriya. ag, B-47 Stratojet. ah, MiG-15. ai, Saab J35 Draken. aj, B-52 Stratofortress. ak, Boeing 367-80. al, U-2. am, C-130 Hercules. an, F-4 Phantom II. ao, North American X-15. ap, Sikorsky S-61 (HH-3E). aq, Learjet 23. ar, SR-71 Blackbird. as, Boeing 747. at, Concorde. au, Airbus A300. av, MiG-29. aw, F-117A Nighthawk. ax, F/A-22 Raptor.

Perf. 10¼x11¼
2004, Aug. 12   Litho.
839   Sheet of 50   23.00 23.00
a.-ax.   A231 23c Any single   .45   .45

Lewis and Clark Type of 2004

No. 840 — Inscriptions: a, First Fourth of July. b, Death of Sgt. Charles Floyd. c, Setting the prairie on fire.

2004, Aug. 24   Perf. 13½
840   Horiz. strip of 3   2.25 2.25
a.-c.   A225 37c Any single   .75   .75

John Wayne (1907-79), Actor — A232

2004, Sept. 9   Perf. 10¼x11¼
841 A232 37c multi   .75   .75

23rd UPU Congress, Bucharest, Romania — A233

No. 842: a, Great Britain #1. b, Romania #1. c, Marshall Islands #1. d, Marshall Islands #31.

2004, Sept. 15   Litho. Perf. 13½
842 A233 $1 Sheet of 4, #a-d   8.00 8.00

Marine Life — A234

No. 843: a, Emperor angelfish. b, Pink anemonefish. c, Humphead wrasse, Moorish idol. d, Black-spotted puffer. e, Snowflake moray eel. f, Lionfish. g, Bumphead parrotfish, threadfin butterflyfish. h, Hawksbill turtle. i, Triton's trumpet. j, Oriental sweetlips.

2004, Oct. 1
843 A234 37c Sheet of 10, #a-j   7.50 7.50

Christmas — A235

No. 844: a, Angel with bells. b, God Almighty. c, Appears the Star of Bethlehem. d, Three Wise Men. e, Procession of the poor people. f, Pastors with sheep. g, Flight to Egypt. h, Holy Family. i, Animals adoring Jesus.

2004, Oct. 27
844 A235 37c Sheet of 9, #a-i   6.75 6.75

Lewis and Clark Type of 2004

No. 845 — Inscriptions: a, The interpreters. b, Sacred bison calling. c, Teton Sioux robmen.

2004, Nov. 22
845   Horiz. strip of 3   2.25 2.25
a.-c.   A225 37c Any single   .75   .75

Battle of the Bulge, 60th Anniv. A236

No. 846: a, Infantry. b, Armor. c, Aviation. d, Lt. Col. Creighton Abrams and Brig. Gen. Anthony McAuliffe.

2004, Dec. 1
846 A236 37c Block of 4, #a-d   3.00 3.00

United States Presidents — A237

No. 847: a, 1c, George Washington. b, 2c, John Adams. c, 3c, Thomas Jefferson. d, 4c, James Madison. e, 5c, James Monroe. f, 6c, John Quincy Adams. g, 7c, Andrew Jackson. h, 8c, Martin Van Buren. i, 9c, William Henry Harrison. j, 10c, John Tyler. k, 11c, James K. Polk. l, 12c, Zachary Taylor. m, 13c, Millard Fillmore. n, 14c, Franklin Pierce. o, 15c, James Buchanan. p, 16c, Abraham Lincoln. q, 17c, Andrew Johnson. r, 18c, Ulysses S. Grant. s, 19c, Rutherford B. Hayes. t, 20c, James A. Garfield. u, 21c, Chester A. Arthur. v, 22c, Grover Cleveland. w, 23c, Benjamin Harrison. x, 24c, Grover Cleveland. y, 25c, William McKinley. z, 26c, Theodore Roosevelt. aa, 27c, William Howard Taft. ab, 28c, Woodrow Wilson. ac, 29c, Warren G. Harding. ad, 30c, Calvin Coolidge. ae, 31c, Herbert Hoover. af, 32c, Franklin D. Roosevelt. ag, 33c, Harry S Truman. ah, 34c, Dwight D. Eisenhower. ai, 35c, John F. Kennedy. aj, 36c, Lyndon B. Johnson. ak, 37c, Richard M. Nixon. al, 38c, Gerald R. Ford. am, 39c, Jimmy Carter. an, 40c, Ronald W. Reagan. ao, 41c, George H. W. Bush. ap, 42c, William J. Clinton. aq, 43c, George W. Bush. ar, 60c, White House. as, $1, White House.

2005, Jan. 20 Litho. Perf. 13½
847 A237   Sheet of 45, #a-as   31.00 31.00
No. 847 sold for $15.49.

New Year 2005 (Year of the Rooster) A238

2005, Feb. 9 Litho. Perf. 13x13½
848 A238 $1 multi   2.00 2.00

Rotary International, Cent. — A239

2005, Feb. 23   Perf. 13½
849 A239 37c multi   .75   .75

Hibiscus Varieties — A240

Designs: 37c, Burgundy Blush. 60c, Fiesta. 80c, June's Joy. $1, Norman Lee.

Perf. 10¼x11¼
2005, Mar. 15   Litho.
850 A240 37c multi   .75   .75
851 A240 60c multi   1.25 1.25
852 A240 80c multi   1.60 1.60
853 A240 $1 multi   2.00 2.00
       Nos. 850-853 (4)   5.60 5.60
See Nos. 860-863, 878-881.

Hans Christian Andersen (1805-75), Author — A241

No. 854: a, The Princess and the Pea. b, Thumbelina. c, The Little Mermaid. d, The Emperor's New Suit.

2005, Apr. 2   Perf. 13½
854 A241 37c Block of 4, #a-d   3.00 3.00

Lewis and Clark Type of 2004

No. 855 — Inscriptions: a, First grizzly confrontation. b, Lewis reaching the Great Falls. c, Sacajawea and her brother reunite.

2005, Apr. 29
855   Horiz. strip of 3   2.25 2.25
a.-c.   A225 37c Any single   .75   .75

American First Day Cover Society, 50th Anniv. — A242

No. 856: a, George W. Linn first day cover for US No. 610 (Harding Memorial stamp). b, First day cover for Marshall Islands Nos. 31-34. c, First day cover of US No. C76 with Moon Landing cancel. d, First day cover for Marshall Islands No. 856.

2005, May 2
856 A242 37c Block of 4, #a-d   3.00 3.00

V-E Day, 60th Anniv. A243

No. 857: a, German surrender, Reims, France. b, Times Square, New York. c, Victory parade, Moscow. d, Royal family and Winston Churchill, Buckingham Palace, London.

2005, May 9
857 A243 37c Block of 4, #a-d   3.00 3.00
Compare A243 stamps with A81a.

Pope John Paul II (1920-2005) A244

No. 858: a, Wearing red cape, with arm raised. b, Wearing green vestments. c, Closeup. d, Holding crucifix, wearing red vestments. e, Wearing miter.

2005, May 18 Litho. Perf. 13½
858   Vert. strip of 5   3.75 3.75
a.-e.   A244 37c Any single   .75   .75
Exists imperf. Vertical strip of 5, value $250.

United Nations, 60th Anniv. — A245

2005, June 26
859 A245   Horiz. pair   2.40 2.40
  a.   37c Six people   .75   .75
  b.   80c Seven people   1.60 1.60

Hibiscus Varieties Type of 2005

Designs: 1c, Margaret Okano. 24c, Cameo Queen. 39c, Madonna. $4, Estrella Red.

MARSHALL ISLANDS

2005, July 13   *Perf. 10¼x11¼*
860	A240	1c multi	.25	.25
861	A240	24c multi	.50	.50
862	A240	39c multi	.80	.80
863	A240	$4 multi	8.00	8.00
	Nos. 860-863 (4)		9.55	9.55

Space Shuttles — A246

No. 864: a, Columbia. b, Discovery. c, Endeavour. d, Challenger. e, Atlantis.

2005, July 26   *Perf. 13½*
864		Horiz. strip of 5	3.75	3.75
a.-e.	A246	37c Any single	.75	.75

Classic Cars Type of 2001

No. 865: a, 1925 Excelsior (8-1). b, 1912 Adler K (8-2). c, 1920 Thulin (8-3). d, 1913 Palladium (8-4). e, 1926 Minerva (8-5). f, 1922 Elizalde (8-6). g, 1911 Rolls-Royce Silver Ghost (8-7). h, 1931 Invicta (8-8).

2005, Aug. 4
865		Block of 8	6.00	6.00
a.-h.	A195	37c Any single	.75	.75

No. 865b is incorrectly inscribed "1926 Minerva."

V-J Day, 60th Anniv. A247

No. 866: a, Fujiyama and Tokyo Bay. b, USS Missouri. c, US contingent. d, Japanese delegation.

2005, Sept. 2
866	A247	37c Block of 4, #a-d	3.00	3.00

Lewis & Clark Type of 2004

No. 867 — Inscriptions: a, Crossing the Bitterroots. b, Peace agreement. c, Ocean in view.

2005, Sept. 22
867		Horiz. strip of 3	2.25	2.25
a.-c.	A225	37c Any single	.75	.75

Battle of Trafalgar, Bicent. A248

No. 868 — Fighting ships: a, Trireme galley. b, Trireme Romano. c, Viking longship. d, Ming treasure ship. e, Mary Rose. f, Nuestra Senora del Rosario. g, Korean turtle ship. h, Brederode. i, Galera Veneziana. j, Santisima Trinidad. k, VIIIe de Paris. l, HMS Victory. m, Bonhomme Richard. n, USS Constellation. o, USS Hartford. p, Fijian ndrua. q, HMS Dreadnought. r, HMAS Australia. s, HMS Dorsetshire. t, Admiral Graf Spee. u, Yamato. v, USS Tautog. w, Bismarck. x, USS Hornet. y, USS Missouri.
$2, HMS Victory, diff.
Illustration reduced.

2005, Oct. 21   *Litho.*   *Perf. 13½*
868	A248	37c Sheet of 25, #a-y	18.50	18.50

Souvenir Sheet
Imperf
869	A248	$2 multi	4.00	4.00

No. 868 contains twenty-five 40x31mm stamps.

Christmas — A249

No. 870 — Angels with: a, Lute. b, Harp, horn and lute. c, Horn. d, Harp.

2005, Nov. 1   *Perf. 13½*
870	A249	37c Block of 4, #a-d	3.00	3.00

Lewis & Clark Type of 2004

No. 871 — Inscriptions: a, First vote allowed to all. b, Leaving Fort Clatsop. c, At Pompey's Pillar.

2005, Nov. 24
871		Horiz. strip of 3	2.25	2.25
a.-c.	A225	37c Any single	.75	.75

Marshallese Culture — A250

No. 872 — Photographs: a, First Catholic Church on Jabwor, Jaluit Atoll, by Josef Schmidlin. b, Women on Jaluit Atoll, by Richard Deeken. c, Canoes in Jaluit Harbor, by Deeken. d, Nelu and His Wife Ledagoba, by Augustin Kramer. e, An Old Man from Ebon Atoll, by Augustin Erdland.

2005, Dec. 1
872		Horiz. strip of 5	3.75	3.75
a.-e.	A250	37c Any single	.75	.75

See also Nos. 886, 901, 929, 950, 973.

Miniature Sheet

Benjamin Franklin (1706-90), Statesman — A251

No. 873 — Franklin: a, Painting by J. S. Duplessis. b, Painting by David K. Stone. c, Painting by Mason Chamberlain. d, Painting by John Trumbull. e, Sculpture, by James Earle Fraser. f, Painting by David Martin. g, Painting by Benjamin West. h, Painting by J. B. Greuze. i, Painting by C. N. Cochin.

2006, Jan. 17   *Perf. 13½*
873	A251	48c Sheet of 9, #a-i	8.75	8.75

Souvenir Sheet

New Year 2006 (Year of the Dog) A252

2006, Jan. 27   *Perf. 13¼x13½*
874	A252	$1 multi	2.00	2.00

Love — A253

2006, Feb. 14   *Litho.*   *Perf. 13½*
875	A253	39c multi	.80	.80

Butterflies Type of 2000

No. 876: a, Peacock. b, Southern comma. c, Pale clouded yellow. d, Common blue. e, Wood white. f, Baltic grayling. g, Purple emperor. h, Silky ringlet. i, Peak white. j, Idas blue. k, Cleopatra. l, Chequered skipper.

2006, Mar. 20   *Perf. 11¾*
876	A176	84c Sheet of 12, #a-l	21.00	21.00

First Spaceflight by Yuri Gagarin, 45th Anniv. — A254

2006, Apr. 12   *Litho.*   *Perf. 11¾*
877	A254	39c multi	.80	.80

Hibiscus Varieties Type of 2005

Designs: 10c, Butterscotch Sundae. 63c, Magic Moments. 84c, Joanne Boulin. $4.05, Capsicum Red.

2006, May 2   *Perf. 10¼x11¼*
878	A240	10c multi	.25	.25
879	A240	63c multi	1.25	1.25
880	A240	84c multi	1.75	1.75
881	A240	$4.05 multi	8.25	8.25
	Nos. 878-881 (4)		11.50	11.50

Miniature Sheet

Washington 2006 World Philatelic Exhibition — A255

No. 882 — Designs of the United States 1922-25 definitive issue inscribed "Marshall Islands Postage": a, ½c, Nathan Hale. b, 1c, Benjamin Franklin. c, 1½c, Warren G. Harding. d, 2c, George Washington. e, 3c, Abraham Lincoln. f, 4c, Martha Washington. g, 5c, Theodore Roosevelt. h, 6c, James A. Garfield. i, 7c, William McKinley. j, 8c, Ulysses S. Grant. k, 9c, Thomas Jefferson. l, 10c, James Monroe. m, 11c, Rutherford B. Hayes. n, 12c, Grover Cleveland. o, 14c, American Indian chief. p, 15c, Statue of Liberty. q, 20c, Golden Gate, horiz. r, 25c, Niagara Falls, horiz. s, 30c, Buffalo, horiz. t, 50c, Arlington Amphitheater, horiz.

2006, May 27   *Litho.*   *Perf. 13½*
882	A255	Sheet of 20, #a-t	4.75	4.75
u.		Souvenir sheet, #882o, 882s, imperf.	.90	.90

Sharks — A256

No. 883: a, Gray reef shark. b, Silvertip shark. c, Blacktip reef shark. d, Whitetip reef shark.

2006, June 16   *Perf. 13½*
883	A256	39c Block of 4, #a-d	3.25	3.25

Miniature Sheet

Operations Crossroads, 60th Anniv. — A257

No. 884: a, Evacuation of Bikinians. b, Navy preparations. c, "Able" bomb blast. d, "Baker" bomb blast. e, Ghost fleet. f, Effects on the Bikinians.

2006, July 1   *Litho.*   *Perf. 13½*
884	A257	39c Sheet of 6, #a-f, + 6 labels	4.75	4.75

Lewis and Clark Type of 2004

No. 885 — Inscriptions: a, Leaving Sacagawea and Charbonneau. b, Return to St. Louis.

2006, Aug. 24
885		Horiz. pair	1.60	1.60
a.-b.	A225	39c Either single	.80	.80

Marshallese Culture Type of 2005

No. 886 — Photographs: a, Harbor Front of Jabwor, Jaluit Atoll, by L. Sander. b, Irooj with Family, Jabwor, Jaluit Atoll, by Richard Deeken. c, Traditional Voyaging Canoe at Jaluit Atoll, by Sander. d, Mission Sisters and Girls Doing Laundry, Jaluit, by Hildegard von Bunsen. e, Traditional House on Mile Atoll, by Hans Seidel.

2006, Sept. 22   *Litho.*   *Perf. 13½*
886		Horiz. strip of 5	4.00	4.00
a.-e.	A250	39c Any single	.80	.80

Ships in the Marshallese Maritime and Corporate Registry — A258

No. 887: a, Cape Norviega. b, Front Century. c, Ashley. d, TI Africa. e, Discoverer Enterprise. f, Genmar Spyridon. g, Rickmers New Orleans. h, LNG Aquarius. i, Centurion. j, Barkald.

2006, Oct. 9
887	A258	39c Sheet of 10, #a-j	8.00	8.00

MARSHALL ISLANDS

Christmas — A259

2006, Nov. 1
888 A259 39c multi .80 .80

Greetings — A260

No. 889: a, "Happy Birthday." b, "Congratulations." c, "Thank You." d, "Best Wishes."

2007, Jan. 16   *Perf. 11¾*
889 A260 39c Block of 4, #a-d 3.25 3.25

Souvenir Sheet

New Year 2007 (Year of the Pig) A261

2007, Feb. 19   *Litho.*   *Perf. 13x13½*
890 A261 $1 multi 2.00 2.00

Trains — A262

No. 891: a, Art Deco train. b, Pennsylvania. c, Santa Fe Chief. d, Hiawatha. e, 20th Century Limited. f, Daylight.

2007, Mar. 26   *Perf. 13½*
891 A262 39c Block of 6, #a-f 4.75 4.75

Dolphins — A263

No. 892: a, Spotter dolphins. b, Bottlenose dolphins. c, Risso's dolphin. d, Common dolphin.

2007, Apr. 9
892 A263 39c Block of 4, #a-d 3.25 3.25

Fish — A264

Designs: 26c, Achilles tang. 41c, Regal angelfish. 52c, Saddled butterflyfish. 61c, Tinker's butterflyfish.

Perf. 10¼x11¼
2007, June 12   *Litho.*
893 A264 26c multi .55 .55
894 A264 41c multi .85 .85
895 A264 52c multi 1.10 1.10
896 A264 61c multi 1.25 1.25
    Nos. 893-896 (4) 3.75 3.75

Miniature Sheet

Space Age, 50th Anniv. A265

No. 897: a, First man in space. b, First man-made satellite. c, First men on the Moon. d, First docking in space. e, First woman in space. f, First manned lunar vehicle. g, First space walk. h, First landing on Mars. i, First probe of Venus. j, First American in orbit.

2007, June 12   *Perf. 13½*
897 A265 41c Sheet of 10, #a-j 8.25 8.25

Scouting, Cent. A266

No. 898 — Inscriptions: a, Helping others. b, Physically strong. c, Mentally awake. d, Fun and adventure.

2007, June 25
898 A266 41c Block of 4, #a-d 3.50 3.50

Purple Heart, 225th Anniv. — A267

2007, July 30   *Litho.*   *Perf. 13½*
899 A267 41c multi .85 .85

Miniature Sheet

United States Air Force, 60th Anniv. A268

No. 900: a, C-54 Skymaster. b, B-36 Peacemaker. c, F-86 Sabre. d, B-47 Stratojet. e, C-124 Globemaster II. f, C-121 Constellation. g, B-52 Stratofortress. h, F-100 Super Sabre. i, F-104 Starfighter. j, C-130 Hercules. k, F-105 Thunderchief. l, KC-135 Stratotanker. m, B-58 Hustler. n, F-4 Phantom II. o, T-38 Talon. p, C-141 Starlifter. q, F-111 Aardvark. r, SR-71 Blackbird. s, C-5 Galaxy. t, A-10 Thunderbolt II. u, F-15 Eagle. v, F-16 Fighting Falcon. w, F-117 Nighthawk. x, B-2 Spirit. y, C-17 Globemaster III.

2007, Aug. 7
900 A268 41c Sheet of 25, #a-y 21.00 21.00

Marshallese Culture Type of 2005

No. 901 — Photographs by J. Debrum: a, Lonkwon Getting Fish from His Trap. b, Alele Style of Fishing at Bilarek. c, Portrait of Lanju and Family. d, Outrigger with Sail. e, Lien and Litublan Collecting Shells.

2007, Sept. 18   *Litho.*   *Perf. 13½*
901   Horiz. strip of 5 4.25 4.25
   a.-e. A250 41c Any single .85 .85

Miniature Sheet

Marshall Islands Yacht Registry — A269

No. 902 — Registered yachts: a, Domani. b, Excellence III. c, Aquasition. d, Perfect Symmetry 5. e, Happy Days. f, Mystique. g, Halcyon Days. h, Man of Steel. i, Marathon. j, Sinbad.

2007, Oct. 8
902 A269 41c Sheet of 10, #a-j 8.25 8.25

Christmas — A270

No. 903 — Santa Claus: a, Reading list. b, Standing by fireplace. c, Holding gift. d, Waving from sleigh.

2007, Dec. 12
903 A270 41c Block of 4, #a-d 3.50 3.50

Miniature Sheet

Flower Bouquets — A271

No. 904 — Various bouquets with country name at bottom: a, Scotland. b, Jersey. c, Gibraltar. d, Dominica. e, Canada. f, Cyprus. g, Turks and Caicos Islands. h, Bahamas. i, Montserrat. j, Cayman Islands. k, Bangladesh. l, Falkland Islands. m, Grenada. n, Nevis. o, Jamaica. p, Australia. q, Fiji. r, New Hebrides. s, Pitcairn Islands. t, Cook Islands. u, Tonga. v, Seychelles. w, Zimbabwe. x, Christmas Island. y, Antigua.

2008, Jan. 15   *Litho.*   *Perf. 13½*
904 A271 41c Sheet of 25, #a-y 20.50 20.50
  See No. 934.

Miniature Sheet

Chinese New Year Animals and Characters — A272

No. 905: a, Pig. b, Ram. c, Horse. d, Tiger. e, Dog. f, Rabbit. g, Dragon. h, Ox. i, Rooster. j, Monkey. k, Snake. l, Rat.

2008, Feb. 7
905 A272 26c Sheet of 12, #a-l 6.25 6.25

United States Lighthouses — A273

No. 906: a, St. Augustine Lighthouse, Florida. b, Old Cape Henry Lighthouse, Virginia. c, Cape Lookout Lighthouse, North Carolina. d, Tybee Island Lighthouse, Georgia. e, Morris Island Lighthouse, South Carolina. f, Hillsboro Inlet Lighthouse, Florida.

2008, Mar. 6   *Litho.*   *Perf. 13½*
906 A273 41c Block of 6, #a-f 5.00 5.00

Miniature Sheet

Wild Cats A274

No. 907: a, Lion family at rest. b, Ocelot mother with cub sitting in grass. c, White Siberian tiger mother with cubs. d, Mother tiger with cubs lying in grass. e, Serval mother with cubs sitting in tall grass. f, North American cougar mother with cubs. g, Lynx mother with cubs. h, Jaguar with cubs at stream. i, Black panther mother with cubs. j, Clouded leopard mother with cubs. k, Cheetah with cubs lying in grass. l, Snow leopard with cubs.

2008, Mar. 26   *Litho.*   *Perf. 13½*
907 A274 41c Sheet of 12, #a-l 10.00 10.00

Miniature Sheet

Sailing Ships A275

No. 908: a, H.M.S. Victory. b, La Grande Hermine. c, U.S.S. Constitution. d, Fram. e, Tovarisch I. f, Ark and Dove. g, Rainbow. h, Great Republic. i, H.M.S. Resolution. j, La Dauphine. k, Kreuzenshtern. l, Golden Hind.

2008, Apr. 2
908 A275 41c Sheet of 12, #a-l 10.00 10.00

Miniature Sheet

Constellations — A276

No. 909: a, Cassiopeia. b, Ursa Major. c, Corvus. d, Camelopardalis. e, Cygnus. f, Andromeda. g, Capricornus. h, Canis Major. i, Dorado. j, Libra. k, Lynx. l, Serpentarius. m, Eridanus. n, Pavo. o, Orion. p, Leo Minor. q, Pegasus. r, Corona Borealis. s, Phoenix. t, Aquarius.

2008, Apr. 29   *Litho.*   *Perf. 13½*
909 A276 41c Sheet of 20, #a-t 16.50 16.50
  See Nos. 945, 964.

MARSHALL ISLANDS

Miniature Sheet

US Marine Corps A277

No. 910: a, US liberates Marshall Islands. b, John Lejeune. c, Holland Smith. d, Smedley D. Butler. e, Daniel J. Daly. f, Lewis "Chesty" Puller. g, John Basilone. h, Alexander Vandegrift. i, Gregory "Pappy" Boyington. j, Marines raising flag on Iwo Jima.

2008, May 12
910 A277 42c Sheet of 10, #a-j 8.50 8.50

Tropical Fish — A278

Designs: 1c, Banded butterflyfish. 3c, Damselfish. 5c, Pink skunk clownfish. 27c, Copperband butterflyfish. 42c, Threadfin butterflyfish. 60c, Beau Gregory damselfish. 61c, Porkfish. 63c, Goatfish. 94c, Common longnose butterflyfish. $1, Royal gramma. $4.80, Longfin bannerfish. $5, Blue-striped blenny. $16.50, Emperor butterflyfish.

2008 Litho. Perf. 11¼x10¼
911 A278 1c multi .25 .25
912 A278 3c multi .25 .25
913 A278 5c multi .25 .25
914 A278 27c multi .55 .55
915 A278 42c multi .85 .85
916 A278 60c multi 1.25 1.25
917 A278 61c multi 1.25 1.25
918 A278 63c multi 1.25 1.25
919 A278 94c multi 1.90 1.90
920 A278 $1 multi 2.00 2.00
921 A278 $4.80 multi 9.75 9.75
922 A278 $5 multi 10.00 10.00
923 A278 $16.50 multi 33.00 33.00
Nos. 911-923 (13) 62.55 62.55

Issued: Nos. 914, 915, 6/24; Nos. 919, 921, 923, 5/12. Nos. 911-913, 916-918, 920, 922, 9/9.

Miniature Sheet

Birds A279

No. 924: a, Blue-gray tanager. b, St. Vincent parrot. c, Green-throated carib. d, Yellow oriole. e, Blue-hooded euphonia. f, Crested honeycreeper. g, Purple-capped fruit dove. h, Green magpie. i, Bay-headed tanager. j, Bananaquit. k, Cardinal honeyeater. l, Toco toucan. m, Cattle egret. n, Ringed kingfisher. o, Red-necked parrot. p, Purple gallinule. q, Copper-rumped hummingbird. r, Micronesian pigeon. s, Painted bunting. t, Black-naped oriole. u, Channel-billed toucan. v, Saddle billed stork. w, Blood pheasant. x, Gray-crowned crane. y, Little blue heron.

2008, June 3 Litho. Perf. 13½
924 A279 42c Sheet of 25, #a-y 21.00 21.00

Miniature Sheet

Dinosaurs — A280

No. 925: a, Camarasaurus. b, Allosaurus. c, Parasaurolophus. d, Ornithomimus. e, Goniopholis. f, Camptosaurus. g, Edmontia. h, Ceratosaurus. i, Stegosaurus. j, Einiosaurus. k, Brachiosaurus. l, Corythosaurus.

2008, June 19
925 A280 42c Sheet of 12, #a-l 10.50 10.50

Miniature Sheet

Fishing Flies A281

No. 926: a, Lefty's Deceiver (25x35mm). b, Apte Tarpon (25x35mm). c, Royal Wulff (50x48mm). d, Muddler Minnow (25x35mm). e, Jock Scott (25x35mm).

2008, July 20
926 A281 42c Sheet of 5, #a-e 4.25 4.25

Miniature Sheet

Personalities of the Wild West — A282

No. 927: a, Wild Bill Hickok. b, Jim Bridger. c, Geronimo. d, Charles Goodnight. e, Chief Joseph. f, Kit Carson. g, Jim Beckwourth. h, Wyatt Earp. i, Dat Masterson. j, Dill Pickett. k, Bill Tilghman. l, Annie Oakley. m, Buffalo Bill Cody. n, Nellie Cashman. o, Sacagawea. p, John Fremont.

2008, Aug. 14
927 A282 42c Sheet of 16, #a-p 13.50 13.50

Endangered Species — A283

No. 928: a, Blue whale. b, Amazonian manatee. c, Hawaiian monk seal. d, Green turtle. e, Giant clam. f, Killer whale.

2008, Aug. 19 Litho. Perf. 13½
928 A283 42c Block of 6, #a-f 5.25 5.25

Marshallese Culture Type of 2005

No. 929, vert. — Photographs by J. Debrum: a, Lokeinlik Wearing Traditional Mat for Men. b, Limekto Weaving Hat from Kimej. c, Unfinished Outrigger. d, Young Boys in Mejit. e, Lonkoon with Fish Trap.

2008, Sept. 15 Litho. Perf. 13½
929 Horiz. strip of 5 4.25 4.25
a.-e. A250 42c Any single .85 .85

Miniature Sheet

Spacecraft and the Solar System — A284

No. 930: a, Mercury, Mariner 10. b, Uranus, Voyager 2. c, Venus, Mariner 2. d, Pluto, Voyager 2. e, Jupiter, Pioneer 11. f, Earth, Landsat. g, Moon, Lunar Orbiter. h, Saturn, Voyager 2. i, Mars, Viking Orbiter. j, Neptune, Voyager 2.

2008, Oct. 1
930 A284 42c Sheet of 10, #a-j 8.50 8.50

Miniature Sheet

Christmas — A285

No. 931 — Song titles under ornament: a, Silent Night. b, We Three Kings. c, Deck the Halls. d, Hark, the Herald Angels Sing. e, O Little Town of Bethlehem. f, Joy to the World. g, Jingle Bells. h, O Come All Ye Faithful.

2008, Oct. 15 Litho. Perf. 13½
931 A285 42c Sheet of 8, #a-h 6.75 6.75

Owls A286

No. 932: a, Barn owl. b, Barred owl. c, Burrowing owl. d, Snowy owl. e, Great horned owl. f, Spotted owl.

2008, Nov. 5
932 A286 42c Block of 6, #a-f 5.25 5.25

Souvenir Sheet

First United States Airmail Stamp, 90th Anniv. A287

2008, Dec. 10 Perf. 13x13½
933 A287 $1 multi 2.00 2.00

Flower Bouquets Type of 2008
Miniature Sheet

No. 934 — Various bouquets with country name at bottom: a, Isle of Man. b, St. Lucia. c, Grenada. d, Bermuda. e, Anguilla. f, Barbados. g, Belize. h, St. Kitts. i, Hong Kong. j, British Virgin Islands. k, St. Vincent. l, Tristan da Cunha. m, St. Helena. n, British Antarctic Territory. o, St. Vincent and the Grenadines. p, New Zealand. q, Papua New Guinea. r, Western Samoa. s, Solomon Islands. t, Brunei. u, Swaziland. v, Botswana. w, Maldives. x, Ghana. y, Sierra Leone.

2009, Mar. 31 Litho. Perf. 13½
934 A271 42c Sheet of 25, #a-y 21.00 21.00

Pres. Abraham Lincoln (1809-65) — A288

No. 935 — Lincoln and: a, "Honesty." b, "Equality." c, "Unity." d, "Liberty."

2009, Apr. 7 Litho. Perf. 13½
935 A288 $1 Block of 4, #a-d 8.00 8.00

Arctic Explorers — A289

No. 936: a, Elisha Kent Kane, ships. b, Robert E. Peary, Matthew A. Henson, dog sled. c, Vilhjalmur Stefansson, ship, dog sled. d, Adolphus Washington Greely, ship.

2009, Apr. 14
936 A289 42c Block of 4, #a-d 3.50 3.50
Peary Expedition to North Pole, cont.

Miniature Sheet

Famous American Indians — A290

No. 937: a, Black Hawk. b, Colorow. c, Looking Glass. d, Dull Knife. e, Mangas Coloradas. f, Red Cloud. g, Little Raven. h, Black Kettle. i, Standing Bear. j, Little Crow. k, Seattle. l, Washakie.

2009, Apr. 21 Litho. Perf. 13½
937 A290 44c Sheet of 12, #a-l 11.00 11.00
See Nos. 960, 987.

Miniature Sheet

US Military Heroes of the Air A291

No. 938: a, Richard I. Bong. b, Charles "Chuck" Yeager. c, Lauris Norstad. d, William "Billy" Mitchell. e, Curtis E. LeMay. f, Edward Henry O'Hare. g, Claire L. Chennault. h, George C. Kenney. i, James "Jimmy" Doolittle. j, Paul W. Tibbets, Jr. k, Benjamin O. Davis, Jr. l, Carl "Tooey" Spaatz. m, Ira C. Eaker. n, Edward "Eddie" Rickenbacker. o, Henry "Hap" Arnold. p, Map of Marshall Islands, birds, outrigger canoe, dolphin.

MARSHALL ISLANDS

2009, Apr. 28
938 A291 44c Sheet of 16, #a-p   14.50 14.50

Souvenir Sheet

Marshall Islands Postal Service, 25th Anniv. A292

2009, May 2   Litho.   *Perf. 13x13½*
939 A292 44c multi   .90 .90

Marine Life — A293

Designs: 28c, Masked butterflyfish. 44c, Queen angelfish. 88c, Clownfish. 98c, Starfish. $1.22, Orca whale.

2009, May 11   Litho.   *Perf. 11¼x10¼*
940 A293 28c multi   .60 .60
941 A293 44c multi   .90 .90
942 A293 88c multi   1.75 1.75
943 A293 98c multi   2.00 2.00
944 A293 $1.22 multi   2.50 2.50
     Nos. 940-944 (5)   7.75 7.75
     See No. 965.

Constellations Type of 2008
Miniature Sheet

No. 945: a, Antinous. b, Aquila. c, Cancer. d, Canis Major. e, Leo. f, Ara. g, Sextans Uraniae. h, Cepheus. i, Apus. j, Indus. k, Ursa Minor. l, Grus. m, Centaurus. n, Cetus. o, Piscis Volans. p, Lupus. q, Equuleus. r, Draco. s, Boötes. t, Scorpius.

2009, June 1   *Perf. 13½*
945 A276 44c Sheet of 20, #a-t   18.00 18.00

2005-09 Rose Varieties of the Year — A294

No. 946: a, Summertime, 2005. b, Champagne Moment, 2006. c, Tickled Pink, 2007. d, Sweet Haze, 2008. e, Lucky!, 2009.

2009, June 18
946   Horiz. strip of 5   4.50 4.50
a.-e. A294 44c Any single   .90 .90

Hot Air Balloons — A295

No. 947: a, Montgolfier's balloon. b, Intrepid. c, Explorer II. d, Double Eagle. e, Contemporary balloons.

2009, July 13
947   Horiz. strip of 5   4.50 4.50
a.-e. A295 44c Any single   .90 .90

July 22, 2009 Solar Eclipse A296

No. 948 — Eclipse phases: a, Beginning (shown). b, Totality and near-totality. c, Ending.

2009, July 22
948   Horiz. strip of 3   2.75 2.75
a.-c. A296 44c Any single   .90 .90

Steam Locomotives — A297

No. 949: a, Samson. b, Best Friend of Charleston. c, John Bull. d, Gowan & Marx. e, Stourbridge Lion. f, Brother Jonathan.

2009, Aug. 6   Litho.   *Perf. 13½*
949 A297 44c Block of 6, #a-f   5.50 5.50

Marshallese Culture Type of 2005

No. 950 — Photographs by J. Debrum: a, Making Arrowroot Lagoonside. b, Boats in Lagoon, One Capsized for Repair. c, Family Portrait in Front of Wooden Home with Pandanus Roof. d, Man Carrying Fish Trap. e, Portrait of New Year and LemeLali Weaving Baskets.

2009, Sept. 1   Litho.   *Perf. 13½*
950   Horiz. strip of 5   4.50 4.50
a.-e. A250 44c Any single   .90 .90

Eagles A298

No. 951: a, Philippine eagle. b, Tawny eagle. c, Martial eagle. d, Bald eagle. e, African fish eagle. f, Bateleur eagle. g, Golden eagle. h, Harpy eagle.

2009, Sept. 14   Litho.   *Perf. 13½*
951 A298 44c Block of 8, #a-h   7.25 7.25

Dogs — A299

No. 952: a, Beagle and Boston terrier. b, Chesapeake Bay retriever and Cocker spaniel. c, Alaskan malamute and Collie. d, Water spaniel and Basset hound. e, Coonhound and Foxhound.
No. 953, horiz.: a, Old English sheepdog. b, Irish setter. c, Welsh springer spaniel. d, West Highland terrier.

2009, Oct. 5   Litho.   *Perf. 13½*
952   Horiz. strip of 5   4.50 4.50
a.-e. A299 44c Any single   .90 .90
953   Sheet of 4   8.00 8.00
a.-d. A299 98c Any single   2.00 2.00

Christmas — A300

No. 954: a, Chili wreath. b, Christmas wreath. c, Traditional wreath. d, Tropical wreath. e, Colonial wreath.

2009, Oct. 15   Litho.   *Perf. 13½*
954   Horiz. strip of 5   4.50 4.50
a.-e. A300 44c Any single   .90 .90

Miniature Sheet

Endangered Species — A301

No. 955: a, Giant anteater. b, Caracal. c, Wild yak. d, Giant panda. e, Black-footed ferret. f, Black rhinoceros. g, Golden lion tamarin. h, African elephant. i, Persian fallow deer. j, Polar bear. k, Ocelot. l, Gorilla.

2009, Nov. 2   Litho.   *Perf. 13½*
955 A301 44c Sheet of 12, #a-l   11.00 11.00

Prehistoric Animals — A302

No. 956: a, Mastodons on prairie. b, Eohippus. c, Woolly mammoth. d, Saber-toothed cat. e, Mastodons in marsh.

2009, Nov. 24
956   Horiz. strip of 5   4.50 4.50
a.-e. A302 44c Any single   .90 .90

Shells A303

No. 957: a, Paper nautilus. b, Giant tun. c, Pilgrim's scallop. d, Gibbula magus.

2009, Dec. 8
957 A303 44c Block of 4, #a-d   3.75 3.75

Miniature Sheet

Signs of the Zodiac A304

No. 958: a, Aquarius. b, Pisces. c, Aries. d, Taurus. e, Gemini. f, Cancer. g, Leo. h, Virgo. i, Libra. j, Scorpio. k, Sagittarius. l, Capricorn.

2010, Jan. 5   *Perf. 11¾*
958 A304 44c Sheet of 12, #a-l   11.00 11.00

Miniature Sheet

Waterfowl — A305

No. 959: a, European wigeon. b, Tufted ducks. c, Mallards. d, Gadwall. e, Snow geese. f, Pintail ducks. g, Northern shoveler. h, Canvasback ducks.

2010, Feb. 10   Litho.   *Perf. 11¾*
959 A305 44c Sheet of 8, #a-h   7.25 7.25

Famous American Indians Type of 2009
Miniature Sheet

No. 960: a, Osceola. b, Lone Wolf. c, Menawa. d, Wabasha. e, Captain Jack. f, Quanah Parker. g, Ouray. h, Mannelito. i, Cochise. j, Satanta. k, Massasoit. l, Red Eagle.

2010, Mar. 4   Litho.   *Perf. 13½*
960 A290 44c Sheet of 12, #a-l   11.00 11.00

Boy Scouts of America, Cent. A306

No. 961 — Background color: a, Olive green. b, Red. c, Yellow bister. d, Blue.

2010, Mar. 18   Litho.   *Perf. 13½*
961 A306 44c Block of 4, #a-d   3.75 3.75

Shells A307

No. 962: a, Paper nautilus. b, Giant tun. c, Pilgrim's scallop. d, Gibbula magus.

2010, Mar. 29   Litho.   *Perf. 13½*
962 A307 98c Block of 4, #a-d   8.00 8.00
     See Nos. 971-972.

Astronomers A308

No. 963: a, Nicolaus Copernicus. b, Johannes Kepler. c, Galileo Galilei. d, Sir Isaac Newton. e, Sir William Herschel.

2010, Apr. 7
963   Horiz. strip of 5   4.50 4.50
a.-e. A308 44c Any single   .90 .90
No. 963e is incorrectly inscribed "Hirschel."

Constellations Type of 2008

No. 964: a, Columba. b, Virgo. c, Argo Navis. d, Tucana (Toucan). e, Aries. f, Coma Berenices. g, Delphinus. h, Perseus. i, Taurus. j, Monoceros. k, Gemini. l, Vulpecula. m, Lepus. n, Auriga. o, Pisces. p, Sagittarius. q, Crater. r, Lyra. s, Hercules. t, Canes Venatici.

2010, June 1
964 A276 44c Sheet of 20, #a-t   18.00 18.00

Fish Type of 2009

2010, June 1   *Perf. 11¼x10¼*
965 A293 28c Mandarin goby   .60 .60

Marshallese Alphabet A309

No. 966 — Letters and Marshallese words: a, "A," Amata (first name of first Marshallese president). b, "A with macron," Aj (to weave). c, "B," Babbub (butterfly). d, "D," Deo (beautiful young lady). e, "E," Ek (fish). f, "I," Iokwe (rainbow). g, "J," Jaki (mat). h, "K," Imon Kien (house of government). i, "L," Loktanur (star

MARSHALL ISLANDS

Capella). j, "L with cedilla," Lokwajek (red-tailed tropic bird). k, "M," Ma (breadfruit). l, "M with cedilla," Makmok (arrowroot plant). m, "N," Ni (coconut tree). n, "N with cedilla," No (ocean wave). o, "N with macron," Niin-pako (shark tooth). p, "O," Ok (fish net). q, "O with cedilla," Eo (tattoo). r, "O with macron," Oo (lionfish). s, "P," Pejak (visitor's hut). t, "R," Raj (whale). u, "T," Tipnol (outrigger sailing canoe). v, "U," Urur (fire). w, "U with macron," Ulin-raj (dorsal fin of whale). x, "W," Wojla (woven pandanus leaf sail).

2010, June 16   **Litho.**   **Perf. 13½**
966   Sheet of 24   22.00   22.00
   a.-x.   A309 44c Any single   .90   .90

Miniature Sheet

Statue of Liberty — A310

No. 967 — Statue of Liberty: a, Red clouds and water (9-1). b, Blue background (9-2). c, Brown and gray clouds (9-3). d, American flag (9-4). e, Frederic Bartholdi (9-5). f, Blue background, diff. (9-6). g, White background around head (9-7). h, Torch (9-8). i, Brown background around head (9-9).

2010, June 17   **Perf. 11¾**
967   A310 44c Sheet of 9, #a-i, + 7 labels   8.25   8.25

Miniature Sheet

Classic Cars — A311

No. 968: a, 1935 Duesenberg. b, 1932 Packard. c, 1928 Locomobile. d, 1931 Cord. e, 1929 Pierce Arrow.

2010, July 7
968   A311 44c Sheet of 5, #a-e, + 4 labels   4.50   4.50

Carousel Horses — A312

No. 969 — Various carousel horses numberd: a, (6-1). b, (6-2). c, (6-3). d, (6-4). e, (6-5). f, (6-6).

2010, Aug. 12   **Perf. 13½**
969   A312 44c Block of 6, #a-f   5.50   5.50

US Warships of World War II — A313

No. 970: a, USS Nevada. b, USS Missouri. c, USS Wisconsin. d, USS Oregon. e, USS Massachusetts. f, USS North Carolina. g, USS Texas. h, USS Idaho. i, USS New Jersey. j, USS Colorado. k, USS South Dakota. l, USS New Mexico. m, USS Washington. n, USS Iowa. o, USS Alabama.

2010, Sept. 2   **Perf. 13½**
970   Sheet of 15   13.50   13.50
   a.-o.   A313 44c Any single   .90   .90

Shells Type of 2010

Designs: 28c, Pilgrim's scallop. 98c, Gibbula magus.

2010, Sept. 20
971   A307 28c multi   .60   .60
972   A307 98c multi   2.00   2.00

Marshallese Culture Type of 2005

No. 973 — Photographs by L. Debrum: a, Church Buildings in Likiep. b, Ijuran Ready to Launch. c, Group of People, One Man Holding Fish Net. d, Lejek with Fish Trap on Korkor in Likiep. e, Landscape with Outrigger and Sailboat.

2010, Sept.14   **Perf. 13½**
973   Horiz. strip of 5   4.50   4.50
   a.-e.   A250 44c Any single   .90   .90

Christmas A314

No. 974 — Various depictions of Santa Claus numbered: a, (4-1). b, (4-2). c, (4-3). d, (4-4).

2010, Oct. 18
974   Horiz. strip of 4   3.75   3.75
   a.-d.   A314 44c Any single   .90   .90

Miniature Sheet

Pres. John F. Kennedy (1917-63) — A315

No. 975 — Various portraits of Kennedy numbered: a, (6-1). b, (6-2). c, (6-3). d, (6-4). e, (6-5). f, (6-6).

2010, Nov. 3
975   A315 44c Sheet of 6, #a-f, + 6 labels   5.50   5.50

Miniature Sheet

Orchids — A316

No. 976: a, Psygmorchis purilla. b, Cycnoches spp. c, Aerangis modesta. d, Ansellia africana. e, Vanda coerulea. f, Dendrobium cruentum. g, Phragmipedium korachii. h, Cymbidium ensifolium. i, Laelia milleri.

2010, Nov. 17
976   A316 44c Sheet of 9, #a-i   8.00   8.00

Miniature Sheet

Butterflies — A317

No. 977: a, Monarch. b, Brimstone. c, Blue-spot hairstreak. d, Small tortoiseshell. e, Small skipper. f, Large blue. g, Large copper. h, Eastern orange-tip. i, Red admiral. j, American painted lady. k, Great eggfly. l, Dark green fritillary.

2010, Dec. 8
977   A317 44c Sheet of 12, #a-l   11.00   11.00

Tulips — A318

No. 978 — Inscriptions: a, Yellow tulip. b, Tulips. c, Purple tulips. d, Red and black tulips. e, Yellow and orange tulips. f, Red tulips.

2011, Jan. 11
978   Block of 6   5.50   5.50
   a.-f.   A318 44c Any single   .90   .90

Miniature Sheet

New Year 2011 (Year of the Rabbit) A319

No. 979 — Rabbit in: a, Blue. b, Red violet. c, Bister. d, Green.

2011, Feb. 3
979   A319 98c Sheet of 4, #a-d   8.00   8.00

Pres. Ronald Reagan (1911-2004) — A320

No. 980 — Inscription: a, Early years. b, Movie actor. c, Governor of California. d, 40th President. e, Elder statesman/late years.

2011, Feb. 6
980   Horiz. strip of 5   4.50   4.50
   a.-o.   A320 44c Any single   .90   .90

Firsts in Flight — A321

No. 981 — Inscription: a, Centennial of first airmail flight. b, First airmail service in America. c, First U.S. coast-to-coast airmail service. d, First permanent U.S. transcontinental airmail service. e, First international airmail service.

2011, Feb. 18
981   Horiz. strip of 5   4.50   4.50
   a.-e.   A321 44c Any single   .90   .90

See Nos. 988, 994, 1004, 1012.

Turtles — A322

Designs: 1c, Green turtle. 2c, Loggerhead turtle. 5c, Leatherback turtle. $10, Hawksbill turtle.

Perf. 11¼x10¼
2011, Feb. 22   **Litho.**
982   A322 1c multi   .25   .25
983   A322 2c multi   .25   .25
984   A322 5c multi   .25   .25
985   A322 $10 multi   20.00   20.00
   Nos. 982-985 (4)   20.75   20.75

Corals and Fish — A323

No. 986 — Inscriptions: a, Flora & fauna of the Pacific Ocean. b, Chalice coral. c, Elkhorn coral. d, Brain coral. e, Finger coral.

2011, Mar. 10   **Perf. 13½**
986   Horiz. strip of 5   3.00   3.00
   a.-e.   A323 29c Any single   .60   .60

Famous American Indians Type of 2009

No. 987: a, Pontiac. b, Barboncito. c, Geronimo. d, Victorio. e, Sitting Bull. f, Cornplanter. g, Uncas. h, Little Wolf. i, Crazy Horse. j, Gall. k, Joseph. l, Tecumseh.

2011, Mar. 22
987   A290 44c Sheet of 12, #a-l   11.00   11.00

Firsts in Flight Type of 2011

No. 988 — Inscriptions: a, First manned flight. b, First manned flight of semi-controlled airship. c, First powered aircraft leaves the ground. d, First manned flight of powered, controlled airship. e, First controlled powered flight.

2011, Apr. 12
988   Horiz. strip of 5   4.50   4.50
   a.-e.   A321 44c Any single   .90   .90

First Man in Space, 50th Anniv. — A324

No. 989: a, Rocket launch, Yuri Gagarin on medal. b, Gagarin wearing space helmet, spacecraft, Earth. c, Monument, Apollo and Soyuz spacecraft docked, medal.

2011, Apr. 12
989   Strip of 3   6.00   6.00
   a.-c.   A324 $1 Any single   2.00   2.00

Printed in sheets containing three strips and seven labels.

Miniature Sheet

Wedding of Prince William and Catherine Middleton — A325

No. 990 — Various flowers numbered: a, 15-1. b, 15-2. c, 15-3. d, 15-4. e, 15-5. f, 15-6. g, 15-7. h, 15-8. i, 15-9. j, 15-10. k, 15-11. l, 15-12. m, 15-13. n, 15-14. o,15-15.

2011, Apr. 29
990   A325 44c Sheet of 15, #a-o   13.50   13.50

MARSHALL ISLANDS

Miniature Sheet

Apostles of Jesus — A326

No. 991: a, Andrew. b, Philip. c, Simon. d, James the Lesser. e, Paul. f, Matthew. g, James the Greater. h, Thaddeus. i, Peter. j, John. k, Bartholomew. l, Thomas.

2011, May 2
991 A326 44c Sheet of 12, #a-l 11.00 11.00

Miniature Sheet

Garden Life — A327

No. 992: a, Great eggfly butterfly. b, Passionflower. c, Ladybug. d, Emperor dragonfly. e, Sweet white violet. f, Magpie moth. g, Bluets. h, Katydid. i, Painted lady butterfly. j, Bumblebee. k, Stag beetle. l, Large tortoiseshell butterfly.

2011, May 28
992 A327 44c Sheet of 12,
                #a-l   11.00 11.00

Miniature Sheet

Antarctic Treaty, 50th Anniv. — A328

No. 993: a, Penguin and ship (6-1). b, Emperor penguin and juvenile (6-2). c, Penguin and ship (6-3). d, Two penguins on iceberg (6-4). e, King penguin mother and baby (6-5). f, King penguin mothers with babies (6-6). g, Penguin and ship (6-7). h, Two adult Emperor penguins and juvenile (6-8). i, Penguin and ship (6-9).

2011, June 23
993 A328 98c Sheet of 9, #a-i,
             + 7 labels   18.00 18.00

Firsts in Flight Type of 2011

No. 994 — Inscriptions: a, First flight to land on a ship. b, First non-stop North American coast-to-coast flight. c, First non-stop transatlantic flight. d, First round-the-world flight. e, First flight over the North Pole.

2011, July 7
994   Horiz. strip of 5   4.50 4.50
  a.-e. A321 44c Any single   .90   .90

Outrigger Canoes A329

Plumeria Flowers A330

Marshall Islands Flag — A331

Coconut Palm Trees and Coconuts A332

Micronesian Pigeons A333

Triton's Trumpet A334

2011, July 7
995   A329 $4.95 multi   10.00   10.00
996   A330 $10.95 multi   22.00   22.00
997   A331 $13.95 multi   28.00   28.00
998   A332 $14.95 multi   30.00   30.00
999   A333 $18.30 multi   37.00   37.00
1000 A334 $29.95 multi   60.00   60.00
       Nos. 995-1000 (6)   187.00 187.00

Miniature Sheet

End of Space Shuttle Missions A335

No. 1001 — Space Shuttle: a, And schematic diagrams. b, Lifting off. c, And eagle. d, In orbit. e, On approach for landing. f, Lifting off, U.S. flag in background. g, And planets.

2011, July 21
1001 A335 44c Sheet of 7, #a-g,
              + 8 labels   6.25 6.25

The label on No. 1001 with the names of the Challenger astronauts has the name of "Judith Resnik" misspelled as "Judith Resuik." The sheet was reprinted later in 2011 with the corrected spelling.

Marshallese Culture Type of 2005

No. 1002 — Photographs by L. Debrum: a, Celebration of Alfonso Capelle's Kemen. b, Three Women Making Pandanus Thatch. c, Men Spearfishing on Reef Oceaside of Likiep. d, Men in Boathouse Grinding Arrowroot. e, The Boat Vilma Being Launched at Likiep.

2011, July 22
1002   Horiz. strip of 5   4.50 4.50
  a.-e. A250 44c Any single   .90   .90

Miniature Sheet

Fish A336

No. 1003: a, Blue-banded surgeonfish, Bleeker's parrotfish, Achilles tang, Oriental sweetlips. c, Regal angelfish, Orangespine unicornfish. d, Coral grouper, Palette surgeonfish. e, Peacock grouper, Coral grouper. f, Bennett's butterflyfish, Picassofish. g, Bleeker's parrotfish, Flame angelfish. h, Orangespine unicornfish, Peacock grouper. i, Flame angelfish, Regal angelfish. j, Palette surgeonfish, Blue-banded surgeonfish. k, Picassofish, Achilles tang. l, Oriental sweetlips, Bennett's butterflyfish.

2011, Aug. 11
1003 A336 44c Sheet of 12,
              #a-l   11.00 11.00

Firsts in Flight Type of 2011

No. 1004 — Inscriptions: a, First turbojet flight. b, First jet fighter flight. c, First jet passenger service. d, First Transatlantic jet passenger service. e, First supersonic commercial aircraft.

2011, Aug. 21
1004   Horiz. strip of 5   4.50 4.50
  a.-e. A321 44c Any single   .90   .90

National Buildings and Symbols — A337

Designs: No. 1005, 64c, Capitol Building. No. 1006, 64c, Nitijela Building. No. 1007, 64c, National seal, vert. No. 1008, 64c, National flag, vert.

Perf. 11¼x10¼, 10¼x11¼
2011, Aug. 31   Litho.
1005-1008 A337   Set of 4   5.25 5.25

Souvenir Sheet

Marshall Islands No. 411 A338

2011, Sept. 17   Litho.   Perf. 13½
1009 A338 $4.95 multi   10.00 10.00
Admission to the United Nations, 20th anniv.

Miniature Sheet

Christmas — A339

No. 1010: a, 10c, Christmas shopping. b, 20c, Cutting Christmas tree. c, 30c, Putting wreath on door. d, 40c, Caroling in cathedral at Christmas. e, 50c, Bringing home the tree. f, 60c, A winter sleigh ride. g, 70c, Arrival in sleigh at church. h, 80c, A pause in the sleigh ride. i, 90c, Christmas caroling outside church. j, $1, Sleigh ride to get Christmas tree. k, $1.10, Western Christmas. l, $1.20, Christmas caroling.

2011, Oct. 13
1010 A339   Sheet of 12, #a-l   16.00 16.00

Souvenir Sheet

Compact of Free Association, 25th Anniv. — A340

No. 1011: a, Marshall Islands national seal. b, Walap sailing. c, Marshall Islands flag.

2011, Oct. 21
1011 A340 98c Sheet of 3, #a-c,
              + 3 labels   6.00 6.00

Firsts in Flight Type of 2011

No. 1012 — Inscriptions: a, First man to fly faster than sound. b, First man in space. c, First astronaut in space. d, First man to walk in space. e, First man on the Moon.

2011, Nov. 4
1012   Horiz. strip of 5   4.50 4.50
  a.-e. A321 44c Any single   .90   .90

Hanukkah — A341

No. 1013 — Various menorahs on: a, Day 1. b, Day 2. c, Day 3. d, Day 4. e, Day 5. f, Day 6. g, Day 7. h, Day 8.

2011, Nov. 20   Litho.   Perf. 13½
1013 A341 44c Block of 8, #a-h   7.25 7.25

Miniature Sheet

American Entry Into World War II, 70th Anniv. — A342

No. 1014 — Inscriptions: a, Burma Road, 717-mile lifeline to China. b, Roosevelt calls for America's first peacetime draft. c, U.S must become "Great Arsenal" to save democracy. d, Lend-Lease Act, aid to our allies. e, Roosevelt, Churchill draft 8 peace aims, joint steps believed changed at parley. f, U.S. Destroyer Reuben James sunk by German U-boat. g, Civil defense mobilizes the U.S.A. h, Kaiser launches Liberty ships. i, War! Oahu bombed by Japanese planes. j, Congress declares war on Japan, 1500 killed in attack on Hawaii.

2011, Dec. 7
1014 A342 44c Sheet of 10, #a-j,
              + 10 labels   9.00 9.00

See Nos. 1035, 1065, 1089, 1123.

Miniature Sheet

Stained Glass Windows A343

No. 1015 — Stained glass windows of: a, Cathedral of Santa Maria del Fiore, Florence,

MARSHALL ISLANDS

Italy (9-1). b, Nidaros Cathedral, Trondheim, Norway (9-2). c, Canterbury Cathedral, Canterbury, England (9-3). d, Notre Dame Cathedral, Tournai, Belgium (9-4). e, Cathedral of Monaco (9-5). f, St. John's Church, Gouda, Netherlands (9-6). g, St. Florin's Cathedral, Vaduz, Liechtenstein (9-7). h, St. Mary the Crowned Cathedral, Gibraltar (9-8). i, Parish Church of St. Saviour, Jersey (9-9).

2011, Dec. 9
1015 A343 44c Sheet of 9, #a-i   8.00 8.00

Miniature Sheet

Rhododendrons — A344

No. 1016 — Various rhododendrons numbered: a, (9-1). b, (9-2). c, (9-3). d, (9-4). e, (9-5). f, (9-6). g, (9-7). h, (9-8). i, (9-9).

2012, Jan. 10
1016 A344 45c Sheet of 9, #a-i   8.25 8.25

Marine Life — A345

2012, Jan. 22
1017 A345 45c multi   .90 .90

Miniature Sheet

New Year 2012 (Year of the Dragon) A346

No. 1018 — Background color: a, Blue. b, Pink. c, Yellow green. d, Green.

2012, Jan. 23
1018 A346 $1.05 Sheet of 4, #a-d   8.50 8.50

Whales — A347

No. 1019. a, Right whales. b, Killer whales. c, Gervais's whales. d, Blue whales.

2012, Feb. 20 Perf. 13½
1019 A347 32c Horiz. strip of 4   2.60 2.60
a.-d. A347 32c Any single   .65 .65

Chuuk War Canoe A348

Cymbidium Orchid A349

Arrival of Early Inhabitants A350

Mandarinfish A351

Hibiscus Rosa-sinensis — A352

Seahorses A353

2012, Feb. 27
1020 A348 $5.15 multi   10.00 10.00
1021 A349 $11.35 multi   22.50 22.50
1022 A350 $15.45 multi   31.00 31.00
1023 A351 $16.95 multi   34.00 34.00
1024 A352 $18.95 multi   37.50 37.50
1025 A353 $38 multi   75.00 75.00
Nos. 1020-1025 (6)   210.00 210.00
Compare No. 1020 with No. 1042.

Miniature Sheet

Reign of Queen Elizabeth II, 60th Anniv. — A354

No. 1026 — Stamps of Great Britain depicting Queen Elizabeth II: a, #MH206 (10p). b, #MH211 (20p). c, #MH219 (30p). d, #MH266 (40p). e, #MH385 (50p). f, #MH397 (60p).

2012, Feb. 6
1026 A354 $1.05 Sheet of 6, #a-f   13.00 13.00

Birds — A355

Designs: 85c, Black-footed albatross. $1.05, Red-tailed tropic bird.

2012, Feb. 27 Perf. 11¼x10¼
1027 A355 85c multi   1.75 1.75
1028 A355 $1.05 multi   2.10 2.10

Chinese Terra Cotta Warriors A356

No. 1029: a, General figure (6-1). b, Kneeling shooter (6-2). c, Armor warriors (6-3). d, Arrow shooter (6-4). e, General figure (6-5). f, Heavy armor (6-6).

2012, Mar. 15 Perf. 13½
1029 A356 45c Block of 6, #a-f   5.50 5.50

Inuits A357

No. 1030: a, Inuits enjoy a hot drink in their igloo. b, Inuit crafts and sculptures. c, Inuit drummers and dancers. d, Inuit men fishing with harpoons. e, Inuit family in skin tent. f, Inuit hunting.

2012, Mar. 26
1030 A357 45c Block of 6, #a-f   5.50 5.50

Creation of Tobolar Coconut Twine and Rope — A358

No. 1031: a, Husking the ripe coconuts after they come off the tree. b, Soaking the husks in sea water under mat and stones. c, Pounding the husks to separate the twine from the meat. d, Making twine and rope from the husk fibers.

2012, Apr. 8
1031 A358 Horiz. strip of 4   3.75 3.75
a.-d. A358 45c Any single   .90 .90

Miniature Sheet

Scientists — A359

No. 1032: a, Charles Darwin. b, William Harvey. c, Robert Boyle. d, Johannes Kepler. e, Thomas Edison. f, André-Marie Ampère. g, Michael Faraday. h, Jöns Jacob Berzelius. i, James Watt. j, Galileo Galilei. k, Andreas Vesalius. l, Antoine Lavoisier. m, Dmitry Mendeleyev. n, Carl Gauss. o, Isaac Newton. p, Gregor Mendel. q, John Dalton. r, Carl Linnaeus. s, Robert Fulton. t, William Thomson, Baron Kelvin.

2012, Apr. 23 Perf. 13½
1032 A359 45c Sheet of 20, #a-t   18.00 18.00

Miniature Sheet

Clouds A360

No. 1033: a, Altocumulus undulatus. b, Altostratus translucidus. c, Cirrostratus fibratus. d, Cumulus congestus. e, Cumulonimbus incus. f, Cirrus radiatus. g, Cirrocumulus undulatus. h, Cumulonimbus with tornado. i, Cumulus humilis. j, Cumulonimbus mammatus. k, Stratus opacus. l, Altocumulus castellanus. m, Altocumulus stratiformis. n, Altocumulus lenticularis. o, Stratocumulus undulatus.

2012, May 10
1033 A360 45c Sheet of 15, #a-o   13.50 13.50

Birds — A361

No. 1034: a, Masked woodswallow. b, Golden-shouldered parrot. c, Regent bowerbird. d, King parrot. e, Rainbow pitta. f, Rainbow bee-eaters on branch. g, White-tailed kingfisher. h, Spotted catbird. i, Rainbow bee-eater in flight. j, Western magpie.

2012, June 18
1034 A361 45c Block of 10   9.00 9.00
a.-j. A361 45c Any single   .90 .90

World War II Type of 2011
Miniature Sheet

No. 1035 — Inscriptions: a, Tokyo bombed. b, Roosevelt praises U.S. rationing effort. c, U.S. wins great naval battle in Coral Sea. d, Corregidor surrenders under land attack after withstanding 300 raids from the air. e, Japanese make landings in Aleutian Islands; U.S. warships attack Attu Island, defeat Japs. f, Codebreaking: Turning the tide in the Pacific. g, Jap fleet smashed by U.S., 2 carriers sunk at Midway. h, Women in the war: "Rosie the Riveter." i, Marines gain hold on Solomon Islands; ships and planes wage fights. j, American forces land in French Africa.

2012, July 3
1035 A342 45c Sheet of 10, #a-j, + 10 labels   9.00 9.00

Miniature Sheet

Introduction of Euro Currency, 10th Anniv. — A362

No. 1036 — 1-euro coins of: a, Austria. b, Belgium. c, Finland. d, France. e, Germany. f, Greece. g, Ireland. h, Italy. i, Luxembourg. j, Netherlands. k, Portugal. l, Spain.

2012, July 16
1036 A362 45c Sheet of 12, #a-l   11.00 11.00

Miniature Sheet

American Civil War, 150th Anniv. — A363

No. 1037 — U.S. stamps commemorating Civil War centennial: a, #1178 (Fort Sumter, 34x25mm). b, #1179 (Battle of Shiloh, 34x25mm). c, #1180 (Battle of Gettysburg, 34x25mm). d, #1181 (Battle of the Wilderness, 34x25mm). e, #1182 (Surrender at Appomattox, 48x50mm).

2012, July 25
1037 A363 45c Sheet of 5, #a-e   4.50 4.50

American Indian Dances — A364

No. 1038: a, Traditional Dance. b, Raven Dance. c, Fancy Dance. d, Hoop Dance. e, Grass Dance. f, Butterfly Dance.

2012, Aug. 16
1038 A364 45c Block of 6, #a-f   5.50 5.50

Souvenir Sheet

USS Constitution and HMS Guerrière — A365

2012, Aug. 20
1039 A365 $4.95 multi + 4 labels   10.00 10.00
War of 1812, bicent.

MARSHALL ISLANDS

Miniature Sheet

Christmas — A366

No. 1040 — Items from carol *The Twelve Days of Christmas*: a, Partridge in a pear tree (12-1). b, Two turtle doves (12-2). c, Three French hens (12-3). d, Four calling birds (12-4). e, Five golden rings (12-5). f, Six geese a-laying (12-6). g, Seven swans a-swimming (12-7). h, Eight maids a-milking (12-8). i, Nine drummers drumming (12-9). j, Ten pipers piping (12-10). k, Eleven ladies dancing (12-11). l, Twelve lords a-leaping (12-12).

2012, Sept. 28
1040 A366 45c Sheet of 12, #a-l   11.00 11.00

Locomotives of the Fifty States — A367

No. 1041 — Steam locomotive from: a, Alabama. b, Alaska. c, Arizona. d, Arkansas. e, California. f, Colorado. g, Connecticut. h, Delaware. i, Florida. j, Georgia. k, Hawaii. l, Idaho. m, Illinois. n, Indiana. o, Iowa. p, Kansas. q, Kentucky. r, Louisiana. s, Maine. t, Maryland. u, Massachusetts. v, Michigan. w, Minnesota. x, Mississippi. y, Missouri. z, Montana. aa, Nebraska. ab, Nevada. ac, New Hampshire. ad, New Jersey. ae, New Mexico. af, New York. ag, North Carolina. ah, North Dakota. ai, Ohio. aj, Oklahoma. ak, Oregon. al, Pennsylvania. am, Rhode Island. an, South Carolina. ao, South Dakota. ap, Tennessee. aq, Texas. ar, Utah. as, Vermont. at, Virginia. au, Washington. av, West Virginia. aw, Wisconsin. ax, Wyoming.

2012, Nov. 3
1041   Sheet of 50   45.00 45.00
a.-ax. A367 45c Any single   .90   .90

Chuuk War Canoe — A368

2012, Nov. 8   Perf. 11¼x10¼
1042 A368 $5.15 multi   10.00 10.00
Compare No. 1042 and No. 1020.

Birds A369

No. 1043: a, Great hornbill. b, Peregrine falcon. c, Bald eagle. d, Channel-billed toucan. e, Secretary bird. f, Black-bellied bustard. g, Toco toucan. h, Hyacinth macaw. i, Burrowing owl. j, Bald ibis.

2013, Jan. 10   Perf. 13½
1043 A369 45c Sheet of 10, #a-j   9.00 9.00
See Nos. 1056-1058.

Australia, 225th Anniv. — A370

No. 1044 — Stars and: a, Australian settler and land claim. b, Tennis racket, coin showing King George V. c, Sydney Harbour Bridge, Sydney Opera House. d, Cricket player. e, Clipper ship, Southern Cross constellation. f, Clipper ship, sextant markings. g, Australian Parliament, Aboriginal drawings. h, William Shakespeare. i, British Parliament, London. j, Queen Elizabeth II, British coat of arms.

2013, Jan. 25
1044   Sheet of 10   9.50 9.50
a.-j. A370 46c Any single   .95   .95
Inscription on No. 1044b is incorrect.

Marine Life — A371

Designs: 33c, Raccoon butterflyfish. 46c, Dolphins. $1.10, Long-nosed butterflyfish, horiz. $5.60, Tiger shark, horiz. $12.35, Star puffer, horiz. $16.85, Nassau grouper, horiz. $19.95, Starfish, horiz. $23.95, Porkfish, horiz. $44.95, Grouper, horiz.

2013, Jan. 28   Perf. 10¼x11¼
1045 A371 33c multi   .70   .70
1046 A371 46c multi   .95   .95

                                   Perf. 11¼x10¼
1047 A371 $1.10   2.25   2.25
1048 A371 $5.60 multi   11.50 11.50
1049 A371 $12.35 multi   25.00 25.00
1050 A371 $16.85 multi   34.00 34.00
1051 A371 $19.95 multi   40.00 40.00
1052 A371 $23.95 multi   47.50 47.50
1053 A371 $44.95 multi   90.00 90.00

Miniature Sheet

New Year 2013 (Year of the Snake) — A372

No. 1054 — Color of snake: a, Blue (4-1). b, Red Brown (4-2). c, Yellow brown (4-3). d, Green (4-4).

2013, Feb. 10   Perf. 13½
1054 A372 $1.10 Sheet of 4, #a-d   9.00 9.00

Camellias — A373

No. 1055 — Number and color of camellias: a, One white (8-1). b, Two red and white (8-2). c, Three pink (8-3). d, One pink (8-4). e, Three dark pink (8-5). f, Two pink (8-6). g, One red (8-7). h, Three pink (8-8).

2013, Feb. 22
1055 A373 46c Block of 8, #a-h   7.50 7.50

Birds Type of 2013
Miniature Sheets

No. 1056: a, Hadada ibis. b, White-face whistling duck. c, Scarlet ibises. d, Fulvous tree duck. e, Knob-billed goose. f, Egyptian goose. g, Baikal teal. h, Humboldt penguins. i, Whooping cranes. j, Red-breasted goose.
No. 1057: a, Caribbean flamingos. b, Dalmatian pelicans. c, Piping plovers. d, Coscoroba swans. e, Hawaiian goose. f, Brown pelican. g, Jabiru. h, King penguins. i, White spoonbill. j, Blue cranes.
No. 1058: a, Golden conure. b, Major Mitchell's cockatoos. c, Eastern bluebirds. d, Giant scops owl. e, Thick-billed parrot. f, Blue-crowned pigeon. g, American kestrels. h, White-breasted silver-eyes. i, St. Lucia amazon. j, California condors.

2013   Perf. 13½
1056 A369 46c Sheet of 10, #a-j   9.50 9.50
1057 A369 46c Sheet of 10, #a-j   9.50 9.50
1058 A369 46c Sheet of 10, #a-j   9.50 9.50

Issued: No. 1056, 3/9; No. 1057, 5/16; No. 1058, 10/3.

Cats — A374

No. 1059: a, Four cats, pink flower (6-5). b, Three cats, blue flower, butterflies (6-6). c, Three cats, pink flowers, basket (6-1). d, Three cats looking at grasshopper on basket (6-2). e, Three cats, red and yellow flowers (6-3). f, Three cats, two hummingbirds (6-4).

2013, Mar. 27   Litho.   Perf. 13½
1059   Horiz. strip of 6   4.25 4.25
a.-f. A374 33c Any single   .70   .70

Medals — A375

No. 1060 — Inscription below medal: a, George Washington. b, John Adams. c, Thomas Jefferson. d, James Madison. e, James Monroe. f, John Quincy Adams. g, Andrew Jackson. h, Martin Van Buren. i, William H. Harrison. j, John Tyler. k, James K. Polk. l, Zachary Taylor. m, Millard Fillmore. n, Franklin Pierce. o, James Buchanan. p, Abraham Lincoln. q, Andrew Johnson. r, Ulysses S. Grant. s, Rutherford B. Hayes. t, James Garfield. u, Chester Arthur. v, Grover Cleveland. w, Benjamin Harrison. x, Peace and Friendship. y, William McKinley. z, Theodore Roosevelt. aa, William H. Taft. ab, Woodrow Wilson. ac, Warren G. Harding. ad, Calvin Coolidge. ae, Herbert Hoover. af, Franklin Delano Roosevelt. ag, Harry S. Truman. ah, Dwight D. Eisenhower. ai, John F. Kennedy. aj, Lyndon B. Johnson. ak, Richard Milhous Nixon. al, Rerald R. Ford. am, Jimmy Carter. an, Ronald Reagan. ao, Geroge Bush. ap, William Jefferson Clinton. aq, George W. Bush. ar, Presidential Seal. as, The White House.

2013, Apr. 9
1060   Sheet of 45   43.00 43.00
a.-as. A375 46c Any single   .95   .95

Souvenir Sheet

"Ich Bin Ein Berliner" Speech, by Pres. John F. Kennedy, 50th Anniv. A376

2013, June 29   Perf. 13¼x13½
1061 A376 $2 multi   4.00 4.00

British Steam Locomotives A377

No. 1062: a, No. 43 Calugareni. b, Beyer Peacock 2-6-4T. c, Adam Brown. d, Baldwin 4-6-0. e, 15A Class Garratt. f, Enterprise 1845. g, Grahamstown. h, Flying Scotsman. i, Black Hawthorn. j, LNER "Mallard" 4-6-2.

2013, July 3   Perf. 13½
1062   Sheet of 10   9.50 9.50
a.-j. A377 46c Any single   .95   .95

Indian Headdresses — A378

No. 1063 — Inscription: a, Cheyenne Headress. b, Flathead Headress. c, American Indian Headress. d, Shoshone Headress. e, Assiniboine Headress.

2013, Aug. 8
1063   Horiz. strip of 5   4.75 4.75
a.-e. A378 46c Any single   .95   .95
"Headdress" is spelled incorrectly on Nos. 1063a-1063e.

Miniature Sheet

Landmark Events in American Civil Rights Movement — A379

No. 1064: a, Executive Order 9981, 1948. b, Brown v. Board of Education, 1954. c, Montgomery bus boycott, 1955. d, Little Rock Nine, 1957. e, Lunch counter sit-ins, 1960. f, Freedom Riders, 1961. g, Dr. Martin Luther King's "I Have a Dream" speech, 1963. h, Civil Rights Act, 1964. i, Selma March, 1965. j, Voting Rights Act, 1964.

2013, Aug. 28
1064 A379 46c Sheet of 10, #a-j   9.50 9.50

World War II Type of 2011
Miniature Sheet

No. 1065 — Inscriptions: a, Tenth Fleet: Overcoming the U-boat menace. b, U.S. Medical Service saving lives on the front lines. c, Allies invade Sicily: Patton's Seventh Army drives on Palermo. d, B-24 Liberators bomb Ploesti Oilfields. e, V-Mail — Letters from around the globe. f, Allied forces land at Salerno. g, Back the attack. h, Willie and Joe: A classic portrait of the American GI. i, Gold Star — Remembering those who died for a just cause — Freedom. j, U.S. Marines land on Tarawa Atoll.

2013, Sept. 9   Perf. 13½
1065 A342 46c Sheet of 10, #a-j,
             + 10 labels   9.50 9.50

Traditional Marshallese Children's Games — A380

No. 1066: a, Etobobo (4-1). b, Lejonjon (4-2). c, Lodidean (4-3). d, Didmakol (4-4).

2013, Sept. 27
1066   Horiz. strip of 4   4.00 4.00
a.-d. A380 46c Any single   .95   .95

Miniature Sheet

Restarting of Space Shuttle Program, 25th Anniv. — A381

No. 1067: a, Launch of Space Shuttle Discovery mission STS-95 (6-1). b, Launch, diff. (6-2). c, Space Shuttle Discoverey and U.S. flag (6-3). d, Space Shuttle Discovery in orbit (6-4). e, Astronaut working outside of Space Shuttle Discovery (6-5). f, U.S. flag, Space Shuttle Discovery on launch pad, Astronaut John Glenn (6-6).

2013, Sept. 29
1067 A381 46c Sheet of 6, #a-f   5.75 5.75

MARSHALL ISLANDS

World War II Aircraft — A382

No. 1068: a, F4U Corsair. b, C-46 Commando. c, A6M Zero. d, B-29 Superfortress. e, Bf 109. f, Ju 88. g, P-38 Lightning. h, A-26 Invader. i, B-17 Flying Fortress. j, P-51 Mustang. k, IL-2. l, P-40 Warhawk. m, C-47 Skytrain. n, B-24 Liberator. o, Spitfire. p, B-25 Mitchell. q, PBY Catalina. r, B-26 Marauder. s, TBM-1C Avenger. t, Lancaster. u, Yak-9. v, F6F Hellcat. w, C54 Skymaster. x, PB4Y-2 Privateer. y, P-47 Thunderbolt.

2013, Oct. 14
1068 A382 Sheet of 25, 24.00 24.00
a.-y. 46c Any single .95 .95

Christmas — A383

No. 1069: a, Annunciation (6-1). b, Journey to Bethlehem (6-2). c, Holy Family (6-3). d, Angel and shepherds (6-4). e, Magi (6-5). f, Nativity (6-6).

2013, Oct. 31 Litho. Perf. 13½
1069 A383 46c Block of 6, #a-f 5.75 5.75

Miniature Sheet

Gettysburg Address, 150th Anniv. — A384

No. 1070 — Soldiers and: a, U.S. Pres. Abraham Lincoln, U.S. flag (34x25mm). b, Confederate States Pres. Jefferson Davis, Confederate flag (34x25mm). c, Gen. Ulysses S. Grant, U.S. flag (34x25mm). d, Gen. Robert E. Lee, Confederate flag (34x25mm). e, U.S. and Confederate flags (48x50mm).

2013, Nov. 19 Litho. Perf. 13½
1070 A384 46c Sheet of 5, #a-e 4.75 4.75

Souvenir Sheet

Declaration of Thanksgiving Day as U.S. Federal Holiday, 150th Anniv. — A385

Perf. 13¼x13¾
2013, Nov. 28 Litho.
1071 A385 $2 multi 4.00 4.00

Military Aircraft Diagrams — A386

No. 1072: a, B-24D Liberator. b, F-104 Starfighter. c, KC-135 Stratotanker. d, AV-8B Harrier II. e, P40-Warhawk. f, F/A-18 Hornet. g, P-38 Lightning. h, F-100 Super Sabre. i, P-26 Peashooter. j, F-16 Fighting Falcon. k, TBD Devastator. l, F-15 Eagle. m, C-130 Hercules. n, F-105 Thunderchief. o, B-17 Flying Fortress.

2014, Jan. 12 Litho. Perf. 13½
1072 A386 46c Sheet of 15, #a-o 14.00 14.00
See Nos. 1082, 1090.

Souvenir Sheet

Marshall Islands Postal Service Authority, 30th Anniv. A387

2014, Jan. 22 Litho. Perf. 13¼x13½
1073 A387 $5.60 multi 11.50 11.50

Shells — A388

Reticulated helmet, New England neptune and Calico scallop shells, with largest being: 34c, Reticulated helmet. 49c, New England neptune. $1.15, Calico scallop.

2014, Jan. 26 Litho. Perf. 11¼x10¼
1074 A388 34c multi .70 .70
1075 A388 49c multi 1.00 1.00
1076 A388 $1.15 multi 2.40 2.40
Nos. 1074-1076 (3) 4.10 4.10
See Nos. 1083-1084, 1090-1094.

Miniature Sheet

New Year 2014 (Year of the Horse) A389

No. 1077 — Color of horse: a, Blue (4-1). b, Red brown (4-2). c, Golden brown (4-3). d, Green (4-4).

2014, Jan. 31 Litho. Perf. 13½
1077 A389 $1.15 Sheet of 4, #a-d 9.25 9.25

Insects — A390

No. 1078: a, Garden insects, red panels (10-1). b, Checkered beetle (10-2). c, Lacewing (10-3). d, Red admiral butterfly (10-4). e, Honey bee (10-5). f, Leaf skeletonizer (10-6). g, Drone fly (10-7). h, Bumblebee (10-8). i, Lamellicorn beetle (10-9). j, Garden insects, blue panels (10-10).

2014, Mar. 1 Litho. Perf. 13½
1078 Block of 10 10.00 10.00
a.-j. A390 49c Any single 1.00 1.00

Castles in Great Britain — A391

No. 1079: a, Carrickfergus Castle, Northern Ireland (4-1). b, Windsor Castle, England (4-2). c, Caernarfon Castle, Wales (4-3). d, Edinburgh Castle, Scotland (4-4).

2014, Mar. 15 Litho. Perf. 13½
1079 Horiz. strip of 4 9.75 9.75
a.-d. A391 $1.15 Any single 2.40 2.40

Miniature Sheet

Historical Flags of the United States A392

No. 1080: a, Continental flag (15-1). b, Bennington flag (15-2). c, Forster flag (15-3). d, Sons of Liberty flag (15-4). e, Brandywine flag (15-5). f, Pierre L'Enfant flag (15-6). g, Indian Peace flag (15-7). h, Star Spangled Banner (15-8). i, Great Star flag (15-9). j, Fort Sumter flag (15-10). k, Centennial flag (15-11). l, 29-star flag (15-12). m, 38-star flag (15-13). n, 48-star flag (15-14). o, 50-star flag (15-15).

2014, Apr. 4 Litho. Perf. 13½
1080 A392 49c Sheet of 15, #a-o, + 9 labels 15.00 15.00

Miniature Sheet

Traditional Costumes of European Countries — A393

No. 1081: a, Switzerland (20-1). b, Monaco (20-2). c, Luxembourg (20-3). d, Spain (20-4). e, Belgium (20-5). f, Denmark (20-6). g, Italy (20-7). h, Ireland (20-8). i, Norway (20-9). j, Great Britain (20-10). k, Portugal (20-11). l, Turkey (20-12). m, France (20-13). n, Sweden (20-14). o, Iceland (20-15). p, Germany (20-16). q, Netherlands (20-17). r, Greece (20-18). s, Liechtenstein (20-19). t, Finland (20-20).

2014, May 10 Litho. Perf. 13½
1081 A393 49c Sheet of 20, #a-t 20.00 20.00

Military Aircraft Diagrams Type of 2014

Miniature Sheet

No. 1082: a, F-80 Shooting Star. b, SR-71 Blackbird. c, U-2. d, F-86 Sabre. e, F-14 Tomcat. f, F6F Hellcat. g, P-47 Thunderbolt. h, F-117 Nighthawk. i, C-5 Galaxy. j, B-52 Stratofortress. k, F-4 Phantom II. l, P-51 Mustang. m, SBD Dauntless. n, B-1 Lancer. o, PBY-5 Catalina.

2014, June 2 Litho. Perf. 13½
1082 A386 49c Sheet of 15, #a-o 15.00 15.00

Shells Type of 2014

Various shells with largest being: 4c, Hawkwinged conch. $19.99, Frilled dogwinkle.

2014, June 16 Litho. Perf. 11¼x10¼
1083 A388 4c multi .25 .25
1084 A388 $19.99 multi 40.00 40.00

Trees A394

No. 1085: a, White willow (6-1). b, Poplar (6-2). c, Oak (6-3). d, Birch (6-4). e, Maple (6-5). f, Larch (6-6).

2014, July 7 Litho. Perf. 13½
1085 A394 49c Block of 6, #a-f 6.00 6.00

Souvenir Sheet

Opening of Panama Canal, Cent. A395

2014, Aug. 15 Litho. Perf. 13x13½
1086 A395 $5.60 multi 11.50 11.50

Miniature Sheet

Amphibians and Reptiles — A396

No. 1087: a, Golden mantella frog (12-1). b, Carpet chameleon (12-2). c, Emerald tree boa (12-3). d, Dyeing poison dart frog (12-4). e, Golfodulcean poison frog (12-5). f, Peruvian rainbow boa (12-6). g, Panther chameleon (12-7). h, Tomato frog (12-8). i, Red & blue poison frog (12-9). j, Flap-necked chameleon (12-10). k, Amazon tree boa (12-11). l, Yellow-banded poison dart frog (12-12).

2014, Aug. 21 Litho. Perf. 13½
1087 A396 49c Sheet of 12, #a-l 12.00 12.00

Souvenir Sheet

Writing of "The Star-Spangled Banner," 200th Anniv. — A397

2014, Sept. 3 Litho. Perf. 13x13½
1088 A397 $5.60 multi 11.50 11.50

World War II Type of 2011

Miniature Sheet

No. 1089 — Inscriptions: a, Allied Forces retake New Guinea. b, 2,000 U.S. planes attack Berlin and 2 aircraft plants near city. c, Invasion is on! d, Airborne units spearhead ground attacks. e, Submarine warfare cripple Japan's shipping routes. f, Paris and Rome liberated by Allies. g, Operation Forager. h, Red Ball Express speeds vital supplies to allies. i, Battle for Leyte Gulf. j, Battle of the Bulge.

2014, Sept. 15 Litho. Perf. 13½
1089 A342 49c Sheet of 10, #a-j, + 10 labels 10.00 10.00

Shells Type of 2014

Various shells.

MARSHALL ISLANDS

Perf. 11¼x10¼

2014, Sept. 18			Litho.		
1090	A388	$5.75 multi		11.50	11.50
1091	A388	$5.95 multi		12.00	12.00
1092	A388	$6.10 multi		12.50	12.50
1093	A388	$12.65 multi		25.50	25.50
1094	A388	$17.90 multi		36.00	36.00
	Nos. 1090-1094 (5)			97.50	97.50

Movie Monsters — A398

No. 1095: a, Count Dracula holding candle (10-1). b, Frankenstein's Monster near stairway (10-2). c, Phantom of the Opera without mask (10-3). d, The Mummy carrying woman (10-4). e, The Wolf Man crouching (10-5). f, Count Dracula at open window (10-6). g, Frankenstein's Monster in laboratory (10-7). h, Phantom of the Opera wearing mask (10-8). i, The Mummy and skull (10-9). j, The Wolf Man and wolf (10-10).

2014, Oct. 14		Litho.	Perf. 13½		
1095	A398	49c Block of 10, #a-j		10.00	10.00

Christmas — A399

No. 1096: a, Singing angels (6-1). b, Shepherd with flock (6-2). c, Three Kings following star (6-3). d, Three Kings at manger (6-4). e, Mary and Baby Jesus (6-5). f, White doves (6-6).

2014, Oct. 10		Litho.	Perf. 13½		
1096	A399	49c Block of 6, #a-f		6.00	6.00

Seahorses — A400

No. 1097: a, Horned seahorse (4-1). b, Lined seahorse (4-2). c, Lined seahorse, diff. (4-3). d, Lined seahorse, diff. (4-4).

2014, Oct. 20		Litho.	Perf. 13½		
1097		Horiz. strip of 4		4.00	4.00
a.-d.	A400	49c Any single		1.00	1.00

Military Aircraft Diagrams Type of 2014
Miniature Sheet

No. 1098: a, Fokker D VII. b, J35 Draaken. c, Bf 109. d, Yak 9. e, MiG 29. f, A-10 Thunderbolt II. g, Me 262. h, B-2 Spirit. i, Spitfire. j, B-29 Superfortress. k, X-15. l, Lancaster. m, A6M Zero. n, F/A 22. o, J1 Monoplane.

2014, Oct. 28			Perf. 13½		
1098	A386	49c Sheet of 15, #a-o		15.00	15.00

Space Adventure for Children — A404

2014, Nov. 7		Litho.	Perf. 13½		
1099		Strip of 4		4.00	4.00
a.	A401	49c multi		1.00	1.00
b.	A402	49c multi		1.00	1.00
c.	A403	49c multi		1.00	1.00
d.	A404	49c multi		1.00	1.00

Flowers — A405

No. 1100: a, Six flowers including thistle at LL (10-1). b, Lily (10-2). c, Iris (10-3). d, Thistles (10-4). e, Rose (10-5). f, Pansy (10-6). g, Strawberries and blossom (10-7). h, Tulip (10-8). i, Three pansies (10-9). j, Five flowers and strawberry at bottom center (10-10).

2014, Nov. 18		Litho.	Perf. 13½		
1100		Block of 10		10.00	10.00
a.-j.	A405	49c Any single		1.00	1.00

Greetings — A406

No. 1101: a, Happy birthday. b, Thinking of you. c, Love. d, Thank you. e, Best wishes. f, Congratulations.

2015, Jan. 5		Litho.	Perf. 13½		
1101	A406	49c Block of 6, #a-f		6.00	6.00

Dinosaur Skeletons — A407

No. 1102: a, Triceratops. b, Stegosaurus. c, Protoceratops. d, Tyrannosaurus.

2015, Jan. 15		Litho.	Perf. 13½		
1102		Horiz. strip of 4		2.80	2.80
a.-d.	A407	34c Any single		.70	.70

Reef Life Type of 1993
Miniature Sheet

No. 1103: a, Butterflyfish. b, Soldierfish. c, Damselfish. d, Filefish. e, Hawkfish. f, Surgeonfish. g, Parrotfish (75x33mm).

2015, Jan. 28			Perf. 13½		
1103		Sheet of 7		17.00	17.00
a.-f.	A79	$1 Any single		2.00	2.00
g.	A79	$2.50 multi		5.00	5.00

Berries — A408

No. 1104: a, Blueberries. b, Raspberries. c, Blackberries, raspberries, strawberries and blueberries. d, Strawberries. e, Blackberries.

2015, Feb. 14		Litho.	Perf. 13½		
1104		Horiz. strip of 5		5.00	5.00
a.-e.	A408	49c Any single		1.00	1.00

New Year 2015 (Year of the Ram) A409
Miniature Sheet

No. 1105 — Color of ram: a, Blue (4-1). b, Red brown (4-2). c, Yellow brown (4-3). d, Green (4-4).

2015, Feb. 19		Litho.	Perf. 13½		
1105	A409	$1.15 Sheet of 4, #a-d		9.25	9.25

Rays — A410

Designs: 7c, Manta rays. 22c, Spotted eagle rays. 35c, Spotted eagle rays, diff. $1.20, Southern stingray.

Perf. 11¼x10¼

2015, Feb. 23			Litho.		
1106	A410	7c multi		.25	.25
1107	A410	22c multi		.45	.45
1108	A410	35c multi		.70	.70
1109	A410	$1.20 multi		2.40	2.40
	Nos. 1106-1109 (4)			3.80	3.80

Seashells Type of 1998 Redrawn

No. 1110: a, Chicoreus brunneus. b, Cypraea aurantium. c, Lambis chiragra. d, Tridacna squamosa.

2015, Feb. 26		Litho.	Perf. 13½		
Stamps With White Frames					
1110		Horiz. strip of 4		4.00	4.00
a.-d.	A137	49c Any single		1.00	1.00

Canoes Type of 1997 Redrawn

No. 1111: a, Pacific Arts Festival canoe Walap of Enewetak. b, Large voyaging canoe Walap of Jaluit. c, Racing canoe Kôr Kôr. d, Sailing canoe Tipnol of Ailuk.

2015, Mar. 10		Litho.	Perf. 13½		
Stamps With White Frames					
1111		Vert. strip of 4		4.00	4.00
a.-d.	A129	49c Any single		1.00	1.00

Ships Type of 1999

No. 1112: a, Galleon Los Reyes, Spain, 1568. b, Frigate Dolphin, Great Britain, 1767. c, Bark Scarborough, Great Britain, 1788. d, Brig Rurik, Russia, 1817.

2015, Mar. 18		Litho.	Perf. 13½		
Stamps With Tan Frames					
1112	A162	49c Horiz. strip of 4, #a-d		4.00	4.00

Miniature Sheet

Marine Life A411

No. 1113: a, Blue tang. b, Loggerhead turtle. c, Hammerhead shark. d, Commerson's dolphin. e, Humpback whale. f, Seahorse. g, Peale's porpoise. h, Sea anemone. i, Bowhead whale. j, Flying gurnard. k, Spotted trunkfish. l, Foureye butterflyfish. m, Bottlenose dolphin. n, Blue whale. o, Blue shark.

2015, Apr. 13		Litho.	Perf. 13½		
1113	A411	49c Sheet of 15, #a-o		15.00	15.00

Souvenir Sheet

Penny Black, 175th Anniv. A412

2015, May 1		Litho.	Perf. 13¼x13½		
1114	A412	$5.60 black		11.50	11.50

Souvenir Sheet

End of American Civil War, 150th Anniv. — A413

2015, May 1		Litho.	Perf. 13¼x13½		
1115	A413	$5.60 multi		11.50	11.50

Miniature Sheet

Postal Relics A414

No. 1116 — Mailboxes and other postal-related items from: a, Sweden. b, Germany. c, Australia. d, Canada. e, Great Britain. f, Switzerland. g, France. h, United States. i, Austria. j, Japan. k, Brazil. l, China.

2015, June 5		Litho.	Perf. 13½		
1116	A414	49c Sheet of 12, #a-l		12.00	12.00

Miniature Sheet

Birds A415

No. 1117: a, Red-billed hornbill. b, Great black-backed gull. c, Barn owl. d, Eastern white pelican. e, Sea eagle. f, Tibetan eared pheasant. g, Hermit ibis. h, Common heron. i, Bearded vulture. j, Kingfisher. k, White-breasted cormorant. l, White egret. m, Broadwinged hawk. n, Greater flamingo. o, Peregrine falcon.

2015, July 7		Litho.	Perf. 13½		
1117	A415	49c Sheet of 15, #a-o		15.00	15.00

Souvenir Sheet

Apollo-Soyuz Space Mission, 40th Anniv. — A416

2015, July 17		Litho.	Perf. 13x13½		
1118	A416	$3 multi		6.00	6.00
a.		Inscribed "40th Anniversary"		6.00	6.00

No. 1118 is incorrectly inscribed "30th anniversary."

National Buildings and Symbols — A417

MARSHALL ISLANDS

Designs: No. 1119, Capitol Building. No. 1120, Nitijela (Legislature Building). No. 1121, National seal and Nitijela, vert. No. 1122, National flag and Nitijela, vert.

2015, Aug. 3   Litho.   Perf. 11¼x10¼
1119	A417	$1.20 multi	2.40	2.40
1120	A417	$1.20 multi	2.40	2.40

Perf. 10¼x11¼
1121	A417	$1.20 multi	2.40	2.40
1122	A417	$1.20 multi	2.40	2.40
	Nos. 1119-1122 (4)		9.60	9.60

World War II Type of 2011

No. 1123 — Inscriptions: a, Marines take Suribachi, chief point on Iwo. b, MacArthur back in Luzon. c, Marines land on Okinawa, push forward from beachhead. d, U.S. and Russian soldiers link-up at Elbe River. e, Allied forces liberate concentration camps. f, The war in Europe is ended. g, War uproots millions, Europe filled with refugees. h, First atomic bomb dropped on Japan. i, War over, Japan surrenders unconditionally. j, The war is ended! U.S. troops return home.

2015, Aug. 22   Litho.   Perf. 13½
1123	A342	49c Sheet of 10, #a-j, + 10 labels	10.00	10.00

Voyages of Discovery Type of 1992 Redrawn

No. 1124: a, Traditional tipnol (39x32m). b, Reconstructed Santa Maria (39x32mm). c, Constellation Argo Navis (39x32mm). d, Marshallese sailor, tipnol (39x32mm). e, Christopher Columbus, Santa Maria (39x32mm). f, Astronaut, Argo Navis (39x32mm). g, Columbus, sailor, and astronaut (75x32mm).

Perf. 13¼x13½
2015, Sept. 11   Litho.
1124		Sheet of 7	17.00	17.00
a.-f.	A76	$1 Any single	2.00	2.00
g.	A76	$2.50 multi	5.00	5.00

Souvenir Sheet

German Reunification, 25th Anniv. — A418

2015, Oct. 3   Litho.   Perf. 13¼x13¾
1125	A418	$5.60 multi	11.50	11.50

Mammals — A419

No. 1126: a, Snow leopard (15-1). b, Pampas deer (15-2). c, Musk ox (15-3). d, Maned wolf (15-4). e, Okapi (15-5). f, Chinese yellow bull (15-6). g, Chinese porcupine (15-7). h, Arabian oryx (15-8). i, Clawless otter (15-9). j, Siberian tiger (15-10). k, Bridled nail-tailed wallaby (15-11). l, Jaguar (15-12). m, Hairy-nosed wombat (15-13). n, Chimpanzee (15-14). o, Polar bear (15-15).

2015, Oct. 9   Litho.   Perf. 13½
1126		Sheet of 15	15.00	15.00
a.-o.	A419	49c Any single	1.00	1.00

Miniature Sheets

Christmas — A420

No. 1127, vert. — Four identical snowflakes in various sizes with stamp numbered: a, (10-1). b, (10-2). c, (10-3). d, (10-4). e, (10-5). f, (10-6). g, (10-7). h, (10-8). i, (10-9). j, (10-10).

No. 1128 — Five different snowflakes with stamp numbered: a, (4-1). b, (4-2). c, (4-3). d, (4-4).

2015, Oct. 20   Litho.   Perf. 13½
1127	A420	49c Sheet of 10, #a-j	10.00	10.00
1128	A420	$1.20 Sheet of 4, #a-d	9.75	9.75

Legends A421

No. 1129: a, Kijeek An Letao (8-1). b, Mennin Jobwodda (8-2). c, Wa Koñe, Waan Letao (8-3). d, Kouj (8-4). e, The Large Pool of Mejit (8-5). f, The Beautiful Woman of Kwajalein (8-6). g, Sharks and Lowakalle Reef (8-7). h, The Demon of Adrie (8-8).

2015, Nov. 5   Litho.   Perf. 13½
1129	A421	49c Block of 8, #a-h	8.00	8.00

Miniature Sheet

Haiku A422

No. 1130: a, Pebbles in the shoals, barely visible, scattered by the metronome (20-1). b, Unnoticed by the sun, the fishing boat drifts past empty cabanas (20-2). c, The harmony of the waterfall is older than the waterfall (20-3). d, Murmuring dunes hide the land from the sea, keeping their secrets separate (20-4). e, Waving columns of sandpipers parade through the surf for all to see (20-5). f, Sometimes even the sailor mistakes the ocean for oblivion (20-6). g, Left ashore by the tide, a shining parliament of broken coral (20-7). h, Then, a tiny cloud begins to dance. The sun has worn a brand new dress (20-8). i, As noon sang, it was clear in the lagoon as it was in the sky (20-9). j, Under jagged waves, chandeliers of sanded glass sway among the fish (20-10). k, Twice the butterfly knocks at the window, making the quietest noise (20-11). l, To truly reshape the landscape, one must have the patience of water (20-12). m, Always-changing clouds float by, never revealing their white mystery (20-13). n, Above the sunburned beaches, beyond the rainbow fleet to some stars (20-14). o, The fluttering sail, the gathering storm, both with a promise to keep (20-15). p, The stone path leading down to the shore disappears into the ocean (20-16). q, The day passed without a remark from the sun or the wind. Just warm rain. (20-17). r, The canoe holds a bed of pandanus leaves for the journey ahead (20-18). s, Past shimmering reefs, to bluest deep, where even fish need submarines (20-19). t, What the night really wants at the end of the day is to be set free (20-20).

2016, Jan. 5   Litho.   Perf. 13½
1130	A422	49c Sheet of 20, #a-t	20.00	20.00

See No. 1151.

Souvenir Sheet

First Commercial Flight of the Concorde, 40th Anniv. — A423

2016, Jan. 21   Litho.   Perf. 13x13½
1131	A423	$4 multi	8.00	8.00

Miniature Sheet

New Year 2016 (Year of the Monkey) A424

No. 1132 — Color of monkey: a, Deep violet (4-1). b, Red brown (4-2). c, Yellow brown (4-3). d, Green (4-4).

2016, Feb. 8   Litho.   Perf. 13½
1132	A424	$1.20 Sheet of 4, #a-d	9.75	9.75

Miniature Sheet

Wildlife A425

No. 1133: a, Starfish (10-1). b, Common dolphins (10-2). c, Blue whales (10-3). d, Megapode (10-4). e, Leatherback turtle (10-5). f, Doves (10-6). g, Hawksbill turtle (10-7). h, Goruper (10-8). i, Manta rays (10-9). j, Tuna (10-10).

2016, Mar. 3   Litho.   Perf. 13½
1133	A425	49c Sheet of 10, #a-j	10.00	10.00

Miniature Sheets

Seals of the States of the Union A426

No. 1134: a, Delaware (10-1). b, Pennsylvania (10-2). c, New Jersey (10-3). d, Georgia (10-4). e, Connecticut (10-5). f, Massachusetts (10-6). g, Maryland (10-7). h, South Carolina (10-8). i, New Hampshire (10-9). j, Virginia (10-10).
No. 1135: a, New York (10-1). b, North Carolina (10-2). c, Rhode Island (10-3). d, Vermont (10-4). e, Kentucky (10-5). f, Tennessee (10-6). g, Ohio (10-7). h, Louisiana (10-8). i, Indiana (10-9). j, Mississippi (10-10).
No. 1136: a, Illinois (10-1). b, Alabama (10-2). c, Maine (10-3). d, Missouri (10-4). e, Arkansas (10-5). f, Michigan (10-6). g, Florida (10-7). h, Texas (10-8). i, Iowa (10-9). j, Wisconsin (10-10).
No. 1137: a, California (10-1). b, Minnesota (10-2). c, Oregon (10-3). d, Kansas (10-4). e, West Virginia (10-5). f, Nevada (10-6). g, Nebraska (10-7). h, Colorado (10-8). i, North Dakota (10-9). j, South Dakota (10-10).
No. 1138: a, Montana (10-1). b, Washington (10-2). c, Idaho (10-3). d, Wyoming (10-4). e, Utah (10-5). f, Oklahoma (10-6). g, New Mexico (10-7). h, Arizona (10-8). i, Alaska (10-9). j, Hawaii (10-10).

2016   Litho.   Perf. 11¾
1134	A426	49c Sheet of 10, #a-j	10.00	10.00
1135	A426	49c Sheet of 10, #a-j	10.00	10.00
1136	A426	49c Sheet of 10, #a-j	10.00	10.00
1137	A426	49c Sheet of 10, #a-j	10.00	10.00
1138	A426	49c Sheet of 10, #a-j	10.00	10.00
	Nos. 1134-1138 (5)		50.00	50.00

Issued: No. 1134, 4/4; No. 1135, 5/12; No. 1136, 5/24; No. 1137, 6/8; No. 1138, 9/2.

Miniature Sheet

Queen Elizabeth II, 90th Birthday A427

No. 1139 — Hat color: a, Blue (6-1). b, Yellow (6-2). c, Peach (6-3). d, Red violet (6-4). e, Purple (6-5). f, Green gray (6-6).

2016, Apr. 21   Litho.   Perf. 13½
1139	A427	90c Sheet of 6, #a-f	11.00	11.00

Semaphore Symbols — A428

No. 1140 — Flag position for: a, "A" and "1" (30-1). b, "B" and "2" (30-2). c, "C" and "3" (30-3). d, "D" and "4" (30-4). e, "E" and "5" (30-5). f, "F" and "6" (30-6). g, "G" and "7" (30-7). h, "H" and "8" (30-8). i, "I" and "9" (30-9). j, "J" (30-10). k, "K" and "0" (30-11). l, "L" (30-12). m, "M" (30-13). n, "N" (30-14). o, "O" (30-15). p, "P" (30-16). q, "Q" (30-17). r, "R" (30-18). s, "S" (30-19). t, "T" (30-20). u, "U" (30-21). v, "V" (30-22). w, "W" (30-23). x, "X" (30-24). y, "Y" (30-25). z, "Z" (30-26). aa, Numeric (30-27). ab, Attention (30-28). ac, Cancel (30-29). ad, Space (30-30).

2016, July 5   Litho.   Perf. 13½
1140		Sheet of 30	30.00	30.00
a.-ad.	A428	49c Any single	1.00	1.00

Miniature Sheet

Paintings by Howard Koslow (1924-2016), Stamp Designer — A429

No. 1141: a, Montgolfier Hot Air Balloon (20-1). b, Roosevelt and Churchill (20-2). c, Astronaut on Moon (20-3). d, To the Heroes of Desert Storm-Eagle (20-4). e, Marines Raising Flag on Mt. Suribachi (20-5). f, Count Basie (20-6). g, Saturn with Voyager 2 (20-7). h, 15th Anniversary of RMI Constitution (20-8). i, Various Minerals (20-9). j, U.S. Liberates Marshall Islands (20-10). k, Freedom of Worship (20-11). l, Circus Elephant (20-12). m, Woman Kneading Breadfruit Dough (20-13). n, China Folk Houses/View of Village (20-14). o, Morris Island Lighthouse (20-15). p, Firemen Raising the American Flag (20-16). q, MacArthur Evacuated from Corregidor (20-17). r, Freddie Stowers (20-18). s, Montage of U.S. Space Vehicles (20-19). t, James "Jimmy" Doolittle (20-20).

2016, July 20   Litho.   Perf. 13½
1141	A429	49c Sheet of 20, #a-t	20.00	20.00

Peace Doves A430

No. 1142: a, Three doves, Swords into Plowshares statue (6-1). b, Four doves, Japanese Peace Bell (6-2). c, Dove and Earth II (6-3). d, Hands Releasing Dove (6-4). e, Dove and Earth (6-5). f, Peace Dove with Horse and Rider (6-6).

2016, Aug. 5   Litho.   Perf. 13½
1142	A430	49c Block of 6, #a-f	6.00	6.00

MARSHALL ISLANDS

Souvenir Sheet

Marshall Islands Constitution Committee — A431

2016, Sept. 16   Litho.   *Perf. 13x13½*
1143   A431   98c multi   2.00   2.00

Souvenir Sheet

Marshall Islands Sovereignty, 30th Anniv. — A432

2016, Oct. 21   Litho.   *Perf. 13x13½*
1144   A432 $3 multi   6.00   6.00

Miniature Sheets

Christmas — A433

No. 1145 — Ornaments shaped like: a, Star (10-1). b, Gingerbread man (10-2). c, Mitten (10-3). d, Christmas tree (10-4). e, Candy cane (10-5). f, Wreath (10-6). g, Gift (10-7). h, Santa Claus (10-8). i, Christmas stocking (10-9). j, Poinsettia (10-10).

No. 1146, horiz. — Ornaments shaped like: a, Christmas tree (4-1). b, Christmas stocking (4-2). c, Candy cane (4-3). d, Gift (4-4).

2016, Nov. 3   Litho.   *Perf. 13½*
1145   A433   49c Sheet of 10, #a-j   10.00   10.00
1146   A433 $1.20 Sheet of 4, #a-d   9.75   9.75

Souvenir Sheet

Attack on Pearl Harbor, 75th Anniv. A434

2016, Dec. 7   Litho.   *Perf. 13x13½*
1147   A434 $5.75 multi   11.50   11.50

Miniature Sheet

United States National Park Service, Cent. A435

No. 1148 — National Parks: a, Denali (10-1). b, Crater Lake (10-2). c, Haleakala (10-3). d, Yellowstone (10-4). e, Glacier (10-5). f, Everglades (10-6). g, Grand Canyon (10-7). h, Great Smoky Mountains (10-8). i, Yosemite (10-9). j, Isle Royale (10-10).

2016, Dec. 15   Litho.   *Perf. 13½*
1148   A435   49c Sheet of 10, #a-j   10.00   10.00

See Nos. 1156, 1168.

Miniature Sheet

Fireworks — A436

No. 1149 — Various fireworks displays numbered: a, (10-1). b, (10-2). c, (10-3). d, (10-4). e, (10-5). f, (10-6). g, (10-7). h, (10-8). i, (10-9). j, (10-10).

2017, Jan. 2   Litho.   *Perf. 13½*
1149   A436   49c Sheet of 10, #a-j   10.00   10.00

Miniature Sheet

New Year 2017 (Year of the Rooster) A437

No. 1150 — Color of rooster: a, Greenish blue (4-1). b, Chestnut (4-2). c, Ochre (4-3). d, Deep blue green (4-4).

2017, Jan. 28   Litho.   *Perf. 13½*
1150   A437 $1.20 Sheet of 4, #a-d   9.75   9.75

Haiku Type of 2016
Miniature Sheet

No. 1151: a, Because of how light works, everything we see is only reflection (20-1). b, All that remained when the moon broke the clouds was the rabbit's silhouette (20-2). c, The grass has every intention of reaching all the way to the sky (20-3). d, The mountain lake was so still that either bird could have been the real one (20-4). e, As the great river bends, it is not the water that turns but the land (20-5). f, Whatever happens, the sparrows still wing their way every afternoon (20-6). g, The chief dreamed only of the great eagle, who dreamed only of the clouds (20-7). h, From the planets to the humble bees, such divine choreography (20-8). i, The first leaf from the tree is the most tentative, and yet the most brave (20-9). j, There is an endless joy which transcends the finite pain of living things (20-10). k, Imperceptible, the moments between moments make all the difference (20-11). l, The sound of the leaves and the sound of the ocean are from the same song (20-12). m, A subtle madness compels the moon to challenge the sun for the night (20-13). n, Rejoice in small things, let them fill you, as starlight fills the mountain sky (20-14). o, Even clouds holding nothing tend to appear at the right time and place (20-15). p, The fleeting thought which preceded morning flight was known but to the bird (20-16). q, If one could chart the path of but a single cloud, one would know all things (20-17). r, Consider the red leaf, and how it is every color except red (20-18). s, Between two branches, the space where a blackbird once was, or might have been (20-19). t, Each ending has two beginnings: the one before and the one after (20-20).

2017, Feb. 22   Litho.   *Perf. 13½*
Red Brown Stamps
1151   A422   49c Sheet of 20, #a-t   20.00   20.00

Miniature Sheet

Flowers A438

No. 1152: a, Plumeria (10-1). b, Hibiscus (10-2). c, Primrose willow (10-3). d, Annona muricata (10-4). e, Globe amaranth (10-5). f, Arrowleaf elephant's ear (10-6). g, Field pumpkin (10-7). h, Asiatic pennywort (10-8). i, Fire on the mountain (10-9). j, Polynesian arrowroot (10-10).

2017, Mar. 3   Litho.   *Perf. 13½*
1152   A438   49c Sheet of 10, #a-j   10.00   10.00

Miniature Sheet

Paintings of China Clipper Seaplane — A439

No. 1153 — Painting by: a, John Swatsley (6-1). b, Jim Butcher (6-2). c, Steve Ferguson (6-3). d, Basil Smith (6-4). e, Butcher, diff. (6-5). f, Swatsley, diff. (6-6).

2017, Mar. 21   Litho.   *Perf. 13½*
1153   A439   49c Sheet of 6, #a-f   6.00   6.00

Miniature Sheet

Photographs by John Clark Helzer — A440

No. 1154: a, Yosemite Majesty (10-1). b, Tin Mine at St. Agnes (10-2). c, Colorado Sunset (10-3). d, Flatirons (10-4). e, White Cliffs (10-5). f, Cliffs of Moher (10-6). g, Dartmoor (10-7). h, Wyoming Sunrise (10-8). i, The Burren (10-9). j, Brittany Coast (10-10).

2017, Apr. 4   Litho.   *Perf. 13½*
1154   A440   49c Sheet of 10, #a-j   10.00   10.00

Miniature Sheet

Jazz and Blues Instruments — A441

No. 1155: a, Piano (10-1). b, Clarinet (10-2). c, Microphone (10-3). d, Banjo (10-4). e, Trumpet (10-5). f, Saxophone (10-6). g, Bass (10-7). h, Drums (10-8). i, Electric guitar (10-9). j, Vibraphone (10-10).

2017, Apr. 25   Litho.   *Perf. 13½*
1155   A441   49c Sheet of 10, #a-j   10.00   10.00

U.S. National Parks Type of 2016
Miniature Sheet

No. 1156 — National Parks: a, Sequoia (10-1). b, Badlands (10-2). c, Arches (10-3). d, Olympic (10-4). e, Guadalupe (10-5). f, Acadia (10-6). g, Mammoth Cave (10-7). h, Glacier Bay (10-8). i, Petrified Forest (10-9). j, Rocky Mountain (10-10).

2017, May 10   Litho.   *Perf. 13½*
1156   A435   49c Sheet of 10, #a-j   10.00   10.00

Souvenir Sheet

Eternal Flame at Arlington National Cemetery Grave of Pres. John F. Kennedy (1917-63) — A442

2017, May 29   Litho.   *Perf. 13x13½*
1157   A442 $1 multi   2.00   2.00

Souvenir Sheet

Fallingwater, Designed by Frank Lloyd Wright (1867-1959) — A443

2017, June 8   Litho.   *Perf. 13x13½*
1158   A443 $1.50 multi   3.00   3.00

Miniature Sheet

World Youth A444

No. 1159: a, Gathering peat in Ireland (20-1). b, Lapland youth with pet reindeer (20-2). c, Boy fishing with his dog (20-3). d, Children in the mountains (20-4). e, Children listening to woman in garden (20-5). f, Waiting for a parade (20-6). g, Children joined in galloping games (20-7). h, Children walking with a dog (20-8). i, Girl helping care for baby (20-9). j, Watching Punch and Judy puppet play (20-10). k, Family singing around piano (20-11). l, Breaking the piñata (20-12). m, Boys on bicycles (20-13). n, Family walking to work (20-14). o, Family enjoying a new camera (20-15). p, Feeding the farmyard geese (20-16). q, Children running in the mountains (20-17). r, Playing near Mermaid statue (20-18). s, Building a snowman (20-19). t, Children harvesting grapes (20-20).

2017, June 29   Litho.   *Perf. 13½*
1159   A444   49c Sheet of 20, #a-t   20.00   20.00

Miniature Sheet

Atolls of the Marshall Islands A445

No. 1160: a, Ailinglaplap (10-1). b, Arno (10-2). c, Ebon (10-3). d, Jaluit (10-4). e, Kwajalein (10-5). f, Majuro (10-6). g, Maloelap (10-7). h, Mili (10-8). i, Namu (10-9). j, Wotje (10-10).

2017, July 13   Litho.   *Perf. 13½*
1160   A445   49c Sheet of 10, #a-j   10.00   10.00

Miniature Sheet

Art of Paul Calle (1928-2010) — A446

No. 1161: a, Charlie Chaplin's "Little Tramp" (20-1). b, Grand Canyon (20-2). c, Harry Truman and the United Nations (20-3). d, The First Step of Man on the Moon (20-4). e, Sporty Cars (20-5). f, Navajo Indian Portrait (20-6). g, The Vietnam War (20-7). h, In Remembrance of September 11, 2001 (20-8). i, The Quest for a Better Future (20-9). j, Lindbergh Flight (20-10). k, Jets Shrink Time and Distance (20-11). l, Computer Age Dawns (20-12). m, Scientists Probe Secrets of Life (20-13). n, Franklin Roosevelt New Deal (20-14). o, Vietnam Veterans Memorial (20-15). p, Pioneer 10 (20-16). q, 50th Anniversary of the United Nations (20-17). r, First Vote (20-18). s,

MARSHALL ISLANDS

Streamlined Design Symbolizes Bright Future (20-19). t, Kennedy's Dream of Man on the Moon (20-20).

2017, Aug. 4   Litho.   Perf. 13½
1161   A446   49c Sheet of 20, #a-t   20.00   20.00

Miniature Sheet

Steamboats — A447

No. 1162: a, Experiment, flag left of smokestack (10-1). b, Phoenix, sails up (10-2). c, New Orleans, steamship name in white (10-3). d, Washington (10-4). e, Walk in the Water, steamboat name in black (10-5). f, Experiment, flag right of smokestack (10-6). g, Phoenix, sails down (10-7). h, New Orleans, steamship name in black (10-8). i, Washington, rowboat in foreground (10-9). j, Walk in the Water, steamboat name in white (10-10).

2017, Aug. 21   Litho.   Perf. 13½
1162   A447   49c Sheet of 10, #a-j   10.00   10.00

Miniature Sheet

Fire Dancers A448

No. 1163 — Various photographs of fire dancers by John Clark Helzer numbered: a, (6-1). b, (6-2). c, (6-3). d, (6-4). e, (6-5). f, (6-6).

2017, Sept. 1   Litho.   Perf. 13½
1163   A448   49c Sheet of 6, #a-f   6.00   6.00

Souvenir Sheet

Launch of Queen Elizabeth 2 Ocean Liner, 50th Anniv. A449

2017, Sept. 20   Litho.   Perf. 13½x13
1164   A449 $5 multi   10.00   10.00

Miniature Sheet

Eyes of Nature A450

No. 1165 — Eye of: a, Eagle (10-1). b, Gecko (10-2). c, Human (10-3). d, Frog (10-4). e, Macaw (10-5). f, Crocodile (10-6). g, Cat (10-7). h, Fish (10-8). i, Dog (10-9). j, Chameleon (10-10).

2017, Oct. 4   Litho.   Perf. 13½
1165   A450   49c Sheet of 10, #a-j   10.00   10.00

Miniature Sheets

Christmas — A452

No. 1166: a, Shepherd with lamb (6-1). b, Mary and Joseph with Baby Jesus (6-2). c, Wise man offering frankincense (6-3). d, Mary and Baby Jesus (6-4). e, Joseph and Baby Jesus (6-5). f, Animals in the stable (6-6).
No. 1167: a, Horse-drawn sleighs (4-1). b, Couple dragging cut Christmas tree (4-2). c, Family dragging cut Christmas tree (4-3). d, Horse-drawn sleigh transporting cut Christmas tree (4-4).

2017, Nov. 2   Litho.   Perf. 13½
1166   A451   49c Sheet of 6, #a-f   6.00   6.00
1167   A452 $1.20 Sheet of 4, #a-d   9.75   9.75

U.S. National Parks Type of 2016
Miniature Sheet

No. 1168 — National Parks: a, Hot Springs (10-1). b, Carlsbad Caverns (10-2). c, North Cascades (10-3). d, Big Bend (10-4). e, Redwood (10-5). f, Katmai (10-6). g, Bryce Canyon (10-7). h, Great Basin (10-8). i, Black Canyon of the Gunnison (10-9). j, Biscayne (10-10).

2017, Nov. 28   Litho.   Perf. 13½
1168   A435   49c Sheet of 10, #a-j   10.00   10.00

Miniature Sheet

Recovered Birds — A453

No. 1169: a, Bald eagles (10-1). b, Hawaiian Nene geese (10-2). c, Wood stork (10-3). d, California condors (10-4). e, Piping plovers (10-5). f, Palau ground dove (10-6). g, Peregrine falcon (10-7). h, Kirtland's warbler (10-8). i, Whooping cranes (10-9). j, Brown pelican (10-10).

2017, Dec. 11   Litho.   Perf. 13½
1169   A453   49c Sheet of 10, #a-j, + 2 central labels   10.00   10.00

Marine Life — A454

Designs: 1c, Little egg cowry. 50c, Green sea turtle. $10, Variable neon slug. $18.90, Shortfin mako shark.

2018, Jan. 1   Litho.   Perf. 12½x13½
1170   A454   1c multi   .25   .25
1171   A454   50c multi   1.00   1.00
1172   A454 $10 multi   20.00   20.00
1173   A454 $18.90 multi   38.00   38.00
    Nos. 1170-1173 (4)   59.25   59.25

Souvenir Sheet

Engagement of Prince Harry and Meghan Markle — A455

No. 1174 — Photograph of couple: a, Holding hands. b, Smiling at each other.

2018, Jan. 1   Litho.   Perf. 12x12½
1174   A455 $7 Sheet of 2, #a-b   28.00   28.00

New Year 2018 (Year of the Dog) A456

No. 1175 — Various flowers and origamis of dogs: a, 50c. b, $1.50. c, $2.50. d, $3.50.

2018, Feb. 1   Litho.   Perf. 14
1175   A456   Sheet of 4, #a-d   16.00   16.00

Miniature Sheet

2018 Winter Olympics, Pyeongchang, South Korea — A457

No. 1176: a, Snowboarding. b, Skeleton. c, Skiing. d, Bobsledding. e, Figure skating. f, Ice hockey.

2018, Apr. 23   Litho.   Perf. 14
1176   A457 $2 Sheet of 6, #a-f   24.00   24.00

Miniature Sheet

Sharks A458

No. 1177: a, 50c, Pelagic thresher shark. b, $1.25, Silky shark. c, $1.60, Whale shark. d, $1.75, Great white shark. e, $2, Oceanic whitetip shark. f, $2.25, Blue shark.

2018, Apr. 23   Litho.   Perf. 12
1177   A458   Sheet of 6, #a-f   18.50   18.50

Coronation of Queen Elizabeth II, 65th Anniv. — A459

No. 1178 — Queen Elizabeth II: a, $1, Waving. b, $3, Holding orb and scepter.

2018, Apr. 26   Litho.   Perf. 14
1178   A459   Horiz. pair, #a-b   8.00   8.00

No. 1178 was printed in sheets containing two pairs.

Grand Canyon National Park, Cent. (in 2019) A460

No. 1179: a, Toroweap Overlook. b, Horseshoe Bend. c, Havasu Falls. d, South Rim in winter. e, Desert View Watchtower. f, Bright Angel Trail.
$4, Cape Royal Point.

2018, Apr. 26   Litho.   Perf. 14
1179   A460 $1.35 Sheet of 6, #a-f   16.50   16.50

Souvenir Sheet
Perf. 12
1180   A460 $4 multi   8.00   8.00

No. 1180 contains one 50x30mm stamp.

Cat Breeds A461

No. 1181: a, American Shorthair. b, Russian Blue. c, Persian. d, Japanese Bobtail. $4, Bombay, horiz.

2018, Apr. 26   Litho.   Perf. 12
1181   A461 $2 Sheet of 4, #a-d   16.00   16.00

Souvenir Sheet
Perf. 12½
1182   A461 $4 multi   8.00   8.00

No. 1182 contains one 51x38mm stamp.

Miniature Sheet

Visit of Pres. Donald Trump to Israel A462

No. 1183: a, $1, Pres. Trump at Western Wall. b, $1, Melania Trump at Western Wall. c, $1, Ivanka Trump at Western Wall. d, $2, Pres. Trump, Israeli Pres. Reuven Rivlin and Prime Minister Benjamin Netanyahu. e, $2, Pres. Trump and Pres. Rivlin. f, $2, Pres. Trump and wife, Melania.

2018, May 4   Litho.   Perf. 14
1183   A462   Sheet of 6, #a-f   18.00   18.00

A463

A464

MARSHALL ISLANDS

Elvis Presley (1935-77) — A465

No. 1185 — Presley: a, Wearing leather jacket, black-and-white photograph. b, Playing guitar, black-and-white photograph. c, With red and black background. d, Playing guitar, color photograph.
Inscriptions: No. 1186, $4, Fans trap Elvis backstage. No. 1187, $4, Memphis Music Hall of Fame. No. 1188, $4, Hottest thing in Charlotte, vert. No. 1189, $4, International Hotel in Vegas, vert.

2018		Litho.		Perf. 12	
1184	A463	$2 multi		4.00	4.00
				Perf. 13¾	
1185	A464	$2 Sheet of 4, #a-d		16.00	16.00

Souvenir Sheets
Perf. 14

1186-1189	A465	Set of 4	32.00	32.00

Issued: No. 1184, 5/17; No. 1185, 5/4; Nos. 1186-1189, 7/6.
No. 1184 comes in sheets of 3.

Butterflies — A466

Designs: 50c, Brown awl. $1.20, Goliath birdwing. $7, Meadow argus. $13.65, Monarch. $18.90, Peablue. $24.90, Great eggfly.

2018, May 17		Litho.		Perf. 12½	
1190	A466	50c multi		1.00	1.00
1191	A466	$1.20 multi		2.40	2.40
1192	A466	$7 multi		14.00	14.00
1193	A466	$13.65 multi		27.50	27.50
1194	A466	$18.90 multi		38.00	38.00
1195	A466	$24.90 multi		50.00	50.00
	Nos. 1190-1195 (6)		132.90	132.90

Miniature Sheet

Louvre Museum, Paris, 225th Anniv. A467

No. 1196: a, $1, Louvre Pyramid and Louvre Palace. b, $2, Louvre, plaza and trees. c, $3, Cour Marly sculpture exhibit. d, $4, Louvre Pyramid at night.

2018, May 17		Litho.		Perf. 12	
1196	A467	Sheet of 4, #a-d		20.00	20.00

Miniature Sheet

Seabirds A468

No. 1197: a, 50c, Great frigatebird. b, 50c, Ruddy turnstone. c, $1, Black-footed albatross. d, $1, Laysan albatross. e, $2, White tern. f, $2, Brown noddy.

2018, May 17		Litho.		Perf. 14	
1197	A468	Sheet of 6, #a-f		14.00	14.00

Miniature Sheet

Birth of Prince Louis of Cambridge — A469

No. 1198: a, Duke and Duchess of Cambridge with Prince Louis. b, Prince George. c, Princess Charlotte. d, Prince Louis.

2018, June 18		Litho.		Perf. 13¾	
1198	A469	$2 Sheet of 4, #a-d		16.00	16.00

Whales A470

No. 1199: a, Pygmy sperm whale. b, Blainville's beaked whale. c, Killer whale. d, Blue whale.
$4, Humpback whale.

2018, June 18		Litho.		Perf. 12	
1199	A470	$2 Sheet of 4, #a-d		16.00	16.00

Souvenir Sheet

1200	A470	$4 multi	8.00	8.00

Miniature Sheet

First Ladies of the United States A471

No. 1201: a, Michelle Obama. b, Laura Bush. c, Hillary Clinton. d, Barbara Bush (1925-2018). e, Rosalynn Carter.

2018, June 30		Litho.		Perf. 14	
1201	A471	$1.60 Sheet of 5, #a-e		16.00	16.00

Transcontinental Railroad, 150th Anniv. (in 2019) — A472

No. 1202: a, Central Pacific train at Cape Horn, Nevada. b, Completion of Transcontinental Railroad. c, Crews laying railroad tracks in Nevada. d, Central Pacific train in Sierra Nevadas. e, Newspaper editorial cartoon commemorating completion of Transcontinental Railroad. f, Central Pacific train in Argenta, Nevada.
$4, 1867 map of Union Pacific Railroad and its connections.

2018, June 30		Litho.		Perf. 14	
1202	A472	$1.40 Sheet of 6, #a-f		17.00	17.00

Souvenir Sheet

1203	A472	$4 multi	8.00	8.00

No. 1203 contains one 80x30mm stamp.

Wedding of Prince Harry and Meghan Markle A473

No. 1204: a, $1, Markle waving. b,$1, Couple holding hands. c, $3, Couple holding hands, descending steps. d, $3, Prince Harry. $5, Couple waving, vert.

2018, July 13		Litho.		Perf. 12	
1204	A473	Sheet of 4, #a-d		16.00	16.00

Souvenir Sheet
Perf. 11x12½

1205	A473	$5 multi	10.00	10.00

No. 1205 contains one 60x80mm stamp.

Souvenir Sheet

Comets A474

No. 1206: a, Halley's Comet. b, Comet Hale-Bopp. c, Comet Hyakutake.

Die Cut Perf. 12¾x13¼
2018, Apr. 26 Litho.
Self-Adhesive

1206	A474	$2 Sheet of 3, #a-c	12.00	12.00

Souvenir Sheet

Singapore Summit of U.S. Pres. Donald Trump and North Korean Chairman Kim Jong Un — A475

No. 1207: a, Chairman Kim. b, Pres. Trump and Chairman Kim. c, Pres. Trump.

2018		Litho.		Perf. 12	
1207	A475	$2 Sheet of 3, #a-c		12.00	12.00

June 12, the date No. 1207 was allegedly issued, is the same day that the summit took place.

Miniature Sheets

Illustrations of Cats Wearing Uniforms of Characters From Star Trek: The Next Generation — A476

No. 1208: a, 50c, Cat and Star Trek badge. b, 50c, Beverly Crusher. c, $1, Data. d, $1, Geordi La Forge. e, $2, Jean-Luc Picard. f, $2, William T. Riker.

No. 1209: a, 50c, Miles O'Brien. b, 50c, Wesley Crusher. c, $1, Deanna Troi. d, $1, Tasha Yar. e, $2, Worf. f, $2, Reginald Barclay.

2018, July 16		Litho.		Perf. 14	
		Sheets of 6, #a-f			
1208-1209	A476	Set of 2		28.00	28.00

Praga 2018 World Stamp Exhibition, Prague — A477

Designs: No. 1210, Czechoslovakia #1.
No. 1211 — Prague synagogues: a, Spanish Synagogue. b, Old New Synagogue. c, Maisel Synagogue. d, Jubilee Synagogue.

2018, Aug. 15		Litho.		Perf. 13¾	
1210	A477	$2 multi		4.00	4.00
1211	A477	$2 Sheet of 4, #a-d		16.00	16.00

No. 1210 was printed in sheets of 4.

Chinese Zodiac Animals A478

New Year 2019 (Year of the Boar) A479

No. 1212: a, 10c, Rat. b, 20c, Ox. c, 30c, Tiger. d, 40c, Rabbit. e, 50c, Dragon. f, 60c, Snake. g, 70c, Horse. h, 80c, Ram. i, 90c, Monkey. j, $1, Rooster. k, $1.10, Dog. l, $1.20, Boar.

2018, Sept. 8		Litho.		Perf. 13¾	
1212	A478	Sheet of 12, #a-l		16.00	16.00

Souvenir Sheet

1213	A479	$2 multi	4.00	4.00

Diplomatic Relations Between Marshall Islands and Republic of China, 20th Anniv. — A480

No. 1214: a, Marshall Islands Pres. Imata J. Kabua (40x60mm). b, Republic of China Pres. Lee Teng-hui (40x60mm). c, Flags of Marshall Islands and Republic of China (40x30mm).
No. 1215 — 20th anniv. emblem and: a, Pres. Kabua (30x40mm). b, Pres. Lee (30x40mm).
No. 1216: a, Like #1214c. b, Like #1216a, with dark brown shading in frame at right.

Perf. 12½x13¼
2018, Nov. 20 Litho.

1214	A480	$5 Sheet of 4, #1214a, 1214b, 2 #1214c	40.00	40.00

Souvenir Sheets
Perf. 12x12½

1215	A480	$10 Sheet of 2, #a-b	40.00	40.00

Perf. 12½x13¼

1216	A480	$10 Sheet of 2, #a-b	40.00	40.00

MARSHALL ISLANDS

Christmas
A481

Designs: No. 1217, 50c, Rocking horse. No. 1218, 50c, Teddy bear. No. 1218A, $1.20, Christmas ornament. No. 1218B, $18.90, Ssnta Claus.

2018, Nov. 10		Litho.		Perf. 12½
1217-1218B	A481	Set of 4		42.50 42.50

Miniature Sheet

Owls
A482

No. 1219: a, 50c, Striped owl. b, 75c, Barred owl. c, $1, Short-eared owl. d, $1.25, Rufous-legged owl. e, $1.50, Great gray owl. f, $1.75, Long-eared owl.

2018, Dec. 21		Litho.	Perf. 14
1219	A482	Sheet of 6, #a-f	13.50 13.50

Miniature Sheets

A483

World War I, Cent.
A484

No. 1220: a, $1, HMS Rocksand (40x30mm). b, $1.25, RMS Mauritania (40x30mm). c, $1.50, SS Alloway (40x30mm). d, $1.75, USS West Mahomet (40x30mm). e, $2, HMS Argus (80x30mm).
No. 1221: a, $1, FFS Gliore (50x30mm). b, $1.25, RMS Olympic (50x30mm). c, $1.50, USS Nebraska (50x30mm). d, $1.75, USS West Shore (50x30mm). e, USS K-5 (100x30mm).

2018, Dec. 21		Litho.	Perf. 14
1220	A483	Sheet of 5, #a-e	15.00 15.00

		Perf. 12
1221	A484	Sheet of 5, #a-e	15.00 15.00

Miniature Sheet

Mohandas K. Gandhi (1869-1948), Indian Nationalist Leader — A485

No. 1222 — Gandhi: a, 1930 *Time* magazine cover. b, Looking left. c, Looking right. d, 1931 *Time* magazine cover.

2018, Dec. 21		Litho.	Perf. 14
1222	A485	$2 Sheet of 4, #a-d	16.00 16.00

Paintings by Leonardo da Vinci (1452-1519) — A486

No, 1223: a, Benois Madonna. b, Madonna of the Carnation. c, Virgin of the Rocks. d, The Virgin and Child with St. Anne.
$4, La Scapigliata.

2019, Mar. 10		Litho.	Perf. 12½
1223	A486	$2 Sheet of 4, #a-d	16.00 16.00

Imperf
Size: 81x130mm

1224	A486	$4 multi	8.00 8.00

Birds
A487

No. 1225: a, White tern. b, Sacred kingfisher. c, Black noddy. d, Pectoral sandpiper. e, Brown noddy. f, Greater crested tern.
$5, Crimson-crowned fruit dove.

2019, Mar. 10		Litho.	Perf. 14
1225	A487	$1.50 Sheet of 6, #a-f	18.00 18.00

Souvenir Sheet

1226	A487	$5 multi	10.00 10.00

Miniature Sheets

Fish
A488

No. 1227, $1.20: a, Orange-fin anemonefish. b, Achilles tang. c, Scissortail sergeant. d, Spotband butterflyfish. e, Orange band surgeonfish. f, Pink skunk clownfish.
No. 1228, $1.50: a, Chocolate surgeonfish. b, Oval butterflyfish. c, Maroon clownfish. d, Whitecheek surgeonfish. e, Cinnamon clownfish. f, Isonish namsanish.

2019, Mar. 14		Litho.	Perf. 14
		Sheets of 6, #a-f	
1227-1228	A488	Set of 2	32.50 32.50

Marine Life — A489

Designs: 5c, Portuguese man o'war. 11c, Indo-Pacific bottlenose dolphin. 35c, Peacock mantis shrimp. 55c, Lionfish. $1.05, Sperm whale.

2019, Mar. 29		Litho.	Perf. 14
1229	A489	5c multi	.25 .25
1230	A489	11c multi	.25 .25
1231	A489	35c multi	.70 .70
1232	A489	55c multi	1.10 1.10
1233	A489	$1.05 multi	2.10 2.10
		Nos. 1229-1233 (5)	4.40 4.40

Miniature Sheet

Covers of Gold Key *Star Trek* Comic Books
A490

No. 1234 — Comic book edition: a, No. 1. b, No. 2. c, No. 3. d, No. 4. e, No. 5. f, No. 7.

2019, Apr. 30		Litho.	Perf. 12½
1234	A490	$1.20 Sheet of 6, #a-f	14.50 14.50

First Man on the Moon, 50th Anniv.
A491

No. 1235 — Apollo 11 patch and: a, Astronaut Edwin E. "Buzz" Aldrin, Jr. (30x40mm). b, Earth and Moon (30x80mm). c, Aldrin carrying equipment (30x40mm). d, Astronaut Michael Collins and members of ground crew (30x40mm). e, Launch of Apollo 11 (30x40mm).
$4, Crew of Apollo 11, horiz.

2019, May 17		Litho.	Perf. 14
1235	A491	$1.10 Sheet of 5, #a-e	11.00 11.00

Souvenir Sheet
Perf. 12½

1236	A491	$4 multi	8.00 8.00

No. 1236 contains one 51x38mm stamp.

Jellyfish
A492

No. 1237: a, Spotted jellyfish. b, Crown jellyfish. c, Moon jellyfish.
$5, Moon jellyfish, vert.

2019, May 17		Litho.	Perf. 13¾
1237	A492	$2 Sheet of 3, #a-c	12.00 12.00

Souvenir Sheet
Perf. 12½

1238	A492	$5 multi	10.00 10.00

No. 1238 contains one 38x51mm stamp.

Sacred Kingfisher — A493

No. 1239 — Kingfisher facing: a, Left, dark background. b, Right, on perch. c, Left, light background. d, Left, legs not visible.
$5, Kingfisher facing right. diff.

2019, May 22		Litho.	Perf. 14
1239	A493	$2 Sheet of 4, #a-d	16.00 16.00

Souvenir Sheet
Perf. 12½

1240	A493	$5 multi	10.00 10.00

No. 1240 contains one 51x38mm stamp.

Queen Victoria (1819-1901) — A494

No. 1241 — Queen Victoria: a, As child. b, As young woman. c, As older woman, facing forward. d, As older woman, facing left.
$5, Queen Victoria. diff.

2019, May 22		Litho.	Perf. 12
1241	A494	$2 Sheet of 4, #a-d	16.00 16.00

Souvenir Sheet
Perf. 12½

1242	A494	$5 multi	10.00 10.00

No. 1242 contains one 38x51mm stamp.

D-Day, 75th Anniv.
A495

No. 1243: a, Soldiers arriving on landing craft. b, American soldiers arriving on Omaha Beach. c, Troops take cover behind enemy obstacles. d, American assault troops wading ashore on Omaha Beach.
$7.50, Front page of *Worcester Telegram* announcing start of invasion.

2019, June 12		Litho.	Perf. 14
1243	A495	$2 Sheet of 4, #a-d	16.00 16.00

Souvenir Sheet
Perf. 12½

1244	A495	$7.50 multi	15.00 15.00

No. 1244 contains one 51x38mm stamp.

Miniature Sheet

Abdication of Japanese Emperor, Akihito — A496

No. 1245 — Emperor Akihito: a, Wearing suit and tie. b, Wearing robe and ceremonial hat. c, With U.S. Pres. Donald Trump. d, With Empress Michiko and Nelson Mandela.

2019, June 12		Litho.	Perf. 14
1245	A496	$2 Sheet of 4, #a-d	16.00 16.00

299

MARSHALL ISLANDS

Miniature Sheet

Birth of Archie Mountbatten-Windsor — A497

No. 1246: a, Duke and Duchess of Sussex. b, Duke and Duchess of Sussex, with people in background. c, Archie Mountbatten-Windsor in hands of Duke of Sussex. d, Duke and Duchess of Sussex with son, Archie.

2019, June 19		Litho.		Perf. 14
1246	A497	$2 Sheet of 4, #a-d	16.00	16.00

Singpex 2019 International Stamp Exhibition, Singapore — A498

No. 1247 — Singapore attractions: a, $1, Marina Bay Sands. b, $1, Singapore Flyer. c, $2, Supertree Grove. d, $2, Clarke Quay. $5, Singapore Merlion Fountain, vert.

2019, July 31		Litho.		Perf. 14
1247	A498	Sheet of 4, #a-d	12.00	12.00

Souvenir Sheet
Perf. 12½

1248	A498	$5 multi	10.00	10.00

No. 1248 contains one 38x51mm stamp.

Dorje Chang Buddha III, Artist and Religious Leader — A499

Perf. 13¼x12½

2019, Aug. 14				Litho.
1249	A499	$1.50 multi	3.00	3.00

No. 1249 was printed in sheets of 4.

Frangipani Flowers — A500

No. 1250: a, One white flower. b, One pink flower. c, Two pink flowers, white background. d, Two pink flowers, leaves in background. $5, Three flowers, horiz.

2019, Aug. 14		Litho.		Perf. 13¾
1250	A500	$2 Sheet of 4, #a-d	16.00	16.00

Souvenir Sheet
Perf. 12

1251	A500	$5 multi	10.00	10.00

No. 1251 contains one 40x30mm stamp.

Morning Glories A501

No. 1252: a, Two violet flowers and part of pink flower. b, One pink flower. c, Two pink flowers. d, Two purple flowers. $5, Violet flowers, vert.

2019, Aug. 25		Litho.		Perf. 14
1252	A501	$2 Sheet of 4, #a-d	16.00	16.00

Souvenir Sheet
Perf. 12½

1253	A501	$5 multi	10.00	10.00

No, 1253 contains one 38x51mm stamp.

Ocellaris Clownfish — A502

No. 1254 — Various photographs of Ocellaris clownfish: a, Two fish. b, One fish. c, One fish, diff. d, Two fish, diff. $7, Ocellaris clownfish, vert.

2019, Aug. 25		Litho.		Perf. 12
1254	A502	$2 Sheet of 4, #a-d	16.00	16.00

Souvenir Sheet
Perf. 12½

1255	A502	$7 multi	14.00	14.00

No, 1255 contains one 38x51mm stamp.

Visit of Pres. Donald Trump to Japan A503

No. 1256: a, Pres. Trump and Emperor Naruhito wearing suits and ties. b, Pres. Trump and Emperor Naruhito in casual wear. c, Melania Trump with Emperor Naruhito and Empress Masako. d, Pres. Trump, Emperor Naruhito and Empress Masako. $5, Pres, Trump and Emperor Naruhito, diff.

2019, Aug. 25		Litho.		Perf. 14
1256	A503	$2 Sheet of 4, #a-d	16.00	16.00

Souvenir Sheet

1257	A503	$5 multi	10.00	10.00

No. 1257 contains one 80x30mm stamp.

Miniature Sheet

Landscapes — A504

No. 1258: a, $10, Beach, water at right. b, $10, Beach, water at left. c, $15, Beach, water at right, diff. d, $15, Aerial view of island. e, $25, Buildings near beach. f, $25, Road and buildings near beach.

Litho. With Foil Application

2019, May 10				Perf. 14
1258	A504	Sheet of 6, #a-f	200.00	200.00

Birds — A505

Designs: 6c, Crimson-crowned fruit dove. $1.45, Arctic tern, vert. $7.75, Long-tailed koel. $15.50, Tufted duck. $26.35, Sacred kingfisher.

2020, May 22		Litho.		Perf. 14
1259	A505	6c multi	.25	.25
1260	A505	$1.45 multi	3.00	3.00
1261	A505	$7.75 multi	15.50	15.50
1262	A505	$15.50 multi	31.00	31.00
1263	A505	$26.35 multi	53.00	53.00
		Nos. 1259-1263 (5)	102.75	102.75

Marine Life — A506

Designs: 55c, Spinner dolphins. $2.20, Christmas tree worm. $8.80, Spotted eagle ray. $21.10, Vase sponge.

2020, May 22		Litho.		Perf. 14
1264	A506	55c multi	1.10	1.10
1265	A506	$2.20 multi	4.50	4.50
1266	A506	$8.80 multi	18.00	18.00
1267	A506	$21.10 multi	42.50	42.50
		Nos. 1264-1267 (4)	66.10	66.10

Souvenir Sheet

Tsakos Group Oil Tanker M.T. El Junior PNT A507

Perf. 12½x13¼

2020, June 18				Litho.
1268	A507	$5 multi	10.00	10.00

Miniature Sheet

COVID-19 Pandemic — A508

No. 1269: a, Magnifying glass, COVID-19 viruses, "Facts over fear." b, Hand and blood specimen tube. c, Health care workers, protective face mask. d, Ambulance, emergency medical technician and badge.

2020, Aug. 7		Litho.		Perf. 13¼x12½
1269	A508	$2 Sheet of 4, #a-d	16.00	16.00

Vietnam War, 65th Anniv. A509

No. 1270, $2: a, Battle of Khe Sanh, 1968. b, Battle of Ia Drang, 1965. c, Tet Offensive, 1968. d, Gulf of Tonkin Incident, 1964. No. 1271, $2 — Battle of Khe Sanh, 1968: a, Machine gun crew. b, Skyhawk provides fire support. c, Purple Foxes extracting Marines from battle. d, Direct fire support.
$8, Grumman A-6A Intruder bombing run.

2020, Sept. 16		Litho.		Perf. 12½
		Sheets of 4, #a-d		
1270-1271	A509	Set of 2	32.00	32.00

Souvenir Sheet

1272	A509	$8 multi	16.00	16.00

Miniature Sheet

Victory in Europe in World War II (V-E Day), 75th Anniv. A510

No. 1273: a, Joseph Stalin (1878-1953), General Secretary of the Soviet Union, flag of the Soviet Union. b, Winston Churchill (1874-1965), British Prime Minister, flag of Great Britain. c, Dwight D. Eisenhower (1890-1969), Supreme Allied Commander in Europe, flag of the United States. d, Bernard Montgomery (1887-1976), British Field Marshal, flag of Great Britain. e, Europe V-E Day celebration. f, Harry S. Truman (1884-1972), 33rd United States President, flag of the United States.

2020, Oct. 16		Litho.		Perf. 12½
1273	A510	$1.60 Sheet of 6, #a-f	19.50	19.50

Geese A511

Greylag Goose A512

No. 1274: a, Pink-footed goose. b, Swan goose. c, Emperor goose. d, Snow goose. e, Canada goose.

2020, Oct. 16		Litho.		Perf. 13¾
1274	A511	$1.50 Sheet of 5, #a-e	15.00	15.00

MARSHALL ISLANDS

Souvenir Sheet
Perf. 12
1275 A512 $5 multi 10.00 10.00

Hibiscus Flowers A514

No. 1276 — Flower color: a, Red. b, White. c, Yellow. d, Pink.

2020, Oct. 16 Litho. Perf. 13¾
1276 A513 $2 Sheet of 4, #a-d 16.00 16.00

Souvenir Sheet
Perf. 12
1277 A514 $5 multi 10.00 10.00

Miniature Sheets

A515

A516

2020 Candidates for President and Vice-President of the United States — A517

No. 1278: a, Democratic Presidential candidate Joseph R. Biden, Jr. wearing striped tie. b, Democratic Vice-Presidential candidate Kamala Harris with flags in background. c, Harris, diff. d, Biden, wearing patterned tie.
No. 1279: a, Republican Presidential candidate Donald J. Trump, with flag in background. b, Republican Vice-Presidential candidate Michael R. Pence, with flag in background. c, Pence, at podium. d, Trump, behind microphone.
No. 1280 — Stamps with "Marshall Islands" at bottom: a, Like #1279a. b, Like #1278a. c, Like #1279b. d, Like #1278b.

2020, Oct. 16 Litho. Perf. 13¾
1278 A515 $2 Sheet of 4, #a-d 16.00 16.00
1279 A516 $2 Sheet of 4, #a-d 16.00 16.00
1280 A517 $2 Sheet of 4, #a-d 16.00 16.00
Nos. 1278-1280 (3) 48.00 48.00

Butterflies A518

No. 1281: a, Common Mormon butterfly. b, Zebra blue butterfly.
$8, Blue-banded king crow butterfly, vert.

2020, Nov. 2 Litho. Perf. 14
1281 A518 $1.50 Pair, #a-b 6.00 6.00

Souvenir Sheet
Perf. 12
1282 A518 $8 multi 16.00 16.00

Antarctic Wildlife A519

No. 1283: a, Chinstrap penguin. b, Antarctic minke whale. c, Southern elephant seal. d, Leopard seal. e, South polar skua. f, Snow petrel.
$8, Emperor penguins.

2020, Nov. 2 Litho. Perf. 14
1283 A519 $1.50 Sheet of 6, #a-f 18.00 18.00

Souvenir Sheet
Perf. 12½
1284 A519 $8 multi 16.00 16.00
No. 1284 contains one 51x38mm stamp.

Souvenir Sheets

Donald J. Trump, 45th President of the United States — A520

2020, Nov. 3 Litho. Perf. 13¼
Flag With Red Stripes
1285 A520 $4.50 multi 9.00 9.00
Flag With Maroon Stripes and Darker Portrait
1286 A520 $4.50 multi 9.00 9.00
The margin on No. 1286 measures 140x100mm and its images and text in the margin are larger than those on No. 1285.

Souvenir Sheets

Joseph R. Biden, Jr., 46th President of the United States — A521

2020, Nov. 3 Litho. Perf. 13¼
Flag With Red Stripes
1287 A521 $4.60 multi 9.25 9.25

Flag With Maroon Stripes and Darker Portrait Placed Lower Against the Stripes
1288 A521 $4.60 multi 9.25 9.25
The margin on No. 1288 measures 140x100mm and its images and text in the margin are larger than those on No. 1287.

Rabbits A522

Rabbits A523

No. 1289 — Various rabbits with frame color of: a, Blue green. b, Lt. blue. c, Magenta. d, Purple.
No. 1290 — Various rabbits with panel color of: a, Green blue. b, Dark green.

2020, Nov. 30 Litho. Perf. 14
1289 A522 $2 Sheet of 4, #a-d 16.00 16.00

Souvenir Sheet
Perf. 14
1290 A523 $4 Sheet of 2, #a-b 16.00 16.00

Farm Animals A524

No. 1291: a, Donkey. b, Leghorn chicken. c, Holstein cow. d, Sheep.
$5, Horse.

2020, Nov. 30 Litho. Perf. 14
1291 A524 $2 Sheet of 4, #a-d 16.00 16.00

Souvenir Sheet
Perf. 12
1292 A524 $5 multi 10.00 10.00

Starfish A525

No. 1293: a, Common seastar. b, Blue seastar. c, Giant seastar. d, Ochre seastar.
$5, Northern Pacific seastar.

2020, Nov. 30 Litho. Perf. 14
1293 A525 $2 Sheet of 4, #a-d 16.00 16.00

Souvenir Sheet
Perf. 12
1294 A525 $5 multi 10.00 10.00

Sea Turtles A526

Sea Turtles A527

No. 1295 — Sea turtle with: a, Head at right, Prussian blue frame. b, Head at left, overhead view, blue green frame. c, Head at left, side view, blue green frame. d, Diver in background, Prussian blue frame.
No. 1296 — Sea turtle with: a, Blue green frame. b, Yellow frame.

2020, Nov. 30 Litho. Perf. 14
1295 A526 $2 Sheet of 4, #a-d 16.00 16.00

Souvenir Sheet
1296 A527 $3 Sheet of 2, #a-b 12.00 12.00

Reptiles A528

No. 1297: a, Leatherback sea turtle. b, Green anole. c, Eastern indigo snake. d, Komodo dragon.
$5, Common box turtle.

2020, Nov. 30 Litho. Perf. 14
1297 A528 $2 Sheet of 4, #a-d 16.00 16.00

Souvenir Sheet
Perf. 12
1298 A528 $5 multi 10.00 10.00

Souvenir Sheets

Elvis Presley (1935-77) — A529

Inscriptions: No. 1299, $8, "I'm ever grateful to my fans everywhere." No. 1300, $8, "The Army teaches boys to think like men." No. 1301, $8, "Burning Love" jumpsuit. No. 1302, $8, "You can make 'em or break 'em," horiz.

Perf. 13¼x12½, 12½x13¼
2020, Nov. 30 Litho.
1299-1302 A529 Set of 4 64.00 64.00

Miniature Sheet

New Year 2021 (Year of the Ox) A530

No. 1303: a, Ox with flower between ears. b, Dark brown ox with horns. c, Ox holding envelopes, tail at right. d, Pale lavendar and gray ox. e, Orange brown ox with horns. f, Ox with garland of flowers around head and yellow banner below head.

2020, Nov. 30 Litho. Perf. 13¾
1303 A530 $1 Sheet of 6, #a-f 12.00 12.00

MARSHALL ISLANDS

Landing of the Pilgrims in North America, 400th Anniv. (in 2020) A531

No. 1304: a, Washing the Skins and Grading the Wool, painting by Isaac Claesz. van Swanenburg. b, The Puritan, sculpture by Augustus Saint-Gaudens. c, Plymouth Rock. d, The Mayflower at sea.
$5, Interior cabin of Mayflower II replica ship.

2021, Apr. 5	Litho.	Perf. 14
1304 A531 $2 Sheet of 4, #a-d		16.00 16.00

Souvenir Sheet Perf. 12½

1305 A531 $5 multi	10.00 10.00

No. 1305 contains one 51x38mm stamp.

Joseph R. Biden, Jr., 46th President of the United States — A532

No. 1306 — Pres. Biden: a, Standing behind microphones. b, Wearing blue striped tie. c, With wife, Jill. d, Signing papers. e, With flag at right.
$4.60, Pres. Biden wearing striped shirt, horiz.

2021, Apr. 5	Litho.	Perf. 14
1306 A532 $1.60 Sheet of 5, #a-e		16.00 16.00

Souvenir Sheet Perf. 12½

1307 A532 $4.60 multi	9.25 9.25

No. 1307 contains one 51x38mm stamp.

Empire State Building, 90th Anniv. A533

No. 1308: a, Windows of observation deck. b, Empire State Building lit up with red, white and blue lights. c, Empire State Building and surrounding buildings. d, Empire State Building at twilight. e, Sculpted concrete eagle at Fifth Avenue entrance.
$4.90, Empire State Building, vert.

2021, Apr. 5	Litho.	Perf. 14
1308 A533 $1.90 Sheet of 5, #a-e		19.00 19.00

Souvenir Sheet Perf. 12

1309 A533 $4.90 multi	10.00 10.00

No. 1309 contains one 30x80mm stamp.

September 11, 2001 Terrorist Attacks, 20th Anniv. — A534

No. 1310: a, North Pool of September 11 Memorial. b, World Trade Center Twin Towers and Brooklyn Bridge. c, One World Trade Center. d, World Trade Center Twin Towers and surrounding buildings.
$5, White rose at Memorial, vert.

2021, Apr. 5	Litho.	Perf. 14
1310 A534 $2 Sheet of 4, #a-d		16.00 16.00

Souvenir Sheet Perf. 12½

1311 A534 $5 multi	10.00 10.00

No. 1311 contains one 38x51mm stamp.

A535

95th Birthday of Queen Elizabeth II (1926-2022) — A536

No. 1311 — Color of hat and jacket of Queen Elizabeth II: a, Purple. b, Brown. c, Blue. d, Pink. e, Yellow.
$5, Queen Elizabeth II in wedding dress.

2021, Apr. 5	Litho.	Perf. 14
1312 A535 $1.95 Sheet of 5, #a-e		19.50 19.50

Souvenir Sheet Perf.

1313 A536 $5 multi	10.00 10.00

A537

Range Rovers, 50th Anniv. (in 2020) A538

No. 1314: a, 2014 Range Rover Gold Edition. b, 2014 Range Rover Evoque. c, 2016 Range Rover Evoque Cabriolet. d, 2017 Land Range Rover.
$5, 2012 Range Rover Convertible.

2021, Apr. 5	Litho.	Perf. 14
1314 A537 $2 Sheet of 4, #a-d		16.00 16.00

Souvenir Sheet Perf. 12½

1315 A538 $5 multi	10.00 10.00

Dorje Chang Buddha III, Religious Leader — A539

2021, May 24	Litho.	Perf. 13¼
1316 A539 $1.20 multi		2.40 2.40

Birds A540

No. 1317: a, Laysan albatross. b, Black-footed albatross. c, Kermadec petrel. d, Juan Fernández petrel. e, White-necked petrel. f, Flesh-footed shearwater. g, Bulwer's petrel. h, Red-bellied tropicbird. i, Masked booby. j, Great frigatebird.
No. 1318: a, Spectacled tern. b, Franklin's gull.

2021, June 17	Litho.	Perf. 14
1317 A540 75c Sheet of 10, #a-j		15.00 15.00

Souvenir Sheet

1318 A540 $3 Sheet of 2, #a-b	12.00 12.00

Crabs A541

No. 1319: a, Golden king crab. b, Brown crab. c, Atlantic blue crab. d, Chinese mitten crab. e, Red rock crab. f, Tanner crab.
No. 1320: a, Christmas Island red crab. b, Flower crab.

2021, June 17	Litho.	Perf. 14
1319 A541 $1.35 Sheet of 6, #a-f		16.50 16.50

Souvenir Sheet

1320 A541 $3 Sheet of 2, #a-b	12.00 12.00

Mantis Shrimp A542

No. 1321: a, Zebra mantis shrimp. b, Split-thumb mantis shrimp. c, Shortnose mantis shrimp. d, Caribbean rock mantis shrimp. e, Common mantis shrimp. f, Japanese mantis shrimp.
No. 1322: a, Dark green and red mantis shrimp, head at right. b, Olive green mantis shrimp, head at left.

2021, June 17	Litho.	Perf. 14
1321 A542 $1.35 Sheet of 6, #a-f		16.50 16.50

Souvenir Sheet

1322 A542 $3 Sheet of 2, #a-b	12.00 12.00

Miniature Sheet

Elvis Presley (1935-77) — A543

No. 1323 — Presley in military uniform: a, In automobile. b, Standing in front of building (dark uniform with private's insignia). c, Without cap. d, Standing in front of building (khaki uniform without private's insignia).

2021, Aug. 16	Litho.	Perf. 14
1323 A543 $2 Sheet of 4, #a-d		16.00 16.00

Miniature Sheet

2020 Summer Olympics, Tokyo — A544

No. 1324: a, Soccer. b, Cycling. c, Basketball. d, Tennis.

2021, Aug. 16	Litho.	Perf. 13¾
1324 A544 $2 Sheet of 4, #a-d		16.00 16.00

The 2020 Summer Olympics were postponed until 2021 because of the COVID-19 pandemic.

Souvenir Sheets

A545

A546

MARSHALL ISLANDS

303

A547

A548

A549

A550

A551

A552

A553

A554

A555

A556

Queen Elizabeth II (1926-2022) and United States Presidents — A557

No. 1325: a, Queen Elizabeth II. b, Pres. Harry S Truman.
No. 1326: a, Prince Philip and Mamie Eisenhower. b, Queen Elizabeth II and Pres. Dwight D. Eisenhower.
No. 1327: a, Pres. John F. Kennedy and Queen Elizabeth II. b, Jacqueline Kennedy and Prince Philip.
No. 1328 — Queen Elizabeth II and Pres. Richard M. Nixon: a, At Chequers. b, At Buckingham Palace.
No. 1329: a, Queen Elizabeth II. b, Pres. Gerald R. Ford.
No. 1330: a, Queen Elizabeth II. b, Pres. Jimmy Carter.
No. 1331: a, Pres. Ronald Reagan on horse. b, Queen Elizabeth II on horse.
No. 1332 — Pres. George H. W. Bush and Queen Elizabeth II, with Queen at: a, Right. b, Left.
No. 1333: a, Pres. Bill Clinton. b, Queen Elizabeth II.
No. 1334: a, Pres. George W. Bush. b, Queen Elizabeth II.
No. 1335: a, Queen Elizabeth II. b, Pres. Barack Obama.
No. 1336 — Pres. Donald Trump and Queen Elizabeth II, with Queen at: a, Right. b, Left.
No. 1337: a, Queen Elizabeth II. b, Pres. Joseph R. Biden, Jr.

Perf. 12½, 12 (#1327)

2021, Aug. 24   Litho.
1325	A545	$3	Sheet of 2, #a-b	12.00	12.00
1326	A546	$3	Sheet of 2, #a-b	12.00	12.00
1327	A547	$3	Sheet of 2, #a-b	12.00	12.00
1328	A548	$3	Sheet of 2, #a-b	12.00	12.00
1329	A549	$3	Sheet of 2, #a-b	12.00	12.00
1330	A550	$3	Sheet of 2, #a-b	12.00	12.00
1331	A551	$3	Sheet of 2, #a-b	12.00	12.00
1332	A552	$3	Sheet of 2, #a-b	12.00	12.00
1333	A553	$3	Sheet of 2, #a-b	12.00	12.00
1334	A554	$3	Sheet of 2, #a-b	12.00	12.00
1335	A555	$3	Sheet of 2, #a-b	12.00	12.00
1336	A556	$3	Sheet of 2, #a-b	12.00	12.00
1337	A557	$3	Sheet of 2, #a-b	12.00	12.00
	Nos. 1325-1337 (13)			156.00	156.00

Owls — A558

No. 1338: a, Great horned owl. b, Screech owl. c, Barred owl. d, Snowy owl.
$5, Barn owl, vert.

2021, Sept. 1   Litho.   **Perf. 14**
| 1338 | A558 | $2 | Sheet of 4, #a-d | 16.00 | 16.00 |

Souvenir Sheet
Perf. 13¾
| 1339 | A558 | $5 | multi | 10.00 | 10.00 |

No. 1339 contains one 35x35mm stamp.

Crocodylinae — A559

No. 1340   Crocodilo: a, With open mouth, facing right. b, In water. c, Lifting head out of water. d, In water, with open mouth, facing right. e, With open mouth, facing left. f, On foliage.
$5, Crocodile, diff.

2021, Sept. 1   Litho.   **Perf. 14**
| 1340 | A559 | $1.35 | Sheet of 6, #a-f | 16.50 | 16.50 |

Souvenir Sheet
Perf. 12½
| 1341 | A559 | $5 | multi | 10.00 | 10.00 |

No. 1341 contains one 51x38mm stamp.

Space Shuttle Discovery — A560

Hubble Space Telescope — A561

Hubble Space Telescope in Space — A562

Hubble Space Telescope Over Earth — A563

Launch of Space Shuttle Discovery — A564

No. 1342: a, Space Shuttle Discovery landing. b, Photograph of Earth taken from Space Shuttle Discovery. c, Space Shuttle Discovery being transported. d, Space Shuttle Discovery in museum, flag hanging from ceiling. e, Space Shuttle Discovery in museum. f, Space Shuttle Discovery in space with hatch opened.
No. 1343: a, Hubble Space Telescope, Earth in background. b, Side view of Hubble Space Telescope in space. c, View from above Hubble Space Telescope. d, Photograph taken by Hubble Space Telescope.

2021, Oct. 1   Litho.   **Perf. 12¾**
| 1342 | A560 | $1.50 | Sheet of 6, #a-f | 18.00 | 18.00 |
| 1343 | A561 | $1.80 | Sheet of 4, #a-d | 14.50 | 14.50 |

Souvenir Sheets
Perf. 13x13¼
1344	A562	$3.50	multi	7.00	7.00
1345	A563	$3.50	multi	7.00	7.00
1346	A564	$3.50	multi	7.00	7.00
	Nos. 1344-1346 (3)			21.00	21.00

Miniature Sheet

Metropolitan Museum of Art, 150th Anniv. (in 2020) — A565

No. 1347: a, Interior courtyard garden at the Cloisters. b, Breuer Building (945 Madison Avenue). c, Mummy and coffin of Ukhhotep. d, European Paintings Gallery.

2021, Oct. 29   Litho.   **Perf. 14**
| 1347 | A565 | $2 | Sheet of 4, #a-d | 16.00 | 16.00 |

Tenth Wedding Anniversary of the Duke and Duchess of Cambridge — A566

MARSHALL ISLANDS

No. 1348: a, Queen Elizabeth II and Prince William. b, Engagement announcement photograph of Duke and Duchess of Cambridge. c, Duke and Duchess of Cambridge on wedding day. d, Duke and Duchess of Cambridge wearing sunglasses at Kaziranga National Park, India. e, Duke and Duchess of Cambridge near Eiffel Tower, Paris.
$5, Duke and Duchess of Cambridge on wedding day, horiz.

2021, Oct. 29		Litho.	Perf. 14	
1348	A566	$1.60 Sheet of 5, #a-e	16.00	16.00

Souvenir Sheet
Perf. 12

1349	A566	$5 multi	10.00	10.00

No. 1349 contains one 50x30mm stamp.

Third Wedding Anniversary of the Duke and Duchess of Sussex — A567

No. 1350: a, Duke and Duchess of Cambridge on wedding day. b, Queen Elizabeth II and Prince Harry. c, Duke and Duchess of Sussex under umbrella. d, Duke and Duchess of Sussex on wedding day. e, Duke and Duchess of Cambridge. e, Duke and Duchess of Sussex in front of brick wall.
$5, Duke and Duchess of Sussex with son, Archie, vert.

2021, Oct. 29		Litho.	Perf. 14	
1350	A567	$1.60 Sheet of 5, #a-e	16.00	16.00

Souvenir Sheet
Perf. 12½

1351	A567	$5 multi	10.00	10.00

No. 1351 contains one 38x51mm stamp.

Prince Philip (1921-2021) — A568

No. 1352: a, Prince Philip and Queen Elizabeth II (black-and-white photograph). b, Prince Philip and Queen Elizabeth II, Prince wearing medals. c, Prince Philip and Queen Elizabeth II standing in car. d, Prince Philip.
$5, Queen Elizabeth II and Prince Philip, vert.

2021		Litho.	Perf. 14	
1352	A568	$2 Sheet of 4, #a-d	16.00	16.00

Souvenir Sheet
Perf. 12½

1353	A568	$5 multi	10.00	10.00

No. 1353 contains one 38x51mm stamp. Nos. 1352-1353 were alleged to have been issued on April 9, 2021, the day Prince Philip died.

Ducks A569

No. 1354: a, Canvasbacks. b, Eurasian wigeons. c, Garganey ducks. d, Northern shovelers. e, Tufted ducks. f, Northern pintails.
$5, Green-winged teals.

2022, Jan. 10		Litho.	Perf. 14	
1354	A569	$2 Sheet of 6, #a-f	24.00	24.00

Souvenir Sheet
Perf. 12½

1355	A569	$5 multi	10.00	10.00

No. 1355 contains one 51x38mm stamp.

Butterflies — A570

No. 1356: a, Cabbage white butterflies. b, Monarch butterflies. c, Blue morpho butterflies. d, Red admiral butterflies. e, Banded peacock butterflies.
$5, Mourning cloak butterflies, horiz.

2022, Jan. 10		Litho.	Perf. 13¾	
1356	A570	$2 Sheet of 5, #a-e	20.00	20.00

Souvenir Sheet
Perf. 12½

1357	A570	$5 multi	10.00	10.00

No. 1357 contains one 51x38mm stamp.

Miniature Sheet

United Arab Emirates Tourist Attractions — A571

No. 1358: a, Sheikh Zayed Grand Mosque, Abu Dhabi. b, Palm Jumeirah, Dubai. c, Al Fahidi historical District, Dubai. d, Burj Al Arab, Dubai.

2022, Jan. 19		Litho.	Perf. 14	
1358	A571	$1 Sheet of 4, #a-d	8.00	8.00

Souvenir Sheet

Litecoin A572

2022, Jan. 19		Litho.	Perf. 12½	
1359	A572	$20 multi	40.00	40.00

Miniature Sheet

New Year 2022 (Year of the Tiger) A573

No. 1360: a, Head of tiger facing right. b, Tiger, gray background. c, Head of tiger facing left. d, Tiger with open mouth. e, Tiger at left facing forward. f, Tiger at right facing forward.

2022, Feb. 1		Litho.	Perf. 14	
1360	A573	$1 Sheet of 6, #a-f	12.00	12.00

Reign of Queen Elizabeth II (1926-2022), 70th Anniv. — A574

No. 1361 — Queen Elizabeth II: a, As young girl at Windsor Great Park. b, As young woman at Buckingham Palace. c, At Windsor Castle. d, As older woman at Buckingham Palace.
$4.70, Wearing crown, vert.

2022, Feb. 6		Litho.	Perf. 14	
1361	A574	$1.70 Sheet of 4, #a-d	14.00	14.00

Souvenir Sheet
Perf. 12½

1362	A574	$4.70 multi	9.50	9.50

No. 1362 contains one 38x51mm stamp.

Miniature Sheet

Gold Medalists at the 2022 Winter Olympics — A575

No. 1363: a, Eileen Gu, freestyle skiing, flag of People's Republic of China. b, Ryoyu Kobayashi, ski jumping, flag of Japan. c, Nico Porteous, freestyle skiing, flag of New Zealand. d, Chloe Kim, snowboarding, flag of United States.

Perf. 13¼x12½

2022, Mar. 25			Litho.	
1363	A575	$2 Sheet of 4, #a-d	16.00	16.00

Fish — A576

Designs: 9c, Orange clownfish. 50c, Bleeker's parrotfish. 58c, Moorish idol. $1.15, Bennet's butterflyfish. $6.95, Coral grouper. $8.95, Fairy basslet. $9.45, Zebra lionfish. $16.10, Bicolor angelfish. $21.50, Foxface rabbitfish. $26.95, Striped bristletooth.

2022, May 30		Litho.	Perf. 14	
1364	A576	9c multi	.30	.30
1365	A576	50c multi	1.00	1.00
1366	A576	58c multi	1.25	1.25
1367	A576	$1.15 multi	2.40	2.40
1368	A576	$6.95 multi	14.00	14.00
1369	A576	$8.95 multi	18.00	18.00
1370	A576	$9.45 multi	19.00	19.00
1371	A576	$16.10 multi	32.50	32.50
1372	A576	$21.50 multi	43.00	43.00
1373	A576	$26.95 multi	54.00	54.00
		Nos. 1364-1373 (10)	185.45	185.45

Souvenir Sheet

Peace Dove, Ukrainian Parliament Building, Kyiv, and Kremlin, Moscow — A577

2022, May 30		Litho.	Perf. 12½	
1374	A577	$5 multi	10.00	10.00

Endangered Parrots — A578

No. 1375: a, Blue macaw. b, Eclectus parrot. c, Martinique macaw. d, Guadeloupe parrot.
$5, Yellow-crested cockatoo, horiz.

2022, June 14		Litho.	Perf. 14	
1375	A578	$2 Sheet of 4, #a-d	16.00	16.00

Souvenir Sheet
Perf. 12

1376	A578	$5 multi	10.00	10.00

Sharks A579

No. 1377: a, Great hammerhead shark. b, Spiny dogfish. c, Gray reef shark. d, Shortfin mako shark.
$5, Oceanic whitetip shark.

2022, June 14		Litho.	Perf. 14	
1377	A579	$2 Sheet of 4, #a-d	16.00	16.00

Souvenir Sheet
Perf. 12

1378	A579	$5 multi	10.00	10.00

Jellyfish A580

No. 1379: a, Golden jellyfish. b, Pacific sea nettle. c, Moon jellyfish. d, Cannonball jellyfish.
$5, Australian spotted jellyfish.

2022, June 14		Litho.	Perf. 14	
1379	A580	$2 Sheet of 4, #a-d	16.00	16.00

Souvenir Sheet
Perf. 12

1380	A580	$5 multi	10.00	10.00

Corals A581

No. 1381: a, Acropora piamata. b, Acropora cervicornis. c, Pocillopora meandrina. d, Favia fragum. e, Tubastraea coccinea.
No. 1382: a, Paramuricea clavata. b, Turbinaria reniformis.

2022, June 14		Litho.	Perf. 13¾	
1381	A581	$1.60 Sheet of 5, #a-e	16.00	16.00

Souvenir Sheet

1382	A581	$3 Sheet of 2, #a-b	12.00	12.00

MARSHALL ISLANDS

Bromeliads — A582

No. 1383: a, Billbergia pyramidalis. b, Orthophytum amoenum. c, Lindmania navioides. d, Pitcairnia heydlauffii. e, Quesnelia arvensis.
No. 1384: a, Quesnelia quesneliana. b, Canistropsis bilbergiodes.

2022, June 14   Litho.   Perf. 13¾
1383   A582 $1.60 Sheet of 5,
     #a-e   16.00   16.00
Souvenir Sheet
1384   A582 $3 Sheet of 2,
     #a-b   12.00   12.00

Muhammad Ali (1942-2016), Boxer — A583

No. 1385 — Ali: a, With arms crossed. b, Facing left. c, Wearing short-sleeved shirt. d, Wearing white boxing trunks.
$5, Ali wearing robe.

2022, July 4   Litho.   Perf. 14
1385   A583 $2 Sheet of 4, #a-d   16.00   16.00
Souvenir Sheet
Perf. 12½
1386   A583 $5 multi   10.00   10.00
No. 1386 contains one 38x51mm stamp.

Neil Armstrong (1930-2012), First Man on the Moon — A584

No. 1387 — Armstrong: a, With fellow Gemini 8 crewmember, David R. Scott. b, With U.S. flag in background. c, With fellow Apollo 11 astronauts, Michael Collins and Edwin E. "Buzz" Aldrin. d, Wearing glasses. e, Wearing space suit and holding helmet.
$5, Armstrong wearing casual shirt.

2022, Aug. 21   Litho.   Perf. 14
1387   A584 $1.50 Sheet of 5,
     #a-e   15.00   15.00
Souvenir Sheet
Perf. 12½
1388   A584 $5 multi   10.00   10.00
No. 1388 contains one 38x51mm stamp.

King Charles III A585

No. 1389 — King Charles III: a, Wearing military uniform. b, With his mother, Queen Elizabeth II, father, Prince Philip, and son, Prince William. c, As young man in crowd. d, Kissing his mother's hand.
$5, King Charles II wearing pinstriped shirt.

2022, Oct. 10   Litho.   Perf. 14
1389   A585 $2 Sheet of 4, #a-d   16.00   16.00
Souvenir Sheet
Perf. 12½
1390   A585 $5 multi   10.00   10.00
No. 1390 contains one 51x38mm stamp.

Compact of Free Association, 35th Anniv. — A586

No. 1391: a, Amata Kabua (1928-96), President of Marshall Islands. b, Flags of Marshall Islands and the United States. c, Traditional outrigger canoe. d, Ronald Reagan (1911-2004), President of the United States.
No. 1392, horiz.: a, Painting of a traditional outrigger canoe (40x30mm). b, Navigational stick chart (40x30mm). c, Flags of Marshall Islands and the United States (80x30mm).

2022, Oct. 21   Litho.   Perf. 14
1391   A586 $1.35 Sheet of 4,
     #a-d   11.00   11.00
Souvenir Sheet
1392   A586 $1.35 Sheet of 3,
     #a-c   8.25   8.25

Elvis Presley (1935-77) — A587

No. 1393 — Presley: a, Wearing plaid shirt. b, Holding microphone. c, Wearing leather vest. d, Wearing black suit. e, Playing guitar. f, With brick wall in background.
$5, Presley wearing Army uniform.

2022, Nov. 18   Litho.   Perf. 14
1393   A587 $1.35 Sheet of 6,
     #a-f   16.50   16.50
Souvenir Sheet
Perf. 12½
1394   A587 $5 multi   10.00   10.00

Visit of Pres. Joseph R. Biden, Jr. to Italy A588

No. 1395 — Pres. Biden: a, With Italian Pres. Sergio Mattarella. b, Standing in front of flags. c, With wife, Jill, on airplane stairway. d, with Italian Prime Minister Mario Draghi.
$5, Pres. Biden with his wife, Draghi, and Draghi's wife, Maria Serenella Cappello.

2022, Dec. 9   Litho.   Perf. 14
1395   A588 $2 Sheet of 4, #a-d   16.00   16.00
Souvenir Sheet
1396   A588 $5 multi   10.00   10.00
No. 1396 contains one 80x30mm stamp.

Insects A589

No. 1397: a, Dynastes hercules. b, Agrionoptera insignis. c, Graphocephala coccinea. d, Papilio machaon. e, Coccinella magnifica.
No. 1398: a, Apis mellifera. b, Hymenopus coronatus.

2022, Dec. 12   Litho.   Perf. 13¾
1397   A589 $1.60 Sheet of 5,
     #a-e   16.00   16.00
Souvenir Sheet
1398   A589 $3 Sheet of 2,
     #a-b   12.00   12.00

Miniature Sheet

Mikhail Gorbachev (1931-2022), President of the Soviet Union — A590

No. 1399 — Gorbachev: a, With U.S. Pres. Barack Obama, 2009. b, With Japanese Prime Minister Junichiro Koizumi, 2003. c, Facing left, without glasses. d, With the Dalai Lama, 2012. e, With Israeli Prime Minister Shimon Peres, 2003. f, With Queen Elizabeth II, 1991. g, Facing right, wearing glasses. h, With Mayor of London Boris Johnson, 2009. i, With Canadian Prime Minister Brian Mulroney, 1990.

2022   Litho.   Perf. 14
1399   A590 $1 Sheet of 9, #a-i   18.00   18.00
No. 1399 was alleged to have been issued on Aug. 30, the day Gorbachev died, which is inscribed on the sheet margin.

Miniature Sheet

Queen Elizabeth II (1926-2022) — A591

No. 1400 — Queen Elizabeth II: a, Wearing military uniform. b, Without hat. c, Wearing hat and carrying flowers in black and white photograph. d, Wearing pink hat and jacket. e, Wearing white hat and jacket. f, Wearing blue hat and jacket.

2022   Litho.   Perf. 14
1400   A591 $1.96 Sheet of 6,
     #a-f   24.00   24.00
No. 1400 was alleged to have been issued on Sept. 8, the day Queen Elizabeth II died, which is inscribed on the sheet margin.

SEMI-POSTAL STAMPS

Operation Crossroads, Nuclear Testing at Bikini Atoll, 50th Anniv. — SP1

Designs: a, Evacuation of Bikinians. b, Navy preparations. c, Able. d, Baker. e, Ghost fleet. f, Effects on Bikinians.

1996, July 1   Litho.   Perf. 13½
B1   SP1   32c +8c #a.-f. + 6 labels   4.75   4.75
Surtax for the benefit of the people of Bikini.

AIR POST STAMPS

Audubon Type of 1985

1985, Feb. 15   Litho.   Perf. 14
C1   A11   44c Booby Gannet, vert.   .90   .90
C2   A11   44c Esquimaux Curlew, vert.   .90   .90
   a.   Pair, #C1-C2   1.80   1.80

AMERIPEX Type of 1986

Designs: No. C3, Consolidated PBY-5A Catalina Amphibian. No. C4, Grumman SA-16 Albatross. No. C5, McDonnell Douglas DC-6B Super Cloudmaster. No. C6, Boeing 727-100.

1986, May 22   Litho.   Perf. 14
C3   A20   44c multicolored   .85   .85
C4   A20   44c multicolored   .85   .85
C5   A20   44c multicolored   .85   .85
C6   A20   44c multicolored   .85   .85
   a.   Block of 4, #C3-C6   3.50   3.50

Operation Crossroads Type of 1986
Souvenir Sheet

1986, July 1   Litho.   Perf. 14
C7   A21   44c USS Saratoga   1.00   1.00

Statue of Liberty Cent., Intl. Peace Year — AP1

1986, Oct. 28   Litho.
C8   AP1   44c multicolored   1.00   .95

Natl. Girl Scout Movement, 20th Anniv. — AP2

No. C9, Community service. No. C10, Salute. No. C11, Health care. No. C12, Learning skills.

1986, Dec. 8   Litho.
C9   AP2   44c multicolored   .75   .75
C10   AP2   44c multicolored   .75   .75
C11   AP2   44c multicolored   .75   .75
C12   AP2   44c multicolored   .75   .75
   a.   Block of 4, #C9-C12   3.00   3.00
Girl Scout Movement in the US, 75th anniv. (1912-1987).

Marine Birds — AP3

No. C13, Wedge-tailed shearwater. No. C14, Red-footed booby. No. C15, Red-tailed tropic-bird. No. C16, Great frigatebird.

1987, Jan. 12   Litho.   Perf. 14
C13   AP3   44c multicolored   .75   .75
C14   AP3   44c multicolored   .75   .75
C15   AP3   44c multicolored   .75   .75
C16   AP3   44c multicolored   .75   .75
   a.   Block of 4, #C13-C16   3.00   3.00

CAPEX '87 — AP4

Last flight of Amelia Earhart: No. C17, Take-off at Lae, New Guinea, July 2, 1937. No. C18, USCG Itasca cutter at Howland Is. No. C19, Purported crash landing of the Electra at

… Mili Atoll. No. C20, Recovery of the Electra by the Koshu, a Japanese survey ship.

1987, June 15   Litho.   Perf. 14

C17	AP4	44c multicolored	.75	.75
C18	AP4	44c multicolored	.75	.75
C19	AP4	44c multicolored	.75	.75
C20	AP4	44c multicolored	.75	.75
a.		Block of 4, #C17-C20	3.00	3.00

Space Shuttle Type of 1988

Design: 45c, Astronaut, shuttle over Rongelap.

1988, Dec. 23   Litho.   Perf. 14

C21	A38	45c multicolored	.85	.85

Aircraft — AP5

12c, Dornier Do228. 36c, Boeing 737. 39c, Hawker Siddeley 748. 45c, Boeing 727.

1989, Apr. 24   Litho.   Perf. 14x14½

C22	AP5	12c multi	.25	.25
a.		Booklet pane of 10	3.00	—
C23	AP5	36c multi	.75	.75
a.		Booklet pane of 10	8.00	—
C24	AP5	39c multi	.90	.90
a.		Booklet pane of 10	9.00	—
C25	AP5	45c multi	1.00	1.00
a.		Booklet pane of 10	10.00	—
b.		Bklt. pane, 5 each 36c, 45c	8.75	—
		Nos. C22-C25 (4)	2.90	2.90

MARTINIQUE

ˌmär-tən-ˈēk

LOCATION — Island in the West Indies, southeast of Puerto Rico
GOVT. — French Colony
AREA — 385 sq. mi.
POP. — 261,595 (1946)
CAPITAL — Fort-de-France

Formerly a French colony, Martinique became an integral part of the Republic, acquiring the same status as the departments in metropolitan France, under a law effective Jan. 1, 1947.

100 Centimes = 1 Franc

Catalogue values for unused stamps in this country are for Never Hinged items, beginning with Scott 196 in the regular postage section, Scott C1 in the airpost section, and Scott J37 in the postage due section.

See France Nos. 1278 and 1508 for stamps inscribed "Martinique."

Stamps of French Colonies 1881-86 Surcharged in Black

Nos. 1, 7
No. 2
No. 3
No. 4
Nos. 5-6, 8
Nos. 9-20

1886-91   Unwmk.   Perf. 14x13½

1	A9	5 on 20c	65.00	55.00
a.		Double surcharge	750.00	750.00
2	A9	5c on 20c	15,000.	15,000.
3	A9	15c on 20c ('87)	275.00	240.00
a.		Inverted surcharge	2,350.	2,500.
4	A9	15c on 20c ('87)	100.00	100.00
a.		Inverted surcharge	1,500.	1,500.
b.		Se-tenant pair, #3-4	475.00	425.00
c.		Se-tenant pair, #3a-4a	4,750.	4,750.
5	A9	01 on 20c ('88)	20.00	19.00
a.		Inverted surcharge	350.00	350.00
6	A9	05 on 20c	16.00	13.00
7	A9	15 on 20c ('88)	200.00	180.00
c.		Inverted surcharge	700.00	750.00
8	A9	015 on 20c ('87)	60.00	65.00
a.		Inverted surcharge	875.00	825.00
9	A9	01c on 2c ('88)	4.75	3.25
a.		Double surcharge	475.00	475.00
10	A9	01c on 4c ('88)	15.00	4.75
11	A9	05c on 4c ('88)	1,500.	1,375.
12	A9	05c on 10c ('90)	120.00	72.50
a.		Slanting "5"	300.00	240.00
13	A9	05c on 20c ('88)	28.00	20.00
a.		Slanting "5"	150.00	120.00
b.		Inverted surcharge	425.00	375.00
14	A9	05c on 30c ('91)	35.00	28.00
a.		Slanting "5"	160.00	150.00
15	A9	05c on 35c ('91)	20.00	16.00
a.		Slanting "5"	160.00	150.00
b.		Inverted surcharge	325.00	300.00
16	A9	05c on 40c ('91)	65.00	47.50
a.		Slanting "5"	260.00	165.00
17	A9	15c on 4c ('88)	12,000.	11,000.
18	A9	15c on 20c ('87)	150.00	120.00
a.		Slanting "5"	500.00	425.00
b.		Double surcharge	700.00	700.00
19	A9	15c on 25c ('90)	32.50	20.00
a.		Slanting "5"	150.00	130.00
b.		Inverted surcharge	325.00	275.00
c.		Double surcharge	450.00	450.00
20	A9	15c on 75c ('91)	210.00	175.00
a.		Slanting "5"	550.00	450.00

French Colonies No. 47 Surcharged

1891

21	A9	01c on 2c brn, buff	11.00	11.00

French Colonies Nos. J5-J9 Surcharged

1891-92   Black Surcharge   Imperf.

22	D1	05c on 5c blk ('92)	17.50	17.00
a.		Slanting "5"	72.50	65.00
23	D1	05c on 15c blk	16.00	16.00
b.		Slanting "5"	72.50	65.00
24	D1	15c on 20c blk	20.00	16.00
a.		Inverted surcharge	300.00	300.00
b.		Double surcharge	300.00	300.00
25	D1	15c on 30c blk	20.00	16.00
a.		Inverted surcharge	300.00	300.00
b.		Slanting "5"	80.00	72.50
		Nos. 22-25 (4)	73.50	65.00

Red Surcharge

26	D1	05c on 10c blk	14.50	11.00
a.		Inverted surcharge	300.00	300.00
27	D1	05c on 15c blk	16.00	16.00
28	D1	15c on 20c blk	52.50	45.00
a.		Inverted surcharge	450.00	450.00
		Nos. 26-28 (3)	83.00	72.00

French Colonies No. 54 Surcharged in Black

j
k

1892   Perf. 14x13½

29	A9 (j)	05c on 25c	65.00	65.00
a.		Slanting "5"	300.00	300.00
30	A9 (j)	15c on 25c	36.00	36.00
a.		Slanting "5"	275.00	275.00
31	A9 (k)	05c on 25c	65.00	65.00
a.		"1882" instead of "1892"	675.00	600.00
b.		"95" instead of "05"	850.00	800.00
c.		Slanting "5"	300.00	300.00
32	A9 (k)	15c on 25c	32.50	32.50
a.		"1882" instead of "1892"	600.00	600.00
b.		Slanting "5"	160.00	160.00
		Nos. 29-32 (4)	198.50	198.50

Navigation and Commerce — A15

1892-1906   Typo.   Perf. 14x13½

"MARTINIQUE" Colony in Carmine or Blue

33	A15	1c blk, lil bl	1.50	1.40
a.		"MARTINIQUE" in blue	1,000.	1,000.
b.		"MARTINIQUE" omitted	5,500.	
34	A15	2c brn, buff	1.75	1.40
35	A15	4c claret, lav	2.00	1.50
36	A15	5c grn, grnish	2.40	1.50
37	A15	5c yel grn ('99)	3.50	1.10
38	A15	10c blk, lav	11.00	2.00
39	A15	10c red ('99)	5.25	1.50
40	A15	15c blue, quadrille paper	42.50	8.00
41	A15	15c gray ('99)	13.50	2.10
42	A15	20c red, grn	20.00	10.00
43	A15	25c blk, rose	24.00	3.25
44	A15	25c blue ('99)	16.00	14.50
45	A15	30c brn, bis	36.00	19.00
46	A15	35c blk, yel ('06)	16.00	9.50
47	A15	40c red, straw	36.00	19.00
48	A15	50c car, rose	40.00	24.00
49	A15	50c brn, az ('99)	42.50	32.50
50	A15	75c dp vio, org	32.50	20.00
51	A15	1fr brnz grn, straw	32.50	21.00
52	A15	2fr vio, rose ('04)	92.50	75.00
53	A15	5fr lil, lav ('03)	110.00	95.00
		Nos. 33-53 (21)	581.40	363.25

Perf. 13½x14 stamps are counterfeits.
For surcharges see Nos. 54-61, 101-104.

Stamps of 1892-1903 Surcharged in Black

1904

54	A15	10c on 30c brn, bis	14.50	14.50
a.		Double surcharge	525.00	525.00
b.		Inverted surcharge	1,600.	1,600.
55	A15	10c on 5fr lil, lav	16.00	16.00

Surcharged

56	A15	10c on 30c brn, bis	24.00	24.00
57	A15	10c on 40c red, straw	24.00	24.00
a.		Double surcharge	600.00	600.00
58	A15	10c on 50c car, rose	28.00	28.00
59	A15	10c on 75c dp vio, org	20.00	20.00
60	A15	10c on 1fr brnz grn, straw	24.00	24.00
a.		Double surcharge	350.00	350.00
61	A15	10c on 5fr lil, lav	200.00	200.00
		Nos. 54-61 (8)	350.50	350.50

Martinique Woman A16

Girl Bearing Pineapple in Cane Field A18

View of Fort-de-France A17

1908-30   Typo.

62	A16	1c red brn & brn	.25	.25
63	A16	2c ol grn & brn	.30	.25
64	A16	4c vio brn & brn	.30	.30
65	A16	5c grn & brn	1.10	.40
66	A16	5c org & brn ('22)	.50	.40
67	A16	10c car & brn	1.10	.50
68	A16	10c bl grn & grn ('22)	.55	.40
69	A16	10c brn vio & rose ('25)	.55	.40
70	A16	15c brn vio & rose ('17)	.65	.40
71	A16	15c bl grn & gray grn ('25)	.50	.40
72	A16	15c dp bl & red org ('28)	1.60	1.60
73	A16	20c vio & brn	1.40	1.10
74	A17	25c bl & brn	2.25	1.10
75	A17	25c org & brn ('22)	.90	.55
76	A17	30c brn org & brn	2.25	1.10
77	A17	30c dl red & brn ('22)	.75	.65
78	A17	30c rose & ver ('24)	.55	.55
79	A17	30c ol brn & brn ('25)	.55	.55
80	A17	30c sl bl & bl grn ('27)	1.60	1.60
81	A17	35c vio & brn	.90	.65
a.		White chalky paper	4.50	2.75
82	A17	40c gray grn & brn	.90	.65
83	A17	45c dk brn & brn	.90	.65
a.		White chalky paper	2.00	1.60
84	A17	50c rose & brn	2.25	1.10
85	A17	50c bl & brn ('22)	1.40	1.30
86	A17	50c org & grn ('25)	.90	.40
87	A17	60c dk bl & lil rose ('25)	.75	.75
88	A17	65c vio & ol brn ('27)	2.00	2.00
89	A17	75c slate & brn	1.40	1.10
90	A17	75c ind & dk bl ('25)	.90	.90
91	A17	75c org brn & lt bl ('27)	2.75	2.75
92	A17	90c brn red & brt red ('30)	5.50	5.50
93	A18	1fr dl bl & brn	1.20	1.00
94	A18	1fr dk bl ('25)	1.00	.90
95	A18	1fr ver & ol grn ('27)	2.75	2.75
96	A18	1.10fr vio & dk brn ('28)	3.75	4.50
97	A18	1.50fr ind & ultra ('27)	5.50	5.50
98	A18	2fr gray & brn	4.50	2.00
99	A18	3fr red vio ('30)	9.50	9.50
100	A18	5fr org red & brn	10.50	6.00
		Nos. 62-100 (39)	76.90	64.40

For surcharges see Nos. 105-128, B1.

Nos. 41, 43, 47 and 53 Surcharged in Carmine or Black

Spacing between figures of surcharge 1.5mm (5c), 2mm (10c)

1912, Aug.

101	A15	5c on 15c gray (C)	1.00	1.00
102	A15	5c on 25c blk, rose (C)	1.50	1.50
103	A15	10c on 40c red, straw	2.40	2.40
104	A15	10c on 5fr lil, lav	3.00	3.00
		Nos. 101-104 (4)	7.90	7.90

Two spacings between the surcharged numerals are found on Nos. 101 to 104. For detailed listings, see the Scott Classic Specialized Catalogue of Stamps and Covers.

Nos. 62, 63, 70 Surcharged

1920, June 15

105	A16	5c on 1c	2.10	2.10
a.		Double surcharge	45.00	45.00
b.		Inverted surcharge	32.50	32.50
106	A16	10c on 2c	2.10	2.10
a.		Double surcharge	130.00	
b.		Inverted surcharge	45.00	45.00
c.		Double surcharge, one inverted	95.00	
107	A16	25c on 15c	2.25	2.25
a.		Double surcharge	55.00	55.00
b.		Inverted surcharge	55.00	55.00
c.		Double surcharge, one inverted	100.00	
d.		Pair, one stamp without surcharge	160.00	160.00
		Nos. 105-107 (3)	6.45	6.45

No. 70 Surcharged in Various Colors

1922, Dec.

108	A16	1c on 15c (Bk)	.50	.50
a.		Double surcharge	190.00	190.00
109	A16	2c on 15c (Bl)	.50	.50
110	A16	5c on 15c (R)	.65	.65
a.		Imperf., pair	260.00	
		Nos. 108-110 (3)	1.65	1.65

MARTINIQUE

Types of 1908-30 Surcharged

1923-25
111	A17	60c on 75c bl & rose	.65	.65
112	A17	65c on 45c ol brn & brn ('25)	1.45	1.45
113	A17	85c on 75c blk & brn (R) ('25)	1.75	1.75
		Nos. 111-113 (3)	3.85	3.85

Nos. 63, 73, 76-77, 84-85 Surcharged in Brown

Surcharge is horiz. on Nos. 114-115, vert. reading up on Nos. 116, 119 and down on Nos. 117-118.

1924, Feb. 14
114	A16	1c on 2c	3.25	3.25
a.		Double surcharge	550.00	550.00
b.		Inverted surcharge	100.00	100.00
115	A16	5c on 20c	4.00	4.00
a.		Inverted surcharge	100.00	100.00
116	A17	15c on 30c (#76)	16.00	16.00
a.		Surcharge reading down	57.50	57.50
117	A17	15c on 30c (#77)	22.50	22.50
a.		Surcharge reading up	67.50	67.50
118	A17	25c on 50c (#84)	325.00	350.00
119	A17	25c on 50c (#85)	10.50	10.50
a.		Double surcharge	400.00	400.00
b.		Surcharge reading down	47.50	
		Nos. 114-119 (6)	381.25	406.25

Stamps and Types of 1908-30 Surcharged

1924-27
120	A16	25c on 15c brn vio & rose ('25)	.55	.55
121	A18	25c on 2fr gray & brn	.50	.50
122	A18	25c on 5fr org red & brn (Bl)	2.10	1.75
123	A17	90c on 75c brn red & red ('27)	3.75	2.75
124	A18	1.25fr on 1fr dk bl ('26)	1.10	1.00
125	A18	1.50fr on 1fr dk bl & ultra ('27)	2.00	1.10
126	A18	3fr on 5fr dl red & grn ('27)	3.00	3.00
127	A18	10fr on 5fr dl grn & dp red ('27)	12.00	12.00
128	A18	20fr on 5fr org brn & red vio ('27)	18.50	17.50
		Nos. 120-128 (9)	43.50	40.15

Common Design Types pictured following the introduction.

Colonial Exposition Issue
Common Design Types
1931, Apr. 13 — Engr. — Perf. 12½
Name of Country in Black
129	CD70	40c deep green	5.25	5.25
130	CD71	50c violet	5.25	5.25
131	CD72	90c red orange	5.25	5.25
132	CD73	1.50fr dull blue	5.25	5.25
		Nos. 129-132 (4)	21.00	21.00

Village of Basse-Pointe — A19

Government Palace, Fort-de-France — A20

Martinique Women — A21

1933-40 — Photo. — Perf. 13½
133	A19	1c red, pink	.25	.25
134	A20	2c dull blue	.25	.25
135	A20	3c sepia ('40)	.35	.35
136	A19	4c olive grn	.25	.25
137	A20	5c dp rose	.35	.35
138	A19	10c blk, pink	.35	.35
139	A20	15c blk, org	.35	.35
140	A21	20c org brn	.35	.35
141	A19	25c brn vio	.35	.35
142	A20	30c green	.50	.50
143	A20	30c lt ultra ('40)	.40	.40
144	A21	35c dl grn ('38)	1.00	.90
145	A21	40c olive brn	.65	.50
146	A20	45c dk brn	2.00	1.90
147	A20	45c grn ('40)	.65	.60
148	A20	50c red	.50	.30
149	A19	55c brn red ('38)	1.30	1.00
150	A19	60c lt bl ('40)	.95	.95
151	A21	65c red, grn	.50	.50
152	A21	70c brt red vio ('40)	.75	.75
153	A19	75c dk brn	1.10	.90
154	A20	80c vio ('38)	.75	.65
155	A19	90c carmine	1.90	1.75
156	A19	90c brt red vio ('39)	.95	.95
157	A20	1fr blk, grn	1.90	1.40
158	A20	1fr rose red ('38)	.75	.65
159	A21	1.25fr dk vio	.80	.80
160	A21	1.25fr dp rose ('39)	.75	.75
161	A19	1.40fr lt ultra ('40)	.80	.80
162	A21	1.50fr dp bl	.65	.55
163	A20	1.60fr chnt ('40)	.80	.80
164	A21	1.75fr ol grn	9.50	5.25
165	A21	1.75fr dp bl ('38)	.75	.75
166	A19	2fr dk bl, grn	.50	.40
167	A21	2.25fr blue ('39)	.75	.75
168	A19	2.50fr sepia ('40)	.95	.95
169	A21	3fr brn vio	.65	.60
170	A21	5fr red, pink	1.30	1.10
171	A19	10fr dk bl, bl	1.10	.80
172	A20	20fr red, yel	1.35	.95
		Nos. 133-172 (40)	40.05	32.75

For surcharges see Nos. 190-195.
For type A20 without "RF," see Nos. 189A-189E.

Landing of Bélain d'Esnambuc — A22

Freed Slaves Paying Homage to Victor Schoelcher — A23

1935, Oct. 22 — Engr. — Perf. 13
173	A22	40c blk brn	3.25	3.25
174	A22	50c dl red	3.25	3.25
175	A22	1.50fr ultra	12.00	12.00
176	A23	1.75fr lil rose	12.00	12.00
177	A23	3fr brown	12.00	12.00
a.		5fr ultramarine (error)	950.00	
178	A23	10fr blue grn	9.50	9.50
		Nos. 173-178 (6)	52.00	52.00

Tercentenary of French possessions in the West Indies

Colonial Arts Exhibition Issue
Common Design Type
Souvenir Sheet
1937 — Imperf.
179	CD74	3fr brt grn	8.75	10.50
a.		"MARTINIQUE" omitted	3,100.	
b.		Inscriptions inverted	2,200.	

Paris International Exposition Issue
Common Design Types
1937, Apr. 15 — Perf. 13
180	CD74	20c dp vio	2.10	2.10
181	CD75	30c dk grn	1.75	1.75
182	CD76	40c car rose	1.75	1.75
183	CD77	50c dk brn & blk	1.60	1.60
184	CD78	90c red	2.00	2.00
185	CD79	1.50fr ultra	2.00	2.00
		Nos. 180-185 (6)	11.20	11.20

New York World's Fair Issue
Common Design Type
1939, May 10 — Perf. 12½x12
186	CD82	1.25fr car lake	1.10	1.10
187	CD82	2.25fr ultra	1.25	1.25

View of Fort-de-France and Marshal Pétain — A23a

1941 — Engr. — Perf. 12½x12
188	A23a	1fr dull lilac	.80	
189	A23a	2.50fr blue	.80	

Nos. 188-189 were issued by the Vichy government in France, but were not placed on sale in Martinique.
For surcharges, see Nos. B10A-B10B.

Types of 1933-40 without "RF"
1942-44 — Photo. — Perf. 13½
189A	A20	3c sepia	.50	
189B	A20	15c blk, org	.55	
189C	A20	30c yel green	.55	
189D	A20	50c red	1.40	
189E	A20	1.50fr dp bl	.65	
		Nos. 189A-189E (5)	3.65	

Nos. 189A-189E were issued by the Vichy government in France, but were not placed on sale in Martinique.

Nos. 134, 135, 136 and 151 Surcharged in Red, Black or Blue

1945 — Perf. 13½, 13x13½
190	A20	1fr on 2c dl bl (R)	.65	.65
191	A19	2fr on 4c ol grn	.65	.65
192	A20	3fr on 2c dl bl (R)	.65	.65
193	A21	5fr on 65c red, grn	1.40	1.40
194	A21	10fr on 65c red, grn	1.50	1.50
195	A20	20fr on 3c sepia (Bl)	1.50	1.50
		Nos. 190-195 (6)	6.50	6.50

Catalogue values for unused stamps in this section, from this point to the end of the section, are for Never Hinged items.

Eboue Issue
Common Design Type
1945 — Engr. — Perf. 13
196	CD91	2fr black	.75	.55
197	CD91	25fr Prussian green	1.30	1.00

Victor Schoelcher and View of Town of Schoelcher — A24

1945 — Unwmk. — Litho. — Perf. 11½
198	A24	10c dp bl vio & ultra	.35	.25
199	A24	30c dk org brn & lt org brn	.35	.25
200	A24	40c grnsh bl & pale bl	.40	.35
201	A24	50c car brn & rose lil	.40	.35
202	A24	60c org yel & yel	.40	.35
203	A24	70c brn & pale brn	.40	.35
204	A24	80c lt bl grn & pale grn	.40	.35
205	A24	1fr bl & lt bl	.40	.35
206	A24	1.20fr rose vio & rose lil	.40	.35
207	A24	1.50fr red org & org	.40	.35
208	A24	2fr blk & gray	.40	.35
209	A24	2.40fr red & pink	1.75	1.00
210	A24	3fr pink & pale pink	.75	.50
211	A24	4fr ultra & lt ultra	.95	.50
212	A24	4.50fr yel grn & lt grn	1.10	.50
213	A24	5fr org brn & lt grn brn	.95	.50
214	A24	10fr dk vio & lil	1.10	.65
215	A24	15fr rose car & lil rose	1.50	.75
216	A24	20fr ol grn & lt ol grn	2.25	1.25
		Nos. 198-216 (19)	14.65	9.30

Martinique Girl — A25

Mountains — A30

Cliffs — A26

Gathering Sugar Cane — A27

Mount Pelée — A28

Tropical Fruit — A29

1947, June 2 — Engr. — Perf. 13
217	A25	10c red brown	.50	.25
218	A25	30c deep blue	.50	.40
219	A25	50c olive green	.50	.40
220	A26	60c dark green	.55	.50
221	A26	1fr red brown	.55	.35
222	A26	1.50fr purple	.60	.50
223	A27	2fr blue green	1.10	.75
224	A27	2.50fr blk brn	1.10	.65
225	A27	3fr deep blue	1.10	.65
226	A28	4fr dk brown	1.00	.65
227	A28	5fr dark green	1.10	.65
228	A28	6fr lilac rose	1.00	.65
229	A29	10fr indigo	1.75	1.25
230	A29	15fr red brown	1.90	1.25
231	A29	20fr blk brown	2.50	1.50
232	A30	25fr violet	2.50	1.60
233	A30	40fr blue green	3.00	2.00
		Nos. 217-233 (17)	21.25	14.00

SEMI-POSTAL STAMPS

Regular Issue of 1908 Surcharged in Red

Perf. 13½x14
1915, May 15 — Unwmk.
B1	A16	10c + 5c car & brn	2.75	2.00
		Never hinged	4.00	

Curie Issue
Common Design Type
1938, Oct. 24 — Perf. 13
B2	CD80	1.75fr + 50c brt ultra	13.00	13.00
		Never hinged	17.50	

French Revolution Issue
Common Design Type
Photo.; Name & Value Typo. in Black
1939, July 5
B3	CD83	45c + 25c grn	10.50	10.50
		Never hinged	15.00	
B4	CD83	70c + 30c brn	10.50	10.50
		Never hinged	15.00	
B5	CD83	90c + 35c red org	10.50	10.50
		Never hinged	15.00	
B6	CD83	1.25fr + 1fr rose pink	10.50	10.50
		Never hinged	16.00	
B7	CD83	2.25fr + 2fr blue	10.50	10.50
		Never hinged	15.00	
		Nos. B3-B7 (5)	52.50	52.50

Common Design Type and

Colonial Infantry with Machine Gun — SP1

Naval Rifleman — SP2

MARTINIQUE — MAURITANIA

		1941	Photo.	Perf. 13½
B8	SP1	1fr + 1fr red		1.25
B9	CD86	1.50fr + 3fr maroon		1.40
B10	SP2	2.50fr + 1fr blue		1.40
		Nos. B8-B10 (3)		4.05

Nos. B8-B10 were issued by the Vichy government in France, but were not placed on sale in Martinique.

Nos. 188-189 Srchd. in Black or Red

1944		Engr.	Perf. 12½x12
B10A		50c + 1.50fr on 2.50fr blue (R)	.95
B10B		+ 2.50fr on 1fr dull lilac	1.00

Colonial Development Fund. Nos. B10A-B10B were issued by the Vichy government in France, but were not placed on sale in Martinique.

Red Cross Issue
Common Design Type

1944			Perf. 14½x14
B11	CD90	5fr + 20fr dark purple	1.20 1.20

The surtax was for the French Red Cross and national relief.

AIR POST STAMPS

Catalogue values for unused stamps in this section are for Never Hinged items.

Common Design Type

1945	Unwmk.	Photo.	Perf. 14½x14
C1	CD87	50fr dark green	1.25 .80
C2	CD87	100fr olive brown	1.75 .80

Two other values, 8.50fr orange and 18fr red brown, were prepared but not issued. Value, $210 each.

Victory Issue
Common Design Type

1946, May 8		Engr.	Perf. 12½
C3	CD92	8fr indigo	1.30 1.00

European victory of the Allied Nations in WWII.

Chad to Rhine Issue
Common Design Types

1946, June 6			
C4	CD93	5fr orange	1.00 .90
C5	CD94	10fr slate grn	1.40 1.10
C6	CD95	15fr carmine	1.40 1.20
C7	CD96	20fr chocolate	1.40 1.20
C8	CD97	25fr deep blue	1.75 1.40
C9	CD98	50fr gray blk	1.90 1.50
		Nos. C4-C9 (6)	8.85 7.30

Seaplane and Beach Scene AP1

Plane over Tropic Shore — AP2

Albatross AP3

1947, June 2			Perf. 13
C10	AP1	50fr dk brn vio	6.50 2.75
C11	AP2	100fr dk bl grn	8.00 3.75
C12	AP3	200fr violet	45.00 25.00
		Nos. C10-C12 (3)	59.50 31.50

AIR POST SEMI-POSTAL STAMPS

Nurse with Mother & Child SPAP1

1942, June 22	Unwmk.	Engr.	Perf. 13
CB1	SPAP1	1.50fr + 3.50fr green	.90
CB2	SPAP1	2fr + 6fr brn & red	.90

Native children's welfare fund. Nos. CB1-CB2 were issued by the Vichy government in France, but were not placed on sale in Martinique.

Colonial Education Fund
Common Design Type

1942, June 22			
CB3	CD86a	1.20fr + 1.80fr blue & red	1.00

No. CB3 was issued by the Vichy government in France, but was not placed on sale in Martinique.

POSTAGE DUE STAMPS

The set of 14 French Colonies postage due stamps (Nos. J1-J14) overprinted "MARTINIQUE" diagonally in red in 1887 was not an official issue.

Postage Due Stamps of France, 1893-1926 Overprinted

1927, Oct. 10			Perf. 14x13½
J15	D2	5c light blue	1.75 1.75
J16	D2	10c brown	2.10 2.00
J17	D2	20c olive green	2.10 2.00
J18	D2	25c rose	2.75 2.60
J19	D2	30c red	3.75 3.50
J20	D2	45c green	5.25 5.00
J21	D2	50c brn violet	6.50 6.00
J22	D2	60c blue green	6.50 6.00
J23	D2	1fr red brown	8.75 8.25
J24	D2	2fr bright vio	12.00 11.00
J25	D2	3fr magenta	13.00 12.00
		Nos. J15-J25 (11)	64.45 60.10

Tropical Fruit — D3

1933, Feb. 15		Photo.	Perf. 13½
J26	D3	5c dk bl, green	.50 .50
J27	D3	10c orange brown	.50 .50
J28	D3	20c dk blue	.95 .95
J29	D3	25c red, pink	1.40 1.40
J30	D3	30c dk vio	1.40 1.40
J31	D3	45c red, yel	1.10 1.10
J32	D3	50c dk brn	1.75 1.75
J33	D3	60c dl grn	1.75 1.75
J34	D3	1fr blk, org	1.75 1.75
J35	D3	2fr dp rose	1.75 1.75
J36	D3	3fr dk blue, bl	1.75 1.75
		Nos. J26-J36 (11)	14.60 14.60

Type of 1933 Without "RF"

1943			
J36A	D3	10c orange brown	.35
J36B	D3	20c dk blue	.35
J36C	D3	25c red, pink	.50
J36D	D3	30c dk vio	.50
		Nos. J36A-J36D (4)	1.70

Nos. J36A-J36D were issued by the Vichy government in France, but were not placed on sale in Martinique.

Catalogue values for unused stamps in this section, from this point to the end of the section, are for Never Hinged items.

Map — D4

1947, June 2		Engr.	Perf. 14x13
J37	D4	10c ultra	.40 .30
J38	D4	30c brt bl grn	.40 .30
J39	D4	50c slate gray	.40 .30
J40	D4	1fr org red	.40 .30
J41	D4	2fr dk vio brn	.90 .75
J42	D4	3fr lilac rose	.95 .80
J43	D4	4fr dk brn	.95 .95
J44	D4	5fr red	1.20 .95
J45	D4	10fr black	2.10 1.60
J46	D4	20fr olive grn	2.40 1.75
		Nos. J37-J46 (10)	10.10 8.00

PARCEL POST STAMP

Postage Due Stamp of French Colonies Surcharged in Black

1903, Oct.	Unwmk.		Imperf.
Q1	D1	5fr on 60c brn, buff	550.00 675.00
a.		Inverted surcharge	875.00 950.00

MAURITANIA

mor-ə-ta-nē-ə

LOCATION — Northwestern Africa, bordering on the Atlantic Ocean
GOVT. — Republic
AREA — 398,000 sq. mi.
POP. — 4,650,000 (2020 est.)
CAPITAL — Nouakchott

The Islamic Republic of Mauritania was proclaimed Nov. 28, 1958. Stamps of French West Africa were used in the period between the issues of the colony and the republic.

100 Centimes = 1 Franc
Ouguiya ("um") (1973)

Catalogue values for unused stamps in this country are for Never Hinged items, beginning with Scott 114 in the regular postage section, Scott B9 in the semipostal section, Scott C6 in the airpost section, Scott J19 in the postage due section, and Scott O1 in the official section.

See French West Africa No. 65 for additional stamp inscribed "Mauritanie" and "Afrique Occidentale Francaise."

General Louis Faidherbe A1

Oil Palms A2

Dr. Noel Eugène Ballay — A3

			Perf. 14x13½
1906-07		Typo.	Unwmk.
		"Mauritanie" in Red or Blue	
1	A1	1c slate	.70 .70
2	A1	2c chocolate	2.10 2.10
3	A1	4c choc, gray bl	2.75 2.75
4	A1	5c green	1.40 1.40
5	A1	10c carmine (B)	14.00 7.00
7	A2	20c black, azure	27.50 17.50
8	A2	25c blue, pnksh	10.00 7.00
9	A2	30c choc, pnksh	105.00 62.50
10	A2	35c black, yellow	10.00 7.00
11	A2	40c car, az (B)	10.00 10.00
12	A2	45c choc, grnsh ('07)	10.00 10.00
13	A2	50c deep violet	10.00 7.00
14	A2	75c blue, org	10.00 10.00
15	A3	1fr black, azure	27.50 27.50
16	A3	2fr blue, pink	55.00 55.00
17	A3	5fr car, straw (B)	140.00 150.00
		Nos. 1-17 (16)	435.95 377.45

Crossing Desert — A4

1913-38			
18	A4	1c brn vio & brn	.30 .55
19	A4	2c black & blue	.30 .55
20	A4	4c violet & blk	.30 .55
21	A4	5c yel grn & bl grn	1.00 .70
a.		Chalky paper	2.10 1.40
22	A4	5c brn vio & rose ('22)	.35 .35
23	A4	10c rose & red org	2.50 1.75
a.		Chalky paper	3.50 2.50
24	A4	10c yel grn & bl grn ('22)	.35 .70
25	A4	10c lil rose, bluish ('25)	.70 1.00
26	A4	15c dk brn & blk ('17)	.70 .70
a.		Chalky paper	1.00 1.00
27	A4	20c bis brn & org	.70 .70
28	A4	25c blue & vio	1.40 1.00
29	A4	25c grn & rose ('22)	.35 .35
30	A4	30c bl grn & rose	1.40 1.50
31	A4	30c rose & red org ('22)	1.75 2.10
32	A4	30c black & yel ('26)	.35 .35
33	A4	30c bl grn & yel grn ('28)	1.40 1.40
34	A4	35c brown & vio	.70 .75
35	A4	35c dp grn & lt grn ('38)	1.40 1.40
36	A4	40c gray & bl grn	2.75 2.50
37	A4	45c org & bis brn	1.40 1.75
38	A4	50c brn vio & rose	1.00 1.40
39	A4	50c dk bl & ultra ('22)	.70 .70
40	A4	50c gray grn & dp bl ('26)	.35 .70
41	A4	60c vio, pnksh ('25)	.70 1.00
42	A4	65c yel grn & lt bl ('26)	1.00 1.75
43	A4	75c ultra & brown	1.00 1.40
44	A4	85c myr grn & lt brn ('26)	1.40 1.75
45	A4	90c brn red & rose ('30)	2.10 2.10
46	A4	1fr rose & black	1.00 1.40
47	A4	1.10fr vio & ver ('28)	10.00 14.00
48	A4	1.25fr dk bl & blk brn ('33)	2.10 2.50
49	A4	1.50fr lt bl & dp bl ('30)	1.40 1.40
50	A4	1.75fr bl grn & brn red ('33)	2.10 2.50
51	A4	1.75fr dk bl & ultra ('38)	2.10 2.10
52	A4	2fr red org & vio	1.75 2.10
53	A4	3fr red violet ('30)	2.10 2.10
54	A4	5fr violet & blue	3.00 3.75
		Nos. 18-54 (37)	53.90 63.30

Stamp and Type of 1913-38 Srchd.

MAURITANIA

1922-25

55	A4	60c on 75c violet, *pnksh*	1.00	1.40
56	A4	65c on 15c dk brn & blk ('25)	1.75	2.10
57	A4	85c on 75c ultra & brn ('25)	1.75	2.10
		Nos. 55-57 (3)	4.50	5.60

Type of 1913-38 Srchd.

1924-27

58	A4	25c on 2fr red org & vio	1.00	1.40
59	A4	90c on 75c brn red & cer ('27)	2.10	2.75
60	A4	1.25fr on 1fr dk bl & ultra ('26)	.70	.70
61	A4	1.50fr on 1fr bl & dp bl ('27)	1.40	1.75
62	A4	3fr on 5fr ol brn & red vio ('27)	7.00	7.00
63	A4	10fr on 5fr mag & bl grn ('27)	7.00	7.75
64	A4	20fr on 5fr bl vio & dp org ('27)	7.00	8.00
		Nos. 58-64 (7)	26.20	29.35

Common Design Types pictured following the introduction.

Colonial Exposition Issue
Common Design Types
Engr.; Name of Country Typo. In Black

1931, Apr. 13 — Perf. 12½

65	CD70	40c deep green	7.00	7.00
66	CD71	50c violet	5.00	5.00
67	CD72	90c red orange	5.00	5.00
68	CD73	1.50fr dull blue	5.00	5.00
		Nos. 65-68 (4)	22.00	22.00

Paris International Exposition Issue
Common Design Types

1937, Apr. 15 — Perf. 13

69	CD74	20c deep violet	1.75	1.75
70	CD75	30c dark green	1.75	1.75
71	CD76	40c carmine rose	2.10	2.10
72	CD77	50c dk brn & blk	1.40	1.40
73	CD78	90c red	1.40	1.40
74	CD79	1.50fr ultra	2.10	2.10
		Nos. 69-74 (6)	10.50	10.50

Colonial Arts Exhibition Issue
Common Design Type
Souvenir Sheet

1937 — Imperf.

75	CD76	3fr dark blue	10.00	14.00

Camel Rider A5

Mauri Couple A8

Mauris on Camels — A6

Family Before Tent — A7

1938-40 — Perf. 13

76	A5	2c violet blk	.25	.25
77	A5	3c dp ultra	.25	.25
78	A5	4c rose violet	.30	.30
79	A5	5c orange red	.30	.30
80	A5	10c brown car	.35	.35
81	A5	15c dk violet	.35	.35
82	A5	20c red	.35	.35
83	A6	25c deep ultra	.35	.35
84	A6	30c deep brown	.25	.25
85	A6	35c Prus green	.35	.70
86	A6	40c rose car ('40)	.35	.35
87	A6	45c Prus grn ('40)	.35	.35
88	A6	50c purple	.35	.50
89	A7	55c rose violet	.70	1.00
90	A7	60c violet ('40)	.35	.35
91	A7	65c deep green	.70	1.00
92	A7	70c red ('40)	.70	.70
93	A7	80c deep blue	1.40	1.40
94	A7	90c rose vio ('39)	.70	.70
95	A7	1fr red	2.75	2.10
96	A7	1fr dp green ('40)	.70	.70
97	A7	1.25fr rose car ('39)	1.40	1.40
98	A7	1.40fr dp blue ('40)	.70	.70
99	A7	1.50fr violet	.70	1.00
99A	A7	1.50fr red brn ('40)	125.00	
100	A7	1.60fr black brn ('40)	1.75	1.75
101	A8	1.75fr deep ultra	1.40	1.40
102	A8	2fr rose violet	.35	1.00
103	A8	2.25fr dull ultra ('39)	.70	.70
104	A8	2.50fr black brn ('40)	1.40	1.40
105	A8	3fr deep green	.35	.90
106	A8	5fr scarlet	.70	1.00
107	A8	10fr deep brown	1.75	1.90
108	A8	20fr brown car	2.10	2.25
		Nos. 76-108 (34)	150.45	28.30

Nos. 91 and 109 surcharged with new values are listed under French West Africa.
For surcharges see Nos. B9-B12.

Caillie Issue
Common Design Type

1939, Apr. 5 — Engr. — Perf. 12½x12

109	CD81	90c org brn & org	.35	1.00
110	CD81	2fr brt violet	.35	1.40
111	CD81	2.25fr ultra & dk bl	.35	1.40
		Nos. 109-111 (3)	1.05	3.80

New York World's Fair Issue
Common Design Type

1939, May 10

112	CD82	1.25fr carmine lake	.70	1.40
113	CD82	2.25fr ultra	.70	1.40

Catalogue values for unused stamps in this section, from this point to the end of the section, are for Never Hinged items.

Caravan and Marshal Pétain — A9

1941

114	A9	1fr green	.80	1.25
115	A9	2.50fr deep blue	.80	1.25

For surcharges, see Nos. B15A-B15B.

Types of 1938-40 Without "RF"

1943-44

115A	A5	10c brown car		.70
115B	A5	15c dk violet		1.40
115C	A6	40c rose car		1.75
115D	A6	50c purple		1.75
115E	A7	60c violet		1.75
115F	A7	1fr dp green		1.75
		Nos. 115A-115F (6)		9.10

Nos. 115A-115F were issued by the Vichy government in France, but were not placed on sale in Mauritania.

Islamic Republic

Camel and Hands Raising Flag — A10

1960, Jan. 20 — Unwmk. — Engr. — Perf. 13

116	A10	25fr multi, *pink*	.60	.35

Issued to commemorate the proclamation of the Islamic Republic of Mauritania.

Imperforates
Most Mauritania stamps from 1960 onward exist imperforate in issued and trial colors, and also in small presentation sheets in issued colors.

C.C.T.A. Issue
Common Design Type

1960, May 16

117	CD106	25fr bluish grn & ultra	.75	.40

Flag and Map — A11

1960, Dec. 15 — Engr. — Perf. 13

118	A11	25fr org brn, emer & sepia	.60	.30

Proclamation of independence, Nov. 28, 1960.

Pastoral Well — A12

Aoudad — A13

Shoemaker A14

Fishing Boats — A15

Nomad School — A15a

Seated Dance — A15b

Metalworker — A15c

Type I

Type II

Types: Type 1 — Small Overprint. Type 2 — Large Overprint.

Striped Hyena — A15d

Aardvark — A15e

Type I

Type II

Types: Type 1 — 26 leaves on tree. Type 2 — 37 leaves on tree.

Designs: 50c, 1fr, Well. 2fr, Date harvesting. 4fr, Fennecs. 5fr, Millet harvesting. 30fr, Seated dance. No. 130, Religious student. No. 131, Ore Train and Camel Riders. 85fr, Scimitar-horned Oryx.

1960-62 — Unwmk. — Perf. 13

119	A12	50c dp claret, ochre & redsh brn ('61)	.25	.25
120	A12	1fr red brn, yel brn & bl grn	.25	.25
121	A12	2fr dk brn, bl & bl grn	.25	.25
122	A13	3fr bl grn, red brn & brnsh blk ('61)	.40	.25
123	A13	4fr yel grn & ocher ('61)	.40	.25
124	A12	5fr blk, blksh brn & org brn	.35	.25
125	A14	10fr dk bl & org red	.40	.25
126	A15	15fr red, ver, dk brn, dk grn & bl	.50	.25
127	A15a	20fr sl grn & red brn	.50	.25
128	A16b	25fr ultra & gray grn	.65	.25
129	A15b	30fr redsh lil, bis & sl grn	.65	.25
130	A15b	50fr red org & emer	1.10	.40
131	A14	50fr org brn, bl & ol & org ('62)	3.00	.80
132	A15c	60fr bl grn, claret & mar	2.00	.40
133	A13	85fr bl, org brn & sep ('61)	4.75	1.90
		Nos. 119-133 (15)	15.45	6.25

An overprint, "Jeux Olympiques / Rome 1960 / Tokyo 1964," the 5-ring Olympic emblem and a 75fr surcharge was applied to Nos. 126-127 in 1962 in two different sizes. Values, set: small overprint, $20; large overprint, $19.50.

An overprint, "Aide aux Réfugiés" with uprooted oak emblem, was applied in 1962 to No. 132 and to pink-paper printings of Nos. 129-100. Values, set: type 1, $24; type 2, $0.
Other overprints, applied to airmail stamps, are noted after No. C16.

1963, July 6

Designs: 1fr, Spotted Hyena. 1.50fr, Cheetah. 2fr, Guinea baboons. 5fr, Dromedaries. 10fr, Leopard. 15fr, Bongo antelopes. 25fr, Patas monkeys. 30fr, Crested porcupine. 50fr, Dorcas gazelle. 60fr, Common chameleon.

134	A15d	50c sl grn, blk & org brn	.25	.25
135	A14	1fr ultra, blk & yel	.25	.25
136	A15d	1.50fr ol grn, brn & bis	.35	.25
137	A14	2fr dk brn, grn & dp org	.30	.25
138	A14	5fr brn, ultra & bis	.35	.25
139	A14	10fr blk & bis	.75	.25
140	A14	15fr vio bl & red brn	.75	.25
141	A15e	20fr dk red brn, dk bl & bis	.85	.30

MAURITANIA

142	A15e	25fr brt grn, red brn & ol bis	1.25	.30
143	A15e	30fr dk brn, dk bl & ol bis	2.40	.30
144	A15e	50fr grn, ocher & brn	3.00	.90
145	A15e	60fr dk bl, emer & ocher	3.75	1.25
		Nos. 134-145 (12)	14.25	4.80

UN Headquarters, New York, and View of Nouakchott — A15f

1962, June 1 Engr. Perf. 13
167	A15f	15fr blk, ultra & cop red	.30	.30
168	A15f	25fr cop red, sl grn & ultra	.45	.35
169	A15f	85fr dk bl, dl pur & cop red	1.25	1.10
		Nos. 167-169 (3)	2.00	1.75

Mauritania's admission to the UN.

African-Malagasy Union Issue
Common Design Type
1962, Sept. 8 Photo. Perf. 12½x12
170	CD110	30fr multi	.75	.50

Organization Emblem and View of Nouakchott A16

1962, Oct. 15 Perf. 12½
171	A16	30fr dk red brn, ultra & brt grn	.75	.50

8th Conf. of the Organization to Fight Endemic Diseases, Nouakchott, Oct. 15-18.

Map, Mechanized and Manual Farm Work — A17

1962, Nov. 28 Engr. Perf. 13
172	A17	30fr blk, grn & vio brn	.75	.40

2nd anniversary of independence.

People in European and Mauritanian Clothes — A18

1962, Dec. 24 Unwmk.
173	A18	25fr multicolored	.90	.45

First anniversary of Congress for Unity.

Weather and WMO Symbols — A20

1964, Mar. 23 Unwmk. Perf. 13
175	A20	85fr dk brn, dk bl & org	1.50	.85

UN 4th World Meteorological Day, Mar. 23.

IQSY Emblem — A21

1964, July 3 Engr.
176	A21	25fr dk bl, red & grn	.60	.45

International Quiet Sun Year, 1964-65.

Striped Mullet — A22

Designs: 5fr, Mauritanian lobster, vert. 10fr, Royal lobster, vert. 60fr, Maigre fish.

1964, Oct. 5 Engr. Perf. 13
177	A22	1fr org brn, dk bl & grn	.40	.25
178	A22	5fr org brn, sl grn & choc	.50	.25
179	A22	10fr dk bl, bis & sl grn	.80	.25
180	A22	60fr dk brn, dp grn & dl brn	3.00	.80
		Nos. 177-180 (4)	4.70	1.55

Cooperation Issue
Common Design Type
1964, Nov. 7 Unwmk. Perf. 13
181	CD119	25fr mag, sl grn & dk brn	.60	.35

Water Lilies — A23

Tropical Plants: 10fr, Acacia. 20fr, Adenium obesum. 45fr, Caralluma retrospiciens.

1965, Jan. 11 Engr. Perf. 13
182	A23	5fr multi	.25	.25
183	A23	10fr multi, vert.	.25	.25
184	A23	20fr multi	.60	.25
185	A23	45fr multi, vert.	1.00	.50
		Nos. 182-185 (4)	2.10	1.25

Hardine — A24

Musical Instruments: 8fr, Tobol (drums). 25fr, Tidinit (stringed instruments). 40fr, Musicians.

1965, Mar. 8 Perf. 13
186	A24	2fr red brn, brt bl & sep	.25	.25
187	A24	8fr red brn, red & brn	.40	.25
188	A24	25fr red brn, emer & blk	.65	.25
189	A24	40fr vio bl, plum & blk	1.00	.35
		Nos. 186-189 (4)	2.30	1.10

Abraham Lincoln (1809-1865) — A25

1965, Apr. 23 Photo. Perf. 13x12½
190	A25	50fr lt ultra & multi	.80	.40

Palms at Adrar — A26

Designs: 4fr, Chinguetti mosque, vert. 15fr, Clay pit and donkeys. 60fr, Decorated door, Oualata.

1965, June 14 Engr. Perf. 13
191	A26	1fr brn, bl & grn	.25	.25
192	A26	4fr dk red, bl & brn	.25	.25
193	A26	15fr multi	.35	.25
194	A26	60fr grn, dk brn & red brn	1.10	.55
		Nos. 191-194 (4)	1.95	1.30

Issued for tourist publicity.

Tea Service in Inlaid Box — A27

7fr, Tobacco pouch and pipe, vert. 25fr, Dagger, vert. 50fr, Mederdra ornamental chest.

1965, Sept. 13 Unwmk. Perf. 13
195	A27	3fr gray, choc & ocher	.25	.25
196	A27	7fr red lil, Prus bl & org	.25	.25
197	A27	25fr blk, org red & brn	.50	.25
198	A27	50fr brt grn, brn org & mar	1.00	.40
		Nos. 195-198 (4)	2.00	1.15

Choum Railroad Tunnel — A28

10fr, Nouakchott wharf, ships & anchor, horiz. 30fr, as 5fr. 85fr, Nouakchott hospital & caduceus, horiz.

1965, Oct. 18 Engr. Perf. 13
199	A28	5fr dk brn & brt grn	.25	.25
200	A28	10fr dk vio bl, brn red & Prus bl	.25	.25
201	A28	30fr brn red, red & red brn	.70	.25
202	A28	85fr dp bl, rose cl & lil	1.30	.65
		Nos. 199-202 (4)	2.50	1.40

Sculptured Heads — A29

Designs: 30fr, "Music and Dance." 60fr, Movie camera and huts.

1966, Apr. Engr. Perf. 13
203	A29	10fr brt grn, blk & brn	.25	.25
204	A29	30fr brt bl, red lil & blk	.50	.25
205	A29	60fr red, org & dk brn	.90	.45
		Nos. 203-205 (3)	1.65	.95

Intl. Negro Arts Festival, Dakar, Senegal, Apr. 1-24.

Mimosa — A30

Flowers: 15fr, Schouwia purpurea. 20fr, Ipomea asarifolia. 25fr, Grewia bicolor. 30fr, Pancratium trianthum. 60fr, Blepharis linariifolia.

1966, Aug. 8 Photo. Perf. 13x12½
Flowers in Natural Colors
206	A30	10fr dl bl & dk bl	.40	.25
207	A30	15fr dk brn & buff	.50	.30
208	A30	20fr grnsh bl & lt bl	.55	.35
209	A30	25fr brn & buff	.75	.45
210	A30	30fr lil & vio	1.10	.60
211	A30	60fr grn & pale grn	1.50	.90
		Nos. 206-211 (6)	4.80	2.85

Myrina Silenus — A31

Various Butterflies.

1966, Oct. 3 Photo. Perf. 12x12½
212	A31	5fr buff & multi	.90	.45
213	A31	30fr bl grn & multi	3.00	.70
214	A31	45fr yel grn & multi	4.00	1.00
215	A31	60fr dl bl & multi	5.50	1.60
		Nos. 212-215 (4)	13.40	3.75

Hunter, Petroglyph from Adrar — A32

Designs: 3fr, Two men fighting, petroglyph from Tenses (Adrar). 30fr, Copper jug, Le Mreyer (Adrar). 50fr, Camel caravan.

1966, Oct. 24 Engr. Perf. 13
216	A32	2fr dk brn & brn org	.30	.25
217	A32	3fr bl & brn org	.80	.25
218	A32	30fr sl grn & dk red	1.40	.30
219	A32	50fr mag, sl grn & brn	2.40	.70
		Nos. 216-219 (4)	4.90	1.75

Issued for tourist publicity.

UNESCO, 20th Anniv. — A33

1966, Dec. 5 Litho. Perf. 12½x13
220	A33	30fr multi	.60	.40

Plaza of Three Cultures, Mexico City — A34

Olympic Village, Grenoble — A35

Designs: 40fr, Olympic torch and skating rink. 100fr, Olympic Stadium, Mexico City.

1967, Mar. 11 Engr. Perf. 13
221	A34	20fr dl bl, brn & sl grn	.50	.25
222	A35	30fr dl bl, brn & grn	.60	.40
223	A34	40fr brt bl, dk brn & sep	1.00	.55
224	A35	100fr brn, emer & blk	1.75	1.00
		Nos. 221-224 (4)	3.85	2.20

Nos. 221 and 224 commemorate the 19th Olympic Games, Mexico City; Nos. 222 and 223, the 10th Winter Olympic Games, Grenoble.

Trees — A36

1967, May 15 Engr. Perf. 13
225	A36	10fr Prosopis	.45	.25
226	A36	15fr Jujube	.60	.25
227	A36	20fr Date palm	.70	.25
228	A36	25fr Peltophorum	.80	.30
229	A36	30fr Baobob	1.10	.35
		Nos. 225-229 (5)	3.65	1.40

1967 Jamboree Emblem and Campsite — A37

Design: 90fr, 1967 Jamboree emblem and Mauritanian Boy Scouts, horiz.

1967, June 5
230	A37	60fr brn, ultra & slate grn	.95	.35
231	A37	90fr dl red, bl & slate grn	1.40	.50

12th Boy Scout World Jamboree, Farragut State Park, Idaho, Aug. 1-9.

Weavers — A38

10fr, Embroiderer, vert. 20fr, Nurse, mother & infant. 30fr, Laundress, vert. 50fr, Seamstresses.

1967, July 3 Engr. Perf. 13
232	A38	5fr plum, blk & cl	.25	.25
233	A38	10fr plum, brt grn & blk	.25	.25
234	A38	20fr brt bl, plum & blk	.45	.25

MAURITANIA

235 A38 30fr dk bl, brn & blk .55 .30
236 A38 50fr plum, sl & blk .90 .30
Nos. 232-236 (5) 2.40 1.35

Progress made by working women.

Cattle and Hypodermic Syringe — A39

1967, Aug. 21 Engr. Perf. 13
237 A39 30fr sl grn, brt bl & rose cl .90 .40

Campaign against cattle plague.

Monetary Union Issue
Common Design Type

1967, Nov. 4 Engr. Perf. 13
238 CD125 30fr gray & orange .45 .25

Fruit — A40

1967, Dec. 4 Engr. Perf. 13
239 A40 1fr Doom palm .30 .25
240 A40 2fr Bito, horiz. .30 .25
241 A40 3fr Baobob .40 .25
242 A40 4fr Jujube, horiz. .45 .25
243 A40 5fr Daye .55 .30
Nos. 239-243 (5) 2.00 1.30

For surcharges see Nos. 323-327.

Human Rights Flame — A41

1968, Jan. 8 Photo. Perf. 13x12½
244 A41 30fr brt grn, blk & yel .60 .25
245 A41 50fr brn org, blk & yel .70 .40

International Human Rights Year.

Nouakchott Mosque — A42

15fr, Amogjar Pass. 90fr, Cavaliers' Towers.

1968, Apr. 1 Photo. Perf. 12½x13
246 A42 30fr multi .30 .25
247 A42 45fr multi .50 .25
248 A42 90fr multi .80 .50
Nos. 246-248 (3) 1.60 1.00

For surcharges see Nos. 332-333.

UPU Building, Bern, Globe and Map of Africa — A43

1968, June 3 Engr. Perf. 13
249 A43 30fr ver, ultra & olive 1.00 .30

Mauritania's admission to the UPU.

Symbolic Water Cycle — A44

1968, June 24
250 A44 90fr car, lake, grn & sl grn .85 .40

Hydrological Decade (UNESCO), 1965-74.

Land Yacht Racing — A45

40fr, Three land yachts racing, horiz. 60fr, Crew changing wheel of land yacht.

1968, Oct. 7 Engr. Perf. 13
251 A45 30fr ultra, org & ocher .55 .25
252 A45 40fr ultra, dp org & plum .70 .30
253 A45 60fr brt grn, dp org & ocher 1.10 .60
Nos. 251-253 (3) 2.35 1.15

Donkey and Foal — A46

Domestic Animals: 10fr, Ewe and lamb. 15fr, Camel and calf. 30fr, Mare and foal. 50fr, Cow and calf. 90fr, Goat and kid.

1968, Dec. 16 Photo. Perf. 13
254 A46 5fr ocher & multi .30 .25
255 A46 10fr multi .40 .25
256 A46 15fr multi .45 .25
257 A46 30fr multi .85 .30
258 A46 50fr pur & multi 1.25 .40
259 A46 90fr multi 2.40 .60
Nos. 254-259 (6) 5.65 2.05

For surcharge see No. 303.

ILO Emblem and Map — A47

1969, Apr. 14 Photo. Perf. 13x12½
260 A47 50fr dk & lt bl, pur & org .60 .30

ILO, 50th anniversary.

Desert Monitor — A48

Reptiles: 10fr, Horned viper. 30fr, Common spitting cobra. 60fr, Rock python. 85fr, African crocodile.

1969, May 5 Photo. Perf. 13x12½
261 A48 5fr brn, pink & yel .40 .25
262 A48 10fr brn, lt grn & yel .65 .30
263 A48 30fr dk brn, pink & yel 1.55 .50
264 A48 60fr dk brn, lt bl & yel 2.00 1.40
265 A48 85fr brn, yel & red 5.00 1.75
Nos. 261-265 (5) 10.20 4.20

Lady Beetle Eating Noxious Insects — A49

1969, May 26 Engr. Perf. 13
266 A49 30fr indigo, grn & mar 1.50 .70

Natural protection of date palms.

Development Bank Issue
Common Design Type

1969, Sept. 10 Engr. Perf. 13
267 CD130 30fr Prus bl, grn & ocher .60 .25

Pendant — A50

Design: 20fr, Rahla headdress, horiz.

1969, Oct. 13 Engr. Perf. 13
268 A50 10fr dk brn, lil & brn .25 .25
269 A50 20fr blk, Prus bl & mag .50 .25

For surcharges see Nos. 309-310.

Desalination Plant — A51

Designs: 15fr, Fishing harbor, Nouadhibou. 30fr, Meat refrigeration plant, Kaedi.

1969, Dec. 1 Engr. Perf. 13
270 A51 10fr brt rose lil, dk bl & red brn .25 .25
271 A51 15fr dk car, blk & dp bl .25 .25
272 A51 30fr blk, dk bl & rose brn .40 .25
Nos. 270-272 (3) .90 .75

Issued to publicize economic progress.

Lenin (1870-1924) — A52

1970, Feb. 16 Photo. Perf. 12x12½
273 A52 30fr car, lt bl & blk 1.40 .40

Sternocera Interrupta — A53

Insects: 10fr, Anoplocnemis curvipes. 20fr, Julodis aequinoctialis. 30fr, Thermophilum sexmaculatum marginatum. 40fr, Plocaederus denticornis.

1970, Mar. 16 Engr. Perf. 13
274 A53 5fr red brn, buff & blk .40 .25
275 A53 10fr red brn, yel & brn .65 .25
276 A53 20fr red brn, lil & dk ol .85 .30
277 A53 30fr red brn, grn & vio 1.40 .45
278 A53 40fr red brn, lt bl & brn 2.25 .85
Nos. 274-278 (5) 5.55 2.10

For surcharges see Nos. 311-315.

Soccer Players and Hemispheres A54

Hemispheres & various views of soccer play.

1970, May 11 Engr. Perf. 13
279 A54 25fr bl, vio bl & dk brn .45 .25
280 A54 30fr vio bl, brn & ol brn .45 .25
281 A54 70fr brt pink, mar & dk brn .85 .50
282 A54 150fr brn red, grn & dk brn 1.90 .75
Nos. 279-282 (4) 3.65 1.75

9th World Soccer Championships for the Jules Rimet Cup, Mexico City, 5/29-6/21.

UPU Headquarters Issue
Common Design Type

1970, May 20 Engr. Perf. 13
283 CD133 30fr grn, dk brn & red brn .60 .30

Woman Wearing "Boubou" — A55

Various Traditional Costumes: 30fr, 70fr, Men. 40fr, 50fr, Women.

1970, Sept. 21 Engr. Perf. 12½x13
284 A55 10fr red brn & org .95 .40
285 A55 30fr ol, red brn & ind 1.25 .50
286 A55 40fr red brn, plum & dk brn 1.55 .50
287 A55 50fr dk brn & brt bl 1.90 .60
288 A55 70fr bl, brn & dk brn 2.40 1.00
Nos. 284-288 (5) 8.05 3.00

People of Various Races A55a

Design: 40fr, Outstretched hands, vert.

1971, Mar. 22 Engr. Perf. 13
288A A55a 30fr brn vio, ol & brt bl .70 .25
288B A55a 40fr brn red, bl & blk .95 .40

Intl. year against racial discrimination.

Gen. Charles de Gaulle (1890-1970), President of France — A56

Design: 100fr, De Gaulle as President.

1971, June 18 Photo. Perf. 13
289 A56 40fr gold, blk & grnsh bl 2.00 .75
290 A56 100fr lt bl, gold & blk 4.00 1.50
a. Souvenir sheet of 2, #289-290 6.50 6.50

Iron Ore Freight Train of Miferma Mines A57

1971, Nov 8 Photo. Perf. 12½x12
291 35fr ore cars 1.75 .65
292 100fr engines 4.00 1.60
a. A57 Pair. #291-292 7.50 7.50

UNICEF Emblem and Child — A59

1971, Dec. 11 Litho. Perf. 13½
293 A59 35fr lt ultra, blk & brn .60 .25

UNICEF, 25th anniv.

Samuel F. B. Morse and Telegraph — A60

Designs: 40fr, Relay satellite over globes. 75fr, Alexander Graham Bell.

1972, May 17 Engr. Perf. 13
294 A60 35fr lilac, indigo & vio .60 .25
295 A60 40fr bl, ocher & choc .65 .30
296 A60 75fr grn, ol grn & Prus bl 1.00 .60
Nos. 294-296 (3) 2.25 1.15

4th World Telecommunications Day.

MAURITANIA

For surcharge see No. 343.

Fossil Spirifer Shell — A61

1972, July 31   Litho.   Perf. 12½
297 A61 25fr shown   2.25 .90
298 A61 75fr Phacops rana   3.75 1.60
Fossil shells.
For surcharges see Nos. 306, 308.

West African Monetary Union Issue
Common Design Type

1972, Nov. 2   Engr.   Perf. 13
299 CD136 35fr brn, yel grn & gray   .75 .25

Mediterranean Monk Seal and Pup — A63

1973, Feb. 28   Litho.   Perf. 13
300 A63 40fr multi   2.00 .80
See No. C130. For surcharges see Nos. 307, C145.

Food Program Symbols and Emblem — A64

1973, Apr. 30   Photo.   Perf. 12x12½
301 A64 35fr gray bl & multi   .45 .25
World Food Program, 10th anniversary.

UPU Monument and Globe — A65

1973, May 28   Engr.   Perf. 13
302 A65 100fr grn, ocher & bl   1.50 .75
Universal Postal Union Day.

Currency Change to Ouguiya ("um")

No. 258 Surcharged and Overprinted

1973, Aug. 16   Photo.   Perf. 13
303 A46 20um on 50fr multi   .95 .60
African solidarity in drought emergency.

African Postal Union Issue
Common Design Type

1973, Sept. 12   Engr.   Perf. 13
304 CD137 20um org, brn & ocher   1.10 .40

INTERPOL Emblem, Detective, Criminal, Fingerprint — A66

1973, Sept. 24
305 A66 15um brn, ver & vio   .90 .50
50th anniv. of Intl. Criminal Police Org.

Nos. 297-298, 300 and 268-269 Surcharged with New Value and Two Bars in Ultramarine, Red or Black

1973-74   Litho.   Perf. 12½
306 A61 5um on 25fr (U) ('74)   2.50 .40
307 A63 8um on 40fr (R)   .95 .40
308 A61 15um on 75fr (U) ('74)   7.00 1.75

Engr.   Perf. 13
309 A50 27um on 10fr (B) ('74)   1.60 .75
310 A50 28um on 20fr (U) ('74)   1.75 .20
Nos. 306-310 (5)   13.80 4.20

Nos. 274-278 Surcharged in Violet Blue or Red

1974, July 29   Engr.   Perf. 13
311 A53 5um on 5fr (VB)   1.10 .50
312 A53 7um on 10fr (VB)   1.00 .40
313 A53 8um on 20fr (R)   1.10 .45
314 A53 10um on 30fr (R)   1.50 .50
315 A53 20um on 40fr (VB)   3.25 1.40
Nos. 311-315 (5)   7.95 3.25

UPU Emblem and Globes A67

1974, Aug. 5   Photo.   Perf. 13
316 A67 30um multi   2.00 .80
317 A67 50um multi   3.25 1.25
Centenary of Universal Postal Union.
For overprints see Nos. 321-322.

5-Ouguiya Coin and Bank Note — A68

Designs: 8um, 10-ouguiya coin. 20um, 20-ouguiya coin. Each design includes picture of different bank note.

1974, Aug. 12   Engr.
318 A68 7um blk, ultra & grn   .60 .25
319 A68 8um blk, sl grn & mag   .70 .25
320 A68 20um blk, red & bl   1.40 .55
Nos. 318-320 (3)   2.70 1.05
First anniversary of currency reform.

Nos. 316-317 Overprinted in Red: "9 OCTOBRE / 100 ANS D'UNION POSTALE / INTERNATIONALE"

1974, Oct. 9   Photo.   Perf. 13
321 A67 30um multi   2.10 1.00
322 A67 50um multi   3.75 1.50
Centenary of Universal Postal Union.

Nos. 239-243 Srchd. in Black or Violet Blue

1975, Feb. 14   Engr.   Perf. 13
323 A40 1um on 5fr multi (B)   .30 .25
324 A40 2um on 4fr multi (VB)   .30 .25
325 A40 3um on 2fr multi (B)   .35 .25
326 A40 10um on 1fr multi (B)   .90 .25
327 A40 12um on 3fr multi (VB) 1.00 .30
Nos. 323-327 (5)   2.85 1.30

Hunters, Rock Carvings — A69

Rock Carvings from Zemmour Cave: 5um, Ostrich. 10um, Elephant, horiz.

1975, May 26   Engr.   Perf. 13
328 A69 4um lt brn & car   .90 .25
329 A69 5um red lil   1.10 .30
330 A69 10um blue   1.75 .60
Nos. 328-330 (3)   3.75 1.15

Europafrica Issue

White and Black Men, Map of Europe and Africa — A70

1975, July 7   Engr.   Perf. 13
331 A70 40um dk brn & red   2.25 1.00

Nos. 247-248 Surcharged in Red or Black

1975, Aug. 25   Photo.   Perf. 12½x13
332 A42 15um on 45fr (R)   1.25 .50
333 A42 25um on 90fr   2.00 .80
African solidarity in drought emergency.

Map of Africa with Mauritania, Akjoujt Blast Furnace, Camel — A71

1975, Sept. 22   Engr.   Perf. 13
334 A71 10um brt bl, choc & org   .90 .30
335 A71 12um brt bl & multi   1.25 .45
Mining and industry: Somima (Société Minière de Mauritanie) and Snim (Société Nationale Industrielle et Minière).

Fair Emblem — A72

1975, Oct. 5   Litho.   Perf. 12
336 A72 10um multi   .60 .30
National Nouakchott Fair, Nov. 28-Dec. 7.

Commemorative Medal — A73

Design: 12um, Map of Mauritania, vert.

1975, Nov. 28   Litho.   Perf. 12
337 A73 10um sil & multi   .75 .35
338 A73 12um grn, yel & grn 1.00 .35
15th anniversary of independence.

Docked Space Ships and Astronauts A74

Docked Space Ships and: 10um, Soyuz rocket launch.

1975, Dec. 29   Litho.   Perf. 14
339 A74 8um multi   .70 .25
340 A74 10um multi   .85 .25
Nos. 339-340, C156-C158 (5) 7.15 2.65
Apollo Soyuz space test project, Russo-American cooperation, launched July 15, link-up July 17, 1975.

French Legion Infantryman — A75

Uniform: 10um, Green Mountain Boy.

1976, Jan. 26   Perf. 13½x14
341 A75 8um multi   9.00 .25
342 A75 10um multi   1.10 .25
Nos. 341-342, C160-C162 (5) 16.05 2.75
American Bicentennial.

No. 296 Surcharged

1976, Mar. 1   Engr.   Perf. 13
343 A60 12um on 75fr multi   .65 .30
Arab Labor Charter, 10th anniversary.

Map of Mauritania with Spanish Sahara Incorporated A76

1976, Mar. 15   Litho.   Perf. 13x12½
344 A76 10um grn & multi   .80 .30
Reunified Mauritania, Feb. 29, 1976.

LZ-4 over Hangar A77

75th anniv. of the Zeppelin: 10um, Dr. Hugo Eckener and "Schwaben" (LZ-10). 12um, "Hansa" (LZ-13) over Heligoland. 20um, "Bodensee" (LZ-120) and Dr. Ludwig Dürr.

1976, June 28   Litho.   Perf. 11
345 A77 5um multi   .25 .25
346 A77 10um multi   .55 .25
347 A77 12um multi   .65 .25
348 A77 20um multi   1.10 .40
Nos. 345-348, C167-C168 (6) 8.20 3.70

Mohenjo-Daro — A78

1976, Sept. 6   Litho.   Perf. 12
349 A78 15um multi   1.10 .40
UNESCO campaign to save Mohenjo-Daro excavations, Pakistan.

MAURITANIA

A. G. Bell, Telephone and Satellite — A79

1976, Oct. 11		Engr.		Perf. 13
350	A79	10um bl, car & red	.80	.25

Centenary of first telephone call by Alexander Graham Bell, Mar. 10, 1876.

Mohammed Ali Jinnah (1876-1948), Governor General of Pakistan A80

1976, Dec. 25		Litho.		Perf. 13
351	A80	10um multi	.60	.30

NASA Control Room, Houston A81

Design: 12um, Viking components, vert.

1977, Feb. 28				Perf. 14
352	A81	10um multi	.60	.25
353	A81	12um multi	.70	.25
		Nos. 352-353,C173-C175 (5)	7.00	2.15

Viking Mars project.
For surcharge and overprints see Nos. 425-426, C192-C195.

Jackals — A82

Designs: 5um, Wild rabbits. 12um, Warthogs. 14um, Lions. 15um, Elephants.

1977, Mar. 14		Litho.		Perf. 12½
354	A82	5um multi	.40	.25
355	A82	10um multi	.95	.25
356	A82	12um multi	1.30	.50
357	A82	14um multi	1.40	.25
358	A82	15um multi	2.75	.90
		Nos. 354-358 (5)	6.80	2.30

For surcharge see No. 577.

Irene and Frederic Joliot-Curie, Chemistry A83

Nobel prize winners: 15um, Emil A. von Bering, medicine.

1977, Apr. 29		Litho.		Perf. 14
359	A83	12um multi	1.10	.25
360	A83	15um multi	.90	.25
		Nos. 359-360,C177-C179 (5)	9.05	2.10

APU Emblem, Member's Flags A84

1977, May 30		Photo.		Perf. 13
361	A84	12um multi	.80	.40

Arab Postal Union, 25th anniversary.

Oil Lamp — A85

Tegdaoust Pottery: 2um, 4-handled pot. 5um, Large jar. 12um, Jug with filter.

1977, June 13		Engr.		Perf. 13
362	A85	1um multi	.25	.25
363	A85	2um multi	.25	.25
364	A85	5um multi	.30	.25
365	A85	12um multi	.80	.30
		Nos. 362-365 (4)	1.60	1.05

X-ray of Hand — A86

1977, June 27		Engr.		Perf. 12½x13
366	A86	40um multi	2.50	1.25

World Rheumatism Year.

Charles Lindbergh and "Spirit of St. Louis" A87

History of aviation: 14um, Clement Ader and "Eole!" 15um, Louis Bleriot over channel. 55um, Italo Balbo and seaplanes. 60um, Concorde. 100um, Charles Lindbergh and "Spirit of St. Louis."

1977, Sept. 19				
367	A87	12um multi	.60	.25
368	A87	14um multi	.65	.25
369	A87	15um multi	.75	.30
370	A87	55um multi	2.60	.70
371	A87	60um multi	3.25	.75
		Nos. 367-371 (5)	7.85	2.25

Souvenir Sheet

372	A87	100um multi	6.00	1.50

Dome of the Rock, Jerusalem — A88

1977, Oct. 31		Litho.		Perf. 12½
373	A88	12um multi	.65	.25
374	A88	14um multi	.85	.40

Palestinian fighters and their families.

Soccer and Emblems A89

Emblems and: 14um, Alf Ramsey and stadium. 15um, Players and goalkeeper.

1977, Dec. 19		Litho.		Perf. 13½
375	A89	12um multi	.55	.25
376	A89	14um multi	.65	.25
377	A89	15um multi	.80	.25
		Nos. 375-377,C182-C183 (5)	7.00	2.05

Elimination Games for World Cup Soccer Championship, Argentina, 1978.
For overprints see Nos. 399-401, C187-C189.

Helen Fourment and her Children, by Rubens — A90

Paintings by Peter Paul Rubens (1577-1640): 14um, Knight in armor. 67um, Three Burghers. 69um, Landscape, horiz. 100um, Rubens with wife and son.

1977, Dec. 26				
378	A90	12um multi	.65	.25
379	A90	14um multi	.75	.35
380	A90	67um multi	3.25	.70
381	A90	69um multi	3.25	.85
		Nos. 378-381 (4)	7.90	2.15

Souvenir Sheet

382	A90	100um gold & multi	5.50	1.50

Sable Antelope and Wildlife Fund Emblem A91

Endangered Animals: 12um, Gazelles, vert. 14um, Manatee. 55um, Aoudad, vert. 60um, Elephant. 100um, Ostrich, vert.

1978, Feb. 28		Litho.		Perf. 13½x14
383	A91	5um multi	.80	.30
384	A91	12um multi	1.60	.40
385	A91	14um multi	1.75	.60
386	A91	55um multi	6.00	1.75
387	A91	60um multi	7.00	2.00
388	A91	100um multi	9.00	3.25
		Nos. 383-388 (6)	26.15	8.30

Nouakchott-Nema Road — A91a

1978, June 19		Litho.		Perf. 13
388A	A91a	12um multicolored	11.00	8.50
388B	A91a	14um multicolored	12.50	9.00

Soccer and Games' Emblem — A92

14um, Rimet Cup. 20um, Soccer ball & F.I.F.A. flag. 50um, Soccer ball & Rimet Cup, horiz.

1978, June 26		Photo.		Perf. 13
389	A92	12um multi	.60	.25
390	A92	14um multi	.70	.25
391	A92	20um multi	1.00	.30
		Nos. 389-391 (3)	2.30	.85

Souvenir Sheet

392	A92	50um multi	2.40	1.00

11th World Cup Soccer Championship, Argentina, June 1-25.

Raoul Follereau and St. George Slaying Dragon A93

1978, Sept. 4		Engr.		Perf. 13
393	A93	12um brn & dp grn	1.50	.60

25th anniversary of the Raoul Follereau Anti-Leprosy Foundation.

Anti-Apartheid Emblem, Fenced-in People — A94

Design: 30um, Anti-Apartheid emblem and free people, vert.

1978, Oct. 9				
394	A94	25um bl, red & brn	1.25	.65
395	A94	30um grn, bl & brn	1.75	.85

Anti-Apartheid Year.

Charles de Gaulle — A95

14um, King Baudouin. 55um, Queen Elizabeth II.

1978, Oct. 16		Litho.		Perf. 12½x12
396	A95	12um gold & multi	1.10	.40
397	A95	14um multi	1.10	.40
398	A95	55um multi	2.40	1.00
		Nos. 396-398 (3)	4.60	1.80

Rulers who helped in de-colonization. No. 398 also commemorates 25th anniversary of coronation of Queen Elizabeth II.

Nos. 375-377 Overprinted in Arabic and French in Silver: "ARGENTINE-/ PAYS BAS 3-1"

1978, Dec. 11		Litho.		Perf. 13½
399	A89	12um multi	.60	.25
400	A89	14um multi	.65	.30
401	A89	15um multi	.00	.25
		Nos. 399-401,C187-C188 (5)	6.80	3.45

Argentina's victory in World Cup Soccer Championship 1978.

View of Nouakchott A96

1978, Dec. 18		Litho.		Perf. 12
402	A96	12um multi	.65	.30

20th anniversary of Nouakchott.

Flame Emblem — A97

1978, Dec. 26				Perf. 12½
403	A97	55um ultra & red	2.50	1.25

Universal Declaration of Human Rights, 30th anniv.

MAURITANIA

Leather Key Holder — A98

Leather Craft: 7um, Toothbrush case. 10um, Knife holder.

1979, Feb. 5   Litho.   Perf. 13½x14
404	A98	5um multi	.35	.25
405	A98	7um multi	.45	.25
406	A98	10um multi	.65	.30
		Nos. 404-406 (3)	1.45	.80

Farmers at Market, by Dürer — A99

Engravings by Albrecht Dürer (1471-1528): 14um, Young Peasant and Wife. 55um, Mercenary with flag. 60um, St. George Slaying Dragon. 100um, Mercenaries, horiz.

Litho.; Red Foil Embossed
1979, May 3   Perf. 13½x14
407	A99	12um blk, *buff*	.60	.25
408	A99	14um blk, *buff*	.95	.25
409	A99	55um blk, *buff*	2.25	.80
410	A99	60um blk, *buff*	3.00	.95
		Nos. 407-410 (4)	6.80	2.25

Souvenir Sheet
Perf. 14x13½
| 411 | A99 | 100um blk, *buff* | 5.00 | 3.50 |

Buddha, Borobudur Temple and UNESCO Emblem — A100

UNESCO Emblem and: 14um, Hunter on horseback, Carthage. 55um, Caryatid, Acropolis.

1979, May 14   Photo.   Perf. 12½
412	A100	12um multi	.65	.35
413	A100	14um multi	.85	.40
414	A100	55um multi	2.50	1.25
		Nos. 412-414 (3)	4.00	2.00

Preservation of art treasures with help from UNESCO.

Paddle Steamer Sirius, Rowland Hill — A101

Sir Rowland Hill (1795-1879), originator of penny postage, and: 14um, Paddle steamer Great Republic. 55um, S.S. Mauritania. 60um, M.S. Stirling Castle. 100um, Mauritania No. 8.

1979, June 4   Litho.   Perf. 13½x14
415	A101	12um multi	.55	.25
416	A101	14um multi	.65	.25
417	A101	55um multi	2.25	.55
418	A101	60um multi	2.60	.70
		Nos. 415-418 (4)	6.05	1.75

Souvenir Sheet
| 419 | A101 | 100um multi | 5.00 | 1.25 |

Embossed Leather Cushion A102

30um, Satellite, jet, ship, globe & UPU emblem.

1979, June 8   Litho.   Perf. 12½
| 420 | A102 | 12um multi | 1.10 | .50 |

Engr.
Perf. 13
| 421 | A102 | 30um multi, vert. | 3.00 | 1.40 |

Philexafrique II, Libreville, Gabon, June 8-17. Nos. 420, 421 each printed in sheets of 10 and 5 labels showing exhibition emblem.

Mother and Children, IYC Emblem — A103

1979, Oct. 2   Litho.   Perf. 12½
422	A103	12um multi	.55	.25
423	A103	14um multi	.65	.35
424	A103	40um multi	1.90	.85
		Nos. 422-424 (3)	3.10	1.45

International Year of the Child

Nos. 352-353 Overprinted in Silver:
"ALUNISSAGE / APOLLO XI / JUILLET 1969" and Emblem
1979, Oct. 24   Litho.   Perf. 14
425	A81	10um multi	.60	.30
426	A81	12um multi	.60	.30
		Nos. 425-426,C192-C194 (5)	6.95	3.20

Apollo 11 moon landing, 10th anniversary.

Runner, Moscow '80 Emblem — A104

Moscow '80 Emblem and: 14um, 55um, 100um, Running, diff. 60um, Hurdles.

1979, Oct. 26   Litho.   Perf. 13½
427	A104	12um multi	.55	.25
428	A104	14um multi	.70	.25
429	A104	55um multi	2.00	.50
430	A104	60um multi	2.40	.60
		Nos. 427-430 (4)	5.65	1.60

Souvenir Sheet
| 431 | A104 | 100um multi | 4.75 | 1.25 |

Pre-Olympic Year.

Scomberesox Saurus Walbaum A104a

1979, Nov. 12   Photo.   Perf. 14
431A	A104a	1um shown	.75	.35
431B	A104a	2um Xiphias gladius	240.00	90.00
431C	A104a	5um Trigla lucerna	.90	.30

No. 431B exists imperforate and in deluxe sheets and proofs, just like nearly all stamps from Mauritania during this period. Unlike the perforated stamp, these collector items were distributed to the philatelic market and are worth less than genuine perforated examples.

Ice Hockey, Lake Placid '80 Emblem A105

Various ice hockey plays.

1979, Dec. 6   Litho.   Perf. 14½
432	A105	10um multi	.45	.25
433	A105	12um multi	.60	.25
434	A105	14um multi	.60	.25
435	A105	55um multi	2.10	.60
436	A105	60um multi	2.25	.65
437	A105	100um multi	4.00	1.20
		Nos. 432-437 (6)	10.00	3.20

13th Winter Olympic Games. Lake Placid, NY, Feb. 12-24, 1980.
For overprints see Nos. 440-445.

Arab Achievements A106

1980, Mar. 22   Litho.   Perf. 13
438	A106	12um multi	.70	.35
439	A106	15um multi	.80	.35

Nos. 432-437 Overprinted

(a)

(b)

(c)

(d)

(e)

(f)

1980, June 14   Litho.   Perf. 14½
440	A105(a)	10um multi	.50	.25
441	A105(b)	12um multi	.55	.25
442	A105(c)	14um multi	.55	.35
443	A105(d)	55um multi	2.10	.85
444	A105(e)	60um multi	2.25	.95
445	A105(f)	100um multi	4.00	1.50
		Nos. 440-445 (6)	9.95	4.15

Equestrian, Olympic Rings A107

Designs: Equestrian scenes. 10um, 20um, 70um, 100um, vert.

1980, June   Litho.   Perf. 14
446	A107	10um multi	.45	.25
447	A107	20um multi	.80	.25
448	A107	50um multi	2.25	.40
449	A107	70um multi	3.00	.60
		Nos. 446-449 (4)	6.50	1.50

Souvenir Sheet
| 450 | A107 | 100um multi | 5.00 | 1.75 |

22nd Summer Olympic Games, Moscow, July 19-Aug. 3.
For overprints see Nos. 464-468.

Armed Forces Day — A108

1980, July 9   Perf. 13x12½
451	A108	12um multi	.60	.25
452	A108	14um multi	.65	.30

World Red Cross Day — A109

1980, June 14   Perf. 13
| 453 | A109 | 20um multi | 10.00 | 2.00 |

Pilgrimage to Mecca — A110

Design: 50um, Mosque, outside view.

1980
454	A110	10um multi	1.00	.35
455	A110	50um multi	3.00	1.40

Man with Turban, by Rembrandt A111

Rembrandt Paintings: 10um, Self-portrait. 20um, His mother. 70um, His son Titus reading. 100um, Polish knight, horiz.

1980, July   Litho.   Perf. 12½
456	A111	10um multi	.60	.25
457	A111	20um multi	.95	.30
458	A111	50um multi	2.40	.45
459	A111	70um multi	3.00	.80
		Nos. 456-459 (4)	6.95	1.80

Souvenir Sheet
| 460 | A111 | 100um multi | 5.00 | 1.50 |

Tea Time — A112

1980, Mar. 11   Litho.   Perf. 12½
460A	A112	1um multi	.25	.25
461	A112	5um multi	.45	.25
462	A112	12um multi	.90	.30
		Nos. 460A-462 (3)	1.60	.80

MAURITANIA

Arbor Day — A113

1980, Aug. 29
463 A113 12um multi .... 1.25 .40

Nos. 446-450 Overprinted with Winner and Country
1980, Oct.   Litho.   Perf. 14
464 A107 10um multi .... .40 .25
465 A107 20um multi .... .75 .30
466 A107 50um multi .... 2.00 .50
467 A107 70um multi .... 2.60 .80
   Nos. 464-467 (4) 5.75 1.85

Souvenir Sheet
468 A107 100um multi 4.75 2.50

Mastodont Locomotive, 1850 — A114

Various locomotives: 12um, Iron ore train. 14um, Chicago-Milwaukee line, 1900. 20um, Bury, 1837. 67um, Reseau North line, 1870. 100um, Potsdam, 1840.

1980, Nov.   Perf. 12½
469 A114 10um shown .... .60 .25
470 A114 12um multi .... .75 .25
471 A114 14um multi .... .95 .25
472 A114 20um multi .... 1.30 .40
473 A114 67um multi .... 4.25 .70
474 A114 100um multi 6.50 1.00
   Nos. 469-474 (6) 14.35 2.85

20th Anniversary of Independence — A115

1980, Nov. 27   Perf. 13
475 A115 12um multi .... .50 .25
476 A115 15um multi .... .60 .30

El Haram Mosque A116

12um, Medina Mosque. 14um, Chinguetti Mosque.

1981, Apr. 13   Litho.   Perf. 12½
477 A116 2um shown .... .25 .25
478 A116 12um multi .... .55 .30
479 A116 14um multi .... .75 .30
   Nos. 477-479 (3) .... 1.55 .85

Hegira, 1500th anniversary.

Prince Charles and Lady Diana, Coach — A117

Designs: Coaches.

1981, July 8   Litho.   Perf. 14½
480 A117 14um multi .... .55 .25
481 A117 18um multi .... .70 .25
482 A117 77um multi .... 2.50 .90
   Nos. 480-482 (3) 3.75 1.40

Souvenir Sheet
483 A117 100um multi 4.50 1.10

Royal wedding.
For overprints see Nos. 518-521.

Intl. Year of the Disabled — A119

1981, June 29   Litho.   Perf. 13x13½
486 A119 12um multi .... .80 .40

Battle of Yorktown Bicentenary (American Revolution) A120

14um, George Washington, vert. 18um, Admiral de Grasse, vert. 63um, Surrender of Cornwallis. 81um, Battle of Chesapeake Bay.

1981, Oct. 5   Perf. 12½
487 A120 14um multi .... .55 .25
488 A120 18um multi .... .75 .25
489 A120 63um multi 2.25 1.00
490 A120 81um multi 3.25 1.40
   Nos. 487-490 (4) 6.80 2.90

475th Death Anniv. of Christopher Columbus (1451-1506) A121

1981, Oct. 5
491 A121 19um Pinta .... 1.10 .40
492 A121 55um Santa Maria .... 3.00 .80

World Food Day — A122

1981, Oct. 16   Perf. 13
493 A122 19um multi .... .80 .40

Kemal Ataturk Birth Cent. — A123

1981, Oct. 29   Perf. 12½
494 A123 63um multi 2.40 1.25

Scouting Year A124

Designs: Boating scenes. 92um vert.

1982, Jan. 20   Litho.   Perf. 12½
495 A124 14um multi .... .70 .25
496 A124 19um multi .... 1.00 .25
497 A124 22um multi .... 1.10 .25
498 A124 92um multi .... 4.25 .85
   Nos. 495-498 (4) 7.05 1.60

Souvenir Sheet   Perf. 13
499 A124 100um Baden-Powell, scout 4.75 1.25

75th Anniv. of Grand Prix — A125

Winners and their Cars: 7um, Deusenberg, 1921. 12um, Alfa Romeo, 1932. 14um, Juan Fangio, 1949. 18um, Renault, 1979. 19um, Niki Lauda, 1974. 100um, Race.

1982, Jan. 23   Perf. 13½
500 A125 7um multi .... .60 .25
501 A125 12um multi .... .85 .25
502 A125 14um multi .... .90 .25
503 A125 18um multi .... 1.05 .30
504 A125 19um multi .... 1.20 .30
   Nos. 500-504 (5) 4.60 1.35

Souvenir Sheet
505 A125 100um multi 5.50 1.75

Birds of the Arguin Bank — A126

1981, Dec. 17   Photo.   Perf. 13
506 A126 2um White pelicans .... 1.00 .25
507 A126 18um Pink flamingoes .... 4.00 .75

Battle of Karameh — A127

14um, Hand holding tattered flag.

1982, Dec. 19   Litho.
508 A127 14um multi .... .80 .35

Deluth Turtle — A128

Designs: Sea turtles.

1981, Dec. 21   Photo.   Perf. 14x13½
509 A128 1um shown .... 1.00 .25
510 A128 3um Green turtle .... 1.50 .30
511 A128 4um Shell turtle .... 2.50 .50
   Nos. 509-511 (3) 5.00 1.05

APU, 30th Anniv. — A129

1982, May 14   Litho.   Perf. 13
512 A129 14um org & brn .... .85 .40

A130

1982, May 17   Photo.   Perf. 13½x13
513 A130 21um multi .... 1.10 .40

14th World Telecommunications Day.

A131

1982, June 7   Litho.   Perf. 12½
514 A131 14um grnsh bl .... .85 .40

UN Conf. on Human Environment, 10th anniv.

21st Birthday of Princess Diana of Wales A132

Portraits.

1982, July   Perf. 14x13½
515 A132 21um multi .... .75 .40
516 A132 77um multi .... 2.50 .85

Souvenir Sheet
517 A132 100um multi 3.50 1.50

Nos. 480-483 Overprinted in Blue: "NAISSANCE ROYALE 1982"
1982, Aug. 2   Perf. 14½
518 A117 14um multi .... .50 .30
519 A117 18um multi .... .75 .35
520 A117 77um multi 2.50 1.25
   Nos. 518-520 (3) 3.75 1.90

Souvenir Sheet
521 A117 100um multi 4.00 1.50

Birth of Prince William of Wales, June 21.

Agricultural Development — A132a

Designs: 14um, Cattle and camels at watering hole, Hodh el Gharbi. 18um, Irrigation system, Gorgol.

1982, Dec. 13   Litho.   Perf. 14½
521A A132a 14um multi 4.00 1.25
521B A132a 18um multi 6.00 2.00

Manned Flight Bicentenary A133

14um, Montgolfiere balloon, 1783, vert. 18um, Hydrogen balloon, 1783. 19um, Zeppelin, vert. 55um, Nieuport plane. 63um, Concorde. 77um, Apollo II, vert.

1982, Dec. 29   Litho.   Perf. 14
522 A133 14um multi .... .65 .25
523 A133 18um multi .... .85 .25
524 A133 19um multi .... .85 .35
525 A133 55um multi .... 2.25 .45
526 A133 63um multi .... 2.40 .55
527 A133 77um multi .... 2.60 .65
   Nos. 522-527 (6) 9.80 2.50

Preservation of Ancient Cities — A134

14um, City Wall, Ouadane. 18um, Chinguetti. 24um, Staircase, panels, Qualata. 30um, Ruins, Tichitt.

MAURITANIA

1983, Feb. 16   **Litho.**   **Perf. 14x14½**
528	A134	14um multi	.65	.25
529	A134	18um multi	.75	.30
530	A134	24um multi	.95	.40
531	A134	30um multi	1.50	.60
	Nos. 528-531 (4)		3.85	1.55

World Communications Year — A135

1983, June 21   **Litho.**   **Perf. 13**
| 532 | A135 | 14um multi | .65 | .30 |

30th Anniv. of Customs Cooperation Council A136

1983, June 25
| 533 | A136 | 14um multi | .65 | .30 |

Traditional Houses — A137

1983, June 14   **Photo.**   **Perf. 13½**
534	A137	14um Peule	2.00	.35
535	A137	18um Toucouleur	3.00	.50
536	A137	19um Tent	3.25	.75
	Nos. 534-536 (3)		8.25	1.60

Ancient Manuscript Page — A138

5um, Ornamental scrollwork. 7um, Sheath.

1983, June 15   **Photo.**   **Perf. 12½x13**
537	A138	2um shown	.25	.25
538	A138	5um multi	.25	.25
539	A138	7um multi	.40	.25
	Nos. 537-539 (3)		.90	.75

Manned Flight Bicentenary A139

Early Fliers and their Balloons or Dirigibles: 10um, F. Pilatre de Rozier, vert. 14um, John Wise, vert. 25um, Charles Renard. No. 543, Henri Julliot. No. 544, Joseph Montgolfier.

1983, Oct. 17   **Litho.**   **Perf. 13½**
540	A139	10um multi	.60	.25
541	A139	14um multi	.75	.25
542	A139	25um multi	1.50	.30
543	A139	100um multi	4.75	1.10
	Nos. 540-543 (4)		7.60	1.90

Souvenir Sheet
| 544 | A139 | 100um multi | 6.00 | 1.25 |

No. 544 contains one stamp 47x37mm. Nos. 543-544 airmail.

Mortar — A140

Various prehistoric grinding implements.

1983, Dec. 28   **Litho.**   **Perf. 13**
545	A140	10um multi	.95	.35
546	A140	14um multi	1.50	.45
547	A140	18um multi	2.10	.75
	Nos. 545-547 (3)		4.55	1.55

Pre-Olympics — A141

1983, Dec. 31   **Litho.**   **Perf. 13½**
548	A141	1um Basketball	.25	.25
549	A141	20um Wrestling	.75	.40
550	A141	50um Equestrian	1.75	.70
551	A141	77um Running	3.25	.95
	Nos. 548-551 (4)		6.00	2.30

Souvenir Sheet
| 552 | A141 | 100um Soccer | 4.25 | 1.25 |

No. 552 contains one stamp 41x36mm. Nos. 551-552 airmail.

Scouting Year — A142

Artemis, by Rembrandt — A142a

Events & Annivs.: 5um, Flag, Baden-Powell. 14um, Johann Wolfgang von Goethe. 25um, Virgin and Child, by Peter Paul Rubens.

1984, Jan. 24
553	A142	5um multicolored	.50	.25
553A	A142	14um multicolored	1.00	.25
553B	A142	25um multicolored	1.50	.40
	Nos. 553-553B (3)		3.00	.90

Souvenir Sheet
| 553C | A142a | 100um multicolored | 4.00 | 1.50 |

No. 553C is airmail and contains one 42x51mm stamp.

Sand Rose — A143

1984, Mar.   **Litho.**   **Perf. 14**
| 554 | A143 | 21um multi | 13.50 | 1.50 |

Inscribed 1982.

Anniversaries and Events — A145

10um, Albrecht Durer (1471-1528). 12um, Apollo XI, 15th anniv. 50um, Chess.

1984, Apr. 26
555	A145	10um multi	.60	.25
556	A145	12um multi	.85	.30
557	A145	50um multi	2.50	1.25
	Nos. 555-557 (3)		3.95	1.80

1984, Apr. 16   **Litho.**   **Perf. 13½**

Designs: 77um, Prince Charles, Princess Diana. 100um, Prince Charles, Princess Diana, vert.
| 557A | A145 | 77um multi | 3.75 | 1.90 |

Miniature Sheet
| 557B | A145 | 100um multi | 5.50 | 3.50 |

Nos. 557A-557B airmail.

Fishing Industry — A146

1984
558	A146	1um Tuna	.25	.25
559	A146	2um Mackerel	.25	.25
560	A146	5um Haddock	.50	.25
561	A146	14um Black chinchard	1.25	.50
562	A146	18um Boat building	1.60	.60
	Nos. 558-562 (5)		3.85	1.85

Nouakchott Olympic Complex — A148

1984, Sept. 26   **Litho.**   **Perf. 13½**
| 569 | A148 | 14um multi | 1.00 | .40 |

Infant Survival Campaign — A149

1984, Sept. 26   **Litho.**   **Perf. 12½**
570	A149	1um Feeding by glass	.25	.25
571	A149	4um Breastfeeding	.40	.25
572	A149	10um Vaccinating	.60	.25
573	A149	14um Weighing	1.00	.30
	Nos. 570-573 (4)		2.25	1.05

Pilgrimage to Mecca A150

1984, Oct. 3   **Litho.**   **Perf. 13**
| 574 | A150 | 14um Tents, mosque | .70 | .40 |
| 575 | A150 | 18um Tents, courtyard | 1.25 | .60 |

10th Anniv., West African Union A151

1984, Nov.   **Litho.**   **Perf. 13**
| 576 | A151 | 14um multi | .80 | .40 |

14um, Map of member nations.

No. 355 Overprinted "Aide au Sahel 84" and Surcharged

1984   **Litho.**   **Perf. 12½**
| 577 | A82 | 18um on 10um | 1.25 | .50 |

Issued to publicize drought relief efforts.

Technical & Cultural Cooperation Agency, 15th Anniv. A152

1985, Mar. 20   **Litho.**   **Perf. 12½**
| 578 | A152 | 18um Profiles, emblem | .80 | .45 |

League of Arab States, 40th Anniv. A153

1985, May 7   **Perf. 13**
| 579 | A153 | 14um brt yel grn & blk | .70 | .40 |

German Railways 150th Anniv. A154

Anniversaries and events: 12um, Adler, 1st German locomotive, 1835. 18um, Series 10, 1956, last Fed. German Railways locomotive. 44um, European Music Year, Johann Sebastian Bach, composer, and Angels Making Music, unattributed painting. 77um, George Frideric Handel. 90um, Statue of Liberty, cent., vert. 100um, Queen Mother, 85th birthday, vert.

1985, Sept.
580	A154	12um multi	.65	.25
581	A154	18um multi	1.00	.45
582	A154	44um multi	2.00	1.10
583	A154	77um multi	3.50	1.90
584	A154	90um multi	4.00	2.25
	Nos. 580-584 (5)		11.15	5.95

Souvenir Sheet
| 585 | A154 | 100um multi | 4.75 | 2.25 |

World Food Day — A155

1985, Oct. 16   **Perf. 13x12½**
| 586 | A155 | 18um multi | .70 | .40 |

UN Food and Agriculture Org., 40th anniv.

Fight Against Drought — A156

1985, Apr. 10   **Litho.**   **Perf. 13**
586A	A156	10um Tree planting	.75	.30
587	A156	14um Antelope	1.00	.35
588	A156	18um Oasis	1.25	.50

Fight Against Desert Encroachment A157

10um, Grain harvest, vert. 14um, Brush fire. 18um, Planting brush.

1985
589	A157	10um multi	.55	.30
590	A157	14um multi	2.00	.75
591	A157	18um multi	2.00	.75
	Nos. 589-591 (3)		4.55	1.80

Natl. Independence, 25th Anniv. — A158

1985, Nov. 27   **Perf. 15x14½**
| 592 | A158 | 18um multi | 1.00 | .40 |

Intl. Youth Year — A159

MAURITANIA

1986, Feb. 13   Litho.   *Perf. 13*
593 A159 18um Development .75 .30
594 A159 22um Participation .90 .45
595 A159 25um Peace, vert. 1.25 .75
   Nos. 593-595 (3) 2.90 1.50

Toujounine Satellite Station — A160

1986, May 22   Litho.   *Perf. 12½*
596 A160 25um multi 1.25 .60

World Wildlife Fund — A161

Monk seal (Monachus monachus).

1986, June 12   *Perf. 13*
597 A161 2um multi 1.50 .35
598 A161 5um multi 2.40 .60
599 A161 10um multi 3.75 1.00
600 A161 18um multi 6.75 2.00
   Nos. 597-600 (4) 14.40 3.95
Souvenir Sheet
601 A161 50um multi 15.00 5.00

Weaving — A162

1986, July 20   Litho.   *Perf. 12½*
602 A162 18um multi .80 .40

Sabra and Chatila Massacre, 4th Anniv. — A163

1986, Oct. 18
603 A163 22um multi .90 .40

A164

Christopher Columbus — A165

Indians, maps on globe and: 2um, Santa Maria. 22um, Nina. 35um, Pinta. 150um, Columbus.

1986, Oct. 14   Litho.   *Perf. 13½*
604 A164 2um multi .25 .25
605 A164 22um multi .75 .30
606 A164 35um multi 1.10 .55
607 A164 150um multi 5.25 2.25
   Nos. 604-607 (4) 7.35 3.40
Souvenir Sheet
608 A165 100um Columbus, Earth 4.50 4.00
   Nos. 607-608 are airmail.

US Space Shuttle Challenger Explosion, Jan. 28, 1986 — A166

Crew members and: 7um, Space shuttle. 22um, Canadarm. 32um, Sky, moon. 43um, Memorial emblem.

1986, Oct. 14
609 A166 7um multi .25 .25
610 A166 22um multi .80 .30
611 A166 32um multi 1.25 .50
612 A166 43um multi 1.75 .65
   Nos. 609-612 (4) 4.05 1.70
Souvenir Sheet
613 A166 100um Crew, lift-off 4.00 1.50
   Nos. 612-613 are airmail.

Fish — A167

1986, Oct. 16   *Perf. 13*
614 A167 4um Dorade .50 .25
615 A167 98um Truite de mer 5.00 2.25
   See Nos. 631-633.

Birds — A168

1986, Oct. 16
616 A168 22um Spatule blanche 1.75 .60
617 A168 32um Sterne bridee 2.25 .80
   See Nos. 634-635.

World Food Day — A169

1986, Nov. 6   *Perf. 12½*
618 A169 22um multi 1.00 .40

A170

1986, Oct. 14   Litho.   *Perf. 13½*
619 A170 5um multi .25 .25
620 A170 18um multi .55 .25
621 A170 26um multi .90 .40
622 A170 80um multi 3.00 1.25
   Nos. 619-622 (4) 4.70 2.15
Souvenir Sheet
623 A171 100um multi 3.75 1.90
   Nos. 622-623 are airmail.
   No. 619 is misspelled "J.H. Dort."

Halley's Comet — A171

Space probes and portraits: 5um, J.H. Oort, Giotto probe. 18um, Sir William Huggins (1824-1910), English astronomer, and launch of Giotto on Ariane rocket. 26um, E.J. Opik, Giotto and Vega. 80um, F.L. Whipple, Planet-A. 100um, Edmond Halley, Giotto.

Jerusalem Day — A172

22um, Dome of the Rock.

1987, May 21   Litho.   *Perf. 13½*
624 A172 22um multi 1.00 .40

Cordoue Mosque, 1200th Anniv. — A173

1987, Sept. 5   Litho.   *Perf. 13½*
625 A173 30um multi 1.50 .55

Literacy Campaign A174

18um, Classroom. 22um, Family reading, vert.

1907, Sept. 12
626 A174 18um multi .65 .40
627 A174 22um multi .85 .60

World Health Day — A175

1987, Oct. 1   *Perf. 13*
628 A175 18um multi .80 .40

Natl. Population Census — A176

1988, Aug. 21   Litho.   *Perf. 13½*
629 A176 20um multi .80 .40

WHO, 40th Anniv. — A177

1988, Sept. 19   *Perf. 13*
630 A177 30um multi 1.25 .50

Fish Type of 1986

1um, Rascasse blanche. 7um, Baliste. 15um, Bonite a ventre raye.

1988, Sept. 10   Litho.   *Perf. 13*
631 A167 1um multi .50 .25
632 A167 7um multi 1.60 .35
633 A167 15um multi 2.40 .75
   Nos. 631-633 (3) 4.50 1.35

Bird Type of 1986

1988, Sept. 15
634 A168 18um Grand cormorant 1.50 .60
635 A168 80um Royal tern 4.50 2.75

Arab Scouting Movement, 75th Anniv. — A178

1988, Sept. 29   Litho.   *Perf. 13*
636 A178 35um multi 1.75 .60

1st Municipal Elections A179

20um, Men casting ballots. 24um, Woman casting ballot.

1988, Nov. 22   *Perf. 13½*
637 A179 20um multi .70 .30
638 A179 24um multi 1.00 .40

Organization of African Unity, 25th Anniv. (in 1988) — A180

1988, Dec. 7   Litho.   *Perf. 13*
639 A180 40um multi 1.25 .65

Intl. Fund for Agricultural Development, 10th Anniv. (in 1988) — A181

1988, Dec. 15
640 A181 35um multi 1.75 .70

Autonomy of Nouakchott (Amitie) Port, 1st Anniv. A182

1988, Dec. 20   Litho.   *Perf. 13*
641 A182 24um multi 1.30 .60

A183

1989, July 7   Litho.   *Perf. 13*
642 A183 35um multi 1.50 .60

French Revolution bicent., PHILEXFRANCE '89.

MAURITANIA

A184

1989, July 17
643 A184 20um multi .90 .40
1990 World Cup Soccer Championships, Italy.

Pilgrimage to Mecca — A185

1989, Aug. 26 Litho. Perf. 13½
644 A185 20um Mosque .90 .40

African Development Bank, 25th Anniv. — A186

1989, Sept. 2
645 A186 37um lt vio & blk 1.25 .60

Tapestry A187

1989, Oct. 1 Perf. 13
646 A187 50um multicolored 2.00 .85

Locusts, Moths and Ladybugs — A188

No. 647, Heliothis armigera. No. 648, Locust. No. 649, Aphis gossypii. No. 650, Agrotis ypsilon. No. 651, Chilo. No. 652, Two locusts, egg case. No. 653, Locusts emerging. No. 654, Plitella xylostella. No. 655, Henosepilachna elaterii. No. 656, Locust flying. No. 657, Trichoplusia ni. No. 658, Locust, diff.

1989, Dec. 29
647 A188 2um multi .25 .25
648 A188 5um multi .45 .25
649 A188 6um multi .25 .25
650 A188 10um multi .45 .25
651 A188 20um multi .85 .35
652 A188 20um multi .90 .35
653 A188 24um multi .95 .40
654 A188 24um multi .95 .40
655 A188 30um multi 1.40 .50
656 A188 40um multi 1.90 .70
657 A188 42um multi 1.75 .70
658 A188 88um multi 4.75 1.40
  Nos. 647-658 (12) 14.85 5.80
For surcharge see No. 737.

Revolt — A189

1989, Dec. 8 Litho. Perf. 13
659 A189 35um multicolored 1.60 .70
2nd Anniv. of the Palestinian Uprising and 1st anniv. of the declaration of a Palestinian State.

Maghreb Arab Union, 1st Anniv. A190

1990, Feb. 17 Litho. Perf. 13½
660 A190 50um multicolored 1.75 .80

Mineral Resources A191

1990, July 27 Perf. 11½
661 A191 60um multicolored 2.75 1.60

Intl. Literacy Year — A192

1990, July 27
662 A192 60um multicolored 2.25 1.00

1992 Summer Olympics, Barcelona — A193

5um, Equestrian. 50um, Archery. 60um, Hammer throw. 75um, Field hockey. 90um, Handball. 220um, Table tennis. 150um, Runner.

Litho. & Typo.
1990, Sept. 2 Perf. 13½
663 A193 5um multi .25 .25
664 A193 50um multi 1.90 .75
665 A193 60um multi 2.00 1.25
666 A193 75um multi 2.75 1.25
667 A193 90um multi 3.50 1.50
668 A193 220um multi 8.50 3.25
  Nos. 663-668 (6) 18.90 8.25

Souvenir Sheet
669 A193 150um multi 6.25 2.50
Nos. 668-669 airmail.

A194

1990, July 27 Perf. 11½
670 A194 50um multicolored 2.00 .75
Multinational Postal School, 20th anniv.

A195

1990, Nov. 21 Litho. Perf. 11½
671 A195 85um multicolored 3.75 1.60
Declaration of the Palestinian State, 2nd anniv.

1992 Winter Olympics, Albertville — A196

60um, Downhill skiing. 75um, Cross-country skiing. 90um, Ice hockey. 220um, Pairs figure skating.
150um, Slalom skiing.

1990, Dec. 10 Litho. Perf. 13½
672 A196 60um multi 2.10 .75
673 A196 75um multi 2.50 1.40
674 A196 90um multi 3.50 2.00
675 A196 220um multi 7.75 3.25
  Nos. 672-675 (4) 15.85 7.40

Souvenir Sheet
676 A196 150um multi 5.00 2.50
Nos. 675-676 are airmail.

Release of Nelson Mandela — A197

1990, Dec. 10
677 A197 85um multicolored 3.75 1.90

Return of Senegalese Refugees A198

50um, Cooking at encampment. 75um, Women sewing. 85um, Drawing water.

1990, Dec. 10
678 A198 50um multi 2.00 1.00
679 A198 75um multi 3.25 1.75
680 A198 85um multi 3.75 1.75
  Nos. 678-680 (3) 9.00 4.50

Boy Scouts Observing Nature — A199

Scout: 5um, Picking mushrooms. 50um, Holding mushroom. 60um, Drawing butterfly. 75um, Feeding butterfly. 90um, Photographing butterfly. 220um, Drying mushrooms. No. 687, Using microscope.

1991, Jan. 16 Litho. Perf. 13½
681 A199 5um multicolored .50 .25
682 A199 50um multicolored 2.75 .95
683 A199 60um multicolored 2.60 1.10
684 A199 75um multicolored 3.00 1.00
685 A199 90um multicolored 3.00 1.10
  a. Sheet of 3, #683-685 20.00
686 A199 220um multicolored 6.75 2.75
  a. Sheet of 3, #681-682, 686 20.00
  Nos. 681-686 (6) 18.60 7.15

Souvenir Sheet
687 A199 150um multicolored 6.00 4.00
Nos. 684 and 687 are airmail. Nos. 681-686 exist in souvenir sheets of 1. Value, $9 each.

Independence, 30th Anniv. — A200

50um, Satellite dish antennae. 60um, Container ship. 100um, Harvesting rice.

1991, Mar. 5
688 A200 50um multi 1.75 .90
689 A200 60um multi 2.10 1.25
690 A200 100um multi 3.50 1.75
  Nos. 688-690 (3) 7.35 3.90

World Meteorology Day — A201

1991, Mar. 23 Perf. 14x15
691 A201 100um multicolored 3.75 2.10

World Population Day — A202

1991, July 27 Litho. Perf. 13½
692 A202 90um multicolored 3.50 1.75

Domesticated Animals — A203

1991 Litho. Perf. 13½
693 A203 50um Cats 2.25 1.00
693A A203 60um Dog 2.75 1.60

Campaign Against Blindness A204

1991, Nov. 10 Litho. Perf. 13½
694 A204 50um multicolored 2.00 1.00

Doctors Without Borders, 20th Anniv. — A205

1991 Litho. Perf. 13½
695 A205 60um multicolored 2.50 1.25

Installation of Central Electric Service (in 1989) — A206

1991, Dec. 29 Litho. Perf. 13½
696 A206 50um multicolored 2.50 1.00

Mineral Exploration, M'Haoudat — A207

60um, Desert landscape.

1993 Litho. Perf. 13½
697 A207 50um shown 2.10 1.00
698 A207 60um multi 2.50 1.40

MAURITANIA

1994 Winter Olympics, Lillehammer — A208

10um, Bobsled. 50um, Luge. 60um, Figure skating. 80um, Downhill skiing. 220um, Cross-country skiing.
150um, Downhill skiing, diff.

1993
699	A208	10um multi	.40	.25
700	A208	50um multi	1.75	1.05
701	A208	60um multi	2.10	1.25
702	A208	80um multi	2.75	1.75
703	A208	220um multi	7.75	4.50
		Nos. 699-703 (5)	14.75	8.80

Souvenir Sheet
704	A208	150um multi	5.75	3.25

No. 704 is airmail.
No. 700 exists dated "1998."

Intifada, 6th Anniv. — A209

Design: 60um, Palestinian children, horiz.

1993
705	A209	50um multicolored	2.10	1.00
706	A209	60um multicolored	2.50	1.40

First Multiparty Presidential Elections, 1st Anniv. — A209a

Designs: 50um, Ballots entering ballot box. 60um, Line at polling place.

1993 Litho. Perf. 13½
706A	A209a	50um multi	25.00	—
706B	A209a	60um multi		

Caravans — A210

1993
707	A210	50um blue & multi	1.90	1.00
708	A210	60um violet & multi	2.25	1.40

Hut — A210a

1994 Litho. Perf. 13¼x13½
708A	A210a	50um Hut, diff.	30.00	—
708B	A210a	60um multi	45.00	12.00
708C	A210a	80um Hut, diff.	35.00	—
		Nos. 708A-708C (3)	110.00	12.00

1994 World Cup Soccer Championships, U.S. — A211

Designs: 10um, Soldier Field. 50um, Foxboro Stadium. 60um, Robert F. Kennedy Stadium. 90um, Stanford Stadium. 220um, Giants Stadium. 150um, Rose Bowl.

1994, Feb. 10 Litho. Perf. 13
709	A211	10um multicolored	.35	.25
710	A211	50um multicolored	1.45	1.05
711	A211	60um multicolored	1.75	1.25
712	A211	90um multicolored	2.50	1.75
713	A211	220um multicolored	6.25	4.50
a.		Sheet of 5, #709-713 + label	12.50	
		Nos. 709-713 (5)	12.30	8.80

Souvenir Sheet
714	A211	150um multicolored	6.00	3.25

Birds of Banc d'Arguin National Park — A211a

Designs: 10 um, Gulls, horiz. 30um, Various birds. 40um, Terns. 50um, Sandpipers.

1994 Litho. Perf. 13½
714A	A211a	10um lt blue & multi	70.00	—
714B	A211a	30um lt blue & multi	—	11.00
714C	A211a	40um lt blue & multi	70.00	—
714D	A211a	50um lt blue & multi		

UN, 50th Anniv. — A212

1995 Litho. Perf. 11½
715	A212	60um Emblem, #167	1.50	.75

FAO, 50th Anniv. — A213

1995
716	A213	50um Working in field	1.00	.70
717	A213	60um With fishing boat	1.25	.85
718	A213	90um Planting garden	1.90	1.25
		Nos. 716-718 (3)	4.15	2.80

Traditional Handicrafts — A214

1995, Aug. 14 Litho. Perf. 12
719	A214	50um Weaving rug	20.00	10.00

Perf. 11½x12
720	A214	60um Kettle	225.00	20.00

1996 Summer Olympics, Atlanta — A216

Design: 20um, Sprinters crouching at starting line. 30um, Six runners at the starting line, horiz. 40um, Five Runners. 50um, Runners, horiz.

1996, July 19 Litho. Perf. 11¾
725	A216	20um pink & multi	20.00	6.00
726	A216	30um gray & multi	20.00	—
727	A216	40um blue & multi		
728	A216	50um yel & multi	20.00	—
		Nos. 725-728 (4)	60.00	6.00

Traditional Games — A218

Designs: 50um, Three women playing board game with balls, vert. 60um, Two men playing board game. 90um, Shown, women and sticks.

1996, Oct. 25 Litho. Perf. 11¾
731	A218	50um multi	30.00	17.00
732	A218	60um multi	20.00	15.00
733	A218	90um multi	20.00	12.00
		Nos. 731-733 (3)	70.00	44.00

French Pres. Jacques Chirac, Mauritanian Pres. Maaouya Ould Sid Ahmed Taya
A219

1997 Litho. Perf. 13¼x13
735A	A219	60um multi	45.00	—

State visit of Chirac to Mauritania.

Universal Declaration of Human Rights, 50th Anniv. — A220

1998 Litho. Perf. 13x13¼
736	A220	60um multi	19.50	5.00

The editors suspect that other stamps were issued in this set and would like to examine any examples.

No. 649 Surcharged

2000 Method and Perf. As Before
737	A188	50um on 6um #649	30.00	

Independence, 40th Anniv. — A221

2000 Litho. Perf. 13¼
738	A221	50um multi	50.00	—

Education A222

Designs: 50um, Man with tablet, woman at computer. 60um, Open-air class. 90um, Reading class. 100um, Mathematics class.

2000
739-742	A222	Set of 4	110.00	—

Mauritanian postal officials have declared as "illegal" the following items:
Sheets of 9 stamps with 60um denominations depicting Famous actresses (2 different). Classic actresses, Marilyn Monroe, Elvis Presley, The Beatles, Queen, Walt Disney, The Simpsons, Teddy bears.
Sheets of 6 stamps with 80um denominations depicting Birds and Scout emblem (15 different).
Sheets of 6 stamps with 60um denominations depicting Trains (5 different), Penguins and Rotary emblem (2 different), Cats and Rotary emblem (2 different), Elephants and Rotary emblem (2 different), Polar bears and Rotary emblem (2 different), Lighthouses and Rotary emblem (2 different), Firearms and Rotary emblem, Firearms and Scout emblem, Pope John Paul II, Harry Potter, Scooby-Doo.
Sheets of 4 stamps depicting various sports of the Sydney Olympics (2 different).
Souvenir sheet depicting Various sports of the Sydney Olympics.
Se-tenant sets of 4 stamps depicting sports of the Sydney Olympics (2 different).

Flora, Fauna and Mushrooms A223

No. 743: a, Chelonia mydas. b, Octopus vulgaris. c, Coelacanth.
No. 744: a, Lepiota aspera. b, Lactarius camphoratus. c, Clitocybe gibba.
No. 745: a, Harpa costata. b, Voluta lapponica. c, Tellina variegata.
No. 746: a, Akhal-Teke horse. b, Arabian horse. c, Lipizzaner horse.
No. 747: a, Tibetan dog, Balinese cat. b, Shetland sheepdog, Ragdoll cat. c, Cao de Serra de Aires sheepdog, Abyssinian cat.
No. 748: a, Acraea igati. b, Mylotris humbolti. c, Mylotris ngaziya.
No. 749: a, Zosterops maderaspatana. b, Otus rutilus. c, Nelicurvitus nelicourvi.
No. 750: a, Maxillaria tenuifolia. b, Crotalaria. c, Maxillaria marginata.
No. 751, Russula virescens. No. 752, Black Russian cat.

2000, Nov. 5 Litho. Perf. 13½
743		Horiz. strip of 3	2.10	2.10
a.-c.	A223	50um Any single	.70	.70
744		Horiz. strip of 3	2.10	2.10
a.-c.	A223	50um Any single	.70	.70
745		Horiz. strip of 3	2.25	2.25
a.-c.	A223	60um Any single	.75	.75
746		Horiz. strip of 3	3.75	3.75
a.-c.	A223	90um Any single	1.25	1.25
747		Horiz. strip of 3	4.00	4.00
a.-c.	A223	100um Any single	1.30	1.30
748		Horiz. strip of 3	8.00	8.00
a.-c.	A223	200um Any single	2.60	2.60
749		Horiz. strip of 3	0.50	0.50
a.-c.	A223	220um Any single	3.00	3.00
750		Horiz. strip of 3	3.75	3.75
a.	A223	60um multi	.90	.90
b.	A223	90um multi	1.35	1.35
c.	A223	100um multi	1.50	1.50
		Nos. 743-750 (8)	35.45	35.45

Souvenir Sheets
751	A223	300um multi	4.75	4.75
752	A223	300um multi	4.75	4.75

Nos. 746-749 exist in souvenir sheets containing one strip of 3 with light blue frames.
No. 750 exists imperf.

2002 World Cup Soccer Championships, Japan and Korea — A224

No. 753: a, Zinedine Zidane. b, Christian Vieri. c, Alessandro del Piero. d, Lilian Thuram.
No. 754: a, Oliver Bierhoff. b, Jürgen Klinsmann. c, Edgar Davids. d, Dennis Bergkamp.
300um, Jules Rimet Cup, soccer players, horiz.

2000
753		Horiz. strip of 4	14.00	14.00
a.-d.	A224	90um Any single	3.00	3.00

MAURITANIA

754		Horiz. strip of 4	14.00	14.00
a.-d.	A224	100um Any single	3.00	3.00

Souvenir Sheet

| 755 | A224 | 300um multi | 4.00 | 4.00 |

No. 755 contains one 57x51mm stamp. Souvenir sheets of 4 stamps exist with Nos. 753a-753d and 754a-754d with colored stamp frames.

A stamp was prepared for the visit of the King of Morocco, but was never issued. Used examples are from first-day covers. Value, $80 unused.

Theodore Monod (1902-2000), Naturalist — A225

2003, Jan. 1   **Perf. 13¼x13**
756   A225   370um multi   3.50   2.50

Trains — A226

Designs: 100um, Freight train for minerals. 370um, Passenger train. 440um, Desert train.

2003, Jan. 1   **Perf. 13x13¼**
757-759   A226   Set of 3   10.00   10.00

Tourist Attractions A227

Designs: 100um, Sailboats, Banc d'Arguin. 220um, Ben Amera. 370um, Desert warthogs, Diawling Park. 440fr, Palms, Tergit, vert.

2003, Jan. 1   **Perf. 13x13¼, 13¼x13**
760-763   A227   Set of 4   16.00   12.00

Handicrafts A228

Designs: 100um, Wooden chest. 220um, Pipes. 310um, Teapot. 370um, Beads.

2003, Jan. 1   **Perf. 13x13¼**
764-767   A228   Set of 4   10.00   6.00

Historic Towns — A229

Designs: 100um, Mosque, Chinguetti. 220um, Mosque, Ouadane. 660um, Wall design, Oualata. 880um, Mosque, Tichitt.

2003, Jan. 1
768-771   A229   Set of 4   18.00   12.00

Promotion of Books and Reading — A230

Open book and: 100um, Stack of books, chair. 220um, Camel. 280um, Tower. 370um, Man, construction equipment.

2003, Jan. 1   **Litho.**   **Perf. 13**
772-775   A230   Set of 4   12.50   6.00

A231

Flags and: 100um, Ships and crane. 370um, Ship and crane, vert.

Perf. 13x13¼, 13¼x13
2005, July 19   **Litho.**
776-777   A231   Set of 2   19.00   19.00

Diplomatic relations between Mauritania and People's Republic of China, 40th anniv.

Independence, 45th Anniv. — A232

Denominations: 100um, 370um.

2005, Nov. 16   **Perf. 13**
778-779   A232   Set of 2   5.00   5.00

World Summit on the Information Society, Tunis — A233

Denominations: 100um, 370um.

2005, Nov. 16
780-781   A233   Set of 2   5.00   5.00

Musical Instruments A234

Designs: 100um, Tidinit and gambré. 220um, Ardines, vert. 370um, Tom-toms. 440um, Kora and djembé, vert.

2005, Nov. 28
782-785   A234   Set of 4   37.50   13.00

Flora — A235

Designs: 100um, Acacia tree. 220um, Euphorbia, vert. 370um, Jujube tree. 440um, Baobab tree, vert.

2005, Nov. 28
786-789   A235   Set of 4   13.00   10.00

Fauna — A236

Designs: 100um, Starred lizard. 220um, Horned viper, vert. 370um, Lizard. 440um, Scorpion, vert.

2005, Nov. 28
790-793   A236   Set of 4   14.00   13.00

Tourism — A237

Designs: 100um, People, fish and dolphins in water. 220um, Hodh El Gharbi. 370um, Adrar. 440um, Tiris Zemour.

2005, Nov. 28
794-797   A237   Set of 4   13.00   13.00

Jewelry — A238

Designs: 100um, Necklaces. 220um, Khalkhal bracelets. 370um, Strings of beads. 440fr, Bracelets.

2008   **Litho.**   **Perf. 13**
798-801   A238   Set of 4   17.00   17.00

Exploitation of Natural Resources A239

Designs: 100um, Zouerate iron mine. 280um, Chinguitti oil platform, vert. 310um, Akjoujt copper mine. 370um, Taziast gold mine, vert.

2008
802-805   A239   Set of 4   17.00   17.00

Animals — A240

Designs: 100um, Birds. 220um, Dolphins. 370um, Seal. 440um, Sea turtle.

2009   **Litho.**   **Perf. 13**
806-809   A240   Set of 4   11.00   11.00

Saddles — A241

Saddle for: 100um, Horse. 220um, Cow. 370um, Ass. 440um, Camel.

2009
810-813   A241   Set of 4   13.50   13.50

Gear for Nomads — A242

Designs: 100um, Rifle holster. 150um, Tassoufra. 220um, Powder horns. 370um, Palanquin, vert. 440um, Prayer rug.

2009
814-818   A242   Set of 5   16.50   16.50

Necklaces — A243

Designs: 100um, Ebony necklace. 150um, Agate necklace. 220um, Amber necklace. 370um, Traditional necklace. 440um, Stone necklace.

2010   **Perf. 13¼**
819-823   A243   Set of 5   12.00   12.00

Independence, 50th Anniv. — A244

2010   **Perf. 13**
824   A244   370um multi   7.50   7.50

Fish — A245

Designs: 100um, Daisy stingray (pastenague marguerite). 220um, Guitar fish (raie guitare). 370um, Spinner shark (requin tisserand).

2011
825-827   A245   Set of 3   25.00   25.00

Birds — A246

Designs: 150um, Great white pelican (pélican blanc). 220um, Dimorphic egret (aigrette dimorphe). 370um, Little stint (bécasseau minute). 440um, Caspian tern (sterne caspienne).

2011   **Litho.**   **Perf. 13**
828-831   A246   Set of 4   40.00   40.00

Mammals — A247

Designs: 100um, Hyena. 370um, Fennec.

2011   **Litho.**   **Perf. 13**
832-833   A247   Set of 2   13.00   13.00

2012 Festival of Old Towns, Ouadane A248

Designs: 100um, Town. 370um, Festival emblem and names of host towns.

2012
834-835   A248   Set of 2   9.00   7.00

Marine Life — A249

Designs: 100um, King mackerel (Maquereau bonite). 150um, Butterfish (Lippe). 220um, Red-banded sea bream (Pagre rayé). 280um, Blue-spotted sea bream (Merou à points bleus). No. 840, 370um, Dogfish (Chien de mer). No. 841, 370um, Cuttlefish (Seiche commune). 440um, Round sardinella (Sardinelle ronde).

2013   **Litho.**   **Perf. 12¾x13**
836-842   A249   Set of 7   22.50   22.50

Nouadhibou Free Zone, 1st Anniv. — A251

2014   **Litho.**   **Perf. 12¾**
844   A251   370um multi   9.00   2.60

MAURITANIA

Marine Life — A252

Designs: No. 845, 100um, Threadfin (petit capitaine). No. 846, 100um, Sea trout (truite de mer). 220um, Black mullet (mulet noir). 280um, Atlantic horse mackerel (chinchard d'europe). No. 849, 370um, Zebra sea bream (sar tambour). No. 850, 370um, Pink shrimp (crevette rose). 440um, Red mullet (rouget barbet).

	2014	Litho.		Perf. 12¾
845-851	A252	Set of 7	27.50	27.50

Festival of Old Towns — A253

	2014	Litho.		Perf. 12¾
852	A253	370um multi	7.00	4.00

Education Year — A254

Design: No. 860, Globe, computer, mortarboard, diploma, students, teacher and blackboard.

	2015	Litho.		Perf. 12¾
860	A254	370um multi		

Seven additional stamps were issued in this set. The editors would like to examine any examples.

Equipment for Making Tea — A258

Inscriptions: No. 864, 100um, Bouilloire eau (kettle). No. 865, 100um, Fourneau (furnace). No. 866, 100um, Récipient sucre en bronze (bronze sugar container). No. 867, 150um, Récipient sucre en cuir (leather sugar container). No. 868, 150um, Bouquet de menthe (mint). 220um, Récipient thé en bronze (bronze tea container). No. 870, 370um, Récipient thé en cuir (leather tea container). No. 871, 370um, Théière (teapot). No. 872, 370um, Verre de thé (tea glass). No. 873, 370um, Accessoires complets (complete set of accessories).

	2016, May 11	Litho.		Perf. 12¾x13
864-873	A258	Set of 10	—	—

SEMI-POSTAL STAMPS

Nos. 23 and 26 Surcharged in Red

	1915-18	Unwmk.		Perf. 14x13½
B1	A4	10c + 5c rose & red org	1.75	2.10
a.		Double surcharge	225.00	
B2	A4	15c + 5c dk brn & blk ('18)	1.75	2.10
a.		Double surcharge	190.00	
b.		Inverted surcharge	150.00	

Curie Issue
Common Design Type

	1938, Oct. 24			Perf. 13
B3	CD80	1.75fr + 50c brt ultra	7.75	7.75

French Revolution Issue
Common Design Type
Photo.; Name and Value Typographed in Black

	1939, July 5		Unwmk.	
B4	CD83	45c + 25c grn	8.50	8.50
B5	CD83	70c + 30c brn	8.50	8.50
B6	CD83	90c + 35c red org	8.50	8.50
B7	CD83	1.25fr + 1fr rose pink	8.50	8.50
B8	CD83	2.25fr + 2fr bl	8.50	8.50
	Nos. B4-B8 (5)		42.50	42.50

Catalogue values for unused stamps in this section, from this point to the end of the section, are for Never Hinged items.

Stamps of 1938 Surcharged in Red or Black

1941

B9	A6	50c + 1fr pur (R)	7.00	3.50
B10	A7	80c + 2fr dp bl (R)	14.00	7.00
B11	A7	1.50fr + 2fr vio (R)	14.00	10.00
B12	A8	2fr + 3fr rose vio (Bk)	14.00	10.00
	Nos. B9-B12 (4)		49.00	30.50

Common Design Type and

Moorish Goumier SP1

White Goumier SP2

	1941	Photo.		Perf. 13½
B13	SP1	1fr + 1fr red		1.00
B14	CD86	1.50fr + 3fr claret		1.00
B15	SP2	2.50fr + 1fr blue		1.00
	Nos. B13-B15 (3)			3.00

Nos. B13-B15 were issued by the Vichy government in France, but were not placed on sale in Mauritania.

Nos. 114-115 Surcharged in Black or Red

	1944	Engr.		Perf. 12½x12
B15A		50c + 1.50fr on 2.50fr deep blue (R)		.80
B15B		2.50fr on 1fr green		.80

Colonial Development Fund.
Nos. B15A-B15B were issued by the Vichy government in France, but were not placed on sale in Mauritania.

Islamic Republic
Anti-Malaria Issue
Common Design Type

	1962, Apr. 7	Engr.		Perf. 12½x12
B16	CD108	25fr + 5f light olive grn	.50	.50

Freedom from Hunger Issue
Common Design Type

	1963, Mar. 21	Unwmk.		Perf. 13
B17	CD112	25fr + 5fr multi	.60	.60

Nurse Tending Infant — SP3

	1972, May 8	Photo.		Perf. 12½x13
B18	SP3	35fr + 5fr grn, red & brn	1.50	1.50

Surtax was for Mauritania Red Crescent Society.

AIR POST STAMPS

Common Design Type
Perf. 12½x12

	1940, Feb. 8	Engr.		Unwmk.
C1	CD85	1.90fr ultra	.35	.35
C2	CD85	2.90fr dk red	.35	.35
C3	CD85	4.50fr dk gray grn	.70	.70
C4	CD85	4.90fr yel bister	.70	.70
C5	CD85	6.90fr deep org	1.40	1.40
	Nos. C1-C5 (5)		3.50	3.50

Catalogue values for unused stamps in this section, from this point to the end of the section, are for Never Hinged items.

Common Design Types

1942

C6	CD88	50c car & bl	.35
C7	CD88	1fr brn & blk	.35
C8	CD88	2fr dk grn & red brn	.70
C9	CD88	3fr dk bl & scar	.70
C10	CD88	5fr vio & brn red	1.00

Frame Engraved, Center Typo.

C11	CD89	10fr ultra, ind & hn	1.40
a.		Center inverted	1,400.
C12	CD89	20fr rose car, mag & buff	1.75
a.		Center inverted	1,400.
C13	CD89	50fr yel grn, dl grn & org	3.50 3.25
	Nos. C6-C13 (8)		9.75

There is doubt whether Nos. C6-C12 were officially placed in use.
No. C11 exists with violet-blue center. Value $300.

Islamic Republic

Flamingoes — AP1

Designs: 200fr, African spoonbills. 500fr, Slender-billed gull, horiz.

	1961, June 30	Engr.	Unwmk.	Perf. 13
C14	AP1	100fr red org, brn & ultra	3.75	2.00
C15	AP1	200fr red org, sep & sl grn	5.50	3.50
C16	AP1	500fr red org, gray & bl	16.50	8.00
	Nos. C14-C16 (3)		25.75	13.50

An overprint, "Europa / CECA / MIFERMA," was applied in carmine to No. C16 in 1962. Two types exist: type 1, no box around "MIFERMA"; box surrounding "MIFERMA". Values: type 1, $35; type 2, $16.
The anti-malaria emblem, including slogan "Le Monde contre le Paludisme," was overprinted on Nos. C14-C15 in 1962. Two types of overprint: type 1, double lines of latitude and longitude on globe; type single lines of latitude and longitude on globe. Values: type 1, $27.50; type 2, $0.

Air Afrique Issue
Common Design Type

	1962, Feb. 17			
C17	CD107	100fr sl grn, choc & bis	2.40	1.25

UN Headquarters, New York; View of Nouakchott — AP2

	1962, Oct. 27	Engr.		Perf. 13
C18	AP2	100fr bluish grn, dk bl & org brn	1.50	1.00

Mauritania's admission to the UN.

Plane, Nouakchott Airport AP3

	1963, May 3	Unwmk.		Perf. 13
C19	AP3	500fr dp bl, gldn brn & slate grn	11.50	4.00

Miferma Open-pit Mine at Zouerate AP4

Design: 200fr, Ore transport at Port Etienne.

	1963, June	Photo.		Perf. 13x12
C20	AP4	100fr multi	1.90	.55
C21	AP4	200fr multi	4.75	1.00

African Postal Union Issue
Common Design Type

	1963, Sept. 8	Unwmk.		Perf. 12½
C22	CD114	85fr blk brn, ocher & red	1.50	.60

Globe and Telstar AP5

Design: 150fr, Relay satellite and stars.

	1963, Oct. 7	Engr.		Perf. 13
C23	AP5	50fr yel grn, pur & red brn	.75	.40
C24	AP5	150fr red brn & sl grn	2.25	1.10

Communication through space.

Tiros Satellite and Emblem of WMO — AP6

1963, Nov. 4

| C25 | AP6 | 200fr ultra, brn & grn | 3.75 | 1.50 |

Space research for meteorology and navigation.

1963 Air Afrique Issue
Common Design Type

	1963, Nov. 19	Photo.		Perf. 13x12
C26	CD115	25fr multi	.70	.25

UN Emblem, Doves and Sun — AP7

	1963, Dec. 10	Engr.		Perf. 13
C27	AP7	100fr vio, brn, & dk bl	1.60	.90

Universal Declaration of Human Rights, 15th anniv.

MAURITANIA

Europafrica Issue

Symbols of Agriculture and Industry — AP8

1964, Jan. 6   **Photo.**
C28 AP8 50fr multi   1.40 .90

Signing of economic agreement between the European Economic Community and the African and Malgache Union at Yaoundé, Cameroun, July 20, 1963.

Lichtenstein's Sand Grouse — AP9

Birds: 200fr, Long-tailed cormorant. 500fr, Chanting goshawk.

1964, Feb. 3   **Engr.**   **Perf. 13**
C29 AP9 100fr ocher, ol & dk brn   3.25 1.10
C30 AP9 200fr blk, dk bl & brn   5.00 1.90
C31 AP9 500fr rose red, grn & sl   15.00 5.75
Nos. C29-C31 (3)   23.25 8.75

Isis, Temple at Philae and Trajan's Kiosk AP10

1964, Mar. 8   **Unwmk.**   **Perf. 13**
C32 AP10 10fr red brn, Prus bl & blk   .50 .25
C33 AP10 25fr red brn, ind & Prus bl   .80 .40
C34 AP10 60fr blk brn, Prus bl & red brn   1.60 .75
Nos. C32-C34 (3)   2.90 1.40

UNESCO world campaign to save historic monuments in Nubia.

Syncom Satellite, Globe AP11

1964, May 4   **Engr.**
C35 AP11 100fr red, red brn & ultra   1.50 .75

Issued to publicize space communications.

Horse Race on Bowl AP12

Sport Designs from Ancient Pottery: 50fr, Runner, vert. 85fr, Wrestlers, vert. 100fr, Charioteer.

1964, Sept. 27   **Unwmk.**   **Perf. 13**
C36 AP12 15fr ol bis & choc   .45 .30
C37 AP12 50fr bl & org brn   1.10 .55
C38 AP12 85fr crim & brn   1.90 1.10
C39 AP12 100fr emer & dk red brn   2.40 1.40
a. Min. sheet of 4, #C36-C39   7.50 7.50
Nos. C36-C39 (4)   5.85 3.35

18th Olympic Games, Tokyo, Oct. 10-25.

Pres. John F. Kennedy (1917-1963) — AP13

1964, Dec. 7   **Photo.**   **Perf. 12½**
C40 AP13 100fr red brn, bl grn & dk brn   1.60 1.00
a. Souv. sheet of 4   7.00 7.00

ITU Emblem, Induction Telegraph and Relay Satellite AP14

1965, May 17   **Engr.**   **Perf. 13**
C41 AP14 250fr multi   4.75 3.00

ITU, centenary.

Fight Against Cancer — AP15

1965, July 19   **Unwmk.**   **Perf. 13**
C42 AP15 100fr bis, Prus bl & red   1.45 .70

Issued to publicize the fight against cancer.

Winston Churchill — AP16

1965, Dec. 6   **Photo.**   **Perf. 13**
C43 AP16 200fr multi   2.50 1.40

Sir Winston Spencer Churchill (1874-1965), statesman and WWII leader.

Diamant Rocket Ascending — AP17

French achievements in space: 60fr, Satellite A-1 and earth, horiz. 90fr, Scout rocket and satellite FR-1, horiz.

1966, Feb. 7   **Engr.**   **Perf. 13**
C44 AP17 30fr dp bl, red & grn   .50 .30
C45 AP17 60fr mar, Prus grn & bl   1.10 .55
C46 AP17 90fr dp bl, rose cl & vio   1.60 .80
Nos. C44-C46 (3)   3.20 1.65

Dr. Albert Schweitzer and Clinic AP18

1966, Feb. 21   **Photo.**   **Perf. 12½**
C47 AP18 50fr multi   1.50 .65

Schweitzer (1875-1965), medical missionary to Gabon, theologian and musician.

Thomas P. Stafford, Walter M. Schirra and Gemini 6 — AP19

Designs: 100fr, Frank A. Borman, James A. Lovell, Jr., and Gemini 7. 200fr, Pavel Belyayev, Alexei Leonov, Voskhod 2.

1966, Mar. 7   **Photo.**   **Perf. 12½**
C48 AP19 50fr multi   .70 .30
C49 AP19 100fr multi   1.50 .55
C50 AP19 200fr multi   2.50 1.25
Nos. C48-C50 (3)   4.70 2.10

Issued to honor achievements in space.

Map of Africa and Dove — AP20

1966, May 9   **Photo.**   **Perf. 13**
C51 AP20 100fr red brn, sl & yel grn   1.10 .50

Organization for African Unity.

D-1 Satellite over Earth — AP21

1966, June 6   **Engr.**
C52 AP21 100fr bl, dk pur & ocher   1.45 .80

Launching of the D-1 satellite at Hammaguir, Algeria, Feb. 17, 1966.

Bréguet 14 — AP22

Planes: 100fr, Goliath Farman, and camel caravan. 150fr, Couzinet "Arc-en-Ciel." 200fr, Latécoère 28 hydroplane.

1966, July 4   **Engr.**   **Perf. 13**
C53 AP22 50fr sl bl, dl grn & ol bis   1.00 .30
C54 AP22 100fr brt bl, dk grn & dk red brn   2.10 .50
C55 AP22 150fr dl brn, Prus bl & saph   3.00 .80
C56 AP22 200fr dk red brn, bl & ind   4.25 1.25
Nos. C53-C56 (4)   10.35 2.85

Air Afrique Issue
Common Design Type

1966, Aug. 31   **Photo.**   **Perf. 13**
C57 CD123 30fr red, blk & gray   .60 .30

"The Raft of the Medusa," by Théodore Géricault AP23

1966, Sept. 5   **Photo.**   **Perf. 12½**
C58 AP23 500fr multi   11.50 7.00

Sinking of the frigate "Medusa" off Mauritania, July 2, 1816.

Symbols of Agriculture and Industry AP24

1966, Nov. 7   **Photo.**   **Perf. 13x12**
C59 AP24 50fr multi   1.10 .40

Third anniversary, economic agreement between the European Economic Community and the African and Malgache Union.

Crowned Crane — AP25

1967, Apr. 3   **Perf. 12½x13**
C60 AP25 100fr shown   2.60 1.00
C61 AP25 200fr Common egret   5.00 1.50
C62 AP25 500fr Ostrich   13.00 4.75
Nos. C60-C62 (3)   20.60 7.25

For surcharge see No. C129.

Eye, Globe and Rockets — AP26

1967, May 2   **Engr.**   **Perf. 13**
C63 AP26 250fr brn, Prus bl & blk   3.75 1.25

EXPO '67 Intl. Exhibition, Montreal, Apr. 28-Oct. 27.

Emblem of Atomic Energy Commission — AP27

1967, Aug. 7   **Engr.**   **Perf. 13**
C64 AP27 200fr dk red, brt grn & ultra   2.60 1.25

International Atomic Energy Commission.

African Postal Union Issue
Common Design Type

1967, Sept. 9   **Engr.**   **Perf. 13**
C65 CD124 100fr brn org, vio brn & brt grn   1.25 .60

MAURITANIA

Francesca da Rimini, by Ingres — AP28

Paintings by and of Ingres: 100fr, Young man's torso. 150fr, "The Iliad" (seated woman). 200fr, Ingres in his Studio, by Alaux. 250fr, "The Odyssey" (seated woman).

1967-68		Photo.		Perf. 12½
C66	AP28	90fr multi	1.60	.60
C67	AP28	100fr multi ('68)	1.60	.70
C68	AP28	150fr multi ('68)	2.25	1.05
C69	AP28	200fr multi ('68)	3.00	1.10
C70	AP28	250fr multi ('68)	4.00	1.75
		Nos. C66-C70 (5)	12.45	5.20

Jean Dominique Ingres (1780-1867), French painter.
Issued: 90fr, 200fr, 10/2/67; others, 9/2/68. See No. C79.

Konrad Adenauer — AP29

1968, Feb. 5		Photo.		Perf. 12½
C71	AP29	100fr org brn, lt bl & blk	1.50	.70
a.		Souv. sheet of 4	7.00	6.00

Adenauer (1876-1967), chancellor of West Germany (1949-63).

Gymnast — AP30

1968, Mar. 4		Engr.		Perf. 13
C72	AP30	20fr plum, blk & bl	.40	.25
C73	AP30	30fr dl pur, brt grn & brn	.50	.25
C74	AP30	50fr Prus bl, bis & bl grn	.70	.30
C75	AP30	100fr brn, grn & ver	1.50	.45
		Nos. C72-C75 (4)	3.10	1.25

Sports: 20fr, Slalom, horiz. 50fr, Ski jump. 100fr, Hurdling, horiz.

1968 Olympic Games.

WHO Emblem, Man and Insects AP31

1968, May 2		Engr.		Perf. 13
C76	AP31	150fr red lil, dp bl & org red	1.90	.80

WHO, 20th anniversary.

Martin Luther King — AP32

Design: No. C78, Mahatma Gandhi.

1968, Nov. 4		Photo.		Perf. 12½
C77	AP32	50fr sl bl, cit & blk	1.00	.30
C78	AP32	50fr sl bl, lt bl & blk	1.00	.30
a.		Souv. sheet of 4, 2 each #C77-C78	4.25	4.25

Issued to honor two apostles of peace.

PHILEXAFRIQUE Issue
Painting Type of 1967

Design: 100fr, The Surprise Letter, by Charles Antoine Coypel.

1968, Dec. 9		Photo.		Perf. 12½
C79	AP28	100fr multi	3.00	1.50

PHILEXAFRIQUE, Phil. Exhib., Abidjan, Feb. 14-23. Printed with alternating brown red label.

2nd PHILEXAFRIQUE Issue
Common Design Type

50fr, Mauritania #89 & family on jungle trail.

1969, Feb. 14		Engr.		Perf. 13
C80	CD128	50fr sl grn, vio brn & red brn	1.90	.75

Napoleon Installed in Council of State, by Louis Charles Couder — AP33

Paintings: 50fr, Napoleon at Council of the 500, by F. Bouchot. 250fr, Farewell at Fontainebleau, by Horace Vernet.

1969, Feb. 24		Photo.		Perf. 12½
C81	AP33	50fr pur & multi	1.75	.90
C82	AP33	90fr multi	2.25	1.40
C83	AP33	250fr multi	6.25	3.25
		Nos. C81-C83 (3)	10.25	5.55

Napoleon Bonaparte (1769-1821).

Camel, Gazelles, and Tourist Year Emblem AP34

1969, June 9		Engr.		Perf. 13
C84	AP34	50fr org, dk brn & lt bl	1.00	.45

Year of African Tourism.

Dancers and Temple Ruins, Baalbek AP35

1969, June 16				
C85	AP35	100fr Prus bl, ol brn & rose car	1.50	.55

International Baalbek Festival, Lebanon.

Apollo 8 and Moon Surface AP36

Embossed on Gold Foil

1969			Die-cut Perf. 10	
C86	AP36	1000fr gold	20.00	20.00

Man's first flight around the moon, Dec. 21-28, 1968 (US astronauts Col. Frank Borman, Capt. James Lovell and Maj. William Anders).

Mamo Wolde, Ethiopia, Marathon — AP37

Designs: 70fr, Bob Beamon, US, broad jump. 150fr, Vera Caslavska, Czechoslovakia, gymnastics.

1969, July 7		Engr.		Perf. 13
C87	AP37	30fr multi	.40	.25
C88	AP37	70fr multi	.65	.40
C89	AP37	150fr multi	1.75	.80
		Nos. C87-C89 (3)	2.80	1.45

Issued to honor gold medal winners in the 19th Olympic Games, Mexico City.

Map of London-Istanbul Route — AP38

London to Sydney automobile rally: 20fr, Map showing Ankara to Teheran route, and compass rose. 50fr, Map showing Kandahar to Bombay route, arms of Afghanistan and elephant. 70fr, Map of Australia with Perth to Sydney route, and kangaroo.

1969, Aug. 14		Engr.		Perf. 13
C90	AP38	10fr multicolored	.25	.25
C91	AP38	20fr multicolored	.45	.25
C92	AP38	50fr multicolored	.75	.30
C93	AP38	70fr multicolored	1.10	.40
a.		Min. sheet of 4, #C90-C93	2.75	2.75
		Nos. C90-C93 (4)	2.55	1.20

Palette with World Map, Geisha and EXPO '70 Emblem — AP39

EXPO '70 Emblem and: 75fr, Fan & fireworks. 150fr, Stylized bird, map of Japan & boat.

1970, June 15		Photo.		Perf. 12½
C94	AP39	50fr multi	.70	.25
C95	AP39	75fr multi	1.00	.40
C96	AP39	150fr multi	1.75	.80
		Nos. C94-C96 (3)	3.45	1.45

Issued to publicize EXPO '70 International Exhibition, Osaka, Japan, Mar. 15-Sept. 13.

UN Emblem, Balloon, Rocket, Farm Woman, Tractor, Old and New Record Players AP40

1970, June 22		Engr.		Perf. 13
C97	AP40	100fr ultra, dk brn & grn	1.10	.55

25th anniversary of the United Nations.

Elliott See (1927-1966), American Astronaut — AP41

No. C99, Vladimir Komarov (1927-67). No. C100, Yuri Gagarin (1934-68). No. C101, Virgil Grissom (1926-67). No. C102, Edward White (1930-67). No. C103, Roger Chaffee (1935-67).

1970		Engr.		Perf. 13

Portrait in Brown

C98	AP41	150fr gray & brt bl	1.60	.75
C99	AP41	150fr gray & org	1.60	.75
C100	AP41	150fr gray & org	1.60	.75
a.		Souv. sheet of 3, #C98-C100	5.50	5.50
C101	AP41	150fr ultra & grnsh bl	1.60	.75
C102	AP41	150fr ultra & org	1.60	.75
C103	AP41	150fr ultra & grnsh bl	1.60	.75
a.		Souv. sheet of 3, #C101-C103	5.50	5.50
		Nos. C98-C103 (6)	9.60	4.50

American and Russian astronauts who died in space explorations.

Apollo 13 Capsule with Parachutes — AP42

Gold Embossed

1970, Aug. 17			Perf. 12½	
C104	AP42	500fr gold, crim & bl	6.50	6.50

Safe return of Apollo 13 crew.

Parliament, Nouakchott, and Coat of Arms — AP43

1970, Nov. 28		Photo.		Perf. 12½
C105	AP43	100fr multi	1.25	.50

10th anniversary of Independence.

Hercules Wrestling Antaeus AP44

1971, Mar. 8		Engr.		Perf. 13
C106	AP44	100fr red lil, brn & ultra	1.90	.85

Pre-Olympic Year. Design from a vase decoration by Euphronius.

Gamal Abdel Nasser (1918-1970), President of U.A.R. AP46

1971, May 10		Photo.		Perf. 12½
C109	AP46	100fr gold & multi	1.00	.45

Boy Scout, Emblem and Map of Mauritania — AP47

1971, Aug. 16		Photo.		Perf. 12½
C110	AP47	35fr yel & multi	.60	.25
C111	AP47	40fr pink & multi	.65	.25
C112	AP47	100fr multi	1.50	.45
		Nos. C110-C112 (3)	2.75	.95

13th Boy Scout World Jamboree, Asagiri Plain, Japan, Aug. 2-10.

MAURITANIA

African Postal Union Issue
Common Design Type

Design: 100fr, Women musicians and UAMPT building, Brazzaville, Congo.

1971, Nov. 13   Photo.   Perf. 13x13½
C113   CD135   100fr bl & multi   1.10   .65

Letter and Postal Emblem — AP48

1971, Dec. 2   Perf. 13
C114   AP48   35fr bis & multi   .65   .30

10th anniversary of African Postal Union.

Mosul Monarch, from Book of Songs, c. 1218 — AP49

Designs from Mohammedan Miniatures: 40fr, Prince holding audience, Egypt, 1334. 100fr, Pilgrim caravan, from "Maquamat," Baghdad, 1237.

1972, Jan. 10   Photo.   Perf. 13
C115   AP49   35fr gold & multi   .55   .25
C116   AP49   40fr gray & multi   .70   .30
C117   AP49   100fr buff & multi   1.90   .60
     Nos. C115-C117 (3)   3.15   1.15

For surcharges see Nos. C140, C143-C144.

Grand Canal, by Canaletto AP50

Designs: 45fr, Venice Harbor, by Carlevaris, vert. 250fr, Santa Maria della Salute, by Canaletto.

1972, Feb. 14
C118   AP50   45fr gold & multi   .75   .30
C119   AP50   100fr gold & multi   1.90   .70
C120   AP50   250fr gold & multi   3.75   1.10
     Nos. C118-C120 (3)   6.40   2.10

UNESCO campaign to save Venice.

Hurdles and Olympic Rings AP51

1972, Apr. 27   Engr.   Perf. 13
C121   AP51   75fr org, vio brn & blk   .75   .25
C122   AP51   100fr Prus bl, vio brn & brn   1.10   .40
C123   AP51   200fr lake, vio brn & blk   2.40   .60
    a.   Min. sheet of 3, #C121-C123   6.00   6.00
     Nos. C121-C123 (3)   4.25   1.25

20th Olympic Games, Munich, Aug. 26-Sept. 11.
For overprints see Nos. C126-C128.

Luna 17 on Moon AP52

75fr, Luna 16 take-off from moon, vert.

1972, Oct. 9
C124   AP52   75fr vio bl, bis & grn   .80   .25
C125   AP52   100fr dl pur, sl & ol bis   1.10   .40

Russian moon missions, Luna 16, Sept. 12-14, 1970; and Luna 17, Nov. 10-17, 1970.

Nos. C121-C123 Overprinted in Violet Blue or Red:
    a.   110m HAIES / MILBURN MEDAILLE D'OR
    b.   400m HAIES / AKII-BUA MEDAILLE D'OR
    c.   3.000m STEEPLE / KEINO MEDAILLE D'OR

1972, Oct. 16
C126   AP51(a)   75fr multi (VB)   .90   .40
C127   AP51(b)   100fr multi (R)   1.10   .55
C128   AP51(c)   200fr multi (VB)   2.50   1.05
     Nos. C126-C128 (3)   4.50   2.00

Gold medal winners in 20th Olympic Games: Rod Milburn, US, John Akii-Bua, Uganda, and Kipchoge Keino, Kenya.

No. C62 Surcharged with New Value, Two Bars and: "Apollo XVII / December 1972"

1973, Jan. 29   Photo.   Perf. 12½x13
C129   AP25   250fr on 500fr multi   3.00   1.25

Apollo 17 moon mission, Dec. 7-19, 1972.

Seal Type of Regular Issue

1973, Feb. 28   Litho.   Perf. 13
C130   A63   135fr Seal's head   4.50   1.90

For surcharge see No. C145.

Lion Eating Caiman, by Delacroix AP53

Painting: 250fr, Lion Eating Boar, by Delacroix.

1973, Mar. 26   Photo.   Perf. 13x12½
C131   AP53   100fr blk & multi   2.00   .90
C132   AP53   250fr blk & multi   4.50   2.25

For surcharges see Nos. C148-C149.

Villagers Observing Solar Eclipse AP54

40fr, Rocket take-off & Concord, vert. 140fr, Scientists with telescopes observing eclipse.

1973, June 20   Engr.   Perf. 13
C133   AP54   35fr grn & pur   .50   .25
C134   AP54   40fr ultra, pur & scar   .55   .30
C135   AP54   140fr scar & pur   2.00   .80
    a.   Souvenir sheet of 3   3.50   3.50
     Nos. C133-C135 (3)   3.05   1.35

Solar eclipse, June 30, 1973. No. C135a contains 3 stamps similar to Nos. C133-C135 in changed colors (35fr, 140fr in magenta and violet blue; 40fr in magenta, violet blue and orange).
For surcharges see Nos. C141-C142, C146.

Soccer — AP55

1973, Dec. 24   Photo.   Perf. 13
C136   AP55   7um multi   .50   .25
C137   AP55   8um multi   .50   .25
C138   AP55   20um multi   1.60   .60
     Nos. C136-C138 (3)   2.60   1.10

Souvenir Sheet
C139   AP55   30um multi   1.90   1.90

World Soccer Cup, Munich, 1974.

A set of four stamps depicting Jules Verne and Skylab were produced in silver and gold. Scott editors would like to examine any examples.

Nos. C115-C117, C130 and C133-C135 Surcharged with New Value and Two Bars in Red, Black or Ultramarine

1973-74   Photo., Litho. or Engr.
C140   AP49   7um on 35fr (R)   .50   .25
C141   AP54   7um on 35fr (B)   .60   .25
C142   AP54   8um on 40fr (B)   .60   .25
C143   AP49   8um on 40fr (U) ('74)   .50   .25
C144   AP49   20um on 100fr (R) ('74)   1.60   .70
C145   A63   27um on 135fr (R)   2.25   .80
C146   AP54   28um on 140fr (B)   1.90   .80
     Nos. C140-C146 (7)   7.95   3.30

Winston Churchill (1874-1965) — AP56

1974, June 3   Engr.   Perf. 13
C147   AP56   40um blk, brn & hn brn   1.90   1.00

Nos. C131-C132 Surcharged with New Value and Two Bars in Red

1974, July 15   Photo.   Perf. 13x12½
C148   AP53   20um on 100fr multi   1.50   .70
C149   AP53   50um on 250fr multi   4.00   1.80

Lenin (1870-1924) — AP57

1974, Sept. 16   Engr.   Perf. 13
C150   AP57   40um slate grn & red   3.50   1.25

Women, IWY Emblem — AP58

40fr, Woman's head and IWY emblems.

1975, June 16   Engr.   Perf. 13
C151   AP58   12um multi   .60   .25
C152   AP58   40um dk brn, lt brn & bl   2.40   .90

International Women's Year.

Albert Schweitzer and Patients Arriving — AP59

1975, Aug. 4   Engr.   Perf. 13
C153   AP59   60um multi   3.25   1.60

Schweitzer (1875-1965), medical missionary.

Javelin and Olympic Emblem AP60

52um, Running and Olympic emblem.

1975, Nov. 17   Engr.   Perf. 13
C154   AP60   50um sl grn, red & ol   2.40   1.40
C155   AP60   52um car, ocher & ultra   2.40   1.40

Pre-Olympic Year 1975.

Apollo Soyuz Type, 1975

Docked Space Ships and: 20um, Apollo rocket launch. 50um, Handshake in linked-up cabin. 60um, Apollo splash-down. 100um, Astronauts and Cosmonauts.

1975, Dec. 29   Litho.   Perf. 14
C156   A74   20um multi   .90   .40
C157   A74   50um multi   2.10   .75
C158   A74   60um multi   2.60   1.00
     Nos. C156-C158 (3)   6.00   2.15

Souvenir Sheet
C159   A74   100um multi   4.00   1.75

American Bicentennial Type, 1976

Uniforms: 20um, French Hussar officer. 50um, 3rd Continental Artillery officer. 60um, French infantry regiment grenadier. 100um, American infantryman.

1976, Jan. 26
C160   A75   20um multi   .85   .35
C161   A75   50um multi   2.10   .90
C162   A75   60um multi   3.00   1.00
     Nos. C160-C162 (3)   5.95   2.25

Souvenir Sheet
C163   A75   100um multi   4.75   1.60

Running and Olympic Rings — AP61

12um, High jump. 52um, Fencing.

1976, June 14   Engr.   Perf. 13
C164   AP61   10um pur, grn & brn   .80   .25
C165   AP61   12um pur, grn & brn   1.00   .40
C166   AP61   52um pur, grn & brn   3.50   1.50
     Nos. C164-C166 (3)   5.30   2.15

21st Olympic Games, Montreal, Canada, July 17-Aug. 1.

Zeppelin Type, 1976

Designs: 50um, "Graf Zeppelin" (LZ-127) over US Capitol. 60um, "Hindenburg" (LZ-130) over Swiss Alps. 100um, "Führersland" (LZ-129) over 1936 Olympic stadium.

1976, June 28   Litho.   Perf. 11
C167   A77   50um multi   2.40   1.10
C168   A77   60um multi   3.25   1.40

Souvenir Sheet
C169   A77   100um multi   5.50   1.00

Marabou Storks AP62

African Birds: 50um, Sacred ibis, vert. 200um, Long-crested eagles, vert.

1976, Sept. 20   Litho.   Perf. 13½
C170   AP62   50um multi   3.50   1.10
C171   AP62   100um multi   6.50   1.90
C172   AP62   200um multi   13.00   4.00
     Nos. C170-C172 (3)   23.00   7.00

Viking Type, 1977

Designs: 20um, Viking orbiter in flight to Mars. 50um, Viking "B" in descent to Mars. 60um, Various phases of descent. 100um, Viking lander using probe.

MAURITANIA

1977, Feb. 28 — Perf. 14
C173 A81 20um multi .95 .25
C174 A81 50um multi 2.25 .60
C175 A81 50um multi 2.50 .80
Nos. C173-C175 (3) 5.70 1.65
Souvenir Sheet
C176 A81 100um multi 4.50 1.00
For surcharge & overprints see #C192-C195.

Nobel Prize Type, 1977
14um, George Bernard Shaw, literature. 55um, Thomas Mann, literature. 60um, Intl. Red Cross Society, peace. 100um, George C. Marshall, peace.

1977, Apr. 29 Litho. Perf. 14
C177 A83 14um multi .80 .25
C178 A83 55um multi 2.75 .60
C179 A83 60um multi 3.50 .75
Nos. C177-C179 (3) 8.50 1.40
Souvenir Sheet
C180 A83 100um multi 7.00 2.00

Holy Kaaba AP63

1977, July 25 Litho. Perf. 12½
C181 AP63 12um multi 1.50 .50
Pilgrimage to Mecca.

Soccer Type of 1977
50um, Soccer ball. 60um, Eusebio Ferreira. 100um, Players holding pennants.

1977, Dec. 19 Litho. Perf. 13½
C182 A89 50um multi 2.40 .55
C183 A89 60um multi 2.60 .75
Souvenir Sheet
C184 A89 100um multi 4.50 1.40
For overprints see Nos. C187-C189.

Franco-African Co-operation — AP63a

1970, June 7 Embossed Perf. 10½
C184A AP63a 250um silver 10.00 10.00
C184B AP63a 500um gold 25.00 25.00

Philexafrique II — Essen Issue
Common Design Types
No. C185, Hyena and Mauritania #C60. No. C186, Wading bird and Hamburg #1.

1978, Nov. 1 Litho. Perf. 12½
C185 CD138 20um multi 2.25 1.10
C186 CD139 20um multi 2.25 1.10
a. Pair, #C185-C186 + label 5.50 5.00

Nos. C182-C184 Overprinted in Arabic and French in Silver: "ARGENTINE- / PAYS BAS 3-1"

1978, Dec. 11 Litho. Perf. 13½
C187 A89 50um multi 1.90 1.00
C188 A89 60um multi 2.75 1.40
Souvenir Sheet
C189 A89 100um multi 5.00 5.00
Argentina's victory in World Cup Soccer Championship 1978.

Flyer A and Prototype Plane AP64

Design: 40um, Flyer A and supersonic jet.

1979, Jan. 29 Engr. Perf. 13
C190 AP64 15um multi .95 .35
C191 AP64 40um multi 2.00 1.00
75th anniversary of first powered flight.

Nos. C173-C176 Overprinted and Surcharged in Silver: "ALUNISSAGE / APOLLO XI / JUILLET 1969" and Emblem

1979, Oct. 24 Litho. Perf. 14
C192 A81 14um on 20um multi .75 .30
C193 A81 50um multi 2.40 1.00
C194 A81 60um multi 2.60 1.30
Nos. C192-C194 (3) 5.75 2.60
Souvenir Sheet
C195 A81 100um multi 4.00 4.00
Apollo 11 moon landing, 10th anniversary.

Soccer Players AP65

Designs: Various soccer scenes.

1980, Sept. 29 Litho. Perf. 12½
C196 AP65 10um multi .45 .25
C197 AP65 12um multi .55 .25
C198 AP65 14um multi .55 .25
C199 AP65 20um multi 1.00 .30
C200 AP65 67um multi 2.75 .70
Nos. C196-C200 (5) 5.30 1.75
Souvenir Sheet
C201 AP65 100um multi 4.50 1.25
World Soccer Cup 1982.
For overprints see Nos. C212-C217.

Flight of Columbia Space Shuttle AP66

Designs: Views of Columbia space shuttle.

1981, Apr. 27 Litho. Perf. 12½
C202 AP66 12um multi .50 .25
C203 AP66 20um multi .85 .25
C204 AP66 50um multi 1.00 .60
C205 AP66 70um multi 2.75 .80
Nos. C202-C205 (4) 6.00 1.90
Souvenir Sheet
C206 AP66 100um multi 4.75 1.40

Dinard Landscape, by Pablo Picasso AP67

Picasso Birth Centenary. 12um, Harlequin, vert. 20um, Vase of Flowers, vert. 50um, Three Women at the Well. 100um, Picnic.

1981, June 29 Litho. Perf. 12½
C207 AP67 12um multi .70 .25
C208 AP67 20um multi 1.00 .30
C209 AP67 50um multi 2.40 .70
C210 AP67 70um multi 3.50 .95
C211 AP67 100um multi 4.75 1.40
Nos. C207-C211 (5) 12.35 3.60

Nos. C196-C201 Overprinted in Red with Finalists and Score on 1 or 2 Lines

1982, Sept. 18 Litho. Perf. 12½
C212 AP65 10um multi .45 .25
C213 AP65 12um multi .50 .25
C214 AP65 14um multi .50 .30
C215 AP65 20um multi .95 .30
C216 AP65 67um multi 2.60 .75
Nos. C212-C216 (5) 5.00 1.85
Souvenir Sheet
C217 AP65 100um multi 4.25 1.25
Italy's victory in 1982 World Cup.

25th Anniv. of Intl. Maritime Org. — AP68

1983, June 18 Litho. Perf. 12½x13
C218 AP68 18um multi .80 .40

Paul Harris, Rotary Founder — AP69

1984, Jan. 20 Litho. Perf. 13½
C219 AP69 100um multi 4.25 1.10

1984 Summer Olympics AP70

14um, Running, horiz. 18um, Shot put. 19um, Hurdles. 44um, Javelin. 77um, High jump. 100um, Steeplechase.

1984, July 15 Litho. Perf. 14
C223 AP70 14um multi .60 .30
C224 AP70 18um multi .75 .40
C225 AP70 19um multi .85 .40
C226 AP70 44um multi 1.60 1.00
C227 AP70 77um multi 3.50 1.90
Nos. C223-C227 (5) 7.30 4.00
Souvenir Sheet
C228 AP70 100um multi 5.25 2.10

Olympics Winners AP71

14um, Van den Berg, sailboard, Netherlands. 18um, Coutts, Finn sailing, N.Z. 19um, 470 class, Spain. 44um, Soling, US. 100um, Sailing, US.

1984, Dec. 20 Litho. Perf. 13
C229 AP71 14um multi .85 .30
C230 AP71 18um multi 1.00 .45
C231 AP71 19um multi 1.10 .50
C232 AP71 44um multi 2.50 1.10
Nos. C229-C232 (4) 5.45 2.35
Souvenir Sheet
C233 AP71 100um multi 5.00 3.00

PHILEXAFRICA '85, Lome, Togo — AP72

No. C234, Youths, map, IYY emblem. No. C235, Oil refinery, Nouadhibou.

1985, May 23 Litho. Perf. 13
C234 AP72 40um multi .60 .45
C235 AP72 40um multi 1.75 1.20
a. Pair, #C234-C235 + label 3.25 3.25
Exists with two labels showing map of Africa or Lome '85 emblem.

1985, Nov. 12 Perf. 13x12½
C236 AP72 50um Iron mine, train 2.25 1.00
C237 AP72 50um Boy reading, herding sheep 2.25 1.00
a. Pair, #C236-C237 + label 5.50 5.50

Audubon Birth Bicentenary AP73

14um, Passeriformes thraupidae. 18um, Larus philadelphia. 19um, Cyanocitta cristata. 44um, Rhyncops nigra. 100um, Anhinga anhinga.

1985, Aug. 14
C238 AP73 14um multi .75 .30
C239 AP73 18um multi .95 .30
C240 AP73 19um multi 1.20 .40
C241 AP73 44um multi 2.60 .80
Nos. C238-C241 (4) 5.50 1.80
Souvenir Sheet
C242 AP73 100um multi 7.00 4.00

1st South Atlantic Crossing, 55th Anniv. AP74

18um, Comte de Vaux, 1930. 50um, Flight reenactment, 1985.

1986, May 19 Litho. Perf. 13
C243 AP74 18um multi .65 .35
C244 AP74 50um multi 1.75 1.00
a. Pair, #C243-C244 + label 3.25 3.25

1986 World Cup Soccer Championships, Mexico — AP75

Various soccer plays.

1986, June 19 Litho. Perf. 13
C245 AP75 8um No. 279 .30 .25
C246 AP75 18um No. 280 .75 .35
C247 AP75 22um No. 281 .95 .40
C248 AP75 25um No. 282 1.10 .45
C249 AP75 40um Soccer cup 1.75 .80
Nos. C245-C249 (5) 4.85 2.25
Souvenir Sheet
C250 AP75 100um multi 4.50 2.75

Air Africa, 25th Anniv. AP76

1986, Oct. 6 Litho. Perf. 13
C251 AP76 26um multi .90 .45

1988 Summer Olympics, Seoul AP77

1987, Aug. 13 Litho. Perf. 13
C252 AP77 30um Boxing 1.10 .50
C253 AP77 40um Judo 1.50 .65
C254 AP77 50um Fencing 1.90 .85
C255 AP77 75um Wrestling 3.00 1.25
Nos. C252-C255 (4) 7.50 3.25
Souvenir Sheet
C256 AP77 150um Judo, diff. 5.50 2.50

MAURITANIA

1988 Winter Olympics, Calgary — AP78

30um, Women's slalom. 40um, Speed skating. 50um, Ice hockey. 75um, Women's downhill skiing. 150um, Men's cross-country skiing.

1987, Sept.

C257	AP78	30um multi	1.25	.50
C258	AP78	40um multi	1.60	.65
C259	AP78	50um multi	1.90	.85
C260	AP78	75um multi	3.00	1.25
	Nos. C257-C260 (4)		7.75	3.25

Souvenir Sheet

C261	AP78	150um multi	5.50	2.50

For overprints see Nos. C267-C271.

1988 Summer Olympics, Seoul — AP79

1988, Sept. 17   Litho.   Perf. 13

C262	AP79	20um Hammer throw	.85	.35
C263	AP79	24um Discus	.90	.40
C264	AP79	30um Shot put	1.25	.50
C265	AP79	150um Javelin	5.50	2.25
	Nos. C262-C265 (4)		8.50	3.50

Souvenir Sheet

C266	AP79	170um Javelin, diff.	6.00	2.75

Nos. C257-C261 Overprinted "Medaille d'or" in Red or Bright Blue and:

a. "Vreni Schneider (Suisse)"
b. "1500 m / Andre Hoffman (R.D.A.)"
c. "U.R.S.S."
d. "Marina Kiehl (R.F.A.)"
e. "15 km / Mikhail Deviatiarov (U.R.S.S.)"

1988, Sept. 18

C267	AP78(a)	30um multi	1.15	.50
C268	AP78(b)	40um multi (BB)	1.60	.65
C269	AP78(c)	50um multi	1.75	.90
C270	AP78(d)	75um multi	3.25	1.40
	Nos. C267-C270 (4)		7.75	3.45

Souvenir Sheet

C271	AP78(e)	150um multi	6.00	3.00

World Cup Soccer Championships, Italy — AP80

Map of Italy and various soccer plays.

1990   Litho.   Perf. 13

C272	AP80	50um multicolored	1.75	.65
C273	AP80	60um multicolored	1.75	.85
C274	AP80	70um multicolored	2.10	.95
C275	AP80	90um multicolored	3.00	1.25
C276	AP80	150um multicolored	6.50	2.75
	Nos. C272-C276 (5)		15.10	6.45

AIR POST SEMI-POSTAL STAMPS

Maternity Hospital, Dakar — SPAP1

Dispensary, Mopti — SPAP2

Nurse Weighing Baby — SPAP3

Unwmk.

1942, June 22   Engr.   Perf. 13

CB1	SPAP1	1.50fr + 3.50fr green	.80	5.50
CB2	SPAP2	2fr + 6fr brown	.80	5.50
CB3	SPAP3	3fr + 9fr carmine	.80	5.50
	Nos. CB1-CB3 (3)		2.40	16.50

Native children's welfare fund.

Colonial Education Fund
Common Design Type

1942, June 22

CB4	CD86a	1.20fr + 1.80fr bl & red	.80	5.50

POSTAGE DUE STAMPS

D1

Perf. 14x13½

1906-07   Unwmk.   Typo.

J1	D1	5c grn, *grnsh*	3.50	3.50
J2	D1	10c red brn	5.00	5.00
J3	D1	15c dk bl	10.00	7.00
J4	D1	20c blk, *yellow*	12.00	10.00
J5	D1	30c red, *straw*	14.00	11.00
J6	D1	50c violet	20.00	19.00
J7	D1	60c blk, *buff*	16.00	14.00
J8	D1	1fr blk, *pinkish*	26.00	20.00
	Nos. J1-J8 (8)		106.50	89.50

Issue dates: 20c, 1906; others 1907. Regular postage stamps canceled "T" in a triangle were used for postage due.

D2

1914

J9	D2	5c green	.25	.35
J10	D2	10c rose	.30	.50
J11	D2	15c gray	.35	.70
J12	D2	20c brown	.35	.70
J13	D2	30c blue	.70	1.00
J14	D2	50c black	1.75	1.75
J15	D2	60c orange	1.40	1.40
J16	D2	1fr violet	1.40	1.40
	Nos. J9-J16 (8)		6.50	7.80

Type of 1914 Issue Surcharged

1927, Oct. 10

J17	D2	2fr on 1fr lil rose	3.50	3.50
a.		Period after "F" omitted	14.00	15.00
J18	D2	3fr on 1fr org brn	3.50	4.25

Catalogue values for unused stamps in this section, from this point to the end of the section, are for Never Hinged items.

Islamic Republic

Oualata Motif — D3

Perf. 14x13½

1961, July 1   Typo.   Unwmk.
Denominations in Black

J19	D3	1fr plum & org yel	.25	.25
J20	D3	2fr red & gray	.25	.25
J21	D3	5fr mar & pink	.25	.25
J22	D3	10fr dk grn & grn	.25	.25
J23	D3	15fr ol & brn org	.25	.25
J24	D3	20fr red brn & lt blue	.40	.25
J25	D3	25fr grn & vermilion	.60	.50
	Nos. J19-J25 (7)		2.25	2.00

Vulture (Ruppell's Griffon) — D4

Birds: No. J27, Eurasian crane. No. J28, Pink-backed pelican. No. J29, Garganey teal. No. J30, European golden oriole. No. J31, Variable sunbird. No. J32, Shoveler ducks. No. J33, Great snipe. No. J34, Vulturine guinea fowl. No. J35, Black stork. No. J36, Gray heron. No. J37, White stork. No. J38, Red-legged partridge. No. J39, Paradise whydah. No. J40, Sandpiper (little stint). No. J41, Sudan bustard.

1963, Sept. 7   Engr.   Perf. 11

J26	D4	50c blk, yel org & red	.25	.25
J27	D4	50c blk, yel org & red	.25	.25
a.		Pair, #J26-J27	.50	.50
J28	D4	1fr blk, red & yel	.25	.25
J29	D4	1fr blk, red & yel	.25	.25
a.		Pair, #J28-J29	.60	.60
J30	D4	2fr blk, bl grn & yel	.25	.25
J31	D4	2fr blk, bl grn & yel	.25	.25
a.		Pair, #J30-J31	.80	.80
J32	D4	5fr blk, grn & red brn	.35	.35
J33	D4	5fr blk, grn & red brn	.35	.35
a.		Pair, #J32-J33	1.25	1.25
J34	D4	10fr blk, red & tan	.70	.70
J35	D4	10fr blk, red & tan	.70	.70
a.		Pair, #J34-J35	2.50	2.50
J36	D4	15fr blk, emer & red	.75	.75
J37	D4	15fr blk, emer & red	.75	.75
a.		Pair, #J36-J37	2.75	2.75
J38	D4	20fr blk, yel grn & red	1.00	1.00
J39	D4	20fr blk, yel grn & red	1.00	1.00
a.		Pair, #J38-J39	3.25	3.25
J40	D4	25fr blk, yel grn & brn	1.50	1.50
J41	D4	25fr blk, yel grn & brn	1.50	1.50
a.		Pair, #J40-J41	4.50	4.50
	Nos. J26-J41 (16)		10.10	10.10
	Nos. J27a-J41a (8)		16.15	16.15

Ornament — D5

1976, May 10   Litho.   Perf. 12½x13

J42	D5	1um buff & multi	.25	.25
J43	D5	3um buff & multi	.25	.25
J44	D5	10um buff & multi	.45	.45
J45	D5	12um buff & multi	.55	.55
J46	D5	20um buff & multi	.95	.95
	Nos. J42-J46 (5)		2.45	2.45

OFFICIAL STAMPS

Catalogue values for unused stamps in this section are for Never Hinged items.

Islamic Republic

Cross of Trarza — O1

Perf. 14x13½

1961, July 1   Typo.   Unwmk.

O1	O1	1fr lilac & brt pur	.25	.25
O2	O1	3fr red & slate	.25	.25
O3	O1	5fr grn & brown	.25	.25
O4	O1	10fr dl bl & vio bl	.25	.25
O5	O1	15fr blue & org	.35	.25
O6	O1	20fr blk & emer	.45	.25
O7	O1	25fr red org & mar	.50	.30
O8	O1	30fr maroon & grn	.60	.40
O9	O1	50fr dk red & dk brn	1.25	.50
O10	O1	100fr orange & blue	1.90	.90
O11	O1	200fr grn & red org	3.75	1.75
	Nos. O1-O11 (11)		9.80	5.35

Ornament — O2

1976, May 3   Litho.   Perf. 12½x13

O12	O2	1um black & multi	.25	.25
O13	O2	2um black & multi	.25	.25
O14	O2	5um black & multi	.25	.25
O15	O2	10um black & multi	.50	.25
O16	O2	12um black & multi	.70	.30
O17	O2	40um black & multi	2.50	.90
O18	O2	50um black & multi	3.00	1.25
	Nos. O12-O18 (7)		7.45	3.45

MAURITIUS

mo-ˈri-sh ̱ē-ə̱s

LOCATION — Island in the Indian Ocean about 550 miles east of Madagascar
GOVT. — Republic
AREA — 720 sq. mi.
POP. — 1,270,000 (2020 est.)
CAPITAL — Port Louis

12 Pence = 1 Shilling
100 Cents = 1 Rupee (1878)

The British Crown Colony of Mauritius was granted self-government in 1967 and became an independent state on March 12, 1968.

Nos. 1-6, 14-17 unused are valued without gum.
Nos. 3a-8, 14-15 are printed on fragile paper with natural irregularities which might be mistaken for faults.
Very fine examples of Nos. 22-58 will have perforations touching the design on one or more sides. Examples with perfs clear on four sides are scarce and will sell for more. Inferior examples will sell for much reduced prices.

Catalogue values for unused stamps in this country are for Never Hinged items, beginning with Scott 223 in the regular postage section, Scott J1 in the postage due section.

Queen Victoria — A1

1847		Unwmk.	Engr.	Imperf.
1	A1	1p orange	1,250,000.	1,250,000.
2	A1	2p dark blue		1,700,000.

Nos. 1 and 2 were engraved and printed in Port Louis. There is but one type of each value. The initials "J. B." on the bust are those of the engraver, J. Barnard.
All unused examples of the 2p are in museums. There is one unused example of the 1p in private hands. There are two used examples of the 1p in private hands, both of which have small faults and are valued thus.

Queen Victoria — A2

Earliest Impressions

1848			Thick Yellowish Paper	
3	A2	1p orange	65,000.	18,000.
4	A2	2p dark blue	62,500.	24,500.
d.	"PENOE"		125,000.	42,500.

Early Impressions
Yellowish White Paper

3a	A2	1p orange	32,500.	7,250.
4a	A2	2p blue	35,000.	8,500.
e.	"PENOE"		65,000.	16,000.

Bluish Paper

5	A2	1p orange	32,500.	7,250.
6	A2	2p blue	35,000.	8,500.
c.	"PENOE"		65,000.	16,000.

Intermediate Impressions
Yellowish White Paper

3b	A2	1p red orange	21,500.	2,850.
4b	A2	2p blue	22,500.	3,600.
f.	"PENOE"		40,000.	7,500.

Bluish Paper

5a	A2	1p red orange	21,500.	2,900.
6a	A2	2p blue	22,500.	3,750.
d.	"PENOE"		40,000.	7,500.
f.	Double impression			

Worn Impressions
Yellowish White Paper

3c	A2	1p orange red	7,500.	900.
d.	1p brownish red		7,500.	900.
4c	A2	2p blue	9,250.	1,600.
g.	"PENOE"		12,500.	3,000.

Bluish Paper

5b	A2	1p orange red	7,000.	850.
c.	1p brownish red		7,000.	850.
d.	Double impression			

| 6b | A2 | 2p blue | 9,500. | 1,500. |
| e. | "PENOE" | | 12,500. | 3,000. |

Latest Impressions
Yellowish or Grayish Paper

3e	A2	1p orange red	6,000.	750.
f.	1p brownish red		6,000.	750.
4h	A2	2p blue	7,500.	1,100.
i.	"PENOE"		14,000.	2,100.

Bluish Paper

5e	A2	1p orange red	6,000.	750.
f.	1p brownish red		6,000.	750.
6g	A2	2p blue	7,500.	1,100.
h.	"PENOE"		14,000.	2,000.

These stamps were printed in sheets of twelve, four rows of three, and each position differs in details. The "PENOE" error is the most pronounced variety on the plates and is from position 7.
The stamps were in use until 1859. Earliest impressions, Nos. 3-4, show the full background of diagonal and vertical lines with the diagonal lines predominant. Early impressions, Nos. 3a-4a, 5-6, show the full background with the vertical lines predominating. As the plate became worn the vertical lines disappeared, giving the intermediate impressions, Nos. 3b-4b, 5a-6a.
Worn impressions, Nos. 3c-4c, 5b-6b, have little background remaining, and latest impressions, Nos. 3e-4h, 5e-6g, have also lost details of the frame and head. The paper of the early impressions is usually rather thick, that of the worn impressions rather thin. Expect natural fibrous inclusions in the paper of all impressions.

"Britannia" — A3

1849-58

| 7 | A3 | red brown, *blue* | 26.00 |
| 8 | A3 | blue ('58) | 10.00 |

Nos. 7-8 were never placed in use.

1858-59

9	A3	(4p) green, *bluish*	550.00	225.00
10	A3	(6p) red	60.00	125.00
11	A3	(9p) magenta ('59)	850.00	225.00

No. 11 was re-issued in Nov. 1862, as a 1p stamp (No. 11a). When used as such it is always canceled "B53." Price so used, $200.

"Britannia" — A4

1858 | | | **Black Surcharge** | |
| 12 | A4 | 4p green, *bluish* | 1,650. | 525.00 |

Queen Victoria — A5

1859, Mar. | | | **Early Impressions** | |
14	A5	2p blue, *grayish*	16,500.	3,000.
a.	2p deep blue, *grayish*	18,500.	3,500.
14B	A5	2p blue, *bluish*	16,500.	3,000.
c.	Intermediate impression	9,000.	1,300.
d.	Worn impression	4,500.	650.00

Type A5 was engraved by Lapirot, in Port Louis, and was printed locally. There were twelve varieties in the sheet.
Early impressions have clear and distinct background lines. In the intermediate impressions, the lines are somewhat blurred, and white patches appear. In the worn impressions, the background lines are discontinuous, with many white patches. Analogous wear is also obvious in the background of the inscriptions on all four sides. Values depend on the state of wear. One should expect natural fibrous inclusions in the paper on all printings.

A6

1859, Oct.
| 15 | A6 | 2p blue, *bluish* | 210,000. | 11,000. |

No. 15 was printed from the plate of the 1848 issue after it had been entirely re-engraved by Sherwin. It is commonly known as the "fillet head." The plate of the 1p, 1848, was also re-engraved but was never put in use.

A7

1859, Dec. | | **Litho.** | **Laid Paper** |
16	A7	1p vermilion	9,000.	1,350.
a.	1p deep red	15,000.	2,350.
b.	1p red	11,250.	1,675.
17	A7	2p pale blue	5,000.	850.
a.	2p slate blue	9,250.	1,250.
b.	2p blue	5,000.	950.

Lithographed locally by Dardenne.

"Britannia" — A8

1859 | | **Wove Paper** | **Engr.** | **Imperf.** |
| 18 | A8 | 6p blue | 800.00 | 57.50 |
| 19 | A8 | 1sh vermilion | 3,150. | 65.00 |

1861
| 20 | A8 | 6p gray violet | 37.50 | 110.00 |
| 21 | A8 | 1sh green | 675.00 | 160.00 |

1862 | | | | **Perf. 14 to 16** |
22	A8	6p slate	37.50	110.00
a.	Horiz. pair, imperf between	8,500.	
23	A8	1sh deep green	2,750.	350.00

Values for Nos. 22-23 are for examples with perfs. touching the design.

Following the change in currency in 1878, a number of issues denominated in sterling were overprinted "CANCELLED" in serifed type and sold as remainders.

A9

1860-63 | | **Typo.** | **Perf. 14** |
24	A9	1p brown lilac	400.00	42.50
25	A9	2p blue	425.00	60.00
26	A9	4p rose	425.00	42.50
27	A9	6p green ('62)	1,050.	175.00
28	A9	6p lilac ('63)	425.00	125.00
29	A9	9p dull lilac	190.00	42.50
30	A9	1sh buff ('62)	400.00	100.00
31	A9	1sh green ('63)	900.00	200.00

For surcharges see Nos. 43-45.

1863-72 | | | **Wmk. 1** |
32	A9	1p lilac brown	85.00	17.00
a.	1p bister brown	150.00	17.00
b.	1p brown	110.00	13.00
33	A9	2p blue	100.00	13.00
a.	Imperf., pair	1,850.	2,350.
34	A9	3p vermilion	90.00	21.00
35	A9	4p rose	100.00	4.00
36	A9	6p lilac ('64)	425.00	45.00
37	A9	6p blue grn ('65)	235.00	7.00
a.	6p yellow green ('65)	300.00	17.00

38	A9	9p green ('72)	190.00	375.00
39	A9	1sh org yel ('64)	365.00	29.00
a.	1sh yellow	285.00	13.50
40	A9	1sh blue ('70)	140.00	29.00
41	A9	5sh red violet	260.00	60.00
a.	5sh bright violet	325.00	60.00
	Nos. 32-41 (10)	1,990.	600.00

For surcharges see Nos. 48-49, 51-58, 87.

A10

1872
| 42 | A10 | 10p claret | 375.00 | 57.50 |

For surcharges see Nos. 46-47.

No. 29 Surcharged in Black or Red

HALF PENNY (a)   ½d HALF PENNY (b)

1876 | | | | **Unwmk.** |
43	A9(a)	½p on 9p	24.00	24.00
a.	Inverted surcharge	800.00	
b.	Double surcharge		2,350.
44	A9(b)	½p on 9p	5,000.	
45	A9(b)	½p on 9p (R)	3,400.	

Nos. 44 and 45 were never placed in use. No. 45 is valued with perfs cutting into the design.

Stamps of 1863-72 Surcharged in Black

HALF PENNY (c)   One Penny (d)

1876-77 | | | | **Wmk. 1** |
46	A10(a)	½p on 10p claret	4.75	29.00
47	A10(c)	½p on 10p cl ('77)	12.00	50.00
48	A9(d)	1p on 4p rose ('77)	25.00	27.50
49	A9(d)	1sh on 5sh red vio ('77)	350.00	125.00
a.	1sh on 5sh violet ('77)	340.00	160.00
	Nos. 46-49 (4)	391.75	231.50

A16   2 CENTS

MAURITIUS

1878		Black Surcharge		
50	A16	2c claret	17.50	12.50

Stamps and Type of 1863-72 Surcharged in Black — e

51	A9	4c on 1p bister brn	27.50	10.00
52	A9	8c on 2p blue	90.00	4.25
53	A9	13c on 3p org red	26.00	52.50
54	A9	17c on 4p rose	200.00	4.50
55	A9	25c on 6p sl blue	275.00	8.00
56	A9	38c on 9p violet	50.00	100.00
57	A9	50c on 1sh green	100.00	5.75
58	A9	2r50c on 5sh violet	22.50	26.00
		Nos. 50-58 (9)	808.50	223.50

For surcharge see No. 87.

Queen Victoria — A18, A19, A20, A21, A22, A23, A24, A25, A26

1879-80			Wmk. 1	
59	A18	2c red brn ('80)	55.00	27.50
60	A19	4c orange	72.50	4.25
61	A20	8c blue ('80)	40.00	4.50
62	A21	13c slate ('80)	180.00	325.00
63	A22	17c rose ('80)	95.00	10.00
64	A23	25c bister	475.00	18.00
65	A24	38c violet ('80)	200.00	375.00
66	A25	50c green ('80)	6.50	5.50
67	A26	2r50c brn vio ('80)	57.50	85.00
		Nos. 59-67 (9)	1,182.	854.75

Nos. 59-67 are known imperforate.
For surcharges & overprints see Nos. 76-78, 83-86, 122-123.

1882-93			Wmk. 2	
68	A18	1c violet ('93)	2.50	.55
69	A18	2c red brown	40.00	7.00
70	A18	2c green ('85)	4.75	.75
71	A19	4c orange	95.00	7.00
72	A19	4c rose ('85)	5.50	1.25
73	A20	8c blue ('91)	5.00	1.80
74	A23	25c bister ('83)	14.00	4.00
75	A25	50c dp orange ('87)	45.00	20.00
		Nos. 68-75 (8)	211.75	42.35

For surcharges and overprint see Nos. 88-89, 121.

Nos. 63 and Type of 1882 Surcharged in Black

f — 16 CENTS
g — SIXTEEN CENTS

1883			Wmk. 1	
		Surcharge Measures 14x3½mm		
76	A22(f)	16c on 17c rose	180.00	60.00
a.		Double surcharge		2,900.
		Surcharge Measures 15½x3½mm		
77	A22(f)	16c on 17c rose	190.00	60.00
a.		Double surcharge		3,150.
		Surcharge Measures 15½x2¾mm		
78	A22(f)	16c on 17c rose	375.00	140.00
		Wmk. 2		
79	A22(g)	16c on 17c rose	115.00	2.40
		Nos. 76-79 (4)	860.00	262.40

Queen Victoria — A29

1885-94				
80	A29	15c orange brown ('92)	9.00	1.50
81	A29	15c blue ('94)	10.00	1.50
82	A29	16c orange brown	9.50	2.75
		Nos. 80-82 (3)	28.50	5.75

For surcharges see Nos. 90, 116.

Various Stamps Surcharged in Black or Red

h — 2 CENTS
j — 2 CENTS

1885-87			Wmk. 1	
83	A24(h)	2c on 38c violet	170.00	47.50
a.		Inverted surcharge	1,250.	1,000.
b.		Double surcharge	1,350.	
c.		Without bar		275.00
84	A21(j)	2c on 13c sl (R) ('87)	80.00	130.00
a.		Inverted surcharge	260.00	300.00
b.		Double surcharge	975.00	850.00
c.		As "b," one on back	1,000.	
d.		Double surcharge, both inverted		1,750.

k — TWO CENTS
l — TWO CENTS / 36 CENTS

1891				
85	A22(k)	2c on 17c rose	145.00	155.00
a.		Inverted surcharge	575.00	575.00
b.		Double surcharge	950.00	950.00
86	A24(k)	2c on 38c vio	11.50	16.00
a.		Double surcharge	240.00	260.00
b.		Dbl. surch., one invtd.	260.00	300.00
c.		Inverted surcharge	1,250.	—
87	A9(e+l)	2c on 38c on 9p vio	15.00	6.75
a.		Double surcharge	850.00	850.00
b.		Inverted surcharge	625.00	
c.		Dbl. surch., one invtd.	200.00	225.00
		Wmk. 2		
88	A19(k)	2c on 4c rose	2.50	1.00
a.		Double surcharge	95.00	90.00
b.		Inverted surcharge	90.00	
c.		Dbl. surch., one invtd.	95.00	90.00
		Nos. 85-88 (4)	174.00	178.75

m — ONE CENT
n — ONE CENT

1893, Jan.				
89	A18(m)	1c on 2c violet	2.75	1.75
90	A29(n)	1c on 16c org brown	3.25	4.50

Coat of Arms — A38

1895-1904			Wmk. 2	
91	A38	1c lilac & ultra	.90	1.80
92	A38	1c gray blk & blk	.60	.25
93	A38	2c lilac & orange	7.50	.60
94	A38	2c dull lil & vio	1.00	.25
95	A38	3c lilac	.85	.60
96	A38	3c grn & scar, yel	4.50	1.50
97	A38	4c lilac & green	6.00	.60
98	A38	4c dull lil & car, yel	3.00	.50
99	A38	4c gray grn & pur	3.00	2.40
100	A38	4c blk & car, blue	18.00	.75
101	A38	5c lilac & vio, buff	12.00	100.00
102	A38	5c lilac & blk, buff	3.00	3.00
103	A38	6c grn & rose	5.75	5.00
104	A38	6c vio & scar, red	4.75	1.00
105	A38	8c gray grn & blk, buff	4.50	15.00
106	A38	12c blk & car rose	3.00	3.00
107	A38	15c grn & org	30.00	10.00
108	A38	15c blk & ultra, blue	65.00	1.50
109	A38	18c gray grn & ultra	22.50	4.25
110	A38	25c grn & car, grn, chalky paper	6.00	27.50
111	A38	50c green, yel	20.00	80.00
		Nos. 91-111 (21)	221.85	259.50

The 25c is on both ordinary and chalky paper. Ornaments in lower panel omitted on Nos. 106-111.
Year of issue: Nos. 103, 107, 1899; Nos. 92, 94, 98, 1900; Nos. 96, 99, 101-102, 104-106, 110-111, 1902; Nos. 100, 108, 1904; others, 1895.
See Nos. 128-135. For surcharges and overprints see Nos. 113, 114, 117-120.

Diamond Jubilee Issue

Arms — A39

1898, May 23			Wmk. 46	
112	A39	36c brown org & ultra	13.50	27.50

60th year of Queen Victoria's reign.
For surcharges see Nos. 114 and 127.

No. 109 Surcharged in Red

6 CENTS

1899			Wmk. 2	
113	A38	6c on 18c	1.40	1.25
a.		Inverted surcharge	725.00	340.00

No. 112 Surcharged in Blue

15 CENTS

			Wmk. 46	
114	A39	15c on 36c	3.50	2.10
a.		Without bar	500.00	

Admiral Mahe de La Bourdonnais — A40

1899, Dec.			Engr. Wmk. 1	
115	A40	15c ultra	30.00	5.00

Birth bicent. of Admiral Mahe de La Bourdonnais, governor of Mauritius, 1734-46.
See Nos. E1-E3F.

No. 82 Surcharged in Black

4 Cents

1900			Wmk. 2	
116	A29	4c on 16c org brn	17.50	27.50

No. 109 Surcharged in Black — r

12 CENTS

1902				
117	A38	12c on 18c grn & ultra	3.50	11.00

Preceding Issues Overprinted in Black

Postage & Revenue

1902				
118	A38	4c lil & car, yel	1.50	.30
119	A38	6c green & rose	3.25	3.25
120	A38	15c green & org	6.25	1.35
121	A23	25c bister	8.00	3.25
		Wmk. 1		
122	A25	50c green	20.00	6.25
123	A26	2r50c brown violet	135.00	225.00
		Nos. 118-123 (6)	172.25	239.40

Coat of Arms — A41

1902			Wmk. 1	
124	A41	1r blk & car rose	62.50	60.00
		Wmk. 2 Sideways		
125	A41	2r50c grn & blk, bl	40.00	160.00
126	A41	5r blk & car, red	110.00	180.00
		Nos. 124-126 (3)	212.50	400.00

No. 112 Surcharged type "r" but with longer bar

1902			Wmk. 46	
127	A39	12c on 36c	2.40	1.50
a.		Inverted surcharge	775.00	525.00

Arms Type of 1895-1904

1904-07			Wmk. 3 Chalky Paper	
128	A38	1c gray blk & black ('07)	8.75	5.00
129	A38	2c dl lil & vio ('05)	35.00	3.00
130	A38	3c grn & scar, yel	22.50	13.00
131	A38	4c blk & car, blue	16.00	.25
132	A38	6c vio & scar, red ('06)	14.00	.35
133	A38	15c blk & ultra, bl	4.50	.40
135	A38	50c green, yel	3.00	7.00
136	A41	1r blk & car rose ('07)	50.00	65.00
		Nos. 128-136 (8)	153.75	94.00

The 2c, 4c, 6c also exist on ordinary paper. Ornaments in lower panel omitted on 15c and 50c.

Arms A42 — Edward VII A43

1910			Wmk. 3 Ordinary Paper	
137	A42	1c black	3.25	.30
138	A42	2c brown	3.00	.25
139	A42	3c green	3.25	.25
140	A42	4c ol grn & rose	4.00	.25
141	A43	5c gray & rose	3.00	3.25
142	A42	6c carmine	5.25	.25
143	A43	8c brn org	3.25	1.60
144	A43	12c gray	3.75	3.00
145	A42	15c ultramarine	21.00	.25
		Chalky Paper		
146	A43	25c blk & scar, yel	2.25	13.00
147	A43	50c dull vio & blk	2.60	20.00
148	A43	1r blk, green	17.75	13.00
149	A43	2r50c blk & car, bl	27.50	75.00
150	A43	5r grn & car, yel	42.50	100.00
151	A43	10r grn & car, grn	165.00	250.00
		Nos. 137-151 (15)	307.35	480.40

Numerals of 12c, 25c and 10r of type A43 are in color on plain tablet.
See Nos. 161-178.

King George V — A44

For description of dies I and II see "Dies of British Colonial Stamps" in table of contents.
Numeral tablet of 5c, 50c, 1r, 2.50r and 5r of type A44 has lined background with colorless denomination.

Die I

MAURITIUS

1912-22 Wmk. 3 Ordinary Paper
152	A44	5c gray & rose	3.00 4.50
153	A44	12c gray	8.00 1.10

Chalky Paper
154	A44	25c blk & red, yel	.45 1.50
a.		25c gray black & red, yellow, Die II	1.10 25.00
155	A44	50c dull vio & blk	52.50 125.00
156	A44	1r blk, emer, die II	2.50 8.00
a.		1r black, emer, olive back, die I ('21)	11.50 60.00
b.		1r blk, bl grn, olive back, die I ('21)	6.75 21.00
157	A44	2r50c blk & red, bl	42.50 75.00
158	A44	5r grn & red, yel	115.00 175.00
		Die II ('22)	115.00 200.00
159	A44	10r grn & red, emer, die II ('21)	47.50 180.00
a.		10r grn & red, bl grn, olive back, die I	1,150.
b.		10r green & red, emer, die I	85.00 200.00
c.		10r green & red, emer, olive back, die I	145.00 210.00
d.		10r grn & red, grn, die I	105.00 210.00

Surface-colored Paper
160	A44	25c blk & red, yel ('16)	2.75 21.00
		Nos. 152-160 (9)	274.20 591.10

1921-26 Wmk. 4 Ordinary Paper
161	A42	1c black	1.10 1.10
162	A42	2c brown	1.10 .25
163	A42	2c violet, yel ('25)	3.50 2.00
164	A42	3c green ('25)	3.50 3.50
165	A42	4c ol grn & rose	1.60 2.00
166	A42	4c green	1.10 .25
167	A42	4c brown ('25)	4.50 2.50
168	A42	6c rose red	13.50 7.25
169	A42	6c violet	1.35 .25
170	A42	8c brown org ('25)	2.50 24.00
171	A42	10c gray ('22)	2.25 3.75
172	A42	10c rose ('25)	12.00 6.75
173	A42	12c rose red	1.70 1.60
174	A42	12c gray ('25)	1.90 5.00
175	A42	15c ultramarine	6.00 5.50
176	A42	15c dull blue	1.60 .25
177	A42	20c ultra ('22)	2.25 .40
178	A42	20c dull vio ('25)	9.50 16.00
		Nos. 161-178 (18)	70.95 82.85

Ornaments in lower panel omitted on Nos. 171-178.

For surcharges see Nos. 201-203.

Die II
1922-34 Ordinary Paper
179	A44	1c black	2.40 3.00
180	A44	2c brown	1.10 .25
181	A44	3c green	2.10 .45
182	A44	4c ol grn & red ('27)	3.25 .30
a.		Die I ('32)	18.00 62.50
183	A44	4c grn, die I ('33)	13.50 .50
184	A44	5c gray & car	1.10 .25
a.		Die I ('32)	10.00 6.50
185	A44	6c ol brn ('28)	5.50 .65
186	A44	8c orange	2.10 15.50
187	A44	10c red ('26)	4.25 .25
a.		Die I ('32)	15.50 16.75
188	A44	12c gray, small "c" ('22)	5.00 23.00
189	A44	12c gray, "c" larger & thinner ('34)	17.50 .35
190	A44	12c rose red	.70 3.75
191	A44	15c dk blue ('28)	4.75 .25
192	A44	20c dull vio	4.75 .45
193	A44	20c dk blue ('34)	28.00 .45
a.		Die I ('27)	11.00 2.60

Chalky Paper
194	A44	25c blk & red, yel	1.10 .25
a.		Die I ('32)	7.25 67.50
195	A44	50c dull vio & blk	8.00 3.75
196	A44	1r blk, emerald	6.75 .55
197	A44	2r50c blk & red, bl	22.00 19.00
198	A44	5r grn & red, yel	47.50 95.00
199	A44	10r grn & red, emer ('28)	145.00 340.00
		Nos. 179-199 (21)	326.35 507.85

A45

1924
200	A45	50r lilac & green	1,100. 2,750.

Nos. 166, 173, 177 Surcharged

1925
201	A42	3c on 4c green	8.00 6.25
202	A42	10c on 12c rose red	.50 1.60
203	A42	15c on 20c ultra	.65 1.75
		Nos. 201-203 (3)	9.15 9.60

Common Design Types pictured following the introduction.

Silver Jubilee Issue
Common Design Type
1935, May 6 Engr. Perf. 13½x14
204	CD301	5c gray blk & ultra	.60 .25
205	CD301	12c indigo & grn	5.25 .25
206	CD301	20c blue & brown	6.25 .25
207	CD301	1r brt vio & indigo	32.50 57.50
		Nos. 204-207 (4)	44.60 58.25
		Set, never hinged	67.50

Coronation Issue
Common Design Type
1937, May 12 Wmk. 4 Perf. 13½x14
208	CD302	5c dark purple	.25 .25
209	CD302	12c carmine	.40 2.25
210	CD302	20c bright ultra	1.10 1.00
		Nos. 208-210 (3)	1.75 3.50
		Set, never hinged	2.50

King George VI — A46

1938-43 Typo. Perf. 14
211	A46	2c gray ('43)	.25 .25
a.		Perf. 15x14 ('43)	.60 .25
212	A46	3c rose vio & car ('43)	1.15 1.60
213	A46	4c green ('43)	1.60 1.60
214	A46	5c violet ('43)	1.90 .25
a.		Perf. 15x14 ('43)	34.00
215	A46	10c carmine ('43)	1.45 .25
a.		Perf. 15x14 ('43)	24.00 2.50
216	A46	12c sal pink ('43)	.60 .25
a.		Perf. 15x14 ('43)	31.00 1.10
217	A46	20c blue ('43)	.60 .25
218	A46	25c maroon ('43)	5.25 .25
219	A46	1r brn blk ('43)	11.50 1.50
220	A46	2.50r pale vio ('43)	24.00 24.00
221	A46	5r ol grn ('43)	21.00 37.50
222	A46	10r rose vio ('43)	9.75 42.50
		Nos. 211-222 (12)	79.05 110.20
		Set, never hinged	127.00

Nos. 218-222 exist on both chalky and ordinary papers. Values above are for stamps on ordinary paper. For detailed listings, see Scott Classic Specialized Catalogue of Stamps & Covers.

Catalogue values for unused stamps in this section, from this point to the end of the section, are for Never Hinged items.

Peace Issue
Common Design Type
1946, Nov. 20 Engr. Perf. 13½x14 Wmk. 4
223	CD303	5c lilac	.25 .80
224	CD303	20c deep blue	.25 .25

"Post Office" Stamp of 1847 — A47

1948, Mar. 22 Perf. 11½
225	A47	5c red vio & orange	.25 .40
226	A47	12c green & orange	.25 .40
227	A47	20c blue & dp blue	.25 .25
228	A47	1r lt red brn & dp blue	1.10 .35
		Nos. 225-228 (4)	1.85 1.40

Cent. of the 1st Mauritius postage stamps.

Silver Wedding Issue
Common Design Types
1948, Oct. 25 Photo. Perf. 14x14½
229	CD304	5c violet	.25 .25

Perf. 11½x11
Engraved; Name Typographed
230	CD305	10r lilac rose	19.00 45.00

UPU Issue
Common Design Types
Engr.; Name Typo. on 20c, 35c
Perf. 13½, 11x11½
1949, Oct. 10   Wmk. 4
231	CD306	12c rose carmine	.50 3.00
232	CD307	20c indigo	2.10 2.40
233	CD308	35c rose violet	.60 1.40
234	CD309	1r sepia	.50 .25
		Nos. 231-234 (4)	3.70 7.05

Sugar Factory — A48   Aloe Plant — A49

Designs: 2c, Grand Port. 4c, Tamarind Falls. 5c, Rempart Mountain. 10c, Transporting cane. 12c, Map and dodo. 20c, "Paul et Virginie." 25c, Statue of Mahe La Bourdonnais. 35c, Government House. 50c, Pieter Both Mountain. 1r, Sambar. 2.50r, Port Louis. 5r, Beach scene. 10r, Arms.

Perf. 13½x14½, 14½x13½
1950, July 1   Photo.
235	A48	1c red violet	.25 .40
236	A48	2c cerise	.25 .25
237	A49	3c yel green	.70 3.50
238	A49	4c green	.25 2.50
239	A48	5c greenish blue	.25 .25
240	A48	10c red	.30 .60
241	A48	12c olive green	1.60 2.25
242	A49	20c brt ultra	1.10 .25
243	A49	25c vio brown	2.10 .35
244	A48	35c rose violet	.45 .25
245	A49	50c emerald	3.00 .40
246	A49	1r sepia	9.75 .25
247	A48	2.50r orange	21.00 16.50
248	A48	5r red brown	22.00 16.50
249	A48	10r gray blue	17.50 37.50
		Nos. 235-249 (15)	80.50 81.75

Coronation Issue
Common Design Type
1953, June 2 Engr. Perf. 13½x13
250	CD312	10c dk green & black	1.10 .25

Sugar Factory — A50   Tamarind Falls — A51

Designs: 2c, Grand Port. 3c, Aloe plant. 5c, Rempart Mountain. 15c, Museum, Mahebourg. 20c, Statue of Mahe La Bourdonnais. 25c, "Paul et Virginie." 35c, Government House. 50c, Pieter Both Mountain. 60c, Map and dodo. 1r, Sambar. 2.50r, Port Louis. 5r, Beach scene. 10r, Arms.

Perf. 13½x14½, 14½x13½
1953-54   Photo.   Wmk. 4
251	A50	2c rose car ('54)	.30 .25
252	A51	3c yel green ('54)	.30 .25
253	A50	4c red violet	.30 .75
254	A50	5c grnsh blue ('54)	.30 .25
255	A51	10c dk green	.30 .25
256	A50	15c scarlet	.30 .25
257	A51	20c violet brown	.30 .25
a.		Imperf., pair	
258	A50	25c brt ultra	1.60 .25
259	A51	35c rose vio ('54)	.30 .25
260	A51	50c emerald	.75 .75
261	A51	60c gray grn ('54)	12.00 .25
262	A50	1r sepia	.35 .25
a.		Imperf., pair	
263	A50	2.50r orange ('54)	16.00 9.25
264	A51	5r red brn ('54)	16.00 10.00
265	A50	10r gray blue ('54)	16.00 1.25
		Nos. 251-265 (15)	65.15 24.50

See Nos. 273-275.

King George III and Queen Elizabeth II — A52

1961, Jan. 11 Wmk. 314 Litho. Perf. 13½
266	A52	10c dk red & dk brown	.25 .25
267	A52	20c lt blue & dk blue	.25 .25
268	A52	35c org yel & brown	.25 .25
269	A52	1r yel green & dk brn	.60 .60
		Nos. 266-269 (4)	1.40 1.40

Sesquicentenary of postal service under British administration.

Freedom from Hunger Issue
Common Design Type
1963, June 4 Photo. Perf. 14x14½
270	CD314	60c lilac	.45 .25

Red Cross Centenary Issue
Common Design Type
1963, Sept. 2 Litho. Perf. 13
271	CD315	10c black & red	.25 .25
272	CD315	60c ultra & red	.60 .25

Types of 1953-54
Perf. 14½x13½, 13½x14½
1963-64   Photo.   Wmk. 314
273	A50	10c dark green ('64)	.25 .30
274	A50	60c gray green ('64)	3.50 .30
275	A50	2.50r orange	11.00 10.50
		Nos. 273-275 (3)	14.75 11.10

Gray White-Eye A53

Birds of Mauritius: 3c, Rodriguez fody. 4c, Olive white-eye. 5c, Mauritius paradise flycatcher. 10c, Mauritius fody. 15c, Rose-ringed parakeet. 20c, Cuckoo shrike. 25c, Mauritian kestrel. 35c, Pink pigeon. 50c, Mauritius olivaceous bulbul. 60c, Mauritius blue pigeon. 1r, Dodo. 2.50r, Rodriguez solitaire. 5r, Van den Broeck's red rail. 10r, Broad-billed Mauritian parrot.

Wmk. 314
1965, Mar. 16 Photo. Perf. 14½
Birds in Natural Colors
276	A53	2c brt yel & brn	.30 .25
a.		Gray (leg, etc.) omitted	375.00
277	A53	3c brn & dk brn	.75 .25
a.		Black (eye, beak) omitted	450.00
278	A53	4c dl rose lil & blk	.25 .25
a.		Rose lilac omitted	80.00
279	A53	5c gray & ultra	2.75 .25
a.		Wmkd. sideways ('66)	.80
280	A53	10c dl grn & dk brn	.25 .25
281	A53	15c lt gray & dk brn	1.50 .30
a.		Carmine (beak) omitted	900.00
282	A53	20c pale yel & dk brown	1.50 .25
283	A53	25c gray & brown	1.50 .25
284	A53	35c vio bl & blk	2.75 .25
a.		Wmkd. sideways ('67)	.40 .25
285	A53	50c pale yel & blk	.40 .45
286	A53	60c pale cit & brn	.45 .25
287	A53	1r yel grn & blk	6.00 .25
a.		Palo gray (ground) omitted	475.00 475.00
b.		Pale orange omitted	325.00
288	A53	2.50r pale grn & brn	3.75 6.75
289	A53	5r pale blue & blk	11.00 11.50
290	A53	10r pale grn & ultra	26.00 25.00
		Nos. 276-290 (15)	62.15 46.50

On No. 278 the background was printed in two colors. The rose lilac tint is omitted on No. 278a.

See Nos. 327-332. For overprints see Nos. 306-320.

ITU Issue
Common Design Type
Perf. 11x11½
1965, May 17 Litho. Wmk. 314
291	CD317	10c dp org & apple grn	.30 .25
292	CD317	60c yellow & violet	.80 .25

Intl. Cooperation Year Issue
Common Design Type
1965, Oct. 25 Perf. 14½
293	CD318	10c lt green & claret	.25 .25
294	CD318	60c lt violet & green	.40 .25

MAURITIUS

Churchill Memorial Issue
Common Design Type
1966, Jan. 24   Photo.   *Perf. 14*
Design in Black, Gold and Carmine Rose
295	CD319	2c brt blue	.25	3.00
296	CD319	10c green	.45	.25
297	CD319	60c brown	1.50	.25
298	CD319	1r violet	1.50	.25
		Nos. 295-298 (4)	3.70	3.75

UNESCO Anniversary Issue
Common Design Type
1966, Dec. 1   Litho.   *Perf. 14*
299	CD323	5c "Education"	.35	.35
300	CD323	10c "Science"	.35	.35
301	CD323	60c "Culture"	1.40	.80
		Nos. 299-301 (3)	2.10	1.50

Red-Tailed Tropic Bird — A54

Birds of Mauritius: 10c, Rodriguez bush warbler. 60c, Newton's parakeet. 1r, Mauritius swiftlet.

1967, Sept. 1   Photo.   *Perf. 14½*
302	A54	2c lt ultra & multi	.30	2.00
303	A54	10c emerald & multi	.85	.25
304	A54	60c salmon & multi	.90	.25
305	A54	1r yellow & multi	.95	.25
		Nos. 302-305 (4)	3.00	2.75

Attainment of self-government, Sept. 1, 1967.

Bird Issue of 1965-67 and Type Overprinted: "SELF GOVERNMENT 1967"
1967, Dec. 1   Photo.   *Wmk. 314*
306	A53	2c multicolored	.25	.40
307	A53	3c multicolored	.25	.40
308	A53	4c multicolored	.25	.40
309	A53	5c multicolored	.25	.25
310	A53	10c multicolored	.25	.25
311	A53	15c multicolored	.25	.30
312	A53	20c multicolored	.25	.25
313	A53	25c multicolored	.25	.25
314	A53	35c multicolored	.25	.25
315	A53	50c multicolored	.30	.25
316	A53	60c multicolored	.30	.25
317	A53	1r multicolored	1.00	.25
318	A53	2.50r multicolored	1.00	2.25
319	A53	5r multicolored	4.25	4.25
320	A53	10r multicolored	8.00	12.00
		Nos. 306-320 (15)	17.10	22.00

5c, 10c, 35c watermarked sideways.

Independent State

Flag of Mauritius A55

Designs: 3c, 20c, 1r, Dodo emerging from egg and coat of arms.

1968, Mar. 12   Litho.   *Perf. 13½x13*   Unwmk.
321	A55	2c brt violet & multi	.25	1.00
322	A55	3c red brown & multi	.25	1.00
323	A55	15c brown & multi	.25	.25
324	A55	20c multicolored	.50	.25
325	A55	60c dk green & multi	.65	.25
326	A55	1r brt violet & multi	1.00	.25
		Nos. 321-326 (6)	2.90	3.00

Independence of Mauritius.

Bird Type of 1965 in Changed Background Colors
Wmk. 314
1968, July 12   Photo.   *Perf. 14½*
Birds in Natural Colors
327	A53	2c lemon & brown	.30	3.25
328	A53	3c ultra & dk brown	.30	6.25
329	A53	15c tan & dk brown	.90	.25
330	A53	20c dull yel & dk brn	1.40	2.75
331	A53	60c pink & black	3.50	.90
332	A53	1r rose lilac & black	5.50	1.00
		Nos. 327-332 (6)	11.90	14.40

Domingue Rescuing Paul and Virginie A56

Designs: 15c, Paul and Virginie crossing river, vert. 50c, La Bourdonnais visiting Madame de 1a Tour. 60c, Paul and Virginie, vert. 1r, Departure of Virginie for Europe. 2.50r, Bernardin de St. Pierre, vert. The designs are from old prints illustrating "Paul et Virginie."

Perf. 13½
1968, Dec. 2   Unwmk.   Litho.
333	A56	2c multicolored	.25	1.00
334	A56	15c multicolored	.50	.25
335	A56	50c multicolored	.95	.25
336	A56	60c multicolored	.95	.25
337	A56	1r multicolored	.95	.25
338	A56	2.50r multicolored	1.40	2.90
		Nos. 333-338 (6)	5.00	4.90

Bicent. of the visit of Bernardin de St. Pierre (1737-1814), author of "Paul et Virginie."

Batardé Fish — A57

Marine Life: 3c, Red reef crab. 4c, Episcopal miter shell. 5c, Bourse fish. 10c, Starfish. 15c, Sea urchin. 20c, Fiddler crab. 25c, Spiny shrimp. 30c, Single and double harp shells. 35c, Argonaut shell. 40c, Nudibranch (seaslug). 50c, Violet and orange spider shells. 60c, Blue marlin. 75c, Conus clytospira. 1r, Dorad. 2.50r, Spiny lobster. 5r, Sacré chien rouge fish. 10r, Moonfish.

Wmk. 314 Sideways (#339-344, 351-352), others Upright
1969, Mar. 12   Photo.   *Perf. 14*
339	A57	2c pink & multi	.25	1.60
340	A57	3c yellow & multi	.25	2.00
341	A57	4c multicolored	2.00	2.60
342	A57	5c lt blue & multi	.25	.25
343	A57	10c salmon & multi	1.60	.25
344	A57	15c pale blue & multi	.25	.25
345	A57	20c pale gray & multi	.55	.45
346	A57	25c multicolored	.25	2.10
347	A57	30c multicolored	1.25	1.05
348	A57	35c multicolored	6.50	10.50
349	A57	40c tan & multi	.30	.75
350	A57	50c lt vio & multi	.85	.25
351	A57	60c ultra & multi	1.25	.25
352	A57	75c lemon & multi	1.25	1.60
353	A57	1r cream & multi	.50	.25
354	A57	2.50r lt vio & multi	2.40	5.00
355	A57	5r multicolored	9.75	7.00
356	A57	10r multicolored	2.00	3.00
		Nos. 339-356 (18)	31.45	39.15

For overprints see Nos. 368-369.

Wmk. 314 Upright (#339a-344a, 351a-352a), others Sideways
1972-74
339a	A57	2c multi ('74)	1.10	1.10
340a	A57	3c multi ('74)	1.10	1.10
341a	A57	4c multi ('74)	1.10	1.10
342a	A57	5c multi ('74)	1.10	1.10
343a	A57	10c multicolored	1.10	1.10
344a	A57	15c multi ('74)	1.10	1.10
345a	A57	20c multicolored	1.10	1.10
346a	A57	25c multi ('73)	1.10	1.10
347a	A57	30c multicolored	1.40	1.25
348a	A57	35c multicolored	1.60	1.40
349a	A57	40c multi ('73)	1.60	1.60
350a	A57	50c multi ('73)	1.60	1.60
351a	A57	60c multi ('74)	2.10	1.60
352a	A57	75c multicolored	2.75	2.10
353a	A57	1r multicolored	3.50	3.00
354a	A57	2.50r multi ('73)	8.25	7.50
355a	A57	5r multi ('73)	16.50	14.00
356a	A57	10r multicolored	31.00	26.00
		Nos. 339a-356a (18)	79.10	68.85

1975-77   *Wmk. 373*
339b	A57	2c multi ('77)	.75	.75
340b	A57	3c multi ('77)	.75	.75
341b	A57	4c multi ('77)	.75	.75
342b	A57	5c multicolored	.75	.75
343b	A57	10c multicolored	.75	.75
344b	A57	15c multicolored	.75	.75
345b	A57	20c multi ('76)	.75	.75
346b	A57	25c multicolored	.95	.75
347b	A57	30c multicolored	1.10	.95
348b	A57	35c multi ('76)	1.10	.95
349b	A57	40c multi ('76)	1.10	1.10
350b	A57	50c multi ('76)	1.50	1.10
351b	A57	60c multi ('77)	1.90	1.50
352b	A57	75c multi ('77)	1.90	1.90
353b	A57	1r multi ('76)	3.00	2.75
354b	A57	2.50r multi ('77)	12.50	7.50
355b	A57	5r multicolored	21.00	16.00
356b	A57	10r multicolored	50.00	32.50
		Nos. 339b-356b (17)	100.55	71.50

Gandhi as Law Student in London — A58

Portraits of Gandhi: 15c, as stretcher bearer during Zulu rebellion. 50c, as member of nonviolent movement in South Africa (Satyagrahi). 60c, wearing Indian garment at No. 10 Downing Street, London. 1r, wearing turban in Mauritius, 1901. 2.50r, as old man.

1969, July 1   Litho.   *Perf. 13½*
357	A58	2c dull org & multi	.30	.30
358	A58	15c brt blue & multi	.30	.30
359	A58	50c multicolored	.30	.30
360	A58	60c brick red & multi	.40	.40
361	A58	1r multicolored	.75	.75
362	A58	2.50r olive & multi	1.90	1.90
a.		Souvenir sheet of 6, #357-362	8.50	8.50
		Nos. 357-362 (6)	3.95	3.95

Mohandas K. Gandhi (1869-1948), leader in India's struggle for independence.

Vertical Cane Crusher (19th Century) A59

Dr. Charles Telfair (1778-1833) A60

Designs: 15c, The Frangourinier, 18th century cane crusher. 60c, Beau Rivage sugar factory, 1867, painting by Numa Desjardin. 1r, Mon Desert-Alma sugar factory, 1969.

Perf. 11x11½, 11½x11
1969, Dec. 22   Photo.   *Wmk. 314*
363	A59	2c multicolored	.25	.25
364	A59	15c multicolored	.25	.25
365	A59	60c multicolored	.25	.25
366	A59	1r multicolored	.25	.25
367	A60	2.50r multicolored	.40	1.00
a.		Souvenir sheet of 5	2.25	2.50
		Nos. 363-367 (5)	1.40	2.00

150th anniv. of Telfair's improvements of the sugar industry.

No. 367a contains one each of Nos. 363-367. The 2.50r in the sheet is imperf., the others are perf. 11x11½.

Nos. 351 and 353 Overprinted: "EXPO '70 / OSAKA"
1970, Apr. 7   *Perf. 14*
368	A57	60c ultra & multi	.25	.25
369	A57	1r cream & multi	.30	.30

EXPO '70 Intl. Exhib., Osaka, Japan, Mar. 15-Sept. 13.

Lufthansa Plane over Mauritius — A61

25c, Brabant Hotel, Morne Beach, horiz.

1970, May 2   Litho.   *Perf. 14*
370	A61	25c multicolored	.35	.25
371	A61	50c multicolored	.35	.25

Lufthansa's inaugural flight from Mauritius to Frankfurt, Germany, May 2, 1970.

Lenin as Student, by V. Tsigal — A62

Design: 75c, Bust of Lenin.

1970, May 15   Photo.   *Perf. 12x11½*
372	A62	15c dk slate blue & sil	.25	.25
373	A62	75c dk brown & gold	.35	.25

Birth cent. of Lenin (1870-1924), Russian communist leader.

UN Emblem and Symbols of UN Activities A63

1970, Oct. 24   Litho.   *Perf. 14*
374	A63	10c blue black & multi	.25	.25
375	A63	60c blue black & multi	.40	.25

25th anniversary of the United Nations.

Mauritius No. 2, and Post Office before 1870 — A64

Designs: 15c, General Post Office Building, 1870-1970. 50c, Mauritius mail coach, 1870. 75c, Port Louis harbor, 1970. 2.50r, Arrival of Pierre André de Suffren de St. Tropez in Port Louis harbor, 1783.

1970, Oct. 15   Litho.   *Perf. 14*
376	A64	5c multicolored	.25	.25
377	A64	15c multicolored	.25	.25
378	A64	50c multicolored	.70	.25
379	A64	75c multicolored	.80	.25
380	A64	2.50r multicolored	.85	2.50
a.		Souvenir sheet of 5	5.00	8.00
		Nos. 376-380 (5)	2.85	3.50

Centenary of the General Post Office and to show the improvements of Port Louis harbor. No. 380a contains one each of Nos. 376-380 and a label showing map of Mauritius.

Waterfall — A65

15c, Trois Mamelles Mountains. 60c, Beach scene with sailboats. 2.50r, Marine life.

1971, Apr. 12   Litho.   *Perf. 14*
381	A65	10c multicolored	.25	.25
382	A65	15c multicolored	.25	.25
383	A65	60c multicolored	.30	.30
384	A65	2.50r multicolored	1.25	1.25
		Nos. 381-384 (4)	2.05	2.05

Tourist publicity. Each stamp has a different 6-line message printed in black on back.

Mauritius at Crossroads of Indian Ocean — A66

60c, Plane at Plaisance Airport. 1r, Stewardesses on plane ramp. 2.50r, Roland Garros' airplane, Choisy Airfield, 1937.

1971, Oct. 23   *Wmk. 314*   *Perf. 14½*
385	A66	15c multicolored	.25	.25
386	A66	60c multicolored	.50	.50
387	A66	1r multicolored	.60	.60
388	A66	2.50r multicolored	2.40	2.40
		Nos. 385-388 (4)	3.75	3.75

25th anniversary of Plaisance Civil Airport.

MAURITIUS

Princess Margaret Orthopedic Center — A67

75c, Operating room, National Hospital.

1971, Nov. 2   Perf. 14x14½
389 A67 10c multicolored   .25   .25
390 A67 75c multicolored   .30   .30
3rd Commonwealth Medical Conf., Nov. 1971.

Elizabeth II and Prince Philip — A68

Design: 2.50r, Queen Elizabeth II, vert.

1972, Mar.   Litho.   Perf. 14½
391 A68 15c brown & multi   .25   .25
392 A68 2.50r ultra & multi   2.50   2.50
Visit of Elizabeth II and Prince Philip.

Port Louis Theater and Masks — A69

Design: 1r, Interior view and masks of Comedy and Tragedy.

1972, June 26
393 A69 10c brown & multi   .25   .25
394 A69 1r multicolored   .40   .40
Sesquicentennial of Port Louis Theater.

Pirate Dhow Entering Tamarind River — A70

60c, Treasure chest, vert. 1r, Lememe and brig Hirondelle, vert. 2.50r, Robert Surcouf.

Perf. 14x14½, 14½x14
1972, Nov. 17   Litho.
395 A70 15c shown   .30   .30
396 A70 60c multi   .75   .75
397 A70 1r multi   1.60   1.60
398 A70 2.50r multi   6.00   6.00
   Nos. 395-398 (4)   8.65   8.65
Pirates and privateers.

Mauritius University A71

60c, Tea development plant. 1r, Bank of Mauritius.

1973, Apr. 10   Perf. 14½
399 A71 10c green & multi   .25   .25
400 A71 60c yellow & multi   .25   .25
401 A71 1r red & multi   .25   .25
   Nos. 399-401 (3)   .75   .75
5th anniversary of independence.

OCAM Emblem — A72

Design: 2.50r, Handshake, map of Africa; inscriptions in French, vert.

1973, Apr. 25
402 A72 10c multicolored   .25   .25
403 A72 2.50r lt blue & multi   .30   .30
Conference of the Organisation Commune Africaine, Malgache et Mauricienne (OCAM), Mauritius, Apr. 25-May 6.

WHO Emblem — A73

Perf. 14½x14
1973, Nov. 20   Wmk. 314
404 A73 1r green & multi   .40   .40
25th anniv. of WHO.

Meteorological Station, Vacoas — A74

1973, Nov. 27
405 A74 75c multicolored   .40   .40
Cent. of intl. meteorological cooperation.

Surcouf and Capture of the "Kent" — A75

1974, Mar. 21   Litho.   Perf. 14½x14
406 A75 60c sepia & multi   1.00   1.00
Bicentenary of the birth of Robert Surcouf (1773-1827), French privateer.

Philibert Commerson & Bougainvillaea — A76

1974, Apr. 18   Perf. 14
407 A76 2.50r slate grn & multi   .45   .45
Philibert Commerson (1727-1773), French physician and naturalist.

FAO Emblem, Woman Milking Cow — A77

1974, Oct. 23   Perf. 14½
408 A77 60c multicolored   .35   .35
8th FAO Regional Conference, Aug. 1-17.

Mail Train and UPU Emblem — A78

Design: 1r, New General Post Office Building, Port Louis, and UPU emblem.

1974, Dec. 4   Litho.   Perf. 14½
409 A78 15c multicolored   .30   .30
410 A78 1r multicolored   .75   .75
Centenary of Universal Postal Union.

Cottage Life, by F. Leroy A79

Paintings: 60c, Milk Seller, by A. Richard, vert. 1r, Entrance to Port Louis Market, by Thuillier. 2.50r, Washerwomen, by Max Boullé, vert.

1975, Mar. 6   Wmk. 373
411 A79 15c multicolored   .25   .25
412 A79 60c multicolored   .35   .35
413 A79 1r multicolored   .50   .50
414 A79 2.50r multicolored   1.25   1.25
   Nos. 411-414 (4)   2.35   2.35
Artistic views of life on Mauritius.

Mace, Map and Arms of Mauritius, Association Emblem — A80

1975, Nov. 21   Litho.   Wmk. 373
415 A80 75c multicolored   .55   .55
French-speaking Parliamentary Association, conf.

Woman and Aladdin's Lamp — A81

1975, Dec. 5   Perf. 14½
416 A81 2.50r multicolored   .50   .50
International Women's Year.

Parched Land — A82

Drought in Africa: 60c, Map of Africa, carcass and desert, vert.

1976, Feb. 26   Litho.   Wmk. 373
417 A82 50c vermilion & multi   .25   .25
418 A82 60c blue & multi   .25   .25

Pierre Loti, 1953-1970 A83

Mail Carriers: 15c, Secunder, 1907. 50c, Hindoostan, 1842. 60c, St. Geran, 1740. 2.50r, Maen, 1638.

1976, July 2   Litho.   Wmk. 373
419 A83 10c multicolored   .60   .60
420 A83 15c multicolored   .60   .60
421 A83 50c multicolored   .85   .85
422 A83 60c multicolored   1.20   1.20
423 A83 2.50r multicolored   5.00   5.00
  a. Souvenir sheet of 5, #419-423   13.50   13.50
   Nos. 419-423 (5)   8.25   8.25

Flame, and "Hindi Carried Across the Sea" — A84

Designs: 75c, like 10c. 1.20r, Flame and tablet with Hindi inscription.

1976, Aug. 28   Perf. 14½x14
424 A84 10c multicolored   .25   .25
425 A84 75c lt blue & multi   .25   .25
426 A84 1.20r multicolored   .30   .30
   Nos. 424-426 (3)   .80   .80
2nd World Hindi Convention.

Commonwealth Emblem, Map of Mauritius — A85

2.50r, Commonwealth emblem twice.

1976, Sept. 22   Litho.   Perf. 14x14½
427 A85 1r multicolored   .40   .40
428 A85 2.50r multicolored   .80   .80
22nd Commonwealth Parliamentary Association Conference, Mauritius, Sept. 17-30.

King Priest and Steatite Pectoral — A86

Designs: 1r, House with well, and goblet. 2.50r, Terracotta goddess and necklace.

1976, Dec. 15   Wmk. 373   Perf. 14
429 A86 60c multicolored   .35   .35
430 A86 1r multicolored   .75   .75
431 A86 2.50r multicolored   1.75   1.75
   Nos. 429-431 (3)   2.85   2.85
UNESCO campaign to save Mohenjo-Daro excavations.

Sega Dance — A87

1977, Jan. 20   Litho.   Perf. 13
432 A87 1r multicolored   .50   .50
2nd World Black and African Festival, Lagos, Nigeria, Jan. 15-Feb. 12.

Elizabeth II at Mauritius Legislative Assembly — A88

Designs: 75c, Queen holding scepter and orb. 5r, Presentation of scepter and orb.

1977, Feb. 7   Perf. 14½x14
433 A88 50c multicolored   .25   .25
434 A88 75c multicolored   .25   .25
435 A88 5r multicolored   .75   .75
   Nos. 433-435 (3)   1.25   1.25
25th anniv. of the reign of Elizabeth II.

Hugonia Tomentosa A89

Flowers: 1r, Oehna mauritiana, vert. 1.50r, Dombeya acuntangula. 5r, Trochetia blackburniana, vert.

1977, Sept. 22   Wmk. 373   Perf. 14
436 A89 20c multicolored   .25   .25
437 A89 1r multicolored   .40   .40
438 A89 1.50r multicolored   .60   .60
439 A89 5r multicolored   1.75   1.75
  a. Souvenir sheet of 4, #436-439   5.00   5.00
   Nos. 436-439 (4)   3.00   3.00

Twin Otter of Air Mauritius — A90

Designs: 50c, Air Mauritius emblem (red tailed tropic bird) and Twin Otter. 75c, Piper Navajo and Boeing 747. 5r, Air Mauritius Boeing 707 in flight.

1977, Oct. 31   Litho.   Perf. 14½
440 A90 25c multicolored   .55   .55
441 A90 50c multicolored   .85   .85
442 A90 75c multicolored   .95   .95

MAURITIUS

443	A90	5r multicolored	5.00	5.00
a.		Souvenir sheet of 4, #440-443	12.00	12.00
		Nos. 440-443 (4)	7.35	7.35

Air Mauritius International Inaugural Flight.

Mauritius, Portuguese Map, 1519 — A91

Dutch Occupation, 1638-1710 — A92

Designs: 20c, Mauritius, map by Van Keulen, c. 1700. 25c, 1st settlement of Rodrigues, 1708. 35c, Proclamation, arrival of French settlers, 1715. 50c, Construction of Port Louis, c. 1736. 60c, Pierre Poivre and nutmeg tree. 70c, Map by Belin, 1763. 75c, First coin minted in Mauritius, 1810. 90c, Naval battle of Grand Port, 1810. 1r, Landing of the British, Nov. 1810. 1.20r, Government House, c. 1840. 1.25r, Invitation with No. 1 and ball of Lady Gomm, 1847. 1.50r, Indian immigration in Mauritius, 1835. 2r, Champ de Mars race course, c. 1870. 3r, Place D'Armes, c. 1880. 5r, Postal card commemorating visit of Prince and Princess of Wales, 1901. 10r, Curepipe College, 1914. 15r, Raising flag of Mauritius, 1968. 25r, Raman Osman, first Governor General and Seewoosagur Ramgoolan, first Prime Minister.

1978, Mar. 12 Wmk. 373 Perf. 13½

444	A91	10c multicolored	.25	.25
a.		Wmk. 373. perf. 13½, dated "1985"	—	—
445	A92	15c multicolored	.25	.25
446	A92	20c multicolored	.25	.25
a.		Wmk. 384, perf. 14½, dated "1987"	.65	.65
447	A91	25c multicolored	.25	.25
a.		Wmk. 384, perf. 14½, dated "1987"	.65	.65
b.		Wmk. 373, perf. 13 ½, dated "1985"	—	—
448	A91	35c multicolored	.25	.25
a.		Wmk. 384, perf. 14½, dated "1986"	.65	.65
b.		Wmk. 373, perf. 13½, dated "1983"	8.00	8.00
c.		Wmk. 373, perf. 13½, dated "1985"	8.00	8.00
449	A92	50c multicolored	.25	.25
a.		Wmk. 373, perf. 13½, dated "1985"	.65	.65
b.		Wmk. 384, perf. 14½, dated "1989"	.65	.65
450	A91	60c multicolored	.35	.35
451	A92	70c multicolored	.40	.35
452	A92	75c multicolored	.40	.40
a.		Wmk. 373, perf. 13½, dated "1983"	—	—
b.		Wmk. 373, perf. 13½, dated "1985"	—	—
453	A92	90c multicolored	.40	.40
454	A92	1r multicolored	.40	.40
a.		Wmk. 373, perf. 13½, dated "1985"	—	—
455	A92	1.20r multicolored	.40	.40
456	A91	1.25r multicolored	.40	.40
a.		Wmk. 373, perf. 13½, dated "1983"	—	—
b.		Wmk. 373, perf. 13½, dated "1985"	—	—
457	A92	1.50r multicolored	.50	.60
458	A92	2r multicolored	.70	.80
a.		Wmk. 384, perf. 14½, dated "1987"	.65	.65
b.		Wmk. 384, perf. 14½, dated "1989"	—	—
c.		Wmk. 373, perf. 13½, dated "1983"	—	—
d.		Wmk. 373, perf. 13½, dated "1985"	—	—
459	A92	3r multicolored	1.00	1.25
a.		Wmk. 384, perf. 14½, dated "1989"	1.05	1.05
460	A92	5r multicolored	1.75	2.00
a.		Wmk. 384, perf. 14½, dated "1989"	1.75	1.75
b.		Wmk. 373, perf. 13½, dated "1985"	—	—
461	A92	10r multicolored	3.50	4.00
462	A91	15r multicolored	4.75	6.00
463	A92	25r multicolored	8.00	9.75
a.		Wmk. 384, perf. 14½, dated "1989"	9.00	9.00
		Nos. 444-463 (20)	24.45	28.60

Issued: Nos. 446a, 447a, 458a, 1/11/87; Nos. 459a, 460a, 463a, 1/19/89.

Elizabeth II Coronation Anniv. Issue
Common Design Types
Souvenir Sheet

1978, Apr. 21 Unwmk. Perf. 15

464		Sheet of 6	2.10	2.10
a.		CD326 3r Antelope of Bohun	.25	.25
b.		CD327 3r Elizabeth II	.25	.25
c.		CD328 3r Dodo	.25	.25

No. 464 contains 2 se-tenant strips of Nos. 464a-464c, separated by horizontal gutter with commemorative and descriptive inscriptions and showing central part of coronation procession with coach.

Dr. Fleming, WWI Casualty, Bacteria — A93

1r, Microscope & 1st mold growth, 1928. 1.50r, Penicillium notatum, close-up. 5r, Alexander Fleming & nurse administering penicillin.

Wmk. 373
1978, Aug. 3 Litho. Perf. 13½

465	A93	20c multicolored	.70	.70
466	A93	1r multicolored	1.40	1.40
467	A93	1.50r multicolored	2.40	2.40
468	A93	5r multicolored	3.25	3.25
a.		Souvenir sheet of 4, #465-468	11.00	11.00
		Nos. 465-468 (4)	7.75	7.75

Discovery of penicillin by Dr. Alexander Fleming, 50th anniversary.

Citrus Butterfly A94

Wildlife Protection (Wildlife Fund Emblem and): 1r, Geckos. 1.50r, Flying foxes. 5r, Mauritius kestrels.

1978, Sept. 21 Perf. 13½x14

469	A94	20c multicolored	3.25	3.25
470	A94	1r multicolored	3.00	3.00
471	A94	1.50r multicolored	3.00	3.00
472	A94	5r multicolored	15.00	15.00
a.		Souvenir sheet of 4, #469-472	100.00	80.00
		Nos. 469-472 (4)	24.25	24.25

Le Reduit — A95

1978, Dec. 21 Perf. 14½x14

473	A95	15c multicolored	.25	.25
474	A95	75c multicolored	.25	.25
475	A95	6r multicolored	.75	.75
		Nos. 473-475 (3)	1.25	1.25

Reconstruction of Chateau Le Reduit, 200th anniversary.

Whitcomb, 1949 — A96

Locomotives: 1r, Sir William, 1922. 1.50r, Kitson, 1930. 2r, Garratt, 1927.

1979, Feb. 1 Perf. 14½

476	A96	20c multicolored	.25	.25
477	A96	1r multicolored	.45	.45
478	A96	1.50r multicolored	.90	.90
479	A96	2r multicolored	1.15	1.15
a.		Souvenir sheet of 4, #476-479	5.00	5.00
		Nos. 476-479 (4)	2.75	2.75

Father Laval and Crucifix — A97

Designs: 1.50r, Jacques Desire Laval. 5r, Father Laval's sarcophagus, horiz.

1979, Apr. 30 Wmk. 373 Perf. 14

480	A97	20c multicolored	.25	.25
481	A97	1.50r multicolored	.30	.30
482	A97	5r multicolored	.95	.95
a.		Souvenir sheet of 3, #480-482	3.75	3.75
		Nos. 480-482 (3)	1.50	1.50

Beatification of Father Laval (1803-1864), physician and missionary.

Souvenir Booklet

10th Anniv. of Apollo 11 Moon Landing A98

Imperf. x Roulette 5
1979, July 20 Litho.
Self-adhesive

483	A98	Booklet of 9	10.00	
a.		20c Astronaut and Lunar Module	.20	
b.		3r Buzz Aldrin erecting solar wind experiment	.90	
c.		5r Astronaut walking on moon	3.75	
d.		Bklt. pane of 3 (20c, 5r, 3r)	5.00	
e.		Bklt. pane of 6 (3 each 20c, 3r)	3.50	

No. 483 contains 2 panes printed on peelable paper backing showing map of moon (d) and details of uniform and spacecraft (e).

Rowland Hill and Great Britain No. 23 — A99

Rowland Hill and: 2r, Mauritius No. 261. 3r, Mauritius No. 2. 5r, Mauritius No. 1.

1979, Aug. 29 Perf. 14½

484	A99	25c multicolored	.25	.25
485	A99	2r multicolored	.55	.55
486	A99	5r multicolored	1.40	1.40
		Nos. 484-486 (3)	2.20	2.20

Souvenir Sheet
Perf. 14½

487	A99	3r multicolored	2.00	2.00

Sir Rowland Hill (1795-1879), originator of penny postage. No. 487 contains one stamp.

Infant Vaccination A100

IYC Emblem and: 25c, Children playing. 1r, Coat of arms, vert. 1.50r, Children in laboratory. 3r, Teacher and student working lathe.

Wmk. 373
1979, Oct. 11 Litho. Perf. 14

488	A100	15c multicolored	.25	.25
489	A100	25c multicolored	.25	.25
490	A100	1r multicolored	.25	.25
491	A100	1.50r multicolored	.35	.35
492	A100	3r multicolored	.70	.70
		Nos. 488-492 (5)	1.80	1.80

International Year of the Child.

Lienard Obelisk — A101

Designs: 25c, Poivre Avenue, 1r, Pandanus. 2r, Giant water lilies, 5r, Mon Plaisir.

1980, Jan. 24 Perf. 14x14½

493	A101	20c multicolored	.25	.25
494	A101	25c multicolored	.25	.25
495	A101	1r multicolored	.25	.25
496	A101	2r multicolored	.45	.45
497	A101	5r multicolored	1.05	1.05
a.		Souvenir sheet of 5, #493-497	4.25	4.25
		Nos. 493-497 (5)	2.25	2.25

Pamplemousses Botanical Gardens.

"Emirne," 19th Century, London 1980 Emblem A102

1r, Boissevain, 1930's. 2r, La Boudeuse, 18th cent. 5r, Sea Breeze, 19th cent.

1980, May 6 Litho. Perf. 14½

498	A102	25c shown	.25	.25
499	A102	1r multi	.50	.50
500	A102	2r multi	1.00	1.00
501	A102	5r multi	2.25	2.25
		Nos. 498-501 (4)	4.00	4.00

London 80 Intl. Stamp Exhib., May 6-14.

Helen Keller Reading Braille — A103

25c, Blind men weaving baskets. 1r, Teacher and deaf girl. 5r, Keller graduating college.

1980, June 27 Litho. Perf. 14½

502	A103	25c multicolored	.25	.25
503	A103	1r multicolored	.50	.50
504	A103	2.50r shown	1.25	1.25
505	A103	5r multicolored	1.75	1.75
		Nos. 502-505 (4)	3.75	3.75

Helen Keller (1880-1968), blind and deaf writer and lecturer.

Prime Minister Seewoosagur Ramgoolan, 80th Birthday — A104

Litho.; Gold Embossed
1980, Sept. 18 Perf. 13½

506	A104	15r multicolored	1.75	1.75

Mauritius Institute, Centenary A105

2r, Rare Veda copy. 2.50r, Rare cone. 5r, Landscape, by Henri Harpignies.

1980, Oct. 1 Litho. Perf. 13

507	A105	25c shown	.25	.25
508	A105	2r multicolored	.50	.50
509	A105	2.50r multicolored	.60	.60
510	A105	5r multicolored	1.25	1.25
		Nos. 507-510 (4)	2.60	2.60

Hibiscus Liliiflorus — A106

2r, Erythrospermum monticolum. 2.50r, Chasalia boryana. 5r, Hibiscus columnaris.

1981, Jan. 15 Litho. Perf. 14

511	A106	25c shown	.25	.25
512	A106	2r multicolored	.70	.70
513	A106	2.50r multicolored	.90	.90
514	A106	5r multicolored	1.75	1.75
		Nos. 511-514 (4)	3.60	3.60

MAURITIUS

Arms of Curepipe — A107

City coats of arms: 25c, Beau-Bassin / Rose Hill. 2r, Quatre-Bornes. 2.50r, Vacoas / Phoenix. 5r, Port Louis.

			Perf. 13½x13		
1981, Apr. 10		Litho.	Wmk. 373		
515	A107	25c multicolored		.25	.25
516	A107	1.50r shown		.25	.25
517	A107	2r multicolored		.25	.25
518	A107	2r multicolored		.35	.35
519	A107	5r multicolored		.65	.65
a.	Souv. sheet of 5, #515-519, perf. 14			2.90	2.90
	Nos. 515-519 (5)			1.75	1.75

Royal Wedding Issue
Common Design Type

1981, July 22		Litho.	Perf. 14		
520	CD331	25c Bouquet		.25	.25
521	CD331	2.50r Charles		.40	.40
522	CD331	10r Couple		1.50	1.50
	Nos. 520-522 (3)			2.15	2.15

Emmanuel Anquetil and Guy Rozemont A108

Famous Men: 25c, Remy Ollier, Sookdeo Bissoondoyal. 1.25r, Maurice Cure, Barthelemy Ohsan. 1.50r, Guy Forget, Renganaden Seeneevassen. 2r, Abdul Razak Mohamed, Jules Koenig. 2.50r, Abdoollatiff Mahomed Osman, Dazzi Rama. 5r, Thomas Lewis.

1981, Aug. 13			Perf. 14½		
523	A108	20c black & red		.25	.25
524	A108	25c black & yellow		.25	.25
525	A108	1.25r black & green		.35	.35
526	A108	1.50r black & vermilion		.40	.40
527	A108	2r black & ultra		.55	.55
528	A108	2.50r black & red brn		.65	.65
529	A108	5r black & blue grn		1.40	1.40
	Nos. 523-529 (7)			3.85	3.85

Chinese Pagoda — A109

20c, Tamil Women. 2r, Swami Sivananda, vert.

1981, Sept. 16			Perf. 13½		
530	A109	20c multicolored		.25	.25
531	A109	2r multicolored		.75	.75
532	A109	5r shown		2.00	2.00
	Nos. 530-532 (3)			3.00	3.00

World Tamil Culture Conférence, 1980 (20c).

A110

25c, Pottery making. 1.25r, Dog grooming. 5r, Hiking. 10r, Duke of Edinburgh.

1981, Oct. 26		Litho.	Perf. 14		
533	A110	25c multicolored		.25	.25
534	A110	1.25r multicolored		.25	.25
535	A110	5r multicolored		.45	.45
536	A110	10r multicolored		.85	.85
	Nos. 533-536 (4)			1.80	1.80

Duke of Edinburgh's Awards, 25th anniv.

Hegira, 1,500th Anniv. — A111

25c, Holy Ka'aba, Mecca. 2r, Prophet's Mosque. 5r, Holy Ka'aba, Prophet's Mosque.

1981, Nov. 26		Wmk. 373	Perf. 14½		
537	A111	25c multicolored		.30	.30
538	A111	2r multicolored		.80	.80
539	A111	5r multicolored		1.90	1.90
	Nos. 537-539 (3)			3.00	3.00

Scouting Year — A112

1982, Feb. 25		Litho.	Perf. 14x14½		
540	A112	25c Emblem		.25	.25
541	A112	2r Baden-Powell		.60	.60
542	A112	5r Grand howl, sign		1.35	1.35
543	A112	10r Scouts, mountain		2.60	2.60
	Nos. 540-543 (4)			4.80	4.80

Darwin Death Centenary A113

1982, Apr. 19		Litho.	Perf. 14		
544	A113	25c Portrait		.30	.30
545	A113	2r Telescope		.55	.55
546	A113	2.50r Riding elephant		.65	.65
547	A113	10r The Beagle		2.60	2.60
	Nos. 544-547 (4)			4.10	4.10

Princess Diana Issue
Common Design Type

1982, July 1		Litho.	Perf. 13		
548	CD333	25c Arms		.25	.25
549	CD333	2.50r Diana		.70	.70
550	CD333	5r Wedding		1.30	1.30
551	CD333	10r Portrait		2.75	2.75
	Nos. 548-551 (4)			5.00	5.00

Birth of Prince William of Wales, June 21 — A114

1982, Sept. 22		Litho.	Perf. 14½		
552	A114	2.50r multicolored		1.00	1.00

Issued in sheets of 9.

TB Bacillus Centenary — A115

25c, Aphloia theiformis. 1.25r, Central Market, Port Louis. 2r, Gaertnera psychotrioides. 5r, Selaginella deliquescens. 10r, Koch.

1982, Dec. 15			Perf. 14		
553	A115	25c multicolored		.30	.30
554	A115	1.25r multicolored		.60	.60
555	A115	2r multicolored		.90	.90
556	A115	5r multicolored		1.35	1.35
557	A115	10r multicolored		4.00	4.00
	Nos. 553-557 (5)			7.15	7.15

100th Anniversary of Robert Koch's Discovery of Tubercle Bacillus.

A116

25c, Flag, arms. 2.50r, Satellite view. 5r, Sugar cane harvest. 10r, Port Louis Harbor.

1983, Mar. 14			Perf. 13x13½		
558	A116	25c multi		.25	.25
559	A116	2.50r multi		.35	.35
560	A116	5r multi		.75	.75
561	A116	10r multi		1.40	1.40
	Nos. 558-561 (4)			2.75	2.75

Commonwealth Day.

World Communications Year — A117

25c, Antique telephone, vert. 1.25r, Early telegraph apparatus. 2r, Earth satellite station, vert. 10r, 1st hot air balloon in Mauritius, 1784.

1983, June 24		Wmk. 373	Perf. 14		
562	A117	25c multi		.25	.25
563	A117	1.25r multi		.35	.35
564	A117	2r multi		.50	.50
565	A117	10r multi		2.40	2.40
	Nos. 562-565 (4)			3.50	3.50

Namibia Day — A118

25c, Map. 2.50r, Breaking chains. 5r, Family, village. 10r, Diamond mining.

1983, Aug. 26					
566	A118	25c multi		.65	.65
567	A118	2.50r multi		1.50	1.50
568	A118	5r multi		3.00	3.00
569	A118	10r multi		5.50	5.50
	Nos. 566-569 (4)			10.65	10.65

Fishery Resources A119

1983, Oct. 7					
570	A119	25c Fish trap, vert.		.25	.25
571	A119	1r Fishermen in boat		.35	.35
572	A119	5r Game fishing, vert.		1.50	1.50
573	A119	10r Octopus drying		3.50	3.50
	Nos. 570-573 (4)			5.60	5.60

Swami Dayananda, Death Centenary — A120

35c, Last meeting with father. 2r, Receiving instruction. 5r, Demonstrating strength. 10r, Religious gathering.

1983, Nov. 3		Litho.	Wmk. 373		
574	A120	25c shown		.25	.25
575	A120	25c multi		.25	.25
576	A120	2r multi		.30	.30
577	A120	5r multi		.75	.75
578	A120	10r multi		1.60	1.60
	Nos. 574-578 (5)			3.15	3.15

Adolf von Plevitz (1837-1893), Social Reformer — A121

1.25r, Government school. 5r, Addressing Commission of Enquiry. 10r, Indian field workers.

1983, Dec. 8					
579	A121	25c shown		.30	.30
580	A121	1.25r multi		.60	.60
581	A121	5r multi		1.10	1.10
582	A121	10r multi		2.25	2.25
	Nos. 579-582 (4)			4.25	4.25

Mauritius Kestrels — A122

25c, Courtship chase. 2r, Side view, vert. 2.50r, Fledgling. 10r, Bird, diff., vert.

1984, Mar. 26		Wmk. 373	Perf. 14		
583	A122	25c multi		.40	.40
584	A122	2r multi		2.25	2.25
585	A122	2.50r multi		2.60	2.60
586	A122	10r multi		11.50	11.50
	Nos. 583-586 (4)			16.75	16.75

Lloyd's List Issue
Common Design Type

25c, Tayeb, Port Lewis. 1r, Taher. 5r, East Indiaman Triton. 10r, Astor.

1984, May 23		Litho.	Perf. 14½x14		
587	CD335	25c multi		.40	.40
588	CD335	1r multi		.75	.75
589	CD335	5r multi		2.50	2.50
590	CD335	10r multi		5.75	5.75
	Nos. 587-590 (4)			9.40	9.40

Palm Trees — A123

25c, Blue latan. 50c, Hyophorbe vaughanii. 2.50r, Tectiphiala ferox. 5r, Round Isld. bottle-palm. 10r, Hyophorbe amaricaulis.

1984, July 23		Litho.	Perf. 14		
591	A123	25c multi		.30	.30
592	A123	50c multi		.30	.30
593	A123	2.50r multi		1.20	1.20
594	A123	5r multi		2.40	2.40
595	A123	10r multi		5.00	5.00
	Nos. 591-595 (5)			9.20	9.20

Slave Sale A124

25c, Woman. 2r, Family, horiz. 10r, Immigrant arrival, horiz.

1984, Aug.			Perf. 14½		
596	A124	25c brn ochre & brn pur		.30	.30
597	A124	1r ochre & brn pur		.90	.90
598	A124	2r mar & brn pur		1.40	1.40
599	A124	10r brown purple		7.00	7.00
	Nos. 596-599 (4)			9.60	9.60

Alliance Francaise Centenary A125

25c, Production of Faust, 1959. 1.25r, Award ceremony. 5r, Headquarters. 10r, Lion Mountain.

1984, Sept. 10			Perf. 14½		
600	A125	25c multi		.25	.25
601	A125	1.25r multi		.65	.65
602	A125	5r multi		2.25	2.25
603	A125	10r multi		4.75	4.75
	Nos. 600-603 (4)			7.90	7.90

Queen Mother 85th Birthday
Common Design Type

25c, Portrait, 1926. 2r, With Princess Margaret. 5r, On Clarence House balcony. 10r, Holding Prince Henry.

15r, On Royal Barge, reopening Stratford Canal, 1964.

MAURITIUS

Perf. 14½x14
1985, June 7   **Wmk. 384**
604	CD336	25c multi	.25	.25
605	CD336	2r multi	.55	.55
606	CD336	5r multi	1.50	1.50
607	CD336	10r multi	2.75	2.75
	Nos. 604-607 (4)		5.05	5.05

Souvenir Sheet
| 608 | CD336 | 15r multi | 6.25 | 6.25 |

2nd Annual Indian Ocean Islands Games — A126

1985, Aug. 24   **Wmk. 373**   **Perf. 14½**
609	A126	25c High jump	.40	.40
610	A126	50c Javelin	.80	.80
611	A126	1.25r Cycling	5.00	5.00
612	A126	10r Wind surfing	8.75	8.75
	Nos. 609-612 (4)		14.95	14.95

Pink Pigeon — A127

25c, Adult and young. 2r, Nest site display. 2.50r, Nesting. 5r, Preening.

1985, Sept. 2   **Wmk. 384**   **Perf. 14**
613	A127	25c multi	6.25	1.25
614	A127	2r multi	11.00	2.75
615	A127	2.50r multi	12.50	4.25
616	A127	5r multi	20.00	6.00
	Nos. 613-616 (4)		49.75	14.25

World Wildlife Fund.

World Tourism Org., 10th Anniv. — A128

25c, Patates Caverns. 35c, Colored Earth, Chamarel. 5r, Serpent Island. 10r, Coin de Mire Island.

1985, Sept. 20   **Perf. 14½**
617	A128	25c multi	.60	.60
618	A128	35c multi	.60	.60
619	A128	5r multi	2.75	2.75
620	A128	10r multi	10.00	10.00
	Nos. 617-620 (4)		13.95	13.95

Port Louis, 250th Anniv. — A129

25c, Old Town Hall. 1r, Al-Aqsa Mosque. 2.50r, Tamil-speaking Indians, settlement. 10r, Port Louis Harbor.

1985, Nov. 22   **Perf. 13½**
621	A129	25c multi	.30	.30
622	A129	1r multi	.90	.90
623	A129	2.50r multi	1.75	1.75
624	A129	10r multi	6.50	6.50
	Nos. 621-624 (4)		9.45	9.45

Halley's Comet — A130

25c, Halley, map. 1.25r, Newton's telescope, 1682 sighting. 3r, Mauritius from space. 10r, Giotto space probe.

1986, Feb. 21   **Wmk. 384**   **Perf. 14**
625	A130	25c multi	.55	.55
626	A130	1.25r multi	.75	.75
627	A130	3r multi	1.50	1.50
628	A130	10r multi	5.00	5.00
	Nos. 625-628 (4)		7.80	7.80

Queen Elizabeth II 60th Birthday
Common Design Type

Designs: 25c, In uniform, Grenadier Guards, 1942. 75c, Investiture of the Prince of Wales, 1969. 2r, State visit with Prince Philip. 3r, State visit to Germany, 1978. 15r, Visiting Crown Agents' offices, 1983.

1986, Apr. 21   **Litho.**   **Perf. 14½x14**
629	CD337	25c scar, black & sil	.25	.25
630	CD337	75c ultra & multi	.25	.25
631	CD337	2r green & multi	.40	.40
632	CD337	3r violet & multi	.50	.50
633	CD337	15r rose vio & multi	2.10	2.10
	Nos. 629-633 (5)		3.50	3.50

Intl. Events — A131

Designs: 25c, World Food Day, FAO emblem, corn. 1r, African Regional Industrial Property Organization, 10th anniv., ARIPO emblem. 1.25r, Intl. Peace Year, IPY emblem. 10r, 1986 World Cup Soccer Championships, Athlete, MFA.

1986, July 25   **Litho.**   **Perf. 14**
634	A131	25c multi	.30	.30
635	A131	1r multi	.65	.65
636	A131	1.25r multi	.90	.90
637	A131	10r multi	6.75	6.75
	Nos. 634-637 (4)		8.60	8.60

Orchids — A132

25c, Cryptopus elatus. 2r, Jumellea recta. 2.50r, Angraecum mauritianum. 10r, Bulbophyllum longiflorum.

1986, Oct. 3   **Litho.**   **Perf. 14½**
638	A132	25c multi	.60	.60
639	A132	2r multi	1.00	1.00
640	A132	2.50r multi	1.60	1.60
641	A132	10r multi	6.00	6.00
	Nos. 638-641 (4)		9.20	9.20

Bridges — A133

25c, Hesketh Bell. 50c, Sir Colville Deverell. 2.50r, Cavendish. 5r, Tamarin. 10r, Grand River North West.

1987, May 22   **Wmk. 373**
642	A133	25c multi	.25	.25
643	A133	50c multi	.60	.60
644	A133	2.50r multi	1.50	1.50
645	A133	5r multi	3.00	3.00
646	A133	10r multi	6.00	6.00
	Nos. 642-646 (5)		11.35	11.35

The Bar, Bicent. — A134

25c, Port Louis Supreme Court. 1r, Flacq District Court. 1.25r, Statue of Justice. 10r, Barristers, 1787-1987.

Perf. 14x14½
1987, June 2   **Wmk. 384**
647	A134	25c multi	.25	.25
648	A134	1r multi	.50	.50
649	A134	1.25r multi	.50	.50
650	A134	10r multi	3.00	3.00
	Nos. 647-650 (4)		4.25	4.25

Intl. Festival of the Sea — A135

25c, Dodo mascot, vert. 1.50r, Sailboats. 3r, Water-skier. 5r, Tall ship Svanen, vert.

1987, Sept. 5   **Wmk. 373**
651	A135	25c multi	.85	.85
652	A135	1.50r multi	1.90	1.90
653	A135	3r multi	3.25	3.25
654	A135	5r multi	5.25	5.25
	Nos. 651-654 (4)		11.25	11.25

Industrialization A136

1987, Oct. 30   **Perf. 14**
655	A136	20c Toy	.30	.30
656	A136	35c Spinning	.30	.30
657	A136	50c Rattan	.30	.30
658	A136	2.50r Optical	.95	.95
659	A136	10r Stone carving	3.25	3.25
	Nos. 655-659 (5)		5.10	5.10

Art & Architecture A137

Designs: 25c, Maison Ouvriere, Intl. Year of Shelter for the Homeless emblem. 1r, Paul et Virginie, a lithograph. 1.25r, Chateau Rosney. 2r, Old Farmhouse, Boulle. 5r, Three Peaks, watercolor.

1988, June 29   **Wmk. 384**   **Perf. 14½**
660	A137	25c multicolored	.25	.25
661	A137	1r gray & black	.40	.40
662	A137	1.25r multicolored	.45	.45
663	A137	2r multicolored	.55	.55
664	A137	5r multicolored	1.45	1.45
	Nos. 660-664 (5)		3.10	3.10

Natl. Independence, 20th Anniv. — A138

Designs: 25c, University of Mauritius. 75c, Calisthenics at sunset in stadium. 2.50r, Runners, Sir Maurice Rault Stadium. 5r, Air Mauritius jet at gate, Sir Seewoosagur Ramgoolam Intl. Airport. 10r, Gov.-Gen. Veerasamy Ringadoo and Prime Minister Aneerood Jugnauth.

1988, Mar. 11   **Wmk. 373**   **Perf. 14**
665	A138	25c multicolored	.25	.25
666	A138	75c multicolored	.25	.25
667	A138	2.50r multicolored	.90	.90
668	A138	5r multicolored	1.60	1.60
669	A138	10r multicolored	3.25	3.25
	Nos. 665-669 (5)		6.25	6.25

WHO, 40th Anniv. — A139

1988, July 1   **Wmk. 373**   **Perf. 13½**
670	A139	20c Breast-feeding	.30	.30
671	A139	2r Immunization	.90	.90
672	A139	3r Nutrition	1.75	1.75
673	A139	10r Emblem	5.00	5.00
	Nos. 670-673 (4)		7.95	7.95

Mauritius Commercial Bank, Ltd., 150th Anniv. — A140

25c, Bank, 1981, vert. 1r, Bank, 1897. 1.25r, Coat of arms, vert. 25r, 15-Dollar bank note, 1838.

1988, Sept. 1   **Wmk. 373**   **Perf. 14**
674	A140	25c multi	.30	.30
675	A140	1r multi	.40	.40
676	A140	1.25r multi	.50	.50
677	A140	25r multi	7.50	7.50
	Nos. 674-677 (4)		8.70	8.70

1988 Summer Olympics, Seoul — A141

1988, Oct. 1
678	A141	25c shown	.25	.25
679	A141	35c Wrestling	.35	.35
680	A141	1.50r Running	.65	.65
681	A141	10r Swimming	4.00	4.00
	Nos. 678-681 (4)		5.25	5.25

Environmental Protection A142

15c, Tropical reef. 30c, Greenshank. 50c, Round Island, vert. 75c, Bassin Blanc. 1r, Mangrove, vert. 1.50r, Whimbrel. 2r, Le Morne. 3r, Fish. 4r, Fern tree, vert. 5r, Riviere du Poste Estuary. 6r, Ecological scenery, vert. 10r, Phelsuma ornata, vert. 15r, Benares surf. 25r, Migratory birds, vert.

Wmk. 384 (20c, 40c, 50c, 1r, 10r), 373 (Others)
1989-97   **Litho.**   **Perf. 14**
682	A142	15c multi	.45	.45
a.		Dated "1994"	1.00	1.00
b.		Dated "1995"	3.00	3.00
683	A142	20c like #682	.45	.45
684	A142	30c multi	.45	.45
a.		Wmk. 384	.45	.45
b.		As No. 684, dated "1995"	3.00	3.00
685	A142	40c shown	.45	.45
a.		Wmk. 373	3.00	3.00
b.		As a, dated "1994	1.60	1.60
c.		As a, dated "1997	3.25	3.25
686	A142	50c multi	.45	.45
687	A142	60c like #686	.45	.45
a.		Dated "1997"	1.60	1.60
688	A142	75c multi	.45	.45
689	A142	1r multi	.45	.45
a.		Dated "1998"	2.10	2.10
690	A142	1.50r multi	.50	.50
691	A142	2r multi	.50	.50
692	A142	3r multi	.95	.95
693	A142	4r multi	1.25	1.25
a.		Dated "1994"	1.60	1.60
b.		Dated "1998"	3.00	3.00
694	A142	5r multi	1.25	1.25
a.		Dated "1998"	3.00	3.00
695	A142	6r multi	1.90	1.90
a.		Dated "1998"	3.00	3.00
696	A142	10r multi	3.00	3.00
a.		Wmk. 373 ('97)	3.00	3.00
b.		As a, dated "1995"	3.00	3.00
c.		As a, dated "1997"	3.00	3.00
d.		As a, dated "1998"	3.00	3.00
697	A142	15r multi	4.00	4.00
a.		Wmk. 384	4.00	4.00
b.		As No. 697, dated "1998"	4.00	4.00
698	A142	25r multi	6.75	6.75
a.		Wmk. 384 ('96)	10.50	10.50
b.		As a, dated "1997"	10.50	10.50
c.		As No. 698, dated "1998"	10.50	10.50
	Nos. 682-698 (17)		23.70	23.70

Issued: 40c, 3r-10r, 3/11/89; No. 685a, 2/19/91; 50c, 75c, 2r, 5r, 15r, 10/4/91; 20c, 60c, 3/96; others, 11/22/90.

For surcharge see No. 781.

A143

French Revolution, Bicent.: 30c, La Tour Sumeire, Place Du Theatre Municipal. 1r, Salle De Spectacle Du Jardin. 8r, Le Comte De Malartic. 15r, Anniv. emblem.

1989, July 14   **Wmk. 373**
702	A143	30c multicolored	.25	.25
703	A143	1r multicolored	.25	.25
704	A143	8r multicolored	2.25	2.25
705	A143	15r multicolored	4.50	4.50
	Nos. 702-705 (4)		7.25	7.25

A144

Visit of Pope John Paul II: 30c, Cardinal Jean Margeot. 40c, Pope welcoming Prime

MAURITIUS

Minister Aneerood Jugnauth to the Vatican, 1988. 3r, Mother Mary Magdalene of the Cross (1810-1889) and Filles des Marie Chapel, Port Louis, 1864. 6r, St. Francis of Assisi Church, 1756, Pamplemousses. 10r, Pope John Paul II.

1989, Oct. 13 — Perf. 14x13½
706	A144	30c multicolored	.30	.30
707	A144	40c multicolored	1.00	1.00
708	A144	3r multicolored	2.00	2.00
709	A144	6r multicolored	4.25	4.25
710	A144	10r multicolored	6.75	6.75
	Nos. 706-710 (5)		14.30	14.30

Jawaharlal Nehru, 1st Prime Minister of India — A145

Designs: 1.50r, Nehru and Indira, Rajiv and Sanjay Gandhi. 3r, With Mahatma Gandhi. 4r, With Nasser and Tito. 10r, With children.

1989, Oct. 13 — Wmk. 384 — Perf. 14
711	A145	40c shown	1.50	1.50
712	A145	1.50r multicolored	1.75	1.75
713	A145	3r multicolored	3.75	3.75
714	A145	4r multicolored	4.75	4.75
715	A145	10r multicolored	11.00	11.00
	Nos. 711-715 (5)		22.75	22.75

Sugar Cane Industry, 350th Anniv. — A146

30c, Cutting cane. 40c, Refinery, 1867. 1r, Mechanically loading cane. 25r, Modern refinery.

1990, Jan. 10 — Perf. 13½x14 — Litho. — Wmk. 384
716	A146	30c multi	.30	.30
717	A146	40c multi	.30	.30
718	A146	1r multi	.75	.75
719	A146	25r multi	13.00	13.00
	Nos. 716-719 (4)		14.35	14.35

Prime Minister Jugnauth's 60th Birthday — A147

Jugnauth: 35c, And symbols of the industrial estate. 40c, At his desk. 1.50r, And stock exchange emblem. 4r, And Gov.-Gen. Ramgoolam. 10r, And Pope John Paul II, map.

Wmk. 373
1990, Mar. 29 — Litho. — Perf. 14
720	A147	35c multicolored	.50	.50
721	A147	40c multicolored	.50	.50
722	A147	1.50r multicolored	2.10	2.10
723	A147	4r multicolored	4.75	4.75
724	A147	10r multicolored	11.50	11.50
	Nos. 720-724 (5)		19.35	19.35

Mauritian Television, 25th Anniv. — A148

Anniversaries and Events: 30c, Death of Desjardins, naturalist, 150th anniversary, vert. 6r, Line barracks, 250th anniversary, vert. 8r, Municipality of Curepipe, centenary.

1990, July 5
725	A148	30c lt orange & multi	.50	.50
726	A148	35c pink & multi	.50	.50
727	A148	6r lt blue & multi	5.25	5.25
728	A148	8r lt green & multi	6.50	6.50
	Nos. 725-728 (4)		12.75	12.75

Intl. Literacy Year — A149

1r, Blind girl printing braille. 3r, Globe, open book. 10r, Open book, world map.

Wmk. 373
1990, Sept. 28 — Litho. — Perf. 14
729	A149	30c shown	.45	.45
730	A149	1r multi	1.60	1.60
731	A149	3r multi	3.00	3.00
732	A149	10r multi	10.50	10.50
	Nos. 729-732 (4)		15.55	15.55

Elizabeth & Philip, Birthdays
Common Design Types

Wmk. 384
1991, June 17 — Litho. — Perf. 14½
733	CD345	8r multicolored	1.60	1.60
734	CD346	8r multicolored	1.60	1.60
a.	Pair, #733-734 + label		4.00	4.00

Port Louis, City Incorporation, 25th Anniv. — A150

Anniversaries and Events: 4r, Col. Draper, 150th death anniv., vert. 6r, Joseph Barnard, engraver of first Mauritius stamps, 175th birth anniv., vert. 10r, Spitfire, Mauritius' contribution to Allied war effort, 1939-1945.

Wmk. 373
1991, Aug. 18 — Litho. — Perf. 14
735	A150	40c multicolored	.30	.30
736	A150	4r multicolored	2.10	2.10
737	A150	6r multicolored	3.25	3.25
738	A150	10r multicolored	5.25	5.25
	Nos. 735-738 (4)		10.90	10.90

Phila Nippon '91 — A151

Butterflies: 40c, Euploea euphon. 3r, Hypolimnas misippus, female. 8r, Papilio manlius. 10r, Hypolimnas misippus, male.

Perf. 14x14½
1991, Nov. 15 — Litho. — Wmk. 373
739	A151	40c multicolored	.90	.90
740	A151	3r multicolored	2.00	2.00
741	A151	8r multicolored	4.75	4.75
742	A151	10r multicolored	5.50	5.50
	Nos. 739-742 (4)		13.15	13.15

Flora and Fauna From Mauritius A152

Designs: 40c, Chelonia mydas, Tromelin. 1r, Ibis, Agalega. 2r, Takamaka flowers, Chagos Archipelago. 15r, Lambis violacea, St. Brandon.

1991, Dec. 13 — Perf. 14
743	A152	40c multicolored	.75	.75
744	A152	1r multicolored	1.25	1.25
745	A152	2r multicolored	1.60	1.60
746	A152	15r multicolored	9.50	9.50
	Nos. 743-746 (4)		13.10	13.10

Republic

Proclamation of the Republic of Mauritius A153

40c, President. 4r, Prime Minister. 8r, Mauritian children. 10r, President's flag.

1992, Mar. 12
747	A153	40c multi	.40	.40
748	A153	4r multi	1.75	1.75
749	A153	8r multi	4.00	4.00
750	A153	10r multi	4.50	4.50
	Nos. 747-750 (4)		10.65	10.65

8th African Track and Field Championships — A154

Designs: 40c, Games mascot, Tricolo. 4r, Sir Aneroord Jugnauth Stadium, horiz. 5r, High jumper, horiz. 6r, Torch, emblem of games.

1992, June 25 — Perf. 13½
751	A154	40c multicolored	.25	.25
752	A154	4r multicolored	.85	.85
753	A154	5r multicolored	1.25	1.25
754	A154	6r multicolored	1.50	1.50
	Nos. 751-754 (4)		3.85	3.85

Anniversaries and Events — A155

Designs: 40c, Flower, vert. 1r, Swami Krishnanandji Maharaj, vert. 2r, Boy and dog. 3r, Building, flags. 15r, Radio telescope antennae.

1992, Aug. 13
755	A155	40c multicolored	.30	.30
756	A155	1r multicolored	.65	.65
757	A155	2r multicolored	1.00	1.00
758	A155	3r multicolored	1.50	1.50
759	A155	15r multicolored	6.75	6.75
	Nos. 755-759 (5)		10.20	10.20

Fleurir Maurice, 25th anniv. (No. 755). 25th anniv. of Swami Maharaj's arrival (No. 756). Humane education (No. 757). Indian Ocean Commission, 10th anniv. (No. 758). Inauguration of radio telescope project (No. 759).

Bank of Mauritius, Silver Jubilee — A156

Designs: 40c, Bank of Mauritius building, vert. 4r, Dodo gold bullion coin. 8r, First bank note issues. 15r, Foreign exchange reserves 1967-1992.

Perf. 14½x14, 14x14½
1992, Oct. 29 — Litho. — Wmk. 373
760	A156	40c multicolored	.30	.30
761	A156	4r multicolored	1.60	1.60
762	A156	8r multicolored	3.50	3.50
763	A156	15r multicolored	5.75	5.75
	Nos. 760-763 (4)		11.15	11.15

National Day, 25th Anniv. — A157

30c, Housing development. 40c, Computer showing gross domestic product. 3r, Flag in shape of map of Mauritius. 4r, Ballot box. 15r, Medal for Grand Commander of the Order of the Star & Key of the Indian Ocean.

1993, Mar. 12 — Perf. 15x14
764	A157	30c multicolored	.25	.25
765	A157	40c multicolored	.25	.25
766	A157	3r multicolored	.55	.55
767	A157	4r multicolored	.75	.75
768	A157	15r multicolored	2.60	2.60
	Nos. 764-768 (5)		4.40	4.40

Air Mauritius Ltd., 25th Anniv. — A158

40c, Bell 206B Jet Ranger. 3r, Boeing 747SP. 4r, ATR 42. 10r, Boeing 767-200ER.

1993, June 14 — Perf. 14
769	A158	40c multicolored	.95	.95
770	A158	3r multicolored	1.60	1.60
771	A158	4r multicolored	2.25	2.25
772	A158	10r multicolored	5.25	5.25
a.	Souvenir sheet of 4, #769-772		12.50	12.50
	Nos. 769-772 (4)		10.05	10.05

5th Francophone Summit — A159

Designs: 1r, 1715 Act of French Seizure of Mauritius, 1810 Act of Surrender. 5r, Signs. 6r, Page from Napoleonic Code. 7r, French publications.

1993, Oct. 16
773	A159	1r multicolored	.25	.25
774	A159	5r multicolored	3.00	3.00
775	A159	6r multicolored	3.75	3.75
776	A159	7r multicolored	4.25	4.25
	Nos. 773-776 (4)		11.25	11.25

Telecommunications — A160

Designs: 40c, SS Scotia, cable laying. 3r, Morse code, Morse key. 4r, Signal mountain station. 8r, Communications satellite.

1993, Nov. 25 — Perf. 13
777	A160	40c multicolored	.70	.70
778	A160	3r multicolored	1.20	1.20
779	A160	4r multicolored	1.90	1.90
780	A160	8r multicolored	3.75	3.75
	Nos. 777-780 (4)		7.55	7.55

No. 686 Surcharged

1993, Sept. 15 — Litho. — Perf. 14
781	A142	40c on 75c multi	2.50	2.50

Mammals A161

Wmk. 384
1994, Mar. 9 — Litho. — Perf. 14½
782	A161	40c Mongoose	.30	.30
783	A161	2r Hare	1.25	1.25
784	A161	8r Monkey	4.00	4.00
785	A161	10r Tenrec	4.50	4.50
	Nos. 782-785 (4)		10.05	10.05

Anniversaries and Events — A162

40c, Dr. E. Brown-Sequard (1817-94). 4r, Silhouettes of family. 8r, World Cup trophy, US map. 10r, Control Tower, SSR Intl. Airport.

Wmk. 373
1994, June 16 — Litho. — Perf. 14
786	A162	40c multicolored	.30	.30
787	A162	4r multicolored	.85	.85
788	A162	8r multicolored	1.75	1.75
789	A162	10r multicolored	2.10	2.10
	Nos. 786-789 (4)		5.00	5.00

Intl. Year of the Family (No. 787). 1994 World Cup Soccer Championships, US (No. 788). ICAO, 50th anniv. (No. 789).

MAURITIUS

Wreck of the St. Geran, 250th Anniv. — A163

Wmk. 384
1994, Aug. 18   Litho.   Perf. 14
790	A163	40c Leaving L'Orient	.35	.35
791	A163	5r In rough seas	1.40	1.40
792	A163	6r Ship's bell	1.60	1.60
793	A163	10r Relics from ship	2.75	2.75
		Nos. 790-793 (4)	6.10	6.10

Souvenir Sheet
794	A163	15r St. Geran, vert.	9.50	9.50

Children's Paintings of Leisure Activities A164

Designs: 30c, "Ring Around the Rosey." 40c, Playing with balls, jump rope. 8r, Water sports. 10r, "Blindman's Buff."

Wmk. 373
1994, Oct. 25   Litho.   Perf. 13½
795	A164	30c multicolored	.25	.25
796	A164	40c multicolored	.25	.25
797	A164	8r multicolored	1.60	1.60
798	A164	10r multicolored	2.00	2.00
		Nos. 795-798 (4)	4.10	4.10

Spices — A165

Perf. 13x14
1995, Mar. 10   Litho.   Wmk. 373
799	A165	40c Nutmeg	.30	.30
800	A165	4r Coriander	.85	.85
801	A165	5r Cloves	1.25	1.25
802	A165	10r Cardamon	2.40	2.40
		Nos. 799-802 (4)	4.80	4.80

End of World War II
Common Design Type
Designs: No. 803, HMS Mauritius. No. 804, Mauritian servicemen, map of North Africa. No. 805, Catalina, Tombeau Bay.

Wmk. 373
1995, May 8
Size: 35x28mm   Perf. 14
803	CD351	5r multicolored	2.50	2.50
804	CD351	5r multicolored	2.50	2.50
805	CD351	5r multicolored	2.50	2.50
		Nos. 803-805 (3)	7.50	7.50

Anniversaries & Events — A166

1995, May 8
806	A166	40c multicolored	.25	.25
807	A166	4r multicolored	1.50	1.50
808	A166	10r multicolored	3.25	3.25
		Nos. 806-808 (3)	5.00	5.00

Construction of Mare Longue Reservoir, 50th anniv. (No. 806). Construction of Mahebourg-Curepipe Road, bicent. (No. 807). Great fire of Port Louis, cent. (No. 808).

Lighthouses — A167

Designs: 30c, Ile Plate. 40c, Pointe aux Caves. 8r, Ile aux Fouquets. 10r, Pointe aux Canonniers.

Perf. 13x14
1995, Aug. 28   Litho.   Wmk. 373
809	A167	30c multi	.85	.85
810	A167	40c multi	.85	.85
811	A167	8r multi	4.00	4.00
812	A167	10r multi	5.00	5.00
a.		Souvenir sheet of 4, #809-812	13.00	13.00
		Nos. 809-812 (4)	10.70	10.70

UN, 50th Anniv.
Common Design Type
Designs: 40c, Silhouettes of children under UNICEF umbrella. 4r, ILO contruction site. 8r, WMO satellite view of hurricane. 10r, Bread, grain representing FAO.

Wmk. 373
1995, Oct. 24   Litho.   Perf. 14
813	CD353	40c multicolored	.30	.30
814	CD353	4r multicolored	.75	.75
815	CD353	8r multicolored	1.60	1.60
816	CD353	10r multicolored	1.90	1.90
		Nos. 813-816 (4)	4.55	4.55

A168

1995, Dec. 8   Litho.   Perf. 13
817	A168	60c pink & multi	.30	.30
818	A168	4r blue & multi	.65	.65
819	A168	8r yellow & multi	1.60	1.60
820	A168	10r green & multi	1.75	1.75
		Nos. 817-820 (4)	4.30	4.30

Common Market for Eastern and Southern Africa (COMESA).

Snails — A169

Designs: 60c, Pachystyla bicolor. 4r, Gonidomus pagodus. 5r, Harmogenanina implicata. 10r, Tropidophora eugeniae.

Wmk. 373
1996, Mar. 11   Litho.   Perf. 13
821	A169	60c multicolored	.35	.35
822	A169	4r multicolored	1.00	1.00
823	A169	5r multicolored	1.25	1.25
824	A169	10r multicolored	2.50	2.50
		Nos. 821-824 (4)	5.10	5.10

Modern Olympic Games, Cent. — A170

Wmk. 384
1996, June 26   Litho.   Perf. 13½
825	A170	60c Boxing	.30	.30
826	A170	4r Badminton	.75	.75
827	A170	5r Basketball	.95	.95
828	A170	10r Table tennis	2.00	2.00
		Nos. 825-828 (4)	4.00	4.00

Ships — A171

Wmk. 373
1996, Sept. 30   Litho.   Perf. 14
829	A171	60c SS Zambesia	.35	.35
830	A171	4r MV Sir Jules	.90	.90
831	A171	5r MV Mauritius	1.10	1.10
832	A171	10r MS Mauritius Pride	2.25	2.25
a.		Souvenir sheet of 4, #829-832	6.25	6.25
		Nos. 829-832 (4)	4.60	4.60

Post Office Ordinance, 150th Anniv. — A172

60c, Pillar box. 4r, Early handstamp cancel. 5r, Mobile post office. 10r, Carriole.

Wmk. 384
1996, Dec. 2   Litho.   Perf. 13½
833	A172	60c multi	.30	.30
834	A172	4r multi	1.10	1.10
835	A172	5r multi	1.50	1.50
836	A172	10r multi	3.00	3.00
		Nos. 833-836 (4)	5.90	5.90

Fruit — A173

Designs: 60c, Vangueria madagascariensis. 4r, Mimusops coriacea. 5r, Syzgium jambos. 10r, Diospyros digyna.

Perf. 14x13½
1997, Mar. 10   Litho.   Wmk. 373
837	A173	60c multicolored	.25	.25
838	A173	4r multicolored	.55	.55
839	A173	5r multicolored	.70	.70
840	A173	10r multicolored	1.50	1.50
		Nos. 837-840 (4)	3.00	3.00

Anniversaries and Events — A174

Designs: 60c, Ile de France, Mahé de La Bourdonnais. 1r, Exploration, La Perouse. 4r, Lady Gomm's Ball, Sir William Maynard Gomm. 6r, Skeleton of the Dodo, George Clark. 10r, Professor Brian Abel-Smith.

Wmk. 373
1997, June 9   Litho.   Perf. 13½
841	A174	60c multicolored	.70	.70
842	A174	1r multicolored	.70	.70
843	A174	4r multicolored	1.30	1.30
844	A174	6r multicolored	1.90	1.90
845	A174	10r multicolored	3.00	3.00
		Nos. 841-845 (5)	7.60	7.60

First Postage Stamps of Mauritius, 150th Anniv. — A175

Stamps: 60c, #1. 4r, #2. 5r, #2, #1, gold background. 10r, #1, #2, silver background. 20r, #2, #1 on "The Bordeaux Cover."

Wmk. 373
1997, Sept. 22   Litho.   Perf. 13½
846	A175	60c multicolored	.50	.50
847	A175	4r multicolored	1.60	1.60
a.		Sheet of 12, 7 #846, 5 #847	8.25	8.25
848	A175	5r multicolored	1.90	1.90
849	A175	10r multicolored	4.25	4.25
		Nos. 846-849 (4)	8.25	8.25

Souvenir Sheet
850	A175	20r multicolored	7.75	7.75

Booklet Panes and Booklets
846a		Booklet pane of 10	5.00	
		Complete booklet, #846a	5.00	
847b		Booklet pane of 10	16.00	
		Complete booklet, #847b	16.00	
848a		Booklet pane of 10	19.00	
		Complete booklet, #848a	19.00	
849a		Booklet pane of 10	42.50	
		Complete booklet, #849a	42.50	

Local Occupations A176

Wmk. 373
1997, Dec. 1   Litho.   Perf. 14½
851	A176	60c Wheelwright	.50	.50
852	A176	4r Washerman	.85	.85
853	A176	5r Shipwright	1.10	1.10
854	A176	15r Quarryman	3.25	3.25
		Nos. 851-854 (4)	5.70	5.70

Geckos — A177

Designs: 1r, Phelsuma guentheri. 6r, Nactus serpensinula. 7r, Nactus coindemirensis. 8r, Phelsuma edwardnewtonii.

Wmk. 373
1998, Mar. 11   Litho.   Perf. 13½
855	A177	1r multicolored	.45	.45
856	A177	6r multicolored	1.10	1.10
857	A177	7r multicolored	1.25	1.25
858	A177	8r multicolored	1.60	1.60
		Nos. 855-858 (4)	4.40	4.40

Inland Transportation A178

40c, Railroad. 5r, Truck. 6r, Bus, bicycles, cars. 10r, Boat.

Wmk. 373
1998, June 15   Litho.   Perf. 13½
859	A178	40c multi	.60	.60
860	A178	5r multi	1.25	1.25
861	A178	6r multi	1.60	1.60
862	A178	10r multi	2.50	2.50
		Nos. 859-862 (4)	5.95	5.95

Dutch Landing, 400th Anniv. — A179

50c, Maurits van Nassau, landing scene. 1r, Otaheite sugar cane, Frederik Hendrik Fort. 7r, Dutch map, 1670. 8r, Landing fleet. 25r, Ships of landing fleet.

Wmk. 373
1998, Sept. 18   Litho.   Perf. 13½
863	A179	50c multicolored	.40	.40
864	A179	1r multicolored	.40	.40
865	A179	7r multicolored	1.90	1.90
866	A179	8r multicolored	2.50	2.50
		Nos. 863-866 (4)	5.20	5.20

Souvenir Sheet
867	A179	25r multicolored	5.75	5.75

State Visit of South African Pres. Nelson Mandela — A180

1998, Sept. 10   Litho.   Perf. 14
868	A180	25r multicolored	3.75	3.75

Waterfalls A181

1r, Balfour Falls. 5r, Rochester Falls. 6r, GRSE Falls, vert. 10r, 500-Foot Falls, vert.

1998   Litho.   Wmk. 384   Perf. 13½
869	A181	1r multicolored	.55	.55
870	A181	5r multicolored	1.10	1.10
871	A181	6r multicolored	1.50	1.50
872	A181	10r multicolored	2.25	2.25
		Nos. 869-872 (4)	5.40	5.40

Creation of Presidential Residence "Le Réduit," 250th Anniv. — A182

Designs: 1r, Drawing of floor plan, 1823. 4r, Exterior view, by P.A.F. Thuillier, 1814. 5r, "Le Réduit," by Hassen Edun, 1998. 15r, Commemorative monument, 1998.

MAURITIUS

1998	Litho.	Wmk. 373	Perf. 14½
873	A182	1r multicolored	.45 .45
874	A182	4r multicolored	.80 .80
875	A182	5r multicolored	1.00 1.00
876	A182	15r multicolored	2.75 2.75
	Nos. 873-876 (4)		5.00 5.00

Admiral Mahé de la Bourdonnais, 300th Birth Anniv. — A183

Wmk. 373

1999, Feb. 11	Litho.	Perf. 13
877 A183 7r No. 115		1.90 1.90

Native Flowers — A184

Designs: 1r, Clerodendron laciniatum. 2r, Senecio lemarckianus. 5r, Cylindrocline commersonii. 9r, Psiadia pollicina.

1999, Mar. 10		Perf. 13½
878 A184 1r multicolored		.40 .40
879 A184 2r multicolored		.40 .40
880 A184 5r multicolored		.70 .70
881 A184 9r multicolored		1.25 1.25
Nos. 878-881 (4)		2.75 2.75

Paintings A185

Designs: 1r, "The Washerwomen," by Hervé Masson. 3r, "The Casino," by Gaetan de Rosnay. 4r, "The Four Elements," by Andrée Poilly. 6r, "Coming out of Mass," by Xavier Le Juge de Segrais.

1999, June 18		Perf. 14x15
882 A185 1r multicolored		.55 .55
883 A185 3r multicolored		.65 .65
884 A185 4r multicolored		.75 .75
885 A185 6r multicolored		1.20 1.20
Nos. 882-885 (4)		3.15 3.15

Old Sugar Mill Chimneys — A186

Wmk. 384

1999, Sept. 17	Litho.	Perf. 14¼
886 A186 1r Alma		.45 .45
887 A186 2r Antoinette		.65 .65
888 A186 5r Belle Mare		.95 .95
889 A186 7r Grande Rosalie		1.00 1.00
a. Souvenir sheet of 4, #886-889, Wmk. 373		3.25 3.25
Nos. 886-889 (4)		3.05 3.05

Achievements in the 20th Century A187

Designs: 1r, Eradication of malaria. 2r, Emancipation of women. 5r, International Conference Center. 9r, Special sugars.

Perf. 13¼x13

1999, Dec. 7	Litho.	Wmk. 373
890 A187 1r multi		.45 .45
891 A187 2r multi		.70 .70
892 A187 5r multi		1.25 1.25
893 A187 9r multi		2.25 2.25
Nos. 890-893 (4)		4.65 4.65

Chamber of Commerce & Industry, 150th Anniv. — A188

1r, Emblem. 2r, Computer chip. 7r, Francis Channell, 1st sec. 15r, Louis Léchelle, 1st pres.

2000, Jan. 25	Litho.	Perf. 13¼
894 A188 1r multi		.45 .45
895 A188 2r multi		.70 .70
896 A188 7r multi		1.25 1.25
897 A188 15r multi		2.25 2.25
Nos. 894-897 (4)		4.65 4.65

Insects — A189

Designs: 1r, Cratopus striga. 2r, Cratopus armatus. 3r, Cratopus chrysochlorus. 15r, Cratopus nigrogranatus.

Wmk. 373

2000, Mar. 29	Litho.	Perf. 14¼
898 A189 1r multi		.40 .40
899 A189 2r multi		.40 .40
900 A189 3r multi		.50 .50
901 A189 15r multi		2.40 2.40
a. Souvenir sheet of 4, #898-901		4.00 4.00
Nos. 898-901 (4)		3.70 3.70

2000 Summer Olympics, Sydney — A190

Wmk. 373

2000, June 28	Litho.	Perf. 14½
902 A190 1r Handball		.40 .40
903 A190 2r Archery		.60 .60
904 A190 5r Sailing		.80 .80
905 A190 15r Judo		2.40 2.40
Nos. 902-905 (4)		4.20 4.20

Sir Seewoosagur Ramgoolam, Birth Cent. — A191

Designs: 1r, Ramgoolam with Mother Teresa. 2r, As elected member of legislative council, vert. 5r, As student, 1926, vert. 15r, As Prime Minister, 1968, vert.

Perf. 13¼x13, 13x13¼

2000, Sept. 18	Litho.	Wmk. 373
906-909 A191 Set of 4		5.25 5.25

Fish — A192

Designs: 50c, Scarus ghobban. 1r, Cephalopholis sonnerati. 2r, Mulloidichthys brevirostris. 3r, Lethrinus nebulosus. 4r, Centropyge debelius. 5r, Amphiprion chrysogaster. 6r, Forcipiger flavissimus. 7r, Acanthurus leucosternon. 8r, Pterois volitans. 10r, Siderea grisea. 15r, Carcharhinus wheeleri. 25r, Istiophorus platypterus.

Perf. 14½x14¼

2000, Oct. 9	Litho.	Wmk. 373
910 A192 50c multi		.45 .45
911 A192 1r multi		.45 .45
912 A192 2r multi		.45 .45
913 A192 3r multi		.45 .45
914 A192 4r multi		.55 .55
915 A192 5r multi		.70 .70
916 A192 6r multi		.85 .85
917 A192 7r multi		.90 .90
918 A192 8r multi		1.10 1.10
919 A192 10r multi		1.20 1.20
a. Souvenir sheet, #914, 917-919		3.75 3.75
b. As #919, perf. 13½ ('08)		1.10 1.10
920 A192 15r multi		2.10 2.10
a. Souvenir sheet of #913, 915-916, 920		4.25 4.25
921 A192 25r multi		3.00 3.00
a. Souvenir sheet, #910-912, 921		4.50 4.50
Nos. 910-921 (12)		12.20 12.20

No. 919b issued 5/28/08.

Famous People — A193

Designs: 1r, Affan Tank Wen (1842-1900). 5r, Alphonse Ravaton (1900-92), musician. 7r, Dr. Idrice Goumany (1859-89). 9r, Anjalay Coopen (d. 1943), martyr.

Perf. 14¼x14½

2000, Dec. 13		Wmk. 373
922-925 A193 Set of 4		4.25 4.25

Textile Industry A194

Designs: 1r, Finished sweater. 3r, Computer-aided machinery. 6r, T-shirt folder. 10r, Embroidery machine.

2001, Jan. 10		Perf. 14½x14¼
926-929 A194 Set of 4		3.75 3.75

End of Slavery and Indentured Labor, 166th Anniv. — A195

2001, Feb. 1		Perf. 14x13½
930 A195 7r multi		2.10 2.10

Trees — A196

Designs: 1r, Foetida mauritana. 3r, Diospyros tessellaria. 5r, Sideroxylon puberulum. 15r, Gastonia mauritana.

2001, Mar. 21	Wmk. 373	Perf. 14¼
931-934 A196 Set of 4		5.25 5.25

Expedition of Nicholas Baudin, Bicent. — A197

Designs: 1r, Ships Géographe and Naturaliste. 4r, Baudin and map of itinerary. 7r, Phedina borbonica. 10r, Napoleon Bonaparte and account of expedition, vert.

Wmk. 373

2001, June 13	Litho.	Perf. 14¼
935-938 A197 Set of 4		4.50 4.50

20th Century Achievements A198

Designs: 2r, Hotel School of Mauritius. 3r, Steel bar milling. 6r, Solar energy, Agalega. 10r, Indian Ocean Rim Association for Regional Cooperation.

Wmk. 373

2001, Sept. 12	Litho.	Perf. 13½
939-942 A198 Set of 4		3.75 3.75

Mahatma Gandhi's Visit to Mauritius, Cent. — A199

2001, Oct. 2		Perf. 14¾x14
943 A199 15r No. 361		3.25 3.25

Copra Industry — A200

Designs: 1r, Dehusking of coconuts, vert. 5r, Deshelling of coconuts. 6r, Drying copra. 10r, Oil extraction, vert.

2001, Dec. 5		Perf. 13½
944-947 A200 Set of 4		5.00 5.00

Republic, 10th Anniv. — A201

Designs: 1r, Port development. 4r, Financial services. 5r, Water storage. 9r, Road development.

Perf. 13½x13¾

2002, Mar. 12	Litho.	Wmk. 373
948-951 A201 Set of 4		4.50 4.50

Cicadas — A202

Designs: 1r, Abricta brunnea. 6r, Fractuosella darwini. 7r, Distantada thomaseti. 8r, Dinarobia claudeae.

Wmk. 373

2002, June 12	Litho.	Perf. 13½
952-955 A202 Set of 4		3.50 3.50
a. Souvenir sheet, #952-955		4.50 4.50

Maps of the Southwest Indian Ocean — A203

Maps by: 1r, Alberto Cantino, 1502. 3r, Jorge Reinel, 1520. 4r, Diogo Ribeiro, 1529. 10r, Gerard Mercator, 1569.

2002, Sept. 18		
956-959 A203 Set of 4		6.00 6.00

Constellations — A204

Designs: 1r, Orion. 7r, Sagittarius. 8r, Scorpius. 9r, Crux.

Perf. 14¼x14½

2002, Dec. 18	Litho.	Wmk. 373
960-963 A204 Set of 4		4.00 4.00

MAURITIUS

2nd U.S. — Sub-Saharan Africa Trade and Economic Forum — A205

Panel color: 1r, Violet blue. 25r, Red.

2003, Jan.		Perf. 14¼
964-965 A205	Set of 2	3.25 3.25

Worldwide Fund for Nature (WWF) — A206

Echo parakeet: 1r, Chick. 2r, Fledgling. 5r, Female. 15r, Male.

	Wmk. 373		
2003, Mar. 19	Litho.		Perf. 13½
966-969 A206	Set of 4		4.25 4.25

Flowers — A207

Designs: 1r, Trochetia boutoniana. 4r, Trochetia uniflora. 7r, Trochetia triflora. 9r, Trochetia parviflora.

	Wmk. 373		
2003, June 18	Litho.		Perf. 13½
970-973 A207	Set of 4		4.00 4.00

Anniversaries and Events — A208

Designs: 2r, Sixth Indian Ocean Games, Mauritius. 6r, Mauritius Chamber of Agriculture, 150th anniv. 9r, Visit of Abbé de la Caille, 250th anniv. 10r, Mauritius Sugar Industry Research Institute, 50th anniv.

2003, Aug. 20		
974-977 A208	Set of 4	5.75 5.75

Fortresses A209

Designs: 2r, Batterie de la Pointe du Diable. 5r, Donjon St. Louis. 6r, Martello tower. 12r, Fort Adelaide.

2003, Dec. 10		
978-981 A209	Set of 4	4.50 4.50

Indian Ocean Commission, 20th Anniv. — A210

	Wmk. 373		
2004, Feb. 16	Litho.		Perf. 13½
982 A210 10r multi			2.25 2.25

Mountains A211

Designs: 2r, Le Pouce. 7r, Corps de Garde. 8r, Le Chat et La Souris. 25r, Piton du Milieu.

2004, Mar. 11		Perf. 14½x14¼
983-986 A211	Set of 4	6.50 6.50

Traditional Trades — A212

Designs: 2r, Tinsmith. 7r, Cobbler. 9r, Blacksmith. 15r, Basket weaver.

	Wmk. 373		
2004, June 30	Litho.		Perf. 13½
987-990 A212	Set of 4		5.00 5.00

24th Southern Africa Development Community Summit A213

Emblem, woman at computer, building and panel in: 2r, Gray. 50r, Red.

	Wmk. 373		
2004, Aug. 16	Litho.		Perf. 13½
991-992 A213	Set of 2		7.00 7.00

Rodrigues Regional Assembly A214

Designs: 2r, Plaine Corail Airport. 7r, Ecotourism. 8r, Agricultural products. 10r, Coat of arms.

	Wmk. 373		
2004, Oct. 12	Litho.		Perf. 13½
993-996 A214	Set of 4		5.75 5.75

Anthurium Andreanum Varieties — A215

Designs: 2r, Acropolis. 8r, Tropical. 10r, Paradisio. 25r, Fantasia.

2004, Dec. 1		Perf. 13¼
997-1000 A215	Set of 4	7.50 7.50

Round Island Flora and Fauna — A216

Designs: 2r, Juvenile keel scale boa. 8r, Hurricane palm. 9r, Round Island petrel. 25r, Mazambron.

	Wmk. 373		
2005, Mar. 18	Litho.		Perf. 13¼
1001-1004 A216	Set of 4		7.50 7.50

Postal Services — A217

Designs: 2r, Counter services. 7r, Mail sorting. 8r, Mail distribution. 10r, Mail transfer.

	Wmk. 373		
2005, July 14	Litho.		Perf. 13¼
1005-1008 A217	Set of 4		4.00 4.00

Stone Buildings A218

Designs: 2r, Vagrant Depot, Grand River North West. 7r, Postal Museum, Port Louis. 16r, Carnegie Library, Curepipe.

	Wmk. 373		
2005, Oct. 9	Litho.		Perf. 13½
1009-1011 A218	Set of 3		4.00 4.00

Ship Models — A219

Designs: 7r, 100-gun ship. 8r, Sampan. 9r, Roman galley. 16r, Drakkar. 25r, Drakkar, horiz.

	Perf. 13¾x13½		
2005, Dec. 20			Litho.
1012-1015 A219	Set of 4		6.00 6.00

Souvenir Sheet
Perf. 13½x13¾

1016 A219 25r multi		4.25 4.25

Mahebourg, Bicent. — A220

Designs: 2r, Market. 7r, Regattas. 8r, Le Lavoir. No. 1020, 16r, Pointe des Régates. No. 1021, vert.: a, 16r, Mahé de la Bourdonnais. b, 16r, Gen. Charles Decaen.

	Wmk. 373		
2006, Feb. 4	Litho.		Perf. 13½
1017-1020 A220	Set of 4		5.25 5.25

Souvenir Sheet

1021 A220 16r Sheet of 2, #a-b	5.50 5.50

Professor Basdeo Bissoondoyal (1906-91), Educator — A221

	Wmk. 373		
2006, Apr. 15	Litho.		Perf. 13¾
1022 A221 10r multi			1.40 1.40

Ecological History — A222

Designs: 2r, Biological control of locusts with introduction of mynah birds, 1763. 8r, Fish repopulation with artificial reefs, 1980. 10r, Erosion control with terraces in Rodrigues, 1958. 25r, First captive breeding of giant tortoises, 1881.

2006, June 5		Perf. 13½
1023-1026 A222	Set of 4	5.50 5.50

Crabs — A223

Designs: 2r, Tourloulou crab. 7r, Land crab. 8s, Freshwater crab. 25r, Coconut crab.

	Wmk. 373		
2006, Oct. 9	Litho.		Perf. 13¼
1027-1030 A223	Set of 4		4.50 4.50

Traditional Children's Activities — A224

Designs: 5r, Sapsiwaye. 10r, Marbles, horiz. 15r, Hop Scotch, horiz. 25r, Kite flying.

Perf. 13¾x13½, 13½x13¾

2006, Dec. 7		
1031-1034 A224	Set of 4	3.75 3.75

Corals — A225

Designs: 3r, Rodrigues endemic coral. 5r, Soft coral. 10r, Chagos coral. 15r, Head coral. 22r, Table coral. 25r, Tube coral.

	Wmk. 373		
2007, Apr. 30	Litho.		Perf. 13½
1035-1040 A225	Set of 6		5.25 5.25

Drawings of Dodo Birds — A226

Drawing: 5r, From Journal of the Gelderland, 1601. 10r, By Adrian van de Venne, 1626. 15r, Published by Harrison, 1798. No. 1044, 25r, By J. W. Frohawk, 1905. No. 1045, By Julian Pender Hume, 2001, vert.

	Wmk. 373		
2007, June 25	Litho.		Perf. 13½
1041-1044 A226	Set of 4		4.25 4.25

Souvenir Sheet
Perf. 13x13¼

1045 A226 25r multi		1.90 1.90

No. 1045 contains one 28x45mm stamp.

24th UPU Congress, Nairobi — A227

	Wmk. 373		
2007, Oct. 9	Litho.		Perf. 13¼
1046 A227 50r multi			3.50 3.50

Due to political unrest in Kenya, the UPU Congress was moved to Geneva, Switzerland.

Anniversaries A228

Designs: 5r, Ministerial System, 50th anniv. 10r, Arrival in Mauritius of Manilall Doctor, cent., vert. 15r, Scouting, cent., vert. 25r, First meteorological observatory in Mauritius, 175th anniv.

2007, Dec. 4		Perf. 13½
1047-1050 A228	Set of 4	3.75 3.75

Ministerial System, 50th Anniv. (With Corrected Photograph) — A229

2007, Dec. 4   Litho.   Perf. 13½
1051   A229   5r multi   .35   .35

The photo in the LR corner on No. 1051 differs from the photo in the LR corner on No. 1047.

Authors Who Mentioned Mauritius — A230

Author and work: 5r, Bernardin de St. Pierre (1737-1814), Paul et Virginie. 10r, Alexandre Dumas (père) (1802-70), Georges. 15r, Charles Baudelaire (1821-67), A une Dame Creole. 22r, Mark Twain (1835-1910), Following the Equator. 25r, Joseph Conrad (1857-1924), A Smile of Fortune.

Wmk. 406
2008, Dec. 8   Litho.   Perf. 13½
1052-1056   A230   Set of 5   5.00   5.00

Flowers — A231

Designs: 3r, Myonima obovata. 4r, Cylindrocline lorencei. 5r, Crinum mauritianum. 6r, Elaeocarpus bojeri. 7r, Bremeria landia. 8r, Distephanus populifolius. 9r, Gaertnera longifolia. 10r, Dombeya acutangula. 15r, Aphloia theiformis. 22r, Barleria observatrix. 25r, Roussea simplex. 50r, Hibiscus fragilis.

Wmk. 406
2009, Apr. 9   Litho.   Perf. 13½
1057   A231   3r multi   .25   .25
1058   A231   4r multi   .25   .25
1059   A231   5r multi   .30   .30
1060   A231   6r multi   .35   .35
1061   A231   7r multi   .45   .45
  a.   Dated "2010"   .50   .50
  b.   Dated "2015"   .40   .40
1062   A231   8r multi   .50   .50
  a.   Dated "2010"   .55   .55
  b.   Dated "2016"   .45   .45
1063   A231   9r multi   .55   .55
1064   A231   10r multi   .60   .60
1065   A231   15r multi   .90   .90
  a.   Dated "2010"   1.00   1.00
1066   A231   22r multi   1.40   1.40
1067   A231   25r multi   1.50   1.50
  a.   Dated "2010"   1.75   1.75
  b.   Dated "2016"   1.40   1.40
1068   A231   50r multi   3.00   3.00
  Nos. 1057-1068 (12)   10.05   10.05

Issued: Nos. 1057a, 1062b, 1067b, 6/1/16.

Extinct Mauritian Giant Tortoises A232

Designs: 5r, Cylindraspis peltastes. 10r, Cylindraspis vosmaeri, vert. 15r, Cylindraspis inepta. 25r, Cylindraspis triserrata, vert. 50r, Cylindraspis peltastes, diff.

Wmk. 406
2009, July 16   Litho.   Perf. 13½
1069-1072   A232   Set of 4   3.50   3.50
Souvenir Sheet
1073   A232   50r multi   3.50   3.50

New Mauritius Travel Slogan — A233

No. 1074 — New slogan on: a, Yellow background. b, Mountain background.

Perf. 13½x13
2009, Oct. 9   Litho.   Wmk. 406
1074   A233   7r Vert. pair, #a-b   .95   .95

Chinese Chamber of Commerce, Cent. (in 2008) — A234

Dr. Kissoonsingh Hazareesingh, Historian, Birth Cent. A235

Capture of Rodrigues Island by British, Bicent. — A236

Teeluckpersad Callychurn, Postmaster General, Birth Cent. — A237

Wmk. 406
2009, Nov. 30   Litho.   Perf. 13½
1075   A234   7r multi   .50   .50
1076   A235   14r multi   1.00   1.00
1077   A236   20r multi   1.40   1.40
1078   A237   21r multi   1.50   1.50
  Nos. 1075-1078 (4)   4.40   4.40

Muhammad al-Idrisi (c.1100-c.1165), Geographer and Cartographer — A238

Wmk. 406
2010, Aug. 2   Litho.   Perf. 13½
1079   A238   27r multi   1.90   1.90

Mauritius No. 2 — A239

2010, Aug. 20
1080   A239   30r multi   2.00   2.00
Expo 2010, Shanghai.

Battle of Grand Port, Bicent. — A240

Designs: 14r, Battle scene. 21r, Ile de la Passe.

2010, Aug. 20
1081-1082   A240   Set of 2   2.25   2.25

Sir Seewoosagur Ramgoolam (1900-85), Prime Minister A241

Litho. & Embossed With Foil Application
2010, Sept. 18   Wmk. 406
1083   A241   100r multi   6.75   6.75

British Conquest of Isle de France, Bicent. — A242

Designs: 2r, Capitulation document. 7r, British landing on Isle de France, horiz.

Wmk. 406
2010, Dec. 3   Litho.   Perf. 13½
1084-1085   A242   Set of 2   .60   .60

2010 World Cup Soccer Championships, South Africa — A243

Perf. 14x13½
2010, Apr. 9   Litho.   Unwmk.
1086   A243   7r multi   4.00   4.00

Values are for stamps with surrounding selvage. A sheet of nine stamps containing No. 1086 and eight other 7r stamps on gold-faced paper bearing the flags of the other countries involved the joint issue (see below) was produced in limited quantities.
See Botswana Nos. 896-901, Lesotho No. , Malawi No. 753, Namibia No. 1188, South Africa No. 1403, Swaziland Nos. 794-803, Zambia Nos. 1115-1118, Zimbabwe Nos. 1112-1121.

UNESCO World Heritage Sites — A244

Designs: 7r, Steps, Aapravasi Ghat. 14r, Mountain, Le Morne, horiz. 15r, Monument, Le Morne, horiz. 25r, Hospital kitchen, Aapravasi Ghat.

Wmk. 406
2011, Apr. 11   Litho.   Perf. 13½
1087-1090   A244   Set of 4   4.50   4.50
1090a   Souvenir sheet of 4, #1087-1090   4.50   4.50

19th Century Census Form A245

Sir Moilin Jean Ah Chuen (1911-91), Politician A246

Dr. Maurice Curé (1886-1977), Co-Founder of Labor Party — A247

Médine Sugar Estates, Cent. — A248

2011, June 30
1091   A245   7r multi   .50   .50
1092   A246   14r multi   1.00   1.00
1093   A247   21r multi   1.50   1.50
1094   A248   25r multi   1.75   1.75
  Nos. 1091-1094 (4)   4.75   4.75

Observation of Transit of Venus From Rodrigues by Alexandre Guy Pingré — A249

Intl. Year of Chemistry A250

Intl. Year of Forests A251

2011, Sept. 8
1095   A249   11r multi   .80   .80
1096   A250   12r multi   .85   .85
1097   A251   17r multi   1.25   1.25
  Nos. 1095-1097 (3)   2.90   2.90

HIV and AIDS Awareness A252

Post Office in Rodrigues, 150th Anniv. A253

2011, Oct. 9
1098   A252   7r multi   .50   .50
1099   A253   21r multi   1.50   1.50

Tea Industry — A254

MAURITIUS

Designs: 7r, Tea flushes. 8r, Tea pickers, horiz. 15r, Loose tea on saucer, spoon, tea bags, horiz. 25r, Tea pot and cup.

2011, Dec. 19
1100-1103 A254 Set of 4   3.75 3.75

Law Day — A255

Designs: 7r, Grand Port District Court. 8r, Interior of Court of Justice. 15r, Sir Michel Rivalland, 1967-70 Chief Justice, vert. 20r, Gavel.

2012, Apr. 4   **Perf. 13¼**
1104-1107 A255 Set of 4   3.50 3.50

Mauritius postal officials have declared sheets of four and six 9r stamps depicting Michael Jackson as "illegal."

Mauritius Turf Club, 200th Anniv. — A256

Designs: 7r, Horse race. 10r, Aerial view of Champ de Mars Race Track. 14r, Grandstand, 1917. 21r, Emblem of Mauritius Turf Club, vert. 50r, Jockey on horse in paddock.

2012, June 25   **Perf. 13½**
1108-1111 A256 Set of 4   3.50 3.50
            Souvenir Sheet
1112 A256 50r multi   3.25 3.25

Customs Department A257

Designs: 7r, Old and new Custom Houses. 8r, Customs officer scanning packages. 20r, Dog sniffing packages, vert. 25r, Customs officers on boat.

2012, Sept. 10
1113-1116 A257 Set of 4   4.00 4.00

Intl. Year of Cooperatives A258

Diplomatic Relations Between Mauritius and People's Republic of China, 40th Anniv. — A259

Scouting in Mauritius, Cent. — A260

2012, Oct. 9
1117 A258 6r multi   .40   .40
1118 A259 14r multi   .90   .90
1119 A260 21r multi   1.40 1.40
        Nos. 1117-1119 (3)   2.70 2.70

Famous Men — A261

Designs: 6r, Marcel Cabon (1912-72), musician. 10r, Goolam Mahomed Dawjee Atchia, newspaper publisher.

2012, Nov. 9
1120-1121 A261 Set of 2   1.10 1.10

Methods of Mail Conveyance — A262

Early Mauritius Stamps A263

No. 1122: a, Foot messenger, 1772. b, Packet mail landing, 1915. c, Express letter messenger, 1930. d, Inland mail arrival, 1935. e, Delivery of mail bags by van, 2012.
No. 1123: a, Mauritius #1 and copper plate cliché. b, Mauritius #2 and copper plate cliché.

2012, Dec. 21   **Perf. 12½x13**
1122   Horiz. strip of 5 2.25 2.25
  a.-e. A262 7r Any single   .45   .45
        Souvenir Sheet
                              Perf. 13½
1123 A263 25r Sheet of 2, #a-b,
            + label   3.25 3.25
Postal services in Mauritius, 240th anniv.

Sites and Monuments A264

Designs: 5r, Belle Mare Prison. 9r, Bel Ombre Château. 10r, IBL Building, Bowen Square. 18r, Le Batelage.

                Wmk. 406
2013, Apr. 18 Litho.   Perf. 13½
1124-1127 A264 Set of 4   2.75 2.75

Intl. Red Cross, 150th Anniv. — A265

2013, May 30
1128 A265 3r multi   .25   .25

63rd FIFA Congress, Mauritius — A266

2013, May 30
1129 A266 18r multi   1.25 1.25

Renewable Energy — A267

Designs: 2r, Solar energy. 6r, Wind energy.

2013, May 30
1130-1131 A267 Set of 2   .55   .55

Flora and Fauna — A268

Designs: 3r, Hurricane palm. 10r, Oeoniella polystachys orchid. 18w, Mascarene swallow.

                Wmk. 406
2013, Aug. 30 Litho.   Perf. 13½
1132-1134 A268 Set of 3   2.00 2.00

Famous Men — A269

Designs: 9r, Hervé Masson (1919-90), painter. 26r, Prof. Stanley Alexander de Smith (1922-74), Constitiutional Commissioner of Mauritius.

                Wmk. 406
2013, Dec. 11 Litho.   Perf. 13½
1135-1136 A269 Set of 2   2.40 2.40

Flora and Fauna — A270

Designs: 7r, Dragonfly. 14r, Roussette de Rodrigues. 25r, Pignon d'Inde, vert.

                Wmk. 406
2014, Mar. 28 Litho.   Perf. 13½
1137-1139 A270 Set of 3   3.00 3.00

Father Jacques-Désiré Laval (1803-64), Missionary — A271

Children's Office Ombudsperson, 10th Anniv. — A272

Arrival in Mauritius of Rev. Jean Joseph Lebrun as Missionary, 200th Anniv. A273

Introduction of Mobile Telephones in Mauritius, 25th Anniv. A274

                Wmk. 406
2014, May 28 Litho.   Perf. 13½
1140 A271 8r multi   .55   .55
1141 A272 14r multi   .95   .95
1142 A273 15r multi   1.00 1.00
1143 A274 25r multi   1.60 1.60
        Nos. 1140-1143 (4)   4.10 4.10

Green Turtle — A275

            Unwmk.
2014, Oct. 9   Litho.   Perf. 14
1144 A275 14r multi   .90   .90

See Comoro Islands No. , France No. 4695, French Southern and Antarctic Territories No. 511, Malagasy Republic No. 1637, Seychelles No. 904.

Disaster Risk Reduction A276

                Wmk. 406
2015, June 29 Litho.   Perf. 13½
1145 A276 17r multi   .95   .95

Ninth Indian Ocean Games, Réunion A277

                Wmk. 406
2015, Aug. 1   Litho.   Perf. 13½
1146 A277 17r multi   .95   .95

Landing of French on Mauritius, 300th Anniv. — A278

                          Perf. 13¼
2015, Sept. 25 Litho.   Unwmk.
1147 A278 17r multi   .95   .95
See France No. 4874.

National Archives, 200th Anniv. — A279

            Perf. 13x13½
2015, Dec. 7   Litho.   Wmk. 406
1148 A279 10r multi   .55   .55

United Nations Sustainable Development Goals — A280

                Wmk. 406
2016, May 9   Litho.   Perf. 13½
1149 A280 27r multi   1.60 1.60

Freshwater Fauna — A281

Designs: 1r, Giant mottled eel. 10r, Water scorpion. 18r, Nile tilapia. 32r, Freshwater shrimp.

                Wmk. 406
2016, June 6   Litho.   Perf. 13½
1150-1153 A281 Set of 4   3.50 3.50

MAURITIUS

Maritime Air Squadron's New Dornier MPCG 04 — A282

Wmk. 406
2016, July 13   Litho.   *Perf. 13½*
1154   A282   11r multi   .65 .65

Nature Walks — A283

Designs: 2r, Powder Mills Nature Walk. 20r, Sophie Nature Walk.

Wmk. 406
2016, Sept. 15   Litho.   *Perf. 13½*
1155-1156   A283   Set of 2   1.25 1.25

Flowers — A284

Designs: 11r, Bacopa monnieri. 13r, Ludwigia octovalvis. 16r, Nelumbo nucifera. 31r, Nelumbo nucifera, diff.

Wmk. 406
2016, Oct. 18   Litho.   *Perf. 13½*
1157-1160   A284   Set of 4   4.00 4.00

World Diabetes Day — A285

2016, Nov. 14   Litho.   *Perf. 13½*
1161   A285   10r multi   .55 .55

Republic of Mauritius, 25th Anniv. — A286

Wmk. 406
2017, Mar. 12   Litho.   *Perf. 13½*
1162   A286   25r multi   1.50 1.50

Kwan Tee Pagoda, 175th Anniv. — A287

Wmk. 406
2017, June 20   Litho.   *Perf. 13½*
1163   A287   10r multi   .60 .60

Mauritius Police Force, 250th Anniv. — A288

Perf. 13½x13¾
2017, Aug. 1   Litho.   Wmk. 406
1164   A288   25r multi   1.50 1.50

Aunauth Beejadhur, First Governor of Bank of Mauritius — A289

Wmk. 406
2017, Sept. 6   Litho.   *Perf. 13½*
1165   A289   275r multi   1.75 1.75

Bank of Mauritius, 50th anniv.

Nightfall, Belle Etoile, by Serge Constantin A290

Wmk. 406
2017, Sept. 28   Litho.   *Perf. 13½*
1166   A290   18r multi   1.10 1.10

Shells — A291

Designs: Nos. 1167, 1171a, 3r, Cone shells. Nos. 1168, 1171b, 4r, Cowrie shell. Nos. 1169, 1171c, 23r, Violet sea snail. Nos. 1170, 1171d, 33r, Trapezium horse conch.

Wmk. 406
2017, Oct. 9   Litho.   *Perf. 13½*
Size: 45x30mm
1167-1170   A291   Set of 4   3.75 3.75
Souvenir Sheet
Perf. 14
1171   A291   Sheet of 4, #a-d   3.75 3.75

No. 1171 contains four 45x33mm stamps.

Maps — A292

Designs: 10r, Seafloor map of Chagos Archipelago. 18r, Map of Mauritius maritime zones, horiz. (50x35mm). 25r, Map of Tromelin Island.

Perf. 13¼, 14¼ (18r)
2017, Dec. 11   Litho.   Wmk. 406
1172-1174   A292   Set of 3   3.25 3.25

Independence, 50th Anniv. — A293

Designs: Nos. 1175, 1178a, 1r, Past and present photographs of Port Louis Harbor. Nos. 1176, 1178b, 6r, National anthem, vert. Nos. 1177, 1178c, 13r, Clasped hands, national flag and "50."

Perf. 13½x13¼, 13¼x13½
2018, Mar. 12   Litho.   Wmk. 406
Sizes: 45x30mm (1r), 30x45mm
1175-1177   A293   Set of 3   1.25 1.25
Souvenir Sheet
Sizes: 45x33mm (1r), 33x45mm
Perf. 13¾x14, 14x13¾
1178   A293   Sheet of 3, #a-c   1.25 1.25

Lions International in Mauritius, 50th Anniv. — A294

Wmk. 406
2018, May 30   Litho.   *Perf. 14*
1179   A294   3r multi   .25 .25

Pandit Cashinath Kistoe Aryan Vedic Hindu Aided School, Vacoas-Phoenix, Cent. — A295

Wmk. 406
2018, May 30   Litho.   *Perf. 14*
1180   A295   5r multi   .30 .30

Diplomatic Relations Between Mauritius and Russia, 50th Anniv. — A296

Wmk. 406
2018, May 30   Litho.   *Perf. 14*
1181   A296   14r multi   .85 .85

Chamarel Colored Earth, Painting by Du Benji — A297

Wmk. 406
2018, June 29   Litho.   *Perf. 14*
1182   A297   33r multi   1.90 1.90

Art and Science A298

Designs: 2r, Nicéphoro Niópoo (1765-1833), inventor of photography, and his earliest surviving photograph. 33r, Nicolas Pike (1818-1905), United States Consul to Mauritius, naturalist and writer, damselfish.

Wmk. 406
2018, July 23   Litho.   *Perf. 14*
1183-1184   A298   Set of 2   2.10 2.10

Diplomatic Relations Between Mauritius and India, 70th Anniv. — A299

Designs: 8r, Flags of Mauritius and India. 20r, Emblem of 11th World Hindi Congress, Port Louis.

Perf. 13½x13½
2018, Aug. 18   Litho.   Wmk. 406
1185-1186   A299   Set of 2   1.75 1.75

Emblem of St. John Ambulance A300

Mauritius Fire and Rescue Service — A301

Wmk. 406
2018, Oct. 9   Litho.   *Perf. 14*
1187   A300   3r multi   .25 .25
1188   A301   13r multi   .75 .75

World War I Memorial, Curepipe — A302

Wmk. 406
2018, Nov. 12   Litho.   *Perf. 14*
1189   A302   25r multi   1.50 1.50

End of World War I, cent.

Police Helicopter A303

Wmk. 406
2019, Mar. 13   Litho.   *Perf. 13½*
1190   A303   13r multi   .75 .75

Radar Station, Trou aux Cerfs — A304

Wmk. 406
2019, Apr. 30   Litho.   *Perf. 13½*
1191   A304   13r multi   .75 .75

Diplomatic relations between Mauritius and Japan, 50th anniv.

International Day of Families — A305

Wmk. 406
2019, May 15   Litho.   *Perf. 13½*
1192   A305   38r multi   2.25 2.25

2019 Indian Ocean Games, Mauritius — A306

Designs: Nos. 1193, 1196a, 7r, Parrot mascot. Nos. 1194, 1196b, 21r, Sailboats, horiz. No. 1195, 1196c, 24r, 2019 Indian Ocean Games emblem.

Wmk. 406
2019, June 19   Litho.   *Perf. 13½*
Sizes: 30x45mm, 45x30mm (21r)
1193-1195   A306   Set of 3   3.00 3.00
Souvenir Sheet
Sizes: 33x45mm, 45x33mm (21r)
Perf. 14x13¾, 13¾x14
1196   A306   Sheet of 3, #a-c   3.00 3.00

MAURITIUS — MAYOTTE

Pierre Poivre (1719-86), Botanist, and Black Ebony Tree — A307

Perf. 14x14¼
2019, Aug. 23　Litho.　Wmk. 406
1197　A307　33r multi　　　1.90　1.90

Maps of Islands in Chagos Archipelago A308

International Court of Justice, The Hague, Netherlands A309

Perf. 14x14¼
2019, Aug. 23　Litho.　Wmk. 406
1198　A308　13r multi　　　.70　.70

Perf. 14¼x14
1199　A309　25r multi　　　1.40　1.40
　a.　Souvenir sheet of 2, #1198-1199　　2.10　2.10

Decision by International Court of Justice in favor of Mauritius taking control of Chagos Archipelago islands from Great Britain.

Visit of Pope Francis to Mauritius — A310

Wmk. 406
2019, Sept. 9　Litho.　Perf. 13¼
1200　A310　13r multi　　　.70　.70

Mohandas K. Gandhi (1869-1948), Indian Nationalist Leader — A311

Perf. 14¼x14½
2019, Oct. 2　Litho.　Wmk. 406
1201　A311　13r brown black　.75　.75

International Civil Aviation Organization, 75th Anniv. — A312

Wmk. 406
2019, Dec. 7　Litho.　Perf. 14
1202　A312　25r multi　　　1.40　1.40

Inauguration of Metro Express Light Rail Line — A313

Perf. 13½x13¼
2019, Dec. 18　Litho.　Wmk. 406
1203　A313　25r multi　　　1.40　1.40

Diplomatic Relations Between Mauritius and Australia, 50th Anniv. — A314

Wmk. 406
2020, Sept. 24　Litho.　Perf. 13¼
1204　A314　33r multi　　　1.75　1.75

Port Louis Central Post Office, 150th Anniv. — A315

Wmk. 406
2020, Oct. 20　Litho.　Perf. 13¼
1205　A315　16r multi　　　.80　.80

SPECIAL DELIVERY STAMPS

No. 115 Surcharged in Red

1903　Wmk. 1　Perf. 14
Red Surcharge
E1　SD1　15c on 15c ultra　14.50　37.50

No. 115 Surcharged in Red

New Setting with Smaller "15c" without period

To make No. E2 the word "INLAND" was printed on No. E1.
Nos. E3 and E3F, new settings of the surcharge of No. E2 were made with different spacing between the words.

1904
E2　SD2　15c on 15c ultra　62.50　95.00
　a.　"INLAND" inverted　　　3,400.
　b.　Inverted "A" in "INLAND"　1,700.　1,250.
E3　SD3　15c on 15c ultra　9.00　3.75
　a.　Double surcharge, both inverted　1,875.　1,900.
　b.　Inverted surcharge　1,250.　800.00
　c.　Vert. pair, imperf between　　　6,250.
E3F　SD3　15c on 15c ultra　840.00　800.00
　g.　Inverted surcharge　　　1,775.
　h.　Double surcharge　　　3,750.
　i.　Double surcharge, inverted　—　5,500.
　j.　"c" omitted　　　2,750.

SD4　　　　SD5

E4　SD4　15c green & red　18.00　6.25
　a.　Double surcharge　800.00　800.00
　b.　Inverted surcharge　1,000.　900.00
　c.　"LNIAND."
　d.　As "c," double surcharge　900.00　800.00
E5　SD5　18c green & black　3.00　32.50
　a.　Exclamation point (!) instead of "I" in "FOREIGN"　　800.00

POSTAGE DUE STAMPS

Catalogue values for unused stamps in this section are for Never Hinged items.

Numeral — D1

Perf. 14½x14
1933-54　Typo.　Wmk. 4
J1　D1　2c black　1.50　.60
J2　D1　4c violet　.60　.80
J3　D1　6c red　.70　.95
J4　D1　10c green　.85　2.40
J5　D1　20c ultramarine　.75　2.60
J6　D1　50c dp red lilac ('54)　.65　19.00
J7　D1　1r orange ('54)　.85　19.00
　Nos. J1-J7 (7)　5.90　45.35

1966-68　Wmk. 314　Perf. 14
J8　D1　2c black ('67)　3.00　3.75

Perf. 14½x14
J9　D1　4c rose violet ('68)　2.00　8.50
J10　D1　6c dp orange ('68)　7.25　27.50
J11　D1　10c yel green ('67)　.40　2.10
J12　D1　20c ultramarine　2.50　5.75
J13　D1　50c dp red lilac ('68)　.85　13.00
　Nos. J8-J13 (6)　16.00　60.60

Nos. 445-446, 450, 455, 457, 462 Surcharged "POSTAGE/ DUE" and New Value
Wmk. 373
1982, Oct. 25　Litho.　Perf. 13½
J14　A92　10c on 15c multi　.40　.45
J15　A92　20c on 20c multi　.40　1.00
J16　A91　50c on 60c multi　.60　.60
J17　A92　1r on 1.20r multi　.75　.60
J18　A92　1.50r on 1.50r multi　.95　1.40
J19　A91　5r on 15r multi　1.75　4.25
　Nos. J14-J19 (6)　4.85　8.30

MAYOTTE

mä-'yät

LOCATION — One of the Comoro Islands situated in the Mozambique Channel midway between Madagascar and Mozambique (Africa)
GOVT. — French Colony
AREA — 144 sq. mi.
POP. — 149,336 (1999 est.)
CAPITAL — Mamoutzou
See Comoro Islands.

100 Centimes = 1 Franc
100 Cents = 1 Euro (2002)

Stamps of Mayotte were replaced successively by those of Madagascar, Comoro Islands and France. Individual issues were resumed in 1997.

See France No. 2271 for French stamp inscribed "Mayotte."

Catalogue values for unused stamps in this country are for Never Hinged items, beginning with Scott 75 in the regular postage section, and Scott C1 in the airpost section.

Navigation and Commerce — A1

Perf. 14x13½
1892-1907　Typo.　Unwmk.
Name of Colony in Blue or Carmine
1　A1　1c blk, lil bl　1.40　.90
2　A1　2c brn, buff　1.90　1.40
　a.　Name double　575.00　500.00
3　A1　4c claret, lav　2.40　1.75
4　A1　5c grn, grnsh　4.75　3.25
5　A1　10c blk, lavender　9.00　4.75
6　A1　10c red ('00)　75.00　52.50
7　A1　15c blue, quadrille paper　17.50　10.50
8　A1　15c gray ('00)　140.00　110.00
9　A1　20c red, grn　13.50　10.50
10　A1　25c blk, rose　14.50　9.75
11　A1　25c blue ('00)　16.00　13.50
12　A1　30c brn, bis　22.00　16.00
13　A1　35c blk, yel ('00)　11.00　8.00
14　A1　40c red, straw　22.50　16.00
15　A1　45c blk, gray grn ('07)　21.00　20.00
16　A1　50c carmine, rose　32.00　22.50
17　A1　50c brn, az ('00)　30.00　30.00
18　A1　75c dp vio, org　30.00　21.00
19　A1　1fr brnz grn, straw　32.00　22.50
20　A1　5fr red lil, lav ('99)　135.00　130.00
　Nos. 1-20 (20)　631.45　504.80

Perf. 13½x14 stamps are counterfeits.

Issues of 1892-1907 Surcharged in Black or Carmine

1912
22　A1　5c on 2c brn, buff　3.25　4.00
23　A1　5c on 4c cl, lav (C)　2.00　2.00
24　A1　5c on 15c bl (C)　2.00　2.00
25　A1　5c on 20c red, grn　2.00　2.40
26　A1　5c on 25c blk, rose (C)　1.60　1.60
　a.　Double surcharge　360.00
　b.　Pair, one stamp without surcharge　1,000.
27　A1　5c on 30c brn, bis (C)　2.00　2.00
28　A1　10c on 40c red, straw　2.00　2.40
　a.　Double surcharge　360.00
29　A1　10c on 45c blk, gray grn (C)　2.00　2.00
　a.　Double surcharge　360.00　325.00
30　A1　10c on 50c car, rose　4.50　5.00
31　A1　10c on 75c dp vio, org　3.50　4.25
32　A1　10c on 1fr brnz grn, straw　3.50　4.25
　Nos. 22-32 (11)　28.35　31.90

Two spacings between the surcharged numerals are found on Nos. 22-32. For detailed listings, see the Scott Classic Specialized Catalogue of Stamps and Covers.
Nos. 22-32 were available for use in Madagascar and the entire Comoro archipelago.

Catalogue values for unused stamps in this section, from this point to the end of the section, are for Never Hinged items.

Marianne Type of France Overprinted

1997, Jan. 2　Engr.　Perf. 13
Design A1161
75　10c on #2179　.25　.30
76　20c on #2180　.25　.30
77　50c on #2181　.25　.30
78　1fr on #2182　.45　.45
79　2fr on #2333　.90　.90
80　(2.50fr) on #2340　1.00　1.00
81　2.70fr on #2335　1.20　1.20
82　3.80fr on #2337　1.60　1.60
83　5fr on #2194　2.25　2.25
84　10fr on #2195　4.50　4.50
　Nos. 75-84 (10)　12.65　12.80

Ylang Ylang — A5

1997, Jan. 2　Litho.　Perf. 13½x13
85　A5　2.70fr multicolored　1.50　1.50

MAYOTTE

Coat of Arms — A6

1997, Jan. 2 *Perf. 13x13½*
86 A6 3fr multicolored 1.60 1.60
  a. Sheet of 4 7.25 7.25
No. 86a issued 6/19/99 for Philex France 99.

Le Banga — A7

1997, May 31 *Litho.* *Perf. 13*
87 A7 3.80fr multicolored 1.90 1.90

Dzen Dzé Musical Instrument — A8

1997, May 31 *Perf. 12½*
88 A8 5.20fr multicolored 2.50 2.50

Lemur — A9

1997, Aug. 30 *Engr.* *Perf. 12*
89 A9 3fr red & dk brown 1.60 1.60

Face of a Woman — A10

1997, Aug. 30 *Litho.* *Perf. 13*
90 A10 3.50fr multicolored 1.75 1.75

Marine Life — A11

1997, Nov. 29 *Litho.* *Perf. 13*
91 A11 3fr multicolored 1.75 1.75

Longoni Port — A12

1998, Jan. 31 *Litho.* *Perf. 13*
92 A12 2.70fr multicolored 1.40 1.40

Chelonia Mydas A13

1998, Jan. 31
93 A13 3fr multicolored 1.75 1.75

Family Planning — A14

1998, Apr. 1 *Litho.* *Perf. 13¼x13*
94 A14 1fr multicolored .75 .75

France Nos. 2594, 2595 and 2597 Overprinted "MAYOTTE"

1997, Aug. 18 *Engr.* *Perf. 13*
95 A1409 2.70fr brt grn (#2594) 1.00 1.00
96 A1409 (3fr) red (#2495) 1.00 1.00
97 A1409 3.80fr blue (#2497) 1.00 1.00

France No. 2604 Ovptd. "MAYOTTE"
Die Cut x Serpentine Die Cut 7

1998, Apr. 15 *Engr.*
Self-Adhesive
104 A1409 (3fr) red 1.40 1.40
  a. Booklet pane of 10 14.00
No. 104a is a complete booklet, the peelable backing serves as a booklet cover.

Children's Carnival — A15

1998, May 30 *Litho.* *Perf. 13*
105 A15 3fr multicolored 1.50 1.50

Ferry, "Salama Djema II" — A16

1998, May 30
106 A16 3.80fr multicolored 1.75 1.75

Mosque of Tsingoni — A17

1998, Sept. 5 *Litho.* *Perf. 13*
107 A17 3fr multicolored 1.50 1.50

Mariama Salim — A18

Photo. & Engr.
1998, Oct. 3 *Perf. 13*
108 A18 2.70fr multicolored 1.25 1.25

Traditional Fishing, Djarifa A19

1998, Nov. 7 *Litho.* *Perf. 13*
109 A19 2fr multicolored 1.25 1.25

Pomacanthus A20

1998, Nov. 7
110 A20 3fr multicolored 1.75 1.75
See Nos. 121-124.

Agricultural Tools — A21

1998, Dec. 19 *Litho.* *Perf. 13*
111 A21 3fr multicolored 1.50 1.50

France Nos. 2589-2593, 2601, 2603 Ovptd. "MAYOTTE"

1999, Jan. 1 *Engr.* *Perf. 13*
112 A1409 10c brn (#2589) .25 .25
113 A1409 20c brt bl grn (#2590) .30 .30
114 A1409 50c purple (#2591) .50 .50
115 A1409 1fr brt orange (#2592) .65 .65
116 A1409 2fr brt blue (#2593) 1.00 1.00
117 A1409 5fr brt grn bl (#2601) 2.25 2.25
118 A1409 10fr violet (#2603) 4.75 4.75
  Nos. 112-118 (7) 9.70 9.70

Map of Mayotte — A22

1999, Feb. 6 *Perf. 12x13*
119 A22 3fr multicolored 1.50 1.50

Combani Dam — A23

1999, Feb. 6 *Litho.* *Perf. 13*
120 A23 8fr multicolored 3.50 3.50

Fish Typo of 1998
Designs: 2.70fr, Cephalopholis miniatus, vert. 3fr, Pterois volitans. 5.20fr, Pygoplites diacanthus. 10fr, Acanthurus leucosternon.

Perf. 13¼x13, 13x13¼
1999, Apr. 3 *Litho.*
121 A20 2.70fr multicolored 1.25 1.25
122 A20 3fr multicolored 1.40 1.40
123 A20 5.20fr multicolored 2.50 2.50
124 A20 10fr multicolored 4.25 4.25
  Nos. 121-124 (4) 9.40 9.40

France No. 2691 Ovptd. "MAYOTTE"

1999, May 25 *Engr.* *Perf. 13*
125 A1470 3fr red & blue 1.25 1.25

Founga — A24

Photo. & Engr.
1999, June 5 *Perf. 13*
126 A24 5.40fr multicolored 2.50 2.50

Baobab Tree — A25

1999, June 5 *Litho.* *Perf. 13x13½*
127 A25 8fr multicolored 3.50 3.50

Dzaoudzi Prefecture — A26

1999, Sept. 25 *Litho.* *Perf. 13x13¼*
128 A26 3fr multicolored 1.40 1.40

Souvenir Sheet

Pirogues — A27

Designs: a, Pirogues on beach, shown. b, Pirogues, vert. c, Pirogues, close-up.

1999, Sept. 25 *Perf. 13*
129 A27 5fr Sheet of 3, #a.-c. 10.50 10.50

Vanilla — A28

1999, Nov. 6 *Litho.* *Perf. 13*
130 A28 4.50fr multi 1.75 1.75

Soulou Waterfalls — A29

1999, Dec. 11 *Perf. 13½x13*
131 A29 10fr multi 4.00 4.00

Year 2000 — A30

1999, Dec. 11 *Perf. 13*
132 A30 3fr multi 1.25 1.25

MAYOTTE

Indian Ocean Boat — A31

2000, Feb. 5   Litho.   *Perf. 13x13¼*
133   A31   3fr multi   1.90   1.90

Whales — A32

2000, Feb. 5   Litho.   *Perf. 13x13¼*
134   A32   5.20fr multi   2.75   2.75

Inner Wheel Rotary District — A33

2000, Mar. 24   *Perf. 13¼x13*
135   A33   5.20fr multi   2.50   2.50

Lagoon — A34

2000, Apr. 29   Litho.   *Perf. 13x13¼*
136   A34   3fr multi   1.40   1.40

Souvenir Sheet

Mahoraise Women — A35

Woman in: a, 3fr, red. b, 5.20fr, white.

2000, Apr. 29   *Perf. 13¼x13*
137   A35   Sheet of 2, #a-b   5.25   5.25

Tire Race — A36

2000, June 24   *Perf. 13x13¼*
138   A36   3fr multi   1.40   1.40

Tomb of Sultan Andriantsouli A37

2000, June 24
139   A37   5.40fr multi   2.75   2.75

Souvenir Sheet

Sea Shells A38

No. 140: a, Cassis cornuta. b, Charonia tritonis. c, Cyraecassis rufa. d, Cyprae mauritania, Cyprae tigris.

2000, Sept. 23   Litho.   *Perf. 13x13½*
140   A38   3fr Sheet of 4, #a-d   8.00   8.00

Zéna M'Déré (1917-99), Politician — A39

2000, Oct. 27   *Perf. 13*
141   A39   3fr multi   1.40   1.40

Ylang Distillery — A40

2000, Nov. 25   Litho.   *Perf. 13x13½*
142   A40   2.70fr multi   1.40   1.40

New Hospital — A41

2000, Nov. 25   *Perf. 13½x13*
143   A41   10fr multi   5.00   5.00

Map of Mayotte — A42

2001, Jan. 1   Litho.   *Perf. 13*
144   A42   2.70fr grn & blk   1.90   1.90
145   A42   (3fr) red & blk   1.90   1.90

Breastfeeding — A43

2001, Jan. 27   *Perf. 13¼x13*
146   A43   3fr multi   1.75   1.75

Return of Pilgrims to Mecca — A44

2001, Mar. 10   *Perf. 13x13¼*
147   A44   2.70fr multi   1.40   1.40

Bush Taxi — A45

2001, Mar. 10   *Perf. 13*
148   A45   3fr multi   1.75   1.75

Soccer — A46

2001, May 26   Litho.   *Perf. 13¼x13*
149   A46   3fr multi   1.40   1.40

Fish Type of 1998

Design: Pajama fish (gaterin, plectorhinchus orientalis).

2001, May 26   *Perf. 13x13¼*
150   A20   10fr multi   5.00   5.00

Foreign Legion Detachment in Mayotte, 25th Anniv. — A47

2001, Apr. 30   Litho.   *Perf. 13*
151   A47   5.20fr multi   2.75   2.75

Souvenir Sheet

Flying Foxes A48

No. 152: a, 3fr, Hanging from branch. b, 5.20fr, In flight.

2001, July 7   Litho.   *Perf. 13x13½*
152   A48   Sheet of 2, #a-b   6.50   6.50

Adapted Military Service Group, 1st Anniv. — A49

2001, Sept. 1   Litho.   *Perf. 13x13½*
153   A49   3fr multi   1.60   1.60

Flowers — A50

Designs: 3fr, Shown. 5.40fr, Fruits.

2001, Sept. 22   *Perf. 13*
154-155   A50   Set of 2   4.75   4.75

Lake Dziani Dzaha A51

2001, Nov. 17
156   A51   5.20fr multi   2.25   2.25

Mayotte Post Office — A52

2001, Nov. 17
157   A52   10fr multi   5.00   5.00

100 Cents = 1 Euro (€)

Arms — A53

2002, Jan. 1   Litho.   *Perf. 13x13½*
158   A53   46c multi   1.75   1.75

France Nos. 2835, 2849-2863 Overprinted

2002, Jan. 1   Engr.   *Perf. 13*
159   A1583   1c yellow   .25   .25
160   A1583   2c brown   .25   .25
161   A1583   5c brt bl grn   .30   .30
162   A1583   10c purple   .40   .40
163   A1583   20c brt org   .70   .70
164   A1583   41c brt green   1.25   1.25
165   A1409   (46c) red   1.40   1.40
166   A1583   50c dk blue   1.50   1.50
167   A1583   53c apple grn   1.60   1.60
168   A1583   58c blue   1.75   1.75
169   A1583   64c dark org   2.00   2.00
170   A1583   67c brt blue   2.10   2.10
171   A1583   69c brt pink   2.25   2.25
172   A1583   €1 Prus blue   3.00   3.00
173   A1583   €1.02 dk green   3.00   3.00
174   A1583   €2 violet   6.00   6.00
Nos. 159-174 (16)   27.75   27.75

Athletics A54

2002, Mar. 23   Litho.   *Perf. 13*
175   A54   41c multi   1.50   1.50

Kawéni Mangrove Swamp A55

2002, Mar. 25
176   A55   €1.52 multi   5.00   5.00

Mayotte Communes, 25th Anniv. — A56

2002, June 3   Litho.   *Perf. 13¼x13*
177   A56   46c multi   1.60   1.60

Salt Drying A57

2002, June 3   *Perf. 13x13¼*
178   A57   79c multi   3.00   3.00

MAYOTTE

2002 Census — A58

2002, July 29 Litho. Perf. 13¼x13
179 A58 46c multi   1.75 1.75

Abandoned Sugar Processing Equipment A59

2002, Sept. 21 Litho. Perf. 13
180 A59 82c multi   2.75 2.75

Miniature Sheet

Birds A60

No. 181: a, Souimanga. b, Drongo. c, Oiseau-lunette. d, Foudy.

2002, Sept. 21 Perf. 13x13¼
181 A60 46c Sheet of 4, #a-d   7.50 7.50

Mt. Choungui — A61

2002, Nov. 16 Litho. Perf. 13¼x13
182 A61 46c multi   1.75 1.75

Breadfruit — A62

2002, Nov. 16
183 A62 €1.22 multi   4.00 4.00

Vanilla and Ylang Museum — A63

2003, Jan. 1 Litho. Perf. 13x13½
184 A63 46c multi   1.75 1.75

Banana Tree — A64

2003, Feb. 1 Perf. 13½x13
185 A64 79c multi   2.50 2.50

Holiday Face Decorations A65

2003, Apr. 5 Litho. Perf. 13
186 A65 46c multi   1.75 1.75

Swordfish A66

2003, Apr. 5
187 A66 79c multi   2.75 2.75

Gecko A67

2003, June 14 Litho. Perf. 13
188 A67 50c multi   1.90 1.90

Mraha Game A68

2003, June 14 Engr. Perf. 13x12½
189 A68 €1.52 claret & brown   5.25 5.25

Mtzamboro College — A69

2003, Sept. 6 Litho. Perf. 13x13¼
190 A69 45c multi   1.75 1.75

Ziyara de Pole — A70

2003, Sept. 6 Perf. 13¼x13
191 A70 82c multi   3.00 3.00

Basketball — A71

2003, Nov. 15 Litho. Perf. 13¼x13
192 A71 50c multi   1.75 1.75

Wadaha — A72

2004, Jan. 3 Perf. 13
193 A72 50c multi   1.75 1.75

Map Type of 2001 Inscribed "RF" and With Euro Denominations Only
2004
194 A42 1c yel & blk   .25   .25
195 A42 2c gray & blk   .25   .25
196 A42 5c greenish bl & blk .25 .25
197 A42 10c red vio & blk   .25   .25
198 A42 20c org & blk   .40   .40
199 A42 45c green & black   1.00 1.00
200 A42 50c dk bl & blk   1.00 1.00
201 A42 €1 Prus bl & blk   1.90 1.90
202 A42 €2 violet & blk   4.00 4.00
     Nos. 194-202 (9)   9.30 9.30

Issued: 1c, 2c, 50c, €2, 3/10; 5c, 10c, 20c, €1, 4/17; 45c, 7/17.

Sada Bay — A73

2004, Apr. 3 Litho. Perf. 13
203 A73 90c multi   2.75 2.75

Souvenir Sheet

Butterflies — A74

No. 204: a, Junonia rhadama. b, Papilio demodocus. c, Acraea ranavalona. d, Danaus chrysippus.

2004, Apr. 3 Perf. 13x13¼
204 A74 50c Sheet of 4, #a-d   7.00 7.00

Papaya and Papaya Tree — A75

2004, June 12 Litho. Perf. 13x13¼
205 A75 50c multi   1.75 1.75

Gold Jewelry — A76

2004, June 12 Litho. Perf. 13
206 A76 €2.40 multi   7.50 7.50

Kwalé River Bridge — A77

2004, Sept. 25 Litho. Perf. 13x13¼
207 A77 50c multi   1.75 1.75

Maki and Young — A78

2004, Sept. 25 Perf. 13
208 A78 75c multi   3.00 3.00

Woman Cooking Food — A79

2004, Nov. 13 Perf. 13x13¼
209 A79 45c multi   1.50 1.50

Domino Players A80

2004, Nov. 13 Perf. 13
210 A80 75c multi   2.10 2.10

Ylang-ylang Trees A81

2005, Jan. 3 Litho. Perf. 13
211 A81 50c multi   1.75 1.75

Traditional Women's Clothing — A82

2005, Mar. 14 Litho. Perf. 13
212 A82 53c multi   1.90 1.90

Breadfruit and Tree — A83

2005, Mar. 14 Perf. 13¼x13
213 A83 64c multi   2.25 2.25

Rotary International, Cent — A84

2005, May 13 Perf. 13
214 A84 90c multi   3.25 3.25

Souvenir Sheet

Marine Mammals — A85

MAYOTTE

No. 215: a, Humpback whale (Baleine à bosse). b, Dolphins. c, Sperm whale (grand cachalot). d, Dugongs.

2005, May 13   **Perf. 13x13¼**
215 A85 53c Sheet of 4, #a-d   7.50   7.50

Stick Figure Drawings — A86

2005, July 4   **Perf. 13**
216 A86 48c multi   1.75   1.75

Mamoudzou A87

2005, Sept. 10   **Litho.**   **Perf. 13**
217 A87 48c multi   1.50   1.50

Fisherman in Pirogue — A88

2005, Sept. 10
218 A88 75c multi   2.00   2.00

Blacksmith A89

2005, Nov. 12   **Litho.**   **Perf. 13x13¼**
219 A89 53c multi   1.75   1.75

Tam-tam Boeuf Celebration A90

2005, Nov. 12   **Perf. 13**
220 A90 53c multi   1.75   1.75

Woman Grating Coconuts — A91

2006, Jan. 14   **Litho.**   **Perf. 13x13¼**
221 A91 53c multi   1.75   1.75

Moya Beach A92

2006, Mar. 18   **Litho.**   **Perf. 13**
222 A92 48c multi   1.75   1.75

Souvenir Sheet

Turtle Protection — A93

No. 223: a, Turtle swimming. b, Turtle laying eggs. c, Hatchlings.

2006, Mar. 18   **Perf. 13x13¼**
223 A93 53c Sheet of 3, #a-c   6.00   6.00

Farmer's Market A94

Ferries A95

2006, May 15   **Litho.**   **Perf. 13x12¾**
224 A94 53c multi   1.75   1.75
225 A95 €1.07 multi   3.50   3.50

Aloe Mayottensis — A96

2006, July 3   **Litho.**   **Perf. 13¼x13**
226 A96 53c multi   1.75   1.75

Frangipani Shrub and Flowers — A97

2006, Sept. 9   **Perf. 13x13¼**
227 A97 53c multi   1.75   1.75

Moulidi Dance A98

2006, Sept. 9   **Perf. 13**
228 A98 75c multi   2.75   2.75

Tropic Birds — A99

2006, Nov. 18   **Litho.**   **Perf. 13**
229 A99 54c multi   2.00   2.00

Resumption of Stamp Issues, 10th Anniv. — A100

2007, Jan. 20   **Litho.**   **Perf. 13½x13**
230 A100 54c multi   1.75   1.75

Phanelopsis Orchid — A101

2007, Jan. 20   **Perf. 13x13½**
231 A101 54c multi   1.90   1.90

Audit Office, Bicent. — A102

2007, Mar. 17   **Engr.**   **Perf. 13¼**
232 A102 54c multi   2.00   2.00

Phyllostachys Edulis — A103

2007, Mar. 19   **Litho.**   **Perf. 13¼x13**
233 A103 €1.01 multi   3.50   3.50

Traditional House — A104

2007, May 14   **Perf. 13¼**
234 A104 54c multi   1.90   1.90

General Council, 30th Anniv. — A105

2007, May 12   **Litho.**   **Perf. 13¼x13**
235 A105 54c multi   1.90   1.90

Souvenir Sheet

Corals A106

No. 236: a, Corail corne d'elan. b, Gorgone eventail. c, Corail corne de cerf. d, Cerveau de Neptune.

2007, June 16   **Perf. 13x13¼**
236 A106 54c Sheet of 4, #a-d   7.75   7.75

Mangos and Mango Tree — A107

2007, Sept. 17   **Litho.**   **Perf. 13x13¼**
237 A107 54c multi   1.90   1.90

Chameleon A108

2007, Sept. 17
238 A108 54c multi   1.90   1.90

Beach Grill and Shelter A109

2007, Nov. 10   **Perf. 13**
239 A109 54c multi   1.90   1.90

N'Gouja Beach A110

2007, Nov. 10   **Perf. 13x13¼**
240 A110 54c multi   3.00   3.00

Zebu — A111

2008, Jan. 28   **Litho.**   **Perf. 13x13½**
241 A111 54c multi   2.00   2.00

Coconuts and Coconut Palm — A112

2008, Jan. 28   **Perf. 13x13¼**
242 A112 54c multi   1.90   1.90

Miniature Sheet

Spices A113

No. 243: a, Cinnamon (cannelle). b, Nutmeg (muscade). c, Turmeric (curcuma). d, Ginger (gingembre).

2008, Mar. 22   **Litho.**   **Perf. 13x13¼**
243 A113 55c Sheet of 4, #a-d   7.75   7.75

MAYOTTE

Hibiscus — A114

2008, May 26   Perf. 13¼x13
244 A114 55c multi   2.00 2.00

Wedding Ceremony A115

2008, May 26   Perf. 13
245 A115 55c multi   2.00 2.00

Younoussa Bamana (1935-2007), Politician — A116

2008, June 23   Litho.   Perf. 13¼x13
246 A116 55c multi   1.90 1.90

M'Biwi Dance — A117

2008, Sept. 22   Litho.   Perf. 13x13¼
247 A117 55c multi   2.00 2.00

Embroidery A118

2008, Nov. 10   Litho.   Perf. 13x13¼
248 A118 55c multi   1.75 1.75

Mamoudzou Town Hall — A119

2008, Dec. 8   Perf. 13
249 A119 55c multi   1.75 1.75

Longoni Power Station A120

2009, Jan. 12
250 A120 55c multi   2.10 2.10

Cardinals — A121

2009, Jan. 12   Litho.   Perf. 13
251 A121 55c multi   2.00 2.00

Tamarind Tree and Fruit — A122

2009, Mar. 9   Perf. 13x13¼
252 A122 56c multi   1.75 1.75

Fishing by Kerosene Lantern A123

2009, Mar. 9   Perf. 13
253 A123 56c multi   1.75 1.75

Miniature Sheet

Citrus Fruits A124

No. 254: a, Oranges. b, Grapefruit (pampiemousse). c, Lemons (citron). d, Kaffir limes (combava).

2009, May 18   Perf. 13x13¼
254 A124 56c Sheet of 4, #a-d   8.25 8.25

Souvenir Sheet

Les Quatres Freres A125

No. 255: a, Close-up view (blue sky). b, Distant view (yellow sky).

2009, June 29   Litho.   Perf. 13x13¼
255 A125 56c Sheet of 2, #a-b   4.50 4.50

Jasmine Flowers — A126

2009, Sept. 21   Litho.   Perf. 13
256 A126 56c multi   2.10 2.10

Gaboussi Player — A127

2009, Nov. 16   Perf. 13x13¼
257 A127 56c multi   2.10 2.10

Welcome to Travelers — A128

2010, Jan. 11   Litho.   Perf. 13
258 A128 56c multi   1.75 1.75

Basket Weaver A129

2010, Mar. 8   Litho.   Perf. 13
259 A129 56c multi   1.75 1.75

Governor's House A130

2010, Mar. 8
260 A130 56c multi   1.75 1.75

Sparrow Hawk — A131

2010, May 17   Engr.   Perf. 13¼
261 A131 56c multi   1.90 1.90

Platycerium Alcicorne — A132

2010, May 17   Litho.   Perf. 13¼
262 A132 56c multi   1.75 1.75

Decorated Book Rest — A133

2010, July 5   Engr.   Perf. 12¼
263 A133 58c multi   1.75 1.75

Customs Department Building — A134

2010, July 30   Litho.   Perf. 13x13½
264 A134 58c multi   1.50 1.50

Chigoma Dance A135

2010, Sept. 13
265 A135 95c multi   2.60 2.60

Mail Carrier on All-Terrain Vehicle A136

2010, Nov. 8   Perf. 13¼x13
266 A136 58c multi   1.60 1.60

Miniature Sheet

Women's Hairstyles — A137

No. 267 — Various hairstyles of women wearing: a, Lilac clothing, woman facing right. b, Yellow brown clothing. c, Red clothing. d, Lilac clothing, woman facing left.

2011, Jan. 17   Perf. 13½x13
267 A137 58c Sheet of 4, #a-d   6.50 6.50

Grand Mosque of Mtsapéré — A138

2011, Feb. 14   Perf. 13¼x13
268 A138 58c multi   1.75 1.75

Woman Carrying Laundry — A139

2011, Mar. 14   Perf. 13
269 A139 58c multi   1.75 1.75

Bee-eaters A140

2011, Mar. 14
270 A140 58c multi   1.75 1.75

Mayotte's Association With France, 170th Anniv. A141

2011, Apr. 4   Engr.   Perf. 13x12¼
271 A141 58c brown   1.75 1.75

White Sand Island — A142

2011, May 16   Litho.   Perf. 13x13¼
272 A142 58c multi   1.75 1.75

Kingfisher — A143

2011, May 16   Perf. 13¼x13
273 A143 58c multi   1.75 1.75

Kapok Tree — A144

2011, June 20
274 A144 58c multi   1.75 1.75

MAYOTTE — MEMEL

Mtzamboro Island Oranges and Orange Tree — A145

2011, June 20
275 A145 58c multi ... 1.75 1.75

Majlis Ceremony A146

2011, June 20 *Perf. 13*
276 A146 58c multi ... 1.75 1.75

Skin Divers A147

2011, July 4 *Litho. Perf. 13¼x13*
277 A147 60c multi ... 1.75 1.75

Karehani Lake A148

2011, July 4
278 A148 60c multi ... 1.75 1.75

Marketplace A149

2011, Sept. 5 *Perf. 13x13½*
279 A149 60c multi ... 1.75 1.75

Flycatchers A150

2011, Sept. 5
280 A150 60c multi ... 1.75 1.75

Indian Ocean Philatelic Show — A151

2011, Sept. 19 *Perf. 13*
281 A151 60c multi ... 1.75 1.75

Change of Mayotte's Political Status A152

2011, Sept. 1
282 A152 60c multi ... 1.75 1.75

The Overseas Collectivity of Mayotte became France's 101st department on Mar. 31, 2011.

Pottery — A153

2011, Oct. 3 *Perf. 13¼x13*
283 A153 60c multi ... 1.75 1.75

Aquaculture A154

2011, Nov. 14 *Perf. 13x13¼*
284 A154 60c multi ... 1.60 1.60

Padza of Dapani — A155

2011, Nov. 14
285 A155 60c multi ... 1.60 1.60

Fishermen Returning with Catch — A156

2011, Dec. 5 *Perf. 13*
286 A156 60c multi ... 1.60 1.60

Northern Islets — A157

2011, Dec. 12 *Perf. 13x13¼*
287 A157 60c multi ... 1.60 1.60

Ship Marion Dufresne in Mamoudzou Lagoon A158

2011, Dec. 31 *Perf. 13*
288 A158 60c multi ... 2.75 2.75

See French Southern & Antarctic Territories No. 453.
Mayotte began to use the postage stamps of France as of Jan. 1, 2012.

AIR POST STAMPS

Catalogue values for unused stamps in this section are for Never Hinged items.

Opening of New Air Terminal AP1

1997, Mar. 1 *Engr. Perf. 13x12½*
C1 AP1 20fr multicolored ... 11.00 11.00

First Mayotte-Réunion Flight, 20th Anniv. — AP2

Photo. & Engr.
1997, Nov. 29 *Perf. 13x12½*
C2 AP2 5fr multicolored ... 3.00 3.00

Pique-boeuf Bird, Zebu — AP3

1998, Apr. 1 *Litho. Perf. 13*
C3 AP3 30fr multicolored ... 13.00 13.00

Deba Religious Festival AP4

1999, Nov. 6 *Litho. Perf. 13*
C4 AP4 10fr multicolored ... 5.00 5.00

Dzaoudzi Aero Club — AP5

2001, July 7 *Litho. Perf. 13*
C5 AP5 20fr multi ... 9.50 9.50

Dzaoudzi Rock — AP6

2003, Nov. 15 *Litho. Perf. 13*
C6 AP6 €1.50 multi ... 5.75 5.75

MEMEL
ˈmä-məl

LOCATION — In northern Europe, bordering on the Baltic Sea
GOVT. — Special commission (see below)
AREA — 1099 sq. mi.
POP. — 151,960

Following World War I this territory was detached from Germany and by Treaty of Versailles assigned to the government of a commission of the Allied and Associated Powers (not the League of Nations), which administered it until January, 1923, when it was forcibly occupied by Lithuania. In 1924 Memel became incorporated as a semi-autonomous district of Lithuania with the approval of the Allied Powers and the League of Nations.

100 Pfennig = 1 Mark
100 Centu = 1 Litas (1923)

Excellent counterfeits of all Memel stamps exist.

Stamps of Germany, 1905-20, Overprinted

Wmk. Lozenges (125)
1920, Aug. 1 *Perf. 14, 14½*
1 A16 5pf green 1.50 15.00
2 A16 10pf car rose 1.90 9.00
3 A16 10pf orange .30 3.25
4 A22 15pf violet brown 2.60 12.00
5 A16 20pf blue violet 1.10 5.25
6 A16 30pf org & blk, *buff* 1.25 8.25
7 A16 30pf dull blue .40 3.25
8 A16 40pf lake & blk .25 3.25
9 A16 50pf pur & blk, *buff* .30 3.25
10 A16 60pf olive green 1.50 6.00
11 A16 75pf grn & blk 2.60 22.50
12 A16 80pf blue violet 1.35 9.75

Overprinted
13 A17 1m car rose .30 3.25
14 A17 1.25m green 13.00 50.00
15 A17 1.50m yel brn 4.50 30.00
16 A21 2m blue 7.50 13.50
17 A21 2.50m red lilac 11.50 60.00
Nos. 1-17 (17) 51.85 257.50

Stamps of France types A18 and A22 were printed in 1916-20 on paper of poor quality, usually grayish and containing bits of fiber. This is called G. C. (Grande Consommation) paper. These wartime printings are noted (GC) in the descriptions.

Stamps of France, Surcharged in Black

On A22   On A18

1920 *Unwmk. Perf. 14x13½*
18 A22 5pf on 5c green .75 3.25
  a. Grayish paper (GC) 3.00 17.50
19 A22 10pf on 10c red .60 2.60
  a. Grayish paper (GC) 28.00 105.00
20 A22 20pf on 25c blue 1.10 3.75
21 A22 30pf on 30c org .75 3.25
  a. Grayish paper (GC) 7.00 14.00
22 A22 40pf on 20c red brn 1.10 3.25
  a. Grayish paper (GC) 7.00 14.00
23 A22 50pf on 35c vio .30 3.25
  a. Grayish paper (GC) 97.50 500.00
24 A18 60pf on 40c red & pale bl .40 3.75
  a. Grayish paper (GC) 4.50 17.50
25 A18 80pf on 45c grn & bl 1.10 4.50
  a. Grayish paper (GC) 6.50 28.00
26 A18 1m on 50c brn & lav .50 3.75
  a. Grayish paper (GC) 17.50 11.00
27 A18 1m 25pf on 60c vio & ultra 1.20 9.00
  a. Grayish paper (GC) 8.50 50.00
28 A18 2m on 1fr cl & gr orn .60 3.50
  a. Grayish paper (GC) 2.50 14.00
29 A18 3m on 5fr bl & buff 22.50 67.50
Nos. 18-29 (12) 30.90 111.35

For stamps with additional surcharges and overprints see Nos. 43-49, C1-C4.

French Stamps of 1900-20 Surcharged like Nos. 24 to 29 in Red or Black

On A18

4 mark — Type I
4 mark — Type II

1920-21 *Unwmk. Perf. 14x13½*
30 A18 3m on 2fr org & pale bl 22.50 67.50
  a. Grayish paper (GC) 62.50 275.00

MEMEL

31	A18	4m on 2fr org & pale bl (I) (Bk)	.45	3.75
a.		Type II	95.00	160.00
b.		As "#31," grayish paper (GC)	10.00	70.00
c.		As "a," grayish paper (GC)	4.50	32.50
32	A18	10m on 5fr bl & buff	3.00	15.00
33	A18	20m on 5fr bl & buff	37.50	150.00
		Nos. 30-33 (4)	63.45	236.25

For stamps with additional overprints see Nos. C5, C19.

New Value with Initial Capital
1921

39	A18	60Pf on 40c red & pale bl	4.50	19.00
40	A18	3M on 60c vio & ultra	2.25	7.50
41	A18	10M on 5fr bl & buff	8.25	
42	A18	20M on 45c grn & bl	4.50	26.00
		Nos. 39-42 (4)	13.50	60.75

The surcharged value on No. 40 is in italics. For stamps with additional overprints see Nos. C6-C7, C18.

Stamps of 1920 Surcharged with Large Numerals in Dark Blue or Red

No. 43 — MEMEL 15
No. 49 — MEMEL 5,00

1921-22

43	A22	15pf on 10pf on 10c	.40	1.90
a.		Inverted surcharge	55.00	225.00
44	A22	15pf on 20pf on 25c	.40	3.00
a.		Inverted surcharge	55.00	
45	A22	15pf on 50pf on 35c (R)	.40	3.00
a.		Inverted surcharge	55.00	
46	A22	60pf on 40pf on 20c, grayish paper (GC)	.40	1.90
a.		Inverted surcharge	55.00	225.00
b.		As "#46," grayish paper (GC)	.35	1.75
47	A18	75pf on 60pf on 40c	.75	3.75
48	A18	1.25m on 1m on 50c	.60	3.00
49	A18	5.00m on 2m on 1fr	.90	4.50
a.		Inverted surcharge	150.00	
		Nos. 43-49 (7)	3.85	21.05

Stamps of France Surcharged in Black or Red

On A20, A22

1922

50	A22	5pf on 5c org	.25	1.35
51	A22	10pf on 10c red	.75	5.25
52	A22	10pf on 10c bl	.25	1.35
53	A22	15pf on 10c grn	.25	1.35
54	A22	20pf on 20c red brn	7.50	37.50
55	A22	20pf on 25c bl	7.50	37.50
56	A22	25pf on 5c org	.25	1.35
57	A22	30pf on 30c red	1.10	5.25
58	A22	35pf on 35c vio	.25	.75
59	A20	40pf on 50c vio	.25	1.35
60	A20	50pf on 50c dl bl	.25	1.35
60	A20	75pf on 15c grn	.30	.75
61	A20	75pf on 35c vio	.30	1.35
62	A22	1m on 25c blue	.30	.75
63	A22	1¼m on 30c red	.25	.75
64	A22	3m on 5c org	.40	5.00
65	A20	6m on 15c grn (R)	.75	5.00
66	A22	8m on 30c red	.75	13.00

On A18 — MEMEL 40 Pfennig

67	A18	40pf on 40c red & pale bl	.25	1.35
68	A18	80pf on 45c grn & bl	.30	1.35
69	A18	1m on 40c red & pale bl	.30	2.25
70	A18	1.25m on 60c vio & ultra (R)	.30	2.25
71	A18	1.50m on 45c grn & bl (R)	.30	2.25
72	A18	2m on 45c grn & bl	.30	2.25
73	A18	2m on 1fr cl & ol grn	.75	2.60
74	A18	2¼m on 60c vio & pale bl	.25	.75
75	A18	2½m on 60c vio & ultra	.75	2.50
76	A18	3m on 60c vio & ultra (R)	1.10	5.25
77	A18	4m on 45c grn & bl	.25	.75
78	A18	5m on 1fr cl & ol grn	.30	3.00
79	A18	6m on 60c vio & ultra	.25	.75
80	A18	6m on 2fr org & pale bl	.30	3.00
81	A18	9m on 1fr cl & ol grn	.25	.75
82	A18	9m on 5fr bl & buff (R)	.40	3.00
83	A18	10m on 45c grn & bl (R)	.75	5.00
84	A18	12m on 40c red & pale bl	.40	2.25
85	A18	20m on 40c red & pale bl	.75	5.00
86	A18	20m on 2fr org & pale bl	.25	2.00
87	A18	30m on 60c vio & ultra	.75	5.00
88	A18	30m on 5fr dk bl & buff	2.60	19.00
89	A18	40m on 1fr cl & ol grn	.75	6.50
90	A18	50m on 2fr org & pale bl	7.50	45.00
91	A18	80m on 2fr org & pale bl (R)	.75	6.50
92	A18	100m on 5fr bl & buff	1.10	12.00
		Nos. 50-92 (43)	43.35	261.90

A 500m on 5fr dark blue and buff was prepared, but not officially issued. Value: unused $800; never hinged $2,000.
For stamps with additional surcharges and overprints see Nos. 93-99, C8-C17, C20-C29.

Nos. 52, 54, 67, 59 Surcharged "Mark"

1922-23

93	A22	10m on 10pf on 10c	.75	7.00
a.		Double surcharge	100.00	500.00
94	A22	20m on 20pf on 20c	.40	1.50
95	A18	40m on 40pf on 40c ('23)	.75	5.00
96	A20	50m on 50pf on 50c	2.25	14.50
		Nos. 93-96 (4)	4.15	31.00

Nos. 72, 61, 70 Srchd. in Red or Black
MEMEL 10 Mark

1922-23

97	A18	10m on 2m on 45c	1.90	13.00
98	A22	25m on 1m on 25c	1.90	13.00
99	A18	80m on 1.25m on 60c (Bk) ('23)	1.10	7.00
		Nos. 97-99 (3)	4.90	33.00

For No. 99 with additional surcharges see Nos. N28-N30.

AIR POST STAMPS

FLUGPOST

Nos. 24-26, 28, 31, 39-40 Ovptd. in Dark Blue

1921, July 6   Unwmk.   Perf. 14x13½

C1	A18	60pf on 40c	30.00	150.00
C2	A18	80pf on 45c	3.75	13.00
C3	A18	1m on 50c	4.00	13.00
C4	A18	2m on 1fr	4.50	13.50
a.		"Flugpost" inverted	160.00	375.00
C5	A18	4m on 2fr (I)	3.75	19.00
a.		Type II	75.00	260.00
b.		Pair, type I and type II	100.00	

New Value with Initial Capital

C6	A18	60Pf on 40c	3.75	17.00
a.		Flugpost inverted	150.00	375.00
C7	A18	3M on 60c	2.60	17.00
a.		"Flugpost" inverted	260.00	600.00
		Nos. C1-C7 (7)	52.35	242.50

The surcharged value on No. C7 is in italics.

Nos. 67-71, 73, 76, 78, 80, 82 Ovptd. in Dark Blue
MEMEL Flugpost

1922, May 12

C8	A18	40pf on 40c	.40	3.75
C9	A18	80pf on 45c	.40	3.75
C10	A18	1m on 40c	.40	3.75
C11	A18	1.25m on 60c	.75	6.00
C12	A18	1.50m on 45c	.75	6.00
C13	A18	2m on 1fr	.75	6.00
C14	A18	3m on 60c	.75	6.00
C15	A18	5m on 1fr	1.10	6.00
C16	A18	6m on 2fr	1.10	6.00
C17	A18	9m on 5fr	1.10	6.00

Same Overprint On Nos. 40, 31

C18	A18	3m on 60c	120.00	1,050.
C19	A18	4m on 2fr	.75	6.00
		Nos. C8-C17, C19 (11)	8.25	59.25

Nos. 67, 69-71, 73, 76, 78, 80, 82 Ovptd. in Black or Red

MEMEL FLUGPOST 40 Pfennig

1922, Oct. 17

C20	A18	40pf on 40c	1.25	15.00
C21	A18	1m on 40c	1.25	15.00
C22	A18	1.25m on 60c (R)	1.25	15.00
C23	A18	1.50m on 45c (R)	1.25	15.00
C24	A18	2m on 1fr	1.25	15.00
C25	A18	3m on 60c (R)	1.25	15.00
C26	A18	4m on 2fr	1.25	15.00
C27	A18	5m on 1fr	1.25	15.00
C28	A18	6m on 2fr	1.25	15.00
C29	A18	9m on 5fr (R)	1.25	15.00
		Nos. C20-C29 (10)	12.50	150.00

No. C26 is not known without the "FLUGPOST" overprint.

OCCUPATION STAMPS

Issued under Lithuanian Occupation

Surcharged in Various Colors on Unissued Official Stamps of Lithuania Similar to Type O4

Klaipėda (Memel) 10 Markių — On Nos. N1-N6
KLAIPĖDA (MEMEL) 25 MARKĖS — On Nos. N7-N11

Memel Printing

1923   Unwmk.   Litho.   Perf. 11

N1	O4	10m on 5c bl (Bk)	1.00	10.00
a.		Double overprint	35.00	230.00
b.		"Memel" and bars omitted	7.00	52.50
N2	O4	25m on 5c bl (R)	1.00	10.00
a.		Double overprint	35.00	230.00
N3	O4	50m on 25c red (Bk)	1.00	10.00
a.		Double overprint	35.00	230.00
N4	O4	100m on 25c red (G)	1.00	10.00
a.		Double overprint	35.00	230.00
N5	O4	400m on 1 l brn (R)	1.30	13.00
a.		Double overprint	35.00	230.00
N6	O4	500m on 1 l brn (Bl)	1.30	13.00
a.		Double overprint	35.00	230.00
		Nos. N1-N6 (6)	6.60	66.00

Kaunas Printing
Black Surcharge

N7	O4	10m on 5c blue	.70	6.00
N8	O4	25m on 5c blue	.70	6.00
N9	O4	50m on 25c red	.70	6.00
N10	O4	100m on 25c red	.80	6.00
N11	O4	400m on 1 l brn	1.30	9.25
		Nos. N7-N11 (5)	4.20	33.25

No. N8 has the value in "Markes," others of the group have it in "Markiu."
For additional surcharge see No. N87.

Surcharged in Various Colors on Unissued Official Stamps of Lithuania Similar to Type O4

KLAIPĖDA (Memel) 25 MARKĖS

1923

N12	O4	10m on 5c bl (R)	1.30	8.00
a.		"Markes" instead of "Markiu"	13.00	92.50
N13	O4	20m on 5c bl (R)	1.30	8.00
N14	O4	25m on 25c red (Bl)	1.30	10.50
N15	O4	50m on 25c red (Bl)	2.60	10.50
a.		Inverted surcharge	32.50	130.00
N16	O4	200m on 1 l brn (Bk)	2.60	15.00
a.		Inverted surcharge	32.50	130.00
N17	O4	200m on 1 l brn (Bk)	4.00	17.00
		Nos. N12-N17 (6)	13.10	69.00

No. N14 has the value in "Markes," others of the group have it in "Markiu."

"Vytis" — O4   O5

1923, Mar.

N18	O4	10m lt brown	.35	5.50
N19	O4	20m yellow	.35	5.50
N20	O4	25m orange	.35	5.50
N21	O4	40m violet	.35	5.50
N22	O4	50m yellow grn	1.00	12.00
N23	O5	100m carmine	.45	6.00
N24	O5	300m olive grn	5.00	120.00
N25	O5	400m olive brn	.45	6.00
N26	O5	500m lilac	5.00	120.00
N27	O5	1000m blue	.85	10.00
		Nos. N18-N27 (10)	14.15	297.50

No. N20 has the value in "Markes."
For surcharges see Nos. N44-N69, N88-N114.

No. 99 Surcharged in Green — Klaipėda 100 M

1923, Apr. 13

N28	A18	100m on No. 99	3.00	60.00
a.		Inverted overprint	70.00	
N29	A18	400m on No. 99	4.00	60.00
a.		Inverted overprint	70.00	
N30	A18	500m on No. 99	3.00	60.00
a.		Inverted overprint	70.00	
		Nos. N28-N30 (3)	10.00	180.00

The normal position of the green surcharge is sideways, up-reading, with the top at the left. Inverted varieties are reversed, with the overprint down-reading.

KLAIPĖDA Ship — O7
KLAIPĖDA Seal — O8
Lighthouse — O9

1923, Apr. 12   Litho.

N31	O7	40m olive grn	3.75	32.50
N32	O7	50m brown	3.75	32.50
N33	O7	80m green	3.75	32.50
N34	O7	100m red	3.75	32.50
N35	O8	200m deep blue	3.75	32.50
N36	O8	300m brown	3.75	32.50
N37	O8	400m lilac	3.75	32.50
N38	O8	500m orange	3.75	32.50
N39	O8	600m olive grn	3.75	32.50
N40	O9	800m deep blue	3.75	32.50
N41	O9	1000m lilac	3.75	32.50
N42	O9	2000m red	3.75	32.50
N43	O9	3000m green	3.75	32.50
		Nos. N31-N43 (13)	48.75	422.50

Union of Memel with Lithuania. Forgeries exist.
For surcharges see Nos. N70-N86.

Nos. N20, N24, N26 Surcharged in Various Colors

10 CENTŲ

1923   Thin Figures

N44	O5	2c on 300m (R)	5.25	13.00
a.		Double surcharge	70.00	325.00
N45	O5	3c on 300m (R)	6.00	17.00
a.		Double surcharge	145.00	400.00
N46	O4	10c on 25m (Bk)	6.00	13.00
a.		Double surcharge	70.00	260.00
b.		Inverted surcharge	92.50	260.00
N47	O4	15c on 25m (Bk)	6.00	13.00
N48	O5	20c on 500m (Bl)	9.25	26.00
N49	O5	30c on 500m (Bk)	7.25	13.00
a.		Double surcharge		
N50	O5	50c on 500m (G)	11.00	26.00
a.		Inverted surcharge	52.50	200.00
b.		Double surcharge	130.00	600.00
		Nos. N44-N50 (7)	50.75	121.00

Nos. N19, N21-N27 Surcharged

2 CENT.
1 LITAS

N51	O4	2c on 20m yellow	3.25	13.00
N52	O4	2c on 50c yel grn	3.25	13.00
a.		Double surcharge	50.00	260.00
b.		Vert. pair, imperf between	70.00	300.00

MEMEL — MESOPOTAMIA

N53	O4 3c on 40m violet	5.50	12.00
a.	Double surcharge	57.50	260.00
N54	O5 3c on 300m ol grn	3.25	10.00
a.	Double surcharge	130.00	450.00
N55	O5 5c on 100m carmine	8.00	10.00
N56	O5 5c on 300m ol grn (R)	3.25	17.00
a.	Double surcharge	92.50	325.00
N57	O5 10c on 400m ol brn	17.00	20.00
N58	O5 30c on 500m lilac	5.25	22.50
a.	Double surcharge	92.50	325.00
b.	Inverted surcharge	100.00	360.00
N59	O5 1 l on 1000m blue	22.50	65.00
a.	Double surcharge	130.00	460.00
	Nos. N51-N59 (9)	71.25	182.50

There are several types of the numerals in these surcharges. Nos. N56 and N58 have "CENT" in short, thick letters, as on Nos. N44 to N50.

Nos. N18-N23, N25, N27 Surcharged

Thick Figures

N60	O4 2c on 10m lt brn	5.25	65.00
N61	O4 2c on 20m yellow	17.00	120.00
N62	O4 2c on 50m yel grn	6.50	80.00
N63	O4 3c on 40m lt brn	17.00	110.00
a.	Double surcharge	130.00	525.00
N64	O4 3c on 40m violet	20.00	190.00
N65	O5 5c on 100m car	10.00	32.50
a.	Double surcharge	92.50	300.00
N66	O5 10c on 400m ol brn	130.00	550.00
N67	O5 15c on 25m orange	130.00	550.00
N68	O5 50c on 1000m blue	5.25	10.00
a.	Double surcharge	92.50	300.00
N69	O5 1 l on 1000m blue	6.50	20.00
	Nos. N60-N69 (10)	347.50	1,728.

No. N69 is surcharged like type "b" in the following group.

Nos. N31-N43 Surcharged

a — 30 CENT
b — 1 LITAS

N70	O7(a) 15c on 40m ol grn	4.25	26.00
N71	O7(a) 30c on 50m brown	4.25	20.00
a.	Double surcharge	52.50	230.00
N72	O7(a) 30c on 80m green	4.25	32.50
N73	O7(a) 30c on 100m red	4.25	13.00
N74	O8(a) 50c on 200m dp blue	4.25	26.00
N75	O8(a) 50c on 300m brn	4.25	13.00
a.	Double surcharge	52.50	230.00
b.	Inverted surcharge	52.50	230.00
N76	O8(a) 50c on 400m lilac	4.25	22.50
a.	Inverted surcharge	60.00	260.00
N77	O8(a) 50c on 500m org	4.25	13.00
a.	Double surcharge	52.50	230.00
N78	O8(b) 1 l on 600m ol grn	4.25	30.00
N79	O9(b) 1 l on 800m dp blue	5.00	30.00
N80	O9(b) 1 l on 1000m lil	4.50	30.00
N81	O9(b) 1 l on 2000m red	5.00	30.00
N82	O9(b) 1 l on 3000m grn	5.00	30.00
	Nos. N70-N82 (13)	57.75	316.00

These stamps are said to have been issued to commemorate the institution of autonomous government.

Nos. N32, N34, N36, N38 Surcharged in Green

60 CENT

1923

N83	O7 15c on 50m brn	165.	1,650.
a.	Thick numerals in surcharge	1,000.	4,000.
N84	O7 25c on 100m red	70.	1,000.
a.	Thick numerals in surcharge	1,000.	2,600.
N85	O8 30c on 300m brn	130.	1,050.
a.	Thick numerals in surcharge	800.	3,000.
N86	O8 60c on 500m org	80.	1,000.
a.	Thick numerals in surcharge	525.	2,000.

Surcharges on Nos. N83-N86 are of two types, differing in width of numerals. Values are for stamps with narrow numerals, as illustrated. Stamps with wide numerals sell for two to four times as much. For detailed listing see the *Scott Classic Specialized Catalogue of Stamps & Covers.*

Nos. N8, N10-N11, N3 Surcharged in Red or Green

N87	O4 10c on 25m on 5c bl (R)	26.00	100.00
N88	O4 15c on 100m on 25c red (G)	32.50	300.00
a.	Inverted surcharge	325.00	1,850.
N89	O4 30c on 400m on 1 l brn (R)	6.50	40.00
N90	O4 60c on 50m on 25c red (G)	32.50	260.00
	Nos. N87-N90 (4)	97.50	700.00

Nos. N18-N22 Surcharged in Green or Red

N91	O4 15c on 10m	26.00	200.00
N92	O4 15c on 20m	2.60	26.00
N93	O4 15c on 25m	5.50	52.50
N94	O4 15c on 40m	1.65	26.00
N95	O4 15c on 50m (R)	2.40	30.00
a.	Inverted surcharge	50.00	
N96	O4 25c on 10m	9.25	100.00
N97	O4 25c on 20m	2.40	26.00
a.	Double surcharge	160.00	
N98	O4 25c on 25m	4.50	40.00
N99	O4 25c on 40m	4.00	40.00
a.	Inverted surcharge	50.00	
N100	O4 25c on 50m (R)	2.40	20.00
a.	Inverted surcharge	50.00	
N101	O4 30c on 10m	26.00	200.00
N102	O4 30c on 20m	4.00	32.50
N103	O4 30c on 25m	4.50	52.50
N104	O4 30c on 40m	3.25	20.00
N105	O4 30c on 50m (R)	2.60	20.00
a.	Inverted surcharge	50.00	
	Nos. N91-N105 (15)	101.05	885.50

Nos. N23, N25, N27 Surcharged in Green or Red

N106	O5 15c on 100m	2.40	20.00
a.	Inverted surcharge	50.00	
N107	O5 15c on 400m	2.00	17.00
N108	O5 15c on 1000m (R)	52.50	400.00
a.	Inverted surcharge	165.00	700.00
N109	O5 25c on 100m	2.00	20.00
N110	O5 25c on 400m	2.00	20.00
a.	Double surcharge	100.00	
N111	O5 25c on 1000m (R)	52.50	400.00
a.	Inverted surcharge	165.00	700.00
N112	O5 30c on 100m	2.60	20.00
a.	Inverted surcharge	50.00	
N113	O5 30c on 400m	2.60	20.00
N114	O5 30c on 1000m (R)	52.50	400.00
a.	Inverted surcharge	165.00	700.00
	Nos. N106-N114 (9)	171.10	1,317.

Nos. N96 to N100 and N109 to N111 are surcharged "Centai," the others "Centu."

MESOPOTAMIA

me-sə-pə-'tā-mē-ə

LOCATION — In Western Asia, bounded on the north by Syria and Turkey, on the east by Persia, on the south by Saudi Arabia and on the west by Trans-Jordan.
GOVT. — A former Turkish Province
AREA — 143,250 (1918) sq. mi.
POP. — 2,849,282 (1920)
CAPITAL — Baghdad

During World War I this territory was occupied by Great Britain. It was recognized as an independent state and placed under British Mandate but in 1932 the Mandate was terminated and the country admitted to membership in the League of Nations as the Kingdom of Iraq. Postage stamps of Iraq are now in use.

16 Annas = 1 Rupee

Watermark

Wmk. 48 — Diagonal Zigzag Lines

Issued under British Occupation

Baghdad Issue
Stamps of Turkey 1901-16 Surcharged

Turkey No. 254 Surcharged

Turkey No. 256 Surcharged — Turkey No. 258 Surcharged

Turkey No. 259 Surcharged — Turkey No. 260 Surcharged

The surcharges were printed from slugs which were arranged to fit the various shapes of the stamps.

1917 Unwmk. Perf. 12, 13½

N1	¼a on 2pa red lil	400.00	425.00
a.	"IN BRITISH" omitted	17,500.	
N2	¼a on 5pa vio brown	300.00	325.00
a.	"¼ An" omitted	20,000.	
N3	½a on 10pa green	1,450.	1,750.
N4	1a on 20pa red	1,000.	1,100.
a.	"BAGHDAD" double	2,600.	
N5	2a on 1pi blue	450.00	500.00
	Nos. N1-N5 (5)	3,600.	4,100.

On Turkey No. 249

N6	A22 2a on 1pi ultra	1,150.	1,375.
a.	"IN BRITISH" omitted	17,500.	

Turkey No. 251 Surcharged

N7	A23 ½a on 10pa green	3,250.	3,500.

On Turkey Nos. 272-273

N8	A29 1a on 20pa red	675.	750.
a.	"OCCUPATION" omitted	20,000.	
b.	"BAGHDAD" double	2,600.	
N9	A30 2a on 1pi blue	5,250.	8,500.

On Turkey Nos. 346-348

N10	A41 ½a on 10pa car, perf 12½	1,000.	1,200.
a.	Perf 13½	2,100.	2,400.
N11	A41 1a on 20pa ultra, perf 13½	2,650.	3,250.
a.	"1 An" omitted	18,500.	
b.	Perf 12½	14,000.	350.00
N12	A41 2a on 1pi vio & black, perf 13½	325.00	200.00
a.	"BAGHDAD" omitted	20,000.	
b.	Perf 12½	650.00	700.00

On Turkey Nos. 297, 300

N13	A17 ¼a on 5pa purple	20,000.	
N14	A17 2a on 1pi blue	450.	500.
a.	"OCCUPATION" omitted	17,500.	

On Turkey No. 306

N15	A18 1a on 20pa car	1,000.	1,150.
a.	Value omitted	17,500.	

On Turkey Nos. 329-331

N16	A22 ½a on 10pa bl grn	300.00	350.00
N17	A22 1a on 20pa car rose	1,000.	1,000.
a.	"1 An" omitted	10,000.	7,500.
b.	With additional "Behie"	11,000.	10,500.
N18	A22 2a on 1pi ultra	325.00	350.00
a.	"BAGHDAD" omitted	—	

On Turkey No. 337

N19	A22 1a on 20pa car rose	9,000.	11,750.

On Turkey No. P125

On Turkey No. B29

N20	A17 1a on 20pa car	—	

On Turkey Nos. B1, B8

Inscription in crescent is obliterated by another crescent handstamped in violet black on Nos. N21-N27.

N21	A18 ½a on 10pa dull grn	325.00	375.00
a.	"OCCUPATION" omitted	16,000.	
N22	A21 1a on 20pa car rose	1,000.	1,100.

On Turkey No. B29

N23	A21 2a on 1pi ultra	3,750.	4,000.

On Turkey Nos. B33-B34

N24	A22 1a on 20pa car rose	325.00	375.00
N25	A22 2a on 1pi ultra	450.00	500.00
a.	"OCCUPATION" omitted	17,500.	
b.	"BAGHDAD" omitted	16,500.	

On Turkey No. B42

N26	A41 ½a on 10pa car, perf 12½	450.00	500.00
a.	"BAGHDAD" double		
b.	Perf 13½	900.00	1,000.

On Turkey No. B38

N27	A11 1a on 20pa on 20pa vio brn	500.00	550.00
a.	"OCCUPATION" omitted	17,500.	

Iraq Issue

N28

MESOPOTAMIA — MEXICO

Turkey Nos. 256, 258-269 Surcharged

		1918-20		Perf. 12
N28		¼a on 5pa vio brn	.55	1.10
N29		½a on 10pa grn	1.00	.25
N30		1a on 20pa red	.55	.25
N31		1½a on 5pa vio brn	16.50	.75
N32		2½a on 1pi blue	1.50	1.50
	a.	Inverted surcharge	11,500.	
N33		3a on 1½pi car & black	1.60	.25
	a.	Double surcharge, red & blk	4,500.	5,500.
N34		4a on 1¾pi slate & red brn	1.60	.30
	a.	Center inverted		37,500.
N35		6a on 2pi grn & black	2.50	2.00
N36		8a on 2½pi org & ol grn	3.75	2.25
N37		12a on 5pi dl vio	2.00	6.50
N38		1r on 10pi red brown	2.75	1.50
N39		2r on 25pi ol grn	12.50	3.25
N40		5r on 50pi car	30.00	32.50
N41		10r on 100pi dp blue	100.00	18.50
		Nos. N28-N41 (14)	176.80	70.90

See #N50-N53. For overprints see #NO1-NO21.

Mosul Issue
On Turkey fiscal stamps

		1919 Unwmk.		Perf. 11½, 12
N42		½a on 1pi grn & brn red	2.40	2.10
N43		1a on 20pa rose	1.50	1.90
	a.	"POSTAGE" omitted		
N44		1a on 20pa rose	4.50	4.50
	a.	Double surcharge	725.00	

Turkish word at right of tughra ("reshad") is large on No. N43, small on No. N44.

Wmk. Turkish Characters Perf. 12½

N45		2½a on 1pi vio & yel	1.60	1.60
N46		3a on 20pa grn & yel	90.00	125.00

Wmk. 48

N47		3a on 20pa green	1.75	4.25
N48		4a on 1pi dull vio	3.50	3.75
	a.	Double surcharge	1,250.	
	b.	"4" omitted	2,000.	
	c.	As "b," double surcharge		
N49		8a on 10pa claret	4.25	5.50
	a.	Double surcharge	750.00	875.00
	b.	Inverted surcharge	900.00	1,000.
	c.	8a on 1pi dull violet	3,500.	
		Nos. N42-N49 (8)	109.50	148.60

Value for No. 49a is for a stamp with the perfs cutting into the design.

Iraq Issue
On Turkey 1918-20 Issue

		1921 Wmk. 4		Perf. 12
N50	A28	½a on 10pa green (#258)	7.50	2.50
N51	A26	1½a on 5pa vio brn (#256)	5.00	1.35
N52	A37	2r on 25pi ol grn (#267)	37.50	14.00
		Nos. N50-N52 (3)	50.00	17.85

Type of 1918-20 without "Reshad"

		1922		Unwmk.
N53	A36	1r on 10pi red brn	350.00	27.50

"Reshad" is the small Turkish word at right of the tughra in circle at top center.
For overprint see No. NO22.

OFFICIAL STAMPS

Nos. N29-N41 Overprinted

		1920 Unwmk.		Perf. 12
NO1	A28	½a on 10pa grn	25.00	2.00
NO2	A29	1a on 20pa red	8.00	1.00
NO3	A26	1½a on 5pa vio brown	60.00	3.00
NO4	A30	2½a on 1pi blue	8.00	8.00
NO5	A31	3a on 1½pi car & black	27.50	1.00
NO6	A32	4a on 1¾pi sl & red brn	55.00	4.75
NO7	A33	6a on 2pi grn & black	42.50	10.00
NO8	A34	8a on 2½pi org & ol grn	55.00	6.00
NO9	A35	12a on 5pi dull vio	32.50	24.00
NO10	A36	1r on 10pi red brown	47.50	12.00
NO11	A37	2r on 25pi ol green	45.00	22.50
NO12	A38	5r on 50pi car	85.00	65.00
NO13	A39	10r on 100pi dp blue	125.00	160.00
		Nos. NO1-NO13 (13)	616.00	319.25

Same Overprint on Types of Regular Issue of 1918-20

		1921-22		Wmk. 4
NO14	A28	½a on 10pa grn	1.10	1.10
NO15	A29	1a on 20pa red	11.50	1.10
NO16	A26	1½a on 5pa dp brn	3.00	1.25
NO17	A32	4a on 1¾pi gray & red brn	2.25	3.25
NO18	A33	6a on 2pi grn & black	42.50	175.00
NO19	A34	8a on 2½pi org & yel grn	3.50	2.25
NO20	A35	12a on 5pi dl vio	42.50	95.00
NO21	A37	2r on 25pi ol grn	125.00	165.00
		Nos. NO14-NO21 (8)	231.35	443.95

Same Overprint on No. N53

		1922		Unwmk.
NO22	A36	1r on 10pi red brn	50.00	7.50

MEXICO

ˈmek-si-ˌkō

LOCATION — Extreme southern part of the North American continent, south of the United States
GOVT. — Republic
AREA — 759,529 sq. mi.
POP. — 128,930,000 (2020 est.)

CAPITAL — Mexico, D.F
8 Reales = 1 Peso
100 Centavos = 1 Peso

Catalogue values for unused stamps in this country are for Never Hinged items, beginning with Scott 792 in the regular postage section, Scott C143 in the airpost section, Scott E8 in the special delivery section, and Scott G4 in the insured letter section.

District Overprints

Nos. 1-149 are overprinted with names of various districts, and sometimes also with district numbers and year dates. Some of the district overprints are rare and command high prices. Values given for Nos. 1-149 are for the more common district overprints.

Watermarks

Wmk. 150 — PAPEL SELLADO in Sheet

Wmk. 151 — R. P. S. in the Sheet (R.P.S. stands for "Renta Papel Sellado")

Wmk. 152 — "CORREOS E U M" on Every Horizontal Line of Ten Stamps

Wmk. 153 — "R M" Interlaced

Wmk. 154 — Eagle and R M

MEXICO

Wmk. 155 — SERVICIO POSTAL DE LOS ESTADOS UNIDOS MEXICANOS

Wmk. 156 — CORREOS MEXICO

Wmk. 248 — SECRETARIA DE HACIENDA MEXICO

Wmk. 260 — Lines and SECRETARIA DE HACIENDA MEXICO (With or Without Lines)

Wmk. 272 — "S. H. C. P. MEXICO" and Eagle in Circle

Wmk. 279 — GOBIERNO MEXICANO and Eagle in Circle

Wmk. 300 — MEX-MEX and Eagle in Circle, Multiple (Letters 6mm)

Wmk. 350 — MEX and Eagle in Circle, Multiple, Letters 8-9mm

Miguel Hidalgo y Costilla — A1

Handstamped with District Name

1856	Unwmk.	Engr.	Imperf.
1	A1 ½r blue	50.00	45.00
	2-4 stamps on cover		150.00
b.	Without overprint	45.00	50.00
2	A1 1r yellow	30.00	5.50
b.	Half used as ½r on cover		10,000.
c.	Without overprint	25.00	30.00
d.	1r green (error)		
3	A1 2r yellow grn	27.50	3.50
a.	2r deep blue green	275.00	40.00
b.	2r emerald	250.00	55.00
c.	Half used as 1r on cover		600.00
d.	Without overprint	40.00	22.50
e.	As "a," without overprint	250.00	45.00
f.	As "b," without overprint		75.00
g.	Printed on both sides (yel green)	300.00	
4	A1 4r red	175.00	110.00
a.	Half used as 2r on cover		250.00
b.	Quarter used as 1r on cover		700.00
c.	Without overprint	140.00	160.00
d.	Three quarters used as 3r on cover		12,000.
5	A1 8r red lilac	350.00	200.00
a.	8r violet	300.00	200.00
b.	Without overprint	225.00	225.00
c.	Eighth used as 1r on cover		20,000.
d.	Quarter used as 2r on cover		225.00
e.	Half used as 4r on cover		900.00
	Nos. 1-5 (5)	632.50	364.00

The 1r and 2r were printed in sheets of 60 with wide spacing between stamps, and in sheets of 190 or 200 with narrow spacing.

No. 3a can be distinguished from the other 2r stamps by the horizontal grain of the paper. The plate for No. 3b has framelines.

All values, except the 1r, have been reprinted, some of them several times. The reprints usually show signs of wear and the impressions are often smudgy. The paper is usually thicker than that of the originals. Reprints are usually on very white paper. Reprints are found with and without overprints and with cancellations made both from the original handstamps and from forged ones.

Counterfeits exist.

See Nos. 6-12. For overprints see Nos. 35-45.

1861			
6	A1 ½r black, *buff*	50.00	45.00
	On cover, 2 or 4 stamps		200.00
a.	Without overprint	34.00	62.50
7	A1 1r black, *green*	20.00	5.50
a.	Impression of 2r on back		1,000.
b.	Without overprint	5.00	22.50
d.	As "b," blk, wmk (error)	8,000	9,000.
f.	Double impression		150.00
8	A1 2r black, *pink*	15.00	6.50
a.	Impression of 1r on back	2,000.	
b.	Half used as 1r on cover		750.00
c.	Without overprint	3.50	22.50
d.	Printed on both sides		2,250.
e.	Double impression		100.00
f.	As "e," without overprint	—	
9	A1 4r black, *yellow*	200.00	100.00
a.	Half used as 2r on cover		190.00
b.	Without overprint	50.00	100.00
c.	Quarter used as 1r on cover		700.00
d.	Three-quarters used as 3r on cover		10,000.
10	A1 4r dull rose, *yel*	200.00	80.00
a.	Half used as 2r on cover		1,050.
b.	Without overprint	110.00	140.00
c.	Printed on both sides		9,000.
d.	Quarter used as 1r on cover		—
11	A1 8r blk, *red brn*	375.00	250.00
a.	⅛ used as 1R on cover front		11,000.
b.	Quarter used as 2r on cover		250.00
c.	Half used as 4r on cover		750.00
d.	Without overprint	110.00	225.00
e.	Three quarters used as 6r on cover		45,000.
12	A1 8r grn, *red brn*	500.00	240.00
a.	Half used as 4r on cover		9,000.
b.	Without overprint	150.00	200.00
c.	Quarter used as 2r on cover		9,000.
d.	Printed on both sides	12,500.	12,500.
	Nos. 6-12 (7)	1,360.	727.00

Nos. 6, 9, 10, 11 and 12 have been reprinted. Most reprints of the ½r, 4r and 8r are on vertically grained paper. Originals are on horizontally grained paper. The original ½r stamps are much worn but the reprints are unworn. The paper of the 4r is too deep and rich in color and No. 10 is printed in too bright red.

Reprints of the 8r can only be told by experts. All these reprints are found in fancy colors and with overprints and cancellations as in the 1856 issue.

Counterfeits exist.

Hidalgo — A3

With District Name

1864			Perf. 12
14	A3 1r red	750.	3,000.
a.	Without District Name	.75	
15	A3 2r blue	1,100.	1,750.
a.	Without District Name	.75	
16	A3 4r brown	1,250.	2,400.
a.	Without District Name	1.25	
b.	Vert. pair, imperf. between		
17	A3 1p black	3,250.	—
a.	Without District Name	2.00	

Nos. 14 to 17 were issued with district overprints of Saltillo or Monterrey on the toned paper of 1864. Overprints on the 1867 white paper are fraudulent. Counterfeits and counterfeit cancellations are plentiful. The 1r red with "½" surcharge is bogus.

Coat of Arms — A4

Overprint of District Name, etc.

Five types of overprints:
I — District name only.
II — District name, consignment number and "1864" in large figures.
III — District name, number and "1864" in small figures.
IV — District name, number and "1865."
V — District name, number and "1866."

1864-66			Imperf.
18	A4 3c brn (IV, V)	1,300.	3,300.
a.	Without overprint	700.00	
b.	Laid paper	4,500.	6,000.
19	A4 ½r brown (I)	400.00	250.00
a.	Type II	2,200.	2,250.
b.	Without overprint	200.00	650.00
20	A4 ½r lilac (IV)	60.00	55.00
a.	Type III	140.00	75.00
b.	Type II	200.00	200.00
c.	Type V		3,000.
d.	½r gray (V)	70.00	80.00
e.	Without overprint	5.75	
f.	½r gray lilac	250.00	100.00
21	A4 1r blue (IV, V)	15.00	9.00
a.	Type III	80.00	40.00
b.	Without overprint	2.50	
c.	Half used as ½r on cover		10,000.
22	A4 1r ultra (I, II)	120.00	30.00
a.	Type III	90.00	40.00
b.	Without overprint	160.00	150.00
c.	Half used as ½r on cover		7,250.
23	A4 2r org (III, IV, V)	10.00	6.00
a.	Type II	20.00	10.00
b.	Type I	50.00	10.00
c.	2r dp org, without ovpt., early plate	175.00	65.00
d.	Without ovpt., late plate	2.00	
e.	Half used as 1r on cover		6,000.
24	A4 4r grn (III, IV, V)	100.00	50.00
a.	Types I, II	160.00	125.00
b.	4r dk grn, without ovpt.	4.75	1,700.
d.	Half used as 2r on cover		700.00
25	A4 8r red (IV, V)	150.00	90.00
a.	Types II, III	175.00	125.00
b.	Type I	400.00	175.00
c.	8r dk red, without ovpt.	7.00	575.00
f.	Quarter used as 2r on cover		15,000.
g.	Three-quarters used as 6r on cover		

The 2r printings from the early plates are 25½mm high; those from the late plate, 24½mm.

Varieties listed as "Without overprint" in unused condition are remainders.

Besides the overprints of district name, number and date, Nos. 18-34 often received, in the district offices, additional overprints of numbers and sometimes year dates. Stamps with these "sub-consignment numbers" sell for more than stamps without them.

Genuine examples of No. 20c should bear Mexico district name overprint, together with consignment numbers 1-1866 or 17-1866. Gray lilac stamps of other consignments are examples of No. 20f.

Value unused for No. 18 is for an example without gum. Examples with original gum sell for more. Examples of No. 18a on laid paper are forgeries.

No. 25c does not exist on full cover.

Faked quarterings and bisects of 1856-64 are plentiful.

The 3c has been reprinted from a die on which the words "TRES CENTAVOS," the outlines of the serpent and some of the background lines have been retouched.

Emperor Maximilian — A5

Overprinted with District Name, Number and Date 1866 or 866; also with Number and Date only, or with Name only

1866			Litho.
26	A5 7c lilac gray	65.00	125.00
a.	7c deep gray	85.00	140.00
27	A5 13c blue	35.00	35.00
a.	Half used as 7c on cover		—
b.	13c cobalt blue	25.00	25.00
c.	Without overprint	2,500.	
28	A5 25c buff	12.50	9.00
a.	Half used as 13c on cover		
b.	Without overprint	2,500.	
29	A5 25c orange	12.00	12.00
a.	25c red orange	20.00	27.50
b.	25c red brown	85.00	47.50
c.	25c brown	110.00	85.00
30	A5 50c green	25.00	30.00
	Nos. 26-30 (5)	149.50	211.00

Litho. printings have round period after value numerals.

Overprinted with District Name, Number and Date 866 or 867; also with Number and Date only

			Engr.
31	A5 7c lilac	450.00	5,500.
a.	Without overprint	3.50	
32	A5 13c blue	12.00	12.00
a.	Without overprint	1.25	
33	A5 25c orange brown	12.00	11.00
a.	Without overprint	1.25	
34	A5 50c green	700.00	70.00
a.	Without overprint	2.50	

See "sub-consignment" note after No. 25.
Engraved printings have square period after value numerals.

Varieties listed as "Without overprint" in unused condition are remainders.

1867			
35	A1 ½r blk, *buff*	4,000.	5,000.
36	A1 1r blk, *green*	60.00	10.00
37	A1 2r blk, *pink*	22.50	5.00
a.	Printed on both sides		140.00
38	A1 4r red, *yel*	625.00	50.00
a.	Printed on both sides		175.00
39	A1 4r red	6,000.	3,250.
40	A1 8r blk, *red brn*	3,500.	275.00
41	A1 8r grn, *red brn*		4,000.

Dangerous counterfeits exist of the "Mexico" overprint.

Examples of No. 38 with yellow removed are offered as No. 39.

Same Overprint Thin Gray Blue Paper Wmk. 151

42	A1 ½r gray	275.00	190.00
a.	Without overprint	175.00	175.00
43	A1 1r blue	400.00	65.00
b.	Without overprint	300.00	125.00
44	A1 2r green	200.00	30.00
a.	Printed on both sides	6,000.	3,500.
b.	Without overprint	300.00	50.00
45	A1 4r rose	3,000.	75.00
a.	Without overprint	5,000.	225.00

Most examples of Nos. 42-45 do not show the watermark. Values are for such stamps. Examples showing the watermark sell for more.

Reprints of the ½r and 4r exist on watermarked paper. Reprints of ½r and 8r also exist in gray on thick grayish wove paper, unwatermarked.

Hidalgo — A6

Thin Figures of Value, without Period after Numerals

6 CENT. 12 CENT.
25 CENT. 50 CENT.
100 CENT.

MEXICO

Overprinted with District Name, Number and Abbreviated Date
1868 Unwmk. Litho. Imperf.

46	A6	6c blk, *buff*	40.00	20.00
47	A6	12c blk, *green*	45.00	20.00
a.		Period after "12"	65.00	55.00
48	A6	25c bl, *pink*	75.00	20.00
a.		Without overprint	125.00	
49	A6	50c blk, *yellow*	600.00	60.00
50	A6	100c blk, *brown*	775.00	140.00
a.		Half used as 50c on cover		5,750.
51	A6	100c brn, *brn*	1,750.	500.00

Perf.

52	A6	6c blk, *buff*	35.00	35.00
a.		Without overprint	150.00	
b.		Period after "6"	100.00	75.00
53	A6	12c blk, *green*	35.00	12.00
a.		Period after "12"	85.00	30.00
b.		Very thick paper	50.00	25.00
c.		Without overprint	110.00	
54	A6	25c blue, *pink*	55.00	10.00
a.		Without overprint	150.00	
55	A6	50c blk, *yellow*	325.00	45.00
a.		Half used as 50c on cover		3,000.
56	A6	100c blk, *brown*	375.00	110.00
c.		Without overprint	350.00	
57	A6	100c brn, *brn*	1,000.	375.00
a.		Printed on both sides	1,250.	1,000.

Four kinds of perforation are found in the 1868 issue: serrate, square, pin and regular. The narrow spacing between stamps was inadequate for some of these perforation types.

Thick Figures of Value, with Period after Numerals

6. CENT.   12. CENT.
25. CENT.   50. CENT.
100. CENT.

Overprinted with District Name, Number and Abbreviated Date
Imperf

58	A6	6c blk, *buff*	9.50	4.50
59	A6	12c blk, *green*	4.25	1.25
a.		Very thick paper		10.00
c.		12c black, *buff* (error)	575.00	575.00
d.		Printed on both sides		3,000.
e.		No period after "12"	—	
61	A6	25c blue, *pink*	8.00	1.25
a.		No period after "25"		90.00
c.		Very thick paper	25.00	6.00
d.		"85" for "25"	75.00	50.00
e.		"35" for "25"		75.00
f.		Printed on both sides	—	
62	A6	50c blk, *yellow*	125.00	15.00
a.		No period after "50"	225.00	35.00
b.		50c blue, *lt pink* (error)	3,000.	2,000.
c.		Half used as 25c on cover		1,000.
d.		Very thick paper		50.00
e.		"30" for "50"	750.00	750.00
64	A6	100c blk, *brown*	150.00	90.00
a.		No period after "100"	175.00	100.00
b.		Very thick paper		75.00
c.		Quarter used as 25c on cover		5,450.
d.		Bisect used as 50c on cover		4,000.
		Nos. 58-64 (5)	296.75	112.00

Perf.

65	A6	6c blk, *buff*	40.00	20.00
a.		Very thick paper	60.00	35.00
66	A6	12c blk, *green*	5.50	5.50
a.		Very thick paper	20.00	15.00
b.		12c black, *buff* (error)	575.00	575.00
c.		No period after "12"		
68	A6	25c blue, *pink*	20.00	2.50
a.		No period after "25"	80.00	80.00
b.		Thick paper	30.00	15.00
d.		"85" for "25"	80.00	40.00
69	A6	50c blk, *yellow*	200.00	25.00
a.		No period after "50"	200.00	30.00
b.		50c blue, *lt pink* (error)	2,500.	1,500.
c.		Thick paper		60.00
70	A6	100c blk, *brown*	200.00	60.00
a.		No period after "100"	200.00	65.00
b.		Very thick paper		80.00
		Nos. 65-70 (5)	465.50	113.00

Postal forgeries of Nos. 58-70 were printed from original plates with district name overprints forged. These include the pelure paper varieties and some thick paper varieties. The "Anotado" handstamp was applied to some of the confiscated forgeries and they were issued, including Nos. 73a and 78a.

Stamps of 1868 Handstamped

Overprinted with District Name, Number and Abbreviated Date
Thick Figures with Period

1872 Imperf.

71	A6	6c blk, *buff*	650.00	675.00
72	A6	12c blk, *green*	85.00	75.00
73	A6	25c bl, *pink*	40.00	45.00
a.		Pelure paper	55.00	65.00
b.		"85" for "25"		125.00
74	A6	50c blk, *yellow*	850.00	475.00
a.		No period after "50"	900.00	475.00
75	A6	100c blk, *brown*	1,250.	1,000.
a.		No period after "100"		1,100.

Perf.

76	A6	6c blk, *buff*		750.00
77	A6	12c blk, *green*	90.00	80.00
78	A6	25c blue, *pink*	35.00	42.50
a.		Pelure paper	65.00	90.00
79	A6	50c blk, *yellow*	850.00	600.00
a.		No period after "50"		550.00
80	A6	100c blk, *brown*		1,200.

Counterfeit "Anotado" overprints abound. Genuine cancellations other than Mexico City or of the Diligencias de Puebla are unknown. It is recommended that these be purchased accompanied by certificates of authenticity from competent experts.

The stamps of the 1872 issue are found perforated with square holes, pin-perf. 13, 14 or 15, and with serrate perforation.

Counterfeits of the 1868 6c, 12c buff, 50c and 100c (both colors) from new plates have clear, sharp impressions and more facial shading lines than the originals. These counterfeits are found perf. and imperf., with thick and thin numerals, and with the "Anotado" overprint.

Hidalgo — A8

Moiré on White Back Overprinted with District Name, Number and Abbreviated Date
White Wove Paper

1872 Litho. Wmk. 150 Imperf.

81	A8	6c green	325.00	275.00
82	A8	12c blue	250.00	125.00
a.		Laid paper	2,000.	350.00
83	A8	25c red	400.00	125.00
a.		Laid paper	2,000.	350.00
84	A8	50c yellow	2,000.	850.00
a.		50c blue (error)		3,000.
b.		Laid paper		4,000.
c.		As "a," without ovpt.	130.00	
86	A8	100c gray lilac	1,000.	650.00
		Nos. 81-86 (5)	3,975.	2,025.

Wmk. "LA + F"

81a	A8	6c green	2,000.	1,000.
82b	A8	12c blue	450.00	325.00
83b	A8	25c red	575.00	575.00
c.		Without overprint	500.00	
84d	A8	50c yellow	3,500.	2,000.
86a	A8	100c gray lilac	4,000.	1,500.

1872 Wmk. 150 Pin-perf.

87	A8	6c green	2,500.	2,000.
88	A8	12c blue	475.00	175.00
89	A8	25c red	550.00	275.00
b.		Laid paper		1,000.
90	A8	50c yellow	1,500.	950.00
a.		50c blue (error)	1,000.	1,250.
b.		As "a," without overprint	£00.00	
92	A8	100c gray lilac	1,200.	1,200.
		Nos. 87-92 (5)	6,225.	4,600.

Wmk. "LA + F"

87a	A8	6c green	2,500.	2,000.
88a	A8	12c blue	450.00	400.00
89a	A8	25c red	950.00	350.00
90c	A8	50c yellow	1,000.	2,500.
92a	A8	100c gray lilac	3,600.	2,750.

The watermark "LA+F" stands for La Croix Frères, the paper manufacturers, and is in double-lined block capitals 13mm high. A single stamp will show only part of this watermark.

Values for Nos. 87-92a are for examples with visible perfs on all sides.

1872 Unwmk. Imperf.

93	A8	6c green	12.50	12.50
a.		Without moiré on back, without overprint	60.00	65.00
b.		Vertically laid paper	3,000.	1,300.
c.		Bottom label retouched	100.00	90.00
d.		Very thick paper	37.50	37.50
94	A8	12c blue	2.00	1.75
a.		Without moiré on back, without overprint	30.00	35.00
b.		Vertically laid paper	350.00	210.00
c.		Thin gray bl paper of 1867 (Wmk 151)		2,000.
95	A8	25c red	8.50	2.00
a.		Without moiré on back, without overprint	30.00	35.00
b.		Vertically laid paper	450.00	500.00
c.		Thin gray bl paper of 1867 (Wmk 151)		1,500.
96	A8	50c yellow	140.00	35.00
a.		50c orange	140.00	35.00
b.		Without moiré on back, without overprint	50.00	70.00
c.		Vertically laid paper	2,000.	
d.		50c blue (error)		650.00
e.		As "d," without overprint	45.00	
f.		As "e," without moiré on back	65.00	
g.		Half used as 25c on cover		5,000.
98	A8	100c gray lilac	90.00	50.00
a.		100c lilac	100.00	42.50
b.		Without moiré on back, without overprint	50.00	110.00
c.		Vertically laid paper		1,250.
		Nos. 93-98 (5)	253.00	101.25

Counterfeits of these stamps are 24½mm high instead of 24mm. The printing is sharper and more uniform than the genuine. Forged district names and consignment numbers exist.

Pin-perf. and Serrate Perf.

99	A8	6c green	90.00	75.00
100	A8	12c blue	3.50	3.00
a.		Vertically laid paper		350.00
b.		Horiz. pair, imperf. vert.	100.00	100.00
c.		Vert. pair, imperf. between		150.00
101	A8	25c red	3.25	1.50
a.		Vertically laid paper		500.00
b.		Horiz. pair, imperf. vert.	100.00	100.00
102	A8	50c yellow	175.00	50.00
a.		50c orange	160.00	50.00
b.		50c blue (error)	475.00	500.00
c.		As "b," without overprint	45.00	
104	A8	100c lilac	150.00	80.00
a.		100c gray lilac	125.00	80.00
		Nos. 99-104 (5)	421.75	209.50

Values for Nos. 99-104a are for examples with visible perfs on all sides.

Hidalgo
A9   A10

A11
A12
A13
A14

Mexican Stamps and British Commonwealth

FROM

Gregg Nelson Stamps

Box 7430, Santa Rosa, CA 95407
Phone: (707) 852-4022
gnmexstmps@aol.com

A wider selection of classics and new inventory, including Worldwide

We have an excellent stock of...
• Early Classics
• 20th Century
• Postal History
• Worldwide

...for Beginners to Advanced Collectors!

www.greggnelsonstamps.com

MEXICO

Overprinted with District Name and Number and Date; also with Number and Date only
Thick Wove Paper, Some Showing Vertical Ribbing

		1874-80	Unwmk.	Engr.	Perf. 12	
105	A9	4c org ('80)		12.50	12.00
a.		Vert. pair, imperf. btwn.		60.00	
		Without overprint		6.50	12.50
		Half used as 2c on cover			1,000.
106	A10	5c brown		4.50	3.00
a.		Horizontally laid paper		100.00	55.00
b.		Imperf., pair		60.00	
c.		Horiz. pair, imperf. btwn.		50.00	300.00
d.		Vert. pair, imperf. btwn.		110.00	110.00
e.		Without overprint		37.50	37.50
f.		As "a," wmkd. "LACROIX"		1,750.	1,000.
107	A11	10c black		2.00	1.25
a.		Horizontally laid paper		2.50	2.50
b.		Horiz. pair, imperf. btwn.		75.00	75.00
c.		Without overprint		35.00	27.50
d.		Half used as 5c on cover			2,000.
e.		Imperf., pair			
f.		As "a," wmkd. "LACROIX"		350.00	250.00
108	A11	10c org ('78)		2.00	1.25
a.		10c yellow bister		7.50	4.25
b.		Imperf., pair			
c.		Without overprint		50.00	50.00
d.		Half used as 5c on cover			100.00
109	A12	25c blue		.85	.70
a.		Horizontally laid paper		2.25	1.75
c.		Imperf., pair		50.00	25.00
d.		Without overprint		35.00	20.00
e.		Horiz. pair, imperf. btwn.		125.00	
f.		As "b," horiz. pair, imperf. vert.			200.00
g.		As "b," wmkd. "LACROIX"		300.00	250.00
h.		Printed on both sides			1,500.
i.		Half used as 10c on cover			2,000.
110	A13	50c green		13.00	13.00
a.		Without overprint		50.00	
b.		Half used as 25c on cover			2,500.
111	A14	100c carmine		18.00	15.00
a.		Imperf., pair		200.00	200.00
b.		Without overprint		50.00	
c.		Quarterf used as 25c on cover			3,000.
		Nos. 105-111 (7)		52.85	46.20

The "LACROIX" watermark is spelled out "LACROIX FRERES" in 2 lines of block capitals with serifs once to a sheet of horiz. laid paper. 6-12 stamps may have a portion of the wmk.

1875-77			Wmk. 150	
112	A10	5c brown	110.00	70.00
113	A11	10c black	110.00	70.00
114	A12	25c blue	110.00	70.00
115	A13	50c green	650.00	450.00
116	A14	100c carmine	600.00	400.00
		Nos. 112-116 (5)	1,580.	1,060.

1881	Unwmk.		Thin Wove Paper	
117	A9	4c orange	70.00	70.00
a.		Without overprint	20.00	20.00
118	A10	5c brown	10.00	6.50
a.		Without overprint	.50	20.00
b.		As "a," vert. pair, imperf. horiz.	1,000.	
119	A11	10c orange	6.00	3.50
a.		Imperf., pair		
b.		Vert. pair, imperf. horiz.		
c.		Without overprint	.75	4.50
d.		Vert. pair, imperf. btwn.		
e.		Half used as 5c on cover		1,500.
120	A12	25c blue	4.00	2.25
a.		Imperf., pair	100.00	
b.		Without overprint	.50	8.00
c.		Double impression		65.00
d.		Printed on both sides		1,500.
121	A13	50c green	45.00	40.00
a.		Without overprint	4.00	30.00
122	A14	100c carmine	50.00	50.00
a.		Without overprint	6.00	300.00

The stamps of 1874-81 are found with number and date wide apart, close together or omitted, and in various colors.

The thin paper is fragile and easily damaged. Values for Nos. 117-122 are for undamaged, fine examples.

Benito Juárez — A15

Overprinted with District Name and Number and Date; also with Number and Date only
Thick Wove Paper, Some Showing Vertical Ribbing

1879				Perf. 12	
123	A15	1c brown		4.00	4.00
a.		Without overprint		75.00	140.00
b.		1c gray		20.00	15.00
124	A15	2c dk violet		4.00	4.50
a.		Without overprint		75.00	150.00
b.		Printed on both sides			
c.		2c dark gray		20.00	14.00
125	A15	5c orange		2.25	1.50
a.		Without overprint		75.00	90.00
b.		Double impression			500.00
126	A15	10c blue		3.00	2.50
a.		Without overprint		75.00	150.00
b.		10c ultra		160.00	160.00
127	A15	25c rose		8.00	30.00
a.		Without overprint		1.75	150.00
128	A15	50c green		15.00	50.00
a.		Without overprint		1.25	150.00
b.		Printed on both sides			165.00
129	A15	85c violet		20.00	250.00
a.		Without overprint		2.50	
130	A15	100c black		25.00	75.00
a.		Without overprint		3.00	150.00
		Nos. 123-130 (8)		81.25	417.50

Used values for Nos. 127-130 are for stamps with postal cancellations. Pen cancelled examples are worth the same as unused stamps.

Forged cancellations on Nos. 127-130 are plentiful.

1882			Thin Wove Paper	
131	A15	1c brown	40.00	37.50
a.		Without overprint	125.00	
132	A15	2c dk violet	27.50	24.00
a.		2c slate	47.50	50.00
b.		Without overprint	110.00	
c.		Half used as 1c on cover		
133	A15	5c orange	9.00	6.00
a.		Without overprint	1.25	
b.		Half used as 2c on cover		
c.		As "a," vert. pair, imperf. btwn.		
134	A15	10c blue	9.00	6.00
a.		Without overprint	1.25	
b.		Half used as 5c on cover		
135	A15	10c brown	9.00	
a.		Imperf., pair	3.00	
136	A15	12c brown	7.50	8.00
a.		Without overprint	2.50	22.50
b.		Imperf., pair	75.00	
c.		Half used as 6c on cover		
137	A15	18c orange brn	9.00	15.00
a.		Horiz. pair, imperf. btwn.	100.00	
b.		Without overprint	2.25	18.00
138	A15	24c violet	9.00	11.00
a.		Without overprint	2.25	17.50
139	A15	25c rose	45.00	250.00
a.		Without overprint	4.50	
140	A15	25c orange brn	5.50	
141	A15	50c green	45.00	75.00
a.		Without overprint	6.25	
142	A15	50c yellow	80.00	350.00
a.		Without overprint	150.00	
143	A15	85c red violet	55.00	
144	A15	100c black	75.00	250.00
a.		Without overprint	5.00	
b.		Vert. pair, imperf. btwn.	165.00	165.00
145	A15	100c orange	95.00	400.00
		Nos. 131-145 (15)	520.50	1,433.

No. 135, 140 and 143 exist only without overprint. They were never placed in use.

Used values for Nos. 139, 141, 142, 144 and 145 are for postally used stamps. Forged cancellations are plentiful. Pen cancelled examples are worth the same as unused stamps.

See note on thin paper after No. 122.

A16

Overprinted with District Name, Number and Abbreviated Date

1882-83				
146	A16	2c green	11.00	8.00
a.		Without overprint	27.50	20.00
147	A16	3c car lake	11.00	8.00
a.		Without overprint	5.25	8.50
148	A16	6c blue ('83)	30.00	40.00
a.		Without overprint	30.00	50.00
149	A16	6c ultra	6.00	8.50
a.		Without overprint	3.50	6.00
b.		As "a," imperf pair	50.00	
		Nos. 146-149 (4)	58.00	64.50

See note on thin paper after No. 122.

Hidalgo — A17

1884	Wove or Laid Paper		Perf. 12	
150	A17	1c green	4.00	.75
a.		Imperf., pair	125.00	
b.		1c blue (error)	600.00	475.00
151	A17	2c green	6.75	1.25
a.		Imperf., pair	200.00	225.00
b.		Half used as 1c on cover		
152	A17	3c green	12.50	2.00
a.		Imperf., pair	200.00	250.00
b.		Horiz. pair, imperf. vert.	225.00	250.00
153	A17	4c green	16.00	2.00
a.		Imperf., pair		
b.		Half used as 2c on cover		400.00
c.		Horiz. pair, imperf. btwn.	200.00	250.00
154	A17	5c green	17.50	1.50
a.		Imperf., pair	200.00	250.00
b.				250.00
d.		Vert. pair, imperf. btwn.		275.00
155	A17	6c green	15.00	1.50
a.		Imperf., pair	200.00	250.00
156	A17	10c green	16.00	.75
a.		Imperf., pair	125.00	150.00
157	A17	12c green	30.00	3.50
a.		Vert. pair, imperf. between	250.00	350.00
b.		Half used as 6c on cover		300.00
158	A17	20c green	90.00	2.50
a.		Diagonal half used as 10c on cover		300.00
b.		Imperf., pair	350.00	350.00
159	A17	25c green	150.00	5.00
a.		Imperf., pair	300.00	300.00
160	A17	50c green	.60	5.00
a.		Imperf., pair	150.00	150.00
b.		Horiz. pair, imperf. btwn.	300.00	
c.		Double impression	200.00	200.00
161	A17	1p blue	.60	11.00
a.		Imperf., pair	250.00	250.00
b.		Vert. pair, imperf. between	100.00	
c.		1p with 1c printed on back	300.00	
d.		Horiz. pair, imperf. btwn.	250.00	
162	A17	2p blue	.60	22.50
a.		Imperf., pair	175.00	200.00
163	A17	5p blue	350.00	300.00
164	A17	10p blue	500.00	225.00
		Nos. 150-162 (13)	359.55	60.00

Imperforate varieties should be purchased in pairs or larger. Single imperforates are usually trimmed perforated stamps.

Beware of examples of No. 150 that have been chemically changed to resemble No. 150b.

Bisects were not officially authorized. Nos. 155 and 160 exist as bisects on piece.

Forged cancels on Nos. 161-162 are plentiful.

Some values exist perf. 11.

See Nos. 165-173, 230-231.

1885				
165	A17	1c pale green	35.00	7.00
166	A17	2c carmine	25.00	3.50
a.		Diagonal half used as 1c on cover		400.00
167	A17	3c orange brn	25.00	6.00
a.		Imperf., pair	250.00	250.00
b.				300.00
168	A17	4c red orange	42.50	19.00
169	A17	5c ultra	27.50	3.50
170	A17	6c dk brown	32.50	6.00
a.		Half used as 3c on cover		350.00
171	A17	10c green	27.50	1.50
a.		10c yellow	30.00	1.50
b.		Horiz. pair, imperf. btwn.	250.00	250.00
c.		Without overprint	300.00	
172	A17	12c olive brn	57.50	9.00
a.		Printed on both sides	300.00	
173	A17	25c grnsh blue	225.00	22.50
		Nos. 165-173 (9)	497.50	78.00

Numeral of Value — A18

1886			Perf. 12	
174	A18	1c yellow green	2.25	.75
a.		1c blue grn	5.50	4.50
b.		Horiz. pair, imperf. btwn.	200.00	200.00
c.		Perf. 11	45.00	45.00
175	A18	2c carmine	2.60	.90
a.		Horiz. pair, imperf. btwn.	80.00	75.00
b.		Vert. pair, imperf. between	200.00	200.00
c.		Perf. 11	45.00	45.00
d.		Half used as 1c on cover		100.00
176	A18	3c lilac	12.00	7.50
177	A18	4c lilac	18.00	5.25
a.		Perf. 11	50.00	55.00
b.		Horiz. pair, imperf. btwn.	450.00	
178	A18	5c ultra	2.25	1.00
a.		5c blue	2.25	.75
179	A18	6c lilac	30.00	7.50
180	A18	10c lilac	22.50	1.10
a.		Perf. 11		125.00
181	A18	12c lilac	25.00	14.00
182	A18	20c lilac	190.00	110.00
183	A18	25c lilac	75.00	19.00
		Nos. 174-183 (10)	379.60	167.00

Nos. 175, 191, 194B, 196, 202 exist with blue or black surcharge "Vale 1 Cvo." These were made by the Colima postmaster.

1887				
184	A18	3c scarlet	1.90	.60
a.		Imperf., pair	75.00	
185	A18	4c scarlet	7.50	2.25
a.		Imperf., pair	500.00	
b.		Horiz. pair, imperf. btwn.	400.00	
186	A18	6c scarlet	12.50	2.25
a.		Imperf., pair	200.00	
187	A18	10c scarlet	2.75	.60
a.		Imperf., pair	75.00	
b.		Horiz. pair, imperf. btwn.		
188	A18	20c scarlet	18.00	1.50
a.		Imperf., pair	275.00	
b.		Vert. pair, imperf. btwn.	350.00	
189	A18	25c scarlet	15.00	4.00
		Nos. 184-189 (6)	57.65	11.20

			Perf. 6	
190	A18	1c blue grn	45.00	45.00
191	A18	2c brown car	22.50	42.00
192	A18	5c ultra	15.00	4.50
a.		5c blue	15.00	4.50
193	A18	10c lilac	15.00	4.25
193A	A18	10c brown lilac	15.00	3.00
194	A18	10c scarlet	35.00	15.00

			Perf. 6x12	
194A	A18	1c blue grn	62.50	42.50
194B	A18	2c brown car	85.00	75.00
194C	A18	3c scarlet	300.00	350.00
194D	A18	5c ultra	60.00	45.00
194E	A18	10c lilac	90.00	75.00
194F	A18	10c scarlet	80.00	60.00
194G	A18	10c brown lilac	90.00	75.00

Many shades exist.

Paper with colored ruled lines on face or reverse of stamp

1887			Perf. 12	
195	A18	1c green	75.00	45.00
196	A18	2c brown car	190.00	47.50
198	A18	5c ultra	110.00	30.00
199	A18	10c scarlet	110.00	25.00

			Perf. 6	
201	A18	1c green	60.00	20.00
202	A18	2c brown car	60.00	24.00
204	A18	5c ultra	50.00	12.00
205	A18	10c brown lil	42.50	10.00
206	A18	10c scarlet	250.00	40.00
		Nos. 201-206 (5)	462.50	106.00

			Perf. 6x12	
207	A18	1c green	225.00	140.00
208	A18	2c brown car	325.00	140.00
209	A18	5c ultra	225.00	140.00
210	A18	10c brown lil	290.00	135.00
211	A18	10c scarlet	350.00	225.00
		Nos. 207-211 (5)	1,415.	780.00

1890-95	Wmk. 152		Perf. 11 & 12	
		Wove or Laid Paper		
212	A18	1c yellow grn	.75	.35
a.		1c blue green	.75	.35
b.		Horiz. pair, imperf. btwn.	125.00	125.00
c.		Laid paper	2.50	2.50
d.		Horiz. pair, imperf. vert.	125.00	125.00
213	A18	2c carmine	1.50	.75
a.		2c brown car	1.25	1.00
b.		Vert. pair, imperf. btwn.	150.00	
c.		Imperf., pair	200.00	
214	A18	3c vermilion	1.00	.60
a.		Horiz. pair, imperf. btwn.	200.00	
215	A18	4c vermilion	3.25	2.10
a.		Horiz. pair, imperf. btwn.	200.00	
216	A18	5c ultra	.60	.50
a.		5c dull blue	1.00	.50
217	A18	6c vermilion	3.75	2.75
a.		Horiz. pair, imperf. btwn.	300.00	
218	A18	10c vermilion	.50	.35
b.		Horiz. or vert. pair, imperf. btwn.	175.00	175.00
c.		Vert. pair, imperf. horiz.	175.00	
d.		Imperf., pair	200.00	
219	A18	12c ver ('95)	14.00	18.00
a.		Horiz. pair, imperf. btwn.	450.00	
220	A18	20c blue	3.00	1.50
220A	A18	20c dk violet	160.00	190.00
221	A18	25c carmine	5.00	2.50
		Nos. 212-220,221 (10)	33.85	29.40

No. 219 has been reprinted in slightly darker shade than the original.

1892				
222	A18	3c orange	4.00	2.00
223	A18	4c orange	4.25	3.00
224	A18	6c orange	5.75	2.00
225	A18	10c orange	27.50	2.00
226	A18	20c orange	50.00	6.00
227	A18	25c orange	16.00	4.50
		Nos. 222-227 (6)	107.50	19.50

1892				
228	A18	5p carmine	1,250.	900.
229	A18	10p carmine	1,900.	1,250.
230	A17	5p blue green	3,500.	1,200.
231	A17	10p blue green	7,000.	2,700.

1894			Perf. 5½, 6	
232	A18	1c yellow grn	3.00	3.00
233	A18	3c vermilion	9.00	9.00
234	A18	4c vermilion	40.00	37.50
235	A18	5c ultra	12.50	6.00
236	A18	10c vermilion	7.50	3.00
236A	A18	20c vermilion	110.00	110.00
237	A18	25c vermilion	62.50	62.50
		Nos. 232-237 (7)	244.50	230.00

			Perf. 5½x11, 11x5½, Compound and Irregular	
238	A18	1c yellow grn	7.00	7.00
238A	A18	2c brown car	16.00	16.00
238B	A18	3c vermilion	47.50	32.50
238C	A18	4c vermilion	55.00	55.00
239	A18	5c ultra	17.50	12.50
a.		5c blue	12.50	12.50
239C	A18	6c vermilion	75.00	75.00
240	A18	10c vermilion	20.00	7.00
240A	A18	20c vermilion	200.00	200.00
241	A18	25c vermilion	62.50	62.50
		Nos. 238-241 (9)	500.50	467.50

The stamps of the 1890 to 1895 issues are also to be found unwatermarked, as part of the sheet frequently escaped the watermark.

MEXICO

Letter Carrier A20

Mounted Courier with Pack Mule A21

Statue of Cuauhtémoc A22

Mail Coach A23

Mail Train — A24

Regular or Pin Perf. 12
1895   **Wmk. 152**
Wove or Laid Paper

242	A20	1c green	3.00	.75
a.		Vert. pair, imperf. horiz.	175.00	
d.		Watermarked sideway ('97)	125.00	15.00
243	A20	2c carmine	3.75	1.00
a.		Half used as 1c on cover		250.00
c.		Watermarked sideways ('97)	80.00	10.00
244	A20	3c orange brown	3.75	1.00
a.		Vert. pair, imperf. horiz.		250.00
d.		Watermarked sideways ('97)	125.00	10.00
e.		Horiz. or vert. pair, imperf. between		300.00
246	A21	4c orange	12.50	1.50
a.		4c orange red	7.50	1.25
247	A22	5c ultra	7.00	.35
a.		Imperf., pair	175.00	200.00
b.		Horiz. or vert. pair, imperf. between	175.00	200.00
e.		Half used as 2c on cover		2,100.
f.		Watermarked sideways ('97)	15.00	5.00
248	A23	10c lilac rose	4.50	1.00
a.		Horiz. or vert. pair, imperf. between		250.00
b.		Half used as 5c on cover		250.00
249	A21	12c olive brown	50.00	12.50
251	A23	15c brt blue	27.50	3.00
b.		Watermarked sideways ('97)		100.00
c.		Imperf., pair		300.00
252	A23	20c brown rose	32.50	3.00
b.		Half used as 10c on cover		200.00
c.		Watermarked sideways ('97)	1,100.	750.00
253	A23	50c purple	70.00	16.00
254	A24	1p brown	90.00	35.00
a.		Watermarked sideways ('97)	750.00	900.00
255	A24	5p scarlet	300.00	190.00
256	A24	10p deep blue	650.00	350.00
		Nos. 242-256 (13)	1,255.	615.10

No. 248 exists in perf. 11.

Nos. 242d, 243c, 244d, 247f, 251b, 252c and 254a was a special printing, made in Jan. 1897. The watermark is sideways, the grain of the paper is horizontal (rather than vertical, as appears on Nos. 242-256), and the design is somewhat shorter than the other stamps in this series. The sideways orientation of the watermark is the most easily identifiable feature of this printing.

Important: For unwatermarked examples of Nos. 242-256, see the footnote after No. 291.

Perf. 6

242b	A20	1c green	60.00	35.00
243b	A20	2c carmine	125.00	60.00
244h	A20	3c orange brown	90.00	50.00
247a	A22	5c ultra	60.00	40.00
248c	A23	10c lilac rose	125.00	55.00
249a	A21	12c olive brown	100.00	50.00

Perf. 6x12, 12x6 & Compound or Irregular

242c	A20	1c green	30.00	20.00
244c	A20	3c orange brown	35.00	20.00
246b	A21	4c orange	75.00	50.00
247d	A22	5c ultra	75.00	50.00
248c	A23	10c lilac rose	35.00	20.00
249b	A21	12c olive brown	50.00	25.00
251a	A23	15c brt blue	60.00	40.00
252a	A23	20c brown rose	100.00	70.00
253b	A23	50c purple	150.00	100.00

See Nos. 257-291. For overprints see Nos. O10-O48A.

"Irregular" Perfs.
Some stamps perf. 6x12, 12x6, 5½x11 and 11x5½ have both perf. 6 and 12 or perf. 5½ and 11 on one or more sides of the stamp. These are known as irregular perfs.

1896-97   **Wmk. 153**   **Perf. 12**

257	A20	1c green	14.00	1.25
c.		Imperf., pair		250.00
258	A20	2c carmine	17.50	1.50
a.		Horiz. pair, imperf. vert.		
259	A20	3c orange brn	20.00	1.50
c.		Horiz. pair, imperf. between		300.00
260	A21	4c orange	32.50	1.75
c.		4c deep orange	30.00	6.00
261	A22	5c ultra	9.00	1.25
a.		Imperf., pair	200.00	200.00
b.		Vert. pair, imperf. btwn.	200.00	
262	A21	12c olive brn	160.00	80.00
263	A23	15c brt blue	200.00	13.00
264	A23	20c brown rose	750.00	275.00
265	A23	50c purple	175.00	110.00
266	A24	1p brown	300.00	250.00
267	A24	5p scarlet	800.00	600.00
268	A24	10p dp blue	900.00	525.00
		Nos. 257-268 (12)	3,378.	1,860.

Perf. 6

257a	A20	1c green	35.00	25.00
259a	A20	3c orange brown	35.00	20.00
260a	A21	4c orange	40.00	25.00
261c	A22	5c ultra	110.00	70.00
263a	A23	15c bright blue	75.00	35.00

Perf. 6x12, 12x6 and Compound or Irregular

257b	A20	1c green	25.00	20.00
258b	A20	2c carmine	50.00	25.00
259b	A20	3c orange brown	40.00	20.00
260b	A21	4c orange	45.00	20.00
261d	A22	5c ultra	10.00	20.00
262a	A21	12c olive brown	125.00	80.00
263b	A23	15c bright blue	250.00	125.00
264a	A23	20c brown rose		
265a	A23	50c purple		

1897-98   **Wmk. 154**   **Perf. 12**

269	A20	1c green	20.00	3.00
270	A20	2c scarlet	35.00	4.50
c.		Horiz. pair, imperf. btwn.		250.00
271	A21	4c orange	52.50	3.75
a.		Horizontal pair, imperf. vertical	—	
272	A22	5c ultra	50.00	3.75
a.		Imperf., pair	85.00	
273	A21	12c olive brown	200.00	45.00
275	A23	15c brt blue	275.00	85.00
276	A23	20c brown rose	175.00	15.00
c.		Horiz. pair, imperf. btwn.		300.00
277	A23	50c purple	375.00	75.00
278	A24	1p brown	425.00	200.00
278A	A24	5p scarlet	—	4,000.
		Nos. 269-278 (9)	1,608.	435.00

Perf. 6

269a	A20	1c green	45.00	25.00
270a	A20	2c scarlet	45.00	25.00
272b	A22	5c ultra	60.00	25.00
273a	A21	12c olive brown	110.00	60.00
276a	A23	20c brown rose		650.00

Perf. 6x12, 12x6 and Compound or Irregular

269b	A20	1c green	25.00	15.00
270b	A20	2c scarlet	30.00	22.50
271b	A21	4c orange	65.00	12.50
272c	A22	5c ultra	50.00	15.00
273b	A21	12c olive brown	125.00	65.00
275a	A23	15c bright blue	125.00	65.00
276b	A23	20c brown rose	240.00	30.00
277a	A23	50c purple	125.00	50.00

1898   **Unwmk.**   **Perf. 12**

279	A20	1c green	3.00	.50
a.		Horiz. pair, imperf. vert	300.00	
b.		Imperf., pair	250.00	
280	A20	2c scarlet	6.25	.75
a.		2c green (error)	175.00	
281	A20	3c orange brn	6.00	.75
a.		Imperf., pair	250.00	250.00
b.		Pair, imperf. between	80.00	80.00
282	A21	4c orange	30.00	3.00
b.		4c deep orange	37.50	7.00
c.		Imperf., pair		300.00
283	A22	5c ultra	2.00	.50
a.		Imperf., pair	200.00	200.00
b.		Pair, imperf. between	200.00	
284	A23	10c lilac rose	550.00	175.00
285	A21	12c olive brn	80.00	27.50
a.		Imperf., pair	200.00	
286	A23	15c brt blue	175.00	8.00
287	A23	20c brown rose	35.00	3.00
a.		Imperf., pair	250.00	
288	A23	50c purple	150.00	42.50
289	A24	1p brown	175.00	80.00
290	A24	5p carmine rose	550.00	425.00
291	A24	10p deep blue	800.00	575.00
		Nos. 279-291 (13)	2,562.	1,342.

Warning: Sheets of Nos. 242-256 (watermarked "CORREOS E U M") have a column of stamps without watermarks, because the watermark did not fit the sheet size. As a result, be careful not to confuse unwatermarked examples of Nos. 242-256 with Nos. 279-291. This is especially important for No. 284. Nos. 242-256 and the watermarked 1895-97 overprinted Officials, Nos. O10-O39, have a vertical grain or mesh to the paper. Nos. 279-291 and the unwatermarked 1898 overprinted Officials, Nos. O40-O48B, have a horizontal grain or mesh to the paper. Be careful not to confuse unwatermarked examples of Nos. O10-O39 with Nos. O40-O48B.

Perf. 6

279c	A20	1c green	85.00	35.00
280b	A20	2c scarlet	75.00	30.00
281c	A20	3c orange brown	50.00	35.00
283c	A22	5c ultra	65.00	30.00
287b	A23	20c brown rose	125.00	75.00
291a	A24	10p deep blue		

Perf. 6x12, 12x6 and Compound or Irregular

279d	A20	1c green	25.00	20.00
280c	A20	2c scarlet	25.00	20.00
281d	A20	3c orange brown	30.00	20.00
282a	A21	4c orange	40.00	25.00
283d	A22	5c ultra	20.00	10.00
284a	A23	10c lilac rose	125.00	85.00
285b	A21	12c olive brown	90.00	60.00
286a	A23	15c bright blue	75.00	50.00
287a	A23	20c brown rose	100.00	50.00
288a	A23	50c purple	575.00	575.00

Forgeries of the 6 and 6x12 perforations of 1895-98 are plentiful.

Coat of Arms A25

A26

A27

A28

A29

A30

A31

Juanacatlán Falls — A32

View of Mt. Popocatépetl A33

Cathedral, Mexico, D. F. A34

1899, Nov. 1   **Wmk. 155**   **Perf. 14, 15**

294	A25	1c green	1.90	.35
295	A26	2c vermilion	4.50	.35
296	A27	3c orange brn	3.00	.35
297	A28	5c dark blue	4.75	.35
298	A29	10c violet & org	6.00	.35
299	A30	15c lav & claret	8.00	.35
300	A31	20c rose & dk bl	9.00	.40
301	A32	50c red lil & blk	35.00	2.25
a.		50c lilac & black	42.50	2.25
302	A33	1p blue & blk	80.00	3.50
303	A34	5p carmine & blk	275.00	12.00
		Nos. 294-303 (10)	427.15	20.25
		Set, never hinged	1,500.	

See Nos. 304-305, 307-309. For overprints see Nos. 420-422, 439-450, 452-454, 482-483, 515-516, 539, 550, O49-O60, O62-O66, O68-O74, O101.

A35

1903

304	A25	1c violet	1.50	.35
305	A26	2c green	2.00	.35
306	A35	4c carmine	5.00	.45
307	A28	5c orange	1.25	.35
308	A29	10c blue & org	5.00	.35
309	A32	50c carmine & blk	75.00	6.50
		Nos. 304-309 (6)	89.75	8.35
		Set, never hinged	350.00	

For overprints see Nos. 451, O61, O67.

Independence Issue

Josefa Ortiz A36

Leona Vicario A37

López Rayón A38

Juan Aldama A39

Miguel Hidalgo A40

Ignacio Allende A41

Epigmenio González A42

Mariano Abasolo A43

MEPSI

MEXICO ELMHURST PHILATELIC SOCIETY INTERNATIONAL

- Quarterly Journal MEXICANA
- MEPSI Circuit Books
- Expertization Committee
- MEPSI Library and Publications
- Local Chapters
- MEPSI Website – www.mepsi.org

For Membership Applications contact:
treasurer@mepsi.org
Eric Stovner, Treasurer
P.O. Box 10097
Santa Ana, CA 92711-0097

MEXICO

Declaration of Independence — A44

Mass on the Mount of Crosses — A45

Capture of Granaditas — A46

1910   **Perf. 14**
310	A36	1c dull violet	.35	.35
311	A37	2c green	.35	.35
312	A38	3c orange brn	.60	.35
313	A39	4c carmine	2.50	.45
314	A40	5c orange	.35	.35
315	A41	10c blue & org	1.50	.35
316	A42	15c gray bl & cl	8.00	1.85
317	A43	20c red & bl	5.00	.40
318	A44	50c red brn & blk	12.00	1.60
319	A45	1p blue & blk	15.00	2.00
320	A46	5p car & blk	57.50	16.50
		Nos. 310-320 (11)	103.15	23.20
		Set, never hinged	325.00	

Independence of Mexico from Spain, cent.

For overprints and surcharges see Nos. 370-380, 423-433, 455-465, 484-494, 517-538, 540-549, 551-558, 577-590, O75-O85, O102-O112, O191-O192, O195, RA13, Merida 1.

CIVIL WAR ISSUES

During the Mexican Civil War, provisional issues with various handstamped overprints were circulated in limited areas, between 1910 and 1916.

Sonora

A47

Seal

Typeset in a row of five varieties. Two impressions placed tête bêche (foot to foot) constitute a sheet. The settings show various wrong font and defective letters, "!" for "1" in "1913," etc. The paper occasionally has a manufacturer's watermark.

a   b   c   d

Four Types of the Numerals.
a — Wide, heavy-faced numerals.
b — Narrow Roman numerals.
c — Wide Roman numerals.
d — Gothic or sans-serif numerals.

Nos. 321-346 Issued Without Gum Embossed "CONSTITUCIONAL"

1913   **Typeset**   **Unwmk.**   **Perf. 12**
321	A47(a)	5c blk & red	4,250.	800.00
a.		"CENTAVOB"	4,750.	850.00

Colorless Roulette
322	A47(b)	1c blk & red	22.00	25.00
a.		With green seal	1,500.	1,250.
323	A47(a)	2c blk & red	18.00	15.00
a.		With green seal	2,000.	2,000.
324	A47(c)	2c blk & red	87.50	72.50
a.		With green seal	5,000.	5,000.
325	A47(a)	3c blk & red	97.50	77.50
a.		With green seal	750.00	750.00
326	A47(a)	5c blk & red	190.00	77.50
a.		"CENTAVOB"	200.00	50.00
327	A47(a)		1,200.	350.00
a.		With green seal		1,000.
328	A47(b)	10c blk & red	35.00	37.50

Black Roulette
329	A47(d)	5c blk & red	300.00	140.00
a.		"MARO"	400.00	225.00

Stamps are known with the embossing double or omitted.

The varieties with green seal are from a few sheets embossed "Constitucional" which were in stock at the time the green seal control was adopted.

Nos. 322-329 are known with papermakers' watermark ("Peerless Mills" or "Yukon Aurora").

No. 339

Without Embossing With Green Seal

Colorless Roulette
336	A47(b)	1c blk & red	15.00	10.00
337	A47(a)	3c blk & red	14.50	9.00
a.		Imperf.	350.00	
338	A47(a)	5c blk & red	750.00	250.00
a.		"CENTAVOB"	800.00	275.00
339	A47(b)	10c blk & red	8.00	7.50

Colored Roulette
340	A47(d)	5c brnsh blk & red	25.00	6.00
a.		5c lilac brown & red	75.00	22.50
b.		Double seal		1,250.
c.		Red printing omitted		1,000.

Nos. 336-340 are known with papermaker's watermark ("Peerless Mills" or "Yukon Aurora").

1913-14   **Black Roulette With Green Seal**
341	A47(a)	1c black & red	4.00	4.00
b.		"erano" ('14)	100.00	60.00
342	A47(d)	2c black & red	4.50	4.00
a.		"erano" ('14)	30.00	35.00
343	A47(a)	3c black & red	4.75	4.00
a.		"CENTAVO"	25.00	25.00
b.		"erano" ('14)	35.00	35.00
344	A47(d)	5c black & red	4.75	4.00
b.		Heavy black penetrating roulette	2.75	1.75
c.		As "b," "MARO"	10.50	8.50
d.		Without green seal	2,250.	
		Nos. 341-344 (4)	18.00	16.00

Stamps without seal are unfinished remainders.

On Nos. 341-344 the rouletting cuts the paper slightly or not at all. On Nos. 344b-344c the rouletting is heavy, cutting deeply into the paper.

1914
345	A47(a)	5c black & red	5.00	5.00
346	A47(b)	10c black & red	4.25	5.00

Coat of Arms — A49

Revenue Stamps Used for Postage

1913   **Litho.**   **Rouletted 14, 14x7**
347	A49	1c yellow grn	2.00	2.50
a.		With coupon	7.00	6.00
348	A49	2c violet	3.50	4.00
a.		With coupon	19.50	14.50
349	A49	5c brown	.60	.75
a.		With coupon	9.00	7.00
350	A49	10c claret	2.50	3.50
a.		With coupon	15.00	12.00
351	A49	20c gray grn	3.00	3.50
a.		With coupon	20.00	18.00
352	A49	50c ultra	11.00	16.00
a.		With coupon	70.00	47.50
353	A49	1p orange	45.00	55.00
a.		With coupon	175.00	120.00
		Nos. 347-353 (7)	67.60	85.25
		Set, never hinged	275.00	

For a short time these stamps (called "Ejercitos") were used for postage with coupon attached. Later this was required to be removed unless they were to be used for revenue. Stamps overprinted with district names are revenues. Values above 1p were used for revenue. Imperfs exist of all values, but were not issued.

Many examples do not have gum because of a flood.

Use of typeset Sonora revenue stamps for postage was not authorized or allowed.

A50

Coat of Arms — A50a

5c (A50): "CINCO CENTAVOS" 14x2mm

1914   **Rouletted 9½x14**
354	A50	1c blue	.45	.45
355	A50	2c yellow grn	.60	.35
a.		2c green	3.00	1.75
356	A50	4c blue vio	11.00	2.50
a.		Horiz. pair, imperf. btwn.	250.00	
357	A50a	5c gray grn	11.00	3.00
a.		Horiz. pair imperf. btwn.	250.00	
358	A50	10c red	.45	.45
359	A50	20c yellow brn	.60	.60
a.		20c deep brown	2.25	2.25
b.		Horiz. pair, imperf. btwn.	250.00	
360	A50	50c claret	2.50	3.50
a.		Horiz. pair, imperf. btwn.	250.00	
361	A50	1p brt violet	14.00	16.00
a.		Horiz. pair, imperf. btwn.	250.00	
		Nos. 354-361 (8)	40.60	26.85
		Set, never hinged	175.00	

Nos. 354-361 (called "Transitorios") exist imperf. but were not regularly issued.

Many examples do not have gum because of a flood.

See Note after No. 465.

See No. 369. For overprints see Nos. 362-368, 559-565.

Overprinted in Black

1914
362	A50	1c deep blue	200.00	175.00
a.		"1912" for "1914"	2,000.	
363	A50	2c yellow green	225.00	200.00
364	A50	4c blue violet	250.00	300.00
365	A50	5c gray green	35.00	50.00
a.		Horiz. pair, imperf. btwn.	550.00	
366	A50	10c red	150.00	150.00
a.		"1912" for "1914"	2,000.	
367	A50	20c yellow brn	2,500.	2,500.
a.		"1912" for "1914"	7,000.	
368	A50	50c claret	3,500.	3,500.

Values are for stamps with design close to, or just touching, the perfs.

Excellent counterfeits of this overprint exist.

Redrawn

Coat of Arms — A51

"CINCO CENTAVOS" 16x2½mm

1914   **Perf. 12**
369	A51	5c gray green	1.00	.35

Imperfs are printers' waste.

Regular Issue of 1910 Overprinted in Violet, Magenta, Black or Green

1914   **Wmk. 155**   **Perf. 14**
370	A36	1c dull violet	1.50	.60
371	A37	2c green	3.00	1.25
372	A38	3c orange brn	3.00	1.25
373	A39	4c carmine	5.00	2.00
374	A40	5c orange	1.00	.35
375	A41	10c blue & org	6.00	2.00
376	A42	15c gray bl & cl	10.00	3.00
377	A43	20c red & blue	20.00	6.00
378	A44	50c red brn & blk	25.00	8.00
379	A45	1p blue & blk	55.00	11.00
380	A46	5p carmine & blk	190.00	160.00
		Nos. 370-380 (11)	319.50	195.45
		Set, never hinged	1,000.	

Overprinted On Postage Due Stamps of 1908
381	D1	1c blue	27.50	30.00
382	D1	2c blue	27.50	30.00
383	D1	4c blue	27.50	30.00
384	D1	5c blue	27.50	30.00
385	D1	10c blue	27.50	30.00
		Nos. 381-385 (5)	137.50	150.00
		Set, never hinged	375.00	

This overprint is found double, inverted, sideways and in pairs with and without the overprint.

There are two or more types of this overprint.

The Postage Due Stamps and similar groups of them which follow were issued and used as regular postage stamps.

Values are for stamps where the overprint is clear enough to be expertised.

Counterfeits abound.

A52

1914   **Unwmk.**   **Litho.**   **Perf. 12**
386	A52	1c pale blue	.35	.35
387	A52	2c light green	.35	.45
388	A52	3c orange	.50	.50
389	A52	5c deep rose	.50	.35
390	A52	10c red	.70	.85
391	A52	15c rose lilac	1.20	1.75
392	A52	50c yellow	2.00	2.50
a.		50c ocher	1.75	
393	A52	1p violet	8.50	12.00
		Nos. 386-393 (8)	14.10	18.90
		Set, never hinged	50.00	

Nos. 386-393, are known imperforate.

This set is usually called the Denver Issue because it was printed there.

See Note after No. 465.

For overprints and surcharges see Nos. 566-573, 591-592.

A53

Revenue Stamps Used for Postage

1914, July   **Perf. 12**
393A	A53	1c rose		40.00
393B	A53	2c lt green		35.00
393C	A53	3c lt orange		75.00
393D	A53	5c red		15.00
393E	A53	10c gray green		70.00
393F	A53	25c blue		150.00
		Nos. 393A-393F (6)		385.00

Nos. 393A-393F were used in the northeast. Values are for examples with postal cancellations.

Unused examples are to be considered as revenues.

Pres. Madero

Stamps in this design, featuring Pres. Madero, within a frame very similar to that of the Denver Issue (Nos. 386-393), were ordered in 1915 by Francisco Villa, to be used by the Constitutionalist government. Five values (1c green, 2c brown, 3c carmine, 5c blue, and 10c yellow) were printed by Ellis Brothers & Co., El Paso, Texas. By the time of the stamps' arrival in Mexico City, the Constitutionalist regime had fallen, and the new Conventionist government returned them to the printer, who later sold the unissued stamps within the philatelic market. Value, set $10.

Background as A55 — A54

MEXICO

Nos. 394-413 Issued Without Gum

1914   **Imperf.**

Values and Inscriptions in Black

Inscribed "SONORA"

394	A54	1c blue & red	.35	.35
a.		Double seal		
b.		Without seal	20.00	
395	A54	2c green & org	.35	.35
a.		Without seal	100.00	
396	A54	5c yellow & grn	.35	.35
a.		5c orange & green	1.50	1.25
b.		Without seal		300.00
397	A54	10c lt bl & red	3.50	1.75
a.		10c blue & red	40.00	15.00
398	A54	20c yellow & grn	1.75	2.00
399	A54	20c orange & bl	15.00	17.50
400	A54	50c green & org	1.25	1.25
		Nos. 394-400 (7)	22.55	23.55

Shades. Stamps of type A54 are usually termed the "Coach Seal Issue."

Inscribed "DISTRITO SUR DE LA BAJA CAL"

401	A54	1c yellow & blue	2.00	30.00
a.		Without seal	50.00	
402	A54	2c gray & ol grn	2.50	25.00
403	A54	5c olive & rose	2.00	20.00
a.		Without seal	50.00	
404	A54	10c pale red & dl vio	2.00	20.00
a.		Without seal	50.00	
		Nos. 401-404 (4)	8.50	95.00

Counterfeit cancellations exist.

A55

Inscribed "SONORA"

405	A55	1c blue & red	6.00	
a.		Without seal	50.00	
406	A55	2c green & org	.50	
407	A55	5c yellow & grn	.50	2.50
a.		Without seal	75.00	
408	A55	10c blue & red	.50	2.50
409	A55	20c yellow & grn	75.00	15.00
a.		Without seal	95.00	
b.		Double seal	80.00	
		Nos. 405-409 (5)	82.50	20.00

With "PLATA" added to the inscription

410	A55	1c blue & red	1.00	
a.		"PLATA" inverted	60.00	
b.		Pair, one without "PLATA"	15.00	
411	A55	10c blue & red	1.00	
412	A55	20c yellow & grn	2.50	
a.		"PLATA" double	50.00	
413	A55	50c gray grn & org	1.75	
a.		Without seal	50.00	
b.		As "a," "P" of "PLATA" missing	150.00	
		Nos. 410-413 (4)	6.25	

Stamps of type A55 are termed the "Anvil Seal Issue".

Nos. 410-413 were not placed in use.

Oaxaca

Coat of Arms — A56

5c:
Type I — Thick numerals, 2mm wide.
Type II — Thin numerals, 1½mm wide.

Perf. 8½ to 14

1915   **Typo.**   **Unwmk.**

414	A56	1c dull violet	2.00	1.25
415	A56	2c emerald	3.00	2.25
a.		Inverted numeral	30.00	
e.		Numeral omitted	35.00	
416	A56	3c red brown	4.00	3.50
b.		Inverted numeral	30.00	
417	A56	5c org (type I)	77.50	77.50
a.		Tête bêche pair	175.00	175.00
418	A56	5c org (type II)	.50	.75
a.		Types I and II in pair	250.00	
419	A56	10c blue & car	4.00	4.00
		Nos. 414-419 (6)	91.00	89.25
		Set, never hinged	275.00	

Many printing errors, imperfs and part perfs exist. Mostly these are printers' waste, private reprints or counterfeits.

Nos. 414-419 printed on backs of post office receipt forms.

Regular Issues of 1899-1910 Overprinted in Black

1914   **Wmk. 155**   **Perf. 14**

On Issues of 1899-1903

420	A28	5c orange		
421	A30	15c lav & claret	250.00	250.00
		Never hinged	700.00	
422	A31	20c rose & dk bl	1,000.	500.00

Counterfeits exist.

The listing of No. 420 is being re-evaluated. The Catalogue Editors would appreciate any information on the stamp.

On Issue of 1910

423	A36	1c dull violet	.35	.35
424	A37	2c green	.35	.35
425	A38	3c orange brown	.40	.40
426	A39	4c carmine	.50	.50
427	A40	5c orange	.35	.35
428	A41	10c blue & orange	.35	.35
429	A42	15c gray bl & claret	.70	.60
430	A43	20c red & blue	.75	.70

Overprinted

431	A44	50c red brn & blk	1.75	1.50
432	A45	1p blue & blk	8.00	5.50
433	A46	5p carmine & blk	42.50	32.50
		Nos. 423-433 (11)	56.00	43.10
		Set, never hinged	170.00	

In the first setting of the overprint on 1c to 20c, the variety "GONSTITUCIONALISTA" occurs 4 times in each sheet of 100. In the second setting it occurs on the last stamp in each row of 10.

The overprint exists reading downward on Nos. 423-430; inverted on Nos. 431-433; double on Nos. 423-425, 427.

See Note after No. 465.

For overprints see Nos. 528-538.

Postage Due Stamps of 1908 Overprinted

434	D1	1c blue	4.75	5.00
435	D1	2c blue	6.00	5.00
436	D1	4c blue	25.00	25.00
437	D1	5c blue	25.00	25.00
438	D1	10c blue	5.50	5.00
a.		Double overprint		
		Nos. 434-438 (5)	66.25	65.00
		Set, never hinged	200.00	

Preceding Issues Overprinted

This is usually called the "Villa" monogram. Counterfeits abound.

1915   **On Issue of 1899**

439	A25	1c green	210.00
440	A26	2c vermilion	210.00
441	A27	3c orange brn	175.00
442	A28	5c dark blue	210.00
443	A29	10c violet & org	210.00
444	A30	15c lav & claret	750.00 750.00
445	A31	20c rose & bl	1,000.
446	A32	50c red lil & blk	500.00
447	A33	1p blue & blk	500.00
448	A34	5p car & blk	750.00
		Nos. 439-448 (10)	4,515.

On Issue of 1903

449	A25	1c violet	200.00
450	A26	2c green	200.00
451	A35	4c carmine	200.00
452	A28	5c orange	45.00
a.		Inverted overprint	75.00
453	A29	10c blue & org	750.00
454	A32	50c car & blk	—
		Nos. 449-453 (5)	1,395.

In Sept. 1915 Postmaster Hinojosa ordered a special printing of Nos. 439-454 (as valued) for sale to collectors. Earlier a small quantity of Nos. 444-445, 448 and 452-454 was regularly issued. They are hard to distinguish and sell for much more. Counterfeits abound.

On Issue of 1910

455	A36	1c dull violet	.85	1.00
456	A37	2c green	.40	.60
457	A38	3c orange brown	.60	.75
458	A39	4c carmine	4.00	4.50
459	A40	5c orange	.35	.35
460	A41	10c blue & orange	7.00	7.50
461	A42	15c gray bl & cl	3.00	4.00
462	A43	20c red & blue	5.50	7.00
463	A44	50c red brn & blk	13.00	14.00
464	A45	1p blue & blk	17.00	20.00
465	A46	5p carmine & blk	150.00	
		Nos. 455-464 (10)	51.70	59.70
		Set, never hinged	175.00	

Nos. 455-465 are known with overprint inverted, double and other variations. Most were ordered by Postmaster General Hinojosa for philatelic purposes. They were sold at a premium. This applies to Nos. 354-361, 386-393, 431-433 with this monogram as well.

Overprinted On Postage Due Stamps of 1908

466	D1	1c blue	15.00	20.00
467	D1	2c blue	15.00	20.00
468	D1	4c blue	15.00	20.00
469	D1	5c blue	15.00	20.00
470	D1	10c blue	15.00	20.00
		Nos. 466-470 (5)	75.00	100.00
		Set, never hinged	225.00	

Nos. 466 to 470 are known with inverted overprint. All other values of the 1899 and 1903 issues exist with this overprint. See note after No. 465.

Issues of 1899-1910 Overprinted

This is called the "Carranza" or small monogram. Counterfeits abound.

On Issues of 1899-1903

482	A28	5c orange	55.00	20.00
		Never hinged	115.00	
483	A30	15c lav & claret	200.00	80.00
		Never hinged	650.00	

On Issue of 1910

484	A36	1c dull violet	.70	.70
485	A37	2c green	.70	.60
486	A38	3c orange brn	.75	.75
487	A39	4c carmine	2.00	2.00
488	A40	5c orange	.35	.35
489	A41	10c blue & org	1.50	1.50
a.		Double ovpt., one invtd.	25.00	
490	A42	15c gray bl & cl	1.50	1.50
491	A43	20c red & blue	1.50	1.50
492	A44	50c red brn & blk	10.00	10.00
493	A45	1p blue & blk	15.00	15.00
494	A46	5p car & blk	150.00	150.00
		Nos. 484-494 (11)	184.00	183.90
		Set, never hinged	550.00	

All values exist with inverted overprint; all but 5p with double overprint.

Overprinted On Postage Due Stamps of 1908

495	D1	1c blue	22.00	25.00
496	D1	2c blue	22.00	25.00
497	D1	4c blue	22.00	25.00
498	D1	5c blue	22.00	25.00
499	D1	10c blue	22.00	25.00
		Nos. 495-499 (5)	110.00	125.00
		Set, never hinged	325.00	

Nos. 495-499 exist with inverted overprint.

It is stated that, in parts of Mexico occupied by the revolutionary forces, instructions were given to apply a distinguishing overprint to all stamps found in the post offices. This overprint was usually some arrangement or abbreviation of "Gobierno Constitucionalista". Such overprints as were specially authorized or were in general use in large sections of the country are listed. Numerous other handstamped overprints were used in one town or locality. They were essentially military faction control marks necessitated in most instances by the chaotic situation following the split between Villa and Carranza. The fact that some were often struck in a variety of colors and positions suggests the influence of philatelists.

Coat of Arms A57

Statue of Cuauhtémoc A58

Ignacio Zaragoza A59

José María Morelos A60

Francisco Madero A61

Benito Juárez A62

1915   **Unwmk. Litho.**   **Rouletted 14**

500	A57	1c violet	.30	.30
501	A58	2c green	.30	.30
502	A59	3c brown	.50	.30
503	A60	4c carmine	.50	.30
504	A61	5c orange	.75	.30
505	A62	10c ultra	.35	.30
		Nos. 500-505 (6)	2.70	1.80
		Set, never hinged	4.00	

Nos. 500-505 exists imperf.; some exist imperf. vertically or horizontally; some with rouletting and perforation combined. These probably were not regularly issued in these forms.

See Nos. 506-511. For overprints see Nos. O86-O97.

Map of Mexico A63

Veracruz Lighthouse A64

Post Office, Mexico, D.F. — A65

TEN CENTAVOS:
Type I — Size 19½x24mm. Crossed lines on coat.
Type II — Size 19x23½mm. Diagonal lines only on coat.

MEXICO

1915-16 — **Perf. 12**

506	A57	1c violet	.40	.25
507	A58	2c green	.40	.30
508	A59	3c brown	.50	.30
509	A60	4c carmine	.50	.35
a.		"CEATRO"	7.75	7.50
510	A61	5c orange	.75	.35
511	A62	10c ultra, type I	1.00	.35
a.		10c ultra, type II	.50	.30

Engr.

512	A63	40c slate	.75	.35
513	A64	1p brown & blk	1.00	.75
a.		Inverted center	200.00	275.00
514	A65	5p cl & ultra ('16)	12.00	4.00
a.		Inverted center	450.00	
		Nos. 506-514 (9)	17.30	7.00
		Set, never hinged	60.00	

Nos. 507-508, 510-514, exist imperf; Nos. 513-514 imperf with inverted center. These varieties were not regularly issued.

See Nos. 626-628, 647. For overprints see Nos. O92-O100, O121-O123, O132-O133, O142-O144, O153-O154, O162-O164, O174, O188, O193, O207, O222.

Issues of 1899-1910 Overprinted in Blue, Red or Black

On Issues of 1899-1903

1916 — **Wmk. 155** — **Perf. 14**

515	A28	5c orange (Bl)	125.00	175.00
		Never hinged	400.00	
516	A30	15c lav & cl (Bl)	775.00	775.00
		Never hinged	2,250.	

On Issue of 1910

517	A36	1c dull vio (R)	10.00	10.00
518	A37	2c green (R)	.50	.35
519	A38	3c orange brn (Bl)	.55	.40
a.		Double overprint	500.00	
520	A39	4c carmine (Bl)	6.00	8.00
521	A40	5c orange (Bl)	.25	.25
a.		Double overprint	75.00	
522	A41	10c blue & org (R)	1.25	1.50
523	A42	15c gray bl & cl (Bk)	1.75	3.00
524	A43	20c red & bl (Bk)	1.75	3.00
525	A44	50c red brn & blk (R)	8.50	5.00
526	A45	1p blue & blk (R)	15.00	6.50
527	A46	5p car & blk (R)	175.00	175.00
		Nos. 517-527 (11)	220.55	213.00
		Nos. 517-527, never hinged	650.00	

Nos. 519-524 exist with this overprint (called the "Corbata") reading downward and Nos. 525-527 with it inverted. Of these varieties only Nos. 519-521 were regularly issued.

On Nos. 423-430

528	A36	1c dull vio (R)	2.50	4.00
529	A37	2c green (R)	.75	.60
530	A38	3c orange brn (Bl)	.60	.60
531	A39	4c carmine (Bl)	.60	.60
532	A40	5c orange (Bl)	1.00	.30
533	A41	10c blue & org (R)	.75	.60
534	A42	15c gray bl & cl (Bk)	.80	.80
535	A43	20c red & bl (Bk)	.80	.80

On Nos. 431-433 in Red

536	A44	50c red brn & blk	7.50	6.00
537	A45	1p blue & blk	16.00	16.00
538	A46	5p carmine & blk	150.00	140.00
a.		Tablet inverted	300.00	
		Nos. 528-538 (11)	181.30	170.30
		Set, never hinged	550.00	

Nos. 529 to 535 are known with the overprint reading downward and Nos. 536 to 538 with it inverted.

On No. 482

539	A28	5c orange (Bl)	400.00	400.00

On Nos. 484-494

540	A36	1c dull vio (R)	6.00	6.00
541	A37	2c green (R)	.75	.75
a.		Monogram inverted	100.00	
542	A38	3c orange brn (Bl)	.75	.75
543	A39	4c carmine (Bl)	8.50	10.00
544	A40	5c orange (Bl)	1.25	.35
545	A41	10c blue & org (R)	2.00	2.50
546	A42	15c gray bl & cl (Bk)	1.75	3.00
a.		Tablet double	750.00	750.00
b.		Monogram double		750.00
547	A43	20c red & bl (Bk)	1.75	1.50
548	A44	50c red brn & blk (R)	9.00	10.00
a.		Monogram inverted	75.00	
b.		Tablet inverted	85.00	
549	A45	1p blue & blk (R)	13.00	14.00
a.		Tablet double	200.00	
b.		Monogram inverted	70.00	
		Nos. 539-549 (11)	444.75	446.60
		Set, never hinged	1,300.	

Nos. 541-547 exist with overprint reading downward. A few 5p were overprinted for the Post Office collection.

On No. 452

550	A28	5c orange (Bl)	125.00	125.00

On Nos. 455-462

551	A36	1c dull vio (R)	11.00	15.00
552	A37	2c green (R)	1.50	.90
553	A38	3c org brn (R)	3.25	4.50
554	A39	4c carmine (Bl)	13.00	15.00
555	A40	5c orange (Bl)	4.50	6.00
556	A41	10c bl & org (R)	12.00	14.00
a.		Monogram inverted	250.00	
557	A42	15c gray bl & cl (Bk)	12.00	14.00
a.		Monogram inverted	250.00	
558	A43	20c red & bl (Bk)	12.00	14.00
a.		Monogram inverted	250.00	
		Nos. 550-558 (9)	194.25	208.40
		Set, never hinged	650.00	

Stamps of 50c, 1p and 5p were overprinted for the Post Office collection but were not regularly issued.

Issues of 1914 Overprinted

On "Transitorio" Issue
Rouletted 9½x14
Unwmk.

559	A50	1c dp blue (R)	24.00	24.00
		Never hinged	75.00	
560	A50	2c yellow grn (R)	12.00	18.00
		Never hinged	27.50	
561	A50	4c blue vio (R)	425.00	375.00
		Never hinged	1,200.	
562	A50	10c red (Bl)	2.00	6.00
		Never hinged	4.00	
a.		Vertical overprint	125.00	
563	A50	20c yellow brn (R)	3.00	6.00
		Never hinged	7.50	
564	A50	50c claret (Bl)	15.00	20.00
		Never hinged	45.00	
565	A50	1p violet (Bl)	27.50	27.50
		Never hinged	100.00	
a.		Horiz. pair, imperf. btwn.		
		Nos. 559-565 (7)	508.50	476.50

Overprinted in Blue
On "Denver" Issue
Perf. 12

566	A52	1c pale blue	3.75	
567	A52	2c lt green	3.75	
568	A52	3c orange	.45	5.00
569	A52	5c deep rose	.45	5.00
570	A52	10c rose	.45	5.00
571	A52	15c rose lilac	.45	5.00
572	A52	50c yellow	1.10	15.00
573	A52	1p violet	9.50	25.00
		Nos. 566-573 (8)	19.90	
		Set, never hinged	65.00	

Many of the foregoing stamps exist with the "G. P. DE M." overprint printed in other colors than those listed. These "trial color" stamps were not regularly on sale at post offices but were available for postage and used stamps are known.

There appears to have been speculation in Nos. 516, 517, 520, 528, 539, 540, 543, 566, and 567. A small quantity of each of these stamps was sold at post offices but subsequently they could be obtained only from officials or their agents at advanced prices.

Venustiano Carranza — A66

1916, June 1 — **Engr.** — **Perf. 12**

574	A66	10c blue	1.75	1.00
a.		Imperf., pair	25.00	
575	A66	10c lilac brown	15.00	15.00
a.		Imperf., pair	50.00	
		Nos. 574-575, never hinged	32.50	

Entry of Carranza into Mexico, D.F. Stamps of type A66 with only horizontal lines in the background of the oval are essays.

Coat of Arms — A67

1916

576	A67	1c lilac	.35	.35
		Never hinged	.80	

Issue of 1910 Surcharged in Various Colors

This overprint is called the "Barril."

1916 — **Wmk. 155** — **Perf. 14**

577	A36	5c on 1c dl vio (Br)	.50	.50
a.		Vertical surcharge	1.25	1.25
b.		Double surcharge	150.00	
578	A36	10c on 1c dl vio (Bl)	.50	.50
a.		Double surcharge	100.00	
579	A40	20c on 5c org (Br)	.50	.50
a.		Double surcharge	90.00	
580	A40	25c on 5c org (G)	.40	.50
581	A37	60c on 2c grn (R)	27.50	20.00
		Nos. 577-581 (5)	29.40	22.00
		Set, never hinged	100.00	

On Nos. 423-424, 427

582	A36	5c on 1c (Br)	.50	.50
a.		Double tablet, one vertical	100.00	
b.		Inverted tablet	250.00	250.00
583	A36	10c on 1c (Bl)	1.00	1.00
584	A40	25c on 5c (G)	.50	.50
a.		Inverted tablet	225.00	225.00
585	A37	60c on 2c (R)	650.00	425.00
		Nos. 582-584, never hinged	4.50	

No. 585 was not regularly issued.
The variety "GONSTITUCIONALISTA" is found on Nos. 582 to 585.

On No. 459

586	A40	25c on 5c org (G)	.35	.35
		Never hinged	.70	

On Nos. 484-485, 488

587	A36	5c on 1c (Br)	15.00	20.00
a.		Vertical surcharge	100.00	125.00
588	A36	10c on 1c (Bl)	5.00	7.50
589	A40	25c on 5c (G)	1.00	1.50
a.		Inverted tablet	225.00	
590	A37	60c on 2c (R)	450.00	
		Nos. 587-589, never hinged	60.00	

No. 590 was not regularly issued.

Surcharged on "Denver" Issue of 1914

1916 — **Unwmk.** — **Perf. 12**

591	A52	60c on 1c pale bl (Br)	3.00	6.00
592	A52	60c on 2c lt grn (Br)	3.00	6.00
a.		Inverted surcharge	1,250.	
		Set, never hinged	18.00	

Postage Due Stamps Surcharged Like Nos. 577-581

1916 — **Wmk. 155** — **Perf. 14**

593	D1	5c on 1c blue (Br)	2.50	
594	D1	10c on 2c blue (V)	2.50	
595	D1	20c on 4c blue (Br)	2.50	
596	D1	25c on 5c blue (G)	2.50	
597	D1	60c on 10c blue (R)	1.50	
598	D1	1p on 1c blue (C)	1.50	
599	D1	1p on 2c blue (C)	1.50	
600	D1	1p on 4c blue (C)	.80	.80
601	D1	1p on 5c blue (C)	2.50	
602	D1	1p on 10c blue (C)	2.50	
		Nos. 593-602 (10)	20.30	
		Set, never hinged	60.00	

There are numerous "trial colors" and "essays" of the overprints and surcharges on Nos. 577 to 602. They were available for postage though not regularly issued.

Postage Due Stamps Surcharged

1916

603	D1	2.50p on 1c blue	1.25	1.25
604	D1	2.50p on 2c blue	10.00	
605	D1	2.50p on 4c blue	10.00	250.00
606	D1	2.50p on 5c blue	10.00	
607	D1	2.50p on 10c blue	10.00	
a.		Inverted surcharge	1,500.	
		Nos. 603-607 (5)	41.25	
		Set, never hinged	125.00	

Regular Issue

Ignacio Zaragoza — A68
Ildefonso Vázquez — A69
J. M. Pino Suárez — A70
Jesús Carranza — A71
Maclovio Herrera — A72
F. I. Madero — A73
Belisario Domínguez — A74
Aquiles Serdán — A75

Rouletted 14½

1917-20 — **Engr.** — **Unwmk.**
Thick Paper

608	A68	1c dull violet	2.00	1.00
		Never hinged	4.00	
609	A68	1c lilac gray ('20)	5.00	.75
		Never hinged	9.50	
a.		1c gray ('20)	5.00	5.00
610	A69	2c gray green	1.50	.50
		Never hinged	3.00	
611	A70	3c bister brn	1.50	1.00
		Never hinged	3.00	
612	A71	4c carmine	2.50	1.00
		Never hinged	7.50	
613	A72	5c ultra	2.50	.50
		Never hinged	5.00	
a.		Horiz. pair, imperf. btwn.	75.00	
b.		Imperf., pair	35.00	75.00
614	A73	10c blue	4.00	.50
		Never hinged	10.00	
a.		Without imprint	7.50	1.00
		Never hinged	16.00	
615	A74	20c brown rose	40.00	2.00
		Never hinged	90.00	
a.		20c rose	40.00	2.00
		Never hinged	80.00	
616	A75	30c gray brown	90.00	3.00
		Never hinged	250.00	
617	A75	30c gray blk ('20)	100.00	4.00
		Never hinged	250.00	
		Nos. 608-617 (10)	249.00	14.25

Perf. 12
Thick or Medium Paper

618	A68	1c dull violet	35.00	25.00
		Never hinged	100.00	
619	A69	2c gray green	10.00	6.00
		Never hinged	20.00	
620	A70	3c bis brn ('17)	200.00	200.00
		Never hinged	400.00	
622	A72	5c ultra	5.00	.35
		Never hinged	10.00	
623	A73	10c blue ('17)	5.00	.35
		Never hinged	10.00	
a.		Without imprint ('17)	20.00	15.00
		Never hinged	40.00	
624	A74	20c rose ('20)	140.00	3.00
		Never hinged	350.00	
625	A75	30c gray blk ('20)	140.00	2.00
		Never hinged	350.00	

Thin or Medium Paper

626	A63	40c violet	65.00	1.00
		Never hinged	200.00	
627	A64	1p blue & blk	50.00	1.50
		Never hinged	150.00	
a.		With center of 5p	800.00	
b.		1p bl & dark blue (error)	500.00	25.00
c.		Vert. pair, imperf. btwn.		250.00
628	A65	5p green & blk	1.50	10.00
		Never hinged	3.00	
a.		With violet or red control number	25.00	10.00
b.		With center of 1p	800.00	

The 1, 2, 3, 5 and 10c are known on thin paper perforated. It is stated they were printed for Postal Union and "specimen" purposes.

All values exist imperf; these are not known to have been regularly issued. Nos. 627a and 628b were not regularly issued.

All values except 3c have an imprint.

For overprints and surcharges see Nos. B1-B2, O113-O165.

MEXICO

Meeting of Iturbide and Guerrero — A77

Entering City of Mexico — A78

1921
632	A77	10c blue & brn	25.00 3.00
		Never hinged	82.50
a.		Center inverted	40,000.
633	A78	10p black brn & blk	22.50 37.50
		Never hinged	75.00

Commemorating the meeting of Agustín de Iturbide and Vicente Guerrero and the entry into City of Mexico in 1821.
For overprint see No. O194.

"El Salto de Agua," Public Fountain A79

Pyramid of the Sun at Teotihuacán A80

Chapultepec Castle A81

Columbus Monument A82

Medallion A90

Map of Americas A91

Juárez Colonnade, Mexico, D. F. A83

Monument to Josefa Ortiz de Dominguez A84

Francisco García y Santos A92

Post Office, Mexico, D. F. A93

Cuauhtémoc Monument — A85

1923 — Unwmk. — Rouletted 14½
634	A79	2c scarlet	2.00 .35
635	A80	3c bister brn	2.00 .35
636	A81	4c green	2.50 .75
637	A82	5c orange	5.00 .35
638	A83	10c brown	3.75 .35
639	A85	10c claret	3.50 .35
640	A84	20c dk blue	52.50 1.75
641	A85	30c dk green	52.50 2.00
		Nos. 634-641 (8)	123.75 6.25
		Set, never hinged	300.00

See Nos. 642-646, 650-657, 688-692, 727A, 735A-736. For overprints see Nos. O166-O173, O178-O181, O183-O187, O196-O197, O199-O206, O210, O212-O214, O217-O222.

Communications Building — A87

Palace of Fine Arts (National Theater) — A88

Type I
Type II

Two types of 1p:
I — Eagle on palace dome.
II — Without eagle.

1923 — Wmk. 156 — Perf. 12
642	A79	2c scarlet	10.00 10.00
643	A81	4c green	1.40 .35
644	A82	5c orange	10.00 7.00
645	A85	10c brown lake	12.50 6.00
646	A83	30c dark green	.95 .35
647	A63	40c violet	1.25 .35
648	A87	50c olive brn	1.00 .35
649	A88	1p red brn & bl (I)	1.00 1.00
a.		Type II	3.00 10.00
		Nos. 642-649 (8)	38.10 25.40
		Set, never hinged	90.00

Most of Nos. 642-649 are known imperforate or part perforate but probably were not regularly issued.
For overprints see Nos. O175-O176, O189-O190, O208-O209, O223.

1923-34 — Rouletted 14½
650	A79	2c scarlet	.35 .35
651	A80	3c bis brn ('27)	.35 .35
652	A81	4c green	47.50 35.00
653	A82	4c green ('27)	.35 .35
654	A82	5c orange	.35 .35
655	A85	10c lake	.35 .35
656	A84	20c deep blue	.75 .35
657	A83	30c dk green ('34)	.75 .35
		Nos. 650-657 (8)	50.75 37.45
		Set, never hinged	125.00

Nos. 650 to 657 inclusive exist imperforate.

1926 — Perf. 12
658	A90	2c red	2.50 1.00
659	A91	4c green	2.50 1.00
660	A90	5c orange	2.50 .75
661	A91	10c brown red	4.00 1.00
662	A92	20c dk blue	4.00 1.25
663	A92	30c dk green	7.50 4.00
664	A92	40c violet	13.50 3.00
665	A93	1p brown & blue	27.50 10.00
a.		1p red brown & blue	37.50 15.00
		Nos. 658-665 (8)	64.00 22.00
		Set, never hinged	150.00

Pan American Postal Congress.
Nos. 658-665 were also printed in black, on unwatermarked paper, for presentation to delegates to the Universal Postal Congress at London in 1929. Remainders were overprinted in 1929 for use as airmail official stamps, and are listed as Nos. CO3-CO10.
For overprints see Nos. 667-674, 675A-682, CO3-CO10.

Benito Juárez — A94

1926 — Rouletted 14½
666	A94	8c orange	.35 .35
		Never hinged	.70

For overprint see No. O182.

Nos. 658-665 Overprinted

1930 — Perf. 12
667	A90	2c red	4.00 2.25
a.		Reading down	16.00 15.00
668	A91	4c green	4.00 2.50
a.		Reading down	15.00 15.00
669	A90	5c orange	4.00 2.00
a.		Reading down	15.00 35.00
b.		Double overprint	75.00 75.00
670	A91	10c brown red	7.50 2.50
671	A92	20c dk blue	9.50 3.50
672	A92	30c dk green	8.50 4.00
a.		Reading down	10.00 12.00
673	A92	40c violet	12.50 8.50
a.		Reading down	47.50 50.00
674	A93	1p red brn & bl	11.00 7.00
a.		Double overprint	250.00
b.		Triple overprint	200.00
		Nos. 667-674 (8)	61.00 32.25
		Set, never hinged	150.00

Overprint horizontal on 1p.

Arms of Puebla — A95

1931, May 1 — Engr.
675	A95	10c dk bl & dk brn	3.00 .50
		Never hinged	7.50

400th anniversary of Puebla.

Nos. 658-665a Overprinted

1931
676	A91	4c green	70.00 75.00
a.		Inverted overprint	750.00
677	A90	5c orange	13.00 17.00
678	A91	10c brown red	13.00 14.00
679	A92	20c dk blue	13.00 18.00
680	A92	30c dk green	22.50 25.00
681	A92	40c violet	32.50 35.00
682	A93	1p brown & bl	30.00 35.00
a.		1p red brown & blue	42.50 45.00
		Nos. 676-682 (7)	194.00 219.00
		Set, never hinged	475.00

Overprint horizontal on 1p.
Nos. 676 and 682 are not known to have been sold to the public through post offices. Forgeries of overprint exist.

Bartolomé de las Casas — A96

1933, Mar. 3 — Engr. — Rouletted 14½
683	A96	15c dark blue	.35 .35
		Never hinged	.70

For overprint see No. O215.

Emblem of Mexican Society of Geography and Statistics — A97

1933, Oct. — Rouletted 14½
684	A97	2c deep green	1.50 .60
685	A97	5c dark brown	1.75 .50
686	A97	10c dark blue	.35 .35
687	A97	1p dark violet	100.00 65.00
		Nos. 684-687 (4)	103.60 66.45
		Set, never hinged	250.00

XXI Intl. Congress of Statistics and the 1st centenary of the Mexican Society of Geography and Statistics.

Types of 1923 and PT1
1934 — Perf. 10½, 11 (4c)
687A	PT1	1c brown	1.00 .35
688	A79	2c scarlet	.35 .35
689	A82	4c green	.35 .35
690	A85	10c brown lake	.35 .35
691	A84	20c dark blue	.75 .35
692	A83	30c dk blue grn	1.00 1.25
		Nos. 687A-692 (6)	3.80 3.00
		Set, never hinged	9.00

See 2nd note after Postal Tax stamp No. RA3.

Indian Archer A99

Indian A100

Woman Decorating Pottery A101

Peon A102

Potter A103

Sculptor A104

Craftsman A105

Offering to the Gods A106

Worshiper — A107

1934, Sept. 1 — Wmk. 156 — Perf. 10½
698	A99	5c dk green	10.00 3.00
699	A100	10c brown lake	17.00 4.00
700	A101	20c ultra	30.00 20.00
701	A102	30c black	60.00 42.50
702	A103	40c black brn	37.50 25.00
703	A104	50c dull blue	175.00 160.00
704	A105	1p brn lake & blk	350.00 175.00
705	A106	5p brn blk & red brn	750.00 725.00
706	A107	10p brown & vio	2,000. 2,500.
a.		Unwatermarked	3,250.
		Never hinged	5,000.
		Nos. 698-706 (9)	3,430. 3,655.
		Set, never hinged	7,500.

National University.
The design of the 1p is wider than the rest of the set. Values are for examples with perfs just touching the design.
See Nos. C54-C61, RA13B.

Yalalteca Indian A108

Tehuana Indian A109

Arch of the Revolution A110

Tower of Los Remedios A111

Cross of Palenque A112

Independence Monument A113

359

MEXICO

Independence Monument, Puebla A114
Monument to the Heroic Cadets A115
Stone of Tizoc A116
Ruins of Mitla A117
Coat of Arms A118
Charro A119

Imprint: "Oficina Impresora de Hacienda-Mexico"

1934-40		Wmk. 156	Perf. 10½
		Size: 20x26mm	
707	A108	1c orange	.65 .35
a.		Unwmkd.	
708	A109	2c green	.65 .35
a.		Unwmkd.	3.75 3.75
709	A110	4c carmine	.90 .35
710	A111	5c olive brn	.65 .35
a.		Unwmkd.	400.00 350.00
711	A112	10c dk blue	.80 .35
712	A112	10c violet ('35)	1.25 .35
a.		Unwmkd.	200.00 40.00
713	A113	15c lt blue	4.00 .35
714	A114	20c gray green	1.90 .35
a.		20c olive green	2.00 .35
715	A114	20c ultra ('35)	1.40 .30
a.		Unwmkd.	150.00
716	A115	30c lake	.90 .35
a.		Unwmkd.	350.00
716B	A115	30c lt ultra ('40)	1.00 .35
717	A116	40c red brown	1.00 .35
718	A117	50c grnsh black	.90 .30
a.		Imperf., pair	110.00
b.		Unwmkd.	375.00
719	A118	1p dk brn & org	2.50 .35
a.		Imperf., pair	350.00
720	A119	5p org & vio	7.75 .75
		Nos. 707-720 (15)	26.25 5.55
		Set, never hinged	70.00

No. 718a was not regularly issued. The existence of No. 707a has been questioned.
See Nos. 729-733, 733B, 735, 784-788, 795A-800A, 837-838, 840-841, 844, 846-851. For overprints see Nos. 728, O224-O232.

Tractor A120

1935, Apr. 1		Wmk. 156	Perf. 10½
721	A120	10c violet	4.00 .50
		Never hinged	9.00

Industrial census of Apr. 10, 1935.

Arms of Chiapas A121

1935, Sept. 14			
722	A121	10c dark blue	.50 .25
		Never hinged	1.40
a.		Unwmkd.	125.00 100.00

The 111th anniversary of the joining of the state of Chiapas with the federal republic of Mexico. See No. 734.

Emiliano Zapata — A122

1935, Nov. 20			Wmk. 156
723	A122	10c violet	.75 .35
		Never hinged	2.00

25th anniversary of the Plan of Ayala.

US and Mexico Joined by Highways A123
Matalote Bridge A124
View of Nuevo Laredo Highway — A125

1936		Wmk. 248	Perf. 14
725	A123	5c blue grn & rose	.35 .35
726	A124	10c slate bl & blk	.50 .35
727	A125	20c brn & dk grn	1.50 1.00
		Nos. 725-727,C77-C79 (6)	3.60 2.70
		Set, never hinged	8.50

Opening of the Mexico City - Nuevo Laredo Highway.

Monument Type of 1923

1935		Wmk. 248 Engr.	Perf. 10½
727A	A85	10c brown lake	2,500. 650.00

No. 712 Overprinted in Green

1936, Dec. 15			Wmk. 156
728	A112	10c violet	.60 .50
		Never hinged	1.50

1st National Congress of Industrial Hygiene and Medicine.

Type of 1934
Redrawn size: 17½x21mm
Imprint: "Talleres de Imp. de Est. y Valores-Mexico"

1937		Photo. Wmk. 156	Perf. 14
729	A108	1c orange	.60 .35
a.		Imperf., pair	12.50 12.50
		Never hinged	25.00
730	A109	2c dull green	.60 .35
a.		Imperf., pair	12.50 12.50
		Never hinged	30.00
731	A110	4c carmine	.90 .35
a.		Imperf., pair	12.50 12.50
		Never hinged	30.00
732	A111	5c olive brn	.80 .35
a.		Unwmkd.	300.00
733	A112	10c violet	.70 .35
a.		Imperf., pair	10.00 12.50
		Never hinged	12.00
		Nos. 729-733 (5)	3.60 1.75
		Set, never hinged	9.00

The imperfs were not regularly issued.

Types of 1934-35

1937		Wmk. 260	Size: 17½x21mm
733B	A111	5c olive brown	4,000. 250.00
		Never hinged	6,000.

1937		Engr.	Perf. 10½
734	A121	10c dark blue	35.00 35.00
		Never hinged	75.00

1937			Size: 20x26mm
735	A112	10c violet	350.00 55.00

Types of 1923

1934-37		Wmk. 260	Perf. 10½
735A	A79	2c scarlet	6,000.
735B	A85	10c brown lake	—

Forged perforations exist.

Rouletted 14½

| 736 | A85 | 10c claret | 5,500. 175.00 |

Blacksmith A126
Revolutionary Soldier A127
Revolutionary Envoy — A128

1938, Mar. 26		Photo.	Wmk. 156 Perf. 14
737	A126	5c black & brn	.80 .25
738	A127	10c red brown	.35 .25
739	A128	20c maroon & org	6.00 1.00
		Nos. 737-739,C82-C84 (6)	13.15 5.00
		Set, never hinged	32.00

Plan of Guadalupe, 25th anniv.

Arch of the Revolution A129
Independence Monument A131

Design: 10c, National Theater.

1938, July 1			
740	A129	5c bister brn	4.25 .60
741	A129	5c red brown	25.00 2.25
742	A129	10c orange	15.00 11.00
743	A129	10c chocolate	1.00 .25
744	A131	20c brown lake	6.00 4.00
745	A131	20c black	18.00 15.00
		Nos. 740-745 (6)	69.25 33.10
		Nos. 740-745,C85-C90 (12)	129.60 63.35
		Set, never hinged	275.00

16th Intl. Congress of Planning & Housing.

Arch of the Revolution A132

1939, May 1			
746	A132	10c Prus blue	.65 .25
		Nos. 746,C91-C93 (4)	4.75 3.00
		Set, never hinged	11.00

New York World's Fair.

Indian — A133

1939, May 17			
747	A133	10c red orange	.45 .25
		Nos. 747,C94-C96 (4)	5.55 2.80
		Set, never hinged	13.00

Tulsa World Philatelic Convention.

Juan Zumárraga A134
First Printing Shop in Mexico, 1539 A135

Design: 10c, Antonio de Mendoza.

1939, Sept. 1		Engr.	Perf. 10½
748	A134	2c brown blk	.75 .25
749	A135	5c green	.75 .25
750	A134	10c red brown	.25 .25
		Nos. 748-750,C97-C99 (6)	3.75 1.95
		Set, never hinged	11.50

400th anniversary of printing in Mexico.

View of Taxco A137
Allegory of Agriculture A138

10c, Two hands holding symbols of commerce.

1939, Oct. 1		Photo.	Perf. 12x13
751	A137	2c dark carmine	1.25 .25
752	A138	5c sl grn & gray grn	.75 .25
753	A138	10c org brn & buff	.25 .25
		Nos. 751-753,C100-C102 (6)	6.75 2.00
		Set, never hinged	14.00

Census Taking.

"Penny Black" of 1840 — A140

1940, May			Perf. 14
754	A140	5c black & lemon	.90 .50
755	A140	10c dark violet	.25 .25
756	A140	20c lt blue & car	.25 .25
757	A140	1p gray & red org	7.00 4.00
758	A140	5p black & Prus bl	50.00 50.00
		Nos. 754-758,C103-C107 (10)	141.00 116.05
		Set, never hinged	340.00

Postage stamp centenary.

Roadside Monument — A141

1940			Wmk. 156
759	A141	6c deep green	.50 .35
		Never hinged	1.25

Opening of the highway between Mexico, D. F., and Guadalajara. See Nos. 789, 842.

Vasco de Quiroga A142
Melchor Ocampo A143

MEXICO

College Seal — A144

1940, July 15 Engr. Perf. 10½
760	A142	2c violet	1.50	.50
761	A143	5c copper red	.80	.25
762	A144	10c olive bister	.80	.30
	a.	Imperf., pair	150.00	
		Nos. 760-762,C108-C110 (6)	5.30	2.60
		Set, never hinged	11.00	

Founding of the National College of San Nicolas de Hidalgo, 400th anniv.

Coat of Arms of Campeche — A145

1940, Aug. 7 Photo. Perf. 12x13
763	A145	10c bis brn & dk car	5.00	1.25
		Nos. 763,C111-C113 (4)	12.60	6.70
		Set, never hinged	30.00	

400th anniversary of the founding of Campeche.

Man at Holm — A146

1940, Dec. 1
764	A146	2c red org & blk	1.60	1.50
765	A146	5c peacock bl & red brn	8.00	1.00
766	A146	10c gray grn & choc	4.00	.85
		Nos. 764-766,C114-C116 (6)	21.00	7.85
		Set, never hinged	45.00	

Inauguration of Pres. Manuel Avila Camacho.

Alternated Perforations

Nos. 763-766, 774-779, 792-795, 801-804, 806-811, 813-818, C100-C102, C111-C116, C123-C128, C143-C162, C430-C431 have alternating small and large perforations.

Javelin Thrower — A147

1941, Nov. 4 Perf. 14
767	A147	10c dull yellow grn	5.00	.50

National Athletic Games of the Revolution, Nov. 4-20, 1941.

Serpent Columns, Chichén Itzá A148

Mayan Sculpture A149

Coat of Arms of Merída — A150

1942, June 30
768	A148	2c dk olive bis	1.10	.75
769	A149	5c deep orange	1.75	.60
770	A150	10c dark violet	1.20	.25
		Nos. 768-770,C117-C119 (6)	11.40	6.35
		Set, never hinged	12.25	

400th anniversary of the founding of Merida.

Independence Monument to Hidalgo A151

Government Palace A152

View of Guadalajara — A153

1942, Feb. 11 Engr. Perf. 10x10½
771	A151	2c bl vio & vio brn	.35	.30
772	A152	5c black & cop red	.95	.50
773	A153	10c red org & ultra	.95	.40
		Nos. 771-773,C120-C122 (6)	7.85	4.20
		Set, never hinged	11.25	

Founding of Guadalajara, 400th anniv.
No. 773 exists imperf on unwatermarked paper as a color proof.

Black Cloud in Orion — A154

Designs: 5c, Total solar eclipse. 10c, Spiral galaxy in the "Hunting Dogs."

1942, Feb. 17 Photo. Perf. 12x13
774	A154	2c lt vio & indigo	7.75	3.00
775	A154	5c blue & indigo	11.50	1.00
776	A154	10c red org & indigo	11.50	.75
		Nos. 774-776,C123-C125 (6)	95.75	16.25
		Set, never hinged	150.00	

Astrophysics Congress and the inauguration of an observatory at Tonanzintla, Feb. 17, 1942.

"Mother Earth" — A157

Sowing Wheat — A158

Western Hemisphere Carrying a Torch A159

1942, July 1
777	A157	2c chestnut	1.60	.40
778	A158	5c turq blue	2.90	1.10
779	A159	10c red orange	1.20	.55
		Nos. 777-779,C126-C128 (6)	12.90	5.50
		Set, never hinged	19.50	

2nd Inter-American Agricultural Conference.

Fuente Academy — A160

1942, Nov. 16 Perf. 14
780	A160	10c grnsh black	2.50	.75

75th anniversary of Fuente Academy.

Las Monjas Church A161

Generalissimo Ignacio José de Allende A163

Design: 5c, San Miguel Church.

1943, May 11
781	A161	2c intense blue	.80	.35
782	A109	5c deep brown	.90	.30
783	A163	10c dull black	2.90	1.00
		Nos. 781-783,C129-C131 (6)	10.60	5.35
		Set, never hinged	15.75	

400th anniv. of the founding of San Miguel de Allende.

Types of 1937

1944 Photo. Wmk. 272
784	A108	1c orange	2.00	.35
785	A109	2c dull green	2.00	.35
786	A110	4c carmine	4.00	.35
787	A111	5c olivo brown	4.00	.35
788	A112	10c violet	2.00	.35

Type of 1940
789	A141	6c green	2.00	.35
		Nos. 784-789 (6)	16.00	2.10
		Set, never hinged	24.00	

"Liberty" — A164

1944 Photo.
790	A164	12c violet brown	.35	.35

See No. 845.

Juan M. de Castorena — A165

1944, Oct. 12 Engr. Perf. 10
791	A165	12c dark brown	.60	.35

Third Book Fair. See No. C142.

> **Catalogue values for unused stamps in this section, from this point to the end of the section, are for Never Hinged items.**

Hands Holding Globe Showing Western Hemisphere A166

1945, Feb. 27 Photo. Perf. 12x13
792	A166	12c dark carmine	.60	.25
793	A166	1p slate green	1.00	.25
794	A166	5p olive brown	6.00	4.50
795	A166	10p black	18.00	8.00
		Nos. 792-795,C143-C147 (9)	57.35	33.80

Inter-American Conf. held at Chapultepec, Feb. 1945.

Types of 1934-40
Wmk. 272

1945-46 Engr. Perf. 10½
795A	A113	15c lt grnsh bl ('46)	325.00	60.00
796	A114	20c gray grn	2.50	.25
797	A115	30c lt ultra	3.25	.25
798	A116	40c brown	2.50	.25
799	A117	50c grnsh blk	1.60	.25
800	A118	1p dk brn & org	7.00	.25
	b.	Imperf., pair		
800A	A119	5p grn & vio ('46)	17.00	6.00
		Nos. 795A-800A (7)	358.85	67.25

Theater of Peace, San Luis Potosi — A167

1945, July 27 Photo. Perf. 12x13
801	A167	12c blk & vio brn	.45	.25
802	A167	1p blk & bl gray	.60	.40
803	A167	5p blk & brn lake	5.75	5.00
804	A167	10p blk & grnsh bl	17.50	12.00
		Nos. 801-804,C148-C152 (9)	53.65	35.50

Reconstruction of the Peace Theater (Teatro de la Paz), San Luis Potosi.

Fountain of Diana, the Huntress — A168

1945 Perf. 14
805	A168	3c violet blue	.80	.35

See No. 839.

Removing Blindfold — A169

1945, Nov. 2 Perf. 12x13
806	A169	2c bluish grn	.40	.25
807	A169	6c orange	.40	.25
808	A169	12c ultra	.40	.25
809	A169	1p olive	.60	.25

MEXICO

810	A169	5p gray & pale rose	3.50	3.00
811	A169	10p bl & yel grn	28.50	22.00
		Nos. 806-811 (6)	33.80	26.00
		Nos. 806-811,C153-C157 (11)	70.55	58.05

Issued to publicize the national literacy campaign.

M. E. de Almanza — A170

1946   *Perf. 14*

812	A170	8c black	1.50	.35

Martines Enriquez de Almanza, founder of the Mexican posts. See No. 843.

Allegory of World Peace — A171

1946, Apr. 10   *Perf. 12x13*

813	A171	2c dk olive bis	.35	.25
814	A171	6c red brown	.30	.25
815	A171	12c Prus green	.25	.25
816	A171	1p lt green	.60	.40
817	A171	5p dull red vio	6.25	5.00
818	A171	10p lt ultra	32.00	20.00
		Nos. 813-818 (6)	39.75	26.15
		Nos. 813-818,C158-C162 (11)	68.35	40.95

United Nations.

Arms of Zacatecas A173
Monument to Gen. Gonzalez Ortega A174
Ramón Lopez Velarde A175
Francisco Garcia Salinas A176

Wmk. 279

1946, Sept. 1   *Photo.*   *Perf. 14*

820	A173	2c orange brn	.55	.25
821	A173	12c Prus blue	.25	.25

Engr.
Perf. 10x10½

822	A174	1p lilac rose	.70	.25
823	A175	5p red	6.25	3.00
824	A176	10p dk blue & blk	40.00	10.00
		Nos. 820-824 (5)	47.75	13.75
		Nos. 820-824,C163-C166 (9)	80.25	32.45

400th anniversary of the founding of the city of Zacatecas.

A177

1947   *Photo.*   *Perf. 14*

825	A177	15c Postman	.60	.35
a.		Imperf., pair	110.00	

A178

10c, F. D. Roosevelt and Stamp of 1st Mexican Issue. 15c, Arms of Mexico and Stamp of 1st US Issue.

1947, May 16

826	A178	10c yellow brown	2.00	1.00
827	A178	15c green	.30	.25
		Nos. 826-827,C167-C169 (5)	6.25	2.40

Cent. Intl. Phil. Exhib., NYC, 5/17-25/47.

Justo Sierra — A180
Communications Building — A181

Perf. 10x10½, 10½x10

1947   *Engr.*   *Wmk. 279*

828	A180	10p brown & dl grn	175.00	40.00
829	A181	20p dk green & lil	1.60	2.00

Cadet Juan Escutia A182
Gen. Manuel Rincón A186
Flag of San Blas Battalion — A188

Designs: 2c, Cadet Francisco Márquez. 5c, Cadet Fernando Montes de Oca. 10c, Cadet Juan Escutia. 15c, Cadet Agustin Melgar. 1p, Gen. Lucas Balderas.

1947, Sept. 8   *Photo.*   *Perf. 14*

830	A182	2c brown black	.65	.25
831	A182	5c red orange	.40	.25
832	A182	10c dk brown	.40	.25
833	A182	15c dk Prus green	.40	.25
834	A186	30c dull olive grn	.50	.25

Engr.
Perf. 10x10½

835	A186	1p aqua	.65	.45
836	A188	5p dk blue & claret	2.60	1.90
		Nos. 830-836 (7)	5.60	3.60
		Nos. 830-836,C180-C184 (12)	10.25	6.60

Centenary of the battles of Chapultepec, Churubusco and Molino del Rey.

Types of 1934-46

1947-50   **Wmk. 279**   *Photo.*   *Perf. 14*

837	A108	1c orange	1.25	.30
a.		Imperf., pair	150.00	
838	A109	2c dk green	.85	.25
839	A168	3c violet blue	.85	.25
840	A110	4c dull red	2.10	.25
841	A111	5c olive brown	2.75	.25
842	A141	6c deep green	.60	.25
a.		Imperf., pair	150.00	
843	A170	8c black	.60	.25
844	A112	10c violet	2.00	.25
845	A164	12c violet brn	12.00	.75

Types A108 to A112 are in the redrawn size of 1937.

Size: 19x25mm
Engr.   *Perf. 10½*

846	A114	20c olive green	1.25	.25
a.		20c green	3.00	.30
847	A115	30c lt ultra	12.25	.40
848	A116	40c red brown	1.40	.25
849	A117	50c green	2.10	.25
a.		Imperf., pair	110.00	
850	A118	1p dk brn & org	45.00	9.00
851	A119	5p org & vio ('50)	40.00	11.00
		Nos. 837-851 (15)	124.90	23.95

A189

Designs: 3c, Modernistic church, Nuevo Leon. 5c, Modern building, Mexico City. 10c, Convent, Morelos. 15c, Benito Juarez. 20c, Puebla Cathedral. 30c, Indian dancer, Michoacan. 40c, Stone head, Tabasco. 50c, Carved head, Veracruz. 1p, Convent and carved head, Hidalgo. 5p, Galleon, arms of Campeche. 10p, Francisco I. Madero. 20p, Modern building, Mexico City.

1950-52   **Wmk. 279**   *Photo.*   *Perf. 14*

856	A189	3c blue vio ('51)	.50	.25
857	A189	5c dk red brn	.75	.25
858	A189	10c dk green	3.75	.25
859	A189	15c dk green ('51)	1.90	.25
860	A189	20c blue violet	15.00	.25
861	A189	30c red	.50	.25
862	A189	40c red orange ('51)	1.00	.25
863	A189	50c blue	1.25	.25

Engr.

864	A189	1p dull brown	5.00	.25
865	A189	5p ultra & bl grn	7.75	4.00
866	A189	10p blk & dp ultra ('52)	7.75	6.50
867	A189	20p pur & grn ('52)	11.50	9.00
		Nos. 856-867 (12)	56.65	21.75

See Nos. 875-885, 909, 928-931, 943-952, 1003-1004, 1054-1055, 1072, 1076, 1081, 1090-1091, 1094-1102.

Highway Bridge A190
Symbolical of Construction in 1950 A191

Perf. 10½x10, 10x10½

1950, May 5   *Engr.*

868	A190	15c purple	.75	.35
869	A191	20c deep blue	.50	.35
		Nos. 868-869,C199-C200 (4)	4.90	1.40

Completion of the International Highway between Ciudad Juarez and the Guatemala border.

Railroad Laborer — A192
Map and Locomotive — A192a

Inscribed: "Ferrocarril del Sureste 1950"

1950, May 24   *Perf. 10x10½*

870	A192	15c chocolate	1.75	.35
871	A192a	20c dp carmine	.55	.35
		Nos. 870-871,C201-C202 (4)	3.50	1.40

Opening of the Southeastern Railroad between Veracruz, Coatzocoalcos and Yucatan, 1950.

Postal Service — A193

1950, June 25   *Perf. 10x10½*

872	A193	50c purple	.65	.35
		Nos. 872,C203-C204 (3)	2.00	1.05

75th anniv. (in 1949) of the UPU.

Miguel Hidalgo y Costilla — A194

Wmk. 300

1953, May 8   *Photo.*   *Perf. 14*

873	A194	20c grnsh bl & dk brn	2.10	.35
		Nos. 873,C206-C207 (3)	4.30	1.05

Bicentenary of birth of Miguel Hidalgo y Costilla. See Nos. C206-C207.

Type of 1950-52

Designs as before.
Two types of 5p:
Type I — Imprint ½mm high and blurred.
Type II — Imprint ¾mm high and clear.

1954-67   *Photo.*   *Perf. 14*

875	A189	5c red brown	.55	.25
876	A189	10c green, redrawn	2.75	.25
a.		10c dark green	2.75	.25
877	A189	15c dk green	.45	.25
878	A189	20c bluish blk, white paper, colorless gum ('67)	.65	.25
a.		20c dark blue	3.75	.25
879	A189	30c brown red	.80	.25
a.		30c redsh brn	.95	.25
880	A189	40c red orange	1.60	.25
881	A189	50c lt blue	1.10	.25

Engr.

882	A189	1p olive grn, perf. 11, vert. wmk. ('58)	13.00	.25
a.		1p olive grn, perf. 14	7.25	.25
b.		olive brown	13.00	.25
883	A189	5p ultra & bl grn, I	7.75	1.00
a.		Type II	525.00	7.00
884	A189	10p sl & dp ultra ('56)	9.00	5.00
a.		10p slate green & ultra	35.00	5.00
885	A189	20p purple & grn	11.50	9.00
a.		20p brn vio & yel grn	77.50	20.00
		Nos. 875-885 (11)	49.15	17.00

Nos. 875-881 come only with watermark vertical, and in various shades. Watermark inverted on Nos. 884, 885.
On No. 876, imprint extends full width of stamp.
Vert. pairs, imperf. horiz. of Nos. 878, 880 are noted after No. 1004.

Aztec Messenger of the Sun — A195

1954, Mar. 6

886	A195	20c rose & bl gray	1.40	.35
		Nos. 886,C222-C223 (3)	3.60	1.05

7th Central American and Caribbean Games.

Symbolizing Adoption of National Anthem — A196

1954, Sept. 16   *Photo.*

887	A196	5c rose lil & dk bl	1.10	.35
888	A196	20c yel brn & brn vio	1.25	.25
889	A196	1p gray grn & cerise	.95	.40
		Nos. 887-889,C224-C226 (6)	4.90	2.15

Centenary of the adoption of Mexico's National Anthem.

Torch-Bearer and Stadium — A197

MEXICO

1955, Mar. 12   Wmk. 300   Perf. 14
890 A197 20c dk grn & red brn   1.10 .75
  Nos. 890,C227-C228 (3)   3.10 1.45
Second Pan American Games, 1955.

Aztec Designs — A198

1956, Aug. 1
891 A198 5c "Motion"   .70 .35
892 A198 10c Bird   .70 .35
893 A198 30c Flowers   .55 .35
894 A198 50c Corn   .70 .35
895 A198 1p Deer   .80 .35
896 A198 5p Man   3.00 3.00
  a. Souv. sheet, #891-896, imperf.   75.00 75.00
  Nos. 891-896,C229-C234 (12)   10.80 8.25
Centenary of Mexico's 1st postage stamps. No. 896a sold for 15p.

Stamp of 1856 — A199

1956, Aug. 1
897 A199 30c brn & intense bl   1.00 .35
Cent. of 1st Mexican Stamp Intl. Philatelic Exhibition, Mexico City, Aug. 16, 1956.

Francisco Zarco — A200

Portraits: 25c, 45c, Guillermo Prieto. 60c, Ponciano Arriaga.

1956-63
897A A200 25c dk brown ('63)   .90 .50
898   A200 45c dk blue green   .45 .35
899   A200 60c red lilac   .45 .35
900   A200 70c violet blue   .50 .35
  Nos. 897A-900,C236-C237A (7)   5.60 3.00
Centenary of the constitution (in 1957). See Nos. C289, 1075, 1092-1093.

"Mexico" — A201

Design: 1p, National Assembly.

1957, Aug. 31   Photo.   Perf. 14
901 A201 30c maroon & gold   .90 .35
902 A201 1p pale brn & metallic grn   .50 .35
  Nos. 901-902,C239-C240 (4)   2.85 1.40
Constitution, centenary.

Mexican Eagle and Oil Derrick — A202

Design: 5p, Map of Mexico and refinery.

1958, Aug. 30   Wmk. 300   Perf. 14
903 A202 30c lt blue & blk   .55 .35
904 A202 5p hn brn & Prus grn   6.75 4.00
  Nos. 903-904,C243-C244 (4)   8.10 5.05
20th anniv. of the nationalization of Mexico's oil industry.

UNESCO Building and Eiffel Tower — A203

1959, Jan. 20
905 A203 30c dull lilac & blk   .75 .35
UNESCO Headquarters opening, Paris, Nov. 9.

UN Headquarters, New York — A204

1959, Sept. 7   Litho.   Perf. 14
906 A204 30c org yel & bl   .75 .35
Meeting of UNESCO.

Carranza — A205

1960, Jan. 15   Photo.   Wmk. 300
907 A205 30c pale grn & plum   .60 .35
Birth centenary of Pres. Venustiano Carranza. See No. C246.

Humboldt Statue — A206

1960, Mar. 16   Wmk. 300   Perf. 14
908 A206 40c bis brn & grn   .60 .35
Cent. of the death (in 1859) of Alexander von Humboldt, German naturalist and geographer.

Type of 1950-52 Inscribed: "HOMENAJE AL COLECCIONISTA DEL TIMBRE DE MEXICO-JUNIO 1960"

1960, June 8   Engr.   Wmk. 300
909 A189 10p lil, brn & grn   100.00 75.00
Visit of the Elmhurst (Ill.) Philatelic Society of Mexico Specialists to Mexico, 25th anniv. See No. C249.

Independence Bell & Monument
A207   A208

5p, Bell of Dolores and Miguel Hidalgo.

Wmk. 300
1960, Sept. 15   Photo.   Perf. 14
910 A207 30c grn & rose red   3.50 .25
911 A208 1p dl grn & dk brn   .75 .25
912 A208 5p maroon & dk bl   6.00 5.00
  Nos. 910-912,C250-C252 (6)   18.00 8.45
150th anniv. of Mexican independence. See US No. 1157.

Agricultural Reform A209

Symbols of Health Education A210

Designs: 20c, Sailor and Soldier, 1960, and Fighter of 1910. 30c, Electrification. 1p, Political development (schools). 5p, Currency stability (Bank and money).

1960-61   Photo.   Perf. 14
913 A209 10c sl grn, blk & red org   .75 .25
914 A210 15c grn & org brn   3.00 .50
915 A210 20c brt bl & lt brn ('61)   1.25 .25
916 A210 30c vio brn & sep   .50 .25
917 A210 1p redsh brn & slate   .75 .25
918 A210 5p maroon & gray   7.00 3.50
  Nos. 913-918,C253-C256 (10)   22.00 9.05
50th anniversary (in 1960) of the Mexican Revolution.
Issued: No. 913, 11/20/60; No. 914, 916-918, 12/23/60; No. 915, 3/14/61.

Tunnel — A211

1961, Dec. 7   Wmk. 300   Perf. 14
919 A211 40c blk & brt grn   .70 .35
  Nos. 919,C258-C259 (3)   1.90 1.05
Opening of the railroad from Chihuahua to the Pacific Ocean.

Microscope, Mosquito and Globe — A212

1962, Apr. 7
920 A212 40c dl bl & maroon   .65 .35
WHO drive to eradicate malaria.

President Joao Goulart of Brazil — A213

Wmk. 300
1962, Apr. 11   Photo.   Perf. 14
921 A213 40c brown olive   1.25 .35
Visit of Joao Goulart, president of Brazil, to Mexico.

Insurgent at Marker for Battle of Puebla — A214

1962, May 5
922 A214 40c sepia & dk grn   .50 .35
Centenary of the Battle of May 5 at Puebla and the defeat of French forces by Gen. Ignacio Zaragoza. See No. C260.

Draftsman and Surveyor — A215

1962, June 11
923 A215 40c slate grn & dk bl   1.25 .35
25th anniversary of the National Polytechnic Institute. See No. C261.

Plumbline — A216

1962, June 21
924 A216 20c dp blue & blk   1.85 .35
Issued to publicize the importance of mental health.

"Space Needle" and Gear Wheels — A217

1962, July 6
925 A217 40c dk grn & gray   .65 .35
"Century 21" International Exposition, Seattle, Wash., Apr. 21-Oct. 12.

Globe — A218

1962, Oct. 1   Perf. 14
926 A218 40c gray & brn   .50 .35
1962 meeting of the Inter-American Economic and Social Council. See No. C263.

Pres. Alessandri of Chile — A219

1962, Dec. 20   Wmk. 300   Perf. 14
927 A219 20c olive black   1.10 .35
Visit of President Jorge Alessandri Rodriguez of Chile to Mexico, Dec. 17-20.

Type of 1950-52
Designs as before.

Wmk. 300, Vertical
1962-74   Photo.   Perf. 14
928 A189 1p ol gray ('67)   1.25 .25
  a. 1p green   4.00 .25
929 A189 5p dl bl & dk grn   3.50 .75
  a. 5p bluish gray & dark green, white paper ('67)   3.50 .50
930 A189 10p gray & bl ('63)   8.50 5.00
  a. 10p green & deep blue ('74)   8.50 5.50
931 A189 20p lil & blk ('63)   9.25 7.50
  a. Redrawn, white paper   10.25 10.00
  Nos. 928-931 (4)   22.50 13.50
No. 928 is on thick, luminescent paper. No. 929 is 20½mm high; No. 929a, 20¾mm. Nos. 931a and 1102 (unwmkd.) have more shading in sky and spots on first floor windows.

MEXICO

Pres. Betancourt of Venezuela — A220

1963, Feb. 23   **Wmk. 300**
932 A220 20c slate   .95   .35
Visit of President Romulo Betancourt of Venezuela to Mexico.

Congress Emblem — A221

1963, Apr. 22   **Wmk. 300**   *Perf. 14*
933 A221 40c fawn & blk   .90   .35
19th International Chamber of Commerce Congress. See No. C271.

Wheat Emblem — A222

1963, June 23   **Wmk. 300**   *Perf. 14*
934 A222 40c crim & dk bl   .90   .35
FAO "Freedom from Hunger" campaign.

Mercado Mountains and Arms of Durango — A223

1963, July 13   *Photo.*
935 A223 20c dk bl & choc   .90   .35
400th anniv. of the founding of Durango.

Belisario Dominguez — A224

1963, July 13   *Photo.*
936 A224 20c dk grn & ol gray   .90   .35
Centenary of the birth of Belisario Dominguez, revolutionary leader.

Mexico. No. 897, depicting Mexico No. 1 — A225

1963, Oct. 9   **Wmk. 350**   *Perf. 14*
937 A225 1p int blue & brn   1.60   .75
77th Annual Convention of the American Philatelic Society, Mexico City, Oct. 7-13. See No. C274.

Tree of Life — A226

1963, Oct. 26   **Wmk. 350**   *Perf. 14*
938 A226 20c dl bl grn & car   .60   .35
Intl. Red Cross, cent. See No. C277.

José Morelos — A227

1963, Nov. 9
939 A227 40c grn & dk sl grn   .90   .35
150th anniv. of the 1st congress of Anahuac.

Pres. Victor Paz Estenssoro — A228

1963, Nov. 9   **Wmk. 350**   *Perf. 14*
940 A228 40c dk brn & dk red brn   .90   .35
Visit of President Victor Paz Estenssoro of Bolivia.

Arms of Sinaloa University — A229

1963   *Photo.*
941 A229 40c slate grn & ol bister   .90   .35
90th anniversary of the founding of the University of Sinaloa.

Diesel Train, Rail Cross Section and Globe — A230

1963, Nov. 29   *Photo.*
942 A230 20c black & dk brn   1.10   .50
11th Pan-American Railroad Congress. See No. C279.

Type of 1950-52
Designs as before.

1963-66   **Wmk. 350**   *Photo.*   *Perf. 14*
943 A189 5c red brn ('65)   .60   .25
944 A189 10c dk green ('64)   .65   .25
945 A189 15c dk green ('66)   .60   .25
946 A189 20c dark blue   .60   .25
948 A189 40c red orange   .70   .25
949 A189 50c blue ('64)   2.00   .25
950 A189 1p olive grn ('64)   4.00   .25
951 A189 5p dl bl & dk grn ('66)   100.00   30.00
952 A189 10p gray & Prus bl ('65)   35.00   25.00
Nos. 943-952 (9)   144.15   56.75
The 20c is redrawn; clouds almost eliminated and other slight variations.

"F.S.T.S.E." Emblem — A231

1964, Feb. 15
954 A231 20c red org & dk brn   .70   .35
25th anniv. (in 1963) of the Civil Service Statute affecting federal employees.

Academy of Medicine Emblem — A232

1964, May 18   **Wmk. 350**   *Perf. 14*
955 A232 20c gold & blk   .70   .35
National Academy of Medicine, cent.

José Rizal — A233

40c, Miguel Lopez de Legaspi, Spanish navigator.

1964, Nov. 10   *Photo.*   *Perf. 14*
956 A233 20c dk bl & dp grn   .65   .35
957 A233 40c dk bl & brt vio   .75   .35
Nos. 956-957,C300-C301 (4)   7.25   2.05
Issued to honor 400 years of Mexican-Philippine friendship.

View of Zacatecas — A234

1964, Nov. 10   **Wmk. 350**
958 A234 40c slate grn & red   .85   .35
50th anniv. of the capture of Zacatecas.

Col. Gregorio Mendez — A235

1964, Nov. 10
959 A235 40c grysh blk & dk brn   .80   .35
Cent. of the Battle of Jahuactal, Tabasco.

Morelos Theater, Aguascalientes — A236

1965, Jan. 9   *Photo.*   *Perf. 14*
960 A236 20c dl cl & dk gray   .60   .35
50th anniversary of the Aguascalientes Convention, Oct. 1-Nov. 9, 1914.

Andrés Manuel del Río — A237

1965, Feb. 18   **Wmk. 350**   *Perf. 14*
961 A237 30c gray   .65   .35
Bicentenary of the birth of Andrés Manuel del Río, founder of the National School of Mining and discoverer of vanadium.

José Morelos and Constitution — A238

1965, Apr. 24   *Photo.*   *Perf. 14*
962 A238 40c brt grn & dk red brn   .70   .35
Sesquicentennial (in 1964) of the 1st Mexican constitution.

Trees — A239

1965, July 14   **Wmk. 350**   *Perf. 14*
963 A239 20c blue & green   .60   .35
Issued to commemorate Tree Day, July 8.

ICY Emblem — A240

1965, Sept. 13   *Photo.*
964 A240 40c olive gray & slate grn   .60   .35
International Cooperation Year, 1965.

Athlete with Sling, Clay Figure — A241

Design: 40c, Batter. Clay figures on 20c and 40c found in Colima, period 300-650 A.D.

1965, Dec. 17   **Wmk. 350**   *Perf. 14*
965 A241 20c olive & vio bl   3.75   .35
966 A241 40c pink & black   1.20   .35
Nos. 965-966,C309-C311 (5)   7.80   1.75
19th Olympic Games, Mexico, 1968.

José Morelos by Diego Rivera — A242

1965, Dec. 22
967 A242 20c lt vio bl & blk   .65   .35
José Maria Morelos y Pavon (1765-1815), priest and patriot in 1810 revolution against Spain.

MEXICO

Emiliano Zapata — A243

20c, Corn, cotton, bamboo, wheat and cow.

1966, Jan. 10   *Photo.*
968 A243 20c carmine rose .55 .35
969 A243 40c black .85 .35

50th anniv. of the Agrarian Reform Law.

Mexican Postal Service Emblem — A244

1966, June 24   *Wmk. 300*   *Perf. 14*
970 A244 40c brt green & blk .70 .35
   Nos. 970,C314,C315 (3) 1.00 1.05

Congress of the Postal Union of the Americas and Spain, UPAE, Mexico City, June 24-July 23.

Bartolomé de Las Casas — A245

1966, Aug. 1   *Photo.*   *Wmk. 300*
971 A245 20c black & buff .65 .35

400th anniv. of the death of Bartolomé de Las Casas (1474-1566), "Apostle of the Indies."

Mechanical Drawings and Cogwheels A246

1966, Aug. 15   *Photo.*   *Perf. 14*
972 A246 20c gray & grn .65 .40

50th anniversary of the founding of the School of Mechanical and Electrical Engineering (ESIME).

FAO Emblem — A247

1966, Sept. 30   *Wmk. 300*   *Perf. 14*
973 A247 40c green .60 .35

FAO International Rice Year.

Wrestling, by Diego Rivera — A248

20c, Running and Jumping.

1966, Oct. 15   *Size: 35x21mm*
974 A248 20c multicolored 1.50 .35
975 A248 40c shown 1.20 .35
   a. Souvenir sheet 4.50 4.50
   Nos. 974-975,C318-C320 (5) 6.85 1.85

Issued to publicize the 19th Olympic Games, Mexico City, D.F., 1968. No. 975a contains 2 imperf. stamps similar to Nos. 974-975 with simulated perforations. Sold for 90c.

First Page of Constitution — A249

Wmk. 300
1967, Feb. 5   *Photo.*   *Perf. 14*
976 A249 40c black .80 .35

Constitution, 50th anniv. See No. C322.

Oil Refinery and Pyramid of the Sun — A250

1967, Apr. 2   *Wmk. 300*   *Perf. 14*
977 A250 40c lt bl & blk .60 .35

7th Intl. Oil Congress, Mexico City, Sept. 1967.

Nayarit Indian — A251

Wmk. 300
1967, May 1   *Photo.*   *Perf. 14*
978 A251 20c pale grn & blk .60 .35

50th anniversary of Nayarit Statehood.

Degollado Theater, Guadalajara A252

Wmk. 300
1967, June 12   *Photo.*   *Perf. 14*
979 A252 40c pink & black .65 .35

Centenary of the founding of the Degollado Theater, Guadalajara.

Mexican Eagle over Imperial Crown — A253

Perf. 10x10½
1967, June 19   *Litho.*   *Wmk. 350*
980 A253 20c black & ocher .60 .35

Centenary of the victory of the Mexican republican forces and of the execution of Emperor Maximilian I.

Canoeing — A254

Designs: 40c, Basketball. 50c, Hockey. 80c, Bicycling. 2p, Fencing.

Wmk. 300
1967, Oct. 12   *Photo.*   *Perf. 14*
981 A254 20c blue & blk .65 .35
982 A254 40c brick red & blk .65 .35
983 A254 50c brt yel grn & blk .65 .35
   a. Souvenir sheet of 3, #981-983, imperf. 5.00 3.50

984 A254 80c brt pur & blk 1.60 .35
985 A254 2p orange & blk 2.75 .35
   a. Souvenir sheet of 2, #984-985, imperf. 7.00 4.00
   Nos. 981-985,C328-C331 (9) 10.90 3.60
   Nos. 981-985 (5) 6.30 1.75

Issued to publicize the 19th Olympic Games, Mexico City, Oct. 12-27, 1968. No. 983a sold for 1.50p; No. 985a sold for 3.50p. Both sheets are watermark 350.
See Nos. 990-995, C335-C338.

Artemio de Valle-Arizpe — A255

1967, Nov. 1   *Photo.*
986 A255 20c brown & slate .60 .35

Centenary of the Ateneo Fuente, a college at Saltillo, Coahuila.

Pedro Moreno — A256

1967, Nov. 18   *Wmk. 300*   *Perf. 14*
987 A256 40c blk & lt bl .60 .35

Moreno (1775-1817), revolutionary leader.

Gabino Barreda A257

Staircase, Palace of Mining A258

1968, Jan. 27   *Photo.*   *Perf. 14*
988 A257 40c dk bl & rose claret .65 .35
989 A258 40c blk & bl gray .65 .35

Centenary of the founding of the National Preparatory and Engineering Schools.

Type of Olympic Issue, 1967

20c, Wrestling. 40c, Pentathlon. 50c, Water polo. 80c, Gymnastics. 1p, Boxing. 2p, Pistol shoot.

1968, Mar. 21   *Wmk. 300*   *Perf. 14*
990 A254 20c olivo & blk .90 .35
991 A254 40c red lil & blk .90 .35
992 A254 50c brt green & blk .90 .35
   a. Souvenir sheet of 3, #990-992, imperf. 7.00 4.00
993 A254 80c brt pink & blk 1.20 .35
994 A254 1p org brn & blk 4.50 3.50
995 A254 2p gray & blk 6.50 5.50
   a. Souvenir sheet of 3, #993-995, imperf. 7.50 4.00
   Nos. 990-995,C335-C338 (10) 18.05 10.55

19th Olympic Games, Mexico City, Oct. 12-27. No. 992a sold for 1.50p; No. 995a sold for 5p. Both sheets are watermark 350.

Map of Mexico, Peace Dove A259

Symbols of Cultural Events A260

40c, University City Olympic stadium. 50c, Telecommunications tower. 2p, Sports Palace. 10p, Pyramid of the Sun, Teotihuacan, & Olympic torch.

Wmk. 350
1968, Oct.   *Photo.*   *Perf. 14*
996 A259 20c blue, yel & grn .75 .25
997 A259 40c multicolored .75 .25
998 A259 50c multicolored .75 .25
   a. Souv. sheet of 3, #996-998, imperf. 25.00 10.00
999 A260 2p multicolored 4.50 .50
1000 A260 5p silver & blk 11.50 1.25
   a. Souv. sheet of 2, #999-1000, imperf. 30.00 20.00
1001 A259 10p multicolored 7.75 2.00
   Nos. 996-1001,C340-C344 (11) 35.65 8.60

19th Olympic Games, Mexico City, Oct. 12-27 (Nos. 996-1000). Arrival of the Olympic torch in Veracruz (No. 1001).
#998a sold for 1.50p. No. 1000a sold for 9p.
Issued: Nos. 996-1000, 10/12; No. 1001, 10/6.

Arms of Veracruz — A261

1969, May 20   *Wmk. 350*   *Perf. 14*
1002 A261 40c multicolored .60 .35

450th anniv. of the founding of Veracruz.

Type of 1950-52 Coil Stamps
Perf. 11 Vert.
1969   *Wmk. 300*   *Photo.*
1003 A189 20c dk blue 4.25 2.00
1004 A189 40c red orange 5.25 3.00

Vert. pairs, imperf. horiz. may be from uncut rolls of coils.

Subway Train — A262

1969, Sept. 4   *Wmk. 350*   *Perf. 14*
1005 A262 40c multicolored .60 .35

Inauguration of Mexico City subway.

Honeycomb, Bee and ILO Emblem — A263

1969, Oct. 18   *Photo.*   *Perf. 14*
1006 A263 40c multicolored .60 .35

50th anniversary of the ILO.

Gen. Allende, by Diego Rivera — A264

1969, Nov. 15   *Wmk. 350*   *Perf. 14*
1007 A264 40c multicolored .60 .35

Gen. Ignacio Allende Unzaga (1769-1811), hero of Mexican independence.

Tourist Issue

Pyramid of Niches at El Tajín, Veracruz, and Dancers Swinging from Pole — A265

Anthropology Museum, Mexico City — A266

MEXICO

Deer Dance, Sonora — A267

Designs: No. 1010, View of Puerto Vallarta. No. 1011, Puebla Cathedral. No. 1012, Calle Belaunzaran. No. 1014, Ocotlan Cathedral, horiz.

1969-73   **Photo.**   **Wmk. 350**
1008	A265	40c shown	.65	.35
1009	A266	40c shown ('70)	.65	.35
1010	A266	40c Jalisco ('70)	.65	.35
1011	A266	40c Puebla ('70)	.65	.35
1012	A266	40c Guanajuato ('70)	.65	.35

Wmk. 300
1013	A267	40c shown ('73)	.50	.35
1014	A267	40c Tlaxcala ('73)	.50	.35
Nos. 1008-1014,C354-C358 (12)			9.15	4.20
Nos. 1008-1014 (7)			4.25	2.45

No. 1010 is inscribed "1970" below the design. Copies inscribed "1969" are from an earlier, unissued printing. Value $500.
Issued: No. 1008, 12/13/69; Nos. 1009-1012, 1/17/70; Nos. 1013-1014, 3/6/73.

Luminescence
Fluorescent stamps include Nos. 1013-1014, 1035, 1038, 1039, 1043-1045, 1047-1050, 1054-1059. (See Luminescence note over No. C527.)

"How Many, Who and What are We?" — A268

40c, "What, How & How Much do we produce?" (horse's head & symbols of agriculture).

1970, Jan. 26   **Wmk. 350**   **Perf. 14**
1024	A268	20c multicolored	.60	.35
1025	A268	40c blue & multi	.60	.35

Issued to publicize the 1970 census.

Human Eye and Spectrum A269

1970, Mar. 8   **Photo.**   **Wmk. 350**
1026	A269	40c multicolored	.60	.35

21st International Congress of Ophthalmology, Mexico City, Mar. 8-14.

Helmets of 1920 and 1970 — A270

1970, Apr. 11   **Wmk. 350**   **Perf. 14**
1027	A270	40c dk car rose, blk & lt brn	.60	.35

50th anniversary of the Military College.

José Maria Pino Suarez — A271

1970, Apr. 25   **Photo.**
1028	A271	40c black & multi	.60	.35

Centenary of the birth of José Maria Pino Suarez (1869-1913), lawyer, poet and Vice President of Mexico.

Coat of Arms of Celaya — A272

1970, Oct. 12   **Photo.**   **Perf. 14**
1029	A272	40c black & multi	.60	.35

City of Celaya, 400th anniversary.

Eclipse of Sun — A273

1970, Nov. 27   **Wmk. 350**   **Perf. 14**
1030	A273	40c black & gray	.60	.35

Total eclipse of the sun, Mar. 7, 1970.

Spheres with Dates 1970-1770 A274

1971, June 26   **Photo.**   **Perf. 14**
1031	A274	40c emerald & blk	.60	.35

Bicentenary of National Lottery.

Vasco de Quiroga, Mural by O'Gorman A275

1971, July 10   **Photo.**
1032	A275	40c multicolored	.60	.35

500th anniversary of the birth of Vasco de Quiroga (1470-1565), Archbishop of Michoacan, founder of hospitals and schools.

Amado Nervo (1870-1919), Poet — A276

1971, Aug. 7   **Wmk. 350**   **Perf. 14**
1033	A276	40c multicolored	.60	.35

Waves and Transformer A277

1971, Oct. 8
1034	A277	40c blk, lt bl & lt grn	.60	.35

50th anniversary of Mexican radio.

Pres. Lazaro Cardenas (1895-1970) — A278

1971, Oct. 19   **Wmk. 300**
1035	A278	40c blk & pale lil	.60	.35

Keyboard and Lara's Signature — A279

1971, Nov. 6   **Wmk. 350**
1036	A279	40c blk, buff & pale bl	.60	.35

Agustin Lara (1900-70), composer.

Arms of Monterrey — A280

1971, Dec. 18
1037	A280	40c black & multi	.60	.35

375th anniv. of the founding of Monterrey.

Cardiology Institute and WHO Emblems — A281

1972, Apr. 8   **Wmk. 300**
1038	A281	40c multicolored	.60	.35

"Your heart is your health," World Health Day 1972. See No. C395.

Gaceta de Mexico, Jan. 1, 1722 — A282

1972, June 24   **Wmk. 350**
1039	A282	40c multicolored	.60	.35

250th anniv. of 1st Mexican newspaper.

Lions Intl. Emblem — A283

1972, June 28
1040	A283	40c black & multi	.60	.35

55th Lions International Convention.

Sailing Ship Zaragoza — A284

1972, July 1
1041	A284	40c blue & multi	.60	.35

75th anniv. of the Naval School of Veracruz.

Olive Tree and Branch — A285

1972, July 18   **Wmk. 350**   **Perf. 14**
1042	A285	40c bl grn, ocher & blk	.60	.35
a.		40c blue green, yellow & black	3.00	3.00

Centenary of Chilpancingo as capital of Guerrero State.

Margarita Maza de Juárez — A286

Design: 40c, Benito Juárez, by Diego Rivera.

1972, Sept. 15   **Photo.**   **Wmk. 300**
1043	A286	20c pink & multi	.75	.35
1044	A286	40c dp yellow & multi	.75	.35
Nos. 1043-1044,C403-C405 (5)			3.00	1.75

Benito Juárez (1806-1872), revolutionary leader and president of Mexico.

Emperor Justinian I, Mosaic — A287

1972, Sept. 30   **Wmk. 300**
1045	A287	40c multicolored	.90	.35

Mexican Bar Association, 50th anniv.

Caravel — A288

1972, Oct. 12   **Wmk. 350**
1046	A288	80c buff, pur & ocher	.65	.35

Stamp Day of The Americas.

Olympic Emblems — A289

1972, Dec. 9   **Wmk. 300**
1047	A289	40c multicolored	1.25	.35

20th Olympic Games, Munich, Aug. 26-Sept. 11. See Nos. C410-C411.

Library, Book Year Emblem — A290

1972, Dec. 16
1048	A290	40c black & multi	.60	.35

International Book Year 1972.

Fish in Clean Water — A291

1972, Dec. 16
1049	A291	40c blk & lt bl	.60	.35

Anti-pollution campaign. See No. C412.

MEXICO

Metlac Railroad Bridge — A292

1973, Feb. 2   **Perf. 14**
1050 A292 40c multicolored   1.10   .35
Centenary of Mexican railroads.

Cadet — A293

1973, Oct. 11   **Photo.**   **Wmk. 300**
1051 A293 40c black & multi   .70   .35
Sesquicentennial of Military College.

Madero, by Diego Rivera — A294

1973, Nov. 9   **Wmk. 350**   **Perf. 14**
1052 A294 40c multicolored   .60   .35
Pres. Francisco I. Madero (1873-1913).

Antonio Narro — A295

1973, Nov. 9   **Photo.**
1053 A295 40c steel gray   .60   .35
50th anniversary of the Antonio Narro Agriculture School in Saltillo.

Type of 1950-52
Designs as before.

1973   **Unwmk.**   **Perf. 14**
1054 A189 20c blue violet   5.25   2.00
1055 A180 40c red orange   5.25   2.00
Fluorescent printing on back consisting of network pattern and diagonal inscription. Flourescent printing on front of No. 1055, value, $20.

Unsaturated Hydrocarbon Molecule — A296

Wmk. 300
1973, Dec. 7   **Photo.**   **Perf. 14**
1056 A296 40c blk, dk car & yel   .60   .35

Pointing Hand Emblem of Foreign Trade Institute — A297

1974, Jan. 11   **Photo.**   **Wmk. 300**
1057 A297 40c dk green & blk   .60   .35
Export promotion.

A298

1974, Jan. 18   **Litho.**   **Wmk. 300**
1058 A298 40c black   .60   .35
EXMEX 73 Philatelic Exhibition, Cuernavaca, Apr. 7-15. See No. C424.

Manuel M. Ponce at Keyboard — A299

1974, Jan. 18   **Photo.**   **Wmk. 300**
1059 A299 40c gold & multi   .55   .30
Manuel M. Ponce (1882-1948), composer.

Silver Statuette of Mexican Woman — A300

1974, Mar. 23   **Photo.**   **Perf. 14**
1060 A300 40c red & multi   .60   .35
First World Silver Fair.

Mariano Azuela — A301

1974, Apr. 26   **Wmk. 300**   **Perf. 14**
1061 A301 40c multicolored   .60   .35
Mariano Azuela (1873-1952), writer.

Dancing Dogs, Pre-Columbian — A302

1974, Apr. 10
1062 A302 40c multicolored   .60   .35
6th Traveling Dog Exhibition, Mexico City, Nov. 23-Dec. 1.

Aqueduct, Tepotzotlan — A303

1974, July 1   **Photo.**   **Wmk. 300**
1063 A303 40c brt blue & blk   .70   .45
National Engineers' Day, July 1.

Dr. Rodolfo Robles — A304

1974, July 19   **Perf. 14**
1064 A304 40c bister & grn   .60   .35
25th anniv. of WHO (in 1973).

EXFILMEX 74 Emblem — A305

1974, July 26   **Perf. 13x12**
1065 A305 40c buff, grn & blk   .60   .35
EXFILMEX 74, 5th Inter-American Philatelic Exhibition honoring UPU cent, Mexico City, 10/26-11/3. See No. C429.

Demosthenes — A306

1974, Aug. 2   **Photo.**   **Perf. 14**
1066 A306 20c green & brn   .60   .35
2nd Spanish-American Cong. for Reading and Writing Studies, Mexico City, May 7-14.

Map of Chiapas and Head — A307

1974, Sept. 14   **Wmk. 300**   **Perf. 14**
1067 A307 20c black & grn   .60   .35
Sesquicentenary of Chiapas statehood.

Law of 1824 — A308

1974, Oct. 11   **Wmk. 300**
1068 A308 40c gray & grn   .60   .35
Sesquicentennial of the establishment of the Federal Republic of Mexico.

Sebastian Lerdo de Tejada — A309

1974, Oct. 11   **Photo.**
1069 A309 40c black & lt bl   .60   .35
Centenary of restoration of the Senate.

UPU Monument, Bern — A310

1974, Dec. 13   **Wmk. 300**   **Perf. 14**
1070 A310 40c ultra & org brn   .60   .35
Nos. 1070, C437-C438 (3)   1.80 1.05
Cent. of UPU.

Types of 1950-56
Designs (as 1951-56 issues): 80c, Michoacan dance of the Moors. 2.30p, Guillermo Prieto. 3p, Modernistic church, Nuevo Leon. 50p, Benito Juarez.

1975   **Photo.**   **Wmk. 300**   **Perf. 14**
1072 A189 80c green   .60   .35
1075 A200 2.30p dp violet bl   .95   .35
1076 A189 3p brick red   .95   .35
1081 A189 50p orange & grn   10.50   7.50
Nos. 1072-1081 (4)   13.00   8.55
See No. 1097 for unwmkd. 3p with no shading under "Leon."

Gov. José Maria Mora — A312

1975, Feb. 21   **Photo.**   **Wmk. 300**
1084 A312 20c yellow & multi   .60   .35
Sesquicentennial (in 1974) of establishment of the State of Mexico.

Merchants with Pre-Columbian Goods — A313

1975, Apr. 18   **Photo.**   **Unwmk.**
1085 A313 80c multicolored   .60   .35
Centenary (in 1974) of the National Chamber of Commerce in Mexico City. Design from Florentine Codex.

Juan Aldama, by Diego Rivera — A314

1975, June 6   **Perf. 14**
1086 A314 80c multicolored   .60   .35
Juan Aldama (1774-1811), officer and patriot, birth bicentenary.

Indians and Eagle on Cactus Destroying Serpent, from Duran Codex — A315

1975, Aug. 1   **Photo.**   **Unwmk.**
1087 A315 80c multicolored   .60   .35
650th anniv. of Tenochtitlan (Mexico City). See No. C465.

MEXICO

Julián Carrillo — A316

1975, Sept. 12   Photo.   Unwmk.
1088 A316 80c brt grn & red brn .60 .35

Julián Carrillo (1875-1965), violinist and composer, birth centenary.

Academy Emblem — A317

1975, Sept. 13   Perf. 14
1089 A317 80c brown & ocher .60 .35

Cent. of Mexican Academy of Languages.

Types of 1950-56

Designs (as 1950-56 issues): 80c, Indian dancer, Michoacan. 2p, Convent, Morelos.

1975-76   Photo.   Unwmk.
1090	A189	40c orange	.40	.35
1091	A189	50c blue	.45	.35
1092	A200	60c red lilac	.55	.35
1093	A200	70c violet blue	.55	.35
1094	A189	80c green	.55	.35
1095	A189	1p olive green	.55	.35
1096	A189	2p scarlet	1.10	.50
1097	A189	3p brick red	1.10	.50
1099	A189	5p gray bl & grn	2.40	1.00
1101	A189	10p grn & dp ultra ('76)	5.50	2.00
1102	A189	20p lilac & blk ('76)	11.00	4.00
	Nos. 1090-1102 (11)		24.15	10.10

University of Guadalajara A318

1975, Oct. 1   Photo.   Perf. 14
1107 A318 80c multicolored .60 .35

University of Guadalajara, 50th anniversary.

Road Workers — A319

1975, Oct. 17   Photo.   Unwmk.
1108 A319 80c gray grn, grn & blk .60 .35

50 years of road building for progress.

Pistons — A320

Designs: Export Emblem and 5c, 6p, Steel pipes. 20c, Chemistry flasks. 40c, Cup of coffee. 80c, Meat cuts marked on steer. 1p, Electrical conductor. 2p, Abalone. 3p, Men's shoes. 4p, Tiles. 5p, Minerals. 7p, 8p, 9p, Overalls. 10p, Tequila. 15p, Honey. 20p, Wrought iron. 25p, Copper vase. 35p, 40p, No. 1133, 80p, Books. No. 1132, Jewelry. 100p, Strawberry. 200p, Citrus fruit. 300p, Motor vehicles. 400p, Circuit board. 500p, Cotton.

Some stamps have a gray burelage;
Type I — Burelage lines run lower left to upper right with arch towards lower right.
Type II — Burelage lines run lower left to upper right with arch towards upper left.

1975-87   Photo.   Unwmk.   Perf. 14
1109	A320	5c slate bl ('77)	1.10	.25
1110	A320	20c blk ('76)	.30	.25
1111	A320	40c dk brn ('76)	1.00	.25
a.		40c claret brown ('81)	2.25	.25
1112	A320	50c slate, thin paper ('81)	.80	.25
a.		50c slate blue ('76)	1.10	.25
b.		50c black ('83)	.85	.25
c.		50c dull blue ('75)	1.10	.25
1113	A320	80c brt car ('76)	6.00	.25
a.		Perf. 11	.65	.30
b.		Perf. 11 ½x11	1.00	.25
c.		As "a," thin paper ('81)	1.60	.75
d.		As "b," thin paper ('81)	1.00	.75
1114	A320	1p vio bl & org ('78)	1.00	.25
1115	A320	1p lt vio & org ('83)	1.60	.25
1116	A320	1p black & org ('84)	.30	.25
1117	A320	2p grn & brt bl ('81)	1.40	.25
a.		2p bl grn & dk bl ('76)	1.75	.25
1118	A320	3p red brown	3.00	.25
a.		3p brn, perf 11½x11 ('82)	3.25	.25
b.		Golden brn, thin paper ('81)	.85	.25
1119	A320	4p tan & dk brn ('80)	.30	.25
1120	A320	5p gray olive ('78)	2.50	.25
a.		Perf 11½x11 ('84)	.60	.25
1121	A320	6p brt org ('83)	.35	.25
a.		Perf 11½x11 ('83)	.55	.25
b.		Perf 11 ('84)	3.50	.25
1121C	A320	6p gray, perf. 11½x11 ('84)	.30	.25
1122	A320	7p Prus blue ('84)	.30	.25
a.		7p blue gray ('84)	5.25	.25
1123	A320	8p bis brn, perf 11½x11 ('84)	.35	.25
a.		Perf 11 ('84)	8.25	.25
1124	A320	9p dk bl ('84)	.30	.25
1125	A320	10p dk & lt grn ('78)	.40	.25
a.		Thin paper ('81)	1.10	.30
b.		Dk ol grn & yel grn ('86)	2.25	.25
c.		Dk ol grn & brt ol grn ('87)	.60	.35
1126	A320	15p yel org & red brn ('84)	.35	.25
1127	A320	20p black ('78)	1.40	.25
1128	A320	20p dk gray ('84)	.30	.25
1129	A320	25p org brn ('84)	.45	.25
1130	A320	35p brt cer & yel ('84)	.30	.25
1131	A320	40p org brn & lt yel ('84)	.35	.25
1132	A320	50p gray, sil, brt vio & pur ('80)	6.50	.75
1133	A320	50p brt bl & lt yel ('83)	1.60	.25
1133A	A320	80p pink & gold ('85)	1.75	.35
1134	A320	100p scar & brt grn, I ('83)	1.60	.80
1135	A320	200p emer & yel grn, I ('83)	5.00	.50
a.		Emer & lemon, I ('87)	6.25	1.25
b.		Emer & yel grn, II ('83)	5.25	2.00
1136	A320	300p brt bl & red, I ('83)	4.00	2.00
a.		Type II ('87)	125.00	20.00
1137	A320	400p lem & red brn, I ('84)	3.25	.75
1138	A320	500p lt ol grn & yel org, I ('84)	4.50	.75
	Nos. 1109-1138 (32)		52.65	12.15

No. 1125b is 2mm wider than No. 1125. Size of No. 1125b: 37x21mm.
Nos. 1117, 1119, 1126, 1135 exist with one or more colors missing. These were not regularly issued.
See Nos. 1166-1176, 1465-1470A, 1491-1505, 1583-1603, 1763-1776, C486-C508, C594-C603.

Aguascalientes Cathedral — A323

1975, Nov. 28
1140 A323 50c bl grn & blk 1.00 .35

400th anniversary of Aguascalientes.

Jaime Torres Bodet — A324

1975, Nov. 28
1141 A324 80c blue & brn .60 .35

Jaime Torres Bodet (1920-1974), writer, director general of UNESCO (1958-1962).

Allegory, by José Clemente Orozco A325

1975, Dec. 9   Perf. 14
1142 A325 80c multicolored .60 .35

Sesquicentennial of Supreme Court.

The Death of Cuauhtemoc, by Chavez Morado — A326

1975, Dec. 12   Photo.
1143 A326 80c multicolored .60 .35

450th anniv. of the death of Cuauhtemoc (1495?-1525), last Aztec emperor.

Netzahualcoyotl (Water God) — A327

1976, Jan. 9   Unwmk.   Perf. 14
1144 A327 80c blue & vio bl .60 .35

50th anniv. of Mexican irrigation projects.

Arch, Leon — A328

1976, Jan. 20
1145 A328 80c dk brn & ocher .60 .35

400th anniversary of León, Guanajuato.

Forest Fire — A329

1976, July 8   Photo.   Perf. 14
1146 A329 80c blk, grn & red .60 .35

Prevent fires!

Hat and Scout Emblem — A330

1976, Aug. 24   Photo.   Unwmk.
1147 A330 80c olive & red brn .60 .35

Mexican Boy Scout Assoc., 50th anniv.

Exhibition Emblem — A331

1976, Sept. 2
1148 A331 80c black, red & grn .60 .35

Mexico Today and Tomorrow Exhibition.

New Building, Military College — A332

1976, Sept. 13   Perf. 14
1149 A332 50c red brn & ocher .60 .35

Military College, new installations.

Dr. Ricardo Vertiz — A333

1976, Sept. 24   Photo.   Perf. 14
1150 A333 80c blk & redsh brn .60 .35

Our Lady of Light Ophthalmological Hospital, centenary.

National Basilica of Guadeloupe A334

1976, Oct. 12
1151 A334 50c black & ocher .60 .35

Inauguration of the new National Basilica of Our Lady of Guadeloupe.

"40" and Emblem — A335

1976, Oct. 28   Photo.   Perf. 14
1152 A335 80c blk, lt grn & car .60 .35

Natl. Polytechnic Institute, 40th anniv.

MEXICO

Blast Furnace — A336

1976, Nov. 4
1153 A336 50c multicolored   .60   .35
Inauguration of the Lazaro Cardenas Steel Mill, Las Truchas.

Saltillo Cathedral — A337

1977, July 25   Photo.   Perf. 14
1154 A337 80c yel & dk brn   .60   .35
400th anniversary of the founding of Saltillo.

Electrification — A338

1977, Aug. 14   Photo.   Perf. 14
1155 A338 80c multicolored   .60   .35
40 years of Mexican development program.

Flags of Spain and Mexico — A339

1977, Oct. 8   Photo.   Wmk. 300
1156 A339 50c multicolored   .60   .35
1157 A339 80c multicolored   .60   .35
Nos. 1156-1157,C537-C539 (5)   3.00 1.75
Resumption of diplomatic relations with Spain.

Aquiles Serdan (1877-1910), Martyr of the Revolution — A340

1977, Nov. 18   Photo.   Perf. 14
1158 A340 80c lt & dk grn & blk   .60   .35

Poinsettia — A341

1977, Dec. 2   Wmk. 300   Perf. 14
1159 A341 50c multicolored   .60   .35
Christmas 1977.

Old and New Telephones — A342

1978, Mar. 15   Photo.   Perf. 14
1160 A342 80c salmon & maroon   .60   .35
Centenary of first telephone in Mexico.

Oil Derrick — A343

1978, Mar. 18
1161 A343 80c dp org & mar   .60   .35
Nos. 1161,C556-C557 (3)   1.80 1.05
Nationalization of oil industry, 40th anniv.

Institute Emblem — A344

1978, July 21   Photo.   Perf. 14
1162 A344 80c blue & black   .60   .35
Nos. 1162,C574-C575 (3)   1.80 1.05
Pan-American Institute for Geography and History, 50th anniv.

Dahlias — A345

1978, Sept. 29   Photo.   Wmk. 300
1163 A345 50c shown   .60   .50
1164 A345 80c Frangipani   .90   .50
See No. 1196.

Decorations and Candles — A346

1978, Nov. 22   Photo.   Perf. 14
1165 A346 50c multicolored   .60   .35
Christmas 1978.

Export Type of 1975
Designs as before. 50p, Jewelry.

1979-81   Photo.   Wmk. 300   Perf. 14
1166 A320 20c black ('81)   .45   .35
1167 A320 50c slate blue   .60   .35
  a.   50c bluish black   .60   .35
1168 A320 80c brt car, perf 11   1.25   .35
  a.   Perf. 14   1.25   .35
1169 A320 1p ultra & org   .40   .35
1170 A320 2p brt grn & bl   .60   .35
1171 A320 3p dk brown   .70   .35
1172 A320 4p tan & dk brn ('80)   .85   .35
1173 A320 5p gray olive   1.20   .35
1174 A320 10p dk & lt green   3.25   .75
1175 A320 20p black   3.25   .75
1176 A320 50p gray, sil, brt vio & pur   7.75 2.50
Nos. 1166-1176 (11)   20.30 6.80

A347

1979, Apr. 26   Wmk. 300   Perf. 14
1177 A347 80c multicolored   .60   .35
Centenary of Hermosillo, Sonora.

Soccer Ball — A348

Designs: 80c, Aztec ball player. 1p, Wall painting showing athletes. 5p, Runners, horiz.

1979, June 15   Photo.   Wmk. 300
1178 A348 50c blue & blk   .60   .35
1179 A348 80c multicolored   .60   .35
1180 A348 1p multicolored   .60   .35
Nos. 1178-1180,C606-C607 (5)   3.00 1.75

Souvenir Sheet
Imperf
1181 A348 5p multicolored   3.75 3.75
Universiada '79, World Games, Mexico City, 9/79. No. 1181 has simulated perforations.

Josefa Ortiz de Dominguez, Wife of the Mayor of Queretaro (Miguel Dominguez), 150th Death Anniv. — A349

1979, July 6   Perf. 14
1182 A349 80c multicolored   .66   .35

Allegory of National Culture, by Alfaro Siqueiros A350

3p, Conquest of Energy, by Chavez Morado.

1979, July 10
1183 A350 80c multicolored   .60   .35
1184 A350 3p multicolored   .60   .35
Nos. 1183-1184,C609-C610 (4)   2.40 1.40
National University, 50th anniv. of autonomy.

Emiliano Zapata, by Diego Rivera — A351

1979, Aug. 8   Photo.   Perf. 14
1185 A351 80c multicolored   .60   .35
Emiliano Zapata (1879-1919), revolutionist.

Soccer — A352

Designs: 80c, Women's volleyball. 1p, Basketball. 5p, Fencing.

1979, Sept. 2
1186 A352 50c multicolored   .60   .35
1187 A352 80c multicolored   .60   .35
1188 A352 1p multicolored   .60   .35
Nos. 1186-1188,C612-C613 (5)   3.00 1.75

Souvenir Sheet
Imperf
1189 A352 5p multicolored   3.25 3.25
Universiada '79 World University Games, Mexico City. No. 1189 has simulated perforations.

Tepoztlan, Morelos — A353

Tourism: No. 1191, Mexcaltitan, Nayarit.

1979, Sept. 28   Photo.   Perf. 14
1190 A353 80c multicolored   .60   .35
1191 A353 80c multicolored   .60   .35
Nos. 1190-1191,C615-C616 (4)   2.40 1.40
See Nos. 1274-1277, 1318-1321, 1513-1516.

Postmaster Martin de Olivares — A354

1979, Oct. 26   Wmk. 300   Perf. 14
1192 A354 80c multicolored   .60   .35
Royal proclamation of mail service in the New World (New Spain), 400th anniversary. See Nos. C618-C620.

Shepherd and Sheep — A355

1979, Nov. 15
1193 A355 50c multicolored   .60   .35
Christmas 1979. See No. C623.

Serpent, Mayan Temple — A356

1980, Feb. 16   Photo.   Perf. 14x14½
1194 A356 80c multicolored   .60   .35
Nos. 1194,C625-C626 (3)   1.80 1.05
Pre-Hispanic monuments.

North American Turkey A357

Tajetes Erecta A358

Wmk. 300
1980, Mar. 8   Photo.   Perf. 14
1195 A357 80c multicolored   .60   .35
1196 A358 80c multicolored   .60   .35
Nos. 1195-1196,C632-C633 (4)   2.40 1.40
See Nos. 1163-1164, 1234-1237.

A359

Designs: 50c, China Poblana (woman's costume), Puebla. 80c, Jarocha, Veracruz.

MEXICO

Wmk. 300
1980, Apr. 26 Photo. Perf. 14
1197 A359 50c multicolored .60 .35
1198 A359 80c multicolored .60 .35
Nos. 1197-1198, C636 (3) 1.80 1.05
See Nos. 1231-1233.

10th National Census — A360

1980, June 4
1200 A360 3p silver & blk .60 .35

Cuauhtemoc (Last Aztec Emperor), 1520, Matritense Codex — A361

Pre-Hispanic Art (Leaders): 1.60p, Nezahualcoyotl (1402-1472), governor of Tetzcoco, poet, Azcatitlan Codex. 5.50p, Eight Deer Tiger's Claw (1011-1063), 11th king of Mixtec, Nuttall Codex.

1980, June 21
1201 A361 80c multicolored .60 .35
1202 A361 1.60p multicolored .60 .35
1203 A361 5.50p multicolored .60 .35
Nos. 1201-1203 (3) 1.80 1.05
See Nos. 1285-1287, 1510-1512.

Xipe (Aztec God of Medicine), Bourbon Codex — A362

1980, June 29
1204 A362 1.60p multicolored .60 .35
22nd Intl. Biennial Cong. of the Intl. College of Surgeons, Mexico City, 6/29-7/4.

Moscow '80 Bronze Medal, Emblem, Misha, Olympic Rings — A363

1980, July 19 Photo. Perf. 14
1205 A363 1.60p shown .60 .35
1206 A363 3p Silver medal .60 .35
1207 A363 5.50p Gold medal .60 .35
Nos. 1205-1207 (3) 1.80 1.05
22nd Summer Olympic Games, Moscow, July 19-Aug. 3.

Ceremonial Vessel, Tenochtitlan Temple — A364

Wmk. 300
1980, Aug. 23 Photo. Perf. 14
1208 A364 80c shown .60 .35
1209 A364 1.60p Caracol .60 .35
1210 A364 5.50p Chacmool .60 .35
Nos. 1208-1210 (3) 1.80 1.05
Pre-Columbian Art.

Sacromonte Sanctuary, Amecameca A365

Colonial Monuments: No. 1212, St. Catherine's Convent, Patzcuaro. No. 1213, Basilica, Cuilapan, vert. No. 1214, Calvary Hermitage, Cuernavaca.

1980, Sept. 26 Photo. Perf. 14
1211 A365 2.50p black .60 .35
1212 A365 2.50p black .60 .35
1213 A365 3p black .60 .35
1214 A365 3p black .60 .35
Nos. 1211-1214 (4) 2.40 1.40
See Nos. 1260-1263, 1303-1306, 1338-1341.

Quetzalcoatl (God) — A366

1980, Sept. 27
1215 A366 2.50p multicolored .60 .35
World Tourism Conf., Manila, Sept. 27.

Sinaloa Coat of Arms — A367

1980, Oct. 13
1216 A367 1.60p multicolored .60 .35
Sinaloa state sesquicentennial.

Straw Angel — A368

Christmas 1980: 1.60p, Poinsettias.

1980 Photo. Perf. 14
1217 A368 50c multicolored .60 .35
1218 A368 1.60p multicolored .60 .35
Issued: No. 1217, 11/15; No. 1218, 10/15.

Congress Emblem — A369

1980, Dec. 1
1219 A369 1.60p multicolored .60 .35
4th International Civil Justice Congress.

Glass Vase and Animals — A370

1p, Poncho. 3p, Wooden mask, 17th century.

1980, Dec. 13 Wmk. 300
1220 A370 50c shown .60 .35
1221 A370 1p multi .60 .35
1222 A370 3p multi .60 .35
Nos. 1220-1222 (3) 1.80 1.05
See Nos. 1267-1269.

Simon Bolivar, by Paulin Guerin — A371

1980, Dec. 17
1223 A371 4p multicolored .65 .35
Simon Bolivar death sesquicentennial.

Vicente Guerrero — A372

1981, Feb. 14
1224 A372 80c multicolored .60 .35
Vicente Guerrero (1783-1831), statesman.

Valentin Gomez Farias — A373

1981, Feb. 14
1225 A373 80c brt grn & gray .60 .35

First Latin-American Table Tennis Cup — A374

Wmk. 300
1981, Feb. 27 Photo. Perf. 14
1226 A374 4p multicolored .65 .35

Jesus Gonzalez Ortega, Politician, Birth Cent. — A375

Wmk. 300
1981, Feb. 28 Photo. Perf. 14
1227 A375 80c brn & yel org .60 .35

Gabino Barreda (1818-1881), Physician — A376

1981, Mar. 10
1228 A376 80c multicolored .60 .35

Benito Juarez, 175th Birth Anniv. — A377

1981, Mar. 21
1229 A377 1.60p multicolored .60 .35

450th Anniv. of Puebla City — A378

1981, Apr. 16 Unwmk.
1230 A378 80c multicolored .60 .35
a. Wmk. 300 3.25 .35

Costume Type of 1980
50c, Purepecha, Michoacan. 80c, Charra, Jalisco. 1.60p, Mestiza, Yucatan.

1981, Apr. 25 Unwmk.
1231 A359 50c multi .60 .35
1232 A359 80c multi .60 .35
1233 A359 1.60p multi .60 .35
Nos. 1231-1233 (3) 1.80 1.05

Flora and Fauna Types of 1980
No. 1234, Mimus polyglottos. No. 1235, Persea americana. No. 1236, Trogon mexicanus. No. 1237, Theobromo cacao.

Wmk. 300 (#1235), Unwmkd.
1981, May 30
1234 A357 80c multi .85 .35
1235 A358 80c multi .85 .35
1236 A357 1.60p multi .85 .35
1237 A358 1.60p multi .85 .35
Nos. 1234-1237 (4) 3.40 1.40

Workers' Strike, by David Alfaro Siqueiros A379

Wmk. 300
1981, June 10 Photo. Perf. 14
1238 A379 1.60p multicolored .60 .35
Labor strike martyrs of Cananea, 75th anniv.

Intl. Year of the Disabled — A380

1981, July 4 Unwmk. Perf. 14
1239 A380 4p multicolored .65 .35

450th Anniv. of Queretaro City — A381

1981, July 25 Unwmk.
1240 A381 80c multicolored .60 .35
a. Wmk. 300 3.25 .35

MEXICO

Alexander Fleming (1881-1955), Discoverer of Penicillin — A382

1981, Aug. 6   Unwmk.
1241   A382   5p blue & orange   .65   .35

No. 1 — A383

1981, Aug. 12
1242   A383   4p multicolored   .60   .35
   a.   Wmk. 300   3.25   .35
   125th anniv. of Mexican stamps.

St. Francis Xavier Clavijero, 250th Birth Anniv. — A384

1981, Sept. 9   Unwmk.   Perf. 14
1243   A384   80c multicolored   .60   .35

Union Congress Building Opening A385

1981, Sept. 1
1244   A385   1.60p red & brt grn   .60   .35

1300th Anniv. of Bulgarian State — A386

1.60p, Desislava, mural, 1259. 4p, Thracian gold cup. 7p, Horseman.

1981, Sept. 19   Photo.   Perf. 14
1245   A386   1.60p multi   .60   .35
1246   A386   4p multi   .60   .35
1247   A386   7p multi   .60   .35
   Nos. 1245-1247 (3)   1.80   1.05

Pre-Hispanic Art — A387

1981, Sept. 26
1248   A387   80c Squatting diety   .60   .35
1249   A387   1.60p Animal head   .60   .35
1250   A387   4p Fish   .60   .35
   Nos. 1248-1250 (3)   1.80   1.05

Pablo Picasso (1881-1973) A388

1981, Oct. 5
1251   A388   5p lt ol grn & grn   .65   .35

Christmas 1981 — A389

1981, Oct. 15
1252   A389   50c Shepherd   .60   .35
1253   A389   1.60p Girl   .60   .35

World Food Day — A390

1981, Oct. 16
1254   A390   4p multicolored   .60   .35

50th Death Anniv. of Thomas Edison — A391

1981, Oct. 18
1255   A391   4p multicolored   .60   .35

Intl. Meeting on Cooperation and Development A392

1981, Oct. 22
1256   A392   4p multicolored   .60   .35

Pan-American Railway Congress — A393

1981, Oct. 25   Unwmk.
1257   A393   1.60p multicolored   .60   .35

50th Anniv. of Mexican Sound Movies — A394

1981, Nov. 3   Photo.   Perf. 14
1258   A394   4p multicolored   .60   .35

Inauguration of Zip Codes — A395

1981, Nov. 12
1259   A395   80c multicolored   .60   .35

Colonial Monument Type of 1980

No. 1260, Mascarones House. No. 1261, La Merced Order Convent. No. 1262, Third Order Chapel, Texoco. No. 1263, Friar Tembleque Aqueduct, Otumba.

1981, Nov. 28
1260   A365   4p black   .60   .35
1261   A365   4p black   .60   .35
1262   A365   5p black   .60   .35
1263   A365   5p black   .60   .35
   Nos. 1260-1263 (4)   2.40   1.40

Martyrs of Rio Blanco, 75th Anniv. — A396

1982, Jan. 7   Photo.   Perf. 14
1264   A396   80c multicolored   .60   .35

Death Sesquicentennial of Ignacio Lopez Rayon — A397

1982, Feb. 2
1265   A397   1.60p multicolored   .60   .35

75th Anniv. of Postal Headquarters A398

1982, Feb. 17
1266   A398   4p green & ocher   .60   .35

Crafts Type of 1980

50c, Huichole art. 1p, Ceramic snail. 3p, Tiger mask, Madera.

1982, Mar. 6   Photo.   Perf. 14
1267   A370   50c multi   .60   .35
1268   A370   1p multi   .60   .35
1269   A370   3p multi   .60   .35
   Nos. 1267-1269 (3)   1.80   1.05

"Use Zip Codes" — A399

1982, Mar. 20
1270   A399   80c multicolored   .60   .35

TB Bacillus Centenary and World Health Day — A400

1982, Apr. 7   Photo.   Perf. 14
1271   A400   4p multicolored   .60   .35

50th Anniv. of Military Academy — A401

1982, Apr. 15
1272   A401   80c multicolored   .60   .35

Oaxaca City, 450th Anniv. — A402

1982, Apr. 25
1273   A402   1.60p multicolored   1.00   .35

Tourism Type of 1979

No. 1274, Basaseachic Cascade, Chihuahua. No. 1275, Silence Zone, Durango. No. 1276, Ruins, Maya city of Edzna, Campeche. No. 1277, Olmec sculpture, Tabasco.

1982, May 29   Photo.   Perf. 14
1274   A353   80c multicolored   .60   .35
1275   A353   80c multicolored   .60   .35
1276   A353   1.60p multicolored   .60   .35
1277   A353   1.60p multicolored   .60   .35
   Nos. 1274-1277 (4)   2.40   1.40

1982 World Cup — A403

Designs: Various soccer players.

1982, June 13
1278   A403   1.60p multicolored   1.25   .35
1279   A403   4p multicolored   1.25   .35
1280   A403   7p multicolored   1.25   .35
   Nos. 1278-1280 (3)   3.75   1.05

Turtles and Map — A404

1982, July 3
1281   A404   1.60p shown   1.25   .35
1282   A404   4p Gray whales   2.25   .35

Gen. Vicente Guerrero (1783-1831) A405

1982, Aug. 9   Photo.   Perf. 14
1283   A405   80c multicolored   .60   .35

MEXICO

A406

1982, Aug. 14
1284 A406 4p multicolored   .60   .35
2nd UN Conference on Peaceful Uses of Outer Space, Vienna, Aug. 9-21.

Pre-Hispanic Art Type of 1980
Designs: 80c, Tariacuri, founder of Tarasco Kingdom, Chronicle of Michoacan, 16th cent. 1.60p, Acamapichtli, Aztec emperor, 1376-1396, Azcatitlan Codex. 4p, 10-Deer Tiger's Breastplate, wife of Lord 13-Eagle Tlaloc Copal Ball, 12th cent., Nuttal Mixtec Codex.

1982, Sept. 4
1285 A361 80c multicolored   .60   .35
1286 A361 1.60p multicolored   .60   .35
1287 A361 4p multicolored   .60   .35
   Nos. 1285-1287 (3)   1.80 1.05

Papaya — A407

1982, Sept. 18   Unwmk.   Perf. 14
1288 A407 80c shown   .60   .35
1289 A407 1.60p Corn   .60   .35

Florentine Codex Illustrations A408

1982, Oct. 2
1290 A408 80c Astrologer .60   .35
1291 A408 1.60p School   .60   .35
1292 A408 4p Musicians   .60   .35
   Nos. 1290-1292 (3)   1.80 1.05
   See Nos. 1520-1522.

Manuel Gamio (1883-1960) Anthropologist A409

Scientists: No. 1294, Isaac Ochoterena (1855-1950), biologist. No. 1295, Angel Maria Garibay K. (1892-1976), philologist. No. 1296, Manuel Sandoval Vallarta (1899-), nuclear physicist. No. 1297, Guillermo Gonzalez Camarena (b. 1917), electronic engineer.

1982, Oct. 16   Photo.   Perf. 14
1293 A409 1.60p multicolored .60   .35
1294 A409 1.60p multicolored .60   .35
1295 A409 1.60p multicolored .60   .35
1296 A409 1.60p multicolored .60   .35
1297 A409 1.60p multicolored .60   .35
   a. Strip of 5, #1293-1297 5.25 5.25

Natl. Archives Opening, Aug. 27 — A410

1982, Oct. 23   Perf. 14
1298 A410 1.60p brt grn & blk .60   .35

Christmas 1982 — A411

1982, Oct. 30   Perf. 14
1299 A411 50c Dove   .60   .35
1300 A411 1.60p Dove, diff. .60   .35

Mexican Food System — A412

1982, Nov. 13   Photo.   Perf. 14
1301 A412 1.60p multicolored .60   .35

Opening of Revolutionary Museum, Chihuahua A413

1982, Nov. 17   Perf. 14
1302 A413 1.60p No. C232 .60   .35

Colonial Monument Type of 1980
Designs: 1.60p, College of Sts. Peter and Paul, Mexico City, 1576. 8p, Convent of Jesus Maria, Mexico City, 1603. 10p, Open Chapel, Tlalmanalco, 1585. 14p, Convent at Actopan, Hidalgo State, 1548.

1982, Nov. 27
1303 A365 1.60p black & gray .60   .35
1304 A365 8p black & gray   .60   .35
1305 A365 10p black & gray   .60   .35
1306 A365 14p black & gray   .65   .35
   a. Vert. strip of 4, #1303-1306 + label 16.00 16.00
   Nos. 1303-1306 (4)   2.45 1.40

Alfonso Garcia Robles, 1982 Nobel Peace Prize Winner — A414

1982, Dec. 10   Unwmk.   Perf. 14
1307 A414 1.60p gold & blk   .60   .35
1308 A414 14p multicolored   .60   .35

Jose Vasconcelos, Philosopher — A415

1982, Dec. 11   Perf. 14
1309 A415 1.60p bl & blk   .60   .35

World Communications Year — A416

1983, Feb. 12   Photo.   Perf. 14
1310 A416 16p multicolored   .60   .35

First Philatelic Exposition of the Mexican Revolution A417

1983, Mar. 13   Photo.   Perf. 14
1311 A417 6p No. 326   .60   .35

25th Anniv. of Intl. Maritime Org. — A418

1983, Mar. 17
1312 A418 16p multicolored   .60   .35

Year of Constitutional Right to Health Protection A419

1983, Apr. 7
1313 A419 6p red & olive   .60   .35

Society of Geography and Statistics Sesquicentennial A420

1983, Apr. 18
1314 A420 6p Founder Gomez Farias   .60   .35

2nd World Youth Soccer Championships — A421

1983, June 2   Photo.   Perf. 14
1315 A421 6p green & blk   .60   .35
1316 A421 13p red & blk   .60   .35
1317 A421 14p blue & blk   .60   .35
   Nos. 1315-1317 (3)   1.80 1.05

Tourism Type of 1979
Designs: No. 1318, Federal Palace Building, Queretaro. No. 1319, Fountain, San Luis Potosi. 13p, Cable car, Zacatecas. 14p, Mayan stone head, Quintana Roo.

1983, June 24   Photo.   Perf. 14
1318 A353 6p multicolored   .60   .35
1319 A353 6p multicolored   .60   .35
1320 A353 13p multicolored .60   .35
1321 A353 14p multicolored .60   .35
   a. Vert. strip of 4, #1318-1321 + label 3.25 3.25
   Nos. 1318-1321 (4) 2.40 1.40

Simon Bolivar (1783-1830) A422

1983, July 24
1322 A422 21p multicolored   .65   .35

Angela Peralta, Opera Singer (1845-1883) — A423

1983, Aug. 30   Photo.   Perf. 14
1323 A423 9p multicolored   .60   .35

Mexican Flora — A424

1983, Sept. 23   Photo.   Perf. 14
1324 A424 9p Achras zapota   .60   .35
1325 A424 9p Agave atrovirens .60   .35

Mexican Fauna — A425

No. 1326, Boa constrictor imperator. No. 1327, Papilio machaon.

1983, Sept. 23   Photo.   Perf. 14
1326 A425 9p multi   2.25   .35
1327 A425 9p multi   2.25   .35

Christmas 1983 — A426

1983, Oct. 15   Photo.   Perf. 14
1328 A426 9p multicolored   .60   .35
1329 A426 20p multicolored   .60   .35

Integral Communications and Transportation Systems — A427

1983, Oct. 17   Photo.   Perf. 14
1330 A427 13p brt blue & blk   .60   .35

Carlos Chavez (1899-1978), Musician, Composer A428

Contemporary Artists: No. 1332, Francisco Goitia (1882-1960), Painter. No. 1333, Salvador Diaz Miron (1853-1927), Lyrical Poet. No. 1334, Carlos Bracho (1899-1966), Sculptor. No. 1335, Fanny Anitua (1887-1968), Singer.

1983, Nov. 7   Photo.   Perf. 14
1331 A428 9p brown & multi   .60   .35
1332 A428 9p brown & multi   .60   .35
1333 A428 9p brown & multi   .60   .35
1334 A428 9p brown & multi   .60   .35
1335 A428 9p brown & multi   .60   .35
   a. Horiz. strip of 5, #1331-1335 5.25 5.25

MEXICO

Jose Clemente Orozco (1883-1949), Painter — A429

1983, Nov. 23   Photo.   Perf. 14
1336   A429   9p multicolored   .60   .35

35th Anniv. of Human Rights Declaration A430

1983, Dec. 10   Perf. 14
1337   A430   20p multicolored   .60   .35

Colonial Monument Type of 1980

9p, Convent Garden, Malinalco, 16th cent. 20p, Open Chapel, Cuernavaca Cathedral, Morelos. 21p, Tepeji del Rio Convent, Hidalgo. 24p, Atlatlahuacan Convent, Morelos.

1983, Dec. 16   Photo.   Perf. 14
1338   A365   9p black & gray   .00   .35
1339   A365   20p black & gray   .65   .35
1340   A365   21p black & gray   .65   .35
1341   A365   24p black & gray   .65   .35
     a. Vert. strip of 4, #1338-1341 + label   5.00   5.00

Antonio Caso (1883-1946), Philosopher A431

1983, Dec. 19   Granite Paper
1342   A431   9p multicolored   .60   .35

Royal Mining Decree Bicentenary A432

9p, Joaquin Velazquez Leon, reform author.

1983, Dec. 21
1343   A432   9p multi   .60   .35

Postal Code Centenary A433

1984, Jan. 2   Photo.   Perf. 14
1344   A433   12p Envelopes   .60   .35

Fight Against Polio — A434

1984, Apr. 7   Photo.   Perf. 14
1345   A434   12p Children dancing   .60   .35

Aquatic Birds — A435

12p, Muscovy duck. 20p, Black-bellied whistling tree duck.

1984, May 4   Photo.   Perf. 14
1346   12p multi   .85   .35
1347   20p multi   .85   .35
   a. A435 Pair, #1346-1347   4.00   2.50
   b. A435 Pair, #1346-1347 + label   8.00   8.00

World Dog Exposition, Mexico City — A436

1984, May 27
1348   A436   12p multicolored   1.50   .35

Natl. Bank of Mexico Centenary A437

1984, June 2
1349   A437   12p multicolored   .60   .35

Forest Protection and Conservation — A438

1984, July 12   Photo.   Perf. 14
1350   A438   20p Hands holding trees   .65   .35

1984 Summer Olympics — A439

1984, July 28
1351   A439   14p Shot put   1.25   .35
1352   A439   20p Equestrian   1.25   .35
1353   A439   23p Gymnastics   1.25   .35
1354   A439   24p Diving   1.25   .35
1355   A439   25p Boxing   1.25   .35
1356   A439   26p Fencing   1.25   .35

Size: 56x62mm   *Imperf*
1357   A439   40p Rings   3.75   1.75
   Nos. 1351-1357 (7)   11.25   3.85

Mexico-USSR Diplomatic Relations, 60th Anniv. — A440

1984, Aug. 4
1358   A440   23p Flags   .65   .35

Intl. Population Conference, Aug. 5-14 — A441

20p, UN emblem, hand.

1984, Aug. 6
1359   A441   20p multicolored   .65   .35

Economic Culture Fund, 50th Anniv. — A442

1984, Sept. 3
1360   A442   14p multicolored   .60   .35

Gen Francisco J. Mugica — A443

1984, Sept. 3
1361   A443   14p black & brown   .60   .35

Red Cactus, by Sebastian A444

Airline Emblem — A445

1984, Sept. 14   Photo.   Perf. 14
1362   A444   14p multicolored   .60   .35
1363   A445   20p blk & org   .60   .35

Aeromexico (airline), 50th anniv.

Palace of Fine Arts, 50th Anniv. — A446

1984, Sept. 29
1364   A446   14p multicolored   .60   .35

275th Anniv. of Chihuahua City — A447

14p, Cathedral exterior detail.

1984, Oct. 12
1365   A447   14p multicolored   .60   .35

Coatzacoalcos Bridge Inauguration — A448

1984, Oct. 17   Perf. 14
1366   A448   14p Aerial view   .60   .35

UN Disarmament Week — A449

1984, Oct. 24   Photo.   Perf. 14
1367   A449   20p multicolored   .60   .35

Christmas 1984 — A450

14p, Toy train & tree. 20p, Pinata breaking, vert.

1984, Oct. 31   Photo.   Perf. 14
1368   A450   14p multi   .60   .35
1369   A450   20p multi   .60   .35

Politician-Journalist Ignacio M. Altamirano (1834-1893) — A451

1984, Nov. 13   Photo.   Perf. 14
1370   A451   14p blk & lt red brn   .60   .35

State Audit Office, 160th Anniv. — A452

1984, Nov. 16
1371   A452   14p multicolored   .60   .35

1986 World Cup Soccer Championships, Mexico — A453

1984, Nov. 19
1372   A453   20p multicolored   2.50   .35
1373   A453   24p multicolored   3.00   .35
   a. Pair, #1372-1373   10.50   10.50
   b. Pair, #1372-1373 + label   20.00   20.00

Romulo Gallegos (1884-1969), Author and Former Pres. of Venezuela — A454

1984, Dec. 6
1374   A454   20p blue & gray   .60   .35

State Registry Office, 125th Anniv. — A455

1984, Dec. 13
1375   A455   24p slate blue   .60   .35

MEXICO

Natl. Flag, 50th Anniv. — A456

1985, Feb. 24
1376 A456 22p multicolored .75 .35

Johann Sebastian Bach — A457

1985, Mar. 21 Photo. *Perf. 14*
1377 A457 35p dl red brn, gold & blk .70 .35

Intl. Youth Year — A458

1985, Mar. 28 Photo. *Perf. 14*
1378 A458 35p rose vio, gold & blk .70 .35

Health Education Campaign A459

1985, Apr. 7 Photo. *Perf. 14*
1379 A459 36p multicolored .70 .35

Mexican Mint, 450th Anniv. — A460

1985, May 11 Photo. *Perf. 14*
1380 A460 35p 1st gold & copper coins .70 .35

Victor Hugo — A461

1985, May 22 Photo. *Perf. 14*
1381 A461 35p slate .70 .35

MEXFIL '85 — A462

1985, June 9 Photo. *Perf. 14*
1382 A462 22p No. 5 .65 .65
1383 A462 35p No. 574 .65 .65
1384 A462 36p No. 1081 .65 .65
  Nos. 1382-1384 (3) 1.95 1.95

Souvenir Sheet

1985, June 27 *Imperf.*
1385 A462 90p No. 111 on cover 3.75 3.75

Morelos Telecommunications Satellite Launch — A463

22p, Shuttle launch. 36p, Ground receiver. 90p, Modes of communication.

1985, June 17 *Perf. 14*
1386 A463 22p multi .60 .35
1387 A463 36p multi .60 .35
1388 A463 90p multi .75 .50
  a. Strip of 3, #1386-1388 + 2 labels 5.00 5.00
  Nos. 1386-1388 (3) 1.95 1.20

Souvenir Sheet
Imperf
1389 A463 100p multicolored 3.75 2.25

Nos. 1386-1388 has continuous design. No. 1389 pictures uninscribed continuous design of Nos. 1386-1388.

9th World Forestry Congress, Mexico City, July 1-9 — A464

1985, July 1 *Perf. 14*
1390 A464 22p Conifer .60 .35
1391 A464 35p Silk-cotton tree .60 .35
1392 A464 36p Mahogany .60 .35
  a. Strip of 3, #1390-1392 + 2 labels 5.75 5.75
  Nos. 1390-1392 (3) 1.80 1.05

Martin Luis Guzman (1887-1977), Journalist, Politician — A465

Contemporary writers: No. 1394, Agustin Yanez (1904-1980), politician. No. 1395, Alfonso Reyes (1889-1959), diplomat. No. 1396, Jose Ruben Romero (1890-1952), diplomat. No. 1397, Artemio de Valle Arizpe (1888-1961), historian.

1985, July 19 *Perf. 14*
1393 A465 22p multicolored .60 .35
1394 A465 22p multicolored .60 .35
1395 A465 22p multicolored .60 .35
1396 A465 22p multicolored .60 .35
1397 A465 22p multicolored .60 .35
  a. Strip of 5, #1393-1397 6.25 6.25
  Nos. 1393-1397 (5) 3.00 1.75

Heroes of the Mexican Independence, 1810 — A466

1985, Sept. 15
1398 A466 22p Miguel Hidalgo .60 .35
1399 A466 35p Jose Morelos .60 .35
1400 A466 35p Ignacio Allende .60 .35
1401 A466 36p Leona Vicario .60 .35
1402 A466 110p Vicente Guerrero .60 .35
  Nos. 1398-1402 (5) 3.00 1.75

Souvenir Sheet
Imperf
1403 A466 90p Bell, church 3.00 2.50

175th anniv. of independence from Spanish rule. No. 1403 contains one 56x49mm stamp.

University of Mexico, 75th Anniv. — A467

No. 1404, San Ildefonso, 1910. No. 1405, University emblem. No. 1406, Rectory, 1985. No. 1407, 1st Rector Justo Sierra, crest, 1910. No. 1408, Crest, 1985.

1985, Sept. 22 Photo. *Perf. 14*
1404 A467 26p multi .60 .35
1405 A467 26p multi .60 .35
1406 A467 40p multi .60 .35
1407 A467 45p multi .60 .35
1408 A467 90p multi 1.00 .65
  a. Strip of 5, #1404-1408 10.25 10.25
  Nos. 1404-1408 (5) 3.40 2.05

Interamerican Development Bank, 25th Anniv. A468

1985, Oct. 23 Photo. *Perf. 14*
1409 A468 26p multicolored .60 .35

UN Disarmament Week — A469

1985, Oct. 24 *Perf. 14*
1410 A469 36p Guns, doves .60 .35

UN, 40th Anniv. — A470

1985, Oct. 25 *Perf. 14*
1411 A470 26p Hand, dove .60 .35

Christmas 1985 — A471

Children's drawings.

1985, Nov. 15 Photo. *Perf. 14*
1412 A471 26p multicolored .60 .35
1413 A471 35p multicolored .60 .35

1910 Revolution, 75th Anniv. — A472

26p, Soldadera. 35p, Francisco Villa. 40p, Emiliano Zapata. 45p, Venustiano Carranza. 110p, Francisco Madero. 90p, Liberty bell.

1985, Nov. 18 *Perf. 14*
1414 A472 26p multi .60 .35
1415 A472 35p multi .60 .35
1416 A472 40p multi .60 .35
1417 A472 45p multi .60 .35
1418 A472 110p multi .60 .35
  Nos. 1414-1418 (5) 3.00 1.75

Souvenir Sheet
Imperf
1419 A472 90p multi 3.25 2.75

No. 1419 contains one 48x40mm stamp.

Astronaut, by Sebastian A473

The Watchman, by Federico Silva — A474

Mexican Astronaut, Rodolfo Neri, by Cauduro A475

Morelos and Telecommunications Satellite Launch — A476

1985, Nov. 26 *Perf. 14*
1420 A473 26p multicolored .60 .35
1421 A474 35p multicolored .60 .35
1422 A475 45p multicolored .60 .35
  Nos. 1420-1422 (3) 1.80 1.05

Miniature Sheet
Imperf
1423 A476 100p multicolored 3.25 2.75

1986 World Cup Soccer Championships, Mexico — A477

1985, Dec. 15 Photo. *Perf. 14*
1424 A477 26p Olympic Stadium 1.75 .35
1425 A477 45p Aztec Stadium 2.25 .35

1st Free Textbook for Primary Education, 25th Anniv. A478

1985, Dec. 16
1426 A478 26p Book cover .60 .35

Colonial Monuments A479

Landmarks in Mexico City: 26p, College of the Vizcainas, c. 1735. 35p, Palace of the Counts of Heras and Soto. 40p, Palace of the Counts of Calimaya, 16th cent. 45p, San Carlos Academy, 16th cent.

MEXICO

1985, Dec. 27 *Perf. 14*
1427 A479 26p grnsh blk & fawn .60 .35
1428 A479 35p grnsh blk & fawn .60 .35
1429 A479 40p grnsh blk & fawn .60 .35
1430 A479 45p grnsh blk & fawn .60 .35
  a. Strip of 4, #1427-1430 + label 5.00 5.00
    Nos. 1427-1430 (4) 2.40 1.40

Natl. Polytechnic Institute, 50th Anniv. — A480

40p, Luis Enrique Erro Planetarium. 65p, School of Arts & Communications. 75p, Emblem, founders.

1986, Feb. 7 *Perf. 14*
1431 A480 40p multi .60 .35
1432 A480 65p multi .60 .35
1433 A480 75p multi .60 .35
  a. Strip of 3, #1431-1433 + 2 labels 7.75 7.75
    Nos. 1431-1433 (3) 1.80 1.05

Fruit — A481

40p, Cucurbita pepo. 65p, Nopalea coccinellifera.

1986, Feb. 21 *Perf. 14*
1434 A481 40p multi .60 .35
1435 A481 65p multi .60 .35

World Health Day — A482

1986, Apr. 7 *Photo. Perf. 14*
1436 A482 65p Doll .60 .35

Halley's Comet — A483

1986, Apr. 25
1437 A483 90p multicolored .75 .35

Natl. Geology Institute, Cent. — A484

1986, May 26
1438 A484 40p multicolored .60 .35

1986 World Cup Soccer Championships A485

Paintings by Angel Zarraga (1886-1946) and Sergio Guerrero Morales: 30p, Three Soccer Players with Cap. 40p, Portrait of Ramon Novaro. 65p, Dimanche. 70p, Portrait of Ernest Charles Gimpel. 90p, Three Soccer Players. 110p, Poster for 1986 championships, by Morales.

1986, May 31
1439 A485 30p multicolored .75 .35
1440 A485 40p multicolored .75 .35
1441 A485 65p multicolored .75 .35
1442 A485 70p multicolored .75 .35
1443 A485 90p multicolored .75 .35

Size: 120x91mm
Imperf
1444 A485 110p multicolored 6.25 3.25
    Nos. 1439-1444 (6) 10.00 5.00

Independence War Heroes — A486

175th Death anniv. of: 40p, Ignacio Allende (1769-1811). 65p, Juan Aldama (1774-1811). 75p, Mariano Jimenez (1781-1811).

1986, June 26 *Photo. Perf. 14*
1445 A486 40p multicolored .60 .35
1446 A486 65p multicolored .60 .35
1447 A486 75p multicolored .60 .35
    Nos. 1445-1447 (3) 1.80 1.05

Miguel Hidalgo y Costilla (1753-1811), Mural by Jose Clemente Orozco — A487

1986, July 30 *Photo. Perf. 14*
1448 A487 40p multicolored .60 .35

Federal Tax Court, 50th Anniv. — A488

1986, Aug. 27 *Perf. 14*
1449 A488 40p gray, bl & blk .60 .35

Gen. Nicolas Bravo (1786-1854) A489

1986, Sept. 10 *Perf. 14*
1450 A489 40p multicolored .65 .35

Paintings by Diego Rivera A490

Designs: 50p, Paisaje Zapatista, 1915, vert. 80p, Desnudo con Alcatraces, 1944, vert. 110p, Sueño de una Tarde Dominical en la Alameda Central, 1947-48.

1986, Sept. 26 *Perf. 14*
1451 A490 50p multicolored .60 .35
1452 A490 80p multicolored .75 .35
1453 A490 110p multicolored .65 .35
    Nos. 1451-1453 (3) 2.00 1.05
    See Nos. 1571-1573.

Guadalupe Victoria (1786-1843), 1st President A491

1986, Sept. 29 *Perf. 14*
1454 A491 50p multicolored .60 .35

Natl. Storage Warehouse, 50th Anniv. A492

1986, Oct. 3
1455 A492 40p multicolored .60 .35

Intl. Post Day — A493

1986, Oct. 9 *Perf. 14*
1456 A493 120p multicolored .75 .35

Natl. Committee Commemorating the 500th Anniv. (1992) of the Meeting of Two Worlds — A494

1986, Oct. 12 *Perf. 14*
1457 A494 50p black & lake .60 .35

15th Pan American Highways Congress, Mexico City — A495

80p, Palacio de Mineria.

1986, Oct. 17 *Photo. Perf. 14*
1458 A495 80p multicolored .60 .35

Franz Liszt, Composer, 175th Birth Anniv. — A496

1986, Oct. 22 *Perf. 14*
1459 A496 100p black & brown .70 .35

Intl. Peace Year — A497

1986, Oct. 24
1460 A497 80p blk, bl & dk red .65 .35

Interment of Pino Suarez in the Rotunda of Illustrious Men — A498

1986, Nov. 6
1461 A498 50p multicolored .60 .35

Jose Maria Pino Suarez, vice-president of 1st revolutionary government, 1911.
See Nos. 1472, 1475, 1487, 1563.

Christmas — A499

Clay figurines from Tonala, Jalisco.

1986, Nov. 28
1462 A499 50p King .60 .35
1463 A499 80p Angel .60 .35

Diego Rivera (1886-1957), Painter — A500

1986, Dec. 8 *Photo. Perf. 14*
1464 A500 80p Self-portrait .60 .35

Export Type of 1975

Designs as before and: 60p, Men's shoes. 70p, Copperware. 80p, Denim overalls. 90p, Abalone. 100p, Cup of coffee.

1986-87 *Unwmk. Perf. 11½x11*
1465 A320 20p gray .35 .35
    Perf. 14
1466 A320 40p pale grn & gold .45 .35
    Perf. 11½x11
1467 A320 60p brown .70 .35
1468 A320 70p orange brn 1.40 .35
  a. Perf. 14 1.90 .35
    Perf. 14
1469 A320 80p blue .70 .35
1470 A320 90p green & blue 1.00 .35
1470A A320 100p brown ('88) .70 .35
  a. 100p dark brown, perf. 11½x11 ('87) 1.00 .35
    Nos. 1465-1470A (7) 5.30 2.45

Natl. Polio Vaccination Program, Jan. 24-Mar. 28 — A501

1987, Jan. 20 *Photo. Perf. 14*
1471 A501 50p Oral vaccine .60 .35

375

MEXICO

Rotunda of Illustrious Men Type of 1986

1987, Feb. 4
1472 A498 100p multicolored .65 .35
Jose Maria Iglesias (1823-1891), president in 1876.

Natl. Teachers' College, 100th Anniv. — A503

1987, Feb. 24 *Perf. 14*
1473 A503 100p multicolored .75 .35

Exploration of Pima Indian Territory by Eusebio Francisco Kino, 300th Anniv. A504

1987, Feb. 27 *Perf. 14*
1474 A504 100p multicolored .75 .35

Rotunda of Illustrious Men Type of 1986

100p, Pedro Sainz de Baranda.

1987, Mar. 20 Photo. *Perf. 14*
1475 A498 100p multi .65 .35

World Health Day, UN Child Survival Program — A505

1987, Apr. 7
1476 A505 100p blue & slate blue .75 .35

Autonomous University of Puebla, 50th Anniv. — A506

1987, Apr. 23
1477 A506 200p multicolored 1.00 .50

Battle of Puebla, 125th Anniv. — A507

1987, May 5 Photo. *Perf. 14*
1478 A507 100p multicolored .65 .35

METROPOLIS '87 — A508

1987, May 19
1479 A508 310p gray blk, grn & red 1.50 .75
Cong. of metropolitan areas, Mexico City.

Handicrafts A509

100p, Lacquerware tray, Uruapan, Michoacan. 200p, Blanket, Santa Ana Chiautempan, Tlaxcala. 230p, Lidded jar, Puebla, Pue.

1987, May 29 Photo. *Perf. 14*
1480 A509 100p multicolored .40 .30
1481 A509 200p multicolored .85 .35
1482 A509 230p multicolored 1.40 .50
Nos. 1480-1482 (3) 2.65 1.15

Genaro Estrada, (1887-1937) Political Reformer — A510

1987, June 2
1483 A510 100p pale pink, blk & pale rose .60 .35
See Nos. 1509, 1568-1569.

Native Traders, 1961, Mural by P. O'Higgins A511

1987, June 8
1484 A511 100p multicolored .60 .35
Nat'l. Bank of Int'l. Commerce, 50th anniv.

Publication of the 1st Shipbuilding Manual in the Americas, by Diego Garcia Palacio, 400th Anniv. — A512

1987, June 15
1485 A512 100p multicolored .60 .35

Nat'l. Food Program, 50th Anniv. — A513

1987, June 22
1486 A513 100p multicolored .65 .35

Rotunda of Illustrious Men Type of 1986

1987, June 22
1487 A498 100p multicolored .60 .35
Leandro Valle (1833-1861), General.

Paintings by Saturnino Herran (1887-1918) A514

1917 paintings: No. 1488, Self-portrait with Skull. No. 1489, The Offering. No. 1490, Creole Woman with Mantilla.

1987, July 9
1488 A514 100p black & red brn .50 .35
1489 A514 100p multicolored .50 .35
1490 A514 400p multicolored 1.50 .75
Nos. 1488-1490 (3) 2.50 1.45

Export Type of 1975

Designs: 10p, Meat cuts marked on steer. 20p, Bicycle. 50p, Tomatoes. 300p, Motor vehicle. 500p, Petroleum valves. 600p, Jewelry. 700p, Film. 800p, Construction materials. 900p, Pistons. 1,000p, Agricultural machinery. 2,000p, Wrought iron. 3,000p, Electric wiring. 4,000p, Honey. 5,000p, Cotton.

1987-88 Photo. Unwmk. *Perf. 14*
1491 A320 10p brt carmine .35 .25
1492 A320 20p black & org .35 .25
1493 A320 50p ver & yel grn .45 .25
1494 A320 300p chalky blue & scar, type I .45 .25
1495 A320 300p Prus blue & brt rose .60 .25
 a. Thin paper 1.40 .25
 b. Brt blue & brt rose .85 .25
1496 A320 500p dark gray & Prus blue .95 .25
1497 A320 600p multicolored 1.90 .30
 a. Thin paper 3.25 .25
1498 A320 700p brt yel grn, dark red & blk 1.60 .75
 a. Brt yel grn, lilac rose & blk 2.00 .85
1499 A320 800p dark org brn & org brn .260 1.25
1500 A320 900p black 5.25 2.10

Wmk. 300 Granite Paper
Type I Burelage in Gray
1501 A320 1000p dk red & blk 6.25 1.10
1502 A320 2000p black 5.75 1.75
1503 A320 3000p gray blk & org 5.75 1.75
1504 A320 4000p yel org & red brn 5.25 2.50
1505 A320 5000p apple grn & org 7.00 3.25
Nos. 1491-1505 (15) 42.16 16.25

Issue years: 10p-50p, 1987; others, 1988.

A515

10th Pan American Games, Indianapolis A516

Unwmk.
1987, Aug. 7 Photo. *Perf. 14*
1506 A515 100p multicolored .60 .35
1507 A516 200p blk, brt grn & dk red .60 .35

Federal Power Commission, 50th Anniv. — A517

1987, Aug. 14 Photo. *Perf. 14*
1508 A517 200p multicolored .65 .35

Art and Science Type of 1987

Design: J.E. Hernandez y Davalos (1827-1893), historian.

1987, Aug. 25 *Perf. 14*
1509 A510 100p buff, blk & dull red brn .60 .35

Pre-Hispanic Art Type of 1980

Designs: 100p, Xolotl (d. 1232), king of Amaquemecan. 200p, Nezahualpilli (1460-1516), king of Texcoco, conqueror. 400p, Motecuhzoma Ilhuicamina (Montezuma I d. 1469), emperor of Tenochtitlan (1440-1469).

1987, Aug. 31 *Perf. 14*
1510 A361 100p multicolored .45 .35
1511 A361 200p multicolored .70 .30
1512 A361 400p multicolored 1.30 .35
Nos. 1510-1512 (3) 2.45 1.00

Tourism Type of 1979

Designs: 100p, Central Public Library, Mexico State. No. 1514, Patzcuaro Harbor, Michoacan. No. 1515, Garcia Caverns, Nuevo Leon. No. 1516, Beach resort, Mazatlan, Sinaloa.

1987 *Perf. 14*
1513 A353 100p multicolored .60 .35
1514 A353 150p multicolored .60 .35
1515 A353 150p multicolored .60 .35
1516 A353 150p multicolored .60 .35
Nos. 1513-1516 (4) 2.40 1.40

Issue dates: 100p, Sept. 11; others, Oct. 19.

Formula 1 Grand Prix Race, Oct. 18 — A518

1987, Sept. 11
1517 A518 100p multicolored .60 .35

13th Intl. Cartography Conference A519

1987, Oct. 12
1518 A519 150p Map, 16th cent. .60 .35

Discovery of America, 500th Anniv. (in 1992) — A520

Design: Santa Maria, emblem of the Discovery of America Festival to be held in 1992.

1987, Oct. 12 *Perf. 14*
1519 A520 150p multicolored 3.75 .35
For overprint see No. 1698.

Illuminated Codices Type of 1982

Mendocino Codex (c. 1541): No. 1520, Founding of Tenochtitlan by the Aztecs, 1324. No. 1521, Pre-Hispanic wedding. No. 1522, Montezuma's Council.

1987, Nov. 3
1520 A408 150p multicolored .60 .35
1521 A408 150p multicolored .60 .35
1522 A408 150p multicolored .60 .35
Nos. 1520-1522 (3) 1.80 1.05

Christmas 1987 — A521

1987, Nov. 6
1523 A521 150p brt pink .60 .35
1524 A521 150p dull blue .60 .35

MEXICO

World Post Day — A522

Documents: 150p, Ordinance for expediting mail by sea, 1777. 600p, Roster of correspondence transported by coach, 1857.

1987, Nov. 12
| 1525 | A522 | 150p pale gray & slate gray | .60 | .35 |

Size: 129x102mm
Imperf
| 1526 | A522 | 600p rose lake & yel bis | 3.25 | 1.25 |

Meeting of Eight Latin American Presidents, 1st Anniv. — A523

500p, Flags, peace doves.

1987, Nov. 26 *Perf. 14*
| 1527 | A523 | 250p shown | .70 | .35 |
| 1528 | A523 | 500p multi | .90 | .45 |

Dualidad 1964, by Rufino Tamayo (b. 1899) — A524

1987, Dec. 9
| 1529 | A524 | 150p multicolored | .60 | .35 |

Nationalization of Mexican Railroads, 50th Anniv. — A525

1987, Dec. 15
| 1530 | A525 | 150p Metlac Bridge | 1.25 | .35 |

Antonio Stradivarius (c. 1644-1737), Italian Violin Maker — A526

1987, Dec. 18 *Perf. 14*
| 1531 | A526 | 150p bluish lilac | .65 | .35 |

Constitutional Tribunal of the Supreme Court, Plenum Hall, Jan. 15 — A527

Design: Statue of Manuel Rejon, author of the Mexican constitution.

1988, Jan. 15 *Photo.* *Perf. 14*
| 1532 | A527 | 300p multicolored | .75 | .35 |

Fauna — A528

No. 1533, Ambystoma mexicanum. No. 1534, Trichechus manatus.

1988, Feb. 29 *Photo.* *Perf. 14*
| 1533 | A528 | 300p multi | 1.25 | .45 |
| 1534 | A528 | 300p multi | 1.25 | .45 |

A529

Nationalization of the Petroleum Industry, 50th Anniv. — A530

No. 1536, PEMEX emblem, vert.

1988, Mar. 18
1535	A529	300p blue & blk	.80	.35
1536	A530	300p multi	.80	.35
1537	A530	300p shown	.90	.35
		Nos. 1535-1537 (3)	2.50	1.05

Vaccination, Detroit, 1932, Mural (detail) by Diego Rivera — A531

1988, Apr. 7
| 1538 | A531 | 300p olive grn & henna brn | .60 | .35 |

World Health Day: child immunization.

The People in Pursuit of Health, 1953, by Diego Rivera A532

1988, Apr. 7
| 1539 | A532 | 300p multicolored | .65 | .35 |

World Health Organization, 40th anniv.

Vallejo in Repose (Large) A533

Vallejo in Repose (Small) A534

1988, Apr. 15
1540	A533	300p shown	.60	.35
1541	A533	300p Portrait, diff. (large)	.60	.35
a.	Pair, #1540-1541		3.75	3.75
b.	Pair, #1540-1541 + label		7.50	7.50
c.	Bklt. pane of 4 (2 each #1540-1541) + label		500.00	
1542	A534	300p shown	.60	.35
1543	A534	300p As #1541 (small)	.60	.35
a.	Pair, #1542-1543		3.75	3.75
b.	Pair, #1542-1543 + label		7.50	7.50
		Nos. 1540-1543 (4)	2.40	1.40

Cesar Vallejo (1892-1938), Peruvian poet. Stamps of the same type printed se-tenant in sheets of 20 stamps containing 10 pairs plus 5 labels between inscribed with various Vallejo quotes or commemorative text.

Issued: No. 1541b, 11/9/90. Label in No. 1541b is overprinted in red with Mexican Chicagopex '90 souvenir cancel, and had limited distribution.

Sketch of Carlos Pellicer Camara (1897-1977), Poet, by Fontanelly — A535

1988, Apr. 23
| 1544 | A535 | 300p pale vio, blk & sal | .70 | .35 |

MEPSIRREY '88 Philatelic Exhibition, Monterrey, May 27-29 — A536

No. 1545, Youth collectors. No. 1546, Hand-stamped cover. No. 1547, Alfa Planetarium.

1988, May 27
1545	A536	300p multicolored	.60	.35
1546	A536	300p multicolored	.60	.35
1547	A536	500p multicolored	1.10	.60
		Nos. 1545-1547 (3)	2.30	1.30

Mexico-Elmhurst Philatelic Society Intl. (MEPSI).

1988 Formula I Grand Prix of Mexico A537

Design: Layout of Hermanos Rodriguez race track, Mexico City, and car.

1988, May 28 *Photo.* *Perf. 14*
| 1548 | A537 | 500p multicolored | 1.00 | .35 |

A538

Birth Centenary of Ramon Lopez Velarde — A539

No. 1549, Drawing and watercolor art outlined in plaster. No. 1550, Ramon Lopez Velarde (1888-1921), Poet.

1988, June 15
1549	A538	300p multicolored	.70	.35
1550	A539	300p multicolored	.70	.35
a.	Pair, #1549-1550 + label		5.00	5.00
b.	Bklt. pane of 4 + label		250.00	

Issue date: No. 1550a, Nov. 9, 1990. Label in No. 1550a is overprinted in red with Mexican Chicagopex '90 souvenir cancel, and had limited distribution.

University Military Pentathlon, 50th Anniv. — A540

1988, July 9 *Photo.* *Perf. 14*
| 1551 | A540 | 300p multicolored | .70 | .35 |

1st Mexico-Japan Friendship, Commerce and Navigation Treaty, Cent. — A541

1988, Aug. 16
| 1552 | A541 | 500p multicolored | 1.00 | .35 |

Joint Oceanographic Assembly, Acapulco, Aug. 23-31 — A542

1988, Aug. 23
| 1553 | A542 | 500p multicolored | 1.00 | .35 |

1988 Summer Olympics, Seoul — A543

700p, Emblems, Olympic flame.

1988, Aug. 31 *Photo.* *Perf. 14*
| 1554 | A543 | 500p multicolored | 1.25 | .35 |

Size: 71x55mm
Imperf
| 1555 | A543 | 700p multi | 0.75 | .60 |

World Boxing Council, 25th Anniv. — A544

1988, Sept. 9
| 1556 | A544 | 500p multi | 1.00 | .35 |

Intl. Red Cross and Red Crescent Organizations, 125th Annivs. — A545

1988, Sept. 23 *Photo.* *Perf. 14*
| 1557 | A545 | 300p blk, gray & scar | .75 | .35 |

Jose Guadalupe Posada (1852-1913), Painter, Illustrator — A546

1988, Sept. 29
| 1558 | A546 | 300p sil & blk | .70 | .35 |

MEXICO

World Wildlife Fund — A547

Various monarch butterflies, *Danaus plexippus*: No. 1560, Three adults. No. 1561, Larva, adult, pupa. No. 1562, Five adults.

1988, Sept. 30			Perf. 14	
1559	A547	300p shown	3.25	.65
1560	A547	300p multi	3.25	.65
1561	A547	300p multi	3.25	.65
1562	A547	300p multi	3.25	.65
	Nos. 1559-1562 (4)		13.00	2.60

Rotunda of Illustrious Men Type of 1986

Portrait and eternal flame: Manuel Sandoval Vallarta (1899-1977), physicist.

1988, Oct. 5				
1563	A498	300p multi	.70	.35

World Post Day — A548

500p, World map. 700p, Envelope, doves, Earth.

1988, Oct. 9			Perf. 14	
1564	A548	500p multi	.95	.35
	Size: 75x44mm		Imperf	
1565	A548	700p multi	3.75	1.00

Discovery of America, 500th Anniv. (in 1992) — A549

Illuminations: Aztec painter Tlacuilo from the Mendocine Codex, 1541, and Dominican scribe from the Yanhuitlan Codex, 1541-50.

1988, Oct. 12			Perf. 14	
1566	A549	500p multi	.95	.35

World Food Day — A550

1988, Oct. 16			Perf. 14	
1567	A550	500p multi	.95	.35

Art and Science Type of 1987

No. 1568, Alfonso Caso (1896-1970), educator, founder of the Natl. Museum of Anthropology. No. 1569, Vito Alessio Robles (1879-1957), historian.

1988, Oct. 24			Perf. 14	
1568	A510	300p gray & blk	.65	.35
1569	A510	300p pale yel, blk & red brn	.75	.35

Act of Independence, 175th Anniv. — A551

1988, Nov. 9				
1570	A551	300p claret brn & fawn	.70	.35

Art Type of 1986

Paintings by Antonio M. Ruiz (1895-1964): No. 1571, *Parade*, 1936. No. 1572, *La Malinche*, 1939. No. 1573, *Self-portrait*, 1925, vert.

1988, Nov. 21			Perf. 14	
1571	A490	300p multi	.65	.35
1572	A490	300p multi	.65	.35
1573	A490	300p multi	.65	.35
	Nos. 1571-1573 (3)		1.95	1.05

Tempera and Oil Paintings by Jose Reyes (b. 1924) — A552

1988, Nov. 25			Perf. 14	
1574	A552	300p Feast	.60	.35
1575	A552	300p Pinata, vert.	.60	.35

Christmas.

Municipal Workers' Trade Union, 50th Anniv. — A553

1988, Dec. 5			Perf. 14	
1576	A553	300p pale bister & blk	.65	.35

Flora — A554

No. 1577, Ustilago maydis. No. 1578, Mimosa tenuiflora.

1988, Dec. 20			Perf. 14	
1577	A554	300p multi	.65	.30
1578	A554	300p multi	.65	.30

Exporta Type of 1975

Designs: 40p, 1400p, Chemistry flasks. 200p, Citrus fruit. 450p, Circuit board. 750p, Film. 950p, Pistons. 1000p, Agricultural machinery. 1100p, Minerals. 1300p, Strawberries. 1500p, Copper vase. 1600p, Steel pipes. 1700p, Tequila. 1900p, Abalone. 2000p, Wrought iron. 2100p, Bicycles. 2500p, Overalls. 5000p, Cotton. Nos. 1588A, 1589, 1592, 1598A, 1599, 1601, 1603 have gray burelage Type I.

1988-92	Photo. Unwmk. Design A320		Perf. 14	
1583	40p black		.30	.25
1584	200p emer & brt yel		.55	.25
	a. Thin paper		1.40	.40
1585	450p yel bister & mag		.80	.25
	a. Thin paper		1.50	.40
1586	750p brt yel grn, dark red & dark gray		2.25	.40
1587	950p indigo		1.90	.60
	a. Thin paper		2.50	.75
1588	1000p dark red & blk		1.20	.25
1588A	1000p dark red & blk, type 1		2.75	.25
1589	1100p dark gray, type I		2.50	.50
1590	1100p dark gray		2.50	.50
1591	1300p red & grn		2.50	.55
1592	1300p red & grn, type I		2.25	.55
	a. Thin paper		3.25	.75
1593	1400p black		1.90	.50
1594	1500p tan		1.90	.60
	a. 1500p orange brown		2.00	.60
1595	1600p red orange		1.75	.55
1596	1700p dk grn & yel grn		1.75	.60
1597	1900p bl grn & bl		1.90	.65
1598	2000p black		3.00	.75
1598A	2000p black, type 1		2.50	.25
1599	2100p black & orange, type I		8.50	.85
1600	2100p black & ver		8.25	1.00
1601	2500p dark blue, type I		4.50	1.00
1602	2500p slate blue		4.50	.90
1603	5000p apple grn & org, type I		5.00	1.90
	Nos. 1583-1603 (23)		64.35	13.80

Issued: 40p, 1/5/88; 200p, 2/27/89; 450p, 2/10/89; No. 1585a, 950p, No. 1587a, 1589, 3/30/89; 1,000p, 1989; Nos. 1590, 1599, 1601, 1991; Nos. 1600, 1602, 5000p, 1992; others, 1990.

Graphic Arts Workshop, 50th Anniv. — A555

1989, Feb. 9			Photo.	Perf. 14
1604	A555	450p yel bis, red & blk	.85	.35

Coat of Arms and *E Santo Domingo*, the Natl. Hymn — A556

1989, Feb. 27				
1605	A556	450p multicolored	.80	.35

Dominican Republic independence, 145th anniv.

Intl. Border and Territorial Waters Commission of Mexico and the US, Cent. — A557

1989, Mar. 1				
1606	A557	1100p multi	1.75	.80

10th Intl. Book Fair — A558

450p, UNAM School of Engineering.

1989, Mar. 4				
1607	A558	450p multi	.90	.35

Lyricists and Composers Soc., 25th Anniv. — A559

1989, Mar. 17				
1608	A559	450p multi	.90	.35

World Day for the Fight Against AIDS — A560

1989, Apr. 7				
1609	A560	450p multi	.90	.35

Leona Vicario (1779-1842), Heroine of the Independence Movement — A561

1989, Apr. 20			Photo.	Perf. 14
1610	A561	450p blk, sepia & golden brn	.90	.35

Alfonso Reyes (1889-1959), Author, Educator — A562

1989, May 17				
1611	A562	450p multi	.85	.35

Formula 1 Grand Prix of Mexico — A563

1989, May 28			Perf. 14	
1612	A563	450p multi	.85	.35

14th Tourism Congress, Acapulco — A564

1989, June 11			Perf. 14	
1613	A564	1100p multi	1.60	.80

14th Intl. Gerontology Congress, Mexico — A565

Statue: The god Huehueteotl as an old man bearing the weight of the world on his shoulders.

1989, June 18				
1614	A565	450p multi	.85	.35

Battle of Zacatecas, 75th Anniv. A566

1989, June 23				
1615	A566	450p black	.85	.35

Baseball Hall of Fame of Mexico — A567

No. 1616, Umpire, catcher. No. 1617, Batter.

1989, June 25				
1616	550p multi		5.00	.45
1617	550p multi		5.00	.45
	a. Pair, #1616-1617		15.50	15.50
	b. A567 Pair, #1616-1617 + label		40.00	40.00

No. 1617a has continuous design.

MEXICO

35th World Archery Championships, Lausanne, Switzerland, July 4-8 — A568

No. 1618, Bows and arrows. No. 1619, Arrows, target.

1989, July 2
1618 A568 650p multi 5.00 .50
1619 A568 650p multi 5.00 .50
 a. Pair, #1618-1619 15.50 15.50
 b. Pair, #1618-1619 + label 40.00 40.00

No. 1619a has continuous design.

Tijuana, Cent. — A569

1989, July 11   Photo.   Perf. 14
1620 A569 1100p Municipal arms 1.60 .70

French Revolution, Bicent. — A570

1989, July 14
1621 A570 1300p blue, blk & dark red 2.00 .80

Gen. Francisco Xavier Mina (1789-1817), Independence Hero A571

1989, Sept. 7
1622 A571 450p green, blk & dark red .85 .35

Natl. Museum of Anthropology, Chapultepec, 25th Anniv. — A572

1989, Sept. 17   Perf. 14
1623 A572 450p multicolored 1.00 .35

7th Mexico City Marathon A573

1989, Sept. 24
1624 A573 450p multicolored 1.40 .35

Printing in America, 450th Anniv. A574

1989, Sept. 28
1625 A574 450p multicolored 1.40 .35

World Post Day — A575

1989, Oct. 9   Photo.   Perf. 14
1626 A575 1100p multicolored 1.60 .65

Sovereign Revolutionary Convention of Aguascalientes, 75th Anniv. — A576

1989, Oct. 10
1627 A576 450p multicolored 1.40 .35

Exploration and Colonization of the Americas by Europeans A577

1989, Oct. 12
1628 A577 1300p multicolored 2.40 .75

America Issue — A578

UPAE emblem and symbols like those produced on art by pre-Columbian peoples.

1989, Oct. 12
1629 A578 450p shown .75 .35
1630 A578 450p multi, diff., vert. .75 .35

Natl. Tuberculosis Foundation, 50th Anniv. — A579

1989, Nov. 10
1631 A579 450p multicolored .65 .35

Mask of the Bat God, Zapoteca Culture, c. 200-300 — A580

1989, Nov. 28
1632 A580 450p multicolored .85 .35

Serfin Commercial Bank of Mexico, 125th Anniv. — A581

1989, Nov. 29
1633 A581 450p deep blue, gold & blk .85 .35

Pres. Adolfo Ruiz Cortines (1889-1973) A582

1989, Dec. 3
1634 A582 450p multicolored .85 .35

Christmas A583

No. 1635, Candlelight vigil. No. 1636, Man sees star, vert.

1989, Dec. 11
1635 A583 450p multi .85 .35
1636 A583 450p multi .85 .35

Natl. Institute of Anthropology and Natural History, 50th Anniv. — A584

1989, Dec. 13
1637 A584 450p dark red, gold & black .85 .35

Nationalization of the Railway System in Mexico, 80th Anniv. A585

1989
1638 A585 450p multicolored .95 .35

Issue dates for some 1990-1991 issues are based on First Day cancels. Original printings were small. Later printings, made in 1991, were distributed to the stamp trade and seem to be the ones used for "First Day Covers."

Tampico Bridge A586

1990, Jan. 11   Photo.   Perf. 14
1639 A586 600p gold, blk & red 1.00 .60

Eradication of Polio — A587

1990, Feb. 1
1640 A587 700p multicolored 1.10 .55

Natl. Census — A588

1990, Mar. 12
1641 A588 700p lt grn & yel 1.10 .60

Mexican Philatelic Assoc., 10th Anniv. A589

1990, Apr. 19
1642 A589 700p multicolored 1.10 .60

Natl. Archives, Bicentennial A590

1990, Apr. 21
1643 A590 700p pale violet 1.10 .60

Intl. Conf. of Advertising Agencies A591

1990, Apr. 27
1644 A591 700p multicolored 1.10 .60

Stamp World London '90 — A592

1990, May 3
1645 A592 700p multicolored 1.10 .60

First Postage Stamps, 150th Anniv. A593

1990, May 6
1646 A593 700p lake, gold & blk 1.10 .60

MEXICO

1990, May 6
1647 A594 700p multicolored 1.00 .60

15th Tourism Exposition — A594

1990, May 6
1648 A595 700p multicolored 1.10 .60

Visit of Pope John Paul II — A595

1990, May 10
1649 A596 700p multicolored 1.00 .60

Health of Young Mothers — A596

1990, May 31
1650 A597 700p multicolored .90 .60

Fight Against Smoking — A597

1990, June 5
1651 A598 700p multicolored 1.00 .60

World Environment Day — A598

1990, June 24
1652 A599 700p grn, red & blk 1.00 .60

Formula 1 Grand Prix of Mexico A599

1990, June 25 Photo. Perf. 14
1653 A600 700p multicolored 1.00 .35

Airport & Auxiliary Services, 25th Anniv. A600

1990, June 26
1654 A601 700p multicolored 1.00 .35

Fight Against Drugs A601

1990, July 6
1655 A602 700p multicolored 1.00 .35

Protection of Rain Forests A602

1990, Aug. 8
1656 A603 700p multicolored 1.00 .35

Solidarity with Poor People A603

Solidarity is a governmental social program of Pres. Salinas de Gortari. See No. 1704.

1990, Aug. 10
1657 A604 700p multicolored 1.00 .60

Oaxaca Cultural Heritage A604

1990, Aug. 21
1658 A605 700p blk, gray & org 1.10 .65

Nature Conservation A605

1990, Aug. 23
1659 A606 700p black & blue 1.10 .60

Mexican Institute of Petroleum, 25th Anniv. — A606

1990, Aug. 24
1660 A607 700p blk, red & grn 1.10 .60

8th Mexico City Marathon A607

1990, Sept. 16
1661 A608 700p gray, bister, red & grn 1.00 .55

University of Colima, 50th Anniv. — A608

1990, Sept. 17
1662 A609 700p sil, yel, blk & org 1.00 .55

Mexico City Advisory Council, Founded in 1929 — A609

1990, Sept. 27
1663 A610 700p gray, grn, red & blk 1.00 .60

Nationalization of Electric Industry, 30th Anniv. — A610

1990, Oct. 4
1664 A611 700p multicolored 1.00 .60

City of Campeche, 450th Anniv. — A611

1990, Oct. 4
1665 A612 700p multicolored 1.00 .45

Silvestre Revueltas (1899-1940), Musician — A612

1990, Oct. 5
1666 A613 700p multicolored 1.00 .45

Plan of San Luis, 80th Anniv. — A613

14th World Conference of Supreme Counselors — A614

1990, Oct. 8
1667 A614 1500p vio, sil, gold & grn 1.90 .85

Discovery of America, 498th Anniv. A615

1990, Oct. 12
1668 A615 700p multicolored .95 .40

Mexican Archaeology, Bicentennial A616

1990, Nov. 18
1669 A616 1500p multicolored 2.10 1.15

16th Central American and Caribbean Games A617

No. 1671, Mayan ball player. No. 1672, Mayan ball player, vert. No. 1673, Ball court, stone ring, vert.

1990, Nov. 20
1670 A617 750p shown 1.00 .60
1671 A617 750p multi 1.00 .60
1672 A617 750p multi 1.00 .60
1673 A617 750p multi 1.00 .60
  a. Strip of 4, #1670-1673 5.50 5.50
  Nos. 1670-1673 (4) 4.00 2.40

Christmas A618 A619

1990, Dec. 3
1674 A618 700p Poinsettias 1.00 .55
1675 A619 700p Candles 1.00 .55

Mexican Canine Federation, 50th Anniv. — A620

1990, Dec. 9
1676 A620 700p multicolored 1.00 .60

World Post Day — A621

1990, Oct. 9 Photo. Perf. 14
1677 A621 1500p multicolored 2.10 1.15

MEXICO

America Issue — A622

No. 1678, Flowers, galleon. No. 1679, Galleon, parrot.

1990, Oct. 12
1678	A622	700p multicolored	.85	.65
1679	A622	700p multicolored	.85	.65
a.		Pair, #1678-1679	5.50	5.50
b.		Pair, #1678-1679 + blank label	15.00	15.00

No. 1679a has continuous design.

Mexican Brewing Industry, Cent. — A623

1990, Nov. 8   *Perf. 14*
1680 A623 700p multicolored   1.00   .60

National Chamber of Industrial Development, 50th Anniv. A624

1990, Dec. 5   *Perf. 14*
1681 A624 1500p multicolored   1.90   1.05

Naval Secretariat, 50th Anniv. — A625

1991, Jan. 4   *Photo.*   *Perf. 14*
1682 A625 1000p bl, blk & gold   1.30   .70

Prevent Transportation Accidents A626

1991, Jan. 11   *Photo.*   *Perf. 14*
1683 A626 700p multicolored   1.00   .60

Natl. Consumers Institute, 15th Anniv. — A627

1991, Feb. 11
1684 A627 1000p multicolored   1.30   .60

Voter Registration A628

1991, Feb. 13   *Perf. 14*
1685 A628 1000p org, blk & grn   1.30   .60

Olympic Basketball — A629

1991, Feb. 25   *Perf. 14*
1686 A629 1000p black & yellow   1.30   .75

Campaign Against Polio — A630

1991, Mar. 8
1687 A630 1000p multicolored   1.50   .95

Nos. 1688-1691, 1697 with "NP" and Post Office eagle head logo or just the logo, are specimens.

Childrens' Day for Peace and Development A631

Health and Family Life A632

1991, Apr. 16   *Perf. 14*
1688 A631 1000p multicolored   1.30   .75
1689 A632 1000p multicolored   1.30   .75

Mining in Mexico, 500th Anniv. — A633

1991, Apr. 25   *Perf. 14*
1690 A633 1000p multicolored   1.30   .60

Promotion of Breastfeeding A634

1991, May 10   *Perf. 14*
1691 A634 1000p multicolored   1.30   .60

16th Tourism Exposition — A635

1991, May 12   *Perf. 14*
1692 A635 1000p brt grn & dk grn   1.40   .65

Rotary Intl. Convention A636

1991, June 2   *Rouletted 6½*
1693 A636 1000p blue & gold   1.40   .65

Integrated Communications and Transportation Systems (SCT), Cent. — A637

Designs: No. 1695a, 1000p, Jet landing. b, 1500p, Airport control tower. c, 1000p, FAX machine. d, 1500p, Upper floors, SCT headquarters. e, 1000p, Communications van. f, 1500p, Satellite. g, 1000p, Satellite in orbit, earth. h, 1000p, Boxcars. i, 1500p, Locomotives. j, 1000p, People using telephones. k, 1500p, Lower floors, SCT headquarters. l, 1000p, Hillside road, left section, highway bridge. m, 1500p, Center section, highway bridge. n, 1000p, Right section of bridge. o, 1000p, Cranes loading cargo ship. p, 1500p, Bow of cargo ship. q, 1000p, Television camera. r, 1500p, Bus. s, 1000p, Truck. t, 1500p, Trailers passing through toll plaza. u, 1000p, Bridge construction. Continuous design.

1991, June 11   *Rouletted 6½*
1694 A637 1000p gray & multi   1.50   .75
1695 A637 Block of 21, #a.-u.   55.00   55.00

Jaguar A638

1991, June 12   *Perf. 14*
1696 A638 1000p black & orange   2.25   1.50
Conservation of the rain forests.

Formula 1 Grand Prix of Mexico — A639

1991, June 16   *Litho.*   *Rouletted 6½*
1697 A639 1000p multicolored   1.30   .65

No. 1519 Ovptd. In Red

1991, June 14   *Photo.*   *Perf. 14*
1698 A520 150p multicolored   21.00   14.00

No. 1698 was available in strips of 5 only in booklets with limited distribution, also containing a strip of 3 Scott No. 1693 and with 2 different booklet covers. No.1698 and complete booklets are speculative.

Total Solar Eclipse A640

Designs: No. 1699a, 1000p, Denomination at lower right. b, Globe showing Mexico. c, 1000p, Denomination at lower left. Continuous design.

1991, July 5   *Rouletted 6½*
1699 A640 Strip of 3, #a.-c.   7.25   6.50

First Latin American Presidential Summit, Guadalajara A641

1991, July 18
1700 A641 1500p blk, org & yel   1.75   .85

Solidarity Bridge — A642

1991, July 31
1701 A642 2000p multicolored   2.40   1.35

Ninth Mexico City Marathon — A643

1991, Aug. 22
1702 A643 1000p multicolored   1.30   .65

Federal Tax Court, 55th Anniv. — A644

1991, Aug. 27
1703 A644 1000p blue & silver   1.40   .65

Solidarity Type of 1990 and

A645

1991   *Perf. 14*
1704 A603 1000p multicolored   1.30   .65
   Rouletted 6½
1705 A645 1000p multicolored   1.30   .65
Issued: No. 1704, 12/17; No. 1705, 9/9.

World Post Day — A646

1991, Oct. 9   *Rouletted 6½*
1706 A646 1000p multicolored   1.30   .65

Voyages of Discovery — A647

MEXICO

Discovery of America, 500th Anniv. (in 1992) — A648

Design: No. 1708, Sailing ship, storm.

1991, Oct. 12
1707	A647	1000p multicolored	2.25	1.35
1708	A647	1000p multicolored	2.25	1.35
a.	Pair, #1707-1708		4.50	3.50
1709	A648	1000p multicolored	2.75	1.90
	Nos. 1707-1709 (3)		7.25	4.60

No. 1708a has continuous design. Printed in sheets of 20 + 5 labels.

A649

Christmas — A650

1991, Nov. 26
| 1710 | A649 | 1000p multicolored | 1.10 | .65 |
| 1711 | A650 | 1000p multicolored | 1.10 | .65 |

Carlos Merida, Birth Cent. — A651

1991, Dec. 2   Photo.   Rouletted 6½
| 1712 | A651 | 1000p multicolored | 1.30 | .65 |

Wolfgang Amadeus Mozart, Death Bicent. — A652

1991, Dec. 5
| 1713 | A652 | 1000p multicolored | 1.30 | .65 |

Self-sufficiency in Corn and Bean Production A653

1991, Dec. 11   Photo.   Rouletted 6½
| 1714 | A653 | 1000p multicolored | 1.30 | .60 |

City of Morelia, 450th Anniv. — A654

1991, Dec. 13
| 1715 | A654 | 1000p multicolored | 1.30 | .60 |

Merida, 450th Anniv. — A655

1992, Jan. 6   Photo.   Rouletted 6½
| 1716 | A655 | 1300p multicolored | 1.60 | .85 |

Engineering Education in Mexico, Bicent. — A656

1992, Jan. 15
| 1717 | A656 | 1300p blue & red | 1.60 | .85 |

1992 Summer Olympics, Barcelona A657

Design: No. 1719, Stylized Olympic Rings.

1992   Photo.   Rouletted 6½
| 1718 | A657 | 2000p multicolored | 2.25 | 1.15 |
| 1719 | A657 | 2000p multicolored | 2.25 | 1.15 |

Issued: No. 1718, Feb. 10; No. 1719, Mar. 1.

Guadalajara, 450th Anniv. — A658

No. 1720: a, 1300p, Coat of arms. b, 1300p, Municipal buildings. c, 1300p, Guadalajara Cathedral. d, 1900p, Allegory of the city's founding. e, 1900p, Anniversary emblem.

1992, Feb. 14
| 1720 | A658 | Strip of 5, #a.-e. | 16.00 | 16.00 |

Healthy Child Development — A659

1992, Feb. 26
| 1721 | A659 | 2000p multicolored | 2.00 | 1.15 |

Formula 1 Grand Prix of Mexico — A660

1992, Mar. 22
| 1722 | A660 | 1300p multicolored | 1.50 | .75 |

Introduction of the wheel and domesticated horses to America, 500th anniv.

Telecom '92 — A661

1992, Apr. 6
| 1723 | A661 | 1300p multicolored | 1.50 | .75 |

World Health Day — A662

1992, Apr. 7
| 1724 | A662 | 1300p blk, red & bl | 1.50 | .75 |

War College, 60th Anniv. — A663

1992, Apr. 15
| 1725 | A663 | 1300p multicolored | 1.50 | .75 |

Discovery of America, 500th Anniv. — A664

Paintings: No. 1726, Inspiration of Christopher Columbus, by Jose Maria Obregon. No. 1727, Meeting of the Races, by Jorge Gonzalez Camarena. No. 1728, Spanish, Indian and Mestizo, from the Natl. Historical Museum. No. 1729, Origin of the Sky, from Selden Codex. No. 1730, Quetzalcoatl and Tezcatlipoca, from Borbonico Codex. No. 1731, Human Culture by Camarena.

1992, Apr. 24   Litho.   Perf. 14
1726	A664	1300p multicolored	2.50	1.75
1727	A664	1300p multicolored	2.50	1.75
1728	A664	2000p multicolored	3.75	2.60
1729	A664	2000p multicolored	3.75	2.60
1730	A664	2000p multicolored	3.75	2.60
	Nos. 1726-1730 (5)		16.25	11.30

Size: 107x84mm
Imperf
| 1731 | A664 | 7000p multicolored | 20.00 | 15.00 |

Granada '92. For overprints see Nos. 1752-1757.

Natl. Medical Center in the 21st Cent. — A665

1992, Apr. 27   Photo.   Rouletted 6½
| 1732 | A665 | 1300p multicolored | 1.50 | .75 |

Rights of the Child — A666

1992, Apr. 30
| 1733 | A666 | 1300p multicolored | 1.50 | .75 |

Midwives in Mexico — A667

1992, May 10
| 1734 | A667 | 1300p multicolored | 1.50 | .75 |

Discovery of America, 500th Anniv. — A668

1992, May 22   Litho.   Imperf.
| 1735 | A668 | 7000p multicolored | 9.25 | 6.75 |

World Columbian Stamp Expo, Chicago.

Notary College of Mexico, Mexico City, Bicent. — A669

1992, June 18   Litho.   Rouletted 6½
| 1736 | A669 | 1300p multicolored | 1.40 | .75 |

Arbor Day — A670

1992, July 9   Rouletted 5
| 1737 | A670 | 1300p multicolored | 1.40 | .75 |

1992 Summer Olympics, Barcelona A671

1992, July 30   Perf. 14
1738	A671	1300p Boxing	1.40	.95
1739	A671	1300p Fencing	1.40	.95
1740	A671	1300p High jump	1.40	.95
1741	A671	1300p Gymnastics	1.40	.95
1742	A671	1300p Shooting	1.40	.95
1743	A671	1900p Swimming	2.75	1.90
1744	A671	1900p Running	2.75	1.90
1745	A671	1900p Rowing	2.75	1.90
1746	A671	1900p Soccer	2.75	1.90
1747	A671	2000p Equestrian	2.75	1.90
	Nos. 1738-1747 (10)		20.75	14.25

Souvenir Sheet
Perf. 10
| 1748 | A671 | 7000p Torch bearer | 15.50 | 11.50 |

10th Intl. Marathon of Mexico City — A672

1992, Aug. 26   Litho.   Rouletted 5
| 1749 | A672 | 1300p multicolored | 1.50 | .75 |

Solidarity, United for Progress A673

1992, Sept. 8   Perf. 10
| 1750 | A673 | 1300p multicolored | 1.50 | .75 |

Souvenir Sheet

Discovery of America, 500th Anniv. — A674

1992, Sept. 18   Perf. 10
| 1751 | A674 | 7000p multicolored | 10.25 | 7.50 |

Genoa '92.

Nos. 1726-1731 Ovptd. with emblem of World Columbian Stamp Expo '92, Chicago

1992, Apr. 24   Litho.   Perf. 14
1752	A664	1300p on #1726	17.00	15.00
1753	A664	1300p on #1727	17.00	15.00
1754	A664	2000p on #1728	17.00	15.00
1755	A664	2000p on #1729	17.00	15.00
1756	A664	2000p on #1730	17.00	15.00
	Nos. 1752-1756 (5)		85.00	75.00

Size: 107x84mm
Imperf
| 1757 | A664 | 7000p on #1731 | 87.50 | 75.00 |

Nos. 1752-1757 were produced in limited quantities and had limited distribution with no advance release information available.

Natl. Council of Radio and Television, 50th Anniv. — A675

1992, Oct. 5   Litho.   Perf. 10
| 1758 | A675 | 1300p multicolored | 1.50 | .75 |

MEXICO

World Post Day — A676

1992, Oct. 9   **Litho.**   **Perf. 10**
1759   A676   1300p multicolored   1.40   .75

Communications System of the Americas — A677

1992, Oct. 12
1760   A677   2000p multicolored   2.25   1.50

Discovery of America, 500th Anniv. — A678

Designs: No. 1761, Aztec calendar stone. No. 1762, Snake, fish, compass.

1992, Oct. 12
1761   A678   2000p shown   2.00   1.50
1762   A678   2000p multicolored   2.00   1.50
   a.   Pair, #1761-1762   5.00   3.50
   b.   Pair, #1761-1762 + label   10.00   10.00

Exporta Type of 1975

Designs: 2200p, Cuts of meat marked on steer. 2800p, Chemistry flasks. 3600p, Pistons. 3900p, Petroleum valves. 4000p, Honey. 4800p, Tomatoes. 6000p, Citrus fruit. 7200p, Film.

1992   **Photo.**   **Perf. 14**
1763   A320   2200p red   1.60   1.20
1764   A320   2800p black   2.50   1.90

With Gray Burelage
1765   A320   3600p blk, I   2.75   2.10
1766   A320   3900p gray & bl, II   3.50   2.60
1767   A320   4000p yel org & red brn, I   3.50   2.60
1768   A320   4800p red & grn, I   4.00   3.00
1768A   A320   4800p red & green, II   25.00   19.00
1769   A320   6000p yel & grn, I   5.00   0.75
1770   A320   7200p grn, red & blk, I   6.00   4.50
   Nos. 1763-1770 (9)   53.85   40.65

San Luis Potosi, 400th Anniv. — A679

1992, Nov. 3   **Litho.**   **Perf. 10**
1777   A679   1300p multicolored   1.50   .75

Values are for copies with perfs touching the design.

United for Conservation A680

1992, Nov. 17
1778   A680   1300p multicolored   2.25   1.50

Navy Day — A681

1992, Nov. 23
1779   A681   1300p multicolored   1.50   .75

Values are for copies with perfs touching the design.

Christmas A682

1300p, Christmas tree, children, pinata, vert.

1992, Nov. 26
1780   A682   1300p multicolored   1.25   .75
1781   A682   2000p multicolored   2.40   1.50

Tourism in States of Mexico — A683

No. 1782, Campeche. No. 1783, Guanajuato. No. 1784, Guanajuato. No. 1785, Colima. No. 1786, Coahuila. No. 1787, Campeche. No. 1788, Colima. No. 1789, Chiapas. No. 1790, Michoacan, vert. No. 1791, Coahuila. No. 1792, Colima. No. 1793, Queretaro. No. 1794, Sinaloa. No. 1795, Yucatan. No. 1796, Sonora. No. 1797, Mexico. No. 1798, Zacatecas, vert. No. 1798A, Campeche. No. 1799, Sinaloa. No. 1800, Sinaloa. No. 1801, Yucatan. No. 1802, Yucatan. No. 1803, Chiapas. No. 1804, Mexico. No. 1805, Sonora.

1993-96   **Photo.**   **Unwmk.**   **Perf. 14**
1782   A683   90c multi   1.40   .50
1783   A683   1p multi   1.60   .60
1784   A683   1.10p multi   1.90   .25
1785   A683   1.30p multi   2.10   .70
1786   A683   1.80p multi   1.50   .45
1787   A683   1.80p multi   1.10   .40
1788   A683   1.80p multi   1.10   .40
1789   A683   1.80p multi   1.10   .30
1790   A683   1.90p multi   3.25   1.10
1791   A683   2p multi   3.00   1.10
1792   A683   2p multi   3.00   .25
1793   A683   2.20p multi   3.50   1.25
1794   A683   2.30p multi   1.60   .35
1795   A683   2.40p multi   1.90   .40
1796   A683   2.50p multi   5.00   1.40
1797   A683   2.70p multi   3.25   .60
1798   A683   2.80p multi   5.25   1.50
1798A   A683   3p multi   4.00   .30
1799   A683   3.40p multi   4.00   .80
1800   A683   3.70p multi   11.00   1.90
1801   A683   3.80p multi   3.25   .85
1802   A683   4.40p multi   7.50   2.40
1803   A683   4.80p multi   8.50   2.50
1804   A683   6p multi   11.00   3.25
1805   A683   6.50p multi   5.50   1.50
   Nos. 1782-1805 (25)   90.00   25.05

A 2nd printing of No. 1797 exists. This printing appears crude, with missing and misregistered color dots.

Issued: 90c, 1p, 1.30p, 1.90p, No. 1791, 2.20p, 2.30p, 2.40p, 2.50p, 2.80p, 3.70p, 4.40p, 4.80p, 6p, 1993; 1.10p, 1.80p, 2.70p, 3.40p, 3.80p, 6.50p, 1995; No. 1792, 3p, 1996.

See Nos. 1960-1980, 2119-2140.

A685   A686

Designs: No. 1807, Doctor, child. No. 1808, Child's drawing, ball, blocks. No. 1809, Hands.

1993, Jan. 19   **Litho.**   **Perf. 10**
1807   A685   1.30p multicolored   1.30   .70
1808   A685   1.30p multicolored   1.50   .75
1809   A685   1.30p multicolored   1.50   .75
1810   A686   1.50p multicolored   1.60   1.10
   Nos. 1807-1810 (4)   5.90   3.30

Mexican Social Security Institute, 50th anniv. Medical Services (No. 1807), Day Nursery Social Security Service (No. 1808), security and solidarity (No. 1809).

Issued: 1.50p, 1/19; No. 1807, 5/11; others, 12/7.

Mexican Society of Ophthalmolgists, Cent. — A687

1993, Feb. 16   **Litho.**   **Perf. 10**
1811   A687   1.30p multicolored   1.50   .75

Children's Month — A688

1993, Feb. 23
1812   A688   1.30p multicolored   1.50   .75

A689

1993, Apr. 19   **Litho.**   **Perf. 10**
1813   A689   1.30p blue, blk & red   1.50   .75

Mexican Geography and Statistics Society, 160th Anniv.

Miguel Ramos Arizpe (1776-1843), Proponent of Mexican Federalism — A690

1993, Apr. 28
1814   A690   1.30p multicolored   1.50   .75

Federico Gomez Children's Hospital, 50th Anniv. — A691

1993, Apr. 29
1815   A691   1.30p multicolored   1.50   .75

Health Begins at Home — A692

1993, May 31
1816   A692   1.30p multicolored   1.50   .75

Upper Gulf of California, Nature Preserve — A693

1993, June 10   **Litho.**   **Perf. 10**
1817   A693   1.30p multicolored   1.50   .75

Mario Moreno (Cantinflas), Film Actor — A694

1993, June 24   **Photo.**   **Perf. 14**
1818   A694   1.30p black & blue   1.50   .95

See Nos. 1847-1851.

Secretariat of Health, 50th Anniv. — A695

Designs: No. 1819, Dr. Maximiliano Ruiz Castaneda. No. 1820, Dr. Bernardo Sepulveda Gutierrez. No. 1821, Dr. Ignacio Chavez Sanchez. No. 1822, Dr. Mario Salazar Mallen. No. 1823, Dr. Gustavo Baz Prada.

1993   **Litho.**   **Perf. 10**
1819   A695   1.30p multicolored   1.50   .75
1820   A695   1.30p multicolored   1.50   .75
1821   A695   1.30p multicolored   1.50   .75
1822   A695   1.30p multicolored   1.50   .75
1823   A695   1.30p multicolored   1.50   .75
   Nos. 1819-1823 (5)   7.50   3.75

Issued: No. 1819, 6/29; No. 1820, 7/26; No. 1821, 8/31; No. 1822, 9/23; No. 1823, 10/26.

First Postage Stamps of Brazil, 150th Anniv. — A696

1993, July 30
1824   A696   2p multicolored   2.10   1.15

Runners — A697

1993, Aug. 25
1825   A697   1.30p multi   1.50   .75

11th Intl. Marathon of Mexico City.

A698

1.30p, Open book, lightning bolt. 2p, Buildings.

1993, Sept. 6
1826   1.30p multicolored   1.00   .75
1827   2p multicolored   1.75   1.05
   a.   A698 Pair, #1826-1827   3.50   3.50

Monterrey Institute of Technology and Higher Studies, 50th anniv.

Solidarity Week — A699

1993, Sept. 6
1828   A699   1.30p multicolored   1.50   .75

Confederation of Mexican Chambers of Industry, 75th Anniv. — A700

1993, Sept. 13   **Litho.**   **Perf. 10**
1829   A700   1.30p multicolored   1.50   .75

City of Torreon, Cent. — A701

1993, Sept. 15
1830   A701   1.30p multicolored   1.50   .75

MEXICO

Europalia '93 — A702

1993, Sept. 22
1831 A702 2p multicolored 2.25 1.15

World Post Day — A703

1993, Oct. 9
1832 A703 2p multicolored 2.10 1.15

A704

1993, Oct. 10
1833 A704 1.30p multicolored 1.50 .75
Guadalupe Victoria (1786-1843), first president of Mexico.

Natl. Civil Protection System — A705

1993, Oct. 13
1834 A705 1.30p multicolored 1.50 .75
Intl. Day for Reduction of Natural Disasters.

UN Decade for Intl. Law — A706

1993, Oct. 19
1835 A706 2p multicolored 2.10 1.15

20th Natl. Wheelchair Games — A707

1993, Oct. 21
1836 A707 1.30p multicolored 1.60 .75

Jose Peon y Contreras, Poet, 150th Anniv. of Birth — A708

1993, Oct. 22   Litho.   Perf. 10
1837 A708 1.30p purple & black 1.60 .75

Endangered Species A709

1993, Oct. 25   Litho.   Perf. 10
1838 A709 2p Quetzal 2.75 1.90
1839 A709 2p Pavon, vert. 2.75 1.90

Christmas A710

Designs: No. 1840, Adoration of the Magi. No. 1841, Christmas trees, presents, vert.

1993, Nov. 26   Litho.   Perf. 10
1840 A710 1.30p multicolored 1.50 .75
1841 A710 1.30p multicolored 1.50 .75

Solidarity — A711

1993, Nov. 20
1842 A711 1.30p multicolored 1.60 .75

Natl. Preparatory School, 125th Anniv. — A712

1993, Dec. 2   Litho.   Perf. 10
1843 A712 1.30p multicolored 1.50 .75

FSTSE, 55th Anniv. — A713

1993, Dec. 6   Photo.
1844 A713 1.30p multicolored 1.50 .75

Mescala Bridge — A714

1993, Dec. 7
1845 A714 1.30p multicolored 1.50 .75

Highway of the Sun — A715

1993, Dec. 7
1846 A715 1.30p multicolored 1.50 .75

Film Actor Type of 1993
No. 1847, Pedro Armendariz. No. 1848, Pedro Infante. No. 1849, Jorge Negrete. No. 1850, Maria Felix. No. 1851, Dolores del Rio.

1993, Dec. 9   Perf. 14
1847 A694 1.30p black & light blue 1.50 .75
1848 A694 1.30p black & green 1.50 .75
1849 A694 1.30p black & purple 1.50 .75
1850 A694 1.30p black & orange 1.50 .75
1851 A694 1.30p black & rose 1.50 .75
Nos. 1847-1851 (5) 7.50 3.75

Secretariat of Education, 72nd Anniv. — A716

Famous educators: No. 1852, Jose Vasconcelos. No. 1853, Rafael Ramirez Castaneda. No. 1854, Estefania Castaneda Nunez. No. 1855, Moises Saenz Garza. No. 1856, Rosaura Zapata Cano. No. 1857, Gregorio Torres Quintero. No. 1858, Lauro Aguirre Espinosa.

1994, Jan. 26   Litho.   Perf. 10
1852 A716 1.30p multicolored 1.50 .75
1853 A716 1.30p multicolored 1.50 .75
1854 A716 1.30p multicolored 1.50 .75
1855 A716 1.30p multicolored 1.50 .75
1856 A716 1.30p multicolored 1.50 .75
1857 A716 1.30p multicolored 1.50 .75
1858 A716 1.30p multicolored 1.50 .75
Nos. 1852-1858 (7) 10.50 5.25

Emiliano Zapata, (1879-1919), Revolutionary A717

1994, Apr. 10   Litho.   Perf. 10
1859 A717 1.30p multicolored 1.50 .75

ILO, 75th Anniv. — A718

1994, Apr. 18   Perf. 14
1860 A718 2p multicolored 2.10 1.05

School Construction by CAPFCE, 50th Anniv. — A719

1994, Apr. 19
1861 A719 1.30p multicolored 1.50 .90

Children for Peace — A720

1994, Apr. 28
1862 A720 1.30p multicolored 1.40 .90

Youth Services — A721

1994, May 12   Rouletted 12
1863 A721 1.30p green & black 1.40 .90

United for Conservation A722

1994, May 6   Perf. 10
1864 A722 1.30p multicolored 2.75 1.90

Rouletting on many of the 1994 issues leaves individual stamps with rough, unattractive edges. Some examples are separated by scissors because of the difficulty in separating stamps.
The gum on many issues is poorly applied, often having a rough feel and appearance, due to air bubbles. Gum may not cover the entire back side.
Serial numbers are found on the back of some examples of No. 1896. These may appear on other stamps.

Francisco Zuniga — A723

1994, Apr. 26   Rouletted 12
1865 A723 1.30p multicolored 1.50 .95
 a. Thin paper 25.00 25.00

A724

1994, May 16   Litho.   Rouletted 13
1866 A724 2p multicolored 2.00 1.05
34th World Advertising Congress, Cancun.

World Telecommunications Day — A725

1994, May 17   Litho.   Rouletted 13
1867 A725 2p multicolored 2.00 1.05

ANIERM (Natl. Assoc. of Importers & Exporters of the Republic of Mexico), 50th Anniv. — A726

1994, May 17   Rouletted 12½
1868 A726 1.30p multicolored 1.40 .90

Yumka Natural Wildlife Center — A727

1994, May 21   Litho.   Rouletted 13
1869 A727 1.30p multicolored 1.50 .90

City of Zacatecas A728

1994, May 26   Rouletted 12½
1870 A728 1.30p multicolored 1.50 .90
 a. Thin paper 25.00 25.00

Prevention of Mental Retardation — A729

1994, June 1   Litho.   Perf. 14
1871 A729 1.30p multicolored 1.40 .90
Month of the Child.

Friendship Hospital — A730

MEXICO

1.30p, Mother and child.

1994, June 1 Litho. Perf. 14
1872 A730 1.30p multicolored 1.50 .90

A731

Stylized soccer players: a, Kicking ball. b, Behind net.

1994, June 7 Rouletted 13
1873 A731 2p Pair, #a.-b. 4.25 2.40

1994 World Cup Soccer Championships, US.

Intl. Fish Fair, Vera Cruz — A732

1994, June 8
1874 A732 1.30p multicolored 1.50 .90

A733

Wildlife conservation: a, Silhouettes of ornamental songbirds (green). b, Silhouettes of cynegetic birds (blue). c, Silhouettes of fierce-looking wildlife (brown). d, Silhouettes of endangered wildlife (red). e, Perico frente-anaranjada. f, Calandria cola amarilla. g, Cardenal torito. h, Sastrecillo americano. i, Cenzontle norteno. j, Guajolote norteno. k, Paloma de ala blanca. l, Pato pijiji de ala blanca. m, Ganso blanco. n, Codorniz de gambel. o, Peregrin falcon. p, Jaguar. q, Jaguarundi. r, Mono saraguato. s, Lobo fino de guadalupe. t, Berrendo peninsular. u, Guacamaya roja. v, Mexican prairie dog. w, Mexican wolf. x, Manati.

1994, June 5 Perf. 14
1875 A733 1.30p Block of 24, #a.-x. + label 56.00 56.00

Juvenile Integration Centers, 25th Anniv. — A734

Rouletted 12½
1994, June 29 Litho.
1876 A734 1.30p multicolored 1.60 1.05
  a. Thin paper 25.00 25.00

Mexican-Canadian Diplomatic Relations, 50th Anniv. — A735

1994, July 1
1877 A735 2p multicolored 2.10 1.40
  a. Thin paper 25.00 25.00

Natl. Population Council, 20th Anniv. — A736

1994, July 15
1878 A736 1.30p multicolored 1.40 .90

Intl. Year of the Family — A737

1994, July 20
1879 A737 2p multicolored 2.10 1.05

Arbor Day — A738

Rouletted 12½
1994, Aug. 22 Photo.
1880 A738 1.30p multi 1.40 .90

12th Mexico City Marathon — A739

1994, July 27
1881 A739 1.30p multicolored 2.00 .90
  a. Thin paper 25.00 25.00

Chapultepec Zoo — A740

1994, Aug. 1
1882 A740 1.30p Giant panda 2.00 .95

Metro System, 25th Anniv. — A741

1994, Sept. 5 Perf. 13x13½
1883 A741 1.30p multicolored 1.40 .90

A742

1994, Sept. 5
1884 A742 1.00p multicolored 1.40 .90
Economic Cultural Foundation, 60th Anniv.

A743

1994, Sept. 22
1885 A743 1.30p multicolored 1.40 .90
Don Adolfo Lopez Mateos, 25th Death Anniv.

Solidarity Week — A744

1994, Sept. 22
1886 A744 1.30p multicolored 1.40 .90

City University, 40th Anniv. — A745

1994, Sept. 21 Litho. Perf. 13½
1887 A745 1.30p blue & yellow 1.40 .90

Opening of the Natl. Medical Center — A746

1994, Oct. 3
1888 A746 1.30p multicolored 1.40 .90

Natl. Week of Patriot Symbols — A747

1994, Sept. 16
1889 A747 1.30p multicolored 1.40 .90

Intl. Olympic Committee, Cent. — A748

1994, Sept. 29
1890 A748 2p multicolored 2.75 1.90

America Issue — A749

Mail delivery vehicles: a, bicycle. b, Railroad cycle.

1994, Oct. 12
1891 A749 2p Pair, #a.-b. 4.25 3.00

City of Salvatierra Guanajuato, 350th Anniv. — A750

1994, Sept. 12
1892 A750 1.30p multicolored 1.40 .90

Horses — A751

Designs: a, Saddled Aztec racer. b, Light brown quarter horse. c, Black quarter horse. d, Charro on horseback. e, Aztec racer. f, Chinaco riding galloping horse.

1994, Sept. 30 Perf. 14
1893 A751 1.30p Block of 6, #a.-f. 16.50 16.50

Issued in sheets of 3 No. 1893 + 7 labels.

Grandparents' Day — A752

1994, Oct. 15 Perf. 13½
1894 A752 1.30p multicolored 1.40 .90

Palace of Fine Arts, Mexico City, 60th Anniv. — A753

1994, Sept. 29 Litho. Perf. 13½
1895 A753 1.30p multicolored 1.40 .90

Antoine de Saint-Exupery (1900-44), Writer — A754

1994, Oct. 6 Rouletted 13
1896 A754 2p multicolored 2.10 1.05

World Post Day — A755

1994, Oct. 9 Perf. 13½
1897 A755 2p multicolored 2.10 1.05

Natl. Clean Water Program — A756

1994, Oct. 17
1898 A756 1.30p multicolored 1.40 .90

Dr. José Luis Mora (1794-1850), Politician — A757

1994, Oct. 27
1899 A757 1.30p multicolored 1.40 .00

City Theater, Saltillo, 50th Anniv. — A758

1994, Nov. 3
1900 A758 1.30p multicolored 1.40 .90

ICAO, 50th Anniv. — A759

1994, Nov. 3
1901 A759 2p multicolored 2.25 1.50

MEXICO

Natl. Museum of Anthropology, 30th Anniv. — A760

1994, Nov. 8
1902 A760 1.30p multicolored 1.40 .90

Natl. Assoc. of Actors, 60th Anniv. — A761

1994, Nov. 9
1903 A761 1.30p multicolored 1.40 .90

Ignacio Allende (1769-1811), Independence Hero — A762

1994, Nov. 10
1904 A762 1.30p multicolored 1.40 .90

Natl. Museum of History, 50th Anniv. A763

1994, Nov. 22 *Perf. 14*
1905 A763 1.30p multicolored 1.40 .90

Coahuila Teachers' College, Cent. — A764

1994, Nov. 23 *Perf. 13½*
1906 A764 1.30p multicolored 1.40 .90

Pumas UNAM Soccer Team, 40th Anniv. — A765

1994, Nov. 23
1907 A765 1.30p blue & gold 1.40 .90

Christmas A766

1994, Nov. 29
1908 A766 2p shown 2.00 1.05
1909 A766 2p Tree, vert. 2.00 1.05

Chalco Valley Solidarity — A767

1994, Nov. 30
1910 A767 1.30p multicolored 1.40 .90

Sr. Juana Ines de la Cruz (1648-95), Writer — A768

1995, Apr. 17 *Litho.* *Perf. 13½*
1911 A768 1.80p multicolored 1.25 .75

Wilhelm Roentgen (1845-1923), Discovery of the X-Ray, Cent. — A769

1995, May 8
1912 A769 2p multicolored 1.30 .70

Teachers' Day — A770

1.80p, Ignacio M. Altamirano.

1995, May 15
1913 A770 1.80p multicolored 1.30 .65

World Telecommunications Day — A771

1995, May 17 *Perf. 14x14½*
1914 A771 2.70p multicolored 1.75 1.10

A772

1995, May 18 *Perf. 13½*
1915 A772 1.80p multicolored 1.30 .70
Natl. Institute of Public Administration, 40th anniv.

A773

Jose Marti (1853-95), Cuban patriot.

1995, May 19 *Perf. 14x14½*
1916 A773 2.70p multicolored 1.75 1.10

A774

1.80p, Venustiano Carranza (1859-1920), politician, President of Mexico, 1917-20.

1995, May 23 *Perf. 13½*
1917 A774 1.80p multicolored 1.25 .75

A775

1995, June 11
1918 A775 2.70p multicolored 1.75 1.10
Tianguis Turistico, travel trade show, 20th anniv.

A776

a, Face becoming skull with pills, needle. b, Person as puppet. c, Faces behind bars.

1995, June 26
1919 A776 1.80p Strip of 3, #a.-c. 3.25 2.25
    d. Strip of 3, #a.-c. + label 9.00 9.00
Intl. Day Against Illegal Drugs.

A777

1995, June 28
1920 A777 1.80p black 1.25 .75
Lazaro Cardenas (1895-1970), soldier, politician, President of Mexico, 1934-40.

Natl. School for the Blind, 125th Anniv. — A778

1995, July 18 *Litho.* *Perf. 13½*
1921 A778 1.30p sepia & black 1.10 .70

Migratory Wildlife — A781

Designs: a, Danaus plexippus. b, Lasiurus cinereus. c, Anas acuta. d, Ceryle alcyon.

1995, Aug. 15 *Litho.* *Perf. 13½*
1924 A781 2.70p Block or strip of 4, #a.-d. 9.00 9.00
See Canada Nos. 1563-1567.

13th Mexico City Marathon — A782

1995, Aug. 22 *Litho.* *Perf. 13½*
1925 A782 2.70p multicolored 1.50 .75

16th Congress of UPAEP — A783

1995, Sept. 15
1926 A783 2.70p multicolored 1.30 .75

Louis Pasteur (1822-95) — A784

1995, Sept. 26 *Perf. 14*
1927 A784 2.70p multicolored 1.30 .75

World Post Day — A785

1995, Oct. 9
1928 A785 2.70p multicolored 1.50 .75

World Food Day — A786

1995, Oct. 16 *Perf. 14x14½*
1929 A786 1.80p multicolored 1.10 .65

FAO, 50th Anniv. — A787

1995, Oct. 16 *Perf. 14*
1930 A787 2.70p multicolored 1.30 .75

Plutarco Elias Calles (1877-1945), President of Mexico 1924-28 — A788

1995, Oct. 19 *Perf. 13½*
1931 A788 1.80p multicolored 1.10 .65

Birth of Cuauhtemoc, 500th Anniv. — A789

1995, Oct. 21
1932 A789 1.80p multicolored 1.10 .65

A790

National Symbols: 1.80p, Natl. flag, Constitution of Apatzingan, words of Natl. Anthem.

1995, Oct. 22
1933 A790 1.80p multicolored 1.10 .65

UN, 50th Anniv. — A791

1995, Oct. 24 *Litho.* *Perf. 14½x14*
1934 A791 2.70p multicolored 1.30 .75

Intl. Year of Travel — A792

1995, Nov. 14 *Litho.* *Perf. 13½*
1935 A792 2.70p multicolored 1.30 .85

MEXICO

Viceregal Gallery of Art Painting, The Holy Family, by Andres de Conchas — A793

1995, Nov. 16 — Perf. 14
1936 A793 1.80p multicolored 1.00 .60

Famous Generals — A794

Designs: No. 1937, Ignacio Zaragoza (1829-62). No. 1938, Sóstenes Rocha (1831-97). No. 1939, Felipe B. Berriozábal (1829-1900). No. 1940, Pedro María Anaya (1795-1854). No. 1941, Leandro Valle (1833-61). No. 1942, Santos Degollado (1811-61).

1995, Nov. 23 — Perf. 13½
1937 A794 1.80p yel, blk & bister 1.00 .60
1938 A794 1.80p yel, blk & bister 1.00 .60
1939 A794 1.80p yel, blk & bister 1.00 .60
1940 A794 1.80p yel, blk & bister 1.00 .60
1941 A794 1.80p yel, blk & bister 1.00 .60
1942 A794 1.80p yel, blk & bister 1.00 .60
　　Nos. 1937-1942 (6) 6.00 3.60

Christmas A795

Children's paintings: 1.80p, Family celebrating Christmas inside house. 2.70p, Adoration of the Magi.

1995, Nov. 27
1943 A795 1.80p multicolored .75 .45
1944 A795 2.70p multicolored 1.00 .85
　　a. Pair, Nos. 1943-1944 2.25 2.25

Mexican Health Foundation, 10th Anniv. — A796

1995, Nov. 30 — Litho. Perf. 14
1945 A796 1.80p multicolored 1.00 .60

Wildlife Conservation A797

1995, Dec. 4 — Perf. 14
1946 A797 1.80p Ocelot 2.25 1.90

Motion Pictures, Cent. — A798

1995, Dec. 12
1947 A798 1.80p violet & black 1.00 .60

Natl. Library of Education — A799

1995, Dec. 13 — Perf. 13½
1948 A799 1.80p bl grn & yel 1.00 .60

A800

1995, Dec. 15
1949 A800 1.80p multicolored 1.00 .60
Natl. Arts and Sciences Awards, 50th anniv.

A801

Radio personalities: a, Pedro Vargas. b, Agustin Lara. c, Hermanas Aguila. d, Toña "La Negra." e, "Cri-Cri," (F. Gabilondo Soler). f, Emilio Tuero. g, Gonzalo Curiel. h, Lola Beltrán.

1995, Dec. 19 — Perf. 14
1950 A801 1.80p Strip or block of 8, #a.-h. 12.00 10.00

Natl. Council of Science and Technology, 25th Anniv. — A802

1995, Dec. 20 — Perf. 13½
1951 A802 1.80p multicolored 1.00 .60

Plaza de Toros, Mexico City, 50th Anniv. — A803

Matadors: 1.80p, Silverio Perez, Carlos Arruza, Manolo Martinez. 2.70p, Rodolfo Gaona, Fermin Espinosa "Armillita," Lorenzo Garza.

1996, Feb. 5 — Litho. Perf. 13½
1952 　1.80p multicolored .70 .45
1953 　2.70p multicolored 1.00 .85
　　a. A803 Pair, Nos. 1952-1953 2.00 2.00
No. 1953a is a contiuuous design.

Mexican Aviation Day — A804

Designs: a, 2.70p, Patrol jet. b, 2.70p, Jet landing, airport terminal. c, 1.80p, Fighter plane, Squadron 201 (1945), map. d, 1.80p, Commercial biplane (1921), commerical jet.

1996, Jan. 20 — Litho. Perf. 13½
1954 A804 Strip or block of 4, #a.-d. 8.50 8.50

Dr. Alfonso Caso (1896-1970), Archaeologist A805

1996, Feb. 1
1955 A805 1.80p multicolored 1.00 .60

Natl. Consumer Agency, 20th Anniv. — A806

1996, Feb. 9 — Perf. 14
1956 A806 1.80p multicolored 1.00 .60

Tourism Type of 1993
Denomination Shown As $
Nos. 1960, 1962, 1976, Colima. Nos. 1961, 1964, Chiapas. No. 1963, Guanajuato. Nos. 1965, 1975, Queretaro. Nos. 1966, 1970, 1980, Mexico. Nos. 1967, 1972, Campeche. No. 1968, Coahuila. Nos. 1969, 1978, Sinaloa. Nos. 1971, 1979, Sonora. No. 1973, Michoacan, vert. No. 1974, Yucatan. No. 1977, Zacatecas, vert.

1996-99 — Photo. Unwmk. Perf. 14
Design A683
1960 1p multi ('97) 1.10 .25
1961 1.80p multi 1.10 .25
1962 2p multi 1.10 .25
1963 2p multi ('97) 1.10 .25
1964 2.30p multi ('97) 1.60 .30
1965 2.50p multi ('97) 1.60 .40
1966 2.70p multi 2.25 .35
1967 3p multi 2.25 .40
1968 3.10p multi ('97) 2.25 .35
1969 3.40p multi 2.75 .45
　　a. Pair, #1799, 1969 125.00 125.00
1970 3.50p multi ('97) 2.75 .60
1971 3.60p multi ('99) 2.75 .35
1972 3.75p multi ('98) 2.75 .35
1973 4p multi ('97) 3.25 .50
1974 4.40p multi ('97) 3.25 .50
1975 5p multi 3.25 .65
1976 5p multi ('98) 4.50 .50
1977 6p multi ('97) 4.50 .70
1978 6.50p multi ('98) 5.50 .65
1979 7p multi ('97) 6.50 .80
1980 8.50p multi ('97) 8.25 1.00
　　Nos. 1960-1980 (21) 64.35 9.85
Denomination on Nos. 1782-1805 was shown as N$.
Two additional printings of the 3.50p appear crude with missing and mis-registered dots. One of these printings is perf 12.
Two additional printings of No. 1975 exist. These appear crude, with missing and mis-registered color dots. One of the reprints is perf 12.

Orthopedics Society, 50th Anniv. — A807

1996, Apr. 29 — Litho. Perf. 13½
1981 A807 1.80p multicolored 1.00 .60

Juan Rulfo (1917-86), Writer — A808

1996, May 3
1982 A808 1.80p multicolored 1.00 .60

Natl. Polytechnical Institute, 60th Anniv. — A809

1996, May 21
1983 A809 1.80p multicolored 1.00 .60

A810

Stylized designs: a, 1.80p, Hands reaching toward one another. b, 1.80p, Person helping another out of hole. c, 2.70p, Two people.

1996, June 26 — Litho. Perf. 13½
1984 A810 Strip of 3, #a.-c. 3.75 3.00
Decade of United Nations Against Illegal Drug Abuse and Trafficking.

A811

1996 Summer Olympic Games, Atlanta: a, Women's gymnastics. b, Soccer. c, Marathon race. d, Hurdles. e, Equestrian show jumping.

1996, July 19 — Perf. 14x14½
1985 A811 Strip of 5, #a.-e. 7.25 7.25

Motion Pictures, Cent. — A812

1996, Aug. 6 — Litho. Perf. 13½
Color of Film Cells
1986 A812 1.80p grn, ocher & vio .55 .45
1987 A812 1.80p pur, grn & red .55 .45
　　a. Pair, #1986-1987 2.75 2.75

Justice Dept., 60th Anniv. — A813

1996, Aug. 18
1988 A813 1.80p multicolored 1.00 .60

14th Mexico City Marathon — A814

1996, Aug. 20
1989 A814 2.70p multicolored 1.10 .70

City of Zacatecas, 450th Anniv. — A815

1996, Sept. 8
1990 A815 1.80p multicolored 1.10 .70

Natl. Council to Promote Education, 25th Anniv. — A816

1996, Sept. 17
1991 A816 1.80p multicolored 1.10 .70

Souvenir Sheet

City of Monterrey, 400th Anniv. — A817

1996, Sept. 20
1992 A817 7.40p multicolored 4.75 4.75

Family Planning — A818

1996, Sept. 26
1993 A818 1.80p multicolored 1.10 .70

Independence, 175th Anniv. — A819

1996, Sept. 27
1994 A819 1.80p multicolored 1.10 .70

MEXICO

Endangered Species — A820

Designs show a wide variety of species, one from each stamp is: a, Aguila arpia. b, Tortola serrana. c, Monarch butterflies. d, Vernado bura. e, Guacamaya roja. f, Quetzal. g, Venado cola blanca. h, Puma. i, Coyote. j, Jaguar. k, Martucha. l, Woodpecker. m, Cuco canelo. n, Lince. o, Oso hormiguero. p, Ocelote. q, Encino. r, Chachalaca. s, Liebre. t, Tapir. u, Crocodile. v, Armadillo. w, Pecari. x, Cacomixtle.

1996, Oct. 2 Sheet of 24
1995 A820 1.80p #a.-x. + label 32.50 32.50
See US No. 3105.

World Post Day — A821
1996, Oct. 9
1996 A821 2.70p multicolored 1.10 .70

Salvador Zubirán Natl. Nutrition Institute, 50th Anniv. — A822
1996, Oct. 12
1997 A822 1.80p multicolored 1.10 .70

Radio in Mexico, 75th Anniv. — A823
1996, Oct. 13
1998 A823 1.80p multicolored 1.10 .70

Paintings in Viceregal Gallery — A824

Designs: a, 1.80p, Portrait of a Woman, by Baltasar de Echave Ibia. b, 2.70p, Archangel Michael, by Luis Juarez. c, 1.80p, Portrait of young Joaquín Manuel Fernández of Santa Cruz, by Nicolas Rodriguez Xuarez. d, 2.70p. The Virgin of the Apocalypse, by Miguel Cabrera. e, 1.80p, Portrait of Dona Maria Luisa Gonzaga Foncerrada y Labarrieta, by Jose Maria Vazquez.

1996, Oct. 14 Perf. 14
1999 A824 Strip of 5, #a.-e. 6.00 6.00

World Food Day — A825
1996, Oct. 31 Perf. 13½
2000 A825 2.70p multicolored 1.10 .70

Mexican Science — A826
1996, Sept. 2
2001 A826 1.80p multicolored 1.10 .70

Intl. Subway Conference A828
1996, Nov. 12 Litho. Perf. 13½
2003 A828 2.70p multicolored 1.10 .70

Christmas A829

1p, Star pinata. 1.80p, Man carrying pinatas.

1996, Nov. 14 Litho. Perf. 13½
2004 A829 1p multi .50 .30
2005 A829 1.80p multi .95 .45

Andres Henestrosa, Writer — A830
1996, Nov. 23 Litho. Perf. 14
2006 A830 1.80p multicolored 1.10 .70

Natl. Cancer Institute, 50th Anniv. — A831
1996, Nov. 25 Litho. Perf. 13½
2007 A831 1.80p multicolored 1.10 .70

Paisano Program — A832
1996, Nov. 28 Litho. Perf. 13½
2008 A832 2.70p multicolored 1.10 .70

David Alfaro Siqueiros (1896-1974), Painter — A833
1996, Dec. 5 Litho. Perf. 13½
2009 A833 1.80p multicolored 1.10 .70

32nd Natl. Assembly of Surgeons — A834

Dr. José Ma. Barceló de Villagrán

1996, Dec. 6 Litho. Perf. 13½
2010 A834 1.80p multicolored 1.10 .70

Wildlife Conservation A835

1.80p, Black bear, cubs.

1996, Dec. 11 Litho. Perf. 14
2011 A835 1.80p multi 2.50 1.75

UNICEF, 50th Anniv. — A836
1996, Dec. 11 Litho. Perf. 13½
2012 A836 1.80p multicolored 1.10 .70

Palafoxiana Library, Puebla, 350th Anniv. — A837
1996, Dec. 17 Litho. Perf. 13½
2013 A837 1.80p multicolored 1.10 .70

Natl. Institute of Nuclear Research — A838
1996, Dec. 19 Litho. Perf. 13½
2014 A838 1.80p multicolored 1.10 .70

A839
1996, Dec. 19 Litho. Perf. 13½
2015 A839 1.80p multicolored 1.10 .70
Intl. Day for Preservation of the Ozone Layer.

A840
1996, Dec. 20 Litho. Perf. 13½
2016 A840 1.80p multicolored 1.10 .70
30 year career of plastic arts sculptor Sebastian.

Mexican Diplomats A841

Design: Isidro Fabela (b. 1882), lawyer, and Genaro Estrada (1887-1977), journalist, politician.

1996, Oct. 24 Litho. Perf. 13½
2017 A841 1.80p multicolored 1.10 .70

Carlos Pellicer (1897-1977), Poet, Museum Founder — A842
1997, Jan. 16
2018 A842 2.30p multicolored 1.25 .75

Andres Eloy Blanco (1896-1955), Poet — A843
1997, Feb. 6 Litho. Perf. 13½
2019 A843 3.40p multicolored 1.60 1.05

A844
1997, Feb. 10
2020 A844 3.40p multicolored 1.60 1.05
UNESCO Intl. Summit on Education, Confederation of American Educators.

A845
1997, Feb. 14
2021 A845 3.40p multicolored 1.60 1.05
Treaty of Tlatelolco prohibiting nuclear weapons in Latin America & Caribbean.

Souvenir Sheet

Mexican Central Post Office, 90th Anniv. — A846
1997, Feb. 20
2022 A846 7.40p multicolored 6.25 6.25

A847

Generals: No. 2023, Francisco L. Urquizo. No. 2024, Mariano Escobedo. No. 2025, Jacinto B. Trevino Gonzalez. No. 2026, Felipe Angeles. No. 2027, Candido Aguilar Vargas. No. 2028, Joaquin Amaro Dominguez.

1997, Mar. 5
2023 A847 2.30p multicolored 1.10 .70
2024 A847 2.30p multicolored 1.10 .70
2025 A847 2.30p multicolored 1.10 .70
2026 A847 2.30p multicolored 1.10 .70
2027 A847 2.30p multicolored 1.10 .70
2028 A847 2.30p multicolored 1.10 .70
Nos. 2023-2028 (6) 6.60 4.20

Intl. Women's Day — A848
1997, Mar. 8
2029 A848 2.30p multicolored 1.00 .60

1st Intl. Congress for Spanish Language A849

MEXICO

Painting: Allegory, "La Gramatica," by Juan Correa.

1997, Apr. 7   Litho.   Perf. 13½
2030 A849 3.40p multicolored   1.25 .70

A850

1997, Apr. 23
2031 A850 2.30p multicolored   1.00 .60
Dr. Ignacio Chávez, Pres. of National Academy of Medicine, Birth Cent.

Mexican Constitution, 80th Anniv. — A851

2.30p, Venustiano Carranza.

1997, Apr. 29
2032 A851 2.30p multi   1.00 .60

First Edition of "Al Filo Del Agua," by Agustín Yáñez, 50th Anniv. — A852

1997, May 9
2033 A852 2.30p multicolored   1.00 .60

Prof. Rafael Ramírez (1855-1959), Educator — A853

1997, May 15
2034 A853 2.30p green & gray   1.00 .60

Japanese Emigration to Mexico, Cent. — A854

1997, May 12
2035 A854 3.40p multicolored   2.00 1.35
See Japan No. 2569.

A855

1997, May 31
2036 A855 2.30p multicolored   1.00 .60
Autonomous University of Baja California, 40th Anniv.

A856

Intl. Day to Stop Use of Illegal Drugs: a, 2.30p, Dove, clouds, sunlight. b, 3.40p, Man with one hand on bars, one hand raised toward sky. c, 3.40p, Dove in window behind bars.

1997, June 26
2037 A856 Strip of 3, #a.-c.   6.25 6.25
  a. Strip of 3, #a.-c. + label   12.00 12.00

Sigmund Freud — A857

1997, June 28
2038 A857 2.30p multicolored   1.00 .60

Naval Military School, Cent. — A858

1997, July 1
2039 A858 2.30p multicolored   1.00 .60

Natl. Bank of Foreign Commerce, 60th Anniv. — A859

1997, July 4   Litho.   Perf. 13½
2040 A859 3.40p multicolored   1.50 .95

United for Conservation A860

1997, July 16
2041 A860 2.30p Vaquita, calf   2.25 1.75

Mexican College of Aviation Pilots, 50th Anniv. — A861

1997, July 17
2042 A861 2.30p multicolored   1.10 .70

15th Mexico City Marathon — A862

1997, Aug. 6
2043 A862 3.40p multicolored   1.50 .95

Juarez Hospital of Mexico, 150th Anniv. — A863

1997, Aug. 18
2044 A863 2.30p multicolored   1.10 .70

Battles of 1847 — A864

No. 2045, Battle of Padierna. No. 2046, Battle of Churubusco. No. 2047, Battle of Molino del Rey. No. 2047A, Defense of the Castle of Chapultepec.

1997
2045 A864 2.30p multicolored   .75 .70
2046 A864 2.30p multicolored   .75 .70
2047 A864 2.30p multicolored   .75 .70
2047A A864 2.30p multicolored   2.75 1.50
  Nos. 2045-2047A (4)   5.00 3.60
Issued: No. 2045, 8/19; No. 2046, 8/20; No. 2047, 9/8; No. 2047A, 9/13.

A865

1997, Sept. 3
2048 A865 2.30p multicolored   1.10 .70
Guillermo Prieto, poet, death cent.

A866

1997, Sept. 12   Litho.   Perf. 13½
2049 A866 3.40p multicolored   1.50 .95
Battalion of St. Patrick, 150th anniv. See Ireland No. 1085.

A867

1997, Oct. 6
2050 A867 2.30p multicolored   1.10 .70
Reproductive health for adolescents month.

Stamp Day — A868

1997, Oct. 9
2051 A868 3.40p multi   1.50 .95

Heinrich von Stephan (1831-97) — A869

1997, Oct. 9
2052 A869 3.40p multicolored   1.50 .95

Manuel Gómez Morin (1897-1949), Politician — A870

1997, Oct. 14
2053 A870 2.30p multicolored   1.10 .70

Dr. Manuel Gea González General Hospital, 50th Anniv. — A871

1997, Oct. 14
2054 A871 2.30p multicolored   1.10 .70

Mexican Bar Assoc. College of Law, 75th Anniv. — A872

1997, Oct. 30
2055 A872 2.30p multicolored   1.10 .70

Christmas A873

Children with piñatas: No. 2056, By Ana R. Botello. No. 2057, By Adrián Laris.

1997, Nov. 19
2056 A873 2.30p multicolored   1.10 .70
2057 A873 2.30p multicolored   1.10 .70

New Law on Social Security — A874

1997, Dec. 10
2058 A874 2.30p multicolored   1.10 .70

Central University Hospital, Chihuahua, Cent. — A875

1997, Dec. 5   Litho.   Perf. 13½
2059 A875 2.30p multicolored   1.10 .70

A876

1997, Dec. 8
2060 A876 3.40p multicolored   1.50 .95
Dr. Mario José Molina Henríquez, 1995 Nobel Prize Recipient in Chemistry.

Baking Industry Granary, 50th Anniv. — A877

Baked goods and: a, Storage shelves. b, Man working at oven. c, Basic ingredients, man working with dough.

1997, Dec. 10
2061 A877 2.30p Vert. strip of 3, #a.-c.   5.75 5.75
  a. Vert. strip of 3, #a.-c. + label   12.00 12.00

A878

Modern Mexican art, by Jose Chavez Morado.

1997, Dec. 19
2062 A878 2.30p multicolored   1.10 .70
Cervantes Festival, Guanajuato, 45th anniv.

MEXICO

City of Loreto, 300th Anniv. — A879

1997, Dec. 20
2063 A879 2.30p multicolored 1.10 .70

Military School of Arms, 50th Anniv. — A880

1998, Mar. 1   Litho.   Perf. 13½
2064 A880 2.30p multicolored 1.10 .70

Intl. Mother's Day — A881

1998, Mar. 8
2065 A881 2.30p multicolored 1.10 .70

Cinco de Mayo — A882

1998, Apr. 16
2066 A882 3.50p multicolored 1.50 .95
See US No. 3203.

1998 World Cup Soccer Championships, France — A883

Eiffel Tower, national colors of France and Mexico and: No. 2067, Soccer player. No. 2068, Mexican Eagle mascot.
No. 2069: a, 8.60p, like #2067. b, 6.20p, like #2068.

1998
2067 A883 2.30p multicolored 1.75 1.50
2068 A883 2.30p multicolored 1.75 1.50
Souvenir Sheet
2069 A883 Sheet of 2, #a.-b. 8.50 8.50
Issued: No. 2067, 4/20; No. 2068, 5/11; No. 2069, 5/25. No. 2069 contains two 24x40mm stamps with a continuous design.

Justo Sierra, Educator, 150th Birth Anniv. — A884

1998, Apr. 23
2070 A884 2.30p multicolored 1.10 .70

Dr. Salvador Zubiran, Birth Cent. — A885

1998, Apr. 24
2071 A885 2.30p multicolored 1.10 .70

Organization of American States, 50th Anniv. — A886

1998, Apr. 27
2072 A886 3.40p multicolored 1.30 .75

University of Puebla, 25th Anniv. — A887

1998, May 6
2073 A887 2.30p multicolored 1.10 .70

Teacher's Day — A888

2.30p, Soledad Anaya Solorzano.

1998, May 15
2074 A888 2.30p multi 1.10 .70

State of Tamaulipas (New Santander), 250th Anniv. — A889

1998, May 31
2075 A889 2.30p multicolored 1.10 .70

Sports Lottery, 20th Anniv. — A890

1998, June 2
2076 A890 2.30p multicolored 1.10 .70

Universal Declaration of Human Rights, 50th Anniv. — A891

1998, June 5   Litho.   Perf. 13½
2077 A891 3.40p multicolored 1.25 .75

Federico García Lorca (1898-1936), Poet — A892

1998, June 5
2078 A892 3.40p multicolored 1.30 .75

Philippine Independence, Cent. — A893

3.40p, Mexican flag, sailing ship. 7.40p, Mexican, Philippine flags, sailing ship.

1998, June 3   Litho.   Perf. 13½
2079 A893 3.40p multicolored 1.30 .75
Souvenir Sheet
2080 A893 7.40p multicolored 5.00 5.00
See Philippines Nos. 2537-2539, Spain No. 2949.

Intl. Day Against Drugs — A894

1998, June 26
2081 A894 2.30p multicolored 1.10 .70

Chapultepec Zoological Park, 7th Anniv. — A895

Design: Alfonso L. Herrera, jaguar.

1998, July 6
2082 A895 2.30p multicolored 1.10 .70

Arbor Day — A896

1998, July 9
2083 A896 2.30p multicolored 1.10 .70

Opening of the Philatelic Museum, Oaxaca — A897

Designs: No. 2084, Convent of St. Peter and St. Paul, Teposcolula. No. 2085, Burnished vase with carving. No. 2086, San Bartolo Coyotepec, "El Camino," by Francisco Toledo. No. 2087, Golden breast plate from Tomb 7, Monte Alban.

1998, July 9
2084 A897 2.30p multicolored 1.00 .70
2085 A897 2.30p multicolored 1.00 .70
2086 A897 3.40p multicolored 2.10 1.35
2087 A897 3.40p multicolored 2.10 1.35
Nos. 2084-2087 (4) 6.20 4.10

A898

1998, July 18   Perf. 14
2088 A898 2.30p multicolored 1.10 .70
Precinct in Natl. Palace Honoring Benito Juárez (1806-72).

Santo Domingo Cultural Center, Oaxaca — A899

a, Entire complex. b, Portals of museum. c, Francisco da Burgoa Library. d, Ethnobotanical Garden.

1998, July 24   Perf. 13½
2089 A899 2.30p Block of 4, #a.-d. 5.25 5.25

Marine Life — A900

a, Frigatebird, gray whale. b, Albatross. c, Whale's tail flukes. d, Dolphins, flamingos. e, Turtles. f, Sea lions. g, Elegant swallows, dolphin. h, Killer whale. i, Flamingos. j, Alligator. k, Sardines. l, Squid, loggerhead turtle. m, Bluefin tuna, jellyfish. n, Barracudas. o, Manatee. p, Garibaldi. q, Hammerhead shark. r, Huachinango, shrimp, ray. s, Octopus, mero. t, Blowfish, turtle. u, Crab, sandollars. v, Seahorse, angelfish. w, Crab, turtle, moray eel. x, Mariposa de cuatro ojos. y, Shark, coral.

1998, Aug. 14   Sheet of 25
2090 A900 2.30p #a.-y. 31.00 31.00
No. 2090 is a continuous design showing many different species of marine life, aquatic birds, and surrounding vegetation. Just a few species from each stamp are described in the above design note.

16th Mexico City Marathon — A901

1998, Aug. 19   Litho.   Perf. 13½
2091 A901 3.40p multicolored 1.30 .75

World Tourism Day — A902

1998, Sept. 25
2092 A902 3.40p multicolored 1.30 .75

Natl. Archives, 175th Anniv. — A903

1998, Sept. 29   Perf. 14
2093 A903 2.30p multicolored 1.10 .70

Interpol, 75th Anniv. — A904

1998, Oct. 1   Perf. 13½
2094 A904 3.40p multicolored 1.30 .75

Reproductive Health Month — A905

1998, Oct. 5
2095 A905 2.30p multicolored .95 .45

MEXICO

Luis Nishizawa (b. 1918), Painter — A906

1998, Oct. 9
2096 A906 2.30p multicolored   .95 .45

World Post Day — A907

1998, Oct. 9
2097 A907 3.40p multicolored   1.30 .75

Heroic Military College, 175th Anniv. — A908

1998, Oct. 11
2098 A908 2.30p multicolored   .95 .45

District of Tamaulipas, 250th Anniv. — A909

1998, Oct. 12
2099 A909 2.30p multicolored   .95 .45

United for Conservation A910

1998, Oct. 13
2100 A910 2.30p Aguila real   .95 .45

World Food Day — A911

1998, Oct. 16
2101 A911 3.40p multicolored   1.30 .75

Natl. Mexican Migration Week — A912

1998, Oct. 19
2102 A912 2.30p multicolored   .95 .45

José Alfredo Jiménez (1926-72), Composer A913

1998, Nov. 11
2103 A913 2.30p multicolored   .95 .45

College of Petroleum Engineers, 25th Anniv. — A914

1998, Nov. 11
2104 A914 3.40p multicolored   1.30 .75

A915

1998, Nov. 12
2105 A915 3.40p multicolored   1.30 .75

Cultural and Economic Cooperation Between Mexico and France.

City of Colima, 175th Anniv. — A916

1998, Nov. 16
2106 A916 2.30p multicolored   .95 .45

Christmas A917

Children's drawings: 2.30p, Nativity scene. 3.40p, Pinata, candy, vert.

1998, Nov. 17 Self-Adhesive
2107 A917 2.30p multicolored   .85 .45
2108 A917 3.40p multicolored   1.40 .75

Latin American Civil Aviation Commission, 25th Anniv. — A918

1998, Dec. 14 Litho. Perf. 13½
2109 A918 3.40p multicolored   1.30 .75

Natl. Institute of Native People, 50th Anniv. — A919

1998, Dec. 4
2110 A919 2.30p multicolored   .95 .45

Federation of Govt. Workers, 60th Anniv. — A920

1998, Dec. 7
2111 A920 2.30p multicolored   .95 .45

State University of Sinaloa, 125th Anniv. — A921

1998, Dec. 18
2112 A921 2.30p multicolored   .95 .45

Mexico's Natl. Program for Women — A922

1999, Mar. 8 Litho. Perf. 13½
2113 A922 4.20p multicolored   1.50 .95

Carnaval '99, Veracruz — A923

1999, Feb. 9
2114 A923 3p multicolored   1.25 .70

A924

1999, Feb. 27
2115   3p Hammock   .75 .50
2116   4.20p Divers   1.00 .70
  a. A924 Pair, #2115-2116   1.50 1.50

Acapulco, 200th Anniv.

Launching of SATMEX 5 — A925

1999, Feb. 9
2117 A925 3p multicolored   1.30 .70

Souvenir Sheet

Visit of Pope John Paul II A926

1999, Jan. 22
2118 A926 10p multicolored   5.25 5.25

Tourism Type of 1993
Denomination Shown As $

Nos. 2119, 2122, 2126, 2136, Coahuila. Nos. 2120, 2128, Yucatan. Nos. 2121, 2130, 2139A, 2141A, Chiapas. No. 2124, Colima. Nos. 2125, 2131, 2134, 2141B, Michoacan, vert. No. 2127, Guanajuato. Nos. 2128, 2137, 2140, Zacatecas, vert. No. 2129, Mexico. No. 2130, Sonora. Nos. 2132, 2135, 2141C-2141D, Queretaro. Nos. 2133, 2138, Sinaloa. No. 2141, Campeche.

Unwmk.

		Photo.		Perf. 14
1999-2001				
2119	A683	50c multi	.80	.25
2120	A683	70c multi	1.00	.25
2121	A683	1.50p multi	1.00	.25
2122	A683	2p multi	1.00	.25
2123	A683	2.50p multi	1.30	.25
2124	A683	2.60p multi	2.10	.30
2125	A683	3p multi	1.75	.30
2126	A683	3.60p multi	1.75	.40
2127	A683	4.20p multi	1.75	.45
2128	A683	4.20p multi	3.00	.45
2129	A683	4.50p multi	3.00	.50
2130	A683	4.90p multi	3.00	.50
2131	A683	5.30p multi	4.00	.55
2132	A683	5.90p multi	3.50	.55
2133	A683	6p multi	3.50	.70
2134	A683	6p multi	4.25	.70
2135	A683	6.50p multi	4.75	.70
2136	A683	7p multi	4.75	.75
2137	A683	8p multi	9.50	.85
2138	A683	8p multi	5.00	.85
2139	A683	8.50p multi	5.00	.90
2139A	A683	8.50p denom. upright	5.75	1.10
2140	A683	8.50p multi	2.00	.95
2141	A683	10p multi	19.00	13.50
2141A	A683	10p multi	8.00	5.75
2141B	A683	10.50p multi	7.25	5.25
2141C	A683	11.50p multi	9.00	6.50
2141D	A683	30p multi	20.00	14.50
Nos. 2119-2141D (28)			139.50	58.25

Issued: Nos. 2122, 2124, 2126, 2127, 2130-2133, 2137, 1999; No. 2120, 2000; Nos. 2119, 2121, 2123, 2125, 2128, 2129, 2134-2136, 2138-2141D, 2001.
The denomination of No. 2139 is in italics.

Natl. Commission to Distribute Free Textbooks, 40th Anniv. — A927

1999, Mar. 11 Litho. Perf. 13½
2142 A927 3p gold & multi   1.30 .75

See Nos. 2155-2156, 2172.

Natl. Population Commission, 25th Anniv. — A928

1999, Mar. 26
2143 A928 3p multicolored   1.25 .75

Souvenir Sheet

Ponciano Díaz Salinas (1856-99), Bullfighter — A929

Sheet Size: 95x240mm

1999, Apr. 17
2144 A929 10p Sheet of 1   5.25 5.25

Ceniceros de Pérez (1908-68), Teacher — A930

1999, May 15
2145 A930 3p multicolored   1.25 .70

Teacher's Day.

AAA Mexican Baseball League, 75th Anniv. — A931

MEXICO

Designs: a, Skeleton pitcher, skeleton batter. b, Stylized pitcher. c, Pitcher lifting up large foot, sun. d, Catcher.

1999, May 31
2146 A931 3p Block of 4, #a.-d. 6.00 6.00
Also available in strip of 4 + label.

National Bank of Mexico, 115th Anniv. — A932

Designs: No. 2147, Old, new bank buildings. No. 2148, 10p bill.

1999, June 2
2147 A932 3p multicolored 1.10 .70
2148 A932 3p multicolored 1.10 .70

World Dog Show — A933

a, 4.20p, Chihuahua. b, 4.20p, Xoloitzcuintle. c, 3p, German shepherd. d, 3p, Rottweiler.

1999, June 2
2149 A933 Sheet of 4, #a.-d. 8.50 8.50

A934

Perf. 13¼x13½ Litho.
1999, June 25
2150 A934 4.20p multicolored 1.50 .95
Intl. Day Against Illegal Drugs.

National Bank, 65th Anniv. — A935

1999, July 2 Litho. *Perf. 13¼x13½*
2151 A935 3p multicolored 1.10 .70

Arbor Day — A936

1999, July 26 *Perf. 13½x13¼*
2152 A936 3p multicolored 1.10 .70

Civil Register, 140th Anniv. — A937

1999, July 27
2153 A937 3p multicolored 1.10 .70

17th Mexico City Marathon — A938

1999, Aug. 11
2154 A938 4.20p multicolored 2.00 1.35

Free Textbook Type of 1999
Designs: No. 2155, Children, book, flag, cacti. No. 2156, "Tsuni tsame."

1999 Litho. *Perf. 13¼x13½*
2155 A927 3p green & multi 1.10 .70
2156 A927 3p orange & multi 1.10 .70
Issued: No. 2155, 8/23; No. 2156, 10/28.

Self-portrait, by Rufino Tamayo (1899-1991) — A939

1999, Aug. 28 *Perf. 13¼x13½*
2157 A939 3p multicolored 1.10 .70

City of Toluca, Bicent. — A940

1999, Sept. 12 *Perf. 13½x13¼*
2158 A940 3p copper & brown 1.10 .70

State of Mexico, 175th Anniv. — A941

1999, Sept. 14
2159 A941 3p multicolored 1.25 .75

Union of Latin American Universities, 50th Anniv. — A942

1999, Sept. 22 *Perf. 13¼x13½*
2160 A942 4.20p multicolored 1.50 .95

Institute of Security & Social Services of State Workers, 40th Anniv. — A943

1999, Oct. 1 *Perf. 13½x13¼*
2161 A943 3p multicolored 1.25 .75

State of Baja California Sur, 25th Anniv. — A944

1999, Oct. 4
2162 A944 3p multicolored 1.25 .75

Family Planning, 25th Anniv. — A945

1999, Oct. 4
2163 A945 3p multicolored 1.25 .75

Nature Conservation A946

1999, Oct. 5
2164 A946 3p Harpy eagle 1.25 1.50

State of Quintana Roo, 25th Anniv. — A947

1999, Oct. 8 Litho. *Perf. 13¼x13½*
2165 A947 3p multicolored 1.25 .75

UPU, 125th Anniv. — A948

1999, Oct. 9
2166 A948 4.20p multicolored 1.75 1.15

World Post Day — A949

1999, Oct. 9
2167 A949 4.20p multicolored 1.75 1.15

12th General Assembly of the Int'l Council on Monuments and Sites — A950

1999, Oct. 17 *Perf. 13½x13¼*
2168 A950 4.20p multicolored 1.75 1.15

Carlos Chavez (1899-1978) & Silvestre Revueltas (1899-1940), Composers A951

1999, Oct. 21
2169 A951 3p multicolored 1.25 .75

Autonomous Metropolitan University, 25th Anniv. — A952

1999, Oct. 25 *Perf. 13¼x13½*
2170 A952 3p multicolored 1.25 .75

State of Guerrero, 150th Anniv. — A953

1999, Oct. 27 Litho. *Perf. 13½x13¼*
2171 A953 3p multicolored 1.25 .75

Free Textbook Type of 1999
Design: "Ciencias Naturales."

Perf. 13¼x13½
1999, Nov. 12 Litho.
2172 A927 3p multi 1.25 .75

Christmas
A954 A955

Designs: 3p, Piñata surrounded by children. 4.20p, Piñata and various fruits.

1999, Nov. 29
2173 A954 3p multi 1.25 .75
2174 A955 4.20p multi 2.50 1.35

Natl. Commission of Professional Education, 20th Anniv. — A956

1999, Dec. 1 *Perf. 13½x 13¼*
2175 A956 3p multi 1.25 .75

Scientific Voyage of Alexander von Humboldt to Americas, Bicent. — A957

1999, Dec. 1
2176 A957 3p multi 1.25 .75

The 20th Century — A958

Education: a, 3p, Natl. Autonomous University of Mexico. b, 3p, Justo Sierra, José Vasconcelos. c, 3p, Natl. Poytechnic Institute. d, 3p, Free text books. e, 4.20p, Reading programs.

Litho. & Embossed
1999, Dec. 15 *Perf. 14x14½*
2177 A958 Sheet of 5, #a.-e. 11.25 11.25
Nos. 2177c-2177d are 79x25mm, No. 2177e is oval-shaped and 39x49mm.
See Nos. 2180-2181, 2191-2196.

2000 Census — A959

2000, Jan. 24 Litho. *Perf. 13¼x13½*
2178 A959 3p multi 1.25 1.00

International Women's Day — A960

2000, Mar. 8 Litho. *Perf. 13¼x13½*
2179 A960 4.20p multi 1.75 1.50

MEXICO

The 20th Century Type of 1999
Building Democracy — No. 2180: a, 3p, Mexican presidents from Porfirio Díaz to Lázaro Cárdenas, Mexican Constitution. b, 3p, Pancho Villa, Emiliano Zapata. c, 3p, Mexican presidents from Manuel Avila Camacho to Gustavo Díaz Ordaz. d, 3p, Political figures, protestors, newspaper boy. e, 4.20p, Voter registration card, child at ballot box.
10p, People writing and at computers.

2000, Mar. 16   **Litho. & Embossed**   **Perf. 14x14½**
2180   A958   Sheet of 5, #a-e   11.25   11.25

Souvenir Sheet
Litho.   **Perf. 13½**
2181   A958   10p multi   7.75   7.75

Nos. 2180a and 2180b are 79x25mm, and No. 2180e is oval-shaped and 39x49mm.

A961

Perf. 13½x13¼   **Litho.**
2000, Mar. 24
2182   A961   3p multi   1.25   1.00

National Assoc. of Universities and Institutions of Higher Learning, 50th Anniv.

26th Mexican Travel Trade Show, Acapulco — A962

2000, Apr. 9
2183   A962   4.20p multi   1.75   1.50

Discovery of Brazil, 500th Anniv. — A963

2000, Apr. 22
2184   A963   4.20p multi   1.75   1.50

Luis Alvarez Barret (1901-71), Educator — A964

2000, May 15   **Perf. 13¼x13½**
2185   A964   3p multi   1.25   1.00

Teacher's Day.

A965

Art by: 3p, Alejandro Guerra Millán. 4.20p, Carlos Hernández García.

2000, May 17   **Perf. 13½x13¼**
2186   A965   3p multi   1.25   1.00
2187   A965   4.20p multi   1.75   1.50

Stampin' the Future Children's Stamp Design Contest Winners.

A966

2000, May 24
2188   A966   4.20p multi   1.75   1.50

Fourth Meeting of Telecommunications Ministers and Information Industry Leaders.

Intl. Day Against Illegal Drugs — A967

Perf. 13¼x13½
2000, June 26   **Litho.**
2189   A967   4.20p multi   1.75   1.50

National Worker's Housing Fund Institute A968

No. 2190, Sculptures: a, 3p, Pre-Hispanic building. b, 3p, Pre-Hispanic building with stairway. c, 10p, Pre-Hispanic natives in circle.

2000, June 27   **Perf. 14¼x13¼**
2190   A968   Sheet of 3, #a-c   7.50   7.00

The 20th Century Type of 1999
Cultural Identity and Diversity — No. 2191: a, Xóchitl Incuícatl. b, Corre y se va. c, Tercera llamada. . . Cácado! d, Al Hablar como al guisar, su granito de sal. e, Children.
Health — No. 2192: a, Six men, certificate, man in tuberculosis prevention truck. b, Children on line. c, Nine men, posters. d, Poster showing tractor, health care. e, Modern medical equipment.
Art — No. 2193: a, El sello de la casa. b, Espíritu del siglo. c, La luz de México. d, Los nostros en que nos reconocemos. e, Building dome, artists and artwork.
Photography — No. 2194: a, Colchón enrollado, by Manuel Alvarez Bravo. b, Roses, by Tina Modotti. c, Four vertical photos, four horizontal photos. d, Two vertical photos, six horizontal photos. e, Three photos.
Commercial Development and Industrialization — No. 2195: a, Tractor. b, Truck cab. c, Store. d, Automobile. e, Globe.
Communications — No. 2196: a, Telephones and telegraph. b, Roads and bridges. c, Postal services. d, Railroads. e, Satellite, satellite dish, train.

Litho. & Embossed
2000   **Perf. 14x14¼**
2191   Sheet of 5   11.00 11.00
   a.-d.   A958 3p Any single   1.00 1.00
   e.   A958 4.20p multicolored   1.50 1.50
2192   Sheet of 5   11.00 11.00
   a.-d.   A958 3p Any single   1.00 1.00
   e.   A958 4.20p multicolored   1.50 1.50
2193   Sheet of 5   11.00 11.00
   a.-d.   A958 3p Any single   1.00 1.00
   e.   A958 4.20p multicolored   1.50 1.50
2194   Sheet of 5   11.00 11.00
   a.-d.   A958 3p Any single   1.00 1.00
   e.   A958 4.20p multicolored   1.50 1.50
2195   Sheet of 5   11.00 11.00
   a.-d.   A958 3p Any single   1.00 1.00
   e.   A958 4.20p multicolored   1.50 1.50
2196   Sheet of 5   11.00 11.00
   a.-d.   A958 3p Any single   1.00 1.00
   e.   A958 4.20p multicolored   1.50 1.50
   Nos. 2191-2196 (6)   66.00 66.00

Issued: No. 2191, 7/18; No. 2192, 10/24; No. 2193, 11/10; No. 2194, 12/9; No. 2195, 12/20; No. 2196, 12/21.
Nos. 2191c-2196c, 2191d-2196d are 79x25mm and Nos. 2191e-2196e are oval shaped and 39x49mm.

Natl. Program for Development of Handicapped People, 5th Anniv. — A969

2000, Aug. 2   **Litho.**   **Perf. 13¼x13½**
2197   A969   3p multi   1.25   1.00

Latin American Integration Association, 20th Anniv. — A970

2000, Aug. 11   **Perf. 13½x13¼**
2198   A970   4.20p multi   1.75   1.50

Restoration of the Senate, 125th Anniv. — A971

2000, Aug. 17   **Perf. 13¼x13½**
2199   A971   3p multi   1.25   1.00

Souvenir Sheet

Expo 2000, Hanover A972

a, 1p, Mexican soul. b, 1p, Natl. mosaic. c, 1.80p, Future construction. d, 1.80p, Plaza pyramid. e, 2p, Creation of towns. f, 2p, Millennial construction. g, 3p, Naturea. h, 3p, Humanity. i, 3p, Technology. j, 3.60p, Expo 2000, Hanover. k, 4.20p, Emblem.

Litho. & Embossed
2000, Aug. 20   **Perf. 14½x14**
2200   A972   Sheet of 11, #a-k   15.00 15.00

No. 2200k is oval shaped and 39x49mm.

Bank of Mexico, 75th Anniv. A973

2000, Aug. 23   **Litho.**   **Perf.**
2201   A973   10p multi   5.25 5.25

Stamp is oval-shaped and 49x39mm.

18th Mexico City Marathon — A974

2000, Aug. 24   **Perf. 13½x13¼**
2202   A974   4.20p multi   1.75   1.50

2000 Summer Olympics, Sydney — A975

2000, Sept. 15
2203   A975   4.20p multi   1.75   1.50

Paisano Program — A976

2000, Sept. 21
2204   A976   4.20p multi   1.75   1.50

2nd Intl. Memory of the World Conference A977

2000, Sept. 12
2205   A977   4.20p multi   1.75   1.50

Women's Reproductive Health Month — A978

2000, Oct. 5   **Perf. 13¼x13½**
2206   A978   3p multi   1.25   1.00

Ciudad Victoria, 250th Anniv. — A979

2000, Oct. 6   **Perf. 13½x13¼**
2207   A979   3p multi   1.25   1.00

World Post Day — A980

2000, Oct. 9   **Perf. 13¼x13½**
2208   A980   4.20p multi   1.75   1.50

Natl. Human Rights Commission, 10th Anniv. — A981

2000, Oct. 23   **Perf. 13½x13¼**
2209   A981   3p multi   1.25   1.00

World Meteorological Organization, 50th Anniv. — A982

2000, Oct. 27
2210   A982   3p multi   1.25   1.00

Intl. Diabetes Federation, 50th Anniv. — A983

2000, Nov. 6
2211   A983   4.20p multi   1.75   1.50

Telegraphy in Mexico, 150th Anniv. — A984

2000, Nov. 11
2212   A984   3p multi   1.25   1.00

Luis Buñuel (1900-83), Film Director — A985

2000, Nov. 21
2213   A985   3p multi   1.25   1.00

MEXICO

Electrical Research Institute, 25th Anniv. — A986

2000, Nov. 25
2214 A986 3p multi 1.25 1.00

Customs Administration, Cent. — A987

2000, Nov. 28
2215 A987 3p multi 1.25 1.00

Christmas A988

2000, Nov. 29
2216 A988 3p shown 1.25 1.00
2217 A988 4.20p Poinsettias 1.75 1.50

Television in Mexico, 50th Anniv. — A989

2000, Nov. 30
2218 A989 3p multi 1.25 1.00

Souvenir Sheet

Postal Headquarters — A990

No. 2219: a, 3p, Adamo Boari (1863-1928), architect. b, 3p, Roofline. c, 3p, Gonzalo Garita y Frontera (1867-1922), engineer. d, 10p, Headquarters building.

Litho. & Embossed
2000, Nov. 30 Perf. 14¼x13½
2219 A990 Sheet of 4, #a-d 10.00 10.00

Pre-Hispanic City of El Tajín — A991

Perf. 13½x13¼
2000, Dec. 14 Litho.
2220 A991 3p multi 1.25 1.00

Nature Conservation A992

2000, Dec. 15
2221 A992 3p Manatee 1.25 1.00
Stamps inscribed 'Aquila Real / Unidos Para Conservacion' with white, yellow or gray backgrounds and 20c denominations have no postal validity.

Francisco Sarabia (1900-39), Aviator — A993

2000, Dec. 20 Perf. 13¼x13½
2222 A993 3p multi 1.25 1.00

Law Faculty of National Autonomous University of Mexico, 50th Anniv. — A994

2001, Mar. 7 Litho. Perf. 13½x13¼
2223 A994 3p multi 1.25 1.00

Intl. Women's Day — A995

2001, Mar. 8
2224 A995 4.20p multi 1.75 1.50

National Cement Council, 53rd Anniv. — A996

2001, Mar. 27
2225 A996 3p multi 1.25 1.00

Teacher's Day — A997

2001, May 15 Perf. 14
2226 A997 3p José Vasconcelos 1.25 1.00

World Refugee Day — A998

2001, June 20
2227 A998 4.20p multi 1.75 1.50

Frida Kahlo (1907-54), Painter — A999

2001, June 21
2228 A999 4.20p multi 1.75 1.50

Intl. Day Against Illegal Drugs — A1000

2001, June 26
2229 A1000 4.20p multi 1.75 1.50

Mario de la Cueva, Educator, Cent. of Birth — A1001

2001, July 11 Litho. Perf. 14
2230 A1001 3p multi 1.25 1.00

Intl. Volunteers Year — A1002

2001, July 25
2231 A1002 4.20p multi 1.75 1.50

Souvenir Sheet

Rodolfo Morales (1925-2001), Painter — A1003

2001, Aug. 4 Perf. 14¼x13½
2232 A1003 10p multi 4.75 4.75

A1004

2001, Aug. 23 Perf. 14
2233 A1004 3p multi 1.25 1.00
Federal Fiscal and Administrative Justice Tribunal, 65th Anniv.

University of Mexico, 450th Anniv. — A1005

2001, Sept. 3
2234 A1005 3p multi 1.25 1.00

Adela Formoso de Obregón Santcilia (1907-81), Woman's Rights Activist — A1006

2001, Sept. 6
2235 A1006 3p multi 1.25 1.00

Daniel Cosío Villegas (1898-1976), Historian — A1007

2001, Sept. 6
2236 A1007 3p multi 1.25 1.00

Mexican Pharmacies A1008

2001, Sept. 27 Litho. Perf. 14
2237 A1008 3p multi 1.25 1.00

Intl. Day of the Elderly — A1009

2001, Oct. 1
2238 A1009 3p multi 1.25 1.00

Year of Dialogue Among Civilizations — A1010

2001, Oct. 9
2239 A1010 3p multi 1.25 1.00

World Post Day — A1011

2001, Oct. 9
2240 A1011 3p multi 1.25 1.00

Women's Health Day — A1012

2001, Oct. 31
2241 A1012 3p multi 1.25 1.00

Ophthalmology Institute, 25th Anniv. — A1013

2001, Nov. 23
2242 A1013 4.20p multi 1.75 1.50

United for Conservation A1014

2001, Nov. 26
2243 A1014 5.30p Chara pinta 2.75 2.50

Christmas A1015

2001, Dec. 3
2244 A1015 3p shown 1.25 1.00
2245 A1015 4.20p Candles 1.75 1.50

Souvenir Sheet

Fund for Indigenous People's Health and Education — A1016

2001, Dec. 4 Perf. 13½x14¼
2246 A1016 3p multi 1.75 1.50

MEXICO

Souvenir Sheet

National Scholarship Fund — A1017

2001, Dec. 4
2247 A1017 3p multi   1.75 1.45

Children's Protection — A1018

2001, Dec. 11   *Perf. 14*
2248 A1018 3p multi   1.25 1.00

World Food Day — A1019

2001, Dec. 17
2249 A1019 3p multi   1.25 1.00

United For Conservation A1020

2002, Jan. 24   *Litho.*   *Perf. 14*
2250 A1020 6p Borrego cimarrón   2.75 2.50

Manuel Alvarez Bravo, Photographer, Cent. of Birth — A1021

2002, Feb. 3
2251 A1021 6p gray & blk   2.50 2.25

Mexico — People's Republic of China — A1022

Designs: No. 2252, green panel at UL and brown panel at LL. No. 2252A, Like #2252, but with brown panel at UL, green panel at LL.

2002, Feb. 14   *Litho.*   *Perf. 14*
2252   A1022 6p multi   2.25 2.00
2252A A1022 6p multi   2.25 2.00
   b. Vert. pair, #2252-2252A 5.50 5.50

Conservation A1023

Designs: 50c, Mangrove swamps. No. 2254, Rivers. No. 2255, Forests. 1.50p No. 2267, Land mammals. No. 2257, Rain forests. No. 2258, Cacti. 4.50p, Birds. No. 2260, Sea turtles. No. 2261, Reptiles. No. 2262, Butterflies. No. 2263, Eagles. 7p, Reefs. 8.50p, 12p, Tropical forests. No. 2266, Marine mammals. No. 2268, Orchids. No. 2269, Cats. No. 2270, Oceans. No. 2271, Coastal birds. No. 2273, Deserts. No. 2274, Lakes and lagoons.

2002, Feb. 18   *Litho.*   *Perf. 14*
2253 A1023 50c multi   .50   .25
2254 A1023 1p multi   .50   .25
2255 A1023 1p multi   .40   .25
2256 A1023 1.50p multi   .80   .25
2257 A1023 2p multi   .85   .25
2258 A1023 2p multi   .85   .25
2259 A1023 4.50p multi   1.75   .50
2260 A1023 5p multi   2.10   .55
2261 A1023 5p multi   2.10   .55
2262 A1023 6p multi   2.10   .65
2263 A1023 6p multi   2.10   .65
2264 A1023 7p multi   2.60   .75
2265 A1023 8.50p multi   2.90   .95
2266 A1023 10p multi   4.25 1.10
2267 A1023 10p multi   4.25 1.10
2268 A1023 10.50p multi   4.50 1.25
2269 A1023 10.50p multi   4.50 1.25
2270 A1023 11.50p multi   6.25 1.25
2271 A1023 11.50p multi   4.75 1.25
2272 A1023 12p multi   6.50 1.25
2273 A1023 30p multi   16.00 3.25
2274 A1023 30p multi   16.00 3.25
      Nos. 2253-2274 (22)   86.55 21.05

2003   *Perf. 13x13¼*
2253a A1023 50c multi   .50   .25
2254a A1023 1p multi   1.20   .25
2255a A1023 1p multi   .50   .25
2259a A1023 4.50p multi   3.75   .40
2260a A1023 5p multi   2.10   .45
2261a A1023 5p multi   2.10   .45
2262a A1023 6p multi   2.00   .55
2263a A1023 6p multi   2.10   .55
2264a A1023 7p multi   2.60   .65
2265a A1023 8.50p multi   4.00   .75
2266a A1023 10p multi   6.25   .90
2267a A1023 10p multi   6.25   .90
2268a A1023 10.50p multi   7.50   .95
2269a A1023 10.50p multi   7.50   .95
2270a A1023 11.50p multi   7.50 1.00
2271a A1023 11.50p multi   7.50 1.00
      Nos. 2253a-2271a (16)   63.05 10.25

See Nos. 2321-2330, 2362-2377, 2394-2436, 2452-2473.

2002 Winter Olympics, Salt Lake City — A1024

2002, Feb. 20   *Litho.*   *Perf. 14*
2275 A1024 8.50p multi   3.00 2.75

Veracruz Port Modernization, Cent. — A1025

2002, Mar. 4
2276 A1025 6p multi   2.50 2.25

Mexico — South Korea Diplomatic Relations, 40th Anniv. — A1026

2002, Mar. 5
2277 A1026 8.50p multi   3.00 2.75

Council for the Restoration of Historic Central Mexico City — A1027

2002, Mar. 7
2278 A1027 6p multi   2.50 2.25

Natl. Women's Institute — A1028

2002, Mar. 8
2279 A1028 8.50p multi   3.00 2.75

José Guadalupe Posada (1851-1913), Printmaker — A1029

2002, Mar. 18
2280 A1029 6p gold & black   2.50 2.25

Justo Sierra Mendez (1848-1912), Writer — A1030

2002, May 15   *Litho.*   *Perf. 14*
2281 A1030 6p multi   2.50 2.25

UN General Assembly Special Session on Children — A1031

2002, May 27
2282 A1031 6p multi   2.50 2.25

Discovery of the Tomb of Pakal, 50th Anniv. — A1032

2002, June 14
2283 A1032 6p multi   2.50 2.25

2002 World Cup Soccer Championships, Japan and Korea — A1033

2002, June 15
2284 A1033 8.50p multi   3.00 2.75

Intl. Day Against Illegal Drugs — A1034

2002, June 26
2285 A1034 6p multi   2.50 2.25

5th Mexico-Central American Summit — A1035

2002, June 27
2286 A1035 6p multi   2.50 2.25

Intl. Year of Mountains A1036

2002, July 24   *Litho.*   *Perf. 14*
2287 A1036 6p multi   2.50 2.25

Intl. Day of Indigenous People — A1037

2002, Aug. 9   *Perf. 13¼x14*
2288 A1037 6p multi   2.50 2.25

Federal Electricity Commission A1038

2002, Aug. 14   *Perf. 14*
2289 A1038 6p multi   2.50 2.25

Natl. Blood Donor Day — A1039

2002, Aug. 23   *Perf. 13¼x13*
2290 A1039 6p multi   2.50 2.25

Campaign Against Corruption A1040

2002, Sept. 12   *Litho.*   *Perf. 13x13¼*
2291 A1040 6p multi   2.50 2.25

Code of Ethics for Public Servants — A1041

2002, Sept. 12   *Perf. 13¼x13*
2292 A1041 6p multi   2.50 2.25

World Tourism Day — A1042

2002, Sept. 27   *Perf. 13x13¼*
2293 A1042 8.50p multi   3.60 2.75

Natl. Organ Transplant and Donation Week — A1043

2002, Oct. 7   *Perf. 13¼x13*
2294 A1043 6p multi   2.50 2.25

World Post Day — A1044

2002, Oct. 9   *Perf. 13x13¼*
2295 A1044 8.50p multi   3.00 2.75

State of Baja California, 50th Anniv. — A1045

2002, Nov. 1
2296 A1045 6p multi   2.50 2.25

Luis Barragan (1902-88), Architect — A1046

2002, Nov. 7   *Perf. 13¼x13*
2297 A1046 6p multi   2.50 2.25

MEXICO

A1047

2002, Nov. 19   *Perf. 13x13¼*
2298 A1047 8.50p multi   3.00   2.75
Renewal of Diplomatic Relations Between Mexico and Spain, 25th Anniv.

Mexico City Intl. Airport, 50th Anniv. — A1048

Details from mural "The Conquest of the Air by Man": a, Indian chief at left, Montgolfier balloon flight at right. b, Charles Lindbergh at left, parachutist at center. c, Wright Brothers at left, Mexico City at center.

2002, Nov. 19   *Perf. 13¼x13*
2299   Horiz. strip of 3   8.25   8.25
a.-b. A1048 6p Either single   2.50   2.50
c. A1048 8.50p multi   3.00   3.00

Information Technology Development in Mexico, 75th Anniv. — A1049

2002, Nov. 21
2300 A1049 6p multi   2.00   1.75

Anti-Violence Campaign A1050

2002, Nov. 25   *Perf. 13x13¼*
2301 A1050 8.50p multi   2.75   2.50

Pan-American Health Organization, Cent. — A1051

2002, Dec. 2   *Perf. 13¼x13*
2302 A1051 8.50p multi   2.00   1.75

Acolmiztli Nezahualcóyotl (1402-72), Poet — A1052

2002, Dec. 10
2303 A1052 6p multi   2.00   1.75

Christmas A1053

Children's art: 6p, Nativity, by Sara Elisa Miranda Alcaraz. 8.50p, Children with Nativity Scene, by Alejandro Ruíz Sampedro.

2002, Dec. 19   *Perf. 13x13¼*
2304 A1053   6p multi   2.00   1.75
2305 A1053 8.50p multi   2.75   2.50

Powered Flight, Cent. — A1054

2003, Mar. 6   *Litho.*   *Perf. 13x13¼*
2306 A1054 8.50p multi   2.75   2.50

Iberoamerican University, 60th Anniv. — A1055

2003, Mar. 7   *Perf. 13¼x13*
2307 A1055 6p multi   2.00   1.75

Intl. Women's Day — A1056

2003, Mar. 8
2308 A1056 8.50p multi   2.75   2.50

Mexicali, Cent. — A1057

2003, Mar. 14   *Perf. 13x13¼*
2309 A1057 6p multi   2.00   1.75

Mexican Chamber of Industry and Construction, 50th Anniv. — A1058

2003, Mar. 26
2310 A1058   6p multi   1.75   1.75

Federico Gomez Children's Hospital, 60th Anniv. — A1059

2003, Apr. 30   *Litho.*   *Perf. 13x13¼*
2311 A1059 6p multi   2.00   1.75

Miguel Hidalgo y Costilla (1753-1811), Independence Leader — A1060

2003, May 8   *Perf. 13¼x13*
2312 A1060 6p multi   2.00   1.75
a.   Perf 14   350.00   350.00

Gregorio Torres Quintero (1866-1934), Educator — A1061

2003, May 15
2313 A1061 6p multi   2.00   1.75
a.   Perf 14   150.00   —

Natl. Astronomical Observatory, 125th Anniv. — A1062

2003, May 20   *Perf. 13¼x13*
2314 A1062 6p multi   2.00   1.75

World Day Against Tobacco — A1063

2003, May 30   *Perf. 13¼x13*
2315 A1063 8.50p multi   2.75   2.50

Inauguration of Satellite Internet Network — A1064

2003, June 5
2316 A1064 6p multi   2.00   1.75

Intl. Day Against Illegal Drugs — A1065

2003, June 26   *Litho.*   *Perf. 13x13¼*
2317 A1065 8.50p multi   2.75   2.50

Mexican Baseball Hall of Fame, 30th Anniv. — A1066

2003, July 21
2318 A1066 6p multi   2.75   1.75

Xavier Villaurrutia (1903-51), Poet — A1067

2003, July 24
2319 A1067 6p multi   2.00   1.75

Veterinary Medicine Education in Mexico, 150th Anniv. — A1068

2003, Aug. 16
2320 A1068 6p multi   2.00   1.75

Conservation Type of 2002

Designs: 50c, Oceans. 1p, Reptiles. No. 2323, Land mammals. No. 2324, Rain forests. No. 2325, Coastal birds. 4.50p, Orchids. 6p, Rivers. 8.50p, Cacti. No. 2329, Lakes and lagoons. No. 2330, Sea turtles.

Perf. 13x13¼, 13½ (#2328)
2003-04   *Litho.*
2321 A1023   50c multi ('04)   .60   .25
2322 A1023   1p multi ('04)   .60   .25
2323 A1023   2.50p multi   1.75   .25
2324 A1023   2.50p multi   1.75   .25
2325 A1023   2.50p multi ('04)   1.50   .25
2326 A1023   4.50p multi ('04)   1.90   .40
2327 A1023   6p multi ('04)   2.40   .55
2328 A1023   8.50p multi ('04)   4.00   .75
2329 A1023   10.50p multi ('04)   5.25   .95
2330 A1023   10.50p multi ('04)   5.00   .95
Nos. 2321-2330 (10)   24.75   4.85

National Pedagogical University, 25th Anniv. — A1069

2003, Aug. 29   *Litho.*   *Perf. 13¼x13*
2331 A1069 6p multi   2.00   1.75

Federico Silva Museum, San Luis Potosí — A1070

2003, Sept. 18   *Perf. 13x13¼*
2332 A1070 6p multi   2.00   1.75

National Organ and Tissue Donation Week — A1071

2003, Sept. 26
2333 A1071 6p multi   2.00   1.75

World Post Day — A1072

2003, Oct. 9   *Perf. 13¼x13*
2334 A1072 8.50p multi   2.50   2.25

Woman Suffrage, 50th Anniv. — A1073

2003, Oct. 16
2335 A1073 6p multi   2.00   1.75

Health Ministry, 60th Anniv. — A1074

2003, Oct. 23   *Perf. 13x13¼*
2336 A1074 6p multi   1.75   1.75

Juarez Theater, Cent. — A1075

2003, Oct. 27
2337 A1075 6p multi   1.75   1.75

Teaching of Law in the Americas, 450th Anniv. — A1076

2003, Nov. 4   *Perf. 13¼x13*
2338 A1076 8.50p multi   2.50   2.25

Central Power and Light, Cent. — A1077

2003, Nov. 18   *Litho.*   *Perf. 13¼x13*
2339 A1077 6p multi   2.00   1.75

Christmas A1078

Children's drawings of Nativity by: 6p, Valeria Báez. 8.50p, Octavio Alemán.

MEXICO

2003, Dec. 3
2340 A1078 6p multi 2.00 1.50
2341 A1078 8.50p multi 2.75 2.25

Children's Rights — A1079

2003, Dec. 5 Perf. 13¼x13
2342 A1079 6p multi 1.75 1.50

Intl. Year of Fresh Water — A1080

2003, Dec. 11
2343 A1080 8.50p multi 2.50 2.25

National Technical Education College, 25th Anniv. — A1081

2003, Dec. 15 Perf. 13x13¼
2344 A1081 6p multi 1.75 1.50

First Visit of Pope John Paul II to Mexico, 25th Anniv. — A1082

2004, Jan. 28 Litho. Perf. 13x13¼
2345 A1082 6p multi 2.25 1.10

Agustín Yáñez (1904-80), Novelist — A1083

2004, May 4
2346 A1083 8.50p multi 1.95 1.50

Enrique Aguilar González — A1084

2004, May 15 Perf. 13¼x13
2347 A1084 8.50p multi 1.75 1.50

Teacher's Day.

Cable Television in Mexico, 50th Anniv. A1085

2004, May 19
2348 A1085 6p multi 1.30 1.10

Mexican Geological Society, Cent. — A1086

2004, June 2 Perf. 13x13¼
2349 A1086 8.50p multi 1.90 1.50

Intl. Day Against Illegal Drugs — A1087

2004, June 25 Perf. 13¼x13
2350 A1087 8.50p multi 1.90 1.50

Salvador Novo (1904-74), Poet — A1088

2004, July 30 Perf. 13x13¼
2351 A1088 7p multi 1.60 1.25

Gilberto Owen (1905-52), Poet — A1089

2004, Aug. 8 Litho. Perf. 13x13¼
2352 A1089 7p multi 1.60 1.25

FIFA (Fédération Internationale de Football Association), Cent. — A1090

2004, Aug. 11
2353 A1090 11.50p multi 2.25 2.00

Mexican Cartooning — A1091

2004, Aug. 13 Perf. 13¼x13
2354 A1091 6p multi 1.40 1.10

2004 Summer Olympics, Athens — A1092

2004, Aug. 13
2355 A1092 10.50p multi 2.50 1.90

Celestino Gorostiza (1904-67), Writer — A1093

2004, Aug. 16 Litho. Perf. 13x13¼
2356 A1093 7p multi 1.60 1.25

Fresnillo, 450th Anniv. — A1094

2004, Sept. 2 Perf. 13¼x13
2357 A1094 7p multi 1.60 1.25

Economic Culture Fund, 70th Anniv. — A1095

2004, Sept. 6 Perf. 13x13¼
2358 A1095 8.50p multi 1.90 1.50

Autonomy of National Autonomous University of Mexico, 75th Anniv. A1096

2004, Sept. 6 Perf. 13¼x13
2359 A1090 11.50p multi 2.50 2.00

Autonomous University of Chihuahua, 50th Anniv. — A1097

2004, Sept. 8 Perf. 13x13¼
2360 A1097 7p multi 1.60 1.25

Palace of Fine Arts, 70th Anniv. — A1098

2004, Sept. 29
2361 A1098 7p multi 1.60 1.25

Conservation Type of 2002
Designs: 50c, Cats. No. 2363, Oceans. No. 2364, Rain forests. 2.50p, No. 2374, Reefs. 4.50p, Forests. 5p, No. 2370, Land mammals. Nos. 2368, 2376, Reptiles. No. 2369, Birds. Nos. 2371, 2375, Deserts. No. 2372, Cacti. No. 2373, Tropical forests. No. 2377, Coastal birds.

2004		Litho.	Perf. 13x13¼	
2362	A1023	50c multi	.55	.25
2363	A1023	1p multi	3.00	.25
2364	A1023	1p multi	.55	.25
2365	A1023	2.50p multi	1.00	.25
2366	A1023	4.50p multi	1.75	.40
2367	A1023	6p multi	2.25	.45
2368	A1023	6p multi	2.25	.55
2369	A1023	6p multi	1.90	.55
2370	A1023	6p multi	2.25	.55
2371	A1023	7p multi	2.25	.60
2372	A1023	7p multi	2.25	.60
2373	A1023	10p multi	3.75	.90
2374	A1023	10p multi	3.75	.90
2375	A1023	10.50p multi	4.50	.95
a.	Microprinting at top in black		4.50	1.00
2376	A1023	30p multi	8.75	2.25
2377	A1023	30p multi	8.75	2.25
Nos. 2362-2377 (16)			49.50	11.95

Microprinting at top on No. 2375 is in gray.

State Workers' Institute of Social Services and Security A1099

2004, Oct. 1 Litho. Perf. 13¼x13
2378 A1099 6p multi 1.40 1.10

Termination of Walled District of Campeche, 300th Anniv. — A1100

2004, Oct. 6 Perf. 13x13¼
2379 A1100 6p multi 1.40 1.10

National Anthem, 150th Anniv. — A1101

2004, Oct. 8
2380 A1101 6.50p multi 1.50 1.25

World Post Day — A1102

2004, Oct. 11
2381 A1102 6p bright rose lilac 1.50 1.10

Admission to UPU, 125th Anniv. — A1103

2004, Oct. 29
2382 A1103 8.50p multi 1.90 1.50

Channel 11 Television — A1104

2004, Nov. 10 Perf. 13¼x13
2383 A1104 8.50p multi 1.75 1.50

Superior Federation Audit, 180th Anniv. A1105

2004, Nov. 16
2384 A1105 6.50p multi 1.50 1.25

Health Secretary's Building, 75th Anniv. — A1106

2004, Nov. 22 Perf. 13x13¼
2385 A1106 8.50p multi 2.00 1.60

Culture on the Radio — A1107

2004, Nov. 30 Perf. 13¼x13
2386 A1107 6.50p multi 1.50 1.25

MEXICO

2004, Nov. 30 — Perf. 13¼x13
2387 A1108 6.50p multi 1.50 1.25

Souvenir Sheet
Perf. 14¼x14
2388 A1108 7.50p multi 1.75 1.40

Natl. Communications and Transportation Department Center, 50th Anniv.

Town of General Escobedo, 400th Anniv. — A1109

2004, Dec. 3 — Perf. 13x13¼
2389 A1109 8.50p multi 1.80 1.60

Natl. Free Textbook Commission, 45th Anniv. — A1110

2004, Dec. 6
2390 A1110 10.50p multi 2.10 1.90

A1111

Christmas — A1112

2004, Dec. 13 — Perf. 13x13¼
2391 A1111 7.50p multi 1.20 1.20

Perf. 13¼x13
2392 A1112 10.50p multi 1.60 1.60

Traffic Accident Prevention — A1113

2004, Dec. 17 Litho. Perf. 13¼x13
2393 A1113 8.50p multi 1.90 1.60

Conservation Type of 2002

Designs: Nos. 2394, 2404, Deserts. Nos. 2395, 2406, 2408, 2411, Orchids. Nos. 2396, 2410, 2419, 2435, Sea turtles. Nos. 2397, 2416, Birds. Nos. 2398, 2401, 2421, 2433, Marine mammals. Nos. 2399, 2425, Oceans. Nos. 2400, 2402, 2424, Cats. Nos. 2403, 2430, Rain forests. Nos. 2405, 2412, Eagles. Nos. 2407, 2415, Lakes and lagoons. Nos. 2409, 2436, Butterflies. Nos. 2413, 2423, Tropical forests. Nos. 2414, 2431, Rivers. Nos. 2417, 2429, Reefs. Nos. 2418, 2427, Forests. Nos. 2420, 2434, Coastal birds. No. 2422, Reptiles. Nos. 2426, 2428, Land mammals. No. 2432, Mangrove swamps.

2004-05 Litho. Perf. 13½x13¼
Inscribed "ROMO" at Lower Right
2394 A1023 50c multi .60 .30
2395 A1023 1p multi .50 .25
2396 A1023 2.50p multi 1.00 .50
2397 A1023 6.50p multi 2.00 1.00
2398 A1023 6.50p multi 190.00 —
2399 A1023 7p multi 3.00 1.50
2400 A1023 7.50p multi 3.00 1.50
2401 A1023 8.50p multi 3.50 1.75
    Complete booklet, 6 #2401 21.00
2402 A1023 10.50p multi 6.50 3.25
    Complete booklet, 6 #2402 39.00
2403 A1023 13p multi 10.00 5.00

Inscribed "TIEV" at Lower Right
Perf. 13x13¼
2404 A1023 50c multi .50 .25
2405 A1023 50c multi .50 .25
2406 A1023 50p multi .75 .40
2407 A1023 1p multi .50 .25
2408 A1023 1p multi .50 .25
  a. Perf. 14 2.00 .80
2409 A1023 2p multi .90 .45
2410 A1023 2.50p multi .90 .45
2411 A1023 2.50p multi .90 .45
2412 A1023 2.50p multi 1.00 .50
2413 A1023 5p multi 2.00 1.00
2414 A1023 5p multi 2.00 1.00
2415 A1023 5p multi 2.00 1.00
2416 A1023 6.50p multi 2.00 1.00
2417 A1023 6.50p multi 2.00 1.00
2418 A1023 6.50p multi 2.00 1.00
  a. Perf. 14x13 350.00 —
  b. Perf. 13x14 350.00 —
2419 A1023 6.50p multi 2.25 1.10
2420 A1023 6.50p multi 2.25 1.10
2421 A1023 6.50p multi 10.00 5.00
2422 A1023 6.50p multi 2.00 1.00
2423 A1023 7p multi 2.00 1.00
2424 A1023 7.50p multi 2.50 1.25
2425 A1023 7.50p multi 2.50 1.25
2426 A1023 7.50p multi, denom. in black 2.50 1.25
  a. Denomination in gray 10.25 5.00
2427 A1023 8.50p multi 3.50 1.75
2428 A1023 10.50p multi 4.25 2.10
2429 A1023 10.50p multi 4.25 2.10
2430 A1023 13p multi 6.50 3.25
2431 A1023 13p multi 6.50 3.25
2432 A1023 13p multi 6.50 3.25
2433 A1023 14.50p multi 7.50 3.75
2434 A1023 14.50p multi 7.50 3.25
2435 A1023 30.50p multi 15.00 7.50
2436 A1023 30.50p multi 15.00 7.50
    Nos. 2394-2436 (43) 341.05 74.95

Issued: Nos. 2401, 2402, 2004. Others, 2005. Colors are duller on stamps inscribed "TIEV" than those on similar stamps inscribed "ROMO."

Mexico General Hospital, Cent. A1114

2005, Feb. 4 Litho. Perf. 13¼x13
2437 A1114 6.50p multi 1.50 1.25

Intl. Women's Day — A1115

2005, Mar. 8 Perf. 13x13¼
2438 A1115 6.50p multi 1.50 1.25

Publication of Pedro Paramo by Juan Rulfo, 50th Anniv. — A1116

2005, Mar. 13
2439 A1116 6.50p multi 1.50 1.25

Natl. University Games — A1117

2005, Apr. 18 Perf. 13¼x13
2440 A1117 7.50p multi 1.60 1.40

World Without Polio — A1118

2005, Apr. 29
2441 A1118 10.50p multi 2.40 1.90

Eulalia Guzmán A1119

2005, May 15 Perf. 13x13¼
2442 A1119 6.50p multi 1.60 1.25

Teacher's Day.

Souvenir Sheet

Publication of Don Quixote, 400th Anniv. — A1120

No. 2443: a, 6.50p, Silhouette of Don Quixote. b, 10.50p, Crowd, horse and rider. c, 10.50p, Don Quixote.

2005, May 23 Perf. 13¼x13
2443 A1120 Sheet of 3, #a-c 5.75 5.75

Intl. Year of Physics A1121

2005, May 26
2444 A1121 7.50p multi 1.75 1.40

Natl. Human Rights Commission A1122

2005, June 5 Perf. 13x13¼
2445 A1122 6.50p multi 1.50 1.25

Society of Mexican Architects, Cent. — A1123

2005, June 8 Perf. 13¼x13
2446 A1123 6.50p multi 1.50 1.25

Intl. Day Against Illegal Drugs — A1124

2005, June 24
2447 A1124 10.50p multi 2.40 2.00

Baseball A1125

2005, June 27
2448 A1125 7.50p multi 1.75 1.40

Information Access and Transparency — A1126

2005, June 27
2449 A1126 6.50p multi 1.50 1.25

Memin Pinguin, by Yolanda Vargas Dulche — A1127

2005, June 28 Perf. 13
2450   Horiz. strip of 5 16.00 16.00
  a.-e. A1127 6.50p Any single 1.90 1.90

Memin Pinguin: a, And comic book page. b, Holding flower. c, Holding open comic book. d, Wearing tuxedo. e, Holding closed book.

Multiple Self-portrait, by Juan O'Gorman (1905-82) — A1128

2005, June 29 Perf. 13¼x13
2451 A1128 7.50p multi 1.60 1.40

Conservation Type of 2002

Designs: No. 2452, Butterflies. Nos. 2453, 2473, Sea turtles. No. 2454, Coastal birds. Nos. 2456, 2463, Marine mammals. Nos. 2457, 2459, Rivers. Nos. 2458, 2462, 2466, Oceans. No. 2460, Lakes and lagoons. Nos. 2461, 2469, Cats. No. 2464, Reptiles. No. 2465, Mangrove swamps. No. 2467, Birds. No. 2468, Cacti. No. 2470, Reefs. No. 2471, Eagles. No. 2472, Tropical forests.

2005 Litho. Perf. 13x13¼
Inscribed "TIEV" at Lower Right
2452 A1023 50c multi .55 .25
2453 A1023 50c multi .55 .25
2454 A1023 1p multi .55 .25
2456 A1023 1p multi .55 .25
2457 A1023 2.50p multi .90 .40
2458 A1023 5p multi 2.25 1.00
2459 A1023 6.50p multi 2.25 1.00
2460 A1023 6.50p multi 1.90 .90
2461 A1023 6.50p multi 1.90 .90
2462 A1023 7p multi 2.25 1.00
2463 A1023 7p multi 2.25 1.00
2464 A1023 7.50p multi 2.25 1.00
2465 A1023 7.50p multi 2.75 1.25
2466 A1023 10.50p multi 4.50 2.10
2467 A1023 10.50p multi 4.50 2.10
2468 A1023 13p multi 7.75 3.50
2469 A1023 13p multi 7.75 3.50
2470 A1023 13p multi 7.75 3.50
2471 A1023 14.50p multi 8.25 3.75
2472 A1023 30.50p multi 17.50 8.00

MEXICO

Inscribed "ROMO" at Lower Right
Booklet Stamp

2473	A1023 (15.75p) multi	5.50	2.50
a.	Booklet pane of 4 #2473	22.00	—
	Complete booklet, 4 #2473	22.00	
	Nos. 2452-2473 (21)	84.40	38.40

See No. 2399 for 7p Oceans stamp with "ROMO" inscription. No. 2473 is inscribed "Porte mundial" at lower left.

Minerals — A1129

No. 2474: a, Silver. b, Argentite. c, Marcasite, quartz and galena. d, Allende meteorite. e, Gold. f, Galena. g, Pyrargyrite. h, Gypsum. i, Manganocalcite. j, Barite. k, Stephanite. l, Red calcite. m, Calcite. n, Asbestos. o, Valencianite. p, Livingstoneite. q, Beryl. r, Smithsonite. s, Fluorite. t, Amethyst quartz. u, Azurite. v, Hemimorphite. w, Apatite. x, Pyromorphite. y, Actinolite with talc.

2005, Aug. 3 — Perf. 13¼x13
2474	Sheet of 25	40.00	40.00
a.-y.	A1129 6.50p Any single	1.25	1.25

Ignacio L. Vallarta (1830-94), Chief Justice — A1130

2005, Aug. 23 — Perf. 13x13¼
| 2475 | A1130 7.50p multi | 1.75 | 1.40 |

Judicial Anniversaries A1131

Designs: No. 2476, Federal Justice Council, 10th anniv. No. 2477, Supreme Court, 180th anniv. 10.50p, Supreme Justice Tribunal, 190th anniv.

2005, Aug. 23
2476	A1131 6.50p multi	1.40	1.25
2477	A1131 6.50p multi	1.40	1.25
2478	A1131 10.50p multi	2.25	2.00
a.	Souvenir sheet, #2476-2478	5.25	5.25

Expo 2005, Aichi, Japan — A1132

2005, Sept. 15 — Perf. 13¼x13
| 2479 | A1132 13p multi | 2.75 | 2.40 |

Federal District Superior Court, 150th Anniv. A1133

No. 2480 — Buildings from: a, 1855. b, 2005. c, 1964.

2005, Oct. 6
2480	Horiz. strip of 3	5.00	5.00
a.-b.	A1133 6.50p Either single	1.50	1.50
c.	A1133 7.50p multi	2.00	2.00

World Post Day — A1134

2005, Oct. 10
| 2481 | A1134 10.50p multi | 2.40 | 2.00 |

United Nations Day — A1135

2005, Oct. 24 — Perf. 13x13¼
| 2482 | A1135 10.50p multi | 2.40 | 2.00 |

Jalisco Philatelic Organization, Cent. — A1136

2005, Oct. 27
| 2483 | A1136 6.50p multi | 2.40 | 1.25 |

Lebanese in Mexico, 125th Anniv. A1137

2005, Nov. 11 — Perf. 13¼x13
| 2484 | A1137 10.50p multi | .250 | 2.00 |

Rodolfo Usigli (1905-79), Playwright — A1138

2005, Nov. 15
| 2485 | A1138 7.50p multi | 1.75 | 1.50 |

San Juan de Ulua, Last Spanish Redoubt A1130

2005, Nov. 23
| 2486 | A1139 7.50p multi | 1.90 | 1.50 |

Gómez Palacio, Cent. A1140

2005, Nov. 24
| 2487 | A1140 6.50p multi | 1.60 | 1.25 |

Folk Art — A1141

Designs: Nos. 2488, 2491M, 2501J, Legged earthen pot. Nos. 2488L, 2491, Black clay jug. Nos. 2489, 2491N, 2501I, Lacquered wooden chest. Nos. 2489L, 2493O, 2500, Copper jar. Nos. 2489N, 2490, 2493M, Horn comb. Nos. 2490M, 2493, Silk shawl. Nos. 2492, 2500M, 2505I, Paper bull. Nos. 2492L, 2501, Embroidered tablecloth. No. 2494, Model. No. 2495, Glazed basin. No. 2496, Vase. No. 2497, Wooden mask. No. 2498, Tin rooster. 7p, Doll. 10.50p, 11.50p, Woven basket. 13p, No. 2503D, Silver pear, with inscription reading "Distrito Federal." No. 2503N, Silver pear, with inscription reading "Ciudad de México." 14.50p, 15p, Amber marimba. No. 2505, Obsidian and opal turtle.

2005-20 — Litho. — Perf. 13¼x13

2488	A1141 50c multi	.25	.25
a.	Dated "2006"	.25	.25
b.	Dated "2007"	.25	.25
c.	Dated "2008"	.25	.25
d.	Magenta panel, dated "2010"		
e.	Dated "2011"	.25	.25
f.	Dated "2012"	.25	.25
g.	Dated "2013"	.25	.25
h.	Dated "2014"	.25	.25
i.	Dated "2015"	.25	.25
j.	Dated "2016"	.25	.25
k.	Dated "2017"	.25	.25
2488L	A1141 50c multi, dated "2018"	.25	.25
m.	Dated "2019"	.25	.25
n.	Dated "2020"	.25	.25
2489	A1141 1p multi	.30	.25
a.	Dated "2006"	.30	.25
b.	Dated "2007"	.30	.25
c.	Dated "2008"	.30	.25
d.	Dated "2010"	.30	.25
e.	Dated "2011"	.30	.25
f.	Dated "2012"	.30	.25
g.	Dated "2013"	.35	.25
h.	Dated "2014"	.40	.25
i.	Dated "2015"	.40	.25
j.	Dated "2016"	.25	.25
k.	Dated "2017"	.25	.25
2489L	A1141 1p multi, dated "2018"	.25	.25
m.	Dated "2019"	.25	.25
2489N	A1141 1p multi, dated "2020"	.25	.25
2490	A1141 1.50p multi	.40	.25
a.	Dated "2006"	.40	.25
b.	Dated "2007"	.40	.25
c.	Dated "2008"	.40	.25
d.	Dated "2009"	.35	.25
e.	Dated "2010"	.40	.25
f.	Dated "2011"	.40	.25
g.	Dated "2012"	.45	.25
h.	Dated "2013"	.60	.26
i.	Dated "2014"	.60	.25
j.	Dated "2015"	.60	.25
k.	Dated "2016"	.30	.25
l.	Dated "2017"	.30	.25
2490M	A1141 1.50p multi, dated "2018"		
n.	Dated "2019"	.30	.25
o.	Dated "2020"	.25	.25
2491	A1141 2p multi	.55	.25
a.	Dated "2006"	.55	.25
b.	Dated "2007"	.55	.25
c.	Dated "2008"	.55	.25
d.	Dated "2009"	.45	.25
e.	Dated "2010"	.55	.25
f.	Dated "2011"	.55	.25
g.	Dated "2012"	.55	.25
h.	Dated "2013"	.65	.35
i.	Dated "2014"	.80	.40
j.	Dated "2015"	.80	.40
k.	Dated "2016"	.25	.25
l.	Dated "2017"	.35	.25
2491M	A1141 2p multi, dated "2018"	.25	.25
2491N	A1141 2p multi, dated "2019"		
o.	Dated "2020"	.35	.25
		.25	.25
2492	A1141 2.50p multi	.65	.35
a.	Dated "2006"	.70	.35
b.	Dated "2007"	.70	.35
c.	Dated "2008"	.70	.35
d.	Dated "2010"	.70	.35
e.	Dated "2011"	.70	.35
f.	Dated "2012"	.70	.35
g.	Dated "2013"	.80	.40
h.	Dated "2014"	1.00	.50
i.	Dated "2015"	1.00	.50
j.	Dated "2016"	.45	.25
k.	Dated "2017"	.45	.25
2492L	A1141 2.50p multi, dated "2018"	.25	.25
m.	Dated "2019"	.25	.25
n.	Dated "2020"	.25	.25
2493	A1141 5p multi	1.30	.65
a.	Dated "2006"	1.35	.70
b.	Dated "2007"	1.35	.70
c.	Dated "2008"	1.35	.70
d.	Dated "2009"	1.15	.60
e.	Dated "2010"	1.35	.70
f.	Dated "2011"	1.35	.70
g.	Dated "2012"	1.40	.70
h.	Dated "2013"	1.60	.80
i.	Dated "2014"	1.90	.95
j.	Dated "2015"	1.90	.95
k.	Dated "2016"	.90	.45
l.	Dated "2017"	.90	.45
2493M	A1141 5p multi, dated "2018"	.55	.55
n.	Dated "2019"	.70	.35
2493O	A1141 5p multi, dated "2020"	.45	.25
2494	A1141 6.50p multi	1.60	.80
a.	Dated "2006"	1.75	.90
b.	Dated "2007"	1.75	.90
c.	Dated "2008"	1.75	.90

2495	A1141 6.50p multi	1.60	.80
a.	Dated "2006"	1.75	.90
b.	Dated "2007"	1.75	.90
c.	Dated "2008"	1.75	.90
2496	A1141 6.50p multi	1.60	.80
a.	Dated "2006"	1.75	.90
b.	Dated "2007"	1.75	.90
c.	Dated "2008"	1.75	.90
2497	A1141 6.50p multi	1.60	.80
a.	Dated "2006"	1.75	.90
b.	Dated "2007"	1.75	.90
c.	Dated "2008"	1.75	.90
2498	A1141 6.50p multi	1.60	.80
a.	Horiz. or vert. strip of 5, #2494-2498	8.00	8.00
b.	Dated "2006"	1.75	.90
c.	Horiz. or vert. strip of 5, #2494a, 2495a, 2496a, 2497a, 2498b	8.75	8.75
d.	Dated "2007"	1.75	.90
e.	Horiz. or vert. strip of 5, #2494b, 2495b, 2496b, 2497b, 2498d	8.75	8.75
f.	Dated "2008"	1.75	.90
g.	Horiz. or vert. strip of 5, #2494c, 2495c, 2496c, 2497c, 2498f	8.75	8.75
2499	A1141 7p multi	1.75	.90
a.	Dated "2006"	1.90	.95
b.	Dated "2007"	1.90	.95
c.	Dated "2008"	1.90	.95
d.	Dated "2010"	1.90	.95
e.	Dated "2011"	1.90	.95
f.	Dated "2012"	1.90	.95
g.	Dated "2013"	2.25	1.15
h.	Dated "2017"	1.20	.60
i.	Dated "2018"	.75	.75
j.	Dated "2019"	.75	.35
k.	Dated "2020"	.65	.30
2500	A1141 7.50p multi	1.90	.95
a.	Dated "2006"	2.00	1.00
b.	Dated "2007"	2.00	1.00
c.	Dated "2008"	2.00	1.00
d.	Dated "2009"	1.60	.80
e.	Dated "2010"	2.00	1.00
f.	Dated "2011"	2.00	1.00
g.	Dated "2012"	2.00	1.00
h.	Dated "2013"	2.40	1.20
i.	Dated "2014"	3.00	1.50
j.	Dated "2015"	3.00	1.50
k.	Dated "2016"	1.35	.70
l.	Dated "2017"	1.20	.66
2500M	A1141 7.50p multi, dated "2018"	.75	.75
n.	Dated "2019"	.80	.40
2501	A1141 9p multi	2.25	1.15
a.	Dated "2010"	2.40	1.20
b.	Dated "2011"	2.40	1.20
c.	Dated "2012"	2.50	1.25
d.	Dated "2013"	3.00	1.50
e.	Dated "2014"	3.50	1.75
f.	Dated "2015"	3.50	1.75
g.	Dated "2016"	1.60	.80
h.	Dated "2017"	1.60	.80
2501I	A1141 9p multi, dated "2018"	.95	.95
2501J	A1141 9p multi, dated "2019"	.95	.45
k.	Dated "2020"	.80	.40
2502	A1141 10.50p multi	2.75	1.40
a.	Dated "2006"	3.00	1.50
b.	Dated "2007"	3.00	1.50
c.	Dated "2008"	3.00	1.50
d.	Dated "2009"	2.40	1.20
2502E	A1141 11.50p multi	3.25	1.60
f.	Dated "2011"	3.25	1.60
g.	Dated "2012"	3.25	1.60
h.	Dated "2013"	3.75	1.90
i.	Dated "2014"	4.50	2.25
j.	Dated "2015"	4.50	2.25
k.	Dated "2016"	2.00	1.00
l.	Dated "2017"	2.00	1.00
m.	Dated "2018"	1.25	1.25
n.	Dated "2019"	1.25	.65
o.	Dated "2020"	1.00	.50
2503	A1141 13p multi	3.50	1.75
a.	Dated "2006"	3.50	1.75
b.	Dated "2007"	3.50	1.75
c.	Dated "2008"	3.50	1.75
2503D	A1141 13.50p multi	3.75	1.90
e.	Dated "2011"	3.75	1.90
f.	Dated "2012"	3.75	1.90
g.	Dated "2013"	4.50	2.25
h.	Dated "2014"	5.25	2.60
i.	Dated "2015"	5.25	2.60
j.	Dated "2016"	2.40	1.20
k.	Dated "2017"	2.25	1.15
l.	Dated "2018"	1.45	.75
m	Dated "2019"	1.50	.75
2503N	A1141 13.50p multi, dated "2019"	7.50	7.50
o.	Dated "2020"	1.25	.60
2504	A1141 14.50p multi	3.75	1.90
a.	Dated "2006"	1.00	0.00
b.	Dated "2007"	4.00	2.00
c.	Dated "2008"	4.00	2.00
2504D	A1141 15p multi	4.00	2.00
e.	Dated "2011"	4.00	2.00
f.	Dated "2012"	4.25	2.10
g.	Dated "2013"	4.75	2.40
h.	Dated "2014"	6.00	3.00
i.	Dated "2015"	6.00	3.00
j.	Dated "2016"	2.60	1.30
k.	Dated "2017"	2.60	1.30
l.	Dated "2018"	1.60	.80
m.	Dated "2019"	1.60	.80
n.	Dated "2020"	1.40	.70
2505	A1141 30.50p multi	8.00	4.00
a.	Dated "2006"	8.25	4.25
b.	Dated "2007"	8.25	4.25
c.	Dated "2008"	8.25	4.25
d.	Dated "2012"	8.50	4.25
e.	Dated "2016"	5.50	2.75
f.	Dated "2017"	5.25	2.60
g.	Dated "2018"	3.25	1.60
h.	Dated "2019"	3.25	1.60
2505I	A1141 30.50p multi, dated "2020"	2.75	1.40
	Nos. 2488-2505I (35)	62.10	37.15

Issued: Nos. 2488, 2489, 2490, 2491, 2492, 2493, 2494, 21495, 2496, 2497, 2498, 2499,

2500, 2501, 2502, 2503, 2504, 2505, 11/30/05.
Nos. 2502E, 2503D and 2504D are dated "2010." Nos. 2488L, 2489L, 2490M, 2491M, 2492L, 2493M, 2500M, 2501I are dated "2018".
For stamps of type A1141 with hyphen-hole perforations, see Nos. 3229-3241. For self-adhesive stamps of type A1141, see Nos. 3161-3173. Any perf. 13¼x13 stamps of type A1141 dated "2022" or after will be minors in these two sets.

Christian Brothers in Mexico, Cent. — A1142

2005, Dec. 2   Perf. 13¼x13
2506   A1142   6.50p multi   1.60   1.25

Jews in Mexico, Cent. — A1143

2005, Dec. 6
2507   A1143   7.50p multi   1.90   1.40

Indigenous Popular Culture — A1144

2005, Dec. 16   Perf. 13x13¼
2508   A1144   6.50p multi   1.60   1.25

A1145

Christmas A1146

2005, Dec. 20
2509   A1145   6.50p multi   1.60   1.25
2510   A1146   7.50p multi   1.90   1.40

Souvenir Sheet

National Polytechnic Institute, 70th Anniv. — A1147

2006, Feb. 27   Litho.   Perf. 13¼x13
2511   A1147   10.50p multi   2.50   2.50

Wolfgang Amadeus Mozart (1756-91), Composer — A1148

2006, Mar. 31
2512   A1148   7.50p multi   1.75   1.40

Central Library of National Autonomous University of Mexico, 50th Anniv. A1149

2006, Apr. 5
2513   A1149   6.50p multi   1.75   1.25

Latin American Tower, 50th Anniv. — A1150

2006, Apr. 26   Perf. 13x13¼
2514   6.50p multi   1.50   1.25
2515   10.50p multi   2.50   2.00
   a.   A1150 Vert. pair, #2514-2515   4.25   4.25

Isidro Castillo Pérez, Educator — A1151

2006, May 15   Perf. 13¼x13
2516   A1151   6.50p multi   1.75   1.25

Vasconcelos Library A1152

2006, May 16
2517   A1152   6.50p multi   1.75   1.25

Intl. Women's Day — A1153

2006, May 31   Perf. 13x13¼
2518   A1153   6.50p multi   1.50   1.25

2006 World Cup Soccer Championships, Germany — A1154

2006, June 9   Perf. 13¼x13
2519   A1154   13p multi   3.00   2.40

Souvenir Sheet

President Benito Juarez (1806-72) — A1155

2006, June 22   Perf. 13x13¼
2520   A1155   13p multi   3.00   3.00

Navy Qualification Center, 50th Anniv. — A1156

2006, Aug. 11   Litho.
2521   A1156   6.50p multi   1.50   1.25

Popular Television Characters — A1157

No. 2522: a, El Chavo del Ocho and barrel. b, El Chapulín Colorado with arms crossed. c, El Chavo del Ocho, door and window d, El Chapulín Colorado with arms spread. e, El Chavo del Ocho holding suspenders.

2006, Aug. 21   Perf. 13¼x13
2522   Horiz. strip of 5   12.00 12.00
   a.   A1157 6.50p multi   1.50   1.50
   b.   A1157 7.50p multi   1.60   1.60
   c.   A1157 10.50p multi   2.10   2.10
   d.   A1157 13p multi   2.60   2.60
   e.   A1157 14.50p multi   3.00   3.00

Intl. Year of Deserts and Desertification — A1158

2006, Sept. 20
2523   A1158   6.50p multi   1.60   1.25

Souvenir Sheet

Dinosaurs — A1159

No. 2524: a, 6.50p, Muzzy (40x24mm). b, 7.50p, Sabinosaurus (40x48mm). c, 10.50p, Aramberri Monster (40x48mm).

2006, Sept. 29   Perf. 13x13¼
2524   A1159   Sheet of 3, #a-c   5.75   5.75

A1160

2006, Oct. 5   Perf. 13¼x13
2525   A1160   6.50p multi   1.75   1.25
Engineering Institute of National Autonomous University of Mexico, 50th Anniv.

Miniature Sheet

First Mexican Stamps, 150th Anniv. A1161

No. 2526 — Miguel Hidalgo y Costilla and inscription: a, Aguascalientes. b, Colima. c, Edo. de México. d, Michoacán. e, Nayarit. f, Quintana Roo. g, Tamaulipas. h, Baja California. i, Chiapas. j, Guanajuato. k, Morelos. l, Nuevo León. m, San Luis Potosí. n, Tlaxcala. o, Baja California Sur. p, Chihuahua. q, Guerrero. r, Oaxaca. s, Sinaloa. t, Veracruz. u, Campeche. v, Distrito Federal. w, Hidalgo. x, Puebla. y, Sonora. z, Yucatán. aa, Coahuila. ab, Durango. ac, Jalisco. ad, Querétaro. ae, Tabasco. af, Zacatecas. ag, Estados Unidos Mexicanos (70x22mm).

Litho., Litho. & Embossed (50p)
2006, Oct. 9
2526   A1161   Sheet of 33   75.00   75.00
   a.-g.   6.50p Any single   1.10   1.10
   h.-n.   7.50p Any single   1.10   1.10
   o.-t.   9p Any single   1.40   1.40
   u.-z.   10.50p Any single   1.50   1.50
   aa.-af.   13p Any single   1.75   1.75
   ag.   50p multi   7.00   7.00

World Post Day — A1162

2006, Oct. 9   Litho.
2527   A1162   13p multi   3.00   2.40

MEXICO

401

Popular Television Characters A1163

Xavier López "Chabelo": 6.50p, Boy with ice cream cone. 10.50p, Man seated.

2006, Oct. 30
2528		6.50p multi	1.50	1.25
2529		10.50p multi	2.50	2.00
a.	A1163 Horiz. pair, #2528-2529		4.00	4.00

Letter Carrier's Day A1164

2006, Nov. 10
2530	A1164 6.50p multi	1.60	1.25

A1165

2006, Nov. 17 — Perf. 13x13¼
2531	A1165 10.50p multi	2.40	1.90

Transformation of the Autonomous Scientific and Literary Institute, Autonomous University of the State of Mexico, 50th Anniv.

"Children, The Future of Mexico" — A1166

2006, Nov. 22
2532	A1166 10.50p multi + label	2.40	1.90

Andrés Henestrosa, Writer, Cent. of Birth A1167

2006, Nov. 23 — Perf. 13¼x13
2533	A1167 9p multi	2.25	1.75

Edmundo O'Gorman (1906-95), Historian A1168

2006, Nov. 28 — Perf. 13x13¼
2534	A1168 10.50p multi	2.25	1.90

Mexico in Intl. Telecommunications Union, Cent. — A1169

2006, Nov. 30 — Perf. 13¼x13
2535	A1169 7p multi	1.90	1.40

Christmas A1170

Children's art by: 7.50p, Ricardo Salas Pineda. 10.50p, María José Goytia.

2006, Dec. 6 Litho. Perf. 13x13¼
2536		7.50p multi	1.75	1.40
2537		10.50p multi	2.50	2.00
a.	A1170 Pair, #2536-2537		4.25	4.25

El Universal Newspaper, 90th Anniv. A1171

2006, Dec. 22 — Perf. 13¼x13
2538	A1171 10.50p multi + label	2.50	2.00

Teacher's Day — A1172

2007, May 15
2539	A1172 7.50p multi	2.00	1.40

Frida Kahlo (1907-54), Painter — A1173

2007, June 13 — Perf. 13x13¼
2540	A1173 13p multi	2.60	2.40

Scouting, Cent. A1174

Designs: 6.50p, Dove and compass. 10.50p, Centenary emblem, compass.

2007, June 30 — Perf. 13¼x13
2541		6.50p multi	1.75	1.25
2542		10.50p multi	2.75	2.00
a.	A1174 Pair, #2541-2542		4.50	4.50

Miniature Sheet

Chichén Itzá A1175

No. 2543: a, Pelota ring, Jaguar Temple, serpent head. b, Colonnade. c, Observatory. d, Castillo, jaguar head. e, Chac Mool.

2007, July 13
2543	A1175	Sheet of 5 + label	13.00	13.00
a.-b.		6.50p Either single	1.60	1.60
c.		10.50p multi	2.50	2.50
d.-e.		13p Either single	3.00	3.00

State of Colima, 150th Anniv. A1176

2007, July 19
2544	A1176 10.50p multi	2.75	1.90

Miniature Sheet

Postal Headquarters Building, Cont. A1177

No. 2545: a, Nude boy writing (40x23mm). b, Nude boy touching item on pedestal (40x23mm). c, Two nude boys, chalice (40x23mm). d, Two nude boys, press (40x23mm). e, Boy, gear (40x23mm). f, Clock and machinery (40x23mm). g, Sculpture of UPU emblem, photographs (80x23mm). h, Mercury and caduceus (40x23mm). i, Two nude boys (40x23mm). j, Two nude boys, diff. (40x23mm). k, Seated nude boy with arms extended, holding bird (40x23mm). l, Seated nude boy holding bird (40x23mm). m, Stairway (40x48mm). n, Glass ceiling (40x48). o, Stairways (80x48mm). p, Building exterior (80x48mm).

2007, Aug. 1 — Perf. 13x13¼
2545	A1177	Sheet of 16	47.00	47.00
a.-b.		5.50p Either single	1.30	1.30
c.-g.		6.50p Any single	1.60	1.60
h.-i.		9p Either single	2.25	2.25
j.		10.50p multi	2.50	2.50
k.-l.		13p Either single	3.25	3.25
m.-n.		14.50p Either single	3.50	3.50
o.		15.50p multi	4.00	4.00
p.		39.50p multi	9.75	9.75

Torreón, Cent. — A1178

No. 2546: a, Locomotive, Torreón Station Museum. b, Bridge, church spires. c, Isauro Martínez Theater. d, Statue of Jesus Christ. e, Bilbao Dunes, Tower.

2007, Sept. 5
2546	A1178	Horiz. strip of 5	12.50	12.50
a.		A1178 9p multi	1.25	1.25
b.-c.		A1178 6.50p Either single	1.75	1.75
d.-e.		A1178 14.50p Either single	3.75	3.75

Cultural Forum, Monterrey A1179

No. 2547: a, Dove and hand. b, Child and books. c, Children, windmill, hand picking orange. d, Woman and artist. e, Sculpture and figurines.

2007, Aug. 20 Litho. Perf. 13x13¼
2547		Horiz. strip of 5	12.50	12.50
a.		A1179 7p multi	1.75	1.75
b.-c.		A1179 7.50p Either single	1.90	1.90
d.-e.		A1179 13p Either single	3.25	3.25

Central University City Campus of National Autonomous University of Mexico World Heritage Site — A1180

No. 2548: a, Olympic Stadium and artwork. b, University building, University Library. c, Rectory Building.

2007, Sept. 21
2548		Horiz. strip of 3	7.50	7.50
a.		A1180 6.50p multi	1.75	1.75
b.		A1180 9p multi	2.25	2.25
c.		A1180 13p multi	3.25	3.25

University of Baja California, 50th Anniv. — A1181

2007, Oct. 1
2549	A1181 7.50p multi	2.00	1.40

Ozone Layer Protection A1182

No. 2550: a, Doves, tree, leaves. b, Doves, Earth in hands.

2007, Oct. 1
2550	A1182	Vert. pair	5.50	5.50
a.		7p multi	1.75	1.75
b.		14.50p multi	3.75	3.75

St. Christopher, by Nicolás Rodríguez Juárez — A1183

2007, Oct. 3
2551	A1183 6.50p multi	1.80	1.25

Autonomous University of Coahuila, 50th Anniv. A1184

2007, Oct. 4 — Perf. 13¼x13
2552	A1184 7.50p multi	2.00	1.40

World Post Day — A1185

No. 2553 — Envelope with denomination in: a, Yellow. b, Black.

2007, Oct. 9 — Perf. 13x13¼
2553	A1185	Vert. pair	4.50	4.50
a.		7p multi	1.75	1.75
b.		10.50p multi	2.75	2.75

MEXICO

Rights of People With Disabilities — A1186

2007, Oct. 11
2554 A1186 6.50p multi 1.80 1.25

Miniature Sheet

Francisco Gabilondo Soler (1907-90), Composer of Children's Songs — A1187

No. 2555: a, Turtle, giraffe, peacock (Caminito de la Escuela). b, Dog, camel, mouse (Caminito de la Escuela). c, Duck and ducklings (La Patita). d, Girl and mouse (La Muñeca Fea). e, Cat with guitar (Gato de Barrio). f, King and cakes (Bombón I). g, Three pigs and cakes (Cochinitos Dormilones). h, Three pigs in bed (Cochinitos Dormilones). i, Old woman and cat (Di Por Que). j, Mouse in cowboy's clothes (El Ratón Vaquero). k, Boy eating watermelon (Negrito Sandía). l, Cricket holding stick (Cri-Cri). m, Soler. n, Cricket at music stand (Cri-Cri). o, Ant and fountain (El Chorrito).

2007, Oct. 11   *Perf. 13¼x13*
2555 A1187 Sheet of 15 ..... 26.00 26.00
  a.-b.   5p Either single 1.25 1.25
  c.-k.   6.50p Any single 1.75 1.75
  l.-n.   7p Any single 1.75 1.75
  o.   7.50p multi 2.00 2.00

Degrees in Administration, 50th Anniv. — A1188

2007, Oct. 19   *Perf. 13x13¼*
2556 A1188 7.50p multi 2.00 1.40

Cuauhtemoc Sailing School A1189

2007, Nov. 4   *Perf. 13¼x13*
2557 A1189 7.50p multi 2.00 1.40

A1190

A1191

Letter Carrier's Day A1192

No. 2559: a, Girl writing letter, letter carrier on bicycle. b, Girl mailing letter in mailbox. c, Letter carrier on bicycle. d, Letter carrier delivering letter.
No. 2560: a, Female letter carrier. b, Letter carrier on bicycle. c, Letter carrier on motorcycle. d, Letter carrier with mail bag. e, Three letter carriers. f, Five letter carriers. g, Letter carriers on rowboat. h, Horse-drawn carriage. i, Letter carrier and mail bag on railway hand car.

2007, Nov. 12   *Perf. 13*
2558 A1190 10.50p multi 2.75 2.00
2559 A1191 Block of 4 ..... 13.00 5.00
  a.-d.   6.50p Any single 3.00 3.00
2560 A1192 Sheet of 9 ..... 19.00 19.00
  a.-c.   6.50p Any single 1.75 1.75
  d.-f.   7p Any single 1.75 1.75
  g.-i.   10.50p Any single 2.50 2.50

Mountains A1193

Designs: No. 2561, Mt. Minya Konka, People's Republic of China. No. 2562, Popocatépetl, Mexico.

2007, Nov. 22   *Litho.*   *Perf. 13¼x13*
2561 A1193 6.50p multi 1.80 1.25
2562 A1193 6.50p multi 1.80 1.25

See People's Republic of China Nos. 3635-3636.

Intl. Day Against Violence Towards Women — A1194

2007, Nov. 26
2563 A1194 7p multi 2.00 1.40

Mariano Otero (1817-50), Judicial and Constitutional Reformer A1195

2007, Nov. 27   *Perf. 13¼x13*
2564 A1195 10.50p multi 2.75 2.00

Trials of Amparo, legal protection of individual constitutional guarantees in federal courts.

Miniature Sheet

Monte Albán Archaeological Site — A1196

No. 2565: a, Scribe of Cuilapan. b, Head with jaguar helmet. c, Building II, Cocijo urn. d, Building I, Central Plaza, Cocijo urn. e, Observatory, Southern Platform, Central Plaza.

2007, Dec. 11   *Perf. 13¼x13*
2565 A1196 Sheet of 5 + label 13.00 13.00
  a.-b.   6.50p Either single 1.60 1.25
  c.   10.50p multi 2.60 2.00
  d.-e.   13p Either single 3.00 2.40

Christmas A1197

2007, Dec. 12   *Perf. 13*
2566   Horiz. strip of 5 ..... 13.50 13.50
  a.   A1197 6.50p Candle 1.60 1.25
  b.   A1197 7p Bell 1.90 1.40
  c.   A1197 10.50p Angel 2.75 2.00
  d.   A1197 13.50p Magi 3.25 2.50
  e.   A1197 14.50p Holy Family 3.75 2.75

Miniature Sheet

Dogs A1198

No. 2567: a, Two English bulldogs. b, Two rottweilers. c, Two boxers. d, Two beagles. e, Head of English Bulldog. f, Head of Rottweiler. g, Head of boxer. h, Head of beagle. i, English bulldog. j, Rottweiler. k, Boxer. l, Beagle.

2007, Dec. 14
2567 A1198 Sheet of 12 ..... 25.00 25.00
  a.-d.   6.50p Any single 1.60 1.25
  e.-h.   7p Any single 1.75 1.40
  i.-l.   10.50p Any single 2.60 2.00

See Nos. 2762-2763.

Jesús García Corona (1883-1907), Heroic Railroad Engineer — A1199

2007, Dec. 17   *Perf. 13¼x13*
2568 A1199 10.50p multi 2.75 2.00

Satélite Towers, Naucalpan, 50th Anniv. — A1200

2007, Dec. 19   *Perf. 13x13¼*
2569 A1200 6.50p multi 1.80 1.25

El Cajón Dam A1201

Aerial view of: 7p, Open spillway. 13p, Dam.

2007, Dec. 28   *Perf. 13¼x13*
2570 A1201 7p multi 1.75 1.40
2571 A1201 13p multi 3.50 2.40

Letter and Heart — A1202

2008, Jan. 29   *Litho.*   *Perf. 13½x13¼*
2572 A1202 6.50p multi 1.80 1.25

Mother's Day — A1203

2008, May 2   *Perf. 13x13¼*
2573 A1203 6.50p multi 1.80 1.25

Pres. Miguel Alemán Valdés (1900-83) A1204

2008, May 14   *Perf. 13x13¼*
2574 A1204 6.50p multi 1.80 1.25

The Fruits, by Diego Rivera — A1205

2008, May 15
2575 A1205 6.50p multi 1.80 1.25

Teacher's Day.

Miniature Sheet

El Santo and El Hijo del Santo A1206

No. 2576: a, El Santo wearing silver mask and robe. b, El Santo in ring. c, El Hijo del Santo with hands outstretched. d, El Santo with automobile. e, El Hijo del Santo in ring. f, El Hijo del Santo with arms crossed.

2008, June 17   *Perf. 13*
2576 A1206 Sheet of 6 ..... 10.75 10.75
  a.-f.   6.50p Any single 1.60 1.25

El Santo (Rodolfo Guzmán Huerta, 1917-84), El Hijo del Santo (Jorge Guzmán), wrestling legends and film stars.

2008 Summer Olympics, Beijing — A1207

Designs: No. 2577, Rowing. No. 2578, Weight lifting. No. 2579, Rhythmic gymnastics.

2008, Aug. 8   *Perf. 13*
2577 A1207 6.50p multi 1.75 1.25
2578 A1207 6.50p multi 1.75 1.25
2579 A1207 6.50p multi 1.75 1.25
    Nos. 2577-2579 (3) 5.25 3.75

Electoral Justice A1208

2008, Aug. 19   *Litho.*   *Perf. 13¼x13*
2580 A1208 6.50p multi 1.80 1.25

MEXICO

Mexico Post Emblem — A1209

2008, Sept. 8
2581 A1209 6.50p multi 1.80 1.25

Fight for Mexican Independence, Bicent. — A1210

Designs: No. 2582, Ignacio Allende (1769-1811), revolutionary leader. No. 2583, Josefa Ortíz de Dominguez (1768-1829), revolutionary leader. No. 2584, José María Morelos y Pavón (1765-1815), revolutionary leader. No. 2585, Battle of Monte de las Cruces, 1810, horiz. No. 2586, Battle of Alhóndiga de Grandaitas, 1810, horiz. No. 2587, Meeting of Miguel Hidalgo and Morelos, horiz. No. 2588, Querétaro Conspiracy, horiz. No. 2589, Francisco Primo de Verdad y Ramos (1760-1808), promoter of Mexican independence, horiz. No. 2590, Miguel Hidalgo and Cry of Independence. No. 2591, Crowd on Mexico City Alameda.

2008, Sept. 15 **Perf. 13x13¼**
2582 A1210 6.50p multi 1.00 1.25
2583 A1210 6.50p multi 1.80 1.25
2584 A1210 6.50p multi 1.80 1.25
 a.   Country name in black (pos. 6) 100.00 —

Perf. 13¼x13
2585 A1210 6.50p multi 1.80 1.25

Size: 71x30mm
2586 A1210 6.50p multi 1.80 1.25
2587 A1210 6.50p multi 1.80 1.25
2588 A1210 6.50p multi 1.80 1.25
2589 A1210 6.50p multi 1.80 1.25
 Nos. 2582-2589 (8) 14.40 10.00

Imperf
Size: 80x80mm
2590 A1210 10.50p multi 2.75 1.90
2591 A1210 10.50p multi 2.75 1.90
  See Nos. 2627-2636.

Miniature Sheet

Autonomous University of Nuevo León, 75th Anniv. — A1211

No. 2592 — Stained-glass windows by Roberto Montenegro: a, Top of "La Historia." b, Top of "La Agricultura." c, Top of "La Ciencia y la Sabiduría." d, Bottom of "La Historia." e, Bottom of "La Agricultura." f, Bottom of "La Ciencia y la Sabiduría."

2008, Sept. 25 **Perf. 13**
2592 A1211 Sheet of 6 10.50 10.50
 a.-f. 6.50p Any single 1.80 1.25

World Post Day — A1212

2008, Oct. 9 **Perf. 13x13¼**
2593 A1212 10.50p multi 2.25 1.60

Flowers A1213

No. 2594: a, Hylocereus undulatus. b, Curcubita pepo.

2008, Oct. 10 **Perf. 13**
2594 A1213 Horiz. pair 3.00 2.00
 a.-b. 6.50p Either single 1.25 1.00

Juarez Autonomous University of Tabasco, 50th Anniv. — A1214

2008, Nov. 3 **Litho.** **Perf. 13x13¼**
2595 A1214 6.50p multi 1.50 1.00

Miniature Sheet

Letter Carrier's Day A1215

No. 2596: a, Letter carrier with large shoulder pouch. b, Letter carrier on bicycle. c, Letter carrier on motorcycle with sidecar. d, Letter carrier on motor scooter. e, Postal service automobile. f, Postal truck. g, Letter carriers, bicycles and truck. h, Postal van, letter carrier on bicycle.

2008, Nov. 12 **Perf. 13**
2596 A1215 Sheet of 8 11.50 11.50
 a.-h. 6.50p Any single 1.25 .95

National Employment Service A1216

2008, Nov. 19 **Perf. 13¼x13½**
2597 A1216 6.50p multi 1.50 .95

Mexican Revolution, Cent. (in 2011) — A1217

Designs: No. 2598, José María Pino Suárez (1869-1913), politician. No. 2599, Aquiles Serdán (1876-1910), politician. No. 2600, Ricardo Flores Magón (1874-1922), anarchist, and Regeneración Newspaper. No. 2601, Mexican Liberal Party. No. 2602, Cananea Strike. No. 2603, Railway system. No. 2604, Rio Blanco Strike. No. 2605, Revolutionary Junta of Puebla.
 No. 2606, Triumphal Entry of Francisco I. Madero. No. 2607, Tienda de raya (company store).

2008, Nov. 20 **Perf. 13x13¼**
2598 A1217 6.50p multi 1.50 .95
2599 A1217 6.50p multi 1.50 .95
2600 A1217 6.50p multi 1.50 .95

Size: 71x30mm
Perf. 13¼x13
2601 A1217 6.50p multi 1.50 .95
2602 A1217 6.50p multi 1.50 .95
2603 A1217 6.50p multi 1.50 .95
2604 A1217 6.50p multi 1.50 .95
2605 A1217 6.50p multi 1.50 .95
 Nos. 2598-2605 (8) 12.00 7.60

Imperf
Size: 80x80mm
2606 A1217 10.50p multi 2.25 1.60
2607 A1217 10.50p multi 2.25 1.60
 See Nos. 2647-2656.

Parque La Venta Archaeological Museum, La Venta — A1218

2008, Dec. 4 **Perf. 13**
2608 A1218 6.50p multi 1.50 .95

Christmas — A1219

Designs: 6.50p, Adoration of the Shepherds, by Cristóbal de Villalpando. 10.50p, Adoration of the Magi, by unknown artist.

2008, Dec. 10 **Perf. 13x13¼**
2609   6.50p multi 1.50 1.00
2610   10.50p multi 2.25 1.60
 a.   A1219 Horiz. pair, #2609-2610 3.75 3.75

Dr. Gonzalo Aguirre Beltrán (1908-96), Anthropologist — A1220

2008, Dec. 16 **Perf. 13¼x13**
2611 A1220 6.50p multi 1.50 .95

Miniature Sheet

Palenque Archaeological Site — A1221

No. 2612: a, Mayan hieroglyphic cartouche, tomb, seated figure. b, Jade mask, skull mask, tablet. c, Palace and tower. d, Temple of the Sun, Temples 14 and 15. e, Temple of Inscriptions, incense holder.

2008, Dec. 19 **Litho.**
2612 A1221 Sheet of 5 + label 10.00 10.00
 a.-b. 6.50p Either single .95 .95
 c.   10.50p multi 1.50 1.50
 d.-e. 13p Either single 1.90 1.90

Mexican Academy of Film Ariel Awards, 50th Anniv. — A1222

2008, Dec. 24 **Perf. 13¼x13**
2613 A1222 6.50p multi 1.50 .95

St. Valentine's Day — A1223

2009, Feb. 9 **Litho.** **Perf. 13x13¼**
2614 A1223 6.50p multi 1.50 .90

Veracruz Carnival — A1224

2009, Feb. 18
2615 A1224 6.50p multi 1.50 .90

Miniature Sheet

Tajín Archaeological Site — A1225

No. 2616: a, Yoke, eagle-shaped hatchet. b, Decorated panel. c, Terracotta pelota player and pelota pyramid. d, Pyramid, bird's head hatchet, lightning bolt. e, Temple, temple diagram, decorated handle.

2009, Mar. 21 **Perf. 13¼x13**
2616 A1225 Sheet of 5 + label 10.00 10.00
 a.-b. 6.50p Either single .95 .95
 c.   10.50p multi 1.00 1.60
 d.-e. 13p Either single 1.90 1.90

Channel 11 Television, 50th Anniv. A1226

2009, Mar. 27
2617 A1226 6.50p multi 1.50 .95

Teacher's Day — A1227

2009, May 15 **Perf. 13x13¼**
2618 A1227 6.50p multi 1.50 1.00

Miniature Sheet

National Bank of Mexico, 125th Anniv. A1228

No. 2619: a, Palacio de los Condes de San Mateo de Valparaiso, Mexico City. b, Main patio, Palacio de los Condes de San Mateo de Valparaiso. c, Column and main door, Palacio de Iturbide, Mexico City. d, Casa Montejo, Mérida. e, Doors, Casa del Mayorazgo de la Canal, San Miguel de Allende. f, Main patio, Palacio de los Condes del Valle de Súchil, Durango.

MEXICO

2009, June 2 — *Perf. 13*
2619 A1228 Sheet of 6   9.00   9.00
  a.-f.   6.50p Any single   1.50   1.00

World Environment Day — A1229

2009, June 5 — *Perf. 13¼x13*
2620 A1229 10.50p multi   2.25   1.60

Aguascalientes Autonomous University — A1230

2009, June 19
2621 A1230 10.50p multi   2.25   1.60

Gymnogyps Californianus A1231

2009, July 27 — *Perf. 13x13¼*
2622 A1231 10.50p multi   2.25   2.25

Intl. Day of Indigenous People — A1232

2009, Aug. 11
2623 A1232 6.50p multi   1.50   1.00

The Country, by Jorge González Camarena A1233

2009, Aug. 20   Litho.   *Perf. 13¼x13*
2624 A1233 6.50p multi   1.50   1.00
  National Free Textbook Commission, 50th anniv.

Preservation of Polar Regions and Glaciers — A1234

Designs: 10.50p, Mts. Popocatépetl and Iztaccíhuatl. 13p, Mt. Citlaltépetl.

2009, Sept. 14 — *Perf. 13*
2625   10.50p multi   2.00   1.60
2626   13p multi   2.75   1.90
  a. A1234 Vert. pair, #2625-2626   4.75   4.75

Fight For Mexican Independence Type of 2008

Designs: No. 2627, Congress of Chilpancingo. No. 2628, Establishment of the Supreme Junta. No. 2629, Leona Vicario (1789-1842), supporter of independence movement, and husband, Andrés Quintana Roo (1787-1851), independence movement leader and politician. No. 2630, Execution of José María Morelos y Pavón, horiz. No. 2631, Capture of Miguel Hidalgo and insurgents, horiz. No. 2632, Execution of Hidalgo, horiz. No. 2633, Siege of Cuautla, horiz. No. 2634, Constitution of Apatzingán, horiz.
No. 2635, Map of campaign of Morelos, portraits of compatriots Hermenegildo Galeana, Mariano Matamoros, Pablo Galeana, and Nicolás Bravo. No. 2636, Abolition of slavery.

2009, Sept. 16 — *Perf. 13x13¼*
2627 A1210 6.50p multi   1.50   1.00
2628 A1210 6.50p multi   1.50   1.00
2629 A1210 6.50p multi   1.50   1.00
  Perf. 13¼x13
2630 A1210 6.50p multi   1.50   1.00
2631 A1210 6.50p multi   1.50   1.00
2632 A1210 6.50p multi   1.50   1.00
  Size: 71x30mm
2633 A1210 6.50p multi   1.50   1.00
2634 A1210 6.50p multi   1.50   1.00
  Nos. 2627-2634 (8)   12.00   8.00
  Imperf Size: 80x80mm
2635 A1210 10.50p multi   2.25   1.60
2636 A1210 10.50p multi   2.25   1.60

UNI Global Union Post and Logistics Conference, Mexico City — A1235

2009, Sept. 30 — *Perf. 13x13¼*
2637 A1235 6.50p multi   1.50   1.00

A1236

2009, Oct. 5 — *Perf. 13¼x13*
2638 A1236 6.50p multi   1.50   1.00
  Autonomous University of San Luis Potosí Scientific and Literary Institute, 150th Anniv.

World Post Day — A1237

2009, Oct. 9 — *Perf. 13x13¼*
2639 A1237 10.50p multi   2.25   1.60

City of Chihuahua, 300th Anniv. A1238

2009, Oct. 12 — *Perf. 13¼x13*
2640 A1238 6.50p multi   1.50   1.00

Day of the Dead (All Souls' Day) A1239

Figurines: No. 2641, Woman honoring dead. No. 2642, Ferris wheel with skeleton riders.

2009, Nov. 2 — *Perf. 13*
2641   6.50p multi   1.50   1.00
2642   6.50p multi   1.50   1.00
  a. A1239 Horiz. pair, #2641-2642   3.75   3.75

Juan Bosch (1909-2001), President of Dominican Republic A1240

2009, Nov. 4 — *Perf. 13x13¼*
2643 A1240 10.50p multi   2.60   1.60

Wilderness Areas — A1241

No. 2644: a, El Carmen Mountains, Mexico. b, Nahanni National Park, Canada. c, Zion National Park, US. d, Kronotsky Reserve, Russia. e, Baviaanskloof Reserve, South Africa.

2009, Nov. 6   Litho.   *Perf. 13*
2644   Horiz. strip of 5   13.50   13.50
  a. A1241 6.50p multi   1.50   1.00
  b.-c. A1241 10.50p Either single   2.50   1.60
  d. A1241 13p multi   3.00   2.00
  e. A1241 14.50p multi   3.00   2.25

Letter Carrier's Day A1242

Letter carrier on: No. 2645, Bicycle. No. 2646, Motorcycle.

2009, Nov. 12 — *Perf. 13*
2645   6.50p multi   1.50   1.00
2646   6.50p multi   1.50   1.00
  a. A1242 Horiz. pair, #2645-2646   3.00   3.00

Mexican Revolution Type of 2008

Designs: No. 2647, Emiliano Zapata (1879-1919), General of Liberation Army of the South. No. 2648, Pres. Francisco I. Madero (1873-1913). No. 2649, Proclamation of the Plan of Ayala. No. 2650, Taking of Zacatecas, horiz. No. 2651, Women revolution fighters, horiz. No. 2652, Francisco "Pancho" Villa (1878-1923), General of the Division of the North, horiz. No. 2653, Railroads in the revolution, horiz. No. 2654, The "Ten Tragic Days," horiz.
No. 2655, Venustiano Carranza (1859-1920), revolution leader, and proclamation of Plan of Guadalupe. No. 2656, Revolutionaries, painting by David Alfaro Siqueiros.

2009, Nov. 20 — *Perf. 13x13¼*
2647 A1217 6.50p multi   1.75   1.10
2648 A1217 6.50p multi   1.75   1.10
2649 A1217 6.50p multi   1.75   1.10
  Perf. 13¼x13
2650 A1217 6.50p multi   1.75   1.10
2651 A1217 6.50p multi   1.75   1.10
  Size: 71x30mm
2652 A1217 6.50p multi   1.75   1.10
2653 A1217 6.50p multi   1.75   1.10
2654 A1217 6.50p multi   1.75   1.10
  Nos. 2647-2654 (8)   14.00   8.80
  Imperf Size: 80x80mm
2655 A1217 10.50p multi   2.50   1.75
2656 A1217 10.50p multi   2.50   1.75

Traffic Safety A1243

2009, Nov. 23 — *Perf. 13¼x13*
2657 A1243 6.50p multi   1.60   1.10

Jaíme Sabínes (1926-99), Poet — A1244

2009, Nov. 27   Litho.
2658 A1244 6.50p multi   1.60   1.10

Federal Fiscal Auditor, 50th Anniv. A1245

2009, Nov. 30
2659 A1245 6.50p multi   1.60   1.10

Christmas   A1246   A1247

2009, Dec. 1 — *Perf. 13¼x13*
2660 A1246 6.50p Melchior   1.60   1.10
2661 A1246 6.50p Gaspar   1.60   1.10
2662 A1246 6.50p Balthazar   1.60   1.10
2663 A1247 6.50p Santa Claus   1.60   1.10
  Nos. 2660-2663 (4)   6.40   4.40

Oportunidades Human Development Program — A1248

2009, Dec. 15 — *Perf. 13x13¼*
2664 A1248 6.50p multi   1.60   1.00

Energy Conservation — A1249

No. 2665 — Children's drawings: a, Child connecting power cord from house to sun. b, Light bulbs in daytime and nighttime. c, Light bulb people in room.

2009, Dec. 16 — *Perf. 13¼x13*
2665   Horiz. strip of 3   5.00   5.00
  a.-c. A1249 6.50p Any single   1.60   1.00

Paisano Program — A1250

2009, Dec. 18 — *Perf. 13x13¼*
2666 A1250 6.50p multi   1.60   1.00

Pres. Venustiano Carranza (1859-1920) A1251

2009, Dec. 21
2667 A1251 6.50p multi   1.60   1.00

MEXICO

Aviation in Mexico, Cent. — A1252

2010, Jan. 8   Litho.   Perf. 13¼x13
2668   A1252   7p multi   1.80   1.10

State Workers' Security and Social Services Institute, 50th Anniv. A1253

2010, Jan. 19
2669   A1253   7p multi   2.00   1.10

St. Valentine's Day — A1254

2010, Feb. 3
2670   A1254   7p multi   2.00   1.10

New Year 2010 (Year of the Tiger) — A1255

2010, Feb. 11   Perf. 13x13¼
2671   A1255   7p multi   2.60   1.10

Mexican Red Cross, Cent. — A1256

2010, Feb. 21   Perf. 13
2672   A1256   10.50p multi   2.75   1.75

Inter-America Development Bank Assembly of Governors, Cancun — A1257

2010, Mar. 19   Perf. 13x13¼
2673   A1257   11.50p multi   3.00   1.90

Souvenir Sheet

Mexico City Red Devils Baseball Players A1258

2010, Apr. 11   Perf. 13
2674   A1258   Sheet of 3   6.00   6.00
a.-c.   7p Any single   2.00   1.10

No. 2674: a, José Luis Sandoval. b, Miguel Ojeda. c, Roberto Saucedo.

Mother's Day — A1259

2010, Apr. 23   Perf. 13x13¼
2675   A1259   7p multi   2.00   1.10

Teacher's Day — A1260

2010, May 15
2676   A1260   7p multi   2.00   1.10

2010 World Cup Soccer Championships, South Africa — A1261

No. 2677 — 2010 World Cup emblem and: a, Mexican team. b, Gerardo Torrado, Giovani Dos Santos. c, Andrés Guardado, Guillermo Ochoa.

2010, May 15   Perf. 13¼x13
2677   Horiz. strip of 3   7.25   7.25
a.-b.   A1261 7p Either single   2.00   1.10
c.   A1261 11.50p multi   2.75   1.75

Intl. Mother Language Day — A1262

2010, May 21
2678   A1262   11.50p multi   3.25   1.75

Pres. Adolfo López Mateos (1909-69) A1263

2010, May 26
2679   A1263   7p multi   2.00   1.10

Natl. Human Rights Commission — A1264

2010, June 7   Litho.
2680   A1264   7p multi   2.00   1.10

Scouting in Mexico, 90th Anniv. — A1265

2010, July 17   Perf. 13
2681   A1265   7p multi   2.00   1.10

Grandparent's Day — A1266

2010, Aug. 16
2682   A1266   7p multi   2.00   1.10

Mexican Petroleum Institute — A1267

2010, Aug. 23   Perf. 13¼x13
2683   A1267   7p multi   2.00   1.10

Mexican Independence, Bicent. — A1268

Designs: No. 2684, Pres. Guadalupe Victoria (1789-1843). No. 2685, Pedro Moreno (1775-1817), revolutionary leader. No. 2686, Father Servando Teresa de Mier (1765-1827), politician. No. 2687, Xavier Mina (1789-1817), revolutionary leader. No. 2688, Vicente Guerrero (1783-1831), soldier and politician. No. 2689, Flag of the Army of the Three Guarantees. No. 2690, Gen. Manuel de Mier y Terán (1789-1832), Nicolás Bravo (1786-1854), soldier and politician, horiz. No. 2691, Ignacio López Rayón (1773-1832), leader of revolutionary government, Gen. Ramón Rayón (1775-1839), horiz. No. 2692, O'Donojú Conference, horiz.
No. 2693, Miguel Hidalgo y Costilla (1753-1811), revolutionary leader; Lieutenant Colonel Mariano Jiménez (1781-1811); Juan Aldama (1774-1811), soldier; Leona Vicario (1789-1842), revolution supporter; José María Morelos y Pavón (1765-1815), revolutionary leader; Ignacio Allende (1769-1811), revolutionary leader; Josefa Ortiz de Domínguez (1768-1829), revolution supporter; and Miguel Domínguez (1756-1830), revolutionary leader. No. 2694, Entrance into Mexico City of the Army of the Three Guarantees.

2010, Sept. 16   Perf. 13x13¼
2684   A1268   7p multi   2.00   1.10
2685   A1268   7p multi   2.00   1.10
2686   A1268   7p multi   2.00   1.10
2687   A1268   7p multi   2.00   1.10
2688   A1268   7p multi   2.00   1.10
2689   A1268   7p multi   2.00   1.10
     Perf. 13¼x13
2690   A1268   7p multi   2.00   1.10
2691   A1268   7p multi   2.00   1.10
2692   A1268   7p multi   2.00   1.10
   Nos. 2684-2692 (9)   18.00   9.90
     Imperf
     Size: 80x80mm
2693   A1268   11.50p multi   3.25   1.90
2694   A1268   11.50p multi   3.25   1.90

Miniature Sheet

National University of Mexico, Cent. — A1269

No. 2695: a, University founder Justo Sierra, opening of National University. b, National Preparatory School, College of San Ildefonso. c, National School of Law, Academy of San Carlos, National School of Higher Studies. d, Murals by José Clemente Orozco and David Alfaro Siqueiros. e, National University of Mexico Symphonic Orchestra in Nezahualcoyotl Hall, Olympic Stadium, Dancers of National University of Mexico Choreographic Studio. f, University Museum of Contemporaneous Art.

2010, Sept. 21   Litho.   Perf. 13
2695   A1269   Sheet of 6   13.00   13.00
a.-f.   7p Any single   2.00   1.10

Girl Guides of Mexico — A1270

2010, Sept. 25
2696   A1270   7p multi   2.00   1.10

Plenipotentiary Conference of the Intl. Telecommunications Union, Guadalajara — A1271

2010, Oct. 4   Perf. 13¼x13
2697   A1271   11.50p multi   3.25   1.90

World Post Day — A1272

2010, Oct. 9   Perf. 13x13¼
2698   A1272   11.50p multi   3.25   1.90

Souvenir Sheet

Temples A1273

No. 2699: a, Pyramid of the Sun, Teotihuacan, Mexico. b, Ateshgah, Baku, Azerbaijan.

2010, Oct. 12
2699   A1273   Sheet of 2   4.00   4.00
a.-b.   7p Either single   2.00   1.10

See Azerbaijan No. 934.

National Center for Disaster Prevention, 20th Anniv. — A1274

2010, Oct. 13
2700   A1274   7p multi   2.00   1.25

All Souls' Day (Day of the Dead) — A1275

2010, Oct. 25
2701   A1275   7p multi   2.00   1.25

MEXICO

A1276

Christmas
A1277

Designs: No. 2702, Santa Claus, children, Christmas tree, toys.
No. 2703 — Red ribbon and: a, Holy Family and angel. b, Candle, children hitting piñata. c, Three Magi.

2010, Nov. 4		Litho.		Perf. 13
2702	A1276	7p multi	2.00	1.25
2703		Horiz. strip of 3	6.25	6.25
a.-c.	A1277 7p Any single		2.00	1.25

Letter Carrier's Day
A1278

Designs: 7p, Postman and old postal truck. 11.50p, Postman on motorcycle, row of postal trucks.

2010, Nov. 11			
2704	7p multi	2.00	1.25
2705	11.50p multi	3.00	1.90
a.	A1278 Horiz. pair, #2704-2705	5.25	5.25

Rodolfo Neri Vela, First Mexican in Space, 25th Anniv. — A1279

Neri Vela and: No. 2706, Space equipment. No. 2707, Mexican flag, Space Shuttles.

2010, Nov. 16		Perf. 13x13¼
2706	7p multi	2.00 1.25
2707	7p multi	2.00 1.25
a.	A1279 Vert. pair, #2706-2707	4.00 4.00

Palace of Fine Arts, Mexico City — A1280

2010, Nov. 19		Perf. 13¼x13
2708	A1280 7p multi	2.00 1.25

Mexican Revolution, Cent. — A1281

Designs: No. 2709, Pres. Venustiano Carranza (1859-1920), Carranza and crowd. No. 2710, Luis Cabrera (1876-1954), politician, and Agricultural Law. No. 2711, 1917 Constitution, detail of painting by Jorge González Camarena depicting Pres. Carranza and papers. No. 2712, 1917 Constitution, by Camarena, detail depicting Constitutional Congress and eagle. No. 2713, The Convention of Aguascalientes, detail of painting by Oswaldo Barra Cunningham, horiz. No. 2714, Battle of Celaya, horiz. No. 2715, Provisional Presidents Eulalio Gutiérrez (1881-1939), Roque González Garza (1885-1962), and Francisco Lagos Cházaro (1878-1932), Provisional Government one-peso banknote, horiz. No. 2716, Women fighters in the Mexican Revolution, horiz.
No. 2717, Revolution leaders Carranza, Francisco "Pancho" Villa (1878-1923), and Emiliano Zapata (1879-1919) on horseback. No. 2718, 1910 Revolution, detail of mural by Diego Rivera depicting revolution leaders.

2010, Nov. 20			Perf. 13x13¼
2709	A1281	7p multi	2.00 1.25
2710	A1281	7p multi	2.00 1.25
2711	A1281	7p multi	2.00 1.25
2712	A1281	7p multi	2.00 1.25
		Perf. 13¼x13	
2713	A1281	7p multi	2.00 1.25
2714	A1281	7p multi	2.00 1.25
		Size: 71x30mm	
2715	A1281	7p multi	2.00 1.25
2716	A1281	7p multi	2.00 1.25
	Nos. 2709-2716 (8)		16.00 10.00
		Imperf	
		Size: 80x80mm	
2717	A1281	11.50p multi	3.25 1.90
2718	A1281	11.50p multi	3.25 1.90

Monumental Clock, Pachuca, Cent. — A1282

2010, Nov. 25		Perf. 13
2719	A1282 7p multi	2.00 1.25

Campaign Against Violence Towards Women — A1283

2010, Dec. 1		Perf. 13¼x13
2720	A1283 11.50p multi	3.25 1.90

2010 United Nations Climate Change Conference, Cancún — A1284

2010, Dec. 6		Perf. 13x13¼
2721	A1284 7p multi	2.00 1.25

National Council of Science and Technology (CONACYT), 40th Anniv. A1285

2010, Dec. 9		Perf. 13¼x13
2722	A1285 7p multi	2.00 1.25

Awarding of Nobel Prize for Literature to Octavio Paz, 20th Anniv. A1286

2010, Dec. 10		Litho.
2723	A1286 7p multi	2.00 1.25

National Week of Small and Medium Enterprises — A1287

2010, Dec. 13		
2724	A1287 7p multi	2.00 1.25

Ardea Herodias
A1288

2010, Dec. 15		
2725	A1288 11.50p multi	3.25 2.50

Souvenir Sheet

Dances
A1289

No. 2726: a, Ballet Folklorico de Mexico de Amalia Hernandez. b, Kalbelia Dance, India.

2010, Dec. 15		Perf. 13
2726	A1289 Sheet of 2	4.00 4.00
a.-b.	7p Either single	2.00 1.25

See India Nos. 2473-2474.

Miniature Sheet

Teotihuacan Archaeological Site — A1290

No. 2727: a, Detail from mural, onyx carving. b, Columns from Quetzalpapalotl Palace, Sun sculpture. c, Censer and vessel. d, Pyramid of the Sun and mask. e, Pyramid of the Moon

2010, Dec. 16		Perf. 13¼x13
2727	A1290 Sheet of 5 + label	14.00 14.00
a.-b.	7p Either single	2.00 1.25
c.	11.50p multi	2.60 1.90
d.-e.	13.50p Either single	3.00 2.25

Miniature Sheet

Orchids
A1291

No. 2728: a, Cypripedium irapeanum. b, Sobralia macrantha. c, Prosthechea Ionophlebia. d, Laelia anceps subspecies dawsonii f. chilapensis. e, Trichocentrum oerstedii. f, Laelia rubescens.

2010, Dec. 17		Perf. 13
2728	A1291 Sheet of 6	11.50 11.50
a.-f.	7p Any single	1.75 1.25

Trust For Electrical Energy Conservation, 20th Anniv.
A1292

2010, Dec. 20		Perf. 13¼x13
2729	A1292 7p multi	2.00 1.25

A1293

Love — A1294

2011, Jan. 31		Perf. 13
2730	A1293 7p multi	2.00 1.25
2731	A1294 7p multi	2.00 1.25

Postal Union of the Americas, Spain and Portugal (UPAEP), Cent. — A1295

2011, Mar. 23		Litho.
2732	A1295 13.50p multi	3.75 2.40

Mother's Day — A1296

2011, Apr. 13		
2733	A1296 7p multi	2.00 1.25

National Seed Inspection and Certification Service, 50th Anniv. — A1297

No. 2734: a, Corn kernels, hands holding seed corn. b, Flowers, flower testers. c, Bananas, prickly pear fruit, flower, agave, avocado, citrus fruit, poinsettia, map of Mexico, corn cobs and kernels.

2011, Apr. 29		Perf. 13x13¼
2734	Vert. strip of 3	6.25 6.25
a.-c.	A1297 7p Any single	2.00 1.25

MEXICO

Main Post Office, Mexico City — A1298

2011, May 4 Litho.
2735 A1298 7p multi 2.00 1.25

Souvenir Sheet

Mil Mascaras (Man of a Thousand Masks), Professional Wrestler — A1299

No. 2736 — Mil Mascaras (Aaron Rodríguez Arellano) wearing: a, Yellow, black and red mask with red "M," and match scene c, Black and white mask with red "M" and cape, Mil Mascaras with outer masks. d, Yellow and black mask with red "M," Mil Mascaras leaping in ring.

2011, May 11 Perf. 13
2736 A1299 Sheet of 3 6.25 6.25
a.-c. 7p Any single 2.00 1.25

The Rural Teacher, by Diego Rivera A1300

2011, May 15 Perf. 13¼x13
2737 A1300 7p multi 2.10 1.25

Teacher's Day.

Armillita (Fermín Espinosa, 1911-78), Matador — A1301

2011, May 17 Perf. 13x13¼
2738 A1301 7p multi 2.10 1.25

Under-17 World Soccer Championships, Mexico — A1302

Tournament emblem, trophy, stadia and various soccer players.

2011, June 15 Litho. Perf. 13¼x13
2739 Horiz. strip of 3 9.50 9.50
a. A1302 7p multi 2.10 1.25
b. A1302 11.50p multi 3.25 2.00
c. A1302 13.50p multi 4.00 2.40

Grandparent's Day — A1303

2011, Aug. 3 Perf. 13
2740 A1303 7p multi 2.25 1.25

Intl. Year of Forests — A1304

2011, Aug. 5 Perf. 13x13¼
2741 A1304 11.50p multi 3.50 1.90

Promotion of Philately — A1305

2011, Aug. 8 Perf. 13
2742 A1305 7p multi 2.25 1.25

National Defense College, 30th Anniv. A1306

2011, Aug. 12 Perf. 13¼x13
2743 A1306 7p multi 2.25 1.25

Mario Moreno (Cantinflas) (1911-93), Film Actor — A1307

Cantinflas: 7p, Photographs. 11.50p, Caricatures.

2011, Aug. 12 Perf. 13x13¼
2744 7p multi 2.25 1.25
2745 11.50p multi 3.25 1.90
a. A1307 Vert pair #2744-2745 5.50 5.50

Natl. Institute of Adult Education, 30th Anniv. — A1308

2011, Aug. 18 Perf. 13¼x13
2746 A1308 7p multi 2.25 1.10

Sepomex (Mexican Postal Service), 25th Anniv. A1309

2011, Aug. 22
2747 A1309 7p multi 1.60 1.10

Law of Fiscal Justice, 75th Anniv. A1310

2011, Aug. 24
2748 A1310 7p multi 2.25 1.10

Mexico Tourism Year — A1311

2011, Aug. 24 Perf. 13x13¼
2749 A1311 11.50p multi 3.50 1.75

Cardiology Hospital, Mexico City, 50th Anniv. A1312

2011, Sept. 13
2750 A1312 7p multi 2.00 1.10

National System of Civil Protection, 25th Anniv. — A1313

2011, Sept. 19 Perf. 13x13¼
2751 A1313 11.50p multi 3.25 1.75

Souvenir Sheet

Highway Projects A1314

No. 2752: a, Highway interchange north of Mexico City. b, Piedra Colorada Tunnel. c, Texcapa Bridge.

2011, Sept. 26 Perf. 13
2752 A1314 Sheet of 3 8.75 8.75
a. 7p multi 1.90 1.10
b. 11.50p multi 3.00 1.75
c. 13.50p multi 3.50 2.10

World Post Day — A1315

2011, Oct. 7 Perf. 13¼x13
2753 A1315 11.50p multi 3.25 1.75

Miniature Sheet

Secretary of Public Education, 90th Anniv. — A1316

No. 2754: a, First Secretary of Public Education José Vasconcelos in chair, man standing next to chair, cover of 1917 Mexican Constitution. b, Man reading to child, teacher in school. c, Building and murals. d, Child reading book, family, children in school. e, Scenes of school laboratories. f, Murals.

2011, Oct. 12 Perf. 13
2754 A1316 Sheet of 6 12.00 12.00
a.-f. 7p Any single 2.00 1.10

2011 Pan American Games, Guadalajara — A1317

No. 2755 — Emblem and: a, Diamonds. b, Mascots. c, Agave plants.

2011, Oct. 14 Perf. 13¼x13
2755 Horiz. strip of 3 8.75 8.75
a. A1317 7p multi 2.00 1.10
b. A1317 11.50p multi 3.00 1.75
c. A1317 13.50p multi 3.50 2.00

National Polytechnic Institute Center for Research and Advanced Studies (CINVESTAV), 50th Anniv. — A1318

2011, Oct. 17 Perf. 13x13¼
2756 A1318 7p multi 2.00 1.10

Miniature Sheet

Agricultural and Food Safety in Mexico — A1319

No. 2757: a, Alfonso Luis Herrera López (1868-1942), biologist, insect specimens, microscope. b, Cattle, packaged meats, butchers, emblem of Mexican food inspection agency (TIF). c, Dr. Dieter Enkerlin (1926-95), entomologist, and insects. d, Food workers using safe food handling practices. e, Map of Mexico, ship, airplane, birds, food inspectors, dog, shipping containers. f, Scientists in laboratory, insect, cotton plant.

2011, Oct. 18 Perf. 13
2757 A1319 Sheet of 6 12.00 12.00
a.-f. 7p Any single 2.00 1.10

All Souls' Day (Day of the Dead) A1320

2011, Oct. 25 Perf. 13¼x13
2758 A1320 7p multi 2.00 1.10

MEXICO

National Council for Educational Development (CONAFE), 40th Anniv. — A1321

2011, Oct. 27			Perf. 13x13¼
2759	A1321	7p multi	2.00 1.10

A1322

2011, Oct. 27			Litho.
2760	A1322	7p multi	2.00 1.10

State Employees' Social Security and Social Services Institute of Zacatecas, 25th Anniv.

Letter Carrier's Day — A1323

2011, Nov. 11			
2761	A1323	7p multi	2.00 1.10

Dogs Type of 2007

Designs: 7p, German shepherd (Pastor Alemán). 13.50p, English cocker spaniel (Cocker spaniel Inglés).

2011, Nov. 17			Perf. 13
2762	A1198	7p multi	2.00 1.10
2763	A1198	13.50p multi	3.75 2.00

Christmas — A1324

Designs: No. 2764, Santa Claus, letters, silhouette of Santa's sleigh in front of Moon. No. 2765, vert.: a, Children, Christmas piñata. b, Creche, candle, fruit and cup. c, Letters, Magi, Christmas gifts.

2011, Nov. 18			Perf. 13¼x13
2764	A1324	11.50p multi	3.00 1.75
2765		Vert. strip of 3	8.25 4.75
a.		A1324 7p multi	2.00 1.10
b.-c.		A1324 11.50p Either single	3.00 1.75

A1326

2011, Nov. 30			Perf. 13x13¼
2766	A1326	7p multi	2.00 1.10

Veracruz Delegation of Mexican Social Security Institute, 50th Anniv.

Intl. Day for Elimination of Violence Toward Women — A1327

2011, Nov. 30			Perf. 13¼x13
2767	A1327	11.50p multi	2.25 1.75

National Voluntary Action and Solidarity Prize — A1328

2011, Dec. 7			Perf. 13x13¼
2768	A1328	11.50p multi	3.00 1.75

Mexican Urban UNESCO World Heritage Sites — A1329

2011, Dec. 8			Perf. 13¼x13
2769	A1329	11.50p multi	3.00 1.75

State Workers' Security and Social Services Institute, 50th Anniv. — A1330

2011, Dec. 16			Perf. 13x13¼
2770	A1330	7p multi	2.00 1.10

Diplomatic Relations Between Mexico and South Korea, 50th Anniv. — A1331

Designs: No. 2771, Adult gray whale, denomination at left. No. 2772, Juvenile gray whale, denomination at right.

2012, Jan. 26	Litho.	Perf. 13¼x13
2771	13.50p multi	3.50 2.10
2772	13.50p multi	3.50 2.10
a.	A1331 Horiz. pair, #2771-2772	7.00 7.00

See South Korea No. 2377.

St. Valentine's Day — A1332

2012, Feb. 2			Perf. 13
2773	A1332	7p multi	2.00 1.10

Intl. Women's Day — A1333

2012, Mar. 8			Perf. 13¼x13
2774	A1333	11.50p multi	3.25 1.75

World Down Syndrome Day — A1334

2012, Mar. 21			Perf. 13¼x13
2775	A1334	13.50p multi	4.00 2.10

National Bioethics Commission, 20th Anniv. — A1335

2012, Mar. 27			Litho.
2776	A1335	7p multi	2.10 1.10

Campaign Against Human Trafficking A1336

2012, Mar. 29			Perf. 13x13¼
2777	A1336	7p multi	2.10 1.10

Linares, 300th Anniv. A1337

2012, Apr. 10			Perf. 13¼x13
2778	A1337	7p multi	2.10 1.10

Mother's Day — A1338

Designs: No. 2779, Mother receiving card and breakfast from two children. No. 2780, Mothers and children.

2012, Apr. 26			Perf. 13
2779	A1338	7p grn & multi	2.10 1.10
2780	A1338	7p pink & multi	2.10 1.10

Interior Stairway of Postal Palace (Main Post Office), Mexico City — A1339

2012, May 4			Perf. 13x13¼
2781	A1339	7p multi	2.10 1.00

Souvenir Sheet

Battle of Puebla, 150th Anniv. — A1340

No. 2782: a, Map of Mexico, flags of France, Great Britain and Spain. b, General Ignacio Zaragoza, soldiers. c, Army of the East.

2012, May 5			Perf. 13
2782	A1340	Sheet of 3	6.00 3.00
a.-c.		7p Any single	2.00 1.00

Teacher's Day — A1341

2012, May 15			Perf. 13x13¼
2783	A1341	7p multi	2.10 1.00

Traditional Foods of Mexico and Brazil — A1342

Designs: No. 2784, Pozole. No. 2785, Milho e mandioca.

2012, June 1	Litho.	Perf. 13
2784	13.50p multi	3.75 1.90
2785	13.50p multi	3.75 1.90
a.	A1342 Horiz. pair, #2784-2785	7.75 7.75

See Brazil No. 3217.

Mexican Wolves A1343

2012, June 4			Perf. 13¼x13
2786	A1343	11.50p multi	3.25 2.25

World Anti-Tobacco Day — A1344

2012, July 5			Perf. 13¼x13
2787	A1344	7p multi	2.10 1.10

Escuela Libre de Derecho (Law School), Mexico City, Cent. — A1345

2012, July 24			Litho.
2788	A1345	7p multi	2.10 1.10

Grandparent's Day — A1346

2012, Aug. 13			Perf. 13
2789	A1346	7p multi	2.10 1.10

MEXICO

Miniature Sheet

Federal Electricity Commission, 75th Anniv. — A1347

No. 2790: a, El Cajón Dam, Nayarit. b, Guaycora Solar Farm, Sonora. c, La Venta Wind Generators, Oaxaca. d, Lineman and electrical lines. e, National Energy Control Center. f, Transmission towers, Colima.

2012, Aug. 14		Perf. 13	
2790	A1347 Sheet of 6	11.50	11.50
a.-f.	7p Any single	1.75	1.10

Mexican Petroleum Congress A1348

Designs: No. 2791, PEMEX Refinery, Ciudad Madera. No. 2792, PEMEX offshore oil platform.

2012, Sept. 9		Perf. 13x13¼	
2791	7p multi	2.10	1.10
2792	7p multi	2.10	1.10
a.	A1348 Vert. pair, #2791-2792	4.25	4.25

40th Intl. Cervantes Festival, Guanajuato A1349

2012, Sept. 25		Perf. 13¼x13	
2793	A1349 13.50p multi	4.00	2.10

National Polytechnic Institute Center for Research and Advanced Studies (CINVESTAV), Saltillo, 50th Anniv. A1350

2012, Oct. 2			
2794	A1350 7p multi	2.25	1.10

University of Sonora, 70th Anniv. — A1351

No. 2795: a, Rector's Building (denomination at UR). b, Stained-glass window depicting Don Quixote. c, University Library and Museum (denomination at UL).

2012, Oct. 2		Perf. 13x13¼	
2795	Horiz. strip of 3	6.50	3.50
a.-c.	A1351 7p Any single	2.10	1.10

World Post Day — A1352

2012, Oct. 9		Perf. 13¼x13	
2796	A1352 11.50p multi	3.50	1.75

Minaret, Agua Caliente — A1353

2012, Oct. 11			
2797	A1353 11.50p multi	3.50	1.75

School Counseling, 20th Anniv. — A1354

2012, Oct. 15		Perf. 13x13¼	
2798	A1354 7p multi	2.25	1.10

Sacred Art of the Viceroys A1355

Paintings by unknown artists of crowned nuns: No. 2799, Sister María Engracia Josefa del Santísimo Rosario (holding candlestick with flowers). No. 2800, Sister from Order of the Immaculate Conception (with round breastplate).

2012, Oct. 25			
2799	7p multi	2.10	1.10
2800	7p multi	2.10	1.10
a.	A1355 Horiz. pair, #2799-2800	4.50	2.25

All Souls' Day (Day of the Dead) A1356

2012, Oct. 29		Perf. 13¼x13	
2801	A1356 7p multi	2.25	1.10

Miniature Sheet

Tulum Archaeological Site — A1357

No. 2802: a, Interior of Temple of the Paintings. b, View of cliffs and the side of the Castillo. c, Front view of the Castillo. d, Temple of the Paintings. e, Building ruins and sculpture of Itzamná from corner of Temple of the Paintings.

2012, Oct. 31		Litho.	
2802	A1357 Sheet of 5 + label	15.00	15.00
a.-b.	7p Either single	1.60	1.10
c.	11.50p multi	2.60	1.75
d.-e.	13.50p Either single	3.25	2.10

Christmas A1358

No. 2803: a, Elves packing toys in boxes. b, People celebrating Christmas. c, Magi on camels.

2012, Nov. 8		Perf. 13	
2803	Horiz. strip of 3	10.00	10.00
a.-c.	A1358 11.50p Any single	3.00	1.75

Letter Carrier's Day — A1359

2012, Nov. 12		Perf. 13x13¼	
2804	A1359 7p multi	2.25	1.10

Lebanese Center, Mexico City, 50th Anniv. A1360

2012, Nov. 13		Perf. 13¼x13	
2805	A1360 13.50p multi	4.00	2.10

Public Housing Authority (FOVISSSTE), 40th Anniv. — A1361

2012, Nov. 28		Perf. 13¼x13	
2806	A1361 7p multi	2.25	1.10

University of Guanajuato, 280th Anniv. — A1362

2012, Dec. 3		Perf. 13¼x13	
2807	A1362 7p multi	2.25	1.10

Justo Sierra (1848-1912), Writer A1363

2012, Dec. 7		Litho.	
2808	A1363 7p multi	2.25	1.10

Sacred Mayan Canoe Crossing A1364

No. 2809 — Rowers at: a, Rear of canoe. b, Center of canoe. c, Front of canoe.

2012, Dec. 21		Perf. 13¼x13	
2809	Horiz. strip of 3	9.50	9.50
a.	A1364 7.50p multi	2.25	1.25
b.	A1364 11.50p multi	3.25	1.90
c.	A1364 13.50p multi	3.75	2.10

St. Valentine's Day — A1365

2013, Feb. 8		Perf. 13	
2810	A1365 7p multi	2.25	1.10

President's Day — A1366

2013, Feb. 15		Perf. 13¼x13	
2811	A1366 7p multi	2.25	1.10

Iberoamericana University, Mexico City, 70th Anniv. — A1367

No. 2812: a, Statue and building. b, Buildings. c, Covered steps.

2013, Mar. 7		Perf. 13¼x13	
2812	A1367 Horiz. strip of 3	7.00	7.00
a.-c.	7p Any single	2.25	1.10

National Association of Supermarkets and Department Stores, 30th Anniv. — A1368

2013, Mar. 13		Perf. 13¼x13	
2813	A1368 7p multi	2.25	1.25

Intl. Mother Language Day — A1369

2013, Mar. 13			
2814	A1369 11.50p multi	3.50	1.90

Expropriation of Foreign-Owned Petroleum Rights and Facilities, 75th Anniv. — A1370

2013, Mar. 17		Litho.	
2815	A1370 7p multi	2.25	1.25

Guillermo Haro Barraza (1913-88), Astronomer A1371

2013, Mar. 21		Perf. 13¼x13	
2816	A1371 7p multi	2.25	1.25

MEXICO

Promulgation of Plan of Guadalupe, Cent. A1372

2013, Mar. 26   Perf. 13¼x13
2817 A1372 7p multi   2.25 1.25

Diplomatic Relations Between Mexico and Indonesia, 60th Anniv. — A1373

Designs: No. 2818, Neofelis diardi borneensis. No. 2819, Panthera onca.

2013, Apr. 6   Perf. 13
2818 15p multi   4.50 2.50
2819 15p multi   4.50 2.50
  a. A1373 Horiz. pair, #2818-2819   9.00 9.00

See Indonesia No. 2345.

Mexican Army, Cent. — A1374

2013, Apr. 17   Perf. 13x13¼
2820 A1374 7p multi   2.25 1.25

Federico Gómez Children's Hospital, Mexico City, 70th Anniv. — A1375

2013, Apr. 30   Litho.   Perf. 13¼x13
2821 A1375 7p multi   2.25 1.25

Children's Day — A1376

2013, Apr. 30   Perf. 13¼x13
2822 A1376 7p multi   2.25 1.25

Mother's Day — A1377

2013, May 10   Litho.   Perf. 13
2823 A1377 11.50p multi   2.25 1.90

Teacher's Day — A1378

2013, May 15   Litho.   Perf. 13x13¼
2824 A1378 7p multi   2.25 1.10

Mexican Army, Cent. A1379

2013, Aug. 13   Litho.   Perf. 13¼x13
2825 A1379 7p multi   2.25 1.10

Veterinary Education in Mexico, 160th Anniv. A1380

2013, Aug. 16   Litho.   Perf. 13¼x13
2826 A1380 7p multi   2.25 1.10

Manuel Acuña (1849-73), Writer A1381

2013, Aug. 27   Litho.   Perf. 13¼x13
2827 A1381 7p multi   2.25 1.10

Grandparent's Day — A1382

2013, Aug. 28   Litho.   Perf. 13
2828 A1382 7p multi   2.25 1.10

First Congress of Anáhuac, 200th Anniv. — A1383

2013, Sept. 5   Litho.   Perf. 13¼x13
2829 A1383 7p multi   2.25 1.10

Metropolitan Cathedral, Mexico City, 200th Anniv. — A1384

2013, Sept. 11   Litho.   Perf. 13x13¼
2830 A1384 7p multi   2.25 1.10

Confederation of Industrial Chambers of Mexico, 95th Anniv. A1385

2013, Sept. 20   Litho.   Perf. 13¼x13
2831 A1385 7p multi   2.25 1.10

Miniature Sheet

Autonomous University of Nuevo León, 80th Anniv. — A1386

No. 2832: a, Las Informantes de Sahagún, by Federico Cantú (head at center top facing right). b, Las Informantes de Sahagún (head at center top facing left). c, Espejos Comunicantes, by Guillermo Ceniceros (compass rose at right). d, Espejos Comunicantes (heads at right). e, Einstein, by Sebastián Xavier Treviño (head of Albert Einstein). f, Einstein (faceless figure and geometric shapes).

2013, Sept. 25   Litho.   Perf. 13
2832 A1386 Sheet of 6   13.00 13.00
  a.-f. 7p Any single   2.25 1.10

World Post Day — A1387

2013, Oct. 9   Litho.   Perf. 13¼x13
2833 A1387 13.50p multi   4.25 2.10

Woman Suffrage in Mexico, 60th Anniv. — A1388

2013, Oct. 11   Litho.   Perf. 13x13¼
2834 A1388 7p multi   2.25 1.10

Secretary of Health, 70th Anniv. — A1389

2013, Oct. 18   Litho.   Perf. 13x13¼
2835 A1389 7p multi   2.40 1.10

All Souls' Day (Day of the Dead) A1390

2013, Oct. 22   Litho.   Imperf.
2836 A1390 15p multi   4.50 2.25

Gran Café de la Parroquia Restaurant, Veracruz, 205th Anniv. — A1391

2013, Oct. 23   Litho.   Perf. 13x13¼
2837 A1391 7p multi   2.25 1.10

Bilateral Relations Between Mexico and South Africa, 20th Anniv. — A1392

2013, Oct. 24   Litho.   Perf. 13¼x13¼
2838 A1392 15p multi   4.50 2.25

National Institute for Rural Development, 40th Anniv. — A1393

2013, Nov. 5   Litho.   Perf. 13x13¼
2839 A1393 7p multi   2.25 1.10

Federal Conciliation and Arbitration Tribunal, 50th Anniv. — A1394

2013, Nov. 8   Litho.   Perf. 13x13¼
2840 A1394 7p multi   2.40 1.10

Letter Carrier's Day — A1395

2013, Nov. 12   Litho.   Perf. 13x13¼
2841 A1395 7p multi   2.40 1.10

Casino Español Restaurant, Mexico City, 150th Anniv. — A1396

2013, Nov. 14   Litho.   Perf. 13x13¼
2842 A1396 13.50p multi   4.25 2.10

Mexican Army, Cent. A1397

2013, Nov. 15   Litho.   Perf. 13¼x13
2843 A1397 7p multi   2.25 1.10

Interior of Postal Palace (Main Post Office), Mexico City — A1398

2013, Nov. 19   Litho.   Perf. 13x13¼
2844 A1398 7p multi   2.40 1.10

A1399

2013, Nov. 21   Litho.   Perf. 13¼x13
2845 A1399 15p multi   4.50 2.40
  a. Tete-beche pair   10.00 10.00

San Matías Jalatlaco Temple, Former Convent of San Pablo, Historical Center of Oaxaca UNESCO World Heritage Site.

MEXICO

Migrant's Protection Program — A1400

2013, Nov. 27	Litho.	Perf. 13x13¼
2846 A1400 7p multi		2.25 1.10

Christmas A1401

Poinsettia and: No. 2847, Magi. No. 2848, Santa Claus. 11.50p, Christmas tree. 13.50p, Holy Family.

2013, Nov. 28	Litho.	Perf. 13
2847 A1401 7p multi		2.25 1.10
2848 A1401 7p multi		2.25 1.10
2849 A1401 11.50p multi		3.50 1.75
a. Pair, #2847, 2849		6.25 6.25
2850 A1401 13.50p multi		4.25 2.10
a. Pair, #2848, 2850		6.50 6.50
Nos. 2847-2850 (4)		12.25 6.05

Morelos State Autonomous University, 60th Anniv. — A1402

2013, Dec. 6	Litho.	Perf. 13¼x13
2851 A1402 7p multi		2.25 1.10

National Education Worker's Union, 70th Anniv. — A1403

2013, Dec. 7	Litho.	Perf. 13x13¼
2852 A1403 7p multi		2.25 1.10

Mexican Institute of Industrial Property, 20th Anniv. — A1404

2013, Dec. 12	Litho.	Perf. 13x13¼
2853 A1404 7p multi		2.25 1.10

National Commission for Sports and Physical Culture, 25th Anniv. — A1405

2013, Dec. 13	Litho.	Perf. 13¾x13
2854 A1405 7p multi		2.25 1.10

Paintings by Francisco Eppens (1913-90), Stamp Designer A1406

No. 2855: a, La Danza de la Media Luna, 1984. b, Alcatraces, 1988. c, Cactáceas, 1988. d, Guerrero Aguila y Guerrero Tiger, 1980. e, Caballos de Colores, 1985.

2013, Dec. 13	Litho.	Perf. 13x13¼
2855 Horiz. strip of 5		17.00 17.00
a.-b. A1406 7p Either single		2.10 1.10
c. A1406 11.50p multi		3.50 1.75
d. A1406 13.50p multi		4.00 2.10
e. A1406 15p multi		4.75 2.40

Promotion of philately.

Industrial Labor Training Centers, 50th Anniv. — A1407

2013, Dec. 17	Litho.	Perf. 13x13¼
2856 A1407 7p multi		2.25 1.10

Federal Police, 85th Anniv. — A1408

2013, Dec. 19	Litho.	Perf. 13x13¼
2857 A1408 7p multi		2.25 1.10

Pipe Organs — A1409

No. 2858 — Organs in Oaxaca: a, Santa Maria Tiltepec Temple. b, San Jerónimo Tlacochahuaya Church. c, San Andrés Zautla Church. d, Santa María de la Natividad Tamazulapan. e, Santo Domingo Yanhuitlán Church. f, Oaxaca Cathedral.

2013, Dec. 20	Litho.	Perf. 13¼x13
2858 Horiz. strip of 6		20.00 20.00
a.-b. A1409 7p Either single		2.10 1.10
c.-d. A1409 11.50p Either single		3.50 1.75
e.-f. A1409 13.50p Either single		4.00 2.10

National Water Commission 25th Anniv. — A1410

No. 2859: a, Weir at Los Mochis, Abelardo Rodríguez Dam, Rosales Canal. b, San Pedro Piedra Gorda Dam, San José I Dam. c, Francisco I. Madero Dam, "El Manantial," sculpture by José Sacal. d, Los Berros Water Purification Plant, La Principal Water Treatment Plant. e, Water tunnel, Atotonilco Water Treatment Plant.

2014, Jan. 16	Litho.	Perf. 13x13¼
2859 Horiz. strip of 5		14.00 14.00
a.-e. A1410 7p Any single		2.25 1.10

St. Valentine's Day — A1411

2014, Jan. 31	Litho.	Perf. 13
2860 A1411 7p multi		2.75 1.10

National Chamber of the Mexican Publishing Industry, 50th Anniv. — A1412

2014, Feb. 28	Litho.	Perf. 13¼x13
2861 A1412 7p multi		2.75 1.10

Octavio Paz (1914-98), 1990 Nobel Laureate in Literature A1413

2014, Mar. 20	Litho.	Perf. 13x13¼
2862 A1413 7p multi		2.75 1.10

National Fund for Tourism Development, 40th Anniv. A1414

2014, Apr. 1	Litho.	Perf. 13¼x13
2863 A1414 7p multi		2.75 1.10

Second Battle of Torreón, Cent. A1415

2014, Apr. 3	Litho.	Perf. 13¼x13
2864 A1415 7p multi		2.75 1.10

Mexican Pres. Adolfo López Mateos and French Pres. Charles de Gaulle — A1416

2014, Apr. 11	Litho.	Perf. 13x13¼
2865 A1416 13.50p multi		5.00 2.10

Visit of Pres. de Gaulle to Mexico, 50th anniv.

Miniature Sheet

American Occupation of Veracruz, Cent. — A1417

No. 2866: a, Veracruz citizens face the intervention. b, Naval Academy cadets. c, General Rubio Navarrete prepares to contain the American advance. d, Venustiano Carranza makes his triumphal entry into Mexico City. e, Cadet José Virgilio Uribe Robles, Lieutenant Luis Felipe José Azueta Abad. f, Naval Academy parade after the intervention.

2014, Apr. 21	Litho.	Perf. 13
2866 A1417 Sheet of 6		16.00 16.00
a.-f. 7p Any single		2.50 1.10

City of General Escobedo, 410th Anniv. — A1418

2014, Apr. 25	Litho.	Perf. 13x13¼
2867 A1418 7p multi		2.75 1.10

Intl. Day of Intellectual Property — A1419

2014, Apr. 28	Litho.	Perf. 13x13¼
2868 A1419 15p multi		5.50 2.40

Children's Day — A1420

2014, Apr. 30	Litho.	Perf. 13
2869 A1420 7p multi		2.75 1.10

City of Misantla, 450th Anniv. — A1421

2014, May 3	Litho.	Perf. 13¼x13
2870 A1421 7p multi		2.75 1.10

Mother's Day — A1422

2014, May 9	Litho.	Perf. 13
2871 A1422 11.50p multi		4.50 1.75

National Fund for Workers Consumption (FONACOT), 40th Anniv. A1423

2014, May 14	Litho.	Perf. 13¼x13
2872 A1423 7p multi		2.75 1.10

Autonomous University of the State of Mexico, 70th Anniv. — A1424

2014, May 14	Litho.	Perf. 13x13¼
2873 A1424 7p multi		2.75 1.10

MEXICO

Laura Mendez de Cuenca (1853-1928), Teacher and Writer — A1425

2014, May 15 Litho. Perf. 13¼x13
2874 A1425 7p multi   2.75 1.10
Teacher's Day.

Mexican National Soccer Team — A1426

2014, May 27 Litho. Perf. 13¼x13
2875 A1426 7p multi   2.75 1.10

Diplomatic Relations Between Mexico and Portugal, 150th Anniv. — A1427

Mexican and Portuguese flags with denomination color of: No. 2876, White. No. 2877, Black.

2014, June 6 Litho. Perf. 13
2876 13.50p multi   4.50 2.10
2877 13.50p multi   4.50 2.10
a. A1427 Horiz. pair, #2876-2877   10.00 10.00
See Portugal Nos. 3605-3606.

Signing of the Treaties of Teoloyucan, Cent. — A1428

2014, Aug. 13 Litho. Perf. 13x13¼
2878 A1428 7p multi   2.75 1.10

National Association of Engineering Schools, 50th Anniv. — A1429

2014, Aug. 22 Litho. Perf. 13¼x13
2879 A1429 7p multi   2.75 1.10

Firefighter's Day — A1430

2014, Aug. 22 Litho. Perf. 13¼x13
2880 A1430 7p multi   2.75 1.10

Technological Institute of Ciudad Juárez, 50th Anniv. — A1431

2014, Sept. 4 Litho. Perf. 13x13¼
2881 A1431 7p multi   2.75 1.10

Greetings — A1432

No. 2882: a, Graduates and diploma. b, Doves and stained-glass window. c, Flowers. d, Clown candle. e, Cupcakes.

2014, Sept. 5 Litho. Perf. 13¼x13
2882 Horiz. strip of 5   17.00 17.00
a.-c. A1432 7p Any single   2.75 1.10
d.-e. A1432 11.50p Either single   4.50 1.75

National Bank of Mexico, 130th Anniv. — A1433

2014, Sept. 9 Litho. Perf. 13
2883 A1433 11.50p multi   4.50 1.75

Veracruz University, 70th Anniv. — A1434

2014, Sept. 10 Litho. Perf. 13¼x13
2884 A1434 7.50p multi   3.00 1.10

Postal Palace (Main Post Office), Mexico City — A1435

2014, Sept. 11 Litho. Perf. 13¼x13
2885 A1435 7p multi   2.75 1.10

La Jornada Newspaper, 30th Anniv. A1436

2014, Sept. 18 Litho. Perf. 13¼x13
2886 A1436 7p multi   2.75 1.10

Palace of Fine Arts, 80th Anniv. — A1437

2014, Sept. 29 Litho. Perf. 13¼x13
2887 A1437 7p multi   2.75 1.10

Resolution of Chamizal Border Dispute With United States, 50th Anniv. — A1438

2014, Sept. 30 Litho. Perf. 13¼x13
2888 A1438 11.50p multi   4.50 1.75

Creation of State of Quintana Roo, 40th Anniv. — A1439

2014, Oct. 1 Litho. Perf. 13¼x13
2889 A1439 7p multi   2.75 1.10

Autonomous Metropolitan University, 40th Anniv. — A1440

2014, Oct. 8 Litho. Perf. 13¼x13
2890 A1440 7p multi   2.75 1.10

World Post Day — A1441

2014, Oct. 9 Litho. Perf. 13x13¼
2891 A1441 13.50p multi   5.00 2.00

A1442

2014, Oct. 10 Litho. Perf. 13x13¼
2892 A1442 13.50p multi   5.00 2.00
2014 Latin American Integration Association Expo, Montevideo, Uruguay.

Battle of Zacatecas, Cent. A1443

2014, Oct. 14 Litho. Perf. 13¼x13
2893 A1443 7p multi   2.75 1.10

Institute of Epidemiological Diagnosis and Reference, 75th Anniv. — A1444

2014, Oct. 17 Litho. Perf. 13x13¼
2894 A1444 7p multi   2.75 1.10
Dated 2012.

Air Traffic Controller's Day — A1445

2014, Oct. 20 Litho. Perf. 13x13¼
2895 A1445 7p multi   2.75 1.50

Constitution of Apatzingán, 200th Anniv. A1446

2014, Oct. 22 Litho. Perf. 13¼x13
2896 A1446 7p multi   2.75 1.10

Philips Mexico, 75th Anniv. — A1447

2014, Oct. 22 Litho. Perf. 13x13¼
2897 A1447 13.50p multi   5.00 2.00

Miniature Sheet

Paquimé Archaeological Site — A1448

No. 2898: a, Pottery, denomination at LR. b, Pottery, denomination at LL. c, Casa de los Cranéos. d, Casa de las Guacamayas, denomination at UR. e, Casa de las Guacamayas, denomination at UL.

2014, Oct. 25 Litho. Perf. 13¼x13
2898 A1448 Sheet of 5 + label   21.00 21.00
a.-b. 7p Either single   2.25 1.10
c. 11.50p multi   3.50 1.75
d.-e. 13.50p Either single   4.00 2.00

All Souls' Day (Day of the Dead) A1449

2014, Oct. 29 Litho. Perf. 13¼x13
2899 A1449 11.50p multi   4.50 1.75

First Performance of Mexican National Anthem, 160th Anniv. — A1450

2014, Oct. 30 Litho. Perf. 13x13¼
2900 A1450 13.50p multi   5.25 2.00

Inventor's Day — A1451

2014, Nov. 4 Litho. Perf. 13¼x13
2901 A1451 7p multi   3.00 1.10

Souvenir Sheet

Alberto Córdova Stadium, Autonomous University of Mexico State, 50th Anniv. — A1452

No. 2902: a, Aerial view of area, stadium in inset. b, Hill overlooking decorated stadium seats. c, Aerial view of stadium and other buildings.

MEXICO

2014, Nov. 5   Litho.   Perf. 13x13¼
2902 A1452   Sheet of 3   8.00 8.00
a.-c.   7p Any single   2.75 1.10

Letter Carrier's Day — A1453

2014, Nov. 10   Litho.   Perf. 13¼x13
2903 A1453 7p multi   3.00 1.00

Crabs A1454

Designs: 13.50p, Isostichopus fuscus. 15p, Danielum ixbauchac.

2014, Nov. 18   Litho.   Perf. 13¼x13
2904   13.50p multi   5.00 1.90
2905   15p multi   6.00 2.10
a.   A1454 Horiz. pair, #2904-2905   11.00 11.00

Ciudad Madero Technological Institute, 60th Anniv. A1455

2014, Nov. 19   Litho.   Perf. 13¼x13
2906 A1455 7p multi   2.90 1.00

Intl. Year of Crystallography — A1456

2014, Nov. 19   Litho.   Perf. 13¼x13
2907 A1456 13.50p multi   5.25 1.90

Ministry of Health, 85th Anniv. A1457

2014, Nov. 20   Litho.   Perf. 13¼x13
2908 A1457 7p multi   2.90 1.00

World Food Day — A1458

Designs: 7p, Shrimp boat, hand holding shrimp. 13.50p, Hand holding tilapia.

2014, Nov. 24   Litho.   Perf. 13x13¼
2909   7p multi   2.75 1.00
2910   13.50p multi   5.00 1.90
a.   A1458 Pair, #2909-2910   8.25 8.25

Anáhuac University, 50th Anniv. — A1459

No. 2911: a, Building and plaza. b, Commemorative pillar, building. c, Fountain.

2014, Nov. 26   Litho.   Perf. 13x13¼
2911   Horiz. strip of 3   8.50 8.50
a.-c.   A1459 7p Any single   2.75 1.00

Autonomous University of Chihuahua, 60th Anniv. — A1460

2014, Dec. 3   Litho.   Perf. 13¼x13
2912 A1460 11.50p multi   4.50 1.60

Christmas — A1461

Designs: No. 2913, Magi. No. 2914, Santa Claus. 11.50p, Christmas tree. 13.50p, Holy Family, shepherd and lambs.

2014, Dec. 5   Litho.   Perf. 13
2913 A1461   7p multi   2.75 .95
2914 A1461   7p multi   2.75 .95
2915 A1461 11.50p multi   4.50 1.60
a.   Pair, #2913, 2915   7.50 7.50
2916 A1461 13.50p multi   5.50 1.90
a.   Pair, #2914, 2916   10.50 10.50
Nos. 2913-2916 (4)   15.50 5.40

General Eulalio Gutiérrez (1881-1939), Provisional President A1462

2014, Dec. 8   Litho.   Perf. 13x13¼
2917 A1462 7p multi   2.90 .95
Sovereign Revolutionary Convention, cent.

Latin American Parliament, 50th Anniv. — A1463

2014, Dec. 9   Litho.   Perf. 13¼x13
2918 A1463 13.50p multi   5.25 1.90

Fernando Hiriart Baldorrama (1914-2005), Secretary of Energy, Mines and State Industry — A1464

2014, Dec. 10   Litho.   Perf. 13x13¼
2919 A1464 7p multi   2.90 .95

Taking of San Pedro, Cent. A1465

2014, Dec. 11   Litho.   Perf. 13¼x13
2920 A1465 7p multi   2.90 .95

National College of Professsional Technical Education, 35th Anniv. A1466

2014, Dec. 11   Litho.   Perf. 13¼x13
2921 A1466 7p multi   2.90 .95

North American Free Trade Agreement, 20th Anniv. A1467

2014, Dec. 18   Litho.   Perf. 13¼x13
2922 A1467 11.50p multi   4.50 1.60

Diplomatic Relations Between Mexico and Iran, 50th Anniv. — A1468

2014, Dec. 18   Litho.   Perf. 13¼x13
2923 A1468 15p multi   6.00 2.10
See Iran No. 3131.

Philately and Postal Culture A1469

2014, Dec. 19   Litho.   Perf. 13¼x13
2924 A1469 7p multi   2.90 .95

St. Valentine's Day — A1470

2015, Jan. 30   Litho.   Perf. 13
2925 A1470 7p multi   2.90 .95

Postal Palace (Main Post Office), Mexico City — A1471

2015, Feb. 17   Litho.   Perf. 13¼x13
2926 A1471 13.50p multi   5.25 1.90

First Supreme Court, 200th Anniv. — A1472

2015, Mar. 7   Litho.   Perf. 13x13¼
2927 A1472 7p multi   2.90 .95

National Livestock Convention, 80th Anniv. — A1473

2015, Mar. 30   Litho.   Perf. 13x13¼
2928 A1473 7p multi   2.90 .95

Battle of Celaya, Cent. — A1474

2015, Apr. 15   Litho.   Perf. 13x13¼
2929 A1474 7p multi   2.90 .95

National Public Administration Institute, 60th Anniv. — A1475

2015, Apr. 16   Litho.   Perf. 13x13¼
2930 A1475 7p multi   2.90 .95

Sister Juana Inés de la Cruz (1651-95), Poet — A1476

2015, Apr. 17   Litho.   Perf. 13x13¼
2931 A1476 13.50p multi   5.25 1.75

2015 Mexican Aerospace Fair, Santa Lucia A1477

2015, Apr. 22   Litho.   Perf. 13¼x13
2932 A1477 13.50p multi   5.25 2.25

Children's Day — A1478

2015, Apr. 30   Litho.   Perf. 13
2933 A1478 7p multi   2.90 .95

Mother's Day — A1479

2015, May 11   Litho.   Perf. 13
2934 A1479 13.50p multi   5.25 1.75

MEXICO

Dolores Correa Zapata (1853-1924), Teacher — A1480

2015, May 15 Litho. Perf. 13¼x13
2935 A1480 7p multi   2.90 .90
Teacher's Day.

Airports and Auxiliary Services, 50th Anniv. A1481

2015, June 10 Litho. Perf. 13¼x13
2936 A1481 7p multi   2.90 1.25

World Intellectual Property Day — A1482

2015, July 7 Litho. Perf. 13¼x13
2937 A1482 15p multi   5.75 1.90

National Human Rights Commision, 25th Anniv. — A1483

2015, July 9 Litho. Perf. 13x13¼
2938 A1483 7p multi   2.90 .90

Guelaguetza Festival — A1484

2015, July 10 Litho. Perf. 13x13¼
2939 A1484 13.50p multi 5.25 1.75

Gilberto Bosques (1892-1995), Mexican Diplomat Who Saved Jews In World War II — A1485

Bosques and: 7p, Notre Dame de la Garde Basilica, Marseilles and signed travel visa. 13.50p, Embassy, Mexican consular handstamp.

2015, July 16 Litho. Perf. 13
2940 A1485 7p multi   2.90 .90
2941 A1485 13.50p multi 5.00 1.75
  a. Horiz. pair, #2940-2941 8.00 8.00
See France Nos. 4839-4840.

Autonomous University of Campeche, 50th Anniv. A1486

Designs: No. 2942, Painting. No. 2943, University building.

2015, Aug. 19 Litho. Perf. 13¼x13
2942 A1486 7p multi   2.75 .85
2943 A1486 7p multi   2.75 .85
  a. Horiz. pair, #2942-2943 5.75 5.75

Mexican Petroleum Institute, 50th Anniv. — A1487

2015, Aug. 24 Litho. Perf. 13¼x13
2944 A1487 7p multi   2.90 .85

University of the Americas, Puebla, 75th Anniv. A1488

2015, Sept. 2 Litho. Perf. 13¼x13
2945 A1488 13.50p multi 5.25 1.60

University of Colima, 75th Anniv. — A1489

2015, Sept. 3 Litho. Perf. 13x13¼
2946 A1489 7p multi   2.90 .85

International Balloon Festival A1490

2015, Sept. 10 Litho. Perf. 13¼x13
2947 A1490 11.50p multi 4.50 1.40

Technological Institute of La Laguna, 50th Anniv. A1491

2015, Sept. 25 Litho. Perf. 13¼x13
2948 A1491 7p multi   2.90 .85

Cacti — A1492

Designs: 7p, Lophophora williamsii. 11.50p, Mammillaria mystax.

2015, Sept. 29 Litho. Perf. 13
2949 A1492 7p multi   2.90 .85
2950 A1492 11.50p multi 4.50 1.40
  a. Vert. pair, #2949-2950 7.25 7.25

José María Morelos (1765-1815), Priest and Patriot — A1493

2015, Sept. 30 Litho. Perf. 13¼x13
2951 A1493 7p multi   2.90 .85

Miniature Sheet

Xochicalco Archaeological Site — A1494

No. 2952: a, Plaza de la Estela and pillar. b, Observatory and sculpture. c, Temple of the Feathered Serpent. d, Archaeological zone (denomination at UR). e, Archaeological zone and pelota goal (denomination at UL).

2015, Oct. 1 Litho. Perf. 13¼x13
2952 A1494 Sheet of 5 + label 20.00 20.00
  a.-b. 7p Either single   2.10 .85
  c. 11.50p multi   3.50 1.40
  d.-e. 13.50p Either single 4.00 1.60

World Post Day — A1495

2015, Oct. 9 Litho. Perf. 13x13¼
2953 A1495 7p multi   2.90 .85

Mexico City Red Devils Baseball Team, 75th Anniv. — A1496

2015, Oct. 17 Litho. Perf. 13x13¼
2954 A1496 7.50p multi   3.00 .90
2954a Tete-beche pair   6.00 6.00

Diplomatic Relations Between Mexico and Russia, 125th Anniv. — A1497

Designs: 7p, Saints Peter and Paul Cathedral, St. Petersburg, Russia. 13.50p, Chapultepec Castle, Mexico City.

2015, Oct. 19 Litho. Perf. 13
2955 7p multi   2.90 .85
2956 13.50p multi   4.50 1.75
  a. A1497 Horiz. pair, #2955-2956 8.00 8.00
See Russia No. 7685.

Cynomys Mexicanus A1498

2015, Oct. 22 Litho. Perf. 13
2957 A1498 13.50p multi 5.25 1.75

Mexican Constitution A1499

Designs: No. 2958, 1823 Plan for Constitution. No. 2959, 1824 Constitution.

2015, Oct. 28 Litho. Perf. 13¼x13
2958 7p multi   2.90 .85
2959 7p multi   2.90 .85
  a. A1499 Horiz. pair, #2958-2959 5.75 5.75

All Souls' Day (Day of the Dead) — A1500

2015, Oct. 30 Litho. Perf. 13x13¼
2960 A1500 9p multi   3.50 1.10

UNESCO International Hydrological Program, 50th Anniv. — A1501

2015, Nov. 10 Litho. Perf. 13¼x13
2961 A1501 13.50p multi 5.25 1.75

Letter Carrier's Day — A1502

2015, Nov. 11 Litho. Perf. 13x13¼
2962 A1502 7p multi   2.90 .85

Philately and Postal Culture A1503

2015, Nov. 19 Litho. Perf. 13¼x13
2963 A1503 13.50p multi 5.25 1.75

A1504

2015, Nov. 23 Litho. Perf. 13x13¼
2964 A1504 7p multi   2.90 .85
National Bank for Savings and Financial Services, 65th Anniv.

Rock Paintings, Baja California A1505

2015, Nov. 23 Litho. Perf. 13x13¼
2965 A1505 13.50p multi 5.25 1.75

College of Mechanical Engineers and Electricians, 70th Anniv. — A1506

2015, Nov. 26 Litho. Perf. 13¼x13
2966 A1506 9p multi   3.50 1.10

Mexican Acceptance of Treaty of the Meter, 125th Anniv. — A1507

2015, Dec. 1 Litho. Perf. 13x13¼
2967 A1507 13.50p multi 5.25 1.75

MEXICO

Christmas — A1508

Designs: No. 2968, Magi and Star of Bethlehem. No. 2969, Santa Claus and Christmas tree. 11.50p, Piñata. 13.50p, Holy Family, angel, lamb, poinsettia.

2015, Dec. 1   Litho.   Perf. 13
2968	A1508	7p multi	2.90	.85
2969	A1508	7p multi	2.90	.85
2970	A1508	11.50p multi	4.00	1.40
a.		Pair, #2968, 2970	7.50	7.50
2971	A1508	13.50p multi	5.25	1.75
a.		Pair, #2969, 2971	8.00	8.00
		Nos. 2968-2971 (4)	15.05	4.85

A1509

2015, Dec. 9   Litho.   Perf. 13x13¼
| 2972 | A1509 | 7p multi | 2.90 | .80 |

National Council for Standardization and Certification of Labor Skills, 20th Anniv.

National Council for Science and Technology, 45th Anniv. A1510

2015, Dec. 10   Litho.   Perf. 13¼x13
| 2973 | A1510 | 11.50p multi | 2.00 | 1.40 |

A1511

2015, Dec. 18   Litho.   Perf. 13¼x13
| 2974 | A1511 | 13.50p multi | 5.25 | 1.60 |

Fourth World Conference on Women and Beijing Declaration and Platform for Action, 20th Anniv.

Phocoena Sinus — A1512

No. 2975: a, Three vaquitas. b, Vaquita, aerial view of Baja California and Gulf of California. c, Two vaquitas.

2015, Dec. 21   Litho.   Perf. 13¼x13
2975		Horiz. strip of 3	5.25	3.75
a.		A1512 7.50p multi	1.90	.90
b.-c.		A1512 11.50p Either single	3.25	1.40

Reforms A1513

Inscriptions at bottom: No. 2976, Reforma Hacendaria. No. 2977, Código Nacional de Procedimientos Penales. No. 2978, Pacto por México. No. 2979, En Materia de Disciplina Financiera de las Entidades Federativas y los Municipios. No. 2980, Reforma Anticorrupción. No. 2981, Nueva Ley de Amparo. No. 2982, Reforma en Materia de Transparencia. No. 2983, Reforma Educativa. No. 2984, Reforma Financiera. No. 2985, Reforma en Materia de Telecomunicaciones y Radiodifusión. No. 2986, Reforma Política-Electoral.

No. 2987, Reforma Laboral. No. 2988, Reforma de Competencia Económica. No. 2989, Reforma Energética.

2015, Dec. 21   Litho.   Perf. 13¼x13
2976	A1513	7p multi	1.30	.80
2977	A1513	7p multi	1.30	.80
2978	A1513	7p multi	1.30	.80
2979	A1513	7p multi	1.30	.80
2980	A1513	7p multi	1.30	.80
2981	A1513	7p multi	1.30	.80
2982	A1513	7p multi	1.30	.80

Size: 72x40mm
2983	A1513	7p multi	1.30	.80
2984	A1513	7p multi	1.30	.80
2985	A1513	7p multi	1.30	.80
2986	A1513	7p multi	1.30	.80
2987	A1513	7p multi	1.30	.80
2988	A1513	7p multi	1.30	.80
2989	A1513	7p multi	1.30	.80
		Nos. 2976-2989 (14)	18.20	11.20

José María Morelos y Pavón (1765-1815), Priest and Leader in War of Independence A1514

2015, Dec. 22   Litho.   Perf. 13x13¼
| 2990 | A1514 | 7p multi | 1.30 | .80 |

Adding of Value to Women in the History of Mexico — A1515

2016, Jan. 21   Litho.   Perf. 13x13¼
| 2991 | A1515 | 7p multi | 2.00 | .80 |

End of International Year of Light — A1516

2016, Feb. 3   Litho.   Perf. 13¼x13
| 2992 | A1516 | 13.50p multi | 2.25 | 1.50 |

A1517

2016, Feb. 5   Litho.   Perf. 13¼x13
| 2993 | A1517 | 9p multi | 1.60 | 1.00 |

Chamber of Deputies, 1840 and 1857 Federal Constitution of the United Mexican States.

St. Valentine's Day — A1518

2016, Feb. 10   Litho.   Perf. 13
| 2994 | A1518 | 11.50p multi | 2.00 | 1.40 |

Visit of Pope Francis to Mexico — A1519

2016, Feb. 13   Litho.   Perf. 13¼x13
| 2995 | A1519 | 15p multi | 2.50 | 1.75 |

Postal Palace (Main Post Office), Mexico City — A1520

2016, Feb. 17   Litho.   Perf. 13¼x13
| 2996 | A1520 | 11.50p multi | 2.00 | 1.40 |

Autonomous University of the State of Mexico, 60th Anniv. — A1521

2016, Mar. 3   Litho.   Perf. 13x13¼
| 2997 | A1521 | 7p multi | 1.30 | .80 |

College of Civil Engineers of Mexico, 70th Anniv. — A1522

2016, Mar. 8   Litho.   Perf. 13x13¼
| 2998 | A1522 | 11.50p multi | 2.00 | 1.40 |

World Intellectual Property Day — A1523

2016, Apr. 28   Litho.   Perf. 13¼x13
| 2999 | A1523 | 13.50p multi | 2.40 | 1.60 |

Children's Day — A1524

2016, Apr. 29   Litho.   Perf. 13¼x13
3000	A1524	7p Doll	1.30	.85
3001	A1524	7p Top	1.30	.85
a.		Horiz. pair, #3000-3001	2.60	2.60

National Livestock Day A1525

2016, May 6   Litho.   Perf. 13¼x13
| 3002 | A1525 | 7p multi | 1.30 | .75 |

Mother's Day — A1526

2016, May 9   Litho.   Perf. 13
| 3003 | A1526 | 13.50p multi | 2.40 | 1.50 |

Communications and Transportation Secretariat, 125th Anniv. — A1527

2016, May 13   Litho.   Perf. 13¼x13
| 3004 | A1527 | 7p silver | 1.30 | .75 |

Jaime Torres Bodet (1902-74), Secretary of Public Education A1528

2016, May 15   Litho.   Perf. 13x13¼
| 3005 | A1528 | 7p multi | 1.30 | .75 |

Teacher's Day.

National Polytechnic Institute, 80th Anniv. A1529

2016, May 20   Litho.   Perf. 13¼x13
| 3006 | A1529 | 7p multi | 1.40 | .75 |

University of Quintana Roo, 25th Anniv. — A1530

2016, May 24   Litho.   Perf. 13¼x13
| 3007 | A1530 | 11.50p multi | 2.00 | 1.25 |

Torre Latinoamericana, Mexico City, 60th Anniv. — A1531

2016, May 31   Litho.   Perf. 13¼x13
| 3008 | A1531 | 13.50p multi | 2.25 | 1.50 |

Supreme Court Building, 75th Anniv. — A1532

2016, June 2   Litho.   Perf. 13x13¼
| 3009 | A1532 | 7p multi | 1.30 | .80 |

New Criminal Justice System — A1533

2016, June 17   Litho.   Perf. 13¼x13
| 3010 | A1533 | 7p multi | 1.30 | .80 |

Technological Institute of Saltillo, 65th Anniv. A1534

2016, June 23   Litho.   Perf. 13¼x13
| 3011 | A1534 | 7.50p multi | 1.30 | .85 |

Clean and Safe Energy Industry A1535

2016, July 27   Litho.   Perf. 13¼x13
| 3012 | A1535 | 9p multi | 1.50 | .95 |

MEXICO

First Mexican Stamps, 160th Anniv. — A1536

2016, Aug. 1	Litho.		Perf. 13¼x13	
3013	A1536	9p multi	1.50	.95

Promotion of Breastfeeding — A1537

2016, Aug. 5	Litho.		Perf. 13¼x13	
3014	A1537	11.50p multi	1.90	1.25

El Universal Newspaper, Cent. — A1538

2016, Aug. 15	Litho.		Perf. 13x13¼	
3015	A1538	13.50p multi	2.25	1.50

Mexico Post, 30th Anniv. A1539

2016, Aug. 19	Litho.		Perf. 13¼x13	
3016	A1539	7p multi	1.30	.75

School of Mechanical and Electrical Engineering, Mexico City, Cent. — A1540

2016, Aug. 23	Litho.		Perf. 13x13¼	
3017	A1540	9p multi	1.30	.95

Federal Institute of Telecommunications — A1541

2016, Sept. 9	Litho.		Perf. 13¼x13	
3018	A1541	7p multi	1.30	.75

National Institute for Adult Education, 35th Anniv. — A1542

2016, Sept. 26	Litho.		Perf. 13¼x13	
3019	A1542	7p multi	1.30	.75

State of Mexico Symphony Orchestra, 45th Anniv. — A1543

2016, Sept. 27	Litho.		Perf. 13x13¼	
3020	A1543	7p multi	1.30	.75

Lozano Brothers Group, 50th Anniv. — A1544

2016, Oct. 5	Litho.		Perf. 13x13¼	
3021	A1544	7p multi	1.30	.75

World Space Week — A1545

2016, Oct. 6	Litho.		Perf. 13x13¼	
3022	A1545	11.50p multi	1.75	1.25

Confederation of Mexican Workers, 80th Anniv. — A1546

2016, Oct. 7	Litho.		Perf. 13¼x13	
3023	A1546	7.50p multi	1.30	.80

World Post Day — A1547

2016, Oct. 10	Litho.		Perf. 13¼x13	
3024	A1547	13.50p multi	2.00	1.40

Civilian Disaster Aid Plan, 50th Anniv. — A1548

2016, Oct. 11	Litho.		Perf. 13¼x13	
3025	A1548	7p multi	1.30	.75

Engineering Institute of the National Autonomous University of Mexico, 60th Anniv. — A1549

2016, Oct. 11	Litho.		Perf. 13¼x13	
3026	A1549	9p multi	1.50	.95

Souvenir Sheet

Military Industry, Cent. A1550

No. 3027: a, Pres. Venustiano Carranza (1859-1920), bullets, factory gate. b, Gun maker. c, Military vehicle.

2016, Oct. 18	Litho.		Perf. 13	
3027	A1550	Sheet of 3	3.50	3.50
a.-c.		7p Any single	1.10	.75

Miniature Sheet

Sharks A1551

No. 3028: a, Prionace glauca. b, Sphyrna zygaena. c, Carcharodon carcharia. d, Carcharhinus falciformis.

2016, Oct. 20	Litho.		Perf. 13	
3028	A1551	Sheet of 12, 3 each #3028a-3028d	17.00	17.00
a.-b.		7p Either single	.75	.75
c.-d.		11.50p Either single	1.25	1.25

Diplomatic Relations Between Mexico and Jamaica, 50th Anniv. — A1552

Design: 7p, Papilio cresphontes. 11.50p, Danaus plexippus.

2016, Oct. 28	Litho.		Perf. 13	
3029		7p multicolored	1.00	.75
3030		11.50p multicolored	1.75	1.25
a.	A1552 Horiz. pair, #3029-3030		2.90	2.90

See Jamaica No. 1126.

All Souls' Day (Day of the Dead) — A1553

2016, Oct. 31	Litho.		Perf. 13¼x13	
3031	A1553	15p multi	2.10	1.60

Letter Carrier's Day — A1554

2016, Nov. 14	Litho.		Perf. 13¼x13	
3032	A1554	7p multi	1.10	.70

Rondalla de Saltillo Musical Group, 50th Anniv. — A1555

2016, Nov. 22	Litho.		Perf. 13x13¼	
3033	A1555	7.50p multi	1.25	.75

Roberto Kobeh González, Former President of Council of Intl. Civil Aviation Organization A1556

2016, Nov. 29	Litho.		Perf. 13¼x13	
3034	A1556	7p multi	1.10	.70

Jesús F. Contreras (1866-1902), Sculptor — A1557

2016, Nov. 30	Litho.		Perf. 13¼x13	
3035	A1557	11.50p multi	2.25	1.10

Christmas — A1558

No. 3036: a, Magi creche figurines. b, Star of Bethlehem. c, Poinsettia. d, Holy Family creche figurines.

2016, Dec. 2	Litho.		Perf. 13	
3036	A1558	Block of 4	5.25	5.25
a.-b.		7p Either single	1.10	.70
c.-d.		11.50p Either single	2.25	1.10

Battle of Juchitán, 150th Anniv. A1559

2016, Dec. 7	Litho.		Perf. 13¼x13	
3037	A1559	13.50p multi	2.00	1.40

Samalayuca Rock Paintings — A1560

2016, Dec. 9	Litho.		Perf. 13¼x13	
3038	A1560	13.50p multi	2.00	1.40

Federal Consumer Attorney's Office, 40th Anniv. — A1561

2016, Dec. 22	Litho.		Perf. 13¼x13	
3039	A1561	7p multi	1.10	.70

St. Valentine's Day — A1562

2017, Jan. 30	Litho.		Perf. 13	
3040	A1562	7p multi	1.30	.70

1917 Constitution, Cent. — A1563

2017, Feb. 5	Litho.		Perf. 13¼x13	
3041	A1563	7p multi	1.30	.70

MEXICO

Postal Palace (Main Post Office), Mexico City — A1564

2017, Feb. 17	Litho.		Perf. 13¼x13	
3042	A1564	7p multi	1.30	.70

Mariana Trinitaria Congregation, 20th Anniv. — A1565

2017, Feb. 17	Litho.		Perf. 13¼x13	
3043	A1565	15p multi	2.50	1.50

State of Nayarit, Cent. — A1566

2017, Mar. 3	Litho.		Perf. 13x13¼	
3044	A1566	7p multi	1.30	.70

Inter-American Defense Board, 75th Anniv. — A1567

2017, Mar. 27	Litho.		Perf. 13¼x13	
3045	A1567	7p multi	1.30	.75

General Health Council, Cent. — A1568

2017, Apr. 7	Litho.		Perf. 13¼x13	
3046	A1568	11.50p multi	2.00	1.25

2017 Aerospace Fair — A1569

2017, Apr. 26	Litho.		Perf. 13¼x13	
3047	A1569	7p multi	1.30	1.00

Children's Day — A1570

2017, Apr. 26	Litho.		Perf. 13¼x13	
3048	A1570	15p multi	2.50	1.60

World Intellectual Property Day — A1571

Designs: 7.50p, Color television, tubes, screen. 13.50p, Scorpion and vial of antivenom.

2017, Apr. 26	Litho.		Perf. 13x13¼	
3049		7.50p multi	1.30	.80
3050		13.50p multi	2.25	1.50
a.	Vert. pair, #3049-3050		3.50	2.40

Enforcement of Labor Regulations of Article 123 of Mexican Constitution of 1917, Cent. — A1572

2017, May 5	Litho.		Perf. 13x13¼	
3051	A1572	13.50p multi	2.25	1.50

Mother's Day — A1573

2017, May 9	Litho.		Perf. 13	
3052	A1573	7p multi	1.30	.75

A1574

2017, May 9	Litho.		Perf. 13x13¼	
3053	A1574	11.50p multi	2.00	1.25

University of Michoacan of San Nicolás de Hidalgo, Cent.

Teacher's Day — A1575

2017, May 15	Litho.		Perf. 13¼x13	
3054	A1575	11.50p multi	2.00	1.25

Military Medical School, Cent. — A1576

2017, May 24	Litho.		Perf. 13¼x13	
3055	A1576	15p multi	2.50	1.60

Telecommunication and Broadcasting Reforms, 4th Anniv. — A1577

2017, June 26	Litho.		Perf. 13x13¼	
3056	A1577	7p multi	1.30	.80

Agrarian Tribunals, 25th Anniv. — A1578

2017, July 7	Litho.		Perf. 13x13¼	
3057	A1578	7p multi	1.30	.80

World Population Day — A1579

2017, July 12	Litho.		Perf. 13x13¼	
3058	A1579	7p multi	1.30	.80

The Reformation and the Fall of the Empire, by José Clemente Orozco A1580

2017, July 14	Litho.		Perf. 13¼x13	
3059	A1580	7.50p multi	1.40	.85

Restoration of the Mexican Republic, 150th anniv.

National Army and Navy Bank (Banjercito), 70th Anniv. — A1581

No. 3060: a, Bank building, people in parking lot. b, Two bank buildings, sign with digital clock. c, Bank building and charter document.

2017, July 14	Litho.		Perf. 13¼x13	
3060	A1581	Horiz. strip of 3	4.50	4.50
a.-b.		7p Either single	1.25	.80
c.		11.50p multi	2.25	1.40

Golden Eagle A1582

2017, July 21	Litho.		Perf. 13¼x13	
3061	A1582	7p multi	1.30	.80

Secretariat of Environment and National Resources Federal Office of Environmental Protection, 25th anniv.

Railroads in Mexico, 180th Anniv. A1583

2017, Aug. 22	Litho.		Perf. 13¼x13	
3062	A1583	7.50p multi	1.40	.85

Avocados A1584

2017, Sept. 4	Litho.		Perf. 13¼x13	
3063	A1584	9p multi	1.60	1.00

Banco de Mexico — A1585

2017, Sept. 7	Litho.		Perf. 13x13¼	
3064	A1585	7p multi	1.30	.80

23rd Congress of Postal Union of the Americas, Spain and Portugal — A1586

2017, Sept. 18	Litho.		Perf. 13¼	
3065	A1586	13.50p multi	2.25	1.50
a.		Souvenir sheet of 1	13.00	13.00

Breast Cancer Prevention Month — A1587

2017, Oct. 4	Litho.		Perf. 13¼x13	
3066	A1587	7p multi	1.30	.80

World Post Day — A1588

2017, Oct. 9	Litho.		Perf. 13¼x13	
3067	A1588	13.50p multi	2.25	1.50

Public Housing Authority (FOVISSTE), 45th Anniv. — A1589

2017, Oct. 16	Litho.		Perf. 13¼x13	
3068	A1589	9p multi	1.60	.95

National Day Against Discrimination A1590

2017, Oct. 19	Litho.		Perf. 13¼x13	
3069	A1590	7p multi	1.30	.75

Mechanical and Electrical Engineering Faculty of Autonomous University of Nuevo León, 70th Anniv. A1591

2017, Oct. 21	Litho.		Perf. 13¼x13	
3070	A1591	11.50p multi	2.00	1.25

A1592

Design: Juan Antonio de la Fuente (1814-67), Politician and Ateneo Fuente, Saltillo.

2017, Oct. 26	Litho.		Perf. 13x13¼	
3071	A1592	7p multi	1.30	.75

Ateneo Fuente, 150th anniv.

All Souls' Day (Day of the Dead) A1593

2017, Oct. 31	Litho.		Perf. 13¼x13	
3072	A1593	7p multi	1.30	.75

First Airmail in Mexico, Cent. — A1594

2017, Nov. 8	Litho.		Perf. 13¼x13	
3073	A1594	7.50p gold & multi	1.40	.80

Protection of the Ozone Layer, 30th Anniv. — A1595

2017, Nov. 10	Litho.		Perf. 13¼x13	
3074	A1595	7p multi	1.30	.75

MEXICO

Letter Carrier's Day — A1596

2017, Nov. 10 Litho. Perf. 13¼x13
3075 A1596 7p multi   1.30 .75

National System of Integral Family Development, 40th Anniv. — A1597

2017, Nov. 14 Litho. Perf. 13x13¼
3076 A1597 7p gold & multi 1.30 .75

Mariano Otero (1817-50), Jurist — A1598

2017, Nov. 14 Litho. Perf. 13x13¼
3077 A1598 11.50p gold & multi 2.00 1.25

Assistance for Recipients of Services of Mexican Institute of Social Security, 40th Anniv. A1599

2017, Nov. 22 Litho. Perf. 13¼x13
3078 A1599 7p multi   1.30 .75

Meritorious Autonomous University of Puebla (BUAP), 80th Anniv. — A1600

2017, Nov. 23 Litho. Perf. 13x13¼
3079 A1600 7.50p multi   1.40 .80

Battle of Molino del Rey, 170th Anniv. — A1601

2017, Nov. 24 Litho. Perf. 13x13¼
3080 A1601 11.50p multi   2.00 1.25

Christmas A1602

Designs: No. 3081, Santa Claus and reindeer in flight. No. 3082, Magi and Star of Bethlehem.

2017, Dec. 1 Litho. Perf. 13
3081 7p multi   1.30 .75
3082 7p multi   1.30 .75
  a. A1602 Vert. pair, #3081-3082 2.75 1.50

Regional Office of the International Civil Aviation Organization, Mexico City, 60th Anniv. — A1603

2017, Dec. 7 Litho. Perf. 13¼x13
3083 A1603 7p multi   1.30 .75

Association for Standardization and Certification, 25th Anniv. — A1604

2017, Dec. 11 Litho. Perf. 13x13¼
3084 A1604 13.50p multi   2.40 1.40

First Encounter of European and American Cultures in Mexico, 500th Anniv. — A1605

2017, Dec. 18 Litho. Perf. 13x13¼
3085 A1605 15p multi   2.50 1.60

Jaime Torres Bodet (1902-74), Politician — A1606

2017, Dec. 20 Litho. Perf. 13¼x13
3086 A1606 7p multi   1.30 .75

Secretariat of Social Development, 25th Anniv. — A1607

2017, Dec. 20 Litho. Perf. 13¼x13
3087 A1607 7p silver & multi 1.30 .75

Mexican Institute of Transportation, 30th Anniv. — A1608

2017, Dec. 21 Litho. Perf. 13x13¼
3088 A1608 7p multi   1.30 .75

National Workers' Housing Fund Institute (INFONAVIT), 45th Anniv. A1609

2017, Dec. 21 Litho. Perf. 13¼x13
3089 A1609 7p multi   1.30 .75

National Preparatory School, 150th Anniv. — A1610

2018, Feb. 1 Litho. Perf. 13x13¼
3090 A1610 13.50p multi   2.10 1.50

St. Valentine's Day — A1611

2018, Feb. 9 Litho. Perf. 13¼x13
3091 A1611 7.50p multi   1.30 .80

"Our Children, Our Future" — A1612

2018, Feb. 12 Litho. Perf. 13x13¼
3092 A1612 9p multi   1.50 .95

Mexican Customs Brokers, Cent. — A1613

2018, Feb. 21 Litho. Perf. 13x13¼
3093 A1613 7p multi   1.25 .75

Postal Palace (Main Post Office), Mexico City A1614

2018, Feb. 22 Litho. Perf. 13¼x13
3094 A1614 15p multi   2.25 1.60

Mexican Petroleum (PEMEX), 80th Anniv. — A1615

2018, Mar. 16 Litho. Perf. 13x13¼
3095 A1615 9p multi   1.50 1.00

Reopening of Main Entrance of Benito Juárez Autonomous University of Oaxaca Faculty of Medicine And Surgery Building — A1616

2018, Mar. 28 Litho. Perf. 13¼x13
3096 A1616 7p multi   1.25 .80

World Intellectual Property Day — A1617

2018, Apr. 26 Litho. Perf. 13¼x13
3097 A1617 11.50p multi   1.90 1.25

Children's Day — A1618

2018, Apr. 30 Litho. Perf. 13x13¼
3098 A1618 13.50p multi   2.10 1.50

Labor Day — A1619

2018, May 1 Litho. Perf. 13¼x13
3099 A1619 7p multi   1.25 .75

Mother's Day — A1620

2018, May 9 Litho. Perf. 13x13¼
3100 A1620 7.50p multi   1.30 .75

Ramón Guillermo Bonfil Viveros (1905-97), Teacher and Union Leader A1621

2018, May 15 Litho. Perf. 13¼x13
3101 A1621 7p multi   1.30 .70
  Teacher's Day.

Mexican National Soccer Team — A1622

Designs: No. 3102, Five team members, soccer ball. No. 3103, Six team members.

2018, June 4 Litho. Perf. 13¼x13
3102 7p multi   1.25 .70
3103 7p multi   1.25 .70
  a. A1622 Horiz. pair, #3102-3103 2.50 2.50

Butterflies — A1623

Designs: No. 3104, Danaus plexippus. No. 3105, Nymphalidae (Morpho blue butterfly).

2018, June 15 Litho. Perf. 13¼x13
3104 15p multi   2.25 1.50
3105 15p multi   2.25 1.50
  a. A1623 Horiz. pair, #3104-3105 4.75 4.75
  See Colombia No. 1481.

Roche Mexico, 70th Anniv. — A1624

2018, June 21 Litho. Perf. 13¼x13
3106 A1624 7p multi   1.30 .70

World Day Against Human Trafficking A1625

2018, July 30 Litho. Perf. 13x13¼
3107 A1625 7p multi   1.25 .70

MEXICO

Ninth Meeting of the Organization of American States Inter-American Committee on Ports — A1626

Designs: No. 3108, Map showing world ports. No. 3109, Lighthouse.

2018, Aug. 2   Litho.   Perf. 13¼x13
3108		13.50p multi	2.10	1.40
3109		13.50p multi	2.10	1.40
a.	A1626 Horiz. pair, #3108-3109		4.25	4.25

Puerto Vallarta, Cent. — A1627

2018, Aug. 20   Litho.   Perf. 13x13¼
3110 A1627 13.50p multi   2.10 1.40

Chiranthodendron Pentadactylon — A1628

2018, Aug. 24   Litho.   Perf. 13¼x13
3111 A1628 7.50p multi   1.30 .80

Gilberto Rincón Gallardo (1939-2008), Politician — A1629

2018, Aug. 30   Litho.   Perf. 13x13¼
3112 A1629 7p multi   1.25 .75

Oaxaca Philately Museum, 20th Anniv. — A1630

Mailbox and: No. 3113, Building, cactus, post office counter. No. 3114, Building with open door, hallway inside building.

2018, Aug. 30   Litho.   Perf. 13x13¼
3113		7p multi	1.25	.75
3114		7p multi	1.25	.75
a.	A1630 Vert. pair, #3113-3114		2.50	2.50

Dogs From Naval Canine Unit — A1631

2018, Sept. 18   Litho.   Perf. 13¼x13
3115 A1631 15p brnz & multi   2.40 1.60

Mexican Society of Geotechnical Engineering A1632

2018, Sept. 20   Litho.   Perf. 13x13¼
3116 A1632 9p gold & multi   1.50 1.00

Victory of Pedro Rodríguez (1940-71) and Lucien Bianchi (1934-69) in 1968 24 Hours at Le Mans Race, 50th Anniv. A1633

2018, Sept. 29   Litho.   Perf. 13¼x13
3117 A1633 13.50p multi   2.10 1.50

National Autonomous University of Mexico Institute of Geography, 75th Anniv. — A1634

2018, Oct. 1   Litho.   Perf. 13x13¼
3118 A1634 7p multi   1.25 .75

National Institute of Migration, 25th Anniv. — A1635

2018, Oct. 5   Litho.   Perf. 13¼x13
3119 A1635 7p multi   1.25 .70

World Post Day — A1636

2018, Oct. 9   Litho.   Perf. 13¼x13
3120 A1636 13.50p multi   2.25 1.40

Military School of Sergeants, 70th Anniv. — A1637

2018, Oct. 11   Litho.   Perf. 13x13¼
3121 A1637 7.50p multi   1.30 .75

Ministry of Health, 75th Anniv. — A1638

2018, Oct. 18   Litho.   Perf. 13x13¼
3122 A1638 7p multi   1.25 .70

Naval Aviation School, 75th Anniv. A1639

2018, Oct. 18   Litho.   Perf. 13¼x13
3123 A1639 11.50p multi   2.00 .60

All Souls' Day (Day of the Dead) A1640

2018, Oct. 31   Litho.   Perf. 13¼x13
3124 A1640 11.50p multi   2.00 1.25

Rural Section Capitalization and Investment Fund, 25th Anniv. — A1641

2018, Nov. 8   Litho.   Perf. 13¼x13
3125 A1641 15p multi   2.50 2.25

Letter Carrier's Day — A1642

2018, Nov. 12   Litho.   Perf. 13¼x13
3126 A1642 11.50p multi   2.00 .60

Mexico Tourism Emblem — A1643

2018, Nov. 13   Litho.   Perf. 13x13¼
3127 A1643 7p multi   1.25 .35

Gopherus Flavomarginatus A1644

2018, Nov. 16   Litho.   Perf. 13x13¼
3128 A1644 15p multi   2.40 .75

Caldo de Piedra (Stone Soup) A1645

Designs: No. 3129, Cook heating broth on hot stones. No. 3130, Bowl of soup, vegetables and seafood.

2018, Dec. 7   Litho.   Perf. 13¼x13
3129		7p multi	1.25	.35
3130		7p multi	1.25	.35
a.	A1645 Horiz. pair, #3129-3130		2.50	1.25

Christmas A1646

Designs: No. 3131, Stylized flower. No. 3132, Magi.

2018, Dec. 14   Litho.   Perf. 13x13¼
3131		7p multi	1.25	.35
3132		7p multi	1.25	.35
a.	A1646 Pair, #3131-3132		2.50	1.25

Opening of New Mexican Baseball Hall of Fame Building, Monterrey — A1647

2018, Dec. 20   Litho.   Perf. 13¼x13
3133 A1647 7p multi   1.25 .35

Translation of the Bible into Spanish, 450th Anniv. — A1648

2019, Jan. 18   Litho.   Perf. 13x13¼
3134 A1648 11.50p multi   1.90 .60

National Commission for Free Textbooks, 60th Anniv. — A1649

2019, Feb. 13   Litho.   Perf. 13x13¼
3135 A1649 7p multi   1.25 .35

Postal Palace A1650

2019, Feb. 15   Litho.   Perf. 13¼x13
3136 A1650 9p multi   1.60 .45

Channel Eleven (Educational Broadcast Television Network), 60th Anniv. — A1651

2019, Mar. 4   Litho.   Perf. 13¼x13
3137 A1651 9p multi   1.60 .45

A1652

A1653

Opening of Alfredo Harp Helú Baseball Stadium, Mexico City A1654

2019, Mar. 23   Litho.   Perf. 13¼x13
3138		Horiz. strip of 3	3.75	1.10
a.	A1652 7p multi		1.25	.35
b.	A1653 7p multi		1.25	.35
c.	A1654 7p multi		1.25	.35

Jaguar A1655

2019, Mar. 27   Litho.   Perf. 13¼x13
3139 A1655 15p multi   2.25 .80

MEXICO

Gen. Emiliano Zapata (1817-1919), Leader of Peasant Revolution — A1656

2019, Apr. 10   Litho.   Perf. 13x13¼
3140 A1656 7.50p multi   1.30 .40

Veracruz, 500th Anniv. — A1657

2019, Apr. 17   Litho.   Perf. 13¼x13
3141 A1657 13.50p multi   2.10 .75

2019 Mexico Aerospace Fair — A1658

2019, Apr. 24   Litho.   Perf. 13x13¼
3142 A1658 7p multi   1.25 .35

Children's Day — A1659

2019, Apr. 29   Litho.   Perf. 13x13¼
3143 A1659 7p multi   1.25 .35

Estefanía Castañeda (1872-1937), Founder of Kindergartens — A1660

2019, May 15   Litho.   Perf. 13¼x13
3144 A1660 15p multi   2.40 .80

Teacher's Day.

University of Veracruz, 75th Anniv. — A1661

2019, Sept. 11   Litho.   Perf. 13x13¼
3145 A1661 7p multi   1.25 .35

Mexiquense Public Radio and Television System, 35th Anniv. — A1662

2019, Sept. 26   Litho.   Perf. 13¼x13
3146 A1662 9p multi   1.50 .45

World Post Day — A1663

2019, Oct. 9   Litho.   Perf. 13x13¼
3147 7p multi   1.25 .35
3148 7p multi   1.25 .35
  a. A1663 Vert. pair, #3147-3148   2.50 1.25

Universal Postal Union emblem and: No. 3147, Hand inserting letter into slot. No. 3148, Hand holding letter.

Autonomy of Autonomous University of the State of Mexico, 75th Anniv. — A1664

2019, Oct. 17   Litho.   Perf. 13x13¼
3149 A1664 13.50p multi   2.25 .70

All Souls' Day (Day of the Dead) — A1665

2019, Oct. 30   Litho.   Perf. 13¼x13
3150 A1665 7.50p multi   1.60 .40

Letter Carrier's Day — A1666

Designs: No. 3151, Mail carrier, old mail car, postal workers and mail sacks. No. 3151, Letter carrier on bicycle, mail van, letter carrier holding envelopes.

2019, Nov. 12   Litho.   Perf. 13¼x13
3151   11.50p multi   1.75 .60
3152   11.50p multi   1.75 .60
  a. A1666 Horiz. pair, #3151-3152   3.75 1.75

Mexican Stock Exchange, 125th Anniv. — A1667

2019, Nov. 19   Litho.   Perf. 13¼x13
3153 A1667 7p multi   1.25 .35

Christmas A1668

Designs: No. 3154, Poinsettia and air mail envelopes. No. 3155, Piñata and Nativity scene.

2019, Dec. 6   Litho.   Perf. 13x13¼
3154   7p multi   1.25 .35
3155   7p multi   1.25 .35
  a. A1668 Vert. pair, #3154-3155   2.50 1.25

Candelaria (Candlemas) Festival — A1669

2020, Jan. 29   Litho.   Perf. 13¼x13
3156 A1669 13.50p multi   2.00 .75

Postal Palace Clock — A1670

2020, Feb. 17   Litho.   Perf. 13
3157 A1670 15p multi   2.10 .80

Deployment of AzTechSat-1 Nanosatellite From International Space Station — A1671

2020, Feb. 25   Litho.   Perf. 13¼
3158 A1671 7p sil & multi   1.10 .35

A souvenir sheet containing No. 3158 was produced in limited quantities.

Cancún, 50th Anniv. — A1672

2020, Mar. 3   Litho.   Perf. 13x13¼
3159 A1672 11.50p gold & multi 1.75 .60

Benita Galeana (1903-95), Feminist Writer and Activist A1673

2020, Mar. 6   Litho.   Perf. 13¼x13
3160 A1673 7p multi   1.10 .30

International Women's Day.

Folk Art Type of 2005

Designs: No. 3161, Black clay jug. No. 3162, Horn comb. No. 3163, Silk shawl. No. 3164, Lacquered wooden chest. No. 3165, Embroidered tablecloth. No. 3166, Copper jar. No. 3167, Doll. No. 3168, Obsidian and opal turtle. No. 3169, Legged earthen pot. No. 3170, Woven basket. No. 3171, Silver pear, with "Ciudad de México" inscription. No. 3172, Amber marimba. No. 3173, Paper bull.

2020   Litho.   Hyphen Hole Perf. 10
Self-Adhesive
3161 A1141 50c multi   .35   .25
  a. Dated "2021"   .35   .25
  b. Dated "2022," hyphen hole perf. 6¾   .25   .30
  c. Dated "2023," hyphen hole perf. 6¾   .30   .30
3162 A1141 1p multi   .35   .25
  a. Dated "2021"   .35   .25
  b. Dated "2022," hyphen hole perf. 6¾   .30   .30
  c. Dated "2023," hyphen hole perf. 6¾   .30   .30
3163 A1141 1.50p multi   .35   .25
  a. Dated "2021"   .35   .25
  b. Dated "2022," hyphen hole perf. 6¾   .30   .30
  c. Dated "2023," hyphen hole perf. 6¾   .30   .30
3164 A1141 2p multi   .35   .25
  a. Dated "2021"   .35   .25
  b. Dated "2022," hyphen hole perf. 6¾   .30   .30
  c. Dated "2023," hyphen hole perf. 6¾   .30   .30
3165 A1141 2.50p multi   .35   .25
  a. Dated "2021"   .35   .25
  b. Dated "2022," hyphen hole perf. 6¾   .30   .30
  c. Dated "2023," hyphen hole perf. 6¾   .30   .30
3166 A1141 5p multi   .75   .25
  a. Dated "2021"   .80   .25
  b. Dated "2022," hyphen hole perf. 6¾   .50   .30
  c. Dated "2023," hyphen hole perf. 6¾   .60   .30
3167 A1141 7p multi   1.00 .30
  a. Dated "2021"   1.10 .35
  b. Dated "2022," hyphen hole perf. 6¾   .75   .35
  c. Dated "2023," hyphen hole perf. 6¾   .85   .40
3168 A1141 7.50p multi   1.10 .35
  a. Dated "2021"   1.25 .35
  b. Dated "2022," hyphen hole perf. 6¾   .80   .40
  c. Dated "2023," hyphen hole perf. 6¾   .90   .45
3169 A1141 9p multi   1.30 .40
  a. Dated "2021"   1.50 .45
  b. Dated "2022," hyphen hole perf. 6¾   .95   .45
  c. Dated "2023," hyphen hole perf. 6¾   1.10 .55
3170 A1141 11.50p multi   1.60 .50
  a. Dated "2021"   1.80 .55
  b. Dated "2023," hyphen hole perf. 6¾   1.40 .70
3171 A1141 13.50p multi   2.00 .60
  a. Dated "2021"   2.10 .65
  b. Dated "2022," hyphen hole perf. 6¾   1.40 .70
  c. Dated "2023," hyphen hole perf. 6¾   1.60 .80
3172 A1141 15p multi   2.25 .70
  a. Dated "2021"   2.50 .75
  b. Dated "2022," hyphen hole perf. 6¾   1.60 .80
  c. Dated "2023," hyphen hole perf. 6¾   1.75 .90
3173 A1141 30.50p multi   4.50 1.40
  a. Dated "2021"   5.00 1.50
  b. Dated "2023," hyphen hole perf. 6¾   3.75 1.90
  Nos. 3161-3173 (13)   16.25 5.75

Nos. 3161-3173 are each dated "2020." For stamps with water-activated gum, see Nos. 3229-3241.

National Commission for Regulatory Improvement, 20th Anniv. — A1674

2020, July 26   Litho.   Perf. 13x13¼
3174 A1674 7p multi   1.10 .30

Pres. Venustiano Carranza (1859-1920) A1675

Hyphen Hole Perf. 10
2020, Aug. 27   Litho.
Self-Adhesive
3175 A1675 15p multi   2.25 .75

José Santos Valdés (1905-90), Educator — A1676

Hyphen Hole Perf. 10
2020, Sept. 11   Litho.
Self-Adhesive
3176 A1676 7p multi   1.10 .30

Teacher's Day.

Leona Vicario (1789-1842), Journalist and Independence Movement Heroine, and Mexico No. 311 — A1677

Hyphen Hole Perf. 10
2020, Sept. 28   Litho.
Self-Adhesive
3177 A1677 7p multi   1.10 .30

Diplomatic Relations Between Mexico and Lebanon, 75th Anniv. A1678

Designs: 7p, Templo Mayor and Metropolitan Cathedral, Mexico City. 15p, Temple of Bacchus, Baalbek, Lebanon.

MEXICO

Hyphen Hole Perf. 10
2020, Sept. 30   Litho.
Self-Adhesive

3178	7p multi	1.25	.30
3179	15p multi	2.00	.70
a.	A1678 Horiz. pair, #3178-3179	3.25	1.60

See Lebanon No. 827.

World Post Day — A1679

Envelopes and half of globe showing: No. 3180, North and Central America, Australia. No. 3181, Greenland, Europe, Africa and South America.

Hyphen Hole Perf. 10
2020, Oct. 9   Litho.
Self-Adhesive

3180	7p multi	1.10	.35
3181	7p multi	1.10	.35
a.	A1679 Horiz. pair, #3180-3181	2.25	1.10

Lázaro Cárdenas del Río (1895-1970), General and President of Mexico — A1680

Hyphen Hole Perf. 10
2020, Oct. 19   Litho.
Self-Adhesive

3182	A1680 11.50p multi	1.90	.55

The Offering, Painting by Manuel Muñoz Olivares (1925-2011) — A1681

Hyphen Hole Perf. 10
2020, Oct. 28   Litho.
Self-Adhesive

3183	A1681 13.50p multi	2.00	.65

All Souls' Day (Day of the Dead).

Workers in the COVID-19 Pandemic A1682

Hyphen Hole Perf. 10
2020, Nov. 3   Litho.
Self-Adhesive

3184	A1682 7p multi	1.10	.35

A1683   A1684
A1685   A1686

Letter Carrier's Day — A1687

Hyphen Hole Perf. 10
2020, Nov. 11   Litho.
Self-Adhesive

3185	Horiz. strip of 5	5.75	3.50
a.	A1683 7p multi	1.10	.35
b.	A1684 7p multi	1.10	.35
c.	A1685 7p multi	1.10	.35
d.	A1686 7p multi	1.10	.35
e.	A1687 7p multi	1.10	.35
f.	Souvenir sheet of 5, #3185a-3185e	—	—

Tribute to Postal Workers During COVID-19 Pandemic A1688

Hyphen Hole Perf. 10
2020, Nov. 11   Litho.
Self-Adhesive

3186	A1688 7p multi	1.10	.35

Sister Juana Inés de la Cruz (1648-95), Writer — A1689

2020, Nov. 12   Litho.   Perf. 13

3187	A1689	Block of 4 + 2 labels	7.25	3.50
a.		7p blue violet & black	1.10	.35
b.		11.50p green & black	1.90	.60
c.		13.50p redsh purple & black	2.00	.70
d.		15p purple & black	2.25	.75

Municipality of Mineral de la Reforma, Cent. — A1690

2020, Nov. 12   Litho.   Perf. 13¼x13

3188	A1690 7p multi	1.10	.35

Christmas A1691

Children: No. 3189, Swinging at piñata. No. 3190, Holding candles and carrying creche.

Hyphen Hole Perf. 10
2020, Nov. 27   Litho.
Self-Adhesive

3189	15p multi	2.25	.75
3190	15p multi	2.25	.75
a.	A1691 Horiz. pair, #3189-3190	4.50	2.25

A1692

Crops A1693

Nos. 3191 and 3192: a, Phaseolus vulgaris "Sangre toro." b, Opuntia ficus-indica. c, Capsicum annuum "Serrano." d, Amaranthus hypochondriacus.

Hyphen Hole Perf. 10
2020, Dec. 7   Litho.
Self-Adhesive

3191	A1692	Block of 4	8.00	8.00
a.		7p multi	1.10	.35
b.		11.50p multi	1.90	.60
c.		13.50p multi	2.00	.70
d.		15p multi	2.25	.75
e.		Souvenir sheet of 4, #3191a-3191d	8.00	8.00

Miniature Sheet

3192	A1693	Sheet of 4	8.00	8.00
a.		7p multi	1.10	.35
b.		11.50p multi	1.90	.60
c.		13.50p multi	2.00	.70
d.		15p multi	2.25	.75

Ludwig van Beethoven (1770-1827), Composer — A1695

Hyphen Hole Perf. 10
2020, Dec. 11   Litho.
Self-Adhesive

3194	A1695 13.50p multi	2.10	.70

Space Flight of Rodolfo Neri Vela, First Mexican Astronaut, and Launch of Morelos II Satellite, 35th Anniv. A1696

Hyphen Hole Perf. 10
2020, Dec. 17   Litho.
Self-Adhesive

3195	A1696 7p gold & multi	1.25	.35

Postal Palace — A1697

Hyphen Hole Perf. 10
2021, Feb. 17   Litho.
Self-Adhesive

3196	A1697 11.50p multi	1.90	.55

Flag Day — A1698

No. 3197 — La Patria, Painting by Jesús Helguera (1910-71), with frame color of: a, Red. b, Maroon. c, Dull brown. d, Dark red. e, Green.

Hyphen Hole Perf. 10
2021, Feb. 24   Litho.
Self-Adhesive

3197	Horiz. strip of 5	6.00	6.00
a.-e.	A1698 7p Any single	1.00	.35

Benito Juárez (1806-72), 26th President of Mexico — A1699

Hyphen Hole Perf. 10
2021, Mar. 21   Litho.
Self-Adhesive

3198	A1699 15p brnz & multi	2.40	.75

Astor Piazzolla (1921-92), Tango Composer and Musician A1700

Hyphen Hole Perf. 10
2021, Apr. 29   Litho.
Self-Adhesive

3199	A1700 7.50p multi	1.30	.35

1847-1901 Mayan Caste War — A1701

Hyphen Hole Perf. 10
2021, May 4   Litho.
Self-Adhesive

3200	A1701 9p multi	1.60	.45

World Philatelist's Day — A1702

Hyphen Hole Perf. 10
2021, May 12   Litho.
Self-Adhesive

3201	A1702 7p multi	1.30	.35

Capitulation of San Juan de Ulúa, Painting by Patrick O'Brien — A1703

Hyphen Hole Perf. 10
2021, May 25   Litho.
Self-Adhesive

3202	A1703 13.50p multi	2.25	.70

Mexican Navy, 200th anniv.

MEXICO

Geometric Projection, Painting by Vicente Rojo (1932-2021) — A1704

Hyphen Hole Perf. 10
2021, June 10 Litho.
Self-Adhesive
3203 A1704 7p multi 1.30 .35

A1705

Ministry of Communications and Transportation, 130th Anniv. — A1706

Hyphen Hole Perf. 10
2021, July 23 Litho.
Self-Adhesive
3204 A1705 15p multi 2.50 .75
3205 A1706 15p multi 2.50 .75
  a. Horiz. pair, #3204-3205 5.00 5.00
  b. Souvenir sheet of 2, #3204-3205 — —

Simón Bolívar (1783-1830), Liberator of Latin American Countries A1707

Hyphen Hole Perf. 10
2021, July 24 Litho.
Self-Adhesive
3206 A1707 7.50p multi 1.40 .40

Rosaura Zapata Cano (1876-1963), Educator A1708

Hyphen Hole Perf. 10
2021, Aug. 3 Litho.
Self-Adhesive
3207 A1708 7p multi 1.30 .35
Teachers' Day.

Allegory of General Vicente Guerrero and the Homeland, Painting by Jaime Antonio Gomez del Payan Medina A1709

Hyphen Hole Perf. 10
2021, Aug. 9 Litho.
Self-Adhesive
3208 A1709 13.50p multi 2.25 .70
Independence of Mexico, 200th anniv.

Autonomy of Mexican Postal Service, 35th Anniv. A1710

Hyphen Hole Perf. 10
2021, Aug. 20 Litho.
Self-Adhesive
3209 A1710 9p multi 1.50 .45

Federal Court of Administrative Justice, 85th Anniv. — A1711

Hyphen Hole Perf. 10
2021, Aug. 27 Litho.
Self-Adhesive
3210 A1711 15p multi 2.50 .75

Fall of Tenochtitlan, 500th Anniv. — A1712

Hyphen Hole Perf. 10
2021, Aug. 30 Litho.
Self-Adhesive
3211 A1712 7p multi 1.30 .35

Founding of Tenochtitlan, 700th Anniv. A1713

Resistance of Indigenous People to Spanish Rule, 500th Anniv. A1714

Mexican Independence, 200th Anniv. — A1715

Hyphen Hole Perf. 10
2021, Sept. 15 Litho.
Self-Adhesive
3212 Horiz. strip of 3 6.25 3.00
  a. A1713 13.50p multi 2.00 .65
  b. A1714 13.50p multi 2.00 .65
  c. A1715 13.50p multi 2.00 .65
  d. Souvenir sheet of 3, #3212a-3212c 6.25 6.25

Crest and Motto of National Autonomous University of Mexico, Cent. — A1716

Hyphen Hole Perf. 10
2021, Sept. 22 Litho.
Self-Adhesive
3213 A1716 15p multi 2.25 .75

Citizen Council for Security and Justice of Mexico City — A1717

Hyphen Hole Perf. 10
2021, Sept. 30 Litho.
Self-Adhesive
3214 A1717 7p multi 1.25 .35

National Financial Education Week — A1718

Hyphen Hole Perf. 10
2021, Oct. 4 Litho.
Self-Adhesive
3215 A1718 13.50p multi 2.00 .65

Secretary of Public Education, Cent. — A1719

Hyphen Hole Perf. 10
2021, Oct. 9 Litho.
Self-Adhesive
3216 A1719 7p multi 1.25 .35

World Post Day — A1720

Hyphen Hole Perf. 10
2021, Oct. 9 Litho.
Self-Adhesive
3217 A1720 15p multi 2.25 .75

National Guard — A1721

Hyphen Hole Perf. 10
2021, Oct. 14 Litho.
Self-Adhesive
3218 A1721 11.50p multi 1.90 .55

All Souls' Day (Day of the Dead) A1722

Hyphen Hole Perf. 10
2021, Oct. 29 Litho.
Self-Adhesive
3219 A1722 7.50p multi 1.40 .35

Telegraphy in Mexico, 170th Anniv. — A1723

Hyphen Hole Perf. 10
2021, Nov. 4 Litho.
Self-Adhesive
3220 A1723 7p multi 1.25 .35

National Institute of Astrophysics, Optics and Electronics, 50th Anniv. — A1724

Hyphen Hole Perf. 10
2021, Nov. 11 Litho.
Self-Adhesive
3221 A1724 7p multi 1.25 .35

Letter Carriers' Day — A1725

No. 3222: a, Female letter carrier on bicycle. b, Male letter carrier on punt. c, Letter carrier's whistle. d, Helmeted carrier delivering mail. e, Envelope.

Hyphen Hole Perf. 10
2021, Nov. 13 Litho.
Self-Adhesive
3222 Horiz. strip of 5 6.25 6.25
  a.-e. A1725 7p Any single 1.25 .35
  f. Souvenir sheet of 5, #3222a-3222e 7.00 7.00

Huawei Technologies Co. in Mexico, 20th Anniv. — A1726

No. 3223 — Huawei 20th anniv. emblem and: a, Parachutist. b, Hand reaching out to robotic hand. c, Lighthouse. d, Mayan calendar.

Hyphen Hole Perf. 10
2021, Nov. 18 Litho.
Self-Adhesive
3223 Horiz. strip of 4 9.50 5.00
  a.-d. A1726 15p Any single 2.25 .75

College of Sciences and Humanities, Naucalpan, 50th Anniv. — A1727

Hyphen Hole Perf. 10
2021, Nov. 22 Litho.
Self-Adhesive
3224 A1727 7p multi 1.25 .35

Christmas A1728

Designs: No. 3225, Christmas star piñata. No. 3226, Magi creche figures and stained glass window.

MEXICO

Hyphen Hole Perf. 10
2021, Dec. 10   Litho.
Self-Adhesive

3225	7.50p multi	1.25	.35
3226	7.50p multi	1.25	.35
a.	A1728 Horiz. pair, #3225-3226	2.75	1.40

Diplomatic Relations Between Mexico and Colombia, 200th Anniv. — A1729

Stylized butterfly at: No. 3227, Left. No. 3228, Right.

Hyphen Hole Perf. 10
2021, Dec. 20   Litho.
Self-Adhesive

3227	13.50p multi	2.25	.65
3228	13.50p multi	2.25	.65
a.	A1729 Pair, #3227-3228	4.50	2.25

See Colombia No. 1593.

Folk Art Type of 2005

Designs: No. 3229, Black clay jug. No. 3230, Horn comb. No. 3231, Silk shawl. No. 3232, Lacquered wooden chest. No. 3233, Embroidered tablecloth. No. 3234, Copper jar. No. 3235, Doll. No. 3236, Obsidian and opal turtle. No. 3237, Legged earthen pot. No. 3238, Woven basket. No. 3239, Silver pear, with "Ciudad de México" inscription. No. 3240, Amber marimba. No. 3241, Paper bull.

2022   Litho.   Hyphen Hole Perf. 10
Water-Activated Gum

3229	A1141	50c multi, dated "2022"	.30	.30
3230	A1141	1p multi, dated "2022"	.30	.30
3231	A1141	1.50p multi, dated "2022"	.30	.30
3232	A1141	2p multi, dated "2022"	.30	.30
3233	A1141	2.50p multi, dated "2022"	.30	.30
3234	A1141	5p multi, dated "2022"	.50	.30
3235	A1141	7p multi, dated "2022"	.75	.35
3236	A1141	7.50p multi, dated "2022"	.80	.40
a.		Perf. 13¼x13, dated "2022"	.80	.40
3237	A1141	9p multi, dated "2022"	.95	.45
3238	A1141	11.50p multi, dated "2022"	1.25	.60
a.		Perf. 13¼x13, dated "2022"	1.25	.60
3239	A1141	13.50p multi, dated "2022"	1.40	.70
a.		Perf. 13¼x13, dated "2022"	1.40	.70
3240	A1141	15p multi, dated "2022"	1.60	.80
3241	A1141	30.50p multi, dated "2022"	3.25	1.60
a.		Perf. 13¼x13, dated "2022"	3.25	1.60
	Nos. 3229-3241 (13)		12.00	6.70

Carlos Pellicer (1897-1977), Poet — A1730

Hyphen Hole Perf. 10
2022, Jan. 16   Litho.
Self-Adhesive

3242	A1730 7p multi	.70	.35

Diplomatic Relations Between Mexico and People's Republic of China, 50th Anniv. — A1731

Designs: No. 3243, Temple of Kukulkán, Chichén Itzá, Mexico. No. 3244, Dengfeng Observatory, Gaocheng, People's Republic of China.

2022, Feb. 14   Litho.   Perf. 13x13¼

3243	15p multi	1.50	.75
3244	15p multi	1.50	.75
a.	A1731 Horiz. pair, #3243-3244	3.00	1.50

Postal Palace, Mexico City, 115th Anniv. — A1755

2022, Feb. 17   Litho.   Perf. 13

3245	Sheet of 24 + central label	17.00	17.00
a.	A1732 7p multi	.70	.35
b.	A1733 7p multi	.70	.35
c.	A1734 7p multi	.70	.35
d.	A1735 7p multi	.70	.35
e.	A1736 7p multi	.70	.35
f.	A1737 7p multi	.70	.35
g.	A1738 7p multi	.70	.35
h.	A1739 7p multi	.70	.35
i.	A1740 7p multi	.70	.35
j.	A1741 7p multi	.70	.35
k.	A1742 7p multi	.70	.35
l.	A1743 7p multi	.70	.35
m.	A1744 7p multi	.70	.35
n.	A1745 7p multi	.70	.35
o.	A1746 7p multi	.70	.35
p.	A1747 7p multi	.70	.35
q.	A1748 7p multi	.70	.35
r.	A1749 7p multi	.70	.35
s.	A1750 7p multi	.70	.35
t.	A1751 7p multi	.70	.35
u.	A1752 7p multi	.70	.35
v.	A1753 7p multi	.70	.35
w.	A1754 7p multi	.70	.35
x.	A1755 7p multi	.70	.35

International Women's Day — A1756

2022, Mar. 8   Litho.   Perf. 13¼x13
3246	A1756 9p multi	.95	.45

National Week to Combat Sanitary Risks — A1757

2022, Apr. 30   Litho.   Perf. 13x13¼
3247	A1757 7p multi	.70	.35

First Phase of the Battle, Painting by Patricio Ramos y Ortega A1758

2022, May 2   Litho.   Perf. 13¼x13
3248	A1758 7p multi	.70	.35

Battle of Puebla, 160th anniv.

MEXICO

Children's Day — A1759

2022, May 3   Litho.   Perf. 13x13¼
3249   A1759   7.50p multi   .80   .40

School of Public Health of Mexico, Cent. A1760

2022, May 13   Litho.   Perf. 13¼x13
3250   A1760   7.50p multi   .80   .40

International Day of Women in Maritime Trades — A1761

2022, May 18   Litho.   Perf. 13¼x13
3251   A1761   11.50p multi   1.25   .60

Institute of the National Housing Fund for Workers, 50th Anniv. — A1762

2022, May 24   Litho.   Perf. 13x13¼
3252   A1762   7p multi   .75   .35

Foundation of Villa del Espíritu Santo, 500th Anniv. — A1763

2022, June 8   Litho.   Perf. 13¼x13
3253   A1763   15p multi   1.50   .75

Mexican Embassy, Rome, Italy, Cent. — A1764

2022, June 27   Litho.   Perf. 13¼x13
3254   A1764   13.50p multi   1.40   .70

Tax Administration Service, 25th Anniv. — A1765

2022, July 1   Litho.   Perf. 13¼x13
3255   A1765   7p multi   .70   .35

State of Baja California, 70th Anniv. — A1766

2022, July 11   Litho.   Perf. 13x13¼
3256   A1766   7p multi   .70   .35

Banjercito (National Army and Navy Bank), 75th Anniv. — A1767

2022, July 15   Litho.   Perf. 13x13¼
3257   A1767   7p multi   .70   .35

Benito Juárez (1806-72), 26th President of Mexico, and Mexico No. 859 — A1768

2022, July 21   Litho.   Perf. 13¼x13
3258   A1768   7.50p multi   .75   .35

Escuela Libre de Derecho (Law School), Mexico City, 110th Anniv. — A1769

2022, July 24   Litho.   Perf. 13¼x13
3259   A1769   7p sil & multi   .70   .35

Leona Vicario (1789-1842) and Manuela Sáenz (1797-1856), Heroines of Latin American Liberation Movements A1770

2022, July 28   Litho.   Perf. 13¼x13
3260   A1770   13.50p multi   1.40   .70
See Ecuador No.

José María Vigil (1829-1909), Writer, Educator and Judge — A1771

2022, Aug. 12   Litho.   Perf. 13¼x13
3261   A1771   7p multi   .70   .35
Teacher's Day.

Retirement Savings System, 25th Anniv. — A1772

2022, Aug. 15   Litho.   Perf. 13¼x13
3262   A1772   7p multi   .70   .35

Technological Institute of Puebla, 50th Anniv. — A1773

2022, Sept. 1   Litho.   Perf. 13x13¼
3263   A1773   7p multi   .70   .35

Diplomatic Relations Between Mexico and Israel, 70th Anniv. — A1774

Designs: No. 3264, Birds, cacti and flowers. No. 3265, Flowers and "70."

2022, Sept. 13   Litho.   Perf. 13x13¼
3264   7.50p multi   .75   .35
3265   7.50p multi   .75   .35
   a.   A1774 Vert. pair, #3264-3265   1.50   .70
See Israel No. 2321.

A1775

A1776

A1777

Mexican Independence Day — A1778

2022, Sept. 15   Litho.   Perf. 13¼x13
3266   Horiz. strip of 4   5.75   2.80
   a.   A1775 13.50p multi   1.40   .70
   b.   A1776 13.50p multi   1.40   .70
   c.   A1777 13.50p multi   1.40   .70
   d.   A1778 13.50p multi   1.40   .70
   e.   Souvenir sheet of 4, #3266a-3266d   5.75   5.75

An additional example of No. 3266d having a slightly different frame is printed at the right side of the strip of 4. Stamps on No. 3266e have different frames than those found in the horizontal strip.

Seaport and Emblem of General Directorate of Port Development and Administration — A1779

2022, Sept. 26   Litho.   Perf. 13¼x13
3267   A1779   15p multi   1.50   .75
   a.   Souvenir sheet of 1   1.50   .75

Pánuco, 500th Anniv. — A1780

2022, Sept. 30   Litho.   Perf. 13x13¼
3268   A1780   7.50p multi   .75   .35

Institute of Security and Social Services for State Workers' Day — A1781

2022, Oct. 3   Litho.   Perf. 13¼x13
3269   A1781   7.50p multi   .75   .35

World Post Day — A1782

2022, Oct. 9   Litho.   Perf. 13¼x13
3270   A1782   15p multi   1.50   .75
   a.   Miniature sheet of 6   9.00   9.00

Gabriela Mistral (1889-1957), 1945 Nobel Laureate in Literature — A1783

2022, Oct. 25   Litho.   Perf. 13¼x13
3271   A1783   11.50p multi   1.25   .60
See Chile No. 1690.

Berta Singerman (1901-98), Singer and Actress — A1784

2022, Oct. 26   Litho.   Perf. 13¼x13
3272   A1784   11.50p multi   1.25   .60
See Argentina No. 2969.

Ricardo Flores Magón (1874-1922), Editor of Anarchist Newspaper A1785

Denomination in: No. 3273, Bister. No. 3274, Brown.

2022, Nov. 21   Litho.   Perf. 13x13¼
3273   7p multi   .75   .35
3274   7p multi   .75   .35
   a.   A1785 Vert. pair, #3273-3274   1.50   .70

Electoral Judicial School — A1786

2022, Nov. 24   Litho.   Perf. 13¼x13
3275   A1786   7p multi   .70   .35

A1787

Mexican National Soccer Team A1788

MEXICO

2022, Nov. 24   Litho.   Perf. 13¼x13
3276	A1787 15p multi	1.50	.75
3277	A1788 15p multi	1.50	.75
a.	Horiz. pair, #3276-3277	3.00	1.50

2022 World Cup Soccer Championships, Qatar.

Christmas A1789

Gifts and: No. 3278, Bird, Christmas tree. No. 3279, Magi on bicycles.

2022, Dec. 8   Litho.   Perf. 13¼x13
3278	7.50p multi	.80	.40
3279	7.50p multi	.80	.40
a.	A1789 Horiz. pair, #3278-3279	1.60	.80

Diplomatic Relations Between Mexico and Vatican City, 30th Anniv. — A1790

2022, Dec. 12   Litho.   Perf. 13¼x13
3200	A1790 10.50p multi	1.40	.70

See Vatican City No. 1810.

Association for Standardization and Certification, 30th Anniv — A1791

2022, Dec. 14   Litho.   Perf. 13¼x13
3281	A1791 13.50p multi	1.40	.70

Allegory of Work, Painting by Saturnino Herrán (1887-1918) — A1792

2022, Dec. 16   Litho.   Perf. 13¼x13
3282	A1792 9p multi	.95	.45

National Polytechnic Institute.

International Migrants Day — A1793

2022, Dec. 16   Litho.   Perf. 13¼x13
3283	A1793 11.50p multi	1.25	.60

Mexican Army, 110th Anniv. — A1794

2023, Feb. 15   Litho.   Perf. 13x13¼
3284	A1794 7p multi	.80	.40

Assassinations of Pres. Francisco I. Madero (1873-1913) and Vice President José María Pino Suárez (1869-1913), 110th Anniv. — A1795

2023, Feb. 23   Litho.   Perf. 13¼x13
3285	A1795 11.50p multi	1.25	.65

Military School of Sergeants, Puebla, 75th Anniv. — A1796

Hyphen Hole Perf. 6¾
2023, Mar. 1   Litho.
Self-Adhesive
3286	A1796 7p multi	.80	.40

Antonio Narro Autonomous Agrarian University, Saltillo, Cent. — A1797

Hyphen Hole Perf. 6¾
2023, Mar. 4   Litho.
Self-Adhesive
3287	A1797 7.50p multi	.85	.40

Housing Fund for the Institute for Social Security and Services for State Workers, 50th Anniv. — A1798

Hyphen Hole Perf. 6¾
2023, Mar. 15   Litho.
Self-Adhesive
3288	A1798 7p multi	.80	.40

TV4 Guanjuato (State-Owned Public Television Broadcaster), 40th Anniv. A1799

Hyphen Hole Perf. 10
2023, Apr. 25   Litho.
Self-Adhesive
3289	A1799 15p multi	1.75	.85

Cosmogony of the Indigenous Peoples of Oaxaca, Mural by Arturo García Bustos (1926-2017) — A1800

Hyphen Hole Perf. 6¾
2023, May 15   Litho.
Self-Adhesive
3290	A1800 7p multi	.80	.40

Teacher's Day.

Mexican Social Security Institute, 80th Anniv. A1801

Hyphen Hole Perf. 10
2023, May 30   Litho.
Self-Adhesive
3291	A1801 15p multi	1.75	.85

A souvenir sheet of 1 of No. 3291 was produced in limited quantities.

Mexican State-Owned Petroleum Company (PEMEX), 85th Anniv. — A1802

Hyphen Hole Perf. 6¾
2023, June 5   Litho.
Self-Adhesive
3292	A1802 7p multi	.85	.40

Father's Day — A1803

Hyphen Hole Perf. 6¾
2023, June 16   Litho.
Self-Adhesive
3293	A1803 15p multi	1.75	.90

General Francisco "Pancho" Villa (1878-1923). Governor of Chihuahua A1804

Hyphen Hole Perf. 6¾
2023, June 21   Litho.
Self-Adhesive
3294	A1804 7.50p multi	.90	.45

Channel 22 (Mexico City Public Television Station), 30th Anniv. — A1805

Hyphen Hole Perf. 6¾
2023, June 22   Litho.
Self-Adhesive
3295	A1805 13.50p multi	1.60	.80

World Health Organization, 75th Anniv. — A1806

Hyphen Hole Perf. 6¾
2023, July 3   Litho.
Self-Adhesive
3296	A1806 9p multi	1.10	.55

Bison Bison, Chapultepec Zoo Centenary Emblem, and Zoo Founder Alfonso L. Herrera (1868-1942) — A1807

Hyphen Hole Perf. 10
2023, July 6   Litho.
Self-Adhesive
3297	A1807 15p multi	1.75	.90
a.	Souvenir sheet of 1	1.75	.90

Frida Kahlo Museum, Mexico City, 65th Anniv. — A1808

2023, July 17   Litho.   Perf. 13x13¼
3298	A1808 7.50p multi	.90	.45

Prehistoric Animals A1809

No. 3299: a, Coahuilaceratops magnacuerna. b, Aquilolamna milarcae. c, Acantholipan gonzalezi.

2023, July 23   Litho.   Perf. 13¼x13
3299	Horiz. strip of 3	5.25	2.75
a.-c.	A1809 15p Any single	1.75	.90
d.	Souvenir sheet of 3, #3299a-3299c	5.25	2.75

Veterinary Education in Mexico, 170th Anniv. — A1810

2023, Aug. 16   Litho.   Perf. 13x13¼
3300	A1810 7p multi	.85	.40

Federal Telecommunications Institute, 10th Anniv. — A1811

2023, Sept. 11   Litho.   Perf. 13x13¼
3301	A1811 7p multi	.80	.40

A1812   A1813

A1814   A1815

Autonomous University of Nuevo León, 90th Anniv. — A1816

2023, Sept. 14   Litho.   Perf. 13¼x13
3302	Horiz. strip of 5	4.00	2.00
a.	A1812 7p multi	.80	.40
b.	A1813 7p multi	.80	.40
c.	A1814 7p multi	.80	.40
d.	A1815 7p multi	.80	.40
e.	A1816 7p multi	.80	.40
f.	Souvenir sheet of 5, #3302a-3302e	4.00	2.00

Diplomatic Relations Between Mexico and Guatemala, 175th Anniv. — A1817

Designs: No. 3303, Pyramid of the Sun, Teotihuacan, Mexico. No. 3304, Temple of the Gret Jaguar, Tikal, Guatemala.

2023, Sept. 18   Litho.   Perf. 13x13¼
3303	7.50p multi	.90	.45
3304	7.50p multi	.90	.45
a.	A1817 Vert. pair, #3303-3304	1.80	.90

MEXICO

Heroic Military College, 200th Anniv. — A1818

2023, Sept. 20   Litho.   Perf. 13x13¼
3305 A1818 7p multi   .80 .40

Textile Art From State of Nayarit A1819
Textile Art From State of Durango A1820
Textile Art From State of Puebla A1821
Textile Art From State of Oaxaca A1822
Textile Art From State of México A1823
Textile Art From State of Tlaxcala A1824
Textile Art From State of Yucatán A1825
Textile Art From State of Michoacán A1826
Textile Art From State of San Luis Potosí A1827
Textile Art From State of Sonora A1828
Textile Art From State of Guerrero A1829
Textile Art From State of Chihuahua A1830

Textile Art From State of Chiapas — A1831

2023, Oct. 13   Litho.   Perf. 13¼x13
3306	A1819	50c multi	.30	.30
3307	A1820	1p multi	.30	.30
3308	A1821	1.50p multi	.30	.30
3309	A1822	2p multi	.30	.30
3310	A1823	2.50p multi	.30	.30
3311	A1824	5p multi	.55	.30
3312	A1825	7p multi	.80	.40
3313	A1826	7.50p multi	.85	.40
3314	A1827	9p multi	1.00	.50
3315	A1828	11.50p multi	1.30	.65
3316	A1829	13.50p multi	1.50	.75
3317	A1830	15p multi	1.75	.85
3318	A1831	30.50p multi	3.50	1.75
a.		Souvenir sheet of 13, #3306-3318	13.00	6.50
		Nos. 3306-3318 (13)	12.75	7.10

Elvia Carrillo Puerto (1881-1965), Suffragist, and Newspaper Announcing Woman Suffrage — A1832

2023, Oct. 24   Litho.   Perf. 13x13¼
3319 A1832 7p multi   .80 .40

Woman suffrage in Mexico, 70th anniv.

City of San Luis Potosí, 430th Anniv. (in 2022) — A1833

2023, Nov. 3   Litho.   Perf. 13x13¼
3320 A1833 7p multi   .80 .40

Famous Mexicans From State of Guanajuato A1834

2023, Nov. 6   Litho.   Perf. 13x13¼
3321 A1834 7p multi   .80 .40

Diego Rivera (1886-1957), muralist; María Grever (1885-1951), composer; José Alfredo Jiménez (1926-73), singer; Miguel Hidalgo (1753-1811), priest and leader of independence movement.

First Railway in Mexico, 150th Anniv. A1835

2023, Nov. 7   Litho.   Perf. 13¼x13
3322 A1835 11.50p multi   1.40 .70

Doll and Santa María Parish Church, Amealco de Bonfil — A1836

2023, Nov. 18   Litho.   Perf. 13¼x13
3323 A1836 7p multi   .80 .40

Christmas — A1837

2023, Dec. 1   Litho.   Perf. 13¼x13
3324 A1837 15p multi   1.75 .85

B'nai B'rith International, 180th Anniv. — A1838

2023, Dec. 6   Litho.   Perf. 13x13¼
3325 A1838 9p multi   1.10 .55

Cozumel Carnivals, 150th Anniv. — A1839

2023, Dec. 6   Litho.   Perf. 13¼x13
3326 A1839 7.50p multi   .90 .45

National Educational Workers Union, 80th Anniv. — A1840

2023, Dec. 7   Litho.   Perf. 13¼x13
3327 A1840 7.50p multi   .90 .45

High School of the State of Morelos, 35th Anniv. — A1841

2023, Dec. 8   Litho.   Perf. 13x13¼
3328 A1841 7p multi   .85 .40

Historic Center of Zacatecas UNESCO World Heritage Site, 30th Anniv. A1842

2023, Dec. 11   Litho.   Perf. 13¼x13
3329 A1842 11.50p multi   1.40 .70

SEMI-POSTAL STAMPS

Nos. 622, 614 Surcharged in Red

1918, Dec. 25   Unwmk.   Perf. 12
B1 A72 5c + 3c ultra   20.00 25.00

Rouletted 14½
B2 A73 10c + 5c blue   25.00 25.00
   Set, never hinged   57.50

AIR POST STAMPS

Eagle — AP1

1922, Apr. 2   Unwmk.   Engr.   Perf. 12
C1 AP1 50c blue & red brn   67.50 50.00
   Never hinged   160.00
a. 50c dark blue & claret ('29)   90.00 90.00
   Never hinged   200.00

See Nos. C2-C3. For overprints and surcharges see Nos. C47-C48, CO1-CO2B, CO18-CO19, CO29.

1927, Oct. 13   Wmk. 156
C2 AP1 50c dk bl & red brn   .75 .35
   Never hinged   2.50
a. 50c dark blue & claret ('29)   .75 .35
   Never hinged   3.00
b. Vert. strip of 3, imperf. btwn.   7,500.

The vignettes of Nos. C1a and C2a fluoresce a bright rose red under UV light.

1928
C3 AP1 25c brn car & gray brn   .45 .35
C4 AP1 25c dk grn & gray brn   .45 .35
   Set, never hinged   2.50

On May 3, 1929, certain proofs or essays were sold at the post office in Mexico, D. F. They were printed in different colors from those of the regularly issued stamps. There were 7 varieties perf. and 2 imperf. and a total of 225 copies. They were sold with the understanding that they were for collections but the majority of them were used on air mail sent out that day.

Capt. Emilio Carranza and his Airplane "México Excelsior" — AP2

1929, June 19
C5	AP2	5c ol grn & sepia	1.10	.65
C6	AP2	10c sep & brn red	1.25	.70
C7	AP2	15c vio & dk grn	3.00	1.25
C8	AP2	20c brown & blk	1.25	.75
C9	AP2	50c brn red & blk	7.50	5.00
C10	AP2	1p black & brn	15.00	10.00
		Nos. C5-C10 (6)	29.10	18.35
		Set, never hinged	75.00	

1st anniv. of death of Carranza (1905-28).
For overprints see Nos. C29-C36, C40-C44.

Coat of Arms and Airplane — AP3

1929-34   Perf. 11½, 12
C11	AP3	10c violet	.35	.25
C12	AP3	15c carmine	1.35	.25
C13	AP3	20c brown olive	37.50	1.25
C14	AP3	30c gray black	.25	.25
C15	AP3	35c blue green	.35	.25
a.		Imperf., pair	1,200.	
C16	AP3	50c red brn ('34)	1.25	.65
C17	AP3	1p blk & dk bl	1.25	.65
C18	AP3	5p claret & dp bl	4.00	3.50
C19	AP3	10p vio & ol brn	6.00	7.00
		Nos. C11-C19 (9)	52.30	14.05
		Set, never hinged	130.00	

1930-32   Rouletted 13, 13½
C20	AP3	5c lt blue ('32)	.35	.25
C21	AP3	10c violet	.35	.25
C22	AP3	15c carmine	.35	.25
a.		15c rose carmine	.40	.25
C23	AP3	20c brown olive	1.50	.25
a.		20c brown	.50	.25
b.		20c yellow brown	.50	.25
c.		Horiz. pair, imperf. btwn.	100.00	
C24	AP3	25c violet	.95	.80
C25	AP3	50c red brown	.90	.75
		Nos. C20-C25 (6)	4.40	2.55
		Set, never hinged	13.00	

Trial impressions of No. C20 were printed in orange but were never sold at post offices.
See Nos. C62-C64, C75. For overprints and surcharges see Nos. C28, C38-C39, C46, C49-C50, CO17, CO20-CO28, CO30.

Plane over Plaza, Mexico City — AP4

1929, Dec. 10   Wmk. 156   Perf. 12
C26 AP4 20c black violet   1.25 1.00
C27 AP4 40c slate green   85.00 75.00
   Set, never hinged   210.00

Aviation Week, Dec. 10-16.
For overprint see No. CO11.

MEXICO

No. C21 Overprinted in Red

1930, Apr. 20   **Rouletted 13, 13½**
C28 AP3 10c violet   2.00   1.25
     Never hinged   5.50

National Tourism Congress at Mexico, D. F., Apr. 20-27, 1930.

Nos. C5 and C7 Overprinted

1930, Sept. 1   **Perf. 12**
C29 AP2 5c ol grn & sepia   5.50   4.50
   a. Double overprint   225.00   250.00
C30 AP2 15c violet & dk grn   9.00   7.75
     Set, never hinged   45.00

Nos. C5-C10 Overprinted

1930, Dec. 18
C31 AP2 5c ol grn & sepia   7.00   6.50
C32 AP2 10c sep & brn red   3.50   4.00
   a. Double overprint   60.00   60.00
C33 AP2 15c vio & dk grn   7.50   7.00
C34 AP2 20c brown & blk   7.00   5.50
C35 AP2 50c brn red & blk   14.00   10.00
C36 AP2 1p black & brn   4.00   2.75
     Nos. C31-C36 (6)   43.00   35.75
     Set, never hinged   130.00

Plane over Flying Field — AP5

1931, May 15   **Engr.**   **Perf. 12**
C37 AP5 25c lake   4.00   4.50
     Never hinged   11.00
   a. Imperf., pair   80.00   72.50
     Never hinged   175.00

Aeronautic Exhibition of the Aero Club of Mexico. Of the 25c, 15c paid air mail postage and 10c went to a fund to improve the Mexico City airport.
For surcharge see No. C45.

Nos. C13 and C23 Srchd. in Red

1931
C38 AP3 15c on 20c brn ol   32.50   39.00
     Never hinged   80.00

Rouletted 13, 13½
C39 AP3 15c on 20c brn ol   .35   .35
     Never hinged   1.00
   a. Inverted surcharge   150.00   200.00
   b. Double surcharge   150.00   200.00
   c. Pair, one without surcharge   350.00

Nos. C5 to C9 Overprinted

1932, July 13   **Perf. 12**
C40 AP2 5c ol grn & sep   6.00   5.00
   a. Imperf., pair   60.00   60.00
C41 AP2 10c sep & brn red   5.00   3.00
   a. Imperf., pair   60.00   60.00
C42 AP2 15c vio & bk grn   6.00   4.00
   a. Imperf., pair   60.00   60.00
C43 AP2 20c brn & blk   5.00   2.75
   a. Imperf., pair   60.00   60.00

C44 AP2 50c brn red & blk   35.00   35.00
   a. Imperf., pair   60.00   60.00
     Nos. C40-C44 (5)   57.00   49.75
     Set, never hinged   170.00
     Set, C40a-C44a never hinged   650.00

Death of Capt. Emilio Carranza, 4th anniv.

No. C37 Surcharged

1932
C45 AP5 20c on 25c lake   .70   .35
     Never hinged   2.50
   a. Imperf., pair   72.50   72.50
     Never hinged   150.00

No. C13 Surcharged

C46 AP3 30c on 20c brn ol   30.00   30.00
     Never hinged   75.00

Similar Surcharge on Nos. C3 and C4
C47 AP1 40c on 25c (#C3)   .90   .90
     Never hinged   3.00
   a. Inverted surcharge   11,000.
C48 AP1 40c on 25c (#C4)   50.00   50.00
     Never hinged   125.00

Surcharged on Nos. C23 and C24
Rouletted 13, 13½
C49 AP3 30c on 20c brn ol   .35   .25
     Never hinged   1.00
   a. Inverted surcharge   2,750.
C50 AP3 80c on 25c dl vio   1.75   1.25
     Never hinged   5.00
     Nos. C45-C50 (6)   83.70   82.75

Palace of Fine Arts — AP6

1933, Oct. 1   **Engr.**   **Perf. 12**
C51 AP6 20c dk red & dl vio   3.50   1.40
C52 AP6 30c dk brn & dl vio   7.00   6.00
C53 AP6 1p grnsh blk & dl vio   72.50   70.00
     Nos. C51-C53 (3)   83.00   77.40
     Set, never hinged   190.00

21st Intl. Cong. of Statistics and the cent. of the Mexican Soc. of Geography and Statistics.

National University Issue

Nevado de Toluca — AP7

Pyramids of the Sun and Moon — AP8

View of Ajusco — AP9

Volcanoes Popocatepetl and Iztaccíhuatl AP10

Bridge over Tepecayo — AP11

Chapultepec Fortress — AP12

Orizaba Volcano (Citlaltépetl) AP13

Mexican Girl and Aztec Calendar Stone — AP14

1934, Sept. 1   **Wmk. 156**   **Perf. 10½**
C54 AP7 20c orange   15.00   10.00
C55 AP8 30c red lilac & vio   20.00   20.00
C56 AP9 50c ol grn & bis brn   20.00   25.00
C57 AP10 75c blk & yel grn   25.00   25.00
C58 AP11 1p blk & pck bl   30.00   30.00
C59 AP12 5p bis brn & dk bl   225.00   250.00
C60 AP13 10p indigo & mar brn   550.00   525.00
C61 AP14 20p brn & brn lake   1,800.   1,800.
     Nos. C54-C61 (8)   2,685.   2,685.
     Set, never hinged   4,750.

Type of 1929-34
1934-35   **Perf. 10½, 10½x10**
C62 AP3 20c olive green   .35   .25
   a. 20c slate   500.00   500.00
     Never hinged   600.00
C63 AP3 30c slate   .40   .40
C64 AP3 50c red brn ('35)   2.00   2.00
     Nos. C62-C64 (3)   2.75   2.65
     Set, never hinged   7.00

Symbols of Air Service — AP15

Tláloc, God of Water (Quetzalcóatl Temple) — AP16

Orizaba Volcano (Citlaltépetl) AP17

"Eagle Man" — AP18

Symbolical of Flight AP19

Aztec Bird-Man AP20

Allegory of Flight and Pyramid of the Sun — AP21

"Eagle Man" and Airplanes AP22

Natives Looking at Airplane and Orizaba Volcano AP23

Imprint: "Oficina Impresora de Hacienda-Mexico"
Perf. 10½x10, 10x10½
1934-35   **Engr.**   **Wmk. 156**
C65 AP15 5c black   .45   .35
   a. Imperf., pair
C66 AP16 10c red brown   .90   .35
C67 AP17 15c gray green   1.25   .35
   a. Imperf., pair   400.00
C68 AP18 20c brown car   3.00   .35
   a. 20c lake   4.00   .35
   b. Imperf., pair
C69 AP19 30c brown olive   .70   .35
C70 AP20 40c blue ('35)   1.25   .35
C71 AP21 50c green   2.50   .35
   a. Imperf., pair   275.00
C72 AP22 1p gray grn & red brn   3.50   .35
C73 AP23 5p dk car & blk   7.25   .70
     Nos. C65-C73 (9)   20.80   3.50
     Set, never hinged   45.00

See Nos. C76A, C80, C81, C132-C140, C170-C177A. For overprint see No. C74.

No. C68 Overprinted in Violet

1935, Apr. 16
C74 AP18 20c lake   3,250.   4,000.
     Never hinged   6,000

Amelia Earhart's goodwill flight to Mexico. No. C74 with "Muestra" to left of "Mexico" was not issued for postage.

Arms-Plane Type of 1929-34
1935   **Wmk. 248**   **Perf. 10½x10**
C75 AP3 30c slate   3.00   5.00
     Never hinged   5.00

Francisco I. Madero — AP24

1935, Nov. 20   **Wmk. 156**
C76 AP24 20c scarlet   .30   .25
     Never hinged   .75

Plan of San Luis, 25th anniv. See No. C76B.

Eagle Man Type of 1934-35
1936   **Wmk. 260**
C76A AP18 20c lake   4,500.   60.00
     Never hinged   7,500.

Madero Type of 1935
1936
C76B AP24 20c scarlet   12,500.

Tasquillo Bridge — AP25

Corona River Bridge — AP26

Bridge on Nuevo Laredo Highway — AP27

MEXICO

Wmk. 248

1936, July 1		**Photo.**	**Perf. 14**
C77	AP25 10c slate bl & lt bl	.35	.25
C78	AP26 20c dl vio & org	.35	.25
C79	AP27 40c dk bl & dk grn	.55	.50
	Nos. C77-C79 (3)	1.25	.90
	Set, never hinged	2.75	

Opening of Nuevo Laredo Highway.

Eagle Man Type of 1934-35
Perf. 10½x10

1936, June 18		**Engr.**	**Unwmk.**
C80	AP18 20c brown carmine	10.00	7.00
	Never hinged	25.00	

Imprint: "Talleres de Imp. de Est. y Valores-Mexico"

1937	**Wmk. 156**	**Photo.**	**Perf. 14**
C81	AP18 20c rose red	1.25	.35
	Never hinged	2.50	
a.	20c brown carmine	1.50	
	Never hinged	3.00	
b.	20c dark carmine		.35
	Never hinged	4.50	
c.	Imperf., pair	37.50	50.00
	Never hinged	75.00	

There are two sizes of watermark 156. No. C81c was not regularly issued.

Cavalryman — AP28

Early Biplane over Mountains — AP29

Venustiano Carranza on Horseback — AP30

1938, Mar. 26			
C82	AP28 20c org red & bl	.50	.25
C83	AP29 40c bl & org red	.75	1.00
C84	AP30 1p bl & bis brn	4.75	2.25
	Nos. C82-C84 (3)	6.00	3.45
	Set, never hinged	18.00	

Plan of Guadalupe, 25th anniversary.

Reconstructed edifices of Chichén Itzá — AP31

Designs: Nos. C85, C86, The Zócalo and Cathedral, Mexico City. Nos. C89, C90, View of Acapulco.

1938, July 1			
C85	AP31 20c carmine rose	.35	.25
C86	AP31 20c purple	20.00	10.00
C87	AP31 40c brt green	10.00	5.00
C88	AP31 40c dark green	10.00	5.00
C89	AP31 1p light blue	10.00	5.00
C90	AP31 1p slate blue	10.00	5.00
	Nos. C85-C90 (6)	60.35	30.25
	Set, never hinged	130.00	

16th Intl. Cong. of Planning & Housing.

Statue of José María Morelos — AP34

1939		**Engr.**	**Perf. 10½**
C91	AP34 20c green	.70	.50
	Never hinged	1.00	
C92	AP34 40c red violet	2.00	1.25
	Never hinged	5.00	

C93	AP34 1p vio brn & car	1.40	1.00
	Never hinged	1.75	
	Nos. C91-C93 (3)	4.10	2.75
	Set, never hinged	9.50	

New York World's Fair. Released in New York May 2, in Mexico May 24.

Type of 1939 Overprinted in Cerise

1939, May 23			
C93A	AP34 20c blue & red	425.00	425.00
	Never hinged	800.00	

Issued for the flight of Francisco Sarabia from Mexico City to New York on May 25.

Statue of Pioneer Woman, Ponca City, OK — AP35

1939, May 17			
C94	AP35 20c gray brown	1.00	.40
	Never hinged	2.00	
C95	AP35 40c slate green	2.50	1.25
	Never hinged	7.00	
C96	AP35 1p violet	1.60	.90
	Never hinged	3.00	
	Nos. C94-C96 (3)	5.10	2.55
	Set, never hinged	12.00	

Tulsa World Philatelic Convention.

First Engraving Made in Mexico, 1544 — AP36

First Work of Legislation Printed in America, 1563 — AP37

Designs: 1p, Reproduction of oldest preserved Mexican printing.

1939, Sept. 7			**Wmk. 156**
C97	AP36 20c slate blue	.25	.25
a.	Unwmkd.	50.00	25.00
C98	AP37 40c slate green	.65	.25
a.	Imperf., pair	700.00	
C99	AP37 1p dk brn & car	1.10	.70
	Nos. C97-C99 (3)	2.00	1.10
	Set, never hinged	8.00	

400th anniversary of printing in Mexico.

Alternated Perforations
Nos. 763-766, 774-779, 792-795, 801-804, 806-811, 813-818, C100-C102, C111-C116, C123-C128, C143-C162, C430-C431 have alternating small and large perforations.

Transportation — AP39

Designs: 40c, Finger counting and factory. 1p, "Seven Censuses."

Perf. 12x13, 13x12			
1939, Oct. 2			**Photo.**
C100	AP39 20c dk bl & bl	1.00	.25
C101	AP39 40c red org & org	.75	.75
C102	AP39 1p ind & vio bl	2.75	.75
	Nos. C100-C102 (3)	4.50	1.20
	Set, never hinged	10.00	

National Census of 1939-40.

Penny Black Type of Regular Issue, 1940

1940, May			**Perf. 14**
C103	A140 5c blk & dk grn	.65	.55
C104	A140 10c bis brn & dp bl	.55	.25
C105	A140 20c car & bl vio	.40	.25
C106	A140 1p car & choc	6.00	5.00
C107	A140 5p gray grn & red brn	75.00	55.00
	Nos. C103-C107 (5)	82.60	61.00
	Set, never hinged	200.00	

Issue dates: 5c-1p, May 2; 5p, May 15.

Part of Original College at Pátzcuaro — AP43

College at Morelia (18th Century) — AP44

College at Morelia (1940) — AP45

1940, July 15		**Engr.**	**Perf. 10½**
C108	AP43 20c brt green	.45	.25
C109	AP44 40c orange	.50	.30
C110	AP45 1p dp pur, red brn & org	1.25	1.00
	Nos. C108-C110 (3)	2.20	1.50
	Set, never hinged	5.00	

400th anniv. of the founding of the National College of San Nicolas de Hidalgo.

Pirate Ship — AP46

Designs: 40c, Castle of San Miguel. 1p, Temple of San Francisco.

Perf. 12x13, 13x12			
1940, Aug. 7			**Photo.**
C111	AP46 20c red brn & bis brn	1.10	.70
C112	AP46 40c blk & sl grn	1.50	.75
C113	AP46 1p vio bl & blk	5.00	4.00
	Nos. C111-C113 (3)	7.60	5.45
	Set, never hinged	20.00	

400th anniversary of Campeche.

Inauguration Type of Regular Issue, 1940

1940, Dec. 1			**Perf. 12x13**
C114	A146 20c gray blk & red org	1.90	1.00
C115	A146 40c chnt brn & dk sl	2.00	1.50
C116	A146 1p brt vio bl & rose	3.50	2.00
	Nos. C114-C116 (3)	7.40	4.50
	Set, never hinged	20.00	

Tower of the Convent of the Nuns — AP50

Casa de Montejo — AP51

1p, Campanile of Cathedral at Mérida.

1942, Jan. 2			**Perf. 14**
C117	AP50 20c Prus blue	1.75	.75
C118	AP51 40c grnsh blk (C)	2.60	2.00
a.	Without overprint	8.00	8.00
C119	AP50 1p carmine	3.00	2.00
	Nos. C117-C119 (3)	7.35	4.75

400th anniversary of Mérida.
No. C118 bears the overprint "Servicio Aereo" in carmine.

Church of Zapopan — AP53

Our Lady of Guadalupe Church — AP54

Guadalajara Arms — AP55

1942, Feb. 11		**Engr.**	**Perf. 10½x10**
C120	AP53 20c green & blk	1.90	.75
C121	AP54 40c ol & yel grn	2.10	1.00
C122	AP55 1p purple & sepia	1.60	1.25
	Nos. C120-C122 (3)	5.60	3.00

400th anniversary of Guadalajara.

Astrophysics Type of Regular Issue

Designs: 20c, Spiral Galaxy NGC 4594. 40c, Planetary Nebula in Lyra. 1p, Russell Diagrams.

1942, Feb. 17		**Photo.**	**Perf. 12x13**
C123	A154 20c dk grn & ind	23.00	3.00
C124	A154 40c car lake & ind	17.00	4.00
C125	A154 1p orange & blk	25.00	4.50
	Nos. C123-C125 (3)	65.00	11.50

Corn — AP59

1942, July 1			
C126	AP59 20c shown	2.40	.70
C127	AP59 40c Coffee	1.80	.75
C128	AP59 1p Bananas	3.00	2.00
	Nos. C126-C128 (3)	7.20	3.45

2nd Inter-American Agricultural Conf.

View of San Miguel de Allende — AP62

Designs: 40c, Birthplace of Allende. 1p, Church of Our Lady of Health.

1943, May 18			**Perf. 14**
C129	AP62 20c dk slate grn	1.25	.60
C130	AP62 40c purple	1.50	.60
C131	AP62 1p dp carmine	3.25	2.50
	Nos. C129-C131 (3)	6.00	3.70

400th anniversary of the founding of San Miguel de Allende.

Types of 1934-35

1944		**Photo.**	**Wmk. 272**
C132	AP18 20c brown carmine	.75	.35

		Perf. 10½x10	
1944-46		**Engr.**	**Wmk. 272**
C133	AP15 5c black	.80	.25
C134	AP16 10c red brn ('45)	2.00	.25
C135	AP17 15c gray grn ('45)	1.40	.25
C136	AP19 30c brown ol ('45)	20.00	.75
C137	AP20 40c gray bl ('45)	1.75	.25
C138	AP21 50c green	1.40	.25
C139	AP22 1p gray grn & red brn ('45)	9.50	1.50
C140	AP23 5p dk car & blk ('46)	7.50	2.00
	Nos. C133-C140 (8)	44.35	5.50

MEXICO

Symbol of Flight — AP65

1944		Photo.		Perf. 14
C141	AP65	25c chestnut brown	.35	.35

See No. C185.

Microphone, Book and Camera — AP66

1944, Nov. 8			Wmk. 272
C142	AP66	25c dull slate grn	.65	.35

Issued to commemorate the third Book Fair.

Catalogue values for unused stamps in this section, from this point to the end of the section, are for Never Hinged items.

Globe-in-Hands Type

1945, Feb. 27			Perf. 12x13
C143	A166	25c red orange	.40	.25
C144	A166	1p brt green	.50	.35
C145	A166	5p indigo	2.60	2.00
C146	A166	10p brt rose	7.25	5.25
C147	A166	20p brt vio bl	21.00	13.00
Nos. C143-C147 (5)			31.75	20.80

Theater Type

1945, July 27				
C148	A167	30c slate & ol	.35	.25
C149	A167	1p slate & lil	.50	.35
C150	A167	5p slate & blk	3.25	2.50
C151	A167	10p sl & lt ultra	6.25	4.25
C152	A167	20p blk & gray grn	19.00	10.50
Nos. C148-C152 (5)			29.35	17.85

Blindfold Type

1945, Nov. 21				
C153	A169	30c slate green	.25	.25
C154	A169	1p brown red	.50	.30
C155	A169	5p red brn & pale bl	3.75	2.50
C156	A169	10p sl blk & pale lil	6.25	5.00
C157	A169	20p grn & lt brn	26.00	24.00
Nos. C153-C157 (5)			36.75	32.05

Torch, Laurel and Flag-decorated ONU — AP70

1946, Apr. 10				
C158	AP70	30c chocolate	.25	.25
C159	AP70	1p slate grn	.50	.30
C160	AP70	5p chnt & dk grn	2.10	1.25
C161	AP70	10p dk brn & chnt	6.75	4.00
C162	AP70	20p sl grn & org red	19.00	9.00
Nos. C158-C162 (5)			28.60	14.80

Issued to honor the United Nations.

Father Margil de Jesus and Plane over Zacatecas AP71

Zacatecas scene and: 1p, Genaro Codina. 5p, Gen. Enrique Estrada. 10p, Fernando Villalpando.

			Perf. 10½x10
1946, Sept. 13		Engr.	Wmk. 279
C163	AP71	30c gray	.40	.35
C164	AP71	1p brn & Prus grn	.60	.35
C165	AP71	5p red & olive	4.50	3.00
C166	AP71	10p Prus grn & dk brn	27.00	15.00
Nos. C163-C166 (4)			32.50	18.70

400th anniversary of Zacatecas.

Franklin D. Roosevelt and Stamp of 1st Mexican Issue — AP72

30c, Arms of Mexico & Stamp of 1st US Issue.

1947, May 16		Photo.	Perf. 14
C167	AP72	25c lt violet bl	1.10	.50
C168	AP72	30c gray black	.75	.25
a.	Imperf., pair		325.00	
C169	AP72	1p blue & car	2.10	.40
Nos. C167-C169 (3)			3.95	1.15

Centenary International Philatelic Exhibition, New York, May 17-25, 1947.

Types of 1934-35

Perf. 10½x10, 10x10½

1947		Engr.	Wmk. 279
C170	AP15	5c black	1.80	.35
C171	AP16	10c red brown	3.50	.30
C172	AP17	15c olive grn	3.50	.30
C173	AP19	30c brown ol	2.40	.25
C174	AP20	40c blue gray	2.40	.25
C175	AP21	50c green	19.00	.30
a.	Imperf., pair		450.00	
C176	AP22	1p gray grn & red brn	4.25	.25
a.	Imperf., pair		500.00	
C177	AP23	5p red & blk	11.00	1.25
c.	5p dark car & black		200.00	2.00

Photo. Perf. 14
Imprint: "Talleres de Imp. de Est. y Valores-Mexico"

C177A	AP18	20c brown car	2.75	.50
b.	Imperf., pair		250.00	
Nos. C170-C177A (9)			50.60	3.75

Emilio Carranza — AP74

Douglas DC-4 — AP75

1947, June 25		Engr.	Perf. 10½x10
C178	AP74	10p red & dk brn	2.00	1.50
a.	10p dark carmine & brown		8.00	
C179	AP75	20p bl & red brn	3.00	2.75

Cadet Vicente Suárez — AP76

Chapultepec Castle — AP78

30c, Lieut. Juan de la Barrera. 1p, Gen. Pedro M. Anaya. 5p, Gen. Antonio de Leon.

1947, Sept. 8		Photo.	Perf. 14
C180	AP76	25c dull violet	.35	.25
C181	AP76	30c brown	.35	.25

Engr. Perf. 10x10½

C182	AP78	50c deep green	.50	.25
C183	AP78	1p violet	.70	.25
C184	AP78	5p aqua & brn	2.75	2.00
a.	Imperf., pair		600.00	
Nos. C180-C184 (5)			4.65	3.00

Centenary of the battles of Chapultepec, Churubusco and Molino del Rey.

Flight Symbol Type of 1944

1947	Wmk. 279	Photo.	Perf. 14
C185	AP65	25c chestnut brn	.75	.35
a.	Imperf., pair		250.00	

Puebla, Dance of the Half Moon — AP81

Designs: 5c, Guerrero, Acapulco waterfront. 10c, Oaxaca, dance. 20c, Chiapas, musicians (Mayan). 25c, Michoacan, masks. 30c, Cuauhtemoc. 35c, Guerrero, view of Taxco. 40c, San Luis Potosi, head. 50c, Chiapas, bas-relief profile, Mayan culture. 80c, Mexico City University Stadium. 5p, Queretaro, architecture. 10p, Miguel Hidalgo. 20p, Modern building.

Two types of 20p:
Type I — Blue gray part 21¼mm wide. Child's figure touching left edge.
Type II — Blue gray part 21¾mm wide; "LQ" at lower left corner. Child's figure 1mm from left edge.

Imprint: "Talleres de Impresion de Estampillas y Valores-Mexico"
Perf. 10½x10

1950-52			Wmk. 279	Engr.
C186	AP81	5c aqua ('51)	.70	.25
C187	AP81	10c brn org ('51)	3.25	.50
C188	AP81	20c carmine	1.50	.25
C189	AP81	25c redsh brown	1.50	.25
C190	AP81	30c olive bister	.60	.25
C191	AP81	35c violet	3.25	.25
a.	Retouched die		19.00	.30
b.	As "a", imperf., pair		300.00	
C192	AP81	40c dk gray bl ('51)	2.75	.25
a.	Imperf., pair		300.00	
C193	AP81	50c green	4.50	.25
C194	AP81	80c claret ('52)	2.75	.50
a.	Imperf., pair		300.00	
C195	AP81	1p blue gray	1.60	.25
C196	AP81	5p dk brn & org ('51)	6.00	1.00
a.	Imperf., pair			1,800.
C197	AP81	10p blk & aqua ('52)	110.00	20.00
C198	AP81	20p car & bl gray, I ('52)	10.00	9.00
a.	Type II		400.00	100.00
Nos. C186-C198 (13)			148.40	33.00

No. C191a: A patch of heavy shading has been added at right of "MEXICO;" lines in sky increased and strengthened. On Nos. C191, C191a, the top of the highest tower is even with the top of the "o" in "Guerrero," and has no frame line at right. No. C220C has frame line at right and tower top is even with "Arquitectura."
Many shades exist of Nos. C186-C198.
See Nos. C208-C221, C249, C265-C268, C285-C288, C290-C298, C347-C349, C422, C444, C446-C450, C471-C480.

AP82

Design: 25c, Pres. Aleman and Highway Bridging Map of Mexico. 35c, Pres. Juarez and map.

1950, May 21			Engr.
C199	AP82	25c lilac rose	3.25	.35
C200	AP82	35c deep green	.40	.35

Completion of the Intl. Highway between Ciudad Juarez and the Guatemala border.

Trains Crossing Isthmus of Tehuantepec AP83

Pres. Aleman and Bridge — AP83a

1950, May 24			
C201	AP83	25c green	.70	.35
C202	AP83a	35c ultra	.50	.35

Opening of the Southeastern Railroad between Veracruz, Coatzocoalcos and Yucatan, 1950.

Aztec Courier, Plane, Train — AP84

80c, Symbols of universal postal service.

1950, June 15			
C203	AP84	25c red orange	.55	.35
C204	AP84	80c blue	.80	.35

75th anniv. (in 1949) of the UPU.

Miguel Hidalgo — AP86

Design: 35c, Hidalgo and Mexican Flag.

		Wmk. 300		
1953, May 8		Photo.	Perf. 14
C206	AP86	25c gray bl & dk red brn	1.10	.35
C207	AP86	35c slate green	1.10	.35
a.	Wmk. 279			

Bicentenary of birth of Miguel Hidalgo y Costilla (1753-1811), priest and revolutionist.

Type of 1950-52

Designs as before.

Imprint: "Talleres de Impresion de Estampillas y Valores-Mexico"
Wmk. 300, Horizontal

1953-56		Engr.	Perf. 10½x10
C208	AP81	5c aqua	.55	.25
C209	AP81	10c orange brn	5.75	3.50
a.	10c orange		4.75	2.50
C210	AP81	30c gray olive	18.00	10.00
C211	AP81	40c gray bl ('56)	18.00	1.50
C212	AP81	50c green	400.00	250.00
C213	AP81	80c claret	100.00	10.00
C214	AP81	1p blue gray	3.25	.30
C215	AP81	5p dk brn & org	3.00	.60
C216	AP81	10p blk & aqua	6.50	1.25
C217	AP81	20p car & bl gray (II) ('56)	75.00	8.00
Nos. C208-C211, C213-C217 (9)			230.05	35.40

Printed in sheets of 30.

Type of 1950-52

Designs as in 1950-52. 2p, Guerrero, view of Taxco. 2.25p, Michoacan, masks.

Two types of 2p:
I — No dots after "Colonial". Frame line at right broken near top.
II — Three dots in a line after "Colonial". Right frame line unbroken.

Wmk. 300, Vertical

1955-65			Perf. 11½x11
		Design AP81	
C218		5c bluish grn ('56)	.60	.35
		Perf. 11	
C219		10c org brn ('60)	.60	.35
a.	Perf. 11½x11		1.30	.40
C220		20c carmine ('60)	.60	.35
k.	Perf. 11½x11 ('57)		1.90	.35
C220A		25c vio brn, perf. 11½x11	2.00	.35
C220B		30c olive gray ('60)	.60	.35
l.	Perf. 11½x11		1.10	.35
C220C		35c dk vio, perf. 11½x11	1.10	.35
C220D		40c slate bl ('60)	.60	.35
m.	Perf. 11½x11		10.00	.35
C220E		50c green, perf. 11½x11	1.10	.35
n.	Perf. 11 ('60)		1.40	.35
q.	50c yellow green		1.40	.35
C220F		80c claret ('60)	5.25	.70
o.	Perf. 11½x11		5.25	.60
C220G		1p grn gray ('60)	1.30	.35
p.	Perf. 11½x11		12.50	.35
C220H		2p dk org brn, II ('63)	1.30	.60
i.	2p lt org brn, perf. 11½x11 ('65)		150.00	40.00
j.	2p org brn, I, perf. 11		8.75	1.25
C221		2.25p maroon ('63)	.90	.70
Nos. C218-C221 (12)			15.95	5.15

Printed in sheets of 45 and 50. Nos. C218-C221 have been re-engraved.

No. C218 has been redrawn and there are many differences. "CTS" measures 7mm; it is 5½mm on No. C208.
Nos. C208-C221 exist in various shades.
For No. C220C, see note after No. C198.

MEXICO

No. C220En was privately overprinted in red: "25vo Aniversario / Primer Cohete Internacional / Reynosa, Mexico-McAllen, U.S.A. / 1936-1961." Value $50.

Mayan Ball Court and Player — AP87

Design: 35c, Modern Stadium, Mexico.

1954, Mar. 6 — Photo. — Perf. 14
C222	AP87	25c brn & dk bl grn	1.25	.35
C223	AP87	35c dl sl grn & lil rose	.95	.35

7th Central American & Caribbean Games.

Allegory — AP88

1954, Sept. 15
C224	AP88	25c red brn & dp bl	.70	.35
C225	AP88	35c dk bl & vio brn	.45	.35
C226	AP88	80c blk & bl grn	.45	.35
	Nos. C224-C226 (3)		1.60	1.05

Centenary of national anthem.

Aztec God Tezcatlipoca and Map — AP89

Design: 35c, Stadium and map.

1955, Mar. 12
C227	AP89	25c dk Prus grn & red brn	1.00	.35
C228	AP89	35c carmine & brn	1.00	.35

2nd Pan American Games, 1955.

Ornaments and Mask, Archeological Era — AP90

Designs: 10c, Virrey Enriquez de Almanza, bell tower and coach, colonial era. 50c, Jose Maria Morelos and cannon, heroic Mexico. 1p, Woman and child and horse back rider, revolutionary Mexico. 1.20p, Sombrero and Spurs, popular Mexico. 5p, Pointing hand and school, modern Mexico.

Perf. 11½x11
1956, Aug. 1 — Engr. — Wmk. 300
C229	AP90	5c black	.55	.35
C230	AP90	10c lt blue	.55	.35
C231	AP90	50c violet brn	.40	.35
C232	AP90	1p blue gray	.55	.35
C233	AP90	1.20p magenta	.55	.35
C234	AP90	5p blue grn	1.75	1.75
a.	Souv. sheet of 6, #C229-C234, perf. 10½x10		70.00	70.00
	Nos. C229-C234 (6)		4.35	3.50

Centenary of Mexico's 1st postage stamps. No. C234a sold for 15 pesos.

Paricutín Volcano — AP91

1956, Sept. 5 — Photo. — Perf. 14
C235	AP91	50c dk violet bl	.75	.35

20th Intl. Geological Cong., Mexico City.

Valentin Gomez Farias and Melchor Ocampo — AP92

1.20p, Leon Guzman and Ignacio Ramirez.

1956-63 — Wmk. 300 — Perf. 14
C236	AP92	15c intense blue	.60	.35
C237	AP92	1.20p dk grn & pur	1.10	.35
b.	Dark green omitted		110.00	
c.	Purple omitted		125.00	
C237A	AP92	2.75p purple ('63)	1.60	.75
	Nos. C236-C237A (3)		3.30	1.45

Centenary of the constitution (in 1957). See Nos. C289, C445, C451, C471A.

Map — AP93

1956, Dec. 1
C238	AP93	25c gray & dk bl	.60	.35

4th Inter-American Regional Tourism Congress of the Gulf of Mexico and the Caribbean (in 1955).

Eagle Holding Scales — AP94

1p, Allegorical figure writing the law.

1957, Aug. 31 — Photo. — Perf. 14
C239	AP94	50c metallic red brn & green	.50	.35
C240	AP94	1p metallic lilac & ultra	.75	.35

Centenary of 1857 Constitution.

Globe, Weights and Measure — AP95

1957, Sept. 21
C241	AP95	50c metallic bl & blk	.65	.35

Centenary of the adoption of the metric system in Mexico.

Death of Jesus Garcia — AP96

1957, Nov. 7 — Wmk. 300 — Perf. 14
C242	AP96	50c car rose & dk vio	.60	.35

50th anniversary of the death of Jesus Garcia, hero of Nacozari.

Oil Industry Symbols — AP97

Design: 1p, Oil refinery at night.

1958, Aug. 30
C243	AP97	50c emerald & blk	.35	.35
C244	AP97	1p car & bluish blk	.45	.35

Nationalization of Mexico's oil industry, 20th anniv.

Independence Monument Figure — AP98

1958, Dec. 15 — Engr. — Perf. 11
C245	AP98	50c gray blue	.60	.35

10th anniversary of the signing of the Universal Declaration of Human Rights.

Pres. Venustiano Carranza — AP99

1960, Jan. 15 — Photo. — Perf. 14
C246	AP99	50c salmon & dk bl	.60	.35

Centenary of the birth of President Venustiano Carranza.

Alberto Braniff's 1910 Plane, Douglas DC-7 and Mexican Airlines Map — AP100

1960, May 15 — Wmk. 300 — Perf. 14
C247	AP100	50c lt brn & vio	.75	.35
C248	AP100	1p lt brn & bl grn	.65	.35

50th anniversary of Mexican aviation.

Type of 1950-52 inscribed: "HOMENAJE AL COLECCIONISTA DEL TIMBRE DE MEXICO-JUNIO 1960"

1960, June 8 — Engr. — Perf. 10½x10
C249	AP81	20p lil, brn & lt grn	100.00	100.00

See note below No. 909.

Flag — AP101

Designs: 1.20p, Bell of Dolores and eagle. 5p, Dolores Church.

Wmk. 300
1960, Sept. 16 — Photo. — Perf. 14
C250	AP101	50c dp grn & brt red	.50	.35
C251	AP101	1.20p grnsh bl & dk brn	.75	.35
C252	AP101	5p sepia & green	6.50	2.25
	Nos. C250-C252 (3)		7.75	2.95

150th anniversary of independence.

Aviation (Douglas DC-8 Airliner) — AP102

Designs: 1p, Oil industry. 1.20p, Road development. 5p, Water power (dam).

1960, Nov. 20 — Photo. — Perf. 14
C253	AP102	50c gray bl & blk	.50	.35
C254	AP102	1p dk grn & rose car	.60	.35
C255	AP102	1.20p dk grn & sep	.65	.35
C256	AP102	5p blue & lilac	7.00	3.00
	Nos. C253-C256 (4)		8.75	4.05

50th anniversary of Mexican Revolution.

Count de Revillaggigedo — AP103

1960, Dec. 23
C257	AP103	60c dk car & blk	.85	.35

80th census and to honor Juan Vicente Güemez Pacheco de Padilla Horcasitas, Count de Revillaggigedo, who conducted the 1st census in America, 1793.

Railroad Tracks and Map — AP104

Design: 70c, Railroad bridge.

1961, Nov. — Wmk. 300 — Perf. 14
C258	AP104	60c chlky bl & dk grn	.60	.35
C259	AP104	70c dk blue & gray	.60	.35

Opening of the railroad from Chihuahua to the Pacific Ocean.

Gen. Ignacio Zaragoza and View of Puebla — AP105

1962, May 5
C260	AP105	1p gray grn & slate grn	.90	.35

Centenary of the Battle of May 5 at Puebla and the defeat of French forces by Gen. Ignacio Zaragoza.

Laboratory AP106

1962, June 11
C261	AP106	1p olive & vio bl	.80	.35

National Polytechnic Institute, 25th anniv.

Pres. John F. Kennedy AP107

1962, June 29
C262	AP107	80c brt blue & car	2.00	.40

Commemorates visit of President John F. Kennedy to Mexico, June 29-30.

Globe — AP108

1962, Oct. 20
C263	AP108	1.20p violet & dk brn	.90	.35

Inter-American Economic and Social Council meeting.

Balloon over Mexico City, 1862 — AP109

1962, Dec. 21 — Wmk. 300 — Perf. 14
C264	AP109	80c lt blue & blk	1.90	.60

Cent. of the 1st Mexican balloon ascension by Joaquin de la Cantolla y Rico.

Type of 1950-52

Designs as before.

Two sizes of 80c:
I — 35½x20mm.
II — 37x20½mm.

Imprint: "Talleres de Imp. de Est. y Valores-Mexico"

Wmk. 300, Vertical
1962-72 — Photo. — Perf. 14
C265	AP81	80c cl, I ('63)	1.40	.30
a.	Perf. 11½x11, size II ('63)		4.25	.35
b.	Perf. 11, size II ('63)		3.75	.35
c.	Perf. 11, size I ('72)		2.75	.35
C266	AP81	5p dk brn & yel org	4.00	1.00
C267	AP81	10p blk & lt grn ('63)	7.00	3.75
C268	AP81	20p car & bl gray	15.00	3.50
a.	20p carmine & aqua		17.00	4.75
	Nos. C265-C268 (4)		27.40	8.55

Vert. pairs, imperf. horiz. of No. C265, perf. 11, may be from uncut rolls of No. C348.

MEXICO

ALALC Emblem — AP110

1963, Feb. 15   **Wmk. 300**
C269   AP110   80c orange & dl pur   1.30   .35
2nd general session of the Latin American Free Trade Assoc. (ALALC), held in 1962.

Mexican Eagle and Refinery AP111

1963, Mar. 23
C270   AP111   80c red org & slate   .85   .35
Nationalization of the oil industry, 25th anniv.

Polyconic Map — AP112

1963, Apr. 22   **Photo.**   **Perf. 14**
C271   AP112   80c blue & blk   1.10   .35
19th Intl. Chamber of Commerce Congress.

EXMEX Emblem and Postmark AP113

1963, Oct. 9   **Wmk. 350**   **Perf. 14**
C274   AP113   5p rose red   3.00   1.75
77th Annual Convention of the American Philatelic Society, Mexico City, Oct. 7-13.

Marshal Tito — AP114

1963, Oct. 15   **Wmk. 350**   **Perf. 14**
C275   AP114   2p dk grn & vio   2.25   .70
Visit of Marshal Tito of Yugoslavia.

Modern Architecture — AP115

1963, Oct. 19
C276   AP115   80c dk blue & gray   .95   .35
Intl. Architects' Convention, Mexico City.

Dove — AP116

1963, Oct. 26
C277   AP116   80c dl bl grn & car   1.60   .35
Centenary of the International Red Cross.

Don Quixote by José Guadalupe Posada — AP117

1963, Nov. 9   **Engr.**   **Perf. 10½x10**
C278   AP117   1.20p black   2.00   .50
50th anniversary of the death of José Guadalupe Posada, satirical artist.

Horse-drawn Rail Coach, Old and New Trains — AP118

1963, Nov. 29   **Wmk. 350**   **Photo.**   **Perf. 14**
C279   AP118   1.20p violet bl & bl   1.10   .35
11th Pan-American Railroad Congress.

Eleanor Roosevelt, Flame and UN Emblem — AP119

1964, Feb. 22   **Wmk. 350**   **Perf. 14**
C280   AP119   80c lt ultra & red   1.10   .35
15th anniversary (in 1963) of the Universal Declaration of Human Rights and to honor Eleanor Roosevelt.

Gen. Charles de Gaulle — AP120

1964, Mar. 16   **Photo.**
C281   AP120   2p dl vio bl & brn   2.75   .80
Visit of President Charles de Gaulle of France to Mexico, Mar. 16-19.

AP121

Design: Pres. John F. Kennedy and Pres. Adolfo López Mateos and Map.

1964, Apr. 11   **Photo.**
C282   AP121   80c vio bl & gray   1.10   .35
Ratification of the Chamizal Treaty, returning the Chamizal area of El Paso, Texas, to Mexico, July 18, 1963.

Queen Juliana — AP122

1964, May 8   **Wmk. 350**   **Perf. 14**
C283   AP122   80c bister & vio bl   1.50   .35
Visit of Queen Juliana of the Netherlands.

Lt. José Azueta and Cadet Virgilio Uribe — AP123

1964, June 18   **Wmk. 350**   **Perf. 14**
C284   AP123   40c dk brn & blk   .80   .35
50th anniversary of the defense of Veracruz (against US Navy).

Types of 1950-62

Designs as before.

Perf. 11 (20c, 40c, 50c, 80c, 2p); 14 Photo.; Engr. (C296-C298)

1964-73			Wmk. 350	
C285	AP81	20c car ('71)	1.00	1.25
C286	AP81	40c gray bl ('71)	140.00	100.00
C287	AP81	50c grn ('71)	.75	.50
C288	AP81	80c claret, I ('73)	.75	.50
C289	AP92	1.20p dk grn & pur	6.75	2.50
C290	AP81	2p red brn, II ('71)	2.00	1.40
C296	AP81	5p brn & org ('66)	11.25	9.00
C297	AP81	10p blk & aqua	40.00	17.50
C298	AP81	20p car & bl gray	55.00	40.00
Nos. C285-C290, C296-C298 (9)			257.50	172.65

AP124

Design: National emblem, Cahill's butterfly world map, sword and scales of justice.

1964, July 29   **Photo.**
C299   AP124   40c sepia & dp bl   .85   .35
10th conference of the International Bar Association, Mexico City, July 27-31.

Galleon — AP125

Map Showing 16th Century Voyages Between Mexico and Philippines AP126

1964, Nov. 10   **Wmk. 350**   **Perf. 14**
C300   AP125   80c ultra & indigo   2.60   .35
C301   AP126   2.75p brt yel & blk   3.25   1.00
400 years of Mexican-Philippine friendship.

Netzahualcoyotl Dam, Grijalva River — AP127

1965, Feb. 19   **Photo.**   **Perf. 14**
C302   AP127   80c vio gray & dk brn   .60   .35

Radio-electric Unit of San Benito, Chiapas — AP128

80c, Microwave tower, Villahermosa, Tabasco.

1965, June 19   **Wmk. 350**   **Perf. 14**
C303   AP128   80c lt bl & dk bl   2.75   .65
C304   AP128   1.20p dk grn & blk   2.75   .65
Centenary of the ITU.

Campfire, Tent and Scout Emblem — AP129

1965, Sept. 27   **Photo.**   **Perf. 14**
C305   AP129   80c lt ultra & vio bl   .90   .35
20th World Scout Conference, Mexico City, Sept. 27-Oct. 3.

King Baudouin, Queen Fabiola and Arms of Belgium — AP130

1965, Oct. 18   **Wmk. 350**   **Perf. 14**
C306   AP130   2p slate grn & dl bl   1.25   .40
Visit of the King and Queen of Belgium.

Mayan Antiquities and Unisphere AP131

1965, Nov. 9   **Photo.**
C307   AP131   80c lemon & emer   .75   .35
Issued for the NY World's Fair, 1964-65.

Dante by Raphael — AP132

Perf. 10x10½
1965, Nov. 23   **Wmk. 350**   **Engr.**
C308   AP132   2p henna brown   1.50   .65
700th anniv. of the birth of Dante Alighieri.

AP133

AP133a

AP133b

Designs: 80c, Runner in Starting Position, Terra Cotta Found in Colima, 300-650 A.D. 1.20p, Chin cultic disk, ball game scoring stone with ball player in center, Mayan culture, c. 500 A.D., found in Chiapas. 2p, Clay sculpture of ball court, players, spectators and temple.
Pieces on 80c and 2p from 300-650 A.D.

1965, Dec. 17   **Photo.**   **Perf. 14**

Size: 35x21mm
C309   AP133   80c orange & sl   .95   .35
C310   AP133a   1.20p bl & vio bl   1.00   .35
  a.   Souv. sheet of 4, #965-966, C309-C310, imperf.   4.25   4.25

Size: 43x36mm
C311   AP133b   2p brt bl & dk brn   .90   .35
  a.   Souv. sheet, imperf.   4.00   4.00
Nos. C309-C311 (3)   2.85   1.05

19th Olympic Games, Mexico, 1968. No. C310a sold for 3.90p. No. C311a sold for 3p. Nos. C310a and C311a have large watermark of national arms (diameter 54mm) and "SECRETARIA DE HACIENDA Y CREDITO PUBLICO." Issued without gum.

Ruben Dario — AP134

1966, Mar. 17   **Wmk. 350**   **Perf. 14**
C312   AP134   1.20p sepia   .85   .35
Ruben Dario (pen name of Felix Ruben Garcia Sarmiento, 1867-1916), Nicaraguan poet, newspaper correspondent and diplomat.

Father Andres de Urdaneta and Compass Rose — AP135

Perf. 10½x10
1966, June 4   **Engr.**   **Wmk. 350**
C313   AP135   2.75p bluish blk   1.50   .60
4th centenary of Father Urdaneta's return trip from the Philippines.

UPAE Type of Regular Issue

Designs: 80c, Pennant and post horn. 1.20p, Pennant and UPAE emblem, horiz.

MEXICO

Wmk. 300
1966, June 24 Photo. Perf. 14
C314 A244 80c magenta & blk .45 .35
C315 A244 1.20p lt ultra & blk .65 .35

U Thant and UN Emblem — AP136

1966, Aug. 24 Photo. Wmk. 300
C316 AP136 80c black & ultra 1.00 .35

Visit of U Thant, Secretary General of the UN.

AP137

1966, Aug. 26 Perf. 14
C317 AP137 80c green & red .60 .35

Issued to publicize the year of friendship between Mexico and Central America.

Olympic Type of Regular Issue

Designs by Diego Rivera: 80c, Obstacle race. 2.25p, Football. 2.75p, Lighting Olympic torch.

1966, Oct. 15 Wmk. 300 Perf. 14
Size: 57x21mm
C318 A248 80c org brn & blk .65 .35
C319 A248 2.25p green & blk 1.10 .35
C320 A248 2.75p dp pur & blk 2.40 .45
  a. Souvenir sheet of 3 4.25 4.25
Nos. C318-C320 (3) 4.15 1.15

Issued to publicize the 19th Olympic Games, Mexico City, D.F., 1968. No. C320a contains 3 imperf. stamps similar to Nos. C318-C320 with simulated perforations. Sold for 8.70p.

UNESCO Emblem — AP138

Litho. & Engr.
1966, Nov. 4 Perf. 11
C321 AP138 80c blk, car, brt grn & org .60 .35
  a. Perf. 10½ 5.25 2.00
  b. Perf. 10½x11 26.00
  c. Perf. 11x10½ 12.50 5.00

UNESCO 20th anniv. The 4th color varies from yellow to orange. A number of perforation varieties exist on the perf 11 stamps.

Venustiano Carranza — AP139

1967, Feb. 5 Photo. Perf. 14
C322 AP139 80c dk red brn & ocher .55 .35

Constitution, 50th anniv. Venustiano Carranza (1859-1920), was president of Mexico 1917-20.

Tiros Satellite over Earth — AP140

1967, Mar. 23 Photo. Wmk. 300
C323 AP140 80c blk & dk bl .70 .35

World Meteorological Day, Mar. 23.

Medical School Emblem — AP141

1967, July 10 Wmk. 300 Perf. 14
C324 AP141 80c black & ocher .60 .35

Mexican Military Medical School, 50th anniv.

Captain Horacio Ruiz Gaviño — AP142

Design: 2p, Biplane, horiz.

1967, July 17 Photo.
C325 AP142 80c black & brown .40 .35
C326 AP142 2p black & brown .80 .35

50th anniv. of the 1st Mexican airmail flight, from Pachuca to Mexico City, July 6, 1917.

Marco Polo and ITY Emblem — AP143

1967, Sept. 9 Wmk. 300 Perf. 14
C327 AP143 80c rose cl & blk .60 .35

Issued for International Tourist Year, 1967.

Olympic Games Type of Regular Issue, 1967

Designs: 80c, Diving. 1.20p, Runners. 2p, Weight lifters. 5p, Soccer.

1967, Oct. 12 Photo. Perf. 14
C328 A254 80c dp lil rose & blk .55 .35
C329 A254 1.20p brt grn & blk .55 .35
  a. Souv. sheet of 2, #C328-C329, imperf. 5.50 3.75
C330 A254 2p yellow & blk 1.60 .40
C331 A254 5p olive & blk 1.90 .75
  a. Souv. sheet of 2, #C330-C331, imperf. 7.50 4.00
Nos. C328-C331 (4) 4.60 1.85

No. C329a sold for 2.50p; No. C331a sold for 9p. Both sheets are watermark 350.

Heinrich Hertz and James Clerk Maxwell — AP144

1967, Nov. 15 Photo. Wmk. 300
C332 AP144 80c brt grn & blk .60 .35

2nd Intl. Telecommunications Plan Conf., Mexico City, Oct. 30-Nov. 15.

EFIMEX Emblem, Showing Official Stamp of 1884 — AP145

1968, Feb. 24 Wmk. 300 Perf. 14
C333 AP145 80c black & grn .70 .35
C334 AP145 2p black & ver .70 .35

EFIMEX '68, International Philatelic Exhibition, Mexico City, Nov. 1-9, 1968.

Olympic Games Type of Regular Issue, 1967

Designs: 80c, Sailing. 1p, Rowing. 2p, Volleyball. 5p, Equestrian.

1968, Mar. 21 Photo. Perf. 14
C335 A254 80c ultra & blk .35 .35
C336 A254 1p brt bl grn & blk .40 .35
  a. Souv. sheet of 2, #C335-C336, imperf. 3.50 2.75
C337 A254 2p yellow & blk .80 .35
C338 A254 5p red brn & blk 1.60 1.10
  a. Souv. sheet of 2, #C337-C338, imperf. 7.50 4.50
Nos. C335-C338 (4) 3.15 2.15

No. C336a sold for 2.40p; No. C338a sold for 9p. Both sheets are watermark 350.

Martin Luther King, Jr. — AP146

1968, June 8 Photo. Wmk. 300
C339 AP146 80c black & gray .60 .35

Rev. Dr. Martin Luther King, Jr. (1929-1968), American civil rights leader.

Olympic Types of Regular Issue, 1968

Designs: 80c, Peace dove and Olympic rings. 1p, Discobolus. 2p, Olympic medals. 5p, Symbols of Olympic sports events. 10p, Symbolic design for Mexican Olympic Games.

1968, Oct. 12 Wmk. 350 Perf. 14
C340 A259 80c green, lil & org .40 .35
C341 A259 1p green, bl & blk .50 .35
C342 A259 2p multicolored 1.00 .50
  a. Souvenir sheet of 3, #C340-C342, imperf. 25.00 17.50
C343 A260 5p multicolored 4.50 1.40
C344 A260 10p black & multi 3.25 1.50
  a. Souvenir sheet of 2, #C343-C344, imperf. 25.00 17.50
Nos. C340-C344 (5) 9.65 4.10

19th Olympic Games, Mexico City, Oct. 12-27. No. C342a sold for 5p. No. C344a sold for 20p.

Souvenir Sheet

EFIMEX Emblem AP147

1968, Nov. 1 Photo. Imperf.
C345 AP147 5p black & ultra 3.75 2.50

EFIMEX '68 International philatelic exhibition, Mexico City, Nov. 1-9. No. C345 contains one stamp with simulated perforations.

Father Francisco Palóu (See footnote) AP148

1969, July 16 Wmk. 350 Perf. 14
C346 AP148 80c multicolored .65 .35

Issued to honor Father Junipero Serra (1713-1784), Franciscan missionary, founder of San Diego, Calif. The portrait was intended to be that of Father Serra. By error the head of Father Palóu, his coworker, was taken from a painting (c. 1785) by Mariano Guerrero which also contains a Serra portrait.

Type of 1950-52 Redrawn
Imprint: "T.I.E.V."
Coil Stamps
Wmk. 300 Vert.
1969 Photo. Perf. 11 Vert.
C347 AP81 20c carmine 3.00 2.00

Imprint: "Talleres de Imp de Est y Valores-Mexico"
C348 AP81 80c claret 4.25 2.00

Imprint: "T.I.E.V."
C349 AP81 1p gray grn 4.25 2.25
Nos. C347-C349 (3) 11.50 6.25

Soccer Ball — AP149

Design: 2p, Foot and soccer ball.

1969, Aug. 16 Wmk. 350 Perf. 14
C350 AP149 80c red & multi 1.50 .35
C351 AP149 2p green & multi 1.50 .35

9th World Soccer Championships for the Jules Rimet Cup, Mexico City, May 30-June 21, 1970.

Mahatma Gandhi — AP150

1969, Sept. 27 Photo. Perf. 14
C352 AP150 80c multicolored .60 .35

Mohandas K. Gandhi (1869-1948), leader in India's fight for independence.

Astronaut's Footprint — AP151

1969, Sept. 29 Photo.
C353 AP151 2p black .60 .35

Man's 1st landing on the moon, July 20, 1969. See note after US No. C76.

Tourist Type of Regular Issue, 1969-73 and

"Sound and Light" at Pyramid, Teotihuacan AP152

Designs: No. C355, Acapulco Bay. No. C356, El Caracol Observatory, Yucatan. No. C357, Dancer with fruit basket, Oaxaca. No. C358, Sports fishing, Lower California, horiz.

1969-73 Wmk. 350 Perf. 14
C354 AP152 80c shown 1.30 .35
C355 AP152 80c multicolored 1.30 .35
C356 AP152 80c multicolored 1.30 .35

Wmk. 300
C357 A267 80c multicolored .50 .35
C358 A267 80c multicolored .50 .35
Nos. C354-C358 (5) 4.90 1.75

Issue dates: Nos. C354-C356, Nov. 1, 1969. Nos. C357-C358, Mar. 16, 1973.

Red Crosses — AP154

1969, Nov. 8 Photo. Wmk. 350
C370 AP154 80c black & multi .60 .35
  a. Red omitted 150.00

50th anniv. of the League of Red Cross Societies.

AP155

1969, Dec. 6 Wmk. 350 Perf. 14
C371 AP155 80c multicolored .60 .35

Installation of the ground station for communications by satellite at Tulancingo, Hidalgo.

MEXICO

AP156

Design: 80c, Soccer Ball, and Mexican Masks. 2p, Pre-Columbian sculptured heads and soccer ball.

1970, May 31   Wmk. 350   Perf. 14
C372 AP156 80c blue & multi   1.50   .35
C373 AP156 2p multicolored   1.50   .35

World Soccer Championships for the Jules Rimet Cup, Mexico City, May 30-June 21, 1970. The design of Nos. C372-C373 is continuous.

SPORTMEX '70 Emblem — AP157

1970, June 19   Rouletted 13
C374 AP157 2p gray & car   5.25   3.00

SPORTMEX '70 philatelic exposition devoted to sports, especially soccer, on stamps. Mexico City, June 19-28. The 2p stamp of No. C374 is imperf.

Ode to Joy and Beethoven's Signature AP158

1970, Sept. 26   Wmk. 350   Perf. 14
C375 AP158 2p multicolored   .75   .35

200th anniversary of the birth of Ludwig van Beethoven (1770-1827), composer.

UN General Assembly Floor Plan — AP159

1970, Oct. 24   Photo.   Perf. 14
C376 AP159 80c multicolored   .60   .35

25th anniversary of United Nations.

Isaac Newton — AP160

1971, Feb. 27   Wmk. 350   Perf. 14
C377 AP160 2p shown   .70   .35
C378 AP160 2p Galileo   .70   .35
C379 AP160 2p Johannes Kepler   .70   .35
   Nos. C377-C379 (3)   2.10   1.05

Mayan Warriors, Dresden Codex — AP161

Designs: No. C381, Sister Juana, by Miguel Cabrera (1695-1768). No. C382, José Maria Velasco (1840-1912), self-portrait. No. C383, El Paricutin (volcano), by Gerardo Murillo ("Dr. Atl," 1875-1964). No. C384, Detail of mural, Man in Flames, by José Clemente Orozco (1883-1949).

Imprint includes "1971"
1971, Apr. 24   Photo.   Wmk. 350
C380 AP161 80c multicolored   1.60   .35
C381 AP161 80c multicolored   1.60   .35
C382 AP161 80c multicolored   1.60   .35
C383 AP161 80c multicolored   .60   .35
C384 AP161 80c multicolored   .60   .35
   Nos. C380-C384 (5)   6.00   1.75

Mexican art and science through the centuries. See Nos. C396-C400, C417-C421, C439-C443, C513-C517, C527-C531.

Stamps of Venezuela, Mexico and Colombia AP162

1971, May 22   Photo.   Wmk. 350
C385 AP162 80c multicolored   .60   .35

EXFILCA 70, 2nd Interamerican Philatelic Exhibition, Caracas, Venezuela, Nov. 27-Dec. 6, 1970.

Francisco Javier Clavijero AP163

1971, July 10   Wmk. 350   Perf. 14
C386 AP163 2p lt ol bis & dk brn   .75   .35

Francisco Javier Clavijero (1731-1786), Jesuit and historian, whose remains were returned from Italy to Mexico in 1970.

Waves — AP164

1971, Aug. 7   Wmk. 350   Perf. 14
C387 AP164 80c multicolored   .60   .35

3rd World Telecommunications Day, May 17.

Mariano Matamoros, by Diego Rivera — AP165

1971, Aug. 28   Photo.
C388 AP165 2p multicolored   .70   .35

Bicentenary of the birth of Mariano Matamoros (1770-1814), priest and patriot.

Vicente Guerrero — AP166

1971, Sept. 27
C389 AP166 2p multicolored   .65   .35

Vicente Guerrero (1783-1831), independence leader, president of Mexico. Painting by Juan O'Gorman.

Circles — AP167

1971, Nov. 4   Wmk. 300
C390 AP167 80c grnsh bl, dk bl & blk   .60   .35

25th anniv. of UNESCO.

Stamps of Venezuela, Mexico, Colombia and Peru — AP168

1971, Nov. 4
C391 AP168 80c multicolored   .70   .35

EXFILIMA '71, 3rd Interamerican Philatelic Exhibition, Lima, Peru, Nov. 6-14.

Faces and Hand — AP169

1971, Nov. 29
C392 AP169 2p blk, dk bl & pink   .70   .35

5th Congress of Psychiatry, Mexico City, Nov. 28-Dec. 4.

Ex Libris by Albrecht Dürer — AP170

1971, Dec. 18
C393 AP170 2p blk & buff   .90   .35

Albrecht Dürer (1471-1528), German painter and engraver.

Retort, Pulley and Burner — AP171

1972, Feb. 26   Wmk. 300   Perf. 14
C394 AP171 2p lilac, blk & yel   .60   .35

Anniversary of the National Council on Science and Technology.

Scientists and WHO Emblem — AP172

1972, Apr. 8
C395 AP172 80c multicolored   .60   .35

World Health Day 1972. Stamp shows Willem Einthoven and Frank Wilson.

Art and Science Type of 1971

Designs: No. C396, King Netzahuacoyotl (1402-1472) of Texcoco, art patron. No. C397, Juan Ruiz de Alarcon (c. 1580-1639), dramatist. No. C398, Jocó Joaquin Fernandez de Lizardi (1776-1827), author. No. C399, Ramon Lopez Velarde (1888-1921), writer. No. C400, Enrique Gonzalez Martinez (1871-1952), poet.

Imprint includes "1972"
1972, Apr. 15   Wmk. 350
Black Inscriptions
C396 AP161 80c ocher   1.50   .35
C397 AP161 80c green   1.50   .35
C398 AP161 80c brown   1.50   .35
C399 AP161 80c carmine   1.50   .35
C400 AP161 80c gray blue   1.50   .35
   Nos. C396-C400 (5)   7.50   1.75

Mexican art and science through the centuries.

Rotary Emblem — AP173

1972, Apr. 15
C401 AP173 80c multicolored   .60   .35

Rotary Intl. in Mexico, 50th anniv.

Tire Treads — AP174

1972, May 11   Wmk. 300
C402 AP174 80c gray & blk   .60   .35

74th Assembly of the International Tourism Alliance, Mexico City, May 8-11.

Benito Juárez — AP175

Designs: 80c, Page of Civil Register. 1.20p, Juárez, by Pelegrin Clavé.

1972   Photo.   Perf. 14
C403 AP175 80c gray bl & blk   .50   .35
C404 AP175 1.20p multi   .50   .35
C405 AP175 2p yellow & multi   .50   .35
   Nos. C403-C405 (3)   1.50   1.05

Benito Juárez (1806-1872), revolutionary leader and president of Mexico. Issue dates: 80c, 2p, July 18; 1.20p, Sept. 15.

Atom Symbol, Olive Branch — AP176

1972, Oct. 3   Photo.   Wmk. 300
C406 AP176 2p gray, bl & blk   .65   .35

16th Conference of the Atomic Energy Commission, Mexico City, Sept. 26.

"Over the Waves," by Juventino Rosas — AP177

1972, Oct. 16   Perf. 14
C407 AP177 80c olive bister   .60   .35

28th Intl. Cong. of the Societies of Authors and Composers, Mexico City, Oct. 16-21.

MEXICO

Child with Doll, by Guerrero Galvan, UNICEF Emblem — AP178

1972, Nov. 4
C408 AP178 80c multicolored   1.00 .35
25th anniv. (in 1971) of UNICEF.

Pedro de Gante, by Rodriguez y Arangorti — AP179

1972, Nov. 22   *Perf. 14*
C409 AP179 2p multicolored   .60 .35
Brother Pedro de Gante (Pedro Moor or van der Moere; 1480?-1572), Franciscan brother who founded first school in Mexico, and writer.

Olympic Games Type of Regular Issue, 1972
Designs: 80c, Olympic emblems and stylized soccer game. 2p, Olympic emblems, vert.

1972, Dec. 9   *Photo.*   *Wmk. 300*
C410 A289 80c green & multi   .50 .35
C411 A289 2p yel grn, blk & bl 1.00 .35
20th Olympic Games, Munich, Aug. 26-Sept. 11.

Anti-pollution Type of Regular Issue
80c, Bird sitting on ornamental capital, vert.

1972, Dec. 16
C412 A291 80c lt blue & blk   .60 .35
Anti-pollution campaign.

Map of Americas with Tourists' Footprints — AP180

1972, Dec. 23
C413 AP180 80c black, yel & grn   .60 .35
Tourism Year of the Americas.

Mexico #O1, Brazil #992, Colombia #130, Venezuela #22, Peru #C320 — AP181

1973, Jan. 19   *Perf. 14*
C414 AP181 80c multicolored   .60 .35
4th Interamerican Philatelic Exhibition, EXFILBRA 72, Rio de Janeiro, Brazil, Aug. 26-Sept. 2, 1972.

Aeolus, God of Winds AP182

1973, Sept. 14 *Photo.* *Wmk. 300*
C415 AP182 80c brt pink, blk & bl .85 .35
Cent. of intl. meteorological cooperation.

Nicolaus Copernicus — AP183

1973, Oct. 10 *Photo.*   *Perf. 14*
                  Wmk. 300
C416 AP183 80c slate green   .40 .35
500th anniversary of the birth of Nicolaus Copernicus (1473-1543), Polish astronomer.

Art and Science Type of 1971
Designs: No. C417, Aztec calendar stone. No. C418, Carlos de Sigüenza y Gongora (1645-1700), mathematician, astronomer. No. C419, Francisco Diaz Covarrubias (1833-1889), topographer. No. C420, Joaquin Gallo (1882-1965), geographer, astronomer. No. C421, Luis Enrique Erro (1897-1955), founder of Tonanzintla Observatory.

Imprint includes "1973"

1973, Nov. 21   *Wmk. 350*
C417 AP161 80c car & sl grn   .60 .35
C418 AP161 80c multicolored   .60 .35
C419 AP161 80c multicolored   .60 .35
C420 AP161 80c multicolored   .60 .35
C421 AP161 80c multicolored   .60 .35
    Nos. C417-C421 (5) 3.00 1.75

Type of 1950-52
Design: Mexico City University Stadium.

Imprint: "Talleres de Imp. de Est. y Valores-Mexico"

1973   *Unwmk.*   *Perf. 11*
C422 AP81 80c claret, I   3.25 .95
Fluorescent printing on front or back of stamps consisting of beehive pattern and diagonal inscription.

San Martin Monument — AP184

Wmk. 350
1973, Dec. 14 *Photo.*   *Perf. 14*
C423 AP184 80c org, indigo & yel .60 .35
Erection of a monument to San Martin in Mexico City, a gift of Argentina.

Palace of Cortes, Cuernavaca AP185

Wmk. 300
1974, Feb. 22 *Litho.*   *Perf. 14*
C424 AP185 80c black & multi .60 .35
EXMEX 73 Philatelic Exhibition, Cuernavaca, Apr. 7-15.

Gold Brooch, Mochica Culture — AP186

1974, Mar. 6 *Photo.* *Wmk. 300*
C425 AP186 80c gold & multi .60 .35
Exhibition of Peruvian gold treasures, Mexico City, 1973-74.

Luggage — AP187

1974, Mar. 22   *Perf. 14*
C426 AP187 80c multicolored .60 .35
16th Convention of the Federation of Latin American Tourist Organizations (COTAL), Acapulco, May 1974.

CEPAL Emblem — AP188

1974, Mar. 22
C427 AP188 80c black & multi .60 .35
  a.   Red omitted   100.00
25th anniversary (in 1973) of the Economic Commission for Latin America (CEPAL).

"The Enameled Casserole," by Picasso AP189

1974, Mar. 29   *Wmk. 300*
C428 AP189 80c multicolored .60 .35
Pablo Ruiz Picasso (1881-1973), painter and sculptor.

EXFILMEX Type of 1974
1974, July 26   *Perf. 13x12*
C429 A305 80c buff, red brn & blk .60 .35
See note after No. 1065.

Biplane AP190

Perf. 13x12
1974, Aug. 20 *Photo.* *Wmk. 300*
C430 AP190 80c shown   .60 .35
C431 AP190 2p Jet plane   .60 .35
50th anniversary of Mexican Airlines (MEXICANA).

Transmitter and Waves Circling Globe AP191

1974, Oct. 4 *Wmk. 300* *Perf. 14*
C432 AP191 2p multicolored .60 .35
First International Congress of Electric and Electronic Communications, Sept. 17-21.

Volleyball AP192

1974, Oct. 12   *Perf. 13x12*
C433 AP192 2p orange, bis & blk .60 .35
8th World Volleyball Championship. Perforation holes are of two sizes.

Souvenir Sheet

Mexico #O1, Colombia #130, Venezuela #22, Peru #C320, Brazil #992, Mexico #123 — AP193

Wmk. 300
1974, Oct. 26 *Photo.* *Imperf.*
C434 AP193 10p multicolored 3.75 1.50
EXFILMEX 74, 5th Inter-American Philatelic Exhibition, Mexico City, Oct. 26-Nov. 3. Exists with red omitted.

Felipe Carrillo Puerto — AP194

1974, Nov. 8   *Perf. 14*
C435 AP194 80c grn & gldn brn .60 .35
Birth centenary of Felipe Carrillo Puerto (1874-1924), politician and journalist.

Mask, Bat and Catcher's Mitt — AP195

1974, Nov. 29 *Wmk. 350* *Perf. 14*
C436 AP195 80c multi   .60 .35
Mexican Baseball League, 50th anniversary.

Man's Face, Mailbox, Colonial Period — AP196

Design: 2p, Heinrich von Stephan, contemporary engraving.

1974, Dec. 13 *Photo.* *Wmk. 300*
C437 AP196 80c multicolored .60 .35
C438 AP196 2p green & ocher .60 .35
Centenary of Universal Postal Union.

MEXICO

Art and Science Type of 1971

Designs: No. C439, Mayan mural (8th century), Bonampak, Chiapas. No. C440, First musical score printed in Mexico, 1556. No. C441, Miguel Lerdo de Tejada (1869-1941), composer. No. C442, Silvestre Revueltas (1899-1940), composer (bronze bust). No. C443, Angela Peralta (1845-1883), singer.

Imprint includes "1974"

1974, Dec. 20		Wmk. 300		
C439	AP161	80c multi	.60	.35
C440	AP161	80c multi	.60	.35
C441	AP161	80c multi	.60	.35
C442	AP161	80c multi	.60	.35
C443	AP161	80c multi	.60	.35
	Nos. C439-C443 (5)		3.00	1.75

Types of 1950-56

Designs (as 1950-56 issues): 40c, San Luis Potosi, head. 60c, Leon Guzman and Ignacio Ramirez. 1.60p, Chiapas, Mayan bas-relief. 1.90p, Guerrero, Acapulco waterfront. 4.30p, Oaxaca, dance. 5.20p, Guerrero, view of Taxco. 5.60p, Michoacan, masks. 50p, Valentin Gomez Farias and Melchor Ocampo.

Engraved (40c), Photogravure
Perf. 11 (40c, 1.60p), 14

1975			Wmk. 300	
C444	AP81	40c bluish gray	.35	.35
C445	AP92	60c yellow grn	.95	.35
C446	AP81	1.60p red	3.25	.35
C447	AP81	1.90p rose red	3.25	
C448	AP81	4.30p ultra	1.10	.25
C449	AP81	5.20p purple	1.90	.40
C450	AP81	5.60p blue grn	2.40	.50
C451	AP92	50p dk bl & brick red	16.00	3.50
	Nos. C444-C451 (8)		29.20	6.05

Women's Year Emblem — AP199

1975, Jan. 3		Wmk. 300	Perf. 14	
C456	AP199	1.60p brt pink & blk	.60	.35

International Women's Year 1975.

Declaration, UN Emblem, Mexican Flag — AP200

1975, Feb. 7		Photo.	Wmk. 300	
C457	AP200	1.60p multi	.60	.35

Declaration of Economic Rights and Duties of Nations.

Balsa Raft "Acali" AP201

1975, Mar. 7		Wmk. 300	Perf. 14	
C458	AP201	80c multicolored	.60	.35

Trans-Atlantic voyage of the "Acali" from Canary Islands to Yucatan, May-Aug. 1973.

Dr. Miguel Jimenez, by I. Ramirez — AP202

1975, Mar. 24		Unwmk.	Perf. 14	
C459	AP202	2p multicolored	.60	.35

Fifth World Gastroenterology Congress.

Miguel de Cervantes — AP203

1975, Apr. 26		Photo.	Unwmk.	
C460	AP203	1.60p bl blk & dk car	.60	.35

Third International Cervantes Festival, Guanajuato, Apr. 26-May 11.

Four-reales Coin, 1535 AP204

1975, May 2				
C461	AP204	1.60p bl, gold & blk	.60	.35

Intl. Numismatic Convention, Mexico City, Mar. 28-30, 1974.

Salvador Novo, by Roberto Montenegro AP205

1975, May 9				
C462	AP205	1.60p multi	.60	.35

Salvador Novo (1904-1974), author.

Mural, Siqueiros AP206

1975, May 16				
C463	AP206	1.60p multi	.60	.35

David Alfaro Siqueiros (1896-1974), painter.

UN and IWY Emblems AP207

1975, June 19				
C464	AP207	1.60p ultra & pink	.60	.35

International Women's Year World Conference, Mexico City, June 19-July 2.

Mexico City Coat of Arms — AP208

		Unwmk.		
1975, Aug. 1		Photo.	Perf. 14	
C465	AP208	1.60p multi	.60	.35

650th anniv. of Tenochtitlan (Mexico City).

Domingo F. Sarmiento — AP209

		Unwmk.		
1975, Aug. 9		Photo.	Perf. 14	
C466	AP209	1.60p brown & sl grn	.60	.35

1st International Congress of Third World Educators, Acapulco, Aug. 5-9. Domingo Faustino Sarmiento (1811-1888), Argentinian statesman, writer and educator.

Teachers' Monument — AP210

1975, Aug. 9				
C467	AP210	4.30p green & ocher	.60	.35

Mexican-Lebanese friendship. The monument in Mexico City, by I Naffa al Rozzi, shows Cadmus, a mythical Phoenician, teaching the alphabet.

7th Pan American Games' Emblem — AP211

1975, Aug. 29				
C468	AP211	1.60p multi	.60	.35

Pan American Games, Mexico City, Oct. 13-26.

Dr. Atl, Self-portrait AP212

		Unwmk.		
1975, Oct. 3		Photo.	Perf. 14	
C469	AP212	4.30p multi	.60	.35

Geraldo Murillo ("Dr. Atl," 1875-1924), painter and writer, birth centenary.

Globe and Traffic Circle — AP213

1975, Oct. 17				
C470	AP213	1.60p bl, blk & gray	.60	.35

15th World Road Congress, Mexico City, Oct. 12-26.

Type of 1950-52

Designs: 40c, San Luis Potosi, head. 60c, Leon Guzman & Ignacio Ramirez. 80c, Mexico City University stadium. 1p, Puebla, Half Moon dance. 1.60p, Chiapas, Mayan bas-relief. 5p, Queretaro, architecture. 5.60p, Michoacan, masks. 10p, Miguel Hidalgo. 20p, Modern building.

Engraved (40c, 1p), Photogravure
Perf. 11 (40c, 80c, 1p, 1.60p), 14

1975-76			Unwmk.	
C471	AP81	40c bluish gray	.40	.35
C471A	AP92	60c yel grn	1,200.	
C472	AP81	80c claret, II	.65	.50
C473	AP81	1p grysh grn	1.10	.80
C474	AP81	1.60p red	1.90	1.00
C476	AP81	5p dk brn & org ('76)	1.60	1.00
a.		5p dark brown & red orange	2.00	2.00
C477	AP81	5.60p bluish grn ('76)	5.25	3.25
C479	AP81	10p blk & grn	4.25	2.50
C480	AP81	20p red & dl grn ('76)	8.25	4.00
	Nos. C471,C472-C480 (8)		23.40	13.40

Bicycle and Export Emblem — AP214

Designs: Export Emblem and 30c, Copper vase. 80c, Overalls. 1.90p, Oil valves. 2p, Books. 4p, Honey. 4.30p, Strawberry. 5p, Motor vehicles. 5.20p, Farm machinery. 5.60p, Cotton. 20p, Film. 50p, Cotton thread.

1975-82		Unwmk.	Photo.	Perf. 14
C486	AP214	30c copper ('76)	.35	.35
C489	AP214	80c dull blue ('76)	.35	.35
C491	AP214	1.60p black & org	.45	.35
a.		Thin paper ('81)	1.25	.35
C492	AP214	1.90p ver & dk grn	.45	.35
C493	AP214	2p ultra & gold ('76)	.80	.35
C495	AP214	4p yel bis & brn ('82)	1.60	.35
C496	AP214	4.30p brt pink & ol	.65	.35
C497	AP214	5p dk bl & ocher ('76)	1.90	.35
C498	AP214	5.20p red & blk ('76)	.95	.40
C499	AP214	5.60p yel grn & org ('76)	.45	.35
C503	AP214	20p multi, thin paper ('81)	1.25	.35
C508	AP214	50p multi ('82)	5.00	2.00
	Nos. C486-C508 (12)		14.20	5.90

See Nos. C594-C603.

Art and Science Type of 1971

Designs: No. C513, Title page of "Medical History of New Spain," by Francisco Hernandez, 1628. No. C514, Alfonso L. Herrera (1868-1942), biologist. No. C515, Title page, Aztec Herbal, 1552. No. C516, Arturo S. Rosenblueth (1900-1970). No. C517, Alfredo Augusto Duges (1826-1910) French-born naturalist.

Imprint includes "1975"

1975, Nov. 21		Unwmk.	Perf. 14	
C513	AP161	1.60p buff, red & blk	.60	.35
C514	AP161	1.60p vio bl & multi	.60	.35
C515	AP161	1.60p black & multi	.60	.35
C516	AP161	1.60p gray & multi	.60	.35
C517	AP161	1.60p green & multi	.60	.35
a.		Thin paper	400.00	
	Nos. C513-C517 (5)		3.00	1.75

Telephone — AP216

1976, Mar. 10			Photo.	
C518	AP216	1.60p gray & blk	.60	.35

Centenary of first telephone call by Alexander Graham Bell, Mar. 10, 1876.

60-peso Gold Coin, Oaxaca, 1917 — AP217

1976, Mar. 25		Photo.	Unwmk.	
C519	AP217	1.60p black, ocher & yel	.60	.35

4th International Numismatic Convention, Mexico City, March 1976.

MEXICO

Rain God Tlaloc and Calles Dam — AP218

1976, Mar. 29   *Perf. 14*
C520 AP218 1.60p vio brn & dk grn   .60   .35

12th International Great Dams Congress, Mar. 29-Apr. 2.

Perforation Gauge — AP219

1976, May 7   *Photo.*   *Unwmk.*
C521 AP219 1.60p blk, red & bl   .60   .35

Interphil 76 International Philatelic Exhibition, Philadelphia, Pa., May 29-June 6.

Rainbow over City — AP220

1976, May 31   *Unwmk.*   *Perf. 14*
C522 AP220 1.60p black & multi   .60   .35

Habitat, UN Conf. on Human Settlements, Vancouver, Canada, May 31-June 11.

Liberty Bell — AP221

1976, July 4   *Photo.*   *Perf. 14*
C523 AP221 1.60p ultra & red   .60   .35

American Bicentennial.

"Peace" — AP222

Design: "Peace" written in Chinese, Japanese, Hebrew, Hindi and Arabic.

1976, Aug. 3   *Photo.*   *Perf. 14*
C524 AP222 1.60p multi   .60   .35

30th Intl. Cong. of Science and Humanities of Asia and North Africa, Mexico, Aug. 3-8.

Television Screen — AP223

1976, Aug. 24   *Photo.*   *Unwmk.*
C525 AP223 1.60p multi   .60   .35

1st Latin-American Forum on Children's Television.

Luminescence

Fluorescent airmail stamps include Nos. C265, C265c, C288, C357-C358, C390-C415, C422-C423.
Airmail stamps issued on both ordinary and fluorescent paper include Nos. C220, C220D-C220E, C220G-C220H, C265b, C266-C268, C286.

Sky, Sun, Water and Earth — AP224

1976, Nov. 8   *Photo.*   *Perf. 14*
C526 AP224 1.60p multi   .60   .35

World Conservation Day.

Art and Science Type of 1971

Designs: No. C527, Coatlicue, Mother of Earth, Aztec sculpture. No. C528, El Caballito, statue of Charles IV of Spain, by Manuel Tolsá. No. C529, Chief Tlahuicole, bronze statue by Manuel Vilar. No. C530, Today's God, Money, seated ceramic figure, by L. Ortiz Monasterio. No. C531, Signal, abstract sculpture by Angela Gurria.

Imprint includes "1976"

1976, Dec. 10   *Photo.*   *Perf. 14*
C527 AP161 1.60p black & yel   .60   .35
C528 AP161 1.60p blk & red brn   .60   .35
C529 AP161 1.60p black & multi   .60   .35
C530 AP161 1.60p car & multi   .60   .35
C531 AP161 1.60p carmine & blk   .60   .35
    Nos. C527-C531 (5)   3.00   1.75

Score for El Pesebre by Casals — AP225

1976, Dec. 29
C532 AP225 4.30p lt bl, blk & brn   .60   .35

Pablo Casals (1876-1973), cellist and composer, birth centenary.

Mankind Destroyed by Nuclear Power — AP226

1977, Feb. 14   *Photo.*   *Perf. 14*
C533 AP226 1.60p multi   .60   .35
    a. Wmk. 300   50.00   40.00

10th anniv. of the Agreement of Tlatelolco, banning nuclear arms in Latin America.

Soccer — AP227

Anniversary Emblem AP228

1977, Aug. 23   *Wmk. 300*   *Perf. 14*
C534 AP227 1.60p multicolored   .60   .35
C535 AP228 4.30p black, bl & yel   .60   .35

Mexican Soccer Fed., 50th anniv.

Hands and Scales — AP229

1977, Sept. 23   *Photo.*   *Perf. 14*
C536 AP229 1.60p org, brn & blk   .35   .25

Federal Council of Reconciliation and Arbitration, 50th anniversary.

Arms of Mexico and Spain — AP230

1977, Oct. 8   *Perf. 14*
C537 AP230 1.60p dull bl & blk   .60   .35
C538 AP230 1.90p lt grn & maroon   .60   .35
C539 AP230 4.30p tan, grn & brn   .60   .35
    Nos. C537-C539 (3)   1.80   1.05

Resumption of diplomatic relations with Spain.

1.90p, Maps of Mexico & Spain. 4.30p, Pres. José López Portillo & King Juan Carlos.

Tlaloc, the Rain God — AP231

Wmk. 300
1977, Nov. 4   *Photo.*   *Perf. 14*
C540 AP231 1.60p multi   .60   .35

National Central Observatory, centenary.

Ludwig van Beethoven — AP232

1977, Nov. 10   *Photo.*
C541 AP232 1.60p brt grn & brn   .60   .35
C542 AP232 4.30p lilac rose & bl   .60   .35

Tractor and Dam AP233

1977, Nov. 25   *Photo.*   *Perf. 14*
C543 AP233 1.60p multi   .60   .35

United Nations Desertification Conference.

Mexico City-Cuernavaca Highway — AP234

1977, Nov. 30
C544 AP234 1.60p multi   .60   .35

25th anniversary of first national highway.

Arms of Campeche — AP235

1977, Dec. 3
C545 AP235 1.60p multi   .60   .35

200th anniv. of the naming of Campeche.

Congress Emblem — AP236

1977, Dec. 9
C546 AP236 1.60p multi   .60   .35

20th World Congress for Education, Hygiene and Recreation, July 18-24, 1977.

Freighter Navimex AP237

1977, Dec. 16
C547 AP237 1.60p multi   .60   .35

60th anniv. of National Merchant Marine.

Mayan Dancer, Jaina — AP238

Pre-Columbian Sculptures: No. C549, Aztec dance god. No. C550, Snake dancer, bas-relief. No. C551, Monte Alban, bas-relief. No. C552, Totonaca figurine.

1977, Dec. 26   *Perf. 14*
C548 AP238 1.60p sal, blk & car   .60   .35
C549 AP238 1.60p lt & dk bl & blk   .60   .35
C550 AP238 1.60p yel, blk & gray   .60   .35
C551 AP238 1.60p bl grn, blk & grn   .60   .35
C552 AP238 1.60p gray, blk & red brn   .60   .35
    Nos. C548-C552 (5)   3.00   1.75

Mexican art.

Tumor Clinic, by David A. Siqueiros AP239

4.30p, La Raza Medical Center, by Diego Rivera.

1978, Jan. 19   *Photo.*   *Wmk. 300*
C553 AP239 1.60p multi   .60   .35
C554 AP239 4.30p multi   .60   .35

Mexican Social Security Institute, 35th anniv.

Moorish Fountain AP240

1978, Mar. 1   *Photo.*   *Perf. 14*
C555 AP240 1.60p multi   .60   .35

Founding of Chiapa de Corzo, Chiapas, 450th anniv.

Oil Industry Type of 1978

Designs: 1.60p, Gen. Lazaro Cardenas. 4.30p, Offshore oil rig.

Wmk. 300
1978, Mar. 18   *Photo.*   *Perf. 14*
C556 A343 1.60p brt bl & lil rose   .60   .35
C557 A343 4.30p bl, brt bl & blk   .60   .35

Oil industry nationalization, 40th anniv.

Arms of Diego de Mazariegos AP241

Wmk. 300
1978, Apr. 3   *Photo.*   *Perf. 14*
C558 AP241 1.60p pink, blk & pur   .60   .35

400th anniversary of the founding of San Cristobal de las Casas, Chiapas, by Diego de Mazariegos.

MEXICO

Blood Pressure Gauge, Map of Mexico — AP242

Globe, Snake, Hand Holding Stethoscope — AP243

1978, Apr. 7
C559 AP242 1.60p dk bl & car .60 .35
C560 AP243 4.30p org & dk bl .60 .35

Drive against hypertension and World Health Day.

X-ABC1 Plane — AP244

1978, Apr. 15
C561 AP244 1.60p ultra & multi .60 .35
C562 AP244 4.30p ultra & multi .60 .35

1st Mexican airmail route, 50th anniv.

Globe, Cogwheel, UN Emblem — AP245

4.30p, Globe, flags, cogwheel, UN emblem.

1978, Apr. 21
C563 AP245 1.60p multi .60 .35
C564 AP245 4.30p multi .60 .35

World Conference on Technical Cooperation of Underdeveloped Countries.

Soccer — AP246

Designs: 1.90p, Goalkeeper catching ball. 4.30p, Soccer player.

Wmk. 300
1978, June 1 Photo. Perf. 14
C565 AP246 1.60p multi .60 .35
C566 AP246 1.90p multi .60 .35
C567 AP246 4.30p multi .60 .35
Nos. C565-C567 (3) 1.80 1.05

11th World Cup Soccer Championship, Argentina, June 1-25.

Francisco (Pancho) Villa — AP247

1978, June 5
C568 AP247 1.60p multi .60 .35

Pancho Villa (1878-1923), revolutionary leader.

Mexico No. C6, Independence Monument, Washington Monument AP248

1978, June 11
C569 AP248 1.60p ol gray & red .60 .35

50th anniversary of flight Mexico to Washington by Emilio Carranza (1905-1928).

Woman and Calendar Stone — AP249

Wmk. 300
1978, July 15 Photo. Perf. 14
C570 AP249 1.60p rose, blk & brn .60 .35
C571 AP249 1.90p brt grn, blk & brn .60 .35
C572 AP249 4.30p org, blk & brn .60 .35
Nos. C570-C572 (3) 1.80 1.05

Miss Universe contest, Acapulco, July 1978.

Alvaro Obregón AP250

1978, July 17
C573 AP250 1.60p multi .60 .35

Obregón (1880-1928), president of Mexico.

Geographical Institute Type of 1978

Institute emblem in different arrangements.

1978, July 21 Photo. Wmk. 300
C574 A344 1.60p emerald & blk .60 .35
C575 A344 4.30p ocher & blk .60 .35

Pan-American Institute for Geography and History, 50th anniversary.

Sun Rising over Ciudad Obregón AP251

1978, Aug. 4 Perf. 14
C576 AP251 1.60p multi .60 .35

Founding of the city of Obregón, 50th anniv.

Mayan Figure, Castle and Pawn — AP252

1978, Aug. 19 Photo. Perf. 14
C577 AP252 1.60p multi .60 .35
C578 AP252 4.30p multi .60 .35

World Youth Team Chess Championship, Ajedrez, Aug. 19-Sept. 7.

Aristotle (384-322 B.C.), Philosopher — AP253

Design: 4.30p, Statue of Aristotle.

1978, Aug. 25
C579 AP253 1.60p multi .60 .35
C580 AP253 4.30p multi .60 .35

Mule Deer — AP254

1978, Sept. 8 Photo. Wmk. 300
C581 AP254 1.60p shown 1.00 .35
C582 AP254 1.60p Ocelot 1.50 .35

Protected animals.

Man's Head, Dove, UN Emblem — AP255

4.30p, Woman's head, dove, UN emblem.

1978, Sept. 22 Perf. 14
C583 AP255 1.60p ver, gray & blk .60 .35
C584 AP255 4.30p lil, gray & blk .60 .35

Anti-Apartheid Year.

Emblem — AP256

Wmk. 300
1978, Oct. 23 Photo. Perf. 14
C585 AP256 1.60p multi .60 .35

13th Congress of International Union of Architects, Mexico City, Oct. 23-27.

Dr. Rafael Lucio (1819-1886) — AP257

1978, Nov. 13 Wmk. 350
C586 AP257 1.60p yellow grn .60 .35

11th International Anti-Leprosy Congress.

Franz Schubert, "Death and the Maiden" — AP258

1978, Nov. 19 Photo. Perf. 14
C587 AP258 4.30p brn, grn & blk .60 .35

Schubert (1797-1828), Austrian composer.

Children, Christmas Decorations — AP259

Wmk. 350
1978, Nov. 22 Photo. Perf. 14
C588 AP259 1.60p multi .60 .35

Christmas 1978.

Antonio Vivaldi — AP260

1978, Dec. 1
C589 AP260 4.30p multi .60 .35

Antonio Vivaldi (1675-1741), Italian violinist and composer.

Wright Brothers' Flyer — AP261

Design: 4.30p, Flyer, different view.

1978, Dec. 17
C590 AP261 1.60p multi .60 .35
C591 AP261 4.30p multi .60 .35

75th anniversary of 1st powered flight.

Einstein and his Equation AP262

Wmk. 300
1979, Apr. 20 Photo. Perf. 14
C592 AP262 1.60p multi .60 .35

Albert Einstein (1879-1955), theoretical physicist.

Rowland Hill — AP263

1979, Apr. 27
C593 AP263 1.60p multi .60 .35

Sir Rowland Hill (1795-1879), originator of penny postage.

Export Type of 1975

Designs: Export Emblem and 50c, Circuit board. 1.60p, Bicycle. 1.90p, Oil valves. 2.50p, Tomato. 4p, Honey. 5p, Motor vehicles. 10p, Citrus fruit. 50p, Cotton thread.

1979-81 Photo. Wmk. 300
C594 AP214 50c ocher & red brn .40 .35
C596 AP214 1.60p black & org .40 .35
C597 AP214 1.90p ver & dk grn ('81) .55 .40
C599 AP214 2.50p ver & grn .40 .35
C600 AP214 4p yel bis & brn ('81) .40 .35
C601 AP214 5p dk bl & dl org 5.25 .50
C602 AP214 10p grn & yel grn ('81) 1.10 .75
C603 AP214 50p multicolored 6.25 1.50
Nos. C594-C603 (8) 14.75 4.55

No. C600 exists with brown omitted.

Children, Child's Drawing AP264

1979, May 16
C604 AP264 1.60p multi .60 .35

International Year of the Child.

437

MEXICO

Registered Letter from Mexico to Rome, 1880 — AP265

Wmk. 300
1979, June 7   Photo.   *Perf. 14*
C605 AP265 1.60p multi   .60   .35
MEPSIPEX '79, 3rd Intl. Exhibition of Elmhurst Philatelic Society, Mexico City, 6/7-10.

Sports Type of 1979
Designs: 1.60p, Games emblem. 4.30p, Symbolic flame and birds. 10p, Women gymnasts, horiz.

1979, June 15
C606 A348 1.60p multi   .60   .35
C607 A348 4.30p multi   .60   .35

Souvenir Sheet
Imperf
C608 A348 10p multi   2.25   2.25
No. C608 has simulated perforations.

University Type of 1979
Paintings: 1.60p, The Return of Quetzalcoatl, by Chavez Morado. 4.30p, Students Reaching for Culture, by Alfaro Siqueiros.

1979, July 10   *Perf. 14*
C609 A350 1.60p multi   .60   .35
C610 A350 4.30p multi   .60   .35

Messenger and UPU Emblem — AP266

1979, July 27   Photo.   Wmk. 300
C611 AP266 1.60p multi   .60   .35
Cent. of Mexico's membership in UPU.

Sports Type of 1979
1979, Sept. 2   Wmk. 300   *Perf. 14*
C612 A352 1.60p multi Tennis   .60   .35
C613 A352 5.50p multi Swimming   .60   .35

Souvenir Sheet
Imperf
C614 A352 10p Various sports   2.50   2.50

Tourism Type of 1979
No. C615, Agua Azul Waterfall, Chiapas. No. C616, King Coliman statue, Colima.

Wmk. 300
1979, Sept. 28   Photo.   *Perf. 14*
C615 A353 1.60p multi   .60   .35
C616 A353 1.60p multi   .60   .35

Graphic Design — AP267

1979, Oct. 14   Photo.   Wmk. 300
C617 AP267 1.60p multi   .60   .35
ICSID, 11th Congress and Assembly of the Intl. Industrial Design Council, Oct. 1979.

Mail Service Type of 1979
Designs: 1.60p, Martin Enriquez de Almanza, Viceroy of New Spain. 5.50p, King Philip II of Spain. 10p, Sailing ship, horiz.

1979, Oct. 26
C618 A354 1.60p multi   .60   .35
C619 A354 5.50p multi   .60   .35

Souvenir Sheet
Imperf
C620 A354 10p multi   4.75   1.50
No. C620 contains stamp with simulated perfs.

Early Lamp — AP268

1979, Oct. 21   Wmk. 300
C621 AP268 1.60p multi   .60   .35
Centenary of invention of electric light.

Union Emblem — AP269

1979, Nov. 12   Wmk. 300   Photo.   *Perf. 14*
C622 AP269 1.60p multi   .60   .35
Latin American Universities Union, 8th general assembly.

Christmas Type of 1979
Design: 1.60p, Girl and Christmas tree.

1979, Nov. 15
C623 A355 1.60p multi   .60   .35

Moon Symbol from Mexican Codex — AP270

1979, Nov. 30
C624 AP270 2.50p multi   .60   .35
Apollo 11 moon landing, 10th anniversary.

Monument Type of 1980
Stone Sculptures: 1.60p, Tlaloc, water god. 5.50p, Coyolxauqui, goddess.

1980, Feb. 16   Photo.   *Perf. 14*
C625 A356 1.60p multi   .60   .35
C626 A356 5.50p multi   .60   .35

16th Century Church, Acolman — AP271

16th Century Churches in: No. C628, Actopan Convent. No. C629, Tlayacapan. No. C630, Yanhuitlan. No. C631, Yuriria. No. C628 actually shows Tlayacapan; No. C629, Actopan convent (inscriptions reversed).

1980, Feb. 1
C627 AP271 1.60p multi   .60   .35
C628 AP271 1.60p multi   .60   .35
C629 AP271 1.60p multi   .60   .35
C630 AP271 1.60p multi   .60   .35
C631 AP271 1.60p multi   .60   .35
   Nos. C627-C631 (5)   3.00   1.75

Flora and Fauna Types of 1980
1980, Mar. 8   *Perf. 14*
C632 A357 1.60p multi Flamingo   .60   .35
C633 A358 1.60p multi Vanilla plant   .60   .35

Jules Verne — AP272

Wmk. 300
1980, Mar. 24   Photo.   *Perf. 14*
C634 AP272 5.50p blk & red brn   .60   .35
Jules Verne (1828-1905) French science fiction writer.

Skeleton Smoking Cigar, UN Emblem — AP273

1980, Apr. 7   *Perf. 14*
C635 AP273 1.60p multi   .60   .35
World Health Day/Fight against cigarette smoking.

Costume Type
1.60p, Chiapaneca, Chiapas.

1980, Apr. 26   *Perf. 14*
C636 A359 1.60p multi   .60   .35

Items inscribed "MEXICO" and "correo aereo" picturing Emiliano Zapata are not postage stamps.

AIR POST OFFICIAL STAMPS

Nos. C4 and C3 Overprinted in Black or Red

1929   Wmk. 156   *Perf. 12*
CO1   AP1   25c dk grn & gray brn   4.50   3.25
   a.   Without period   20.00   20.00
CO2   AP1   25c dk grn & gray brn (R)   4.00   5.00
   a.   Without period   21.00   21.00
CO2B   AP1   25c brn car & gray brn   10.00   12.50
   c.   Without period   25.00   25.00
   Nos. CO1-CO2B (3)   18.50   20.75
   Set, never hinged   35.00

Types of Regular Issue of 1926 Overprinted in Red

1929, Oct. 15   Unwmk.
CO3   A90   2c black   75.00   90.00
CO4   A91   4c black   75.00   90.00
CO5   A90   5c black   75.00   90.00
CO6   A91   10c black   75.00   90.00
CO7   A92   20c black   75.00   90.00
CO8   A92   30c black   75.00   90.00
CO9   A92   40c black   75.00   90.00
   Nos. CO3-CO9 (7)   525.00   630.00
   Set, never hinged   1,100.

Horizontal Overprint
CO10   A93   1p black   2,250.   2,250.
   Never hinged   4,000.
Nos. CO3-CO9 also exist with overprint reading up.

No. C26 Overprinted in Black

1930   Wmk. 156
CO11   AP4   20c black violet   1.10   1.75
   Never hinged   1.65
   a.   Without period   20.00   20.00
   b.   Inverted overprint   18.00   18.00
   c.   As "a," inverted overprint   210.00   210.00
No. CO11 with red overprint is believed not to have been issued for postal purposes.

Plane over Mexico City — OA1

1930   Engr.
CO12   OA1   20c gray black   6.50   6.50
CO13   OA1   35c lt violet   1.10   1.90
CO14   OA1   40c ol brn & dp bl   1.25   1.75
CO15   OA1   70c vio & ol gray   1.50   1.75
   Nos. CO12-CO15 (4)   10.35   11.90
   Set, never hinged   23.50

No. CO12 Surcharged in Red

1931
CO16   OA1   15c on 20c   .85   1.40
   Never hinged   1.20
   a.   Inverted surcharge   140.00
   b.   Double surcharge   140.00

No. C20 Overprinted

1932   Rouletted 13, 13½
CO17   AP3   5c light blue   .80   .90
   Never hinged   1.20

Air Post Stamps of 1927-32 Overprinted

On No. C1a
1932   Unwmk.   *Perf. 12*
CO18   AP1   50c dk bl & cl   1,000.   1,000.
   Never hinged   2,000.

On Nos. C2, C2a
Wmk. 156
CO19   AP1   50c dk bl & red brn   1.25   1.50
   Never hinged   2.25
   a.   50c dark blue & claret   1.40   1.60
See note after No. C2.

On Nos. C11 and C12
1932   *Perf. 12*
CO20   AP3   10c violet   22.50   25.00
   Never hinged   45.00
CO21   AP3   15c carmine   350.00   375.00
   Never hinged   700.00

On Nos. C21 to C23
Rouletted 13, 13½
CO22   AP3   10c violet   .35   .55
CO23   AP3   15c carmine   1.40   2.00
CO24   AP3   20c brn olive   1.40   2.00

Nos. C20, C21 C23 and C25 Overprinted

1933-34   Rouletted 13½
CO25   AP3   5c light blue   .50   .55
CO26   AP3   10c violet ('34)   .50   .90
CO27   AP3   20c brown olive   1.60   1.25
CO28   AP3   50c red brn ('34)   1.25   1.90

MEXICO

On No. C2
Perf. 12
CO29	AP1	50c dk bl & red brn	1.10	2.00
a.		50c dark blue & claret	1.60	2.50

On No. C11
Perf. 12
CO30	AP3	10c violet ('34)	140.00	175.00
a.		Double overprint	325.00	

Forgeries exist.

SPECIAL DELIVERY STAMPS

Motorcycle Postman — SD1

1919 Unwmk. Engr. Perf. 12
E1	SD1	20c red & black	100.00	2.75

1923 Wmk. 156
E2	SD1	20c blk car & blk	.35	.35

For overprint see No. E7

Messenger with Quipu — SD2

1934
E3	SD2	10c brn red & blue	.35	.50

Indian Archer — SD3

Imprint: "Oficina Impresora de Hacienda Mexico."

1934 Perf. 10x10½
E4	SD3	10c black violet	1.50	.50

See Nos. E5-E6, E8-E9.

Redrawn
Imprint: "Talleres de Imp. de Est. y Valores-Mexico."

1938-41 Photo. Perf. 14
E5	SD3	10c slate violet	.75	.35
a.		Unwatermarked	50.00	
E6	SD3	20c orange red ('41)	.50	.35
		Set of 2, never hinged	1.95	

Imperforate examples of No. E6 were not regularly issued.

No. E2 Overprinted "1940" in Violet
1940 Engr. Perf. 12
E7	SD1	20c red & black	.40	.05

Catalogue values for unused stamps in this section, from this point to the end of the section, are for Never Hinged items.

Redrawn Archer Type of 1941
1944-47 Wmk. 272 Photo. Perf. 14
E8	SD3	20c orange red	1.25	.25

Wmk. 279
E9	SD3	20c orange red ('47)	2.10	.25

Special Delivery Messenger SD4

Messengers' Hands Transferring Letter — SD5

1950-51 Photo. Wmk. 279
E10	SD4	25c bright red	.45	.25
E11	SD5	60c dk bl grn ('51)	2.40	.95

Redrawn
1951
E12	SD4	25c bright red	60.00	5.00

Sharper Impression, heavier shading; motorcycle sidecar ½mm from "s" of "centavos;" imprint wider, beginning under "n" of "inmediata."

Second Redrawing
1952
E13	SD4	25c bright red	15.00	2.00

Design 35½mm wide (33mm on Nos. E10 and E12); finer lettering at left, and height of letters in imprint reduced 50 per cent; three distinct lines in tires.

Redrawn Type of 1951
1954 Wmk. 300
E14	SD4	25c red orange	.55	.35

Type of 1951
1954
E15	SD5	60c dk blue grn	.80	1.10

Hands and Pigeon — SD6

Plane Circling Globe — SD7

1956 Wmk. 300 Photo. Perf. 14
E16	SD6	35c red lilac	.40	.30
E17	SD7	80c henna brown	.80	1.40

1962
E18	SD6	50c green	1.00	.30
E19	SD7	1.20p dark purple	1.50	1.40

1964 Wmk. 350
E20	SD6	50c green	.75	.30
E21	SD7	1.20p dk purple	1.75	1.00

1973 Unwmk.
E22	SD6	50c green	3.75	3.25

Fluorescent printing on front or back consists of beehive pattern and diagonal inscription.

1975 Wmk. 300
E23	SD6	2p orange	.40	1.00
E24	SD7	5p vio bl	1.60	.90

1976 Unwmk.
E25	SD6	2p red org	.40	.40
E26	SD7	5p dk vio bl	1.10	1.00

Watch — SD8

1976 Unwmk. Photo. Perf. 14
E27	SD8	2p org & blk	.60	1.00

INSURED LETTER STAMPS

Insured Letters IL1

Registered Mailbag IL2

Safe — IL3

1935 Engr. Wmk. 156 Perf. 10½
G1	IL1	10c vermilion	1.75	.75
a.		Perf. 10x10½		
G2	IL2	50c dk bl	10.00	.60
G3	IL3	1p turq grn	1.25	.85
		Nos. G1-G3 (3)	13.00	2.20
		Set, never hinged	19.50	

Nos. G1 and G4 were issued both with and without imprint.

Catalogue values for unused stamps in this section, from this point to the end of the section, are for Never Hinged items.

1944-45 Wmk. 272 Perf. 10x10½
G4	IL1	10c ver ('45)	13.00	1.50
G5	IL2	50c dk bl	2.00	.50
G6	IL3	1p turq grn	3.75	.65
		Nos. G4-G6 (3)	18.75	2.65

1947 Wmk. 279 Perf. 10x10½
G7	IL1	10c vermilion	10.50	.85
G8	IL2	50c dark blue	13.00	1.50
G9	IL3	1p turq grn	4.50	1.00
		Nos. G7-G9 (3)	28.00	3.35

Vault — IL4

1950-51 Photo. Perf. 14
G10	IL4	20c blue	4.00	.45
G11	IL4	40c purple	.45	.35
G12	IL4	1p yel grn	1.90	.50
G13	IL4	5p dk bl & gray grn ('51)	1.60	1.00
G14	IL4	10p car & ultra ('51)	4.50	4.00
		Nos. G10-G14 (5)	12.45	6.30

1954-71 Wmk. 300
G15	IL4	20c blue ('56)	.35	.35
G16	IL4	40c lt pur ('56)	.35	.35
G17	IL4	1p yel grn	.45	.35
a.		Size: 37x21¼mm ('71)	2.25	1.10
G18	IL4	5p bl & grn ('59)	1.40	1.00
G19	IL4	10p car & ultra ('63)	5.25	2.50
		Nos. G15-G19 (5)	7.80	4.55

No. G17 measures 35x19½mm. Vertical measurement excludes imprint.

1967 Wmk. 350 Perf. 14
G21	IL4	40c light purple	2.25	1.50
G22	IL4	1p yellow green	2.25	1.50

1975 Photo. Wmk. 300
G23	IL4	2p lilac rose	.50	.35
G24	IL4	20p orange & gray	3.50	3.00

Padlock — IL5

1976-81 Unwmk. Photo. Perf. 14
G25	IL5	40c black & blue	.35	.30
G26	IL5	1p black & blue	.35	.30
G26A	IL5	2p blk & bl ('81)	.45	.30
G27	IL5	5p black & blue	1.90	.50
G28	IL5	10p black & blue	1.90	.50
G28A	IL5	20p black & blue	2.75	.55
		Nos. G25-G28A (6)	7.70	2.45

1979 Photo. Wmk. 300
G29	IL5	40c black & blue	1.10	.40
G30	IL5	1p black & blue	1.10	.30
G31	IL5	5p black & blue	1.90	.45
G32	IL5	10p black & blue	5.00	.40
G33	IL5	20p black & blue	5.00	.75
		Nos. G29-G33 (5)	14.10	2.30

Perf. 14½x14
1983-86 Photo. Unwmk.
Size of Lock: 20x31mm
G36	IL5	5p black & blue	1.40	.40
G37	IL5	10p black & blue	1.10	.40
G38	IL5	20p black & blue	1.10	.40
G39	IL5	50p black & blue	2.75	.45
G40	IL5	100p blk & bl ('86)	5.50	3.00
		Nos. G36-G40 (5)	11.85	4.65

POSTAGE DUE STAMPS

D1

1908 Engr. Wmk. 155 Perf. 14
J1	D1	1c blue	1.00	3.00
J2	D1	2c blue	1.00	3.00
J3	D1	4c blue	1.00	3.00
J4	D1	5c blue	1.00	3.00
J5	D1	10c blue	1.00	3.00
		Nos. J1-J5 (5)	5.00	15.00

For overprints and surcharges see Nos. 381-385, 434-438, 466-470, 495-499, 593-607.

PORTE DE MAR STAMPS

These stamps were used to indicate the amount of cash to be paid to the captains of the mail steamers taking outgoing foreign mail. Used values are for stamps canceled on cover, on piece or with expert certificates.

PM2

1875 Unwmk. Litho. Imperf.
JX9	PM2	2c black	.60	50.00
a.		"5" added to make 25c	12.00	100.00
JX10	PM2	10c black	.80	30.00
JX11	PM2	12c black	.80	50.00
JX12	PM2	20c black	1.00	50.00
JX13	PM2	25c black	3.25	50.00
JX14	PM2	35c black	3.25	60.00
JX15	PM2	50c black	3.00	60.00
JX16	PM2	60c black	3.00	75.00
JX17	PM2	75c black	3.50	75.00
JX18	PM2	85c black	3.25	100.00
JX19	PM2	100c black	4.00	100.00
		Nos. JX9-JX19 (11)	26.45	700.00

Same, Numerals Larger
JX20	PM2	5c black	1.00	50.00
JX21	PM2	25c black	1.65	50.00
JX22	PM2	35c black	250.00	
JX23	PM2	50c black	1.00	50.00
JX24	PM2	60c black	125.00	
JX25	PM2	100c black	.60	100.00
		Nos. JX20-JX25	379.25	

In Nos. JX9-JX19 the figures of value are 7mm high and "CENTAVOS" is 7½mm long. On Nos. JX20-JX25 the figures of value are 8mm high and "CENTAVOS" is 9½mm long. Nos. JX9-JX25 exist with overprints of district names.
Counterfeits exist of Nos. JX9-JX31.

PM3

1879
JX26	PM3	2c brown	.50	
JX27	PM3	5c yellow	.50	
JX28	PM3	10c red	.50	
JX29	PM3	25c blue	.50	
JX30	PM3	50c green	.50	
JX31	PM3	100c violet	.50	
		Nos. JX26-JX31 (6)	3.00	

Nos. JX26-JX31 were never put in use. Nos. JX26-JX31 were printed on paper watermarked "ADMINISTRACION GENERAL DE CORREOS MEXICO." Approximately ¾ of the stamps do not show any of the watermark.

MEXICO

Stamps of this design were never issued. Examples appeared on the market in 1884. Value, set, $75. Value, full sheet $400.

All were printed in same sheet of 49 (7x7). Sheet consists of 14 of 10c; 7 each of 25c, 35c, 50c; 4 each of 60c, 85c; 3 each of 75c, 100c. There are four varieties of 10c, two of 25c, 35c and 50c.

OFFICIAL STAMPS

Hidalgo — O1

Wove or Laid Paper
1884-93 Unwmk. Engr. Perf. 12

O1	O1	red	1.40	1.00
a.		Vert. pair, imperf. betwn.	120.00	
O1B	O1	scarlet ('85)	1.40	1.00
O2	O1	olive brn ('87)	.90	.70
a.		Horiz. pair, imperf. betwn.		
b.		Blue ruled lines on paper		
O3	O1	orange ('88)	2.50	.90
a.		Vert. pair, imperf. betwn.	110.00	
		Perf. 11	15.00	12.00
O4	O1	blue grn ('93)	1.40	.80
a.		Imperf., pair	15.00	12.00
b.		Perf. 11	15.00	12.00
		Nos. O1-O4 (5)	7.60	4.40

Pin-perf. 6

O5	O1	olive brown ('87)	100.00	50.00

Wmk. "Correos E U M" on every Vertical Line of Ten Stamps (152)
1894 Perf. 5½

O6	O1	ultra	3.00	2.75
a.		Vert. pair, imperf. horiz.	35.00	
b.		Imperf., pair	45.00	

Perf. 11, 12

O7	O1	ultra	1.75	1.60

Perf. 5½x11, 11x5½

O9	O1	ultra	12.00	8.00
		Nos. O6-O9 (3)	16.75	12.35

Regular Issues with Handstamped Overprint in Black

1895 Wmk. 152 Perf. 12

O10	A20	1c green	17.50	6.00
O11	A20	2c carmine	20.00	6.00
O12	A20	3c orange brn	17.50	6.00
O13	A21	4c red orange	26.00	6.00
a.		4c orange	42.50	14.00
O14	A22	5c ultra	45.00	12.00
O15	A23	10c lilac rose	32.50	3.00
O16	A21	12c olive brn	100.00	30.00
O17	A23	15c brt blue	60.00	18.00
O18	A23	20c brown rose	42.50	18.00
O19	A23	50c purple	90.00	42.50
O20	A24	1p brown	200.00	90.00
O21	A24	5p scarlet	475.00	250.00
O22	A24	10p deep blue	750.00	500.00
		Nos. O10-O22 (13)	1,876.	993.50

Similar stamps with red overprint were not officially placed in use. Nos. O10-O22 have a vertical grain or mesh to the paper.

1896-97 Wmk. 153
Black Overprint

O23	A20	1c green	60.00	10.00
O24	A20	2c carmine	60.00	12.00
O25	A20	3c orange brn	60.00	12.00
O26	A21	4c red orange	60.00	10.00
a.		4c orange	75.00	22.50
O27	A22	5c ultra	60.00	10.00
O28	A21	12c olive brn	80.00	30.00
O29	A23	15c brt blue	100.00	30.00
O29A	A23	50c purple	650.00	650.00
		Nos. O23-O29A (8)	1,130.	768.00

Nos. O23-O29A have a vertical grain or mesh to the paper.

1897 Wmk. 154 Black Overprint

O30	A20	1c green	100.00	30.00
O31	A20	2c scarlet	90.00	35.00
O33	A21	4c orange	125.00	60.00
O34	A22	5c ultra	100.00	35.00
O35	A21	12c olive brn	125.00	42.50
O36	A23	15c brt blue	160.00	42.50
O37	A23	20c brown rose	110.00	18.00
O38	A23	50c purple	150.00	30.00
O39	A24	1p brown	375.00	125.00
		Nos. O30-O39 (9)	1,335.	418.00

Nos. O30-O39 have a vertical grain or mesh to the paper.

1898 Unwmk. Black Overprint

O40	A20	1c green	35.00	9.50
O41	A20	2c scarlet	35.00	9.50
O42	A20	3c orange brn	35.00	9.50
O43	A21	4c orange	60.00	12.00
O44	A22	5c ultra	60.00	20.00
O46	A21	12c olive brn	125.00	30.00
O47	A23	15c brt blue	125.00	45.00
O48	A23	20c brown rose	225.00	75.00
O48A	A23	50c purple	375.00	150.00
O48B	A24	10p deep blue	5,500.	5,500.
		Nos. O40-O48A (9)	1,075.	345.50

See note following No. 291.

1900 Black Overprint
Wmk. 155 Perf. 14, 15

O49	A25	1c green	37.50	2.50
O50	A26	2c vermilion	50.00	4.00
O51	A27	3c yellow brn	50.00	2.50
O52	A28	5c dark blue	60.00	4.50
O53	A29	10c violet & org	65.00	5.50
O54	A30	15c lavender & cl	65.00	5.50
O55	A31	20c rose & dk bl	75.00	2.50
O56	A32	50c red lil & blk	150.00	25.00
O57	A33	1p blue & blk	300.00	25.00
O58	A34	5p carmine & blk	575.00	75.00
		Nos. O49-O58 (10)	1,418.	152.00

1903 Black Overprint

O59	A25	1c violet	35.00	4.00
O60	A26	2c green	35.00	4.00
O61	A25	4c carmine	65.00	2.50
O62	A28	5c orange	65.00	13.00
O63	A29	10c blue & org	70.00	4.00
O64	A32	50c carmine & blk	200.00	25.00
		Nos. O59-O64 (6)	470.00	52.50

Regular Issues Overprinted

1910 On Issues of 1899-1903

O65	A26	2c green	175.00	6.50
O66	A27	3c orange brn	175.00	4.00
O67	A35	4c carmine	200.00	10.00
O68	A28	5c orange	225.00	50.00
O69	A29	10c blue & org	200.00	4.00
O70	A30	15c lav & claret	275.00	6.50
O71	A31	20c rose & dk bl	275.00	3.00
O72	A32	50c carmine & blk	375.00	35.00
O73	A33	1p blue & blk	575.00	125.00
O74	A34	5p carmine & blk	200.00	125.00
		Nos. O65-O74 (10)	2,675.	369.00

1911 On Issue of 1910

O75	A36	1c violet	5.00	5.00
O76	A37	2c green	3.75	2.25
O77	A38	3c orange brn	5.00	2.50
O78	A39	4c carmine	5.50	2.25
O79	A40	5c orange	12.50	7.00
O80	A41	10c blue & org	5.50	2.50
O81	A42	15c gray bl & cl	13.00	8.50
O82	A43	20c red & blue	10.00	2.50
O83	A44	50c red brn & blk	35.00	15.00
O84	A45	1p blue & blk	60.00	25.00
O85	A46	5p carmine & blk	300.00	125.00
		Nos. O75-O85 (11)	455.25	197.50

Nos. 500 to 505 Overprinted

1915 Unwmk. Rouletted 14½

O86	A57	1c violet	1.00	2.00
O87	A58	2c green	1.00	2.00
O88	A59	3c brown	1.25	2.00
O89	A60	4c carmine	1.00	2.00
O90	A61	5c orange	1.00	2.00
O91	A62	10c ultra	1.25	2.00
		Nos. O86-O91 (6)	6.50	12.00

All values are known with inverted overprint. All values exist imperforate and part perforate but were not regularly issued in these forms.

On Nos. 506 to 514
1915-16 Perf. 12

O92	A57	1c violet	1.50	2.00
O93	A58	2c green	1.50	2.00
O94	A59	3c brown	1.50	2.00
O95	A60	4c carmine	1.50	2.00
a.		"CEATRO"	21.00	30.00
O96	A61	5c orange	1.50	2.00
O97	A62	10c ultra, type II	1.50	2.00
a.		Double overprint	475.00	
O98	A63	40c slate	8.00	14.50
a.		Inverted overprint	24.00	25.00
b.		Double overprint	40.00	
O99	A64	1p brown & blk	10.00	14.50
a.		Inverted overprint	27.50	27.50
O100	A65	5p claret & ultra	60.00	60.00
a.		Inverted overprint	80.00	
		Nos. O92-O100 (9)	87.00	101.00

Nos. O98 and O99 exist imperforate but probably were not issued in that form.

Preceding Issues Overprinted in Red, Blue or Black

On No. O74
1916 Wmk. 155

O101	A34	5p carmine & blk	900.00	

On Nos. O75 to O85

O102	A36	1c violet	6.50	
O103	A37	2c green	1.25	
O104	A38	3c orange brn (Bl)	1.75	
O105	A39	4c carmine (Bl)	7.00	
O106	A40	5c orange (Bl)	1.75	
O107	A41	10c blue & org	1.75	
O108	A42	15c gray bl & cl (Bk)	1.75	
O109	A43	20c red & bl (Bk)	1.90	
O110	A44	50c red brn & blk	200.00	
O111	A45	1p blue & blk	11.00	
O112	A46	5p carmine & blk	3,250.	
		Nos. O102-O111 (10)	234.65	

No. O102 with blue overprint is a trial color. Counterfeits exist of Nos. O110, O112.

Nos. 608, 610 to 612, 615 and 616 Overprinted Vertically in Red or Black

Thick Paper
1918 Unwmk. Rouletted 14½

O113	A68	1c violet (R)	60.00	35.00
O114	A69	2c gray grn (R)	65.00	35.00
O115	A70	3c bis brn (R)	60.00	35.00
O116	A71	4c carmine (Bk)	60.00	35.00
O117	A74	20c rose (Bk)	125.00	90.00
O118	A75	30c gray brn (R)	190.00	175.00

On Nos. 622-623
Medium Paper Perf. 12

O119	A72	5c ultra (R)	40.00	40.00
O120	A73	10c blue (R)	35.00	25.00
a.		Double overprint	400.00	400.00
		Nos. O113-O120 (8)	635.00	470.00

Overprinted Horizontally in Red

On Nos. 626-628
Thin Paper

O121	A63	40c violet (R)	35.00	27.50
O122	A64	1p bl & blk (R)	85.00	85.00
O123	A65	5p grn & blk (R)	575.00	600.00
		Nos. O121-O123 (3)	695.00	712.50

Nos. 608 and 610 to 615 Ovptd. Vertically Up in Red or Black

Thick Paper
1919 Rouletted 14½

O124	A68	1c dull vio (R)	6.00	6.00
a.		"OFICIAN"	70.00	80.00
O125	A69	2c gray grn (R)	9.50	3.50
a.		"OFICIAN"	70.00	80.00
O126	A70	3c bis brn (R)	14.00	6.00
a.		"OFICIAN"	95.00	100.00
O127	A71	4c car (Bk)	29.00	13.00
a.		"OFICIAN"		
O127A	A72	5c ultra	200.00	125.00
b.		"OFICIAN"	500.00	
O128	A73	10c blue (R)	9.50	2.50
a.		"OFICIAN"	85.00	60.00
O129	A74	20c rose (Bk)	60.00	47.50
a.		"OFICIAN"		140.00

On Nos. 618, 622
Perf. 12

O130	A68	1c dull violet (R)	47.50	47.50
a.		"OFICIAN"	140.00	100.00
O131	A72	5c ultra (R)	47.50	22.50
a.		"OFICIAN"	140.00	100.00

Overprinted Horizontally On Nos. 626-627
Thin Paper

O132	A63	40c violet (R)	47.50	35.00
O133	A64	1p bl & blk (R)	60.00	50.00
		Nos. O124-O133 (11)	530.50	358.50

Nos. 608 to 615 and 617 Ovptd. Vertically down in Black, Red or Blue

Size: 17½x3mm
1921 Rouletted 14½

O134	A68	1c gray (Bk)	30.00	12.00
a.		1c dull violet (Bk)	17.00	7.00
O135	A69	2c gray grn (R)	5.00	3.00
O136	A70	3c bis brn (R)	8.50	4.50
O137	A71	4c carmine (Bk)	27.50	21.00
O138	A72	5c ultra (R)	25.00	12.00
O139	A73	10c bl, reading down (Bk)	32.50	12.00
a.		Overprint reading up	60.00	60.00
O140	A74	20c rose (Bl)	47.50	27.50
O141	A75	30c gray blk (R)	25.00	25.00

Overprinted Horizontally On Nos. 626-628
Perf. 12

O142	A63	40c violet (R)	32.50	32.50
O143	A64	1p bl & blk (R)	25.00	25.00
O144	A65	5p grn & blk (Bk)	600.00	600.00
		Nos. O134-O144 (11)	858.50	774.50

Nos. 609 to 615 Overprinted Vertically Down in Black

1921-30 Rouletted 14½

O145	A68	1c gray	5.00	2.50
a.		1c lilac gray	1.00	.70
O146	A69	2c gray green	1.75	.70
O147	A70	3c bister brn	.80	.70
a.		"OFICAL"	47.50	25.00
b.		"OIFCIAL"	47.50	25.00
c.		Double overprint	140.00	
O148	A71	4c carmine	22.50	2.50
O149	A72	5c ultra	1.00	.70
O150	A73	10c blue	1.00	.70
a.		"OIFCIAL"	50.00	
O151	A74	20c brown rose	9.00	9.50
a.		20c rose	5.00	2.50

On No. 625
Perf. 12

O152	A75	30c gray black	7.25	2.50

Overprinted Horizontally On Nos. 626, 628

O153	A63	40c violet	7.00	5.00
a.		"OFICAL"	60.00	60.00
b.		"OICIFAL"	60.00	60.00
c.		Inverted overprint	90.00	125.00
O154	A65	5p grn & blk ('30)	375.00	375.00
		Nos. O145-O154 (10)	430.30	399.80

Ovptd. Vertically Down in Red On Nos. 609, 610, 611, 613 and 614

1921-24 Rouletted 14½

O155	A68	1c lilac	1.60	1.00
O156	A69	2c gray green	1.50	.90
O157	A70	3c bister brown	4.00	1.00
O158	A72	5c ultra	1.60	.80
O159	A73	10c blue	35.00	3.50
a.		Double overprint		

On Nos. 624-625
Perf. 12

O160	A74	20c rose	7.25	1.60
O161	A75	30c gray black	19.00	5.00

MEXICO

Overprinted Horizontally On Nos. 626-628

O162	A63	40c violet	14.00	7.50
a.		Vert. pair, imperf. btwn.		
O163	A64	1p blue & blk	35.00	25.00
O164	A65	5p green & blk	300.00	300.00

Overprinted Vertically Down in Blue on No. 612
Rouletted 14½

O165	A71	4c carmine	7.00	3.50
		Nos. O155-O165 (11)	425.95	349.80

Same Overprint Vertically Down in Red on Nos. 635 and 637

1926-27   **Rouletted 14½**

O166	A80	3c bis brn, ovpt. horiz.	12.00	12.00
a.		Period omitted	30.00	30.00
O167	A82	5c orange	27.50	30.00

Same Overprint Vertically Down in Blue or Red on Nos. 650, 651, 655 and 656
Wmk. 156

O168	A79	2c scarlet (Bl)	20.00	20.00
a.		Overprint reading up	30.00	30.00
O169	A80	3c bis brn, ovpt. horiz. (R)	5.00	5.00
a.		Inverted overprint	60.00	
O170	A85	10c claret (Bl)	35.00	16.00
O171	A84	20c deep blue (R)	14.00	12.00
a.		Overprint reading up	14.00	12.00

Overprinted Horizontally in Red On Nos. 643, 646-649
Perf. 12

O172	A81	4c green	6.00	6.00
O173	A83	30c dk grn	6.00	6.00
O174	A63	40c violet	16.00	16.00
a.		Inverted overprint	80.00	
O175	A87	50c olive brn	1.50	1.50
a.		50c yellow brown	18.00	18.00
O176	A88	1p red brn & bl	15.00	15.00
		Nos. O168-O176 (9)	118.50	97.50

Same Overprint Horizontally on No. 651, Vertically Up on Nos. 650, 653-656, 666, RA1

1927-31   **Rouletted 14½**

O177	PT1	1c brown ('31)	.70	1.00
O178	A79	2c scarlet	.70	1.00
a.		"OFICAIL"	30.00	30.00
b.		Overprint reading down	1.50	2.00
O179	A80	3c bis brn	2.00	1.50
a.		"OFICAIL"	40.00	30.00
O180	A82	4c green	1.50	1.00
a.		"OFICAIL"	40.00	40.00
b.		Overprint reading down	10.00	2.00
O181	A82	5c orange	4.00	3.00
a.		Overprint reading down	4.00	2.50
O182	A94	8c orange	12.00	8.00
a.		Overprint reading down	7.00	6.00
O183	A85	10c lake	2.00	2.00
a.		Overprint reading down	2.00	2.00
O184	A84	20c dark blue	10.00	4.00
a.		"OFICAIL"	40.00	40.00
b.		Overprint reading down	20.00	20.00
		Nos. O177-O184 (8)	32.90	21.50

Overprinted Vertically Up on #O186, Horizontally On Nos. 643 and 645 to 649

1927-33   **Perf. 12**

O185	A81	4c green	6.00	5.00
a.		Inverted overprint	60.00	30.00
O186	A85	10c brown lake	55.00	45.00
O187	A83	30c dark green	1.40	1.00
a.		Inverted overprint	30.00	30.00
b.		Pair, tête bêche overprints	35.00	35.00
c.		"OFICAIL"	35.00	35.00
O188	A63	40c violet	12.00	8.00
O189	A87	50c olive brn ('33)	3.25	4.00
O190	A88	1p red brn & bl	24.00	20.00
		Nos. O185-O190 (6)	101.65	83.00

The overprint on No. O186 is vertical.

Nos. 320, 628, 633 Overprinted Horizontally

On Stamp No. 320

1927-28   **Wmk. 155**   **Perf. 14, 15**

O191	A46	5p car & blk (R)	175.00	250.00
O192	A46	5p car & blk (Bl)	175.00	250.00

Unwmk.   Perf. 12

O193	A65	5p grn & blk (Bk)	375.00	500.00
a.		Inverted overprint	—	—
O194	A78	10p blk brn & blk (Bl)	200.00	300.00

No. 320 Overprinted Horizontally

Wmk. 155   Perf. 14

| O195 | A46 | 5p carmine & blk | 300.00 | |

Nos. 650 and 655 Overprinted Horizontally

1928-29   **Wmk. 156**   **Rouletted 14½**   **Size: 16x2½mm**

O196	A79	2c dull red	18.00	12.00
O197	A85	10c rose lake	27.50	12.00

Nos. RA1, 650-651, 653-656 Overprinted

1932-33

O198	PT1	1c brown	.70	1.00
O199	A79	2c dull red	.80	1.00
O200	A80	3c bister brn	3.00	3.00
O201	A82	4c green	10.00	8.00
O202	A82	5c orange	12.00	8.00
O203	A85	10c rose lake	3.25	3.00
O204	A84	20c dark blue	15.00	10.00
a.		Double overprint	200.00	90.00
		Nos. O198-O204 (7)	44.75	34.00

Nos. 651, 646-649 Overprinted Horizontally

1933   **Rouletted 14½**

| O205 | A80 | 3c bister brn | 3.00 | 3.00 |

Perf. 12

O206	A83	30c dk green	8.00	3.00
O207	A63	40c violet	15.00	6.00
O208	A87	50c olive brn	2.50	3.00
a.		"OFICIAL OFICIAL"	50.00	50.00
O209	A88	1p red brn & bl, type I	3.00	3.00
a.		Type II	2.75	3.50

Overprinted Vertically On No. 656
Rouletted 14½

O210	A84	20c dark blue	18.00	10.00
		Nos. O205-O210 (6)	49.50	28.00

Nos. RA1, 651, 653, 654, 683 Overprinted Horizontally

1934-37   **Rouletted 14½**   **Size: 13x2mm**

O211	PT1	1c brown	5.00	6.00
O212	A80	3c bister brn	.70	.70
O213	A82	4c green	12.00	10.00
O214	A82	5c orange	.70	.70
O215	A86	15c dk blue ('37)	1.00	1.00
		Nos. O211-O215 (5)	19.40	18.40

See No. O217a.

Same Overprint on Nos. 687A-692

1934-37   **Perf. 10½**

O216	PT1	1c brown ('37)	1.00	1.25
O217	A79	2c scarlet	1.00	1.50
a.		On No. 650 (error)	350.00	
b.		Double overprint	275.00	
O218	A82	4c green ('35)	1.40	1.60
O219	A85	10c brown lake	1.00	1.00
O220	A84	20c dk blue ('37)	1.25	1.25
O221	A83	30c dk bl grn ('37)	2.00	2.00

On Nos. 647 and 649
Perf. 12, 11½x12

O222	A63	40c violet	3.00	3.50
O223	A88	1p red brn & bl (I)	5.00	6.00
a.		Type II	4.00	4.00
		Nos. O216-O223 (8)	15.65	18.10

On Nos. 707 to 709, 712, 715, 716, 717, 718 and 719

O224	A108	1c orange	2.00	4.00
O225	A109	2c green	1.25	2.00
O226	A110	4c carmine	1.25	1.40
O227	A112	10c violet	1.25	2.50
O228	A114	20c ultra	1.60	2.50
O229	A115	30c lake	2.00	4.00
O230	A116	40c red brown	2.50	4.00
O231	A117	50c black	2.75	2.75
O232	A118	1p dk brn & org	8.00	12.00
		Nos. O224-O232 (9)	22.60	35.15

PARCEL POST STAMPS

Railroad Train — PP1

1941   **Photo.**   **Wmk. 156**   **Perf. 14**

Q1	PP1	10c brt rose	2.75	.35
Q2	PP1	20c dk vio bl	1.75	.35

1944-46   **Wmk. 272**

Q3	PP1	10c brt rose	1.75	1.00
Q4	PP1	20c dk vio bl ('46)	5.00	2.50

1947-49   **Wmk. 279**

Q5	PP1	10c brt rose	1.25	.60
Q6	PP1	20c dk vio bl ('49)	1.60	.60

Streamlined Locomotive PP2

1951

Q7	PP2	10c rose pink	5.00	.40
Q8	PP2	20c blue violet	4.00	.70

1954   **Wmk. 300**

Q9	PP2	10c rose pink	4.25	.60
Q10	PP2	20c blue violet	4.25	1.50

POSTAL TAX STAMPS

Morelos Monument — PT1

Rouletted 14½

1925   **Engr.**   **Wmk. 156**

RA1	PT1	1c brown	.35	.25
a.		Imperf.	30.00	

1926   **Perf. 12**

RA2	PT1	1c brown	.75	5.00
a.		Booklet pane of 2	12.50	

1925   **Unwmk.**   **Rouletted 14½**

| RA3 | PT1 | 1c brown | 75.00 | 19.00 |

It was obligatory to add a stamp of type PT1 to the regular postage on every article of domestic mail matter. The money obtained from this source formed a fund to combat a plague of locusts.

In 1931, 1c stamps of type PT1 were discontinued as Postal Tax stamps. It was subsequently used for the payment of postage on drop letters (announcement cards and unsealed circulars) to be delivered in the city of cancellation. See No. 687A.

For overprints see Nos. O177, O198, O211, O216, RA4.

No. RA1 Overprinted in Red

1929   **Wmk. 156**

RA4	PT1	1c brown	.35	.25
a.		Overprint reading down	75.00	75.00

There were two settings of this overprint. They may be distinguished by the two lines being spaced 4mm or 6mm apart.

The money from sales of this stamp was devoted to child welfare work.

Mother and Child — PT3

1929   **Litho.**   **Rouletted 13, 13½**

| RA5 | PT3 | 1c violet | .35 | .35 |

PT4

1929   **Size: 18x24½mm**   **Unwmk.**

RA6	PT4	2c deep green	.40	.35
RA7	PT4	5c brown	.40	.35
a.		Imperf., pair	60.00	60.00
		Set of 2, never hinged	1.30	

For surcharges see Nos. RA10-RA11.

PT5

Two types of 1c:
Type I — Background lines continue through lettering of top inscription. Denomination circle hangs below second background line. Paper and gum white.
Type II — Background lines cut away behind some letters. Circle rests on second background line. Paper and gum yellowish.

1929   **Size: 19x25¼mm**

RA8	PT5	1c violet, type I	.35	.35
a.		Booklet pane of 4	10.00	
b.		Booklet pane of 2	18.00	
c.		Typo II	.40	.35
d.		Imperf., pair	50.00	50.00
RA9	PT5	2c deep green	.65	.05
a.		Imperf., pair		

The use of these stamps, in addition to the regular postage, was compulsory. The money obtained from their sale was used for child welfare work.

For surcharge see No. RA12.

Nos. RA6, RA7, RA9 Surcharged

1930

RA10	PT4	1c on 2c dp grn	.75	.40
RA11	PT4	1c on 5c brown	1.00	.60
RA12	PT5	1c on 2c dp grn	2.00	1.00
		Nos. RA10-RA12 (3)	3.75	2.00

Used stamps exist with surcharge double or reading down.

No. 423 Overprinted

1931, Jan. 30   **Wmk. 155**   **Perf. 14**

RA13	A36	1c dull violet	.40	.40
a.		"PRO INFANCIA" double	50.00	

Indian Mother and Child — PT6

1934, Sept. 1   **Wmk. 156**   **Engr.**   **Perf. 10½**

| RA13B | PT6 | 1c dull orange | .35 | .35 |

Mosquito Attacking Man — PT7

MEXICO

1939	Photo.	Wmk. 156	Perf. 14
RA14	PT7	1c Prus blue	1.50 .30
a.	Imperf.		3.00 3.00

This stamp was obligatory on all mail, the money being used to aid in a drive against malaria.
See Nos. RA16, RA19.

Miguel Hidalgo y Costilla — PT8

1941			
RA15	PT8	1c brt carmine	.45 .35

	Type of 1939		
1944	Wmk. 272		Perf. 14
RA16	PT7 1c Prus blue		1.00 .35

Learning Vowels — PT9

1946	Photo.		Wmk. 279
RA17	PT9 1c black brown		.45 .35
a.	1c green black		1.00 1.00

1947			Wmk. 272
RA18	PT9 1c black brown		65.00 5.00

	Type of 1939		
	Wmk. 279		
RA19	PT7 1c Prus blue		3.50 .35

PROVISIONAL ISSUES

During the struggle led by Juarez to expel the Emperor Maximilian, installed June, 1864 by Napoleon III and French troops, a number of towns when free of Imperial forces issued provisional postage stamps. Maximilian was captured and executed June 19, 1867, but provisional issues continued current for a time pending re-establishment of Republican Government.

Campeche

A southern state in Mexico, comprising the western part of the Yucatan peninsula.

**White Paper
Numerals in Black**

1876	Handstamped	Imperf.
1	A1 5c gray blue & blue	2,000.
2	A1 25c gray blue & blue	1,100.
3	A1 50c gray blue & blue	4,500.

The stamps printed in blue-black and blue on yellowish paper, formerly listed as issued in 1867, are now known to be an unofficial production of later years. They are reprints, but produced without official sanction.

Chiapas

A southern state in Mexico, bordering on Guatemala and the Pacific Ocean.

1866		Typeset
1	A1 ½r blk, gray bl	2,000. 1,300.
2	A1 1r blk, lt grn	850.
3	A1 2r blk, rose	1,600.
4	A1 4r blk, lt buff	2,000.
a.	Vertical half used as 2r on cover	3,000.
5	A1 8r blk, rose	15,000.
a.	Quarter used as 2r on cover	4,000.
b.	Half used as 4r on cover	5,000.

Chihuahua

A city of northern Mexico and capital of the State of Chihuahua.

1872	Handstamped	
1	A1 12(c) black	3,000.
2	A2 25(c) black	3,000.

Cuautla

A town in the state of Morelos.

1867	Handstamped	
1	A1 (2r) black	7,000.

All known examples on cover are uncancelled. Examples are known without the "73" inside the oval.

Cuernavaca

A city of Mexico, just south of the capital, and the capital of the State of Morelos.

1867	Handstamped	
1	A1 (1r) black	2,500.
2	A1 (2r) black	40,000.

No. 1 was canceled at Cuernavaca with the district name overprint. Supplies of overprinted stamps were sent to the Tetecala and Yquala sub-offices, where they were canceled with the usual local postmarks.
No. 2 was created by doubling the impression of the basic stamp and applying the district name overprint twice.
Unused examples of Nos. 1 and 2 do not exist.
Counterfeits exist.

Guadalajara

A city of Mexico and capital of the State of Jalisco.

**Dated "1867"
1st Printing
Medium Wove Paper**

1867	Handstamped	Imperf.
1	A1 Medio r blk, white	350.00 900.00
2	A1 un r blk, gray bl	750.00 350.00
a.	Overprinted "Cd. Guzman"	1,000.
3	A1 un r blk, dk bl	450.00
4	A1 un r blk, white	250.00
a.	Overprinted "Cd. Guzman"	750.00
5	A1 2r blk, dk grn	250.00 21.00
a.	Overprinted "Cd. Guzman"	2,400. 500.00
6	A1 2r blk, white	125.00
a.	Overprinted "Cd. Guzman"	400.00
b.	Double print	250.00
7	A1 4r blk, rose	250.00 300.00
a.	Half used as 2r on cover	500.00
b.	Overprinted "Cd. Guzman"	900.00
8	A1 4r blk, white	500.00
a.	Half used as 2r on cover	2,500.
9	A1 un p blk, lilac	250.00 300.00

Serrate Perf.

10	A1 un r blk, gray bl	900.00
11	A1 2r blk, dk grn	700.00
12	A1 4r blk, rose	350.00
12A	A1 un p blk, lilac	1,750.

**2nd Printing
No Period after "2" or "4"
Thin Quadrille Paper
Imperf**

| 13 | A1 2r blk, green | 30.00 20.00 |
| a. | Half used as 1r on cover | 400.00 |

Serrate Perf.

| 14 | A1 2r blk, green | 1,500. |

**Thin Laid Batonné Paper
Imperf**

| 15 | A1 2r blk, green | 45.00 24.00 |

Serrate Perf.

| 16 | A1 2r blk, green | 1,100. |

**3rd Printing
Capital "U" in "Un" on 1r, 1p
Period after "2" and "4"
Thin Wove Paper
Imperf**

16A	A1 Un r blk, white	125.00
17	A1 Un r blk, blue	90.00
17A	A1 Un r blk, lilac	100.00
18	A1 2r blk, rose	50.00
18A	A1 4r blk, blue	8,500. 1,000.
18B	A1 Un p blue	1,750.

Serrate Perf.

19	A1 Un r blk, blue	300.00
19A	A1 2r blk, rose	750.00
19B	A1 4r blue	500.00

**Thin Quadrille Paper
Imperf**

20	A1 2r blk, rose	42.50 42.50
21	A1 4r blk, blue	15.00 30.00
22	A1 4r blk, white	200.00
23	A1 Un p blk, lilac	15.00 60.00
24	A1 Un p blk, rose	65.00
24A	A1 Un p blk, white	1,500.

Serrate Perf

24B	A1 2r blk, rose	500.00
25	A1 Un p blk, lilac	750.00 750.00
25A	A1 Un p blk, rose	700.00 300.00

**Thin Laid Batonné Paper
Imperf**

26	A1 Un r blk, green	22.50 17.50
27	A1 2r blk, rose	27.50 22.50
27A	A1 2r blk, green	47.50
28	A1 4r blk, blue	17.50 42.50
29	A1 4r blk, white	3,400.
30	A1 Un p blk, lilac	30.00 52.50
31	A1 Un p blk, rose	65.00

Serrate Perf.

32	A1 Un r blk, green	300.00
33	A1 2r blk, rose	400.00 200.00
34	A1 4r blk, blue	425.00
34A	A1 4r blk, white	1,750.
34B	A1 Un p blk, lilac	700.00

**Thin Oblong Quadrille Paper
Imperf**

35	A1 Un r blk, blue	250.00 22.50
35A	A1 Un r blk, white	1,500.
36	A1 4r blk, blue	600.00

Serrate Perf.

| 37 | A1 Un r blk, blue | 300.00 |

**4th Printing
Dated "1868"
Wove Paper**

1868		Imperf.
38	A1 2r blk, lilac	30.00 14.00
a.	Half used as 1r on cover	500.00
39	A1 2r blk, rose	52.50 65.00

Serrate Perf.

| 40 | A1 2r blk, lilac | 300.00 |
| 41 | A1 2r blk, rose | 750.00 300.00 |

**Laid Batonné Paper
Imperf**

42	A1 un r blk, green	12.50 12.50
43	A1 2r blk, lilac	12.50 12.50
a.	Half used as 1r on cover	1,500.
43A	A1 2r blk, rose	750.00

Serrate Perf.

| 44 | A1 un r blk, green | 250.00 200.00 |
| 44A | A1 2r blk, rose | 500.00 |

**Quadrille Paper.
Imperf**

| 45 | A1 2r blk, lilac | 25.00 14.00 |

Serrate Perf.

| 46 | A1 2r blk, lilac | 300.00 300.00 |

**Laid Paper
Imperf**

47	A1 un r blk, green	13.00 17.00
a.	Watermarked "LA + F"	750.00 1,000.
b.	"nu" instead of "un"	750.00
c.	Dated "1863"	300.00
48	A1 2r blk, lilac	32.50 32.50
49	A1 2r blk, rose	37.50 37.50

Serrate Perf.

| 50 | A1 un r blk, green | 750.00 300.00 |
| 51 | A1 2r blk, rose | 475.00 |

Counterfeits of Nos. 1-51 abound.

Merida

A city of southeastern Mexico, capital of the State of Yucatan.

Mexico No. 521 Surcharged **25**

1916	Wmk. 155	Perf. 14
1	A40 25(c) on 5c org, on cover	500.00

The G.P.DE.M. overprint reads down.

Authorities consider the Monterrey, Morelia and Patzcuaro stamps to be bogus.

Tlacotalpan

A village in the state of Veracruz.

Handstamped Monogram, Value in Manuscript

1856, Oct.		
1	A1 ½(r) black	30,000.

Research suggests that this stamp was not an officially sanctioned issue, but was instead part of a postal fraud orchestrated by Tlacotalpan postmaster Angel Fernando and his assistant Ignacio Crespo to cover theft of funds in that post office. The initials IMC in the stamp are most likely those of Crespo.

REVOLUTIONARY ISSUES

SINALOA

A northern state in Mexico, bordering on the Pacific Ocean. Stamps were issued by a provisional government.

Coat of Arms — A1

1929	Unwmk.	Litho.	Perf. 12
1	A1 10c blk, red & bl		5.00
a.	Tête bêche pair		35.00
2	A1 20c blk, red & gray		5.00
a.	Inverted center		600.00
	Set of 2, never hinged		20.00

Just as Nos. 1 and 2 were ready to be placed on sale the state was occupied by the Federal forces and the stamps could not be used. At a later date a few stamps were canceled by favor.
A recent find included a number of errors or printer's waste.
No. 2a was created by the printing of the 10c center onto a 20c frame.

YUCATAN

A southeastern state of Mexico.

Chalchihuitlicue, Nahuatl Water Goddess — A1

"Casa de Monjas" — A2

Temple of the Tigers — A3

Without Gum

1924   Unwmk.   Litho.   Imperf.

1	A1	5c violet	10.00 15.00
2	A2	10c carmine	40.00 50.00
3	A3	50c olive green	175.00

Perf. 12

4	A1	5c violet	50.00 60.00
5	A2	10c carmine	50.00 75.00
6	A3	50c olive green	200.00

Nos. 3 and 6 were not regularly issued.

MICRONESIA

ˌmī-krə-ˈnē-zhə

LOCATION — A group of over 600 islands in the West Pacific Ocean, north of the Equator.
GOVT. — Republic
AREA — 271 sq. miles
POP. — 115,000 (2020 est.)
CAPITAL — Palikir

These islands, also known as the Caroline Islands, were bought by Germany from Spain in 1899. Caroline Islands stamps issued as a German territory are listed in Vol. 2 of this Catalogue. Seized by Japan in 1914, they were taken by the US in WWII and became part of the US Trust Territory of the Pacific in 1947. By agreement with the USPS, the islands began issuing their own stamps in 1984, with the USPS continuing to carry the mail to and from the islands.

On Nov. 3, 1986 Micronesia became a Federation as a Sovereign State in Compact of Free Association with the US.

100 Cents = 1 Dollar

Catalogue values for all unused stamps in this country are for Never Hinged items.

Postal Service Inauguration — A1

1984, July 12   Litho.   Perf. 14

1	A1	20c Yap	.45 .45
2	A1	20c Truk	.45 .45
3	A1	20c Pohnpei	.45 .45
4	A1	20c Kosrae	.45 .45
a.	Block of 4, #1-4		1.90 1.90

For surcharges see Nos. 48-51.

Fernandez de Quiros — A2

Men's House, Yap — A3

Designs: 1c, 19c, Pedro Fernandez de Quiros, Spanish explorer, first discovered Pohnpei, 1595. 2c, 20c, Louis Duperrey, French explorer. 3c, 30c, Fyodor Litke, Russian explorer. 4c, 37c, Dumont d'Urville. 10c, Sleeping Lady, Kosrae. 13c, Liduduhriap Waterfall, Pohnpei. 17c, Tonachau Peak, Truk. 50c, Devil mask, Truk. $1, Sokeh's Rock, Pohnpei. $2, Canoes, Kosrae. $5, Stone money, Yap.

1984, July 12   Perf. 13½x13

5	A2	1c Prussian blue	.25 .25
6	A2	2c deep claret	.25 .25
7	A2	3c dark blue	.25 .25
8	A2	4c green	.25 .25
9	A3	5c yellow brown	.25 .25
10	A3	10c dark violet	.25 .25
11	A3	13c dark blue	.25 .25
12	A3	17c brown lake	.25 .25
13	A2	19c dark violet	.30 .30
14	A2	20c olive green	.30 .30
15	A2	30c rose lake	.45 .45
16	A2	37c deep violet	.55 .55
17	A3	50c brown	.75 .75
18	A3	$1 olive	1.75 1.75
19	A3	$2 Prussian blue	3.50 3.50
20	A3	$5 brown lake	8.50 8.50
	Nos. 5-20 (16)		18.10 18.10

See Nos. 33, 36, 38.

Ausipex '84 — A4

1984, Sept. 21   Litho.   Perf. 13½

21	A4	20c Truk Post Office	.40 .40
	Nos. 21,C4-C6 (4)		3.00 3.00

Christmas — A5

Child's drawing.

1984, Dec. 20

22	A5	20c Child in manger	.90 .90
	Nos. 22,C7-C9 (4)		3.55 3.55

Ships — A6

22c, U.S.S. Jamestown.

1985, Aug. 19

23	A6	22c multi	.55 .55
	Nos. 23,C10-C12 (4)		3.00 3.00

Christmas — A7

22c, Lelu Protestant Church, Kosrae.

1985, Oct. 15   Litho.   Perf. 13½

24	A7	22c multi	.75 .60
	Nos. 24,C13-C14 (3)		2.90 2.75

Audubon Birth Bicentenary — A8

1985, Oct. 30   Perf. 14½

25	A8	22c Noddy tern	.60 .60
26	A8	22c Turnstone	.60 .60
27	A8	22c Golden plover	.60 .60
28	A8	22c Black-bellied plover	.60 .60
a.	Block of 4, #25-28		2.60 2.60
	Nos. 25-28,C15 (5)		3.40 3.40

Types of 1984 and

Birds — A9

Tall Ship Senyavin — A10

Natl. Seal — A11

No. 31, Long-billed white-eye. No. 32, Truk monarch. No. 33, Liduduhriap Waterfall, Pohnpei. No. 35, Pohnpei mountain starling. No. 36, Tonachau Peak, Truk. No. 38, Sleeping Lady, Kosrae.

Perf. 13½ (A8a), 13½x13

1985-88   Litho.

31	A9	3c multi	.25 .25
32	A9	14c multi	.30 .30
33	A3	15c dark red	.30 .30
a.	Booklet pane of 10		6.00 —
34	A10	22c bright blue green	.35 .35
35	A9	22c multi	.45 .45
36	A3	25c ochre	.50 .50
a.	Booklet pane of 10		6.50 —
b.	Booklet pane, 5 15c + 5 25c		7.50 —
37	A10	36c ultramarine	.70 .70
38	A3	45c emerald	.90 .90
39	A11	$10 bright ultra	15.00 15.00
	Nos. 31-39,C34-C36 (12)		21.75 21.75

Issued: $10, 10/15; No. 34, 4/14/86; 3c, 14c, No. 35, 8/1/88; 15c, 25c, 36c, 45c, 9/1/88.

Nan Madol Ruins, Pohnpei — A16

22c, Land of the Sacred Masonry.

1985, Dec.   Litho.   Perf. 13½

45	A16	22c multicolored	.60 .60
	Nos. 45,C16-C18 (4)		3.00 3.00

Intl. Peace Year — A17

1986, May 16

46	A17	22c multicolored	.65 .60

Nos. 1-4 Surcharged

1986, May 19   Litho.   Perf. 14

48	A1	22c on 20c No. 1	.40 .40
49	A1	22c on 20c No. 2	.40 .40
50	A1	22c on 20c No. 3	.40 .40
51	A1	22c on 20c No. 4	.40 .40
a.	Block of 4, #48-51		1.75 1.75

AMERIPEX '86 — A18

Bully Hayes (1829-1877), Buccaneer.

1986, May 22   Perf. 13½

52	A18	22c At ship's helm	.50 .50
	Nos. 52,C21-C24 (5)		4.00 4.00

First Passport — A19

1986, Nov. 4   Litho.   Perf. 13½

53	A19	22c multicolored	.60 .60

Christmas — A20

Virgin and child paintings: 5c, Italy, 18th cent. 22c, Germany, 19th cent.

1986, Oct. 15   Litho.   Perf. 14½

54	A20	5c multicolored	.25 .25
55	A20	22c multicolored	.75 .75
	Nos. 54-55,C26-C27 (4)		3.40 3.40

Anniversaries and Events — A21

22c, Intl. Year of Shelter for the Homeless. $1, CAPEX '87.

1987, June 13   Litho.   Perf. 14½

56	A21	22c multicolored	.50 .50
	Nos. 56,C28-C30 (4)		3.20 3.20

Souvenir Sheet

57	A21	$1 multicolored	3.25 3.25

Christmas — A22

22c, Archangel Gabriel appearing before Mary.

1987, Nov. 16   Litho.   Perf. 14½

58	A22	22c multicolored	.60 .60
	Nos. 58,C31-C33 (4)		3.30 3.30

Colonial Eras — A23

1988, July 20   Litho.   Perf. 13x13½

59	A23	22c German	.60 .60
60	A23	22c Spanish	.60 .60
61	A23	22c Japanese	.60 .60
62	A23	22c US Trust Territory	.60 .60
a.	Block of 4, #59-62		2.40 2.40
	Nos. 59-62,C37-C38 (6)		4.30 4.30

Printed se-tenant in sheets of 28 plus 4 center labels picturing flags of Spain (UL), Germany (UR), Japan (LL) and the US (LR).

1988 Summer Olympics, Seoul — A24

1988, Sept. 1   Litho.   Perf. 14

63	A24	25c Running	.50 .50
64	A24	25c Women's hurdles	.50 .50
a.	Pair, #63-64		1.00 .94
65	A24	45c Basketball	.80 .80
66	A24	45c Women's volleyball	.80 .80
a.	Pair, #65-66		1.65 1.65
	Nos. 63-66 (4)		2.60 2.60

Christmas — A25

Children decorating tree: No. 67, Two girls, UL of tree. No. 68, Boy, girl, dove, UR of tree. No. 69, Boy, girl, LL of tree. No. 70, Boy, girl, LR of tree. Se-tenant in a continuous design.

1988, Oct. 28   Litho.   Perf. 14

67	A25	25c multicolored	.45 .45
68	A25	25c multicolored	.45 .45
69	A25	25c multicolored	.45 .45
70	A25	25c multicolored	.45 .45
a.	Block of 4, #67-70		1.90 1.90

MICRONESIA

Miniature Sheet

Truk Lagoon State Monument — A26

a, Sun and stars angelfish. b, School of fish. c, 3 divers. d, Goldenjack. e, Blacktip reef shark. f, 2 schools of fish. g, Squirrelfish. h, Batfish. i, Moorish idols. j, Barracudas. k, Spot banded butterflyfish. l, Three-spotted damselfish. m, Foxface. n, Lionfish. o, Diver. p, Coral. q, Butterflyfish. r, Bivalve, fish, coral.

1988, Dec. 19   Litho.   *Perf. 14*
| 71 | A26 | Sheet of 18 | 9.50 | 9.50 |
| a.-r. | | 25c any single | .50 | .50 |

Mwarmwarms A27

1989, Mar. 31   Litho.   *Perf. 14*
72	A27	45c Plumeria	.65	.65
73	A27	45c Hibiscus	.65	.65
74	A27	45c Jasmine	.65	.65
75	A27	45c Bougainvillea	.65	.65
a.		Block of 4, #72-75	2.75	2.75

Souvenir Sheet

Pheasant and Chrysanthemum, 1830s, by Hiroshige (1797-1858) — A28

1989, May 15   Litho.   *Perf. 14½*
| 76 | A28 | $1 multicolored | 1.60 | 1.60 |

Hirohito (1901-1989), emperor of Japan.

Sharks — A29

1989, July 7
77	A29	25c Whale	.40	.40
78	A29	25c Hammerhead	.40	.40
a.		Pair, #77-78	.80	.80
79	A29	45c Tiger, vert.	.75	.75
80	A29	45c Great white, vert.	.75	.75
a.		Pair, #79-80	1.50	1.50
		Nos. 77-80 (4)	2.30	2.30

Miniature Sheet

First Moon Landing, 20th Anniv. A30

Space achievements: a, X-15 rocket plane, 1959. b, *Explorer 1* launched into orbit, 1958. c, Ed White, 1st American to walk in space, Gemini 4 mission, 1965. d, Apollo 18 command module, 1975. e, Gemini 4 capsule. f, Space shuttle *Challenger*, 1983-86. g, *San Marco 2*, satellite engineered by Italy. h, Soyuz 19 spacecraft, 1975. i, *Columbia* command module and Neil Armstrong taking man's first step onto the Moon during the Apollo 11 mission, 1969.

1989, July 20   Litho.   *Perf. 14*
| 81 | A30 | Sheet of 9 | 5.25 | 4.50 |
| a.-i. | | 25c any single | .50 | .45 |

Earth and Lunar Module, by William Hanson, 1st Art Transported to the Moon — A31

1989, July 20   *Perf. 13½x14*
| 82 | A31 | $2.40 multicolored | 4.50 | 4.00 |

First Moon landing, 20th anniv.

Seashells — A32

1c, Horse's hoof. 3c, Rare spotted cowrie. 15c, Commercial trochus. 20c, General cone. 25c, Triton's trumpet. 30c, Laciniated conch. 36c, Red-mouthed olive. 45c, Map cowrie. 50c, Textile cone. $1, Orange spider conch. $2, Golden cowrie. $5, Episcopal miter.

1989, Sept. 26   *Perf. 14*
83	A32	1c multi	.25	.25
84	A32	3c multi	.25	.25
85	A32	15c multi	.25	.25
a.		Booklet pane of 10	5.00	
87	A32	20c multi	.30	.30
88	A32	25c multi	.40	.40
a.		Booklet pane of 10	7.50	
b.		Booklet pane, 5 each 15c, 25c	7.50	—
90	A32	30c multi	.45	.45
91	A32	36c multi	.55	.55
93	A32	45c multi	.70	.70
95	A32	50c multi	.75	.75
100	A32	$1 multi	1.75	1.75
101	A32	$2 multi	3.50	3.50
102	A32	$5 multi	8.50	8.50
		Nos. 83-102 (12)	17.65	17.65

Booklet panes issued Sept. 14, 1990.

Miniature Sheet

Fruits and Flowers Endemic to Kosrae — A33

Designs: a, Orange. b, Lime. c, Tangerine. d, Mango. e, Coconut. f, Breadfruit. g, Sugar cane. h, Thatched dwelling. i, Banana. j, Girl, boy. k, Pineapple picker. l, Taro. m, Hibiscus. n, Ylang ylang. o, White ginger. p, Plumeria. q, Royal poinciana. r, Yellow allamanda.

1989, Nov. 18   Litho.   *Perf. 14*
| 103 | A33 | Sheet of 18 | 9.00 | 9.00 |
| a.-r. | | 25c any single | .45 | .45 |

Margin inscribed for World Stamp Expo '89.

Christmas A34

1989, Dec. 14   Litho.   *Perf. 14½*
| 104 | A34 | 25c Heralding angel | .50 | .50 |
| 105 | A34 | 45c Three wise men | .90 | .90 |

World Wildlife Fund — A35

Micronesian kingfishers and pigeons.

1990, Feb. 19   Litho.   *Perf. 14*
106	A35	10c Kingfisher (juvenile)	.55	.55
107	A35	15c Kingfisher (adult)	1.25	1.25
108	A35	20c Pigeon	1.75	1.75
109	A35	20c Pigeon, diff.	2.50	2.50
		Nos. 106-109 (4)	6.05	6.05

Stamp World London '90 — A36

Exhibition emblem, artifacts and whaling vessels: No. 110, Wooden whale stamp, *Lyra*, 1826. No. 111, Harpoons, *Prudent*, 1827. No. 112, Scrimshaw (whale), *Rhone*, 1851. No. 113, Scrimshaw on whale tooth, *Sussex*, 1843. $1, Whalers at kill.

1990, May 3   Litho.   *Perf. 14*
110	A36	45c multicolored	.80	.80
111	A36	45c multicolored	.80	.80
112	A36	45c multicolored	.80	.80
113	A36	45c multicolored	.80	.80
a.		Block of 4, #110-113	3.25	3.25

Souvenir Sheet
| 114 | A36 | $1 multicolored | 2.00 | 2.00 |

Souvenir Sheet

Penny Black, 150th Anniv. A37

1990, May 6   *Perf. 14*
| 115 | A37 | $1 Great Britain No. 1 | 2.00 | 2.00 |

Main Building A38

Fr. Hugh Costigan, School Founder A39

Designs: No. 117, Fr. Costigan, students. No. 119, Fr. Costigan, Isaphu Samuel Hadley. No. 120, New York City Police Badge.

1990, July 31   Litho.   *Perf. 14*
116	A38	25c multicolored	.50	.50
117	A38	25c multicolored	.50	.50
118	A39	25c multicolored	.50	.50
119	A38	25c multicolored	.50	.50
120	A38	25c multicolored	.50	.50
a.		Strip of 5, #116-120	2.50	2.50

Pohnpei Agriculture and Trade School, 25th anniversary. Printed in sheets of 15.

Souvenir Sheet

Expo '90, Intl. Garden and Greenery Exposition, Osaka, Japan — A40

1990, July 31   Litho.   *Perf. 14*
| 121 | A40 | $1 multicolored | 1.75 | 1.75 |

Loading Mail, Pohnpei Airport, 1990 — A41

Pacifica Emblem and: 45c, Japanese mail boat, Truk Lagoon, 1940.

1990, Aug. 24
| 122 | A41 | 25c multicolored | .50 | .50 |
| 123 | A41 | 45c multicolored | 1.25 | 1.25 |

Canoe, Flag of Federated States of Micronesia — A42

Designs: No. 124, Stick chart, canoe, flag of Marshall Islands. No. 125, Frigate bird, eagle, USS Constitution, flag of US.

1990, Sept. 28   *Perf. 13½*
124	A42	25c multicolored	.55	.55
125	A42	25c multicolored	.55	.55
126	A42	25c multicolored	.55	.55
a.		Strip of 3, #124-126	1.75	1.75

Compact of Free Association with the US. Printed in sheets of 15. See No. 253, US No. 2506, Marshall Islands No. 381.

Moths — A43

No. 127, Gracillariidae. No. 128, Yponomeatidae. No. 129 Cosmopterigidae, full moon. No. 130, Cosmopterigidae, three-quarter moon.

1990, Nov. 10   Litho.   *Perf. 14*
127	A43	45c multi	.80	.80
128	A43	45c multi	.80	.80
129	A43	45c shown	.80	.80
130	A43	45c multi	.80	.80
a.		Block of 4, #127-130	3.25	3.25

Miniature Sheet

Christmas — A44

Designs: a, Cherub. b, Star of Bethlehem. c, Cherub blowing horn. d, Goats. e, Nativity scene. f, Children, outrigger canoe. g, Messenger blowing a conch shell. h, Family walking. i, People carrying bundles.

1990, Nov. 19   Litho.   *Perf. 14*
| 131 | A44 | Sheet of 9 | 4.50 | 4.50 |
| a.-i. | | 25c any single | .50 | .50 |

Souvenir Sheets

New Capital of Micronesia — A45

1991, Jan. 15   Litho.   *Perf. 14x13½*
132	A45	Sheet of 2	1.40	1.40
a.		25c Executive Branch	.50	.50
b.		45c Legislative, Judicial Branches	.90	.90
133	A45	$1 New Capitol	2.00	2.00

Turtles — A46

MICRONESIA

1991, Mar. 14   Litho.   Perf. 14
134	A46	29c Hawksbill on beach	1.10	1.10
135	A46	29c Green	1.10	1.10
a.		Pair, #134-135	2.25	2.25
136	A46	50c Hawksbill	1.40	1.40
137	A46	50c Leatherback	1.40	1.40
a.		Pair, #136-137	2.75	2.75
		Nos. 134-137 (4)	5.00	5.00

Operation Desert Storm — A47

No. 138, Battleship Missouri. No. 139, Multiple launch rocket system. No. 140, F-14 Tomcat. No. 141, E-3 Sentry (AWACS). No. 142, Frigatebird, flag.

1991, July 30   Litho.   Perf. 14
138	A47	29c multicolored	.60	.60
139	A47	29c multicolored	.60	.60
140	A47	29c multicolored	.60	.60
141	A47	29c multicolored	.60	.60
a.		Block or strip of 4, #138-141	2.40	2.40

Size: 51x38mm
142	A47	$2.90 multicolored	5.00	5.00
a.		Souvenir sheet of 1	5.50	5.50
		Nos. 138-142 (5)	7.40	7.40

Miniature Sheets

Micronesian Ukiyo-e Prints of Paul Jacoulet (1902-1960)

Phila Nippon '91 — A48

Ukiyo-e prints by Paul Jacoulet (1902-1960) — No. 143: a, Evening Flowers, Toloas, Truk, 1941. b, The Chief's Daughter, Mogomog, 1953. c, Yagourouh and Mio, Yap, 1938. No. 144a, Yap Beauty and Orchids, 1934. b, The Yellow-eyed Boys, Ohlul, 1940. c, Violet Flowers, Tomil, 1937. $1, First Love, Yap, 1937, horiz.

1991, Sept.   Litho.   Perf. 14
143	A48	Sheet of 3	2.25	2.25
a.-c.		29c any single	.75	.75
144	A48	Sheet of 3	3.50	3.50
a.-c.		50c any single	1.25	1.25

Souvenir Sheet
| 145 | A48 | $1 multicolored | 2.40 | 2.40 |

Christmas A49

Handicraft scenes: 29c, Nativity. 40c, Adoration of the Magi. 50c, Adoration of the Shepherds.

1991, Oct. 30   Perf. 14x13½
146	A49	29c multicolored	.50	.50
147	A49	40c multicolored	.75	.75
148	A49	50c multicolored	1.00	1.00
		Nos. 146-148 (3)	2.25	2.25

Pohnpei Rain Forest — A50

Designs: a, Pohnpei fruit bat. b, Purple capped fruit-dove. c, Micronesian kingfisher. d, Birdnest fern. e, Island swiftlet. f, Long-billed white-eye. g, Brown noddy. h, Pohnpei lory. i, Pohnpei flycatcher. j, Caroline ground-dove. k, White-tailed tropicbird. l, Micronesian honeyeater. m, Ixora. n, Pohnpei fantail. o, Gray white-eye. p, Blue-faced parrotfinch. q, Cicadabird. r, Green skink.

1991, Nov. 18
| 149 | | Sheet of 18 | 13.00 | 13.00 |
| a.-r. | | A50 29c any single | .65 | .65 |

Peace Corps — A51

Designs: a, Learning crop planting techniques. b, Education. c, John F. Kennedy. d, Public health nurses. e, Recreation.

1992, Apr. 10   Litho.   Perf. 14
| 150 | A51 | 29c Strip of 5, #a.-e. | 2.50 | 2.50 |

Printed in sheets of 15.

Discovery of America, 500th Anniv. — A52

Designs: a, Queen Isabella I. b, Santa Maria. c, Columbus.

1992, May 23   Litho.   Perf. 13½
| 151 | | Strip of 3 | 5.00 | 5.00 |
| a.-c. | | A52 29c any single | 1.65 | 1.65 |

Admission to the UN, First Anniv. — A53

1992, Sept. 24   Perf. 11x10½
152	A53	29c multicolored	1.50	1.50
153	A53	50c multicolored	2.25	2.25
a.		Souvenir sheet of 2, #152-153	3.60	3.60

Christmas — A54

1992, Dec. 4   Perf. 13½
| 154 | A54 | 29c multicolored | 1.90 | 1.90 |

Pioneers of Flight — A55

a, Andrei N. Tupolev. b, John A. Macready. c, Edward V. Rickenbacker. d, Manfred von Richtofen. e, Hugh M. Trenchard. f, Glenn H. Curtiss. g, Charles E. Kingsford-Smith. h, Igor I. Sikorsky.

1993, Apr. 12
| 155 | A55 | 29c Block of 8, #a.-h. | 4.75 | 4.75 |

See Nos. 178, 191, 200, 210, 233, 238, 249.

Fish — A56

Designs: 10c, Bigscale soldierfish. 19c, Bennett's butterflyfish. 20c, Peacock grouper. 22c, Great barracuda. 25c, Coral grouper. 29c, Regal angelfish. 30c, Bleeker's parrotfish. 35c, Picassofish. 40c, Mandarinfish. 45c, Bluebanded surgeonfish. 50c, Orange-striped triggerfish. 52c, Palette surgeonfish. 75c, Oriental sweetlips. $1, Zebra moray. $2, Foxface rabbitfish. $2.90, Orangespine unicornfish.

1993-94   Litho.   Perf. 10½
156	A56	10c multicolored	.25	.25
157	A56	19c multicolored	.35	.35
158	A56	20c multicolored	.35	.35
159	A56	22c multicolored	.40	.40
160	A56	25c multicolored	.45	.45
161	A56	29c multicolored	.55	.55
162	A56	30c multicolored	.55	.55
162A	A56	35c multicolored	.65	.65
163	A56	40c multicolored	.70	.70
163A	A56	45c multicolored	.75	.75
164	A56	50c multicolored	.90	.90
164A	A56	52c multicolored	1.00	1.00
164B	A56	75c multicolored	1.40	1.40
165	A56	$1 multicolored	1.75	1.75
166	A56	$2 multicolored	3.50	3.50
167	A56	$2.90 multicolored	5.50	5.50
		Nos. 156-167 (16)	19.05	19.05

Issued: 19c, 29c, 50c, $1, 5/14/93; 22c, 30c, 40c, 45c, 8/26/93; 10c, 20c, 35c, $2.90, 5/20/94; 25c, 52c, 75c, $2, 8/5/94.

See Nos. 213-227, 250.

A57

Sailing Ships: a, Great Republic. b, Benjamin F. Packard. c, Stag Hound. d, Herald of the Morning. e, Rainbow. f, Flying Cloud. g, Lightning. h, Sea Witch. i, Columbia. j, New World. k, Young America. l, Courier.

1993, May 21   Litho.   Perf. 13½
| 168 | A57 | 29c Sheet of 12, #a.-l. | 15.00 | 15.00 |

A59

1993, July 4   Litho.   Perf. 13½
| 172 | A59 | 29c multicolored | .80 | .80 |

Thomas Jefferson, 250th anniv. of birth.

Pacific Canoes A60

1993, July 21   Litho.   Perf. 13½
173	A60	29c Yap	.80	.80
174	A60	29c Kosrae	.80	.80
175	A60	29c Pohnpei	.80	.80
176	A60	29c Chuuk	.80	.80
a.		Block of 4, #173-176	3.25	3.25

Local Leaders — A61

Designs: a, Ambilos Iehsi, (1935-81), educator. b, Andrew Roboman (1905-92), Yap chief. c, Joab N. Sigrah (1932-88), first vice-speaker of Congress. d, Petrus Mailo (1902-71), Chuuk leader.

1993, Sept. 16   Litho.   Perf. 13½
| 177 | | Strip of 4 | 2.50 | 2.50 |
| a.-d. | | A61 29c any single | .65 | .65 |

See Nos. 204-207.

Pioneers of Flight Type of 1993

Designs: a, Hugh L. Dryden. b, Theodore von Karman. c, Otto Lilienthal. d, Thomas O.M. Sopwith. e, Lawrence B. Sperry. f, Alberto Santos-Dumont. g, Orville Wright. h, Wilbur Wright.

1993, Sept. 25   Litho.   Perf. 13½
| 178 | A55 | 50c Block of 8, #a.-h. | 6.75 | 6.75 |

Tourist Attractions, Pohnpei — A62

1993, Oct. 5
| 179 | A62 | 29c Kepirohi Falls | .75 | .75 |
| 180 | A62 | 50c Spanish Wall | 1.50 | 1.50 |

Souvenir Sheet
| 181 | A62 | $1 Sokehs Rock | 2.00 | 2.00 |

No. 181 contains one 80x50mm stamp.
See Nos. 187-189.

Butterflies — A63

No. 182: a, Great eggfly female (typical). b, Great eggfly female (local variant).
No. 183: a, Monarch. b, Great eggfly male.

1993, Oct. 20   Litho.   Perf. 13½
182		Pair	1.40	1.40
a.-b.		A63 29c Any single	.70	.70
183		Pair	2.00	2.00
a.-b.		A63 50c Any single	1.00	1.00

See No. 190.

Christmas — A64

29c, We Three Kings. 50c, Silent Night, Holy Night.

1993, Nov. 11
| 184 | A64 | 29c multicolored | .75 | .75 |
| 185 | A64 | 50c multicolored | 1.25 | 1.25 |

Miniature Sheet

Yap Culture — A65

Designs: a, Baby basket. b, Bamboo raft. c, Baskets, handbag. d, Fruit bat. e, Forest. f, Outrigger canoe. g, Dioscorea yams. h, Mangroves. i, Manta ray. j, Cyrtosperma taro. k, Fish weir. l, Seagrass, fish. m, Taro bowl. n, Thatched house. o, Coral reef. p, Lavalava. q, Dance. r, Stone money.

1993, Dec. 15   Litho.   Perf. 13½x14
| 186 | A65 | 29c Sheet of 18, #a.-r. | 12.50 | 12.50 |

Tourist Attractions Type of 1993

Sites on Kosrae: 20c, Sleeping Lady Mountain. 40c, Walung. 50c, Lelu Ruins.

1994, Feb. 11   Litho.   Perf. 13½
187	A62	29c multicolored	.55	.55
188	A62	40c multicolored	.75	.75
189	A62	50c multicolored	.95	.95
		Nos. 187-189 (3)	2.25	2.25

Butterfly Type of 1993 with Added Inscription

Souvenir Sheet

a, 29c, like No. 182a. b, 29c, like No. 182b. c, 50c, like No. 183a. d, 50c, like No. 183b.

1994, Feb. 18
| 190 | A63 | Sheet of 4, #a.-d. | 4.25 | 4.25 |

Inscription reads "Hong Kong '94 Stamp Exhibition" in Chinese on Nos. 190a, 190d, and in English on Nos. 190b-190c.
Inscriptions on Nos. 190a-190d are in black.

Pioneers of Flight Type of 1993

Designs: a, Edwin E. Aldrin, Jr. b, Neil A. Armstrong. c, Michael Collins. d, Wernher von

MICRONESIA

Braun. e, Octave Chanute. f, T. Claude Ryan. g, Frank Whittle. h, Waldo D. Waterman.

1994, Mar. 4   Litho.   *Perf. 13½*
191   A55   29c Block of 8, #a.-h.   5.75   5.75

1994 Micronesian Games — A66

Designs: a, Spearfishing. b, Basketball. c, Coconut husking. d, Tree climbing.

1994, Mar. 26   *Perf. 13½x14*
192   Block of 4   2.75   2.75
   a.-d.   A66 29c any single   .70   .70

Native Costumes — A67

a, Pohnpei. b, Kosrae. c, Chuuk. d, Yap.

1994, Mar. 31   *Perf. 13½*
193   Block of 4, #a.-d.   2.75   2.75
   a.-d.   A67 29c any single   .70   .70

Constitution, 15th Anniv. — A68

1994, May 10   Litho.   *Perf. 11x10½*
194   A68   29c multicolored   1.50   1.50

Flowers — A69

Designs: a, Fagraea berteriana. b, Pangium edule. c, Pittosporum ferrugineum. d, Sonneratia caseolaris.

1994, June 6   Litho.   *Perf. 13½*
195   Strip of 4   2.75   2.75
   a.-d.   A69 29c any single   .70   .70

1994 World Cup Soccer Championships, US — A70

Design: No. 197, Soccer players, diff.

1994, June 17   Litho.   *Perf. 13½*
196   A70   50c red & multi   2.25   2.25
197   A70   50c blue & multi   2.25   2.25
   a.   Pair, #196-197   4.50   4.50

No. 197a has a continuous design.

Micronesian Postal Service, 10th Anniv. — A71

Stamps: a, #39, 45, 54 (c), 159, 189, 192 (b). b, #58 (d), 151, 161 (d), 176a, 183a (d). c, #4a, 137a, 184 (a), C12 (c), C39, C41. d, #161 (b), 183a (b), 183b, 193, C12, C40, C42.

1994, July 12   Litho.   *Perf. 13½*
198   Block of 4   5.00   5.00
   a.-d.   A71 29c any single   1.25   1.25

No. 198 is a continuous design.

Souvenir Sheet

PHILAKOREA '94 — A72

Dinosaurs: a, 29c, Iguanodons (b). b, 52c, Coelurosaurs (c). c, $1, Camarasaurus.

1994, Aug. 16   Litho.   *Perf. 13½*
199   A72   Sheet of 3, #a.-c.   5.25   5.25

Pioneers of Flight Type of 1993

a, William A. Bishop. b, Karel J. Bossart. c, Marcel Dassault. d, Geoffrey de Havilland. e, Yuri A. Gagarin. f, Alan B. Shepard, Jr. g, John H. Towers. h, Hermann J. Oberth.

1994, Sept. 20   Litho.   *Perf. 13½*
200   A55   50c Block of 8, #a.-h.   6.75   6.75

Migratory Birds — A73

Designs: a, Oriental cuckoo. b, Long-tailed cuckoo. c, Short-eared owl. d, Dollarbird.

1994, Oct. 20   Litho.   *Perf. 13½*
201   Block of 4   2.50   2.50
   a.-d.   A73 29c any single   .65   .65

Christmas — A74

1994, Nov. 2
202   A74   29c Doves   .60   .60
203   A74   50c Angels   1.00   1.00

Local Leaders Type of 1993

Pioneers of island unification: No. 204, Johnny Moses (1900-91), Pohnpei. No. 205, Belarmino Hatheylul (1907-93), Yap. No. 206, Anton Ring Buas (1907-79), Chuuk. No. 207, Paliknoa Sigrah (King John) (1875-1957), Kosrae.

1994, Dec. 15   Litho.   *Perf. 13½*
204   A61   32c multicolored   .65   .65
205   A61   32c multicolored   .65   .65
206   A61   32c multicolored   .65   .65
207   A61   32c multicolored   .65   .65
   Nos. 204-207 (4)   2.60   2.60

Souvenir Sheet

New Year 1995 (Year of the Boar) A75

1995, Jan. 2
208   A75   50c multicolored   1.00   1.00

Chuuk Lagoon — A76

Underwater scenes: a, Photographer with light. b, Various species of fish, coral. c, Diver. d, Two gold fish.

1995, Feb. 6
209   Block of 4   2.50   2.50
   a.-d.   A76 32c any single   .65   .65

Pioneers of Flight Type of 1993

Designs: a, Robert H. Goddard. b, Leroy R. Grumman. c, Hugo Junkers. d, James A. Lovell, Jr. e, Louis-Charles Breguet. f, Juan de la Cierva. g, Donald W. Douglas. h, Reginald J. Mitchell.

1995, Mar. 4   Litho.   *Perf. 13½*
210   A55   32c Block of 8, #a.-h.   5.25   5.25

Dogs — A77

a, West Highland white terrier. b, Welsh springer spaniel. c, Irish setter. d, Old English sheepdog.

1995, Apr. 5   Litho.   *Perf. 13½*
211   Block of 4   2.50   2.50
   a.-d.   A77 32c any single   .65   .65

Fish Type of 1993

Designs: 23c, Yellow-fin tuna. 32c, Saddled butterflyfish. 46c, Achilles tang. 55c, Moorish idol. 60c, Skipjack tuna. 78c, Square-spot fairy basslet. 95c, Bluelined snapper. $3, Flame angelfish. $5, Cave grouper.
No. 227: a, like #157. b, like #161. c, like #164. d, like #165. e, like #159. f, like #162. g, like #163. h, like #163A. i, like #156. j, like #158. k, like #162A. l, like #167. m, like #217. n, like #160. o, like #164A. p, like #164B. q, like #166. r, like #214. s, like #218. t, like #222. u, like #225. v, like #213. w, like #219. x, like #223. y, like #226.

1996   Litho.   *Perf. 13½*
213   A56   23c multicolored   .45   .45
214   A56   32c multicolored   .65   .65
217   A56   46c multicolored   .95   .95
218   A56   55c multicolored   1.10   1.10
219   A56   60c multicolored   1.25   1.25
222   A56   78c multicolored   1.50   1.50
223   A56   95c multicolored   1.90   1.90
225   A56 $3 multicolored   6.00   6.00
226   A56 $5 multicolored   10.00   10.00
   Nos. 213-226 (9)   23.80   23.80

Miniature Sheet

227   A56   32c Sheet of 25, #a.-y.   16.00   16.00

Issued: 32c, 55c, 78c, $3, 5/15/95. 23c, 60c, 95c, $5, 8/4/95; 46c, 4/10/96.

Hibiscus — A78

a, Tiliaceus. b, Huegelii. c, Trionum. d, Splendens.

1995, June 1   Litho.   *Perf. 13½*
228   Strip of 4   2.50   2.50
   a.-d.   A78 32c any single   .65   .65

No. 228 is a continuous design.

Souvenir Sheet

UN, 50th Anniv. A79

1995, June 26   Litho.   *Perf. 13½*
229   A79 $1 multicolored   2.00   2.00

Miniature Sheet

Singapore '95 — A80

Orchids: a, Paphiopedilum henrietta fujiwara. b, Lycaste virginalis. c, Thunia alba. d, Laeliocattleya prism palette.

1995, Sept. 1   Litho.   *Perf. 13½*
230   Sheet of 4   2.60   2.60
   a.-d.   A80 32c any single   .65   .65

End of World War II, 50th Anniv. — A81

US warships: a, USS Portland. b, USS Tillman. c, USS Soley. d, USS Hyman.

1995, Sept. 2
231   Block of 4   5.00   5.00
   a.-d.   A81 60c any single   1.25   1.25

Souvenir Sheet

Intl. Stamp & Coin Expo, Beijing '95 A82

1995, Sept. 14
232   A82   50c Temple of Heaven   1.00   1.00

Pioneers of Flight Type of 1993

Designs: a, Hugh C.T. Dowding. b, William Mitchell. c, John K. Northrop. d, Frederick Handley Page. e, Frederick H. Rohr. f, Juan T. Trippe. g, Konstantin E. Tsiolkovsky. h, Ferdinand Graf von Zeppelin.

1995, Sept. 21   Litho.   *Perf. 13½*
233   A55   60c Block of 8, #a.-h.   9.50   9.50

Christmas Poinsettias — A83

1995, Oct. 30   Litho.   *Perf. 13½*
234   A83   32c gray & multi   .65   .65
235   A83   60c bister & multi   1.25   1.25

Yitzhak Rabin (1922-95), Israeli Prime Minister — A84

1995, Nov. 30   Litho.   *Perf. 13½*
236   A84   32c multicolored   .65   .65

No. 236 was issued in sheets of 8.

Souvenir Sheet

New Year 1996 (Year of the Rat) A85

1996, Jan. 5   Litho.   *Perf. 13½*
237   A85   50c multicolored   1.00   1.00

Pioneers of Flight Type of 1993

Designs: a, James H. Doolittle. b, Claude Dornier. c, Ira C. Eaker. d, Jacob C.H. Ellehammer. e, Henry H. Arnold. f, Louis Blériot. g, William E. Boeing. h, Sydney Camm.

1996, Feb. 21   Litho.   *Perf. 13½*
238   A55   32c Block of 8, #a.-h.   5.25   5.25

MICRONESIA

Tourism in Yap — A86

a, Meeting house. b, Stone money. c, Churu dancing. d, Traditional canoe.

1996, Mar. 13	Litho.		Perf. 13½	
239	Block of 4		2.50	2.50
a.-d.	A86 32c any single		.65	.65

Sea Stars — A87

Designs: a, Rhinoceros. b, Necklace c, Thick-skinned. d, Blue.

1996, Apr. 26	Litho.		Perf. 12	
240	Block of 4		4.50	4.50
a.-d.	A87 55c any single		1.15	1.15

Olympic Games, Cent. — A88

First Olympic stamps, Greece: a, #120. b, #122. c, #121. d, #128.

1996, Apr. 27				
241	Block of 4		4.75	4.75
a.-d.	A88 60c any single		1.20	1.20

Souvenir Sheet

China '96, 9th Asian Intl. Philatelic Exhibition — A89

Design: The Tarrying Garden, Suzhou.

1996, May 15			Perf. 13x13½	
242	A89 50c multicolored		1.00	1.00

Patrol Boats — A90

1996, May 3	Litho.		Perf. 13¼	
243	A90 32c FSS Palikir		.65	.65
244	A90 32c FSS Micronesia		.65	.65
a.	Pair, #243-244		1.30	1.30

No. 244a is a continuous design.

First Ford Automobile, Cent. — A91

a, 1896 Quadricycle. b, 1917 Model T truck. c, 1928 Model A Tudor Sedan. d, 1932 V-8 Sport Roadster. e, 1941 Lincoln Continental. f, 1953 F-100 Truck. g, 1958 Thunderbird convertible. h, 1996 Mercury Sable.

1996, June 4			Perf. 13½	
245	Sheet of 8		8.75	8.75
a.-h.	A91 55c any single		1.10	1.10

Officer Reza, Member of Natl. Police Drug Enforcement Unit — A93

1996, July 31	Litho.		Perf. 13½	
247	A93 32c multicolored		.65	.65

Citrus Fruit — A94

a, Orange. b, Lime. c, Lemon. d, Tangerine.

1996, Aug. 24	Litho.		Perf. 13½	
248	Strip of 4		4.00	4.00
a.-d.	A94 50c any single		1.00	1.00

Pioneers of Flight Type of 1993

Designs: a, Gianni Caproni. b, Henri Farman. c, Curtis E. LeMay. d, Grover Loening. e, Sergey P. Korolyov. f, Isaac M. Laddon. g, Glenn L. Martin. h, Alliott Verdon Roe.

1996, Sept. 18				
249	A55 60c Block of 8, #a.-h.		12.50	12.50

Fish Type of 1993

Designs: a, like #157. b, like #165. c, like #162A. d, like #218.

1996, Oct. 21	Litho.		Perf. 13½	
250	A56 32c Block of 4, #a.-d.		2.50	2.50

Taipei '96, 10th Asian Intl. Philatelic Exhibition. Nos. 250a, 250d have English inscriptions. Nos. 250b-250c have Chinese inscriptions.

Magi Following Star to Bethlehem — A95

1996, Oct. 30	Litho.		Perf. 13½	
251	A95 32c dark blue & multi		.65	.65
252	A95 60c lt. blue & multi		1.25	1.25

Christmas.

Canoe, Flag of Federated States of Micronesia Type of 1990

1996, Nov. 3			Perf. 11x10½	
253	A42 $3 like #124		6.00	6.00

No. 253 inscribed "Free Association United States of America."

Deng Xiaoping (1904-97) — A96

Portraits: a, Wearing white-collared shirt. b, Looking left. c, Looking right. d, Wearing hat. $3, Looking left, diff.

1997	Litho.		Perf. 14	
254	Sheet of 4		4.75	4.75
a.-d.	A96 60c any single		1.20	1.20

Souvenir Sheet

255	A96 $3 multicolored		6.00	6.00

Souvenir Sheet

Bridge to the Future — Hong Kong A97

1997				
256	A97 $2 multicolored		4.00	4.00

New Year 1997 (Year of the Ox) — A98

1997	Litho.		Perf. 14	
257	A98 32c multicolored		.65	.65

Souvenir Sheet

258	A98 $2 like #257		4.00	4.00

Return of Hong Kong to China — A99

Flowers, Victoria Harbor: a, Melia azedarach. b, Sail from ship, Victoria Peak. c, Sail from ship, dendrobium chrysotoxum. d, Bauhinia blakeana. e, Cassia surattensis, Chinese junk. f, Junk, nelumbo nucifera. $3, Strongylodon macrobatrys, pagoda.

1997, July 1				
259	Sheet of 6		7.25	7.25
a.-f.	A99 60c any single		1.20	1.20

Souvenir Sheet

260	A99 $3 multicolored		6.00	6.00

Sea Goddesses of the Pacific — A100

a, Giant serpent, woman holding child, Walutahanga of Melanesia. b, Sailing ship in storm, woman holding lantern, Tien-Hou of China. c, Woman swimming to bottom of sea gathering fish into basket, Lorop of Micronesia. d, Woman swimming to man in canoe, Oto-Hime of Japan. e, Woman holding seashell, Nomoi of Micronesia. f, Three women in canoe, Junkgowa sisters of Australia.

1997, May 29	Litho.		Perf. 14	
261	A100 32c Sheet of 6, #a.-f.		3.75	3.75

PACIFIC 97.

Paintings by Hiroshige (1797-1858) A101

Whirlpools at Naruto in Awa Province, 1857: No. 262: a, Sailboats in distance. b, Island of trees at left. c, Island of trees at right.
Tale of Genji: Viewing the Plum Blossoms, 1852: No. 263: a, Small evergreen trees in front of woman. b, Woman. c, Trees, house in distance with woman.
Snow on the Sumida River, 1847: No. 264: a, House, river. b, Two women under umbrella. c, Woman with folded umbrella.
Each $2: No. 265, Rapids in Bitchu Province, 1854. No. 266, Fuji from Satta Point, 1858.

1997, July 25			Perf. 13½x14	
262	Sheet of 3		1.25	1.25
a.-c.	A101 20c any single		.40	.40
263	Sheet of 3		3.00	3.00
a.-c.	A101 50c any single		1.00	1.00
264	Sheet of 3		3.50	3.50
a.-c.	A101 60c any single		1.20	1.20

Souvenir Sheets

265-266	A101 Set of 2		8.00	8.00

Second Federated States of Micronesia Games — A102

a, Tennis. b, Discus. c, Swimming. d, Canoeing.

1997, Aug. 15	Litho.		Perf. 14	
267	A102 32c Block of 4, #a.-d.		2.50	2.50

No. 267 was issued in sheets of 16 stamps.

Elvis Presley (1935-77) A103

Various portraits.

1997, Aug. 16				
268	Sheet of 6		6.00	6.00
a.-f.	A103 50c any single		1.00	1.00

Ocean Exploration A104

No. 269: a, Simon Lake, Argonaut, 1897. b, William Beebe, Bathysphere, 1934. c, Auguste Piccard, Bathyscaphe, 1954. d, Harold Edgerton, deep-sea camera, 1954. e, Jacques Piccard, Trieste, 1960. f, Edwin Link, Man-in-Sea Project, 1962. g, Melvin Fisher, search for treasure, 1971. h, Robert Ballard, Alvin, 1978. i, Sylvia Earle, Deep Rover, 1979.
Each $2: No. 270, C. Wyville Thomson, deep sea dredge, vert. No. 271, Shinkai 6500 exploring bottom of sea, vert. No. 272, Jacques-Yves Cousteau, vert.

1997, Oct. 6	Litho.		Perf. 14	
269	Sheet of 9		4.25	4.25
a.-i.	A104 32c any single		.45	.45

Souvenir Sheets

270-272	A104 Set of 3		30.00	30.00

Diana, Princess of Wales (1961-97) — A105

1997, Nov. 26	Litho.		Perf. 14	
273	A105 60c multicolored		1.25	1.25

No. 273 was issued in sheets of 6.

447

MICRONESIA

World Wildlife Fund — A106

Butterfly fish: a, Blackback. b, Saddled. c, Threadfin. d, Bennett's.

1997, Nov. 24	Litho.		Perf. 14	
274	A106	50c Block of 4, #a.-d.	8.00	8.00

No. 274 was issued in sheets of 16 stamps.

Christmas Paintings — A107

Christ Glorified in the Court of Heaven, by Fra Angelico: No. 275, Angels playing musical instruments. No. 276, Choir of Angels.
A Choir of Angels, by Simon Marmion: No. 277, Two angels blowing long horns. No. 278, One angel blowing horn.

1997, Nov. 25				
275	A107	32c multicolored	.65	.65
276	A107	32c multicolored	.65	.65
a.		Horiz. pair, Nos. 275-276	1.30	1.30
277	A107	60c multicolored	1.25	1.25
278	A107	60c multicolored	1.25	1.25
a.		Vert. pair, Nos. 277-278	2.50	2.50

Nos. 276a, 278a were each issued in sheets of 8 pairs.

Souvenir Sheets

New Year 1998 (Year of the Tiger) A108

1998, Jan. 2	Litho.		Perf. 14	
279	A108	50c shown	1.00	1.00
280	A108	50c Chinese toy (face)	1.00	1.00

Souvenir Sheet

Micronesia's Admission to United Nations, 7th Anniv. — A109

1998, Feb. 13			Perf. 13½	
281	A109	$1 multicolored		2.00 2.00

Winnie the Pooh A110

No. 282: a, Rabbit. b, Owl. c, Eeyore. d, Kanga and Roo. e, Piglet. f, Tigger. g, Pooh. h, Christopher Robin.
Each $2: No. 283, Piglet, Pooh, and Tigger. No. 284, Rabbit and Pooh.

1998, Feb. 16			Perf. 14x14½	
282		Sheet of 8	5.25	5.25
a.-h.	A110 32c any single		.65	.65

Souvenir Sheets

| 283-284 | A110 Set of 2 | 8.00 | 8.00 |

1998 World Cup Soccer Championships, France — A111

Various soccer plays, color of foreground player's shirt & shorts — No. 285: a, White & black. b, Green & white. c, Yellow & blue, socks with colored stripes. d, Green & black. e, Yellow & black. f, Red & blue. g, Yellow & blue, plain socks. h, Red & white.
Each $2: No. 286, Red & blue. No. 287, Green, black & white.

1998, Mar. 20	Litho.		Perf. 13½	
285		Sheet of 8	5.00	5.00
a.-h.	A111 32c any single		.65	.65

Souvenir Sheets

| 286-287 | A111 Set of 2 | 8.00 | 8.00 |

Souvenir Sheet

Micronesia's Recognition by Intl. Olympic Committee — A112

1998, Mar. 20				
288	A112	$3 multicolored	6.00	6.00

Old Testament Bible Stories — A113

Adam and Eve — No. 289: a, Land of plenty. b, Adam, Eve before the fall. c, Serpent of temptation.
Joseph and his brethren — No. 290: a, Brothers plan to sell Joseph. b, Joseph in his many-colored coat. c, Ishmaelites take Joseph.
Rebekah — No. 291: a, Rebekah at the well. b, Abraham's servant Eliezer. c, Angel sent to prosper Eliezer's way.
Each $2: No. 292, Adam and Eve sent forth from Eden. No. 293, Joseph forgives his brothers. No. 294, Isaac takes Rebekah to wife.

1998, May 13	Litho.		Perf. 13½x14	
289		Sheet of 3	1.90	1.90
a.-c.	A113 32c any single		.65	.65
290		Sheet of 3	2.50	2.50
a.-c.	A113 40c any single		.85	.85
291		Sheet of 3	3.50	3.50
a.-c.	A113 60c any single		1.20	1.20

Souvenir Sheets

| 292-294 | A113 Set of 3 | 12.00 | 12.00 |

Israel '98.

Intl. Year of the Ocean — A114

Deep sea research — No. 295: a, Marine observation satellite. b, Support vessel, Natsushima. c, Research vessel, Kaiyo. d, Deep sea anemone. e, Shinkai 2000. f, Deep tow. g, Tripod fish. h, Towed deep survey system. i, Black smokers.

Each $2: No. 296, Communications satellite. No. 297, Ocean observation buoy, vert. No. 298, Weather satellite.

1998, June 2	Litho.		Perf. 13	
295		Sheet of 9	5.75	5.75
a.-i.	A114 32c any single		.65	.65

Souvenir Sheets

| 296-298 | A114 Set of 3 | 12.00 | 12.00 |

Native Birds — A115

No. 299: a, Kosrae white-eye. b, Chuuk monarch. c, Yap monarch. d, Pohnpei lory.
$3, Pohnpei mountain starling.

1998, June 30			Perf. 14x14½	
299	A115	50c Block or strip of 4, a.-d.	4.00	4.00

Souvenir Sheet

| 300 | A115 | $3 multicolored | 6.00 | 6.00 |

No. 299 was issued in sheets of 16 stamps.

Fish — A116

Designs: 1c, White-tipped soldierfish. 2c, Red-breasted wrasse. 3c, Bicolor angelfish. 4c, Falco hawkfish. 5c, Convict tang. 10c, Square-spot fairy basslet. 13c, Orangeband surgeonfish. 15c, Multibarred goatfish. 17c, Masked rabbitfish. 20c, White-spotted surgeonfish. 22c, Blue-girdled angelfish. 32c, Wedge picassofish. 39c, Red parrotfish. 40c, Lemonpeel angelfish. 60c, Humphead wrasse. 78c, Sapphire damselfish. $1, Bluefin travally. $3, Whitespot hawkfish. $5, Spotted trunkfish. $10.75, Pinktail triggerfish.

1998		Litho.	Perf. 14½	
301	A116	1c multi	.25	.25
302	A116	2c multi	.25	.25
303	A116	3c multi	.25	.25
304	A116	4c multi	.25	.25
305	A116	5c multi	.25	.25
306	A116	10c multi	.25	.25
307	A116	13c multi	.25	.25
308	A116	15c multi	.30	.30
309	A116	17c multi	.35	.35
310	A116	20c multi	.40	.40
311	A116	22c multi	.45	.45
312	A116	32c multi	.65	.65
313	A116	39c multi	.75	.75
314	A116	40c multi	.80	.80
315	A116	60c multi	1.25	1.25
316	A116	78c multi	1.50	1.50
317	A116	$1 multi	1.90	1.90
318	A116	$3 multi	5.75	5.75
319	A116	$5 multi	10.00	10.00
319A	A116	$10.75 multi	21.00	21.00
	Nos. 301-319A (20)		46.85	46.85

Issued: $10.75, 9/8; others, 7/20.
See Nos. 328-333.

Fala, Franklin D. Roosevelt's Scottish Terrier — A117

Designs: a, Roosevelt's hand petting dog. b, Radio at right. c, Radio at left. d, In car with FDR. e, Presidential seal. f, Closeup of Fala looking left.

1998, Aug. 27	Litho.		Perf. 13½	
320		Sheet of 6	3.75	3.75
a.-f.	A117 32c any single		.65	.65

Christmas — A118

Twentieth cent. art — No. 321: a, Eskimo Madonna, by Claire Fejes. b, Madonna, by Man Ray. c, Peasant Mother, by David Siqueiros.
No. 322: a, Mother and Child, by Pablo Picasso. b, Gypsy Woman with Baby, by Amedeo Modigliani. c, Mother and Child, by José Orozco.
$2, Detail from The Family, by Marisol, horiz.

1998, Sept. 15	Litho.		Perf. 13½x14	
321		Sheet of 3	1.90	1.90
a.-c.	A118 32c any single		.65	.65
322		Sheet of 3	3.75	3.75
a.-c.	A118 60c any single		1.25	1.25

Souvenir Sheet

Perf. 14x13½

| 323 | A118 | $2 multicolored | 4.00 | 4.00 |

John Glenn's Return to Space — A119

Each 60c: No. 324: Various photos of Friendship 7 mission, 1962.
Each 60c: No. 325: Various photos of Discovery space shuttle mission, 1998.
Each $2: No. 326, Launch of Friendship 7. No. 327, Portrait of Glenn, 1998.

1998, Oct. 29	Litho.		Perf. 14	
		Sheets of 8		
324-325		Set of 2	19.00	19.00
a.-h.	A119 60c any single		1.20	1.20

Souvenir Sheets

| 326-327 | A119 Set of 2 | 8.00 | 8.00 |

Fish Type of 1993

Designs: 33c, Black jack. 50c, Whitecheek surgeonfish. 55c, Long-jawed squirrelfish. 77c, Onespot snapper. $3.20, Tan-faced parrotfish. $11.75, Yellow-faced angelfish.

1999		Litho.	Perf. 14½	
328	A116	33c multicolored	.65	.65
329	A116	50c multicolored	1.00	1.00
330	A116	55c multicolored	1.10	1.10
331	A116	77c multicolored	1.50	1.50
332	A116	$3.20 multicolored	6.50	6.50

Perf. 14
Size: 45x21mm

| 333 | A116 | $11.75 multicolored | 22.50 | 22.50 |
| | Nos. 328-333 (6) | | 33.25 | 33.25 |

Issued: $11.75, 3/31; others, 2/22.

Russian Space Exploration — A120

No. 334: a, Sputnik 1, 1957. b, Laika in Sputnik 2, 1957. c, Luna 1, 1959. d, Luna 3, 1959. e, Yuri Gagarin in Vostok 1, 1961. f, Venera 1, 1961. g, Mars 1, 1962. h, Valentina Tereshkova in Vostok 6, 1963. i, Voskhod 1, 1964. j, Aleksei Leonov in Voskhod 2, 1965. k, Venera 3, 1966. l, Luna 10. m, Luna 9. n, Luna 16, 1970. o, Luna 17, 1970. p, Mars 3, 1971. q, Leonid Popov, Valeri Ryumin, Soyuz 35, 1980. r, Vega 1, 1985. s, Vega 1, Halley's Comet, 1986. t, Mir, 1986-98.
Each $2: No. 335, Russian Space Station, Mir, 1998. No. 336, Docking of USSR Soyuz 19 and Apollo 18, horiz.

1999, Mar. 15			Perf. 14	
334		Sheet of 20	13.50	13.50
a.-t.	A120 33c any single		.70	.70

Souvenir Sheets

| 335-336 | A120 Set of 2 | 8.00 | 8.00 |

See Nos. 344-346.

MICRONESIA

"Romance of the Three Kingdoms," by Lo Kuan-Chung
A121

No. 337: a, Men, women conferring. b, Four men, one grabbing on clothes of another. c, Two men jousting. d, Four men looking down at one man. e, Man kneeling before another man in wheelchair.
No. 338: a, Mounted warriors approaching drawbridge. b, Warriors fighting in front of fire, banners. c, Warrior fighting off others, smoke. d, Man, woman kneeling before old man. e, Two men looking up at smoke coming from boiling pot.
No. 339, Three men in boat, raging fire.

1999, Mar. 19 Litho. Perf. 13½
Sheets of 5
337 A121 33c #a.-e. 3.25 3.25
338 A121 50c #a.-e. 5.00 5.00
Souvenir Sheet
339 A121 $2 multicolored 4.00 4.00
No. 339 contains one 52x79mm stamp.

IBRA '99, World Stamp Exhibition, Nuremberg, Germany — A122

Designs: No. 340, The Leipzig-Dresden Railway, Caroline Islands #4. No. 341, Gölsdorf 4-4-0, Caroline Islands #16. $2, Exhibition emblem, Caroline Islands #6, vert.

1999, Apr. 27 Perf. 14x14½
340 A122 55c multicolored 1.10 1.10
341 A122 55c multicolored 1.10 1.10
Souvenir Sheet
342 A122 $2 multicolored 4.00 4.00

Voyages of the Pacific — A123

Designs: a, Map of Pacific Ocean. b, Parrot. c, Bird in flight, leaves. d, Map, ship's stern. e, Part of ship, various blocks. f, Flower. g, Sailing ship, side view. h, Three flowers, compass rose. i, Fish over ship's drawing. j, Map, flag LL. k, Map, flag UR. l, Map, flag LR. m, Three sections of coconut. n, Three flowers, plant. o, Fish. p, Flag, UL, "Equator." q, Sextant. r, Bottom of plant. s, Fish, compass rose. t, Sailing ship, bow on.

1999, Mar. 19 Litho. Perf. 13½
343 A123 33c Sheet of 20,
#a.-t. 13.50 13.50

Space Achievements Type of 1999
US space achievements — No. 344: a, Explorer 1, 1958. b, OSO 1, 1962. c, Mariner 2 to Venus, 1962. d, Mariner 2, 1962. e, Apollo 8, 1968. f, First step onto moon, Apollo 11, 1969. g, First samples from moon, Apollo 11, 1969. h, Apollo 15, 1971. i, Mariner 9, 1971. j, Pioneer 10, 1973. k, Mariner 10, 1974. l, Viking 1, 1976. m, Pioneer 11, 1970. n, STS 1, 1981. o, Pioneer 10, 1983. p, Solar Maximum Mission, 1984. q, Cometary Explorer, 1985. r, Voyager 2, 1989. s, Gallileo to Gaspra, 1992. t, Sojourner, 1997.
Each $2: No. 345, International space station. No. 346, Shuttle mission to repair Hubble Telescope, 1993.

1999, Mar. 15 Litho. Perf. 14
344 A120 33c Sheet of 20,
#a.-t. 13.50 13.50
Souvenir Sheets
345-346 A120 Set of 2 8.00 8.00
Illustrations on Nos. 344p and 344q are incorrect.

Earth Day — A124

Endangered, extinct, and prehistoric species — No. 347: a, Black rhinoceros. b, Cheetah. c, Jackass penguin. d, Blue whale. e, Red-headed woodpecker. f, African elephant. g, Aurochs. h, Dodo bird. i, Tasmanian wolf. j, Giant lemur. k, Quagga. l, Steller's sea cow. m, Pteranodon. n, Shonisaurus. o, Stegosaurus. p, Galliminus. q, Tyrannosaurus. r, Archelon. s, Brachiosaurus. t, Triceratops.
Each $2: No. 348, Moa. No. 349, Suchominus tenerensis, horiz.

1999
347 Sheet of 20 13.50 13.50
a.-t. A124 33c any single .70 .70
Souvenir Sheets
348-349 A124 Set of 2 8.00 8.00
Nos. 348-349 contain one 50x38mm and one 38x50mm stamp, respectively.

Paintings by Hokusai (1760-1849)
A125

Details or entire paintings — No. 350, each 33c: a, Ghost of O-Iwa. b, Horse Drawings (head down). c, Abe Nakamaro. d, Ghost of Kasane. e, Horse Drawings (head up). f, The Ghost of Kiku and the Priest Mitazuki.
No. 351, each 33c: a, Belly Band Float. b, Drawing of Women (facing left). c, Swimmers. d, Eel Climb. e, Drawings of Women (facing right). f, Kimo Ga Imo Ni Naru.
Each $2: No. 352, Whaling off Goto. No. 353, Fishing by Torchlight.

1999, July 20 Litho. Perf. 13¾x14
Sheets of 6
350-351 Set of 2 8.00 8.00
a.-f. A125 33c any single .65 .65
Souvenir Sheets
352-353 A125 Set of 2 8.00 8.00

Flowers — A126

Various flowers making up a photomosaic of Princess Diana.

1999 Litho. Perf. 13¼
354 A126 50c Sheet of 8, #a.-h. 8.00 8.00
See No. 393, 403.

Millennium — A127

No. 355 — Highlights of the 12th Century: a, Death of Emperor Henry IV. b, Taira and Minamoto clans. c, Order of the Knights of the Hospital of St. John founded. d, Nautical compass invented. e, "White Ship" disaster. f, Pope Calixtus and Henry V end dispute. g, Death of Omar Khyyam. h, Death of Duke William IX. i, Roger II crowned King of Sicily. j, Stephen of Blois, Matilda. k, Birth of Maimonides. l, Church condemns Peter Abelard. m, Crusaders defeated at Damascus. n, Fall of city of Tula. o, Completion of Angkor Wat. p, Chimu culture flourishes (60x40mm). q, Honen becomes hermit.
No. 356 — Science and Technology of Ancient China: a, Well drilling. b, Chain pump. c, Magic lantern. d, Seismograph. e, Dial and pointer devices. f, Refined value of pi. g, Porcelain. h, Water mill. i, Stirrup. j, Tea. k, Umbrella. l, Brandy and whiskey. m, Printing. n, Paper money. o, Gunpowder. p, Arch bridge (60x40mm). q, Mercator map projection.

1999, Oct. 4 Perf. 12¾x12½
Sheets of 17
355 A127 20c #a.-q. + label 7.00 7.00
356 A127 33c #a.-q. + label 11.50 11.50
Inscriptions on Nos. 355g, 355o, and perhaps others, are incorrect or misspelled.
See No. 377.

Costumes — A128

Designs: a, French princess gown (head at R). b, As "a," (head at B). c, As "a," (bust). d, As "a," (umbrella). e, Scissors. f, Tools for fabric making. g, Micronesian wedding costume (head at R). h, As "g," (midriff). i, As "g," (feet). j, Japanese fabrics. k, Masai warrior costume (head at L). l, As "k," (head at R). m, African fabric details. n, Kabuki theater costume. o, As "n," (midriff). p, French Renaissance costume (head at B). q, Textile patterns. r, As "p," (head at R). s, Rulers. t, Iron.

1999, Nov. 22 Perf. 14¾
357 A128 33c Sheet of 20,
#a.-t. 13.50 13.50
Vertical strips of 2, 3 or 5 have continuous designs.

Christmas — A129

Paintings by Anthony Van Dyck: 33c, Holy Family with St. John. 60c, Madonna with Child. No. 360, The Virgin and Child with Two Donors (detail).
No. 361, The Adoration of the Shepherds.

1999, Dec. 1 Litho. Perf. 13¾
358 A129 33c multi .65 .65
359 A129 60c multi 1.25 1.25
360 A129 $2 multi 4.00 4.00
Nos. 358-360 (3) 5.90 5.90
Souvenir Sheet
361 A129 $2 multi 4.00 4.00

Millennium — A130

Airplanes — No. 362: a, Wright Flyer I. b, Blériot XI. c, Fokker D VII. d, Dornier Komet I. e, Ryan NYP. f, Mitsubishi A6M. g, Boeing B-29. h, Messerschmitt 262A. i, Bell X-1. j, MiG-19. k, Lockheed U-2. l, Boeing 707. m, Concorde. n, McDonnell Douglas DC-10. o, B-2.
No. 363, P38. No. 364, Dornier Do X.

1999, Dec. 9 Perf. 14
362 A130 33c Sheet of 15,
#a.-o. 10.00 10.00
Souvenir Sheets
Perf. 13¾
363 A130 $2 multi 4.00 4.00
364 A130 $2 multi 4.00 4.00
No. 363 contains one 32x48mm stamp. No. 364 contains one 48x32mm stamp.

Orchids — A131

No. 365: a, Baptistonia echinata. b, Bulbophyllum lobbii. c, Cattleya bicolor. d, Cischweinfia dasyandra. e, Cochleanthes discolor. f, Dendrobium bellatulum.
No. 366: a, Esmeralda clarkei. b, Gomesa crispa. c, Masdevallia elephanticeps. d, Maxillaria variabilis. e, Mitoniopsis roezlii. f, Oncidium cavendishianum.
No. 367: a, Oncidium obryzatum. b, Oncidium phalaenopsis. c, Oncidium pulvinatum. d, Paphiopedilum armeniacum. e, Paphiopedilum dayanum. f, Paphiopedilum druryi.
No. 368, Paphiopedilum hirutissimum. No. 369, Licoglossum oerstedii.

2000, Jan. 5 Perf. 14¼x14
Sheets of 6
365 A131 33c #a.-f. 4.00 4.00
366 A131 33c #a.-f. 4.00 4.00
367 A131 33c #a.-f. 4.00 4.00
Souvenir Sheets
Perf. 14x14¼
368 A131 $1 multi 2.00 2.00
369 A131 $1 multi 2.00 2.00
Nos. 368-369 each contain one 31x53mm stamp.

Leaders of the 20th Century — A132

Designs: a, Martin Luther King, Jr. b, Albert Schweitzer. c, Pope John Paul II. d, Sarvepalli

MICRONESIA

Radhakrishnan. e, Toyohiko Kagawa. f, Mahatma Gandhi. g, Mother Teresa. h, Khyentse Rinpoche. i, Desmond Tutu. j, Chiara Lubich. k, 14th Dalai Lama. l, Abraham Heschel.

2000, Jan. 18   Litho.   Perf. 14¼
370 A132 33c Sheet of 12, #a.-l.   8.00 8.00

Souvenir Sheet

New Year 2000 (Year of the Dragon) A133

2000, Feb. 5   Perf. 13¾
371 A133 $2 multi   4.00 4.00

Butterflies — A134

No. 372: a, Salamis parhassus. b, Morpho rhetenor. c, Danaus plexippus. d, Phyciodes actinote. e, Idea leucone. f, Actinote negra.
No. 373: a, Graphium sarpedon. b, Papilio machaon. c, Ornithoptera priamus. d, Ornithoptera chimaerea. e, Graphium antiphates. f, Pachliopta aristochiae.
Each $2: No. 374, Hamadryas amphinome, vert. No. 375, Colias croceus, vert. No. 376, Butterfly collector, vert.

2000, Feb. 28   Litho.   Perf. 14
Sheets of 6
372 A134 20c #a.-f.   2.40 2.40
373 A134 55c #a.-f.   6.75 6.75
Souvenir Sheets
374-376 A134 Set of 3   12.00 12.00

Millennium Type of 1999

Highlights of the 1920s: a, Mahatma Gandhi leads non-violent reform in India. b, International Dada Fair in Berlin. c, American women win right to vote. d, Sacco and Vanzetti case. e, Hermann Rorshach develops inkblot test. f, Thomas J. Watson incorporates IBM. g, First successful commercial 35mm camera. h, Scopes "Monkey Trial." i, Charles Lindbergh makes first solo transatlantic flight. j, George Lemaitre develops "Big Bang" theory of cosmology. k, Chiang Kai-shek becomes generalissimo of China. l, Werner Heisenberg states "uncertainty principle" of physics. m, Alexander Fleming isolates Penicillium mold. n, Hirohito enthroned as Japanese emperor. o, Stock market crash starts Great Depression. p, First round-the-world flight (60x40mm). q, "All Quiet on the Western Front" published.

2000, Mar. 13   Perf. 12¾x12½
Sheet of 17
377 A127 20c #a.-q. + label   7.00 7.00

Inscriptions are incorrect or misspelled on Nos. 377a, 377f and 377m.

Millennium Type of 1999 with "Millennium 2000" Inscription
Perf. 13¼x13½
2000, Mar. 13   Litho.
378 A127 33c Like #356o   .65 .65

Peacemakers — A135

a, Mikhail Gorbachev. b, Ending the Cold War. c, Ronald Reagan. d, Le Duc Tho. e, Resolving the conflict in Viet Nam. f, Henry Kissinger. g, Linus Pauling. h, Protest against nuclear weapons. i, Peter Benenson. j, Amnesty Intl. k, Mahatma Gandhi. l, Fasting for peace. m, Initiating the Peace Corps. n, John F. Kennedy. o, Praying for peace. p, The 14th Dalai Lama. q, The UN. r, Cordell Hull. s, F. W. De Klerk. t, Ending apartheid. u, Nelson Mandela. v, Franklin Roosevelt. w, Yalta Conference. x, Winston Churchill.
Illustration reduced.

2000, Mar. 28   Perf. 14
379 A135 33c Sheet of 24, #a-x   16.00 16.00

Philanthropists — A136

a, Andrew Carnegie. b, John D. Rockefeller. c, Henry Ford. d, Madam C. J. Walker. e, James B. Duke. f, Andrew Mellon. g, Charles F. Kettering. h, Robert W. Woodruff. i, Brooke Astor. j, Howard Hughes. k, Jesse H. Jones. l, Paul Mellon. m, J. Paul Getty. n, George Soros. o, Phyllis Wattis. p, Ted Turner.

2000, May 1   Perf. 14¼x14½
380 A136 33c Sheet of 16, #a-p   11.00 11.00

Mushrooms — A137

No. 381, each 33c: a, Fairies' bonnets. b, Black bulgar. c, Amethyst deceiver. d, Common morel. e, Bird's nest fungus. f, Trumpet clitocybe.
No. 382, each 33c: a, Bonnet mycena. b, Horse mushroom. c, Velvet boletus. d, Oyster. d, Aztec mandala. e, Fly agaric.
Each $2: No. 383, Magpie ink cap. No, 384, Brown birch bolete.

2000, May 15   Perf. 13¾x14¼
Sheets of 6, #a-f
381-382 A137 Set of 2   8.00 8.00
Souvenir Sheets
383-384 A137 Set of 2   8.00 8.00

Flowers of the Pacific A138

Wildflowers — A139

No. 385: a, Freycinetia arborea. b, Mount Cook lily. c, Sun orchid. d, Bossiaea ensata. e, Swamp hibiscus. f, Gardenia brighamii.
No. 386: a, Eleagant brodiaea. b, Skyrocket. c, Hedge bindweed. d, Woods' rose. e, Swamp rose. f, Wake robin.
No. 387, Black-eyed Susan. No. 388, Yellow meadow lily.

2000, May 29   Perf. 14x13¾
385 A138 33c Sheet of 6, #a-f   4.00 4.00
386 A139 33c Sheet of 6, #a-f   4.00 4.00
Souvenir Sheets
387 A138 $2 multi   4.00 4.00
388 A139 $2 multi   4.00 4.00

Souvenir Sheet

2000 Summer Olympics, Sydney — A140

No. 389: a, Henry Taylor. b, Cycling. c, Olympic Stadium, Munich and German flag. d, Ancient Greek wrestling.

2000, July 10   Litho.   Perf. 14
389 A140 33c Sheet of 4, #a-d   2.75 2.75

Zeppelins and Airships — A141

No. 390: a, Zodiac Capitaine Ferber. b, Astra Adjutant Reau. c, Italian dirigible IA. d, Astra-Torres XIV. e, Schuttle-Lanz SL3. f, Siemens-Schukert.
Each $2: No. 391, Graf Zeppelin. No. 392, Dupuy de Lome airship.

2000, Aug. 7   Litho.   Perf. 14
390 A141 33c Sheet of 6, #a-f   4.00 4.00
Souvenir Sheets
391-392 A141 Set of 2   8.00 8.00

First Zeppelin flight, cent. (Nos. 390, 391).

Flower Photomosaic Type of 1999

Various flowers making up a photomosaic of the Queen Mother.

2000, Sept. 5   Litho.   Perf. 13¾
393 A126 33c Sheet of 8, #a-h   5.25 5.25

Souvenir Sheet

2000 Summer Olympics, Sydney — A142

No. 394: a, 33c, Weight lifting. b, 33c, Basketball. c, $1, Weight lifting.

2000, Sept. 11   Perf. 14
394 A142 Sheet of 3, #a-c   3.50 3.50

Olymphilex 2000, Sydney.

Fish — A143

Designs: No. 395, Rock beauty. No. 396, Bluestreak cleaner wrasse. No. 397, Chevroned butterflyfish (with frame). No. 398, Longfin bannerfish (with frame).
No. 399: a, Mandarinfish. b, Emperor snapper. c, Copper-banded butterflyfish. d, Chevroned butterflyfish (no frame). e, Lemonpeel angelfish. f, Harlequin tuskfish. g, Clown triggerfish. h, Coral hind. i, Longfin bannerfish (no frame).
No. 400: a, Six-spot grouper. b, Common jellyfish. c, Palette surgeonfish. d, Bicolor angelfish. e, Threadfin butterflyfish. f, Clown anemonefish. g, Three-banded demoiselle. h, Reef shark. i, Starfish.
No. 401, Long-nosed butterflyfish. No. 402, Emperor angelfish.

2000, Nov. 1
395-398 A143 33c Set of 4   2.60 2.60
Sheets of 9, #a-i
399-400 A143 33c Set of 2   12.00 12.00
Souvenir Sheets
401-402 A143 $2 Set of 2   8.00 8.00

Flower Photomosaic Type of 1999

Various photos with religious themes making up a photomosaic of Pope John Paul II.

2000, Nov. 1   Litho.   Perf. 13¾x14
403 A126 50c Sheet of 8, #a-h   8.00 8.00

Christmas — A144

Designs: 20c, The Holy Trinity, by Titian. 33c, The Adoration of the Magi, by Diego Velazquez. 60c, The Holy Nereus, by Peter Paul Rubens. $3.20, St. Gregory With Saints Around Him, by Rubens.

2000, Dec. 1   Perf. 14¼
404-407 A144 Set of 4   8.75 8.75

Dogs and Cats A145

No. 408, 33c: a, Afghan hound. b, Yellow Labrador retriever. c, Greyhound. d, German shepherd. e, King Charles spaniel. f, Jack Russell terrier.
No. 409, 33c: a, Siamese. b, Mackerel tabby. c, British shorthair. d, Persian. e, Turkish angora. f, Calico.
No. 410, $2, Dog in field. No. 411, $2, Cat stalking bird.

2000, June 26   Litho.   Perf. 14
Sheets of 6, #a-f
408-409 A145 Set of 2   8.00 8.00
Souvenir Sheets
410-411 A145 Set of 2   8.00 8.00

Souvenir Sheets

New Year 2001 (Year of the Snake) A146

Designs: No. 412, 60c, Snake on ground. No. 413, 60c, Snake in bamboo, vert.

2001, Jan. 2
412-413 A146 Set of 2   2.40 2.40

MICRONESIA

Pokémon — A147

No. 414: a, Weepinbell. b, Snorlax. c, Seel. d, Hitmonchan. e, Jynx. f, Ponyta.

2001, Feb. 13 — Perf. 13¾
414 A147 50c Sheet of 6, #a-f   6.00 6.00
Souvenir Sheet
415 A147 $2 Farfetch'd   4.00 4.00

Whales — A148

No. 416, 50c: a, Fin. b, Right. c, Pygmy right. d, Humpback. e, Blue. f, Bowhead.
No. 417, 60c: a, True's beaked. b, Cuvier's beaked. c, Shepherd's beaked. d, Baird's beaked. e, Northern bottlenose. f, Pygmy sperm.
No. 418, $2, Killer. No. 419, $2, Sperm.

2001, Feb. 27 — Perf. 13¼x13¾
Sheets of 6, #a-f
416-417 A148 Set of 2   13.50 13.50
Souvenir Sheets
418-419 A148 Set of 2   8.00 8.00

Ecology — A149

No. 420: a, Coral reef in peril. b, Galapagos Islands tortoise. c, Tasmanian tiger. d, Yanomani. e, Bird from Florida Keys. f, Eagle, Endangered species act.
No. 421: a, Pollution. b, Deforestation. c, Acid rain. d, Greenhouse effect.
No. 422, $2, Bird in flight. No. 423, Chimpanzee, vert.

Perf. 13¼x13¾, 13¾x13¼
2001, Feb. 27 — Litho.
420 A149 34c Sheet of 6, #a-f   4.25 4.25
421 A149 60c Sheet of 4, #a-d   5.00 5.00
Souvenir Sheets
422-423 A149 $2 Set of 2   8.00 8.00

Fish Type of 1998

Designs: 11c, Yellow damselfish. 34c, Rainbow runner. 70c, Whitelined grouper. 80c, Purple queen anthias. $3.50, Eibl's angelfish. $12.25, Blue-spotted boxfish.

2001, Mar. 28 — Perf. 11½x14¾
424 A116 11c multi   .25 .25
425 A116 34c multi   .70 .70
426 A116 70c multi   1.40 1.40
427 A116 80c multi   1.60 1.60
428 A116 $3.50 multi   7.00 7.00
429 A116 $12.25 multi   25.00 25.00
Nos. 424-429 (6)   35.95 35.95

Japanese Art — A150

Designs: No. 430, 34c, Parody of the Allegory of the Sage Chin Kao Riding a Carp, by Suzuki Harunobu. No. 431, 34c, The Courtesan Hinazuru of the Choji-Ya, by Chokosai Eisho. No. 432, 34c, Girl Tying Her Hair Ribbon, by Torii Kiyomine. No. 433, 34c, The Iris Garden, by Kiyonaga Torii. No. 434, 34c, The Courtesan Mayuzumi of the Daimonji-Ya, by Shunsho Katsukawa. No. 435, 34c, Bath House Scene, by Toyokuni Utagawa.
No. 436 — Paintings by Utamaro: a, Dance of a Kamisha. b, The Courtesan Hinazura at the Keizetsuro. c, Toilet Scene. d, Applying Lip Rouge. e, Beauty Reading a Letter. f, The Geisha Kamekichi.
No. 437, $2, Allegory of Ariwara No Narihira, by Kikugawa Eizan, horiz. No. 438, $2, Girl Seated by a Brook, by Harunobu, horiz.

2001, Apr. 20 — Perf. 14
430-435 A150 Set of 6   4.25 4.25
436 A150 34c Sheet of 6, #a-f   4.25 4.25
Imperf
Size: 118x88mm
437-438 A150 Set of 2   8.00 8.00
Phila Nippon '01, Japan (Nos. 436-438).

Toulouse-Lautrec Paintings — A151

No. 439. a, Oscar Wilde. b, Doctor Tapie in a Theater Corridor. c, Monsieur Delaporte. $2, The Clowness Cha-U-Kao.

2001, May 15 — Perf. 13¾
439 A151 60c Sheet of 3, #a-c   3.75 3.75
Souvenir Sheet
440 A151 $2 multi   4.00 4.00

Queen Victoria (1819-1901) — A152

Various portraits.

2001, May 15 — Perf. 14
441 A152 60c Sheet of 6, #a-f   7.25 7.25
Souvenir Sheet
Perf. 13¼
442 A152 $2 shown   4.00 4.00
No. 441 contains six 28x42mm stamps.

Queen Elizabeth II, 75th Birthday — A153

No. 443: a, With necklace and brooch. b, Color photograph. c, As girl. d, As child. e, With dog. f, Facing left.
$2, Portrait in color.

2001, May 15 — Perf. 14
443 A153 60c Sheet of 6, #a-f   7.25 7.25
Souvenir Sheet
444 A153 $2 multi   4.00 4.00

Marine Life — A154

No. 445, 60c, horiz.: a, Striped dolphin. b, Olive Ridley turtle. c, Goldrim tang. d, Blue shark. e, Picasso triggerfish. f, Polkadot grouper.
No. 446, 60c, horiz.: a, Loggerhead turtle. b, Striped marlin. c, Bicolor cherub. d, Clown wrasse. e, Clown triggerfish. f, Japanese tang.
No. 447, $2, Adult and juvenile emperor angelfish. No. 448, $2, Harlequin tuskfish, horiz.

2001, July 16 — Perf. 14
Sheets of 6, #a-f
445-446 A154 Set of 2   14.50 14.50
Souvenir Sheets
Perf. 13¼
447-448 A154 Set of 2   8.00 8.00
Nos. 445-446 each contain six 42x28mm stamps.

Prehistoric Animals — A155

Designs: No. 449, 60c, Allosaurus (with frame). No. 450, 60c, Psittacosaurus. No. 451, 60c, Triceratops. No. 452, 60c, Archaeopteryx (with frame).
No. 453, 60c: a, Tyrannosaurus. b, Pteranodon. c, Brachiosaurus. d, Spinosaurus. e, Deinonychus. f, Teratosaurus.
No. 454, 60c: a, Parasaurolophus. b, Plateosaurus. c, Archaeopteryx (no frame). d, Allosaurus (no frame). e, Torosaurus. f, Euoplocephalus.
No. 455, $2, Tyrannosaurus. No. 456, $2, Parasaurolophus, horiz.

2001, Aug. 12 — Litho. Perf. 14
449-452 A155 Set of 4   4.75 4.75
Sheets of 6, #a-f
453-454 A155 Set of 2   14.50 14.50
Souvenir Sheets
455-456 A155 Set of 2   8.00 8.00

Shells — A156

No. 457, 50c: a, Bat volute. b, Horned helmet. c, Troschel's murex. d, Lotorium triton. e, Orange-mouthed olive. f, Phos whelk.
No. 458, 50c, vert.: a, Oblique nutmeg. b, Imperial volute. c, Pontifical miter. d, Eburneus cone. e, Variegated sundial. f, Heart cockle.
No. 459, $2, Eyed auger. No. 460, $2, Geography cone.

2001, Oct. 15 — Litho. Perf. 14
Sheets of 6, #a-f
457-458 A156   Set of 2   12.00 12.00
Souvenir Sheets
459-460 A156   Set of 2   8.00 8.00
On Nos. 485a-458f, the descriptions of the shells are transposed. Our descriptions are those of the stamps as they are printed.

Birds — A157

Designs: 5c, Malleefowl. 22c, Corncrake. 23c, Hooded merganser. $2.10, Purple gallinule.
No. 465, 60c: a, Fairy wren. b, Golden-crowned kinglet warbler. c, Flame-tempered babbler. d, Golden-headed cisticola. e, White-browed babbler. f, White-breasted dipper.
No. 466, 60c: a, Logrunner. b, Eurasian treecreeper. c, Goldfinch. d, Rufous fantail. e, Orange-billed flowerpecker. f, American goldfinch.
No. 467, $2, Emperor bird of paradise. No. 468, $2, Yellow-eyed cuckooshrike, vert.

2001, Oct. 29 — Litho. Perf. 14
461-464 A157   Set of 4   5.25 5.25
Sheets of 6, #a-f
465-466 A157   Set of 2   14.50 14.50
Souvenir Sheets
467-468 A157   Set of 2   8.00 8.00

Nobel Prizes, Cent. — A158

No. 469, 60c — Physiology or Medicine laureates: a, Alexis Carrel, 1912. b, Max Theiler, 1951. c, Niels Finsen, 1903. d, Philip S. Hench, 1950. e, Sune Bergström, 1982. f, John R. Vane, 1982.
No. 470, 60c — Laureates: a, Bengt Samuelsson, Physiology or Medicine, 1982. b, Johannes Fibiger, Physiology or Medicine, 1926. c, Theodore Richards, Chemistry, 1914. d, Tadeus Reichstein, Physiology or Medicine, 1950. e, Frederick Soddy, Chemistry, 1921. f, Albert Szent-Györgyi, 1937.
No. 471, $2, Irving Langmuir, Chemistry, 1932. No. 472, $2, Artturi Ilmari Virtanen, Chemistry, 1945.

Sheets of 6, #a-f
469-470 A158   Set of 2   14.50 14.50
Souvenir Sheets
471-472 A158   Set of 2   8.00 8.00

Christmas — A159

Santa Claus: 22c, On cat. 34c, Between Christmas trees. 60c, In sleigh. $1, On dog. $2, Entering chimney, vert.

2001, Dec. 5
473-476 A159   Set of 4   4.50 4.50
Souvenir Sheet
477 A159 $2 multi   4.00 4.00

MICRONESIA

Attack on Pearl Harbor, 60th Anniv. A160

No. 478, 60c: a, Rollover of USS Oklahoma. b, Japanese attack Wheeler Air Field. c, Japanese sailors loading bombs onto planes. d, Destroyer USS Ward sinks a Japanese submarine. e, USS Arizona sunk by Japanese bombs. f, Ewa Marine Base attacked by Japanese.

No. 479, 60c: a, Memorial poster showing attack. b, Japanese Prime Minister Hideki Tojo. c, Rescue at Bellows Field. d, Rescue of USS Arizona crew. e, Admiral Isoroku Yamamoto. f, Memorial poster showing soldier and flag.

No. 480, $2, USS Arizona Memorial. No. 481, $2, Pres. Franklin D. Roosevelt.

2001, Dec. 7		Sheets of 6, #a-f		
478-479	A160	Set of 2	14.50	14.50
Souvenir Sheets				
480-481	A160	Set of 2	8.00	8.00

Souvenir Sheet

New Year 2002 (Year of the Horse) A161

Various horses.

2002, Jan. 24			Perf. 13¾x13¼	
482	A161	60c Sheet of 5, #a-e	6.00	6.00

Reign of Queen Elizabeth II, 50th Anniv. A162

No. 483: a, Queen wearing flowered dress. b, Prince Philip. c, Queen waving, holding flowers. d, Queen with children.
$2, Queen wearing scarf.

2002, Feb. 6			Perf. 14¼	
483	A162	80c Sheet of 4, #a-d	6.50	6.50
Souvenir Sheet				
484	A162	$2 multi	4.00	4.00

United We Stand — A163

2002, Feb. 20		Perf. 13¾x13¼	
485	A163	$1 multi	2.00 2.00

Issued in sheets of 4.

2002 Winter Olympics, Salt Lake City — A164

Designs: No. 486, $1, Luge. No. 487, $1, Ice hockey.

2002, Mar. 18			Perf. 14	
486-487	A164	Set of 2	4.00	4.00
487a		Souvenir sheet, #486-487	4.00	4.00

Compare with Nos. 502-503.

Japanese Art — A165

Birds and Flowers of the Twelve Months, by Hoitsu Sakai — No. 488, 60c: a, January. b, February. c, March. d, April. e, May. f, June.
No. 489, 60c: a, July. b, August. c, September. d, October. e, November. f, December.
No. 490, $2, Seashells and Plums by Kiitsu Suzuki. No. 491, Peacock and Peonies, by Rosetsu Nagasawa.

2002, Mar. 25		Litho.	Perf. 14x14¾	
		Sheets of 6, #a-f		
488-489	A165	Set of 2	14.50	14.50
		Imperf		
490-491	A165	Set of 2	8.00	8.00

Nos. 488-489 each contain six 77x26mm stamps.

Intl. Year of Mountains — A166

No. 492: a, Matterhorn, Switzerland. b, Maroonbells, U.S. c, Wetterhorn, Switzerland. d, Mt. Tsaranora, Africa.
$2, Cerro Fitzroy, South America.

2002, Mar. 30			Perf. 14	
492	A166	80c Sheet of 4, #a-d	6.50	6.50
Souvenir Sheet				
493	A166	$2 multi	4.00	4.00

Pres. John F. Kennedy (1917-63) — A167

No. 494: a, Dark blue background. b, Lilac background, name at left. c, Tan background, name at right. d, Light blue background.
$2, Purple background.

2002, Mar. 30				
494	A167	60c Sheet of 4, #a-d	5.00	5.00
Souvenir Sheet				
495	A167	$2 multi	4.00	4.00

Princess Diana (1961-97) — A168

No. 496: a, Wearing wedding veil. b, Wearing tiara and necklace. c, Wearing brimless hat. d, Wearing scarf. e, Hatless. f, Wearing tiara and large collar.
$2, Wearing hat with brim.

2002, Mar. 30				
496	A168	60c Sheet of 6, #a-f	7.25	7.25
Souvenir Sheet				
497	A168	$2 multi	4.00	4.00

Intl. Year of Ecotourism — A169

No. 498: a, Lizard. b, Canoes. c, Micronesian house. d, Three children in costume. e, Woman. f, Two dancers, house.
$2, Fishermen.

		Perf. 13¼x13½		
2002, June 17		Litho.		
498	A169	80c Sheet of 6, #a-f	9.75	9.75
Souvenir Sheet				
499	A169	$2 multi	4.00	4.00

20th World Scout Jamboree, Thailand — A170

No. 500: a, Thai temple. b, American scout insignia. c, Scout cap.
$2, Merit badges.

2002, June 17			Perf. 13½x13¼	
500	A170	$1 Sheet of 3, #a-c	6.00	6.00
Souvenir Sheet				
501	A170	$2 multi	4.00	4.00

Winter Olympics Type of 2002 Redrawn With White Panel Behind Olympic Rings

Designs: No. 502, $1, Luge. No. 503, $1, Ice hockey.

2002, July 15				
502-503	A164	Set of 2	4.00	4.00
503a		Souvenir sheet, #502-503	4.00	4.00

Xavier High School, 50th Anniv. — A171

2002, July 31		Perf. 13½x13¾	
504	A171	37c multi	.75 .75

Queen Mother Elizabeth (1900-2002) — A172

No. 505, horiz.: a, At age 7. b, At wedding. c, At birth of Princess Elizabeth. d, At coronation of King George VI, 1937.
$2, As elderly lady.

2002, Aug. 12			Perf. 14	
505	A172	80c Sheet of 4, #a-d	6.50	6.50
Souvenir Sheet				
506	A172	$2 multi	4.00	4.00

Teddy Bears, Cent. A173

No. 507: a, Burglar bear. b, White bear with heart. c, Blue bear with flowers. d, Brown bear with heart.

2002, Sept. 23		Litho.	Perf. 14	
507	A173	80c Sheet of 4, #a-d	6.50	6.50

Elvis Presley (1935-77) — A174

Presley with: a, Hand below guitar. b, Head on guitar. c, Hat. d, Checked shirt, no hat. e, Arms raised. f, Microphone.

2002, Oct. 7			Perf. 13¾	
508	A174	37c Sheet of 6, #a-f	4.50	4.50

Christmas A175

Paintings: 21c, Madonna and Child, by Filippino Lippi, vert. 37c, Madonna and Child, by Giovanni Bellini, vert. 70c, Madonna and Child Between St. Stephen and St. Ladislaus, by Simone Martini. 80c, Holy Family, by Bronzino, vert. No. 513, $2, Holy Family, by Martini, vert.
No. 514, Sacred Conversation, by Bellini, vert.

2002, Nov. 4			Perf. 14	
509-513	A175	Set of 5	8.25	8.25
Souvenir Sheet				
		Perf. 14x14¼		
514	A175	$2 multi	4.00	4.00

MICRONESIA

Flora, Fauna and Mushrooms — A176

No. 515, 37c — Moths: a, White-lined sphinx. b, Tropical fruit-piercer. c, Coppery dysphania. d, Large agarista. e, Indian moon moth. f, Croker's frother.
No. 516, 55c — Mushrooms: a, Phellinus robustus. b, Purple coincap. c, Shaggy parasol. d, King bolete. e, Boletus crocipodius. f, Sharp-scaled parasol.
No. 517, 60c — Orchids: a, Eria javanica. b, Cymbidium finlaysonianum. c, Coelogyne asperata. d, Spathoglottis affinis. e, Vanda tricolor. f, Calanthe rosea.
No. 518, 60c — Butterflies: a, Meadow argus. b, Cairns birdwing. c, Large green-banded blue. d, Beak butterfly. e, Palmfly. f, Broad-bordered grass yellow.
No. 519, 80c — Insects and spiders: a, Stag beetle. b, Honeybee. c, Black widow spider. d, Mosquito. e, Black ant. f, Cicada.
No. 520, $2, Zodiac moth. No. 521, $2, Lepiota acutesquamosa mushroom. No. 522, $2, Dendrobium phalaenopsis orchid. No. 523, $2, Yamfly butterfly. No. 524, $2, Dragonfly, horiz.

2002, Dec. 16   *Perf. 14*
Sheets of 6, #a-f
515-519 A176   Set of 5   35.00 35.00
Souvenir Sheets
520-524 A176   Set of 5   20.00 20.00

Birds — A177

Designs: 3c, Greater flame-backed woodpecker. 5c, Red-tailed tropicbird. 21c, Hair-crested drongo. 22c, Pale white-eye. 23c, White-backed munia. 37c, Yap monarch. 60c, Eclectus parrot. 70c, Sulphur-crested cockatoo. 80c, Giant white-eye. $2, Green magpie. $3.85, Dollarbird. $5, Great frigatebird. $13.65, Micronesian pigeon.

2002, Dec. 30   *Perf. 14¼x14*
525 A177 3c multi .25 .25
526 A177 5c multi .25 .25
527 A177 21c multi .40 .40
528 A177 22c multi .45 .45
529 A177 23c multi .45 .45
530 A177 37c multi .75 .75
531 A177 60c multi 1.25 1.25
532 A177 70c multi 1.40 1.40
533 A177 80c multi 1.60 1.60
534 A177 $2 multi 4.00 4.00

Perf. 13¾
535 A177 $3.85 multi 7.75 7.75
536 A177 $5 multi 10.00 10.00
537 A177 $13.65 multi 27.50 27.50
   Nos. 525-537 (13)   56.05 56.05

First Non-stop Solo Transatlantic Flight, 75th Anniv. (in 2002) — A178

No. 538: a, Charles Lindbergh, Donald Hall, Spirit of St. Louis. b, Spirit of St. Louis, Apr. 28, 1927. c, Towing of Spirit of St. Louis, May 20. d, Lindbergh taking off from Roosevelt Field, May 20. e, Lindbergh's arrival in Paris, May 21. f, Lindbergh in ticker tape parade, New York.

2003, Jan. 13   *Litho.*   *Perf. 14*
538 A178 60c Sheet of 6, #a-f   7.25 7.25

New Year 2003 (Year of the Ram) A179

No. 539: a, Black ram facing left, country name at left. b, Black ram facing left, country name at right. c, White ram facing right, country name at left. d, White ram facing forward, country name at right.

2003, Feb. 1   *Litho.*   *Perf. 14¼x14*
539 A179 37c Sheet of 6, #a-b, 2 each #c-d   4.50 4.50

Astronauts Killed in Space Shuttle Columbia Accident — A180

No. 540: a, Mission Specialist 1 David M. Brown. b, Commander Rick D. Husband. c, Mission Specialist 2 Laurel Blair Salton Clark. d, Mission Specialist 4 Kalpana Chawla. e, Payload Commander Michael P. Anderson. f, Pilot William C. McCool. g, Payload Specialist Ilan Ramon.

2003, Apr. 7   *Perf. 13½x13¼*
540 A180 37c Sheet of 7, #a-g   5.25 5.25

Coronation of Queen Elizabeth II, 50th Anniv. — A181

No. 541: a, Wearing pearl necklace. b, Wearing sash and tiara. c, Wearing robe. $2, Wearing crown.

2003, May 13   *Perf. 14x14¼*
541 A181 $1 Sheet of 3, #a-c   6.00 6.00
Souvenir Sheet
542 A181 $2 multi   4.00 4.00

Prince William, 21st Birthday A182

No. 543: a, Wearing checked shirt and striped sweater. b, Facing right, wearing sweater, shirt and tie. c, Wearing suit and tie. $2, Wearing raincoat.

2003, May 14
543 A182 $1 Sheet of 3, #a-c   6.00 6.00
Souvenir Sheet
544 A182 $2 multi   4.00 4.00

Operation Iraqi Freedom — A183

No. 545, 37c: a, B-52 Bomber. b, F-16 Fighter. c, Cobra Helicopter. d, Apache Helicopter. e, T8000 Tow Missile. f, Bradley Tank.
No. 546, 37c: a, Stealth Fighter. b, AC-130 Cargo plane. c, MH-53j Pave Low II Helicopter. d, Predator. e, Challenger Two Tank. f, Aegis Cruiser.

2003, May 14   *Perf. 14*
Sheets of 6, #a-f
545-546 A183   Set of 2   9.00 9.00

Tour de France Bicycle Race, Cent. A184

No. 547: a, Greg LeMond, 1990. b, Miguel Indurain, 1991. c, Indurain, 1992. d, Indurain, 1993.
$2, Marco Pantani, 1998.

2003, July 1   *Perf. 13½*
547 A184 60c Sheet of 4, #a-d   5.00 5.00
Souvenir Sheet
548 A184 $2 multi   4.00 4.00

Intl. Year of Fresh Water A185

No. 549: a, Kosrae mangroves. b, Chuuk Lagoon. c, Pohnpei's waterfalls.
$2, Pohnpei Lagoon.

2003, July 21   *Perf. 13½*
549 A185 $1 Sheet of 3, #a-c   6.00 6.00
Souvenir Sheet
550 A185 $2 multi   4.00 4.00

Powered Flight, Cent. A186

No. 551: a, Mach 2 Concorde. b, Boeing 757. c, Junkers F13a. d, Martin M-130 China Clipper. e, Handley Page H.P.42W. f, Wright Flyer II.
$2, Boeing 747.

2003, Aug. 7   *Perf. 14*
551 A186 55c Sheet of 6, #a-f   6.75 6.75
Souvenir Sheet
552 A186 $2 multi   4.00 4.00
2003 APS Stampshow, Columbus, Ohio (No. 551).

Circus Performers — A187

No. 553, 80c: Clowns — a, Glen Little. b, Joseph Grimaldi. c, Beverly Rebo Bergeron. d, Coco Michael Polakov.
No. 554, 80c: a, Jana Mandana. b, Maxim Papazov. c, Harry Keaton. d, Giraffe.

2003, Aug. 25   *Perf. 14*
Sheets of 4, #a-d
553-554 A187   Set of 2   13.00 13.00

Paintings of Boy Scouts by Norman Rockwell (1894-1978) — A188

No. 555: a, Scout with plaid neckerchief, from 1963 Boy Scout Calendar. b, A Scout is Helpful. c, The Scoutmaster. d, Scout with red neckerchief, from 1963 Boy Scout Calendar.
$2, No Swimming.

2003, Sept. 8   *Perf. 14*
555 A188 80c Sheet of 4, #a-d   6.50 6.50
Imperf
556 A188 $2 multi   4.00 4.00
No. 555 contains four 28x42mm stamps.

Paintings by Paul Gauguin (1848-1903) — A189

No. 557: a, Vahine No Te Tiare. b, Les Amants. c, Trois Tahitiens Conversation. d, Arearea.
$2, Ta Matete.

2003, Sept. 8   *Perf. 13¾*
557 A189 80c Sheet of 4, #a-d   6.50 6.50
Imperf
558 A189 $2 multi   4.00 4.00
No. 557 contains four 51x38mm stamps.

Paintings of James McNeill Whistler (1834-1903) — A190

MICRONESIA

Designs: 37c, Blue and Silver Blue: Wave, Biarritz. 55c, Brown and Silver: Old Battersea Bridge. 60c, Nocturne in Blue and Silver: The Lagoon, Venice. 80c, Crepuscule in Flesh Color and Green: Valparaiso.
No. 563: a, Symphony in White No. 2: The Little White Girl, vert. b, At the Piano (75x50mm). c, Symphony in White No. 1: The White Girl, vert.
$2, Portrait of Thomas Carlyle: Arrangement in Gray and Black No. 2, vert.

2003, Oct. 6   **Perf. 14¼**
559-562 A190   Set of 4   4.75 4.75
563 A190 $1 Sheet of 3, #a-c   6.00 6.00

Size: 83x104mm
Imperf
564 A190 $2 multi   4.00 4.00

Christmas — A191

Designs: 37c, Madonna of the Carnation, by Leonardo da Vinci. 60c, Madonna with Yarn Winder, by da Vinci. 80c, Litta Madonna, by da Vinci. $1, Madonna of the Grand Duke, by Raphael.
$2, The Adoration of the Magi, by Giambattista Tiepolo.

2003, Nov. 5   **Perf. 14¼**
565-568 A191   Set of 4   5.75 5.75

Souvenir Sheet
569 A191 $2 multi   4.00 4.00

Cats, Dogs, Birds, Reptiles & Amphibians — A192

No. 570, 80c — Cats: a, Ragdoll. b, Calico Shorthaired Japanese Bobtail. c, Blue Mackerel Taffy Exotic Shorthair. d, Dilute Calico.
No. 571, 80c — Dogs: a, Australian shepherd. b, Greyhound. c, English bulldog. d, Schnauzer.
No. 572, 80c, horiz. — Birds: a, Greenwinged macaw. b, American flamingo. c, Blue and gold macaw. d, Abyssinian ground hornbill.
No. 573, 80c, horiz. — Reptiles and amphibians: a, Leopard gecko. b, Red-eyed tree frog. c, Panther chameleon. d, Green and black poison frog.
No. 574, 80c, Lynx Point Colorpoint Shorthair. No. 575, $2, Toy poodle. No. 576, $2, American flamingo. No. 577, $2, Madagascan chameleon, horiz.

2003, Dec. 22   **Perf. 14**
Sheets of 4, #a-d
570-573 A192   Set of 4   26.00 26.00

Souvenir Sheets
574-577 A192   Set of 4   16.00 16.00

Pres. Bailey Olter (1932-99) — A193

2004, Feb. 16   **Litho.**   **Perf. 14**
578 A193 37c multi   .75 .75

Paintings by Pablo Picasso (1881-1973) — A194

No. 579: a, Marie-Thérèse Leaning on One Elbow. b, Portrait of Jaime Sabartés. c, Portrait of Emilie Marguerite Walter (Mémé). d, Bust of a Woman Leaning on One Elbow.
$2, Seated Bather (Olga).

2004, Mar. 8   **Perf. 14¼**
579 A194 80c Sheet of 4, #a-d   6.50 6.50

Imperf
580 A194 $2 multi   4.00 4.00
No. 579 contains four 37x50mm stamps.

Paintings in the Hermitage, St. Petersburg, Russia — A195

Designs: 22c, A Young Lady in a Theatrical Costume, by Alexis Grimou. 37c, Portrait of Mrs. Harriet Greer, by George Romney. 80c, Portrait of Prince Nikolai Yusupov, by Friedrich Heinrich Füger. $1, Portrait of Richard Brinsley Sheridan, by John Hoppner.
$2, Spanish Concert (Conversation Espagnole), by Carle Vanloo.

2004, Mar. 8   **Perf. 14¼**
581-584 A195   Set of 4   5.00 5.00

Imperf
Size: 64x81mm
585 A195 $2 multi   4.00 4.00

New Year 2004 (Year of the Monkey) — A196

Designs: 50c, Moon-struck Gibbon, by Gao Qi-feng. $1, Detail from Moon-struck Gibbon.

2004, Mar. 9   **Perf. 13¼**
586 A196 50c multi   1.00 1.00

Souvenir Sheet
Perf. 13¼x13
587 A196 $1 multi   2.00 2.00
No. 587 contains one 30x40mm stamp. No. 586 printed in sheets of four.

Election of Pope John Paul II, 25th Anniv. (in 2003) A197

No. 588 — Pope John Paul II: a, Visiting Monaco, 1990. b, With Bill and Hillary Clinton, 1999. c, Visiting Ukraine, 2001. d, Visiting Spain, 2003.

2004, Sept. 1   **Perf. 14¼x14**
588 A197 80c Sheet of 4, #a-d   6.50 6.50

2004 European Soccer Championships, Portugal — A198

No. 589: a, Lars Olsen. b, Juergen Klinsmann. c, Peter Schmeichel. d, Nya Ullevi Stadium.
$2, 1992 Denmark team, horiz.

2004, Sept. 1   **Perf. 14**
589 A198 80c Sheet of 4, #a-d   6.50 6.50

Souvenir Sheet
Perf. 14¼
590 A198 $2 multi   4.00 4.00
No. 589 contains four 28x42mm stamps.

D-Day, 60th Anniv. A199

No. 591: a, Landing craft vehicle personnel. b, Destroyer Thompson. c, LST-391. d, Rhino Ferry 2, Rhino Tug 3. e, HMS Mauritius. f, Battleship Arkansas.
$2, LCI 1539.

2004, Sept. 1   **Perf. 14**
591 A199 50c Sheet of 6, #a-f   6.00 6.00

Souvenir Sheet
592 A199 $2 multi   4.00 4.00

Souvenir Sheet

Deng Xiaoping (1904-97), Chinese Leader — A200

2004, Sept. 1   **Litho.**   **Perf. 14**
593 A200 $2 multi   4.00 4.00

Locomotives, Bicent. — A201

No. 594, 80c: a, CFL N5520. b, Inter-region trains. c, SW-600. d, WSOR 3801.
No. 595, 80c: a, Baldwin 2-8-0. b, F-10 #1114 Diesel. c, BNSF locomotive (incorrectly inscribed "Okinawa Hitachi trains". d, Shinkansen.
No. 596, 80c: a, RS-1 #22. b, Diesel class 630. c, Okinawa Hitachi train. d, Eurostar.
No. 597, $2, Eurostar, diff. No. 598, $2, Locomotive 231-065. No. 599, $2, Michigan Central locomotive.

2004, Sept. 1   **Sheets of 4, #a-d**
594-596 A201   Set of 3   19.50 19.50

Souvenir Sheets
597-599 A201   Set of 3   12.00 12.00

Birds Type of 2002

Designs: 2c, Blue-gray gnatcatcher. 10c, Clapper rail.

2004, Nov. 1   **Perf. 13¼**
600 A177 2c multi   .25 .25
601 A177 10c multi   .25 .25

Miniature Sheet

Intl. Year of Peace A202

No. 602: a, Nelson Mandela. b, Dalai Lama. c, Pope John Paul II.

2004, Nov. 1   **Perf. 14**
602 A202 80c Sheet of 3, #a-c   5.00 5.00

2004 Summer Olympics, Athens A203

Designs: 37c, Ancient bronze sculpture of horse and rider. 55c, Pin from 1912 Stockholm Olympics, vert. 80c, Baron Pierre de Coubertin, Intl. Olympic Committee President, vert. $1, Poster from 1968 Mexico City Olympics, vert.

2004, Nov. 1   **Perf. 14¼**
603-606 A203   Set of 4   5.50 5.50

Miniature Sheets

Elvis Presley's First Recording, 50th Anniv. — A204

No. 607, 80c — Presley with: a, Beard. b, Boxing gloves. c, Kaffiyeh. d, Cowboy hat.
No. 608, 80c, vert. — Presley with denomination in: a, Red. b, Purple. c, Blue. d, Orange yellow.

MICRONESIA

2004, Nov. 1   Perf. 14
Sheets of 4, #a-d
607-608   A204   Set of 2   13.00   13.00

Flowers — A205

No. 609, horiz.: a, Epiphytic aeschynanthus. b, Darwinia collina. c, Rhododendron. d, Rhododendron retusum. e, Eucryphia lucida. f, Microporus xanthopus. $2, Grevillea.

2004, Nov. 1   Perf. 13¼x13½
609   A205   55c Sheet of 6, #a-f   6.75   6.75
Souvenir Sheet   Perf. 13½x13¼
610   A205 $2 multi   4.00   4.00

FIFA (Fédération Internationale de Football Association), Cent. — A206

No. 611: a, Herman Crespo. b, Peter Shilton. c, Klaus Augenthaler. d, Bryan Robson. $2, Ruud Gullit.

2004, Nov. 1   Perf. 12¾x12½
611   A206   80c Sheet of 4, #a-d   6.50   6.50
Souvenir Sheet
612   A206 $2 multi   4.00   4.00

National Basketball Association Players — A207

Designs: No. 613, 20c, Dirk Nowitzki, Dallas Mavericks. No. 614, 20c, Vince Carter, Toronto Raptors.

2004   Perf. 14
613-614   A207   Set of 2   .80   .80
Issued: No. 613, 11/2; No. 614, 11/3. Each stamp issued in sheets of 12.

Prehistoric Animals — A208

No. 615, 80c: a, Indricotheres. b, Hyaenodons. c, Deinotherium. d, Chalicotheres.

No. 616, 80c: a, Apatosaurus. b, Pachyrhinosaurus. c, Kentrosaurus. d, Saltasaurus.
No. 617, 80c, vert.: a, Allosaurus. b, Tyrannosaurus. c, Troodon. d, Carnotaurus.
No. 618, $2, Moeritherium. No. 619, $2, Coelophysis. No. 620, $2, Deinonychus.

Perf. 14½x14, 14x14½
2004, Dec. 13   Litho.
Sheets of 4, #a-d
615-617   A208   Set of 3   19.50   19.50
Souvenir Sheets
618-620   A208   Set of 3   12.00   12.00

Fish and Coral — A209

No. 621: a, Clown triggerfish. b, Striped-face unicornfish. c, Firefish. d, Longnose hawkfish. e, Annella mollis. f, Dendronephthya. $2, Great barracuda.

2004, Nov. 1   Litho.   Perf. 13½
621   A209   55c Sheet of 6, #a-f   6.75   6.75
Souvenir Sheet
622   A209 $2 multi   4.00   4.00

Reptiles and Amphibians — A210

No. 623: a, Blue coral snake. b, Solomon Islands horned frog. c, Levuka wrinkled ground frog. d, Flying lizard. e, Platymantis vitensis. f, Pacific ground boa. $2, Loggerhead turtle.

2004, Nov. 1
623   A210   55c Sheet of 6, #a-f   6.75   6.75
Souvenir Sheet
624   A210 $2 multi   4.00   4.00
No. 623c has incorrect inscription as stamp depicts a lizard.

Birds — A211

No. 625, vert.: a, Black-faced woodswallows. b, Brown boobies. c, Rainbow lorikeets. d, Wandering albatross. e, Kagu. f, Great frigatebird. $2, Golden whistler.

2004, Nov. 1
625   A211   55c Sheet of 6, #a-f   6.75   6.75
Souvenir Sheet
626   A211 $2 multi   4.00   4.00

Christmas — A212

Madonna and Child paintings by: 37c, Giovanni Battista Tiepolo. 60c, Raphael. 80c, Jan Gossaert (Mabuse). $1, Fra Filippo Lippi. $2, Unknown artist.

2004, Dec. 27   Perf. 14¼
627-630   A212   Set of 4   5.75   5.75
Souvenir Sheet
631   A212 $2 multi   4.00   4.00

A212a

Designs: No. 631A, FSM-China Friendship Sports Center. No. 631B, Arms of People's Republic of China and Micronesia.

2004, Dec. 29   Litho.   Perf. 13x13¼
631A   A212a   37c multi   —
631B   A212a   37c multi   —
   c.   Horiz. pair, #631A-631B

Diplomatic Relations Between Micronesia and People's Republic of China, 15th Anniv.

New Year 2005 (Year of the Rooster) — A213

2005, Jan. 17   Perf. 12¾
632   A213   50c multi   1.00   1.00
Printed in sheets of 4.

Basketball Players Type of 2004
Design: Luke Walton, Los Angeles Lakers.

2005, Feb. 24   Perf. 14
633   A207   20c multi   .40   .40

Pres. Ronald Reagan (1911-2004) — A214

No. 634: a, With British Prime Minister Margaret Thatcher. b, With Israeli Prime Minister Yitzhak Shamir.

2005, Mar. 21   Perf. 13¼x13½
634   A214   55c Horiz. pair, #a-b   2.25   2.25
Printed in sheets containing 3 each Nos. 634a and 634b.

Elvis Presley (1935-2005) — A215

No. 635, 60c — Photos from: a, 1955. b, 1956. c, 1960 (with arm outstretched). d, 1968. e, 1970. f, 1973.
No. 636, 60c — Photos from: a, 1957. b, 1960 (in army uniform). c, 1963. d, 1965. e, 1967. f, 1969.

2005, Mar. 21   Perf. 13½x13¼
Sheets of 6, #a-f
635-636   A215   Set of 2   14.50   14.50

End of World War II, 60th Anniv. A216

No. 637, 60c: a, U.S. soldiers marching in Ireland. b, British troops cross Volturno River, Italy. c, Hawker Typhoon attacks enemy on the Rhine River. d, Damaged Remagen Bridge. e, Meeting of Russian and American armies near Torgau, Germany.
No. 638, 60c: a, Poster remembering Pearl Harbor. b, Chula Beach, Tinian Island. c, Paul Tibbets and the Enola Gay. d, Hiroshima atomic bomb mushroom cloud. e, Newspaper announcing Japanese surrender.

2005, Mar. 31   Perf. 14
Sheets of 5, #a-e
637-638   A216   Set of 2   12.00   12.00

Friedrich von Schiller (1759-1805), Writer — A217

No. 639: a, Wearing red cape. b, Statue. c, With head on hand.

2005, Mar. 31
639   A217 $1 Sheet of 3, #a-c   6.00   6.00
Souvenir Sheet
640   A217 $2 shown   4.00   4.00

Battle of Trafalgar, Bicent. A218

Various depictions of ships in battle: 37c, 55c, 80c, $1. $2, Death of Admiral Horatio Nelson.

2005, Mar. 31   Perf. 14¼
641-644   A218   Set of 4   5.50   5.50
Souvenir Sheet
645   A218 $2 multi   4.00   4.00

Pope John Paul II (1920-2005) — A219

2005, June 27   Perf. 13½x13¼
646   A219 $1 multi   2.00   2.00
Printed in sheets of 6.

MICRONESIA

Rotary International, Cent. — A220

No. 647, vert.: a, Child. b, Emblem. c, 2004-05 Rotary International President Glenn E. Estess, Sr.
$2, 2002-03 Rotary International President Bhichai Rattakul.

	2005, July 12		Perf. 12¾
647	A220 $1 Sheet of 3, #a-c	6.00	6.00

Souvenir Sheet

648	A220 $2 multi	4.00	4.00

Jules Verne (1828-1905), Writer — A221

No. 649, vert.: a, Around the World in 80 Days. b, Phineas Fogg in India. c, Phineas Fogg, explorer and adventurer.
$2, Nautilus.

	2005, June 7	Litho.	Perf. 12¾
649	A221 $1 Sheet of 3, #a-c	6.00	6.00

Souvenir Sheet

650	A221 $2 multi	4.00	4.00

Souvenir Sheet

Expo 2005, Aichi, Japan A222

No. 651: a, Gray nurse shark. b, Surfer. c, Krakatoa Volcano. d, Yellow coral.

	2005, June 27		Perf. 12x12¼
651	A222 80c Sheet of 4, #a-d	6.50	6.50

Boats A223

No. 652: a, 37c, Papyrus boat. b, 55c, Outrigger canoe. c, 80c, Papyrus sailboat. d, $1, Arab dhow.
$2, Lateen-rigged Nile riverboat.

	2005, June 27		Perf. 12¾
652	A223 Sheet of 4, #a-d	5.50	5.50

Souvenir Sheet

653	A223 $2 multi	4.00	4.00

Kosrae Government Building Complex A224

Views of various buildings with frame colors of: 4c, Light yellow. 10c, Light blue. 22c, Pink. 37c, Light green.

	2005, July 8		Perf. 14
654-657	A224 Set of 4	1.50	1.50

Vatican City No. 67 — A225

	2005, Aug. 9		Perf. 13x13¼
658	A225 37c multi	.75	.75

Pope John Paul II (1920-2005). Printed in sheets of 12.

Worldwide Fund for Nature (WWF) — A226

No. 659: a, Stephanometra echinus. b, Oxycomanthus bennetti. c, Alloeocomatella polycaldia. d, Dichrometra flagellata.

	2005, Aug. 31		Perf. 14
659	A226 50c Block or vert. strip of 4, #a-d	4.00	4.00
e.	Souvenir sheet, 2 each #659a-659d	8.00	8.00

Souvenir Sheet

Albert Einstein (1879-1955), Physicist — A227

No. 660 — Various portraits with "Albert Einstein (1879-1955)" in: a, Orange. b, Blue. c, Red. d, Black.

	2005, Sept. 20		Perf. 12¾
660	A227 $1 Sheet of 4, #a-d	8.00	8.00

Bananas A228

Designs: 4c, Mother feeding banana to child. 10c, Four bananas. 22c, Bunch of bananas. 37c, Banana plant.

	2005, Oct. 14		Perf. 14
661-664	A228 Set of 4	1.50	1.50

Hans Christian Andersen (1805-75), Author — A229

No. 665: a, Bust of Andersen. b, Statue of seated Andersen. c, Bust of Andersen on pedestal.
$2, Statue of standing Andersen.

	2005, Nov. 15		Perf. 12¾
665	A229 80c Sheet of 3, #a-c	5.00	5.00

Souvenir Sheet

666	A229 $2 multi	4.00	4.00

Pope Benedict XVI — A230

	2005, Nov. 21	Litho.	Perf. 13½
667	A230 80c multi	1.60	1.60

Printed in sheets of 4.

Christmas — A231

Painting details: 37c, Kanigani Madonna, by Raphael. 60c, Madonna with the Fish, by Raphael. 80c, The Holy Family, by Bartolomé Esteban Murillo. $1, Madonna with the Book, by Raphael.
$2, The Holy Family, by Murillo, diff.

	2005, Dec. 1	Litho.	Perf. 14
668-671	A231 Set of 4	5.75	5.75

Souvenir Sheet

672	A231 $2 multi	4.00	4.00

Flowers — A232

Designs: 4c, Tecoma stans. 10c, Ipomoea fistulosa. 22c, Hibiscus rosa-sinensis. 37c, Gerbera jamesonii. No. 677, 80c, Helianthus annuus. $1, Ixora casei.
No. 679, 80c: a, Tapeinochilos ananassae. b, Bauhinia monandra. c, Galphimia gracilis. d, Hibiscus rosa-sinensis, diff.
No. 680, $2, Helianthus annuus, diff. No. 681, $2, Phinia variegata.

	2005, Nov. 15	Litho.	Perf. 12
673-678	A232 Set of 6	5.25	5.25
679	A232 80c Sheet of 4, #a-d	6.50	6.50

Souvenir Sheets

680-681	A232 Set of 2	8.00	8.00

New Year 2006 (Year of the Dog) — A233

Paintings by Liu Jiyou: 50c, Wolf Dog. $1, Wolf Dog, horiz.

	2006, Jan. 3		Perf. 13¼
682	A233 50c multi	1.00	1.00

Souvenir Sheet

683	A233 $1 multi	2.00	2.00

No. 683 contains one 48x35mm stamp.
No. 682 was issued in sheets of 4.

Birds — A234

Designs: No. 684, Glaucous-winged gull. No. 685, Slaty-headed parakeet. No. 686, Harlequin duck. No. 687, Purple sunbird. 75c, Plum-headed parakeet. 84c, Yellow-wattled lapwing. $4.05, Eurasian collared dove, horiz.

	2006		Perf. 12
684	A234 24c multi	.50	.50
685	A234 24c multi	.50	.50
686	A234 39c multi	.80	.80
687	A234 39c multi	.80	.80
688	A234 75c multi	1.50	1.50
689	A234 84c multi	1.75	1.75
690	A234 $4.05 multi	8.25	8.25
	Nos. 684-690 (7)	14.10	14.10

Issued: Nos. 684, 686, 2/21; others, 4/20.

Vice-President Petrus Tun (1936-99) — A235

	2006, Mar. 19		Perf. 12¾
691	A235 39c multi	.80	.80

Printed in sheets of 4.

Rembrandt (1606-69), Painter — A236

No. 692: a, Saskia as Flora. b, Young Girl at a Window. c, Girl with a Broom. d, Prodigal Son in the Tavern.
$2, Man in Oriental Costume.

	2006, June 22		Perf. 13¼
692	A236 $1 Sheet of 4, #a-d	8.00	8.00

Imperf

693	A236 $2 multi	4.00	4.00

No. 692 contains four 38x50mm stamps.

Queen Elizabeth II, 80th Birthday A237

No. 694 — Dogs and Queen in: a, Red violet dress. b, Beige dress. c, Purple dress. d, Light blue dress.

MICRONESIA

$2, Green dress.

2006, June 22 — Perf. 14¼
694 A237 84c Sheet of 4, #a-d   6.75 6.75
Souvenir Sheet
695 A237 $2 multi   4.00 4.00

Space Achievements — A238

No. 696 — Various views of Venus Express: a, Text in black. b, Country name in black, denomination in white. c, Country name in white, denomination in black. d, Country name and denomination in white. e, Country name and denomination in red, "Venus Express" at left. f, Country name and denomination in red, "Venus Express" at right.
No. 697, $1, horiz. — Return to space of Space Shuttle Discovery: a, Denomination in white. b, Shuttle arm. c, Shuttle with cargo bay open. d, Shuttle tail.
No. 698, $1, horiz. — Spacecraft for future trips to: a, Moon, black denomination. b, Moon, blue denomination. c, Mars, red denomination. d, Mars, white denomination.
No. 699, $2, Space Shuttle Discovery astronaut space-walking. No. 700, $2, Mars Reconnaissance Orbiter. No. 701, $2, Stardust probe, horiz.

2006, July 11 — Perf. 14¼
696 A238 75c Sheet of 6, #a-f   9.00 9.00
Sheets of 4, #a-d
697-698 A238 Set of 2   16.00 16.00
Souvenir Sheets
699-701 A238 Set of 3   12.00 12.00

Butterflies A239

Designs: 1c, Papilio euchenor. 2c, Golden birdwing. 4c, Delias henningia. 5c, Bassarona duda. 10c, Common bluebottle. 19c, Arhopala cleander. 20c, Arhopala argentea. 22c, Danaus aspasia. 75c, Arhopala aurea. 84c, Caleta mindaurus. $1, Black and white tit. $4.05, Grand imperial. $5, Jamides abdul. $10, Paralaxita lacoon.

2006, Nov. 15 — Perf. 12
702 A239 1c multi   .25 .25
703 A239 2c multi   .25 .25
704 A239 4c multi   .25 .25
705 A239 5c multi   .25 .25
706 A239 10c multi   .25 .25
707 A239 19c multi   .40 .40
708 A239 20c multi   .40 .40
709 A239 22c multi   .45 .45
710 A239 75c multi   1.50 1.50
711 A239 84c multi   1.75 1.75
712 A239 $1 multi   2.00 2.00
713 A239 $4.05 multi   8.25 8.25
714 A239 $5 multi   10.00 10.00
715 A239 $10 multi   20.00 20.00
  Nos. 702-715 (14)   46.00 46.00

Christmas — A240

Designs: 22c, Christmas tree. 24c, Stocking. 39c, Snowman. 75c, Candle. 84c, Ornament.

2006, Dec. 4 — Perf. 13½
716-720 A240 Set of 5   5.00 5.00

Concorde — A241

No. 721, 75c — Concorde's Jubilee Flypast: a, With statue. b, Without statue.
No. 722, 75c — Concorde 001: a, In flight. b, On ground.

Perf. 13¼x13½
2006, Dec. 20 — Litho.
Pairs, #a-b
721-722 A241 Set of 2   6.00 6.00

New Year 2007 (Year of the Pig) — A242

2007, Jan. 3 — Perf. 13¼
723 A242 75c multi   1.50 1.50
  Printed in sheets of 4.

Souvenir Sheet

Wolfgang Amadeus Mozart (1756-91), Composer — A243

2007, Jan. 11
724 A243 $2 multi   4.00 4.00

Souvenir Sheet

Ludwig Durr (1878-1956), Engineer — A244

No. 725 — Durr and: a, Walrus Hula airship. b, Walrus heavy transport blimp. c, Hindenburg.

2007, Jan. 11
725 A244 $1 Sheet of 3, #a-c   6.00 6.00

Souvenir Sheet

Marilyn Monroe (1926-62), Actress — A245

No. 726: a, Looking right. b, With puckered lips. c, Wearing beret. d, With eyes closed, facing left.

2007, Jan. 11
726 A245 $1 Sheet of 4, #a-d   8.00 8.00

Scouting, Cent. — A246

2007, Jan. 11
727 A246 $1 shown   2.00 2.00
Souvenir Sheet
728 A246 $2 Scouts, flag   4.00 4.00
  No. 727 was printed in sheets of 3. No. 728 contains one 37x50mm stamp.

Pope Benedict XVI, 80th Birthday — A247

2007, May 25
729 A247 50c multi   1.00 1.00
  Printed in sheets of 8.

Miniature Sheet

Wedding of Queen Elizabeth II and Prince Philip, 60th Anniv. A248

No. 730 — Queen and Prince: a, Standing, red frame. b, Seated, red frame. c, Seated, white frame. d, Standing, white frame. e, Standing, blue frame. f, Seated, blue frame.

2007, May 25
730 A248 60c Sheet of 6, #a-f   7.25 7.25

Princess Diana (1961-97) — A249

No. 731 — Various portraits with background color of: a, Pink. b, Lilac. c, Bister. d, Light green.
$2, Diana wearing tiara.

2007, May 25
731 A249 90c Sheet of 4, #a-d   7.25 7.25
Souvenir Sheet
732 A249 $2 multi   4.00 4.00

Bananas — A250

Inscriptions: 22c, Utim was. 26c, Utin lap. 41c, Mangat. 58c, Ipali. 80c, Daiwang. 90c, Akadahn Weitahta, horiz. $1.14, Peleu. $4.60, Utin Kerenis.

Perf. 14x14¾, 14¾x14
2007, June 12
733 A250 22c multi   .45 .45
734 A250 26c multi   .55 .55
735 A250 41c multi   .85 .85
736 A250 58c multi   1.25 1.25
737 A250 80c multi   1.60 1.60
738 A250 90c multi   1.90 1.90
739 A250 $1.14 multi   2.40 2.40
740 A250 $4.60 multi   9.25 9.25
  Nos. 733-740 (8)   18.25 18.25

Miniature Sheet

Elvis Presley (1935-77) — A251

No. 741 — Various portraits with denomination color of: a, Blue (country name in gray). b, Pink. c, Blue (country name in blue). d, Green. e, Buff. f, Lilac.

2007, June 20 — Perf. 14¼
741 A251 75c Sheet of 6, #a-f   9.00 9.00

Fish A252

No. 742: a, Longnose hawkfish. b, Fingerprint sharpnose puffer. c, Ornate butterflyfish. d, Longnose filefish.
$2, Multi-barred goatfish.

2007, June 21 — Perf. 13¼
742 A252 90c Sheet of 4, #a-d   7.25 7.25
Souvenir Sheet
743 A252 $2 multi   4.00 4.00

Flowers A253

No. 744: a, White plumeria. b, Yellow plumeria. c, White lily. d, Yellow ginger lily.
$2, Bougainvillea glabra.

2007, June 21
744 A253 90c Sheet of 4, #a-d   7.25 7.25
Souvenir Sheet
745 A253 $2 multi   4.00 4.00

MICRONESIA

Souvenir Sheet

Peace Corps in Micronesia, 40th Anniv. (in 2006) — A254

No. 746 — Inscriptions: a, Yap State. b, Kosrae State. c, Pohnpei State. d, Chuuk State.

2007, June 22
746 A254 90c Sheet of 4, #a-d   7.25 7.25

Miniature Sheet

Pres. Gerald R. Ford (1913-2006) — A255

No. 747 — Ford: a, With hand raised. b, Seated, reading documents. c, With Pres. Richard Nixon, denomination at UL. d, With Nixon, denomination at UR. e, With wife, Betty. f, Signing Nixon's pardon.

2007, Aug. 7
747 A255 $1 Sheet of 6, #a-f   12.00 12.00

Intl. Polar Year A256

No. 748: a, African penguins. b, Emperor penguins. c, Galapagos penguin. d, Humboldt penguin. e, Magellanic penguin. f, Rockhopper penguin.
$3.50, Gentoo penguins.

2007, Aug. 7
748 A256 75c Sheet of 6, #a-f   9.00 9.00
Souvenir Sheet
749 A256 $3.50 multi   7.00 7.00

Souvenir Sheet

Micronesian Red Cross, 9th Anniv. — A257

No. 750 — Various pictures of relief efforts with denomination at: a, LR. b, LL. c, UR. d, UL.

2007, Aug. 20
750 A257 90c Sheet of 4, #a-d   7.25 7.25

Cats — A258

Designs: 22c, Scottish Fold. 26c, Munchkin. 41c, Abyssinian. 90c, Somali, horiz.

$2, Blue Silver Shaded Tiffanie.
Perf. 13½x13, 13x13½
2007, Sept. 24   Litho.
751-754 A258 Set of 4   3.75 3.75
Souvenir Sheet
Perf. 12½x12¾
755 A258 $2 multi   4.00 4.00
No. 755 contains one 29x42mm stamp.

Christmas — A259

Churches: 22c, Mother Church, United Church of Christ, Pohnpei. 26c, St. Mary's Church, Yap, horiz. 41c, Sapore Bethesca Church, Fefan, Chuuk, horiz. 90c, Lelu Congregational Church, Kosrae, horiz.

Perf. 14¼x14¾, 14¾x14¼
2007, Nov. 12
756-759 A259 Set of 4   3.75 3.75

America's Cup Yachting Races, Valencia, Spain — A260

Sails of various sailboats.

2007, Dec. 12   *Perf. 13¼*
760   Strip of 4   8.50 8.50
 a. A260 26c aquamarine & multi   .50 .50
 b. A260 80c red & multi   1.60 1.60
 c. A260 $1.14 yellow & multi   2.40 2.40
 d. A260 $2 orange & multi   4.00 4.00

First Helicopter Flight, Cent. — A261

No. 761: a, AH-1 Huey Cobra. b, 206 Jet Ranger. c, H-43 Huskie. d, AS-350 Ecureuil.
$2.50, Fa 223 Drache.

2007, Dec. 12   *Perf. 13¼*
761 A261 $1 Sheet of 4, #a-d   8.00 8.00
Souvenir Sheet
762 A261 $2.50 multi   5.00 5.00

Princess Diana (1961-97) — A262

Serpentine Die Cut 7¾
2007, Dec. 12   Litho. & Embossed
Without Gum
763 A262 $8 multi   16.00 16.00

Miniature Sheet

Pres. John F. Kennedy (1917-63) — A263

No. 764 — Kennedy: a, With curtain at left. b, Color portrait. c, With Presidential Seal. d, At microphones.

2008, Jan. 2   Litho.   *Perf. 14*
764 A263 90c Sheet of 4, #a-d   7.25 7.25

New Year 2008 (Year of the Rat) — A264

2008, Jan. 2   Litho.   *Perf. 12*
765 A264 90c multi   1.90 1.90
Printed in sheets of 4.

Miniature Sheet

2008 Olympic Games, Beijing A265

No. 766: a, Cover of book with music from 1904 World's Fair. b, Poster for 1904 Olympic Games and World's Fair. c, Jim Lightbody. d, Martin Sheridan.

2008, Jan. 8   *Perf. 14*
766 A265 50c Sheet of 4, #a-d   4.00 4.00

Souvenir Sheet

Breast Cancer Awareness — A266

2008, Mar. 12
767 A266 $2 multi   4.00 4.00

Hummer Vehicles A267

No. 768: a, Front bumper of Hummer H3x, denomination at UR. b, Side view of Hummer H3x, denomination at LR. c, Front view of Hummer H3x, denomination at LR. d, Rear view of Hummer H3x, denomination at UR. $2, Hummer H3.

2008, May 6   *Perf. 13¼*
768 A267 90c Sheet of 4, #a-d   7.25 7.25
Souvenir Sheet
769 A267 $2 multi   4.00 4.00

Jerusalem — A268

2008, May 14   *Imperf.*
770 A268 $3 multi   6.00 6.00
World Stamp Championship, Israel, 2008.

Miniature Sheet

Elvis Presley (1935-77) — A269

No. 771 — Presley: a, With head on hand, buff background. b, Sitting in director's chair, gray background. c, Wearing striped jacket, brown background. d, Wearing brown shirt, red brown background. e, Wearing gray suit, yellow orange background. f, Wearing gray suit, blue gray background.

2008, June 12   *Perf. 13¼*
771 A269 75c Sheet of 6, #a-f   9.00 9.00

Miniature Sheet

Members of Phoenix Suns Basketball Team — A270

No. 772 — Emblem of National Basketball Association and: a, Amare Stodemire. b, Boris Diaw. c, Brian Skinner. d, D. J. Strawberry. e, Shaquille O'Neal. f, Grant Hill. g, Leandro Barbosa. h, Raja Bell. i, Steve Nash.

2008, June 19
772 A270 42c Sheet of 9, #a-i   7.75 7.75

Miniature Sheet

Royal Air Force, 90th Anniv. A271

No. 773 — Aircraft: a, Tornado. b, Harrier. c, Typhoon. d, Hawk.

2008, May 6   Litho.   *Perf. 13¼*
773 A271 90c Sheet of 4, #a-d   7.25 7.25

Miniature Sheet

Visit of Pope Benedict XVI to United States A272

No. 774 — Pope Benedict XVI and one quarter of Papal arms at: a, LR. b, LL. c, UR. d, UL.

2008, Sept. 9   *Perf. 13¼*
774 A272 94c Sheet of 4, #a-d   7.75 7.75

MICRONESIA

Miniature Sheets

A273

Muhammad Ali, Boxer — A274

No. 775 — Ali: a, Wearing protective headgear. b, Receiving adjustment of headgear. c, Looking right. d, In boxing ring, looking right. e, In boxing ring, looking left. f, With trainer, looking at hands.
No. 776 — Ali fighting: a, Throwing left jab. b, Ready to deliver punch. c, With hands in front of his chest. d, With opponent's punch missing.

2008, Sept. 9   **Perf. 11½x11¼**
775 A273 75c Sheet of 6, #a-f   9.00   9.00
             Perf. 13¼
776 A274 94c Sheet of 4, #a-d   7.75   7.75

Star Trek A275

No. 777: a, U.S.S. Enterprise. b, Mr. Spock and woman. c, Captain Kirk. d, Uhura and Chekov. e, Starbase 11. f, Dr. McCoy and Mr. Spock.
No. 778: a, Scotty. b, Captain Kirk. c, Dr. McCoy and Uhura. d, Chekov.

2008, Sept. 9   **Perf. 12x11½**
777 A275 75c Sheet of 6, #a-f   9.00   9.00
             Perf. 13¼
778 A275 94c Sheet of 4, #a-d   7.75   7.75
No. 778 contains four 38x60mm stamps.

Christmas — A276

Ornaments: 22c, Angel. 27c, Snowflake. 42c, Cross. 94c, Angel, diff.

2008, Sept. 9   **Perf. 14x14¾**
779-782 A276 Set of 4   3.75   3.75

Famous Men A277

No. 783: a, Ioanis Artui, Palikiri chief. b, Dr. Eluel K. Pretrick, Human Resources Secretary.

2008, Oct. 17   **Perf. 13¼**
783 A277 94c Pair, #a-b   3.75   3.75

Miniature Sheet

Inauguration of US Pres. Barack Obama — A278

No. 784: a, 42c, Obama facing right. b, 42c, Obama facing left, one side of shirt collar showing. c, 42c, Obama facing left, both sides of shirt collar showing. d, 75c, As "c." e, 75c, As "b." f, 75c, As "a."

2009, Jan. 20   **Litho.**   **Perf. 11½**
784 A278 Sheet of 6, #a-f   7.25   7.25

Miniature Sheet

Marilyn Monroe (1926-62), Actress — A279

No. 785: a, Monroe in dressing gown. b, Head of Monroe. c, Monroe in lilac sweater. d, Monroe in automobile.

2009, Jan. 22
785 A279 94c Sheet of 4, #a-d   7.75   7.75

Surfing — A280

Ocean waves and various surfers. Waves only on 20c, 22c, 59c, 83c.

2009, Jan. 26   **Perf. 14x14¾**
786 A280   1c multi   .25   .25
787 A280   2c multi   .25   .25
788 A280   17c multi   .35   .35
789 A280   20c multi   .40   .40
790 A280   22c multi   .45   .45
791 A280   27c multi   .55   .55
792 A280   42c multi   .85   .85
793 A280   59c multi   1.25   1.25
794 A280   72c multi   1.50   1.50
795 A280   83c multi   1.75   1.75
796 A280   94c multi   1.90   1.90
797 A280 $1.17 multi   2.40   2.40
798 A280 $4.80 multi   9.75   9.75
799 A280 $16.50 multi   33.00   33.00
   Nos. 786-799 (14)   54.65   54.65

Miniature Sheet

New Year 2009 (Year of the Ox) A281

No. 800: a, Denomination next to yellow arc, three leaves at top. b, Denomination even with yellow curlicues, two tan arcs going beneath denomination. c, Denomination next to yellow arc, one leaf between yellow and pink curlicues at top. d, Denomination even with yellow curlicues, tip of brown leaf touching "9" in denomination.

2009, Jan. 26   **Perf. 11½**
800 A281 94c Sheet of 4, #a-d   7.75   7.75

Peonies — A282

2009, Apr. 10   **Perf. 13¼**
801 A282 42c multi   .85   .85
Printed in sheets of 6.

Miniature Sheets

A283

China 2009 World Stamp Exhibition — A284

No. 802 — Olympic sports: a, Triathlon. b, Diving. c, Equestrian. d, Table tennis.
No. 803 — Tang Dynasty art: a, Portrait of Emperor Taizong (Li Shih-min). b, Portrait of Emperor Taizong and his subjects. c, Calligraphy of Emperor Taizong. d, Mural of Emperor Taizong, Dunhuang.

2009, Apr. 10   **Perf. 12**
802 A283 59c Sheet of 4, #a-d   4.75   4.75
803 A284 50c Sheet of 4, #a-d   1.75   1.75

Souvenir Sheets

A285

A286

A287

Elvis Presley (1935-77) — A288

2009, June 10   **Perf. 13¼**
804 A285 $2.50 multi   5.00   5.00
805 A286 $2.50 multi   5.00   5.00
806 A287 $2.50 multi   5.00   5.00
807 A288 $2.50 multi   5.00   5.00
   Nos. 804-807 (4)   20.00   20.00

Miniature Sheets

A289

Michael Jackson (1958-2009) — A290

No. 808 — Shirt color: a, 28c, Yellow. b, 28c, Black. c, 75c, Yellow. d, 75c, Black.
No. 809 — Shirt color: a, 28c, Tan. b, 28c, White. c, 75c, Tan. d, 75c, White.

2009, July 7   **Litho.**   **Perf. 13¼x13**
808 A289 Sheet of 4, #a-d   4.25   4.25
809 A290 Sheet of 4, #a-d   4.25   4.25

Miniature Sheets

A291

MICRONESIA

First Man on the Moon, 40th Anniv. A292

No. 810: a, Apollo 11 lift-off. b, Neil Armstrong in space. c, Bust of Armstrong by Paula Slater. d, Apollo 11 Command Module. e, Apollo 11 Lunar Module. f, Buzz Aldrin on moon.
No. 811: a, Apollo 11 Lunar and Command Modules. b, Apollo 11 Command Module. c, Armstrong. d, Silicon disc left on Moon.

2009, July 20			Perf. 13¼	
810	A291	75c Sheet of 6, #a-f	9.00	9.00
811	A292	98c Sheet of 4, #a-d	8.00	8.00

Butterflies A293

Designs: 28c, Great orange tip. 44c, Red pierrot. 98c, Plains cupid. $1.05, Blue admiral.
No. 816: a, Tree nymph sinharaja. b, Great Mormon. c, Blue Mormon. d, Tailed jay. e, Gladeye bushbrown. f, Ceylon rose.

2009, Sept. 4			Perf. 12	
812-815	A293	Set of 4	5.50	5.50
816	A293	75c Sheet of 6, #a-f	9.00	9.00

Fish — A294

Designs: 22c, Powder blue surgeon. 28c, Maroon clownfish. 61c, Flame angelfish. 78c, Moon wrasse. $1.24, Regal angelfish. $2.30, Firefish.
No. 823: a, Clown triggerfish. b, Wreckfish. c, Purple firefish. d, Regal tang.

2009, Sept. 4				
817-822	A294	Set of 6	11.00	11.00
823	A294	94c Sheet of 4, #a-d	7.75	7.75

A295

Dolphins A296

Designs: 22c, Indo-Pacific bottlenose dolphin. 88c, Chinese white dolphin. 95c, Southern right whale dolphin. $2.80, Northern right whale dolphin.
No. 828: a, Bottlenose dolphin. b, Costero. c, Tucuxi. d, Short-beaked common dolphin. e, Long-beaked common dolphin. f, Indo-Pacific humpbacked dolphin.

2009, Sept. 4				
824-827	A295	Set of 4	9.75	9.75
828	A296	75c Sheet of 6, #a-f	9.00	9.00

A297

Shells A298

Designs: 22c, Clea nigericans. 79c, Achatina fulica. $1.39, Pomacea canaliculata. $1.56, Cyclophorus diplochilus.
No. 833: a, Thais bitubercularis. b, Conus caracteristicus. c, Amphidromus glaucolarynx. d, Anadara pilula. e, Cypraea erronea pyriformis. f, Thais aculeata.

2009, Sept. 4				
829-832	A297	Set of 4	8.00	8.00
833	A298	75c Sheet of 6, #a-f	9.00	9.00

Corals — A299

Designs: 27c, Flat leather coral. 55c, Strawberry coral. 83c, Discosoma sp. 3. $1.44, Porous lettuce coral.
No. 838, vert.: a, Lobophytum sp. 1. b, Nara nematifera. c, Leuconia palaoensis. d, Dendronepithya sp. 1.
No. 839, vert.: a, Sarcophyton sp. 1. b, Echinopora lamellosa.

2009, Sept. 24			Perf. 14¾x14	
834-837	A299	Set of 4	5.75	5.75
			Perf. 14x14¾	
838	A299	98c Sheet of 4, #a-d	8.00	8.00

Souvenir Sheet

839	A299	98c Sheet of 2, #a-b	4.00	4.00

Miniature Sheet

Pres. Abraham Lincoln (1809-65) — A300

No. 840 — Photographs of Lincoln: a, Without beard. b, With beard, top of head not showing. c, With beard, looking right. d, With beard, profile.

2009, Oct. 16			Perf. 13¼	
840	A300	98c Sheet of 4, #a-d	8.00	8.00

Chinese Aviation, Cent. A301

No. 841 — Airplanes: a, CJ-5. b, CJ-6. c, JJ-5. d, JJ-6.
$2, JL-8.

2009, Nov. 12		Litho.	Perf. 14¼	
841	A301	75c Sheet of 4, #a-d	6.00	6.00

Souvenir Sheet

842	A301	$2 multi	4.00	4.00

No. 841 contains four 42x28mm stamps. Aeropex 2009 Philatelic Exhibition, Beijing.

Christmas — A302

Designs: 22c, Santa Claus and palm tree. 44c, Christmas ornaments. 98c, Christmas stocking. $4.80, Decorated Christmas tree.

2009, Nov. 30			Perf. 14x14¾	
843-846	A302	Set of 4	13.00	13.00

Miniature Sheet

Visit of Pope Benedict XVI to Czech Republic A303

No. 847: a, Pope and Czech Pres. Vaclav Klaus. b, Pope in red vestments. c, Pope and Miroslav Cardinal Vlk. d, Pope in green vestments.

2009, Dec. 2			Perf. 13x13¼	
847	A303	98c Sheet of 4, #a-d	8.00	8.00

Worldwide Fund for Nature (WWF) — A304

No. 848 — Mandarinfish: a, Male. b, Female. c, Unspecified gender. d, Unspecified gender, diff.

2009, Dec. 2			Perf. 13½	
848		Block or strip of 4	4.25	4.25
a.	A304	28c orange & multi	.60	.60
b.	A304	35c yellow & multi	.70	.70
c.	A304	44c green & multi	.90	.90
d.	A304	98c blue & multi	2.00	2.00
e.		Sheet of 8, 2 each #848a-848d	8.50	8.50

Turtles — A305

Designs: 22c, Hawksbill turtle. 88c, Australian flatback turtle. 95c, Loggerhead turtle. $2.80, Green sea turtle.
No. 853: a, Kemp's ridley turtle. b, Leatherback turtle. c, Loggerhead turtle, diff. d, Olive ridley turtle.
No. 854: a, Green sea turtle, diff. b, Hawksbill turtle, diff.

2009, Sept. 4		Litho.	Perf. 14¾x14	
849-852	A305	Set of 4	9.75	9.75
853	A305	98c Sheet of 4, #a-d	8.00	8.00

Souvenir Sheet

854	A305	$1.56 Sheet of 2, #a-b	6.25	6.25

Birds — A306

Designs: 28c, Brown booby. 44c, Sacred kingfisher. 98c, White-face heron. $1.05, Rainbow lorikeet.
No. 859, horiz.: a, Brandt's cormorant. b, Red-footed booby. c, Beach thick-knee. d, Common noddy.
No. 860, horiz.: a, Blue-footed booby. b, Australian pelican.

2009, Sept. 4			Perf. 14x14¾	
855-858	A306	Set of 4	5.50	5.50
			Perf. 14¾x14	
859	A306	98c Sheet of 4, #a-d	8.00	8.00

Souvenir Sheet

860	A306	$1.56 Sheet of 2, #a-b	6.25	6.25

A306a
A306b
A306c
A306d
A306e
A306f
A306g

Diplomatic Relations Between Micronesia and People's Republic of China, 20th Anniv. — A306h

2009		Litho.	Perf. 12	
860C	A306a	44c multi	—	
860D	A306b	44c multi	—	
860E	A306c	44c multi	—	
860F	A306d	44c multi	—	
860G	A306e	44c multi	—	
860H	A306f	44c multi	—	
860I	A306g	44c multi	—	
860J	A306h	44c multi	—	
k.		Block of 8, #860C-860J	—	

Litho. Affixed to 3-Dimensional Plastic
Souvenir Sheet
Without Gum

860L		Sheet of 2, #860l-860m	—	—
m.	A306a	44c multi	—	—
n.	A306b	44c multi	—	—

Miniature Sheet

Chinese Zodiac Animals A307

No. 861: a, Rat. b, Ox. c, Tiger. d, Rabbit. e, Dragon. f, Snake. g, Horse. h, Ram. i, Monkey. j, Cock. k, Dog. l, Pig.

2010, Jan. 4			Perf. 13¼	
861	A307	22c Sheet of 12, #a-l	5.50	5.50

MICRONESIA

Souvenir Sheet

New Year 2010 (Year of the Tiger) A308

No. 862: a, Tiger. b, Chinese character for "tiger."

2010, Jan. 4   **Perf. 11½**
862 A308 $2 Sheet of 2, #a-b   8.00 8.00

Miniature Sheet

Charles Darwin (1809-82), Naturalist — A309

No. 863: a, Photograph of Darwin. b, Human and gorilla skulls. c, Gorilla. d, Human evolution. e, Darwin's notes. f, Darwin's drawings of finch beaks.

2010, Feb. 17   **Perf. 13¼**
863 A309 75c Sheet of 6, #a-f   9.00 9.00

Miniature Sheet

Pope John Paul II (1920-2005) — A310

No. 864 — Pope John Paul II with: a, Faint vertical line at left, white area at right. b, White area at left and top. c, White area at UL corner and at left, gray area at right. d, Gray area at left and bottom, faint vertical line at right.

2010, Apr. 23   **Perf 11½**
864 A310 75c Sheet of 4, #a-d   6.00 6.00

A311

Mushrooms — A312

Designs: 28c, Galerina decipiens. 44c, Amanita pekeoides. 75c, Rhodocollybia laulaha. 98c, Amanita nothofagi.
No. 869: a, Hygrocybe aff. minutula. b, Hygrocybe pakelo. c, Amanita nehuta. d, Amanita muscaria. e, Amanita australis. f, Hygrocybe constrictospora.

2010, June 8   **Perf. 11½**
865-868 A311 Set of 4   5.00 5.00
     Perf. 12x11½
869 A312 75c Sheet of 6, #a-f   9.00 9.00

Pres. Tosiwo Nakayama (1931-2007) — A313

No. 870 — Photos of Pres. Nakayama: a, On Saipan, 1970. b, In Washington, DC, 1986. c, On Pohnpei, 1970. d, On Saipan, 1975. $2, Color photograph.

2010, June 8   **Perf. 11½**
870 A313 80c Sheet of 4, #a-d   6.50 6.50

Souvenir Sheet
     Perf. 13½
871 A313 $2 multi   4.00 4.00

No. 870 contains four 30x40mm stamps.

Girl Guides, Cent. A314

No. 872, horiz.: a, Two Girl Guides holding hands. b, Two Girl Guides with yellow neckerchiefs. c, Three Girl Guides with balloons. d, Three Girl Guides writing.
$2.50, Two Rainbows.

2010, June 8   **Perf. 11½x12**
872 A314 94c Sheet of 4, #a-d   7.75 7.75

Souvenir Sheet
     Perf. 11½
873 A314 $2.50 multi   5.00 5.00

Flowers and Fruit — A315

Designs: 1c, Bougainvillea. 2c, Yellow plumeria. 4c, White ginger. 5c, Guettardia speciosa. 10c, Mangat bananas. 19c, Akadahn Weitahta bananas. 20c, Peleu bananas. 22c, Three unopened coconuts. 28c, Utin Kerenis bananas. 40c, Unopened coconut. 44c, Opened coconut. 70c, Coconut out of shell. $1, Opened and unopened coconuts. $3.85, Opened coconut, diff. $4.60, Soursop. $4.80, Partially opened soursop.

2010, June 18   **Perf. 13¼**
874 A315 1c multi   .25 .25
875 A315 2c multi   .25 .25
876 A315 4c multi   .25 .25
877 A315 5c multi   .25 .25
878 A315 10c multi   .25 .25
879 A315 19c multi   .40 .40
880 A315 20c multi   .40 .40
881 A315 22c multi   .45 .45
882 A315 28c multi   .60 .60
883 A315 40c multi   .80 .80
884 A315 70c multi   .90 .90
885 A315 70c multi   1.40 1.40
886 A315 $1 multi   2.00 2.00
887 A315 $3.85 multi   7.75 7.75
888 A315 $4.60 multi   9.25 9.25
889 A315 $4.80 multi   9.75 9.75
   Nos. 874-889 (16)   34.95 34.95

Miniature Sheet

British Monarchs — A316

No. 890: a, Queen Anne. b, King George I. c, King George II. d, King George III. e, King George IV. f, King George V.

2010, Aug. 26   **Perf. 11½**
890 A316 75c Sheet of 6, #a-f   9.00 9.00

Miniature Sheet

Paintings by Sandro Botticelli (1445-1510) — A317

No. 891: a, Madonna and Two Angels. b, Pallas and the Centaur. c, Portrait of a Man with the Medal. d, St. Augustine in His Cell. e, Scenes from the Life of Moses. f, Adoration of the Magi.

2010, Aug. 26   **Litho.**
891 A317 75c Sheet of 6, #a-f   9.00 9.00

Henri Dunant (1828-1910), Founder of the Red Cross — A318

No. 892 — Various depictions of the Battle of Solferino and Dunant's photograph in: a, Gray green. b, Brown. c, Red violet. d, Gray blue.
$2.50, Violet.

2010, Aug. 26   **Perf. 11½x12**
892 A318 94c Sheet of 4, #a-d   7.75 7.75

Souvenir Sheet
     Perf. 11½
893 A318 $2.50 multi   5.00 5.00

Miniature Sheet

Princess Diana (1961-97) — A319

No. 894 — Princess Diana: a, In beige dress, embracing child. b, In plaid suit, meeting child. c, In blue green suit, meeting child. d, In pink suit.

2010, Aug. 26   **Litho.**   **Perf. 12x11½**
894 A319 75c Sheet of 4, #a-d   6.00 6.00

Souvenir Sheet

Issuance of the Penny Black, 170th Anniv. A320

No. 895: a, Great Britain #1. b, Micronesia #2.

2010, Oct. 6   **Perf. 13x13¼**
895 A320 $2 Sheet of 2, #a-b   8.00 8.00

Christmas — A321

Paintings: 22c, Adoration of the Magi, by Corrado Giaquinto. 28c, Polyptych with the Nativity, by Rogier van der Weiden. 44c, The Nativity, by Federico Barocci. 98c, The Newborn Christ, by Georges de La Tour. $4.95, The Flight into Egypt, by Giotto di Bondone.

2010, Nov. 1   **Perf. 13¼x13**
896-900 A321 Set of 5   14.00 14.00

Pope John Paul II (1920-2005) — A322

2010, Dec. 16   **Perf. 12**
901 A322 75c multi   1.50 1.50
Printed in sheets of 4.

Miniature Sheet

Pope Benedict XVI A323

No. 902 — Pope Benedict XVI with lower panel: a, In solid black. b, In black and dark gray at LR. c, In brown and black with "d" over black area, finger partially visible at right. d, In brown and black with "of" over black area.

2010, Dec. 16
902 A323 75c Sheet of 4, #a-d   6.00 6.00

Miniature Sheet

Pres. Abraham Lincoln (1809-65) — A324

MICRONESIA

No. 903 — Lincoln: a, Giving Gettysburg Address. b, With wife, Mary. c, Reading draft of the Emancipation Proclamation. d, Meeting General George McClellan in tent at Antietam.

2010, Dec. 16		Perf. 12½x12		
903	A324	75c Sheet of 4, #a-d	6.00	6.00

Miniature Sheets

2010 World Cup Soccer Championships, South Africa — A325

No. 904, 61c: a, Dani Alves. b, Dirk Kuyt. c, Lucio. d, Gregory Van Der Wiel. e, Robinho. f, Mark Van Bommel.
No. 905, 61c: a, Diego Perez. b, Isaac Vorsah. c, Egidio Arevalo. d, Kevin-Prince Boateng. e, Luis Suarez. f, Kwadwo Asamoah.

2010, Dec. 30		Litho.	Perf. 12	
		Sheets of 6, #a-f		
904-905	A325	Set of 2	15.00	15.00

Souvenir Sheet

New Year 2011 (Year of the Rabbit) A326

2011, Jan. 27				
906	A326	Sheet of 2 #906a	6.00	6.00
a.		$1.50 Single stamp	3.00	3.00

Miniature Sheet

Inauguration of Pres. John F. Kennedy, 50th Anniv. — A327

No. 907: a, Kennedy taking oath. b, Kennedy pointing. c, Kennedy on reviewing stand. d, Kennedy with wife, Jacqueline.

2011, Jan. 27				
907	A327	75c Sheet of 4, #a-d	6.00	6.00

Miniature Sheet

Elvis Presley (1935-77) — A328

No. 908 — Presley: a, Without guitar. b, Playing guitar, wearing jacket with plain shoulders. c, Holding guitar. d, Playing guitar, wearing shirt with decorated shoulders.

2011, Jan. 27				
908	A328	75c Sheet of 4, #a-d	6.00	6.00

Mohandas K. Gandhi (1869-1948) — A329

2011, Jan. 27		Perf. 13 Syncopated		
909	A329	95c shown	1.90	1.90

Souvenir Sheet

910	A329	$2.50 Gandhi, horiz.	5.00	5.00

Indipex 2011, New Delhi (No. 910). No. 909 was printed in sheets of four.

A330

Beijing 2010 Intl. Philatelic Exhibition — A331

No. 911 — Three Gorges Dam and: a, Reservoir, denomination in red. b, Fountain, denomination in white. c, Denomination in black. d, Boats, denomination in white.
$2, Face of terra cotta warrior, Xi'an.

2011, Jan. 27			Perf. 12	
911	A330	75c Sheet of 4, #a-d	6.00	6.00

Souvenir Sheet

912	A331	$2 multi	4.00	4.00

Engagement of Prince William and Catherine Middleton — A332

No. 913: a, Royal arms of the United Kingdom, blue background. b, Arms of Prince William of Wales, blue background. c, Couple, Middleton without hat.
No. 914: a, Royal arms of the Untied Kingdom, brown background. b, Arms of Prince William of Wales, brown background. c, Couple, Middleton with hat.
No. 915, $1.50: a, Couple. b, Royal arms of the Untied Kingdom.
No. 916, $1.50: a, Arms of Prince William of Wales. b, Prince William.

2011, Jan. 27		Perf. 13 Syncopated		
913	A332	94c Sheet of 4, #913a-913b, 2 #913c	7.75	7.75
914	A332	94c Sheet of 4, #914a-914b, 2 #914c	7.75	7.75

Souvenir Sheets of 2, #a-b

915-916	A332	Set of 2	12.00	12.00

Miniature Sheets

A333

A334

Travels of U.S. Pres. Barack Obama A335

No. 917 — Pres. Obama at United Nations General Assembly with: a, Viet Nam Pres. Nguyen Minh Triet, Philippines Pres. Benigno Aquino III. b, Azerbaijan Pres. Ilham Aliyev. c, Colombia Pres. Juan Manuel Santos Calderón. d, Kyrgyzstan Pres. Roza Otunbayeva.
No. 918 — Pictures from 2010 G20 Summit in Seoul: a, Pres. Obama waving. b, Pres. Obama with France Pres. Nicolas Sarkozy. c, Pres. Obama with South Korea Pres. Lee Myung-bak. d, Pres. Obama with Russia Pres. Dmitry Medvedev.
No. 919 — Pictures from 2010 G20 Summit: a, Pres. Obama facign right. b, South Korea Pres. Lee. c, Pres. Obama and others holding certificate. d, Pres. Obama at lectern, flags in background.

2011, Jan. 27		Litho.	Perf. 12	
917	A333	75c Sheet of 4, #a-d	6.00	6.00
918	A334	75c Sheet of 4, #a-d	6.00	6.00
		Perf. 13 Syncopated		
919	A335	75c Sheet of 4, #a-d	6.00	6.00
		Nos. 917-919 (3)	18.00	18.00

Miniature Sheet

Roald Amundsen's Expedition to the South Pole, Cent. — A336

No. 920: a, Lake Fryxell, Antarctica. b, Amundsen. c, Emperor penguins. d, Aurora Australis at Amundsen-Scott South Pole Station.

2011, Apr. 6			Perf. 12	
920	A336	98c Sheet of 4, #a-d	8.00	8.00

Miniature Sheets

U.S. Civil War, 150th Anniv. A337

No. 921, 98c — Eagle, shield, Union and Confederate flags, Commodore George N. Hollins and Capatin John Pope from Battle of the Head of Passes, Oct. 12, 1861, and: a, The CSS Manassas attacks the USS Richmond. b, USS Richmond. c, CSS Manassas. d, USS Water Witch.
No. 922, 98c — Eagle, shield, Union and Confederate flags, Colonel Nathan G. Evans and General Charles F. Stone from Battle of Ball's Bluff, Oct. 21, 1861, and: a, General Stone's forces at Ball's Bluff. b, Union artillery fires shells across Potomac River. c, Battle map of Ball's Bluff. d, Death of Col. Edward D. Baker.

2011, Apr. 6		Perf. 13 Syncopated		
		Sheets of 4, #a-d		
921-922	A337	Set of 2	16.00	16.00

U.S. Pres. Abraham Lincoln (1809-65) — A338

2011, Apr. 6		Perf. 13 Syncopated		
923	A338	75c shown	1.50	1.50

Souvenir Sheet
Perf. 12½

924	A338	$2.50 Lincoln, diff.	5.00	5.00

No. 923 was printed in sheets of 4. No. 924 contains one 38x51mm stamp.

Beatification of Pope John Paul II — A339

No. 925 — Pope John Paul II: a, With archway in background at left. b, Waving. c, With man's head in background at left. d, Holding child.
$2.50, Pope John Paul II wearing miter, vert.

2011, Apr. 6			Perf. 12	
925	A339	75c Sheet of 4, #a-d	6.00	6.00

Souvenir Sheet

926	A339	$2.50 multi	5.00	5.00

A340

A341

A342

MICRONESIA

A343

A344

Elvis Presley (1935-77) — A345

No. 927 — Presley: a, With drums in background. b, Wearing suit with handkerchief in pocket. c, Playing double-necked guitar. d, Singing, holding microphone, wearing spotted and decorated jacket and pants. e, With red guitar. f, Singing, wearing decorated shirt and pants.
No. 928 — Presley: a, Wearing Western shirt with flower on shoulder. b, With hand in front of mouth. c, Wearing light-colored jacket. d, Wearing necklaces. e, Singing, with sign in background. f, With spotlight behind head.

2011			Perf. 13½	
927	A340	75c Sheet of 6, #a-f	9.00	9.00
928	A341	75c Sheet of 6, #a-f	9.00	9.00

Souvenir Sheets
Perf. 12½

929	A342	$2.50 multi	5.00	5.00
930	A343	$2.50 multi	5.00	5.00
931	A344	$2.50 multi	5.00	5.00
932	A345	$2.50 multi	5.00	5.00
		Nos. 929-932 (4)	20.00	20.00

Issued: Nos. 927-928, 5/16; Nos. 929-932, 4/6.

Wedding of Prince William and Catherine Middleton — A346

No. 933, 98c — Couple kissing with: a, Light gray design above denomination, white area to left of denomination. b, Dark gray design below and around denomination. c, Light gray design under and around denomination. d, White area under and around denomination.
No. 934, 98c: a, Groom, light gray design above denomination, white area to left of denomination. b, Bride, dark gray design under and around denomination. c, Groom, light gray design under and around denomination. d, Bride, white area under and around denomination.
$2.50, Couple, diff.

2011, Aug. 29 *Perf. 13 Syncopated*
Sheets of 4, #a-d

933-934	A346	Set of 2	16.00	16.00

Souvenir Sheet

935	A346	$2.50 multi	5.00	5.00

A347

Princess Diana (1961-97) — A348

No. 936 — Princess Diana wearing: a, Black dress, holding clutch purse. b, White blouse covering shoulders. c, Strapless white dress. d, Purple dress.
No. 937 — Princess Diana: a, As child, wearing red headband. b, Wearing black and white dress. c, Wearing red dress and hat. d, Wearing beige hat and beige checked jacket.

2011, July 14 *Perf. 12*

936	A347	98c Sheet of 4, #a-d	8.00	8.00
937	A348	98c Sheet of 4, #a-d	8.00	8.00

Reptiles A349

No. 938: a, Stripe-necked turtle. b, Oceanic gecko. c, Tropical gecko. d, Four-clawed gecko. e, Mourning gecko.
No. 939: a, Marianas blue-tailed skink. b, Green sea turtle.

2011, July 14 *Litho.*

938	A349	50c Sheet of 5, #a-e	5.00	5.00

Souvenir Sheet

939	A349	$1.25 Sheet of 2, #a-b	5.00	5.00

September 11, 2011 Terrorist Attacks, 10th Anniv. — A350

No. 940 — American flag and: a, Silhouette of Pentagon Building. b, World Trade Center in black. c, World Trade Center in gray. d, Map of Stonycreek Township, Pennsylvania.
$2.50, World Trade Center, horiz.

2011, Sept. 9 *Perf. 13¼x13*

940	A350	98c Sheet of 4, #a-d	8.00	8.00

Souvenir Sheet
Perf. 12

941	A350	$2.50 multi	5.00	5.00

Miniature Sheets

Japanese Team, Winners of 2011 Women's World Cup Soccer Tournament — A351

Finalists of 2011 Women's World Cup Soccer Tournament — A352

No. 942: a, Two women, woman at right wearing black headband. b, Woman wearing headband. c, Two women, woman at left wearing head bandage, woman at ridght wearing headband. d, Woman wearing yellow and black uniform. e, Woman in front of players wearing uniform numbers 10 and 7. f, Two women in front of player wearing uniform number 6. g, Woman in front of player wearing uniform number 17. h, Woman in front of woman wearing yellow and black uniform.
No. 043: a, Japan goalie Ayumi Kaihori. b, Team Japan. c, Team USA. d, USA goalie Hope Solo.

2011, Sept. 21 *Perf. 13½x13*

942	A351	50c Sheet of 8, #a-h	8.00	8.00

Perf. 12x12½

943	A352	98c Sheet of 4, #a-d	8.00	8.00

Whales A353

No. 944: a, Physeter polycyphus. b, Physeter macrocephalus. c, Sei whale.
No. 945: a, Tail of sperm whale. b, Head of sperm whale.

2011, Sept. 21 *Perf. 12½x12*

944	A353	$1 Sheet of 3, #a-c	6.00	6.00

Souvenir Sheet
Perf.

945	A353	$1.25 Sheet of 2, #a-b	5.00	5.00

No. 945 contains two 35mm diameter stamps.

A354

A355

Dr. Sun Yat-sen (1866-1925), President of Republic of China — A355a

No. 946: a, Blue background. b, Pink background.
No. 947: a, Denomination at UR. b, Denomination at UL.
No. 947C: a, Dr. Sun Yat-sen. b, Flag of Wuchang Uprising.

2011, Sept. 27 *Perf. 13 Syncopated*

946	A354	63c Horiz. pair, #a-b	2.60	2.60
947	A355	63c Pair, #a-b	2.60	2.60

Souvenir Sheet
Imperf
Without Gum

947C	A355a	$2 Sheet of 2, #d-e	8.00	8.00

No. 946 was printed in sheets containing two pairs. No. 947 was printed in sheets containing three pairs.

Sharks A356

No. 948: a, Sharpnose seven-gill shark. b, Basking shark. c, Porbeagle. d, Bluntnose six-gill shark.
$2.50, Sand tiger shark.

2011, Oct. 6 *Perf. 13x13¼*

948	A356	75c Sheet of 4, #a-d	6.00	6.00

Souvenir Sheet

949	A356	$2.50 multi	5.00	5.00

Game Fish A357

No. 950: a, Houndfish. b, Pacific agujon needlefish. c, Keeltail needlefish.
No. 951, $2.50, Swordfish. No. 952, $2.50, Rainbow runner.

2011, Oct. 6 *Perf. 12*

950	A357	$1 Sheet of 3, #a-c	6.00	6.00

Souvenir Sheets
Perf. 13x13¼

951-952	A357	Set of 2	10.00	10.00

Christmas — A358

Designs: 22c, Fish and sea anemone. 44c, Perfume flower tree branch. 98c, Palm tree. $4.95, Sea shell.

2011, Nov. 1 *Perf. 12*

953-956	A358	Set of 4	13.50	13.50

MICRONESIA

Chinese Pottery A359

No. 957: a, Tang Dynasty ceramic offering plate with six eaves. b, Song Dynasty Celadon vase. c, Ming Dynasty porcelain plate. d, Qing Dynasty porcelain vase.
$2.50, Ming Dynasty blue and white porcelain plate.

2011, Nov. 7		Perf. 12
957 A359 $1.25 Sheet of 4, #a-d		10.00 10.00

Souvenir Sheet

958 A359 $3.50 multi	7.00 7.00

Chinal 2011 Intl. Philatelic Exhibition, Wuxi.

New Year 2012 (Year of the Dragon) A360

2011, Nov. 7	Embroidered	Imperf. Self-Adhesive
959 A360 $8 red & yellow		16.00 16.00

Miniature Sheet

Peace Corps, 50th Anniv. A361

No. 960 — Winning art in children's stamp design contest: a, People in canoe, by Arvin Helgenberger. b, People with sign, by Alex Alexander. c, Trees, people in canoe, and fish, by Ashly-Ann Alfons. d, Ship and flag, by Leonard Klingen.

2011, Nov. 15	Litho.	Perf. 12½x12
960 A361 44c Sheet of 4, #a-d		3.75 3.75

Erhart Aten (1932-2004), Governor of Chuuk State — A362

2011, Nov. 28	Perf. 11¼x11½
961 A362 44c multi	.90 .90

Independence, 25th Anniv. (in 2011) — A363

2012, Mar. 1	Perf. 12
962 A363 25c multi	.50 .50

Pope Benedict XVI — A364

No. 963: a, Denomination at R. b, Denomination at L.
$3.50, Pope Benedict XVI, vert.

2012, Apr. 4	Perf. 14
963 A364 $1.25 Horiz. pair, #a-b	5.00 5.00

Souvenir Sheet Perf. 12

964 A364 $3.50 multi	7.00 7.00

No. 963 was printed in sheets containing two pairs.

Pres. Ronald Reagan (1911-2004) — A365

2012, Apr. 4	Perf. 12
965 A365 $1.25 shown	2.50 2.50

Souvenir Sheet

966 A365 $3.50 Reagan, diff.	7.00 7.00

No. 965 was printed in sheets of 4.

Reign of Queen Elizabeth II, 60th Anniv. — A366

No. 967 — Queen Elizabeth II wearing Army uniform in 1945: a, Wearing cap, looking right. b, Wearing cap, looking left. c, Without cap. d, Wearing cap, hands visible.
$3.50, Queen Elizabeth II wearing cap, vert.

2012, Apr. 4	Perf. 13 Syncopated
967 A366 $1.25 Sheet of 4, #a-d	10.00 10.00

Souvenir Sheet

968 A366 $3.50 multi	7.00 7.00

Sinking of the Titanic, Cent. A367

No. 969, horiz.: a, Titanic sinking. b, People waiting for survivors. c, Last known photograph of the Titanic.
$3.50, Passengers on deck.

2012, Apr. 4	Perf. 12
969 A367 $1.25 Sheet of 3, #a-c	7.50 7.50

Souvenir Sheet

970 A367 $3.50 multi	7.00 7.00

Hindenburg Disaster, 75th Anniv. — A368

No. 971 — Hindenburg in color and: a, "D-LZ129" and Olympic rings on side of zeppelin. b, Name "Hindenburg" on side of zeppelin. c, Mooring mast.
$3.50, Hindenburg, diff.

2012, Apr. 4	Perf. 13 Syncopated
971 A368 $1.50 Sheet of 3, #a-c	9.00 9.00

Souvenir Sheet

972 A368 $3.50 multi	7.00 7.00

Hybrid Dogs — A369

No. 973: a, Mal-shi. b, Puggle. c, Labradoodle. d, Chiweenie.
$3.50, Schnoodle.

2012, Apr. 4	Litho.
973 A369 $1.25 Sheet of 4, #a-d	10.00 10.00

Souvenir Sheet

974 A369 $3.50 multi	7.00 7.00

Mother Teresa (1910-97), Humanitarian — A370

Designs: $1.25, Mother Teresa. $3.50, Mother Teresa holding infant.

2012, Apr. 11	Perf. 12
975 A370 $1.25 Sheet of 4, #a-d	2.50 2.50

Souvenir Sheet

976 A370 $3.50 multi	7.00 7.00

No. 975 was printed in sheets of 4.

Premiere of Movie "The Three Stooges" — A371

No. 977, vert.: a, Sean Hayes as Larry. b, Chris Diamantopoulos as Moe. c, Will Sasso as Curly. d, Moe grabbing Curly and Larry. e, Stooges on bicycle.
$3.50, Stooges with hands against faces.

2012, Apr. 17	Perf. 13 Syncopated
977 A371 $1 Sheet of 5, #a-e	10.00 10.00

Souvenir Sheet

978 A371 $3.50 multi	7.00 7.00

Miniature Sheet

2012 Summer Olympics, London — A372

No. 979: a, Weight lifting. b, Archery. c, Tennis. d, Equestrian.

2012, May 30	Perf. 14
979 A372 80c Sheet of 4, #a-d	6.50 6.50

Turtles A373

No. 980: a, Hawksbill turtle. b, Leatherback turtle. c, Green sea turtle. d, Olive ridley turtle.
No. 981: a, Loggerhead turtle. b, Flatback turtle.

2012, June 27	Perf. 13 Syncopated
980 A373 $1.25 Sheet of 4, #a-d	10.00 10.00

Souvenir Sheet

981 A373 $1.25 Sheet of 2, #a-b	5.00 5.00

Souvenir Sheets

Elvis Presley (1935-77) — A374

Presley: No. 982, $3.50, On Heartbreak Hotel record cover. No. 983, $3.50, On Hound Dog record cover. No. 984, $3.50, On Teddy Bear record cover. No. 985, $3.50, Playing guitar. No. 986, $3.50, Wearing striped shirt.

2012, Aug. 7	Perf. 12½
982-986 A374 Set of 5	35.00 35.00

Miniature Sheets

A375

Pope Benedict XVI A376

No. 987 — Pope Benedict XVI: a, Holding Bible. b, Waving, microphone visible. c, With white horizontal panel in background. d, With white vertical panel in background.

MICRONESIA

No. 988 — Pope Benedict XVI: a, Wearing miter. b, Waving, cross in background. c, With brown, black and gray areas in background. d, Wearing red hat.

2012, Aug. 28   *Perf. 12*
987   A375 $1.25 Sheet of 4, #a-d   10.00   10.00
988   A376 $1.25 Sheet of 4, #a-d   10.00   10.00

Space Flight Speech of Pres. John F. Kennedy, 50th Anniv. — A377

No. 989, $1.25: a, Astronaut on Moon. b, Kennedy behind microphones and Presidential seal. c, Mercury capsule. d, Gemini capsule.
No. 990, $1.25: a, Lunar Module orbiting Moon. b, Apollo service and command modules orbiting moon. c, Lunar Module and astronaut on Moon. d, Kennedy and flag.

2012, Aug. 28   *Perf. 12*
Sheets of 4, #a-d
989-990   A377   Set of 2   20.00   20.00

Ranger Moon Program, 50th Anniv. — A378

No. 991, $1.25: a, Atlas Agena rocket lifting off. b, Moon targets. c, Ranger Lander above Moon, denomination at LL. d, Ranger 3 above Moon, country name at bottom.
No. 992, $1.25: a, Ranger 3 above Moon, country name at top. b, Ranger 7. c, Ranger lander above Moon, denomination at LR. d, Ranger 4.

2012, Aug. 28   *Perf. 13 Syncopated*
Sheets of 4, #a-d
991-992   A378   Set of 2   20.00   20.00

Carnivorous Plants — A379

No. 993: a, Pitcher plant. b, Fairy apron. c, Spoon-leaved sundew. d, Tropical sundew.
No. 994: a, Bladderwort. b, Common swamp pitcher plant.

Perf. 13 Syncopated
2012, Aug. 28   *Litho.*
993   A379 $1.25 Sheet of 4, #a-d   10.00   10.00
Souvenir Sheet
994   A379 $1.25 Sheet of 2, #a-b   5.00   5.00

Christmas — A380

Inscriptions: No. 995, 25c, Kosrae. No. 996, 25c, Yap Stone Money, vert. No. 997, 45c, Chuuk. No. 998, 45c, Pohnpei, vert.

2012, Nov. 1   *Litho.*   *Perf. 12½*
995-998   A380   Set of 4   2.80   2.80

Miniature Sheet
Octopi — A381

No. 999: a, Longarm octopus. b, Common octopus. c, Giant octopus. d, Red octopus. e, Day octopus.

2012, Nov. 28   *Perf. 13¾*
999   A381 $1 Sheet of 5, #a-e   10.00   10.00

Raphael Paintings — A382

No. 1000: a, Saint John in the Wilderness. b, The Sistine Madonna. c, Cardinal Bernardo Dovizi da Bibbiena. d, Madonna dell'Impannata.
$3.50, The Transfiguration.

2012, Nov. 28   *Perf. 12½*
1000   A382 $1 Sheet of 4, #a-d   8.00   8.00
Souvenir Sheet
1001   A382 $3.50 multi   7.00   7.00

A383, A384, A385, A386

New Year 2013 (Year of the Snake) — A387

2012, Oct. 10   *Litho.*   *Perf. 13¼*
1002   Sheet of 20, #1002a-1002d, 16 #1002e   8.00   8.00
   a. A383 18c multi   .40   .40
   b. A384 18c multi   .40   .40
   c. A385 18c multi   .40   .40
   d. A386 18c multi   .40   .40
   e. A387 18c multi   .40   .40

Michelangelo's Completion of the Sistine Chapel Ceiling Paintings, 500th Anniv. — A388

No. 1003 — Details from *The Creation of Adam*: a, Adam. b, Hands of Adam and God. c, Head of God. d, Feminine figure.
No. 1004: a, Separation of Land and Water. b, Creation of the Sun, Moon and Earth. c, Separation of Light and Darkness.

2012, Nov. 28   *Litho.*   *Perf. 12½*
1003   A388 $1.25 Sheet of 4, #a-d   10.00   10.00

Souvenir Sheet
1004   A388 $1.25 Sheet of 3, #a-c   7.50   7.50

World Radio Day — A389

No. 1005: a, Alexanderson alternator. b, Brant Rock Radio Tower, Massachusetts. c, Vacuum tube. d, Crystal radio receiver.
$3.50, Telstar communications satellite.

2013, Jan. 8   *Litho.*   *Perf. 12½*
1005   A389 $1.25 Sheet of 4, #a-d   10.00   10.00
Souvenir Sheet
Perf.
1006   A389 $3.50 multi   7.00   7.00
No. 1006 contains one 38mm diameter stamp.

Paintings by Vincent van Gogh (1853-90) — A390, A391

No. 1007 — Details from: a, Self-portrait, 1889. b, Starry Night, 1889. c, Still Life: Vase with Irises, 1889. d, Willows at Sunset, 1888.
No. 1008: a, Entrance Hall of Saint-Paul Hospital, 1889. b, Café Terrace at Night, 1888. c, Still Life with Oranges, Lemons and Blue Gloves (Früchtekorb und Handschuhe), 1889. d, Vincent's Bedroom in Arles, 1888.
$3.50, The Painter on His Way to Work, 1888.

2013, Jan. 8   *Litho.*   *Perf. 13¾*
1007   A390 $1.20 Sheet of 4, #a-d   9.75   9.75
Perf. 12½
1008   A391 $1.20 Sheet of 4, #a-d   9.75   9.75
Souvenir Sheet
1009   A391 $3.50 multi   7.00   7.00

Sarah Bernhardt (1844-1923), Actress — A392

No. 1010 — Illustrations by Alfons Mucha showing Bernhardt with: a, Vase. b, Staff. c, Dagger. d, Palm frond.
$3.50, Bernhardt with lilies in hair.

2013, Feb. 20   *Litho.*   *Perf. 12*
1010   A392 $1.20 Sheet of 4, #a-d   9.75   9.75
Souvenir Sheet
Perf. 12½
1011   A392 $3.50 multi   7.00   7.00
No. 1011 contains one 38x51mm stamp.

Pres. John F. Kennedy (1917-63) — A393

No. 1012 — Pres. Kennedy: a, Facing right. b, Pointing. c, Facing slightly left, chin above top of diamond. d, Facing slightly left, chin even with top of diamond.
$3.50, Pres. Kennedy, diff.

2013, Apr. 3   *Litho.*   *Perf. 12*
1012   A393 $1.20 Sheet of 4, #a-d   9.75   9.75
Souvenir Sheet
1013   A393 $3.50 multi   7.00   7.00

Details of Stained Glass Windows by Louis Comfort Tiffany — A394

No. 1014 — Stained-glass window with: a, Green piece of glass just below "MIC." b, Pink and red flower. c, Numerous green pieces of glass. d, Purple and yellow pieces of glass.
$3.50, Stained-glass window, vert.

2013, Apr. 4   *Litho.*   *Perf. 13¾*
1014   A394 $1.20 Sheet of 4, #a-d   9.75   9.75
Souvenir Sheet
Perf. 12½
1015   A394 $3.50 multi   7.00   7.00
No. 1015 contains one 38x51mm stamp.

History of Art — A395

No. 1016, $1.50 — Neoclassical paintings: a, The Daughter of Jephthah, by Alexandre Cabanel. b, Raphael and the Fornarina, by Jean Auguste Dominique Ingres. c, Portrait of Cornelia Knott Miltenberger, by Jacques Amans.
No. 1017, $1.50 — Neoclassical paintings: a, Nanna, by Anselm Feuerbach. b, Portrait of Madame de Verninac, by Jacques-Louis David. c, François Marius Gronet, by Ingres.
No. 1018, $3.50, Wanderer Above the Sea of Fog, by Caspar David Friedrich. No. 1019, $3.50, Caspar David Friedrich in his Studio, by Georg Friedrich Kersting, horiz.

2013, Apr. 4   *Litho.*   *Perf. 12½*
Sheets of 3, #a-c
1016-1017   A395   Set of 2   18.00   18.00
Souvenir Sheets
1018-1019   A395   Set of 2   14.00   14.00

MICRONESIA

Pope Benedict XVI Resignation, 2013 — A396

Resignation of Pope Benedict XVI — A397

No. 1020 — Pope Benedict XVI: a, Behind lectern. b, Waving, wristwatch visible. c, Kissing person. d, Waving, person wearing red cap in background.
No. 1021 — Pope Benedict XVI: a, Seated in chair. b, Facing forward, white background. c, Waving, grass in background. d, Waving, hand above eyes.
No. 1022, $3.50, In arched doorway, waving. No. 1023, $3.50, Facing right, waving.

Perf. 13 Syncopated
2013, Apr. 29   Litho.
1020 A396 $1.20 Sheet of 4, #a-d   9.75 9.75
1021 A397 $1.20 Sheet of 4, #a-d   9.75 9.75
Souvenir Sheets
1022-1023 A397 Set of 2   14.00 14.00

Dolphins A398

No. 1024, $1.20: a, Long-beaked common dolphin. b, Short-beaked common dolphin. c, Pygmy killer whale. d, Short-finned pilot whale.
No. 1025, $1.20: Dusky dolphin. b, Hector's dolphin. c, Bottlenose dolphin. d, Pantropical spotted dolphin.
No. 1026, $3.50, Spinner dolphin, horiz. No. 1027, $3.50, Rough-toothed dolphin, horiz.

2012, May 7   Litho.   Perf. 13¾
Sheets of 4, #a-d
1024-1025 A398 Set of 2   19.50 19.50
Souvenir Sheets
1026-1027 A398 Set of 2   14.00 14.00

Fish A399

No. 1028, $1.20: a, Mandarinfish. b, Neon damselfish. c, Man-of-war fish. d, Banggai cardinalfish.
No. 1029, $1.20: a, Australasian snapper. b, Australian herring. c, Saddletail grouper. d, Tasmanian clingfish.
No. 1030, $3.50, Slender-spined porcupine fish. No. 1031, $3.50, Ocellaris clownfish.

Perf. 13 Syncopated
2013, May 7   Litho.
Sheets of 4, #a-d
1028-1029 A399 Set of 2   19.50 19.50
Souvenir Sheets
1030-1031 A399 Set of 2   14.00 14.00

Dr. Lois Englberger (1948-2011), Acting Director and Research Advisor of Island Food Community — A400

Perf. 13 Syncopated
2013, May 8   Litho.
1032 A400 $1.20 multi   2.40 2.40
Souvenir Sheet
1033 A400 $3.50 multi   7.00 7.00
No. 1032 was printed in sheets of 4.

Mushrooms — A401

No. 1034, $1.25: a, Psilocybe subaeruginosa. b, Gymnopilus luteofolius. c, Gymnopilus junonius. d, Panaeolus cyanescens.
No. 1035, $1.25: a, Psilocybe aucklandii. b, Entoloma hochstetteri. c, Amanita citrina. d, Agaricus bernardii.
No. 1036, $3.50, Panaeolus subbalteatus. No. 1037, $3.50, Weraroa novae, vert.

2013, June 3   Litho.   Perf. 12
Sheets of 4, #a-d
1034-1035 A401 Set of 2   20.00 20.00
Souvenir Sheets
1036-1037 A401 Set of 2   14.00 14.00

John De Avila Mangefel (1932-2007), First Governor of Yap — A402

Perf. 13¼x12½
2013, June 13   Litho.
1038 A402 46c multi   .95 .95
No. 1038 was printed in sheets of 4.

Shells A403

No. 1039: a, Haliotis sorenseni. b, Melongena corona. c, Lyropecten nodosus. d, Pleurotomaria rumphii. e, Lioconcha castrensis. f, Conus ammiralis.
$3.50, Echinus melo, vert.

2013, July 7   Litho.   Perf. 13¾
1039 A403 $1 Sheet of 6, #a-f   12.00 12.00
Souvenir Sheet
Perf. 12½
1040 A403 $3.50 multi   7.00 7.00
No. 1040 contains one 38x51mm stamp.

Wildlife of Thailand A404

No. 1041: a, Banded pitta. b, Dhole. c, Wrinkled hornbill. d, Nicobar pigeon. e, Lar gibbon. f, Leopard. g, Malaysian tapir. h, Red-footed booby.
No. 1042, vert.: a, Dugong. b, Red-breasted parakeet.

2013, July 7   Litho.   Perf. 13¾
1041 A404 75c Sheet of 8, #a-h   12.00 12.00
Souvenir Sheet
Perf. 12½
1042 A404 $1.75 Sheet of 2, #a-b   7.00 7.00
2013 Thailand World Stamp Exhibition, Bangkok. No. 1042 contains two 38x51mm stamps.

Internet, 30th Anniv. A405

No. 1043 — Inscriptions: a, The World Wide Web. b, A series of tubes. c, Information super-highway.
3.50, Computer, vert.

2013, Aug. 12   Litho.   Perf. 13¾
1043 A405 $1.50 Sheet of 3, #a-c   9.00 9.00
Souvenir Sheet
Perf. 12½
1044 A405 $3.50 multi   7.00 7.00
No. 1044 contains one 38x51mm stamp.

Souvenir Sheet

Elvis Presley (1935-77) — A406

Litho., Margin Embossed With Foil Application
2013, Aug. 12   Imperf.
Without Gum
1045 A406 $10 black   20.00 20.00

Dogs A407

No. 1046: a, Basset hounds. b, Jack Russell terrier. c, Alaskan huskies. d, Yorkshire terrier.
$3.50, German shepherds.

2014, Mar. 24   Litho.   Perf. 14
1046 A407 $1.20 Sheet of 4, #a-d   9.75 9.75
Souvenir Sheet
Perf. 12
1047 A407 $3.50 multi   7.00 7.00

Parrots A408

No. 1048: a, Alisterus amboinensis. b, Geoffroyus geoffroyi geoffroyi. c, Loriculus camiguinensis. d, Loriculus calculus. e, Psittacula alexandri alexandri. f, Psittacula alexandri.
$3.50, Alisterus amboinensis, diff.

2014, Mar. 24   Litho.   Perf. 12½
1048 A408 $1 Sheet of 6, #a-f   12.00 12.00
Souvenir Sheet
1049 A408 $3.50 multi   7.00 7.00

World War I, Cent. A409

No. 1050, $1.20: a, Belgian soldier throwing Mills grenade. b, Head of Belgian soldier. c, Head of German soldier. d, German soldier charging.
No. 1051, $1.20, horiz.: a, HMS C1 submarine. b, HMS E5 submarine. c, HMS K17 submarine. d, HMS R3 submarine.
No. 1052, $2: a, King Albert I of Belgium. b, Kaiser Wilhelm II of Germany.
No. 1053, $2, horiz.: a, HMS B11 submarine. b, HMS C27 submarine.

2014, Mar. 24   Litho.   Perf. 14
Sheets of 4, #a-d
1050-1051 A409 Set of 2   19.50 19.50
Souvenir Sheets of 2, #a-b
Perf. 12½
1052-1053 A409 Set of 2   16.00 16.00
No. 1052 contains two 38x51mm stamps.
No. 1053 contains two 51x38mm stamps.

MICRONESIA
467

Paintings — A410

No. 1054, $1.50: a, Maria Magdalena, by Carlo Crivelli. b, Madonna of the Goldfinch, by Crivelli. c, The Gentleman in Pink, by Giovanni Battista Moroni.
No. 1055, $1.50: a, Portrait of a Woman with a Winged Bonnet, by Rogier van der Weyden. b, Annunciation, by Peter Paul Rubens. c, St. Augustine, by Caravaggio.
No. 1056, $4, Henry VII, by Hans Holbein the Younger. No. 1057, $4, The Dance Lesson, by Edgar Degas.

2014, Mar. 24   Litho.   Perf. 12½
Sheets of 3, #a-c
| 1054-1055 | A410 | Set of 2 | 18.00 | 18.00 |

Size: 100x100
Imperf
| 1056-1057 | A410 | Set of 2 | | 16.00 |

A411
A412
Pope Francis — A413
Pope Francis — A414

No. 1058. a, One ear visible. b, Both ears visible.
No. 1059, Pope wearing zucchetto.
No. 1060: a, Pink area in background. b, White area in background.
No. 1061: a, Denomination in black. b, Denomination in white.

2014, Mar. 24   Litho.   Perf. 14
1058	A411	$1.75 Horiz. pair, #a-b	7.00	7.00
1059	A412	$1.75 multi	3.50	3.50
a.		Horiz. pair, #1058b, 1059	7.00	7.00

Souvenir Sheets
Perf. 12
| 1060 | A413 | $3.50 Sheet of 2, #a-b | 14.00 | 14.00 |
| 1061 | A414 | $3.50 Sheet of 2, #a-b | 14.00 | 14.00 |

No. 1058 and 1059a each were printed in sheets containing two pairs.

A415
College of Micronesia, 20th Anniv. — A416

2014, Apr. 5   Litho.   Perf. 12½
| 1062 | A415 | 49c multi | 1.00 | 1.00 |
| 1063 | A416 | 49c multi | 1.00 | 1.00 |

Birth of Prince George of Cambridge — A417

No. 1064: a, Prince George in arms of Duchess of Cambridge. b, Duchess of Cambridge and Prince George. c, Prince George, Duke and Duchess of Cambridge. d, Prince, Duke and Duchess, face of Duchess not visible.
$4, Prince, Duke and Duchess, horiz.

2014, Apr. 29   Litho.   Perf. 13¾
| 1064 | A417 | $1.20 Sheet of 4, #a-d | 9.75 | 9.75 |

Souvenir Sheet
Perf. 12½
| 1065 | A417 | $4 multi | 8.00 | 8.00 |

No. 1065 contains one 51x38mm stamp.

Birds — A418

Designs: 1c, Black tern. 2c, Black-headed gull. 4c, Sabine's gull. 5c, Caspian tern. 10c, Common gull. 49c, White-winge black tern. 50c, Wilson's storm petrel. $1, Great skua.

2014, May 8   Litho.   Perf. 13¾
| 1066-1073 | A418 | Set of 8 | 4.50 | 4.50 |

Canonization of Pope John Paul II — A419

No. 1074, $1.20: a, Pope John Paul II in red robe. b, Coat of arms of Pope John Paul II. c, Pope John Paul II wearing miter, color photograph. d, Emblem of the papacy.
No. 1075, $1.20: a, St. Peter's Basilica clock. b, Pope John Paul II wearing miter, black-and-white photograph. c, Papal arms on St. Peter's Basilica. d, Pope John Paul wearing zucchetto.
No. 1076, $2: a, Pope John Paul II in red robe, diff. b, Dome of St. Peter's Basilica.
No. 1077, $2, horiz.: a, Pope John Paul II, color photograph. b, Pope John Paul II, black-and-white photograph.

Perf. 14, 12 (#1077)
2014, May 12   Litho.
Sheets of 4, #a-d
| 1074-1075 | A419 | Set of 2 | 19.50 | 19.50 |

Souvenir Sheets of 2, #a-b
| 1076-1077 | A419 | Set of 2 | 16.00 | 16.00 |

A420
Nelson Mandela (1918-2013), President of South Africa — A421

No. 1078 — Mandela: a, Wearing shirt and sweater. b, Wearing black shirt with white polka dots. c, In black-and-white photograph. d, Wearing suit and tie.
No. 1079 — Mandela: a, On book cover at left, in black-and white photograph at right. b, In black-and-white photograph at left, in color photograph wearing sweater at right. c, Wearing tribal neck covering in black-and-white photograph at left, wearing jacket with Olympic emblem in color photograph at right. d, In two color photographs.
No. 1080, $7, Mandela wearing green shirt, waving. No. 1081, $7, Mandela wearing blue and white shirt.

2014, May 12   Litho.   Perf. 13¾
| 1078 | A420 | $1.75 Sheet of 4, #a-d | 14.00 | 14.00 |
| 1079 | A421 | $1.75 Sheet of 4, #a-d | 14.00 | 14.00 |

Souvenir Sheets
| 1080-1081 | A421 | Set of 2 | 28.00 | 28.00 |

Keitani Graham (1980-2012), Wrestler — A422

Graham: No. 1082, $1, Close-up. No. 1083, $1, With numbered sign in background. No. 1084, $1, Wrestling opponent.

2014, June 4   Litho.   Perf. 14
| 1082-1084 | A422 | Set of 3 | 6.00 | 6.00 |

South Korean Tourist Attractions — A423

No. 1085: a, Gwanghwamun Palace, Seoul. b, Seongsan Sunrise Peak, Jeju Island. c, Seorak Mountain, Gangwon Province. d, Bulguksa, Gyeongju.
No. 1086, vert.: a, N Seoul Tower, Seoul. b, Gwangan Bridge, Busan.

2014, June 30   Litho.   Perf. 14
| 1085 | A423 | $1.20 Sheet of 4, #a-d | 9.75 | 9.75 |

Souvenir Sheet
| 1086 | A423 | $2 Sheet of 2, #a-b | 8.00 | 8.00 |

Philakorea 2014 World Stamp Exhibition, Seoul.

A424
A425
A426
Caroline Kennedy, U.S. Ambassador to Japan — A427

Various photographs of Caroline Kennedy, as shown.

2014, June 30   Litho.   Perf. 12
| 1087 | A424 | $1.20 Sheet of 4, #a-d | 9.75 | 9.75 |
| 1088 | A425 | $1.20 Sheet of 4, #a-d | 9.75 | 9.75 |

Souvenir Sheets
| 1089 | A426 | $2 Sheet of 2, #a-b | 8.00 | 8.00 |

Perf. 14
| 1090 | A427 | $2 Sheet of 2, #a-b | 8.00 | 8.00 |

Miniature Sheet

Fruit — A428

No. 1091: a, Strawberries. b, Limes. c, Pears. d, Red currants. e, Blueberries. f, Tomatoes. g, Grapes. h, Oranges. i, Guavas.

2014, July 9   Litho.   Perf.
| 1091 | A428 | 75c Sheet of 9, #a-i | 13.50 | 13.50 |

MICRONESIA

Polar Bears A429

No. 1092 — Polar bear: a, Underwater, denomination at UR. b, Underwater, head at right, denomination at UL. c, With nose above water, denomination at UR. d, Underwater, head at left, denomination at UL. $2.50, Head of polar bear.

2014, July 31	Litho.		Perf. 14	
1092	A429	75c Sheet of 4, #a-d	6.00	6.00

Souvenir Sheet
Perf. 12½
| 1093 | A429 | $2.50 multi | 5.00 | 5.00 |

No. 1093 contains one 51x38mm stamp.

Tropical Fish A430

Tropical Fish A431

No. 1094, 75c: a-d, Various depictions of clownfish in anemone, as shown.
No. 1095, 75c: a, Barcheek unicornfish. b, Discus. c, Old woman angelfish. d, Lined surgeonfish.
No. 1096, $2: a-b, Various depictions of clownfish in anemone, as shown.
No. 1097, $2, vert.: a, Clownfish, anemone at right of fish. b, Clownfish, anemone at left and right of fish

2014, Aug. 27	Litho.	Perf. 14
Sheets of 4, #a-d		
1094-1095	A430 Set of 2	12.00 12.00
Souvenir Sheets of 2, #a-b		
Perf. 12½		
1096-1097	A431 Set of 2	16.00 16.00

Bodyboarding — A432

2014, Sept. 6	Litho.		Perf. 14	
1098	A432	$2 multi	4.00	4.00

Seaglass A433

Seaglass A434

Nos. 1099, 1100, Various depictions of seaglass, as shown.
No. 1101, $4, Seaglass with black rock at left. No. 1102, $4, Seaglass with black rock at top.

Perf. 12, 14 (#1100)
2014, Sept. 15		Litho.	
1099	A433	75c Sheet of 4, #a-d	6.00 6.00
1100	A434	75c Sheet of 6, #a-f	9.00 9.00

Souvenir Sheets
| 1101-1102 | A434 | Set of 2 | 16.00 16.00 |

A435

Paintings by Qi Baishi (1864-1957) — A436

No. 1103: a, Flowers on branch. b, Flowers and cricket. c, Basket of fruit. d, Mushrooms and flowers.
No. 1104: a, Flowers and beetle. b, Flowers and dragonfly. c, Flowers and dragonfly, diff. d, Flowers and grsasshopper.
No. 1105, $4, Flowers. No. 1106, $4, Rocks and boats.

2014, Sept. 15	Litho.	Perf. 14
1103	A435 $1.20 Sheet of 4, #a-d	9.75 9.75
1104	A436 $1.20 Sheet of 4, #a-d	9.75 9.75

Souvenir Sheets
Perf. 12
| 1105-1106 | A436 | Set of 2 | 16.00 16.00 |

Nos. 1105-1106 each contain one 30x50mm stamp.

Sharks A437

No. 1107, $1: a, Blacktip reef shark. b, Dogfish shark. c, Lemon shark. d, Tiger shark.
No. 1108, $1 — Whale shark with: a, Tail fin touching edge of design below "M" in "Micronesia." b, Tail fin not near edge of design. c, Mouth open, tail fin not visible. d, Tail fin at right.
No. 1109, $3, Great white shark. No. 1110, $3, Great hammerhead shark.

Perf. 12, 14 (#1108, 1110)
2014, Oct. 14		Litho.	
Sheets of 4, #a-d			
1107-1108	A437 Set of 2	16.00 16.00
Souvenir Sheets			
1109-1110	A437 Set of 2	12.00 12.00

Miniature Sheets

A438

Illustrations by Alphonse Mucha (1860-1939) — A439

Various unnamed illustrations, as shown.

2014, Oct. 14		Litho.	Perf. 14
1111	A438 $1 Sheet of 4, #a-d	8.00 8.00
1112	A439 $1 Sheet of 4, #a-d	8.00 8.00

Butterflies — A440

No. 1113, $1: a, Milbert's tortoise-shell butterfly. b, Blue morpho butterfly. c, Tiger swallowtail butterfly. d, Monarch butterfly. e, Goliath birdwing butterfly. f, Striped albatross butterfly.
No. 1114, $1: a, Emerald swallowtail butterfly. b, Gold rim swallowtail butterfly. c, Scalloped grass yellow butterfly. d, European peacock butterfly. e, Blue mountain butterfly. f, Orange-tip butterfly.
No. 1115, $3.50, Postman butterfly, horiz. No. 1116, $3.50, Richmond birdwing butterfly, horiz.

2014, Oct. 20	Litho.	Perf. 13¾
Sheets of 6, #a-f		
1113-1114	A440 Set of 2	24.00 24.00
Souvenir Sheets		
Perf. 12½		
1115-1116	A440 Set of 2	14.00 14.00

Nos. 1115-1116 each contain one 51x38mm stamp.

Worldwide Fund for Nature (WWF) — A441

Nos. 1117 and 1118 — Orbicular batfish: a, School. b, One yellow fish. c, Two fish. d, One gray and black fish.

2014, Nov. 11	Litho.	Perf. 14
1117	A441 40c Block or horiz. strip of 4, #a-d	3.25 3.25
1118	A441 90c Block or horiz. strip of 4, #a-d	7.25 7.25

Souvenir Sheets

Elvis Presley (1935-77) — A442

Inscriptions: No. 1119, $4, Elvis' network television debut. No. 1120, $4, Elvis' fist live concert in NYC. No. 1121, $4, "Heartbreak Hotel" goes gold. No. 1122, $4, Elvis named honorary colonel.

2014, Nov. 11	Litho.	Perf. 14
1119-1122	A442 Set of 4	32.00 32.00

Christmas — A446

Designs: No. 1123, 49c, Boat and presents (shown). No. 1124, 49c, Boat and presents, side view of boat. $1, Presents under palm tree. $2, Boat and presents inside boat, gold garland.

2014, Nov. 24	Litho.	Perf. 14
1123-1126	A446 Set of 4	8.00 8.00

A447

New Year 2015 (Year of the Ram) — A448

No. 1127 — Various depictions of rams as shown.

MICRONESIA

2014, Nov. 24   Litho.   Perf. 14
1127 A447 90c Sheet of 4, #a-d   7.25 7.25

Embossed
Imperf
Without Gum
1128 A448 $8 gold   16.00 16.00

Trans-Siberian Railway — A449

No. 1129 — Inscriptions: a, Construction between Yekaterinburg and Chelyabinsk. b, Convicts, as well as soldiers, worked to build the railroad. c, Construction of the Trans-Siberian Railroad by the Angara River. d, The Trans-Siberian Railway undergoing construction in 1929.
$3.50, Workers layin the last ties for the Trans-Siberian Railway.

2014, Dec. 31   Litho.   Perf. 12
1129 A449 $1 Sheet of 4, #a-d   8.00 8.00

Souvenir Sheet
1130 A449 $3.50 multi   7.00 7.00

A450

A451

Coral Reefs A452

Coral Reefs A453

Nos. 1131 and 1132 — Various corals as shown.

2014, Dec. 31   Litho.   Perf. 12
1131 A450 $1 Sheet of 4, #a-d   8.00 8.00
1132 A451 $1 Sheet of 4, #a-d   8.00 8.00

Souvenir Sheets
1133 A452 $3.50 multi   7.00 7.00
1134 A453 $3.50 multi   7.00 7.00

Sharks — A454

Designs: 26c, Scalloped hammerhead shark. 49c, Oceanic whitetip shark. $1.15, Tiger shark. $3, Gray reef shark.

2015, Jan. 1   Litho.   Perf. 14¾x14¼
1135-1138 A454 Set of 4   10.00 10.00

Miniature Sheet

St. John Paul II (1920-2005) — A455

No. 1139 — St. John Paul II with: a, White area to right of "Pope" in red. b, White area at UR corner. c, White area at UL corner. d, Dark gray area under left part of country name.

2015, Feb. 2   Litho.   Perf. 14
1139 A455 75c Sheet of 4, #a-d   6.00 6.00

Meeting of Duke of Cambridge and U.S. Pres. Barack Obama — A456

No. 1140: a, Duke of Cambridge. b, Pres. Obama. c, Coat of arms of Duke of Cambridge. d, Presidential seal.
No. 1141: a, Duke of Cambridge, diff. b, Pres. Obama, diff.

2015, Mar. 2   Litho.   Perf. 12
1140 A456 $1 Sheet of 4, #a-d   8.00 8.00

Souvenir Sheet
Perf. 14
1141 A456 $1.75 Sheet of 2, #a-b   7.00 7.00

World War I Airships A457

No. 1142: a, British Beta II airship. b, Astra Torres airship. c, Caquot dirigible. d, German LZ-18 Zeppelin. e, British SS Class airship. f, German LZ-3 Zeppelin.
$3.50, WWI Reconnaisance balloon, vert.

2015, Mar. 2   Litho.   Perf. 14
1142 A457 $1 Sheet of 6, #a-f   12.00 12.00

Souvenir Sheet
Perf. 12
1143 A457 $3.50 multi   7.00 7.00

No. 1143 contains one 30x50mm stamp.

BMX Cycling A458

No. 1144 — Rider: a, With black shirt and helmet. b, With white shirt and black helmet, seated on bicycle. c, With black stocking cap. d, With yellow helmet. e, Without helmet. f, With white shirt and black helmet, not on bicycle seat.
$3.50, Rider with blue shirt and helmet, horiz.

2015, Mar. 9   Litho.   Perf. 14
1144 A458 $1 Sheet of 6, #a-f   12.00 12.00

Souvenir Sheet
Perf. 12½
1145 A458 $3.50 multi   7.00 7.00

No. 1145 contains one 51x38mm stamp.

Marine Life — A459

Designs: 1c, Achilles surgeonfish. 2c, Yellow finger sponge. 4c, Spotted eagle ray. 5c, Green sea turtle. 10c, Box jellyfish.

2015, Apr. 1   Litho.   Perf. 12½
1146-1150 A459 Set of 5   .45 .45

A460

A461

A462

A463

A464

A465

A466

A467

A468

Hibiscus Flowers — A469

Various hibiscus flowers: No. 1151, 20c. No. 1152, 25c. No. 1153, 26c. No. 1154, 27c.

2015, Apr. 1   Litho.   Perf. 13¼x12½
1151-1154 A460 Set of 4   2.00 2.00
1155 Vert. strip of 5   5.00 5.00
  a. A460 50c multi   1.00 1.00
  b. A461 50c multi   1.00 1.00
  c. A462 50c multi   1.00 1.00
  d. A463 50c multi   1.00 1.00
  e. A464 50c multi   1.00 1.00
  f. Souvenir sheet of 5, #1155a-1155e   5.00 5.00
1156 Vert. strip of 5   10.00 10.00
  a. A465 $1 multi   2.00 2.00
  b. A466 $1 multi   2.00 2.00
  c. A467 $1 multi   2.00 2.00
  d. A468 $1 multi   2.00 2.00
  e. A469 $1 multi   2.00 2.00
  f. Souvenir sheet of 5, #1156a-1156e   10.00 10.00

Illustrations of British Warblers by Henrik Grönvold (1858-1940) — A470

No. 1157: a, Common chiffchaff. b, Lesser whitethroat. c, Great reed warbler. d, Aquatic warbler. e, Common whitethroat. f, Melodious warbler.
$3.50, Radde's bush warblers, horiz.

2015, Apr. 16   Litho.   Perf. 13¼x12½
1157 A470 $1 Sheet of 6, #a-f   12.00 12.00

Souvenir Sheet
Perf. 13¼
1158 A470 $3.50 multi   7.00 7.00

Europhilex 2015 Stamp Exhibition, London.
No. 1158 contains one 51x38mm stamp.

Queen Elizabeth II and World Leaders A471

No. 1159 — Queen Elizabeth II with: a, British Prime Minister Sir Winston Churchill and Baroness Spencer-Churchill. b, Irish Pres. Mary McAleese. c, Pope John Paul II. d, Pope Francis. e, South African Pres. Nelson Mandela. f, U.S. Pres. John F. Kennedy and wife, Jacqueline.
$3.50, Queen Elizabeth II and U.S. Pres. Barack Obama, vert.

2015, May 25   Litho.   Perf. 14
1159 A471 $1 Sheet of 6, #a-f   12.00 12.00

Souvenir Sheet
Perf. 12
1160 A471 $3.50 multi   7.00 7.00

Masks A472

No. 1161: a, K'inich Janaab' Pakal death mask. b, Japanese demon mask. c, Tapuanu mask. d, Sicán mask. e, Alutiiq mask. f, Mask of Anubis.
$3.50, Mask of Agamemnon.

MICRONESIA

2015, June 1 Litho. Perf. 14
1161 A472 $1 Sheet of 6, #a-f, + 6 labels   12.00 12.00

Souvenir Sheet
Perf. 12
1162 A472 $3.50 multi   7.00 7.00

Miniature Sheets

A473

Submarines — A474

No. 1163: a, Barbarigo, Italy. b, USS George Washington, United States. c, Type C (I-16), Japan. d, Brin, Italy.
No. 1164: a, General Mola, Spain. b, C Class HMS, Great Britain. c, India Class Rescue, Russia. d, HMS B1, Great Britain.

2015, July 13 Litho. Perf. 14
1163 A473 $1 Sheet of 4, #a-d   8.00 8.00
1164 A474 $1 Sheet of 4, #a-d   8.00 8.00

Sir Winston Churchill (1874-1965), British Prime Minister — A475

No. 1165 — Photograph of Churchill from: a, 1895. b, 1904. c, 1914. d, 1924. e, 1940. f, 1951.
No. 1166 — Photograph of Churchill from: a, 1881. b, 1960.

2015, July 13 Litho. Perf. 14
1165 A475 $1 Sheet of 6, #a-f   12.00 12.00

Souvenir Sheet
Perf. 12
1166 A475 $1.75 Sheet of 2, #a-b   7.00 7.00

Birth of Princess Charlotte of Cambridge — A476

No. 1167: a, King George VI, Queen Mother and Princess Elizabeth. b, Princess Elizabeth and Prince Charles. c, Prince Charles, Princess Diana and Prince William. d, Duke and Duchess of Cambridge with Princess Charlotte.
$3.50, Duke and Duchess of Cambridge with Princess Charlotte, diff.

2015, July 13 Litho. Perf. 12
1167 A476 $1 Sheet of 4, #a-d   8.00 8.00

Souvenir Sheet
Perf. 14
1168 A476 $3.50 multi   7.00 7.00

Birds A477

No. 1169: a, White tern. b, Red junglefowl. c, Little pied cormorant. d, Purple swamphen. e, Chestnut munia. f, Reunion gray white-eye.
$3.50, Blue-faced parrotfinch.

2015, July 13 Litho. Perf. 12
1169 A477 $1 Sheet of 6, #a-f   12.00 12.00

Souvenir Sheet
1170 A477 $3.50 multi   7.00 7.00

Miniature Sheets

Stamps of United Nations Countries — A478

No. 1171, $1: a, Great Britain #1. b, Brunei #1. c, Bulgaria #1. d, Burkina Faso #1. e, Burundi #1. f, Cape Verde #1.
No. 1172, $1: a, Cambodia #1. b, Cameroun #1. c, Canada #1. d, Central African Republic #1. e, Chad #1. f, Chile #1.
No. 1173, $1: a, People's Republic of China #1. b, Colombia #6. c, Comoros Islands #30. d, Congo Democratic Republic #323. e, Congo Republic #89. f, Costa Rica #1.
No. 1174, $1: a, Croatia #1. b, Cuba #1. c, Cyprus #1. d, Czech Republic #2877. e, Denmark #1. f, Djibout #439.
No. 1175, $1: a, Dominica #1. b, Dominican Republic #1. c, Ecuador #2. d, Egypt #1. e, El Salvador #1. f, Equatorial Guinea #1.
No. 1176, $1: a, Eritrea #1. b, Estonia #1. c, Ethiopia #1. d, Fiji #1. e, Finland #83. f, France #1.
No. 1177, $1: a, Gabon #1. b, Gambia #1. c, Georgia #7. d, Germany #1. e, Ghana #1. f, Greece #1.
No. 1178, $1: a, Grenada #1. b, Guatemala #1. c, Guinea-Bissau #345. d, Guinea #168. e, British Guiana #13. f, Haiti #1.
$3.50, United States #1.

2015, July 13 Litho. Perf. 12½
Sheets of 6, #a-f
1171-1178 A478 Set of 8   96.00 96.00
1178G A478 $3.50 multi   7.00 7.00

Pope Benedict XVI A479

No. 1179: a, Crowd at St. Peter's Square (70x35mm). b, Pope Benedict XVI waving, microphone at right (35x35mm). c, Head of Pope Benedict XVI (35x35mm). d, Crowd watching Pope Benedict XVI in Popemobile (35x35mm). e, Pope Benedict XVI waving under roof of Popemobile (35x35mm).
$3.50, Pope Benedict XVI on balcony.

2015, Sept. 8 Litho. Perf. 13¾
1179 A479 $1 Sheet of 5, #a-e   10.00 10.00

Souvenir Sheet
1180 A479 $3.50 multi   7.00 7.00
No. 1180 contains one 35x35mm stamp.

New Horizons Space Probe A480

No. 1181 — Inscriptions: a, Solar system card. b, New Horizons. c, Kuiper Belt. d, Oort Cloud.
$3.50, Jan. 19, 2006 launch of New Horizons.

2015, Sept. 8 Litho. Perf. 12
1181 A480 $1 Sheet of 4, #a-d   8.00 8.00

Souvenir Sheet
1182 A480 $3.50 multi   7.00 7.00

Paintings by Vincent van Gogh (1853-90) — A481

No. 1183: a, Cypresses with Two Women, 1889. b, Vase with Red Poppies, 1886. c, Avenue of Poplars in Autumn, 1884. d, The Good Samaritan (after Delacroix), 1890. e, Plaster Statuette of a Female Torso, 1886. f, Portrait of a Man (Joseph-Michel Ginoux), 1888.
$3.50, Wheat Field with Cypresses, 1889, horiz.

2015, Sept. 8 Litho. Perf. 12
1183 A481 $1 Sheet of 6, #a-f   12.00 12.00

Souvenir Sheet
Perf. 12½
1184 A481 $3.50 multi   7.00 7.00
No. 1184 contains one 51x38mm stamp.

Orchids A482

No. 1185: a, Phalaenopsis violacea. b, Pigeon orchid. c, Calanthe triplicata. d, Phalaenopsis venosa.
$3.50, Moth orchid.

2015, Sept. 8 Litho. Perf. 12
1185 A482 $1 Sheet of 4, #a-d   8.00 8.00

Souvenir Sheet
Perf. 13¾
1186 A482 $3.50 multi   7.00 7.00
No. 1186 contains one 35x35mm stamp.

Flowers A483

No. 1187: a, Spider lily. b, Garden croton. c, Sea hibiscus. d, Frangipani. e, Wild ginger. f, Dauerleng.
$3.50, Frangipani, diff.

2015, Sept. 8 Litho. Perf. 14
1187 A483 $1 Sheet of 6, #a-f   12.00 12.00

Souvenir Sheet
Perf. 12½
1188 A483 $3.50 multi   7.00 7.00
No. 1188 contains one 51x38mm stamp.

Marine Mammals — A484

No. 1189: a, Killer whale. b, Bryde's whale. c, Bottlenose dolphins. d, Spinner dolphins. e, Risso's dolphin. f, Sperm whale.
$3.50, Dugong, vert.

2015, Sept. 8 Litho. Perf. 12
1189 A484 $1 Sheet of 6, #a-f   12.00 12.00

Souvenir Sheet
Perf. 12½
1190 A484 $3.50 multi   7.00 7.00
No. 1190 contains one 38x51mm stamp.

Battle of Waterloo, 200th Anniv. — A485

No. 1191 — Lion's Mound Monument with outer frame color of: a, Dull scarlet. b, Blue black. c, light blue. d, Blue green. e, Carmine. f, Yellow orange.
$3.50, Purple brown.

2015, Sept. 30 Litho. Perf. 13¾
1191 A485 $1 Sheet of 6, #a-f   12.00 12.00

Souvenir Sheet
1192 A485 $3.50 multi   7.00 7.00

Christmas — A486

Paintings by Bartolomé Esteban Murillo (1617-82): 34c, Adoration of the Shepherds, 1657. 49c, Adoration of the Shepherds, 1646-50. $1, Adoration of the Magi, 1655-60. $2, Madonna and Child, 1670.

2015, Nov. 2 Litho. Perf. 12½
1193-1196 A486 Set of 4   7.75 7.75

AIR POST STAMPS

Boeing 727, 1968 — AP1

35c, SA-16 Albatross, 1960. 40c, PBY-5A Catalina, 1951.

MICRONESIA — MIDDLE CONGO

1984, July 12	**Litho.**	**Perf. 13½**	
C1 AP1	28c shown	.60	.60
C2 AP1	35c multi	.80	.80
C3 AP1	40c multi	1.00	1.00
	Nos. C1-C3 (3)	2.40	2.40

Ausipex Type of 1984
Ausipex '84 emblem and: 28c, Caroline Islands No. 4. 35c, No. 7. 40c, No. 19.

1984, Sept. 21	**Litho.**	**Perf. 13½**	
C4 A4	28c multicolored	.65	.65
C5 A4	35c multicolored	.85	.85
C6 A4	40c multicolored	1.10	1.10
	Nos. C4-C6 (3)	2.60	2.60

Christmas Type
Children's drawings: 28c, Illustrated Christmas text. 35c, Decorated palm tree. 40c, Feast preparation.

1984, Dec. 20			
C7 A5	28c multi	.65	.65
C8 A5	35c multi	.90	.90
C9 A5	40c multi	1.10	1.10
	Nos. C7-C9 (3)	2.65	2.65

Ships Type

1985, Aug. 19			
C10 A6	33c L'Astrolabe	.65	.65
C11 A6	39c La Coquille	.80	.80
C12 A6	44c Shenandoah	1.00	1.00
	Nos. C10-C12 (3)	2.45	2.45

Christmas Type
33c, Dublon Protestant Church. 44c, Pohnpei Catholic Church.

1985, Oct. 15	**Litho.**	**Perf. 13½**	
C13 A7	33c multi	.90	.90
C14 A7	44c multi	1.25	1.25

Audubon Type

1985, Oct. 31		**Perf. 14½**	
C15 A8	44c Sooty tern	1.00	1.00

Ruins Type
33c, Nan Tauas inner courtyard. 39c, Outer wall. 44c, Tomb.

1985, Dec.	**Litho.**	**Perf. 13½**	
C16 A16	33c multi	.70	.70
C17 A16	39c multi	.80	.80
C18 A16	44c multi	.90	.90
	Nos. C16-C18 (3)	2.40	2.40

Halley's Comet — AP2

1986, May 16			
C19 AP2	44c dk bl, bl & blk	1.40	1.25

Return of Nauruans from Truk, 40th Anniv. — AP3

1986, May 16			
C20 AP3	44c Ship in port	1.40	1.25

AMERIPEX '86 Type
Bully Hayes (1829-1877), buccaneer: 33c, Forging Hawaiian stamp. 39c, Sinking of the Leonora, Kosrae. 44c, Hayes escapes capture. 75c, Biography, by Louis Becke. $1, Hayes ransoming chief.

1986, May 22			
C21 A18	33c multi	.55	.55
C22 A18	39c multi	.70	.70
C23 A18	44c multi	.75	.75
C24 A18	75c multi	1.50	1.50
	Nos. C21-C24 (4)	3.50	3.50

Souvenir Sheet

C25 A18	$1 multi	3.25	3.25

Christmas Type
Virgin and child paintings: 33c, Austria, 19th cent. 44c, Italy, 18th cent., diff.

1986, Oct. 15	**Litho.**	**Perf. 14½**	
C26 A20	33c multicolored	1.00	1.00
C27 A20	44c multicolored	1.40	1.40

Anniversaries and Events Type
33c, US currency, bicent. 39c, 1st American in orbit, 25th anniv. 44c, US Constitution, bicent.

1987, June 13	**Litho.**	**Perf. 14½**	
C28 A21	33c multi	.60	.60
C29 A21	39c multi	1.00	1.00
C30 A21	44c multi	1.10	1.10
	Nos. C28-C30 (3)	2.70	2.70

Christmas Type

1987, Nov. 16	**Litho.**	**Perf. 14½**	
C31 A22	33c Holy Family	.80	.80
C32 A22	39c Shepherds	.90	.90
C33 A22	44c Three Wise Men	1.00	1.00
	Nos. C31-C33 (3)	2.70	2.70

Bird Type
33c, Great truk white-eye. 44c, Blue-faced parrotfinch. $1, Yap monarch.

1988, Aug. 1	**Litho.**	**Perf. 13½**	
C34 A9	33c multi	.55	.55
C35 A9	44c multi	.70	.70
C36 A9	$1 multi	1.75	1.75
	Nos. C34-C36 (3)	3.00	3.00

Colonial Era Type
No. C37, Traditional skills (boat-building). No. C38, Modern Micronesia (tourism).

1988, July 20		**Perf. 13x13½**	
C37 A23	44c multi	.95	.95
C38 A23	44c multi	.95	.95
a.	Pair, #C37-C38	1.90	1.90

Printed se-tenant in sheets of 28 plus 4 center labels picturing flags of Kosrae (UL), Truk (UR), Pohnpei (LL) and Yap (LR).

Flags of the Federated States of Micronesia — AP4

1989, Jan. 19	**Litho.**	**Perf. 13x13½**	
C39 AP4	45c Pohnpei	.70	.70
C40 AP4	45c Truk	.70	.70
C41 AP4	45c Kosrae	.70	.70
C42 AP4	45c Yap	.70	.70
a.	Block of 4, #C39-C42	2.80	2.80

This issue exists with 44c denominations but was not issued.

Aircraft Serving Micronesia — AP5

1990, July 16	**Litho.**	**Perf. 14**	
C43 AP5	22c shown	.40	.40
C44 AP5	36c multi, diff.	.65	.65
C45 AP5	39c multi, diff.	.75	.75
C46 AP5	45c multi, diff.	.85	.85

No. C47, Propeller plane, outrigger canoe. No. C48, Passenger jet, sailboat.

1992, Mar. 27			
C47 AP5	40c multicolored	.70	.70
C48 AP5	50c multicolored	.85	.85
	Nos. C43-C48 (6)	4.20	4.20

Souvenir Sheet
First Manned Moon Landing, 25th Anniv. AP6

1994, July 20	**Litho.**	**Perf. 13½**	
C49 AP6	$2.90 US #C76	4.25	4.25

MIDDLE CONGO
ˈmi-dəl ˈkäŋˌgō

LOCATION — Western Africa at the Equator, bordering on the Atlantic Ocean
GOVT. — Former French Colony
AREA — 166,069
POP. — 746,805 (1936)
CAPITAL — Brazzaville

In 1910 Middle Congo, formerly a part of French Congo, was declared a separate colony. It was grouped with Gabon and the Ubangi-Shari and Chad Territories and officially designated French Equatorial Africa. This group became a single administrative unit in 1934. See Gabon.

See Congo People's Republic for issues of 1959 onward.

100 Centimes = 1 Franc

See French Equatorial Africa No. 191 for additional stamp inscribed "Moyen Congo" and "Afrique Equatoriale Francaise."

Leopard A1

Bakalois Woman A2

Coconut Grove — A3

Perf. 14x13½

1907-22		**Typo.**	**Unwmk.**	
1	A1	1c ol gray & brn	.55	.55
2	A1	2c vio & brn	.55	.55
3	A1	4c blue & brn	1.10	1.10
4	A1	5c dk grn & bl	1.40	.85
5	A1	5c yel & bl ('22)	1.10	1.10
6	A1	10c car & bl	1.60	.85
7	A1	10c dp grn & bl grn ('22)	5.00	5.00
a.		Imperf pair	300.00	
8	A1	15c brn vio & rose ('17)	3.25	1.25
9	A1	20c brown & bl	4.25	4.00
10	A2	25c blue & grn	2.25	1.50
11	A2	25c bl grn & gray ('22)	1.40	1.40
12	A2	30c scar & grn	3.25	2.40
13	A2	30c car ver & rose ('22)	2.25	2.25
14	A2	35c vio brn & bl	2.75	1.75
15	A2	40c dl grn & brn	2.75	1.75
16	A2	45c violet & red	7.50	5.00
17	A2	50c bl grn & red	3.00	2.50
18	A2	50c bl & grn ('22)	2.25	2.25
19	A2	75c brown & bl	9.75	6.75
20	A3	1fr dp grn & vio	15.00	12.50
21	A3	2fr vio & gray grn	16.00	11.00
22	A3	5fr blue & rose	47.50	35.00
		Nos. 1-22 (22)	134.45	101.30

For stamps of types A1-A3 in changed colors, see Chad and Ubangi-Shari. French Congo A4-A6 are similar but inscribed "Congo Francais."

For overprints and surcharges see Nos. 33-60, B1-B2.

Stamps and Types of 1907-22 Overprinted in Black, Blue or Red

1924-30

23	A1	1c ol gray & brn	.35	.35
a.		Double surcharge	150.00	
24	A1	2c violet & brn	.35	.35
25	A1	4c blue & brn	.35	.35
b.		Imperf pair	350.00	
26	A1	5c yellow & bl	.50	.50
27	A1	10c grn & bl grn (R)	1.40	.45
28	A1	10c car & gray ('25)	.50	.50
29	A1	15c brn vio & rose (Bl)	1.00	.65
a.		Double surcharge	175.00	
30	A1	20c brown & blue	.75	.75
31	A1	20c bl grn & yel grn ('26)	.50	.50
32	A1	20c dp brn & rose lil ('27)	1.60	.75

Nos. 10-22 Overprinted in Black, Red (R), and Blue (Bl)

33	A2	25c bl grn & gray	1.25	.65
34	A2	30c car ver & rose (Bl)	1.90	.70
35	A2	30c lil brown & vio bl (R) ('25)	1.00	.85
36	A2	30c dk grn & grn ('27)	2.10	1.60
37	A2	35c choc & bl	1.00	1.00
38	A2	40c ol grn & brn	2.10	1.25
a.		Double overprint	300.00	
39	A2	45c vio & pale red (Bl)	2.10	1.50
a.		Inverted overprint	200.00	
40	A2	50c blue & grn (R)	2.10	1.00
41	A2	50c org & blk ('25)	1.00	.85
a.		Without overprint	220.00	225.00
42	A2	65c org brn & bl ('27)	3.25	2.25
43	A2	75c brown & blue	1.90	1.40
44	A2	90c brn red & pink ('30)	5.75	4.75
45	A3	1fr green & vio	2.25	1.75
a.		Double overprint	275.00	
46	A3	1.10fr vio & brn ('28)	4.75	4.25
47	A3	1.50fr ultra & bl ('30)	7.00	5.75
48	A3	2fr vio & gray grn	2.10	1.75
b.		Imperf pair	300.00	
49	A3	3fr red violet ('30)	8.00	6.75
50	A3	5fr blue & rose	6.25	5.00
		Nos. 23-50 (28)	63.10	48.75

Nos. 48 and 50 Surcharged with New Values

1924

51	A3	25c on 2fr vio & gray grn	1.10	1.10
52	A3	25c on 5fr bl & rose (Bl)	1.25	1.25

Types of 1924-27 Surcharged with New Values in Black or Red

1925-27

53	A3	65c on 1fr red org & ol brn	1.20	1.20
a.		Without surcharge	275.00	
54	A3	85c on 1fr red org & ol brn	1.20	1.20
a.		Double surcharge	175.00	
55	A2	90c on 75c brn red & rose ('27)	2.00	2.40
56	A3	1.25fr on 1fr dl bl & ultra (R)	1.10	1.10
a.		Without surcharge	200.00	200.00
57	A3	1.50fr on 1fr ultra & bl ('27)	2.00	2.00
a.		Without surcharge	200.00	200.00
58	A3	3fr on 5fr org brn & dl red ('27)	4.00	4.00
a.		Without surcharge	275.00	
59	A3	10fr on 5fr ver & bl grn ('27)	13.00	13.00
60	A3	20fr on 5fr org brn & vio ('27)	13.50	13.50
		Nos. 53-60 (8)	38.00	38.40

Bars cover old values on Nos. 56-60.

Common Design Types pictured following the introduction.

Colonial Exposition Issue
Common Design Types

1931 Engr. **Perf. 12½**

Name of Country in Black

61	CD70	40c deep green	5.25	4.50
62	CD71	50c violet	4.25	4.00
63	CD72	90c red orange	4.25	4.50
64	CD73	1.50fr dull blue	6.25	5.50
		Nos. 61-64 (4)	20.00	18.50

Viaduct at Mindouli — A4

Pasteur Institute at Brazzaville — A5

MIDDLE CONGO — MOHELI — MOLDOVA

MIDDLE CONGO

Government Building, Brazzaville — A6

		1933	Photo.	Perf. 13½	
65	A4	1c lt brown		.25	.25
66	A4	2c dull blue		.25	.25
67	A4	4c olive grn		.30	.30
68	A4	5c red violet		.50	.35
69	A4	10c slate		.70	.40
70	A4	15c dk violet		1.50	1.00
71	A4	20c red, *pink*		12.00	7.00
72	A4	25c orange		1.40	.40
73	A4	30c yellow grn		2.50	1.75
74	A5	40c orange brn		3.00	1.40
75	A5	45c blk, *green*		2.00	1.75
76	A5	50c black violet		1.00	1.00
77	A5	65c brn red, *grn*		2.00	1.00
78	A5	75c black, *pink*		17.00	9.50
79	A5	90c carmine		2.50	1.75
80	A5	1fr dark red		1.25	1.00
81	A5	1.25fr Prus blue		2.75	1.25
82	A5	1.50fr dk blue		14.00	4.25
83	A6	1.75fr dk violet		3.00	1.25
84	A6	2fr grnsh blk		2.75	1.40
85	A6	3fr orange		7.00	4.00
86	A6	5fr slate blue		20.00	17.50
87	A6	10fr black		65.00	35.00
88	A6	20fr dark brown		35.00	27.50
		Nos. 65-88 (24)		197.65	121.85

SEMI-POSTAL STAMPS

No. 6 Surcharged in Black

		1916	Unwmk.	Perf. 14x13½	
B1	A1	10c + 5c car & blue		1.60	1.60
a.		Double surcharge		140.00	140.00
b.		Inverted surcharge		120.00	120.00
e.		As "a," One inverted		175.00	175.00
f.		In pair with unsurcharged stamp		360.00	

A printing with the surcharge placed lower and more to the left was made and used in Ubangi.

No. 6b Surcharged in Red

| B2 | A1 | 10c + 5c car & blue | 1.60 | 1.60 |

POSTAGE DUE STAMPS

Postage Due Stamps of France Overprinted A. E. F.

		1928	Unwmk.	Perf. 14x13½	
J1	D2	5c light blue		.50	.50
J2	D2	10c gray brn		.75	.75
J3	D2	20c olive grn		1.40	1.40
J4	D2	25c brt rose		1.75	1.75
J5	D2	30c lt red		1.75	1.75
J6	D2	45c blue grn		1.75	1.75
J7	D2	50c brown vio		1.90	1.90
J8	D2	60c yellow brn		2.75	2.75
J9	D2	1fr red brn		2.75	2.75
J10	D2	2fr orange red		4.00	4.00
J11	D2	3fr brt violet		6.50	7.00
		Nos. J1-J11 (11)		25.80	26.30

Village on Ubangi, Dance Mask — D3

Steamer on Ubangi River — D4

		1930		Typo.	
J12	D3	5c dp bl & ol		.90	1.40
J13	D3	10c dp red & brn		1.40	1.40
J14	D3	20c green & brn		3.00	3.00
J15	D3	25c lt bl & brn		4.00	4.00
J16	D3	30c bis brn & Prus bl		5.00	5.00
J17	D3	45c Prus bl & ol		6.50	6.50
J18	D3	50c red vio & brn		6.75	6.75
J19	D3	60c gray lil & bl blk		8.50	9.00
J20	D4	1fr bis brn & bl blk		12.50	14.00
J21	D4	2fr violet & brn		14.00	14.00
J22	D4	3fr dk red & brn		14.00	14.00
		Nos. J12-J22 (11)		76.55	79.05

Rubber Trees and Djoué River — D5

		1933	Photo.	Perf. 13½	
J23	D5	5c apple green		.90	.90
J24	D5	10c dk bl, *bl*		.90	.90
J25	D5	20c red, *yel*		1.50	1.50
J26	D5	25c chocolate		1.50	1.50
J27	D5	30c orange red		2.25	2.25
J28	D5	45c dk violet		2.25	2.25
J29	D5	50c gray black		3.00	3.00
J30	D5	60c blk, *orange*		5.00	5.00
J31	D5	1fr brown rose		6.25	6.25
J32	D5	2fr orange yel		8.00	8.50
J33	D5	3fr Prus blue		12.50	15.00
		Nos. J23-J33 (11)		44.05	47.05

MOHELI

mō-ˈä-lē

LOCATION — One of the Comoro Islands, situated in the Mozambique Channel midway between Madagascar and Mozambique (Africa)
GOVT. — French Colony
AREA — 89 sq. mi.
POP. — 4,000
CAPITAL — Fomboni
See Comoro Islands

100 Centimes = 1 Franc

Navigation and Commerce — A1

Perf. 14x13½

		1906-07	Typo.	Unwmk.	
		Name of Colony in Blue or Carmine			
1	A1	1c blk, *lil bl*		3.75	2.40
2	A1	2c brn, *buff*		2.50	1.75
3	A1	4c claret, *lav*		3.75	2.40
4	A1	5c yellow grn		4.25	2.40
5	A1	10c carmine		6.00	2.40
6	A1	20c red, *green*		13.00	7.25
7	A1	25c blue		13.00	5.50
8	A1	30c brn, *bister*		17.50	14.50
9	A1	35c blk, *yellow*		10.50	4.00
10	A1	40c red, *straw*		17.50	13.50
11	A1	45c blk, *gray grn*		75.00	60.00
a.		Perf 11 ('07)		300.00	
12	A1	50c brn, *az*		24.00	14.50
13	A1	75c dp vio, *org*		27.50	24.00
14	A1	1fr brnz grn, *straw*		24.00	17.50
15	A1	2fr vio, *rose*		35.00	35.00
16	A1	5fr lil, *lavender*		140.00	140.00
a.		Imperf pair		700.00	
		Nos. 1-16 (16)		417.25	347.10

Perf. 13½x14 stamps are counterfeits.
No. 12, affixed to pressboard with animals printed on the back, was used as emergency currency in the Comoro Islands in 1920.

Issue of 1906-07 Surcharged in Carmine or Black

1912

17	A1	5c on 4c cl, *lav* (C)	2.40	3.25
18	A1	5c on 20c red, *grn*	3.50	3.50
19	A1	5c on 30c brn, *bis* (C)	2.25	3.50
20	A1	10c on 40c red, *straw*	2.00	3.50
21	A1	10c on 45c blk, *gray grn* (C)	2.00	2.00
a.		"Moheli" double	475.00	
b.		"Moheli" triple	475.00	
22	A1	10c on 50c brn, *az* (C)	3.50	4.50
		Nos. 17-22 (6)	15.90	20.25

Two spacings between the surcharged numerals are found on Nos. 17 to 22. For detailed listings, see the *Scott Classic Specialized Catalogue of Stamps and Covers.*
The stamps of Moheli were supposed to have been superseded by those of Madagascar, January, 1908. However, Nos. 17-22 were surcharged in 1912 to use up remainders. These were available for use in Madagascar and the entire Comoro archipelago. In 1950 stamps of Comoro Islands came into use.

MOLDOVA

mäl-ˈdō-və

(Moldavia)

LOCATION — Southeastern Europe, bounded by Romania and the Ukraine
GOVT. — Independent republic, member of the Commonwealth of Independent States
AREA — 13,012 sq. mi.
POP. — 4,030,000 (2020 est.)
CAPITAL — Chisinau

With the breakup of the Soviet Union on Dec. 26, 1991, Moldova and ten former Soviet republics established the Commonwealth of Independent States.

100 Kopecks = 1 Ruble
100 Bani = 1 Leu (1993)

Catalogue values for all unused stamps in this country are for Never Hinged items.

Coat of Arms — A1

Flag — A2

		1991, June 23	Litho.	Imperf.	
		Without Gum			
1	A1	7k grn & multi		.25	.25
2	A1	13k blue & multi		.25	.25
3	A2	30k multi		.25	.35
		Nos. 1-3 (3)		.75	.85

Codrii Nature Preserve — A6

		1992, Feb. 8	Litho.	Perf. 12	
25	A6	25k multicolored		.40	.40

For surcharge see No. 547.

Natl. Arms — A7

		1992, May 24	Photo.	Perf. 13½	
26	A7	35k green		.25	.25
27	A7	50k red		.25	.25
28	A7	65k brown		.25	.25
29	A7	1r purple		.25	.25
30	A7	1.50r blue		.25	.25
		Nos. 26-30 (5)		1.25	1.25

Birds — A8

Designs: 50k, Merops apiaster. 65k, Oriolus oriolus. 2.50r, Picus viridis. 6r, Coracias garrulus. 7.50r, Upupa epops. 15r, Cuculus canorus.

		1992, Aug. 5	Litho.	Perf. 13½x14	
31	A8	50k multicolored		.25	.25
32	A8	65k multicolored		.25	.25
33	A8	2.50r multicolored		.35	.35
34	A8	6r multicolored		.60	.60
35	A8	7.50r multicolored		.80	.80
36	A8	15r multicolored		1.75	1.75
		Nos. 31-36 (6)		4.00	4.00

No. 31 incorrectly inscribed "ariaster."
See Nos. 75-81.

Church of St. Panteleimon, Cent. — A9

		1992, Aug. 10	Photo.	Perf. 11½	
37	A9	1.50r multicolored		.40	.40

She-Wolf Suckling Romulus and Remus — A10

		1992, Aug. 10		Perf. 12x11½	
38	A10	5r multicolored		.90	.90

Russia Nos. 4598-4599, 5839 Surcharged "MOLDOVA" and New Value in Black or Red

		1992, Aug. 31	Litho.	Perf. 12x12½	
39	A2138	2.50r on 4k #4599		.30	.30
40	A2139	6r on 3k #4598		.55	.55
41	A2138	8.50r on 4k #4599		.70	.70
42	A2765	10r on 3k #5839 (R)		.80	.80
a.		Black surcharge		.80	.80
b.		Brown red surcharge		.80	.80
		Nos. 39-42 (4)		2.35	2.35

Sheets of Nos. 39, 41 had row 5 inverted. On No. 40 only the 1st 5 stamps of row 5 were inverted. Counterfeit inverts were made using the original plates but with all 100 surcharges inverted. All inverts on No. 42 are fakes.

Russia Nos. 4596-4598 Surcharged in Black, Green or Red

		1992, Oct. 20	Litho.	Perf. 12x12½	
43	A2138	45k on 2k #4597 (G)		.80	.80
44	A2138	46k on 2k #4597		.80	.80
45	A2138	63k on 1k #4596 (R)		.80	.80
46	A2138	63k on 3k #4598		1.40	1.40
47	A2138	70k on 1k #4596 (R)		.80	.80
50	A2138	4r on 1k #4596		1.40	1.40
a.		Red surcharge		1.40	1.40
		Nos. 43-50 (6)		6.00	6.00

Nos. 45-46 exist with overprint inverted (6th row of sheet).

1992 Summer Olympics, Barcelona A11

		1992, Oct. 24	Litho.	Perf. 13	
53	A11	35k High jump		.30	.30
54	A11	65k Wrestling		.30	.30
55	A11	1r Archery		.30	.30
56	A11	2.50r Swimming		.65	.65
57	A11	10r Equestrian		2.50	2.50
a.		Souvenir sheet, #53-57 + label		3.50	3.50
		Nos. 53-57 (5)		4.05	4.05

Nos. 55-56 Ovptd. with Name of Medalist, Medal and Olympic Rings in Bronze or Silver

		1992, Oct. 24			
58	A11	1r "NATALIA VALEEV / bronz" (BR)		.50	.50
59	A11	2.50r "IURIE BASCATOV / argint"		.90	.90

MOLDOVA

Souvenir Sheet

Tudor Casapu, 1992 Weight Lifting Gold Medalist — A12

1992, Oct. 24			Perf. 14½	
60	A12	25r multicolored	3.50	3.50

Admission of Moldova to UN — A13

Designs: 12r, UN Headquarters at left, Statue of Liberty, UN emblem, Moldovan flag.

1992, Oct. 24			Perf. 13	
61	A13	1.30r multicolored	.45	.45
62	A13	12r multicolored	.90	.90

Moldovan Participation in Conference on European Security and Cooperation — A14

2.50r, Flag, Prague Castle. 25r, Helsinki Cathedral, flag.

1992, Oct. 24				
63	A14	2.50r multi	.65	.65
64	A14	25r multicolored	1.60	1.60

Traditional Folk Art — A15

1992, Nov. 21			Perf. 12x11½	
65	A15	7.50r Rug, pottery	.70	.70

Admission of Moldova to UPU — A16

1992, Dec. 26			Perf. 12	
66	A16	5r Train, flag, emblem	.40	.40
67	A16	10r Plane, flag, emblem	.80	.80

Discovery of America, 500th Anniv. — A17

1992, Dec. 26			Litho.	Perf. 12
68	A17	1r Galleon	.30	.30
69	A17	6r Carrack	.70	.70
70	A17	6r Caravel	.70	.70
a.	Pair, #69-70		2.00	2.00
	Nos. 68-70 (3)		1.70	1.70

Souvenir Sheet

| 71 | A17 | 25r Columbus | 2.75 | 2.75 |

Elaphe Longissima — A18

Denominations at: a, UL. b, UR. c, LL. d, LR.

1993, July 3			Litho.	Perf. 13½
72	A18	3r Block of 4, #a.-d.	1.50	1.50
73	A18	15r Natrix natrix	.60	.60
74	A18	25r Vipera berus	.85	.85
	Nos. 72-74 (3)		2.95	2.95

Bird Type of 1992

1993, July 24			Litho.	Perf. 13x13½
75	A8	2r like #31	.30	.30
76	A8	3r like #32	.30	.30
77	A8	5r like #33	.30	.30
78	A8	10r like #34	.30	.30
79	A8	15r like #35	.35	.35
80	A8	50r like #36	.80	.80
81	A8	100r Hirundo rustica	1.60	1.60
	Nos. 75-81 (7)		3.95	3.95

Nos. 75-81 exist imperf. Value, set $100.

Natl. Arms — A19

1993, Aug. 7			Photo.	Perf. 12x12½
82	A19	2k blue	.25	.25
83	A19	3k purple	.25	.25
84	A19	6k green	.25	.25
85	A19	10k olive & purple	.25	.25
86	A19	15k olive & purple	.25	.25
87	A19	20k gray & purple	.25	.25
88	A19	30k yellow & purple	.25	.25
89	A19	50k pink & purple	.40	.40

Size: 21x32½mm
Perf. 12½x12

90	A19	100k multicolored	.40	.40
91	A19	250k multicolored	.95	.95
	Nos. 82-91 (10)		3.50	3.50

For surcharges see Nos. 558-559.

Butterflies — A20

1993, Dec. 22			Litho.	Perf. 13
94	A20	6b Pyrameis atalanta	.30	.30
95	A20	10b Papilio machaon	.30	.30
96	A20	50b Vanessa jo	.50	.50
97	A20	250b Saturnia pavonia	2.25	2.25
	Nos. 94-97 (4)		3.35	3.35

Flowers — A21

Designs: 6b, Tulipa bibersteiniana. 15b, Convallaria majalis. 25b, Galanthus nivalis. 30b, Paeonia peregrina. 50b, Galanthus plicatus. 90b, Pulsatilla grandis. 250b, Cypripedium calceolus.

1993, Dec. 25			Litho.	Perf. 13½
98	A21	6b multicolored	.25	.25
99	A21	15b multicolored	.25	.25
100	A21	25b multicolored	.30	.30
101	A21	30b multicolored	.35	.35
102	A21	50b multicolored	.40	.40
103	A21	90b multicolored	.65	.65
	Nos. 98-103 (6)		2.20	2.20

Souvenir Sheet

| 104 | A21 | 250b multicolored | 1.80 | 1.80 |

No. 104 contains one 30x45mm stamp.

A22

Famous Men: 6b, Dragos Voda. 25b, Bogdan Voda I. 50b, Latcu Voda. 100b, Petru I Musat. 150b, Roman Voda Musat. 200b, Stefan I.

1993, Dec. 29			Litho.	Perf. 13
105	A22	6b multicolored	.30	.30
106	A22	25b multicolored	.30	.30
107	A22	50b multicolored	.30	.30
108	A22	150b multicolored	.40	.40
109	A22	150b multicolored	.55	.55
110	A22	200b multicolored	.90	.90
	Nos. 105-110 (6)		2.75	2.75

A23

Europa (Contemporary art): 3b, History of Man, by M. Grecu. 150b, Springtime, by I. Vieru.

1993, Dec. 29			Litho.	Perf. 13
111	A23	3b multicolored	.40	.40
112	A23	150b multicolored	3.75	3.75
a.	Souvenir sheet, 4 each #111-112 + label		17.50	17.50

1994 Winter Olympics, Lillehammer — A24

1994, Feb. 12			Litho.	Perf. 13½
113	A24	3b Biathlete, skiiers	.75	.75
114	A24	150b Biathlete, diff.	1.25	1.25

Russia No. 4596 Surcharged in Dark Blue

1994, Apr. 11			Litho.	Perf. 12x12½
114A	A2138	3b on 1k olive grn	.25	.25
114B	A2138	25b on 1k olive grn	.25	.25
114C	A2138	50b on 1k olive grn	.30	.30
	Nos. 114A-114C (3)		.80	.80

First Manned Moon Landing, 25th anniv. — A25

Europa: 1b, Gemini space mission, Titan II rocket. 45b, Ed White, Gemini IV. 2.50 l, Lunar landing module.

1994, June 18			Litho.	Perf. 14
115	A25	1b multicolored	.50	.50
116	A25	45b multicolored	2.40	2.40
117	A25	2.50 l multicolored	5.25	5.25
	Nos. 115-117 (3)		8.15	8.15

Natl. Arms — A26

1994				Perf. 13½x14
118	A26	1b multicolored	.25	.25
119	A26	10b multicolored	.25	.25
120	A26	30b multicolored	.25	.25
121	A26	38b multicolored	.25	.25
122	A26	45b multicolored	.55	.55
123	A26	75b multicolored	.65	.65
125	A26	1.50 l multicolored	1.20	1.20
126	A26	1.80 l multicolored	1.20	1.20
127	A26	2.50 l multi, size: 23½x29mm	1.90	1.90
128	A26	4.50 l multicolored	3.75	3.75
128A	A26	5.40 l multicolored	4.00	4.00
128B	A26	6.90 l multicolored	5.00	5.00

Size: 23½x29mm

128C	A26	7.20 l multicolored	5.00	5.00
129	A26	13 l multicolored	9.25	9.25
130	A26	24 l multicolored	17.50	17.50
	Nos. 118-130 (15)		51.00	51.00

Issued: 1b, 45b, 1.50 l, 4.50 l, 6/11/94; 10b, 30b, 5.40 l, 6.90 l, 13 l, 7/16/94; 38b, 75b, 1.80 l, 2.50 l, 7.20 l, 8/13/94.

Stamp Card A27

Designs: 1.50 l, 4.50 l, Map of Moldova.

Rouletted 26 on 2 or 3 Sides

1994, Dec. 22				Litho.
Self-Adhesive				
Cards of 6 + 6 labels				
131	A27	1.50 l #a.-f., lt vio & multi		6.00
132	A27	4.50 l #a.-f., dp red vio & multi		15.00

Individual stamps measure 70x9mm and have a card backing. Se-tenant labels inscribed "AIR MAIL."

Famous People — A28

Designs: 3b, Maria Cibotari (1910-49), singer. 90b, Dumitru Caraciobanu (1937-80), actor. 150b, Eugeniu Coca (1893-1954), composer. 250b, Igor Vieru (1923-83), painter.

1994, June 30			Litho.	Perf. 13½
133	A28	3b multicolored	.30	.30
134	A28	90b multicolored	.35	.35
135	A28	150b multicolored	.45	.45
136	A28	250b multicolored	.90	.90
	Nos. 133-136 (4)		2.00	2.00

Stamp Day — A29

Designs: 10b, Designing stamp. 45b, Printing stamps. 2 l, Inspecting finished sheets.

1994, July 22			Litho.	Perf. 14
137	A29	10b multicolored	.30	.30
138	A29	45b multicolored	.60	.60
139	A29	2 l multicolored	1.75	1.75
	Nos. 137-139 (3)		2.65	2.65

Intl. Olympic Committee, Cent. — A30

60b, Pierre de Coubertin. 1.50 l, Olympic rings, symbol.

1994, Aug. 29			Litho.	Perf. 13½x14
140	A30	60b multi	.40	.40
141	A30	1.50 l multi	1.00	1.00

Moldova's Entrance into NATO — A31

Designs: 60b, Moldova Pres. Mircea Snegur, NATO Secretary General Manfred Worner signing documents. 2.50 l, World map centered on Europe.

1994, Nov. 8			Litho.	Perf. 13½
142	A31	60b multicolored	.85	.85
143	A31	2.50 l multicolored	3.25	3.25

Intl. Year of the Family — A32

MOLDOVA

30b, Family. 60b, Mother breast-feeding. 1.50 l, Child painting.

1994, Nov. 26			Perf. 14	
144	A32	30b multi	.50	.50
145	A32	60b multi	1.00	1.00
146	A32	1.50 l multi	1.75	1.75
	Nos. 144-146 (3)		3.25	3.25

1996 European Soccer Championships, England — A33

Designs: 10b, Handshaking. 40b, Players legs, soccer ball. 1.20 l, Goalie.
No. 150: a, 1.10 l, Soccer federation, German flags. b, 2.20 l, Soccer ball, German, Moldovan flags. c, 2.40 l, Players.

1994, Dec. 10				
147	A33	10b multicolored	.30	.30
148	A33	40b multicolored	.60	.60
149	A33	2.40 l multicolored	2.75	2.75
	Nos. 147-149 (3)		3.65	3.65

Souvenir Sheet

150	A33	Sheet of 3, #a.-c.	5.00	5.00

Christmas — A34

Paintings of Birth of Christ by: 20b, unknown artist, 18th cent. 3.60 l, Gherasim, 1808.

1994, Dec. 29				
151	A34	20b multicolored	.40	.40
152	A34	3.60 l multicolored	3.50	3.50

Mushrooms — A35

4b, Russula virescens. 10b, Boletus luridus. 20b, Cantherellus cibarius. 90b, Leccinum aurantiacum. 1.80 l, Leccinum duriusculum.

1995, Feb. 8				
153	A35	4b multi	.50	.50
154	A35	10b multi	.80	.80
155	A35	20b multi	1.60	1.60
156	A35	90b multi	4.75	4.75
157	A35	1.80 l multi	8.75	8.75
	Nos. 153-157 (5)		16.40	16.40

European Nature Conservation Year — A36

Designs: 4b, Hieraaetus pennatus. 45b, Capreolus capreolus. 90b, Sus scrofa.

1995, Mar. 18		Litho.	Perf. 14	
158	A36	4b multicolored	.75	.75
159	A36	45b multicolored	3.50	3.50
160	A36	90b multicolored	7.50	7.50
	Nos. 158-160 (3)		11.75	11.75

Museum of Natural Sciences A37

Designs: 4b, Jars. 10b+2b, Dinotherium giganteum. 1.80 l+30b, Silver coin, 3rd-2nd cent. BC.

1995		Litho.	Perf. 14	
161	A37	4b multicolored	.50	.50
162	A37	10b +2b multi	1.00	1.00
163	A37	1.80 l +30b multi	7.00	7.00
	Nos. 161-163 (3)		8.50	8.50

Peace & Freedom A38

Paintings: 10b, May 1945, by Igor Vieru. 40b, Linistea, by Sergiu Cuciuc. 2.20 l, Primavara 1944, by Cuciuc.

1995, May 9		Litho.	Perf. 14	
164	A38	10b multicolored	.45	.45
165	A38	40b multicolored	2.60	2.60
166	A38	2.20 l multicolored	5.00	5.00
	Nos. 164-166 (3)		8.05	8.05

Europa.

A39

Famous People: 9b, Constantin Stere (1865-1936), writer. 10b, Tamara Ceban (1914-90), musician. 40b, Alexandru Plamadeala (1888-1940), sculptor. 1.80 l, Lucian Blaga (1895-1961), writer.

1995, June 17		Litho.	Perf. 14	
167	A39	9b dp cl & gray	.35	.35
168	A39	10b brt mag & gray	.35	.35
169	A39	40b violet & gray	1.40	1.40
170	A39	1.80 l dk grn & gray	6.00	6.00
	Nos. 167-170 (4)		8.10	8.10

A40

Kings of Moldova, reign: No. 171, Alexandru Cel Bun, 1400-32. No. 172, Petru Aron, 1451-52, 1454-57. No. 173, Stefan Cel Mare, 1457-1504. 45b, Petru Rares, 1527-38, 1541-46. 90b, Alexandru Lapusneanu, 1552-61, 1564-68. 1.80 l, Ion Voda Cel Cumplit, 1572-74. 5 l, Stefan Cel Mare, 1457-1504.

1995, July 2		Litho.	Perf. 14	
171	A40	10 b multicolored	.40	.40
172	A40	10 b multicolored	.40	.40
173	A40	10 b multicolored	.40	.40
174	A40	45 b multicolored	1.50	1.50
175	A40	90 b multicolored	2.50	2.50
176	A40	1.80 l multicolored	7.00	7.00
	Nos. 171-176 (6)		12.20	12.20

Souvenir Sheet

177	A40	5 l multicolored	3.25	3.25

No. 177 contains one 24x29mm stamp.

Citadels of Moldova — A41

1995, July 29				
178	A41	10 b Soroca	.35	.35
179	A41	20 b Tighina	.70	.70
180	A41	60 b Alba	1.50	1.50
181	A41	1.30 l Hotin	4.25	4.25
	Nos. 178-181 (4)		6.80	6.80

A42

UN, 50th Anniv. A43

Designs inside of stylized eye: No. 182, Forest stream. No. 183, Fighter plane. No. 184, Black child, barbed wire fence.
Nos. 185-186: a, 1. b, 2. c, 3. d, 4. e, 5. f, 6. g, 7. h, 8. i, 9. j, 10.

1995, Oct. 24		Litho.	Perf. 14	
182	A42	10b yellow & multi	.40	.40
183	A42	10b blue & multi	.40	.40
184	A42	1.50 l green & multi	6.00	6.00
	Nos. 182-184 (3)		6.80	6.80

Stamp Cards
Rouletted 15 on 2 or 3 Sides
Self-Adhesive
Cards of 10

185	A43	90b #a.-j.	17.50	17.50
186	A43	1.50 l #a.-j.	30.00	30.00

Background color of stamps gradually shifts from light blue (#1) to dark blue (#10). Each stamp is individually numbered.

Motion Pictures, Cent. — A44

Films: 10b, Last Moon of Autumn. 40b, Lautarii. 2.40 l, Dimitrie Cantemir.

1995, Dec. 28		Litho.	Perf. 14	
187	A44	10b red brn & blk	.60	.60
188	A44	40b olive & black	1.75	1.75
189	A44	2.40 l ultra & black	6.00	6.00
	Nos. 187-189 (3)		8.35	8.35

Mushrooms — A45

No. 190, Amanita muscaria. No. 191, Boletus satanas. 65b, Amanita phalloides. 1.30 l, Hypholoma fasciculare. 2.40 l, Amanita virosa.

1996, Mar. 23		Litho.	Perf. 14	
190	A45	10b multicolored	.85	.85
191	A45	10b multicolored	.85	.85
192	A45	65b multicolored	1.25	1.25
193	A45	1.30 l multicolored	2.00	2.00
194	A45	2.40 l multicolored	5.75	5.75
	Nos. 190-194 (5)		10.70	10.70

1996 Summer Olympic Games, Atlanta — A46

1996, Mar. 30				
195	A46	10b Weight lifting	.45	.45
196	A46	20b +5b Judo	.45	.45
197	A46	45b +10b Running	.85	.85
198	A46	2.40 l +30b Canoeing	4.75	4.75
	Nos. 195-198 (4)		6.50	6.50

Souvenir Sheet

199	A46	2.20 l Archery	3.00	3.00
a.		With added inscription in sheet margin	3.75	3.75

No. 199 contains one 34x29mm stamp.

No. 199a inscribed "Nicolae JURAVSCHI Victor RENEISCHI / -canoe, argint- / Serghei MUREICO/ -lupte greco-romane,bronz-".

Monasteries — A47

10b, Rudi, 18th cent. 90b, Japca, 17th cent. 1.30 l, Curchi, 18th cent. 2.80 l, Saharna, 18th cent. 4.40 l, Capriana, 16th cent.

1996, Apr. 26				
200	A47	10b multi	.45	.45
201	A47	90b multi	.80	.80
202	A47	1.30 l multi	1.40	1.40
203	A47	2.80 l multi	3.00	3.00
204	A47	4.40 l multi	4.75	4.75
	Nos. 200-204 (5)		10.40	10.40

Birds — A48

Designs: 9b, Gallinula chloropus. 10b, Anser anser. No. 207, Streptopelia turtur. 4.40 l, Anas platyrhynchos.
No. 209, Phasianus colchicus.

1996, May 17				
205	A48	9b multicolored	.35	.35
206	A48	10b multicolored	.35	.35
207	A48	2.20 l multicolored	2.50	2.50
208	A48	4.40 l multicolored	4.25	4.25
	Nos. 205-208 (4)		7.45	7.45

Souvenir Sheet

209	A48	2.20 l multicolored	2.50	2.50

Europa

A49

Famous Women: 10b, Elena Alistar (1873-1955), president of women's league. 3.70 l, Marie Curie (1867-1934), chemist, physicist. 2.20 l, Julia Hasdeu (1869-1888), writer.

1996, June 21		Litho.	Perf. 14	
210	A49	10b multicolored	.50	.50
211	A49	3.70 l multicolored	4.75	4.75

Souvenir Sheet

212	A49	2.20 l multicolored	4.75	4.75

A50

Famous Men: No. 213, Gavriil Banulescu-Bodoni (1746-1821), Metropolitan of Moldavia. No. 214, Mihail Eminescu (1850-69), poet. 2.20 l, Ion Creanga (1837-89), writer. 3.30 l, Vasile Alecsandri (1821-90), writer. 5.40 l, Petru Movila (1596-1646), theologian. 1.80 l, Eminescu, diff., vert.

1996, July 30		Litho.	Perf. 14	
213	A50	10b gray vio & brn	.35	.35
214	A50	10b lt brn & dk brn	.35	.35
215	A50	2.20 l gray & brn	2.00	2.00
216	A50	3.30 l ol & brn	2.75	2.75
217	A50	5.40 l red brn & brn	4.50	4.50
	Nos. 213-217 (5)		9.95	9.95

Souvenir Sheet

218	A50	1.80 l brn	2.00	2.00

City of Chisinau, 560th Anniv. — A51

Building, year erected: 10b, City Hall, 1902. 1.30 l, Palace of Culture, 1911. 2.40 l, Mazarache Church, 1752.

MOLDOVA

1996, Oct. 6   Litho.   *Perf. 14*
219	A51	10b multicolored	.75	.75
220	A51	1.30 l multicolored	2.50	2.50
221	A51	2.40 l multicolored	5.75	5.75
		Nos. 219-221 (3)	9.00	9.00

A52

Christmas: 10b, Children carrying star. 2.20 l+30b, Mother and child in center of star. 2.80 l+50b, Children decorating Christmas tree.

1996, Dec. 12   Litho.   *Perf. 14*
222	A52	10b multicolored	.35	.35
223	A52	2.20 l +30b multicolored	2.25	2.25
224	A52	2.80 l +50b multicolored	3.00	3.00
		Nos. 222-224 (3)	5.60	5.60

A53

Wines of Moldova: 10b, Feteasca. 45b, Cabernet-Sauvignon. 65b, Sauvignon. 3.70 l, Rara neagra.

1997, Jan. 17   Litho.   *Perf. 14*
225	A53	10b multi	.35	.35
226	A53	45b multi	.45	.45
227	A53	65b multi	.75	.75
228	A53	3.70 l multi	3.75	3.75
		Nos. 225-228 (4)	5.30	5.30

Easter — **A54**

Designs: 3.30b, Colored eggs, grass on plate. 5 l, Basket of eggs, food.

1997, Apr. 25   Litho.   *Perf. 13½*
| 229 | A54 | 10b multicolored | .35 | .35 |
| 230 | A54 | 3.30 l multicolored | 3.00 | 3.00 |

Souvenir Sheet
| 231 | A54 | 5 l multicolored | 5.00 | 5.00 |

Composers **A55**

Designs: No. 232, Franz Schubert (1797-1828). No. 233, Gavriil Musicescu (1847-1903). 45b, Sergei Rachmaninoff (1873-1943). 4.40 l, Georges Enescu (1881-1955).

1997, Feb. 22   Litho.   *Perf. 14*
232	A55	10b slate & bl grn	.35	.35
233	A55	10b slate & bl grn	.35	.35
234	A55	45b slate & bl grn	.50	.50
235	A55	4.40 l slate & bl grn	4.00	4.00
		Nos. 232-235 (4)	5.20	5.20

Stories and Legends — **A56**

Europa: 10b, Man holding up arms, goose flying, arrows from fortress. 2.80 l, Man upside down, church, sun in sky with stars and eye. 5 l, Angel touching flowers during winter.

1997, June 20   Litho.   *Perf. 13½*
| 236 | A56 | 10b multicolored | 1.00 | 1.00 |
| 237 | A56 | 2.80 l multicolored | 6.50 | 6.50 |

Souvenir Sheet
| 238 | A56 | 5 l multicolored | 8.50 | 8.50 |

Red Book Insects — **A57**

Insects on plants, flowers: 25b, Mantis religiosa. 80b, Ascalphus macaronius scop. 1 l, Calosoma sycophanta. 2.20 l, Liometopum microcephalum. 5 l, Scolia maculata drury.

1997, July 26   Litho.   *Perf. 14*
239	A57	25b multicolored	.35	.35
240	A57	80b multicolored	.95	.95
241	A57	1 l multicolored	1.10	1.10
242	A57	2.20 l multicolored	2.50	2.50
		Nos. 239-242 (4)	4.90	4.90

Souvenir Sheet
| 243 | A57 | 5 l multicolored | 5.00 | 5.00 |

World Post Day — **A58**

Designs: 10b, Chisinau post office building, 1997. 2.20 l, Mail coach, Chisinaupost office building. 3.30 l, Heinrich von Stephan (1831-97), vert.

1997, Oct. 18   Litho.   *Perf. 14*
244	A58	10b multicolored	.40	.40
245	A58	2.20 l multicolored	2.00	2.00
246	A58	3.30 l multicolored	4.00	4.00
		Nos. 244-246 (3)	6.40	6.40

Christmas — **A59**

Designs: 10b, Noul Neamt Monastery. 45b, "Adoration of the Shepherds," Noul Neamt Monastery. 5 l, "Nativity", Natl. Museum of Plastic Arts.

1997, Dec. 17   Litho.   *Perf. 13½*
247	A59	10b multicolored	.30	.30
248	A59	45b multicolored	.40	.40
249	A59	5 l multicolored	3.50	3.50
		Nos. 247-249 (3)	4.20	4.20

A60

Cultural Heritage Sites: 7b, Nicolai Zelinski High School, Tiraspol. No. 251, Railway station, Tighina. No. 252, Cathedral, Balti. 90b, Church, Causeni. 1.30 l, Cathedral, Ragul. 3.30 l, Art Institute, Chisinau.

1997, Dec. 16   Litho.   *Perf. 14*
250	A60	7b black & lilac	.40	.40
251	A60	10b black & red violet	.40	.40
252	A60	10b black & grn blue	.40	.40
253	A60	90b black & yel org	.80	.80
254	A60	1.30 l black & blue	1.25	1.25
255	A60	3.30 l black & gray	3.00	3.00
		Nos. 250-255 (6)	6.25	6.25

A61

Princes of Moldova, reign: No. 256, Petru Schiopul (1574-77, 78-79, 82-91). No. 257, Ieremia Movila (1595-1606). 45b, Stefan Tomsa (1611-15, 1621-23). 1.80 l, Radu Mihnea (1616-19, 1623-26). 2.20 l, Miron Barnovschi Movila (1626-29, 1633). 2.80 l, Bogdan Orbul (1504-17). 5 l, Mihai Viteazul, 1600.

1997, Dec. 17
256	A61	10b multicolored	.30	.30
257	A61	10b multicolored	.30	.30
258	A61	45b multicolored	.40	.40
259	A61	1.80 l multicolored	1.50	1.50
260	A61	2.20 l multicolored	2.00	2.00
261	A61	2.80 l multicolored	2.50	2.50
		Nos. 256-261 (6)	7.00	7.00

Souvenir Sheet
| 262 | A61 | 5 l multicolored | 4.75 | 4.75 |

No. 262 contains one 23x29mm stamp.

1998 Winter Olympic Games, Nagano — **A62**

1998, Feb. 28
263	A62	10b Slalom skiing	.40	.40
264	A62	45b Figure skating	.80	.80
265	A62	2.20 l Biathlon	3.00	3.00
		Nos. 263-265 (3)	4.20	4.20

A63

Famous People: 10b, Alexei Mateevici (1888-1917). 40b, Pantelimon Halippa (1883-1979). 60b, Stefan Ciobanu (1883-1950). 2 l, Constantin Stamati-Ciurea (1828-98). 5 l, Nicolae Milescu-Spatarul (1636-1708).

1998, May 9   Litho.   *Perf. 14*
266	A63	10b multicolored	.25	.25
267	A63	40b multicolored	.45	.45
268	A63	60b multicolored	.60	.60
269	A63	2 l multicolored	1.80	1.80
		Nos. 266-269 (4)	3.10	3.10

Souvenir Sheet
| 270 | A63 | 5 l multicolored | 4.50 | 4.50 |

A64

Monuments and Works of Art: 10b, Monument to Stefan cel Mare, by Alexandru Plamadeala. 60b, The Resurrected Christ, by 19th cent. artist. 1 l, Steel column, by Constantin Brancusi. 2.60 l, Trajan's Column, by Apollodorus of Damascus, Rome.

1998, May 13   *Perf. 14½x14*
271	A64	10b multicolored	.25	.25
272	A64	60b multicolored	.65	.65
273	A64	1 l multicolored	.90	.90
274	A64	2.60 l multicolored	2.50	2.50
		Nos. 271-274 (4)	4.30	4.30

Natl. Holidays and Festivals — **A65**

Europa: 10b, Eugène Ionesco biennial Theater Festival. 2.20 l, Lurceni ceramics, Nisporeni. 5 l, Music Festival, Martisor.

1998, July 18   Litho.   *Perf. 14*
| 275 | A65 | 10b multicolored | .75 | .75 |
| 276 | A65 | 2.20 l multicolored | 4.75 | 4.75 |

Souvenir Sheet
| 277 | A65 | 5 l multicolored | 8.25 | 8.25 |

Fruit — **A66**

1998, Aug. 15
278	A66	7b Cerasus avium	.35	.35
279	A66	10b Prunus domestica	.35	.35
280	A66	1 l Malus domestica	.90	.90
281	A66	2 l Cydonia oblonga	1.80	1.80
		Nos. 278-281 (4)	3.40	3.40

Diana, Princess of Wales (1961-97) — **A67**

Various portraits: a, 10b. b, 90b. c, 1.80 l. d, 2.20 l. e, 1.80 l.

1998, Aug. 31   Litho.   *Perf. 14*
| 282 | A67 | Sheet of 5, #a.-e. + label | 6.50 | 6.50 |

First Stamps Used in Moldova, 140th Anniv. — **A68**

Stamps on stamps: 10b, Romania #1-2, Type A2. 90b, Romania #2, #329, Type A177. 2.20 l, Romania #4, Russia #4132, #5916. 2.40 l, Moldova #122, #214, Romania #3.

Photo. & Engr.

1998, Oct. 9   *Perf. 14*
283	A68	10b multicolored	.30	.30
284	A68	90b multicolored	.50	.45
285	A68	2.20 l multicolored	2.00	2.00
286	A68	2.40 l multicolored	2.50	2.50
		Nos. 283-286 (4)	5.30	5.25

Medieval Fortresses **A69**

1998, Sept. 26   Litho.   *Perf. 14*
287	A69	10b Chilia	.40	.40
288	A69	60b Orhei	.70	.70
289	A69	1 l Suceava	1.10	1.10
290	A69	2 l Ismail	2.40	2.40
		Nos. 287-290 (4)	4.60	4.60

Birds **A70**

25b, Bubo bubo, vert. 2 l, Anthropoides virgo.

1998, Oct. 31
| 291 | A70 | 25b multicolored | .55 | .55 |
| 292 | A70 | 2 l multicolored | 3.50 | 3.50 |

Regional Costumes — **A71**

1998, Nov. 28   Litho.   *Perf. 14*
293	A71	25b Vara	.35	.35
294	A71	90b Vara, diff.	.80	.80
295	A71	1 l Iarna	2.10	2.10
296	A71	2 l Iarna, diff.	2.25	2.25
		Nos. 293-296 (4)	5.50	5.50

Annexation of Bessarabia to Romania, 80th Anniv. — **A72**

1998, Dec. 10
| 297 | A72 | 90b multicolored | 1.00 | 1.00 |

MOLDOVA

Universal Declaration of Human Rights, 50th Anniv. — A73

1998, Dec. 10
298 A73 2.40 l multicolored 3.25 3.25

UPU, 125th Anniv. — A74

1999, Apr. 9 *Litho.* *Perf. 14*
299 A74 25b multicolored .55 .55

Council of Europe, 50th Anniv. — A75

1999, Apr. 9
300 A75 2.20 l multicolored 3.00 3.00

Nature Reserves A76

Europa: 25b, Prutul de Jos. 2.40 l, Padurea Domneasca. 5 l, Codru.

1999, May 5 *Litho.* *Perf. 14*
301 A76 25b multicolored .60 .60
302 A76 2.40 l multicolored 3.25 3.25

Souvenir Sheet
303 A76 5 l multicolored 7.00 7.00

Honoré de Balzac (1799-1850), Writer — A77

1999, May 20
304 A77 90b multicolored 1.00 1.00

Aleksandr Pushkin (1788-1837), Poet — A78

1999, June 6
305 A78 65b brown & black .80 .80

National Sports — A79

1999, June 26 *Litho.* *Perf. 13¾*
306 A79 25b Wrestling .40 .40
307 A79 1.80 l Oina 2.10 2.10

First Manned Moon Landing, 30th Anniv. — A80

1999, July 20 *Litho.* *Perf. 14*
308 A80 25b Michael Collins .30 .30
309 A80 25b Neil Armstrong .30 .30
310 A80 5 l Edwin Aldrin 4.50 4.50
Nos. 308-310 (3) 5.10 5.10

Medals — A81

1999, July 31 *Litho.* *Perf. 14*
311 A81 25b Meritul Militar .30 .30
312 A81 25b Pentru Vitejie .30 .30
313 A81 25b Meritul Civic .30 .30
314 A81 90b Mihai Eminescu .30 .30
315 A81 1.10 l Gloria Muncii .90 .90
316 A81 2.40 l Stefan cel Mare 2.25 2.25
Nos. 311-316 (6) 4.35 4.35

Souvenir Sheet
317 A81 5 l Ordinul Republicii 4.50 4.50

Crafts — A82

1999, Aug. 7
318 A82 5b Wood carving .25 .25
319 A82 30b Embroidery .30 .30
320 A82 95b Pottery .55 .55
321 A82 1.80 l Wicker furniture 1.60 1.60
Nos. 318-321 (4) 2.70 2.70

Johann Wolfgang von Goethe (1749-1832), German Poet — A83

1999, Aug. 20
322 A83 1.10 l multicolored 1.50 1.50

Return to Use of Latin Letters for Moldavian Language, 10th Anniv. — A84

1999, Aug. 31 *Perf. 13¾*
323 A84 25b multicolored .50 .50

A85

Metropolitans: 25b, Varlaam (1590-1657). 2.40 l, Gurie Grosu (1877-1943).

1999, Sept. 12 *Litho.* *Perf. 14*
324 A85 25b multicolored .30 .30
325 A85 2.40 l multicolored 2.75 2.75

A86

Moldavian Rulers, dates ruled: No. 326, Bogdan II (1449-51). No. 327, Bogdan IV (1568-72). No. 328, Constantin Cantemir (1685-93). 1.50 l, Simion Movila (1606-07). 3 l, Duke Gheorghe III (1665-66, 1668-72, 1678-84). 3.90 l, Ilias Alexandru (1666-68). 5 l, Vasile Lupu (1634-53).

1999, Oct. 16 *Litho.* *Perf. 14¼x14*
326 A86 25b multi .30 .30
327 A86 25b multi .30 .30
328 A86 25b multi .30 .30
329 A86 1.50 l multi 1.00 1.00
330 A86 3 l multi 2.10 2.10
331 A86 3.90 l multi 3.50 3.50
Nos. 326-331 (6) 7.50 7.50

Souvenir Sheet
Perf. 13¾x14
332 A86 5 l multi 5.00 5.00

No. 332 contains one 24x30mm stamp. Compare with Type A110.

Fauna — A87

Designs: 25b, Lutra lutra. 1.80 l, Huso huso. 3.60 l, Rhinolophus ferrumequinum.

1999, Nov. 20 *Perf. 14x14¼*
333 A87 25b multi .35 .35
334 A87 1.80 l multi 1.75 1.75
335 A87 3.60 l multi 3.25 3.25
Nos. 333-335 (3) 5.35 5.35

1999 Women's Chess Championships, Chisinau — A88

1999, Nov. 27 *Perf. 13¾*
336 A88 25b Woman .25 .25
337 A88 2.20 l Building 2.50 2.50

A89

Items From National History Museum: 25b, Helmet, candleholder. 1.80 l, Ceramic jug. 3.60 l, Bible.

Perf. 14¼x13¾
1999, Dec. 11 *Litho.*
338 A89 25b multi .30 .30
339 A89 1.80 l multi 1.25 1.25
340 A89 3.60 l multi 3.50 3.50
Nos. 338-340 (3) 5.05 5.05

A90

a, 20b, Raluca Eminovici. b, 5 l, Mihail Eminescu (1850-89), Poet. c, 25b, Gheorghe Eminovici. d, 3 l, Veronica Micle. e, 1.50 l, Iosif Vulcan.

2000, Jan. 15 *Litho.* *Perf. 13¾x14*
341 A90 Sheet of 5, #a.-e., + label 6.75 6.75

Fairy Tales — A91

Designs: 25b, Ileana Cosinzeana. 1.50 l, Fat Frumos. 1.80 l, Harap Alb.

2000, Feb. 15 *Litho.* *Perf. 14*
342 A91 25b multi .25 .25
343 A91 1.50 l multi 1.50 1.50
344 A91 1.80 l multi 1.90 1.90
Nos. 342-344 (3) 3.65 3.65

Famous People — A92

Designs: No. 345, Henri Coanda (1886-1972), physicist. No. 346, Toma Ciorba (1864-1936), doctor. 2 l, Guglielmo Marconi (1874-1937), physicist. 3.60 l, Norbert Wiener (1894-1964), mathematician.

2000, Feb. 26 *Perf. 13¾x14*
345 A92 25b multi .25 .25
346 A92 25b multi .25 .25
347 A92 2 l multi 1.50 1.50
348 A92 3.60 l multi 3.00 3.00
Nos. 345-348 (4) 5.00 5.00

Events of the 20th Century — A93

Designs: 25b, Moon landing. 1.50 l, Nuclear fission. 3 l, Global computerization. 3.90 l, Reconciliation between Partiarch Teoctist and Pope John Paul II, horiz.

2000, Apr. 12 *Perf. 14*
349 A93 25b multi .30 .30
350 A93 1.50 l multi 1.20 1.20
351 A93 3 l multi 2.50 2.50
352 A93 3.90 l multi 4.00 4.00
Nos. 349-352 (4) 8.00 8.00

Easter — A94

Religious artwork from: 25b, 1841. 3 l, 19th cent.

2000, Apr. 30 *Perf. 14x13¾*
353 A94 25b multi .25 .25
354 A94 3 l multi 3.25 3.25

Europa, 2000 Common Design Type

2000, May 9 *Litho.* *Perf. 14¼x14*
355 CD17 3 l multi 3.50 3.50
Booklet, 6 #355 19.00

Exhibitions — A95

Designs: 25b, Faces, Expo 2000 emblem. 3.60 l+25b, WIPA 2000 Emblem, No. 118.

2000, May 30 *Litho.* *Perf. 14x13¾*
356 A95 25b multi .35 .35
357 A95 3.60 l +25b multi 1.75 1.75

Churches and Monasteries A96

Designs: 25b, Monastery, Tipova, 16th-17th Cent. 1.50 l, Church, Heciul Vechi, 1791. 1.80 l, Church, Palanca, 18th-19th Cent. 3 l, Monastery, Butuceni, 15th-16th Cent.

2000, Aug. 12 *Litho.* *Perf. 14*
358-361 A96 Set of 4 4.75 4.75

2000 Summer Olympics, Sydney — A97

Olympic flag and: 25b, Judo. 1.80 l, Wrestling. 5 l, Weight lifting.

2000, Sept. 15 *Litho.* *Perf. 14x13¾*
362-364 A97 Set of 3 4.50 4.50

MOLDOVA

Teacher's Day — A98

25b, Child, teacher, class. 3.60 l, Teacher.

2000, Oct. 5   *Perf. 14x14¼*
365-366 A98   Set of 2   3.00 3.00

Christmas — A99

Icons: 25b, Adoration of the Shepherds. 1.50 l, Nativity.

2000, Nov. 11   *Litho.*   *Perf. 13¾*
367-368 A99   Set of 2   1.50 1.50

Souvenir Sheet
Perf. 13¾x14
369 A99   5 l Madonna and Child   4.00 4.00
No. 369 contains one 27x33mm stamp.

UN High Commissioner for Refugees, 50th Anniv. — A99a

2001, Jan. 19   *Perf. 14*
369A A99a   3 l multi   2.00 2.00

Worldwide Fund for Nature (WWF) — A100

Crex crex: a, On rock. b, With mouth open. c, With eggs. d, With chicks.

2001, Mar. 31   *Litho.*   *Perf. 14x14¼*
370 A100   3 l Block of 4, #a-d   7.00 7.00

First Manned Spaceflight, 40th Anniv. — A101

2001, Apr. 12   *Perf. 14*
371 A101   1.80 l Yuri Gagarin   1.50 1.50
See No. 377. For surcharge, see No. 903.

Famous Women — A102

Designs: 25b, Maria Dragan (1947-86), singer. 1 l, Marlene Dietrich (1901-92), actress. 2 l, Ruxandra Lupu (1630?-87). 3 l, Lidia Lipkovski (1884-1958).

2001, Apr. 28   *Perf. 14x14¼*
372-375 A102   Set of 4   4.75 4.75

Europa — A103

2001, May 5   *Perf. 14*
376 A103   3 l multi   2.00 2.00
Booklet, 6 #376   16.50

Space Anniversary Type of 2001
Design: Dumitru Prunariu, first Romanian cosmonaut.

2001, May 14
377 A101   1.80 l multi   1.40 1.40
Prunariu's flight, 20th anniv.

Children's Art — A104

Art by: No. 378, 25b, Cristina Mereacre. No. 379, 25b, Ion Sestacovschi. No. 380, 25b, Aliona-Valeria Samburic. 1.80 l, Andrei Sestacovschi.

2001, June 1
378-381 A104   Set of 4   2.75 2.75

Souvenir Sheet

Moldovan Stamps, 10th Anniv. — A105

Pre-independence era stamps: a, 40b, 7c Arms stamp (27x32mm). b, 2 l, 13c Arms stamp (27x32mm). c, 3 l, 30c Flag stamp (42x25mm).

2001, June 23   *Perf. 13¾x14, 14 (3 l)*
382 A105   Sheet of 3, #a-c   4.00 4.00

Animals in Chisinau Zoo — A106

Designs: 40b, Panthera tigris tigris. 1 l, Equus quagga. 1.50 l, Ursus arctos. 3 l+30b, Boselaphus tragocamelus. 5 l, Panthera leo.

2001, July 14   *Perf. 13¾*
383-386 A106   Set of 4   6.25 6.25

Souvenir Sheet
387 A106   5 l multi   4.75 4.75

Declaration of Independence, 10th Anniv. — A107

2001, Aug. 27   *Litho.*   *Perf. 14x13¾*
388 A107   1 l multi   1.25 1.25

Musical Instruments — A108

Designs: 40b, Cimpol. 1 l, Fluier. 1.00 l, Nai. 3 l, Taragot.

2001, Oct. 6   *Perf. 14x13¾*
389-392 A108   Set of 4   6.00 6.00

A109

Year of Dialogue Among Civilizations — A109a — 394

Designs: 40b, Heads, spacecraft, horiz. 3.60b, Emblem.

2001, Oct. 9   *Perf. 14x14¼, 14¼x14*
393 A109   40b multicolored   2.00 2.00
394 A109a   3.60b multicolored   2.00 2.00

A110

Moldavian Rulers — A111

Ruler, dates ruled: No. 395, 40b, Mihai Racovita (1703-05, 1707-09, 1716-26). No. 396, 40b, Nicolae Mavrocordat (1709-10, 1711-15). No. 397, 40b, Constantin Mavrocordat (1733-35, 1741-43, 1748-49, 1769). No. 398, 40b, Grigore Callimachi (1761-64, 1767-69). 1 l, Grigore Alexandru Ghica (1764-67, 1774-77). 3 l, Antion Cantemir (1695-1700, 1705-07).
5 l, Dimitrie Cantemir (1710-11).

2001, Oct. 27   *Perf. 14¼x14*
395-400 A110   Set of 6   4.75 4.75

Souvenir Sheet
Perf. 14x14¼
401 A111   5 l multi   4.75 4.75
Compare with type A86.

Christmas A112

Designs: 40b, Church, 1821. 1 l, Church, 1841. 3 l, Church, 1836. 3.90 l, Cathedral, 1836.

2001, Nov. 10   *Perf. 13¾x14*
402-405 A112   Set of 4   7.25 7.25

Commonwealth of Independent States, 10th Anniv. — A113

2001, Dec. 14   *Perf. 14¼x14*
406 A113   1.50 l multi   1.40 1.40

2002 Winter Olympics, Salt Lake City — A114

Designs: 40b, Cross-country skiing. 5 l, Biathlon.

2002, Feb. 8   *Litho.*   *Perf. 13¾x14*
407-408 A114   Set of 2   3.25 3.25

Dances — A115

Designs: 40b, Hora. 1.50 l, Sirba.

2002, Mar. 16   *Perf. 14x14¼*
409-410 A115   Set of 2   2.50 2.50

Paintings — A116

Designs: No. 411, 40b, Fetele din Ceadir-lunga, by Mihai Grecu. No. 412, 40b, Meleag Natal, by Eleonora Romanescu. 1.50 l, Fata la Fereastra, by Valentina Rusu-Ciobanu. 3 l, In Doi, by Igor Vieru.

2002, Apr. 20   *Litho.*   *Perf. 13¾*
411-414 A116   Set of 4   4.50 4.50

Europa — A117

2002, May 9   *Perf. 14*
415 A117   3 l multi   1.50 1.50
Booklet, 6 #415   9.00 9.00

Souvenir Sheet

Botanical Gardens, Chisinau A118

No. 416: a, 40b, Rose. b, 40b, Peony. c, 1.50 l, Aster. d, 3 l, Iris.

2002, June 14   *Perf. 13¾x14*
416 A118   Sheet of 4, #a-d   4.00 4.00

Souvenir Sheet

Leonardo da Vinci (1452-1519) — A119

No. 417: a, 40b, Lady with an Ermine. b, 1.50 l, Virgin and Child with St. Anne. c, 3 l, Mona Lisa.

2002, July 25
417 A119   Sheet of 3, #a-c   3.25 3.25

Famous Men — A120

Designs: No. 418, 40b, Grigore Ureche (1590-1647), chronicler. No. 419, 40b, Nicolae Costin (1660-1712). No. 420, 40b, Ion Neculce (1672-1745), chronicler. No. 421, 40b, Nicolae Testemiteanu (1927-86). 1.50 l,

MOLDOVA

Sergiu Radautan (1926-98), scientist. 3.90 l, Alexandre Dumas (father) (1802-70), novelist.

2002, Aug. 24
418-423 A120 Set of 6   5.00 5.00

Horses — A121

Designs: 40b, Vladimir. 1.50 l, Orlov. 3 l, Arabian.

2002, Sept. 20 *Perf. 14*
424-426 A121 Set of 3   4.00 4.00

The Post in Children's Art — A122

Art by: 40b, Alexandry Catranji. 1.50 l, Natalia Corcodel. 2 l, Dana Lungu.

2002, Oct. 3 *Litho.* *Perf. 14*
427-429 A122 Set of 3   5.75 5.75

Commonwealth of Independent States Summit — A123

CIS emblem and: 1.50 l, National leaders and flags. 3.60 l, Handshake.

2002, Oct. 6 *Litho.* *Perf. 13½*
430-431 A123 Set of 2   4.00 4.00

Cricova Wine Industry, 50th Anniv. — A124

Designs: No. 432, 40b, Truck in warehouse. No. 433, 40b, Entrance to underground warehouse. 1.50 l, Wine glasses on table, vert. 2 l, Dusty wine bottles, wine cellar, statue. 3.60 l, Wine glasses and bottles, vert.

2002, Oct. 11 *Perf. 13¼x13, 13x13¼*
432-436 A124 Set of 5   5.50 5.50

Dirigibles — A125

Designs: 40b, Tissandier dirigible, France, 1883. 2 l, Ucebnii dirigible, Russia, 1908. 5 l, Graf Zeppelin, Germany, 1928.

2003, Apr. 22 *Litho.* *Perf. 13¼*
437-439 A125 Set of 3   4.50 4.50

Butterflies — A126

Designs: 40b, Iphiclides podalirius. 2 l, Callimorpha quadripunctaria. 3 l, Marumba quercus. 5 l, Polyommatus daphnis.

2003, Apr. 30 *Perf. 13¼x13*
440-443 A126 Set of 4   6.50 6.50
443a   Souvenir sheet, #440-443   6.50 6.50
443b   Booklet pane, #441-442, 2 each #440, 443   11.00
       Complete booklet, #443b   11.00

Europa — A127

Poster art: 3 l, Popular Dance Ensemble poster. 5 l, Eminescu Exhibition poster.

2003, June 12 *Perf. 13¼*
444-445 A127 Set of 2   5.00 5.00
445a   Booklet pane, 3 each #444-445   15.00 —
       Complete booklet, #445a   15.00

Souvenir Sheet

Moldovan Europa Stamps, 10th Anniv. — A128

No. 446: a, 1.50 l, Rural landscape. b, 5 l, Chisinau.

2003, June 12 *Perf. 13½*
446 A128 Sheet of 2, #a-b + label   3.75 3.75

Red Cross — A129

Emblem and: 40b, Flag. 5 l, Red Cross workers at disaster site.

2003, July 4 *Perf. 13¼x13*
447-448 A129 Set of 2   2.75 2.75

Youth Olympics, Paris — A130

Designs: 40b, Runner. 3 l, Cyclists. 5 l, Gymnast.

2003, July 25 *Perf. 13½*
449-451 A130 Set of 3   4.00 4.00

Battle Against Terrorism — A131

Art: 40b, Luminari, by A. Ahlupin. 3.90 l, Pax Cultura, by N. Roerich, horiz.

2003, Oct. 21
452-453 A131 Set of 2   3.00 3.00

Dimitrie Cantemir (1673-1723), Historian — A132

2003, Oct. 24 *Perf. 13*
454 A132 3.60 l multi   2.25 2.25

Visit of Pres. Vladimir Voronin to European Union — A133

2003, Nov. 5 *Perf. 13½*
455 A133 3 l multi   2.25 2.25

Famous Men — A134

Designs: 40b, Nicolae Donici (1874-1956), astronomer. 1.50 l, Nicolae Dimo (1873-1959), agronomist. 2 l, Nicolai Costenco (1913-93), writer. 3.90 l, Lewis Milestone (1895-1980), film director. 5 l, Vincent van Gogh (1853-90), painter.

2003, Nov. 14
456-460 A134 Set of 5   7.00 7.00

Birds From Red Book of Moldova A135

Designs: 40b, Cygnus olor. 2 l, Egretta alba. 3 l, Aquila rapax, vert. 5 l, Tetrax tetrax, vert.

2003, Dec. 18 *Litho.* *Perf. 13¾*
461-464 A135 Set of 4   6.00 6.00
464a   Souvenir sheet, #461-464, perf. 13   6.00 6.00

Famous People — A136

Designs: 40b, Natalia Gheorghiu (1914-2001), surgeon. 1.50 l, Metropolitan Dosoftei (1624-93).

2004, Apr. 30 *Litho.* *Perf. 14x14½*
465-466 A136 Set of 2   1.75 1.75

Europa — A137

Designs: 40b, Archaeological dig. 4.40 l, Tourists at winery.

2004, June 25 *Litho.* *Perf. 14x14½*
467-468 A137 Set of 2   4.50 4.50
468a   Booklet pane, 2 each #467-468   9.00 —
       Complete booklet, #468a   9.00

Stephen the Great (1437-1504), Prince of Moldavia — A138

Stephen the Great and: 40b, Soroca Fortress. 2 l, Capriana Monastery. 4.40 l, Map of Moldova.

2004, July 2 *Perf. 14½x14*
469-470 A138 Set of 2   2.00 2.00

Souvenir Sheet
471 A138 4.40 l multi + 2 labels   3.25 3.25

FIFA (Fédération Internationale de Football Association), Cent. — A139

No. 472: a, 2 l, Goalie catching ball. b, 4.40 l, Player dribbling ball.

2004, Aug. 14
472 A139 Horiz. pair, #a-b, + central label   4.00 4.00

Souvenir Sheet

Iasi-Chisinau Operation Memorial — A140

2004, Aug. 22
473 A140 2 l multi + label   1.50 1.50

Iasi-Chisinau Operation, 60th anniv.

2004 Summer Olympics, Athens — A141

Designs: 40b, Boxing. 4.40 l, Weight lifting.

2004, Dec. 28 *Perf. 14x14½*
474-475 A141 Set of 2   3.25 3.25

Ancient Jewelry A142

Designs: 40b, Earrings, 4th cent. B.C. 1 l, Necklace, 4th-3rd cent. B.C. 1.50 l, Silver temple earring, 14th-15th cent. 2 l, Bronze bracelet, 4th cent. B.C.

2004, Dec. 28
476-479 A142 Set of 4   3.25 3.25

Flowering Bushes — A143

Designs: 40b, Ephedra distachya. 1.50 l, Pyrus elaeagrifolia. No. 482, 2 l, Padus avium. No. 483, 2 l, Crataegus pentagyna.

2004, Dec. 29 *Perf. 14½x14*
480-483 A143 Set of 4   4.25 4.25

Locomotives A144

Designs: 60b, ER. 1 l, ChME3. 1.50 l, D 777-3. 4.40 l, 3TE10M.

2005, Apr. 2 *Litho.* *Perf. 14x14½*
484-487 A144 Set of 4   4.75 4.75

MOLDOVA

St. George's Church, Capriana Monastery — A145

2005, May 6   Perf. 14½x14
488 A145 40b multi   .65 .65

End of World War II, 60th Anniv. — A146

2005, May 9
489 A146 1.50 l multi   1.25 1.25

Europa — A147

Designs: 1.50 l, Cheese, corn meal mush, pitcher and cup. 4.40 l, Pies, stein and bottle of wine.

2005, May 20   Perf. 14x14½
490-491 A147   Set of 2   3.75 3.75
491a   Miniature sheet, 3 each
    #490-491   14.50 —

No. 491a was sold with, but not attached to, a booklet cover.

European Women's Chess Championships, Chisinau — A148

2005, June 10   Perf. 14½x14
492 A148 4.40 l multi   3.25 3.25

Composers A149

Designs: 40b, Serghei Lunchevici (1934-95). 1 l, Valeriu Cupcea (1929-89). 2 l, Anton Rubinstein (1829-94).

2005, July 1   Perf. 14x14½
493-495 A149   Set of 3   2.75 2.75

First Europa Stamps, 50th Anniv. (in 1996) — A150

Designs: No. 496, 1.50 l, Moldovan landmarks, flag and map. 15 l, Vignette of 1956 Europa stamps.
No. 498a, Moldoveanca, by Anatol Silitkii.

2005, July 20   Litho.   Perf. 14½x14
496-497 A150   Set of 2   5.00 5.00
Souvenir Sheet
498   Sheet, #497, 498a   5.00 5.00
   a. A150 1.50 l multi   .55 .55

World Summit on the Information Society, Tunis — A151

2005, Sept. 14
499 A151 4.40 l multi   2.75 2.75

Souvenir Sheet

Moldovan Passports, 10th Anniv. — A152

No. 500: a, 40b, Three passport pages with pictures. b, 1.50 l, Two closed passports. c, 4.40 l, Two passport pages with pictures.

2005, Sept. 16
500 A152   Sheet of 3, #a-c   4.00 4.00

Endangered Reptiles and Amphibians A153

Designs: Nos. 501, 505a, 40b, Emys orbicularis. Nos. 502, 505b, 1 l, Eremias arguta. Nos. 503, 505c, 1.50 l, Pelobates fuscus. Nos. 504, 505d, 2 l, Vipera ursini.

2005, Sept. 29   Perf. 14x14½
With White Frames
501-504 A153   Set of 4   3.50 3.50
Souvenir Sheet
Without White Frames
505 A153   Sheet of 4, #a-d, + 2 labels   3.50 3.50

St. Nicholas Church — A154

2005, Oct. 30   Perf. 14½x14
506 A154 40b multi   .80 .80

Christmas A155

Designs: 40b, St. Ierarh Nicolae Church, Falesti. 0 l, Varzaresti Monastery.

2005, Dec. 19   Litho.   Perf. 14x14½
507-508 A155   Set of 2   3.50 3.50

Makler Newspaper, 15th Anniv. — A156

2006, Jan. 20
509 A156 60b multi   .70 .70

2006 Winter Olympics, Turin — A157

Designs: 60b, Luge. 6.20 l, Skiing.

2006, Feb. 10
510-511 A157   Set of 2   3.25 3.25

Buildings — A158

Designs: 22b, Post Office No. 21, Balti. 40b, Saint Gates, Chisinau. 53b, Museum of History, Cahul. 57b, Old Post and Telegraph Office, Soroca. 60b, Adormirea Maicii Domnului Church, Copceac. 3.50 l, National Museum of Fine Arts, Chisinau.

2006, Mar. 23   Perf. 14½x14
512 A158   22b dark blue   .65 .65
513 A158   40b brown   .65 .65
514 A158   53b dark blue   .65 .65
515 A158   57b green   .65 .65
516 A158   60b olive green   .65 .65
517 A158   3.50 l red brown   2.25 2.25
   Nos. 512-517 (6)   5.50 5.50

Textile Arts and Native Costumes A159

Designs: 40b, Crocheting. 60b, Moldavian woman, 19th cent., vert. 3 l, Moldavian man, 19th cent., vert. 4.50 l, Embroidery.

2006, Apr. 14   Perf. 14x14½, 14½x14
518-521 A159   Set of 4   3.75 3.75

Gheorghe Mustea, Conductor A160

2006, Apr. 28   Perf. 14x14½
522 A160 60b multi   .60 .60

Europa A161

Designs: 60b, Children and town on globe. 4.50 l, Artist and musicians, vert.

2006, May 6   Perf. 14x14½, 14½x14
523-524 A161   Set of 2   2.75 2.75
524a   Miniature sheet, 3 each
    #523-524   8.25 8.25

No. 524a was sold with, but not attached to, a booklet cover.

37th Chess Olympiad, Turin — A162

2006, May 24   Perf. 14x14½
525 A162 4.50 l multi   3.00 3.00

2006 World Cup Soccer Championships, Germany — A163

World Cup, emblem and: 2 l, Players. 3 l, Mascot. 4.50 l, Players, diff.

2006, June 28
526-528 A163   Set of 3   4.00 4.00

Famous People — A164

Designs: 40b, Ion Halippa (1871-1941), archaeologist. 1 l, Eufrosinia Cuza (1856-1910), singer. 2 l, Petre Stefanuca (1906-42), folklorist. 4.50 l, Wolfgang Amadeus Mozart (1756-91), composer.

2006, Aug. 11   Perf. 14½x14
529-532 A164   Set of 4   14.50 14.50

Endangered Animals A165

Designs: 60b, Martes martes. 1 l, Mustela erminea. 2 l, Mustela lutreola. 3 l, Mustela eversmanni.
6.20 l, Felis silvestris, vert.

2006, Aug. 16   Perf. 14x14½
533-536 A165   Set of 4   3.75 3.75
Souvenir Sheet
Perf. 14½x14
537 A165 6.20 l multi + label   3.75 3.75

Independence, 15th Anniv. — A166

2006, Aug. 27   Perf. 14½x14
538 A166 2.60 l multi   1.35 1.35

Dogs — A167

Designs: 40b, German shepherd. 60b, Collie. 2 l, Standard poodle. 6.20 l, Hungarian greyhound.

2006, Sept. 8   Perf. 14x14½
539-542 A167   Set of 4   4.25 4.25
542a   Sheet, 2 each #539-542   8.50 8.50

National Wine Day — A168

2006, Oct. 7
543 A168 60b multi   .75 .75

Christmas A169

Paintings by: 40b, Valerii, Metleaev, 1988. 3 l, Mihail Statnii, 1986, vert. 6.20 l, Elena Bontea, 1973.

Perf. 14x14½, 14½x14
2006, Dec. 12   Litho.
544 A169   40b multi   .30 .30
545 A169   3 l multi   1.30 1.30
546 A169   6.20 l multi   2.40 2.40
   a. Strip of 3, #544-546   4.00 4.00

Nos. 544 and 545 were each printed in sheets of 10 and in sheets of 9 containing 3 each of Nos. 544-546.

No. 25 Surcharged

Methods and Perfs As Before
2007, Jan. 11
547 A6 85b on 25k #547   1.25 1.25

MOLDOVA

Portraits in Natl. Art Museum — A170

Designs: 65b, Petrarch, by Raphael Morghen. 85b, Napoleon Bonaparte, by unknown artist. 2 l, Friedrich von Schiller, by Johann Gotthard Muller. 4.50 l, Johann Wolfgang von Goethe by James Hopwood.

2007, Feb. 28   Litho.   *Perf. 14½x14*
548-551   A170   Set of 4   2.75   2.75

Mushrooms A171

Designs: 65b, Morchella steppicola. 85b, Phylloporus rhodoxanthus. 2 l, Amanita solitaria. 6.20 l, Boletus aereus.

2007, Apr. 23   Litho.   *Perf. 14x14½*
552-555   A171   Set of 4   2.75   2.75

Europa A172

Designs: 2.85 l, Scouts with pencil and paint brush. 4.50 l, Scouts examining butterfly.

2007, May 8
556-557   A172   Set of 2   2.25   2.25
Scouting, cent.

No. 83 Surcharged in Blue or Black

Methods and Perfs As Before
2007, June 7
558   A19   25b on 3k #83 (Bl)   .30   .30
559   A19   85b on 3k #83 (Bk)   .70   .70

Cats — A173

Designs: 65b, Mixed breed. 1 l, Siamese, vert. 1.50 l, Birman, vert. 6.20 l, Persian.

Perf. 14x14½, 14½x14
2007, June 20   Litho.
560-563   A173   Set of 4   3.00   3.00

Birds — A174

Designs: 75b, Otis tarda. 1 l, Neophron percnopterus. 2.50 l, Lyrurus tetrix. 5 l, Gyps fulvus. 6.20 l, Tetrao urogallus.

2007, Aug. 14   Litho.   *Perf. 14x14½*
564-567   A174   Set of 4   3.25   3.25
Souvenir Sheet
568   A174   6.20 l multi + label   2.25   2.25

Dniester River Fish Preservation A175

No. 569: a, Acipenser gueldenstaedtii. b, Zingel zingel.

2007, Sept. 6
569   Horiz. pair + central label   1.40   1.40
  a.   A175   1 l multi   .35   .35
  b.   A175   3 l multi   1.05   1.05
See Ukraine No. 694.

Famous People A176

Designs: 75b, Ion Luca Caragiale (1852-1912), writer. 1 l, Anastasia Dicescu (1887-1945), opera singer. 3 l, Mircea Eliade (1907-86), historian. 6.20 l, Maria Biesu, opera singer, vert.

2007, Sept. 15   *Perf. 14x14½*
570-572   A176   Set of 3   1.60   1.60
Souvenir Sheet
Perf. 14½x14
573   A176   6.20 l multi + label   2.25   2.25

World Chess Championships, Mexico — A177

2007, Sept. 29   *Perf. 14x14½*
574   A177   6.20 l multi   1.90   1.90

A178   **Christmas — A179**

2007, Dec. 1   Litho.   *Perf. 14x14½*
575   A178   1 l multi   .30   .30
576   A179   4.50 l multi   1.50   1.50
  a.   Miniature sheet, 6 #575, 3 #576   6.00   6.00

Covered Wells — A180

Well in: 10b, Peresecina. 75b, Duruitoarea. 1 l, Ciripcau, vert. 3 l, Ocnita, vert.

2008, Feb. 19   *Perf. 14½x14, 14x14½*
577-580   A180   Set of 4   2.00   2.00

2008 Summer Olympics, Beijing A181

Designs: 1 l, Cycling. 6.20 l, Boxing. 15 l, Weight lifting.

2008, Mar. 5   *Perf. 14x14½*
581-583   A181   Set of 3   8.00   8.00
For overprint see No. 607.

Europa A182

Designs: 3.50 l, Post rider, scroll, castle. 4.50 l, Letters, computer screen.

2008, Apr. 30   Litho.   *Perf. 14x14½*
584-585   A182   Set of 2   3.00   3.00
585a   Sheet, 2 each #584-585   6.00   6.00
No. 585a was sold with, but not attached to, a booklet cover.

First Postage Stamps of Moldavia, 150th Anniv. — A183

Designs: 1 l, Romania #1-2. 3 l, Romania #3-4.

2008, May 23
586-587   A183   Set of 2   1.50   1.50
587a   Booklet pane of 4, 2 each #586-587   3.00   3.00
   Complete booklet, #587a   3.00

UEFA Euro 2008 Soccer Championships, Austria and Switzerland — A184

2008, June 28
588   A184   4.50 l multi   1.75   1.75

Flowers A185

Designs: 1 l, Maianthemum bifolium. 3 l, Hepatica nobilis. 5 l, Nymphaea alba.

2008, Aug. 19   Litho.   *Perf. 14x14½*
589-591   A185   Set of 3   3.25   3.25
591a   Souvenir sheet of 3, #589-591, + 3 labels   3.25   3.25

Famous People — A186

Designs: 1.20 l, Onisifor Ghibu (1883-1972), teacher. 1.50 l, Ciprian Porumbescu (1853-83), composer. 3 l, Leo Tolstoy (1828-1910), author. 4.50 l, Maria Tanase (1913-63), singer.

2008, Sept. 5
592-595   A186   Set of 4   4.00   4.00

Deer A187

No. 596: a, Cervus nippon. b, Cervus elaphus sibiricus.

2008, Sept. 18
596   A187   3 l Horiz. pair, #a-b   2.25   2.25
See Kazakhstan No. 577.

Souvenir Sheet

Bender (Tighina), 600th Anniv. — A188

2008, Oct. 8
597   A188   4.20 l brn & buff + 3 labels   1.60   1.60

Princes — A189

Designs: 1.20 l, Prince Antiokh Cantemir (1708-44). 3 l, Prince Dimitrie Cantemir (1673-1723).

2008, Oct. 27   *Perf. 14½x14*
598   A189   1.20 l brown   .45   .45
Souvenir Sheet
599   A189   3 l brown + label   1.10   1.10

Princes — A190

Designs: 85b, Prince Mihail Grigore Sutu (1784-1864). 1.20 l, Prince Grigore Alexandru Ghica (1807-57). 1.50 l, Prince Mihail Sturza (1795-1884). 2 l, Prince Alexandru Ipsilanti (1726-1807). 3 l, Prince Ioan Sandu Sturza (1761-1842). 4.50 l, Prince Scarlat Callimachi (1773-1821). 6.20 l, Prince Alexandru Ioan Cuza (1820-73).

2008, Nov. 14
600-605   A190   Set of 6   4.75   4.75
Souvenir Sheet
606   A190   6.20 l multi + 5 labels   2.25   2.25

No. 582 Overprinted in Bronze

2008, Nov. 21   *Perf. 14x14½*
607   A161   6.20 l multi   2.25   2.25

Souvenir Sheet

Moldovan Presidency of the Central European Initiative — A191

No. 608 — CEI emblems and map of: a, 1.20 l, Western Europe. b, 4.50 l, Eastern Europe.

2008, Nov. 27   *Perf. 14½x14*
608   A191   Sheet of 2, #a-b   2.10   2.10

A192

Christmas — A193

2008, Dec. 5   Litho.   *Perf. 14x14½*
609   A192   1.20 l multi   .45   .45
Souvenir Sheet
610   A193   6.20 l multi   2.25   2.25

MOLDOVA

Universal Declaration of Human Rights, 60th Anniv. — A194

2008, Dec. 10
611 A194 4.50 l multi   1.60 1.60

Moldavian State, 650th Anniv. — A195

Designs: 1.20 l, Moldovan arms and flag, Presidential offices. 6.20 l, Bogdan I Voda, Prince of Moldavia.

2009, Jan. 20
612 A195 1.20 l multi   .45 .45
Souvenir Sheet
613 A195 6.20 l multi + label   2.00 2.00

Ancient Weapons A196

Weapons from: 1.20 l, 10th-14th cents. 4.50 l, 8th-13th cents.

2009, Feb. 24
614-615 A196 Set of 2   1.75 1.75

Preservation of Polar Regions and Glaciers — A197

Question mark, emblem and: 1.20 l, Penguin. 6.20 l, Polar bear.

2009, Mar. 18 Litho. Perf. 14½x14
616-617 A197 Set of 2   2.75 2.75

Easter — A198

Decorated Easter eggs: 1.20 l, In basket. 3 l, In bowl.

2009, Apr. 2   Perf. 14x14½
618-619 A198 Set of 2   1.40 1.40

Council of Europe, 60th Anniv. — A199

2009, Apr. 15   Perf. 14½x14
620 A199 4.50 l multi   1.45 1.45

Europa A200

Designs: 4.20 l, Nicolae Donici (1874-1956), astrophysicist, observatory, planetary diagram and eclipse. 4.50 l, Galileo Galilei (1564-1642), astronomer, armillary sphere and star.

2009, May 7   Perf. 14x14½
621-622 A200 Set of 2   3.25 3.25
622a   Sheet, 3 each #621-622   10.00 10.00

Intl. Year of Astronomy. No. 622a was sold with, but not attached to, a booklet cover.

Children's Art — A201

Children's art on clean environment theme by: 1.20 l, Olesea Curteanu. 1.50 l, Iulia Struta, vert. 5 l+20b, Irina Simion, vert.

2009, June 1 Perf. 14x14½, 14½x14
623-625 A201 Set of 3   2.40 2.40

Flowers — A202

Designs: 1.20 l, Viola suavis. 1.50 l, Adonis vernalis. 3 l, Campanula persicifolia. 4.50 l, Papaver rhoeas.

2009, June 18 Perf. 13 Syncopated
626-628 A202 Set of 3   1.75 1.75
Souvenir Sheet
629 A202 4.50 l multi + label   1.50 1.50
  a. Sheet of 4, #626-629, + 2 labels   3.25 3.25

Insects — A203

Designs: 1.20 l, Bombus paradoxus. 1.50 l, Xylocopa valga. 3 l, Carabus clathratus. 4.50 l, Coenagrion lindeni.

Perf. 13 Syncopated
2009, Sept. 24   Litho.
630-633 A203 Set of 4   2.75 2.75

A204

Personalizable Stamps — A205

Designs: No. 636, Statue of Prince Stephen the Great. No. 637, Cathedral. No. 638, Roses, wedding rings. No. 639, Basket of flowers.

2009, Aug. 5   Perf. 13 Syncopated
634 A204 1.20 l lt bl & dk bl   1.40 1.40
635 A204 1.20 l red & dk red   1.40 1.40
636 A205 1.20 l multi + label   1.40 1.40
637 A205 1.20 l multi + label   1.40 1.40
638 A205 1.20 l multi + label   1.40 1.40
639 A205 1.20 l multi + label   1.40 1.40
     Nos. 634-639 (6)   8.40 8.40

Vignettes of Nos. 634-635 and labels of Nos. 636-639 could be personalized. The vignette image shown in illustration A204 and label image shown in illustration A205 are generic.

Nuts and Fruit — A206

Designs: 50b, Walnuts. 85b, Mulberries. 1.20 l, Pears. 5 l, Apricots.

2009, Aug. 28   Perf. 14½x14
640-643 A206 Set of 4   2.00 2.00

Houses A207

House in: 1.20 l, Briceni. 4.50 l, Comrat. 7 l, Orhei.

2009, Oct. 1   Perf. 14x14½
644-646 A207 Set of 3   3.00 3.00

Moldova Grapes — A208

2009, Oct. 9   Perf. 14½x14
647 A208 4.50 l multi   1.10 1.10

European Day Against Human Trafficking A209

2009, Oct. 18   Perf. 14x14½
648 A209 4.50 l multi   1.60 1.60

Famous People — A210

Designs: No. 649, 1.20 l, Eugene Ionescu (1909-94), playwright. No. 650, 1.20 l, Eufrosinia Kersnovskaia (1907-95), writer. 4.50 l, Nicolai Gogol (1809-52), writer. 7 l, Charles Darwin (1809-92), naturalist.

2009, Nov. 26   Litho. Perf. 14x14½
649-652 A210 Set of 4   4.00 4.00

Christmas A211

Designs: 1.20 l, Capra. 4.50 l, Plugusorul.

2009, Dec. 1
653-654 A211 Set of 2   1.40 1.40

Famous People — A212

Designs: No. 655, 1.20 l, Grigore Vieru (1935-2009), writer. No. 656, 1.20 l, Natalia Dadiani (1865-1903), founder of school for girls. 5.40 l, Ivan Zaikin (1880-1948), wrestler and aviator. 7 l, Maria Cebotari (1910-49), singer and actress. 4.50 l, Mihai Eminescu (1850-89), writer, vert.

2010, Jan. 15   Litho. Perf. 14x14½
655-658 A212 Set of 4   3.75 3.75
Souvenir Sheet
Perf. 14½x14
659 A212 4.50 l multi + label   1.10 1.10

2010 Winter Olympics, Vancouver A213

Designs: 1.20 l, Alpine skiing. 8.50 l, Biathlon, vert.

2010, Feb. 12 Perf. 14x14½, 14½x14
660-661 A213 Set of 2   2.25 2.25

Jewelry in National Museum of Archaeology and History — A214

Designs: 1.20 l, Shell necklace, 5th cent. B.C. 7 l, Headband and pendant, 5th cent. B.C.

2010, Feb. 23   Perf. 13 Syncopated
662-663 A214 Set of 2   2.25 2.25

Frédéric Chopin (1810-49), Composer A215

2010, Mar. 1   Perf. 14x14½
664 A215 5.40 l multi   1.25 1.25

Mushrooms — A216

Designs: 1.20 l, Lactarius piperatus. 2 l, Amanita pantherina. 5.40 l, Russula sanguinea. 7 l, Coprinus picaceus.

2010, Mar. 27   Perf. 14½x14
665-668 A216 Set of 4   4.00 4.00
668a   Souvenir sheet, #665-668   4.00 4.00

Birds — A217

Designs: 85b, Carduelis carduelis. 1 l, Passer domesticus. 1.20 l, Strix uralensis. 4.50 l, Pica pica. 8.50 l, Columba livia.

2010, Apr. 8   Perf. 13 Syncopated
669-672 A217 Set of 4   2.25 2.25
Souvenir Sheet
673 A217 8.50 l multi   2.25 2.25

Europa — A218

Children's books: 1.20 l, Punguta cu doi Dani, by Ion Creanga. 5.40 l, Guguta si Prietenii Sai, by Spiridon Vangheli.

2010, Apr. 30   Perf. 14x14½
674-675 A218 Set of 2   1.50 1.50
675a   Sheet, 3 each #674-675   9.00 9.00

No. 675a was sold with, but unattached to, a booklet cover.

End of World War II, 65th Anniv. — A219

2010, May 9   Perf. 14½x14
676 A219 4.50 l multi   1.40 1.40

481

MOLDOVA

2010 World Cup Soccer Championships, South Africa — A220

Soccer player and: 1.20 l, Mascot. 8.50 l, Emblem, vert.

Perf. 14x14½, 14½x14
2010, June 11
677-678 A220 Set of 2 2.50 2.50

Campaign Against AIDS — A221

2010, July 1 **Perf. 14x14½**
679 A221 1.20 l multi .55 .55

Paintings Depicting Flowers — A222

Designs: 1 l, Flowers, by Ion Tabirta. 1.20 l, Bouquet of Poppies, by Oleg Cojocari. 2 l, Flowers, by Mihail Statnii. 5.40 l, Chrysanthemums, by Leonid Grigorasenco.

Perf. 13 Syncopated
2010, Aug. 6 **Litho.**
680-683 A222 Set of 4 2.50 2.50

Dances A223

Designs: 85b, Moldovanesca. 5.40 l, Calusarii, vert.

Perf. 14x14½, 14½x14
2010, Sept. 18
684-685 A223 Set of 2 2.40 2.40

Feteasca Grapes — A224

2010, Oct. 9 **Perf. 14½x14**
686 A224 4.50 l multi 1.25 1.25

National Symbols — A225

Perf. 13 Syncopated at Top
2010, Nov. 3
687 A225 1.20 l Arms .25 .25
  a. Perf. 13, syncopation at sides .30 .30
688 A225 4.50 l Flag 1.00 1.00
  a. Perf. 13, syncopation at sides 1.10 1.00
  b. Sheet of 6, 3 each #687a, 688a 4.25 4.25

Prehistoric Animals A226

Designs: 85b, Mammuthus. 1 l, Ursus spelaeus. No. 691, 1.20 l, Panthera leo spelaea. 4.20 l, Bison.

No. 693: a, 1.20 l, Pontoceros. b, 1.50 l, Anancus. c, 5.40 l, Stephanorhinus. d, 8.50 l, Homotherium.

2010, Nov. 30 **Litho.** **Perf. 14x14½**
689-692 A226 Set of 4 1.60 1.60
Souvenir Sheet
693 A226 Sheet of 4, #a-d, + 2 labels 3.75 3.75

Christmas — A227

Designs: 1.20 l, Child at window, angel holding gift. 5.40 l, Cathedral.

2010, Dec. 7 **Perf. 13 Syncopated**
694 A227 1.20 l multi .35 .35
Souvenir Sheet
695 A227 5.40 l multi 1.25 1.25

Items in National Museum of Archaeology and History — A228

Designs: 85b, Amphora with lid, 5th cent. B.C. 1.20 l, Vessel with animal design, 4th cent. B.C. 8.50 l, Vessel depicting person, 4th cent. B.C.

2011, Jan. 25
696-698 A228 Set of 3 2.50 2.50
698a Sheet of 4, #696, 698, 2 #697 + 2 labels 3.00 3.00

Buildings — A229

Designs: 10b, Ralli family house, 19th cent., Dolna. 25b, Mirzoian family house, 19th cent., Hincesti. 85b, Balioz family house, 1847, Ivancea. 1 l, High school, 1916, Soroca. 1.20 l, Pommer family house, 20th cent., Taul. 1.50 l, Hasnas family house, 19th cent., Sofia.

2011, Feb. 15 **Perf. 14½x14**
699 A229 10b chocolate .25 .25
700 A229 25b deep blue .25 .25
701 A229 85b greenish blue .25 .25
702 A229 1 l plum .25 .25
703 A229 1.20 l dark blue .25 .25
704 A229 1.50 l dark green .30 .30
Nos. 699-704 (6) 1.55 1.55

Handicrafts — A230

Designs: 1.20 l, Decorated rope, by Ludmila Berezin. 4.20 l, Straw head, by Natalia Cangea. 7 l, Rug, by Ecaterina Popescu.

2011, Mar. 1
705-707 A230 Set of 3 3.25 3.25

Self-Portraits A231

Self-portrait of: 85b, Eugenia Maleseveshi (1866-1942). 1.20 l, Nicolae Grigorescu (1838-1907). 2 l, Alexandru Piamadeala (1888-1940). 5.40 l, Mihail Grecu (1916-98).

2011, Apr. 1 **Perf. 13 Syncopated**
708-711 A231 Set of 4 2.50 2.50

First Manned Space Flight, 50th Anniv. — A232

No. 712 — Pioneer cosmonauts and astronauts: a, 1.20 l, Yuri Gagarin. b, 5.40 l, Gherman Titov. c, 7 l, Virgil I. Grissom. d, 8.50 l, Alan B. Shepard, Jr.

2011, Apr. 9 **Perf. 14½x14**
712 A232 Sheet of 4, #a-d, + 2 labels 7.00 7.00

Europa A233

Designs: 4.20 l, Leaf depicting forest fire, healthy forest and buck. 5.40 l, Owl, forest, cut tree.

2011, May 7 **Perf. 13 Syncopated**
713-714 A233 Set of 2 2.50 2.50
714a Sheet of 6, 3 each #713-714 8.50 8.50

No. 714a was sold with, but unattached to, a booklet cover.

Flowers — A234

2011, May 20 **Perf. 14½x14**
715 A234 70b Hyacinth .25 .25
716 A234 85b Tulips .25 .25
717 A234 1.20 l Narcissi .30 .30
718 A234 2 l Violas .45 .45
Nos. 715-718 (4) 1.25 1.25

Deportation of Moldovans to Siberia by the Soviet Union, 70th Anniv. — A235

2011, June 12 **Perf. 14½x14**
719 A235 1.20 l multi .45 .45

Souvenir Sheet

First Moldovan Stamps, 20th Anniv. — A236

No. 720: a, 85b, Moldova #1. b, 1.20 l, Moldova #2. c, 4.20 l, Moldova #3.

2011, June 23 **Perf. 13 Syncopated**
720 A236 Sheet of 3, #a-c 1.50 1.50

Mammals and Birds — A237

Designs: No. 721, 85b, Meles meles. No. 722, 1.20 l, Erinaceus europaeus. 3 l, Canis lupus. 4.20 l, Vulpes vulpes.
No. 725: a, 85b, Plegadis falcinellus. b, 1.20 l, Pelecanus onocrotalus. c, 5.40 l, Platalea leucorodia. d, 8.50 l, Aythya nyroca.

2011, July 29
721-724 A237 Set of 4 2.25 2.25
725 A237 Sheet of 4, #a-d, + 2 labels 4.00 4.00

Souvenir Sheet

Independence, 20th Anniv. — A238

2011, Aug. 27 **Perf. 14½x14**
726 A238 4.20 l multi + 2 labels 1.40 1.40

Campaign Against Smoking — A239

2011, Sept. 10
727 A239 1.20 l multi .45 .45

Diplomatic Relations Between Moldova and Romania, 20th Anniv. — A240

Designs: 1.20 l, Holy Gates, Chisinau. 4.50 l, Arch of Triumph, Bucharest, Romania.

2011, Oct. 11 **Perf. 13 Syncopated**
728-729 A240 Set of 2 1.50 1.50
729a Sheet of 2, #728-729, + 4 labels 1.50 1.50

See Romania Nos. 5301-5302.

Miniature Sheet

Chisinau, 575th Anniv. A241

No. 730: a, 85b, Palace of Culture. b, 1.20 l, National Opera and Ballet Theater. c, 2 l, Mihai Emenscu National Theater. d, 3.85 l, National Palace. e, 5.40 l, Patria Movie Theater.

2011, Oct. 13 **Perf. 14x14½**
730 A241 Sheet of 5, #a-e, + label 3.50 3.50

UN High Commisioner for Refugees, 60th Anniv. — A242

2011, Nov. 25 **Perf. 14½x14**
731 A242 1.20 l multi .50 .50

MOLDOVA

Christmas — A244

2011, Dec. 3			Perf. 14½x14
732	A243	1.20 l multi	.40 .40

Souvenir Sheet
Perf. 14x14½

| 733 | A244 | 4.50 l multi | 1.10 1.10 |

Famous People A245

Designs: 85b, Magda Isanos (1916-44), poet. 1.20 l, Nicolae Sulac (1936-2003), musician. 3 l, Cleopatra Hrsanovschi (1861-1939), musician. 4.50 l, Franz Liszt (1811-86), composer.

2011, Dec. 17			Perf. 14x14½
734-737	A245	Set of 4	2.25 2.25

Paintings Depicting Children — A246

Designs: 85b, Pokrovka Boy, by Igor Vieru. 1.20 l, Orphan, by Pavel Piscariov. 2.85 l, Portrait of a Child, by Lidia Arionescu-Baillayre. 4.50 l, Boy with Hat, by Constantin Kitaika.

2012, Feb. 4			Perf. 13 Syncopated
738-741	A246	Set of 4	2.25 2.25

Souvenir Sheet

Ion (1954-92) and Doina (1958-92) Aldea-Teodorovici, Musicians — A247

2012, Mar. 3			Perf. 14x14½
742	A247	7 l multi + label	1.75 1.75

Souvenir Sheet

Mihai Dolgan (1942-2008), Musician — A248

2012, Mar. 14			Perf. 14½x14
743	A248	4.50 l multi + label	1.10 1.10

Traditional Costumes — A249

Designs: 85b, Woman. 1.20 l, Man. 3 l, Woman, diff. 8.50 l, Man and woman.

2012, Apr. 7			
744-746	A249	Set of 3	1.25 1.25

Souvenir Sheet

| 747 | A249 | 8.50 l multi + label | 1.90 1.90 |

Regional Communications Commonwealth, 20th anniv.

Europa — A250

Designs: 4.20 l, Curchi Monastery. 5.40 l, Winery.

2012, Apr. 18			Perf. 14x14½
748	A250	4.20 l multi	1.00 1.00
a.		Souvenir sheet of 3 + label	3.00 3.00
749	A250	5.40 l multi	1.40 1.40
a.		Souvenir sheet of 3 + label	4.25 4.25

Nos. 748a and 749a were sold with, but unattached to, a booklet cover.

Medieval Military Scenes A251

Designs: 85b, Battering ram. 1.20 l, Soldier with spear and shield, vert. 1.50 l, Military commander on horseback, vert. 5.40 l, Catapult.

Perf. 14x14½, 14½x14

2012, May 31			Litho.
750-753	A251	Set of 4	2.25 2.25

Pigeons A252

Designs: 85b, Jucator de Chisinau. 1.20 l, Jucator de Balti. 3 l, Jucator basarbean. 4.20 l, Roller de Chisinau.

2012, June 21			Perf. 14x14½
754-757	A252	Set of 4	2.25 2.25

2012 Summer Olympics, London A253

Designs: 4.50 l, Wrestling. 5.40 l, Cycling.

2012, July 21			
758-759	A253	Set of 2	2.00 2.00

Rose Varieties — A254

Designs: 85b, Mildred Scheel. 1.20 l, Friesia. 3 l, Priscilla. 4.20 l, Caribia.

2012, Aug. 10		Perf. 13 Syncopated
760-763	A254	Set of 4	2.10 2.10
763a		Sheet of 6, #762-763, 2 each #760-761	3.00 3.00

Famous Men — A255

Designs: 85b, Eugeniu Ureche (1917-2005), actor. 1.20 l, Spiridon Mocanu (1932-2007), dancer. 4.50 l, George Emil Palade (1912-2008), 1974 Nobel laureate for Physiology or Medicine. 8.50 l, Jean-Jacques Rousseau (1712-78), political philosopher.

2012, Aug. 27			Perf. 14x14½
764-767	A255	Set of 4	3.25 3.25

Maria Biesu (1935-2012), Opera Singer — A256

2012, Sept. 7			Litho.
768	A256	1.20 l multi	.35 .35

Natural Monuments A257

Designs: 1.20 l, Cheile Butesti Canyon. 4.20 l, Suta de Movile. 7 l, Emil Racovita Caves.

2012, Sept. 21			Perf. 14x14½
769-771	A257	Set of 3	3.50 3.50

Christmas — A258

Icons from: 1.75 l, 1903. 5.40 l, 19th cent.

2012, Dec. 1			Perf. 13 Syncopated
772-773	A258	Set of 2	1.60 1.60

Nos. 772-773 each were printed in sheets of 8 + central label.

Zero Kilometer Marker, Chisinau — A259

2012, Dec. 12			Perf. 14½x14
774	A259	1.75 l multi	.55 .55

Paintings Depicting Mihai Eminescu (1850-89), Poet — A260

Designs: 1.75 l, Mihai Eminescu, by Emil Childescu. 5.75 l, Dedication, by Vasile Nascu.

2013, Jan. 15			Perf. 13 Syncopated
775-776	A260	Set of 2	1.75 1.75

Nos. 775-776 each were printed in sheets of 8 + label.

Regional Communications Commonwealth Emblem, Communications Tower, Map of Moldova — A261

2013, Feb. 28			Perf. 14½x14
777	A261	4.50 l multi	1.10 1.10

Berries — A262

Designs: 55b, Ribes uva-crispa. 1.50 l, Vaccinium myrtillus. No. 780, Rubus idaeus. No. 781, Viburnum opulus. 2 l, Hippophae rhamnoides. 4 l, Ribes rubrum.

2013, Mar. 30			Perf. 14x14½
778	A262	55b multi	.30 .30
779	A262	1.50 l multi	.35 .35
780	A262	1.75 l multi	.40 .40
781	A262	1.75 l multi	.40 .40
782	A262	2 l multi	.45 .45
783	A262	4 l multi	.85 .85
	Nos. 778-783 (6)		2.75 2.75

Europa — A263

Postal vehicles: 4.50 l, Van. 5.75 l, Horse-drawn carriage.

2013, Apr. 30			
784	A263	4.50 l multi	.95 .95
a.		Souvenir sheet of 4	4.00 4.00
785	A263	5.75 l multi	1.25 1.25
a.		Souvenir sheet of 4	5.00 5.00

Nos. 784a and 785a were sold with, but unattached to, a booklet cover.

Animals in the Chisinau Zoo — A264

Designs: 1.75 l, Panthera uncia. 2 l, Maoropuo rufogriscus, vert. 5.75 l, Pavo cristatus.

2013, May 18	Perf. 14x14½, 14½x14
786-787	A264	Set of 2	.90 .90

Souvenir Sheet

| 788 | A264 | 5.75 l multi + label | 1.40 1.40 |

Illustrations From Guguta Stories by Spiridon Vangheli — A265

Designs: No. 789, 1.75 l, Cusma. No. 790, 1.75 l, Datoria.

2013, June 1			Perf. 14½x14
789-790	A265	Set of 2	.80 .80

Folk Traditions A266

Designs: No. 791, 1.75 l, Cleaning of the well. No. 792, 1.75 l, Rain dance, vert.

Perf. 14x14½, 14½x14

2013, June 20			
791-792	A266	Set of 2	.80 .80

Butterflies A267

Designs: 1 l, Thysania agrippina. No. 794, 1.75 l, Papilio blumei. No. 795, 1.75 l, Salamis temora. 5.75 l, Cymothoe excelsa.

MOLDOVA

Perf. 13 Syncopated
2013, July 5   Litho.
793-796   A267   Set of 4   2.40   2.40
796a   Souvenir sheet of 8, 2 each
     #793-796, + label   5.00   5.00

Famous People — A268

Designs: No. 797, 1.75 l, Adrian Paunescu (1943-2010), poet and politician. No. 798, 1.75 l, Anton Crihan (1893-1993), politician. No. 799, 1.75 l, Ion Bass (1933-2005), folk singer. No. 800, 1.75 l, Angela Paduraru (1938-95), folk singer. 4.50 l, Giuseppe Verdi (1813-1901), composer. 5.40 l, Richard Wagner (1813-83), composer.

2013   Litho.   Perf. 14x14½
797-802   A268   Set of 6   4.00   4.00

Issued: Nos. 797-798, 7/20; Nos. 799-802, 8/2.

Souvenir Sheet

Alexei Mateevici (1888-1917), Poet — A269

2013, Aug. 28   Litho.   Perf. 14½x14
803   A269   5.75 l multi + label   1.25   1.25

Muscat Grapes — A270

2013, Sept. 13   Litho.   Perf. 14½x14
804   A270   1.75 l multi   .60   .60

Urban Mass Transportation A271

Designs: 1.75 l, Bus. 3 l, Trolleybus. 5.75 l, Tram.

2013, Oct. 12   Litho.   Perf. 14x14½
805-806   A271   Set of 2   1.10   1.10

Souvenir Sheet
807   A271   5.75 l multi + label   1.25   1.25

First tram in Chisinau, cent. (No. 807).

Christmas A272

2013, Nov. 22   Litho.   Perf. 14x14½
808   A272   1.75 l multi   .65   .65

Forget-me-nots — A273

Tree of Life Embroidery Design — A274

A275   A276

2013, Dec. 20   Litho.   Perf. 14x14½
809   A273   1.75 l multi + label   1.15   1.15
810   A274   1.75 l multi + label   1.15   1.15

Perf. 13 Syncopated
811   A275   1.75 l multi   1.15   1.15
812   A276   1.75 l multi   1.15   1.15
     Nos. 809-812 (4)   4.60   4.60

Nos. 809-810 each were printed in sheets of 8 + 8 labels that could be personalized. The labels shown are generic.

Nos. 811-812 each were printed in sheets of 8 stamps + 4 labels that could not be personalized. The image areas of Nos. 811-812 could be personalized. Illustrations show a generic image in the image area.

The frame portion of No. 811 has eight slightly different types. Values are for any of the frame types.

Traditional Crafts — A277

Designs: 1.20 l, Pottery. 1.75 l, Basket weaving. 5.75 l, Carpet weaving.

2014, Jan. 18   Litho.   Perf. 14x14½
813-815   A277   Set of 3   1.75   1.75

2014 Winter Olympics, Sochi, Russia — A278

Designs: 4.50 l, Skiing, bobsledding, snowboarding. 5.40 l, Ice hockey, figure skating, biathlon.

2014, Feb. 7   Litho.   Perf. 14x14½
816-817   A278   Set of 2   2.10   2.10

Europa — A279

Musical instruments: 3 l, Tambal (dulcimer). 5.75 l, Cobza (lute).

2014, Mar. 22   Litho.   Perf. 14x14½
818-819   A279   Set of 2   1.75   1.75
818a   Sheet of 3 + label   2.10   2.10
819a   Sheet of 3 + label   4.00   4.00

Nos. 818a and 819a were sold with, but unattached, to a booklet cover.

Easter — A280

Perf. 13 Syncopated
2014, Apr. 5   Litho.
820   A280   1.75 l multi   .70   .70

No. 820 was printed in sheets of 8 + central label.

Museums A281

Designs: 1.20 l, National Museum of Ethnography and Natural History. 2 l, National History Museum. 4 l, National Art Museum.

2014, May 3   Litho.   Perf. 14x14½
821-823   A281   Set of 3   1.50   1.50

Nos. 821-823 each were printed in sheets of 10 + 5 labels.

Arrival of German Settlers in Bessarabia, 200th Anniv. — A282

2014, May 15   Litho.   Perf. 14x14½
824   A282   1.75 l multi   .60   .60

Famous People — A283

Designs: 1.20 l, Tamara Ceban (1914-90), singer. 1.75 l, Dumitru Matcovschi (1939-2013), writer. 3 l, Toma Ciorba (1864-1936), physician. 8.50 l, Elena Cernei (1924-2000), opera singer.

Perf. 13 Syncopated
2014, June 7   Litho.
825-828   A283   Set of 4   2.75   2.75

Souvenir Sheet

Mihai Eminescu and Ion Creanga, Painting by Mihai Grecu — A284

Perf. 13 Syncopated
2014, June 14   Litho.
829   A284   5.75 l multi   1.10   1.10

Deportation of Germans from Bessarabia, 65th Anniv. — A285

2014, July 5   Litho.   Perf. 14x14½
830   A285   1.75 l multi   .60   .60

Association Agreement Between Moldova and European Union — A286

2014, Aug. 9   Litho.   Perf. 14x14½
831   A286   1.75 l multi   .60   .60

Sheep Breeds — A287

Designs: 1.20 l, Karakul sheep. 5.75 l, Tigaie sheep.

Perf. 13 Syncopated
2014, Aug. 16   Litho.
832-833   A287   Set of 2   1.40   1.40

Traditional Dishes — A288

Designs: 1 l, Fried fish with garlic sauce. 1.20 l, Bean soup with thyme. 4 l, Cheese and dill pies. 7 l, Chicken broth with parsley.

2014, Sept. 30   Litho.   Perf. 14x14½
834-837   A288   Set of 4   2.75   2.75

Fauna — A289

Designs: 1.20 l, Helix pomatia. 1.50 l, Ciconia ciconia (46x28mm). 1.75 l, Stizostedion lucioperca (46x28mm). 2 l, Cyprinus carpio (46x28mm). 3 l, Viviparus viviparus. 8.50 l, Motacilla flava (46x28mm).

2014, Nov. 7   Litho.   Perf. 14x14½
838-843   A289   Set of 6   3.50   3.50
843a   Souvenir sheet of 6, #838-843   3.50   3.50

Famous Men In World War I — A290

Designs: 1.75 l, Dimitrie Bogos (1889-1946), politician. 4 l, General Constantin Braescu (1873-1927). 5.75 l, Marshal Alexandru Averescu (1859-1938).

2014, Nov. 22   Litho.   Perf. 14x14½
844-846   A290   Set of 3   2.10   2.10

New Year 2015 — A291

Designs: 1.75 l, Snowman. 5.75 l, Santa Claus in sleigh.

2014, Dec. 12   Litho.   Perf. 14½x14
847-848   A291   Set of 2   1.40   1.40

Souvenir Sheet

Grigore Vieru (1935-2009), Poet — A292

2015, Feb. 14   Litho.   Perf. 14½x14
849   A292   5.75 l multi + label   1.10   1.10

International Year of Soils — A293   International Year of Light — A294

Perf. 13 Syncopated
2015, Feb. 21   Litho.
850   A293   1.75 l multi   .35   .35
851   A294   4.50 l multi   .85   .85

MOLDOVA

Design: Composer Eugen Doga, Dancers and Musical Score for Movie *My Sweet and Tender Beast*.

2015, Mar. 1 Litho. Perf. 14x14½
852 A295 1.75 l multi .60 .60

Coats of Arms — A296

Arms of: 10b, Causeni. 25b, Hîncesti. 1 l, Ungheni. 1.20 l, Orhei. 3 l, Balti. 5 l, Chisinau.

2015, Mar. 7 Litho. Perf. 14½x14
853-858 A296 Set of 6 2.00 2.00

Europa — A297

Old toys: 5.75 l, Wooden rocking horse and stackable rings. 11 l, Clay bird and ram figurines.

2015, Apr. 15 Litho. Perf. 14x14½
859-860 A297 Set of 2 2.60 2.60
860a Booklet pane of 4, 2 each
 #859-860 5.50 —
 Complete booklet, #860a 5.50

International Telecommunication Union, 150th Anniv. — A298

2015, Apr. 29 Litho. Perf. 14x14½
861 A298 1.75 l multi .60 .60

End of World War II, 70th Anniv. — A299

2015, May 5 Litho. Perf. 14½x14
862 A299 1.75 l multi .60 .60

Intl. Children's Day — A300

Children's art by: 1.20 l, Catalina Munteanu. 1.75 l, Cristina Isacov. 5.75 l, Ana Vlas, vert.

Perf. 14x14½, 14½x14
2015, June 1 Litho.
863-865 A300 Set of 3 1.25 1.25

Traditional Embroidered Blouses — A301

Blouse from: 1.75 l, 20th century. 11 l, 1925.

Perf. 13 Syncopated
2015, June 24 Litho.
866-867 A301 Set of 2 1.75 1.75

Famous People — A302

Designs: 1.20 l, Constanta Tirtau (1930-2014), actress. 1.75 l, Gica Petrescu (1915-2006), composer and singer. 4 l, Nicolae Corlateanu (1915-2005), linguist. 11 l, Pyotr Ilich Tchaikovsky (1840-93), composer. 5.75 l, Alexandru Cristea (1890-1942), composer of Moldovan national anthem.

Perf. 13 Syncopated
2015, July 17 Litho.
868-871 A302 Set of 4 2.40 2.40
Souvenir Sheet
872 A302 5.75 l multi .90 .90

Helsinki Accords, 40th Anniv. — A303

Perf. 13 Syncopated
2015, July 30 Litho.
873 A303 11 l multi 1.50 1.50

Paintings — A304

Designs: 1.75 l, Rocks, by Veniamin Slobodzinschi, 1978. 3 l, Evening in the Field, by Eleonora Romanescu, 1967. 5.75 l, On the Outskirts of the Village of Dolna, by Dimitrie Peicev, 2008. 9.50 l, Landscape, by Vasile Nascu, 2004.

Perf. 13 Syncopated
2015, Aug. 15 Litho.
874-877 A304 Set of 4 3.00 3.00

Birds — A305

Designs: 1.20 l, Sturnus vulgaris. 1.75 l, Pyrrhula pyrrhula. 4 l, Parus caeruleus. No. 881, 5.75 l, Bombycilla garrulus. No. 882, 5.75 l, Alauda arvensis.

2015, Sept. 25 Litho. Perf. 14x14½
878-881 A305 Set of 4 1.75 1.75
Souvenir Sheet
882 A305 5.75 l multi 1.00 1.00

Dancers A306

No. 883: a, 1.75 l, Dancers from Moldova. b, 11 l, Dancers from Azerbaijan.

2015, Oct. 16 Litho. Perf. 14x14½
883 A306 Horiz. pair, #a-b 1.90 1.90
See Azerbaijan No. 1094.

Mihai Volontir (1934-2015), Actor — A307

2015, Oct. 21 Litho. Perf. 14x14½
884 A307 1.75 l multi .35 .35

United Nations, 70th Anniv. — A308

Perf. 13 Syncopated
2015, Oct. 24 Litho.
885 A308 15.50 l multi 2.25 2.25

A309

Personalized Stamps A310

Perf. 13 Syncopated
2015, Nov. 17 Litho.
Panel Color
886 A309 1.75 l lt bl green 1.25 1.25
887 A309 1.75 l dark green 1.25 1.25
888 A309 1.75 l dark blue 1.25 1.25
889 A309 1.75 l pinkish org 1.25 1.25

Perf. 14x14½
890 A310 1.75 l light green 1.25 1.25
891 A310 1.75 l pink 1.25 1.25
892 A310 1.75 l light blue 1.25 1.25
Nos. 886-892 (7) 8.75 8.75

Vignette portions could be personalized for an additional fee. Vignette images shown are generic.

Motor Sports A311

No. 893: a, 1.20 l, Motocross. b, 5.75 l, Autocross.

2015, Nov. 27 Litho. Perf. 14x14½
893 A311 Horiz. pair, #a-b .90 .90

Christmas — A312

Designs: 1.75 l, Star procession. 9.50 l, Plugusorul carolers.

Perf. 13 Syncopated
2015, Dec. 4 Litho.
894-895 A312 Set of 2 1.50 1.50

Blood Donation Campaign — A313

2016, Feb. 2 Litho. Perf. 14½x14
896 A313 1.75 l multi .35 .35

Souvenir Sheet

Struve Geodetic Arc UNESCO World Heritage Site, 200th Anniv. — A314

2016, Feb. 11 Litho. Perf. 14½x14
897 A314 5.75 l multi + label .75 .75

Martisor (Spring Celebration) — A315

Martisor string on: 1.20 l, Snowdrops. 5.75 l, Cherry blossoms.

Perf. 13 Syncopated
2016, Mar. 1 Litho.
898-899 A315 Set of 2 .90 .90

Nos. 898-899 were both printed in sheets of 8 + central label.

1951 Soviet Deportation of Bessarabians, 65th Anniv — A316

2016, Mar. 31 Litho. Perf. 14½x14
900 A316 1.75 l multi .25 .25

A317

Europa A318

2016, Apr. 5 Litho. Perf. 14x14½
901 A317 5.75 l multi .90 .90
902 A318 9.50 l multi 1.60 1.60
a. Souvenir sheet of 6, 3 each
 #901-902 7.50 7.50
Think Green Issue.
No. 902a was sold with, but unattached to, a booklet cover.

No. 371 Surcharged in Gold

2016, Apr. 12 Litho.
903 A101 11 l on 1.80 l #371 1.60 1.60
First space flight by Yuri Gagarin, 55th anniv.

Flowers — A319

Designs: 10b, Xeranthemum annuum. 25b, Matricaria recutita. 1 l, Cichorium intybus. 2 l, Taraxacum officinale. 3 l, Achillea millefolium. 5 l, Salvia nemorosa.

MOLDOVA

2016, Apr. 15 Litho. Perf. 14x14½
904-909 A319 Set of 6 1.60 1.60
909a Souvenir sheet of 6, #904-909, + 3 labels 1.60 1.60

Palm Sunday — A320

2016, Apr. 24 Litho. Perf. 14x14½
910 A320 1.75 l multi .30 .30

Worldwide Fund for Nature (WWF) — A321

No. 911 — Gladiolus imbricatus: a, Sky and flowers on seven stems. b, Sky and flowers on one stem. c, Five flowers on one stem, no sky. d, Two flowers on one stem, no sky.

Perf. 13 Syncopated
2016, May. 27 Litho.
911 A321 11 l Block of 4, #a-d 6.00 6.00

Pentecost A322

2016, June 19 Litho. Perf. 14x14½
912 A322 1.75 l multi .30 .30

Famous Men — A323

Designs: No. 913, 1.20 l, Carol Schmidt (1846-1928), mayor of Chisinau. No. 914, 1.20 l, Nicolae Anestiadi (1916-68), surgeon. 1.75 l, Grigore Grigoriu (1941-2003), actor. 5.75 l, Emil Loteanu (1936-2003), film director.

2016, June 29 Litho. Perf. 14x14½
913-916 A323 Set of 4 1.25 1.25

Souvenir Sheet

Putna Monastery, 550th Anniv. — A324

Perf. 13 Syncopated
2016, July 2 Litho.
917 A324 5.75 l multi .75 .75

Nativity of St. John the Baptist — A325

2016, July 7 Litho. Perf. 14x14½
918 A325 1.75 l multi .30 .30

2016 Summer Olympics, Rio de Janeiro A326

Designs: 5.75 l, Women's discus and hammer throw. 15.50 l, Rowing.

2016, July 25 Litho. Perf. 14x14½
919-920 A326 Set of 2 2.75 2.75

Souvenir Sheet

Independence, 25th Anniv. — A327

No. 921: a, 1 l, Flags and words from national anthem. b, 5.75 l, Triumphal Arch, Chisinau, and words from Moldovan Declaration of Independence. c, 11 l, Moldova coat of arms.

Litho. With Foil Application
2016, Aug. 27 Perf. 14½x14
921 A327 Sheet of 3, #a-c 2.60 2.60

Woodworking — A328

No. 922 — Woodworker with mallet and: a, 1.75 l, Wooden flasks. b, 11 l, Carving of a bull.

2016, Sept. 8 Litho. Perf. 14x14½
922 A328 Horiz. pair, #a-b 1.75 1.75
See Belarus No. 1010.

International Year of Pulses — A329

No. 923: a, 1.20 l, Cicer arietinum. b, 1.75 l, Phaseolus vulgaris. c, 5.75 l, Vicia faba. d, 9.50 l, Pisum sativum.

Perf. 13 Syncopated
2016, Sept. 27 Litho.
923 A329 Block of 4, #a-d 2.50 2.50

Extinct Animals of Moldova A330

Designs: 1.20 l, Tapir. 1.75 l, Dolichopithecus ruscinensis. 4 l, Crocuta crocuta spelaea. 5.75 l, Paracamelus alexejevi. 15.50 l, Megaloceros giganteus.

2016, Oct. 29 Litho. Perf. 14x14½
924-927 A330 Set of 4 1.75 1.75
Souvenir Sheet
928 A330 15.50 l multi 2.10 2.10

Souvenir Sheet

Mihail Grecu (1916-98), Painter — A331

2016, Nov. 22 Litho. Perf. 14x14½
929 A331 5.75 l multi .80 .80

New Year 2017 — A332

Ornaments: 1.75 l, Spherical with snowflakes. 5.75 l, Bells.

Perf. 13 Syncopated
2016, Dec. 2 Litho.
930-931 A332 Set of 2 1.00 1.00
Nos. 930-931 were each printed in sheets of 8 + label.

Souvenir Sheet

Months of the Year A333

No. 932: a, January (Januarie). b, February (Februarie). c, March (Martie).

Perf. 13 Syncopated
2017, Jan. 5 Litho.
932 A333 5.75 l Sheet of 3, #a-c, + label 2.25 2.25

Coats of Arms — A334

Arms of: 10b, Briceni. 25b, Rezina. 1 l, Sângerei. 1.20 l, Floresti. 1.75 l, Ialoveni. 3 l, Leova.

2017, Feb. 10 Litho. Perf. 14x14½
933-938 A334 Set of 6 .95 .95

International Year of Sustainable Tourism for Development A335

2017, Mar. 10 Litho. Perf. 14x14½
939 A335 5.75 l multi .75 .75

Easter A336

No. 940 — Easter egg and: a, 1.75 l, Girl holding two eggs. b, 15.50 l, Hands of girl holding two eggs.

2017, Apr. 5 Litho. Perf. 14x14½
940 A336 Horiz. pair, #a-b 2.25 2.25

Mimi Castle, Anenii Noi — A337

2017, Apr. 28 Litho. Perf. 14x14½
941 A337 11 l multi 1.50 1.50
 a. Miniature sheet of 4 6.00 6.00
Europa. No. 941a was sold with, but unattached to, a booklet cover.

Ancient Jewelry — A338

Designs: 1.20 l, Earrings, Scythian culture. 1.75 l, Moon pendant, Sântana de Mures Cerneahov culture. 5.75 l, Ring, Sarmatic culture. 9.50 l, Brooch, Sântana de Mures Cerneahov culture.

Perf. 13 Syncopated
2017, May 18 Litho.
942-945 A338 Set of 4 2.50 2.50
Nos. 942-945 were each printed in sheets of 8 + central label.

Flowers A339

No. 946: a, 1.75 l, Digitalis purpurea. b, 4 l+10b, Aquilegia hybrida. c, 5.20 l, Paeonia lactiflora. d, 5.75 l, Hemerocallis hybrida.

Perf. 13 Syncopated
2017, May 30 Litho.
946 A339 Block of 4, #a-d 2.40 2.40

Emergency Rescue Crew Killed in 2016 Helicopter Crash in Haragîs — A340

Perf. 13 Syncopated
2017, June 4 Litho.
947 A340 9.50 l multi 1.40 1.40

Traditional Clothing of Gagauz Men and Women — A341

Perf. 13 Syncopated
2017, June 21 Litho.
948 A341 1.75 l multi .25 .25

Bats — A342

Designs: 1.75 l, Myotis myotis. 2 l, Vespertilio murinus. 5.75 l, Nyctalus lasiopterus. 15.50 l, Plecotus austriacus.

Perf. 13 Syncopated
2017, July 29 Litho.
949-952 A342 Set of 4 3.50 3.50

MOLDOVA

Sports — A343

Designs: 1.75 l, Volleyball. 9.50 l, Tennis.

2017, Aug. 23 Litho. Perf. 14½x14
953-954 A343 Set of 2 1.60 1.60

Paintings Depicting Animals — A344

Designs: 1.20 l, Turkeys, by Vilhelmina Zazerskaia. 4 l, Expectations, by Alexandr Grigorashenko. 5.20 l, The Plow, by Vladimir Ocusco. 5.75 l, Chicks, by Nicolae Gumalic.

Perf. 13 Syncopated
2017, Sept. 15 Litho.
955-958 A344 Set of 4 2.40 2.40

Souvenir Sheet

Country Council, Cent. A345

Litho. With Foil Application
2017, Oct. 23 Perf. 13 Syncopated
959 A345 9.50 l gold & multi 1.40 1.40

Famous Men — A346

Designs: 1.20 l, Vladimir Andrunachievici (1917-97), mathematician. 1.75 l, Leonid Fitov (1917-98), sculptor. 2 l, Dumitru Gheorghita (1917-87), composer. 5.20 l, Alexandru Stuart (1842-1917), founder of National Museum of Ethnography and Natural History. 5.75 l, Mihail Kogalniceanu (1817-91), historian and Prime Minister of Romania. 9.50 l, Jonathan Swift (1667-1745), writer.

2017, Nov. 15 Litho. Perf. 14x14½
960-965 A346 Set of 6 3.75 3.75

Christmas — A347

Icons: 1.75 l, Birth of Christ, Church of St. Michael and Gavriil, Durlesti. 5.75 l, Nativity of Jesus Christ, Nativity Cathedral, Chisinau.

Litho. with Foil Application
2017, Dec. 7 Perf. 13 Syncopated
966-967 A347 Set of 2 1.10 1.10

Organ Donation — A348

Perf. 13 Syncopated
2018, Jan. 11 Litho.
968 A348 1.75 l multi .25 .25

Europa — A349

Designs: 5.75 l, Eiffel Bridge, Ungheni. 11 l, Pohorniceni Wooden Bridge. Orhei.

2018, Feb. 8 Litho. Perf. 14½x14
969 A349 5.75 l multi .90 .90
  a. Sheet of 4 3.75 3.75
970 A349 11 l multi 1.75 1.75
  a. Sheet of 4 7.00 7.00

Nos. 969a and 970a were sold with, but unattached to, a booklet cover.

Trees — A350

Designs: 1.20 l, Populus. 1.75 l, Aesculus hippocastanum. 5 l, Acer platanoides. 5.75 l, Quercus robur.

2018, Mar. 1 Litho. Perf. 14½x14
971-974 A350 Set of 4 2.10 2.10
974a Sheet of 8, 2 each #971-974 + 2 labels 4.25 4.25

Fauna of Padurea Domneasca Nature Reserve A351

Designs: 1.20 l, Nycticorax nycticorax. 1.75 l, Ardea cinerea. 4 l, Sus scrofa. 5.75 l, Bison bonasus. 9.50 l, Dryocopus martius.

2018, Mar. 29 Litho. Perf. 14x14½
975-978 A351 Set of 4 1.90 1.90

Souvenir Sheet
979 A351 9.50 l multi 1.50 1.50

Months of the Year A352

No. 932: a, April (Aprilie). b, May (Mai). c, June (Junie).

Perf. 13 Syncopated
2018, Apr. 13 Litho.
980 A352 5.75 l Sheet of 3, #a.-c. + label 2.75 2.75

Traditional Clothing of Romas — A353

Perf. 13 Syncopated
2018, Apr. 20 Litho.
981 A353 1.75 l multi .30 .30

Scientists A354

Designs: 5.75 l, Nikola Tesla (1856-1943), and electric induction motor. 9.50 l, Alexander Fleming (1881-1955), and molecular structure of penicillin.

2018, May 3 Litho. Perf. 14x14½
982-983 A354 Set of 2 2.40 2.40

A355

Designs: 1.20 l, Bowl and obverse and reverse of coin, c. 359-336 B.C. 1.75 l, Obverse and reverse of 2 coins, c. 336-323 B.C. 5.75 l, Obverse and reverse of coin, c. 323-317 B.C.

2018, May 18 Litho. Perf. 14x14½
984-986 A355 Set of 3 1.40 1.40

Ancient Coins From the Larguta Treasure, Museum of Ethnography and Natural History of Moldova.

Children's Day — A356

Children's drawings of fairy tale characters: 1.20 l, Fat-Frumos and Ileana Cosânzeana, by Anastasia Voitenko. 5.75 l, The Bear Tricked by the Fox, by Corina Jdanova.

2018, June 1 Litho. Perf. 14x14½
987-988 A356 Set of 2 1.10 1.10

Postcrossing — A357

2018, June 23 Litho. Perf. 14½x14
989 A357 11 l multi 1.75 1.75

Tourism A358

Designs: 1.75 l, Soroca Fort. 5.75 l, Archaeological Ruins of Old Orhei.

2018, July 5 Litho. Perf. 14x14½
990-991 A358 Set of 2 1.10 1.10

Stamp Day A359

2018, July 22 Litho. Perf. 14x14½
992 A359 9.50 l multi 1.40 1.40

Poultry — A360

Designs: 1.75 l, Anas platyrhynchos. 4 l, Anser anser. 5.75 l, Gallus gallus. 15.50 l, Meleagris gallopavo.

2018, Aug. 23 Litho. Perf. 14x14½
993-996 A360 Set of 4 4.25 4.25

Nos. 993-996 were each printed in sheets of 8 + 2 labels.

Moldova, 2018 World Capital of Wine Tourism — A361

2018, Sept. 6 Litho. Perf. 14½x14
997 A361 5.75 l multi .85 .85

Moldova Postal Service, 25th Anniv. — A362

Perf. 13 Syncopated
2018, Oct. 9 Litho.
998 A362 1.75 l multi .25 .25

Clocks of Chisinau — A363

Clock from: 1.75 l, Chisinau City Hall. 5.75 l, Triumphal Arch.

Perf. 13 Syncopated
2018, Oct. 12 Litho.
999-1000 A363 Set of 2 1.10 1.10

Famous People — A364

Designs: No. 1001, 1.20 l, George Meniuc (1918-87), writer. No. 1002, 1.20 l, Mihail Berezovschi (1868-1940), composer. No. 1003, 1.75 l, Eugenia Malesevschi (1868-1942), painter. No. 1004, 1.75 l, Constantin Mimi (1868-1935), politician.

2018, Nov. 13 Litho. Perf. 14½x14
1001-1004 A364 Set of 4 .85 .85

Union of Bessarabia With Romania, Cent. — A365

2018, Nov. 27 Litho. Perf. 14x14½
1005 A365 5.75 l multi .85 .85

New Year 2019 — A366

Designs: 1.75 l, Christmas tree. 5.75 l, Snowflake.

Litho. With Foil Application
2018, Dec. 4 Perf. 13 Syncopated
1006-1007 A366 Set of 2 1.10 1.10

Famous Men — A367

Designs: 1.75 l, Alexandru Mosanu (1932-2017), President of Parliament. 5.75 l, Vladimir

MOLDOVA

Curbet (1930-2017), choreographer. 9.50 l, King Michael of Romania (1921-2017).

2018 Litho. Perf. 13 Syncopated
1008-1010 A367 Set of 3 2.50 2.50

Issued: 1.75 l, 12/7, 5.75 l, 12/8; 9.50 l, 12/5. Nos. 1008-1010 were each printed in sheets of 5 + label.

Souvenir Sheet

Church Bells A368

No. 1011: a, Bell, Cathedral of the Nativity, Chisinau, 1838. b, Mazepa Bell, St. Sophia's Cathedral, Kyiv, Ukraine, 1705.

Litho. & Silk-screened
2018, Dec. 26 Perf. 13 Syncopated
1011 A368 9.50 l Sheet of 2, #a-
 b 2.75 2.75

See Ukraine No. 1195.

Emergency Number 112 — A369

2019, Jan. 3 Litho. Perf. 14x14½
1012 A369 1.75 l multi .25 .25

Famous People — A370

Designs: No. 1013, 1.20 l, Domnica Darienco (1919-2010), actress. No. 1014, 1.20 l, Alexei Stârcea (1919-74), composer. 1.75 l, Gheorge Asachi (1788-1869), writer. 2 l, Constantin Stamati (1786-1869), writer. No. 1017, 5.75 l, Glebus Sainciuc (1919-2012), painter. No. 1018, 5.75 l, Alecu Russo (1819-59), writer.

Perf. 13 Syncopated
2019, Jan. 15 Litho.
1013-1018 A370 Set of 6 2.60 2.60

Man and Woman in Traditional Ukrainian Clothing — A371

Perf. 13 Syncopated
2019, Feb. 1 Litho.
1019 A371 1.75 l multi .25 .25

World Radio Day — A372

Designs: 1.75 l, 1934 Telefunken radio. 5.75 l, 1943 Philips radio.

Perf. 13 Syncopated
2019, Feb. 13 Litho.
1020-1021 A372 Set of 2 1.10 1.10

Martisor Music Festival, Chisinau — A373

Perf. 13 Syncopated
2019, Mar. 1 Litho.
1022 A373 5.75 l multi .85 .85

Flowering Shrubs — A374

Designs: 1.20 l, Viburnum opulus roseum. 2 l, Syringa vulgaris. 4 l, Forsythia. 5.75 l, Jasminus communis.

Perf. 13 Syncopated
2019, Mar. 14 Litho.
1023-1026 A374 Set of 4 1.90 1.90

Endangered Animals A375

Designs: 1.20 l, Rosalia alpina. 1.75 l, Lucanus cervus. 2 l, Cricetus cricetus. 9.50 l, Spermophilus suslicus.

2019, Apr. 11 Litho. Perf. 14x14½
1027-1030 A375 Set of 4 2.10 2.10

Europa A376

Birds: No. 1031, Ciconia ciconia. No. 1032, Aquila chrysaetos.

Perf. 13 Syncopated
2019, Apr. 19 Litho.
1031 A376 11 l multi 1.60 1.60
 a. Sheet of 3 + label 5.00 5.00
1032 A376 11 l multi 1.60 1.60
 a. Sheet of 3 + label 5.00 5.00

Nos. 1031a and 1032a were sold with, but unattached to, a booklet cover.

Water Lilies — A377

Designs: 25b, Nuphar lutea. 1 l, Nymphaea Rose Arey. 5.75 l, Nymphaea alba.

2019, May 7 Litho. Perf. 14½x14
1033-1035 A377 Set of 3 1.00 1.00

International Year of Indigenous Languages — A378

International Year of The Periodic Table of Elements — A379

2019, May 23 Litho. Perf. 14x14½
1036 A378 15.50 l multi 2.25 2.25
1037 A379 15.50 l multi 2.25 2.25

2019 European Games, Minsk — A380

Designs: 1.75 l, Canoeing. 9.50 l, Wrestling.

2019, June 21 Litho. Perf. 14x14½
1038-1039 A380 Set of 2 1.60 1.60

Domesticated Animals A381

Designs: 1.20 l, Capra aegagrus hircus. 1.75 l, Oryctolagus cuniculus domesticus. 4 l, Bos taurus domesticus. 5.75 l, Equus caballus.

2019, June 28 Litho. Perf. 14x14½
1040-1043 A381 Set of 4 1.75 1.75

Nos. 1040-1043 were each printed in sheets of 9 + label.

Souvenir Sheet

Months of the Year A382

No. 1044: a, July (Julie). b, August. c, September (Septembrie).

Perf. 13 Syncopated
2019, July 10 Litho.
1044 A382 5.75 l Sheet of 3, #a-
 c, + label 2.50 2.50

Souvenir Sheet

First Man on the Moon, 50th Anniv. A383

2019, July 20 Litho. Perf. 14x14½
1045 A383 15.50 l multi 2.25 2.25

Food Crops — A384

Designs: 1.75 l, Helianthus annuus. 2 l, Triticum. 5.75 l, Zea mays.

Perf. 13 Syncopated
2019, Aug. 15 Litho.
1046-1048 A384 Set of 3 1.40 1.40

Maria Biesu International Opera and Ballet Festival, Chisinau — A385

Perf. 13 Syncopated
2019, Sept. 6 Litho.
1049 A385 5.75 l multi .85 .85

Council of Europe, 70th Anniv. — A386

2019, Oct. 9 Litho. Perf. 14½x14
1050 A386 9.50 l multi 1.40 1.40

Universal Postal Union, 145th Anniv. — A387

2019, Oct. 9 Litho. Perf. 14x14½
1051 A387 15.50 l multi 2.25 2.25

Famous Men — A388

Designs: No. 1052, 1.75 l, Louis Braille (1809-52), educator of the blind. No. 1053, 1.75 l, Albert Einstein (1879-1955), physicist. 5.75 l, Mohandas K. Gandhi (1869-1948), Indian nationalist leader. 9.50 l, Leonardo da Vinci (1452-1519), sculptor and painter.

Perf. 13 Syncopated
2019, Oct. 28 Litho.
1052-1055 A388 Set of 4 2.75 2.75
1055a Souvenir sheet of 4,
 #1052-1055 2.75 2.75

Nos. 1052-1055 were each printed in sheets of 8 + label.

Paintings in National Museum of Fine Arts — A389

Designs: 1.20 l, Venus and Mars, by Jean-Baptiste van Loo (1684-1745). 1.75 l, The Holy Family, by Andrea Sacchi (1599-1661), vert. 5.20 l, Bathsheba, by unknown artist, vert. 5.75 l, Angelica and Medoro, by Michele Desubleo (1602-76).

Perf. 14x14½, 14½x14
2019, Nov. 26 Litho.
1056-1059 A389 Set of 4 2.00 2.00

New Year 2020 A390

No. 1060: a, Forest. b, House and snowman.

Litho. With Foil Application
2019, Dec. 10 Perf. 13 Syncopated
1060 A390 5.75 l Horiz. pair, #a-
 b 1.75 1.75

Victims of Fascism Monument, Chisinau — A391

Perf. 13 Syncopated
2020, Jan. 27 Litho.
1061 A391 15.50 l multi 2.25 2.25

International Holocaust Remembrance Day.

Europa — A392

Map of old postal route from: 9.50 l, 1812 and wagon wheel. 11 l, 1926 and biplane.

2020, Aug. 17 Litho. Perf. 14x14½
1062-1063 A392 Set of 2 3.25 3.25
1063a Souvenir sheet of 4, 2
 each #1062-1063 6.50 6.50

MOLDOVA

International Year of Plant Health — A393

Perf. 13 Syncopated   Litho.
2020, Aug. 25
1064 A393 15.50 l multi   2.40   2.40

Desserts A394

Designs: 1.20 l, Cusma lui guguta (crepe cake). 4 l, Baba neagra (cake with yogurt and vodka).

2020, Sept. 14   Litho.   Perf. 14x14½
1065-1066 A394   Set of 2   .80   .80

Varzareshti Monastery, 600th Anniv. — A395

2020, Sept. 21   Litho.   Perf. 14x14½
1067 A395 5.75 l multi   .85   .85
No. 1067 was printed in sheets of 5.

St. Stephen the Great Public Garden A396

Rose Valley Park A397

Morilor Valley Park A398

Dendrariu Park — A399

Perf. 13¾x14¼   Litho.
2020, Sept. 29
1068 A396 1.75 l multi   .25   .25
1069 A397 1.75 l multi   .25   .25
1070 A398 5.75 l multi   .90   .90
1071 A399 5.75 l multi   .90   .90
Nos. 1068-1071 (4)   2.30   2.30
Parks and gardens of Chisinau.

Famous People — A400

Designs: 1.20 l, St. Teresa of Calcutta (1910-97). 1.75 l, Raphael (1483-1520), painter. 9.50 l + 3 l, Florence Nightingale (1820-1910), nurse. 11 l, Ludwig van Beethoven (1770-1827), composer.

Perf. 13 Syncopated   Litho.
2020, Oct. 13
1072-1075 A400   Set of 4   4.00   4.00

Souvenir Sheet

Ferdinand Magellan (1452-1519), Explorer — A401

Perf. 13 Syncopated   Litho.
2020, Oct. 13
1076 A401 15.50 l multi + label   2.25   2.25
Circumnavigation of the globe by expedition led by Magellan, 500th anniv.

United Nations, 75th Anniv. — A402

2020, Oct. 24   Litho.   Perf. 14x14½
1077 A402 15.50 l multi   2.25   2.25

Souvenir Sheet

Months of the Year A403

No. 1078: a, October (Octombrie). b, November (Noiembrie). c, December (Decembrie).

Perf. 13 Syncopated   Litho.
2020, Oct. 30
1078 A403 5.75 l Sheet of 3, #a-c, + label   2.60   2.60

Adoption of Flag of Moldova, 30th Anniv. A404

Adoption of Coat of Arms of Moldova, 30th Anniv. A405

2020, Nov. 3   Litho.   Perf. 14x14½
1079 A404 1.75 l multi   .25   .25

Perf. 14½x14
1080 A405 5.75 l multi   .85   .85

International Day for the Elimination of Violence Against Women A406

2020, Nov. 25   Litho.   Perf. 14x14½
1081 A406 1.20 l multi   .25   .25

Christmas — A407

2020, Dec. 22   Litho.   Perf. 14½x14
1082 A407 1.75 l multi   .25   .25

Valeriu Gafencu (1921-52), Theologian Tortured by Communists A408

2021, Jan. 24   Litho.   Perf. 14x14½
1083 A408 1.75 l multi   .25   .25

Toma Ciorba Hospital for Infectious Diseases, 125th Anniv. — A409

2021, Feb. 25   Litho.   Perf. 14x14½
1084 A409 1.20 l multi   .25   .25
Campaign against COVID-19 pandemic.

Gavril Banulescu-Bodoni (1746-1821), Metropolitan of Moldavia — A410

Perf. 13 Syncopated   Litho.
2021, Mar. 30
1085 A410 5.75 l multi   .80   .80

Coat of Arms of Moldova — A411

2021, Apr. 8   Litho.   Perf. 14x14½
1086 A411   25b light blue   .25   .25
1087 A411   1.20 l blue green   .25   .25
1088 A411   1.75 l rose   .25   .25
Nos. 1086-1088 (3)   .75   .75

Easter — A412

Paintings: 1.75 l, Carrying the Cross, by Frans Francken (1581-1642). 5.75 l, Resurrection of Christ, by Agostino Gaetano Ugolini (1755-1824), vert.

Perf. 14x14½, 14½x14
2021, Apr. 23   Litho.
1089-1090 A412   Set of 2   1.10   1.10

Souvenir Sheet

Balti, 600th Anniv. A413

2021, May 22   Litho.   Perf. 14x14½
1091 A413 5.75 l multi   .85   .85

Endangered Animals — A414

Designs: 5.75 l, Ciconia nigra. 11 l, Bubo bubo.

Perf. 13 Syncopated   Litho.
2021, May 28
1092-1093 A414   Set of 2   2.40   2.40
1093a   Souvenir sheet of 4, 2 each #1092-1093   4.80   4.80
Europa.

Nicolae Iorga (1871-1940), Writer and Prime Minister of Romania A415

2021, June 24   Litho.   Perf. 14x14½
1094 A415 5.75 l multi   .80   .80

Vasile Alecsandri (1821-90), Writer and Romanian Minister of Foreign Affairs — A416

2021, July 21   Litho.   Perf. 14x14½
1095 A416 5.75 l multi   .80   .80

2020 Summer Olympics, Tokyo — A417

Designs: 1.75 l, Wrestling. 15.50 l, Canoeing.

2021, Aug. 7   Litho.   Perf. 14x14½
1096-1097 A417   Set of 2   2.50   2.50

The 2020 Summer Olympics were postponed until 2021 because of the COVID-19 pandemic. Compare No. 1097 with No. 1105.

Souvenir Sheet

Independence, 30th Anniv. — A418

Perf. 13 Syncopated   Litho.
2021, Aug. 27
1098 A418 5.75 l multi   .85   .85

Souvenir Sheet

Moldova Nos. 1-3 — A419

2021, Aug. 27   Litho.   Perf. 14½x14
1099 A419 5.75 l multi   .85   .85
First Moldova postage stamps, 30th anniv.

Souvenir Sheet

Moldovan Army, 30th Anniv. — A420

2021, Sept. 3   Litho.   Perf. 14½x14
1100 A420 5.75 l multi + label   .85   .85

MOLDOVA

Birds of the Lower Prut Biosphere Reserve — A421

Designs: 1.20 l, Phalacrocorax pygmaeus. 1.75 l, Botaurus stellaris, horiz. No. 1103, 5.75 l, Haliaeetus albicilla. No. 1104, 5.75 l, Tadorna tadorna, horiz.

Perf. 14½x14, 14x14½
2021, Sept. 30   Litho.
1101-1104 A421   Set of 4

Canoer and Olympic Bronze Medal — A422

2021, Oct. 22   Litho.   *Perf. 14x14½*
1105 A422   15.50 l multi   2.25   2.25

Third-place finish of Serghei Tarnovschi in men's 1000-meter canoe sprint event at 2020 Summer Olympics, which was postponed until 2021 because of the COVID-19 pandemic. Compare No. 1105 with No. 1097.

Souvenir Sheet

Mihai Eminescu National Theater, Chisinau, Cent. — A423

Perf. 13 Syncopated
2021, Oct. 30   Litho.
1106 A423   5.75 l multi + label   .85   .85

Viticulture — A424

Designs: 1.75 l, Rara neargra grapes and flask. 11 l, Zghihara grapes and wine pitcher.

Perf. 13 Syncopated
2021, Nov. 24   Litho.
1107-1108 A424   Set of 2   1.90   1.90
See Romania Nos. 6659-6660.

Self-portrait of Valentina Rusu Ciobanu (1920-2021) — A425

2021, Dec. 29   Litho.   *Perf. 14½x14*
1109 A425   1.75 l multi   .30   .30

International Year of Glass — A426

Perf. 13 Syncopated
2022, Jan. 31   Litho.
1110 A426   1.75 l multi   .30   .30

2022 Winter Olympics, Beijing — A427

Designs: 5.75 l, Bobsled. 15.50 l, Biathlon.

Perf. 13 Syncopated
2022, Feb. 16   Litho.
1111-1112 A427   Set of 2   3.00   3.00

Famous Men — A428

Designs: No. 1113, 1.75 l, Ion Creanga (1837-89), writer of children's literature. No. 1114, 1.75 l, Ion Neculce (1672-1745), chronicler.

2022, Mar. 1   Litho.   *Perf. 14x14½*
1113-1114 A428   Set of 2   .50   .50

The Grieving Mother, Sculpture by Iurie Canasin A429

2022, Mar. 2   Litho.   *Perf. 14x14½*
1115 A429   1.75 l multi   .30   .30
Day of Remembrance.

Admission of Moldova to United Nations, 30th Anniv. — A430

Perf. 13 Syncopated
2022, Mar. 2   Litho.
1116 A430   15.50 l multi   2.10   2.10

Peace Dove — A431

2022, Apr. 19   Litho.   *Perf. 14x14½*
1117 A431   1.75 l multi   .30   .30

Europa — A432

Designs: 9.50 l, Legend of the Moldavian Aurochs. 11 l, Legend of the Poor Man and the Dragons.

2022, Apr. 29   Litho.   *Perf. 14x14½*
1118-1119 A432   Set of 2   2.75   2.75

Items in National Museum of Ethnography and Natural History, Chisinau — A433

Designs: 3 l, Clay pot, 13th cent. 9.50 l, Hunnic bronze container, 5th cent. 11 l, Painted vessel, 3rd millenium B.C.

2022, May 18   Litho.   *Perf. 14½x14*
1120-1122 A433   Set of 3   3.25   3.25

Painters and Their Paintings in the National Museum of Art A434

Designs: 3 l, Dniester at Criuleni, by Pavel Piscariov (1875-1949). 9.50 l, Dniester, by Pavel Sillingovski (1881-1942). 15.50 l, Morning on the Dniester, by Mihai Petric (1923-2005).

2022, May 18   Litho.   *Perf. 14x14½*
1123-1125 A434   Set of 3   3.75   3.75

Municipal Coats of Arms — A435

Arms of: 1 l, Ocnita. 2.80 l, Calarasi. 5.35 l, Nisporeni. 8.15 l, Cimislia. 10.95 l, Falesti. 45 l, Anenii Noi.

2022, June 1   Litho.   *Perf. 14x14½*
1126 A435   1 l multi   .30   .30
1127 A435   2.80 l multi   .40   .40
1128 A435   5.35 l multi   .70   .70
1129 A435   8.15 l multi   1.10   1.10
1130 A435   10.95 l multi   1.50   1.50
1131 A435   45 l multi   6.00   6.00
Nos. 1126-1131 (6)   10.00   10.00

DescOpera Classical Music Festival, Butuceni A436

2022, June 17   Litho.   *Perf. 14x14½*
1132 A436   3.20 l multi   .45   .45

Mansions A437

Mansion of: 3.40 l, The Lazo Family. 8.35 l, Manuc Bey.

2022, June 21   Litho.   *Perf. 14x14½*
1133-1134 A437   Set of 2   1.60   1.60

Traditional Costumes of Bessarabian Bulgarian Men and Women — A438

Perf. 13 Syncopated
2022, July 22   Litho.
1135 A438   2.80 l multi   .40   .40

Butterflies and Moths — A439

Designs: 2.80 l, Glaucopsyche alexis. 5.50 l, Zerynthia polyxena. 8.15 l, Anthocharis cardamines. 11.15 l, Zygaena filipendulae.

Perf. 13 Syncopated
2022, July 29   Litho.
1136-1139 A439   Set of 4   3.75   3.75

Cactus Flowers — A440

Designs: 2.80 l, Cryptocereus anthoyanus. 3.20 l, Opuntia phaeacantha. 11.35 l, Mammillaria magnimamma.

Perf. 13 Syncopated
2022, Aug. 12   Litho.
1140-1142 A440   Set of 3   2.25   2.25

Mushrooms — A441

Designs: 2.80 l, Macrolepiota procera. 3.40 l, Xerocomus chrysenteron. 8.75 l, Lactarius volemus. 16.30 l, Russula delica.

2022, Sept. 15   Litho.   *Perf. 14½x14*
1143-1146 A441   Set of 4   4.00   4.00

Souvenir Sheet

Wineries A442

No. 1147: a, 2.80 l, Milesti Mici Winery. b, 3.20 l, Cricova Winery. c, 8.55 l, Purcari Winery.

2022, Oct. 1   Litho.   *Perf. 14x14½*
1147 A442   Sheet of 3, #a-c   1.90   1.90

Souvenir Sheet

Coronation of King Ferdinand (1865-1927) and Queen Marie (1875-1938) of Romania, Cent. — A443

Perf. 13 Syncopated
2022, Oct. 15   Litho.
1148 A443   9.50 l multi   1.25   1.25

Famous Men — A445

Designs: 2.80 l, Louis Pasteur (1822-95), microbiologist. 8.15 l, Franz Schubert (1797-1828), composer. 9.50 l, Roald Amundsen (1872-1928), polar explorer. 11 l, Thomas Edison (1847-1931), inventor.

Perf. 13 Syncopated
2022, Nov. 29   Litho.
1152-1155 A445   Set of 4   4.25   4.25

Christmas A446   **New Year 2023 A447**

Perf. 13 Syncopated
2022, Dec. 9   Litho.
1156 A446   2.80 l multi   .40   .40
1157 A447   8.15 l multi   1.10   1.10

MOLDOVA

Paintings by Ion Daghi (1936-2022) — A448

Designs: 2.80 l, Interferenta Suferintelor (The Interference of Sufferers), 2003. 8.15 l, Rasai Asupra Mea (Fall On Me), 2011.

2023, Jan. 15 Litho. Perf. 14½x14
1158-1159 A448 Set of 2 1.50 1.50

Healthy Living — A453

2023, Mar. 29 Litho. Perf. 14x14½
1164 A453 3.20 l multi .45 .45

Firefighters — A454

Designs: 2.80 l, Two firefighters on ladder. 8.15 l, Four firefighters, car in background.

Perf. 13 Syncopated
2023, Apr. 5 Litho.
1165-1166 A454 Set of 2 1.60 1.60

Earth Day — A455

2023, Apr. 22 Litho. Perf. 14x14½
1167 A455 10 l multi 1.40 1.40

Europa — A456

No. 1168: 10 l, Interlocking hands. No. 1169: 10 l, Dove with multicolored hearts.

2023, Apr. 28 Litho. Perf. 14x14½
1168-1169 A456 Set of 2 3.00 3.00

PostEurop, 30th Anniv. — A457

Perf. 13 Syncopated
2023, May 20 Litho.
1170 A457 10 l multi 1.40 1.40

Campaign for Bee and Wildlife Protection — A458

Perf. 13½x13 Syncopated
2023, May 23 Litho.
1171 A458 3.40 l multi .50 .50

Animals in Chisinau Zoo — A459

Designs: 3.30 l, Lama glama. 7 l, Ara ararauna, horiz. 10.30 l, Crocodylus rhombifer, horiz. 13.60 l, Dromaius novaehollandiae. 12 l, Cygnus atratus, horiz.

Perf. 14½x14, 14x14½
2023, May 30 Litho.
1172-1175 A459 Set of 4 5.00 5.00
Souvenir Sheet
1176 A459 12 l multi 1.75 1.75

Summit of the European Political Community A460

Litho. With Foil Application
2023, June 1 Perf. 14½x14
1177 A460 55 l multi + label 7.75 7.75

Garden Flowers — A461

Designs: 50b, Chrysanthemum. 3.30 l, Dahlia. 10.30 l, Gladiolus.

2023, June 20 Litho. Perf. 14x14½
1178-1180 A461 Set of 3 2.00 2.00

Famous People — A464

Designs: 3.30 l, Ludovic Daus (1873-1954), novelist. 3.40 l, Alexey Shchusev (1873-1949), architect. 3.50 l, Ariadna Salari (1923-2016), writer. 7 l, Zamfir Ralli Arbore (1848-1933), journalist. 10.30 l, Elena Alistar (1873-1956), physician. 13.60 l, Eugen Cioclea (1948-2013), poet.

Perf. 13 Syncopated
2023, July 28 Litho.
1183-1188 A464 Set of 6 5.75 5.75

Protected Reptiles and Batrachians From Red Book of Moldova A465

Designs: 3.30 l, Hyla arborea. 3.40 l, Podarcis tauricus. 10.30 l, Triturus cristatus. 13.60 l, Coluber caspius.

2023, Aug. 11 Litho. Perf. 14x14½
1189-1192 A465 Set of 4 4.50 4.50

Romanian Folklore A466

Designs: 3.30 l, "Pacala and Tandala," fairy tale. 7 l, "Toma Alimos," ballad. 13.60 l, "The Sun and the Moon," ballad.

2023, Aug. 25 Litho. Perf. 14x14½
1193-1195 A466 Set of 3 3.50 3.50

Composers A467

Designs: 3.30 l, Aram Khachaturian, (1903-78). 10 l, György Ligeti, (1923-2006).

2023, Sept. 22 Litho. Perf. 14x14½
1196-1197 A467 Set of 2 1.90 1.90

Items from the National History Museum of Moldova — A469

No. 1199: 3.30 l, Needham harmonium. No. 1200: 3.30 l, Monarch Junior phonograph.

2023, Oct. 20 Litho. Perf. 14½x14
1199-1200 A469 Set of 2 1.00 1.00

Famous Men — A471

Designs: 3.30 l, Ion Druta, (1928-2023), writer. 3.40 l, Pres. Mircea Snegur (1940-2023).

2023, Nov. 15 Litho. Perf. 14x14½
1202-1203 A471 Set of 2 1.00 1.00

Introduction of Moldovan Leu, 30th Anniv. — A472

2023, Nov. 29 Litho. Perf. 14x14½
1204 A472 10.30 l multi 1.50 1.50

A473 / Children's Art — A474

2023, Dec. 8 Litho. Perf. 14x14½
1205 A473 3.30 l multi .50 .50
1206 A474 3.30 l multi .50 .50

Traditional Food — A475

Designs: 3.30 l, Bread, stuffed peppers, cabbage, and grape leaves; red panel. 10.30 l, Meats; green panel.

2023, Dec. 19 Litho. Perf. 14x14½
1207-1208 A475 Set of 2 2.00 2.00

SEMI-POSTAL STAMPS

Flood Relief — SP1

2010, Sept. 11 Litho. Perf. 14x14½
B1 SP1 1.20 l + 50b multi .35 .35

Serghei Lunchevici National Philharmonic Before and After Fire — SP2

2020, Nov. 18 Litho. Perf. 14x14½
B2 SP2 5.75 l +3 l multi 1.30 1.30

Surtax for reconstruction of the fire-damaged building.

AIR POST STAMPS

TU-144 — AP1

1992-93 Litho. Perf. 12
C1 AP1 1.75r maroon .30 .30
C2 AP1 2.50r red vio .35 .35
C3 AP1 7.75r blue 1.15 1.15
C4 AP1 8.50r blue green 1.40 1.40
C5 AP1 25r red brown .35 .35
C6 AP1 45r brown .55 .55
C7 AP1 50r olive green .65 .65
C8 AP1 90r blue 1.40 1.40
Nos. C1-C8 (8) 6.15 6.15

Issued: #C1-C4, 7/20/92; #C5-C8, 7/24/93.

POSTAGE DUE STAMPS

Dove, Envelope — D1

1994, Nov. 12 Litho. Perf. 14
J1 D1 30b lt olive & brown .65 .65
J2 D1 40b pale vio & slate .75 .75

In use, Nos. J1-J2 were torn apart, one half being affixed to the postage due item and the other half being pasted into the postman's record book. Values are for unused and canceled-to-order pairs.

MONACO

'mä-nə-ˌkō

LOCATION — Southern coast of France, bordering on the Mediterranean Sea
GOVT. — Principality
AREA — 481 acres
POP. — 39,000 (2020 est.)
CAPITAL — Monaco

100 Centimes = 1 Franc
100 Cents = 1 Euro (2002)

Catalogue values for unused stamps in this country are for Never Hinged items, beginning with Scott 182 in the regular postage section, Scott B51 in the semi-postal section, Scott C2 in the airpost section, Scott CB1 in the airpost semi-postal section, and Scott J28 in the postage due section.

Values for unused stamps are for examples with original gum as defined in the catalogue introduction. Very fine examples of Nos. 1-181, B1-B50, C1 and J1-J27 will have perforations clear of the design and/or frameline. Very well centered are worth more than the values quoted.

Prince Charles III — A1

1885 Unwmk. Typo. Perf. 14x13½

1	A1	1c olive green	25.00	17.50
2	A1	2c dull lilac	57.50	27.50
3	A1	5c blue	70.00	35.00
4	A1	10c brown, *straw*	85.00	40.00
5	A1	15c rose	350.00	18.00
6	A1	25c green	700.00	75.00
7	A1	40c slate, *rose*	85.00	45.00
8	A1	75c black, *rose*	275.00	125.00
9	A1	1fr black, *yellow*	1,750.	500.00
10	A1	5fr rose, *green*	3,000.	2,000.

Prince Albert I — A2

1891-1921

11	A2	1c olive green	.70	.70
12	A2	2c dull violet	.80	.80
13	A2	5c blue	50.00	6.00
14	A2	5c yel grn ('01)	.50	.35
15	A2	10c brown, *straw*	100.00	16.00
16	A2	10c carmine ('01)	4.00	.70
17	A2	15c rose	175.00	8.00
a.	Double impression		1,400.	
18	A2	15c vio brn, *straw* ('01)	3.00	1.00
19	A2	15c gray grn ('21)	2.00	2.50
20	A2	25c green	275.00	32.50
21	A2	25c dp blue ('01)	15.00	5.00
22	A2	40c slate, *rose* ('94)	4.00	2.40
23	A2	50c vio brn (shades), *org*	7.00	4.75
24	A2	75c vio brn, *buff* ('94)	27.50	18.00
25	A2	75c ol brn, *buff* ('21)	20.00	24.00
26	A2	1fr black, *yellow*	19.00	11.00
27	A2	5fr rose, *grn*	100.00	87.50
c.	Double impression		1,500.	
28	A2	5fr dull vio ('21)	200.00	250.00
29	A2	5fr dk grn ('21)	22.50	27.50
	Nos. 11-29 (19)		1,026.	498.70

The handstamp "OL" in a circle of dots is a cancellation, not an overprint.
For shades, see the *Scott Classic Specialized Catalogue of Stamps and Covers.*
See No. 1782. For overprints and surcharges see Nos. 30-35, 57-59, B1.

Stamps of 1901-21 Overprinted or Surcharged

1921, Mar. 5

30	A2	5c lt green	.70	.70
31	A2	75c brown, *buff*	5.25	6.25
32	A2	2fr on 5fr dull vio	32.50	52.50
	Nos. 30-32 (3)		38.45	59.45

Issued to commemorate the birth of Princess Antoinette, daughter of Princess Charlotte and Prince Pierre, Comte de Polignac.

Stamps and Type of 1891-1921 Surcharged

1922

33	A2	20c on 15c gray green	1.10	1.40
34	A2	25c on 10c rose	.70	.90
35	A2	50c on 1fr black, *yel*	6.00	6.50
	Nos. 33-35 (3)		7.80	8.80

Prince Albert I — A5

Oceanographic Museum — A6

"The Rock" of Monaco — A7

Royal Palace — A8

1922-24 Engr. Perf. 11

40	A5	25c deep brown	4.00	4.75
41	A6	30c dark green	.90	.90
42	A6	30c scarlet ('23)	.50	.45
43	A6	50c ultra	4.25	4.25
44	A7	60c black brown	.35	.35
45	A7	1fr black, *yellow*	.25	.25
46	A7	2fr scarlet ver	.50	.45
47	A8	5fr red brown	32.50	37.50
48	A8	5fr green, *bluish*	10.50	10.50
49	A8	10fr carmine	14.00	18.00
	Nos. 40-49 (10)		67.75	77.40

Nos. 40-49 exist imperf.
For shades, see the *Scott Classic Specialized Catalogue of Stamps and Covers.*

Prince Louis II
A9   A10

St. Dévote Viaduct ("Bridge of Suicides") — A11

1923-24 Engr.

50	A9	10c deep green	.35	.55
51	A9	15c car rose ('24)	.45	.70
52	A9	20c red brown	.35	.55
53	A9	25c violet	.25	.45
a.	Without engraver's name		27.50	27.50
54	A11	40c orange brn ('24)	.65	.55
55	A10	50c ultra	.35	.45
	Nos. 50-55 (6)		2.40	3.25

The 25c comes in 2 types, one with larger "5" and "c" touching frame of numeral tablet.
Stamps of the 1922-24 issues sometimes show parts of the letters of a papermaker's watermark.
The engraved stamps of type A11 measure 31x21½mm. The typographed stamps of that design measure 36x21½mm.

Stamps and Type of 1891-1921 Surcharged

1924, Aug. 5 Perf. 14x13½

57	A2	45c on 50c brn ol, *buff*	.60	.70
a.	Double surcharge		775.00	775.00
58	A2	75c on 1fr blk, *yel*	.60	.70
a.	Double surcharge		550.00	550.00
59	A2	85c on 5fr dk green	.60	.70
a.	Double surcharge		650.00	650.00
	Nos. 57-59 (3)		1.80	2.10
Set, never hinged			2.25	

Grimaldi Family Coat of Arms A12

Prince Louis II A13

Louis II — A14

View of Monaco — A15

1924-33 Typo.

60	A12	1c gray black	.25	.25
61	A12	2c red brown	.25	.25
62	A12	3c brt violet ('33)	2.75	1.90
63	A12	5c orange ('26)	.35	.30
64	A12	10c blue	.25	.25
65	A13	15c apple green	.25	.25
66	A13	15c dull vio ('29)	2.75	1.90
67	A13	20c violet	.25	.25
68	A13	20c rose	.35	.25
69	A13	25c rose	.25	.25
70	A13	25c red, *yel*	.25	.25
71	A13	30c orange	.25	.25
72	A13	40c black brown	.25	.25
73	A13	40c lt bl, *bluish*	.35	.35
74	A13	45c gray blk ('26)	.90	.70
75	A14	50c myrtle grn ('25)	.25	.25
76	A13	50c brown, *org*	.25	.25
77	A14	60c yel brn ('25)	.25	.25
78	A13	60c ol grn, *grnsh*	.25	.25
79	A13	75c ol grn, *grnsh* ('26)	.70	.35
80	A13	75c car, *straw* ('26)	.35	.25
81	A13	75c slate	.90	.55
82	A13	80c red, *yel* ('26)	.40	.30
83	A13	90c rose, *straw* ('27)	2.00	1.60
84	A13	1.25fr bl, *bluish* ('26)	.25	.25
85	A13	1.50fr bl, *bluish* ('27)	3.75	1.90

Size: 36x21½mm

86	A11	1fr blk, *orange*	.25	.25
87	A11	1.05fr red violet ('26)	.25	.25
88	A11	1.10fr blue grn ('27)	8.00	6.00
89	A15	2fr vio & ol brn ('25)	2.75	1.00
90	A15	3fr rose & ultra, *yel* ('27)	22.50	11.00
91	A15	5fr grn & rose ('25)	8.50	6.00
92	A15	10fr yel brn & bl ('25)	25.00	17.50
	Nos. 60-92 (33)		86.30	55.85
Set, never hinged			175.00	

Nos. 60 to 74 and 76 exist imperforate.
For surcharges see Nos. 93-94, 97-99, C1.

Type of 1924-33 Surcharged in Black

1926-31

93	A13	30c on 25c rose	.30	.25
94	A13	50c on 60c ol grn, *grnsh* ('28)	1.50	.35
95	A11	50c on 1.05fr red vio ('28)	1.10	.70
a.	Double surcharge		65.00	
96	A11	50c on 1.10fr bl grn ('31)	14.00	8.75
97	A13	50c on 1.25fr bl, *bluish* (R) ('28)	1.60	.65
98	A13	1.25fr on 1fr bl, *bluish*	.80	.50

See #86-88. For surcharges see #95-96.

99	A15	1.50fr on 2fr vio & ol brn ('28)	7.00	5.25
	Nos. 93-99 (7)		26.30	16.45
Set, never hinged			40.00	

Princes Charles III, Louis II and Albert I — A17

1928, Feb. 18 Engr. Perf. 11

100	A17	50c dull carmine	2.50	4.75
101	A17	1.50fr dark blue	2.50	4.75
102	A17	3fr dark violet	2.50	4.75
	Nos. 100-102 (3)		7.50	14.25
Set, never hinged			18.00	

Nos. 100-102 were sold exclusively at the Intl. Phil. Exhib. at Monte Carlo, Feb., 1928. One set was sold to each purchaser of a ticket of admission to the exhibition which cost 5fr. Exist imperf. Value, set $27.50.

Old Watchtower A20

Royal Palace A21

Church of St. Dévote A22

Prince Louis II — A23

"The Rock" of Monaco — A24

Gardens of Monaco — A25

Fortifications and Harbor — A26

1932-37 Perf. 13, 14x13½

110	A20	15c lilac rose	.80	.25
111	A20	20c orange brn	.80	.25
112	A21	25c olive blk	1.10	.35
113	A22	30c yellow grn	1.40	.35
114	A23	40c dark brown	3.25	1.40
115	A24	45c brown red	3.50	1.10
a.	45c red		425.00	425.00
116	A23	50c purple	3.25	.85
117	A25	65c blue green	3.50	1.10
118	A26	75c deep blue	4.00	1.75
119	A23	90c red	9.50	3.25
120	A22	1fr red brn ('33)	27.50	7.75
121	A26	1.25fr rose lilac	6.75	4.50
122	A23	1.50fr ultra	40.00	10.50
123	A21	1.75fr rose lilac	35.00	9.50
124	A21	1.75fr car rose ('37)	24.00	13.00
125	A24	2fr dark blue	13.50	4.75
126	A20	3fr purple	20.00	9.00
127	A21	3.50fr orange ('35)	47.50	32.50
128	A22	5fr violet	27.50	20.00
129	A21	10fr deep blue	125.00	70.00
130	A25	20fr black	175.00	140.00
	Nos. 110-130 (21)		572.85	332.15
Set, never hinged			1,150.	

Postage Due Stamps of 1925-32 Surcharged or Overprinted in Black

MONACO

1937-38 — Perf. 14x13
No.	Type	Description	Unused	Used
131	D3	5c on 10c violet	1.00	1.00
132	D3	10c violet	1.00	1.00
133	D3	15c on 30c bister	1.00	1.00
134	D3	20c on 30c bister	1.00	1.00
135	D3	25c on 60c red	1.50	1.50
136	D3	30c bister	2.40	2.40
137	D3	40c on 60c red	2.40	2.40
138	D3	50c on 60c red	2.40	2.40
139	D3	65c on 1fr lt bl	2.25	2.00
140	D3	85c on 1fr lt bl	5.00	4.50
141	D3	1fr light blue	7.75	7.75
142	D3	2.15fr on 2fr dl red	7.75	7.75
143	D3	2.25fr on 2fr dl red ('38)	19.00	19.00
144	D3	2.50fr on 2fr dl red ('38)	29.00	29.00
		Nos. 131-144 (14)	83.45	82.70
		Set, never hinged	175.00	

Grimaldi Arms — A27

Prince Louis II — A28

1937-43 — Engr.
No.	Type	Description	Unused	Used
145	A27	1c dk vio brn ('38)	.25	.25
146	A27	2c emerald	.25	.25
147	A27	3c brt red violet	.25	.25
148	A27	5c red	.25	.25
149	A27	10c ultra	.25	.25
149A	A27	10c black ('43)	.25	.25
150	A27	15c violet ('39)	1.75	1.50
150A	A27	30c dull grn ('43)	.25	.25
150B	A27	40c rose car ('43)	.25	.25
150C	A27	50c brt vio ('43)	.25	.25
151	A28	55c red brn ('38)	5.75	2.25
151A	A27	60c Prus blue ('43)	.25	.25
152	A28	65c violet ('38)	30.00	13.00
153	A28	70c red brn ('39)	.35	.35
153A	A27	70c red brn ('43)	.25	.25
154	A28	90c violet ('39)	.35	.30
155	A28	1fr rose red ('38)	18.50	10.50
156	A28	1.25fr rose red ('39)	.35	.35
157	A28	1.75fr ultra ('38)	18.50	10.50
158	A28	2.25fr ultra ('39)	.35	.25
		Nos. 145-158 (20)	78.65	41.75
		Set, never hinged	150.00	

Nos. 151, 152, 155, 157 exist imperf.

Souvenir Sheet
Prince Louis II — A29

1938, Jan. 17 — Unwmk. — Imperf.
| 159 | A29 | 10fr magenta | 65.00 | 65.00 |
| | | Never hinged | 175.00 | |

"Fête Nationale" 1/17/38. Size: 99x120mm.

Cathedral of Monaco A30

St. Nicholas Square A31

Palace Gate A32

Palace of Monaco A34

Panorama of Monaco — A33

Harbor of Monte Carlo — A35

1939-46 — Perf. 13
No.	Type	Description	Unused	Used
160	A30	20c rose lilac	.25	.25
161	A31	25c gldn brown	.45	.30
162	A32	30c dk blue grn	.35	.30
162A	A32	30c brn red ('40)	.35	.25
163	A31	40c henna brn	.70	.50
164	A33	45c brt red vio	.50	.50
165	A32	50c dk blue grn	.40	.35
166	A32	60c rose carmine	.40	.35
166A	A32	60c dk grn ('40)	.90	.70
166B	A35	70c brt red vio ('41)	.40	.25
167	A35	75c dark green	.40	.25
167A	A30	80c dull grn ('43)	.25	.25
168	A33	1fr brown black	.40	.25
168A	A34	1fr claret ('43)	.25	.25
168B	A35	1.20fr ultra ('43)	.25	.35
168C	A34	1.30fr brn blk ('41)	.40	.35
168D	A31	1.50fr ultra ('46)	.40	.40
169	A31	2fr rose violet	.40	.30
169A	A35	2fr lt ultra ('43)	.25	.25
169B	A34	2fr green ('46)	.35	.25
170	A33	2.50fr red	27.50	17.50
171	A33	2.50fr dp green ('40)	1.75	1.75
172	A35	3fr brown red	.45	.25
172A	A31	3fr black ('43)	.25	.25
172B	A30	4fr rose lil ('46)	1.25	.55
172C	A34	4.50fr brt vio ('43)	.25	.25
173	A30	5fr Prus blue	5.25	4.00
173A	A35	5fr dp grn ('43)	.25	.25
173B	A34	6fr lt violet ('46)	.70	.55
174	A33	10fr green	1.40	1.60
174A	A30	10fr dp blue ('43)	.25	.25
174B	A35	15fr rose pink ('43)	.40	.25
175	A32	20fr brt ultra	1.60	1.25
175A	A33	20fr sepia ('43)	.40	.25
175B	A35	25fr blue grn ('46)	1.40	1.25
		Nos. 160-175B (35)	51.10	36.85
		Set, never hinged	100.00	

See Nos. 214-221, 228-232, 274-275, 319-320, 407-408, 423, 426, 428-429, B36-B50.

Louis II Stadium — A36

1939, Apr. 23 — Engr.
| 176 | A36 | 10fr dark green | 100.00 | 110.00 |
| | | Never hinged | 175.00 | |

Inauguration of Louis II Stadium.

Louis II Stadium — A37

1939, Aug. 15
177	A37	40c dull green	1.25	1.25
178	A37	70c brown black	1.60	1.60
179	A37	90c dark violet	2.25	2.25
180	A37	1.25fr copper red	3.00	3.00
181	A37	2.25fr dark blue	4.25	4.25
		Nos. 177-181 (5)	12.35	12.35
		Set, never hinged	22.50	

8th International University Games.

Imperforates
Many Monaco stamps from 1940 to 1999 exist imperforate. Officially 20 sheets, ranging from 25 to 100 subjects, were left imperforate.

Catalogue values for unused stamps in this section, from this point to the end of the section, are for Never Hinged items.

Prince Louis II — A38

1941-46 — Perf. 14x13
182	A38	40c brown carmine	.65	.50
183	A38	80c deep green	.65	.50
184	A38	1fr rose violet	.25	.25
185	A38	1.20fr green ('42)	.25	.25
186	A38	1.50fr rose	.25	.25
187	A38	1.50fr violet ('42)	.25	.25
187A	A38	2fr lt green ('46)	.65	.35
188	A38	2.40fr red ('42)	.25	.25
189	A38	2.50fr deep ultra	1.10	1.25
190	A38	4fr blue ('42)	.25	.25
		Nos. 182-190 (10)	4.55	4.10

Prince Louis II — A39

1943 — Perf. 13
| 191 | A39 | 50fr violet | 2.00 | 1.10 |

A40

Prince Louis II — A41

1946 — Unwmk. — Engr. — Perf. 14x13
192	A40	2.50fr dk blue green	.70	.25
193	A40	3fr brt red violet	.70	.25
194	A40	6fr brt red	.70	.35
195	A40	10fr brt ultra	.70	.35

Perf. 13
196	A41	50fr dp Prus green	4.00	2.10
197	A41	100fr red	5.25	2.75
		Nos. 192-197 (6)	12.05	6.05

Nos. 196-197 exist imperforate.
See Nos. 222-227, 233-236. For overprints see Nos. C8-C9.

Franklin D. Roosevelt A42

Harbor of Monte Carlo — A43

Palace of Monaco A44

Map of Monaco A45

Prince Louis II — A46

1946, Dec. 13 — Unwmk. — Perf. 13
198	A42	10c red violet	.50	.45
199	A43	30c deep blue	.50	.45
200	A44	60c blue black	.50	.45
201	A45	1fr sepia	1.50	1.25
202	A45	3fr lt violet	2.25	1.75
		Nos. 198-202,B93,C14-C15,CB6 (9)	10.35	8.65

Issued in tribute to the memory of Franklin D. Roosevelt.

1947, May 15
| 203 | A46 | 10fr dark blue green | 3.50 | 3.50 |

25th anniv. of the reign of Prince Louis II.
See Nos. B94, C20a.

Hurdler A47

Runner A48

Designs: 2fr, Discus thrower. 2.50fr, Basketball. 4fr, Swimmer.

1948, July 1 — Perf. 13
204	A47	50c blue green	.25	.25
205	A48	1fr rose brown	.25	.25
206	A48	2fr grnsh blue	1.00	.75
207	A48	2.50fr vermilion	2.75	2.00
208	A48	4fr slate gray	3.25	3.00
		Nos. 204-208,CB7-CB10 (9)	72.00	70.75

Issued to publicize Monaco's participation in the 1948 Olympic Games held at Wembley, England, during July and August.

MONACO PRICE LIST AVAILABLE

Monaco 1885-2010
Sets, Singles, S/S, B-O-B
Year Sets Starting 1958

556var Soccer stadium w/o Surcharge
$475.00

Also available: Covers and Specialized including Imperfs & Trial Color Proofs

Large stock of Monaco Artist Die Proofs Available on our 26-page Worldwide Artist Die Proofs price list!

For Buying or Selling Monaco
1-800-94-STAMP
(1-800-947-8267)

Henry Gitner Philatelists, Inc. HGPI
P.O. Box 3077-S, Middletown, NY 10940
Tel: 845-343-5151 Fax: 845-343-0068
Toll Free: 1-800-947-8267
E-mail: hgitner@hgitner.com
PHILATELY - THE QUIET EXCITEMENT!

MONACO

Nymph Salmacis — A49
Hercules — A50
Aristaeus — A51
Hyacinthus — A52
François J. Bosio and Louis XIV Statue — A53

1948, July 12

209	A49	50c dark green		.55	.35
210	A50	1fr red		.55	.35
211	A51	2fr deep ultra		1.90	.75
212	A52	2.50fr deep violet		4.75	2.25
213	A53	4fr purple		4.75	2.50
		Nos. 209-213,CB11-CB14 (9)		94.50	88.20

Issued to honor François J. Bosio (1768-1845), sculptor. No. 213 inscribed "J F Bosio."

Scenic Types of 1939

1948 — Engr.

214	A30	50c sepia	.35	.25
215	A31	60c rose pink	.35	.25
216	A32	3fr violet rose	1.10	.35
217	A31	4fr emerald	1.10	.35
218	A34	8fr red brown	4.25	2.00
219	A34	10fr brown red	6.00	2.00
220	A33	20fr carmine rose	1.50	.65
221	A35	25fr gray black	35.00	17.50
		Nos. 214-221 (8)	49.65	23.35

Louis II Type of 1946

1948, July — Perf. 14x13

222	A40	30c black	.30	.25
223	A40	5fr orange brown	.45	.30
224	A40	6fr purple	5.00	1.75
225	A40	10fr orange	.45	.30
226	A40	12fr deep carmine	6.00	2.50
227	A40	18fr dark blue	9.50	6.00
		Nos. 222-227 (6)	21.70	11.10

Scenic Types of 1939

1949 — Perf. 13

228	A33	5fr blue green	.85	.35
229	A35	10fr orange	1.75	.65
230	A32	25fr blue	52.50	16.00
231	A30	40fr brown red	9.25	4.75
232	A30	50fr purple	5.75	1.00
		Nos. 228-232 (5)	70.10	22.75

Louis II Type of 1946

1949, Mar. 10 — Perf. 14x13

233	A40	50c olive	.35	.25
234	A40	1fr dk violet bl	.25	.25
235	A40	12fr dk slate grn	10.00	7.00
236	A40	15fr brown carmine	10.00	3.75
		Nos. 233-236 (4)	20.60	11.25

Hirondelle I — A54
Cactus Plants — A55

Designs: 4fr, Oceanographic Museum. 5fr, Princess Alice II at Spitzbergen. 6fr, Albert I Monument. 10fr, Hirondelle II. 12fr, Albert I whaling. 18fr, Bison.

1949, Mar. 5 — Perf. 13

237	A54	2fr brt blue	.25	.25
238	A55	3fr dark green	.25	.25
239	A54	4fr blk brn & bl	.25	.25
240	A54	5fr crimson	1.00	1.00
241	A55	6fr dark violet	.90	.90
242	A54	10fr black brown	1.10	1.10
243	A54	12fr brt red violet	2.50	2.50
244	A54	18fr dk brn & org brn	3.50	3.50
		Nos. 237-244 (8)	9.75	9.75

See Nos. C21-C26.

Palace, Globe and Pigeon — A56

1949-50 — Engr. — Unwmk.

245	A56	5fr blue green	.60	.60
245A	A56	10fr orange	7.00	7.00
246	A56	15fr carmine	.60	.60
		Nos. 245-246,C30-C33 (7)	16.70	16.70

75th anniversary of the UPU.
Nos. 245, 245A and 246 exist imperf.
Issued: 5fr, 15fr, 12/27; 10fr, 9/12/50.

Prince Rainier III — A57

1950, Apr. 11

247	A57	10c red & blk brn	.25	.25
248	A57	50c dp yel & dk brn	.25	.25
249	A57	1fr purple	.45	.35
250	A57	5fr dark green	3.50	1.90
251	A57	15fr carmine	5.25	5.25
252	A57	25fr ultra, ol grn & ind	5.25	5.25
		Nos. 247-252,C34-C35 (8)	27.45	25.75

Enthronement of Prince Rainier III.

Prince Rainier III — A58

1950, Apr. — Engr. — Perf. 14x13

253	A58	50c purple	.35	.25
254	A58	1fr orange brown	.35	.30
255	A58	8fr blue green	9.00	2.40
256	A58	12fr blue	2.25	.50
257	A58	15fr crimson	4.25	.70
		Nos. 253-257 (5)	16.20	4.15

1951, Apr. 31 — Typo.

258	A58	5fr emerald	12.00	4.75
259	A58	10fr orange	20.00	7.75

See Nos. 276-279.

Statue of Prince Albert I — A59

1951, Apr. 11 — Engr. — Perf. 13

260	A59	15fr deep blue	11.00	6.50

Edmond and Jules de Goncourt — A60

1951, Apr. 11

261	A60	15fr violet brown	8.00	5.00

50th anniversary of the foundation of Goncourt Academy.

St. Vincent de Paul — A61
Judgment of St. Dévote — A62
Symbolizing Monaco's Adoption of Catholicism — A63
Mosaic of the Immaculate Conception — A64
Blessed Rainier of Westphalia — A65

Holy Year, 1951: 50c, Pope Pius XII. 12fr, Prince Rainier III at Prayer. 15fr, St. Nicholas de Patare. 20fr, St. Roman. 25fr, St. Charles Borromée. 40fr, Cross, arms and Roman Coliseum. 50fr, Chapel of St. Dévote.

Inscribed: "Anno Santo"

1951, June 4 — Unwmk. — Perf. 13

262	A61	10c ultra, dk blue & red	.25	.25
263	A61	50c dk rose lake & pur	.25	.25
264	A62	1fr brown & dk grn	.30	.30
265	A63	2fr vio brn & ver	.35	.35
266	A64	5fr blue green	.45	.45
267	A63	12fr rose violet	.70	.70
268	A63	15fr vermilion	4.00	4.00
269	A63	20fr red brown	6.00	6.00
270	A63	25fr ultra	8.00	8.00
271	A63	40fr dk car rose & pur	9.50	9.50
272	A63	50fr ol grn & dk vio brn	12.50	12.50
273	A65	100fr dk violet brn	25.00	25.00
		Nos. 262-273 (12)	67.30	67.30

Scenic Types of 1939-46

1951, Dec. 22 — Perf. 13

274	A31	3fr deep turq green	2.75	.90
275	A32	30fr slate black	8.50	3.50

Rainier Type of 1950

1951, Dec. 22 — Perf. 14x13

276	A58	6fr blue green	1.75	.75
277	A58	8fr orange	1.75	.75
278	A58	15fr indigo	2.50	.45
279	A58	18fr crimson	6.25	1.50
		Nos. 276-279 (4)	12.25	3.45

Radio Monte Carlo — A66

1951, Dec. 22 — Perf. 13

280	A66	1fr blue, car & org	1.00	.35
281	A66	15fr pur, car & rose vio	4.00	1.25
282	A66	30fr indigo & red brn	17.50	6.50
		Nos. 280-282 (3)	22.50	8.10

Knight in Armor — A67

1951, Dec. 22

283	A67	1fr purple	1.10	.50
284	A67	5fr gray black	3.50	2.00
285	A67	8fr deep carmine	7.00	3.50
286	A67	15fr emerald	11.50	6.50
287	A67	30fr slate black	19.00	13.50
		Nos. 283-287 (5)	42.10	26.00

See Nos. 328-332, 2025-2026.

Nos. B96-B99a Surcharged with New Values and Bars in Black

1951, Dec. — Perf. 13½x13, Imperf.

288	SP51	1fr on 10fr + 5fr	12.50	12.50
289	SP52	3fr on 15fr + 5fr	12.50	12.50
290	SP52	3fr on 25fr + 5fr	13.00	12.50
291	SP51	6fr on 40fr + 5fr	13.00	12.50
b.		Block of 4, #288-291	51.00	50.00

Gallery of Hercules, Royal Palace — A68

1952, Apr. 26 — Engr. — Perf. 13

292	A68	5fr red brn & brn	2.00	.55
293	A68	15fr purple & lil rose	2.50	.60
294	A68	30fr indigo & ultra	2.90	.75
		Nos. 292-294 (3)	7.40	1.90

Opening of a philatelic museum at the royal palace, Apr. 26, 1952.

Basketball — A69

2fr, Soccer. 3fr, Sailing. 5fr, Cyclist. 8fr, Gymnastics. 15fr, Louis II Stadium.

1953, Feb. 23 — Unwmk. — Perf. 11

295	A69	1fr dk purple & mag	.25	.25
296	A69	2fr dk grn & sl bl	.25	.25
297	A69	3fr blue & lt blue	.25	.25
298	A69	5fr dk brn & grnsh blk	.80	.25
299	A69	8fr brown lake & red	2.00	1.00
300	A69	15fr bl, brn blk & dk grn		
		Nos. 295-300,C36-C39 (10)	70.55	37.90

Issued to publicize Monaco's participation in the Helsinki Olympic Games.

Books, Pens and Proof Pages — A70

1953, June 29 — Perf. 13

301	A70	5fr dark green	.55	.45
302	A70	15fr red brown	3.75	.70

Publication of a first edition of the unexpurgated diary of Edmond and Jules Goncourt.

Physalia and Laboratory Ship Hirondelle II — A71

1953, June 29

303	A71	2fr Prus grn, pur & choc	.25	.25
304	A71	5fr dp mag, red & Prus grn	.80	.30
305	A71	15fr ultra, vio brn & Prus grn	2.90	1.60
		Nos. 303-305 (3)	3.95	2.15

50th anniversary of the discovery of anaphylaxis by Charles Richet and Paul Portier.

MONACO

Frederic Ozanam — A72
Nun — A73

1954, Apr. 12		Engr.	Perf. 13	
306	A72	1fr bright red	.25	.25
307	A73	5fr dark blue	.50	.50
308	A72	15fr black	2.10	1.90
		Nos. 306-308 (3)	2.85	2.65

Centenary of the death of Frederic Ozanam, founder of the Society of Saint Vincent de Paul.

Jean Baptiste de la Salle — A74, A75

1954, Apr. 12				
309	A74	1fr dark carmine	.25	.25
310	A75	5fr black brown	.50	.50
311	A74	15fr bright ultra	2.10	1.90
		Nos. 309-311 (3)	2.85	2.65

Jean Baptiste de la Salle, founder of the Christian Brothers Institute and saint.

A76, A77

Grimaldi Arms — A78

Various Forms of Grimaldi Arms in Black and Red or Black, Red and Deep Plum (5fr)

Perf. 13½x14, 14x13½

1954, Apr. 12			Typo.	
312	A76	50c black & mag	.25	.25
313	A77	70c black & aqua	.25	.25
314	A76	80c black, red & dk grn	.25	.25
315	A77	1fr violet blue	.25	.25
316	A77	2fr black & dp org	.25	.25
317	A77	3fr black & green	.25	.25
318	A78	5fr black & lt grn	.25	.25
		Nos. 312-318 (7)	1.75	1.75

Scenic Typo of 1939-46

1954, Apr. 12		Engr.	Perf. 13	
319	A34	25fr bright red	3.25	.50
320	A31	75fr dark green	23.00	7.50

Knight in Armor — A79

1954, Apr. 12		Unwmk.	Perf. 13	
321	A79	4fr dark red	1.50	.40
322	A79	8fr dark green	1.50	.80
323	A79	12fr dark purple	6.00	1.75
324	A79	24fr dark maroon	11.00	4.75
		Nos. 321-324 (4)	20.00	7.70

Nos. 321-324 were issued precanceled only. Values for precanceled stamps in first column are for those which have not been through the post and have original gum. Values in the second column are for postally used, gumless stamps.

See Nos. 400-404, 430-433, 466-469.

Lambarene Landing, Gabon — A80
Dr. Albert Schweitzer — A81

Design: 15fr, Lambarene hospital.

1955, Jan. 14			Perf. 11x11½	
325	A80	2fr ol grn, bl grn & ind	.30	.25
326	A81	5fr dk grnsh bl & grn	1.25	.90
327	A81	15fr dk bl grn, dp cl & brn blk	3.50	2.50
		Nos. 325-327 (3)	5.05	3.65

Issued to honor Dr. Albert Schweitzer, medical missionary. See No. C40.

Knight Type of 1951

1955, Jan. 14			Perf. 13	
328	A67	5fr purple	3.25	.75
329	A67	6fr red	5.00	1.50
330	A67	8fr red brown	6.00	3.00
331	A67	15fr ultra	13.00	4.50
332	A67	30fr dark green	22.50	14.00
		Nos. 328-332 (5)	49.75	23.75

Automobile and Representation of Eight European Cities — A82

1955, Jan. 14			Unwmk.	
333	A82	100fr dk brown & red	75.00	50.00

25th Monte Carlo Automobile Rally.

Prince Rainier III — A83

1955, June 7		Engr.	Perf. 13	
334	A83	6fr green & vio brn	.70	.40
335	A83	8fr red & violet	.70	.40
336	A83	12fr carmine & green	.70	.40
337	A83	15fr purple & blue	1.40	.40
338	A83	18fr orange & blue	4.50	.40
339	A83	30fr ultra & gray	14.00	7.75
		Nos. 334-339 (6)	22.00	9.75

See Nos. 405-406, 424-425, 427, 462-465, 586, 603-604A, 725-728, 730, 789, 791.

"Five Weeks in a Balloon" — A84
"A Floating City" and Jules Verne — A85
"Michael Strogoff" — A86
"Around the World in 80 Days" — A87
USS Nautilus and Verne — A88

Designs (Scenes from Jules Verne's Books): 3fr, The House of Vapors. 6fr, The 500 Millions of the Begum. 8fr, The Magnificent Orinoco. 10fr, A Journey to the Center of the Earth. 25fr, Twenty Thousand Leagues under the Sea.

1955, June 7				
340	A84	1fr red brn & bl gray	.25	.25
341	A85	2fr blue, ind & brn	.25	.25
342	A85	3fr red brn, gray & sl	.25	.25
343	A86	5fr car & blk brn	.25	.25
344	A84	6fr blk brn & bluish gray	.45	.45
345	A86	8fr ol grn & aqua	.35	.35
346	A85	10fr indigo, turq & brn	1.25	1.00
347	A87	15fr rose brn & ver	1.00	.70
348	A85	25fr bl grn, grn & gray	2.50	1.75
349	A88	30fr violet, turq & blk	6.25	5.25
		Nos. 340-349,C45 (11)	37.80	35.50

50th anniv. of the death of Jules Verne.

Virgin by Francois Brea — A89
Blessed Rainier — A90

Marian Year: 10fr, Pieta by Louis Brea.

1955, June 7				
350	A89	5fr vio brn, gray & dk grn	.25	.25
351	A89	10fr vio brn, gray & dk grn	.40	.35
352	A90	15fr black brn & org brn	.60	.55
		Nos. 350-352 (3)	1.25	1.15

Rotary Emblem, World Map — A91

1955, June 7				
353	A91	30fr blue & orange	1.00	1.00

50th anniv. of the founding of Rotary Intl.

George Washington — A92
Franklin D. Roosevelt — A93
Dwight D. Eisenhower — A94
Palace of Monaco, c. 1790 — A95
Palace of Monaco, c. 1750 — A96

Designs: 3fr, Abraham Lincoln. 30fr, Columbus landing in America. 40fr, Prince Rainier III. 100fr, Early Louisiana scene.

1956, Apr. 3		Engr.	Perf. 13	
354	A92	1fr dark purple	.25	.25
355	A93	2fr claret & dk pur	.25	.25
356	A93	3fr vio & dp ultra	.25	.25
357	A94	5fr brown lake	.25	.25
358	A95	15fr brn blk & vio brn	.25	.25
359	A95	30fr ind, blk & ultra	3.75	2.00
360	A94	40fr dk brn & vio brn	5.00	2.50
361	A96	50fr vermilion	5.00	2.50
362	A96	100fr Prus green	5.00	3.50
a.		Strip of 3, #360-362	19.00	19.00
		Nos. 354-362 (9)	20.00	11.75

5th Intl. Phil. Exhib. (FIPEX), NYC, Apr. 28-May 6, 1956.

Ski Jump, Cortina d'Ampezzo — A97

Design: 30fr, Olympic Scenes.

1956, Apr. 3				
363	A97	15fr brn vio, brn & dk grn	1.10	.55
364	A97	30fr red orange	2.25	1.60

Issued to publicize Monaco's participation in the 1956 Olympic Games.

MONACO

"Glasgow to Monte Carlo" — A98

1956, Apr. 3   **Unwmk.**
365 A98 100fr red brn & red   20.00 20.00
The 26th Monte Carlo Automobile Rally.
See Nos. 411, 437, 460, 483, 500, 539, 549, 600, 629.

Princess Grace and Prince Rainier III — A99

1956, Apr. 19   **Engr.**   **Perf. 13**
Portraits in Black
366 A99 1fr dark green   .25 .25
367 A99 2fr dark carmine   .25 .25
368 A99 3fr ultra   .40 .25
369 A99 5fr brt yellow grn   .90 .55
370 A99 15fr redsh brown   1.25 .65
   Nos. 366-370,C46-C48 (8)   8.55 5.15
Wedding of Prince Rainier III to Grace Kelly, Apr. 19, 1956.

Nos. J41-J47, J50-J56 Overprinted with Bars and Surcharged in Indigo, Red or Black
Designs: Early Transportation.
Unwmk.
1956, Apr. 3   **Engr.**   **Perf. 11**
371 D6 2fr on 4fr (I)   .45 .45
   a. Pair, #371, 381   1.00 1.00
372 D6 3fr (R)   .45 .45
   a. Pair, #372, 382   1.00 1.00
373 D6 5fr on 4fr   .65 .65
   a. Pair, #373, 383   1.40 1.40
374 D6 10fr on 4fr (R)   1.25 1.25
   a. Pair, #374, 384   2.75 2.75
375 D6 15fr on 5fr (I)   1.60 1.60
   a. Pair, #375, 385   3.50 3.50
376 D6 20fr (R)   2.50 2.50
   a. Pair, #376, 386   5.50 5.50
377 D6 25fr on 20fr   4.50 4.50
   a. Pair, #377, 387   10.00 10.00
378 D6 30fr on 10fr (I)   8.50 8.50
   a. Pair, #378, 388   19.00 19.00
379 D6 40fr on 50fr (R)   12.00 12.00
   a. Pair, #379, 389   27.00 27.00
380 D6 50fr on 100fr   14.00 14.00
   a. Pair, #380, 390   32.00 32.00

Designs: Modern Transportation.
381 D7 2fr on 4fr (I)   .45 .45
382 D7 3fr (R)   .45 .45
383 D7 5fr on 4fr   .65 .65
384 D7 10fr on 4fr (R)   1.25 1.25
385 D7 15fr on 5fr (I)   1.60 1.60
386 D7 20fr (R)   2.50 2.50
387 D7 25fr on 20fr   4.50 4.50
388 D7 30fr on 10fr (I)   8.50 8.50
389 D7 40fr on 50fr (R)   12.00 12.00
390 D7 50fr on 100fr   14.00 14.00
   Nos. 371-390,C49-C50 (22)   109.80 109.80
Pairs se-tenant at the base.

Princess Grace — A100

1957, May 11   **Engr.**   **Perf. 13**
391 A100 1fr blue violet   .25 .25
392 A100 2fr lt olive grn   .25 .25
393 A100 3fr yellow brown   .25 .25
394 A100 5fr magenta   .30 .25
395 A100 15fr pink   .60 .25
396 A100 25fr Prus blue   .75 .65
397 A100 30fr purple   1.00 .90
398 A100 50fr scarlet   1.60 .90
399 A100 75fr orange   2.75 2.90
   Nos. 391-399 (9)   7.75 6.20
Birth of Princess Caroline of Monaco.

Knight Type of 1954
1957   **Unwmk.**   **Perf. 13**
400 A79 5fr dark blue   .40 .25
401 A79 10fr yellow green   .30 .25
402 A79 15fr brt orange   1.40 .90
403 A79 30fr brt blue   2.00 .90
404 A79 45fr crimson   3.25 1.75
   Nos. 400-404 (5)   7.35 4.05
Nos. 400-404 were issued precanceled only. See note after No. 324.

Types of 1955 and 1939-46
1957
405 A83 20fr greenish blue   2.00 .50
406 A83 35fr red brown   4.00 1.60
407 A83 65fr brt violet   10.00 6.50
408 A30 70fr orange yellow   9.50 6.00
   Nos. 405-408 (4)   25.50 14.60

Princesses Grace and Caroline — A101

1958, May 15   **Engr.**   **Perf. 13**
409 A101 100fr black   6.50 5.00
Birth of Prince Albert Alexander Louis, Mar. 14.

Order of St. Charles — A102

1958, May 15
410 A102 100fr carmine, grn & bis   1.75 1.50
Cent. of the Natl. Order of St. Charles.

Rally Type of 1956
Design: 100fr, "Munich to Monte Carlo."
1958, May 15
411 A98 100fr red, grn & sepia   7.00 6.00
27th Monte Carlo Automobile Rally.

Virgin Mary, Popes Pius IX and XII A103

Bernadette Soubirous A104

Tomb of Bernadette, Nevers A105

Designs: 3fr, Shepherdess Bernadette at Bartres. 5fr, Bouriette kneeling (first miracle). 8fr, Stained glass window showing apparition. 10fr, Empty grotto at Lourdes. 12fr, Grotto with statue and altar. 20fr, Bernadette praying. 35fr, High Altar at St. Peter's during canonization of Bernadette. 50fr, Bernadette, Pope Pius XI, Mgr. Laurence and Abbe Peyramale.

1958, May 15   **Unwmk.**
412 A103 1fr lilac gray & vio brn   .25 .25
413 A104 2fr lt blue & violet   .25 .25
414 A104 3fr green & sepia   .25 .25
415 A104 5fr gray brn & vio bl   .25 .25
416 A104 8fr blk, ol bis & ind   .25 .25
417 A105 10fr multicolored   .25 .25
418 A105 12fr ind, ol bis & ol grn   .25 .25
   a. Strip of 3, #416-418   3.50 3.50
419 A104 20fr dk sl grn & rose   .40 .35
420 A104 35fr ol, gray ol & dk sl grn   .50 .45
421 A103 50fr lake, ol grn & ind   .80 .55
422 A105 65fr indigo & grnsh bl   1.10 .75
   Nos. 412-422,C51-C52 (13)   8.80 7.75
Centenary of the apparition of the Virgin Mary at Lourdes.
Sizes: Nos. 413-415, 419-420 26x36mm. No. 416 22x36mm. Nos. 417-418 48x36mm. No. 422 36x26mm.

Types of 1939-46 and 1955
1959   **Engr.**   **Perf. 13**
423 A32 5fr copper red   1.10 .55
424 A83 25fr orange & blk   1.10 .55
425 A83 30fr dark violet   4.25 2.10
426 A34 35fr dark blue   8.50 3.25
427 A83 50fr bl grn & rose cl   5.50 2.10
428 A31 85fr dk carmine rose   12.50 6.50
429 A33 100fr brt grnsh blue   12.50 6.50
   Nos. 423-429 (7)   45.45 21.55

Knight Type of 1954
1959
430 A79 8fr deep magenta   .75 .35
431 A79 20fr bright green   1.40 1.25
432 A79 40fr chocolate   2.75 1.10
433 A79 55fr ultra   4.50 2.75
   Nos. 430-433 (4)   9.40 5.45
Nos. 430-433 were issued precanceled only. See note after No. 324.

Princess Grace Polyclinic A106

1959, May 16
434 A106 100fr gray, brn & grn   3.00 2.00
Opening of Princess Grace Hospital.

UNESCO Building, Paris, and Cultural Emblems A107

50fr, UNESCO Building, children of various races.

1959, May 16
435 A107 25fr multicolored   .30 .30
436 A107 50fr ol, bl grn & blk brn   .40 .40
Opening of UNESCO Headquarters in Paris, Nov. 3, 1958.

Rally Type of 1956
Design: 100fr, "Athens to Monaco."
1959, May 16
437 A98 100fr vio bl, red & sl grn, bl   5.50 5.00
28th Monte Carlo Automobile Rally.

Carnations — A108

Bougainvillea A109

Flowers: 10fr on 3fr, Princess Grace Carnations. 15fr on 1fr, Mimosa, vert. 25fr on 6fr, Geranium, vert. 35fr, Oleander. 50fr, Jasmine. 85fr on 65fr, Lavender. 100fr, Grace de Monaco Rose.

1959, May 16
438 A108 5fr brn, Prus grn & rose car   .25 .25
439 A108 10fr on 3fr brn, grn & rose   .25 .25
440 A109 15fr on 1fr dk grn & cit   .30 .25
441 A109 20fr ol grn & mag   .75 .55
442 A109 25fr on 6fr yel grn & red   1.25 .75
443 A109 35fr dk grn & pink   2.00 1.75
444 A109 50fr dk brn & dk grn   2.75 2.10
445 A109 85fr on 65fr ol grn & gray vio   3.00 3.00
446 A108 100fr green & pink   4.00 4.00
   Nos. 438-446 (9)   14.55 12.90
Nos. 439-440, 442 and 445 were not issued without surcharge.

View of Monaco and Uprooted Oak Emblem — A110

1960, June 1   **Unwmk.**   **Perf. 13**
447 A110 25c bl, olive grn & sepia   .35 .25
World Refugee Year, 7/1/59-6/30/60.

Entrance to Oceanographic Museum — A111

Museum and Aquarium A112

Designs: 15c, Museum conference room. 20c, Arrival of equipment, designed by Prince Albert I. 25c, Research on electrical qualities of cephalopodes. 50c, Albert I and vessels Hirondelle I and Princesse Alice.

1960, June 1   **Engr.**   **Perf. 13**
448 A111 5c blue, sepia & cl   .55 .25
449 A112 10c multicolored   .70 .35
450 A112 15c sep, ultra & bis   .70 .35
451 A112 20c rose lil, blk & bl   1.00 .55
452 A112 25c grnsh blue   1.50 1.00
453 A112 50c lt ultra & brown   2.50 1.75
   Nos. 448-453 (6)   6.95 4.25
Inauguration of the Oceanographic Museum of Monaco, 50th anniv. See #475.

Horse Jumping A113

Sports: 10c, Women swimmers. 15c, Broad jumper. 20c, Javelin thrower. 25c, Girl figure skater. 50c, Skier.

1960, June 1
454 A113 5c dk brn, car & emer   .25 .25
455 A113 10c red brn, bl & grn   .25 .25
456 A113 15c dl red brn, ol & mag   .35 .35
457 A113 20c black, bl & grn   2.75 2.75
458 A113 25c dk grn & dull pur   .70 .70
459 A113 50c dk bl, grnsh bl & dl pur   1.10 1.10
   Nos. 454-459 (6)   5.40 5.40
Nos. 454-457 for the 17th Olympic Games, Rome, Aug. 25-Sept. 11; Nos. 458-459 for the 8th Winter Olympic Games, Squaw Valley, Feb. 18-29.

MONACO

Rally Type of 1956
Design: 25c, "Lisbon to Monte Carlo."
1960, June 1
460 A98 25c bl, brn & car, *bluish* 2.00 2.00
29th Monte Carlo Automobile Rally.

A114

Design: Stamps of Sardinia and France, 1860, and Stamp of Monaco, 1885.

1960, June 1   Engr. & Embossed
461 A114 25c violet, blue & ol   .75 .65
75th anniv. of postage stamps of Monaco.

Prince Rainier Type of 1955
1960   Engr.   Perf. 13
462 A83 25c orange & blk   .55 .25
463 A83 30c dark violet   .55 .25
464 A83 50c bl grn & rose lil   2.25 .35
465 A83 65c yel brn & slate   14.00 4.25
  Nos. 462-465 (4)   17.35 5.10

Knight Type of 1954
1960
466 A79 8c deep magenta   1.60 .55
467 A79 20c brt green   2.75 .55
468 A79 40c chocolate   4.50 1.10
469 A79 55c ultra   6.75 1.60
  Nos. 466-469 (4)   15.60 3.80
Nos. 466-469 were issued precanceled only. See note after No. 324.

Sea Horse — A115

#471 Cactus (Cereanee). #472, Cactus (Nopalea dejecta). #473, Scorpion fish, horiz.

1960, June 1
470 A115 15c org brn & sl grn   .80 .25
471 A115 15c ol grn, yel & brn   .95 .25
472 A115 20c maroon & ol grn   .95 .25
473 A115 20c brn, red brn, red & ol   .80 .35
  Nos. 470-473 (4)   3.50 1.10
See Nos. 581-584.

Type of 1960 and

Palace of Monaco — A116

Designs: 10c, Type A111 without inscription. 45c, Aerial view of Palace. 85c, Honor court. 1fr, Palace at night.

1960, June 1
474 A116 5c green & sepia   .25 .25
475 A111 10c dk bl & vio brn   .55 .35
476 A116 45c dk bl, sep & grn   6.75 .70
477 A116 85c slate, gray & bis   8.75 2.10
478 A116 1fr dk bl, red brn & sl grn   1.10 .40
  Nos. 474-478 (5)   17.40 3.80
See #585, 602, 729, 731, 731A, 790, 792.

Sphinx of Wadi-es-Sebua — A117

1961, June 3   Unwmk.   Perf. 13
479 A117 50c choc, dk bl & ocher   1.25 .80
Issued as publicity to save historic monuments in Nubia.

Murena, Starfish, Sea Urchin, Sea Cucumber and Coral — A118

1961, June 3
480 A118 25c vio buff & dk red   .25 .25
Issued to commemorate the World Congress of Aquariology, Monaco, Nov. 1960.

Medieval Town and Leper — A119

1961, June 3
481 A119 25c ol gray, ocher & car   .25 .25
Issued to honor the Sovereign Order of the Knights of Malta.

Hand and Ant — A120

1961, June 3
482 A120 25c magenta & dp car   .40 .40
Issued to publicize "Respect for Life."

Rally Type of 1956
Design: 1fr, "Stockholm to Monte Carlo."
1961, June 3
483 A98 1fr multicolored   1.50 1.50
30th Monte Carlo Automobile Rally.

Turcat-Mery, 1911 Winner, and 1961 Car — A121

1961, June 3
484 A121 1fr org brn, vio & rose red   1.50 1.50
50th anniv. of the founding of the Monte Carlo Automobile Rally.

Chevrolet, 1912 — A122

Automobiles (pre-1912): 2c, Peugeot. 3c, Fiat. 4c, Mercedes. 5c, Rolls Royce. 10c, Panhard-Levassor. 15c, Renault. 20c, Ford. 25c, Rochet-Schneider. 30c, FN-Herstal. 45c, De Dion Bouton. 50c, Buick. 65c, Delahaye. 1fr, Cadillac.

1961, June 13   Engr.
485 A122 1c org brn, dk brn & grn   .25 .25
486 A122 2c org red, dk bl & brn   .25 .25
487 A122 3c multicolored   .25 .25
488 A122 4c multicolored   .25 .25
489 A122 5c ol bis, sl grn & car   .25 .25
490 A122 10c brn, sl & red   .25 .25
491 A122 15c grnsh bl & dk sl grn   .25 .25
492 A122 20c pur, blk & red   .25 .25
493 A122 25c dk brn lil & red   .75 .75
494 A122 30c ol grn & dl pur   .95 .95
495 A122 45c multicolored   1.25 1.25
496 A122 50c brn blk, red & ultra   1.75 1.75
497 A122 65c multicolored   2.00 2.00
498 A122 1fr brt pur, ind & red   2.75 2.75
  Nos. 485-498 (14)   11.45 11.45
See Nos. 648-661.

Bugatti, First Winner, and Course A123

1962, June 6   Unwmk.   Perf. 13
499 A123 1fr lilac rose   1.50 1.50
20th Automobile Grand Prix of Monaco.

Rally Type of 1956
Design: 1fr, "Oslo to Monte Carlo."
1962, June 6
500 A98 1fr multicolored   1.50 1.50
31st Monte Carlo Automobile Rally.

Louis XII and Lucien Grimaldi — A124

50c, Document granting sovereignty. 1fr, Seals of Louis XII & Lucien Grimaldi.

1962, June 6   Engr.
501 A124 25c ver, blk & vio bl   .30 .30
502 A124 50c dk bl, brn & mag   .40 .40
503 A124 1fr dk brn, grn & car   .60 .60
  Nos. 501-503 (3)   1.30 1.30
450th anniversary of Monaco's reception of sovereignty from Louis XII.

Mosquito and Swamp — A125

1962, June 6
504 A125 1fr brn ol & lt grn   .60 .60
WHO drive to eradicate malaria.

Aquatic Stadium at Night — A126

1962, June 6
505 A126 10c dk bl, ind & grn   .25 .25

Sun, Flowers and Hope Chest — A127

1962, June 6
506 A127 20c multicolored   .25 .25
Issued to publicize the National Multiple Sclerosis Society of New York.

Wheat Harvest — A128

1962, June 6
507 A128 25c dk bl, red brn & brn   .30 .30
508 A128 50c ind, ol bis & dk bl grn   .50 .35
509 A128 1fr red lil & olive bister   1.00 .65
  Nos. 507-509,C61 (4)   3.30 2.30
Europa. See No. C61.

Blood Donor's Arm and Globe — A129

1962, Nov. 15   Engr.   Perf. 13
510 A129 1fr dk red, blk & orange   .90 .90
3rd International Blood Donors' Congress, Nov. 15-18 at Monaco.

Yellow Wagtails — A130

Birds: 10c, European robins. 15c, European goldfinches. 20c, Blackcaps. 25c, Great spotted woodpeckers. 30c, Nightingale. 45c, Barn owls. 50c, Common starlings. 85c, Red crossbills. 1fr, White storks.

1962, Dec. 12   Unwmk.
511 A130 5c green, sep & yel   .25 .25
512 A130 10c bis, dk pur & red   .25 .25
513 A130 15c multicolored   .25 .25
514 A130 20c mag, grn & blk   .35 .35
515 A130 25c multicolored   .70 .70
516 A130 30c brn, sl grn & bl   .90 .90
517 A130 45c vio & gldn brn   1.10 1.10
518 A130 50c bl grn, blk & yel   1.50 1.50
519 A130 85c multicolored   1.75 1.75
520 A130 1fr blk, grn & red   2.75 2.75
  Nos. 511-520 (10)   9.80 9.80
Protection of useful birds.

Divers — A131

10c, Galeazzi's turret, vert. 25c, Williamson's photosphere, 1914 & bathyscape "Trieste," 1962. 45c, Diving suits. 50c, Diving chamber. 85c, Fulton's "Nautilus," 1800 and modern submarine. 1fr, Alexander the Great's underwater chamber and bathysphere of the N. Y. Zoological Society.

1962, Dec. 12
521 A131 5c bluish grn, vio & blk   .25 .25
522 A131 10c multicolored   .25 .25
523 A131 25c bis, bluish grn & sl grn   .25 .25
524 A131 45c green, ind & blk   .45 .45
525 A131 50c blt & dk bl   .70 .70
526 A131 85c Prus grn & dk vio bl   1.25 1.25
527 A131 1fr dk bl, dk brn & dk grn   2.00 2.00
  Nos. 521-527 (7)   5.15 5.15

Issued in connection with an exhibition at the Oceanographic Museum "Man Under Water," showing ancient and modern methods of under-water exploration.

MONACO

Dancing Children and UN Emblem — A132

Children on Scales — A133

Designs: 10c, Bird feeding nestlings, vert. 20c, Sun shining on children of different races, vert. 25c, Mother and child, vert. 50c, House and child. 95c, African mother and child, vert. 1fr, Prince Albert and Princess Caroline.

1963, May 3   Unwmk.   Perf. 13

528	A132	5c ocher, dk red & ultra	.25	.25
529	A133	10c vio bl, emer & ol gray	.25	.25
530	A133	15c ultra, red & grn	.25	.25
531	A133	20c multicolored	.25	.25
532	A133	25c blue, brn & pink	.25	.25
533	A133	50c multicolored	.40	.40
534	A133	95c multicolored	.80	.80
535	A132	1fr multicolored	1.60	1.60
		Nos. 528-535 (8)	4.05	4.05

Publicizing the UN Children's Charter.

Figurehead with Red Cross, Red Crescent and Red Lion and Sun — A134

1fr, Centenary emblem, Gustave Moynier, Henri Dunant and Gen. Henri Dufour, horiz.

1963, May 3   Engr.

536	A134	50c bluish grn, red & red brn	.50	.50
537	A134	1fr blue, sl grn & red	.50	.50

Centenary of International Red Cross.

Racing Cars on Monte Carlo Course and Map of Europe — A135

1963, May 3

538	A135	50c multicolored	.70	.45

European Automobile Grand Prix.

Rally Type of 1956

Design: 1fr, "Warsaw to Monte Carlo."

1963, May 3

539	A98	1fr multicolored	1.50	1.50

32nd Monte Carlo Auto Race.

Lions International Emblem — A136

1963, May 3

540	A136	50c bis, lt vio & bl	.60	.60

Issued to commemorate the founding of the Lions Club of Monaco, Mar. 24, 1962.

Hôtel des Postes, Paris, and UPU Allegory — A137

1963, May 3

541	A137	50c multicolored	.60	.40

1st Intl. Postal Conference, Paris, 1863.

Globe and Telstar — A138

1963, May 3

542	A138	50c grn, dk pur & maroon	.60	.50

1st television connection of the US and Europe through the Telstar satellite, July 11-12, 1962.

Holy Spirit over St. Peter's and World — A139

1963, May 3

543	A139	1fr grn, red brn & bl	.60	.60

Vatican II, the 21st Ecumenical Council of the Roman Catholic Church.

Wheat Emblem and Dove Feeding Nestlings — A140

1963, May 3   Engr.

544	A140	1fr multicolored	.70	.70

FAO "Freedom from Hunger" campaign.

Henry Ford and 1903 Model A — A141

1963, Dec. 12   Unwmk.   Perf. 13

545	A141	20c slate grn & lil rose	.75	.50

Centenary of the birth of Henry Ford, American automobile manufacturer.

Bicycle Racer in Town — A142

Design: 50c, Bicyclist on country road.

1963, Dec. 12

546	A142	25c bl, sl grn & red brn	.30	.30
547	A142	50c bl, gray grn, & blk brn	.60	.60

50th anniv. of the Bicycle Tour de France.

Pierre de Coubertin and Myron's Discobolus — A143

1963, Dec. 12

548	A143	1fr dp cl, car & ocher	.75	.75

Baron Pierre de Coubertin, organizer of the modern Olympic Games, birth cent.

Rally Type of 1956

Design: 1fr, "Paris to Monte Carlo."

1963, Dec. 12

549	A98	1fr multicolored	1.10	1.10

33rd Monte Carlo Automobile Rally.

Children with Stamp Album and UNESCO Emblem — A144

1963, Dec. 12

550	A144	50c dp ultra, red & vio	.45	.45

International Philatelic and Educational Exposition, Monaco, Nov.-Dec., 1963.

Europa Issue

Woman, Dove and Lyre — A145

1963, Dec. 12

551	A145	25c brn, grn & car	1.50	.35
552	A145	50c dk brn, bl & car	2.00	.60

Wembley Stadium and British Football Association Emblem — A146

Overhead Kick — A147

Soccer Game, Florence, 16th Century — A148

Tackle — A149

Designs: 3c, Goalkeeper. 4c, Louis II Stadium and emblem of Sports Association of Monaco, with black overprint: "Championnat /1962-1963/Coupe de France." 15c, Soule Game, Brittany, 19th century. 20c, Soccer, England, 1827. 25c, Soccer, England, 1890. 50c, Clearing goal area. 95c, Heading the ball. 1fr, Kicking the ball.

1963, Dec. 12

553	A146	1c grn, vio & dk red	.25	.25
554	A147	2c black, red & grn	.25	.25
555	A147	3c gray ol, org & red	.25	.25
556	A146	4c bl, red, grn, pur & blk	.25	.25
557	A148	10c dk bl, car & sep	.25	.25
558	A148	15c sepia & car	.25	.25
559	A148	20c sepia & dk bl	.25	.25
560	A148	25c sepia & lilac	.25	.25
a.		Block of 4	1.00	1.00
561	A149	30c green, sep & red	.45	.45
562	A149	50c sepia, grn & red	.70	.70
563	A149	95c sepia, grn & red	1.00	1.00
564	A149	1fr sepia, grn & red	1.25	1.25
a.		Block of 4	4.00	4.00
		Nos. 553-564 (12)	5.40	5.40

Cent. of British Football Assoc. (organized soccer). No. 556 also for the successes of the soccer team of Monaco, 1962-63 (overprint typographed). No. 556 was not regularly issued without overprint. Value $750.

The 4 stamps of No. 560a are connected by an 1863 soccer ball in red brown; the stamps of No. 564a by a modern soccer ball.

Design from 1914 Rally Post Card A150

Farman Biplane over Monaco A151

Designs: 3c, Nieuport monoplane. 4c, Breguet biplane. 5c, Morane-Saulnier monoplane. 10c, Albatros biplane. 15c, Deperdussin monoplane. 20c, Vickers-Vimy biplane and map (Ross Smith's flight London-Port Darwin, 1919). 25c, Douglas Liberty biplane (first American around-the-world flight. 4 planes, 1924). 30c, Savoia S-16 hydroplane (De Pinedo's Rome-Australia-Japan-Rome flight, 1925). 45c, Trimotor Fokker F-7 monoplane (first aerial survey of North Pole, Richard E. Byrd and James Gordon Bennett, 1925). 50c, Spirit of St. Louis (first crossing of Atlantic, New York-Paris, Charles Lindbergh, 1927). 65c, Breguet 19 (Paris-New York, Coste and Bellonte, 1930). 95c, Laté 28 hydroplane (first South Atlantic airmail route, Dakar-Natal, 1930). 1fr, Dornier DO-X, (Germany-Rio de Janeiro, 1930).

1964, May 22   Engr.   Perf. 13

565	A150	1c green, bl & ol	.25	.25
566	A151	2c bl, bis & red brn	.25	.25
567	A151	3c olive, grn & bl	.25	.25
568	A151	4c red brn, bl & Prus grn	.25	.25
569	A151	5c gray ol, vio & mag	.25	.25
570	A151	10c violet, bl & ol	.25	.25
571	A151	15c blue, org & brn	.25	.25
572	A151	20c brt grn, blk & bl	.35	.25
573	A151	25c red, bl & ol	.35	.25
574	A151	30c bl, sl grn & dp cl	.45	.45
575	A151	45c red brn, grnsh bl & blk	.75	.55
576	A151	50c purple, ol & bis	.90	.75
577	A151	65c steel bl, blk & red	1.20	1.00
578	A151	95c ocher, sl grn & red	1.60	1.25
579	A151	1fr sl grn, bl & vio brn	2.25	1.60
		Nos. 565-579,C64 (16)	12.35	10.70

50th anniv. of the 1st airplane rally of Monte Carlo. Nos. 565-571 show planes which took part in the 1914 rally, Nos. 572-579 and C64 show important flights from 1919 to 1961.

Ancient Egyptian Message Transmitters and Rocket A152

1964, May 22   Unwmk.

580	A152	1fr dk bl, indigo & org brn	.70	.70

Issued to publicize "PHILATEC", International Philatelic and Postal Techniques Exhibition, Paris, June 5-21, 1964.

Types of 1955-60

1c, Crab (Macrocheira Kampferi), horiz. 2c, Flowering cactus (Selenicereus Gr.). 12c, Shell (Fasciolaria trapezium). 18c, Aloe ciliaris. 70c, Honor court of palace (like #477). 95c, Prince Rainier III.

MONACO

1964, May 19   *Perf. 13*

581	A115	1c bl grn & dk red	.25	.25
582	A115	2c dk grn & multi	.25	.25
583	A115	12c vio & brn red	.50	.25
584	A115	18c grn, yel & car	.55	.25
585	A116	70c lt grn, choc & red org	.70	.40
586	A83	95c ultra	1.50	.50
		Nos. 581-586 (6)	3.75	1.90

Rainier III Aquatic Stadium — A153

1964-67   *Engr.*   *Perf. 13*

587	A153	10c dk car, rose, bl & blk	1.75	.25
587A	A153	15c dk car, rose, brt bl & blk ('67)	1.00	.25
588	A153	25c dl grn, dk bl & blk	1.00	.25
589	A153	50c lil, bl grn & blk	1.75	1.00
		Nos. 587-589 (4)	5.50	1.75

Nos. 587-589 were issued precanceled only. See note after No. 324. The "1962" date has been obliterated with 2 bars. See Nos. 732-734, 793-796, 976-979.

Common Design Types pictured following the introduction.

Europa Issue, 1964
Common Design Type

1964, Sept. 12   Size: 22x34½mm

590	CD7	25c brt red, brt grn & dk grn	1.00	.25
591	CD7	50c ultra, ol bis & dk red brn	1.50	.45

Weight Lifter A154

1964, Dec. 3   *Unwmk.*   *Perf. 13*

592	A154	1c shown	.25	.25
593	A154	2c Judo	.25	.25
594	A154	3c Pole vault	.25	.25
595	A154	4c Archery	.25	.25
		Nos. 592-595 (4)	1.00	1.00

18th Olympic Games, Tokyo, 10/10-25. See #C65.

Pres. John F. Kennedy and Mercury Capsule A155

1964, Dec. 3

596	A155	50c brt bl & indigo	.60	.60

Pres. John F. Kennedy (1917-63).

Television Set and View of Monte Carlo — A156

1964, Dec. 3

597	A156	50c dk car rose, dk bl & brn	.50	.50

Fifth International Television Festival.

Frédéric Mistral, (1830-1914), Provençal Poet — A157

1964, Dec. 3   *Engr.*

598	A157	1fr gray olive & brn red	.55	.55

Scales of Justice and Code — A158

1964, Dec. 3

599	A158	1fr gldn brn & slate grn	.60	.60

Universal Declaration of Human Rights.

Rally Type of 1956

Design: 1fr, "Minsk to Monte Carlo."

1964, Dec. 3

600	A98	1fr bl grn, ocher & brn	.90	.90

34th Monte Carlo Automobile Rally.

International Football Association Emblem — A159

1964, Dec. 3

601	A159	1fr red, bl & ol bister	.85	.85

60th anniv. of FIFA, the Federation Internationale de Football (soccer).

Types of 1955 and 1960

Designs: 40c, Aerial view of palace. 60c, 1.30fr, 2.30fr, Prince Rainier III.

1965-66   *Engr.*   *Perf. 13*

602	A116	40c sl grn, dl cl & brt grn	.75	.25
603	A83	60c sl grn & blk	1.10	.35
604	A83	1.30fr dk red & blk	3.25	.75
604A	A83	2.30fr org & rose lil ('66)	2.75	.75
		Nos. 602-604A (4)	7.85	2.10

Telstar and Pleumeur-Bodou Relay Station — A160

Alexander Graham Bell and Telephone A161

Designs (ITU Emblem and): 5c, Syncom II and Earth. 10c, Echo II and Earth. 12c, Relay satellite and Earth, vert. 18c, Lunik III and Moon. 50c, Samuel Morse and telegraph. 60c, Edouard Belin, belinograph and newspaper. 70c, Roman signal towers and Chappe telegraph. 95c, Cable laying ships; "The Great Eastern" (British, 1858) and "Alsace" (French, modern). 1fr, Edouard Branly, Guglielmo Marconi and map of English Channel.

1965, May 17

605	A161	5c vio bl & slate grn	.25	.25
606	A161	10c dk bl & sepia	.25	.25
607	A161	12c gray, brn & dk car	.25	.25
608	A161	18c ind, dk car & plum	.25	.25
609	A160	25c vio, ol & rose brn	.25	.25
610	A161	30c dk brn, ol & bis brn	.25	.25
611	A161	50c green & indigo	.25	.25
612	A161	60c dl red brn & brt bl	.25	.25
613	A160	70c brn blk, org & dk bl	.55	.55
614	A160	95c indigo, blk & bl	.55	.55
615	A160	1fr brn, blk & ultra	.75	.75
		Nos. 605-615,C66 (12)	7.35	7.35

International Telecommunication Union, cent.

Europa Issue, 1965
Common Design Type

1965, Sept. 25   *Engr.*   *Perf. 13*

Size: 36x22mm

616	CD8	30c red brn & grn	1.25	.65
617	CD8	60c violet & dk car	2.00	1.00

Palace of Monaco, 18th Century — A162

Views of Palace: 12c, From the Bay, 17th century. 18c, Bay with sailboats, 18th century. 30c, From distance, 19th century. 60c, Close-up, 19th century. 1.30fr, Aerial view, 20th century.

1966, Feb. 1   *Engr.*   *Perf. 13*

618	A162	10c vio, dl grn & ind	.25	.25
619	A162	12c bl, bis brn & dk brn	.25	.25
620	A162	18c blk, grn & bl	.25	.25
621	A162	30c vio bl, sep & red brn	.25	.25
622	A162	60c bl, grn & brn	.65	.65
623	A162	1.30fr dk grn & red brn	.80	.80
		Nos. 618-623 (6)	2.45	2.45

750th anniversary of Palace of Monaco.

Dante Alighieri A163

Designs: 60c, Dante facing Panther of Envy. 70c, Dante and Virgil boating across muddy swamp of 5th Circle. 95c, Dante watching the arrogant and Cross of Salvation. 1fr, Invocation of St. Bernard; Dante and Beatrice.

1966, Feb. 1

624	A163	30c crimson & dp grn	.35	.35
625	A163	60c dl grn, Prus bl & ind	.50	.50
626	A163	70c black, sep & car	.70	.70
627	A163	95c red lilac & blue	.75	.75
628	A163	1fr ultra & bluish grn	1.10	1.10
		Nos. 624-628 (5)	3.40	3.40

700th anniv. (in 1965) of the birth of Dante (1265-1321), poet.

Rally Type of 1956

Design: 1fr, "London to Monte Carlo."

1966, Feb. 1

629	A98	1fr purple, red & indigo	.95	.75

The 35th Monte Carlo Automobile Rally.

Nativity by Gerard van Honthorst — A164

1966, Feb. 1

630	A164	30c brown	.30	.30

Issued to honor the World Association for the Protection of Children.

Casino, Monte Carlo — A165

View of La Condamine, 1860, and François Blanc A166

Designs: 12c, Prince Charles III, vert. 40c, Charles III monument, Bowling Green Gardens. 60c, Seaside Promenade and Rainier III. 70c, René Blum, Sergei Diaghilev and "Petroushka." 95c, Jules Massenet and Camille Saint-Saens. 1.30fr, Gabriel Fauré and Maurice Ravel.

1966, June 1   *Engr.*   *Perf. 13*

631	A165	12c dp blue, blk & mag	.25	.25
632	A165	25c multicolored	.25	.25
633	A166	30c bl, plum, grn & org	.25	.25
634	A165	40c multicolored	.25	.25
635	A166	60c multicolored	.25	.25
636	A165	70c rose cl & ind	.25	.25
637	A165	95c purple & blk	.25	.25
638	A165	1.30fr brn org, ol bis & brn	.65	.65
		Nos. 631-638,C68 (9)	5.15	5.15

Centenary of founding of Monte Carlo.

Europa Issue, 1966
Common Design Type

1966, Sept. 26   *Engr.*   *Perf. 13*

Size: 21½x35½mm

639	CD9	30c orange	.75	.25
640	CD9	60c light green	1.25	.40

Prince Albert I, Yachts Hirondelle I and Princess Alice A167

1966, Dec. 12   *Engr.*   *Perf. 13*

641	A167	1fr ultra & dk vio brn	.75	.75

1st Intl. Congress of the History of Oceanography, Monaco, Dec. 12-17. Issued in sheets of 10.

Red Chalk Drawing by Domenico Zampieri — A168

1966, Dec. 12

642	A168	30c brt rose & dk brn	.25	.25
643	A168	60c brt bl & yel brn	.35	.35

20th anniv. of UNESCO.

Television Screen and Cross over Monaco — A169

1966, Dec. 12

644	A169	60c dk car rose, lil & red	.35	.25

10th meeting of "UNDA," the International Catholic Association for Radio and Television.

Precontinent III and Divers on Ocean Floor A170

1966, Dec. 12

645	A170	1fr Prus bl, yel & dk brn	.60	.35

First anniversary of the submarine research station Precontinent III.

MONACO

WHO Headquarters, Geneva — A171

1966, Dec. 12
| 646 | A171 | 30c dp bl, ol brn & dp grn | .25 | .25 |
| 647 | A171 | 60c dk grn, crim & dk brn | .35 | .35 |

Opening of WHO Headquarters, Geneva.

Automobile Type of 1961

Automobiles (Previous Winners): 1c, Bugatti, 1931. 2c, Alfa Romeo, 1932. 5c, Mercedes, 1936. 10c, Maserati, 1948. 18c, Ferrari, 1955. 20c, Alfa Romeo, 1950. 25c, Maserati, 1957. 30c, Cooper-Climax, 1958. 40c, Lotus-Climax, 1960. 50c, Lotus-Climax, 1961. 60c, Cooper-Climax, 1962. 70c, B.R.M., 1963-66. 1fr, Walter Christie, 1907. 2.30fr, Peugeot, 1910.

1967, Apr. 28 Engr. Perf. 13x12½
648	A122	1c ind, red & brt bl	.25	.25
649	A122	2c green, red & blk	.25	.25
650	A122	5c red, ind & gray	.25	.25
651	A122	10c violet, red & ind	.25	.25
652	A122	18c indigo & red	.25	.25
653	A122	20c dk grn, red & ind	.25	.25
654	A122	25c ultra, red & ind	.25	.25
655	A122	30c brown, ind & grn	.25	.25
656	A122	40c car rose, ind & grn	.40	.40
657	A122	50c lilac, ind & grn	.60	.60
658	A122	60c carmine, ind & grn	.60	.60
659	A122	70c dl yel, bl grn & ind	.80	.80
660	A122	1fr brn red, blk & gray	1.20	1.20
661	A122	2.30fr multicolored	2.00	2.00
		Nos. 648-661,C73 (15)	10.35	10.35

25th Grand Prix of Monaco, May 7.

Dog, Egyptian Statue — A172

1967, Apr. 28 Perf. 12½x13
| 662 | A172 | 30c dk grn, brn & blk | .55 | .40 |

Congress of the International Dog Fanciers Federation, Monaco, Apr. 5-9.

View of Monte Carlo A173

1967, Apr. 28 Perf. 13
| 663 | A173 | 30c slate grn, brt bl & brn | .40 | .40 |

International Tourist Year, 1967.

Chessboard and Monte Carlo Harbor A174

1967, Apr. 28
| 664 | A174 | 60c brt bl, dk pur & blk | .85 | .85 |

International Chess Championships, Monaco, Mar. 19-Apr. 1.

Melvin Jones, View of Monte Carlo and Lions Emblem A175

1967, Apr. 28
| 665 | A175 | 60c ultra, slate bl & choc | .60 | .40 |

50th anniversary of Lions International.

Rotary Emblem and View of Monte Carlo A176

1967, Apr. 28
| 666 | A176 | 1fr brt bl & lt ol grn | .60 | .50 |

Issued to publicize the Rotary International Convention, Monaco, May 21-26.

EXPO '67 Monaco Pavilion A177

1967, Apr. 28
| 667 | A177 | 1fr multicolored | .55 | .45 |

EXPO '67, International Exhibition, Montreal, Apr. 28-Oct. 27, 1967.

Map of Europe — A178

1967, Apr. 28
| 668 | A178 | 1fr choc, lemon & Prus bl | .55 | .45 |

Issued to publicize the International Committee for European Migration, CIME.

Europa Issue, 1967
Common Design Type

1967, Apr. 28 Perf. 12½x13
| 669 | CD10 | 30c brt car, rose lil & brt vio | 1.00 | .30 |
| 670 | CD10 | 60c grn ol & bl grn | 1.75 | .40 |

Skier and Olympic Emblem A179

1967, Dec. 7 Engr. Perf. 13
| 671 | A179 | 2.30fr red brn, gray & brt bl | 1.25 | 1.25 |

10th Winter Olympic Games, Grenoble, France, Feb. 6-18, 1968.

Sounding Line and Map A180

1967, Dec. 7
| 672 | A180 | 1fr dk bl, grn & ol | .55 | .45 |

9th International Hydrographic Conference, Monte Carlo, April-May, 1967.

Marie Curie, Chemical Apparatus and Atom Symbol A181

1967, Dec. 7
| 673 | A181 | 1fr brn, ultra & ol | .70 | .50 |

Marie Curie (1867-1934), discoverer of radium and polonium.

Princes of Monaco Issue

Rainier I, by Eugene Charpentier A182

#675, Lucien Grimaldi, by Ambrogio di Predis.

1967, Dec. 7 Perf. 12x13
| 674 | A182 | 1fr multicolored | .75 | .75 |
| 675 | A182 | 1fr multicolored | .75 | .75 |

See Nos. 710-711, 735-736, 774-775, 813-814, 860-861, 892-893, 991-992, 1035-1036, 1093, 1135-1136, 1187-1188, 1246-1247, 1302-1303.

Shot Put — A183

1968, Apr. 29 Engr. Perf. 13
676	A183	20c brt bl, grn & brn	.25	.25
677	A183	30c vio bl, sep & brn vio	.25	.25
678	A183	60c car, brt rose lil & dp bl	.25	.25
679	A183	70c ocher, brn org & Prus bl	.25	.25
680	A183	1fr brn org, brn & ind	.45	.45
681	A183	2.30fr dk car, vio bl & ol	.95	.95
		Nos. 676-681,C74 (7)	3.65	3.65

19th Olympic Games, Mexico City, 10/12-27.

Sport: 30c, High jump. 60c, Gymnast on rings. 70c, Water polo. 1fr, Wrestling. 2.30fr, Gymnast.

St. Martin and the Beggar — A184

1968, Apr. 29
| 682 | A184 | 2.30fr brn red, Prus bl & blk brn | 1.25 | 1.00 |

Red Cross of Monaco, 20th anniversary.

Anemones, by Raoul Dufy — A185

1968, Apr. 29 Photo. Perf. 12x13
| 683 | A185 | 1fr lt blue & multi | .75 | .60 |

International Flower Show in Monte Carlo. See Nos. 766, 776, 815-816, 829, 865.

Arms of Pope Pius IX and Prince Charles III A186

St. Nicholas A187

St. Benedict — A187a

Designs: 60c, Benedictine Monastery, Subiaco (Italy). 1fr, Church of St. Nicholas, Monaco, 13th century, horiz.

Perf. 12½x13, 13x12½

1968, Apr. 29 Engr.
684	A186	10c red & brown	.25	.25
685	A187	20c sl grn, ocher & car	.25	.25
686	A187a	30c ultra & ol grn	.25	.25
687	A187	60c lt bl, brn & dk grn	.30	.30
688	A187	1fr ind, bl & ol bis	.35	.35
		Nos. 684-688 (5)	1.40	1.40

Centenary of the elevation of St. Nicholas Church to an Abbey *Nullius*, directly subject to the Holy See.

Europa Issue, 1968
Common Design Type

1968, Apr. 29 Perf. 13
Size: 36x22mm
689	CD11	30c dp orange & car	.90	.25
690	CD11	60c carmine & ultra	2.25	.30
691	CD11	1fr green & red brn	2.25	.40
		Nos. 689-691 (3)	5.40	.95

Locomotive 030, 1868 A188

Locomotives and Views: 30c, Type "C"-220, 1898. 60c, Type 230-"C", 1910. 70c, Type 231-"F," 1925. 1fr, Type 241-"A," 1932. 2.30fr, Type "BB," 1968.

1968, Dec. 12 Engr. Perf. 13
692	A188	20c vio bl, brn & blk	.45	.45
693	A188	30c dk ol grn, bl & blk	.45	.45
694	A188	60c bl, bis & blk	2.25	1.90
695	A188	70c vio, red brn & blk	2.25	1.90
696	A188	1fr bl, brn red & blk	3.25	2.25
697	A188	2.30fr sal pink, brt bl & blk	3.25	2.25
		Nos. 692-697 (6)	11.90	9.20

Centenary of the Nice-Monaco Railroad.

MONACO

Chateaubriand and Combourg Castle — A189

Scenes from Chateaubriand Novels: 20c, The Genius of Christianity. 25c, René. 30c, The Last Abencerage. 60c, The Martyrs. 2.30fr, Atala.

1968, Dec. 12

698	A189	10c dk grn, grn & pur	.25	.25
699	A189	20c brt bl, vio & mag	.25	.25
700	A189	25c slate, pur & brn	.25	.25
701	A189	30c dp brn, brn & pur	.25	.25
702	A189	60c brn red, bl grn & dk brn	.35	.35
703	A189	2.30fr dk bl, ol & mag	1.10	1.10
		Nos. 698-703 (6)	2.45	2.45

Vicomte François René de Chateaubriand (1768-1848), novelist and statesman.

"France" and "Fidelity" by Bosio A190

François Joseph Bosio (1768-1845), Sculptor — A191

25c, Henri IV as a boy. 60c, Louis XIV on horseback, Place des Victoires. 2.30fr, Busts of Louis XVIII, Napoleon I and Charles X.

1968, Dec. 12

704	A190	20c brown	.25	.25
705	A191	25c sal pink & dk brn	.25	.25
706	A191	30c slate & vio bl	.25	.25
707	A191	60c dk ol grn & gray grn	.40	.40
708	A190	2.30fr black & slate	.90	.90
		Nos. 704-708 (5)	2.05	2.05

WHO Emblem A192

1968, Dec. 12   Photo.

709	A192	60c multicolored	.35	.25

World Health Organization, 20th anniv.

Princes of Monaco Type of 1967

Designs: 1fr, Charles II (1581-89). 2.30fr, Jeanne Grimaldi (1596-1620).

1968, Dec. 12   Engr.   Perf. 12x13

710	A182	1fr multicolored	.70	.70
711	A182	2.30fr multicolored	.70	.70

Faust and Mephistopheles — A193

Scenes from "Damnation of Faust" by Berlioz: 10c, Rakoczy March. 25c, Auerbach's Cellar. 30c, Dance of the Sylphs. 40c, Dance of the Sprites. 50c, Faust and Marguerite. 70c, Woods and Meadows. 1fr, The Ride to the Abyss. 1.15fr, Heaven.

1969, Apr. 26   Engr.   Perf. 13

712	A193	10c bl grn, pur & org brn	.25	.25
713	A193	20c mag, dk ol & lt brn	.25	.25
714	A193	25c ind, brn & mag	.25	.25
715	A193	30c yel grn, sl & blk	.25	.25
716	A193	40c org red, sl & blk	.25	.25
717	A193	50c ol, plum & sl	.25	.25
718	A193	70c dp grn, sl & lt brn	.25	.25
719	A193	1fr mag, blk & ol bis	.40	.40
720	A193	1.15fr Prus bl, blk & ultra	.40	.40
		Nos. 712-720,C75 (10)	3.30	3.30

Hector Berlioz (1803-69), French composer.

St. Elizabeth and Husband, Louis IV, Landgrave of Thuringia — A194

1969, Apr. 26

721	A194	3fr dk red, slate & gray	1.40	1.40

Issued for the Red Cross.

See Nos. 767, 812, 830, 905, 963, 1037, 1094, 1189.

Europa Issue, 1969
Common Design Typo

1969, Apr. 26
Size: 36x26mm

722	CD12	40c scarlet & purple	2.00	.30
723	CD12	70c brt blue & blk	4.25	.85
724	CD12	1fr yel bis, brn & bl	4.25	.85
		Nos. 722-724 (3)	10.50	2.00

Prince Rainier Type of 1955 and Palace Type of 1960

Designs: 80c, Aerial view of Palace. 1.15fr, 1.30fr, Honor Court.

1969-70   Engr.   Perf. 13

725	A83	40c olive & rose red	.30	.25
726	A83	45c slate & ocher	.50	.25
727	A83	50c ocher & mar	.70	.35
728	A83	70c dk pur & brt vio bl	.70	.70
729	A116	80c bl, red brn & grn	1.10	.70
730	A83	85c dk vio & brt grn	1.10	.70
731	A116	1.15fr blk, bl & mar	1.75	.75
731A	A116	1.30fr ol brn, lt bl & dl grn ('70)	.75	.75
		Nos. 725-731A (8)	6.90	4.45

Aquatic Stadium Type of 1964-67, "1962" Omitted

1969   Engr.   Perf. 13

732	A153	22c choc, brt bl & blk	.50	.25
733	A153	35c Prus bl, brt bl & blk	.60	.25
734	A153	70c black & vio bl	.80	.35
		Nos. 732-734 (3)	1.80	.85

Nos. 732-734 were issued precanceled only. See note after No. 324.

Princes of Monaco Type of 1967

Designs: 1fr, Honoré II (1604-1662), by Philippe de Champaigne. 3fr, Louise-Hippolyte (1697-1731), by Pierre Gobert.

1969, Nov. 25   Engr.   Perf. 12x13

735	A182	1fr multicolored	.60	.60
736	A182	3fr multicolored	1.25	1.25

Woman's Head, by Leonardo da Vinci — A195

Drawings by Leonardo da Vinci: 40c, Self-portrait. 70c, Head of old man. 80c, Study for head of St. Magdalene. 1.15fr, Man's head. 3fr, Professional soldier.

1969, Nov. 25   Perf. 13

737	A195	30c dull brown	.25	.25
738	A195	40c brn & rose red	.25	.25
739	A195	70c gray green	.30	.30
740	A195	80c dk brown	.40	.35
741	A195	1.15fr orange brn	.75	.55
742	A195	3fr olive brown	1.10	.90
		Nos. 737-742 (6)	3.05	2.60

Leonardo da Vinci (1452-1519), Florentine painter, sculptor and scientist.

Alphonse Daudet and Scenes from "Letters from My Windmill" A196

Various Scenes from "Letters from My Windmill" (Lettres de Mon Moulin).

1969, Nov. 25

743	A196	30c blue grn & multi	.25	.25
744	A196	40c brn, vio bl & ol	.40	.40
745	A196	70c pur, brn & ol gray	.40	.40
746	A196	80c sl grn, vio bl & mar	.40	.40
747	A196	1.15fr ocher, sep & blk	.55	.55
		Nos. 743-747 (5)	2.00	2.00

Centenary of publication of "Letters from My Windmill," by Alphonse Daudet (1840-1897).

ILO Emblem — A197

1969, Nov. 25   Perf. 13x12½

748	A197	40c dk blue & dk pur	.35	.30

50th anniv. of the ILO.

World Map and JCI Emblem — A198

1969, Nov. 25

749	A198	40c olive, dk bl & bl	.35	.25

25th anniversary of the Junior Chamber of Commerce in Monaco.

Television Camera and View of Monte Carlo — A199

1969, Nov. 25

750	A199	40c red brn, lil & bl	.35	.25

10th International Television Festival in 1970.

King Alfonso XIII, Prince Albert I and Underwater Scene — A200

1969, Nov. 25   Perf. 12½x13

751	A200	40c dk brn, blk & grnsh bl	.45	.45

50th anniv. of the International Commission for the Scientific Exploration of the Mediterranean.

Congress Building, Princes Albert I and Rainier III — A201

1970, Feb. 21   Engr.   Perf. 13

752	A201	40c gray & carmine	.35	.25

Meeting of the Interparliamentary Union, Monaco, Mar. 30-Apr. 5.

EXPO '70 Emblem, Japanese Scroll — A202

Designs (EXPO '70 Emblem and): 30c, Red-crowned crane. 40c, Torii. 70c, Cherry blossoms, horiz. 1.15fr, Palace and arms of Monaco, Osaka Castle and arms, horiz.

1970, Mar. 16

753	A202	20c brn, yel grn & car	.25	.25
754	A202	30c brn, yel grn & buff	.30	.30
755	A202	40c olive bis & pur	.35	.35
756	A202	70c lt gray & red	.45	.45
757	A202	1.15fr red & multi	.50	.50
		Nos. 753-757 (5)	1.85	1.85

Issued to publicize EXPO '70 International Exposition, Osaka, Japan, Mar. 15-Sept. 13.

Harbor Seal Pup — A203

1970, Mar. 16

758	A203	40c red lil, bl & gray	.75	.55

Protection of seal pups.

Doberman Pinscher — A204

1970, Apr. 25

759	A204	40c ocher & black	1.40	.75

International Dog Show, Monte Carlo, Apr. 25. See No. 996.

Basque Ponies — A205

Designs: 30c, Parnassius Apollo butterfly. 50c, Harbor seal in Somme Bay. 80c, Pyrenean chamois, vert. 1fr, White-tailed eagles, vert. 1.15fr, European otter, vert.

1970, May 4

760	A205	30c Prus bl & multi	.40	.25
761	A205	40c blue & multi	.65	.35
762	A205	50c grnsh bl, bis & brn	.90	.50
763	A205	80c gray grn, sl bl & brn	1.90	1.00
764	A205	1fr gray, brown & bis	2.50	2.00
765	A205	1.15fr dk brn, lt bl & yel grn	3.25	2.25
		Nos. 760-765 (6)	9.60	6.35

20th anniversary of the International Federation of Animal Protection.

MONACO

Flower Type of 1968
Roses and Anemones, by Vincent van Gogh.

1970, May 4   **Photo.**   **Perf. 12x13**
766 A185 3fr black & multi   2.00   1.75
International Flower Show, Monte Carlo.

Red Cross Type of 1969
3fr, St. Louis giving alms to the poor.

1970, May 4   **Engr.**   **Perf. 13**
767 A194 3fr dk gray, ol gray & slate grn   1.50   1.50
Issued for the Red Cross.

Europa Issue, 1970
Common Design Type

1970, May 4   Size: 26x36mm
768 CD13 40c deep rose lilac   .85   .30
769 CD13 80c bright green   2.75   .90
770 CD13 1fr deep blue   2.75   .90
   Nos. 768-770 (3)   6.35   2.10

UPU Headquarters and Monument, Bern — A206

1970, May 4
771 A206 40c brn ol, gray & bl grn   .25   .25
New UPU Headquarters in Bern opening.

Plaque and Flag on the Moon, Presidents Kennedy and Nixon — A207

Design: 80c, Astronauts and landing module on moon, and Apollo 11 emblem.

1970, May 4   **Photo.**
772 A207 40c multicolored   .60   .50
773 A207 80c multicolored   .80   .70

Man's first landing on moon, July 20, 1969. US astronauts Neil A. Armstrong and Col. Edwin E. Aldrin, Jr., with Lt. Col. Michael Collins piloting Apollo 11.

Princes of Monaco Type of 1967
Designs: 1fr, Louis I (1662-1701), by Jean Francois de Troy. 3fr, Charlotte de Gramont (1639-1678), by Sebastian Bourdon.

1970, Dec. 15   **Engr.**   **Perf. 12x13**
774 A182 1fr multicolored   .55   .55
775 A182 3fr multicolored   1.25   1.25

Painting Type of 1968
Design: 3fr, Portrait of Dédie, by Amedeo Modigliani (1884-1920).

1970, Dec. 15
776 A185 3fr multicolored   2.00   2.00

Beethoven and "Ode to Joy" — A208

1970, Dec. 15
777 A208 1.30fr brown & maroon   1.50   1.10
Ludwig van Beethoven (1770-1827), composer.

Dumas and Scene from "Three Musketeers" A209

Designs: 40c, Henri Rougier and biplane over Monaco. 80c, Alphonse de Lamartine and scenes from his works.

1970, Dec. 15
778 A209 30c blue, brown & gray   .35   .25
779 A209 40c blue, sepia & gray   .35   .25
780 A209 80c multicolored   .35   .35
   Nos. 778-780 (3)   1.05   .85

Alexandre Dumas, père (1802-70), novelist; 1st flight over the Mediterranean by Henri Rougier, 60th anniv.; publication of "Méditations Poétiques" by Alphonse de Lamartine (1790-1869), poet, 150th anniv.

Camargue Horse — A210

Horses: 20c, Anglo-Arabian thoroughbred. 30c, French saddle horse. 40c, Lippizaner. 50c, Trotter. 70c, English thoroughbred. 85c, Arabian. 1.15fr, Barbary.

1970, Dec. 15   **Engr.**   **Perf. 13**
781 A210 10c bl, ol bis & dk bl   .25   .25
782 A210 20c vio bl, brn & ol   .25   .25
783 A210 30c blue, brn & grn   .25   .25
784 A210 40c gray, ind & ol bis   .35   .25
785 A210 50c blue, dk brn &   .85   .45
786 A210 70c dk grn, ol brn & red brn   1.00   .85
787 A210 85c dk grn, ol & sl   1.75   1.50
788 A210 1.15fr blue, emer & blk   2.10   1.75
   Nos. 781-788,C77 (9)   11.05   8.55

Prince Rainier Type of 1955 and Palace Type of 1960
90c, Honor Court. 1.40fr, Aerial view of Palace.

1971   **Engr.**   **Perf. 13**
789 A83 60c plum & blk   1.75   1.00
790 A116 90c dk car, ultra & blk   1.75   1.00
791 A83 1.10fr gray & ultra   2.50   1.75
792 A116 1.40fr pur, org & grn   2.50   1.75
   Nos. 789-792 (4)   8.50   5.50

Aquatic Stadium Type of 1964-67, "1962" Omitted

1971
793 A153 26c pur, ultra & blk   .45   .25
794 A153 30c cop red, bl, lil & blk   .55   .25
795 A153 45c sl grn, vio bl & blk   .90   .35
796 A153 90c ol, Prus bl & blk   1.40   .55
   Nos. 793-796 (4)   3.30   1.40

Nos. 793-796 were issued precanceled only. See note after No. 324.
For surcharges, see Nos. 976-979.

Europa Issue, 1971
Common Design Type

1971, Sept. 6
797 CD14 50c carmine rose   2.50   .50
798 CD14 80c brt blue   6.25   .80
799 CD14 1.30fr slate green   6.25   1.50
   Nos. 797-799 (3)   15.00   2.80

Old Bridge at Sospel A211

80c, Roquebrune Castle. 1.30fr, Grimaldi Castle. 3fr, Roman Monument, La Turbie, vert. All views in Alpes-Maritimes Department, France.

1971, Sept. 6
800 A211 50c sl grn, bl & ol brn   .35   .35
801 A211 80c sl grn, sl & brn   .40   .40
802 A211 1.30fr brn, sl grn & red   .65   .65
803 A211 3fr brt bl, sl & olive   1.10   1.10
   Nos. 800-803 (4)   2.50   2.50

Protection of historic monuments.

Theodolite, Underwater Scene and Coast Line A212

1971, Sept. 6
804 A212 80c blue grn & multi   .55   .45
International Hydrographic Bureau, 50th anniv.

Sea Bird Covered with Oil — A213

1971, Sept. 6
805 A213 50c dp blue & indigo   .55   .45
Against pollution of the seas.

"Arts" (Organ Pipes and Michelangelo's Creation of Adam) A214

"Science" (Alchemist, Radar and Rocket) A215

Design: 80c, "Culture" (medieval scholar, book, film and television).

1971, Sept. 6   **Engr.**   **Perf. 13**
806 A214 30c brt bl, pur & brn   .25   .25
807 A215 50c slate & brn org   .25   .25
808 A214 80c emerald & brn   .25   .25

Prince Pierre of Monaco — A216

1971, Sept. 6   **Photo.**   **Perf. 12½x13**
809 A216 1.30fr gray green   .50   .25
   Nos. 806-809 (4)   1.25   1.00
25th anniv. of UNESCO.

Cocker Spaniel — A217

1971, Sept. 6   **Perf. 13x12½**
810 A217 50c multicolored   2.50   1.60
Intl. Dog Show. See Nos. 826, 879, 910.

Hand Holding Blood Donor Emblem — A218

1971, Sept. 6   **Engr.**   **Perf. 13**
811 A218 80c red, violet & gray   .45   .45
7th International Blood Donors Congress, Monaco, Oct. 21-24.

Red Cross Type of 1969
3fr, St. Vincent de Paul appearing to prisoners.

1971, Sept. 6
812 A194 3fr bl grn, ol grn & dp grn   1.40   1.25

Princes of Monaco Type of 1967
Designs: 1fr, Antoine I (1701-1731), by Hyacinthe Rigaud. 3fr, Marie de Lorraine (1674-1724), French School.

1972, Jan. 18   **Perf. 12x13**
813 A182 1fr multicolored   .70   .70
814 A182 3fr multicolored   1.40   1.40

Painting Type of 1968
Designs: 2fr, The Cradle, by Berthe Morisot. 3fr, Clown, by Jean Antoine Watteau.

1972, Jan. 18
815 A185 2fr green & multi   .50   .50
816 A185 3fr multicolored   1.40   1.40
No. 815 issued for 25th anniv. (in 1971) of UNICEF.

Christ Before Pilate, by Dürer — A219

1972, Jan. 18   **Perf. 13**
817 A219 2fr lt brown & blk   1.25   1.00
500th anniv. of the birth of Albrecht Dürer (1471-1528), German painter and engraver.

La Fontaine and Animals — A220

Saint-Saens and "Samson et Dalila" A221

1.30fr, Charles Baudelaire, nudes and cats.

1972, Jan. 18
818 A220 50c brn, grn & sl grn   .65   .35
819 A221 90c dk brn & yel brn   .60   .45
820 A220 1.30fr blk, red & vio brn   .95   .70
   Nos. 818-820 (3)   2.20   1.50

350th anniv. of the birth of Jean de La Fontaine (1621-1695), fabulist; 50th anniv. of the death of Camille Saint-Saens (1835-1921), composer; 150th anniv. of the birth of Charles Baudelaire (1821-1867), poet.

Father Christmas — A222

1972, Jan. 18
821 A222 30c bis, slate bl & red   .25   .25
822 A222 50c vio brn, grn & red   .25   .25
823 A222 90c ocher, indigo & red   .55   .35
   Nos. 821-823 (3)   1.05   .85

Christmas 1971.

MONACO

Battle of Lepanto — A223

1972, Jan. 18
824 A223 1fr dull bl, red & brn .65 .45

400th anniversary of the Battle of Lepanto against the Turks.

Steam and Diesel Locomotives, UIC Emblem — A224

1972, Apr. 27   Engr.   Perf. 13
825 A224 50c dk car, lilac & choc 1.00 .75

50th anniversary of the founding of the International Railroad Union (UIC).

Dog Type of 1971

1972, Apr. 27   Photo.   Perf. 13x12½
826 A217 60c Great Dane 2.50 1.60

International Dog Show.

Serene Landscape, Pollution, Destruction A225

1972, Apr. 27   Engr.   Perf. 13
827 A225 90c grn, brn & blk .60 .45

Anti-pollution fight.

Ski Jump, Sapporo '72 Emblem A226

1972, Apr. 27
828 A226 90c bl grn, dk red & blk .60 .50

11th Winter Olympic Games, Sapporo, Japan, Feb. 3-13.

Flower Type of 1968

3fr, Flowers in Vase, by Paul Cezanne.

1972, Apr. 27   Photo.   Perf. 12x13
829 A185 3fr multicolored 2.75 2.75

International Flower Show, Monte Carlo.

Red Cross Type of 1969

3fr, St. Francis of Assisi comforting poor man.

1972, Apr. 27   Engr.   Perf. 13
830 A194 3fr dk purple & brn 1.75 1.40

For the Red Cross.

Europa Issue 1972
Common Design Type

1972, Apr. 27   Perf. 12½x13
Size: 26x36mm
831 CD15 50c vio blue & org 1.75 .60
832 CD15 90c vio blue & emer 3.25 .80

Church of Sts. John and Paul (detail), by Canaletto A227

Designs: 60c, Church of St. Peter of Castello, by Francesco Guardi. 2fr, St. Mark's Square, by Bernardo Bellotto.

1972, Apr. 27   Perf. 13
Sizes: 36x48mm (30c, 2fr);
26½x48mm (60c)
833 A227 30c rose red .40 .25
834 A227 60c brt purple .50 .35
835 A227 2fr Prus blue 1.90 1.25
  Nos. 833-835 (3) 2.80 1.85

UNESCO campaign to save Venice.

Dressage — A228

Equestrian Events: 90c, Jump over fences. 1.10fr, Jump over wall. 1.40fr, Jump over gates.

1972, Apr. 27
836 A228 60c rose car, vio bl & brn .85 .85
837 A228 90c vio bl, rose car & brn 1.10 1.10
838 A228 1.10fr brn, rose car & vio bl 1.75 1.75
839 A228 1.40fr vio bl, rose car & brn 2.75 2.75
  a. Block of 4 + 2 labels 10.00 10.00

20th Olympic Games, Munich, Aug. 26-Sept. 10. Nos. 836-839 printed se-tenant in sheets of 24 stamps and 6 labels.

Auguste Escoffier and his Birthplace A229

1972, May 6   Engr.   Perf. 13
840 A229 45c black & olive .50 .25

125th anniversary of the birth of Georges Auguste Escoffier (1846-1935), French chef.

Young Drug Addict A230

1972, July 3
841 A230 50c carmine, sep & org .40 .25
842 A230 90c slate grn, sep & ind .60 .45

Fight against drug abuse.

Congress Emblem, Birds and Animals — A231

Designs: 50c, Congress emblem, Neptune, sea, earth and land creatures, horiz. 90c, Globe, land, sea and air creatures.

1972, Sept. 25
843 A231 30c ol, brt grn & car .25 .25
844 A231 50c ocher, brn & org brn .35 .25
845 A231 90c org brn, bl & ol .55 .45
  Nos. 843-845 (3) 1.15 .95

17th Intl. Zoology Cong., Monaco, 9/24-30.

Arrangement of Lilies and Palm — A232

Designs: Floral arrangements.

1972, Nov. 13   Photo.   Perf. 13
846 A232 30c orange red & multi .65 .40
847 A232 50c multicolored 1.00 .60
848 A232 90c black & multi 1.50 1.00
  Nos. 846-848 (3) 3.15 2.00

International Flower Show, Monte Carlo, May, 1973. See Nos. 894-896.

Child and Adoration of the Kings — A233

1972, Nov. 13   Engr.
849 A233 30c gray, vio bl & brt pink .25 .25
850 A233 50c dp car, lil & brn .25 .25
851 A233 90c violet bl & pur .45 .35
  Nos. 849-851 (3) .95 .85

Christmas 1972.

Louis Bleriot and his Monoplane A234

50c, Roald Amundsen & Antarctic landscape. 90c, Louis Pasteur & laboratory.

1972, Dec. 4
852 A234 30c choc & brt blue .25 .25
853 A234 50c Prus blue & ind .35 .30
854 A234 90c choc & ocher .70 .55
  Nos. 852-854 (3) 1.30 1.10

Louis Bleriot (1872-1936), French aviation pioneer (30c); Roald Amundsen (1872-1928), Norwegian polar explorer (50c); Louis Pasteur (1822-1895), French chemist and bacteriologist (90c).

Gethsemane, by Giovanni Canavesio A235

Frescoes by Canavesio, 15th century, Chapel of Our Lady of Fountains at La Brigue: 50c, Christ Stripped of His Garments. 90c, Christ Carrying the Cross. 1.40fr, Resurrection. 2fr, Crucifixion.

1972, Dec. 4
855 A235 30c bright rose .25 .25
856 A235 50c indigo .35 .25
857 A235 90c slate green .50 .50
858 A235 1.40fr bright red .65 .65
859 A235 2fr purple 1.00 .70
  Nos. 855-859 (5) 2.75 2.35

Protection of historic monuments.

Princes of Monaco Type of 1967

1fr, Jacques I, by Nicolas de Largillière. 3fr, Louise Hippolyte (1697-1731), by Jean Baptiste Vanloo.

1972, Dec. 4   Perf. 12x13
860 A182 1fr multicolored .75 .55
861 A182 3fr multicolored 1.50 1.25

Girl, Syringe, Addicts — A236

1973, Jan. 5   Engr.   Perf. 13
862 A236 50c brt bl, claret & sl grn .35 .25
863 A236 90c orange, lil & emer .55 .45

Fight against drug abuse.

Souvenir Sheet

Sts. Barbara, Dévote and Agatha, by Louis Brea A237

1973, Apr. 30
864 A237 5fr dull red 10.00 10.00

Red Cross of Monaco, 25th anniv.

Flower Type of 1968

Flowers in Vase, by Ambrosius Bosschaert.

1973, Apr. 30   Photo.   Perf. 12x13
865 A185 3.50fr multicolored 4.75 3.25

International Flower Show, Monte Carlo.

Europa Issue 1973
Common Design Type

1973, Apr. 30   Engr.   Perf. 13
Size: 36x26mm
866 CD16 50c orange 6.00 .90
867 CD16 90c blue green 9.00 1.50

Molière, Scene from "Le Malade Imaginaire" — A238

1973, Apr. 30
868 A238 20c red, blue & brn .45 .35

Tricentenary of the death of Molière (1622-1673), French actor and writer.

Costumed Players and Mask — A239

1973, Apr. 30
869 A239 60c red, lilac & blue .50 .35

5th International Amateur Theater Festival.

Virgin Mary, St. Teresa, Lisieux Basilica A240

1973, Apr. 30
870 A240 1.40fr indigo, ultra & brn .80 .55

Centenary of the birth of St. Teresa of Lisieux (Thérèse Martin, 1873-1897), Carmelite nun.

MONACO

Charles Peguy and Cathedral of Chartres — A241

1973, Apr. 30
871 A241 50c dp claret, ol brn & sl .40 .35

Centenary of the birth of Charles Pierre Peguy (1873-1914), French writer.

Colette, Books and Cat — A242

Designs: No. 873, Eugene Ducretet and transmission from Eiffel Tower to Pantheon. 45c, Jean Henri Fabre and insects. 50c, Blaise Pascal, vert. 60c, Radar installation and telegraph wire insulators. No. 877, William Webb Ellis and rugby. No. 878, Sir George Cayley and early model plane.

1973, Apr. 30
872	A242	30c dp org, bl & dk bl	.80	.50
873	A242	30c brown & multi	.25	.25
874	A242	45c dp blue & multi	1.25	1.25
875	A242	50c vio bl, lil & dk pur	.25	.25
876	A242	60c brn, bl blk & brt bl	.35	.35
877	A242	90c brown & car rose	.50	.50
878	A242	90c red & multi	.50	.50
		Nos. 872-878 (7)	3.90	3.60

Anniversaries: Colette (1873-1954), French writer (#872); 75th anniv. of 1st Hertzian wave transmission (#873); Fabre (1823-1915), entomologist (45c); Pascal (1623-1662), scientist and philosopher (50c); 5th Intl. Telecommunications Day (60c); Sesquicentennial of the invention of rugby (#877); Cayley (1821-95), aviation pioneer (#878).

Dog Type of 1971

45c, German shepherd.

1973, Apr. 30 Photo. Perf. 13x12½
879 A217 45c multicolored 9.00 5.00

International Dog Show.

The First Crèche, by Giotto — A243

Paintings of the Nativity by: 45c, School of Filippo Lippi. 50c, Giotto. 1fr, 15th century miniature, vert. 2fr, Fra Angelico, vert.

Perf. 13x12, 12x13
1973, Nov. 12 Engr.
880	A243	30c purple	.40	.35
881	A243	45c rose magenta	.60	.60
882	A243	50c brown orange	.75	.75
883	A243	1fr slate green	.90	.90
884	A243	2fr olive green	2.25	1.90
		Nos. 880-884, C78 (6)	7.65	6.75

750th anniversary of the first crèche assembled by St. Francis of Assisi.

Picnic and View of Monte Carlo — A244

Designs: 20c, Dance around maypole, vert. 30c, "U Brandi" folk dance. 45c, Dance around St. John's fire. 50c, Blessing of the Christmas bread. 60c, Blessing of the sea. 1fr, Good Friday procession.

1973, Nov. 12 Perf. 13
885	A244	10c sl grn, dk bl & sep	.25	.25
886	A244	20c blue, ol & lil	.25	.25
887	A244	30c lt grn, bl & brn	.25	.25
888	A244	45c dk brn, vio & red brn	.25	.25
889	A244	50c black, brn & ver	.25	.25
890	A244	60c blue, mag & vio bl	.50	.50
891	A244	1fr ind, vio & ol bis	.65	.65
		Nos. 885-891 (7)	2.40	2.40

Monegasque customs.

Princes of Monaco Type of 1967

Paintings of Charlotte Grimaldi, by Pierre Gobert, 1733: No. 892, in court dress, No. 893, in nun's habit.

1973, Nov. 12 Perf. 12x13
892	A182	2fr multicolored	1.75	1.50
893	A182	2fr multicolored	1.75	1.50

Flower Type of 1972

Designs: Floral arrangements.

1973, Nov. 12 Photo. Perf. 13
894	A232	45c vio blue & multi	1.25	.80
895	A232	60c dk brown & multi	2.00	1.10
896	A232	1fr brown org & multi	3.50	2.00
		Nos. 894-896 (3)	6.75	3.90

Intl. Flower Show, Monte Carlo, May 1974.

Children, Syringes, Drug Addicts — A245

1973, Nov. 12 Engr.
897	A245	50c blue, grn & brn	.25	.25
898	A245	90c red, brn & indigo	.70	.45

Fight against drug abuse.

Souvenir Sheet

Prince Rainier III — A246

1974, May 8 Engr. Imperf.
899 A246 10fr black 6.50 6.50

25th anniv. of the accession of Prince Rainier III.

Art from Around the World — A247

70c, Hands holding letters. 1.10fr, Famous buildings, Statue of Liberty and Sphinx.

1974, May 8 Perf. 13
900	A247	50c choc & org brn	.35	.25
901	A247	70c aqua & multi	.35	.45
902	A247	1.10fr indigo & multi	.80	.70
		Nos. 900-902 (3)	1.50	1.40

Centenary of the Universal Postal Union.

King of Rome (Napoleon's Son), by Bosio — A248

Europa: 1.10fr, Madame Elisabeth (sister of Louis XVI), by Francois Josef Bosio.

1974, May 8
903	A248	45c slate grn & sep	1.50	.50
904	A248	1.10fr brn & ol brn	3.00	.85
a.		Souv. sheet, 5 #903, 5 #904	45.00	25.00

Red Cross Type of 1969

Design: St. Bernard of Menthon rescuing mountain traveler.

1974, May 8
905 A194 3fr Prus bl & vio brn 1.50 1.25

For the Red Cross.

Henri Farman and Farman Planes — A249

Designs: 40c, Guglielmo Marconi, circuit diagram and ships which conducted first tests. 45c, Ernest Duchesne and penicillin. 50c, Fernand Forest and 4-cylinder motor.

1974, May 8
906	A249	30c multicolored	.25	.25
907	A249	40c multicolored	.35	.25
908	A249	45c multicolored	.35	.25
909	A249	50c multicolored	.35	.25
		Nos. 906-909 (4)	1.30	1.00

Farman (1874-1934), French aviation pioneer; Marconi (1874-1937), Italian inventor; Duchesne (1874-1912), French biologist; Forest (1851-1914), inventor.

Dog Type of 1971

1974, May 8 Photo. Perf. 13x12½
910 A217 60c Schnauzer 5.00 3.25

Intl. Dog Show, Monte Carlo, Apr. 6-7.

Ronsard and Scenes from his Sonnet à Hélène — A250

1974, May 8 Engr. Perf. 13
911 A250 70c choc & dk car .55 .25

450th anniversary of the birth of Pierre de Ronsard (1524-1585), French poet.

Winston Churchill — A251

1974, May 8
912 A251 1fr gray & brn .65 .45

Centenary of the birth of Sir Winston Churchill (1874-1965), statesman.

Palaces of Monaco and Vienna — A252

1974, May 8
913 A252 2fr multicolored 1.40 1.00

60th anniversary of the first International Police Congress, Monaco, Apr. 1914.

The Box, by Auguste Renoir — A253

Rising Sun, by Claude Monet — A254

Impressionist Paintings: No. 915, Dancing Class, by Edgar Degas. No. 917, Entrance to Voisins Village, by Camille Pissarro. No. 918, House of the Hanged Man, by Paul Cezanne. No. 919, The Flooding of Port Marly, by Alfred Sisley.

Perf. 12x13, 13x12
1974, Nov. 12 Engr.
914	A253	1fr multicolored	3.00	2.50
915	A253	1fr multicolored	3.00	2.50
916	A254	2fr multicolored	3.00	2.50
917	A254	2fr multicolored	3.00	2.50
918	A254	2fr multicolored	3.00	2.50
919	A254	2fr multicolored	3.00	2.50
		Nos. 914-919 (6)	18.00	15.00

Trainer and Tigers — A255

Prancing Horses — A256

Perf. 13x12½, 12½x13
1974, Nov. 12
920	A255	2c shown	.25	.25
921	A256	3c shown	.25	.25
922	A256	5c Elephants	.25	.25
923	A256	45c Equestrian act	.25	.25
924	A255	70c Clowns	.70	.70
925	A256	1.10fr Jugglers	1.75	1.75
926	A256	5fr Trapeze act	3.50	3.50
		Nos. 920-926 (7)	6.95	6.95

International Circus Festival.

Honoré II Coin — A257

1974, Nov. 12 Perf. 13
927 A257 60c rose red & blk .50 .35

350th anniversary of coins of Monaco.

Underwater Fauna and Flora — A258

Designs: 45c, Fish, and marine life. 1.10fr, Coral.

1974, Nov. 12 Photo. Perf. 13x12½
Size: 35x25mm
928 A258 45c multicolored 1.00 .65
Size: 48x27mm
Perf. 13
929	A258	70c multicolored	1.25	1.10
930	A258	1.10fr multicolored	1.90	1.50
		Nos. 928-930 (3)	4.15	3.25

Congress of the International Commission for the Scientific Exploration of the Mediterranean, Monaco, Dec. 6-14.

A259

MONACO

Floral Arrangements — A260

1974, Nov. 12   Perf. 13x12½
931	A259	70c multicolored	.85	.60
932	A260	1.10fr multicolored	1.25	.90

International Flower Show, Monte Carlo, May 1975. See Nos. 1003-1004, 1084-1085.

Prince Rainier III — A261

1974-78   Engr.   Perf. 13
933	A261	60c slate green	1.25	.35
934	A261	80c red	1.25	.45
935	A261	80c brt green	.45	.25
936	A261	1fr brown	2.00	.90
937	A261	1fr scarlet	.50	.30
938	A261	1fr slate green	.50	.35
939	A261	1.20fr violet bl	5.00	1.25
940	A261	1.20fr red	.65	.40
941	A261	1.25fr blue	.90	.75
942	A261	1.50fr black	.80	.65
943	A261	1.70fr dp blue	1.00	.70
944	A261	2fr dk purple	3.50	2.25
945	A261	2.10fr olive bister	1.25	.75
946	A261	2.50fr indigo	2.00	1.50
947	A261	9fr brt violet	4.50	3.50
		Nos. 933-947 (15)	25.55	14.35

Issued: 60c, #934, 936, 939, 2fr, Dec. 23; #935, 937, 1.25fr, 2.50fr, Jan. 10, 1977; #938, 940, 1.50fr, 1.70fr, 2.10fr, 9fr, Aug. 18, 1978. See Nos. 1200-1204, 1255-1256.

Monte Carlo Beach A262

Prince Albert I Statue and Museum A264

948	A262	25c shown	.90	.40
949	A264	50c multi	1.40	.80
950	A262	1.10fr Like #948 ('77)	2.25	1.10
951	A264	1.40fr shown	1.75	1.00
952	A262	1.70fr multi	2.25	2.00
953	A264	3fr multi	5.50	3.00
954	A262	5.50fr multi	11.00	5.00
		Nos. 948-954 (7)	25.05	13.30

1974-77

50c, Clock tower. 1.70fr, All Saints' Tower. 3fr, Fort Antoine. 5.50fr, La Condamine (view).

Issue: 1.10fr, Jan. 10; others, Dec. 23. See Nos. 1005-1008, 1030-1033, 1069-1072, 1095-1098, 1138-1152.

Haageocereus — A265

1974, Dec. 23   Photo.   Perf. 12½x13
955	A265	10c shown	.40	.40
956	A265	20c Matucana	.40	.40
957	A265	30c Parodia	.40	.40
958	A265	85c Mediolobivia	2.25	1.50
959	A265	1.90fr Matucana	3.00	2.25
960	A265	4fr Echinocereus	5.75	4.50
		Nos. 955-960 (6)	12.20	9.45

Plants from Monaco Botanical Gardens.

Europa Issue

Sailor, by Philibert Florence A266

St. Dévote, by Ludovic Brea A267

1975, May 13   Engr.   Perf. 13
961	A266	80c brt red lilac	1.75	.50
962	A267	1.20fr brt blue	2.25	.85
a.		Souv. sheet, 5 ea #961-962	40.00	20.00

Red Cross Type of 1969

Design: St. Bernardino of Siena (1380-1444) burying the dead.

1975, May 13
963	A194	4fr pur & Prus bl	2.75	1.75

For the Red Cross.

Carmen, at the Tavern — A268

Scenes from Carmen: 30c, Prologue, vert. 80c, The smugglers' hide-out. 1.40fr, Entrance to bull ring.

1975, May 13
964	A268	30c multicolored	.25	.25
965	A268	60c multicolored	.35	.25
966	A268	80c multicolored	.55	.45
967	A268	1.40fr multicolored	1.00	.90
		Nos. 964-967 (4)	2.15	1.85

Centenary of first performance of opera Carmen by George Bizet (1838-1875).

Louis de Saint-Simon A269

Albert Schweitzer A270

1975, May 13
968	A269	40c bluish black	.35	.30
969	A270	60c black & dull red	.65	.50

300th birth anniversary of Louis de Saint-Simon (1675-1755), statesman and writer, and birth centenary of Albert Schweitzer (1875-1965), medical missionary.

ARPHILA 75 Emblem, G Clef — A271

1975, May 13
970	A271	80c sepia & org brn	.70	.45

ARPHILA 75 International Philatelic Exhibition, Paris, June 6-16.

Seagull and Rising Sun — A272

1975, May 13   Photo.
971	A272	85c multicolored	.85	.65

Oceanexpo 75, International Exhibition, Okinawa, July 20, 1975-Jan. 1976.

Charity Label and "1f" Destroying Cancer — A273

1975, May 13   Engr.
972	A273	1fr multicolored	.85	.60

Fight against cancer.

Jesus with Crown of Thorns, Holy Year Emblem — A274

1975, May 13
973	A274	1.15fr lilac, bis & ind	1.00	.70

Holy Year 1975.

Villa Sauber, by Charles Garnier — A275

1975, May 13
974	A275	1.20fr multicolored	1.10	.70

European Architectural Heritage Year 1975.

Woman, Globe, IWY Emblem — A276

1975, May 13
975	A276	1.20fr multicolored	1.10	.70

International Women's Year.

Nos. 793-796 Surcharged

1975, Apr. 1   Engr.   Perf. 13
976	A153	42c on 26c multi	2.50	1.10
977	A153	48c on 30c multi	3.25	1.75
978	A153	70c on 45c multi	3.75	2.25
979	A153	1.35fr on 90c multi	5.75	3.00
		Nos. 976-979 (4)	15.25	8.10

Nos. 976-979 were issued precanceled only. See note after No. 324.

Rolls Royce "Silver Ghost" 1907 A277

10c, Hispano Suiza, 1926. 20c, Isotta Fraschini, 1928. 30c, Cord L. 29. 50c, Voisin, 1930. 60c, Duesenberg, 1933. 80c, Bugatti, 1938. 85c, Delahaye, 1940. 1.20fr, Cisitalia, 1940. 1.40fr, Mercedes Benz, 1955. 5.50fr, Lamborghini, 1974.

1975, Nov.   Engr.   Perf. 13
980	A277	5c shown	.45	.45
981	A277	10c multi	.45	.45
982	A277	20c multi	.45	.45
983	A277	30c multi	.45	.45
984	A277	50c multi	.90	.90
985	A277	60c multi	1.40	1.40
986	A277	80c multi	1.60	1.60
987	A277	85c multi	1.60	1.60
988	A277	1.20fr multi	2.75	2.75
989	A277	1.40fr multi	3.50	3.50
990	A277	5.50fr multi	9.00	9.00
		Nos. 980-990 (11)	22.55	22.55

Development of the automobile.

Princes of Monaco Type of 1967

Paintings (Unknown Artists): 2fr, Prince Honoré III (1733-1795). 4fr, Princess Catherine de Brignole (1759-1813).

1975, Nov.
991	A182	2fr multicolored	1.90	1.10
992	A182	4fr multicolored	3.75	3.00

Caged Dog — A278

Designs: 80c, Cat chased up a tree, vert. 1.20fr, Horses pulling heavy load.

1975, Nov.
993	A278	60c black & brown	.90	.70
994	A278	80c blk, gray & brn	1.40	1.00
995	A278	1.20fr mag & sl grn	2.25	1.60
		Nos. 993-995 (3)	4.55	3.30

125th anniv. of the Grammont (J. P. Delmas Grammont) Law against cruelty to animals.

Dog Type of 1970

1975, Nov.
996	A204	60c Poodle	4.00	3.25

International Dog Show, Monte Carlo.

Maurice Ravel — A279

1.20fr, Johann Strauss and dancers.

1975, Nov.
997	A279	60c maroon & sepia	1.00	.60
998	A279	1.20fr maroon & indigo	2.10	1.40

Maurice Ravel (1875-1937), birth centenary, and Johann Strauss (1804-1849), sesquicentennial of birth, composers.

Clown — A280

1975, Nov.   Photo.   Perf. 12½x13
999	A280	80c multicolored	1.25	.55

2nd Intl. Circus Festival, Monte Carlo, Dec. 1975.

Honoré II Florin, 1640 A281

1975, Nov.   Engr.   Perf. 13
1000	A281	80c slate & gray	.75	.55

See Nos. 1040, 1088, 1234.

Ampère and Ampère Balance — A282

1975, Nov.
1001	A282	85c ultra & indigo	.75	.60

André Marie Ampère (1775-1836), physicist, birth bicentennial.

Lamentation for the Dead Christ, by Michelangelo A283

1975, Nov.
1002	A283	1.40fr black & ol gray	1.25	.80

Michelangelo Buonarroti (1475-1564), Italian sculptor, painter and architect.

MONACO

Flower Types of 1974
Designs: Floral arrangements.

1975, Nov.	Photo.	Perf. 13x12½
1003 A259	60c multicolored	1.10 .60
1004 A260	80c multicolored	1.60 .85

Intl. Flower Show, Monte Carlo, May 1976.

Clock Tower Type, 1974

1976, Jan. 26	Engr.	Perf. 13
1005 A263	50c brown lake	.65 .35
1006 A263	60c olive green	.75 .50
1007 A263	90c purple	1.10 .75
1008 A263	1.60fr brt blue	1.60 1.40
Nos. 1005-1008 (4)		4.10 3.00

Nos. 1005-1008 were issued precanceled only. See note after No. 324.

Prince Pierre — A284

André Maurois and Colette A285

Writers: 25c, Jean and Jerome Tharaud. 30c, Emile Henriot, Marcel Pagnol, Georges Duhamel. 50c, Philippe Heriat, Jules Supervielle, L. Pierard. 60c, Roland Dorgeles, Marcel Achard, G. Bauer. 80c, Franz Hellens, André Billy, Msgr. Grente. 1.20fr, Jean Giono, Louis Pasteur-Vallery-Radot, Maurice Garcon.

1976, May 3	Engr.	Perf. 13
1009 A284	10c black	.25 .25
1010 A285	20c red & slate	.30 .25
1011 A285	25c red, dk bl & blk	.30 .25
1012 A285	30c brown	.30 .30
1013 A285	50c brn, red & vio bl	.30 .25
1014 A285	60c grn, brn & lt brn	.35 .30
1015 A285	80c blk & mag	.70 .55
1016 A285	1.20fr blk, vio & cl	1.10 .85
Nos. 1009-1016 (8)		3.60 3.00

Literary Council of Monaco, 25th anniv.

Dachshunds A286

1976, May 3		Photo.
1017 A286	60c multicolored	5.00 4.25

International Dog Show, Monte Carlo.

Bridge Table, Coast — A287

1976, May 3		Engr.
1018 A287	60c multicolored	.60 .45

Fifth Bridge Olympiade, Monte Carlo.

A. G. Bell, Telephone, 1876, Satellite Dish — A288

1976, May 3		
1019 A288	80c multicolored	.55 .35

Centenary of first telephone call by Alexander Graham Bell, Mar. 10, 1876.

Federation Emblem A289

1976, May 3		
1020 A289	1.20fr multicolored	.85 .55

International Federation of Philately (F.I.P.), 50th anniversary.

US Liberty Bell Type of 1926 A290

1976, May 3		
1021 A290	1.70fr carmine & blk	1.40 .95

American Bicentennial.

Fritillaria, by Vincent van Gogh — A291

1976, May 3	Photo.	Perf. 12x13
1022 A291	3fr multicolored	8.00 5.50

Intl. Flower Show, Monte Carlo, May 1976.

Plate with Lemon Branch — A292

1976, May 3		Perf. 12½x13
1023 A292	80c sal & multi	1.25 .35
1024 A292	1.20fr ultra & multi	1.75 .50
a. Souv. sheet of 10, 5 each #1023-1024		32.50 25.00

Europa: 1.20fr, The Peddler, 19th century figurine, and CEPT emblem.

21st Summer Olympic Games, Montreal, Canada — A293

60c, Diving. 80c, Athlete on parallel bars. 85c, Hammer throw. 1.20fr, Rowing, horiz. 1.70fr, Boxing, horiz.

1976, May 3	Engr.	Perf. 13
1025 A293	60c multicolored	.35 .35
1026 A293	80c multicolored	.45 .35
1027 A293	85c multicolored	.55 .45
1028 A293	1.20fr multicolored	.80 .60
1029 A293	1.70fr multicolored	1.40 1.10
a. Souv. sheet of 5, #1025-1029, perf. 14		4.25 4.25
Nos. 1025-1029 (5)		3.55 2.85

Clock Tower Type, 1974

1976, Sept. 1	Engr.	Perf. 13
1030 A263	52c bister	.45 .25
1031 A263	62c red lilac	.55 .45
1032 A263	95c scarlet	1.10 .55
1033 A263	1.70fr blue green	1.75 1.00
Nos. 1030-1033 (4)		3.85 2.25

Nos. 1030-1033 were issued precanceled only. See note after No. 324.

Princes of Monaco Type of 1967

Paintings: 2fr, Honoré IV (1815-1819), by Francois Lemoyne. 4fr, Louise d'Aumont-Mazarin (1750-1826), by Marie Verroust.

1976, Nov. 9		Perf. 12½x13
1035 A182	2fr violet brown	2.00 1.50
1036 A182	4fr multicolored	3.00 2.00

Red Cross Type of 1969
Design: St. Louise de Marillac and children.

1976, Nov. 9		Perf. 13
1037 A194	4fr grn, gray & plum	2.50 2.00

St. Vincent de Paul, View of Monaco — A294

1976, Nov. 9		
1038 A294	60c multicolored	.45 .35

St. Vincent de Paul Conference, Monaco, July 31, 1876, centenary.

Marquise de Sevigné — A295

1976, Nov. 9		
1039 A295	80c multicolored	.55 .35

Marie de Rabutin-Chantal, Marquise de Sevigné (1626-1696), writer.

Coin Type of 1975
Design: 80c, Honoré II 2-gros coin.

1976, Nov. 9		
1040 A281	80c grn & steel bl	.75 .45

Richard E. Byrd, Roald Amundsen, North Pole — A296

1976, Nov. 9		
1041 A296	85c olive, blk & bl	1.75 1.25

1st flights over the North Pole, 50th anniv.

Gulliver Holding King, Queen and Enemy Fleet — A297

1976, Nov. 9		
1042 A297	1.20fr indigo, bl & brn	.80 .55

250th anniversary of the publication of Gulliver's Travels, by Jonathan Swift.

Child and Christmas Decorations A298

1976, Nov. 9		Perf. 13x12½
1043 A298	60c multicolored	.40 .25
1044 A298	1.20fr multicolored	.85 .50

Christmas 1976.

"Trapped by Drugs" — A299

1976, Nov. 9		
1045 A299	80c grn, ultra & org	.60 .35
1046 A299	1.20fr red brn, vio & car	.85 .50

Fight against drug abuse.

Floral Arrangement — A300

Design: 1fr, Floral arrangement. Designs by Princess Grace.

1976, Nov. 9	Photo.	Perf. 13½x13
1047 A300	80c yellow grn & multi	1.50 .90
1048 A300	1fr lt blue & multi	2.25 1.50

International Flower Show, Monte Carlo, May 1977. See Nos. 1124-1125, 1191.

Clown and Circus Acts — A301

1976, Nov. 9		
1049 A301	1fr multi	1.90 1.10

3rd Intl. Circus Festival, Dec. 26-30.

L'Hirondelle I — A302

Prince Albert I — A303

Designs (Gouaches by Louis Tinayre): 30c, Crew of L'Hirondelle. 80c, L'Hirondelle in Storm. 1fr, The Helmsman, vert. 1.25fr, L'Hirondelle in Storm. 1.40fr, Shrimp Fishermen in Boat. 1.90fr, Hauling in the Net, vert. 2.50fr, Catching Opah Fish.

1977, May 3	Engr.	Perf. 13
1050 A302	10c multicolored	.25 .25
1051 A303	20c multicolored	.25 .25
1052 A302	30c multicolored	.25 .25
1053 A302	80c multicolored	.35 .35
1054 A302	1fr multicolored	.90 .90
1055 A302	1.25fr multicolored	1.10 1.10
1056 A302	1.40fr multicolored	1.40 .75
1057 A302	1.90fr multicolored	1.75 1.75
1058 A302	2.50fr multicolored	2.75 2.75
Nos. 1050-1058 (9)		9.00 8.35

75th anniversary of publication of "The Career of a Sailor," by Prince Albert I. See Nos. 1073-1081.

Pyreneean Mountain Dogs A304

1977, May 3		Photo.
1059 A304	80c multicolored	5.00 3.75

International Dog Show, Monte Carlo. See No. 1199.

MONACO

Motherhood, by Mary Cassatt — A305

1977, May 3   Engr.
1060   A305   80c multicolored   .90   .90

World Association of the Friends of Children.

Archers, Target and Monte Carlo — A306

1977, May 3
1061   A306   1.10fr multicolored   .80   .55

10th Intl. Rainier III Archery Championships.

Spirit of St. Louis and Lindbergh — A307

1977, May 3
1062   A307   1.90fr multicolored   1.75   1.25

50th anniversary of first transatlantic flight by Charles Lindbergh.

The Dock at Deauville, by Dufy — A308

1977, May 3   Photo.
1063   A308   2fr multicolored   4.50   3.00

Raoul Dufy (1877-1953), painter, birth centenary.

Young Girl, by Rubens — A309

Rubens Paintings: 1fr, Duke of Buckingham. 1.40fr, Rubens' son Nicolas, 2 years old.

1977, May 3   Engr.
1064   A309   80c multicolored   .65   .55
1065   A309   1fr multicolored   .95   .70
1066   A309   1.40fr multicolored   1.75   1.25
    Nos. 1064-1066 (3)   3.35   2.50

Peter Paul Rubens (1577-1640).

Helmet Tower, Monaco — A310

Europa: 1.40fr, St. Michael's Church, Menton.

1977, May 3
1067   A310   1fr multicolored   1.25   .50
1068   A310   1.40fr multicolored   3.00   .80
    a. Souv. sheet, 5 each #1067-1068   35.00   25.00

Clock Tower Type of 1974

1977, Apr. 1   Engr.   Perf. 13
1069   A263   54c brt green   .45   .35
1070   A263   68c orange   .55   .45
1071   A263   1.05fr olive   1.10   .55
1072   A263   1.85fr brown   1.75   1.00
    Nos. 1069-1072 (4)   3.85   2.35

Nos. 1069-1072 were issued precanceled only. See note after No. 324.

Career of a Sailor Types of 1977

Designs (Gouaches by Louis Tinayre): 10c, Yacht Princess Alice II, Kiel harbor. 20c, Laboratory on board ship. 30c, Yacht amidst ice floes. 80c, Crew in arctic outfits. 1fr, Yacht in polar region. 1.25fr, Yacht in snow storm. 1.40fr, Building camp on ice. 1.90fr, Yacht under steam amidst ice floes. 3fr, Yacht passing iceberg.

1977, Nov.   Engr.   Perf. 13
1073   A302   10c blk & brt bl   .25   .25
1074   A302   20c Prus blue   .25   .25
1075   A302   30c blk & brt bl   .25   .25
1076   A303   80c multicolored   .55   .45
1077   A302   1fr brt grn & blk   .70   .55
1078   A302   1.25fr vio, sep & blk   1.00   .75
1079   A302   1.40fr ol, bl & pur   1.60   1.25
1080   A302   1.90fr blk & brt bl   2.75   2.25
1081   A302   3fr dk grn, ol & brt bl   4.00   3.00
    Nos. 1073-1081 (9)   11.35   9.00

75th anniversary of publication of "The Career of a Sailor," by Prince Albert I.

Santa Claus — A311

1977, Nov.
1082   A311   80c multicolored   .60   .25
1083   A311   1.40fr multicolored   .80   .40

Christmas 1977.

Flowers Types of 1974

Designs: 80c, Snapdragons and bellflowers. 1fr, Ikebana arrangement.

1977, Nov.   Photo.   Perf. 13½x13
1084   A259   80c multicolored   1.25   .70
1085   A260   1fr multicolored   1.75   1.10

Intl. Flower Show, Monte Carlo, May 1978.

Face (Van Gogh), Syringe, Hallucination Pattern — A312

1977, Nov.   Engr.   Perf. 13
1086   A312   1fr multicolored   .75   .45

Fight against drug abuse.

Clown, Flags of Participants — A313

1977, Nov.   Photo.   Perf. 13½x13
1087   A313   1fr multicolored   1.75   1.25

Fourth International Circus Festival. Monte Carlo, December 1977.

Coin Type of 1975

Design: 80c, Doubloon of Honoré II, 1648.

1977, Nov.   Engr.   Perf. 13
1088   A281   80c lil & brn   .70   .45

Mediterranean Landscape and Industrial Pollution — A314

1977, Nov.
1089   A314   1fr multicolored   .85   .50

Protection of the Mediterranean. Meeting of the UN Mediterranean Environmental Protection Group, Monte Carlo, Nov. 28-Dec. 6.

Men Spreading Tar, Dr. Guglielminetti, 1903 Car — A315

1977, Nov.
1090   A315   1.10fr multicolored   .80   .45

75th anniversary of first tarred roads, invented by Swiss Dr. Guglielminetti.

View of Monaco and Tennis Emblem — A316

First Match at Wimbledon and Stadium — A317

1977, Nov.
1091   A316   1fr multicolored   1.25   .70
1092   A317   1.40fr multicolored   1.50   1.00

Lawn Tennis Federation of Monaco, 50th anniv. and cent. of 1st intl. tennis match at Wimbledon.

Prince of Monaco Type of 1967

Honoré V (1819-1841), by Marie Verroust.

1977, Nov.   Perf. 12½x13
1093   A182   6fr multicolored   4.50   3.25

Red Cross Type of 1969

Design: 4fr, St. John Bosco and boys.

1977, Nov.   Perf. 13
1094   A194   4fr multicolored   2.50   2.00

Nos. 1069-1072 Surcharged

1978, Jan. 17
1095   A263   58c on 54c brt grn   .55   .40
1096   A263   73c on 68c orange   .90   .55
1097   A263   1.15fr on 1.05fr olive   1.25   .90
1098   A263   2fr on 1.85fr brn   2.10   1.40
    Nos. 1095-1098 (4)   4.80   3.25

See note after No. 324.

Illustrations, Novels by Jules Verne — A318

5c, Shipwreck. 25c, The Abandoned Ship, from "Mysterious Island". 30c, Secret of the Island. 80c, Robur, the Conqueror. 1fr, Master Zacharius. 1.40fr, The Castle in the Carpathians. 1.70fr, The Children of Capt. Grant. 5.50fr, Jules Verne and allegories.

1978, May 2   Engr.   Perf. 13
1099   A318   5c multicolored   .25   .25
1100   A318   25c multicolored   .30   .25
1101   A318   30c multicolored   .30   .25
1102   A318   80c multicolored   .55   .50
1103   A318   1fr multicolored   1.00   .60
1104   A318   1.40fr multicolored   1.20   .85
1105   A318   1.70fr multicolored   1.75   1.40
1106   A318   5.50fr multicolored   4.25   3.25
    Nos. 1099-1106 (8)   9.60   7.35

Jules Verne (1828-1905), science fiction writer, birth sesquicentennial.

Congress Center and Monte Carlo — A319

1.40fr, Congress Center, view from the sea.

1978, May 2
1107   A319   1fr multicolored   .60   .50
1108   A319   1.40fr multicolored   .80   .50

Inauguration of Monaco Congress Center.

Soccer Players and Globe — A320

1978, May 2
1109   A320   1fr multicolored   .75   .75

11th World Soccer Cup Championship, Argentina, June 1-25.

Vivaldi and St. Mark's Place, Venice — A321

1978, May 2
1110   A321   1fr dk brown & red   .90   .80

Antonio Vivaldi (1675?-1741), Italian violinist and composer.

Control Ship and Grimaldi Palace — A322

1fr, Map of coastal area and city emblems.

1978, May 2   Size: 26x36mm
1111   A322   80c multi   .60   .50
    Size: 48x27mm
1112   A322   1fr multi, horiz.   .60   .50

Protection of the environment, signing of "Ra Mo Ge" agreement for the protection of the Mediterranean Coast between Saint-Raphael, France, and Genoa, Italy (including Monaco).

Monaco Cathedral — A323

Europa: 1.40fr, View of Principality from East.

1978, May 2   Perf. 12½x13
1113   A323   1fr multicolored   1.75   .40
1114   A323   1.40fr multicolored   3.25   .70
    a. Souv. sheet, 5 each #1113-1114   40.00   25.00

Cinderella — A324

MONACO

Mother Goose Tales: 25c, Puss in Boots. 30c, Sleeping Beauty. 80c, Fairy tale princess. 1fr, Little Red Riding Hood. 1.40fr, Bluebeard. 1.70fr, Tom Thumb. 1.90fr, Riquet with the Tuft of Hair. 2.50fr, The Fairies.

1978, Nov. 8		Engr.		Perf. 13	
1115	A324	5c multicolored		.25	.25
1116	A324	25c multicolored		.25	.25
1117	A324	30c multicolored		.25	.25
1118	A324	80c multicolored		.60	.50
1119	A324	1fr multicolored		.80	.60
1120	A324	1.40fr multicolored		1.00	.85
1121	A324	1.70fr multicolored		1.25	1.10
1122	A324	1.90fr multicolored		1.75	1.25
1123	A324	2.50fr multicolored		2.40	1.75
		Nos. 1115-1123 (9)		8.55	6.80

Charles Perrault (1628-1703), compiler of Mother Goose Tales.

Flower Type of 1976

Van Gogh Paintings: 1fr, Sunflowers. 1.70fr, Iris.

1978, Nov. 8		Photo.		Perf. 12½x13	
1124	A300	1fr multicolored		2.50	2.25
1125	A300	1.70fr multicolored		3.50	2.25

Intl. Flower show, Monte Carlo, May 1979, and 125th birth anniv. of Vincent van Gogh (1853-1890), Dutch painter.

Afghan Hound — A325

Design: 1.20fr, Russian wolfhound.

1978, Nov. 8				Perf. 13x12½	
1126	A325	1fr multicolored		3.00	2.40
1127	A325	1.20fr multicolored		4.50	3.00

International Dog Show, Monte Carlo.

Child Holding Gift of Shoes — A326

1978, Nov. 8		Engr.		Perf. 12½x13	
1128	A326	1fr multicolored		.80	.50

Christmas 1978.

Catherine and William Booth, Salvation Army Band — A327

1978, Nov. 8		Engr.		Perf. 13	
1129	A327	1.70fr multicolored		1.20	1.00

Centenary of founding of Salvation Army.

Trained Seals — A328

1fr, Lions, vert. 1.40fr, Equestrian act. 1.90fr, Monkey music band. 2.40fr, Trapeze act.

1978, Nov. 8				Perf. 13x12½	
1130	A328	80c multicolored		.70	.50
1131	A328	1fr multicolored		1.00	.80
1132	A328	1.40fr multicolored		1.60	1.00
1133	A328	1.90fr multicolored		2.00	2.00
1134	A328	2.40fr multicolored		2.75	2.40
		Nos. 1130-1134 (5)		8.05	6.70

5th Intl. Circus Festival, Monte Carlo.

Princes of Monaco Type of 1967

Paintings: 2fr, Florestan I (1841-1856), by G. Dauphin. 4fr, Caroline Gilbert de Lametz (1793-1879), by Marie Verroust.

1978, Nov. 8		Engr.		Perf. 12½x13	
1135	A182	2fr multicolored		2.00	1.40
1136	A182	4fr multicolored		3.00	3.00

Souvenir Sheet

Henri Dunant and Battle Scene — A329

1978, Nov. 8		Engr.		Perf. 13	
1137	A329	5fr multicolored		4.25	4.25

Henri Dunant (1828-1910), founder of Red Cross.

View Types of 1974

25c, All Saints' Tower. 65c, Monte Carlo Beach. 70c, Exotic Garden, cacti. 1.10fr, Palais de Justice. 1.30fr, Cathedral. 1.50fr, Prince Albert Statue and Museum. 1.80fr, La Condamine. 2.30fr, Palace. 6.50fr, Monte Carlo Auditorium.

1978-80

1138	A262	25c multi		.25	.25
1139	A262	65c multi		.25	.25
1140	A264	70c multi ('80)		.55	.35
1142	A262	1.10fr multi ('80)		.60	.35
1144	A264	1.30fr multi		.75	.40
1145	A264	1.50fr multi ('80)		1.10	1.10
1146	A262	1.80fr multi		1.10	.90
1148	A262	2.30fr multi ('80)		1.90	1.50
1152	A262	6.50fr multi		3.00	2.75
		Nos. 1138-1152 (9)		9.50	7.85

Convention Center, Monte Carlo — A330

1978-79

1154	A330	61c vermilion		.30	.25
1155	A330	64c green		.35	.25
1156	A330	68c brt blue		.30	.25
1157	A330	78c dp rose lilac		.35	.25
1158	A330	83c violet blue		.30	.25
1159	A330	88c orange		.35	.25
1160	A330	1.25fr brown		.60	.45
1161	A330	1.30fr purple		.75	.35
1162	A330	1.40fr brt yel grn		.55	.35
1163	A330	2.10fr violet blue		1.00	.75
1164	A330	2.25fr brown org		.75	.60
1165	A330	2.35fr lilac rose		.80	.65
		Nos. 1154-1165 (12)		6.40	4.65

Issued precanceled only. See note after No. 324.

Issue dates: 61c, 78c, 1.25fr, 2.10fr, July 10, 1978. Others, 1979.

Souvenir Sheet

Prince Albert — A331

1979, Apr. 30		Engr.		Perf. 12½x13	
1166	A331	10fr multicolored		6.50	6.50

21st birthday of Hereditary Prince Albert.

The Juggler of Notre Dame, by Jules Massenet — A332

1.20fr, Hans, the Flute Player, by Gaston L. Ganne. 1.50fr, Don Quichotte, by Massenet. 1.70fr, L'Aiglon, by Jacques Ibert & Arthur Honegger, vert. 2.10fr, The Child & the Sorcerer, by Maurice Ravel. 3fr, Monte Carlo Opera & Charles Garnier, architect.

1979, Apr. 30				Perf. 13	
1167	A332	1fr multicolored		.80	.45
1168	A332	1.20fr multicolored		.80	.55
1169	A332	1.50fr multicolored		1.20	.90
1170	A332	1.70fr multicolored		1.50	1.25
1171	A332	2.10fr multicolored		1.50	1.50
1172	A332	3fr multicolored		2.25	2.25
		Nos. 1167-1172 (6)		8.05	6.90

Centenary of the Salle Garnier, Monte Carlo Opera.

Flower, Bird, Butterfly, IYC Emblem — A333

Children's Drawings (IYC Emblem and): 1fr, Horse and child. 1.20fr, Children shaking hands, and heart. 1.50fr, Children of the world for peace. 1.70fr, Children against pollution.

1979, Apr. 30					
1173	A333	50c multicolored		.25	.25
1174	A333	1fr multicolored		.45	.35
1175	A333	1.20fr multicolored		.70	.50
1176	A333	1.50fr multicolored		1.00	.80
1177	A333	1.70fr multicolored		1.00	.80
		Nos. 1173-1177 (5)		3.40	2.70

International Year of the Child.

Armed Messenger, 15th-16th Centuries — A334

Europa (designs similar to 1960 postage dues); 1.50fr, Felucca, 18th cent. 1.70fr, Arrival of 1st train, Dec. 12, 1868.

1979, Apr. 30					
1178	A334	1.20fr multicolored		1.25	.40
1179	A334	1.50fr multicolored		5.00	.60
1180	A334	1.70fr multicolored		5.00	.85
a.	Souv. sheet of 6, 2 each #1178-1180, perf. 13x12½			27.50	18.00
		Nos. 1178-1180 (3)		11.25	1.85

Les Biches, by Francis Poulenc — A335

Ballets: 1.20fr, Les Matelots, by George Auric. 1.50fr, Le Spectre de 1a Rose, by Carl Maria Weber, vert. 1.70fr, Gaieté Parisienne, by Jacques Offenbach. 2.10fr, Dance of Salomé, by Richard Strauss, vert. 3fr, Instrumental Music, ceiling decoration of Salle Garnier.

1979, Nov. 12					
Size: 26x36mm, 36x26mm					
1181	A335	1fr multicolored		.70	.50
1182	A335	1.20fr multicolored		.85	.65
1183	A335	1.50fr multicolored		1.25	1.00
1184	A335	1.70fr multicolored		1.60	1.40
1185	A335	2.10fr multicolored		2.75	2.25
Size: 48x27mm					
1186	A335	3fr multicolored		4.00	3.25
		Nos. 1181-1186 (6)		11.15	9.05

Salle Garnier, Monte Carlo Opera, cent.

Princes of Monaco Type of 1967

Paintings: 3fr, Charles III (1856-1889). 4fr, Antoinette de Merode (1828-1864).

1979, Nov. 12				Perf. 12½x13	
1187	A182	3fr multicolored		2.25	1.75
1188	A182	4fr multicolored		3.25	2.40

Red Cross Type of 1969

5fr, St. Peter Claver preaching to slaves.

1979, Nov. 12				Perf. 13	
1189	A194	5fr multicolored		3.25	2.40

Princess Grace Orchid — A336

1979, Nov. 12				Photo.	
1190	A336	1fr multicolored		2.75	1.75

Intl. Orchid Exhibition, Monte Carlo, Apr. 1980.

Flower Type of 1976

Design: 1.20fr, Princess Grace rose.

1979, Nov. 12					
1191	A300	1.20fr multicolored		2.75	1.75

Intl. Flower Show, Monte Carlo, May 1980.

Clown Balancing on Globe — A337

1979, Nov. 12					
1192	A337	1.20fr multicolored		2.00	1.25

6th International Circus Festival, Monte Carlo, Dec. 6-10.

Rowland Hill, Penny Black — A338

1979, Nov. 12		Engr.		Perf. 13	
1193	A338	1.70fr multicolored		1.00	.65

Sir Rowland Hill (1795-1879), originator of penny postage.

Albert Einstein, Equations — A339

1979, Nov. 12					
1194	A339	1.70fr multicolored		1.40	.80

Albert Einstein (1879-1955), theoretical physicist.

St. Patrick's Cathedral, New York City, Cent. — A340

1979, Nov. 12					
1195	A340	2.10fr multicolored		1.25	.75

Nativity — A341

1979, Nov. 12					
1196	A341	1.20fr multicolored		.80	.65

Christmas 1979.

MONACO

Bugatti, Monte Carlo, 1929 Winner — A342

1979, Nov. 12
1197 A342 1fr multicolored 1.10 .70

50th anniv. of Grand Prix auto race, Monte Carlo.

Arms of Charles V and Monaco, View of Monaco A343

1979, Nov. 12
1198 A343 1.50fr multicolored .90 .65

Emperor Charles V visit to Monaco, 450th anniversary.

Dog Type of 1977
Design: 1.20fr, Setter and pointer.

1979, Nov. 12 Photo.
1199 A304 1.20fr multicolored 5.00 3.50

International Dog Show, Monte Carlo.

Prince Rainier Type of 1974

1980, Jan. 17 Engr. Perf. 13
1200 A261 1.10fr emerald .70 .25
1201 A261 1.30fr rose red .70 .25
1202 A261 1.60fr dk blue gray 1.25 .55
1203 A261 1.80fr grnsh blue 2.00 1.90
1204 A261 2.30fr red lilac 2.50 1.40
  Nos. 1200-1204 (5) 7.15 4.35

Chestnut Branch in Spring — A344

Designs of 1980, 1981 stamps show chestnut branch. 1982 stamps show peach branch. 1983 stamps show apple branch.

1980-83 Engr. Perf. 13x12½
1205 A344 76c shown .50 .40
1206 A344 88c Spring ('81) .50 .40
1207 A344 97c Spring ('82) .50 .40
1208 A344 99c Summer .80 .60
1209 A344 1.05fr Spring ('83) .80 .60
1210 A344 1.14fr Summer ('81) .80 .60
1211 A344 1.25fr Summer ('83) .80 .60
1212 A344 1.35fr Summer .85 .60
1213 A344 1.60fr Autumn 1.25 .85
1214 A344 1.91fr Autumn ('81) 1.25 .85
1215 A344 2.03fr Autumn ('82) 1.25 .85
1216 A344 2.19fr Autumn ('83) 1.40 1.00
1217 A344 2.65fr Winter 1.75 1.20
1218 A344 3.05fr Winter ('81) 1.60 1.25
1219 A344 3.36fr Winter ('82) 1.75 1.25
1220 A344 3.63fr Winter ('83) 1.60 1.60
  Nos. 1205-1220 (16) 17.40 13.05

Issued precanceled only. See note after No. 324. See Nos. 1406-1409, 1457-1460.

Gymnast A345

1980, Apr. 28
1221 A345 1.10fr shown .40 .25
1222 A345 1.30fr Handball .50 .35
1223 A345 1.60fr Shooting .65 .45
1224 A345 1.80fr Volleyball .85 .60
1225 A345 2.30fr Ice hockey 1.00 .85
1226 A345 4fr Slalom 1.60 1.25
  Nos. 1221-1226 (6) 5.00 3.75

22nd Summer Olympic Games, Moscow, July 19-Aug. 3; 13th Winter Olympic Games, Lake Placid, NY, Feb. 12-24.

Colette, Novelist — A346

Europa: 1.80fr, Marcel Pagnol (1895-1974), French playwright.

1980, Apr. 28 Perf. 12½x13
1227 A346 1.30fr multicolored 1.00 .35
1228 A346 1.80fr multicolored 1.50 .35
  a. Souv. sheet, 5 each #1227-1228 15.00 10.00

The Source, by Ingres — A347

1980, Apr. 28
1229 A347 4fr multicolored 7.00 5.50

Jean Auguste Dominique Ingres (1780-1867).

Michel Eyquem de Montaigne — A348

1980, Apr. 28 Perf. 13
1230 A348 1.30fr multicolored .65 .45

Essays of Montaigne (1533-1592), 400th anniversary of publication.

Guillaume Apollinaire (1880-1918), French Writer — A349

1980, Apr. 28
1231 A349 1.10fr multicolored .65 .45

Paul P. Harris, Chicago Skyline, Rotary Emblem A350

1980, Apr. 28
1232 A350 1.80fr multicolored .65 .55

Rotary International, 75th anniversary.

Convention Center, Map of Europe, Kiwanis Emblem A351

1980, Apr. 28
1233 A351 1.30fr multicolored .65 .50

Kiwanis International, European Convention, Monte Carlo, June.

Coin Type of 1975
Design: 1.50fr, Honoré II silver ecu, 1649.

1980, Apr. 28
1234 A281 1.50fr multicolored .75 .55

Lhasa Apso and Shih-Tzu A352

1980, Apr. 28 Photo.
1235 A352 1.30fr multicolored 4.00 3.25

International Dog Show, Monte Carlo.

The Princess and the Pea — A353

Hans Christian Andersen (1805-1875) Fairy Tales: 1.30fr, The Little Mermaid. 1.50fr, The Chimneysweep and the Shepherdess. 1.60fr, The Brave Little Tin Soldier. 1.80fr, The Little Match Girl. 2.30fr, The Nightingale.

1980, Nov. 6 Engr. Perf. 13
1236 A353 70c multicolored .35 .25
1237 A353 1.30fr multicolored .65 .60
1238 A353 1.50fr multicolored .95 .85
1239 A353 1.60fr multicolored 1.10 .85
1240 A353 1.80fr multicolored 1.40 1.10
1241 A353 2.30fr multicolored 1.75 1.20
  Nos. 1236-1241 (6) 6.20 4.85

Women on Balcony, by Van Dongen A354

Paintings from 1905 Paris Fall Salon: 2fr, The Road, by de Vlaminck. 4fr, Woman Reading in the Grass, by André Derain.

1980, Nov. 6 Perf. 13x12
1242 A354 2fr multicolored 2.75 1.75
1243 A354 3fr multicolored 3.25 2.50
1244 A354 4fr multicolored 4.75 4.25
1245 A354 5fr multicolored 5.00 5.00
  Nos. 1242-1245 (4) 15.75 13.50

Princes of Monaco Type of 1967
Paintings: No. 1246, Prince Albert I (1848-1922), by Leon Bonnat. No. 1247, Princess Alice (1857-1925), by L. Maeterlinck.

1980, Nov. 6 Perf. 12½x13
1246 A182 4fr multicolored 2.75 2.40
1247 A182 4fr multicolored 2.75 2.40

Sun and Birds, by Perrette Lambert A355

1980, Nov. 6 Perf. 13
1248 A355 6fr multicolored 3.50 3.25

Red Cross.

7th International Circus Festival — A356

1980, Nov. 6 Perf. 13x12½
1249 A356 1.30fr multicolored 2.00 1.25

Christmas 1980 — A357

1980, Nov. 6
1250 A357 1.10fr multicolored .50 .35
1251 A357 2.30fr multicolored 1.00 .75

Princess Stephanie of Monaco Rose — A358

1980, Nov. 6 Photo. Perf. 12½x13
1252 A358 1.30fr shown 1.00 .65
1253 A358 1.80fr Ikebana 1.50 1.40

International Flower Show, Monte Carlo, May 1981.

Prince Rainier Type of 1974

1980 Engr. Perf. 13
1255 A261 1.20fr bright green .90 .25
1256 A261 1.40fr red 1.10 .25

Issue dates: 1.20fr, Aug. 19; 1.40fr, Aug. 11.

Spirographis Spallanzanii — A359

Paramuricea Clavata — A359a

10c, Anemonia sulcata. 15c, Leptosammia pruvoti. 20c, Pteroides. 40c, Alcyonium. 50c, Corallium rubrum. 60c, Caliactis parisitica. 70c, Cerianthus membranaceus. 1fr, Actinia equina. 2fr, Protula.

1980, Nov. 6 Perf. 13x12½
1259 A359 5c multi .25 .25
1260 A359 10c multi .25 .25
1261 A359 15c multi .25 .25
1262 A359 20c multi .25 .25
1263 A359a 30c shown .25 .25
1264 A359 40c multi .35 .25
1265 A359 50c multi .55 .25
1266 A359a 60c multi 1.00 .65
1267 A359a 70c multi 1.25 .90
1268 A359a 1fr multi 1.25 .90
1269 A359 2fr multi 2.50 1.10
  Nos. 1259-1269 (11) 8.15 5.50

See Nos. 1316-1321, 1380.

25th Wedding Anniversary of Prince Rainier and Princess Grace A360

1981, May 4 Perf. 13
1270 A360 1.20fr green & blk 1.50 1.00
1271 A360 1.40fr carmine & blk 2.00 1.50
1272 A360 1.70fr olive grn & blk 2.50 1.90
1273 A360 1.80fr brown & blk 2.75 2.25
1274 A360 2fr brt blue & blk 3.75 2.75
  Nos. 1270-1274 (5) 12.50 9.40

Mozart with his Father and Sister, by Carmontelle A361

509

MONACO

Wolfgang Amadeus Mozart (1756-1791), 225th Birth Anniversary (Paintings): 2fr, Portrait, by Lorenz Vogel (26x36mm). 3.50fr, Conducting his Requiem Two Days Before his Death, by F.C. Baude.

1981, May 4	Engr.	Perf. 13½x13		
1275	A361	2fr multicolored	1.65	1.50
1276	A361	2.50fr multicolored	2.40	2.00
1277	A361	3.50fr multicolored	3.25	2.50
a.		Strip of 3, #1275-1277	8.50	8.50

Cross of Palms — A362

Europa (Palm Sunday Traditions): 2fr, Children with palms at benediction.

1981, May 4		Perf. 12½x13		
1278	A362	1.40fr multicolored	.75	.35
1279	A362	2fr multicolored	1.25	.55
a.		Souv. sheet, 5 ea #1278-1279	18.00	9.00

European Soccer Cup, 25th Anniversary A363

1981, May 4		Perf. 13		
1280	A363	2fr black & blue	1.25	.85

International Year of the Disabled — A364

1981, May 4				
1281	A364	1.40fr brt grn & bl	1.00	.60

Monegasque National Pavilion Centenary A365

1981, May 4				
1282	A365	2fr multicolored	1.25	.85

Oceanographic Institute, Monaco and Museum, Paris — A366

1981, May 4				
1283	A366	1.20fr multicolored	.95	.80

75th anniversary of the Oceanographic Institute (Monaco-France).

50th Anniversary of the International Hydrographic Bureau — A367

1981, May 4				
1284	A367	2.50fr multicolored	1.75	1.25

Rough Collies and Shetland Sheepdogs A368

1981, May 4		Photo.		
1285	A368	1.40fr multicolored	5.00	4.00

International Dog Show, Monte Carlo.

Marine Life Preservation — A369

1981, Mar. 21		Photo.		
1286	A369	1.20fr multicolored	1.00	.70

Prince Rainier III and Hereditary Prince Albert — A370

1981-84		Engr.	Perf. 13	
1287	A370	1.40fr dark green	1.00	.25
1288	A370	1.60fr carmine	1.40	.25
1289	A370	1.60fr ol grn ('82)	1.00	.25
1290	A370	1.70fr bluish grn ('84)	1.00	.25
1291	A370	1.80fr mag ('82)	1.20	.25
1292	A370	2fr red ('83)	1.50	.25
1293	A370	2.10fr red ('84)	1.50	.25
1294	A370	2.30fr blue	2.00	1.10
1295	A370	2.60fr violet bl ('82)	1.75	.80
1296	A370	2.80fr steel bl ('83)	2.00	1.25
1297	A370	3fr sky blue ('84)	3.00	1.60
1298	A370	4fr brown	1.75	.75
1299	A370	5.50fr black	2.50	1.50
		Nos. 1287-1299 (13)	21.60	8.75

See Nos. 1505-1515.

Hauling Ice Floes, 17th Cent. Map Arctic — A371

1981, Oct. 5				
1301	A371	1.50fr multicolored	1.60	1.25

First Intl. Arctic Committee Congress, Rome, Oct. 5-9.

Princes of Monaco Type of 1967

Paintings by P.A. de Laszlo, 1929: 3fr, Prince Louis II. 5fr, Princess Charlotte.

1981, Nov. 5		Engr.	Perf. 12½x13	
1302	A182	3fr multicolored	2.50	1.25
1303	A182	5fr multicolored	3.50	2.40

Ettore Bugatti, Auto Designer and Racer, Birth Centenary — A372

1981, Nov. 5		Perf. 13		
1304	A372	1fr multicolored	1.25	.85

George Bernard Shaw (1856-1950) — A373

2.50fr, Fernand Leger, painter, birth cent.

1981, Nov. 5				
1305	A373	2fr multicolored	1.25	1.00
1306	A373	2.50fr multicolored	1.25	1.00

Self-portrait, by Pablo Picasso (1881-1973) A374

#1308, Self-portrait, by Rembrandt (1606-69).

1981, Nov. 5		Perf. 12½x13		
1307	A374	4fr multicolored	4.50	3.25
1308	A374	4fr multicolored	4.50	3.25

Ikebana, Painting by Ikenobo, 1673 — A375

Intl. Flower Show, Monte Carlo, 1982: 1.40fr, Elegantines, morning glories.

1981, Nov. 5	Photo.	Perf. 12½		
1309	A375	1.40fr multicolored	1.40	1.00
1310	A375	2fr multicolored	2.25	1.75

Catherine Deneuve Rose — A376

1981, Nov. 5		Perf. 13x12½		
1311	A376	1.80fr multicolored	4.00	2.50

First Intl. Rose Competition, Monte Carlo, June 12-14.

8th Intl. Circus Festival, Monte Carlo, Dec. 10-14 — A377

1981, Nov. 5		Engr.	Perf. 13	
1312	A377	1.40fr multicolored	2.50	1.40

Christmas 1981 — A378

1981, Nov. 5				
1313	A378	1.20fr multicolored	.65	.60

50th Monte Carlo Auto Race A379

1981, Nov. 5				
1314	A379	1fr Lancia-Stratos	1.25	.90

Souvenir Sheet

Persimmon Branch in Different Seasons — A380

1981, Nov. 5		Perf. 13x12½		
1315	A380	Sheet of 4	8.50	8.50
a.		1fr Spring	.80	.80
b.		2fr Summer	1.50	1.50
c.		3fr Autumn	2.50	2.50
d.		4fr Winter	3.00	3.00

Coral Type of 1980

Exotic Plants. 1.40fr, Hoya bella, vert. 1.60fr, Bolivicereus sam-aipatanus, vert. 1.80fr, Trichocereus grandi-florus. 2.30fr, Euphorbia milii, vert. 2.60fr, Echinocereus fitchii. 2.90fr, Rebutia heliosa. 4.10fr, Echinopsis multiplex.

		Perf. 12½x13, 13x12½		
1981-82			Photo.	
1316	A359	1.40fr multi	3.25	1.60
1317	A359	1.60fr multi	2.75	1.10
1317A	A359a	1.80fr multi	2.25	1.10
1318	A359a	2.30fr multi	2.75	1.10
1319	A359a	2.60fr multi	2.75	1.10
1320	A359a	2.90fr multi	2.75	1.10
1321	A359a	4.10fr multi	3.25	2.75
		Nos. 1316-1321 (7)	19.75	9.85

Issued: 1.80fr, 6/7; others 12/10.

Miniature Sheet

1982 World Cup — A381

Designs: Various soccer players.

1982, May 3			Perf. 13	
1322	A381	Sheet of 4	8.00	8.00
a.		1fr multicolored	.75	.75
b.		2fr multicolored	1.50	1.50
c.		3fr multicolored	2.25	2.25
d.		4fr multicolored	2.75	2.75

Mercantour Natl. Park Birds — A382

60c, Nutcracker. 70c, Black grouse. 80c, Rock partridge. 90c, Wall creeper, horiz. 1.40fr, Ptarmigan, horiz. 1.60fr, Golden eagle.

1982, May 3		Perf. 12½x13, 13x12½		
1323	A382	60c multi	1.00	.85
1324	A382	70c multi	1.20	1.10
1325	A382	80c multi	1.20	1.10
1326	A382	90c multi	2.25	1.75
1327	A382	1.40fr multi	3.00	2.40
1328	A382	1.60fr multi	3.75	2.40
		Nos. 1323-1328 (6)	12.40	9.60

Europa — A383

1.60fr, Guelph attacking Fortress of Monaco, 1297. 2.30fr, Treaty of Peronne, 1641.

1982, May 3		Perf. 12½x13		
1329	A383	1.60fr multi	1.50	.40
1330	A383	2.30fr multi	1.50	.50
a.		Souv. sheet, 5 ea #1329-1330	18.00	9.00

MONACO

Fontvieille Landfill Project — A384

1982, May 3			Perf. 13x12½	
1331	A384	1.40fr Old coastline	1.00	.50
1332	A384	1.60fr Landfill site	1.00	.60
1333	A384	2.30fr Completed site	1.50	1.00
		Nos. 1331-1333 (3)	3.50	2.10

Fontvielle Stadium A385

1982, May 3			Perf. 13	
1334	A385	2.30fr multicolored	1.25	1.00

PHILEXFRANCE '82 Stamp Exhibition, Paris, June 11-21 — A386

1982, May 3				
1335	A386	1.40fr multicolored	1.00	.80

Intl. Dog Show, Monte Carlo — A387

60c, Old English sheepdog. 1fr, Briard terrier.

1982, May 3	Photo.		Perf. 13x12½	
1336	A387	60c multi	3.25	1.75
1337	A387	1fr multi	3.25	1.75

See Nos. 1366, 1431, 1479, 1539, 1676, 1704, 1756, 1806, 1855, 1900, 1940, 1990, 2035, 2108.

Monaco Cathedral, Arms of Pope John Paul II and Monaco — A388

1982, May 3			Engr.	
1338	A388	1.60fr multicolored	.85	.80

Creation of archbishopric of Monaco, July 25, 1981.

800th Birth Anniv. of St. Francis of Assisi — A389

1982, May 3			Perf. 12½x13	
1339	A389	1.40fr multicolored	.75	.75

TB Bacillus Cent. — A390

1982, May 3				
1340	A390	1.40fr multicolored	1.10	.85

Scouting Year — A391

1982, May 3				
1341	A391	1.60fr dk brown & blk	1.60	1.00

Intl. Hunting Council, 29th Meeting — A392

1982, June 11	Photo.		Perf. 12½	
1342	A392	1.60fr St. Hubert	1.20	1.00

Intl. Bibliophile Assoc. General Assembly A393

1982, Sept. 30		Engr.	Perf. 13	
1343	A393	1.60fr multicolored	.80	.60

Monte Carlo and Monaco During the Belle Epoch (1870-1925), by Hubert Clerissi — A394

1982, Nov. 8	Engr.		Perf. 13x12½	
1344	A394	3fr Casino, 1870	1.75	1.25
1345	A394	5fr Palace, 1893	3.25	2.00

See Nos. 1385-1386, 1436-1437, 1488-1489, 1546-1547, 1605-1606, 1638-1639, 1695-1696.

Niccolo Paganini (1782-1840), Composer and Violinist — A395

1.80fr, Anna Pavlova (1881-1931), ballerina. 2.60fr, Igor Stravinsky (1882-1971), composer.

1982, Nov. 8	Engr.		Perf. 12½x13	
1346	A395	1.60fr multicolored	1.25	1.00
1347	A395	1.80fr multicolored	1.76	1.20
1348	A395	2.60fr multicolored	2.00	1.40
		Nos. 1346-1348 (3)	5.00	3.60

In a Boat, by Manet (1832-1883) A396

Design: No. 1350, Les Poissons Noir, by Georges Braque (1882-1963).

1982, Nov. 8	Engr.		Perf. 13x12½	
1349	A396	4fr multicolored	3.50	3.00
1350	A396	4fr multicolored	3.50	3.00

Intl. Flower Show, Monte Carlo — A397

Designs: Various floral arrangements.

1982, Nov. 8	Photo.		Perf. 12½x13	
1351	A397	1.60fr multicolored	1.50	1.00
1352	A397	2.60fr multicolored	2.00	1.25

Bouquet — A398

1982			Perf. 13	
1353	A398	1.60fr multicolored	2.00	1.50

Christmas 1982 — A399

1982, Nov. 8	Engr.		Perf. 12½x13	
1354	A399	1.60fr Three Kings	.60	.35
1355	A399	1.80fr Holy Family	.75	.35
1356	A399	2.60fr Shepherds	1.10	.50
a.		Souv. sheet of 3, #1354-1356	3.25	3.25
		Nos. 1354-1356 (3)	2.45	1.20

Intl. Polar Year Centenary A400

1.60fr, Prince Louis, Discovery.

1982, Nov. 8		Engr.	Perf. 13	
1358	A400	1.60fr multi	2.25	1.60

Discovery of Greenland Millenium A401

1.60fr, Erik the Red's longship.

1982, Nov. 8				
1359	A401	1.60fr multi	2.25	1.60

Death Bimillenium of Virgil A402

1.80fr, Scene from Aeneid, Book 6.

1982, Nov. 8				
1360	A402	1.80fr multi	2.00	1.50

50th Anniv. of Botanical Garden — A403

1.80fr, Cacti, vert. 2fr, Exotic plants, vert. 2.30fr, Intl. exhibits, vert. 2.60fr, Cave. 3.30fr, Prehistoric Anthropology Museum.

1983, Feb. 11	Photo.		Perf. 12½x13	
1361	A403	1.80fr multi	1.50	1.10
1362	A403	2fr multi	1.75	1.20
1363	A403	2.30fr multi	2.00	1.75
1364	A403	2.60fr multi	2.25	1.75
1365	A403	3.30fr multi	2.50	2.75
		Nos. 1361-1365 (5)	10.00	8.55

Monte Carlo Dog Show Type

1983, Apr. 13			Perf. 13x12½	
1366	A387	1.80fr Alaskan malamute	6.50	4.00

Souvenir Sheet

Princess Grace (1929-1982) — A405

1983, Apr. 19		Engr.	Perf. 13	
1367	A405	10fr black	7.00	7.00

Europa — A406

1.80fr, Montgolfiere balloon flight, 1783. 2.60fr, Columbia space shuttle.

1983, Apr. 27			Perf. 12½x13	
1368	A406	1.80fr multi	1.75	.35
1369	A406	2.60fr multi	1.75	.50
a.		Souv. sheet, 5 ea #1368-1369	20.00	8.00

St. Charles' Church, Monte Carlo, Cent. — A407

2.60fr, St. Charles Borromeo.

1983, Apr. 27			Engr.	
1370	A407	2.60fr multi	1.00	.90

Franciscan College Centenary A408

1983, Apr. 27			Perf. 13x12½	
1371	A408	2fr Church, medallion	.90	.70

Fontvielle Stadium Interior A409

1983, Apr. 28			Perf. 13	
1372	A409	2fr multicolored	.90	.70

Automobile Centenary A410

2.90fr, Benz, 1883, Formula One racer.

1983, Apr. 27				
1373	A410	2.90fr multi	3.25	1.90

511

MONACO

Save the Whales Campaign — A411

1983, Apr. 27
1374 A411 3.30fr Blue whale 3.75 3.00

World Communications Year — A412

1983, Apr. 27
1375 A412 4fr lil rose & brn vio 1.60 1.20

Souvenir Sheet

Fig Branch in Different Seasons — A413

1983, Nov. 9   Engr.   Perf. 13x12½
1376 A413 Sheet of 4 8.00 8.00
  a. 1fr Spring .75 .75
  b. 2fr Summer 1.40 1.40
  c. 3fr Autumn 2.25 2.25
  d. 4fr Winter 2.75 2.75

Exotic Plant Type of 1980

2fr, Argyroderma roseum.

1983, Nov. 9   Photo.   Perf. 13
1380 A359 2fr multi 1.75 .65

Belle Epoch Type of 1982

Paintings by Hubert Clerissi: 3fr, Thermes Valentia from the Beach, 1902. 5fr, Cafe de Paris and Place du Casino, 1905.

1983, Nov. 9   Engr.   Perf. 13x12½
1385 A394 3fr multicolored 3.00 2.40
1386 A394 5fr multicolored 4.25 3.50

Portrait of a Young Man, by Raphael (1483-1520) A414

Passage Cottin, by Maurice Utrillo (1883-1955) A415

1983, Nov. 9   Engr.   Perf. 13
1387 A414 4fr multicolored 3.00 2.25
1388 A415 4fr multicolored 3.00 2.25

Johannes Brahms (1833-1897), Composer A416

#1390, Giacomo Puccini (1858-1924), composer, scene from Madame Butterfly.

1983, Nov. 9   Engr.   Perf. 13½x13
1389 A416 3fr multicolored 1.75 1.25
1390 A416 3fr multicolored 1.75 1.25

9th Intl. Circus Festival, Monte Carlo, Dec. 8-12 — A417

1983, Nov. 9   Perf. 13
1391 A417 2fr multicolored 1.75 1.40

Intl. Flower Show, Monte Carlo — A418

1.60fr, Pansies, convolvulus, carnations. 2.60fr, Oriental poppies.

1983, Nov. 9   Photo.
1392 A418 1.60fr multi 1.50 1.00
1393 A418 2.60fr multi 2.25 1.50

Christmas 1983 — A419

2fr, Provencal creche figures.

1983, Nov. 9   Photo.
1394 A419 2fr multi 1.60 1.10

Alfred Nobel (1833-1896), Literature Medal — A420

1983, Nov. 9   Engr.
1395 A420 2fr multicolored 1.00 .80

Sesquicentenary of Society of St. Vincent de Paul — A421

1.80fr, F. Ozanam, founder, Paris headquarters.

1983, Nov. 9   Engr.
1396 A421 1.80fr multi 1.00 .60

Offshore Petroleum Plant — A422

1983, Nov. 9
1397 A422 5fr multi 2.25 1.25

19th Cent. Figurines, Galea Toy Collection — A423

50c, Water pipe smoker. 60c, Clown with yo-yo. 70c, Smoking monkey. 80c, Farmer and pig. 90c, Buffalo Bill. 1fr, Snake charmer. 1.50fr, Piano and harp player. 2fr, Girl powdering her face.

1983, Nov. 9   Photo.   Perf. 12½x13
1398 A423 50c multi .25 .25
1399 A423 60c multi .40 .25
1400 A423 70c multi .40 .25
1401 A423 80c multi .50 .50
1402 A423 90c multi .60 .60
1403 A423 1fr multi .60 .60
1404 A423 1.50fr multi 1.00 .80
1405 A423 2fr multi 1.75 1.00
  Nos. 1398-1405 (8) 5.50 4.25

Quince Branch in Spring — A424

1984, May 10   Photo.   Perf. 13x12½
1406 A424 1.14fr shown .40 .40
1407 A424 1.47fr Summer .50 .50
1408 A424 2.38fr Autumn 1.00 1.00
1409 A424 3.95fr Winter 1.75 1.50
  Nos. 1406-1409 (4) 3.65 3.40

Issued precanceled only. See note after No. 324.

Place de la Visitation, by Hubert Clerissi — A425

Drawings by Hubert Clerissi: 10c, Town Hall. 15c, Rue Basse. 20c, Place Saint-Nicolas. 30c, Quai du Commerce. 40c, Rue des Iris. 3fr, Bandstand. 6fr, Opera House.

1984, May 10   Engr.   Perf. 12½x13
1410 A425 5c brown .25 .25
1411 A425 10c claret .25 .25
1412 A425 15c violet .25 .25
1413 A425 20c dark blue .25 .25
1414 A425 30c deep blue .25 .25
1415 A425 40c dark green .70 .25
1416 A425 3fr red brown 2.25 .90
1417 A425 6fr yellow green 1.25 1.10
  Nos. 1410-1417 (8) 5.45 3.50

See #1516-1524, 1750-1755, 1821-1825.

Souvenir Sheet

1984 Los Angeles Olympics — A426

Rhythmic Gymnastics.

1984, May 10   Perf. 13
1418 A426 Sheet of 4 7.50 7.50
  a. 2fr Ball .95 .95
  b. 3fr Clubs 1.40 1.40
  c. 4fr Ribbon 1.75 1.75
  d. 5fr Hoop 2.40 2.40

1984 Winter Olympics A427

1984, May 10
1422 A427 2fr Rink, speed skater .90 .55
1423 A427 4fr Skater, snowflake 1.60 1.10

Europa (1959-84) — A428

1984, May 10   Perf. 13x12½
1424 A428 2fr blue 1.50 .40
1425 A428 3fr yel grn 2.50 .85
  a. Souv. sheet, 4 ea #1424-1425 20.00 8.50

Butterflies and Rare Flowers, Mercantour Natl. Park — A429

1.60fr, Boloria graeca tendensis, ranunculus montanus. 2fr, Zygaena vesubiana, saxifraga aizoides. 2.80fr, Erebia aethiopella, myosotis alpestris. 3fr, Parnassius phoebus gazeli, rhododendron ferrugineum. 3.60fr, Papilio alexanor, myrrhis odorata. Nos. 1426-1428 vert.

Perf. 12½x13, 13x12½
1984, May 10   Photo.
1426 A429 1.60fr multicolored 1.75 1.25
1427 A429 2fr multicolored 1.75 1.40
1428 A429 2.80fr multicolored 2.60 1.75
1429 A429 3fr multicolored 2.60 2.25
1430 A429 3.60fr multicolored 2.60 2.50
  Nos. 1426-1430 (5) 11.30 9.15

Monte Carlo Dog Show Type

1.60fr, Auvergne pointer.

1984, May 10   Perf. 13x12½
1431 A387 1.60fr multi 3.00 2.50

Sanctuary of Our Lady of Laghet — A431

2fr, Statue, rosary, pilgrimage sanctuary.

1984, May 10   Engr.   Perf. 12½x13
1432 A431 2fr multi .90 .45

Auguste Piccard, Birth Cent. — A432

2.80fr, Stratosphere balloon. 4fr, Bathyscaphe.

1984, May 10
1433 A432 2.80fr multi 1.00 .60
1434 A432 4fr multi 1.50 .85

25th Anniv. of Princely Palace Concerts — A433

1984, May 10   Perf. 13x12½
1435 A433 3.60fr Orchestra 1.50 .90

Belle Epoch Type of 1982

Paintings by Hubert Clerissi: 4fr, Rue Grimaldi, 1908. 5fr, Train Entering Monte Carlo Station, 1910.

1984, Nov. 8   Engr.   Perf. 12½x13
1436 A394 4fr multicolored 3.00 2.40
1437 A394 5fr multicolored 5.00 3.75

25th Intl. Television Festival, Monte Carlo, Feb. 1985 A434

2.10fr, Lights. 3fr, Golden nymph (prize).

1984, Nov. 8   Engr.   Perf. 13
1438 A434 2.10fr multi 1.00 .60
1439 A434 3fr multi 1.40 .85

MONACO

Intl. Flower Show, Monte Carlo — A435

1984, Nov. 8 Photo. Perf. 12½x13
| 1440 | A435 | 2.10fr Mixed bouquet | 1.60 | 1.00 |
| 1441 | A435 | 3fr Ikebana | 2.40 | 1.25 |

See Nos. 1491-1492, 1552-1553.

Pharmaceuticals, Cosmetics Industry — A436

1984, Nov. 8 Engr. Perf. 13
| 1442 | A436 | 2.40fr multicolored | 1.00 | .85 |

Illustration from Gargantua, by Rabelais — A437

Francois Rabelais (1490-1553), 17th Cent. Drawing — A438

No. 1443, With animals. No. 1444, With sheep of Panurge.

1984, Nov. 8 Perf. 13x12½, 12½x13
1443	A437	2fr multicolored	1.10	.60
1444	A437	2fr multicolored	1.10	.60
1445	A438	4fr multicolored	2.50	1.25
		Nos. 1443-1445 (3)	4.70	2.45

Souvenir Sheet

10th Intl. Circus Festival, Dec. 6-10 A439

1984, Nov. 8 Photo. Perf. 13
| 1446 | A439 | 5fr Poster | 4.00 | 4.00 |

La Femme a la Potiche, by Degas — A440

1984, Nov. 8 Engr. Perf. 12x13
| 1447 | A440 | 6fr multicolored | 5.00 | 2.75 |

Christmas 1984 — A441

Figurines from Provence: 70c, Shepherd. 1fr, Blind man. 1.70fr, Happy man. 2fr, Woman spinning. 2.10fr, Angel. 2.40fr, Garlic seller. 3fr, Drummer. 3.70fr, Knife grinder. 4fr, Elderly couple.

1984, Nov. 8 Perf. 12½x13
1448	A441	70c multi	.45	.40
1449	A441	1fr multi	.55	.50
1450	A441	1.70fr multi	1.20	1.00
1451	A441	2fr multi	1.25	1.10
1452	A441	2.10fr multi	1.40	1.20
1453	A441	2.40fr multi	1.60	1.40
1454	A441	3fr multi	1.90	1.60
1455	A441	3.70fr multi	2.40	2.00
1456	A441	4fr multi	2.75	2.40
		Nos. 1448-1456 (9)	13.50	11.60

See Nos. 1737-1739, 1766-1768, 1838-1840, 1883-1885, 1919-1921, 1976-1978.

Cherry Tree — A442

1985, Mar. 1 Engr. Perf. 13
1457	A442	1.22fr Spring	.50	.50
1458	A442	1.57fr Summer	.50	.50
1459	A442	2.55fr Fall	1.10	.80
1460	A442	4.23fr Winter	2.00	1.50
		Nos. 1457-1460 (4)	4.10	3.30

Issued precanceled only. See note after No. 324.

No. 1 in Green — A443

1985, Mar. 25
1461	A443	1.70fr shown	.85	.50
1462	A443	2.10fr #1 in scarlet	1.00	.25
1463	A443	3fr #1 in lt peacock bl	1.20	.85
		Nos. 1461-1463 (3)	3.05	1.60

Stamp centenary, Natl. Stamp Exhibition, Dec. 5-8, Monte Carlo.

Europa 1985 — A444

Portraits. 2.10fr Prince Antoine I (1661-1731), Founder of Monaco Palace, music library. 3fr, Jean-Baptiste Lully (1632-1687), composer, violinist, superintendent of music to King Louis XIV.

1985, May 23 Perf. 12½x13
1464	A444	2.10fr brt blue	1.75	.50
1465	A444	3fr dark carmine	3.00	.75
a.		Souv. sheet, 5 #1464, 5 #1465	25.00	15.00

Flowers in Mercantour Park — A444a

1.70fr, Berardia subacaulis. 2.10fr, Saxifraga florulenta, vert. 2.40fr, Fritillaria moggridgei, vert. 3fr, Sempervivum allionii, vert. 3.60fr, Silene cordifolia, vert. 4fr, Primula allionii.

Perf. 13x12½, 12½x13
1985, May 23 Photo.
1466	A444a	1.70fr multi	.85	.80
1467	A444a	2.10fr multi	1.00	.85
1468	A444a	2.40fr multi	1.20	1.00
1469	A444a	3fr multi	1.75	1.20
1470	A444a	3.60fr multi	2.40	1.60
1471	A444a	4fr multi	3.00	2.00
		Nos. 1466-1471 (6)	10.20	7.45

Japanese Medlar — A445

1985, May 23 Engr. Perf. 13x12½
1472		Sheet of 4	6.50	6.50
a.	A445	1fr Spring	.55	.55
b.	A445	2fr Summer	1.25	1.25
c.	A445	3fr Autumn	1.90	1.90
d.	A445	4fr Winter	2.40	2.40

Nadia Boulanger (1887-1979), Musician, Composer, Conductor — A446

Portraits, manuscripts and music: 2.10fr, Georges Auric (1899-1983), composer of film, ballet music, Music Foundation council president.

1985, May 23 Perf. 13
| 1473 | A446 | 1.70fr brown | 1.00 | .60 |
| 1474 | A446 | 2.10fr brt ultra | 1.25 | .90 |

Prince Pierre de Monaco Music Foundation composition prize, 25th anniv.

Natl. Oceanographic Museum, 75th Anniv. — A447

1985, May 23
| 1475 | A447 | 2.10fr brt bl, grn & blk | 1.00 | .80 |

Graphs, Fish, Molecular Structures, Lab Apparatus A448

1985, May 23
| 1476 | A448 | 3fr dk bl grn, blk & dk rose lil | 1.25 | .70 |

Prince Rainier III Scientific Research Center, 25th anniv.

Intl. Athletic Championships, May 25-26 — A449

1985, May 23
| 1477 | A449 | 1.70fr Running | .70 | .55 |
| 1478 | A449 | 2.10fr Swimming | 1.00 | .55 |

Opening of Louis II Stadium, May 25.

Monte Carlo Dog Show Type

1985, May 3 Photo. Perf. 13x12½
| 1479 | A387 | 2.10fr Boxer | 3.25 | 2.00 |

Intl. Youth Year — A450

1985, May 23 Engr. Perf. 13
| 1480 | A450 | 3fr fawn, sepia & dp grn | 1.25 | .75 |

Fish, Natl. Oceanographic Museum Aquarium — A451

1.80fr, Pygoplites diacanthus. 2.20fr, Acanthurus leucosternon. 3.20fr, Chaetodon collare. 3.90fr, Balistoides conspicillum. 7fr, Aquarium.

1985, Aug. 13 Photo. Perf. 12½x13
1481	A451	1.80fr multi	1.40	1.10
1482	A451	2.20fr multi	1.40	1.10
1483	A451	3.20fr multi	2.25	1.60
1484	A451	3.90fr multi	2.75	2.25

Size: 40x52mm
Perf. 13
| 1485 | A451 | 7fr multi | 4.75 | 3.50 |
| | | Nos. 1481-1485 (5) | 12.55 | 9.55 |

See Nos. 1560-1561, 1610-1615.

Souvenir Sheet

Transatlantic Yachting Race, Oct. 13 — A452

Yacht classes: a, Catamaran. b, Monocoque. c, Trimaran.

1985, Oct. Engr. Perf. 13
| 1486 | A452 | Sheet of 3 | 6.00 | 6.00 |
| a.-c. | | 4fr, any single | 1.75 | 1.75 |

Monaco-New York competition.

ITALIA '85, Rome, Oct. 25-Nov. 3 — A453

Design: Exhibition emblem, St. Peter's Cathedral and Temple of Castor ruins.

1985, Oct. 25 Perf. 13½x13
| 1487 | A453 | 4fr int blk, brt grn & red rose | 1.60 | 1.00 |

Belle Epoch Type of 1982

Illustrations by Hubert Clerissi: 4fr, Port of Monaco, 1912. 6fr, La Gare Vers Avenue, 1920.

1985, Nov. 7 Engr. Perf. 13x12½
| 1488 | A394 | 4fr multi | 3.00 | 1.75 |
| 1489 | A394 | 6fr multi | 3.50 | 3.00 |

11th Intl. Circus Festival, Dec. 5-9 — A454

1985, Nov. 7 Photo. Perf. 13
| 1490 | A454 | 1.80fr multi | 1.50 | 1.10 |

Intl. Flower Show Type of 1984

2.20fr, Roses, tulips, jonquils. 3.20fr, Ikebana of chrysanthemums, bryony.

1985, Nov. 7
| 1491 | A435 | 2.20fr multi | 1.40 | 1.00 |
| 1492 | A435 | 3.20fr multi | 2.10 | 1.90 |

Dated 1986.

MONACO

Factory, Ship, Fish, Crustaceans — A455

1985, Nov. 7   Engr.   Perf. 13x13½
1493 A455 2.20fr brt bl, dp brn & dk grnsh bl   1.00   .60

Monagasque fishing industry, Fontvieille District. See No. 1555.

Christmas 1985 — A456

1985, Nov. 7   Photo.   Perf. 12½x13
1494 A456 2.20fr multi   1.25   .50

EUTELSAT Orbiting Earth A457

1985, Nov. 7   Engr.   Perf. 13
1495 A457 3fr int blk, dp rose lil & dk bl   1.40   1.00

European Telecommunications Satellite Org.

Sacha Guitry (1885-1957), Actor, Dramatist — A458

Authors, composers: 4fr, Brothers Grimm. 5fr, Frederic Chopin and Robert Schumann, composers. 6fr, Johann Sebastian Bach and George Frideric Handel, composers.

1985, Nov. 7
1496 A458 3fr brn blk & gldn brn   1.50   1.20
1497 A458 4fr dp rose lil, sep & turq bl   2.00   1.20
1498 A458 5fr stl bl, dp bl & grnsh bl   2.50   1.90
1499 A458 6fr blk, brn & stl bl   3.00   2.40
       Nos. 1496-1499 (4)   9.00   6.70

Souvenir Sheet

Natl. Postage Stamp Cent. — A459

Altered designs: a, Type A1. b, Type A2. c, Type A13. d, Type A83.

1985, Dec. 5
1500 A459 Sheet of 4   8.00   8.00
a.-d.   5fr, any single   2.00   2.00

Rainier and Albert Type of 1981-84

1985-88   Engr.   Perf. 13
1505 A370 1.80fr brt grn   1.10   .25
1506 A370 1.90fr ol grn ('86)   1.90   .55
1507 A370 2fr emer grn ('87)   1.25   .25
1508 A370 2.20fr red rose   1.25   .25
1509 A370 2.50fr dk brn   1.50   .75
1510 A370 3.20fr brt bl   2.75   2.25
1511 A370 3.40fr ind ('86)   4.25   2.25
1512 A370 3.60fr dp ultra ('87)   2.75   1.25
1513 A370 10fr claret ('86)   4.75   1.10
1514 A370 15fr dk bl grn ('86)   9.25   2.25
1515 A370 20fr brt blue ('88)   11.00   2.75
       Nos. 1505-1515 (11)   41.75   13.90

Views of Old Monaco Type of 1984

Illustrations by Hubert Clerissi: 50c, Port of Monaco. 60c, St. Charles Church. 70c, Promenade. 80c, Harbor, olive trees. 90c, Quay. 1fr, Palace Square. 2fr, Ships, harbor mouth. 4fr, Monaco Train Station. 5fr, Mail coach.

1986, Jan. 23
1516 A425 50c red   .25   .25
1517 A425 60c Prus blue   .25   .25
1518 A425 70c orange   .55   .35
1519 A425 80c brt yel grn   .35   .25
1520 A425 90c rose violet   .35   .25
1521 A425 1fr brt blue   .45   .25
1522 A425 2fr black   .95   .45
1523 A425 4fr ultramarine   1.90   .75
1524 A425 5fr olive green   2.40   .75
       Nos. 1516-1524 (9)   7.45   3.55

Hazel Nut Tree — A460

1986, Feb. 24   Engr.   Perf. 13x12½
1525 A460 1.28fr Spring   .70   .45
1526 A460 1.65fr Summer   .90   .55
1527 A460 2.67fr Fall   1.40   1.00
1528 A460 4.44fr Winter   2.00   1.60
       Nos. 1525-1528 (4)   5.00   3.60

Nos. 1525-1528 known only precanceled. See note after No. 324.
See Nos. 1580-1583, 1616-1619, 1685-1688, 1719-1722, 1809-1812.

Port of Monaco, 18th Cent. — A461

1986, Feb. 24
1529 A461 2.20fr ultra, gray & brown   1.10   .45

Publication of Annales Monegasques, 10th anniv.

Europa 1986 — A462

2.20fr, Ramoge Nature Protection Treaty. 3.20fr, Natl. marine reserve.

1986, May 22   Engr.   Perf. 12½x13
1530 A462 2.20fr multi   1.75   .40
1531 A462 3.20fr multi   2.25   .75
a.   Souv. sheet, 5 each #1530-1531   25.00   14.00

Souvenir Sheet

1986 World Cup Soccer Championships, Mexico — A463

1986, May 22
1532 A463 Sheet of 2   6.50   6.50
a.   5fr Player   2.50   2.50
b.   7fr Goalie   3.50   3.50

Ovis Musimon — A464

2.50fr, Capra ibex. 3.20fr, Rupicapra rupicapra. 3.90fr, Marmota marmota. 5fr, Lepus timidus varronis. 7.20fr, Mustela erminea.

1986, May 22
1533 A464 2.20fr shown   1.25   .60
1534 A464 2.50fr multi   1.25   1.00
1535 A464 3.20fr multi   1.75   1.60
1536 A464 3.90fr multi   2.50   2.00
1537 A464 5fr multi   3.00   2.75
1538 A464 7.20fr multi   3.75   3.25
       Nos. 1533-1538 (6)   13.50   11.20

Nos. 1536-1538 vert.

Monte Carlo Dog Show Type

1986, May 22   Photo.   Perf. 13x12½
1539 A387 1.80fr Terriers   5.00   3.25

Prince Albert I, Parliament A465

1986, May 22   Perf. 13
1540 A465 2.50fr brn & ol grn   1.10   .75

First Constitution, 75th anniv.

Serge Diaghilev, Founder A466

1986, May 22   Perf. 13
1541 A466 3.20fr brn blk, carm rose & blk   1.90   1.60

Diaghilev's first permanent ballet company, 75th anniv., and creation of Monte Carlo Ballet Company, 1986.

1st Monte Carlo Auto Rally, 75 Anniv. A467

Winner Henri Rougier and Turcat-Mery, 1911.

1986, May 22
1542 A467 3.90fr rose mag & car   2.50   2.00

Statue of Liberty, Cent. — A468

1986, May 22
1543 A468 5fr multi   2.00   1.40

Halley's Comet A469

10fr, Sightings, 1986, 1532.

1986, May 22
1544 A469 10fr multi   3.50   3.00

AMERIPEX '86, Chicago, May 22-June 1 — A470

1986, May 22
1545 A470 5fr US flag, skyline   2.00   1.20

Belle Epoch Type of 1982

Illustrations by Hubert Clerissi: 6fr, Pavilion, 1920, vert. 7fr, Beau Rivage Avenue, 1925, vert.

1986, Oct. 28   Engr.   Perf. 12½x13
1546 A394 6fr multi   4.00   2.40
1547 A394 7fr multi   5.00   3.00

Premiere of El Cid, by Pierre Corneille, 350th Anniv. A471

1986, Oct. 28   Engr.   Perf. 13
1548 A471 4fr Scenes   1.50   1.20

Franz Liszt, Composer A472

1986, Oct. 28
1549 A472 5fr dk red brn & brt ultra   2.00   1.40

The Olympic Diver, 1961, by Emma de Sigaldi — A473

1986, Oct. 28   Perf. 12½x13
1550 A473 6fr multi   2.50   1.60

Intl. Insurers Congress, Monte Carlo, Sept. 30 — A474

1986, Oct. 28   Perf. 13½x13
1551 A474 3.20fr brn, dp grn & brt bl   1.50   1.00

Intl. Flower Show Type of 1984

2.20fr, Bouquet of roses, acidenthera. 3.90fr, Ikebana of lilies, beech branches.

1986, Oct. 28   Photo.   Perf. 12½x13
1552 A435 2.20fr multi   1.40   .80
1553 A435 3.90fr multi   2.25   1.75

Dated 1987.

12th Intl. Circus Festival, Dec. 4-8 — A475

1986, Oct. 28   Perf. 13
1554 A475 2.20fr multi   1.75   1.00

Industries Type of 1985

Design: 3.90fr, Plastics industry.

1986, Oct. 28   Engr.
1555 A455 3.90fr dk red, dk gray & bl grn   1.75   1.20

MONACO

Christmas — A476

1986, Oct. 28 Photo. Perf. 12½x13
1556 A476 1.80fr Holly .60 .30
1557 A476 2.50fr Poinsettia 1.25 .50

Ascent of Mt. Blanc by J. Balmat and M.G. Paccard, Bicent. A477

1986, Oct. 28 Engr. Perf. 13
1558 A477 5.80fr red, brt bl & slate bl 2.50 1.75

Miniature Sheet

Arbutus Tree — A478

1986, Oct. 28 Perf. 13x12½
1559 A478 Sheet of 4 9.50 9.50
  a. 3fr Spring 1.25 1.25
  b. 4fr Summer 1.00 1.00
  c. 5fr Fall 2.75 2.75
  d. 6fr Winter 2.50 2.50
See Nos. 1645, 1680, 1736, 1775, 1804, 1852, 1934, 1943.

Aquarium Type of 1985

1986, Sept. 25 Photo. Perf. 12½x13
1560 A451 1.90fr like No. 1481 2.25 1.00
1561 A451 3.40fr like No. 1483 4.00 2.50

Prince Rainier III — A479

Villa Miraflores, Seat of the Philatelic Bureau A480

#1562b, Prince Louis II, founder of the bureau.

1987, Apr. 23 Engr. Perf. 12½x13
1562 Strip of 3 8.50 8.50
  a. A479 4fr bright blue 1.90 1.90
  b. A479 4fr dark red 1.90 1.90
  c. A480 8fr black 3.75 3.75
Philatelic Bureau, 50th anniv.
See No. 1607.

Louis II Stadium — A481

1987, Apr. 23 Perf. 13x12½
1563 A481 2.20fr Exterior 1.75 .40
1564 A481 3.40fr Interior 2.00 .75
  a. Min. sheet, 5 each #1563-1564 25.00 13.00
Europa 1987.

Insects — A482

1fr, Carabe de solier. 1.90fr, Guepe dorec. 2fr, Cicindele. 2.20fr, Grande aeschne. 3fr, Chrysomele. 3.40fr, Grande sauterelle verte.

1987, Apr. 23 Photo.
1565 A482 1fr multi .55 .55
1566 A482 1.90fr multi 1.00 .90
1567 A482 2fr multi 1.25 1.00
1568 A482 2.20fr multi 1.50 1.00
1569 A482 3fr multi 2.40 1.75
1570 A482 3.40fr multi 3.25 2.50
Nos. 1565-1570 (6) 9.95 7.70
Nos. 1565, 1567 and 1569 horiz.

St. Devote Parish, Cent. — A483

1987, Apr. 23 Engr. Perf. 12½x13
1571 A483 1.90fr black .90 .45

Monaco Diocese, Cent. — A484

1987, Apr. 23
1572 A484 2.50fr dk yellow grn 1.00 .55

50th Intl. Dog Show, Monte Carlo — A485

1987, Apr. 23 Perf. 13x12½
1573 A485 1.90fr Dog breeds 2.00 1.25
1574 A485 2.70fr Poodle 3.50 1.90

Stamp Day — A486

1987, Apr. 23 Perf. 13
1575 A486 2.20fr multi 1.00 .45

Red Curley Tail, Mobile by Alexander Calder (1898-1976), Sculptor — A487

1987, Apr. 23 Photo.
1576 A487 3.70fr multi 1.60 1.00
Sculpture Exhibition, Monte Carlo.

2nd Small European Countries Games, May 14-17 A488

1987, Apr. 23 Engr.
1577 A488 3fr Tennis 2.00 1.60
1578 A488 5fr Windsurfing 2.50 1.75

Miniature Sheet

Grape Vines — A489

1987, Apr. 23 Perf. 13x12½
1579 A489 Sheet of 4 11.00 11.00
  a. 3fr Spring 1.50 1.50
  b. 4fr Summer 1.50 1.50
  c. 5fr Autumn 2.00 2.00
  d. 6fr Winter 2.50 2.50

Four Seasons Type of 1986

Life cycle of the chestnut tree.

1987, Mar. 17 Engr. Perf. 13x12½
1580 A460 1.31fr Spring .50 .45
1581 A460 1.69fr Summer .80 .70
1582 A460 2.74fr Fall 1.25 1.10
1583 A460 4.56fr Winter 2.00 1.60
Nos. 1580-1583 (4) 4.55 3.85
Nos. 1580-1583 known only precanceled.
See note after No. 324.

The Life of St. Devote, Patron Saint of Monaco — A490

Text: 4fr, Born in 283, in Quercio, Devote was martyred in Mariana, Corsica. 5fr, Devote's nurse teaches the saint about Christianity.

1987, Nov. 13 Photo. Perf. 13x12½
1584 A490 4fr multi 1.25 .85
1585 A490 5fr multi 1.60 1.10
Red Cross of Monaco.
See Nos. 1643-1644, 1692-1693, 1714-1715, 1776-1777, 1836-1837.

Philately — A491

Butterflies and butterflies on simulated stamps.

1987, July 28 Engr.
1586 A491 1.90fr brt grn & dk gray .90 .40
1587 A491 2.20fr rose red & rose lake .95 .50
1588 A491 2.50fr red lil & vio 1.25 .80
1589 A491 3.40fr brt bl & bluish blk 1.90 .85
Nos. 1586-1589 (4) 5.00 2.55

13th Int'l. Circus Festival, Monte Carlo, Jan. 28-Feb. 1 — A492

1987, Nov. 13 Photo. Perf. 12½x13
1590 A492 2.20fr multi 1.90 1.00

1988 Int'l Flower Show — A493

1987, Nov. 13
1591 A493 2.20fr Ikebanas 1.00 .60
1592 A493 3.40fr multi, horiz. 1.40 1.20
Dated 1988. See Nos. 1651, 1749.

Christmas A494

1987, Nov. 13 Engr. Perf. 13x12½
1593 A494 2.20fr crimson 1.00 .50

5-Franc Prince Honoré V Coin — A495

1987, Nov. 13 Perf. 13
1594 A495 2.50fr scar & dk gray .90 .45
Recapture of the Mint, 150th anniv.

Electronics Industry A496

1987, Nov. 13
1595 A496 2.50fr henna brn, vio bl & grn .90 .80

Int'l. Marine Radioactivity Laboratory, 25th Anniv. — A497

Design: Monaco Oceanographic Museum and Int'l. Agency of Atomic Energy, Vienna.

1987, Nov. 13
1596 A497 5fr brt bl, red brn & blk 2.00 1.40

Louis Jouvet (b 1887), French Actor — A498

1987, Nov. 16 Perf. 13x12½
1597 A498 3fr black 1.25 1.10

The River Crossing — A499

1987, Nov. 16
1598 A499 3fr multi 1.25 1.10
Paul and Virginia, by Bernardin de Saint-Pierre, first edition bcent. (in 1988).

Marc Chagall (1887-1985), Painter — A500

1987, Nov. 16 Perf. 13
1599 A500 4fr terra cotta & bl gray 1.75 1.25

MONACO

Jean Jenneret (Le Corbusier, 1887-1965), French Architect — A501

4fr, Architect, Ronchamp Chapel.

1987, Nov. 16
1600 A501 4fr multi 1.60 1.20

Newton's Theory of Gravity, 300th Anniv. A502

Invention of the Telegraph by Samuel Morse, 150th Anniv. A503

1987, Nov. 16
1601 A502 4fr magenta & dk bl 1.75 1.10
1602 A503 4fr brt vio, turq bl & brn 1.75 1.10

Don Juan, Opera by Mozart, Bicent. A504

Mass of the Dead, by Berlioz A505

1987, Nov. 16
1603 A504 5fr ind, vio brn & sage grn 2.00 1.50
1604 A505 5fr sl grn, vio brn & bl 2.00 1.50

Belle Epoch Type of 1982
Illustrations by Hubert Clerissi. 6fr, Rampe Major, vert. 7fr, Old Monte Carlo Station, vert.

1987, Nov. 16 Engr. Perf. 12½x13
1605 A394 6fr multi 3.75 2.50
1606 A394 7fr multi 4.50 3.75

Philatelic Bureau Type of 1987

1987, Nov. 13 Engr. Perf. 12½x13
1607 Sheet of 3 7.50 7.50
a. A479 4fr blk vio, like #1562a 1.75 1.75
b. A479 4fr blk vio, like #1562b 1.75 1.75
c. A480 8fr blk vio, like #1562c 3.50 3.50

Postage Due Arms Type of 1985 Booklet Stamps

1987-88 Photo. Perf. 13 on 3 Sides Size: 17x23mm
1608 D10 2fr multi ('88) 1.00 .40
a. Bklt. pane of 10 11.00
1609 D10 2.20fr multi 1.00 .60
a. Bklt. pane of 10 11.00
Issued: 2fr, Jan. 15; 2.20fr, Nov. 13.

Aquarium Type of 1985
2fr, Bodianus rufus. 2.20fr, Chelmon rostratus. 2.50fr, Oxymonacanthus longirostris. 3fr, Ostracion lentiginosum. 3.70fr, Pterois volitans, horiz. 7fr, Thalassoma lunare, horiz.

Perf. 13x12½, 12½x13
1988, Jan. 15 Photo.
1610 A451 2fr multi 1.00 .80
1611 A451 2.20fr multi 1.50 .50
1612 A451 2.50fr multi 2.00 1.10
1613 A451 3fr multi 1.50 .80
1614 A451 3.70fr multi 2.50 2.10
1615 A451 7fr multi 3.50 2.25
Nos. 1610-1615 (6) 12.00 7.55

Four Seasons Type of 1986
Life cycle of the pear tree.

1988, Feb. 15 Perf. 13x12½
1616 A460 1.36fr Spring .45 .45
1617 A460 1.75fr Summer .45 .45
1618 A460 2.83fr Fall 1.40 1.10
1619 A460 4.72fr Winter 2.25 1.60
Nos. 1616-1619 (4) 4.55 3.60
Nos. 1616-1619 known only precanceled. See note after No. 324.

Souvenir Sheet

Biathlon, 1988 Winter Olympics, Calgary — A506

1988, Feb. 15 Engr. Perf. 13
1620 A506 Sheet of 2 12.00 12.00
a. 4fr Skiing 4.00 4.00
b. 6fr Shooting 4.00 4.00

51st Intl. Dog Show, Monte Carlo — A507

1988, Mar. 30 Photo. Perf. 12½x13
1621 A507 3fr Dachshunds 3.00 2.00

World Assoc. of the Friends of Children (AMADE), 25th Anniv. — A508

1988, Mar. 30 Engr. Perf. 13
1622 A508 5fr dk vio bl, dk brn & brt ol grn 2.50 1.75

Europa 1988 — A509

Transport and communication: 2.20fr, Globe picturing hemispheres, man, brain, telecommunications satellite. 3.60fr, Plane propeller and high-speed locomotive.

1988, Apr. 21 Perf. 12½x13
1623 A509 2.20fr multi 1.50 .50
1624 A509 3.60fr multi 2.75 1.00
a. Souv. sheet, 5 each #1623-1624 27.50 12.50

Mushrooms of Mercantour Natl. Park — A510

2fr, Leccinum rotundifoliae. 2.20fr, Hygrocybe punicea. 2.50fr, Pholiota flammans. 2.70fr, Lactarius lignyotus. 3fr, Cortinarius traganus. 7fr, Russula olivacea.

Perf. 13x12½, 12½x13
1988, May 26 Photo.
1625 A510 2fr multicolored 1.25 .90
1626 A510 2.20fr multicolored 1.50 .85
1627 A510 2.50fr multicolored 1.75 1.50
1628 A510 2.70fr multicolored 2.10 1.75
1629 A510 3fr multicolored 2.50 2.25
1630 A510 7fr multicolored 4.25 4.25
Nos. 1625-1630 (6) 13.35 11.50
Nos. 1629-1630 vert.

Nautical Soc., Cent. A511

1988, May 26 Engr. Perf. 13
1631 A511 2fr dk red, lt blue & dk grn 1.00 .70

5th Year of Restoration of Our Lady of Laghet Sanctuary — A512

1988, May 26 Perf. 12½
1632 A512 5fr multicolored 2.00 1.40

World Health Organization, 40th Anniv. — A513

1988, May 26 Perf. 13
1633 A513 6fr brt blue & lake 2.50 1.75

Intl. Red Cross and Red Crescent Organizations, 125th Anniv. — A514

1988, May 26 Photo. Perf. 13x12½
1634 A514 6fr dull red, blk & gray 2.50 1.75

Jean Monnet (1888-1979), Nobel Peace Prize Winner in 1922 — A515

Maurice Chevalier (1888-1972), Actor — A516

1988, May 26 Engr. Perf. 12½x13
1635 A515 2fr brt blue, dk ol bister & blk 3.00 1.75
1636 A516 2fr blk & dark blue 3.25 1.75

1st Crossing of Greenland by Fridtjof Nansen (1861-1930), Cent. — A517

1988, May 26 Perf. 13
1637 A517 4fr bright violet 2.25 1.60

Belle Epoch Type of 1982
Illustrations by Hubert Clerissi: 6fr, Packet in Monte Carlo Harbor, 1910. 7fr, Monte Carlo Station, c. 1910.

1988, Sept. 8 Engr. Perf. 13x12½
1638 A394 6fr multi 3.25 2.50
1639 A394 7fr multi 4.00 3.25

Souvenir Sheet

1988 Summer Olympics, Seoul — A518

Woman wearing Korean regional costume, Games emblem and event: 2fr, Women's tennis. 3fr, Women's table tennis. 5fr, Women's yachting. 7fr, Women's cycling.

1988, Sept. 8 Engr.
1640 A518 Sheet of 4 9.50 9.50
a. 2fr blk, light ultra & brown 1.10 1.10
b. 3fr blk, light ultra & brown 1.40 1.40
c. 5fr blk, light ultra & brown 2.40 2.40
d. 7fr blk, light ultra & brown 3.25 3.25

Monte Carlo Congress Center, 10th Anniv. — A519

1988, Sept. 8 Perf. 13
1641 2fr dark blue grn 1.00 1.00
1642 3fr henna brn 1.25 1.25
a. A519 Pair, #1641-1642 2.50 2.50

Monegasque Red Cross Type of 1987
The Life of St. Devote, patron saint of Monaco: 4fr, Devote witnessing the arrival of the governor of Rome. 5fr, Devote and the governor.

1988, Oct. 20 Photo. Perf. 13x12½
1643 A490 4fr multicolored 2.00 1.00
1644 A490 5fr multicolored 2.50 1.50

Tree Type of 1986
Life cycle of the olive tree.

1988, Oct. 20 Engr. Perf. 13x12½
1645 A478 Sheet of 4 12.00 12.00
a. 3fr Spring 2.00 2.00
b. 4fr Summer 2.50 2.50
c. 5fr Fall 3.00 3.00
d. 6fr Winter 3.50 3.50

Le Nain and Brothers, Detail of a Painting in the Louvre, by Antoine Le Nain (c. 1588-1648) A521

1988, Oct. 20 Perf. 12½x13
1646 A521 5fr ol brn, dull brn & car rose 3.25 1.90

Les Grands Archeologues, Bronze Sculpture by Giorgio De Chirico (1888-1978), Italian Painter and Sculptor — A522

1988, Oct. 20 Perf. 13
1647 A522 5fr ol bis, blk brn & dark bl 3.25 1.90

MONACO

Pierre Carlet de Chamblain de Marivaux (1688-1763), French Playwright, Novelist — A523

1988, Oct. 20
1648 A523 3fr dull ol & ultra 1.50 1.00

Lord Byron (1788-1824), English Poet — A524

1988, Oct. 20
1649 A524 3fr grnsh bl, brn & blk 1.75 .85

14th Intl. Circus Festival, Monte Carlo, Feb 2-6, 1989 — A525

1988, Oct. 20 Photo. Perf. 12½x13
1650 A525 2fr multi 1.75 1.00

Intl. Flower Show Type of 1987
1988, Oct. 20
1651 A493 3fr Ikebana 1.75 1.25

22nd Intl. Flower Show and Flower Arranging Contest, Monte Carlo.

Textile Industry (Ready-to-Wear Clothes by Bettina and Le Squadra) — A526

1988, Oct. 20 Engr. Perf. 13
1652 A526 3fr blk, yel org & dk ol grn 1.50 1.00

Christmas — A527

1988, Oct. 20 Litho. Perf. 12½x13
1653 A527 2fr black & lemon 1.25 .70

Petroglyphs, Mercantour Natl. Park — A528

2fr, Magician. 2.20fr, Team of oxes. 3fr, Tools. 3.60fr, Chieftain. 4fr, Jumping jack, vert. 5fr, Christ., vert.

Perf. 13x12½, 12½x13
1989, Feb. 8 Litho.
1654 A528 2fr multi 1.00 .80
1655 A528 2.20fr multi 1.00 .80
1656 A528 3fr multi 1.40 1.20
1657 A528 3.60fr multi 2.00 1.50
1658 A528 4fr multi 2.00 1.75
1659 A528 5fr multi 2.50 2.00
Nos. 1654-1659 (6) 9.90 8.05

St. Nicolas Place — A528a

2fr, Rue des Spelugues.

Booklet Stamps
1989, Feb. 8 Litho. Perf. 13½x13
1660 A528a 2fr multi 1.00 .50
  b. Booklet pane of 10 12.00
1660A A528a 2.20fr shown 1.25 .60
  c. Booklet pane of 10 14.00
See Nos. 1702-1703, 1826-1827.

Prince Rainier III — A529

1989-91 Engr. Perf. 13
1661 A529 2fr pale blue grn & Prus grn .80 .35
1662 A529 2.10fr lt blue & Prus blue 1.00 .25
1663 A529 2.20fr pink & rose brn 1.00 .25
1664 A529 2.20fr pale grnsh bl & grnsh bl 1.00 .35
1665 A529 2.50fr pale pink & car lake 1.00 .25
1666 A529 2.50fr pale rose & rose lake 1.00 .25
1667 A529 3.20fr pale blue & brt blue 1.50 .90
1668 A529 3.40fr lt bl & dk bl 1.50 1.00
1669 A529 3.60fr lt blue & sapphire 1.50 1.25
1670 A529 3.80fr pale pink & dk lil rose 1.75 .55
1671 A529 4fr pale vio & rose vio 1.90 1.25
1672 A529 5fr buff & dark vio brn 2.00 .55
1673 A529 15fr pale vio & indigo 6.00 1.75
1673A A529 20fr pink & rose car 7.50 2.75
1674 A529 25fr pale gray & blk 8.00 2.00
Nos. 1661-1674 (15) 37.45 13.70

Issued: 2fr, #1663, 3.60fr, 5fr, 15fr, 3/14; 2.10fr, 2.30fr, 25fr 1/11/90; 3.20fr, 3.80fr, 3/15/90; 20fr, 4/26/91; #1664, 2.50fr, 3.40fr, 4fr, 9/24/91

See Nos. 1790-1799.

5th Magic Grand Prix, Monte Carlo, Mar. 17-19 — A530

1989, Mar. 14 Engr. Perf. 13x12½
1675 A530 2.20fr multi 1.25 .80

Dog Show Type of 1982
1989, Mar. 14 Photo.
1676 A387 2.20fr Yorkshire terrier 2.00 1.10

Our Lady of Mercy Soc., 350th Anniv. — A531

1989, Mar. 14 Engr. Perf. 13
1677 A531 3fr choc, dark red & blk 1.25 .75

Theater & Film A532

Designs: 3fr, Jean Cocteau (1889-1963), French writer, artist. 4fr, Charlie Chaplin (1889-1977), English actor, film producer.

1989, Mar. 14
1678 A532 3fr Prus grn, olive grn & dp rose lil 1.40 1.10
1679 A532 4fr dk grn, dk vio & dk red 2.75 1.60

Tree Type of 1986
Life cycle of the pomegranate tree.

1989, Mar. 14 Perf. 13x12½
Miniature Sheet
1680 A478 Sheet of 4 10.00 10.00
  a. 3fr Spring 1.40 1.40
  b. 4fr Summer 2.00 2.00
  c. 5fr Fall 2.75 2.75
  d. 6fr Winter 3.00 3.00

Souvenir Sheet

Reign of Prince Rainier III, 40th Anniv. A533

1989, May 9 Engr. Perf. 13
1681 A533 20fr rose vio 11.00 11.00
See No. 2128.

Europa 1989 — A534

Children's games: 2.20fr, Marbles. 3.60fr, Jumping rope.

1989, May 9 Perf. 12½x13
1682 A534 2.20fr multi 1.50 .40
1683 A534 3.60fr multi 2.75 .70
  a. Souv. sheet, 5 each #1682-1000 27.50 14.00

Souvenir Sheet

French Revolution, Bicent., PHILEXFRANCE '89 — A535

a, Liberty. b, Equality. c, Fraternity.

1989, July 7 Engr. Perf. 12½x13
1684 A535 Sheet of 3 6.50 6.50
  a. 5fr sapphire 2.00 2.00
  b. 4fr multi 1.00 1.00
  c. 5fr dark red 2.00 2.00

Four Seasons Type of 1986
Life cycle of the pear tree.

1989, July 27 Photo. Perf. 13x12½
1685 A460 1.39fr like No. 1616 .50 .50
1686 A460 1.79fr like No. 1617 .60 .60
1687 A460 2.90fr like No. 1618 1.25 1.25
1688 A460 4.84fr like No. 1619 2.25 1.75
Nos. 1685-1688 (4) 4.60 4.10

Nos. 1685-1688 known only precanceled. See note after No. 324.

Portrait of the Artist's Mother, by Philibert Florence — A536

Regatta at Molesey, by Alfred Sisley (1839-1899) A537

Paintings: 8fr, Enclosed Courtyard, Auvers, by Paul Cezanne (1839-1906), vert.

Perf. 13, 13x12½ (6fr), 12½x13 (8fr)
1989, Sept. 7 Engr.
1689 A536 4fr olive black 2.50 1.75
1690 A537 6fr multi 3.00 2.00
1691 A537 8fr multi 4.50 3.00
Nos. 1689-1691 (3) 10.00 6.75

Birth sesquicentennials of painters.

Monegasque Red Cross Type of 1987

The life of St. Devote, patron saint of Monaco: 4fr, Eutychius refuses to betray Devote to Barbarus and is poisoned. 5fr, Devote is condemned to torture by Barbarus when she refuses to make sacrifices to the Gods.

1989, Sept. 7 Photo. Perf. 13x12½
1692 A490 4fr multi 1.75 1.20
1693 A490 5fr multi 2.50 1.40

Interparliamentary Union, Cent. — A538

1989, Oct. 26 Engr. Perf. 13
1694 A538 4fr multi 1.75 1.00

Belle Epoch Type of 1982
Illustrations by Hubert Clerissi: 7fr, Ship in Monaco Port. 8fr, Gaming hall, Monte Carlo Casino.

1989, Oct. 26 Perf. 12½x13
1695 A394 7fr multi 3.50 2.50
1696 A394 8fr multi 4.25 3.00

Souvenir Sheet

Princess Grace Foundation, 25th Anniv. — A539

1989, Oct. 26
1697 A539 Sheet of 2 9.00 9.00
  a.-b. 5fr any single 3.50 3.50

a, Princess Grace. b, Princess Caroline.

20th UPU Congress A540

Design: Views of the Prince of Monaco's palace and the White House.

1989, Oct. 26 Perf. 13
1698 A540 6fr multicolored 2.50 1.75

MONACO

Christmas — A541

1989, Oct. 26   Litho.   Perf. 12½x13
1699 A541 2fr Poinsettia   2.25   .80

15th Intl. Circus Festival, Monte Carlo, Feb. 1-5, 1990 — A542

1989, Dec. 7   Photo.   Perf. 12½x13
1700 A542 2.20fr multicolored   3.50 1.00

Monaco Aid and Presence, 10th Anniv. — A543

1989, Dec. 7   Engr.   Perf. 13x12½
1701 A543 2.20fr brown & red   2.25 1.00

Avenues Type of 1989
2.10fr, The Great Stairs. 2.30fr, Mayoral Court of Honor.

1990, Feb. 8   Litho.   Perf. 13½x13
1702 A528a 2.10fr multi   .90   .50
  a. Bklt. pane of 10 + 2 labels 9.50
1703 A528a 2.30fr multi   1.00   .50
  a. Bklt. pane of 10 + 2 labels 11.00

Dog Show Type of 1982
1990, Mar. 15   Perf. 13x12½
1704 A387 2.30fr Bearded collie 2.25 1.25

Sir Rowland Hill, Great Britain No. 1 — A544

1990, Mar. 15   Engr.   Perf. 13
1705 A544 5fr royal bl & blk   2.75 2.00
Penny Black, 150th anniv.

Flowers Named for Members of the Royal Family — A545

1990, Mar. 15   Litho.   Perf. 12½x13
1706 A545 2fr Princess Grace   .95   .55
1707 A545 3fr Prince Rainier III 1.40 .70
1708 A545 3fr Grace Patricia   1.40   .90
1709 A545 4fr Principessa Grace 1.90 1.10
1710 A545 5fr Caroline of Monaco 2.50 1.75
  Nos. 1706-1710 (5)   8.15 5.00

Intl. Telecommunications Union, 125th Anniv. — A546

1990, Mar. 15   Engr.   Perf. 13
1711 A546 4fr pink, dp vio & dull blue grn 1.75 1.50

Antony Noghes (1890-1978), Creator of the Monaco Grand Prix and Monte Carlo Rally — A547

1990, Mar. 15
1712 A547 3fr deep vio, blk & dark red   1.25 1.00

Automobile Club, Cent. — A548

1990, Mar. 15
1713 A548 4fr brt pur, sepia & brt blue 2.10 1.40

Monegasque Red Cross Type of 1987
The life of St. Devote, patron saint of Monaco: 4fr, Devote tortured to death (whipped). 5fr, Body layed out in a small boat.

1990, Mar. 15   Litho.   Perf. 13x12½
1714 A490 4fr multicolored   1.90 1.25
1715 A490 5fr multicolored   2.50 1.75

Europa — A549

1990, May 3   Engr.   Perf. 12½x12
1716 A549 2.30fr multicolored   1.50   .35
1717 A549 3.70fr multicolored   2.25   .55
  a. Souv. sheet, 4 each, perf. 12½x13 27.50 13.00

Souvenir Sheet

World Cup Soccer Championships, Italy — A550

1990, May 3   Perf. 13x12½
1718 A550 Sheet of 4   13.00 13.00
  a. 5fr Players, trophy   3.25 3.25
  b. 5fr Player dribbling ball   3.25 3.25
  c. 5fr Ball   3.25 3.25
  d. 5fr Players, stadium   3.25 3.25

Four Seasons Type of 1986
Life cycle of the plum tree.

1990, Sept. 17   Perf. 13
1719 A460 1.46fr Spring   .80   .50
1720 A460 1.89fr Summer   1.00   .80
1721 A460 3.06fr Fall   1.60 1.25
1722 A460 5.10fr Winter   2.25 1.75
  Nos. 1719-1722 (4)   5.65 4.30
Nos. 1719-1722 known only precanceled. See note after No. 324.

Minerals, Mercantour Natl. Park — A551

Perf. 13x12½, 12½x13
1990, Sept. 4   Litho.
1723 A551 2.10fr Anatase   1.00   .50
1724 A551 2.30fr Albite   1.00   .50
1725 A551 3.20fr Rutile   1.50 1.10
1726 A551 3.80fr Chlorite   2.00 1.25
1727 A551 4fr Brookite   2.00 1.00
1728 A551 6fr Quartz   3.50 2.75
  Nos. 1723-1728 (6)   11.00 7.85
Nos. 1727-1728 vert.

Pierrot Ecrivain — A552

1990, Sept. 4   Engr.   Perf. 12½x13
1729 A552 3fr dark blue   1.50   .80

Helicopter, Monaco Heliport — A553

5fr, Helicopters, Monte Carlo skyline.

1990, Sept. 4   Perf. 13
1730 A553 3fr red, brn & blk   1.25   .60
1731 A553 5fr blk, gray bl & brn 2.00 1.40
30th World Congress of Civilian Airports, Monte Carlo.

C. Samuel Hahnemann (1755-1843), Physician — A554

1990, Sept. 4
1732 A554 3fr multicolored   1.40   .85
Homeopathic medicine, bicentennial.

Jean-Francois Champollion (1790-1832), Egyptologist — A555

1990, Sept. 4
1733 A555 5fr blue & brown   2.25 1.25

Offshore Power Boating World Championships — A556

1990, Sept. 4
1734 A556 2.30fr brt ultra, brn & red   1.00   .70
1735 A556 6fr brn org, brn & bl   2.50 1.60

Tree Type of 1986
Miniature Sheet
Life cycle of the lemon tree.

1990, Oct. 17   Litho.   Perf. 13x12½
1736 A478 Sheet of 4   9.50 9.50
  a. 3fr Spring   1.25 1.25
  b. 4fr Summer   1.75 1.75
  c. 5fr Fall   2.40 2.40
  e. 6fr Winter   2.75 2.75

Type of 1984
2.30fr, Miller riding donkey. 3.20fr, Woman carrying firewood. 3.80fr, Baker.

1990, Oct. 17   Litho.   Perf. 12½x13
1737 A441 2.30fr multi   1.00   .45
1738 A441 3.20fr multi   1.50   .80
1739 A441 3.80fr multi   2.00 1.25
  Nos. 1737-1739 (3)   4.50 2.50

The Cathedral, by Auguste Rodin (1840-1917) — A558

1990, Oct. 17   Engr.   Perf. 12½
1740 A558 5fr bl & cream   2.25 1.25

La Pie by Claude Monet (1840-1926) — A559

1990, Oct. 17   Perf. 13x12
1741 A559 7fr multicolored   4.00 4.00

Peter Ilich Tchaikovsky (1840-1893), Composer — A560

1990, Oct. 17   Perf. 12½x13
1742 A560 5fr dark grn & bl   2.25 1.25

16th Intl. Circus Festival, Monte Carlo — A561

1991, Jan. 2   Photo.   Perf. 13
1743 A561 2.30fr multicolored   1.50   .85
See No. 1801.

Intl. Symposium on Migratory Birds — A562

Migratory birds and their continents: 2fr, Ciconia abdimii, Africa. 3fr, Selasphorus platycercus, America. 4fr, Anas querquedula, Asia. 5fr, Eurystomus orientalis, Australia. 6fr, Merops apiaster, Europe.

1991, Feb. 22   Litho.   Perf. 12½x13
1744 A562 2fr multicolored   1.00   .60
1745 A562 3fr multicolored   1.25 1.00
1746 A562 4fr multicolored   2.00 1.25
1747 A562 5fr multicolored   2.50 2.00
1748 A562 6fr multicolored   3.25 2.50
  Nos. 1744-1748 (5)   10.00 7.35

Intl. Flower Show Type of 1987
1991, Feb. 22
1749 A493 3fr Cyclamen   1.50   .85

Views of Old Monaco Type of 1984
Designs: 20c, Cliffs of Monaco, Port de Fontvieille. 40c, Place du Casino. 50c, Place de la Cremaillere. 70c, Prince's Palace. 80c, Avenue du Beau Rivage. 1fr, Place d'Armes.

1991, Feb. 22   Engr.
1750 A425 20c rose violet   .25   .25
1751 A425 40c dk green   .25   .25
1752 A425 50c claret   .25   .25
1753 A425 70c ol green   .25   .25

MONACO

1754	A425	80c ultramarine	.30	.25
1755	A425	1fr dk blue	.40	.25
		Nos. 1750-1755 (6)	1.70	1.50

Dog Show Type of 1982
1991, Feb. 22 Litho. Perf. 12
1756	A387	2.50fr Schnauzer	2.00	1.40

Oceanographic Museum — A563

1991, Feb. 22
1757	A563	2.10fr Phytoplankton	1.25	.80

1992 Olympics — A564

Design: No. 1758b, Cross country skiiers, diff. No. 1759a, Relay runner receiving baton. No. 1759b, Runner passing baton.

1991, Apr. 26 Engr. Perf. 13x12½
1758		Pair	3.50	3.50
a.	A564	3fr dark green, blue & olive	1.40	1.25
b.	A564	4fr dark green, blue & olive	1.75	1.50
1759		Pair	4.00	4.00
a.	A564	3fr brown & Prussian blue	1.40	1.25
b.	A564	5fr brown & Prussian blue	2.50	2.00

Nos. 1758 and 1759 have continuous designs.

Europa — A565

1991, Apr. 26
1760	A565	2.30fr Eutelsat	1.75	.45
1761	A565	3.20fr Inmarsat	3.00	.60
a.		Min. sheet, 5 ea. #1760-1761	30.00	13.00

25th Intl. Contemporary Art Competition — A566

1991, Apr. 26 Engr. Perf. 12½x13
1762	A566	4fr multicolored	2.00	1.25

Prince Pierre Foundation, 25th Anniv. — A567

1991, Apr. 26
1763	A567	5fr multicolored	2.25	1.25

Coral — A568

1991, Apr. 26 Photo. Perf. 12
1764	A568	2.20fr shown	1.00	.80
1765	A568	2.40fr Coral necklace	1.25	.85

Christmas Type of 1984
2.50fr, Consul. 3.50fr, Woman from Arles. 4fr, Mayor.

1991, Nov. 7 Litho. Perf. 12
1766	A441	2.50fr multi	1.25	.50
1767	A441	3.50fr multi	2.00	1.10
1768	A441	4fr multi	2.25	1.40
		Nos. 1766-1768 (3)	5.50	3.00

Conifers, Mercantour Natl. Park — A569

2.50fr, Epicea. 3.50fr, Sapin. 4fr, Pin a crochets. 5fr, Pin sylvestre, vert. 6fr, Pin cembro. 7fr, Meleze, vert.

1991, Nov. 7
1769	A569	2.50fr multi	.95	.35
1770	A569	3.50fr multi	1.40	.70
1771	A569	4fr multi	1.50	.90
1772	A569	5fr multi	1.90	1.10
1773	A569	6fr multi	2.25	1.50
1774	A569	7fr multi	2.75	1.75
		Nos. 1769-1774 (6)	10.75	6.30

Tree Type of 1986
Miniature Sheet
Life cycle of an orange tree.

1991, Nov. 7 Engr. Perf. 13x12½
1775	A478	Sheet of 4	9.50	9.50
a.		3fr Spring	1.25	1.25
b.		4fr Summer	1.75	1.75
c.		5fr Fall	2.50	2.50
d.		6fr Winter	2.75	2.75

Monagasque Red Cross Type of 1907
Life of St. Devote, Monaco's Patron Saint: 4.50fr, The Storm is Rising. 5.50fr, Arrival of the Rock of Monaco.

1991, Nov. 7 Photo.
1776	A490	4.50fr multicolored	2.00	.90
1777	A490	5.50fr multicolored	2.25	1.25

Testudo Hermanni — A570

No. 1778, Two crawling right. No. 1779, Peering from shell. No. 1780, Walking in grass. No. 1781, Walking amid plants.

1991, Nov. 7 Litho. Perf. 12
1778	A570	1.25fr multi	1.40	.80
1779	A570	1.25fr multi	1.40	.80
1780	A570	1.25fr multi	1.40	.80
1781	A570	1.25fr multi	1.40	.80
a.		Block or strip of 4, #1778-1781	7.00	7.00

Prince Albert I Type of 1891
Miniature Sheet

1991, Nov. 7 Engr. Perf. 13
Stamp size: 22½x28mm
1782		Sheet of 3	12.00	12.00
a.	A2	10fr dark red	3.50	3.50
b.	A2	10fr dark blue green	3.50	3.50
c.	A2	10fr deep violet	3.50	3.50

Portrait of Claude Monet by Auguste Renoir — A571

1991, Nov. 7 Engr. Perf. 12½x13
1783	A571	5fr multicolored	2.40	1.75

Treaty of Peronne, 350th Anniv. — A572

Portraits by Philippe de Champaigne (1602-1674): 6fr, Honore II (1604-1662), Monaco. 7fr, Louis XIII (1610-1643), France.

1991, Nov. 7
1784	A572	6fr multicolored	3.00	2.50
1785	A572	7fr multicolored	3.75	2.50

Princess Grace Theatre, 10th Anniv. — A573

1991, Nov. 7 Litho.
1786	A573	8fr Princess Grace	4.25	3.75

Prince Rainier III Type of 1989
1991-96 Engr. Perf. 13
1790	A529	2.40fr pale grnsh bl & dk Prus bl	.80	.50
1791	A529	2.70fr palo bl grn, dk bl grn	1.60	.80
1791A	A529	(2.70fr) pale & Prus grn	1.00	.50
b.		With strengthened lines in military ribbon at LR	1.00	.50
1792	A529	2.80fr pale rose & rose lake	1.00	.60
1793	A529	3fr pale red, red brn	1.00	.90
1793A	A529	(3fr) pink & red	1.10	.55
1794	A529	3.70fr pale bl & dk bl	1.25	.80
1795	A529	3.80fr pale bl & dk bl	1.50	1.10
1796	A529	(3.80fr) pale & dk bl	1.50	.70
1797	A529	10fr lt bl grn & dp bl grn	3.25	1.90
1799	A529	40fr pale brn & dk brn	13.00	8.25
		Nos. 1790-1799 (11)	27.00	16.60

Nos. 1791A, 1793A, 1796 are dated "1999."
Issued: 10fr, 11/7/91; 2.40fr, 2.80fr, 3.70fr, 40fr, 7/28/93; 2.70fr, 3/18/96; 3fr, 3.80fr, 7/8/96; #1791A, 1793A, 1796, 11/28/98. No. 1791Ab, Apr. 2003.
No. 1791Ab sold for 41c on day of issue and has other strengthened lines other than those in the military ribbon.
See No. 1863b.

16th Intl. Circus Festival Type
1992, Jan. 6 Photo. Perf. 12½x13
1801	A561	2.50fr multicolored	1.60	1.00

1992 Winter and Summer Olympics, Albertville and Barcelona A574

Designs: 7fr, Two-man bobsled. 8fr, Soccer.

1992, Feb. 7 Engr. Perf. 13
1802	A574	7fr multicolored	3.25	1.50
1803	A574	8fr multicolored	3.75	2.00

Tree Type of 1986
Miniature Sheet
Life cycle of a cactus plant.

1992, Apr. 24 Photo. Perf. 13x12½
1804	A478	Sheet of 4	10.00	10.00
a.		3fr Spring	1.25	1.25
b.		4fr Summer	1.75	1.75
c.		5fr Fall	2.50	2.50
d.		6fr Winter	3.50	3.50

60th Monte Carlo Rally — A575

1992, Mar. 13 Engr. Perf. 13x12½
1805	A575	4fr dk bl grn, blk & red	1.75	1.25

Intl. Dog Show Type of 1982
2.20fr, Labrador retriever.

1992, Mar. 13 Litho. Perf. 13x12½
1806	A387	2.20fr multi	1.75	1.00

50th Grand Prix of Monaco — A576

1992, Mar. 13 Engr.
1807	A576	2.50fr vio brn, blk & brt bl	1.50	.80

25th Intl. Flower Show, Monte Carlo — A577

1992, Mar. 13 Photo. Perf. 12½x13
1808	A577	3.40fr multicolored	1.75	1.25

See No. 1848.

Four Seasons Type of 1986
Life cycle of a walnut tree.

1992, Mar. 13 Photo.
1809	A460	1.60fr Spring	.80	.50
1810	A460	2.08fr Summer	1.00	.80
1811	A460	2.98fr Fall	1.25	1.25
1812	A460	5.28fr Winter	2.00	1.75
		Nos. 1809-1812 (4)	5.05	4.30

Nos. 1809-1812 known only precanceled. See the note after No. 324.

Souvenir Sheet

Dolphins A578

1992, Mar. 13
1813	A578	Sheet of 4	11.50	11.50
a.		4fr Steno bredanensis	1.90	1.90
b.		5fr Delphinus delphis	2.40	2.40
c.		6fr Tursiops truncatus	3.00	3.00
d.		7fr Stenella coeruleoalba	3.50	3.50

See Nos. 1853, 1898.

Discovery of America, 500th Anniv. — A579

1992, Apr. 24
1814	A579	2.50fr Pinta	1.00	.45
1815	A579	3.40fr Santa Maria	2.00	.80
1816	A579	4fr Nina	3.00	1.25
a.		Sheet, 2 each #1814-1816	15.00	13.50
		Nos. 1814-1816 (3)	6.00	2.50

Europa.

Ameriflora Intl. Flower Show, Columbus, Ohio — A580

4fr, Fruits & vegetables. 5fr, Vase of flowers.

1992, Apr. 24 Litho. Perf. 12½x13
1817	A580	4fr multi	2.00	1.10
1818	A580	5fr multi	2.50	1.75

MONACO

Columbus Exposition, Genoa '92 — A581

1992, Apr. 24	Engr.		Perf. 13	
1819	A581	6fr multicolored	3.00	1.75

Expo '92, Seville A582

1992, Apr. 24				
1820	A582	7fr multicolored	3.25	2.00

Views of Old Monaco Type of 1984

Illustrations by Hubert Clerissi: 60c, National Council. 90c, Port of Fontvieille. 2fr, Condamine Market. 3fr, Sailing ship. 7fr, Oceanographic Museum.

1992, May 25	Engr.		Perf. 12½x13	
1821	A425	60c dark blue	.25	.25
1822	A425	90c violet brown	.25	.25
1823	A425	2fr vermilion	.35	.30
1824	A425	3fr black	1.10	.60
1825	A425	7fr gray blue & blk	2.50	1.40
		Nos. 1821-1825 (5)	4.45	2.80

Avenues Type of 1989

2.20fr, Porte Neuve, horiz. 2.50fr, Placette Bosio, horiz.

1992, May 25	Litho.		Perf. 13x13½	
		Booklet Stamps		
1826	A528a	2.20fr multi	1.00	.40
a.		Bklt. pane of 10 + 2 labels	10.00	
1827	A528a	2.50fr multi	1.00	.45
a.		Bklt. pane of 10 + 2 labels	10.00	

Genoa '92 — A583

Roses: 3fr, Christopher Columbus. 4fr, Prince of Monaco.

1992, Sept. 18	Litho.		Perf. 12	
1828	A583	3fr multicolored	1.75	1.10
1829	A583	4fr multicolored	1.75	1.10

Gypaetus Barbatus, Mercantour Natl. Park — A584

1992, Oct. 20	Engr.		Perf. 13x12½	
1830	A584	2.20fr grn, org & blk	1.50	1.00

Seabus — A585

1992, Oct. 20				
1831	A585	4fr multicolored	1.75	1.40

Phytoplankton — A586

Designs: 2.20fr, Ceratium ranipes. 2.50fr, Ceratium hexacanthum.

1992, Oct. 20	Litho.		Perf. 12	
1832	A586	2.20fr multicolored	1.40	.80
1833	A586	2.50fr multicolored	1.40	.40

Baron de Coubertin's Call for Modern Olympics, Cent. A587

1992, Oct. 20	Engr.		Perf. 13	
1834	A587	10fr blue	4.00	2.50

Chapel of St. Catherine A588

Prince of Monaco, the Marquisat of Baux-de-Provence.

1992, Oct. 20	Litho. & Engr.			
1835	A588	15fr multicolored	6.00	3.50

Monagasque Red Cross Type of 1987

The life of St. Devote, patron saint of Monaco: 6fr, Fire aboard ship. 8fr, Procession of the reliquary.

1992, Oct. 20	Engr.			
		Size: 48x36mm		
1836	A490	6fr multicolored	2.25	1.75
1837	A490	8fr multicolored	3.25	2.50

Christmas Type of 1984

1992, Oct. 20	Litho.		Perf. 12	
1838	A441	2.50fr Basket maker	1.25	.50
1839	A441	3.40fr Fishmonger	1.75	.85
1840	A441	5fr Drummer	2.25	1.50
		Nos. 1838-1840 (3)	5.25	2.85

Miniature Sheet

Postal Museum A589

1992, Oct. 20	Litho. & Engr.		Perf. 13	
1841	A589	Sheet of 2	9.00	9.00
a.		10fr Sardinia Type A4	4.25	4.25
b.		10fr France Type A3	4.25	4.25

17th Intl. Circus Festival, Monte Carlo — A590

1993, Jan. 5	Litho.		Perf. 13½x13	
1842	A590	2.50fr multicolored	1.40	.60

Birds, Mercantour Natl. Park — A591

Designs: 2fr, Circaetus gallicus, horiz. 3fr, Falco peregrinus, horiz. 4fr, Bubo bubo. 5fr, Pernis apivorus. 6fr, Aegolius funereus.

	Perf. 13x12½, 12½x13			
1993, Feb. 15			Engr.	
1843	A591	2fr multicolored	.95	.55
1844	A591	3fr multicolored	1.40	.70
1845	A591	4fr multicolored	1.75	1.10
1846	A591	5fr multicolored	2.10	1.50
1847	A591	6fr multicolored	2.60	1.75
		Nos. 1843-1847 (5)	8.80	5.60

Intl. Flower Show Type of 1992

1993, Mar. 1	Photo.		Perf. 12½x13	
1848	A577	3.40fr multicolored	1.50	.85

10th World Amateur Theater Festival A592

1993, Mar. 1	Litho.		Perf. 13	
1849	A592	4.20fr multicolored	2.00	.85

Intl. Civil Protection Day — A593

1993, Mar. 1	Engr.		Perf. 12½x13	
1850	A593	6fr multicolored	3.50	1.75

Princess Grace — A594

1993, Mar. 24	Engr.		Perf. 13	
1851	A594	5fr Prus blue	2.40	1.40

See US No. 2749.

Tree Type of 1986
Miniature Sheet

Life cycle of an almond tree: a, Spring. b, Summer. c, Autumn. d, Winter.

1993, Feb. 15	Photo.		Perf. 13x12½	
1852	A478	Sheet of 4	10.50	10.50
a.-d.		5fr any single	2.40	2.40

Marine Mammals Type of 1992
Miniature Sheet

1993, Mar. 24				
1853	A578	Sheet of 4	11.50	11.50
a.		4fr Balaenoptera physalus	1.90	1.90
b.		5fr Balaenoptera acutorostrata	2.40	2.40
c.		6fr Physeter catodon	3.00	3.00
d.		7fr Ziphius cavirostris	3.25	3.25

10th Monte Carlo Open Golf Tournament — A595

1993, Mar. 24	Photo.		Perf. 12	
1854	A595	2.20fr multicolored	1.00	.70

Dog Show Type of 1982

1993, Mar. 24	Litho.		Perf. 13x13½	
1855	A387	2.20fr Newfoundland	1.75	1.10

10th Biennial of Antique Dealers of Monte Carlo — A596

1993, Mar. 24			Perf. 12	
1856	A596	7fr multicolored	2.60	1.60

Flowering Cacti — A597

No. 1857, Echinopsis multiplex. No. 1858, Zygocactus truncatus. No. 1859, Echinocereas procumbens. No. 1860, Euphorbia virosa.

1993, May 4	Engr.		Perf. 13x13½	
		Booklet Stamps		
1857	A597	2.50fr multicolored	1.00	.70
1858	A597	2.50fr multicolored	1.00	.70
1859	A597	2.50fr multicolored	1.00	.70
1860	A597	2.50fr multicolored	1.00	.70
a.		Booklet pane, 2 each #1857-1860	8.50	
		Nos. 1857-1860 (4)	4.00	2.80

See Nos. 1889-1892, 1914-1918, 2007-2009, 2086-2089.

Europa — A598

2.50fr, Monte Carlo Ballet. 4.20fr, Sigaldi sculpture.

1993, May 4			Perf. 12½x12	
1861	A598	2.50fr multicolored	.90	.40
1862	A598	4.20fr multicolored	1.25	.70
a.		Souvenir sheet, 3 each, #1861-1862, perf. 13x12½	7.50	7.50

Souvenir Sheet

Admission to the UN — A599

1993, July 28	Engr.		Perf. 13	
1863	A599	Sheet of 3	12.50	12.50
a.		10fr light blue	4.00	4.00
b.		10fr brn vio (Design A529)	4.00	4.00
c.		10fr brown violet & red	4.00	4.00

Intl. Olympic Committee, 101st Session — A600

1993, Sept. 20	Litho. & Engr.		Perf. 13½x13	
		Booklet Stamps		
1864	A600	2.80fr Coat of arms	1.00	1.00
1865	A600	2.80fr Bobsledding	1.00	1.00
1866	A600	2.80fr Skiing	1.00	1.00
1867	A600	2.80fr Sailing	1.00	1.00
1868	A600	2.80fr Rowing	1.00	1.00
1869	A600	2.80fr Swimming	1.00	1.00
1870	A600	2.80fr Cycling	1.00	1.00
1871	A600	2.80fr shown	1.00	1.00
a.		Bklt. pane of 8, #1864-1871	8.00	
1872	A600	4.50fr like #1864	1.50	1.50
1873	A600	4.50fr Gymnastics	1.50	1.50
1874	A600	4.50fr Judo	1.50	1.50
1875	A600	4.50fr Fencing	1.50	1.50
1876	A600	4.50fr Hurdles	1.50	1.50
1877	A600	4.50fr Archery	1.50	1.50
1878	A600	4.50fr Weight lifting	1.50	1.50
1879	A600	4.50fr like #1871	1.50	1.50
a.		Bklt. pane of 8, #1872-1879	12.00	

See No. 1899.

Red Cross of Monaco — A601

Design: 6fr, Red, white crosses.

1993, Nov. 10	Litho.		Perf. 13½x13	
1880	A601	5fr red, black & yellow	2.10	1.25
1881	A601	6fr red & black	2.50	2.00

MONACO

Monaco Philatelic Union, Cent. — A602

1993, Nov. 10 — Perf. 13x13½
1882 A602 2.40fr multicolored 1.00 .45

Christmas Type of 1984
1993, Nov. 10 — Perf. 13½x13
1883 A441 2.80fr Donkey 1.00 .50
1884 A441 3.70fr Shepherd 1.50 .85
1885 A441 4.40fr Cow 1.50 1.25
Nos. 1883-1885 (3) 4.00 2.60

Edvard Grieg (1843-1907), Composer — A603

Joan Miro (1893-1943), Artist — A604

Georges de La Tour (1593-1652), Painter — A605

Litho. (#1887), Engr.
1993, Dec. 10 — Perf. 13
1886 A603 4fr blue 2.50 1.25
1887 A604 5fr multicolored 2.50 1.60
— Perf. 12x13
1888 A605 6fr multicolored 2.75 1.75

Flowering Cacti Type of 1993
1994, Jan. 7 Engr. Perf. 13
1889 A597 20c like #1857 .25 .25
1890 A597 30c like #1858 .25 .25
1891 A597 40c like #1860 .25 .25
1892 A597 4fr like #1859 1.25 .40
Nos. 1889-1892 (4) 2.00 1.15

18th Intl. Circus Festival, Monte Carlo — A606

1994, Jan. 7 Litho. Perf. 13½x13
1893 A606 2.80fr multicolored 1.40 .60

Figurines, Natl. Museum — A607

Designs: No. 1894, Poet. No. 1895, Japanese geisha. No. 1896, Shepherdess with lamb. No. 1897, Parisian woman.

1994, Jan. 7 Engr. Perf. 12½x13
1894 A607 2.80fr blue 1.00 .60
1895 A607 2.80fr magenta 1.00 .60
1896 A607 2.80fr purple 1.00 .60
1897 A607 2.80fr blue green 1.00 .60
Nos. 1894-1897 (4) 4.00 2.40

Marine Mammals Type of 1992
Miniature Sheet
1994, Feb. 11 Photo. Perf. 13x12½
1898 A578 Sheet of 4 12.00 12.00
 a. 4fr Orcinus orca 2.10 2.10
 b. 5fr Grampus griseus 2.50 2.50
 c. 6fr Pseudorca crassidens 2.90 2.90
 d. 7fr Globicephala melas 3.50 3.50

Intl. Olympic Committee Type of 1993
Souvenir Sheet
1994, Feb. 11 Engr. Perf. 13
1899 Sheet of 2 10.00 10.00
 a. A600 10fr like #1866 4.50 4.50
 b. A600 10fr like #1865 4.50 4.50
1994 Winter Olympics, Lillehammer.

Intl. Dog Show Type of 1982
2.40fr, King Charles spaniel.
1994, Mar. 14 Litho. Perf. 13x13½
1900 A387 2.40fr multi 1.50 .80

27th Intl. Flower Show — A608

1994, Mar. 14 — Perf. 13½x13
1901 A608 4.40fr Iris 2.00 1.25
See Nos. 1941, 1989, 2028.

10th Grand Prix of Magic, Monte Carlo — A609

1994, Mar. 14 Engr. Perf. 13x12½
1902 A609 5fr lake, black & blue 2.00 1.50

25th Conference of the Grand Cordon of French Cuisine — A610

1994, Mar. 14 — Perf. 12½
1903 A610 6fr multicolored 2.50 1.75

Prince Albert I, Research Ship Princess Alice II — A611

Europa: 4.50fr, Opisthoproctus Grimaldii, Eryoneicus Alberti, Oceanographic Museum, Monaco.

1994, May 5 Engr. Perf. 13x12½
1904 A611 2.80fr multicolored 1.25 .75
1905 A611 4.50fr multicolored 2.10 1.10
 a. Min. sheet, 3 each #1904-1905 12.00 9.00

Intl. Olympic Committee, Cent. — A612

1994, May 17 Engr. Perf. 12½x12
1906 A612 3fr multicolored 1.40 .75

Institute for Preservation of the Sea — A613

1994, May 17 Litho. Perf. 13
1907 A613 6fr multicolored 2.25 1.75

Intl. Year of the Family — A614

1994, May 17 Engr. Perf. 13
1908 A614 7fr multicolored 2.75 2.00

1994 World Cup Soccer Championships, US — A615

1994, May 17 — Perf. 12½x13
1909 A615 8fr red & black 3.25 2.25

Intl. Amateur Athletic Federation A616

1994, June 10 — Perf. 13
1910 A616 8fr multicolored 3.00 2.25

1903 De Dion Bouton — A617

1994, Aug. 22 Engr. Perf. 13x12½
1911 A617 2.80fr lil, blk & brn 1.25 .85

Intl. Assoc. of Philatelic Catalogue Editors (ASCAT) — A618

1994, Aug. 22 Litho. Perf. 13
1912 A618 6fr blk, lil rose & grn 1.25 .75

21st UPU Congress, Seoul, Korea — A619

1994, Aug. 22
1913 A619 4.40fr bl, red & blk 2.25 1.25

Flowering Cacti Type of 1993
50c, Selenicereus grandiflorus. 60c, Opuntia basilaris. 70c, Aloe plicatilis. 80c, Opuntia hybride. 2fr, Aporocactus flagelliformis.

1994, Oct. 17 Engr. Perf. 13
1914 A597 50c multi .40 .25
1915 A597 60c multi .40 .25
1916 A597 70c multi .40 .25
1917 A597 80c multi .40 .25
1918 A597 2fr multi .40 .40
Nos. 1914-1918 (5) 2.00 1.40

Christmas Type of 1984
1994, Oct. 17 Litho. Perf. 13
1919 A441 2.80fr Mary 1.25 .55
1920 A441 4.50fr Christ child 2.10 .90
1921 A441 6fr Joseph 2.75 1.10
Nos. 1919-1921 (3) 6.10 2.55

Currency Museum — A620

3fr, Prince Albert. 4fr, Arms of Grimaldi. 7fr, Prince Rainier III.

1994, Oct. 17 Engr. Perf. 12½
1922 A620 3fr multi 1.00 .85
1923 A620 4fr multi 1.50 1.25
1924 A620 7fr multi 3.00 2.00
Nos. 1922-1924 (3) 5.50 4.10

Souvenir Sheet
Perf. 12½x13
1925 Sheet of 3 14.00 14.00
 a. A620 10fr like #1922 4.50 4.50
 b. A620 10fr like #1923 4.50 4.50
 c. A620 10fr like #1924 4.50 4.50

Red Cross Campaigns A621

Designs: 6fr, Fight against cancer. 8fr, Fight against AIDS.

1994, Oct. 17 Litho. Perf. 13
1926 A621 6fr lake, blue & black 1.75 1.40
1927 A621 8fr lake, grn & blk 2.50 1.75
See Nos. 1983-1984.

ICAO, 50th Anniv. — A622

Helicopters and: 5fr, Monaco Heliport. 7fr, Monaco skyline.

1994, Oct. 17 Engr. Perf. 13
1928 A622 5fr multicolored 2.00 1.50
1929 A622 7fr multicolored 3.00 2.00

Voltaire (1694-1778), Writer — A623

Sarah Bernhardt (1844-1923), Actress — A624

Publication of Robinson Crusoe, by Daniel Defoe, 275th Anniv. A625

The Snake Charmer, by Henri Rousseau (1844-1910) A626

MONACO

1994, Oct. 17   Engr.   *Perf. 13*
| 1930 | A623 | 5fr olive green | 2.00 | 1.25 |
| 1931 | A624 | 6fr multicolored | 2.25 | 1.50 |

Litho.
1932	A625	7fr multicolored	2.75	1.90
1933	A626	9fr multicolored	3.75	2.25
	Nos. 1930-1933 (4)		10.75	6.90

Tree Type of 1986
Miniature Sheet
Life cycle of an apricot tree.

1994, Oct. 17   Photo.   *Perf. 13x12½*
1934	A478	Sheet of 4	12.00	12.00
a.		6fr Spring	2.50	2.50
b.		7fr Summer	2.75	2.75
c.		8fr Autumn	3.25	3.25
d.		9fr Winter	3.50	3.50

19th Intl. Circus Festival, Monte Carlo — A627

1995, Jan. 3   Litho.   *Perf. 13½x13*
| 1935 | A627 | 2.80fr multicolored | 1.40 | .60 |

Monte Carlo Television, 35th Festival — A628

1995, Feb. 13   Engr.   *Perf. 12½x13*
| 1936 | A628 | 8fr Prince Albert | 3.00 | 1.75 |

European Nature Conservation Year — A629

1995, Apr. 3   Litho.   *Perf. 13x13½*
| 1937 | A629 | 2.40fr multicolored | 1.10 | .55 |

Intl. Special Olympics — A630

1995, Apr. 3
| 1938 | A630 | 3fr multicolored | 1.10 | .80 |

Rotary Intl. Convention, Nice — A631

1995, Apr. 3   Engr.   *Perf. 13x12½*
| 1939 | A631 | 4fr blue | 1.75 | 1.00 |

Intl. Dog Show Type of 1982
4fr, American cocker spaniel.

1995, Apr. 3   Litho.   *Perf. 13x13½*
| 1940 | A387 | 4fr multi | 2.25 | 1.25 |

Intl. Flower Show Type of 1993
1995, Apr. 3   *Perf. 13½x13*
| 1941 | A608 | 5fr Perroquet tulips | 2.00 | 1.25 |

European Bonsai Congress — A632

1995, Apr. 3   *Perf. 12*
| 1942 | A632 | 6fr Acer palmatum | 2.50 | 1.40 |

Tree Type of 1986
Miniature Sheet
Life cycle of a jujube tree.

1995, Apr. 3   Photo.   *Perf. 12x12½*
1943	A478	Sheet of 4	10.50	10.50
a.		4fr Spring	1.90	1.90
b.		5fr Summer	2.40	2.40
c.		6fr Fall	2.75	2.75
d.		7fr Winter	3.25	3.25

Peace & Liberty — A633

Photo. & Engr.
1995, May 8   *Perf. 12x12½*
| 1944 | A633 | 2.80fr multicolored | 1.25 | .80 |
| 1945 | A633 | 5fr multicolored | 2.40 | 1.25 |

Europa: 2.80fr, Dove with olive branch, Alfred Nobel. 5fr, Chain broken over concentration camp, flowers.

50th anniversaries: End of World War II (#1944), liberation of the concentration camps (#1945).

A634

Designs: 5fr, Jean Giono (1895-1970), writer. 6fr, Marcel Pagnol (1895-1974), film producer, writer.

1995, May 8   Engr.   *Perf. 12½x13*
| 1946 | A634 | 5fr multicolored | 1.75 | 1.00 |
| 1947 | A634 | 6fr multicolored | 2.00 | 1.40 |

Princess Caroline, Pres. of World Assoc. of Friends of Children — A635

1995, May 8   Photo.   *Perf. 13½x13*
| 1948 | A635 | 7fr blue | 2.50 | 2.00 |

Intl. Council of Wildlife Conservation A636

1995, May 8   Engr.   *Perf. 13*
| 1949 | A636 | 6fr St. Hubert, stag | 2.00 | 1.25 |

IAAF Track & Field Championships, Louis II Stadium — A637

1995, May 8
| 1950 | A637 | 7fr multicolored | 2.50 | 1.60 |

Alps Monument A638

1995, May 8
| 1951 | A638 | 8fr multicolored | 3.00 | 2.00 |

Prince Pierre of Monaco (1895-1964) — A639

1995, May 8
| 1952 | A639 | 10fr lake | 3.50 | 2.40 |

Souvenir Sheet
Stamp & Coin Museum A640

a, #927. b, Museum entrance. c, #294.

1995, May 8
| 1953 | A640 | Sheet of 3, #a.-c. | 13.50 | 13.50 |
| a.-c. | | 10fr any single | 4.50 | 4.50 |

St. Anthony of Padua (1195-1231) — A641

1995, Sept. 25   Litho.   *Perf. 13½*
| 1954 | A641 | 2.80fr multicolored | 1.00 | .60 |

UN, 50th Anniv. — A642

Designs: #1955, 1963a, Soldiers, UN Charter. #1956, 1963b, Grain, child. #1957, 1963c, Childrens' faces. #1958, 1963d, Musical notes, temple of Abu Simbel. #1959, 1963e, UN Security Council. #1960, 1963f, Hand holding grain, field. #1961, 1963g, Letters from various languages. #1962, 1963h, UNESCO Headquarters.

1995, Oct. 24   Engr.   *Perf. 13*
1955	A642	2.50fr multicolored	1.00	.50
1956	A642	2.50fr multicolored	1.00	.50
1957	A642	2.50fr multicolored	1.00	.50
1958	A642	2.50fr multicolored	1.00	.50
1959	A642	3fr multicolored	1.25	.70
1960	A642	3fr multicolored	1.25	.70
1961	A642	3fr multicolored	1.25	.70
1962	A642	3fr multicolored	1.25	.70
	Nos. 1955-1962 (8)		9.00	4.80

Miniature Sheet
1963		Sheet of 8	15.00	15.00
a.-d.		A642 3fr any single	1.25	1.25
e.-h.		A642 4.50fr any single	2.00	2.00

A643

Flowers: No. 1964, Rose *Grace of Monaco*. No. 1965, Fuschia *Lakeland Princess*. No. 1966, Carnation *Century of Monte Carlo*. No. 1967, Fuschia *Grace*. No. 1968, Rose *Princess of Monaco*. No. 1969, Alstroemeria *Gracia*. No. 1970, Lily *Princess Grace*. No. 1971, Carnation *Princess Caroline*. No. 1972, Rose *Stephanie of Monaco*. No. 1973, Carnation *Prince Albert*. No. 1974, Sweet pea *Grace of Monaco*. No. 1975, Gerbera *Gracia*.

1995, Oct. 24   Litho.   *Perf. 13½*
Booklet Stamps
1964	A643	3fr multicolored	1.20	.80
1965	A643	3fr multicolored	1.20	.80
1966	A643	3fr multicolored	1.20	.80
1967	A643	3fr multicolored	1.20	.80
1968	A643	3fr multicolored	1.20	.80
1969	A643	3fr multicolored	1.20	.80
1970	A643	3fr multicolored	1.40	.80
1971	A643	3fr multicolored	1.20	.80
1972	A643	3fr multicolored	1.20	.80
1973	A643	3fr multicolored	1.20	.80
1974	A643	3fr multicolored	1.20	.80
1975	A643	3fr multicolored	1.20	.80
a.		Bklt. pane, #1964-1975 + 2 labels	15.00	
		Complete booklet, #1975a	16.00	

Christmas Type of 1984
1995, Oct. 24   Litho.   *Perf. 13½x13*
1976	A441	3fr Balthazar	1.00	.65
1977	A441	5fr Gaspard	1.50	1.10
1978	A441	6fr Melchior	2.00	1.25
	Nos. 1976-1978 (3)		4.50	3.00

Monagasque Assoc. for Protection of Nature, 20th Anniv. — A644

1995, Oct. 24   Engr.   *Perf. 13*
| 1980 | A644 | 4fr green, black & red | 1.50 | .85 |

Wilhelm Röntgen (1845-1923), Discovery of X-Rays, Cent. — A645

1995, Oct. 24
| 1981 | A645 | 6fr multicolored | 2.50 | 1.25 |

Motion Pictures, Cent. A646

1995, Oct. 24
| 1982 | A646 | 7fr dark blue | 3.00 | 1.75 |

Red Cross Campaigns Type of 1994
Designs: 7fr, World fight against leprosy. 8fr, Drs. Prakash and Mandakini Amte, Indian campaign against leprosy.

1995, Oct. 24   Litho.
| 1983 | A621 | 7fr multicolored | 2.00 | 1.50 |
| 1984 | A621 | 8fr multicolored | 3.00 | 1.75 |

Pneumatic Automobile Tires, Cent. A647

1995, Oct. 24   Engr.
| 1985 | A647 | 8fr claret & dk purple | 3.00 | 1.75 |

MONACO

Springtime, by Sandro Botticelli (1445-1510) — A648

1995, Oct. 24
| 1986 | A648 | 15fr blue | 9.25 | 5.25 |
| a. | Souvenir sheet of 1 | | 9.25 | 5.25 |

No. 1986 printed in sheets of 10 + 5 labels.
No. 1986a inscribed in sheet margin as a winner of the 4th World Cup of Stamps, portrait of Botticelli. Issued 11/6/97.

20th Intl. Circus Festival, Monte Carlo — A649

1996, Jan. 10 Litho. Perf. 13
| 1987 | A649 | 2.40fr multicolored | 1.10 | .50 |

Compare with No. 2825b.

Magic Festival, Monte Carlo — A650

1996, Jan. 10 Engr.
| 1988 | A650 | 2.80fr black & gray | 1.25 | .55 |

Intl. Flower Show Type of 1994

1996, Jan. 26 Litho.
| 1989 | A608 | 3fr Rhododendron | 1.25 | .65 |

Intl. Dog Show Type of 1982

1996, Jan. 26
| 1990 | A387 | 4fr Fox terrier | 1.75 | 1.00 |

Opening of Chapel of Notre Dame of Miséricorde, 350th Anniv. — A651

1996, Jan. 26 Engr. Perf. 12x13
| 1991 | A651 | 6fr multicolored | 2.40 | 2.00 |

Oceanographic Voyages of Prince Albert I of Monaco and King Charles I of Portugal, Cent. — A652

3fr, Fish in sea, net, Prince Albert I holding binoculars, ship. 4.50fr, Ship, King Charles I holding sextant, microscope, sea life.

1996, Feb. 1 Litho. Perf. 12
| 1992 | A652 | 3fr multicolored | 1.40 | .70 |
| 1993 | A652 | 4.50fr multicolored | 2.10 | 1.25 |

See Portugal Nos. 2084-2085.

Prince Rainer III Type of 1974 Inscribed "MUSEE DES TIMBRES ET DES MONNAIES"

1996, Mar. 11 Engr. Perf. 13
1994	AP37	10fr purple	3.00	2.00
1995	AP37	15fr henna brown	5.00	3.50
1996	AP37	20fr ultra	7.00	4.75
	Nos. 1994-1996 (3)	15.00	10.25

Stamp and Currency Museum.

Princess Grace — A653

1996, Apr. 29
| 1997 | A653 | 3fr red & brown | 2.00 | .70 |

Europa.

RAMOGE Agreement Between France, Italy, Monaco, 20th Anniv. — A654

Photo. & Engr.
1996, May 14 Perf. 13
| 1998 | A654 | 3fr multicolored | 1.25 | .65 |

See France #2524, Italy #2077.

Annales Monegasques, 20th Anniv. — A655

Famous people: a, Saint Nicolas of Myra, by Louis Brea. b, Guillaume Apollinaire (1880-1918), poet. c, Jean-Baptiste Francois Bosio (1764-1827), painter. d, Francois-Joseph Bosio (1768-1845), sculptor. e, Hector Berlioz (1803-69), composer. f, Niccolo Machiavelli (1469-1527), writer. g, Sidonie-Gabrielle Colette (1873-1954), writer. h, Michael Montaigne (1533-92), essayist.

1996, May 14 Engr. Perf. 12½x13
1999	A655	Sheet of 8	15.00	15.00
a., e.		3fr any single	1.00	1.00
b., f.		4fr any single	1.50	1.50
c., g.		5fr any single	1.75	1.75
d., h.		6fr any single	2.00	2.00

Souvenir Sheet

CHINA '96, 9th Asian Intl. Philatelic Exhibition — A656

Designs: a, Chinese acrobats in Monaco. b, Fuling Tomb, Shenyang.

1996, May 14 Litho. Perf. 13
| 2000 | A656 | Sheet of 2 | 4.00 | 4.00 |
| a.-b. | | 5fr any single | 1.50 | 1.50 |

Introduction of Telephone Area Code 377 for Monaco — A657

1996, June 21 Engr. Perf. 13
| 2001 | A657 | 3fr dark blue | 1.00 | .75 |
| 2002 | A657 | 3.80fr vermilion | 1.50 | 1.00 |

1996 Summer Olympic Games, Atlanta — A658

No. 2003, Javelin, 1896. No. 2004, Women's softball, 1996. No. 2005, Runners, 1896. No. 2006, Cycling, 1996.

1996, July 19 Litho. Perf. 13½x13
2003	A658	3fr multi	1.00	.90
2004	A658	3fr multi	1.00	.90
2005	A658	4.50fr multi	1.60	1.40
2006	A658	4.50fr multi	1.60	1.40
	Nos. 2003-2006 (4)	5.20	4.60

Flowering Cacti Type of 1993

Designs: 10c, Bromelia brevifolia. 1fr, Stapelia flavirostris. 5fr, Cereus peruvianus.

1996, Sept. 16 Engr. Perf. 13
2007	A597	10c multicolored	.25	.25
2008	A597	1fr multicolored	.40	.25
2009	A597	5fr multicolored	1.50	.75
	Nos. 2007-2009 (3)	2.15	1.25

Tree Type of 1986

Life cycle of thorn (ronce) tree.

1996, Oct. 14 Photo. Perf. 13
2010	A478	Sheet of 4	11.00	11.00
a.		4fr Spring	1.75	1.75
b.		5fr Summer	2.25	2.25
c.		6fr Fall	2.75	2.75
d.		7fr Winter	3.25	3.25

Red Cross Campaigns Type of 1994

Designs: 7fr, Fight against tuberculosis. 8fr, Camille Guérin, Albert-Leon C. Calmette, developers of BCG vaccine against tuberculosis.

1996, Oct. 14
| 2011 | A621 | 7fr multicolored | 3.00 | 1.50 |
| 2012 | A621 | 8fr multicolored | 3.00 | 2.00 |

UNICEF, 50th Anniv. — A658a

1996, Oct. 14 Engr. Perf. 12½x13
| 2013 | A658a | 3fr multicolored | 1.25 | .70 |

Discovery of the Planet, Neptune, 150th Anniv. — A659

Photo. & Engr.
1996, Oct. 14 Perf. 13x12½
| 2014 | A659 | 4fr multicolored | 2.00 | .80 |

René Descartes (1596-1650), Philosopher, Mathematician — A660

1996, Oct. 14 Engr. Perf. 13
| 2015 | A660 | 5fr blue & carmine | 2.25 | 1.25 |

Christmas — A661

1996, Oct. 14 Litho. Perf. 13
| 2016 | A661 | 3fr Angel | 1.25 | .65 |
| 2017 | A661 | 6fr Angels | 2.50 | 1.25 |

Self-Portrait, by Corot (1796-1875) — A662

7fr, Self-portrait (detail), by Goya (1746-1828).

Photo. & Engr.
1996, Oct. 14 Perf. 12x13
| 2018 | A662 | 6fr multicolored | 2.50 | 1.50 |
| 2019 | A662 | 7fr multicolored | 3.25 | 1.75 |

Stamp and Coin Museum — A663

Designs: No. 2020, Printing and engraving stamps. No. 2021, Coins, screw press. 10fr, Front entrance to museum.

1996, Oct. 14 Engr. Perf. 13
2020	A663	5fr dk olive & violet	2.00	2.00
2021	A663	5fr dk ol & dk bl	2.00	2.00
2022	A663	10fr dk ol & dk bl	4.00	4.00
a.	Souvenir sheet, #2020-2022	8.50	8.50
	Nos. 2020-2022 (3)	8.00	8.00

No. 2022 is 48x36mm.

Grimaldi Dynasty, 700th Anniv. — A664

No. 2023: a, Francois Grimaldi, 1297. b, Rainier I, d. 1314. c, Charles I, d. 1357. d, Rainier II, 1350-1407. e, Jean I, 1382-1454. f, Catalan, d. 1457. g, Lambert, d. 1494. h, Jean II, 1468-1505. i, Lucien, 1481-1523. j, Augustin, d. 1532. k, Honoré I, 1522-1581. l, Charles II, 1555-1589. m, Hercule I, 1562-1604.
No. 2024: a, Honoré II (1597-1662). b, Louis I (1642-1701). c, Antoine (1661-1731). d, Louise-Hippolyte (1697-1731). e, Jacques I (1689-1751). f, Honoré III (1720-95). g, Honoré IV (1758-1819). h, Honoré V (1778-1841). i, Florestan I (1785-1856). j, Charles III (1818-89). k, Albert I (1848-1922). l, Louis II (1870-1949). m, Rainier III.

1997 Litho. Perf. 13
2023		Sheet of 13 + 2 labels	30.00	30.00
a.	A664	1fr multicolored	2.50	2.50
b.-d.	A664	1fr multi, each	.30	.30
e., g.	A664	2fr multi, each	.75	.75
f.	A664	9fr multicolored	3.50	3.50
h.-j.	A664	9fr multi, each	3.50	3.50
k.-m.	A664	9fr multi, each	2.50	2.50
2024		Sheet of 13 + 2 labels	30.00	30.00
a.-c.	A664	1fr multi, each	.35	.35
d.	A664	1fr multicolored	3.50	3.50
e.	A664	2fr multicolored	.75	.75
f.-i.	A664	2fr multi, each	3.50	3.50
j.-m.	A664	7fr multi, each	2.50	2.50

Portions of the designs on Nos. 2023-2024 were applied by a thermographic process producing a shiny, raised effect.
Issued: #2023, 1/9; #2024, 7/3.

Knight in Armor Type of 1951 Inscribed "1297-1997"

1996-97 Engr. Perf. 13
| 2025 | A67 | 2.70fr bl, brn & red | 1.00 | .60 |

Sheet of 8
2026		2 ea #a.-c., 2025	9.00	9.00
a.	A67	2.70fr red	1.25	1.25
b.	A67	2.70fr brown	1.25	1.25
c.	A67	2.70fr blue	1.25	1.25

Issued: #2025, 12/19/96; #2026, 1/8/97.

MONACO

Yacht Club of Monaco — A665

1996, Dec. 12	Litho.	Perf. 13
2027	A665 3fr multicolored	1.25 .70

Intl. Flower Show Type of 1993

1996, Dec. 19		Perf. 13½x13
2028	A608 3.80fr Camellia	1.50 .75

Tennis Tournaments in Monaco, Cent. — A666

1997, Feb. 1	Litho.	Perf. 13
2029	A666 4.60fr multicolored	1.90 1.00

Portions of the design on No. 2029 were applied by a thermographic process producing a shiny, raised effect.
For overprint see No. 2049.

37th Festival of Television in Monte Carlo — A667

1996, Dec. 19		Perf. 13½x13
2030	A667 4.90fr multicolored	2.00 1.00

Campanula "Medium" — A668

1996, Dec. 19	Litho.	Perf. 13
2031	A668 5fr multicolored	2.00 1.10

Auto Sports in Monaco — A669

1996, Dec. 19	Litho.	Perf. 13
2032	A669 3fr multicolored	1.40 .65

Philatelic Events — A670

Stamp & Coin Museum and: No. 2033, Pictures, engraving tools, picture on stamps. No. 2034, Stamp, magnifying glass, envelopes.

1996, Dec. 19	Engr.	Perf. 13
2033	A670 3fr multicolored	2.00 .60
2034	A670 3fr multicolored	2.00 .60
a.	Pair, #2033-2034	5.00 5.00

Monaco Philatelic Office, 60th anniv. (#2033). Monaco Intl. Philatelic Exhibition (#2034).

Dog Show Type of 1982

1996, Dec. 19	Litho.	Perf. 13x13½
2035	A387 4.40fr Afghan hound	2.40 1.00

21st Intl. Circus Festival, Monte Carlo — A671

1996, Dec. 19	Litho.	Perf. 13½x13
2036	A671 3fr multicolored	1.50 .60

Intl. Grand Prix of Philately — A672

1997, Apr. 5	Litho.	Perf. 13
2041	A672 4.60fr multicolored	1.75 1.25

Red Cross Campaign Against Drug Abuse — A673

1997, May 5		Perf. 13½x13
2042	A673 7fr multicolored	3.25 1.60

Europa (Stories and Legends) — A674

No. 2043, Legend of St. Devote. No. 2044, Port Hercules named for mythological Hercules.

1997, May 5	Engr.	Perf. 12½x13
2043	A674 3fr multicolored	1.50 .65
2044	A674 3fr multicolored	1.50 .65
a.	Pair, #2043-2044	3.00 3.00

PACIFIC 97 Intl. Philatelic Exhibition — A675

Design: US types A2 & A1, Monaco #1995.

1997, May 29		Perf. 13x12½
2045	A675 4.90fr multicolored	2.25 1.25

Uniforms of the Carabiniers (Palace Guards) — A676

Years uniforms used: 3fr, 1997. 3.50fr, 1750-1853. 5.20fr, 1865-1935.

1997, May 31	Litho.	Perf. 13x13½
2046	A676 3fr multicolored	1.25 .50
2047	A676 3.50fr multicolored	1.40 .60
2048	A676 5.20fr multicolored	2.25 .90
	Nos. 2046-2048 (3)	4.90 2.00

No. 2029 Ovptd. "M. RIOS"

1997		Perf. 13
2049	A666 4.60fr multicolored	2.10 1.40

13th Grand Prix of Magic, Monte Carlo — A677

1997	Litho.	Perf. 13½x13
2050	A677 4.40fr multicolored	1.75 1.25

Monaco Soccer Assoc., 1996 French Division 1 Champions — A678

1997		Perf. 13
2051	A678 3fr multicolored	1.40 .80

François Grimaldi, by Ernando Venanzi — A679

9fr, Saint Peter and Saint Paul, by Rubens.

1997, Sept. 8	Engr.	Perf. 13½x13
2052	A679 8fr multicolored	2.25 2.00
2053	A679 9fr multicolored	3.25 2.50

Evolution of the Geographic Territory of Monaco — A680

Designs: a, 13th century. b, 15th-19th century. c, Map of western half of Monaco, panoramic view. d, Map of eastern half of Monaco, panoramic view.

1997, Oct. 6	Litho. & Engr.	Perf. 13
2054	A680 5fr Sheet of 4, #a.-d.	8.00 8.00

Grimaldi Dynasty, 700th anniv.

49th Session of Intl. Whaling Commission — A681

1997, Oct. 20	Photo.	Perf. 13x13½
2055	A681 6.70fr multicolored	2.25 1.75

22nd Intl. Circus Festival, Monte Carlo — A682

1997, Nov. 30	Litho.	Perf. 13½x13
2057	A682 3fr multicolored	1.75 .70

Princess Charlotte (1898-1977) — A683

1997, Nov. 28	Engr.	Perf. 13x12½
2058	A683 3.80fr brown	1.50 .90

Designs by Monagasque Students — A685
A684

Perf. 13½x13, 13x13½

1997, Nov. 29		Litho.
2059	A684 4fr Under 13 group	1.40 .90
2060	A685 4.50fr Over 13 group	1.75 .90

31st Intl. Flower Show — A686

1997, Nov. 30		Perf. 13½x13
2061	A686 4.40fr multicolored	1.50 1.00

1998 Winter Olympic Games, Nagano — A687

Designs: No. 2062, 4-Man bobsled, speed skating, ice hockey, figure skating. No. 2063, Downhill skiing, biathlon, luge, ski jumping, slalom skiing.

1997, Nov. 28	Photo.	Perf. 12½
2062	4.90fr multicolored	1.90 1.25
2063	4.90fr multicolored	1.90 1.25
a.	A687 Pair, #2062-2063	4.00 4.00

Moscow '97 — A688

Ballet Russes de Monte Carlo.

1997, Nov. 28	Photo.	Perf. 13½x13
2064	A688 5fr multicolored	2.10 1.25

J.L. David (1748-1825), Painter — A689

1997, Nov. 30	Engr.	Perf. 12½x13
2065	A689 5.20fr red brn & dk grn	2.00 1.10

MONACO

Papal Bull for the Parish of Monaco, 750th Anniv. — A690

7.50fr, Pope Innocent IV.

1997, Nov. 30   Perf. 12½x13
2066   A690   7.50fr brn, lt blue   3.00   1.90

Prince Albert I (1848-1922) — A691

1997, Nov. 29   Photo.   Perf. 13x12½
2067   A691   8fr multicolored   3.00   2.40

38th Television Festival — A692

1998, Feb. 4   Litho.   Perf. 13½x13
2068   A692   4.50fr multicolored   1.75   1.00

Marcel Kroenlein Arboretum, 10th Anniv. A693

1997, Nov. 28   Photo.   Perf. 13
2069   A693   9fr multicolored   3.50   2.50

No. 2069 was issued in sheets of 2.

Boxer, Doberman — A693a

1998, Mar. 19   Litho.   Perf. 13x13½
2069A   A693a   2.70fr multi   1.25   .80

International Dog Show, Monte Carlo.

Intl. Academy of Peace — A694

1998, Mar. 19   Litho.   Perf. 13
2070   A694   3fr green & blue   1.25   .70

Portions of the design of No. 2070 were applied by a thermographic process producing a shiny, raised effect.

15th Spring Arts Festival — A695

1998, Mar. 19   Litho.   Perf. 13x13½
2071   A695   4fr multicolored   1.40   .90

Pierre and Marie Curie, Discovery of Radium, Cent. — A696

1998, Mar. 19   Engr.   Perf. 13x12½
2072   A696   6fr lilac & green blue   2.25   1.40

Monegasque Red Cross, 50th Anniv. — A697

Prince Albert, Prince Louis II, Princess Grace, Prince Rainier III.

1998, Mar. 3   Litho.   Perf. 13
2073   A697   5fr sepia, red & dk brown   2.00   1.25

Prince Albert I (1848-1922) — A698

1998, May 6   Engr.
2074   A698   7fr dark brown   3.25   1.50

Charles Garnier (1825-98), Architect, Designer of Casino of Monte Carlo — A699

1998, May 6   Litho.
2075   A699   10fr multicolored   4.00   2.25

Festival of St. Dévote A700

1998, May 6   Litho.   Perf. 13x13½
2076   A700   3fr multicolored   1.25   .65
   a.   Tete-beche pair   2.50   1.30

Europa. Portions of the design on No. 2076 were applied by a thermographic process producing a shiny, raised effect.

Joseph Kessel (1898-1979), Writer and Journalist — A701

1998, May 6   Engr.   Perf. 13½
2077   A701   3.90fr multicolored   1.40   .90

Expo '98, Lisbon — A702

1998, May 6   Litho.   Perf. 13x13½
2078   A702   2.70fr multicolored   1.10   .60

1st Formula 3000 Grand Prix in Monaco — A703

1998, May 20   Engr.   Perf. 12
2079   A703   3fr red & black   1.40   .70

European Conference of the Youth Chamber of Economics — A705

1998, May 6   Litho.   Perf. 13½x13
2081   A705   3fr multicolored   1.25   .70

World Music Awards — A706

1998, May 6
2082   A706   10fr multicolored   4.00   2.75

Porcelain A707

1998, June 24   Perf. 13
2083   A707   8fr multicolored   2.75   1.75

Publication of Monaco's Works of Art — A708

1998, June 24
2084   A708   9fr multicolored   3.25   2.00

National Festival A709

Europa: Prince Albert, Prince Rainier III, national palace.

1998, May 31   Litho.   Perf. 13
2085   A709   3fr multicolored   1.40   .70

Portions of the design on No. 2085 were applied by a thermographic process producing a shiny, raised effect.

Flowering Cacti Type of 1993

2.70fr, Opuntia dejecta. 4fr, Echinocereus blanckii. 6fr, Euphorbia milii. 7fr, Stapelia variegata.

1998, Aug. 3   Engr.   Perf. 13
2086   A597   2.70fr multicolored   1.00   .50
2087   A597   4fr multicolored   1.50   .75
2088   A597   6fr multicolored   2.00   1.10
2089   A597   7fr multicolored   2.50   1.25
    Nos. 2086-2089 (4)   7.00   3.60

1998 World Cup Soccer Championships, France — A710

1998, Aug. 3
2090   A710   15fr multicolored   6.00   3.50

No. 2090 contains hexagonal perforated label in center.

Enzo Ferrari (1898-1988), Automobile Manufacturer A711

1998, Aug. 14   Litho.
2091   A711   7fr multicolored   2.50   1.75

George Gershwin (1898-1937), Composer A712

1998, Aug. 14   Engr.   Perf. 13x12½
2092   A712   7.50fr bl, bl grn & blk   3.00   1.75

Intl. College for Study of Marine Pollution, Marine Environment Laboratory A713

1998, Sept. 4   Litho.   Perf. 13x13½
2093   A713   4.50fr multicolored   1.75   .90

Plenary Assembly of the European Post, Monte Carlo — A714

1998, Sept. 4
2094   A714   5fr multicolored   1.90   .90

Expo '98, World Philatelic Exhibition, Lisbon — A715

1998, Sept. 4   Litho. & Engr.
2095   A715   6.70fr multicolored   2.50   1.50

Intl. Assoc. Against Violence in Sports, 30th Anniv. — A716

Photo. & Engr.
1998, Sept. 14   Perf. 13x13½
2096   A716   4.20fr multicolored   1.60   1.00

MONACO

Magic Stars Magic Festival, Monte Carlo — A717

1998, Sept. 26	Litho.	Perf. 13½x13
2097 A717 3.50fr red & bister		1.40 .80

See No. 2140.

Giovanni Lorenzo Bernini (1598-1680), Architect, Sculptor — A718

1998, Sept. 26	Engr.	Perf. 13x12½
2098 A718 11.50fr blue & brown		4.50 3.25

Italia '98, Intl. Philatelic Exhibition, Milan — A719

1998, Oct. 23		Perf. 12½x13
2099 A719 4.90fr Milan Cathedral		2.00 1.10

Christmas — A720

3fr, Ornament. 6.70fr, Nativity scene, horiz. 15fr, Icon of Madonna and Child, 18th cent.

Perf. 13½x13, 13x13½		
1998, Oct. 26		Litho.
2100 A720 3fr multicolored		1.25 .50
2101 A720 6.70fr multicolored		2.25 1.25

Souvenir Sheet
Engr.
Perf. 13

2102 A720 15fr multicolored	5.75 5.75

No. 2102 contains one 36x49mm stamp.

23rd Intl. Circus Festival, Monte Carlo — A721

1998, Nov. 20	Litho.	Perf. 13½x13
2103 A721 2.70fr multicolored		1.25 .50

Grimaldi Seamounts A722

1998, Nov. 20		Perf. 13
2104 A722 10fr multicolored		3.50 2.00

Reign of Prince Rainier III, 50th Anniv. A723

1998, Nov. 20		Engr.
2105 A723 25fr red & yel bister		9.00 9.00

Congress Center Auditorium of Monaco, 20th Anniv. — A724

1999, Feb. 12	Litho.	Perf. 13x13½
2106 A724 2.70fr multicolored		1.25 .50

39th Intl. Television Festival, Monte Carlo — A725

1999, Jan. 18	Litho.	Perf. 13½x13
2107 A725 3.80fr multicolored		1.75 .80

Dog Show Type of 1982

Cocker spaniel and American cocker spaniel.

1999, Jan. 18	Litho.	Perf. 13x13½
2108 A387 4fr multicolored		2.00 1.10

Geneva Conventions, 50th Anniv. — A726

1999, Jan. 18	Engr.	Perf. 13½x13
2109 A726 4.40fr black & red		1.90 .80

32nd Intl. Flower Show, Monte Carlo — A727

1999, Jan. 18	Litho.	Perf. 13½x13
2110 A727 4.50fr multicolored		1.90 1.10

Monaco '99, Intl. Philatelic Exhibition A728

Photo. & Engr.

1999, Jan. 18		Perf. 13x12
2111 A728 3fr multicolored		1.25 .50

Beginning with No. 2112, denominations are indicated on the stamps in both Francs and Euros. The listing value is shown in Francs.

10th Piano Masters Competition, Monte Carlo — A729

1999, Feb. 12		Perf. 13x13½
2112 A729 4.60fr multicolored		1.75 .80

Flowers — A730

Designs: 4.90fr, Prince of Monaco Jubilee Rose. 6fr, Paphiopedilum Prince Rainier III, Prince of Monaco and Grimaldi Roses.

1999	Litho.	Perf. 13½x13
2113 A730 4.90fr multicolored		1.75 1.25
2114 A730 6fr multicolored		2.25 1.40

Issued: 4.90fr, 2/14; 6fr, 2/13.

Monaco Charity Assoc., 20th Anniv. — A731

1999, Jan. 28	Litho.	Perf. 13
2115 A731 6.70fr multicolored		2.50 1.50

Formula 1 Grand Prix of Monaco, 70th Anniv. A732

1999, Apr. 16	Photo.	Perf. 12¼
2116 A732 3fr multicolored		1.25 .80

Intl. Grand Prix of Philately, Monaco — A733

1999, Apr. 16		Perf. 13¼
2117 A733 4.40fr multicolored		1.75 1.10

Fifth Intl. Show Jumping Championships, Monte Carlo — A734

1999, Apr. 16	Engr.	Perf. 13x12½
2118 A734 5.20fr blk, dk grn & red		2.00 1.50

ASM Sports Club, 75th Anniv.

Cutouts of soccer players over: No. 2119, Palace. No. 2120, Aerial view of city.

1999, Apr. 16	Litho.	Perf. 13x12¾
2119 A735 7fr multicolored		2.75 1.90
2120 A735 7fr multicolored		2.75 1.90
a. Pair, #2119-2120		6.00 6.00

Grimaldi Forum — A736

1999, Apr. 25	Photo.	Perf. 13¼
2121 A736 3fr multicolored		1.10 .50

Oceanography Museum, Cent. — A737

1999, Apr. 25	Engr.	Perf. 13¼x13
2122 A737 5fr multicolored		2.00 1.25

Philexfrance '99, Intl. Philatelic Exhibition — A738

France #1, Eiffel Tower, map of France, exhibition emblem, arms of Monaco.

1999, May 5	Engr.	Perf. 13¼
2123 A738 2.70fr multicolored		1.00 .60

See No. 2133.

Europa — A739

No. 2124, Casino, Cliffs. No. 2125, Park in Fontvieille.

1999, May 5	Photo.	Perf. 13
2124 A739 3fr multi		1.25 .65
	Size: 51x28mm	
2125 A739 3fr multi		1.25 .65
a. Pair, #2124-2125		3.00 3.00

Monegasque Economic Growth — A740

Chart and: No. 2126, Fontveille and underground train station. No. 2127, Larvotto and Grimaldi Forum.

1999, May 5	Photo.	Perf. 13x13¼
2126 5fr multi		1.75 .95
2127 5fr multi		1.75 .95
a. A740 Pair, #2126-2127		4.00 4.00

MONACO

Souvenir Sheet

Reign of Prince Rainier III, 50th Anniv. — A741

1999, May 9	**Engr.**		**Perf. 13**	
2128	A741	20fr blue & gold	8.00	8.00

See No. 1681.

Honoré de Balzac (1799-1850), Writer — A742

Design: 5.20fr, Countess of Ségur (1799-1874), children's storyteller.

			Perf. 12¾x13	
1999				
2129	A742	4.50fr red & blue	1.90	1.10
2130	A742	5.20fr multicolored	2.10	1.25

Reign of Prince Rainier III, 50th Anniv. — A743

Design: #256, 337, 427, 937, 1287, 1669.

1999	**Engr.**		**Perf. 12¾x13**	
2131	A743	30fr multicolored	12.00	12.00

UNESCO, 50th Anniv. — A744

1999, July 2	**Engr.**		**Perf. 13x12½**	
2132	A744	4.20fr multicolored	1.60	.80

PhilexFrance Type of 1999

7fr, Franco #1, 02, Monaco #3.

1999, July 2	**Engr.**		**Perf. 13¼**	
2133	A738	7fr multi	2.50	1.50

Sportel, 10th Anniv. — A745

1999, July 2	**Litho.**		**Perf. 12¼**	
2134	A745	10fr multicolored	3.50	2.40

Sovereign Military Order of Malta, 900th Anniv. — A746

1999, July 2	**Engr.**		**Perf. 11**	
2135	A746	11.50fr multicolored	4.50	2.75

UPU, 125th Anniv. — A747

1999, July 2	**Engr.**		**Perf. 13¼**	
2136	A747	3fr multicolored	1.10	.70

Rose, Iris Named After Prince Rainier III — A748

1999, July 2	**Litho.**		**Perf. 13¼x13**	
2137	A748	4fr multicolored	1.60	.90

Stamp, Coin and Postcard Show, Fontvieille — A749

3fr, Aerial photograph, coin obverse, No. 1793A. 6.50fr, Aerial photograph, 100fr coin, #257.

1999		**Photo.**	**Perf. 13¼**	
2138	A749	3fr multicolored	1.10	.50
			Perf. 13¼x13½	
2139	A749	6.50fr multicolored	2.50	1.75

Jubiloo Bourso (#2139). Issued: 3fr, 7/3; 6.50fr, 9/26.

Magic Stars Type of 1998
Inscribed "99"

Litho. & Typo.				
1999, Sept. 6			**Perf. 13¼x13**	
2140	A717	4.50fr red & gold	1.60	1.00

Development Projects — A750

Designs: a, Fontvieille 1 & 2. b, La Digue (with jetty). c, Grimaldi Forum. d, La Gare.

1999, Sept. 26		**Photo.**	**Perf. 13**	
2141		Sheet of 4 + label	15.00	15.00
a.		A750 4fr multicolored	1.50	1.50
b.-c.		A750 9fr Any single	3.00	3.00
d.		A750 19fr multicolored	6.00	6.00

No. 2141d is 80x40mm.

24th Intl. Circus Festival, Monte Carlo — A751

1999, Dec. 13	**Litho.**		**Perf. 13¼x13**	
2142	A751	2.70fr multi	1.40	.55

A752

1999, Dec. 13	**Engr.**		**Perf. 13¼**	
2143	A752	3fr Christmas	1.10	.60

Holy Year 2000 — A753

1999, Dec. 13	**Litho.**		**Perf. 13x13¼**	
2144	A753	3.50fr multi	1.25	.95

33rd Intl. Flower Show — A754

1999, Dec. 13			**Perf. 13¼x13**	
2145	A754	4.50fr multi	1.75	1.00

Monaco 2000 Intl. Philatelic Exposition — A755

1999, Dec. 23	**Engr.**		**Perf. 13¼x13**	
2146	A755	3fr multi	1.10	.55

Bust of Napoleon, by Antonio Canova — A756

Litho. & Embossed				
2000, Jan. 17			**Perf. 13¼**	
2147	A756	4.20fr multi	2.00	.90

40th Intl. Television Festival, Monte Carlo — A757

2000, Jan. 17	**Litho.**		**Perf. 13¼x13**	
2148	A757	4.90fr multi	2.00	.95

The Twelve Apostles — A758

Saints: 4fr, Peter and James the Great. 5fr, John and Andrew. 6fr, Philip and Bartholomew. 7fr, Matthew and Thomas. 8fr, James the Less and Judas. 9fr, Simon and Matthias.

Engr. with Foil Application				
2000, Apr. 3			**Perf. 13¼**	
2149	A758	4fr multi	1.50	.80
2150	A758	5fr multi	2.00	.95
2151	A758	6fr multi	2.00	1.25
2152	A758	7fr multi	3.00	1.50
2153	A758	8fr multi	3.00	2.00
2154	A758	9fr multi	3.50	2.40
Nos. 2149-2154 (6)			15.00	8.90

Intl. Dog Show, Monte Carlo — A759

6.50fr, Labrador Retriever and Golden Retriever.

2000, Apr. 3	**Engr.**		**Perf. 13¼**	
2155	A759	6.50fr multi	3.00	1.50

A760

2000, Apr. 25			**Photo.**	
2156	A760	7fr multi	2.50	1.50

1993 Intl. Olympic Committee Meeting Awarding 2000 Games to Sydney.

Souvenir Sheet

Art Depicting Monaco and the Sea — A761

Artwork by: a, Adami. b, Arman. c, Cane. d, Folon. e, Fuchs. f, E. De Sigaldi. g, Sosno. h, Verkade.

2000, Apr. 25			**Perf. 13x12½**	
2157	A761	Sheet of 8 + label	20.00	20.00
a.-h.		6.55fr Any single	2.50	1.50

2nd Historic Automobile Grand Prix — A762

2000, May 9	**Litho.**		**Perf. 13½x13**	
2158	A762	4.40fr multi	1.90	1.00

Monaco Pavilion, Expo 2000, Hanover — A763

2000, May 9			**Perf. 13x13¼**	
2159	A763	5fr multi	2.00	1.25

Saints Mark, Matthew, John and Luke — A764

2000, May 9	**Engr.**		**Perf. 12¾x13**	
2160	A764	20fr multi	8.00	8.00

MONACO

Europa, 2000
Common Design Type and
Flags and Map of Europe — A765

2000, May 9   Litho.   *Perf. 13¼x13*
2161   CD17   3fr multi   1.40   .70
2162   A765   3fr multi   1.40   .70
   a.   Pair, #2161-2162   3.00   3.00

WIPA 2000 Philatelic Exhibition, Vienna — A766

2000, May 30   Engr.   *Perf. 13¼*
2163   A766   4.50fr multi   1.40   1.00

Professional-Celebrity Golf Tournament, Monte Carlo — A767

2000, June 19   Photo.   *Perf. 13¼*
2164   A767   4.40fr multi   1.75   1.00

Club de Monte Carlo Exhibition of Rare Philatelic Material — A768

2000, June 23
2165   A768   3.50fr multi   1.40   .75

Red Cross — A769

2000, June 23
2166   A769   10fr multi   3.50   2.00

2000 Summer Olympics, Sydney — A770

Olympic rings and: 2.70fr, Fencing, emblem of Monegasque Fencing Federation. 4.50fr, Rowers, flag of Monegasque Nautical Society.

2000, June 23   Engr. & Embossed
2167-2168   A770   Set of 2   2.50   1.75

Automobiles in Prince Rainier III Collection — A771

Woman and: 3fr, 1911 Humber Type Beeston. 6.70fr, 1947 Jaguar 4 cylinder. 10fr, 1956 Rolls-Royce Silver Cloud. 15fr, 1986 Lamborghini Countach.

2000, June 23   Engr.   *Perf. 13x13¼*
2169-2172   A771   Set of 4   13.00   10.50
See Nos. 2186-2188.

World Stamp Expo 2000, Anaheim — A772

2000, July 7   Litho.   *Perf. 13¼x13*
2173   A772   4.40fr multi   1.50   .90

Magic Stars Magic Festival, Monte Carlo — A773

2000, Sept. 4   Photo.   *Perf. 13¼*
2174   A773   4.60fr multi   1.75   1.25

Intl. Mathematics Year — A774

2000, Sept. 4   Engr.
2175   A774   6.50fr brown   2.50   1.50

Souvenir Sheet

Retable of St. Nicholas, by Ludovic Bréa, Monaco Cathedral — A775

No. 2176: a, Two figures, (31x52mm). b, Three figures, (53x52mm).

2000, Sept. 4   Photo.
2176   A775   Sheet of 2   12.00   12.00
   a.   10fr multicolored   3.50   1.75
   b.   20fr multicolored   6.50   4.50

New Aquarium, Oceanographic Museum — A776

2000, Oct. 2   Engr.
2177   A776   3fr multi   2.00   .70

España 2000 Intl. Philatelic Exhibition A777

2000, Oct. 2
2178   A777   3.80fr multi   1.50   .80

Observatory Grotto, 50th Anniv. and Anthropological Museum, 40th Anniv. — A778

2000, Oct. 2
2179   A778   5.20fr multi   2.00   .80

Fish — A779

5fr, Fish, coral. 9fr, Fish, starfish, seaweed.

2000, Oct. 2   Photo.
2180-2181   A779   Set of 2   5.50   3.00
Fifth Congress of Aquariums (No. 2180), Monegasque Nature Protection Association, 25th anniv. (No. 2181).

Fifth Congress of Aquariums — A780

2000, Nov. 25   Photo.   *Perf. 13x12¾*
2182   A780   7fr multi   2.50   1.75

Christmas — A781

2000, Dec. 1   Photo.   *Perf. 13¼*
2183   A781   3fr multi   1.40   .50

Princess Stephanie, President of AMAPEI — A782

2000, Dec. 1   Engr.
2184   A782   11.50fr red & slate   4.25   3.00

Souvenir Sheet

Monaco 2000 Intl. Philatelic Exhibition — A783

2001, Dec. 1   Photo.   *Imperf.*
2185   A783   Sheet of 2 #2185a   17.00   17.00
   a.   20fr multi   8.00   8.00

Prince's Automobiles Type of 2000

Woman and: 5fr, 1989 Ferrari F1. 6fr, 1955 Fiat 600 Type Jolly. 8fr, 1929 Citroen C4F Autochenille.

2000, Dec. 1   Engr.   *Perf. 13x13¼*
2186-2188   A771   Set of 3   7.50   4.50

Exhibit of Chinese Terra-cotta Figures, Grimaldi Forum — A784

2000, Dec. 2   Photo.   *Perf. 13¼*
2189   A784   2.70fr multi   1.00   .40

Postal Museum, 50th Anniv. — A785

2000, Dec. 2
2190   A785   3fr multi   1.25   .50

Coat of Arms — A786

Serpentine Die Cut 11
2000, Dec. 4   Photo.
Booklet Stamp
Self-Adhesive
2191   A786   (3fr) red & black   1.25   .30
   a.   Booklet of 10   12.50
See Nos. 2389, 2410, 2673, 2775, 2863, 2994. Compare with Types A1076 and A1597.

Princess Caroline of Monaco Iris — A787

2000, Dec. 2   Photo.   *Perf. 13¼*
2192   A787   3.80fr multi   1.50   .70
34th Intl. Flower Show.

Sardinian Postage Stamps, 150th Anniv. (in 2001) — A788

2000, Dec. 2   Engr.   *Perf. 13x12½*
2193   A788   6.50fr Sardinia #1-3   2.50   1.75

RAMOGE Agreement, 25th Anniv. — A789

2000, Dec. 2
2194   A789   6.70fr multi   2.50   1.75

Awarding of ASCAT Grand Prize to Bertrand Piccard — A790

2000, Dec. 2   Photo.   *Perf. 13¼*
2195   A790   9fr Balloon, #1433   3.50   2.00

Monaco Team, 2000 French Soccer Champions — A791

2000, Dec. 3
2196   A791   4.50fr multi   1.75   .90

MONACO

French, Italian and Monegasque Marine Mammal Sanctuary A792

2000, Dec. 3
2197 A792 5.20fr multi — 2.25 1.25

Neapolitan Creche, Natl. Museum — A793

2000, Dec. 3 Perf. 13x12½
2198 A793 10fr multi — 3.50 3.00

25th Intl. Circus Festival, Monte Carlo — A794

No. 2200: a, Clown with guitar. b, Clown. c, Tiger and tent top. d, Acrobats, tiger, lion, horses, clowns. e, Chimpanzee and high-wire acrobat.

2000, Dec. 3 Perf. 13¼
2199 A794 2.70fr shown 1.25 .60
2200 A794 6fr Sheet of 5, #a-e + label 12.00 12.00

41st Intl. Television Festival, Monte Carlo — A795

2001, Feb. 5 Photo. Perf. 13½x13
2201 A795 3.50fr multi 1.75 .90

Leonberger and Newfoundland A796

2001, Apr. 14 Litho. Perf. 13x13¼
2202 A796 6.50fr multi 2.50 1.25
International Dog Show, Monte Carlo.

Euroflora Flower Show — A797

2001, Apr. 21 Photo. Perf. 13¼
2203 A797 0.70fr multi 2.50 1.25

Europa — A798

Designs: No. 2204, 3fr, Palace of Monaco, water droplets. No. 2205, 3fr, Wash house.

2001, May 7 Litho. Perf. 13½x13
2204-2205 A798 Set of 2 2.75 1.10

Prince Rainier III Literary Prize, 50th Anniv. — A799

2001, May 14 Engr. Perf. 13¼
2206 A799 2.70fr multi 1.00 .45

André Malraux (1901-76), Novelist — A800

2001, May 14 Litho. Perf. 13¼x13
2207 A800 10fr black & red 3.50 1.75

Belgica 2001 Intl. Stamp Exhibition, Brussels — A801

2001, June 9 Engr. Perf. 13¼
2208 A801 4fr brt blue & red 1.50 .70

2001 Philatelic and Numismatic Bourse — A802

2001, July 2 Photo. Perf. 13¼
2209 A802 2.70fr multi 1.00 .45

Princess Grace Dance Academy, 25th Anniv. — A803

2001 July 2 Photo. Perf. 13¼
2210 A803 4.40fr multi 1.75 .90

Naval Museum — A804

2001, July 2 Photo. Perf. 13¼
2211 A804 4.50fr multi 1.75 .90

37th Petanque World Championships — A805

2001, July 2 Perf. 13x13¼
2212 A805 5fr multi 1.90 .80

Emile Littré, Denis Diderot, and Reference Books — A806

2001, Aug. 1 Engr. Perf. 13¼
2213 A806 4.20fr multi 1.50 .95

Prince Albert I Oceanography Prize, 30th Anniv. — A807

2001, Aug. 1 Engr. Perf. 13¼
2214 A807 9fr bright blue 3.50 1.50

David, by Michelangelo, 500th Anniv. — A808

2001, Aug. 1 Engr. Perf. 13
2215 A808 20fr multi 7.50 7.50

Palace of Monaco A809

Designs: 3fr, Fireplace, Throne Hall. 4.50fr, Blue Hall. 6.70fr, York Chamber. 15fr, Fresco, ceiling of Throne Hall.

2001, Aug. 1 Photo. Perf. 13x13¼
2216-2219 A809 Set of 4 10.00 6.50

A810

Nobel Prizes, Cent. — A811

Designs: 5fr, Alfred Nobel. 8fr, Jean-Henri Dunant, 1901 Peace laureate. 11.50fr, Enrico Fermi, 1938 Physics laureate.

2001, Sept. 3 Engr. Perf. 13¼
2220 A810 5fr multi 2.00 .95
2221 A810 8fr multi 3.00 1.50
2222 A811 11.50fr multi 4.00 3.25
Nos. 2220-2222 (3) 9.00 5.70

36th Meeting of Intl. Commission for Scientific Exploration of the Mediterranean — A812

2001, Oct. 1 Photo. Perf. 13x13¼
2223 A812 3fr multi 1.25 .50

Christmas — A813

2001, Oct. 1 Perf. 13¼
2224 A813 3fr multi 1.25 .50

100 Cents = 1 Euro (€)

Flora & Fauna — A814

Designs: 1c, Arctia caja, vert. 2c, Luria lurida. 5c, Thunbergia grandiflora, vert. 10c, Parus major. 20c, Anthias anthias. 50c, Charaxes jasius, vert. €1, Mitra zonata. €2, Datura sanguinea, vert. €5, Parus cristatus, vert. €10, Macroamphosus scolopax.

2002, Jan. 1 Engr. Perf. 13¼
2225 A814 1c multi .25 .25
2226 A814 2c multi .25 .25
2227 A814 5c multi .25 .25
2228 A814 10c multi .25 .25
2229 A814 20c multi .45 .25
2230 A814 50c multi 1.10 .75
2231 A814 €1 multi 2.25 1.50
2232 A814 €2 multi 4.50 3.00
2233 A814 €5 multi 11.00 7.50
2234 A814 €10 multi 22.50 16.00
Nos. 2225-2234 (10) 42.80 29.00
See Nos. 2275, 2323-2324.

Palace of Monaco — A815

Designs: 41c, Gallery of Mirrors, vert. 46c, Throne room. 58c, Painting in Gallery of Mirrors.

2002, Jan. 1 Photo.
2235-2237 A815 Set of 3 3.50 2.00

26th Intl. Circus Festival — A816

2002, Jan. 1
2238 A816 41c multi 1.00 .60

35th Intl. Flower Show — A817

2002, Jan. 1
2239 A817 53c multi 1.25 .75

Souvenir Sheet

Automobile Club of Monaco — A818

No. 2240: a, Old and new cars, emblem of 70th Monte Carlo Rally. b, Racing cars in 3rd Historic Grand Prix and 60th Grand Prix races.

2002, Jan. 16 Perf. 13¼x13
2240 A818 Sheet of 2 5.50 5.50
a. €1.07 multi 2.25 1.50
b. €1.22 multi 3.00 1.75

529

MONACO

Prehistoric Anthropology Museum, Cent. — A819

2002, Feb. 8		Perf. 13¼
2241 A819 64c multi		1.60 .95

La Carrière d'un Navigateur, by Prince Albert I, Cent. — A820

2002, Feb. 8	
2242 A820 67c multi	1.75 1.00

2002 Winter Olympics, Salt Lake City — A821

No. 2243: a, Denomination at UL. b, Denomination at UR.

2002, Feb. 8		Perf. 12¼
2243 A821 Horiz. pair		1.00 1.00
a.-b. 23c Either single		.50 .50

Jules Cardinal Mazarin (1602-61) — A822

2002, Feb. 18	
2244 A822 69c multi	2.00 1.00

Legion of Honor, Bicent. — A823

2002, Feb. 18		Perf. 13¼
2245 A823 70c multi		1.75 1.00

Cetacean Conservation Accord — A824

2002, Feb. 18		Engr.
2246 A824 75c multi		2.25 1.10

Leonardo da Vinci (1452-1519) A825

2002, Mar. 21		Photo.
2247 A825 76c multi		2.25 1.10

St. Bernard and Swiss Bouvier — A826

2002, Mar. 21		Engr.
2248 A826 99c multi		2.50 1.50

Intl. Dog Show. See Nos. 2286, 2491.

Police, Cent. — A827

2002, Apr. 23		Photo.
2249 A827 53c multi		1.50 .70

European Academy of Philately, 25th Anniv. — A828

2002, Apr. 27		Engr.
2250 A828 58c multi		1.25 .85

20th Intl. Swimming Meet — A829

2002, May 3	Photo.	Perf. 13¼
2251 A829 64c multi		1.60 .95

Europa — A830

Designs: No. 2252, 46c, Clown on globe, juggler, elephant, tent tops. No. 2253, 46c, "Jours de Cirque," circus acts.

2002, May 3	
2252-2253 A830 Set of 2	2.75 1.25

First Experiment with Tar Roads, Cent. — A831

2002, May 31		Engr.
2254 A831 41c multi		1.00 .60

MonacoPhil 2002 Intl. Philatelic Exhibition — A832

2002, May 31		
2255 A832 46c multi		1.00 .65

42nd Intl. Television Festival, Monte Carlo — A833

2002, May 31	Photo.	Perf. 13¼x13
2256 A833 70c multi		1.50 1.00

2002 World Cup Soccer Championships, Japan and Korea — A834

2002, May 31	Engr.	Perf. 13¼
2257 A834 75c multi		1.50 1.10

"Pelléas et Mélisande," Opera by Claude Debussy, Cent. of Debut — A835

2002, June 21	
2258 A835 69c multi	1.40 1.00

Saint Dévote, Dove and Boat — A836

2002, June 21	
2259 A836 €1.02 multi	2.50 1.50

Red Cross.

Intl. Year of Mountains — A837

2002, June 21	Litho.	Perf. 13x13¼
2260 A837 €1.37 multi		3.25 2.00

Euro Coinage A838

No. 2261: a, Obverse of 1c, 2c, and 5c coins and reverse. b, Obverse of 10c, 20c, and 50c coins and reverse.
No. 2262: a, Obverse and reverse of €1 coin. b, Obverse and reverse of €2 coin.

Litho. & Embossed

2002, June 21		Perf. 13¼
2261 A838 Horiz. pair		3.00 3.00
a.-b. 46c Either single		1.40 .70
2262 A838 Horiz. pair		9.25 9.25
a.-b. €1.50 Either single		4.50 4.50

Victor Hugo (1802-85), Writer — A839

No. 2263: a, Hugo and illustration from Notre-Dame de Paris. b, Hugo and illustration from La Légende de Siécles.

2002, July 1	Engr.	Perf. 13¼
2263 A839 Horiz. pair		2.50 2.50
a. 50c multi		1.25 .75
b. 57c multi		1.25 .85

Alexandre Dumas (Father) (1802-70), Writer — A840

No. 2264: a, Dumas. b, Characters, manuscript.

2002, July 1		Photo.
2264 A840 Horiz. pair		2.50 2.50
a.-b. 61c Either single		1.25 .85

26th Publication of "Annales Monegasques" — A841

2002, July 15	
2265 A841 €1.75 multi	4.25 2.50

Christmas — A842

2002, Sept. 2	
2266 A842 50c multi	1.25 .75

Debut of Movie "Le Voyage dans le Lune," by Georges Méliès, Cent. — A843

2002, Sept. 2		Perf. 13¼
2267 A843 76c multi		1.75 1.10

17th Magic Stars Magic Festival, Monte Carlo — A844

2002, Sept. 2	
2268 A844 €1.52 multi	3.50 2.25

Awarding of ASCAT Grand Prize to Luis Figo — A845

2002, Nov. 29		Engr.
2269 A845 91c multi		1.90 1.25

Automobiles in Prince Rainier III Collection — A846

Designs: 46c, 1949 Mercedes 220A Cabriolet. 69c, 1956 Rolls-Royce Silver Cloud I. €1.40, 1974 Citroen DS 21.

2002, Nov. 29		Photo.
2270-2272 A846 Set of 3		6.50 3.75

Souvenir Sheet

The Four Seasons, Frescos in Prince's Palace A847

2002, Nov. 29		Perf. 13x13¼
2273 A847 Sheet of 4		12.00 12.00
a. 50c Spring		1.00 .75
b. €1 Summer		2.00 1.50
c. €1.50 Autumn		3.00 2.25
d. €2 Winter		4.00 3.00

MONACO

Souvenir Sheet

MonacoPhil 2002 Intl. Philatelic Exhibition — A848

No. 2274: a, Monaco attractions. b, Emblem of Club de Monte Carlo.

2002, Nov. 29			Imperf.
2274	A848	Sheet of 2	14.00 14.00
a.-b.		€3 Either single	6.00 6.00

Flora & Fauna Type of 2002

41c, Helix aspersa, vert.

2002, Nov. 30		Engr.	Perf. 13¼
2275	A814	41c multi	1.00 .60

36th Intl. Flower Show — A849

2002, Nov. 30			Photo.
2276	A849	67c multi	1.75 1.00

World Association of Friends of Children, 40th Anniv. (in 2003) — A850

2002, Nov. 30			
2277	A850	€1.25 multi	3.00 1.75

Martyrdom of St. George, 1700th Anniv. — A851

2002, Dec. 1			
2278	A851	53c multi	1.30 .70

Saint Cyr Military School, Bicent. — A852

2002, Dec. 1			
2279	A852	61c multi	1.50 .85

27th Intl. Circus Festival — A853

2003, Jan. 2		Photo.	Perf. 13¼
2280	A853	59c multi	1.25 .70

15th New Circus Artists' Festival — A854

2003, Feb. 1			
2281	A854	€2.82 multi	6.50 4.00

10th World Bobsled Push Championships, Ilsenberg, Germany — A855

2003, Feb. 3			
2282	A855	80c multi	1.75 .95

Monaco Yacht Club, 50th Anniv. — A856

2003, Feb. 5			
2283	A856	46c multi	1.00 .60

Intl. Institute for Peace, Cent. — A857

2003, Mar. 3			
2284	A857	€1.19 multi	2.75 1.75

Tennis Tournament at Monte Carlo Country Club, 75th Anniv. — A858

2003, Mar. 3			
2285	A858	€1.30 multi	3.00 2.00

Dog Show Type of 2002

2003, Mar. 24		Litho.	Perf. 13x13½
2286	A826	79c Rough collie	2.00 1.25

Junior Economic Chamber of Monaco, 40th Anniv. — A859

2003, Apr. 5		Photo.	Perf. 13¼
2287	A859	41c multi	1.00 .60

Monte Carlo Country Club, 75th Anniv. — A860

2003, Apr. 12			
2288	A860	46c multi	1.00 .70

General Bathymetric Charts of the Oceans, Cent. — A861

No. 2289: a, Prince Albert I, map of Arctic region, chart of Northern hemisphere. b, Oceanographic museum, map of Antarctica, chart of Southern hemisphere.

2003, Apr. 14			Perf. 13x12½
2289	A861	€1.25 Vert. pair, #a-b	5.50 5.50

Poster by Alfons Mucha A862

Poster by Jean-Gabriel Domergue A863

2003, May 5			Perf. 13¼
2290	A862	50c multi	1.50 .75
2291	A863	50c multi	1.50 .75

Europa.

Grand Bourse 2003 — A864

2003, June 2			
2292	A864	45c multi	1.00 .70

43rd Intl. Television Festival, Monte Carlo — A865

2003, June 2			Perf. 13¼x13
2293	A865	90c multi	2.00 1.25

15th Antiques Biennale — A866

2003, June 2			Perf. 13¼
2294	A866	€1.80 multi	4.00 2.75

Navigation of Northwest Passage by Roald Amundsen, Cent. — A867

2003, June 30			
2295	A867	90c multi	2.00 1.40

Powered Flight, Cent. — A868

2003, June 30			
2296	A868	€1.80 multi	4.00 2.75

Hector Berlioz (1803-69), Composer — A869

2003, July 21			Engr.
2297	A869	75c red & black	1.75 1.10

Aram Khatchaturian (1903-78), Composer A870

2003, July 21			
2298	A870	€1.60 multi	4.00 2.40

Portrait of a Woman, by François Boucher (1703-70) — A871

Self-portrait, by Vincent van Gogh (1853-90) — A872

Self-portrait, by Francesco Mazzola, "Il Parmigianino" (1503-40) — A873

2003, Aug. 6			Perf. 13¼x13
2299	A871	€1.30 multi	3.00 1.90
2300	A872	€3 black & pink	7.00 4.25
2301	A873	€3.60 black & tan	8.00 5.00
Nos. 2299-2301 (3)			18.00 11.15

Discovery of Structure of DNA Molecule, 50th Anniv. — A874

2003, Sept. 1			Perf. 13¼
2302	A874	58c multi	1.25 .85

Nostradamus (1503-66), Astrologer — A875

2003, Sept. 1			Photo.
2303	A875	70c multi	1.60 1.00

2003 Magic Stars Festival, Monte Carlo — A876

2003, Sept. 1		Litho.	Perf. 13½x13
2304	A876	75c multi	1.75 1.10

MONACO

Discovery of Penicillin by Alexander Fleming, 75th Anniv. — A877

2003, Sept. 1	Engr.		Perf. 13¼
2305	A877	€1.11 multi	2.50 1.60

Awarding of Nobel Physics Prize to Pierre and Marie Curie, Cent. — A878

2003, Sept. 1		Photo.
2306	A878 €1.20 multi	2.75 1.75

Conquest of Mt. Everest, by Sir Edmund Hillary, 50th Anniv. — A879

2003, Sept. 29	Engr.		Perf. 13¼
2307	A879	€1 multi	2.25 1.50

Saint Dévote A880

No. 2308: a, Kneeling before cross. b, Standing before soldiers. c, Boat and dove. d, Standing in front of church.

2003, Sept. 29			
2308	A880 45c Block of 4, #a-d		4.00 4.00

Christmas — A881

2003, Oct. 13		Photo.
2309	A881 50c multi	1.25 .75

MonacoPhil 2004 Intl. Philatelic Exhibition — A882

2003, Dec. 15		
2310	A882 50c multi	1.25 .75

28th Intl. Circus Festival, Monte Carlo — A883

2003, Dec. 15		
2311	A883 70c multi	1.60 1.00

Beausoleil, France, Cent. — A884

2004, Jan. 5	Photo.	Perf. 13¼
2312	A884 75c multi	1.75 1.10

Saint Dévote — A885

Designs: 50c, Arrest of St. Dévote, vert. 75c, Proceedings against St. Dévote. 90c, Stoning of St. Dévote. €1, St. Dévote in boat, vert. €4, Protection of St. Dévote.

2004, Jan. 5		Engr.	
2313	A885	50c red brn & red	1.10 .75
2314	A885	75c brn & orange	1.75 1.10
2315	A885	90c dk brn & brn	2.00 1.50
2316	A885	€1 dk brn & yel brn	2.50 1.50
2317	A885	€4 dk brn & red brn	9.00 6.00
	Nos. 2313-2317 (5)		16.35 10.85

6th Monegasque Biennale of Cancerology A886

2004, Jan. 29	Photo.	Perf. 13¼
2318	A886 €1.11 multi	2.50 1.50

Princess Grace Foundation, 40th Anniv. — A887

Princess Grace Irish Library, 20th Anniv. — A888

Statue of Princess Grace, by Daphné du Barry — A889

Princess Grace Rose Garden, 20th Anniv. — A890

Photo., Litho. (#2320-2321)

2004, Jan. 29			
2319	A887	50c multi	1.25 .75
2320	A888	€1.11 grn & brown	2.50 1.50
2321	A889	€1.45 multi	3.25 2.00
2322	A890	€1.90 multi	4.50 2.75
	Nos. 2319-2322 (4)		11.50 7.00

Flora & Fauna Type of 2002

Designs: 75c, Hyla meridionalis, vert. €4.50, Lacerta viridis, vert.

2004, Mar. 8	Engr.	Perf. 13¼
2323	A814 75c multi	2.00 1.10
2324	A814 €4.50 multi	10.00 6.75

20th Spring of Arts — A891

2004, Apr. 2		
2325	A891 €1 multi	2.50 1.50

Cathedral Choir School, Cent. — A892

2004, Apr. 5		Photo.
2326	A892 45c multi	1.00 .70

37th Intl. Flower Show — A893

2004, Apr. 5		
2327	A893 58c multi	1.40 .85

Cavalier King Charles Spaniel — A893a

2004, Apr. 9	Litho.	Perf. 13x13¼
2328	A893a 90c multi	2.00 1.40

International Dog Show, Monte Carlo.

Monaco Grand Prix, 75th Anniv. — A894

2004, Apr. 14	Photo.	Perf. 13¼
2329	A894 €1.20 multi	2.75 1.75

International School of Monaco, 10th Anniv. — A895

2004, Apr. 26	Litho.	Perf. 13x13¼
2330	A895 50c multi	1.25 .75

Europa — A896

Travel posters: No. 2331, 50c, Shown. No. 2332, 50c, Women in bathing suits at beach.

2004, May 3	Photo.	Perf. 13¼
2331-2332 A896 Set of 2		3.00 1.50

Order of Grimaldi, 50th Anniv. — A897

Litho. & Embossed

2004, May 3		Perf. 13¼x13
2333	A897 90c multi	2.25 1.40

2004 Summer Olympics, Athens — A898

No. 2334: a, Stadium, modern runners. b, Stadium, ancient runners.

2004, May 3		Perf. 13x13¼
2334	A898 45c Vert. pair, #a-b	2.25 1.40

Napoleon I and Monegasque Princes in Imperial Army — A899

Stéphanie de Beauharnais, by Baron Gérard — A900

Designs: 75c, Imperial symbols of Napoleon I, horiz. €2.40, Napoleon I, by Gérard.

Perf. 12¼x13, 13x13¼ (75c)

2004, May 28			Photo.
2335	A899	58c multi	1.40 .85
2336	A899	75c multi	1.75 1.10
2337	A900	€1.90 multi	4.50 2.75
2338	A900	€2.40 multi	5.50 3.50
	Nos. 2335-2338 (4)		13.15 8.20

Sergey Diaghilev (1872-1929), George Balanchine (1904-83) and Dancers of Ballet Russes de Monte Carlo — A901

2004, June 14	Engr.	Perf. 13¼
2339	A901 €1.60 multi	4.00 2.40

44th Television Festival, Monte Carlo — A902

2004, June 14	Litho.	Perf. 13¼x13
2340	A902 €1.80 multi	4.25 2.75

Frédéric Mistral (1830-1914), 1904 Nobel Laureate in Literature A903

2004, June 26	Engr.	Perf. 13¼
2341	A903 45c multi	1.10 .70

MONACO

23rd UPU Congress, Bucharest, Romania — A904

2004, June 26
2342 A904 50c multi 1.25 .75

Marco Polo (1254-1324), Explorer — A905

2004, June 26
2343 A905 50c multi 1.25 .75

Salon du Timbre, Paris — A906

2004, June 26
2344 A906 75c multi 1.75 1.10

Translation into French of *A Thousand and One Nights*, 300th Anniv. — A907

Litho. & Silk Screened
2004, June 26   **Perf. 13x13¼**
2345 A907 €1 deep blue & gray 2.50 1.50

Monte Carlo Beach Hotel, 75th Anniv. — A908

2004, July 5   **Photo.**   **Perf. 13¼**
2346 A908 45c multi 1.00 .70

FIFA (Fédération Internationale de Football Association), Cent. — A909

2004, Aug. 2
2347 A909 €1.80 multi 4.00 2.40

Magic Stars Magic Festival, Monte Carlo — A910

2004, Sept. 6   **Litho.**   **Perf. 13x13¼**
2348 A910 45c multi 1.10 .70

Souvenir Sheet

Princess Grace (1929-82) — A911

Portraits of Princess Grace engraved by: a, 75c, Pierre Albuisson. b, €1.75, Czesław Slania. c, €3.50, Martin Mörck.

2004, Oct. 4   **Engr.**   **Perf. 13¼x13**
2349 A911 Sheet of 3 + label 14.00 14.00
 a. 75c green & blue 1.75 1.10
 b. €1.75 green & blue 4.00 2.50
 c. €3.50 green & blue 7.50 5.25
See No. 2367.

Christmas — A912

2004, Oct. 4   **Photo.**   **Perf. 13¼**
2350 A912 50c multi 1.25 .75

Admission to Council of Europe — A913

2004, Oct. 5   **Engr.**   **Perf. 13x12½**
2351 A913 50c red & blue 1.25 .75

29th Intl. Circus Festival, Monte Carlo — A914

2004, Dec. 3   **Photo.**   **Perf. 13¼**
2352 A914 45c multi 1.10 .70

Louis II Stadium, 20th Anniv. — A915

2004, Dec. 3   **Engr.**   **Perf. 12½x13**
2353 A915 50c multi 1.25 .75

University of Paris Student Hostel, 70th Anniv. — A916

2004, Dec. 3   **Perf. 13¼**
2354 A916 58c multi 1.40 .85

Palace of Justice, 75th Anniv. — A917

2004, Dec. 3   **Photo.**
2355 A917 75c multi 1.75 1.10

French Alliance of Monaco, 25th Anniv. — A918

2004, Dec. 3
2356 A918 75c multi 1.75 1.10

38th Intl. Flower Show — A919

2004, Dec. 3   **Photo.**   **Perf. 13¼**
2357 A919 90c multi 2.25 1.40

Luigi Valentino Brugnatelli (1761-1818), Inventor of Electroplating A920

Litho. & Engr.
2004, Dec. 3   **Perf. 13¼**
2358 A920 €1 blk & brn 2.50 1.50

Jean-Paul Sartre (1905-80), Author — A921

2004, Dec. 3   **Photo.**
2359 A921 €1.11 multi 2.50 1.60

Invention of Safety Matches by Johan Edvard Lundstrom, 150th Anniv. — A922

2004, Dec. 3
2360 A922 €1.20 multi 2.75 1.75

Publication of Don Quixote, by Miguel de Cervantes, 400th Anniv. — A923

2004, Dec. 3   **Engr.**
2361 A923 €1.20 multi 3.00 1.75

Léo Ferré (1916-93), Singer — A924

2004, Dec. 3   **Photo.**
2362 A924 €1.40 multi 3.50 2.10

Invention of Hypodermic Syringe by Alexander Wood, 150th Anniv. — A925

2004, Dec. 3   **Engr.**
2363 A925 €1.60 multi 3.75 2.40

Development of Carbon 14 Dating by Willard F. Libby, 50th Anniv. — A926

2004, Dec. 3   **Perf. 12½x13**
2364 A926 €1.80 multi 4.25 2.75

Princes and Palace of Monaco A927

No. 2365: a, Prince Rainier III (30x31mm). b, Palace of Monaco (60x31mm). c, Hereditary Prince Albert (30x31mm).

2004, Dec. 3   **Perf. 13¼**
2365 A927 50c Horiz. strip of 3, #a-c 3.50 3.00

First World Cup Soccer Championships, 75th Anniv. — A928

No. 2366: a, World Cup, goalie catching soccer ball. b, Flag of Uruguay, player dribbling ball.

2004, Dec. 3   **Photo.**   **Perf. 13¼**
2366 A928 €1 Horiz. pair, #a-b 4.50 3.00

Princess Grace Type of 2004 in Changed Colors with "MonacoPhil 2004" Added in Sheet Margin
Souvenir Sheet
Designs like No. 2349.

2004, Dec. 3   **Engr.**   **Imperf.**
2367 A911 Sheet of 3 14.00 14.00
 a. 75c blue & emerald 1.75 2.25
 b. €1.75 blue & emerald 4.00 5.25
 c. €3.50 blue & emerald 8.50 10.50

Rotary International, Cent. — A929

Designs: 55c, Rotary emblem, founder, president, treasurer and secretary of original club. 70c, Rotary emblem, vert.

Litho. & Engr., Litho. (70c)
Perf. 13¼, 13¼x13 (70c)
2005, Feb. 23
2368-2369 A929 Set of 2 2.75 1.90

UNESCO Fine Arts Committee, 50th Anniv. — A930

2005, Mar. 1   **Photo.**   **Perf. 13¼**
2370 A930 48c multi 1.25 .70

Publication of Albert Einstein's Theory of Relativity, Cent. — A931

2005, Mar. 1
2371 A931 53c multi 1.25 .80

First Awarding of Diplomas From School of Fine Arts — A932

2005, Mar. 1   **Litho.**   **Perf. 13¼x13**
2372 A932 64c black & red 1.60 .95

MONACO

Dog Show Type of 2002
82c, Dachshund (teckel).

2005, Mar. 1	Photo.		Perf. 13¼
2373	A826	82c multi	2.00 1.25

Intl. Automobile Federation, Cent. — A933

2005, Apr. 1	Photo.		Perf. 13¼
2374	A933	55c multi	1.25 1.60

21st World Exhibition of Hybrid and Electric Vehicles — A934

Designs, 75c, Fetish, first electric sports car. €1.30, Stylized automobile with electric plug.

2005, Apr. 1			
2375-2376	A934	Set of 2	5.00 5.00

Tenth Horse Jumping International, Monte Carlo — A935

2005, Apr. 1	Engr.		Perf. 13¼
2377	A935	90c multi	2.25 1.40

Food A936

No. 2378, 53c: a, Pissaladière. b, Barbaguians.
No. 2379, 55c: a, Tourte de blettes. b, Desserts.

2005, May 3	Photo.		
	Horiz. Pairs, #a-b		
2378-2379	A936	Set of 2	5.00 4.00

Europa (#2378).

Monegasque Special Olympics, 25th Anniv. — A937

2005, June 3	Litho.		Perf. 13x13¼
2380	A937	€1.20 multi	3.00 1.75

Early 20th Century Advertising Art — A938

Advertisements for: 77c, Bains de Mer de Monaco. €2.50, English Sanitary Co. €3.10, Scapini Biscuits.

2005, June 3	Photo.		Perf. 12¼x13
2381-2383	A938	Set of 3	15.00 9.50

Monaco Yacht Show — A939

2005, July 4			Perf. 13¼
2384	A939	82c multi	2.00 1.25

Admission to UPU, 50th Anniv. — A940

2005, July 4			Engr.
2385	A940	€3.03 multi	7.50 4.50

Astronomers — A941

Designs: €1.22, Edmond Halley (1656-1742). €1.98, Gerard P. Kuiper (1905-73). €3.80, Clyde Tombaugh (1906-97).

2005, July 4			Perf. 12½x13
2386-2388	A941	Set of 3	17.00 10.50

Coat of Arms Type of 2000
Inscribed "20g Ecopli" at Top
Serpentine Die Cut 11

2005, July 12			Photo.
	Booklet Stamp		
	Self-Adhesive		
2389	A786	(48c) grn, blk & red	1.10 1.10
a.	Booklet pane of 10		11.00
b.	(49c) Dated 2007		65.00 32.50
c.	As b, booklet pane of 10		650.00
d.	(50c) Dated 2008		6.00 3.00
e.	As d, booklet pane of 10		60.00

No. 2389 is inscribed "ITVF 2005" in the bottom margin of the stamp. No. 2389b is inscribed "Phil@poste 2007." No. 2389d is inscribed "Phil@poste 2008."

10th European Patrimony Day — A942

2005, Sept. 5	Engr.		Perf. 13¼
2390	A942	48c multi	1.10 1.00

20th Magic Stars Festival, Monte Carlo — A943

2005, Sept. 5	Litho.		Perf. 13x13¼
2391	A943	€1.45 red, gold & blk	3.50 3.00

Christmas — A944

2005, Oct. 3	Engr.		
2392	A944	53c blk & red	1.40 1.10

Monte Carlo Bay Hotel and Resort — A945

2005, Oct. 7			Photo.
2393	A945	55c multi	1.40 1.10

Nadia Boulanger (1887-1979), Conductor, and Lili Boulanger (1893-1918), Composer A946

2005, Oct. 21			Engr.
2394	A946	90c multi	2.25 1.75

Miniature Sheet

Restoration of Garnier Hall, Monte Carlo Opera — A947

No. 2395: a, "Song." b, Garnier Hall. c, "Comedy." d, "Dance." e, Charles Garnier (1825-98), architect. f, "Music."

2005, Nov. 16			
2395	A947	82c Sheet of 6, #a-f	14.50 14.50

Souvenir Sheet

Prince Rainier III (1923-2005) — A948

2005, Nov. 19			Perf. 13
2396	A948	€4 black	12.00 12.00

Prince Albert II — A949

2005, Nov. 19			Perf. 13x13¼
2397	A949	(48c) green	1.10 1.10
2398	A949	(53c) red	1.25 1.25
2399	A949	(75c) blue	1.75 1.75
		Nos. 2397-2399 (3)	4.10 4.10

National Day A950

No. 2400: a, Fontveille (26x27mm, country name at UL). b, Palace (56x27mm, country name at UL). c, La Condamine and Monte Carlo (26x27mm, country name at UR).

2005, Nov. 19	Photo.		Perf. 13¼
2400	A950	€1.01 Horiz. strip of 3, #a-c	7.00 7.00

MonacoPhil 2006 Philatelic Exhibition — A951

2005, Dec. 12			
2401	A951	55c multi	1.25 1.25

30th Intl. Circus Festival, Monte Carlo — A952

No. 2403: a, Charles Rivel, 1974 Golden Clown. b, Fredy Knie, 1977 Golden Clown. c, Alexis Gruss, Sr., 1975 Golden Clown. d, Golden Clown award. e, Georges Carl, 1979 Golden Clown.

2005, Dec. 14			
2402	A952	64c shown	1.75 1.40
2403	A952a	75c Sheet of 5, #a-e, + label	11.00 11.00

The label on No. 2403 has the same vignette as No. 2402, lacking country name and denomination, but with a gray background. Compare No. 2402 with No. 2825c.

A953

2006 Winter Olympics, Turin — A954

No. 2404: a, Red mascot. b, Blue mascot.

2006, Jan. 9	Photo.		Perf. 13¼
2404	A953	55c Horiz. pair, #a-b	2.75 2.75
2405	A954	82c multi	2.40 1.75

Museum of Postage Stamps and Money, 10th Anniv. — A955

2006, Jan. 30			Engr.
2406	A955	53c multi	1.25 1.25

5th Intl. Film and Literature Forum — A956

2006, Feb. 6	Photo.		Perf. 13¼
2407	A956	82c multi	2.00 1.75

MONACO

Léopold Sédar Senghor (1906-2001), First President of Senegal — A957

Litho. & Engr.
2006, Mar. 6 Perf. 13x13¼
2408 A957 €1.45 multi 3.25 3.00

100th Monte Carlo Tennis Tournament — A958

2006, Mar. 8 Photo. Perf. 13¼
2409 A958 55c multi 1.25 1.25

Coat of Arms Type of 2000 Inscribed "20g Zone A" at Top
Serpentine Die Cut 11
2006, Apr. 6 Photo.
Self-Adhesive Booklet Stamp
2410 A786 (55c) red & black 1.25 1.25
 a. Booklet pane of 10 12.50

Monte Carlo Philharmonic Orchestra, 150th Anniv. — A959

2006, Apr. 6 Perf. 13¼
2411 A959 64c multi 1.75 1.40

Arctic Oceanographic Expeditions of Prince Albert I, Cent. — A960

Litho. & Engr.
2006, Apr. 10 Perf. 13x13¼
2412 A960 €1.60 multi 4.00 3.50

Dog Show Type of 2002
64c, Special schnauzer.
2000, Apr. 14 Photo. Perf. 13¼
2413 A826 64c multi 1.75 1.25

39th Intl. Flower Show — A961

2006, Apr. 18
2414 A961 77c multi 2.00 1.60

2006 World Cup Soccer Championships, Germany — A962

No. 2415: a, World Cup, stadium. b, Stadium and 2006 World Cup emblem.

2006, Apr. 18
2415 A962 90c Horiz. pair, #a-b 4.50 3.00

A963

Europa — A964

2006, May 5 Photo. Perf. 13¼
2416 A963 53c multi 1.25 1.25
2417 A964 55c multi 1.40 1.40

RAMOGE Agreement, 30th Anniv. — A965

2006, May 9 Perf. 12¼x13
2418 A965 €1.75 multi 4.50 4.50

Washington 2006 World Philatelic Exhibition — A966

2006, May 27 Engr. Perf. 13¼
2419 A966 90c blue & red 2.25 1.75

John Huston (1906-87), Film Director A967

2006, May 27 Perf. 13x12¼
2420 A967 €1.80 blk & hen brn 4.50 3.50

Prince Albert Challenge Sabre Tournament A968

2006, June 6 Photo. Perf. 13¼
2421 A968 48c multi 1.20 1.00

Pierre Corneille (1606-84), Dramatist A969

2006, June 17
2422 A969 55c multi 1.40 1.00

46th Intl. Television Festival, Monte Carlo — A970

2006, June 17
2423 A970 82c multi 2.00 1.75

Wolfgang Amadeus Mozart (1756-91), Composer A971

2006, June 17 Engr. Perf. 13x12¼
2424 A971 €1.22 org red & blue 3.00 2.50

Prince Pierre Foundation, 40th Anniv. — A972

2006, June 20 Perf. 12½x13
2425 A972 €2.50 multi 6.25 5.50

Dino Buzzati (1906-72), Writer — A973

2006, July 17 Photo. Perf. 13¼
2426 A973 55c multi 1.40 1.10

Cetacean Conservation Accord, 10th Anniv. — A974

2006, July 17 Perf. 13x12¼
2427 A974 90c multi 2.25 1.75

Luchino Visconti (1906-76), Film Director — A975

2006, July 17 Engr. Perf. 12¼x13
2428 A975 €1.75 henna brn 4.50 3.50

Rolls-Royce Automobiles, Cent. — A976

2006, Sept. 4 Engr. Perf. 13¼
2429 A976 64c multi 1.75 1.40

2006 Magic Stars Festival, Monte Carlo — A977

2006, Sept. 4 Photo.
2430 A977 77c multi 2.00 1.50

Monaco Red Cross — A978

2006, Oct. 2
2431 A978 48c multi 1.20 1.00

Christmas — A979

Perf. 13½x13¼
2006, Oct. 2 Litho. & Engr.
2432 A979 53c multi 1.40 1.00

Prince Albert II — A980

2006, Dec. 1 Engr. Perf. 13x13¼
2433 A980 (49c) green 1.10 .75
2434 A980 (54c) red 1.50 1.10
 a. Dated "2009" 1.50 1.10
2435 A980 (60c) blue 1.60 1.60
 Nos. 2433-2435 (3) 4.20 3.45
 Dated 2007.
No. 2434a sold for 56c when issued.

Prince Albert II and Coat of Arms — A981

2006, Dec. 1 Photo. Perf. 13¼x13
2436 A981 60c multi 1.50 1.20
Souvenir Sheet
Perf. 13x13¼
2437 A981 €6 multi 15.00 15.00
MonacoPhil 2006 Intl. Philatelic Exhibition. Dated 2007.

World AIDS Day — A982

2006, Dec. 1 Litho. Perf. 13x13¼
2438 A982 49c multi 1.20 1.00
Dated 2007.

Josephine Baker (1906-75), Singer and Dancer — A983

2006, Dec. 1 Perf. 13¼x13
2439 A983 49c multi 1.20 1.00
Princess Grace Theater, 25th anniv. Dated 2007.

MONACO

Philatelic Anniversaries — A984

2006, Dec. 1 Photo. Perf. 13¼
2440 A984 54c multi 1.40 1.10
Creation of Philatelic Bureau, 70th anniv. (in 2007), Consultative Commission of the Prince's Philatelic Collection, 20th anniv. (in 2007). Dated 2007.

Les Enfants de Frankie Children's Charity, 10th Anniv. (in 2007) — A985

2006, Dec. 1
2441 A985 70c multi 1.75 1.50
Dated 2007.

Albert Camus (1913-60), 1957 Nobel Literature Laureate — A986

2006, Dec. 1 Engr.
2442 A986 84c multi 2.25 1.75
Dated 2007.

Auguste Escoffier (1846-1935), Chef — A987

2006, Dec. 1
2443 A987 85c multi 2.25 1.75
Dated 2007.

Daniel Bovet (1907-92), 1957 Nobel Medicine Laureate — A988

2006, Dec. 1
2444 A988 86c dk blue & red 2.25 1.75
Dated 2007.

Cardiothoracic Center, 20th Anniv. (in 2007) — A989

2006, Dec. 1
2445 A989 €1.15 multi 3.00 2.50
Dated 2007.

Rudyard Kipling (1865-1936), 1907 Nobel Literature Laureate — A990

2006, Dec. 1
2446 A990 €1.57 multi 4.00 3.25
Dated 2007.

Opening of Institute of Sports Medicine and Surgery — A991

2006, Dec. 1
2447 A991 €1.70 multi 4.25 3.50
Dated 2007.

Meeting of Prince Albert II and Pope Benedict XVI, 1st Anniv. A992

2006, Dec. 1 Photo. Perf. 13x13¼
2448 A992 €1.70 multi 4.25 4.00
Dated 2007.

Paul-Emile Victor (1907-95), Explorer A993

2006, Dec. 1 Engr. Perf. 13x12¼
2449 A993 €2.11 multi 5.25 4.50
Dated 2007.

European Philatelic Academy, 30th Anniv. (in 2007) A994

2006, Dec. 1 Photo. Perf. 13x13¼
2450 A994 €2.30 multi 5.75 5.00
Dated 2007.

Awarding of 2006 Grand Prix of Philately to Alexander D. Kroo — A995

2006, Dec. 1 Litho. Perf. 13¼x13
2451 A995 €3 multi 7.50 6.50
Dated 2007.

Auto Racing A996

No. 2452: a, 65th Monaco Grand Prix. b, 75th Monte Carlo Rally.
2006, Dec. 1
2452 A996 60c Horiz. pair, #a-b 3.00 2.75
Dated 2007.

Art in Grimaldi Forum by Nall A997

No. 2453: a, Purple Flower. b, Yellow Flower.
2006, Dec. 1 Photo. Perf. 13¼
2453 A997 €1.70 Pair, #a-b 8.00 7.00
Printed in panes of 2 pairs. Dated 2007.

A998

31st Intl. Circus Festival, Monte Carlo — A999

2006, Dec. 1 Photo. Perf. 13¼
2454 A998 60c multi 1.50 1.20
Litho. Perf. 13¼x13
2455 A999 84c multi 2.25 1.75
Dated 2007.

Souvenir Sheet

40th Intl. Flower Show A1000

No. 2456: a, Classic composition. b, Modern composition. c, Contemporary composition. d, Japanese composition.
2006, Dec. 1 Photo. Perf. 13¼
2456 A1000 €1.30 Sheet of 4, #a-d 16.00 16.00
Dated 2007.

Stenella Coeruleoalba A1001

2007, Jan. 2 Litho. Perf. 13x13¼
2457 A1001 (36c) multi .95 .95
Issued precanceled only. See note after No. 324.

Giuseppe Garibaldi (1807-82), Italian Nationalist Leader — A1002

2007, Mar. 16 Engr. Perf. 13¼
2458 A1002 €1.40 ol brn & red 3.50 3.25

Carlo Goldoni (1707-93), Playwright A1003

Litho. & Silk-screened
2007, Mar. 16 Perf. 13x13¼
2459 A1003 €4.54 multi 11.00 10.00

Monaco Olympic Committee, Cent. — A1004

2007, Apr. 2 Photo. Perf. 13¼
2460 A1004 60c multi 1.40 1.20

Dalmatian A1005

2007, Apr. 2 Perf. 13x13¼
2461 A1005 70c multi 1.75 1.40
Intl. Dog Show.

12th Games of Small European States — A1006

2007, Apr. 2 Perf. 13¼
2462 A1006 86c multi 2.00 1.75

Princess Grace Exposition, Grimaldi Forum — A1007

2007, May 4 Litho. Perf. 13
2463 A1007 85c multi 2.00 1.75

First Flight of Helicopter Designed by Maurice Leger, Cent. — A1008

2007, May 4 Engr. Perf. 12½x13
2464 A1008 €1.15 multi 2.75 2.25

47th Television Festival, Monte Carlo — A1009

2007, May 4 Litho. Perf. 13¼x13
2465 A1009 €2.90 multi 6.75 6.00

Scouting, Cent. A1010

No. 2466: a, Scouts and campfire. b, Lord Robert Baden-Powell.
2007, May 4 Photo. Perf. 13¼
2466 A1010 60c Horiz. pair, #a-b 3.75 3.75

Cartophily, Numismatics and Philately Grand Bourse — A1011

MONACO

Litho. & Silk-Screened
2007, June 25   *Perf. 13¼x13*
2467   A1011   49c multi   1.20   1.00

22nd Magic Stars Festival, Monte Carlo — A1012

2007, June 25   *Litho.*
2468   A1012   €1.30 red & black   3.00   2.50

Monaco Harbor — A1013

2007, Oct. 1   *Engr.*   *Perf. 13x12½*
2469   A1013   85c multi   2.00   1.75

Christmas — A1014

Litho. & Silk-screened
2007, Oct. 1   *Perf. 13¼x13*
2470   A1014   54c multi   1.25   1.10

32nd Intl. Circus Festival, Monte Carlo — A1015

2007, Oct. 15   *Photo.*   *Perf. 13¼*
2471   A1015   60c multi   1.40   1.25

Giacomo Puccini (1858-1924), Composer — A1016

2007, Dec. 7   *Engr.*   *Perf. 13¼*
2472   A1016   €1.40 blue & red   3.25   2.75

41st Intl. Flower Show — A1017

2008, Jan. 3   *Photo.*
2473   A1017   49c multi   1.10   1.00

Reformed Church of Monaco, 50th Anniv. — A1018

2008, Jan. 3   *Engr.*   *Perf. 13¼*
2474   A1018   49c blue & brown   1.10   1.10

Consecration of St. Charles Church, 125th Anniv. — A1019

2008, Mar. 3
2475   A1019   54c gray blue & red   1.25   1.10

A1020

Design: Arc de Triomphe du Carrousel Quadriga, Paris, by François Joseph Bosio.

2008, Jan. 3
2476   A1020   54c multi   1.25   1.10

Andrea Palladio (1508-80), Architect — A1021

2008, Jan. 3   *Photo.*   *Perf. 13¼*
2477   A1021   60c multi   1.25   1.25

10th Special Session of United Nations Environment Program, Monaco — A1022

2008, Jan. 3   *Photo.*   *Perf. 13¼*
2478   A1022   85c multi   2.00   1.75

Johannes Brahms (1833-97), Composer — A1023

2008, Jan. 3   *Engr.*   *Perf. 13¼*
2479   A1023   €1.15 Prus grn & red   2.75   2.25

Return of Comet Predicted by Edmond Halley, 250th Anniv. — A1024

2008, Jan. 3   *Photo.*   *Perf. 13¼*
2480   A1024   €1.57 multi   3.50   3.00

Marcel Kroenlein Arboretum, Roure, France, 20th Anniv. — A1025

2008, Jan. 3   *Engr.*   *Perf. 13¼*
2481   A1025   €2.11 multi   4.75   4.00

Poster for Monte Carlo Country Club, by Raymond Gid — A1026

Poster for Monte Carlo Beach Hotel, by Raymond Gid — A1027

Poster for Monte Carlo Golf Club, by Raymond Gid — A1028

Poster for Monte Carlo Tourism, by Louis Rué — A1029

Perf. 12¼x13, 13 (#2483)
2008, Jan. 3   *Photo., Litho.*
2482   A1026   70c multi   1.60   1.25
2483   A1027   85c multi   2.00   1.50
2484   A1028   €1.15 multi   2.75   2.25
2485   A1029   €2.90 multi   6.50   5.50
Nos. 2482-2485 (4)   12.85   10.50

Gen. André Massena (1758-1817) — A1030

2008, Jan. 21   *Engr.*   *Perf. 13¼*
2486   A1030   86c grn & yel brown   2.00   1.50

Apparition at Lourdes, France, 150th Anniv. — A1031

2008, Feb. 11   *Engr.*   *Perf. 13x12¾*
2487   A1031   €1.30 dark blue & blue   3.00   2.25

Introduction of the Ford Model T, Cent. — A1032

2008, Mar. 10   *Perf. 13¼*
2488   A1032   €1.70 multi   3.75   3.25

National Aeronautics and Space Administration, 50th Anniv. — A1033

2008, Mar. 10
2489   A1033   €2.30 multi   5.00   4.00

Alfred Nobel (1833-1906), Inventor and Philantropist — A1034

2008, Mar. 10
2490   A1034   €4 blk & claret   9.00   6.50

Dog Show Type of 2002
2008, Mar. 17   *Photo.*   *Perf. 13¼*
2491   A826   88c Greyhound, vert.   2.00   1.50

Expo Zaragoza 2008 — A1035

2008, Mar. 18   *Litho.*   *Perf. 13x13¼*
2492   A1035   65c multi   1.50   1.00

Mother's Day — A1036

2008, Apr. 8   *Perf. 13¼x13*
2493   A1036   55c multi   1.25   .90

Stendhal (Marie-Henri Beyle) (1783-1842), Writer — A1037

2008, Apr. 8   *Engr.*   *Perf. 13¼*
2494   A1037   €1.33 multi   3.00   2.25

Boris Pasternak (1890-1960), Writer — A1038

2008, Apr. 8
2495   A1038   €2.18 multi   5.00   3.50

2008 Summer Olympics, Beijing — A1039

No. 2496 — Olympic rings and: a, Pagoda, basketball, tennis, javelin. b, Beijing Olympics emblem, baseball, fencing, shooting.

2008, Apr. 8   *Perf. 13x12½*
2496   A1039   Horiz. pair   3.25   3.25
   a.   55c red & black   1.25   1.00
   b.   85c red & black   1.90   1.25

Cap d'Ail, France, Cent. — A1040

2008, Apr. 21   *Litho.*   *Perf. 13x13¼*
2497   A1040   55c multi   1.25   1.00

MONACO

Exotic Garden, 75th Anniv. — A1041
2008, May 2   Engr.   Perf. 13¼
2498 A1041 50c multi   1.20 .90

2008 Magic Stars Festival, Monte Carlo — A1042
2008, May 5   Photo.
2499 A1042 72c multi   1.60 1.10

Europa — A1043
Designs: 55c, Letters encircling globe. 65c, Postmen, letter, means of postal communication.
2008, May 5   Engr.
2500-2501 A1043   Set of 2   2.75 2.00

Intl. Skating Union, 52nd Congress — A1044
2008, May 16   Litho.   Perf. 13¼x13
2502 A1044 50c multi   1.25 1.00

Prince Albert II of Monaco Foundation A1045
Litho. & Engr.
2008, May 16   Perf. 13x13¼
2503 A1045 88c multi   2.00 1.50

48th Intl. Television Festival, Monte Carlo — A1046
2008, June 2   Photo.   Perf. 13¼
2504 A1046 €2.80 multi   6.25 4.50

Monegasque International Cooperation A1047
Designs: 65c, Education. €1, Health. €1.25, Campaign against poverty. €1.70, Campaign against desertification.
2008, June 5   Engr.
2505-2508 A1047   Set of 4   10.00 7.50

Monaco 2008 Intl. Numismatic Exhibition — A1048
Litho. & Embossed With Foil Application
2008, June 16   Perf. 13½x13
2509 A1048 65c multi   1.50 1.00

Schönbrunn Palace, Vienna — A1049
2008, Sept. 18   Engr.   Perf. 13¼
2510 A1049 65c multi   1.50 1.00
WIPA 2008 Intl. Philatelic Exhibition, Vienna.

Order of Saint Charles, 150th Anniv. — A1050
Photo. & Embossed With Foil Application
2008, Sept. 18   Perf. 13x13¼
2511 A1050 €1.50 multi   3.50 2.75

Coins of Monaco — A1051
Obverse and reverse of: 50c, 1837 Franc. 55c, 1943 Franc. 72c, 1950 Franc. €1.25, 1960 Franc. €1.64, Euro coinage of 2002. €1.70, Euro coinage of 2006.
Litho. & Embossed With Foil Application
2008, Sept. 18
2512-2517 A1051   Set of 6   14.00 10.00

Christmas — A1052
2008, Sept. 19   Photo.   Perf. 13¼
2518 A1052 55c multi   1.25 1.00

33rd Intl. Circus Festival, Monte Carlo — A1053
2008, Dec. 19   Photo.   Perf. 13¼
2519 A1053 85c multi   2.00 1.50

Prince Albert I — A1054

Flag of Monaco and Intl. Polar Year Emblem A1055

Prince Albert II — A1056

2008, Dec. 19   Perf. 13x12¼
2520   Horiz. strip of 3   6.00 6.00
   a. A1054 85c multi   1.90 1.50
   b. A1055 85c multi   1.90 1.50
   c. A1056 85c multi   1.90 1.50

Admiral Robert E. Peary (1856-1920), Arctic Explorer, and Dog Sleds — A1057

Peary, Flag of US and Map of Arctic Area — A1058

Matthew Henson (1866-1955), Arctic Explorer and Ship — A1059

Litho. & Engr.
2008, Dec. 19   Perf. 13¼
2521   Horiz. strip of 3   6.00 6.00
   a. A1057 87c multi   2.00 1.50
   b. A1058 87c multi   2.00 1.50
   c. A1059 87c multi   2.00 1.50

Monaco Firefighting Corps, Cent. — A1060
Designs: 50c, Railway and road emergency vehicle. 72c, Ladder truck, 1909. 87c, Fireman, ladder truck.
2009, Jan. 5   Photo.   Perf. 13¼
2522-2524 A1060   Set of 3   4.75 3.50

Princess Grace Rose Garden, 25th Anniv. — A1061
2009, Jan. 5   Perf. 13¼x13
2525 A1061 €1.25 multi   2.75 2.25

Spring Arts Festival, 25th Anniv. — A1062
2009, Jan. 5
2526 A1062 €1.33 multi   3.00 2.50

First Flight Across English Channel by Louis Blériot, Cent. — A1063
Litho. & Engr.
2009, Jan. 29   Perf. 13x12½
2527 A1063 87c multi   2.00 1.50

Felix Mendelssohn Bartholdy (1809-47), Composer — A1064
2009, Jan. 29   Engr.   Perf. 13¼
2528 A1064 €1.50 ol grn & blue   3.50 2.50

Beatification of Joan of Arc, Cent. — A1065
2009, Jan. 29
2529 A1065 €2.22 multi   5.00 4.00

MonacoPhil 2009 Philatelic Exhibition — A1066
2009, Feb. 7   Litho.   Perf. 13¼x13
2530 A1066 56c multi   1.25 1.00

Chihuahua and Cavalier King Charles Spaniel — A1067
2009, Feb. 7   Photo.   Perf. 13¼
2531 A1067 72c multi   1.60 1.25
Intl. Dog Show.

2009 Intl. Cat Show — A1068
2009, Feb. 7   Litho.   Perf. 13x13¼
2532 A1068 88c multi   2.00 1.50

MONACO

Association of Members of the Order of Academic Palms World Conference A1069

2009, Feb. 7   Engr.   Perf. 13x12½
2533 A1069 88c multi   2.00 1.50

Barbie Doll, 50th Anniv. — A1070

2009, Feb. 7   Photo.   Perf. 13¼
2534 A1070 88c multi   2.00 1.50

42nd Intl. Flower Show — A1071

2009, Feb. 7   Photo.   Perf. 13¼
2535 A1071 89c multi   2.00 1.50

Monaco Fencing and Handgun Club, Cent. — A1072

2009, Feb. 16   Litho. & Engr.
2536 A1072 55c multi   1.25 1.00

Giro d'Italia Bicycle Race, Cent. — A1073

2009, Feb. 16   Photo.
2537 A1073 70c multi   1.60 1.25

Sir Arthur Conan Doyle (1859-1930), Writer — A1074

2009, Feb. 16   Engr.   Perf. 12¼
2538 A1074 85c multi   2.00 1.50

Edgar Allan Poe (1809-49), Writer A1075

2009, Feb. 16
2539 A1075 €1.70 red & dk grn   3.75 2.75

Coat of Arms — A1076

Serpentine Die Cut 11
2009, Apr. 6   Photo.
Booklet Stamp
Self-Adhesive
2540 A1076 (70c) multi   1.60 1.25
  a. Booklet pane of 10   16.00
Compare type A1086 with types A786 and A1597.

Louis Notari Library, Cent. — A1077

2009, Apr. 29   Engr.   Perf. 13x12½
2541 A1077 51c red & purple   1.20   .90

Monaco Grand Prix Auto Race, Cent. — A1078

2009, Apr. 29   Photo.   Perf. 13x13¼
2542 A1078 70c multi   1.60 1.20

Monaco's Admission to UNESCO, 60th Anniv. A1079

2009, Apr. 29
2543 A1079 €1.70 multi   3.75 2.75

Louis Braille (1809-52), Educator of the Blind — A1080

2009, Apr. 29   Engr.   Perf. 12¼x13
2544 A1080 €3.80 multi   8.50 6.50

Concerts at the Prince's Palace, 50th Anniv. — A1081

2009, May 4   Perf. 13x13¼
2545 A1081 51c purple & black   1.20   .90

Europa — A1082

Astronomers: 56c, Francesco Maria Grimaldi (1618-63), map of Moon showing crater named after Grimaldi. 70c, Galileo Galilei (1564-1642), telescope.

Litho. & Engr.
2009, May 4   Perf. 13x12½
2546-2547 A1082 Set of 2   2.75 2.25
Intl. Year of Astronomy.

Ballets de Monte-Carlo A1083

2009, May 11   Photo.   Perf. 13¼x13
2548 A1083 73c multi   1.60 1.25

Ballets Russes, Cent. — A1084

Designs: 89c, Fifteen performers. €1.35, Nine performers.

2009, May 11
2549-2550 A1084 Set of 2   5.00 4.00

Georges Seurat (1859-91), Painter — A1085

Litho. & Engr.
2009, May 14   Perf. 13x13¼
2551 A1085 73c multi   1.60 1.25

St. Francis of Assisi (c. 1181-1226) — A1086

2009, May 14   Engr.   Perf. 13¼
2552 A1086 90c blue & black   2.00 1.50
Franciscan Order, 800th anniv.

John Calvin (1509-64), Theologian and Religious Reformer A1087

2009, May 14   Perf. 13x13¼
2553 A1087 €1.67 multi   3.75 2.75

49th Intl. Television Festival, Monte Carlo — A1088

2009, May 29   Photo.   Perf. 13¼
2554 A1088 €1.60 multi   3.50 2.75

Italian Writers — A1089

Emblem of Monaco Dante Alighieri Society and: 70c, Niccolò Machiavelli (1469-1527). 85c, Giovanni Boccaccio (1313-75). €1.30, Francesco Petrarca (Petrarch) (1304-74).

2009, June 3   Engr.   Perf. 12¼x13
2555-2557 A1089 Set of 3   6.25 4.50
Monaco Dante Alighieri Society, 30th anniv.

Grande Bourse 2009 — A1090

2009, June 17   Photo.   Perf. 13¼
2558 A1090 51c multi   1.20   .90

Youth Hostels, Cent. — A1091

2009, June 17   Litho.   Perf. 13x13¼
2559 A1091 90c multi   2.00 1.50

Tuiga, Flagship of Monaco Yacht Club, Cent. — A1092

2009, June 18   Photo.   Perf. 13¼
2560 A1092 70c multi   1.50 1.10

Start of Tour de France Bicycle Race in Monaco — A1093

2009, July 2   Litho.   Perf. 13¼x13
2561 A1093 56c multi   1.25 1.00

2009 Magic Stars Festival, Monte Carlo — A1094

2009, Sept. 16   Litho.   Perf. 13¼x13
2562 A1094 73c multi   1.60 1.20

Place de la Mairie — A1095

2009, Sept. 16   Photo.
2563 A1095 85c multi   1.90 1.25

MONACO

Big Ben, 150th Anniv. — A1096

2009, Sept. 16   Engr.
2564   A1096   €1 red & black   2.25   1.50

Christmas A1097

2009, Oct. 5   Perf. 13x13¼
2565   A1097   56c multi   1.25   1.00

2010 Intl. Cat Show — A1098

2009, Dec. 4   Photo.   Perf. 13¼
2566   A1098   56c multi   1.25   1.00
Dated 2010.

Jean Anouilh (1910-87), Playwright A1099

2009, Dec. 4   Engr.   Perf. 13x12¼
2567   A1099   73c multi   1.50   1.25
Dated 2010.

Ayrton Senna (1960-94), Race Car Driver A1100

2009, Dec. 4   Engr.   Perf. 13x12¼
2568   A1100   73c multi   1.50   1.25
Dated 2010.

Auguste Rodin (1840-1917), Sculptor — A1101

2009, Dec. 4   Engr.   Perf. 13x12¼
2569   A1101   85c multi   1.90   1.50
Dated 2010.

Princess Grace (1929-82) A1102

2009, Dec. 4   Engr.   Perf. 12¼x13
2570   A1102   89c red & black   2.00   1.50
Dated 2010.

Gustav Mahler (1860-1911), Composer A1103

2009, Dec. 4
2571   A1103   90c brown & blue   2.00   1.50
Dated 2010.

2010 Winter Olympics, Vancouver — A1104

No. 2572 — 2010 Winter Olympics emblem and: a, Slalom skier. b, Snowboarder and figure skater.

2009, Dec. 4   Engr.   Perf. 13¼x13½
2572   A1104   Horiz. pair   4.00   4.00
a.-b.   90c Either single   2.00   1.50
Dated 2010.

Monte Carlo Vu de Roquebrune, by Claude Monet (1840-1926) — A1105

2009, Dec. 4   Photo.   Perf. 13x13¼
2573   A1105   €1.30 multi   3.00   2.25
Dated 2010.

US No. 85A, Trophy — A1106

2009, Dec. 4   Litho.
2574   A1106   €1.35 multi   3.00   2.25
Awarding of Intl. Association of Stamp Catalogue Publishers Grand Prix for Philately to William H. Gross. Dated 2010.

The Birth of Venus, by William Bouguereau (1825-1905) A1107

2009, Dec. 4   Photo.   Perf. 13¼x13
2575   A1107   €1.60 multi   3.50   2.75
Dated 2010.

Anton Chekhov (1860-1904), Writer — A1108

2009, Dec. 4   Engr.   Perf. 13x12¼
2576   A1108   €1.67 multi   3.50   2.75
Dated 2010.

Souvenir Sheet

Prince Albert II A1109

Litho. (Margin) & Engr.
2009, Dec. 4   Perf. 13¼x13
2577   A1109   €4 red & black   9.00   7.00
MonacoPhil 2009 Intl. Philatelic Exhibition. Dated 2010.

Souvenir Sheet

Automobile Club of Monaco, 120th Anniv. — A1110

No. 2578: a, Race car. b, Formula 1 race car.

2009, Dec. 4   Photo.   Perf. 13x13¼
2578   A1110   Sheet of 2   6.50   6.50
a.   €1.30 multi   3.00   2.50
b.   €1.70 multi   3.00   2.50
Dated 2010.

34th Intl. Circus Festival, Monte Carlo — A1111

2009, Dec. 10   Photo.   Perf. 13¼
2579   A1111   70c multi   1.50   1.10
Dated 2010.

Australian Shepherd A1112

2010, Feb. 8   Photo.   Perf. 13¼
2580   A1112   51c multi   1.10   .80
Intl. Dog Show.

Intl. Flower Arrangement Festival — A1113

2010, Feb. 8
2581   A1113   70c multi   1.50   1.10

Five Nations Rugby Championships, Cent. — A1114

2010, Feb. 8   Litho.   Perf. 13¼x13
2582   A1114   70c multi   1.50   1.10

Scenes From "The Seven Samurai," Film by Akira Kurosawa (1910-98) A1115

2010, Feb. 24   Engr.   Perf. 13x12¼
2583   A1115   51c ol grn & black   1.10   .80

Monte Carlo Rolex Masters Tennis Tournament — A1116

2010, Mar. 4   Photo.   Perf. 13¼
2584   A1116   85c multi   1.90   1.50

2010 World Cup Soccer Championships, South Africa — A1117

No. 2585 — Flag of South Africa, players in stadium with denomination at: a, LL. b, UR.

2010, Mar. 4
2585   A1117   Horiz. pair   4.00   4.00
a.-b.   89c Either single   2.00   1.50

Souvenir Sheet

2008 Monaco Coin A1118

MONACO

Litho. & Embossed With Foil Application
2010, Mar. 4 — Perf. 13½
2586 A1118 €1 multi — 2.25 1.75
Expo 2010, Shanghai.

Miniature Sheet

Oceanographic Museum of Monaco, Cent. — A1119

No. 2587: a, Prince Albert I. b, Stuffed Ursus maritimus. c, Pterapogon kauderni, horiz. d, Hands pointing at starfish, horiz.

Litho. & Engr.
2010, Mar. 29 — Perf. 13¼x13
2587 A1119 Sheet of 4 — 6.00 6.00
 a. 51c multi — 1.10 .80
 b. 56c multi — 1.25 1.00
 c. 73c multi — 1.60 1.20
 d. 90c multi — 2.00 1.50

Miniature Sheet

Former Grimaldi Family Fiefs in France A1120

No. 2588: a, County of Thann. b, Barony of Altkirch. c, County of Rosemont. d, County of Ferrette.

2010, Apr. 23 Photo. Perf. 13x13¼
2588 A1120 €1 Sheet of 4, #a-d — 9.00 9.00

Flora and Fauna — A1121

Designs: 2c, Pinna nobilis, Submarine Reserve of Larvotto. €2, Lis martagon, Mercantour National Park, France.

2010, Apr. 29 Engr. Perf. 13¼
2589 A1121 2c multi — .25 .25
2590 A1121 €2 multi — 4.00 3.00

Mother Teresa (1910-97), Humanitarian A1122

2010, Apr. 29 Photo. Perf. 13¼
2591 A1122 €1.70 multi — 3.75 2.75

UNAIDS Program, 15th Anniv. — A1123

2010, May 5 Photo. Perf. 13¼
2592 A1123 89c multi — 2.00 1.50

Europa — A1124

Map of Europe, books and: 56c, Five children. 70c, One child.

2010, May 5 Engr. Perf. 13x13¼
2593-2594 A1124 Set of 2 — 2.75 2.25

London 2010 Festival of Stamps A1125

2010, May 7
2595 A1125 €1.30 multi — 2.75 2.25

50th Television Festival, Monte Carlo — A1126

Litho. With Foil Application
2010, May 26 — Perf. 13¼x13
2596 A1126 €2.80 multi — 5.75 3.75

Human Paleontology Institute, Paris, Cent. — A1127

2010, June 1 Engr. Perf. 13x12¾
2597 A1127 56c multi — 1.25 1.00
See France No. 3821.

Grimaldi Forum, 10th Anniv. — A1128

2010, June 22 Litho. Perf. 13x13¼
2598 A1128 75c multi — 1.60 1.25

Youth Olympic Games, Singapore A1129

2010, June 22 Photo.
2599 A1129 87c multi — 1.90 1.50

Maritime and Airport Police Division, 50th Anniv. — A1130

2010, July 1 Engr. Perf. 13¼
2600 A1130 53c multi — 1.10 .75

Invention of the Food Canning Process, by Nicholas Appert, Bicent. — A1131

2010, July 1 Perf. 12¼
2601 A1131 95c red & purple — 2.10 1.60

Invention of First Practical Internal Combustion Engine by Jean-Joseph-Etienne Lenoir, 150th Anniv. — A1132

2010, July 1
2602 A1132 €1.75 multi — 4.00 3.00

Little Africa Gardens, Monaco A1133

2010, July 1 Perf. 13x13¼
2603 A1133 €2.30 multi — 5.00 4.00

First International Electric Postal Flight, Monaco to Nice — A1134

2010, Aug. 23 Litho. Perf. 13
2604 A1134 95c multi — 2.00 1.50

Monaco Scientific Center, 50th Anniv. — A1135

2010, Sept. 17 Photo. Perf. 13¼
2605 A1135 58c multi — 1.25 1.00

25th Magic Stars Festival, Monte Carlo — A1136

2010, Sept. 17 Litho. Perf. 13¼x13
2606 A1136 €1.40 multi — 3.00 2.25

Monaco Regional Express Transport A1137

2010, Sept. 19 Engr. Perf. 13x13¼
2607 A1137 €1.35 multi — 3.00 2.25

Albert I High School, Cent. — A1138

2010, Oct. 4 Perf. 13x13¼
2608 A1138 75c multi — 1.60 1.20

Christmas — A1139

2010, Oct. 4 Photo. Perf. 13¼
2609 A1139 58c multi — 1.25 1.00

35th Intl. Circus Festival, Monte Carlo — A1140

2010, Dec. 20 Perf. 13¼
2610 A1140 75c multi — 1.60 1.10

Constitution of Monaco, Cent. — A1141

2011, Jan. 4
2611 A1141 53c multi — 1.20 .90

Egyptian Mau Cat — A1142

2011, Jan. 4
2612 A1142 87c multi — 1.90 1.25
Intl. Cat Show.

Juan Manuel Fangio (1911-95), Race Car Driver A1143

Indianapolis 500, Cent. — A1144

541

MONACO

Monte Carlo Rally, Cent. — A1145

2011, Jan. 12		Engr.	Perf. 13x13¼
2613	A1143	95c multi	2.00 1.50
		Photo.	
2614	A1144	€1.35 multi	3.00 2.25
2615	A1145	€1.40 multi	3.00 2.25
	Nos. 2613-2615 (3)		8.00 6.00

Marine Laboratory of the Intl. Atomic Energy Agency, 50th Anniv. — A1146

2011, Jan. 20		Photo.	Perf. 13¼
2616	A1146	87c multi	1.90 1.25

Renewable Energy — A1147

2011, Jan. 20		Litho.	Perf. 13x13¼
2617	A1147	€1.80 multi	4.00 3.00

Mission Enfance Association, 20th Anniv. — A1148

2011, Jan. 28			
2618	A1148	53c multi	1.10 .75

Labrador Retriever A1149

2011, Feb. 7		Photo.	Perf. 13¼
2619	A1149	53c multi	1.10 .75
		Intl. Dog Show.	

Sculptors and Their Sculptures — A1151

A1150

No. 2620: a, Antoine Bourdelle (1861-1929). b, Horse's head from Monument to General Alvear.
No. 2621: a, Aristide Maillol (1861-1944). b, The Night.

2011, Feb. 21		Engr.	Perf. 13¼
2620	A1150	Horiz. pair	3.25 3.25
a.-b.		75c Either single	1.60 1.60
2621	A1151	Horiz. pair	4.25 4.25
a.-b.		95c Either single	2.00 1.50

State Visit of Prince Albert II to Ireland — A1152

2011, Feb. 21		Photo.	Perf. 13¼
2622	A1152	€1.40 multi	3.00 2.25

Monte Carlo Rolex Masters Tennis Tournament — A1153

2011, Mar. 2			
2623	A1153	75c multi	1.60 1.10

Napoleon II (1811-32), Titular King of Rome — A1154

2011, Mar. 2		Engr.	
2624	A1154	€1 brown & blue	2.25 1.60

44th Intl. Flower Show, Monte Carlo A1155

Chelsea Flower Show, London A1156

Japanese Garden of Monaco — A1157

	Photo., Litho. (#2626)		
2011, Mar. 24			Perf. 13¼
2625	A1155	95c multi	2.00 1.50
		Perf. 13¼x13	
2626	A1156	€1.75 multi	3.75 2.75
		Perf. 13x13¼	
2627	A1157	€2.35 multi	5.00 3.50
	Nos. 2625-2627 (3)		10.75 7.75

Consecration of Monaco Cathedral, Cent. — A1158

2011, Mar. 31		Engr.	Perf. 13x13¼
2628	A1158	58c red & black	1.25 1.00

Lions Club of Monaco, 50th Anniv. — A1159

2011, Mar. 31		Photo.	Perf. 13¼
2629	A1159	75c multi	1.60 1.10

Former Grimaldi Family Fiefs in Provence A1160

No. 2630: a, Saint-Rémy-de-Provence. b, Les Baux-de-Provence.

2011, Apr. 4			Perf. 13x13¼
2630	A1160	Sheet of 2	8.00 8.00
a.		€1.75 multi	3.75 2.75
b.		€1.80 multi	3.75 2.75

Aquilegia Bertolonii, Mercantour National Park A1161

Tarentola Mauritanica A1162

2011, Apr. 20		Photo.	Perf. 13¼
2631	A1161	3c multi	.25 .25
		Engr.	
		Perf. 13¼x13	
2632	A1162	€2.30 multi	5.00 3.50

Europa — A1163

Designs: 58c, Alpine forest. 75c, Mediterranean forest.

2011, May 3		Photo.	Perf. 13¼
2633-2634	A1163	Set of 2	3.00 2.25
		Intl. Year of Forests.	

Winning Artwork in Environment and Ecology in Monaco Children's Stamp Design Contest — A1164

2011, May 18		Litho.	Perf. 13x13¼
2635	A1164	53c multi	1.20 .90

A1165

Wedding of Prince Albert II and Charlene Wittstock A1166

	Engr. With Foil Application		
2011, July 1			Perf. 13x13¼
2636	A1165	55c blk & grn	1.25 1.00
2637	A1165	60c blk & red	1.25 1.00
2638	A1165	77c blk & pur	1.75 1.25
2639	A1165	89c blk & blue	2.00 1.50
2640	A1165	€4.10 brn, gold & red	9.00 7.00
	Nos. 2636-2640 (5)		15.25 11.75
	Souvenir Sheet		
	Photo.		
2641	A1166	€5 multi	11.00 8.00

Prince's Company of Carabiniers A1167

2011, July 18		Photo.	Perf. 13¼
2642	A1167	77c multi	1.75 1.25

Monte Carlo Golf Club, Cent. — A1168

2011, Aug. 9		Litho.	Perf. 13¼
2643	A1168	60c multi	1.25 .90

Monegasque Alpine Club, Cent. — A1169

2011, Aug. 9			Photo.
2644	A1169	60c multi	1.25 .90

2011 Grande Bourse, Salle du Canton — A1170

2011, Aug. 12			
2645	A1170	60c multi	1.25 .90

Zeus Faber — A1171

2011, Aug. 16			Litho.
2646	A1171	(39c) multi	.85 .65

No. 2646 was issued precanceled only. See note after No. 324.

MonacoPhil 2011 Intl. Philatelic Exhibition — A1172

2011, Aug. 29			Perf. 13¼
2647	A1172	55c multi	1.25 .90

MONACO

543

Paris Institute of Oceanography, Cent. — A1173

2011, Sept. 19		Engr.		Perf. 13x13¼	
2648	A1173	77c multi		1.75	1.25

Exotic Garden, Monaco A1174

2011, Sept. 28		Photo.		Perf. 13¼	
2649	A1174	75c multi		1.75	1.25

First Man in Space, 50th Anniv. — A1175

2011, Sept. 28		Engr.		Perf. 13x13¼	
2650	A1175	€2.78 blue		6.00	4.50

Georges Méliès (1861-1938), Film Maker — A1176

2011, Sept. 28					
2651	A1176	€1.45 multi		3.25	2.40

Franz Liszt (1811-86), Composer A1177

2011, Oct. 10				Perf. 13x12¼	
2652	A1177	€1 multi		2.25	1.75

Théophile Gautier (1811-72), Poet A1178

2011, Oct. 10		Litho.		Perf. 13	
2653	A1178	€1.75 multi		4.00	3.00

Prince Antoine I (1661-1731) A1179

Litho. & Embossed With Foil Application

2011, Oct. 10					
2654	A1179	€1.80 multi		4.00	3.00

Henri Troyat (1911-2007), Writer — A1180

2011, Oct. 10		Engr.		Perf. 12¼x13	
2655	A1180	€2.40 multi		5.25	3.75

Christmas A1181

2011, Oct. 17		Litho.		Perf. 13¼	
2656	A1181	60c multi		1.25	.90

25th Telethon A1182

2011, Dec. 2					
2657	A1182	60c multi		1.25	.90

Intl. Association of Philatelic Catalogue Editors (ASCAT) Grand Prix — A1183

2011, Dec. 2				Photo.	
2658	A1183	78c multi		1.75	1.25

Souvenir Sheet

Prince Albert II and Princess Charlene A1184

2011, Dec. 2					
2659	A1184	€5 multi		11.00	11.00

MonacoPhil 2011 Intl. Philatelic Exhibition.

36th Intl. Circus Festival, Monte Carlo A1185

2011, Dec. 19					
2660	A1185	77c multi		1.75	1.25

Intl. Flower Arrangement Festival — A1186

2012, Jan. 10				Litho.	
2661	A1186	55c multi		1.25	.90

2012 Intl. Cat Show — A1187

2012, Jan. 10		Photo.		Perf. 13¼	
2662	A1187	77c multi		1.75	1.25

St. Martin's Gardens A1188

2012, Jan. 10					
2663	A1188	89c multi		2.00	1.50

Miniature Sheet

Frescoes of the Monte Carlo Opera A1189

No. 2664: a, Comedy, by Frédéric Lix. b, Music, by Gustave Boulanger. c, Dance, by Georges Clairin. d, Song and Eloquence, by François Feyen-Perrin.

2012, Jan. 25				Perf. 13x13¼	
2664	A1189	€1.45 Sheet of 4, #a-d		13.00	13.00

2012 Monte Carlo Rolex Masters Tennis Tournament — A1190

2012, Feb. 2				Perf. 13¼	
2665	A1190	89c multi		2.00	1.50

Collie — A1191

2012, Feb. 2				Engr.	
2666	A1191	89c multi		2.00	1.50

Intl. Dog Show.

Florestan Company, 25th Anniv. — A1192

2012, Feb. 20		Litho.		Perf. 13¼	
2667	A1192	55c multi		1.25	.90

Recognition by France of Monaco's Independence, 500th Anniv. — A1193

2012, Feb. 20		Engr.		Perf. 13x13¼	
2668	A1193	55c red & black		1.25	.90

Carabine de Monaco (Rifle Shooting Association), Cent. — A1194

2012, Feb. 20					
2669	A1194	€1.35 multi		3.00	2.25

75th Bazaar for the Work of Sister Mary — A1195

2012, Mar. 16		Litho.		Perf. 13¼	
2670	A1195	60c multi		1.25	.90

70th Monaco Grand Prix — A1196

2012, Mar. 20		Engr.		Perf. 13x13¼	
2671	A1196	77c multi		1.75	1.25

First Seaplane Competition, Cent. — A1197

2012, Mar. 20					
2672	A1197	€1.80 multi		4.00	3.00

Coat of Arms Type of 2000 Inscribed "20g écopli" at Top

Serpentine Die Cut 11

2012, Apr. 20				Photo.	
Booklet Stamp					
Self-Adhesive					
2673	A786	(55c) blue & multi		1.25	.90
a.	Booklet pane of 10			12.50	

Compare with No. 2863.

Arrival of PlanetSolar Boat in Monaco — A1198

2012, Apr. 20		Engr.		Perf. 13x13¼	
2674	A1198	77c multi		1.75	1.25

Expo 2012, Yeosu, South Korea — A1199

2012, Apr. 20		Photo.		Perf. 13¼	
2675	A1199	78c multi		1.75	1.25

Europa — A1200

MONACO

Rooms in the Prince's Palace: 60c, Louis XV Bedroom. 77c, Mazarin Room.

2012, May 9   Litho.
2676-2677 A1200   Set of 2   3.00   2.25

Rotary Club of Monaco, 75th Anniv. — A1201

2012, June 9
2678 A1201 77c multi   1.75 1.25

United Nations Rio + 20 Conference on Sustainable Development, Rio de Janeiro — A1202

2012, June 9
2679 A1202 78c multi   1.75 1.25

Prince of Monaco Islands, French Southern and Antarctic Territories — A1203

No. 2680: a, Giant Antarctic petrel. b, Coastline of Prince of Monaco Islands.

2012, June 9   Litho. & Engr.
2680 A1203   Sheet of 2   4.50 4.50
a.-b.   €1 Either single   2.25 1.60

See French Southern and Antarctic Territories No. 467.

Souvenir Sheet

Cabaret on the Banks of the River, by Jan Breughel A1204

2012, June 25   Photo.
2681 A1204 €3 multi   6.50 5.00

Exhibition of philatelic collection of Prince Albert II, Bruges, Belgium. See Belgium No. 2577.

Fort-la-Laffe, Matignon, France — A1205

2012, July 5   Engr.   Perf. 13x13¼
2682 A1205 €1.75 multi   3.75 2.75

Visit of Prince Albert II to Matignon.

Intl. Association of Athletics Federations, Cent. — A1206

2012, July 17   Photo.   Perf. 13¼
2683 A1206 89c multi   2.00 1.50

2012 Summer Olympics, London — A1207

2012, July 17   Litho. & Engr.
2684 A1207 €1.35 multi   3.00 2.25

Tenth World Council of Consuls, Monaco A1208

2012, Aug. 22   Photo.   Perf. 12¼
2685 A1208 55c multi   1.25 .90

Claude Debussy (1862-1918), Composer — A1209

2012, Aug. 22   Engr.   Perf. 13x12¼
2686 A1209 €1 red & black   2.25 1.60

Crucifixion, by Louis Brea — A1210

2012, Aug. 22   Litho.   Perf. 12¼x13
2687 A1210 €1.35 multi   3.00 2.25

Bird Protection League, Cent. — A1211

2012, Sept. 10   Engr.   Perf. 13¼
2688 A1211 €1 multi   2.25 1.60

Opening of New National Council Building A1212

2012, Sept. 12   Perf. 13x13¼
2689 A1212 78c brown & black   1.75 1.25

Great Organ, Monaco Cathedral A1213

2012, Sept. 12   Litho. & Engr.   Perf. 13¼
2690 A1213 €1.80 multi   4.00 3.00

Title of Prince of Monaco, 400th Anniv. — A1214

2012, Sept. 12   Engr.   Perf. 13x13¼
2691 A1214 €2.40 multi   5.25 3.75

Consecration of St. Charles Church, Monaco, Cent. — A1215

2012, Oct. 19   Perf. 13¼
2692 A1215 €1.45 multi   3.25 2.50

Auguste Lumière (1862-1954), Filmmaker A1216

2012, Oct. 19   Perf. 12¼
2693 A1216 €2.35 multi   5.25 4.00

Discovery of Bust of Nefertiti, Cent. — A1217

2012, Oct. 19
2694 A1217 €3.78 multi   8.50 6.50

Timbres Passion 2012 Philatelic Exhibition, Belfort, France — A1218

No. 2695 — Coat of arms and: a, Duchess Louise d'Aumont Mazarin (1759-1826), wife of Prince Honoré IV. b, Prince Honoré IV of Monaco (1758-1819).

2012, Nov. 2   Litho.   Perf. 13¼
2695 A1218   Horiz. pair   2.40 1.75
a.-b.   55c Either single   1.20 .90

Christmas — A1219

2012, Nov. 2   Photo.
2696 A1219 60c multi   1.25 .90

Release of Third Volume of Adventures of Tintin A1220

2012, Nov. 21   Perf. 13x13¼
2697 A1220 77c multi   1.75 1.25

Prince Albert II — A1221

Inscription: (56c) Ecopli 20g. (63c), Prioritaire 20g. No. 2700, Europa 20g. No. 2701, Ecopli 50g. (€1.05), Prioritaire 50g.

2012, Dec. 1   Engr.   Perf. 13x13¼
2698 A1221   (56c) blue   1.25 .90
2699 A1221   (63c) red   1.40 1.10
a.   Dated "2015"   1.40 1.10
2700 A1221   (80c) red violet   1.75 1.25
2701 A1221   (80c) emerald   1.75 1.25
2702 A1221   (€1.05) black   2.40 1.75
   Nos. 2698-2702 (5)   8.55 6.25

Issued: No. 2699a, 1/2/15. No. 2699a sold for 76c on day of issue. See Nos. 2826-2828, 2995, 3124.

Painting by Patients of Speranza-Albert II Alzheimer's Disease Day Care Center — A1222

2012, Dec. 3   Photo.   Perf. 13¼x13
2703 A1222 €1.35 multi   3.00 2.25

Olympia, by Edouard Manet A1223

2012, Dec. 3   Litho.   Perf. 13x13¼
2704 A1223 €1.80 multi   4.00 3.00

37th Intl. Circus Festival, Monte Carlo — A1224

2013, Jan. 2   Photo.   Perf. 13¼
2705 A1224 63c multi   1.40 1.10

Pierre de Coubertin (1863-1937), Founder of Intl. Olympic Committee A1225

2013, Jan. 2   Engr.   Perf. 13x13¼
2706 A1225 €2.55 multi   5.75 4.50

MONACO

Turkish Angora Cat — A1226

2013, Jan. 16   Photo.   Perf. 13¼
2707 A1226 56c multi   1.25 .90
Intl. Cat Show.

Nautical Society of Monaco, 125th Anniv. — A1227

2013, Jan. 16   Engr.
2708 A1227 95c multi   2.00 1.50

Intl. Flower Arrangement Festival — A1228

2013, Jan. 16   Photo.
2709 A1228 €1.75 multi   3.75 3.00

French Bulldog — A1229

2013, Feb. 7   Engr.
2710 A1229 80c red & black   1.75 1.25
Intl. Dog Show.

Monte Carlo Casino Terraces A1230

2013, Feb. 7   Photo.
2711 A1230 80c multi   1.75 1.25

Monte Carlo Rolex Masters Tennis Tournament — A1231

2013, Feb. 7
2712 A1231 €1.05 multi   2.25 1.60

World Association of Children's Friends, 50th Anniv. — A1232

2013, Feb. 18
2713 A1232 €1.55 multi   3.25 2.50

Intl. Red Cross, 150th Anniv. — A1233

2013, Feb. 18   Engr.   Perf. 13x13¼
2714 A1233 €4.10 red & blk   9.00 7.00

Formula 1 Race Cars — A1234

Designs: €1.05, Maserati 250F. €1.75, Tyrrell P34.

2013, Mar. 14   Litho.   Perf. 13¼
2715-2716 A1234 Set of 2   6.00 4.50

Clean Transportation — A1235

No. 2717: a, Solar-powered shuttle boat. b, Electric bicycle.

Litho. & Silk-screened
2013, Apr. 5
2717 A1235 Horiz. pair   8.00 8.00
   a.-b. €1.85 Either single   4.00 3.00

Archconfraternity of Misericordia, Bicent. — A1236

2013, Apr. 27   Photo.   Perf. 13¼
2718 A1236 80c multi   1.75 1.25

Junior Chamber International Monaco, 50th Anniv. — A1237

2013, May 10   Litho.
2719 A1237 56c multi   1.25 .90

Europa — A1238

2013, May 10
2720 A1238 63c multi   1.40 1.00

Grimaldi Family Coat of Arms and Tower of Crest, France — A1239

2013, May 17   Photo.
2721 A1239 €1.05 multi   2.25 1.60
Visit of Prince Albert II to Duchy of Valentinois and Crest, France.

Giuseppe Verdi (1813-1901), Composer — A1240

Richard Wagner (1813-83), Composer A1241

Premiere of *The Rite of Spring*, Ballet by Igor Stravinsky, Cent. A1242

2013, May 22   Engr.   Perf. 13x12¼
2722 A1240 €1.55 multi   3.25 2.50
2723 A1241 €1.85 multi   4.00 3.00
2724 A1242 €2.55 multi   5.50 4.00
Nos. 2722-2724 (3)   12.75 9.50

Admission to United Nations, 20th Anniv. — A1243

2013, May 28   Litho.   Perf. 13¼
2725 A1243 80c multi   1.75 1.25

15th World Festival of Amateur Theater — A1244

2013, June 5
2726 A1244 63c multi   1.40 1.00

Larus Michahellis A1245

2013, June 5
2727 A1245 80c multi   1.75 1.25

Discovery of Otiorhynchus Monoecirupus in Monaco — A1246

2013, June 5
2728 A1246 €1 multi   2.00 1.50

Miniature Sheet

Sharks A1247

No. 2729: a, Blacktip shark (requin bordé). b, Tiger shark (requin-tigre). c, Whale shark (requin-baleine). d, Great white shark (grand requin blanc).

2013, June 8   Photo.
2729 A1247 Sheet of 4   7.50 7.50
   a.-b. 63c Either single   1.40 1.00
   c.-d. €1.05 Either single   2.25 1.60

Miniature Sheet

Monte Carlo Société des Bains de Mer, 150th Anniv. A1248

No. 2730 — Monte Carlo Casino with: a, Beige background and white dots. b, Beige background. c, Black background. d, Black background and white dots.

Photo., (Sheet Margin Photo., Silk-screened and Embossed)
2013, July 5
2730 A1248 Sheet of 4   8.00 8.00
   a.-b. 80c Either single   1.75 1.25
   c. €1.05 multi   2.25 1.60
   d. €1.35 multi   3.00 2.25

2013 Grande Bourse — A1249

2013, July 10   Photo.   Perf. 13¼
2731 A1249 63c multi   1.40 1.00

MonacoPhil 2013 Intl. Philatelic Exhibition, Fontvieille Terraces A1250

2013, July 10   Litho.
2732 A1250 80c multi   1.75 1.25

First Trans-Mediterranean Flight by Roland Garros, Cent. — A1251

2013, Sept. 23   Litho. & Engr.
2733 A1251 €1.35 multi   3.00 2.25

Yachts A1252

2013, Sept. 23   Engr.   Perf. 13x13¼
2734 A1252 Horiz. pair   5.50 5.50
   a. €1 Yacht without sails   2.00 1.50
   b. €1.55 Yacht with sails   3.25 2.50

Jules Richard (1863-1945), Director of Monaco Oceanographic Museum — A1253

2013, Oct. 9   Perf. 13¼
2735 A1253 €1 multi   2.00 1.50

Charles Pathé (1863-1957), Sound Recording and Film Entrepreneur — A1254

2013, Oct. 9
2736 A1254 €1.85 pur & black   4.00 3.00

MONACO

Crossword Puzzles, Cent. — A1255

2013, Oct. 9		Perf. 13x13¼
2737	A1255 €2.78 black & red	6.00 4.50

Christmas — A1256

2013, Oct. 30	Photo.	Perf. 13¼
2738	A1256 63c multi	1.40 1.00

A1257

Design: Awarding of 2013 ASCAT Grand Prix of philately to Jacques Rogge, Pres. of Intl. Olympic Committee.

2013, Dec. 5	Litho.	Perf. 13¼
2739	A1257 95c multi	2.00 1.50

Automobiles — A1258

No. 2740: a, Sunbeam Alpine. b, ZIL-111V.

2013, Dec. 5	Litho.	Perf. 13
2740	A1258 Horiz. pair	4.00 4.00
a.-b.	95c Either single	2.00 1.50

See Russia No. 7501.

Miniature Sheet

MonacoPhil 2013 Intl. Philatelic Exhibition — A1259

No. 2741: a, Prince Albert II facing right, country name at LL. b, Prince Albert II facing forward. c, Prince Albert II facing right, country name at bottom center. d, Monogram of Prince Albert II.

Engr. With Foil Application

2013, Dec. 5		Perf. 13
2741	A1259 Sheet of 4	8.50 8.50
a.-d.	€1 Any single	2.00 1.50

38th Intl. Circus Festival, Monte Carlo — A1260

2014, Jan. 6	Photo.	Perf. 13¼
2742	A1260 83c multi	1.75 1.25

Posters for Movies Starring Grace Kelly — A1261

Designs: €1.38, The Country Girl (Une Fille de la Province). €2.40, Dial M for Murder (Le Crime Etait Presque Parfait).

2014, Jan. 16	Litho.	Perf. 13¼
2743-2744	A1261 Set of 2	8.00 6.00

See Nos. 2783-2784, 2845-2846, 2865-2866, 2911-2912, 2953-2954.

British Shorthair Cat — A1262

2014, Jan. 30	Litho.	Perf. 13¼
2745	A1262 61c multi	1.25 .90

Intl. Cat Show.

2014 Winter Olympics, Sochi, Russia — A1263

2014, Jan. 30	Engr.	Perf. 13x13¼
2746	A1263 €1.78 multi	3.75 3.00

Monte Carlo Rolex Masters Tennis Tournament — A1264

2014, Feb. 5	Photo.	Perf. 13¼
2747	A1264 €1.10 multi	2.25 1.60

Bull Terrier — A1265

2014, Feb. 20	Litho.	Perf. 13¼
2748	A1265 87c multi	1.75 1.25

Intl. Dog Show.

Intl. Flower Arrangement Festival — A1266

2014, Feb. 20	Photo.	Perf. 13¼
2749	A1266 €2.10 multi	4.50 3.50

Gilles Villeneuve (1950-82), Formula 1 Race Car Driver — A1267

Ayrton Senna (1960-94), Formula 1 Race Car Driver — A1268

No. 2750: a, Villeneuve (31x31mm). b, Villeneuve (52x31mm).
No. 2751: a, Senna (31x31mm). b, Senna (52x31mm).

2014, Mar. 5	Photo.	Perf. 13
2750	A1267 Horiz. pair	2.75 2.75
a.-b.	66c Either single	1.25 .90
2751	A1268 Horiz. pair	3.50 3.50
a.-b.	83c Either single	1.75 1.25

Princess Grace Foundation, 50th Anniv. — A1269

2014, Mar. 14	Litho.	Perf. 13¼
2752	A1269 66c multi	1.25 .90

Printemps des Arts Festival (Spring Arts Festival), 30th Anniv. — A1270

2014, Mar. 14	Litho.	Perf. 13¼
2753	A1270 €1.20 multi	2.50 1.75

Marsupilami, Comic Book Character by André Franquin — A1271

2014, Apr. 1	Photo.	Perf. 13x13¼
2754	A1271 83c multi	1.75 1.25

Diana at the Bath, by Carlo Maratti A1272

No. 2755: a, 18th cent. engraving of painting (denomination at LR). b, Painting, 1684 (denomination at LL).

2014, Apr. 1	Litho.	Perf. 13¼
2755	A1272 Horiz. pair	7.00 7.00
a.-b.	€1.65 Either single	3.50 2.75

Monaco Air Rally, Cent. — A1273

2014, Apr. 1	Engr.	Perf. 13¼
2756	A1273 €2.65 multi	5.75 4.25

Old Tram and Modern Bus A1274

Litho. & Silk-Screened

2014, Apr. 30		Perf. 13
2757	A1274 59c multi	1.25 .90

Europa — A1275

2014, May 7	Litho.	Perf. 13¼
2758	A1275 83c multi	1.75 1.25

Souvenir Sheet

Ancient Grimaldi Fiefdoms in France A1276

No. 2759: a, House of the Princes of Monaco, Vic-sur-Cère, France. b, Rocher de Carlat.

2014, May 14	Photo.	Perf. 13¼
2759	A1276 Sheet of 2	8.00 8.00
a.	€1.65 multi	3.50 2.75
b.	€2.10 multi	4.50 3.50

2014 World Cup Soccer Tournament, Brazil — A1277

2014, May 30	Photo.	Perf. 13
2760	A1277 98c multi	2.00 1.50

Values are for stamp with surrounding selvage.

Prince Honoré IV (1758-1819) A1278

2014, May 30	Engr.	Perf. 13x13¼
2761	A1278 €2.10 multi	4.50 3.50

Treaty of Paris, 200th anniv., which restored Prince Honoré IV to Monegasque throne.

Souvenir Sheet

Sharks A1279

No. 2762: a, Blacktip reef shark and diver. b, Hammerhead shark and diver, horiz. c, Gray reef sharks.

2014, June 10	Photo.	Perf. 13¼
2762	A1279 Sheet of 3	7.50 7.50
a.	66c multi	1.25 .90
b.	€1.10 multi	2.25 1.60
c.	€1.65 multi	3.50 2.75

Princess Grace Rose Garden, 30th Anniv. — A1280

Litho. & Silk-Screened

2014, June 14		Perf. 13¼
2763	A1280 66c multi	1.25 .90

No. 2763 is impregnated with a rose scent.

MONACO

2014, June 14 Litho. Perf. 13¼
2764 A1281 83c multi 1.75 1.25
Protea Flowers — A1281

New Clubhouse of Yacht Club of Monaco — A1282

2014, June 20 Litho. & Engr. Perf. 13¼
2765 A1282 83c multi 1.75 1.25

Scorpionfish — A1283

2014, June 25 Litho. Perf. 13¼
2766 A1283 (40c) multi .85 .65

No. 2766 is known only precanceled. See note after No. 324.

Ceratonia Siliqua — A1284

2014, July 12 Photo. Perf. 13¼
2767 A1284 61c multi 1.25 .90

Princess Stephanie and Elephants Baby and Nepal — A1285

2014, July 12 Engr. Perf. 13x13¼
2768 A1285 €1.10 multi 2.25 1.60
Baby & Nepal Association, 1st anniv.

World War I, Cent. — A1286

Designs: €1.85, Hotel Alexandra (military hospital during war). €2.40, Prince Louis II, volunteer in French Army, and soldiers.

2014, Aug. 1 Engr. Perf. 13x13¼
2769-2770 A1286 Set of 2 9.00 7.50

2014 Grande Bourse — A1287

2014, Aug. 22 Litho. Perf. 13¼x13
2771 A1287 59c multi 1.25 .90

Opera Set Designed by Eugène Frey (1864-1930) — A1288

Litho., Silk-Screened & Embossed
2014, Aug. 22 Perf. 13x13¼
2772 A1288 €1.38 multi 3.00 2.25

Sportel Monaco (World Sports Content Media Convention), 25th Anniv. — A1289

2014, Sept. 1 Litho. Perf. 13¼
2773 A1289 59c multi 1.25 .90

Children's Day — A1290

2014, Sept. 1 Engr. Perf. 13¼
2774 A1290 66c multi 1.40 1.00
Intl. Convention on the Rights of the Child, 25th Anniv.

Coat of Arms Type of 2000
Inscribed "20g prioritaire" at Top
Serpentine Die Cut 11
2014, Sept. 17 Photo.
Booklet Stamp
Self-Adhesive
2775 A786 (66c) red & black 1.40 1.00
  a. Booklet pane of 10 14.00

83rd Interpol General Assembly, Monaco — A1291

2014, Nov. 3 Litho. Perf. 13¼x13
2776 A1291 66c multi 1.40 1.00

Adoration of the Magi, by Taddeo di Bartolo — A1292

2014, Nov. 3 Photo. Perf. 13¼
2777 A1292 66c multi 1.40 1.00
Christmas.

Exhibition on Prince Albert I's Exploration of Morocco, Rabat — A1293

2014, Nov. 7 Photo. Perf. 13¼
2778 A1293 Horiz. pair 3.50 3.50
  a. 66c multi 1.40 1.00
  b. 98c multi 2.00 1.50
See Morocco No. 1193.

127th International Olympic Committee Session, Monaco — A1294

2014, Dec. 1 Litho. & Engr.
2779 A1294 66c multi 1.40 1.00

Fight AIDS Monaco, 10th Anniv. — A1295

Litho. & Silk-Screened With Flocking Application
2014, Dec. 1 Perf. 13¼
2780 A1295 €1 red & black 2.00 1.50

39th Intl. Circus Festival, Monte Carlo — A1296

2015, Jan. 7 Photo. Perf. 13¼
2781 A1296 95c multi 2.00 1.50

Russian Year in Monaco — A1297

No. 2782: a, Text (30x30mm). b, Buildings in Russia and Monaco (41x30mm).

2015, Jan. 7 Photo. Perf. 13¼
2782 A1297 Horiz. pair 5.00 5.00
  a.-b. €1.20 Either single 2.50 1.75

Posters for Movies Starring Grace Kelly Type of 2014
Designs: €1.50, The Swan (Le Cygne). €2, To Catch a Thief (La Main au Collet).

2015, Jan. 14 Litho. Perf. 13¼
2783-2784 A1261 Set of 2 7.50 6.00

Posidonia Oceanica — A1298

2015, Jan. 21 Photo. Perf. 13¼
2785 A1298 68c multi 1.50 1.10

Kiwanis International, Cent. — A1299

2015, Jan. 21 Litho. Perf. 13¼
2786 A1299 95c multi 2.00 1.50

Princess Antoinette Park — A1300

2015, Jan. 21 Photo. Perf. 13¼
2787 A1300 €1.45 multi 3.00 2.25

German Shorthaired Pointer — A1301

2015, Feb. 5 Litho. Perf. 13¼
2788 A1301 €1.05 multi 2.25 1.60
Intl. Dog Show.

Monte Carlo Rolex Masters Tennis Tournament — A1302

2015, Feb. 5 Litho. Perf. 13¼
2789 A1302 €1.25 multi 2.75 1.75

Intl. Flower Arrangement Festival — A1303

2015, Feb. 5 Engr. Perf. 13¼
2790 A1303 €1.45 multi 3.00 2.25

Souvenir Sheet

Jellyfish — A1304

No. 2791: a, Phyllorhiza punctata. b, Pelagia noctiluca.

2015, Feb. 25 Photo. Perf. 13¼
2791 A1304 Sheet of 2 4.50 4.50
  a.-b. €1 Either single 2.25 2.25

Monaco Pavilion at Expo Milan 2015 — A1305

2015, Mar. 5 Litho. Perf. 13¼
2792 A1305 €1 multi 2.25 2.25

Michele Alboreto (1956-2001), Formula 1 Race Car Driver — A1306

Graham Hill (1929-75), Formula 1 Race Car Driver — A1307

No. 2793: a, Alboreto wearing helmet (31x31mm). b, Alboreto in race car (52x31mm).
No. 2794: a, Hill wearing helmet (31x31mm). b, Hill in race car (52x31mm).

2015, Mar. 5 Engr. Perf. 13
2793 A1306 Horiz. pair 4.00 4.00
  a. 76c multi 1.75 1.75
  b. 95c multi 2.10 2.10
2794 A1307 Horiz. pair 5.50 5.50
  a. 95c multi 2.10 2.10
  b. €1.50 multi 3.25 3.25

Monacosat — A1308

2015, Mar. 23 Litho. Perf. 13¼
2795 A1308 76c multi 1.75 1.75

MONACO

Caritas Monaco, 25th Anniv. — A1309

2015, Mar. 23	Litho.	Perf. 13¼
2796	A1309 76c multi	1.75 1.75

La Nymphe Salamacis, Sculpture by François-Joseph Bosio (1768-1845) — A1310

2015, Apr. 9	Engr.	Perf. 13x12¼
2797	A1310 €1.25 red & black	3.00 3.00

Dante Alighieri (1265-1321), Writer — A1311

Litho. & Engr.

2015, Apr. 9		Perf. 13x13¼
2798	A1311 €1.90 dp car, blk & brn	4.25 4.25

Souvenir Sheet

Birth of Prince Jacques and Princess Gabriella A1312

No. 2799 — Prince Albert II, Princess Charlène and twins: a, Color photograph. b, Sepia-toned photograph.

2015, Apr. 27	Litho.	Perf. 13¼
2799	A1312 Sheet of 2	9.00 9.00
a.-b.	€2 Either single	4.50 4.50

Formula E Race Car — A1313

2015, May 9	Litho.	Perf. 13¼
2800	A1313 €1.05 multi	2.40 2.40

2015 Monaco ePrix race for electric cars.

Europa — A1314

2015, May 11	Litho.	Perf. 13¼
2801	A1314 95c multi	2.10 2.10

International Telecommunications Union, 150th Anniv. — A1315

2015, May 11	Litho.	Perf. 13¼
2802	A1315 €1.25 purple	2.75 2.75

Miniature Sheet

Old Travel Posters for Granville, France A1316

No. 2803 — Poster by: a, Jacquier. b, Pazy. c, Commarmond. d, Dorival.

2015, June 15	Photo.	Perf. 13¼x13
2803	A1316 Sheet of 4	6.50 6.50
a.-b.	66c Either single	1.50 1.50
c.-d.	76c Either single	1.75 1.75

Visit of Prince Albert II to Grimaldi Family fiefdom of Granville.

Rainier III Academy for Music and Theater — A1317

2015, June 17	Litho.	Perf. 13¼
2804	A1317 66c multi	1.50 1.50

Dancers, Building and Theater Curtains — A1318

2015, June 17	Litho.	Perf. 13¼
2805	A1318 €1.20 multi	2.75 2.75

Miniature Sheet

Automobile Club of Monaco, 125th Anniv. — A1319

No. 2806 — Club emblem and race car in: a, Red. b, Blue. c, Yellow brown. d, Green.

2015, June 25	Photo.	Perf. 13x13¼
2806	A1319 Sheet of 4	11.00 11.00
a.-d.	€1.25 Any single	2.75 2.75

Monaco Oceanographic Museum — A1320

2015, July 1	Photo.	Perf. 13x13¼
2807	A1320 76c multi	1.75 1.75

50,000,000th visitor at Monaco Oceanographic Museum.

Fortress of Monaco (Prince's Residence), 800th Anniv. — A1321

2015, July 11	Litho.	Perf. 13¼
2808	A1321 95c multi	2.10 2.10

Souvenir Sheet

Reign of Prince Albert II, 10th Anniv. A1322

No. 2809: a, Prince Albert II, whales, map, flag on ice sheet (41x30mm). b, Fortress, flags, monogram of Prince Albert II (30x30mm). c, Monaco skyline (41x30mm).

2015, July 11	Photo.	Perf. 13¼
2809	A1322 Sheet of 3	6.75 6.75
a.-c.	€1 Any single	2.25 2.25

2015 Rugby World Cup, Great Britain — A1323

2015, Aug. 17	Photo.	Perf. 13
2810	A1323 €1.20 multi	2.75 2.75

Values are for stamps with surrounding selvage.

MonacoPhil 2015 Intl. Philatelic Exhibition A1324

2015, Sept. 3	Litho.	Perf. 13¼
2811	A1324 76c multi	1.75 1.75

2015 Grand Bourse — A1325

2015, Sept. 3	Litho.	Perf. 13¼
2812	A1325 76c multi	1.75 1.75

25th Monaco Yacht Show, Port Hercule — A1326

2015, Sept. 3	Litho.	Perf. 13¼
2813	A1326 €1.20 multi	2.75 2.75

Alliance Between Grimaldi and Matignon Families, 300th Anniv. — A1327

2015, Sept. 3	Engr.	Perf. 13x13¼
2814	A1327 €1.50 multi	3.50 3.50

Pyotr Ilyich Tchaikovsky (1840-93), Composer — A1328

2015, Sept. 10	Engr.	Perf. 13¼
2815	A1328 €2 multi	4.50 4.50

Francesco Tamagno (1850-1905), Opera Singer — A1329

Adelina Patti (1843-1919), Opera Singer — A1330

2015, Sept. 10	Engr.	Perf. 13x12¼
2816	A1329 €2.60 multi	6.00 6.00
2817	A1330 €3.05 multi	7.00 7.00

United Nations, 70th Anniv. — A1331

2015, Oct. 24	Litho.	Perf. 13¼
2818	A1331 76c multi	1.75 1.75

Publication of Albert Einstein's Works on General Relativity, Cent. — A1332

2015, Oct. 24	Litho.	Perf. 13¼
2819	A1332 €1 multi	2.25 2.25

Christmas — A1333

2015, Nov. 3	Litho.	Perf. 13¼
2820	A1333 76c multi	1.60 1.60

MONACO

Princess Charlene of Monaco Rose — A1334

2015, Dec. 3	Photo.	Perf. 13¼
2821 A1334	68c multi	1.50 1.50

Princess Charlene — A1335

2015, Dec. 3	Engr.	Perf. 13¼
2822 A1335	€1.60 brn pur	3.50 3.50

Souvenir Sheet

MonacoPhil 2015 — A1336

No. 2823: a, Prince Albert I's Arctic expedition. b, Prince Albert I (1848-1922), vert.

Engr., Sheet Margin Litho. & Engr.		
2015, Dec. 3	Perf. 13x13¼, 13¼x13	
2823 A1336	Sheet of 2	11.00 11.00
a.-b.	€2.50 Either single	5.50 5.50

5th New Generation Circus Festival — A1337

40th Intl Circus Festival, Monte Carlo A1338

No. 2825 — Posters for: a, 10th Intl. Circus Festival. b, 20th Intl. Circus Festival. c, 30th Intl. Circus Festival. d, 40th Intl. Circus Festival.

2016, Jan. 5	Litho.	Perf. 13¼
2824 A1337	80c multi	1.75 1.75
2825 A1338	Sheet of 4	8.00 8.00
a.-b.	80c Either single	1.75 1.75
c.-d.	€1 Either single	2.25 2.25

Prince Albert II Type of 2012

Inscription: (68c), Ecopli. (80c), Prioritaire. (€1), Europe.

2016, Jan. 15	Engr.	Perf. 13x13¼
2826 A1221	(68c) blue	1.50 1.50
2827 A1221	(80c) scarlet	1.75 1.75
2828 A1221	(€1) dp claret	2.25 2.25
	Nos. 2826-2828 (3)	5.50 5.50

2016 Winter Youth Olympics, Lillehammer, Norway — A1339

2016, Feb. 3	Photo.	Perf. 13¼
2829 A1339	€1.25 multi	2.75 2.75

Monte Carlo Rolex Masters Tennis Tournament — A1340

2016, Feb. 3	Litho.	Perf. 13¼
2830 A1340	€1.60 multi	3.50 3.50

Princess Grace Rose Garden — A1341

2016, Feb. 5	Litho.	Perf. 13¼
2831 A1341	70c multi	1.50 1.50

Continental Toy Spaniel — A1342

2016, Feb. 5	Litho.	Perf. 13¼
2832 A1342	€1.25 multi	2.75 2.75

Intl. Dog Show.

Sciaena Umbra — A1343

2016, Feb. 5	Engr.	Perf. 13x13¼
2833 A1343	€1.60 multi	3.50 3.50

Race Cars — A1344

Designs: 80c, March 711. €1.36, Auto Union Type C.

2016, Mar. 1	Photo.	Perf. 13¼
2834-2835 A1344	Set of 2	4.75 4.75

Ronnie Peterson (1944-78), Formula 1 Race Car Driver — A1345

No. 2836: a, Peterson (31x31mm). b, Peterson (52x31mm).

2016, Mar. 1	Photo.	Perf. 13
2836 A1345	Horiz. pair	4.00 4.00
a.	80c multi	1.75 1.75
b.	€1 multi	2.25 2.25

Prince Pierre of Monaco (1895-1964) — A1346

2016, Mar. 16	Engr.	Perf. 13¼
2837 A1346	68c multi	1.60 1.60

Prince Pierre of Monaco Foundation, 50th anniv.

Orchestra of the Palace Guards, 50th Anniv. — A1347

2016, Mar. 16	Photo.	Perf. 13¼
2838 A1347	€1 multi	2.25 2.25

Prince Charles III (1818-89) and Sovereign Order Creating Monte Carlo A1348

2016, Mar. 16	Engr.	Perf. 13x13¼
2839 A1348	€1.36 multi	3.25 3.25

Foundation of Monte Carlo, 150th anniv.

Visit of Prince Albert II to Belfort, France — A1349

2016, Apr. 1	Engr.	Perf. 13x13¼
2840 A1349	€1 multi	2.25 2.25

Miniature Sheet

Lifecycle of Caretta Caretta A1350

No. 2841: a, Juvenile at sea, denomination at UR. b, Adult at sea, denomination at UL. c, Hatchlings leaving shell. d, Female laying eggs, vert.

Photo. & Thermography		
2016, Apr. 1		Perf. 13¼
2841 A1350	Sheet of 4	10.00 10.00
a.-b.	80c multi	1.90 1.90
c.	€1 multi	2.25 2.25
d.	€1.60 multi	3.75 3.75

Intl. Flower Arrangement Festival — A1351

2016, Apr. 29	Litho.	Perf. 13¼
2842 A1351	80c multi	1.90 1.90

Europa — A1352

2016, May 9	Litho.	Perf. 13¼
2843 A1352	€1 multi	2.25 2.25

Think Green Issue.

Mercury Teaching Geography to Love, by Louis-Jean-François Lagrenée, the Elder (1725-1805) — A1353

2016, May 12	Litho.	Perf. 13¼
2844 A1353	€2 multi	4.50 4.50

Posters for Movies Starring Grace Kelly Type of 2014

Designs: €1.60, Rear Window (Fenêtre sur Cour). €2, The Bridges at Toko-Ri (Les Ponts do Toko Ri).

2016, May 19	Litho.	Perf. 13¼
2845-2846 A1261	Set of 2	8.00 8.00

Nellie Melba (1861-1931), Opera Singer A1354

Enrico Caruso (1873-1921), Opera Singer A1355

2016, May 19	Engr.	Perf. 13x13¼
2847 A1354	€1.36 multi	3.00 3.00
		Perf. 13¼
2848 A1355	€2.50 multi	5.75 5.75

2016 European Soccer Championships, France — A1356

2016, June 1	Photo.	Perf. 13
2849 A1356	€1 multi	2.25 2.25

Values are for stamps with surrounding selvage.

2016 Summer Olympics, Rio de Janeiro — A1357

2016, June 1	Litho.	Perf. 13¼
2850 A1357	€1.25 multi	2.75 2.75

Tree, La Rocher — A1358

2016, June 24	Litho.	Perf. 13¼
2851 A1358	€1 multi	2.25 2.25

MONACO

Prince Albert I, Observatory Cave Archaeological Excavations — A1359

2016, June 24	Engr.	Perf. 13x13¼
2852 A1359 €1.60 multi		3.75 3.75

Observatory Cave archaeological excavations, cent.

Emblem of Prince Albert II Foundation — A1360

Conservation Efforts of Prince Albert II Foundation — A1361

	Litho. & Silk-Screened	
2016, June 30		Perf. 13¼
2853 A1360 70c multi		1.60 1.60
2854 A1361 Sheet of 4		11.00 11.00
a.-d. €1.25 Any single		2.75 2.75

10th Anniv. of Prince Albert II of Monaco Foundation.

No. 2854: a, Polar bear. b, Desert landscape. c, Tiger. d, Forest.

Princess Grace and Child — A1362

2016, July 5	Litho.	Perf. 13¼
2855 A1362 68c multi		1.50 1.50

Association Mondial des Amis de l'Enfance, 50th anniv.

2016 World Rowing Coastal Championships, Monaco — A1363

2016, July 21	Litho.	Perf. 13¼
2856 A1363 €2 multi		4.50 4.50

Monte Carlo Ballet Company Dancer A1364

2016, July 21	Litho.	Perf. 13x13¼
2857 A1364 €2.72 multi		6.25 6.25

24th Grande Bourse — A1365

2016, Aug. 24	Litho.	Perf. 13¼
2858 A1365 80c multi		1.90 1.90

Léo Ferré (1916-93), Singer — A1366

2016, Aug. 24	Engr.	Perf. 13¼
2859 A1366 €1.36 red & brnish blk		3.00 3.00

Miniature Sheet

Worldwide Fund for Nature (WWF) — A1367

No. 2860 — Thalassoma pavo: a, One facing right. b, One facing left. c, Two facing left and coral. d, Two fish and starfish.

	Perf. 13¼x13½
2016, Sept. 15	Photo.
2860 A1367 Sheet of 4	9.00 9.00
a.-d. €1 Any single	2.25 2.25

Monégasque Annals, 40th Anniv. of Publication A1368

2016, Nov. 4	Litho.	Perf. 13¼x13
2861 A1368 80c multi		1.75 1.75

Christmas A1369

2016, Nov. 4	Litho.	Perf. 13¼
2862 A1369 80c multi		1.75 1.75

Coat of Arms Type of 2000 Inscribed "écopli" at Top
Serpentine Die Cut 11

2017-22		Photo.
Booklet Stamp		
Self-Adhesive		
2863 A786 (71c) blue & multi		1.50 1.50
a. Booklet pane of 10		15.00
b. As #2863, dated "2019"		2.00 2.00
c. Booklet pane of 10 #2863b		20.00
d. As #2863, dated "2022"		2.60 2.60
e. Booklet pane of 10 #2863d		26.00

Issued: No. 2863, 1/3; No. 2863b, 5/6/19; No. 2863d, 1/4/22. On day of issue, No. 2863b sold for 86c; No. 2863d, for €1.14. Compare with No. 2673.

41st Intl. Circus Festival, Monte Carlo — A1370

	Photo. & Embossed With Foil Application	
2017, Jan. 3		Perf. 13¼
2864 A1370 €1.10 multi		2.40 2.40

Grace Kelly Movie Posters Type of 2014

Designs: €1.42, Mogambo. €2.20, High Noon (Le Train Siffera 3 Fois).

2017, Jan. 16	Litho.	Perf. 13¼
2865-2866 A1261 Set of 2		7.75 7.75

Monte Carlo Rolex Masters Tennis Tournament — A1371

2017, Feb. 9	Litho.	Perf. 13¼
2867 A1371 €1.70 multi		3.75 3.75

Great Dane — A1372

2017, Feb. 27	Litho.	Perf. 13¼
2868 A1372 71c multi		1.50 1.50

International Dog Show.

Anthony Burgess (1917-93), Writer — A1373

	Litho. & Engr.	
2017, Feb. 27		Perf. 13x13¼
2869 A1373 €1.30 multi		2.75 2.75

Aimé Barelli (1917-95), Trumpet Player — A1374

2017, Feb. 27	Engr.	Perf. 13x13¼
2870 A1374 €1.42 blue & red		3.00 3.00

Race Cars — A1375

Designs: 85c, Matra MS80. €1.10, Ferrari 156.

2017, Mar. 8	Litho.	Perf. 13¼
2871-2872 A1375 Set of 2		4.25 4.25

James Hunt (1947-93), Formula 1 Race Car Driver — A1376

No. 2873: a, Hunt wearing helmet (31x31mm). b, Hunt in car (52x31mm).

2017, Mar. 8	Photo.	Perf. 13
2873 A1376 Horiz. pair		4.25 4.25
a. 85c multi		1.75 1.75
b. €1.10 multi		2.40 2.40

Prince's Carabiniers (Palace Guards), 200th Anniv. — A1377

2017, Mar. 10	Photo.	Perf. 13
2874 A1377 85c multi		1.90 1.90

Values are for stamps with surrounding selvage.

Prince Louis II at Battle of Chemin des Dames — A1378

2017, Mar. 10	Engr.	Perf. 13x13¼
2875 A1378 €2.60 multi		5.50 5.50

Second Battle of the Aisne, cent.

Ships Used in Scientific Studies — A1379

Designs: €1.30, The Yersin. €1.70, The Calypso.

	Litho. & Engr.	
2017, Mar. 22		Perf. 13x13¼
2876-2877 A1379 Set of 2		6.50 6.50

Princess Charlene of Monaco Foundation, 5th Anniv. — A1380

Princess Charlene with: 71c, One swimmer. 85c, Two swimmers.

2017, Apr. 10	Litho.	Perf. 13¼
2878-2879 A1380 Set of 2		3.50 3.50

Miniature Sheet

75th Grand Prix de Monaco Formula I Race A1381

No. 2880 — Old and new race cars with car at right, country name and denomination in: a, Green. b, Blue. c, Yellow. d, Purple.

2017, Apr. 10	Photo.	Perf. 13¼
2880 A1381 Sheet of 4		9.25 9.25
a.-b. 85c Either single		1.90 1.90
c. €1.10 multi		2.40 2.40
d. €1.30 multi		3.00 3.00

MONACO

Souvenir Sheet

50th Intl. Flower Arrangement Festival — A1382

No. 2881 — Color of flowers in arrangement: a, Red. b, Blue. c, Yellow.

Photo., Sheet Margin Photo. & Silk-Screened

			Perf. 13¼	
2017, Apr. 28				
2881	A1382	Sheet of 3	5.75	5.75
a.-c.		85c Any single	1.90	1.90

Corallium Rubrum A1383

Campanula Macrorhiza A1384

2017, May 2 Litho. Perf. 13¼
2882 A1383 5c multi .25 .25
2883 A1384 €5 multi 11.50 11.50

Peace and Sport Organization, 10th Anniv. — A1385

2017, May 9 Litho. Perf. 13¼
2884 A1385 85c multi 1.90 1.90

Prince's Palace — A1386

2017, May 9 Litho. Perf. 13¼
2885 A1386 €1.10 multi 2.50 2.50
Europa.

Saint-Martin Gardens A1387

2017, May 16 Litho. Perf. 13¼
2886 A1387 73c multi 1.75 1.75

Monaco Pavilion, Expo 2017, Astana, Kazakhstan A1388

2017, May 16 Litho. Perf. 13¼
2887 A1388 €1.30 multi 3.00 3.00

Pottery — A1389

2017, June 1 Litho. Perf. 13¼
2888 A1389 71c multi 1.60 1.60

Melvin Jones (1879-1961), Founder of Lions Clubs International A1390

2017, June 1 Litho. Perf. 13¼
2889 A1390 85c multi 1.90 1.90
Lions Clubs International, cent.

25th Prince Albert II Challenge Fencing Tournament — A1391

2017, June 1 Litho. & Engr. Perf. 13¼
2890 A1391 €1.42 multi 3.25 3.25

Arturo Toscanini (1867-1957), Conductor A1392

2017, June 21 Engr. Perf. 13x13¼
2891 A1392 €2.60 multi 6.00 6.00

Titta Ruffo (1877-1953), Opera Singer — A1393

Emma Calvé (1858-1942), Opera Singer — A1394

2017, June 21 Engr. Perf. 13x12¼
2892 A1393 €2.60 multi 6.00 6.00
Perf. 12¼x13
2893 A1394 €2.84 multi 6.50 6.50

Herculis International Track Meet — A1395

2017, July 4 Litho. Perf. 13¼
2894 A1395 85c multi 2.00 2.00

Visit of Prince Albert II to Chateau de Duras — A1396

2017, July 4 Engr. Perf. 13x13¼
2895 A1396 €1.70 multi 4.00 4.00

Jacques II de Goyon, Marshal of Matignon and Mayor of Bordeaux, France — A1397

2017, July 4 Engr. Perf. 13x13¼
2896 A1397 €2.20 multi 5.25 5.25
Visit of Prince Albert II to Bordeaux.

Souvenir Sheet

Grimaldi Forum Exhibition on China's Forbidden City — A1398

2017, July 13 Photo. Perf. 13¼x13
2897 A1398 €3.40 multi 8.00 8.00

Audiovisual Archives of Monaco, 20th Anniv. — A1399

2017, July 24 Litho. Perf. 13x13¼
2898 A1399 71c multi 1.75 1.75

Ecoute Cancer Réconfort, 25th Anniv. — A1400

2017, July 24 Litho. Perf. 13¼
2899 A1400 71c multi 1.75 1.75

Princess Grace (1929-82) — A1401

2017, July 24 Litho. Perf. 13¼
2900 A1401 85c multi 2.00 2.00
MonacoPhil 2017.

25th Numismatic and Post Card Grande Bourse — A1402

2017, Aug. 21 Litho. Perf. 13¼
2901 A1402 71c multi 1.75 1.75

Souvenir Sheet

2017-20 Monaco Exploration Initiative — A1403

No. 2902: a, Diver. b, Submarine. c, Research vessel Yersin.

2017, Aug. 21 Photo. Perf. 13¼
2902 A1403 Sheet of 3 7.25 7.25
a.-b. 85c Either single 2.00 2.00
c. €1.30 multi 3.25 3.25

AS Monaco Soccer Team, 2016-17 Champions of French Ligue 1 — A1404

2017, Sept. 18 Litho. Perf. 13¼
2903 A1404 85c multi 2.00 2.00

Armand Lunel (1892-1977), Writer — A1405

2017, Sept. 18 Engr. Perf. 13x13¼
2904 A1405 €1.10 multi 2.60 2.60

Christmas — A1406

Litho. & Engr.
2017, Nov. 3 Perf. 13¼
2905 A1406 85c multi 2.10 2.10

Mediterrranean Dusky Grouper — A1407

2017, Nov. 30 Litho. Perf. 13¼
2906 A1407 (42c) multi 1.00 1.00
No. 2906 is known only precanceled. See note after No. 324.

Souvenir Sheet

MonacoPhil 2017 International Philatelic Exhibition, Monte Carlo — A1408

No. 2907: a, Princess Grace (1929-82). b, Hercule Florence (1804-79), explorer of Brazil and inventor.

Litho. & Engr.
2017, Nov. 30 Perf. 13¼
2907 A1408 Sheet of 2 12.50 12.50
a.-b. €2.60 Either single 6.25 6.25

Christmas — A1409

Designs: 85c, Annunciation. €1.10, Madonna and Child.
2017, Nov. 30 Litho. Perf. 13¼
2908-2909 A1409 Set of 2 4.75 4.75
Joint Issue between Monaco and Vatican City.
See Vatican City Nos. 1670-1671.

42nd Intl. Circus Festival, Monte Carlo — A1410

2018, Jan. 3 Litho. Perf. 13¼
2910 A1410 €1.20 multi 3.00 3.00

Posters for Movies Starring Grace Kelly Type of 2014
Designs: €1.56, High Society (La Haute Société). €2.40, Green Fire (L'émeraude Tragique).
2018, Jan. 17 Litho. Perf. 13¼
2911-2912 A1261 Set of 2 10.00 10.00

German Spitz — A1411

2018, Feb. 8 Litho. Perf. 13¼
2913 A1411 78c multi 1.90 1.90
Intl. Dog Show.

2018 Winter Olympics, PyeongChang, South Korea — A1412

2018, Feb. 8 Litho. Perf. 13¼
2914 A1412 95c multi 2.40 2.40

Rolex Monte Carlo Masters Tennis Tournament — A1413

2018, Feb. 8 Litho. Perf. 13¼
2915 A1413 €1.90 multi 4.75 4.75

Race Cars — A1414

Designs: 95c, Lotus 49. €1.20, Mercedes-Benz W196.
2018, Feb. 19 Photo. Perf. 13¼
2916-2917 A1414 Set of 2 5.25 5.25

Jim Clark (1936-68), Formula 1 Race Car Driver — A1415

No. 2918: a, Clark wearing helmet (31x31mm). b, Clark driving car (52x31mm).
2018, Feb. 19 Photo. Perf. 13
2918 A1415 Horiz. pair 5.25 5.25
 a. 95c multi 2.25 2.25
 b. €1.20 multi 3.00 3.00

Monegasque Red Cross, 70th Anniv. — A1416

 Litho. & Silk-Screened
2018, Mar. 5 Perf. 13¼
2919 A1416 78c multi 2.00 2.00

International Flower Arrangement Festival — A1417

2018, Mar. 7 Litho. Perf. 13¼
2920 A1417 78c multi 2.00 2.00

Sea Turtle Care Center A1418

2018, Mar. 7 Litho. Perf. 13
2921 A1418 €1.20 multi 3.00 3.00

Garden Club of Monaco, 50th Anniv. — A1419

 Litho. & Silk-Screened
2018, Mar. 7 Perf. 13¼
2922 A1419 €1.90 multi 4.75 4.75

Quadriga of the Carousel Triumphal Arch, by François-Joseph Bosio (1768-1845) — A1420

2018, Mar. 19 Engr. Perf. 13x12¼
2923 A1420 95c red & blksh vio 2.40 2.40

Opera Singers A1421

Designs: €2.40, Selma Kurz (1874-1933). €3, Feodor Chaliapin (1873-1938), vert.
 Perf. 13x12¼, 12¼x13
2018, Mar. 19 Engr.
2924-2925 A1421 Set of 2 13.50 13.50

The Night, by Kees Van Dongen (1877-1968) A1422

2018, Mar. 19 Photo. Perf. 13x12¼
2926 A1422 €3.12 multi 7.75 7.75

2018 World Cup Soccer Championships, Russia — A1423

2018, Apr. 10 Litho. Perf. 13¼
2927 A1423 €1.30 multi 3.25 3.25

Ecole des Frères, 150th Anniv. — A1424

2018, Apr. 10 Engr. Perf. 13
2928 A1424 €1.56 multi 3.75 3.75

Exotic Garden of Monaco Botanical Center — A1425

2018, Apr. 30 Litho. Perf. 13¼
2929 A1425 80c multi 1.90 1.90

Sainte Dévote Bridge — A1426

2018, May 3 Litho. Perf. 13¼
2930 A1426 €1.20 multi 2.75 2.75
Europa.

Visit of Prince Albert II to Bardi Castle, Italy — A1427

2018, May 15 Engr. Perf. 13
2931 A1427 €2.40 multi 5.75 5.75

St. Roman Feast Committee, 150th Anniv. — A1428

2018, May 28 Engr. Perf. 13¼x13
2932 A1428 78c multi 1.90 1.90

Admission of Monaco to the United Nations, 25th Anniv. — A1429

2018, May 28 Litho. Perf. 13¼
2933 A1429 €1.30 multi 3.00 3.00

Monaco Covered in Snow — A1430

2018, June 7 Litho. Perf. 13¼
2934 A1430 95c multi 2.25 2.25

Mediterranean Shag — A1431

2018, June 7 Engr. Perf. 13¼
2935 A1431 €1.30 multi 3.00 3.00

Visit of Prince Albert II to Chilly-Mazarin, France — A1432

2018, June 19 Engr. Perf. 13x13¼
2936 A1432 €1.90 multi 4.50 4.50

Arrival of First Train in Monaco, 150th Anniv. — A1433

2018, June 19 Engr. Perf. 13
2937 A1433 €1.90 brn & scar 4.50 4.50

Miniature Sheet

Exhibition of Historical Sites of the Grimaldis of Monaco — A1434

No. 2938 — Inscriptions under arms: a, Sites Historiques Grimaldi de Monaco. b, Baux-de-Provence. c, Menton. d, Carladès.

 Litho., Engr. Sheet Margin
2018, June 23 Perf. 13¼
2938 A1434 Sheet of 4 9.00 9.00
 a.-d. 95c Any single 2.25 2.25

Funerary Mask of King Psusennes I — A1435

 Litho. & Embossed
2018, July 6 Perf. 13¼x13
2939 A1435 95c multi 2.25 2.25
Grimaldi Forum exhibition of "The Golden Treasures of the Pharaohs - 2500 Years of the Goldsmith's Art in Ancient Egypt."

MONACO

Souvenir Sheet

Princes of Monaco — A1436

No. 2940: a, Prince Albert I (1848-1922). b, Prince Rainier III (1923-2005). c, Prince Albert II.

Engr., Sheet Margin Litho.
2018, July 6 Perf. 13¼x13
2940 A1436 Sheet of 3 10.50 10.50
a. €1.20 blue gray 2.75 2.75
b. €1.30 blue gray 3.00 3.00
c. €1.90 blue gray 4.50 4.50

Oceanographic Museum of Monaco exhibit of "Monaco and the Ocean, from Exploration to Protection."

P.E.N. Club of Monaco, 50th Anniv. — A1437

Litho. & Engr.
2018, July 18 Perf. 13¼x13
2941 A1437 95c multi 2.25 2.25

Nelson Mandela (1918-2013), President of South Africa — A1438

2018, July 18 Engr. Perf. 13¼
2942 A1438 €1.20 scar & yel brn 2.75 2.75

Prince Charles III (1818-89) — A1439

2018, July 18 Engr. Perf. 13¼
2943 A1439 €2.60 multi 6.00 6.00

26th Grande Bourse — A1440

2018, Aug. 9 Litho. Perf. 13¼
2944 A1440 95c multi 2.25 2.25

International Union of Modern Pentathlon, 20th Anniv. in Monaco — A1441

2018, Aug. 9 Litho. Perf. 13¼
2945 A1441 €1.30 multi 3.00 3.00

Souvenir Sheet

Princes and Princesses of Monaco Exhibit, Beijing — A1442

Photo., Sheet Margin Photo. With Foil Application
2018, Sept. 7 Perf. 13
2946 A1442 €3.80 gold & multi 9.00 9.00

Yachts — A1443

Designs: €2.40, Malizia II. €2.60, Viola.

Litho. & Engr.
2018, Sept. 10 Perf. 13x13¼
2947-2948 A1443 Set of 2 11.50 11.50

Dove and Monte Carlo — A1444

2018, Sept. 20 Litho. Perf. 13¼
2949 A1444 €1.56 multi 3.75 3.75

After downloading an app to a smartphone, taking a photo of No. 2949 will play a recording of Monegasque songs performed by the children of the choir of the Académie Rainier III and the Monte Carlo Philharmonic Orchestra.

Christmas A1445

2018, Nov. 5 Litho. Perf. 13¼
2950 A1445 95c multi 2.25 2.25

World Circus Federation, 10th Anniv. — A1446

2019, Jan. 4 Litho. Perf. 13¼
2951 A1446 €1.05 multi 2.40 2.40

43rd Intl. Circus Festival, Monte Carlo — A1447

2019, Jan. 4 Litho. Perf. 13¼
2952 A1447 €1.30 multi 3.00 3.00

Posters for Movies Starring Grace Kelly Type of 2014

Designs: €1.72, 14 Hours. €2.10, The Wedding in Monaco.

2019, Jan. 14 Litho. Perf. 13¼
2953-2954 A1261 Set of 2 8.75 8.75

Alberto Ascari (1918-55), Formula 1 Race Car Driver — A1448

No. 2955: a, Ascari wearing helmet (31x31mm). b, Ascari and entire car (52x31mm).

2019, Feb. 5 Photo. Perf. 13
2955 A1448 Horiz. pair 6.50 6.50
a. €1.05 multi 2.40 2.40
b. €1.72 multi 4.00 4.00

Race Cars — A1449

Designs: €1.05, BRM P57. €1.30, Renault Turbo RS01.

2019, Feb. 5 Litho. Perf. 13¼
2956-2957 A1449 Set of 2 5.50 5.50

Monte Carlo Rolex Masters Tennis Tournament — A1450

2019, Feb. 5 Litho. Perf. 13¼
2958 A1450 €2.10 multi 4.75 4.75

Intl. Flower Arrangement Festival — A1451

2019, Feb. 18 Engr. Perf. 13¼x13
2959 A1451 88c multi 2.00 2.00

Tibetan Mastiff — A1452

2019, Feb. 18 Litho. Perf. 13x13¼
2960 A1452 €1.05 multi 2.40 2.40

Intl. Dog Show.

Accession to the Throne of Prince Honoré V, 200th Anniv. — A1453

2019, Feb. 18 Engr. Perf. 13
2961 A1453 €2.10 multi 4.75 4.75

Paintings of Nudes by Paul Gervais (1859-1944) — A1454

Designs: €2.60, Florentine Graces. €3.44, Les Naïades (Le Jardin des Hespérides).

Litho. & Embossed With Foil Application
2019, Mar. 4 Perf. 13
2962-2963 A1454 Set of 2 14.00 14.00

Opera Singers — A1455

Designs: €2.60, Maurice Renaud (1861-1933). €3.44, Geraldine Farrar (1882-1967).

2019, Mar. 4 Engr. Perf. 13¼x13
2964-2965 A1455 Set of 2 14.00 14.00

Convalescence of United States Troops in Monaco, Cent. — A1456

2019, Mar. 15 Engr. Perf. 13x13¼
2966 A1456 €1 multi 2.25 2.25

Mediterranean Science Commission (CIESM), Cent. — A1457

Litho. & Silk-Screened
2019, Mar. 15 Perf. 13
2967 A1457 €1.30 multi 3.00 3.00

Atlantic Bluefin Tuna — A1458

2019, Mar. 15 Engr. Perf. 13x13¼
2968 A1458 €2 multi 4.50 4.50

Miniature Sheet

Monaco Grand Prix, 90th Anniv. — A1459

No. 2969: a, 90th anniv. emblem and race track layout. b, Louis Chiron in Bugatti 51, 1931. c, Graham Hill in Lotus 49B, 1969. d, Ayrton Senna in McLaren MP4, 1988.

Perf. 12¾x13¼
2019, Mar. 22 Photo.
2969 A1459 Sheet of 4 14.00 14.00
a.-b. €1.05 Either single 2.40 2.40
c.-d. €2 Either single 4.50 4.50

Council of Europe, 70th Anniv. — A1460

2019, Apr. 30 Litho. Perf. 13¼
2970 A1460 86c multi 2.00 2.00

MONACO

Peregrine Falcon — A1461

2019, May 6	Litho.	Perf. 13¼
2971 A1461 €1.30 multi		3.00 3.00

Europa.

36th Conference of Francophone Ministers, Monaco — A1462

2019, May 29	Litho.	Perf. 13¼
2972 A1462 86c multi		2.00 2.00

Fausto Coppi (1919-60), Cyclist — A1463

	Litho. & Engr.	Perf. 13¼
2019, May 29		
2973 A1463 86c multi		2.00 2.00

2019 Women's World Cup Soccer Championships, France — A1464

2019, May 29	Litho.	Perf. 13¼
2974 A1464 €1.05 multi		2.40 2.40

Zonta Club of Monaco, 25th Anniv. — A1465

2019, June 18	Litho.	Perf. 13¼
2975 A1465 88c multi		2.00 2.00

Souvenir Sheet

Princess Grace (1929-82) — A1466

No. 2976 — Princess Grace wearing: a, Jeweled necklace, facing right. b, Dress, holding handbag. c, Chain necklace, facing left.

Litho.; Sheet Margin Litho. & Engr. With Foil Application

2019, June 18		Perf. 13
2976 A1466 Sheet of 3		13.50 13.50
a.-c. €2 Any single		4.50 4.50

House in Monaco-Ville — A1467

2019, June 20	Litho.	Perf. 13¼
2977 A1467 86c multi		2.00 2.00

MonacoPhil 2019 Philatelic Exhibition — A1468

2019, June 20	Litho.	Perf. 13¼
2978 A1468 €1.05 multi		2.40 2.40

Reopening of Hôtel de Paris, Monte Carlo A1469

2019, June 20	Litho.	Perf. 13¼x13
2979 A1469 €1.05 multi		2.40 2.40

Jacques Offenbach (1819-80), Composer A1470

2019, June 20	Engr.	Perf. 13x12¼
2980 A1470 €3.44 multi		7.75 7.75

Miniature Sheet

Exhibition of Historical Sites of the Grimaldis of Monaco — A1471

No. 2981 — Inscriptions under arms: a, Crest (Valentinois). b, Roquebrune-Cap-Martin. c, Dolceacqua. d, Matignon.

Litho.; Sheet Margin Litho. & Engr.

2019, June 22		Perf. 13
2981 A1471 Sheet of 4		9.75 9.75
a.-d. €1.05 Any single		2.40 2.40

First Man on the Moon, 50th Anniv. — A1472

2019, July 5	Litho.	Perf. 13¼
2982 A1472 €1 multi		2.25 2.25

Grimaldi Forum Exhibition of Art by Salvador Dalí (1904-89) A1473

2019, July 5	Litho.	Perf. 13
2983 A1473 €1.05 red & black		2.40 2.40

2019 Grande Bourse — A1474

2019, Aug. 5	Litho.	Perf. 13¼
2984 A1474 86c multi		1.90 1.90

Henri Matisse (1869-1954), Painter — A1475

2019, Aug. 5	Engr.	Perf. 12¼x13
2985 A1475 €1.72 multi		3.75 3.75

Visit of Prince Albert II to Valmont Château, France — A1476

Visit of Prince Albert II to Romans-sur-Isère, France — A1477

2019, Sept. 2	Engr.	Perf. 13x13¼
2986 A1476 €1 multi		2.25 2.25
		Perf. 13¼x13
2987 A1477 €1.30 multi		3.00 3.00

Circumnavigation by Ferdinand Magellan's Expedition, 500th Anniv. — A1478

2019, Sept. 2	Engr.	Perf. 13x13¼
2988 A1478 €2.60 multi		5.75 5.75

Mohandas K. Gandhi (1869-1948), Indian Nationalist Leader — A1479

2019, Oct. 2	Engr.	Perf. 13x13¼
2989 A1479 €2.10 brn lake		4.75 4.75

Christmas — A1480

2019, Nov. 4	Litho.	Perf. 13¼
2990 A1480 €1.05 multi		2.40 2.40

Committee on Women's Rights, 1st Anniv. — A1481

2019, Nov. 28	Litho.	Perf. 13x13¼
2991 A1481 €1.16 multi		2.60 2.60

Bather Arranging Her Hair, by Pierre-Auguste Renoir (1841-1919) A1482

2019, Nov. 28	Litho.	Perf. 13
2992 A1482 €2.80 multi		6.25 6.25

Souvenir Sheet

MonacoPhil 2019 Philatelic Exhibition — A1483

No. 2993: a, MonacoPhil 2019 emblem. b, Pyramid, horiz.

2019, Nov. 28	Litho.	Perf. 13¼
2993 A1483 Sheet of 2		12.50 12.50
a.-b. €2.80 Either single		6.25 6.25

Coat of Arms Type of 2000 With "Prioritaire" Inscribed at Upper Right

Serpentine Die Cut 11

2020, Jan. 6		Photo.

Booklet Stamp Self-Adhesive

2994 A786 (€1.16) red & black		2.60 2.60
a. Booklet pane of 10		26.00

Prince Albert II Type of 2012 Inscribed "International"

2020, Jan. 6	Litho.	Perf. 13x13¼
2995 A1221 (€1.40) red violet		3.25 3.25

44th Intl. Circus Festival, Monte Carlo — A1484

Litho, Silk-Screened & Embossed

2020, Jan. 6		Perf. 13¼
2996 A1484 €1.40 multi		3.25 3.25

Opera Singers A1485

Designs: €2.32, Fidès Devriès (1852-1941). €3.80, Tito Schipa (1889-1965).

2020, Jan. 20	Engr.	Perf. 13x12¼
2997-2998 A1485 Set of 2		13.50 13.50

Expo 2020, Dubai, United Arab Emirates — A1486

MONACO

Litho. & Embossed With Foil Application

2020, Feb. 10 — Perf. 13¼
2999 A1486 €1.16 multi — 2.60 2.60

Irish Wolfhound — A1487

2020, Feb. 10 — Litho. — Perf. 13¼
3000 A1487 €1.90 multi — 4.25 4.25
Intl. Dog Show.

Council of Europe Anti-Doping Convention, 30th Anniv. — A1488

2020, Feb. 28 — Litho. — Perf. 13¼
3001 A1488 95c multi — 2.10 2.10

Marcel Pagnol (1895-1974), Writer and Filmmaker — A1489

2020, Feb. 28 — Engr. — Perf. 13¼
3002 A1489 €2 multi — 4.50 4.50

Race Cars — A1490

Designs: €1.16, Cooper Climax T53. €1.40, McLaren M23.

2020, Mar. 4 — Litho. — Perf. 13¼
3003-3004 A1490 Set of 2 — 5.50 5.50

International Flower Arrangement Festival — A1491

2020, Mar. 27 — Litho. — Perf. 13¼
3005 A1491 97c multi — 2.10 2.10

Rolex Monte Carlo Masters Tennis Tournament — A1492

2020, Mar. 27 — Litho. — Perf. 13¼
3006 A1492 €2.32 multi — 5.00 5.00
The tennis tournament was canceled because of the coronavirus pandemic.

Niki Lauda (1949-2019), Formula 1 Race Car Driver — A1493

No. 3007: a, Lauda wearing helmet (31x31mm). b, Lauda and entire race car (52x31mm).

2020, Mar. 27 — Photo. — Perf. 13
3007 A1493 Horiz. pair — 6.25 6.25
a. 95c multi — 2.00 2.00
b. €1.90 multi — 4.25 4.25

Prince Louis II (1870-1949) — A1494

2020, Apr. 29 — Engr. — Perf. 13
3008 A1494 95c multi — 2.10 2.10

18th Century Mail Carrier — A1495

2020, May 6 — Engr. — Perf. 13x13¼
3009 A1495 €1.40 multi — 3.25 3.25
Europa.

Prince Albert II Holding Globe — A1496

2020, June 3 — Litho. — Perf. 13¼
3010 A1496 €1.16 multi — 2.00 2.00
Coronavirus pandemic solidarity.

Ludwig van Beethoven (1770-1827), Composer — A1497

2020, June 11 — Engr. — Perf. 13
3011 A1497 €2.80 blk vio & reddish pur — 6.25 6.25

Souvenir Sheet

Coral Reef A1498

No. 3012: a, Coral and fish. b, Coral, fish and diver. c, Corals.

2020, June 11 — Photo. — Perf. 13½x13
3012 A1498 Sheet of 3 — 10.50 10.50
a. €1.16 multi — 2.60 2.60
b. €1.40 multi — 3.25 3.25
c. €1.90 multi — 4.25 4.25
"Immersion," temporary exhibit at Oceanographic Museum of Monaco.

L'Indolence, by Eva Gonzalès (1849-83) — A1499

2020, June 25 — Litho. — Perf. 13¼x13
3013 A1499 €1.90 multi — 4.25 4.25

Crest of the Historic Sites of the Grimaldi Family — A1500

2020, June 25 — Engr. — Perf. 13¼x13
3014 A1500 €2 multi — 4.50 4.50

Siberian Cat — A1501

2020, July 7 — Litho. — Perf. 13¼
3015 A1501 97c multi — 2.25 2.25
International Cat Show.

18th Century Residence of the Princes of Monaco in Torigny-sur-Vire, France — A1502

2020, July 7 — Engr. — Perf. 12¾x13¼
3016 A1502 €3.80 multi — 9.00 9.00

Fort Antoine Theater, 50th Anniv. — A1503

2020, Aug. 3 — Litho. — Perf. 13¼
3017 A1503 95c multi — 2.25 2.25

Visit of Prince Albert II to Grimaldi Family Holdings in Terlizzi, Italy — A1504

2020, Sept. 8 — Litho. — Perf. 13¼
3018 A1504 €1.40 multi — 3.25 3.25

Opening of Redesigned Place du Casino — A1505

2020, Sept. 14 — Litho. — Perf. 13¼
3019 A1505 €1.40 multi — 3.25 3.25

Prince Honoré III (1720-95) — A1506

No. 3020 — Prince Honoré III as: a, Young man. b, Old man.

2020, Sept. 14 — Engr. — Perf. 13¼
3020 A1506 Horiz. pair — 9.50 9.50
a.-b. €2 Either single — 4.75 4.75

Films Shot in Monaco — A1507

Designs: €1.90, Spanish poster for L'Amour et la Veine (El Amor y la Suerte), 1932. €2, Swedish poster for The Story of a Cheat (Jag ar en Falskspelare), 1936. €2.32, Swedish poster for Quadrille of Love (En Csardas i Monte Carlo), 1935. €3, French poster for Unknown of Monte Carlo (L'Inconnue de Monte Carlo), 1939 (31x52mm).

2020, Oct. 2 — Litho. — Perf. 13
3021-3024 A1507 Set of 4 — 21.50 21.50

United Nations, 75th Anniv. A1508

No. 3025: a, Emblems of the 17 Sustainable Development Goals. b, Aerial view of Monaco.

2020, Oct. 23 — Litho. — Perf. 13¼
3025 A1508 Horiz. pair — 6.50 6.50
a.-b. €1.40 Either single — 3.25 3.25

New Boat of Monaco Marine and Airport Police Division — A1509

Litho. & Engr.
2020, Oct. 23 — Perf. 13¼
3026 A1509 €2 multi — 4.75 4.75

2020 Summer Olympics, Tokyo — A1510

2020, Nov. 3 — Litho. — Perf. 13¼
3027 A1510 €1.40 multi — 3.50 3.50
The 2020 Summer Olympics were postponed until 2021 because of the coronavirus pandemic.

Christmas A1511

Litho. With Foil Application
2020, Nov. 3 — Perf. 13¼
3028 A1511 €1.16 gold & multi — 2.75 2.75

Prince Rainier III (1923-2005) and Mariana Museum of Archaeology, Lucciana, France — A1512

2020, Nov. 4 — Engr. — Perf. 13¼
3029 A1512 €1.40 multi — 3.50 3.50

Ballons Montés (Letters Sent from Paris by Balloons) of the Franco-Prussian War, 150th Anniv. — A1513

2020, Nov. 4 — Engr. — Perf. 13x13¼
3030 A1513 €1.90 multi — 4.50 4.50

MONACO

Souvenir Sheets

Charlie Rivel (1896-1983), Circus Clown — A1514

Yuri Nikulin (1921-97), Circus Clown — A1515

Photo., Sheet Margin Photo. & Embossed With Foil Application
2021, Jan. 7   Perf.
3031 A1514 €4 gold & multi   9.75 9.75
Photo. With Foil Application
3032 A1515 €4 gold & multi   9.75 9.75

Opera Singers — A1516

Designs: €2.56, Julian Gayarre (1844-90). €3.86, Caroline Miolan-Carvalho (1827-95).

2021, Jan. 25   Perf. 13¼x13
3033 A1516 €2.56 dp blue grn & sepia   6.25 6.25
     Perf. 12¼x12¾
3034 A1516 €3.86 multi   9.50 9.50

2021 Rolex Monte Carlo Masters Tennis Tournament — A1517

2021, Feb. 12   Litho.   Perf. 13¼
3035 A1517 €2.12 multi   5.25 5.25

Acis Nicaeensis — A1518

2021, Feb. 12   Engr.   Perf. 13¼
3036 A1518 €5 multi   12.00 12.00

International Hydrographic Organization, Cent. — A1519

Speech on State of the Oceans by Prince Albert I (1848-1922) at Smithsonian Museum of Natural History, Cent. — A1520

Prince Albert I and German Emperor Wilhelm II (1859-1941) at 1914 Kiel Regatta — A1521

Camille Saint-Saens (1835-1921), Composer and Friend of Prince Albert I — A1522

2021, Feb. 26   Photo.   Perf. 13x13¼
3037 A1519 €1.28 multi   3.25 3.25
     Litho. & Engr.
     Perf. 13¼
3038 A1520 €2.12 multi   5.25 5.25
3039 A1521 €2.56 multi   6.25 6.25
3040 A1522 €3 multi   7.25 7.25
     Nos. 3037-3040 (4)   22.00 22.00

Race Cars — A1523

Designs: €1.28, Honda RA271. €1.50, Williams Renault FW14B.

2021, Mar. 5   Litho.   Perf. 13¼
3041-3042 A1523 Set of 2   6.50 6.50

Stirling Moss (1929-2020), Formula 1 Race Car Driver — A1524

No. 3043: a, Moss wearing helmet (31x31mm). b, Moss in race car (52x31mm).

2021, Mar. 5   Photo.   Perf. 13¼x13
3043 A1524 Horiz. pair   7.50 7.50
   a. €1.06 multi   2.50 2.50
   b. €2.12 multi   5.00 5.00

Intl. Flower Arrangement Festival — A1525

2021, Mar. 15   Litho.   Perf. 13¼
3044 A1525 €1.06 multi   2.50 2.50

Afghan Hound — A1526

2021, Mar. 15   Litho.   Perf. 13¼
3045 A1526 €1.06 multi   2.50 2.50
Intl. Dog Show.

Prince Rainier III and Princess Grace Awarding Golden Nymph Trophy — A1527

2021, Mar. 25   Litho.   Perf. 13¼
3046 A1527 €1.28 multi   2.50 2.50
60th Monte Carlo Television Festival.

2020 European Soccer Championships A1528

2021, Mar. 25   Litho.   Perf. 13¼
3047 A1528 €1.50 multi   3.50 3.50
The 2020 European Soccer Championships were postponed until 2021 because of the COVID-19 pandemic.

Prince Albert II, Princess Charlene, Hereditary Prince Jacques and Princess Gabriella A1529

2021, Apr. 12   Litho.   Perf. 13¼x13
3048 A1529 €2.56 multi   6.25 6.25

Miniature Sheet

Tenth Anniversary of Wedding of Prince Albert II and Princess Charlene — A1530

No. 3049: a, Monogram of Prince Albert II. b, Prince Albert II and Princess Charlene on wedding day. c, Princes Albert II and Jacques, Princesses Charlene and Gabriella, horiz. d, Prince Albert II and Princess Charlene waving, horiz.

Photo. With Foil Application (#3049a), Photo. (others)
2021, Apr. 30   Perf. 13¼
3049 A1530 Sheet of 4   15.00 15.00
   a.-d. €1.50 Any single   3.75 3.75

Hippocampus Guttulatus A1531

2021, May 6   Litho.   Perf. 13¼
3050 A1531 €1.50 multi   3.75 3.75
Europa.

Agreement on the Conservation of Cetaceans of the Black Sea, Mediterranean Sea and the Contiguous Atlantic Area, 25th Anniv. — A1532

Photo. & Embossed
2021, May 6   Perf. 13x13¼
3051 A1532 €1.50 dp ultra   3.75 3.75

Gustave Flaubert (1821-80), Writer — A1533

2021, May 25   Engr.   Perf. 13x13¼
3052 A1533 €2.12 multi   5.25 5.25

Fyodor Dostoyevsky (1821-81), Writer — A1534

2021, May 25   Engr.   Perf. 13¼
3053 A1534 €2.56 multi   6.25 6.25

Marcel Proust (1871-1922), Writer — A1535

Litho. & Engr.
2021, May 25   Perf. 13¼
3054 A1535 €3 multi   7.50 7.50

Jean de La Fontaine (1621-95), Fabulist and Poet — A1536

2021, May 25   Engr.   Perf. 13x13¼
3055 A1536 €3.86 multi   9.50 9.50

Walking Man, Sculpture by Alberto Giacometti (1901-66) — A1537

2021, June 17   Litho.   Perf. 13¼
3056 A1537 €1.06 multi   2.50 2.50
Exhibition of works by Giacometti at Grimaldi Forum.

Tenth Monaco Literary Show — A1538

2021, June 17   Litho.   Perf. 13¼
3057 A1538 €1.08 multi   2.60 2.60

MONACO

15th International Show Jumping Event, Monte Carlo — A1539

2021, June 17	Litho.	Perf. 13¼
3058 A1539 €1.28 multi		3.00 3.00

Burin and Czeslaw Slania (1921-2005), Stamp and Banknote Engraver A1540

2021, June 17	Engr.	Perf. 12¼x13
3059 A1540 €2 multi		4.75 4.75

Effiat Castle, Effiat, France — A1541

2021, June 28	Engr.	Perf. 13x13¼
3060 A1541 €2.56 multi		6.25 6.25

Grimaldi family properties outside of Monaco.

Calipers and 1914 Map of Monaco — A1542

2021, July 10	Litho.	Perf. 13¼
3061 A1542 €1.50 multi		3.75 3.75

Heracles and the Cretan Bull, Fresco in Prince's Palace A1543

2021, July 10	Litho.	Perf. 13x13¼
3062 A1543 €2.12 multi		5.00 5.00

Maine Coon Cats — A1544

2021, Sept. 7	Litho.	Perf. 13¼
3063 A1544 €1.50 multi		3.50 3.50

International Cat Show.

Therapeutic Art From Princess Grace Hospital Center's Unit of Psychiatry and Medical Psychology A1545

2021, Sept. 7	Litho.	Perf. 13x13¼
3064 A1545 €3 multi		7.00 7.00

Carl Jung (1875-1961), psychoanalyst.

28th Grand Bourse — A1546

2021, Sept. 15	Litho.	Perf. 13¼
3065 A1546 €1.06 multi		2.50 2.50

Posters for Movies Made in Monaco — A1547

Designs: €2.12, The Racers (Le Cercle Infernal). €2.56, The Red Shoes (De Rode Schoentjes). €3, Bay of Angels (La Baie des Anges). €4.71, Monte Carlo Madness (En Natt i Monte Carlo).

2021, Oct. 5	Litho.	Perf. 13¼x13
3066-3069 A1547 Set of 4		29.00 29.00

Miniature Sheet

Opening of the Monaco Museum of Stamps and Coins, 25th Anniv. A1548

No. 3070: a, 2015 coin commemorating 800th anniv. of the fortress on the Rock of Monaco, gold pistole coin depicting Prince Honoré II, Monaco No. 1229. b, Coins and 1648 letter to the Marquis de Courbon. c, Coin press, lion's head, Monaco No. 1813b, horiz. d, Stamp printing press, coin, Monaco No. 1861, horiz.

Perf. 13¼x13 (vert. stamps), 13x13¼ (horiz. stamps)

2021, Oct. 15	Litho. & Engr.	
3070 A1548 Sheet of 4		13.00 13.00
a.-b. €1.28 Either single		3.00 3.00
c.-d. €1.50 Either single		3.50 3.50

Christmas A1549

Litho. With Foil Application

2021, Nov. 5		Perf. 13¼x13
3071 A1549 €1.28 gold & multi		3.00 3.00

2022 Winter Olympics, Beijing — A1550

2022, Jan. 17	Litho.	Perf. 13¼
3072 A1550 €1.65 multi		3.75 3.75

Molière (1622-73), Playwright and Actor — A1551

2022, Jan. 17	Engr.	Perf. 12¼x13
3073 A1551 €2.28 multi		5.25 5.25

Les Enfants de Frankie Charity, 25th Anniv. — A1552

2022, Feb. 2	Litho.	Perf. 13¼
3074 A1552 €1.43 multi		3.25 3.25

Prince Albert I (1848-1922) — A1553

Litho. & Engr.

2022, Feb. 2		Perf. 13¼
3075 A1553 €2.86 multi		6.50 6.50

Admission of Prince Albert I to Paris Academy of Sciences of the French Institue as foreign associate member, 113th anniv.

Art'Ochtones Association, 10th Anniv. — A1554

2022, Feb. 18	Litho.	Perf. 13¼
3076 A1554 €1.14 multi		2.60 2.60

2022 Rolex Monte Carlo Masters Tennis Tournament — A1555

2022, Feb. 18	Litho.	Perf. 13¼
3077 A1555 €1.05 multi		0.75 0.75

London 2022 International Stamp Exhibition A1556

2022, Feb. 18	Engr.	Perf. 13x13¼
3078 A1556 €2 multi		4.50 4.50

Race Cars — A1557

Designs: €1.43, Vanwall VW5. €1.65, Benetton B195.

2022, Mar. 8	Litho.	Perf. 13¼
3079-3080 A1557 Set of 2		7.00 7.00

Jochen Rindt (1942-70), Formula 1 Race Car Driver — A1558

No. 3081: a, Rindt wearing helmet (31x31mm). b, Rindt in race car (52x31mm).

2022, Mar. 8	Photo.	Perf. 13¼x13
3081 A1558 Horiz. pair		7.50 7.50
a. €1.14 multi		2.50 2.50
b. €2.28 multi		5.00 5.00

Restoration of The Abduction of Europa by Jupiter, Ceiling Fresco in Prince's Palace A1559

2022, Mar. 17	Litho.	Perf. 13x13¼
3082 A1559 €2.86 multi		6.50 6.50

Opera Singers — A1560

Designs: €3.30, Victor Maurel (1848-1923). €3.92, Felia Litvinne (1860-1936).

2022, Mar. 17	Engr.	Perf. 13¼x13
3083 A1560 €3.30 multi		7.25 7.25
3084 A1560 €3.92 multi		8.75 8.75

Rainier III Academy, Cent. — A1561

Litho. With Foil Application

2022, Mar. 25		Perf. 13¼
3085 A1561 €1.14 gold & multi		2.50 2.50

Dalmatian — A1562

2022, Mar. 25	Litho.	Perf. 13¼
3086 A1562 €1.16 multi		2.60 2.60

International Dog Show.

A1563 / A1564

Design: €1.43, Column gifted by people of Monaco to Prince Albert I on the 25th anniv. of his reign. €2.28, Jules Massenet (1842-1912), composer and friend of Prince Albert I.

Litho. & Engr.

2022, Apr. 12		Perf. 13¼
3087 A1563 €1.43 multi		3.00 3.00
3088 A1564 €2.28 multi		4.75 4.75

MONACO

Visit of Prince Albert II to Former Grimaldi Family Holdings — A1565

No. 3089: a, Terlizzi, Italy (30x30mm). b, Chateau de Garagnone (40x30mm).

2022, Apr. 20		**Photo.**		**Perf. 13¼**	
3089	A1565	Horiz. pair		6.50	6.50
a.		€1.43 multi		3.00	3.00
b.		€1.65 multi		3.50	3.50

Police Department of Monaco, 120th Anniv. — A1566

2022, Apr. 29	**Litho. & Silk-Screened**		**Perf. 13¼**	
3090	A1566	€1.65 multi	3.50	3.50

MonacoPhil 2022 International Philatelic Exhibition — A1567

2022, Apr. 29	**Litho.**		**Perf. 13¼**	
3091	A1567	€1.65 multi	3.50	3.50

Legend of the 1297 Seizure of Monaco by François Grimaldi — A1568

2022, May 9	**Litho.**		**Perf. 13¼**	
3092	A1568	€1.65 multi	3.50	3.50

Europa.

Serge Diaghilev (1872-1929), Founder of Ballets Russes — A1569

2022, May 9	**Engr.**		**Perf. 13x13¼**	
3093	A1569	€2.86 multi	6.25	6.25

International Flower Arrangement Festival — A1570

2022, May 23	**Litho.**		**Perf. 13¼**	
3094	A1570	€1.14 multi	2.75	2.75

Polar Bear — A1571

2022, May 23	**Litho.**		**Perf. 13¼**	
3095	A1571	€1.43 multi	3.50	3.50

Polar Mission Exhibition at the Oceanographic Museum of Monaco.

Souvenir Sheet

Federation of Grimaldi of Monaco Historic Sites, 1st Anniv. — A1572

2022, June 3	**Litho., Sheet Margin Engr.**		**Perf. 13**	
3096	A1572	€3.30 multi	8.00	8.00

Black Smoke Egyptian Mau Cat — A1573

2022, June 14	**Litho.**		**Perf. 13¼**	
3097	A1573	€1.43 multi	3.50	3.50

International Cat Show.

Brewery of Monaco — A1574

2022, June 14	**Engr.**		**Perf. 13x13¼**	
3098	A1574	€1.65 multi	4.00	4.00

Bee Hives on Roof of the Museum of Stamps and Coins — A1575

2022, June 23	**Litho.**		**Perf. 13¼**	
3099	A1575	€1.65 multi	4.00	4.00

Louis Blériot (1872-1936), Aviator, Blériot XI, and His House in Monaco — A1576

2022, June 23	**Engr.**		**Perf. 13¼**	
3100	A1576	€2.28 multi	5.50	5.50

1907 Topographical Expedition to Spitsbergen, Norway, of Prince Albert I — A1577

2022, June 23	**Litho. & Engr.**		**Perf. 13¼**	
3101	A1577	€3.30 multi	8.00	8.00

Grimaldi Forum Exhibition of Shoes Designed by Christian Louboutin — A1578

2022, July 1	**Litho.**		**Perf. 13¼**	
3102	A1578	€1.65 multi	4.00	4.00

Prince Albert II as President of Monaco Red Cross, 40th Anniv. — A1579

2022, July 11	**Litho.**		**Perf. 13¼**	
3103	A1579	€1.43 multi	3.50	3.50

Nekya, Fresco from Ceiling of Throne Room of the Prince's Palace — A1580

2022, July 11	**Litho.**		**Perf. 13¼**	
3104	A1580	€1.43 multi	3.50	3.50

Exhibition of Paintings by Louis Tinayre (1861-1942), Painter of Works Depicting Prince Albert I — A1581

2022, July 18	**Litho.**		**Perf. 13¼**	
3105	A1581	€1.43 multi	3.50	3.50

Prince Albert I (1848-1922), Museum of Prehistoric Anthropology of Monaco — A1582

Prince Albert I on Wicker Sled in Madeira — A1583

2022, Sept. 6	**Litho. & Engr.**		**Perf. 13¼**	
3106	A1582	€1.65 multi	3.25	3.25
3107	A1583	€2.86 multi	5.75	5.75

Museum of Prehistoric Anthropology of Monaco, 120th anniv.

International Motorboating Union, Cent. — A1584

2022, Sept. 19	**Litho. & Engr.**		**Perf. 13¼**	
3108	A1584	€1.65 multi	3.25	3.25

Inauguration of Prince Albert I Avenue in Ponta Delgada, Azores, Painting by Louis Tinayre (1861-1942) A1585

Prince Albert I of Monaco (1848-1922) and King Carlos I of Portugal (1863-1908), Patrons of Oceanography A1586

2022, Sept. 19	**Litho.**		**Perf. 13¼**	
3109	A1585	€2 multi	4.00	4.00
	Litho. & Engr.			
3110	A1586	€2.28 multi	4.50	4.50

Posters for Movies Made in Monaco — A1588

Designs: No. 3111, German poster for *Ich Warte in Monte Carlo (I'll Be Waiting in Monte Carlo)*, 1969. No. 3112, American poster for *Charlie Chan at Monte Carlo*, 1937. €3.30, Polish poster for *Grand Prix*, 1966. €3.92, American poster for *Seven Thieves*, 1960.

2022, Oct. 4	**Litho.**		**Perf. 13**	
3111	A1587	€2 multi	4.00	4.00
3112	A1588	€2 multi	4.00	4.00
3113	A1588	€3.30 multi	6.50	6.50
3114	A1588	€3.92 multi	7.75	7.75
		Nos. 3111-3114 (4)	22.25	22.25

2022 World Cup Soccer Championships, Qatar — A1589

2022, Oct. 17	**Litho.**		**Perf. 13¼**	
3115	A1589	€1.65 multi	3.25	3.25

Honoré I (1522-81), Lord of Monaco — A1590

2022, Oct. 17	**Engr.**		**Perf. 13x13¼**	
3116	A1590	€2.86 multi	5.75	5.75

Christmas — A1591

2022, Nov. 3	**Litho. & Engr.**		**Perf. 13¼x13**	
3117	A1591	€1.43 multi	3.00	3.00

Princess Charlene of Monaco Foundation, 10th Anniv. — A1592

2022, Nov. 24	**Litho.**		**Perf. 13¼**	
3118	A1592	€1.16 multi	2.40	2.40

MONACO

2022 Monaco Explorations Mission in the Indian Ocean — A1593

2022, Nov. 24	Litho.	Perf. 13
3119	A1593	€2.32 multi	5.00 5.00

Souvenir Sheet

Prince Albert I of Monaco (1848-1922) — A1594

No. 3120: a, Prince Albert I, map of Antarctica (52x31mm). b, Pourquoi-Pas, ship from the second Charcot expedition to Antarctica (30x40mm).

Perf. 13 (#3120a), 13¼x13 (#3120b)

2022, Nov. 24		Litho.	
3120	A1594	Sheet of 2	8.50 8.50
a.-b.		€2 Either single	4.25 4.25

See French Southern & Antarctic Territories No. 689.

Souvenir Sheet

Prince Albert II and Queen Elizabeth II (1926-2022) — A1595

2022, Nov. 24	Litho.	Perf. 13x13¼
3121	A1595	€4 multi	8.25 8.25

Souvenir Sheet

MonacoPhil 2022 — A1596

No. 3122: a, Prince Honoré V of Monaco (1778-1841). b, Napoleon Bonaparte (1769-1821), Emperor of France, horiz.

Perf. 13¼x13 (#3122a), 13x13¼ (#3122b)
Engr., Sheet Margin Litho. & Engr.

2022, Nov. 24			
3122	A1596	Sheet of 2	12.50 12.50
a.-b.		€3 Either single	6.25 6.25

Coat of Arms and "Lettre Verte" — A1597

Serpentine Die Cut 11

2023, Jan. 2		Photo.	
Booklet Stamp			
Self-Adhesive			
3123	A1597	(€1.16) green & multi	2.50 2.50
a.		Booklet pane of 10	25.00

Compare type A1597 with types A786 and A1076.

Prince Albert II Type of 2012
Inscribed "Lettre Verte"

2023, Jan. 3	Engr.	Perf. 13x13¼
3124	A1221	(€1.16) emerald	2.50 2.50

St. Thérèse of Lisieux (1873-97) — A1598

2023, Jan. 3	Engr.	Perf. 13x13¼
3125	A1598	€2.32 multi	5.00 5.00

10th New Generation Circus A1599

45th Intl. Circus Festival, Monte Carlo A1600

2023, Jan. 9	Litho.	Perf. 13¼
3126	A1599	€1.16 multi	2.60 2.60
3127	A1600	€1.80 multi	4.00 4.00

Colette (1873-1954), Writer — A1601

2023, Jan. 30	Engr.	Perf. 13x13¼
3128	A1601	€3.70 multi	8.00 8.00

Bearded Collie — A1602

2023, Feb. 9	Litho.	Perf. 13¼
3129	A1602	€1.16 multi	2.50 2.50

Intl. Dog Show.

Rolex Monte Carlo Masters Tennis Tournament — A1603

2023, Feb. 9	Litho.	Perf. 13¼
3130	A1603	€2.32 multi	5.00 5.00

Race Cars — A1604

Designs: €1.16, Brabham BT26. €1.80, Brawn GP 001.

2023, Mar. 7	Litho.	Perf. 13¼
3131-3132	A1604	Set of 2	6.50 6.50

Jack Brabham (1926-2014), Formula 1 Race Car Driver — A1605

No. 3133: a, Brabham wearing helmet (31x31mm). b, Brabham in race car (52x31mm).

2023, Mar. 7	Photo.	Perf. 13¼x13
3133	A1605	Horiz. pair	4.50 4.50
a.-b.		€1 Either single	2.25 2.25

Scouting in Monaco, Cent. — A1606

2023, Mar. 22	Photo.	Perf. 13¼
3134	A1606	€1.16 multi	2.60 2.60

Values are for stamps with surrounding selvage.

Sergei Rachmaninoff (1873-1943), Composer A1607

2023, Mar. 22	Engr.	Perf. 13¼x13
3135	A1607	€2.32 multi	5.00 5.00

Marcel Marceau (1923-2007), Mime — A1608

2023, Mar. 22	Engr.	Perf. 13¼x13
3136	A1608	€3.70 multi	8.00 8.00

80th Monaco Formula 1 Grand Prix Automobile Race — A1609

2023, Apr. 28	Litho.	Perf. 13¼
3137	A1609	€1.80 multi	4.00 4.00

Europa — A1610

2023, May 9	Litho.	Perf. 13¼
3138	A1610	€1.80 multi	4.00 4.00

Enzo Ferrari (1898-1988), Race Car Driver and Automobile Manufacturer A1611

2023, May 9	Engr.	Perf. 13¼
3139	A1611	€1.80 multi	4.00 4.00

Larvotto Seaside Complex A1612

2023, May 17	Litho.	Perf. 13¼
3140	A1612	€1.16 multi	2.50 2.50

Maria Callas (1923-77), Opera Singer — A1613

2023, May 17	Engr.	Perf. 12¼x13
3141	A1613	€3.70 multi	8.00 8.00

Portrait of Prince Rainier III (1923-2005), by Hélier Cosson (1897-1976) — A1614

2023, May 31	Litho.	Perf. 13¼
3142	A1614	€1.16 multi	2.50 2.50

Prince Rainier III (1923-2005) at Lectern at United Nations Headquarters A1615

2023, May 31	Litho. & Engr.	Perf. 13¼
3143	A1615	€1.80 multi	4.00 4.00

Admission of Monaco to United Nations, 30th anniv.

Achievements of Prince Rainier III (1923-2005), Fresco by Claude Gauthier — A1616

2023, May 31	Litho.	Perf. 13x13¼
3144	A1616	€2.32 multi	5.00 5.00

No. 3144 is shown sideways.

Prince Rainier III (1923-2005) and Marine Life A1617

Killer Whale, Map of Area Near Monaco, and Scientific Researcher A1618

2023, May 31	Litho.	Perf. 13
3145		Horiz. pair	5.00 5.00
a.	A1617	€1.16 multi	2.50 2.50
b.	A1618	€1.16 multi	2.50 2.50

Environmental protection activities of Prince Rainier III.

MONACO

Visit of Prince Albert II to Fortress of Polignac, France — A1619

2023, June 1	Engr.	Perf. 13x13¼
3146	A1619 €2.32 multi	5.00 5.00

Souvenir Sheet

Fourth Meeting of the Historical Sites of the Grimaldis of Monaco — A1620

2023, June 1	Litho.	Perf. 13x13¼
3147	A1620 €3.70 multi	8.00 8.00

World Association of Children's Friends (AMADE), 60th Anniv. — A1621

2023, June 19	Litho.	Perf. 13¼
3148	A1621 €1.16 gold	2.60 2.60

Yacht Club of Monaco, 70th Anniv. A1622

No. 3149: a, Prince Rainier III (1923-2005), founder of Yacht Club (31x31mm). b, Yacht Club Building (52x31mm).

2023, June 17	Photo.	Perf. 13
3149	A1622 Horiz. pair	4.50 4.50
a.-b.	€1 Either single	2.25 2.25

Blaise Pascal (1623-62), Mathematician and Philosopher — A1623

2023, June 19	Engr.	Perf. 13x13¼
3150	A1623 €2.32 multi	5.00 5.00

La Condamine Market — A1624

2023, July 3	Litho.	Perf. 13¼
3151	A1624 €1.80 multi	4.00 4.00

Grimaldi Forum Exhibition of Art by Claude Monet (1840-1926) — A1625

2023, July 3	Litho.	Perf. 13¼
3152	A1625 €1.16 multi	2.60 2.60

AS Monaco, 2022-23 Winners of French Basketball Cup — A1626

2023, July 17	Litho.	Perf. 13¼
3153	A1626 €1.16 multi	2.60 2.60

Souvenir Sheet

Territorial Development of Prince Rainier III (1923-2005) — A1627

Designs: No. 3154: a, Aerial view of Port Hercule. b, Map of Port Hercule.
No. 3155: a, Map of Larvotto. b, Aerial view of Larvotto.
No. 3156: a, Aerial view of Fontvieille. b, Map of Fontvieille.

Litho. & Engr. With Foil Application

2023, July 19		Perf. 13¼x13
3154	A1627 Sheet of 2	9.00 9.00
a.-b.	€2 Either single	4.50 4.50
3155	A1627 Sheet of 2	11.50 11.50
a.	€2 red, silver & blk	4.50 4.50
b.	€3 red, silver & blk	6.75 6.75
3156	A1627 Sheet of 2	13.50 13.50
a.-b.	€3 Either single	6.75 6.75
	Nos. 3154-3156 (3)	34.00 34.00

International Flower Arrangement Festival — A1628

2023, Sept. 4	Litho.	Perf. 13¼
3157	A1628 €1 multi	2.25 2.25

Bengal Cat — A1629

2023, Sept. 4	Litho.	Perf. 13¼
3158	A1629 €1.80 multi	4.00 4.00

International Cat Show.

Promulgation of 1962 Constitution by Prince Rainier III (1923-2005) — A1630

Litho. & Engr.

2023, Sept. 8		Perf. 13¼
3159	A1630 €1.16 multi	2.50 2.50

Prince Rainier III (1923-2005) and European Union Flag — A1631

Litho. & Engr.

2023, Oct. 5		Perf. 13¼
3160	A1631 €1.16 multi	2.50 2.50

Application of Monaco for admission to Council of Europe, 25th anniv.

Posters for Movies Made in Monaco — A1632

Designs: No. 3161, Italian poster for *The Monte-Carlo Story*, 1957. No. 3162, French poster for *Trente et Quarante (Thirty and Forty)*, 1946.

2023, Oct. 16	Litho.	Perf. 13¼x13
3161	A1632 €1.80 multi	4.00 4.00
3162	A1632 €2 multi	4.25 4.25

Doria Castle, Dolceacqua, Italy — A1633

2023, Nov. 3	Engr.	Perf. 13x13¼
3163	A1633 €1.80 multi	4.00 4.00

Historical relationship between Monaco and Dolceacqua, Italy, 500th anniv.

Christmas — A1634

2023, Nov. 3	Litho.	Perf. 13¼
3164	A1634 €1.16 multi	2.50 2.50

SEMI-POSTAL STAMPS

No. 16 Surcharged in Red

1914, Oct.	Unwmk.	Perf. 14x13½
B1	A2 10c + 5c carmine	5.00 5.00

View of Monaco — SP2

1919, Sept. 20		Typo.
B2	SP2 2c + 3c lilac	32.50 32.50
B3	SP2 5c + 5c green	17.50 17.50
B4	SP2 15c + 10c rose	17.50 17.50
B5	SP2 25c + 15c blue	37.50 37.50
B6	SP2 50c + 50c brn, buff	175.00 150.00
B7	SP2 1fr + 1fr blk, yel	275.00 150.00
B8	SP2 5fr + 5fr dull red	925.00 1,050.
	Nos. B2-B8 (7)	1,480. 1,455.

Nos. B4-B8 Surcharged

1920, Mar. 20		
B9	SP2 2c + 3c on #B4	37.50 37.50
a.	"c" of "3c" inverted	1,500. 1,500.
b.	Pair, Nos. 9, 9a	2,250. 2,250.
B10	SP2 2c + 3c on #B5	37.50 37.50
a.	"c" of "3c" inverted	1,500. 1,500.
b.	Pair, Nos. 10, 10a	2,250. 2,250.
B11	SP2 2c + 3c on #B6	37.50 37.50
a.	"c" of "3c" inverted	1,500. 1,500.
b.	Pair, Nos. 11, 11a	2,250. 2,250.
B12	SP2 5c + 5c on #B7	37.50 37.50
B13	SP2 5c + 5c on #B8	37.50 37.50

Overprinted

B14	SP2 15c + 10c rose	25.00 25.00
B15	SP2 25c + 15c blue	10.50 10.50
B16	SP2 50c + 50c brn, buff	50.00 50.00
B17	SP2 1fr + 1fr blk, yel	67.50 67.50
B18	SP2 5fr + 5fr red	5,800. 5,800.
	Nos. B9-B17 (9)	340.50 340.50

Marriage of Princess Charlotte to Prince Pierre, Comte de Polignac.

Palace Gardens — SP3

"The Rock" of Monaco — SP4

Bay of Monaco — SP5

Prince Louis II — SP6

1937, Apr.	Engr.	Perf. 13
B19	SP3 50c + 50c green	2.10 2.10
B20	SP4 90c + 90c car	2.10 2.10
B21	SP5 1.50fr + 1.50fr blue	5.00 5.00
B22	SP6 2fr + 2fr violet	8.50 8.50
B23	SP6 5fr + 5fr brn red	60.00 60.00
	Nos. B19-B23 (5)	77.70 77.70
	Set, never hinged	225.00

The surtax was used for welfare work.

Pierre and Marie Curie SP7

Monaco Hospital, Date Palms SP8

1938, Nov. 15		Perf. 13
B24	SP7 65c + 25c dp bl grn	9.00 9.00
B25	SP8 1.75fr + 50c dp ultra	9.00 9.00
	Set, never hinged	35.00

B24 and B25 exist imperforate.
The surtax was for the International Union for the Control of Cancer.

Lucien SP9

Honoré II SP10

MONACO

Louis I SP11
Charlotte de Gramont SP12
Antoine I SP13
Marie de Lorraine SP14
Jacques I SP15
Louise-Hippolyte SP16
Honoré III — SP17
"The Rock," 18th Century — SP18

1939, June 26

B26	SP9	5c + 5c brn blk	1.25	.75
B27	SP10	10c + 10c rose vio	1.25	.75
B28	SP11	45c + 15c brt grn	4.50	3.50
B29	SP12	70c + 30c brt red vio	6.75	6.00
B30	SP13	90c + 35c vio	6.75	6.00
B31	SP14	1fr + 1fr ultra	17.00	16.00
B32	SP15	2fr + 2fr brn org	17.00	16.00
B33	SP16	2.25fr + 1.25fr Prus bl	20.00	20.00
B34	SP17	3fr + 3fr dp rose	27.50	27.50
B35	SP18	5fr + 5fr red	50.00	50.00
		Nos. B26-B35 (10)	152.00	146.50
		Set, never hinged	400.00	

Types of Regular Issue, 1939 Surcharged in Red

1940, Feb. 10 Engr. Perf. 13

B36	A30	20c + 1fr violet	1.75	1.75
B37	A31	25c + 1fr dk grn	1.75	1.75
B38	A32	30c + 1fr brn red	1.75	1.75
B39	A31	40c + 1fr dk blue	1.75	1.75
B40	A33	45c + 1fr rose car	1.75	1.75
B41	A34	50c + 1fr brown	1.75	1.75
B42	A32	60c + 1fr dk grn	2.25	2.25
B43	A35	75c + 1fr brn blk	2.25	2.25
B44	A34	1fr + 1fr scarlet	3.00	3.00
B45	A31	2fr + 1fr indigo	3.00	3.00
B46	A33	2.50fr + 1fr dk grn	7.00	7.00
B47	A35	3fr + 1fr dk blue	7.00	7.00
B48	A30	5fr + 1fr brn blk	9.50	9.50
B49	A33	10fr + 5fr lt blue	18.00	18.00
B50	A32	20fr + 5fr brn vio	18.00	18.00
		Nos. B36-B50 (15)	80.50	80.50
		Set, never hinged	240.00	

The surtax was used to purchase ambulances for the French government.

Catalogue values for unused stamps in this section, from this point to the end of the section, are for Never Hinged items.

Symbol of Charity and View of Monaco SP19
Symbol of Charity and View of Monaco SP20

1941, May 15

B51	SP19	25c + 25c brt red vio	3.25	1.60
B52	SP20	50c + 25c dk brn	3.25	1.60
B53	SP20	75c + 50c rose vio	5.75	2.00
B54	SP19	1fr + 1fr dk blue	5.75	2.00
B55	SP19	1.50fr + 1.50fr rose red	6.00	2.00
B56	SP19	2fr + 2fr Prus grn	6.25	2.75
B57	SP20	2.50fr + 2fr brt ultra	7.75	3.50
B58	SP19	3fr + 3fr dl red brn	10.00	4.00
B59	SP20	5fr + 5fr dk bl grn	14.50	5.75
B60	SP19	10fr + 8fr brn blk	21.00	11.50
		Nos. B51-B60 (10)	83.50	36.70

The surtax was for various charities.

Rainier Grimaldi SP21

Designs: 5c, Charles II. 10c, Jeanne Grimaldi. 20c, Charles-August Goyon de Matignon. 30c, Jacques I. 40c, Louise-Hippolyte. 50c, Charlotte Grimaldi. 75c, Marie-Charles Grimaldi. 1fr, Honoré III. 1.50fr, Honoré IV. 2.50fr, Honoré V. 3fr, Florestan I. 5fr, Charles III. 10fr, Albert I. 20fr, Marie-Victoire. Frames differ.

1942, Dec. 10

B61	SP21	2c + 3c ultra	.35	.35
B62	SP21	5c + 5c org ver	.35	.35
B63	SP21	10c + 5c blk	.35	.35
B64	SP21	20c + 10c brt grn	.35	.35
B65	SP21	30c + 30c brn vio	.35	.35
B66	SP21	40c + 40c rose red	.35	.35
B67	SP21	50c + 50c vio	.35	.35
B68	SP21	75c + 75c brt red vio	.35	.35
B69	SP21	1fr + 1fr dk grn	.35	.35
B70	SP21	1.50fr + 1.50fr ear brn	.35	.35
B71	SP21	2.50fr + 2.50fr pur	4.25	3.50
B72	SP21	3fr + 3fr turq bl	4.50	3.50
B73	SP21	5fr + 5fr sepia	5.00	4.50
B74	SP21	10fr + 5fr rose lil	5.50	5.00
B75	SP21	20fr + 5fr ultra	6.50	5.75
		Nos. B61-B75 (15)	29.25	25.75

Saint Dévote SP36
Procession SP37
Procession SP38
Church of St. Dévote SP39
Burning of Symbolic Boat SP40
Blessing of the Sea SP41
Church of St. Dévote SP42
Trial of St. Barbara SP43
Arrival of St. Dévote at Monaco SP44

1944, Jan. 27 Unwmk. Perf. 13

B76	SP36	50c + 50c sepia	.25	.25
B77	SP37	70c + 80c dp ultra	.25	.25
B78	SP38	80c + 70c green	.25	.25
B79	SP39	1fr + 1fr rose vio	.25	.25
B80	SP40	1.50fr + 1.50fr red	.35	.35
B81	SP41	2fr + 2fr brn vio	.65	.65
B82	SP42	5fr + 2fr violet	.65	.65
B83	SP43	10fr + 40fr royal bl	.65	.65
B84	SP44	20fr + 60fr chlky bl	4.50	4.50
		Nos. B76-B84 (9)	7.80	7.80

Issued in honor of St. Dévote. Type SP43 is inscribed "Jugement de Sainte Dévote," but actually shows the trial of St. Barbara in 235 A.D.

Needy Child — SP45

1946, Feb. 18 Engr.

B85	SP45	1fr + 3fr dp bl grn	.30	.30
B86	SP45	2fr + 4fr rose pink	.30	.30
B87	SP45	4fr + 0fr dk bl	.90	.75
B88	SP45	5fr + 40fr dk vio	.90	.75
B89	SP45	10fr + 60fr brn vio	.90	.75
B90	SP45	15fr + 100fr indigo	1.40	1.10
		Nos. B85-B90 (6)	4.10	3.50

The surtax was for child welfare.

Nurse and Child — SP46

1946, Feb. 18

B91	SP46	2fr + 8fr brt blue	.75	.70

The surtax was used for prevention of tuberculosis.

19th Century Steamer and Map — SP47

1946

B92	SP47	3fr + 2fr deep blue	.50	.50

Stamp Day, June 23, 1946.

Harbor of Monte Carlo — SP48

1946, Dec. 13

B93	SP48	2fr + 3fr dk bluish grn	1.40	1.40

Issued in tribute to the memory of Franklin D. Roosevelt. The surtax was for a fund to erect a monument in his honor.

Prince Louis II Type
Souvenir Sheet
Unwmk.

1947, May 15 Engr. Imperf.

B94	A46	200fr + 300fr dk red & choc	30.00	19.00

Prince Charles III — SP50

1948, Mar. 6 Perf. 14x13

B95	SP50	6fr + 4fr dk bl grn, lt bl	.50	.50

Issued for Stamp Day, Mar. 6.

Princess Charlotte SP51
Prince Rainier III SP52

Perf. 13½x13, Imperf.
1949, Dec. 27 Engr.
Cross Typo. in Red

B96	SP51	10fr + 5fr red brown	10.00	10.00
B97	SP52	15fr + 5fr brt red	10.00	10.00
B98	SP52	25fr + 5fr dk vio bl	10.00	10.00
B99	SP51	40fr + 5fr dull green	10.00	10.00
a.		Block of 4, #B96-B99	45.00	45.00

Printed in sheets measuring 151x173mm, perf. and imperf., containing 4 of No. B99a. The surtax was for the Red Cross. For surcharges see Nos. 288-291.

Hercules Strangling the Lion of Nemea SP53

Twelve Labors of Hercules: No. B101, Killing the Hydra of Lerna. No. B102, Capturing the Erymanthean boar. No. B103, Killing Stymphalian birds. No. B104, Hercules and the Ceryneian Hind. No. B105, The Augean Stables. No. B106, Hercules and the Cretan Bull. No. B107, Wild horses of Diomedes. No. B108, Hercules and the Oxen of Geryon. No. B109, Hercules and the Belt of Hippolytus. No. B110, Winning the golden apple of Hesperides. No. B111, Battling Cerberus.

1981, Nov. 5 Perf. 13

B100	SP53	2.50fr + 50c multi	1.25	1.25
B101	SP53	3.50fr + 50c multi	1.25	1.25

1982, Nov. 8

B102	SP53	2.50fr + 50c multi	1.25	1.25
B103	SP53	3.50fr + 50c multi	1.25	1.25

1983, Nov. 9

B104	SP53	2.50fr + 50c multi	1.25	1.25
B105	SP53	3.50fr + 50c multi	1.25	1.25

1984, Nov. 8

B106	SP53	3fr + 50c multi	1.25	1.25
B107	SP53	4fr + 50c multi	1.25	1.25

MONACO

1985, Nov. 7
B108 SP53 3fr + 70c multi 1.25 1.25
B109 SP53 4fr + 80c multi 1.25 1.25

1986, Oct. 28
B110 SP53 3fr + 70c multi 1.25 1.25
B111 SP53 4fr + 80c multi 1.25 1.25
Nos. B100-B111 (12) 15.00 15.00

Surtax on #B100-B111 for the Red Cross.

Monegasque Committee to Fight Tuberculosis and Respiratory Diseases — SP54

1994, Mar. 14   Litho.   Perf. 13½x13
B112 SP54 2.40fr +60c multi 1.00 1.00

AIR POST STAMPS

No. 91 Srchd. in Black

Perf. 14x13½
1933, Aug. 22   Unwmk.
C1 A15 1.50fr on 5fr 16.00 16.00
a. Imperf., pair 350.00

Catalogue values for unused stamps in this section, from this point to the end of the section, are for Never Hinged items.

Plane over Monaco AP1
Plane Propeller and Buildings AP2
Pegasus AP3
Sea Gull AP4
Plane, Globe and Arms of Monaco — AP5

1942, Apr. 15   Engr.   Perf. 13
C2 AP1 5fr blue green .30 .30
C3 AP1 10fr ultra .30 .30
C4 AP2 15fr sepia .60 .60
C5 AP3 20fr henna brown .85 .85
C6 AP4 50fr red violet 4.25 3.50
C7 AP5 100fr red & vio brn 4.25 3.50
Nos. C2-C7 (6) 10.55 9.05

For surcharges see Nos. CB1-CB5.

Nos. 196-197 Overprinted in Blue

1946, May 20
C8 A41 50fr dp Prus green 4.00 4.00
C9 A41 100fr red 4.00 4.00
a. Inverted overprint 37,500.
b. Double overprint 22,500.

Douglas DC-3 and Arms — AP6

1946, May 20
C10 AP6 40fr red 1.00 .50
C11 AP6 50fr red brown 2.00 .70
C12 AP6 100fr dp blue grn 2.50 1.25
C13 AP6 200fr violet 2.75 2.00
Nos. C10-C13 (4) 8.25 4.45

Exist imperforate. See Nos. C27-C29.

Harbor of Monte Carlo AP7
Map of Monaco AP8

1946, Dec. 13
C14 AP7 5fr carmine rose .40 .40
C15 AP8 10fr violet black .55 .55

Issued in tribute to the memory of Franklin D. Roosevelt.

Franklin D. Roosevelt Examining his Stamp Collection — AP9

Main Post Office, New York City — AP10

Oceanographic Museum, Monaco — AP11

Harbor of Monte Carlo AP12

Statue of Liberty and New York City Skyline AP13

1947, May 15   Unwmk.
C16 AP9 50c violet 1.25 1.25
C17 AP10 1.50fr rose violet .55 .55
C18 AP11 3fr henna brown .55 .55
C19 AP12 10fr deep blue 3.00 3.00
C20 AP13 15fr rose carmine 6.00 6.00
a. Strip of 3, #C20, 203, C19 13.00 13.00
Nos. C16-C20 (5) 11.35 11.35

Monaco's participation in the Centenary Intl. Philatelic Exhibition, NYC, May, 1947.

Crowd Acclaiming Constitution of 1911 AP14
Anthropological Museum AP15

Designs: 25fr, Institute of Human Paleontology, Paris. 50fr, Albert I. 100fr, Oceanographic Institute, Paris. 200fr, Albert I medal.

1949, Mar. 5   Engr.   Perf. 13
C21 AP14 20fr brown red .85 .85
C22 AP14 25fr indigo .85 .85
C23 AP15 40fr blue green 1.40 1.40
C24 AP15 50fr blk, brn & grn 2.10 2.10
C25 AP15 100fr cerise 6.50 6.50
C26 AP14 200fr deep orange 9.00 9.00
Nos. C21-C26 (6) 20.70 20.70

Plane-Arms Type of 1946
1949, Mar. 10
C27 AP6 300fr dp ultra & ind 45.00 45.00
C28 AP6 500fr grnsh blk & bl grn 37.50 30.00
C29 AP6 1000fr black & red vio 67.50 45.00
Nos. C27-C29 (3) 150.00 120.00

UPU Type of Regular Issue
1949-50
C30 A56 25fr deep blue .50 .50
C31 A56 40fr red brown & sep 1.00 1.00
C32 A56 50fr dk green & ultra 2.00 2.00
C33 A56 100fr dk car & dk grn 5.00 5.00
Nos. C30-C33 (4) 8.50 8.50

75th anniv. of the UPU.
Nos. C30-C33 exist imperforate, also No. C30 in deep plum and violet, imperforate.
Issued: 25fr, 12/27; others, 9/12/50.

Rainier Type of Regular Issue
1950, Apr. 11   Unwmk.
C34 A57 50fr black & red brn 4.50 4.50
C35 A57 100fr red brn, sep & ind 8.00 8.00

Enthronement of Prince Rainier III.

Runner AP18

Designs: 50fr, Fencing. 100fr, Target Shooting. 200fr, Olympic Torch.

1953, Feb. 23   Perf. 11
C36 AP18 40fr black 11.00 8.00
C37 AP18 50fr brt purple 13.50 9.00
C38 AP18 100fr dk slate grn 17.50 9.00
C39 AP18 200fr deep carmine 24.00 9.00
Nos. C36-C39 (4) 66.00 35.00

Issued to publicize Monaco's participation in the Helsinki Olympic Games.

Dr. Albert Schweitzer and Ogowe River Scene, Gabon AP19

1955, Jan. 14   Perf. 13
C40 AP19 200fr multicolored 28.00 21.00

Dr. Albert Schweitzer, medical missionary.

Mediterranean Sea Swallows — AP20

Birds: 200fr, Sea gulls. 500fr, Albatross. 1000fr, Great cormorants.

1955-57   Perf. 11
C41 AP20 100fr dp blue & indigo 21.00 11.00
a. Perf. 13 24.00 19.00
C42 AP20 200fr bl & blk 21.00 11.00
a. Perf. 13 300.00 150.00
C43 AP20 500fr gray & dk grn 37.50 30.00
Perf. 13
C44 AP20 1000fr dk bl grn & blk brn 90.00 60.00
a. Perf. 11 240.00 190.00
Nos. C41-C44 (4) 169.50 112.00

Issued: Perf. 11, 1/14/55; Perf. 13, 1957.

"From the Earth to the Moon" and Jules Verne AP21

1955, June 7   Unwmk.
C45 AP21 200fr dp blue & slate 25.00 25.00

50th anniv. of the death of Jules Verne.

Wedding Type of Regular Issue
1956, Apr. 19   Engr.
Portraits in Brown
C46 A99 100fr purple 1.00 .45
C47 A99 200fr carmine 1.25 .75
C48 A99 500fr gray violet 3.25 2.00
Nos. C46-C48 (3) 5.50 3.20

Wedding of Prince Rainier III to Grace Kelly, Apr. 19, 1956.

Nos. J45 and J54 Surcharged and Overprinted "Poste Aerienne" and bars

1956, Apr.   Perf. 11
C49 D6 100fr on 20fr 9.00 9.00
a. Double surcharge 475.00
C50 D7 100fr on 20fr 9.00 9.00
a. Double surcharge 475.00
b. Pair, #C49, C50 22.50 22.50

See footnote after No. 390.

Basilica of Lourdes AP23

200fr, Pope Pius X, underground basilica.

1958, May 15   Unwmk.   Perf. 13
C51 AP23 100fr dk bl, grn & gray 1.75 1.40
C52 AP23 200fr red brn & sepia 2.50 2.50

Centenary of the apparition of the Virgin Mary at Lourdes.

Prince Rainier III and Princess Grace — AP24

1959, May 16
C53 AP24 300fr dark purple 9.00 6.00
C54 AP24 500fr blue 13.00 10.50

MONACO

St. Dévote — AP25

1960, June 1   Engr.   Perf. 13
C55   AP25   2fr green, bl & vio   1.00   .65
C56   AP24   3fr dark purple   34.00   16.00
C57   AP24   5fr blue   34.00   24.00
C58   AP25   10fr green & brown   5.75   3.50
     Nos. C55-C58 (4)   74.75   44.15

1961, June 3
C59   AP25   3fr ultra, grn & gray ol   2.10   1.10
C60   AP25   5fr rose carmine   4.50   2.10

Europa Issue

Mercury over Map of Europe — AP26

1962, June 6   Unwmk.   Perf. 13
C61   AP26   2fr dk grn, sl grn & brn   1.50   1.00

Oceanographic Museum, Atom Symbol and Princes Albert I and Rainier III — AP27

1962, June 6
C62   AP27   10fr violet, bl & bis   5.50   6.00
Establishment of a scientific research center by agreement with the Intl. Atomic Energy Commission.

Roland Garros — AP28

1963, Dec. 12   Engr.   Perf. 13
C63   AP28   2fr dk blue & dk brn   1.25   1.25
50th anniversary of the first airplane crossing of the Mediterranean by Roland Garros (1888-1918).

Type of Regular Issue, 1964
Design: 5fr, Convair B-58 Hustler (New York-Paris in 3 hours, 19 minutes, 41 seconds, Maj. William R. Payne, USAF, 1961).

1964, May 22   Unwmk.   Perf. 13
C64   A151   5fr brown, blk & bl   2.75   2.75
1st airplane rally of Monte Carlo, 50th anniv.

Bobsledding — AP29

1964, Dec. 3   Engr.   Perf. 13
C65   AP29   5fr multicolored   2.50   2.50
9th Winter Olympic Games, Innsbruck, Austria, Jan. 29-Feb. 9, 1964.

ITU Type of Regular Issue
Design: 10fr, ITU Emblem and Monte Carlo television station on Mount Agel, vert.

1965, May 17   Engr.   Perf. 13
C66   A161   10fr bis brn, sl grn & bl   3.50   3.50

Princess Grace with Albert Alexander Louis, Caroline and Stephanie AP30

1966, Feb. 1   Engr.   Perf. 13
C67   AP30   3fr pur, red brn & Prus bl   2.00   1.25
Birth of Princess Stephanie, Feb. 1, 1965.

Opera House Interior — AP31

1966, June 1   Engr.   Perf. 13
C68   AP31   5fr Prus bl, bis & dk car rose   2.75   2.75
Centenary of founding of Monte Carlo.

Prince Rainier III and Princess Grace — AP32

1966-71   Engr.   Perf. 13
C69   AP32   2fr pink & slate   1.10   .40
C70   AP32   3fr emer & slate   2.10   .80
C71   AP32   5fr lt blue & slate   2.75   1.10
C72   AP32   10fr lemon & sl ('67)   4.00   3.50
C72A   AP32   20fr org & brn ('71)   42.50   35.00
     Nos. C69-C72A (5)   52.45   40.80
Issue dates: 10fr, Dec. 7, 1967; 20fr, Sept. 6, 1971. Others, Dec. 12, 1966.

Panhard-Phenix, 1895 — AP33

1967, Apr. 28   Engr.   Perf. 13
C73   AP33   3fr Prus blue & blk   2.75   2.75
25th Grand Prix of Monaco.

Olympic Games Type of Regular Issue

1968, Apr. 29   Engr.   Perf. 13
C74   A183   3fr Field hockey   1.25   1.25

Berlioz Monument, Monte Carlo — AP34

1969, Apr. 26   Engr.   Perf. 13
C75   AP34   2fr green, blk & ultra   .75   .75
Hector Berlioz (1803-69), French composer.

Napoleon, by Paul Delaroche AP35

1969, Apr. 26   Photo.   Perf. 12x13
C76   AP35   3fr multicolored   1.60   1.60
Bicentenary of birth of Napoleon I.

Horses, Prehistoric Drawing from Lascaux Cave — AP36

1970, Dec. 15   Engr.   Perf. 13
C77   AP36   3fr multicolored   4.25   3.00

Nativity Type of Regular Issue
Design: 3fr, Nativity, Flemish School, 15th century, vert.

1973, Nov. 12   Engr.   Perf. 12x13
C78   A243   3fr Prus green   2.75   2.25

Prince Rainier III — AP37

1974, Dec. 23   Engr.   Perf. 12½x13
C81   AP37   10fr dark purple   4.50   2.00
C82   AP37   15fr henna brown   6.00   4.00
C83   AP37   20fr ultra   10.00   5.50
     Nos. C81-C83 (3)   20.50   11.50
See Nos. 1994-1996.

Prince Rainier and Hereditary Prince Albert — AP38

1982-84   Engr.   Perf. 13x13½
C84   AP38   5fr deep violet   1.60   .60
C85   AP38   10fr red   5.00   1.10
C86   AP38   15fr dk blue grn   6.00   1.75
C87   AP38   20fr brt blue   7.00   2.25
C88   AP38   30fr brown ('84)   11.00   4.50
     Nos. C84-C88 (5)   30.60   10.20

AIR POST SEMI-POSTAL STAMPS

Catalogue values for unused stamps in this section are for Never Hinged items.

Types of 1942 Air Post Stamps Surcharged with New Values and Bars
Unwmk.

1945, Mar. 27   Engr.   Perf. 13
CB1   AP1   1fr + 4fr on 10fr rose red   .60   .60
CB2   AP2   1fr + 4fr on 15fr red brn   .60   .60
CB3   AP3   1fr + 4fr on 20fr sepia   .60   .60
CB4   AP4   1fr + 4fr on 50fr ultra   .60   .60
CB5   AP5   1fr + 4fr on 100fr brt red vio   .60   .60
     Nos. CB1-CB5 (5)   3.00   3.00
Surtax for the benefit of prisoners of war.

Franklin D. Roosevelt Type
1946, Dec. 13
CB6   A42   15fr + 10fr red   2.25   1.50
The surtax was for a fund to erect a monument in his honor.

1948 Olympic Type
1948, July
CB7   A48   5fr +5fr Rowing   9.00   9.00
CB8   A48   6fr +9fr Skiing   12.00   12.00
CB9   A48   10fr +15fr Tennis   17.50   17.50
CB10   A47   15fr +25fr Sailing   26.00   26.00
     Nos. CB7-CB10 (4)   64.50   64.50

Salmacis Nymph — SPAP4

Designs similar to regular issue.

1948, July
CB11   A50   5fr + 5fr blk bl   11.00   11.00
CB12   A51   6fr + 9fr dk grn   11.00   11.00
CB13   A52   10fr + 15fr crim   22.50   22.50
CB14   SPAP4   15fr + 25fr red brown   37.50   37.50
     Nos. CB11-CB14 (4)   82.00   82.00
François J. Bosio (1769-1845), sculptor.

POSTAGE DUE STAMPS

D1

Perf. 14x13½
1905-43   Unwmk.   Typo.
J1   D1   1c olive green   .45   .55
J2   D1   5c green   .45   .55
J3   D1   10c rose   .45   .55
J4   D1   10c brn ('09)   350.00   125.00
J5   D1   15c vio brn, *straw*   3.50   1.75
J6   D1   20c bis brn, *buff* ('26)   .35   .35
J7   D1   30c blue   .45   .55
J8   D1   40c red vio ('26)   .35   .35
J9   D1   50c brn, *org*   4.50   4.00
J10   D1   50c blue grn ('27)   .35   .35
J11   D1   60c gray blk ('26)   .35   .65
J12   D1   60c brt vio ('34)   21.00   27.50
J13   D1   1fr red brn, *straw* ('26)   .35   .25
J14   D1   2fr red org ('27)   1.00   1.50
J15   D1   3fr mag ('27)   1.00   1.50
J15A   D1   5fr ultra ('43)   .80   1.00
     Nos. J1-J15A (16)   385.35   166.40
For surcharge see No. J27.

Prince Albert I — D2

1910
J16   D2   1c olive green   25   45
J17   D2   10c light violet   .45   .60
J18   D2   30c bister   190.00   160.00
In January, 1917, regular postage stamps overprinted "T" in a triangle were used as postage due stamps.

Nos. J17 and J18 Surcharged

1918
J19   D2   20c on 10c lt vio   3.75   7.50
     a. Double surcharge   1,000.
J20   D2   40c on 30c bister   4.50   8.50

MONACO — MONGOLIA

1925-32
J21	D3	1c gray green	.40	.50
J22	D3	10c violet	.40	.55
J23	D3	30c bister	.50	.75
J24	D3	60c red	.70	.75
J25	D3	1fr lt bl ('32)	75.00	75.00
J26	D3	2fr dull red ('32)	75.00	75.00
		Nos. J21-J26 (6)	152.00	152.55

Nos. J25 and J26 have the numerals of value double-lined.

"Recouvrements" stamps were used to recover charges due on undelivered or refused mail which was returned to the sender.

No. J9 Surcharged

1925
J27	D1	1fr on 50c brn, *org*	.75	.50
a.		Double surcharge	750.00	

Catalogue values for unused stamps in this section, from this point to the end of the section, are for Never Hinged items.

1946-57 Engr. Perf. 14x13, 13
J28	D4	10c sepia	.25	.25
J29	D4	30c dark violet	.25	.25
J30	D4	50c deep blue	.25	.25
J31	D4	1fr dark green	.25	.25
J32	D4	2fr yellow brn	.25	.25
J33	D4	3fr brt red vio	.30	.30
J34	D4	4fr carmine	.45	.45
J35	D5	5fr chocolate	.35	.35
J36	D5	10fr deep ultra	.65	.65
J37	D5	20fr grnsh blue	.70	.70
J38	D5	50fr red vio & red ('50)	55.00	55.00
J38A	D5	100fr dk grn & red ('57)	12.00	12.00
		Nos. J28-J38A (12)	70.70	70.70

Sailing Vessel D6

S. S. United States D7

Early Postal Transport (D6): 1fr, Carrier pigeons. 3fr, Old railroad engine. 4fr, Old monoplane. 5fr, Steam automobile. 10fr, daVinci's flying machine. 20fr, Balloon. 50fr, Post rider. 100fr, Old mail coach.

Modern Postal Transport (D7): 1fr, Sikorsky S-51 helicopter. 3fr, Modern locomotive. 4fr, Comet airliner. 5fr, Sabre sports car. 10fr, Rocket. 20fr, Graf Zeppelin. 50fr, Motorcyclist. 100fr, Railroad mail car.

1953-54 Perf. 11
J39	D6	1fr dk grn & brt red ('54)	.25	.25
a.		Pair, Nos. J39, J48	.25	.25
J40	D6	2fr dp ultra & bl grn		
			.40	.40
a.		Pair, Nos. J40, J49		
J41	D6	3fr Prus grn & brn lake		
			.25	.25
a.		Pair, Nos. J41, J50	.40	.40
J42	D6	4fr dk brn & Prus grn		
			.25	.25
a.		Pair, Nos. J42, J51	.55	.55
J43	D6	5fr ultra & pur	.60	.60
			1.40	1.40
J44	D6	10fr dp ultra & dk bl		
			6.00	6.00
a.		Pair, Nos. J44, J53	15.00	15.00
J45	D6	20fr indigo & pur	4.00	4.00
			9.50	9.50

J46	D6	50fr red & dk brn	8.00	8.00
a.		Pair, Nos. J46, J55	19.00	19.00
J47	D6	100fr vio brn & dp grn	13.50	13.50
a.		Pair, Nos. J47, J56	32.50	32.50
J48	D7	1fr brt red & dk grn ('54)	.25	.25
J49	D7	2fr bl grn & dp ultra	.25	.25
J50	D7	3fr brn lake & Prus grn	.25	.25
J51	D7	4fr Prus grn & dk brn	.25	.25
J52	D7	5fr purple & ultra	.60	.60
J53	D7	10fr dk bl & dp ultra	6.00	6.00
J54	D7	20fr purple & indigo	4.00	4.00
J55	D7	50fr dk brn & red	8.00	8.00
J56	D7	100fr dp grn & vio brn	13.50	13.50
		Nos. J39-J56 (18)	66.20	66.20

Pairs se-tenant at the base.
For overprints see Nos. 371-390.

Felucca, 18th Century — D8

2c, Paddle steamer La Palmaria, 19th cent. 5c, Arrival of 1st train. 10c, Armed messenger, 15th-16th cent. 20c, Monaco-Nice courier, 18th cent. 30c, "Charles III," 1866. 50c, Courier on horseback, 17th cent. 1fr, Diligence, 19th cent.

1960-69 Engr. Perf. 13
J57	D8	1c bl grn, bis brn & bl	.25	.25
J58	D8	2c sl grn, sep & ultra	.25	.25
J59	D8	5c grnsh bl, gray & red brn	.25	.25
J60	D8	10c vio bl, blk & grn	.25	.25
J61	D8	20c blue, brn & grn	.90	.90
J62	D8	30c brn, brt grn & brt bl ('69)	1.40	1.40
J63	D8	50c dk bl, brn & sl grn	1.90	1.90
J64	D8	1fr sl grn, bl & brn	2.50	2.50
		Nos. J57-J64 (8)	7.70	7.70

Knight in Armor — D9

1980-83 Engr. Perf. 13
J65	D9	5c red & gray	.25	.25
J66	D9	10c salmon & red	.25	.25
J67	D9	15c violet & red	.25	.25
J68	D9	20c lt green & red	.25	.25
J69	D9	30c blue & red	.25	.25
J70	D9	40c lt brown & red	.25	.25
J71	D9	50c lilac & red	.35	.35
J72	D9	1fr black & blue	.55	.55
J73	D9	2fr dk brn & org ('82)	.85	.85
J74	D9	3fr sl bl & rose car ('83)	1.20	1.20
J75	D9	4fr red & dk grn ('82)	1.75	1.75
J76	D9	5fr magenta & brn ('83)	2.00	2.00
		Nos. J65-J76 (12)	8.20	8.20

Nos. J65-J76 printed in horizontal rows with princely coat of arms between stamps. Sold in strips of 3 only.
Issued: #J65-J72, 2/8; #J73, J75, 2/15; 3/J74, J76, 1/3.

Natl. Coat of Arms — D10

1985-86 Photo. Perf. 13x12½
J77	D10	5c multicolored	.25	.25
J78	D10	10c multicolored	.25	.25
J79	D10	15c multicolored	.40	.40
J80	D10	20c multicolored	.25	.25
J81	D10	30c multicolored	.25	.25
J82	D10	40c multicolored	.25	.25
J83	D10	50c multicolored ('86)	.25	.25
J84	D10	1fr multicolored ('86)	.35	.35
J85	D10	2fr multicolored ('86)	.55	.55
J86	D10	3fr multicolored	.95	.95
J87	D10	4fr multicolored ('86)	1.20	1.20
J88	D10	5fr multicolored	1.75	1.75
		Nos. J77-J88 (12)	6.55	6.55

See Nos. 1608-1609.

MONGOLIA

män-'gōl-yə

(Mongolian People's Republic)

(Outer Mongolia)

LOCATION — Central Asia, bounded on the north by Siberia, on the west by Sinkiang, on the south and east by China proper and Manchuria
GOVT. — Republic
AREA — 604,250 sq. mi.
POP. — 3,280,000 (2020 est.)
CAPITAL — Ulan Bator

Outer Mongolia, which had long been under Russian influence although nominally a dependency of China, voted at a plebescite on October 20, 1945, to sever all ties with China and become an independent nation. See Tannu Tuva.

100 Cents = 1 Dollar
100 Mung = 1 Tugrik (1926)

Catalogue values for unused stamps in this country are for Never Hinged items, beginning with Scott 149 in the regular postage section, Scott B1 in the semipostal section, Scott C1 in the airpost section, and Scott CB1 in the airpost semi-postal section.

Watermark

Wmk. 170 — Greek Border and Rosettes

Scepter of Indra — A1

1924 Litho. Unwmk. Perf. 10, 13½
Surface Tinted Paper
1	A1	1c multi, *bister*	20.00	20.00
2	A1	2c multi, *brnsh*	17.50	9.50
a.		Perf. 13½	82.50	70.00
3	A1	5c multi	70.00	42.50
a.		Perf. 10	82.50	60.00
4	A1	10c multi, *gray bl*	35.00	27.50
a.		Perf. 10	35.00	27.50
5	A1	20c multi, *gray*	47.50	30.00
6	A1	50c multi, *salmon*	70.00	42.50
7	A1	$1 multi, *yellow*	150.00	70.00
b.		Perf. 10	1,000.	300.00
		Nos. 1-7 (7)	410.00	242.00

These stamps vary in size from 19x25mm (1c) to 30x39mm ($1). They also differ in details of the design.
Errors of perforating and printing exist.
Some quantities of Nos. 1-2, 4-7 were defaced with horizontal perforation across the center. Value, set of six: $75.
The 5c exists perf 11½. Value, $500 unused, hinged, $200 used.

Revenue Stamps Handstamp

A2

Sizes: 1c to 20c: 22x36mm
50c, $1: 26x43½mm
$5: 30x45½mm

Overprinted in Violet
1926 Perf. 11
16	A2	1c blue	35.00	35.00
17	A2	2c orange	21.00	21.00
18	A2	5c plum	27.50	14.00
19	A2	10c green	21.00	21.00
20	A2	20c yel brn	35.00	27.50
21	A2	50c brn & ol grn	300.00	260.00
22	A2	$1 brn & salmon	550.00	475.00
23	A2	$5 red, yel & gray	650.00	—
		Nos. 16-23 (8)	1,640.	860.00

Black Overprint
16a	A2	1c blue	55.00	25.00
17a	A2	2c orange	42.50	27.50
18a	A2	5c plum	50.00	27.50
19a	A2	10c green	70.00	35.00
20a	A2	20c yellow brown	100.00	50.00
21a	A2	50c brown & olive grn	1,200.	325.00
22a	A2	$1 brown & salmon	600.00	400.00
23a	A2	$5 red, yellow & gray	500.00	
		Nos. 16a-22a (7)	2,118.	890.00

Red Overprint
16b	A2	1c blue		
17b	A2	2c orange		
18b	A2	5c plum		
19b	A2	10c green		
20b	A2	20c yellow brown		

The preceding handstamped overprints may be found inverted, double, etc. Counterfeits abound.
For overprints and surcharges see #48-61.

Soyombo

A3   A4

TYPE I — The pearl above the crescent is solid. The devices in the middle of the stamp are not outlined.
TYPE II — The pearl is open. The devices and panels are all outlined in black.

1926-29 Perf. 11
Type I
Size: 22x28mm
32	A3	5m lilac & blk	50.00	40.00
33	A3	20m blue & blk	125.00	120.00

Type II
Size: 22x29mm
34	A3	1m yellow & blk	8.00	5.00
35	A3	2m brn org & blk	10.00	5.00
36	A3	5m lilac & blk	12.00	6.00
37	A3	10m lt blue & blk	10.00	3.00
a.		Imperf, pair		
39	A3	25m yel grn & blk	20.00	6.00
a.		Imperf, pair	300.00	160.00

Size: 26x34mm
40	A3	40m lemon & blk	27.50	7.00
41	A3	50m buff & blk	40.00	9.50

Size: 28x37mm
42	A4	1t brown, grn & blk	80.00	17.50
43	A4	3t red, yel & blk	175.00	70.00
44	A4	5t brn vio, rose & blk	250.00	90.00
		Nos. 32-44 (12)	807.50	379.00

In 1929 a change was made in the perforating machine. Every fourth pin was removed, which left the perforation holes in groups of three with blank spaces between the groups. Nos. 44A-44D have only this interrupted perforation. Nos. 37 and 39 are found with both perforations.
For overprints and surcharges see #45-47.

Soyombo — A5

1929, July Interrupted Perf 11
44A	A5	5m lilac & black	35.00	20.00
44B	A5	10m lt grnish blue & black	100.00	65.00
a.		imperf, pair		
44C	A5	20m blue & black	55.00	50.00
b.		Horiz. pair, imperf btwn.		
44D	A5	25m yel grn & black	55.00	50.00
a.		imperf, pair		

See note after No. 44.

MONGOLIA 565

Nos. 34, 35, 40 Handstamped With New Values in Black

1930
45	A3	10m on 1m	55.00	55.00
46	A3	20m on 2m	75.00	70.00
47	A3	25m on 40m	90.00	90.00
		Nos. 45-47 (3)	220.00	215.00

Soyombo — A6

Violet Overprint, Handstamped
1931
48	A6	1c blue	50.00	50.00
a.		Blue overprint	110.00	60.00
49	A6	2c orange	35.00	12.00
50	A6	5c brown vio	40.00	12.00
a.		Blue overprint	90.00	40.00
51	A6	10c green	40.00	12.00
a.		Blue overprint	90.00	65.00
52	A6	20c bister brn	60.00	15.00
53	A6	50c brown & ol yel	275.00	125.00
54	A6	$1 brown & salmon	250.00	175.00
		Nos. 48-54 (7)	750.00	401.00

Soyombo — A7

Revenue Stamps Surcharged in Black, Red or Blue
1931
59	A7	5m on 5c brn vio (Bk)	55.00	25.00
a.		Inverted surcharge		50.00
b.		Imperf., pair	300.00	300.00
60	A7	10m on 10c grn (R)	70.00	35.00
a.		Inverted surcharge	125.00	65.00
b.		Imperf., pair	300.00	300.00
61	A7	20m on 20c bis brn (Bl)	85.00	50.00
a.		Inverted surcharge		75.00
b.		Imperf., pair	300.00	300.00
		Nos. 59-61 (3)	210.00	110.00

On Nos. 59-61, "Postage" is always diagonal, and may read up or down.

Weaver at Loom A8

Telegrapher A9

Sukhe Bator — A10

Lake and Mountains A11

Designs: 5m, Mongol at lathe. 10m, Government building, Ulan Bator. 15m, Young Mongolian revolutionary. 20m, Studying Latin alphabet. 25m, Mongolian soldier. 50m, Monument to Sukhe Bator. 3t, Sheep shearing. 5t, Camel caravan. 10t, Chasing wild horses.

1932 Perf. 12½x12 Photo. Wmk. 170
62	A8	1m brown	3.25	—
63	A9	2m red violet	3.25	—
64	A8	5m indigo	2.00	—
65	A8	10m dull green	2.00	—
66	A9	15m dp brown	2.00	—
67	A9	20m rose red	2.40	—
68	A9	25m dull violet	2.40	—
69	A10	40m gray black	2.00	—
70	A10	50m dull blue	2.40	—

Perf. 11x12
71	A11	1t dull green	2.75	—
72	A11	3t dull violet	5.50	—
73	A11	5t brown	19.50	—
74	A11	10t ultra	40.00	—
		Nos. 62-74 (13)	89.45	

Nos. 70-74 Handstamped With New Values in Black or Violet

1941 Black handstamp
74A	A11	5m on 5t	—	—
74B	A10	10m on 50m	—	—
74C	A11	10m on 10t	900.00	120.00
74D	A11	15m on 5t	125.00	—
74E	A11	20m on 1t	—	—
74F	A11	30m on 3t	—	—

Violet handstamp
74G	A11	5m on 5t	—	—
74H	A11	15m on 5t	—	—
74I	A11	20m on 1t	—	—
74J	A11	30m on 3t	—	—

Mongolian Man A12

Mongolian Woman A13

Soldier A14

Camel Caravan A15

Modern School A16

Arms of the Republic A17

Sukhe Bator — A18

Pasture Scene — A19

Paper with network as in italics
1943 Typo. Perf. 12½
75	A12	5m green, *green*	12.00	10.00
76	A13	10m dp blue, *lt bl*	60.00	33.00
77	A14	15m rose, *lt rose*	67.50	45.00
78	A15	20m org brn, *org*	97.50	82.50
79	A16	25m red brn, *buff*	97.50	97.50
80	A17	30m carmine, *red*	110.00	110.00
81	A18	45m purple, *mauve*	150.00	150.00
82	A19	60m dp green, *grn*	3,000.	3,000.
		Nos. 75-82 (8)	3,595.	3,528.

Marshal Kharloin Choibalsan — A21

1945 Unwmk. Perf. 12½
83	A21	1t black brown	60.00	70.00

Choibalsan A22

Victory Medal A24

Sukhe Bator and Choibalsan — A23

Designs: #86, Choibalsan as young man. #87, Choibalsan University, Ulan Bator. 1t, Anniversary medal. 2t, Sukhe Bator.

1946, July Photo. Perf. 12½
84	A22	30m olive bister	10.00	10.00
85	A23	50m dull purple	21.00	21.00
86	A24	60m black	22.50	22.50
87	A23	60m orange brown	37.50	37.50
88	A24	80m dk orange brn	35.00	35.00
89	A24	1t indigo	45.00	45.00
90	A24	2t deep brown	62.50	62.50
		Nos. 84-90 (7)	241.50	241.50

25th anniversary of independence.

New Housing — A25

School Children A26

Mongolian Arms and Flag — A27

Sukhe Dator — A28

Flags of Communist Countries A29

Lenin — A30

Designs: 15m, Altai Hotel. No. 94, State Store. No. 95, Like 30m. 25m, University. 40m, National Theater. 50m, Pedagogical Institute. 60m, Sukhe Bator monument. Sizes of type A25: Nos. 91, 93-94, 98-99, 32½x22mm. 25m, 55x26mm.

1951, July
91	A25	5m brn, *pink*	37.50	37.50
92	A26	10m dp bl, *pink*	45.00	45.00
93	A25	15m grn, *grnsh*	55.00	55.00
94	A25	20m red org	55.00	55.00
95	A27	20m dk bl & multi	55.00	55.00
96	A25	25m bl, *bluish*	55.00	55.00
97	A27	30m red & multi	55.00	55.00
98	A25	40m pur, *pink*	55.00	55.00
99	A25	50m brn, *grysh*	110.00	110.00
100	A28	60m brn blk	110.00	110.00
101	A29	1t multi	110.00	110.00
102	A28	2t dk brn & org brn	22.50	22.50
103	A30	3t multi	22.50	22.50
		Nos. 91-103 (13)	787.50	787.50

30th anniversary of independence.

Choibalsan A31

Choibalsan and Farmer A32

Choibalsan in uniform — A32a

Choibalsan and Sukhe Bator — A33

Designs: No. 108, 30m, Choibalsan and factory worker (47x33mm). 50m, Choibalsan and Young Pioneer. No. 112, 2t, Choibalsan in uniform.

MONGOLIA

1953, Dec.   Photo.   Perf. 12½
104	A31	15m dull blue	210.00	210.00
105	A32	15m dull green	210.00	210.00
106	A31	20m dull green	210.00	210.00
107	A32	20m sepia	210.00	210.00
108	A32	20m violet blue	210.00	210.00
109	A32	30m dark brown	210.00	210.00
110	A33	50m orange brn	210.00	210.00
111	A33	1t carmine rose	210.00	210.00
112	A32a	1t sepia	125.00	125.00
113	A32a	2t red	125.00	125.00
114	A33	3t sepia	20.00	20.00
115	A33	5t red	40.00	40.00
		Nos. 104-115 (12)	1,990.	1,990.

First anniversary of death of Marshal Karloin Choibalsan (1895-1952).

Arms of Mongolia — A34

1954, Mar.   Litho.   Perf. 12½
116	A34	10m carmine	25.00	15.00
117	A34	20m carmine	120.00	100.00
118	A34	30m carmine	25.00	17.50
119	A34	40m carmine	80.00	80.00
120	A34	60m carmine	25.00	20.00
		Nos. 116-120 (5)	275.00	232.50

Sukhe Bator and Choibalsan A35

Lake Hubsugul A36

Guard with Dog — A37

#122, Lenin Statue, Ulan Bator. 50m, Choibalsan University. 1t, Arms and flag of Mongolia.

1955, June   Photo.   Perf. 12½
121	A35	30m green	7.00	7.00
122	A35	30m orange ver	12.50	7.00
123	A36	30m brt blue	11.00	8.00
124	A37	40m dp red lilac	25.00	12.50
125	A36	50m ocher	25.00	15.00
126	A37	1t red & multi	45.00	45.00
		Nos. 121-126 (6)	125.50	94.50

35th anniversary of independence.

1955

Design: 2t, Lenin.

127	A35	2t bright blue	10.00	5.00

85th anniversary of birth of Lenin.

Flags of Communist Countries — A38

1955
128	A38	60m blue & multi	5.00	4.00

Fight for peace.

Arms of Mongolia — A39

1956   Photo.   Perf. 12½
129	A39	20m dark brown	7.00	4.50
130	A39	30m dark olive	9.00	7.00
131	A39	40m bright blue	11.00	9.00
132	A39	60m blue green	14.00	10.00
133	A39	1t deep carmine	22.50	17.50
		Nos. 129-133 (5)	63.50	48.00

Kremlin, Moscow, Train and Sukhe Bator Monument — A40

Design: 2t, Flags of Mongolia and USSR.

1956
134	A40	1t dk blue & multi	25.00	15.00
135	A40	2t red & multi	10.00	8.00

Establishment of railroad connection between Moscow and Ulan Bator.

Mongolian Arms and Flag A41

Hunter with Golden Eagle A42

Wrestlers — A43

Designs: No. 138, 3 children (33x26½mm).

1956, July   Typo.   Perf. 9
136	A41	30m blue	20.00	10.00
137	A42	30m pale brown	100.00	50.00
138	A42	60m orange	40.00	40.00
139	A43	60m yellow green	40.00	40.00
		Nos. 136-139 (4)	200.00	140.00

35th anniversary of independence.

Types A41 and A43 without "XXXV"

1958
140	A41	20m red	5.00	3.00
141	A43	50m brown, *pink*	12.50	3.00

Nos. 140-143 were issued both with and without gum.

Poster — A44

1958, Mar.   Litho.   Perf. 9
142	A44	30m maroon & salmon	5.00	4.00

13th Congress of Mongolian People's Party.

Globe and Dove — A45

1958, May
143	A45	60m deep blue	5.00	4.00

4th Congress of International Democratic Women's Federation, Vienna, June, 1958. Nos. 142-143 exist imperf.

Yak — A46

No. 144, Pelicans, vert. No. 145, Siberian ibex, vert. No. 147, Yak. No. 148, Camels.

1958, July   Typo.   Perf. 9
144	A46	30m lt blue	17.50	5.00
145	A46	30m brt green	5.00	5.00
146	A46	60m orange	5.00	5.00
147	A46	1t blue	5.00	5.00
148	A46	1t rose	5.00	5.00
		Nos. 144-148 (5)	37.50	25.00

Shades exist.

Canceled to Order
Some quantity of all issues not printed by the State Printing Works, Ulan Bator, except Nos. 296-303, were canceled to order. Used values are for c-t-o. Postally used stamps sell for considerably more.

Catalogue values for unused stamps in this section, from this point to the end of the section, are for Never Hinged items.

Stallion — A47

Designs: 5m, 40m, Goat. 10m, 30m, Ram. 15m, 60m, Stallion. 20m, 50m, Bull. 25m, 1t, Bactrian camel.

Perf. 10½x11½

1958, Nov. 11   Litho.
149	A47	5m yellow & brn	.25	.25
150	A47	10m lt grn & brn	.25	.25
151	A47	15m lilac & brn	.35	.25
152	A47	20m lt bl & brn	.35	.25
153	A47	25m rose & brn	.40	.25
154	A47	30m lilac & pur	.50	.25
155	A47	40m lt & dk green	.50	.25
156	A47	50m salmon & brn	.55	.25
157	A47	60m lt blue & ind	.95	.25
158	A47	1t yellow & brn	1.75	.50
		Nos. 149-158 (10)	5.85	2.75

Holy Flame (Tulaga) — A48

1959, May 1   Litho.   Perf. 9
159	A48	1t multi	4.50	3.50

See No. C36.

Archer A49

Mongol Sports: 5m, Taming wild horse. 10m, Wrestlers. 15m, Horseback riding. 25m, Horse race. 30m, Archers. 70m, Hunting wild horse. 80m, Proclaiming a champion.

1959, June 6   Photo.   Perf. 11
160	A49	5m multi	.25	.25
161	A49	10m multi	.25	.25
162	A49	15m multi	.25	.25
163	A49	20m multi	.25	.25
164	A49	25m multi	.40	.25
165	A49	30m multi	.55	.25
166	A49	70m multi	.75	.25
167	A49	80m multi	1.10	.55
		Nos. 160-167 (8)	3.80	2.30

Young Wrestlers A50

Youth Festival Emblem A51

Designs: 5m, Young musician, horiz. 20m, Boy on horseback. 25m, Two opera singers. 40m, Young Pioneers with flags, horiz.

Photo.; Litho. (30m)

1959, July   Perf. 12, 11 (30m)
168	A50	5m vio bl & rose car	.25	.25
169	A50	10m bl grn & brn	.25	.25
170	A50	20m claret & grn	.25	.25
171	A50	25m green & vio bl	.35	.25
172	A51	30m lil & lt bl	.35	.25
173	A50	40m green & pur	1.25	.50
		Nos. 168-173 (6)	2.70	1.75

Mongolian Youth Festival.
The 30m was printed by State Printing Works, Ulan Bator.
Issue dates: 30m, July 11; others July 10.

"Mongol" in Stylized Uighur Script — A52

"Mongol" in Various Scripts: 40m, Soyombo. 50m, Kalmuck. 60m, Square (Pagspa). 1t, Cyrillic.
Printed by State Printing Works, Ulan Bator.

1959, Sept. 1   Litho.   Perf. 11
Size: 29x42½mm
174	A52	30m black & multi	6.00	6.00
175	A52	40m black & multi	6.00	6.00
a.		Horiz. pair, imperf between and at right	150.00	
176	A52	50m black & multi	7.50	7.50
177	A52	60m black & multi	12.50	12.50

Size: 21x31mm
Perf. 9
178	A52	1t black & multi	16.00	16.00
		Nos. 174-178 (5)	48.00	48.00

1st Intl. Mongolian Language Congress.

Battle Emblem A53

Battle Monument A54

1959, Sept. 15   Photo.   Perf. 12½x12
179	A53	40m yellow, brn & car	.60	.25
180	A54	50m multicolored	.60	.25

Ha-lo-hsin (Khalka) River Battle, 20th anniv.

Congress Emblem — A55

Printed by State Printing Works, Ulan Bator.

1959, Dec.   Litho.   Perf. 11
181	A55	30m green	4.50	4.50

2nd meeting of rural economy cooperatives of Mongolia.

Sable A56

Pheasants — A57

MONGOLIA

Perf. 15, 11x13
1959, Dec. 21 — Photo.
182	A56	5m shown	.25	.25
183	A57	10m shown	.25	.25
184	A56	15m Muskrat	.25	.25
185	A57	20m Otter	.55	.25
186	A56	30m Argali	.55	.25
187	A57	50m Saigas	1.00	.35
188	A57	1t Musk deer	2.00	.75

Nos. 182-188 (7)   4.85   2.35

Lunik 3 — A58

50m, Lunik 3 with path around moon, horiz.

1959, Dec. 30   Photo.   Perf. 12
189	A58	30m violet & yel grn	.80	.80
190	A58	50m red, dk bl & grn	1.25	1.25

Lunik 3 Russian moon mission, Oct. 7, 1959.

Motherhood Badge — A59

Flower Emblem — A60

1960, Mar. 8   Perf. 11, 12½x11½
191	A59	40m blue & bister	.75	.25
192	A60	50m blue, grn & yel	1.10	.40

International Women's Day.

Lenin — A61

1960, Apr. 22   Photo.   Perf. 11½x12
193	A61	40m dk rose car	.60	.25
194	A61	50m rose violet	.80	.35

90th anniversary, birth of Lenin.

Jacob's-ladder — A62

1960, May 31   Perf. 11½x12
195	A62	5m Larkspur	.25	.25
196	A62	10m Tulips	.25	.25
197	A62	15m shown	.25	.25
198	A62	20m Globeflowers	.25	.25
199	A62	30m Bellflowers	.35	.25
200	A62	40m Parnassia	.55	.25
201	A62	50m Geranium	.80	.35
202	A62	1t Begonia	1.00	.65

Nos. 195-202 (8)   3.70   2.50

For overprints see Nos. 296-303.

Equestrian — A63

Running A64

15m, Diving. 20m, Wrestling. 30m, Hurdling. 50m, Gymnastics, women's. 70m, High jump. 1t, Discus, women's.

1960, Aug. 1   Perf. 15, 11
203	A63	5m shown	.25	.25
204	A64	10m shown	.25	.25
205	A63	15m multi	.25	.25
206	A64	20m multi	.25	.25
207	A63	30m multi	.40	.25
208	A64	50m multi	.50	.25
209	A63	70m multi	.60	.30
210	A64	1t multi	1.00	.40

Nos. 203-210 (8)   3.50   2.20

17th Olympic Games, Rome, 8/25-9/11.

Red Cross — A65

1960, Aug. 29   Perf. 11
211	A65	20m blue, red & yel	1.00	.40

Newspaper "Unen" (Truth) — A66

1960, Dec. 19   Perf. 12x11½
212	A66	20m red, yel & sl grn	.35	.25
213	A66	30m grn, yel & red	.45	.25

40th anniversary of Mongolian press.

Golden Orioles A67

Songbirds: 5m, Rose-colored starling. 10m, Hoopoe. 20m, Black-billed capercaillie. 50m, Oriental broad-billed roller. 70m, Tibetan sandgrouse. 1t, Mandarin duck.
Triangle points down on 5m, 50m, 70m, 1t.

1961, Jan. 3   Perf. 11
214	A67	5m multi	.50	.25
215	A67	10m multi	.60	.25
216	A67	15m multi	.70	.25
217	A67	20m multi	.90	.25
218	A67	50m multi	1.25	.45
219	A67	70m multi	1.60	.60
220	A67	1t multi	1.90	.85

Nos. 214-220 (7)   7.50   2.90

Federation Emblem — A68

Design: 30m, Worker and emblem, vert.

Perf. 11½x12, 12x11½
1961, Jan. 29   Photo.
221	A68	30m dk gray & rose	.35	.25
222	A68	50m ultra & red	.45	.25

World Federation of Trade Unions, 15th anniv.

Patrice Lumumba (1925-1961), Premier of Congo — A69

1961, Apr. 8   Perf. 11½x12
223	A69	30m brown	1.75	1.00
224	A69	50m violet gray	2.25	1.40

Bridge — A70

Designs: 10m, Shoemaker. 15m, Department Store, Ulan Bator. 20m, Government building. 30m, State Theater, Ulan Bator. 50m, Machinist. 1t, Modern and old buildings.

Sizes: 31½x21mm, 59x20mm (20m)

1961, Apr. 30   Perf. 11½x12, 15
225	A70	5m emerald	.25	.25
226	A70	10m blue	.25	.25
227	A70	15m rose red	.25	.25
228	A70	20m brown	.25	.25
229	A70	30m blue	.25	.25
230	A70	50m olive green	.35	.25
231	A70	1t violet	.60	.35

Nos. 225-231 (7)   2.20   1.85

40th anniversary of independence; modernization of Mongolia.

Yuri Gagarin and Globe A71

Designs: 20m, Gagarin with rocket, vert. 50m, Gagarin making parachute descent, vert. 1t, Gagarin wearing helmet, globe.

1961, May 31   Perf. 15
232	A71	20m multi	.50	.25
233	A71	30m multi	.80	.40
234	A71	50m multi	1.00	.60
235	A71	1t multi	1.50	.65

Nos. 232-235 (4)   3.80   1.90

Yuri A. Gagarin, 1st man in space, 4/12/61.

Postman on Reindeer — A72

15m, #241a, Postman on camel. 10m, 20m, Postman with yaks. 25m, #241c, Postman with ship. 30m, 50m, Diesel train.

1961, June 5   Perf. 15
236	A72	10m multi	.25	.25
237	A72	15m multi	.25	.25
238	A72	20m multi	.25	.25
239	A72	25m multi	.25	.25
240	A72	30m multi	4.00	2.00

Nos. 236-240,C1-C3 (8)   7.00   3.90

Souvenir Sheet
Perf. 11

241		Sheet of 4	—	—
a.		A72 5m light blue & brown	—	—
b.		A72 10m green, brown & blue	—	—
c.		A72 15m green, violet & brown	—	—
d.		A72 25m violet, green & black	—	—

40th anniv. of independence; postal modernization. See No. C4b for 25m, perf. 11.

Souvenir Sheet

Ornamental Column — A73

1961, June 20   Perf. 12
242	A73	Sheet of 2 + label	—	—
a.		2t blue, red & gold	—	—

40th anniversary of the Mongolian People's Revolution. No. 242 contains two No. 242a and label, imperf. between.

Herdsman and Oxen — A74

Designs: Herdsmen and domestic animals (except 1t and No. 252a).

1961, July 10   Perf. 13
243	A74	5m Rams	.25	.25
244	A74	10m shown	.25	.25
245	A74	15m Camels	.25	.25
246	A74	20m Pigs and geese	.30	.25
247	A74	25m Angora goats	.30	.25
248	A74	30m Horses	.30	.25
249	A74	40m Sheep	.35	.25
250	A74	50m Cows	.50	.25
251	A74	1t Combine harvester	.75	.50

Nos. 243-251 (9)   3.25   2.50

Souvenir Sheets
Perf. 12

252		Sheet of 3	—	—
a.		A74 5m Combine harvester	—	—
b.		A74 15m Angora goats	—	—
c.		A74 40m Oxen	—	—
253		Sheet of 3	—	—
a.		A74 10m Pigs and geese	—	—
b.		A74 20m Horses	—	—
c.		A74 50m Cows	—	—
254		Sheet of 3	—	—
a.		A74 25m Camels	—	—
b.		A74 50m Rams	—	—
c.		A74 1t Sheep	—	—

40th anniversary of independence. Nos. 252-254 each contain 3 stamps imperf. between.

Horseback Riders A75

5m, Young wrestlers & instructor. 15m, Camel & pony riders. 20m, Falconers. 30m, Skier. 50m, Archers. 1t, Male dancers.

1961, Aug. 10   Perf. 11
255	A75	5m multi	.25	.25
256	A75	10m multi	.25	.25
257	A75	15m multi	.25	.25
258	A75	20m multi	.80	.25
259	A75	30m multi	.35	.25
260	A75	50m multi	.45	.35
261	A75	1t multi	.75	.50

Nos. 255-261 (7)   3.10   2.20

Independence, 40th anniv.; Mongolian youth sports.

Statue of Sukhe Bator — A76

MONGOLIA

Designs: 5m, Mongol youth. 10m, Mongol chieftain. 20m, Singer. 30m, Dancer. 50m, Dombra player. 70m, Musicians. 1t, Gymnast. 5m, 10m, 70m, 1t, horiz.

Perf. 12x11½, 11½x12
1961, Sept. 16
262	A76	5m brt grn & red lil	.25	.25
263	A76	10m red & dk bl	.25	.25
264	A76	15m bl & lt brn	.25	.25
265	A76	20m pur & brt grn	.25	.25
266	A76	30m vio bl & car	.30	.25
267	A76	50m ol & vio	.50	.25
268	A76	70m brt lil rose & ol	.60	.35
269	A76	1t dk bl & ver	1.10	.75
	Nos. 262-269 (8)		3.50	2.60

40th anniv. of independence; Mongolian culture.

Arms of Mongolia — A77

1961, Nov. 17 **Perf. 11½x12**
270	A77	5m multi	.25	.25
271	A77	10m multi	.25	.25
272	A77	15m multi	.25	.25
273	A77	20m multi	.25	.25
274	A77	30m multi	.25	.25
275	A77	50m multi	.35	.25
276	A77	70m multi	.45	.35
277	A77	1t multi	.50	.45
	Nos. 270-277 (8)		2.55	2.30

For surcharges see Nos. 2144A, 2302D.

Congress Emblem — A78

1961, Dec. 4 **Litho.** **Perf. 11½**
278	A78	30m vio bl, yel & red	.30	.25
279	A78	50m brn, yel & red	.40	.30

5th World Congress of Trade Unions, Moscow, Dec. 4-16.

UN Emblem and Arms of Mongolia A79

10m, Globe, map of Mongolia, dove. 50m, Flags of UN & Mongolia. 60m, UN Headquarters, New York. Parliament, Ulan Bator. 70m, UN assembly, UN & Mongolian flags.

1962, Mar. 15 **Photo.** **Perf. 11**
280	A79	10m gold & multi	.25	.25
281	A79	30m gold & multi	.25	.25
282	A79	50m gold & multi	.50	.30
283	A79	60m gold & multi	.60	.30
284	A79	70m gold & multi	.65	.45
	Nos. 280-284 (5)		2.25	1.55

Mongolia's admission to UN.

Soccer A80

Designs: 10m, Soccer ball, globe and flags. 30m, Soccer players, globe and ball. 60m, Goalkeeper. 70m, Stadium.

1962, May 15 **Litho.** **Perf. 10½**
285	A80	10m multi	.25	.25
286	A80	30m multi	.30	.25
287	A80	40m multi	.40	.25
288	A80	60m multi	.50	.35
289	A80	70m multi	.70	.35
	Nos. 285-289 (5)		2.15	1.45

World Soccer Championship, Chile, 5/30-6/17.

D. Natsagdorji — A81

1962, May 15 **Photo.** **Perf. 15x14½**
290	A81	30m brown	.30	.25
291	A81	50m bluish grn	.40	.25

Mongolian writers' congress. For overprints see Nos. 430-431.

Solidarity Emblem — A82

1962, May 22 **Litho.** **Perf. 11½x10½**
292	A82	20m yel grn & multi	.30	.25
293	A82	30m bl & multi	.40	.25

Afro-Asian Peoples' solidarity.

Flags of USSR and Mongolia — A83

Perf. 11½x10½
1962, June 25 **Litho.**
294	A83	30m brn & multi	.30	.25
295	A83	50m vio bl & multi	.40	.25

Mongol-Soviet friendship.

Nos. 195-202 Overprinted

1962, July 20 **Photo.** **Perf. 11½x12**
296	A62	5m multi	.60	.30
297	A62	10m multi	.65	.35
298	A62	15m multi	.75	.35
299	A62	20m multi	.75	.35
300	A62	30m multi	.80	.50
301	A62	40m multi	.90	.50
302	A62	50m multi	1.10	.50
303	A62	1t multi	1.75	.90
	Nos. 296-303 (8)		7.30	3.75

WHO drive to eradicate malaria.

Military Field Emblem — A84

Designs: 30m, Tablets with inscriptions. 50m, Stone column. 60m, Genghis Khan.

1962, July 20 **Perf. 11½x12**
304	A84	20m blue & multi	1.50	1.50
305	A84	30m red & multi	1.50	1.50
306	A84	50m pink, brn & blk	3.50	3.50
307	A84	60m blue & multi	3.50	3.50
	Nos. 304-307 (4)		10.00	10.00

Genghis Khan (1162-1227), Mongol conqueror.
For overprints see Nos. 1846-1849. For surcharge, see No. 2378A.

River Perch — A85

10m, Burbot. 15m, Arctic grayling. 20m, Shorthorn sculpin. 30m, Marine zander. 50m, Siberian sturgeon. 70m, Waleck's chub minnow. 1.50t, Cottocomephorid.

1962, Dec. 28 **Perf. 11**
308	A85	5m shown	.25	.25
309	A85	10m multi	.25	.25
310	A85	15m multi	.25	.25
311	A85	20m multi	.35	.25
312	A85	30m multi	.50	.25
313	A85	50m multi	.70	.30
314	A85	70m multi	1.00	.50
315	A85	1.50t multi	1.75	.75
	Nos. 308-315 (8)		5.05	2.80

Sukhe Bator (1893-1923), National Hero — A86

1963, Feb. 2 **Photo.** **Perf. 11½x12**
316	A86	30m blue	.25	.25
317	A86	60m rose car	.40	.25

Laika and Rocket A87

Designs: 15m, Rocket launching, vert. 25m, Lunik 2, vert. 70m, Andrian G. Nikolayev and Pavel R. Popovich. 1t, Mars rocket.

1963, Apr. 1 **Litho.** **Perf. 12½x12**
Size: 46x32mm
318	A87	5m multicolored	.25	.25

Size: 20x68mm
319	A87	15m multicolored	.25	.25
320	A87	25m multicolored	.40	.25

Size: 46x32mm
321	A87	70m multicolored	.75	.30
322	A87	1t multicolored	1.00	.60
	Nos. 318-322 (5)		2.65	1.65

Soviet space explorations.

Blood Transfusion — A88

20m, Packing Red Cross parcels. 50m, Vaccination. 60m, Ambulance service. 1.30t, Centenary emblem.

1963, Aug. 15 **Perf. 10½**
323	A88	20m multi	.25	.25
324	A88	30m shown	.25	.25
325	A88	50m multi	.50	.30
326	A88	60m multi	.60	.40
327	A88	1.30t multi	.90	.50
	Nos. 323-327 (5)		2.50	1.70

Red Cross centenary.

Karl Marx — A89

1963, Sept. 16 **Photo.** **Perf. 11½x12**
328	A89	30m blue	.30	.25
329	A89	60m dk car rose	.40	.30

145th anniversary of birth of Karl Marx.

Mongolian Woman — A90

1963, Sept. 26
330	A90	30m blue & multi	.50	.25

5th Intl. Women's Cong., Moscow, 6/24-29.

Inachis — A91

Mongolian butterflies: 10m, Gonepteryxrhamni. 15m, Aglais urticae. 20m, Parnassius apollo. 30m, Papilio machaon. 60m, Agrodiaetus damon. 1t, Limenitis populi.

1963, Nov. 7 **Litho.** **Perf. 11½**
331	A91	5m shown	.45	.25
332	A91	10m multi	.50	.25
333	A91	15m multi	.70	.25
334	A91	20m multi	.75	.25
335	A91	30m multi	1.20	.25
336	A91	60m multi	1.75	.50
337	A91	1t multi	2.25	.75
	Nos. 331-337 (7)		7.60	2.50

UNESCO Emblem, Globe and Scales — A92

1963, Dec. 10 **Photo.** **Perf. 12**
338	A92	30m multicolored	.40	.25
339	A92	60m multicolored	.60	.40

Universal Declaration of Human Rights, 15th anniversary.

Mushrooms — A93

Designs: 5m, Coprinus Comatus. 10m, Lactarius torminosus. 15m, Psalliota campestris. 20m, Russula delica. 30m, Ixocomus granulatus. 50m, Lactarius scrobiculatus. 70m, Lactarius deliciosus. 1t, Ixocomus variegatus.

1964, Jan. 1 **Litho.** **Perf. 10½**
340	A93	5m shown	.50	.25
341	A93	10m multi	.75	.40
342	A93	15m multi	.95	.50
343	A93	20m multi	1.10	.60
344	A93	30m multi	1.25	.60
345	A93	50m multi	1.50	.70

MONGOLIA

346	A93	70m multi	1.75	.90
347	A93	1t multi	2.25	2.10
		Nos. 340-347 (8)	10.05	6.05

Souvenir Sheet

Skier A94

1964, Feb. 12 Photo. Perf. 12x11½

348	A94	4t gray	4.50	4.50

9th Winter Olympic Games, Innsbruck, Jan. 29-Feb. 9.

Lenin — A95

1964 Photo. Perf. 11½x12

349	A95	30m salmon & multi	.60	.25
350	A95	50m blue & multi	.80	.40

60th anniversary of Communist Party. Nos. 349-350 printed with alternating label showing Lenin quotation.

Javelin A96

351	A96	5m multi	.25	.25
352	A96	10m shown	.25	.25
353	A96	15m multi	.25	.25
354	A96	20m multi	.25	.25
355	A96	30m multi	.40	.25
356	A96	50m multi	.60	.25
357	A96	60m multi	.80	.30
358	A96	1t multi	1.00	.60
		Nos. 351-358 (8)	3.60	2.40

1964, Apr. 30 Litho. Perf. 10½

5m, Gymnastics, women's. 15m, Wrestling. 20m, Running, women's. 30m, Equestrian. 50m, Diving, women's. 60m, Bicycling. 1t, Olympic Games emblem. 4t, Wrestling.

Souvenir Sheet

Perf. 12x11½

359	A96	4t multi	3.50	3.50

18th Olympic Games, Tokyo, Oct. 10-25. No. 359 contains one horizontal stamp, 37x27½mm. Issued Sept. 1.

Congress Emblem A97

1964, Sept. 30 Photo. Perf. 11

360	A97	30m multicolored	.40	.30

4th Mongolian Women's Congress.

Lunik 1 — A98

Space Research: 10m, Vostok 1 and 2. 15m, Tiros weather satellite, vert. 20m, Cosmos circling earth, vert. 30m, Mars probe, vert. 60m, Luna 4, vert. 80m, Echo 2. 1t, Radar and rockets.

1964, Oct. 30

361	A98	5m multicolored	.25	.25
362	A98	10m multicolored	.25	.25
363	A98	15m multicolored	.25	.25
364	A98	20m multicolored	.30	.25
365	A98	30m multicolored	.40	.30
366	A98	60m multicolored	.50	.30
367	A98	80m multicolored	.75	.40
368	A98	1t multicolored	1.00	.45
		Nos. 361-368 (8)	3.70	2.45

Rider Carrying Flag — A99

1964, Nov. 26 Photo. Perf. 11½x12

369	A99	25m multicolored	.40	.25
370	A99	50m multicolored	.50	.40

40th anniversary of Mongolian constitution.

Weather Balloon — A100

Designs: 5m, Oceanographic exploration. 60m, Northern lights and polar bears. 80m, Geomagnetism. 1t, I.Q.S.Y. emblem and Mercator map.

1965, May 15 Photo. Perf. 13½

371	A100	5m gray & multi	.25	.25
372	A100	10m grn & multi	.25	.30
373	A100	60m blue, blk & pink	.70	.25
374	A100	80m citron & multi	.85	.35
375	A100	1t brt green & multi	1.25	.60
		Nos. 371-375,C6-C8 (8)	7.10	2.75

International Quiet Sun Year.

Horses A101

Designs: Mares and Foals.

1965, Aug. 25 Perf. 11

376	A101	5m shown	.25	.25
377	A101	10m Falconers	.25	.25
378	A101	15m Taming wild horse	.25	.25
379	A101	20m Horse race	.30	.25
380	A101	30m Hurdles	.45	.30
381	A101	60m Wolf hunt	.60	.35
382	A101	80m Milking a mare	.85	.40
383	A101	1t Mare and foal	1.10	.50
		Nos. 376-383 (8)	4.05	2.55

Girl Holding Lambs A102

10m, Boy and girl drummers. 20m, Camp fire. 30m, Wrestlers. 50m, Emblem.

1965, Oct. 10 Photo. Perf. 11

384	A102	5m shown	.25	.25
385	A102	10m multi	.25	.25
386	A102	20m multi	.30	.25
387	A102	30m multi	.40	.30
388	A102	50m multi	.70	.50
		Nos. 384-388 (5)	1.90	1.55

40th anniv. of Mongolian Youth Org.

Chinese Perch A103

1965, Nov. 25

389	A103	5m shown	.25	.25
390	A103	10m Lenok trout	.25	.25
391	A103	15m Siberian sturgeon	.25	.25
392	A103	20m Amur salmon	.40	.25
393	A103	30m Bagrid catfish	.60	.25
394	A103	60m Siluri catfish	.95	.25
395	A103	80m Northern pike	1.10	.45
396	A103	1t River perch	1.50	.65
		Nos. 389-396 (8)	5.30	2.60

Marx and Lenin — A104

1965, Dec. 15 Perf. 11½x12

397	A104	10m red & blk	.35	.25

6th Conference of Postal Ministers of Communist Countries, Peking, June 21-July 15.

Sable A105

10m, Fox. 15m, Otter, vert. 20m, Cheetah, vert. 30m, Pallas's cat. 60m, Stone marten. 80m, Ermine, vert. 1t, Woman in mink coat, vert.

1966, Feb. 15 Photo. Perf. 12½

398	A105	5m shown	.25	.25
399	A105	10m multi	.25	.25
400	A105	15m multi	.30	.25
401	A105	20m multi	.30	.25
402	A105	30m multi	.40	.25
403	A105	60m multi	.60	.30
404	A105	80m multi	.80	.40
405	A105	1t multi	1.25	.75
		Nos. 398-405 (8)	4.15	2.70

Opening of WHO Headquarters, Geneva — A106

1966, May 3 Photo. Perf. 12x11½

406	A106	30m bl grn, bl & gold	.30	.25
407	A106	50m red, bl & gold	.50	.30

For overprints see Nos. 483-484.

Soccer A107

Designs: 30m, 60m, 80m, Various soccer plays. 1t, British flag and World Soccer Cup emblem. 4t, Wembley Stadium, horiz.

1966, May 31 Photo. Perf. 11

408	A107	10m multicolored	.25	.25
409	A107	30m multicolored	.25	.25
410	A107	60m multicolored	.35	.30
411	A107	80m multicolored	.55	.40
412	A107	1t multicolored	.75	.50
		Nos. 408-412 (5)	2.15	1.70

Souvenir Sheet

Perf. 12½, Imperf.

413	A107	4t gray & brown	2.75	2.00

World Soccer Championship for Jules Rimet Cup, Wembley, England, July 11-30. No. 413 contains one stamp 61x83mm.

Sukhe Bator, Parliament Building, Ulan Bator — A108

1966, June 7 Litho. Perf. 12x12½

414	A108	30m red, bl & brn	.40	.25

15th Congress of Mongolian Communist Party.

Wrestling — A109

Designs: Various wrestling holds.

1966, June 15 Photo. Perf. 11½x12

415	A109	10m multicolored	.25	.25
416	A109	30m multicolored	.25	.25
417	A109	60m multicolored	.40	.25
418	A109	80m multicolored	.45	.25
419	A109	1t multicolored	.60	.25
		Nos. 415-419 (5)	1.95	1.25

World Wrestling Championship, Toledo, Spain.

Emblem and Map of Mongolia A110

Sukhe Bator, Grain and Factories A111

Perf. 11½x12, 12x11½

1966, July 11 Litho.

420	A110	30m red & multi	1.10	.60
421	A111	50m red & multi	2.50	.75

45th anniversary of independence. For overprints see Nos. 552-553.

Lilium Tenuifolium A112

5m, Physochlaena physaloides. 10m, Allium polyrrchizum. 20m, Thermopsis lanceolata. 30m, Amygdalus mongolica. 60m, Caryopteris mongolica. 80m, Piptanthus mongolicus. 1t, Iris bungei.

1966, Oct. 15 Photo. Perf. 12x11½

422	A112	5m multi	.25	.25
423	A112	10m multi	.30	.25
424	A112	15m shown	.40	.25
425	A112	20m multi	.50	.25
426	A112	30m multi	.60	.30
427	A112	60m multi	.85	.40
428	A112	80m multi	1.00	.55
429	A112	1t multi	1.25	.75
		Nos. 422-429 (8)	5.15	3.00

**Nos. 290-291 Overprinted:
"1906/1966"**

1966, Oct. 26 Photo. Perf. 15x14½

430	A81	30m brown	8.00	8.00
431	A81	50m bluish grn	10.00	10.00

60th anniv. of birth of D. Natsagdorji, writer. 50m exists double, one inverted.

MONGOLIA

Children's Day — A113

10m, Child with dove. 15m, Children with reindeer. 20m, Boys wrestling, vert. 30m, Horseback riding. 60m, Children riding camel, vert. 80m, Child with sheep. 1t, Boy archer, vert.

1966, Dec. 2 Perf. 11½x12, 12x11½
432	A113	10m shown	.25	.25
433	A113	15m multi	.25	.25
434	A113	20m multi	.30	.25
435	A113	30m multi	.40	.25
436	A113	60m multi	.60	.25
437	A113	80m multi	.80	.30
438	A113	1t multi	1.00	.40
		Nos. 432-438 (7)	3.60	1.95

Proton 1 — A114

Perf. 11½x12½, 12½x11½
1966, Dec. 28 Photo.
439	A114	5m Vostok 2, vert.	.25	.25
440	A114	10m shown	.25	.25
441	A114	15m Telstar 1, vert.	.25	.25
442	A114	20m Molniya 1, vert.	.30	.25
443	A114	30m Syncom 3, vert.	.40	.30
444	A114	60m Luna 9	.50	.30
445	A114	80m Luna 12, vert.	.60	.40
446	A114	1t Mariner 4	.80	.50
		Nos. 439-446 (8)	3.35	2.50

Space exploration.

Tarbosaurus A115

1967, Mar. 31 Perf. 12x11½
447	A115	5m shown	.35	.25
448	A115	10m Talarurus	.40	.25
449	A115	15m Proceratops	.45	.25
450	A115	20m Indricotherium	.45	.25
451	A115	30m Saurolophus	.70	.30
452	A115	60m Mastodon	1.60	.40
453	A115	80m Mongolotherium	1.75	.60
454	A115	1t Mammoth	2.00	.90
		Nos. 447-454 (8)	7.70	3.20

Prehistoric animals.

A116

Congress emblem.

1967, June 9 Litho. Perf. 12
455	A116	30m lt blue & multi	.40	.25
456	A116	50m pink & multi	.60	.40

9th Youth Festival for Peace and Friendship, Sofia.

A117

Design: 40m, Sukhe Bator and soldiers. 60m, Lenin and soldiers.

1967, Oct. 25 Litho. Perf. 11½x12
457	A117	40m red & multi	.45	.25
458	A117	60m red & multi	.75	.35

Russian October Revolution, 50th anniv.

Ice Hockey and Olympic Rings — A118

5m, Figure skating. 10m, Speed skating. 20m, Ski jump. 30m, Bobsledding. 60m, Figure skating, pair. 80m, Slalom. 4t, Women's figure skating.

1967, Dec. 29 Perf. 12x12½
459	A118	5m multi	.25	.25
460	A118	10m multi	.25	.25
461	A118	15m shown	.25	.25
462	A118	20m multi	.30	.25
463	A118	30m multi	.45	.25
464	A118	60m multi	.65	.30
465	A118	80m multi	.80	.40
		Nos. 459-465 (7)	2.95	1.95

Souvenir Sheet
Perf. 12
466	A118	4t multi	3.00	3.00

10th Winter Olympic Games, Grenoble, France, Feb. 6-18.

Bactrian Camels — A119

1968, Jan. 15 Photo. Perf. 12
467	A119	5m shown	.25	.25
468	A119	10m Yak	.25	.25
469	A119	15m Lamb	.25	.25
470	A119	20m Foal	.35	.25
471	A119	30m Calf	.40	.25
472	A119	60m Bison	.55	.25
473	A119	80m Roe deer, horiz.	.80	.35
474	A119	1t Reindeer	1.40	.45
		Nos. 467-474 (8)	4.25	2.30

Young animals.

Black Currants A120

Berries: 5m, Rosa acicularis. 15m, Gooseberries. 20m, Malus. 30m, Strawberries. 60m, Ribes altissimum. 80m, Blueberries. 1t, Hippophae rhamnoides.

Lithographed & Engraved
1968, Feb. 15
475	A120	5m blue & ultra	.25	.25
476	A120	10m buff & brn	.25	.25
477	A120	15m lt grn & grn	.25	.25
478	A120	20m yel & red	.25	.25
479	A120	30m pink & car	.40	.25
480	A120	60m sal & org brn	.45	.25
481	A120	80m pale & dl bl	.80	.30
482	A120	1t lt yel & red	.95	.45
		Nos. 475-482 (8)	3.60	2.25

Nos. 406-407 Overprinted

1968, Apr. 16 Photo. Perf. 12x11½
483	A106	30m bl grn, bl & gold	6.00	4.00
484	A106	50m red, blue & gold	6.00	4.00

WHO, 20th anniversary.

Human Rights Flame — A121

1968, June 20 Litho. Perf. 12
485	A121	30m turq & vio bl	.50	.25

International Human Rights Year.

"Das Kapital," by Karl Marx — A122

Design: 50m, Karl Marx.

1968, July 1 Litho. Perf. 12
486	A122	30m blue & multi	.30	.25
487	A122	50m red & multi	.50	.25

Karl Marx (1818-1883).

Artist, by A. Sangatzohyo A123

Paintings: 10m, On Remote Roads, by Sangatzohyo. 15m, Camel calf, by B. Avarzad. 20m, Milk, by Avarzad. 30m, The Bowman, by B. Gombosuren. 80m, Girl Sitting on Yak, by Sangatzohyo. 1.40t, Cagan Dara Eke, by Janaivajara. 4t, Meeting, by Sangatzohyo, horiz.

1968, July 11 Litho. Perf. 12
488	A123	5m brown & multi	.25	.25
489	A123	10m brown & multi	.25	.25
490	A123	15m brown & multi	.25	.25
491	A123	20m brown & multi	.40	.25
492	A123	30m brown & multi	.55	.25
493	A123	80m brown & multi	1.10	.55
494	A123	1.40t brown & multi	2.10	1.00
		Nos. 488-494 (7)	4.90	2.90

Miniature Sheets
Perf. 11½, Imperf.
495	A123	4t brown & multi	5.00	5.00

Paintings from national museum, Ulan Bator. #495 contains one 54x84mm stamp.

Volleyball A124

Olympic Rings and: 10m, Wrestling. 15m, Bicycling. 20m, Javelin, women's. 30m, Soccer. 60m, Running. 80m, Gymnastics, women's. 1t, Weight lifting. 4t, Equestrian.

1968, Sept. 1 Litho. Perf. 12
496	A124	5m multicolored	.25	.25
497	A124	10m multicolored	.25	.25
498	A124	15m multicolored	.25	.25
499	A124	20m multicolored	.25	.25
500	A124	30m multicolored	.25	.25
501	A124	60m multicolored	.40	.30
502	A124	80m multicolored	.60	.30
503	A124	1t multicolored	.80	.40
		Nos. 496-503 (8)	3.05	2.30

Souvenir Sheets
Perf. 11½, Imperf.
504	A124	4t orange & multi	3.00	3.00

19th Olympic Games, Mexico City, Oct. 12-27. #504 contains one 52x44mm stamp.

A125

Hammer, spade & cogwheel.

1968, Sept. 17 Litho. Perf. 11½
505	A125	50m blue & vermilion	.40	.25

Industrial development in town of Darhan.

A126

1968, Nov. 6 Litho. Perf. 12
506	A126	60m turquoise & sepia	.40	.25

Maxim Gorki (1868-1936), Russian writer.

Madonna and Child, by Boltraffio — A127

Paintings: 10m, St. Roch Healed by an Angel, by Brescia. 15m, Madonna and Child with St. Anne, by Macchietti. 20m, St. John on Patmos, by Cano. 30m, Lady with Viola da Gamba, by Kupetzky. 80m, Boy, by Amerling. 1.40t, Death of Adonis, by Furini. 4t, Portrait of a Lady, by Renoir.

1968, Nov. 20 Litho. Perf. 12
507	A127	5m gray & multi	.25	.25
508	A127	10m gray & multi	.25	.25
509	A127	15m gray & multi	.30	.25
510	A127	20m gray & multi	.35	.25
511	A127	30m gray & multi	.45	.30
512	A127	80m gray & multi	.85	.40
513	A127	1.40t gray & multi	1.25	.75
		Nos. 507-513 (7)	3.70	2.45

Miniature Sheet
514	A127	4t gray & multi	4.00	4.00

UNESCO, 22nd anniv.

Jesse Owens, US — A128

Olympic Gold Medal Winners: 5m, Paavo Nurmi, Finland. 15m, Fanny Blankers-Koen, Netherlands. 20m, Laszlo Papp, Hungary. 30m, Wilma Rudolph, US. 60m, Boris Shakhlin, USSR. 80m, Donald Schollander, US. 1t Akinori Nakayama, Japan. 4t, Jigjidin Munkhbat, Mongolia.

1969, Mar. 25 Litho. Perf. 12
515	A128	5m multicolored	.25	.25
516	A128	10m multicolored	.25	.25
517	A128	15m multicolored	.25	.25
518	A128	20m multicolored	.25	.25
519	A128	30m multicolored	.25	.25
520	A128	60m multicolored	.50	.30
521	A128	80m multicolored	.65	.35
522	A128	1t multicolored	.80	.40
		Nos. 515-522 (8)	3.20	2.30

Souvenir Sheet
523	A128	4t green & multi	3.50	3.50

MONGOLIA

Bayit Woman — A129

Regional Costumes: 10m, Torgut man. 15m, Dzakhachin woman. 20m, Khalkha woman. 30m, Dariganga woman. 60m, Mingat woman. 80m, Khalkha man. 1t, Bargut woman.

1969, Apr. 20		Litho.	Perf. 12	
524	A129	5m multicolored	.25	.25
525	A129	10m multicolored	.25	.25
526	A129	15m multicolored	.25	.25
527	A129	20m multicolored	.35	.25
528	A129	30m multicolored	.35	.25
529	A129	60m multicolored	.50	.25
530	A129	80m multicolored	.65	.25
531	A129	1t multicolored	1.00	.45
		Nos. 524-531 (8)	3.60	2.20

Red Cross Emblem and Helicopter A130

50m, Emblem, Red Cross car, shepherd.

1969, May 15		Litho.	Perf. 12	
532	A130	30m multicolored	.70	.25
533	A130	50m multicolored	.55	.25

30th anniversary of Mongolian Red Cross.

Landscape and Edelweiss — A131

Mongolian landscapes and flowers: 10m, Pinks. 15m, Dianthus superbus. 20m, Geranium. 30m, Dianthus ramosissimus. 60m, Globeflowers. 80m, Delphinium. 1t, Haloxylon.

1969, May 20				
534	A131	5m shown	.25	.25
535	A131	10m multi	.25	.25
536	A131	15m multi	.25	.25
537	A131	20m multi	.25	.25
538	A131	30m multi	.35	.25
539	A131	60m multi	.45	.25
540	A131	80m multi	.60	.25
541	A131	1t multi	.75	.35
		Nos. 534-541 (8)	3.15	2.20

See No. 1105.

Bull Fight, by Tsewegdjaw — A132

Paintings from National Museum: 10m, Fighting Colts, by O. Tsewegdjaw. 15m, Horseman and Herd, by A. Sangatzohyo. 20m, Camel Caravan, by D. Damdinsuren. 30m, On the Steppe, by N. Tsultem. 60m, Milking Mares, by Tsewegdjaw. 80m, Going to School, by B. Avarzad. 1t, After Work, by G. Odon. 4t, Horses, by Damdinsuren.

1969, July 11		Litho.	Perf. 12	
542	A132	5m multicolored	.25	.25
543	A132	10m multicolored	.25	.25
544	A132	15m multicolored	.25	.25
545	A132	20m multicolored	.25	.25
546	A132	30m multicolored	.25	.25
547	A132	60m multicolored	.35	.25
548	A132	80m multicolored	.50	.35
549	A132	1t multicolored	1.00	.40
		Nos. 542-549 (8)	3.10	2.25

Souvenir Sheet

| 550 | A132 | 4t multicolored | 2.50 | 2.50 |

10th anniversary of cooperative movement. No. 550 contains one stamp 65x42mm.

Mongolian Flag and Emblem — A133

1969, Sept. 20		Litho.	Perf. 11½	
551	A133	50m multicolored	.50	.30

Battle of Ha-lo-hsin (Khalka) River, 30th anniversary.
For surcharge, see No. 2384A.

Nos. 420-421 Overprinted

Perf. 11½x12, 12x11½

1969, Nov. 26			Photo.	
552	A110	30m red & multi	8.00	8.00
553	A111	50m red & multi	10.00	10.00

45th anniv. of Mongolian People's Republic.

Mercury 7 — A134

Designs: 5m, Sputnik 3. 10m, Vostok 1. 20m, Voskhod 2. 30m, Apollo 8. 60m, Soyuz 5. 80m, Apollo 12.

1969, Dec. 6		Photo.	Perf. 12x11½	
554	A134	5m multicolored	.25	.25
555	A134	10m multicolored	.25	.25
556	A134	15m multicolored	.25	.25
557	A134	20m multicolored	.25	.25
558	A134	30m multicolored	.25	.25
559	A134	60m multicolored	.45	.25
560	A134	80m multicolored	.60	.25
		Nos. 554-560 (7)	2.30	1.75

Souvenir Sheet

| 561 | A134 | 4t multicolored | 3.00 | 2.00 |

Space achievements of US and USSR.

Wolf A135

Designs: 10m, Brown bear. 15m, Lynx. 20m, Wild boar. 30m, Moose. 60m, Bobac marmot. 80m, Argali. 1t, Old wall carpet showing hunter and dog.

1970, Mar. 25		Photo.	Perf. 12	
562	A135	5m multicolored	.25	.25
563	A135	10m multicolored	.25	.25
564	A135	15m multicolored	.25	.25
565	A135	20m multicolored	.35	.25
566	A135	30m multicolored	.45	.25
567	A135	60m multicolored	.50	.30
568	A135	80m multicolored	.75	.45
569	A135	1t multicolored	1.10	.60
		Nos. 562-569 (8)	3.90	2.60

Lenin and Mongolian Delegation, by Sangatzohyo A136

Designs: 20m, Lenin, embroidered panel, by Cerenhuu, vert. 1t, Lenin, by Mazhig, vert.

1970, Apr. 22		Photo. & Litho.		
570	A136	20m multicolored	.30	.25
571	A136	50m multicolored	.40	.25
572	A136	1t lt bl, blk & red	.60	.30
		Nos. 570-572 (3)	1.30	.80

Centenary of the birth of Lenin.

Souvenir Sheet

EXPO '70 Pavilion of Matsushita Electric Co. and Time Capsule — A137

1970, May 26		Photo.	Perf. 12½	
573	A137	4t gold & multi	4.00	4.00

EXPO '70 International Exposition, Osaka, Japan, Mar. 15-Sept. 13.

Sumitomo Fairy Tale Pavilion — A138

1970, June 5		Photo.	Perf. 12x11½	
574	A138	1.50t multi + label	.80	.80

EXPO '70 International Exposition, Osaka. No. 574 printed in sheets of 20 (5x4) with alternating horizontal rows of tabs showing various fairy tales and EXPO '70 emblem.

Soccer, Rimet Cup A139

1970, June 20			Perf. 12½x11½	
575	A139	10m multi	.25	.25
576	A139	20m multi	.25	.25
577	A139	30m multi	.25	.25
578	A139	50m multi	.30	.25
579	A139	60m multi	.35	.25
580	A139	1t multi	.60	.25
581	A139	1.30t multi	.75	.30
		Nos. 575-581 (7)	2.75	1.80

Souvenir Sheet
Perf. 12½

| 582 | A139 | 4t multi | 2.50 | 2.50 |

World Soccer Championship for Jules Rimet Cup, Mexico City, May 30-June 21. No. 582 contains one stamp 51x37mm.

Old World Buzzard — A140

Birds of Prey: 20m, Tawny owls. 30m, Northern goshawk. 50m, White-tailed sea eagle. 60m, Peregrine falcon. 1t, Old world kestrel. 1.30t, Black kite.

1970, June 30		Litho.	Perf. 12	
583	A140	10m bl & multi	.75	.25
584	A140	20m pink & multi	1.00	.25
585	A140	30m yel grn & multi	1.10	.25
586	A140	50m bl & multi	1.20	.25
587	A140	60m yel & multi	1.60	.50
588	A140	1t grn & multi	2.00	.50
589	A140	1.30t bl & multi	2.50	.65
		Nos. 583-589 (7)	10.15	2.65

Russian War Memorial, Berlin — A141

1970, July 11		Litho.	Perf. 12	
590	A141	60m blue & multi	.60	.30

25th anniversary of end of World War II.

Bogdo-Gegen Palace — A142

Designs: 10m, Archer. 30m, Horseman. 40m, "White Mother" Goddess. 50m, Girl in national costume. 60m, Lion statue. 70m, Dancer's mask. 80m, Detail from Bogdo-Gegen Palace, Ulan Bator.

1970, Sept. 20		Litho.	Perf. 12	
591	A142	10m multi	.35	.25
592	A142	20m multi	.35	.25
593	A142	30m multi	.35	.25
594	A142	40m multi	.35	.30
595	A142	50m multi	.75	.65
596	A142	60m multi	.90	.75
597	A142	70m multi	1.00	.85
598	A142	80m multi	1.25	1.10
a.		Block of 4, #595-598		
		Nos. 591-598 (8)	5.30	4.40

Souvenir Sheet

Recovery of Apollo 13 Capsule A143

1970, Nov. 1		Litho.	Perf. 12	
599	A143	4t blue & multi	4.50	4.50

Space missions of Apollo 13, Apr. 11-17, and Soyuz 9, June 1-10, 1970.

Mongolian Flag, UN and Education Year Emblems A144

1970, Nov. 7				
600	A144	60m multi	.60	.30

International Education Year.

Mounted Herald — A145

1970, Nov. 7		Litho.	Perf. 12	
601	A145	30m gold & multi	.50	.30

50th anniv. of newspaper Unen (Truth).

571

MONGOLIA

Apollo 11 Lunar Landing Module — A146

Designs: 10m, Vostok 2 & 3. 20m, Voskhod 2, space walk. 30m, Gemini 6 & 7 capsules. 50m, Soyuz 4 & 5 docking in space. 60m, Soyuz 6, 7 & 8 group flight. 1t, Apollo 13 with damaged capsule. 1.30t, Luna 16 unmanned moon landing. 4t, Radar ground tracking station.

1971, Feb. 25	Litho.	Perf. 12		
602	A146	10m multi	.25	.25
603	A146	20m multi	.25	.25
604	A146	30m multi	.25	.25
605	A146	50m multi	.25	.25
606	A146	60m multi	.40	.25
607	A146	80m multi	.50	.25
608	A146	1t multi	.60	.30
609	A146	1.30t multi	.75	.40
		Nos. 602-609 (8)	3.25	2.20

Souvenir Sheet

| 610 | A146 | 4t vio bl & multi | 3.00 | 3.00 |

US and USSR space explorations.

Rider with Mongolian Flag — A147

Designs: 30m, Party meeting. 90m, Lenin with Mongolian leader. 1.20t, Marchers, pictures of Lenin and Marx.

1971, Mar. 1	Photo.	Perf. 12½		
611	A147	30m gold & multi	.25	.25
612	A147	60m gold & multi	.30	.25
613	A147	90m gold & multi	.35	.25
614	A147	1.20t gold & multi	.45	.30
		Nos. 611-614 (4)	1.35	1.05

Mongolian Revolutionary Party, 50th anniv.

Souvenir Sheet

Lunokhod 1 on Moon — A148

Design: No. 615b, Apollo 14 on moon.

1971, Apr. 15	Photo.	Perf. 14		
615	A148	Sheet of 2	3.00	3.00
a.-b.		2t any single	1.25	1.25

Luna 17 unmanned automated moon mission, Nov. 10-17, 1970, and Apollo 14 moon landing, Jan. 31-Feb. 9, 1971.

Dancer's Mask — A149

Designs: Various masks for dancers.

1971, Apr. 25	Litho.	Perf. 12		
616	A149	10m gold & multi	.25	.25
617	A149	20m gold & multi	.30	.25
618	A149	30m gold & multi	.40	.25
619	A149	50m gold & multi	.40	.25
620	A149	60m gold & multi	.50	.30
621	A149	1t gold & multi	.90	.40
622	A149	1.30t gold & multi	1.00	.55
		Nos. 616-622 (7)	3.75	2.25

Red Flag and Emblems — A150

1971, May 31	Photo.	Perf. 12x11½		
623	A150	60m bl, red & gold	.40	.25

16th Congress of Mongolian Revolutionary Party.

Steam Locomotive — A151

1971, July 11	Litho.	Perf. 12		
624	A151	20m shown	.50	.25
625	A151	30m Diesel locomotive	.60	.25
626	A151	40m Truck	.65	.25
627	A151	50m Automobile	.75	.25
628	A151	60m Biplane PO-2	.85	.30
629	A151	80m AN-24 plane	1.00	.40
630	A151	1t Fishing boat	1.75	1.00
		Nos. 624-630 (7)	6.10	2.70

50th anniversary of modern transportation. For overprints and surcharge, see Nos. 850A-850G, 2825.

Arms of Mongolia and Soldier — A152

Design: 1.50t, Arms, policeman and child.

1971, July 11	Litho.	Perf. 12		
631	A152	60m multi	.50	.25
632	A152	1.50t multi	.65	.30

50th anniversary of the people's army and police.

Mongolian Flag and Emblem — A153

1971, Aug. 25	Photo.	Perf. 12x11½		
633	A153	60m lt bl & multi	.40	.25

International Year Against Racial discrimination.

Flag of Youth Organization — A154

1971, Aug. 25	Litho.	Perf. 12		
634	A154	60m org & multi	.60	.30

50th anniversary of Mongolian revolutionary youth organization.

The Woodsman and the Tiger — A155

Designs: Various Mongolian fairy tales.

1971, Sept. 15	Litho.	Perf. 12		
635	A155	10m gold & multi	.25	.25
636	A155	20m gold & multi	.25	.25
637	A155	30m gold & multi	.25	.25
638	A155	50m gold & multi	.30	.25
639	A155	60m gold & multi	.40	.25
640	A155	80m gold & multi	.55	.25
641	A155	1t gold & multi	.75	.30
642	A155	1.30t gold & multi	.95	.40
		Nos. 635-642 (8)	3.70	2.20

Bactrian Camel — A156

1971, Nov. 1	Litho.	Perf. 12½		
643	A156	20m Yaks	.25	.25
644	A156	30m shown	.25	.25
645	A156	40m Sheep	.25	.25
646	A156	50m Goats	.35	.25
647	A156	60m Cattle	.50	.25
648	A156	80m Horses	.55	.30
649	A156	1t White horse	.90	.40
		Nos. 643-649 (7)	3.05	1.95

Mongolian livestock breeding.

Cross-country Skiing — A157

Designs (Sapporo Olympic Emblem and): 20m, Bobsledding. 30m, Women's figure skating. 50m, Slalom. 60m, Speed skating. 80m, Downhill skiing. 1t, Ice hockey. 1.30t, Figure skating, pairs. 4t, Ski jump.

1972, Jan. 20	Photo.	Perf. 12½x11½		
650	A157	10m multi	.25	.25
651	A157	20m ol & multi	.25	.25
652	A157	30m ultra & multi	.25	.25
653	A157	50m brt bl & multi	.30	.25
654	A157	60m multi	.35	.25
655	A157	80m grn & multi	.45	.25
656	A157	1t bl & multi	.55	.25
657	A157	1.30t vio & multi	.70	.30
		Nos. 650-657 (8)	3.10	2.05

Souvenir Sheet
Perf. 12½

| 658 | A157 | 4t lt bl & multi | 2.00 | 2.00 |

11th Winter Olympic Games, Sapporo, Japan, Feb. 3-13.

Taming Wild Horse — A158

Paintings: 20m, Mythological animal in winter. 30m, Lancer on horseback. 50m, Athletes. 60m, Waterfall and horses. 80m, The Wise Musician, by Sarav. 1t, Young musician. 1.30t, Old sage with animals.

1972, Apr. 15	Litho.	Perf. 12		
659	A158	10m multi	.25	.25
660	A158	20m multi	.25	.25
661	A158	30m multi	.25	.25
662	A158	50m multi	.30	.25
663	A158	60m multi	.35	.25
664	A158	80m multi	.55	.30
665	A158	1t multi	.60	.30
666	A158	1.30t multi	.85	.35
		Nos. 659-666 (8)	3.40	2.20

Paintings by contemporary artists in Ulan Bator Museum.

Calosoma Fischeri — A159

Designs: Various insects.

1972, Apr. 30	Litho.	Perf. 12		
667	A159	10m multi	.25	.25
668	A159	20m multi	.25	.25
669	A159	30m multi	.30	.25
670	A159	50m multi	.35	.25
671	A159	60m multi	.50	.25
672	A159	80m multi	.80	.25
673	A159	1t multi	.90	.25
674	A159	1.30t multi	1.40	.50
		Nos. 667-674 (8)	4.75	2.35

UN Emblem — A160

1972, Aug. 30	Photo.	Perf. 12		
675	A160	60m multi	.60	.40

ECAFE (UN Economic Commission for Asia and the Far East), 25th anniv.

Slow Lizard — A161

Designs: 15m, Radd's toad. 20m, Pallas's viper. 25m, Toad-headed agamid. 30m, Siberian wood frog. 60m, Przewalski's lizard. 80m, Taphrometopon lineolatum (snake). 1t, Stoliczka's agamid.

1972, Sept. 5	Litho.	Perf. 12		
676	A161	10m multi	.25	.25
677	A161	15m multi	.25	.25
678	A161	20m multi	.25	.25
679	A161	25m multi	.40	.25
680	A161	30m multi	.45	.25
681	A161	60m multi	.60	.30
682	A161	80m multi	.95	.45
683	A161	1t multi	1.50	.55
		Nos. 676-683 (8)	4.65	2.55

Symbols of Technical Knowledge — A162

Design: 60m, University of Mongolia.

1972, Sept. 25				
684	A162	50m org & multi	.40	.25
685	A162	60m lil & multi	.50	.25

30th anniversary of Mongolian State University.

Virgin and Child with St. John, by Bellini — A163

Paintings by Venetian Masters: 20m, Transfiguration, by Bellini, vert. 30m, Virgin and Child, by Bellini, vert. 50m, Presentation in the Temple, by Bellini. 60m, St. George, by Mantegna, vert. 80m, Departure of St. Ursula, by Carpaccio, vert. 1t, Departure of St. Ursula, by Carpaccio.

MONGOLIA

1972, Oct. 1

686	A163	10m multi	.25	.25
687	A163	20m multi	.25	.25
688	A163	30m multi	.25	.25
689	A163	50m multi	.35	.25
690	A163	60m multi	.50	.25
691	A163	80m multi	.55	.25
692	A163	1t multi	.80	.50
	Nos. 686-692 (7)		2.95	2.05

Save Venice campaign. See No. B3.

Manlay Bator Damdinsuren — A164

Designs: 20m, Ard Ayus, horiz. 50m, Hatan Bator Magsarzhav. 60m, Has Bator, horiz. 1t, Sukhe Bator.

1972, Oct. 20 — Litho. — Perf. 12

693	A164	10m gold & multi	.25	.25
694	A164	20m gold & multi	.25	.25
695	A164	50m gold & multi	.30	.25
696	A164	80m gold & multi	.40	.25
697	A164	1t gold & multi	.75	.30
	Nos. 693-697 (5)		1.95	1.30

Paintings of national heroes. For surcharge, see No. 2986.

Spasski Tower, Moscow — A165

1972, Nov. 7 — Photo. — Perf. 11

| 698 | A165 | 60m multi + label | .70 | .25 |

50th anniversary of USSR.

Mark Spitz, US, Gold Medal — A166

Designs (Medal and): 10m, Ulrike Meyfarth, Germany. 20m, Sawao Kato, Japan. 30m, Andras Balczo, Hungary. 60m, Lasse Viren, Finland. 80m, Shane Gould, Australia. 1t, Anatoli Bondarchuk, USSR. 4t, Khorloo Baianmunk, Mongolia.

1972, Dec. 15 — Photo. — Perf. 12½

699	A166	5m grn & multi	.25	.25
700	A166	10m ver & multi	.25	.25
701	A166	20m bl & multi	.25	.25
702	A166	30m multi		.25 .25
703	A166	60m lt vio & multi	.35	.25
704	A166	80m ol & multi	.50	.25
705	A166	1t lem & multi	.70	.30
	Nos. 699-705 (7)		2.55	1.80

Souvenir Sheet

| 706 | A166 | 4t red & multi | 2.25 | 2.25 |

Winners in 20th Olympic Games, Munich.

Chimpanzee on Bicycle — A167

Circus Scenes: 10m, Seal playing ball. 15m, Bear riding wheel. 20m, Woman acrobat on camel. 30m, Woman equestrian. 50m, Clown playing flute. 60m, Woman gymnast. 1t, Circus building, Ulan Bator, horiz.

1973, Jan. 29 — Litho. — Perf. 12

707	A167	5m multi	.25	.25
708	A167	10m multi	.25	.25
709	A167	15m multi	.25	.25
710	A167	20m multi	.30	.25
711	A167	30m multi	.40	.25
712	A167	50m multi	.45	.25
713	A167	60m multi	.60	.30
714	A167	1t multi	.80	.50
	Nos. 707-714 (8)		3.30	2.30

Postrider — A168

Designs: 60m, Diesel locomotive. 1t, Truck.

1973, Jan. 31 — Photo. — Perf. 12x11½

715	A168	50m brown	.55	.25
716	A168	60m green	2.00	1.00
717	A168	1t rose claret	1.00	.30
	Nos. 715-717, C34 (4)		5.15	1.20

For surcharges, see Nos. 2405-2407.

Sukhe Bator and Merchants — A169

Paintings of Sukhe Bator: 20m, With eldero. 50m, Leading partisans. 60m, With revolutionary council. 1t, Receiving deputation, horiz.

1973, Feb. 2 — Photo. — Perf. 11½x12

718	A169	10m gold & multi	.25	.25
719	A169	20m gold & multi	.25	.25
720	A169	50m gold & multi	.35	.25
721	A169	60m gold & multi	.40	.25
722	A169	1t gold & multi	.65	.25
	Nos. 718-722 (5)		1.90	1.25

Sukhe Bator (1893-1923).

Nicolaus Copernicus — A170

1973, Mar. — Litho. — Perf. 12

723	A170	50m gold & multi	.40	.25
724	A170	60m gold & multi	.50	.25
725	A170	1t gold & multi	.80	.30
	Nos. 723-725 (3)		1.70	.80

Souvenir Sheet

726		Sheet of 3	4.00	3.00
a.	A170	1t multi	.60	.60
b.	A170	1t multi	.60	.60
c.	A170	2t multi	1.50	1.50

500th anniversary of the birth of Nicolaus Copernicus (1473-1543), Polish astronomer.

Marx and Lenin — A171

1973, July 15 — Photo. — Perf. 11½x12

| 727 | A171 | 60m gold, car & ultra | .75 | .40 |

9th meeting of postal administrations of socialist countries, Ulan Bator.

Aquatic Birds — A172

Designs: 5m, Common Shelducks. 10m, Arctic loons. 15m, Bar-headed geese. 30m, Great crested grebe. 50m, Mallards. 60m, Mute swans. 1t, Greater scaups.

1973, Aug. 10 — Litho. — Perf. 12x11

728	A172	5m shown	.45	.25
729	A172	10m multi	.60	.25
730	A172	15m multi	1.00	.25
731	A172	30m multi	1.20	.30
732	A172	50m multi	1.60	.40
733	A172	60m multi	1.90	.45
734	A172	1t multi	2.25	.60
	Nos. 728-734 (7)		9.00	2.50

1973, Aug. 25 — Litho. — Perf. 12x11

Designs: Fur-bearing animals: 5m, Siberian weasel. 10m, Siberian chipmunk. 15m, Flying squirrel. 20m, Eurasian badger. 30m, Eurasian red squirrel. 60m, Wolverine. 80m, Mink. 1t, White hare.

735	A172	5m multi	.25	.25
736	A172	10m multi	.25	.25
737	A172	15m multi	.25	.25
738	A172	20m multi	.35	.25
739	A172	30m multi	.50	.25
740	A172	60m multi	.85	.40
741	A172	80m multi	1.00	.60
742	A172	1t multi	1.50	.70
	Nos. 735-742 (8)		4.95	2.95

1973, Dec. 15 — Litho. — Perf. 12x11

Designs: Flowers: 5m, Alpine aster. 10m, Mongolian silene. 15m, Rosa davurica. 20m, Mongolian dandelion. 30m, Rhododendron dahuricum. 50m, Clematis tangutica. 60m, Siberian primula. 1t, Pasqueflower.

743	A172	5m multi	.25	.25
744	A172	10m multi	.25	.25
745	A172	15m multi	.25	.25
746	A172	20m multi	.30	.25
747	A172	30m multi	.45	.25
748	A172	50m multi	.75	.35
749	A172	60m multi	.90	.50
750	A172	1t multi	1.50	.65
	Nos. 743-750 (8)		4.65	2.75

Globe and Red Flag Emblem — A173

1973, Dec. 10 — Photo. — Perf. 12x12½

| 751 | A173 | 60m gold, red & blue | .60 | .25 |

15th anniversary of the review "Problems of Peace and Socialism," published in Prague.

Limenitis Populi — A174

Butterflies: 10m, Arctia hebe. 15m, Rhyparia purpurata. 20m, Catocala pacta. 30m, Isoceras kaszabi. 50m, Celerio costata. 60m, Arctia caja. 1t, Diacrisia sannio.

1974, Jan. 15 — Litho. — Perf. 11

752	A174	5m lil & multi	.30	.25
753	A174	10m brn & multi	.35	.25
754	A174	15m bl & multi	.35	.25
755	A174	20m brn org & multi	.55	.25
756	A174	30m lt vio & multi	.75	.25
757	A174	50m dl red & multi	1.00	.30
758	A174	60m yel grn & multi	1.20	.40
759	A174	1t ultra & multi	1.50	.50
	Nos. 752-759 (8)		6.00	2.45

"Hehe Namshil" by L. Merdorsh — A175

Designs (Various Scenes from): 20m, "Sive Hiagt," by D. Luvsansharav. 25m, 80m, 1t, "Edre," by D. Namdag. 30m, "The 3 Khans of Sara-Gol" (legend). 60m, "Amarsana," by B. Damdinsuren. 20m and 30m horizontal.

1974, Feb. 20 — Litho. — Perf. 12

760	A175	15m sil & multi	.25	.25
761	A175	20m sil & multi	.25	.25
762	A175	25m sil & multi	.30	.25
763	A175	30m sil & multi	.40	.25
764	A175	60m sil & multi	.45	.25
765	A175	80m sil & multi	.60	.25
766	A175	1t sil & multi	.75	.60
	Nos. 760-766 (7)		3.00	2.10

Mongolian operas and dramas. Stamps dated 1973 in the bottom left margin.

Government Building and Sukhe Bator — A176

1974, Mar. 1 — Photo. — Perf. 11

| 767 | A176 | 60m gold & multi | .75 | .40 |

50th anniv. of renaming capital Ulan Bator.

Juggler — A177

10m, Circus horses, horiz. 30m, Trained elephant. 40m, Yak pushing ball, horiz. 60m, Acrobats with ring. 80m, Woman acrobat on unicycle.

1974, May 4 — Litho. — Perf. 12

768	A177	10m multi	.25	.25
769	A177	20m multi	.40	.25
770	A177	30m multi	.50	.30
771	A177	40m multi	.80	.40
772	A177	60m multi	1.00	.50
773	A177	80m multi	1.60	.75
	Nos. 768-773, C65 (7)		5.80	3.05

Mongolian Circus. No. 773 has se-tenant label, with similar design.

Girl on Bronco — A178

MONGOLIA

Children's Activities: 20m, Boy roping calf. 30m, 40m, Boy taming horse (different designs). 60m, Girl with doves. 80m, Wrestling. 1t, Dancing.

1974, June 2		Litho.	Perf. 12	
774	A178	10m dl yel & multi	.25	.25
775	A178	20m lt bl & multi	.25	.25
776	A178	30m grn & multi	.25	.25
777	A178	40m yel & multi	.35	.25
778	A178	60m pink & multi	.50	.25
779	A178	80m bl & multi	.65	.30
780	A178	1t dl bl & multi	.80	.45
		Nos. 774-780 (7)	3.05	2.00

Children's Day.
For surcharges see Nos. 2577-2578.

Archer — A179

National Sports: 20m, Two horsemen fighting for goatskin. 30m, Archer on horseback. 40m, Horse race. 60m, Riding wild horse. 80m, Rider chasing riderless horse. 1t, Boys wrestling.

1974, July 11		Photo.	Perf. 11	
781	A179	10m vio bl & multi	.25	.25
782	A179	20m yel & multi	.25	.25
783	A179	30m lil & multi	.25	.25
784	A179	40m multi	.30	.25
785	A179	60m multi	.50	.25
786	A179	80m multi	.65	.30
787	A179	1t multi	.80	.45
		Nos. 781-787 (7)	3.00	2.00

Nadom, Mongolian national festival.

Grizzly Bear — A180

20m, Common panda. 30m, Giant panda. 40m, Two brown bears. 60m, Sloth bear. 80m, Asiatic black bears. 1t, Giant brown bear.

1974, July		Litho.	Perf. 12	
788	A180	10m shown	.25	.25
789	A180	20m multi	.30	.25
790	A180	30m multi	.35	.25
791	A180	40m multi	.50	.35
792	A180	60m multi	.75	.35
793	A180	80m multi	1.00	.50
794	A180	1t multi	1.50	.75
		Nos. 788-794 (7)	4.65	2.70

Stag in Zuun Araat Wildlife Preserve A181

20m, Beaver. 30m, Leopard. 40m, Great black-backed gull. 60m, Deer. 80m, Mouflon. 1t, Deer and entrance to Bogd-uul Preserve.

1974, Sept.		Litho.	Perf. 12	
795	A181	10m shown	.25	.25
796	A181	20m multi	.30	.25
797	A181	30m multi	.35	.25
798	A181	40m multi	.50	.35
799	A181	60m multi	.75	.35
800	A181	80m multi	1.00	.50
801	A181	1t multi	1.50	.75
		Nos. 795-801 (7)	4.65	2.70

Protected fauna in Mongolian wildlife preserves.

Buddhist Temple, Bogdo Gegen Palace A182

Mongolian Architecture: 15m, Buddhist Temple, now Museum. 30m, Entrance to Charity Temple, Ulan Bator. 50m, Mongolian yurta. 80m, Gazebo in convent yard.

1974, Oct. 15		Litho.	Perf. 12	
802	A182	10m bl & multi	.30	.25
803	A182	15m multi	.30	.25
804	A182	30m grn & multi	.30	.25
805	A182	50m multi	.50	.25
806	A182	80m yel & multi	.80	.30
		Nos. 802-806 (5)	2.20	1.30

Spasski Tower, Sukhe Bator Statue — A183

1974, Nov. 26		Photo.	Perf. 11½x12	
807	A183	60m multi	.75	.40

Visit of General Secretary Brezhnev and a delegation from the USSR to participate in celebration of 50th anniversary of People's Republic of Mongolia.

Sukhe Bator Proclaiming Republic — A184

Designs: No. 808, "First Constitution," symbolic embroidery. No. 809, Flag over landscape, plane and communications tower.

1974, Nov. 28			Litho.	
808	A184	60m multi	.35	.25
809	A184	60m multi	.35	.25
810	A184	60m multi	.35	.25
		Nos. 808-810 (3)	1.05	.75

50th anniv. of People's Republic of Mongolia.

Decanter — A185

Designs: 20m, Silver jar. 30m, Night lamp. 40m, Tea jug. 60m, Candelabra. 80m, Teapot. 1t, Silver bowl on 3-legged stand.

1974, Dec. 1			Photo.	
811	A185	10m blue & multi	.25	.25
812	A185	20m claret & multi	.25	.25
813	A185	30m multi	.30	.25
814	A185	40m dp bl & multi	.40	.25
815	A185	60m multi	.45	.25
816	A185	80m grn & multi	.60	.30
817	A185	1t lilac & multi	.75	.45
		Nos. 811-817 (7)	3.00	2.00

Mongolian 19th century goldsmiths' work.

Lapwing (plover) A186

1974, Dec.		Litho.	Perf. 11	
818	A186	10m shown	.35	.25
819	A186	20m Fish	.45	.25
820	A186	30m Marsh marigolds	.50	.25
821	A186	40m White pelican	.70	.25
822	A186	60m Perch	.70	.30
823	A186	80m Mink	.85	.40
		Nos. 818-823,C66 (7)	4.55	2.20

Water and nature protection.

American Mail Coach, UPU Emblem — A187

Designs (UPU Emblem and): 20m, French two-wheeled coach. 30m, Changing horses, Russian coach. 40m, Swedish caterpillar mail truck. 50m, First Hungarian mail truck. 60m, German Daimler-Benz mail truck. 1t, Mongolian dispatch rider.

1974, Dec.		Litho.	Perf. 12	
824	A187	10m multi	.25	.25
825	A187	20m multi	.25	.25
826	A187	30m multi	.30	.25
827	A187	40m multi	.35	.25
828	A187	50m multi	.55	.30
829	A187	60m multi	.70	.35
830	A187	1t multi	.90	.55
		Nos. 824-830 (7)	3.30	2.20

Cent. of the UPU and Stockholmia 74.

Soviet Flag, Broken Swastika — A188

1975, May 9		Photo.	Perf. 11½x12	
832	A188	60m multi	.75	.40

30th anniversary of the end of World War II and victory over fascism.

Mongolian Woman — A189

1975, May				
833	A189	60m multi	.75	.45

International Women's Year 1975.

Zygophyllum Xanthoxylon — A190

Medicinal Plants: 20m, Ingarvillea potaninii. 30m, Lancea tibetica. 40m, Jurinea mongolica. 50m, Saussurea involucrata. 60m, Allium mongolicum. 1t, Adonis mongolica.

1975, May 24		Photo.	Perf. 11x11½	
834	A190	10m dp org & multi	.25	.25
835	A190	20m grn & multi	.25	.25
836	A190	30m yel & multi	.40	.25
837	A190	40m vio & multi	.55	.25
838	A190	50m brn & multi	.60	.25
839	A190	60m bl & multi	.80	.30
840	A190	1t multi	1.25	.45
		Nos. 834-840 (7)	4.10	2.00

12th International Botanists' Conference.

Shepherd A191

Puppet Theater: 20m, Boy on horseback. 30m, Boy and disobedient bull calf. 40m, Little orphan camel's tale. 50m, Boy and obedient little yak. 60m, Boy riding swan. 1t, Children's choir.

1975, June 30		Litho.	Perf. 12	
841	A191	10m multi	.25	.25
842	A191	20m multi	.25	.25
843	A191	30m multi	.30	.25
844	A191	40m multi	.45	.25
845	A191	50m multi	.50	.25
846	A191	60m multi	.55	.30
847	A191	1t multi	.90	.40
		Nos. 841-847 (7)	3.20	1.95

For surcharges see Nos. 2575-2576.

Pioneers Tending Fruit Tree — A192

60m, Pioneers studying, and flying model plane. 1t, New emblem of Mongolian Pioneers.

1975, July 15			Perf. 12x11½	
848	A192	50m multi	.30	.25
849	A192	60m multi	.40	.25
850	A192	1t multi	.55	.30
		Nos. 848-850 (3)	1.25	.80

Mongolian Pioneers, 50th anniversary.

Nos. 624-630 Overprinted

1975, July 15		Litho.	Perf. 12	
850A	A151	20m multi	5.00	5.00
850B	A151	30m multi	5.00	5.00
850C	A151	40m multi	4.00	4.00
850D	A151	50m multi	4.00	4.00
850E	A151	60m multi	5.00	5.00
850F	A151	80m multi	5.00	5.00
850G	A151	1t multi	6.00	6.00
		Nos. 850A-850G (7)	34.00	34.00

Fifty years of communication.

Golden Eagle Hunting Fox A193

Hunting Scenes: 20m, Dogs treeing lynx, vert. 30m, Hunter stalking marmots. 40m, Hunter riding reindeer, vert. 50m, Boar hunt. 60m, Trapped wolf, vert. 1t, Bear hunt.

1975, Aug. 25		Litho.	Perf. 12	
851	A193	10m multi	.30	.25
852	A193	20m multi	.35	.25
853	A193	30m multi	.40	.25
854	A193	40m multi	.45	.25
855	A193	50m multi	.50	.30

MONGOLIA

856	A193	60m multi	.55	.30
857	A193	1t multi	.70	.40
		Nos. 851-857 (7)	3.25	2.00

Hunting in Mongolia.

Mesocottus Haitej — A194

Various Fish: 20m, Pseudaspius leptocephalus. 30m, Oreoleuciscus potanini. 40m, Tinca tinca. 50m, Coregonus lavaretus pidschian. 60m, Erythroculter mongolicus. 1t, Carassius auratus.

1975, Sept. 15   Photo.   Perf. 11

858	A194	10m multi	.25	.25
859	A194	20m multi	.25	.25
860	A194	30m multi	.35	.25
861	A194	40m bl & multi	.50	.25
862	A194	50m grn & multi	.60	.30
863	A194	60m lil & multi	.75	.35
864	A194	1t vio bl & multi	1.25	.50
		Nos. 858-864 (7)	3.95	2.15

Neck and Bow of Musical Instrument (Morin Hur) — A195

National Handicraft: 20m, Saddle. 30m, Silver headgear. 40m, Boots. 50m, Tasseled Woman's cap. 60m, Pipe and tobacco pouch. 1t, Sable cap.

1975, Oct. 10   Litho.   Perf. 11½x12½

865	A195	10m multi	.25	.25
866	A195	20m multi	.25	.25
867	A195	30m multi	.30	.25
868	A195	40m multi	.35	.25
869	A195	50m multi	.45	.25
870	A195	60m multi	.55	.25
871	A195	1t multi	.90	.45
		Nos. 865-871 (7)	3.05	1.95

Revolutionists with Flags — A196

1975, Nov. 15   Litho.   Perf. 11½x12

872	A196	60m multi	.60	.25

70th anniversary of Russian Revolution.

Ski Jump, Olympic Games Emblem — A197

Winter Olympic Games Emblem and: 20m, Ice hockey. 30m, Skiing. 40m, Bobsled. 50m, Biathlon. 60m, Speed skating. 1t, Figure skating, women's. 4t, Skier carrying torch.

Perf. 11½x12½

1975, Dec. 20   Litho.

873	A197	10m multi	.25	.25
874	A197	20m multi	.25	.25
875	A197	30m brn & multi	.30	.25
876	A197	40m grn & multi	.40	.25
877	A197	50m multi	.45	.25
878	A197	60m ol & multi	.55	.25
879	A197	1t multi	.90	.40
		Nos. 873-879 (7)	3.10	1.90

Souvenir Sheet

880	A197	4t multi	2.75	2.75

12th Winter Olympic Games, Innsbruck, Austria, Feb. 4-15, 1976.

Taming Wild Horse — A198

Mongolian Paintings: 20m, Camel caravan, horiz. 30m, Man playing lute. 40m, Woman adjusting headdress, horiz. 50m, Woman wearing ceremonial costume. 60m, Women fetching water. 1t, Woman musician. 4t, Warrior on horseback.

1975, Nov. 30   Perf. 12

881	A198	10m brown & multi	.25	.25
882	A198	20m blue & multi	.25	.25
883	A198	30m olive & multi	.30	.25
884	A198	40m lilac & multi	.40	.25
885	A198	50m blue & multi	.45	.25
886	A198	60m lilac & multi	.55	.25
887	A198	1t silver & multi	.90	.45
		Nos. 881-887 (7)	3.10	1.95

Souvenir Sheet

888	A198	4t bl & multi	3.50	3.00

House of Young Technicians — A199

Designs: 60m, Hotel Ulan Bator. 1t, Museum of the Revolution.

1975, Dec. 30   Photo.   Perf. 12x11½

893	A199	50m ultra	.40	.25
894	A199	60m bl grn	.45	.25
895	A199	1t brick red	.75	.30
		Nos. 893-895 (3)	1.60	.80

Camels in Gobi Desert A200

20m, Horse taming. 30m, Herding. 40m, Pioneers' camp. 60m, Young musician. 80m, Children's festival. 1t, Mongolian wrestling.

1976, June 1   Litho.   Perf. 12

896	A200	10m multi	.25	.25
897	A200	20m multi	.30	.25
898	A200	30m multi	.35	.25
899	A200	40m multi	.50	.25
900	A200	60m multi	.60	.25
901	A200	80m multi	.90	.40
902	A200	1t multi	1.00	.50
		Nos. 896-902 (7)	3.90	2.15

International Children's Day.

Red Star — A201

1976, May 1   Photo.   Perf. 11x12½

903	A201	60m red, maroon & silver	.75	.40

17th Congress of the Mongolian People's Revolutionary Party, June 14.

Archery, Montreal Games' Emblem, Canadian Flag A202

20m, Judo. 30m, Boxing. 40m, Vaulting. 60m, Weight lifting. 80m, High Jump. 1t, Target shooting.

1976, May 20   Litho.   Perf. 12½x11½

904	A202	10m yel & multi	.25	.25
905	A202	20m yel & multi	.25	.25
906	A202	30m yel & multi	.25	.25
907	A202	40m yel & multi	.35	.25
908	A202	60m yel & multi	.50	.25
909	A202	80m yel & multi	.70	.30
910	A202	1t yel & multi	.90	.40
		Nos. 904-910 (7)	3.20	1.95

21st Olympic Games, Montreal, Canada, July 17-Aug. 1. See No. C81.

Partisans — A203   Fighter and Sojombo Independence Symbol — A204

Perf. 12x11½, 11½x12

1976, June 15   Litho.

911	A203	60m multi	.45	.25
912	A204	60m multi	.45	.25

55th anniversary of Mongolia's independence. See No. C82.

Souvenir Sheet

Sukhe Bator Medal A205

1976, July 11   Perf. 11½

913	A205	4t multi	4.00	4.00

Mongolian honors medals.

Osprey A206

Protected Birds: 20m, Griffon vulture. 30m, Bearded lammergeier. 40m, Marsh harrier. 60m, Black vulture. 80m, Golden eagle. 1t, Tawny eagle.

1976, Aug. 16   Litho.   Perf. 12

914	A206	10m multi	.60	.25
915	A206	20m multi	.90	.25
916	A206	30m multi	1.10	.30
917	A206	40m multi	1.40	.30
918	A206	60m multi	1.75	.40
919	A206	80m multi	1.90	.50
920	A206	1t multi	2.25	.60
		Nos. 914-920 (7)	9.90	2.60

"Nadom" Military Game A207

Paintings by O. Cevegshava: 10m, Taming Wild Horse, vert. 30m, Hubsugul Lake Harbor. 40m, The Steppe Awakening. 80m, Wrestlers. 1.60t, Yak Descending in Snow, vert.

1976, Sept.   Litho.   Perf. 12

921	A207	10m multi	.25	.25
922	A207	20m multi	.25	.25
923	A207	30m multi	.30	.25
924	A207	40m multi	.35	.25
925	A207	80m multi	.65	.30
926	A207	1.60t multi	.60	.70
		Nos. 921-926 (6)	2.40	2.00

Interlocking Circles, Industry and Transport A208

1976, Oct. 15   Photo.   Perf. 12x11½

927	A208	60m brn, bl & red	1.50	.25

Soviet-Mongolian friendship.

John Naber, US Flag, Gold Medals — A209

Designs: 20m, Nadia Comaneci, Romanian flag. 30m, Kornelia Ender, East German flag. 40m, Mitsuo Tsukahara, Japanese flag. 60m, Gregor Braun, German flag. 80m, Lasse Viren, Finnish flag. 1t, Nikolai Andrianov, Russian flag.

1976, Nov. 30   Litho.   Perf. 12

928	A209	10m multi	.25	.25
929	A209	20m multi	.25	.25
930	A209	30m multi	.25	.25
931	A209	40m multi	.35	.25
932	A209	60m multi	.50	.25
933	A209	80m multi	.75	.30
934	A209	1t multi	.90	.45
		Nos. 928-934 (7)	3.15	2.00

Gold medal winners, 21st Olympic Games, Montreal. See No. C83.

Stone Tablet on Tortoise A210   Carved Tablet, 6th-8th Centuries A211

1976, Dec. 15   Litho.   Perf. 11½x12

935	A210	50m brn & lt bl	.75	.25
936	A211	60m gray & brt grn	1.00	.25

Intl. Archaeological Conference, Ulan Bator.

R-1 Plane A212

Designs: Various Mongolian planes.

1976, Dec. 22   Perf. 12

937	A212	10m multi	.25	.25
938	A212	20m multi	.25	.25
939	A212	30m multi	.30	.25
940	A212	40m multi	.35	.25
941	A212	60m multi	.50	.25
942	A212	80m multi	.65	.30
943	A212	1t multi	.75	.40
		Nos. 937-943 (7)	3.05	1.95

Dancers A213

MONGOLIA

Folk Dances: 20m, 13th century costumes. 30m, West Mongolian dance. 40m, "Ekachi," or horse-dance. 60m, "Bielge," West Mongolian trunk dance. 80m, "Hodak," or friendship dance. 1t, "Dojarka."

1977, Mar. 20	Litho.	Perf. 12½		
944	A213	10m multi	.25	.25
945	A213	20m multi	.30	.25
946	A213	30m multi	.45	.25
947	A213	40m multi	.55	.25
948	A213	60m multi	.75	.25
949	A213	80m multi	1.00	.40
950	A213	1t multi	1.10	.45
	Nos. 944-950 (7)		4.40	2.10

For surcharges, see Nos. 2938-2939.

Miniature Sheet

A214 & A215 Designs

a, Path of Pioneer from Earth to Jupiter, deflected by Mars. b, Apple tree. c, Sextant and planets. d, Astronauts in space. e, Isaac Newton. f, Prism and spectrum. g, Rain falling on earth. h, Motion of celestial bodies. i, Pioneer 10 over Jupiter.

1977, Mar. 31	Litho.	Perf. 11½x12		
951		Sheet of 9	4.00	1.75
a.	A214 60m multi		.30	.25
b.	A215 60m multi		.30	.25
c.	A214 60m multi		.30	.25
d.	A215 60m multi		.30	.25
e.	A214 60m multi		.30	.25
f.	A215 60m multi		.30	.25
g.	A214 60m multi		.30	.25
h.	A215 60m multi		.30	.25
i.	A214 60m multi		.30	.25

Sir Isaac Newton (1642-1727), English natural philosopher and mathematician.
Nos. 951a-951i arranged in 3 rows of 3. Nos. 951d and 951i inscribed AIR MAIL.

D. Natsagdorji, Writer, and Quotation — A216

Design: No. 953, Grazing horses, landscape, ornament and quotation.

1977		Perf. 11½x12		
952	A216 60m multi		.60	.25
953	A216 60m multi		.60	.25

D. Natsagdorji, founder of modern Mongolian literature. Label and vignette separated by simulated perforations.

Primitive Tortoises A217

Prehistoric Animals: 20m, Ungulate (titanothere). 30m, Beaked dinosaurs. 40m, Entelodon (swine). 60m, Antelope. 80m, Hipparion. 1t, Aurochs.

1977, May 7	Photo.	Perf. 12½		
954	A217 10m multi		.30	.25
955	A217 20m multi		.45	.25
956	A217 30m multi		.45	.25
957	A217 40m multi		.70	.25
958	A217 60m multi		1.10	.25
959	A217 80m multi		1.40	.35
960	A217 1t multi		1.75	.50
	Nos. 954-960 (7)		6.15	2.10

Souvenir Sheet

Mongolia, Type A2 and Netherlands No. 1 — A218

1977, May 20				
961	A218 4t multi		2.50	2.00

AMPHILEX '77 International Philatelic Exhibition, Amsterdam, May 27-June 5. No. 961 contains one 37x52mm stamp.

Boys on Horseback — A219

20m, Girl on horseback. 30m, Hunter on horseback. 40m, Grazing horses. 60m, Mare & foal. 80m, Grazing horse & student. 1t, White stallion.

1977, June 15	Litho.	Perf. 12		
962	A219 10m multi		.25	.25
963	A219 20m multi		.30	.25
964	A219 30m multi		.35	.25
965	A219 40m multi		.45	.25
966	A219 60m multi		.55	.25
967	A219 80m multi		.80	.30
968	A219 1t multi		.90	.40
	Nos. 962-968 (7)		3.60	1.95

Copper and Molybdenum Plant, Vehicles — A220

1977, June 15	Litho.	Perf. 12		
969	A220 60m multi		1.50	.50

Erdenet, a new industrial town.

Bucket Brigade Fighting Fire A221

Fire Fighting: 20m, Horse-drawn fire pump. 30m, Horse-drawn steam pump. 40m, Men in protective suits fighting forest fire. 60m, Modern foam extinguisher. 80m, Truck and ladder. 1t, Helicopter fighting fire on steppe.

1977, Aug.	Litho.	Perf. 12		
970	A221 10m multi		.25	.25
971	A221 20m multi		.25	.25
972	A221 30m multi		.40	.25
973	A221 40m multi		.55	.25
974	A221 60m multi		.65	.30
975	A221 80m multi		.85	.35
976	A221 1t multi		1.10	.50
	Nos. 970-976 (7)		4.05	2.15

Radar and Molniya Satellite on TV Screen — A222

1977, Sept. 12	Photo.	Perf. 12x11½		
977	A222 60m gray, bl & blk		.50	.30

40th anniversary of Technical Institute.

Lenin Museum, Ulan Bator — A223

1977, Oct. 1	Litho.	Perf. 12		
978	A223 60m multi		.60	.30

Inauguration of Lenin Museum in connection with the 60th anniversary of the Russian October Revolution.

Dove, Globe, Decree of Peace — A224

Designs: 50m, Cruiser Aurora and Russian flag, vert. 1.50t, Globe and "Freedom."

1977, Oct. 1	Perf. 11½x12, 12x11½	Photo.		
979	A224 50m gold & multi		.65	.25
980	A224 60m gold & multi		.55	.25
981	A224 1.50t gold & multi		1.00	.40
	Nos. 979-981 (3)		2.20	.90

60th anniversary of the Russian Revolution.

Aporia Crataegi A225

Moths: 20m, Gastropacha quercifolia. 30m, Colias chrysoteme. 40m, Dasychira fascelina. 60m, Malocosoma neustria. 80m, Diacrisia sanno. 1t, Heodes virgaureae.

1977, Sept. 25	Photo.	Perf. 12½		
982	A225 10m multi		.25	.25
983	A225 20m multi		.40	.25
984	A225 30m multi		.50	.25
985	A225 40m multi		.80	.25
986	A225 60m multi		.70	.25
987	A225 80m multi		1.40	.35
988	A225 1t multi		1.75	.50
	Nos. 982-988 (7)		5.80	2.10

Giant Pandas A226

Pandas: 10m, Eating bamboo, vert. 30m, Female and cub in washtub, vert. 40m, Male and cub playing with bamboo. 60m, Female and cub, vert. 80m, Family. 1t, Male, vert.

1977, Nov. 25	Litho.	Perf. 12		
989	A226 10m multi		.25	.25
990	A226 20m multi		.25	.25
991	A226 30m multi		.40	.25
992	A226 40m multi		.50	.25
993	A226 60m multi		.80	.30
994	A226 80m multi		1.25	.45
995	A226 1t multi		1.60	.60
	Nos. 989-995 (7)		5.05	2.35

Souvenir Sheet

Helen Fourment and her Children, by Rubens — A227

1977, Dec. 5		Perf. 11½x10½		
996	A227 4t multi		4.50	4.50

Peter Paul Rubens (1577-1640).

Ferrari Racing Car A228

Experimental Racing Cars: 30m, Ford McLaren. 40m, Madi, USSR. 50m, Mazda. 60m, Porsche. 80m, Russian model car. 1.20t, The Blue Flame, US speed car.

1978, Jan. 28	Litho.	Perf. 12		
997	A228 20m multi		.25	.25
998	A228 30m multi		.25	.25
999	A228 40m multi		.30	.25
1000	A228 50m multi		.40	.30
1001	A228 60m multi		.60	.30
1002	A228 80m multi		.80	.25
1003	A228 1.20t multi		1.25	.50
	Nos. 997-1003 (7)		3.85	2.25

Boletus Variegatus — A229

Mushrooms: 30m, Russula cyanoxantha. 40m, Boletus aurantiacus. 50m, Boletus scaber. 60m, Russula flava. 80m, Lactarius resimus. 1.20t, Flammula spumosa.

1978, Feb. 28	Photo.	Perf. 11x11½		
1004	A229 20m yel & multi		.35	.25
1005	A229 30m yel & multi		.55	.25
1006	A229 40m yel & multi		.80	.30
1007	A229 50m yel & multi		1.00	.35
1008	A229 60m yel & multi		1.40	.40
1009	A229 80m yel & multi		1.90	.45
1010	A229 1.20t yel & multi		2.50	.75
	Nos. 1004-1010 (7)		8.50	2.75

Young Couple with Youth Flag — A230

1978, Apr.	Litho.	Perf. 11½x12		
1011	A230 60m multi		.60	.25

17th Congress of Mongolian Youth Organization, Ulan Bator, Apr. 1978.

Soccer, Sugar Loaf Mountain, Rio de Janeiro, Brazil 1950 Emblem — A231

Designs (Various Soccer Scenes and): 30m, Old Town Tower, Bern, Switzerland, 1954. 40m, Town Hall, Stockholm, Sweden, 1958. 50m, University of Chile, Chile, 1962. 60m,

MONGOLIA

Parliament and Big Ben, London, 1966. 80m, Degolladeo Theater, Guadalajara, Mexico, 1970. 1.20t, Town Hall and TV Tower, Munich, Germany.

1978, Apr. 15		Perf. 12	
1012 A231	20m multi	.25	.25
1013 A231	30m multi	.25	.25
1014 A231	40m multi	.30	.25
1015 A231	50m multi	.35	.30
1016 A231	60m multi	.45	.30
1017 A231	80m multi	.60	.30
1018 A231	1.20t multi	.90	.50
Nos. 1012-1018 (7)		3.10	2.15

11th World Cup Soccer Championship, Argentina, June 1-25. See No. C109.

Capex Emblem, Eurasian Beaver and Canada #336 — A232

30m, Tibetan sand grouse & Canada #478. 40m, Red-throated loon & Canada #369. 50m, Argali & Canada #324. 60m, Eurasian brown bear & Canada #322. 80m, Moose & Canada #323. 1.20t, Great black-backed gull & Canada #343.

1978, June	Litho.	Perf. 12	
1019 A232	20m multi	.25	.25
1020 A232	30m multi	.35	.25
1021 A232	40m multi	.50	.25
1022 A232	50m multi	.75	.30
1023 A232	60m multi	.85	.35
1024 A232	80m multi	.90	.45
1025 A232	1.20t multi	1.40	.70
Nos. 1019-1025 (7)		5.00	2.55

CAPEX '78 International Philatelic Exhibition, Toronto, June 9-18. See No. C110.

Marx, Engels and Lenin — A233

1978, July 11 Photo. *Perf. 12x11½*
1026 A233 60m gold, blk & red .60 .25

50th anniversary of publication in Prague of "Problems of Peace and Socialism."

Souvenir Sheet

Outdoor Rest, by Amgalan — A234

Paintings by D. Amgalan: No. 1027b, Winter Night (dromedary and people in snow). No. 1027c, Saddling up.

1978, Aug. 10 Litho. *Perf. 12*
1027 A234 Sheet of 3 3.25 3.25
a.-c. 1.50t any single 1.00

Philatelic cooperation between Hungary and Mongolia, 20th anniversary. No. 1027 contains 3 stamps and 3 labels.

Papillon — A235

Dogs: 20m, Black Mongolian sheepdog. 30m, Puli. 40m, St. Bernard. 50m, German shepherd. 60m, Mongolian watchdog. 70m, Samoyed. 80m, Laika (1st dog in space) and rocket. 1.20t, Cocker spaniel and poodles.

1978, Sept. 25	Litho.	Perf. 12	
1028 A235	10m multi	.25	.25
1029 A235	20m multi	.25	.25
1030 A235	30m multi	.35	.25
1031 A235	40m multi	.40	.25
1032 A235	50m multi	.50	.25
1033 A235	60m multi	.60	.25
1034 A235	70m multi	.70	.35
1035 A235	80m multi	.85	.35
1036 A235	1.20t multi	1.10	.55
Nos. 1028-1036 (9)		5.00	2.75

Open Book and Pen — A236

1978, Oct. 20 Photo. *Perf. 12x11½*
1037 A236 60m car & ultra .50 .25

Mongolian Writers' Association, 50th anniversary.

Souvenir Sheets

Paintings — A237

Melancholy, by Dürer — A238

Paintings: No. 1038a, Clothed Maya, by Goya. No. 1038b, "Ta Matete," by Gauguin. No. 1038c, Bridge at Arles, by Van Gogh.

1978, Oct. 30 Litho. *Perf. 12*
1038 A237 Sheet of 3 + 3 labels 4.50 4.50
a.-c. 1.50t any single + label 1.25 1.25

Perf. 11½
1039 A238 4t black 4.50 4.50

Anniversaries of European painters: Francisco Goya; Paul Gauguin; Vincent van Gogh; Albrecht Dürer.

Camel and Calf — A239

Bactrian Camels: 30m, Young camel. 40m, Two camels. 50m, Woman leading pack camel. 60m, Old camel. 80m, Camel pulling cart. 1.20t, Race.

1978, Nov. 30	Litho.	Perf. 12	
1040 A239	20m multi	.25	.25
1041 A239	30m multi	.25	.25
1042 A239	40m multi	.40	.25
1043 A239	50m multi	.50	.25
1044 A239	60m multi	.65	.30
1045 A239	80m multi	.85	.30
1046 A239	1.20t multi	1.20	.55
Nos. 1040-1046 (7)		4.10	2.25

Flags of Comecon Members, Globe — A240

1979, Jan. 2 Litho. *Perf. 12*
1047 A240 60m multi + label .50 .25

30th anniversary of the Council of Mutual Assistance (Comecon). Label and vignette separated by simulated perforations.

Silver Tabby — A241

Domestic Cats: 30m, White Persian. 50m, Red Persian. 60m, Cream Persian. 70m, Siamese. 80m, Smoky Persian. 1t, Burmese.

1979, Feb. 10			
1048 A241	10m multi	.25	.25
1049 A241	30m multi	.35	.25
1050 A241	50m multi	.45	.25
1051 A241	60m multi	.65	.25
1052 A241	70m multi	.80	.35
1053 A241	80m multi	.85	.35
1054 A241	1t multi	1.00	.45
Nos. 1048-1054 (7)		4.35	2.10

Potaninia Mongolica — A242

Flowers: 30m, Sophora alopecuroides. 50m, Halimodendron halodendron. 60m, Forget-me-nots. 70m, Pincushion flower. 80m, Leucanthemum Sibiricum. 1t, Edelweiss.

1979, Mar. 10	Litho.	Perf. 12	
1055 A242	10m multi	.25	.25
1056 A242	30m multi	.35	.25
1057 A242	50m multi	.45	.25
1058 A242	60m multi	.50	.25
1059 A242	70m multi	.55	.30
1060 A242	80m multi	.65	.35
1061 A242	1t multi	.70	.50
Nos. 1055-1061 (7)		3.45	2.15

Finland-Czechoslovakia, Finnish Flag — A243

Ice Hockey Games and 1980 Olympic Emblems: 30m, German Fed. Rep. Sweden, German flag. 50m, US-Canada, US flag. 60m, USSR-Sweden, Russian flag. 70m, Canada-USSR, Canadian flag. 80m, Swedish goalie and flag. 1t, Czechoslovakia-USSR, Czechoslovak flag.

1979, Apr. 10	Litho.	Perf. 12	
1062 A243	10m multi	.25	.25
1063 A243	30m multi	.25	.25
1064 A243	50m multi	.25	.25
1065 A243	60m multi	.40	.25
1066 A243	70m multi	.50	.25
1067 A243	80m multi	.60	.30
1068 A243	1t multi	.80	.35
Nos. 1062-1068 (7)		3.05	1.90

Ice Hockey World Championship, Moscow, Apr. 14-27.

Lambs — A244

Paintings: 30m, Milking, camels. 50m, Plane bringing supplies in winter. 60m, Herdsmen and horses. 70m, Milkmaids, vert. 80m, Summer Evening (camels). 1t, Landscape with herd. 4t, After the Storm.

Perf. 12x11½, 11½x12
1979, May 3 Litho.
1069 A244	10m multi	.25	.25
1070 A244	30m multi	.25	.25
1071 A244	50m multi	.35	.25
1072 A244	60m multi	.40	.25
1073 A244	70m multi	.45	.30
1074 A244	80m multi	.65	.30
1075 A244	1t multi	.85	.35
Nos. 1069-1075 (7)		3.20	1.95

Souvenir Sheet
1076 A244 4t multi 3.00 3.00

20th anniv. of 1st agricultural cooperative.

Souvenir Sheet

A245

Designs (Rowland Hill and): No. 1077a, Mongolia No. 4, Bulgaria No. 1, Philaserdica Emblem. No. 1077b, American mail coach. No. 1077c, Mail car, London-Birmingham railroad, 1838. 1077d, Packet leaving Southampton, Sept. 24, 1842, opening Indian mail service.

1979, May 15 Litho. *Perf. 12*
1077 A245 Sheet of 4, multi 4.50 4.50
a.-d. 1t any single 1.00 .90

Philaserdica '79, Sofia, May 18-27, and Rowland Hill (1795-1879), originator of penny postage.

Rocket, Manchester, 1829 — A246

Locomotives: 20m, "Adler" Nuremberg-Furth, 1835. 30m, American engine, 1860. 40m, Ulan Bator-Nalajh run, 1931. 50m, Moscow-Ulan Bator run, 1936. 60m, Moscow-Ulan Bator, 1970. 70m, Tokyo-Osaka run, 1963. 80m, Orleans Aerotrain, 1967. 1.20t, Soviet Rapidity, experimental train.

1979, June 8	Litho.	Perf. 12	
1078 A246	10m multi	.25	.25
1079 A246	20m multi	.25	.25
1080 A246	30m multi	.35	.25
1081 A246	40m multi	.45	.25
1082 A246	50m multi	.50	.25
1083 A246	60m multi	.55	.30
1084 A246	70m multi	.75	.30
1085 A246	80m multi	.80	.40
1086 A246	1.20t multi	.85	.50
Nos. 1078-1086 (9)		4.75	2.75

Intl. Transportation Exhibition, Hamburg. For surcharge see No. 2144B.

MONGOLIA

Mongolian and Russian Flags — A247
Battle Scene and Emblem — A248

1979, Aug. 10   Photo.   Perf. 11½x12
1087   A247   60m multi   .60   .25
1088   A248   60m multi   .60   .25
Battle of Ha-lo-hsin River, 40th anniversary.

Manuls — A249

Wild Cats: 30m, Lynx. 50m, Tigers. 60m, Snow leopards. 70m, Black panthers. 80m, Cheetahs. 1t, Lions.

1979, Sept. 10   Litho.   Perf. 12
1089   A249   10m multi   .25   .25
1090   A249   30m multi   .30   .25
1091   A249   50m multi   .50   .25
1092   A249   60m multi   .60   .25
1093   A249   70m multi   .75   .30
1094   A249   80m multi   .80   .35
1095   A249   1t multi   1.10   .45
   Nos. 1089-1095 (7)   4.30   2.10

Souvenir Sheet

A250

a, Brazil No. 1582. b, Brazil #1144 (Pele). c, Mongolia #C1.

1979, Sept. 15   Litho.   Perf. 11
1096   A250   Sheet of 3 + 3 labels   6.00   6.00
  a.-c.   1.50t any single + label   1.75   1.75

Brasiliana '79, 3rd World Thematic Stamp Exhibition, Rio de Janeiro, Sept. 15-23.

Cross-Country Skiing, Lake Placid '80 Emblem — A251

30m, Biathlon. 40m, Ice hockey. 50m, Ski jump. 60m, Downhill skiing. 80m, Speed skating. 1.20t, Bobsledding. 4t, Figure skating.

1980, Jan. 20   Litho.   Perf. 11½x12½
1097   A251   20m multi   .25   .25
1098   A251   30m multi   .30   .25
1099   A251   40m multi   .30   .25
1100   A251   50m multi   .40   .25
1101   A251   60m multi   .50   .25
1102   A251   80m multi   .60   .30
1103   A251   1.20t multi   .70   .35
   Nos. 1097-1103 (7)   3.05   1.90

Souvenir Sheet
1104   A251   4t multi   2.25   2.25
13th Winter Olympic Games, Lake Placid, NY, Feb. 12-24.

Flower Type of 1969
Souvenir Sheet
Design: Landscape and edelweiss.

1980, May 5   Litho.   Perf. 11
1105   A131   4t multi   2.00   1.75
London 1980 Intl. Stamp Exhib., May 6-14. No. 1105 contains one stamp 43x26mm.

Weightlifting, Moscow '80 Emblem — A252

1980, June 2   Litho.   Perf. 12
1106   A252   20m shown   .25   .25
1107   A252   30m Archery   .25   .25
1108   A252   40m Gymnast   .25   .25
1109   A252   50m Running   .40   .25
1110   A252   60m Boxing   .50   .25
1111   A252   80m Judo   .60   .25
1112   A252   1.20t Bicycling   .70   .35
   Nos. 1106-1112 (7)   2.95   1.85

Souvenir Sheet
1113   A252   4t Wrestling   2.00   1.75
22nd Summer Olympic Games, Moscow, July 19-Aug. 3.

Gold Medal, Swimmer, Moscow '80 Emblem — A253

Gold Medal, Moscow '80 Emblem and Number of Medals won by Top Countries: 30m, Fencing. 50m, Judo. 60m, Track. 80m, Boxing. 1t, Weight lifting. 1.20t, Kayak.

1980, Sept. 15   Litho.   Perf. 12½
1114   A253   20m multi   .25   .25
1115   A253   30m multi   .25   .25
1116   A253   50m multi   .30   .25
1117   A253   60m multi   .40   .25
1118   A253   80m multi   .50   .30
1119   A253   1t multi   .70   .40
1120   A253   1.20t multi   .90   .50
   Nos. 1114-1120 (7)   3.30   2.20
   See No. C144.

A254

No. 1121, Jumdshaigiin Zedenbal. No. 1122, Zedenbal, 1941. No. 1123, Zedenbal, 1979. No. 1124, With Brezhnev, horiz. No. 1125, With children. No. 1126, Sukhe Bator. No. 1127, Choibalsan.

1980, Sept. 17   Perf. 11½x12
1121   A254   60m blue green   .30   .25
1122   A254   60m gray green   .30   .25
1123   A254   60m blk, gray   .30   .25
1124   A254   60m reddish brown   .30   .25
1125   A254   60m carmine   .30   .25
1126   A254   60m brown purple   .30   .25
1127   A254   60m ultra   .30   .25
   Nos. 1121-1127 (7)   2.10   1.75

Miniature Sheet

A255

Cosmonauts from various Intercosmos flights: a, A. Gubarjev. b, Czechoslovakia No.2222. c, P. Klimuk. d, Poland No.2270. e, V. Bykovsky. f, DDR No.1947. g, N. Rukavishnikov. h, Bulgaria No.2576. i, V. Kubasov. j, Hungary No.C417.

1980, Oct. 10   Litho.   Perf. 12
1128   A255   Sheet of 10   3.50   3.50
  a.-j.   40m any single   .30   .30
Intercosmos cooperative space program. See No. 1232.

Benz, Germany, 1885 — A256

Antique Cars: 30m, President, Austria-Hungary, 1897. 40m, Armstrong Siddley, 1904. 50m, Russo-Balt, 1909. 60m, Packard, United States, 1909. 80m, Lancia, Italy, 1911. 1.60t, Marne taxi, France, 1914. 4t, Nami-1, Russia, 1927.

1980, Nov. 20   Litho.   Perf. 12½
1129   A256   20m multi   .25   .25
1130   A256   30m multi   .25   .25
1131   A256   40m multi   .45   .25
1132   A256   50m multi   .50   .35
1133   A256   60m multi   .60   .40
1134   A256   80m multi   .80   .50
1135   A256   1.60t multi   1.75   .75
   Nos. 1129-1135 (7)   4.60   2.75

Souvenir Sheet
1136   A256   4t multi   3.50   3.50

Penguins — A257

30m, Giant blue whale. 40m, Albatross. 50m, Weddell seals. 60m, Emperor penguins. 70m, Skua. 80m, Grampus. 1.20t, Penguins, Soviet plane. 4t, World map showing continental drift.

1980, Dec. 1   Perf. 12
1137   A257   20m shown   .65   .25
1138   A257   30m multi   .90   .25
1139   A257   40m multi   1.10   .30
1140   A257   50m multi   1.40   .30
1141   A257   60m multi   1.60   .35
1142   A257   70m multi   1.90   .45
1143   A257   80m multi   2.25   .60
1144   A257   1.20t multi   3.00   .90
   Nos. 1137-1144 (8)   12.80   3.40

Souvenir Sheet
1145   A257   4t multi   6.50   6.50
Antarctic animals and exploration. No. 1145 contains one 44mm circular stamp.

Souvenir Sheet

A258

1980, Dec. 20   Litho.   Perf. 11
1146   Sheet of 2   2.50   2.00
  a.   A258 2t shown   1.10   .75
  b.   A258 2t Old Marketplace   1.10   .75

The Shepherd Speaking the Truth, IYC Emblem — A259

IYC Emblem and Nursery Tales: 30m, Above Them the Sky is Always Clear. 40m, Winter's Joys. 50m, Little Musicians. 60m, Happy Birthday. 80m, The First Day of School. 1.20t, May Day. 4t, The Wonderworking Squirrels.

1980, Dec. 29   Perf. 12
1147   A259   20m multi   .25   .25
1148   A259   30m multi   .25   .25
1149   A259   40m multi   .30   .25
1150   A259   50m multi   .40   .25
1151   A259   60m multi   .50   .30
1152   A259   80m multi   .60   .40
1153   A259   1.20t multi   .75   .50
   Nos. 1147-1153 (7)   3.05   2.20

Souvenir Sheet
1154   A259   4t multi   2.50   2.00
Intl. Year of the Child (1979).

60th Anniversary of People's Army — A260

1981, Jan. 31   Litho.   Perf. 12
1155   A260   60m multi   .60   .25

60th Anniversary of People's Revolutionary Party — A261

1981, Feb. 2
1156   A261   60m multi   .60   .25

Ice Racing A262

Designs: Various racing motorcycles.

1981, Feb. 28   Perf. 12½
1157   A262   10m multi   .25   .25
1158   A262   20m multi   .25   .25
1159   A262   30m multi   .25   .25
1160   A262   40m multi   .35   .25
1161   A262   50m multi   .35   .25
1162   A262   60m multi   .45   .25
1163   A262   70m multi   .45   .25
1164   A262   80m multi   .50   .25
1165   A262   1.20t multi   .50   .25
   Nos. 1157-1165 (9)   3.35   2.25

Rocket Designer Koroljov — A263

Designs: 20m, Cosmonauts boarding Soyuz 39. 40m, Vostok I, Yuri Gagarin. 50m, Salyut space station. 60m, Satellite photographing earth. 80m, Light crystallization from Salyut spacecraft. 1.20t, Salyut, Kremlin, Sukhe Bator statue. 4t, Soviet and Mongolian cosmonauts.

MONGOLIA

1981, Mar. 22	Litho.	Perf. 12		
1166	A263	20m multi	.25	.25
1167	A263	30m multi	.30	.25
1168	A263	40m multi	.30	.25
1169	A263	60m multi	.40	.30
1170	A263	80m multi	.40	.30
1171	A263	1t multi	.60	.40
1172	A263	1.20t multi	.80	.60
		Nos. 1166-1172 (7)	3.05	2.35

Souvenir Sheet
Perf. 11½

| 1173 | A263 | 4t multi | 2.25 | 2.25 |

Intercosmos cooperative space program (Mongolia-USSR). No. 1173 contains one 29x39mm stamp.

A264

1981, Apr. 28	Litho.	Perf. 12		
1174		Sheet of 4 + 4 labels	6.00	6.00
a.	A264	1t No. 240, Ulan Bator + label	1.40	1.25
b.	A264	1t Germany #8N4, 8NB10 + label	1.40	1.25
c.	A264	1t Austria #B110 + label	1.40	1.25
d.	A264	1t Japan #827 + label	1.40	1.25

1981 Stamp Exhibitions: Mongolian Natl., Ulan Bator; Naposta, Stuttgart; WIPA, Vienna; Japex, Tokyo.

Star Shining on Factories and Sheep — A265

1981, May 5				
1175	A265	60m multi	.60	.25

18th Congress of Revolutionary People's Party, May.

Souvenir Sheet

Statue of Sukhe Bator, Mongolian Flag — A266

1981, May 20		Perf. 12½		
1176	A266	4t multi	2.50	1.50

Mongolian Revolutionary People's Party, 60th anniv.

Sheep Farming (Economic Development) — A267

30m, Transportation. 40m, Telecommunications. 50m, Public health service. 60m, Agriculture. 80m, Power plant. 1.20t, Public housing.

1981, June 1		Perf. 12½x11½		
1177	A267	20m shown	.25	.25
1178	A267	30m multi	.30	.25
1179	A267	40m multi	.40	.25
1180	A267	50m multi	.50	.35
1181	A267	60m multi	.60	.30
1182	A267	80m multi	.80	.40
1183	A267	1.20t multi	1.25	.60
		Nos. 1177-1183 (7)	4.10	2.40

Souvenir Sheet

A268

1981, July 11	Litho.	Perf. 12½x11½		
1184	A268	4t multi	2.50	2.50

20th anniv. of UN membership.

A269

Designs: Sailing ships: 10m, Egyptian, 15th cent. BC, horiz. 20m, Mediterranean, 9th cent., horiz. 40m, Hansa Cog, 12th cent. 50m, Venitian, 13th cent. 60m, Santa Maria. 80m, Endeavor. 1t, Poltava, 18th cent. 1.20t, US schooner, 19th cent.

1981, Aug. 1		Perf. 12		
1185	A269	10m multi	.25	.25
1186	A269	20m multi	.25	.25
1187	A269	40m multi	.35	.30
1188	A269	50m multi	.50	.30
1189	A269	60m multi	.60	.40
1190	A269	80m multi	.70	.40
1191	A269	1t multi	.85	.45
1192	A269	1.20t multi	1.00	.50
		Nos. 1185-1192 (8)	4.50	2.85

Mongolian-USSR Friendship Pact — A270

1981, Sept. 1		Perf. 11½x12		
1193	A270	60m multi	.60	.25

Flora, by Rembrandt — A271

30m, Hendrickje in the Bed. 40m, Young woman with Earrings. 50m, Young Girl in the Window. 60m, Hendrickje like Flora. 80m, Saskia with Red Flower. 1.20t, Holy Family with Drape. 4t, Self-portrait with Saskia.

1981, Sept. 1		Perf. 11½x12½		
1194	A271	20m shown	.25	.25
1195	A271	30m multi	.25	.25
1196	A271	40m multi	.30	.25
1197	A271	50m multi	.45	.25
1198	A271	60m multi	.60	.25
1199	A271	80m multi	.85	.30
1200	A271	1.20t multi	1.10	.35
		Nos. 1194-1200 (7)	3.80	1.90

Souvenir Sheet

| 1201 | A271 | 4t multi | 4.00 | 4.00 |

375th birth anniv. of Rembrandt.

Goat (Pawn) A272

Designs: Wood chess pieces.

1981, Sept. 30	Litho.	Perf. 12½		
1202	A272	20m shown	.25	.25
1203	A272	40m Cart (castle)	.45	.25
1204	A272	50m Camel (bishop)	.55	.25
1205	A272	60m Horse (knight)	.60	.30
1206	A272	80m Lion (queen)	.85	.35
1207	A272	1.20t Man and dog (king)	1.10	.60
		Nos. 1202-1207 (6)	3.80	2.00

Souvenir Sheet

| 1208 | A272 | 4t Men playing | 4.00 | 4.00 |

Camel and Circus Tent — A273

1981, Oct. 30	Litho.	Perf. 12		
1209	A273	10m shown	.25	.25
1210	A273	20m Horsemen	.25	.25
1211	A273	40m Wrestlers	.35	.25
1212	A273	50m Archers	.40	.25
1213	A273	60m Folksinger	.50	.30
1214	A273	80m Girl playing jat-ga	.65	.30
1215	A273	1t Ballet dancers	.90	.50
1216	A273	1.20t Statue	1.10	.50
		Nos. 1209-1216 (8)	4.40	2.60

Wolfgang Amadeus Mozart and Scene from his Magic Flute — A274

Composers and Scenes from their Works: 30m, Beethoven, Fidelio. 40m, Bartok, Miraculous Mandarin. 50m, Verdi, Aida. 60m, Tchaikovsky, Sleeping Beauty. 80m, Dvorak, New World Symphony score. 1.20t, Chopin, piano.

1981, Nov. 16				
1217	A274	20m shown	.30	.25
1218	A274	30m multi	.40	.25
1219	A274	40m multi	.40	.25
1220	A274	50m multi	.50	.30
1221	A274	60m multi	.50	.30
1222	A274	80m multi	.80	.40
1223	A274	1.20t multi	1.25	.50
		Nos. 1217-1223 (7)	4.15	2.25

Ribbon Weaver — A275

Designs: Mongolian women.

Perf. 11½x12½

1981, Dec. 10	Litho.			
1224	A275	20m multi	.25	.25
1225	A275	30m multi	.35	.25
1226	A275	40m multi	.45	.25
1227	A275	50m multi	.50	.25
1228	A275	60m multi	.60	.40
1229	A275	80m multi	.60	.50
1230	A275	1.20t multi	1.25	.75
		Nos. 1224-1230 (7)	4.00	2.65

Souvenir Sheet

| 1231 | A275 | 4t multi | 3.50 | 3.50 |

For surcharge, see No. 2728.

Intercosmos Type of 1980

Designs: a, V. Gorbatko. b, Y. Romanenko. c, V. Dzhanibekov. d, L. Popov. e, Vietnamese stamp. f, Cuban stamp. g, No. 1173. h, Romania No. C241.

1981, Dec. 28		Perf. 12		
1232	A255	Sheet of 8, multi	4.50	4.50
a.-h.		50m, any single	.50	.35

Historic Bicycles — A276

10m, Germany, 1816. 20m, Scotland, 1838. 40m, US, 1866. 50m, France, 1863. 60m, "Kangaroo", 1877. 80m, England, 1870. 1t, 1878. 1.20t, Modern bike. 4t, Racing.

1982, Mar. 25	Litho.	Perf. 11		
1233	A276	10m multi	.25	.25
1234	A276	20m multi	.25	.25
1235	A276	40m multi	.30	.25
1236	A276	50m multi	.40	.25
1237	A276	60m multi	.50	.30
1238	A276	80m multi	.60	.30
1239	A276	1t multi	.70	.40
1240	A276	1.20t multi	.80	.40
		Nos. 1233-1240 (8)	3.80	2.40

Souvenir Sheet
Perf. 12½

| 1241 | A276 | 4t multi | 2.75 | 2.75 |

No. 1241 contains one stamp 47x47mm.

1982 World Cup — A277

10m, Brazil, 1950. 20m, Switzerland, 1954. 40m, Sweden, 1958. 50m, Chile, 1962. 60m, England, 1966. 80m, Mexico, 1970. 1t, Germany, 1974. 1.20t, Argentina, 1978. 4t, Spain, 1982.

1982, Apr. 20		Perf. 12		
1242	A277	10m multi	.25	.25
1243	A277	20m multi	.25	.25
1244	A277	40m multi	.30	.25
1245	A277	50m multi	.40	.25
1246	A277	60m multi	.50	.25
1247	A277	80m multi	.60	.30
1248	A277	1t multi	.70	.40
1249	A277	1.20t multi	.80	.40
		Nos. 1242-1249 (8)	3.80	2.40

Souvenir Sheet
Perf. 11

| 1250 | A277 | 4t multi | 3.00 | 3.00 |

No. 1250 contains one stamp 40x40mm.

12th Trade Union Congress, Ulan Bator — A278

1982, May 20	Litho.	Perf. 11½x12½		
1251	A278	60m multi	1.25	.35

Souvenir Sheet

PHILEXFRANCE Intl. Stamp Exhibition, Paris, June 11-21 — A279

1982, June 11		Imperf.		
1252	A279	4t No. B13 design	2.50	2.50

MONGOLIA

George Dimitrov (1882-1949), First Prime Minister of Bulgaria — A280

1982, June 18   *Perf. 12*
1253 A280 60m gold & blk .60 .25

Chicks A281

1982, June 25   *Perf. 11*
1254 A281 10m shown .25 .25
1255 A281 20m Colt .25 .25
1256 A281 30m Lamb .40 .25
1257 A281 40m Fawn .45 .25
1258 A281 50m Camel calf .55 .25
1259 A281 60m Kid .60 .25
1260 A281 70m Calf .70 .30
1261 A281 1.20t Young boar .90 .30
Nos. 1254-1261 (8) 4.10 2.10

Coal Mining Industry A282

1982, July 5   *Perf. 12*
1262 A282 60m Mine, truck .60 .25

18th Mongolian Youth Org. Congress — A283

1982, Aug. 14   *Perf. 11½x12*
1263 A283 60m multi .60 .25

Siberian Pine — A284

30m, Abies sibirica. 40m, Populus diversifolia. 50m, Larix sibirica. 60m, Pinus silvestris. 80m, Betula platyphylla. 1.20t, Picea obovata.

1982, Aug. 16
1264 A284 20m shown .25 .25
1265 A284 30m multi .25 .25
1266 A284 40m multi .30 .25
1267 A284 50m multi .40 .25
1268 A284 60m multi .50 .25
1269 A284 80m multi .60 .25
1270 A284 1.20t multi .90 .30
Nos. 1264-1270 (7) 3.20 1.80

60th Anniv. of Mongolian Youth Org. — A285

1982, Aug. 30
1271 A285 60m multi .60 .25

Iseki-6500 Tractor, Japan A286

20m, Deutz-DX-230, Germany. 40m, Bonser, Gt. Britain. 50m, Intl.-884, US. 60m, Renault TX-145-14, France. 80m, Belarus-611, USSR. 1t, K-7100, USSR. 1.20t, DT-75, USSR.

1982, Oct. 1   *Litho.*   *Perf. 12½*
1272 A286 10m shown .25 .25
1273 A286 20m multi .25 .25
1274 A286 40m multi .30 .25
1275 A286 50m multi .40 .25
1276 A286 60m multi .50 .30
1277 A286 80m multi .60 .30
1278 A286 1t multi .70 .40
1279 A286 1.20m multi .80 .40
Nos. 1272-1279 (8) 3.80 2.40

Scenes from The Foal and The Hare Folktale A287

1983, Jan. 1   *Litho.*   *Perf. 14*
1280 A287 10m multi .25 .25
1281 A287 20m multi .25 .25
1282 A287 30m multi .25 .25
1283 A287 40m multi .35 .25
1284 A287 50m multi .40 .25
1285 A287 60m multi .50 .30
1286 A287 70m multi .80 .35
1287 A287 80m multi .90 .35
1288 A287 1.20t multi 1.10 .40
Nos. 1280-1288 (9) 4.80 2.65

Souvenir Sheet
Imperf.
1289 A287 7t multi 4.00 4.00
No. 1289 contains one stamp 58x58mm.

Scenes from Walt Disney's The Sorcerer's Apprentice A288

1983, Jan. 1
1290 A288 25m multi .25 .25
1291 A288 35m multi .30 .25
1292 A288 45m multi .35 .25
1293 A288 55m multi .45 .30
1294 A288 65m multi .55 .30
1295 A288 75m multi .65 .30
1296 A288 85m multi .85 .30
1297 A288 1.40t multi 1.00 .40
1298 A288 2t multi 1.10 .45
Nos. 1290-1298 (9) 5.50 2.80

Souvenir Sheet
1299 A288 7t multi 4.50 4.50

Fish, Lake Hevsgel A289

30m, Sheep, Zavhan Highlands. 40m, Beaver, Lake Hovd. 50m, Horses, Lake Uvs. 60m, Chamois, Bajanhongor Steppe. 80m, Mounted hunter, eagle, Bajan-Elgij Highlands. 1.20t, Camels, Gobi Desert.

1982, Nov. 30   *Perf. 12*
1300 A289 20m shown .25 .25
1301 A289 30m multi .25 .25
1302 A289 40m multi .30 .25
1303 A289 50m multi .40 .35
1304 A289 60m multi .50 .45
1305 A289 80m multi 1.40 .45
1306 A289 1.20t multi 1.40 .50
Nos. 1300-1306 (7) 4.50 2.50

Mongolian Skin Tent (Yurt) A290

20m, Antonov AN-24B plane. 40m, Deer. 50m, Bighorn sheep. 60m, Eagle. 80m, Museum of the Khans, Ulan Bator. 1.20t, Sukhe Bator monument, Ulan Bator.

1983, Mar. 30   *Litho.*   *Perf. 14*
1307 A290 20m multi .25 .25
1308 A290 30m shown .25 .25
1309 A290 40m multi .30 .25
1310 A290 50m multi .45 .25
1311 A290 60m multi 1.25 .35
1312 A290 80m multi .75 .30
1313 A290 1.20t multi .85 .35
Nos. 1307-1313 (7) 4.10 2.00

For surcharge, see No. 2670.

Souvenir Sheet

90th Birth Anniv. of Sukhe Bator A291

1983   *Perf. 13x14*
1314 A291 4t multi 2.50 2.50

No. 1314 with "1893-1993" overprinted in the sheet margin was produced in limited quantities.

Local Flowers A292

20m, Rose. 30m, Dahlias. 40m, Tagetes faula. 50m, Narcissus. 60m, Violets. 80m, Tulips. 1.20t, Heliopsis helianthoides.

1983, Feb. 4   *Photo.*   *Perf. 13*
1315 A292 20m multi .25 .25
1316 A292 30m multi .25 .25
1317 A292 40m multi .25 .25
1318 A292 50m multi .40 .25
1319 A292 60m multi .50 .25
1320 A292 80m multi .55 .25
1321 A292 1.20t multi .70 .30
Nos. 1315-1321 (7) 2.90 1.80

50th Anniv. of Border Forces — A293

1983, Feb. 9   *Litho.*   *Perf. 14*
1322 A293 60m multi .60 .25

Souvenir Sheet

BRASILIANA, Philatelic Exhibition — A294

1983, July 10   *Litho.*   *Perf. 14*
1323 A294 4t multi 2.50 2.00

Karl Marx — A295

1983, Oct. 1   *Litho.*   *Perf. 14*
1324 A295 60m gold, dp car & bl .60 .25

18th Party Congress, Ulan Bator A296

10m, Cattle. 20m, Coal. 30m, Garment. 40m, Agricultural. 60m, Communications. 80m, Transportation. 1t, Educational System.

1983, Nov. 1   *Litho.*   *Perf. 14*
1325 A296 10m multi .25 .25
1326 A296 20m multi .25 .25
1327 A296 30m multi .25 .25
1328 A296 40m multi .25 .25
1329 A296 60m multi .35 .25
1330 A296 80m multi 1.50 .40
1331 A296 1t multi .60 .35
Nos. 1325-1331 (7) 3.45 2.00

Souvenir Sheet

Sistine Madonna, by Raphael (1483-1520) — A297

1983, Dec. 15   *Litho.*   *Perf. 14x13½*
1332 A297 4t multi 4.00 4.00

A298

Children in Various Activities.

1984, Jan. 1   *Photo.*   *Perf. 13*
1333 A298 10m multi .25 .25
1334 A298 20m multi .25 .25
1335 A298 30m multi .30 .25
1336 A298 40m multi .45 .25
1337 A298 50m multi .75 .35
1338 A298 70m multi 1.10 .50
1339 A298 1.20t multi 1.50 .75
Nos. 1333-1339 (7) 4.60 2.60

Rodents A299

Various rodents.

1984, Jan. 15   *Litho.*   *Perf. 13½x13*
1340 A299 20m multi .25 .25
1341 A299 30m multi .45 .25
1342 A299 40m multi .55 .25
1343 A299 50m multi .70 .35
1344 A299 60m multi .85 .40
1345 A299 80m multi 1.10 .60
1346 A299 1.20t multi 1.40 .90
Nos. 1340-1346 (7) 5.30 3.05

MONGOLIA

1984 Winter Olympics
A300

20m, Bobsledding. 30m, Cross-country skiing. 40m, Hockey. 50m, Speed skating. 60m, Downhill skiing. 80m, Figure skating. 1.20t, Biathlon. 4t, Ski jumping.

1984, Feb. 15	Litho.	Perf. 14
1347 A300 20m multi	.25	.25
1348 A300 30m multi	.25	.25
1349 A300 40m multi	.25	.25
1350 A300 50m multi	.25	.25
1351 A300 60m multi	.40	.25
1352 A300 80m multi	.50	.25
1353 A300 1.20t multi	.60	.40
Nos. 1347-1353 (7)	2.50	1.90

Souvenir Sheet

| 1354 A300 4t multi | 2.50 | 2.50 |

Size of No. 1354: 134x106mm. Nos. 1347-1352 vert.

Children Feeding Lambs
A301

20m, Ice skating. 40m, Planting tree. 50m, Playing on beach. 60m, Carrying pail. 80m, Three dancers. 1.20t, Two dancers. 4t, Boy, girl.

1984, Mar. 1	Litho.	Perf. 12
1355 A301 20m multi	.25	.25
1356 A301 30m shown	.30	.25
1357 A301 40m multi	.40	.25
1358 A301 50m multi	.40	.25
1359 A301 60m multi	.50	.30
1360 A301 80m multi	.60	.30
1361 A301 1.20t multi	1.00	.40
Nos. 1355-1361 (7)	3.45	2.00

Souvenir Sheet

| 1362 A301 4t multi | 3.00 | 3.00 |

No. 1362 contains one stamp 48x46mm. Compare with Type SP3. For surcharges, see Nos. 2656-2657.

Mail Car, Communications Emblems — A302

20m, Earth satellite receiving station. 40m, Airplane. 50m, Central PO. 1t, Radar station. 1.20t, Train. 4t, Dish antenna.

1984, Apr. 15		Perf. 13½x14
1363 A302 10m shown	.25	.25
1364 A302 20m multi	.30	.25
1365 A302 40m multi	.40	.25
1366 A302 60m multi	.60	.30
1367 A302 1t multi	.90	.40
1368 A302 1.20t multi	2.00	1.00
Nos. 1363-1368 (6)	4.35	2.50

Souvenir Sheet
Imperf

| 1369 A302 4t multi | 2.50 | 2.50 |

1984 Summer Olympics
A303

1984, June 1	Photo.	Perf. 14
1370 A303 20m Gymnastics	.25	.25
1371 A303 30m Bicycling	.25	.25
1372 A303 40m Weight lifting	.35	.25
1373 A303 50m Judo	.35	.25
1374 A303 60m Archery	.50	.25
1375 A303 80m Boxing	.50	.25
1376 A303 1.20t High jump	.75	.35
Nos. 1370-1376 (7)	2.95	1.85

Souvenir Sheet

| 1377 A303 4t Wrestling | 3.25 | 2.25 |

Souvenir Sheet

AUSIPEX '84 and ESPANA '84 — A304

1984, May	Litho.	Perf. 14
1378 A304 4t Jet	3.50	3.50

Cuban Revolution, 25th Anniv. — A304a

1984, June 2	Litho.	Perf. 14
1378A A304a 60m multi	.60	.25

State Bank, 60th Anniv. — A304b

60m, Commemorative coins, 1981.

1984, Sept. 25		Perf. 13½x13
1378B A304b 60m multi	.50	.25

Radio Broadcasting in Mongolia, 50th Anniv. — A304c

1984, Sept. 1	Litho.	Perf. 13x13½
1378C A304c 60m multicolored	.75	.25

Scenes from Walt Disney's Mickey and the Beanstalk
A305

1984, Dec. 20	Litho.	Perf. 11
1379 A305 25m multi	.30	.25
1380 A305 35m multi	.40	.25
1381 A305 45m multi	.55	.25
1382 A305 55m multi	.65	.25
1383 A305 65m multi	.75	.30
1384 A305 75m multi	.85	.40
1385 A305 85m multi	.95	.50
1386 A305 1.40t multi	1.10	.65
1387 A305 2t multi	1.40	.80
Nos. 1379-1387 (9)	6.95	3.65

Miniature Sheet
Perf. 14

| 1388 A305 7t multi | 4.00 | 4.00 |

Fairy Tales
A306

1984, Dec. 20	Litho.	Perf. 13½
1389 A306 10m multi	.25	.25
1390 A306 20m multi	.30	.25
1391 A306 30m multi	.35	.25
1392 A306 40m multi	.40	.25
1393 A306 50m multi	.45	.25
1394 A306 60m multi	.50	.25
1395 A306 70m multi	.60	.35
1396 A306 80m multi	.75	.40
1397 A306 1.20t multi	.90	.55
Nos. 1389-1397 (9)	4.50	2.80

Miniature Sheet

| 1398 A306 4t multi | 4.00 | 4.00 |

Souvenir Sheet

60th Anniv. of Mongolian Stamps — A308

1984, Dec. 20	Litho.	Perf. 14
1400 A308 4t No. 1	3.00	3.00

Ulan Bator, 60th Anniv.
A309

Mongolian People's Republic, 60th Anniv.
A310

1984, Nov. 26	Litho.	Perf. 13x13½
1401 A309 60m multicolored	.75	.40

Perf. 14

| 1402 A310 60m multicolored | .75 | .40 |

Mongolian People's Party, 60th Anniv. — A311

1984, Nov. 26	Litho.	Perf. 14
1403 A311 60m multi	.60	.25

Native Masks — A312

1984, Dec. 31	Litho.	Perf. 14
1404 A312 20m multi	.25	.25
1405 A312 30m multi	.30	.25
1406 A312 40m multi	.45	.25
1407 A312 50m multi	.55	.25
1408 A312 60m multi	.75	.30
1409 A312 80m multi	1.00	.30
1410 A312 1.20t multi	1.25	.50
Nos. 1404-1410 (7)	4.55	2.10

Souvenir Sheet

| 1411 A312 4t multi | 4.00 | 4.00 |

Dogs — A313

20m, Collie. 30m, German Sheepdog. 40m, Papillon. 50m, Cocker Spaniel. 60m, Puppy. 80m, Dalmatians. 1.20t, Mongolian Sheepdog.

1984, Dec. 31	Litho.	Perf. 13
1412 A313 20m multi	.25	.25
1413 A313 30m multi	.25	.25
1414 A313 40m multi	.35	.25
1415 A313 50m multi	.55	.25
1416 A313 60m multi	.65	.30
1417 A313 80m multi	.80	.35
1418 A313 1.20t multi	1.25	.50
Nos. 1412-1418 (7)	4.10	2.10

Cattle
A314

20m, Shar tarlan. 30m, Bor khaliun. 40m, Sarlag. 50m, Dornod taliin bukh. 60m, Char tarlan. 80m, Nutgiin uulderiin unee. 1.20t, Tsagaan tolgoit.

1985, Jan.		Perf. 14
1419 A314 20m multi	.25	.25
1420 A314 30m multi	.35	.25
1421 A314 40m multi	.45	.25
1422 A314 50m multi	.50	.25
1423 A314 60m multi	.60	.25
1424 A314 80m multi	.80	.35
1425 A314 1.20t multi	.95	.35
Nos. 1419-1425 (7)	3.90	1.95

1984 Olympic Winners
A315

Gold medalists: 20m, Gaetan Boucher, Canada, 1500-meter speed skating. 30m, Eirik Kvalfoss, Norway, 10-kilometer biathlon. 40m, Marja-Lissa Haemaelainen, Finland, 5-kilometer Nordic skiing. 50m, Max Julen, Switzerland, men's giant slalom. 60m, Jens Weissflog, German Democratic Republic, 70-meter ski jump. 80m, W. Hoppe and D. Schauerhammer, German Democratic Republic, 2-man bobsled. 1.20t, Elena Valova and Oleg Vasiliev, USSR, pairs figure skating. 4t, USSR, ice hockey. Nos. 1430-1432 vert.

1985, Apr. 25		
1426 A315 20m multi	.25	.25
1427 A315 30m multi	.30	.25
1428 A315 40m multi	.40	.30
1429 A315 50m multi	.40	.30
1430 A315 60m multi	.60	.40
1431 A315 80m multi	.70	.50
1432 A315 1.20t multi	.80	.60
Nos. 1426-1432 (7)	3.45	2.60

Souvenir Sheet

| 1433 A315 4t multi | 3.00 | 3.00 |

Souvenir Sheet

Girl, Fawn
A316

1985, Apr. 25		
1434 A316 4m multi	4.00	4.00

MONGOLIA

Birds — A317

20m, Ciconia nigra. 30m, Haliaetus albicilla. 40m, Grus leucogeranus. 50m, Paradoxornis heudei. 60m, Grus monacha. 80m, Grus vipio. 1.20t, Buteo lagopus.

1985, May 1			Perf. 12½x13	
1435	A317	20m multi	.25	.25
1436	A317	30m multi	.25	.25
1437	A317	40m multi	.40	.25
1438	A317	50m multi	.50	.25
1439	A317	60m multi	.65	.30
1440	A317	80m multi	.80	.35
1441	A317	1.20t multi	1.25	.40
	Nos. 1435-1441 (7)		4.10	2.05

National Wildlife Preservation Association.

World Youth Festival, Moscow — A318

60m, Girls in folk costumes.

1985, June			Perf. 14	
1442	A318	60m multi	.60	.25

Camelus Bactrianus A319

Panthera Unicias A320

Cervus Elaphus A321

Camels, leopards and deer.

1985
1443	A319	50m Adults, young	1.00	.30
1444	A319	50m Facing right	1.00	.30
1445	A319	50m Facing left	1.00	.30
1446	A319	50m Trotting	1.00	.30
1447	A320	50m Hunting	.40	.25
1448	A320	50m Standing in snow	.40	.25
1449	A320	50m Female, young	.40	.25
1450	A320	50m Adults	.40	.25
1451	A321	50m Fawn	.90	.25
1452	A321	50m Doe in woods	.90	.25
1453	A321	50m Adult male	.90	.25
1454	A321	50m Adults, fawn	.90	.25
	Nos. 1443-1454 (12)		9.20	3.20

#1443-1446 show the World Wildlife Fund emblem, #1447-1454 the Natl. Wildlife Preservation emblem. Issue dates: #1443-1446, July 1; #1447-1454, Aug. 1.

UN, 40th Anniv. — A322

60m, Flags, UN building.

1985, Aug. 1			Perf. 13½x13	
1455	A322	60m multi	.75	.40

Indigenous Flowering Plants — A323

20m, Rosa davurica. 30m, Matricaria chamomilla. 40m, Taraxacum officinale. 50m, Saxzifraga hirculus. 60m, Vaccinium vitis idaea. 80m, Sanguisorba officinalis. 1.20t, Plantago major. 4t, Hippophae rhamnoides.

1985, Aug. 1			Perf. 14	
1456	A323	20m multi	.25	.25
1457	A323	30m multi	.30	.25
1458	A323	40m multi	.45	.25
1459	A323	50m multi	.55	.25
1460	A323	60m multi	.60	.25
1461	A323	80m multi	.80	.30
1462	A323	1.20t multi	1.10	.35
	Nos. 1456-1462 (7)		4.05	1.90

Souvenir Sheet
| 1463 | A323 | 4t multi | 4.00 | 4.00 |

Defeat of Nazi Germany, 40th Anniv. — A324

1985, Sept. 15			Perf. 13x13½	
1464	A324	60m Monument	.60	.25

A325

Various soccer plays. No. 1472 horiz.

1985, Oct. 1			Perf. 14	
1465	A325	20m multi	.25	.25
1466	A325	30m multi	.25	.25
1467	A325	40m multi	.25	.25
1468	A325	50m multi	.35	.25
1469	A325	60m multi	.40	.25
1470	A325	80m multi	.50	.25
1471	A325	1.20t multi	.55	.25
	Nos. 1465-1471 (7)		2.55	1.75

Souvenir Sheet
| 1472 | A325 | 4t multi | 2.50 | 2.50 |

1985 Junior World Soccer Championships, Moscow.

Souvenir Sheet

ITALIA '85 A326

1985, Oct. 1				
1473	A326	4t Horseman	2.50	2.00

Conquest of Space A327

Russian spacecraft.

1985, Nov. 1				
1474	A327	20m Soyuz	.25	.25
1475	A327	30m Cosmos	.25	.25
1476	A327	40m Venera 9	.25	.25
1477	A327	50m Salyut	.30	.25
1478	A327	60m Luna 9	.40	.25
1479	A327	80m Train	.45	.55
1480	A327	1.20t Dish receiver	.80	.25
	Nos. 1474-1480 (7)		2.70	2.05

Souvenir Sheet
1985, Dec. 15				
1481	A327	4t Cosmonaut on space walk	2.50	2.50

Mushrooms A328

20m, Tricholoma mongolica. 30m, Cantharellus cibarius. 40m, Armillariella mellea. 50m, Amanita caesarea. 70m, Xerocomus badius. 80m, Agaricus silvaticus. 1.20t, Boletus edulis.

1985, Dec. 1			Perf. 13½	
1482	A328	20m multi	.30	.25
1483	A328	30m multi	.45	.25
1484	A328	40m multi	.50	.25
1485	A328	50m multi	.60	.25
1486	A328	70m multi	.80	.30
1487	A328	80m multi	.95	.30
1488	A328	1.20t multi	1.50	.35
	Nos. 1482-1488 (7)		5.10	1.95

Souvenir Sheet

Phalacrocorax Penicillatus — A329

1986, Jan. 15			Perf. 12½x13	
1489	A329	4t multi	3.50	3.50

No. 1489 contains one stamp plus 2 labels picturing various bird species.

Young Pioneers — A330

1985, Dec. 31		Litho.	Perf. 13x13½	
1490	A330	60m multi	.60	.25

Victory Monument — A331

1985, Dec. 31			Perf. 12½x13	
1491	A331	60m multi	.60	.25

Victory over Japan ending WWII, 40th anniv.

Natl. Costumes — A332

1986, Mar. 1		Litho.	Perf. 14	
		Background Color		
1492	A332	60m yel grn, shown	.50	.25
1493	A332	60m red	.50	.25
1494	A332	60m pale yel grn	.50	.25
1495	A332	60m violet	.50	.25
1496	A332	60m ultra	.50	.25
1497	A332	60m bluish grn	.50	.25
1498	A332	60m pale org brn	.50	.25
	Nos. 1492-1498 (7)		3.50	1.75

Ernst Thalmann (1886-1944) — A333

1986, May 15		Litho.	Perf. 14	
1499	A333	60m gold, redsh brn & dk brn	.60	.25

Natl. Revolution, 65th Anniv. — A334

60m, Statue of Sukhe Bator.

1986, May 15				
1500	A334	60m multi	.60	.25

19th Socialist Party Congress — A335

1986, May 15				
1501	A335	60m multi	.60	.25

1986 World Cup Soccer Championships, Mexico — A336

FIFA emblem and various soccer plays. Nos. 1502-1503, 1505-1508 vert.

1986, May 31				
1502	A336	20m multi	.25	.25
1503	A336	30m multi	.25	.25
1504	A336	40m multi	.35	.25
1505	A336	50m multi	.40	.25
1506	A336	60m multi	.50	.25
1507	A336	80m multi	.60	.25
1508	A336	1.20t multi	.80	.30
	Nos. 1502-1508 (7)		3.15	1.80

Souvenir Sheet
| 1509 | A336 | 4t multi | 2.50 | 2.00 |

Mink, Wildlife Conservation — A337

MONGOLIA

1986, June 15
1510	A337	60m Spring	.55	.25
1511	A337	60m Summer	.55	.25
1512	A337	60m Autumn	.55	.25
1513	A337	60m Winter	.55	.25
	Nos. 1510-1513 (4)		2.20	1.00

Flowers — A338

20m, Valeriana officinalis. 30m, Hyoscymus niger. 40m, Ephedra sinica. 50m, Thymus gobica. 60m, Paeonia anomala. 80m, Achilea millefolium. 1.20t, Rhododendron adamsii.

1986, June 1   Litho.   Perf. 14
1514	A338	20m multi	.25	.25
1515	A338	30m multi	.30	.25
1516	A338	40m multi	.35	.25
1517	A338	50m multi	.40	.25
1518	A338	60m multi	.50	.25
1519	A338	80m multi	.75	.30
1520	A338	1.20t multi	1.00	.40
	Nos. 1514-1520 (7)		3.55	1.95

Butterflies — A339

20m, Neptis coenobita. 30m, Colias tycha. 40m, Leptidea amurensis. 50m, Oeneis tarpenledevi. 60m, Mesoacidalia charlotta. 80m, Smerinthus ocellatus. 1.20t, Pericalia matronula.

1986, Aug. 1   Perf. 13½
1521	A339	20m multi	.25	.25
1522	A339	30m multi	.25	.25
1523	A339	40m multi	.35	.25
1524	A339	50m multi	.40	.25
1525	A339	60m multi	.45	.25
1526	A339	80m multi	.55	.30
1527	A339	1.20t multi	.85	.40
	Nos. 1521-1527 (7)		3.10	1.95

Circus A340

Animal trainers & acrobats. #1531-1534 vert.

1986, Aug. 1   Perf. 14
1528	A340	20m multi	.25	.25
1529	A340	30m multi	.30	.25
1530	A340	40m multi	.35	.25
1531	A340	50m multi	.40	.25
1532	A340	60m multi	.50	.25
1533	A340	80m multi	.75	.25
1534	A340	1.20t multi	1.00	.30
	Nos. 1528-1534 (7)		3.55	1.80

Przewalski's Horses — A341

No. 1535, Two horses, foal. No. 1536, One facing left, two facing right. No. 1537, Three facing right. No. 1538, Four in storm.

1986, Aug. 1   Litho.   Perf. 14
1535	A341	50m multi	.75	.25
1536	A341	50m multi	.75	.25
1537	A341	50m multi	.75	.25
1538	A341	50m multi	.75	.25
	Nos. 1535-1538 (4)		3.00	1.00

Pelicans (Pelecanus) — A341a

No. 1538A, Crispus feeding. No. 1538B, Crispus wading. No. 1538C, Onocrotalus flying. No. 1538D, Onocrotalus on land.

1986, Sept. 1   Litho.   Perf. 14
1538A	A341a	60m multi	.75	.25
1538B	A341a	60m multi	.75	.25
1538C	A341a	60m multi	.75	.25
1538D	A341a	60m multi	.75	.25
	Nos. 1538A-1538D (4)		3.00	1.00

Saiga Tatarica Mongolica A341b

No. 1538E, Spring (doe, fawn). No. 1538F, Summer (buck, doe). No. 1538G, Fall (buck). No. 1538H, Winter (buck, doe).

1986, Sept. 15
1538E	A341b	60m multi	.75	.25
1538F	A341b	60m multi	.75	.25
1538G	A341b	60m multi	.75	.25
1538H	A341b	60m multi	.75	.25
	Nos. 1538E-1538H (4)		3.00	1.00

Musical Instruments — A342

1986, Sept. 4
1539	A342	20m Morin khuur	.25	.25
1540	A342	30m Bishguur	.30	.25
1541	A342	40m Ever buree	.35	.25
1542	A342	50m Shudarga	.40	.25
1543	A342	60m Khiil	.50	.25
1544	A342	80m Janchir	.75	.30
1545	A342	1.20t Jatga	1.00	.30
	Nos. 1539-1545 (7)		3.55	1.85

Souvenir Sheet
1546	A342	4t like 20m, vert.	3.50	3.50

STOCKHOLMIA '86. Nos. 1539-1543 vert.

Intl. Peace Year A342a

1986, Sept. 20   Litho.   Perf. 13x13½
1546A	A342a	10m multicolored	.60	.25

North American Bird Species A343

No. 1547, Anthus spinoletta. No. 1548, Aythya americana. No. 1549, Bonasa umbellus. No. 1550, Olor columbianus.

1986, Oct. 1
1547	A343	60m multi	.80	.50
1548	A343	60m multi	.80	.50
1549	A343	60m multi	.80	.50
1550	A343	60m multi	.80	.50
	Nos. 1547-1550 (4)		3.20	2.00

Eastern Architecture — A343a

Various two-story buildings.

1986, Oct. 1   Color of Border
1551	A343a	60m dark grn & blk	.75	.40
1552	A343a	60m beige & blk	.75	.40
1553	A343a	60m apple grn & blk	.75	.40
1554	A343a	60m red brn & blk	.75	.40
	Nos. 1551-1554 (4)		3.00	1.60

Classic Automobiles — A344

20m, 1922 Alfa Romeo RL Sport, Italy. 30m, 1912 Stutz Bearcat, US. 40m, 1902 Mercedes Simplex, Germany. 50m, 1923 Tatra 11, Czechoslovakia. 60m, 1908 Ford Model T, US. 80m, 1905 Vauxhall, England. 1.20t, 1913 Russo-Baltik, Russia.

1986, Oct. 1   Litho.   Perf. 14
1554A	A344	20m multi	.25	.25
1554B	A344	30m multi	.30	.25
1554C	A344	40m multi	.35	.25
1554D	A344	50m multi	.40	.25
1554E	A344	60m multi	.50	.25
1554F	A344	80m multi	.75	.25
1554G	A344	1.20t multi	1.00	.40
	Nos. 1554A-1554G (7)		3.55	1.95

Souvenir Sheet
1554H	A344	4t like 1.20t	3.00	3.00

Woodpeckers A344a

20m, Picus canus. 30m, Jynx torquilla. 40m, Dryobates major. 50m, Dryobates leucotos. 60m, Dryobates minor. 80m, Dryocopus martius. 1.20t, Picoides tridactylus. 4t, Saphopipo noguchi.

1986, Nov. 1
1555	A344a	20m multi	.25	.25
1556	A344a	30m multi	.30	.25
1557	A344a	40m multi	.35	.25
1558	A344a	50m multi	.40	.25
1559	A344a	60m multi	.50	.25
1560	A344a	80m multi	.75	.30
1561	A344a	1.20t multi	1.00	.40
	Nos. 1555-1561 (7)		3.55	1.95

Souvenir Sheet
1562	A344a	4t multi	4.00	4.00

Chess Champions A345

Portraits and chessmen on boards in match-winning configurations: 20m, Steinitz, Austria. 30m, Lasker, Germany. 40m, Alekhine, France. 50m, Botvinnik, USSR. 60m, Karpov, USSR. 80m, N. Gaprin-dashvili. 1.20t, M. Chibur-danidze. No. 1562H, Chess champions Gary Kasparov, Jose R. Capablanca, Max Euwe, Vassily Smyslow, Mikhail Tal, Tigran Petrosian, Boris Spassky and Bobby Fischer; W. Menchik, L. Rudenko, E. Bykowa and O. Rubzowa.

1986, Nov. 1   Perf. 14
1562A	A345	20m multi	.25	.25
1562B	A345	30m multi	.25	.25
1562C	A345	40m multi	.35	.25
1562D	A345	50m multi	.35	.25
1562E	A345	60m multi	.45	.25
1562F	A345	80m multi	.55	.25
1562G	A345	1.20t multi	.90	.30

Size: 110x100mm
Imperf
1562H	A345	4t multi	3.50	3.50
	Nos. 1562A-1562H (8)		6.50	5.30

Souvenir Sheet

Halley's Comet A346

1986, Nov. 30   Litho.   Perf. 14
1563	A346	4t multicolored	3.00	2.00

Ovis Ammon Ammon A347

No. 1565, In the mountains. No. 1566, Close-up of head. No. 1567, Male, female, lamb.

1987, Jan. 1
1564	A347	60m shown	.75	.25
1565	A347	60m multi	.75	.25
1566	A347	60m multi	.75	.25
1567	A347	60m multi	.75	.25
	Nos. 1564-1567 (4)		3.00	1.00

For surcharges, see Nos. 2779-2782.

Children's Activities — A348

20m, Backpacking, hunting butterflies. 30m, Playing with calves. 40m, Chalk-writing on cement. 50m, Playing soccer. 60m, Go-cart, model rocket, boat. 80m, Agriculture. 1.20t, Playing the morin khuur, dancing.

1987, Feb. 1
1568	A348	20m multi	.25	.25
1569	A348	30m multi	.30	.25
1570	A348	40m multi	.35	.25
1571	A348	50m multi	.40	.25
1572	A348	60m multi	.45	.25
1573	A348	80m multi	.55	.25
1574	A348	1.20t multi	.80	.30
	Nos. 1568-1574 (7)		3.10	1.80

Int'l. Peace Year (40m); Child Survival Campaign (50m).

13th Trade Unions Congress A349

1987, Feb. 15   Perf. 13½x13
1575	A349	60m multi	1.00	.35

Equestrian Sports A350

1987, Mar. 1
1576	A350	20m Lassoer	.25	.25
1577	A350	30m Breaking horse	.25	.25
1578	A350	40m Shooting bow	.30	.25
1579	A350	50m Race	.40	.25
1580	A350	60m Retrieving flags	.45	.25
1581	A350	80m Tug-of-war	.55	.25
1582	A350	1.20t Racing wolf	.85	.30
	Nos. 1576-1582 (7)		3.05	1.80

583

MONGOLIA

Admission into Comecon, 25th Anniv. — A351

1987, Apr. 15   *Perf. 13x13½*
1583   A351   60m multi   .60   .25

Fruit — A352   A353

20m, Hippophae rhamnoides. 30m, Ribes nigrum. 40m, Ribes rubrus. 50m, Ribes altissimum. 60m, Rubus sachalinensis. 80m, Padus asiatica. 1.20t, Fragaria orientalis. 4t, Malus domestica.

1987, June 1   *Perf. 13½*
1584   A352   20m multi   .25   .25
1585   A352   30m multi   .35   .25
1586   A352   40m multi   .45   .25
1587   A352   50m multi   .50   .25
1588   A352   60m multi   .60   .25
1589   A352   80m multi   .70   .25
1590   A352   1.20t multi   .90   .25
    Nos. 1584-1590 (7)   3.75   1.75

Souvenir Sheet
Perf. 14
1591   A353   4t multicolored   3.00   3.00

Soviet-Mongolian Diplomatic Relations, 50th Anniv. — A354

1987, July 1   *Perf. 13x13½*
1592   A354   60m multi   .60   .25

Russian Revolution, 70th Anniv. — A355

1987, July 1
1593   A355   60m multi   .60   .25

Folk Dances A356

1987, Aug. 1   *Perf. 14*
1594   A356   20m multi   .25   .25
1595   A356   30m multi, diff.   .25   .25
1596   A356   40m multi, diff.   .25   .25
1597   A356   50m multi, diff.   .40   .25
1598   A356   60m multi, diff.   .50   .25
1599   A356   80m multi, diff.   .60   .25
1600   A356   1.20t multi, diff.   .70   .30
    Nos. 1594-1600 (7)   2.95   1.80

Antiques — A357

Full costume and accessories: 20m, Folk costumes. 30m, Gilded nunchaku. 40m, Brooches. 50m, Draw-string pouch, rice bowl. 60m, Headdress. 80m, Pouches, bottle, pipe. 1.20t, Sash, brooch.

1987, Aug. 10
1601   A357   20m multi   .25   .25
1602   A357   30m multi   .25   .25
1603   A357   40m multi   .25   .25
1604   A357   50m multi   .40   .25
1605   A357   60m multi   .50   .25
1606   A357   80m multi   .60   .25
1607   A357   1.20t multi   .70   .30
    Nos. 1601-1607 (7)   2.95   1.80

Souvenir Sheet

HAFNIA '87 A358

1987, Aug. 10
1608   A358   4t multi   3.00   2.75

Swans A359

No. 1609, Cygnus olor on land. No. 1610, Cygnus olor in water. No. 1611, Cygnus bewickii. No. 1612, Cygnus bewickii, gunus and olor.

1987, Aug. 15
1609   A359   60m multi   .75   .25
1610   A359   60m multi   .75   .25
1611   A359   60m multi   .75   .25
1612   A359   60m multi   .75   .25
    Nos. 1609-1612 (4)   3.00   1.00

Domestic and Wild Cats — A360

1987, Oct. 1   *Litho.*   *Perf. 14*
1613   A360   20m multi, vert.   .30   .25
1614   A360   30m multi   .35   .25
1615   A360   40m multi, vert.   .40   .25
1616   A360   50m shown   .50   .25
1617   A360   60m multi   .60   .25
1618   A360   80m multi   .75   .25
1619   A360   1.20t multi   1.10   .30
    Nos. 1613-1619 (7)   4.00   1.85

Miniature Sheet
1620   A360   4t multi, vert.   3.00   2.75

Helicopter A361

20m, B-12. 30m, Westland-WG-30. 40m, Bell-S-206L. 50m, Kawasaki-369HS. 60m, KA-32. 80m, MI-17. 1.20t, MI-10K.

1987, Oct. 3   *Perf. 12½x11½*
1621   A361   20m multi   .25   .25
1622   A361   30m multi   .25   .25
1623   A361   40m multi   .25   .25
1624   A361   50m multi   .40   .25
1625   A361   60m multi   .50   .25
1626   A361   80m multi   .60   .25
1627   A361   1.20t multi   .70   .30
    Nos. 1621-1627 (7)   2.95   1.80

Disney Cartoons A362

The Brave Little Tailor (25m-55m, 2t, No. 1637), and The Celebrated Jumping Frog of Calaveras County (65m-1.40t, No. 1638).

1987, Nov. 23   *Perf. 14*
1628   A362   25m multi   .25   .25
1629   A362   35m multi   .25   .25
1630   A362   45m multi   .40   .25
1631   A362   55m multi   .50   .25
1632   A362   65m multi   .60   .25
1633   A362   75m multi   .70   .25
1634   A362   85m multi   .80   .30
1635   A362   1.40t multi   .90   .45
1636   A362   2t multi   1.20   .65
    Nos. 1628-1636 (9)   5.60   2.90

Souvenir Sheets
1637   A362   7t multi   4.00   4.00
1638   A362   7t multi   4.00   4.00

A363

Tropical Fish A364

20m, Betta splendens. 30m, Carassius auratus. 40m, Rasbora hengeli. 50m, Aequidens. 60m, Xiphophorus macalatus. 80m, Xiphophorus helleri. 1.20t, Pterophyllum scalare, vert. 4t, Crenuchus spilurus.

1987, Oct.   *Perf. 13x12½, 12½x13*
1639   A363   20m multi   .25   .25
1640   A363   30m multi   .25   .25
1641   A363   40m multi   .35   .25
1642   A363   50m multi   .40   .25
1643   A363   60m multi   .50   .25
1644   A363   80m multi   .60   .25
1645   A363   1.20t multi   .80   .30
    Nos. 1639-1645 (7)   3.15   1.80

Miniature Sheet
Perf. 14
1646   A364   4t multi   3.75   3.25

19th Communist Party Congress — A365

1987, Dec.   *Perf. 14*
1647   A365   60m Family   .40   .25
1648   A365   60m Construction   .75   .25
1649   A365   60m Jet, harvesting, produce   .40   .25
1650   A365   60m Education   .40   .25
1651   A365   60m Transportation   .40   .25
1652   A365   60m Heavy industry   .40   .25
1653   A365   60m Science and technology   .40   .25
    Nos. 1647-1653 (7)   3.15   1.75

Vulpes Vulpes (Fox) A366

1987, Dec.
1654   A366   60m Adult in snow   .65   .25
1655   A366   60m Adult, young   .65   .25
1656   A366   60m Adult in field   .65   .25
1657   A366   60m Close-up of head   .65   .25
    Nos. 1654-1657 (4)   2.60   1.00

Souvenir Sheet

INTERCOSMOS — A367

1987, Dec. 15   *Litho.*   *Perf. 14*
1658   A367   4t multi   2.75   2.25

Souvenir Sheet

PRAGA '88 A368

1988, Jan. 30
1659   A368   4t 1923 Tatra 11   2.75   2.25

Sukhe Bator — A369

1988, Feb. 2   *Perf. 13x13½*
1660   A369   60m multi   .60   .25

For surcharge, see footnote after No. 2764.

Roses — A370

1988, Feb. 20   *Perf. 14*
1661   A370   20m Invitation   .25   .25
1662   A370   30m Meilland   .30   .25
1663   A370   40m Pascali   .30   .25
1664   A370   50m Tropicana   .40   .25
1665   A370   60m Wendy Cussons   .40   .25

MONGOLIA

1666	A370	80m Blue moon	.45	.25
1667	A370	1.20t Diorama	.60	.30
		Nos. 1661-1667 (7)	2.70	1.80

Souvenir Sheet

1668	A370	4t multicolored	2.50	2.00

19th Communist Youth Congress — A371

1988, Apr. 15   Perf. 12½x13

1669	A371	60m multicolored	.80	.25

Puppets A372

Folk tales: 20m, Ukhaant Ekhner. 30m, Altan Everte Mungun Turuut. 40m, Aduuchyn Khuu. 50m, Suulenkhuu. 60m, Khonchyn Khuu. 80m, Argat Byatskhan Baatar. 1.20t, Botgochyn Khuu.

1988, Apr. 1   Litho.   Perf. 14

1670	A372	20m multi	.25	.25
1671	A372	30m multi	.25	.25
1672	A372	40m multi	.25	.25
1673	A372	50m multi	.40	.25
1674	A372	60m multi	.50	.25
1675	A372	80m multi	.60	.25
1676	A372	1.20t multi	.70	.30
		Nos. 1670-1676 (7)	2.95	1.80

1988 Summer Olympics, Seoul — A373

20m, Judo. 30m, Women's archery. 40m, Weight lifting. 50m, Women's gymnastics. 60m, Cycling. 80m, Running. 1.20t, Wrestling. 4t, Boxing.

1988, Feb. 15

1677	A373	20m multi	.25	.25
1678	A373	30m multi	.25	.25
1679	A373	40m multi	.30	.25
1680	A373	50m multi	.35	.25
1681	A373	60m multi	.45	.25
1682	A373	80m multi	.50	.25
1683	A373	1.20t multi	.55	.30
		Nos. 1677-1683 (7)	2.65	1.80

Souvenir Sheet

1684	A373	4t multi	2.75	2.25

Soviet Space Achievements A374

1988, May 15

1685	A374	20m Cosmos	.25	.25
1686	A374	30m Meteor	.25	.25
1687	A374	40m Salyut-Soyuz	.40	.25
1688	A374	50m Prognoz-6	.45	.25
1689	A374	60m Molniya-1	.50	.25
1690	A374	80m Soyuz	.60	.25
1691	A374	1.20t Vostok	1.00	.25
		Nos. 1685-1691 (7)	3.45	1.75

Effigies of Buddhist Deities — A375

Various statues.

1988, June 15   Litho.   Perf. 14

1692	A375	20m multi	.25	.25
1693	A375	30m multi, diff.	.25	.25
1694	A375	40m multi, diff.	.30	.25
1695	A375	50m multi, diff.	.40	.25
1696	A375	60m multi, diff.	.50	.25
1697	A375	70m multi, diff.	.60	.25
1698	A375	80m multi, diff.	.70	.30
1699	A375	1.20t multi, diff.	.80	.30
		Nos. 1692-1699 (8)	3.80	2.10

Wildlife Conservation — A376

Eagles — Haliaeetus albicilla: No. 1700, Eagle facing left, diff., vert. No. 1701, Landing on branch, vert. No. 1702, Facing right, vert.

1988, Aug. 1   Litho.   Perf. 14

1700	A376	60m multi	.70	.25
1701	A376	60m multi	.70	.25
1702	A376	60m multi	.70	.25
1703	A376	60m shown	.70	.25
		Nos. 1700-1703 (4)	2.80	1.00

Souvenir Sheet

Cosmos A377

1988, Sept. 15   Litho.   Perf. 14

1704	A377	4t Satellite links	3.50	3.50

Opera A378

1988, Oct. 1   Litho.   Perf. 13x12½

1705	A378	60m multi + label	1.50	.75

Equus hemionus A380

1988, May 3

1713	A380	60m Mare, foal	.55	.25
1714	A380	60m Ass's head	.55	.25
1715	A380	60m Ass galloping	.55	.25
1716	A380	60m Ass cantering	.55	.25
		Nos. 1713-1716 (4)	2.20	1.00

Winners of the 1988 Winter Olympics, Calgary A381

No. 1717, Matti Nykänen, Finland. No. 1718, Bonnie Blair, US, vert. No. 1719, Alberto Tomba, Italy, vert. No. 1720, USSR hockey team, vert. No. 1721, Katarina Witt, DDR.

1988, July 1

1717	A381	1.50t multicolored	.50	.25
1718	A381	1.50t multicolored	.50	.25
1719	A381	1.50t multicolored	.50	.25
1720	A381	1.50t multicolored	.50	.25
		Nos. 1717-1720 (4)	2.00	1.00

Souvenir Sheet

1721	A381	4t multicolored	2.75	2.75

A382

20m, Horsemanship. 30m, Archery. 40m, Wrestling. 50m, Archery, diff. 70m, Horsemanship, diff. 1.20t, Horsemanship, wrestling, archery.

1988, Sept. 1

1722	A382	10m shown	.25	.25
1723	A382	20m multi	.25	.25
1724	A382	30m multi	.30	.25
1725	A382	40m multi	.35	.25
1726	A382	50m multi	.50	.25
1727	A382	70m multi	.55	.25
1728	A382	1.20t multi	.65	.30
		Nos. 1722-1728 (7)	2.85	1.80

Socialism and Peace — A383

1988, Dec. 1   Perf. 13x13½

1729	A383	60m multicolored	.75	.25

Goats A384

Various species.

1989, Jan. 15   Perf. 14

1730	A384	20m multi	.30	.25
1731	A384	30m multi	.35	.25
1732	A384	40m multi	.45	.25
1733	A384	50m multi	.50	.25
1734	A384	60m multi	.60	.25
1735	A384	80m multi	.75	.25
1736	A384	1.20t multi	1.00	.30
		Nos. 1730-1736 (7)	3.95	1.80

Souvenir Sheet

1737	A384	4t multi, vert.	3.25	3.25

Souvenir Sheet

Child Survival A385

4t, Drawing by H. Jargalsuren.

1989, Jan. 28   Litho.   Perf. 14

1738	A385	4t multicolored	3.50	2.00

Karl Marx — A386

1989, Feb. 25   Litho.   Perf. 13x13½

1739	A386	60m multicolored	.75	.25

Miniature Sheet

A387

Mongolian Airline Jet — A388

1989, July 1   Perf. 14

1740	A387	Sheet of 3	5.50	5.50
a.		20m Concorde jet	.65	.40
b.		60m TGV high-speed train	1.50	1.25
c.		1.20t Statue of Sukhe Bator	3.50	3.00

Souvenir Sheet

1741	A388	4t multicolored	3.50	3.50

PHILEXFRANCE '89, BULGARIA '89.
For overprint see No. 1756.

World War II Memorial — A389

1989, Sept. 2

1742	A389	60m multicolored	.75	.50

For surcharge, see No. 2384B.

Cacti — A390

20m, O. microdasys. 30m, E. multiplex. 40m, R. tephracanthus. 50m, B. haselbergii. 60m, G. mihanovichii. 80m, C. strausii. 1.20t, Horridocactus tuberisvicatus. 4t, Astrophytum ornatum.

1989, Sept. 7

1743	A390	20m multi	.25	.25
1744	A390	30m multi	.25	.25
1745	A390	40m multi	.35	.25
1746	A390	50m multi	.40	.25
1747	A390	60m multi	.50	.25
1748	A390	80m multi	.65	.25
1749	A390	1.20t multi	.80	.30
		Nos. 1743-1749 (7)	3.20	1.80

Souvenir Sheet

1750	A390	4t multi	2.75	2.50

MONGOLIA

A391

Winners at the 1988 Summer Olympics, Seoul: No. 1751, Kristin Otto, East Germany. No. 1752, Florence Griffith-Joyner, US. No. 1753, Gintaoutas Umaras, USSR. No. 1754, Stefano Cerioni, Italy. No. 1755, N. Enkhbat, Mongolia.

1989, Oct. 1

1751	A391	60m multi	.50	.25
1752	A391	60m multi	.50	.25
1753	A391	60m multi	.50	.25
1754	A391	60m multi	.50	.25
		Nos. 1751-1754 (4)	2.00	1.00

Souvenir Sheet

1755	A391	4t multi	3.00	2.00

No. 1740 Overprinted for WORLD STAMP EXPO '89

1989, Nov. 17   Miniature Sheet

1756	A387	Sheet of 3	8.00	8.00
a.		20m multicolored	.75	.50
b.		60m multicolored	2.00	1.50
c.		1.20t multicolored	4.50	4.00

Books, Fountain Pen — A392

1989, Dec. 1

1757	A392	60m multicolored	.75	.25

Beavers (Castor fiber birulai) A393

No. 1758, Cutting down saplings. No. 1759, Rolling wood across ground. No. 1760, Beaver on land, in water. No. 1761, Beaver and young.

1989, Dec. 10

1758	A393	60m multi	.65	.25
1759	A393	60m multi	.65	.25
1760	A393	60m multi	.65	.25
1761	A393	60m multi	.65	.25
		Nos. 1758-1761 (4)	2.60	1.00

Medals and Military Decorations — A394

1989, Dec. 31   Perf. 13x13½

1762	A394	60m pink & multi	.60	.25
1763	A394	60m lt blue grn & multi	.60	.25
1764	A394	60m vio & multi	.60	.25
1765	A394	60m org & multi	.60	.25
1766	A394	60m brt blue & multi	.60	.25
1767	A394	60m ver & multi	.60	.25
1768	A394	60m vio & multi	.60	.25
		Nos. 1762-1768 (7)	4.20	1.75

Bears and Giant Pandas A395

20m, Ursus pruinosis. 30m, Ursus arctos syriacus. 40m, Ursus thibetanus. 50m, Ursus maritimus. 60m, Ursus arctos bruinosus. 80m, Ailuropus melanoleucus. 1.20t, Ursus arctos isabellinus.
4t, Ailuropus melanoleucus, diff.

1990, Jan. 1   Perf. 14

1769	A395	20m multi	.25	.25
1770	A395	30m multi	.25	.25
1771	A395	40m multi	.30	.25
1772	A395	50m multi	.35	.30
1773	A395	60m multi	.55	.45
1774	A395	80m multi	.75	.60
1775	A395	1.20t multi	1.10	1.00
		Nos. 1769-1775 (7)	3.55	3.10

Souvenir Sheet

1776	A395	4t multi	5.00	3.00

Winter Sports — A396

20m, 4-man bobsled. 30m, Luge. 40m, Women's figure skating. 50m, 1-man bobsled. 60m, Pairs figure skating. 80m, Speed skating. 1.20t, Ice speedway.
4t, Ice hockey.

1990, Jan. 6

1777	A396	20m multi	.25	.25
1778	A396	30m multi	.25	.25
1779	A396	40m multi	.30	.25
1780	A396	50m multi	.35	.25
1781	A396	60m multi	.45	.25
1782	A396	80m multi	.55	.25
1783	A396	1.20t multi	.85	.30
		Nos. 1777-1783 (7)	3.00	1.80

Souvenir Sheet

1784	A396	4t multi	4.00	3.00

Space Exploration A397

Rockets and spacecraft: 20m, Soyuz, USSR. 30m, Apollo-Soyuz, US-USSR. 40m, Columbia space shuttle, US, vert. 50m, Hermes, France. 60m, Nippon, Japan, vert. 80m, Energy, USSR, vert. 1.20t, Buran, USSR, vert.
4t, Sanger, West Germany.

1990, Jan. 30

1785	A397	20m shown	.25	.25
1786	A397	30m multicolored	.25	.25
1787	A397	40m multicolored	.35	.25
1788	A397	50m multicolored	.45	.25
1789	A397	60m multicolored	.55	.30
1790	A397	80m multicolored	.75	.30
1791	A397	1.20t multicolored	1.10	.40
		Nos. 1785-1791 (7)	3.70	2.00

Souvenir Sheet

1792	A397	4t multicolored	4.00	4.00

Jawaharlal Nehru, 1st Prime Minister of Independent India — A398

1990, Feb. 10

1793	A398	10m gold, blk & dark red brn	1.50	.75

Statue of Sukhe Bator — A399

1990, Feb. 27

1794	A399	10m multicolored	1.50	.75

Mongolian Ballet A400

Dancers in scenes from various ballets. 40m, 80m, 1.20t vert.

1990, Feb. 28

1795	A400	20m shown	.25	.25
1796	A400	30m multi	.25	.25
1797	A400	40m multi	.40	.25
1798	A400	50m multi	.50	.25
1799	A400	60m multi	.60	.25
1800	A400	80m multi	.65	.25
1801	A400	1.20t multi	.90	.30
		Nos. 1795-1801 (7)	3.55	1.80

Dated 1989.

Automobiles — A401

20m, Citroen, France. 30m, Volvo 760 GLF, Sweden. 40m, Honda, Japan. 50m, Volga, USSR. 60m, Ford Granada, US. 80m, VAZ 21099, USSR. 1.20t, Mercedes Class 190, West Germany.

1990, Mar. 26

1802	A401	20m multi	.25	.25
1803	A401	30m multi	.25	.25
1804	A401	40m multi	.35	.25
1805	A401	50m multi	.45	.25
1806	A401	60m multi	.50	.25
1807	A401	80m multi	.55	.25
1808	A401	1.20t multi	.85	.30
		Nos. 1802-1808 (7)	3.20	1.80

Souvenir Sheet

1809	A401	4t like 50m	3.50	2.50

Lenin — A402

1990, Mar. 27   Perf. 13x13½

1810	A402	60m gold, black & ver	1.00	.50

Unen Newspaper, 70th Anniv. — A403

1990, Apr. 1   Perf. 14

1811	A403	60m multicolored	.90	.50

End of World War II, 45th Anniv. — A404

1990, Apr. 1

1812	A404	60m multicolored	1.00	.60

Buddhist Deities (18th-20th Cent. Paintings) — A405

20m, Damdin Sandub. 30m, Pagwa Lama. 40m, Chu Lha. 50m, Agwanglobsan. 60m, Dorje Dags Dan. 80m, Wangchikdorje. 1.20t, Buddha.
4t, Migjed Jang-Rasek.

1990, Apr. 1

1813	A405	20m multi	.25	.25
1814	A405	30m multi	.25	.25
1815	A405	40m multi	.35	.25
1816	A405	50m multi	.85	.30
1817	A405	60m multi	.65	.30
1818	A405	80m multi	.80	.40
1819	A405	1.20t multi	1.10	.50
		Nos. 1813-1819 (7)	4.25	2.25

Souvenir Sheet

1820	A405	4t multi	6.50	6.50

A406

Aspects of a Cooperative Settlement — A407

Paintings: 20m, Animals on plain, rainbow. 30m, Workers, reindeer, dog, vert. 40m, Two men, mountains, Bactrian camels. 50m, Man, Bactrian camels. 60m, Huts, animal shelter, corral. 80m, Breaking horses, vert. 1.20t, Sheep, shepherd girl on horse. 4t, Wrestling match.

1990, Apr. 1

1821	A406	20m shown	.25	.25
1822	A406	30m multicolored	.30	.25
1823	A406	40m multicolored	.50	.25
1824	A406	50m multicolored	.60	.30
1825	A406	60m multicolored	.70	.40
1826	A406	80m multicolored	.90	.50
1827	A406	1.20t multicolored	1.40	.55
		Nos. 1821-1827 (7)	4.65	2.50

Souvenir Sheet

1828	A407	4t shown	4.00	4.00

Scenes from Various Mongolian-made Films — A408

1990, Apr. 1

1829	A408	20m shown	.25	.25
1830	A408	30m multi, diff.	.35	.25
1831	A408	40m multi, diff.	.50	.30
1832	A408	50m multi, diff.	.65	.40
1833	A408	60m multi, diff.	.80	.50
1834	A408	80m multi, diff.	1.00	.65
1835	A408	1.20t multi, diff.	1.40	.90
		Nos. 1829-1835 (7)	4.95	3.25

Souvenir Sheet

1836	A408	4t multi, diff., vert.	3.50	2.00

MONGOLIA

Souvenir Sheet

Stamp World London '90 — A409

1990, Apr. 1
| 1837 | A409 | 4t multicolored | 4.00 | 4.00 |

1990 World Cup Soccer Championships, Italy — A410

Trophy and various athletes.

1990, Apr. 30
1838	A410	20m multicolored	.25	.25
1839	A410	30m multicolored	.25	.25
1840	A410	40m multicolored	.30	.25
1841	A410	50m multicolored	.40	.25
1842	A410	60m multicolored	.45	.25
1843	A410	80m multicolored	.65	.25
1844	A410	1.20t multicolored	.95	.25
		Nos. 1838-1844 (7)	3.25	1.75

Souvenir Sheet
| 1845 | A410 | 4t Trophy, vert. | 3.00 | 2.00 |

Nos. 304-307 Ovptd.

1990, May 1 Photo. Perf. 11½x12
1846	A84	20m multicolored	3.50	
1847	A84	30m multicolored	4.00	
1848	A84	50m multicolored	5.00	
1849	A84	60m multicolored	6.00	
		Nos. 1846-1849 (4)	18.50	

Coronation of Genghis Khan, 800th anniv. (in 1989).

Souvenir Sheet

Genghis Khan A411

1990, May 8 Litho. Perf. 13½
| 1850 | A411 | 7t multicolored | 5.00 | 5.00 |

Stamp World London '90. Exists imperf. Exists without "Stamp World London '90" and Great Britain No. 1.

Cranes (Grus vipio pallas) A412

1990, May 23 Perf. 14
1851	A412	60m brt blue & multi	.75	.35
1852	A412	60m brt rose lil & multi	.75	.35
1853	A412	60m red lil & multi	.75	.35
1854	A412	60m car rose & multi	.75	.35
		Nos. 1851-1854 (4)	3.00	1.40

Nos. 1853-1854 are vert.

Marine Mammals A413

20m, Balaenoptera physalus. 30m, Megaptera novaeangliae. 40m, Monodon monoceros. 50m, Grampus griseus. 60m, Tursiops truncatus. 80m, Lagenorhynchus acutius. 1.20t, Balaena mysticetus. 4t, Killer whale.

1990, June 20 Litho. Perf. 14
1855	A413	20m multi	.25	.25
1856	A413	30m multi	.30	.25
1857	A413	40m multi	.45	.25
1858	A413	50m multi	.55	.30
1859	A413	60m multi	.70	.35
1860	A413	80m multi	.90	.45
1861	A413	1.20t multi	1.10	.45
		Nos. 1855-1861 (7)	4.25	2.30

Souvenir Sheet
| 1861A | A413 | 4t multi | 4.00 | 4.00 |

Cultural Heritage — A415

No. 1864, Fire ring. No. 1865, Genghis Khan. No. 1866, Tent. No. 1867, Horses. No. 1868, Royal family. No. 1869, Royal court.

1990, Aug. 13 Perf. 13x12½
1862	A414	10m shown	.25	.25
1863	A414	10m Like No. 1862, arrows at left	.25	.25
1864	A415	40m multi	.45	.25
1865	A415	60m multi	.65	.25
1866	A414	60m multi	.65	.25
1867	A415	60m multi	.65	.25
1868	A414	80m green panel	.95	.40
1869	A414	80m dk bl panel	.95	.40
	a.	Souv. sheet, #1862-1869 + label	8.00	8.00
		Nos. 1862-1869 (8)	4.80	2.30

20th Party Congress — A416

1990, Mar. 1 Litho. Perf. 14
| 1870 | A416 | 60m multicolored | .90 | .50 |

Dinosaurs A417

1990, Aug. 25
1871	A417	20m shown	.25	.25
1872	A417	30m multi, diff.	.35	.25
1873	A417	40m multi, diff.	.50	.25
1874	A417	50m multi, diff	.65	.30
1875	A417	60m multi, vert.	.80	.35
1876	A417	80m multi, diff.	1.00	.45

Size: 60x21mm Perf. 13
| 1877 | A417 | 1.20t multi, diff. | 1.40 | .55 |
| | | Nos. 1871-1877 (7) | 4.95 | 2.40 |

Souvenir Sheet
| 1878 | A417 | 4t multi, diff. | 5.00 | 5.00 |

Giant Pandas A418

10m, Adult on rock, vert. 20m, Adult, eating, vert. 30m, Adult and cub, vert. 50m, Adult and cub, resting. 60m, Adult, mountains. 80m, Adult and cub, playing. 1.20t, Adult, in winter. 4t, Family.

1990, Aug. 15 Litho. Perf. 14
1879	A418	10m multi	.25	.25
1880	A418	20m multi	.30	.25
1881	A418	30m multi	.40	.25
1882	A418	40m shown	.45	.30
1883	A418	50m multi	.60	.35
1884	A418	60m multi	.70	.40
1885	A418	80m multi	.95	.60
1886	A418	1.20t multi	1.40	.80
		Nos. 1879-1886 (8)	5.05	3.20

Souvenir Sheet
| 1887 | A418 | 4t multi | 5.00 | 5.00 |

Pyramids of Egypt A419

Seven wonders of the ancient world: 20m, Lighthouse of Alexander, vert. 40m, Statue of Zeus, vert. 50m, Colossus of Rhodes, vert. 60m, Mausoleum of Hallcarnassus, vert. 80m, Temple of Artemis. 1.20t, Hanging gardens of Babylon, vert. 4t, Pyramids of Egypt, vert.

1990, Sept. 25
1888	A419	20m multicolored	.35	.25
1889	A419	30m shown	.45	.25
1890	A419	40m multicolored	.65	.25
1891	A419	50m multicolored	.75	.25
1892	A419	60m multicolored	1.00	.25
1893	A419	80m multicolored	1.25	.40
1894	A419	1.20t multicolored	1.75	.65
		Nos. 1888-1894 (7)	6.20	2.30

Souvenir Sheet
| 1895 | A419 | 4t multi | 6.00 | 6.00 |

Moschus Moschiferus — A419a

No. 1895B, In snow. No. 1895C, Facing left. No. 1895D, Two, one on ground.

1990, Sept. 26 Litho. Perf. 14
1895A	A419a	60m shown	.75	.35
1895B	A419a	60m multi	.75	.35
1895C	A419a	60m multi	.75	.35
1895D	A419a	60m multi	.75	.35
		Nos. 1895A-1895D (4)	3.00	1.40

Parrots — A420

1990, Oct. 25 Litho. Perf. 14
1896	A420	20m shown	.25	.25
1897	A420	30m multi, diff.	.25	.25
1898	A420	40m multi, diff.	.40	.25
1899	A420	50m multi, diff.	.55	.30
1900	A420	60m multi, diff.	.70	.35
1901	A420	80m multi, diff.	.95	.45
1902	A420	1.20t multi, diff.	1.40	.50
		Nos. 1896-1902 (7)	4.50	2.35

Souvenir Sheet
| 1903 | A420 | 4t multi, diff. | 4.25 | 3.75 |

Butterflies A421

Designs: 20m, Purpurbar. 30m, Grosses nachtpfauenauge. 40m, Grosser C-Falter. 50m, Stachelbeerspanner. 60m, Damenbrett. 80m, Schwalbenschwanz. 1.20t, Aurorafalter. 4t, Linienschwarmer, vert.

1990, Nov. 25 Litho. Perf. 14
1904	A421	20m multicolored	.25	.25
1905	A421	30m multicolored	.30	.25
1906	A421	40m multicolored	.45	.25
1907	A421	50m multicolored	.55	.30
1908	A421	60m multicolored	.70	.40
1909	A421	80m multicolored	.80	.40
1910	A421	1.20t multicolored	1.00	.50
		Nos. 1904-1910 (7)	4.05	2.35

Souvenir Sheet
| 1911 | A421 | 4t multicolored | 4.00 | 3.50 |

For surcharges, see Nos. 2910-2912.

Flintstones Visit Mongolia A422

Designs: 25m, Dino, Bamm-Bamm. 35m, Dino, Bamm-Bamm, diff., vert. 45m, Betty, Wilma, Bamm-Bamm, Pebbles. 55m, Fred, Barney, Dino. 65m, Flintstones & Rubbles. 75m, Bamm-Bamm riding Dino. 85m, Fred, Barney, Bamm-Bamm. 1.40t, Flintstones, Rubbles in car. 2t, Fred, Barney. No. 1921, Wilma, Betty & Bamm-Bamm. No. 1922, Bamm-Bamm, Pebbles riding Dino.

1991, Feb. 10 Litho. Perf. 14
1912	A422	25m multicolored	.30	.25
1913	A422	35m multicolored	.30	.25
1914	A422	45m multicolored	.45	.25
1915	A422	55m multicolored	.50	.25
1916	A422	65m multicolored	.70	.25
1917	A422	75m multicolored	.70	.30
1918	A422	85m multicolored	.85	.30
1919	A422	1.40t multicolored	1.20	.40
1920	A422	2t multicolored	1.75	.40
		Nos. 1912-1920 (9)	6.75	2.65

Souvenir Sheets
| 1921 | A422 | 7t multicolored | 4.50 | 4.50 |
| 1922 | A422 | 7t multicolored | 4.50 | 4.50 |

The Jetsons — A423

Designs: 20m, Jetsons blasting off in spaceship. 25m, Jetsons on planet, horiz. 30m, George, Jane, Elroy & Astro. 40m, George, Judy, Elroy & Astro. 50m, Jetsons in spaceship, horiz. 60m, George, Jane, Elroy & Mr. Spacely, horiz. 70m, George, Elroy wearing jet packs. 80m, Elroy. 1.20t, Elroy, Judy & Astro. No. 1932, Elroy, red flowers. No. 1933, Elroy, blue flowers.

1991, Feb. 10
1923	A423	20m multicolored	.25	.25
1924	A423	25m multicolored	.25	.25
1925	A423	30m multicolored	.35	.25
1926	A423	40m multicolored	.45	.25
1927	A423	50m multicolored	.50	.30
1928	A423	60m multicolored	.55	.30
1929	A423	70m multicolored	.65	.30
1930	A423	80m multicolored	.70	.40
1931	A423	1.20t multicolored	1.10	.40
		Nos. 1923-1931 (9)	4.80	2.70

Souvenir Sheets
| 1932 | A423 | 7t multicolored | 4.50 | 4.50 |
| 1933 | A423 | 7t multicolored | 4.50 | 4.50 |

587

MONGOLIA

Mongolian People's Revolutionary Party, 70th Anniv. — A423a

1991, Mar. 1		Litho.		Perf. 14	
1933A	A423a	60m multicolored		.90	.40

A424

Stamp World London '90 — A425

Various birds: 25m, Black-capped Chickadee (Poecile atricapillus). 35m, Northern Cardinal (Cardinalis cardinalis). 45m, Crested Shelduck (Tadorna cristata). 55m, Mountain Bluebird (Sialia currucoides). 65m, Baltimore Oriole (Icterus galbula). 75m, Bluethroat (Luscinia svecica), horiz. 85m, Eastern Bluebird (Sialia sialis). 1.40t, Great Reed Warbler (Acrocephalus arundinaceus). 2t, Golden Eagle (Aquila chrysaetos).
No. 1943, Greater Scaup (Aythya marila). No. 1944, Common Pheasant (Phasianus colchicus), horiz.

1991, Mar. 3		Litho.		Perf. 14½	
1934	A424	25m multicolored		.25	.25
1935	A424	35m multicolored		.35	.25
1936	A424	45m multicolored		.50	.25
1937	A424	55m multicolored		.60	.25
1938	A424	65m multicolored		.75	.25
1939	A424	75m multi, horiz.		.80	.30
1940	A424	85m multicolored		1.00	.40
1941	A424	1.40t multicolored		1.50	.50
1942	A424	2t multicolored		2.25	.55
		Nos. 1934-1942 (9)		8.00	3.00
		Souvenir Sheets			
1943	A424	7t multicolored		7.00	7.00
1944	A425	7t multicolored		7.00	7.00

Butterflies and Flowers of Mongolia — A426

Designs: 20m, 30m-60m, various butterflies. Others, various flowers.

1991, Mar. 3		Litho.		Perf. 14½	
1945	A426	20m multicolored		.25	.25
1946	A426	25m multicolored		.25	.25
1947	A426	30m multicolored		.30	.25
1948	A426	40m multicolored		.40	.25
1949	A426	50m multicolored		.50	.25
1950	A426	60m multicolored		.60	.25
1951	A426	70m multicolored		.70	.30
1952	A426	80m multicolored		.80	.30
1953	A426	1.20t multicolored		1.10	.40
		Nos. 1945-1953 (9)		4.90	2.50

Nos. 1945-1953 and Types Overprinted

1991, Mar. 3

1954	A426	20m multicolored		.45	.25
1955	A426	25m multicolored		.50	.25
1956	A426	30m multicolored		.65	.25
1957	A426	40m multicolored		.85	.25
1958	A426	50m multicolored		1.00	.25
1959	A426	60m multicolored		1.25	.25
1960	A426	70m multicolored		1.50	.30
1961	A426	80m multicolored		1.75	.30
1962	A426	1.20t multicolored		2.25	.40
		Nos. 1954-1962 (9)		10.20	2.50
		Souvenir Sheets			
1963	A426	7t Butterfly		10.00	10.00
1964	A426	7t Flower		10.00	10.00

Nos. 1963-1964 were not issued without overprint which appears in sheet margin only.

Mongolian People's Army, 70th Anniv. — A426a

People's Army — A426b

1991, Mar. 18		Litho.		Perf. 14	
1964A	A426a	60m multicolored		.90	.40
		Souvenir Sheet			
1964B	A426b	4t multicolored		3.00	3.00

Issue date: No. 1964B 7/11/91.

Birds — A427

20m, Lururus tetrix. 30m, Tadorna tadorna. 40m, Phasianus colchicus. 50m, Clangula byemalis. 60m, Tetrastes bonasia. 80m, Mergus serrator. 1.20t, Bucephaia clangula. 4t, Anas crecca, vert.

1991, Apr. 1				Perf. 14	
1965	A427	20m multi		.25	.25
1966	A427	30m multi		.40	.25
1967	A427	40m multi		.45	.25
1968	A427	50m multi		.60	.30
1969	A427	60m multi		.80	.45
1970	A427	80m multi		1.20	.45
1971	A427	1.20t multi		1.40	.65
		Nos. 1965-1971 (7)		5.10	2.55
		Souvenir Sheet			
1972	A427	4t multi		4.50	4.50

Flowers — A428

20m, Dianthus superbus. 30m, Gentiana puenmonanthe. 40m, Taraxacum officinale. 50m, Iris sibrica. 60m, Lilium martagon. 80m, Aster amellus. 1.20t, Cizsium rivulare. 4t, Campanula persicifolia.

1991, Apr. 15					
1973	A428	20m multi		.25	.25
1974	A428	30m multi		.30	.25
1975	A428	40m multi		.45	.25
1976	A428	50m multi		.60	.30
1977	A428	60m multi		.60	.40
1978	A428	80m multi		.80	.40
1979	A428	1.20t multi		1.20	.50
		Nos. 1973-1979 (7)		4.20	2.35
		Souvenir Sheet			
1980	A428	4t multi		4.00	4.00

Buddhist Effigies — A429

20m, Defend. 30m, Badmasanhava. 40m, Avalokitecvara. 50m, Buddha. 60m, Mintugwa. 80m, Shyamatara. 1.20t, Samvara. 4t, Lamidhatara.

1991, May 1					
1981	A429	20m multi		.25	.25
1982	A429	30m multi		.25	.25
1983	A429	40m multi		.45	.25
1984	A429	50m multi		.60	.30
1985	A429	60m multi		.75	.40
1986	A429	80m multi		1.00	.45
1987	A429	1.20t multi		1.10	.50
		Nos. 1981-1987 (7)		4.40	2.40
		Souvenir Sheet			
1988	A429	4t multi		4.50	4.50
a.		With Phila Nippon '91 emblem overprinted in sheet margin		4.00	4.00

For surcharge, see No. 2658.

Insects — A430

20m, Neolamprima adolphinae. 30m, Chelorrhina polyphemus. 40m, Coptolabrus coelestis. 50m, Epepeotes togatus. 60m, Cicindela chinensis. 80m, Macrodontia cervicornis. 1.20t, Dynastes hercules. 4t, Cercopis sanguinolenta, vert.

1991, May 22					
1989	A430	20m multi		.25	.25
1990	A430	30m multi		.30	.25
1991	A430	40m multi		.45	.25
1992	A430	50m multi		.60	.30
1993	A430	60m multi		.70	.40
1994	A430	80m multi		.85	.45
1995	A430	1.20t multi		1.25	.50
		Nos. 1989-1995 (7)		4.40	2.40
		Souvenir Sheet			
1995A	A430	4t multi		4.25	4.25

African Animals — A431

1991, May 23					
1996	A431	20m Zebras		.25	.25
1997	A431	30m Cheetah		.35	.25
1998	A431	40m Black rhinos		.50	.25
1999	A431	50m Giraffe, vert.		.65	.30
2000	A431	60m Gorilla		.75	.40
2001	A431	80m Elephants		.90	.45
2002	A431	1.20t Lion, vert.		1.25	.50
		Nos. 1996-2002 (7)		4.65	2.40
		Souvenir Sheet			
2003	A431	4t Gazelle		5.00	5.00

No. 1997 is incorrectly spelled "Cheetan."

Exhibition of Meiso Mizuhara's Mongolian Stamp Collection — A432

1991, June		Litho.		Perf. 13½	
2004	A432	1.20t multicolored		3.00	1.00

Lizards — A433

20m, Iguana iguana. 30m, Ptychozoon kihli. 40m, Chlamydosaurus kingii. 50m, Cordylus cordylus. 60m, Basiliscus basilicus. 80m, Tupinambis teguixin. 1.20t, Amblyrhynchus cristatus. 4t, Varanus bengalensis, vert.

1991, Oct. 29				Perf. 14	
2005	A433	20m multi		.25	.25
2006	A433	30m multi		.30	.25
2007	A433	40m multi		.45	.25
2008	A433	50m multi		.60	.30
2009	A433	60m multi		.75	.40
2010	A433	80m multi		.90	.45
2011	A433	1.20t multi		1.40	.50
		Nos. 2005-2011 (7)		4.65	2.40
		Souvenir Sheet			
2012	A433	4t multi		4.25	4.25

Masks and Costumes — A434

Various masks and costumes.

1991, Oct. 1					
2013	A434	35m multicolored		.40	.25
2014	A434	45m multicolored		.50	.25
2015	A434	55m multicolored		.65	.25
2016	A434	65m multicolored		.75	.30
2017	A434	85m multicolored		1.00	.50
2018	A434	1.40t multicolored		1.65	.80
2019	A434	2t multicolored		2.35	1.00
		Nos. 2013-2019 (7)		7.30	3.35
		Souvenir Sheet			
2020	A434	4t multicolored		5.50	5.50

Phila Nippon '91 — A435

1991, Oct. 29					
2021	A435	1t Pagoda		.55	.50
2022	A435	2t Japanese beauty		.80	.75
2023	A435	3t Mongolian woman		1.10	.75
2024	A435	4t Mongolian building		1.50	1.00
		Nos. 2021-2024 (4)		3.95	3.00

Fantasia, 50th Anniv. — A436

Designs: 1.70t, Poster, 1985. 2t, Poster, 1940. 2.30t, Poster, 1982. 2.60t, Poster, 1981. 4.20t, Poster, 1969. 10t, Poster, 1941. 15t, Drawing of Mlle. Upanova, 1940. 16t, Sketch of Mickey as Sorcerer's Apprentice.
No. 2033, Mickey as Sorcerer's Apprentice. No. 2034, Dinosaurs from "The Rite of Spring," horiz. No. 2035, Thistles and orchids from "Russian Dance," horiz. No. 2036, Dancing mushrooms from "Chinese Dance," horiz.

1991, Dec. 31		Perf. 13½x14, 14x13½			
2025	A436	1.70t multicolored		.25	.25
2026	A436	2t multicolored		.35	.25
2027	A436	2.30t multicolored		.40	.25
2028	A436	2.60t multicolored		.55	.25
2029	A436	4.20t multicolored		.80	.35
2030	A436	10t multicolored		1.50	.50
2031	A436	15t multicolored		1.75	1.10
2032	A436	16t multicolored		2.50	1.10
		Nos. 2025-2032 (8)		8.10	4.05
		Souvenir Sheets			
2033	A436	30t multicolored		5.00	5.00
2034	A436	30t multicolored		5.00	5.00
2035	A436	30t multicolored		5.00	5.00
2036	A436	30t multicolored		5.00	5.00

MONGOLIA

1992 Winter Olympics, Albertville — A437

60m, Speed skating, vert. 80m, Ski jumping, vert. 1t, Hockey, vert. 1.20t, Figure skating, vert. 1.50t, Biathlon. 2t, Downhill skiing. 2.40t, Two-man bobsled.
8t, Four-man bobsled, vert.

1992, Feb. 1			Perf. 14	
2037	A437	60m multi	.25	.25
2038	A437	80m multi	.35	.25
2039	A437	1t multi	.40	.25
2040	A437	1.20t multi	.50	.25
2041	A437	1.50t multi	.65	.25
2042	A437	2t multi	.90	.25
2043	A437	2.40t multi	1.10	.25
	Nos. 2037-2043 (7)		4.15	1.75

Souvenir Sheet
2044	A437	8t multi	4.00	2.50

Dogs — A438

Various breeds of dogs.

1991, Dec. 1		Litho.	Perf. 14	
2045	A438	20m multi	.25	.25
2046	A438	30m multi, vert.	.30	.25
2047	A438	40m multi, vert.	.45	.25
2048	A438	50m multi	.55	.30
2049	A438	60m multi	.70	.35
2050	A438	80m multi	.85	.45
2051	A438	1.20t multi	1.25	.65
	Nos. 2045-2051 (7)		4.35	2.50

Souvenir Sheet
2052	A438	4t multi	4.50	4.50

Cats — A439

Various breeds of cats.

1991, Dec. 27				
2053	A439	20m multi	.25	.25
2054	A439	30m multi, vert.	.30	.25
2055	A439	40m multi	.45	.25
2056	A439	50m multi, vert.	.55	.30
2057	A439	60m multi, vert.	.70	.35
2058	A439	80m multi, vert.	.85	.45
2059	A439	1.20t multi, vert.	1.25	.65
	Nos. 2053-2059 (7)		4.35	2.50

Souvenir Sheet
2060	A439	4t multi	4.50	4.50

Alces Alces — A440

1992, May 1		Litho.	Perf. 14	
2061	A440	0t Male	1.00	.50
2062	A440	3t Two females	1.00	.50
2063	A440	3t One female, vert.	1.00	.50
2064	A440	3t Male's head, vert.	1.00	.50
	Nos. 2061-2064 (4)		4.00	2.00

Souvenir Sheet

Ferdinand von Zeppelin (1838-1917), Airship Designer — A441

1992, May 1				
2065	A441	16t multicolored	4.00	4.00

Souvenir Sheets

People and Events — A442

No. 2066, Pres. Punsalmaagiin Ochirbat visiting Pres. George Bush at White House. No. 2067, Mother Teresa helping poor in Calcutta. No. 2068, Pope John Paul II at mass. Nos. 2069-2070, Boy Scout blowing bugle.

1992, May 22		Perf. 14x13½	
2066	A442	30t silver & multi	5.00	4.50

		Perf. 14	
2067	A442	30t silver & multi	5.00	4.50
2068	A442	30t silver & multi	5.00	4.50
2069	A442	30t silver & multi	5.00	4.50
2070	A442	30t silver & multi	5.00	4.50
	Nos. 2066-2070 (5)		25.00	22.50

Nos. 2067-2070 each contain one 43x28mm stamp. Nos. 2069-2070 exist with gold inscription and border. No. 2069, 17th World Boy Scout Jamboree, Korea. No. 2070, 18th World Boy Scout Jamboree, Netherlands, 1995.

Souvenir Sheet

Discovery of America, 500th Anniv. — A443

Designs: a, Columbus. b, Sailing ship.

1992, May 22				
2071	A443	30t Sheet of 2, #a.-b.	7.50	6.00

World Columbian Stamp Expo '92, Chicago, Genoa '92.

Miniature Sheets

Railways of the World — A444

Designs: No. 2072a, 3t, Tank locomotive, Darjeeling-Himalaya Railway, India. b, 3t, Royal Scot, Great Britain. c, 6t, Bridge on the River Kwai, Burma-Siam Railway. d, 6t, Baltic tank engine, Burma. e, 8t, Baldwin locomotive, Thailand. f, 8t, Western Railway locomotive, Pakistan. g, 16t, P.36 class locomotive, USSR. h, 16t, Shanghai-Beijing Express, China.
Orient Express: No. 2073a, 3t, 1931 Advertising poster. b, 3t, 1928 poster. c, 6t, Dawn departure. d, 6t, Golden Arrow departing Victoria Station. e, 8t, Waiting at station in Yugoslavia. f, 8t, Turn of the century picture of train. g, 16t, Fleche d'Or locomotive approaching Étaples, France. h, 16t, Arrival in Istanbul, Turkey.
No. 2074, New Tokaido line, Japan. No. 2075, TGV, France. No. 2076a, Emblem of Pullman Car Company. b, Emblem of Intl. Wagons-lits Company. No. 2077, Passengers waiting to board Orient Express.

1992, May 24				
2072	A444	Sheet of 8, #a.-h.	12.00	9.00
2073	A444	Sheet of 8, #a.-h.	12.00	9.00

Souvenir Sheets
2074	A444	30t multicolored	6.00	5.00
2075	A444	30t multicolored	6.00	5.00
2076	A444	30t Sheet of 2, #a.-b.	12.00	11.00
2077	A444	30t black & gold	6.00	5.00

Nos. 2074-2075 contain one 58x42mm stamp.

Miniature Sheet

Birds — A445

Various birds: a, 3t. b, 3t, Owl. c, 6t, Gull, horiz. d, 6t, horiz. e, 8t. f, 8t, horiz. g, 16t. h, 16t, horiz.

1992, May 24				
2078	A445	Sheet of 8, #a.-h.	10.00	7.50

Souvenir Sheet
		Perf. 14x13½	
2079	A445	30t Ducks, 30t in UR	4.50	4.50
2080	A445	30t Duck, 30t in LR	4.50	4.50

Nos. 2079-2080 contain one 50x38mm stamp.

Miniature Sheet

Butterflies and Moths — A446

Various butterflies or moths and: a, 3t, Mountains. b, 3t, Desert. c, 6t, Grass. d, 6t, Lake. e, 8t, Mountain, diff. f, 8t, Flowers. g, 16t, Rocks. h, 16t, Lake, diff.

1992, May 24		Perf. 14	
2081	A446	Sheet of 8, #a.-h.	15.00	10.00

Souvenir Sheet
		Perf. 14x13½	
2082	A446	30t pink & multi	6.00	5.00
2083	A446	30t blue & multi	6.00	5.00

Nos. 2082-2083 contain one 50x38mm stamp.

1992 Summer Olympics, Barcelona — A447

Designs: a, Gold medal. b, Torch.

1992, Jan. 22		Litho.	Perf. 14	
2084	A447	30t Sheet of 2, #a.-b.	8.75	8.75

Souvenir Sheet

Genghis Khan — A448

1992, June 15		Litho.	Perf. 14	
2085	A448	16t multicolored	20.00	20.00

Mushrooms — A449

Designs: 20m, Marasmius oreades. 30m, Boletus luridus. 40m, Hygrophorus marzuelus. 50m, Cantharellus cibarius. 60m, Agaricus campester. 80m, Boletus aereus. 1.20t, Amanita caesarea. 2t, Tricholoma terreum. 4t, Mitrophora hybrida.

1991, June 18		Litho.	Perf. 13	
2086	A449	20m multicolored	.25	.25
2087	A449	30m multicolored	.25	.25
2088	A449	40m multicolored	.40	.25
2089	A449	50m multicolored	.45	.25
2090	A449	60m multicolored	.50	.30
2091	A449	80m multicolored	.65	.40
2092	A449	1.20t multicolored	1.00	.50
2093	A449	2t multicolored	1.40	.65
	Nos. 2086-2093 (8)		4.90	2.85

Souvenir Sheet
| 2094 | A449 | 4t multicolored | 5.00 | 4.50 |

Dated 1990. No. 2094 contains one 32x40mm stamp.

Discovery of America, 500th Anniv. — A450

Columbus and: 3t, Two sailing ships. 7t, Natives approaching Santa Maria. 10t, Pinta. 16t, Santa Maria, vert. 30t, Santa Maria, diff. 40t, Santa Maria, dolphins. 50t, Nina.
#2102, Ship, vert. #2103, Portrait, vert.

1992, Aug.		Litho.	Perf. 14	
2095	A450	3t multicolored	.25	.25
2096	A450	7t multicolored	.30	.25
2097	A450	10t multicolored	.45	.25
2098	A450	16t multicolored	.75	.30
2099	A450	30t multicolored	1.40	.80
2100	A450	40t multicolored	2.00	1.40
2101	A450	50t multicolored	2.25	1.75
	Nos. 2095-2101 (7)		7.40	5.00

Souvenir Sheets
		Perf. 13½x14	
2102	A450	80t multicolored	4.00	4.00
2103	A450	80t multicolored	4.00	4.00

Nos. 2102-2103 each contain one 38x52mm stamp.

Miniature Sheet

Butterflies — A451

#2104: a, 3t, Anthocharis cardamines. b, 8t, Inachis io. c, 10t, Fabriciana adippe. d, 16t, Limenitis reducta. e, 30t, Agrumaenia carniolica. f, 40t, Polyommatus icarus. g, 50t, Parnassius apollo. h, 60t, Saturnia pyri.
No. 2105, Limenitis populi. No. 2106, Heodes virgaureae.

MONGOLIA

1992, Dec.	Litho.	Perf. 14
2104 A451	Sheet of 8, #a.-h.	12.00 11.00

Souvenir Sheets
Perf. 14x13½

| 2105 | A451 | 80t multicolored | 5.00 | 4.00 |
| 2106 | A451 | 80t multicolored | 5.00 | 4.00 |

Nos. 2105-2106 each contain one 51x38mm stamp.

1992 Summer Olympics, Barcelona — A452

1993, Jan.	Litho.	Perf. 13½
2107	A452	3t Long jump	.25 .25
2108	A452	6t Pommel horse	.25 .25
2109	A452	8t Boxing	.35 .25
2110	A452	16t Wrestling	.35 .25
2111	A452	20t Archery, vert.	.55 .25
2112	A452	30t Cycling	.60 .25
2113	A452	40t Equestrian	.70 .30
2114	A452	50t High jump	.90 .30
2115	A452	60t Weight lifting	1.10 .40
	Nos. 2107-2115 (9)	5.05 2.50

Souvenir Sheet
Perf. 15x14

| 2116 | A452 | 80t Judo | 4.00 3.50 |
| 2117 | A452 | 80t Javelin | 4.00 3.50 |

Nos. 2116-2117 contain one 40x30mm stamp.

Miniature Sheet

Birds — A453

Designs: No. 2118a, 3t, Tetrae tetrix. b, 8t, Gallinula chloropus. c, 10t, Regulus satrapa. d, 16t, Alcede atthis. e, 30t, Gavia stellata. f, 40t, Ardes cinerea. g, 50t, Upupa epops. h, 60t, Niltava rubeculoides. No. 2119, Gyps fulvus. No. 2120, Podiceps cristatus.

1993, Feb.	Litho.	Perf. 14
2118 A453	Sheet of 8, #a.-h.	11.00 10.00

Souvenir Sheets
Perf. 14x13½

| 2119 | A453 | 80t multicolored | 4.50 4.00 |
| 2120 | A453 | 80t multicolored | 4.50 4.00 |

Nos. 2119-2120 each contain one 51x38mm stamp.

Souvenir Sheets

Polska '93 — A454

#2121a, 2122, Copernicus. #2121b, Chopin. #2121c, 2123, Pope John Paul II.

1993, May 1	Litho.	Perf. 13½x14
2121 A454	30t Sheet of 3, #a.-c.	8.00 7.00
2122	A454	80t multicolored	7.00 7.00
2123	A454	80t multicolored	7.00 7.00
	Nos. 2121-2123 (3)	22.00 21.00

Animals, Sports, & Transportation — A455

Designs in gold: No. 2124, Cats, dogs. No. 2125, Turtle, bee, wildcat, butterfly. No. 2126, Owl, butterfly, mushroom, dinosaur. Nos. 2127, Chessmen, archer, baseball player, wrestlers, horse and rider. Nos. 2128, Modern transportation.

No. 2129, Dinosaur, whales, butterflies. No. 2130, Mushroom, turtle, flowers.

1993, Jan. 5	Embossed	Perf. 9
2124-2128 A455	200t Set of 5	75.00 75.00

Nos. 2124-2128 exist in silver and in either gold or silver imperf. souvenir sheets of 1.

Embossed
1993, June 1   Perf. 8½x9
Size: 79x53mm

| 2129 | A455 | 200t silver | 15.00 15.00 |

Souvenir Sheet
Imperf
Litho. & Embossed

| 2130 | A455 | 200t gold | 25.00 20.00 |

No. 2130, Topex '93, Madison, WI. No. 2129 exists in imperf. souvenir sheet of 1. No. 2130 exists in silver.

Souvenir Sheets

Taipei '93 — A456

1993, Aug. 14	Litho.	Perf. 13½x14
2137	A456	80t Genghis Khan	15.00 —
2138	A456	80t Sun Yat-Sen	20.00 —

Dirigible Flight Over Ulan Bator — A457

1993, Aug. 27	Litho.	Perf. 14
2139	A457	80t multicolored	3.00 3.00

No. 2139 has a holographic image. Soaking in water may affect the hologram. Issued in sheets of 4.

Buddhist Deities — A458

Various statues and paintings.

1993, Oct. 3		Perf. 13½x14
2140	A458	50t multicolored	.35 .25
2141	A458	100t multicolored	.70 .30
2142	A458	150t multicolored	1.00 .50
2143	A458	200t multicolored	1.40 .65
a.	Miniature sheet of 4	5.25 5.25
	Nos. 2140-2143 (4)	3.45 1.70

Souvenir Sheet

| 2144 | A458 | 300t multicolored | 2.00 2.00 |

Bangkok '93.

Nos. 276 & 1084 Surcharged

1993	Perfs., Etc. as Before
2144A	A77	8t on 70m #276	7.50 —
2144B	A246	15t on 70m #1084	— —

No. 2144A exists with double surcharge. The surcharge on No. 2144B exists with four different type fonts.

New Year 1994 (Year of the Dog) — A459

No. 2146, Stylized dog running, vert.

1994, Jan. 10	Perf. 14x13½, 13½x14
2145	A459	60t multicolored	1.50 .75
2146	A459	60t multicolored	1.50 .75

1994 World Cup Soccer Championships, U.S. — A460

Championship teams: #2147, Uruguay, 1930, 1950. #2148, Italy, 1954. #2149, Brazil, 1959. #2150, West Germany, 1954. #2151, Argentina, 1978, 1986. #2152, Italy, 1938. #2153, Brazil, 1962. #2154, West Germany, 1974. #2155, Brazil, 1970. #2156, Italy, 1982. #2157, West Germany, 1990.

1994, Jan. 15		Perf. 14x13½
2147	A460	150t multicolored	.70 .25
2148	A460	150t multicolored	.70 .25
2149	A460	150t multicolored	.70 .25
2150	A460	150t multicolored	.70 .25
2151	A460	150t multicolored	.70 .25
a.	Souv. sheet of 2, #2147, 2151	2.00 2.00
2152	A460	200t multicolored	.90 .40
2153	A460	200t multicolored	.90 .40
2154	A460	200t multicolored	.90 .40
2155	A460	250t multicolored	1.20 .55
a.	Souvenir sheet of 3, #2149, 2153, 2155	3.50 3.50
2156	A460	250t multicolored	1.20 .55
a.	Souvenir sheet of 3, #2148, 2152, 2156	3.50 3.50
2157	A460	250t multicolored	1.20 .55
a.	Souvenir sheet of 3, #2150, 2154, 2157	3.50 3.50
b.	Miniature sheet of 4, #2151, 2155-2157	5.50 6.25
	Nos. 2147-2157 (11)	9.80 4.10

Souvenir Sheet

Punsalmaagiin Ochirbat, First President of Mongolia — A461

1994, Apr. 1		Perf. 14
2158	A461	150t multicolored	2.00 2.00

1994 Winter Olympics, Lillehammer — A462

50t, Biathlon. 60t, Two-man bobsled. 80t, Slalom skiing. 100t, Ski jumping. 120t, Pairs figure skating. 200t, Speed skating. 400t, Ice hockey.

1994, Apr. 10	Litho.	Perf. 13½
2159	A462	50t multi	.35 .25
2160	A462	60t multi	.45 .25
2161	A462	80t multi	.60 .40
2162	A462	100t multi	.75 .50
2163	A462	120t multi	.80 .55
2164	A462	200t multi	1.10 .90
	Nos. 2159-2164 (6)	4.05 2.85

Souvenir Sheet

| 2165 | A462 | 400t multi | 4.00 4.00 |

Souvenir Sheet

Dalai Lama, 1989 Nobel Peace Prize Winner — A463

1994, June 27	Litho.	Perf. 13½
2166	A463	400t multicolored	30.00

Miniature Sheet of 18

Wildlife — A466

Designs: a, Brown raptor. b, Woodpecker. c, Cranes in flight. d, White raptor. e, Yellow bird on tree branch (i). f, Two birds flying left. g, Raptor perched on rock. h, Two birds flying right. i, Squirrel. j, Dragonfly (f). k, Water bird standing near pond (o). l, Duck in flight over pond. m, Brown bird. n, Ground hog. o, Ladybug on flower. p, Bird's eggs. q, Grasshopper (m). r, Butterfly.

1994, July 15		
2169	A466	60t #a.-r. + 2 labels	10.00 7.00

First Manned Moon Landing, 25th Anniv. — A467

No. 2170, Trans-lunar injection. No. 2171, Astronaut on moon. No. 2172, Space shuttle, earth. No. 2173, Astronaut, shuttle.

1994, July 20	Litho.	Perf. 13½
2170	A467	200t multi	.90 .50
2171	A467	200t multi	.90 .50
2172	A467	200t multi	.90 .50
2173	A467	200t multi	.90 .50
a.	Miniature sheet of 4, #2170-2173	4.50 2.50
	Nos. 2170-2173 (4)	3.60 2.00

Singpex '94 — A468

1994, Aug. 31		
2174	A468	300t Butterfly	1.50 1.00

Souvenir Sheet

| 2175 | A468 | 400t Dog | 6.00 5.00 |

New Year 1994 (Year of the Dog)

A469

MONGOLIA

PHILAKOREA '94 — A470

1994   Litho.   Perf. 14
2176	A469	600t Korea #1749	2.25	.75
2177	A469	600t Korea #433	2.25	.75
2178	A470	600t #1	2.25	.75
2179	A470	600t Korea #1	2.25	.75
		Nos. 2176-2179 (4)	9.00	3.00

Souvenir Sheets
Perf. 13½x14
2180	A470	400t #5	4.00	4.00

Perf. 14
2181	A469	600t Yong Sik Hong	4.50	4.00

First Mongolian Stamp, 70th anniv. (#2180). No. 2180 contains one 34x46mm stamp. Issued: No. 2180, 11/23, others, 8/16. For surcharges see #2247C-2247G.

Dinosaurs A471

60t, Mammuthus, vert. 80t, Stegosaurus, vert. 100t, Talarurus. 120t, Gorythosaurus. 200t, Tyrannosaurus. 400t, Triceratops.

1994, Nov. 30   Perf. 14
2182	A471	60t multi	.40	.25
2183	A471	80t multi	.50	.30
2184	A471	100t multi	.55	.40
2185	A471	120t multi	.75	.55
2186	A471	200t multi	1.10	.90
		Nos. 2182-2186 (5)	3.30	2.40

Souvenir Sheet
2187	A471	400t multi	3.50	3.50

Nos. 2182-2187 exist in imperf. sheets of 1. Value, set: $20.
No. 2182 is misspelled.

Mongolian-Japanese Friendship — A472

1994, Dec. 15   Perf. 14x13½
2188	A472	20t multicolored	.75	.30

New Year 1995 (Year of the Boar) — A474

1995, Jan. 1   Perf. 14x13½, 13½x14
2190	A474	200t shown	.75	.30
2191	A474	200t Boar, diff., vert.	.75	.30

A475

Nos. 2192, 2192A, Flower. Nos. 2193, 2196-2197 Ram. Nos. 2194-2195, Airplane.

Litho. & Typo.
1994, July 25   Perf. 15x14
Denomination in Black
2192	A475	10t green	2.00	.25
2192A	A475	10t grn, red denomination	2.00	.75
2193	A475	18t magenta	1.00	.25
2194	A475	22t blue	3.00	.25
2195	A475	22t blue, red denomination	3.00	1.00
2196	A475	44t like #2193	2.00	.25
2197	A475	44t magenta, blue denomination	4.00	1.25
		Nos. 2192-2197 (7)	17.00	4.00

Dated 1993.
No. 2192A issued 1994(?).

Religious Masked Dancing — A476

Various masked dancers in traditional costumes.

1995, Feb. 25   Litho.   Perf. 14
2201	A476	20t multicolored	.25	.25
2202	A476	50t multicolored	.30	.25
2203	A476	60t multicolored	.35	.25
2204	A476	100t multicolored	.60	.30
2205	A476	120t multicolored	.70	.30
2206	A476	150t multicolored	1.00	.35
2207	A476	200t multicolored	1.00	.40
		Nos. 2201-2207 (7)	4.20	2.10

Souvenir Sheet
2208	A476	400t multicolored	4.00	4.00

Saiga Tatarica — A477

1995, Mar. 30   Litho.   Perf. 14
2209	A477	40t shown	.35	.25
2210	A477	55t Two adults	.45	.25
2211	A477	70t One running left	.60	.30
2212	A477	200t One up close	1.60	.80
a.		Block of 4, #2209-2212	3.00	3.00

World Wildlife Fund.

First Philately & Collections Fair, Hong Kong '95 — A478

Designs: a, Butterfly. b, Flowers.

1995, June 6   Litho.   Perf. 14
2213	A478	200t Sheet of 2, #a.-b. + 2 labels	4.25	4.25

Goldfish A479

Designs: 20t, Yellow oranda. 50t, Red and white wen-yu. 60t, Brown oranda with red head. 100t, Calico pearl-scale with phoenix tail. 120t, Red lion-head. 150t, Brown oranda. 200t, Red and white oranda with narial. 400t, White and gold unidentified fish.

1995, Sept. 1   Litho.   Perf. 14
2214-2220	A479	Set of 7	5.50	4.00

Souvenir Sheet
2221	A479	400t multicolored	5.50	4.00

No. 2221 contains one 50x38mm stamp.

Motion Pictures, Cent. — A480

Various portraits of Marilyn Monroe (1926-62): No. 2222a, 60t. b, 80t. c, 100t. d, 120t. e, 150t. f, 200t. g, 250t. h, 300t. i, 350t.
No. 2223, In white-collared blouse. No. 2224, With lion. No. 2225, In black lace dress. No. 2226, In scene from movie, Niagara.

1995, Oct. 20
2222	A480	Sheet of 9, #a.-i.	8.50	7.00

Souvenir Sheets
2223	A480	200t multi	4.50	4.50
2224-2226	A480	300t each	4.50	4.50

UN, 50th Anniv. — A481

Exterior views of UN complexes, Secretaries General: a, Trygve Lie. b, Dag Hammarskjold. c, U Thant. d, Kurt Waldheim. e, Jose Perez de Cuellar. f, Boutros Boutros-Ghali.

1995, Oct. 15
2227	A481	60t Sheet of 6, #a.-f.	6.50	5.00

Elvis Presley (1935-77) — A482

Various portaits: No. 2228a, 60t. b, 80t. c, 100t. d, 120t. e, 150t. f, 200t. g, 250t. h, 300t. i, 350t.
No. 2229, Wearing yellow sweater. No. 2230, With dancing girl. No. 2231, With guitar. No. 2232, In army uniform, wife Priscilla.

1995, Oct. 20
2228	A482	Sheet of 9, #a.-i.	9.00	8.00

Souvenir Sheets
2229	A482	200t multi	5.00	5.00
2230	A482	300t multi	5.00	5.00
2231-2232	A482	400t each	6.50	5.00

X-Men Comic Characters — A483

Designs: No. 2233a, 30t, Bishop. b, 50t, Beast. c, 60t, Rogue. d, 70t, Gambit. e, 80t, Cyclops. f, 100t, Storm. g, 200t, Professor X. h, 250t, Wolverine.
No. 2234: a, Wolverine, horiz. b, Magneto, horiz.

1995, Sept. 15
2233	A483	Sheet of 8, #a.-h.	3.50	3.00

Souvenir Sheet of 2
2234	A483	250t #a.-b.	3.50	3.00

New Year 1996 (Year of the Rat) — A484

1996, Jan. 1   Litho.   Perf. 14
2235	A484	150t Rat, diff., vert.	.75	.45
2236	A484	200t shown	1.25	.65

CHINA '96 — A485

Designs: a, Monument of Sukhe Bator. b, Temple of Heaven, Beijing. c, Migjed Jang-Rasek. d, Great Wall.

1996, Apr. 25   Litho.   Perf. 13½x14
2237	A485	65t Sheet of 4, #a.-d.	8.00	8.00

1996 Summer Olympic Games, Atlanta — A486

30t, Cycling. 60t, Women's shooting. 80t, Weight lifting. 100t, Boxing. 120t, Women's archery, vert. 150t, Rhythmic gymnastics, vert. 200t, Hurdles, vert. 350t, Equestrian. 400t, Wrestling.
500t, Basketball. 600t, Judo.

1996   Litho.   Perf. 14
2238	A486	30t multicolored	.25	.25
2239	A486	60t multicolored	.25	.25
2240	A486	80t multicolored	.25	.25
2241	A486	100t multicolored	.25	.25
2242	A486	120t multicolored	.25	.25
2243	A486	150t multicolored	.35	.25
2244	A486	200t multicolored	.45	.30
2245	A486	350t multicolored	.90	.70
2246	A486	400t multicolored	1.00	.80
		Nos. 2238-2246 (9)	3.95	3.30

Souvenir Sheets
2246A	A486	500t multicolored	3.00	2.50
2246B	A486	600t multicolored	3.50	3.50

No. 2246A contains one 37x53mm stamp, No. 2246B one 52x39mm stamp.
Olymphilex '96 (#2246A-2246B).

Mongolian postal authorities have declared as "unauthorized" two sheets of nine 350t Train stamps similar to Nos. 2442-2443, two souvenir sheets of one 2000t Train stamps similar to Nos. 2444-2445, and one sheet of six 300t Ferrari stamps similar to No. 2446.

MONGOLIA

Genghis Khan
A486a

Die Cut Perf. 7½
1996, Aug. 28   **Embossed**
Self-Adhesive
2246C   A486a   10,000t gold   50.00   50.00

CAPEX '96
A487

Designs: a, 350t, #2. b, 400t, Canada #1.

1996   **Litho.**   **Perf. 12½**
2247   A487   Sheet of 2, #a.-b.   8.00   8.00

No. 2247b is 40x30mm. No. 2247 exists with blue at upper right margin corner and different colored margin picture of CN Tower.

Nos. 2176-2179, 2181 Overprinted

1996, Sept. 8	**Litho.**		**Perf. 14**
2247C	A469	600t On #2176	2.50 2.50
2247D	A469	600t On #2177	2.50 2.50
2247E	A470	600t On #2178	2.50 2.50
2247F	A470	600t On #2179	2.50 2.50
	Nos. 2247C-2247F (4)		10.00 10.00

Souvenir Sheet
2247G   A469   600t On No. 2181   4.00   4.00

Mongolian National Democratic and Social Democratic Parties — A487a

1996, Sept. 25   **Litho.**   **Perf. 13¾**
2247H   A487a   100t multicolored   .50   .25

Souvenir Sheet

Taipei '96
A487b

1996, Oct. 21   **Litho.**   **Perf. 12¾**
2247I   A487b   750t multicolored   5.00   5.00
   r.   Overprinted "Taipei 2005" in margin in silver   5.00   5.00

No. 2247Ir issued 8/19/2005.

Children & Scouting Emblem — A487c

1996, Dec. 16   **Litho.**   **Perf. 14**
Country Flags
2247J	A487c	250t Mongolia	1.25 .40
2247K	A487c	250t US	1.25 .40
2247L	A487c	250t Germany	1.25 .40
2247M	A487c	250t Russia	1.25 .40
2247N	A487c	250t Japan	1.25 .40
2247O	A487c	250t PRC	1.25 .40
q.	Souvenir sheet, #2247J-2247O		12.00 3.00
	Nos. 2247J-2247O (6)		7.50 2.40

Souvenir Sheet
Perf. 12¾x12¾
2247P   A487c   700t No flag   4.25   4.25
UNICEF (#2247P).

New Year 1997 (Year of the Ox) — A488

1997   **Litho.**   **Perf. 14**
2248   A488   300t Ox, vert.   1.00   1.00
2249   A488   350t shown   1.25   1.25

Souvenir Sheet

Total Solar Eclipse Over Mongolia, Mar. 9, 1997 — A489

1997   **Litho.**   **Perf. 12½**
2250   A489   1000t Map of Mongolia   5.00   4.75

Return of Hong Kong to China — A490

Designs: 200t, Former Chinese Pres. Deng Xioaping, Queen Elizabeth II. 250t, Chinese Pres. Jiang Zemin and Chief Executive of the Special Administrative Region of Hong Kong, Tung Chee-hwa.

1997   **Litho.**   **Perf. 13½**
2251   A490   200t multicolored   1.00   1.00
2252   A490   250t multicolored   1.25   1.25
   a.   Pair, #2251-2252   2.40   2.40

Seven Joys — A491

Designs: a, Wheel. b, Gem. c, Minister. d, Queen. e, Elephant. f, Horse. g, General.

1997   **Litho.**   **Perf. 11**
2253   A491   200t Sheet of 7, #a.-g., + 2 labels   6.00   6.00

Souvenir Sheet

Moscow '97
A492

1997   **Perf. 12½x11½**
2254   A492   1000t No. 264   5.00   5.00
   a.   With Irkutsk 2007 emblem and inscription added in sheet margin ('07)   1.75   1.75

No. 2254a issued 6/8/2007.

Monument to the Politically Repressed — A493

1997   **Perf. 13x13½**
2255   A493   150t black & gray   .95   .60

Trains — A493a

Designs: 20t, VL-80 electric locomotive. 40t, Japanese high speed electric train. 120t, BL-80 Diesel locomotive. 200t, German steam locomotive. 300t, Lass "FDp" steam locomotive. 350t, 0-6-0 tank locomotive. 400t, Diesel locomotive. 500t, T6-106 Diesel locomotive. 600t, Magnetic train.
No. 2255K, "Rocket." No. 2255L, London-Paris train.

1997, Dec. 5   **Litho.**   **Perf. 14x14¼**
2255A	A493a	20t multi	.45 .25
2255B	A493a	40t multi	.55 .25
2255C	A493a	120t multi	.65 .25
2255D	A493a	200t multi	.85 .30
2255E	A493a	300t multi	.90 .40
2255F	A493a	350t multi	1.00 .60
2255G	A493a	400t multi	1.25 .70
2255H	A493a	500t multi	1.40 .75
2255I	A493a	600t multi	1.75 1.00
j.	Sheet of 9, #2255A-2255I		11.00 11.00
	Nos. 2255A-2255I (9)		8.80 4.50

Souvenir Sheets
Perf. 11¼
2255K   A493a   800t multi   3.75   2.50
2255L   A493a   800t multi   3.75   2.50

Nos. 2255K, 2255L each contain one 59x43mm stamp.

Emperors of Mongolia — A494

a, Genghis Khan. b, Ogadai Khan. c, Guyuk Khan. d, Mangu Khan. e, Kublai Khan.

1997, Dec. 25   **Perf. 11½x12½**   **Litho.**
2256   A494   1000t Strip of 5, #a.-e.   15.00   15.00

Nos. 2256a-2256e exist in souvenir sheets containing 1 or 2 21x33mm stamps.

New Year 1998 (Year of the Tiger) — A495

Various stylized tigers.

1998, Feb. 1   **Perf. 12**
2257   A495   150t multicolored   1.00   1.00
2258   A495   200t multicolored   1.50   1.50
2259   A495   300t multicolored   2.00   2.00
   Nos. 2257-2259 (3)   4.50   4.50

Design on No. 2259 is oriented point down.

Mongolian Yaks — A496

Various yaks: 20t, Three. 30t, One white. 50t, With carts. 100t, One male. 150t, Female with calf. 200t, Three, campsite. 300t, One with horns, flowing hair. 400t, Brown yak looking back.
800t, Carrying children and supplies.

1998, Mar. 15   **Litho.**   **Perf. 12**
2260   A496   20t multicolored   .25   .25
2261   A496   30t multicolored   .25   .25
2262   A496   50t multicolored   .25   .25
2263   A496   100t multicolored   .35   .35
2264   A496   150t multicolored   .55   .55
2265   A496   200t multicolored   .75   .75

Size: 50x36mm
2266   A496   300t multicolored   1.10   1.10
2267   A496   400t multicolored   1.50   1.50
   Nos. 2260-2267 (8)   5.00   5.00

Souvenir Sheet
Perf. 11
2268   A496   800t multicolored   5.50   5.50

No. 2268 contains one 60x47mm stamp.

Butterflies and Orchids — A497

Designs: 100t, Adonis blue, dendrobium cunninghamii. 150t, Brown hairstreak, oncidium ampliatum. 200t, Large skipper, maxillaria triloris. 250t, Orange tip, calypso bulbosa. 300t, Painted lady, catasetum pileatum. 350t, Purple hairstreak, epidendrum fimbratum. 400t, Red admiral, cleistes rosea. 450t, Small copper, ponthieva maculata. 500t, Small tortoiseshell, cypripeium calceolus.
Each 800t: No. 2278, Red admiral, c. macranthum. No. 2279, Adonis blue, c. guttatum.

1997, Dec. 5   **Litho.**   **Perf. 14**
2269-2277   A497   Set of 9   5.00   3.50

Souvenir Sheets
2278-2279   A497   Set of 2   8.50   5.00

Souvenir Sheet

1998 World Cup Soccer Championships, France — A498

1998, June 1   **Perf. 13**
2280   A498   1000t multicolored   5.00   5.00

MONGOLIA

Souvenir Sheet

Pres. Natsagyn Bagabandi — A499

1998, July 15	Litho.	Perf. 12½
2281	A499 1000t multicolored	4.00 3.50

Greenpeace, 26th Anniv. — A500

Designs: 200t, Penguin in snow. 400t, Six penguins, water, mountain. 500t, Two penguins at water's edge. 800t, Large group of penguins.
No. 2286: a, like #2282. b, like #2283. c, like #2284. d, like #2285. e, like #2287.
1000t, Greenpeace ship.

1997, Sept. 15	Litho.	Perf. 13½
2282-2285	A500 Set of 4	5.50 5.50
2286	A500 Sheet of 5, #a.-e.	8.00 8.00

Souvenir Sheet

| 2287 | A500 1000t multicolored | 6.00 6.00 |

Country name, denominations, "Greenpeace" in red on No. 2286. Nos. 2282-2287 exist imperf.

Diana, Princess of Wales (1961-97) — A501

Various portraits with bister background — No. 2288: a, 50t. b, 100t. c, 150t. d, 200t. e, 250t. f, 300t. g, 350t. h, 400t. i, 450t.
Various portraits with pale brown background — No. 2289: a, 50t. b, 100t. c, 150t. d, 200t. e, 250t. f, 300t. g, 350t. h, 400t. i, 450t.
Each 1000t: No. 2290, Diana holding infant son. No. 2291, Diana wearing tiara. No. 2292, Diana in pink dress. No. 2293, Diana in white (Mother Teresa in margin).

1997, Dec. 15		Sheets of 9, #a-i
2288-2289	A501 Set of 2	15.00 15.00

Souvenir Sheets

| 2290-2293 | A501 Set of 4 | 14.00 14.00 |

Nos. 2288-2289 exist imperf.

Genghis Khan's Soldiers — A502

Various soldiers in traditional attire, background color: 100t, tan. 150t, pale violet. 200t, green blue. 250t, green. 300t, gray. 350t, pink. 400t, blue. 600t, pale brown.
Army on the march — #2302: a, 600t, One standing, others on horses. b, 1000t, Leaders riding decorated horses. c, 600t, Two standing, leopards, others on horses.

1997, Dec. 20		Perf. 12
2294-2301	A502 Set of 8	10.00 10.00

Souvenir Sheet

| 2302 | A502 Sheet of 3, #a.-c. | 8.50 8.50 |

No. 2302b is 65x56mm.

No. 276 Surcharged

1996, Dec. 25	Photo.	Perf. 11½x12
2302D	A77 200t on 70m multi	8.50 2.00

National Symbols — A503

1998, Jan. 1		
2303	A503 300t Natl. flag, horiz.	.90 .75
2304	A503 300t shown	.90 .75

Ursus Arctos Gobiensis A504

100t, Adult looking forward. 150t, Adult walking left. 200t, Two bears. 250t, Mother, cubs.

1998, July 20		
2305-2308	A504 Set of 4	6.00 6.00
2307a	Sheet of 2, #2305, 2307	3.00 3.00
2308a	Sheet of 2, #2306, 2308	4.00 4.00

Fish — A505

Designs: 20t, Lebistes reticulatus. 30t, Goldfish. 50t, Balistes conspicillum. 100t, Goldfish, diff. 150t, Synchirops splendidus. 200t, Auratus. 300t, Xiphophorus helleri. 400t, Pygoplites diacanthus. 600t, Chaetodon auriga.
Various fish, denomination (800t): No. 2318, At top. No. 2319, At bottom.

1998, July 20		Perf. 12½
2309-2317	A505 Set of 9	5.50 5.50

Souvenir Sheets
Perf. 11

| 2318-2319 | A505 Set of 2 | 10.00 10.00 |

Nos. 2318-2319 each contain one 95x49mm stamp.

Domestic Cats — A506

Designs: 50t, Red Persian. 100t, Manx cat. 150t, Smoke Persian. 200t, Long-haired white Persian. 250t, Silver tabby. 300t, Siamese. 1000t, Kittens, basket.

1998, Sept. 1		Perf. 12
2320-2325	A506 Set of 6	5.00 5.00

Souvenir Sheet

| 2326 | A506 1000t multicolored | 5.00 5.00 |

Jerry Garcia (1942-95) and The Grateful Dead — A507

Nos. 2327-2328, Various portraits of Jerry Garcia.
No. 2328A — Black and white photos: f, 100t. g, 150t. h, 50t.
No. 2328B — Blue guitar: i, 150t. j, 200t. k, 100t.
No. 2328C — Red guitar: l, 200t. m, 250t. n, 150t.
No. 2328D — White guitar: o, 200t. p, 250t. q, 150t.
No. 2328E — Dark background: r, 300t. s, 350t. t, 250t.
No. 2329: Various portraits of Garcia: a, 50t. b, 100t. c, 150t. d, 200t. e, 250t. f, 300t. g, 350t. h, 400t. i, 450t.
No. 2330: Various pictures of bears (Grateful Dead emblem) in sports activities: a, 50t, Dirt biking. b, 100t, Soccer. c, 150t, Basketball. d, 200t, Golf. e, 250t, Baseball. f, 300t, Roller blading. g, 350t, Ice hockey. h, 400t, Football. i, 450t, Skiing.
Each 1000t: No. 2331, Garcia holding guitar. No. 2331A, Garcia with left hand on guitar, right hand in air.

1998-99		Perf. 12½
2327	A507 100t multicolored	1.00 .50
2328	A507 200t multicolored	1.00 .50

Strips of 3

| 2328A-2328E | A507 Set of 5 | 15.00 15.00 |

Sheets of 9, #a-i

| 2329-2330M | A507 Set of 2 | 11.50 11.50 |

Souvenir Sheets

| 2331-2331A | A507 Set of 2 | 5.00 5.00 |

Nos. 2327-2328 were each issued in sheets of 9. Nos. 2331-2331A contain one 51x76mm. Dot of "I" in Garcia is a diamond on Nos. 2327-2329, 2331-2331A. "Jerry Garcia" is in pink letters with rose shadowing on Nos. 2328A-2328E.
Issued: No. 2331A, 1/1/99; #2328A-2328E, 1999; others 10/15/98.
See Nos. 2385-2389.

Bob Marley (1947-81) — A508

Portraits: 200t, Up close. 1000t, At microphone.

1998, Oct. 15		
2332	A508 200t multicolored	1.25 1.25

Souvenir Sheet

| 2333 | A508 1000t multicolored | 3.00 3.00 |

No. 2332 was issued in sheets of 9. No. 2333 contains one 51x76mm stamp.

Carlos Santana — A509

1998, Oct. 15		
2334	A509 200t multicolored	1.50 1.50

No. 2334 was issued in sheets of 9.

The Three Stooges A510

Scenes from "The Three Stooges" motion pictures — #2335: a, 50t, Guns, cigars. b, 100t, Road signs. c, 150t, Dynamite. d, 200t, Golf clubs. e, 240t, Medals on uniform. f, 300t, Dove. g, 350t, Flower bouquets. h, 400t, Bright green cap. i, 450t, Whisk broom, cigar.
No. 2336: a, 50t, Doctor's equipment. b, 100t, Musical instruments. c, 150t, Clothes press. d, 200t, Long cord. e, 250t, Vise. f, 300t, Brick wall. g, 350t, Pliers. h, 400t, Turkey. i, 450t, Door.
No. 2337: a, 50t, Union soldiers. b, 100t, French Foreign Legion. c, 150t, Confederate soldiers, women. d, 200t, Horse. e, 250t, Army uniform, grenade. f, 300t, Cannon. g, 350t, Confederate soldiers, whiskey flask. 400t, Army uniforms, officer. 450t, Scarecrow.
Each 800t: No. 2338, like #2335b. No. 2339, like #2336c, vert. No. 2340, With football.

1998, Nov. 25	Litho.	Perf. 13½
	Sheets of 9, #a-i	
2335-2337	A510 Set of 3	22.50 22.50

Souvenir Sheets

| 2338-2340 | A510 Set of 3 | 9.00 9.00 |

Nos. 2335-2340 exist imperf. Nos. 2338-2340 each contain one 51x41mm stamp.

Eight Offerings of Buddha — A511

#2341, The White Sign of Luck. #2342, The Auspicious Wheel. #2343, The Auspicious Cup. #2344, The White Couch. #2345, The White Umbrella. #2346, The Duaz of Victory. #2347, The White Lotus. #2348, The Auspicious Fish.

1998, Dec. 10	Litho.	Perf. 12
2341-2348	A511 200t Set of 8	5.00 5.00

Howdy Doody Television Show — A512

No. 2349: a, 50t, Chief Thunderthud. b, 100t, Princess Summerfall Winterspring. c, 150t, Howdy in Mexican outfit. d, 150t, Buffalo Bob in gray shirt, Howdy. e, 200t, Buffalo Bob in red and white shirt, Howdy. f, 250t, Howdy, Buffalo Bob rubbing noses. g, 450t, Howdy in military uniform. h, 250t, Clarabell the Clown. i, 450t, Howdy lying down.
Each 800t: No. 2350, Howdy. No. 2351, Buffalo Bob, Howdy, horiz. No. 2352, Howdy, Buffalo Bob.

Perf. 13½x14, 14x13½x14

1999, Apr. 1		
2349	A512 Sheet of 9, #a.-i.	7.00 7.00

Souvenir Sheets
Perf. 14 (#2352)

| 2350-2352 | A512 Set of 3 | 10.00 10.00 |

No. 2352 contains one 48x61mm stamp.

Prime Ministers of Mongolia — A513

a, T. Namnansuren. b, Badamdorj. c, D. Chagdarjav. d, D. Bodoo. e, S. Damdinbazar. f, B. Tserendorj. g, A. Amar. h, Ts. Jigjidjav. i, P. Genden. j, Kh. Ghoibalsan. k, Yu.

MONGOLIA

Tsedenbal. l, J. Batmunkh. m, D. Sodnom. n, Sh. Gungaadorj. o, D. Byambasuren. p, P. Jasrai. q, M. Enkhsaikhan. r, Ts. Elbegdorj.

1998, Dec. 1 — *Perf. 12*
2353 A513 200t Sheet of 18, #a.-r. 15.00 15.00

Natl. Wrestling Champions — A514

Designs: a, D. Damdin. b, S. Batsuury. c, J. Munkhbat. d, H. Bayanmunkh. e, B. Tubdendorj. f, D. Tserentogtokh. g, B. Baterdne.

1998, Dec. 26 — *Perf. 12½*
2354 A514 200t Sheet of 7, #a.-g. 6.50 6.50

John Glenn's Return to Space — A515

Mercury Friendship 7 — #2355: a, 50t, Mercury capsule in outer space. b, 100t, NASA emblem. c, 150t, Friendship 7 mission patch. d, 150t, Launch of Friendship 7. e, 200t, Glenn, 1962. f, 250th, Recovery of capsule. g, 450t, Moon. h, 250t, Capsule re-entering atmosphere. i, 450t, Stars.
Shuttle Discovery mission — #2356: a, 50t, NASA emblem. b, 100t, Glenn in red launch suit. c, 150t, Discovery mission patch. d, 150t, Launch of Discovery. e, 200t, Glenn, 1998. f, 250t, Discovery landing. g, 450t, Sun. h, 250t, Discovery in outer space. i, 450t, NASA "40" emblem.

Sheets of 9

1998, Dec. 31 — *Perf. 14*
2355-2356 A515 #a.-i., each 11.00 11.00

Postal Delivery — A516

Post office: a, 100t, Brown. b, 200t, Blue. c, 200t, Blue green. d, 400t, Red lilac. e, 400t, Violet.
Electronic services: f, 100t, Blue. g, 200t, Blue green. h, 200t, Red lilac. i, 400t, Violet. j, 400t, Brown.
EMS delivery: k, 100t, Blue green. l, 200t, Red lilac. m, 200t, Violet. n, 400t, Brown. o, 400t, Blue.
Mail train: p, 100t, Red lilac. q, 200t, Violet. r, 200t, Brown. s, 400t, Blue. t, 400t, Blue green.
Jet plane: u, 100t, Violet. v, 200t, Brown. w, 200t, Blue. x, 400t, Blue green. y, 400t, Red lilac.

1998, Nov. 15 — *Perf. 12*
2357 A516 Sheet of 25, #a.-y. 22.50 22.50

Universal Declaration of Human Rights, 50th Anniv. — A517

1998, Dec. 25 — *Litho.* *Perf. 12*
2358 A517 450t multi + label 1.75 1.75

New Year 1999 (Year of the Rabbit) — A518

1999, Feb. 17
2359 A518 250t Rabbit, vert. 1.40 1.00
2360 A518 300t shown 1.75 1.20

Buddha Migjed Jankraisig, Ulan Bator — A519

Designs: 200t, Temple. Each 1000t: No. 2363, Statue. No. 2364, Statue, drawing of Temple.

1999, Apr. 15
2361 A519 200t multicolored 1.00 .75
2362 A519 400t multicolored 1.75 1.50

Souvenir Sheets
Perf. 11
2363-2364 A519 Set of 2 7.00 7.00
Nos. 2363-2364 each contain one 49x106mm stamp.

Falcons — A520

Falcon: a, 300t, Subbuteo. b, 250t, Naumanni. c, 200t, Tinnunculus. d, 170t, Peregrinus. e, 800t, Rusticolus by nest. f, 600t, Rusticolus in flight. g, 400t, Pelegrinoides over kill. h, 350t, Pelegrinoides on branch. i, 150t, Columbarius. j, 100t, Vespertinus. k, 50t, Cherrug. l, 30t, Amurensis.

1999, Mar. 20 — *Perf. 12*
2365 A520 Sheet of 12, #a.-l. 12.00 12.00

"I Love Lucy" Television Show — A521

Various scenes — #2366: a, 50t. b, 100t. c, 150t. d, 150t. e, 200t. f, 250t. g, 450t. h, 250t. i, 450t.
Each 800t: No. 2367, Lucy talking with woman. No. 2368, Ethel looking at Lucy locked in cold storage locker.

1999, July 15 — *Litho.* *Perf. 13½x14*
2366 A521 250t Sheet of 9, #a.-i. 6.00 6.00

Souvenir Sheets
2367-2368 A521 Set of 2 7.00 7.00
Nos. 2367-2368 each contain one 38x51mm stamp.

Betty Boop Cartoon Character — A522

Various pictures of Betty Boop — #2369: a, 50t. b, 100t. c, 150t. d, 150t. e, 200t. f, 250t. g, 450t. h, 250t. i, 450t.
Each 800t: No. 2370, Betty in dog's eyes, horiz. No. 2371, Up close, horiz.

1999, July 15
2369 A522 Sheet of 9, #a.-i. 6.00 6.00

Souvenir Sheets
Perf. 14x13½
2370-2371 A522 Set of 2 6.00 6.00
Nos. 2370-2371 each contain one 51x38mm stamp.

Folk Tales — A523

Designs: 50t, Man, yurt, two demons. 150t, Chess players. 200t, Lion carrying logs. 250t, Flying horse. 300t, Archer, bird, sun. 450t, Horses, cranes. 1000t, Birds, camel in flight.

1999, June 15 — *Litho.* *Perf. 13x13¼*
2372-2377 A523 Set of 6 6.50 6.50

Souvenir Sheet
Perf. 12½
2378 A523 1000t multicolored 6.50 6.50
No. 2378 contains one 41x32mm stamp.

No. 307 Surcharged

Methods and Perfs as Before
1999, June 15
2378A A84 810t on 60m bl & multi 16.00 16.00

Miniature Sheet

Ram A524

Panel color: a, 250t, Blue. b, 450t, Red.

1999, Aug. 21 — *Litho.* *Perf. 12½*
2379 A524 Miniature sheet of 2, #a.-b. 2.25 2.25
China 1999 World Philatelic Exhibition. No. 2379 is cut from a larger sheet of alternating stamps and labels. The cutting is through the labels along the diagonal axes.

UPU, 125th Anniv. — A525

Designs: No. 2380, Rider, two horses. No. 2381, Rider, one horse. No. 2382, Train and truck. No. 2382, Airplane and computer. 800t, Ogodei Khan (1186-1241).

1999, Oct. 9
2380-2383 A525 250t Set of 4 3.50 3.50

Souvenir Sheet
2384 A525 800t multi 4.00 4.00
No. 2384 contains one 31x41mm stamp.

Nos. 551, 1742 Surcharged

Methods and Perfs. as Before
1999, Aug. 25
2384A A133 250t on 50m multi 10.00 10.00
2384B A389 250t on 60m multi 10.00 10.00
Victory in Khalkh-gol War, 60th anniv.

Genghis Khan — A525a

Die Cut Perf. 11½
1999, Sept. 27 — *Embossed Self-Adhesive*
2384C A525a 15,000t gold & sil 60.00

Jerry Garcia Type of 1998

No. 2385 — Rose and blue speckled background: a, 50t. b, 100t. c, 150t.
No. 2386 — Pink-toned vignette extension backgrounds: a, 100t. b, 150t. c, 200t.
No. 2387 — Pink, blue and purple curved line backgrounds: a, 150t. b, 200t. c, 250t.
No. 2388 — Dark blue and purple straight line backgrounds: a, 150t. b, 200t. c, 250t.
No. 2389 — Blue green and green backgrounds: a, 250t. b, 300t. c, 350t.

1999 — *Litho.* *Perf. 12½*
"Jerry Garcia" In Black-Shadowed Letters
2385-2389 A507 Set of 5 strips of 3 9.00 9.00

Stone Carvings — A526

Designs: 50t, Stele with Uigur inscriptions, vert. 150t, Turtle, 13th cent. 200t, Kul Tegin burial site, 7th-8th cent., vert. 250t, Kul Tegin, 8th cent., vert. 300t, Dragon, 8th-9th cent. 450t, Man, 5th-7th cent., vert.

2000, Jan. 17 — *Litho.* *Perf. 12*
2390-2395 A526 Set of 6 5.00 5.00

A527

World Teachers' Day — A528

Academicians: #2396, 2398, Dr. Tsendiin Damdinsuren (1908-86). #2397, 2399, Dr. B. Rinchin (1905-77).

MONGOLIA

1999, Dec. 5
2396	A527	250t blue & blk	.50	.50
2397	A527	250t grn & blk	.50	.50
2398	A527	450t pur & blk	.85	.85
2399	A527	450t brn & blk	.85	.85
2400	A528	600t multi	1.10	1.10
	Nos. 2396-2400 (5)		3.80	3.80

Souvenir Sheet

Sanjaasuregin Zorig (1962-98), Politician — A529

Designs: a, 600t, Zorig in 1968. b, 1000t, Three people, flag. c, 600t, Zorig in 1998.

1999, Oct. 1 — Perf. 13¼x13
| 2401 | A529 | Sheet of 3, #a.-c. | 5.50 | 5.50 |

Size of No. 2401b: 59x39mm.

World Intellectual Property Organization, 20th Anniv. — A529a

No. 2401D: e, 250t, Satellite, airplane. f, 450t, Statue, television. g, 250t, Cauldron, toy. h, 250t, Copier, stamps. i, 450t, Camera, yurt, Mongolian couple. j, 250t, Red automobile. k, 250t, Grille of antique auto, bottles, cellular phones, wristwatch. l, 450t, Perfume bottles. m, 250t, Pack of cigarettes, soccer ball, volley ball, basketball, bottle of motor oil, boom box.

1999, Dec. 24 — Litho. — Perf. 12
| 2401D | A529a | Sheet of 9, #e-m | 8.00 | 8.00 |

Souvenir Sheet

Japan-Mongolia Friendship — A530

a, Sumo wrestler. b, Symbols of countries.

1999, Dec. 28 — Perf. 13½
| 2402 | A530 | 450t Sheet of 2, #a.-b. | 4.50 | 4.50 |

New Year 2000 (Year of the Dragon) A531

Background color: 250t, Red. 450t, Blue, vert.

2000, Jan. 10 — Litho. — Perf. 12
| 2403-2404 | A531 | Set of 2 | 4.00 | 4.00 |

For overprint, see Nos. 2733-2734.

Nos. 715-717, C34 Surcharged

Methods and Perfs as Before
2000, Jan. 19
| 2405 | A168 | 1000t on 50m brn | 7.00 | 7.00 |
| 2406 | A168 | 2000t on 60m grn | 8.00 | 8.00 |

2407	A168	5000t on 1t rose claret	15.00	15.00
2408	AP12	10,000t on 1.50t bl	30.00	30.00
	Nos. 2405-2408 (4)		60.00	60.00

Wolves A532

Designs: 150t, Pair, one with snout up. 250t, Eating deer. 300t, Nursing young. 450t, Snarling.

2000, Jan. 17 — Litho. — Perf. 12
| 2409-2412 | A532 | Set of 4 | 4.00 | 4.00 |

Souvenir Sheet
| 2413 | A532 | 800t Pair baying | 4.00 | 4.00 |

No. 2413 contains one 50x30mm stamp.

Sheep A533

Breeds: 50t, Sumber. 100t, Orkhon. 150t, Baidrag. 250t, Barga. 400t, Uzemchin. 450t, Bayad.

2000, Jan. 20
| 2414-2419 | A533 | Set of 6 | 4.00 | 4.00 |

Souvenir Sheet
| 2420 | A533 | 800t Govi-Altai | 4.00 | 4.00 |

One Day of Mongolia, by Balduugiin Sharav — A534

Various parts of painting: a, 50t. b, 100t, c, 150t. d, 200t. e, 250t. f, 300t. g, 350t. h, 450t. i, 600t.

2000, Jan. 24
| 2421 | A534 | Sheet of 9, #a-i | 9.00 | 9.00 |

Huts and Yurts — A535

Designs: 50t, Hunters returning to hut. 100t, Mother, daughter, animals near hut. 150t, Yurt near hill. 250t, Two yurts, motorcycle, and satellite dish. 450t, Yurt construction.
No. 2427, 800t, Yurt's furnishings. No. 2428, 800t, Yurt and wagon.

2000, Jan. 25
| 2422-2426 | A535 | Set of 5 | 4.00 | 4.00 |

Souvenir Sheets
| 2427-2428 | A535 | Set of 2 | 8.00 | 8.00 |

Union of Mongolian Production and Service Cooperatives, 10th Anniv. — A536

Panel colors: 300t, Blue. 450t, Green.

2000, Mar. 27 — Perf. 12
| 2429-2430 | A536 | Set of 2 | 4.00 | 4.00 |

Costumes of Mongolian Lords — A544

2000, May 11 — Perf. 13¼
2431	A537	550t multi	5.00	1.00
2432	A538	550t multi	5.00	1.00
2433	A539	550t multi	5.00	1.00
2434	A540	550t multi	5.00	1.00
2435	A541	550t multi	5.00	1.00
2436	A542	550t multi	5.00	1.00
2437	A543	550t multi	5.00	1.00
2438	A544	550t multi	5.00	1.00
	Nos. 2431-2438 (8)		40.00	8.00

Buddhas — A545

No. 2439: a, Jigjid. b, Gombo. c, Tsamba. d, Jamsran. e, Baldanlkham. f, Ochirvani. g, Namsrai. h, Gongor. i, Damdinchoijoo. j, Shalshi.

2000, July 1 — Perf. 13x13½
| 2439 | | Block of 10 | 15.00 | 11.00 |
| a.-j. | A545 | 550t Any single | 1.50 | 1.10 |

Worldwide Fund for Nature (WWF) — A546

Two Przewalski's horses: No. 2440a, 300t, Standing apart. No. 2441a, 100t, Standing apart. No. 2440b, 150t, No. 2441b, 250t, Galloping. No. 2440c, 100t, No. 2441d, 200t, Grazing. No. 2440d, 200t, No. 2441c, 50t, Standing together.

2000, July 5 — Litho. — Perf. 13½
| 2440 | A546 | Block or strip of 4, #a-d | 4.50 | 4.50 |

Litho. & Holography
Size: 50x35mm
| 2441 | A546 | Block of 4, #a-d | 6.00 | 6.00 |

Illustrations on No. 2441 are mirror images of those on No. 2440.

Trains A547

No. 2442: a, 200t, Guaari-Current electric locomotive, France. b, 400t, 2-10-0 Austerity, Great Britain. c, 300t, ALG Bo-Bo electric locomotive, Great Britain. d, 400t, Diesel-electric locomotive, Australia. e, 300t, E-10 Bo Bo electric locomotive, Germany. f, 200t, C30 Class Pacific, US. g, 300t, 46 Class electric locomotive, US. h, 200t, Bo-Bo electric locomotive, New Zealand. i, 400t, Bo Bo electric locomotive, Netherlands.
No. 2443: a, 300t, Italian second-class carriage. b, 400t, Bodmin & Wadebridge Railway composite carriage. c, 200t, Stephenson 2-2-2, Russia. d, 200t, 2-2-2 Walt, US. e, 300t, The General, US. f, 400t, 4-4-0 Washington, US. g, 400t, Braithwaite 0-4-0, Great Britain. h, 200t, Ross Winans Muddigger locomotive, US. i, 300t, 4-4-0 Ramapo, US.
No. 2444, 800t, The Ringmaster, US. No. 2445, 800t, Deltic electric locomotive, Great Britain.

2000, July 7 — Litho. — Perf. 14
Sheets of 9, #a-i
| 2442-2443 | A547 | Set of 2 | 15.00 | 15.00 |

Souvenir Sheets
| 2444-2445 | A547 | Set of 2 | 8.00 | 8.00 |

Ferrari Race Cars A548

No. 2446: a, 1975 312 T. b, 1961 156 F1. c, 1979 312 T4. d, 1964 158 F1. e, 1981 126 CK. f, 1974 312 B3.

MONGOLIA

2000, July 15
2446 A548 350t Sheet of 6, #a-f 16.00 16.00

2000 Summer Olympics, Sydney — A549

Designs: 100t, Boxing. 200t, Wrestling. 300t, Judo. 400t, Shooting.

2000, July 21   Perf. 13x13¼
2447-2450 A549 Set of 4 .... 4.00 4.00

Albert Einstein (1879-1955) — A550

Einstein: a, 100t, At blackboard. b, 300t, Wearing hat. c, 200t, Wearing green sweater. d, 200t, With violin. e, 550t, Close-up. f, 100t, At lectern. g, 100t, Holding pipe. h, 400t, Receiving award. i, 300t, Holding clock.

2000, Aug. 10   Perf. 12½
2451 A550 Sheet of 9, #a-i 7.50 7.50

I Love Lucy A551

No. 2452, vert.: a, 100t, Lucy, wiping hands, and Ethel. b, 400t, Lucy, reading letter, and Ethel. c, 200t, Lucy, setting table, and Fred. d, 200t, Lucy on telephone. e, 300t, Lucy with chin on fist. f, 100t, Lucy with head on hands. g, 100t, Lucy and Ethel waving. h, 550t, Lucy, holding bowl, and Ethel. i, 300t, Lucy, wearing brown sweater and holding jar, and Ethel.
No. 2453, 800t, Lucy, with mouth open, holding jar, and Ethel. No. 2454, 800t, Lucy. wearing stole, and Ethel.

2000, Aug. 15   Litho.   Perf. 12½
2452 A551 Sheet of 9, #a-i 8.00 8.00
         Souvenir Sheets
2453-2454 A551 Set of 2 .... 7.00 7.00

The Three Stooges A552

No. 2455, horiz.: a, 100t, Moe, Larry and woman. b, 400t, Moe, Shemp and Larry attempting jail escape. c, 300t, Moe, with blow torch, Shemp and Larry. d, 200t, Moe, Larry and Joe Besser with musical instruments. e, 300t, Man knocking together heads of Shemp, Larry and Moe. f, 100t, Man with hammer, Moe, Larry and Shemp. g, 100t, Larry, Joe Besser and Moe in kitchen. h, 550t, Moe, Shemp and Larry with large wrench. i, 200t, Larry, Moe and Shemp in kitchen.

No. 2456, 800t, Moe, with fingers in ears, and Shemp. No. 2457, 800t, Shemp and Larry in army uniforms.

2000, Aug. 17
2455 A552 Sheet of 9, #a-i 8.00 8.00
         Souvenir Sheets
2456-2457 A552 Set of 2 .... 7.00 7.00

20th Century Events in Mongolia A553

No. 2458: a, Independence, 1911. b, National revolution, 1921. c, Declaration of Mongolian People's Republic, 1924. d, Political repression, 1937. e, War years, 1939-45. f, Voting for independence, 1945. g, Agricultural reform, 1959. h, Member of UN, 1961. i, Space flight, 1981. j, Democratic revolution, 1990.

2000, Sept. 13   Litho.   Perf. 13½x13
2458 A553 300t Sheet of 10, #a-j
       + 2 labels 8.00 8.00
See No. 2482.

Marmota Sidisica — A554

Number of marmots: 100t, One. 200t, Three. 300t, Two. 400t, Three, diff.

2000, Sept. 15   Perf. 13¼x13
2459-2462 A554 Set of 4 .... 5.00 5.00
         Souvenir Sheet
         Perf. 13x13¼
2463 A554 800t One marmot, horiz. 5.50 5.50

Traditional Patterns — A555

Various designs: 50t, 200t, 250t, 300t, 400t, 550t.
50t, 250t, 550t are horiz.

Perf. 13¼x13, 13x13¼
2000, Sept. 20
2464-2469 A555 Set of 6 .... 8.50 8.50

John F. Kennedy, Jr. (1960-99) — A556

2000, Sept. 25   Perf. 14
2470 A556 300t multi 1.50 1.00
Printed in sheets of 6.

Millennium — A557

Exploration: a, 100t, Charles Darwin. b, 200t, Mollusk. c, 300t, HMS Beagle. d, 400t, Peacock. e, 400t, Dinosaur. f, 100t, Clematis. g, 200t, Orchid. h, 300t, Giant tortoise. i, 200t, Reduviid bug. j, 100t, Down House. k, 300t, Duck. l, 550t, The Origin of Species. m, 100t, Chimpanzee. n, 300t, Turkey. o, 550t, Horse. p, 600t, Ram (60x40mm). q, Vormela peregusna.

2000, Oct. 5   Perf. 12¾x12½
2471 A557 Sheet of 17, #a-q
       + label 17.00 17.00

State Symbols A558

No. 2472: a, Headdress on spike. b, Horn. c, Bow, arrows and quiver. d, Robe. e, Crossed swords. f, Saddle. g, Belt. h, Seated man. i, Throne.

2000, Oct. 25   Litho.   Perf. 12
2472 A558 300t Sheet of 9, #a-i 13.00 6.50

Queens — A559

No. 2473: a, Oulen. b, Borteujin. c, Turakana. d, Caymish. e, Chinbay.

2000, Oct. 30
2473   Horiz. strip of 5 .... 7.50 4.00
a.-e. A559 300t Any single .... 1.50 .75

Trains A560

No. 2474: a, 200t, TGV, France. b, 100t, X200, Sweden. c, 300t, Regio Runner, Netherlands. d, 100t, Deltic, Great Britain. e, 300t, Type M1200, Burma. f, 200t, ICE, Germany. g, 300t, G Class, Australia. h, 200t, Class E444, Italy. i, 100t, GM F7 Warbonnet, US.
No. 2475: a, 200t, Class 18 4-6-2, Germany. b, 100t, Class GS-4 4-8-4, US. c, 300t, Class 25 4-8-4, South Africa. d, 100t, Class 685 2-6-2, Italy. e, 300t, Class HP, India. f, 200t, Class SY 2-8-2, China. g, 300t, Liner A3 Pacific, Great Britain. h, 200t, Class 231C 4-6-2, France. i, 100t, Class 3700, Netherlands.

No. 2476, 800t, Rocket 0-2-2, Great Britain. No. 2477, 800t, Eurostar, France and Great Britain, vert.

2000, Nov. 25   Perf. 14
         Sheets of 9, #a-i
2474-2475 A560 Set of 2 .... 13.50 13.50
         Souvenir Sheets
2476-2477 A560 Set of 2 .... 9.00 9.00
Nos. 2474-2475 each contain nine 42x28mm stamps.

Endangered Animals of Gobi Desert — A561

No. 2478: a, 100t, Scarabaeus typhon (40x30mm). b, 400t, Ursus arctos gobiensis (40x40mm). c, 300t, Camelus bactrianus ferus (40x40mm). d, 300t, Saiga tatarica mongolica (40x40mm). e, 550t, Ovis ammon (40x40mm). f, 550t, Uncia uncia (40x40mm). g, 100t, Phrynosephalus heliosopicus (40x30mm). h, 200t, Coliber spinalus (40x40mm). i, 200t, Euchoreutes paso (40x40mm). j, 300t, Chlamydotis undulata (40x40mm).

2000, Dec. 25   Perf. 12½
2478 A561 Sheet of 10, #a-j 15.00 15.00

         Souvenir Sheet

Advent of New Millennium — A562

     Litho. & Embossed with Foil Application
2001, Jan. 1   Perf. 13½
2479 A562 5000t multi 15.00 15.00

New Year 2001 (Year of the Snake) A563

Color behind snake: 300t, Pink. 400t, green, vert.

2001, Jan. 15   Litho.   Perf. 13¼
2480-2481 A563 Set of 2 .... 3.50 3.00

20th Century Events Type of 2000

World events: a, First World War, 1914. b, October Revolution, 1917. c, Power seized by Fascists, 1933. d, Second World War, 1939. e, Nuclear weapons, 1945. f, Establishment of the United Nations, 1945. g, End of colonialism, 1940. h, Space travel, 1961. i, Downfall of socialism, 1989. j, Establishment of Mongolia, 1911.

2001, Mar. 15   Perf. 13½x13
2482 A553 300t Sheet of 10, #a-
       j, + 2 labels 8.00 8.00

Armed Forces, 80th Anniv. — A564

Designs: No. 2483, 300t, Marshal G. Demid (blue green). No. 2484, 300t, Marshal J.

MONGOLIA

Lhagvasuren (dark green). No. 2485, 300t, L. Dandar (olive green).

2001, Mar. 18			Perf. 13¾x13¼
2483-2485	A564	Set of 3	3.00 3.00

Souvenir Sheet

Mountaineers — A565

No. 2486: a, Mountaineer waving. b, Mountaineers starting climb.

2001, Apr. 1		Perf. 13¼x13
2486	A565	400t Sheet of 2, #a-b 4.00 4.00

I Love Lucy — A566

No. 2487, horiz.: a, 100t, Lucy drinking from cup, Ricky reading newspaper. b, 400t, Ricky and Fred. c, 300t, Lucy, Ethel and two candy factory workers. d, 200t, Lucy with arms outstretched, candy factory worker. e, 300t, Lucy looking at candy factory worker. f, 100t, Lucy smearing chocolate on worker's face. g, 100t, Worker smearing Lucy's face with chocolate. h, 250t, Ricky holding stocking, Fred. i, 200t, Ethel and Lucy.
No. 2488, 800t, Lucy wrapping chocolates.
No. 2489, 800t, Fred and Ricky preparing dinner.

2001, Apr. 15			Perf. 12½
2487	A566	Sheet of 9, #a-i	7.00 7.00

Souvenir Sheets

2488-2489	A566	Set of 2	7.00 7.00

The Three Stooges — A567

No. 2490: a, 100t, Larry. b, 400t, Larry and Shemp inserting instrument into man's mouth. c, 200t, Moe and Shemp. d, 200t, Moe, Larry and Shemp on telephones. e, 300t, Moe with chef's toque, Shemp, Larry. f, 100t, Moe looking in tube. g, 100t, Moe hitting Larry, Shemp. h, 550t, Shemp, Larry, Moe and woman. i, 200t, Moe with gavel, Curly on telephone.
No. 2491, 800t, Shemp and Larry as shown on #2490e. No. 2492, 800t, Shemp as angel, vert.

2001, Apr. 15			
2490	A567	Sheet of 9, #a-i	7.00 7.00

Souvenir Sheets

| 2491-2492 | A567 | Set of 2 | 7.00 7.00 |

Philatelic Exhibitions — A568

Nomading, by T.S. Minjuur and exhibition emblem of: a, Hong Kong 2001. b, Hafnia 01. c, Phila Nippon '01. d, Belgica 2001.

2001, May 15		Perf. 13½
2493	A568	400t Sheet of 4, #a-d 5.00 5.00

Souvenir Sheet

Expo 2001, Kitakyushu, Japan — A569

No. 2494: a, Roses from Gobi Dream, by Shosaku Tasaki (52x24mm). b, Dreamer from Gobi Dream, vert. (32x42mm). c, Tarbosaurus (48x35mm). d, Iguanodon, vert. (30x41mm). e, Triceratops (48x25mm).

Serpentine Die Cut 10¾, 12¼ (#2494c-2494e)

2001, July 1		Self-Adhesive
2494	A569	500t Sheet of 5, #a-e 9.00 9.00

Children and Sports — A570

No. 2495: a, Chess. b, Bicycling. c, Baseball.
No. 2496: a, 200t, Mongolian children on horses. b, 350t, Ice hockey. c, 500t, Flag, Mongolian boy on horse. d, 150t, Children playing soccer. e, 300t, Mongolian girl on horse. f, 450t, Boy playing soccer. g, 100t, Mongolian children on horses. h, 250t, Golf. i, 400t, Mongolian children on horses.

2001, Sept. 1			Perf. 12½
2495	A570	500t Horiz. strip of 3, #a-c	4.00 4.00
2496	A570	Sheet of 9, #a-i	12.00 12.00

Scouting and Nature — A571

No. 2497: a, 100t, Salpingotus. b, 200t, Uncia uncia. c, 300t, Haliaeetus albicilla. d, 400t, Pandion haliatus. e, 450t, Panciawus colchicus.
No. 2498: a, 50t, Butterfly. b, 100t, Bat. c, 200t, Butterfly, diff. d, 300t, Mushrooms. e, 400t, Dinosaur. f, 450t, Puffin.
No. 2499, vert.: a, 150t, Sea shell. b, 300t, Owl. c, 450t, Sea turtle. d, 100t, Frog. e, 250t, Butterfly. f, 400t, Orchid. g, 50t, Penguins. h, 200t, Elephant. i, 350t, Whale.

2001, Sept. 1			
2497	A571	Sheet of 5, #a-e, + label	5.00 5.00
2498	A571	Sheet of 6, #a-f	5.00 5.00
2499	A571	Sheet of 9, #a-i	7.50 7.50

Modern Transportation — A572

No. 2500: a, 50t, Zeppelin. b, 100t, Balloon. c, 150t, Apollo 11 command module. d, 200t, Apollo Lunar Module. e, 250t, Concorde. f, 300t, Train. g, 350t, Motorcycle. h, 400t, Race car. i, 450t, Sailboat.

2001, Sept. 15			
2500	A572	Sheet of 9, #a-i	9.00 9.00

Admission to United Nations, 40th Anniv. — A573

No. 2501: a, Dove, map. b, UN and Mongolian flags.

2001, Oct. 27		Perf. 13
2501	A573	400t Horiz. pair, #a-b 3.00 3.00

Year of Dialogue Among Civilizations — A574

2001, Dec. 20		Perf. 13¼x13
2502	A574	300t multi 2.50 2.50

Endangered Species in Steppe Zone — A575

No. 2503: a, 300t, Vespertilio superans (40x40mm). b, 200t, Podoces hendersoni (40x30mm). c, 300t, Capra sibirica (40x40mm). d, 100t, Gazella subgutturosa (40x30mm). e, 400t, Equus przewalskii (40x40mm). f, 300t, Equus hemionus hemionus (40x40mm). g, 550t, Erinaceus dauricus (40x30mm). h, 200t, Papilio machaon (40x30mm). i, 550t, Vormela peregusna (40x30mm). j, 100t, Rana chensinensis (40x30mm).

2001, Dec. 30		Perf. 13½x13¼
2503	A575	Sheet of 10, #a-j 10.00 10.00

History of Humanity — A576

Prominent features of stamps: a, Leaning Tower of Pisa, Romulus and Remus suckling she-wolf. b, Eagle, warrior with shield. c, Great Wall of China. d, Mosque, warrior on horseback. e, Celtic cross, castle, warrior with shield. f, Mona Lisa, by Leonardo da Vinci, David, by Michelangelo, other sculptures and religious paintings. g, Mask, Easter Island statues, boomerang, native, hut. h, Sir Isaac Newton, telescope, planets, Nicolaus Copernicus. i, Eiffel tower, Napoleon bonaparte on horseback, French flag, Arc de Triomphe. j, Astronaut, Earth, DNA molecule, computer. k, Greek soldier and amphora. l, Taj Mahal, Asoka pillar. m, Statue of Buddha. n, Genghis Khan. o, Yurt, Buddhist statue. p, Jesus Christ, Madonna and Child. q, Globe, ship, Christopher Columbus. r, Statue of Liberty, U.S. Capitol, Indian chief, U.S. flag, George Washington, city skyline. s, Printing press, man on horseback, letters of alphabet. t, Tower Bridge, British flag, Penny Black.

2001, Dec. 30		Perf. 13½
2504		Sheet of 20	20.00 20.00
a.-j.	A576	200t Any single	1.00 1.00
k.-t.	A576	300t Any single	1.00 1.00

New Year 2002 (Year of the Horse) — A577

Mane color: 300t, Gray, vert. 400t, Yellow brown.

2002, Feb. 13	Perf. 13¼x13, 13x13¼
2505-2506	A577 Set of 2 4.00 4.00

Birds of Prey — A578

Designs: 100t, Gyps himalayensis. 150t, Gyps fulvus. 300t, Neophron percnopterus. 400t, Aegypius monachus. 550t, Gypaetus barbatus.

2002, Apr. 1			Perf. 12½
2507-2511	A578	Set of 5	5.00 5.00

Souvenir Sheets

Mongolia - Japan Diplomatic Relations, 30th Anniv. — A579

No. 2512, 550t: a, Camel. b, Przewalski's horse.
No. 2513, 550t, vert. (38x50mm): a, Rider on horseback. b, Face of cartoon character.

2002, Apr. 27			Perf. 12
2512-2513	A579	Set of 2	8.00 8.00

Dogs — A580

Dogs with: 100t, Sheep. 200t, Cattle. 300t, Camel and yurt. 400t, Camels. 800t, Dog.

2002, May 1			Perf. 13¼x13
2514-2517	A580	Set of 4	4.00 4.00

Souvenir Sheet

2518	A580	800t multi	3.50 3.50

2002 World Cup Soccer Championships, Japan and Korea — A581

No. 2519: a, 300t, Stadium, Seoul. b, 400t, 1998 French team and flag, World Cup trophy. c, 400t, 1966 English team and flag, Jules Rimet Cup. d, 300t, Stadium, Yokohama.

2002, May 31			Perf. 12
2519	A581	Sheet of 4, #a-d	4.50 4.50

Flowers — A582

Designs: 100t, Thermopsis. No. 2521, 150t, Chelidonium. No. 2522, 150t, Hypencum. 200t, Plantago. 250t, Saussurea. 300t, Rosa acicularis. 450t, Lilium.

2002, June 15		Litho.	Perf. 12
2520-2526	A582	Set of 7	7.00 7.00

597

MONGOLIA

Rock Paintings A583

Various paintings with background colors of: 50t, Pink. 100t, Beige. 150t, Greenish blue. 200t, Green. 300t, Blue. 400t, Blue. 800t, Dark blue.

2002, July 1
2527-2532	A583	Set of 6	6.00	6.00

Souvenir Sheet
2533	A583	800t multi	3.50	3.50

New Year 2003 (Year of the Sheep) — A584

Sheep with background colors of: 300t, Yellow. 400t, Green, horiz.

2003, Jan. 1
2534-2535	A584	Set of 2	4.00	4.00

Mushrooms and Birds — A585

Designs: 50t, Russula aeruginosa, Coccothraustes coccothraustes. 100t, Boletus edulis, Loxia curvirostra. 150t, Boletus badius, Carpodacus erythrinus. 200t, Agaricus campester, Garrulus glandarius. 250t, Marasmius onreades, Luscinia megarhynchos. 300t, Cantharellus cibarius, Locustella certhiola. 400t, Amanita phalloides, Ardea cinerea. 550t, Suillus granulatus, Accipter gentilis.
No. 2544, 800t, Lactarius tormmosus, Aeqithalos caudatus. No. 2545, 800t, Tricholoma pertentosum, Lanius collurio.

2003, Feb. 1   **Perf. 13¼x13**
2536-2543	A585	Set of 8	8.00	8.00

Souvenir Sheets
2544-2545	A585	Set of 2	10.00	10.00

Nos. 2544-2545 each contain one 60x40mm stamp.

Visit Mongolia A586

No. 2546: a, 100t, Statue of Sukhe Bator. b, 200t, City buildings. c, 300t, Rock formation. d, 400t, Yurts.
No. 2547: a, 100t, Camels. b, 200t, Yaks. c, 300t, Hunter with eagle. d, 400t, Snow leopard.

2003, July 11   **Perf. 12**
Sheets of 4, #a-d
2546-2547	A586	Set of 2	8.00	8.00

Endangered Species in Khangai Zone — A587

No. 2548: a, 300t, Pandion haliaetus (40x30mm). b, 200t, Dryomys nitedula (40x30mm). c, 300t, Rangifer tarandus (40x40mm). d, 100t, Moschus moschiferus (40x40mm). e, 550t, Alces alces pfizenmayeri (40x40mm). f, 400t, Alces alces cameloides (40x40mm). g, 300t, Sus scrofa nigripes (40x40mm). h, 550t, Phasianus colchicus (40x30mm). i, 200t, Lutra lutra (40x30mm). j, 100t, Castor fiber birulai (40x30mm).

2003, Aug. 15   **Perf. 13½**
2548	A587	Sheet of 10, #a-j	10.00	10.00

Birds, Butterflies, Orchids and Mushrooms — A588

No. 2549, 800t — Birds: a, Common bush tanager. b, Black-headed hemispingus. c, Scarlet-rumped tanager. d, Band-tailed seedeater.
No. 2550, 800t — Butterflies: a, Thecla teresina. b, Theritas cypria. c, Theritas coronata. d, Thecla phaleros.
No. 2551, 800t — Orchids: a, Vanda rothschildiana. b, Paphiopedium parishii. c, Dendrobium nobile. d, Cattleya loddigesii.
No. 2552, 800t — Mushrooms: a, Hypholoma fasciculare. b, Marasmiellus ramealis. c, Collybia fusipes. d, Kuehneromyces mutabilis.
No. 2553, 2500t, Andean hillstar. No. 2554, 2500t, Thecla pedusa. No. 2555, 2500t, Barkeria skinnerii. No. 2556, 2500t, Psathyrella multipedata, vert.

Perf. 13¼x13½, 13½x13¼
2003, Dec. 10
Sheets of 4, #a-d
2549-2552	A588	Set of 4	25.00	25.00

Souvenir Sheets
2553-2556	A588	Set of 4	20.00	20.00

Souvenir Sheet

Yang Liwei, First Chinese Astronaut — A589

2003, Dec. 25   **Litho.**   **Perf. 12**
2557	A589	800t multi	4.00	4.00

New Year 2004 (Year of the Monkey) — A590

Monkey and background in: 300t, Blue. 400t, Red.

2004, Feb. 21
2558-2559	A590	Set of 2	4.00	4.00

Peace Mandala A591

No. 2560: a, 50t, Tushita Heaven. b, 100t, Elephant and Lady Maya. c, 150t, Birth of Buddha. d, 200t, Buddha as prince of Shakya clan. e, 250t, Prince shaving off hair. f, 300t, Buddha beating the devil. g, 400t, Buddha preaching for first time. h, 550t, Great Nirvana Sutra. i, 5000t, Various scenes in Buddha's life.
No. 2561, Central details of No. 2560i.
Size of Nos. 2560a-2560h, 41x38mm; No. 2560i, 132x182mm.

Serpentine Die Cut 10, 6¾ (#2560i, 2561)
2004, June 3   **Litho.**
Self-Adhesive
2560	A591	Sheet of 9, #a-i	18.00	18.00

Souvenir Sheet
Litho. With Foil Application
2561	A591	5000t gold & brn	20.00	20.00

Mammals — A592

Designs: (100t), Equus przewalskii. (300t), Camelus bactrianus ferus. (400t), Ovis ammon. (550t), Capra sibirica.

2004, July 1   **Litho.**   **Perf. 13¼x13**
2562	A592	(100t) multi	.65	.65
2563	A592	(300t) multi	1.00	1.00
2564	A592	(400t) multi	1.60	1.60
2565	A592	(550t) multi	2.00	2.00
	Nos. 2562-2565 (4)		5.25	5.25

Genghis Khan (c. 1162-1227) A593

Various depictions of Genghis Khan: 200t, 300t, 350t, 550t. 300t is horiz.

2004, July 11   **Perf. 13**
2566-2569	A593	Set of 4	4.00	4.00

Unification of Mongolia, 800th anniv. (in 2006).

2004 Summer Olympics, Athens — A594

Designs: 100t, Judo. 200t, Wrestling, horiz. 300t, Boxing. 400t, Pistol shooting, horiz.

2004, Aug. 13   **Perf. 12**
2570-2573	A594	Set of 4	3.50	3.00

UPU, 130th Anniv. — A595

2004, Sept. 15   **Perf. 12¾**
2574	A595	300t multi	1.50	1.00

Nos. 776, 778, 841, 842 Surcharged

Methods and Perfs as Before
2004, Oct. 5
2575	A191	550t on 10m #841	—	—
2576	A191	550t on 20m #842	—	—
2577	A178	550t on 30m #776	—	—
2578	A178	550t on 60m #778	—	—

Soccer — A599

Designs: No. 2581, Goalie making save. No. 2582, Player kicking ball. No. 2583, Three players. No. 2584, Player and goalie.

2004, Oct. 15   **Litho.**   **Perf. 12¾x13**
2579	A596	50t multi	.25	.25
2580	A597	50t multi	.25	.25
2581	A597	100t multi	.40	.40
2582	A597	100t multi	.40	.40
2583	A597	150t multi	.55	.55
2584	A597	150t multi	.55	.55
2585	A598	200t multi	.80	.80
2586	A599	200t multi	.80	.80
	Nos. 2579-2586 (8)		4.00	4.00

Souvenir Sheet

First Mongolian Stamp, 80th Anniv. — A600

2004, Dec. 4   **Perf. 13¼x13**
2587	A600	800t multi	3.50	3.50

Miniature Sheets

Insects and Flowers A601

No. 2588: a, 100t, Mantis religiosa. b, 100t, Aster alpina. c, 200t, Echinops humilis. d, 200t, Apis mellifera. e, 300t, Angaraeris barabensis. f, 300t, Nymphaea candida.
No. 2589: a, 100t, Lytta caraganae. b, 100t, Rosa acicularis. c, 200t, Aguilegia sibirica. d, 200t, Tabanus bovinus. e, 300t, Corizus hyoscyami. f, 300t, Lilium pumilum.

2004, Dec. 25   **Perf. 13**
Sheets of 6, #a-f
2588-2589	A601	Set of 2	10.00	10.00

Women's Headdresses — A602

No. 2590: a, Kazakh headdress, denomination at left. b, Mongol headdress, denomination at right.

2004, Dec. 31   **Perf. 11½x11¾**
2590	A602	550t Horiz. pair, #a-b	5.00	5.00

See Kazakhstan No. 472.

MONGOLIA

New Year 2005 (Year of the Rooster) — A603

Roosters with frame color of: 300t, Red violet. 400t, Blue, vert.

2005, Jan. 1   Perf. 12
2591-2592   A603   Set of 2   3.50   2.00

Souvenir Sheet

Expo 2005, Aichi, Japan — A604

No. 2593: a, 100t, Butterfly on flower. b, 150t, Flower. c, 200t, Puppy. d, 550t, Kitten.

2005, Mar. 25
2593   A604   Sheet of 4, #a-d   4.50   4.50

World Vision — A605

2005, Apr. 1
2594   A605   550t multi   3.00   1.50

Native Costumes — A606

No. 2595, 200t — Blue frame: a, Man with white and blue costume. b, Woman with green and white costume.
No. 2596, 200t — Green frame: a, Man with stringed instrument. b, Woman with red costume.
No. 2597, 200t — Rose pink frame: a, Man with white and blue costume. b, Woman with green costume.

2005, June 20   Perf. 13½x13
                 Horiz. pairs, #a-b
2595-2597   A606   Set of 3   5.00   5.00

Maharanza A607

No. 2595 — Color of face: a, White. b, Blue. c, Red. d, Yellow brown.

2005, July 8   Perf. 13x12¾
2598   Horiz. strip of 4   4.00   4.00
a.-d.   A607   400t Any single   1.00   1.00

Souvenir Sheet

Asashoryu, Sumo Wrestling Champion — A608

No. 2599 — Asashoryu: a, 600t, Wearing baseball cap. b, 700t, On horse, vert. c, 800t, In wrestling loincloth, vert.

2005, July 18   Perf. 13
2599   A608   Sheet of 3, #a-c   6.00   6.00

World Vision — A609

2005, Sept. 20   Perf. 12
2600   A609   550t multi   2.50   1.50

Headdresses — A610

People wearing various headdresses: 50t, 100t, 150t, 200t, 250t, 300t, 800t, National headdress.

2005, Oct. 3   Perf. 12¾x13
2601-2606   A610   Set of 6   4.00   4.00

Souvenir Sheet
             Perf. 12
2607   A610   800t multi   3.50   3.50

No. 2607 contains one 37x56mm stamp.

Souvenir Sheets

Shenzhou VI Space Flight — A611

No. 2608, 800t, Astronauts waving. No. 2609, 800t, Astronauts in spacecraft.

2005, Dec. 9   Perf. 12
2608-2609   A611   Set of 2   8.00   8.00

Souvenir Sheet

Coins of the Mongolian Empire — A612

No. 2610 — Various coins with background color of: a, Blue. b, Grayish lilac. c, Deep bister.

2006, Jan. 11   Perf. 13x12¾
2610   A612   550t Sheet of 3, #a-c   5.00   5.00

New Year 2006 (Year of the Dog) — A613

Mongolian emblem and "Year of the Dog" at: 300t, Right. 400t, Left.

2006, Jan. 27   Perf. 13x13¼
2611-2612   A613   Set of 2   3.50   2.00

Miniature Sheet

Europa Stamps, 50th Anniv. A614

No. 2613: a, Archer. b, Camels. c, Boys herding livestock. d, Goat. e, Rocks. f, Building spire. g, Dinosaur skeleton. h, Circus performers. i, Yurt. j, Two men in native costumes. k, Airplane. l, Ox.

2006, Feb. 1   Perf. 12½x13
2613   A614   200t Sheet of 12, #a-l   8.00   8.00
   m.   Souvenir sheet, #2613a-2613b, perf. 13   1.50   1.50
   n.   Souvenir sheet, #2613c-2613d, perf. 13   1.50   1.50
   o.   Souvenir sheet, #2613e-2613f, perf. 13   1.50   1.50
   p.   Souvenir sheet, #2613g-2613h, perf. 13   1.50   1.50
   q.   Souvenir sheet, #2613i-2613j, perf. 13   1.50   1.50
   r.   Souvenir sheet, #2613k-2613l, perf. 13   1.50   1.50

World Vision A615

No. 2614: a, Children riding ox. b, Child riding horse.

2006, May 5   Litho.   Perf. 12
2614   A615   550t Horiz. pair, #a-b   3.50   3.50

Souvenir Sheet

Morin Khuur A616

2006, June 16
2615   A616   550t multi   2.50   2.50

Souvenir Sheet

Pres. Nambaryn Enkhbayar — A617

2006, June 21
2616   A617   800t multi   3.50   3.50

Souvenir Sheet

2006 World Cup Soccer Championships, Germany — A618

No. 2617 — Various stylized players: a, 200t. b, 250t. c, 300t. d, 400t.

2006, June 23
2617   A618   Sheet of 4, #a-d   5.00   5.00

Souvenir Sheet

State Visit of US Pres. George W. Bush A619

2006, June 30   Perf. 13x13¼
2618   A619   600t multi   3.00   3.00

Souvenir Sheets

A620

Famous Mongols A621

No. 2619 — Various unnamed Mongols: a, 50t (23x33mm). b, 100t (23x33mm). c, 300t (23x33mm). d, 400t (23x33mm). e, 500t (80x56mm).

2006   Perf. 13, 11½ (#2619e)
2619   A620   Sheet of 5, #a-e   6.00   6.00
   f.   As #2619, with sheet margin overprinted in gold with Mongolian text   1.90   1.90
           Perf. 11½x11¾
2620   A621   3800t shown   12.00   12.00

Mongolian stamps, 85th anniv. (#2619). Issued: No. 2619, 7/0; No. 2619f, 7/10/09. No. 2620, 9/19. Mongolian State, 800th anniv.

Souvenir Sheet

Horse Sculptures — A622

No. 2621: a, 300t, Horse and rider. b, 400t, Horse only.

2006, Sept. 28   Perf. 12
2621   A622   Sheet of 2, #a-b   3.50   3.50

See India No. 2167.

Miniature Sheet

Friendly Exchange Philatelic Exhibition — A623

No. 2622: a, 150t, Olympic Stadium, Beijing. b, 200t, Waterfalls. c, 250t, City street at night.

2006, Oct. 25   Litho.   Perf. 12
2622   A623   Sheet of 3, #a-c   2.25   1.50

Hucho Taimen Fish A624

No. 2623 — Various depictions of fish: a, 100t. b, 200t. c, 300t. d, 400t.

2006, Dec. 17
2623   A624   Block of 4, #a-d   3.00   3.00

MONGOLIA

New Year 2007 (Year of the Pig) A625

Designs: 300t, Two pigs. 400t, Two pigs, diff.

2006, Dec. 17
2624-2625 A625 Set of 2   2.25 2.25

Dutch Royalty — A625a

No. 2625A: b, Prince Willem-Alexander. c, Prince Willem-Alexander and Princess Máxima. d, Princess Máxima.

2007, Jan. 7   *Perf. 13¼x13½*
2625A Vert. strip of 3   10.00 10.00
   b.-d. A625a 700t Any single   2.00 2.00

Printed in sheets containing 2 each of Nos. 2625Ab-2625Ad.

Miniature Sheet

Marilyn Monroe (1926-62), Actress — A625b

No. 2625E — Monroe with: f, Background in orange in white, country name and denomination in orange. g, Background and denomination in orange, country name in white. h, Background in rose and white, country name and denomination in white. i, Background in claret, country name and denomination in white.

2007, Jan. 26
2625E A625b 1050t Sheet of 4, #f-i   10.00 10.00

Miniature Sheet

Elvis Presley (1935-77) — A625c

No. 2625J — Presley: k, Facing right, holding microphone. l, Facing forward, country name at top. m, Facing right, without microphone. n, Facing forward, country name at bottom.

2007, Jan. 26   *Perf. 13¼*
2625J A625c 1050t Sheet of 4, #k-n   10.00 10.00

Betty Boop — A625d

No. 2625O — Betty Boop: p, Holding down dress in breeze. q, With both hands in air. r, With hands clasped. s, With one arm raised, parts of "B," "E," and "T" at top. t, Winking, with leg lifted. u, With one arm raised, parts of "B," "O," and "P" at top.
No. 2625V — Betty Boop lifting dress to expose garter: a, Without part of heart to left of "GO" in country name. b, With part of heart to left of "GO" in country name.

2007, Jan. 26   *Perf. 13¼x13½*
2625O A625d 700t Sheet of 6, #p-u   10.00 10.00

Souvenir Sheet
2625V A625d 1500t Sheet of 2, #w-x   7.00 7.00

Souvenir Sheet

Diplomatic Relations Between Mongolia and the United States, 20th Anniv. — A626

No. 2626: a, 400t, Statue of Genghis Khan, Ulan Bator. b, 550t, Statue of Abraham Lincoln, Washington, DC.

2007, Jan. 29   *Perf. 12*
2626 A626 Sheet of 2, #a-b   3.25 3.25

Lama Tsonghapa (1357-1419), Buddhist Teacher — A627

2007, Jan. 30   *Perf. 12¾*
2627 A627 100t multi   4.00 4.00

Souvenir Sheet

Diplomatic Relations Between Mongolia and Japan, 35th Anniv. — A628

No. 2628: a, 550t, Mt. Fuji, Japan. 700t, Mt. Otgontenger, Mongolia.

2007, Feb. 23   *Perf. 12*
2628 A628 Sheet of 2, #a-b   3.50 3.50

Calligraphy — A629

Designs: 50t, Light of wisdom. 100t, Butterfly. 150t, Flower. 200t, Horse. 250t, Spring. 300t, Leaves. 400t, Wow. 550t, Wild camel. 800t, Sky.

2007, Aug. 2   *Perf. 13x12¾*
2629-2636 A629 Set of 8   7.00 7.00

Souvenir Sheet   *Perf. 12¾*
2637 A629 800t multi   3.50 3.50

No. 2637 contains one 43x57mm stamp.

Souvenir Sheets

Modern Art — A630

Art by: No. 2638, 400t, Ts. Tsegmid. No. 2639, 400t, S. Sarantsatsralt. No. 2640, 400t, Ts. Enkhjin. No. 2641, 400t, Do. Bold, horiz. No. 2642, 400t, Sh. Chimeddorj, horiz.

2007, Aug. 21   *Perf. 13*
2638-2642 A630 Set of 5   7.50 7.50

Miniature Sheet

Naotoshi Yamada, Olympic Cheerleader, and Mongolian Sumo Wrestlers — A631

No. 2643 — Yamada and various wrestlers with Mongolian emblem and inscriptions at: a, 500t, Right. b, 500t, Left. c, 600t, Right. d, 600t, Left. e, 700t, Right. f, 700t, Left.

2007, Oct. 3   *Die Cut*
   Self-Adhesive
2643 A631 Sheet of 6, #a-f, + 10 labels   9.00 9.00

Genghis Khan (c. 1162-1227) — A632

   Perf. 12½x12¾
2007, Nov. 29   *Litho.*
2644 Horiz. strip of 5   7.50 7.50
   a. A632 230t black   .50 .50
   b. A632 400t brown   1.00 1.00
   c. A632 650t blue   1.50 1.50
   d. A632 800t green   2.00 2.00
   e. A632 1000t violet   2.50 2.50

New Year 2008 (Year of the Rat) — A633

No. 2645 — Rat with denomination at: a, UR. b, LL.

2008, Jan. 1   *Perf. 12¾*
2645 A633 800t Vert. pair, #a-b   4.00 4.00

Wedding of Queen Elizabeth II and Prince Philip, 50th Anniv. A634

No. 2646: a, Queen. b, Queen and Prince.

2008, Jan. 25   *Perf. 13¼*
2646 A634 400t Pair, #a-b   1.60 1.60

Printed in sheets of 6 containing 2 each of Nos. 2646a-2646b.

Princess Diana (1961-97) — A635

No. 2647, vert. — Princess Diana wearing: a, Necklace and black gown. b, Red hat and coat. c, Black and white dress. d, Black and white hat and jacket.
3000t, Prince Charles and Princess Diana.

2008, Jan. 25
2647 A635 1150t Sheet of 4, #a-d   8.00 8.00

Souvenir Sheet
2648 A635 3000t multi   5.25 5.25

First Helicopter Flight, Cent. — A636

No. 2649: a, Belvedere. b, AS 565 Dauphin/Panther. c, Explorer. d, Shark. 3000t, Scout.

2008, Jan. 25
2649 A636 1150t Sheet of 4, #a-d   9.00 9.00

Souvenir Sheet
2650 A636 3000t multi   5.25 5.25

Muhammad Ali, Boxer — A637

No. 2651, 1150t — Ali: a, Wearing shirt. b, Shadow-boxing. c, Punching bag. d, Punching at opponent.
No. 2652, 1150t, horiz. — Ali with: a, Black boxing gloves punching at opponent. b, Red boxing gloves with left arm extended. c, Red boxing gloves, ring rope in background. d, Red boxing gloves, lights and ring rope in background.
No. 2653, 3000t, Ali wearing robe. No. 2654, 3000t, Close-up photograph.

   Perf. 13¼, 11½ (#2652)
2008, Jan. 25
   Sheets of 4, #a-d
2651-2652 A637 Set of 2   18.00 18.00
   Souvenir Sheets
2653-2654 A637 Set of 2   11.00 11.00

MONGOLIA

Pope John Paul II (1920-2005) — A637a

2008, Jan. 25 Litho. Perf. 13½x13¼
2654A A637a 880t multi 2.50 2.50

Miniature Sheet

Photomosaic of Pope Benedict XVI — A638

No. 2655 — Part of photomosaic with frame around it: a, At left and top in green. b, At left in green. c, At left in green and white. d, At left and bottom in white.

2008, Jan. 25 Perf. 13¼
2655 A638 1150t Sheet of 4, #a-d 8.00 8.00

Nos. 1355 and 1359 Surcharged

Methods and Perfs As Before
2008, Feb. 29
2656 A301 1000t on 20m #1355 2.00 2.00
2657 A301 1000t on 60m #1359 2.00 2.00

No. 1983 Surcharged

Method and Perf. As Before
2008, Mar. 7
2658 A429 250t on 40m #1983 1.25 1.25

Campaign Against AIDS — A639

2008, Apr. 10 Litho. Perf. 12¾x13
2659 A639 500t multi 1.40 1.40

Handcrafted Items — A640

Designs: No. 2660, 500t, Pipe and tobacco pouch (shown). No. 2661, 500t, Jar and cloth. No. 2662, 500t, Silver bowls. No. 2663, 500t, Sword and sheath. No. 2664, 500t, Saddle.

2008, June 8 Perf. 12¾
2660-2664 A640 Set of 5 6.50 6.50

Miniature Sheet

2008 Summer Olympics, Beijing — A641

No. 2665: a, Canoe-kayak. b, Fencing. c, Handball. d, Modern pentathlon.

2008, July 8 Perf. 12¾x12½
2665 A641 600t Sheet of 4, #a-d 5.00 5.00

Wild Boars — A642

No. 2666: a, Head of boar. b, Sow and piglets. c, Boar. d, Boar and sow.

2008, Sept. 10 Perf. 12½x12¾
2666 Horiz. strip of 4 7.00 7.00
a.-d. A642 800t Any single 1.75 1.75

New Year 2009 (Year of the Ox) — A643

Ox with background color of: 200t, Yellow. 300t, Blue.

2009, Jan. 19 Perf. 12
2667-2668 A643 Set of 2 1.75 1.75

National Coat of Arms A644

Great White Banner A645

National Flag A646

Soyombo A647

2009, Jan. 28 Litho.
2669 Horiz. strip of 4 5.00 5.00
a. A644 400t multi .75 .75
b. A645 500t multi 1.00 1.00
c. A646 800t multi 1.50 1.50
d. A647 1000t multi 1.75 1.75

No. 1307 Surcharged

Method and Perf. As Before
2009, Apr. 6
2670 A290 1000t on 20m #1307 2.75 2.75

People in Yurt — A648

2009, Apr. 6 Litho. Perf. 13x12¾
2671 A648 1000t multi 2.00 2.00

China 2009 World Stamp Exhibition, Luoyang — A649

No. 2672: a, Giant panda. b, Ursus arctos gobiensis.

2009, Apr. 10 Perf. 12¾x12½
2672 A649 300t Pair, #a-b 1.75 1.75
Printed in sheets of 14, 7 each Nos. 2672a-2672b, + 2 labels.

Peonies — A650

2009, Apr. 23 Perf. 13½x13¼
2673 A650 700t multi 1.75 1.75
Printed in sheets of 6.

Earrings From Korea, 5th-6th Cent. — A651

Earrings From Mongolia, 18th-19th Cent. — A652

Earring From Kazakhstan, 2nd-1st Cent. B.C. — A653

2009, June 12 Perf. 12
2674 Horiz. strip of 3 5.00 5.00
a. A651 800t multi 1.60 1.60
b. A652 800t multi 1.60 1.60
c. A653 800t multi 1.60 1.60
See Kazakhstan No. 595, South Korea No. 2313.

Battles of Khalkhiin Gol, 70th Anniv. A654

2009, Aug. 20 Perf. 13x12½
2675 A654 500t lil & pur 1.25 1.25

Souvenir Sheet

Taras A655

No. 2676: a, White Tara. b, Green Tara.

2009, Oct. 9 Perf. 12
2676 A655 800t Sheet of 2, #a-b 3.50 3.50

Diplomatic Relations Between Mongolia and People's Republic of China, 60th Anniv. — A656

No. 2677 — Buildings with frame and denomination in: a, Blue. b, Red.

2009, Oct. 9 Perf. 12¾
2677 Horiz. pair with central label 4.00 4.00
a.-b. A656 1000t Either single 2.00 2.00

APU Company, 85th Anniv. — A657

2009, Dec. 1 Perf. 12¾x13
2678 A657 800t multi 1.75 1.75

Camel Polo — A658

2010, Jan. 26 Litho. Perf. 11½
2679 A658 1000t multi 2.00 2.00

A659

A660

A661

A662

A663

MONGOLIA

A664

Secrets of the Mongols A665

Designs: No. 2686, Black banner. No. 2687, Five arrows.

2010, Feb. 5   *Perf. 13x12¾*
2680	A659	1000t multi	2.00	2.00
2681	A660	1000t multi	2.00	2.00
2682	A661	1000t multi	2.00	2.00
2683	A662	1000t multi	2.00	2.00
2684	A663	1000t multi	2.00	2.00
2685	A664	1000t multi	2.00	2.00
	Nos. 2680-2685 (6)		8.40	8.40

Souvenir Sheets
Perf. 12
2686	A665	1500t pur & multi	3.00	3.00
2687	A665	1500t grn & multi	3.00	3.00

Compare with Types A677-A683.

New Year 2010 (Year of the Tiger) — A666

No. 2688 — Tiger with background color of: a, Green. b, Blue.

2010, Feb. 14   *Perf. 12*
2688	A666	1000t Vert. pair, #a-b	4.00	4.00

Children — A667

Children with stringed instruments and: 800t, Horse. 1000t, Camel.

2010, Apr. 20   *Perf. 13½*
2689-2690	A667	Set of 2	3.50	3.50

Mountains — A668

No. 2691: a, Sutai Khairkhan. b, Altan Khokhii. c, Khan Khokhii. d, Suvarga Khairkhan.
No. 2692: a, Burkhan Khaldun. b, Bogd Khairkhan. c, Dariganga, Dari Ovoo. d, Otgontenger.

2010   *Litho.*   *Perf. 13¼*
2691	A668	500t Block or horiz. strip of 4, #a-d	4.00	4.00

Perf. 12
2692	A668	500t Block of 4, #a-d	4.00	4.00

Issued: No. 2691, 5/27; No. 2692, 6/15.

Flag of Mongolia — A669

2010, June 15   *Perf. 13*
2693	A669	800t multi	1.50	1.50

2010 World Cup Soccer Championships, South Africa — A670

No. 2694: a, Emblem. b, Mascot.

2010, July 11   *Perf. 13¼x13*
2694	A670	800t Horiz. pair, #a-b, + central label	3.00	3.00

Souvenir Sheet

Chingunjav (1710-57), Leader of Rebellion Against Manchus — A671

2010, Aug. 27   *Perf. 12¼x12*
2695	A671	800t multi	1.50	1.50

Souvenir Sheet

Pres. Tsakhiagiin Elbegdorj — A672

2010, Oct. 22   *Perf. 12½x13*
2696	A672	500t multi	2.50	2.50

Butterflies — A673

Designs: 100t, Ornithoptera croesus. 200t, Papilio antimachus. 400t, Ornithoptera priamus urvilleanus. 500t, Papilio zalmoxis. 800t, Troides rhadamantius. 1000t, Ornithoptera victoriae epiphanes.

2010, Dec. 8   *Litho.*   *Perf. 12*
2697-2702	A673	Set of 6	7.50	7.50

Souvenir Sheet

Taras A674

No. 2703: a, Green tara. b, Red tara.

2010, Dec. 8   *Perf. 13x13¼*
2703	A674	800t Sheet of 2, #a-b	3.50	3.50

New Year 2011 (Year of the Rabbit) — A675

2011, Jan. 12   *Perf. 11½*
2704	A675	1000t multi	2.00	2.00

First Man in Space, 50th Anniv. — A676

2011, Apr. 12   *Perf. 13¼*
2705	A676	500t multi	1.10	1.10

Printed in sheets of 10 + 2 labels.

A677

A678

A679

A680

A681

A682

Secrets of the Mongols A683

Designs: No. 2712, White banner. No. 2713, Khan's seal of Great Mongol.

2011, May 29   *Litho.*   *Perf. 13x12¾*
2706	A677	1000t multi	1.90	1.90
2707	A678	1000t multi	1.90	1.90
2708	A679	1000t multi	1.90	1.90
2709	A680	1000t multi	1.90	1.90
2710	A681	1000t multi	1.90	1.90
2711	A682	1000t multi	1.90	1.90
	Nos. 2706-2711 (6)		11.40	11.40

Souvenir Sheets
Perf. 12
2712	A683	1500t blue & multi	2.75	2.75
2713	A683	1500t brown & multi	2.75	2.75

Compare with Types A659-A665.

Livestock — A684

Designs: No. 2714, 1000t, Yak. No. 2715, 1000t, Camel. No. 2716, 1200t, Mongolian horse. No. 2717, 1200t, Reindeer.

2011, June 13   *Perf. 13x12¾*
2714-2717	A684	Set of 4	8.00	8.00

Souvenir Sheet

Motor Sports A685

No. 2718: a, 300t, Road rally. b, 400t, Motorcycle racing. c, 600t, Auto racing.

2011, July 8   *Perf. 13x13¼*
2718	A685	Sheet of 3, #a-c	2.50	2.50

Miniature Sheet

Mongolian People's Revolution, 90th Anniv. — A686

No. 2719: a, 600t, Kharloin Choibalsan (1895-1952), Prime Minister, 1939-52 (30x30mm). b, 600t, Dogsomyn Bodoo (1895-1922), Prime Minister, 1921-22 (30x30mm). c, 600t, Soliin Danzan (1885-1924), Central Committee chairman (30x30mm). d, 600t, Dambyn Chagdarjav (1880-1922), Prime Minister, 1921 (30x30mm). e, 600t, Dansrabilegiin Dogsom (1884-1939), President, 1936-39 (30x30mm). f, 600t, D. Losol (1898-1940), revolutionist (30x30mm). g, 1200t, Sukhe Bator (1893-1923), leader of revolution (30x40mm).

2011, July 11   *Perf. 12*
2719	A686	Sheet of 7, #a-g	9.00	9.00

Souvenir Sheets

Reign of Genghis Khan, 805th Anniv. A687

Designs: No. 2720, 2000t, Genghis Khan (c. 1162-1227). No. 2721, 2000t, Order of Genghis Khan.

2011, July 11   *Litho.*
2720-2721	A687	Set of 2	7.50	7.50

Hunnu Culture, 2200th Anniv. A688

No. 2722: a, Pottery. b, Jewelry depicting horse. c, Jewelry depicting bird. d, Wolf attacking buck. e, Arrowheads.
5000t, Modun Shanyu (c. 234 B.C.-174 B.C.), emperor.

2011, July 25   *Perf. 11¾x11½*
2722	A688	1000t Sheet of 5, #a-e	9.50	9.50

MONGOLIA

Souvenir Sheet
Perf. 12¾
2723 A688 5000t multi   9.50 9.50
No. 2723 contains one 60x65mm stamp.

Wildlife — A689

Wildlife of: 400t, Antarctic and Arctic regions. 600t, Mongolia. 1000t, Australia. 1200t, Africa.

2011, July 27		Perf. 12
2724-2727 A689	Set of 4	6.00 6.00

No. 1231 Surcharged in Gold

Method and Perf. As Before
2011, July 28
2728 A275 800t on 4t #1231   1.50 1.50
PhilaNippon '11, Intl. Philatelic Exhibition, Yokohama.

Wedding of Prince William and Catherine Middleton — A690

Designs: 1200t, Couple.
No. 2730: a, Prince William. b, Catherine Middleton.

2011, Aug. 22	Litho.	Perf. 12
2729 A690 1200t multi		2.25 2.25

Souvenir Sheet
Perf. 13½x13
2730 A690 1500t Sheet of 2, #a-b   5.50 5.50

Souvenir Sheet

Education in Mongolia, 90th Anniv. — A691

No. 2731: a, Students, bugler, building. b, Girl, children at computers. c, Mongolian flag, graduates, building.

2011, Sept. 9		Perf. 12
2731 A691 1200t Sheet of 3, #a-c		6.50 6.50

Souvenir Sheet

Admission to the United Nations, 50th Anniv. — A692

2011, Oct. 27	Litho.	Perf. 12¾
2732 A692 1000t multi		2.00 2.00

Nos. 2403-2404 Overprinted in Gold

Methods and Perfs As Before
2011, Nov. 11
2733 A531 250t multi on #2403   .60 .60
2734 A531 450t multi on #2404   1.10 1.10
China 2011 Intl. Philatelic Exhibition, Wuxi.

Souvenir Sheet

Mongolian Diplomatic Service, Cent. — A693

No. 2735: a, Mijiddorjiin Khanddorj (1869-1915), first Mongolian Foreign Minister (30x65mm). b, Flag of Mongolia, United Nations Building, dove (50x38mm). c, Golden gerege (30x65mm).

Perf. 12¾, 13¼ (#2735b)
2011, Dec. 1		Litho.
2735 A693 600t Sheet of 3, #a-c		3.50 3.50

Souvenir Sheet

United Nations Secretary General Ban Ki-Moon and Mongolian Prime Minister Sukhbaatar Batbold — A694

2011, Dec. 13		Perf. 13x13¼
2736 A694 500t multi		1.00 1.00

Admission to United Nations, 50th anniv.

Souvenir Sheet

Mongolian Government Palace and Flag — A695

2011, Dec. 17		Perf. 12¾
2737 A695 1000t multi		2.00 2.00

Mongolian government, cent.

Souvenir Sheet

Mongolian Revolution, Cent. — A696

No. 2738: a, Bogdo Jebtsundamba VIII (Bogd Khan, 1869-1924), Emperor. b, Tögs-Ochiryn Namnansuren (1878-1919), Prime Minister.

2011, Dec. 29		Perf. 13¼x13
2738 A696 1000t Sheet of 2, #a-b, + label		4.00 4.00

New Year 2012 (Year of the Dragon) — A697

2012, Jan. 1		Perf. 13x13¼
2739 A697 600t multi		1.25 1.25

Souvenir Sheet

Fleet of Kublai Khan — A698

No. 2740: a, 1000t, Kublai Khan (1215-94), Emperor. b, 1200t, Warship.

2012, Mar. 4		Perf. 12
2740 A698 Sheet of 2, #a-b		4.50 4.50

Souvenir Sheet

Diplomatic Relations Between Mongolia and Japan, 40th Anniv. — A699

No. 2741: a, Mongolian doll. b, Japanese doll.

2012, Mar. 12		Perf. 12¾x13
2741 A699 600t Sheet of 2, #a-b, + label		2.50 2.50

Mythological Creatures A700

Cats — A701

Designs: 100t, Dragon. 200t, Lion. 400t, Tiger. 600t, Khan Garuda.

2012, Apr. 22	Litho.	Perf. 13¼
2742 A700 100t multi		.25 .25
2743 A701 200t multi		.40 .40
2744 A701 400t multi		.75 .75
2745 A700 600t multi		1.25 1.25
Nos. 2742-2745 (4)		2.65 2.65

Souvenir Sheet

Antarctic Explorers — A702

No. 2746: a, Fabian von Bellingshausen (1778-1852). b, Mikhail P. Lazarev (1788-1851).

2012, June 17		Perf. 13
2746 A702 800t Sheet of 2, #a-b		3.25 3.25

2012 Summer Olympics, London — A703

No. 2747 — Emblem of 2012 Summer Olympics, British flag and: a, London tourist attractions. b, Athletes.

2012, July 5		Perf. 13¼
2747	Pair	3.00 3.00
a. A703 700t multi		1.40 1.40
b. A703 800t multi		1.60 1.60

Women in Modern National Costumes — A704

Various costumes: 100t, 200t, 300t, 400t, 500t, 600t.
No. 2754: a, 700t. b, 800t.

2012, Aug. 24		Perf. 12
2748-2753 A704	Set of 6	4.25 4.25

Souvenir Sheet
Perf. 13x13¼
2754 A704 Sheet of 2, #a-b   3.00 3.00
No. 2754 contains two 38x50mm stamps.

Miniature Sheet

Guardians of the Days — A705

No. 2755 — Guardian and inscription: a, 100t, Moon. b, 200t, Mars. c, 300t, Mercury. d, 400t, Jupiter. e, 500t, Venus. f, 600t, Saturn. g, 700t, Sun.

Self-Adhesive
2012, Oct. 14		Die Cut Perf.
2755 A705 Sheet of 7, #a-g		5.50 5.50

Souvenir Sheet

Customs Department, Cent. — A706

MONGOLIA

No. 2756: a, 800t, Three Mongolian customs officials. b, 1000t, Two modern Mongolian customs officials, flag, horiz. 1200t, Customs dog, marijuana.

2012, Oct. 20			Perf. 13¼x13
2756	A706	Sheet of 3, #a-c	6.00 6.00

Souvenir Sheet

Genghis Khan (1162-1227), Mongol Conqueror — A707

No. 2757: a, 350t, Horse. b, 850t, Genghis Khan.

2012, Nov. 14			Perf. 12
2757	A707	Sheet of 2, #a-b	2.50 2.50

Birds — A708

Designs: 100t, Amazona aestiva, Ara chloroptera, Ara ararauna. 200t, Paradisaea raggiana, Paradisaea rudolphi. 300t, Cygnus atratus, Cygnus olor, Phoenicopterus roseus. 400t, Aix galericulata, Aix sponsa. 800t, Erythrura gouldiae, Pteridophora albertus, Euplectes orix. 1000t, Pavo cristatus, Chrysolophus pictus.

2012, Dec. 24			Perf. 13¼
2758-2763	A708	Set of 6	5.50 5.50

Flag and Emblem of Mongolia — A709

2012, Dec. 29			Perf. 13x13¼
2764	A709	1200t multi	2.50 2.50

No. 1660 with this 500t surcharge in gold, released in Feb. 2013, was produced in limited quantities. Value, $3.

New Year 2013 (Year of the Snake) — A710

2013, Feb. 6		Litho.	Perf. 12
2765	A710	600t multi	1.25 1.25

No. 2765 was printed in sheets of 16 + 4 labels.

Gazelles — A711

Designs: 200t, Gazella subgutturosa. 400t, Procapra gutturosa. 800t, Procapra gutturosa, diff. 1000t, Gazella subgutturosa, diff.

2013, June 4			Perf. 13x13¼
2766-2769	A711	Set of 4	5.00 5.00
2769a		Sheet of 8, 2 each #2766-2769, + central label	10.00 10.00

Miniature Sheet

Falcons A712

No. 2770: a, 100t, Falcon in flight (60x30mm). b, 200t, Two Falco cherrug in flight (60x30mm). c, 300t, Falcon chicks and eggs (60x30mm). d, 400t, Falcon on rock (60x30mm). e, 800t, Falcon and Mongolian regalia (40x60mm). f, 1000t, Falcon on hand of Mongolian falconer (40x60mm).

Litho., Margin Litho. With Foil Application

2013, June 19			Perf. 12
2770	A712	Sheet of 6, #a-f	6.00 6.00

Animals on Elephant A713

Musician A714

Mongolian Woman A715

Yurt A716

2013, July 21		Litho.	Perf. 12½x12¾
2771	A713	1000t multi	2.00 2.00
2772	A714	1000t multi	2.00 2.00
2773	A715	1000t multi	2.00 2.00
2774	A716	1000t multi	2.00 2.00
		Nos. 2771-2774 (4)	8.00 8.00

No. 2363 Srchd. in Red With Thailand 2013 World Stamp Exhibition Emblem Added

Souvenir Sheet

2013, Aug. 2			Perf. 11
2775	A519	1500t on 1000t #2363	3.00 3.00

Thailand 2013 World Stamp Exhibition, Bangkok.

Batu Khan (c. 1207-55), Mongol Ruler — A717

2013, Oct. 16		Litho.	Perf. 12
2776	A717	1000t multi	2.25 2.25

The Beatles A718

2013, Dec. 6		Litho.	Perf. 13
2777	A718	Sheet of 3, #a-c	4.50 4.50

No. 2777: a, 500t, Ringo Starr (38x50mm). b, 500t, John Lennon (38x50mm). c, 1000t, Paul McCartney and George Harrison (60x50mm).

New Year 2014 (Year of the Horse) — A719

No. 2778 — Horse facing: a, Right. b, Left.

2013, Dec. 22	Litho.	Perf. 13xx12¾
2778	Horiz. pair + central label	2.75 2.75
a.-b.	A719 650t Either single	1.25 1.25

Nos. 1564-1567 Surcharged

Methods and Perfs As Before

2014, Jan. 6			
2779	A347	1300t on 60m #1564	2.75 2.75
2780	A347	1300t on 60m #1565	2.75 2.75
2781	A347	1300t on 60m #1566	2.75 2.75
2782	A347	1300t on 60m #1567	2.75 2.75
		Nos. 2779-2782 (4)	11.00 11.00

Mongolian postage stamps, 90th anniv.

Flowers — A720

Designs: 200t, Lilium dahuricum, Cypripedium calceolus and bee. 300t, Saussurea involucrata and bird. 400t, Iris sibirica, Lilium pumilum and butterfly. 900t, Trollius asiaticus, Tulipa uniflora and dragonfly. 1000t, Cypripedium macranthum, Adonis sibirica and ladybug.

2014, Feb. 15		Litho.	Perf. 13x12¾
2783-2787	A720	Set of 5	6.00 6.00
2787a		Sheet of 10, 2 each #2783-2387, + 2 central labels	12.50 12.50

Scientists — A721

Designs: No. 2788, 100t, Charles Darwin (1809-82), naturalist. No. 2789, 100t, Albert Einstein (1879-1955), physicist. No. 2790, 300t, Leonardo da Vinci (1452-1519). No. 2791, 300t, Isaac Newton (1642-1727), physicist. No. 2792, 500t, Galileo Galilei (1564-1642), astronomer. No. 2793, 500t, Niels Bohr (1885-1962), physicist.

2014, Mar. 25		Litho.	Perf. 13¼x13
2788-2793	A721	Set of 6	4.00 4.00

No. 1400 Surcharged in Metallic Red

Method and Perf. As Before

2014, May 16			
2794	A308	2000t on 4t #1400	20.00 20.00

Mongolian postage stamps, 90th anniv.

Threatened Species From Red Book of Mongolia A722

Designs: 200t, Lynx pardinus. 300t, Podoces hendersoni. 400t, Phasianus colchicus. 500t, Vormela peregusna.

2014, May 16		Litho.	Perf. 12
2795-2798	A722	Set of 4	4.00 4.00
2798a		Souvenir sheet of 4, #2795-2798	4.00 4.00

Souvenir Sheet

Bank of Mongolia, 90th Anniv. — A723

No. 2799: a, Mongolian man. b, Bank of Mongolia emblem.

2014, May 30		Litho.	Perf. 13¼x13
2799	A723	2000t Sheet of 2, #a-b	10.00 10.00

A724 A725
A726 A727
A728 A729
A730

MONGOLIA

Items at Bogd Khan Palace Museum — A731

Design: 2000t, Bogd Khan (1869-1924), 8th Jebtsundamba, Khagan of Mongolia.

2014, June 13   Litho.   Perf. 13x13¼

2800	A724	1000t multi	2.00	2.00
2801	A725	1000t multi	2.00	2.00
2802	A726	1000t multi	2.00	2.00
2803	A727	1000t multi	2.00	2.00
2804	A728	1000t multi	2.00	2.00
2805	A729	1000t multi	2.00	2.00
2806	A730	1000t multi	2.00	2.00
2807	A731	1000t multi	2.00	2.00
	Nos. 2800-2807 (8)		16.00	16.00

Souvenir Sheet

2808	A731	2000t multi	4.00	4.00

No. 2808 contains one 40x60mm stamp.

A732

Tarbosaurus bataar — A733

Designs: No. 2809, 1000t, Tarbosaurus bataar. No. 2810, 1000t, Tarbosaurus bataar skeleton.
No. 2811: a, 200t, Tarbosaurus bataar, diff. b, 400t, Tarbosaurus bataar skull. c, 500t, Tarbosaurus bataar skeleton, diff. d, 800t, Tarbosaurus bataar, map of Mongolia highlighted on globe.

2014, July 24   Litho.   Perf. 13x13¼

2809-2810	A732	Set of 2	4.00	4.00

Miniature Sheet
Perf. 12

2811	A733	Sheet of 4, #a-d	4.00	4.00

Souvenir Sheets

Visits to Mongolia by World Leaders A734

No. 2812: a, Mongolia Pres. Tsakhiagiin Elbegdorj. b, Xi Jinping, President of People's Republic of China.
No. 2813a, Russian Pres. Vladimir Putin.

2014   Litho.   Perf. 12¾

2812	A734	800t Sheet of 2, #a-b	4.00	4.00
2813	A734	Sheet of 2, #2812a, 2813a		4.00	4.00
a.		800t multi	2.00	2.00

Issued: No. 2812, 8/21; No. 2813, 9/3.

Genghis Khan (c. 1162-1227) — A735

2014, Aug. 28   Litho.   Perf. 12½

2814	A735	100t brn & multi	.30	.30
2815	A735	1300t red & multi	3.00	3.00

Battles of Khalkhiin Gol, 75th Anniv. A736

2014, Aug. 28   Litho.   Perf. 13¼

2816	A736	750t multi	2.50	2.50

See Russia No. 7562.

Souvenir Sheet

Mongolian Postage Stamps, 90th Anniv. — A737

No. 2817: a, Mongolian flag, Mongolia #7. b, Great White Banner, Mongolia #1-6.

Litho., Sheet Margin Litho. With Foil Application

2014, Oct. 7   Perf. 13¼x13

2817	A737	1000t Sheet of 2, #a-b		5.00	5.00

Souvenir Sheet

Ulan Bator, 375th Anniv. A738

2014, Oct. 27   Litho.   Perf. 13¼

2818	A738	1000t multi	3.25	3.25

New Year 2015 (Year of the Ram) — A739

No. 2819 — Ram with head at: a, Right. b, Left.

2014, Dec. 28   Litho.   Perf. 13x12½

2819		Horiz. pair + central label		3.00	3.00
a.-b.	A739	650t Either single	1.50	1.50

Miniature Sheet

Snow Leopards A740

No. 2820: a, 1000t, Two leopards, green panel. b, 1000t, Two leopards, blue panel. c, 1300t, One leopard, purple panel. d, 1300t, Three leopards, magenta panel.

2015, Jan. 21   Litho.   Perf. 12¾x13

2820	A740	Sheet of 4, #a-d	10.00	10.00

Souvenir Sheet

3,000,000th Citizen of Mongolia — A741

No. 2821: a, Close-up of horseman on globe sculpture. b, Entire sculpture.

2015, Jan. 28   Litho.   Perf. 13¼x13

2821	A741	1000t Sheet of 2, #a-b		4.50	4.50

Water Conservation — A742

2015, Mar. 20   Litho.   Perf. 13¼x13

2822	A742	1300t multi	3.00	3.00

Freedom Online Coalition Emblem — A743

2015, Apr. 29   Litho.   Perf. 13¼x13

2823	A743	1300t multi	3.00	3.00

End of World War II, 70th Anniv. — A744

2015, May 9   Litho.   Perf. 11½

2824	A744	800t multi	1.75	1.75

No. 626 Surcharged in Black and Gold

Methods and Perfs. As Before
2015, July 19

2825	A151	900t on 40m #626	3.00	3.00

Transportation Department, 90th anniv.

Dogs and Yaks — A745

Designs: 300t, Tibetan mastiff and yak. 500t, Two Tibetan mastiffs. 800t, Mongolian bankhar and yak. 1000t, Mongolian bankhar and taiga.

2015, Aug. 3   Litho.   Perf. 12¾

2826-2829	A745	Set of 4	5.50	5.50

Kublai Khan (1215-94) — A746

Designs: 300t, Hand cannons. 400t, Banknote. 500t, Gereege. 800t, Golden goblet. 2000t, Portrait of Kublai Khan.

2015, Sept. 16   Litho.   Perf. 13¼x13

2830-2833	A746	Set of 4	4.00	4.00

Souvenir Sheet
Perf. 13x13¼

2834	A746	2000t multi	4.00	4.00

No. 2834 contains one 38x50mm stamp.

Horses A747

No. 2835: a, 800t, Gray horse, brown horse with white mane. b, 800t, Light brown horse galloping, black and white horse. c, 800t, Dappled gray horse, brown horse with saddle. d, 1000t, Dark gray horse galloping, dark brown horse. e, 1000t, Brown horse with blue ribbon. f, 1000t, Horse and foal.

2015, Dec. 4   Litho.   Perf. 12

2835	A747	Block of 6, #a-f	11.00	11.00

Dashichoiling Monastery A748

Designs: 100t, Traditional ger temples. 500t, Khuree Maidar procession. 800t, Khuree Tsam ritual, two people in costume. 1000t, Khuree Tsam ritual, 5 people in costume.
No. 2840, vert. a, Drawing of Maidar. b, Maidar sculpture.

2015, Dec. 14   Litho.   Perf. 12½

2836-2839	A748	Set of 4	5.00	5.00

Souvenir Sheet
Perf. 13x13¾

2840	A748	1300t Sheet of 2, #a-b		5.50	5.50

No. 2840 contains two 40x60mm stamps.

United Nations, 70th Anniv. — A749

2015, Dec. 20   Litho.   Perf. 13¼

2841	A749	500t multi	1.10	1.10

Paintings A750

Paintings by unknown artists: No. 2842, 1000t, Dating. No. 2843, 1000t, Goatherd. No. 2844, 1000t, Migration. No. 2845, 1000t, Clatter. No. 2846, 1000t, Girls, vert. No. 2847, 1000t, Gorge, vert.

2015, Dec. 25   Litho.   Perf. 12¾

2842-2847	A750	Set of 6	12.50	12.50

New Year 2016 (Year of the Monkey) — A751

No. 2848 — Three monkeys with "Year of the Monkey" inscription at: a, Left. b, Right.

2015, Dec. 28   Litho.   Perf. 13x12½

2848		Horiz. pair + central label		2.75	2.75
a.-b.	A751	650t Either single	1.25	1.25

Souvenir Sheet

Traditional Mongolian Life — A752

No. 2849: a, 1000t, Man and woman in traditional costumes, denomination at LL (30x40mm). b, 1000t, Man and woman in traditional costumes, denomination at LR

MONGOLIA

(30x40mm). c, 2000t, Yurts and horses (60x40mm).

2016, Mar. 20	Litho.	Perf. 13¼x13		
2849	A752	Sheet of 3, #a-c	6.50	6.50

Mongol Information Technology, Post and Telecommunications System, 95th Anniv. — A753

2016, Mar. 30	Litho.	Perf. 13x13¼		
2850	A753	1300t multi	2.75	2.75

Souvenir Sheet

11th Asia-Europe Meeting, Ulan Bator — A754

No. 2851: a, 1300t, Emblem. b, 1500t, Statue of Genghis Khan.

2016, Apr. 15	Litho.	Perf. 12		
2851	A754	Sheet of 2, #a-b	4.00	4.00

Folklore — A755

Designs: No. 2852, 900t, Woman, elephant, bulls, goats, camels and horses. No. 2853, 900t, Bearded man, birds, deer. No. 2854, 1200t, Camel, deer, swans, man holding tiger. No. 2855, 1200t, Tree, bird, rabbit, monkey, elephant.

2016, July 1	Litho.	Perf. 12¾		
2852-2855	A755	Set of 4	8.50	8.50

Privatization, 25th Anniv. — A755a

2016, July 5	Litho.	Perf. 12		
2855A	A755a	800t multi	1.75	1.75

Anandyn Amar (1886-1941), Prime Minister — A756

2016, July 8	Litho.	Perf. 12		
2856	A756	500t multi	1.10	1.10

People's Revolution, 95th Anniv. — A757

2016, July 10	Litho.	Perf. 13x13¼		
2857	A757	400t multi	.90	.90

2016 Summer Olympics, Rio de Janeiro — A758

2016, July 28	Litho.	Perf. 13¼x13		
2858	A758	1000t multi	2.50	2.50

Souvenir Sheet

Genghis Khan (c. 1162-1227) — A759

2016, Oct. 23	Litho.	Perf. 12		
2859	A759	2000t multi	5.00	5.00

Mongol Empire, 810th Anniv.

Mammals A760

Designs: 600t, Ram. 700t, Goat. 800t, Bull. 900t, Stallion. 1000t, Camel.

2016, Oct. 30	Litho.	Perf. 12		
2860-2864	A760	Set of 5	6.50	6.50

Souvenir Sheet

Harps A761

No. 2865: a, 1000t, Ahu harp. b, 1500t, Altai bow harp.

2016, Nov. 11	Litho.	Perf. 12		
2865	A761	Sheet of 2, #a-b	4.00	4.00

Transportation With Animals — A762

Designs: 100t, Reindeer-drawn sled. 200t, Horse-drawn cart. 300t, Ox-drawn cart. 400t, Camel-drawn cart.

2016, Dec. 11	Litho.	Perf. 13x13¼		
2866-2869	A762	Set of 4	2.50	2.50

Yumjaagiin Tsedenbal (1916-91), Prime Minister — A763

Litho., Sheet Margin Litho. With Foil Application

2016, Dec. 21		Perf. 13¼		
2870	A763	2000t multi	4.00	4.00

New Year 2017 (Year of the Rooster) — A764

No. 2871 — Rooster and chicks with chicks at: a, Right. b, Left.

2017, Jan. 8	Litho.	Perf. 13x12½		
2871		Horiz. pair + central label	2.50	2.50
a.-b.	A764	650t Either single	1.25	1.25

Miniature Sheet

Nine Traditional Treasures — A765

No. 2872: a, Gold. b, Coral. c, Turquoise. d, Silver. e, Pearl. f, Steel. g, Nacre. h, Lazurite. i, Copper.

2017, Apr. 30	Litho.	Perf. 12		
2872	A765	400t Sheet of 9, #a-i	7.50	7.50

Miniature Sheet

Locomotives — A766

No. 2873: a, TE2. b, TEM3. c, 2TE116YM. d, M62YM. e, 2 ZAGAL. f, DASH 7.

2017, June 16	Litho.	Perf. 13x13¼		
2873	A766	800t Sheet of 6, #a-f	9.00	9.00

Owls — A767

Designs: 300t, Bubo bubo. 400t, Strix nebulosa, horiz. 500t, Surnia ulula, horiz. 800t, Bubo scandiaca.

Perf. 13¼x13, 13x13¼

2017, July 6			Litho.	
2874-2877	A767	Set of 4	4.00	4.00
2877a		Souvenir sheet of 4, #2874-2877	4.00	4.00

Saddles — A768

No. 2878 — Saddle from: a, 8th cent. b, 13th cent. c, 19th cent. d, 20th cent.

2017, Aug. 30	Litho.	Perf. 14¼		
2878		Horiz. strip of 4	9.00	9.00
a.-d.	A768	1300t Any single	2.25	2.25

Television Broadcasting in Mongolia, 50th Anniv. — A769

2017, Sept. 8	Litho.	Perf. 13x13¼		
2879	A769	400t multi	.75	.75

Training of Information and Communication Technology Engineers, 50th Anniv. — A770

2017, Oct. 6	Litho.	Perf. 13x13¼		
2880	A770	800t multi	1.25	1.25

No. 2880 was printed in sheets of 10 + central label.

Souvenir Sheet

Scabiosa Comosa A771

No. 2881 — Scabiosa comosa and: a, Flag of Mongolia. b, Mongolian woman in traditional costume, butterfly.

2017, Nov., 15	Litho.	Perf. 13¼		
2881	A771	1500t Sheet of 2, #a-b	5.00	5.00

Souvenir Sheet

Coins of the Silk Road A772

2017, Dec. 3	Litho.	Perf. 13¼		
2882	A772	1300t multi	2.25	2.25

New Year 2018 — A773

2017, Dec. 8	Litho.	Perf. 13¼		
2883	A773	100t multi	.50	.50

New Year 2018 (Year of the Dog) — A774

No. 2884 — Three dogs with "Year of the Dog" inscription at: a, UL. b, UR.

2018, Jan. 5	Litho.	Perf. 13¼		
2884		Horiz. pair + central label	2.25	2.25
a.-b.	A774	650t Either single	1.10	1.10

Souvenir Sheet

Gangaamaa Badamgarav, First Mongolian Climber to Ascend the Seven Summits — A775

2018, Mar. 19	Litho.	Perf. 14x13¾		
2885	A775	1500t multi	2.50	2.50

MONGOLIA

A776

A777

A778

Mongolian Cuisine — A779

2018, Apr. 22   Litho.   Perf. 13x13¼
2886 A776 1300t multi   2.25 2.25
2887 A777 1300t multi   2.25 2.25
2888 A778 1300t multi   2.25 2.25
2889 A779 1300t multi   2.25 2.25
Nos. 2886-2889 (4)   9.00 9.00

Tsendiin Damdinsuren (1908-86), Writer — A780

2018, May 4   Litho.   Perf. 13¼x13
2890 A780 800t multi   1.40 1.40

Mongolian Pride, by Ts. Bolortsetseg A781

National Tradition and Race Horses, by E. Yeruult A782

2018, June 1   Litho.   Perf. 13¼
2891 A781 800t multi   1.40 1.40
2892 A782 800t multi   1.40 1.40

Mongolian Scripts — A783

Various Mongolian scripts with background color of: 200t, Brown. 300t, Blue. 400t, Red. 1300t, Green.

2018, June 21   Litho.   Perf. 13¼x13
2893-2896 A783 Set of 4   4.00 4.00

Landscapes A784

Designs: No. 2897, 1300t, Urantogoo Mountain, Marmota sibirica, Trollius asiaticus. No. 2898, 1300t, Otgontenger Mountain, Canis lupus, Saussurea involucrata. No. 2899, 1300t, Bayanzag-Flaming Cliffs, Podoces hendersoni, Cynomorium songaricum. No. 2900, 1300t, Khar Zurkhnii Khukh Lake, Alces alces, Rhododendron aureum. No. 2901, 1300t, Rock of Ergeliin Zoo Natural Reserve,

Iris bungei maxim, Ovis ammon. No. 2902, 1300t, Terkhiin Tsagaan Lake, leontopodium ochroleucum, Sus scrofa. No. 2903, 1300t, Burenkhaan Mountain, Adonis mongolica simonovicz, Rangifer tarandus.

2018, July 27   Litho.   Perf. 13¼x13½
2897-2903 A784 Set of 7   15.00 15.00
See Nos. 2921-2927, 2945-2951.

Ethnic People and Their Costumes — A785

No. 2904: a, Khalkh man and woman. b, Buryat man and woman. c, Uzemchin man and woman. d, Kalmyk man and woman.

2018, Oct. 15   Litho.   Perf. 13½x13¼
2904   Vert. strip of 4   1.60 1.60
a.-d. A785 500t Any single   .40   .40

New Year 2019 (Year of the Pig) — A786

No. 2905 — Three pigs and piglet with "Year of the Pig" at: a, UL. b, UR.

2019, Jan. 4   Litho.   Perf. 13¼x13½
2905   Horiz. pair + central label   1.00 1.00
a.-b. A786 650t Either single   .50   .50

Souvenir Sheet

Miner and Dump Truck A787

Litho. & Embossed With Foil Application
2019, Feb. 20   Perf. 13½
2906 A787 20,000t gold   15.50 15.50
Erdenet, 40th anniv.

Souvenir Sheet

Baldugiin Sharav (1869-1939), Painter — A788

2019, Mar. 22   Litho.   Perf. 14
2907 A788 2000t multi   1.60 1.60
Mongolian postage stamps, 95th anniv.

Puzzles — A789

Various puzzles with denomination in: No. 2908, 800t, Olive gray. No. 2909, 800t, Red orange.

2019, Apr. 26   Litho.   Perf. 13½x13
2908-2909 A789 Set of 2   1.25 1.25

Nos. 1904, 1907 and 1908 Surcharged in Black, Gold and Multicolored

Methods and Perfs. As Before
2019, June 30
2910 A421 100t on 20m #1904   .25 .25
2911 A421 100t on 60m #1908   .25 .25
2912 A421 1300t on 50m #1907   1.00 1.00
Nos. 2910-2912 (3)   1.50 1.50
Mongolian postage stamps, 95th anniv.

Items Made in Mongolia — A790

Various items made in Mongolia with panel at left in: No. 2913, 1300t, Dark blue. No. 2914, 1300t, Dark red.

2019, July 8   Litho.   Perf. 13x13¼
2913-2914 A790 Set of 2   2.00 2.00

Souvenir Sheet

Neil Armstrong (1931-2012), First Man on the Moon — A791

2019, Aug. 30   Litho.   Perf. 13¾
2915 A791 1500t multi   1.25 1.25
Space flight of Apollo 11, 50th anniv.

Battles of Khalkhin Gol, 80th Anniv. — A792

2019, Sept. 2   Litho.   Perf. 13x13½
2916 A792 400t multi   .30 .30

A 2000t souvenir sheet commemorating the Saints and Reincarnations of the Great Mongols was produced in limited quantities and issued on Sept. 9, 2019.

Express Mail Service, 20th Anniv. — A793

2019, Sept. 10   Litho.   Perf. 13½
2917 A793 1300t multi   1.00 1.00

Mohandas K. Gandhi (1869-1948), Indian Nationalist Leader — A794

2019, Oct. 2   Litho.   Perf. 13½x13
2918 A794 800t multi   .60 .60

Diplomatic Relations Between Mongolia and People's Republic of China, 70th Anniv. — A795

No. 2919 — Boy and girl in traditional costumes of: a, Mongolia. b, People's Republic of China.

2019, Oct. 16   Litho.   Perf. 13½
2919 A795 1000t Horiz. pair, #a-b, + central label   1.50 1.50

Souvenir Sheet

Ulan Bator, 380th Anniv. A796

No. 2920 — Photographs of Ulan Bator from: a, 1874. b, 1929. c, 1984.

2019, Oct. 21   Litho.   Perf. 13½
2920 A796 1000t Sheet of 3, #a-c   2.25 2.25

Landscapes Type of 2018

Designs: No. 2921, 1300t, Altan Ovoo Mountain, Cygnus cygnus, Cymbaria dahurica. No. 2922, 1300t, Ikh Bogd Mountain, Haloxylon ammodendron, Ursus arctos gobiensis. No. 2923, 1300t, Scarp of Tsagaan Suvarga, Allium mongolicum, Otocolobus manul. No. 2924, 1300t, Zorgol Khairkhan Mountain, Thymus gobicus, Equus przewalskii. No. 2925, 1300t, Saikhnii Khutul, Hucho taimen, Pinus sylvestris. No. 2926, 1300t, Choiriin Bogd Mountain, Falco cherrug, Amygdalus pedunculatus. No. 2927, 1300t, Alag Khairkhan Mountain, Arnebia guttata, Camelus ferus.

Perf. 13¼x13½
2019, Nov. 18   Litho.
2921-2927 A784 Set of 7   6.75 6.75

UNESCO Intangible Heritage — A797

Designs: 100t, Mongolian calligraphy. 200t, Falconry. 300t, Mongolian knuckle-bone shooting. 400t, Mongol Biyelgee traditional folk dance. 700t, Traditional music of the Tsuur. No. 2933, 2000t, Traditional music of the Morin Khuur, horiz. No. 2934, 2000t, Urtiin Duu, traditional folk song, horiz.

2019, Nov. 22   Litho.   Perf. 13
2928-2932 A797 Set of 5   1.25 1.25

Souvenir Sheets
Perf. 13½x14
2933-2934 A797 Set of 2   3.00 3.00
Nos. 2933-2934 each contain one 45x33mm stamp.

607

MONGOLIA

Gadinbal Chagdarjav (1869-1915) — A798

2019, Nov. 29 Litho. Perf. 13¼
2935 A798 800t multi .60 .60

Souvenir Sheet

Bogd Khan (1869-1924), Buddhist Spiritual Leader — A799

2019, Dec. 17 Litho. Perf. 13x13½
2936 A799 4000t multi 3.00 3.00
No. 2936 is impregnated with a floral scent.

New Year 2020 (Year of the Rat) — A800

No. 2905 — Two rats eating with "Year of the Rat" at: a, UL. b, UR.

2020, Jan. 6 Litho. Perf. 13x13¼
2937 Horiz. pair + central label 1.00 1.00
a.-b. A800 650t Either single .50 .50

Nos. 944-945 Surcharged in Gold or Silver and Black

Methods and Perfs As Before
2020, May 1
2938 A213 200t on 10m #944 (G) .25 .25
2939 A213 1300t on 20m #945 (S) .95 .95
Issuance of the Penny Black, 180th anniv.

Architecture A801

Designs: 300t, Wedding Palace. 400t, Mongolian State Academic Theater of Opera and Ballet. 500t, Chojin Lama Temple Museum, Perfect Benefit and Bliss Temple. 800t, Asia-Europe Summit Meeting Ger (yurt).

2020, June 4 Litho. Perf. 13x13¼
2940-2943 A801 Set of 4 1.40 1.40
2943a Souvenir sheet of 4, #2940-2943 1.40 1.40

End of World War II, 75th Anniv. — A802

2020, June 19 Litho. Perf. 13x13¼
2944 A802 800t multi .60 .60

Landscapes Type of 2018
Designs: No. 2945, 1300t, Khuisiin Naiman Lake, Allactaga sibirica, Campanula turczaninovii. No. 2946, 1300t, Khetsuu Khad, Uncia uncia, Oxygraphis glacialis. No. 2947, 1300t, Tsambagarav Mountain, Nymphaea candida, pelecanus crispus. No. 2948, 1300t, Potanin Glacier, Saussurea glacialis, Aquila chrysaetos. No. 2949, 1300t, Darkhan Khairkhan Mountain, Cervus elaphus, Cypripedium calceolus. No. 2950, 1300t, Zurkhen Island, Lilium pensylvanicum, Procapra gutturosa. No. 2951, 1300t, Bayan-Undur Mountain, Sciurus vulgaris, Lilium martagon.

2020, July 8 Litho. Perf. 13¼x13½
2945-2951 A784 Set of 7 6.50 6.50

Olympic and Paralympic Medalists of Mongolia — A803

No. 2952: a, Damdinsharav Chimedbazar, 1968 wrestling bronze medalist. b, Sereeter Danzandarjaa, 1968 wrestling bronze medalist. c, Artag Tumur, 1968 wrestling bronze medalist. d, Munkhbat Jigjid, 1968 wrestling silver medalist. e, Bayanmunkh Khorloo, 1972 wrestling silver medalist. f, Oidov Zeveg, 1976 wrestling silver medalist. g, Davaadalai Ravdan, 1980 judo bronze medalist. h, Damdin Tsend, 1980 judo silver medalist. i, Oyunbold Dugarsuren, 1980 wrestling bronze medalist. j, Davaajav Jamts, 1980 wrestling silver medalist. k, Enkhbat Nergui, 1988 boxing bronze medalist. l, Munkhbayar Dorjsuren, 1992 shooting bronze medalist. m, Bayarsaikhan Namjil, 1992 boxing bronze medalist. n, Narmandakh Dorjpalam, 1996 judo bronze medalist.

No. 2953: a, Tsagaanbaatar Khashbaatar, 2004 judo bronze medalist. b, Gundegmaa Otryad, 2008 shooting silver medalist. c, Tuvshinbayar Naidan, 2008 judo gold medalist and 2012 judo silver medalist. d, Serdamba Purevdorj, 2008 boxing silver medalist. e, Badar-Uugan Enkhbat, 2008 boxing gold medalist. f, Baatarjav Dambadondog, 2008 archery gold medalist. g, Nyam-Ochir Sainjargal, 2012 judo bronze medalist. h, Battsetseg Soronzonbold, 2012 wrestling bronze medalist. i, Munkh-Erdene Uranchimeg, 2012 boxing bronze medalist. j, Tugstsogt Nyambayar, 2012 boxing silver medalist. k, Sumiya Dorjsuren, 2016 judo silver medalist. l, Otgondalai Dorjnyambuu, 2016 boxing bronze medalist. m, Uugankhuu Bolormaa, 2016 judo bronze medalist. n, Sodnompiljee Enkhbayar, 2016 powerlifting bronze medalist.

2020, Nov. 11 Litho. Perf. 13¾
2952 Sheet of 14 10.00 10.00
a.-n. A803 1000t Any single .70 .70
2953 Sheet of 14 10.00 10.00
a.-n. A803 1000t Any single .70 .70
No. 2953b has incorrect year and host city.

A804
A805
A806
A807
A808
A809

Writing of *The Secret History of the Mongols*, 780th Anniv. A810

Designs: No. 2960, 2000t, Genghis Khan (1162-1227), founder and emperor of Mongol Empire. No. 2961, 2000t, Ogedei Khan (1186-1241), second emperor of Mongol Empire.

2020, Nov. 16 Litho. Perf. 13¼
2954 A804 1500t multi 1.10 1.10
2955 A805 1500t multi 1.10 1.10
2956 A806 1500t multi 1.10 1.10
2957 A807 1500t multi 1.10 1.10
2958 A808 1500t multi 1.10 1.10
2959 A809 1500t multi 1.10 1.10
Nos. 2954-2959 (6) 6.60 6.60

Souvenir Sheets
Perf. 13½
2960 A810 2000t multi 1.40 1.40
2961 A810 2000t multi 1.40 1.40

Mongolian Monument to Falconry — A811

2020, Nov. 20 Litho. Perf. 13½
2962 A811 1000t multi .70 .70
Joint issue between Mongolia and Slovakia. See Slovakia No. 857.

Souvenir Sheet

Diplomatic Relations Between Mongolia and Singapore, 50th Anniv. — A812

No. 2963: a, Endless knot, Mongolia. b, Bird and flowers, Singapore.

2020, Dec. 1 Litho. Perf. 13¼x13
2963 A812 1300t Sheet of 2, #a-b 1.90 1.90
See Singapore Nos. 2056-2057.

Souvenir Sheet

Ludwig van Beethoven (1770-1827), Composer — A813

No. 2964 — Various depictions of Beethoven: a, 1000t. b, 1300t.

2020, Dec. 12 Litho. Perf. 13¼x13
2964 A813 Sheet of 2, #a-b 1.75 1.75

Diplomatic Relations Between Mongolia and India, 65th Anniv. — A814

2020, Dec. 24 Litho. Perf. 13¼x13
2965 A814 1000t multi .70 .70

Souvenir Sheet

Khurelsukh Ukhnaa, Prime Minister of Mongolia — A815

2020, Dec. 29 Litho. Perf. 13½
2966 A815 2000t multi 1.40 1.40

New Year 2021 (Year of the Ox) — A816

No. 2967 — Ox facing: a, Left. b, Right.

2021, Jan. 3 Litho. Perf. 13¼x13½
2967 Horiz. pair + central label .90 .90
a.-b. A816 650t Either single .45 .45

Souvenir Sheet

Soyuz 39 Cosmonauts Vladimir Dzhanibekov and Jügderdemidiin Gürragchaa, flags of Soviet Union and Mongolia — A817

2021, Apr. 12 Litho. Perf. 13¾x14
2968 A817 2000t multi 1.40 1.40
Flight of Soyuz 39, 40th anniv.

Souvenir Sheet

State Great Khural (Mongolian Parliament), 30th Anniv. — A818

No. 2969: a, Parliamentary Chairman at rostrum (24x30mm). b, Parliament in session (48x30mm).

2021, July 8 Litho. Perf. 13½x13¼
2969 A818 1500t Sheet of 2, #a-b 2.10 2.10

A819
A820

MONGOLIA

Mongolian Tax Administration, 30th Anniv. — A821

2021, Aug. 2   Litho.   **Perf. 13¼**
2970   Horiz. strip of 3   2.10   2.10
  a.   A819 1000t multi   .70   .70
  b.   A820 1000t multi   .70   .70
  c.   A821 1000t multi   .70   .70

Souvenir Sheet

Hunnu Empire, 2230th Anniv. A822

No. 2971 — Symbol of: a, Sun (40x40mm). b, Dragons (60x40mm). c, Moon (40x40mm).

2021, Sept. 2   Litho.   **Perf. 14**
2971   A822 1000t Sheet of 3, #a-c   2.10   2.10

Souvenir Sheet

People's Revolution, Cent. — A823

2021, Sept. 2   Litho.   **Perf. 13¾x14**
2972   A823 2000t multi   1.40   1.40

Souvenir Sheet

Communications and Information Technology Sector, Cent. — A824

Litho. & Embossed With Foil Application

2021, Sept. 17   **Perf. 13¾**
2973   A824 15,000t multi   10.50   10.50

Equus Przewalskii A825

2021, Oct. 5   Litho.   **Perf. 13¾**
2974   A825 1000t multi   .70   .70

Souvenir Sheet

Mongolian Youth Organization, Cent. — A826

2021, Oct. 15   Litho.   **Perf. 13¾x14**
2975   A826 2000t multi   1.40   1.40

Miniature Sheet

Mongolian Admission to the United Nations, 60th Anniv. — A827

No. 2976: a, Khorloogiin Choibalsan (1895-1952), Mongolian leader who signed first application to join the United Nations. b, Gold gerege, United Nations headquarters, New York. c, 1961 ceremony for Mongolia's admittance to the United Nations. d, Mongolian initiatives in the United Nations. e, Emblems of United Nations organizations and 60th anniversary emblem. f, United Nations Sustainable Development Goals.

2021, Oct. 26   Litho.   **Perf. 13¼**
2976   A827 1000t Sheet of 6, #a-f   4.25   4.25

Souvenir Sheet

Mongolian Police, Cent. — A828

2021, Oct. 29   Litho.   **Perf. 13¾x14**
2977   A828 2000t multi   1.40   1.40

Balalaika and Morin Khuur A829

2021, Nov. 5   Litho.   **Perf. 13½x13¼**
2978   A829 2000t multi   1.40   1.40
  a.   Souvenir sheet of 1   1.40   1.40

Diplomatic relations between Mongolia and Russia, cent. See Russia No. 8317.

Souvenir Sheet

Central Military Hospital, Cent. A830

2021, Nov. 11   Litho.   **Perf. 13¾x14**
2979   A830 2000t multi   1.40   1.40

Souvenir Sheet

Modern Mongolian Armed Forces, Cent. — A831

2021, Nov. 15   Litho.   **Perf. 13¾x14**
2980   A831 2000t multi   1.40   1.40

Souvenir Sheet

Memory of the World Registry Item, Kanjur Written With Seven Precious Stones A832

2021, Nov. 18   Litho.   **Perf. 13¾x14**
2981   A832 2000t multi   1.40   1.40

Miniature Sheet

Mongolian Popular Music — A833

No. 2982: a, Trumpet, saxophone, musical score. b, Emblem of Haranga rock band, musical score. c, Guitars, musical score. d, Bayan Mongol Variety Group. e, Soyol Erdene vocal and instrumental group. f, Drum set, musical score. g, Mongolian zither, microphone, musical score. h, Piano, electric organ, musical score.

2021, Nov. 25   Litho.   **Perf. 13¼**
2982   A833 400t Sheet of 8, #a-h, + central label   2.25   2.25

Souvenir Sheet

Women in Store A834

2021, Dec. 16   Litho.   **Perf. 13¾x14**
2983   A834 2000t multi   1.40   1.40

Mongolian trade and service sector, cent.

Peace Corps Presence in Mongolia, 30th Anniv. — A835

2021, Dec. 23   Litho.   **Perf. 13¾x14**
2984   A835 1000t multi   .70   .70

Souvenir Sheet

Scientists — A836

2021, Dec. 24   Litho.   **Perf. 13¾x14**
2985   A836 2000t multi   1.40   1.40

Modern science in Mongolia, cent.

No. 693 Surcharged in Red and Black

Methods and Perfs. As Before

2021, Dec. 30
2986   A164 1500t on 10m #693   1.10   1.10

Souvenir Sheet

Modern Education in Mongolia, Cent. — A837

2021, Dec. 30   Litho.   **Perf. 13¾x14**
2987   A837 2000t multi   1.40   1.40

New Year 2022 (Year of the Tiger) — A838

No. 2988 — Tigers with "Year of the Tiger" at: a, UL. b, UR.

2022, Jan. 3   Litho.   **Perf. 13½x13¾**
2988   Horiz. pair + central label   .90   .90
  a.-b.   A838 650t Either single   .45   .45

Souvenir Sheet

Mongolian Constitution, 30th Anniv. — A839

2022, Jan. 7   Litho.   **Perf. 13¾x13½**
2989   A839 2000t multi   1.40   1.40

Souvenir Sheet

Galdan Boshugtu Khan (1644-97), Khan of the Dzungar Khanate — A840

2022, Feb. 22   Litho.   **Perf. 14¼**
2990   A840 2000t multi   1.40   1.40

MONGOLIA

Miniature Sheet

Gombojav Gombosuren (1918-2004), Actor — A841

No. 2991 — Gombosuren in: a, 500t, Othello, 1955 (30x40mm). b, 500t, On the Barley Field, 1961 (30x40mm). c, 500t, King Lear, 1964 (30x40mm). d, 1000t, Oedipus the King, 1972 (60x40mm).

2022, Mar. 27   Litho.   Perf. 14x14¼
2991 A841   Sheet of 4, #a-d   1.75 1.75

Souvenir Sheet

Diplomatic Relations Between Mongolia and Japan, 50th Anniv. — A842

No. 2992: a, Horses and riders. b, Cranes.

2022, May 19   Litho.   Perf. 13½
2992 A842   1500t Sheet of 2, #a-b   1.90 1.90

Dinosaurs — A843

Fossils of: No. 2993, 500t, Citipati on nest. No. 2994, 500t, Deinocheirus mirificus. No. 2995, 1000t, Citipati osmolskae embryo in egg, horiz. No. 2996, 1000t, Gobihadros mongoliensis, horiz. 2000t, Protoceratops andrewsi and Velociraptor mongoliensis fighting, horiz.

Perf. 14x13¾, 13¾x14
2022, May 23   Litho.
2993-2996 A843   Set of 4   1.90 1.90

Souvenir Sheet
2997 A843   2000t multi   1.30 1.30

Souvenir Sheet

Bakula Rinpoche (1918-2003), Religious Leader and Indian Ambassador to Mongolia — A844

2022, June 15   Litho.   Perf. 13¼x13
2998 A844   2000t multi   1.30 1.30

Souvenir Sheet

Mongolian Intelligence Services, Cent. — A845

2022, June 23   Litho.   Perf. 13¾x14
2999 A845   2000t multi   1.30 1.30

Miniature Sheet

Carved Statues by Legshid Chuvaamed (1934-2011) — A846

No. 3000: a, 500t, Lion (30x40mm). b, 500t, Maitreya (30x40mm). c, 500t, Flower (30x40mm). d, 1000t, Camel Bull in Rut (60x40mm).

2022, June 29   Litho.   Perf. 14x14¼
3000 A846   Sheet of 4, #a-d   1.60 1.60

Souvenir Sheet

Mongolian Audit Office, Cent. — A847

2022, Aug. 25   Litho.   Perf. 13¾x14
3001 A847   2000t multi   1.25 1.25

A848

A849

A850

A851

A852

A853

Mongolian Cartoons — A854

2022, Sept. 12   Litho.   Perf. 13¾x14
3002 A848   1000t multi   .60   .60
3003 A849   1000t multi   .60   .60
3004 A850   1000t multi   .60   .60
3005 A851   1000t multi   .60   .60
3006 A852   1000t multi   .60   .60
3007 A853   1000t multi   .60   .60
Nos. 3002-3007 (6)   3.60 3.60

Souvenir Sheet
3008 A854   2000t multi   1.25 1.25

Souvenir Sheet

Diplomatic Relations Between Mongolia and Australia, 50th Anniv. — A855

No. 3009: a, Saiga borealis. b, Macropus rufus.

2022, Sept. 23   Litho.   Perf. 13½
3009 A855   1500t Sheet of 2, #a-b   1.90 1.90

Friendship A856

The Five Jewels A857

Sri Devi A858

Green Tara A859

2022, Sept. 24   Litho.   Perf. 14x13¾
3010 A856   1000t multi   .60   .60
3011 A857   1000t multi   .60   .60

Souvenir Sheets
3012 A858   2000t multi   1.25 1.25
3013 A859   2000t multi   1.25 1.25

Silk appliqué.

Camels — A860

Camel: No. 3014, 500t, With calf. No. 3015, 500t, Calf. No. 3016, 1000t, Head, horiz. No. 3017, 1000t, Bull with two humps, horiz. 2000t, Gelded camel, horiz.

Perf. 14x13¾, 13¾x14
2022, Oct. 31   Litho.
3014-3017 A860   Set of 4   1.90 1.90

Souvenir Sheet
3018 A860   2000t multi   1.25 1.25

Obverse and Reverse of Gold Coin from Reign of Genghis Khan A861

Front and Back of Golden Gerege A862

Monument Depicting Genghis Khan — A863

Mongolia No. 307 — A864

Nine White Banners A865

Genghis Khan Museum, Ulan Bator A866

MONGOLIA

Genghis Khan (c. 1162-1227) — A867

2022, Dec. 22   Litho.   *Perf. 13½x13*
3019	A861	1000t	multi	.60	.60
3020	A862	1000t	multi	.60	.60
3021	A863	1000t	multi	.60	.60
3022	A864	3000t	multi	1.75	1.75
3023	A865	3000t	multi	1.75	1.75
3024	A866	3000t	multi	1.75	1.75
	Nos. 3019-3024 (6)			7.05	7.05

Souvenir Sheet
| 3025 | A867 | 3000t | multi | | 1.75 | 1.75 |

No. 3025 contains one 38x45mm stamp.

Miniature Sheets

Flora and Fauna From Red Book of Mongolia — A868

No. 3026: a, Paeonia lactiflora and Emberiza aureola. b, Spongiocarpella grubovii and Camelus ferus. c, Acorus calamus and Mesocottus haitej. d, Chesneya mongolica and Cyrtopodion elongatus.

No. 3027: a, Cypripedium macranthos and Alces alces. b, Drosera anglica and Salamandrella keyserlingii. c, Swertia banzragczii and Saxicola insignis. d, Cistanche deserticola and Stylodipus sungorus.

2022, Dec. 28   Litho.   *Perf. 13¾*
| 3026 | A868 | 1000t | Sheet of 4, #a-d | 2.50 | 2.50 |
| 3027 | A868 | 3000t | Sheet of 4, #a-d | 7.00 | 7.00 |

New Year 2023 (Year of the Rabbit) — A869

No. 3028 — Rabbits with "Year of the Rabbit" at: a, UL. b, UR.

2023, Jan. 13   Litho.   *Perf. 13½*
| 3028 | | Horiz. pair + central label | 1.75 | 1.75 |
| a.-b. | A869 | 1500t Either single | .85 | .85 |

Souvenir Sheet

Diplomatic Relations Between Mongolia and the United Kingdom, 60th Anniv. — A870

No. 3029: a, Mongolia No. 1. b, Great Britain No. 1.

2023, Jan. 23   Litho.   *Perf. 13½*
| 3029 | A870 | 3000t Sheet of 2, #a-b | 3.50 | 3.50 |

Souvenir Sheet

Mongolian Ice Festival — A871

No. 3030: a, Ankle shooting on ice. b, Archery on ice.

2023, Feb. 12   Litho.   *Perf. 13x13½*
| 3030 | A871 | 3000t Sheet of 2, #a-b | 3.50 | 3.50 |

Miniature Sheet

Precious Stones A872

No. 3031: a, Garnet. b, Chalcedony. c, Tourmaline. d, Ruby. e, Topaz. d, Quartz.

2023, Mar. 1   Litho.   *Perf. 13½*
| 3031 | A872 | 1000t Sheet of 6, #a-f | 3.50 | 3.50 |

Souvenir Sheet

Astrology A873

Designs: No. 3032, Sun, Moon, Western zodiac symbols. No. 3033, Dragon and Chinese zodiac symbols.

2023, Mar. 10   Litho.   *Perf.*
| 3032 | A873 | 3000t | multi | 1.75 | 1.75 |
| 3033 | A873 | 3000t | multi | 1.75 | 1.75 |

Cultural Relations Between Mongolia and Japan — A874

2023, May 29   Litho.   *Perf. 13½x13*
| 3034 | A874 | 1500t | multi | .90 | .90 |

Souvenir Sheet

The Hu Folk Metal Band A875

2023, May 31   Litho.   *Perf. 13½*
| 3035 | A875 | 3000t | multi | 1.75 | 1.75 |

Dulmaa Shagdar, Writer — A876

2023, June 2   Litho.   *Perf. 13½x13*
| 3036 | A876 | 1000t | multi | .60 | .60 |

Souvenir Sheet

Khentii Province, Cent. A877

2023, June 23   Litho.   *Perf. 13¼*
| 3037 | A877 | 3000t | multi | 1.75 | 1.75 |

Souvenir Sheet

Arkhangai Province, Cent. — A878

2023, July 1   Litho.   *Perf. 13¼*
| 3038 | A878 | 3000t | multi | 1.75 | 1.75 |

Souvenir Sheet

Zavkhan Province, Cent. A879

2023, July 3   Litho.   *Perf. 13¼*
| 3039 | A879 | 3000t | multi | 1.75 | 1.75 |

Souvenir Sheet

Tuv Province, Cent. A880

2023, July 5   Litho.   *Perf. 13¼*
| 3040 | A880 | 3000t | multi | 1.75 | 1.75 |

Miniature Sheet

International Mongolian Scholars and Their Publications — A881

No. 3041: a, Tseveen Jamsran (1881-1942). b, Boris Yakovlevich Vladimirtsov (1884-1931). c, Owen Lattimore (1900-89). d, Walther Heissig (1913-2005). e, Ozawa Shigeo (1926-2017). f, Igor de Rachewiltz (1929-2016).

2023, Aug. 11   Litho.   *Perf. 13½*
| 3041 | A881 | 1000t Sheet of 6, #a-f | 3.50 | 3.50 |

Visit of Pope Francis to Mongolia — A882

2023, Aug. 31   Litho.   *Perf. 14x13¾*
| 3042 | A882 | 3000t | multi | 1.75 | 1.75 |
| a. | | Souvenir sheet of 1 | 1.75 | 1.75 |

Souvenir Sheet

First Secondary School in Ulan Bator, Cent. — A883

2023, Sept. 20   Litho.   *Perf. 13½*
| 3043 | A883 | 3000t | multi | 1.75 | 1.75 |

Space Exploration A884

Designs: No. 3044, 500t, Tiangong space station. No. 3045, 500t, Juno space probe. No. 3046, 1000t, Orion spacecraft. No. 3047, 1000t, James Webb space telescope. 3000t, Zhurong rover.

2023, Oct. 4   Litho.   *Perf. 13¼x13½*
| 3044-3047 | A884 | Set of 4 | 1.75 | 1.75 |

Souvenir Sheet
| 3048 | A884 | 3000t | multi | 1.75 | 1.75 |

Souvenir Sheet

Tsevegjav Purevdorj (1929-2007), Opera Singer — A885

2023, Oct. 14   Litho.   *Perf. 13¼x13*
| 3049 | A885 | 3000t | multi | 1.75 | 1.75 |

MONGOLIA

Mongolian Membership in the Food and Agriculture Organization, 50th Anniv. — A886

2023, Oct. 16	Litho.	Perf. 13¾x14
3050 A886 1000t multi		.60 .60

Souvenir Sheet

Diplomatic Relations Between Mongolia and Canada, 50th Anniv. — A887

No. 3051: a, Mongolian flag. b, Canadian flag.

2023, Nov. 15	Litho.	Perf. 13½
3051 A887 3000t Sheet of 2, #a-b		3.50 3.50

Horses — A888

Designs: No. 3052, 500t, Stallion. No. 3053, 500t, Horse with tied mane. No. 3054, 1000t, Mare with foal, horiz. No. 3055, 1000t, Two foals, horiz. 3000t, Horse with saddle, horiz.

Perf. 14x13¾, 13¾x14

2022, Oct. 31	Litho.	
3052-3055 A888 Set of 4		1.75 1.75

Souvenir Sheet

| 3056 A888 3000t multi | 1.75 1.75 |

Miniature Sheet

Ice Age Animals A889

No. 3057: a, Bison priscus. b, Mammuthus primigenius. c, Struthio anderssoni. d, Coelodonta antiquitatis.

2023, Dec. 21	Litho.	Perf. 13¼
3057 A889 1500t Sheet of 4, #a-d		3.50 3.50

Stone Monument Inscriptions — A890

Designs: No. 3058, 1000t, Sogdian script, Bugat Stone Monument, 585. No. 3059, 1000t, Brahmi script, Khuis Tolgoi, 601. No. 3060, 1000t, Runic script, Nomgon, 692. No. 3061, 1000t, Khitan script, Buleen Ovoo, 926. No. 3062, 1000t, Mongolian script, Karakorum, 1348. No. 3063, 1000t, Soyombo script, Erdene Zuu, 1686.

Perf. 13½x13¼

2023, Dec. 21	Litho.	
3058-3063 A890 Set of 6		3.50 3.50

Miniature Sheets

Mongolian Porcelain — A891

No. 3064: a, Vases decorated in Mongolian style (40x52mm). b, Porcelain vessel for Airag (40x30mm). c, Plates decorated in Mongolian style (40x30mm). d, Mongolian wine vessels (40x52mm).
No. 3065: a, Figurine of Great Khaan (40x52mm). b, Mongolian snuff bottles (40x30mm). c, Bowls decorated in Mongolian style (40x30mm). d, Figurines of first Bogd Gegeen and Green Tara (40x52mm).

2023, Dec. 24	Litho.	Perf. 13x13¼
3064 A891 1000t Sheet of 4, #a-d		2.50 2.50
3065 A891 1500t Sheet of 4, #a-d		3.50 3.50

Souvenir Sheet

Dulduit Dansanravjaa (1803-56), Buddhist Monk — A892

2023, Dec. 28	Litho.	Perf. 13¼
3066 A892 3000t multi		1.75 1.75

SEMI-POSTAL STAMPS

Catalogue values for unused stamps in this section are for Never Hinged items.

Vietnamese Mother and Child — SP1

1967, Dec. 22	Photo.	Perf. 12x11½
B1 SP1 30m + 20m multi		.40 .25
B2 SP1 50m + 30m multi		.60 .35

Solidarity with Vietnam.

Save Venice Type of Regular Issue
Souvenir Sheet
Departure of St. Ursula, by Carpaccio.

1972, Oct. 1	Litho.	Perf. 12
B3 A163 3t + 1t multi		4.00 4.00

Save Venice Campaign. No. B3 contains one horizontal stamp.

Girl Feeding Lambs — SP2

UNICEF Emblem and: 20m+5m, Boy playing flute and dancing girl. 30m+5m, Girl chasing butterflies. 40m+5m, Girl with ribbon. 60m+5m, Girl with flowers. 80m+5m, Girl carrying bucket. 1t+5m, Boy going to school.

1977, June 1	Litho.	Perf. 12
B4 SP2 10m + 5m multi		.25 .25
B5 SP2 20m + 5m multi		.25 .25
B6 SP2 30m + 5m multi		.35 .25
B7 SP2 40m + 5m multi		.45 .30
B8 SP2 60m + 5m multi		.65 .35
B9 SP2 80m + 5m multi		.85 .55
B10 SP2 1t + 5m multi		1.10 .70
Nos. B4-B10 (7)		3.90 2.65

Surtax was for Mongolian Children's Village. See No. CB1.

Boys on Horseback — SP3

Children and IYC Emblem: 30m+5m, Raising chickens. 50m+5m, With deer. 60m+5m, With flowers. 70m+5m, Planting tree. 80m+5m, Studying space project. 1t+5m, Dancing. 4t+50m, Girl on horseback.

1979, Jan. 10		
B11 SP3 10m + 5m multi		.25 .25
B12 SP3 30m + 5m multi		.25 .25
B13 SP3 50m + 5m multi		.35 .25
B14 SP3 60m + 5m multi		.45 .25
B15 SP3 70m + 5m multi		.60 .25
B16 SP3 80m + 5m multi		.65 .35
B17 SP3 1t + 5m multi		.75 .40
Nos. B11-B17 (7)		3.30 2.00

Souvenir Sheet

| B18 SP3 4t + 50m multi | 3.00 3.00 |

International Year of the Child. Compare with Type A301.

1998 Winter Olympic Games, Nagano SP4

No. B19, Speed skating. No. B20, Ski jumping. No. B21, Snowboarding. No. B22, Freestyle skiing.

1998	Litho.	Perf. 12
B19 SP4 150t +15t multi		.65 .50
B20 SP4 200t +20t multi		.80 .60
B21 SP4 300t +30t multi		1.30 1.00
B22 SP4 600t +60t multi		2.25 1.75
Nos. B19-B22 (4)		5.00 3.85

Ulan Bator, 360th Anniv. — SP5

Designs, 300t +30t each: No. B23, Flags and arms. No. B24, Seated man. No. B25, Arms.
No. B26, Various views of Ulan Bator.

1999	Litho.	Perf. 12½
B23-B25 SP5 Set of 3		3.00 3.00

Sheet of 9
Perf. 12½x12¼

| B26 SP5 200t +20t #a.-i. | 8.00 8.00 |

No. B26 contains nine 45x27mm stamps.

Unity Against Terrorism — SP6

World Trade Center, Statue of Liberty, American flag and country name in: 300t+50t, Red. 400t+50t, Blue.

2001, Nov. 11	Litho.	Perf. 13½x13¼
B27-B28 SP6 Set of 2		3.00 3.00

Together Against Cancer Campaign — SP7

Designs: 700t+100t, Green ribbon, surgery, radiation and chemotherapy. 1200t+100t, Togerther Against Cancer emblem.

2018, Sept. 28	Litho.	Perf. 13¼x13
B29-B30 SP7 Set of 2		1.75 1.75

AIR POST STAMPS

Catalogue values for unused stamps in this section are for Never Hinged items.

Postal Modernization Type of Regular Issue

Designs: 10m, 20m, Postman with horses. 25m, Postman with reindeer. 30m, 50m, Plane over map of Mongolia. 1t, Post horn and flag of Mongolia.

1961, June 5	Photo.	Perf. 15
C1 A72 10m multicolored		.30 .25
C2 A72 50m multicolored		.60 .25
C3 A72 1t multicolored		1.10 .40
Nos. C1-C3 (3)		2.00 .80

Souvenir Sheet
Perf. 11

C4	Sheet of 4	— —
a.	A72 20m lt blue grn & multi	— —
b.	A72 25m light blue & multi	— —
c.	A72 30m light green & multi	— —
d.	A72 1t rose carmine & multi	— —

40th anniversary of independence; postal modernization. No. C4b is not inscribed Airmail.

Souvenir Sheet

Austria Type SP55, Austrian and Mongolian Stamps Circling Globe — AP1

1965, May 1	Engr.	Perf. 11½
C5 AP1 4t brown carmine		3.50 3.50

Vienna Intl. Philatelic Exhibition, WIPA, June 4-13. #C5 contains one 61x38mm stamp.

Weather Satellite — AP2

Designs: 20m, Antarctic exploration. 30m, Space exploration.

MONGOLIA

1965, May 15 Photo. Perf. 13½
C6 AP2 15m lilac, gold & blk .45 .25
C7 AP2 20m blue & multi 2.75 .50
C8 AP2 30m rose & multi .60 .25
   Nos. C6-C8 (3) 3.80 1.00
International Quiet Sun Year, 1964-65.

ITU Emblem — AP3

Design: 4t, Communications satellite.

1965, Dec. 20 Perf. 11½x12
C9 AP3 30m blue & bister .40 .25
C10 AP3 50m red & bister .60 .25

Souvenir Sheet
Perf. 11, Imperf.
C11 AP3 4t gold, bl & blk 4.00 3.00
ITU, centenary. No. C11 contains one stamp, 38x51mm. Exists imperf. Values: unused or used, $4.

Souvenir Sheet

Luna 10, Moon and Earth AP4

1966, July 10 Photo. Imperf.
C12 AP4 4t multicolored 3.50 3.50
Luna 10 Russian moon mission, Apr. 3, 1966.

Souvenir Sheet

Astronaut and Landing Module — AP5

1969, Aug. 20 Litho. Perf. 11½
C13 AP5 4t ultra & multi 4.00 3.00
Apollo 11 US moon mission, first man landing on moon.

Souvenir Sheet

Apollo 16 AP6

Perf. 12½x11½
1972, Apr. 16 Photo.
C14 AP6 4t multicolored 3.50 2.50
Apollo 16 moon mission, Apr. 15-27.

Souvenir Sheet

Mongolian Horse — AP7

1972, May 10 Photo. Perf. 12½
C15 AP7 4t multicolored 5.00 3.00
Centenary of the discovery of the Przewalski wild horse, bred in captivity in Berlin Zoo.

Telecommunication — AP8

Designs: 30m, Horse breeding. 40m, Train and plane. 50m, Corn and farm machinery. 60m, Red Cross ambulance and hospital. 80m, Actors. 1t, Factories.

1972, July 11 Litho. Perf. 12
C16 AP8 20m olive & multi .25 .25
C17 AP8 30m violet & multi .35 .25
C18 AP8 40m rose & multi 1.00 .25
C19 AP8 50m red & multi .40 .25
C20 AP8 60m multicolored .55 .25
C21 AP8 80m lt blue & multi .70 .30
C22 AP8 1t green & multi .86 .35
   Nos. C16-C22 (7) 4.10 1.90
Mongolian Achievements.

Mongolian Flag, Globe and Radar — AP9

Perf. 12½x11½
1972, July 20 Photo.
C23 AP9 60m olive & multi 1.00 .50
Intl. Telecommunications Day, May 17, 1972.

Running and Olympic Rings AP10

Olympic Rings and: 15m, Boxing. 20m, Judo. 25m, High jump. 30m, Rifle shooting. 60m, Wrestling. 80m, Weight lifting. 1t, Mongolian flag and sport emblem. 4t, Woman archer, vert.

Perf. 12½x11½
1972, July 30 Photo.
C24 AP10 10m multicolored .25 .25
C25 AP10 15m multicolored .25 .25
C26 AP10 20m multicolored .25 .25
C27 AP10 25m multicolored .25 .25
C28 AP10 30m multicolored .25 .25
C29 AP10 60m multicolored .30 .25
C30 AP10 80m multicolored .35 .30
C31 AP10 1t multicolored .45 .40
   Nos. C24-C31 (8) 2.35 2.20

Souvenir Sheet
Perf. 11½x12½
C32 AP10 4t orange & multi 2.50 2.50
20th Olympic Games, Munich, 8/26-9/11.

U.S./U.S.S.R. Space Achievements — AP11

Astrological Signs of the Eastern Calendar and Space Project: a, Snake, Mars 1. b, Dragon and Mariner 2. c, Hare, Soyuz 5. d, Monkey, Explorer 6. e, Cock, Venera 1. f, Rat, Apollo 15. g, Horse, Apollo 8. h, Boar, Cosmos 110. i, Tiger, Gemini 7. j, Sheep, Electron 2. k, Dog, Ariel 2. l, Ram, Venera 4.

1972, Dec. 4 Photo. Perf. 12
C33 Sheet of 12 7.00 5.00
a.-f. AP11 60m any single, size: 55x35mm .50 .30
g.-l. AP11 60m any single, size: 35x35mm .50 .30

Airliner — AP12

1973, Jan. Photo. Perf. 12
C34 AP12 1.50t blue 1.60 .40
For surcharge, see No. 2408.

Weather Satellite, Earth Station, WMO Emblem AP13

1973, Feb. Photo. Perf. 12x11½
C35 AP13 60m multicolored .50 .25
Intl. meteorological cooperation, cent.

Holy Flame Type of 1959
Souvenir Sheet
1973, Apr. 15 Photo. Perf. 12½
C36 A48 4t gold & multi 3.00 2.50
IBRA München 1973 Intl. Stamp Exhibition, Munich, May 11-20. No. C36 contains one 40x63mm stamp in redrawn design of A48 with simulated perforations and wide gold margin.

Mongolia #236 AP14

Designs: Stamps (with mail-connected designs) of participating countries: No. C37, Russia No. 3100. No. C38, Bulgaria #1047. No. C39, Hungary #B202. No. C40, Czechoslavia #C72. No. C41, German Dem. Rep. #369. No. C42, Cuba #C31. No. C43, Romania #2280. No. C44, Poland #802.

1973, July 31 Litho. Perf. 12½
C37 AP14 30m multi .50 .25
C38 AP14 30m shown .50 .25
C39 AP14 30m multi .50 .25
C40 AP14 30m multi .50 .25
C41 AP14 30m multi .50 .25
C42 AP14 30m multi .50 .25
C43 AP14 30m multi .50 .25
C44 AP14 30m multi .50 .25
C45 AP14 30m multi .50 .25
   Nos. C37-C45 (9) 4.50 2.25
Conference of Permanent Committee for Posts and Telecommunications of Council for Economic Aid (COMECON), Ulan Bator, Aug. 1973.

Launching of Soyuz Spacecraft — AP15

10m, Apollo 8. 15m, Soyuz 4 & 5 docking. 20m, Apollo 11 lunar module. 30m, Apollo 14 splashdown. 50m, Soyuz 6, 7 & 8. 60m, Apollo 16 moon rover. 1t, Lunokhod 1 on moon. 4t, Soyuz and Apollo.

1973, Oct. 26 Litho. Perf. 12½
C46 AP15 5m shown .25 .25
C47 AP15 10m multi .25 .25
C48 AP15 15m multi .25 .25
C49 AP15 20m multi .25 .25
C50 AP15 30m multi .25 .25
C51 AP15 50m multi .40 .25
C52 AP15 60m multi .60 .25
C53 AP15 1t multi .60 .30
   Nos. C46-C53 (8) 2.85 2.05

Souvenir Sheet
C54 AP15 4t multi 2.50 2.00
US and Russian achievements in space.

Comecon Building, Moscow — AP16

1974, Feb. 28 Photo. Perf. 11½x12
C55 AP16 60m blue & multi .50 .25
25th anniversary of the Council of Mutual Economic Assistance.

Souvenir Sheet

Mongolia No. 4 AP17

1974, Mar. 15 Photo. Perf. 12½
C56 AP17 4t multicolored 3.50 2.50
50th anniv. of 1st stamps of Mongolia.

Postrider and UPU Emblem AP18

UPU emblem & means of transportation: No. C58, Reindeer post. No. C59, Mail coach. No. C60, Balloon post. No. C61, Steamship and AN-2 plane. No. C62, Train, truck and city. No. C63, Rocket over North Pole. No. C64, Globe and post horn, vert.

1974, Apr. Litho. Perf. 12
C57 AP18 50m shown .90 .35
C58 AP18 50m multi .90 .35
C59 AP18 50m multi .90 .35
C60 AP18 50m multi 1.00 .35
C61 AP18 50m multi 1.25 .35
C62 AP18 50m multi 1.25 .35
C63 AP18 50m multi 1.00 .35
   Nos. C57-C63 (7) 7.20 2.45

Souvenir Sheet
C64 AP18 4t multi 10.00 9.00
Centenary of Universal Postal Union.

Circus Type of 1974
Design: 1t, Two women contortionists.

1974, May 4 Litho. Perf. 12
C65 A177 1t multicolored 1.25 .60
No. C65 has se-tenant label, with similar design.

MONGOLIA

Nature Type of Regular Issue
1t, Scientist checking water, globe. 4t, Wild rose.

1974, Dec.	Litho.	Perf. 11		
C66	A186	1t multicolored	1.00	.50

Souvenir Sheet
Perf. 12½

C67	A186	4t multicolored	3.50	2.50

UPU Type of 1974
Souvenir Sheet
Design: UPU Emblem, vert.

1974, Dec.		Perf. 11½x12		
C68	A187	4t multicolored	4.50	4.50

Soyuz on Launching Pad, Project Emblem AP19

Project Emblem and: 20m, Radar and Apollo. 30m, Apollo, Soyuz and earth. 40m, Spacecraft before docking. 50m, Spacecraft after docking. 60m, Soyuz circling earth. 1t, Spacecraft, space station and earth. 4t, Russian and American astronauts.

1975, June 14	Litho.	Perf. 12		
C69	AP19	10m blue & multi	.25	.25
C70	AP19	20m multicolored	.25	.25
C71	AP19	30m sepia & multi	.25	.25
C72	AP19	40m silver & multi	.40	.25
C73	AP19	50m multicolored	.55	.30
C74	AP19	60m multicolored	.70	.30
C75	AP19	1t multicolored	1.00	.60
	Nos. C69-C75 (7)		3.40	2.20

Souvenir Sheet

C76	AP19	4t black & multi	2.75	2.75

Apollo Soyuz space test project (Russo-American space cooperation), launching July 15; link-up July 17.

Mongolian Mountain Sheep — AP20

1975, Aug. 4	Litho.	Perf. 12		
C77	AP20	1.50t multi + label	1.40	.60

South Asia Tourism Year.

Satellite over Weather Map of Mongolia AP21

1976, Mar. 20		Perf. 12x11½		
C78	AP21	60m blue & yellow	.60	.25

40th anniversary of meteorological service.

Souvenir Sheet

Girl with Books and Flowers AP22

1976, Mar. 30		Perf. 12		
C79	AP22	4t multicolored	3.50	3.00

30th anniversary of UNESCO.

Souvenir Sheet

The Wise Musician, by Sarav — AP23

1976, May 3	Litho.	Perf. 11½x12½		
C80	AP23	4t multicolored	3.50	3.00

Interphil 76 Phil. Exhib., Philadelphia, Pa., May 29-June 6.

Olympic Games Type of 1976
Souvenir Sheet

1976, May 20		Perf. 12½x11½		
C81	A202	4t Wrestling	2.25	2.00

Independence Type of 1976
60m, Progress in agriculture and industry.

1976, June 20	Litho.	Perf. 12x11½		
C82	A203	60m multicolored	.45	.25

Olympic Medalists Type, 1976
Souvenir Sheet
Design: 4t, Oidov Zeveg, Mongolian flag.

1976, Nov. 30	Litho.	Perf. 11x11½		
C83	A209	4t multicolored	2.50	2.50

Mounting Carrier Rocket with Bell-shaped Gear — AP24

Designs: 20m, Launching of Intercosmos 3. 30m, Marine Observatory Gagarin (ship). 40m, Satellite observation of lunar eclipse. 60m, Observatory with multiple antenna system. 80m, Examination of Van Allen Zone, magnetosphere. 1t, Meteorological earth satellite. 4t, Intercosmos satellite with lines showing participating countries on globe.

1977, June 20	Litho.	Perf. 12		
C84	AP24	10m multicolored	.25	.25
C85	AP24	20m multicolored	.25	.25
C86	AP24	30m multicolored	.25	.25
C87	AP24	40m multicolored	.40	.25
C88	AP24	60m multicolored	.60	.30
C89	AP24	80m multicolored	.80	.40
C90	AP24	1t multicolored	1.00	.45
	Nos. C84-C90 (7)		3.55	2.15

Souvenir Sheet
Perf. 12½

C91	AP24	4t multicolored	2.50	2.50

11th anniv. of Intercosmos program, cooperation of 9 socialist countries for space research. No. C91 contains one stamp 58x37mm.

Trade Union Emblem, Factory and Sheep — AP25

1977, June		Perf. 12x11½		
C92	AP25	60m multicolored	.75	.25

11th Cong. of Mongolian Trade Unions, May 12.

Montgolfier's Balloon — AP26

Dirigibles: 30m, Zeppelin over North Pole, 1931. 40m, Osoaviahim, Russian Arctic cargo. 50m, North, Russian heavy duty cargo. 60m, Aeron-340, Russian planned. 80m, Machinery transport, Russian planned. 1.20t, Flying crane, French planned. 4t, Russia No. C26 (stamp) and Sukhe Bator statue.

1977, Dec.	Litho.	Perf. 12		
C93	AP26	20m multicolored	.25	.25
C94	AP26	30m multicolored	.25	.25
C95	AP26	40m multicolored	.25	.25
C96	AP26	50m multicolored	.35	.25
C97	AP26	60m multicolored	.50	.25
C98	AP26	80m multicolored	.65	.40
C99	AP26	1.20t multicolored	1.00	.45
	Nos. C93-C99 (7)		3.25	2.10

Souvenir Sheet
Perf. 12½x11½

C100	AP26	4t multicolored	2.50	2.50

History of airships.

A. F. Mozhaiski and his Plane, 1884 AP27

Designs: 30m, Henry Farman and his plane, 1909. 40m, Geoffrey de Havilland and D. H. 66 Hercules, 1920's. 50m, Charles A. Lindbergh, Spirit of St. Louis and route New York to Paris, 1927. 60m, Mongolian pilots Shagdarsuren and Demberel and plane over Altai Mountains, 1935. 80m, Soviet aviators Chkalov, Baidukov, Beliakov, plane and route Moscow to Vancouver, 1937. 1.20t, A. N. Tupolev, supersonic plane TU 154, route Moscow to Alma-Ata, 1968. 4t, Wilbur and Orville Wright and their plane.

1978, Mar. 25	Litho.	Perf. 12½x11		
C101	AP27	20m multi	.25	.25
C102	AP27	30m multi	.25	.25
C103	AP27	40m multi	.30	.25
C104	AP27	50m multi	.35	.25
C105	AP27	60m multi	.45	.25
C106	AP27	80m multi	.55	.30
C107	AP27	1.20t multi	.85	.40
	Nos. C101-C107 (7)		3.00	1.95

Souvenir Sheet

C108	AP27	4t multi	2.75	2.75

75th anniversary of first powered flight, Wright brothers, 1903.

Soccer Type of 1978
Souvenir Sheet
Design: 4t, Two soccer players.

1978, Apr. 15		Perf. 11½		
C109	A231	4t multi	3.25	3.25

World Soccer Championships, Argentina 78, June 1-25. #C109 contains 1 45x38mm stamp.

Souvenir Sheet

Canada No. 553 and Mongolia No. 549 AP28

1978, June	Litho.	Perf. 12½		
C110	AP28	4t multi	3.00	3.00

CAPEX '78, Intl. Phil. Exhibition, Toronto, June 9-18.

Map of Cuba, Ship, Plane and Festival Emblem AP29

1978, July 28	Litho.	Perf. 12		
C111	AP29	1t multicolored	1.50	.30

11th World Youth Festival, Havana, 7/28-8/5.

Souvenir Sheet

Aleksei Gubarev and Vladimir Remek, PRAGA '78 Emblem AP30

1978, Sept. 5	Litho.	Perf. 12		
C112	AP30	4t multicolored	3.00	3.00

PRAGA '78 Intl. Phil. Exhib., Prague, Sept. 8-17, and Russian-Czechoslovak space cooperation, Intercosmos.

DDR Flag, TV Tower, Berlin, Satellite — AP31

1979, Oct. 9	Litho.	Perf. 11½x12		
C113	AP31	60m multicolored	.60	.25

German Democratic Republic, 30th anniv.

Demoiselle Crane — AP32

Protected Birds: 30m, Hawk warbler. 50m, Ruddy shelduck. 60m, Blue magpie. 70m, Goldfinch. 80m, Titmouse. 1t, Golden oriole.

1979, Oct. 25				
C114	AP32	10m multi	.30	.25
C115	AP32	30m multi	.45	.25
C116	AP32	50m multi	.55	.25
C117	AP32	60m multi	.70	.25
C118	AP32	70m multi	.85	.30
C119	AP32	80m multi	1.00	.30
C120	AP32	1t multi	1.10	.35
	Nos. C114-C120 (7)		4.95	1.95

Venera 5 and 6 — AP33

American and Russian Space Missions: 30m, Mariner 5. 50m, Mars 3. 60m, Viking 1 and 2. 70m, Luna 1, 2 and 3. 80m, Lunokhod 2. 1t, Apollo 15. 4t, Apollo 11, astronauts on moon.

Perf. 12½x11½

1979, Nov. 24		Litho.		
C121	AP33	10m multi	.25	.25
C122	AP33	30m multi	.25	.25
C123	AP33	50m multi	.30	.25
C124	AP33	60m multi	.40	.25
C125	AP33	70m multi	.50	.25
C126	AP33	80m multi	.60	.30
C127	AP33	1t multi	.70	.30
	Nos. C121-C127 (7)		3.00	1.85

Souvenir Sheet

C128	AP33	4t multi	2.50	2.50

Apollo 11 moon landing, 10th anniversary.

Andrena Scita AP34

Insects: 30m, Paravespula germanica. 40m, Perilampus ruficornis. 50m, Bumblebee. 60m, Honey bee. 80m, Stilbum cyanurum. 1.20t, Ruby tail.

MONGOLIA

1980, Feb. 25　Litho.　Perf. 11x12
C129	AP34	20m multi	.25	.25
C130	AP34	30m multi	.30	.25
C131	AP34	40m multi	.35	.25
C132	AP34	45m multi	.45	.25
C133	AP34	60m multi	.50	.35
C134	AP34	80m multi	.75	.35
C135	AP34	1.20t multi	1.00	.45
	Nos. C129-C135 (7)		3.60	2.15

Z-526 AFS Stunt Planes, Czechoslovakia — AP35

30m, RS-180 "Sportsman," Germany. 40m, Yanki-Anu, US. 50m, MJ-2 "Tempete," France. 60m, "Pits," Canada. 80m, "Acrostar," Switzerland. 1.20t, JAK-50, USSR.
4t, JAK-52, USSR.

1980, Aug. 4　Litho.　Perf. 12
C136	AP35	20m shown	.25	.25
C137	AP35	30m multi	.25	.25
C138	AP35	40m multi	.25	.25
C139	AP35	50m multi	.40	.25
C140	AP35	60m multi	.50	.25
C141	AP35	80m multi	.60	.35
C142	AP35	1.20t multi	.90	.40
	Nos. C136-C142 (7)		3.15	2.00

Souvenir Sheet
C143	AP35	4t multi	3.00	2.50

10th World Aerobatic Championship, Oshkosh, Wisconsin, Aug 17-30. No. C143 contains one 50x43mm stamp.

Olympic Type of 1980
Souvenir Sheet

1980, Sept. 15　Litho.　Perf. 12½
C144	A253	4t Wrestlers	2.50	2.00

J. Davaajav, Mongolian silver medalist, 22nd Summer Olympic Games, Moscow. Inscribed "Los Angeles '84".

Souvenir Sheet

AP36

1980, Dec. 10　Litho.　Perf. 11½x11
C145	AP36	4t multi	3.00	2.50

Johannes Kepler (1571-1630), German astronomer.

AP37

Graf Zeppelin and: 20m, Germany #C40, sea eagle. 30m, Germany #C41, polar fox. 40m, Germany #C42, walrus. 50m, Russia #C26, polar bear. 60m, Russia #C27, snowy owl. 80m, Russia #C28, puffin. 1.20t, Russia #C29, seal. 4t, Icebreaker Maligin.

1981, Oct. 5　Litho.　Perf. 12x11½
C146	AP37	20m multi	.40	.25
C147	AP37	30m multi	.50	.25
C148	AP37	40m multi	.60	.25
C149	AP37	50m multi	.75	.25
C150	AP37	60m multi	.85	.30
C151	AP37	80m multi	1.10	.30
C152	AP37	1.20t multi	1.50	.35
	Nos. C146-C152 (7)		5.70	1.95

Souvenir Sheet
C153	AP37	4t multi	4.00	3.50

Graf Zeppelin polar flight, 50th anniv. No. C153 contains one stamp 36x51mm.

ITU Plenipotentiaries Conference, Nairobi, Sept. — AP38

1982, Sept. 27　Litho.　Perf. 12
C154	AP38	60m Map	.80	.30

2nd UN Conference on Peaceful Uses of Outer Space, Vienna, Aug. 9-21 — AP39

No. C155, Sputnik 1. No. C156, Sputnik 2. No. C157, Vostok 1. No. C158, Venera 8. No. C159, Vostok 6. No. C160, Voskhod 2. No. C161, Apollo II. No. C162, Soyuz T-6. No. C163, Soyuz 39, Salyut 6.

1982, Dec. 15　Litho.　Perf. 12
C155	AP39	60m multi	.40	.25
C156	AP39	60m multi	.40	.25
C157	AP39	60m multi	.40	.25
C158	AP39	60m multi	.40	.25
C159	AP39	60m multi	.40	.25
C160	AP39	60m multi	.40	.25
C161	AP39	60m multi	.40	.25
C162	AP39	60m multi	.40	.25
	Nos. C155-C162 (8)		3.20	2.00

Souvenir Sheet
Perf. 12½x12
C163	AP39	4t multi	3.00	3.00

Balloon Flight Bicentenary — AP40

20m, Montgolfiere, 1783. 30m, Blanchard, 1785. 40m, Royal-Vauzhall, 1836. 50m, Oernen, 1897. 60m, Gordon Bennett Race, 1906. 80m, Paris, 1931. 1.20t, USSR-VR-62, 1033.
4t, Mongolia, 1977.

1982, Dec. 31　Perf. 11½x12½
C164	AP40	20m multi	.25	.25
C165	AP40	30m multi	.25	.25
C166	AP40	40m multi	.25	.25
C167	AP40	50m multi	.40	.25
C168	AP40	60m multi	.50	.25
C169	AP40	80m multi	.60	.25
C170	AP40	1.20t multi	1.00	.30
	Nos. C164-C170 (7)		3.25	1.80

Souvenir Sheet
C171	AP40	4t multi	3.00	3.00

Souvenir Sheet

Revolutionary Mongolia Monument — AP41

1983　Litho.　Imperf.
C172	AP41	4t multi	2.50	2.50

Concorde AP42

20m, DC-10, vert. 30m, Airbus A-300 B-2. 50m, Boeing 747. 60m, IL-62. 80m, TU-154. 1.20t, IL-86.
4t, Yak-42.

1984, Aug. 15　Litho.　Perf. 14
C173	AP42	20m multi	.25	.25
C174	AP42	30m multi	.25	.25
C175	AP42	40m shown	.35	.25
C176	AP42	50m multi	.45	.35
C177	AP42	60m multi	.55	.35
C178	AP42	80m multi	.75	.45
C179	AP42	1.20t multi	1.10	.55
	Nos. C173-C179 (7)		3.70	2.45

Souvenir Sheet
C180	AP42	4t multi	3.50	3.50

1988 Winter Olympics, Calgary — AP43

20m, Bobsled. 30m, Ski jumping. 40m, Downhill skiing. 50m, Biathlon. 60m, Speed skating. 80m, Women's figure skating. 1.20t, Ice hockey.
4t, Cross-country skiing.

1988, Jan. 20　Litho.　Perf. 14
C181	AP43	20m multi	.25	.25
C182	AP43	30m multi	.25	.25
C183	AP43	40m multi	.35	.25
C184	AP43	50m multi	.40	.25
C185	AP43	60m multi	.55	.30
C186	AP43	80m multi	.65	.30
C187	AP43	1.20t multi	.75	.40
	Nos. C181-C187 (7)		3.20	2.00

Souvenir sheet
C188	AP43	4t multi	3.25	2.50

Souvenir Sheet

Hong Kong '94 AP44

1994, Feb. 18　Litho.　Perf. 14½x15
C189	AP44	600t multicolored	4.00	4.00
a.		With Hong Kong '97 emblem in sheet margin	4.00	4.00

Issued: #C189a, 1/12/97.

No. C163 Surcharged in Red
Souvenir Sheet

2001, Mar. 22　Litho.　Perf. 12½x12
C190	AP39	400t on 4t multi	25.00	25.00

Joint Soviet-Mongolian space flight, 20th anniv.

Souvenir Sheet

Diplomatic Relations with Turkey, 50th Anniv. — AP45

No. C191: a, Mongolian Airlines jet over bridge, tulip. b, Turkish Airlines jet, Mongolian woman, flower.

Litho. & Embossed
2019, July 29　Perf. 13¾
C191	AP45	2500t Sheet of 2, #a-b	3.75	3.75

AIR POST SEMI-POSTAL STAMP

Catalogue values for unused stamps in this section are for Never Hinged items.

UNICEF Type of 1977
Souvenir Sheet

Design: 4t+50m, Balloon with Mongolian flag, children and UNICEF emblem.

1977, June 1　Litho.　Perf. 12
CB1	SP2	4t + 50m multi	4.00	4.00

First balloon flight in Mongolia. Surtax was for Children's Village.

MONTENEGRO

,män-tə-'nē-ˌgrō

LOCATION — Southern Europe, bordering on the Adriatic Sea
GOVT. — Republic in southern Europe.
AREA — 5,415 sq. mi.
POP. — 628,000 (2020 est.)
CAPITAL — Podgorica

Montenegro maintained a precarious independence from the Ottoman Turks during the 16th-19th centuries as a theocracy, under a succession of bishop princes. In 1852 it became an independent principality. On December 1, 1918, Montenegro, along with Bosnia and Herzegovina, Croatia, Dalmatia and Slovenia, was absorbed by Serbia to form the Kingdom of the Serbs, Croats and Slovenes, which became the Kingdom of Yugoslavia in 1929.

All stamps of the Kingdom of Montenegro were printed at the State Printing Works, Vienna. Later, overprints were applied at Cetinje.

During World War II, an Italian satellite regime was established in an enlarged Montenegrin state, but after the war, Montenegro became one of the constituent republics of the Socialist Federal Republic of Yugoslavia.

In 1992, with the dissolution of the greater Yugoslav republic, only Montenegro remained associated with Serbia, first in the Federal Republic of Yugoslavia and, after 2002, in the looser federation of Serbia & Montenegro.

On May 21, 2006, Montenegrins endorsed independence and complete separation from Serbia in a national referendum, and the Republic of Montenegro declared independence on June 3. On June 7, Serbia officially recognized Montenegro's independence.

100 Novcic = 1 Florin
100 Helera = 1 Kruna (1902)
100 Para = 1 Kruna (1907)
100 Para = 1 Perper (1910)
100 cents = 1 euro (2003)

Canceled to Order

Used values for Nos. 1-110, H1-H5, and J1-J26 are for canceled-to-order stamps. Postally used examples sell for considerably more.

Watermarks

Wmk. 91 — "BRIEF-MARKEN" (#1-14) or "ZEITUNGS-MARKEN" (#15-21) in Double-lined Capitals once across sheet

Wmk. 140 — Crown

Prince Nicholas I — A1

Early Printings
Narrow Spacing (2-2½mm)
Perf. 10½ Large Holes, pointed teeth

1874		Typo.	Wmk. 91	
1	A1	2n yellow	40.00	45.00
2	A1	3n green	55.00	45.00
3	A1	5n rose red	50.00	45.00
4	A1	7n lt lilac	50.00	37.50
5	A1	10n blue	140.00	92.50
6	A1	15n yel bister	160.00	140.00
7	A1	25n lilac gray	325.00	225.00
		Nos. 1-7 (7)	820.00	630.00

Middle Printings (1879)
Narrow spacing
Perf. 12, 12½, 13 and Compound

8	A1	2n yellow	11.50	7.50
a.		Perf. 12-13x10½	190.00	140.00
9	A1	3n green	9.25	6.00
10	A1	5n red	9.25	6.00
11	A1	7n rose lilac	9.25	6.00
a.		7n lilac	19.00	14.00
12	A1	10n blue	19.00	8.00
a.		Perf. 12-13x10½	65.00	52.50
13	A1	15n bister brn	19.00	11.00
14	A1	25n gray lilac	25.00	16.00
		Nos. 8-14 (7)	102.25	60.50

Late Printings (1893?)
Narrow and wide spacing (2¾-3½mm)
Perf. 10½, 11½ Small holes, broad teeth
(Perf. 11½ also with pointed teeth)

15	A1	2n yellow	4.50	3.00
e.		Perf. 11 ('94)	32.50	23.00
16	A1	3n green	4.50	3.00
17	A1	5n red	3.50	2.75
18	A1	7n rose	3.50	2.75
e.		Perf. 11 ('94)	14.50	13.50
19	A1	10n blue	4.50	3.25
20	A1	15n brown	4.50	3.50
21	A1	25n brown violet	5.75	4.50
		Nos. 15-21 (7)	30.75	22.75

Dates of issue of the late printings are still being researched.

Types of 1874-93 Overprinted in Black or Red

1893			Perf. 10½, 11½	
22	A1	2n yellow	32.50	8.00
a.		Perf. 11	75.00	30.00
23	A1	3n green	6.50	3.25
24	A1	5n red	4.50	2.75
25	A1	7n rose	5.75	4.50
a.		Perf. 12	110.00	72.50
b.		7n rose lilac	5.00	3.00
c.		7n lilac, perf. 12	125.00	
d.		Perf. 11	40.00	30.00
26	A1	10n blue	5.75	4.50
27	A1	10n blue (R)	8.50	6.25
28	A1	15n brown	4.50	3.50
a.		Perf. 12	140.00	92.50
29	A1	15n brown (R)	2,750.	1,900.
30	A1	25n brown violet	4.50	3.50
31	A1	25n brn vio (R)	8.50	5.50
a.		Perf. 12½		275.00
		Nos. 22-28,30-31 (9)	81.00	41.75

Introduction of printing to Montenegro, 400th anniversary.

This overprint had many settings. Several values exist with "1494" or "1495" instead of "1493", or with missing letters or numerals due to wearing of the clichés. Double and inverted overprints exist. Some printings were made after 1893 to supply a philatelic demand, but were available for postage.

The 7n with red overprint was not issued.

1894-98		Wmk. 91	Perf. 10½	
32	A1	1n gray blue	.65	.65
33	A1	2n emerald ('98)	.45	.45
34	A1	3n car rose ('98)	.45	.45
c.		3n analine red ('98)	.45	.75
35	A1	5n orange ('98)	2.75	.65
36	A1	7n gray lilac ('98)	.55	.55
37	A1	10n magenta ('98)	.65	.95
38	A1	15n red brn ('98)	.45	.65
39	A1	20n brown orange	.65	.65
40	A1	25n dull blue ('98)	.45	.65
41	A1	30n maroon	.65	.65
42	A1	50n ultra	.65	.45
43	A1	1fl deep green	.95	4.50
44	A1	2fl red brown	1.50	13.50
		Nos. 32-44 (13)	10.80	24.75

Monastery at Cetinje (Royal Mausoleum) — A3

1896, Sept. 1		Litho.	Unwmk.	
		Perf. 10½		
45	A3	1n dk blue & bis	.40	1.40
46	A3	2n magenta & yel	.40	1.40
47	A3	3n org brn & yel grn	.40	1.40
48	A3	5n bl grn & bis	.40	1.40
49	A3	10n yellow & ultra	.40	1.40
50	A3	15n dk blue & grn	.40	1.40
51	A3	20n bl grn & ultra	.40	1.50
52	A3	25n dk blue & yel	.50	1.50
53	A3	30n magenta & bis	.65	1.50
54	A3	50n red brn & gray bl	.65	1.50
55	A3	1fl rose & gray bl	1.10	1.90
56	A3	2fl brown & black	1.60	2.25
		Nos. 45-56 (12)	7.30	18.55

Perf. 11½

45a	A3	1n dark blue & bister	.95	2.25
46a	A3	2n magenta & yellow	.95	2.25
47a	A3	3n org brn & yel grn	.95	2.25
48a	A3	5n blue green & bister	.95	2.25
49a	A3	10n yellow & ultramarine	.45	1.40
50a	A3	15n dark blue & green	72.50	110.00
51a	A3	20n blue green & ultra	45.00	67.50
52a	A3	25n dk blue & yellow	1.40	2.75
53a	A3	30n magenta & bister	1.40	2.75
54a	A3	50n red brn & gray blue	1.40	2.75
55a	A3	1fl rose & gray blue	2.10	3.50
56a	A3	2fl brown & black	2.75	5.50

Bicentenary of the ruling dynasty, founded by the Vladika, Danilo Petrovich of Nyegosh. Inverted centers and other errors exist, but experts believe these to be printer's waste.

Perf. 11½ counterfeits are common.

Prince Nicholas I — A4

Perf. 13x13½, 13x12½ (2h, 5h, 50h, 2k, 5k); 12½ (1h, 25h)

1902, July 12				
57	A4	1h ultra	.45	.45
58	A4	2h rose lilac	.45	.45
59	A4	5h green	.45	.45
a.		Pair, imperf.	5.75	
60	A4	10h rose	.45	.45
61	A4	25h dull blue	.95	1.10
a.		Perf. 12½	4.50	
62	A4	50h gray green	.95	1.10
63	A4	1k chocolate	.95	.95
64	A4	2k pale brown	.95	1.10
65	A4	5k buff	1.10	2.75
		Nos. 57-65 (9)	6.70	8.80

The 2h black brown and 25h indigo were not issued. Values: 2h, $95; 25h, $65. The 25h, perf. 12½, probably was never issued. Value, $4.50.

Constitution Issue
Same Overprinted in Red or Black

УСТАВ УСТАВ
Type I   Type II

УСТАВ УСТАВ
Type III   Type IV

1905, Dec. 5		"Constitution" 15mm		
66	A4	1h ultra (R)	.45	.45
e.		Double overprint	14.00	14.00
67	A4	2h rose lilac	.45	.45
e.		Double overprint	14.00	14.00
68	A4	5h green (R)	.95	.95
e.		Double overprint	14.00	14.00
f.		Inverted overprint	37.50	
69	A4	10h rose	1.40	1.10
e.		Double overprint	14.00	
70	A4	25h dull blue (R)	.70	.65
e.		Double overprint	14.00	
71	A4	50h gray green (R)	.70	.65
e.		Double overprint	14.00	14.00
72	A4	1k chocolate (R)	.70	.65
e.		Double overprint	14.00	14.00
73	A4	2k pale brown (R)	.95	.95
e.		Double overprint	17.00	17.00
74	A4	5k buff	1.50	1.40
e.		Double overprint	17.00	
		Nos. 66-74 (9)	7.80	7.25

Overprints in other colors are proofs.

1906		"Constitution" 16½mm		
		Type I		
67a	A4	2h rose lilac	45.00	45.00
e.		Double overprint		
f.		Inverted overprint	—	
69a	A4	10h rose	325.00	
70a	A4	25h dull blue (R)	29.00	27.00
e.		Double overprint		
f.		Inverted overprint	—	
71a	A4	50h gray green (R)	29.00	27.00
e.		Double overprint		
f.		Inverted overprint		
72a	A4	1k chocolate (R)	29.00	27.00
73a	A4	2k pale brown (R)	29.00	27.00
f.		Inverted overprint		
74a	A4	5k buff	1.50	1.40
f.		Inverted overprint		
		Nos. 67a-74a (9)	488.90	155.80

Type II

66b	A4	1h ultra (R)	.45	.45
67b	A4	2h rose lilac	.45	.45
f.		Inverted overprint	19.00	
e.		Double overprint	47.50	
68b	A4	5h green (R)	.95	.95
e.		Double overprint	19.00	
69b	A4	10h rose	1.10	1.10
f.		Inverted overprint	47.50	
70b	A4	25h dull blue (R)	.70	.65
e.		Double overprint	19.00	
f.		Inverted overprint	47.50	
71b	A4	50h gray green (R)	.70	.65
e.		Double overprint	19.00	
72b	A4	1k chocolate (R)	.70	.65
73b	A4	2k pale brown (R)	.95	.95
f.		Inverted overprint	47.50	
74b	A4	5k buff	1.50	1.40
f.		Inverted overprint	55.00	
		Nos. 66b-74b (9)	7.50	7.25

Type III

66c	A4	1h ultra (R)	2.75	2.75
67c	A4	2h rose lilac	2.75	2.75
e.		Double overprint	—	
f.		Inverted overprint	—	
68c	A4	5h green (R)	5.75	5.50
e.		Double overprint	—	
69c	A4	10h rose	7.25	6.75
f.		Inverted overprint	—	
70c	A4	25h dull blue (R)	3.75	3.50
e.		Double overprint	—	
f.		Inverted overprint	—	
71c	A4	50h gray green (R)	3.75	3.50
e.		Double overprint	—	
72c	A4	1k chocolate (R)	3.75	3.75
73c	A4	2k pale brown (R)	4.75	4.75
f.		Inverted overprint	—	
74c	A4	5k buff	5.75	5.50
f.		Inverted overprint	—	

Type IV

66d	A4	1h ultra (R)	.95	.95
67d	A4	2h rose lilac	.95	.95
68d	A4	5h green (R)	2.40	2.40
e.		Double overprint	—	
f.		Inverted overprint	—	
69d	A4	10h rose	2.25	6.75
f.		Inverted overprint	—	
g.		"Constitutton"	22.50	
70d	A4	25h dull blue (R)	1.90	1.90
e.		Double overprint	—	
f.		Inverted overprint	—	
71d	A4	50h gray green (R)	2.40	2.40
72d	A4	1k chocolate (R)	2.40	2.40
73d	A4	2k pale brown (R)	3.50	3.25
f.		Inverted overprint	—	
74d	A4	5k buff	3.75	3.50
f.		Inverted overprint		

Prince Nicholas I — A5

1907, June 1		Engr.	Perf. 12½	
75	A5	1pa ocher	.40	.25
76	A5	2pa black	.40	.25
77	A5	5pa yellow green	1.60	.25
78	A5	10pa rose red	2.75	.25
79	A5	15pa ultra	.45	.45
80	A5	20pa red orange	.45	.45
81	A5	25pa indigo	.45	.45
82	A5	35pa bister brown	.70	.45
83	A5	50pa dull violet	.70	.65
84	A5	1kr carmine rose	.70	.65
85	A5	2kr green	.70	.65
86	A5	5kr red brown	1.50	1.10
		Nos. 75-86 (12)	10.80	5.85

Many Montenegro stamps exist imperforate or part perforate. Experts believe these to be printer's waste.

King Nicholas I as a Youth — A6

King Nicholas I and Queen Milena — A7

King Nicholas I — A11

Prince Nicholas — A12

MONTENEGRO

5pa, 10pa, 25pa, 35pa, Nicholas in 1910. 15pa, Nicholas in 1878. 20pa, King and Queen, diff.

1910, Aug. 28   **Engr.**
87	A6	1pa black	.75	.45
88	A7	2pa purple brown	.75	.45
89	A6	5pa dark green	.75	.45
90	A6	10pa carmine	.75	.45
91	A6	15pa slate blue	.75	.45
92	A7	20pa olive green	.95	.65
93	A6	25pa deep blue	.95	.65
94	A6	35pa chestnut	1.40	.95
95	A11	50pa violet	1.40	.95
96	A11	1per lake	1.40	.95
97	A11	2per yellow green	1.75	1.10
98	A12	5per pale blue	1.90	1.40
a.		Perf. 10	25.00	
		Nos. 87-98 (12)	13.50	8.90

Proclamation of Montenegro as a kingdom, the 50th anniv. of the reign of King Nicholas and the golden wedding celebration of the King and Queen.

King Nicholas I — A13

1913, Apr. 1   **Typo.**
99	A13	1pa orange	.45	.65
100	A13	2pa plum	.45	.65
101	A13	5pa deep green	.50	.65
102	A13	10pa deep rose	.50	.65
103	A13	15pa blue gray	.60	.65
104	A13	20pa dark brown	.60	.65
105	A13	25pa deep blue	.95	.95
106	A13	35pa vermilion	.70	.65
107	A13	50pa pale blue	.45	.95
108	A13	1per yellow brown	.95	1.40
109	A13	2per gray violet	.95	1.40
110	A13	5per yellow green	.95	1.40
		Nos. 99-110 (12)	8.05	10.65

SERBIA & MONTENEGRO

100 Cents=1 Euro

Yugoslavia became Serbia & Montenegro Feb. 4, 2003, with each section of the country maintaining and operating their own postal service, and each having their own currency. After a referendum on independence on May 21, 2006, Montenegro seceded from Serbia and Montenegro, declaring independence on June 3. Serbia formally recognized Montenegro's independence on June 7.

The stamps below are inscribed only with euro denominations, used solely within Montenegro. Stamps inscribed with dinar denominations, issued for use in Serbia, and those denominated in both dinar and euro currencies, for use in either region, are found under the Serbia listings.

Budva A20

Durmitor A21

2003, Sept. 15   **Litho.**   **Perf. 12½**
120	A20	25c multi	1.25	1.25
121	A21	40c multi	2.25	2.25

Christmas — A22

2003, Nov. 21   **Perf. 13¼**
122	A22	25c multi	1.75	1.75
		Complete booklet, 10 #122	17.50	

National Symbols — A23

Small coat of arms, outline map of Europe and: 25c, Map of Montenegro. 40c, Parliament Building and map of Montenegro. 50c, Large coat of arms and map of Montenegro. 60c, Flag and map of Montenegro.

2005, Dec. 15   **Litho.**   **Perf. 13**
123-126	A23	Set of 4	9.00	9.00

See Nos. 140-142.

Europa — A24

Designs: 25c, Fish, shrimp, and mussels. 50c, Meat, olives, cheese and fruit.
No. 128C: d, 25c, Bee, honeycomb and honey. e, 50c, Grapes, grapevine, wine.

2005, Dec. 30   **Perf. 13½x13¾**
127	A24	25c multicolored	4.75	4.75
a.		As #127, perf. 13½ x 13¾ x 13½ imperf.	21.50	21.50
128	A24	50c multicolored	10.00	10.00
a.		As #128, perf. 13½x imperf. x 13½ x 13¾	30.00	30.00
b.		Souvenir sheet, #127a, 128a	55.00	55.00

Souvenir Sheet
Perf. 13½x13¾
128C	A24	Sheet of 2, #d-e	42.50	42.50

A25

Europa Stamps, 50th Anniv. A26

No. 129: a, Montenegro #100, common vignette of 1960 Europa stamps. b, Montenegro #101, common vignette of 1961-62 Europa stamps. c, Montenegro #102, bee and honeycomb. d, Montenegro #105, common vignette of 1956 Europa stamps.
No. 129E: f, Like #129a. g, Like #129b. h, Like #129c. i, Like #129d.

2006, Jan. 3   **Litho.**   **Perf. 13½x13¾**

Stamps with Frames
129		Horiz. strip of 4	17.00	17.00
a.		A25 50c multi	1.25	1.25
b.		A25 €1 multi	2.75	2.75
c.-d.		A25 €2 Either single	5.25	5.25

Souvenir Sheet
Stamps Without Frames
129E	A25	Sheet of 4, #f-i	26.00	26.00

Litho. with Foil Application
Imperf
Size: 103x76mm
130	A26	€5.50 multi	19.00	19.00

No. 129E exists imperf. Value, $65.

2006 Winter Olympics, Turin — A27

Designs: 60c, Figure skating. 90c, Ski jumping.

2006, Feb. 7   **Litho.**   **Perf. 13½x13¾**
131-132	A27	Set of 2	4.25	4.25

Flowers — A28

Designs: 25c, Petteria ramentacea. 50c, Viola nikolai.

2006, Mar. 15
133-134	A28	Set of 2	3.00	3.00

Introduction of Perper Currency, Cent. — A29

Central Bank of Montenegro and: 40c, 1906 1-para coin. 50c, 1906 20-para coin.

2006, Apr. 27   **Litho.**   **Perf. 13½x13¾**
135-136	A29	Set of 2	3.00	3.00

2006 World Cup Soccer Championships, Germany — A30

Designs: No. 137, 60c, Players in match. No. 138, 90c, Players in match, diff.
No. 139: a, 60c, Players, empty stadium in background. b, 90c, Players, empty stadium in background, diff.

2006, May 30   **Perf. 13¾x13½**
137-138	A30	Set of 2	5.25	5.25

Souvenir Sheet
139	A30	Sheet of 2, #a-b	5.00	5.00

National Symbols Type of 2005 Redrawn With "Posta Crne Gore" Under Postal Emblem

Designs as before.

2006, June   **Litho.**   **Perf. 13¾**
140	A23	25c multi	1.00	1.00
a.		Perf. 13	3.50	3.50
141	A23	40c multi	1.50	1.50
a.		Perf. 13	5.50	5.50
142	A23	60c multi	2.50	2.50
		Nos. 140-142 (3)	5.00	5.00

Nos. 140a and 141a are dated "2005," while Nos. 140-142 are dated "2006."

Independent Republic

Tourism — A31

Designs: 25c, Durmitor. 50c, Sveti Stefan.

2006, July 5   **Perf. 13½x13¾**
143-144	A31	Set of 2	2.75	2.75

Independence Referendum of May 21 — A32

2006, July 13
145	A32	50c multi	2.00	2.00

Europa — A33

Designs: No. 146, 60c, Women linking chain. No. 147, 90c, People and sun, horiz.
No. 148: a, 60c, Man with suitcase. b, 90c, People of different races.

2006, Aug. 30   **Perf. 13¾**
146-147	A33	Set of 2	5.25	5.25

Souvenir Sheet
148	A33	Sheet of 2, #a-b	5.00	5.00

Capt. Ivo Visin (1806-68), Circumnavigator, and Ship, Splendido — A34

2006, Sept. 5   **Perf. 13½x13¾**
149	A34	40c multi	1.75	1.75

Stamp Day — A35

2006, Oct. 2   **Perf. 13¾**
150	A35	25c multi	1.10	1.10

Mona Lisa, by Leonardo da Vinci, 500th Anniv. — A36

2006, Oct. 18   **Perf. 13¾x13½**
151	A36	50c multi	2.25	2.25

Cultural Heritage — A37

Designs: No. 152, 25c, Ruins, Dukla Archaeological Site. No. 153, 25c, Glassware.

2006, Nov. 3   **Perf. 13¾x13½**
152-153	A37	Set of 2	2.25	2.25

Tara River — A38

2006, Nov. 15   **Litho.**
154	A38	40c multi	1.75	1.75

Gregorian Calendar, 425th Anniv. — A39

2007, Jan. 4   **Perf. 13¾x13**
155	A39	50c multi	2.00	2.00

Printed in sheets of 8 + label.

MONTENEGRO

Wildlife Protection — A40

2007, Feb. 7
156 A40 50c multi 2.00 2.00
Printed in sheets of 8 + label.

Europa — A41

Map of Montenegro and: Nos. 157, 159a, 60c, Montenegro Scouting emblem. Nos. 158, 159b, 90c, Tent and campfire.

2007, Apr. 20 Litho. Perf. 13¾
157 A41 60c multi 2.25 2.25
158 A41 90c multi 3.00 3.00
 a. Souvenir sheet, #157-158 5.50 5.50
Perf. 13¾ (Imperf. Between Stamps)
159 Sheet of 2 6.00 6.00
 a. A41 60c multi, 42x28mm 2.25 2.25
 b. A41 90c multi, 42x28mm 3.00 3.00

Nos. 157 and 158 were each printed in sheets of 8 + label. No. 159 was sold with but not attached to a booklet cover.

Birds — A42

No. 160: a, 25c, Gull. b, 50c, Eagle.

2007, May 11 Litho. Perf. 13¾
160 A42 Pair, #a-b 3.00 3.00

Migration of Montenegrins to Istria, 350th Anniv. — A43

2007, June 21 Perf. 13¾
161 A43 60c multi 2.10 2.10
Printed in sheets of 8 + label.

Postal History — A44

Glagolithic Text — A45

Mountains — A46

Stylized Butterfly — A47

2007, July 3
162 A44 25c multi .85 .85
163 A45 40c multi 1.30 1.30
164 A46 50c multi 1.60 1.60
165 A47 60c multi 2.00 2.00
 Nos. 162-165 (4) 5.75 5.75

Petar Lubarda (1907-74), Painter — A48

2007, July 27 Perf. 13¾
166 A48 40c multi 1.75 1.75

Ship — A49

2007, Aug. 1
167 A49 60c multi 2.10 2.10
Printed in sheets of 8 + label.

Joy of Europe — A50

2007, Oct. 2
168 A50 50c multi 1.90 1.90

Regional Telephone Service, Cent. — A51

Designs: 25c, Telephone dial. 50c, Telephone dial and red dots.

2007, Nov. 9 Litho. Perf. 13¾
169-170 A51 Set of 2 2.75 2.75

New Year's Day — A52

Designs: No. 171, 25c, Twisted ribbon. No. 172, 25c, Christmas ornament on tree branch. 50c, Wreath and bells. €1, Lit candle.

2007, Dec. 5 Perf. 14x13¾
171-174 A52 Set of 4 7.25 7.25

Stabilization and Association Agreement Between Montenegro and the European Union — A53

Jigsaw puzzle pieces with: 60c, Montenegro coat of arms and European Union ring of stars.

No. 176: a, 40c, Montenegro coat of arms. b, 50c, European Union ring of stars.

2008, Feb. 1 Litho. Perf. 13¾
175 A53 60c multi 2.50 2.50
Souvenir Sheet
176 A53 Sheet of 2, #a-b 3.50 3.50

Flowers — A54

Designs: 25c, Draba bertiscea. 40c, Edraianthus wettsteinii. 50c, Protoedriantus tarae. 60c, Dianthus nitidus.

2008, Feb. 20
177-180 A54 Set of 4 7.25 7.25
Nos. 177-180 each were printed in sheets of 5 + label.

2008 Summer Olympics, Beijing — A55

Stylized athletes, Beijing Olympics emblem and: 60c, Map of Montenegro. 90c, Montenegro coat of arms.

2008, Mar. 26
181-182 A55 Set of 2 5.25 5.25

Europa — A56

Designs: No. 183, 60c, Boy, envelope with stamp. No. 184, 90c, Girl, letter.
No. 185: a, 60c, Boy, right half of envelope. b, 90c, Girl, left half of envelope.

2008, Apr. 2
183-184 A56 Set of 2 5.25 5.25
Souvenir Sheet
185 A56 Sheet of 2, #a-b 6.00 6.00
Nos. 183-184 each were printed in sheets of 8 + label.

Marko Miljanov (1833-1901), Writer — A57

2008, Apr. 24
186 A57 60c multi 2.25 2.25

Battle of Grahovac, 150th Anniv. — A58

2008, Apr. 29
187 A58 25c multi 1.10 1.10

Tourism — A59

Designs: 25c, Hillside hut. 40c, Fortress. 50c, Pier and boats. 60c, Boat on lake.

2008, May 21
188-191 A59 Set of 4 6.00 6.00
191a Sheet of 4, #188-191 6.00 6.00

Chess Olympics, Dresden, Germany — A60

2008, June 18 Litho. Perf. 13¾
192 A60 60c multi 2.50 2.50

Ship Jadran, 75th Anniv. — A61

2008, July 16
193 A61 50c multi 2.00 2.00

Victory of Montenegrin Team at European Water Polo Championships, Malaga, Spain — A62

2008, Sept. 15
194 A62 50c multi 2.40 2.40
Printed in sheets of 8 + label.

Roman Art — A63

No. 195: a, 25c, Frieze depicting faces. 50c, Mosaic depicting angel.

2008, Sept. 17
195 A63 Horiz. pair, #a-b 3.00 3.00

Stamp Day — A64

2008, Oct. 2
196 A64 60c multi 2.60 2.60

Automobile A65

Hourglass, Map of Montenegro A66

Eagle and Angel — A67

2008, Oct. 20 Perf. 13¾x13¼
197 A65 40c multi 1.90 1.90
198 A66 50c multi 2.00 2.00
199 A67 60c multi 2.75 2.75
 Nos. 197-199 (3) 6.65 6.65

MONTENEGRO

Alfred Nobel (1833-96), Inventor and Philanthropist — A68

2008, Oct. 21 — *Perf. 13¾*
200 A68 50c multi 2.25 2.25

A69
A70
A71
A72
A73

First Railway in Montenegro, Cent. — A74

2008, Nov. 2
201 A69 25c multi 1.10 1.10
202 A70 25c multi 1.10 1.10
203 A71 25c multi 1.10 1.10
204 A72 25c multi 1.10 1.10
205 A73 25c multi 1.10 1.10
206 A74 25c multi 1.10 1.10
  a. Souvenir sheet of 6, #201-206 6.75 6.75
    Nos. 201-206 (6) 6.60 6.60

Nos. 201-206 each were printed in sheets of 5 + label.

Joy of Europe — A75

Designs: 25c, Shown. 40c, Towers and bridge, horiz.

2008, Nov. 20
207-208 A75 Set of 2 3.00 3.00

Nos. 207-208 each were printed in sheets of 8 + label.

Universal Declaration of Human Rights, 60th Anniv. — A76

2008, Dec. 11 — *Perf. 13¾*
209 A76 50c multi 2.50 2.50

Printed in sheets of 8 + label.

Louis Braille (1809-52), Educator of the Blind — A77

2009, Jan. 30
210 A77 60c multi 2.50 2.50

Kotor Churches Honoring St. Tryphon, 1200th Anniv. — A78

No. 211 — St. Tryphon and denomination in: a, Black. b, White.

2009, Feb. 3 — *Perf. 14*
211 A78 50c Horiz. pair, #a-b 4.00 4.00

First Theatrical Performance in Niksic, 125th Anniv. — A79

Vita Nikolic (1934-94), Poet — A80

Zetski Dom Theater, Cetinje, 125th Anniv. — A81

Crnojevic Monastery, 525th Anniv. — A82

2009 — *Litho.* — *Perf. 13¾*
212 A79 25c multi 1.15 1.15
213 A80 40c multi 1.60 1.60
214 A81 50c multi 1.90 1.90
215 A82 60c multi 2.25 2.25
    Nos. 212-215 (4) 6.90 6.90

Arts through the ages. Issued: 25c, 2/16; others, 4/8.

Fish — A83

Designs: 25c, Alburnus scoranza. 40c, Thymallus thymallus. 50c, Salmothymus obtusirostris zetensis. 60c, Cyprinus carpio.

2009, Apr. 16
216-219 A83 Set of 4 7.00 7.00

Nos. 216-219 each were printed in sheets of 5 + label.

Europa — A84

Designs: No. 220, 60c, Boy and girl looking at celestial objects. No. 221, 90c, Boy looking through telescope. No. 222, vert.: a, 60c, Planets and constellations. b, 90c, Comet, asteroids and constellations.

2009, Apr. 16
220-221 A84 Set of 2 4.50 4.50
Souvenir Sheet
222 A84 Sheet of 2, #a-b 5.50 5.50

Intl. Year of Astronomy.

Tourism — A85

Designs: 25c, Water skiing. 40c, Rock climbing in Nevidio Canyon. 50c, Paragliding. 60c, Rafting on the Tara River.

2009, Apr. 16
223-226 A85 Set of 4 6.50 6.50
226a   Souvenir sheet of 4, #223-226 6.50 6.50

Nos. 223-226 each were printed in sheets of 5 + label.

25th Universiade, Belgrade — A86

2009, June 4 — *Perf. 13¾*
227 A86 50c multi 2.00 2.00

Printed in sheets of 8 + label.

Prince Vasilije Petrovic-Njegos (1709-66), Bishop — A87

2009, June 4 — *Perf. 13¾x13*
228 A87 40c multi 1.50 1.50

Vicko Bujovic (1660-1709), Military Leader, and Ship — A88

2009, July 10 — *Perf. 13¾*
229 A88 60c multi 2.25 2.25

Printed in sheets of 8 + label.

Nature Protection — A89

Bandaged plants and: 25c, Lake Plav. 50c, Lake Crno.

2009, July 10 — *Litho.*
230-231 A89 Set of 2 2.75 2.75

Nos. 230-231 each were printed in sheets of 8 + label.

Stamp Day — A90

2009, Oct. 2 — *Perf. 13x13¾*
232 A90 25c multi 1.00 1.00

Joy of Europe — A91

Children's art with: 40c, Dialogue balloon. 50c, Thought balloon.

2009, Nov. 20 — *Perf. 13¾*
233-234 A91 Set of 2 3.25 3.25

Nos. 233-234 each were printed in sheets of 8 + label.

Valtazar Bogisic (1834-1908), Jurist — A92

2009, Dec. 7 — *Perf. 13x13¾*
235 A92 50c multi 1.75 1.75

700-Year-Old Historical Document in Kotor Archives — A93

2009, Dec. 20 — *Perf. 13¾x13*
236 A93 25c multi 1.00 1.00

Dado Duric (1933-2010), Painter A94

St. Elias, Fresco in Moraca Monastery A95

2010, Jan. 28 — *Perf. 13x13¾*
237 A94 50c multi 1.25 1.25
238 A95 50c multi 1.25 1.25

2010 Winter Olympics, Vancouver A96

Designs: €1, Speed skater. €1.50, Snowboarder.

2010, Feb. 12 — *Perf. 13¾*
239-240 A96 Set of 2 7.25 7.25

Nos. 239-240 each were printed in sheets of 8 + label.

Danilo Kis (1935-89), Writer — A97

2010, Feb. 22 — *Perf. 13¾x13*
241 A97 50c multi 1.60 1.60

MONTENEGRO

Flora — A98

Designs: 25c, Salvia officinalis. 50c, Satureja subspicata. 60c, Tilia tomentosa. €1, Epilobium angustifolium.

2010, Mar. 18   Litho.
242-245   A98   Set of 4   7.75   7.75
Nos. 242-245 each were printed in sheets of 5 + label.

Europa — A99

Stack of books and: No. 246, 60c, Girl, butterfly, castle, rainbow. No. 247, 90c, Boy, car, star, rope ladder.
No. 248: a, 60c, Books, fairy, crown, dress. b, 90c, Books, ship, ladder.

2010, Apr. 22   Perf. 13¾
246-247   A99   Set of 2   4.75   4.75
Souvenir Sheet
248   A99   Sheet of 2, #a-b   4.75   4.75

St. Basil of Ostrog (1610-71) — A100

2010, May 12   Perf. 13x13¾
249   A100   50c multi   1.60   1.60

2010 World Cup Soccer Tournament, South Africa — A101

2010, June 11   Perf. 13¾
250   A101   €1.50 multi   4.25   4.25
Printed in sheets of 8 + label.

Tourism — A102

Designs: 25c, Canoe and trees. 50c, Mountains. 60c, Waterside straw hut. €1, Beach.

2010, June 24   Litho.
251-254   A102   Set of 4   7.00   7.00
254a   Souvenir sheet of 4, #251-254   7.00   7.00
Nos. 251-254 each were printed in sheets of 5 + label.

Ship — A103

2010, July 8
255   A103   25c multi   .90   .90
Printed in sheets of 8 + label.

Balsic Dynasty, 650th Anniv. — A104

2010, July 15
256   A104   25c multi   .90   .90

First Electric Power Network in Montenegro, Cent. — A105

2010, Aug. 19
257   A105   25c multi   .90   .90

Kingdom of Montenegro, Cent. — A106

2010, Aug. 28
258   A106   50c multi   1.60   1.60

Bozidar Vukovic (c. 1466-c. 1540), Printer — A107

2010, Sept. 16   Litho.
259   A107   50c multi   1.60   1.60

Stamp Day — A108

2010, Oct. 2   Perf. 13¾x13
260   A108   30c multi   1.10   1.10

Joy of Europe — A109

2010, Oct. 21   Perf. 13¾
261   A109   90c multi   2.75   2.75
Printed in sheets of 8 + label.

Pasha Husein Mosque, Pljevlja A110

Ivan Mazuranic (1814-90), Poet A111

Reverse of Roman Reduced Sestertius Found in Duklja (Podgorica) A112

Miroslav Gospels A113

Perf. 13¾x13, 13x13¾
2010, Nov. 12
262   A110   30c multi   1.00   1.00
263   A111   40c multi   1.25   1.25
264   A112   80c multi   2.50   2.50
265   A113   90c multi   2.75   2.75
Nos. 262-265 (4)   6.70   6.70
Art through the ages.

Nature Protection — A114

Umbrella over: 30c, Waterfall. 40c, Mountains.

2010, Dec. 16   Perf. 13¾x13
266-267   A114   Set of 2   2.25   2.25

Painting by Vojo Stanic A115

Jovan Ivanisevic (1860-89), Composer A116

2011, Jan. 31   Litho.   Perf. 13
268   A115   30c multi   .85   .85
269   A116   40c multi   1.15   1.15

Tripo Kokolja (1661-1713), Painter — A117

2011, Feb. 22
270   A117   30c multi   .95   .95

Vuk Vrcevic (1811-82), Poetry Translator — A118

2011, Feb. 26
271   A118   30c multi   .95   .95

Fauna — A119

Map of Montenegro and: No. 272, 30c, Pina nobilis. No. 273, 30c, Triturus alpestris montenegrinus. 40c, Pelecanus crispus. 90c, Phalacrocorax pygmaeus.

2011, Mar. 17
272-275   A119   Set of 4   5.50   5.50

Europa — A120

Designs: No. 276, 90c, "EU" in foliage. No. 277, 90c, Map of Europe with leaf veins, white background.
No. 278, 90c, vert.: a, "EU" in foliage. b, Map of Europe with leaf veins, green background.

2011, Apr. 21   Perf. 13¼x13
276-277   A120   Set of 2   5.00   5.00
Souvenir Sheet
Perf. 13x13¼
278   A120   90c Sheet of 2, #a-b   5.00   5.00
Intl. Year of Forests.

Tourism — A121

Designs: No. 279, 30c, Mountains and valley, "Turizam" at left. No. 280, 30c, Mountains and lake, "Turizam" at right. 40c, Mountains and valley, diff. 90c, Beach.

2011, May 12   Perf. 13
279-282   A121   Set of 4   5.00   5.00
282a   Sheet of 4, #279-282   5.00   5.00
No. 282a was sold with a booklet cover but was not attached to it.

Environmental Protection — A122

Butterfly, flowers and: 30c, House, oscilloscope wave pattern. 40c, Smiling face.

2011, May 21
283-284   A122   Set of 2   2.25   2.25

Kazansky Cathedral, St. Petersburg, Russia — A123

Russian Diplomatic Mission, Cetinje — A124

2011, May 26   Perf. 13¼x13
285   A123   30c multi   1.00   1.00
286   A124   30c multi   1.00   1.00
   a.   Horiz. pair, #285-286   2.25   2.25
Nos. 285-286 each were printed in sheets of 8 + label. See Russia No. 7272.

Games of Small European States, Liechtenstein A125

Designs: 30c, Volleyball. 90c, Tennis ball.

2011, June 9
287-288   A125   Set of 2   3.50   3.50
Nos. 287-288 each were printed in sheets of 8 + label.

Belvedere Demonstrations, 75th Anniv. — A126

2011, June 25   Perf. 13
289   A126   30c multi   1.00   1.00

Ship "Brindisi" A127

2011, July 7   Perf. 13¼x13
290   A127   40c multi   1.40   1.40
Printed in sheets of 8 + label.

MONTENEGRO

Concordat Between Montenegro and Vatican City, 125th Anniv. — A128

2011, Oct. 7 — Perf. 13
291 A128 30c multi .95 .95

Joy of Europe — A129

2011, Oct. 21 — Perf. 13¼x13
292 A129 90c multi 2.75 2.75
Printed in sheets of 8 + label.

Fresco of King Michael A130
Crnogorac, First Montenegrin Newspaper A131
Zabljak Crnojevica Fortified Town — A132
Josip Slade (1828-1911), Architect — A133

2011, Nov. 11 — Perf. 13
293 A130 30c multi .90 .90
294 A131 40c multi 1.25 1.25
295 A132 50c multi 1.50 1.50
296 A133 90c multi 2.50 2.50
Nos. 293-296 (4) 6.15 6.15

Stamp Day — A134

2011, Dec. 15 — Litho.
297 A134 40c multi 1.40 1.40

Sculptures by Risto Stijovic (1894-1974) A135
Montenegrin Man, by Ilija Sobajic (1876-1953) A136
Painting by Nikola Vujosevic A137
Montenegrin Army Musicians A138

2012, Jan. 27 — Perf. 13
298 A135 30c multi .80 .80
299 A136 40c multi 1.10 1.10
300 A137 80c multi 2.00 2.00
301 A138 95c multi 2.50 2.50
Nos. 298-301 (4) 6.40 6.40

Ilovik Nomocanon, 750th Anniv. — A139

2012, Feb. 23 — Perf. 13
302 A139 30c multi .95 .95

Enthronement of Durad Balsic as Lord of Zeta, 650th Anniv. — A140

2012, Feb. 27
303 A140 30c multi .95 .95

Flora — A141

Designs: 30c, Nettles (kopriva). 90c, Vranac grapes (vinova loza).

2012, Mar. 16
304-305 A141 Set of 2 3.50 3.50
Nos. 304-305 each were printed in sheets of 5 + label.

Matija Zmajevic (1680-1735), Russian Admiral — A142

2012, May 10
306 A142 30c multi .95 .95

Tourism — A143

Designs: No. 307, 30c, Directional arrows on pole. No. 308, 30c, Ship, sun, town names. 80c, Suitcase with blue handle decorated with travel symbols. 95c, Suitcase with red handle decorated with travel symbols.

2012, May 14
307-310 A143 Set of 4 6.25 6.25
310a Souvenir sheet of 4, #307-310 6.75 6.75
No. 310a was sold with, but unattached to, a booklet cover.

Environmental Protection — A144

Life preserver on: 30c, Duck. 95c, Frog.

2012, May 21 — Litho. Perf. 13
311-312 A144 Set of 2 3.25 3.25

2012 Summer Olympics, London — A145

Designs: 90c, Rhythmic gymnastics. 95c, Discus thrower.

2012, June 8 — Litho. Perf. 13¼x13
313-314 A145 Set of 2 5.00 5.00
314a Souvenir sheet of 2, #313-314 5.00 5.00
Nos. 313-314 each were printed in sheets of 8 + central label.

Battle of Carev Laz, 300th Anniv. — A146

2012, June 25 — Perf. 13
315 A146 30c multi .85 .85

Accession Negotiations with the European Union — A147

2012, June 29
316 A147 95c multi 2.50 2.50

Lighthouses — A148

Designs: No. 317, 30c, Verige Lighthouse. No. 318, 30c, Volujica Lighthouse.

2012, July 6 — Perf. 13x13¼
317-318 A148 Set of 2 1.90 1.90
Nos. 317-318 each were printed in sheets of 8 + central label.

2012 European Championship of ZRK Buducnost Women's Handball Team — A149

2012, July 27 — Litho.
319 A149 30c multi .85 .85
No. 319 was printed in sheets of 8 + central label.

Fixing of Montenegrin Boundaries, 175th Anniv. — A150

2012, Oct. 10 — Perf. 13
320 A150 30c multi .85 .85

Europa — A151

Leaves and: 80c, River gorge. 95c, Sveti Stefan.

2012, Oct. 17 — Perf. 13¼x13
321-322 A151 Set of 2 4.50 4.50
322a Souvenir sheet of 2, #321-322 4.50 4.50
Nos. 321-322 each were printed in sheets of 8 + central label.

Joy of Europe — A152

2012, Oct. 22 — Perf. 13x13¼
323 A152 90c multi 2.25 2.25
No. 323 was printed in sheets of 8 + central label.

Art in Piva Monastery A153
Hieromonk Makarije Printing Works A154
Legend of Pava and Ahmet A155
Battle of Tudjemila A156

2012, Nov. 12 — Perf. 13
324 A153 30c multi .75 .75
325 A154 30c multi .75 .75
326 A155 40c multi 1.10 1.10
327 A156 95c multi 2.50 2.50
Nos. 324-327 (4) 5.10 5.10

Stamp Day — A157

2012, Dec. 14
328 A157 30c multi .80 .80

Success of Montenegro Women's Handball Team — A158

Women's handball team, flag of Montenegro, and: No. 329, 30c, Gold medal from 2012 European championships. No. 330, 30c, Silver medal from 2012 Olympics.

2012, Dec. 28 — Litho. Perf. 13¼x13
329-330 A158 Set of 2 1.60 1.60
Nos. 329-330 each were printed in sheets of 8 + central label.

Camil Sijaric (1913-89), Writer A160
Pero Pocek (1878-1963), Painter A161
Traditional Folk Costume A162
Our Lady of Philerme Icon A163

2013, Jan. 31 — Litho. Perf. 13
331 A160 30c multi .85 .85
332 A161 40c multi 1.10 1.10
333 A162 80c multi 2.25 2.25
334 A163 95c multi 2.60 2.60
Nos. 331-334 (4) 6.80 6.80

MONTENEGRO

Prince Petar II Petrovic-Njegos (1813-51) — A164

2013, Feb. 22　Litho.　Perf. 13x13¼
335　A164　30c multi　.85　.85
No. 335 was printed in sheets of 8 + central label.

Union of Montenegro and Kotor Bay, 200th Anniv. — A165

2013, Feb. 27　Litho.　Perf. 13
336　A165　30c multi　.85　.85

Flora and Fauna — A166

Map of Montenegro and: 80c, Parnassius apollo. 95c, Scabiosa ochroleuca.

2013, Mar. 15　Litho.　Perf. 13
337-338　A166　Set of 2　4.75　4.75

Europa — A167

2013, Apr. 19　Litho.　Perf. 13x13¼
339　A167　95c multi　20.00　20.00
No. 339 was printed in sheets of 8 + central label.

Valtazar Bogisic (1834-1908), Writer of Montenegro's General Property Code — A168

2013, May 10　Litho.　Perf. 13
340　A168　30c multi　.85　.85

Tourism — A169

Designs: 30c, Two hikers. 40c, Cyclist raising bicycle.

2013, May 14　Litho.　Perf. 13
341-342　A169　Set of 2　2.00　2.00
342a　Souvenir sheet of 2, #341-342　2.00　2.00

Stara Maslina, Old Olive Tree, Stari Bar — A170

2013, May 23　Litho.　Perf. 13¼x13
343　A170　30c multi　.85　.85
No. 343 was printed in sheets of 8 + central label.

Sports — A171

Designs: 80c, Basketball. 95c, "100", emblem of Lovcen soccer team, soccer ball.

2013, June 7　Litho.　Perf. 13
344-345　A171　Set of 2　4.75　4.75
345a　Souvenir sheet of 2, #344-345　4.75　4.75
Participation of Montenegrin team in 2013 Euro Basket tournament, Slovenia (No. 344); Lovcen soccer team, cent. (No. 345).

Edict of Milan, 1700th Anniv. — A172

2013, June 21　Litho.　Perf. 13
346　A172　30c multi　.85　.85

Marko Martinovic (1663-1716), Teacher of Naval Navigation A173

2013, June 28　Litho.　Perf. 13¼x13
347　A173　30c multi　.85　.85
No. 347 was printed in sheets of 8 + central label.

First Airplane Flight in Montenegro, Cent. — A174

2013, Sept. 5　Litho.　Perf. 13
348　A174　30c multi　.85　.85

Ljubo Cupic (1913-42), Communist Prisoner Executed by Chetniks — A175

2013, Oct. 8　Litho.　Perf. 13
349　A175　30c multi　.85　.85

Joy of Europe — A176

2013, Oct. 22　Litho.　Perf. 13¼x13
350　A176　95c multi　2.75　2.75
No. 350 was printed in sheets of 8 + central label.

Princess Elena of Montenegro (1873-1952) A177

Map of Stari Bar A178

2013, Nov. 12　Litho.　Perf. 13
351　A177　30c multi　.85　.85
352　A178　40c multi　1.10　1.10

Stamp Day — A179

2013, Dec. 15　Litho.　Perf. 13
353　A179　30c multi　.85　.85

Dobrota Lace A180

Medieval Tombstones A181

2014, Jan. 31　Litho.　Perf. 13
354　A180　30c multi　.80　.80
355　A181　95c multi　2.60　2.60

2014 Winter Olympics, Sochi, Russia — A182

2014, Feb. 17　Litho.　Perf. 13¼x13
356　A182　95c multi　2.75　2.75
No. 356 was printed in sheets of 8 + central label.

Archbishopric of Bar, 925th Anniv. — A183

2014, Feb. 27　Litho.　Perf. 13
357　A183　30c multi　.85　.85

Edraianthus Wetstainii Ssp. Lovcenicus A184

Hypholoma Fasciculare A185

2014, Mar. 14　Litho.　Perf. 13
358　A184　30c multi　.85　.85
359　A185　95c multi　2.60　2.60

Gusle — A186

2014, Apr. 18　Litho.　Perf. 13x13¼
360　A186　95c multi　2.75　2.75
a.　Souvenir sheet of 1　2.75　2.75
Europa. No. 360 was printed in sheets of 8 + central label.

Church, Grahovac, 150th Anniv. — A187

2014, May 9　Litho.　Perf. 13
361　A187　30c multi　.85　.85

Tourism — A188

Designs: 30c, Porto Montenegro, Tivat. 40c, Mount Hajla.

2014, May 14　Litho.　Perf. 13
362-363　A188　Set of 2　1.90　1.90

Crna Poda Forest — A189

2014, May 23　Litho.　Perf. 13x13¼
364　A189　95c multi　2.60　2.60
No. 364 was printed in sheets of 8 + central label.

2014 World Cup Soccer Championships, Brazil — A190

2014, June 9　Litho.　Perf. 13
365　A190　95c multi　2.60　2.60
a.　Souvenir sheet of 1　2.60　2.60

Podgorica Telegraph Station, Cent. — A191

2014, June 20　Litho.　Perf. 13
366　A191　30c multi　.85　.85

Reburial of King Nicholas I and Queen Milena in Montenegro, 25th Anniv. — A192

2014, June 27　Litho.　Perf. 13¼x13
367　A192　30c multi　.85　.85
No. 367 was printed in sheets of 8 + central label.

Lokanda Hotel, Cetinje, 150th Anniv. — A193

2014, Sept. 5　Litho.　Perf. 13
368　A193　30c multi　.85　.85

Mihailo Lalic (1914-92), Writer — A194

2014, Oct. 8　Litho.　Perf. 13
369　A194　30c multi　.85　.85

MONTENEGRO

Joy of Europe — A195

2014, Oct. 22   Litho.   Perf. 13x13¼
370   A195   95c multi   2.60   2.60
No. 370 was printed in sheets of 8 + central label.

Anastas Bocaric (1864-1944), Painter — A196

2014, Nov. 12   Litho.   Perf. 13
371   A196   30c multi   .85   .85

Orlov Krs Mausoleum — A197

2014, Nov. 12   Litho.   Perf. 13
372   A197   80c multi   2.10   2.10

Svac Archaeological Site — A198

2014, Nov. 12   Litho.   Perf. 13
373   A198   95c multi   2.50   2.50

Danilovgrad Library, 125th Anniv. — A199

2014, Nov. 17   Litho.   Perf. 13
374   A199   30c multi   .85   .85

Kotor High School, 150th Anniv. — A200

2014, Nov. 20   Litho.   Perf. 13
375   A200   30c multi   .85   .85

Stamp Day — A201

2014, Dec. 15   Litho.   Perf. 13
376   A201   30c multi   .85   .85
First female postal official, cent.

National Art Museum, Cetinje — A202

2015, Feb. 5   Litho.   Perf. 13¼x13¾
377   A202   30c multi   .80   .80

Jeweled Buckle — A203

2015, Feb. 5   Litho.   Perf. 13¼x13¾
378   A203   40c multi   1.00   1.00

Ostrog Monastery, 350th Anniv. — A204

Perf. 13¾x13¼
2015, Feb. 19   Litho.
379   A204   30c multi   .80   .80

Phoenicopterus Roseus — A205

Perf. 13¼x13¾
2015, Mar. 12   Litho.
380   A205   95c multi   2.40   2.40

Europa — A206

2015, Apr. 16   Litho.   Perf. 13¾
381   A206   95c multi   2.40   2.40
 a.   Souvenir sheet of 1   2.40   2.40
No. 381 was printed in sheets of 8 + central label.

First Written Mention of Cetinje, 575th Anniv. — A207

2015, May 5   Litho.   Perf. 13¼x13¾
382   A207   30c multi   .80   .80

Kitesurfing — A208

2015, May 8   Litho.   Perf. 13¾
383   A208   95c multi   2.40   2.40
No. 383 was printed in sheets of 8 + central label.

Pinus Heldreichii — A209

2015, May 13   Litho.   Perf. 13¾
384   A209   95c multi   2.40   2.40
No. 384 was printed in sheets of 8 + central label.

2015 European Basketball Championships — A210

2015, May 22   Litho.   Perf. 13¼x13¾
385   A210   95c multi   2.40   2.40
 a.   Souvenir sheet of 1   2.40   2.40

Joy of Europe — A211

2015, Oct. 22   Litho.   Perf. 13x13¾
386   A211   95c multi   2.40   2.40

Bar, Montenegro - Bari, Italy Ferry, 50th Anniv. — A212

2015, Oct. 30   Litho.   Perf. 13¾
387   A212   30c multi   .80   .80
No. 387 was printed in sheets of 8 + label.

St. George Monastery, Berane — A213

Ruins, Soko Grad — A214

Perf. 13¼x13¾
2015, Nov. 11   Litho.
388   A213   30c multi   .75   .75
389   A214   95c multi   2.25   2.25

Stamp Day — A215

Perf. 13¾x13¼
2015, Dec. 15   Litho.
390   A215   95c multi   2.40   2.40

Restoration of the Montenegrin Orthodox Church, 25th Anniv. — A216

Perf. 13¾x13¼
2015, Dec. 28   Litho.
391   A216   30c multi   .80   .80

Girl's Cap — A217

Muslim Woman's Cap — A218

2016, Jan. 29   Litho.   Perf. 13x13¾
392   A217   30c multi   .65   .65
393   A218   40c multi   .90   .90

Battle of Mojkovac, Cent. — A219

2016, Feb. 9   Litho.   Perf. 13¼x13¾
394   A219   30c multi   .65   .65

Medovske Disaster, Cent. — A220

2016, Feb. 27   Litho.   Perf. 13¼x13¾
395   A220   30c multi   .65   .65

Gentiana Kochiana — A221

2016, Apr. 19   Litho.   Perf. 13¾
396   A221   95c multi   2.25   2.25
No. 396 was printed in sheets of 8 + central label.

"Reduce Your Carbon Footprint" — A222

2016, Apr. 22   Litho.   Perf. 13x13¾
397   A222   95c multi   2.25   2.25

Europa — A223

2016, May 9   Litho.   Perf. 13¾
398   A223   95c multi   2.25   2.25
 a.   Souvenir sheet of 1   2.25   2.25
Think Green Issue.
No. 398 was printed in sheets of 8 + central label.

Roman Mosaic of Hypnos — A224

2016, May 17   Litho.   Perf. 13x13¾
399   A224   30c multi   .70   .70
Tourism.

Independence, 10th Anniv. — A225

2016, May 21   Litho.   Perf. 13¾
400   A225   €1 multi   2.25   2.25
No. 400 was printed in sheets of 8 + central label.

Ali Pasha Springs — A226

2016, May 27   Litho.   Perf. 13¾
401   A226   95c multi   2.10   2.10
Environmental Protection.
No. 401 was printed in sheets of 8 + central label.

2016 Summer Olympics, Rio de Janeiro — A227

2016, June 9   Litho.   Perf. 13¾
402   A227   95c multi   2.10   2.10
 a.   Souvenir sheet of 1   2.10   2.10
No. 402 was printed in sheets of 8 + central label.

MONTENEGRO

Cathedral of St. Tryphon, Kotor, 850th Anniv. — A228

2016, June 19 Litho. *Perf. 13¾x13*
403 A228 95c multi   2.10 2.10

Diplomatic Relations Between Montenegro and People's Republic of China, 10th Anniv. — A229

2016, July 7 Litho. *Perf. 13¾*
404 A229 40c multi   .90   .90
  No. 404 was printed in sheets of 8 + central label.

July 13th Uprising, 75th Anniv. — A230

2016, July 12 Litho. *Perf. 13¾x13*
405 A230 30c multi   .70   .70

Joy of Europe — A231

2016, Oct. 5 Litho. *Perf. 13¼x13¾*
406 A231 95c multi   2.10 2.10

Marine Navigation School, Perast — A232

2016, Oct. 21 Litho. *Perf. 13¾*
407 A232 30c multi   .70   .70

Flint and Striker A233

Prince Jovan Vladimir of Duklja (c. 990-1016), and Wife, Theodora Kosara A234

2016, Nov. 10 Litho. *Perf. 13x13¾*
408 A233 30c multi   .65   .65
  Perf. 13¾x13
409 A234 95c multi   2.10 2.10

Dejan Zlaticanin, World Boxing Council Lightweight Champion A235

2016, Dec. 8 Litho. *Perf. 14*
410 A235 50c multi   1.10 1.10
  No. 410 was printed in sheets of 8 + central label.

Stamp Day — A236

2016, Dec. 15 Litho. *Perf. 13¾x13*
411 A236 30c multi   .65   .65
  PTT Museum.

Windows From Drago Palace, Kotor — A237

Cap of Boka Navy — A238

2017, Feb. 15 Litho. *Perf. 13*
412 A237 30c multi   .65   .65
413 A238 40c multi   .85   .85

Platalea Leucorodia — A239

2017, Mar. 30 Litho. *Perf. 13x13¼*
414 A239 95c multi   2.10 2.10
  No. 414 was printed in sheets of 8 + central label.

King Nikola's Palace, Cetinje — A240

2017, May 9 Litho. *Perf. 13¼x13*
415 A240 95c multi   2.10 2.10
  a. Souvenir sheet of 1   2.10 2.10
  Europa. No. 415 was printed in sheets of 8 + central label.

Rijeka Crnojevica — A241

2017, May 21 Litho. *Perf. 13*
416 A241 30c multi   .70   .70

Admittance of Montenegro to North Atlantic Treaty Organization A242

2017, June 5 Litho. *Perf. 13¼x13*
417 A242 €1 multi   2.40 2.40
  No. 417 was printed in sheets of 8 + central label.

Cijevna River Canyon — A243

2017, June 16 Litho. *Perf. 13¼x13*
418 A243 95c multi   2.25 2.25
  No. 418 was printed in sheets of 8 + central label.

2017 Under-23 European Judo Championships, Podgorica — A244

2017, July 5 Litho. *Perf. 13x13¼*
419 A244 €1 multi   2.40 2.40
  a. Souvenir sheet of 1   2.40 2.40
  No. 419 was printed in sheets of 8 + central label.

Joy of Europe — A245

2017, Oct. 31 Litho. *Perf. 13*
420 A245 30c multi   .70   .70

Mendra Lighthouse A246

2017, Nov. 10 Litho. *Perf. 13¼x13*
421 A246 95c multi   2.25 2.25
  No. 421 was printed in sheets of 8 + central label.

"The Mountain Wreath," Poem by Petar II Petrovic-Njegos A247

Constantine Bodin, Ruler of Dulja A248

2017, Nov. 29 Litho. *Perf. 13*
422 A247 40c multi   .95   .95
423 A248 50c multi   1.25 1.25
  Statehood of Montenegro, 1000th anniv. (No. 423).

Post Office — A249

2017, Dec. 15 Litho. *Perf. 13*
424 A249 30c multi   .75   .75
  Stamp Day.

Battle Cruiser Sankt Georg — A250

2018, Jan. 25 Litho. *Perf. 13¼x13*
425 A250 30c multi   .75   .75
  No. 425 was printed in sheets of 8 + central label.

Women's Blouse — A251

2018, Feb. 16 Litho. *Perf. 13*
426 A251 30c multi   .75   .75

Snowboarding — A252

2018, Mar. 1 Litho. *Perf. 13*
427 A252 40c multi   1.00 1.00

Sphaerocarpus Texanus — A253

Gentiana Lutea — A254

2018, Apr. 12 Litho. *Perf. 13*
428 A253 30c multi   .75   .75
429 A254 95c multi   2.25 2.25

Mostanica Bridge — A255

2018, May 9 Litho. *Perf. 13¼x13*
430 A255 95c multi   2.25 2.25
  a. Souvenir sheet of 1   2.25 2.25
  Europa. No. 430 was printed in sheets of 8 + central label.

Lake Zminje — A256

2018, May 31 Litho. *Perf. 13x13¼*
431 A256 50c multi   1.25 1.25

2018 Winter Olympics, Pyeongchang, South Korea — A257

2018, June 20 Litho. *Perf. 13¼x13*
432 A257 €1 multi   2.40 2.40
  a. Souvenir sheet of 1   2.40 2.40
  No. 432 was printed in sheets of 8 + central label.

Bijelo Polje House of Risto Ratkovic (1903-54), Writer — A258

Fourth Century Cage Cup — A259

2018, July 4 Litho. *Perf. 13*
433 A258 30c multi   .70   .70
434 A259 95c multi   2.25 2.25

Joy of Europe — A260

2018, Oct. 4 Litho. *Perf. 13*
435 A260 95c multi   2.25 2.25

MONTENEGRO

Self-portrait, by Mario Maskereli (1918-96) — A261

2018, Nov. 8	Litho.	Perf. 13
436	A261 30c multi	.70 .70

Montenegrin Anti-Fascist Assembly of People's Liberation and Boka Kotorska, 75th Anniv. — A262

2018, Nov. 28	Litho.	Perf. 13
437	A262 30c multi	.70 .70

Montenegro No. 28 — A263

2018, Dec. 15	Litho.	Perf. 13
438	A263 40c multi	.90 .90

1893 overprints on stamps of 1874-93, 125th anniv.

Mimosa Festival — A264

2019, Feb. 8	Litho.	Perf. 13¼x13
439	A264 50c multi	1.25 1.25

Painting by Mihailo Jovicevic — A265

2019, Mar. 1	Litho.	Perf. 13¼x13¾
440	A265 30c multi	.70 .70

Dinarolacerta Montenegrina — A266

2019, Apr. 12	Litho.	Perf. 13¾
441	A266 95c multi	2.10 2.10

Tetrao Urogallus — A267

2019, May 9	Litho.	Perf. 13¾
442	A267 95c multi	2.10 2.10
a.	Souvenir sheet of 1	2.10 2.10

Europa. No. 442 was printed in sheets of 8 + label.

Hussein Pasha Mosque, Pljevlja — A268

2019, May 16	Litho.	Perf. 13¾
443	A268 95c multi	2.10 2.10

2019 Games of Small States of Europe, Montenegro — A269

2019, May 27	Litho.	Perf. 13¾
444	A269 €1 multi	2.25 2.25

Lynx Lynx Martinoi A270

Lovcen National Park A271

2019, June 15	Perf. 13¾x13¼ Litho.	
445	A270 30c multi	.70 .70
	Perf. 13¼x13¾	
446	A271 95c multi	2.25 2.25

Nature protection.

Ulcinj — A274

2019, July 4	Litho.	Perf. 13x14
449	A274 40c multi	.90 .90

Joy of Europe — A275

2019, Oct. 4	Litho.	Perf. 13x14
450	A275 95c multi	2.10 2.10

Pobjeda Newspaper, 75th Anniv. — A276

2019, Oct. 24	Litho.	Perf. 14
451	A276 95c multi	2.10 2.10

No. 451 was printed in sheets of 8 + label.

Duke Gavro Vukovic (1852-1928), Politician and Writer — A277

2019, Nov. 4	Litho.	Perf. 14x13
452	A277 30c multi	.70 .70

No. 452 was printed in sheets of 8 + label.

Medun — A278

2019, Nov. 4	Litho.	Perf. 13x14
453	A278 40c multi	.90 .90

St. Nicholas Lighthouse — A279

2019, Nov. 28	Litho.	Perf. 14
454	A279 95c multi	2.10 2.10

No. 454 was printed in sheets of 8 + label.

Mohandas K. Gandhi (1869-1948), Indian Nationalist Leader — A280

2019, Nov. 29	Litho.	Perf. 13¾x13
455	A280 30c multi	.70 .70

Duke Simo Popovic (1846-1921), Politician and Designer of First Montenegro Stamp — A281

2019, Dec. 12	Litho.	Perf. 14x13
456	A281 30c multi	.70 .70

Stamp Day. No. 456 was printed in sheets of 8 + label.

Borislav Pekic (1930-92), Writer A282

Painting by Cvetko Lainovic (1931-2006) A283

2020, Feb. 26	Litho.	Perf. 13x14
457	A282 30c multi	.70 .70
458	A283 40c multi	.90 .90

Geastrum Berkeleyi — A284

2020, Mar. 16	Litho.	Perf. 13¾
459	A284 95c multi	2.10 2.10

No. 459 was printed in sheets of 8 + label.

Cedo Vukovic (1920-2014), Writer — A285

2020, Apr. 15	Litho.	Perf. 13x14
460	A285 30c multi	.65 .65

Cursus Publicus Horse-drawn Wagon — A286

2020, May 9	Litho.	Perf. 13¾
461	A286 95c multi	2.10 2.10
a.	Souvenir sheet of 1	2.10 2.10

No. 461 was printed in sheets of 8 + label.

Biogradska Gora National Park — A287

2020, May 27	Litho.	Perf. 13x14
462	A287 50c multi	1.10 1.10

Church of Our Lady of the Rocks — A288

2020, July 6	Litho.	Perf. 13
463	A288 30c multi	.70 .70

Joy of Europe — A289

2020, Oct. 5	Litho.	Perf. 13
464	A289 95c multi	2.25 2.25

United Nations, 75th Anniv. — A290

2020, Oct. 24	Litho.	Perf. 13
465	A290 30c multi	.70 .70

Princess Xenia (1881-1960) A291

2020, Nov. 17	Litho.	Perf. 13
466	A291 30c multi	.75 .75

Dowry Chest — A292

2020, Nov. 17	Litho.	Perf. 13
467	A292 40c multi	.95 .95

Sextant — A293

2020, Nov. 30	Litho.	Perf. 13¼x13
468	A293 95c multi	2.25 2.25

No. 468 was printed in sheets of 8 + central label.

Telegraphy in Montenegro, 150th Anniv. — A294

2020, Dec. 16	Litho.	Perf. 13
469	A294 50c multi	1.25 1.25

Stamp Day.

MONTENEGRO

Aca Prijic (1920-86)
Painter — A295

2020, Dec. 17	Litho.	Perf. 13
470 A295 30c multi		.75 .75

Svetlana Kana Radevic (1937-2000), Architect — A296

2021, Feb. 28	Litho.	Perf. 13
471 A296 30c multi		.75 .75

Zivko Nikolic (1946-2001), Film Director — A297

2021, Feb. 28	Litho.	Perf. 13
472 A297 40c multi		1.00 1.00

Agency for Electronic Communications and Postal Service Day — A298

2021, Mar. 8	Litho.	Perf. 13
473 A298 30c multi		.70 .70

Lutra Lutra — A299

2021, Mar. 15	Litho.	Perf. 14x14¼
474 A299 95c multi		2.25 2.25

No. 474 was printed in sheets of 8 + central label.

Ilija Plamenac (1821-1916), Military Commander A300

2021, Apr. 15	Litho.	Perf. 13
475 A300 50c multi		1.25 1.25

Endangered Birds in Tivat Saline Wetlands A301

2021, May 8	Litho.	Perf. 14x14¼
476 A301 95c multi		2.40 2.40
a. Souvenir sheet of 1		2.40 2.40

Europa. No. 476 was printed in sheets of 8 + central label.

Lake Trnovacko — A302

2021, May 28	Litho.	Perf. 13
477 A302 30c multi		.75 .75

2020 Summer Olympics, Tokyo — A303

2021, June 16	Litho.	Perf. 14x14¼
478 A303 €1 multi		2.40 2.40

No. 478 was printed in sheets of 8 + central label. The 2020 Summer Olympics were postponed until 2021 because of the COVID-19 pandemic.

Old Town, Budva — A304

2021, July 4	Litho.	Perf. 13
479 A304 40c multi		.95 .95

No. 479 was printed in sheets of 5 + label.

Earrings From Budva, 4th-3rd Century, B.C. — A305

2021, July 12	Litho.	Perf. 14x14¼
480 A305 95c multi		2.25 2.25

No. 480 was printed in sheets of 8 + label.

Joy of Europe — A306

2021, Oct. 7	Litho.	Perf. 13
481 A306 50c multi		1.25 1.25

Montenegrin Academy of Arts and Sciences, 50th Anniv. — A307

2021, Oct. 12	Litho.	Perf. 13
482 A307 50c multi		1.25 1.25

Petar I Petrovic Njegos (1748-1830), Prince-Bishop of Montenegro A308

Clock Tower, Podgorici A309

2021, Nov. 10	Litho.	Perf. 13
483 A308 30c multi		.70 .70
484 A309 40c multi		.90 .90

Battle of Lepanto, 450th Anniv. — A310

2021, Nov. 30	Litho.	Perf. 13
485 A310 95c multi		2.25 2.25

No. 485 was printed in sheets of 8 + central label.

Mladost Children's Home, Bijela, 75th Anniv. — A311

2021, Dec. 1	Litho.	Perf. 13
486 A311 30c multi		.70 .70

Pero Soc (1884-1966), Drector of Yugoslavian Post and Telegraph Service — A312

2021, Dec. 15	Litho.	Perf. 13
487 A312 50c multi		1.25 1.25

Uros Toskovic (1932-2019), Painter — A313

2022, Feb. 25	Litho.	Perf. 13
488 A313 30c multi		.70 .70

Dragan Radulovic (1951-2002), Poet — A314

2022, Feb. 25	Litho.	Perf. 13
489 A314 40c multi		.90 .90

Spartium Junceum — A315

2022, Mar. 15	Litho.	Perf. 13x13¼
490 A315 95c multi		2.10 2.10

No. 490 was printed in sheets of 8 + label.

Milo Milunovic (1897-1967), Painter — A316

2022, Apr. 15	Litho.	Perf. 13
491 A316 50c multi		1.10 1.10

Cehotina River — A317

2022, May 27	Litho.	Perf. 13
492 A317 30c multi		.65 .65

Bozidar "Cikota" Stanisic (1936-2014), Water Polo Player — A318

2022, June 16	Litho.	Perf. 13¼x13
493 A318 €1 multi		2.10 2.10
a. Souvenir sheet of 1		2.10 2.10

No. 493 was printed in sheets of 8 + label.

Legend of Bukumir Lake — A319

2022, June 24	Litho.	Perf. 13¼x13
494 A319 95c multi		2.00 2.00
a. Souvenir sheet of 1		2.00 2.00

Europa. No. 494 was printed in sheets of 8 + label.

Lim River Regatta — A320

2022, July 5	Litho.	Perf. 13
495 A320 40c multi		.85 .85

Ancient Illyrian Coin From Risan Depicting King Ballaios — A321

2022, July 12	Litho.	Perf. 13¼x13
496 A321 95c multi		2.00 2.00

No. 496 was printed in sheets of 8 + label.

Joy of Europe — A322

2022, Oct. 7	Litho.	Perf. 13
497 A322 95c multi		1.90 1.90

Higher Education in Montenegro, 75th Anniv. — A323

2022, Oct. 17	Litho.	Perf. 13
498 A323 30c multi		.60 .60

Historic Religious Buildings — A324

Designs: 30c, Emperor's Mosque, Plav. 40c, Praskvica Monastery, Sveti Stefan, vert. 50c, St, John the Baptist Church, Budva, vert.

2022, Nov. 2	Litho.	Perf. 13
499-501 A324 Set of 3		2.50 2.50

Jadran Water Polo Club, Cent. — A325

2022, Nov. 18	Litho.	Perf. 13
502 A325 30c multi		.65 .65

Yacht Rumija — A326

		Perf. 13¼x12¾
2022, Nov. 28		Litho.
503 A326 95c multi		2.00 2.00

No. 503 was printed in sheets of 8 + label.

MONTENEGRO

Old Mailbox — A327

2022, Dec. 15 Litho. Perf. 13
504 A327 30c multi .65 .65
Stamp Day.

University of Montenegro Faculty of Law, 50th Anniv. — A328

2022, Dec. 23 Litho. Perf. 13
505 A328 50c multi 1.10 1.10

Miodrag Bulatovic (1930-91), Writer A329

Zdravko Velimirovic (1930-2005), Film Director A330

2023, Feb. 28 Litho. Perf. 13
506 A329 30c multi .65 .65
507 A330 40c multi .85 .85

Vipera Ammodytes A331

2023, Mar. 16 Litho. Perf. 13¼x13
508 A331 95c multi 2.10 2.10
No. 508 was printed in sheets of 8 + label.

Sculpture by Drago Ðurovic (1923-86) — A332

2023, Apr. 14 Litho. Perf. 13
509 A332 50c multi 1.10 1.10

Europa — A333

2023, May 9 Litho. Perf. 13¼x13
510 A333 95c multi 2.10 2.10
a. Souvenir sheet of 1 2.10 2.10
No. 510 was printed in sheets of 8 + label.

Ursus Arctos — A334

2023, May 29 Litho. Perf. 13
511 A334 30c multi .65 .65

Mirko Vesovic School of Economics, Podgorica, Cent. — A335

2023, May 31 Litho. Perf. 13
512 A335 30c multi .65 .65

Woman Wearing Xhubleta — A336

Perf. 12¾x13¼
2023, June 23 Litho.
513 A336 95c multi 2.10 2.10
Year of the Xhubleta. No. 513 was printed in sheets of 8 + central label.

Beaches — A337

Designs: 30c, Jaz Beach. 40c, Mogren Beach, horiz. 50c, Becicka Beach, horiz.

Perf. 12¾x13¼, 13¼x12¾
2023, July 5 Litho.
514-516 A337 Set of 3 2.75 2.75
Nos. 514-516 were each printed in sheets of 5 + label.

2023 Montenegro Film Festival, Herceg Novi — A338

2023, July 10 Litho. Perf. 13¼x12¾
517 A338 95c multi 2.10 2.10
No. 517 was printed in sheets of 8 + central label.

Joy of Europe — A339

2023, Oct. 6 Litho. Perf. 13
518 A339 95c multi 2.00 2.00

Danilo I Hospital, Cetinje, 150th Anniv. — A340

2023, Oct. 10 Litho. Perf. 13
519 A340 40c multi .85 .85

Empress Maria Girls' Institute, Cetinje A341

Queen Milena Petrovic Njegos (1847-1923) A342

Item in Polim Museum Collection — A343

2023, Nov. 2 Litho. Perf. 13
520 A341 30c multi .65 .65
521 A342 40c multi .90 .90
522 A343 50c multi 1.10 1.10
Nos. 520-522 (3) 2.65 2.65

Elena of Montenegro (1873-1946), Queen of Italy — A344

Perf. 13¼x12¾
2023, Nov. 17 Litho.
523 A344 €1 multi 2.25 2.25
No. 523 was printed in sheets of 8 + label.

The Wedding of Montenegro with the Sea, Painting by Ivan Zmiric (1842-1929) A345

Perf. 13¼x12¾
2023, Nov. 28 Litho.
524 A345 95c multi 2.10 2.10
No. 524 was printed in sheets of 8 + central label.

ACKNOWLEDGMENT OF RECEIPT STAMPS

Prince Nicholas I — AR1

Perf. 10½, 11½
1895 Litho. Wmk. 91
H1 AR1 10n ultra & rose 1.10 1.10
a. Perf. 11½ 1.10 1.10

Prince Nicholas I — AR2

1902 Unwmk. Perf. 12½
H2 AR2 25h orange & carmine 1.10 1.10
a. Double print 29.00
b. Pair, imperf. 45.00

Constitution Issue

No. H2 Overprinted in Black

1905 "Constitution" 15mm
H3 AR2 25h orange & carmine 1.10 1.10
g. Inverted overprint 85.00
h. Double overprint 24.00

"Constitution" 16½mm ('06)
H3a Overprint Type I 32.50 35.00
H3b Overprint Type II 1.40 1.50
H3c Overprint Type III 5.75 6.50
H3d Overprint Type IV 3.25 3.50
See note after 74a.

AR3
1907 Engr.
H4 AR3 25pa olive .95 1.40

Nicholas I — AR4

1913 Typo.
H5 AR4 25pa olive green .95 3.50

POSTAGE DUE STAMPS

D1

Perf. 10½
1894, Nov. Litho. Wmk. 91
J1 D1 1n red 3.75 3.50
c. Pair, imperf. 42.50
J2 D1 2n yellow green 1.50 1.40
J3 D1 3n orange .95 .95
c. Double impression 8.50
J4 D1 5n olive green .70 .65
J5 D1 10n violet .70 .65
J6 D1 20n ultra .70 .65
c. Double impression 55.00
J7 D1 30n emerald .70 .65
c. Double impression 55.00
J8 D1 50n pale gray grn .70 .65
Nos. J1-J8 (8) 9.70 9.10

Perf. 11
J1a D1 1n red 7.25 6.75
J2a D1 2n yellow green 4.75 4.75
J3a D1 3n orange 5.75 5.50
J5a D1 10n violet 3.75 3.50
J6a D1 20n ultramarine 3.75 3.50
J7a D1 30n emerald 5.75 5.50
J8a D1 50n pale gray green 5.75 5.50
Nos. J1a-J8a (7) 36.75 35.00

Perf. 11½
J1b D1 1n red 3.75 3.50
J2b D1 2n yellow green 1.50 1.40
J3b D1 3n orange .95 .95
J4b D1 5n olive green .70 .65
J5b D1 10n violet .70 .65
J6b D1 20n ultramarine .70 .65
J7b D1 30n emerald .70 .65
J8b D1 50n pale gray green .70 .65
Nos. J1b-J8b (8) 9.70 9.10

D2

1902 Unwmk. Perf. 12½
J9 D2 5h orange .45 .65
J10 D2 10h olive green .45 .65
J11 D2 25h dull lilac .45 .65
J12 D2 50h emerald .45 .65
J13 D2 1k pale gray green .95 1.50
Nos. J9-J13 (5) 2.75 4.10

Constitution Issue
Postage Due Stamps of 1902 Overprinted in Black or Red "Constitution" 15mm

1905
J14 D2 5h orange .65 1.40
a. Inverted overprint 37.50
b. Double overprint 17.00
J15 D2 10h olive green (R) .95 2.75
a. Double overprint 17.00
b. Ovpt. 16¾mm,Type II 1.90 4.00
c. As "b," Type III 1.90 4.00
d. As "b," Type IV 1.90 4.00
J16 D2 25h dull lilac .65 1.40
a. Inverted overprint 37.50
b. Double overprint 17.00
J17 D2 50h emerald .65 1.40
a. Inverted overprint 37.50
b. Double overprint 14.00
J18 D2 1k pale gray green .95 1.90
a. Double overprint 14.00
Nos. J14-J18 (5) 3.85 8.85

D3

1907 Typo. Perf. 13x13½
J19 D3 5pa red brown .45 1.40
J20 D3 10pa violet .45 1.40
J21 D3 25pa rose .45 1.40
J22 D3 50pa green .45 1.40
Nos. J19-J22 (4) 1.80 5.60

D4

1913 Perf. 12½
J23 D4 5pa gray 1.40 1.90
J24 D4 10pa violet .95 1.40
J25 D4 25pa blue gray .95 1.40
J26 D4 50pa lilac rose 1.40 1.90
Nos. J23-J26 (4) 4.70 6.60

MONTENEGRO

ISSUED UNDER AUSTRIAN OCCUPATION

Austrian Military Stamps of 1917 Overprinted

1917		Unwmk.	Perf. 12½
1N1	M1	10h blue	14.50 14.50
1N2	M1	15h car rose	14.50 14.50

Austrian Military Stamps of 1917 Overprinted in Black

1918			
1N3	M1	10h blue	40.00
1N4	M1	15h car rose	1.90

Nos. 1N3-1N4 were never placed in use.
This overprint exists on other stamps of Austria and Bosnia and Herzegovina, and in blue or red.

ISSUED UNDER ITALIAN OCCUPATION

Used values for Italian occupation issues are for postally used examples. Canceled to order stamps sell for much less.

Yugoslavia Nos. 142, 144-154 Overprinted

1941		Unwmk. Typo.	Perf. 12½
2N1	A16	25p black	1.75 3.50
2N2	A16	1d yel grn	1.75 3.50
2N3	A16	1.50d red	1.75 3.50
2N4	A16	2d dp mag	1.75 3.50
2N5	A16	3d dull red brn	1.75 3.50
2N6	A16	4d ultra	1.75 3.50
2N7	A16	5d dark blue	2.50 7.00
2N8	A16	5.50d dk vio brn	2.50 7.00
2N9	A16	6d slate blue	2.50 7.00
2N10	A16	8d sepia	2.50 7.00
2N11	A16	12d brt violet	2.50 7.00
2N12	A16	16d dull violet	2.50 7.00
2N13	A16	20d blue	175.00 300.00
2N14	A16	30d brt pink	75.00 210.00
		Nos. 2N1-2N14 (14)	275.50 573.00
		Set, never hinged	775.00

The 25p, 1d, 3d, 6d and 8d exist with inverted overprint.

Stamps of Italy, 1929, Overprinted in Red or Black

1941		Wmk. 140	Perf. 14
2N15	A90	5c ol brn (R)	.80 2.50
2N16	A92	10c dark brn	.80 2.50
2N17	A93	15c sl grn (R)	.80 2.50
2N18	A91	20c rose red	.80 2.50
2N19	A94	25c deep grn	.80 2.50
2N20	A95	30c ol brn (R)	.80 2.50
2N21	A95	50c pur (R)	.80 2.50
2N22	A95	75c rose red	.80 2.50
2N23	A94	1.25 l dp bl (R)	1.00 2.50
		Nos. 2N15-2N23 (9)	7.40 22.50
		Set, never hinged	20.00

Yugoslavia Nos. 144-145, 147-148, 148B, 149-152 Overprinted in Black

1942		Unwmk. Typo.	Perf. 12½
2N24	A16	1d yel grn	6.25 14.00
2N25	A16	1.50d red	87.50 160.00
2N26	A16	3d dull red brn	6.25 14.00
2N27	A16	4d ultra	6.25 14.00
2N28	A16	5.50d dk vio brn	6.25 14.00
2N29	A16	6d slate blue	6.25 14.00
2N30	A16	8d sepia	6.25 14.00
2N31	A16	12d brt violet	6.25 14.00
2N32	A16	16d dull violet	6.25 14.00
		Nos. 2N24-2N32 (9)	137.50 272.00
		Set, never hinged	375.00

Yugoslavia Nos. 142 and 146 with this overprint in red were not officially issued.

Red Overprint

2N24a	A16	1d	5.00 10.00
2N25a	A16	1.50d	125.00 525.00
2N26a	A16	3d	5.00 10.00
2N27a	A16	4d	5.00 10.00
2N28a	A16	5.50d	5.00 10.00
2N29a	A16	6d	5.00 10.00
2N30a	A16	8d	5.00 10.00
2N31a	A16	12d	5.00 10.00
2N32a	A16	16d	5.00 10.00
		Nos. 2N24a-2N32a (9)	165.00 605.00
		Set, never hinged	460.00

Peter Nyegosh and Mt. Lovchen View — OS1

Mt. Lovchen Scene OS2

Peter Petrovich Nyegosh OS3

Designs: 15c, Mountain Church, Eve of Trinity Feast. 20c, Chiefs at Cetinje Monastery. 25c, Folk Dancing at Cetinje Monastery. 50c, Eagle dance. 1.25 l, Chiefs taking loyalty oath. 2 l, Moslem wedding procession. 5 l, Group sitting up with injured standard bearer.

1943, May 9		Unwmk.	Perf. 14.
			Photo.
2N33	OS1	5c deep violet	1.25 4.25
2N34	OS2	10c dull olive grn	1.25 4.25
2N35	OS1	15c brown	1.25 4.25
2N36	OS1	20c dull orange	1.25 4.25
2N37	OS1	25c dull green	1.25 4.25
2N38	OS1	50c rose pink	1.25 4.25
2N39	OS1	1.25 l sapphire	1.25 4.25
2N40	OS1	2 l blue green	3.75 4.25
2N41	OS1	5 l dark red, sal	6.25 15.00
2N42	OS3	20 l dark vio, gray	15.00 30.00
		Nos. 2N33-2N42 (10)	33.75 79.00
		Set, never hinged	95.00

Quotations from national poem on backs of stamps.
For overprints and surcharges see Nos. 3N10-3N14, 3NB3-3NB8.

OCCUPATION AIR POST STAMPS

Yugoslavia Nos. C7-C14 Overprinted Like Nos. 2N1-2N14

Perf. 12½, 11½x12½, 12½x11½

1941			Unwmk.
2NC1	AP6	50p brown	3.00 9.75
2NC2	AP7	1d yel grn	2.50 9.75
2NC3	AP8	2d blue gray	2.50 9.75
2NC4	AP9	2.50d rose red	3.00 9.75
2NC5	AP6	5d brn vio	22.50 62.50
2NC6	AP7	10 brn lake	22.50 62.50
2NC7	AP8	20d dark grn	47.50 110.00
2NC8	AP9	30d ultra	25.00 62.50
		Nos. 2NC1-2NC8 (8)	128.50 336.50
		Set, never hinged	350.00

Italy No. C13 Overprinted in Red Like Nos. 2N15-2N23

1941		Wmk. 140	Perf. 14
2NC9	AP3	50c olive brn	.75 2.10
		Never hinged	2.25

Yugoslavia Nos. C7-C14 Overprinted in Black

a

b

Perf. 12½, 11½x12½, 12½x11½

1942, Jan. 9			Unwmk.
2NC10	AP6(a)	50p brown	5.00 9.00
2NC11	AP7(a)	1d yel grn	5.00 9.00
2NC12	AP8(b)	2d blue gray	5.00 9.00
2NC13	AP9(b)	2.50d rose red	5.00 9.00
2NC14	AP6(a)	5d brn vio	5.00 9.00
2NC15	AP7(a)	10d brn lake	5.00 9.00
2NC16	AP8(b)	20d dk grn	125.00 275.00
2NC17	AP9(b)	30d ultra	19.00 52.50
		Nos. 2NC10-2NC17 (8)	174.00 381.50
		Set, never hinged	500.00

Nos. 2NC10-2NC17 exist with red overprints. Value, each $125 unused, $240 used.

c

Overprints *a*, *b* or *c* were applied in 1941-42 to the following Yugoslavia stamps under Italian occupation:
 a. or *b*. Nos. B120-B123 (4 values) in black and in red.
 c. Nos. B116-B119 (4 values) in black and in red.

Cetinje AP1

Mt. Durmitor AP6

Designs: 1 l, Seacoast. 2 l, Budus. 5 l, Mt. Lovchen. 10 l, Rieka River.

1943		Photo.	Perf. 14
2NC18	AP1	50c brown	2.50 4.25
2NC19	AP1	1 l ultra	2.50 4.25
2NC20	AP1	2 l rose pink	2.50 4.25
2NC21	AP1	5 l green	3.75 7.00
2NC22	AP1	10 l lake, rose buff	8.75 22.50
2NC23	AP6	20 l indigo, rose	12.50 40.00
		Nos. 2NC18-2NC23 (6)	32.50 82.25
		Set, never hinged	100.00

For overprints and surcharges see Nos. 3NC1-3NC5, 3NCB1-3NCB6.

OCCUPATION POSTAGE DUE STAMPS

Yugoslavia Nos. J28-J32 Overprinted Like Nos. 2N1-2N14

1941		Unwmk. Typo.	Perf. 12½
2NJ1	D4	50p violet	1.25 4.25
2NJ2	D4	1d dp mag	1.25 4.25
2NJ3	D4	2d deep blue	1.25 4.25
2NJ4	D4	5d orange	55.00 175.00
2NJ5	D4	10d chocolate	5.00 28.00
		Nos. 2NJ1-2NJ5 (5)	63.75 215.75
		Set, never hinged	190.00

1934 Postage Due Stamps of Italy Overprinted in Black Like Nos. 2N15-2N23

1942		Wmk. 140	Perf. 14
2NJ6	D6	10c blue	1.25 4.50
2NJ7	D6	20c rose red	1.25 4.50
2NJ8	D6	30c red orange	1.25 4.50
2NJ9	D6	50c violet	1.25 4.50
2NJ10	D7	1 l red orange	1.25 4.50
		Nos. 2NJ6-2NJ10 (5)	6.25 22.50
		Set, never hinged	20.00

ISSUED UNDER GERMAN OCCUPATION

Used values for German occupation issues are for postally used examples. Canceled to order stamps sell for much less.

Yugoslavia Nos. 147-148 Surcharged

1943		Unwmk. Typo.	Perf. 12½
3N1	A16	50c on 3d	4.00 24.00
3N2	A16	1 l on 3d	4.00 24.00
3N3	A16	1.50 l on 3d	4.00 24.00
3N4	A16	2 l on 3d	6.00 47.50
3N5	A16	4 l on 3d	6.00 47.50
3N6	A16	5 l on 4d	6.00 47.50
3N7	A16	8 l on 4d	14.00 95.00
3N8	A16	10 l on 4d	16.00 140.00
3N9	A16	20 l on 4d	40.00 200.00
		Nos. 3N1-3N9 (9)	100.00 649.50
		Set, never hinged	375.00

Montenegro Nos. 2N37-2N41 Ovptd.

1943		Photo.	Perf. 14
3N10	OS1	25c dull green	12.00 160.00
3N11	OS1	50c rose pink	12.00 160.00
3N12	OS1	1.25 l sapphire	12.00 160.00
3N13	OS1	2 l blue green	12.00 160.00
3N14	OS2	5 l dk red, sal	125.00 2,000.
		Nos. 3N10-3N14 (5)	173.00 2,640.
		Set, never hinged	600.00

Counterfeits exist.

SEMI-POSTAL STAMPS

Yugoslavia Nos. 147-148 Surcharged

1944		Unwmk. Typo.	Perf. 12½
3NB1	A16	15pf + 85pf on 3d	11.00 160.00
3NB2	A16	15pf + 85pf on 4d	11.00 160.00

Montenegro Nos. 2N37-2N40 Surcharged

d

1944		Photo.	Perf. 14
3NB3	OS1	15pf +85pf on 25c	11.00 160.00
3NB4	OS1	15pf +1.35m on 50c	11.00 160.00
3NB5	OS1	25pf +1.75m on 1.25 l	11.00 160.00
3NB6	OS1	25pf +1.75m on 2 l	11.00 160.00
		Nos. 3NB1-3NB6 (6)	66.00 960.00
		Set, never hinged	260.00

Surtax on Nos. 3NB1-3NB6 aided refugees.

Montenegro Nos. 2N37-2N38 and Yugoslavia Nos. 147-148 Surcharged

e

f

MONTENEGRO — MONTSERRAT

1944

3NB7	OS1	15pf + 85pf on 25c (e)	9.00	150.00
3NB8	OS1	15pf + 1.35m on 50c (e)	9.00	150.00
3NB9	A16	50pf + 2.50m on 3d (f)	9.00	150.00
3NB10	A16	50pf + 2.50m on 4d (f)	9.00	150.00
	Nos. 3NB7-3NB10 (4)		36.00	600.00
	Set, never hinged			150.00

The surtax on Nos. 3NB7-3NB10 aided the Montenegro Red Cross.

AIR POST STAMPS

Montenegro Nos. 2NC18-2NC22 Overprinted Like Nos. 3N10-3N14

1943 Unwmk. Photo. Perf. 14

3NC1	AP1	50c brown	12.00	160.00
3NC2	AP1	1 l ultra	12.00	160.00
3NC3	AP1	2 l rose pink	12.00	160.00
3NC4	AP1	5 l green	12.00	160.00
3NC5	AP1	10 l lake, rose buff	1,575.	18,000.
	Nos. 3NC1-3NC5 (5)		1,623.	18,640.
	Set, never hinged			5,000.

Counterfeits exist.

AIR POST SEMI-POSTAL STAMPS

Montenegro Nos. 2NC18-2NC20 Surcharged Type "d"

1944 Unwmk. Photo. Perf. 14

3NCB1	AP1	15pf +85pf on 50c	11.00	160.00
3NCB2	AP1	25pf +1.25m on 1 l	11.00	160.00
3NCB3	AP1	50pf +1.50m on 2 l	11.00	160.00
	Nos. 3NCB1-3NCB3 (3)		33.00	480.00
	Set, never hinged			135.00

The surtax aided refugees.

Same Surcharged Type "e"

1944

3NCB4	AP1	25pf +1.75m on 50c	9.00	150.00
3NCB5	AP1	25pf +2.75m on 1 l	9.00	150.00
3NCB6	AP1	50pf +2m on 2 l	9.00	150.00
	Nos. 3NCB4-3NCB6 (3)		27.00	450.00
	Set, never hinged			105.00

The surtax aided the Montenegro Red Cross.

MONTSERRAT

ˌmän(t)-sə-ˈrat

LOCATION — West Indies southeast of Puerto Rico
GOVT. — British Crown Colony
AREA — 39 sq. mi.
POP. — 4,922 (2011 est.)

Montserrat was one of the four presidencies of the former Leeward Islands colony until it became a colony itself in 1956.

Montserrat stamps were discontinued in 1890 and resumed in 1903. In the interim, stamps of Leeward Islands were used. In 1903-50, stamps of Montserrat and Leeward Islands were used concurrently.

12 Pence = 1 Shilling
20 Shillings = 1 Pound
100 Cents = 1 Dollar (1951)

Catalogue values for unused stamps in this country are for Never Hinged items, beginning with Scott 104 in the regular postage section, Scott B1 in the semi-postal section, Scott O45 in the officials section.

Watermark

Wmk. 380 — "POST OFFICE"

Values for unused stamps are for examples with original gum as defined in the catalogue introduction. Very fine examples of Nos. 1-2, 6 and 11 will have perforations touching the design on at least one side due to the narrow spacing of the stamps on the plates. Stamps with perfs clear of the framelines on all four sides are scarce and will command higher prices.

Stamps of Antigua Overprinted in Black — a

1876 Engr. Wmk. 1 Perf. 14

1	A1	1p red	30.00	19.00
a.	Vert. or diag. half used as ½p on cover			1,650.
c.	"S" inverted		1,250.	875.00
2	A1	6p green	75.00	50.00
a.	Vertical half used as 3p on cover			—
b.	Vertical third used as 2p on cover			6,500.
c.	"S" inverted		1,900.	1,350.
d.	6p blue green		1,350.	
e.	As "d," "S" inverted		13,000.	

Some experts consider Nos. 2d, 2e to be from a trial printing

Queen Victoria — A2

1880 Typo.

3	A2	2½p red brown	300.00	225.00
4	A2	4p blue	160.00	47.50

See Nos. 5, 7-10.

1884 Wmk. 2

5	A2	½p green	1.25	11.00

Antigua No. 18 Overprinted type "a"

1884 Engr.

6	A1	1p rose red	28.00	20.00
a.	Vert. half used as ½p on cover			1,550.
b.	"S" inverted		1,100.	1,100.

Type of 1880

1884-85 Typo.

7	A2	2½p red brown	275.00	77.50
8	A2	2½p ultra ('85)	29.00	22.50
9	A2	4p blue	2,100.	300.00
10	A2	4p red lilac ('85)	6.00	0.50

Antigua No. 20 Overprinted type "a"

1884 Engr.

11	A1	1p red	42.50	66.00
a.	"S" inverted		2,350.	1,550.
b.	Vert. half used as ½p on cover			1,900.

Symbol of the Colony A3

King Edward VII A4

1903 Wmk. 2 Typo. Perf. 14

12	A3	½p gray grn & grn	.90	19.00
13	A3	1p car & ol gray	.90	.50
14	A3	2p brown & black	6.50	50.00
15	A3	2½p ultra & black	1.75	2.10
16	A3	3p dk vio & brn orange	8.50	50.00
17	A3	6p ol grn & vio	15.00	65.00
18	A3	1sh vio & brn	12.00	26.00
19	A3	2sh brn org & gray green	42.50	27.50
20	A3	2sh6p blk & gray grn	27.50	60.00

Wmk. 1

21	A4	5sh car & black	160.00	225.00
	Nos. 12-21 (10)		275.55	525.10

1904-08 Wmk. 3 Chalky Paper

22	A3	½p grn & gray grn ('06)	1.00	1.25
a.	Ordinary paper		13.00	4.00
23	A3	1p car & blk ('07)	17.00	30.00
24	A3	2p brown & black ('06)	2.50	1.40
a.	Ordinary paper		3.00	13.00
25	A3	2½p ultra & blk ('05)	3.00	7.75
26	A3	3p dk vio & brn orange ('08)	13.00	2.75
a.	Ordinary paper		13.00	8.00
27	A3	6p ol grn & vio ('08)	16.00	6.50
a.	Ordinary paper		13.00	42.50
28	A3	1sh violet & gray grn ('08)	12.00	8.50
29	A3	2sh brn org & gray grn ('08)	60.00	55.00
30	A3	2sh6p blk & gray grn ('08)	65.00	60.00
31	A4	5sh car & blk ('07)	160.00	190.00
	Nos. 22-31 (10)		349.50	363.15

1908-13 Ordinary Paper

31A	A3	½p deep green	12.00	1.10
32	A3	1p carmine	1.75	.35
33	A3	2p gray	2.00	22.50
34	A3	2½p ultramarine	2.50	4.25

Chalky Paper

35	A3	2p vio, yellow	1.10	22.50
36	A3	6p red vio & gray grn	12.00	60.00
37	A3	1sh blk, green	10.00	55.00
38	A3	2sh bl & vio, bl	50.00	67.50
39	A3	2sh6p car & blk, blue	42.50	87.50
40	A4	5sh grn & scar, yel	65.00	92.50

Surface-colored Paper

41	A3	3p vio, yel ('13)	4.50	40.00
	Nos. 31A-41 (11)		203.35	453.20

King George V — A5

1913 Chalky Paper

42	A5	5sh green & scar, yel	90.00	160.00

King George V — A6

1916-22 Wmk. 3 Perf. 14
Ordinary Paper

43	A6	½p green	.45	2.75
44	A6	1p scarlet	2.50	.90
45	A6	2p gray	2.75	5.00
46	A6	2½p ultramarine	2.50	26.00

Chalky Paper

47	A6	3p violet, yel	1.40	23.00
48	A6	4p blk & red, yel ('22)	8.50	42.50
49	A6	6p dl vio & red violet	3.50	37.50
50	A6	1sh blk, bl grn, ol back	3.50	42.50
51	A6	2sh vio & ultra, bl	22.00	60.00
52	A6	2sh6p blk & red, bl	40.00	90.00
53	A6	5sh grn & red, yel	55.00	95.00
	Nos. 43-53 (11)		142.10	425.15

For overprints see Nos. MR1-MR3.

1922-29 Wmk. 4 Ordinary Paper

54	A6	¼p brown	.35	6.25
55	A6	½p green ('23)	.30	.30
56	A6	1p dp violet ('23)	.80	.70
57	A6	1p carmine ('29)	1.10	1.75
58	A6	1½p orange	2.50	11.00
59	A6	1½p rose red ('23)	.60	5.00
60	A6	1½p fawn ('29)	3.25	.55
61	A6	2p gray	.80	2.25
62	A6	2½p ultramarine	9.25	18.00
63	A6	2½p orange ('23)	2.75	21.00
64	A6	3p ultra ('23)	.80	18.00

Chalky Paper

65	A6	3p vio, yel ('26)	2.00	6.50
66	A6	4p black & red, yel ('23)	1.75	14.00
67	A6	5p dull vio & ol grn	5.50	11.00
68	A6	6p dull vio & red vio ('23)	3.50	8.50
69	A6	1sh blk, emer ('23)	3.50	8.00
70	A6	2sh vio & ultra, bl ('23)	8.00	22.50
71	A6	2sh6p blk & red, bl ('23)	14.00	65.00
72	A6	3sh green & vio	14.00	22.50
73	A6	4sh black & scar	17.50	50.00
74	A6	5sh grn & red, yel ('23)	37.50	65.00
	Nos. 54-74 (21)		129.75	357.80

Tercentenary Issue

New Plymouth and Harbor — A7

1932, Apr. 18 Engr.

75	A7	½p vio, yel ('26)	1.25	16.00
76	A7	1p red	1.25	6.50
77	A7	1½p orange brown	1.40	3.00
78	A7	2p gray	1.90	23.00
79	A7	2½p ultra	1.40	21.00
80	A7	3p orange	1.90	21.00
81	A7	6p violet	2.50	37.50
82	A7	1sh olive green	14.50	50.00
83	A7	2sh6p lilac rose	52.50	87.50
84	A7	5sh dark brown	115.00	200.00
	Nos. 75-84 (10)		193.60	465.50
	Set, never hinged			400.00

300th anniv. of the colonization of Montserrat.

Common Design Types pictured following the introduction.

Silver Jubilee Issue
Common Design Type

1935, May 6 Perf. 11x12

85	CD301	1p car & dk blue	1.25	4.25
86	CD301	1½p gray blk & ultra	2.00	3.75
87	CD301	2½p ultra & brn	2.75	4.25
88	CD301	1sh brn vio & ind	4.25	18.00
	Nos. 85-88 (4)		10.25	30.25
	Set, never hinged			19.00

Coronation Issue
Common Design Type

1937, May 12 Perf. 13½x14

89	CD302	1p carmine	.25	1.50
90	CD302	1½p brown	.40	.35
91	CD302	2½p bright ultra	.35	1.50
	Nos. 89-91 (3)		1.00	3.35
	Set, never hinged			1.75

Carr's Bay — A8
Sea Island Cotton — A9

Botanic Station — A10

1941-48 Perf. 14

92	A8	½p dk grn ('42)	.25	.25
93	A9	1p car ('42)	.40	.35
94	A9	1½p rose vio ('42)	.40	.55
95	A10	2p red orange	1.20	.80
96	A9	2½p brt ultra ('43)	.40	.35
97	A8	3p brown ('42)	1.50	.45
98	A10	6p dull vio ('42)	2.00	.70
99	A8	1sh brn lake ('42)	1.75	.35
100	A10	2sh6p slate bl ('43)	13.50	3.00
101	A8	5sh car rose ('42)	16.00	3.50

Perf. 12

102	A10	10sh blue ('48)	10.00	30.00
103	A8	£1 black ('48)	10.00	35.00
	Nos. 92-103 (12)		57.40	75.30
	Set, never hinged			85.00

1938, Aug. 2 Perf. 13

92a	A8	½p	2.50	2.00
93a	A8	1p	2.50	.40
94a	A9	1½p	11.00	1.00
95a	A10	2p	11.00	1.00
96a	A9	2½p	1.25	1.50
97a	A8	3p	3.00	3.25
98a	A10	6p	11.50	1.25

629

MONTSERRAT

99a	A8	1sh	11.50	1.25
100a	A10	2sh6p	20.00	1.00
101a	A8	5sh	24.00	10.00
	Nos. 92-101a (10)		98.25	22.65
	Set, never hinged		200.00	

Catalogue values for unused stamps in this section, from this point to the end of the section, are for Never Hinged items.

Peace Issue
Common Design Type
1946, Nov. 1 Engr. Perf. 13½x14

104	CD303	1½p deep magenta	.25	.25
105	CD303	3p brown	.25	.25

Silver Wedding Issue
Common Design Types
1949, Jan. 3 Photo. Perf. 14x14½

106	CD304	2½p brt ultra	.25	.25

Engraved; Name Typographed
Perf. 11½x11

107	CD305	5sh rose carmine	8.50	17.00

UPU Issue
Common Design Types
Engr.; Name Typo. on 3p and 6p
Perf. 13½, 11x11½
1949, Oct. 10 Wmk. 4

108	CD306	2½p ultramarine	.40	1.10
109	CD307	3p chocolate	1.50	.85
110	CD308	6p lilac	.70	1.00
111	CD309	1sh rose violet	.70	1.40
	Nos. 108-111 (4)		3.30	4.35

University Issue
Common Design Types
1951, Feb. 16 Engr. Perf. 14x14½

112	CD310	3c rose lil & gray blk	.25	1.00
113	CD311	12c violet & black	.60	1.00

Government House — A11

Designs (portrait at right on 12c, 24c and $2.40): 2c, $1.20, Cotton field. 3c, Map of Presidency. 4c, 24c, Picking tomatoes. 5c, 12c, St. Anthony's Church. 6c, $4.80, Badge of Presidency. 8c, 60c, Cotton ginning.

Perf. 11½x11
1951, Sept. 17 Engr. Wmk. 4

114	A11	1c gray	.30	1.75
115	A11	2c green	.30	1.00
116	A11	3c orange brown	.30	.50
117	A11	4c rose carmine	.30	1.75
118	A11	5c red violet	.30	.30
119	A11	6c dark brown	.40	.30
120	A11	8c dark blue	2.50	.30
121	A11	12c red brn & blue	1.25	.30
122	A11	24c emer & rose car		1.50	.50
123	A11	60c rose car & gray black	10.00	5.00
124	A11	$1.20 dp bl & emer	10.00	10.00
125	A11	$2.40 dp grn & gray black	15.00	15.00
126	A11	$4.80 pur & gray blk	29.00	29.00
	Nos. 114-126 (13)		71.15	65.70

Coronation Issue
Common Design Type
1953, June 2 Perf. 13½x13

127	CD312	2c dark green & black	.60	.45

Type of 1951 with Portrait of Queen Elizabeth II

½c, 3c, "Map of Presidency." 48c, Cotton field.

1953-57 Perf. 11½x11

128	A11	½c violet ('56)	.30	.25
129	A11	1c gray black	.30	.25
130	A11	2c green	.30	.25
131	A11	3c orange brown	.75	.65
132	A11	4c rose car ('55)	.30	.25
133	A11	5c red vio ('55)	.30	.25
134	A11	6c dk brown ('55)	.80	.70
135	A11	8c dp ultra ('55)	.30	.25
136	A11	12c red brn & blue ('55)	.30	.25
137	A11	24c emer & rose car ('55)	.90	.80
138	A11	48c rose violet & olive ('57)	1.75	1.50
139	A11	60c rose car & blk ('55)	2.25	1.75
140	A11	$1.20 bl & emer ('55)	4.50	3.50
141	A11	$2.40 dp green & blk ('55)	9.25	7.00
142	A11	$4.80 pur & gray black ('55)	40.00	30.00
	Nos. 128-142 (15)		62.30	47.65

See Nos. 146-149, 156.

West Indies Federation
Common Design Type
1958, Apr. 22 Engr. Perf. 11½x11 Wmk. 314

143	CD313	3c green	.45	.25
144	CD313	6c blue	.65	.65
145	CD313	12c carmine rose	1.25	.45
	Nos. 143-145 (3)		2.35	1.35

Type of 1953-57

As before, but inscribed: "Map of the Colony" (½c, 3c) "Badge of the Colony" (6c, $4.80).

1958 Wmk. 4 Perf. 11½x11

146	A11	½c violet	.65	.25
147	A11	3c orange brown	.65	.75
148	A11	6c dark brown	.30	.25
149	A11	$4.80 pur & gray blk	14.50	9.00
	Nos. 146-149 (4)		16.10	10.25

Freedom from Hunger Issue
Common Design Type
Perf. 14x14½
1963, June 4 Photo. Wmk. 314

150	CD314	12c lilac	.55	.35

Red Cross Centenary Issue
Common Design Type
1963, Sept. 2 Litho. Perf. 13

151	CD315	4c black & red	.25	.25
152	CD315	12c ultra & red	.75	.50

Shakespeare Issue
Common Design Type
1964, Apr. 23 Photo. Perf. 14x14½

153	CD316	12c slate blue	.35	.25

Type of 1953-57
Perf. 11½x11
1964, Oct. 30 Engr. Wmk. 314

156	A11	2c green	1.00	.25

ITU Issue
Common Design Type
Perf. 11x11½
1965, May 17 Litho. Wmk. 314

157	CD317	4c ver & lilac	.25	.25
158	CD317	48c emer & rose red	.80	.90

Pineapple — A12

Wmk. 314 Upright
1965, Aug. 16 Photo. Perf. 15x14

159	A12	1c shown	.30	.25
160	A12	2c Avacado	.30	.25
161	A12	3c Soursop	.30	.25
162	A12	4c Peppers	.30	.25
163	A12	5c Mango	.30	.25
164	A12	6c Tomatoes	.30	.25
165	A12	8c Guava	.30	.25
166	A12	10c Okra	.30	.25
167	A12	12c Limes	.30	.25
168	A12	20c Oranges	.40	.25
169	A12	24c Bananas	.65	.40
170	A12	42c Onion	1.00	.75
171	A12	48c Cabbage	1.75	1.00
172	A12	60c Papayas	2.75	1.25
173	A12	$1.20 Pumpkin	2.10	5.00
174	A12	$2.40 Sweet potato	7.00	7.50
175	A12	$4.80 Eggplant	11.00	12.00
	Nos. 159-175 (17)		29.35	30.40

For surcharges see Nos. 193-198.

1969 Wmk. 314 Sideways

159a	A12	1c	.25	.25
160a	A12	2c	.45	.50
161a	A12	3c	.30	.40
162a	A12	4c	.75	.40
163a	A12	5c	.90	1.00
166a	A12	10c	1.75	2.00
168a	A12	20c	2.10	2.40
	Nos. 159a-168a (7)		6.50	6.95

Intl. Cooperation Year Issue
Common Design Type
1965, Oct. 25 Litho. Perf. 14½

176	CD318	2c lt green & claret	.25	.25
177	CD318	12c lt violet & green	.55	.40

Churchill Memorial Issue
Common Design Type
1966, Jan. 24 Photo. Perf. 14
Design in Black, Gold and Carmine Rose

178	CD319	1c bright blue	.25	.25
179	CD319	2c green	.25	.25
180	CD319	24c brown	.35	.30
181	CD319	42c violet	.75	.75
	Nos. 178-181 (4)		1.60	1.55

Royal Visit Issue
Common Design Type
Perf. 11x12
1966, Feb. 4 Litho. Wmk. 314

182	CD320	14c violet blue	.75	.25
183	CD320	24c dk carmine rose	1.25	.75

WHO Headquarters Issue
Common Design Type
1966, Sept. 20 Litho. Perf. 14

184	CD322	12c multicolored	.25	.25
185	CD322	60c multicolored	.75	.75

UNESCO Anniversary Issue
Common Design Type
1966, Dec. 1 Litho. Perf. 14

186	CD323	4c "Education"	.25	.25
a.		Orange omitted	100.00	
187	CD323	60c "Science"	.40	.40
188	CD323	$1.80 "Culture"	1.75	1.75
	Nos. 186-188 (3)		2.40	2.40

On No. 186a, the squares of the lowercase letters appear in yellow.

Sailing and ITY Emblem — A13

ITY Emblem and: 15c, Waterfall, Chance Mountain, vert. 16c, Beach scene. 24c, Golfers.

1967, Dec. 29 Photo. Wmk. 314

189	A13	5c multicolored	.35	.35
190	A13	15c multicolored	.35	.35
191	A13	16c multicolored	.45	.45
192	A13	24c multicolored	1.10	1.10
	Nos. 189-192 (4)		2.25	2.25

Issued for International Tourist Year.

Nos. 167, 169, 171, 173-175 and Type Surcharged

1968, May 6 Perf. 15x14

193	A12	15c on 12c multi	.25	.25
a.		Wmkd. sideways ('69)	1.50	1.75
194	A12	25c on 24c multi	.25	.25
a.		Wmkd. sideways ('69)	2.50	3.00
195	A12	50c on 48c multi	.45	.45
a.		Wmkd. sideways ('69)	6.00	12.00
196	A12	$1 on $1.20 multi	.70	.70
197	A12	$2.50 on $2.40 multi	1.50	1.50
198	A12	$5 on $4.80 multi	3.00	3.00
	Nos. 193-198 (6)		6.15	6.15

The surcharge bars are slightly thinner on the "Wmkd. sideways" varieties.

Woman Runner — A14

Designs: 25c, Weight lifter. 50c, Athlete on rings. $1, Runner and Toltec sculptures, vert.

Perf. 14½x14, 14x14½
1968, July 31 Photo. Wmk. 314

199	A14	15c gold, brt grn & rose claret	.25	.25
200	A14	25c gold, org & blue	.25	.25
201	A14	50c gold, ver & green	.25	.25
202	A14	$1 multicolored	.30	.30
	Nos. 199-202 (4)		1.05	1.05

19th Olympic Games, Mexico City, 10/12-27.

Albert T. Marryshow A15

Portraits and Human Rights Flame: 5c, Alexander Hamilton. 25c, William Wilberforce. 50c, Dag Hammarskjold. $1, Rev. Martin Luther King, Jr.

1968, Dec. 2 Photo. Perf. 14x14½

203	A15	5c multicolored	.25	.25
204	A15	15c multicolored	.25	.25
205	A15	25c multicolored	.25	.25
206	A15	50c multicolored	.25	.25
207	A15	$1 multicolored	.25	.25
	Nos. 203-207 (5)		1.25	1.25

International Human Rights Year.

The Two Trinities, by Murillo — A16

Christmas: 15c, 50c, The Adoration of the Magi, by Botticelli.

1968, Dec. 16 Perf. 14½x14

208	A16	5c red & multi	.25	.25
209	A16	15c dk green & multi	.25	.25
210	A16	25c purple & multi	.25	.25
211	A16	50c brown & multi	.25	.25
	Nos. 208-211 (4)		1.00	1.00

Map of Caribbean — A17

Design: 35c, 50c, "Strength in Unity," horiz.

1969, May 27 Photo. Perf. 14

212	A17	15c green & multi	.25	.25
213	A17	20c brown & multi	.25	.25
214	A17	35c dp carmine & multi	.25	.25
215	A17	50c multicolored	.25	.25
	Nos. 212-215 (4)		1.00	1.00

First anniversary of CARIFTA (Caribbean Free Trade Area).

Telephone and Map — A18

Development Projects (Map and): 25c, Book and "New Schools." 50c, Planes (air transport service). $1, Pylon and power lines.

Wmk. 314
1969, July 29 Litho. Perf. 13½

216	A18	15c multicolored	.25	.25
217	A18	25c multicolored	.25	.25
218	A18	50c multicolored	.25	.25
219	A18	$1 multicolored	.25	.25
	Nos. 216-219 (4)		1.00	1.00

Dolphin — A19

Fish: 15c, Atlantic sailfish. 25c, Blackfin tuna and fishing boat. 40c, Spanish mackerel.

1969, Nov. 1 Photo. Perf. 13x14

220	A19	5c multicolored	.25	.25
221	A19	15c multicolored	.35	.35
222	A19	25c multicolored	.70	.70
223	A19	40c multicolored	1.15	1.15
	Nos. 220-223 (4)		2.45	2.45

MONTSERRAT

King Caspar, Virgin and Child (Stained-glass Window) — A20

Christmas: 50c, Nativity, by Leonard Limosin, horiz.

1969, Dec. 10   Litho.   Perf. 12½x13, 13x12½   Wmk. 314
224	A20	15c violet & multi	.25	.25
225	A20	25c red & multi	.25	.25
226	A20	50c orange & multi	.25	.25
		Nos. 224-226 (3)	.75	.75

Red Cross and Distribution of Hearing Aids — A21

Red Cross and: 3c, Fund raising sale and invalid. 15c, Car bringing handicapped to work. 20c, Instruction for blind worker.

1970, Apr. 13   Litho.   Perf. 14½
227	A21	3c multicolored	.25	.25
228	A21	4c multicolored	.25	.25
229	A21	15c multicolored	.25	.25
230	A21	20c multicolored	.25	.25
		Nos. 227-230 (4)	1.00	1.00

Centenary of British Red Cross Society.

Red-footed Booby — A22

Birds: 2c, Killy hawk, vert. 3c, Frigate bird, vert. 4c, White egret, vert. 5c, Brown pelican, vert. 10c, Bananaquit, vert. 15c, Common ani. 20c, Tropic bird. 25c, Montserrat oriole. 50c, Greenthroated carib, vert. $1, Antillean crested hummingbird. $2.50, Little blue heron, vert. $5, Purple-throated carib. $10, Forest thrush.

Wmk. 314 Upright on Horiz. Stamps, Sideways on Vert. Stamps
Perf. 14x14½, 14½x14

1970-74   Photo.
231	A22	1c yel org & multi	.25	.25
232	A22	2c lt vio & multi	.25	.25
233	A22	3c multicolored	.25	.25
234	A22	4c lt grn & multi	.25	.25
235	A22	5c bister & multi	.25	.25
236	A22	10c gray & multi	.25	.25
237	A22	15c multicolored	.50	.40
238	A22	20c rose brn & multi	.65	.55
239	A22	25c brown & multi	.85	.70
240	A22	50c lt vio & multi	1.75	1.40
241	A22	$1 multicolored	3.00	2.40
242	A22	$2.50 dl bl & multi	6.75	5.50
243	A22	$5 multicolored	13.50	11.00
243A	A22	$10 blue & multi	26.00	22.50
		Nos. 231-243A (14)	54.50	45.95

Issued: $10, 10/30/74; others 7/2/70. For surcharges and overprints see Nos 314, 317, 337-339, O1-O4.

Wmk. Sideways on Horiz. Stamps, Upright on Vert. Stamps

1972-74
231a	A22	1c multicolored	.80	1.10
232a	A22	2c multicolored	1.00	1.10
233a	A22	3c multicolored	1.00	1.10
234a	A22	4c multicolored	1.50	1.50
235a	A22	5c multicolored	2.00	1.75
237a	A22	15c multicolored	5.00	4.50
238a	A22	20c multicolored	7.00	7.50
239a	A22	25c multicolored	9.75	9.50
		Nos. 231a-239a (8)	28.05	28.05

Issued: 1c, 2c, 3c, 7/21/72; 5c, 15c, 3/8/73; 20c, 10/2/73; 4c, 2/4/74; 25c, 5/17/74.

"Madonna and Child with Animals," after Dürer — A23

Christmas: 15c, $1, Adoration of the Shepherds, by Domenichino (Domenico Zampieri).

1970, Sept. 21   Litho.   Perf. 14
244	A23	5c lt blue & multi	.25	.25
245	A23	15c red orange & multi	.25	.25
246	A23	20c ol green & multi	.25	.25
247	A23	$1 multicolored	.40	.40
		Nos. 244-247 (4)	1.15	1.15

War Memorial, Plymouth A24

Tourist Publicity: 15c, Fort St. George and view of Plymouth. 25c, Beach at Carrs Bay. 50c, Golf Course.

1970, Nov. 30   Litho.   Perf. 14
248	A24	5c multicolored	.25	.25
249	A24	15c multicolored	.40	.40
250	A24	25c multicolored	.70	.70
251	A24	$1 multicolored	1.40	1.40
a.		Souvenir sheet of 4, #248-251	6.00	6.00
		Nos. 248-251 (4)	2.75	2.75

Girl Guide — A25

Girl Guides' 60th Anniv.: 15c, 25c, Brownie.

1970, Dec. 31
252	A25	10c orange & multi	.25	.25
253	A25	15c lt blue & multi	.25	.25
254	A25	25c lilac & multi	.25	.25
255	A25	40c multicolored	.30	.30
		Nos. 252-255 (4)	1.05	1.05

"Noli me Tangere," by Orcagna (Andrea di Cione) — A26

Easter: 5c, 20c, Descent from the Cross, by Jan van Hemessen.

1971, Mar. 22   Photo.   Perf. 13½x13   Wmk. 314
256	A26	5c orange brn & multi	.25	.25
257	A26	15c multicolored	.25	.25
258	A26	20c green & multi	.25	.25
259	A26	40c blue green & multi	.25	.25
		Nos. 256-259 (4)	1.00	1.00

Distinguished Flying Cross and Medal — A27

Highest Awards for Military Personnel: 20c, Military Cross and Medal. 40c, Distinguished Service Cross and Medal. $1, Victoria Cross.

1971, July 8   Perf. 14½x14   Wmk. 314
260	A27	10c gray, vio & silver	.25	.25
261	A27	20c green & multi	.25	.25
262	A27	40c lt bl, dk bl & sil	.25	.25
263	A27	$1 red, dk brn & gold	.30	.30
		Nos. 260-263 (4)	1.05	1.05

50th anniversary of the British Commonwealth Ex-services League.

"Nativity with Saints" (detail), by Romanino — A28

Christmas (Paintings): 15c, $1, Angels' Choir, by Simon Marmion.

1971, Sept. 16   Perf. 14x13½
264	A28	5c brown & multi	.25	.25
265	A28	15c emerald & multi	.25	.25
266	A28	20c ultra & multi	.25	.25
267	A28	$1 red & multi	.35	.35
		Nos. 264-267 (4)	1.10	1.10

Piper Apache, First Landing at Olveston Airfield — A29

Designs: 10c, Beech Twin Bonanza. 15c, De Havilland Heron. 20c, Britten Norman Islander. 40c, De Havilland Twin Otter. 75c, Hawker Siddeley 748 and stewardesses.

1971, Dec. 16   Perf. 13½x14
268	A29	5c multicolored	.25	.25
269	A29	10c multicolored	.30	.30
270	A29	15c multicolored	.45	.45
271	A29	20c multicolored	.65	.65
272	A29	40c multicolored	1.25	1.25
273	A29	75c multicolored	2.00	2.00
a.		Souvenir sheet of 6, #268-273	15.00	15.00
		Nos. 268-273 (6)	4.90	4.90

14th anniversary of Leeward Islands Air Transport (LIAT).

Chapel of Christ in Gethsemane, Coventry Cathedral A30

Easter: 10c, 75c, The Agony in the Garden, by Giovanni Bellini.

1972, Mar. 9   Litho.   Perf. 13½x13
274	A30	5c red & multi	.25	.25
275	A30	10c blue & multi	.25	.25
276	A30	20c emerald & multi	.25	.25
277	A30	75c lilac & multi	.75	.75
		Nos. 274-277 (4)	1.50	1.50

Iguana — A31

Designs: 15c, Spotted amelva (lizard), vert. 20c, Frog (mountain chicken), vert. $1, Redfoot tortoises.

1972, June 8   Litho.   Perf. 14½
278	A31	15c lilac rose & multi	.60	.60
279	A31	20c black & multi	.70	.70
280	A31	40c blue & multi	1.50	1.50
281	A31	$1 green & multi	2.75	2.75
		Nos. 278-281 (4)	5.55	5.55

Madonna of the Chair, by Raphael — A32

Christmas (Paintings): 35c, Virgin and Child with Cherubs, by Bernardino Fungai. 50c, Magnificat Madonna, by Botticelli. $1, Virgin and Child with St. John and Angel, by Botticelli.

1972, Oct. 18   Perf. 13½
282	A32	10c violet & multi	.25	.25
283	A32	35c red brn & multi	.25	.25
284	A32	50c red brown & multi	.30	.30
285	A32	$1 olive & multi	.50	.50
		Nos. 282-285 (4)	1.30	1.30

Silver Wedding Issue, 1972
Common Design Type

Design: Queen Elizabeth II, Prince Philip, tomatoes, papayas, limes.

1972, Nov. 20   Photo.   Perf. 14x14½   Wmk. 314
286	CD324	35c car rose & multi	.25	.25
287	CD324	$1 ultra & multi	.25	.25

Passionflower — A33

Designs: 35c, Passiflora vitifolia. 75c, Passiflora amabilis. $1, Passiflora alata caerulea.

1973, Apr. 9   Litho.   Perf. 14x13½
288	A33	20c purple & multi	.45	.45
289	A33	35c multicolored	.80	.80
290	A33	75c brt blue & multi	1.25	1.25
291	A33	$1 multicolored	2.00	2.00
		Nos. 288-291 (4)	4.50	4.50

Easter. Black backprinting gives story of passionflower.

Montserrat Monastery, Spain — A34

35c, Columbus aboard ship sighting Montserrat. 60c, Columbus' ship off Montserrat. $1, Arms and map of Montserrat & neighboring islands.

1973, July 16   Litho.   Perf. 13½x14
292	A34	10c multicolored	.45	.45
293	A34	35c multicolored	1.00	1.00
294	A34	60c multicolored	1.50	1.50
295	A34	$1 multicolored	2.25	2.25
a.		Souvenir sheet of 4, #292-295	16.00	16.00
		Nos. 292-295 (4)	5.20	5.20

480th anniversary of the discovery of Montserrat by Columbus.

Virgin and Child, Studio of David — A35

Christmas (Paintings): 35c, Holy Family with St. John, by Jacob Jordaens. 50c, Virgin and Child, by Bellini. 90c, Virgin and Child by Carlo Dolci.

1973, Oct. 15   Litho.   Perf. 14x13½
296	A35	20c blue & multi	.25	.25
297	A35	35c ol bister & multi	.30	.30
298	A35	50c brt green & multi	.40	.40
299	A35	90c brt rose & multi	.55	.55
		Nos. 296-299 (4)	1.50	1.50

Princess Anne's Wedding Issue
Common Design Type

1973, Nov. 14   Perf. 14
300	CD325	35c brt green & multi	.25	.25
301	CD325	$1 multicolored	.30	.30

MONTSERRAT

Masqueraders — A36

20c, Steel band, horiz. 60c, Girl weaving. $1, University Center, horiz.

1974, Apr. 8
302	A36	20c multi	.25	.25
303	A36	35c shown	.25	.25
304	A36	60c multi	.25	.25
305	A36	$1 multi	.40	.40
a.	Souvenir sheet of 4, #302-305		4.25	4.25
	Nos. 302-305 (4)		1.15	1.15

University of the West Indies, 25th anniv. For surcharge see No. 316.

Hands Holding Letters, UPU Emblem — A37

Designs: 2c, 5c, $1, Hands and figures from UPU Monument, Bern; UPU emblem. 3c, 50c, like 1c.

1974, July 3   Litho.   Perf. 14
306	A37	1c violet & multi	.25	.25
307	A37	2c red & black	.25	.25
308	A37	3c olive & multi	.25	.25
309	A37	5c orange & black	.25	.25
310	A37	50c brown & multi	.25	.25
311	A37	$1 grnsh blue & black	.40	.40
	Nos. 306-311 (6)		1.65	1.65

Centenary of Universal Postal Union. For surcharges see Nos. 315-318.

Churchill, Parliament, Big Ben — A38

Churchill and Blenheim Palace — A39

Perf. 13x13½

1974, Nov. 30   Unwmk.
312	A38	35c ocher & multi	.25	.25
313	A39	70c brt green & multi	.30	.30
a.	Souvenir sheet of 2, #312-313		.70	.70

Sir Winston Churchill (1874-1965).

Nos. 241, 304, 310-311 Surcharged

Perf. 14x14½, 14
Photo., Litho.

1974, Oct. 2   Wmk. 314
314	A22	2c on $1 multi	.30	.30
315	A37	5c on 50c multi	1.40	1.40
316	A36	10c on 60c multi	3.75	3.75
317	A22	20c on $1 multi	1.25	1.25
a.	One bar in surcharge		4.00	4.00
318	A37	35c on $1 multi	2.75	2.75
	Nos. 314-318 (5)		9.45	9.45

Carib Carbet (House) — A40

Carib Artifacts: 20c, Necklace (caracoli). 35c, Club. 70c, Canoe.

Wmk. 314

1975, Mar. 3   Litho.   Perf. 14
319	A40	5c dk red, ocher & blk	.25	.25
320	A40	20c blk, och & dk red	.25	.25
321	A40	35c blk, dk red & och	.25	.25
322	A40	70c ocher, dk red & blk	.35	.35
a.	Souvenir booklet		4.00	
	Nos. 319-322 (4)		1.10	1.10

No. 322a contains 2 self-adhesive panes printed on peelable paper backing with bicolored advertising on back. One pane of 6 contains 3 each similar to Nos. 320-321; the other pane of 4 contains one each similar to Nos. 319-322. Stamps are imperf. x roulette. Panes have commemorative marginal inscription.

One Bitt — A41

Old Local Coinage (1785-1801): 10c, Eighth of a dollar. 35c, Quarter dollars. $2, One dollar.

1975, Sept. 1   Litho.   Perf. 14
323	A41	5c ultra, silver & blk	.25	.25
324	A41	10c brown org, sil & blk	.25	.25
325	A41	35c green, silver & blk	.35	.35
326	A41	$2 brt rose, sil & blk	1.10	1.10
a.	Souvenir sheet of 4, #323-326		2.25	2.25
	Nos. 323-326 (4)		1.95	1.95

Explanation and description of coinage printed in black on back of souvenir sheet.

Montserrat Nos. 1 and 2 — A42

10c, Post Office, Montserrat & #1a with AO8 cancel. 40c, Cover with #1a, 1b. 55c, #A4 (G.B. #27 with AO8 cancel) & #2. 70c, 2 #1, 1 #1a with AO8 cancels. $1.10, Packet "Antelope" & #2.

1976, Jan. 5   Perf. 13½
327	A42	5c multicolored	.25	.25
328	A42	10c multicolored	.25	.25
329	A42	40c multicolored	.50	.50
330	A42	55c multicolored	.65	.65
331	A42	70c multicolored	.85	.85
332	A42	$1.10 multicolored	1.25	1.25
a.	Souvenir sheet of 6, #327-332		4.25	4.25
	Nos. 327-332 (6)		3.75	3.75

Centenary of Montserrat's postage stamps.

Trinity, by Orcagna — A43

Paintings by Orcagna (Andrea di Cione): 40c, Resurrection. 55c, Ascension. $1.10, Pentecost.

Perf. 14x13½

1976, Apr. 5   Wmk. 373
333	A43	15c multicolored	.25	.25
334	A43	40c multicolored	.25	.25
335	A43	55c multicolored	.25	.25
336	A43	$1.10 multicolored	.30	.30
a.	Souvenir sheet of 4		1.90	1.90
	Nos. 333-336 (4)		1.05	1.05

Easter 1976. Nos. 333-336 were prepared, but not issued in 1975. Stamps are surcharged with new values; date "1975" obliterated with heavy bar. No. 336a contains one each of Nos. 333-336; "1975" in margin obliterated with heavy bar.

Nos. 235-236, 233 Surcharged

White Frangipani A44

Designs: Flowering trees of Montserrat.

Perf. 14½x14

1976, Apr. 12   Photo.   Wmk. 314
337	A22	2c on 5c multi	.35	.35
338	A22	30c on 10c multi	.70	.70
339	A22	45c on 3c multi	1.20	1.20
	Nos. 337-339 (3)		2.25	2.25

For overprints see Nos. O3-O4.

Perf. 13½x14

1976, July 5   Litho.   Wmk. 373
340	A44	1c shown	.25	.25
341	A44	2c Cannonball tree	.25	.25
342	A44	3c Lignum vitae	.25	.25
343	A44	5c Malay apple	.25	.25
344	A44	10c Jacaranda	.25	.25
345	A44	15c Orchid tree	.25	.25
346	A44	20c Manjak	.25	.25
347	A44	25c Tamarind	.25	.25
348	A44	40c Flame of the Forest	.25	.25
349	A44	55c Pink cassia	.30	.30
350	A44	70c Long John	.35	.35
351	A44	$1 Saman	.55	.55
352	A44	$2.50 Immortelle	1.40	1.40
353	A44	$5 Yellow poui	2.25	2.25
354	A44	$10 Flamboyant	5.50	5.50
	Nos. 340-354 (15)		12.60	12.60

For surcharges and overprints see Nos. 374-376, 420, 435-440, O10-O44.

Mary and Joseph on Road to Bethlehem — A45

Christmas (Map of Montserrat and): 20c, Shepherds. 55c, Virgin and Child. $1.10, Three Kings.

1976, Oct. 4   Perf. 14½
355	A45	15c vio blue & multi	.25	.25
356	A45	20c green & multi	.25	.25
357	A45	55c lilac & multi	.25	.25
358	A45	$1.10 multicolored	.30	.30
a.	Souvenir sheet of 4, #355-358		2.00	2.00
	Nos. 355-358 (4)		1.05	1.05

Hudson River Review of Opsail 76 A46

Designs: 40c, Raleigh. 75c, HMS Druid (Raleigh attacking Druid, 1776).

1976, Dec. 13   Litho.   Perf. 13
359		15c multicolored	.30	.30
a.	A46 Pair, #359, 362		1.90	1.90
360		40c multicolored	.65	.65
361		75c multicolored	1.10	1.10
a.	A46 Pair, #360-361		1.75	1.75
362		$1.25 multicolored	1.60	1.60
a.	A46 Souvenir sheet of 4, #359-362, perf. 14x13½		4.00	4.00
	Nos. 359-362 (4)		3.65	3.65

American Bicentennial.

Queen Arriving for 1966 Visit, Yacht Britannia A48

Designs: 45c, Firing of cannons at Tower of London. $1, The crowning.

1977, Feb. 7
363	A48	30c multicolored	.25	.25
364	A48	45c multicolored	.25	.25
365	A48	$1 multicolored	.25	.25
	Nos. 363-365 (3)		.75	.75

25th anniv. of the reign of Elizabeth II. #363-365 were issued also in booklet panes of 4.

Epiphyllum Hookeri — A49

Flowers of the Night: 15c, Ipomoea alba, vert. 55c, Cereus hexagonus. $1.50, Cestrum nocturnum, vert.

1977, June 1   Litho.   Perf. 14
366	A49	15c multicolored	.25	.25
367	A49	40c multicolored	.30	.30
368	A49	55c multicolored	.40	.40
369	A49	$1.50 multicolored	1.10	1.10
a.	Souvenir sheet of 4, #366-369		3.25	3.25
	Nos. 366-369 (4)		2.05	2.05

Princess Anne at Ground-breaking Ceremony, Glendon Hospital — A50

Designs: 40c, New deep-water jetty, Plymouth. 55c, Glendon Hospital. $1.50, Freighter unloading at new jetty.

1977, Oct. 3   Wmk. 373   Perf. 14½
370	A50	20c multicolored	.25	.25
371	A50	40c multicolored	.25	.25
372	A50	55c multicolored	.30	.30
373	A50	$1.50 multicolored	.80	.80
a.	Souvenir sheet of 4, #370-373		2.50	2.50
	Nos. 370-373 (4)		1.60	1.60

Development.

Nos. 349-350, 352 Surcharged with New Value and Bars and Overprinted: "SILVER JUBILEE 1977 / ROYAL VISIT / TO THE CARIBBEAN"

1977, Oct.   Litho.   Perf. 13½x14
374	A44	$1 on 55c multi	.30	.30
375	A44	$1 on 70c multi	.30	.30
376	A44	$1 on $2.50 multi	.30	.30
	Nos. 374-376 (3)		.90	.90

Caribbean visit of Queen Elizabeth II. Surcharge has bars of differing thickness and length. No. 374 has two settings.

"Silent Night, Holy Night" — A51

Christmas Carols and Map of Montserrat: 40c, "We Three Kings of Orient Are." 55c, "I Saw Three Ships Come Sailing In." $2, "Hark the Herald Angels Sing."

1977, Nov. 14   Litho.   Perf. 14½
377	A51	5c blue & multi	.25	.25
378	A51	40c bister & multi	.25	.25
379	A51	55c lt blue & multi	.25	.25
380	A51	$2 rose & multi	.40	.40
a.	Souvenir sheet of 4, #377-380		1.25	1.25
	Nos. 377-380 (4)		1.15	1.15

Four-eye Butterflyfish A52

Fish: 40c, French angelfish. 55c, Blue tang. $1.50, Queen triggerfish.

1978, Feb. 27   Wmk. 373   Perf. 14
381	A52	30c multicolored	.40	.40
382	A52	40c multicolored	.50	.50
383	A52	55c multicolored	.70	.70

MONTSERRAT

384	A52	$1.50 multicolored		2.00	2.00
a.	Souvenir sheet of 4, #381-384			5.25	5.25
	Nos. 381-384 (4)			3.60	3.60

Elizabeth II and St. Paul's, London — A53

Designs: 55c, Chichester Cathedral. $1, Lincoln Cathedral. $2.50, Llandaff Cathedral, Cardiff.

1978, June 2   Perf. 13½

385	A53	40c multicolored	.25	.25
386	A53	55c multicolored	.25	.25
387	A53	$1 multicolored	.25	.25
388	A53	$2.50 multicolored	.40	.40
a.	Souvenir sheet of 4, #385-388		1.10	1.10
	Nos. 385-388 (4)		1.15	1.15

25th anniversary of coronation of Elizabeth II, Defender of the Faith. Nos. 385-388 printed in sheets of 10 stamps and 2 labels. Nos. 385-388 also issued in bklt. panes of 2.

Alpinia — A54

Flowering Plants: 55c, Allamanda cathartica. $1, Blue tree petrea. $2, Amaryllis.

1978, Sept. 18   Litho.   Perf. 13½x13

389	A54	40c multicolored	.25	.25
390	A54	55c multicolored	.35	.35
391	A54	$1 multicolored	.65	.65
392	A54	$2 multicolored	1.25	1.25
	Nos. 389-392 (4)		2.50	2.50

Private, 1796 — A55

Uniforms: 40c, Corporal, 1831. 55c, Sergeant, 1837. $1.50, Officer, 1784.

1978, Nov. 20   Litho.   Perf. 14½

393	A55	30c multicolored	.25	.25
394	A55	40c multicolored	.25	.25
395	A55	55c multicolored	.35	.35
396	A55	$1.50 multicolored	1.00	1.00
a.	Souvenir sheet of 4, #393-396		2.25	2.25
	Nos. 393-396 (4)		1.85	1.85

See Nos. 401-404.

Cub Scouts — A56

Boy Scouts: 55c, Signaling. $1.25, Cooking, vert. $2, Flag folding ceremony, vert.

1979, Apr. 2   Litho.   Perf. 14

397	A56	40c multicolored	.25	.25
398	A56	55c multicolored	.30	.30
399	A56	$1.25 multicolored	.70	.70
400	A56	$2 multicolored	.75	.75
a.	Souvenir sheet of 4, #397-400		2.75	2.75
	Nos. 397-400 (4)		2.00	2.00

50th anniversary of Scouting in Montserrat.

Uniform Type of 1978

30c, Private, 1783. 40c, Private, 1819. 55c, Officer, 1819. $2.50, Highlander officer, 1830.

1979, July 4   Wmk. 373   Perf. 14

401	A55	30c multicolored	.25	.25
402	A55	40c multicolored	.25	.25
403	A55	55c multicolored	.25	.25
404	A55	$2.50 multicolored	1.25	1.25
a.	Souvenir sheet of 4, #401-404		2.50	2.50
	Nos. 401-404 (4)		2.00	2.00

IYC Emblem, Learning to Walk — A56a

1979, Sept. 17   Litho.   Perf. 13½x14

405	A56a	$2 brown org & black	.60	.60
a.	Souvenir sheet		1.40	1.40

International Year of the Child.

Hill, Penny Black, Montserrat No. 1 — A57

Designs: 55c, UPU Emblem, charter. $1, UPU Emblem, cover. $2, Hill, Post Office regulations.

1979, Oct. 1   Perf. 14

406	A57	40c multicolored	.25	.25
407	A57	55c multicolored	.25	.25
408	A57	$1 multicolored	.35	.35
409	A57	$2 multicolored	.70	.70
a.	Souvenir sheet of 4, #406-409		2.50	2.50
	Nos. 406-409 (4)		1.55	1.55

Sir Rowland Hill (1795-1879), originator of penny postage; UPU membership, centenary.

Tree Lizard — A58

1980, Feb. 4   Litho.   Perf. 14

410	A58	40c Tree frog	.35	.35
411	A58	55c shown	.50	.50
412	A58	$1 Crapaud	.90	.90
413	A58	$2 Wood slave	1.90	1.90
	Nos. 410-413 (4)		3.65	3.65

Marquis of Salisbury, 1817; Postmarks, 1838, London 1980 Emblem — A59

Ships or Planes, Stamps of Montserrat: 55c, H.S. 748, #349. #416, La Plata, 1901, type A4. #417, Lady Hawkins, 1929, #84. #418, Avon, 1843, Gt Britain #3. #419, Aeronca, #140.

1980, Apr. 14   Litho.   Perf. 14½

414	A59	40c multicolored	.25	.25
415	A59	55c multicolored	.30	.30
416	A59	$1.20 multicolored	.55	.60
417	A59	$1.20 multicolored	.55	.60
418	A59	$1.20 multicolored	.55	.60
419	A59	$1.20 multicolored	.55	.60
a.	Souvenir sheet of 6, #414-419		3.00	3.00
	Nos. 414-419 (6)		2.75	2.95

London 1980 Intl. Stamp Exhib., May 6-14. For surcharges see Nos. 736-740.

No. 352 Overprinted: 75th Anniversary of / Rotary International

1980, July 7   Litho.   Perf. 13½x14

420	A44	$2.50 multicolored	1.25	1.25

Discus Thrower, Stadium, Olympic Rings — A60

Flags of Host Countries: 40c, Greece, 1896; France, 1900; U.S., 1904. 55c, Great Britain, 1908; Sweden, 1912; Belgium, 1920. 70c, France, 1924; Netherlands, 1928; US, 1932. $1, Germany, 1936; Great Britain, 1948; Finland, 1952. $1.50, Australia, 1956; Italy, 1960; Japan, 1964. $2, Mexico, 1968; Fed. Rep. of Germany, 1972; Canada, 1976.

1980, July 7   Litho.   Perf. 14

421	A60	40c multicolored	.25	.25
422	A60	55c multicolored	.25	.25
423	A60	70c multicolored	.30	.30
424	A60	$1 multicolored	.40	.40
425	A60	$1.50 multicolored	.50	.50
426	A60	$2 multicolored	.70	.70
427	A60	$2.50 multicolored	.90	.90
a.	Souv. sheet of 7, #421-427 + 2 labels		3.50	3.50
	Nos. 421-427 (7)		3.30	3.30

22nd Summer Olympic Games, Moscow, July 19-Aug. 3.

Lady Nelson, 1928 — A61

1980   Litho.   Perf. 14

428	A61	40c shown	.25	.25
429	A61	55c Chignecto, 1913	.40	.40
430	A61	$1 Solent, 1878	.75	.75
431	A61	$2 Dee, 1841	1.25	1.25
	Nos. 428-431 (4)		2.65	2.65

Plume Worm — A62

1980   Litho.   Perf. 14

432	A62	40c shown	.50	.50
433	A62	55c Sea fans	.70	.70
434	A62	$2 Coral, sponges	1.75	1.75
	Nos. 432-434 (3)		2.95	2.95

Nos. 340, 342, 345, 348 Surcharged

1980, Sept. 30   Litho.   Perf. 14

435	A44	5c on 3c (#342)	.25	.25
436	A44	35c on 1c (#340)	.25	.25
437	A44	35c on 3c (#342)	.25	.25
438	A44	35c on 15c (#345)	.25	.25
439	A44	55c on 40c (#348)	.25	.25
440	A44	$5 on 40c (#348)	1.40	1.40
	Nos. 435-440 (6)		2.65	2.65

Zebra Butterfly — A63

65c, Tropical checkered skipper. $1.50, Large orange sulphur. $2.50, Monarch.

1981, Feb. 2   Wmk. 373

441	A63	50c shown	.75	.75
442	A63	65c multi	.90	.90
443	A63	$1.50 multi	1.10	1.10
444	A63	$2.50 multi	1.60	1.60
	Nos. 441-444 (4)		4.35	4.35

Spadefish — A64

10c, Hogfish. 15c, Creole wrasse. 20c, Yellow damselfish. 25c, Sergeant major. 35c, Clown wrasse. 45c, Schoolmaster. 55c, Striped parrotfish. 65c, Bigeye. 75c, French grunt. $1, Rock beauty. $2, Blue chromis. $3, Fairy basslet, blueheads. $5, Cherubfish. $7.50, Longspine squirrelfish. $10, Longsnout butterflyfish.

Wmk. 373

1981, Mar. 20   Litho.   Perf. 13½

445	A64	5c shown	.25	.25
446	A64	10c multi	.25	.25
447	A64	15c multi	.25	.25
448	A64	20c multi	.25	.25
449	A64	25c multi	.25	.25
450	A64	35c multi	.25	.25
451	A64	45c multi	.40	.40
452	A64	55c multi	1.25	1.25
453	A64	65c multi	.55	.55
454	A64	75c multi	.60	.60
455	A64	$1 multi	.85	.85
456	A64	$2 multi	1.75	1.75
457	A64	$3 multi	2.75	2.75
458	A64	$5 multi	4.25	4.25
459	A64	$7.50 multi	4.75	4.75
460	A64	$10 multi	7.25	7.25
	Nos. 445-460 (16)		25.90	25.90

For surcharges and overprints see Nos. 507-508, 511-512, 515, O45-O55, O95-O97.

Inscribed 1983

1983   Wmk. 380

445a	A64	5c	.30	.30
446a	A64	10c	.35	.35
449a	A64	25c	.40	.40
450a	A64	35c	.45	.45
454a	A64	75c	.65	.65
455a	A64	$1	.85	.85
458a	A64	$5	3.75	3.75
460a	A64	$10	6.75	6.75
	Nos. 445a-460a (8)		13.50	13.50

Fort St. George (National Trust) — A65

65c, Bird Sanctuary, Fox's Bay. $1.50, The Museum. $2.50, Bransby Point Battery.

1981, May 18   Wmk. 373   Perf. 13½

461	A65	50c shown	.30	.30
462	A65	65c multi	.30	.30
463	A65	$1.50 multi	.70	.70
464	A65	$2.50 multi	1.40	1.50
	Nos. 461-464 (4)		2.70	2.80

Prince Charles, Lady Diana, Royal Yacht — A66

Prince Charles and Lady Diana A67

Wmk. 380

1981, July 13   Litho.   Perf. 14

465	A66	90c Charlotte	.35	.35
a.	Booklet pane of 4, perf. 12		1.75	
466	A67	90c shown	1.25	1.25
467	A66	$3 Portsmouth	.85	.85
468	A67	$3 like #466	2.10	2.10
a.	Booklet pane of 2, perf. 12		3.50	
469	A66	$4 Britannia	1.10	1.10
470	A67	$4 like #466	2.40	2.40
	Nos. 465-470 (6)		8.05	8.05

Royal wedding. Each denomination issued in sheets of 7 (6 type A66, 1 type A67). For surcharges and overprints see Nos. 509-510, 513-514, 578-579, O56-O61.

Souvenir Sheet

1981, Dec.   Perf. 12

471	A67	$5 multicolored	2.75	2.75

50th Anniv. of Airmail Service — A68

50c, Seaplane, Dorsetshire. 65c, Beechcraft Twin Bonanza. $1.50, DeHaviland Dragon Rapide. $2.50, Hawker Siddeley Avro 748.

1981, Aug. 31   Wmk. 373   Perf. 14

472	A68	50c multicolored	.40	.40
473	A68	65c multicolored	.50	.50
474	A68	$1.50 multicolored	1.00	1.00
475	A68	$2.50 multicolored	1.60	1.60
	Nos. 472-475 (4)		3.50	3.50

Methodist Church, Bethel — A69

Christmas (Churches): 65c, St. George's Anglican, Harris. $1.50, St. Peter's Anglican, St. Peter's. $2.50, St. Patrick's Roman Catholic, Plymouth.

1981, Nov. 16   Litho.   Perf. 14

476	A69	50c multicolored	.25	.25
477	A69	65c multicolored	.30	.30
478	A69	$1.50 multicolored	.50	.50

MONTSERRAT

479	A69	$2.50 multicolored	.90	.90
a.		Souvenir sheet of 4, #476-479	2.75	2.75
		Nos. 476-479 (4)	1.95	1.95

Wild Flowers First Discovered on Montserrat — A70

50c, Rondeletia buxifolia, vert. 65c, Heliotropium ternatum. $1.50, Picramnia pentandra, vert. $2.50, Diospyros revoluta.

1982, Jan. 18   Litho.   Perf. 14½

480	A70	50c multicolored	.25	.25
481	A70	65c multicolored	.25	.25
482	A70	$1.50 multicolored	.50	.50
483	A70	$2.50 multicolored	1.10	1.10
		Nos. 480-483 (4)	2.10	2.10

350th Anniv. of Settlement of Montserrat by Sir Thomas Warner — A70a

Jubilee Type of 1932.

Wmk. 373

1982, Apr. 17   Litho.   Perf. 14½

483A	A70a	40c green	.25	.25
483B	A70a	55c red	.25	.25
483C	A70a	65c brown	.30	.30
483D	A70a	75c gray	.30	.30
483E	A70a	85c ultra	.35	.35
483F	A70a	95c orange	.40	.40
483G	A70a	$1 purple	.40	.40
483H	A70a	$1.50 olive	.60	.60
483I	A70a	$2 car rose	.75	.75
483J	A70a	$2.50 sepia	1.05	1.05
		Nos. 483A-483J (10)	4.65	4.65

A70b

75c, Catherine of Aragon, 1501. $1, Aragon arms. $5, Diana.

1982, June   Wmk. 380   Perf. 14

484	A70b	75c multi	.30	.30
485	A70b	$1 multi	.30	.30
486	A70b	$5 multi	1.25	1.25
		Nos. 484-486 (3)	1.85	1.85

21st birthday of Princess Diana, July 1.
For surcharges and overprints see Nos. 574, O62-O64.

Scouting Year — A71

1982, Sept. 13   Litho.   Perf. 14

487	A71	$1.50 Scout	.75	.75
488	A71	$2.50 Baden-Powell	1.10	1.10

Christmas — A72

35c, Annunciation. 75c, Shepherds' vision. $1.50, Virgin and Child. $2.50, Flight into Egypt.

1982, Nov. 18   Wmk. 373   Perf. 14

489	A72	35c multi	.25	.25
490	A72	75c multi	.35	.35
491	A72	$1.50 multi	.60	.60
492	A72	$2.50 multi	1.10	1.10
		Nos. 489-492 (4)	2.30	2.30

Dragonflies — A73

50c, Lepthemis vesiculosa. 65c, Orthemis ferruginea. $1.50, Triacanthagyna trifida. $2.50, Erythrodiplax umbrata.

1983, Jan. 19   Litho.   Perf. 13½x14

493	A73	50c multi	.55	.55
494	A73	65c multi	.70	.70
495	A73	$1.50 multi	1.40	1.40
496	A73	$2.50 multi	2.00	2.00
		Nos. 493-496 (4)	4.65	4.65

Blue-headed Hummingbird — A74

75c, Green-throated carib. $2, Antillean crested hummingbird. $3, Purple-throated carib.

1983, May 24   Wmk. 373   Perf. 14

497	A74	35c shown	.90	.90
498	A74	75c multi	1.25	1.25
499	A74	$2 multi	3.25	3.25
500	A74	$3 multi	4.50	4.50
		Nos. 497-500 (4)	9.90	9.90

Arms — A75

1983, July 25   Litho.   Perf. 14½

501	A75	$12 red & black	5.00	5.00
502	A75	$30 blue & red	15.00	15.00

Manned Flight Bicentenary A76

Designs: 35c, Montgolfiere, 1783, vert. 75c, De Havilland Twin Otter 310, 1981. $1.50, Lockheed Vega's around the world flight, 1933. $2, British R34 airship transatlantic flight, 1919.

1983, Sept. 19   Litho.   Perf. 14

503	A76	35c multicolored	.30	.30
504	A76	75c multicolored	.40	.40
505	A76	$1.50 multicolored	.60	.60
506	A76	$2 multicolored	.90	.90
a.		Souvenir sheet of 4, #503-506	2.75	2.75
		Nos. 503-506 (4)	2.20	2.20

For surcharges see Nos. 573, 577.

Nos. 449, 446, 467-468, 453-454, 469-470, 456 Surcharged

Wmk. 373 (A64), 380

1983, Aug. 15   Litho.   Perf. 13½x14

507	A64	40c on 25c multi	.55	.55
508	A64	70c on 10c multi	.85	.85
509	A66	70c on $3 multi	.75	.75
510	A67	70c on $3 multi	1.75	1.75
511	A64	90c on 65c multi	.95	.95
512	A66	$1.15 on 75c multi	1.20	1.20
513	A66	$1.15 on $4 multi	.95	.95
514	A67	$1.15 on $4 multi	2.25	2.25
515	A64	$1.50 on $2 multi	1.50	1.50
		Nos. 507-515 (9)	10.75	10.75

Christmas Carnival 1983 — A77

1983, Nov. 18   Wmk. 380   Perf. 14

516	A77	55c Clowns	.25	.25
517	A77	90c Star Bursts	.25	.25
518	A77	$1.15 Flower Girls	.30	.30
519	A77	$2 Masqueraders	.45	.45
		Nos. 516-519 (4)	1.25	1.25

See Nos. 547-550.

Nos. 503-506 were overprinted "INAUGURAL FLIGHT Montserrat — Nevis — St. Kitts." These exist on souvenir covers with first day cancel of Dec. 15, 1983. No announcement of this set was made nor were mint stamps generally available.

1984 Summer Olympics — A78

1984, Mar. 6   Litho.   Perf. 14

520	A78	90c Discobolus	.40	.40
521	A78	$1 Torch	.50	.50
522	A78	$1.15 Stadium	.55	.55
523	A78	$2.50 Flags	1.00	1.00
a.		Souvenir sheet of 4, #520-523	3.25	3.25
		Nos. 520-523 (4)	2.45	2.45

Cattle Egret — A79

10c, Carib grackles. 15c, Common gallinule. 20c, Brown boobys. 25c, Black-whiskered vireos. 40c, Scaly-breasted thrashers. 55c, Laughing gulls. 70c, Glossy ibis. 90c, Green heron. $1, Belted kingfisher. $1.15, Bananaquits. $3, Sparrow hawks. $5, Forest thrush. $7.50, Black-crowned night heron. $10, Bridled quail doves.

1984, May 11

524	A79	5c shown	.45	.35
525	A79	10c multi	.45	.35
526	A79	15c multi	.45	.35
527	A79	20c multi	.60	.35
528	A79	25c multi	.60	.50
529	A79	40c multi	.90	.55
530	A79	55c multi	1.10	.35
531	A79	70c multi	1.40	.50
532	A79	90c multi	1.50	.70
533	A79	$1 multi	1.90	.90
534	A79	$1.15 multi	2.40	1.60
535	A79	$3 multi	5.00	6.00
536	A79	$5 multi	7.00	8.00
537	A79	$7.50 multi	9.00	14.50
538	A79	$10 multi	10.50	15.00
		Nos. 524-538 (15)	43.25	50.00

For surcharges see Nos. 651-655, 663-666.
For overprints see Nos. O65-O78.

Packet Boats — A80

1984, July 9   Wmk. 380   Perf. 14

539	A80	55c Tagus, 1907	.30	.30
540	A80	90c Cobequid, 1913	.45	.45
541	A80	$1.15 Lady Drake, 1942	.55	.55
542	A80	$2 Factor, 1948	.90	.90
a.		Souvenir sheet of 4, #539-542	4.25	4.25
		Nos. 539-542 (4)	2.20	2.20

Marine Life — A81

90c, Top shell & hermit crab. $1.15, Rough file shell. $1.50, True tulip snail. $2.50, West Indian fighting conch.

1984, Sept.   Wmk. 380   Perf. 14

543	A81	90c multi	1.60	1.60
544	A81	$1.15 multi	2.00	2.00
545	A81	$1.50 multi	3.25	3.25
546	A81	$2.50 multi	4.25	4.25
		Nos. 543-546 (4)	11.10	11.10

Christmas Carnival Type of 1983

55c, Bull Man. $1.15, Masquerader Captain. $1.50, Carnival Queen contestant. $2.30, Contestant, diff.

1984, Nov. 12

547	A77	55c multi	.65	.65
548	A77	$1.15 multi	1.60	1.60
549	A77	$1.50 multi	1.75	1.75
550	A77	$2.30 multi	2.75	2.75
		Nos. 547-550 (4)	6.75	6.75

National Emblems — A82

1985, Feb. 8   Litho.   Perf. 14

551	A82	$1.15 Mango	.75	.75
552	A82	$1.50 Lobster Claw	1.15	1.15
553	A82	$3 Montserrat Oriole	2.60	2.60
		Nos. 551-553 (3)	4.50	4.50

Indigenous Orchids — A83

90c, Oncidium urophyllum. $1.15, Epidendrum difforme. $1.50, Epidendrum ciliare. $2.50, Brassavola cucullata.

1985, May 9   Wmk. 380   Perf. 14

554	A83	90c multicolored	.90	.90
555	A83	$1.15 multicolored	.90	.90
556	A83	$1.50 multicolored	1.10	1.10
557	A83	$2.50 multicolored	1.30	1.30
a.		Souvenir sheet of 4, #554-557	8.00	8.00
		Nos. 554-557 (4)	4.20	4.20

Queen Mother, 85th Birthday A84

#558a, 564a, Facing right. #558b, 564b, Facing forward. #559a, Facing right. #559b, Facing left. #560a, Facing right. #560b, Glancing right. #561a, 563a, Facing right. #561b, 563b, Facing left. #562a, Facing right. #562b, Facing forward.

1985-86   Unwmk.   Perf. 12½

558	A84	55c Pair, #a.-b.	.45	.45
559	A84	90c Pair, #a.-b.	.75	.75
560	A84	$1.15 Pair, #a.-b.	.85	.85
561	A84	$1.50 Pair, #a.-b.	1.20	1.20
		Nos. 558-561 (4)	3.25	3.25

Souvenir Sheets of 2

562	A84	$2 #a.-b.	1.75	1.75
563	A84	$3.50 #a.-b.	3.50	3.50
564	A84	$6 #a.-b.	5.50	5.50

Issued: Nos. 563-564, 1/10/86; others, 8/7/85.
For surcharges see No. 575.

Cotton Industry — A85

1985, Sept. 23   Unwmk.   Perf. 15

569	A85	90c Cotton plants	.30	.30
570	A85	$1 Carding	.35	.35
571	A85	$1.15 Automated loom	.35	.35
572	A85	$2.50 Hand loom	.50	.50
a.		Souvenir sheet of 4, #569-572	4.50	4.50
		Nos. 569-572 (4)	1.50	1.50

MONTSERRAT

Nos. 504, 485, 560, 505, 469-470 Ovptd. or Surcharged "CARIBBEAN ROYAL VISIT 1985" in 2 or 3 Lines
Perf. 14, 12½ ($1.15)
Wmk. as Before

1985, Nov. 14			Litho.
573	A76	75c multi	4.75 4.75
574	A70b	$1 multi	6.75 6.75
575	A84	$1.15 Pair, #a.-b.	14.50 14.50
577	A76	$1.50 multi	9.25 9.25
578	A66	$1.60 on $4 multi	4.75 4.75
579	A67	$1.60 on $4 multi	18.00 18.00
		Nos. 573-579 (6)	58.00 58.00

No. 579 surcharged but not overprinted.

Audubon Birth Bicentenary — A86

Illustrations of North American bird species by John J. Audubon: No. 580a, Black-throated blue warbler. No. 580b, Palm warbler. No. 581a, Bobolink. No. 581b, Lark sparrow. No. 582a, Chipping sparrow. No. 582b, Northern oriole. No. 583a, American goldfinch. No. 583b, Blue grosbeak.

1985, Nov. 29	Unwmk.		Perf. 12½
580	A86	15c Pair, #a.-b.	.25 .25
581	A86	30c Pair, #a.-b.	.25 .25
582	A86	55c Pair, #a.-b.	.40 .40
583	A86	$2.50 Pair, #a.-b.	1.40 1.40
		Nos. 580-583 (4)	2.30 2.30

Christmas — A87

70c, Angel of the Lord. $1.15, Three wise men. $1.50, Caroling, Plymouth War Memorial. $2.30, Our Lady of Montserrat.

1985, Dec. 2	Wmk. 380		Perf. 15
588	A87	70c multi	.25 .25
589	A87	$1.15 multi	.35 .35
590	A87	$1.50 multi	.40 .40
591	A87	$2.30 multi	.70 .70
		Nos. 588-591 (4)	1.70 1.70

A set of 8 stamps for the 1986 World Cup was printed but not issued. Stamps became available with the liquidation of the printer.

Girl Guides, 50th Anniv. A88

#592a, Lord Baden-Powell. #592b, Guide giving oath. #593a, Lady Baden-Powell. #593b, Guide cutting hair. #594a, Lord and Lady Baden-Powell. #594b, Guides in public service. #595a, Troop inspection, 1936. #595b, Guides saluting.

1986, Apr. 11			
592	A88	20c Pair, #a.-b.	.25 .25
593	A88	75c Pair, #a.-b.	.75 .75
594	A88	90c Pair, #a.-b.	.85 .85
595	A88	$1.15 Pair, #a.-b.	1.10 1.10
		Nos. 592-595 (4)	2.95 2.95

For overprints see Nos. 966-967.

Queen Elizabeth II, 60th Birthday A89

Various portraits.

1986, Apr. 11	Unwmk.		Perf. 12½
600	A89	10c multicolored	.25 .25
601	A89	$1.50 multicolored	.35 .35
602	A89	$3 multicolored	.55 .55
603	A89	$6 multi, vert.	.85 .85
		Nos. 600-603 (4)	2.00 2.00

Souvenir Sheet

| 604 | A89 | $8 multicolored | 5.00 5.00 |

Halley's Comet A90

Designs: 35c, 40c (No. 613a,) Bayeux Tapestry (detail), 1066 sighting. 50c, $1.75 (No. 613b), Adoration of the Magi, by Giotto. 70c, $2 (No. 613c), Edmond Halley, trajectory diagram, 1531 sighting. $1, $3 (No. 613d), Sightings, 1066 and 1910. $1.15, 55c (No. 614a), Sighting, 1910. $1.50, 60c (No. 614b), Giotto space probe, comet, diagram. $2.30, 80c (No. 614c), U.S. Space Telescope, comet. $4, $5 (No. 614d), Computer picture of photograph, 1910.

1986			
605-612	A90	Set of 8	4.00 4.00

Souvenir Sheets

| 613 | A90 | Sheet of 4, #a.-d. | 3.00 3.00 |
| 614 | A90 | Sheet of 4, #a.-d. | 3.00 3.00 |

Issued: Nos. 613-614, 10/10; others, 5/9.
For overprints see Nos. 656-657.

A91

Wedding of Prince Andrew and Sarah Ferguson A92

1986	Litho.	Perf. 12½x13, 13x12½
615	A91	70c Pair, #a.-b.	.70 .70
616	A91	$2 Pair, #a.-b.	1.00 1.00
c.		Souvenir booklet	5.00

Souvenir Sheet

| 617 | A92 | $10 multicolored | 5.00 5.00 |

No. 616c contains 2 imperf panes. One pane contains 2 No. 615; the other 2 No. 616.
Issued: No. 617, 10/15; others, 7/23.
For overprints see Nos. 628-629.

Clipper Ships — A93

90c, Antelope, 1793. $1.15, Montagu, 1840. $1.50, Little Catherine, 1813. $2.30, Hinchinbrook, 1813.

1986, Aug. 29			Perf. 14
618	A93	90c multi	1.25 1.25
619	A93	$1.15 multi	3.00 3.00
620	A93	$1.50 multi	3.25 3.25
621	A93	$2.30 multi	4.75 4.75
a.		Souvenir sheet of 4, #618-621	12.50 12.50
		Nos. 618-621 (4)	12.25 12.25

Communications A94

Designs: 70c, Radio Montserrat, near Dagenham. $1.15, Radio Gem ZGM-FM 94, Plymouth. $1.50, Radio Antilles, O'Garro's, $2.30, Cable & Wireless telegraph office, Plymouth.

1986, Sept. 29	Wmk. 380	Perf. 14
622	A94	70c multicolored	1.10 1.10
623	A94	$1.15 multicolored	1.60 1.60
624	A94	$1.50 multicolored	1.90 1.90
625	A94	$2.30 multicolored	2.40 2.40
		Nos. 622-625 (4)	7.00 7.00

Nos. 615-616 Ovptd. in Silver "Congratulations to T.R.H. The Duke & Duchess of York"
Perf. 12½x13, 13x12½

1986, Nov. 14		Litho.
628	A91	70c Pair, #a.-b.	1.75 1.75
629	A91	$2 Pair, #a.-b.	4.00 4.00

Christmas — A95

70c, Christmas rose. $1.15, Candle flower. $1.50, Christmas tree kalanchoe. $2.30, Snow on the mountain.

1986, Dec. 12	Unwmk.	Perf. 14
632	A95	70c multi	.85 .85
633	A95	$1.15 multi	1.40 1.40
634	A95	$1.50 multi	2.00 2.00
635	A95	$2.30 multi	3.00 3.00
a.		Souvenir sheet of 4, #632-635, perf. 12x12½	11.00 11.00
		Nos. 632-635 (4)	7.25 7.25

Souvenir Sheets

Statue of Liberty, Cent. A96

1986, Nov. 18	Litho.	Perf. 14
636	A96	$3 Statue, pedestal	1.75 1.75
637	A96	$4.50 Head	2.40 2.40
638	A96	$5 Statue, NYC	2.75 2.75
		Nos. 636-638 (3)	6.90 6.90

Sailing — A97

$1.15, Golf. $1.50, Plymouth Public Market. $2.30, Air Studios.

1986, Dec. 10		Perf. 15
639	A97	70c shown	.55 .55
640	A97	$1.15 multi	.80 .80
641	A97	$1.50 multi	.80 .80
642	A97	$2.30 multi	1.60 1.60
		Nos. 639-642 (4)	3.75 3.75

For surcharge see No. B3.

Sharks — A98

1987, Feb. 2	Wmk. 380	Perf. 14
643	A98	40c Tiger	1.75 1.75
644	A98	90c Lemon	3.00 3.00
645	A98	$1.15 White	3.50 3.50
646	A98	$3.50 Whale	7.00 7.00
a.		Souvenir sheet of 4, #643-646, perf. 12½x12	16.00 16.00
		Nos. 643-646 (4)	15.25 15.25

Butterflies — A99

90c, Straight-line sulpher. $1.15, Red rim. $1.50, Hammock skipper. $2.50, Mimic.

1987, Aug. 10	Wmk. 380	Perf. 14
647	A99	90c multi	2.50 2.50
648	A99	$1.15 multi	3.25 3.25
649	A99	$1.50 multi	4.00 4.00
650	A99	$2.50 multi	6.25 6.25
		Nos. 647-650 (4)	16.00 16.00

Nos. 531, 527, 525, 532 and 535 Surcharged

1987, Apr. 6		
651	A79	5c on 70c multi	.80 .80
652	A79	$1 on 20c multi	2.60 2.60
653	A79	$1.15 on 10c multi	3.25 3.25
654	A79	$1.50 on 90c multi	3.75 3.75
655	A79	$2.30 on $3 multi	5.50 5.50
		Nos. 651-655 (5)	15.90 15.90

Nos. 613-614 Ovptd. for CAPEX '87 in Red and Black
Souvenir Sheets of 4

1987, June 13		Unwmk.
656	A90	#a.-d.	3.50 3.50
657	A90	#a.-d.	3.50 3.50

Orchids A100

90c, Oncidium variegatum, vert. $1.15, Vanilla planifolia. $1.50, Gongora quinquenervis, vert. $3.50, Brassavola nodosa. $5, Oncidium lanceanum.

1987, Nov. 13	Unwmk.	Perf. 14
658	A100	90c multi	1.00 1.00
659	A100	$1.15 multi	1.25 1.25
660	A100	$1.50 multi	1.75 1.75
661	A100	$3.50 multi	4.25 4.25
		Nos. 658-661 (4)	8.25 8.25

Souvenir Sheet

| 662 | A100 | $5 multi | 17.00 17.00 |

Christmas.

Nos. 525, 528-529 and 532 Surcharged "40th Wedding Anniversary / HM Queen Elizabeth II / HRH Duke of Edinburgh / November 1987." and New Value
Wmk. 380

1987, Nov. 20	Litho.	Perf. 14
663	A79	5c on 90c No. 532	.55 .55
664	A79	$1.15 on 10c No. 525	.70 .70
665	A79	$2.30 on 25c No. 528	1.50 1.50
666	A79	$5 on 40c No. 529	3.00 3.00
		Nos. 663-666 (4)	5.75 5.75

Prince Philip Edinburgh Visit, set $50.

Tropical Bats — A101

1988, Feb. 8	Wmk. 380	Perf. 14
667	A101	55c Free-tailed bat	1.00 1.00
668	A101	90c Fruit bat	1.75 1.75
669	A101	$1.15 Fisherman bat	2.25 2.25
670	A101	$2.30 Fruit bat, diff.	4.50 4.50
		Nos. 667-670 (4)	9.50 9.50

Souvenir Sheet

| 671 | A101 | $2.50 Funnel-eared bat | 10.50 10.50 |

MONTSERRAT

Marine Birds — A102

90c, Magnificent frigatebird. $1.15, Caribbean elaenia. $1.50, Glossy ibis. $3.50, Purple-throated carib. $5, Brown pelican.

1988, Apr. 2			Unwmk.	
672	A102	90c multi	1.00	1.00
673	A102	$1.15 multi	1.25	1.25
674	A102	$1.50 multi	1.50	1.50
675	A102	$3.50 multi	3.25	3.25
	Nos. 672-675 (4)		7.00	7.00
Souvenir Sheet				
676	A102	$5 multi	5.50	5.50

Easter.

1988 Summer Olympics, Seoul — A103

Eastern architecture and events: 90c, Women's discus. $1.15, High jump. $3.50, Women's 200-meter and Seoul university building. $5, Single scull rowing, pagoda.

1988, July 29		Litho.	Perf. 14	
		Unwmk.		
677	A103	90c multicolored	.95	.95
678	A103	$1.15 multicolored	1.00	1.00
679	A103	$3.50 multicolored	3.25	3.25
	Nos. 677-679 (3)		5.20	5.20
Souvenir Sheet				
680	A103	$5 multicolored	5.25	5.25

Sea Shells — A104

5c, Golden tulip. 10c, Little knobby scallop. 15c, Sozoni's cone. 20c, Globular coral shell. 25c, Sundial. 40c, King helmet. 55c, Channeled turban. 70c, True tulip shell. 90c, Music volute. $1, Flame auger. $1.15, Rooster-tail conch. $1.50, Queen conch. $3, Teramachi's slit shell. $5, Florida crown conch. $7.50, Beau's murex. $10, Triton's trumpet.

1988, Aug. 30				
681	A104	5c multi	.30	.25
682	A104	10c multi	.30	.25
683	A104	15c multi	.30	.25
684	A104	20c multi	.30	.25
685	A104	25c multi	.30	.25
686	A104	40c multi	.45	.45
687	A104	55c multi	.55	.55
688	A104	70c multi	.70	.70
689	A104	90c multi	.90	.90
690	A104	$1 multi	1.00	1.00
691	A104	$1.15 multi	1.25	1.25
692	A104	$1.50 multi	1.50	1.50
693	A104	$3 multi	3.50	3.50
694	A104	$5 multi	5.00	5.00
695	A104	$7.50 multi	7.50	7.50
696	A104	$10 multi	10.50	10.50
	Nos. 681-696 (16)		34.35	34.10

For surcharges see Nos. 698-701, 767-770.
For overprints see Nos. O79-O94.

University of the West Indies, 40th Anniv. — A105

1988, Oct. 4		Litho.	Perf. 14	
697	A105	$5 multicolored	4.00	4.00

Nos. 687, 690, 693 and 694 Surcharged

	Unwmk.			
1988, Nov. 4		Litho.	Perf. 14	
698	A104	40c on 55c No. 687	.50	.50
699	A104	90c on $1 No. 690	1.50	1.50
700	A104	$1.15 on $3 No. 693	1.75	1.75
701	A104	$1.50 on $5 No. 694	2.50	2.50
	Nos. 698-701 (4)		6.25	6.25

Intl. Red Cross, 125th Anniv. A106

1988, Dec. 16				
702	A106	$3.50 multicolored	2.25	2.25

Christmas A107

Birds: 90c, Spotted sandpiper. $1.15, Ruddy turnstone. $3.50, Red-footed booby. $5, Aububon's shearwater.

1988, Nov. 28			Perf. 14x13½	
703	A107	90c multi	1.00	1.00
704	A107	$1.15 multi	1.25	1.25
705	A107	$3.50 multi	3.75	3.75
	Nos. 703-705 (3)		6.00	6.00
Souvenir Sheet				
		Perf. 13½x14		
706	A107	$5 multi	6.00	6.00

Defense Force, 75th Anniv. — A108

Uniforms: 90c, Drum major. $1.15, Fatigue clothing. $1.50, Khaki uniform. $3.50, Dress uniform. $5, Cadet (girl), woman.

1989, Feb. 24		Litho.	Perf. 14	
707	A108	90c multi	1.10	1.10
708	A108	$1.15 multi	1.25	1.25
709	A108	$1.50 multi	1.60	1.60
710	A108	$3.50 multi	4.25	4.25
	Nos. 707-710 (4)		8.20	8.20
Souvenir Sheet				
711	A108	$5 multi	6.25	6.25

Easter Lilies — A109

90c, Amazon. $1.15, Salmon blood, vert. $1.50, Amaryllis, vert. $3.50, Amaryllis, diff., vert. $5, Resurrection, vert.

1989, Mar. 21		Litho.	Perf. 14	
712	A109	90c multi	.75	.75
713	A109	$1.15 multi	.90	.90
714	A109	$1.50 multi	1.10	1.10
715	A109	$3.50 multi	3.00	3.00
	Nos. 712-715 (4)		5.75	5.75
Souvenir Sheet				
716	A109	$5 multi	7.25	7.25

Ships Built in Montserrat A110

Designs: 90c, Schooner Morning Prince, 1942-1948. $1.15, Cargo boat Western Sun. $1.50, Cargo boat Kim G under construction. $3.50, Cargo and passenger boat MV Romaris.

1989, June 30		Litho.	Perf. 13½x14	
717	A110	90c multicolored	1.50	1.50
718	A110	$1.15 multicolored	1.75	1.75
719	A110	$1.50 multicolored	2.25	2.25
720	A110	$3.50 multicolored	5.00	5.00
	Nos. 717-720 (4)		10.50	10.50

For surcharges see Nos. B1-B2.

Making of the Film *The Wizard of Oz*, 50th Anniv. A111

1989, Sept. 22		Litho.	Perf. 14	
721	A111	90c Scarecrow	1.00	1.00
722	A111	$1.15 Cowardly Lion	1.25	1.25
723	A111	$1.50 Tin Man	1.75	1.75
724	A111	$3.50 Dorothy	3.50	3.50
	Nos. 721-724 (4)		7.50	7.50
Souvenir Sheet				
725	A111	$5 shown	7.50	7.50

Nos. 721-724 vert.

1st Moon Landing, 20th Anniv. A112

Designs: $1.15, Armstrong on ladder, descending from lunar module. $1.50, Eagle, astronaut on lunar surface. $3.50, Recovery of command module after splashdown. $5, Astronaut on the Moon, vert.

	Perf. 13½x14, 14x13½			
1989, Dec. 19		Litho.		
726	A112	90c shown	.70	.70
727	A112	$1.15 multicolored	.90	.90
728	A112	$1.50 multicolored	1.20	1.20
729	A112	$3.50 multicolored	2.50	2.50
	Nos. 726-729 (4)		5.30	5.30
Souvenir Sheet				
730	A112	$5 multi	7.50	7.50

For overprints see Nos. 847-850.

World War II Battle Ships — A113

70c, I.J.N. Yamato. $1.15, USS Arizona. $1.50, K.M. Bismarck on fire. $3.50, HMS Hood. $5, K.M. Bismarck, map.

1990, Feb. 12		Litho.	Perf. 14	
731	A113	70c multi	2.25	2.25
732	A113	$1.15 multi	4.25	4.25
733	A113	$1.50 multi	5.50	5.50
734	A113	$3.50 multi	12.50	12.50
	Nos. 731-734 (4)		24.50	24.50
Souvenir Sheet				
735	A113	$5 multi	20.00	20.00

Nos. 414-418 Surcharged in Bright Rose Lilac

1990, May 3			Perf. 14½	
736	A59	70c on 40c #414	1.10	1.10
737	A59	90c on 55c #415	1.40	1.40
738	A59	$1 on $1.20 #416	1.50	1.50
739	A59	$1.15 on $1.20 #417	1.75	1.75
740	A59	$1.50 on $1.20 #418	2.25	2.25
	Nos. 736-740 (5)		8.00	8.00

Stamp World London '90.

Penny Black, 150th Anniv. A114

Designs: 90c, Montserrat #5, General P.O. $1.15, Montserrat #1, postal workers sorting mail, vert. $1.50, Great Britain #1, man and woman mailing letters, vert. $3.50, Great Britain #2, mailman delivering to residence. $5, Chateau Barrack cover of 1836, Great Britain #1, landscape.

1990, June 1		Perf. 13½x14, 14x13½		
741	A114	90c shown	1.25	1.25
742	A114	$1.15 multicolored	1.60	1.60
743	A114	$1.50 multicolored	1.90	1.90
744	A114	$3.50 multicolored	4.25	4.25
	Nos. 741-744 (4)		9.00	9.00
Souvenir Sheet				
745	A114	$5 multicolored	9.75	9.75

Stained-glass Windows — A115

1990, Apr. 12		Litho.	Perf. 14x15	
746	A115	Strip of 3	7.00	7.00
a.	$1.15 The Empty Tomb		1.25	1.25
b.	$1.50 The Ascension		1.75	1.75
c.	$3.50 Risen Christ with Disciples		3.75	3.75
Souvenir Sheet				
747	A115	$5 The Crucifixion	7.50	7.50

World Cup Soccer Championships, Italy — A116

Designs: 90c, Montserrat vs. Antigua. $1.15, U.S. vs. Trinidad. $1.50, Montserrat team. $3.50, West Germany vs. Wales. $5, World Cup trophy.

1990, July 8		Litho.	Perf. 14	
748	A116	90c multicolored	.90	.90
749	A116	$1.15 multicolored	1.25	1.25
750	A116	$1.50 multicolored	1.60	1.60
751	A116	$3.50 multicolored	3.75	3.75
	Nos. 748-751 (4)		7.50	7.50
Souvenir Sheet				
752	A116	$5 multicolored	8.75	8.75

Spinner Dolphin — A117

$1.15, Common dolphin. $1.50, Striped dolphin. $3.50, Atlantic spotted dolphin. $5, Atlantic white-sided dolphin.

1990, Sept. 25		Litho.	Perf. 14	
753	A117	90c shown	2.00	2.00
754	A117	$1.15 multi	2.50	2.50
755	A117	$1.50 multi	3.50	3.50
756	A117	$3.50 multi	5.50	5.50
	Nos. 753-756 (4)		13.50	13.50
Souvenir Sheet				
757	A117	$5 multi	14.50	14.50

MONTSERRAT

Fish — A118

90c, Spotted goatfish. $1.15, Cushion starfish. $1.50, Rock beauty. $3.50, French grunt. $5, Trunkfish.

1991, Feb. 7   Litho.   *Perf. 14*
758	A118	90c multi	1.75	1.75
759	A118	$1.15 multi	2.25	2.25
760	A118	$1.50 multi	3.00	3.00
761	A118	$3.50 multi	6.50	6.50
	Nos. 758-761 (4)		13.50	13.50

Souvenir Sheet
762	A118	$5 multi	14.00	14.00

For surcharges and overprints see Nos. O98-O99, O104, O107.

Birds — A119

90c, Duck. $1.15, Hen, chicks. $1.50, Rooster. $3.50, Helmeted guinea fowl.

1991, Apr. 17   Litho.   *Perf. 14*
763	A119	90c multi	1.00	1.00
764	A119	$1.15 multi	1.40	1.40
765	A119	$1.50 multi	1.60	1.60
766	A119	$3.50 multi	4.00	4.00
	Nos. 763-766 (4)		8.00	8.00

For surcharges and overprints see Nos. O100, O102, O105, O108.

Nos. 684-685, 692, 695 Surcharged

1991   Litho.   *Perf. 14*
767	A104	5c on 20c #684	.40	.40
768	A104	5c on 25c #685	.40	.40
769	A104	$1.15 on $1.50 #692	5.00	5.00
770	A104	$1.15 on $7.50 #695	5.00	5.00
	Nos. 767-770 (4)		10.80	10.80

Mushrooms — A120

90c, Panaeolus antillarum. $1.15, Cantharellus cinnabarinus. $1.50, Gymnopilus chrysopellus. $2, Psilocybe cubensis. $3.50, Leptonia caeruleocapitata.

1991, June 13   Litho.   *Perf. 14*
771	A120	90c multi	1.50	1.50
772	A120	$1.15 multi	1.90	1.90
773	A120	$1.50 multi	2.50	2.50
774	A120	$2 multi	3.50	3.50
775	A120	$3.50 multi	5.75	5.75
	Nos. 771-775 (5)		15.15	15.15

Lilies — A121

1991, Aug. 8
776	A121	90c Red water lily	.95	.95
777	A121	$1.15 Shell ginger	1.25	1.25
778	A121	$1.50 Early day lily	1.50	1.50
779	A121	$3.50 Anthurium	3.50	3.50
	Nos. 776-779 (4)		7.20	7.20

For surcharges and overprints see Nos. O101, O103, O106, O109.

Frogs and Toads — A122

$1.15, Tree frog. $2, Crapaud toad. $3.50, Mountain chicken.

1991, Oct. 9   Litho.   *Perf. 14*
780	A122	$1.15 multi	2.75	2.75
781	A122	$2 multi	5.00	5.00
782	A122	$3.50 multi	8.00	8.00
	Nos. 780-782 (3)		15.75	15.75

Souvenir Sheet   *Perf. 14½x14*
783	A122	$5 Sheet of 1	15.00	15.00

No. 783 contains one 81x48mm stamp that incorporates designs of Nos. 780-782.

Cats — A123

90c, Black British shorthair. $1.15, Seal point siamese. $1.50, Silver tabby persian. $2.50, Birman temple cat. $3.50, Egyptian mau.

1991, Dec. 5
784	A123	90c multi	2.00	2.00
785	A123	$1.15 multi	2.75	2.75
786	A123	$1.50 multi	3.50	3.50
787	A123	$2.50 multi	5.50	5.50
788	A123	$3.50 multi	7.25	7.25
	Nos. 784-788 (5)		21.00	21.00

Discovery of America, 500th Anniv. — A124

No. 789: a, $1.50, Navigating instruments. b, $1.50, Coat of arms, Columbus. c, $1.50, Columbus, Bahamian natives. d, $1.50, Queen Isabella, Columbus with petition. e, $1.50, Exotic birds. f, $1.50, Exotic plants. g, $3.00, Santa Maria, Nina & Pinta.

1992, Jan. 16   Litho.   *Perf. 14*
789	A124	Sheet of 7, #a.-g.	17.00	17.00

No. 789g is 85x28mm. See No. 829.

Dinosaurs A125

$1, Tyrannosaurus. $1.15, Diplodocus. $1.50, Apatosaurus. $3.45, Dimetrodon. $4.60, Owen with bone, vert.

1992, Aug. 1   Litho.   *Perf. 14*
790	A125	$1 multi	2.10	2.10
791	A125	$1.15 multi	2.40	2.40
792	A125	$1.50 multi	3.00	3.00
793	A125	$3.45 multi	7.00	7.00
	Nos. 790-793 (4)		14.50	14.50

Souvenir Sheet
794	A125	$4.60 multi	12.50	12.50

Sir Richard Owen, cent. of death.

1992 Summer Olympics, Barcelona — A126

$1, Torch bearer. $1.15, Flags. $2.30, Olympic flame, map. $3.60, Various events.

1992, Apr. 10
795	A126	$1 multi	1.25	1.25
796	A126	$1.15 multi	1.50	1.50
797	A126	$2.30 multi	2.75	2.75
798	A126	$3.60 multi	4.00	4.00
	Nos. 795-798 (4)		9.50	9.50

Montserrat Oriole A127

$1, Male. $1.15, Male, female. $1.50, Female feeding chicks. $3.60, Map, male.

1992, June 30   Litho.   *Perf. 13½x14*
799	A127	$1 multi	1.50	1.50
800	A127	$1.15 multi	1.75	1.75
801	A127	$1.50 multi	2.25	2.25
802	A127	$3.60 multi	5.50	5.50
	Nos. 799-802 (4)		11.00	11.00

Insects — A128

5c, Grasshopper. 10c, Field cricket. 15c, Dragonfly. 20c, Red skimmer. 25c, Pond skater. 40c, Leaf weevil. 55c, Leaf cutter ants. 70c, Paper wasp. 90c, Bee fly. $1, Lacewing. $1.15, Orange-barred sulphur. $1.50, Painted lady. $3, Bella moth. $5, Plume moth. $7.50, White peacock. $10, Postman.

1992, Aug. 20   Litho.   *Perf. 15x14*
803	A128	5c multi	.30	.30
804	A128	10c multi	.30	.30
805	A128	15c multi	.30	.30
806	A128	20c multi	.30	.30
807	A128	25c multi	.30	.30
808	A128	40c multi	.40	.40
809	A128	55c multi	.55	.55
810	A128	70c multi	.70	.70
811	A128	90c multi	.95	.95
812	A128	$1 multi	1.10	1.10
813	A128	$1.15 multi	1.20	1.20
814	A128	$1.50 multi	1.50	1.50
815	A128	$3 multi	3.00	3.00
816	A128	$5 multi	5.00	5.00
817	A128	$7.50 multi	8.00	8.00
818	A128	$10 multi	10.50	10.50
	Nos. 803-818 (16)		34.40	34.40

For overprints and surcharges see Nos. 871-872, 881A, 881C, O110-O125.

Christmas A129

Designs: $1.15, Adoration of the Magi. $4.60, Angel appearing before shepherds.

1992, Nov. 26   Litho.   *Perf. 13½x14*
819	A129	$1.15 multicolored	1.75	1.75
820	A129	$4.60 multicolored	7.00	7.00

Coins and Bank Notes — A130

Designs: $1, One-dollar coin, twenty-dollar notes. $1.15, Ten-cent, twenty-five cent coins, ten-dollar notes. $1.50, Five-cent coin, five-dollar notes. $3.60, One-cent, two-cent coins, one-dollar notes.

1993, Feb. 10   *Perf. 14x13½*
821	A130	$1 multicolored	1.60	1.60
822	A130	$1.15 multicolored	1.75	1.75
823	A130	$1.50 multicolored	2.25	2.25
824	A130	$3.60 multicolored	5.50	5.50
	Nos. 821-824 (4)		11.10	11.10

Discovery of America, 500th Anniv. (in 1992) — A131

1993, Mar. 10   Litho.   *Perf. 14*
825	A131	$1 Coming ashore	2.25	2.25
826	A131	$2 Natives, ships	4.00	4.00

Organization of East Caribbean States.

Coronation of Queen Elizabeth II, 40th Anniv. A132

Designs: $1.15, Queen, M.H. Bramble. $4.60, Queen riding in Gold State Coach.

1993, June 2   *Perf. 13½x14*
827	A132	$1.15 multicolored	1.40	1.40
828	A132	$4.60 multicolored	5.25	5.25

Columbus Type of 1992 with Added Text

No. 829: a, $1.15, like #789a. b, $1.15, like #789b. c, $1.15, like #789c. d, $1.50, like #789d. e, $1.50, like #789e. f, $1.50, like #789f. g, $3.45, like #789g.

1993, Sept. 7   Litho.   *Perf. 14*
829	A124	Sheet of 7, #a.-g.	27.50	27.50

Nos. 829a-829g each have different added text.

Royal Air Force, 75th Anniv.
Common Design Type

Designs: 15c, Boeing Sentry, 1993. 55c, Vickers Valiant, 1962. $1.15, Handley Page Hastings, 1958. $3, 1943 Lockheed Ventura, 1943.

No. 834: a, Felixstowe F5, 1921. b, Armstrong Whitworth Atlas, 1934. c, Fairey Gordon, 1935. d, Boulton Paul Overstrand, 1936.

Wmk. 373
1993, Nov. 17   Litho.   *Perf. 14*
830	CD350	15c multicolored	.30	.30
831	CD350	55c multicolored	.80	.80
832	CD350	$1.15 multicolored	1.75	1.75
833	CD350	$3 multicolored	4.25	4.25
	Nos. 830-833 (4)		7.10	7.10

Souvenir Sheet
834	CD350	$1.50 Sheet of 4, #a.-d.	7.00	7.00

Beetles — A133

Perf. 15x14
1994, Jan. 21   Litho.   *Unwmk.*
835	A133	$1 Ground beetle	1.25	1.25
836	A133	$1.15 Click beetle	1.60	1.60
837	A133	$1.50 Harlequin beetle	1.90	1.90
838	A133	$3.45 Leaf beetle	4.50	4.50
	Nos. 835-838 (4)		9.25	9.25

Souvenir Sheet
839	A133	$4.50 Scarab beetle	6.00	6.00

Hibiscus Flowers and Fruits — A134

Designs: 90c, Cotton. $1.15, Sorrel. $1.50, Okra. $3.50, Hibiscus rosa sinensis.

1994, Mar. 22   Litho.   *Perf. 14x13½*
840	A134	90c multicolored	1.25	1.25
841	A134	$1.15 multicolored	1.60	1.60
842	A134	$1.50 multicolored	2.00	2.00
843	A134	$3.50 multicolored	4.75	4.75
	Nos. 840-843 (4)		9.60	9.60

MONTSERRAT

Aquatic Dinosaurs — A135

No. 844: a, $1, Elasmosaurus. b, $1.15, Plesiosaurus. c, $1.50, Nothosaurus. d, $3.45, Mosasaurus.

1994, May 6	Litho.	Perf. 15x14
844 A135 Strip of 4, #a.-d.		12.50 12.50

1994 World Cup Soccer Championships, U.S. — A136

No. 845: a, 90c, Montserrat youth soccer. b, $1, 1990 World Cup, US vs. England. c, $1.15, Rose Bowl Stadium, Pasadena, Calif., US. d, $3.45, German team, 1990 World Cup Winners.

No. 846: a, Jules Rimet. b, Bobby Moore, England Team Captain, 1966. c, Lew Jaschin. d, Sepp Herberger, German trainer.

1994, May 20		Perf. 14
845 A136 Vert. strip of 4, #a.-d.		9.50 9.50

Souvenir Sheet
Perf. 14x14½

846 A136 $2 Sheet of 4, #a.-d. 10.50 10.50

No. 845 printed in sheets of 2 strips + 4 labels.

Nos. 726-729 Ovptd. in Red or Srchd. in Red and Black

Inscribed "Space Anniversaries" and: 40c, "Yuri Gagarin / First man in space / April 12, 1961." $1.15, "First Joint US / Soviet Mission / July 15, 1975." $1.50, "25th Anniversary / First Moon Landing / Apollo XI-July 20, 1994." $2.30, "Columbia / First Space Shuttle / April 12, 1981."

1994, July 20		Perf. 13½x14
847 A112	40c on 90c multi	.75 .75
848 A112	$1.15 multi	3.00 3.00
849 A112	$1.50 multi	3.50 3.50
850 A112	$2.30 on $3.50 multi	5.75 5.75
Nos. 847-850 (4)		13.00 13.00

Obliterator on Nos. 847, 850 is black.

Woodstock Festival, 25th Anniv. — A137

1994, Oct. 20		Perf. 12½
851 A137 $1.15 1969 Poster		2.25 2.25
852 A137 $1.50 1994 Poster		2.50 2.50

Souvenir Sheets

853 A137 $4.50 like #851	5.75 5.75
854 A137 $4.50 like #852	5.75 5.75

Sea Vegetation — A138

1995, Feb. 14		Perf. 14x15
855 A138	$1 Sea fan	.85 .85
856 A138	$1.15 Sea lily	1.00 1.00
857 A138	$1.50 Sea pen	1.40 1.40
858 A138	$3.45 Sea fern	3.25 3.25
Nos. 855-858 (4)		6.50 6.50

Souvenir Sheet

859 A138 $4.50 Sea rose 4.50 4.50

Motion Pictures, Cent. — A139

No. 860: a.-i., Various portraits of Marilyn Monroe.
$6, Marilyn Monroe & Elvis Presley.

1995, June 13	Litho.	Perf. 12½
860 A139 $1.15 Sheet of 9, #a-i		11.00 11.00

Souvenir Sheet

861 A139 $6 multicolored 7.50 7.50

No. 861 contains one 51x57mm stamp.

1995 IAAF World Track & Field Championships, Gothenburg, Sweden — A140

No. 862: a, Jesse Owens, U.S. b, Eric Lemming, Sweden. c, Rudolf Harbig, Germany. d, Montserrat youth.

1995, Aug. 3		Perf. 14
862 A140 $1.50 Sheet of 4, #a-d		7.50 7.50

End of World War II, 50th Anniv. — A141

No. 863: a, Atmospheric sounding experiments using V-2 rockets. b, Space Shuttle Challenger.
No. 864: a, 1st successful nuclear reactor. b, Calder Hall Atomic Power Station, England.
No. 865: a, Ju88G-7a nightfighter equipped with SN2 radar. b, NATO Boeing E6 AWACS.
No. 866: a, Gloster Meteor III jet aircraft. b, British Airways Concorde.

1995, Aug. 15		
863 A141 $1.15 Pair, #a.-b.		3.25 3.25
864 A141 $1.15 Pair, #a.-b.		3.25 3.25
865 A141 $1.50 Pair, #a.-b.		4.25 4.25
866 A141 $1.50 Pair, #a.-b.		4.25 4.25
Nos. 863-866 (4)		15.00 15.00

Nos. 812, 818 Ovptd.

1995	Litho.	Perf. 15x14
871 A128 $1 multicolored		1.25 1.25
872 A128 $10 multicolored		11.00 11.00

UN, 50th Anniv. — A142

1995, Sept. 4	Litho.	Perf. 14
873 A142 $1.15 Food		1.25 1.25
874 A142 $1.50 Education		1.50 1.50
875 A142 $2.30 Health		2.50 2.50
876 A142 $3 Peace		3.25 3.25
Nos. 873-876 (4)		8.50 8.50

Souvenir Sheet

877 A142 $6 Justice 7.00 7.00

Natl. Trust, 25th Anniv. — A143

Designs: $1.15, Headquarters building. $1.50, 17th cent. cannon, Bransby Point. $2.30, Painting of original Galways sugar mill, vert. $3, Great Alps Falls, vert.

1995, Nov. 15	Litho.	Perf. 14
878-881 A143 Set of 4		12.50 12.50

Nos. 806 and 809 Surcharged

Methods and Perfs As Before

1995		
881A A128 5c on 55c #809	— —
881C A128 10c on 20c #806	— —

An additional stamp was issued in this set. The editors would like to examine any example of it.

Scavengers of the Sea — A144

1996, Feb. 14	Litho.	Perf. 15x14
882 A144	$1 Bull shark	1.20 1.20
883 A144	$1.15 Sea mouse	1.40 1.40
884 A144	$1.50 Bristleworm	1.75 1.75
885 A144	$3.45 Prawn xiphocaris	3.75 3.75
Nos. 882-885 (4)		8.10 8.10

Souvenir Sheet

886 A144 $4.50 Man o'war 6.50 6.50

Radio, Cent. (in 1995) — A145

Designs: $1.15, Guglielmo Marconi, transmitting equipment, 1901. $1.50, Wireless laboratory, Marconi's yacht, Elettra. $2.30, First transatlantic radio message, Newfoundland, 1901. $3, First air/ground radio station, Croydon, 1920.
$4.50, First radio telescope, Jodrell Bank, Cheshire, England.

1996, Mar. 19	Litho.	Perf. 14
887-890 A145 Set of 4		8.25 8.25

Souvenir Sheet

891 A145 $4.50 multi 5.00 5.00

1996 Summer Olympic Games, Atlanta — A146

1896 Medalists: $1.15, Paul Masson, cycling. $1.50, Robert Garrett, discus. $2.30, Spiridon Louis, marathon. $3, John Boland, tennis.

1996, June 24	Litho.	Perf. 14
892-895 A146 Set of 4		7.50 7.50

Mythical Creatures — A147

1996, Aug. 15	Litho.	Perf. 14
896 A147	5c Leprechaun	.25 .25
897 A147	10c Pegasus	.25 .25
898 A147	15c Griffin	.25 .25
899 A147	20c Unicorn	.25 .25
900 A147	25c Gnome	.25 .25
901 A147	40c Mermaid	.40 .40
902 A147	55c Cockatrice	.50 .50
903 A147	70c Fairy	.65 .65
904 A147	90c Goblin	.80 .80
905 A147	$1 Faun	.90 .90
906 A147	$1.15 Dragon	1.00 1.00
907 A147	$1.50 Giant	1.25 1.25
908 A147	$3 Elf	2.40 2.40
909 A147	$5 Centaur	4.00 4.00
910 A147	$7.50 Phoenix	6.00 6.00
911 A147	$10 Erin	7.50 7.50
Nos. 896-911 (16)		26.65 26.65

For overprints see Nos. O126-O140.

James Dean (1931-55), Actor — A148

Various portraits.

1996, June 28	Litho.	Perf. 12½
912 A148 $1.15 Sheet of 9, #a.-i.		11.00 11.00

Souvenir Sheet

913 A148 $6 multicolored 7.00 7.00

No. 913 contains one 51x57mm stamp.
For overprint see No. 921.

Dancing Bears, Emblem of "The Grateful Dead" A149

Jerry Garcia — A150

No. 914 — Color of bears: a, blue violet, green. b, yellow. c, orange, pink.

1996, Oct. 21	Litho.	Perf. 12½
914 A149 $1.15 Strip of 3, #a.-c.		3.75 3.75
915 A150 $6 multicolored		6.75 6.75

For overprint and surcharge see Nos. 920A, 928. Compare with Nos. 955-956 and 970-83.

Scavenger Birds — A151

1997, Jan. 28	Litho.	Perf. 14½x14
916 A151	$1 Turkey vulture	1.00 1.00
917 A151	$1.15 American crow	1.25 1.25
918 A151	$1.50 Great skua	1.50 1.50
919 A151	$3.45 Kittiwake	3.50 3.50
Nos. 916-919 (4)		7.25 7.25

Souvenir Sheet

920 A151 $4.50 King vulture 5.25 5.25

MONTSERRAT

No. 914 Overprinted "Hong Kong '97" Across Strip in Dark Blue Methods and Perfs as before

1997, Mar. 26
920A A149 $1.15 Strip of 3,
#b-d   4.25 4.25

No. 912 Overprinted

1997, June 2   Litho.   Perf. 12½
921 A148 $1.15 Sheet of 9,
#a.-i.   12.00 12.00

Overprints are placed over vertical perfs separating each column of stamps. Each stamp in the left and right columns has only half the overprint. The stamps in the center column contain two incomplete halves of the overprint. The overprints also appear twice in sheet margin.

Eruption of Mt. Soufriere, Endangered Species — A152

No. 922: a, Heavy ash eruption, Plymouth, 1995. b, First pyroclastic flow entering sea. c, Double venting at Castle Peak. d, Mangrove cuckoo. e, Nocturnal lava flow, Soufriere Hills, 1996. f, Antillean crested hummingbird. g, Ash cloud engulfing Plymouth. h, Lava spine extruded, Soufriere Hills, 1996. i, New land created from pyroclastic flows.

1997, June 23   Perf. 14
922 A152 $1.50 Sheet of 9,
#a.-i.   13.00 13.00
j, Additional inscription in sheet
margin   13.00 13.00

No. 922j is inscribed in sheet margin: "MUSIC FOR" and "IN AID OF THE VICTIMS OF SOUFRIERE HILLS VOLCANO," "ROYAL ALBERT HALL LONDON" and "15th SEPTEMBER 1997."

Elvis Presley (1935-77) — A153

American rock stars: No. 924, Jimi Hendrix (1942-70). No. 925, Jerry Garcia (1942-95). No. 926, Janis Joplin (1943-70).

1997, Aug. 29   Litho.   Perf. 12½
923 A153 $1.15 multicolored   2.25 2.25
924 A153 $1.15 multicolored   2.25 2.25
925 A153 $1.15 multicolored   2.25 2.25
926 A153 $1.15 multicolored   2.25 2.25
Nos. 923-926 (4)   9.00 9.00

Abstract Art — A154

1997, Aug. 29   Litho.   Perf. 12½
927 A154 $1.50 multicolored   2.25 2.25

No. 915 Surcharged in Gold and Black

1997   Litho.   Perf. 12½
928 A150 $1.50 on $6 multi   3.00 3.00

Medicinal Plants — A155

1998, Mar. 30   Litho.   Perf. 15
929 A155 $1 Prickly pear   .75 .75
930 A155 $1.15 Pomme coolie   .85 .85
931 A155 $1.50 Aloe   1.10 1.10
932 A155 $3.45 Bird pepper   2.75 2.75
Nos. 929-932 (4)   5.45 5.45

A156

Famous People of the 20th Cent.: No. 933, Jean-Henri Dunant. No. 934, Mohandas Gandhi. No. 935, Pablo Picasso. No. 936, David Ben-Gurion. No. 937, Dwight D. Eisenhower. No. 938, Wernher von Braun. No. 939, Eva & Juan Perón. No. 940, Konrad Adenauer. No. 941, Mao Tse-tung. No. 942, Lord Mountbatten. No. 943, Charles Lindbergh. No. 944, Anne Frank. $3, John F. Kennedy.

1998, May 18   Litho.   Perf. 12½
933 A156 $1.15 multicolored   2.00 2.00
934 A156 $1.15 multicolored   2.00 2.00
935 A156 $1.15 multicolored   2.00 2.00
936 A156 $1.15 multicolored   2.00 2.00
937 A156 $1.15 multicolored   2.00 2.00
938 A156 $1.15 multicolored   2.00 2.00
939 A156 $1.15 multicolored   2.00 2.00
940 A156 $1.50 multicolored   2.75 2.75
941 A156 $1.50 multicolored   2.75 2.75
942 A156 $1.50 multicolored   2.75 2.75
943 A156 $1.50 multicolored   2.75 2.75
944 A156 $1.50 multicolored   2.75 2.75
Nos. 933-944 (12)   27.75 27.75

Souvenir Sheet
945 A156 $3 multicolored   5.00 5.00

No. 945 contains one 51x38mm stamp.
Issued in sheets of 4 with illustrated right margin.

1998, May 18   Litho.   Perf. 12½

Royalty of the 20th cent.: No. 946, Grand Duchess Charlotte (1896-1985) & Felix, Luxembourg. No. 947, Leopold III (1901-83) & Astrid, Belgium. No. 948, Wilhelmina (1880-1962), Netherlands. No. 949, Gustav V (1858-1950), Sweden. No. 950, Alfonso XIII (1886-1931), Spain. No. 951, Christian X (1870-1947), Denmark. No. 952, Haakon VII (1872-1957) & Olav, Denmark. No. 953, George VI (1895-1952), Great Britain.

946 A156 $1.15 multicolored   1.50 1.50
947 A156 $1.15 multicolored   1.50 1.50
948 A156 $1.50 multicolored   1.75 1.75
949 A156 $1.50 multicolored   1.75 1.75
950 A156 $1.50 multicolored   1.75 1.75
951 A156 $1.50 multicolored   1.75 1.75
952 A156 $1.50 multicolored   1.75 1.75
953 A156 $1.50 multicolored   1.75 1.75
Nos. 946-953 (8)   13.50 13.50

Issued in sheets of 4 with illustrated right margin.

Bob Marley (1947-81) — A157

Various portraits.

1998, Aug. 6
954 A157 $1.15 Sheet of 8,
#a.-h. + label   14.00 14.00

Jerry Garcia (1947-95) — A158

Various portraits.

1998, Aug. 6
955 A158 $1.15 Sheet of 9,
#a.-i.   14.00 14.00

Souvenir Sheet
956 A158 $5 multicolored   8.00 8.00

No. 956 contains one 51x76mm stamp. Compare with Nos. 914-915 and 970-983.

Eclipse of the Sun, Feb. 26, 1998 A159

Views of Mt. Soufriere volcano: No. 957, Homes near water. No. 958, Looking across mountain tops. No. 959, Ash on mountainside, home. No. 960, Ash, steam rising in air. $6, View of eclipse, vert.

1998   Litho.   Perf. 12½
957 A159 $1.15 multicolored   2.00 2.00
958 A159 $1.15 multicolored   2.00 2.00
959 A159 $1.15 multicolored   2.00 2.00
960 A159 $1.15 multicolored   2.00 2.00
Nos. 957-960 (4)   8.00 8.00

Souvenir Sheet
961 A159 $6 multicolored   7.25 7.25

Diana, Princess of Wales (1961-97) — A160

$1.15, As bride. $1.50, Princess of charities. $3, At Royal Ascot.
$6, Rose, Diana.

1998   Litho.   Perf. 12½
962 A160 $1.15 multi   1.75 1.75
963 A160 $1.50 multi   2.00 2.00
964 A160 $3 multi   3.75 3.75
Nos. 962-964 (3)   7.50 7.50

Souvenir Sheet
965 A160 $6 multi   7.00 7.00

No. 965 contains one 51x38mm stamp.

Nos. 592-593 Ovptd. in Red with emblem and "13th WORLD JAMBOREE MONDIALE CHILE 1999"

Wmk. 380

1998, Dec. 29   Litho.   Perf. 15
966 20c Pair, #a.-b.   .75 .75
967 75c Pair, #a.-b.   2.50 2.50

Nos. 873-874 Overprinted

Unwmk.

1999, Apr. 27   Litho.   Perf. 14
968 A142 $1.15 on #873   2.50 2.50
969 A142 $1.50 on #874   3.00 3.00

Jerry Garcia (1947-95) A161

Garcia: No. 970, $1.15, Wearing purple shirt, microphone at right, light blue background. No. 971, $1.15, In red light, dark blue background. No. 972, $1.15, Wearing purple shirt, microphone at left. No. 973, $1.15, Like #971, blue green background. No. 974, $1.15, Wearing black shirt, playing guitar. No. 975, $1.15, Wearing red shirt. No. 976, $1.15, Wearing blue shirt, microphone at right, vert. No. 977, $1.15, Wearing blue shirt, microphone to left of face, vert. No. 978, $1.15, Wearing blue shirt, microphone partially covering face, vert. No. 979, $1.15, Wearing black shirt, orange rectangular frame, vert. No. 980, $1.15, Wearing blue shirt, orange and blue frame, vert. No. 981, $1.15, Wearing black shirt, orange and blue frame, vert.
No. 982, $6, Vignette of #980. No. 983, $6, Wearing black shirt, vert.

1999   Litho.   Unwmk.   Perf. 12½
970-981 A161 Set of 12   19.00 19.00

Souvenir Sheets
982-983 A161 Set of 2   19.00 19.00

Issued in sheets of 9 containing 3 each of Nos. 970-972, 973-975, 976-978, 979-981 respectively. Nos. 982-983 contain one 76x51mm or 51x76mm stamp, respectively. Compare with #914-915 and #955-956.

Fruit — A162

1999   Litho.   Wmk. 380   Perf. 12½
984 A162 $1.15 Mango   1.10 1.10
985 A162 $1.50 Breadfruit   1.50 1.50
986 A162 $2.30 Papaya   2.40 2.40
987 A162 $3 Lime   3.00 3.00
988 A162 $6 Akee   6.25 6.25
a, Sheet of 5, #984-988 +label   15.00 15.00
Nos. 984-988 (5)   14.25 14.25

Dogs — A163

70c, Yorkshire terrier. $1, Welsh corgi. $1.15, King Charles spaniel. $1.50, Poodle. $3, Beagle.

1999
989 A163 70c black   1.30 1.30
990 A163 $1 black   2.25 2.25
991 A163 $1.15 black   2.25 2.25
992 A163 $1.50 black   3.25 3.25
993 A163 $3 black   6.25 6.25
a, Sheet of 5, #989-993 + label   15.00 15.00
Nos. 989-993 (5)   15.30 15.30

MONTSERRAT

World Teachers' Day — A164

World map and: $1, Ruler, scissors, compass, pencil, paint brush. $1.15, Teacher lecturing. $1.50, Compass, flag, camera, globe, plumb bob, theodolite. $5, Pen, flask, funnel, thermometer, calipers, microscope.

1999		Litho.	Perf. 12½
994-997	A164	Set of 4	13.00 13.00

Worldwide Fund for Nature — A165

No. 998 — Great hammerhead shark: a, Pair swimming. b, Pair near ocean floor. c, Trio swimming. d, One swimming.

	Perf. 13¼		
1999, Nov. 29	Litho.		Unwmk.
998	Horiz. strip of 4		5.25 5.25
a.-d.	A165 50c Any single		1.00 1.00

Millennium A166

2000, Jan. 1			Unwmk.
999	A166	$1.50 multi	3.25 3.25

100th Test Cricket Match at Lord's Ground — A167

Designs: $1, Alfred Valentine. $5, George Headley. $6, Lord's Ground, horiz.

2000, May 5	Litho.	Perf. 13½x13¼
1000-1001	A167 Set of 2	7.75 7.75
Souvenir Sheet		
	Perf. 13¼x13½	
1002	A167 $6 multi	10.00 10.00

The Stamp Show 2000, London — A168

Battle of Britain, 60th anniv.: 70c, Scramble. $1.15, Hurricane Mk.1 overhaul. $1.50, Hurricane Mk. 1 and enemy plane. $5, Spitfire Mk. 1a of Flight Lt. Frank Howell. $6, Plane in air.

	Wmk. 373		
2000, May 22	Litho.		Perf. 14
1003	A168	70c multi	.70 .70
1004	A168	$1.15 multi	1.10 1.10
1005	A168	$1.50 multi	1.50 1.50
1006	A168	$5 multi	5.00 5.00
Nos. 1003-1006 (4)			8.30 8.30
Souvenir Sheet			
1007	A168	$6 multi	7.00 7.00

Millennium A169

People of Montserrat and: 90c, Statue of Liberty. $1.15, Great Wall of China. $1.50, Eiffel Tower. $3.50, Millennium Dome, Great Britain.

	Perf. 13½		
2000, July 3	Litho.		Unwmk.
1008-1011	A169	Set of 4	7.50 7.50

Queen Mother, 100th Birthday A170

Queen Mother and various buildings. Panel color under country name in: 70c, Yellow. $1.15, Purple. $3, Green. $6, Orange.

2000, Aug. 4		Perf. 13½x13
1012-1015	A170 Set of 4	11.50 11.50
1015a	Souvenir sheet, #1012-1015	13.00 13.00

Christmas — A171

Designs: $1, The three Magi. $1.15, Cavalla Hill Methodist Church. $1.50, Shepherds. $3, $6, Mary and Joseph arriving in Bethlehem.

	Perf. 14x14¾		
2000, Nov. 29			Wmk. 373
1016-1019	A171	Set of 4	6.75 6.75
Souvenir Sheet			
1020	A171	$6 multi	7.50 7.50

Birds — A172

Designs: $1, Golden swallow, vert. $1.15, Crested quail dove. $1.50, Red-legged thrush. $5, Fernandina's flicker, vert. $8, St. Vincent parrot.

2001, Mar. 26	Litho.	Perf. 13¼
1021-1024	A172 Set of 4	12.00 12.00
Souvenir Sheet		
1025	A172 $8 multicolored	10.00 10.00

Philatelic Personalities A173

Designs: $1, Edward Stanley Gibbons, Charles J. Phillips. $1.15, John Lister. $1.50, Theodore Champion and 19th cent. French postilion. $3, Thomas de la Rue. $8, Sir Rowland Hill, Bruce Castle.

2001, Apr. 30		Perf. 13¼
1026-1029	A173 Set of 4	9.00 9.00
Souvenir Sheet		
1030	A173 $8 multi	10.00 10.00

Queen Elizabeth II, 75th Birthday — A174

Dress color: 90c, Black. $1.15, Yellow. $1.50, Pink. $5, Green. $6, Lilac.

2001, June 22		Perf. 13¼
1031-1034	A174 Set of 4	9.75 9.75
Souvenir Sheet		
1035	A174 $6 multi	8.75 8.75

Buildings A175

Designs: 70c, Lookout community. $1, St. John's Hospital. $1.15, Tropical Mansion Suites. $1.50, Montserrat Secondary School. $3, Golden Years Home.

2001, Aug. 15	Litho.	Perf. 13½
1036-1040	A175 Set of 5	9.50 9.50

Fruit — A176

Designs: 5c, West Indian cherries. 10c Mammee apples. 15c, Limes. 20c, Grapefruits. 25c, Orange. 40c, Passion fruits. 55c, Bananas. 70c, Papayas. 90c, Pomegranates. $1, Guavas. $1.15, Mangos. $1.50, Sugar apple. $3, Cashews. $5, Soursops. $7.50, Watermelon. $10, Pineapple.

2001, Oct. 10	Litho.	Perf. 13½x13¼
1041	A176 5c multi	.25 .25
1042	A176 10c multi	.25 .25
1043	A176 15c multi	.25 .25
1044	A176 20c multi	.25 .25
1045	A176 25c multi	.25 .25
1046	A176 40c multi	.40 .40
1047	A176 55c multi	.50 .50
1048	A176 70c multi	.65 .65
1049	A176 90c multi	.85 .85
1050	A176 $1 multi	1.00 1.00
1051	A176 $1.15 multi	1.10 1.10
1052	A176 $1.50 multi	1.40 1.40
1053	A176 $3 multi	3.00 3.00
1054	A176 $5 multi	4.75 4.75
1055	A176 $7.50 multi	7.50 7.50
1056	A176 $10 multi	9.75 9.75
Nos. 1041-1056 (16)		32.15 32.15

Butterflies A177

Designs: $1, Common long-tail skipper. $1.15, Straight-line skipper. $1.50, Giant hairstreak. $3, Monarch. $10, Painted lady.

2001, Dec. 20	Litho.	Perf. 13¼
1057-1060	A177 Set of 4	8.50 8.50
Souvenir Sheet		
1061	A177 $10 multi	12.50 12.50

2002 Winter Olympics, Salt Lake City — A178

No. 1062: a, $3, Downhill skiing. b, $5, Bobsled.

2002, Mar. 12	Litho.	Perf. 13¼
1062	A178 Horiz. pair, #a-b	9.50 9.50

Fish — A179

Designs: $1, Sergeant major. $1.15, Mutton snapper. $1.50, Lantern bass. $5, Shy hamlet. $8, Queen angelfish.

	Perf. 13¼		
2002, July 29	Litho.		Unwmk.
1063-1066	A179	Set of 4	11.50 11.50
Souvenir Sheet			
1067	A179	$8 multi	10.50 10.50

Nos. 1012-1015 Overprinted

2002, Sept. 23	Litho.	Perf. 13½x13
1068	A170 70c on #1012	.75 .75
1069	A170 $1.15 on #1013	1.00 1.00
1070	A170 $3 on #1014	3.00 3.00
1071	A170 $6 on #1015	6.25 6.25
Nos. 1068-1071 (4)		11.00 11.00

Wild Flowers A180

Designs: 70c, Allamanda cathartica. $1.15, Lantana camara. $1.50, Leonotis nepetifolia. $5, Plumeria rubra. $8, Alpinia purpurata.

	Perf. 13¼		
2002, Nov. 29	Litho.		Unwmk.
1072-1075	A180	Set of 4	12.00 12.00
Souvenir Sheet			
1076	A180	$8 multi	11.00 11.00

Coronation of Queen Elizabeth II, 50th Anniv. — A181

No. 1077: a, Queen wearing crown. b, Crown on pillow. c, Queen wearing tiara and purple sash. $6, Queen wearing crown, diff.

2003, Apr. 30		Perf. 14
1077	A181 $3 Sheet of 3, #a-c	9.50 9.50
Souvenir Sheet		
1078	A181 $6 multi	5.50 5.50

Powered Flight, Cent. A182

No. 1079: a, Wright Flyer II in purple. b, Wright Flyer II in brown. c, Wright Brothers. d, Wright Flyer I. $6, Wright Flyer II.

2003, June 30	Litho.	Perf. 14
1079	A182 $2 Sheet of 4, #a-d	9.25 9.25
Souvenir Sheet		
1080	A182 $6 multi	8.00 8.00

Prince William, 21st Birthday A183

No. 1081 — Prince William in suit and tie with: a, Frame obscured at LL and LR by portrait. b, Frame obscured at LL by portrait. c, Frame not obscured. $6, Wearing sweater and shirt with open collar.

2003, Aug. 20		
1081	A183 $3 Sheet of 3, #a-c	10.00 10.00
Souvenir Sheet		
1082	A183 $6 multi	8.00 8.00

MONTSERRAT

Fauna — A184

No. 1083: a, Piping frog. b, Land hermit crab. c, Spix's pinche. d, Dwarf gecko. e, Green sea turtle. f, Indian mongoose. $6, Sally Lightfoot crab.

2003, Nov. 28
| 1083 | A184 | $1.50 Sheet of 6, #a-f | 10.00 | 10.00 |

Souvenir Sheet
| 1084 | A184 | $6 multi | 7.50 | 7.50 |

Mushrooms — A185

No. 1085: a, Slimy lead milk cap. b, Rosy spike cap. c, Stump puffball. d, Parasol. e, Crab russula. f, Scaly vase chanterelle. $6, Fly agaric.

2003, Nov. 28
| 1085 | A185 | $1.50 Sheet of 6, #a-f | 10.50 | 10.50 |

Souvenir Sheet
| 1086 | A185 | $6 multi | 7.50 | 7.50 |

Birds — A186

Designs: 90c, Belted kingfisher. $1.15, Yellow warbler. No. 1089, $1.50, Hooded warbler. $5, Cedar waxwing.
No. 1091: a, Roseate spoonbill. b, Laughing gull. c, White-tailed tropicbird. d, Bare-eyed thrush. e, Glittering-throated emerald. f, Lesser Antillean grackle.
$6, Bananaquit.

2003, Nov. 28
| 1087-1090 | A186 | Set of 4 | 11.50 | 11.50 |
| 1091 | A186 | $1.50 Sheet of 6, #a-f | 9.00 | 9.00 |

Souvenir Sheet
| 1092 | A186 | $6 multi | 7.00 | 7.00 |

2004 Summer Olympics, Greece — A187

Designs: 90c, 1932 Los Angeles Olympics poster. $1.15, 1972 Munich Olympics pin. $1.50, 1976 Montreal Olympics poster. $5, Pankration, horiz.

2004, June 30   Litho.   Perf. 13¼
| 1093-1096 | A187 | Set of 4 | 9.25 | 9.25 |

Butterflies — A188

No. 1097: a, Lacewing. b, Swallowtail. c, Shoemaker. d, White peacock.
$6, Flashing astraptes.

2004, July 6   Litho.   Perf. 14
| 1097 | A188 | $2.30 Sheet of 4, #a-d | 9.25 | 9.25 |

Souvenir Sheet
| 1098 | A188 | $6 multi | 5.00 | 5.00 |

Cats — A189

Designs: $1.15, Singapura. $1.50, Burmese. $2, Abyssinian. $5, Norwegian.
$6, Russian Blue.

2004, Aug. 23
| 1099-1102 | A189 | Set of 4 | 10.50 | 10.50 |

Souvenir Sheet
| 1103 | A189 | $6 multi | 0.50 | 0.50 |

Fish — A190

No. 1104: a, Blue-girdled angelfish. b, Regal angelfish. c, Emperor angelfish. d, Blotch-eyed soldierfish.
$6, Banded butterflyfish.

2004, Sept. 30
| 1104 | A190 | $2.30 Sheet of 4, #a-d | 10.00 | 10.00 |

Souvenir Sheet
| 1105 | A190 | $6 multi | 8.00 | 8.00 |

Locomotives, 200th Anniv. — A191

No. 1106: a, Austerity. b, Deli Vasut. c, Class 424 No. 424.247/287. d, L-1646. e, Steam locomotive 324.1564. f, Class Ia.
No. 1107: a, Old Class TV. b, Class Va 7111. c, Class 424 No. 424.009. d, Class III.
$6, Class QR1.

2004, Oct. 29   Perf. 14½x14
| 1106 | A191 | $1.50 Sheet of 6, #a-f | 7.50 | 7.50 |
| 1107 | A191 | $2 Sheet of 4, #a-d | 6.75 | 6.75 |

Souvenir Sheet
| 1108 | A191 | $6 multi | 5.00 | 5.00 |

World AIDS Day — A192

2004, Dec. 1   Perf. 13½
| 1109 | A192 | $3 multi | 2.25 | 2.25 |

Printed in sheets of 4.

D-Day, 60th Anniv. — A193

Designs: $1.15, Air assault begins. $1.50, Troops assault beaches of Normandy. $2, Field Marshal Montgomery. $5, HMS Belfast.

2004, Dec. 24   Perf. 14
| 1110-1113 | A193 | Set of 4 | 9.00 | 9.00 |

National Soccer Team — A194

2004, Dec. 24   Litho.   Perf. 12
| 1114 | A194 | $6 multi | 5.00 | 5.00 |

Nos. 1036-1040 Overprinted

THE VISIT OF
HRH THE PRINCESS ROYAL
FEBRUARY 2005

2005, Feb. 21   Litho.   Perf. 13½
1115	A175	70c multi	.65	.65
1116	A175	$1 multi	.90	.90
1117	A175	$1.15 multi	1.05	1.05
1118	A175	$1.50 multi	1.40	1.40
1119	A175	$3 multi	2.75	2.75
		Nos. 1115-1119 (5)	6.75	6.75

Birds — A195

No. 1120: a, Brown pelican. b, Red-billed tropicbird. c, Galapagos Island cormorant. d, Waved albatross.
$6, Common tern.

2005, Apr. 25   Litho.   Perf. 13¼x13½
| 1120 | A195 | $2.30 Sheet of 4, #a-d | 8.25 | 8.25 |

Souvenir Sheet
| 1121 | A195 | $6 multi | 6.00 | 6.00 |

Orchids A196

No. 1122: a, Cattleya lueddemanniana. b, Cattleya luteola. c, Cattleya trianaei. d, Cattleya mossiae.
$6, Cattleya mendelii.

2005, Apr. 25
| 1122 | A196 | $2.30 Sheet of 4, #a-d | 8.00 | 8.00 |

Souvenir Sheet
| 1123 | A196 | $6 multi | 5.50 | 5.50 |

Molluscs and Shells — A197

Designs: $1.15, Liguus virgineus. $1.50, Liguus fasciatus testudineus. $2, Liguus fasciatus. $5, Cerion striatella.
$6, Liguus fasciatus, vert.

2005, June 1   Perf. 13¼x13½
| 1124-1127 | A197 | Set of 4 | 8.75 | 8.75 |

Souvenir Sheet
Perf. 13½x13¼
| 1128 | A197 | $6 multi | 6.00 | 6.00 |

Miniature Sheet

Soufriere Hills Volcanic Eruption, 10th Anniv. A198

No. 1129: a, Dome glow. b, Explosion. c, Tar River Delta. d, Belham River. e, MVO Building. f, Pyroclastic flow entering the sea. g, Blackburne Airport, destroyed in 1997. h, Helicopter maintenance and monitoring. i, Instruments used for monitoring.

2005, July 18   Litho.   Perf. 14
| 1129 | A198 | $2 Sheet of 9, #a-i | 17.50 | 17.50 |

Rotary International, Cent. — A199

Emblem and: $1, Shamrock. $1.15, Heliconia flower. $1.50, Lady and the Harp. $5, Map of Montserrat.
$6, Medical care for children, horiz.

2005, Sept. 12   Perf. 12¾
| 1130-1133 | A199 | Set of 4 | 8.50 | 8.50 |

Souvenir Sheet
| 1134 | A199 | $6 multi | 6.00 | 6.00 |

Battle of Trafalgar, Bicent. A200

No. 1135: a, Napoleon Bonaparte. b, Admiral Horatio Nelson. c, Battle of the Nile. d, Battle of Trafalgar.
$6, Nelson, diff.

2005, Nov. 4   Litho.   Perf. 12
| 1135 | A200 | $2 Sheet of 4, #a-d | 8.75 | 8.75 |

Souvenir Sheet
| 1136 | A200 | $6 multi | 6.50 | 6.50 |

MONTSERRAT

Hans Christian Andersen (1805-75), Author — A201

No. 1137: a, Thumbelina. b, The Flying Trunk. c, The Buckwheat.
$6, The Little Mermaid.

2005, Dec. 23   **Perf. 12¾**
1137 A201 $3 Sheet of 3, #a-c   8.50 8.50
Souvenir Sheet   **Perf. 12**
1138 A201 $6 multi   6.50 6.50

No. 1137 contains three 39x25mm stamps.

Famous People — A202

Designs: No. 1139, $1.15, William Henry Bramble (1901-88), first chief minister. No. 1140, $1.15, Michael Simmons Osborne (1902-67), merchant and parliamentarian. No. 1141, $1.15, Robert William Griffith (1904-96), union leader. No. 1142, $1.15, Patricia Griffin (1907-86), social worker. No. 1143, $1.15, Lilian Cadogan (1907-92), nurse. No. 1144, $1.15, Samuel Aymer (1911-79), folk musician.

2005, Dec. 5   **Litho.**   **Perf. 12¾**
1139-1144 A202 Set of 6   6.50 6.50
1140a   Inscribed "Symmons" instead of "Simmons"   1.10 1.10
1144a   Souvenir sheet, #1139, 1140a, 1141-1144   6.50 6.50

Nos. 1022, 1058-1059, 1072 and 1075 Overprinted

Methods and Perfs As Before
2006, Apr. 1
1145 A180 70c on #1072   .65 .65
1146 A172 $1 on #1022   .95 .95
1147 A177 $1.15 on #1058   1.10 1.10
1148 A177 $1.50 on #1059   1.40 1.40
1149 A180 $5 on #1075   4.50 4.50
Nos. 1145-1149 (5)   8.60 8.60

Overprint is on four lines on No. 1146.

Marine Life A203

No. 1150: a, Giant Caribbean anemone. b, Beadlet anemone. c, Golden crinoid. d, Oval cup coral.
$6, Tube-dwelling anemone.

2006, May 2   **Litho.**   **Perf. 12**
1150 A203 $2.30 Sheet of 4, #a-d   9.50 9.50
Souvenir Sheet
1151 A203 $6 multi   6.00 6.00

Moths A204

No. 1152: a, Cecropia moth. b, Madagascan sunset moth. c, Great peacock moth. d, Zodiac moth.
$6, White-lined sphinx moth.

2006, May 2
1152 A204 $2.30 Sheet of 4, #a-d   9.50 9.50
Souvenir Sheet
1153 A204 $6 multi   6.00 6.00

Dogs — A205

Designs: $1.15, Rottweiler. $1.50, Boxer. $2, Corgi. $5, Great Dane.
$6, St. Bernard.

2006, Aug. 16
1154-1157 A205 Set of 4   9.00 9.00
Souvenir Sheet
1158 A205 $6 multi   5.75 5.75

Worldwide Fund for Nature (WWF) — A206

No. 1159 — Various depictions of Mountain chicken frog: a, 70c. b, $1. c, $1.15. d, $1.50.

2006, Aug. 16   **Perf. 13¼**
1159 A206 Block of 4, #a-d   3.75 3.75
e.   Miniature sheet, 2 #1159   7.50 7.50

Souvenir Sheet

2006 World Cup Soccer Championships, Germany — A207

No. 1160 — World Cup, emblem and: a, $1.15, FIFA World Cup Stadium, Hanover. b, $1.50, Sir Stanley Matthews, England team uniform. c, $2, Sir Ralph "Dixie" Dean, England team uniform. d, $5, Bobby Moore, England team uniform.

2006, Aug. 31   **Perf. 12**
1160 A207 Sheet of 4, #a-d   8.25 8.25

Christopher Columbus (1451-1506), Explorer — A208

Designs: $1.15, Map of North and South America, Columbus's vessels. $1.50, Columbus and map of voyage. $2, Ship, Earth, Columbus. $5, Columbus, vert.
$6, Earth, Columbus and crew with flag, vert.

2006, Oct. 27   **Perf. 12¾**
1161-1164 A208 Set of 4   8.25 8.25
Souvenir Sheet
1165 A208 $6 multi   5.25 5.25

Queen Elizabeth II, 80th Birthday A210
A209

No. 1166: a, Queen wearing crown, country name in black. b, Queen wearing crown, country name in white. c, Queen wearing tiara. d, Queen wearing tiara and sash.

2006, Oct. 27   **Perf. 13¼**
1166 A209 $2.30 Sheet of 4, #a-d   7.25 7.25
Souvenir Sheet
1167 A210 $8 shown   6.25 6.25

2007 Cricket World Cup, West Indies — A211

Designs: $3, 2007 Cricket World Cup emblem, map and flag of Montserrat. $5, Cricket team, horiz.
$8, 2007 Cricket World Cup emblem.

2007, Mar. 9   **Litho.**   **Perf. 13¼**
1168-1169 A211 Set of 2   6.25 6.25
Souvenir Sheet
1170 A211 $8 multi   6.25 6.25

Scouting, Cent. A212

No. 1171, horiz. — Scouts: a, Looking at flower. b, Working at construction site. c, In sailboat. d, Feeding goat. e, Making campfire. f, Installing birdhouse.
$6, Lord Robert Baden-Powell.

2007, Mar. 9
1171 A212 $2 Sheet of 6, #a-f   9.50 9.50
Souvenir Sheet
1172 A212 $6 multi   4.75 4.75

Flowers — A213

Designs: 10c, Poinsettia. 30c, Periwinkle. 35c, Bougainvillea. 50c, Ixora. 70c, Heliconia. 80c, Morning glory. 90c, Poinciana. $1, Cup of gold. $1.10, Chenille plant. $1.50, Oleander. $2.25, Hibiscus. $2.50, Frangipani. $2.75, Bird of paradise. $5, Madagascar jasmine. $10, Yellow poui. $20, Rose.

2007, May 14   **Litho.**   **Perf. 12½**
1173 A213 10c multi   .25 .25
1174 A213 30c multi   .25 .25
1175 A213 35c multi   .25 .25
1176 A213 50c multi   .40 .40
1177 A213 70c multi   .55 .55
1178 A213 80c multi   .60 .60
1179 A213 90c multi   .70 .70
1180 A213 $1 multi   .75 .75
1181 A213 $1.10 multi   .85 .85
1182 A213 $1.50 multi   1.10 1.10
1183 A213 $2.25 multi   1.75 1.75
1184 A213 $2.50 multi   1.90 1.90
1185 A213 $2.75 multi   2.10 2.10
1186 A213 $5 multi   3.75 3.75
1187 A213 $10 multi   7.50 7.50
1188 A213 $20 multi   15.00 15.00
Nos. 1173-1188 (16)   37.70 37.70

Princess Diana (1961-97) — A214

No. 1189 — Diana wearing tiara and: a, Blue dress. b, Black dress. c, White dress. d, White dress with high neck.
$7, Diana without tiara.

2007, Aug. 8   **Litho.**   **Perf. 13¼**
1189 A214 $3.40 Sheet of 4, #a-d   11.00 11.00
Souvenir Sheet
1190 A214 $7 multi   6.00 6.00

Turtles A215

No. 1191: a, Hawksbill turtle. b, Green turtle. c, Leatherback turtle. d, Loggerhead turtle.
$7, Kemp's Ridley sea turtle.

2007, Aug. 8   **Perf. 13¼x13½**
1191 A215 $3.40 Sheet of 4, #a-d   11.50 11.50
Souvenir Sheet
1192 A215 $7 multi   6.00 6.00

Parrots A216

No. 1193: a, Green-winged macaw. b, Mitred conure. c, Sun conure. d, Blue-and-yellow macaw.
$7, Hyacinth macaw.

2007, Oct. 11   **Litho.**   **Perf. 13½x13¼**
1193 A216 $3.40 Sheet of 4, #a-d   13.50 13.50
Souvenir Sheet
1194 A216 $7 multi   9.00 9.00

Lilies A217

No. 1195, horiz.: a, Hippeastrum puniceum. b, Hymenocallis caribaea. c, Zephyranthes puertoricensis. d, Belamcanda chinensis.
$7, Crinum erubescens.

2007, Oct. 11   **Perf. 13¼x13½**
1195 A217 $3.40 Sheet of 4, #a-d   11.50 11.50
Souvenir Sheet   **Perf. 13½x13¼**
1196 A217 $7 multi   6.00 6.00

MONTSERRAT

Miniature Sheet

Charles Wesley (1707-88), Hymn Writer — A218

No. 1197: a, Portrait of Wesley by unknown artist. b, Portrait of Wesley by John Russell. c, Engraving of Wesley by Jonathan Spilsbury. d, Bethany Methodist Church.

2007, Dec. 18   Litho.   Perf. 13¼
1197 A218 $2.50 Sheet of 4, #a-d   8.00   8.00

Whales — A219

No. 1198: a, Sperm whale. b, Minke whale. c, Cuvier's beaked whale. d, Humpback whale.
$7, Blue whale.

2008, May 2   Perf. 12¾
1198 A219 $3.55 Sheet of 4, #a-d   13.00   13.00
Souvenir Sheet
1199 A219 $7 multi   8.00   8.00

Space Exploration, 50th Anniv. — A220

No. 1200, vert.: a, Explorer I on Juno I launch rocket. b, Dr. James Van Allen, Explorer I. c, Explorer I. d, Drs. William Pickering, James Van Allen and Wernher von Braun with Explorer I model.
$7, Explorer I, diff.

2008, May 29   Perf. 13¼
1200 A220 $3.55 Sheet of 4, #a-d   12.00   12.00
Souvenir Sheet
1201 A220 $7 multi   6.00   6.00

Endangered Animals — A221

No. 1202, vert.: a, African elephant. b, Bald eagle. c, Sumatran tiger. d, Hawksbill turtle. e, Indian rhinoceros. f, Western gorilla.
$7, Rock iguana.

2008, July 3
1202 A221 $2.25 Sheet of 6, #a-f   12.00   12.00
Souvenir Sheet
1203 A221 $7 multi   6.50   6.50

Miniature Sheet

Early Postal History — A222

No. 1204: a, "Lady McLeod" stamp, early paddle packet boat. b, Early Montserrat postal card. c, Great Britain #U1-U2. d, Great Britain #1, Sir Rowland Hill. e, Montserrat #1-2. f, Montserrat cancels.

2008, July 31   Litho.   Perf. 13½
1204 A222 $2.75 Sheet of 6, #a-f   13.50   13.50

Miniature Sheets

Royal Air Force, 90th Anniv. A223

No. 1205, $3.55: a, English Electric Lightning P3. b, Hurricane IIC. c, Jet Provost T3A. d, Jaguar GR3A.
No. 1206, $3.55: a, Westland Sea King HAR3 helicopter. b, Gloster Javelin FAW9. c, P-66 Pembroke C1. d, Chinook HC2 helicopter.

2008, Sept. 5   Litho.   Perf. 13¼
Sheets of 4, #a-d
1205-1206 A223 Set of 2   24.00   24.00

University of the West Indies, 60th Anniv. A224

Designs: $2, Building on Montserrat campus. $5, University arms, diploma.

2008, Sept. 30
1207-1208 A224 Set of 2   6.00   6.00

Miniature Sheets

Orchids A225

No. 1209, $2.75: a, Cattleya labiata. b, Phalaenopsis cultivar with pink spots. c, Cymbidium annabelle. d, Phalaenopsis taisuco.
No. 1210, $2.75: a, Phalaenopsis amabilis. b, Cattleya aurantiaca. c, Phalaenopsis culti var with pink lines. d, Dendrobium nobile.

2008, Nov. 27   Perf. 13¼
Sheets of 4, #a-d
1209-1210 A225 Set of 2   19.00   19.00

Dolphins A226

No. 1211: a, Common dolphin. b, Bottlenose dolphin. c, Pantropical spotted dolphin. d, Long-snouted spinner dolphin.
$7, Risso's dolphin.

2008, Nov. 27   Perf. 12¾
1211 A226 $3.55 Sheet of 4, #a-d   12.50   12.50
Souvenir Sheet
1212 A226 $7 multi   5.75   5.75

Miniature Sheet

New Year 2009 (Year of the Ox) A227

No. 1213: a, Yellow orange ox facing right. b, Black ox facing left. c, Gray ox facing right. d, White ox facing left.

2009, Feb. 2   Litho.   Perf. 12¾
1213 A227 $3.55 Sheet of 4, #a-d   13.00   13.00

Miniature Sheets

Dr. Martin Luther King, Jr. (1929-68), Civil Rights Leader — A228

No. 1214, $2.50: a, King. b, King at desk. c, King wearing hat. d, King's wife, Coretta.
No. 1215, $2.50, horiz.: a, March on Washington crowd. b, King meeting Malcolm X. c, King with Pres. John F. Kennedy and other civil rights leaders. d, King waving to March on Washington crowd.

2009, Feb. 26   Perf. 13½
Sheets of 4, #a-d
1214-1215 A228 Set of 2   16.00   16.00

Birds A229

No. 1216: a, Smooth-billed ani. b, American kestrel. c, Common moorhen. d, Cattle egret.
$7, Male Montserrat oriole.

2009, Apr. 1
1216 A229 $2.75 Sheet of 4, #a-d   9.00   9.00
Souvenir Sheet
1217 A229 $7 multi   6.50   6.50

Corals — A230

Designs: $1.10, Staghorn coral. $2.25, Zoanthid coral. $2.50, Blade fire coral. $2.75, Brain coral.
$7, Orange tube coral, vert.

2009, Apr. 29
1218-1221 A230 Set of 4   7.00   7.00
Souvenir Sheet
1222 A230 $7 multi   6.00   6.00
No. 1222 contains one 37x51mm stamp.

Charles Darwin (1809-82), Naturalist — A231

No. 1223, vert.: a, Darwin. b, Coenobita clypeatus. c, Anolis lividus. d, Epidendrum montserratense.
$7, Darwin, waterfall, emblem of Montserrat Centre Hills Project.

2009, July 28
1223 A231 $2.75 Sheet of 4, #a-d   8.50   8.50
Souvenir Sheet
1224 A231 $7 multi   6.00   6.00

Rain Forest Animals A232

No. 1225: a, $1.10, Green iguana. b, $2.25, Galliwasp. c, $2.50, Black snake. d, $2.75, Common agouti.
$5, Yellow-shouldered bat.

2009, Sept. 25   Litho.   Perf. 13¼
1225 A232 Sheet of 4, #a-d   7.50   7.50
Souvenir Sheet
1226 A232 $5 multi   4.25   4.25

Trees A233

Designs: $1.10, Tamarind. $2.25, Dwarf coconut. $2.50, Breadfruit. $2.75, Calabash. $5, Geiger.

2009, Oct. 30   Perf. 14¼x14¾
1227-1231 A233 Set of 5   10.50   10.50

Miniature Sheet

Naval Aviation, Cent. A234

No. 1232 — Aircraft carriers: a, 70c, HMS Ark Royal II. b, $1.10, HMS Furious. c, $2.25, HMS Argus. d, $2.50, HMS Illustrious. e, $2.75, HMS Ark Royal IV. f, $5, HMS Invincible.

2009, Dec. 4   Litho.   Perf. 11½x11¼
1232 A234 Sheet of 6, #a-f   11.00   11.00

MONTSERRAT

Christmas — A236

Designs: $1.10, Snowflake bush. $2.25, Carnival troupe. $2.50, Masquerade. $2.75, St. Patrick's Roman Catholic Church. $6, Creche figurines of Holy Family.

2009, Dec. 18			Perf. 12¾
1233-1236	A235	Set of 4	6.75 6.75
Souvenir Sheet			
1237	A236	$6 multi	5.25 5.25

Marine Life — A237

Designs: $1.10, Basket star. $2.25, Spiny lobster. $2.50, Spotted drum. $2.75, Sea anemone, vert. $5, Batwing coral crab.

2010, Mar. 15			Perf. 14¼
1238-1242	A237	Set of 5	10.50 10.50

Miniature Sheets

World Landmarks — A238

No. 1243: a, $1.10, Jin Mao Tower, Shanghai, China. b, $2.25, Montserrat Cultural Center, Little Bay, Montserrat. c, $2.50, Assumption Cathedral, Moscow, Russia. d, $2.75, Brooklyn Bridge.
No. 1244: a, $1.10, Fishing villages in Shanghai and Hong Kong. b, $2.25, Camelot Villa, Montserrat. c, $2.50, Buildings at Zaanse Schans Windmill Village, Zaandam, Netherlands. d, $2.75, Reichstag, Berlin, Germany.

2010, Apr. 19			Perf. 14¼
		Sheets of 4, #a-d	
1243-1244	A238	Set of 2	15.00 15.00

Miniature Sheets

A239

Michael Jackson (1958-2009), Singer — A240

No. 1245 — Jackson: a, Wearing sunglasses. b, Wearing red jacket and white shirt. c, With microphone near mouth. d, Wearing high-collared red jacket.
No. 1246 — Jackson: a, Facing right, no microphone. b, Facing left, holding microphone. c, Wearing black jacket, holding microphone. d, Facing forward, no microphone.

2010, June 25			Perf. 13½
1245	A239	$2.50 Sheet of 4, #a-d	8.50 8.50
1246	A240	$2.50 Sheet of 4, #a-d	8.50 8.50

A241

Flowers A242

Designs: $1.10, Wild marigold. $2.25, Shrubby toothedthread. $2.50, Wild sweet pea. $2.75, Rosy periwinkle. $5, Measle bush. $7, Pribby.

2010, Aug. 18			
1247-1251	A241	Set of 5	12.00 12.00
Souvenir Sheet			
1252	A242	$7 multi	6.50 6.50

Worldwide Fund for Nature (WWF) — A243

No. 1253 — Reddish egret: a, $1.10, Two birds in water. b, $2.25, Two birds in flight. c, $2.50, Bird preening feathers. d, $2.75, Bird running in water.

2010, Oct. 29			Litho.
1253	A243	Block or strip of 4, #a-d	7.50 7.50
	e.	Souvenir sheet of 8, 2 each #a-d	15.00 15.00

Giant Panda A244

No. 1254 — Panda: a, Eating, brown in background. b, Resting on tree. c, Eating, green in background. d, Walking. $7, Panda, diff.

2010, Nov. 22		Litho.	Perf. 12
1254	A244	$2.50 Sheet of 4, #a-d	3.00 3.00
Souvenir Sheet			
		Perf. 13 Syncopated	
1255	A244	$7 multi	4.50 4.50

Beijing 2010 Intl. Philatelic Exhibition.

Shells — A245

Designs: $1.10, Beaded periwinkle. $2.25, Green star shell. $2.50, Smooth Scotch bonnet. $2.75, Calico scallop. $5, Hawk wing conch. $7, Atlantic partridge tun, vert.

2011, Jan. 10		Perf. 13 Syncopated	
1256-1260	A245	Set of 5	10.50 10.50
Souvenir Sheet			
1261	A245	$7 multi	5.25 5.25

Miniature Sheet

Medicinal Plants — A246

No. 1262: a, Anise. b, Lemon grass. c, Vervain. d, Ram goat bush. e, Rosemary. f, Inflammation bush.

2011, Mar. 15			Perf. 12x11½
1262	A246	$2.25 Sheet of 6, #a-f	10.00 10.00

Engagement of Prince William and Catherine Middleton — A247

No. 1263: a, Couple, door at left. b, Middleton. c, Prince William. d, Couple, picture frame in background.
No. 1264: a, Middleton, diff. b, Prince William, diff.

2011, Mar. 31			Perf. 13¼
1263	A247	$2.75 Sheet of 4, #a-d	8.25 8.25
Souvenir Sheet			
1264	A247	$5 Sheet of 2, #a-b	7.50 7.50

Livestock — A248

Designs: $2.25, Barbados black belly sheep. $2.50, Boer goat, horiz. $2.75, Black donkey. $5, Red cattle, horiz. $7, Arabian horse.

2011, June 6			Perf. 12
1265-1268	A248	Set of 4	9.25 9.25
Souvenir Sheet			
1269	A248	$7 multi	5.25 5.25

Wedding of Prince William and Catherine Middleton — A249

No. 1270: a, Groom wearing hat. b, Couple, groom without hat. c, Bride looking left. d, Groom without hat. e, Couple with groom. f, Bride looking right.
$7, Couple kissing.

2011, June 29			Perf. 13x13¼
1270	A249	$2.25 Sheet of 6, #a-f	10.00 10.00
Souvenir Sheet			
1271	A249	$7 multi	5.25 5.25

Sept. 11, 2001 Terrorist Attacks, 10th Anniv. A250

No. 1272: a, Tribute in Washington Square, New York City, Sept. 14, 2001. b, American flag, chain-link fence, message on piece of wood. c, Messages on pillar in Union Square, New York City, Sept. 13, 2001. d, Memorial, Stonycreek Township, Pennsylvania.
$6, Keithroy Maynard (1971-2001), New York City firefighter killed in attacks.

2011, Sept. 11			Perf. 12
1272	A250	$2.75 Sheet of 4, #a-d	8.25 8.25
Souvenir Sheet			
1273	A250	$6 multi	4.50 4.50

Alphonsus Cassell (1949-2010), Calypso and Soca Singer — A251

Designs: $2.25, Color photograph of Cassell. $2.50, Color photograph, diff.
No. 1276, horiz. — Cassell singing: a, With spotlights in background. b, Wearing headphones. c, With hand raised above head. d, Not holding microphone.

2011, Oct. 15		Set of 2	Perf. 14
1274-1275	A251		3.50 3.50
		Perf. 12	
1276	A251	$2.75 Sheet of 4, #a-d	8.25 8.25

Statue of Liberty, 125th Anniv. A252

No. 1277 — View of: a, $1.10, Head. b, $1.10, Torch. c, $2.25, Head, diff. d, $2.25, Tablet. e, $2.50, Entire statue. f, $2.50, Head and tablet.
$6, Entire statue and base.

2011, Oct. 28			Perf. 12
1277	A252	Sheet of 6, #a-f	8.75 8.75
Souvenir Sheet			
1278	A252	$6 multi	4.50 4.50

No. 1278 contains one 30x80mm stamp.

Miniature Sheets

Flora and Fauna of China A253

MONTSERRAT

No. 1279 — Flora: a, $1.10, Chinese plum. b, $2.25, Opium poppy. c, $2.50, Japanese camellia. d, $2.75, Pomegranate.
No. 1280 — Fauna: a, $1.10, Purple heron. b, $2.25, Indian elephant. c, $2.50, Snub-nosed monkey. d, $2.75, Royal Bengal tiger.

2011, Nov. 11 — Perf. 12
Sheets of 4, #a-d
1279-1280 A253 Set of 2 13.00 13.00
China 2011 Intl. Philatelic Exhibition, Wuxi.

Christmas A254

Designs: $2.25, Choral group Voices. $2.50, Emerald Community Singers. $2.75, Volpanics. $5, New Ebenezer Seventh Day Adventist Church.

2011, Dec. 6 — Perf. 14
1281-1284 A254 Set of 4 9.25 9.25

Ducks A255

No. 1285: a, Northern pintail. b, Green-winged teal. c, Fulvous whistling duck. d, Blue-winged teal.
$6, Northern shoveler.

2012, Feb. 28 — Perf. 14
1285 A255 $3.50 Sheet of 4, #a-d 10.50 10.50
Souvenir Sheet Perf. 12
1286 A255 $6 multi 4.50 4.50

Cacti A256

No. 1287: a, Queen of the night. b, Old man's whiskers. c, Devil cholla. d, Century plant.
No. 1288: Prickly pear cactus. b, Prickly pear fruit.

2012, Feb. 10
1287 A256 $2.75 Sheet of 4, #a-d 8.25 8.25
Souvenir Sheet
1288 A256 $3.50 Sheet of 2, #a-b 5.25 5.25

Reign of Queen Elizabeth II 60th Anniv. A257

No. 1289: a, Head of Queen Elizabeth II. b, Queen Elizabeth II waving, two men in background. c, Queen Elizabeth II on throne. d, Queen Elizabeth II and Prince Philip.
$7, Queen Elizabeth II, vert.

2012, Apr. 18 — Perf. 12
1289 A257 $3.50 Sheet of 4, #a-d 10.50 10.50
Souvenir Sheet Perf. 14
1290 A257 $7 multi 5.25 5.25

Bridges A258

No. 1291, vert.: a, Sydney Harbour Bridge. b, Brooklyn Bridge. c, Golden Gate Bridge. $6, Tower Bridge, London.

2012, June 8 — Perf. 14
1291 A258 $4 Sheet of 3, #a-c 9.00 9.00
Souvenir Sheet
1292 A258 $6 multi 4.50 4.50

Marine Life A259

No. 1293: a, Yellow tang. b, Spotted dolphin. c, Manatee. d, Green sea turtle.
$6, Blue-spotted grouper.

2012, June 20 — Litho.
1293 A259 $3 Sheet of 4, #a-d 9.00 9.00
Souvenir Sheet
1294 A259 $6 multi 4.50 4.50

Ferns A260

No. 1295: a, Argyrochosma jonesii. b, Danaea kalevala. c, Lastreopsis effusa. d, Asplenium serratum.
$6, Phlebodium aureum, vert.

2012, Aug. 20 — Perf. 14
1295 A260 $3 Sheet of 4, #a-d 9.00 9.00
Souvenir Sheet Perf. 12½
1296 A260 $6 multi 4.50 4.50
No. 1296 contains one 38x51mm stamp.

Scenes From China A261

No. 1297 — Great Wall of China: a, Tower at right, denomination in black. b, Four towers, denomination in black. c, Wall turrets, denomination in white. d, Wall walkway, denomination in white.
No. 1298: a, Gate of Heavenly Peace. b, Forbidden City. c, Summer Palace, large rock at LL. d, Summer Palace, stairway at LL. e, Pudong skyline. f, Li River, Quangxi Province.
No. 1299, $5, Sanqingshan National Park, vert. No. 1300, $5, Dragon carving on a temple facade, vert.

2012, Nov. 15 — Perf. 13¾
1297 A261 $2.25 Sheet of 4, #a-d 6.75 6.75
1298 A261 $2.50 Sheet of 6, #a-d 11.50 11.50
Souvenir Sheets Perf. 12½
1299-1300 A261 Set of 2 7.50 7.50
Beijing 2012 Intl. Philatelic Exhibition. Nos. 1299-1300 each contain one 38x51mm stamp.

Minerals A262

No. 1301: a, Amber. b, Chrysoberyl. c, Garnet. d, Microcline. e, Sunstone. f, Lapis lazuli.
$6, Orpiment, vert.

2013, Jan. 31 — Perf. 13¾
1301 A262 $2.50 Sheet of 6, #a-f 11.50 11.50
Souvenir Sheet Perf. 12¾
1302 A262 $6 multi 4.50 4.50
No. 1302 contains one 38x51mm stamp.

Butterflies — A263

Designs: 10c, Pygmy fritillary. 30c, Cloudless sulphur. 35c, Gulf fritillary. 60c, St. Christopher's hairstreak. 70c, Nyctelius skipper. 80c, Cassius blue. 90c, Antillean orcooont. $1, Polydamas swallowtail. $1.10, Flambeau. $1.50, Bronze hairstreak. $2.25, Caribbean buckeye. $2.50, Red rim. $2.75, White peacock. $5, Stub-tailed skipper. $10, Zebra. $20, Manuel's skipper.

2013, Mar. 5 — Perf. 12
1303 A263 10c multi .25 .25
1304 A263 30c multi .25 .25
1305 A263 35c multi .25 .25
1306 A263 50c multi .40 .40
1307 A263 70c multi .55 .55
1308 A263 80c multi .60 .60
1309 A263 90c multi .70 .70
1310 A263 $1 multi .75 .75
1311 A263 $1.10 multi .85 .85
1312 A263 $1.50 multi 1.10 1.10
1313 A263 $2.25 multi 1.75 1.75
1314 A263 $2.50 multi 1.90 1.90
1315 A263 $2.75 multi 2.10 2.10
1316 A263 $5 multi 3.75 3.75
1317 A263 $10 multi 7.50 7.50
1318 A263 $20 multi 15.00 15.00
Nos. 1303-1318 (16) 37.70 37.70

Globe Theater Fire, 400th Anniv. A264

No. 1319 — Plays by William Shakespeare (1564-1616): a, Hamlet. b, Julius Caesar. c, Macbeth. d, Romeo and Juliet.
$7, Shakespeare, vert.

2013, May 29 — Perf. 13¾
1319 A264 $2.75 Sheet of 4, #a-d 8.25 8.25
Souvenir Sheet Perf. 12½
1320 A264 $7 multi 5.25 5.25
No. 1320 contains one 38x51mm stamp.

New Year 2014 (Year of the Horse) A265

No. 1321 — Horse: a, Grazing. b, Pacing, with one front leg lifted. c, Walking, with no feet lifted. d, Galloping, with two front legs lifted.
$7, Horse, diff.

2013, July 17 — Perf. 13¾
1321 A265 $2.75 Sheet of 4, #a-d 8.25 8.25
Souvenir Sheet
1322 A265 $7 multi 5.25 5.25

Caribbean Community, 40th Anniv. — A266

No. 1323: a, Economy. b, Diplomacy. c, Education. d, Conservation.
$7, 40th anniv. emblem.

2013, July 31
1323 A266 $3 Sheet of 4, #a-d 9.00 9.00
Souvenir Sheet
1324 A266 $7 multi 5.25 5.25

Flowers A267

No. 1325: a, $2.75, Black pirate. b, $2.75, Cape blue water lily. c, $3, Angel's trumpet. d, $3, Emerald vine.
$7, Moon vine.

2013, Aug. 27 — Litho. Perf. 12½
1325 A267 Sheet of 4, #a-d 8.50 8.50
Souvenir Sheet
1326 A267 $7 multi 5.25 5.25

Thailand 2013 World Stamp Exhibition, Bangkok — A268

No. 1326: a, $2.75, Coconut trees. b, $2.75, Sanphet Prasat Palace. c, $3, Buddha statues. d, $3, Erawan Waterfall.
$7, Elephant and riders.

2013, Sept. 2 — Litho. Perf. 13¾
1327 A268 Sheet of 4, #a-d 8.50 8.50
Souvenir Sheet
1328 A268 $7 multi 5.25 5.25

Birth of Prince George of Cambridge — A269

No. 1329 — Prince George and: a, Duchess of Cambridge. b, Duke and Duchess of Cambridge.
$7, Prince George and Duke of Cambridge.

MONTSERRAT

2013, Sept. 22	Litho.	Perf. 14
1329 A269 $2.75 Pair, #a-b		4.25 4.25

Souvenir Sheet

1330 A269 $7 multi   5.25 5.25

No. 1329 was printed in sheets containing 2 each of Nos. 1329a and 1329b.

Kittens A270

No. 1331: a, Bicolor tabby. b, Brown-and-white mackerel tabby. c, Calico. d, Gray-and-white mackerel tabby.
$7, Mackerel tabby, diff.

2013, Nov. 7	Litho.	Perf. 13¾
1331 A270 $3 Sheet of 4, #a-d		9.00 9.00

Souvenir Sheet

1332 A270 $7 multi   5.25 5.25

Pres. John F. Kennedy (1917-63) — A271

No. 1333 — Pres. Kennedy: a, Sitting in rocking chair. b, Facing right. c, Facing forward, picture frame in background. d, Signing paper.
$7, Pres. Kennedy at microphone.

2013, Nov. 22	Litho.	Perf. 13¾
1333 A271 $2.25 Sheet of 4, #a-d		6.75 6.75

Souvenir Sheet

1334 A271 $7 multi   5.25 5.25

Reptiles A272

No. 1335: a, Red-footed tortoise. b, Iguana. c, Brown anole. d, House gecko.
$7, Blue-headed anole.

2013, Dec. 23	Litho.	Perf. 12
1335 A272 $2.75 Sheet of 4, #a-d		8.25 8.25

Souvenir Sheet

1336 A272 $7 multi   5.25 5.25

War Memorial, Plymouth A273

Montserrat Coat of Arms A274

2014, Feb. 7	Litho.	Perf. 12
1337 A273 $50 multi		37.50 37.50
1338 A274 $100 multi		75.00 75.00

World War I, Cent. A275

No. 1339: a, Female munitions worker welding, 1915. b, Nurse ironing bandages, 1915. c, Woman at Southwark Hall Army Recruiting Office, London, 1915. d, Delivery woman, 1914. e, Woman cleaning railway car door, 1914. f, Miss D. Milman of the Women's Sevice League, 1918.
$7, French Red Cross poster, 1915, vert.

2014, Feb. 26	Litho.	Perf. 13¾
1339 A275 $2.25 Sheet of 6, #a-f		10.00 10.00

Souvenir Sheet
Perf. 12¾x12½

1340 A275 $7 multi   5.25 5.25

No. 1340 contains one 38x51mm stamp.

Hummingbirds — A276

No. 1341: a, Bronze-tailed plumeleteer. b, White-bellied mountaingem. c, Olivaceous thornbill. d, White-bellied emerald.
No. 1342: a, Chestnut-breasted coronet. b, Collared Inca.

2014, Apr. 22	Litho.	Perf. 13¾
1341 A276 $3 Sheet of 4, #a-d		9.00 9.00

Souvenir Sheet

1342 A276 $3.50 Sheet of 2, #a-b   5.25 5.25

Astronomy — A277

No. 1343 — Various illustrations of Moon by Galileo Galilei, as shown.
$7, Galileo Galilei (1564-1642), astronomer.

2014, June 5	Litho.	Perf. 14
1343 A277 $3 Sheet of 4, #a-d		9.00 9.00

Souvenir Sheet

1344 A277 $7 multi   5.25 5.25

Vegetables — A278

No. 1345: a, Lettuce. b, Corn. c, Eggplants. d, Sweet potatoes.
No. 1346: a, Cauliflower. b, Carrots.

2014, June 24	Litho.	Perf. 13¾
1345 A278 $3 Sheet of 4, #a-d		9.00 9.00

Souvenir Sheet

1346 A278 $3.50 Sheet of 2, #a-b   5.25 5.25

Paintings A279

No. 1347: a, Still Life Vase with Twelve Sunflowers, by Vincent van Gogh. b, Young Woman in the Garden, by Henri Lebasque. c, Dancer Arranging Her Hair, by Edgar Degas. d, The Fruit Seller, by Frederick Childe Hassam.
$7, At the Market, by Félix Vallotton.

2014, Aug. 6	Litho.	Perf. 12½
1347 A279 $3.50 Sheet of 4, #a-d		10.50 10.50

Souvenir Sheet

1348 A279 $7 multi   5.25 5.25

Dogs A280

No. 1349: a, Siberian husky. b, French bulldog. c, Chihuahua. d, Basset hound.
$7, Dalmatian.

2014, Aug. 27	Litho.	Perf. 12
1349 A280 $3 Sheet of 4, #a-d		9.00 9.00

Souvenir Sheet

1350 A280 $7 multi   5.25 5.25

Sports A281

No. 1351: a, Hurdling. b, Relay race. c, Shot put. d, Soccer.
$7, Cricket.

2014, Oct. 13	Litho.	Perf. 12½x12
1351 A281 $3.50 Sheet of 4, #a-d		10.50 10.50

Souvenir Sheet

1352 A281 $7 multi   5.25 5.25

Famous People A282

No. 1353: a, Benjamin Franklin. b, Dr. Martin Luther King, Jr. c, Nelson Mandela. d, Sir Winston Churchill.
$7, Mahatma Gandhi.

2014, Dec. 4	Litho.	Perf. 12x12½
1353 A282 $3.25 Sheet of 4, #a-d		9.75 9.75

Souvenir Sheet
Perf. 13½

1354 A282 $7 multi   5.25 5.25

No. 1354 contains one 38x51mm stamp.

Tropical Fish A283

No. 1355: a, Blue-girdled angelfish. b, Foxface rabbitfish. c, Powder blue tang. d, Clown triggerfish.
$7, Sixspine butterflyfish.

2014, Dec. 22	Litho.	Perf. 12½x12
1355 A283 $3.25 Sheet of 4, #a-d		9.75 9.75

Souvenir Sheet

1356 A283 $7 multi   5.25 5.25

International Year of Light — A284

No. 1357: a, Prism and spectrum. b, Sir Isaac Newton (1643-1727), physicist. c, Wavelengths of violet, blue and green light. d, Wavelengths of yellow, orange and red light.
$7, Wavelengths of ultraviolet and infrared light.

2015, Jan. 29	Litho.	Perf. 12x12½
1357 A284 $3.25 Sheet of 4, #a-d		9.75 9.75

Souvenir Sheet
Perf. 13½

1358 A284 $7 multi   5.25 5.25

No. 1358 contains one 38x51mm stamp.

Leatherback Sea Turtle — A285

No. 1359: a, Turtle in sea. b, Head of hatchling. c, Turtle heading to sea. d, Turtle returning to beach.
$7, Hatchling heading to sea.

2015, Mar. 24	Litho.	Perf. 13¾
1359 A285 $3.25 Sheet of 4, #a-d		9.75 9.75

Souvenir Sheet

1360 A285 $7 multi   5.25 5.25

Great Britain No. O1 and Street Scene — A286

MONTSERRAT

Design: $7, Great Britain No. O1.

2015, May 15   Litho.   Perf. 14
1361   A286 $3.25 multi   2.40   2.40
Souvenir Sheet
Perf. 12
1362   A286 $7 multi   5.25   5.25

Penny Black (not shown on Nos. 1361-1362), 175th anniv. No. 1361 was printed in sheets of 4.

Seahorses — A287

No. 1363: a, Two Longsnout seahorses. b, Lined seahorse and sea grass. c, Lined seahorse. d, Two longsnout seahorses, coral in background.
$7, Dwarf seahorse.

2015, May 28   Litho.   Perf. 13¾
1363   A287 $3.25 Sheet of 4, #a-d   9.75   9.75
Souvenir Sheet
Perf. 14x13¾
1364   A287 $7 multi   5.25   5.25

Roses A288

No. 1365 — Color of rose: a, Yellow. b, Red. c, Pink. d, Pale pink.
$7, Two roses, horiz.

2015, July 20   Litho.   Perf. 14
1365   A288 $3.25 Sheet of 4, #a-d   9.75   9.75
Souvenir Sheet
Perf. 12½
1366   A288 $7 multi   5.25   5.25
No. 1366 contains one 51x38mm stamp.

Photographs of Earth from Space — A289

No. 1367: a, Wildfires in central Chile. b, Kavir Desert, Iran. c, Central Saudi Arabia. d, Cancún, Mexico.
$7, Montserrat.

2015, Sept. 15   Litho.   Perf. 12
1367   A289 $3.25 Sheet of 4, #a-d   9.75   9.75
Souvenir Sheet
1368   A289 $7 multi   5.25   5.25

Bees A290

No. 1369: a, Orange-belted bumblebee. b, American bumblebee. c, Eastern carpenter bee. d, Cuckoo bee.
$7, Common eastern bumblebee.

2015, Sept. 30   Litho.   Perf. 13¾
1369   A290 $3.25 Sheet of 4, #a-d   9.75   9.75
Souvenir Sheet
1370   A290 $7 multi   5.25   5.25

Self-Portraits — A291

No. 1371: a, Jan Van Eyck, 1433. b, Peter Paul Rubens, 1623. c, William Hind, 1862-63. d, Georges Daniel de Monfreid, 1905.
$7, Paul Gauguin, 1885.

2015, Nov. 11   Litho.   Perf. 12x12½
1371   A291 $3.25 Sheet of 4, #a-d   9.75   9.75
Souvenir Sheet
1372   A291 $7 multi   5.25   5.25

Beetles A292

No. 1373: a, Goliathus giganteus. b, Dynastes tityus. c, Lucanus laminifer. d, Penthea pardalis.
$7, Chalcosoma atlas.

2015, Nov. 30   Litho.   Perf. 12½
1373   A292 $3.25 Sheet of 4, #a-d   9.75   9.75
Souvenir Sheet
1374   A292 $7 multi   5.25   5.25

British Royal Family A293

No. 1375 — Queen Elizabeth II: a, Wearing black gloves, no horse. b, Holding flowers. c, Wearing black gloves, with horse. d, Wearing purple coat, with horse.
$7, Prince George and Princess Charlotte.

2016, Jan. 22   Litho.   Perf. 14
1375   A293 $3.25 Sheet of 4, #a-d   9.75   9.75
Souvenir Sheet
Perf. 12½
1376   A293 $7 multi   5.25   5.25
No. 1376 contains one 38x51mm stamp.

Birds A294

No. 1377: a, Brown trembler. b, Black swift. c, Willet. d, Brown noddy.
$7, Montserrat oriole.

2016, Mar. 8   Litho.   Perf. 12½
1377   A294 $3.25 Sheet of 4, #a-d   9.75   9.75
Souvenir Sheet
1378   A294 $7 multi   5.25   5.25

Cricket A295

No. 1379: a, Ball. b, Glove. c, Bat and wickets. d, Helmet.
$7, Ball, vert.

2016, Mar. 17   Litho.   Perf. 13¾
1379   A295 $3.25 Sheet of 4, #a-d   9.75   9.75
Souvenir Sheet
Perf. 12½
1380   A295 $7 multi   5.25   5.25
No. 1380 contains one 38x51mm stamp.

Worldwide Fund for Nature (WWF) — A296

Various depictions of Nassau grouper, as shown.

2016, May 30   Litho.   Perf. 14
1381   A296 $3.75 Block of 4, #a-d   11.00   11.00
e,   Miniature sheet of 8, 2 each #1381a-1381d   22.00   22.00

Waterfalls — A297

No. 1382: a, Bigar Waterfall, Romania. b, Pearl Shoal Waterfall, People's Republic of China. c, Ban Gioc Waterfall, Viet Nam. d, Iguazu Falls, Argentina.
$10, Great Alps Waterfall, Montserrat, vert.

2016, June 8   Litho.   Perf. 14
1382   A297 $3.25 Sheet of 4, #a-d   9.75   9.75
Souvenir Sheet
Perf. 12½
1383   A297 $10 multi   7.50   7.50
No. 1383 contains one 38x51mm stamp.

Elvis Presley (1935-77) — A298

No. 1384: Various photographs of Presley, as shown.
$10, Presley on knee, spreading cape with arms.

2016, July 27   Litho.   Perf. 14
1384   A298 $3.50 Sheet of 4, #a-d   10.50   10.50
Souvenir Sheet
Perf. 12½
1385   A298 $10 multi   7.50   7.50
No. 1385 contains one 51x38mm stamp.

Sea Turtles A299

No. 1386: a, Green sea turtle. b, Loggerhead sea turtle. c, Olive ridley sea turtle. d, Kemp's ridley sea turtle.
$7, Hawksbill sea turtle, horiz.

2016, Sept. 23   Litho.   Perf. 13¾
1386   A299 $3.50 Sheet of 4, #a-d   10.50   10.50
Souvenir Sheet
Perf. 12½
1387   A299 $7 multi   5.25   5.25
No. 1387 contains one 51x38mm stamp.

Transportation — A300

No. 1388: a, Ferry. b, Prison van. c, State automobile. d, Police motorcycle.
$7, Airplane.

2016, Nov. 16   Litho.   Perf. 14
1388   A300 $3.50 Sheet of 4, #a-d   10.50   10.50
Souvenir Sheet
Perf. 12½
1389   A300 $7 multi   5.25   5.25
No. 1389 contains one 51x38mm stamp.

Christmas — A301

MONTSERRAT

No. 1390: a, Three round silver ornaments. b, Small ornaments on Christmas tree. c, Reindeer. d, Gold ornaments.
$7, Ornament with snowflake.

2016, Nov. 29	Litho.	Perf. 14
1390 A301	$3.50 Sheet of 4, #a-d	10.50 10.50

Souvenir Sheet
Perf. 12½

| 1391 | A301 | $7 multi | 5.25 5.25 |

No. 1391 contains one 51x38mm stamp.

Crabs A302

No. 1392: a, Batwing coral crab. b, Caribbean hermit crab. c, Red land crab. d, Blue land crab.
$10, Atlantic ghost crab.

2017, May 11	Litho.	Perf. 14
1392 A302	$5.50 Sheet of 4, #a-d	16.50 16.50

Souvenir Sheet

| 1393 | A302 | $10 multi | 7.50 7.50 |

Miniature Sheets

Soufriere Hills Volcano A303

No. 1394: a, $2.80, Pyroclastic flow, 1995-96. b, $2.95, Ash plume, 2008. c, $3.75, Ash plume, 2008, diff. d, $4.50, Pyroclastic flow, 2010. e, $5, Pyroclastic flow, 1997. f, $6, Ash plume, 1997.
No. 1395: a, $2.80, General Post Office, 1997. b, $2.95, Colony House, 2013. c, $3.75, Bethany Pentacostal Church, 2016. d, $4.50, Cassell's Building, 2016. e, $5, Government House, 2016. f, $6, Court House, 2006.

Perf. 14, 11½x12 (#1395)

2017		Litho.

Sheets of 6, #a-f

| 1394-1395 A303 | Set of 2 | 37.00 37.00 |

Issued: No. 1394, 7/12; No. 1395, 8/15.

Heliconia Flowers of Montserrat — A304

No. 1396: a, Heliconia champneiana. b, Heliconia bihai. c, Heliconia rostrata. d, Heliconia psittacorum x spathocircinata.
$10, Heliconia caribaea, horiz.

2017, July 24	Litho.	Perf. 12x12½
1396 A304	$7 Sheet of 4, #a-d	21.00 21.00

Souvenir Sheet
Perf. 13¼

| 1397 | A304 | $10 multi | 7.50 7.50 |

No. 1397 contains one 51x38mm stamp.

Princess Diana (1961-97) — A305

No. 1398 — Princess Diana wearing: a, Dark blue jacket, spotted hat and dress. b, Blue green dress and white hat. c, Tiara. d, Striped jacket and white hat.
$11, Princess Diana seated in chair.

2017, Aug. 31	Litho.	Perf. 14
1398 A305	$7 Sheet of 4, #a-d	21.00 21.00

Souvenir Sheet

| 1399 | A305 | $11 multi | 8.25 8.25 |

Coral Reef Marine Life A306

No. 1400: a, Staghorn coral. b, Venus sea fan. c, Elkhorn coral. d, Brown tube sponge.
$10, Stovepipe sponge.

2017, Dec. 6	Litho.	Perf. 13¼x12½
1400 A306	$4 Sheet of 4, #a-d	12.00 12.00

Souvenir Sheet
Perf. 13¼

| 1401 | A306 | $10 multi | 7.50 7.50 |

No. 1401 contains one 38x51mm stamp.

Coronation of Queen Elizabeth II, 65th Anniv. — A307

No. 1402: a, Queen Elizabeth II and Prince Philip at coronation. b, Imperial State Crown. c, Gold State Coach. d, Coronation dress.
$11, Portrait of Queen Elizabeth II, by Ralph Heimans, vert.

2018, Mar. 1	Litho.	Perf. 14
1402 A307	$6.50 Sheet of 4, #a-d	19.50 19.50

Souvenir Sheet
Perf. 12

| 1403 | A307 | $11 multi | 8.25 8.25 |

No. 1403 contains one 30x50mm stamp.

Frogs and Toads A308

No. 1404: a, $5, Cane toad (40x30mm). b, $6, Lesser Antillean frog (40x30mm). c, $7, Cane toad, diff. (50x30mm). d, $8, Lesser Antillean frog, diff. (50x30mmm).
$10, Giant ditch frog.

2018, Mar. 1	Litho.	Perf. 12
1404 A308	Sheet of 4, #a-d	19.50 19.50

Souvenir Sheet
Perf. 12½

| 1405 | A308 | $10 multi | 7.50 7.50 |

No. 1405 contains one 51x38mm stamp.

Royal Air Force, Cent. A309

No. 1406 — Members of Falcons Parachute Display Team and: a, $4, Lockheed C-130J Hercules. b, $5, British flag. c, $6, Boeing CH-47 Chinook helicopter. d, $7, Douglas C-47 Dakota.
$10, Falcons Parachute Display team joining hands, Dornier 228.

2018, Apr. 12	Litho.	Perf. 14
1406 A309	Sheet of 4, #a-d	16.50 16.50

Souvenir Sheet
Perf. 12½

| 1407 | A309 | $10 multi | 7.50 7.50 |

No. 1407 contains one 51x38mm stamp.

St. Patrick's Day Celebrations in Montserrat — A310

No. 1408: a, $5, Montserrat woman (30x40mm). b, $5, Montserrat man (30x40mm). c, $7, Original St. Patrick's Roman Catholic Church, Plymouth (60x40mm). d, $7, Costumed revelers (60x40mm).
$10, Montserrat man and woman.

2018, Mar. 29	Litho.	Perf. 14
1408 A310	Sheet of 4, #a-d	18.00 18.00

Souvenir Sheet
Perf. 12½

| 1409 | A310 | $10 multi | 7.50 7.50 |

No. 1409 contains one 51x38mm stamp.

United States Air Mail, Cent. A311

No. 1410: a, 1930 postmark and handstamp from first Montserrat air mail flight. b, Fairey Swordfish floatplane. c, HMS Dorsetshire. d, Stamps and postmark from cover from first Montserrat air mail flight.
$10, Fairey Swordfish floatplane and Curtiss Jenny.

2018, May 15	Litho.	Perf. 14
1410 A311	$5.50 Sheet of 4, #a-d	16.50 16.50

Souvenir Sheet
Perf. 12½

| 1411 | A311 | $10 multi | 7.50 7.50 |

No. 1411 contains one 51x38mm stamp.

World War II, 75th Anniv. A312

No. 1412: a, Avro Lancaster. b, Short Sunderland. c, Infantry tank. d, Rolls-Royce armored car.
$10, Churchill VII Crocodile flame-thrower tank.

2018, Aug. 14	Litho.	Perf. 12
1412 A312	$5.50 Sheet of 4, #a-d	16.50 16.50

Souvenir Sheet
Perf. 14

| 1413 | A312 | $10 multi | 7.50 7.50 |

No. 1413 contains one 80x30mm stamp.

Birds A313

No. 1414: a, $4, Rufous-tailed hummingbird. b, $5, Glittering-throated emerald. c, $6, Cinnamon hummingbird. d, $7, White-necked jacobin.
$11, Montserrat oriole.

2018, Aug. 18	Litho.	Perf. 12
1414 A313	Sheet of 4, #a-d	16.50 16.50

Souvenir Sheet
Perf. 12½

| 1415 | A313 | $11 multi | 8.25 8.25 |

No. 1415 contains one 38x51mm stamp.

Fishing A314

No. 1416: a, Net fishing (60x40mm). b, Northern red snapper (30x40mm). c, Fish pot (30x40mm).
$10, Boat fishing, horiz.

2018, Oct. 10	Litho.	Perf. 14
1416 A314	$6 Sheet of 3, #a-c	13.50 13.50

Souvenir Sheet
Perf. 12

| 1417 | A314 | $10 multi | 7.50 7.50 |

No. 1417 contains one 50x30mm stamp.

MONSERRAT

Last Concorde Flight, 15th Anniv. — A315

No. 1418: a, British Airways Concorde. b, Air France Concorde. c, Geoffroy de Courcel and Julian Amery with an early Concorde model. d, Early Concorde prototype.
$12, Concorde and Red Arrows Aerobatic Team.

			2018, Oct. 24	Litho.	Perf. 14	
1418	A315	$5.50	Sheet of 4, #a-d		16.50	16.50

Souvenir Sheet
Perf. 12

1419	A315	$12 multi	9.00	9.00

No. 1419 contains one 50x30mm stamp.

Trees A316

No. 1420: a, $5, Tamarind tree. b, $5, Cashew tree. c, $6, Starfruit tree. d, $6, Barbados cherry tree.
$10, Guinep tree, vert.

			2018, Dec. 5	Litho.	Perf. 14	
1420	A316		Sheet of 4, #a-d		16.50	16.50

Souvenir Sheet
Perf. 12½

1421	A316	$10 multi	7.50	7.50

No. 1421 contains one 38x51mm stamp.

Birth of Archie Mountbatten-Windsor — A317

No. 1422 — Various pictures of baby and parents, Duke and Duchess of Sussex: a, $4. b, $5. c, $6. d, $7.
$12, Family, vert.

			2019, Aug. 15	Litho.	Perf. 14	
1422	A317		Sheet of 4, #a-d		16.50	16.50

Souvenir Sheet
Perf. 12

1423	A317	$12 multi	9.00	9.00

Caribbean Flamingos — A318

No. 1424: a, $4, Head of flamingo (30x50mm). b, $5, Flamingo feeding (30x50mm). c, $6, Two flamingos in flight (30x40mm). d, $7, Two flamingos in water (30x40mm).
$12, Two flamingos, diff.

			2019, Aug. 15	Litho.	Perf. 14	
1424	A318		Sheet of 4, #a-d		16.50	16.50

Souvenir Sheet
Perf.

1425	A318	$12 multi	9.00	9.00

No. 1425 contains one 44x33mm oval stamp.

Mohandas K. Gandhi (1869-1948), Indian Nationalist Leader — A319

No. 1426: a, $2, Photograph of Gandhi. b, $3, Statue of Gandhi. c, $4, Statue of Gandhi, diff. d, $5, Photograph of Gandhi, diff.
$14, Photograph of Gandhi, diff.

			2019, Oct. 10	Litho.	Perf. 14	
1426	A319		Sheet of 4, #a-d		10.50	10.50

Souvenir Sheet
Perf. 12

1427	A319	$14 multi	10.50	10.50

Orchids A320

No. 1428: a, Singapore orchid. b, Moth orchid with pink petals. c, Moth orchid with white petals.
$14, Boat orchid, vert.

			2019, Dec. 31	Litho.	Perf. 14	
1428	A320	$5	Sheet of 3, #a-c		11.00	11.00

Souvenir Sheet
Perf. 12

1429	A320	$14 multi	10.50	10.50

No. 1429 contains one 30x50mm stamp.

SEMI-POSTAL STAMPS

Catalogue values for unused stamps in this section are for Never Hinged items.

Nos. 719-720 Surcharged

			1989, Oct. 20	Litho.	Perf. 13½x14	
B1	A110	$1.50 +$2.50 multi		2.75	2.75
B2	A110	$3.50 +$2.50 multi		4.25	4.25

Surcharge for hurricane relief.

No. 642 Surcharged

			1995, Dec. 29	Litho.	Perf. 15	
B3	A97	$2.30 +$5 multi		8.50	8.50

Surcharge for volcano relief.

WAR TAX STAMPS

No. 43 Overprinted in Red or Black

		1917-18	Wmk. 3	Perf. 14	
MR1	A6	½p green (R)		.25	1.75
MR2	A6	½p green ('18)		.25	2.00

Type of Regular Issue of 1919 Overprinted

1918

MR3	A6	1½p orange & black	.30	.35

Denomination on No. MR3 in black on white ground. Two dots under "d."

OFFICIAL STAMPS

Nos. O1-O44 used on Post Office and Philatelic Bureau mail. Not sold to public, used or unused.

Nos. 235-236, 338-339 Overprinted

		Perf. 12½x14	
1976, Apr. 12	Photo.	Wmk. 314	
O1	A22	5c multicolored	1.90
O2	A22	10c multicolored	2.50
O3	A22	30c on 10c multi	5.00
O4	A22	45c on 3c multi	6.00
	Nos. O1-O4 (4)		15.40

Nos. 243-243A also received this overprint.

Nos. 343-347, 349-351, 353-354 Overprinted

		Perf. 13½x14	
1976, Oct. 1	Litho.	Wmk. 373	
O10	A44	5c multicolored	.25
O11	A44	10c multicolored	.25
O12	A44	15c multicolored	.25
O13	A44	20c multicolored	.25
O14	A44	25c multicolored	.25
O15	A44	55c multicolored	.40
O16	A44	70c multicolored	.50
O17	A44	$1 multicolored	.70
O18	A44	$5 multicolored	3.25
O19	A44	$10 multicolored	6.50
	Nos. O10-O19 (10)		12.60

Nos. 343-347, 349-351, 353-354 Overprinted

		1980, Sept. 30		Perf. 14
O20	A44	5c multicolored		.25
O21	A44	10c multicolored		.25
O22	A44	15c multicolored		.25
O23	A44	20c multicolored		.25
O24	A44	25c multicolored		.25
O25	A44	55c multicolored		.35
O26	A44	70c multicolored		.45
O27	A44	$1 multicolored		.65
O28	A44	$5 multicolored		2.75
O29	A44	$10 multicolored		5.50
	Nos. O20-O29 (10)			10.95

Nos. 341-351, 353-354 Overprinted or Surcharged

		1980, Sept. 30	Litho.	Perf. 14
O30	A44	5c multicolored		.25
O31	A44	5c on 3c multi		.25
O32	A44	10c multicolored		.25
O33	A44	15c multicolored		.25
O34	A44	20c multicolored		.25
O35	A44	25c multicolored		.25
O36	A44	30c on 15c multi		.25
O37	A44	35c on 2c multi		.40
O38	A44	40c multicolored		.30
O39	A44	55c multicolored		.45
O40	A44	70c multicolored		.60
O41	A44	$1 multicolored		.80
O42	A44	$2.50 on 40c multi		2.00
O43	A44	$5 multicolored		3.75
O44	A44	$10 multicolored		7.50
	Nos. O30-O44 (15)			17.55

Catalogue values for unused stamps in this section, from this point to the end of the section, are for Never Hinged items.

Fish Issue of 1981
Nos. 445-449, 451, 453, 455, 457-458, 460 Overprinted

		1981, Mar. 20	Litho.	Perf. 13½	
O45	A64	5c multicolored		.25	.25
O46	A64	10c multicolored		.25	.25
O47	A64	15c multicolored		.25	.25
O48	A64	20c multicolored		.25	.25
O49	A64	25c multicolored		.25	.25
O50	A64	45c multicolored		.35	.35
O51	A64	65c multicolored		.60	.60
O52	A64	$1 multicolored		.75	.75
O53	A64	$3 multicolored		2.25	2.25
O54	A64	$5 multicolored		3.75	3.75
O55	A64	$10 multicolored		7.50	7.50
	Nos. O45-O55 (11)			16.35	16.35

Nos. 465-470 Surcharged

		1982, Nov. 17	Litho.	Perf. 14	
O56	A66	45c on 90c (#465)		.70	.70
O57	A67	45c on 90c (#466)		.70	.70
O58	A66	75c on $3 (#467)		1.05	1.05
O59	A67	75c on $3 (#468)		1.05	1.05
O60	A66	$1 on $4 (#469)		1.35	1.35
O61	A67	$1 on $4 (#470)		1.35	1.35
	Nos. O56-O61 (6)			6.20	6.20

MONTSERRAT — MOROCCO

Princess Diana Issue, Nos. 484-486 Overprinted or Surcharged

1983, Oct. 19 — Litho. — Perf. 14
O62	A70b	70c on 75c (#484)	1.50 1.50
O63	A70b	$1 (#485)	1.90 1.90
O64	A70b	$1.50 on $5 (#486)	2.50 2.50
		Nos. O62-O64 (3)	5.90 5.90

Nos. 524-536, 538 Overprinted

1985, Apr. 12 — Wmk. 380 — Perf. 14
O65	A79	5c multicolored	.50 .25
O66	A79	10c multicolored	.50 .25
O67	A79	15c multicolored	.50 .25
O68	A79	20c multicolored	.50 .25
O69	A79	25c multicolored	.50 .25
O70	A79	40c multicolored	.80 .40
O71	A79	55c multicolored	.90 .45
O72	A79	70c multicolored	1.25 .65
O73	A79	90c multicolored	1.60 .80
O74	A79	$1 multicolored	1.90 .90
O75	A79	$1.15 multicolored	2.00 1.00
O76	A79	$3 multicolored	5.25 2.50
O77	A79	$5 multicolored	9.25 4.75
O78	A79	$10 multicolored	17.50 9.00
		Nos. O65-O78 (14)	42.95 21.70

Nos. 681-694 and 696 Overprinted

1989, May 9 — Unwmk. — Litho. — Perf. 14
O79	A104	5c multicolored	.25 .25
O80	A104	10c multicolored	.25 .25
O81	A104	15c multicolored	.25 .25
O82	A104	20c multicolored	.25 .25
O83	A104	25c multicolored	.25 .25
O84	A104	40c multicolored	.40 .40
O85	A104	55c multicolored	.60 .55
O86	A104	70c multicolored	.75 .70
O87	A104	90c multicolored	.95 .90
O88	A104	$1 multicolored	1.00 .95
O89	A104	$1.15 multicolored	1.25 1.25
O90	A104	$1.50 multicolored	1.60 1.40
O91	A104	$3 multicolored	3.00 2.75
O92	A104	$5 multicolored	5.25 4.75
O93	A104	$10 multicolored	10.50 9.50
		Nos. O79-O94 (15)	26.55 24.40

Nos. 446, 454a and 456 Surcharged

1989 — Wmk. 373 — Perf. 13½
O95	A64	70c on 10c multi	2.00 2.00
O96	A64	$1.15 on 75c multi	3.75 3.75
O97	A64	$1.50 on $2 multi	4.50 4.50
		Nos. O95-O97 (3)	10.25 10.25

Nos. 758-761, 763-766, 776-779 Surcharged or Overprinted "OHMS"

1992 — Litho. — Perf. 14
O98	A118	70c on 90c #758	1.50 1.50
O99	A118	70c on $3.50 #761	1.50 1.50
O100	A119	70c on 90c #763	1.50 1.50
O101	A121	70c on 90c #776	1.50 1.50
O102	A119	$1 on $3.50 #766	2.00 2.00
O103	A121	$1 on $3.50 #779	2.00 2.00
O104	A118	$1.15 on #759	2.25 2.25
O105	A119	$1.15 on #764	2.25 2.25
O106	A121	$1.15 on #777	2.25 2.25
O107	A118	$1.50 on #760	3.00 3.00
O108	A119	$1.50 on #765	3.00 3.00
O109	A121	$1.50 on #778	3.00 3.00
		Nos. O98-O109 (12)	25.75 25.75

Nos. 803-816, 818 Ovptd. "OHMS" in Red

1993, Apr. 14 — Litho. — Perf. 15x14
O110	A128	5c multicolored	.30 .30
O111	A128	10c multicolored	.30 .30
O112	A128	15c multicolored	.30 .30
O113	A128	20c multicolored	.30 .30
O114	A128	25c multicolored	.30 .30
O115	A128	40c multicolored	.50 .50
O116	A128	55c multicolored	.75 .75
O117	A128	70c multicolored	.85 .85
O118	A128	90c multicolored	1.05 1.05
O119	A128	$1 multicolored	1.20 1.20
O120	A128	$1.15 multicolored	1.40 1.40
O121	A128	$1.50 multicolored	1.75 1.75
O122	A128	$3 multicolored	3.75 3.75
O123	A128	$5 multicolored	6.00 6.00
O125	A128	$10 multicolored	12.00 12.00
		Nos. O110-O125 (15)	30.75 30.75

A number has been reserved for an additional value in this set.

Nos. 896-909, 911 Ovptd. "O.H.M.S." In Red

1997 — Litho. — Perf. 14
O126	A147	5c multicolored	.25 .25
O127	A147	10c multicolored	.25 .25
O128	A147	15c multicolored	.25 .25
O129	A147	20c multicolored	.25 .25
O130	A147	25c multicolored	.25 .25
O131	A147	40c multicolored	.40 .40
O132	A147	55c multicolored	.50 .50
O133	A147	70c multicolored	.70 .70
O134	A147	90c multicolored	.90 .90
O135	A147	$1 multicolored	.95 .95
O136	A147	$1.15 multicolored	1.10 1.10
O137	A147	$1.50 multicolored	1.40 1.40
O138	A147	$3 multicolored	3.00 3.00
O139	A147	$5 multicolored	4.75 4.75
O140	A147	$10 multicolored	9.75 9.75
		Nos. O126-O140 (15)	24.70 24.70

Nos. 1041-1054, 1056 Overprinted

2002, June 14 — Perf. 13½x13¼ — Litho.
O141	A176	5c multi	.30 .30
O142	A176	10c multi	.30 .30
O143	A176	15c multi	.30 .30
O144	A176	20c multi	.30 .30
O145	A176	25c multi	.30 .30
O146	A176	40c multi	.35 .35
O147	A176	55c multi	.45 .45
O148	A176	70c multi	.90 .90
O149	A176	90c multi	1.20 1.20
O150	A176	$1 multi	1.40 1.40
O151	A176	$1.15 multi	1.75 1.75
O152	A176	$1.50 multi	2.00 2.00
O153	A176	$3 multi	4.50 4.50
O154	A176	$5 multi	7.00 7.00
O155	A176	$10 multi	14.00 14.00
		Nos. O141-O155 (15)	35.05 35.05

Nos. 1173-1186, 1188 Overprinted

2007, May 14 — Litho. — Perf. 12½
O156	A213	10c multi	.25 .25
O157	A213	30c multi	.25 .25
O158	A213	35c multi	.25 .25
O159	A213	50c multi	.40 .40
O160	A213	70c multi	.55 .55
O161	A213	80c multi	.60 .60
O162	A213	90c multi	.70 .70
O163	A213	$1 multi	.75 .75
O164	A213	$1.10 multi	.85 .85
O165	A213	$1.50 multi	1.10 1.10
O166	A213	$2.25 multi	1.75 1.75
O167	A213	$2.50 multi	1.90 1.90
O168	A213	$2.75 multi	2.10 2.10
O169	A213	$5 multi	3.75 3.75
O170	A213	$20 multi	15.00 15.00
		Nos. O156-O170 (15)	30.20 30.20

Size and location of overprint varies.

MOROCCO

mə-'rä-ˌkō

LOCATION — Northwest coast of Africa
GOVT. — Kingdom
AREA — 171,953 sq. mi.
POP. — 36,910,000 (2020 est.)
CAPITAL — Rabat

A powerful kingdom from the 8th century, during the Middle Ages, Morocco ruled large areas of northwest Africa and Spain. By the turn of the 20th century, it had contracted to roughly its present borders and was the focus of an intense rivalry between France and Germany, who actively competed for control of the country. In 1912 most of Morocco became a French protectorate, with Spain acting as protector of zones in the extreme northern and southern parts of the country. Tangier was designated an international zone, administered by France, Spain, Britain and, later, Italy.

In 1956 the three zones of Morocco, French, Spanish and Tangier, were united to form an independent nation. Nos. 1-24 and C1-C3 were intended for use only in the southern (French currency) zone. Issues of the northern zone (Spanish currency) are listed after Postage Due stamps.

For earlier issues see French Morocco and Spanish Morocco.

400 Moussonats = 1 Rial (1912)
100 Centimes = 1 Franc (1956)
100 Centimes = 1 Dirham (1962)

Catalogue values for all unused stamps in this country are for Never Hinged items, except for Nos. A1-A14.

CHERIFIAN POST

Aissaouas Mosque, Tangier — A1a

On White Paper Narrow Margins

1912, May 25 — Litho. — Perf. 11
A1	A1a	1m light gray	8.00 8.00
A2	A1a	2m lilac	9.00 8.00
A3	A1a	5m blue green	12.00 8.00
A4	A1a	10m vermilion	20.00 8.50
A5	A1a	25m blue	29.00 24.00
A6	A1a	50m violet	42.50 35.00
		Nos. A1-A6 (6)	120.50 91.50

Aissaouas Mosque, Tangier — A1b

On Lightly Tinted Paper

1913, Feb. — Wide Margins
A7	A1b	1m gray	1.75 1.75
A8	A1b	2m brown lilac	1.75 1.75
A9	A1b	5m blue green	2.00 2.00
A10	A1b	10m vermilion	2.00 2.00
A11	A1b	25m blue	4.25 4.25
A12	A1b	50m gray violet	4.25 4.25
		Nos. A7-A12 (6)	16.00 16.00

On Nos. A1-A12, the 5m and 10m values always have the name of the engraver beneath the design, while the 1m, 25m and 50m always lack name, and the 2m value exists both with and without name.

No. A6 Surcharged

1913, Nov.
A13	A1a	.05 on 50c violet	1,750. 2,000.
A14	A1a	.10 on 50c violet	1,750. 2,000.

All issues of Morocco between 1956 and 2010 exist imperforate. Value between 5 and 10 times that of regular perforated issue.

GENERAL ISSUES

Sultan Mohammed V — A1

1956-57 — Unwmk. — Engr. — Perf. 13
1	A1	5fr brt bl & indigo	.30 .25
2	A1	10fr bis brn & choc	.25 .25
3	A1	15fr dp grn & magenta	.35 .25
4	A1	25fr purple ('57)	.95 .25
5	A1	30fr green ('57)	1.60 .25
6	A1	50fr rose red ('57)	2.40 .25
7	A1	70fr dk brn & brn red ('57)	3.75 .75
		Nos. 1-7 (7)	9.60 2.25

For surcharges see Nos. B1-B5, B8-B9.

Men Reading — A2

Campaign against illiteracy: 15fr, Girls reading. 20fr, Instructor and pupils. 30fr, Old man and child reading. 50fr, Girl pointing out poster.

1956, Nov. 5
8	A2	10fr pur & vio	1.60 1.10
9	A2	15fr car & rose lake	2.10 1.35
10	A2	20fr bl grn & grn	2.50 2.10
11	A2	30fr rose lake & brt red	4.00 2.50
12	A2	50fr dp bl & bl	8.00 4.75
		Nos. 8-12 (5)	18.20 11.80

Sultan Mohammed V — A3

1957, Mar. 2 — Photo. — Perf. 13½x13
13	A3	15fr blue green	1.40 1.00
14	A3	25fr gray olive	1.90 1.00
15	A3	30fr deep rose	3.75 1.75
		Nos. 13-15 (3)	7.05 3.75

Anniversary of independence.

Prince Moulay el Hassan — A4

1957, July 9 — Perf. 13
16	A4	15fr blue	1.50 1.00
17	A4	25fr green	1.90 1.50
18	A4	30fr car rose	3.00 2.10
		Nos. 16-18 (3)	6.40 4.60

Designation of Prince Moulay el Hassan as heir to the throne.

King Mohammed V — A5

MOROCCO

1957, Nov.   **Perf. 12½**
19	A5 15fr blk & brt grn	1.10	.55
20	A5 25fr blk & rose red	1.25	.75
21	A5 30fr blk & vio	2.25	1.00
	Nos. 19-21 (3)	4.60	2.30

Enthronement of Mohammed V, 30th anniv.

Morocco Pavilion, Brussels World's Fair — A6

1958, Apr. 20   **Engr.**   **Perf. 13**
22	A6 15fr brt grnsh bl	.40	.25
23	A6 25fr carmine	.40	.30
24	A6 30fr indigo	.50	.35
	Nos. 22-24 (3)	1.30	.90

World's Fair, Brussels.

UNESCO Building, Paris, and Mohammed V — A7

1958, Nov. 23
25	A7 15fr green	.45	.25
26	A7 25fr lake	.45	.25
27	A7 30fr blue	.65	.30
	Nos. 25-27 (3)	1.55	.80

UNESCO Headquarters opening, Paris, Nov. 3.

Ben Smin Sanatorium — A8

1959, Jan. 18   **Unwmk.**   **Perf. 13**
28	A8 50fr dk brn, car & slate grn	.90	.50

Red Cross-Red Crescent Society.

Mohammed V — A9

1959, Aug. 18   **Engr.**   **Perf. 13**
29	A9 15fr dk car rose	.60	.40
30	A9 25fr brt bl	.85	.55
31	A9 45fr dk grn	1.10	.60
	Nos. 29-31 (3)	2.55	1.55

50th birthday of King Mohammed V.

Princess Lalla Amina — A10

1959, Nov. 17
32	A10 15fr blue	.40	.25
33	A10 25fr green	.45	.25
34	A10 45fr rose lil	.50	.30
	Nos. 32-34 (3)	1.35	.80

Issued for International Children's Week.

Map of Africa and Symbols of Agriculture, Industry and Commerce — A11

1960, Jan. 31   **Perf. 13**
35	A11 45fr vio, ocher & emer	1.10	.65

Issued to publicize the meeting of the Economic Commission for Africa, Tangier.

Refugees and Uprooted Oak Emblem — A12

45fr, Refugee family and uprooted oak emblem.

1960, Apr. 7   **Unwmk.**   **Perf. 13**
36	A12 15fr ocher, blk & grn	.40	.40
37	A12 45fr blk & grn	.60	.60

World Refugee Year, July 1, 1959-June 30, 1960.

Marrakesh — A13

1960, Apr. 25   **Engr.**   **Perf. 13**
38	A13 100fr grn, bl & red brn	1.30	.85

900th anniversary of Marrakesh.

Lamp — A14

Designs: 25fr, Fountain and arched door. 30fr, Minaret. 35fr, Ornamented wall. 45fr, Moorish architecture.

1960, May 12   **Perf. 13½**
39	A14 15fr rose lil	.50	.50
40	A14 25fr dk bl	.55	.55
41	A14 30fr org red	1.25	.65
42	A14 35fr black	1.40	1.10
43	A14 45fr yel grn	2.00	1.50
	Nos. 39-43 (5)	5.70	4.30

1,100th anniv. of Karaouiyne University, Fez.

Arab League Center, Cairo and Mohammed V — A15

1960, June 28   **Photo.**   **Perf. 12½**
44	A15 15fr grn & blk	.50	.25

Opening of the Arab League Center and the Arab Postal Museum, Cairo.

Wrestlers — A16

Sports: 10fr, Gymnast. 15fr, Bicyclist. 20fr, Weight lifter. 30fr, Runner. 40fr, Boxers. 45fr, Sailboat. 70fr, Fencers.

1960, Sept. 26   **Engr.**   **Perf. 13**
45	A16 5fr ol, vio bl & plum	.25	.25
46	A16 10fr org brn, bl & brn	.25	.25
47	A16 15fr amber, bl & red brn	.50	.25
48	A16 20fr ultra, ol & brn	.35	.25
49	A16 30fr vio bl, mar & sep	.40	.25
50	A16 40fr grnsh bl, dk pur & red brn	.65	.25
51	A16 45fr grn, plum & ultra	.80	.30
52	A16 70fr dk brn, bl & gray	1.10	.40
	Nos. 45-52 (8)	4.10	2.20

17th Olympic Games, Rome, 8/25-9/11.

Runner — A17

1961, Aug. 30   **Unwmk.**   **Perf. 13**
53	A17 20fr dk grn	.25	.25
54	A17 30fr dk car rose	.50	.25
55	A17 50fr brt bl	.65	.40
	Nos. 53-55 (3)	1.40	.90

3rd Pan-Arabic Games, Casablanca.

Post Office, Tangier A18

View of Tangier and Gibraltar A19

Design: 30fr, Telephone operator.

1961, Dec. 8   **Litho.**   **Perf. 12½**
56	A18 20fr red vio	.40	.25
57	A18 30fr green	.55	.25
57A	A19 90fr lt bl & vio bl	1.00	.50
	Nos. 56-57A (3)	1.95	1.00

Conference of the African Postal and Telecommunications Union, Tangier.

Mohammed V and Map of Africa — A20

1962, Jan. 4   **Unwmk.**   **Perf. 11½**
58	A20 20c buff & vio brn	.30	.25
59	A20 30c lt & dk bl	.45	.25

1st anniv. of the conference of African heads of state at Casablanca.

Patrice Lumumba and Map of Congo — A21

1962, Feb. 12   **Perf. 12½**
60	A21 20c bis & blk	.30	.25
61	A21 30c dl red brn & blk	.45	.25

1st death anniv. of Patrice Lumumba, Premier of Congo Democratic Republic.

Moroccan Students — A22

1962, Mar. 5   **Engr.**
62	A22 20fr multi	.55	.30
63	A22 30fr multi	.55	.40
64	A22 90fr gray grn, indigo & brn	.90	.70
	Nos. 62-64 (3)	2.00	1.40

Issued to honor the nation's students.

Arab League Building, Cairo — A23

1962, Mar. 22   **Photo.**   **Perf. 13½x13**
65	A23 20c red brn	.50	.25

Arab Propaganda Week, 3/22-28. See #146.

Malaria Eradication Emblem and Swamp — A24

50c, Dagger stabbing mosquito, vert.

1962, Sept. 3   **Engr.**   **Perf. 13**
66	A24 20c dk grn & grnsh blk	.35	.25
67	A24 50c dk grn & mag	.50	.30

WHO drive to eradicate malaria.

Fish and Aquarium — A25

1962, Nov. 5   **Unwmk.**   **Perf. 13**
68	A25 20c shown	.60	.25
69	A25 30c Moray eel	.75	.25

Casablanca Aquarium.

Courier and Sherifian Stamp of 1912 — A26

Designs: 30c, Courier on foot and round Sherifian cancellation. 50c, Sultan Hassan I and octagonal cancellation.

1962, Dec. 15   **Unwmk.**
70	A26 20c Prus grn & redsh brn	.75	.25
71	A26 30c dk car rose & blk	.75	.40
72	A26 50c bl & bister	1.10	.50
	Nos. 70-72 (3)	2.60	1.15

Stamp Day; 1st National Stamp Exhibition, Dec. 15-23; 75th anniv. of the Sherifian Post and the 50th anniv. of its reorganization.

Boy Scout — A27

1962, Aug. 8   **Litho.**   **Perf. 11½**
73	A27 20c vio brn & lt bl	.50	.25

5th Arab Boy Scout Jamboree, Rabat.

King Hassan II — A28

1962   **Engr.**   **Perf. 13½x13**
75	A28 1c gray olive	.25	.25
76	A28 2c violet	.25	.25
77	A28 5c black	.25	.25
78	A28 10c brn org	.30	.25
79	A28 15c Prus grn	.40	.25
80	A28 20c purple	.55	.25
81	A28 30c dp yel grn	.80	.25
82	A28 50c vio brn	1.30	.25
83	A28 70c deep blue	1.75	.25
84	A28 80c magenta	2.10	.25
	Nos. 75-84 (10)	7.95	2.50

"Mazelin" (designer-engraver) reads down on Nos. 75-84. See Nos. 110-114.

King Moulay Ismail — A29

1963, Mar. 3   **Perf. 12½**
85	A29 20c sepia	.50	.25

Tercentenary of Meknes as Ismaili capital.

Al Idrissi, Geographer — A30

MOROCCO

No.87, 88A, Ibn Batota, explorer. No.88, Ibn Khaldoun, historian and sociologist.

1963-66   Engr.
86	A30 20c dk sl grn	.40	.30
87	A30 20c dk car rose	.40	.30
88	A30 20c black	.40	.30
88A	A30 40c dk vio bl ('66)	.50	.30
	Nos. 86-88A (4)	1.70	1.20

Famous medieval men of Morocco (Maghreb). No. 88A also marks the inauguration of the ferryboat "Ibn Batota" connecting Tangier and Malaga.
Issued: #86-88, 5/7/63; #88A, 7/15/66.

Sugar Beet and Sugar Refinery, Sidi Slimane — A31

50c, Tuna fisherman, vert.

1963, June 10   Unwmk.   Perf. 13
89	A31 20c shown	.45	.25
90	A31 50c multicolored	.80	.35

FAO "Freedom from Hunger" campaign.

Heads of Ramses II, Abu Simbel — A32

Designs: 30c, Isis, Kalabsha Temple, vert. 50c, Temple of Philae.

1963, July 15   Engr.   Perf. 11½
91	A32 20c black	.40	.30
92	A32 30c vio, grysh	.70	.30
93	A32 50c maroon, buff	.95	.40
	Nos. 91-93 (3)	2.05	1.00

Campaign to save historic monuments in Nubia.

Agadir Before Earthquake — A33

30c, Like 20c, with "29 Février 1960" and crossed bars added. 50c, Agadir rebuilt.

Engr.; Engr. & Photo. (No. 95)
1963, Oct. 10   Perf. 13½x13
94	A33 20c bl & brn red	.45	.30
95	A33 30c bl, brn red & red	.50	.40
96	A33 50c bl & brn red	1.00	.60
	Nos. 94-96 (3)	1.95	1.30

Issued to publicize the rebuilding of Agadir.

Centenary Emblem and Plan of Agadir Hospital — A34

1963, Oct. 28   Photo.   Perf. 12½x13
97	A34 30c blk, dp car & sil	.50	.25

Centenary of the International Red Cross.

Arms of Morocco and Rabat — A35

1963, Nov. 18   Perf. 13x12½
98	A35 20c gold, red, blk & emer	.50	.25

Installation of Parliament.

Hands Breaking Chain — A36

1963, Dec. 10   Engr.   Perf. 13
99	A36 20c dk brn, grn & org	.55	.25

15th anniversary of the Universal Declaration of Human Rights.

Flag — A37

1963, Dec. 25   Photo.   Perf. 13x12½
100	A37 20c blk, dp car & grn	.50	.25

Evacuation of all foreign military forces from Moroccan territory.

Moulay Abd-er-Rahman, by Delacroix — A38

1964, Mar. 3   Engr.   Perf. 12x13
101	A38 1d multi	2.50	1.60

Coronation of King Hassan II, 3rd anniv.

Weather Map of Africa and UN Emblem — A39

30c, World map and barometer trace, horiz.

1964, Mar. 23   Photo.   Perf. 11½
Granite Paper
102	A39 20c multi	.65	.25
103	A39 30c multi	1.35	.50

UN 4th World Meteorological Day. See No. C10.

Children on Vacation — A40

30c, Heads of boy and girl, buildings.

1964, July 6   Litho.   Perf. 12½
104	A40 20c multi	.40	.40
105	A40 30c multi	.50	.50

Issued for vacation camps for children of P.T.T. employees.

Olympic Torch — A41

1964, Sept. 22   Engr.   Perf. 13
106	A41 20c car lake, dk pur & grn	.35	.25
107	A41 30c bl, dk grn & red brn	.55	.35
108	A41 50c grn, red & brn	.70	.60
	Nos. 106-108 (3)	1.60	1.20

18th Olympic Games, Tokyo, Oct. 10-25.

Cape Spartel Lighthouse, Sultan Mohammed ben Abd-er-Rahman — A42

Perf. 12½x11½
1964, Oct. 15   Photo.
109	A42 25c multi	.55	.25

Centenary of the Cape Spartel lighthouse.

King Type of 1962
1964-65   Engr.   Perf. 12½x13
Size: 17x23mm
110	A28 20c purple (redrawn)	2.00	.30

Perf. 13½x13
Size: 18x22mm
111	A28 25c rose red ('65)	.35	.25
112	A28 35c slate ('65)	.55	.25
113	A28 40c ultra ('65)	.55	.25
114	A28 60c red lilac ('65)	.85	.25
	Nos. 110-114 (5)	4.30	1.30

The Arabic inscription touches the frame on No. 110. "Mazelin" (designer-engraver) reads up on No. 110, down on Nos. 111-114. No. 110 is a coil stamp with red control numbers on the back of some copies.

Iris — A43

40c, Gladiolus segetum. 60c, Capparis spinosa, horiz.

1965   Photo.   Perf. 11½
Granite Paper
115	A43 25c shown	.95	.55
116	A43 40c multi	1.25	.65
117	A43 60c multi	1.50	1.40
	Nos. 115-117 (3)	3.70	2.60

Printed in sheets of 10. Five tête-bêche pairs in every sheet; vertical stamps arranged 5x2, horizontal stamps 2x5.
See Nos. 129-131.

Mohammed V Arriving by Plane — A44

1965, Mar. 15   Litho.   Perf. 12½
118	A44 25c lt bl & dk grn	.50	.30

10th anniv. of the return of King Mohammed V from exile and the restoration of the monarchy.

ITU Emblem, Punched-Tape Writer and Telegraph Wires — A45

Design: 40c, ITU emblem, TIROS satellite, radio waves and "ITU" in Morse code.

Perf. 13x14
1965, May 17   Unwmk.   Typo.
119	A45 25c multi	.45	.25
120	A45 40c lt bl, dp bl & bis	.55	.25

ITU, centenary.

ICY Emblem — A46

1965, June 14   Engr.   Perf. 13
121	A46 25c slate grn	.40	.25
122	A46 60c dk car rose	.85	.25

International Cooperation Year.

Royal Prawn — A47

Designs: No. 123, Triton shell. No. 124, Varnish shell (pitaria chione). No. 125, Great voluted shell (cymbium neptuni). No. 126, Helmet crab, vert. 40c, Mantis shrimp, vert.

1965   Photo.   Perf. 11½
Granite Paper
123	A47 25c vio & multi	1.10	.45
124	A47 25c lt bl & multi	1.10	.45
125	A47 25c org & multi	1.10	.45
126	A47 25c lt grn & multi	1.10	.45
127	A47 40c multi	1.90	.65
128	A47 1d yel & multi	2.60	1.35
	Nos. 123-128 (6)	8.90	3.80

Printed in sheets of 10. Nos. 126-127 (5x2); others (2x5). Five tête bêche pairs in every sheet.

Flower Type of 1965

Orchids: 25c, Ophrys speculum. 40c, Ophrys fusca. 60c, Ophrys tenthredinifera (front and side view), horiz.

1965, Dec. 13   Photo.   Perf. 11½
Granite Paper
129	A43 25c yel & multi	.75	.40
130	A43 40c dl rose & multi	1.40	.40
131	A43 60c lt bl & multi	1.75	1.25
	Nos. 129-131 (3)	3.90	2.05

Note on tête bêche pairs after No. 117 also applies to Nos. 129-131.

Grain — A48

40c, Various citrus fruit. 60c, Olives, horiz.

1966   Photo.   Perf. 11½
Granite Paper
133	A48 25c blk & bister	.50	.25
136	A48 40c multi	.50	.25
137	A48 60c gray & multi	.55	.25
	Nos. 133-137 (3)	1.55	.75

For surcharge see No. 231.

Flag, Map and Dove — A49

1966, Mar. 2   Typo.   Perf. 14x13
139	A49 25c brt grn & red	.45	.25

Tenth anniversary of Independence.

King Hassan II — A50

1966, Mar. 2   Engr.   Perf. 13
140	A50 25c red, brt grn & indigo	.45	.25

Coronation of King Hassan II, 5th anniv.

Cross-country Runner — A51

1966, Mar. 20   Engr.   Perf. 13
141	A51 25c blue green	.50	.25

53rd International Cross-country Race.

MOROCCO

WHO Headquarters from West — A52

40c, WHO Headquarters from the East.

1966, May 3		Engr.		Perf. 13	
142	A52	25c rose lil & blk		.30	.25
143	A52	40c dp bl & blk		.50	.25

Inauguration of the WHO Headquarters, Geneva.

Crown Prince Hassan Kissing Hand of King Mohammed V — A53

25c, King Hassan II and parachutist.

		Perf. 12½x12	
1966, May 14	Photo.		Unwmk.
144 A53 25c gold & blk		.40	.25
145 A53 40c gold & blk		.55	.30
a. Strip of 2, #144-145 + label		1.10	.75

10th anniv. of the Royal Armed Forces.

Type of 1962 Inscribed: "SEMAINE DE LA PALESTINE"

1966, May 16			Perf. 11x11½
146 A23 25c slate blue		.45	.25

Issued for Palestine Week.

Train — A54

1966, Dec. 19		Photo.	Perf. 13½
147 A54 25c shown		.80	.25
148 A54 40c Ship		.75	.35
149 A54 1d Autobus		.95	.25
Nos. 147-149 (3)		2.50	1.10

Twaite Shad — A55

Fish: 40c, Plain bonito. 1d, Bluefish, vert.

1967, Feb. 1	Photo.	Perf. 11½
Granite Paper		
150 A55 25c yel & multi	.75	.30
151 A55 40c yel & multi	.85	.30
152 A55 1d lt grn & multi	1.90	.90
Nos. 150-152 (3)	3.50	1.50

Printed tête bêche in sheets of 10. Nos. 150-151 (2x5); No. 152 (5x2).

Ait Aadel Dam — A56

1967, Mar. 3		Engr.	Perf. 13
153 A56 25c sl grn, Prus bl & gray	.30	.25
154 A56 40c Prus bl & lt brn	.70	.25

Inauguration of Ait Aadel Dam.

Rabat Hilton Hotel, Map of Morocco and Roman Arch — A57

1967, Mar. 3			
155 A57 25c brt bl & blk		.40	.25
156 A57 1d brt bl & pur		.80	.25

Opening of the Rabat Hilton Hotel.

Torch, Globe, Town and Lions Emblem A58

1967, Apr. 22	Photo.	Perf. 12½
157 A58 40c gold & saph bl	.40	.25
158 A58 1d gold & slate grn	1.10	.25

Lions International, 50th anniversary.

Three Hands Holding Pickax — A59

1967, July 9		Engr.	Perf. 13
159 A59 25c slate green		.45	.25

Community Development Campaign.

Intl. Tourism Year Emblem — A60

1967, Aug. 9		Photo.	Perf. 12½
160 A60 1d lt ultra & dk bl		.80	.35

Arrow and Map of Mediterranean — A61

1967, Sept. 8		Perf. 13x12
161 A61 25c dk bl, ultra, red & tan	.50	.25
162 A61 40c blk, bl grn, red & tan	.55	.25

Mediterranean Games, Tunis, Sept. 8-17.

Steeplechase A62

1967, Oct. 14	Photo.	Perf. 12½
163 A62 40c yel grn, blk & brt rose lilac	.50	.25
164 A62 1d lt ultra, blk & brt rose lilac	.80	.35

International Horseshow.

Cotton — A63

1967, Nov. 15	Photo.	Perf. 12½
165 A63 40c lt bl, grn & yel	.50	.25

Human Rights Flame — A64

1968, Jan. 10	Engr.	Perf. 13
166 A64 25c gray	.50	.25
167 A64 1d rose claret	.60	.25

International Human Rights Year.

King Hassan II — A65

1968-74	Litho.	Perf. 13
Portrait in Magenta, Brown and Black		
Size: 23x30mm		
169 A65 1c cream & blk	.25	.25
170 A65 2c lt grnsh bl & blk	.25	.25
171 A65 5c lt ol grn & blk	.25	.25
172 A65 10c pale rose & blk	.25	.25
173 A65 15c gray bl & blk	.25	.25
174 A65 20c pink & blk	.25	.25
175 A65 25c white & blk	.25	.25
176 A65 30c pale rose & blk	.35	.25
177 A65 35c bl & blk	.60	.30
178 A65 40c gray & blk	.60	.25
179 A65 50c lt bl & blk	.70	.25
180 A65 60c salmon & blk	1.00	.25
181 A65 70c gray & blk	4.25	.90
182 A65 75c pale yel ('74)	1.20	.30
183 A65 80c ocher & blk	1.20	.30
Perf. 13½x14		
Size: 26x40mm		
184 A65 90c lt bl grn & blk	1.60	.45
185 A65 1d tan & blk	2.00	.30
186 A65 2d lt ultra & blk	3.00	.60
187 A65 3d bluish lil & blk	6.25	1.10
188 A65 5d apple grn & blk	10.00	3.25
Nos. 169-188 (20)	34.50	10.25

For overprints & surcharges see #224, B17-B18.

Nurse and Child — A66

1968, Apr. 8	Engr.	Perf. 13
189 A66 25c ultra, red & olive	.40	.25
190 A66 40c slate, red & olive	.60	.25

WHO, 20th anniv.

Pendant — A67

1968, May 15	Photo.	Perf. 11½
191 A67 25c shown	.80	.25
192 A67 40c Bracelet	1.25	.30
a. Pair, #191-192, vertically tête-bêche	4.00	2.40

Moroccan Red Crescent Society. See Nos. 373-374.

Map of Morocco and Rotary Emblem A68

1968, May 23		Perf. 13
193 A68 40c multi	.65	.25
194 A68 1d ultra & multi	.90	.30

Rotary Intl. District Conference, Casablanca, May 24-25.

Ornamental Design — A69

Designs: Various patterns used for sashes.

1968, July 12	Photo.	Perf. 11½
195 A69 25c multi	1.60	.80
196 A69 40c multi	2.00	1.00
197 A69 60c multi	3.00	1.75
198 A69 1d multi	5.50	2.75
Nos. 195-198 (4)	12.10	6.30

Berber (Riff), North Morocco — A70

Regional Costumes: 10c, Man from Ait Moussa ou Ali. 15c, Woman from Ait Mouhad. No. 200, Bargeman from Rabat Salé. No. 201, Citadin man. 40c, Citadin woman. 60c, Royal Mokhazni. No. 204, Zemmours man. No. 204A, Man from Meknassa. No. 206, Msouffa woman, Sahara.

1968-74	Litho.	Perf. 13x12½
198A A70 10c multi ('69)	.60	.45
199 A70 15c yel & multi ('69)	1.00	.65
200 A70 25c bis & multi	1.00	.70
201 A70 25c tan & multi ('69)	1.10	.70
202 A70 40c lt bl & multi	1.15	1.00
203 A70 60c emer & multi	1.60	1.30
204 A70 1d lt bl & multi	2.10	1.75
204A A70 1d gray & multi ('69)	1.90	1.15
Perf. 15		
205 A70 1d bis & multi	1.35	.90
206 A70 1d grn & multi	1.35	.90
a. Souvenir sheet of 10, #198A-206, perf. 13	19.50	19.50
b. As "a," with red overprint & surcharge	22.00	20.00
Nos. 198A-206 (10)	13.15	9.50

No. 206a issued June 30, 1970, for the opening of the National P.T.T. Museum, Rabat. Sold for 10d.

No. 206b issued Nov. 22, 1974, for the 8th Cong. of the Intl. Fed. of Blood Donors. Each stamp overprinted vertically "8eme Congres de la F.I.O.D.S." and blood container emblem. Black marginal inscription partially obliterated with lines, new Arabic inscription and price added. Sold for 20d.

Princess Lalla Meryem — A71

Children's Week: 40c, Princess Lalla Asmaa. 1d, Crown Prince Sidi Mohammed.

1968, Oct. 7	Litho.	Perf. 13½
207 A71 25c red & multi	.55	.25
208 A71 40c yel & multi	.70	.40
209 A71 1d lt bl & multi	.85	.70
Nos. 207-209 (3)	2.10	1.35

Wrestling, Aztec Calendar Stone and Olympic Rings A72

1968, Oct. 25	Photo.	Perf. 12x11½
210 A72 15c shown	.30	.25
211 A72 20c Basketball	.40	.25
212 A72 25c Cycling	.60	.25
213 A72 40c Boxing	.75	.25

MOROCCO

214	A72	60c Running	1.15	.25
215	A72	1d Soccer	2.00	.40
		Nos. 210-215 (6)	5.20	1.65

19th Olympic Games, Mexico City, 10/12-27.

10 Dirham Coin of Tetuan, 1780 — A73

Coins: 25c, Dirham, Agmat, c. 1138 A.D. 40c, Dirham, El Alya (Fes), c. 840 A.D. 60c, Dirham, Marrakesh, c. 1248 A.D.

1968, Dec. 17 Photo. Perf. 11½
Granite Paper

216	A73	20c dp plum, sil & blk	.55	.25
217	A73	25c dk rose brn, gold & blk	.65	.35
218	A73	40c dk grn, sil & blk	1.30	.50
219	A73	60c dk red, gold & blk	1.60	.75
		Nos. 216-219,C16-C17 (6)	17.60	8.85

Issued with tabs.

Women from Zagora — A74

Design: 25c, Women from Ait Adidou.

1969, Jan. 21 Litho. Perf. 12

220	A74	15c multi	1.25	.65
221	A74	25c multi	1.60	.95
		Nos. 220-221,C15 (3)	5.25	2.85

Painting by Belkahya — A75

1969, Mar. 27 Litho. Perf. 11½x12

| 222 | A75 | 1d lt grnsh bl, blk & brn | .60 | .40 |

International Day of the Theater.

King Hassan II — A76

1969, July 9 Photo. Perf. 11½

| 223 | A76 | 1d gold & multi | 1.25 | .50 |

40th birthday of King Hassan II. A souvenir sheet contains one No. 223. Size: 75x105mm. Sold for 2.50d.

All issues of Morocco between 1969 and 2010 exist in imperforate deluxe sheets of one. Values are usually between $20 and $40 each.

No. 185 Overprinted

1969, Sept. 22 Litho. Perf. 13

| 224 | A65 | 1d tan & multi | 4.50 | 2.90 |

First Arab Summit Conference, Rabat.

Mahatma Gandhi — A77

1969, Oct. 16 Photo. Perf. 11½

| 225 | A77 | 40c pale vio, blk & gray | 1.00 | .40 |

Mohandas K. Gandhi (1869-1948), leader in India's struggle for independence.

ILO Emblem — A78

1969, Oct. 29

| 226 | A78 | 50c multi | .50 | .25 |

ILO, 50th anniv.

King Hassan II on Way to Prayer — A79

1969, Nov. 20 Photo. Perf. 11½

| 227 | A79 | 1d multi | .90 | .50 |

1st Arab Summit Conference, Rabat, Sept. 1969. For overprint see No. 311.

Spahi Horsemen, by Haram al Glaoui — A80

1970, Jan. 23 Engr. Perf. 12x13

| 228 | A80 | 1d multi | .90 | .50 |

Main Sewer, Fez — A81

1970, Mar. 23 Litho. Perf. 12

| 229 | A81 | 60c multi | .45 | .25 |

50th Congress of Municipal Engineers, Rabat, Mar. 1970.

Guedra Dance, by P. C. Beaubrun — A82

1970, Apr. 15

| 230 | A82 | 40c multi | .55 | .25 |

Folklore Festival, Marrakesh, May 1970. See No. 1284a.

No. 137 Overprinted "1970", "Census" in Arabic in Red and Surcharged in Black

1970, July 9 Photo. Perf. 11½

| 231 | A48 | 25c on 60c multi | .45 | .25 |

Issued to publicize the 1970 census.

Radar Station at Souk El Arba des Sehoul, and Satellite — A83

1970, Aug. 20

| 232 | A83 | 1d lt ultra & multi | 1.00 | .30 |

Revolution of King and People, 17th anniv.

Ruddy Shelduck — A84

1970, Sept. 25 Photo. Perf. 11½

| 233 | A84 | 25c shown | 1.10 | .40 |
| 234 | A84 | 40c Houbara bustard | 1.45 | .45 |

Campaign to save Moroccan wildlife.

Man Reading Book, Intl. Education Year Emblem A85

1970, Oct. 20 Litho. Perf. 12x11½

| 235 | A85 | 60c dl yel & multi | .75 | .25 |

Symbols of Peace, Justice and Progress — A86

1970, Oct. 27 Perf. 13½

| 236 | A86 | 50c multi | .60 | .25 |

United Nations, 25th anniversary.

Arab League Countries and Emblem — A87

1970, Nov. 13 Photo. Perf. 11½

| 237 | A87 | 50c multi | .50 | .25 |

Arab League, 25th anniversary.

Olive Grove, Tree and Branch — A88

1970, Dec. 3 Litho. Perf. 12

| 238 | A88 | 50c red brn & grn | .75 | .40 |

International Olive Year.

Es Sounna Mosque, Rabat — A89

1971, Jan. 5 Engr. Perf. 13

| 239 | A89 | 60c ol bis, bl & sl grn | .50 | .30 |

Restoration of Es Sounna Mosque, Rabat, built in 1785.

Heart and Horse — A90

1971, Feb. 23 Photo. Perf. 12x12½

| 240 | A90 | 50c blk & multi | .55 | .25 |

European heart research week, Feb. 21-28.

Dam and Hassan II — A91

1971, Mar. 3 Perf. 11½

| 241 | A91 | 25c multi | .50 | .25 |
| a. | | Souv. sheet of 4 | 2.50 | 1.75 |

Accession of King Hassan II, 10th anniv. No. 241a issued Mar. 24. Sold for 2.50d.

Black and White Hands with Dove and Emblem — A92

1971, June 16 Photo. Perf. 13

| 242 | A92 | 50c brn & multi | .65 | .25 |

Intl. Year against Racial Discrimination.

Children Around the World — A93

1971, Oct. 4 Litho. Perf. 13x14

| 243 | A93 | 40c emer & multi | .50 | .25 |

International Children's Day.

Shah Mohammed Riza Pahlavi of Iran — A94

1971, Oct. 11 Photo. Perf. 11½

| 244 | A94 | 1d bl & multi | .65 | .45 |

2500th anniv. of the founding of the Persian empire by Cyrus the Great.

Mausoleum of Mohammed V — A95

50c, Mausoleum, close-up view, and Mohammed V. 1d, Decorated interior wall.

MOROCCO

1971, Nov. 10 Litho. *Perf. 14*
245 A95 25c multi .35 .25
246 A95 50c multi .45 .25
247 A95 1d multi, vert. .75 .25
Nos. 245-247 (3) 1.55 .75

Soccer Ball and Games Emblem — A96

1971, Nov. 30 Photo. *Perf. 13x13½*
248 A96 40c shown .55 .25
249 A96 60c Runner .80 .25
Mediterranean Games, Izmir, Turkey, Oct. 6-17.

Arab Postal Union Emblem — A97

1971, Dec. 23 Litho. *Perf. 13x12½*
250 A97 25c dk & lt bl & org .50 .25
25th anniv. of the Conference of Sofar, Lebanon, establishing APU.

Sun over Cultivated Sand Dunes — A98

1971, Dec. 30 Photo. *Perf. 12½*
251 A98 70c blk, bl & yel .50 .25
Sherifian Phosphate Office (fertilizer production and export), 50th anniversary.

Torch and Book Year Emblem — A99

1972, Jan. 12 *Perf. 11½*
252 A99 1d silver & multi 1.10 .25
International Book Year.

National Lottery — A100

1972, Feb. 7 Photo. *Perf. 13*
253 A100 25c tan, blk & gold .45 .25
Creation of a national lottery.

Bridge of Sighs — A101

Designs: 50c, St. Mark's Basilica and waves, horiz. 1d, Lion of St. Mark.
1972, Feb. 25
254 A101 25c multi .25 .25
255 A101 50c red, blk & buff .60 .25
256 A101 1d lt bl & multi .50 .35
Nos. 254-256 (3) 1.35 .85
UNESCO campaign to save Venice.

Bridge, Road, Map of Africa A102

1972, Apr. 21 *Perf. 13*
257 A102 75c blue & multi .55 .25
2nd African Road Conf., Rabat, Apr. 17-22.

Morocco No. 223 — A103

1972, Apr. 27 *Perf. 11½*
258 A103 1d lt ultra & multi .50 .25
Stamp Day.

The Engagement of Imilchil, by Tayeb Lahlou — A104

1972, May 26 Litho. *Perf. 13x13½*
259 A104 60c blk & multi .75 .40
Folklore Festival, Marrakesh, May 26-June 4.

Map of Africa, Dove and OAU Emblem — A105

1972, June 12 Photo. *Perf. 11½*
260 A105 25c multi .35 .25
9th Summit Conference of Organization for African Unity, Rabat, June 12-15.

Landscape, Environment Emblem — A106

1972, July 20 Photo. *Perf. 12½x12*
261 A106 50c bl & multi .45 .25
UN Conference on Human Environment, Stockholm, June 5-16

Olympic Emblems, Running — A107

1972, Aug. 29 Photo. *Perf. 13x13½*
262 A107 25c shown .25 .25
263 A107 50c Wrestling .35 .25
264 A107 75c Soccer .60 .25
265 A107 1d Cycling .75 .50
Nos. 262-265 (4) 1.95 1.25
20th Olympic Games, Munich, 8/26-9/11.

Sow Thistle — A108

40c, Amberboa crupinoides.

1972, Sept. 15 Litho. *Perf. 14*
266 A108 25c shown .75 .25
267 A108 40c multi .85 .25
See No. 305-306.

Mountain Gazelle — A109

1972, Sept. 29 Photo. *Perf. 11½*
268 A109 25c shown .90 .35
269 A109 40c Barbary sheep 1.25 .40
Nos. 266-269 issued for nature protection.

Rabat Rug — A110

25c, High Atlas rug. 70c, Tazanakht rug. 75c, Rabat rug, different pattern.
Perf. 13½ (25fr, 70fr), 11½
1972-73 Photo.
270 A110 25c multi .85 .25
270A A110 50c multi .90 .25
271 A110 70c multi 1.30 .45
271A A110 75c multi 1.35 .45
Nos. 270-271A (4) 4.40 1.40
Issued: 50c, 75c, 10/27; 25c, 70c, 12/28/73.
See Nos. 326-327.

Child and UNICEF Emblem — A111

1972, Dec. 20 Photo. *Perf. 13½x13*
272 A111 75c brt grn & bl .45 .25
International Children's Day.

Symbolic Letter Carrier and Stamp — A112

1973, Jan. 30 Photo. *Perf. 13x13½*
273 A112 25c brn & multi .25 .25
Stamp Day.

Weather Map, Northern Hemisphere — A113

1973, Feb. 23 Photo. *Perf. 13*
274 A113 70c silver & multi .55 .30
Intl. meteorological cooperation, cent.

King Hassan II, Coat of Arms — A114

1973-76 Photo. *Perf. 14*
275 A114 1c pale yel & multi .25 .25
276 A114 2c pale bl & multi .25 .25
277 A114 5c pale ol & multi .25 .25
278 A114 10c brn org & multi .25 .25
279 A114 15c vio gray & multi .25 .25
280 A114 20c pink & multi .25 .25
281 A114 25c pale bl & multi .25 .25
282 A114 30c rose & multi .25 .25
283 A114 35c org yel & multi .35 .25
284 A114 40c lt gray & multi 3.75 .35
285 A114 50c ultra & multi .45 .25
286 A114 60c sal & multi .55 .25
287 A114 70c yel grn & multi .45 .25
288 A114 75c lem & multi .40 .25
289 A114 80c multi .45 .30
290 A114 90c brt grn & multi .50 .25
291 A114 1d beige & multi 1.50 .25
292 A114 2d gray & multi 3.25 .45
293 A114 3d lt lil & multi 4.00 .70
294 A114 5d lt brn & multi ('75) 3.25 .90
294A A114 5d pink & multi ('76) 3.75 .90
Nos. 275-294A (21) 24.65 7.35

Nos. B26-B27 Surcharged to Obliterate Surtax

1973, Mar. 13 *Perf. 11½*
295 SP1 25c multi 2.10 2.10
296 SP1 70c multi 2.25 2.25
a. Pair, #295-296, vert. tête-bêche 5.75 5.75
Tourism Conference 1973. Arabic overprint and date on one line on No. 296.
See Nos. 351-352.

Holy Ka'aba, Mecca, Mosque and Minaret, Rabat — A115

1973, May 3 Photo. *Perf. 13½x14*
297 A115 25c lt bl & multi .25 .25
Mohammed's 1,403rd birthday.

Roses and M'Gouna — A116

1973, May 14 *Perf. 13*
298 A116 25c bl & multi .45 .25
Rose Festival of M'Gouna.

Hands, Torch, OAU Emblem — A117

1973, May 25 Photo. *Perf. 14x13*
299 A117 70c deep claret & multi .45 .25
OAU, 10th anniversary.

Dancers with Tambourines A118

Design: 1d, Dancer with handbells, Marrakesh Minaret, Atlas Mountain.
1973, May 30 *Perf. 12½x13*
300 A118 50c multi .70 .25
301 A118 1d multi .85 .30
Folklore Festival, Marrakesh.

MOROCCO

Copernicus — A119

70c, Heliocentric system.

1973, June 29   *Perf. 13x13½*
302 A119 70c multi   1.25 .30

Microscope, WHO Emblem, World Map — A120

1973, July 16   Photo.   *Perf. 13x12½*
303 A120 70c multi   .50 .25
WHO, 25th anniversary.

INTERPOL Emblem, Fingerprint — A121

1973, Sept. 12   Photo.   *Perf. 13x13½*
304 A121 70c brn, sil & bl   .50 .25
50th anniv. of Intl. Criminal Police Org.

Flower Type of 1972

1973, Oct. 12   Litho.   *Perf. 14*
305 A108 25c Daisies, horiz.   .75 .25
306 A108 1d Thistle   1.50 .50
Nature protection.

Berber Hyena — A122

Design: 50c, Eleonora's falcon, vert.

1973, Nov. 23   Photo.   *Perf. 14*
307 A122 25c multi   1.50 .25
308 A122 50c multi   3.00 .40
Nature protection.

Map and Colors of Morocco, Algeria and Tunisia — A123

1973, Dec. 7   *Perf. 13x13½*
309 A123 25c gold & multi   .50 .25
Maghreb Committee for Coordination of Posts and Telecommunications.

Fairway and Drive over Water Hazard — A124

1974, Feb. 8   Photo.   *Perf. 14x13*
310 A124 70c multi   1.90 .25
International Golf Grand Prix for the Hassan II Morocco trophy.

No. 227 Overprinted in Red

1974, Feb. 25   *Perf. 11½*
311 A79 1d multi   2.75 1.50
Islamic Conference, Lahore, India, 1974.

Map of Africa, Scales, Human Rights Flame — A125

1974, Mar. 15   Photo.   *Perf. 14x13½*
312 A125 70c gold & multi   .50 .25
25th anniversary of the Universal Declaration of Human Rights.

Vanadinite — A126

1974-75   Photo.   *Perf. 13*
313   A126 25c shown   2.25 .60
313A A126 50c Aragonite   2.00 .35
314   A126 70c Erythrine   4.00 .75
314A A126 1d Agate   4.00 .60
Nos. 313-314A (4)   12.25 2.30
Issued: 25c, 70c, 4/30/74; 50c, 1d, 2/14/75.

Minaret, Marrakesh Mosque, Rotary Emblem — A127

1974, May 11   Photo.   *Perf. 14*
315 A127 70c multi   .55 .25
District 173 Rotary International annual meeting, Marrakesh, May 10-12.

UPU Emblem, Congress Dates — A128

1d, Scroll with UPU emblem, Lausanne coat of arms & 17th UPU Congress emblem, horiz.

1974, May 30   Photo.
316 A128 25c lt grn, org & blk   .35 .25
317 A128 1d dk grn & multi   .80 .25
Centenary of Universal Postal Union.

Drummer and Dancers — A129

Design: 70c, Knife juggler and women.

1974, June 7   Photo.   *Perf. 14*
318 A129 25c multi   .50 .25
319 A129 70c multi   1.25 .35
National folklore festival, Marrakesh. See Nos. 1284b-1284c.

Environment Emblem, Polution, Clean Water and Air — A130

1974, June 25   *Perf. 13*
320 A130 25c multi   .40 .25
World Environment Day.

Simulated Stamps, Cancel and Magnifier — A131

1974, Aug. 2   Photo.   *Perf. 13*
321 A131 70c sil & multi   .50 .25
Stamp Day.

No. J5 Surcharged

1974, Sept. 25   Photo.   *Perf. 14*
322 D2 1d on 5c multi   1.90 1.30
Agricultural census.

World Soccer Cup — A132

1974, Oct. 11
323 A132 1d brt bl & multi   1.10 .75
World Cup Soccer Championship, Munich, June 13-July 7.
A stamp similar to No. 323, also issued Oct. 11, has gold inscription: "CHAMPION: R.F.A." in French and Arabic, honoring the German Federal Republic as championship winner. Value $32.50.

Double-spurred Francolin — A133

Perf. 14x13½, 13½x14
1974, Dec. 5   Photo.
324 A133 25c green & multi   .55 .25
325 A133 70c Leopard, horiz.   1.15 .35
Nature protection.

Zemmour Rug — A134

Design: 1d, Beni Mguilo rug.

1974, Dec 20   *Perf. 13*
326 A134 25c multi   .75 .25
327 A134 1d multi   1.50 .30
See Nos. 349-350, 398-400.

Columbine — A135

1975   Photo.   *Perf. 13½*
328 A135 10c Daisies   .25 .25
329 A135 25c Columbine   .45 .25
330 A135 35c Orange lilies   .50 .25
331 A135 50c Anemones   .60 .25
332 A135 60c White starflower   .70 .35
333 A135 70c Poppies   .75 .35
334 A135 90c Carnations   1.05 .45
335 A135 1d Pansies   1.00 .55
Nos. 328-335 (8)   5.30 2.70
Issued: 25c, 35c, 70c, 90c, 1/10; others, 4/29. See Nos. 1285b-1285e.

Water Carrier, by Feu Tayeb Lahlou — A136

1975, Apr. 3   *Perf. 13*
338 A136 1d multicolored   1.20 .50

Stamp Collector, Carrier Pigeon, Globe — A137

1975, May 21   Photo.   *Perf. 13*
339 A137 40c gold & multi   .35 .25
Stamp Day.

Musicians and Dancers — A138

1975, June 12   Photo.   *Perf. 14x13½*
340 A138 1d multicolored   1.05 .30
16th Folklore Festival, Marrakesh, 5/30-6/15. See No. 1284d.

Guitar and Association for the Blind Emblem — A139

1975, July 8   *Perf. 13x13½*
341 A139 1d purple & multi   .95 .50
Week of the Blind. See No. 1265c.

MOROCCO

Animals in Forest — A140

1975, July 25   Photo.   Perf. 13x13½
342   A140   25c multicolored   .50   .25
Children's Week.

Games' Emblem, Runner, Weight Lifter A141

1975, Sept. 4   Photo.   Perf. 13
343   A141   40c gold, maroon & buff   .50   .25
7th Mediterranean Games, Algiers, 8/23-9/6.

Bald Ibis — A142

1975, Oct. 21   Photo.   Perf. 13
344   A142   40c shown   1.60   .50
345   A142   1d Persian lynx, vert.   2.00   1.00
Nature protection.

King Mohammed V Greeting Crowd, Prince Moulay Hassan at Left — A143

King Hassan II — A144

#348, King Mohammed V wearing fez.

1975, Nov. 21   Photo.   Perf. 13½
346   A143   10c blk, oil & dk bl   .50   .25
347   A144   1d blk, gold & dk bl   .75   .45
348   A144   1d blk, gold & dk bl   .75   .45
    a.   Sheet of 3, #346-348   13.00   13.00
20th anniversary of independence.

Rug Type of 1974
25c, Ouled Besseba. 1d, Ait Ouaouzguid.

1975, Dec. 11
349   A134   25c red & multi   .85   .45
350   A134   1d orange & multi   1.30   .50

A number of issues have been printed se-tenant in sheets of 10 (5x2) arranged vertically tête bêche.

Nos. B29-B30 Surcharged in Green to Obliterate Surtax

1975   Perf. 11½
351   SP1   25c blue & multi   2.50   2.50
352   SP1   70c orange & multi   2.75   2.75
    a.   Pair, #351-352, vertically tête-bêche   7.25   7.25
March of Moroccan people into Spanish Sahara, Dec. 1975.

"Green March of the People" — A145

1975, Dec. 30   Photo.   Perf. 13½x13
353   A145   40c multicolored   .45   .25
March of Moroccan people into Spanish Sahara, Dec. 1975.

Copper Coin, Fez, 1883-84 — A146

Coins: 15c, 50c, silver coin, Rabat, 1774-75. 35c, 65c, Gold coin, Sabta, 13th-14th centuries. 1d, Square coin, Sabta, 12th-13th centuries.

1976   Photo.   Perf. 14x13½
354   A146   5c dull rose & multi   .25   .25
355   A146   15c brown & multi   .25   .25
356   A146   35c gray & multi   .50   .25
357   A146   40c ocher & multi   .70   .25
358   A146   50c ultra & blk   .80   .25
359   A146   65c yellow & multi   .95   .30
360   A146   1d multicolored   1.25   .45
    Nos. 354-360 (7)   4.70   2.00
Issued: #354-356, 4/26; #357-360, 1/20.

1976, Sept. 9
Designs: Various Moroccan coins.
361   A146   5c green & multi   .25   .25
362   A146   15c dp rose & multi   .25   .25
363   A146   20c lt bl & multi   .40   .25
364   A146   30c lil rose & multi   .50   .25
365   A146   35c green & multi   .65   .25
366   A146   70c orange & multi   .90   .25
    Nos. 361-366 (6)   2.95   1.50
See Nos. 403-406A, 524B-524C.

Family — A147

1976, Feb. 12   Perf. 14x13½
367   A147   40c multicolored   .45   .25
Family planning.

Arch, Ibn Zaidoun Mosque — A148

40c, Hall, Ibn Zaidoun Mosque, horiz.

  Perf. 13½x14, 14x13½
1976, Feb. 12   Photo.
368   A148   40c multicolored   .40   .25
369   A148   65c multicolored   .70   .25
Ibn Zaidoun Mosque, millennium.

Medersa bou Anania, Fez — A149

1976, Feb. 26   Perf. 13x14½
370   A149   1d multicolored   .65   .25

Borobudur Temple — A150

Design: 40c, Bas-relief, Borobudur.

1976, Mar. 11   Photo.   Perf. 13
371   A150   40c multicolored   .70   .25
372   A150   1d multicolored   1.40   .25
UNESCO campaign to save Borobudur Temple, Java.

Islamic Conference, 6th Anniv. — A151

1976   Litho.   Perf. 13½x13
372A   A151   1d Dome of the Rock   .65   .25

Jewelry Type of 1968
Designs: 40c, Pendant. 1d, Breastplate.

1976, June 29   Photo.   Perf. 14x13½
373   A67   40c blue & multi   .50   .25
374   A67   1d olive & multi   .95   .30
    a.   Pair, #373-374, vertically tête-bêche   2.00   2.00
Moroccan Red Crescent Society.

Bicentennial Emblem, Flags and Map of US and Morocco — A152

Design: 1d, George Washington, King Hassan, Statue of Liberty and Royal Palace, Rabat, vert.

1976, July 27   Photo.   Perf. 14
375   A152   40c multicolored   .45   .25
376   A152   1d multicolored   .85   .35
American Bicentennial.

Wrestling — A153

1976, Aug. 11   Perf. 10x10½
377   A153   35c shown   .25   .25
378   A153   40c Cycling   .25   .25
379   A153   50c Boxing   .60   .30
380   A153   1d Running   1.00   .50
    Nos. 377-380 (4)   2.10   1.30
21st Olympic Games, Montreal, Canada, July 17-Aug. 1.

Old and New Telephones, Radar — A154

1976, Sept. 29   Photo.   Perf. 14
381   A154   1d gold & multi   .65   .25
Centenary of first telephone call by Alexander Graham Bell, Mar. 10, 1876.

Blind Person's Identification A155

1976, Oct. 12   Photo.   Perf. 13½x14
382   A155   50c multicolored   .55   .25
Week of the Blind.

Chanting Goshawk — A156

1976, Oct. 29   Perf. 13x13½
383   A156   40c shown   1.60   .50
384   A156   1d Purple gallinule   2.40   1.00
Nature protection.

King Hassan, Star, Torch, Map of Morocco — A157

1976, Nov. 19   Photo.   Perf. 12½x13
385   A157   40c multicolored   .75   .25
Green March into Spanish Sahara, 1st anniv.

Nos. B34-B35 Ovptd. with 2 Bars over Srch. and 4-line Arabic Inscription

1976, Nov. 29   Photo.   Perf. 13½
386   SP1   25c ultra, blk & org   2.00   2.00
387   SP1   70c red, blk & org   2.40   2.40
    a.   Pair, #386-387, vert. tête-bêche   5.50   5.50
5th African Tuberculosis Conference, Rabat.

Globe and Dove — A158

1976, Dec. 16   Perf. 13
388   A158   1d blue, blk & red   .55   .25
5th Summit Meeting of Non-aligned Countries, Colombo, Aug. 9-19, and 25th anniv. of Org. of Non-aligned Countries.

African Soccer Cup — A159

1976, Dec. 29   Photo.   Perf. 14
389   A159   1d multicolored   .65   .25

Letters Circling Globe, Postmark A160

1977, Jan. 24   Photo.   Perf. 13½
390   A160   40c multicolored   .50   .25
Stamp Day.

MOROCCO

Aeonium Arboreum — A161

Malope Trifida — A162

1d, Hesperolaburnum platyclarpum.

Perf. 13x13½, 14 (A162)
1977, Feb. 22
391	A161	40c multicolored	.75	.40
392	A162	50c multicolored	1.35	.60
393	A161	1d multicolored	1.60	.75
		Nos. 391-393 (3)	3.70	1.75

Ornamental Lamps, View of Salé — A163

1977, Mar. 24   Photo.   Perf. 14
| 394 | A163 | 40c multicolored | .55 | .25 |

Candle procession of Salé.

No. J6 Surcharged in Orange

1977, May 11   Photo.   Perf. 14
| 395 | D2 | 40c on 10c multi | .75 | .40 |

Cherry Festival.

Map of Arab Countries, Emblem — A164

1977, June 2   Photo.   Perf. 14
| 396 | A164 | 50c multicolored | .45 | .25 |

5th Congress of Organization of Arab Cities.

APU Emblem, Members' Flags — A165

1977, June 20
| 397 | A165 | 1d multicolored | .50 | .25 |

Arab Postal Union, 25th anniversary.

Rug Type of 1974
Designs: 35c, No. 399A, Marmoucha rug; diff. No. 399, Ait Haddou rug. 1d, Salé rug.

Perf. 11½x12, 13½ (#399A)
1977-79   Photo.
398	A134	35c multicolored	.45	.25
399	A134	40c multicolored	.55	.25
399A	A134	40c multicolored ('79)	1.10	.40
400	A134	1d multicolored	1.00	.40
		Nos. 398-400 (4)	3.10	1.30

Issued: #399A, 3/8/79; others, 7/21/77.

Cithara — A166

1977, Aug. 18   Photo.   Perf. 14
| 401 | A166 | 1d multi | 1.05 | .30 |

Week of the Blind.

Ali Jinnah and Map of Pakistan — A167

1977, Oct. 10   Photo.   Perf. 13½x13
| 402 | A167 | 70c multi | .55 | .25 |

Mohammed Ali Jinnah (1876-1948), first Governor General of Pakistan.

Coin Type of 1976
Designs: Various Moroccan coins.

1977-81   Perf. 14x13½
403	A146	10c gray & multi	.50	.25
403A	A146	25c ap grn & multi ('81)	1.40	.35
404	A146	60c dk red & multi ('78)	.85	.25
405	A146	75c citron & multi	.95	.25
405A	A146	80c pale vio & mult	7.00	.50
406	A146	2d yel grn & multi	2.25	.35
406A	A146	3d beige & multi ('81)	14.00	1.75
		Nos. 403-406A (7)	26.95	3.70

Marcher with Flag, Map of Morocco and Spanish Sahara — A168

1977, Nov. 6   Photo.   Perf. 14
| 407 | A168 | 1d multi | .60 | .25 |

Green March into Spanish Sahara, 2nd anniv. In 1984, a limited number of examples of No. 407 were overprinted "2ème TRANSAT / DES ALIZES". Value, $60.

Chamber of Representatives — A169

1977, Nov. 6   Perf. 13½
| 408 | A169 | 1d multi | .55 | .25 |
| a. | | Souvenir sheet | 3.00 | 3.00 |

Opening of Chamber of Representatives. No. 408a sold for 3d.

Enameled Silver Brooch — A170

1977, Dec. 14   Photo.   Perf. 11½
| 409 | A170 | 1d multi | 2.50 | .25 |

Moroccan Red Crescent Society.

Copper Vessel — A171

1978, Jan. 5   Photo.   Perf. 13
410	A171	40c gold & multi	.40	.25
411	A171	1d gold & multi	.85	.25
a.		Pair, #410-411, vert. tête-bêche	1.90	1.90

1d, Standing filigree copper bowl with cover.

Map of Sahara, Cogwheel Emblem — A172

1d, Map of North Africa, fish in net, camels.

1978, Feb. 27   Photo.   Perf. 14
| 412 | A172 | 40c multi | .50 | .25 |
| 413 | A172 | 1d multi, horiz | .90 | .25 |

Promotion of the Sahara. See Nos. 441-442 for similar stamps overprinted.

Covered Jar — A173

1978, Mar. 27   Perf. 13½x13
| 414 | A173 | 1d shown | .90 | .50 |
| 415 | A173 | 1d Vase | .90 | .50 |

Week of the Blind.

Red Crescent, Red Cross, Arab Countries — A174

1978, Apr. 14   Perf. 13x13½
| 416 | A174 | 1d multi | .50 | .25 |

10th Conference of Arab Red Crescent and Red Cross Societies, Apr. 10-15.

View of Fez, Rotary Emblem — A175

1978, Apr. 22   Photo.   Perf. 14
| 417 | A175 | 1d multi | .65 | .30 |

Rotary Intl. Meeting, Fez, District 173.

Dome of the Rock, Jerusalem — A176

1978, May 29   Perf. 14½
| 418 | A176 | 5c multi | .30 | .25 |
| 419 | A176 | 10c multi | .30 | .25 |

Palestinian fighters and their families. For overprints see Nos. 502-502A.

Folk Dancers and Flutist — A177

1978, June 15   Perf. 13½x13
| 420 | A177 | 1d multi | 1.75 | .45 |

National Folklore Festival, Marrakesh. See No. 1284h.

Sugar Cane Field, and Conveyor Belt — A178

1978, July 24   Photo.   Perf. 13
| 421 | A178 | 40c multi | .45 | .25 |

Sugar industry.

Games Emblem — A179

1978, Aug. 25
| 422 | A179 | 1d multi | .90 | .25 |

World sailing championships.

Bird, Tree, Tent, Scout Emblem — A180

1978, Sept. 26   Photo.   Perf. 13
| 423 | A180 | 40c multi | .50 | .25 |

Pan-Arab Scout Jamboree, Rabat.

View of Fez — A181

1978, Oct. 10
| 424 | A181 | 40c multi | .45 | .25 |

Moulay Idriss the Great, Festival, Fez.

Flame Emblem — A182

1978, Dec. 21   Photo.   Perf. 14
| 425 | A182 | 1d multi | .65 | .25 |

30th anniversary of Universal Declaration of Human Rights.

Houses, Agadir — A183

1979, Jan. 25   Photo.   Perf. 12
| 426 | A183 | 40c shown | .40 | .25 |
| 427 | A183 | 1d Old Fort, Marrakesh | .80 | .25 |

Soccer and Cup — A184

1979, Mar. 2   Perf. 13
| 428 | A184 | 40c multi | .50 | .25 |

Mohammed V Soccer Cup.

MOROCCO

Vase — A185

1979, Mar. 29   Photo.   Perf. 14
429 A185 1d multi   1.10 .25
Week of the Blind.

Procession — A186

1d, Festival, by Mohamed Ben Ali Rbati, horiz.

1979, Apr. 18   Perf. 13x13½, 13½x13
430 A186 40c multi   .45 .25
431 A186 1d multi   .75 .25

Brass Containers, Red Crescent — A187

1d, Heated coffee urn, vert.

Perf. 13x13½, 13½x13
1979, May 16   Photo.
432 A187 40c shown   .40 .25
433 A187 1d multi   .90 .30
Red Crescent Society.

Dancers — A188

1979, June 1   Photo.   Perf. 13
434 A188 40c multi   .50 .25
National Festival of Marrakech. See No. 1284g.

Silver Dagger — A189

1979, June 20   Perf. 14
435 A189 1d multi   .65 .25

King Hassan II, 50th Birthday — A190

1979, July 9   Photo.   Perf. 14
436 A190 1d multi   .60 .25

4th Arab Youth Festival, Rabat — A191

1979, July 30   Photo.   Perf. 13½x14
437 A191 1d multi   .60 .25

King Hassan II and Crowd — A192

1979, Aug. 20   Perf. 14x13½
438 A192 1d multi   .50 .25
Revolution of the King and the People, 25th anniv.

Intl. Bureau of Education, 50th Anniv. — A193

1979, Sept. 28   Photo.   Perf. 13x13½
439 A193 1d multi   .60 .25

Pilgrimage to Mecca, Mt. Arafat, Holy Ka'aba — A194

1979, Oct. 25   Perf. 13½
440 A194 1d multi   .65 .25

No. 413 Redrawn in Smaller Size and Ovptd. in Red

1979, Nov. 7   Litho.   Perf. 14
Size: 33x23mm
441 A172 40c multi   .55 .25
442 A172 1d multi   1.10 .40
Return of Oued Eddahab province, Aug. 14.

Leucanthemum Catanance — A195

1979, Nov. 21   Photo.   Perf. 14½
443 A195 40c Centaurium   .45 .25
444 A195 1d shown   1.20 .25

Children, Globe, IYC Emblem — A196

1979, Dec. 3   Perf. 14
445 A196 40c multi   .75 .30
International Year of the Child.

Otter — A197

1979, Dec. 18   Perf. 13½x13
446 A197 40d shown   .95 .25
447 A197 1d Redstart   2.00 .25

Traffic Signs and Road — A198

1980, Jan. 3   Photo.   Perf. 14
448 A198 40c shown   .25 .25
449 A198 1d Children at curb   .50 .25

Fortress — A199

1980, Jan. 29   Perf. 13x13½
450 A199 1d multi   .50 .25

Copper Bowl and Lid, Red Crescent — A200

Red Crescent Soc.: 70c, Copper kettle, brazier.

1980, Feb. 28   Photo.   Perf. 14
451 A200 50c multi   1.00 .25
452 A200 70c multi   1.50 .25
  a Pair, #451-452, vert. tête-bêche 2.60 2.60

Week of the Blind — A201

1980, Mar. 19   Photo.   Perf. 14
453 A201 40c multi   .45 .25

Rabat Mechanical Sorting Office — A202

1980, Apr. 17
454 A202 40c multi   .45 .25
Stamp Day.

Rotary Intl., 75th Anniv. — A203

1980, May 14   Photo.   Perf. 14
455 A203 1d multi   .55 .25

Cloth and Leather Goods — A204

1980, May 31   Photo.   Perf. 13½x13
456 A204 1d multi   .65 .25
4th Textile and Leather Exhibition, Casablanca, May 2-9.

Gypsum — A205

1980, June 19   Photo.   Perf. 13½x13
457 A205 40c multi   1.25 .25
See Nos. 477-478.

Falcon — A206

1980, July 26   Perf. 11½
458 A206 40c multi   1.90 .30
Hunting with falcons.

Fight against Heart Disease — A207

1980, Aug. 7   Photo.   Perf. 13x13½
459 A207 1d multi   .65 .25

A208

1980, Aug. 18   Perf. 14
460 A208 40c shown   .60 .25
461 A208 1d Emblems, diff.   1.10 .25
United Nations Decade for Women.

Ornamental Saddle and Harness — A209

40c, Saddle, harness, diff.

1980, Sept. 3   Perf. 14½
462 A209 40c multi   .35 .25
463 A209 1d shown   .90 .25

World Meteorological Day — A210

1980, Sept. 18
464 A210 40c multi   .55 .25

MOROCCO

Hand Holding Dry Gas Pump — A211

40c, Light bulb, gas can.

1980, Oct. 6   Photo.   Perf. 14
465 A211 40c multi   .30 .25
466 A211 1d shown   .65 .25

Energy conservation.

World Tourism Conference, Manila, Sept. 27 — A212

1980, Oct. 22   Perf. 11½x12
467 A212 40c multi   .45 .25

Symbolic Tree Rooted in Europe and Africa — A213

1980, Oct. 30   Perf. 14
468 A213 1d multi   .75 .25

Straits of Gibraltar linking Europe and Africa.

5th Anniversary of the Green March — A214

1980, Nov. 6
469 A214 1d multi   .65 .25

Holy Ka'aba — A215

1980, Nov. 9
470 A215 40c shown   .25 .25
471 A215 1d Mecca Mosque   .70 .25
   a. Souv. sheet of 2, #470-471   2.00 2.00

No. 471a sold for 3d.

Senecio Antheuphorbium A216

1980, Dec. 4   Perf. 13
472 A216 50c shown   1.00 .25
473 A216 1d Periploca laevigata   1.90 .50

Leaves, by Mahjoubi Aherdan — A217

Design: 40c. Untitled painting by Mahjoubi Aherdan (23x38mm).

1980, Dec. 18   Perf. 12
474 A217 40c multicolored   .30 .25
475 A217 1d multicolored   .75 .25

Nejjarine Fountain, Fes — A218

1981, Jan. 22   Perf. 14x13½
476 A218 40c multi   .35 .25

Mineral Type of 1980

1981, Feb. 19   Photo.   Perf. 13½x13
477 A205 40c Onyx   1.00 .25
478 A205 1d Malachite-azurite   2.25 .40

Inscribed 1980.

King Hassan II — A219

1981, Mar. 2   Perf. 14
479 A219 60c shown   .30 .25
480 A219 60c Map of Morocco   .30 .25
481 A219 60c King Mohammed V   .30 .25
   a. Strip of 3, #479-481   1.25 .75

25th anniv. of independence.

25th Anniv. of King Hassan II Coronation A220

1981, Mar. 3
482 A220 1.30d multi   .65 .25

The Source, by Jillali Gharbaoui A221

1981, Apr. 8   Perf. 13x12½
483 A221 1.30d multi   .75 .30

Anagalis Monelli — A222

70c, Bubonium intricatum.

1981, Apr. 23   Perf. 13
484 A222 40c shown   .60 .25
485 A222 70c multicolored   1.20 .25

See No. 1285a.

Army Badge — A223

Moroccan Armed Forces, 25th Anniv: No. 486, King Hassan II as army major general; No. 488, King Mohammed V.

1981, May 14   Photo.   Perf. 14x13½
486 A223 60c multi   .30 .25
487 A223 60c multi   .30 .25
488 A223 60c multi   .30 .25
   a. Strip of 3, #486-488   1.30 1.30

13th World Telecommunications Day — A224

1981, May 18   Perf. 14x13
489 A224 1.30d multi   .65 .25

Hand-painted Plate — A225

1981, June 5   Perf. 14
490 A225 50c shown   .35 .25
491 A225 1.30d Plate, diff.   .80 .25

Week of the Blind.

22nd Marrakesh Arts Festival — A226

1981, June 18   Perf. 13½x13
492 A226 1.30d multi   .90 .25

See No. 1284f. For overprint see No. 579.

Seboula Dagger, Oujda — A227

1981, Sept. 7   Photo.   Perf. 13½
493 A227 1.30d multi   .95 .25

Copper Mortar and Pestle, Red Crescent — A228

1981, Sept. 24   Perf. 14
494 A228 60c shown   .45 .25
495 A228 1.30d Tripod   1.10 .30

Intl. Year of the Disabled — A229

1981, Oct. 15   Perf. 13½
496 A229 60c multi   .55 .25

Iphiclides Feisthamelii — A230

1.30d, Zerynthia rumina.

1981, Oct. 29   Perf. 13½x13
497 A230 60c shown   2.00 .50
498 A230 1.30d multi   3.50 1.00

See Nos. 528-529.

6th Anniv. of Green March — A231

1981, Nov. 6   Perf. 13x13½
499 A231 1.30d multi   .55 .25

Intl. Palestinian Solidarity Day — A232

1981, Nov. 22   Perf. 13½x13
500 A232 60c multi   .55 .25

Congress Emblem A233

1981, Nov. 22   Perf. 13½
501 A233 1.30d multi   .65 .30

World Federation of Twin Cities, 10th Congress, Casablanca, Nov. 15-18.

Nos. 418-419 Surcharged

1981, Nov. 25   Photo.   Perf. 14½
502 A176 40c on 5c multi   6.75 4.75
   b. As #502, with second line of overprint replaced with first line of overprint (position 17)
502A A176 40c on 10c multi   5.25 3.00
   c. As #502A, with second line of overprint replaced with first line of overprint (position 17)

First Anniv. of Mohammed V Airport — A234

1981, Dec. 8   Photo.   Perf. 14x13
503 A234 1.30d multi   .65 .25

Al Massirah Dam Opening — A235

1981, Dec. 17   Perf. 11½
504 A235 60c multi   .40 .25

King Hassan II — A236

1981, Dec. 28   Perf. 13x12½
505 A236 5c multi   .25 .25
506 A236 10c multi   .25 .25
507 A236 15c multi   .25 .25
508 A236 20c multi   .25 .25

MOROCCO

509	A236	25c multi		.25	.25
510	A236	30c multi		.25	.25
511	A236	35c multi		.25	.25
512	A236	40c multi		.40	.25
513	A236	50c multi		.25	.25
514	A236	60c multi		.25	.25
515	A236	65c multi		.25	.25
516	A236	70c multi		.25	.25
a.	Perf 12x11¾, granite paper		8.50	.25
517	A236	75c multi		.25	.25
518	A236	80c multi		.30	.25
519	A236	90c multi		.50	.25

No. 516a is dated 1999 and has the denomination and "Postes" closer to the shoulder than to the chin.

1983, Mar. 1   Photo.   Perf. 14½
Size: 25x32mm

520	A236	1d multi	.30	.25
521	A236	1.40d multi	.40	.25
522	A236	2d multi	.45	.25
523	A236	3d multi	.75	.25
524	A236	5d multi	1.10	.45
524A	A236	10d multi	2.25	.80
e.	Perf 11½, granite paper	30.00	2.50
Nos. 505-524A (21)		9.45	6.00

No. 524Ae is dated 1999 and has the denomination and "Postes" closer to the shoulder than to the chin.
See Nos. 566-575, 715-724.

Coin Type of 1976
1979-81   Photo.   Perf. 12½
Size: 18x23mm

524B	A146	40c ocher & multi	.50	.25
d.	Bklt. pane of 10 with white pane selvage at left, right and bottom	6.00	
Complete booklet, #524Bd	—	
Complete booklet, 10 #524B	—	
524C	A146	50c brt bl, blk & dk brn ('81)	.95	.25
e.	Bklt. pane of 10	10.00	

Equestrian Sports — A237

1981, Dec. 29   Perf. 13x13½
525 A237 1.30d multi   1.25 .40

Traditional Carpet Design — A238

50c, Glaoua pattern. 1.30d, Ouled Besseba pattern.

1982, Jan. 21
526 A238 50c multi   .25 .25
527 A238 1.30d multi   .65 .25

Butterfly Type of 1981
60c, Celerio oken lineata. 1.30d, Mesoacidalia aglaja lyauteyi.

1982, Feb. 25   Perf. 13½x13
528 A230 60c multi   1.40 .45
529 A230 1.30d multi   3.25 .75

World Forest Day — A240

1982, Apr. 8   Perf. 14
531 A240 40c multi   .50 .25

Blind Week — A241

1982, May 10
532 A241 1d Jug   .50 .25

Folk Dancers, Rabat — A242

1982, June 3
533 A242 1.40d multi   .50 .25

Copper Candlestick, Red Crescent — A243

1982, July 1
534 A243 1.40d multi   .65 .25

Women in Traditional Clothing, by M. Mezian — A244

1982, Aug. 16   Photo.   Perf. 14
535 A244 1.40d multi   .65 .30

Natl. Census — A245

1982, Sept. 6   Photo.   Perf. 11½
536 A245 60c multi   .40 .25

ITU Conf., Nairobi, Sept. — A246

1982   Perf. 13½x13
537 A246 1.40d multi   .50 .25

TB Bacillus Centenary — A247

1982, Sept. 30
538 A247 1.40d multi   .90 .30

World Food Day — A248

1982, Oct. 16   Perf. 14
539 A248 60c multi   .55 .25

Unity Railroad — A249

1982, Nov. 6   Perf. 13x13½
540 A249 1.40d multi   1.10 .45

30th Anniv. of Arab Postal Union — A250

1982, Nov. 17   Perf. 14
541 A250 1.40d multi   .50 .25

Intl. Palestinian Solidarity Day — A251

1982, Nov. 29   Perf. 14
542 A251 1.40d sil & multi   .50 .25

Red Coral, Al-Hoceima — A252

1982, Dec. 20   Perf. 13½
543 A252 1.40d multi   1.25 .30

Stamp Day — A253

1983, Jan. 26   Perf. 13½x13
544 A253 1.40d Nos. 3, 178   .60 .25

Week of the Blind — A254

1983, Apr. 20   Photo.   Perf. 14
545 A254 1.40d multi   .65 .25

Popular Arts — A255

1983, June 27   Photo.   Perf. 14
546 A255 1.40d multi   .90 .25

Wrought-Iron Lectern — A256

1983, July 7   Litho.   Perf. 13½
547 A256 1.40d multi   .75 .25

Economic Commission for Africa, 25th Anniv. — A257

1983, July 18   Photo.   Perf. 14
548 A257 1.40d multi   .50 .25

Moroccan Flora — A258

1983, Aug. 1   Litho.   Perf. 14
549 A258 60c Tecoma   .75 .25
550 A258 1.40d Strelitzia   1.30 .30

Kings Mohammed V and Hassan II — A259

1983, Aug. 20   Litho.   Perf. 14
551 A259 80c multi   .45 .25
  a. Souvenir sheet of 1   2.25 2.25

King and People's Revolution, 30th Anniv.
No. 551a sold for 5 dinars.

Mediterranean Games — A260

80c, Stylized sportsmen. 1d, Emblem. 2d, Stylized runner, horiz.

1983, Sept. 3   Photo.   Perf. 14
552 A260 80c multi   .40 .25
553 A260 1d multi   .55 .30
554 A260 2d multi   1.60 .45
  a. Souv. sheet of 3, #552-554, imperf.   3.00 3.00
Nos. 552-554 (3)   2.55 1.00

No. 554a sold for 5d.

Touiza — A261

1983, Sept. 30   Photo.   Perf. 13
555 A261 80c Tractors   .45 .25

Palestinian Solidarity — A262

1983, Nov. 10   Photo.   Perf. 13½x13
556 A262 80c multi   .45 .25

MOROCCO

8th Anniv. of the Green March into Spanish Sahara — A263

1983, Nov. 17   *Perf. 13x13½*
557   A263   80c multi   .45   .25

Ouzoud Waterfall — A264

1983, Nov. 28   *Perf. 14*
558   A264   80c multi   .45   .25

Children's Day — A265

1983, Dec. 5   Photo.   *Perf. 13½x13*
559   A265   2d multi   .65   .25

Zemmouri Carpet — A266

Various carpets.

1983, Dec. 15   *Perf. 13½*
560   A266   60c multi   .45   .25
561   A266   1.40d multi   .90   .35

World Communications Year — A267

1983, Dec. 20   *Perf. 14*
562   A267   2d multi   1.20   .25

Twin Cities, Jerusalem and Fez — A268

1984, Jan. 16   Photo.   *Perf. 13x13½*
563   A268   2d multi   1.00   .25

Desert Fox — A269

2d, Jumping mouse, vert.

1984, Feb. 13   *Perf. 11½x12, 12x11½*
564   A269   80c shown   .90   .40
565   A269   2d multi   2.10   .75

King Hassan II Type of 1981

1984-88   Photo.   *Perf. 14½*
    Size: 25x32mm
566   A236   1.20d multi ('88)   .30   .25
567   A236   1.25d multi   .30   .25
568   A236   1.60d multi ('87)   .45   .25
569   A236   2.50d multi ('87)   .65   .35
570   A236   3.60d multi ('88)   1.25   .40
571   A236   4d multi   1.10   .65
    a.   Dated "1995"   45.00   8.50
572   A236   5.20d multi ('88)   1.75   .75
573   A236   6.50d multi ('87)   1.75   1.10
574   A236   7d multi ('87)   1.90   1.25
575   A236   8.50d multi ('87)   2.25   1.60
    Nos. 566-575 (10)   11.70   6.85

Dated 1986: 1.60d, 2.50d, 6.50d, 7d, 8.50d.
Issued: 1.20d, 3.60d, 5.20d, Dec. 26, 1988.

39th Anniv. of Arab League — A270

1984, May 24   *Perf. 14½x14*
578   A270   2d Emblem   .60   .25

No. 492 Overprinted

1984, June 12   *Perf. 13½x13*
579   A226   1.30d multi   .90   .25

25th Anniv. of Marrakesh Arts Festival.

Local Plants — A271

1984, June 13   *Perf. 14*
580   A271   80c Mentha viridis   .25   .25
581   A271   2d Aloe   .65   .25

See Nos. 602-603.

Week of the Blind — A272

1984, July 10   *Perf. 13x13½*
582   A272   80c Painted bowl   .50   .25

Red Crescent — A273

2d, Octagonal brass container.

1984, July 16   *Perf. 14*
583   A273   2d multi   .70   .35

1984 Summer Olympics — A274

1984, Aug. 8   *Perf. 13½x13*
584   A274   2d Sports   .90   .35

Intl. Child Victims' Day — A275

2d, Children held by dove.

1984, Aug. 22   *Perf. 14*
585   A275   2d multi   .75   .35

UPU Day — A276

1984, Oct. 9   Photo.   *Perf. 13½*
586   A276   2d multi   .60   .25

World Food Day — A277

1984, Oct. 16   *Perf. 14*
587   A277   80c multi   .50   .25

Intl. Civil Aviation Org., 40th Anniv. — A278

1984, Oct. 20   *Perf. 13½*
588   A278   2d multi   .80   .40

Green March, 9th Anniv. — A279

1984, Nov. 6   *Perf. 14*
589   A279   80c Scroll, text   .55   .25

Palestinian Solidarity — A281

2d, Arab Revolt flag, 1918-19.

1984, Nov. 29   *Perf. 13½*
591   A281   2d multi   1.00   .50

UN Human Rights Declaration, 36th Anniv. — A282

1984, Dec. 10   *Perf. 14*
592   A282   2d multi   .50   .25

Native Dogs — A283

1984, Dec. 21   Photo.   *Perf. 14*
593   A283   80c Aidi   .75   .25
594   A283   2d Sloughi   1.50   .50

UN Child Survival Campaign — A284

1985, Mar. 5   Photo.   *Perf. 14*
595   A284   80c Growth monitoring   .55   .25

1st SOS Children's Village in Morocco — A285

1985, Mar. 11   *Perf. 13x13½*
596   A285   2d multi   .65   .25

Sherifian Hand Stamp, 1892 — A287

1985, Mar. 25   Photo.   *Perf. 14*
597   A287   2d dl pink, blk & gray   .65   .25

Souvenir Sheet
Perf. 13½
598   Sheet of 6   3.75   3.75
  a.   A287 80c green, black & gray   .50   .40
  b.   A287 80c yellow, black & gray   .50   .40
  c.   A287 80c blue, black & gray   .50   .40
  d.   A287 80c red, black & gray   .50   .40
  e.   A287 80c purple, black & gray   .50   .40
  f.   A287 80c brown, black & gray   .50   .40

Stamp Day. #598 sold for 5d.
See #615-616, 633-634, 668-669, 684-685, 701-702, 733-734, 756-757, 790-791, 806-807, 821-822, 835-836, 906-907.

World Environment Day — A288

1985, June 5   *Perf. 13*
599   A288   80c Emblem, ecosystem   .55   .25

Susi Dancers from Marrakesh and Kutabia, Minaret — A289

1985, June 7   *Perf. 13x13½*
600   A289   2d multi   .95   .40

Folk Arts Festival. See No. 1284e.

Week of the Blind — A290

1985, June 24   *Perf. 14*
601   A290   80c Ceramic bowl   .50   .25

See type A316.

MOROCCO

Flower Type of 1984
1985, July 1
602 A271 80c Bougainvillea 1.10 .30
603 A271 2d Red hibiscus 1.90 .50

Berber Woman — A291

1985, July 15 *Perf. 14*
604 A291 2d multi 3.25 .50
Red Crescent Society.

6th Pan-Arab Games — A292
2d, Torch, emblem, map.

1985, Aug. 2 *Perf. 14½x13½*
605 A292 2d multi .90 .35

UN, 40th Anniv. — A293

1985, Oct. 7 *Perf. 13*
606 A293 2d multi 2.00 .75

Intl. Youth Year — A294

1985, Oct. 21
607 A294 2d multi 2.25 .75

Green March, 10th Anniv. — A295
2d, Commemorative medal.

1985, Nov. 6 *Perf. 14½x13½*
608 A295 2d multi .65 .25

Palestinian Solidarity — A296

1985, Nov. 29 *Perf. 13½*
609 A296 2d multi .80 .25

Butterflies — A297
80c, Euphydryas desfontainii. 2d, Colotis evagore.

1985, Dec. 16 *Photo. Perf. 14*
610 A297 80c multi 1.60 .65
611 A297 2d multi 4.00 1.60

Accession of King Hassan II, 25th Anniv. — A298

Perf. 13x13½, 13½x13
1986, Mar. 3 *Litho.*
612 A298 80c Natl arms, vert 50 .25
613 A298 2d shown 1.15 .60
  a. Souv. sheet of 2, #612-613, imperf. 1.75 1.75

26th Intl. Military Medicine and Pharmaceutical Congress — A299

1986, Mar. 24 *Photo. Perf. 14*
614 A299 2d multi .60 .45

Hand Stamp Type of 1985
Sherifian postal seals of Maghzen-Safi, 1892.

1986, Apr. 7
615 A287 80c orange & blk .30 .25
616 A287 2d green & blk .70 .30

Week of the Blind — A300

1986, Apr. 21
617 A300 1d multi 1.00 .35

1986 World Cup Soccer Championships, Mexico — A301
1d, Emblems, horiz. 2d, Soccer cup, emblems.

1986, May 31 *Perf. 13½*
618 A301 1d multi .60 .25
619 A301 2d multi 1.10 .35

Red Crescent Soc. — A302

1986, June *Perf. 14*
620 A302 2d multi 1.25 .50

Popular Arts — A303

1986, June
621 A303 2d Folk band, dancers 1.00 .30

Flowers — A304
1d, Warionia saharae. 2d, Mandragora autumnalis.

1986, July 21 *Photo. Perf. 14*
622 A304 1d multi 1.50 .35
623 A304 2d multi 2.75 .65

Intl. Peace Year — A305

1986, Aug. 4 *Perf. 13*
624 A305 2d multicolored .85 .40

18th Skydiving Championships — A306

1986, Aug. 18 *Perf. 13½x13*
625 A306 2d multicolored 1.40 .40

Horse Week — A307

1986, Oct. 10 *Perf. 13*
626 A307 1d multicolored 1.40 .25

Green March, 11th Anniv. — A308

1986, Nov. 6 *Photo. Perf. 14*
627 A308 1d multicolored .95 .25

World Food Day — A309

1986, Nov. 12
628 A309 2d multicolored .60 .40

Aga Khan Architecture Prize — A310

1986, Nov. 24 *Litho. Perf. 13*
629 A310 2d multicolored 2.50 .75

Operation Grain: One Million Hectares — A311

1986, Dec. 8
630 A311 1d multicolored .55 .25

Butterflies — A312
1d, Elphinstonia charlonia. 2d, Anthocharis belia.

1986, Dec. 22 *Perf. 14*
631 A312 1d multi 1.40 .65
632 A312 2d multi 3.50 1.60

Hand Stamp Type of 1985
Stamp Day: Sherifian postal seals of Maghzen-Tetouan, 1892.

1987, Jan. 26 *Photo.*
633 A287 1d blue & blk .60 .30
634 A287 2d red & black 1.20 .55

King Mohammed V, Flag, 1947 — A313
No. 636, King Hassan II, 1987.

1987, Apr. 9 *Photo. Perf. 13½x13*
635 A313 1d shown .50 .25
636 A313 1d multi .50 .25
  a. Souvenir sheet of 2, Nos. 635-636 1.40 1.40
Tangiers Conf., 40th anniv. #636a sold for 3d.

Red Crescent Society — A314

1987, May 1 *Photo. Perf. 14*
637 A314 2d Brass lamp .70 .35

UN Child Survival Campaign — A315
1d, Oral rehydration.

1987, May 25 *Perf. 12½x13*
638 A315 1d multi .55 .30
See No. 647.

MOROCCO

Week of the Blind — A316

1987, June 8   **Perf. 14**
639   A316   1d Porcelain cup   .45   .25

Flowering Plants — A317

1d, Zygophyllum fontanesii. 2d, Otanthus maritimus.

1987, July 6   **Photo.**
640   A317   1d multi   .55   .25
641   A317   2d multi   1.10   .55

See Nos. 661-662.

US-Morocco Diplomatic Relations, 200th Anniv. — A318

1987, July   **Litho & Engr.**
642   A318   1d lt bl, blk & scar   .50   .25

See United States No. 2349.

Give Blood — A319

2d, King Hassan II, map.

1987, Aug. 20   **Photo.**   **Perf. 13x13½**
643   A319   2d multi   .80   .45

Desert Costumes, the Sahara — A320

1d, Woman from Melhfa. 2d, Man from Derraa.

1987, Sept. 14   **Perf. 13**
644   A320   1d multi   1.00   .50
645   A320   2d multi   2.00   1.00

See Nos. 711-712, 740-741.

13th Intl. Cong. on Irrigation and Drainage — A321

1987, Sept. 21
646   A321   1d multi   .55   .30

UN Child Survival Type of 1987

1d, Universal immunization.

1987, Sept. 28
647   A315   1d multicolored   .55   .30

Congress on Mineral Industries, Marrakesh — A322

1987, Oct.   **Perf. 14**
648   A322   1d Azurite   1.40   .50
649   A322   2d Wulfenite   1.90   .75

See No. 769.

Green March, 12th Anniv. — A323

1987, Nov. 6   **Photo.**   **Perf. 14**
650   A323   1d multicolored   .55   .25

See Nos. 667, 683, 695, 727, 750, 769, 802, 820, 834, 848, 862, 885.

Royal Armed Forces Social Services Month — A324

1987, Nov. 13   **Perf. 13x12½**
651   A324   1d multicolored   .55   .25

Birds — A325

1d, Passer simplex saharae. 2d, Alectoris barbara.

1987, Dec. 1   **Litho.**   **Perf. 14**
652   A325   1d multi   1.10   .40
653   A325   2d multi   2.10   .75

Natl. Postage Stamp 75th Anniv. A326

Design: Postmark and Sherifian postage stamp (French Morocco) of 1912.

1987, Dec. 31   **Photo.**   **Perf. 14x13½**
654   A326   3d pale lil rose, blk & blue grn   .95   .50

Cetiosaurus Mogrebiensis A327

1988, Jan. 18   **Photo.**   **Perf. 13½**
655   A327   2d multicolored   3.50   .95

A328

1988, Feb. 16   **Litho.**   **Perf. 14**
656   A328   2d multicolored   .65   .45

Intl. Symposium on Mohammed V, Aug. 16-Nov. 20, 1987.

A329

Perf. 14½x13½
1988, Mar. 13   **Photo.**
657   A329   3d multi   1.00   .75

16th Africa Cup Soccer Championships.

Horse Week — A330

1988, Mar. 20   **Litho.**   **Perf. 14**
658   A330   3d multi   1.75   .75

Intl. Red Cross and Red Crescent Orgs., 125th Anniv. — A331

1988, Apr. 30   **Photo.**   **Perf. 12½x13**
659   A331   3d pink, blk & dark red   .95   .65

Week of the Blind — A332

1988, May 25   **Litho.**   **Perf. 14**
660   A332   3d Pottery bottle   .85   .60

Flower Type of 1987

No. 661, Citrullus colocynthis. No. 662, Calotropis procera.

1988, June 27   **Litho.**   **Perf. 14**
661   A317   3.60d multi   1.60   1.00
662   A317   3.60d multi   1.60   1.00

UN Child Survival Campaign — A333

1988, July 18   **Litho.**   **Perf. 12½x13**
663   A333   3d multi   1.50   1.00

1988 Summer Olympics, Seoul — A334

Perf. 14½x13½
1988, Sept. 17   **Litho.**
664   A334   2d multi   .65   .40

Birds — A335

1988, Oct. 26   **Litho.**   **Perf. 14**
665   A335   3.60d Grande outarde   1.75   .75
666   A335   3.60d Flamant rose   1.75   .75

Green March Anniv. Type of 1987

1988, Nov. 6
667   A323   2d multi   .65   .40

Green March, 13th anniv.

Hand Stamp Type of 1985

Sherifian postal seals of Maghzen-El Jadida, 1892: No. 668, Octagonal. No. 669, Circular.

1988, Nov. 22   **Photo.**   **Perf. 14**
668   A287   3d olive bister & blk   1.10   .60
669   A287   3d violet & blk   1.10   .60

Stamp Day.

Housing of the Ksours and Casbahs — A336

1989, Jan. 23   **Perf. 13x13½**
670   A336   2d multi   .65   .40

Royal Chess Federation, 25th Anniv. — A337

1989, Apr. 17   **Litho.**   **Perf. 14**
671   A337   2d multi   1.00   .40

Red Crescent Society — A338

1989, May 29   **Litho.**   **Perf. 14x13½**
672   A338   2d multi   1.10   .40

Week of the Blind — A339

1989, June 12   **Perf. 14**
673   A339   2d multi   .55   .40

MOROCCO

665

A340

No. 675, King Hassan II, diff.

1989, July 9   **Litho.**   **Perf. 13x13½**
674	A340	2d multi	.80	.40
675	A340	2d multi	.80	.40
a.		Souvenir sheet of 2, #674-675, imperf. & embossed	15.00	15.00

King Hassan II, 60th birthday. No. 675a sold for 5d.

Flowering Plants — A341

No. 676, Narcissus papyraceus. No. 677, Cerinthe major.

1989, Sept. 11   **Litho.**   **Perf. 14**
676	A341	2d multi	.80	.45
677	A341	2d multi	.80	.45

See Nos. 709-710, 742-743.

World Telecommunications Day — A342

1989, Sept. 25   **Perf. 13x12½**
678	A342	2d multicolored	.60	.45

13th World Congress on Fertility and Sterility — A343

1989, Oct. 6   **Perf. 14**
679	A343	2d multicolored	.60	.45

Birds — A344

1989, Oct. 16   **Perf. 14**
680	A344	2d Desert beater	.70	.45
681	A344	3d Gorget lark	1.00	.70

Interparliamentary Union, Cent. — A345

1989, Oct. 27
682	A345	2d multicolored	.65	.50

Green March Anniv. Type of 1987

1989, Nov. 6
683	A323	3d multicolored	.95	.75

Green March, 14th anniv.

Hand Stamp Type of 1985

Sherifian postal seals of Maghzen-Casablanca, 1892: 2d, Circular. 3d, Octagonal.

1990, Jan. 15   **Photo.**   **Perf. 14**
684	A287	2d orange & blk	.65	.45
685	A287	3d green & blk	1.00	.70

Maghreb Union, 1st Anniv. — A346

1990, Feb. 17   **Perf. 13½x14**
686	A346	2d multicolored	.60	.45
a.		Souv. sheet of one, perf. 13½	.95	.95

No. 686a sold for 3d.

3rd World Olive Day — A347

1990, May 14   **Litho.**   **Perf. 14**
688	A347	2d Olive press	.65	.45
689	A347	3d King Hassan II	1.00	.75

Week of the Blind — A348

1990, May 28   **Litho.**   **Perf. 14**
690	A348	2d multicolored	.70	.50

Red Crescent Society — A349

1990, June 11
691	A349	2d multicolored	.55	.35

Intl. Literacy Year — A350

1990, Sept. 17   **Litho.**   **Perf. 14**
692	A350	3d blk, yel grn & grn	1.10	.80

Birds — A351

1990, Oct. 26
693	A351	2d Tourterelle, vert.	1.10	.65
694	A351	3d Huppe fasciee	1.50	.95

Green March Anniv. Type of 1987

1990, Nov. 5
695	A323	3d multicolored	1.10	.80

Green March, 15th anniv.

Independence, 35th Anniv. — A353

1990, Nov. 18
696	A353	3d multicolored	1.20	.85

Dam — A354

1990, Nov. 26
697	A354	3d multicolored	1.20	.85

A355

1990, Dec. 28   **Litho.**   **Perf. 14**
698	A355	3d multicolored	.95	.70

Royal Academy of Morocco, 10th anniv.

A356

Opening of Postal Museum, 20th Anniv.: No. 699, Telegraph machine. No. 700, Horse-drawn mail carriage fording river.

1990, Dec. 31   **Litho.**   **Perf. 13½x13**
699	A356	2d multicolored	.65	.50
700	A356	3d multicolored	1.00	.75
a.		Souv. sheet of 2, #699-700, imperf.	2.10	2.10

No. 700a sold for 6d, has simulated perforations.

Hand Stamp Type of 1985

Sherifian postal seals of Maghzen-Rabat, 1892: 2d, Circular. 3d, Octagonal.

1991, Jan. 25   **Perf. 14**
701	A287	2d ver & blk	.65	.50
702	A287	3d blue & blk	.95	.70

A357

1991, Feb. 18
703	A357	3d multicolored	.85	.65

UN Development Program, 40th anniv.

A358

No. 705, Wearing business suit.

1991, Mar. 3   **Litho.**   **Perf. 14½x13**
704	A358	3d shown	1.40	.40
705	A358	3d multi	1.40	.40
a.		Souv. sheet of 2, #704-705, imperf.	3.50	2.75

Coronation of King Hassan II, 30th anniv. Nos. 704-705 exist tete beche. No. 705a has simulated perforations and sold for 10d.

A359

1991, Mar. 28   **Litho.**   **Perf. 14**
706	A359	3d multicolored	1.00	.75

Phosphate Mining, 70th anniv.

Week of the Blind — A360

1991, May 15   **Photo.**   **Perf. 14**
707	A360	3d multicolored	1.00	.75

Red Crescent Society — A361

1991, May 27   **Litho.**   **Perf. 14**
708	A361	3d multicolored	.95	.70

Flowering Plants Type of 1989

1991, June 27   **Litho.**   **Perf. 14**
709	A341	3d Pyrus mamorensis	.95	.70
710	A341	3d Cynara humilis	.95	.70

Desert Costumes Type of 1987

Costumes of Ouarzazate.

1991, July 31   **Photo.**
711	A320	3d Woman	1.00	.70
712	A320	3d Man	1.00	.70

King Hassan II Type of 1981

1991-98   **Photo.**   **Perf. 14½**
Size: 25x32mm
715	A236	1.35d multicolored	.45	.25
717	A236	1.70d multicolored	.40	.25
719	A236	2.30d multicolored	.50	.25
a.		Perf 11½, granite paper	12.50	.60
722	A236	5.50d multicolored	1.25	1.00
a.		Perf 11½, granite paper	17.50	1.40
723	A236	6d multicolored	1.25	.95
a.		Perf 11½, granite paper	21.00	1.50
724	A236	20d multicolored	5.00	3.50
		Nos. 715-724 (6)	8.85	6.20

Issued: 1.35d, Sept. 2; 1.70d, 1994; 2.30d, 6d, 1998.

Nos. 719a and 722a are dated 1999, and have the denomination and "Postes" closer to the shoulder than to the chin.

A362

1991, Sept. 23   **Litho.**   **Perf. 14**
725	A362	3d multicolored	.95	.70

19th World Congress on Roads, Marrakesh.

MOROCCO

A363

1991, Oct. 30 Litho.
726 A363 3d multicolored .95 .70
4th Session of the Council of Presidents of the Maghreb Arab Union.

Green March Anniv. Type of 1987
1991, Nov. 6 Photo. Perf. 14
727 A323 3d multicolored .95 .70
Green March, 16th anniv.

Birds — A364

1991, Nov. 20 Litho. Perf. 14
728 A364 3d Merops apiaster 1.90 .60
729 A364 3d Ciconia ciconia 1.90 .60
See Nos. 748-749.

Fight Against AIDS — A365

1991, Dec. 16
730 A365 3d multicolored 1.00 .80

Organization of the Islamic Conference, 20th Anniv. — A366

1991, Dec. 16
731 A366 3d multicolored .85 .65

African Tourism Year — A367

1991 Litho. Perf. 14
732 A367 3d multicolored .95 .75

Hand Stamp Type of 1985
Sherifian postal seals of Maghzen-Essaouira, 1892: No. 733, Circular. No. 734, Octagonal.
1992, Jan. 13
733 A287 3d olive & blk 1.00 .80
734 A287 3d purple & blk 1.00 .80

Intl. Space Year — A368

1992, Feb. 17
735 A368 3d multicolored .95 .75

Week of the Blind — A369

1992, Mar. 19 Photo. Perf. 14
736 A369 3d multicolored 1.00 .80

Red Crescent Society — A370

1992, Mar. 30
737 A370 3d multicolored 1.00 .80

Minerals — A371

1992, May 11 Litho. Perf. 14
738 A371 1.35d Quartz .75 .50
739 A371 3.40d Calcite 1.60 1.25

Desert Costumes Type of 1987
Costumes of Tata.
1992, May 25 Photo. Perf. 14
740 A320 1.35d Woman .55 .45
741 A320 3.40d Man 1.40 1.10

Flowering Plants Type of 1989
1.35d, Campanula afra. 3.40d, Thymus broussonetii.
1992, July 13
742 A341 1.35d multi .55 .45
743 A341 3.40d multi 1.40 1.10

A372

1992, July 24
744 A372 3.40d multicolored 1.40 1.10
1992 Summer Olympics, Barcelona.

Modes of Transportation and Communications, Map of Africa — A373

1992, Sept. 14 Litho. Perf. 14
745 A373 3.40d multicolored 1.55 .85

Expo '92, Seville — A374

1992, Oct. 12
746 A374 3.40d multicolored 1.55 .85

Discovery of America, 500th Anniv. — A375

1992, Oct. 12
747 A375 3.40d multicolored 1.55 .85

Bird Type of 1991
1992, Oct. 26 Litho. Perf. 14
748 A364 3d Gyps fulvus 1.60 .75
749 A364 3d Ganga cata, horiz. 1.60 .75

Green March Anniv. Type of 1987
1992, Nov. 6 Litho.
750 A323 3.40d multicolored 1.10 .85
Green March, 17th anniv.

Sherifian Post, Cent. — A377

Designs: 3.40d, Octagonal Sherifian postal seal, scroll, Sultan Moulay Hassan I. 5d, Scroll, various circular and octagonal Sherifian postal seals, Sultan.
1992, Nov. 22 Litho. Perf. 14
751 A377 1.35d multicolored .60 .25
752 A377 3.40d multicolored 1.00 .75
Size: 165x115mm
Imperf
753 A377 5d multicolored 2.25 1.10
Nos. 751-753 (3) 3.85 2.10

Intl. Conference on Nutrition, Rome — A378

1992, Dec. 7 Litho. Perf. 14
754 A378 3.40d multicolored 1.55 .85

Al Massira Airport, Agadir — A379

1992, Dec. 21 Litho. Perf. 14
755 A379 3.40d multicolored 1.40 .90

Hand Stamp Type of 1985
Sherifian postal seals of Maghzen-Tanger, 1892: 1.70, Circular. 3.80d, Octagonal.
1993, Jan. 29 Litho. Perf. 14
756 A287 1.70d green & black .50 .40
757 A287 3.80d orange & black 1.10 .90
Stamp Day.

Week of the Blind — A380

1993, Mar. 15 Litho. Perf. 14
758 A380 4.40d multicolored 1.40 1.10

World Meteorology Day — A381

1993, Mar. 23
759 A381 4.40d multicolored 1.40 1.10

Red Crescent Society — A382

1993, Apr. 26 Litho. Perf. 14
760 A382 4.40d multicolored 1.40 1.10

A383

1993, June 14
761 A383 4.40d multicolored 1.40 1.10
World Telecommunications Day.

Argania Spinosa — A384

1993, July 26 Litho. Perf. 14
762 A384 1.70d Extracting oil .70 .40
763 A384 4.80d Tree branch 1.90 1.10

A385

1993, Aug. 21
764 A385 4.80d multicolored 1.40 1.10
Prince Sidi Mohammed, 30th birthday.

Inauguration of the Hassan II Mosque — A386

1993, Aug. 30 Perf. 13
765 A386 4.80d multicolored 1.40 1.10

A387

1993, Sept. 30 Litho. Perf. 14
766 A387 4.80d multicolored 1.40 1.10
King and People's Revolution, 40th Anniv.

World Post Day — A388

1993, Oct. 15
767 A388 4.80d multicolored 1.40 1.10

MOROCCO

New Islamic University — A389

1993, Nov. 1   Litho.   *Perf. 14*
768   A389   4.80d multicolored   1.40   1.10

Green March Anniv. Type of 1987
1993, Nov. 6
769   A323   4.80d multicolored   1.40   1.10
Green March, 18th anniv.

Water Birds — A390

1993, Dec. 13   Litho.   *Perf. 14*
770   A390   1.70d Sarcelle marbree   .85   .35
771   A390   4.80d Foulque a crete   1.90   .95

Manifest of Independence, 50th Anniv. — A391

1994, Mar. 31   Litho.   *Perf. 14*
772   A391   4.80d multicolored   2.75   .95

A392

General Agreement on Tariffs and Trade (GATT), 1994 Summit, Marrakech — A393

No. 774Ab, 1.70d, like #773. c, 4.00d, like #774.

1994, Apr. 20   Litho.   *Perf. 14*
773   A392   1.70d multicolored   .55   .35
774   A393   4.80d multicolored   1.40   .90

Sheet of 2
Rouletted
774A   A393   #b.-c.   4.00   3.50

Buildings and background are all in shades of claret on Nos. 774b-774c. No. 773 has building and background in shades of green. No. 774 has black building with claret background. No. 774A sold for 10d.

Week of the Blind — A394

1994, May 9
775   A394   4.80d multicolored   3.50   1.25

Red Crescent Society — A395

1994, May 18
776   A395   4.80d multicolored   1.55   .95

Natl. Conference on Children's Rights — A396

4.80d, Boy, girl under sun.

1994, May 25
777   A396   1.70d shown   .55   .35
778   A396   4.80d multi   1.40   .95

1994 World Cup Soccer Championships, US — A397

1994, June 17   *Perf. 13*
779   A397   2.00   .75

King Hassan II, 65th Birthday — A398

Designs: 1.70d, Wearing business suit. 4.80d, Wearing traditional costume, vert.

1994   *Perf. 13x12½, 12½x13*
780   A398   1.70d multicolored   1.00   .35
781   A398   4.80d multicolored   2.50   1.10

A399

1994, June 27   *Perf. 12½x13*
782   A399   4.80d multicolored   1.90   .70
Intl. Olympic Committee, Cent.

A400

1994
783   A400   4.80d multicolored   1.35   .70
Death of Antoine de Saint-Exupery, 50th anniv.

Flowers — A401

1.70d, Chamaelon gummifer. 4.80d, Pancratium maritimum, vert.

1994   *Perf. 13x12½, 12½x13*
784   A401   1.70d multi   .75   .40
785   A401   4.80d multi   1.50   .75

Water Birds — A402

1.70d, Courlis a bec grele. 4.80d, Goeland d'audouin.

1994, Oct. 24   Photo.   *Perf. 13x13½*
786   A402   1.70d multi   1.60   .70
787   A402   4.80d multi   5.00   2.25

A403

Green March, 19th Anniv.: 4.80d, Marchers, map, inscription.

1994, Nov. 6   Litho.   *Perf. 12½*
788   A403   1.70d multicolored   .45   .35
789   A403   4.80d multicolored   1.25   .90

Hand Stamp Type of 1985
Sherifan postal seals of Maghzen-Marrakesh: 1.70d, Circular. 4.80d, Octagonal.

1994, Nov. 22   Litho.   *Perf. 12½*
790   A287   1.70d blue & black   .70   .35
791   A287   4.80d vermilion & black   1.55   .90
Stamp Day.

Week of the Blind — A404

1995, Feb. 27   Litho.   *Perf. 13½*
792   A404   4.80d multicolored   2.25   .90

Arab League, 50th Anniv. — A405

1995, Mar. 22   Litho.   *Perf. 13½*
793   A405   4.80d multicolored   1.55   .90

Red Crescent Society — A406

1995, Apr. 24   Litho.   *Perf. 13½x13*
794   A406   4.80d multicolored   1.55   .90

Flowers — A407

1995, May 29   Litho.   *Perf. 13½x13*
795   A407   2d Malva hispanica   .60   .40
796   A407   4.80d Phlomis crinita   1.60   .90

Birds — A408

1.70d, Coracias garrulus. 4.80d, Carduelis carduelis.

1995, Sept. 18   Litho.   *Perf. 13½x13*
797   A408   1.70d multi   .50   .35
798   A408   4.80d multi   1.25   .95
See Nos. 818-819, 832-833, 846-847.

FAO, 50th Anniv. — A409

1995, Oct. 16   Photo.   *Perf. 13½*
799   A409   4.80d multicolored   1.55   .95

UN, 50th Anniv. — A410

1.70d, "50," Moroccan, UN flags. 4.80d, Moroccan flag, UN emblem, map of Africa.

1995, Oct. 24   *Perf. 12½*
800   A410   1.70d multicolored   .85   .35
801   A410   4.80d multicolored   2.50   .95

Green March Anniv. Type of 1987 and

Green March, 20th Anniv. — A411

1995, Nov. 6   Photo.   *Perf. 12½*
802   A323   1.70d multicolored   .45   .35
803   A411   4.80d multicolored   1.25   .95

A412

Independence, 40th anniv.: 4.80d, Crown, national flag. 10d, King Mohammed V, crown over flag, King Hassan II.

1995, Nov. 18   Litho.   *Perf. 12½*
804   A412   4.80d multicolored   1.40   .95

Size: 112x83mm
Imperf
805   A412   10d multicolored   3.25   2.25

Hand Stamp Type of 1985
Sherifan postal seals of Maghzen-Meknes, 1892: 1.70d, Circular. 4.80d, Octagonal.

1995, Nov. 22   Photo.   *Perf. 12½*
806   A287   1.70d olive & black   .40   .30
807   A287   4.80d violet & black   1.10   .85
Stamp Day.

A413

MOROCCO

1996, Mar. 3   Litho.   Perf. 13½
808 A413 2d Natl. arms   .50 .40
809 A413 5.50d King Hassan II 1.40 1.05
Size: 134x86mm
Imperf
810 A413 10d Crown, King   3.25 1.90
Accession of King Hassan II, 35th anniv.

Traditional Crafts — A414

1996, Mar. 25   Photo.   Perf. 13½x13
811 A414 5.50d Pottery   1.40 1.10
812 A414 5.50d Copper   1.40 1.10

Flowers — A415

2d, Cleonia lusitanica. 5.50d, Tulipa sylvestris.

1996, Apr. 25
813 A415 2d multi   .55 .45
814 A415 5.50d multi   1.40 1.10

A416

King Hassan II: 2d, In uniform. 5.50d, Wearing traditional headpiece.

1996, May 14   Photo.   Perf. 13x13½
815 A416 2d multicolored   .60 .40
816 A416 5.50d multicolored 1.40 1.00
Royal Armed Forces, 40th anniv.

A417

1996, July 19   Photo.   Perf. 13½x13
817 A417 5.50d multicolored 1.40 1.10
1996 Summer Olympics, Atlanta.

Bird Type of 1995
2d, Pandion haliaetus. 5.50d, Egretta garzetta.

1996, Oct. 21   Photo.   Perf. 13½x13
818 A408 2d multi   1.40 .40
819 A408 5.50d multi   3.00 1.00

Green March Anniv. Type of 1987
1996, Nov. 6   Litho.   Perf. 13½
820 A323 5.50d multicolored 1.60 1.10
Green March, 21st anniv.

Hand Stamp Type of 1985
Sherifan postal seals of Maghzen-Fes, 1892: 2d, Circular. 5.50d, Octagonal.

1996, Nov. 22   Photo.   Perf. 13½
821 A287 2d orange & black   .50 .40
822 A287 5.50d green & black 1.50 1.10
Stamp Day.

UNICEF, 50th Anniv. — A418

1996, Dec. 11   Perf. 13x13½
823 A418 5.50d multicolored 1.60 1.10

Moroccan Pottery — A419

1997, Feb. 24   Photo.   Perf. 13x13½
824 A419 5.50d multicolored 1.60 1.10

Flowers — A420

2d, Lupinus luteus. 5.50d, Silybum marianum.

1997, Mar. 24   Photo.   Perf. 13½x13
825 A420 2d multi   .60 .25
826 A420 5.50d multi   1.90 .50

A421

Speakers, 1947: No. 827, Crown Prince Hassan. No. 828, Sultan Mohammed V.

1997, Apr. 9   Litho.   Perf. 13½x13
827 A421 2d multicolored   .70 .25
828 A421 2d multicolored   .70 .25
Speech in Tangier by King Hassan II, 50th anniv.

World Reading and Copyright Day — A422

1997, Apr. 23
829 A422 5.50d multicolored 1.40 .70

Intl. Meeting on Ibn Battuta (1304-77?), Traveler and Writer — A423

1997, May 9   Perf. 13x13½
830 A423 5.50d multicolored 1.40 .70

Moroccan Copper — A424

1997, July 21   Photo.   Perf. 13½
831 A424 5.50d multicolored 1.40 .65

Bird Type of 1995
Designs: 2d, Anthropoides virgo. 5.50d, Parus caeruleus ultramarinus.

1997, Oct. 20   Photo.   Perf. 13½x13
832 A408 2d multicolored   .60 .25
833 A408 5.50d multicolored 1.75 .70

Green March Anniv. Type of 1987
1997, Nov. 6   Perf. 13½
834 A323 5.50d multicolored 1.35 .70
Green March, 22nd anniversary.

Hand Stamp Type of 1985
Sherifan postal seals of Maghzen-Larache, 1892: 2d, Circular. 5.50d, Octagonal.

1997   Photo.   Perf. 13½
835 A287 2d blue & black   .55 .25
836 A287 5.50d vermilion & black 1.40 .70

Flowers — A425

2.30d, Rhus pentaphylla. 6d, Orchis papilionacea.

1998   Photo.   Perf. 13½x13
837 A425 2.30d multi   .65 .30
838 A425 6d multi   1.60 .80

A426

1998
839 A426 6d multicolored   1.60 .80
25th Intl. Road Transportation Congress.

Copper Ornament — A427

1998
840 A427 6d multicolored   1.40 .70

A428

1998
841 A428 6d multicolored   1.60 .80
1998 World Cup Soccer Championships, France.

Pottery — A429

1998   Perf. 13x13½
842 A429 6d multicolored   1.75 .90

Intl. Year of the Ocean — A430

1998
843 A430 6d multicolored   1.60 .80

King & People's Revolution, 45th Anniv. — A431

1998
844 A431 6d multicolored   1.60 .80

World Stamp Day — A432

1998   Photo.   Perf. 13½x13
845 A432 6d multicolored   1.60 .80

Bird Type of 1995
Designs: 2.30d, Luscinia megarhynchos. 6d, Struthio camelus.

1998   Photo.
846 A408 2.30d multicolored .75 .35
847 A408 6d multicolored   1.75 .90

Green March Anniv. Type
1998, Nov. 6   Perf. 13½
848 A323 6d multicolored   1.75 .90
Green March, 23rd anniv.

Public Liberties, 40th Anniv. — A433

1998   Litho.   Perf. 13½x13
849 A433 6d multicolored   1.60 .80

A434

1998   Photo.
850 A434 6d multicolored   1.60 .80
Universal Declaration of Human Rights, 50th anniv.

World Theater Day — A435

1999   Litho.   Perf. 13¼
851 A435 6d multi   1.60 .80

Flora — A436

2.30d, Eryngium triquetrum. 6d, Viscum cruciatum.

1999
852 A436 2.30d multi   .60 .30
853 A436 6d multi   1.50 .75

MOROCCO

Bab Mansour Laalej A437

1999   Perf. 13x13¼
854   A437   6d multi   1.60   .85

Jewelry — A438

1999   Perf. 13¼
855   A438   6d multi   1.60   .85

A439

1999
856   A439   2.30d On throne   .60   .30
857   A439   6d in robes   1.50   .75
   a.   Souvenir sheet, #856-857, imperf., without gum   2.60   1.25

King Hassan II, 70th birthday.

World Environment Day — A440

1999
858   A440   6d multi   1.50   .75

UPU, 125th Anniv. — A441

1999, Oct. 9   Photo.   Perf. 13¼
859   A441   6d multi   1.40   .70

FAO Medal Awarded by King Hassan II — A442

1999, Oct. 16
860   A442   6d multi   1.75   .70
See No. 964.

Anti-poverty Week — A443

1999, Nov. 11   Photo.   Perf. 11¾
    Granite Paper
861   A443   6d multi   1.40   1.00
Compare with type A461.

Green March Anniv. Type of 1987
1999, Nov. 6   Photo.   Perf. 13¼
862   A323   6d multi   1.50   .60
Green March, 24th anniv.

Fish — A444

Designs: 2.30d, Diplodus cervinus. 6d, Lampris guttatus.

1999, Nov. 29   Photo.   Perf. 13¼
863   A444   2.30d multi   .70   .25
864   A444   6d multi   1.50   .75

Miniature Sheet

Morocco Year in France — A445

No. 865: a, Stork on nest. b, People in robes. c, Mandolin, pillars. d, Boat at dock.

1999, Dec. 13   Perf. 13¼x13
865   A445   Sheet of 4   6.25   3.00
   a.-d.   6d Any single   1.50   .75

African Cup Soccer Tournament A446

2000, Jan. 25   Perf. 11¾x11½
    Granite Paper
866   A446   6d multi   1.60   .85

Year 2000 — A447

2000, Jan. 31   Granite Paper
867   A447   6d multi   1.60   .85

Reconstruction of Agadir, 40th Anniv. — A448

2000, Feb. 29   Photo.   Perf. 11¾
    Granite Paper
868   A448   6.50d multi   1.75   .90

Islamic Development Bank — A449

2000, Mar. 6   Photo.   Perf. 11¾x11½
    Granite Paper
869   A449   6.50d multi   1.75   .90

Natl. Day of the Handicapped A450

2000, Mar. 30   Granite Paper
870   A450   6.50d multi   1.75   .90

Flora — A451

Designs: 2.50d, Jasione montana. 6.50d, Pistorica breviflora.

2000, Apr. 27   Photo.   Perf. 11¾
    Granite Paper
871-872   A451   Set of 2   2.75   1.25

World Meteorological Organization, 50th Anniv. — A452

2000, May 15   Granite Paper
873   A452   6.50d multi   1.75   .90

Marrakesh Arts Festival A453

2000, June 5   Photo.   Perf. 11¾
    Granite Paper
874   A453   6.50d multi   1.75   .90

Intl. Peace Year — A454

2000   Photo.   Perf. 11¾
    Granite Paper
875   A454   6.50d multi   1.75   .90

Enthronement of King Mohammed VI, 1st Anniv. — A455

King in: 2.50d, Business suit. 6.50d, Robe.

2000, July 30   Photo.   Perf. 11¾
    Granite Paper
877-878   A455   Set of 2   2.25   1.10
878a   Souvenir sheet of 2, #877-878, imperf.   3.50   1.75
No. 878a sold for 10d.

Intl. Festival, Volubilis — A456

2000, Sept. 8   Perf. 11¾
    Granite Paper
879   A456   6.50d multi   2.10   1.75

2000 Summer Olympics, Sydney — A457

2000, Sept. 15   Granite Paper
880   A457   6.50d multi   2.10   1.75

SOS Children's Villages — A458

2000, Oct. 12   Granite Paper
881   A458   6.50d multi   1.90   .90

World Teacher's Day — A459

2000, Oct. 25   Photo.   Perf. 11¾
    Granite Paper
882   A459   6.50d multi   1.90   .90

Anti-poverty Week A461

2000, Nov. 1   Photo.   Perf. 11¾
    Granite Paper
884   A461   6.50d multi   1.90   .90

Compare with type A443. Value is for stamp with surrounding selvage. See Nos. 911, 928, 953, 997, 1027, 1048, 1076, 1098, 1117, 1144, 1159.

MOROCCO

Green March Anniv. Type of 1987 and

Map and Inscription — A462

2000, Nov. 6   **Photo.**   *Perf. 11¾*
Granite Paper
885   A323   2.50d multi   .75   .25
886   A462   6.50d multi   1.90   .90
Green March, 25th anniv.

Antoine de Saint-Exupéry (1900-44), Aviator, Writer — A463

2000, Nov. 13   **Photo.**   *Perf. 11¾*
Granite Paper
887   A463   6.50d multi   2.25   .90

Independence, 45th Anniv. — A464

2000, Nov. 18   **Granite Paper**
888   A464   6.50d multi   1.75   .90

Fish — A465

Designs: 2.50d, Apogon imberbis. 6.50d, Scorpaena loppei.

2000, Dec. 25   **Granite Paper**
889-890   A465   Set of 2   3.25   1.40

El Gharbi Gate — A466

2001, Mar. 22   **Photo.**   *Perf. 11¾*
Granite Paper
891   A466   6.50d multi   1.90   1.10

World Water Day — A467

2001, Mar. 30   **Granite Paper**
892   A467   6.50d multi   1.90   1.10

Armed Forces, 45th Anniv. — A468

Designs: 2.50d, Soldier and insignia. 6.50d, Soldier in frame.

2001, May 16   **Litho.**   *Perf. 14¼x13¾*
893-894   A468   Set of 2   2.60   1.40

Flora — A469

Designs: 2.50d, Euphorbia rigida. 6.50d, Glaucium flavum.

2001, June 7   **Photo.**   *Perf. 11¾*
Granite Paper
895-896   A469   Set of 2   4.00   2.00

Houses of Worship — A470

Designs: 2.50d, Koekelberg Basilica, Belgium. 6.50d, Hassan II Mosque, Casablanca.

2001, June 10   **Granite Paper**
897-898   A470   Set of 2   3.50   1.60
See Belgium Nos. 1855-1856.

Natl. Diplomacy Day — A471

Perf. 14¼x13¾
2001, June 29   **Litho.**
899   A471   6.50d multi   1.90   .80

A472   A473

A474

King Mohammed VI A475

Perf. 12¾x13¼, 13¼x12¾
2001, July 31   **Litho.**
Size: 24x33mm
900   A472   2.50d multi   .65   .25
901   A473   6d multi   1.60   .60
902   A474   6.50d multi   1.75   .65
Size: 32x24mm
Arms 14mm Tall
903   A475   10d multi   3.00   1.00
     Nos. 900-903 (4)   7.00   2.50
Compare type A472 with type A687; type A473 with types A572 and A688; type A475 with type A573.
See Nos. 934A-934B, 940-943, 960-962, 1007A-1007B, 1020, 1029A.

Marine Life — A476

Designs: 2.50d, Lophius budegassa. 6.50d, Monachus monachus, horiz.

2001, Sept. 28   **Litho.**   *Perf. 11¾*
Granite Paper
904-905   A476   Set of 2   2.50   1.05

Hand Stamp Type of 1985

Hand stamps of Ksar el Kebir, 1892: 2.50d, Round. 6.50d, Octagonal.

2001, Oct. 9   **Litho.**   *Perf. 14¼x13¾*
906   A287   2.50d olive & black   .70   .25
907   A287   6.50d violet & black   1.75   .70

World Day to Combat Desertification — A477

2001, Oct. 29   *Perf. 13¼*
908   A477   6.50d multi   1.55   .70

7th UN Climate Change Conference — A478

2001, Oct. 29
909   A478   6.50d multi   1.55   .70

Green March, 26th Anniv. — A479

2001, Nov. 7   **Photo.**   *Perf. 13x13¼*
910   A479   6.50d multi   1.55   .70

Anti-Poverty Week Type of 2000 and

Anti-Poverty Week — A480

2001, Nov. 8   *Perf. 12½*
911   A461   6.50d multi   1.75   .70
        Perf. 13x13¼
912   A480   6.50d multi   1.75   .70
Value of No. 911 is for stamp with surrounding selvage.

Year of Dialogue Among Civilizations — A481

2001, Dec. 14   *Perf. 13¼x13*
913   A481   6.50d multi   1.55   .70

Fountains — A482

Designs: 2.50d, Wallace Fountain, Paris. 6.50d, Nejjarine Fountain, Fez.

2001, Dec. 14   *Perf. 13¼*
914-915   A482   Set of 2   2.50   .95
See No. 963. See France Nos. 2847-2848.

Chellah Gate — A483

2002, Feb. 28   *Perf. 13x13¼*
916   A483   6.50d multi   1.75   .70

Intl. Women's Day — A484

2002, Mar. 8   *Perf. 13¼x13*
917   A484   6.50d multi   1.75   .70

Cedar Tree — A485

2002, Mar. 29
918   A485   6.50d multi   2.00   1.00

2nd World Assembly on the Elderly — A486

2002, Apr. 30   *Perf. 13x13¼*
919   A486   6.50d multi   1.75   .70

Special Session of UN General Assembly on Children — A487

2002, May 8   *Perf. 13¼x13*
920   A487   6.50d multi   2.00   1.00
Dated 2001.

Flora — A488

Designs: 2.50d, Linaria bipartita. 6.50d, Verbascum pseudocreticum.

2002, June 5   **Photo.**   *Perf. 13¼x13*
921-922   A488   Set of 2   3.25   .90

Intl. Telecommunications Union Plenipotentiary Conference, Marrakesh — A489

2002, Sept. 23   **Photo.**   *Perf. 13¼*
923   A489   6.50d multi   1.75   .70

MOROCCO

Size: 120x90mm
Imperf
Without Gum
924 A489 10d multi   3.25 1.60

Palestinian Intifada — A490

2002, Sept. 28   **Perf. 13¼**
925 A490 6.50d multi   6.00 6.00

Intl. Year of Ecotourism A491

2002, Sept. 30
926 A491 6.50d multi   1.75 .80

Green March, 27th Anniv. — A492

2002, Nov. 7
927 A492 6.50d multi   2.00 1.00

Anti-Poverty Week Type of 2000 and

Anti-Poverty Week — A493

2002, Nov. 8   **Perf. 12½**
928 A461 6.50d multi   1.50 .80
   Perf. 13¼
929 A493 6.50d multi   1.50 .80
Value of No. 928 is for stamp with surrounding selvage.

Maghzen Post, 110th Anniv. — A494

Sultan Moulay Hassan I and: 2.50d, Circular postal seal. 6.50d, Octagonal postal seal.

2002, Nov. 22   **Perf. 12½, 13 (6.50d)**
930-931 A494 Set of 2   2.60 1.00
Value of Nos. 930-931 are for stamps with surrounding selvage. No. 931 is octagonally shaped.

UN Year for Cultural Heritage — A495

2002, Dec. 18   **Perf. 13¼x13**
932 A495 6.50d multi   1.90 .80

Fish — A496

Designs: 2.50d, Alosa alosa. 6.50d, Epinephelus marginatus.

2002, Dec. 30   **Perf. 13¼**
933-934 A496 Set of 2   3.25 1.00

King Mohammed VI Type of 2001
2002   **Litho.**   **Perf. 11½**
Granite Paper
Size: 24x30mm
934A A472 2.50d multi   .85 .40
934B A473 6d multi   2.25 1.10

Bab el Okla, Tetuan — A497

2003, Feb. 28   **Photo.**   **Perf. 13¼**
935 A497 6.50d multi   1.75 .80

Fir Trees — A498

2003, Mar. 28
936 A498 6.50d multi   2.00 1.00

Intl. Year of Fresh Water — A499

2003, Apr. 28   **Perf. 13¼x13**
937 A499 6.50d multi   1.90 .80

Flora — A500

Designs: 2.50d, Limonium sincatum. 6.50d, Echinops spinosus.

2003, May 30   **Perf. 13¼**
938-939 A500 Set of 2   3.00 1.40

King Mohammed VI Type of 2001
2003   **Litho.**   **Perf. 13¼x12¾**
940 A475 70c lt bl & multi   .25 .25
941 A475 80c pur & multi   .25 .25
942 A475 5d yel & multi   1.60 .55
943 A475 20d lil & multi   6.75 2.25
   Nos. 940-943 (4)   8.85 3.30
Coat of arms on Nos. 940 and 941 is 14mm tall. See Nos. 1007A-1007B for stamps with coat of arms 11mm tall.

Salé Grand Mosque, 1000th Anniv. A501

2003, July 11   **Photo.**   **Perf. 13x12¼**
944 A501 6.50d multi   2.00 1.00

World Youth Congress — A502

2003, Aug. 12   **Perf. 13¼**
945 A502 6.50d multi   2.00 1.00

Revolution of the King and People, 50th Anniv. — A503

2003, Aug. 20
946 A503 6.50d multi   2.00 1.00

King Mohammed VI, 40th Birthday — A504

Designs: Nos. 947, 949a, 2.50d, King in suit and tie. Nos. 948, 949b, 6.50d, King in robe.

2003, Aug. 21
947-948 A504 Set of 2   2.75 1.60
Souvenir Sheet
Stamps With Pink Frames
949 A504 Sheet of 2, #a-b   3.25 3.25
No. 949 sold for 10d.
Compare with type A545.

Fish — A505

Designs: 2.50d, Sparisoma cretense. 6.50d, Anthias anthias.

2003, Sept. 30   **Photo.**   **Perf. 13¼**
950-951 A505 Set of 2   3.25 1.75

World Post Day — A506

2003, Oct. 9
952 A506 6.50d multi   2.00 1.00

Anti-Poverty Week Type of 2000 and

King Mohammed VI Visiting Sick Child — A507

2003, Oct. 31   **Photo.**   **Perf. 12¾**
953 A461 6.50d multi   1.90 .95
954 A507 6.50d multi   1.90 .95

Green March, 28th Anniv. — A508

2003, Nov. 5   **Photo.**   **Perf. 13¼**
955 A508 6.50d multi   2.00 1.00

Rabat, 2003 Arab Culture Capital A509

2003, Dec. 19   **Litho.**   **Perf. 13x13¼**
956 A509 6.50d multi   2.25 1.10

Philately at School — A510

2003, Dec. 29   **Perf. 13¼**
957 A510 6.50d multi   2.25 1.10

UN Literacy Decade A511

2003, Dec. 29   **Perf. 13x13¼**
958 A511 6.50d multi   2.00 1.00

Morocco - People's Republic of China Diplomatic Relations, 45th Anniv. A512

2003, Dec. 31   **Perf. 12**
959 A512 6.50d multi   2.00 1.00

Types of 2001 Redrawn With Added Frame Lines
2002-03   **Litho.**   **Perf. 11½**
Size: 24x30mm
960 A474 6.50d multi   2.75 2.75
Size: 32x23mm
Arms 11mm Tall
961 A475 10d multi   4.50 4.50
Booklet Stamps
Self-Adhesive
Serpentine Die Cut 11
Size: 20x23mm
962 A472 2.50d multi ('03)   .85 .45
   a. Booklet pane of 10   8.50
963 A482 6.50d Like #915 ('03)   2.00 1.10
   a. Booklet pane of 10   20.00
Issued: 6.50d, 10d, 2002. 2.50d, 6.50d, 9/3/03.
On No. 903, arms are 9mm tall.

FAO Medal Type of 1999
2003, July   **Photo.**   **Perf. 13x13¼**
Size: 48x38mm
964 A442 6d multi   3.25 3.25

Ibn Battutah (1304-68), Traveler and Author A513

2004, Feb. 24   **Photo.**   **Perf. 13x12¼**
965 A513 6.50d multi   2.25 1.10

Bab Agnaou, Marrakesh — A514

2004, Mar. 18   **Perf. 13¼**
966 A514 6.50d multi   2.00 1.00

MOROCCO

Flowers — A515

Designs: 2.50d, Linaria gharbensis. 6.50d, Nigella damascena.

2004, Mar. 29
967-968 A515 Set of 2 2.75 1.25

16th World Military Equestrian Championships, Témara — A516

2004, Apr. 18
969 A516 6.50d multi 2.25 1.10

Hassan II Tennis Grand Prix, 20th Anniv. — A517

2004, May 14
970 A517 6.50d multi 2.25 1.00

10th World Sacred Music Festival, Fez — A518

2004, May 28 *Perf. 12¼x13*
971 A518 6.50d multi 2.25 1.10

Caftan — A519

2004, June 18 *Perf. 13¼*
972 A519 6.50d multi 2.00 1.00

Dinosaur Fossils Found in Tazouda — A520

2004, July 12
973 A520 6.50d multi 2.25 1.10

30th Intl. Military History Congress — A521

2004, July 29
974 A521 6.50d multi 2.25 1.10

Enthronement of King Mohammed VI, 5th Anniv. — A522

Designs: Nos. 975, 977a, 2.50d, King in suit. Nos. 976, 977b, 6d, King in robe.

2004, July 30
975-976 A522 Set of 2 2.75 2.75
Souvenir Sheet
Stamps With Yellow Frames
977 A522 Sheet of 2, #a-b 3.75 3.75
No. 977 sold for 10d.

Intl. Peace Day — A523

2004, Sept. 21 *Photo.* *Perf. 13¼*
978 A523 6d multi 1.90 .95

Anti-Poverty Week Type of 2000 and

Anti-Poverty Week — A524

2004, Oct. 22 *Perf. 12¾*
979 A461 6.50d multi 2.00 1.00
Perf. 13¼
980 A524 6.50d multi 2.00 1.00
Value for No. 979 is for stamp with surrounding selvage.

Green March, 29th Anniv. — A525

2004, Nov. 6 *Photo.* *Perf. 13¼*
981 A525 6d multi 2.00 1.00

Marine Life — A526

Designs: 2.50d, Xiphias gladius. 6.50d, Octopus vulgaris.

2004, Nov. 16 *Photo.* *Perf. 13¼*
982-983 A526 Set of 2 3.25 1.40

World Children's Day — A527

2004, Nov. 24
984 A527 6.50d multi 2.00 1.00

Rotary International, Cent. — A528

2005, Feb. 23 *Perf. 13x13¼*
985 A528 6.50d multi 2.00 1.00

Arab League, 60th Anniv. — A529

2005, Mar. 22 *Perf. 13¼x13*
986 A529 6.50d multi 2.00 1.00

Bab Boujloud, Fez — A530

2005, Mar. 30 *Perf. 13¼*
987 A530 6.50d multi 2.00 1.00

Amnesty International — A531

2005, May 6 *Photo.* *Perf. 13¼*
988 A531 6.50d multi 2.00 1.00

Flora — A532

Designs: 2.50d, Erodium sebaceum. 6.50d, Linaria ventricosa.

2005, May 26 *Photo.* *Perf. 13¼*
989-990 A532 Set of 2 2.75 1.10

Rock Carvings, Iourarhane A533

2005, May 31
991 A533 6.50d multi 2.00 1.00

13th World Neurosurgery Congress, Marrakesh — A534

2005, June 19
992 A534 6.50d multi 2.00 1.00

Phosphates Office, 80th Anniv. — A535

2005, Aug. 31 *Photo.* *Perf. 13¼*
993 A535 6.50d multi 2.00 1.00

United Nations, 60th Anniv. — A536

2005, Oct. 24
994 A536 6.50d multi 2.00 1.00

Green March, 30th Anniv. — A537

Marchers and "30" in: 2.50d, Light blue. 6d, Green.

2005, Nov. 6
995-996 A537 Set of 2 2.75 2.75

Anti-Poverty Week Type of 2000 and

Anti-Poverty Week — A538

2005, Nov. 7 *Perf. 12¾*
997 A461 6.50d multi 2.00 1.00
Perf. 13¼
998 A538 6.50d multi 2.00 1.00
Values for No. 997 are for stamps with surrounding selvage.

Friendship of Morocco and the Netherlands, 400th Anniv. — A539

Designs: No. 999, 6.50d, Five tourist attractions. No. 1000, 6.50d, Arch and waterway, vert.

2005, Nov. 14 *Perf. 13¼*
999-1000 A539 Set of 2 4.00 1.90

World Summit on the Information Society, Tunis — A540

2005, Nov. 16
1001 A540 6d multi 2.10 1.05

Return from Exile of King Mohammed V, 50th Anniv. — A541

Country name in: No. 1002, Red. No. 1003a, Green.

2005, Nov. 16 *Perf. 13¼x13*
1002 A541 6.50d multi 2.00 1.00

MOROCCO

Souvenir Sheet
1003	Sheet, #1002, 1003a		4.00	2.25
a.	A541 6.50d multi		1.75	.75

Souvenir Sheet

Children's Art — A542

No. 1004: a, Children and flower, by Kaoutar Azizi Alaoui. b, Children and dove, by Sara Bourquiba. c, House and trees, by Mohcine Kahyouchat. d, Sun on horizon, by Anise Anico.

2005, Nov. 21   *Perf. 13x13¼*
1004	A542 2.50d Sheet of 4, #a-d		4.00	2.75

Intl. Year of Microcredit — A543

2005, Nov. 30   *Perf. 13¼*
1005	A543 6.50d multi		2.00	1.00

Marine Life — A544

Designs: 2.50d, Sparus aurata. 6d, Sepia officinalis.

2005, Dec. 22
1006-1007	A544	Set of 2	2.75	1.00

King Mohammed VI Type of 2001 Redrawn With Smaller Coat of Arms

2005   *Litho.*   *Perf. 11½*
Coat of Arms 11mm Tall
1007A	A475 70c multi		5.00	1.00
1007B	A475 80c multi		5.00	1.00

Nos. 1007A and 1007B are dated 2005. Coat of arms is 14mm tall on Nos. 940 and 941.

King Mohammed VI — A545

Designs: No. 1008, King in suit and tie. No. 1009, King in robe.

2005   *Litho.*   *Serpentine Die Cut 11*
Booklet Stamps
Self-Adhesive
1008	A545 2.50d multi		.75	.75
1009	A545 2.50d multi		.75	.75
a.	Booklet pane, 5 each #1008-1009		7.50	

Compare type A545 with A504. See Nos. 1054A-1054B.

Bustard A546

Melierax Metabates A547

Egretta Garzetta A548

Alectoris Barbara A550

Carduelis Carduelis A552

Duck A554

Self-Adhesive

2005   *Serpentine Die Cut 11*
1010	Booklet pane of 10		8.50	
a.	A546 2.50d multi		.85	.40
b.	A547 2.50d multi		.85	.40
c.	A548 2.50d multi		.85	.40
d.	A549 2.50d multi		.85	.40
e.	A550 2.50d multi		.85	.40
f.	A551 2.50d multi		.85	.40
g.	A552 2.50d multi		.85	.40
h.	A553 2.50d multi		.85	.40
i.	A554 2.50d multi		.85	.40
j.	A555 2.50d multi		.85	.40

Two Women A556

Saharaoui Derraa A558

Citadin A560

Tata Woman A562

Meknassa A564

Ait Mouhad A557

Two Women A559

Saharaoui Melhfa A561

Tata Man A563

Mokhazni du Roi A565

Self-Adhesive

2005   *Serpentine Die Cut 11*
1011	Booklet pane of 10		20.00	
a.	A556 6d multi		2.00	1.10
b.	A557 6d multi		2.00	1.10
c.	A558 6d multi		2.00	1.10
d.	A559 6d multi		2.00	1.10
e.	A560 6d multi		2.00	1.10
f.	A561 6d multi		2.00	1.10
g.	A562 6d multi		2.00	1.10
h.	A563 6d multi		2.00	1.10
i.	A564 6d multi		2.00	1.10
j.	A565 6d multi		2.00	1.10

Pandion Haliaetus A549

Porphyrio Porphyrio A551

Bird A553

Falcon A555

Traffic Safety Day — A566

2006, Feb. 18   *Photo.*   *Perf. 13½x13*
1012	A566 6.50d multi		2.00	1.00

OPEC Intl. Development Fund, 30th Anniv. — A567

2006, Feb. 28   *Perf. 13¼*
1013	A567 6.50d multi		2.00	1.00

Bab Marshan, Tangiers — A568

2006, Mar. 30
1014	A568 6.50d multi		2.00	1.00

Foreign Affairs Ministry, 50th Anniv. — A569

2006, Apr. 26
1015	A569 6d multi		1.90	1.10

Flowers — A570

Designs: 2.50d, Narcissus cantabricus. 6.50d, Paeonia mascula.

2006, Apr. 28
1016-1017	A570	Set of 2	2.75	2.75

Royal Armed Forces, 50th Anniv. — A571

Kings Mohammed VI, Hassan II, and Mohammed V, anniversary emblem, airplanes and: 2.50d, Tank. 6.50d, Ships.

2006, May 14
1018-1019	A571	Set of 2	2.75	1.25
1019a	Souvenir sheet, #1018-1019		3.25	3.25

No. 1019a sold for 10d.

Type of 2001 With Added Frameline and

A572

King Mohammed VI — A573

2006, July 1   *Litho.*   *Perf. 11½*
Granite Paper
1020	A472 3.25d blue & multi		.90	.50
1021	A572 7.80d lt grn & multi		2.40	1.20
1022	A573 13d lilac & multi		3.75	1.90
	Nos. 1020-1022 (3)		7.05	3.60

Designs size of No. 1020: 25x32mm.
See No. 1029A for stamp similar to No. 1020, with 22x32mm design without frameline.
See No. 1054D for stamp similar to No. 1021, with 22x32mm design, with country name in white, inscribed "Phil@poste" at bottom. Compare types A572 with types A473 and A688.
Compare type A573 with types A475 and A599a.

Barbary Ape — A574

Atlas Lion — A575

2006, July 31   *Perf. 13¼x13*
1023	A574 3.25d multi		.90	.50
1024	A575 7.80d multi		2.25	1.10

Green March, 31st Anniv. — A576

Designs: No. 1025, 7.80d, King Mohammed VI waving to crowd. No. 1026, 7.80d, Mohammed VI Mosque, Boujdour.

2006, Nov. 7   *Photo.*   *Perf. 13¼*
1025-1026	A576	Set of 2	4.50	2.25

Anti-Poverty Week Type of 2000
2006, Nov. 10
1027	A461 7.80d multi		2.25	.95

Values are for stamps with surrounding selvage.

Stamp Day — A577

2006, Nov. 22
1028	A577 7.80d multi		2.25	1.10

Values are for stamps with surrounding selvage.

Admission to the United Nations, 50th Anniv. — A578

2006, Nov. 24
1029	A578 7.80d multi		2.25	1.10

King Mohammed VI Type of 2001
2006, Nov.   *Litho.*   *Perf. 13¼*
Size: 22x32mm
1029A	A472 3.25d blue & multi		1.10	1.10
b.	Dated 2010		—	—

No. 1020 has a frame line around design while No. 1029A does not. No. 1029A has a printer's imprint of "Phil@poste."

673

MOROCCO

World AIDS Day — A579

2006, Dec. 1   Litho.   Perf. 13¼
1030   A579   7.80d multi   2.25   1.10

Diplomatic Relations Between Morocco and Japan, 50th Anniv. — A580

Designs: 3.25d, Dove, maps and flags. 7.80d, Flags, arches, pottery.

2006, Dec. 20   Photo.   Perf. 13¼
1031-1032   A580   Set of 2   3.25   1.50

Fish — A581

Designs: 3.25d, Thunnus thynnus. 7.80d, Sardina pilchardus.

2006, Dec. 25
1033-1034   A581   Set of 2   3.75   1.60

Flowers — A581a

No. 1034A: b, Pyrus mamorensis. c, Tulipa sylvestris. d, Cleonia lusitanica. e, Thymus broussonetii. f, Silybum marianum. g, Cynara humilis. h, Phlomis crinita ssp. mauritanica. i, Verbascum pseudocreticum. j, Campanula atra. k, Orchis papilionacea.

Serpentine Die Cut 11
2006, Dec.   Litho.
Self-Adhesive
1034A   Booklet pane of 10   —   —
b.-k.   A581a 3.25d Any single

Jewelry — A581b

No. 1034L: m, Brooch, red background. n, Bracelet, orange background. o, Earrings, orange background, country name in red. p, Pendant, diff., yellow background. q, Earrings, olive green background. r, Necklace, black brown background. s, Brooch, violet blue background. t, Pendant, bright blue background. u, Bracelets, bright green background. v, Bracelets, diff., brick red background.

Serpentine Die Cut 11
2006, Dec.   Litho.
Self-Adhesive
1034L   Booklet pane of 10   —   —
m.-v.   A581b 7.80d Any single

Denomination on No. 1034Lp appears twice, with one intermingled in the picture of the pendant.

African Soccer Confederation, 50th Anniv. — A582

2007, Feb. 26   Litho.   Perf. 13¼
1035   A582   7.80d multi   2.40   1.10
Values are for stamps with surrounding selvage.

Mohammed V University, 50th Anniv. — A583

2007, Mar. 15
1036   A583   3.25d multi   1.10   .55

Ibn Khaldun (1332-1406), Philosopher A584

2007, Mar. 28
1037   A584   7.80d multi   2.40   1.10

Souvenir Sheet

Intl. Agricultural Exhibition, Meknès — A585

No. 1038: a, Palm trees. b, Argans. c, Cattle, horiz. d, Olives, horiz.

Perf. 12¾x13¼, 13¼x12¾ (horiz. stamps)

2007, Apr. 19
1038   A585   Sheet of 4   7.25   7.25
   a.-b.   3.25d Either single   1.00   .50
   c.-d.   7.80d Either single   2.40   1.25
No. 1038 sold for 24d.

Couscous A586

2007, June 1   Perf. 13¼x13
1039   A586   7.80d multi   2.40   1.10

Andalusian Music A587

2007, June 8   Perf. 13x13¼
1040   A587   7.80d multi   2.40   1.10

Souvenir Sheet

Paintings A588

No. 1041: a, Fulgurance, by M. Qotbi. vert. b, Horses and Riders, by, H. Glaoui. c, Symphonie d'Eté, by Qotbi. d, Horses, by Glaoui.

2007, June 21   Perf. 13
1041   A588   3.25d Sheet of 4, #a-d   4.50   4.50

Scouting, Cent. — A589

2007, Aug. 7   Litho.   Perf. 13¼
1042   A589   7.80d multi   2.40   1.10

Buildings — A590

Designs: 3.25d, Silves Castle, Portugal. 7.80d, Tower, Arzila, Morocco.

2007, Sept. 26
1043-1044   A590   Set of 2   3.75   1.90
See Portugal Nos. 2955-2956.

World Post Day — A591

2007, Oct. 9
1045   A591   3.25d multi   1.25   .90

Fez, 2007 Islamic Cultural Capital — A592

2007, Oct. 30
1046   A592   7.80d multi   2.40   1.10
Compare with Type A618.

Green March, 32nd Anniv. — A593

2007, Nov. 6
1047   A593   7.80d multi   2.40   1.10

Anti-Poverty Week Type of 2000
2007, Nov. 8
1048   A461   7.80d multi   2.40   1.10
Values are for stamps with surrounding selvage.

National Quality Week — A594

2007, Nov. 12
1049   A594   7.80d multi   2.40   1.10

World Children's Day — A595

2007, Nov. 20
1050   A595   7.80d multi   2.40   1.10

Supreme Court, 50th Anniv. — A596

2007, Nov. 21
1051   A596   3.25d multi   1.10   .55

Bab Lamrissa — A597

2007, Dec. 7   Litho.   Perf. 13¼
1052   A597   7.80d multi   2.40   1.10

Royal Air Morocco, 50th Anniv. — A598

2007, Dec. 19
1053   A598   7.80d multi   2.40   1.10

"Morocco of Champions" — A599

2007, Dec. 28
1054   A599   7.80d multi   2.40   1.10
Values are for stamps with surrounding selvage.

King Mohammed VI Types of 2005, 2006 (Redrawn)

King Mohammed VI — A599a

Designs: Nos. 1054A, 1054K, King in suit and tie. Nos. 1054B, 1054L, King in robe.

Serpentine Die Cut 11
2007-09   Litho.
Booklet Stamps
Self-Adhesive
Denominations in Orange
1054A   A545   3.25d multi   1.00   1.00
   h.   Dated 2009   .85   .85
1054B   A545   3.25d multi   1.00   1.00
   c.   Booklet pane, 5 each
       #1054A-1054B   10.00
   i.   Dated 2009   .85   .85
   j.   Booklet pane of 10, 5 each
       #1054Ah, 1054Bi   8.50

Denomination in Black
Dated 2008
1054K   A545   3.25d multi ('08)   .80   .80
1054L   A545   3.25d multi ('08)   .80   .80
   m.   Booklet pane of 10, 5 each
       #1054K-1054L   8.00

MOROCCO

Size: 22x32mm
Country Name in White
Water-Activated Gum
Perf. 13
1054D A572 7.80d multi 2.25 1.10
  f. Dated 2009 2.25 1.00
  g. Dated 2010 2.25 .95

Compare with No. 1021, which is wider and has country name in blue.

Size: 31x23mm
1054E A599a 13d pink & multi 3.50 1.75

Compare with No. 1022, which is taller and has a lilac background. See No. 1128.

Moroccan Travel Market — A600
2008, Jan. 17
1055 A600 7.80d multi 2.40 1.10

Africa Cup of Nations Soccer Championships A601
2008, Jan. 31
1056 A601 7.80d multi 2.40 1.10

Export Trophy — A602
2008, Apr. 4 Litho. Perf. 13¼
1057 A602 3.25d multi 1.00 .50

Fez, 1200th Anniv. — A603
2008, Apr. 5
1058 A603 3.25d multi 1.00 .50

Flowers — A604

Designs: 3.25d, Calendula stellata. 7.80d, Convolvulus tricolor.

2008, Apr. 30 Litho. Perf. 13¼
1059-1060 A604 Set of 2 3.25 1.60

Buildings in Morocco and Iran A605

No. 1061: a, 3.25d, Flags of Morocco and Iran, Kasbah, Oudayas, Morocco, and Falak-Ol-Aflak Castle, Iran. b, 3.25d, Scroll and Falak-Ol-Aflak Castle. c, 7.80d, Scroll and Kasbah, Oudayas, Morocco.

2008, May 12 Litho. Perf. 13¼
1061 A605 Horiz. strip of 3, #a-c 4.25 2.25
See Iran No. 2955.

Children's Art — A606

No. 1062: a, Earth, by Narjiss Lasfar. b, House and trees, by Chaimae Abbaich, horiz. c, Polluted sphere, by Ahmed Anas Bennis, vert. d, House and sun, by Wassim Chakou, vert.

2008, May 26
1062 Horiz. strip of 4 4.00 2.00
a.-d. A606 3.25d Any single .95 .45

World Environment Day — A607
2008, June 5
1063 A607 7.80d multi 2.40 1.10

Rug From Salé A608

Rug From Ouled Besseba A610

Rug From Ait Haddou A612

Rug From Marmoucha A614

Rug From Ait Ouaouzguit A616

Rug From Marmoucha A609

Rug From Haut Atlas A611

Rug From Tazenakht A613

Rug From Rabat A615

Rug From Rabat A617

Self-Adhesive
2008   **Serpentine Die Cut 11**
1064 Booklet pane of 10 25.00
  a. A608 7.80d multi 2.50 1.10
  b. A609 7.80d multi 2.50 1.10
  c. A610 7.80d multi 2.50 1.10
  d. A611 7.80d multi 2.50 1.10
  e. A612 7.80d multi 2.50 1.10
  f. A613 7.80d multi 2.50 1.10
  g. A614 7.80d multi 2.50 1.10
  h. A615 7.80d multi 2.50 1.10
  i. A616 7.80d multi 2.50 1.10
  j. A617 7.80d multi 2.50 1.10

Fez, 1200th Anniv. — A618
2008, June 23 Perf. 13¼
1065 A618 7.80d multi 2.40 1.10
Compare with Type A592.

Bouregreg Valley Light Rail Line — A619

No. 1066: a, 3.25d, Train, bridge. b, 7.80d, Train, fortress.

2008, July 21
1066 A619 Horiz. pair, #a-b 3.25 1.60

2008 Summer Olympics, Beijing — A620

No. 1067 — Olympic rings and: a, Four runners. b, Three hurdlers. c, Boxers. d, Runner.

2008, Aug. 8 Photo. Perf. 13¼
1067 Horiz. strip of 4 4.00 2.00
a.-d. A620 3.25d Any single 1.00 .45

Arab Post Day A621

No. 1068 — Emblem and: a, World map, pigeon. b, Camel caravan.

2008, Aug. 28 Litho. Perf. 12¾
1068 Sheet of 2 4.50 2.25
a.-b. A621 7.80d Either single 2.25 1.10

Marine Life — A622

Designs: 3.25d, Isurus oxyrinchus. 7.80d, Haliotis tuberculata.

2008, Sept. 18 Perf. 13¼
1069-1070 A622 Set of 2 3.25 1.60

Miniature Sheet

Art and Culture A623

No. 1071: a, Musicians. b, Ezzellij tiles. c, Haik (white garment). d, Koran school.

2008, Oct. 10 Photo. Perf. 13¼x13
1071 A623 3.25d Sheet of 4, #a-d 4.00 2.00

Diplomatic Relations Between Morocco and People's Republic of China A624

Designs: 3.25r, Vases and flags of Morocco and People's Republic of China. No. 1073, 7.80d, Intertwined arabesque and Chinese emblem. No. 1074, 7.80d, Arabic archway and Great Wall of China, vert.

2008, Oct. 30 Photo. Perf. 12
1072-1074 A624 Set of 3 4.50 2.25
1074a Souvenir sheet of 3, #1072-1074 — —

No 1074 exists as souvenir sheets of one on regular paper, silk paper, and on porcelain. Values, $30, $75, and $500, respectively.

Green March, 33rd Anniv. — A625
2008, Nov. 6 Litho. Perf. 13¼
1075 A625 3.25d multi 1.00 .35

Anti-Poverty Week Type of 2000
2008, Nov. 12 Photo. Perf. 13¼
1076 A461 7.80d multi 2.00 .95

Natl. Cancer Prevention Day — A626
2008, Nov. 22 Perf. 13¼
1077 A626 3.25d multi 1.00 .35

Universal Declaration of Human Rights, 60th Anniv. — A627
2008, Dec. 10 Litho. Perf. 13
1078 A627 7.80d multi 2.00 .95

Bab Al Marsa, Essaouira A628
2008, Dec. 26 Photo. Perf. 13¼
1079 A628 7.80d multi 2.00 1.00

Louis Braille (1809-52), Educator of the Blind — A629
2009, Jan. 16
1080 A629 7.80d multi 2.00 .95

Insurance for Artisans and the Self Employed A630
2009, Feb. 16 Perf. 13x13¼
1081 A630 3.25d multi 1.00 .35

25th Hassan II Grand Prix Tennis Tournament — A631
2009, Apr. 6 Perf. 13¼
1082 A631 3.25d multi 1.00 .40

MOROCCO

Cadi Ayyad University, Marrakesh, 30th Anniv. — A632

2009, Apr. 20				
1083	A632	3.25d multi	1.00	.40

Sugar Industry — A633

2009, Apr. 22			Photo.	
1084	A633	3.25d multi	1.00	.40

Cheetah With Mail Bag — A633a

2009, May 6	Litho.	Perf. 13x13¼		
1084A	A633a	5.90d multi	2.00	.75

Natl. Theater Day — A634

2009, May 14	Photo.	Perf. 13¼		
1085	A634	3.25d multi	1.00	.40

Intl. Year of Astronomy A635

2009, May 15				
1086	A635	7.80d multi	2.50	1.00

Protection for Children Using Computers A636

2009, May 17	Litho.	Perf. 13x13¼		
1087	A636	7.80d multi	2.50	1.00

Al-Maghrib Bank, 50th Anniv. — A637

2009, July 2	Photo.	Perf. 13¼		
1088	A637	3.25d multi	1.00	.40

A638

Enthronement of King Mohammed VI, 10th Anniv. — A639

King Mohammed VI: 3.25d, On horse. 7.80d, Wearing suit.
15d, With images of Kings Mohammed V and Hassan II.

Photo. & Embossed With Foil Application

2009, July 30		Perf. 13¼		
Granite Paper (#1089-1090)				
1089	A638	3.25d multi	1.00	.40
1090	A638	7.80d multi	2.50	1.00

Souvenir Sheet
Litho. with Three-Dimensional Plastic Affixed
Serpentine Die Cut 9½
Self-Adhesive

1091	A639	15d multi	11.00	11.00

Nos. 1089-1090 have gold frames with an orange cast. A souvenir sheet containing Nos. 1089-1090 having gold frames with a yellow cast sold for 36d.

Jerusalem, Capital of Arab Culture — A640

2009, Aug. 3	Litho.	Perf. 13¼		
1092	A640	3.25d multi	1.00	.40

Natl. Women's Day — A641

2009, Oct. 10

1093	A641	3.25d multi	1.00	.40

Ait Ouaouzguid Rug — A642

Marmoucha Rug — A643

Ait Haddou Rug — A644

Ouled Besseba Rug — A645

Hénbale de Salé Rug — A646

Rabat Rug — A647

Rabat Rug — A648

Tazenakht Rug — A649

Haut Atlas Rug — A650

Marmoucha Rug — A651

2009 **Litho.** *Serpentine Die Cut 11*
Self-Adhesive

1094		Booklet pane of 10	20.00	
a.	A642	7.80d multi	2.00	2.00
b.	A643	7.80d multi	2.00	2.00
c.	A644	7.80d multi	2.00	2.00
d.	A645	7.80d multi	2.00	2.00
e.	A646	7.80d multi	2.00	2.00
f.	A647	7.80d multi	2.00	2.00
g.	A648	7.80d multi	2.00	2.00
h.	A649	7.80d multi	2.00	2.00
i.	A650	7.80d multi	2.00	2.00
j.	A651	7.80d multi	2.00	2.00

Mohammedia School of Engineering, 50th Anniv. — A652

2009, Oct. 24	Litho.	Perf. 13¼		
1095	A652	3.25d multi	1.00	.40

Mehdia Gate — A653

2009, Oct. 30	Photo.	Perf. 13¾		
1096	A653	7.80d multi	2.50	1.10

Green March, 34th Anniv. — A654

2009, Nov. 6	Litho.	Perf. 13¼		
1097	A654	3.25d multi	1.10	.55

Anti-Poverty Week Type of 2001

2009, Nov. 15	Photo.	Perf. 13		
1098	A461	7.80d multi	2.50	1.10

Value is for stamp with surrounding selvage.

Port of Tangiers A655

No. 1099 — Ship in port, gear wheels in: a, 3.25d, Gray. b, 7.80d, Brown.

2009, Dec. 7	Litho.	Perf. 13¼		
1099	A655	Horiz. pair, #a-b	3.50	1.50

Caisse de Dépot et de Gestion, 50th Anniv. — A656

2009, Dec. 19

1100	A656	7.80d dk blue & gold	2.50	1.00

Fish — A657

Designs: No. 1101, 7.80d, Sarda sarda. No. 1102, 7.80d, Oblada melanura.

2009, Dec. 28				
1101-1102	A657	Set of 2	5.00	2.00

Children's Art — A658

No. 1103: a, Horses. b, Trees. c, Lake, mountain and trees. d, Building with smokestacks.

2009, Dec. 31

1103		Vert. strip of 4	4.00	1.75
a.-d.	A658	3.25d Any single	.85	.40

Rosa Damascena A659

Orange Blossoms A660

2010, Jan. 14		Perf. 13¼x13		
1104	A659	7.80d multi	2.50	1.00
		Perf. 13x13¼		
1105	A660	7.80d multi	2.50	1.00

Nos. 1104-1105 are each impregnated with the scent of the depicted flower.

Reconstruction of Agadir, 50th Anniv. — A661

2010, Feb. 28		Perf. 13¼		
1106	A661	7.80d multi	2.50	.95

Earth Day — A662

2010, Apr. 22				
1107	A662	3.25d multi	1.00	.40

Alfalfa — A663

2010, Apr. 22	Litho. & Embossed			
1108	A663	10d multi	3.50	1.25

No. 1108 has a circle of adhesive tape covering a small embossed circle containing alfalfa seeds.

Miniature Sheet

Art and Culture A664

No. 1109 — Paintings of casbahs in: a, Ibeghouzen. b, Oudaias. c, Ait ben Haddou. d, Tinzouline.

2010, May 12		Perf. 13x13¼		
1109	A664	3.25d Sheet of 4, #a-d	5.00	1.50

Level A Quality Certification for Morocco Post — A665

2010, May 26		Perf. 13¼		
1110	A665	3.25d multi	1.00	.35

MOROCCO

National Day of Resistance — A666

2010, June 18
1111 A666 3.25d multi 1.00 .35

Bab al Bahr, Abilah — A667

2010, July 10
1112 A667 7.80d multi 2.50 .95

OCP Groupe, 90th Anniv. — A668

2010, Aug. 7 — Perf. 12¼
1113 A668 7.80d multi 2.50 .95

Intl. Year of Biodiversity — A669

2010, Oct. 11 Litho. Perf. 13¼
1114 A669 7.80d multi 2.50 1.00

Souvenir Sheet

Green March, 35th Anniv. — A670

No. 1115: a, Marchers. b, Hand holding Moroccan flag.

2010, Nov. 6 Litho. Perf. 14
1115 A670 7.80d Sheet of 2, #a-b 5.00 5.00

Grains of sand were applied to portions of the design by a thermographic process.

Sciaena Umbra — A671

2010, Nov. 10 Photo. Perf. 13¼
1116 A671 7.80d multi 2.50 .95

Anti-Poverty Week Type of 2001

2010, Nov. 19 Photo. Perf. 13
1117 A461 7.80d multi 2.50 .95

Value is for stamp with surrounding selvage.

Numeric 2013 Plan — A672

2010, Nov. 30 Litho. Perf. 13¼x13
1118 A672 7.80d multi 2.50 .95

Tenth Marrakesh Intl. Film Festival — A673

2010, Dec. 3 Photo. Perf. 13¼
1119 A673 7.80d multi 2.50 .95

Train — A674

2010, Dec. 14
1120 A674 3.25d multi 1.00 .40

Greetings — A675

Inscriptions: No. 1121, 3.25d, Bonheur (happiness). No. 1122, 3.25d, Prospérité (prosperity). No. 1123, 3.25d, Santé (health).

2010, Dec. 20
1121-1123 A675 Set of 3 3.00 1.25

King Mohammed VI — A676

Serpentine Die Cut 11
2010, July 6 Litho.
Booklet Stamp
Self-Adhesive
1124 A676 3.25d multi .75 .75
  a. Booklet pane of 10 7.50

A677 A678
A679 A680
A681 A682
A683 A684
A685

Pottery — A686

Serpentine Die Cut 11
2010, July 6 Litho.
Self-Adhesive
1125 Booklet pane of 10 19.00
  a. A677 7.80d multi 1.90 1.90
  b. A678 7.80d multi 1.90 1.90
  c. A679 7.80d multi 1.90 1.90
  d. A680 7.80d multi 1.90 1.90
  e. A681 7.80d multi 1.90 1.90
  f. A682 7.80d multi 1.90 1.90
  g. A683 7.80d multi 1.90 1.90
  h. A684 7.80d multi 1.90 1.90
  i. A685 7.80d multi 1.90 1.90
  j. A686 7.80d multi 1.90 1.90

Week of the Blind.

King Mohammed VI Type of 2007 and

A687 A688

2011-13 Litho. Perf. 13x13¼
1126 A687 3.50d brn org & multi 1.25 .40
  a. Dated "2012," perf. 13x13¼ syncopated — —
  b. Dated "2013," perf. 13x13¼ syncopated — —

Perf. 13x13¼ Syncopated
1126C A687 3.50d Like # 1126, redrawn design — —
  a. Dated "2013" perf. 13x13¼ syncopated — —
1127 A688 8.40d lilac & multi 2.75 1.10
  a. Dated "2013" perf. 13x13¼ syncopated — —

Perf. 13¼x13
1128 A599a 20d lt green & multi 6.50 2.50
  a. Dated 2014, perf. 13¼x13 syncopated — —
  Nos. 1126-1128 (3) 10.50 4.00

Issued: Nos. 1126, 1127, 1128, 2/1. No. 1126a, 12/24/12; Nos. 1126b, 1127a, 4/24/13; No. 1120C, 10/5/12.
No. 1126C has thinner Latin lettering and an Enschede imprint at bottom, and a redrawn Arabic inscription at the top using flatter characters and with the hook at left side of the second word from the left not under the right side of the first word at left.
Compare type A687 with type A472, and type A688 with types A473 and A572.

King Mohammed VI — A689

Serpentine Die Cut 11
2011, May 1 Litho.
Booklet Stamp
Self-Adhesive
1129 A689 3.50d multi .90 .90
  a. Booklet pane of 10 9.00

Leopard With Mail Bag — A690

2011, Apr. 20 Litho. Perf. 13x13¼
1130 A690 6.40d multi 2.25 .85

Miniature Sheet

Tom and Jerry Cartoons — A691

No. 1131: a, Jerry hitting tennis ball through Tom's racquet. b, Tom and Jerry in hammocks on desert island. c, Jerry shooting tennis balls at Tom with machine. d, Tom swimming with Jerry on his chest. e, Tom hitting tennis net with racquet. f, Wave approaching Tom and Jerry. g, Jerry holding tennis ball for Tom. h, Jerry listening to shell, Tom collecting shells. i, Tom slipping on tennis balls thrown by Jerry. j, Tom and Jerry building sand castles.

2011, May 4 Perf. 13¼
1131 A691 3.50d Sheet of 10, #a-j 12.00 12.00

Turkeys — A692 **Henna Plant — A693**

2011, May 30
1132 A692 3.50d multi 1.25 .45
1133 A693 8.40d multi 2.75 1.10

A694 A695
A696 A697
A698 A699
A700 A701

Copperware
A702 A703

Serpentine Die Cut 11
2011, June 16 Self-Adhesive
1134 Booklet pane of 10 25.00
  a. A094 0.40d multi 2.50 1.10
  b. A695 8.40d multi 2.50 1.10
  c. A696 8.40d multi 2.50 1.10
  d. A697 8.40d multi 2.50 1.10
  e. A698 8.40d multi 2.50 1.10
  f. A699 8.40d multi 2.50 1.10
  g. A700 8.40d multi 2.50 1.10
  h. A701 8.40d multi 2.50 1.10
  i. A702 8.40d multi 2.50 1.10
  j. A703 8.40d multi 2.50 1.10

Al Barid Bank — A704

2011, June 27 Perf. 13¼
1135 A704 3.50d multi 1.25 .45

Famous Men — A705

MOROCCO

No. 1136: a, Moulay Abderrahmane Ben Zidane (1873-1946), historian. b, Abou Chouaib Doukkali Essadiki (1878-1938), scientist. c, Mohamed Ben Larbi Alaoui Lamdaghri (1880-1964), Justice Minister. d, Mohamed El Mokhtar Soussi (1900-63), religious scholar. e, Abdellah Ben Abdessamad Guennoune (1908-89), first governor of Tangiers.

2011, June 30 Litho.
1136 Horiz. strip of 5 6.00 6.00
a.-e. A705 3.50d Any single 1.00 .50

Campaign Against AIDS — A706

2011, July 27
1137 A706 8.40d multi 2.75 1.10

National Artisan's Week — A707

2011, Sept. 8 Perf. 13¼
1138 A707 3.50d multi 1.25 .45

First Air Mail in Morocco, Cent. — A708

No. 1139 — Airplane and monument in: a, Color. b, Black-and-white.

2011, Sept. 19
1139 A708 8.40d Vert. pair, #a-b 5.00 3.00

Miniature Sheet

Coins A709

No. 1140: a, Obverse of 1893 bronze 8-fels coin (showing star). b, As "a," reverse (showing "1131" date). c, Obverse of 1609 gold dinar (26mm diameter coin with 20mm diameter inner circle, no horizontal lines). d, As "c," reverse (with long horizontal lines inside inner circle). e, Obverse of gold Almohades dinar (29mm coin with inner square, no long horizontal lines inside square). f, As "e," reverse (with long horizontal line inside square). g, Obverse of 1145 gold dinar (25mm coin with 15mm inner circle, with long horizontal lines inside inner circle). h, As "g," reverse (without long horizontal lines inside inner circle). i, Obverse of 790 silver dirham (Arabic script around edge of coin). j, As "i," reverse (five dots around edge of coin).

Litho. & Embossed
2011, Oct. 20 Perf. 13¼x13¾
1140 A709 3.50d Sheet of 10, #a-j 12.00 12.00

National Campaign on Millennial Development Objectives — A710

2011, Oct. 24 Litho. Perf. 13¼
1141 A710 8.40d multi 2.75 1.10

Children's Art — A711

No. 1142 — Various works of children's art inscribed: a, L'Ecole (school), by Ibtissam Gariate. b, L' Envirommement (environment), by Ramah Damach. c, La Sante (health), by Hanane Aliouan. d, L'Enfance (childhood), by Kenza Najdaoui, horiz.

2011, Oct. 25
1142 A711 3.50d Horiz. strip of 4, #a-d 5.00 5.00

Green March, 36th Anniv. — A712

2011, Nov. 6 Photo.
1143 A712 8.40d multi 2.75 1.10

Anti-Poverty Week Type of 2001
2011, Nov. 28 Photo. Perf. 13
1144 A461 8.40d multi 2.75 1.10
Values are for stamps with surrounding selvage.

Miniature Sheet

Folding Screens — A713

No. 1145 — Screen art by: a, 3.50d, Paula Cardozo. b, 3.50d, Abdellah Yacoubi. c, 8.40d, Yukako Fukuda-Ota, vert. d, 8.40d, Miki Tica, vert.

Perf. 13x13¼, 13¼x13 (vert. stamps)
2011, Dec. 1
1145 A713 Sheet of 4, #a-d 7.00 7.00

National Statistics and Applied Economics Institute, 50th Anniv. — A714

2011, Dec. 15 Perf. 13¼
1146 A714 3.50d multi 1.25 .40

Animals in Rabat Zoo — A715

No. 1147: a, Mouflons. b, Oryx. c, Lions, vert. d, Ibises, vert.

2012, Jan. 9 Photo. Perf. 13¼
1147 Strip of 4 7.00 7.00
a.-b. A715 3.50d Either single 1.00 .40
c.-d. A715 8.40d Either single 2.25 1.00
e. Souvenir sheet of 4, #1147a-1147d 7.00 7.00

2012 African Cup of Nations Soccer Tournament, Equatorial Guinea and Gabon — A716

2012, Jan. 23 Litho. Perf. 13¾
1148 A716 3.50d multi 1.25 .50
Values are for stamps with surrounding selvage.

Mohammed V Theater, Rabat, 50th Anniv. — A717

2012, Mar. 27 Perf. 13x13¼
1149 A717 3.50d multi 1.25 .40

Moroccan Postage Stamps, Cent. — A718

No. 1150: a, 3.50d, Anniversary emblem. b, 8.40d, Horses and riders.

2012, May 22 Perf. 13¼x14
1150 A718 Vert. pair, #a-b 3.75 3.75

Arab Post Day — A719

2012, Aug. 3 Perf. 13x13¼
1151 A719 8.40d multi 2.75 .95

2012 Summer Olympics, London — A720

Perf. 13¼ Syncopated
2012, Aug. 17
1152 A720 8.40d multi 2.75 1.00

15th National Quality Prize — A721

2012, Sept. 27 Litho.
1153 A721 8.40d multi 2.75 1.00

Retirement Allowance Collective Plan, 35th Anniv. — A722

2012, Oct. 4 Perf. 13¼ Syncopated
1154 A722 3.50d multi 1.25 .40

Falcon, Flags of Qatar and Morocco — A723

2012, Oct. 9 Photo. Perf. 13x13¼
1155 A723 8.40d multi — —
See Qatar No. 1085.

Children's Art — A724

No. 1156 — Inscriptions: a, Mon pays (my country), vert. b, Mon environnement (my environment). c, La monnaie (money).

Perf. 13¼ Syncopated
2012, Oct. 10 Litho.
1156 A724 3.50d Vert. strip of 3, #a-c 2.50 2.50

El Jadida Horse Show — A725

Perf. 13¼ Syncopated
2012, Oct. 17 Photo.
1157 A725 8.40d multi 2.75 1.00

Green March, 37th Anniv. — A726

Perf. 13x13¼ Syncopated
2012, Nov. 6 Photo.
1158 A726 3.50d multi — —

Anti-Poverty Week Type of 2001
2012, Nov. 7 Photo. Perf. 13¼
Dated "2012"
1159 A461 8.40d multi 2.75 1.00
Values are for stamps with surrounding selvage.

Official Bulletin, Cent. A727

No. 1160: a, 3.50d, Gray background. b, 8.40d, Red background.

Perf. 13¼x13 Syncopated
2012, Nov. 20 Litho.
1160 A727 Horiz. pair, #a-b — —

Maghzen Post, 120th Anniv. A728

MOROCCO

No. 1161 — Sherifian postal seals and their impressions: a, Purple circular. b, Purple octagonal. c, Blue green circular. d, Blue green octagonal. e, Blue circular. f, Blue octagonal. g, Red circular. h, Red octagonal. i, Black circular. j, Black octagonal. k, Orange circular. l, Orange octagonal.

Perf. 13¼x13 Syncopated
2012, Nov. 22   Photo.
1161   Sheet of 12 + 12 labels   15.00 15.00
a.-l.   A728 3.50d Any single + label   1.00   .45

Intl. Year of Renewable Energy — A729

Perf. 13¼ Syncopated
2012, Dec. 24   Photo.
1163   A729 8.40d multi   2.75   1.00

Postage Stamps of Morocco, Cent. A730

No. 1164: a, Locomotives and map of Morocco. b, Map of Africa, satellite and Morocco Post emblem in space.

2012, Dec. 27   Litho.   **Perf. 14x13½**
1164   A730 3.50d Horiz. pair, #a-b   —   —

A731

High Commission for Water and Forests, Cent. — A732

Perf. 13¼ Syncopated
2013, May 7   Photo.
1165   A731 3.50d multi   .85   .85
1166   A732 8.40d multi   2.00   2.00

Seventh World Congress on Environmental Education, Marrakesh — A733

Perf. 13¼ Syncopated
2013, June 9   Photo.
1167   A733 3.50d multi   .90   .90

El Houssaine Slaoui (1921-51), Singer — A734

Mohammed Ben Ali Rbati (1861-1939), Painter — A735

Abu El Kassem Zayani (1734-1833), Historian — A736

Abu El Hassan Ali El Youssi (1630-91), Writer — A737

Sultan Sidi Mohammed Ben Abdellah (1710-90) — A738

Perf. 13¼ Syncopated
2013, June 28   Photo.
1168   Horiz. strip of 5   4.25   4.25
a.   A734 3.50d multi   .85   .85
b.   A735 3.50d multi   .85   .85
c.   A736 3.50d multi   .85   .85
d.   A737 3.50d multi   .85   .85
e.   A738 3.50d multi   .85   .85

King Mohammed VI
A739   A740

Perf. 13x13¼ Syncopated
2013-14   Photo.
1169   A739 3.50d multi   —   —
a.   Dated "2014"   —   —
1170   A740 8.40d multi   —   —
Issued: Nos. 1169, 1170, 8/6; No. 1169a, 3/4/14.

King Mohammed VI
A741   A742

Serpentine Die Cut 11
2013, Aug. 16   Litho.
Booklet Stamps
Self-Adhesive
1171   A741 3.50d multi   .85   .85
a.   Booklet pane of 10   8.50
1172   A742 8.40d multi   2.00   2.00
a   Booklet pane of 10   20.00

National Day of the Moroccan Community Abroad — A743

Perf. 13¼ Syncopated
2013, Aug. 10   Photo.
1173   A743 8.40d multi   2.00   2.00

Revolution of the King and People, 60th Anniv. — A744

Perf. 13¼ Syncopated
2013, Aug. 20   Photo.
1174   A744 3.50d multi   .85   .85

Souvenir Sheet

King Mohammed VI, 50th Birthday — A745

No. 1175 — King wearing: a, Robe. b, Suit and tie.

2013, Aug. 21   Litho.   Perf. 13¼x13
On Silk-Faced Paper
1175   A745 Sheet of 2   4.00   4.00
a.-b.   8.40d Either single   2.00   2.00

A746

World Summit of Local and Regional Leaders, Rabat — A747

Perf. 13¼ Syncopated
2013, Oct. 1   Photo.
1176   A746 8.40d multi   2.10   2.10
1177   A747 8.40d multi   2.10   2.10

Green March, 38th Anniv. — A748

Perf. 13¼ Syncopated
2013, Nov. 6   Photo.
1178   A748 8.40d multi   2.00   2.00

Anti-Poverty Week Type of 2001
2013, Nov. 8   Photo.   **Perf. 13¼**
Dated "2013"
1179   A461 8.40d multi   2.00   2.00
Values are for stamps with surrounding selvage.

Festival of the Return from Exile of King Mohammed V, End of French Occupation, and Moroccan Independence A749

Perf. 13¼ Syncopated
2013, Nov. 18   Photo.
1180   A749 3.50d multi   .85   .85

Land Registration, Cent. — A750

Perf. 13x13¼ Syncopated
2013, Nov. 29   Photo.
1181   A750 3.50d multi   —   —

Ports of Ukraine and Morocco A751

No. 1182: a, Odessa, Ukraine. b, Tangiers, Morocco.

Perf. 13¼ Syncopated
2013, Dec. 18   Litho.
1182   Horiz. pair   3.00   3.00
a.   3.50d multi   .85   .85
b.   8.40d multi   2.10   2.10
See Ukraine No. 951.

Morocco's Ratification of United Nations Convention on the Rights of the Child, 20th Anniv. — A752

No. 1183: a, 3.50d, Children, white background. b, 8.40d, Children, mauve background.

Perf. 13¼ Syncopated
2013, Dec. 25   Litho.
1183   A752 Horiz. pair, #a-b   3.00   3.00

National Parliament, 50th Anniv. — A753

Perf. 13¼ Syncopated
2013, Dec. 27   Photo.
1184   A753 3.50d multi   .85   .85

National Railways Office, 50th Anniv. — A754

Perf. 13¼ Syncopated
2014, Mar. 6   Photo.
1185   A754 3.50d multi   .85   .85
Dated 2013.

20th World Sacred Music Festival, Fez — A755

Perf. 13¼ Syncopated
2014, June 13   Photo.
1186   A755 3.50d multi   .85   .85

Euromed Postal Emblem and Mediterranean Sea — A756

Perf. 13¼ Syncopated
2014, July 9   Photo.
1187   A756 8.40d multi   2.00   2.00

2014 Continental Cup Track and Field Competition, Marrakesh A757

Emblem and: 3.50d, Runners on track in stadium. 8.40d, Runners and palm tree, vert.

Perf. 13¼ Syncopated
2014, Sept. 12   Photo.
1188-1189 A757 Set of 2   2.75   2.75

Birds and Lakes A758

No. 1190: a, Ruddy shelduck at Lake Isli. b, Gray heron at Lake Tislite.

MOROCCO

Perf. 13¼ Syncopated

2014, Sept. 25 — Photo.
1190 A758 Horiz. pair 2.75 2.75
a. 3.50d multi .80 .80
b. 8.40d multi 1.90 1.90

Opening of Mohammed VI Museum of Modern and Contemporary Art, Rabat — A759

Perf. 13¼ Syncopated

2014, Oct. 7 — Photo.
1191 A759 3.50d multi .80 .80

Green March, 39th Anniv. — A760

Perf. 13¼ Syncopated

2014, Nov. 6 — Photo.
1192 A760 8.40d multi 1.90 1.90

Exhibition on Monaco's Prince Albert I's Exploration of Morocco, Rabat — A761

No. 1193: a, Oceanographic Museum, Monaco. b, Hassan Tower, Rabat.

Perf. 13¼ Syncopated

2014, Nov. 7 — Photo.
1193 A761 Horiz. pair 2.75 2.75
a. 3.50d multi .80 .80
b. 8.40d multi 1.90 1.90

See Monaco No. 2778.

World Human Rights Forum, Marrakesh — A762

Perf. 13¼ Syncopated

2014, Nov. 28 — Photo.
1194 A762 8.40d multi 1.90 1.90

Anti-Poverty Week — A763

2015, Jan. 8 Photo. **Perf. 13¼ Dated "2014"**
1195 A763 (8.40d) multi —

Values are for stamps with surrounding selvage. See Nos. 1220, 1229.

Bodies of Water — A764

No. 1196: a, Aguelmam Azegza. b, Aguelmam Sidi Ali. c, Dayet Aoua. d, Lac Ifni. e, Lac Sidi Boughaba.

Perf. 13¼ Syncopated

2015, Mar. 2 — Photo.
1196 Horiz. strip of 5 — —
a.-e. A764 N Any single — —

Nos. 1196a-1196e each sold for 3.75d on day of issue.

Kasbah Ait Ben Haddou A765

Bab Agnaw Gate, Marrakesh A766

Serpentine Die Cut 11¼ Syncopated

2015, Mar. 2 — Litho.
Booklet Stamps Self-Adhesive
1197 A765 l multi — —
1198 A766 l multi — —
a. Booklet pane of 10, 5 each #1197-1198 —

On day of issue, Nos. 1197-1198 each sold for 9d.

King Mohammed VI — A769

A767   A768

Perf. 13¼ Syncopated

2015-17 — Photo.
1199 A767 3.75d multi .80 .80
a. Dated 2017 .80 .80
b. Dated 2019 — —
c. Dated 2020 — —
1200 A768 9d multi 1.90 1.90
a. Dated 2016 1.90 1.90
b. Dated 2017 2.00 2.00
c. Dated 2019 1.90 1.90
d. Dated 2020 — —

Booklet Stamp Self-Adhesive
Serpentine Die Cut 11 Syncopated
1201 A769 3.75d multi .80 .80
a. Booklet pane of 10 8.00
b. Dated 2016 .75 .75
c. Booklet pane of 10 #1201b 7.50
d. Dated 2021 — —
e. Booklet pane of 10 #1201d —

Issued: Nos. 1199, 1200, 4/9; No. 1201, 6/9; Nos. 1199c, 1200d, 2/21/20; No. 1201d, 5/24/21. Compare types A767 and A769 with types A828 and A859.

Cap Spartel Lighthouse, 150th Anniv. — A770

Perf. 13¼ Syncopated

2015, Apr. 21 — Photo.
1202 A770 9d multi — —

Jidar Festival — A771

Perf. 13¼ Syncopated

2015, May 15 — Photo.
1203 A771 9d multi 2.00 2.00

Stamp Day — A772

Perf. 13¼ Syncopated

2015, May 22 — Photo.
1204 A772 3.75d multi .80 .80

Marine Life — A773

No. 1205: a, Sparus aurata. b, Oblada melanura. c, Sarda sarda. d, Sparisoma cretense. e, Xiphias gladius. f, Haliotis tuberculata. g, Isurus oxyrinchus. h, Sardina pilchardus. i, Octopus vulgaris. j, Sepia officinalis.

Serpentine Die Cut 11 Syncopated

2015, June 9 — Litho.
Self-Adhesive
1205 Booklet pane of 10 19.00
a.-j. A773 9d Any single 1.90 1.90

Xebec — A774

Perf. 13¼ Syncopated

2015, Aug. 12 — Photo.
1206 A774 9d multi 1.90 1.90

2015 World Tourism Cities Federation Summit, Rabat and Fez — A775

Perf. 13¼ Syncopated

2015, Sept. 21 — Photo.
1207 A775 9d multi 1.90 1.90

Rocks and Fossils — A776

Designs: No. 1208, 3.75d, Stromatolite from Amane-n'Tourhart outcrop. No. 1209, 3.75d, Marellomorph fossil from Zagora. No. 1210, 9d, Meteorite found near Tissint, horiz. No. 1211, 9d, Aegirocassis benmoulai fossil, horiz.

Perf. 13¼ Syncopated

2018, Oct. 9 — Photo.
1208-1211 A776 Set of 4 5.25 5.25

United Nations, 70th Anniv. — A777

Perf. 13¼ Syncopated

2015, Oct. 26 — Photo.
1212 A777 9d multi 1.90 1.90

Green March, 40th Anniv. A778

No. 1213: a, Marchers. b, Flag of Morocco and towers.

Perf. 13¼ Syncopated

2015, Nov. 6 — Photo.
1213 A778 9d Horiz. pair, #a-b 3.75 3.75
c. As "a," perf. 13¼x13 — —
d. As "b," perf. 13¼x13 — —
e. Souvenir sheet, #1213c-1213b — —

Flag of Morocco, Cent. — A779

Perf. 13¼ Syncopated

2015, Nov. 17 — Photo.
1214 A779 9d multi 1.90 1.90

Morocco No. 15 and Map of Morocco — A780

Perf. 13¼ Syncopated

2015, Nov. 18 — Photo.
1215 A780 9d multi 1.90 1.90

Independence, 60th anniv.

Rotary International, 110th Anniv. — A781

Perf. 13¼ Syncopated

2015, Nov. 30 — Photo.
1216 A781 9d multi 1.90 1.90

National Artisans' Week — A782

Perf. 13¼ Syncopated

2015, Dec. 17 — Photo.
1217 A782 3.75d multi .75 .75

Famous Men — A783

No. 1218: a, Ahmed Balafrej (1908-90), Prime Minister. b, Mouha Ou Hammou Zayani (1863-1921), Berber military commander. c, Abdelkrim El Khatib (1921-2008), politician. d, Ahmed Tayib Laalaj (1928-2012), actor. e, Larbi Benmbarek (1914-92), soccer player.

Perf. 13¼ Syncopated

2015, Dec. 30 — Photo.
1218 Horiz. strip of 5 3.75 3.75
a.-e. A783 3.75d Any single .75 .75

First Urban Planning Law, Cent. — A784

Perf. 13¼ Syncopated

2016, Jan. 14 — Photo.
1219 A784 3.75d multi — —

Anti-Poverty Week Type of 2015
2016, Feb. 15 Photo. **Perf. 13¼ Dated "2016"**
1220 A763 9d multi — —

Values are for stamps with surrounding selvage.

MOROCCO

International Women's Day — A785

Perf. 13¼ Syncopated
2016, Mar. 8   Photo.
1221 A785 9d multi   1.90 1.90

National Civil Society Day — A786

Perf. 13¼ Syncopated
2016, Mar. 14   Photo.
1222 A786 3.75d multi   .80   .80

Retrospective of Art of Alberto Giacometti (1901-66) at Mohammed VI Museum of Modern and Contemporary Art — A787

Perf. 13¼ Syncopated
2016, Apr. 27   Photo.
1223 A787 9d multi   1.90 1.90

Pagrus Auriga — A788

Perf. 13¼ Syncopated
2016, Sept. 22   Photo.
1224 A788 3.75d multi   .80   .80

African Philatelic Club — A789

Perf. 13¼ Syncopated
2016, Oct. 4   Photo.
1225 A789 9d multi   1.90 1.90

Green March, 41st Anniv. — A790

Perf. 13¼ Syncopated
2016, Nov. 6   Photo.
1226 A790 9d multi   1.90 1.90

United Nations Climate Change Conference, Marrakesh — A791

No. 1227 — Inscription in red: a, "Marrakech 2016." b, "Act Actuemos Agissons 2016."

Perf. 13¼ Syncopated
2016, Nov. 7   Photo.
1227 A791 9d Horiz. pair, #a-b   3.75 3.75

Prionace Glauca — A792

Perf. 13¼ Syncopated
2017, Jan. 25   Photo.
1228 A792 3.75d multi   .75   .75

Anti-Poverty Week Type of 2015
2017, Mar. 15   Photo.   **Perf. 13¼ Dated "2017"**
1229 A763 9d multi   1.90 1.90
Values are for stamps with surrounding selvage.

Minerals — A793

No. 1230: a, Azurite. b, Calcite. c, Wulfenite. d, Quartz. e, Aragonite. f, Agate. g, Vanadinite. h, Erythrine. i, Malachite and Azurite. j, Onyx.

Serpentine Die Cut 11 Syncopated
2017, Mar. 15   Litho.
      Self-Adhesive
1230   Booklet pane of 10   19.00
  a.-j. A793 9d Any single   1.90 1.90

A794

A795

A796

Children's Art — A797

Perf. 13¼ Syncopated
2017, Apr. 28   Photo.
1231   Strip of 4   3.00 3.00
  a. A794 3.75d multi   .75   .75
  b. A795 3.75d multi   .75   .75
  c. A796 3.75d multi   .75   .75
  d. A797 3.75d multi   .75   .75

Tan-Tan Moussem (Festival of Berber Tribes) — A798

Perf. 13¼ Syncopated
2017, May 8   Photo.
1232 A798 9d multi   1.90 1.90

Exhibition of Art by Pablo Picasso (1881-1973) at Mohammed VI Museum of Modern and Contemporary Art — A799

No. 1233 — Drawing of woman with background color of: a, Lt. greenish gray. b, Beige.

Perf. 13¼ Syncopated
2017, May 15   Photo.
1233 A799 Horiz. pair   2.75 2.75
  a. 3.75d multi   .80   .80
  b. 9d multi   1.90 1.90

General Treasury, Cent. — A800

Perf. 13¼ Syncopated
2017, July 4   Photo.
1234 A800 9d multi   1.90 1.90

Cork Oak — A801

Perf. 13¼ Syncopated
2017, Aug. 16   Photo.
1235 A801 9d multi   2.00 2.00

El Jadida Horse Show, 10th Anniv. — A802

Perf. 13¼ Syncopated
2017, Oct. 17   Photo.
1236 A802 9d multi   1.00 1.00

Flora and Fauna A803

No. 1237: a, 3.75d, Dragon tree. b, 9d, Mhorr gazelle.

Perf. 13x13¼ Syncopated
2017, Oct. 31   Litho.
1237 A803 Horiz. pair, #a-b

Green March, 42nd Anniv. — A804

Perf. 13¼ Syncopated
2017, Nov. 6   Photo.
1238 A804 9d multi   1.90 1.90

National Quality Week, 20th Anniv. — A805

Perf. 13¼ Syncopated
2017, Nov. 14   Photo.
1239 A805 9d multi   1.90 1.90

ISO 9001 V 2015 Certification Letter — A806

Perf. 13¼ Syncopated
2017, Dec. 15   Photo.
1240 A806 9d multi   1.90 1.90

Tanger Med Port, 10th Anniv. — A807

No. 1241: a, Drawing of cranes and 10th anniv. emblem. b, Photograph of cranes and containers in port.

Perf. 13¼ Syncopated
2017, Dec. 21   Photo.
1241 A807 Horiz. pair   2.75 2.75
  a. 3.75d multi   .80   .80
  b. 9d multi   1.90 1.90

Jemaa El-Fna, Marrakesh A808

Perf. 13¼ Syncopated
2017, Dec. 27   Photo.
1242 A808 9d multi   1.90 1.90

A809

A810

A811

A812

A813

A814

A815

Children's Art — A816

Serpentine Die Cut 11 Syncopated
2018, Feb. 21   Litho.
      Self-Adhesive
1243   Booklet pane of 8   6.50
  a. A809 3.75d multi   .80   .80
  b. A810 3.75d multi   .80   .80
  c. A811 3.75d multi   .80   .80
  d. A812 3.75d multi   .80   .80
  e. A813 3.75d multi   .80   .80

MOROCCO

f.	A814 3.75d multi		.80	.80
g.	A815 3.75d multi		.80	.80
h.	A816 3.75d multi		.80	.80

International Conference on Justice, Marrakesh — A817

Perf. 13¼ Syncopated
2018, Apr. 2 — Photo.
1244 A817 9d multi — 2.00 2.00

Morocco's Bid to Host 2026 World Cup Soccer Championships — A818

Perf. 13¼ Syncopated
2018, Apr. 17 — Photo.
1245 A818 9d multi — 2.00 2.00

National Soccer Team of Morocco Appearance at 2018 World Cup Soccer Championships, Russia — A819

2018, June 20 — Photo. — Perf. 13¼
1246 A819 9d multi — 1.90 1.90

40th International Cultural Festival, Assilah — A820

Perf. 13¼ Syncopated
2018, June 29 — Photo.
1247 A820 9d multi — 1.90 1.90

A821, A822, A823

Children's Art — A824

Perf. 13¼ Syncopated
2018, June 29 — Photo.
1248 — Horiz. strip of 4 — 3.25 3.25
a. A821 3.75d multi — .80 .80
b. A822 3.75d multi — .80 .80
c. A823 3.75d multi — .80 .80
d. A824 3.75d multi — .80 .80

Mediterranean Houses — A825

No. 1249 — Various houses with Euromed Postal emblem at: a, UR. b, LR.

Perf. 13¼ Syncopated
2018, July 9 — Photo.
1249 A825 3.75d Horiz. pair, #a-b — 1.60 1.60

Mediterranean Houses — A826

No. 1250 — Various house interiors and Euromed Postal emblem at: a, LR. b, UL.

Perf. 13¼ Syncopated
2018, July 9 — Litho.
1250 A826 3.75d Vert. pair, #a-b — 1.60 1.60

General Confederation of Moroccan Enterprises, 70th Anniv. — A827

Perf. 13¼ Syncopated
2018, July 25 — Photo.
1251 A827 9d multi — 1.90 1.90

King Mohammed VI With Coat of Arms at Upper Right — A828

Serpentine Die Cut 11 Syncopated
2018, July 26 — Litho.
Booklet Stamp
Self-Adhesive
1252 A828 3.75d multi — .80
a. Booklet pane of 5 — 4.00

Compare type A828 with types A767, A769 and A859.

City Gates — A829

No. 1253: a, Bab el Okla, Tetuan. b, Bab Marshan, Tangier. c, Bab al Marsa, Essaouira. d, Bab al Bahr, Assilah. e, Bab el Gharbi, Oujda. f, Bab el Kebir, Rabat. g, Bab Lamrissa, Salé. h, Mehdia Gate, Kenitra.

Serpentine Die Cut 11 Syncopated
2018, Aug. — Litho.
Self-Adhesive
1253 — Booklet pane of 8 — 15.50
a.-h. A829 9d Any single — 1.90 1.90

Flora and Fauna — A830

No. 1254: a, Dromedary. b, Lavender flowers.

Perf. 13 Syncopated
2018, Aug. 9 — Photo.
1254 A830 3.75d Horiz. pair, #a-b — 1.60 1.60

Miniature Sheet

Butterflies — A831

No. 1255 — Various unnamed butterflies with background color of: a, Orange and yellow orange (denomination below butterfly). b, Orange brown (denomination to left of butterfly). c, Slate blue. d, Green. e, Blue gray.

Serpentine Die Cut 11
2018, Oct. 1 — Self-Adhesive — Litho.
1255 A831 — Sheet of 5 — —
a.-e. 3.75d Any single — — —

A832

Oujda, 2018 Capital of Arab Culture A833

No. 1256: a, Woman wearing blouza. b, Grand Mosque of Oudja.
No. 1257: a, Rebab. b, Bab Sidi Abdelouahab.

2018, Oct. 9 — Litho. — Perf. 14
1256 A832 3.75d Horiz. pair, #a-b — 1.60 1.60
c. As "a," perf. 13¼x14 — 1.75 1.75
d. As "b," perf. 13¼x14 — 1.75 1.75
1257 A833 3.75d Horiz. pair, #a-b — 1.60 1.60
c. As "a," perf. 14x13¼ — 1.75 1.75
d. As "b," perf. 14x13¼ — 1.75 1.75
e. Souvenir sheet of 4, #1256c, 1256d, 1257c, 1257d — 7.50 7.50

Green March, 43rd Anniv. — A834

Perf. 13¼ Syncopated
2018, Nov. 6 — Litho.
1258 A834 9d multi — 1.90 1.90

Maghzen Hand Stamps A835

No. 1259: a, Rectangular hand stamp, blue background. b, Octagonal hand stamp, red brown background.

Perf. 13¼ Syncopated
2018, Nov. 22 — Litho.
1259 A835 3.75d Horiz. pair, #a-b — 1.60 1.60

Amateur Andalusian Musicians Association, 60th Anniv. — A836

Perf. 13¼ Syncopated
2018, Dec. 14 — Litho.
1260 A836 3.75d multi — .80 .80

Universal Declaration of Human Rights, 70th Anniv. — A837

Perf. 13¼ Syncopated
2018, Dec. 20 — Litho.
1261 A837 9d multi — 1.90 1.90

Al Boraq High-Speed Train — A838

Perf. 13¼x13 Syncopated
2019, Mar. 21 — Litho.
1262 A838 9d multi — 1.90 1.90

A839, A840, A841, A842, A843, A844

A845

Ceramics — A846

Serpentine Die Cut 11 Syncopated
2019, Mar. 22 — Litho.
Self-Adhesive
1263 — Booklet pane of 8 — 15.50
a. A839 9d multi — 1.90 1.90
b. A840 9d multi — 1.90 1.90
c. A841 9d multi — 1.90 1.90
d. A842 9d multi — 1.90 1.90
e. A843 9d multi — 1.90 1.90
f. A844 9d multi — 1.90 1.90
g. A845 9d multi — 1.90 1.90
h. A846 9d multi — 1.90 1.90

A847, A848

MOROCCO

683

A849
A850
A851
A852
A853
A854
A855
A856

Jewelry
A855   A856

Serpentine Die Cut 11 Syncopated
2019, Mar. 29 Litho.
Self-Adhesive
1264	Booklet pane of 10	19.00	
a.	A847 9d multi	1.90	1.90
b.	A848 9d multi	1.90	1.90
c.	A849 9d multi	1.90	1.90
d.	A850 9d multi	1.90	1.90
e.	A851 9d multi	1.90	1.90
f.	A852 9d multi	1.90	1.90
g.	A853 9d multi	1.90	1.90
h.	A854 9d multi	1.90	1.90
i.	A855 9d multi	1.90	1.90
j.	A856 9d multi	1.90	1.90

Musical Instrument Types of 1971-75 Redrawn and

A857

Musical Instruments
A858

Serpentine Die Cut 11 Syncopated
2019, Apr. 1 Litho.
Self-Adhesive
1265	Booklet pane of 5	—
a.	SP4 3.75d multi	—
b.	A857 3.75d multi	—
c.	A139 3.75d multi	—
d.	A858 3.75d multi	—
e.	SP6 3.75d multi	—

King Mohammed VI With Crown at Upper Left — A859

Serpentine Die Cut 11 Syncopated
2019, Apr. 1 Litho.
Booklet Stamp
Self-Adhesive
1265F	A859 3.75d multi	—
g.	Booklet pane of 5	—

Compare type A859 with types A767, A769 and A828.

Portrait of Claude Monet, by Pierre-Auguste Renoir (1841-1919) — A862

Perf. 13¼ Syncopated
2019, Apr. 9 Photo.
| 1266 | A862 9d multi | 1.90 | 1.90 |

Bee on Flower — A863

Lemons and Lemon Blossoms — A864

Perf. 13 Syncopated
2019, Apr. 16 Photo.
| 1267 | A863 3.75d multi | .80 | .80 |
| 1268 | A864 9d multi | 1.90 | 1.90 |

Nos. 1267-1268 are impregnated with a lemon scent.

Paintings A865

No. 1269: a, The Gulf of Marseille Seen From L'Estaque, by Paul Cézanne (1839-1906). b, Mohammed V Square, Casablanca, by Jacques Majorelle (1886-1962).

Perf. 13¼ Syncopated
2019, Apr. 26 Photo.
1269	A865	Horiz. pair	2.75	2.75
a.		3.75d multi	.80	.80
b.		9d multi	1.90	1.90
c.		As "a," perf. 13¼	.80	.80
d.		As "b," perf. 13¼	1.90	1.90
e.		Souvenir sheet of 2, #1269c-1269d	2.75	2.75

See France No. 5641.

Children's Art — A866

No. 1270 — Art by: a, Anas Rabhi. b, Ryan Youssef. c, Ahmed Habbani. d, Mohammed Amine Aqamour.

Perf. 13¼ Syncopated
2019, June 17 Litho.
| 1270 | | Vert. strip of 4 | 3.25 | 3.25 |
| a.-d. | A866 3.75d Any single | .80 | .80 |

Moroccan National Soccer Team — A867

Perf. 13¼ Syncopated
2019, June 24 Photo.
| 1271 | A867 9d multi | 1.90 | 1.90 |

Traditional Costumes — A868

No. 1272: a, Woman's costume. b, Man's costume.

Perf. 13¼ Syncopated
2019, July 8 Photo.
1272	A868	Horiz. pair	2.75	2.75
a.		3.75d multi	.80	.80
b.		9d multi	1.90	1.90

Accession to the Throne of King Mohammed VI, 20th Anniv. — A869

Nos. 1273 and 1274 — King Mohammed VI wearing: a, Suit and tie. b, Robes and red hat.

Perf. 13¼ Syncopated
2019, Aug. 1 Litho.
| 1273 | A869 9d Horiz. pair, #a-b | — | — |

Litho. With Foil Application
Souvenir Sheet
| 1274 | A869 9d Sheet of 2, #a-b | — | — |

Gold foil on No. 1274 is more reflective than the gold ink used on No. 1273.

12th Africa Games, Rabat A870

No. 1275: a, Games emblem. b, Games emblem and map of Africa.

Perf. 13¼ Syncopated
2019, Aug. 19 Photo.
1275	A870	Horiz. pair	—	—
a.		3.75d multi	—	—
b.		9d multi	—	—

Doves, Flag of Palestinian Authority, Dome of the Rock, Jerusalem A871

Perf. 13¼ Syncopated
2019, Oct. 9 Photo.
| 1276 | A871 9d multi | — | — |

Jerusalem, capital of Palestinian Authority.

World Savings Day — A872

Perf. 13¼ Syncopated
2019, Oct. 31 Photo.
| 1277 | A872 9d multi | — | — |

Green March, 44th Anniv. — A873

Perf. 13¼ Syncopated
2019, Nov. 6 Photo.
| 1278 | A873 9d multi | — | — |

Aissaouas Mosque, Tangier — A874

No. 1279 — Stamp color: a, Brown. b, Red. c, Emerald. d, Orange. e, Prus blue. f, Violet.

Perf. 13 Syncopated
2019, Nov. 21 Photo.
1279		Horiz. strip of 6	—	—
a.-f.	A874 3.75d Any single	—	—
g.		Souvenir sheet of 6, #1279a-1279f	—	—

Opening of Barid Al-Maghrib Museum (No. 1279g).

Public Bus Transportation in Morocco, Cent. — A875

Perf. 13¼ Syncopated
2019, Dec. 10 Photo.
| 1280 | A875 3.75d multi | — | — |

Morocco Post Electronic Certification Service — A876

Perf. 13¼ Syncopated
2020, Jan. 14 Photo.
| 1281 | A876 3.75d multi | — | — |

King Mohammed VI — A878

Serpentine Die Cut 11 Syncopated
2020-21 Photo.
Booklet Stamp
Self-Adhesive
1283	A878 9d multi	—	—
a.	Booklet pane of 10	—	—
b.	Dated 2021	—	—
c.	Booklet pane of 10 #1283b	—	—

Issued: No. 1283, 3/20; No. 1283b, 6/17/21.

Folklore Festivals Types of 1970-85 Redrawn
Serpentine Die Cut 11 Syncopated
2020, Feb. 21 Litho.
Self-Adhesive
1284	Booklet pane of 8	—	—
a.	A82 9d Like #230	—	—
b.	A129 9d Like #318	—	—
c.	A129 9d Like #319	—	—
d.	A138 9d Like #340	—	—
e.	A289 9d Like #600	—	—
f.	A226 9d Like #492	—	—
g.	A188 9d Like #434	—	—
h.	A177 9d Like #420	—	—

Flower Types of 1975-81 Redrawn

No. 1285: a, Bubonium intricatum. b, Pansies. c, Poppies. d, Anemones. e, Daisies.

Serpentine Die Cut 11 Syncopated
2020, Feb. 27 Litho.
1285	Booklet pane of 5	—	—
a.	A222 3.75d Like #485	—	—
b.	A135 3.75d Like #335	—	—
c.	A135 3.75d Like #333	—	—
d.	A135 3.75d Like #331	—	—
e.	A135 3.75d Like #328	—	—

Reconstruction of Earthquake-Stricken Agadir, 60th Anniv. — A879

Perf. 13¼ Syncopated
2020, Feb. 29 Photo.
| 1286 | A879 3.75d multi | — | — |

World Environment Day — A880

No. 1287: a, Brown trout (truite fario). b, Atlas pistachio tree.

MOROCCO

Perf. 13¼ Syncopated
2020, June 5 — Litho.
1287 A880 Vert. pair
  a. 3.75d multi
  b. 9d multi
  c. As "a," perf. 13¼
  d. As "b," perf. 13¼
  e. Souvenir sheet of 2, #1287c-1287d

Traditional Dishes — A881

No. 1288: a, Bissara (bean soup). b, Tagine tagra (fish stew).

Perf. 13¼ Syncopated
2020, July 13 — Litho.
1288 A881 9d Horiz. pair, #a-b

Children's Art — A882

No. 1289 — Children's drawings on the theme of plastic pollution by: a, Maram Elkamili. b, Najlaa El Ouafiri. c, Basma Belbahloul. d, Abderrahman Karimine, vert.

Perf. 13¼ Syncopated
2020, Sept. 29 — Photo.
1289 A882 3.75d Strip of 4, #a-d

Moroccan Retirement Fund, 90th Anniv. — A883

Perf. 13¼ Syncopated
2020, Oct. 1 — Photo.
1290 A883 3.75d multi

Noor Ouarzazate Solar Power Station A884

Perf. 13x13¼ Syncopated
2020, Oct. 22 — Photo.
1291 A884 3.75d multi

United Nations, 75th Anniv. — A885

Perf. 13¼ Syncopated
2020, Oct. 24 — Photo.
1292 A885 9d multi

Green March, 45th Anniv. — A886

Perf. 13¼ Syncopated
2020, Nov. 6 — Photo.
1293 A886 9d multi

Sijilmassa, 1300th Anniv. — A887

Perf. 13¼ Syncopated
2020, Nov. 23 — Photo.
1294 A887 3.75d multi

First Moroccan Ceramics School, Safi, Cent. — A888

No. 1295: a, Plate. b, Zir Vase, vert. c, Jug, vert.

Perf. 13¼ Syncopated
2020, Nov. 30 — Photo.
1295 A888 3.75d Strip of 3, #a-c
  d. Souvenir sheet of 3, #1295a-1295c

The sides of the stamps having the syncopation on No. 1295d differ from those on Nos. 1295a-1295c.

National Human Rights Council, 30th Anniv. — A889

Perf. 13¼ Syncopated
2020, Dec. 10 — Photo.
1296 A889 3.75d multi

Al-Barid Bank, 10th Anniv. — A890

Perf. 13¼ Syncopated
2020, Dec. 30 — Photo.
1297 A890 3.75d multi

Diplomatic Relations Between Morocco and Dominican Republic, 60th Anniv. — A891

No. 1298: a, 3.75d, Alcázar de Colón, Santo Domingo, Dominican Republic. b, 9d, Kasbah of the Oudaias, Rabat, Morocco.

Perf. 13¼ Syncopated
2021, Mar. 25 — Photo.
1298 A891 Horiz. pair, #a-b
  Dated 2020. See Dominican Republic No. 1685.

World Day of Work Security and Health — A892

Perf. 13¼ Syncopated
2021, Apr. 28 — Photo.
1299 A892 3.75d multi

Thor Heyerdahl's Ra II Expedition, 50th Anniv. — A893

Perf. 13¼ Syncopated
2021, May 21 — Photo.
1300 A893 9d multi

World Anti-Tobacco Day — A894

Perf. 13¼ Syncopated
2021, May 31 — Photo.
1301 A894 3.75d multi

Painted Screens A895

No. 1302 — Screen depicting: a, People at seaside restaurant, by M'hammad Jirari. b, Rocks on shore, by El Batoul Bargach.

Perf. 13¼ Syncopated
2021, June 21 — Photo.
1302 A895 3.75d Horiz. pair, #a-b

Painting by Abbes Saladi (1950-92) — A896

Perf. 13¼ Syncopated
2021, June 30 — Litho.
1303 A896 9d multi

Earrings — A897

Perf. 13¼ Syncopated
2021, July 12 — Litho.
1304 A897 9d multi

African Philatelic Hub, 5th Anniv. — A898

Perf. 13¼ Syncopated
2021, Aug. 24 — Litho.
1305 A898 9d multi

The Passage of a Guá in Morocco, Painting by Eugène Delacroix (1798-1863) A899

Perf. 13¼ Syncopated
2021, Sept. 22 — Litho.
1306 A899 9d multi

Battle of Annual, Cent. — A900

Perf. 13x13¼ Syncopated
2021, Sept. 30 — Litho.
1307 A900 3.75d multi

Es-Samara Mosque and Map of Morocco — A901

Perf. 13¼ Syncopated
2021, Nov. 6 — Litho.
1308 A901 9d multi
  Green March, 46th anniv.

National Archives of Morocco, 10th Anniv. — A902

Perf. 13¼ Syncopated
2021, Nov. 30 — Litho.
1309 A902 3.75d multi

Musicians — A903

No. 1310: a, 3.75d, Stambali musicians, Tunisia. b, 9d, Gnaoua musicians, Morocco.

Perf. 13¼ Syncopated
2021, Dec. 1 — Litho.
1310 A903 Horiz. pair, #a-b
  Joint issue between Morocco and Tunisia. See Tunisia No. 1770.

International Day of Volunteers — A904

Perf. 13¼ Syncopated
2021, Dec. 6 — Litho.
1311 A904 9d multi

School of Textile and Clothing Industries, 25th Anniv. — A905

Perf. 13¼ Syncopated
2021, Dec. 15 — Litho.
1312 A905 3.75d multi

MOROCCO

International Year of Fruits and Vegetables — A906

Perf. 13¼x13¾ Syncopated
2021, Dec. 31 Litho.
1313 A906 3.75d multi

Rabat Zoo, 10th Anniv. — A907

Perf. 13¼x13¾ Syncopated
2022, Jan. 14 Litho.
1314 A907 3.75d multi

Diplomatic Relations Between Morocco and Serbia, 65th Anniv. — A908

No. 1315: a, Zezelj Bridge over Danube River, Novi Sad, Serbia. b, Mohammed VI Bridge over Bouregreg River, Rabat, Morocco.

Perf. 13¼x14 Syncopated
2022, Mar. 1 Litho.
1315 A908 Horiz. pair
  a. N multi
  b. I multi

On day of issue, No. 1315a sold for 3.75d and No. 1315b sold for 9d. See Serbia No. 1015.

International Women's Day — A909

Perf. 13¼x14 Syncopated
2022, Mar. 9 Litho.
1316 A909 (3.75d) multi

Famous Women A910

No. 1317: a, Malika El Fasi (1919-2007), writer and signer of Independence Proclamation. b, Fatima Mernissi (1940-2015), sociologist. c, Touria Chaoui (1936-56), first Moroccan aviatrix.

Perf. 13¼x14 Syncopated
2022, Mar. 23 Litho.
1317 A910 (3.75d) Horiz. strip of 3, #a-c

Hassania School of Public Works, 50th Anniv. — A911

Perf. 13 Syncopated
2022, June 9 Litho.
1318 A911 3.75d multi

Bank Al-Maghrib Museum, 20th Anniv. — A912

Perf. 14 Syncopated
2022, July 1 Litho.
1319 A912 3.75d multi

Tétouan — A913

Perf. 14 Syncopated
2022, July 11 Litho.
1320 A913 9d multi

Emblem of National Union of Moroccan Women — A914

Perf. 13¼x14 Syncopated
2022, Oct. 10 Litho.
1321 A914 3.75d multi

Marrakech Declaration on Violence Against Women.

Green March, 47th Anniv. — A915

Perf. 14 Syncopated
2022, Nov. 6 Litho.
1322 A915 9d multi

Octagonal Sherifian Handstamps of Azemmour A916

Magnified

Octagonal Sherifian Handstamps of Casablanca A917

Magnified

Octagonal Sherifian Handstamps of El Ksar — A918

Magnified

Octagonal Sherifian Handstamps of Fez — A919

Magnified

Octagonal Sherifian Handstamps of Larache — A920

Magnified

Octagonal Sherifian Handstamps of Marrakech A921

Magnified

Octagonal Sherifian Handstamps of Mazagan — A922

Magnified

Octagonal Sherifian Handstamps of Meknes — A923

Magnified

Octagonal Sherifian Handstamps of Mogador — A924

Magnified

Octagonal Sherifian Handstamps of Rabat — A925

Magnified

Octagonal Sherifian Handstamps of Safi — A926

Magnified

Octagonal Sherifian Handstamps of Tangier — A927

Magnified

Octagonal Sherifian Handstamps of Tétuan — A928

Magnified

Perf. 14 Syncopated
2022, Nov. 24 Litho.
1323 A916 3.75d multi
1324 A917 3.75d multi
1325 A918 3.75d multi
1326 A919 3.75d multi
1327 A920 3.75d multi
1328 A921 3.75d multi
1329 A922 3.75d multi
1330 A923 3.75d multi
1331 A924 3.75d multi

MOROCCO

1332 A925 3.75d multi — —
1333 A926 3.75d multi — —
1334 A927 3.75d multi — —
1335 A928 3.75d multi — —

Round Sherifian Handstamps of Azemmour and Sultan Yusef Ben Hassan — A929

Magnified

Round Sherifian Handstamps of Casablanca and Sultan Yusef Ben Hassan — A930

Magnified

Round Sherifian Handstamps of El Ksar and Sultan Yusef Ben Hassan — A931

Magnified

Round Sherifian Handstamps of Fez and Sultan Yusef Ben Hassan — A932

Magnified

Round Sherifian Handstamps of Larache and Sultan Yusef Ben Hassan — A933

Magnified

Round Sherifian Handstamps of Marrakech and Sultan Yusef Ben Hassan — A934

Magnified

Round Sherifian Handstamps of Mazagan and Sultan Yusef Ben Hassan — A935

Magnified

Round Sherifian Handstamps of Meknes and Sultan Yusef Ben Hassan — A936

Magnified

Round Sherifian Handstamps of Mogador and Sultan Yusef Ben Hassan — A937

Magnified

Round Sherifian Handstamps of Rabat and Sultan Yusef Ben Hassan — A938

Magnified

Round Sherifian Handstamps of Safi and Sultan Yusef Ben Hassan — A939

Magnified

Round Sherifian Handstamps of Tangier and Sultan Yusef Ben Hassan — A940

Magnified

Round Sherifian Handstamps of Tétuan and Sultan Yusef Ben Hassan — A941

Magnified

Perf. 14 Syncopated
2022, Nov. 24 Litho.
1336 A929 3.75d multi — —
   a. Horiz. pair, #1323, 1336
1337 A930 3.75d multi — —
   a. Horiz. pair, #1324, 1337
1338 A931 3.75d multi — —
   a. Horiz. pair, #1325, 1338
1339 A932 3.75d multi — —
   a. Horiz. pair, #1326, 1339
1340 A933 3.75d multi — —
   a. Horiz. pair, #1327, 1340
1341 A934 3.75d multi — —
   a. Horiz. pair, #1328, 1341
1342 A935 3.75d multi — —
   a. Horiz. pair, #1329, 1342
1343 A936 3.75d multi — —
   a. Horiz. pair, #1330, 1343
1344 A937 3.75d multi — —
   a. Horiz. pair, #1331, 1344
1345 A938 3.75d multi — —
   a. Horiz. pair, #1332, 1345
1346 A939 3.75d multi — —
   a. Horiz. pair, #1333, 1346
1347 A940 3.75d multi — —
   a. Horiz. pair, #1334, 1347
1348 A941 3.75d multi — —
   a. Horiz. pair, #1335, 1348

Muhammad V Theater, 60th Anniv. — A942

Perf. 14 Syncopated
2022, Dec. 12 Litho.
1349 A942 3.75d multi — —

Moulay Idris High School, Fez, 107th Anniv. — A943

Perf. 14 Syncopated
2022, Dec. 12 Litho.
1350 A943 3.75d multi — —

Moroccan National Men's Soccer Team for 2022 World Cup Soccer Tournament, Qatar — A944

Perf. 14 Syncopated
2022, Dec. 28 Litho.
1351 A944 9d multi — —

International Data Protection Day — A945

Perf. 14 Syncopated
2023, Jan. 28 Litho.
1352 A945 3.75d multi — —

Office of the Royal Mediator, 20th Anniv. — A946

Perf. 14 Syncopated
2023, Feb. 28 Litho.
1353 A946 3.75d multi — —

SEMI-POSTAL STAMPS

Nos. 1-5 Surcharged

1960, Mar. Unwmk. Engr. Perf. 13
B1 A1 5fr + 10fr brt bl & ind .45 .40
B2 A1 10fr + 10fr bis brn & choc .50 .50
B3 A1 15fr + 10fr dp grn & mag 1.15 1.10
B4 A1 25fr + 15fr purple 1.25 1.15
B5 A1 30fr + 20fr green 2.00 2.00
  Nos. B1-B5 (5) 5.35 5.15

The surtax aided families whose members consumed adulterated cooking oil with crippling or fatal results.

French Morocco Nos. 321 and 322 Surcharged

1960, Sept. 12
B6 A71 15fr + 3fr on 18fr dk grn .75 .75
B7 A71 20fr + 5fr brown lake 1.20 1.20

Nos. 1 and 6 Surcharged in Red or Black

1963, Jan. 28 Engr. Perf. 13
B8 A1 20c + 5c on 5fr brt bl & ind (R) .70 .70
B9 A1 30c + 10c on 50fr rose red .80 .45

The surtax was for flood victims.

MOROCCO

Moroccan Brooch — SP1

Design: 40c+10c, Brooch with pendants.

1966, May 23   Photo.   Perf. 11½
Granite Paper
B10 SP1 25c + 5c ultra, sil, blk & red   .90   .55
B11 SP1 40c + 10c mag, sil, blk, ultra & bl   1.40   .70
  a. Pair, #B10-B11, vertically tête-bêche   3.25   3.25

Meeting in Morocco of the Middle East and North African Red Cross-Red Crescent Seminar. The surtax was for the Moroccan Red Crescent Society.
See Nos. B12-B13, B15-B16, B19-B22, B26-B27, B29-B30, B34-B35.

1967, May 15   Granite Paper
Designs: 60c+5c, Two brooches, by silver drapery. 1d+10c, Two bracelets.
B12 SP1 60c + 5c yel bis & multi   .75   .75
  a. Pair, vertically tête-bêche   3.00   3.00
B13 SP1 1d + 10c emer & multi   1.60   1.60
  a. Pair, vertically tête-bêche   4.75   4.75

Surtax for the Moroccan Red Crescent Society.

Hands Reading Braille and Map of Morocco — SP2

1969, Mar. 21   Photo.   Perf. 12½
B14 SP2 25c + 10c multi   .60   .25

Week of the Blind, Mar. 21-29.

Jewelry Type of 1966
Designs: 25c+5c, Silver earrings. 40c+10c, Gold ear pendant.

1969, May 9   Photo.   Perf. 11½
Granite Paper
B15 SP1 25c + 5c gray grn & multi   1.25   .65
B16 SP1 40c + 10c tan & multi   1.60   .80
  a. Pair, #B15-B16, vert. tête-bêche   5.75   5.75

50th anniv. of the League of Red Cross Societies. Surtax was for Moroccan Red Crescent Society.

Nos. 173-174 Surcharged

1970, Feb. 26   Litho.   Perf. 13
B17 A65 10c + 25c multi   3.00   3.00
B18 A65 15c + 25c multi   3.00   3.00

The surtax was for flood victims.

Jewelry Type of 1966
Designs: 25c+5c, Necklace with pendants. 50c+10c, Earring with 5 pendants.

1970, May 25   Photo.   Perf. 11½
Granite Paper
B19 SP1 25c + 5c gray & multi   1.10   .90
B20 SP1 50c + 10c brt vio & multi   1.40   1.25
  a. Pair, #B19-B20, vert. tête-bêche   3.75   3.75

Surtax for Moroccan Red Crescent Society.

1971, May 10   Granite Paper
25c+5c, Brooch. 40c+10c, Stomacher.
B21 SP1 25c + 5c gray & multi   1.10   .65
B22 SP1 40c + 10c yel & multi   1.90   1.00
  a. Pair, #B21-B22, vertically tête-bêche   3.25   3.25

Globe and Map of Palestine — SP3

1971, Apr. 30   Perf. 13
B23 SP3 25c + 10c multi   .60   .30

Palestine Week, May 3-8.

String Instrument and Bow — SP4

1971, June 28   Photo.   Perf. 12
B24 SP4 40c + 10c multi   .60   .40

Week of the Blind. See No. 1265a.

Mizmar (Double Flute) — SP5

1972, Mar. 31   Photo.   Perf. 13x13½
B25 SP5 25c + 10c multi   .60   .55

Week of the Blind.

Jewelry Type of 1966
Designs: 25c+5c, Jeweled bracelets. 70c+10c, Rectangular pendant with ball drop.

1972, May 8   Photo.   Perf. 11½
Granite Paper
B26 SP1 25c + 5c brn & multi   .75   .75
B27 SP1 70c + 10c dp grn & multi   1.10   1.10
  a. Pair, #B26-B27, vert. tête-bêche   3.00   3.00

For overprints see Nos. 295-296.

Drums — SP6

1973, Mar. 30   Photo.   Perf. 13x14
B28 SP6 70c + 10c multi   .65   .50

Week of the Blind. See No. 1265e.

Jewelry Type of 1966
25c+5c, Silver box pendant. 70c+10c, Bracelet.

1973, June 15   Photo.   Perf. 11½
B29 SP1 25c + 5c bl & multi   1.40   .60
B30 SP1 70c + 10c org & multi   2.00   .95
  a. Pair, #B29-B30, vert. tête-bêche   5.75   5.75

Moroccan Red Crescent Society. For overprints see Nos. 351-352.

Pistol — SP7

70c+10c, Decorated antique powder box.

1974, July 8   Photo.   Perf. 14x13½
B31 SP7 25c + 5c multi   1.15   1.15
B32 SP7 70c + 10c multi   1.75   1.75
  a. Pair, #B31-B32, vert. tête-bêche   3.00   3.00

Moroccan Red Crescent Society.

Erbab (Fiddle) — SP8

1975, Jan. 10   Photo.   Perf. 13
B33 SP8 70c + 10c multi   1.10   .50

Week of the Blind.

Jewelry Type of 1966
25c+5c, Silver pendant. 70c+10c, Earring.

1975, Mar. 13   Photo.   Perf. 13½
B34 SP1 25c + 5c multi   .80   .80
B35 SP1 70c + 10c multi   1.25   1.25
  a. Pair, #B34-B35, vert. tête-bêche   2.50   2.50

Moroccan Red Crescent Society. For overprints see #386-387.

Campaign Against COVID-19 — SP9

Perf. 13¼ Syncopated
2020, May 7   Litho.
B36 SP9 3.75d +5d multi

Surtax was for COVID-19 Special Fund.

AIR POST STAMPS

Sultan's Star over Casablanca — AP1

Unwmk.
1957, May 4   Engr.   Perf. 13
C1 AP1 15fr car & brt grn   1.25   1.00
C2 AP1 25fr brt grnsh bl   1.75   1.25
C3 AP1 30fr red brn   2.60   1.75
  Nos. C1-C3 (3)   5.60   4.00

Intl. Fair, Casablanca, May 4-19.

King Hassan II — AP2

1962
C5 AP2 90c black   .70   .25
C6 AP2 1d rose red   .95   .25
C7 AP2 2d deep blue   1.10   .60
C8 AP2 3d dl bl grn   2.10   1.00
C9 AP2 5d purple   4.25   1.60
  Nos. C5-C9 (5)   9.10   3.70

Meteorological Day Type of Regular Issue

1964, Mar. 23   Photo.   Perf. 11½
Granite Paper
C10 A39 90c Anemometer & globe 1.10   .70

Intl. Fair, Casablanca, 20th Anniv. — AP3

1964, Apr. 30   Photo.   Perf. 12½
C11 AP3 1d bl, bis & org   1.10   .70

Moroccan Pavilion and Unisphere — AP4

1964, May 25   Unwmk.   Perf. 12½
C12 AP4 1d dk grn, red & bl   1.10   .80

New York World's Fair, 1964-65.

Ramses II and UNESCO Emblem — AP5

Litho. & Engr.
1966, Oct. 3   Perf. 12x11½
C13 AP5 1d magenta, yel   1.25   .80

UNESCO, 20th anniv.

Jet Plane — AP6

Perf. 12½x13½
1966, Dec. 19   Photo.
C14 AP6 3d multi   3.50   1.75

Costume Type of Regular Issue
Design: 1d, Women from Ait Ouaouzguit.

1969, Jan. 21   Litho.   Perf. 12
C15 A74 1d multi   2.40   1.25

Coin Type of Regular Issue, 1968
Coins: 1d, King Mohammed V, 1960. 5d, King Hassan II, 1965.

1969, Mar. 3   Photo.   Perf. 11½
Granite Paper
C16 A73 1d brt bl, sil & blk   4.50   1.50
C17 A73 5d vio blk, sil & blk   9.00   5.50

King Hassan II — AP7

1983, Mar. 1   Photo.   Perf. 12
Granite Paper
C18 AP7 1.40d multi   .60   .25
C19 AP7 2d multi   .65   .25
C20 AP7 3d multi   .90   .30
C21 AP7 5d multi   1.40   .50
C22 AP7 10d multi   3.00   .95
  Nos. C18-C22 (5)   6.55   2.25

No. C18 Overprinted

1987, Mar. 23   Photo.   Perf. 12
Granite Paper
C23 AP7 2d multi   1.10   .65

1st World Congress of Friday Preachers, Al Joumouaa.

No. C18 Overprinted

MOROCCO — MOZAMBIQUE

1989, Mar. 27   *Photo.*   *Perf. 12*
Granite Paper
C24   AP7   1.40d multi   .45   .35

Maghreb Union, agreement between Morocco, Algeria and Tunisia.

No. C18 Surcharged

2000, July 6   *Photo.*   *Perf. 12*
Granite Paper
C25   AP7   6.50d on 1.40d multi   2.25   1.10

Intl. Colloquium on King Hassan II.

POSTAGE DUE STAMPS

D1

1965		Unwmk.	Typo.	Perf. 14x13½
J1	D1	5c green	21.00	3.50
J2	D1	10c bister brown	1.00	.30
J3	D1	20c red	1.00	.30
J4	D1	30c brown black	1.50	.65
		Nos. J1-J4 (4)	24.50	4.75

See French Morocco Nos. J27-J34, J46-J56.

Oranges — D2

1974-96		Photo.		Perf. 14
J5	D2	5c shown	.30	.25
J6	D2	10c Cherries	.45	.25
J7	D2	20c Grapes	.60	.25
J8	D2	30c Peaches, horiz.	.90	.25
J9	D2	40c Grapes ('78)	.35	.25
J10	D2	60c Peaches, horiz. ('78)	1.10	.25
J11	D2	80c Oranges ('78)	1.40	.25
J12	D2	1d Apples ('86)	.50	.25
J13	D2	1.20d Cherries ('84)	.90	.25
J14	D2	1.60d Peaches ('85)	.90	.25
J15	D2	2d Strawberries ('86)	.90	.35

Litho.

J16	D2	5d like #J12 ('96)	1.90	1.00
		Nos. J5-J16 (12)	10.20	3.85

For surcharges see Nos. 322, 395.

Strawberries — D3

Strawberries — D3a

Grapes D4

Apples D5

Cherries — D6

2003   *Photo.*   *Perf. 13x13½*

J17	D3	1.50d multi	—	—
J17A	D3a	1.50d multi	.90	.75
J18	D4	2d multi	—	—
J19	D5	5d multi	3.25	2.75
J20	D6	2d multi	1.20	1.10
		Nos. J17-J20 (5)	5.35	4.60

Fruit Type of 1974-96

2005 ?   *Litho.*   *Perf. 14*

J21   D2   60c Peaches   —   —

No. J21 has a background of solid color. No. J10 has a background of dots. The text is thicker and heavier on No. J10 than on No. J21.

Bananas — D7

Serpentine Die Cut 11

2009, Sept. 1   *Litho.*
Self-Adhesive
J24   D7   3.25d multi   .80   .80

NORTHERN ZONE

100 Centimos = 1 Peseta

All Northern Zone issues except Nos. 21-22 were also sold imperforate in limited quantities.

Sultan Mohammed V — A1

Villa Sanjurjo Harbor — A2

Designs: 25c, Polytechnic school. 50c, 10p, Institute of Culture, Tetuan.

Perf. 13x12½, 12½x13

1956, Aug. 23		Photo.		Unwmk.
1	A1	10c deep rose	.30	.25
2	A1	15c yellow brn	.30	.25
3	A2	25c dk bl gray	.30	.25
4	A1	50c dark olive	.40	.25
5	A1	80c brt green	.80	.80
6	A2	2p brt red lil	6.50	6.50
7	A2	3p brt blue	11.00	11.00
8	A1	10p green	25.00	40.00
		Nos. 1-8 (8)	44.60	59.30

Value, set of Nos. 1-8 as imperf. pairs $2,500.

A3

1957, Mar. 2   *Perf. 13½x13*

9	A3	80c blue green	.75	.75
10	A3	1.50p gray olive	1.90	1.90
11	A3	3p deep rose	4.00	4.00
		Nos. 9-11 (3)	6.65	6.65

1st anniv. of independence. See Morocco Nos. 13-15. Value, set of Nos. 9-11 as imperf. pairs $500.

Sultan Mohammed V — A4

1957   *Engr.*   *Perf. 13*

12	A4	30c brt bl & indigo	.25	.25
13	A4	70c bis, brn & choc	.35	.25
14	A4	80c brt violet	1.50	.35
15	A4	1.50p dp grn & mag	.50	.30
16	A4	3p green	.75	.65
17	A4	7p rose red	5.00	1.50
		Nos. 12-17 (6)	8.35	3.30

Value, set of Nos. 12-17 as imperf. pairs $700.

Prince Moulay el Hassan — A5

1957, July 15   *Photo.*   *Perf. 13*

18	A5	80c blue	.60	.60
19	A5	1.50p green	1.50	1.50
20	A5	3p carmine rose	4.50	4.50
		Nos. 18-20 (3)	6.60	6.60

Value, set of Nos. 18-20 as imperf. pairs $600.

Nos. 13 and 15 Surcharged in Carmine or Black

1957   *Engr.*

21	A4	15c on 70c (C)	.75	.75
22	A4	1.20p on 1.50p (Bk)	1.25	1.25

King Mohammed V — A6

1957, Nov.   *Photo.*   *Perf. 12½*

23	A6	1.20p blk & brt grn	.65	.65
24	A6	1.80p blk & rose red	.65	.65
25	A6	3p black & violet	2.00	2.00
		Nos. 23-25 (3)	3.30	3.30

Enthronement of Mohammed V, 30th anniv. Value, set of Nos. 23-25 as imperf. pairs $750.

NORTHERN ZONE AIR POST STAMPS

Plane over Lau Dam — AP1

1.40p, 4.80p, Plane over Nekor bridge.

Perf. 12½x13

1956, Dec. 17		Photo.		Unwmk.
C1	AP1	25c rose violet	.35	.35
C2	AP1	1.40p lilac rose	.90	.90
C3	AP1	3.40p org vermilion	1.90	1.90
C4	AP1	4.80p dull violet	3.25	3.25
		Nos. C1-C4 (4)	6.40	6.40

Value, Nos. C1-C4 as set of imperf. pairs $750.

MOZAMBIQUE

mō-zəm-'bēk

LOCATION — Southeastern Africa, bordering on the Mozambique Channel
GOVT. — Republic
AREA — 308,642 sq. mi.
POP. — 31,260,000 (2020 est.)
CAPITAL — Maputo

Formerly a Portuguese colony, Mozambique, or Portuguese East Africa, was divided into eight districts: Lourenco Marques, Inhambane, Quelimane, Tete, Mozambique, Zambezia, Nyassa and the Manica and Sofala region formerly administered by the Mozambique Company. At various times the districts issued their own stamps which were eventually replaced by those inscribed "Mocambique."

Mozambique achieved independence June 25, 1975, taking the name People's Republic of Mozambique.

1000 Reis = 1 Milreis
100 Centavos = 1 Escudo (1913)
100 Centavos = 1 Metical (1980)

Catalogue values for unused stamps in this country are for Never Hinged items, beginning with Scott 330 in the regular postage section, Scott C29 in the airpost section, Scott J51 in the postage due section, and Scott RA55 in the postal tax section.

Portuguese Crown — A1

Perf. 12½, 13½

1877-85		Typo.		Unwmk.
1	A1	5r black	2.75	1.60
	a.	Perf. 13½	4.50	3.75
2	A1	10r yellow	15.00	7.50
3	A1	10r green ('81)	2.10	1.50
4	A1	20r bister	2.10	1.25
	a.	Perf. 13½	4.50	3.25
5	A1	20r rose ('85)	1,300.	600.00
6	A1	25r rose	1.40	1.10
	a.	Perf. 13½	12.00	4.25
7	A1	25r violet ('85)	5.25	2.75
8	A1	40r blue	32.50	17.50
9	A1	40r yel buff ('81)	5.00	5.25
10	A1	50r green	275.00	150.00
	a.	Perf. 13½	1,100.	800.00
11	A1	50r blue ('81)	1.30	1.20
12	A1	100r lilac	2.00	1.10
13	A1	200r orange	6.25	2.50
	a.	Perf. 12½	7.50	7.50
14	A1	300r chocolate	4.50	2.75
		Nos. 1-4,6-14 (13)	355.15	196.00

The reprints of the 1877-85 issues are printed on a smooth white chalky paper, ungummed, with rough perforation 13½, also on thin white paper, with shiny white gum and clean-cut perforation 13½.

King Luiz — A2

Typographed and Embossed

1886   *Perf. 12½*

15	A2	5r black	2.20	1.40
16	A2	10r green	4.50	2.50
17	A2	20r rose	2.25	1.50
18	A2	25r dull lilac	37.50	5.00
19	A2	40r chocolate	3.50	2.25
20	A2	50r blue	3.75	1.75
21	A2	100r yellow brn	4.00	1.75
22	A2	200r gray violet	7.00	4.50
23	A2	300r orange	8.75	6.00
		Nos. 15-23 (9)	73.45	26.65

Perf. 13½

15a	A2	5r	6.00	5.00
16a	A2	10r	8.00	4.75
17a	A2	20r	19.00	8.50
18a	A2	25r	19.00	8.75
19a	A2	40r	21.00	10.00
20a	A2	50r	16.00	5.25
22a	A2	200r	28.00	19.00
		Nos. 15a-22a (7)	117.00	61.25

Nos. 15, 18, 19, 20, 21 and 23 have been reprinted. The reprints have shiny white gum and clean-cut perforation 13½. Many of the colors are paler than those of the originals. For surcharges and overprints see Nos. 23A, 36-44, 46-48, 72-80, 192, P1-P5.

MOZAMBIQUE

No. 19 Surcharged in Black

Type I, Type II, Type III

There are three varieties of No. 23A:
I — "PROVISORIO" 19mm long, numerals 4½mm high.
II — "PROVISORIO" 19½mm long, numerals 5mm high.
III — "PROVISORIO" 19½mm long, numerals of both sizes.

1893, Jan. — Perf. 12½
Without Gum

23A	A2	5r on 40r choc		325.00	140.00
c.		Double surcharge		375.00	200.00
d.		"5"s doubled		375.00	200.00
e.		Inverted surcharge		375.00	200.00

King Carlos I — A3

1894 — Typo. — Perf. 11½, 12½

24	A3	5r yellow		.90	.70
25	A3	10r red lilac		.90	.70
26	A3	15r red brown		1.75	1.00
27	A3	20r gray lilac		1.75	1.10
28	A3	25r blue green		1.25	.55
29	A3	50r lt blue		6.75	4.00
a.		Perf. 12½		9.50	2.50
b.		Perf. 13½		30.00	7.00
30	A3	75r rose		2.75	2.00
31	A3	80r yellow grn		6.25	2.75
32	A3	100r brown, buff		3.00	2.25
33	A3	150r car, rose		21.00	7.75
a.		Perf. 11½		700.00	700.00
34	A3	200r dk blue, blue		7.00	5.25
35	A3	300r dk blue, salmon		7.00	6.00
		Nos. 24-35 (12)		60.30	32.05

Nos. 28 and 31-33 have been reprinted with shiny white gum and clean-cut perf. 13½.
For surcharges and overprints see Nos. 45, 81-92, 193-198, 201-205, 226-228, 238-239.

Stamps of 1886 Overprinted in Red or Black

1895, July 1 — Perf. 12½
Without Gum

36	A2	5r black (R)		15.00	10.00
37	A2	10r green		18.00	12.50
38	A2	20r rose		20.00	13.00
39	A2	25r violet		23.00	13.00
a.		Double overprint		160.00	160.00
40	A2	40r chocolate		24.00	17.00
41	A2	50r blue		24.00	17.00
a.		Perf. 13½		110.00	100.00
42	A2	100r yellow brown		24.00	17.00
43	A2	200r gray violet		41.00	29.00
a.		Perf. 10½		130.00	100.00
44	A2	300r orange		55.00	33.00
		Nos. 36-44 (9)		244.00	161.50

Birth of Saint Anthony of Padua, 7th cent.

No. 35 Surcharged in Black

1897, Jan. 2 — Perf. 12½
Without Gum

45	A3	50r on 300r dk bl, sal		375.00	225.00

Nos. 17, 19 Surcharged

a, b

c

1898 — Without Gum

46	A2 (a)	2½r on 20r rose		75.00	75.00
a.		Inverted surcharge		150.00	130.00
47	A2 (b)	2½r on 20r rose		37.50	27.50
a.		Inverted surcharge		55.00	45.00
48	A2 (c)	5r on 40r choc		50.00	35.00
a.		Inverted surcharge		150.00	130.00
		Nos. 46-48 (3)		162.50	137.50

King Carlos I — A4

Name and Value in Black except 500r

1898-1903 — Typo. — Perf. 11½

49	A4	2½r gray		.55	.40
50	A4	5r orange		.55	.40
51	A4	10r lt green		.55	.40
52	A4	15r brown		5.75	3.25
53	A4	15r gray grn ('03)		2.25	1.75
54	A4	20r gray violet		1.50	.75
55	A4	25r sea green		1.60	.75
56	A4	25r carmine ('03)		2.25	1.50
57	A4	50r dark blue		2.10	1.00
58	A4	50r brown ('03)		4.00	3.00
59	A4	65r dull blue ('03)		15.00	12.00
60	A4	75r rose		8.75	4.25
61	A4	75r red lilac ('03)		4.25	3.25
62	A4	80r violet		8.25	4.00
63	A4	100r dk blue, bl		4.00	2.50
64	A4	115r org brn, pink ('03)		14.50	8.75
65	A4	130r brown, straw ('03)		14.50	8.75
66	A4	150r brown, straw		4.50	4.50
67	A4	200r red lilac, pnksh		3.75	2.50
68	A4	300r dk blue, rose		9.50	4.75
69	A4	400r dl bl, straw ('03)		19.00	15.00
70	A4	500r blk & red, bl ('01)		20.00	10.00
71	A4	700r vio, yelsh ('01)		32.50	14.00
		Nos. 49-71 (23)		179.60	107.45

For overprints and surcharges see Nos. 94-113, 200, 207-220.

Stamps of 1886-94 Surcharged

On Stamps of 1886 Red Surcharge

1902 — Perf. 12½, 13½

72	A2	115r on 5r blk		2.75	2.30

Black Surcharge

73	A2	65r on 20r rose		7.00	3.75
a.		Double surcharge		28.00	27.50
74	A2	65r on 40r choc		8.25	7.00
75	A2	65r on 200r violet		6.00	3.25
76	A2	115r on 50r blue		2.75	1.80
77	A2	130r on 25r red vio		3.75	2.25
78	A2	130r on 300r orange		4.00	2.50
79	A2	400r on 10r green		7.50	6.50
80	A2	400r on 100r yel brn		55.00	37.50
		Nos. 72-80 (9)		97.00	80.85

The reprints of Nos. 74, 75, 76, 77, 79 and 80 have shiny white gum and clean-cut perforation 13½.

On Stamps of 1894 — Perf. 11½

81	A3	65r on 10r red lil		5.00	4.50
82	A3	65r on 15r red brn		5.00	4.50
83	A3	65r on 20r gray lil		4.50	4.00
84	A3	115r on 5r yel		4.50	4.00
85	A3	115r on 25r bl grn		3.50	3.00
86	A3	130r on 75r rose		3.50	3.00
87	A3	130r on 100r brn, buff		9.75	9.00
88	A3	130r on 150r car, rose		3.50	3.00
89	A3	130r on 200r bl, bl		8.75	8.25
90	A3	400r on 50r lt bl		2.50	2.00
91	A3	400r on 80r yel grn		2.50	2.00
92	A3	400r on 300r bl, sal		2.00	1.50

On Newspaper Stamp of 1893 — Perf. 13½

93	N3	115r on 2½r brn		4.50	4.25
		Nos. 81-93 (13)		59.50	53.00

Reprints of No. 87 have shiny white gum and clean-cut perforation 13½.
For overprints, see Nos. 192-199, 201-206.

Overprinted in Black

On Stamps of 1898 — Perf. 11½

94	A4	15r brown		3.50	1.75
95	A4	25r sea green		3.75	1.75
96	A4	50r blue		7.00	4.00
97	A4	75r rose		10.00	5.00
		Nos. 94-97 (4)		24.25	12.50

For overprints, see Nos. 200 and 207.

No. 59 Surcharged in Black

1905

98	A4	50r on 65r dull blue		5.75	4.50

For overprint, see No. 208.

Stamps of 1898-1903 Overprinted in Carmine or Green

1911

99	A4	2½r gray		.55	.40
a.		Inverted overprint		15.00	15.00
100	A4	5r orange		.55	.40
101	A4	10r lt green		1.65	1.15
102	A4	15r gray grn		.40	.40
103	A4	20r gray vio		1.65	.45
104	A4	25r carmine (G)		.40	.35
a.		25r gray violet (error)		65.00	65.00
105	A4	50r brown		.65	.55
106	A4	75r red lilac		1.35	1.15
107	A4	100r dk blue, bl		1.35	1.15
108	A4	115r org brn, pink		1.65	1.15
109	A4	130r brown, straw		1.65	1.15
a.		Double overprint			
110	A4	200r red lil, pnksh		4.00	1.90
111	A4	400r dull bl, straw		4.70	1.90
112	A4	500r blk & red, bl		4.70	1.90
113	A4	700r vio, straw		4.70	1.90
		Nos. 99-113 (15)		29.95	15.90

King Manuel II — A5

Overprinted in Carmine or Green

1912 — Perf. 11½x12

114	A5	2½r violet		.50	.40
115	A5	5r black		.50	.40
116	A5	10r gray grn		.50	.40
117	A5	20r carmine (G)		1.30	1.05
118	A5	25r vio brn		.50	.40
119	A5	50r dp blue		1.10	.65
120	A5	75r bis brn		1.10	.65
121	A5	100r brn, lt grn		1.10	.65
122	A5	200r dk grn, salmon		3.25	1.50
123	A5	300r black, azure		2.00	1.50

Perf. 14x15

124	A5	500r ol grn & vio brn		6.50	3.40
		Nos. 114-124 (11)		18.35	11.00

Vasco da Gama Issue of Various Portuguese Colonies Common Design Types Surcharged

1913 — On Stamps of Macao

125	CD20	¼c on ½a bl grn		1.80	1.50
126	CD21	½c on 1a red		1.80	1.50
127	CD22	1c on 2a red vlo		1.80	1.50
128	CD23	2½c on 4a yel grn		1.80	1.50
a.		Double surcharge		50.00	40.00
129	CD24	5c on 8a dk bl		2.00	1.85
130	CD25	7½c on 12a vio brn		2.85	2.75
131	CD26	10c on 16a bis brn		2.00	1.70
132	CD27	15c on 24a bis		2.00	1.70
		Nos. 125-132 (8)		16.05	14.00

On Stamps of Portuguese Africa

133	CD20	¼c on 2½r bl grn		1.75	1.25
134	CD21	½c on 5r red		1.75	1.25
135	CD22	1c on 10r red vio		1.75	1.25
a.		Double surcharge		65.00	65.00
136	CD23	2½c on 25r yel grn		1.75	1.25
137	CD24	5c on 50r dk bl		1.75	1.25
138	CD25	7½c on 75r vio brn		2.85	2.10
139	CD26	10c on 100r bis brn		2.15	1.75
140	CD27	15c on 150r bis		2.15	1.95
		Nos. 133-140 (8)		15.90	12.05

On Stamps of Timor

141	CD20	¼c on ½a bl grn		2.40	1.90
142	CD21	½c on 1a red		2.40	1.90
143	CD22	1c on 2a red vio		2.40	1.90
144	CD23	2½c on 4a yel grn		2.40	1.90
145	CD24	5c on 8a dk bl		3.45	2.75
146	CD25	7½c on 12a vio brn		3.45	2.75
147	CD26	10c on 16a bis brn		2.20	1.75
148	CD27	15c on 24a bis		2.20	1.75
		Nos. 141-148 (8)		20.90	16.60
		Nos. 125-148 (24)		52.85	42.65

Ceres — A6

1914 — Typo. — Perf. 15x14
Name and Value in Black
Chalky Paper

149	A6	¼c olive brown		.45	.25
150	A6	½c black		.45	.25
151	A6	1c blue green		.45	.25
152	A6	1½c lilac brown		.45	.25
153	A6	2c carmine		.55	.25
154	A6	2½c lt vio		.55	.25
155	A6	5c deep blue		.55	.25
156	A6	7½c yel brn		1.90	.75
157	A6	8c slate		1.90	.75
158	A6	10c org brn		1.90	.75
159	A6	15c plum		4.00	1.60
160	A6	20c yellow green		1.90	.75
161	A6	30c brown, grn		3.30	1.30
163	A6	40c brn, pink		3.45	1.40
164	A6	50c org, salmon		5.95	2.40
165	A6	1e grn, bl		39.75	15.00
		Nos. 149-165 (16)		67.50	26.45

1919-26 — Ordinary Paper

166	A6	¼c olive brown		.35	.35
a.		Name and value printed twice		27.50	
b.		Name and value printed triple		27.50	
167	A6	½c black		.35	.35
168	A6	1c blue green		.35	.35
169	A6	1½c lilac brown		.35	.35
170	A6	2c carmine		.35	.35
171	A6	2½c lt vio		.35	.35
172	A6	3c org ('21)		.35	.35
173	A6	4c pale rose ('21)		.35	.35
174	A6	4½c gray ('21)		.35	.35
175	A6	5c deep blue		.35	.35
176	A6	7c ultra ('21)		.35	.35
177	A6	7½c yel brn		.35	.35
178	A6	8c slate		.70	.35
179	A6	10c org brn		14.00	8.75
180	A6	30c deep green ('21)		1.05	.70
181	A6	1e rose		1.95	1.15
		Nos. 166-181 (16)		21.90	15.15

Perf. 12x11½

182	A6	¼c olive brown		.40	.35
183	A6	½c black		.35	.35
184	A6	1c blue green		.65	.35
a.		Name and value printed twice		27.50	
185	A6	1½c lilac brown		.35	.35
186	A6	2c carmine		.35	.35
187	A6	2c gray ('26)		.35	.35
188	A6	2½c lt vio		.35	.35
189	A6	3c org ('21)		.35	.35
190	A6	4c pale rose ('21)		.35	.35
191A	A6	6c lilac ('21)		.35	.35
a.		Name and value printed twice			
191B	A6	7c ultra ('21)		.35	.35
191C	A6	7½c yel brn		.35	.35
191D	A6	8c slate		.35	.35
191E	A6	10c org brn		.35	.35
191F	A6	12c gray brn ('21)		.35	.35
191G	A6	12c blue grn ('22)		.35	.35
191H	A6	15c plum		1.85	1.25
191I	A6	15c brn rose ('22)		.40	.35
191J	A6	20c yel grn		.65	.35
191K	A6	24c ultra ('26)		.45	.35
191L	A6	25c choc ('26)		.55	.50
191M	A6	30c deep green ('21)		.45	.35
191N	A6	40c turq blue ('21)		1.30	.45
191O	A6	50c lt violet ('26)		.65	.35
191P	A6	60c dk blue ('22)		1.30	.75
191Q	A6	60c rose ('26)		1.85	1.25
191R	A6	80c brt rose ('22)		2.10	1.80
191S	A6	80c rose ('22)		1.45	.75
191T	A6	1e rose ('22)		2.95	1.25
		Nos. 182-191T (30)		22.25	15.85

For surcharges see Nos. 232-234, 236-237, 240-244, 249-250, J46-50.

MOZAMBIQUE

		1921			**Chalky Paper**
191U	A6	40c brown, *pink* ('21)		3.25	2.25
191V	A6	60c red brn, *pink*		2.25	1.80
191W	A6	80c dk brn, *bl* ('21)		2.00	1.50
191X	A6	1e grn, *bl*,		4.25	2.50
191Y	A6	2e brt vio, *pink*		3.00	1.50

Perf. 15x14

191Z	A6	30c gray bl, *pink* ('21)	2.25	1.80
		Nos. 191U-191Z (6)	17.00	11.35

Stamps of 1902 Overprinted Locally in Carmine

1915
On Provisional Stamps of 1902

192	A2	115r on 5r black	85.00	70.00
193	A3	115r on 5r yellow	2.25	1.75
194	A3	115r on 25r bl grn	2.25	1.75
195	A3	130r on 75r rose	2.25	1.75
196	A3	130r on 100r brn, *buff*	2.25	1.75
197	A3	130r on 150r car, *rose*	2.25	1.75
198	A3	130r on 200r bl, *bl*	2.25	1.75
199	N3	115r on 2½r brn	1.50	1.20

On No. 97

200	A4	75r rose	3.25	1.75
		Nos. 192-200 (9)	103.25	83.45

Stamps of 1902-05 Overprinted in Carmine

1915
On Provisional Stamps of 1902

201	A3	115r on 5r yellow	1.50	1.25
202	A3	115r on 25r bl grn	1.50	1.25
203	A3	130r on 75r rose	1.50	1.25
204	A3	130r on 150r car, *rose*	1.50	1.25
205	A3	130r on 200r bl, *bl*	1.50	1.25
206	N3	115r on 2½r brn	1.50	1.25

On No. 96

| 207 | A4 | 50r blue | 1.50 | 1.25 |

On No. 98

208	A4	50r on 65r dull blue	1.50	1.25
		Nos. 201-208 (8)	12.00	10.00

The overprint on No. 206 reads from upper left to lower right.

Stamps of 1898-1903 Overprinted Locally in Carmine Like Nos. 192-200

1917

209	A4	2½r gray	31.50	22.00
210	A4	15r gray grn	31.50	22.00
211	A4	20r gray vio	31.50	22.00
212	A4	50r brown	26.50	15.75
213	A4	75r red lilac	82.50	62.50
214	A4	100r blue, *bl*	9.50	4.00
215	A4	115r org brn, *pink*	8.75	4.00
216	A4	130r brown, *straw*	9.50	4.00
217	A4	200r red lil, *pnksh*	9.50	4.00
218	A4	400r dull bl, *straw*	9.50	4.00
219	A4	500r blk & red, *bl*	8.75	7.50
220	A4	700r vio, *yelsh*	15.75	7.50
		Nos. 209-220 (12)	274.75	179.25

War Tax Stamps of 1916-18 Surcharged

1918 — Rouletted 7

| 221 | WT2 | 2½c on 5c rose | 3.75 | 2.00 |

Perf. 11, 12

222	WT2	2½c on 5c red	1.75	1.25
a.		"PETRIA"	13.00	13.00
b.		"PEPUBLICA"	13.00	13.00
c.		"1910" for "1916"	13.00	9.50
d.		"TELFGRAFO"	13.00	13.00

War Tax Stamps of 1916-18 Surcharged

1919 — Perf. 11

224	WT1	1c on 1c gray grn	1.25	1.00
a.		"PEPUBLICA"	9.50	7.50
b.		Rouletted 7	21.00	16.00

Perf. 12

225	WT2	1½c on 5c red	1.25	1.00
a.		"PETRIA"	9.75	9.75
b.		"PEPUBLICA"	9.75	9.75
c.		"1910" for "1916"	9.75	9.75
d.		Rouletted	30.00	22.50
e.		"TELFGRAFO"	9.50	9.50

Stamps of 1902 Overprinted Locally in Carmine Like Nos. 192-200

1920

226	A3	400r on 50r lt blue	3.00	2.25
227	A3	400r on 80r yel grn	3.00	2.25
228	A3	400r on 300r bl, *sal*	3.00	2.25
		Nos. 226-228 (3)	9.00	6.75

War Tax Stamp of 1918 Surcharged in Green

1920 — Perf. 12

229	WT2	6c on 5c red	1.50	1.25
a.		"1910" for "1916"	9.50	9.50
b.		"PETRIA"	9.50	9.50
c.		"PEPUBLICA"	9.50	9.50
d.		Pair, imperf.	22.50	22.50
e.		Inverted surcharge	50.00	50.00
f.		"TELFGRAFO"	9.50	9.50

Lourenco Marques Nos. 117, 119 Surcharged in Red or Bue

1921 — Perf. 15x14

230	A4	10c on ½c blk (R)	3.00	1.80
231	A4	30c on 1½c brn (Bl)	3.00	1.80

Same Surcharge on Mozambique Nos. 150, 152, 155 in Red, Blue or Green

232	A6	10c on ½c blk (R)	3.00	1.75
233	A6	30c on 1½c brn (Bl)	3.00	1.75
a.		Double surcharge	40.00	40.00
234	A6	60c on 2½c vio (G)	4.00	2.25
		Nos. 230-234 (5)	16.00	9.35

War Tax Stamp of 1918 Surcharged in Green

1921 — Perf. 12

235	WT2	2e on 5c red	2.40	1.10
a.		"PETRIA"	7.50	5.00
b.		"PEPUBLICA"	9.50	7.50
c.		"1910" for "1916"	11.50	9.50

No. 190 Surcharged

1923 — Perf. 12x11½

| 236 | A6 | 50c on 4c pale rose | 2.00 | 1.60 |

No. 191R Overprinted in Green

1924

| 237 | A6 | 80c bright rose | 2.25 | 1.10 |

4th centenary of the death of Vasco da Gama.

Nos. 90 and 91 Surcharged

1925 — Perf. 11½

238	A3	40c on 400r on 50r	1.50	1.00
239	A3	40c on 400r on 80r	1.50	1.00
a.		"a" omitted	27.50	27.50

Glazed Paper

1922-26 — Perf. 12x11½

240	A6	1e blue ('26)	2.00	1.30
241	A6	2e dk violet ('22)	1.40	.85
242	A6	5e buff ('26)	9.50	6.75
243	A6	10e pink ('26)	15.00	6.50
244	A6	20e pale turq ('26)	57.00	22.50

Postage Due Stamp of 1917 Overprinted in Black and Bars in Red

1929, Jan. — Perf. 12

| 247 | D1 | 50c gray | 2.00 | 1.60 |

No. 191Y Surcharged

1931 — Perf. 11½

249	A6	70c on 2e dk vio	1.50	.75
250	A6	1.40e on 2e dk vio	1.50	.75

"Portugal" Holding Volume of the "Lusiads" — A7

Wmk. Maltese Cross (232)

1933, July 13 — Typo. — Perf. 14
Value in Red or Black

251	A7	1c bister brn (R)	.35	.30
252	A7	5c black brn	.35	.30
253	A7	10c dp violet	.35	.30
254	A7	15c black (R)	.35	.30
255	A7	20c light gray	.35	.30
256	A7	30c blue green	.35	.30
257	A7	40c orange red	.35	.30
258	A7	45c brt blue	.50	.35
259	A7	50c dk brown	.50	.30
260	A7	60c olive grn	.60	.30
261	A7	70c orange brn	.60	.30
262	A7	80c emerald	.60	.30
263	A7	85c deep rose	1.65	.85
264	A7	1e red brown	1.15	.30
265	A7	1.40e dk blue (R)	13.00	3.00
266	A7	2e dk violet	2.75	1.10
267	A7	5e apple green	5.50	1.10
268	A7	10e olive bister	11.00	2.35
269	A7	20e orange	51.50	6.25
		Nos. 251-269 (19)	91.80	18.60

See Nos. 298-299.

Common Design Types pictured following the introduction.

Common Design Types
Perf. 13½x13

1938, Aug. — Engr. — Unwmk.
Name and Value in Black

270	CD34	1c gray green	.35	.30
271	CD34	5c orange brn	.35	.30
272	CD34	10c dk carmine	.35	.30
273	CD34	15c dk vio brn	.35	.30
274	CD34	20c slate	.35	.30
275	CD35	30c rose vio	.35	.30
276	CD35	35c brt green	.45	.30
277	CD35	40c brown	.60	.30
278	CD35	50c brt red vio	.60	.30
279	CD36	60c gray black	.75	.30
280	CD36	70c brown vio	.75	.30
281	CD36	80c orange	1.15	.30
282	CD36	1e red	.105	.30
283	CD37	1.75e blue	2.65	.35
284	CD37	2e brown car	2.30	.35
285	CD37	5e olive green	7.50	.75
286	CD37	10e blue vio	15.00	1.50
287	CD38	20e red brown	34.50	2.15
		Nos. 270-287 (18)	68.46	9.00

For surcharges see Nos. 297, 301.

No. 258 Surcharged in Black

1938, Jan. 16 — Wmk. 232 — Perf. 14

| 288 | A7 | 40c on 45c brt blue | 7.00 | 4.50 |

Map of Africa — A7a

Perf. 11½x12

1939, July 17 — Litho. — Unwmk.

289	A7a	80c vio, *pale rose*	4.35	3.30
290	A7a	1.75e bl, *pale bl*	14.75	7.00
291	A7a	3e grn, *yel grn*	27.00	11.00
292	A7a	20e dk gray	135.00	58.00
		Nos. 289-292 (4)	181.10	79.30

Presidential visit.

New Cathedral, Lourenço Marques A8

Railroad Station A9

Municipal Hall — A10

1944, Dec. — Litho. — Perf. 11½

293	A8	50c dk brown	2.00	.80
294	A8	50c dk green	2.00	.80
295	A9	1.75e ultra	9.50	2.95
296	A10	20e dk gray	24.00	2.95
		Nos. 293-296 (4)	37.50	7.50

4th cent. of the founding of Lourenço Marques. See No. 302. For surcharge see No. 300.

No. 283 Surcharged in Carmine

1946 — Engr. — Perf. 13½x13

| 297 | CD37 | 60c on 1.75e blue | 2.00 | .90 |

Lusiads Type of 1933

1947 — Wmk. 232 — Typo. — Perf. 14
Value in Black

298	A7	35c yellow grn	9.75	3.00
299	A7	1.75e deep blue	8.25	3.00

No. 296 Srchd. in Pink

1946 — Unwmk. — Perf. 11½

| 300 | A10 | 2e on 20e dk gray | 2.50 | 1.40 |

No. 273 Surcharged with New Value and Wavy Lines
Perf. 13½x13

301	CD34	10c on 15c dk vio brn	.90	.75
a.		Inverted surcharge	30.00	

Cathedral Type of 1944
Commemorative Inscription Omitted

1948 — Litho. — Perf. 11½

| 302 | A8 | 4.50e brt vermilion | 3.00 | 1.10 |

Antonio Enes — A11

MOZAMBIQUE

1948, Oct. 4 — Perf. 14
303 A11 50c black & cream 1.10 .75
304 A11 5e vio brn & cream 2.50 2.30
Birth centenary of Antonio Enes.

Gogogo Peak — A12
Zambezi River Bridge — A13
Zumbo River A14
Waterfall at Nhanhangare A15
Lourenço Marques A16
Plantation, Baixa Zambezia A17
Pungwe River at Beira — A18
Lourenço Marques — A19
Polana Beach — A20
Malema River — A21

Perf. 13½x13, 13x13½
1948-49 Typo. Unwmk.
305 A12 5c orange brn .30 .25
306 A13 10c violet brn .30 .25
307 A14 20c dk brown .30 .25
308 A12 30c plum .30 .25
309 A14 40c dull green .40 .25
310 A16 50c slate .40 .25
311 A15 60c brown car .40 .25
312 A16 80c violet blk .40 .25
313 A17 1e carmine .60 .30
314 A13 1.20e slate gray .65 .30
315 A15 1.50e dk purple .90 .35
316 A20 1.75e dk blue ('49) 1.25 .45
317 A18 2e brown 1.20 .35
318 A19 2.50e dk slate ('49) 4.00 .30
319 A20 3e gray ol ('49) 2.50 .30
320 A15 3.50e olive gray 2.60 .30
321 A17 5e blue grn 2.60 .30
322 A19 10e choc ('49) 6.25 .45
323 A21 15e dp carmine ('49) 15.00 3.25
324 A21 20e orange ('49) 30.00 6.00
Nos. 305-324 (20) 70.35 13.65
On No. 320 the "$" is reversed.

Lady of Fatima Issue
Common Design Type
1948, Oct. Litho. Perf. 14½
325 CD40 50c blue 2.50 1.95
326 CD40 1.20e red violet 5.75 3.90
327 CD40 4.50e emerald 22.50 3.65
328 CD40 20e chocolate 42.50 18.00
Nos. 325-328 (4) 73.25 27.50

Symbols of the UPU — A21a

1949, Apr. 11 Perf. 14
329 A21a 4.50e ultra & pale gray 2.75 1.75
75th anniversary of UPU.

Catalogue values for unused stamps in this section, from this point to the end of the section, are for Never Hinged items.

Holy Year Issue
Common Design Types
1950, May Perf. 13x13½
330 CD41 1.50e red orange 1.25 .60
331 CD42 3e brt blue 1.75 1.00

Spotted Triggerfish A22
Pennant Coral Fish A22a

Fish: 10c, Golden butterflyfish. 15c, Orange butterflyfish. 20c, Lionfish. 30c, Sharpnose puffer. 40c, Porky filefish. 50c, Dark brown surgeonfish. 1.50e Rainbow wrasse. 2e, Orange-spotted gray-skin. 2.50e, Kasmir snapper. 3e, Convict fish. 3.50e, Stellar triggerfish. 4e, Cornetfish. 4.50e, Vagabond butterflyfish. 5e, Mail-cheeked fish. 6e, Pinnate batfish. 8e, Moorish idol. 9e, Triangulate boxfish. 10e, Flying gurnard. 15e, Redtooth triggerfish. 20e, Striped triggerfish. 30e, Horned cowfish. 50e, Spotted cowfish.

Photogravure and Lithographed
1951 Unwmk. Perf. 14x14½
Fish in Natural Colors
332 A22 5c dp yellow .35 .90
333 A22 10c lt blue .30 .60
334 A22 15c yellow 1.00 1.20
335 A22 20c pale olive .50 .30
336 A22 30c gray .50 .30
337 A22 40c pale green .35 .30
338 A22 50c pale buff .35 .30
339 A22a 1e aqua .35 .30
340 A22 1.50e olive .30 .30
341 A22 2e blue .35 .30
342 A22 2.50e brnsh lilac .75 .30
343 A22 3e aqua .75 .30
344 A22 3.50e olive grn .75 .30
345 A22 4e blue gray 1.70 1.20
346 A22 4.50e green 1.50 2.45
347 A22 5o buff 1.60 .30
348 A22a 6e salmon pink 1.50 .30
349 A22 8e gray blue 2.60 .30
350 A22 9e lilac rose 5.50 .35
351 A22 10e gray lilac 16.50 2.45
352 A22 15e gray 49.00 10.75
353 A22 20e lemon 30.00 4.75
354 A22 30e yellow grn 30.00 6.75
355 A22 50e gray vio 52.50 14.50
Nos. 332-355 (24) 198.90 49.80
Set, hinged 100.00

Holy Year Extension Issue
Common Design Type
1951, Oct. Litho. Perf. 14
356 CD43 5e carmine & rose + label 3.25 1.75
No. 356 without label attached sells for less.

Victor Cordon — A23

1951, Oct. Perf. 11½
357 A23 1e dk brown 3.00 .75
358 A23 5e black & slate 14.50 1.75
Centenary of the birth of Victor Cordon, explorer.

Medical Congress Issue
Common Design Type
Design: Miguel Bombarda Hospital.
1952, June 19 Litho. Perf. 13½
359 CD44 3e dk bl & brn buff 1.90 .90

Plane and Ship — A24

1952, Sept. 15 Unwmk.
360 A24 1.50e multi 1.10 .80
4th African Tourism Congress.

Missionary — A25

1953
361 A25 10c red brn & pale vio .35 .30
362 A25 1e red brn & pale yel grn 1.10 .30
363 A25 5e blk & lt bl 2.60 .80
Nos. 361-363 (3) 4.05 1.40
Exhibition of Sacred Missionary Art, held at Lisbon in 1951.

Canceled to Order
Certain issues, including Nos. 364-383, were canceled to order under Republican administration.

Papilio Demodocus — A26

Various Butterflies and Moths in Natural Colors
Photogravure and Lithographed
1953, May 28 Perf. 13x14
364 A26 10c lt blue .30 .25
365 A26 15c cream .30 .25
366 A26 20c yellow grn .30 .25
367 A26 30c lt violet .30 .25
368 A26 40c brown .30 .25
369 A26 50c bluish gray .30 .25
370 A26 80c brt blue .30 .25
371 A26 1e gray bl .30 .25
372 A26 1.50e ocher .30 .25
373 A26 2e orange brn 7.50 .50
374 A26 2.30e blue 7.50 .35
375 A26 2.50e citron 7.50 .35
376 A26 3e lilac rose 2.60 .25
377 A26 4e light blue .50 .25
378 A26 4.50e orange .65 .25
379 A26 5e green .65 .25
380 A26 6e pale vio .80 .25
381 A26 7.50e buff 9.00 .90
382 A26 10e pink 12.50 2.25
383 A26 20e grnsh gray 18.00 2.25
Nos. 364-383 (20) 69.90 9.50
Value of set canceled-to-order, $2.75. For overprints see Nos. 517, 527.

Stamps of Portugal and Mozambique — A27

1953, July 23 Litho. Perf. 14
384 A27 1e multicolored 1.70 .65
385 A27 3e multicolored 6.00 1.60
Issued in connection with the Lourenço Marques philatelic exhibition, July 1953.

Stamp of Portugal and Arms of Colonies — A27a

Stamp Centenary Issue
1953 Photo. Perf. 13
386 A27a 50c multicolored 1.25 .75

Map — A28

1954, Oct. 15 Litho.
Color of Colony
387 A28 10c pale rose lilac .30 .25
388 A28 20c pale yellow .30 .25
389 A28 50c lilac .30 .25
390 A28 1e orange yel .30 .25
391 A28 2.30e white .90 .60
392 A28 4e pale salmon 1.00 .40
393 A28 10e lt green 3.00 .35
394 A28 20e brown buff 4.00 .55
Nos. 387-394 (8) 10.10 2.90
For overprints see Nos. 516, 530.

Sao Paulo Issue
Common Design Type
1954, July 2
395 CD46 3.50e dk gray, cream & ol .75 .30

Arms of Beira — A29

Paper with network as in parenthesis
Arms in Silver, Gold, Red and Pale Green
1954, Dec. 1 Perf. 13x13½
396 A29 1.50e dk bl (bl) 60 40
397 A29 3.50e brn (buff) 1.60 .70
Issued to publicize the first philatelic exhibition of Manica and Sofala.

Mousinho de Albuquerque — A30

2.50e, Statue of Mousinho de Albuquerque.
1955, Feb. 1 Litho. Perf. 11½x12
398 A30 1e gray, blk & buff .95 .50
399 A30 2.50e ol bis, blk & bl 2.00 1.00
100th anniversary of the birth of Mousinho de Albuquerque, statesman.

A31

Fight Races Holding Arms of Portugal
1956, Aug. 4 Unwmk. Perf. 14½
Central Design in Multicolored
400 A31 1e pale yellow & multi .60 .25
401 A31 2.50e lt blue & multi 1.25 .60
Issued to commemorate the visit of President Antonio Oscar de Fragoso Carmona.

A32

1957, Aug. 15 Litho.
402 A32 2.50e View of Beira 1.25 .50
50th anniversary of the city of Beira.

MOZAMBIQUE

Brussels Fair Issue

Exhibition Emblems and View — A32a

1958, Oct. 8   **Unwmk.**   *Perf. 14½*
403   A32a   3.50e blk, grn, yel, red & bl   .50   .25

Tropical Medicine Congress Issue
Common Design Type
Design: Strophanthus grandiflorus.

1958, Sept. 14   *Perf. 13½*
404   CD47   1.50e sal brn, grn & red   3.50   1.50

Caravel — A33

1960, June 25   **Litho.**   *Perf. 13½*
405   A33   5e multicolored   1.00   .35

500th anniversary of the death of Prince Henry the Navigator.

Technical Instruction — A34

1960, Nov. 21   **Unwmk.**   *Perf. 14½*
406   A34   3e multicolored   .80   .40

Commission for Technical Co-operation in Africa South of the Sahara (C.C.T.A.), 10th anniv.

Arms of Lourenço Marques — A35

Arms of various cities of Mozambique.

1961, Jan. 30   **Litho.**   *Perf. 13½*
Arms in Original Colors; Black, Ultramarine and Red Inscriptions

407	A35	5c salmon	.35	.25
408	A35	15c pale green	.35	.25
409	A35	20c lt vio gray	.35	.25
410	A35	30c buff	.35	.25
411	A35	50c bluish gray	.35	.25
412	A35	1e pale ol	.35	.25
413	A35	1.50e lt blue	.35	.25
414	A35	2e pale pink	.55	.25
415	A35	2.50e lt bl grn	1.70	.25
416	A35	3e beige	.60	.25
417	A35	4e yellow	.60	.25
418	A35	4.50e pale gray	.60	.25
419	A35	5e pale bluish grn	.60	.25
420	A35	7.50e rose	1.35	.40
a.		"CORREIOS 7$50" omitted		
421	A35	10e lt yel grn	2.15	.40
422	A35	20e beige	4.75	.55
423	A35	50e gray	9.75	1.60
		Nos. 407-423 (17)	25.10	6.20

Sports Issue
Common Design Type

50c, Water skiing. 1e, Wrestling. 1.50e, Woman gymnast. 2.50e, Field hockey. 4.50e, Women's basketball. 15e, Speedboat racing.

1962, Feb. 10   **Unwmk.**   *Perf. 13½*
Multicolored Designs

424	CD48	50c gray green	.35	.25
425	CD48	1e dk gray	.95	.25
426	CD48	1.50e pink	.45	.25
427	CD48	2.50e buff	1.05	.25
428	CD48	4.50e gray	1.45	.45
429	CD48	15e gray green	2.30	1.00
		Nos. 424-429 (6)	6.55	2.45

For overprints see Nos. 522, 526, 529.

Anti-Malaria Issue
Common Design Type
Design: Anopheles funestus.

1962, Apr. 5   *Perf. 13½*
430   CD49   2.50e multicolored   2.00   .50

Planes over Mozambique — A36

1962, Oct. 15   **Litho.**   *Perf. 14½*
431   A36   3e multicolored   1.00   .25

25th anniversary of DETA airlines.

Lourenço Marques 1887 and 1962 — A37

1962, Nov. 1   *Perf. 13*
432   A37   1e multicolored   .65   .25

75th anniversary of Lourenço Marques.

Vasco da Gama Statue and Arms — A38

1963, Apr. 25   **Unwmk.**   *Perf. 14½*
433   A38   3e multicolored   .65   .25

Founding of Mozambique City, 200th anniv.

Airline Anniversary Issue
Common Design Type

1963, Oct. 21   **Litho.**   *Perf. 14½*
434   CD50   2.50e brt pink & multi   .55   .25

Barque, 1430 — A39

Caravel, 1436 — A40

Development of Sailing Ships: 30c, Lateen-rigged caravel, 1460. 50c, "Sao Gabriel," 1497. 1e, Dom Manuel's ship, 1498. 1.50e, Warship, 1500. 2e, "Flor de la Mar," 1511. 2.50e, Redonda caravel, 1519. 3.50e, 800-ton ship, 1520. 4e, Portuguese India galley, 1521. 4.50e, "Santa Tereza," 1639. 5e, "Nostra Senhora da Conceiçao," 1716. 6e, "Nostra Senhora do Bom Sucesso," 1764. 7.50e, Launch with mortar, 1788. 8e, Brigantine, 1793. 10e, Corvette, 1799. 12.50e, Schooner "Maria Teresa," 1820. 15e, "Vasco da Gama," 1841. 20e, Frigate "Dom Fernando II," 1843. 30e, Training Ship "Sagres," 1924.

1963, Dec. 1   **Litho.**   *Perf. 14½*

435	A39	10c multicolored	.30	.25
436	A40	20c multicolored	.30	.25
437	A40	30c multicolored	.30	.25
438	A40	50c multicolored	.30	.25
439	A40	1e multicolored	.65	.25
440	A40	1.50e multicolored	.55	.25
441	A40	2e multicolored	.55	.25
442	A39	2.50e multicolored	.60	.25
443	A40	3.50e multicolored	.55	.30
444	A39	4e multicolored	.70	.25
445	A39	4.50e multicolored	1.30	.25
446	A40	5e multicolored	11.75	.35
447	A39	6e multicolored	1.15	.30
448	A39	7.50e multicolored	1.30	.40
449	A39	8e multicolored	1.30	.40
450	A40	10e multicolored	1.45	.60
451	A39	12.50e multicolored	1.65	.75
452	A39	15e multicolored	2.35	.70
453	A40	20e multicolored	3.50	.70
454	A40	30e multicolored	7.00	2.00
		Nos. 435-454 (20)	37.55	8.95

National Overseas Bank Issue

Modern Bank Building, Luanda — A40a

1964, May 16   *Perf. 13½*
455   A40a   1.50e bl, yel gray & grn   .65   .25

National Overseas Bank of Portugal, cent.

Pres. Americo Rodrigues Thomaz — A41

1964, July 23   **Litho.**   *Perf. 13½x12½*
456   A41   2.50e multicolored   .65   .25

Visit of Pres. Americo Rodrigues Thomaz of Portugal to Mozambique, in July.

Royal Barge of King John V, 1728 — A42

Designs: 35c, Barge of Dom Jose I, 1753. 1e, Customs barge, 1768. 1.50e, Sailor, 1780, vert. 2.50e, Royal barge, 1780. 5e, Barge of Dona Carlota Joaquina, 1790. 9e, Barge of Dom Miguel, 1831.

1964, Dec. 18   **Litho.**   *Perf. 14½*

457	A42	15c multicolored	.30	.25
458	A42	35c lt bl & multi	.30	.25
459	A42	1e gray & multi	.50	.25
460	A42	1.50e gray & multi	.30	.25
461	A42	2.50e multicolored	.30	.25
462	A42	5e multicolored	.75	.25
463	A42	9e multicolored	1.60	.65
		Nos. 457-463 (7)	4.05	2.15

ITU Issue
Common Design Type

1965, May 17   **Unwmk.**   *Perf. 14½*
464   CD52   1e yellow & multi   .65   .25

National Revolution Issue
Common Design Type
Design: 1e, Beira Railroad Station, and Antonio Enes School.

1966, May 28   **Litho.**   *Perf. 11½*
465   CD53   1e multicolored   .65   .30

Harquebusier, 1560 — A42a

30c, Harquebusier, 1640. 40c, Infantry soldier, 1777. 50c, Infantry officer, 1777. 80c, Drummer, 1777. 1e, Infantry sergeant, 1777. 2e, Infantry major, 1784. 2.50e, Colonial officer, 1788. 3e, Infantry soldier, 1789. 5e, Colonial bugler, 1801. 10e, Colonial officer, 1807. 15e, Colonial infantry soldier, 1817.

1967, Jan. 12   **Photo.**   *Perf. 14*

466	A42a	20c multicolored	.30	.25
467	A42a	30c multicolored	.30	.25
468	A42a	40c multicolored	.30	.25
469	A42a	50c multicolored	.30	.25
470	A42a	80c multicolored	.50	.25
471	A42a	1e multicolored	.40	.25
472	A42a	2e multicolored	.40	.25
473	A42a	2.50e multicolored	.60	.25
474	A42a	3e multicolored	.60	.25
475	A42a	5e multicolored	1.25	.30
476	A42a	10e multicolored	1.50	.40
477	A42a	15e multicolored	2.25	.60
		Nos. 466-477 (12)	8.70	3.55

Navy Club Issue
Common Design Type
Designs: 3e, Capt. Azevedo Coutinho and gunboat (stern-wheeler) Tete. 10e, Capt. Joao Roby and gunboat (paddle steamer) Granada.

1967, Jan. 31   **Litho.**   *Perf. 13*
478   CD54   3e multicolored   .50   .25
479   CD54   10e multicolored   1.25   .40

Virgin's Crown, Presented by Portuguese Women — A43

1967, May 13   **Litho.**   *Perf. 12½x13*
480   A43   50c multicolored   .30   .25

50th anniversary of the appearance of the Virgin Mary to 3 shepherd children at Fatima.

Cabral Issue

Raising the Cross at Porto Seguro — A44

Designs: 1.50e, First mission to Brazil. 3e, Grace Church, Santarem, vert.

1968, Apr. 22   **Litho.**   *Perf. 14*

481	A44	1e multicolored	.30	.25
482	A44	1.50e multicolored	.40	.25
483	A44	3e multicolored	1.00	.25
		Nos. 481-483 (3)	1.70	.75

500th birth anniv. of Pedro Alvares Cabral, navigator who took possession of Brazil for Portugal.

Admiral Coutinho Issue
Common Design Type
Design: 70c, Adm. Coutinho and Adm. Gago Coutinho Airport.

1969, Feb. 17   **Litho.**   *Perf. 14*
484   CD55   70c multicolored   .30   .25

Luiz Vaz de Camoens A45

Sailing Ship, 1553 A46

Designs: 1.50e, Map of Mozambique, 1554. 2.50e, Chapel of Our Lady of Baluarte, 1552. 5e, Excerpt from Lusiads about Mozambique (1st Song, 14th Stanza).

Perf. 12½x13, 13x12½
1969, June 10   **Litho.**

485	A45	15c multicolored	.30	.25
486	A46	50c multicolored	.30	.25
487	A45	1.50e multicolored	.30	.25
488	A46	2.50e multicolored	.30	.25
489	A45	5e multicolored	.50	.30
		Nos. 485-489 (5)	1.70	1.30

Visit to Mozambique of Luiz Vaz de Camoens (1524-80), poet, 400th anniv.

Vasco da Gama Issue

Map Showing Voyage to Mozambique and India — A47

1969, Aug. 29   **Litho.**   *Perf. 14*
490   A47   1e multicolored   .30   .25

Vasco da Gama (1469-1524), navigator.

Administration Reform Issue
Common Design Type

1969, Sept. 25   **Litho.**   *Perf. 14*
491   CD56   1.50e multicolored   .30   .25

King Manuel I Issue

Illuminated Miniature of King's Arms — A48

1969, Dec. 1   **Litho.**   *Perf. 14*
492   A48   80c multicolored   .30   .25

500th anniversary of the birth of King Manuel I.

MOZAMBIQUE

Marshal Carmona Issue
Common Design Type
5e, Antonio Oscar Carmona in marshal's uniform.

1970, Nov. 15   Litho.   Perf. 14
493   CD57   5e multicolored   .40   .25

Fossil Fern — A49

Fossils and Minerals: 50c, Fossil snail. 1e, Stibnite. 1.50e, Pink beryl. 2e, Dinosaur. 3e, Tantalocolumbite. 3.50e, Verdelite. 4e, Zircon. 10e, Petrified wood.

1971, Jan. 15   Litho.   Perf. 13
494	A49	15c gray & multi	.30	.25
495	A49	50c lt ultra & multi	.30	.25
496	A49	1e green & multi	.30	.25
497	A49	1.50e multicolored	.40	.25
498	A49	2e multicolored	.75	.25
499	A49	3e lt bl & multi	1.20	.25
500	A49	3.50e lilac & multi	1.50	.25
501	A49	4e multicolored	2.25	.30
502	A49	10e dl red & multi	3.75	.85
		Nos. 494-502 (9)	10.75	2.90

For overprints see Nos. 525, 528.

Mozambique Island — A49a

1972, May 25   Litho.   Perf. 13
503   A49a   4e ultra & multi   .40   .25

4th centenary of publication of The Lusiads by Luiz Camoens.

Olympic Games Issue
Common Design Type
3e, Hurdles and swimming, Olympic emblem.

1972, June 20   Perf. 14x13½
504   CD59   3e multi   .30   .25

For overprint see No. 523.

Lisbon-Rio de Janeiro Flight Issue
Common Design Type
1e, "Santa Cruz" over Recife harbor.

1972, Sept. 20   Litho.   Perf. 13½
505   CD60   1e multi   .30   .25

Sailboats — A50

Designs: Various sailboats.

1973, Aug. 21   Litho.   Perf. 12x11½
506	A50	1e multi	.30	.25
507	A50	1.50e multi	.30	.25
508	A50	3e multi	.40	.25
		Nos. 506-508 (3)	1.00	.75

World Sailing Championships, Vauriens Class, Lourenço Marques, Aug. 21-30.
For overprints see Nos. 519-520, 524.

WMO Centenary Issue
Common Design Type

1973, Dec. 15   Litho.   Perf. 13
509   CD61   2e rose red & multi   .40   .25

For overprint see No. 521.

Satellite Dishes — A51

1974, June 25   Litho.   Perf. 13
510   A51   50c multi   .30   .25

Establishment of satellite communications network via Intelsat among Portugal, Angola and Mozambique.
For overprint see No. 518.

"Bird" Made of Flags of Portugal and Mozambique A52

1975, Jan.   Litho.   Perf. 14½
511	A52	1e pink & multi	.30	.25
512	A52	1.50e yel & multi	.30	.25
513	A52	2e gray & multi	.30	.25
514	A52	3.50e lem & multi	.50	.30
515	A52	6e lt bl & multi	1.25	.30
	a.	Souv. sheet of 5, #511-515 + label	6.75	6.75
		Nos. 511-515 (5)	2.65	1.35

Lusaka Agreement, Sept. 7, 1974, which gave Mozambique independence from Portugal, effective June 25, 1975.
No. 515a sold for 25e.
For overprints see Nos. 543-545.

Republic
Issues of 1953-74 Overprinted in Red or Black

a   b

1975, June 25
516	A28 (a)	10c (R; #387)	.40	.40
517	A26 (a)	40c (R; #368)	.30	.25
518	A51 (b)	50c (B; #510)	.30	.25
519	A50 (b)	1e (B; #506)	.50	.40
520	A50 (b)	1.50e (B; #507)	.95	.80
521	CD61 (a)	2e (R; #509)	2.75	2.75
522	CD48 (b)	2.50e (B; #427)	.55	.45
523	CD59 (a)	3e (R; #504)	.65	.55
524	A50 (b)	3e (B; #508)	.70	.65
525	A49 (b)	3.50e (B; #500)	2.75	2.75
526	CD48 (b)	4.50e (B; #428)	3.75	1.75
527	A26 (a)	7.50e (R; #381)	.90	.45
528	A49 (b)	10e (#502)	1.75	.60
529	CD48 (b)	15e (#429)	2.10	1.75
530	A28 (a)	20e (#394)	2.40	1.40
		Nos. 516-530,C35-C38 (19)	24.95	18.60

Workers, Farmers and Children — A53

Designs: 30c, 50c, 2.50e, like 20c. 4.50e, 5e, 10e, 50e, Dancers, workers, armed family.

1975   Litho.   Perf. 12x11½
531	A53	20c pink & multi	.30	.25
532	A53	30c bis & multi	.30	.25
533	A53	50c bl & multi	.30	.25
534	A53	2.50e grn & multi	.30	.25
535	A53	4.50e brn & multi	.35	.25
536	A53	5e blk & multi	.60	.25
537	A53	10e bl & multi	1.00	.45
538	A53	50e yel & multi	4.25	2.25
	a.	Souvenir sheet of 8	8.50	8.50
		Nos. 531-538 (8)	7.30	4.20

No. 538a contains 8 stamps similar to Nos. 531-538 with simulated perforation. Sold for 75e.
For overprint see No. 554.

Farm Woman — A54

1976, Apr. 7   Litho.   Perf. 14½
539	A54	1e shown	.30	.25
540	A54	1.50e Teacher	.30	.25
541	A54	2.50e Nurse	.30	.25
542	A54	10e Mother	1.10	.70
		Nos. 539-542 (4)	2.00	1.45

Day of the Mozambique Woman, Apr. 7.

Nos. 513-515 Overprinted in Red

1976, Apr. 20   Litho.   Perf. 14½
543	A52	2e gray & multi	.30	.25
544	A52	3.50e lem & multi	.40	.30
545	A52	6e lt bl & multi	.80	.50
		Nos. 543-545 (3)	1.50	1.05

Visit of President Kaunda of Zambia.

Pres. Machel's Arrival at Maputo — A55

Designs: 1e, Independence proclamation ceremony. 2.50e, Pres. Samora Moises Machel taking office. 7.50e, Military parade. 20e, Flame of Unity and festival.

1976, June 25
546	A55	50c multi	.30	.25
547	A55	1e multi	.30	.25
548	A55	2.50e multi	.30	.25
549	A55	7.50e multi	.80	.30
550	A55	20e multi	2.25	1.25
		Nos. 546-550 (5)	3.95	2.30

First anniversary of independence.

Mozambique No. 1 — A56

1976, July   Perf. 11½x12
551	A56	1.50e ocher & multi	.30	.25
552	A56	6e red & multi	.55	.30

Centenary of Mozambique postage stamps.

Flag and Weapons — A57

1976, Sept. 25   Litho.   Perf. 14½
553   A57   3e multi   .40   .25

Army Day 1976.

No. 534 Ovptd. in Silver

1976   Litho.   Perf. 12x11½
554   A53   2.50e multi   .70   .30

FACIM, Industrial Fair.

Bush Baby — A58

Animals: 1e, Honey badger. 1.50e, Pangolin. 2e, Steinbok. 2.50e, Guenon (monkey). 3e, Cape hunting dog. 4e, Cheetah. 5e, Spotted hyena. 7.50e, Wart hog. 8e, Hippopotamus. 10e, Rhinoceros. 15e, Sable antelope. 1e, 2e, 3e, 4e, 7.50e, 8e, 10e horiz.

1977, Jan.   Litho.   Perf. 14½
555	A58	50c multi	.30	.25
556	A58	1e multi	.30	.25
557	A58	1.50e multi	.30	.25
558	A58	2e multi	.30	.25
559	A58	2.50e multi	.30	.25
560	A58	3e multi	.30	.25
561	A58	4e multi	.50	.25
562	A58	5e multi	.70	.25
563	A58	7.50e multi	1.10	.30
564	A58	8e multi	1.20	.40
565	A58	10e multi	1.20	.40
566	A58	15e multi	1.75	.95
		Nos. 555-566 (12)	8.25	4.05

Congress Emblem A59   **Monument in Maputo A60**

Design: 3.50e, Monument in Macheje, site of 2nd Frelimo Congress, horiz.

1977, Feb. 7   Perf. 14½
567   A59   3e multi   .40   .25

Perf. 12x11½, 11½x12
568	A60	3.50e multi	.30	.30
569	A60	20e multi	2.10	.95
		Nos. 567-569 (3)	2.80	1.50

3rd FRELIMO Party Congress, Maputo, Feb. 3-7.

Women, Child's Design — A61

1977, Apr. 7   Litho.   Perf. 14½
570	A61	5e dp org & multi	.30	.25
571	A61	15e lt grn & multi	1.40	.55

Mozambique Women's Day 1977.

Worker and Farmer — A62

1977, May 1   Litho.   Perf. 14½
572   A62   5e red, blk & yel   1.00   .30

Labor Day.

People, Flags and Rising Sun — A63

1977, June 25   Litho.   Perf. 11½x12
573	A63	50c multi	.30	.25
574	A63	1.50e multi	.30	.25
575	A63	3e multi	.30	.25
576	A63	15e multi	1.10	.45
		Nos. 573-576 (4)	2.00	1.20

2nd anniversary of independence.

Bread Palm — A64

MOZAMBIQUE

1977, Dec. 21   Litho.   Perf. 12x11½
| 577 | A64 | 1e shown | | .50 | .25 |
| 578 | A64 | 10e Nyala | | 1.25 | .55 |

Nature protection and Stamp Day.

Chariesthes Bella Rufoplagiata — A65

Beetles: 1e, Tragocephalus variegata. 1.50e, Monochamus leuconotus. 3e, Prospocera lactator meridionalis. 5e, Dinocephalus ornatus. 10e, Tragiscoschema nigroscriptum maculata.

1978, Jan. 20   Litho.   Perf. 11½x12
579	A65	50c multi	.40	.30
580	A65	1e multi	.40	.30
581	A65	1.50e multi	.55	.30
582	A65	3e multi	.60	.30
583	A65	5e multi	.85	.45
584	A65	10e multi	1.40	.45
	Nos. 579-584 (6)	4.20	2.10

Violet-crested Touraco — A66

Birds of Mozambique: 1e, Lilac-breasted roller. 1.50e, Weaver. 2.50e, Violet-backed starling. 3e, Peter's twinspot. 15e, European bee-eater.

1978, Mar. 20   Litho.   Perf. 11½
585	A66	50c multi	.55	.30
586	A66	1e multi	.55	.30
587	A66	1.50e multi	.70	.30
588	A66	2.50e multi	.85	.30
589	A66	3e multi	1.00	.30
590	A66	15e multi	2.00	.55
	Nos. 585-590 (6)	5.65	2.05

Mother and Child, WHO Emblem — A67

1978, Apr. 17   Perf. 12
| 591 | A67 | 15e multi | .70 | .35 |

Smallpox eradication campaign.

Crinum Delagoense — A68

Flowers of Mozambique: 1e, Gloriosa superba. 1.50e, Eulophia speciosa. 3e, Erithrina humeana. 5e, Astripomoea malvacea. 10e, Kigelia africana.

1978, May 16   Perf. 11½x12
592	A68	50c multi	.40	.25
593	A68	1e multi	.40	.25
594	A68	1.50e multi	.40	.25
595	A68	3e multi	.40	.25
596	A68	5e multi	.80	.25
597	A68	10e multi	1.00	.50
	Nos. 592-597 (6)	3.40	1.75

No. 1, Canada No. 1 — A69

1978, June 9
| 598 | A69 | 15e multi | .90 | .50 |

CAPEX Canadian International Philatelic Exhibition, Toronto, Ont., June 9-18.

National Flag — A70

1.50e, Coat of arms. 7.50e, Page of Constitution people. 10e, Music band & natl. anthem.

1978, June 25   Perf. 11½x12
599	A70	1e multi	.30	.25
600	A70	1.50e multi	.30	.25
601	A70	7.50e multi	.45	.25
602	A70	10e multi	.60	.35
a.	Souvenir sheet of 4	2.25	2.25
	Nos. 599-602 (4)	1.65	1.10

3rd anniversary of proclamation of independence. No. 602a contains 4 stamps similar to Nos. 599-602 with simulated perforations. Sold for 30e.

Soldiers, Festival Emblem — A71

2.50e, Student. 7.50e, Farmworkers.

1978, July 28
603	A71	2.50e multi	.30	.25
604	A71	3e multi	.30	.25
605	A71	7.50e multi	.55	.40
	Nos. 603-605 (3)	1.15	.90

11th World Youth Festival, Havana, 7/28-8/5.

Czechoslovakia No. B126 and PRAGA '78 Emblem — A72

1978, Sept. 8   Litho.   Perf. 12x11½
| 606 | A72 | 15e multi | 1.00 | .50 |
| a. | Souvenir sheet | 3.50 | 2.00 |

PRAGA '78 International Philatelic Exhibition, Prague, Sept. 8-17.
No. 606a contains one stamp with simulated perforations. Sold for 30e.

Soccer — A73

Stamp Day: 1.50e, Shotput. 3e, Hurdling. 7.50e, Fieldball. 12.50e, Swimming. 25e, Roller skate hockey.

1978, Dec. 21   Litho.   Perf. 12x11½
607	A73	50c multi	.30	.25
608	A73	1.50e multi	.30	.25
609	A73	3e multi	.30	.25
610	A73	7.50e multi	.50	.35
611	A73	12.50e multi	.70	.45
612	A73	25e multi	1.60	1.10
	Nos. 607-612 (6)	3.70	2.65

Carrier Pigeon, UPU Emblem — A74

1979, Jan. 1   Litho.   Perf. 11x11½
| 613 | A74 | 20e multi | 1.75 | .90 |

Membership in Universal Postal Union.

Soldier Giving Gourd to Woman A75

Designs: 3e, Frelimo soldiers. 7.50e, Mozambique children in school.

1979, Feb. 3   Perf. 11½x11, 11x11½
614	A75	1e multi	.30	.25
615	A75	3e multi	.30	.25
616	A75	7.50e multi	.55	.30
617	A76	12.50e multi	.80	.50
	Nos. 614-617 (4)	1.95	1.30

Dr. Edward Chivambo Mondlane (1920-1969), educator, founder of Frelimo Party.

Edward Chivambo Mondlane — A76

Shaded Silver Cat — A77

Cats: 1.50e, Manx. 2.50e, English blue. 3e, Turkish. 12.50e, Long-haired Mid-East tabby. 20e, African wild cat.

1979, Mar. 27   Litho.   Perf. 11
618	A77	50c multi	.35	.25
619	A77	1.50e multi	.40	.25
620	A77	2.50e multi	.40	.25
621	A77	3e multi	.50	.25
622	A77	12.50e multi	1.10	.50
623	A77	20e multi	1.60	1.00
	Nos. 618-623 (6)	4.35	2.50

Wrestling and Moscow '80 Emblem A78

Sport and Moscow '80 Emblem: 2e, Running. 3e, Equestrian. 5e, Canoeing. 10e, High jump. 15e, Archery.

1979, Apr. 24   Litho.   Perf. 11
624	A78	1e gray grn & blk	.30	.25
625	A78	2e brt bl & blk	.30	.25
626	A78	3e lt brn & blk	.30	.25
627	A78	5e multi	.30	.25
628	A78	10e grn & blk	.50	.30
629	A78	15e lil rose & blk	1.25	.65
	Nos. 624-629 (6)	2.95	1.95

Souvenir Sheet
Imperf
| 630 | A78 | 30e rose & dk brn | 2.50 | 2.50 |

22nd Olympic Games, Moscow, July 10-Aug. 3, 1980. No. 630 contains one 47x37mm stamp.

Garden and IYC Emblem — A79

Children's Drawings and IYC Emblem: 1.50e, Dancers. 3e, City. 5e, Farmers. 7.50e, Village. 12.50e, Automobiles, train and flowers.

1979, June 1   Litho.   Perf. 11
631	A79	50c multi	.30	.25
632	A79	1.50e multi	.30	.25
633	A79	3e multi	.30	.25
634	A79	5e multi	.30	.25
635	A79	7.50e multi	.45	.25
636	A79	12.50e multi	1.10	.45
	Nos. 631-636 (6)	2.75	1.70

International Year of the Child.

Flight from Colonialism A80

Designs: 2e, Founding of FRELIMO and Pres. Eduardo Chivambo Mondlane. 3e, Advance of armed strruggle and death of Mondlane. 7.50e, Final fight for liberation. 15e, Proclamation of victory, Pres. Samora Moises Machel, flag and torch. Designs after mural in Heroes' Square, Maputo. 30e, Building up the country.

1979, June 25
637	A80	50c multi	.30	.25
638	A80	2e multi	.30	.25
639	A80	3e multi	.30	.25
640	A80	7.50e multi	.45	.25
641	A80	15e multi	.95	.70
b.	Strip of 5, #637-641	3.25	3.25

Souvenir Sheet
Imperf
| 641A | A80 | 30e multi | 6.00 | 6.00 |

4th anniversary of independence. No. 641A contains one stamp with simulated perforations. No. 641b has continuous design.

Scorpion Fish — A81

Tropical Fish: 1.50e, King fish. 2.50e, Gobius inhaca. 3e, Acanthurus lineatus. 10e, Gobuchthys lemayi. 12.50e, Variola louti.

1979, Aug. 7   Litho.   Perf. 11
642	A81	50c multi	.30	.25
643	A81	1.50e multi	.30	.25
644	A81	2.50e multi	.30	.25
645	A81	3e multi	.30	.25
646	A81	10e multi	.75	.25
647	A81	12.50e multi	.85	.35
	Nos. 642-647 (6)	2.80	1.60

For surcharge see No. 1254.

Quartz — A82

Mozambique Minerals.

1979, Sept. 10
648	A82	1e shown	.45	.25
649	A82	1.50e Beryl	.60	.25
650	A82	2.50e Magnetite	.85	.25
651	A82	5e Tourmaline	1.25	.35
652	A82	10e Euxenite	1.50	.40
653	A82	20e Fluorite	2.10	.70
	Nos. 648-653 (6)	6.75	2.20

MOZAMBIQUE 695

Citizens Gathering Arms — A83

1979, Sept. 25
654 A83 5e multi .90 .25
15th anniversary of independence.

Locomotive A85

Designs: Historic Locomotives.

1979, Nov. 11 Litho. Perf. 11
656 A85 50c multi .30 .25
657 A85 1.50e multi .30 .25
658 A85 3e multi .35 .25
659 A85 7.50e multi .65 .25
660 A85 12.50e multi .35 .40
661 A85 15e multi 1.20 .50
Nos. 656-661 (6) 3.15 1.90

For surcharge see No. 1298.

Dalmatian A86

50c, Basenji. vert. 3e, Boxer. 7.50e, Blue gasconha braco. 12.50e, Cocker spaniel. 15e, Pointer.

Perf. 11½x11, 11x11½
1979, Dec. 17 Litho.
662 A86 50c multi .30 .25
663 A86 1.50e shown .30 .25
664 A86 3e multi .45 .25
665 A86 7.50e multi .60 .25
666 A86 12.50e multi .95 .35
667 A86 15e multi 1.25 .50
Nos. 662-667 (6) 3.85 1.85

For surcharge see No. 1299.

Nireus Lyaeus A87

Butterflies: 1.50e, Amauris ochlea. 2.50e, Pinacopterix eriphia. 5e, Junonia hierta cebrene. 10e, Nephronia argia. 20e, Catacroptera cloanthe.

1979, Dec. 21
668 A87 1e multi .30 .25
669 A87 1.50e multi .40 .25
670 A87 2.50e multi .50 .25
671 A87 5e multi .65 .25
672 A87 10e multi 1.10 .30
673 A87 20e multi 2.10 .75
Nos. 668-673 (6) 5.05 2.05

Dermacentor Rhinocerinus, Rhinoceros — A88

Ticks and Animals: 50c, Dermacentor circumguttatus cunhasilvai, elephant. 2.50e, Green tick, giraffe. 3e, Red tick, antelope. 5e, Ambloymma theilerae, cattle. 7.50e, Buffalo tick, buffalo.

1980, Jan. 29 Litho. Perf. 11½x11
674 A88 50c multi .30 .25
675 A88 1.50e multi .35 .25
676 A88 2.50e multi .35 .25
677 A88 3e multi .65 .25
678 A88 5e multi 1.00 .25
679 A88 7.50e multi 1.50 .30
Nos. 674-679 (6) 4.15 1.55

Ford Hercules, 1950 — A89

Public Transportation: 1.50e, Scania Marcopolo, 1978. 3e, Bussing Nag, 1936. 5e, Articulated Ikarus, 1978. 7.50e, Ford taxi, 1929. 12.50e, Fiat 131 taxi, 1978.

1980, Feb. 29 Litho. Perf. 11
680 A89 50c multi .30 .25
681 A89 1.50e multi .30 .25
682 A89 3e multi .30 .25
683 A89 5e multi .35 .25
684 A89 7.50e multi .60 .25
685 A89 12.50e multi .80 .40
Nos. 680-685 (6) 2.65 1.65

Marx, Engels, and Lenin — A90

1980, May 1 Litho. Perf. 11
686 A90 10e multi 1.10 .30
Workers' Day.

"Heads," by Malangatana, London 1980 Emblem — A91

Paintings by Mozambique Artists: 1.50e, Crowded Market, by Moises Simbine. 3e, Heads with Helmets, by Malangatana. 5e, Women with Goods, by Machiana. 7.50e, Crowd with Masks, by Malangatana. 12.50e, Man and Woman with Spear, by Mankeu.

1980, May 6
687 A91 50c multi .30 .25
688 A91 1.50e multi .30 .25
689 A91 3e multi .30 .25
690 A91 5e multi .35 .25
691 A91 7.50e multi .50 .25
692 A91 12.50e multi .70 .35
Nos. 687-692 (6) 2.45 1.60

London 1980 Intl. Stamp Exhibition, 5/6-14.

World Telecommunications Day — A92

1980, May 17 Litho. Perf. 12
693 A92 15e multi 1.00 .45

Mueda Massacre, 20th Anniv. — A93

1980, June 16 Litho. Perf. 11
694 A93 15e multi 1.25 .45

People with Weapons and Flag — A94

1e, Development projects, 1975. 3e, Arms, flags, 1977. 4e, Raised fists, 1978. 5e, Hand holding grain, flags, 1979. 10e, Year banners, 1980. 30e, Soldiers.

1980, June 25
695 A94 1e multi .25 .25
696 A94 2e shown .25 .25
697 A94 3e multi .25 .25
698 A94 4e multi .35 .25
699 A94 5e multi .35 .25
700 A94 10e multi .70 .30
Nos. 695-700 (6) 2.15 1.55

Souvenir Sheet
Litho. Imperf.
700A A94 30e multi 3.50 3.50
5th anniv. of independence. No. 700A contains one stamp with simulated perforations.

Gymnast, Moscow '80 Emblem — A95

1980, July 19
701 A95 50c shown .25 .25
702 A95 1.50e Soccer .25 .25
703 A95 2.50e Running .25 .25
704 A95 3e Volleyball .30 .25
705 A95 10e Bicycling .65 .25
706 A95 12.50e Boxing .90 .40
Nos. 701-706 (6) 2.60 1.65

22nd Summer Olympic Games, Moscow, July 19-Aug. 3.

Soldier, Map of Southern Africa Showing Zimbabwe A96

1980, Apr. 18
707 A96 10e multi .65 .30
Establishment of independent Zimbabwe, Apr. 18.

Narina Trogon — A97

1.50m, Crowned crane. 2.50m, Red-necked francolin. 5m, Ostrich. 7.50m, Spur-winged goose. 12.50m, Fish eagle.

1980, July 30 Litho. Perf. 11
708 A97 1m shown .40 .25
709 A97 1.50m multi .55 .25
710 A97 2.50m multi .65 .25
711 A97 5m multi .85 .25
712 A97 7.50m multi 1.25 .25
713 A97 12.50m multi 1.40 .30
Nos. 708-713 (6) 5.10 1.55

For surcharges see Nos. 1253A, 1255.

First Census, Aug. 1-15 — A98

1980, Aug. 12 Perf. 11
714 A98 3.5m multi .40 .25

Brush Fire Control Campaign A99

1980, Sept. 7
715 A99 3.5m multi .80 .25

Harpa Major — A100

1.50m, Lambis chiragra. 2.50m, Murex pecten. 5m, Architectonia perspectiva. 7.50m, Murex ramosus. 12.50m, Strombus aurisdinae.

1980, Dec. 12 Litho. Perf. 11
716 A100 1m shown .35 .25
717 A100 1.50m multi .40 .25
718 A100 2.50m multi .50 .25
719 A100 5m multi .60 .25
720 A100 7.50m multi .75 .25
721 A100 12.50m multi 1.25 .40
Nos. 716-721 (6) 3.85 1.65

Pres. Machel and Symbols of Industry and Transportation A101

Decade of Development, 1981-1990 (Pres. Machel and): 7.50m, Soldiers. 12.50m, Symbols of education.

1981, Jan. 1 Litho. Perf. 11x11½
722 A101 3.50m red & bl .55 .25
723 A101 7.50m grn & red brn 1.00 .25
724 A101 12.50m dk bl & lil rose 1.90 .45
Nos. 722-724 (3) 3.45 .95

Bilbao Soccer Stadium, Soccer Player A102

Soccer players and various stadiums.

1981, Jan. 30 Litho. Perf. 11
725 A102 1m multi .30 .25
726 A102 1.50m multi .30 .25
727 A102 2.50m multi .30 .25
728 A102 5m multi .05 .25
729 A102 7.50m multi .60 .25
730 A102 12.50m multi .95 .40
c Souvenir sheet of 6 2.40 2.40
Nos. 725-730 (6) 2.80 1.65

Souvenir Sheets
Imperf
730A A102 20m multi 3.50 3.50
730B A102 20m multi 3.50 3.50

ESPANA '82 World Cup Soccer Championship. No. 730c contains Nos. 725-730 with simulated perforations. Sizes: No. 730A, 105x85mm; 730B, 141x111mm.

For surcharge see No. 1303.

Giraffe — A103

1.50m, Tsessebe. 2.50m, Aardvark. 3m, African python. 5m, Loggerhead turtle. 10m, Marabou. 12.50m, Saddlebill stork. 15m, Kori bustard.

1981, Mar. 3 Perf. 11
731 A103 50c shown .35 .25
732 A103 1.50m multi .40 .25
733 A103 2.50m multi .60 .25
734 A103 3m multi .65 .25
735 A103 5m multi .70 .25

MOZAMBIQUE

736	A103	10m multi	.90 .35
737	A103	12.50m multi	1.10 .50
738	A103	15m multi	1.75 .60
	Nos. 731-738 (8)		6.45 2.70

Pankwe — A104

50c, Chitende, vert. 2.50m, Kanyembe, vert. 7m, Nyanga. 10m, Likuti and m'petheni.

1981, Apr. 8   Litho.   Perf. 11

739	A104	50c multi	.30 .25
740	A104	2m shown	.30 .25
741	A104	2.50m multi	.30 .25
742	A104	7m multi	.55 .25
743	A104	10m multi	1.20 .45
	Nos. 739-743 (5)		2.65 1.45

International Year of the Disabled A105

1981, Apr. 18

744	A105	5m multi	.50 .25

African Buffalo and Helicopter, Exhibition Emblem A106

5m, Hunters, blue kids. 6m, Hunter, impala. 7.50m, Hunters shooting. 12.50m, Elephants. 20m, Trap.

1981, June 14   Perf. 11

745	A106	2m shown	.35 .25
746	A106	5m multi	.50 .25
747	A106	6m multi	.60 .25
748	A106	7.50m multi	.80 .25
749	A106	12.50m multi	1.00 .35
750	A106	20m multi	1.25 .60
a.	Souv. sheet of 6, #745-750, imperf.		5.50 5.50
	Nos. 745-750 (6)		4.50 1.95

World Hunting Exhibition, Plovdiv, Bulgaria. No. 750a sold for 60m.
For surcharge see No. 1258.

50-centavo Coin, Obverse and Reverse — A107

First Anniversary of New Currency (Coins on stamps of matching denomination).

1981, June 16

751	A107	50c multi	.30 .25
752	A107	1m multi	.30 .25
753	A107	2.50m multi	.30 .25
754	A107	5m multi	.35 .25
755	A107	10m multi	.55 .25
756	A107	20m multi	1.25 .60
a.	Souv. sheet of 6, #751-756, imperf.		3.25 3.25
	Nos. 751-756 (6)		3.05 1.85

No. 756a sold for 40m.

Crops — A108

Designs: 50c, Sunflower (Helianthus annus). 1m, Cotton (Gossypium spp.). 1.50m, Sisal (Agave sisalana). 2.50m, Cashews (Anacardium occidentale). 3.50m, Tea (Camellia sinensis). 4.50m, Sugar cane (Saccharum officianum). 10m, Castor oil plant (Ricinus communis). 12.50m, Coconuts (Cocos nucifera). 15m, Tobacco (Nicotiniana tabacum). 25m, Rice (Oryza sativa). 40m, Corn (Zea mays). 60m, Peanut (Arachis hypogaea).

1981, July 24   Litho.   Perf. 14½

757	A108	50c red & org	.30 .25
758	A108	1m red & black	.30 .25
759	A108	1.50m red & Prus bl	.30 .25
760	A108	2.50m red & bis	.30 .25
761	A108	3.50m red & gray grn	.30 .25
762	A108	4.50m red & gray	.30 .25
763	A108	10m red & blue	.75 .25
764	A108	12.50m red & dk brn	1.00 .35
765	A108	15m red & ol grn	1.10 .40
766	A108	25m red & yel grn	1.50 .60
767	A108	40m red & org brn	2.50 .80
768	A108	60m red & brn	3.75 1.25
	Nos. 757-768 (12)		12.40 5.15

For surcharges see Nos. 1034A, 1185, 1216, 1218, 1252, 1300, 1399, 1420.

9th Cent. Persian Bowl, Chibuene Excavation Site — A109

1m, Manyikeni Museum. 1.50m, Hand ax, Massingir Dam. 7.50m, Pot, Chibuene, 9th cent. 12.50m, Gold beads, Manyikeni. 20m, Iron, Manyikeni, 15th cent.

1981, Aug. 30   Perf. 11

769	A109	1m multi	.30 .25
770	A109	1.50m multi	.30 .25
771	A109	2.50m shown	.30 .25
772	A109	7.50m multi	.50 .25
773	A109	12.50m multi	.85 .30
774	A109	20m multi	1.40 .50
	Nos. 769-774 (6)		3.65 1.80

For surcharge see No. 1213.

Sculptures — A110

50c, Mapiko mask. 1m, Suffering woman. 2.50m, Mother and child. 3.50m, Man making fire. 5m, Chietane and man. 12.50m, Chietane.

1981, Sept. 25   Litho.   Perf. 11

775	A110	50c multi	.30 .25
776	A110	1m multi	.30 .25
777	A110	2.50m multi	.30 .25
778	A110	3.50m multi	.30 .25
779	A110	5m multi	.50 .30
780	A110	12.50m multi	.50 .50
	Nos. 775-780 (6)		2.20 1.80

World Food Day — A111

1981, Oct. 16   Litho.   Perf. 11

781	A111	10m multi	.80 .40

Ocean Tanker Matchedje A112

1.50m, Tugboat Macuti. 3m, Prawn trawler Vega 7. 5m, Freighter Linde. 7.50m, Ocean freighter Pemba. 12.50m, Dredger Rovuma.

1981, Nov. 22   Litho.   Perf. 11

782	A112	50c shown	.30 .25
783	A112	1.50m multi	.30 .25
784	A112	3m multi	.30 .25
785	A112	5m multi	.35 .25
786	A112	7.50m multi	.65 .30
787	A112	12.50m multi	1.25 .50
	Nos. 782-787 (6)		3.15 1.80

Chinaman Crab — A113

50c, Portunus Pelageius. 1.50m, Scylla serrata. 3m, Penaeus indicus. 7.50m, Palinurus delagoae. 12.50m, Lusiosquilla maculata. 15m, Panulirus ornatus.

1981, Dec. 6

788	A113	50c multi	.45 .25
789	A113	1.50m multi	.45 .25
790	A113	3m multi	.45 .25
791	A113	7.50m multi	.65 .25
792	A113	12.50m multi	1.00 .35
793	A113	15m multi	1.40 .40
	Nos. 788-793 (6)		4.40 1.75

For surcharges see Nos. 1214, 1219, 1253, 1392.

Hypoxis Multiceps — A114

1.50m, Pelargonium luridum. 2.50m, Caralluma melananthera. 7.50m, Ansellia gigantea. 12.50m, Stapelia leendertziae. 25m, Adenium multiflorium.

1981, Dec. 21   Litho.   Perf. 11

794	A114	1m shown	.30 .25
795	A114	1.50m multi	.30 .25
796	A114	2.50m multi	.30 .25
797	A114	7.50m multi	.50 .25
798	A114	12.50m multi	.90 .40
799	A114	25m multi	1.75 .75
	Nos. 794-799 (6)		4.05 2.15

For surcharges see Nos. 1215, 1217, 1251, 1301, 1390, 1303A.

First Anniv. of Posts and Telecommunications Dept. — A115

1982, Jan. 1   Litho.   Perf. 11

800	A115	6m Phone, globe	.45 .25
801	A115	15m Envelope	1.25 .60

Gasoline Conservation A116

1982, Jan. 25

802	A116	5m Piston	.35 .25
803	A116	7.50m Car	.55 .30
804	A116	10m Truck	.75 .40
	Nos. 802-804 (3)		1.65 .95

Sea Snake — A117

1.50m, Mozambique spitting cobra. 3m, Savanna vine snake. 6m, Black mamba. 15m, Boomslang. 20m, Bitis arietans.

1982, Feb. 27   Perf. 11

805	A117	50c shown	.45 .25
806	A117	1.50m multi	.45 .25
807	A117	3m multi	.45 .25
808	A117	6m multi	.50 .25
809	A117	15m multi	1.20 .35
810	A117	20m multi	1.60 .55
	Nos. 805-810 (6)		4.65 1.90

TB Bacillus Centenary A118

1982, Mar. 15   Litho.   Perf. 11

811	A118	20m multi	1.50 .75

ITU Plenipotentiary Conference, Nairobi, Sept. 28-Nov. 5 — A119

1982, Mar. 31   Perf. 13½

812	A119	20m multi	1.60 .65

1982 World Cup — A120

Designs: Various soccer players.

1982, Apr. 19   Litho.   Perf. 13½

813	A120	1.5m multi	.30 .25
814	A120	3.5m multi	.30 .25
815	A120	7m multi	.50 .25
816	A120	10m multi	.85 .30
817	A120	20m multi	1.25 .70
	Nos. 813-817 (5)		3.20 1.75

Souvenir Sheet
Imperf

818	A120	50m multi	3.50 .350

Souvenir Sheet

Two Tahitian Women, by Gauguin A121

1982, June 11   Litho.   Imperf.

819	A121	35m multi	5.00 5.00

PHILEXFRANCE '82 Intl. Stamp Exhibition, Paris, June 11-21.

Natl. Liberation Front, 20th Anniv. — A122

4m, Pres. Mondland addressing crowd. 8m, Guarded fields. 12m, Procession.

1982, June 25   Perf. 13

820	A122	4m multi	.30 .25
821	A122	8m multi	.55 .25
822	A122	12m multi	.85 .30
	Nos. 820-822 (3)		1.70 .80

Vangueria Infausta — A123

Designs: Fruits: 2m, Mimusops caffra. 4m, Sclerocarya caffra. 8m, Strychnos spinosa. 12m, Salacia kraussi. 32m, Trichilia emetica.

1982, Sept. 13   Perf. 11

823	A123	1m shown	.30 .25
824	A123	2m multi	.30 .25
825	A123	4m multi	.30 .25
826	A123	8m multi	.50 .25

MOZAMBIQUE

| 827 | A123 | 12m multi | .85 | .35 |
| 828 | A123 | 32m multi | 1.75 | .75 |

Nos. 823-828 (6) 4.00 2.10

25th Anniv. of Sputnik 1 Flight — A124

1m, Sputnik, 1957. 2m, Yuri Gagarin's flight, 1961. 4m, A. Leonov's spacewalk, 1965. 8m, Apollo 11, 1969. 16m, Apollo-Soyuz, 1975. 20m, Salyut-6, 1978.

1982, Oct. 4 Litho. Perf. 11
829	A124	1m multi	.30	.25
830	A124	2m multi	.30	.25
831	A124	4m multi	.30	.25
832	A124	8m multi	.60	.25
833	A124	16m multi	1.25	.60
834	A124	20m multi	1.60	.60
a.		Min. sheet of 6, #829-834	4.50	4.50

Nos. 829-834 (6) 4.35 2.20

People's Vigilance Day — A125

1982, Oct. 11 Perf. 13½
835 A125 4m multi .40 .25

Caique — A126

Traditional boats. 4m, 8m, 12m, 16m horiz.

1982, Nov. 29
836	A126	1m shown	.30	.25
837	A126	2m Machua	.30	.25
838	A126	4m Calaua	.40	.25
839	A126	8m Chitatarro	.75	.25
840	A126	12m Cangaia	1.00	.30
841	A126	16m Chata (flatboat)	1.75	.50

Nos. 836-841 (6) 4.50 1.80

Marine Life — A127

1m, Ophiomastix venosa. 2m, Protoreaster lincki. 4m, Tropiometra carinata. 8m, Holothuria scabra. 12m, Prionocidaris baculosa. 16m, Colobocentrotus atnatus.

1982, Dec. 21 Litho. Perf. 11
842	A127	1m multi	.45	.25
843	A127	2m multi	.45	.25
844	A127	4m multi	.45	.25
845	A127	8m multi	.75	.25
846	A127	12m multi	1.10	.30
847	A127	16m multi	1.25	.45

Nos. 842-847 (6) 4.45 1.65

Frelimo Party 4th Congress — A128

1983, Jan. 17
848	A128	4m Map, soldier	.30	.25
849	A128	8m Voters	.35	.25
850	A128	16m Farm workers	.90	.45

Nos. 848-850 (3) 1.55 .95

Seaweed A129

1m, Codium duthierae. 2m, Halimeda cuncata. 4m, Dictyota liturata. 8m, Encorachne bing hamiae. 12m, Laurencia flexuosa. 20m, Acrosorium sp..

1983, Feb. 28 Litho. Perf. 11
851	A129	1m multi	.30	.25
852	A129	2m multi	.30	.25
853	A129	4m multi	.30	.25
854	A129	8m multi	.55	.25
855	A129	12m multi	.85	.25
856	A129	20m multi	1.10	.50

Nos. 851-856 (6) 3.40 1.75

1984 Olympic Games, Los Angeles — A130

1983, Mar. 31 Litho. Perf. 11
857	A130	1m Diving	.30	.25
858	A130	2m Boxing	.30	.25
859	A130	4m Basketball	.30	.25
860	A130	8m Handball	.55	.25
861	A130	12m Volleyball	.80	.25
862	A130	16m Running	1.10	.25
863	A130	20m Sailing	1.25	.60

Nos. 857-863 (7) 4.60 2.20

Souvenir Sheet
Imperf
864 A130 50m Discus 3.25 3.25

For surcharge see No. 1257.

Steam Locomotives A131

1983, Apr. 29 Litho. Perf. 11
865	A131	1m 1912	.35	.25
866	A131	2m 1947	.35	.25
867	A131	4m 1923	.35	.25
868	A131	8m 1924	.60	.25
869	A131	16m 1924, diff.	1.20	.40
870	A131	32m 1950	2.40	.80

Nos. 865-870 (6) 5.25 2.20

20th Anniv. of Org. of African Unity — A132

1983, May 25 Litho. Perf. 11
871 A132 4m multi .30 .25

Mammals — A133

1m, Petrodromus tetradactylus. 2m, Rhabdomys pumilio. 4m, Paraxerus vincenti. 8m, Cryptomys hottentotus. 12m, Pronolagus crassicaudatus. 16m, Eidolon helvum.

1983, May 30
872	A133	1m multi	.45	.25
873	A133	2m multi	.45	.25
874	A133	4m multi	.45	.25
875	A133	8m multi	.75	.25
876	A133	12m multi	1.10	.30
877	A133	16m multi	1.40	.40

Nos. 872-877 (6) 4.60 1.70

Souvenir Sheet

Marimba Players — A134

1983, July 29 Litho. Perf. 11
878 A134 30m multi 3.50 3.50

BRASILIANA '83 Intl. Stamp Show, Rio de Janeiro, July 29-Aug. 7.

World Communications Year — A135

1983, Aug. 26 Litho. Perf. 11
879 A135 8m multi .60 .25

Fishing Techniques A136

1983, Oct. 29 Litho. Perf. 11
880	A136	50c Line fishing	.30	.25
881	A136	2m Chifonho	.30	.25
882	A136	4m Momba	.30	.25
883	A136	8m Gamboa	.50	.25
884	A136	16m Mono	1.25	.50
885	A136	20m Lema	1.50	.50

Nos. 880-885 (6) 4.15 1.85

World Communications Year, Stamp Day — A137

50c, Horn. 1m, Drum. 4m, Native mail carriers. 8m, Boat. 16m, Truck. 20m, Train.

1983, Dec. 21 Litho.
886	A137	50c multicolored	.30	.25
887	A137	1m multicolored	.30	.25
888	A137	4m multicolored	.40	.25
889	A137	8m multicolored	.95	.25
890	A137	16m multicolored	1.90	.35
891	A137	20m multicolored	2.50	.50

Nos. 886-891 (6) 6.35 1.85

2nd Anniv. of Mozambique Red Cross (July 10) — A138

1983, Oct. 29 Litho. Perf. 11
892	A138	4m Flood relief	.30	.25
893	A138	8m Rescue truck	.55	.25
894	A138	16m First aid	1.25	.25
895	A138	32m Field first aid	2.25	.65

Nos. 892-895 (4) 4.35 1.50

Olympic Games 1984, Los Angeles — A139

1984, Jan. 2 Litho. Perf. 11
896	A139	50c Swimming	.30	.25
897	A139	4m Soccer	.35	.25
898	A139	8m Hurdles	.55	.25
899	A139	16m Basketball	1.10	.35
900	A139	32m Handball	2.40	1.00
901	A139	60m Boxing	3.75	1.00

Nos. 896-901 (6) 8.45 3.10

Indigenous Trees — A140

50c, Trichilia emetica. 2m, Brachystegia spiciformis. 4m, Androstachys johnsonii. 8m, Pterocarpus angolensis. 16m, Milletia stuhlmannii. 50m, Dalbergia melanoxylon.

1984, Mar. 30 Perf. 11
902	A140	50c multicolored	.30	.25
903	A140	2m multicolored	.30	.25
904	A140	4m multicolored	.30	.25
905	A140	8m multicolored	.55	.25
906	A140	16m multicolored	1.00	.35
907	A140	50m multicolored	3.00	1.25

Nos. 902-907 (6) 5.45 2.60

Nkomati Accord, Mar. 16 — A141

1984, Mar. 16
908 A141 4m Dove .40 .25

Natl. Arms — A142

1984, May 1
| 909 | A142 | 4m shown | .30 | .25 |
| 910 | A142 | 8m Natl. flag | .65 | .30 |

Traditional Dances — A143

1984, May 9
911	A143	4m Makway	.30	.25
912	A143	8m Mapiko	.50	.25
913	A143	16m Wadjaba	1.40	.45

Nos. 911-913 (3) 2.20 .95

LUBRAPEX '84, May 9-17.

Museums and Artifacts A144

Designs: 50c, Nampula Museum, African carrying water jar, wooden statue. 4m, Museum of Natural History, preserved bird. 8m, Revolution Museum, guerrilla fighter statue. 16m, Colonial Occupation Museum, fort and cannon. 20m, Numismatic Museum, coins. 30m, Palace of St. Paul, chair, 19th cent.

1984, June 25
914	A144	50c multi	.30	.25
915	A144	4m multi	.35	.25
916	A144	8m multi	.55	.25
917	A144	16m multi	1.10	.40
918	A144	20m multi	1.25	.60
919	A144	30m multi	2.10	.85

Nos. 914-919 (6) 5.65 2.60

MOZAMBIQUE

Freshwater Fish — A145

50c, Alestes imberi. 4m, Labeo congoro. 12m, Syndontis zambezensis. 16m, Notobranchius rachovii. 40m, Barbus paludinosus. 60m, Barilius zambezensis.

1984, Aug. 24
920	A145	50c multi	.30	.25
921	A145	4m multi	.35	.25
922	A145	12m multi	.90	.30
923	A145	16m multi	.90	.40
924	A145	40m multi	2.50	1.10
925	A145	60m multi	3.50	1.50
	Nos. 920-925 (6)		8.45	3.80

For surcharge see No. 1311.

Intl. Fair, Maputo — A145a — 925A

1984, Aug. 24   Litho.   Perf. 11
925A	A145a	16m multicolored	1.60	.50

Traditional Weapons — A146

1984, Sept. 25
926	A146	50c Knife, cudgel	.30	.25
927	A146	4m Axes	.40	.25
928	A146	8m Shield, assagai	.45	.25
929	A146	16m Bow and arrow	2.00	.30
930	A146	32m Muzzleloader	3.00	.80
931	A146	50m Assagai, arrow	4.00	1.25
	Nos. 926-931 (6)		10.15	3.10

Natl. Revolution, 20th anniv.
For surcharge see No. 1256.

Natl. Trade Unions, 1st Anniv. — A147

1984, Oct. 13   Perf. 13½
932	A147	4m Workers, emblem	.40	.25

Stamp Day — A149

Cancellations on altered stamps and stationery: 4m, Barue cancel on 1885 20r postal card. 8m, Zumbo cancel on design similar to No. 52. 12m, Mozambique Co. cancel on design similar to Mozambique Company Type API. 16m, Macequece cancel on design similar to Mozambique Company No. 190.

1984, Dec. 21   Perf. 11½x11
936	A149	4m multi	.35	.25
937	A149	8m multi	.90	.35
938	A149	12m multi	1.50	.60
939	A149	16m multi	1.75	.75
	Nos. 936-939 (4)		4.50	1.95

African Development Bank, 20th Anniv. — A150

1984, Sept. 16   Photo.   Perf. 11½x11
940	A150	4m multi	.40	.25

Apiculture — A151

4m, Beekeeper. 8m, Bee gathering pollen. 16m, Entering nest. 20m, Building honeycomb.

1985, Feb. 3
941	A151	4m multi	.30	.25
942	A151	8m multi	.70	.30
943	A151	16m multi	1.40	.60
944	A151	20m multi	2.00	.90
	Nos. 941-944 (4)		4.40	2.05

OLYMPHILEX '85, Lausanne — A152

1985, Mar. 18   Perf. 11
945	A152	16m Shot putter	1.50	.60

World Meteorology Day — A153

1985, Mar. 23   Litho.   Perf. 11
946	A153	4m multi	.45	.25

Southern African Development Coordination Conference, 5th Anniv. — A154

4m, Map. 8m, Map, transmission tower. 16m, Industry. 32m, Flags.

1985, Apr. 1
947	A154	4m multi	.35	.25
948	A154	8m multi	1.00	.35
949	A154	16m multi	2.00	.75
950	A154	32m multi	3.25	1.25
	Nos. 947-950 (4)		6.60	2.60

Independence, 10th Anniv. — A155

Colonial resistance battles: 1m, Mujenga, 1896. 4m, Mungari, 1917. 8m, Massangano, 1868. 16m, Marracuene, 1895, and Gungunhana (c. 1840-1906), resistance leader.

1985, June 25   Litho.   Perf. 11
951	A155	1m multi	.30	.25
952	A155	4m multi	.30	.25
953	A155	8m multi	.75	.25
954	A155	16m multi	1.60	.65
	Nos. 951-954 (4)		2.95	1.40

UN, 40th Anniv. — A156

1985, June 26
955	A156	16m multi	1.40	.60

Traditional Games — A157

1985, Aug. 28   Litho.   Perf. 11
956	A157	50c Mathacuzana	.30	.25
957	A157	4m Mudzobo	.30	.25
958	A157	8m Muravarava	.50	.30
959	A157	16m N'Tshuwa	1.10	.60
	Nos. 956-959 (4)		2.20	1.40

Frogs and Toads — A158a

Designs: 50c, Rana angolensis. 1m, Hyperolius pictus. 4m, Ptychadena porosissima. 8m, Afrixalus formasinii. 16m, Bufo regularis. 32m, Hyperolius marmoratus. 30m, Afrixalus formasinii, diff.

1985, Oct. 25   Litho.   Perf. 11
960	A158	50c multi	.30	.25
961	A158	1m multi	.35	.25
962	A158	4m multi	.50	.25
963	A158	8m multi	1.00	.25
964	A158	16m multi	2.00	.40
965	A158	32m multi	3.50	.85
	Nos. 960-965 (6)		7.65	2.25

Size: 89x85mm
Imperf
965A	A158a	30m multi	6.00	4.00

For surcharge, see No. 1389.

Souvenir Sheet

Italia '85 Philatelic Exhibition, Rome — A158b

1985, Oct. 25   Litho.   Imperf
965B	A158b	60m multi	7.50	4.50

No. 965B has simulated perforations.

Medicinal Plants — A159

50c, Aloe ferox. 1m, Boophone disticha. 3.50m, Gloriosa superba. 4m, Cotyledon orbiculata. 8m, Homeria breyniana. 50m, Haemanthus coccineus.

1985, Nov. 28   Litho.   Perf. 11
966	A159	50c multi	.30	.25
967	A159	1m multi	.30	.25
968	A159	3.50m multi	.30	.25
969	A159	4m multi	.40	.25
970	A159	8m multi	.90	.25
970A	A159	50m multi	5.00	1.25
	Nos. 966-970A (6)		7.20	2.50

Stamp Day — A160

Stamps: 1m, Mozambique Company No. 126. 4m, Nyassa Type A6. 8m, Mozambique Company No. 110. 16m, Nyassa No. J2.

1985, Dec. 21
971	A160	1m multi	.30	.25
972	A160	4m multi	.45	.25
973	A160	8m multi	1.00	.25
974	A160	16m multi	2.00	.45
	Nos. 971-974 (4)		3.75	1.20

Halley's Comet — A161

Comet and: 4m, Space probe. 8m, Trajectory diagram. 16m, Newton's telescope, observatory, probe. 30m, Earth.

1986, Jan. 2
975	A161	4m multi	.30	.25
976	A161	8m multi	.60	.25
977	A161	16m multi	1.25	.50
978	A161	30m multi	2.25	1.00
	Nos. 975-978 (4)		4.40	2.00

1986 World Cup Soccer Championships, Mexico — A162

Players.

1986, Feb. 28   Litho.   Perf. 11½x11
979	A162	3m Vicente	.30	.25
980	A162	4m Coluna	.30	.25
981	A162	8m Costa Pereira	.45	.25
982	A162	12m Hilario	.80	.35
983	A162	16m Matateu	1.00	.50
984	A162	50m Eusebio	3.50	1.50
	Nos. 979-984 (6)		6.35	3.10

Intl. Peace Year — A163

1986, Mar. 18   Perf. 11
985	A163	16m multi	1.25	.50

Mushrooms — A164

4m, Amanita muscaria. 8m, Lactarius deliciosus. 16m, Amanita phalloides. 30m, Tricholoma nudum.

MOZAMBIQUE

1986, Apr. 8
986	A164	4m multi	.45	.25
987	A164	8m multi	.30	.30
988	A164	16m multi	1.75	.75
989	A164	30m multi	3.50	1.25

Nos. 986-989 (4) 6.00 2.55

Souvenir Sheet

Statue of Liberty, Cent. — A165

1986, May 22 *Imperf.*
| 990 | A165 | 100m multi | 5.50 | 5.50 |

AMERIPEX '86. No. 990 has simulated perfs.

Traditional Women's Hair Styles — A166

1986, June *Litho.* *Perf. 11½x11*
991	A166	1m Tanzanian	.30	.25
992	A166	4m Miriam	.30	.25
993	A166	8m Estrelinhas	.50	.25
994	A166	16m Toto	1.50	.60

Nos. 991-994 (4) 2.00 1.35

Marine Mammals A167

1m, Dugongo dugon. 8m, Delphinus delphis. 16m, Neobalena marginata. 50m, Balaenoptera physalus.

1986, Aug. *Perf. 11*
995	A167	1m multi	.30	.25
996	A167	8m multi	.75	.25
997	A167	16m multi	2.75	.70
998	A167	50m multi	7.25	2.00

Nos. 995-998 (4) 11.05 3.20

Continuing Youth Education Organization, 1st Anniv. A168

1986, Sept. 18 *Litho.* *Perf. 11½x11*
| 999 | A168 | 4m multi | .45 | .25 |

Natl. Savings Campaign A169

Bank notes, front and back.

1986, Oct. 22 *Litho.* *Perf. 11½x11*
1000	A169	4m 50m note	.30	.25
1001	A169	8m 100m note	.55	.25
1002	A169	16m 500m note	1.60	.60
1003	A169	30m 1000m note	2.75	1.25

Nos. 1000-1003 (4) 5.20 2.35

For surcharges, see Nos. 1302, 1392B.

Stamp Day — A170

Post offices.

1986, Dec. 21 *Litho.* *Perf. 11*
1004	A170	3m Quelimane	.30	.25
1005	A170	4m Maputo	.70	.25
1006	A170	8m Beira	1.25	.35
1007	A170	16m Nampula	2.75	.75

Nos. 1004-1007 (4) 5.00 1.60

Minerals — A171

1987, Jan. 2 *Perf. 11x11½*
1008	A171	4m Pyrite	.75	.25
1009	A171	8m Emerald	1.40	.25
1010	A171	12m Agate	2.00	.40
1011	A171	16m Malachite	2.60	.60
1012	A171	30m Garnet	4.50	1.25
1013	A171	50m Amethyst	6.50	2.00

Nos. 1008-1013 (6) 17.75 4.75

For surcharges see Nos. 1304-1305.

Frelimo Party, 10th Anniv. — A172

1987, Feb. 3 *Perf. 11*
| 1014 | A172 | 4m multi | .45 | .25 |

Pequenos Libombos Dam — A173

1987, Feb. 17 *Perf. 11½x11*
| 1015 | A173 | 16m multi | 1.75 | .75 |

World Health Day — A174

1987, Apr. 7 *Litho.* *Perf. 11x11½*
| 1016 | A174 | 50m multi | 1.20 | .50 |

Birds — A175

3m, Granatina granatina. 4m, Halcyon senegalensis. 8m, Mellittophagus bullockoides. 12m, Perinestes minor. 16m, Coracias naevia mosambica. 30m, Cinnyris neergardi.

1987, Apr. 27 *Litho.* *Perf. 11½x11*
1017	A175	3m multi	.30	.25
1018	A175	4m multi	.30	.25
1019	A175	8m multi	.60	.35
1020	A175	12m multi	.95	.45
1021	A175	16m multi	1.10	.65
1022	A175	30m multi	2.25	1.10

Nos. 1017-1022 (6) 5.50 3.05

For surcharge, see No. 1299A.

Souvenir Sheet

CAPEX '87, Toronto, June 13-21 A176

1987, June *Imperf.*
| 1023 | A176 | 200m multi | 4.00 | 4.00 |

No. 1023 contains one stamp having simulated perforations.

1988 Summer Olympics, Seoul — A177

12.50m, Soccer players and ball. 25m, Runner's legs. 50m, Volleyball. 75m, Chess. 100m, Basketball. 200m, Swimming.

1987, May *Litho.* *Perf. 11½x11*
1024	A177	12.50m multi	.30	.30
1025	A177	25m multi	.40	.30
1026	A177	50m multi	.75	.45
1027	A177	75m multi	1.20	.70
1028	A177	100m multi	1.50	.80
1029	A177	200m multi	3.25	1.20

Nos. 1024-1029 (6) 7.40 3.75

Tapestries A178

20m, Incomplete pattern on loom. 40m, Diamond-shaped pattern. 80m, Landscape pattern. 200m, Oriental pattern.

1987, Aug. *Perf. 11*
1030	A178	20m multi	.30	.25
1031	A178	40m multi	.55	.25
1032	A178	80m multi	1.10	.35
1033	A178	200m multi	2.50	1.00

Nos. 1030-1033 (4) 4.45 1.85

Maputo City — A179

Early Portuguese map of Lourenco Marques.

1987, Nov. 10 *Litho.* *Perf. 11*
| 1034 | A179 | 20m multi | .65 | .25 |

No. 762 Surcharged in Silver and Dark Red

1987 *Litho.* *Perf. 14½*
| 1034A | A108 | 4m on 4.50m multi | 1.60 | 1.60 |

1988 Summer Olympics, Seoul — A180

10m, Javelin. 20m, Baseball, horiz. 40m, Boxing, horiz. 80m, Field hockey, horiz. 100m, Gymnastic rings, horiz. 400m, Cycling, horiz.

1988, Feb. 10 *Litho.* *Perf. 11*
1035	A180	10m multi	.30	.25
1036	A180	20m multi	.30	.25
1037	A180	40m multi	.30	.25
1038	A180	80m multi	.65	.45
1039	A180	100m multi	1.00	.90
1040	A180	400m multi	1.25	1.10

Nos. 1035-1040 (6) 3.80 3.20

Flowering Plants — A181

10m, Heamanthus nelsonii. 20m, Crinum polyphyllum. 40m, Boophane disticha. 80m, Cyrtanthus contractus. 100m, Nerine angustifolia. 400m, Cyrtanthus galpinnii.

1988, Mar. 18 *Perf. 11½x11*
1041	A181	10m multi	.30	.25
1042	A181	20m multi	.30	.25
1043	A181	40m multi	.45	.35
1044	A181	80m multi	.95	.55
1045	A181	100m multi	1.25	.65
1046	A181	400m multi	1.90	1.90

Nos. 1041-1046 (6) 5.15 3.95

World Health Organization, 40th Anniv. — A182

1988, Apr. 7
| 1047 | A182 | 20m multi | .85 | .45 |

Anti-smoking campaign.

Wickerwork A183

20m, Mat. 25m, Lidded container. 80m, Market basket. 100m, Fan. 400m, Flat basket. 500m, Funnel basket.

1988, June 16 *Litho.* *Perf. 11*
1048	A183	20m multi	.30	.25
1049	A183	25m multi	.30	.25
1050	A183	80m multi	.55	.25
1051	A183	100m multi	.65	.30
1052	A183	400m multi	1.60	1.25
1053	A183	500m multi	2.25	1.50

Nos. 1048-1053 (6) 5.65 3.80

MOZAMBIQUE

Souvenir Sheet

FINLANDIA '88 — A184

1988, June 12 Litho. Imperf.
1054 A184 500m multi 3.50 3.50
Stamp in No. 1054 has simulated perfs.

Souvenir Sheet

State Visit of Pope John Paul II, Sept. 16-19 — A185

1988 Litho. Perf. 13½
1055 A185 500m multi 4.75 4.75

Horses — A186

1988, Sept. 20 Litho. Perf. 11
1056 A186 20m Percheron .40 .30
1057 A186 40m Arab .80 .30
1058 A186 80m Thoroughbred 1.75 .40
1059 A186 100m Pony 2.50 .50
  Nos. 1056-1059 (4) 5.45 1.50

Pres. Samora Machel (1933-1986) — A187

1988, Oct. 19 Litho. Perf. 11
1060 A187 20m multi .30 .30

Stamp Day — A188

1988, Dec. 21 Perf. 11½x11, 11½x11
1061 A188 20m P.O. trailer .30 .30
1062 A188 40m Mailbox, vert. .30 .30

Ports — A189

25m, Inhambane. 50m, Quelimane, vert. 75m, Pemba. 100m, Beira. 250m, Nacala, vert. 500m, Maputo.

1988, Nov. 30 Perf. 11
1063 A189 25m multi .30 .30
1064 A189 50m multi .30 .30
1065 A189 75m multi .50 .30
1066 A189 100m multi .55 .30
1067 A189 250m multi 1.40 .40
1068 A189 500m multi 3.00 .90
  Nos. 1063-1068 (6) 6.05 2.50

5th Frelimo Party Congress — A190

1989, Jan. 19
1069 A190 Strip of 5 3.50 3.50
  a. 25m Corn .30 .30
  b. 50m Axe .30 .30
  c. 75m Abstract shapes .30 .30
  d. 100m 2½ Gearwheels .35 .35
  e. A190 250m ½ Gearwheel .90 .90
Printed se-tenant in a continuous design.

French Revolution Bicent. — A191

Designs: 100m, *Storming of the Bastille*, by Thevenin. 250m, *Liberty Guiding the People*, by Delacroix. 500m, *Declaration of the Rights of Man and the Citizen*, a print by Blanchard.

1989, Feb. 16 Perf. 11
1070 A191 100m multi .40 .30
1071 A191 250m multi 1.20 .45

Souvenir Sheet
1072 A191 500m multi 2.50 2.50
No. 1072 is a continuous design.

Eduardo Chivambo Mondlane (1920-1969), Frelimo Party Founder, 20th Death Anniv. — A192

1989, Feb. 3 Litho. Perf. 11
1073 A192 25m blk, gold & dark red .30 .30

Venomous Species A193

25m, Pandinus. 50m, Naja haje. 75m, Bombus. 100m, Paraphysa. 250m, Conus marmoreus. 500m, Pterois volitans.

1989, Mar. 23
1074 A193 25m multi .30 .30
1075 A193 50m multi .30 .30
1076 A193 75m multi .60 .30
1077 A193 100m multi 1.00 .30
1078 A193 250m multi 1.75 .45
1079 A193 500m multi 3.50 .75
  Nos. 1074-1079 (6) 7.45 2.40

Coral — A194

25m, Acropora pulchra. 50m, Eunicella papilosa. 100m, Dendrophyla migrantus. 250m, Favia fragum.

1989, May 2 Litho. Perf. 11
1080 A194 25m multi .35 .30
1081 A194 50m multi .35 .30
1082 A194 100m multi .60 .30
1083 A194 250m multi 1.40 .55
  Nos. 1080-1083 (4) 2.70 1.45

1990 World Cup Soccer Championships, Italy — A195

Athletes executing various plays.

1989, June 22 Litho. Perf. 11½x11
1084 A195 30m multi .30 .25
1085 A195 60m multi .30 .25
1086 A195 125m multi .35 .25
1087 A195 200m multi .55 .35
1088 A195 250m multi .70 .40
1089 A195 500m multi 1.60 .80
  Nos. 1084-1089 (6) 3.80 2.30

Lighthouses — A196

1989, July 24 Litho. Perf. 11
1090 A196 30m Macuti .30 .25
1091 A196 60m Pinda .30 .25
1092 A196 125m Cape Delgado .40 .25
1093 A196 200m Isle of Goa .80 .35
1094 A196 250m Caldeira Point 1.00 .40
1095 A196 500m Vilhena 1.60 .90
  Nos. 1090-1095 (6) 4.40 2.40

Filigree Workmanship in Silver — A197

1989, Aug. 30 Litho. Perf. 11x11½
1096 A197 30m shown .30 .25
1097 A197 60m Flower on band .30 .25
1098 A197 125m Necklace .35 .25
1099 A197 200m Decorative box .70 .35
1100 A197 250m Utensils .85 .40
1101 A197 500m Butterfly 1.40 .90
  Nos. 1096-1101 (6) 3.90 2.40

Natl. Liberation War, 25th Anniv. — A198

1989, Sept. 25
1102 A198 30m multicolored .30 .25

Meteorological Instruments — A199

Designs: 30m, Rain gauge. 60m, Weather system on radar. 125m, Instrument shelter. 200m, Computer monitor and keyboard.

1989, Oct. 12 Perf. 11½x11
1103 A199 30m multicolored .30 .25
1104 A199 60m multicolored .30 .25
1105 A199 125m multicolored .45 .25
1106 A199 200m multicolored .90 .35
  Nos. 1103-1106 (4) 1.95 1.10

Souvenir Sheet

World Stamp Expo '89, Washington, DC — A200

500m, Washington Monument.

1989, Nov. 17 Perf. 13½
1107 A200 500m multi 2.50 2.50

Stamp Day — A201

1989, Dec. 21 Litho. Perf. 11½x11
1108 A201 30m UPU emblem .30 .25
1109 A201 60m P.O. emblem .30 .25

Southern African Development Coordination Conf. (SADCC), 10th Anniv. — A201a

1990, Jan. 31 Perf. 11½x11
1109A A201a 35m multicolored .30 .25

Textile Designs — A202

1990, Feb. 28 Litho. Perf. 11x11½
1110 A202 42m multi, diff. .30 .25
1111 A202 90m multi, diff. .35 .25
1112 A202 150m multi, diff. .50 .30
1113 A202 200m multi, diff. .65 .35
1114 A202 400m multi, diff. 1.40 .65
1115 A202 500m multi, diff. 1.75 .90
  Nos. 1110-1115 (6) 4.95 2.70

Forts — A203

45m, Sena. 90m, Santo Antonio. 150m, Santo Sebastiao. 200m, Santo Caetano. 400m, Our Lady of Conceicao. 500m, Santo Luis.

1990, Mar. 20 Perf. 11x11½
1116 A203 45m lt blue .30 .25
1117 A203 90m blue .35 .25
1118 A203 150m multi .50 .30
1119 A203 200m multi .65 .35
1120 A203 400m rose 1.40 .65
1121 A203 500m org red 1.75 .90
  Nos. 1116-1121 (6) 4.95 2.70

MOZAMBIQUE

Souvenir Sheet

Penny Black, Mozambique No. 1 — A204

1990, May 3   Litho.   *Perf. 11½x11*
1122   A204   1000m red, blk & bl   4.00   4.00
Penny Black, 150th anniversary. Stamp World London '90.

Bank of Mozambique, 15th Anniv. — A205

1990, May 17   Litho.   *Perf. 11x11½*
1123   A205   100m multicolored   .40   .25

Natl. Independence, 15th Anniv. — A206

42.50m, Eduardo Mondlane. 150m, Samora Machel.

1990, June 25   *Perf. 11*
1124   A206   42.50m multi   .30   .25
1125   A206   150m multi   .45   .35

Endangered Species — A207

42.50m, Ceratotherium simum. 100m, Dugong dugong. 150m, Loxodonta africana. 200m, Acinonix jubatus. 400m, Lutra maculicollis. 500m, Eretmochelys imbricata.

1990, Aug. 20   Litho.   *Perf. 11x11½*
1126   A207   42.50m multi   .40   .25
1127   A207   100m multi   .55   .25
1128   A207   150m multi   .80   .30
1129   A207   200m multi   1.00   .35
1130   A207   400m multi   2.25   .65
1131   A207   500m multi   2.75   .90
Nos. 1126-1131 (6)   7.75   2.70

Trees and Plants — A208

42.50m, Dichrostachys cinerea. 100m, Queimadas. 150m, Casuariana equisetifolia. 200m, Rhizophora muronata. 400m, Estrato herbaceo. 500m, Atzelia cuanzensis.

1990, Oct. 15   Litho.   *Perf. 11½x11*
1132   A208   42.50m multi   .30   .25
1133   A208   100m multi   .35   .25
1134   A208   150m multi   .50   .30
1135   A208   200m multi   .65   .35
1136   A208   400m multi   1.40   .65
1137   A208   500m multi   1.75   .90
Nos. 1132-1137 (6)   4.95   2.70

Stamp Day — A209

No. 1138: a, Pick-up at letter box. b, Canceling letters. c, Letter carrier. d, Delivery to recipient.

1990, Dec. 21   Litho.   *Perf. 11½x11*
1138   Strip of 4   1.00   1.00
a.-d.   A209 42.50m any single   .30   .25

Governmental Departments — A210

Designs: No. 1139, Post Office Dept., 10th anniv. No. 1140, Telecommunications Dept.

1991, Jan. 2
1139   A210   50m dk bl, red & blk   .30   .25
1140   A210   50m grn, blk & brn   .30   .25

Flowers — A211

50m, Strilitzia reginae. 125m, Anthurium andraeanum. 250m, Zantedeschia pentlandii. 300m, Canna indica.

1991, Feb. 25   Litho.   *Perf. 11½x11*
1141   A211   50m multi   .30   .25
1142   A211   125m multi   .40   .30
1143   A211   250m multi   .80   .60
1144   A211   300m multi   1.00   .70
Nos. 1141-1144 (4)   2.50   1.85

Alcelaphus Lichtensteini — A212

1991, Mar. 27   *Perf. 14*
1145   Strip of 4   0.50   0.50
a.   A212 50m Two adults   .30   .30
b.   A212 100m Adult   .65   .30
c.   A212 250m Adult grazing   1.75   .75
d.   A212 500m Nursing calf   2.75   1.75

Fountains of Maputo — A213

Designs: 50m, Mpompine. 125m, Chinhambanine. 250m, Sao Pedro-Zaza. 300m, Xipamanine.

1991, Apr. 15   Litho.   *Perf. 11½x11*
1146   A213   50m multicolored   .30   .25
1147   A213   125m multicolored   .30   .25
1148   A213   250m multicolored   .60   .30
1149   A213   300m multicolored   .75   .40
Nos. 1146-1149 (4)   1.95   1.20
For surcharge see No. 1394.

Paintings by Mozambican Artists — A214

180m, Samale. 250m, Malangatana. 560m, Malangatana, diff.

1991, May 18   Litho.   *Perf. 11½x11*
1150   A214   180m multicolored   .45   .25
1151   A214   250m multicolored   .60   .30
1152   A214   560m multicolored   1.40   .70
Nos. 1150-1152 (3)   2.45   1.25

1992 Summer Olympics, Barcelona — A215

1991, June 25   Litho.   *Perf. 11½x11*
1153   A215   10m Swimming   .30   .25
1154   A215   50m Roller hockey   .30   .25
1155   A215   100m Tennis   .30   .25
1156   A215   200m Table tennis   .55   .30
1157   A215   500m Running   1.30   .60
1158   A215   1000m Badminton   2.75   1.30
Nos. 1153-1158 (6)   5.50   2.95

For surcharges, see Nos. 1393, 1393A, 1395-1396.

British-Portuguese Agreement on Mozambique Borders, Cent. — A216

1991, Oct. 9   Litho.   *Perf. 11½x11*
1159   A216   600m Map of 1890   1.00   .45
1160   A216   800m Map of 1891   1.25   .70

Souvenir Sheet

Phila Nippon '91 — A217

1991, Nov. 15   Litho.   *Perf. 11½x11*
1161   A217   1500m Map of Japan   3.00   3.00

Children's Games — A218

1991, Dec. 21
1162   A218   40m Jumping rope   .30   .25
1163   A218   150m Spinning top   .30   .25
1164   A218   400m Marbles   .55   .30
1165   A218   900m Hopscotch   1.30   .70
Nos. 1162-1165 (4)   2.45   1.50

Stained Glass Windows A219

No. 1166 — Various designs: a, 40m. b, 150m. c, 400m. d, 900m.

1992, Jan. 22
1166   A219   Block of 4, #a.-d.   1.90   1.90

Plants — A220

300m, Rhisophora mucronata. 600m, Cymodocea ciliata. 1000m, Sophora inhambanensis.

1992, Mar. 23   Litho.   *Perf. 11½x11*
1167   A220   300m multi   .60   .30
1168   A220   600m multi   1.25   .60
1169   A220   1000m multi   2.00   1.00
Nos. 1167-1169 (3)   3.85   1.90

Traditional Tools — A221

100m, Spear, spear-thrower. 300m, Pitchforks. 500m, Hatchet. 1000m, Dagger.

1992, May 9
1170   A221   100m multi   .30   .25
1171   A221   300m multi   .80   .30
1172   A221   500m multi   1.40   .55
1173   A221   1000m multi   2.60   1.00
Nos. 1170-1170 (4)   5.10   2.10

Lubrapex '92, Lisbon.

A222

Birds: 150m, Chalcomitra amethystina. 200m, Ceropis senegalensis. 300m, Cossypha natalensis. 400m, Lamprocolius chloropterus. 500m, Malaconotus poliocephalus. 800m, Oriolus auratus.

1992, July 24   Litho.   *Perf. 11½x11*
1174   A222   150m multicolored   .40   .25
1175   A222   200m multicolored   .45   .25
1176   A222   300m multicolored   .70   .30
1177   A222   400m multicolored   .90   .45
1178   A222   500m multicolored   1.10   .45
1179   A222   800m multicolored   1.75   .90
Nos. 1174-1179 (6)   5.30   2.60

Eduardo Mondlane University, 30th Anniv. — A223

1992, Aug. 21
1180   A223   150m grn, brn & blk   .40   .25

Traditional Musical Instruments — A224

1992, Sept. 18
1181   A224   200m Phiane   .45   .25
1182   A224   300m Xrupe   .60   .25
1183   A224   500m Ngulula   1.10   .35
1184   A224   1500m Malimba   3.25   1.10
a.   Souvenir sheet of 4, #1181-1184, imperf.   3.50   3.50
Nos. 1181-1184 (4)   5.40   1.95

Genoa '92. #1184a has simulated perfs.

No. 757 Surcharged

1992, Oct.   Litho.   *Perf. 14½*
1185   A108   50m on 50c #757   .90   .45

MOZAMBIQUE

Intl. Conference on Nutrition — A225

1992, Oct. 16   Perf. 11½x11
1186 A225 450m multicolored   .90   .45

Parachuting — A226

Various parachutists descending from sky.

1992, Nov. 10   Litho.   Perf. 11½x11
1187 A226   50m multicolored   .30   .25
1188 A226   400m multicolored   .60   .40
1189 A226   500m multicolored   .85   .45
1190 A226   1500m multicolored   2.40   1.30
Nos. 1187-1190 (4)   4.10   2.40

No. 690 Surcharged

Methods and Perfs As Before
1992
1190A A91 200m on 5e #690   —

Medals — A227

400m, Order of Peace & Amity. 800m, Bagamoyo. 1000m, Order of Eduardo Mondlane. 1500m, War veterans.

1993, Feb. 3   Litho.   Perf. 11½x11
1191 A227   400m multi   .30   .25
1192 A227   800m multi   .60   .40
1193 A227   1000m multi   .85   .40
1194 A227   1500m multi   1.20   .60
Nos. 1191-1194 (4)   2.95   1.65

Pollution — A228

200m, Deforestation. 750m, Factory smoke. 1000m, Oil spill from ship. 1500m, Automobile exhaust.

1993, Apr. 8   Perf. 11x11½
1195 A228   200m multi   .40   .25
1196 A228   750m multi   1.10   .40
1197 A228   1000m multi   1.50   .45
1198 A228   1500m multi   2.25   .70
Nos. 1195-1198 (4)   5.25   1.80

Natl. Parks — A229

Park, animal, map: 200m, Gorongosa, lion. 800m, Banhine, giraffes. 1000m, Bazaruto, manatees. 1500m, Zinave, ostriches.

1993, May 25   Litho.   Perf. 11x11½
1199 A229   200m multicolored   .30   .25
1200 A229   800m multicolored   .85   .40
1201 A229   1000m multicolored   1.10   .45
1202 A229   1500m multicolored   1.75   .70
Nos. 1199-1202 (4)   4.00   1.80

Natl. Conference on Culture — A230

1993, Sept. 27   Litho.   Perf. 11½x11
1203 A230 200m multicolored   .45   .25

Union of Portuguese Speaking Capitals — A231

1993, July 30   Litho.   Perf. 11x11½
1204 A231 1500m multicolored   2.40   .60
Brasilana '93.

Forest Plants — A232

Designs: 200m, Cycas cercinalis. 250m, Cycas revoluta. 900m, Encephalartos ferox. 2000m, Equisetum ramosissimum.

1993, Dec. 29   Litho.   Perf. 11½x11
1205 A232   200m multicolored   .30   .25
1206 A232   250m multicolored   .30   .25
1207 A232   900m multicolored   .70   .40
1208 A232   2000m multicolored   1.60   .80
Nos. 1205-1208 (4)   2.90   1.70

Medicinal Plants — A233

200m, Anacardium occidentale. 250m, Sclerocarya caffra. 900m, Annona senegalensis. 2000m, Crinum delagoense.

1994   Litho.   Perf. 11½x11
1209 A233   200m multi   .30   .25
1210 A233   250m multi   .30   .25
1211 A233   900m multi   .80   .30
1212 A233   2000m multi   1.90   .60
Nos. 1209-1212 (4)   3.30   1.40

Nos. 699, 763-764, 772, 791-792, 797-798 Surcharged

1994
Perfs. and Printing Methods as Before
1212A A94   50m on 5e #699   —
1213 A109   50m on 7.50m
     #772   .40   .25
1214 A113   50m on 7.50m
     #791   .40   .25
1215 A114   50m on 7.50m
     #797   .40   .25
1216 A108   100m on 10m #763   .55   .25
1217 A114   100m on 12.50m
     #798   .55   .25
1218 A108   200m on 12.50m
     #764   1.10   .25
1219 A113   250m on 12.50m
     #792   1.30   .25
Nos. 1213-1219 (7)   4.70   1.75

Size and location of surcharge varies. Surcharge on Nos. 1214-1215, 1219 does not contain an obliterator.
For additional surcharge, see No. 1391.

PHILAKOREA '94 — A234

Reptiles: 300m, Ichnotropis squamulosa. 500m, Lepidachelys olivacea. 2000m, Prosyma frontalis. 3500m, Rampholeon marshalli. 4000m, Snake eating a lizard.

1994, Aug. 16   Litho.   Perf. 11½x11
1220 A234   300m multicolored   .30   .25
1221 A234   500m multicolored   .35   .25
1222 A234   2000m multicolored   1.25   .40
1223 A234   3500m multicolored   2.25   .75
Nos. 1220-1223 (4)   4.15   1.65

Souvenir Sheet
1224 A234 4000m multicolored   4.25   3.00

ICAO, 50th Anniv. — A235

Designs: 300d, Crop dusting. 500m, Airport terminal. 2000m, Passenger jet in flight. 3500m, Maintenance man inspecting jet engine.

1994, Oct. 12   Litho.   Perf. 11x11½
1225 A235   300m multicolored   .30   .25
1226 A235   500m multicolored   .40   .25
1227 A235   2000m multicolored   1.50   .60
1228 A235   3500m multicolored   2.75   1.10
Nos. 1225-1228 (4)   4.95   2.20

World Food Day — A236

1994, Oct. 24   Perf. 11½x11
1229 A236 2000m multicolored   2.25   .60
Lubrapex '94.

National Elections — A237

1994, Oct. 26
1230 A237 900m multicolored   1.10   .40

Fight Against Illegal Drugs — A238

Designs: 500m, Couple using drugs. 1000m, Hypodermic needle, couple tied in rope, skeleton. 2000m, Man with drug dependency. 5000m, Dog apprehending man with contraband.

1994, Dec. 7
1231 A238   500m multicolored   .45   .25
1232 A238   1000m multicolored   .85   .30
1233 A238   2000m multicolored   1.60   .70
1234 A238   5000m multicolored   4.25   1.75
Nos. 1231-1234 (4)   7.15   3.00

Lusaka Accord, 20th Anniv. — A239

1994, Nov. 9
1235 A239 1500m multicolored   2.00   .45

Basketry — A240

300m, Two-handled basket. 1200m, Round purse. 5000m, Rectangle purse.

1995, Apr. 15   Litho.   Perf. 11½x11
1236 A240   250m shown   .30   .25
1237 A240   300m multi   .30   .25
1238 A240   1200m multi   .85   .35
1239 A240   5000m multi   3.50   1.25
Nos. 1236-1239 (4)   4.95   2.10

Clothing — A241

Various styles of women's traditional clothing.

1995, May 25
1240 A241   250m blue & multi   .30   .25
1241 A241   300m pink & multi   .30   .25
1242 A241   1200m blue & multi   .85   .35
1243 A241   5000m red & multi   3.50   1.25
Nos. 1240-1243 (4)   4.95   2.10

Inauguration of Pres. Joaquim A. Chissano, Dec. 9, 1994 — A242

No. 1244: a, 900m, Natl. arms. b, 5000m, Pres. Chissano. c, 2500m, Natl. flag.

1995, June 25   Litho.   Perf. 11½x11
1244 A242   Strip of 3, #a.-c.   3.00   1.50
No. 1244 has a common inscription across the bottom.

Wild Animals — A243

Designs: 500m, Crassicadautus lombergi. 2000m, Tragelaphus strepsceros, horiz. 3000m, Potamochoerus porcus nyasae, horiz. 5000m, Tragelaphus scriptus.

Perf. 11½x11, 11x11½
1995, Aug. 29   Litho.
1245 A243   500m multicolored   .30   .25
1246 A243   2000m multicolored   .95   .30
1247 A243   3000m multicolored   1.50   .40
1248 A243   5000m multicolored   2.50   .70
Nos. 1245-1248 (4)   5.25   1.65

MOZAMBIQUE

FAO, 50th Anniv. — A244

1995, Oct. 16   *Perf. 11½x11*
1249   A244   5000m multicolored   1.40   .75

UN, 50th Anniv. — A245

1995, Oct. 24
1250   A245   5000m blue & black   1.60   .85

Nos. 647, 711, 713, 749, 763, 792, 798, 862, 929 Surcharged

Perfs. and Printing Methods as Before

1995, Oct. 4
1251   A114   250m on 12.50m #798   .75   .25
1252   A108   300m on 10m #763   .75   .25
1253   A113   500m on 12.50m #792   .75   .25
1253A   A97   600m on 5m #711   —   .25
1254   A81   900m on 12.50m #647   1.00   .25
1255   A97   1000m on 12.50m #713   1.00   .25
1256   A146   1500m on 16m #929   1.00   .25
1257   A130   2000m on 16m #862   1.00   .30
1258   A106   2500m on 12.50m #749   1.20   .40
     Nos. 1251-1258 (9)   7.45   2.20

UNICEF, 20th Anniv. in Mozambique — A246

1995, Nov. 22   *Litho.*   *Perf. 11½*
1259   A246   5000m multicolored   1.50   .85

Mozambique-South Africa Soccer Match — A247

Various soccer plays.

1996, Apr. 5   *Litho.*   *Perf. 11x11½*
1260   A247   1000m multicolored   .30   .25
1261   A247   2000m multicolored   .45   .30
1262   A247   4000m multicolored   .95   .55
1263   A247   6000m multicolored   1.50   .85
     Nos. 1260-1263 (4)   3.20   1.95

Masks — A248

Various masks.

1996, July 2   *Litho.*   *Perf. 11½x11*
1264   A248   1000m multicolored   .30   .25
1265   A248   2000m multicolored   .45   .30
1266   A248   4000m multicolored   .95   .55
1267   A248   6000m multicolored   1.50   .85
     Nos. 1264-1267 (4)   3.20   1.95

Red Cross of Mozambique, 15th Anniv. — A249

1996, July 10
1268   A249   5000m multicolored   1.25   .85

Endangered Wildlife — A250

1000m, Loxodona africana. 2000m, Ceratotherum simum. 4000m, Panthera pardus. 6000m, Scotopelia peli.

1996, Sept. 3   *Litho.*   *Perf. 11½x11*
1269   A250   1000m multi   .40   .25
1270   A250   2000m multi   .70   .30
1271   A250   4000m multi   1.40   .55
1272   A250   6000m multi   2.25   .85
     Nos. 1269-1272 (4)   4.75   1.95

Removal of Land Mines — A251

Designs: 2000m, Mine, tripwire across path. 6000m, Warning sign posted. 8000m, Using mine detector. 10,000m, Removing mine.

1996, Nov. 9   *Litho.*   *Perf. 11½x11*
1273   A251   2000m multicolored   .45   .25
1274   A251   6000m multicolored   1.30   .80
1275   A251   8000m multicolored   1.90   1.10
1276   A251   10,000m multicolored   2.40   1.30
     Nos. 1273-1276 (4)   6.05   3.45

Keep The City Clean Campaign — A252

1996, Dec. 16   *Litho.*   *Perf. 11½x11*
1277   A252   2000m multicolored   .60   .30

Mozambique Postage Stamps, 120th Anniv. — A253

1996, Dec. 16   *Litho.*   *Perf. 11½x11*
1278   A253   2000m No. 1   .75   .30

Mozambique Boats — A254

1997, Apr. 10   *Litho.*   *Perf. 11x11½*
1279   A254   2000m Mitumbui   .45   .30
1280   A254   6000m Muterere   1.30   .95
1281   A254   8000m Lancha   1.90   1.30
1282   A254   10,000m Dau   2.40   1.60
     Nos. 1279-1282 (4)   6.05   4.15

Children's Day — A255

1997, June 1   *Litho.*   *Perf. 11x11½*
1283   A255   2000m multicolored   .75   .30

Aquatic Birds — A256

Designs: 2000m, Mycteria ibis. 4000m, Himantopus himantopus. 8000m, Calidris subminuta. 10,000m, Pelecanus onocrotalus.

Perf. 11½x11, 11x11½
1997, June 10
1284   A256   2000m multi, vert.   .60   .30
1285   A256   4000m multi, vert.   1.40   .60
1286   A256   8000m multi   2.40   1.30
1287   A256   10,000m multi, vert.   3.00   1.75
     Nos. 1284-1287 (4)   7.40   3.95

Independence of India, 50th Anniv. — A258a

1997   *Litho.*   *Perf. 11x11½*
1287A   A258a   2000m multi   1.20   .55

Insects — A257

Designs: 2000m, Enaretta conifera. 6000m, Zographus heiroglyphicus. 8000m, Tragiscoschema bertolonii. 10,000m, Tragocephala ducalis.

1997, July 5   *Litho.*   *Perf. 11x11½*
1288   A257   2000m multicolored   .65   .30
1289   A257   6000m multicolored   1.75   .80
1290   A257   8000m multicolored   2.40   1.10
1291   A257   10,000m multicolored   2.75   1.40
   a.   Souvenir sheet, #1288-1291   7.50   7.50
     Nos. 1288-1291 (4)   7.55   3.60
Labrapex '97 (No. 1291a).

Joao Ferreira dos Santos Group, Cent. — A258

1997, Sept. 5   *Litho.*   *Perf. 11x11½*
1292   A258   2000m multi   24.00   12.00

Protection of the Ozone Layer — A259

1997, Sept. 16   *Litho.*   *Perf. 11½x11*
1293   A259   2000m multicolored   .45   .30

Peace Accord, 5th Anniv. — A260

1997, Oct. 4   *Litho.*   *Perf. 11½x11*
1294   A260   2000m multi   .55   .30

Anhinga A261

Souvenir Sheet

1997   *Litho.*   *Perf. 11½x11*
1295   A261   5000m multi   8.00   —

Food Products — A262

1998, June 1   *Litho.*   *Perf. 11x11½*
1296   A262   2000m multicolored   1.00   .40

Expo '98, Lisbon — A263

1998, May 22
1297   A263   2000m Coelacanth   .95   .40

Nos. 660, 666, 730, 764, 797, 1002, 1009, 1011, 1021 Surcharged

Printing Methods and Perfs as before

1998 (?)
1298   A85   2000m on 12.50e #660   2.75   2.75
1299   A86   2000m on 12.50e #666   2.75   2.75
1299A   A175   2000m on 1m #1021   —   —
1300   A108   4000m on 12.50m #764   1.90   1.90
1301   A114   6000m on 7.50m #797   3.25   3.25
1302   A169   7500m on 16m #1002   3.50   3.50
1303   A102   10,000m on 12.50m #730   2.50   2.50
1304   A171   12,500m on 8m #1009   5.50   5.50
1305   A171   12,500m on 16m #1011   2.75   2.75
     Nos. 1298-1305 (8)   24.90   24.90
For surcharges, see Nos. 1400-1400A.

703

MOZAMBIQUE

Diana, Princess of Wales (1961-97) — A264

Nos. 1306-1308: Various portraits.
No. 1309, 30,000m, Wearing Red Cross vest. No. 1310, 30,000m, Wearing purple dress.

1998	Litho.		Perf. 13½
1306	A264	2000m Sheet of 9, #a.-i.	4.50 4.50
1307	A264	5000m Sheet of 9, #a.-i.	9.00 9.00
1308	A264	8000m Sheet of 9, #a.-i.	15.00 15.00

Souvenir Sheets

| 1309-1310 | A264 | Set of 2 | 12.00 12.00 |

Nos. 1309-1310 each contain one 42x60mm stamp.

No. 923 Surcharged in Silver

1998	Litho.		Perf. 14
1311	A145	500m on 16m multi	— —

Promotion of Breast Feeding — A265

1998	Litho.		Perf. 11½x11
1312	A265	2000m multi	.95 .30

Mother Teresa (1910-97) — A266

1998			Perf. 11x11½
1313	A266	2000m multi	.95 .30

UPAP, 18th Anniv. — A267

1998, Oct. 9			Perf. 11½x11
1314	A267	2000m multi	.80 .40

Mother's Day — A268

Designs: 2000m, Breast feeding. 4000m, Teacher. 8000m, Using computer. 10,000m, Woman in field.

1998, June 25			Perf. 11½x11
1315-1318	A268	Set of 4	8.00 8.00

For surcharge, see No. 1417.

Plants — A269

Designs: 2000m Garcinia livingstonei. 7500m, Tabernaemontana elegans. 12,500m, Ximenia caffra. 25,000m, Syzygium guineense. 50,000m, Uapaca kirkiana.

1998, Oct. 9			Perf. 11¾x12
1319-1322	A269	Set of 4	12.00 12.00

Souvenir Sheet

| 1323 | A269 | 50,000m multi | 12.00 12.00 |

For surcharges, see Nos. 1418-1419, 1741-1742.

Dwellings — A270

Various dwellings: 2000m, 4000m, 6000m, 8000m, 10,000m, 15,000m, 20,000m, 30,000m, 50,000m, 100,000m.

1998	Litho.		Perf. 11x11¼
1324-1333	A270	Set of 10	20.00 20.00

For surcharges and overprints, see Nos. 1399A-1399C, 1418-1419, 1420D, 420H.

Souvenir Sheets

I Love Lucy — A270a

Designs: No. 1333A, 35,000m, Lucy wearing hat. No. 1333B, 35,000m, Lucy as ballet dancer.

1999	Litho.		Perf. 13½
1333A-1333B	A270a	Set of 2	12.00 12.00

A271

Diana, Princess of Wales (1961-97) A272

No. 1334: a, purple, shown. b, Dull brown, looking left. c, Orange brown, wearing pearls. d, Olive green. e, Purple, wearing feathers & hat, looking right. f, Red brown, wearing round earring.
No. 1335 — Diana with: a, Large white collar, earring (purple vignette). b, Hat, looking left (red violet vignette). c, White dress (red brown vignette). d, Dangling earrings (brown vignette). e, Patterned dress (blue violet vignette). f, Flower bouquet (olive green vignette).

1999			Perf. 14
1334	A271	6500m Sheet of 6, #a.-f.	7.50 7.50
1335	A271	6500m Sheet of 6, #a.-f.	7.50 7.50

Litho. & Embossed
Die Cut Perf. 7

| 1336 | A272 | 25,000m gold & multi | 9.00 9.00 |

Issued: #1336, 6/30.

The Three Stooges — A272a

No. 1336A: b, Joe Besser, Larry, Moe, frying pan. c, Shemp wearing hat. d, Moe and Larry putting pan on Joe Besser's head. e, Moe with pipe. f, Larry and Moe pouring liquids on Curly's head. g, Larry wearing hat. h, Joe Besser and Larry, pulling Moe's tooth. i, Curly. j, Shemp, Larry and Moe.
No. 1336K, 35,000m, Larry in pink shirt. No. 1336L, 35,000m, Larry holding shovel.

1999	Litho.		Perf. 13½
1336A	A272a	5000m Sheet of 9, #b-j	7.00 7.00

Souvenir Sheets

| 1336K-1336L | A272a | Set of 2 | 12.00 12.00 |

Trains — A273

2000m, DE-AC Blue Tiger, Germany. #1338, 2500m, DB 218 (red & black), Germany. #1339, 3000m, Mt. Pilatus inclined railroad car, Switzerland. 3500m, Berlin subway train, Germany.
No. 1341: a, DB V200, Germany. b, Union Pacific, US. c, Class 613, Germany. d, Canadian Pacific 4242, Canada. e, Duchess of Hamilton, Great Britain. f, Pacific Delhi, India. g, ISA, South Africa. h, DR VT 18-16-07, Germany. i, DB-DE, Australia.
No. 1342: a, DB 218 (green & yellow), Germany. b, QJ Class 2-10-2, China. c, 232 232.9, Germany. d, Flying Scotsman, Scotland. e, WR 360 CH, Germany. f, Henschel 2-8-2. g, Santa Fe 39C, US. h, Balkan Express, Greece. i, DB 218 (red & white), Germany.
No. 1343, 25,000m, Steam 2-8-2, Germany. No. 1344, 25,000m, DMU, Germany.

1999, Oct. 12	Litho.		Perf. 14
1337-1340	A273	Set of 4	2.10 2.10
1341	A273	2500m Sheet of 9, #a.-i.	4.00 4.00
1342	A273	3000m Sheet of 9, #a.-i.	4.75 4.75

Souvenir Sheets

| 1343-1344 | A273 | Set of 2 | 10.00 10.00 |

Betty Boop — A273a

No. 1344A: b, Seated on motorcycle, winking, wearing cap. c, Seated on motocycle, winking, without cap. d, Wearing cap. e, Seated on motorcycle, wearing cap, not winking. f, Hands folded across handlebars. g, Riding motorcycle. h, Hitchhiking. i, Seated on motorcycle, wearing bandana. j, Seated on motorcycle, hand raised.
No. 1344K, 35,000m, Seated on motorcycle, hand raised. No. 1344L, 35,000m, Seated next to motorcycle.

1999	Litho.		Perf. 13½
1344A	A273a	3500m Sheet of 9, #b-j	6.50 6.00

Souvenir Sheets

| 1344K-1344L | A273a | Set of 2 | 12.00 12.00 |

Cats A274

No. 1345, 4000m: a, Chartreux. b, Australian Mist. c, Egyptian Mau. d, Scottish Fold. e, Cornish Rex. f, Abyssinian.
No. 1346, 4000m: a, Himalayan. b, Balinese. c, Persian. d, Turkish Van. e, Norwegian Forest Cat. f, Maine Coon Cat.
No. 1347, 25,000m, Ragdoll. No. 1348, 25,000m, Siamese.

2000, Mar. 29	Litho.		Perf. 14
	Sheets of 6, #a-f		
1345-1346	A274	Set of 2	9.50 9.50

Souvenir Sheets

| 1347-1348 | A274 | Set of 2 | 9.50 9.50 |

Dated 1999.

Dogs A275

No. 1349, 4500m, vert.: a, Shetland sheepdog. b, Basenji. c, Poodle. d, St. Bernard. e, Shar Pei. f, Spinone Italiano.
No. 1350, 4500m, vert.: a, Jack Russell terrier. b, Schweizer Laufhund. c, Japanese Spitz. d, Australian Shepherd. e, Saluki. f, Siberian Husky.
No. 1351, 25,000m, Border Collie. No. 1352, 25,000m, Eurasier.

2000, Mar. 29	Litho.		Perf. 14
	Sheets of 6, #a-f		
1349-1350	A275	Set of 2	10.00 10.00

Souvenir Sheets

| 1351-1352 | A275 | Set of 2 | 9.50 9.50 |

Dated 1999.

MOZAMBIQUE

Dinosaurs — A276

No. 1353, 3000m: a, Pteranodon. b, Bothriospondylus. c, Iguanodon. d, Stegosaurus. e, Nodosaurus. f, Elaphrosaurus. g, "Petrolaccisaurus." h, Procompsognathus. i, Dimetrodon.
No. 1354, 3000m: a, Plesiosaur. b, "Ceresiosaurus." c, Cryptoclidus. d, Placochelys. e, Plotosaurus. f, Ichthyosaurus. g, Platecarpus. h, Archelon. i, Mosasaur.
No. 1355, 20,000m, Tyrannosaurus Rex.
No. 1356, 20,000m, "Honodus."

2000, Apr. 28		Sheets of 9, #a-i		
1353-1354	A276	Set of 2	8.50	8.50
		Souvenir Sheets		
1355-1356	A276	Set of 2	6.50	6.50
		Dated 1999.		

A277

Butterflies — A278

Designs: 2000m, Palla ussheri. 2500m, Euschemon rafflesia. No. 1359, 3000m, Buttus philenor. No. 1360, 3000m, Hypolimnas bolina. 3500m, Lycorea cleobaea. 4000m, Dynastor napoleon. No. 1363, 4500m, Callimorpha dominula. 5000m, Pereute leucodrosime.
No. 1365, 4500m: a, Tisiphone abeone. b, Pseudacraea boisduvali. c, Mylothris chloris. d, Papilio glaucus. e, Mimacraea marshalli. f, Gonepteryx cleopatra.
No. 1366, 4500m: a, Palla ussheri, diff. b, Hypolimnas salmacis. c, Pereute leucodrosime, diff. d, Anteos clorinde. e, Colias eurytheme. f, Hebomoia glaucippe.
No. 1367, 4500m, horiz.: a, Thauria aliris. b, Catocala ilia. c, Colotic danao. d, Agrias olaudia. e, Euploe core. f, Scoptes alphaeus.
No. 1368, 4500m, horiz.: a, Phoebis philea. b, Anteos clorinde, diff. c, Arhopala amantes. d, Mesene phareus. e, Euploea mulciber. f, Helianthus (?).
No. 1369, 4500m, vert.: a, Euphaedra neophorn. b, Catopsilia florella. c, Charaxes bohemani. d, Junonia orithya. e, Colotis danae, diff. f, Euryteta dryope.
No. 1370, 4500m, vert.: a, Papilio demodocus. b, Kallimoides rumia. c, Danaus chrysippus. d, Palla ussheri, diff. e, Hypolimnas salmacis, diff. f, Zinina otis.
No. 1371, 20,000m, Papilio glaucus, diff. No. 1372, 20,000m, Delias mysis, horiz. No. 1373, 20,000m, Mylothris chloris, horiz. No. 1374, 20,000m, Loxura atymnus, horiz. No. 1375, 20,000m, Homiolauc coocuiuc. No. 1376, 20,000m, Euxanthe wakefieldii.

2000, Apr. 28				
1357-1364	A277	Set of 8	4.75	4.75
		Sheets of 6, #a-f		
1365-1368	A277	Set of 4	19.00	19.00
1369-1370	A278	Set of 2	9.50	9.50

Souvenir Sheets

1371-1374	A277	Set of 4	16.00	16.00
1375-1376	A278	Set of 2	6.50	6.50
		Dated 1999.		

Worldwide Fund for Nature — A279

No. 1377: a, Two adult gnus. b, Adult and juvenile gnus. c, Lion catching gnu. d, Adult gnu.
Illustration reduced.

2000, Apr. 28
1377	A279	6500m Block of 4, #a-d	5.50	5.50

Dated 1999.

Wild Cats A280

No. 1378, 3000m: a, Leptailurus several. b, Panthera onca. c, Panthera tigris corbetti. d, Puma concolor. e, Panthera leo persica. f, Felis pardina. g, Lepardus pardalia. h, Acinonyx jubatus. i, Felis wrangeli.
No. 1379, 3000m: a, Felis silvestris grampia. b, Felis ourata. c, Panthera tigris tigris. d, Panthera uncia. e, Felis caracal. f, Panthera pardus. g, Panthera tigris amoyensis. h, Panthera onca (spotted). i, Neofelis nabuloso.
No. 1380, 25,000m, Panthera tigris altaica.
No. 1381, 25,000m, Panthera tigris, horiz.

2000, Apr. 28		Sheets of 9, #a-i		
1378-1379	A280	Set of 2	9.50	9.50
		Souvenir Sheets		
1380-1381	A280	Set of 2	8.00	8.00
		Dated 1999.		

Flowers A281

No. 1382, 3000m: a, Laetiocattleya. b, Papaver oriental. c, Anemone blanda. d, Ipomea alba. e, Phalaenopsis luma. f, Iris ensata. g, Coenagrion puella. h, Rosa raubritter. i, Iris x daylilies hybridizers.
No. 1383, 3000m: a, Lilium auratum. b, Oncidium macianthum. c, Dendrobium. d, Cobaea scandens. e, Paphiopedilum gilda. f, Papaver nudicaule. g, Colocasia esculenta. h, Carinatum tricolor. i, Phalaenopsis.
No. 1384, vert.: a, Euanthe sanderiana. b, Torenia fourleri. c, "Amor Perfeito." d, Borboleto matizada. e, Dendrobium primulinum. f, "Lasurstern" Clematite. g, Helianthus annuus. h, Jacinto grana.
No. 1385, 20,000m, Viola x wittrockiana. No. 1386, 20,000m, Nelimbo nucifera. No. 1387, 20,000m, Gerbera jamesonii. No. 1388, 20,000m, Narcissuses and anemones.
Illustration reduced.

2000, Apr. 28		Sheets of 9, #a-i		
1382-1383	A281	Set of 2	9.50	9.50
1384	A281	3500m Sheet of 8, #a-h	5.50	5.50
		Souvenir Sheets		
1385-1388	A281	Set of 4	12.50	12.50
		Dated 1999.		

Nos. 792, 797-798, 964, 1002, 1147, 1153, 1154, 1156, 1214 Surcharged

2000		Methods & Perfs. As Before		
1389	A158	1000m on 16m #964	—	—
1390	A114	10,000m on 7.50m #797	—	—
1391	A113	10,000m on 50m on 7.50m #1214	—	—
1392	A113	10,000m on 12.50m #792	—	—
1392A	A114	10,000m on 12.50m #798	—	—
1392B	A169	10,000m on 16m #1002	—	—
1393	A215	17,000m on 10m #1153	—	—
1393A	A215	17,000m on 50m #1154	—	—
1394	A213	17,000m on 125m #1147	—	—
1395	A215	17,000m on 200m #1156	—	—
1396	A215	17,000m on 1000m #1158	—	—

No. 1393A and 1396 lack "2000" date in surcharge. No. 1391 contains "Correios — 2000)" in surcharge.
The editors suspect that other surcharges may exist and would like to examine any examples.

No. 763 Surcharged in Black and Blue

No. 764 Surcharged in Black and Brown

2000		Litho.	Perf. 14½	
1398	A108	2000m on 10m #763	—	—
1399	A108	2000m on 12.50m #764	—	—

Nos. 1325-1327 Overprinted

No. 1399A

2000		Method and Perf. as Before		
1399A	A270	4000m on #1325	—	—
1399B	A270	6000m on #1326	—	—
1399C	A270	8000m on #1327	—	—

Nos. 1300, 1301 Ovptd. in Brown or Black

2000		Litho.	Perf. 14½	
1400	A108	4000m on 12.50m #1300 (BR)	—	—
1400A	A114	6000m on 7.50m #1301	—	—

Sports and Chess A282

No. 1401, 6500m: a, Cycling. b, Volleyball. c, Boxing. d, Weight lifting. e, Fencing. f, Judo.
No. 1402, 9000m — Chess pieces: a, Six pieces, red queen at left. b, Six pieces, gray bishop fifth from left. c, Five knights. d, Six rooks, elephant rook at left. e, Six pawns. f, Six pawns, spearholder pawn at right.
No. 1403, 9500m — Chess champions: a, Paul Morphy. b, Mikhail Botvinnik. c, Emanuel Lasker. d, Wilhelm Steinitz. e, José Raul Capablanca. f, Howard Staunton.
No. 1404, 12,500m: a, Cricket batsmen and bowler. b, Three cricket batsman, one fielder. c, Polo, rider with red shirt at left. d, Polo, player wearing #1 at right. e, Golf, flag stick at right. f, Golf, woman golfer at right.
No. 1405, 14,000m: a, Tennis, woman with headband at right. b, Table tennis, players with blue shirts. c, Table tennis, player with pink shirt in center. d, Tennis, two men at left. e, Tennis, man with cap at left. f, Table tennis, player with red shirt at left.
No. 1406, 35,000m, Table tennis. No. 1407, 35,000m, Chess player Garry Kasparov.

2000		Litho.	Perf. 13¼	
		Sheets of 6, #a-f		
1401-1405	A282	Set of 5	40.00	40.00
		Souvenir Sheets		
1406-1407	A282	Set of 2	17.50	17.50

Nos. 1401-1405 each contain six 59x29mm stamps.

Marine Life A283

Marine Life A284

No. 1408: a, Threadfin butterflyfish. b, Common clownfish. c, Regal tang. d, Regal angelfish. e, Copperbanded butterflyfish. f, Blue-girdled angelfish. g, Sharpnosed pufferfish. h, Humbug damselfish. i, Tailbar lionfish. j, Forcepsfish. k, Powder blue surgeon. l, Moorish idol.
No. 1409, 9500m: a, Oceanic whitetip shark. b, Gray reef shark. c, Tiger shark. d, Silky shark. e, Basking shark. f, Epaulette shark.

MOZAMBIQUE

No. 1410, 9500m: a, Sperm whale. b, Giant squid. c, Killer whale. d, Great white shark. e, Manta ray. f, Octopus.
No. 1411, 9500m: a, Blue whale. b, Dolphinfish. c, Hammerhead shark. d, Whale shark. e, Leatherback turtle. f, Porkfish.
No. 1412, 35,000m, Wimple fish. No. 1413, 35,000m, Queen angelfish.
No. 1414, 35,000m, Phryniethys wedli. No. 1415, 35,000m, Bull shark. No. 1416, 35,000m, Spotted trunkfish.

2001, Aug. 8   **Perf. 14**

1408	A283	4550m Sheet of 12, #a-l	8.00	8.00

Sheets of 6, #a-f

1409-1411	A284	Set of 3	24.00	24.00

Souvenir Sheets

| 1412-1413 | A283 | Set of 2 | 9.50 | 9.50 |
| 1414-1416 | A284 | Set of 3 | 14.50 | 14.50 |

Nos. 763, 1316-1317, 1325, 1327-1330 Surcharged

Methods and Perfs As Before

2001 ?

1416A	A268	3000m on 4000m #1316	—	—
1417	A268	3000m on 8000m #1317	—	—
1418	A270	3000m on 15,000m #1329	—	—
1419	A270	3000m on 20,000m #1330	—	—
1420	A108	5000m on 10m #763	—	—
1420B	A270	17,000m on 4000m #1325	—	—
1420D	A270	17,000m on 8000m #1327	—	—
1420E	A270	17,000m on 10,000m #1328	—	—
1420F	A270	17,000m on 15,000m #1329	—	—

2000 European Soccer Championships — A285

No. 1421, 10,000m: a, Luis Figo dribbling ball. b, Fernando Couto. c, Figo diving. d, Sergio Conceicao. e, Nuno Gomes. f, Rui Costa.
No. 1422, 17,000m: a, Nicolas Anelka. b, Didier Deschamps. c, Emmanuel Petit. d, Thierry Henry. e, Marcel Desailly. f, Zinedine Zidane.
No. 1422G, 75,000m, Zinedine Zidane. No. 1422H, 75,000m, Rivaldo.

2001   **Litho.**   **Perf. 13¼x12¾**

Sheets of 6, #a-f

1421-1422	A285	Set of 2	17.50	17.50

Souvenir Sheets

| 1422G-1422H | A285 | Set of 2 | 16.00 | 16.00 |

2000 Summer Olympics Medalists — A286

No. 1423, 8500m: a, Domenico Fioravanti. b, Stacy Dragila. c, Pieter van den Hoogenband. d, David O'Connor. e, Venus Williams. f, Maurice Greene. g, Joy Fawcett. h, Marion Jones. i, Patricio Ormazabal and Jeff Agoos.
No. 1424, 10,000m: a, Agnes Kovacs. b, Youila Raskina. c, Kong Linghui and Liu Guoliang. d, Nicolas Gill. e, Anky van Grunsven. f, Brian Olson. g, Wang Nan. h, Megan Quann. i, Venus Williams.
No. 1425, 17,000m: a, Vince Carter. b, Blaine Wilson. c, Steve Keir. d, Wen Xiao Wang and Chris Xu. e, Venus and Serena Williams. f, Gu Jun and Ge Fei.
No. 1426, 20,000m: a, Clara Hughes. b, Martina Hingis. c, Otilla Badescu. d, Isabel Fernandez. e, Coralie Simmons. f, Mia Hamm.
No. 1427, 28,000m: a, Patrick Rafter. b, Tadahiro Nomura. c, Seiko Iseki. d, Michael Dodge. e, Ann Dow. f, David Beckham.
No. 1428, 50,000m, Andre Agassi. No. 1429, 50,000m, Chang Jun Gao and Michelle Do. No. 1430, 50,000m, Kong Linghui. No. 1431, 100,000m, Michelle Do. No. 1432, 100,000m, Serena Williams. No. 1433, 100,000m, Christophe Legout.

2001   **Sheets of 9, #a-i**   **Litho.**

1423-1424	A286	Set of 2	22.50	22.50

Sheets of 6, #a-f

| 1425-1427 | A286 | Set of 3 | 25.00 | 25.00 |

Souvenir Sheets

| 1428-1433 | A286 | Set of 6 | 47.50 | 47.50 |

Chess Champions — A287

No. 1434, 10,000m: a, Mikhail Botvinnik. b, Garry Kasparov. c, Wilhelm Steinitz. d, Emanuel Lasker. e, Paul Morphy. f, Anatoly Karpov. g, Tigran Petrossian. h, Mikhail Tal. i, José Raul Capablanca.
No. 1435, 10,000m: a, Judith Polgar (wearing brown sweater). b, Xie Jun. c, Zsuza Polgar. d, Nana Ioseliani. e, Alisa Galliamova. f, Judith Polgar (head in hands). g, Judith Polgar (wearing blouse). h, Monica Calzetta. i, Anjelina Belakovskaia.
No. 1436, 100,000m, Kasparov. No. 1437, 100,000m, Judith Polgar.

2001   **Perf. 13¼x12¾**

Sheets of 9, #a-i

1434-1435	A287	Set of 2	20.00	20.00

Souvenir Sheets

| 1436-1437 | A287 | Set of 2 | 22.00 | 22.00 |

2002 Winter Olympics, Salt Lake City — A288

No. 1438, 17,000m: a, Martin Brodeur. b, Svetlana Vysokova. c, Ray Bourque and Patrik Elias. d, Rachel Belliveau. e, Scott Gomez and Janne Laukkanen. f, Sonja Nef.
No. 1439, 20,000m: a, Rusty Smith. b, Sandra Schmirler. c, Totmianina and Marinin. d, Brigitte Obermoser. e, Roman Turek. f, Jennifer Heil.
No. 1440, 28,000m: a, Kovarikova and Novotny. b, Li Song. c, Armin Zoeggeler. d, Michael von Gruenigen. e, Tami Bradley. f, Chris Drury, Turner Stevenson and Greg de Vries.
No. 1441, 50,000m, Armin Zoeggeler. No. 1442, 75,000m, Tommy Salo. No. 1443, 100,000m, Jayne Torvill and Christopher Dean.

2001   **Sheets of 6, #a-f**   **Litho.**

1438-1440	A288	Set of 3	25.00	25.00

Souvenir Sheets

| 1441-1443 | A288 | Set of 3 | 24.00 | 24.00 |

On illustrated sheets lacking design information the lettering of minors starts with the upper left stamp, goes right and down and ends with the lower right stamp.

2002 World Cup Soccer Championships, Japan and Korea — A289

No. 1444: a, Filippo Inzaghi. b, Georghe Hagi. c, Gabriel Batistuta pointing. d, Mateja Kezman. e, Ivan Zamorano. f, Michael Owen wearing blue uniform.
No. 1445: a, Marcio Amoroso. b, Alessandro Nesta. c, Robbie Keane. d, Michel Owen kicking ball. e, Stefan Effenberg. f, Oliver Kahn.
No. 1446: a, Zinedine Zidane without ball. b, Zoran Mirkovic. c, Robbie Fowler with fist raised. d, Romario wearing red jersey. e, Francesco Totti. f, Ryan Giggs.
No. 1447: a, Javier Saviola. b, Alan Smith. c, Raul Gonzalez. d, Dwight Yorke. e, Joe Cole. f, David Beckham wearing red jersey.
No. 1448: a, Angelo Peruzzi. b, Jaap Stam. c, Jamie Redknapp. d, Rivaldo with ball at feet. e, Alan Shearer. f, Boudewijn Zenden.
No. 1449: a, Hernan Jorge Crespo. b, Gianluigi Buffon. c, Arnold Bruggink. d, Antonio Cassano. e, Mohamed Kallon. f, Jonathan Bachini.
No. 1450: a, Didier Deschamps. b, Cafu wearing green jersey. c, Dennis Bergkamp. d, Lilian Thuram. e, David Beckham wearing red jersey, diff. f, Francesco Totti, diff. g, Carsten Jancker. h, Martin Palermo. i, Andy Cole running left.
No. 1451: a, David Beckham sitting on ball. b, Edgar Davids wearing orange shirt. c, Michael Owen with hands on ball. d, Andy Cole with one leg raised. e, Ronaldo sitting. f, Emmanuel Petit with ball. g, Rivaldo with ball at chest. h, Robbie Fowler looking at ball. i, Romario wearing blue jacket.
No. 1452: a, César Manuel Rui Costa. b, Hidetoshi Nakata. c, Luis Figo. d, Michael Owen. e, Leonardo. f, Thierry Henry. g, Fabien Barthez. h, Oliver Kahn. i, Antonio Conte.
No. 1453: a, Shinji Ono. b, Rigobert Song. c, Matias Jesus Almeyda. d, Ronaldinho. e, Gabriel Batistuta wearing striped jersey. f, Rivaldo sitting on ground. g, Thierry Henry. h, Zinedine Zidane kicking ball. i, Ronaldo with ball.
No. 1454: a, Florain Maurice. b, Nicolas Anelka. c, Zinedine Zidane without ball, wearing striped jersey. d, Kazuyoshi Miura. e, Patrick Vieira. f, Gianfranco Zola. g, Emmanuel Petit without ball. h, Roberto Carlos. i, Teddy Sheringham.
No. 1455, 75,000m, Fabien Barthez. No. 1456, 75,000m, Edgar Davids wearing striped shirt. No. 1457, 75,000m, Cafu wearing red shirt.
No. 1458, 100,000m, Ronaldo wearing striped uniform. No. 1459, 100,000m, Romario wearing yellow shirt. No. 1460, 100,000m, Rivaldo dribbling ball. No. 1461, 100,000m, Nwankwo Kanu. No. 1462, 100,000m, Michael Owen wearing yellow shirt. No. 1463, 100,000m, Franz Beckenbauer. No. 1464, 100,000m, Pelé. No. 1465, 100,000m, Diego Maradona.

2001   **Litho.**   **Perf. 13¼x12¾**

Sheets of 6, #a-f

1444	A289	5000m multi	3.25	3.25
1445	A289	10,000m multi	6.75	6.75
1446	A289	12,000m multi	8.00	8.00
1447	A289	15,000m multi	10.00	10.00
1448	A289	17,000m multi	11.50	11.50
1449	A289	20,000m multi	13.50	13.50
	Nos. 1444-1449 (6)		53.00	53.00

Sheets of 9, #a-i

1450	A289	5000m multi	5.25	5.25
1451	A289	5000m multi	5.25	5.25
1452	A289	5000m multi	5.25	5.25
1453	A289	8500m multi	8.75	8.75
1454	A289	8500m multi	8.75	8.75
	Nos. 1450-1454 (5)		33.25	33.25

Souvenir Sheets

| 1455-1457 | A289 | Set of 3 | 32.50 | 32.50 |
| 1458-1465 | A289 | Set of 8 | 115.00 | 115.00 |

On illustrated sheets lacking design information, the lettering of minors starts with the upper left stamp, continues right and down and ends with the lower right stamp.

Paintings

Madonna Paintings A290

Alfred Sisley A291

Hieronymus Bosch — A292

Pieter Brueghel A293

Paul Cézanne A294

Salvador Dali A295

Henri Matisse A296

Michelangelo — A297

MOZAMBIQUE

Vincent van Gogh — A298

Johannes Vermeer — A299

Michelangelo — A300

Amadeo Modigliani — A301

Paintings of Angels A302

Gustav Klimt A303

Perf. 13¼x12¾
2001, Dec. 28   **Litho.**
Sheets of 6, #a-f

1466	A290	5000m multi	3.25	3.25
1467	A291	10,000m multi	6.75	6.75
1468	A292	12,000m multi	8.00	8.00
1469	A293	12,000m multi	8.00	8.00
1470	A294	12,000m multi	8.00	8.00
1471	A295	12,000m multi	8.00	8.00
1472	A296	12,000m multi	8.00	8.00
1473	A297	12,000m multi	8.00	8.00
1474	A298	12,000m multi	8.00	8.00
1475	A299	12,000m multi	8.00	8.00
1476	A300	15,000m multi	10.00	10.00
1477	A301	15,000m multi	10.00	10.00
1478	A302	17,000m multi	12.00	12.00
1479	A303	28,000m multi	19.00	19.00
		Nos. 1466-1479 (14)	125.00	125.00

Paintings

Marc Chagall A304

Salvador Dali A305

Edgar Degas A306

Paul Delvaux A307

Paul Gauguin A308

Pablo Picasso A309

Pierre Auguste Renoir A310

Henri de Toulouse-Lautrec — A311

Vincent van Gogh A312

Pablo Picasso A313

Individual stamps depicting various works of art lack titles. On Nos. 1489-1512 artist name is in margin.
No. 1489, Pieter Breughel. No. 1490, Lucas Cranach. No. 1491, Paul Delvaux. No. 1492, El Greco. No. 1493, Wassily Kandinsky. No. 1494, Gustav Klimt. No. 1495, Johannes Vermeer. No. 1496, Paul Cézanne. No. 1497, Marc Chagall. No. 1498, Albrecht Dürer. No. 1499, Thomas Gainsborough. No. 1500, Francisco de Goya. No. 1501, Edouard Manet. No. 1502, Claude Monet. No. 1503, Henri Matisse. No. 1504, Camille Pissarro. No. 1505, Vincent van Gogh. No. 1506, Salvador Dali. No. 1507, Paul Gauguin. No. 1508, Joan Miró. No. 1509, Amadeo Modigliani. No. 1511, Picasso, diff. No. 1512, Henri de Toulouse-Lautrec. No. 1513, Religious icon.

Perf. 13¾x12¾
2001, Dec. 28   **Litho.**
Sheets of 9, #a-i

1480	A304	10,000m multi	8.75	8.75
1481	A305	10,000m multi	8.75	8.75
1482	A306	10,000m multi	8.75	8.75
1483	A307	10,000m multi	8.75	8.75
1484	A308	10,000m multi	8.75	8.75
1485	A309	10,000m multi	8.75	8.75
1486	A310	10,000m multi	8.75	8.75
1487	A311	10,000m multi	8.75	8.75
1488	A312	10,000m multi	8.75	8.75
		Nos. 1480-1488 (9)	78.75	78.75

Souvenir Sheets

1489	A313	50,000m multi	4.00	4.00
1490	A313	50,000m multi	4.00	4.00
1491	A313	50,000m multi	4.00	4.00
1492	A313	50,000m multi	4.00	4.00
1493	A313	50,000m multi	4.00	4.00
1494	A313	50,000m multi	4.00	4.00
1495	A313	50,000m multi	4.00	4.00
1496	A313	75,000m multi	6.25	6.25
1497	A313	75,000m multi	6.25	6.25
1498	A313	75,000m multi	6.25	6.25
1499	A313	75,000m multi	6.25	6.25
1500	A313	75,000m multi	6.25	6.25
1501	A313	75,000m multi	6.25	6.25
1502	A313	75,000m multi	6.25	6.25
1503	A313	75,000m multi	6.25	6.25
1504	A313	75,000m multi	6.25	6.25
1505	A313	75,000m multi	6.25	6.25
1506	A313	100,000m multi	8.25	8.25
1507	A313	100,000m multi	8.25	8.25
1508	A313	100,000m multi	8.25	8.25
1509	A313	100,000m multi	8.25	8.25
1510	A313	100,000m shown	8.25	8.25
1511	A313	100,000m multi	8.25	8.25
1512	A313	100,000m multi	8.25	8.25
1513	A313	100,000m multi	8.25	8.25
		Nos. 1489-1513 (25)	156.50	156.50

Lance Armstrong, Cyclist — A314

2001   **Litho.**   **Perf. 13¼x12¾**
1514 A314 100,000m multi   11.00   11.00
2004 Olympic Games, Athens.

New Year 2002 (Year of the Horse) A315

No. 1515 — Chinese characters in: a, Yellow. b, Purple. c, Pink. d, Brown. 22,000m, Maroon, vert.

2002, May 6   **Litho.**   **Perf. 13¼**
1515 A315 11,000m Sheet of 4,
     #a-d   5.25   5.25

Souvenir Sheet
Perf. 13½x13¼
1516 A315 22,000m multi   2.75   2.75
No. 1516 contains one 28x42mm stamp.

2002 Winter Olympics, Salt Lake City — A316

Designs: 10,000m, Freestyle skiing. 17,000m, Freestyle skiing, vert.

Perf. 13¼x13½, 13½x13¼
2002, May 6
1517-1518 A316   Set of 2   2.75   2.75

Intl. Year of Mountains A317

Designs: No. 1519, 17,000m, Mt. Namuli. No. 1520, 17,000m, Mt. Binga.
No. 1521: a, Mt. Kenya, Kenya. b, Mt. Cook, New Zealand. c, Mt. Ararat, Turkey. d, Mt. Paine, Chile. e, Mt. Everest, Nepal. f, Mt. Kilimanjaro, Tanzania.
50,000m, Zugspitze, Germany.

2002, May 6   **Perf. 13¼x13½**
1519-1520 A317   Set of 2   3.25   3.25
1521 A317 17,000m Sheet of 6,
     #a-f   9.50   9.50

Souvenir Sheet
1522 A317 50,000m multi   4.75   4.75

20th World Scout Jamboree, Thailand — A318

No. 1523, horiz.: a, 1933 Jamboree patch. b, 19th World Jamboree patch. c, Patch and mascot. d, Jamboree emblem, scout.
No. 1524, Scout.

MOZAMBIQUE

2002, May 6		Perf. 13¼x13½		
1523	A318	28,000m Sheet of 4, #a-d	11.50	11.50

Souvenir Sheet
Perf. 13½x13¼

| 1524 | A318 | 28,000m multi | 3.00 | 3.00 |

Amerigo Vespucci (1452-1512), Explorer — A319

No. 1525, horiz.: a, Vespucci observing stars. b, Brotogeris chiriri, ship. c, Huts, ship. 50,000m, Map of voyages to South America.

2002, May 6		Perf. 13¼x13½		
1525	A319	30,000m Sheet of 3, #a-c	8.75	8.75

Souvenir Sheet
Perf. 13½x13¼

| 1526 | A319 | 50,000m multi | 4.75 | 4.75 |

Ships A320

No. 1527, 13,500m: a-f, Various unnamed ships (shown).
No. 1528, 13,500m: a, Viking ship. b, Kayak. c, Gondola, bridge. d, Fishing boat. e, Light ship. f, Tugboat.
No. 1529, 40,000m, Aircraft carrier. No. 1530, 40,000m, Ship's figurehead, vert.

Perf. 13¼x13½, 13½x13¼

2002, May 6		Sheets of 6, #a-f		
1527-1528	A320	Set of 2	14.50	14.50

Souvenir Sheets

| 1529-1530 | A320 | Set of 2 | 7.50 | 7.50 |

2002 World Cup Soccer Championships, Japan and Korea — A321

No. 1531, 28,000m: a, Zico. b, 1958 World Cup poster. c, Flag, player from Nigeria. d, Flag, player from Morocco. e, Gwangju Stadium, Korea, horiz. (56x42mm).
No. 1532, 28,000m: a, 1966 World Cup poster. b, Paolo Rossi. c, Flag, player from Denmark. d, Flag, player from Colombia. e, Inchon Munhak Stadium, Korea, horiz. (56x42mm)
No. 1533, 50,000m, Pele. No. 1534, 50,000m, Morlock, horiz.

Perf. 13½x13¼, 13¼x13½

2002, May 6		Sheets of 5, #a-e		
1531-1532	A321	Set of 2	27.50	27.50

Souvenir Sheets

| 1533-1534 | A321 | Set of 2 | 9.50 | 9.50 |

A322

A323

Princess Diana (1961-97) — A324

No. 1538, 50,000m, Brown background. No. 1539, 50,000m, Purple background. No. 1540, 50,000m, Pink lilac background.

2002, May 6		Perf. 13½x13¼		
1535	A322	28,000m Sheet of 4, #a-d	11.00	11.00
1536	A323	28,000m Sheet of 4, #a-d	11.00	11.00
1537	A324	28,000m Sheet of 4, #a-d	11.00	11.00
		Nos. 1535-1537 (3)	33.00	33.00

Souvenir Sheets

| 1538-1540 | A324 | Set of 3 | 14.50 | 14.50 |

Butterflies — A325

Designs: 5000m, Papilio demoleus. No, 1542, 10,000m, Euschemom rafflesia. 17,000m, Liphyra brassolis. 28,000m, Mimacraea marshalli.
No. 1545, 10,000m: a, Eurema brigitta. b, Loxura atymunus. c, Arhopala amantes. d, Junonia coenia. e, Eurides isabella. f, Hiliconius ricini. g, Zipaetis scylax. h, Cepheuptychia cephus. i, Philaethria dido.
No. 1546, 10,000m: a, Parides coon. b, Delias mysis. c, Troides brookiana. d, Syrmatia dorilas. e, Danis danis. f, Lycaena dispar. g, Mesene phareus. h, Kallima inachus. i, Morpho rhetenor.
No. 1547, 50,000m, Papilio cresphontes. No. 1548, 50,000m, Ornithoptera alexandrae caterpillar.

2002, June 17		Perf. 14		
1541-1544	A325	Set of 4	6.50	6.50

Sheets of 9, #a-i

| 1545-1546 | A325 | Set of 2 | 16.00 | 16.00 |

Souvenir Sheets

| 1547-1548 | A325 | Set of 2 | 11.00 | 11.00 |

Fauna, Flora and Mushrooms — A326

No. 1549, 10,000m: a, Pandion haliaetus. b, Flying squirrel. c, Fox squirrel. d, Agelaius phoeniceus. e, Papilio polyxenes. f, Didelphus virginiana. g, Hyla crucifer. h, Odocoileus virginianus, standing. i, Procyon lotor.
No. 1550, 10,000m: a, Heraclides cresphontes. b, Tyto alba. c, Drocopus pileatus. d, Cypripedium parviflorum, Archilochus colobris. e, Vulpes vulpes. f, Odocoileus virginianus. g, Enallagma sp. h, Amanita muscaria. i, Tamiasciurus hudsonicus.

2002, June 17		Perf. 14		
		Sheets of 9, #a-i		
1549-1550	A326	Set of 2	16.00	16.00

Flowers A327

No. 1551, 10,000m: a, Viola jeannie, Viola cultivar. b, Sunflower Moonshadow. c, Momo botan. d, Schomburgkia orchid. e, Dahlia hybrid. f, Sparaxis elegans harlequin. g, Dianhus. h, Camassia leichtlinii, Tulipa saxatilis. i, Pansy hybrid.
No. 1552, 10,000m, horiz.: a, Hemerocallis. b, Narcissus (Nazcissys). c, Hybrid tea rose. d, Rainbow Promised Cayenne Capers and flying insect. e, Anemone cordnazia. f, Hymenocallis narcissiflora. g, Hymenocallis. h, Tulipa. i, Lachenalia aloides, Meconopsis poppies.
No. 1553, 10,000m, horiz.: a, Narcissus. b, L. bulbiferun var. Croceum. c, Iris purpureobractea. d, Neomarica caerulea. e, Peonia lactiflora, Primula chungensis, Viola cornuta. f, Rainbow Promised Cayenne Capers and beetle. g, Iris purpureobractea (puzpuzeobractea). h, Tuberous begonia cultivar. i, Oriental hybrid lily.

2002, June 17		Perf. 14		
		Sheets of 9, #a-i		
1551-1553	A327	Set of 3	16.00	16.00

Dogs, Cats and Horses A328

No. 1554, 17,000m — Dogs: a, Labrador retriever. b, Bulldog. c, Cocker spaniel. d, Golden retriever. e, Boxer. f, Bloodhound.
No. 1555, 17,000m — Cats: a, Maine Coon. b, Cornish Rex. c, La Perm. d, Sphynx. e, Siamese. f, Persian.
No. 1556, 17,000m — Horses: a, Hanoverian. b, Haflinger. c, Nonius. d, Belgian heavy drafts. e, Australian-bred Arab. f, Thoroughbred.

No. 1557, 40,000m, Basset hound. No. 1558, 50,000m, Chestnut Oriental Longhair cat. No. 1559, 50,000m, Don horses.

2002, June 17		Perf. 13¼		
		Sheets of 6, #a-f		
1554-1556	A328	Set of 3	19.00	19.00

Souvenir Sheets

| 1557-1559 | A328 | Set of 3 | 15.00 | 15.00 |

Dinosaurs A329

Designs: 5000m, Protosaurus. No. 1561, 10,000m, Psittacosaurus. 17,000m, Torosaurus. 28,000m, Triceratops.
No. 1564, 10,000m: a, Diplodocus head. b, Pterosaurs. c, Diplodocuses. d, Afrovenator. e, Parasaurolophus. f, Ramphorhynchus. g, Lambeosaur. h, Euoplocephalus. i, Cynodont.
No. 1565, 10,000m: a, Brachiosaur. b, Monoclonius. c, Homalocephalus. d, Pterodactyl. e, Deinonychus. f, Archaeopteryx. g, Cretaceous landscape. h, Hypsilophodon. i, Lystrosaur.
No. 1566, 50,000m, Baryonyx. No. 1567, 50,000m, Styracosaurus, vert.

2002, June 17		Perf. 14		
1560-1563	A329	Set of 4	5.25	5.25

Sheets of 9, #a-i, + 3 labels

| 1564-1565 | A329 | Set of 2 | 11.00 | 11.00 |

Souvenir Sheets

| 1566-1567 | A329 | Set of 2 | 11.00 | 11.00 |

A330   Birds — A331

Designs: No. 1568, 5000m, Tachymarptis melba. No. 1569, 5000m, Falco tinnunculus. No. 1570, 10,000m, Pitta angolensis. No. 1571, 10,000m, Ardea cinerea. No. 1572, 17,000m, Corythaeola cristata. No. 1573, 28,000m, Butastur rufipennis.
No. 1574, 5000m, Creagrus furcatus. No. 1575, 10,000m, Larosterna inca. No. 1576, 17,000m, Pelecanus crispus. No. 1577, 28,000m, Morus bassanus.
No. 1578, 10,000m: a, Phaeton aethereus. b, Catharacta maccormicki. c, Diomedea bulleri. d, Puffinus ihermineri. e, Oceanites oceanicus. f, Pterodroma hasitata. g, Fregata magnificens. h, Sula nebouxii. i, Uria aagle.
No. 1579, 17,000m: a, Psittacus erithacus. b, Ficedula hypleuca. c, Tchagra senegala. d, Oriolus oriolus. e, Luscinia megarhynchos. f, Halcyon malimbica.
No. 1580, 17,000m: a, Coracias garrulus. b, Estrilda astrild. c, Upupa epops. d, Merops apiaster. e, Ploceus cucullatus. f, Clamator glandarius.
No. 1581, 50,000m, Falco subbuteo. No. 1582, 50,000m, Strix varia. No. 1583, 50,000m, Butorides striatus. No. 1584, 50,000m, Actophilornis africanus, horiz.
No. 1585, 50,000m, Spheniscus demersus. No. 1586, 50,000m, Rhynchops niger, horiz.

2002, June 17				
1568-1573	A330	Set of 6	6.50	6.50
1574-1577	A331	Set of 4	5.25	5.25
1578	A331	10,000m Sheet of 9, #a-i	7.75	7.75

Sheets of 6, #a-f

| 1579-1580 | A330 | Set of 2 | 17.50 | 17.50 |

Souvenir Sheets

| 1581-1584 | A330 | Set of 4 | 17.00 | 17.00 |
| 1585-1586 | A331 | Set of 2 | 8.50 | 8.50 |

For surcharges see Nos. 1739A, 1740, 1748.

Worldwide Fund for Nature (WWF) — A332

African savannah elephant: Nos. 1587a, 1588a, Herd. Nos. 1587b, 1588b, And birds. Nos. 1587c, 1588c, With juvenile. Nos. 1587d, 1588d, With rainbow.

MOZAMBIQUE

2002, Sept. 20   **Perf. 13¼x13½**
Size: 40x26½mm
Large Year
1587		Strip of 4	8.50	8.50
a.-d.	A332 19,000m	Any single	1.90	1.75

Size: 39x25mm
Small Year
1588		Miniature sheet of 4 + 4 labels	12.00	12.00
a.-d.	A332 19,000m	Any single	2.50	2.25

Princess Diana — A333

Pope John Paul II — A334

Elvis Presley — A335

Marilyn Monroe — A336

Marilyn Monroe — A337

Lord Robert Baden-Powell, Scout Emblem, Mushrooms and Flowers — A338

Astronauts and the Concorde — A339

Composers — A340

Louis Pasteur and Dogs — A341

Robert Stephenson and Locomotives — A342

Pope John Paul II — A343

Pope John Paul II, Madonna and Child — A344

Pope John Paul II, Madonna and Child — A345

Robert Stephenson — A346

Robert Stephenson — A347

No. 1593 — Famous men: a, Henri Dunant. b, Theodore Roosevelt. c, Albert Einstein. d, Ernest Hemingway. e, Thomas Nast. f, Albert Camus.
No. 1594 — Egyptian rulers: a, Seti I. b, Djedefre. c, Smekhkare. d, Seti II. e, Senusret III. f, Tutankhamun.
No. 1597: a, Michael Collins. b, Concorde. c, John Glenn. d, Concorde, diff. e, Neil Armstrong. f, Concorde, diff.
No. 1598 — Chess players and pieces: a, Tigran Petrosian, Lions emblem. b, Robert Fischer, Rotary emblem. c, Boris Spassky, Lions emblem. d, Raul Capablanca, Rotary emblem. e, Max Euwe, Lions emblem. f, Emanuel Lasker, Rotary emblem.
No. 1599 — Nobel Prize winners: a, Albert Einstein. b, Dalai Lama. c, Winston Churchill. d, Hideki Yukawa. e, Albert Schweitzer. f, Linus Pauling.
No. 1600 — Scout emblem and: a, Lord Robert Baden-Powell. b, Morpho aega, Baden-Powell. c, Prepona meander, Baden-Powell. d, Charaxes bernardus, Baden-Powell. e, Hypolimnas salmacis, Baden-Powell. f, Morpho rhetenor, Baden-Powell.
No. 1601 — Egyptian rulers: a, Netjenkhet Djoser. b, Tutankhamun. c, Neferefre. d, Amenhotep III. e, Pepi I. f, Amenmesses.
No. 1602 — Composers: a, Antonio Vivaldi. b, Franz Liszt. c, Ludwig van Beethoven. d, Wolfgang Mozart.
No. 1603 — Famous Men: a, Che Guevara. b, Pope John Paul II (blue gray background). c, Dr. Martin Luther King, Jr. d, Mao Zedong.
No. 1604 — Princess Diana and Pope John Paul II: a, Princess Diana in deep blue dress. b, Diana holding flowers. c, Pope John Paul II, hand showing. d, Pope John Paul II.
No. 1605 — Nelson Mandela and: a, Heulandite. b, Adamite. c, Wulfenite. d, Hemimorphite.
No. 1606 — Auto racing: a, Ayrton Senna. b, Modern race car. c, Old race car. d, Juan Manuel Fangio.
No. 1607 — Egyptian queens (tan background): a, Nefertiti facing right. b, Cleopatra VII. c, Nefertiti facing left. d, Nefertiti facing forward.
No. 1608 — Egyptian rulers (gray background): a, Nefertari. b, Tutankhamun. c, Tuthmosis. d, Nefertiti.
No. 1609 — Egyptian rulers (pale green background): a, Amenhotem II. b, Merenptah. c, Amenophis IV. d, Tuthmosis.
No. 1610 — Famous people: a, Dalai Lama. b, Mother Teresa. c, Pope John Paul II. d, Mahatma Gandhi.
No. 1611 — Explorers: a, Vasco da Gama. b, Ferdinand Magellan. c, Christopher Columbus. d, Amerigo Vespucci.
No. 1612 — Aviation: a, Antoine de Saint-Exupéry. b, Charles Lindbergh standing. c, Lindbergh seated. d, Concorde.
No. 1613 — Lions and Rotary Founders: a, Paul Harris (color picture), Rotary emblem. b, Melvin Jones (sepia picture), Lions emblem. c, Harris (sepia picture), Rotary emblem. d, Jones (color picture), Lions emblem.
No. 1614 — Film personalities: a, Charlie Chaplin. b, Frank Sinatra. c, Alfred Hitchcock. d, Walt Disney.
No. 1615: a, Scipionyx. b, Beipiaosaurus. c, Haroun Tazieff and vanadinite. d, Tazieff and adamite.
No. 1616 — Famous men: a, Winston Churchill. b, John F. Kennedy. c, Konrad Adenauer. d, Charles de Gaulle.
No. 1619 — Scientists: a, Charles Darwin, Byronosaurus. b, Alexander Fleming, Tricholoma terreum. c, Fleming, Boletus edulis. d, Darwin, Irratator.

No. 1620 — Famous men: a, Albert Schweitzer. b, Claude Bernard. c, Henri Dunant. d, Raoul Follerau.
No. 1621: a, John J. Audubon. b, Audubon, Aix sponsa. c, Audubon, Toxastoma montanum, Ixoreus naevius. d, Audubon, Loxia leucoptera.
No. 1625, John Glenn. No. 1626, Lord Robert Baden-Powell. No. 1627, Victor Hugo. No. 1628, John F. Kennedy. No. 1629, Princess Diana. No. 1630, Wolfgang Mozart. No. 1631, Alexander Fleming. No. 1632, Garry Kasparov. Nos. 1633, 1634, Marilyn Monroe. No. 1635, Mother Teresa. No. 1636, Henri Dunant. No. 1637, Nelson Mandela. No. 1638, Elvis Presley. No. 1639, Vasco da Gama. No. 1640, Paul Émile Victor. No. 1641, Tutankhamun. No. 1642, Nefertiti. No. 1643, John J. Audubon, Patagioenas leucophal. No. 1644, Audubon, Quiscalus quiscula.

2002, Sept. 30   **Perf. 13¼x12¾**
Sheets of 6, #a-f
1589	A333	15,000m multi	8.50	8.50
1590	A334	15,000m multi	8.50	8.50
1591	A335	15,000m multi	8.50	8.50
1592	A336	15,000m multi	8.50	8.50
1593	A336	15,000m multi	8.50	8.50
1594	A336	15,000m multi	8.50	8.50
1595	A337	17,000m multi	9.50	9.50
1596	A338	17,000m multi	9.50	9.50
1597	A339	17,000m multi	9.50	9.50
1598	A339	17,000m multi	9.50	9.50
1599	A339	17,000m multi	9.50	9.50
1600	A339	17,000m multi	9.50	9.50
1601	A339	17,000m multi	9.50	9.50

Sheets of 4, #a-d
1602	A340	5000m multi	1.90	1.90
1603	A340	20,000m multi	7.75	7.75
1604	A340	20,000m multi	7.75	7.75
1605	A340	20,000m multi	7.75	7.75
1606	A340	20,000m multi	7.75	7.75
1607	A340	20,000m multi	7.75	7.75
1608	A340	20,000m multi	7.75	7.75
1609	A340	20,000m multi	7.75	7.75
1610	A340	22,000m multi	8.50	8.50
1611	A340	22,000m multi	8.50	8.50
1612	A340	22,000m multi	8.50	8.50
1613	A340	25,000m multi	9.25	9.25
1614	A340	25,000m multi	9.25	9.25
1615	A340	25,000m multi	9.25	9.25
1616	A340	25,000m multi	9.25	9.25
1617	A341	25,000m multi	9.25	9.25
1618	A342	25,000m multi	9.25	9.25
1619	A342	33,000m multi	12.50	12.50
1620	A342	33,000m multi	12.50	12.50
1621	A342	33,000m multi	12.50	12.50

Nos. 1589-1621 (33)   292.15   292.15

Souvenir Sheets
1622	A343	88,000m shown	8.50	8.50
1623	A344	88,000m shown	8.50	8.50
1624	A345	88,000m shown	8.50	8.50
1625	A345	88,000m multi	8.50	8.50
1626	A345	88,000m multi	8.50	8.50
1627	A345	88,000m multi	8.50	8.50
1628	A345	88,000m multi	8.50	8.50
1629	A345	88,000m multi	8.50	8.50
1630	A345	88,000m multi	8.50	8.50
1631	A345	88,000m multi	8.50	8.50
1632	A345	88,000m multi	8.50	8.50
1633	A345	88,000m multi	8.50	8.50
1634	A345	110,000m multi	10.50	10.50
1635	A345	110,000m multi	10.50	10.50
1636	A345	110,000m multi	10.50	10.50
1637	A345	110,000m multi	10.50	10.50
1638	A345	110,000m multi	10.50	10.50
1639	A345	110,000m multi	10.50	10.50
1640	A345	110,000m multi	10.50	10.50
1641	A345	110,000m multi	10.50	10.50
1642	A345	110,000m multi	10.50	10.50
1643	A345	110,000m multi	10.50	10.50
1644	A345	110,000m multi	10.50	10.50
1645	A346	110,000m shown	10.50	10.50
1646	A347	110,000m shown	10.50	10.50

Nos. 1622-1646 (25)   238.50   238.50

World of the Sea

Ships — A348

Aircraft — A349

MOZAMBIQUE

Sea Lions A350
Polar Bears A351
Killer Whales A352
Whales A353
Dolphins A354
Fish A355
Fish A356
Fish A357
Fish A358

Sea Horses A359
Penguins A360
Penguins A361
Sea Birds A362
Sea Birds A363
Sea Birds A364
Crustaceans — A365
Snails A366
Jellyfish A367

Coral A368
Submarines — A369
Lighthouses — A370
Ship A371
Ship A372
Fish A373
Fish A374
Sea Horse A375

Sea Horse A376
Penguin A377
Penguin A378
Sea Bird A379
Sea Bird A380
Sea Bird A381

No. 1668 — Marine invertebrates: a, Phyllidia elegans. b, Phyllidia coelestis. c, Hypselodoris bullocki. d, Glossodoris hikuerensis. e, Glossodoris cruentus. f, Chromodoris leopardus.

No. 1669 — Shells: a, Murex brassica (showing shell opening). b, Cassis cornuta. c, Strombus gigas. d, Rapana rapiformis (showing shell opening). e, Chicoreus ramosus. f, Bursa bubo.

No. 1670 — Shells: a, Chicoreus virgineus. b, Tonna galea. c, Murex erythrostomus. d, Strombus gigas. e, Murex brassica (showing front of shell). f, Rapana rapiformis (showing front of shell).

No. 1671 — Tubeworms and seaweed: a, Kallymenia cribosa. b, Ulva lactuca. c, Chondrus crispus. d, Gigartina disticha. e, Palmaria palmata. f, Filogranella elatensis.

No. 1685, Seal flensing. No. 1686, Polar bear. No. 1687, Killer whale breaching surface. No. 1688, Whales underwater. No. 1689, Dolphins with open mouths. No. 1690, Lobster. No. 1691, Jellyfish. No. 1692 Coral and fish. No. 1693, Filogranella elatensis. No. 1694, Chromodoris leopardus. No. 1695, Tonna galea. No. 1696, Turbo marmoratus. No. 1697, Submarine. No. 1698, Christopher Columbus.

Perf. 12¾x13¼, 13¼x12¾

2002, Nov. 1   Sheets of 6, #a-f
1647	A348	5000m multi	3.25	3.25
1648	A349	17,000m multi	9.50	9.50
1649	A350	17,000m multi	9.50	9.50

MOZAMBIQUE

1650	A351	17,000m multi	9.50	9.50
1651	A352	17,000m multi	9.50	9.50
1652	A353	17,000m multi	9.50	9.50
1653	A354	17,000m multi	9.50	9.50
1654	A355	17,000m multi	9.50	9.50
1655	A356	17,000m multi	9.50	9.50
1656	A357	17,000m multi	9.50	9.50
1657	A358	17,000m multi	9.50	9.50
1658	A359	17,000m multi	9.50	9.50
1659	A360	17,000m multi	9.50	9.50
1660	A361	17,000m multi	9.50	9.50
1661	A362	17,000m multi	9.50	9.50
1662	A363	17,000m multi	9.50	9.50
1663	A364	17,000m multi	9.50	9.50
1664	A365	17,000m multi	9.50	9.50
1665	A366	17,000m multi	9.50	9.50
1666	A367	17,000m multi	9.50	9.50
1667	A368	17,000m multi	9.50	9.50
1668	A368	17,000m multi	9.50	9.50
1669	A368	17,000m multi	9.50	9.50
1670	A368	17,000m multi	9.50	9.50
1671	A368	17,000m multi	9.50	9.50
1672	A369	20,000m multi	12.00	12.00
1673	A370	33,000m multi	20.00	20.00
Nos. 1647-1673 (27)			263.25	263.25

Souvenir Sheets

1674	A371	110,000m shown	11.00	11.00
1675	A372	110,000m shown	11.00	11.00
1676	A373	110,000m shown	11.00	11.00
1677	A374	110,000m shown	11.00	11.00
1678	A375	110,000m shown	11.00	11.00
1679	A376	110,000m shown	11.00	11.00
1680	A377	110,000m shown	11.00	11.00
1681	A378	110,000m shown	11.00	11.00
1682	A379	110,000m shown	11.00	11.00
1683	A380	110,000m shown	11.00	11.00
1684	A381	110,000m shown	11.00	11.00
1685	A350	110,000m multi	11.00	11.00
1686	A351	110,000m multi	11.00	11.00
1687	A352	110,000m multi	11.00	11.00
1688	A353	110,000m multi	11.00	11.00
1689	A354	110,000m multi	11.00	11.00
1690	A365	110,000m multi	11.00	11.00
1691	A367	110,000m multi	11.00	11.00
1692	A368	110,000m multi	11.00	11.00
1693	A368	110,000m multi	11.00	11.00
1694	A368	110,000m multi	11.00	11.00
1695	A368	110,000m multi	11.00	11.00
1696	A368	110,000m multi	11.00	11.00
1697	A369	110,000m multi	11.00	11.00
1698	A369	110,000m multi	11.00	11.00
Nos. 1674-1698 (25)			275.00	275.00

Zeppelins — A382

No. 1699, 28,000m, horiz.: a, Ferdinand von Zeppelin, brown and yellow background. b, LZ-2 in flight. c, LZ-10 in flight. d, LZ-1, purple background.
No. 1700, 28,000m, horiz.: a, LZ-1, blue and yellow background. b, LZ-2 tethered. c, LZ-10 above sheep. d, Ferdinand von Zeppelin with binoculars.
No. 1701, 50,000m, Ferdinand von Zeppelin, in military uniform. No. 1702, 50,000m, Ferdinand von Zeppelin, in suit.

2002, Nov. 18   Perf. 13¼x13½
Sheets of 4, #a-d

1699-1700	A382	Set of 2	15.00	15.00

Souvenir Sheets
Perf. 13½x13¼

1701-1702	A382	Set of 2	6.75	6.75

Locomotives — A383

No. 1703, 17,000m, horiz.: a, London, Midland and Scottish Railway, England. b, Great Northern Railway, Ireland. c, Southern Railway, England. d, Great Northern Railway, US. e, Chicago, Milwaukee, St. Paul and Pacific Railroad, US. f, London and Northeastern Railway, England.
No. 1704, 17,000m, horiz.: a, Great Southern Railway, Spain. b, Shantung Railway, China. c, Austrian State Railway. d, Victorian Government Railways, Australia. f, London and Northwester Railways, England.
No. 1705, 17,000m, horiz.: a, Western Railways, France. b, Netherlands State Railway (green locomotive on bridge). c, Great Indian Peninsula Railway. d, Paris-Orleans Railway, France. e, Madras and Southern Mahratta Railway, India. f, Netherlands State Railway (green locomotive).
No. 1706, 50,000m, London, Brighton and South Coast Railway, England. No. 1707, 50,000m, New York Central, US.

2002, Nov. 18   Perf. 13¼x13½
Sheets of 6, #a-f

1703-1705	A383	Set of 3	20.00	20.00

Souvenir Sheets

1706-1707	A383	Set of 2	6.75	6.75

Vintage Cars

A384

Automobiles — A385

No. 1708, 13,000m: a, 1912 Bentley. b, 1914 Delage Grand Prix. c, 1949, Healey Silverstone. d, 1922 Duesenberg. e, Delage 1500cc Grand Prix. f, 1961 Ferrari 375/F1.
No. 1709, 13,000m: a, 1906 Mercedes. b, 1951 Morgan. c, 1912 Sunbeam. d, 1922 Sunbeam. e, 1925 Sunbeam Tiger. f, 1908 Austin 100hp.
No. 1710, 17,000m: a, 1937, Bugatti Type 57 Alalante coupe. b, 1948 Tucker Torpedo. c, 1966 Honda S 800m. d, 1946 Cisitalia 202 GT. e, 1958 Chevrolet Impala. f, 1934 Cadillac LaSalle convertible.
No. 1711, 17,000m: a, 1908 Austin. b, 1937 Studebaker coupe. c, 1930 Bugatti Type 40GP. d, 1931 Ford Model A roadster. e, 1937 Alfa Romeo 2900B. f, 1937 Cord 812.
No. 1712, 40,000m, 1931 Alfa Romeo. No. 1713, 40,000m, 1911 Marmon Wasp.
No. 1714, 50,000m, 1957 Plymouth Fury. No. 1715, 50,000m, 1928 Mercedes-Benz SSK.

Perf. 13¼x13½, 13½x13¼
2002, Nov. 18   Sheets of 6, #a-f

| 1708-1709 | A384 | Set of 2 | 10.00 | 10.00 |
| 1710-1711 | A385 | Set of 2 | 12.50 | 12.50 |

Souvenir Sheets

| 1712-1713 | A384 | Set of 2 | 6.50 | 6.50 |
| 1714-1715 | A385 | Set of 2 | 6.75 | 6.75 |

Pottery — A386

Designs: 1000m, Pote. 2000m, Ohaleira. 4000m, Taças. 5000m, Cantaro. 17,000m, Panela. 28,000m, Alguidar. 50,000m, Jarra. 100,000m, Bilhas.

2002, Dec. 2   Perf. 12¾

1716-1723	A386	Set of 8	8.00	8.00

Dated 2001.
For surcharge see No. 1739.

Justino Chemane, Composer of National Anthem — A387

2003, July 11

1724	A387	6000m multi	.55	.55

Minerals — A388

Designs: 5000m, Bauxite. 14,000m, Marble. 19,000m, shown. 33,000m, Gold.

2004, Apr. 30

1725-1728	A388	Set of 4	6.00	6.00

Dated 2003.

Paintings by Jean-Auguste Ingres — A389

Paintings by James Tissot A390

Paintings by Pierre-Auguste Renoir — A391

Paintings by Edgar Degas A392

Various unnamed paintings.

2004, June 17   Litho.   Perf. 13½x13

1729	A389	6500m Sheet of 6, #a-f	9.50	9.50
1730	A390	6500m Sheet of 6, #a-f	9.50	9.50
g.		Souvenir sheet, #1730e	1.60	1.60
1731	A391	10,000m Sheet of 6, #a-f	11.50	11.50
1732	A392	17,000m Sheet of 6, #a-f	13.00	13.00
Nos. 1729-1732 (4)			43.50	43.50

Diplomatic Relations Between Mozambique and People's Republic of China, 30th Anniv. — A395

No. 1735: a, Flags, buildings and animals. b, Arms, Admiral Zheng He, building, vase, sculpture.

Illustration reduced.

2005, June 25   Litho.   Perf. 13¼

1735	A395	33,000m Pair, #a-b	5.50	5.50

Exists imperf.

Southern African Development Community, 25th Anniv. — A396

2005, Aug. 11   Perf. 11¼x11

1736	A396	8000m multi	.65	.65

Traditional African Medicine Day — A397

2005, Aug. 31   Perf. 11x11¼

1737	A397	8000m multi	.65	.65

World Summit on the Information Society, Tunis — A398

2005, Oct. 9   Perf. 11¼x11

1738	A398	8000m multi	.65	.65

Nos. 1320, 1575, 1576, 1717 Surcharged Like No. 1417 and No. 1321 Surcharged in Black and Silver

Methods and Perfs as Before
2005 ?

1739	A386	6000m on 2000m #1717	.50	.50
1739A	A331	6000m on 10,000m #1575		—
1740	A331	8000m on 17,000m #1576	.70	.70
1741	A269	33,000m on 7500m #1320	2.75	2.75
1742	A269	33,000m on 12,500m #1321 (B&S)	2.75	2.75
Nos. 1739-1742 (4)			6.70	6.70

Mozambique Telecommunications Company, 25th Anniv. — A399

2006, June 10   Litho.   Perf. 11½x11

1743	A399	8000m multi	.65	.65

No. 1743 also has denomination expressed in revalued meticals, which were put into service on July 1.
For surcharge, see No. 1747.

Presidential Initiative Against AIDS — A400

MOZAMBIQUE

Pres. Armando Guebuza: 8m, Holding gavel. 16m, Behind microphones. 33m, With arm raised.

2006, Oct. 9		Perf. 11x11½
1744-1746	A400	Set of 3 4.50 4.50

World Vision — A400a

2006	Litho.	Perf. 11½x11
1746A	A400a	33m multi

An additional stamp was issued in this set. The editors would like to examine any example.

No. 1743 Surcharged

2006	Litho.	Perf. 11½x11
1747	A399	33m on 8000m #1743 — —

The following items inscribed "Moçambique Correios" have been declared "illegal" by Mozambique postal officials:

Sheet of nine stamps of various denominations depicting Princess Diana;
Sheet of six 5000m stamps depicting the art of Paul Delvaux;
Sheet of six 17,000m stamps depicting the art of Edgar Degas;
Stamps depicting the art of Lucas Cranach;
Six different 15,000m souvenir sheets of one depicting Pope John Paul II;
Souvenir sheet of one 30,000m stamp depicting French Pres. Nicolas Sarkozy.
A set of 12 stamps with denominations of 5,000m, 19,000m, and 33,000m depicting Europa stamps, 50th anniv.
Stamps depicting Wolfgang Amadeus Mozart; Pierre Auguste Renoir; Jean Auguste Ingres Bessieres; Marilyn Monroe; Rotary International; Lions International; Formula 1 Racing; Astronauts; 2007 Rugby World Cup.

No. 1575 Surcharged

Methods and Perfs As Before

2006 ?		
1748	A331	33m on 10,000m #1575 6.75 6.75

Cahora Bassa Dam — A401

Designs: 8m, Dam and reservoir. 20m, Dignitaries shaking hands. 33m, Dam and flag of Mozambique.

2007, Nov. 26	Litho.	Perf. 11x11¼
1749-1751	A401	Set of 3 4.75 4.75

Reign of Aga Khan, 50th Anniv. — A402

Designs: 8m, Building. No. 1753, 20m, People on beach. No. 1754, 20m, People under shelter. No. 1755, 33m, Polana Serena Hotel. No. 1756, 33m, Students in classroom, vert. (30x40mm).

Perf. 12¾, 11¼x11 (#1756)

2007, Nov.		
1752-1756	A402	Set of 5 9.00 9.00

Fauna, Flora and Minerals A403

No. 1757 — Map of Africa and wild cats: a, 8m, Acionyx jubatus. b, 8m, Panthera leo with closed mouth. c, 8m, Panthera leo with open mouth. d, 33m, Male Panthera leo. e, 33m, Female Panthera leo, diff. f, 33m, Panthera pardus.
No. 1758 — Map of Africa and elephants: a, 8m, Loxodonta cyclotis facing right. b, 8m, Loxodonta africana. c, 8m, Loxodonta cyclotis facing left. d, 33m, Loxodonta africana facing right. e, 33m, Loxodonta cyclotis, diff. f, 33m, Loxodonta africana facing left.
No. 1759 — Lighthouses and marine mammals: a, 8m, Sousa teuszii. b, 8m, Stenella frontalis. c, 8m, Stenella clymene. d, 33m, Sotalia fluviatilis. e, 33m, Stenella longirostris. f, 33m, Tursiops truncatus.
No. 1760 — Map of Africa and birds of prey: a, 8m, Haliaeetus leucocephalus. b, 8m, Terathopius ecaudatus. c, 8m, Accipiter gentilis. d, 33m, Buteo lagopus. e, 33m, Head of Aquila verreauxii. f, 33m, Aquila verreauxi on branch.
No. 1761 — Hummingbirds and orchids: a, 8m, Tachybaptus, Malaxis uniflora. b, 8m, Fregata magnificus, Coryanthes speciosa. c, 8m, Gallinula, Calochilus robertsonii. d, 33m, Veniliornis, Stanhopea. e, 33m, Basilinna leucotis, Habaneria saccata. f, 33m, Actitis macularia, Diuris filifolia.
No. 1762 — Map of Africa and bees: a, 8m, Polubia. b, 8m, Apis mellifera scutellata. c, 8m, Pompilus. d, 33m, Tiphiidae. e, 33m, Vespula vulgaris. f, 33m, Scoliidae.
No. 1763 — Map of Africa and butterflies: a, 8m, Danaus chrysippus. b, 8m, Libytheana carineta. c, 8m, Papilio morondavana. d, 33m, Danaus gilippus. e, 33m, Amblypodia tyrannus. f, 33m, Lycaena cupreus.
No. 1764 — Map of Africa and crocodiles: a, 8m, Crocodylus porosus. b, 8m, Crocodylus novaeguineae. c, 8m, Crocodylus rhombifer. d, 33m, Crocodylus niloticus. e, 33m, Osteolaemus tetraspis. f, 33m, Crocodylus siamensis.
No. 1765 — Map of Africa and frogs: a, 8m, Gastrotheca. b, 8m, Mantella. c, 8m, Rana esculenta. d, 33m, Litoria rubella. e, 33m, Dendrobatidae. f, 33m, Pyxicephalus.
No. 1766 — Dinosaurs: a, 8m, Aublysodon. b, 8m, Ornithomimus. c, 8m, Coelurus. d, 33m, Velociraptor. e, 33m, Abelisaurus. f, 33m, Saurornithoides.
No. 1767 — Map of Africa and cacti: a, 8m, Hoodia gordonii. b, 8m, Hoodia officinalis. c, 8m, Hoodia ruschii. d, 33m, Hoodia flava. e, 33m, Hoodia officinalis, diff. f, 33m, Hoodia currorii.
No. 1768 — Fruit: a, 8m, Citrus vulgaris. b, 8m, Cola acuminata. c, 8m, Cocos nucifera. d, 33m, Citrus limonum. e, 33m, Cocos nucifera, diff. f, 33m, Citrus bergamia.
No. 1769 — Map of Africa, diamonds and minerals: a, 8m, Fluorite, quartz. b, 8m, Elbaite tourmaline, quartz. c, 8m, Staurolite. d, 33m, Fluorite, pyrite. e, 33m, Benitoite, neptunite. f, 33m, Celestine.
No. 1770, 20m — Map of Africa and primates: a, Cebidae. b, Nomascus leucogenys. c, Borneo proboscis monkey. d, Symphalangus syndactylus. e, Pan troglodytes. f, Cercopithecidae.
No. 1771, 20m — Lighthouses and whales: a, Balaenoptera borealis. b, Orcinus orca. c, Eschrichtius robustus. d, Balaenoptera physalus. e, Three Orcinus orca. f, Megaptera novaeangliae.
No. 1772, 20m — Map of Africa and owls: a, Strix woodfordii. b, Tyto capensis. c, Phodilus badius on thin branch. d, Phodilus badius on thick branch. e, Tytonidae. f, Otus senegalensis.
No. 1773, 20m — Map of Africa and parrots: a, Psittacopes. b, Serudaptus. c, Pseudasturidae. d, Quercypsittidae. e, Xenopsitta. f, Palaeopsittacus.
No. 1774, 20m — Butterflies or moths and unnamed flowers: a, Inachis io. b, Saturnia pavonia. c, Papilio xuthus. d, Prepona praeneste. e, Speyeria cybele. f, Nymphalidae.
No. 1775, 20m — Map of Africa and fish: a, Scorpaenidae. b, Balistodae. c, Antennarius. d, Triglidae. e, Hydrocynus. f, Lophius.
No. 1776, 20m — Map of Africa and marine life: a, Birgus latro. b, Panulirus. c, Gecarcoidea natalis. d, Loligo opalescens. e, Genus ocypode. f, Hapalochlaena.
No. 1777, 20m — Map of Africa and reptiles: a, Vaanus niloticus. b, Chamaeleo jacksonii. c, Veranus exanthematicus. d, Scincus. e, Brookesia. f, Furcifer pardalis.
No. 1778, 20m — Map of Africa and turtles: a, Natator depressus. b, Eretmochelys imbricata. c, Lepidochelys olivacea. d, Lepidochelys olivacea with dark neck. d, Lepidochelys olivacea with light neck. e, Caretta caretta. f, Chelonia mydas.
No. 1779, 20m — Map of Africa and snakes: a, Bitis nasicornis. b, Bitis gabonica. c, Ophiophagus hannah. d, Thelotornis kirtlandii. e, Dendroaspis angusticeps. f, Atheris.
No. 1780, 20m — Dinosaurs: a, Therizinosaurus. b, Heterdontosaurus. c, Prosaurolophus. d, Melanorosaurus. e, Megalosaurus. f, Proceratosaurus.
No. 1781, 20m — Trees: a, Punica granatum, fruit split, and on branch. b, Elaeis guineensis. c, Cola acuminata. d, Areca catechu. e, Hevea brasiliensis. f, Punica granatum, flowers on branches and split.
No. 1782, 20m — Map of Africa and orchids: a, Purple Cattleya lueddemanniana. b, Paphiopedilum delenatii. c, Vanda coerulea. d, Pink Cattleya lueddmanniana. e, Paphiopedilum. f, Spathoglottis.
No. 1783, 20m — Map of Africa and minerals: a, Carrollite. b, Ettringite. c, Cerrusite, barite. d, Malachite. e, Carrollite, calcite. f, Dioptase.
No. 1784, 132m, Map of Africa and Nomascus nasutus. No. 1785, 132m, Map of Africa and Panthera leo. No. 1786, 132m, Loxodonta africana. No. 1787, 132m, Stenella logirostris, diff. No. 1788, 132m, Orcinus orca and lighthouse, diff. No. 1789, 132m, Lepidocolaptes, Spathoglottis plicata. No. 1790, 132m, Pulchrapollia. No. 1791, 132m, Accipiter nisus. No. 1792, 132m, Map of Africa and Polubia. No. 1793, 132m, Arctia hebe. No. 1794, 132m, Papilio homerus, Caladeria reptans. No. 1795, 132m, Map of Africa and Thassophryninae. No. 1796, 132m, Map of Africa and Chauliodus. No. 1797, 132m, Map of Africa and Dendroaspis polylepis. No. 1798, 132m, Map of Africa and Pogona vitticeps. No. 1799, 132m, Map of Africa and Crocodylus niloticus, diff. No. 1800, 132m, Map of Africa and Eretmochelys imbircata, diff. No. 1801, 132m, Map of Africa and Pychicephalus adspersus. No. 1802, 132m, Hadrosaurus. No. 1803, 132m, Adansonia hebe. No. 1804, 132m, Map of Africa and Euphorbia enopla. No. 1805, 132m, Map of Africa, Diuris filifolia, Malaxis uniflora. No. 1806, 132m, Cirtus africana, diff. No. 1807, 132m, Vanadinite, poldervaartite. No. 1808, 132m, Malachite, barite and malachite.

Perf. 12¾x13¼

2007, Dec. 10		Litho.
Sheets of 6, #a-f		
1757-1769	A403	Set of 13 125.00 125.00
1770-1783	A403	Set of 14 130.00 130.00

Souvenir Sheets
Perf. 13¼ Syncopated

| 1784-1808 | A403 | Set of 25   260.00   260.00 |

Minerva Central Publishers, Cent. — A404

Background color: 8m, Red. 20m, Olive green. 33m, Purple.

2008, Apr. 10	Litho.	Perf. 11x11¼
1809-1811	A404	Set of 3 4.75 4.75

Second Frelimo Party Congress, 40th Anniv. — A405

2008, July 25		Perf. 11¼x11
1812	A405	8m multi .65 .65

Miniature Sheets

2008 Summer Olympics, Beijing — A406

No. 1813 Surcharged

Nos. 1813 and 1814: a, Soccer. b, Basketball. c, Swimming. d, Running.

2008		Perf. 13¼x12¾
1813	A406	8m Sheet of 4, #a-d 5.00 5.00
1814	A406	8m on 8m Sheet of 4, #a-d 2.50 2.50

No. 1813 shows an incorrect abbreviation for the currency, which was corrected by the surcharge.

Food — A407

Designs: 8m, Bolo de milho (corn cake). 20m, Mathapa com carangueijo (cassava with crab). 33m, Quiabo com camarao (Okra and shrimp).

2008, Oct. 9		Perf. 11¼x11
1815-1817	A407	Set of 3 4.75 4.75

World Vision — A407a

2008	Litho.	Perf. 11x11½
1817A	A407a	33m multi

Maria de Lurdes Mutola, 800-Meter Gold Medalist in 2000 Summer Olympics — A408

2009, Jan. 21		Perf. 11x11¼
1818	A408	8m multi .65 .65

Mozambique postal officials have declared as "illegal" stamps dated 2008 depicting chess grandmaster Bobby Fischer.

MOZAMBIQUE

Eduardo Mondlane (1920-69), President of Mozambique Liberation Front — A409

2009, June 20　　Litho.　　Perf. 11¼x11
1819　A409　33m black & red　　2.40　2.40

Transportation — A410

No. 1820, 33m — Transportation with animals: a, Elephants and howdah. b, Reindeer pulling sled. c, Camel and rider. d, Horse-drawn carriage. e, Donkey and rider. f, Dog sled.
No. 1821, 33m — Two-wheeled transportation: a, Rickshaw. b, Bicycle. c, Motor scooter. d, Motorcycle. e, Foot-powered scooter. f, Segway.
No. 1822, 33m — Old automobiles: a, Citroen BL 11. b, Jaguar XK-140. c, Chrysler Imperial. d, Dodge Royal Lancer. e, Mercedes-Benz 300 SL. f, Ford Custom.
No. 1823, 33m — Modern automobiles: a, Hyundai QuarmaQ. b, Lamborghini Murcielago. c, Buick Invicta. d, Ford Verve. e, Mazda RX-8. f, Cadillac CTS Sport Wagon.
No. 1824, 33m — Modern electric automobiles: a, Mitsubishi iMiEV Sport. b, Opel Meriva. c, Pickup truck (incorrectly identified as InterCity 225). d, Nissan Navara. e, Opel Insignia. f, Tesla Roadster.
No. 1825, 33m — Ancient sailing vessels: a, Phoenician bark. b, Egyptian sailing ship. c, Arab ship. d, Chinese junk. e, Greek galley. f, Roman galley.
No. 1826, 33m — Ships and maps: a, Independence, map of United States. b, Great Harry, map of Great Britain and Ireland. c, Vespucci, map of Spain. d, Norske Löwe, map of Denmark. e, Brederode, map of Netherlands. f, Madre di Dio, map of Italy.
No. 1827, 33m — Steam-powered ships: a, SS Martha's Vineyard. b, SS America. c, SS Statendam. d, SS Brazil. e, SS Ryndam. f, SS Nieuw Amsterdam.
No. 1828, 33m — Warships: a, Warrior. b, Merrimack. c, Dreadnought. d, Lightning. e, MEKO frigate. f, Yamato.
No. 1829, 33m — Warships: a, HMS Astute. b, NS Yamal. c, USS Harry S Truman. d, Trafalgar. e, Vaygach. f, Nimitz class aircraft carrier.
No. 1830, 33m — Modern ships: a, Surcouf. b, Sea Shadow. c, Skjold class patrol boat. d, MS Radiance of the Seas. e, MS Pacific Princess. f, MS Mariner of the Seas.
No. 1831, 33m — Early locomotives: a, Trevithick. b, Blenkinsop. c, Marc Seguin. d, Puffing Billy. e, Rocket. f, Liverpool.
No. 1832, 33m — Locomotives: a, Evening Star. b, LMS Princess Royal Class. c, Russian 2TE10U. d, Atlantis. e, Cock o' the North. f, LMS Compound 4-4-0.
No. 1833, 33m — Locomotives: a, ALCO RS-1 (bister panel). b, British Rail Class 03. c, 643 Class. d, 661 Class. e, 641 Class. f, Hudswell Clarke 0-4-2ST.
No. 1834, 33m — Locomotives: a, ALCO RS-1 (gray panel). b, Re420. c, TAGAB Re2. d, EuroSprinter DB AG Class 182. e, SKODA 109. f, Re4.
No. 1835, 33m — High-speed trains: a, Thalys. b, Eurostar. c, InterCity 225. d, ICE. e, TGV. f, Pendolino.
No. 1836, 33m — High-speed trains: a, JR-Maglev. b, KTX. c, Maglev. d, 100 Series Shinkansen. e, E1 Series Shinkansen. f, N700 Series Shinkansen.
No. 1837, 33m — Pioneer aircraft: a, 1868 Albatross II glider of Jean-Marie LeBris. b, 1852 Henry Giffard balloon. c, 1849 glider of George Cayley. d, 1897 Avion III airplane of Clément Ader. e, 1874 monoplane of Félix du Temple. f, 1901 flying machine of Traian Vuia.
No. 1838, 33m — Pioneer aircraft: a, 1902 Number 21 airplane of Gustave Whitehead. b, 1904 Wright Flyer II. c, 14 Bis, 1906. d, 1908 Henry Farman biplane. e, 1909 Louis Blériot monoplane. f, 1910 Rumpler Taube.
No. 1839, 33m — Airplanes: a, Fokker D.1. b, Handley Page. c, Winstead Special. d, Boeing P26-B. e, Mitsubishi Ki-15. f, Nakajima Ki-27.
No. 1840, 33m — Military airplanes: a, Messerschmitt Bf-109. b, B-29 Superfortress. c, Yak-9. d, Avro Lancaster. e, Kawasaki Ki-61. f, Northrop P-61 Black Widow.
No. 1841, 33m — Military airplanes: a, Saab J35J. b, Sukhoi SU-30MKI. c, A-7 Corsair. d, Boeing 747 carrying Space Shuttle. e, Myasishchev M-55. f, Aero L-39 Albatros.

No. 1842, 33m — Supersonic airplanes: a, TU-144. b, F-105 Thunderbird. c, North American XB-70A. d, SR-71 Blackbird. e, Concorde 102. f, F16XL.
No. 1843, 33m — Fire vehicles: a, 1963 Magirus-Deutz Mercur 126 DL. b, 1979 Mercedes-Benz LA 1113 BR. c, 1958 Magirus-Deutz V6 Ladder. d, 1976 Dodge K1050 Somati MONIA. e, 2002 Scania 91 G310 Rosenbauer. f, 1984 Renault G300-17 Riffaul.
No. 1844, 33m — Ambulances: a, 1942 Morris Y Series. b, 1974 Citroen HB2AS 1600. c, 1942 Dodge WC54. d, 1981 Land Rover. e, 1966 Cadillac S&S48. f, 1955 Ford Kaiser V8.
No. 1845, 33m — Spacecraft: a, Sputnik I. b, Vostok I. c, Explorer I. d, Skylab. e, Mir. f, Apollo 11.
No. 1846, 33m — Spacecraft: a, Venture Star. b, Ares V. c, Space Shuttle Discovery. d, Dawn. e, SpaceShip One. f, Phoenix.
No. 1847, 175m, Camels and rider. No. 1848, 175m, Rickshaw and Segway. No. 1849, 175m, Cadillac Eldorado. No. 1850, 175m, Citroen 2CV. No. 1851, 175m, Renault Z17. No. 1852, 175m, Egyptian canoe. No. 1853, 175m, Portuguese carrack Santa Catarina do Monte Sinai and map of Portugal. No. 1854, 175m, SS Great Britain. No. 1855, 175m, Italian battleship Littorio. No. 1856, 175m, PFS Polarstern. No. 1857, 175m, F261 Magdeburg. No. 1858, 175m, North Star locomotive. No. 1859, 175m, Pannier locomotive. No. 1860, 175m, 10000 locomotive. No. 1861, 175m, CC7102 locomotive. No. 1862, 175m, Thalys, diff. No. 1863, 175m, KTX, diff. No. 1864, 175m, Triplane of John Stringfellow. No. 1865, 175m, Nieuport 28. No. 1866, 175m, Aichi D3A. No. 1867, 175m, Corsair F4U. No. 1868, 175m, EF-111. No. 1869, 175m, A2 airplane. No. 1870, 175m, 1996-2001 Mercedes Unimog 2450 L38 fire truck. No. 1871, 175m, 1956 Gurkha Red Cross Ambulance. No. 1872, 175m, Salyut 1 and Telstar. No. 1873, 175m, V-2 rocket and SS-6 Sapwood. Nos. 1847-1873 are vert.

Perf. 12¾x13¼
2009, Sept. 30　　Litho.
Sheets of 6, #a-f
1820-1846　A410　Set of 27　425.00　425.00
Souvenir Sheets
Perf. 13¼ Syncopated
1847-1873　A410　Set of 27　375.00　375.00
Nos. 1847-1873 each contain one 37x38mm stamp.

Famous People and Events A411

No. 1874, 8m — Year of the Tiger (in 2010): a, Tiger with head at bottom, Temple of Heaven. b, Tiger running, Forbidden City. c, Tiger with head at top, Temple of Heaven. d, Tiger walking, Forbidden City. e, Tiger, Yong He Gong Lama Temple. f, Tiger, Great Wall of China.
No. 1875, 8m — Shen Chou (1427-1509), painter: a, Painting of forest, sketch of tree branch with calligraphy. b, Shen Chou at R, painting at L. c, 14x19mm landscape and 13x26mm landscape. d, 17x21mm landscape and 16x20mm landscape. e, Shen Chou at L, painting at R. f, 13x15mm landscape and 16x23mm painting of man on bridge.
No. 1876, 8m — Pope John Paul II (1920-2005) and: a, Arms, sculpture. b, Dove, St. Peter's Basilica. c, Arms, dome interior. d, Arms, St. Peter's Basilica. e, Dove in flight, St. Peter's Square. f, Arms, buildings in distance.
No. 1877, 8m — Mohandas Gandhi (1869-1948) and: a, Ganesha. b, Spinning wheel. c, Taj Mahal. d, Naja naja (cobra). e, Meditating woman. f, Panthera tigris tigris (tiger).
No. 1878, 8m — Chinese film personalities: a, Sun Daolin. b, Zhao Dan. c, Ge You. d, Bai Yang. e, Ruan Lingyu. f, Zhang Yu.
No. 1879, 8m — People's Republic of China, 60th Anniv.: a, Hand holding Chinese flag, Chinese soldiers. b, Mao Zedong. c, Qian Sanqiang, Tianwan Nuclear Center. d, Deng Xiaoping, Great Wall of China. e, Hu Jintao, fireworks above Olympic Stadium. f, Jiang Zemin, Hong Kong skyline, ruins of St. Paul's Church, Macao.
No. 1880, 20m — Charlie Chaplin (1889-1977), actor, in scene from film from: a, 1915. b, 1925 (clapboard in background). c, 1918 (film reel in background). d, 1925 (film reel in background). e, 1918 (strip of film in background). f, 1925 (standing next to actress).
No. 1881, 20m — Hirohito (1901-89), emperor of Japan, in suit and tie, and in background: a, Japanese flag, Hirohito in military uniform. b, Hirohito, waving, standing next to Empress Nakano. c, Japanese flag. d, Hirohito

as child, pagoda. e, Hirohito on horse, Japanese flag. f, Hirohito and Empress Nakano in gown.
No. 1882, 20m — Pres. John F. Kennedy (1917-63) and: a, Astronaut on moon. b, Kennedy at typewriter. c, Kennedy presidential campaign button. d, Family. e, Wife, Jacqueline, holding baby. f, Wedding photo.
No. 1883, 20m — Marilyn Monroe (1926-62), actress: a, Wearing costume from 1954 movie, wearing striped blouse. b, Wearing swimsuit, wearing green coat. c, Wearing top hat, wearing necklace. d, Wearing blue shorts. e, Looking through ship's porthole. f, Wearing short skirt and wearing red dress.
No. 1884, 20m — Elvis Presley (1935-77): a, Wearing white jacket and lei. b, Wearing red jacket, and jumping in air wearing cape. c, With four women. d, With arms raised, and with arms at neck. e, On telephone, wearing blue striped jacket. f, With guitar.
No. 1885, 20m — Michael Jackson (1958-2009), singer: a, Holding on to rail. b, Wearing top hat. c, Holding woman. d, As boy, with brothers. e, Speaking into microphone. f, Behind lectern, raising both arms.
No. 1886, 20m — Pope Benedict XVI: a, Facing forward, wearing miter, holding cross, arms at left. b, Wearing red hat, dove in flight. c, Facing left, wearing miter, holding cross, arms at left. d, Waving censer, arms at UR. e, With arms extended, dove on pedestal. f, Wearing red stole and zucchetto, arms at left.
No. 1887, 20m — Expo 2010, Shanghai: a, Nepal Pavilion. b, Africa Pavilion, with text beginning with "O tema." c, United Kingdom Pavilion. d, Romania Pavilion. e, African Pavilion, with text beginning with "A fachada." f, Japan Pavilion.
No. 1888, 33m — Galileo Galilei (1564-1642), astronomer, and: a, Leaning Tower of Pisa. b, Three people around telescope. c, Gear mechanism. d, Galileo's telescope. e, Telescope on wooden stand. f, Globe.
No. 1889, 33m — Johannes Kepler (1571-1630), astronomer, and: a, Moon. b, Kepler's model of the solar system and book, Mysterium Cosmographicum. c, Austrian coin depicting Kepler. d, Horoscope for General Wallenstein. e, Model of solar system. f, Model inscribed with Kepler's name.
No. 1890, 33m — George Frideric Handel (1685-1759), composer, and: a, Bust. b, Sculpture of Handel. c, Musical notes and orchestra hall in background. d, Engraving of Handel. e, Sculpture of lyre player. f, Handel's house in London.
No. 1891, 33m — William Kirby (1759-1850), entomologist: a, Kirby and Hychrysopus epicurus. b, Nicrophorus vespillo and Dytiscus marginalis. c, Kirby and unnamed butterfly. d, Kirby and Delias ninus. e, Polistes dominula and Philanthus triangulum. f, Kirby and Chilasa agestor.
No. 1892, 33m — Napoleon Bonaparte (1769-1821), emperor of France, and: a, French army. b, Battle of the Pyramids, 1798. c, Battle of Borodino, 1812. d, Imperial arms. e, Napoleon's bed. f, Battle of Arcola Bridge, 1796.
No. 1893, 33m — Joseph Haydn (1732-1809), composer, and: a, Haydn's house, Eisenstadt, Germany. b, Piano. c, Musicians. d, Haydn's birthplace. e, Esterházy Theater. f, Pianist.
No. 1894, 33m — Charles Darwin (1809-82), naturalist, and: a, Mimus trifasciatus. b, Allosaurus. c, Darwin's notes and okotohos. d, Desmodus d'Orbignyi. e, Lesothosaurus. f, Microraptor gui.
No. 1895, 33m — Louis Braille (1809-52), educator of the blind: a, Braille, at left, and blind boy reading book, at right. b, Braille Institute. c, Braille, at right, and blind boy writing in Braille, at left. d, Woman and seeing-eye dogs. e, Hands and book in Braille, at left, Braille, at right. f, Braille alphabet.
No. 1896, 33m — Katsushika Hokusai (1760-1849), artist: a, Poppies, ocean waves. b, Man, red mountain. c, Sumo wrestlers. d, Man on horseback. e, Palanquin carriers. f, Man and falcon.
No. 1897, 33m — Alexander von Humboldt (1769-1859), naturalist, and: a, Simia melanocephala. b, Rhexia speciosa. c, Simia leonina. d, Hibiscus. e, Convolvulus. f, Melastoma.
No. 1898, 33m — Georges-Pierre Seurat (1859-91), painter, and paintings on tripod: a, Young woman Powdering Herself (Muher jovem a maquilhar-se). b, The Reaper (O debulhador). c, The Stonebreaker. d, Chahut (O Chabut). e, A Sunday Afternoon on the Island of La Grande Jatte (Tarde de Domingo na Ilha da Grande Jatte). f, The Bridge - View of the Seine (A vista da ponte de Seine).
No. 1899, 33m — Sir Peter Scott (1909-89), founder of Worldwide Fund for Nature: a, Scott holding dog, painting of birds in flight. b, Scott feeding ducks, painting of ducks in flight. c, Scott facing left, painting of birds in flight. d, Scott with camera, painting of birds in flight. e, Scott facing forward, painting of birds in flight. f, Scott with binoculars, painting of ducks on water.
No. 1900, 33m — First man on the Moon, 40th anniv.: a, Neil Armstrong, Moon, Apollo 11 on launch pad. b, Neil Armstrong, Moon, Apollo 11 in flight. c, Apollo 11 Lunar Module above Moon,

Apollo 11 above Moon, Edwin E. Aldrin. e, Apollo 11, astronaut and American flag on Moon. f, Apollo 11 Command Module, Michael Collins.
No. 1901, 33m — International Polar Year: a, Iceberg and Odobenus rosmarus. b, Map of Antarctica, Belgium's Princess Elisabeth Antarctic Station. c, Map of Arctic Ocean and CCGS Amundsen. d, Intl. Polar Year emblem, iceberg, Ovibos moschatus. e, Map of Antarctica, Georg von Neumayer (1826-1909) and Karl Weyprecht (1838-81), polar explorers. f, Intl. Polar Year emblem, iceberg, Ursus maritimus.
No. 1902, 175m, Tiger and Forbidden City. No. 1903, 175m, Shen Chou and painting. No. 1904, 175m, Pope John Paul II giving communion to man. No. 1905, 175m, Gandhi. No. 1906, 175m, Xie Jin (1923-2008), Chinese film director. No. 1907, 175m, Ceremony of founding of the People's Republic of China. No. 1908, 175m, Chaplin. No. 1909, 175m, Emperor Hirohito, Empress Nakano and Queen Elizabeth II. No. 1910, 175m, Pres. Kennedy, White House. No. 1911, 175m, Monroe. No. 1912, 175m, Presley. No. 1913, 175m, Jackson and Slash. No. 1914, 175m, Pope Benedict XVI. No. 1915, 175m, Chinese Pavilion at Expo 2010, Shanghai. No. 1916, 175m, Galileo Galilei and men around globe. No. 1917, 175m, Kepler, telescope, planets. No. 1918, 175m, Handel. No. 1919, 175m, Kirby and Psuedotergumia pisidice. No. 1920, 175m, Map, Napoleon on horse. No. 1921, 175m, Haydn, harpsichord. No. 1922, 175m, Darwin and Rhea darwinii. No. 1923, 175m, Braille, teacher and blind students. No. 1924, 175m, Hokusai paintings of server of sake and mountain. No. 1925, 175m, Humboldt and specimens of flora and fauna. No. 1926, 175m, Artist's palette, Bathers at Asniers, by Seurat. No. 1927, 175m, Scott with camera on tripod, painting of birds in flight. No. 1928, 175m, Astronauts on moon, American flag. No. 1929, 175m, Iceberg, Alopes lagopus.

Perf. 12¾x13¼
2009, Nov. 30　　Litho.
Sheets of 6, #a-f
1874-1901　A411　Set of 28　375.00　375.00
Souvenir Sheets
Perf. 13¼ Syncopated
1902-1929　A411　Set of 28　375.00　375.00
On Nos. 1874-1901, stamps "a," "c," "d" and "f" are 37x38mm, stamps "b" and "e" are 50x38mm. Nos. 1902-1929 each contain one 50x38mm stamp.

Worldwide Fund for Nature (WWF) — A412

No. 1930 — Hippotragus equinus: a, Adult. b, Adult and juvenile. c, Adults at watering hole. d, Adults in grass.
175m, Adult grazing.

2010, Jan. 30　　Perf. 13x13¼
1930　A412　33m Block or strip of 4, #a-d　10.50　10.50
　e.　Souvenir sheet of 8, 2 each #1930a-1930d + 2 labels　21.00　21.00
Souvenir Sheet
Perf. 12¾x13¼
1931　A412　175m multi　13.50　13.50
No. 1931 contains one 37x38mm stamp.

The Natural World A413

No. 1932, 8m — Giraffes (Giraffa camelopardalis): a, Two giraffes, giraffe at right on ground. b, Herd of giraffes. c, Two giraffes, giraffe at left on ground. d, Adult and juvenile giraffes. e, Two giraffes, giraffe at left with front legs extended. f, Two adult giraffes standing.
No. 1933, 8m — Wild pigs: a, Sus scrofa facing right. b, Brown Sus scrofa facing left. c,

MOZAMBIQUE

Souvenir Sheet
Perf. 13¼ Syncopated
2045 A417 175m multi   13.50 13.50
No. 2045 contains one 50x39mm stamp.

French Castles A418

No. 2046 — Castle at: a, Chenonceau (38x39mm). b, Berzé (50x39mm). c, Montaner (38x39mm). d, Chaumont (38x39mm). e, Amboise (50x39mm). f, Brissac (38x39mm). 175m, Chambord Castle.

2010, June 30   *Perf. 13x13¼*
2046 A418 33m Sheet of 6,
      #a-f   15.50 15.50

Souvenir Sheet
Perf. 13¼ Syncopated
2047 A418 175m multi   13.50 13.50
No. 2047 contains one 50x39mm stamp.

Bridges A419

No. 2048: a, Beipanjiang Railroad Bridge, Guizhou, People's Republic of China (38x39mm). b, Sydney Harbour Bridge (50x39mm). c, Apollo Bridge, Bratislava, Slovakia (38x39mm). d, Millau Viaduct, Millau, France (38x39mm). e, Tsing Ma Bridge, Hong Kong (50x39mm). f, Coronado Bridge, San Diego, California (38x39mm). 175m, Tower Bridge, London.

2010, June 30   *Perf. 13x13¼*
2048 A419 33m Sheet of 6,
      #a-f   15.50 15.50

Souvenir Sheet
Perf. 13¼ Syncopated
2049 A419 175m multi   13.50 13.50
No. 2049 contains one 50x39mm stamp.

UNESCO World Heritage Sites — A420

No. 2050, 20m — Sites in Africa: a, Rock-hewn church, Lalibela, Ethiopia (38x39mm). b, Great Zimbabwe National Monument (50x39mm). c, Old towns of Djenné, Mali (38x39mm). d, Stone Circles of Senegambia, Gambia and Senegal (38x39mm). e, Timgad, Algeria (50x39mm). f, Carthage, Tunisia (38x39mm).
No. 2051, 20m — Sites in South America: a, Tiwanaku, Bolivia (38x39mm). b, Sacsayhuamán, Cuzco, Peru (38x39mm). c, Chan Chan, Peru (38x39mm). d, Rapa Nui, Chile (38x39mm). e, Machu Picchu, Peru (50x39mm). f, Jesuit Block and Estancias of Cordoba, Argentina (38x39mm).
No. 2052, 20m — Sites in Asia: a, Kathmandu Valley, Nepal (38x39mm). b, Buddhist ruins, Takht-i-Bati, Pakistan (50x39mm). c, Horyu-ji, Japan (38x39mm). d, Nemrut Dag, Turkey (38x39mm). e, Mogao Caves, People's Republic of China (50x39mm). f, Orkhon Valley Cultural Landscape, Mongolia (38x39mm).
No. 2053, 20m — Sites in Europe: a, Olympia, Greece (38x39mm). b, Bend of the Boyne Archaeological Site, Ireland (50x39mm). c, Trulli of Alberollo, Italy (38x30mm). d, Delos, Greece (38x39mm). e, Santiago de Compostela, Spain (50x39mm). f, Paphos, Cyprus (38x39mm).
No. 2054, 33m — Sites in Africa: a, Osun-Osogbo Sacred Grove, Nigeria (38x39mm). b, Carthage, Tunisia, diff. (50x39mm). c, Gorée Island, Senegal (38x39mm). d, El Jem Amphitheater, Tunisia (38x39mm). e, Dougga, Tunisia, diff. (38x39mm). f, Gebel Barkal, Sudan (38x39mm).
No. 2055, 33m — Sites in Africa: a, Cyrene, Libya (38x39mm). b, Leptis Magna, Libya (50x39mm). c, Aksum, Ethiopia (38x39mm). d,

Dougga, Tunisia, diff (38x39mm). e, Sabratha, Libya (50x39mm). f, Thebes, Egypt (38x39mm).
No. 2056, 33m — Sites in North America: a, Palenque, Mexico (38x39mm). b, Uxmal, Mexico (50x39mm). c, Mesa Verde National Park, U.S. (38x39mm). d, Mayan Ruins of Copan, Honduras (38x39mm). e, Teotihuacan, Mexico (50x39mm). f, Chichen-Itza, Mexico (38x39mm).
No. 2057, 33m — Sites in South America: a, Historic Center of Santa Ana de los Ríos de Cuenca, Ecuador (38x39mm). b, Machu Picchu, Peru, diff. (50x39mm). c, Rapa Nui, Chile, diff. (38x39mm). d, Tiwanaku, Bolivia, diff. (38x39mm). e, Rapa Nui, Chile, diff. (50x39mm). f, Sacsayhuamán, Cuzco, Peru, diff. (38x39mm).
No. 2058, 33m — Sites in Asia: a, Palmyra, Syria (38x39mm). b, Persepolis, Iran (50x39mm). c, Ruins of the Buddhist Vihara, Bangladesh (38x39mm). d, Nemrut Dag, Turkey, diff. (38x39mm). e, Tyre, Lebanon (50x39mm). f, Prambanan Temples, Indonesia (38x39mm).
No. 2059, 33m — Sites in Asia: a, Koguryo Tombs, North Korea (38x39mm). b, Palmyra, Syria, diff. (50x39mm). c, Polonnaruwa, Sri Lanka (38x39mm). d, Ayutthaya, Thailand (38x39mm). e, Bosra, Syria (50x39mm). f, Borobudur, Indonesia (38x39mm).
No. 2060, 33m — Sites in Europe: a, Grand-Place, Belgium (38x39mm). b, Historic Center of Rome, Italy (50x39mm). c, Rila Monastery, Bulgaria (38x39mm). d, Gardens and Castle at Kromeríz, Czech Republic (38x39mm). e, Piazza del Duomo, Pisa, Italy (50x39mm). f, Acropolis, Athens, Greece. (38x39mm).
No. 2061, 33m — Sites in Europe: a, Paphos Castle, Cyprus, diff. (38x39mm). b, Roman Monuments, Arles, France (50x39mm). c, Las Médulas, Spain (38x39mm). d, Megalithic Temples of Malta (38x39mm). e, Pont du Gard, France (50x39mm). f, Segovia Aqueduct, Spain (38x39mm).
No. 2062, 175m, Abu Simbel Temple, Egypt. No. 2063, 175m, Volubilis, Morocco. No. 2064, 175m, Sabratha, Libya, diff. No. 2065, 175m, Monte Albán, Mexico. No. 2066, 175m, Sacsayhuamán, Cuzco, Peru, diff. No. 2067, 175m, Rapa Nui, Chile, diff. No. 2068, 175m, Sanchi Buddhist Monuments, India. No. 2069, 175m, Lakshmana Temple, Khajuraho Group of Monuments, India. No. 2070, 175m, Lesahn Giant Buddha, People's Republic of China. No. 2071, 175m, Mérida, Archaeological Complex, Spain. No. 2072, 175m, Pompeii, Italy. No. 2073, 175m, Olympia, Greece, diff.

2010, June 30   *Perf. 13x13¼*
Sheets of 6, #a-f
2050-2061 A420 Set of 12   160.00 160.00

Souvenir Sheets
Perf. 13¼ Syncopated
2062-2073 A420 Set of 12   162.50 162.50
Nos. 2062-2073 each contain one 50x39mm stamp.

Museums and Art — A421

No. 2074, 20m — Museum of Modern Art, New York, and work of art by: a, Terry Winters (38x39mm). b, Lisa Yuskavage (50x39mm). c, Ken Price (38x39mm). d, Philip Guston (38x39mm). e, Vincent van Gogh (38x39mm). f, Robert Colescott (38x39mm).
No. 2075, 33m — Metropolitan Museum of Art, New York, and work of art by: a, Bernhard Strigel (38x39mm). b, Johannes Vermeer (50x39mm). c, Thomas Couture (38x39mm). d, Jean Baptiste Greuze (38x39mm). e, Giovanni Bellini (38x39mm). f, Adolphe-William Bouguereau (38x39mm).
No. 2076, 33m — Prado Museum, Madrid, and work of art by: a, Diego Velázquez (38x39mm). b, Francisco de Goya (38x39mm). c, Fra Angelico (38x39mm). d, Hieronymus Bosch (38x39mm). e, Bernaert van Orley (50x39mm). f, Raphael (38x39mm).
No. 2077, 33m — Uffizi Gallery (Galeria dos Oficios), Florence, Italy, and work of art by: a, Fra Filippo Lippi (38x39mm). b, Leonardo da Vinci (50x39mm). c, Andrea del Verrocchio (38x39mm). d, Sandro Botticelli (38x39mm). e, Giovanni Bellini (50x39mm). f, Raphael (38x39mm).
No. 2078, 33m — Orsay Museum, Paris, and work of art by: a, Claude Monet (38x39mm). b, Paul Signac (50x39mm). c, Edgar Degas (38x39mm). d, Paul Gauguin (38x39mm). e, Berthe Morisot (50x39mm). f, Vincent van Gogh (38x39mm).
No. 2079, 33m — Louvre Museum, Paris, and work of art by: a, Michelangelo Merisi da

Caravaggio (38x39mm). b, Hyacinthe Rigaud (50x39mm). c, Quentin Massys (38x39mm). d, Nicolas Poussin (38x39mm). e, Johannes Vermeer (38x39mm). f, Rogier van der Weyden (38x39mm).
No. 2080, 33m — National Gallery, London, and work of art by: a, Antonello da Messina (38x39mm). b, Jan van Eyck (50x39mm). c, Raphael (38x39mm). d, Thomas Gainsborough (38x39mm). e, Hans Holbein the Younger (50x39mm). f, Joseph Mallord William Turner (38x39mm).
No. 2081, 33m — National Museum, Amsterdam, and work of art by: a, Pieter Saenredam (38x39mm). b, Pieter Aertsen (50x39mm). c, Pieter de Hooch (38x39mm). d, Floris van Dijck (38x39mm). e, Jan van Scorel (50x39mm). f, Frans Hals (38x39mm).
No. 2082, 33m — Kunsthistorisches Museum, Vienna, and work of art by: a, Lucas Cranach the Elder (38x39mm). b, Jan Steen (50x39mm). c, Giuseppe Arcimboldo (Fogo, 1566) (38x39mm). d, Arcimboldo (Agua, 1566) (38x39mm). e, Pieter Bruegel the Elder (50x39mm). f, Giorgione (38x39mm).
No. 2083, 33m — Alte Pinakothek, Munich, and work of art by: a, Frans Hals (38x39mm). b, Fritz Schider (50x39mm). c, Hans Wertinger (38x39mm). d, Juan Pantoja de la Cruz (38x39mm). e, Philips Koninck (50x39mm). f, Jean Baptiste Siméon Chardin (38x39mm).
No. 2084, 33m — Gemäldegalerie, Berlin, and work of art by: a, Albrecht Dürer (38x39mm). b, Konrad Witz (50x39mm). c, Rogier van der Weyden (38x39mm). d, Raphael (38x39mm). e, Andrea Mantegna (50x39mm). f, Martin Schongauer (38x39mm).
No. 2085, 33m — Pushkin Museum of Fine Arts, Moscow, and work of art by: a, Maurice de Vlaminck (38x39mm). b, Jan Gossaert (50x39mm). c, Albert Marquet (38x39mm). d, Edgar Degas (38x39mm). e, Gustave Courbet (50x39mm). f, André Derain (38x39mm).
No. 2086, 33m — Hermitage State Museum, St. Petersburg, and work of art by: a, Thomas Gainsborough (38x39mm). b, Pieter Hendricksz de Hooch (50x39mm). c, Leonardo da Vinci (38x39mm). d, Paul Cézanne (38x39mm). e, Louis Le Nain (50x39mm). f, Unknown Egyptian sculptor (38x39mm).
No. 2087, 175m, Museum of Modern Art, work of art by Marlene Dumas. No. 2088, 175m, Metropolitan Museum of Art, work of art by Hokusai. No. 2089, 175m, Prado Museum, work of art by Bartolomé Esteban Murillo. No. 2090, 175m, Uffizi Gallery (Galeria dos Oficios), work of art by Agnolo Bronzino. No. 2091, 175m, Orsay Museum, work of art by Maurice Denis. No. 2092, 175m, Louvre Museum, work of art by Jan van Eyck. No. 2093, 175m, National Gallery, London, work of art by William Hogarth. No. 2094, 175m, National Museum, Amsterdam, work of art by Rembrandt. No. 2095, 175m, Kunsthistorisches Museum, work of art by Pieter Bruegel the Elder. No. 2096, 175m, Alte Pinakothek, work of art by Gerard ter Borch. No. 2097, 175m, Gemäldegalerie, work of art by Hans Holbein the Younger. No. 2098, 175m, Pushkin Museum of Fine Arts, work of art by Paul Cézanne. No. 2099, 175m, Hermitage State Museum, work of art by Vincent van Gogh.

2010, June 30   *Perf. 13x13¼*
Sheets of 6, #a-f
2074-2086 A421 Set of 13   195.00 195.00

Souvenir Sheets
Perf. 13¼ Syncopated
2087-2099 A421 Set of 13   175.00 175.00
Nos. 2087-2099 each contain one 50x39mm stamp.

Association of Portuguese-Speaking Postal and Telecommunications Organizations, 20th Anniv. — A422

2010, Nov. 10   *Litho.   Perf. 11x11½*
2100 A422 92m multi   7.25   7.25

People, Anniversaries and Events — A423

No. 2101, 66m — Jean-Henri Dunant (1828-1910), founder of Red Cross, world map, Red Cross and: a, Red Cross nurse holding child. b, Red Cross workers moving supplies. c, Red Cross worker tending to injured child. d, U.S. Naval Hospital Ship Comfort.
No. 2102, 66m — Katharine Hepburn (1907-2003), actress, and scene from: a, Sea of Grass, 1947. b, Mary of Scotland, 1936. c, A Woman Rebels, 1936. d, The Philadelphia Story, 1940.
No. 2103, 66m — Jonh Lennon (1940-80), singer, and: a, Beatles, peace sign. b, Yoko Ono, protest sign. c, Yoko Ono, guitar. d, Cat.
No. 2104, 66m — Lech Kaczynski (1949-2010), President of Poland, Polish flag, and: a, Wife, Maria, and heraldic eagle. b, Pope Benedict XVI. c, Tupelov Tu-154M. d, Wife, Maria.
No. 2105, 66m — Vasily Smyslov (1921-2010), chess player, and chess board with: a, Brown red squares. b, Blue gray squares. c, Dark blue squares, cat. d, Gray squares.
No. 2106, 66m — Marshall Warren Nirenberg (1927-2010), biochemist, and: a, Macrolepiota procerea. b, Boletus luidus. c, Agaricus albus. d, Agaricus nitidus.
No. 2107, 66m — Tsutomu Yamaguchi (1916-2010), survivor of Hiroshima and Nagasaki nuclear blasts, and: a, Mushroom cloud. b, Enola Gay over Hiroshima. c, Ruins of Hiroshima. d, Mushroom cloud, statue.
No. 2108, 66m — Republic of India, 60th anniv.: a, Mother Teresa, crowd, Hindu god Ganesh. b, Statue of Ganesh, people bathing in the Ganges River. c, Cow, Taj Mahal, mangos. d, Lotus flowers, Bengal tiger.
No. 2109, 66m — Armand Razafindratandra (1925-2010), Archbishop of Antananarivo, Madagascar, and: a, St. Peter's Basilica, cross on rosary. b, Church in Madagascar. c, St. Peter's Square. d, Pope John Paul II.
No. 2110, 66m — 2010 Visit of Pope Benedict XVI to Portugal: a, Pope, cardinals. b, Pope, Papal arms. c, Pope, crowd. d, Pope waving from balcony.
No. 2111, 66m — Paintings of Johannes Vermeer (1632-1675): a, Milkmaid, 1660, and Lacemaker, 1669. b, View of Delft, 1660-61, and Girl with a Pearl Earring, 1675. c, The Art of Painting (detail), 1673, painting of a city. d, The Girl with a Wine Glass, 1659-60, The Astronomer, 1668.
No. 2112, 66m — Mask paintings of James Ensor (1860-1949) from: a, 1892, 1925-29. b, 1898, 1892. c, 1888, 1927. d, 1892, 1908.
No. 2113, 175m, Dunant, world map, Red Cross flag. No. 2114, 175m, Hepburn, scene from The Iron Petticoat, 1956. No. 2115, 175m. Lennon and Yoko Ono, diff. No. 2116, 175m, Kaczynski, cross. No. 2117, 175m, Smyslov, chessboard. No. 2118, 175m, Nirenberg, Cortinarius torvus, diagram of ribonucleic acid molecule. No. 2119, 175m, Yamaguchi, mushroom cloud. No. 2120, 175m, Mohandas K. Gandhi, Indian flag, Nelumbo nucifera. No. 2121, 175m, Razafindratandra, arms. No. 2122, 175m, Pope Benedict XVI, crowd, diff. No. 2123, 175m, The Procuress, 1656, and Girl with a Red Hat, 1666, by Vermeer. No. 2124, 175m, Mask paintings from 1890 and 1888 by Ensor.

2010, Nov. 30   *Perf. 12¾x13½*
Sheets of 4, #a-d
2101-2112 A423 Set of 12   250.00 250.00

Souvenir Sheets
Perf. 13¼ Syncopated
2113-2124 A423 Set of 12   162.50 162.50
Nos. 2113-2124 each contain one 50x39mm stamp.

People, Anniversaries and Events — A424

No. 2125 — 70th birthday of Pelé, wearing New York Cosmos soccer jersey: a, 16m, And jacket with green collar, denomination at UR. b, 16m, Dribbling ball, denomination at UR. c, 16m, Scissor kicking, denomination at UL. d, 66m, Playing against players in green and yellow jerseys. e, 66m, Playing against player in blue, white and green uniforms. f, 66m, Playing against player in blue, orange and white uniforms.
No. 2126 — Athletes of Ninth South American Games: a, 16m, Yari Alvear. b, 16m,

MOZAMBIQUE

Facundo Argüello. c, 16m, Gustavo Tsuboi. d, 66m, Betsi Rivas. e, 66m, Mariana Pajon Londoño. f, 66m, Myke Carvalho.

No. 2127 — Princess Diana (1961-97) and: a, 16m, Tower Bridge, London. b, 16m, London Eye. sons William and Harry. c, 16m, Buckingham Palace. d, 66m, Houses of Parliament, sons William and Harry. e, 66m, Arms and British flag. f, 66m, St. Paul's Cathedral, Mother Teresa.

No. 2128 — Wedding of Prince William and Catherine Middleton: a, 16m, Windsor Castle, Prince William, Catherine Middleton. b, 16m, Princes William and Harry, Buckingham Palace. c, 16m, Palace of Westminster, Prince William, Catherine Middleton. d, 66m, Prince William, map of Great Britain. e, 66m, Prince William, Catherine Middleton, Princess Diana. f, 66m, Prince William, Catherine Middleton, Westminster Abbey.

No. 2129 — Alfred Hitchcock (1899-1988), movie director, and scene from: a, 16m, Vertigo, 1958. b, 16m, Dial M for Murder, 1954. c, 16m, Spellbound, 1945. d, 66m, Rear Window, 1954. e, 66m, Rebecca, 1940. f, 66m, The Birds, 1963.

No. 2130 — Japanese high-speed trains: a, 16m, Joetsu Shinkansen E4 Max Toki. b, 16m, Tohoku Akita Shinkansen Komachi. c, 16m, Nagano Shinkansen E2 Asama. d, 66m, Tokaido Shinkansen 700 Nozomi. e, 66m, Tokaido Shinkansen 500 Nozomi. f, 66m, Tokaido Shinkansen N700 Nozomi.

No. 2131 — European high-speed trains: a, 16m, ICE Bombardieer, Germany. b, 16m, Thalys, Belgium. c, 16m, Eurostar, Great Britain. d, 66m, Eurostar, Italy. e, 66m, 103 Velaro E Siemens, Spain. f, 66m, TGV, France.

No. 2132 — Paintings by Amedeo Modigliani (1884-1920) from: a, 16m, 1915-16 and 1898-1920. b, 16m, 1918 and 1916. c, 16m, 1917 and 1918. d, 66m, 1917 and 1898-1920. e, 66m, 1915 and 1918. f, 66m, 1909 and 1898-1920.

No. 2133 — Vitaly Sevastyanov (1935-2010), cosmonaut: a, 16m, Wearing suit and tie, with Soyuz TMA-9. b, 16m, Wearing space suit, with Soyuz TMA-18 in space. c, 16m, Wearing suit, with Soyuz TMA-18 in space. d, 66m, Wearing space suit, with Soyuz TMA-18 in space. e, 66m, Wearing suit and tie, with Soyuz TMA-9 being prepared for launch. f, 66m, Wearing suit with military medals, with Salyut 6.

No. 2134 — IKAROS experimental spacecraft: a, 16m, In space, with text over Venus. b, 16m, With H-IIA rocket lifting off. c, 16m, In space, with Venus cut off at top. d, 66m, With rocket H-IIA lifting off, diff. e, 66m, In space, with Venus partially obscured. f, 66m, Akatsuki Vesus orbiter and Earth.

No. 2135 — World development of electrical energy: a, 16m, Earth and stylized birds. b, 16m, Greek philosopher Thales. c, 16m, Silhouettes of people, clouds. d, 66m, Hand with antique map. e, 66m, Inventor Thomas Alva Edison and lightbulb. f, 66m, Chinese Premier Sun Yat-sen and dam.

No. 2136, 175m, Pelé. No. 2137, 175m, Santiago Botero, cyclist. No. 2138, 175m, Princess Diana with youths, Red Cross. No. 2139, 175m, Prince William, Catherine Middleton, engagement ring. No. 2140, 175m, Hitchcock, scene from Psycho, 1960. No. 2141, 175m, 320 kmh Shinkansen train, 2011. No. 2142, 175m, ALSTOM AGV, France. No. 2143, 175m, Paintings by Modigliani from 1919 and 1918. No. 2144, 175m, Sevastyanov and Salyut 4. No. 2145, 175m, IKAROS and H-IIA rocket lifting off, diff. No. 2146, 175m, Luigi Galvani, and diagram of his experiments with frogs.

2010, Nov. 30 Perf. 12¾x13½
Sheets of 6, #a-f
2125-2135 A424 Set of 11 210.00 210.00

Souvenir Sheets
Perf. 13¼ Syncopated
2136-2146 A424 Set of 11 150.00 150.00

People, Anniversaries and Events — A425

No. 2147, 16m — New Year 2011 (Year of the Rabbit): a, Rabbit sitting, facing right, Chinese character to right or rabbit. b, Rabbit facing left, Chinese character to left of rabbit. c, Rabbit running left, Chinese character above rabbit. d, Rabbit running right, chinese character to right of rabbit, below head, text at UL. e, Rabbit with front legs raised, Chinese character to right of rabbit. f, Rabbit leaping, Chinese character below rabbit's hind legs. g, Rabbit standing, facing left, Chinese character to left of rabbit. h, Rabbit standing, facing right, Chinese character to right of rabbit, text at LR.

No. 2148, 16m — Views of Ocean Park, Hong Kong and: a, Ailurus fulgens. b, Zalophus californianus. c, Delphinus delphis. d, Ailuropoda melanoleuca. e, Ramphastos toco. f, Chrysaora fuescens. g, Phoenicopterus roseus. h, Ara ararauna.

No. 2149, 16m — 2010 Commonwealth Games, Delhi, India: a, Achanta Sharath Kamal, table tennis player. b, Allan Davis, cyclist. c, Anastasia Rodionova, tennis player. d, Christine Girard, weight lifter. e, Paddy Barnes, boxer. f, Alicia Coutts, swimmer. g, Alison Shanks, cyclist. h, Azhar Hussain, wrestler.

No. 2150 — Details from paintings by Caravaggio (1571-1610) dated: a, 16m, 1594-95 and 1593-94. b, 16m, 1600-04 and 1593-94. c, 16m, 1607-08 and 1593-94. d, 16m, 1596 and 1601. e, 16m, 1597 and 1595-96. f, 16m, 1598 and 1596-98. g, 92m, 1598-99 and 1599. h, 92m, 1603 and 1608.

No. 2151 — Tony Curtis (1925-2010), actor, and scenes from: a, 16m, Houdini, 1953. b, 16m, Son of Ali Baba, 1952. c, 16m, The Defiant Ones, 1958. d, 16m, The Black Shield of Falworth, 1954. e, 16m, The Great Race, 1965. f, 16m, Wild and Wonderful, 1964. g, 92m, Some Like it Hot, 1959. h, 92m, Sweet Smell of Success, 1957.

No. 2152 — BP Deepwater Horizon oil spill: a, 16m, Bird standing, burning oil rig. b, 16m, Turtle in net, oil boom on water, burning rig. c, 16m, Bird in flight, ships near burning rig. d, 16m, Pelican, boat with oil boom in oil slick. e, 16m, Bird with head raised in oily water. f, 16m, Ship, bird on piling, oil burning on water's surface. g, 92m, Bird, cleanup workers on beach. h, 92m, Birds, burning rig, map of Gulf of Mexico coastline.

No. 2153 — Details of religious paintings by: a, 16m, Titian, from 1535 and 1540 . b, 16m, Alessandro Botticelli, from 1490 and 1470. c, 16m, El Greco, from 1600 and 1590-95. d, 16m, Giotto, from 1295-1300 and 1304. e, 16m, Rogier van der Weyden, from 1445 and 1435-40. f, 16m, Antonio da Correggio, from 1525 and 1520. g, 92m, Piero della Francesca, from 1450-63 and 1454-69. h, 92m, Giovanni Bellini, from 1465 and 1464-68.

No. 2154, 175m, Rabbit and Chinese character, diff. No. 2155, 175m, Stegostoma fasciatum in Ocean Park tank. No. 2156, 175m, Somdev Devvarman, tennis player. No. 2157, 175m, Painting details by Caravaggio, from 1609 and 1593-94. No. 2158, 175m, Curtis, scene from movie. No. 2159, 175m, Bird in flight near burning BP Deepwater Horizon oil rig. No. 2160, 175m, Painting details by Lorenzo Lotto from 1508 and 1530.

2010, Nov. 30 Perf. 12¾x13½
Sheets of 8, #a-h
2147-2153 A425 Set of 7 120.00 120.00

Souvenir Sheets
Perf. 13¼ Syncopated
2154-2160 A425 Set of 7 95.00 95.00

Intl. Year of Forests A426

No. 2161 — Sheet inscribed "Gibao de maos brancas": a, 16m, Hylobates lar sitting on tree branch. b, 16m, Hylobates lar hanging from tree branch. c, 16m, Hylobates lar walking. d, 16m, Hylobates lar, leaves of palm tree beneath denomination. e, 66m, Hylobates lar seated. f, 66m, Hylobates lar seated on stump.

No. 2162 — Sheet inscribed "Lémur": a, 16m, Lemur catta facing left with tail raised. b, 16m, Lemur catta, tail at bottom. c, 16m, Lemur catta facing right with tail raised. d, 16m, Lemur catta with tail over shoulder. e, 66m, Lemur catta with tail around head. f, 66m, Lemur catta with tail hanging.

No. 2163 — Sheet inscribed "Preguiça": a, 16m, Choloepus didactylus. b, 16m, Bradypus pygmaeus. c, 16m, Choloepus hoffmanni. d, 16m, Bradypus variegatus. e, 66m, Choloepus hoffmanni, diff. f, 66m, Choloepus didactylus, diff.

No. 2164 — Sheet inscribed "Rinoceronte-de-sumatra": a, 16m, Dicerorhinus sumatrensis facing right with head near ground. b, 16m, Dicerorhinus sumatrensis facing left with head raised. c, 16m, Dicerorhinus sumatrensis facing left with head near ground. d, 16m, Dicerorhinus sumatrensis facing left with head raised. e, 66m, Dicerorhinus sumatrensis facing left with head raised, diff. f, 66m, Dicerorhinus sumatrensis facing left, diff.

No. 2165 — Sheet inscribed "Morcego-Vampiro": a, 16m, Desmodus rotundus facing right, in flight . b, 16m, Desmodus rotundus on rock, blue area surrounding denomination. c, 16m, Desmodus rotundus on rock, rock under "16". d, 16m, Desmodus rotundus facing left, in flight. e, 66m, Desmodus rotundus in flight, diff. f, 66m, Desmodus rotundus on rock, diff.

No. 2166 — Sheet inscribed "Jaguar": a, 16m, Panthera onca facing left on cut off tree branch. b, 16m, Panthera onca on fallen log. c, 16m, Panthera onca on grass. d, 16m, Panthera onca walking. e, 66m, Panthera onca walking, facing left. f, 66m, Panthera onca walking, facing forward.

No. 2167 — Sheet inscribed "Peixi-boi": a, 16m, Trichechus inunguis, left fin close to frame line at bottom. b, 16m, Two Trichechus senegalensis. c, 16m, One Trichechus manatus. d, 16m, Trichechus inunguis, right fin close to frame line at bottom. e, 66m, Two Trichecus manatus. f, 66m, One Trichechus senegalensis.

No. 2168 — Sheet inscribed "Harpia": a, 16m, Harpia harpyja facing right on tree branch with leaves. b, 16m, Harpia harpyja in flight near tree. c, 16m, Harpia harpyja facing left on branch without leaves. d, 16m, Harpia harpyja facing left on tree branch with leaves. e, 66m, Harpia harpyja in flight, tree in background. f, 66m, Harpia harpyja in flight, no trees in background.

No. 2169 — Sheet inscribed "Borboleta asas de pássaro": a, 16m, Ornithoptera alexandrae on leaf, name at LL. b, 16m, Ornithoptera alexandrae in flight. c, 16m, Ornithoptera alexandrae on leaf, name at UR. d, 16m, Ornithoptera alexandrae on leaf, name at UL. e, 66m, Ornithoptera alexandrae on leaf, diff. f, 66m, Ornithoptera alexandrae in flight, diff.

No. 2170 — Sheet inscribed "Borboleta azul": a, 16m, Morpho menelaus on leaf with wings closed, name at UL. b, 16m, Morpho menelaus on tree with wings open, name at UR. c, 16m, Morpho memelaus on tree with wings partially open, name at UL. d, 16m, Morpho menelaus on rock with wings open, name at LL. e, 66m, Morpho menelaus on leaf, name at UL on two lines. f, 66m, Morpho menelaus on leaf, name at UL on one line.

No. 2171 — Sheet inscribed "Piranha": a, 16m, Pygocentrus ternetzi. b, 16m, Serrasalmus manueli. c, 16m, Pygocentrus nattereri. d, 16m, Pygocentrus cariba. e, 66m, Pygocentrus nattereri, diff. f, 66m, Pygocentrus ternetzi, diff.

No. 2172 — Sheet inscribed "Cobra-papagaio": a, 16m, Corallus caninus on branch, head at top of stamp. b, 16m, Corallus caninus on branch, head at LL. c, 16m, Corallus caninus, head at LR. d, 16m, Corallus caninus on branch, head at bottom center. e, 66m, Corallus caninus on branch, head in center, tail visible. f, 66m, Corallus caninus on branch, head at left, tail not visible.

No. 2173 — Sheet inscribed "Jacaré-açu": a, 16m, Melanosuchus niger in grass. b, 16m, Melanosuchus niger swimming. c, 16m, Melanosuchus niger standing, facing right. d, 16m, Melanosuchus niger standing, facing forward. e, 66m, Juvenile melanosuchus niger in water. f, 66m, Melanosuchus niger with mouth open.

No. 2174 — Sheet inscribed "Ra de olhos vermelhos": a, 16m, Agalychnis callidryas on vine, name at LR. b, 16m, Agalychnis callidryas facing right with rear leg extended at top, name at UR. c, 16m, Agalychnis callidryas facing left, name at UR. d, 16m, Agalychnis callidryas on vine, name at UL. e, 66m, Agalychnis callidryas on vine, name at LL. f, 66m, Agalychnis callidryas on vine, name at LR.

No. 2175 — Sheet inscribed "Tartaruga": a, 16m, Trachemys scripta elegans. b, 16m, Geochelone sulcata. c, 16m, Malaclemys terrapin. d, 16m, Chelus fimbriatus. e, 66m, Chelonoidis carbonaria. f, 66m, Terrepene carolina carolina.

No. 2176 — Sheet inscribed "Jupará": a, 16m, Potus flavus, head at UL, name at UR. b, 16m, Potos flavus on vine, name at UR. c, 16m, Potos flavus, head at LL, name at UR. d, 92m, Potos flavus standing, name at UR. diff. e, 92m, Potos flavus, name at UL, diff. f, 92m, potos flavus in tree, name at UR.

No. 2177 — Sheet inscribed "Gorila": a, 16m, Gorilla beringei graueri, name at LR. b, 16m, Gorilla beringei. c, 16m, Gorilla gorilla diehli. d, 16m, Gorilla beringei graueri, name at UR. e, 92m, Gorilla gorilla. f, 92m, Gorilla gorilla gorilla.

No. 2178 — Sheet inscribed "Ateles": a, 16m, Ateles hybridus, name at right. b, 16m, Ateles chamek. c, 16m, Trichechus manatus. d, 16m, Ateles hybridus, name at UR. e, 92m, Ateles paniscus. f, 92m, Ateles hybridus, diff.

No. 2179 — Sheet inscribed "Társio": a, 16m, Tarsius syrichta, name at UR. b, 16m, Tarsius bancanus. c, 16m, Tarsius syrichta, name at LR. d, 16m, Tarsius tarsier. e, 16m, Tarsius dentatus. f, 92m, Tarsius syrichta, name at UL.

No. 2180 — Sheet inscribed "Tigris de Bengala": a, 16m, Panthera tigris, name at left. b, 16m, Panthera tigris tigris. c, 16m, Panthera tigris in water, name at right. d, 16m, Panthera tigris in grass, name at UR. e, 92m, Panthera tigrist tigris laying down. f, 92m, Panthera tigris tigris walking.

No. 2181 — Sheet inscribed "Calaubicórnico": a, 16m, Buceros bicornis on branch, name at UR. b, 16m, Buceros bicornis in flight, name at LR. c, 16m, Buceros bicornis on branch on tree at left, name at UR. d, 16m, Buceros bicornis on branch, name at LL. e, 92m, Buceros bicornis in flight, name at UL. f, 92m, Buceros bicornis in flight, name at LR, diff.

No. 2182 — Sheet inscribed "Casuario Austral": a, 16m, Casuarius causarius sitting, name at UL. b, 16m, Casuarius causarius standing, name at right. c, 16m, Casuarius casuarius standing, name at left. d, 16m, Casuarius casuarius with leg lifted, name at left. e, 92m, Cauarius casuarius, name at LL. f, 92m, Casuaraius casuarius, name at UL.

No. 2183 — Sheet inscribed "Coruja": a, 16m, Tyto multipunctata. b, 16m, Ninox connivens. c, 16m, Glaucidium tephronotum. d, 16m, Asio madagascariensis. e, 92m, Ninox novaeseelandiae. f, 92m, Otus rutilus.

No. 2184 — Sheet inscribed "Papagaio": a, 16m, Lorus garrulus. b, 16m, Trichoglossus chlorolepidotus. c, 16m, Trichoglottus flavoviridis. d, 16m, Trichoglossus euteles. e, 92m, Eos reticulata. f, 92m, Trichoglossus haematodus.

No. 2185 — Sheet inscribed "Quetzalresplandecente": a, 16m, Pharomachrus mocinno on brach, name at right. b, 16m, Pharomachrus mocinno on branch, name at UR. c, 16m, Pharomachrus mocinno on branch, name at LR. d, 16m, Pharomachrus mocinno on branch, name at LL. e, 92m, Pharomachrus mocinno on branch, name at LR, diff. f, 92m, Pharomachrus mocinno on branch, name at LL, diff.

No. 2186 — Sheet inscribed "Tucano": a, 16m, Ramphastos dicolorus. b, 16m, Ramphastos toco. c, 16m, Ramphastos vitellinus. d, 16m, Ramphastos swainsonii. e, 92m, Ramphastos torquatus. f, 92m, Ramphastos sulfuratus.

No. 2187 — Sheet inscribed "Libélula": a, 16m, Anax imperator. b, 16m, Libellula depressa. c, 16m, Sympetrum fonscolombii. d, 16m, Libellula quadrimaculata. e, 92m, Ischnura heterosticta. f, 92m, Crocothemis sanguinolenta.

No. 2188 — Sheet inscribed "Borboletamonarca": a, 16m, Danaus plexippus on flower, antennae near flower, name at right. b, 16m, Danaus plexippus on flower, antennae near denomination, name at right. c, 16m, Danaus plexippus on flower, name at UL, denomination at UR. d, 16m, Danaus plexippus on flower, name below denomination at UL. e, 92m, Danaus plexippus on branch, name at UL. f, 92m, Danaus plexippus on flower, name at LL.

No. 2189 — Sheet inscribed "Dendrobatidae": a, 16m, Epipedobates tricolor. b, 16m, Dendrobates auratus. c, 16m, Dendrobates azureus. d, 16m, Dendrobates leucomelas. e, 92m, Phyllobates terribilis. f, 92m, Oophaga pumilio.

No. 2190 — Sheet inscribed "Víbora do Gabao": a, 16m, Bitis gabonica, head at LL, name at LR. b, 16m, Bitis gabonica in grass, head in center, name at LR. c, 16m, Bitis gabonica, name at UL. d, 16m, Bitis gabonica on parched earth, head in center, name at LR. e, 92m, Bitis gabonica, name at LL. f, 92m, Bitis gabonica, name at UR.

No. 2191, 175m, Hylobates lar, diff. No. 2192, 175m, Lemur catta, diff. No. 2193, 175m, Bradypus variegatus, diff. No. 2194, 175m, Three Dicerorhinus sumatrensis. No. 2195, 175m, Desmodus rotundus, diff. No. 2196, 175m, Panthera onca, diff. No. 2197, 175m, Two Trichechus inunguis. No. 2198, 175m, Harpia harpyja in flight, diff. No. 2199, 175m, Ornithoptera alexandrae on leaf, diff. No. 2200, 175m, Two Morpho menelaus on leaves. No. 2201, 175m, Two Pygocentrus nattereri. No. 2202, 175m, Coprallus caninus on tree branch. No. 2203, 175m, Melanosuchus niger, diff. No. 2204, 175m, Agalychnis callidryas, diff. No. 2205, 175m, Geochelone sulcata, diff. No. 2206, 175m, Potos flavus, diff. No. 2207, 175m, Gorilla gorilla, diff. No. 2208, 175m, Ateles hybridus, diff. No. 2209, 175m, Tarsius pumilus, diff. No. 2210, 175m, Panthera tigris, diff. No. 2211, 175m, Buceros bicornis, diff. No. 2212, 175m, Casuarius casuarius, diff. No. 2213, 175m, Asio madagascariensis, diff. No. 2214, 175m, Trichoglossus rubritorquis, diff. No. 2215, 175m, Pharomachrus mocinno, diff. No. 2216, 175m, Ramphastos sulfuratus, diff. No. 2217, 175m, Trithemis kirbyi. No. 2218, 175m, Danaus plexippus on flower, diff. No. 2219, 175m, Dendrobates azureus, diff. No. 2220, 175m, Bitis gabonica, diff.

2011, Jan. 30 Perf. 12¾x13½
Sheets of 6, #a-f
2161-2190 A426 Set of 30 525.00 525.00

MOZAMBIQUE

Souvenir Sheets
Perf. 13½x12¾

2191-2220	A426	Set of 30	400.00	400.00

Television in Mozambique, 30th Anniv. — A427

Denominations: 66m, 92m.

2011, Feb. 28   Litho.   Perf. 11x11¼

2221-2222	A427	Set of 2	12.50	12.50

People, Events and Anniversaries — A428

No. 2223 — George Clooney, actor, and scenes from his films: a, 16m, Solaris. b, 16m, The American. c, 66m, Ocean's 12. d, 92m, The Good German.

No. 2224 — Elizabeth Taylor (1932-2011), actress: a, 16m, Wearing black dress, wearing white dress holding Oscar. b, 16m, Wearing brown dress, wearing white dress. c, 66m, Holding dog. d, 92m, With Michael Jackson.

No. 2225 — Roald Amundsen (1872-1928), Antarctic explorer and scenes from his 1911 expedition: a, 16m, With Norwegian flag at South Pole. b, 16m, With expedition members making scientific observations. c, 66m, Standing in hut. d, 92m, With dog team and Norwegian flag.

No. 2226 — Fridtjof Nansen (1961-1930), polar explorer, and: a, 16m, Arctocephalus gazella. b, 16m, Orcinus orca. c, 66m, Aptenodytes forsteri. d, 92m, Ship named Fridtjof Nansen.

No. 2227 — First airmail flight, cent.: a, 16m, Pilot Henri Pequet, airplane, maps. b, 16m, Pilot Earle Lewis Ovington and airplane. c, 66m, Pilot Fred J. Wiseman and airplane. d, 92m, Airplane of Fred J. Wiseman used in airmail flight from Petaluma to Santa Rosa, California.

No. 2228 — Andor Lilienthal (1911-2010), chess grandmaster, chess board and pieces, and: a, 16m, David Bronstein. b, 16m, Ruslan Ponomariov. c, 66m, Lilienthal playing chess. d, 92m, Lilienthal playing against 121 opponents.

No. 2229 — Maia Chiburdanidze, chess grandmaster, and: a, 16m, Chess board in purple. b, 16m, Chess board in gray blue. c, 66m, Knight. d, 92m, Rook and pawn.

No. 2230 — Japanese earthquake relief: a, 16m, Red Cross worker feeding infant. b, 16m, Workers carrying dead body. c, 66m, Red Cross worker watching fire. d, 92m, Fireman with hose.

No. 2231 — Chiune Sugihara (1900-86), Japanese diplomat who saved Jews in World War II, and: a, 16m, Jews, star of David. b, 16m, Sugihara in chair. c, 66m, Sugihara and his family. d, 92m, Monument to Sugihara in Vilnius, Lithuania.

No. 2232 — Rajiv Gandhi (1944-91), Indian prime minister, and: a, 16m, With Indians and cow. b, 16m, With family. c, 66m, With Mother Teresa. d, 92m, Standing in automobile.

No. 2233 — Paintings by Lucas Cranach, the Younger (1515-86): a, 16m, Portrait of a Woman, 1539. b, 16m, Prince Elector Moritz of Saxony, 1578. c, 66m, Elector Johann Friedrich of Saxony, 1578. d, 92m, Portrait of a Woman, diff.

No. 2234 — Paintings by Giorgio Vasari (1511-74): a, 16m, Lorenzo de Medici, 1533. b, 16m, Battle of Lepanto. c, 66m, St. Luke Painting the Virgin. d, 92m, Entombment.

No. 2235 — Franz Liszt (1811-86), composer, and: a, 16m, Liszt's house in Weimar, Germany from 1869-86. b, 16m, Budapest Opera House. c, 66m, Liszt's residence from 1863-69, Madonna del Rosario Monastery. d, 92m, Birthplace, Dobroján, Hungary.

No. 2236 — Gustav Mahler (1860-1911), composer, and: a, 16m, Hofoper Building, Vienna. c, 66m, Metropolitan Oper, New York. d, 92m, Symphony orchestra, diff.

No. 2237 — Princess Diana (1961-97), and: a, 16m, Elton John. b, 16m, Baroness Chalker. c, 66m, Prince Charles, Ronald and Nancy Reagan. d, 92m, Michael Jackson.

No. 2238 — Human evolution: a, 16m, Australopithecus africanus. b, 16m, Homo habilis. c, 16m, Homo antecessor. d, 92m, Homo heidelbergensis.

No. 2239, 175m, Clooney, director's chair, projector, film reels. No. 2240, 175m, Taylor, diff. No. 2241, 175m, Amundsen and ship trapped in ice. No. 2242, 175m, Nansen, ship and Ursus maritimus. No. 2243, 175m, Pequet and airplane. No. 2244, 175m, Lilienthal playing chess, diff. No. 2245, 175m, Chiburdanidze, diff. No. 2246, 175m, Japanese firefighter holding hose at fire at industrial complex. No. 2247, 175m, Sugihara and refugees. No. 2248, 175m, Rajiv Gandhi and children. No. 2249, 175m, The Ill Matched Lovers, painting by Lucas Cranach, the Younger. No. 2250, 175m, The Walk to Emmaus, painting by Lelio Orsi. No. 2251, 175m, Liszt and Franz Liszt Music Academy, Budapest. No. 2252, 175m, Mahler and symphony orchestra, diff. No. 2253, 175m, Princess Diana, roses, Nepalese children. No. 2254, 175m, Australopithecus afarensis, map of Africa.

2011, Apr. 30   Perf. 13½x12¾
Sheets of 4, #a-d

2223-2238	A428	Set of 16	240.00	240.00

Souvenir Sheets

2239-2254	A428	Set of 16	225.00	225.00

People, Events and Anniversaries — A429

No. 2255 — James Gandolfini, actor, and scenes from: a, 16m, Surviving Christmas, 2004. b, 16m, Lonely Hearts, 2006. c, 16m, The Last Castle, 2001. d, 16m, Welcome to the Rileys, 2010. e, 66m, The Sopranos, 1999-2007. f, 92m, In the Loop, 2009.

No. 2256 — Joseph Barbera (1911-2006), cartoon director, and: a, 16m, Abbott and Costello cartoon characters. b, 16m, Top Cat. c, 16m, William Hanna, production drawings of cartoon characters for Magilla Gorilla. d, 16m, Huckleberry Hound and elephant. e, 00m, Motormouse and Autocat. f, 92m, Huckleberry Hound with guitar.

No. 2257 — Ishiro Honda (1911-93), film director and scene from: a, 16m, Ghidorah, the Three-Headed Monster. b, 16m, Battle in Outer Space, 1959. c, 16m, Godzilla, 1954. d, 16m, Destroy All Monsters, 1968. e, 66m, Frankenstein Conquers the World, 1965. f, 92m, Yog: Monster from Space, 1970.

No. 2258 — American Civil War soldiers: a, 16m, Three Union soldiers and flag, 1864. b, 16m, Three Confederate soldiers with guns, 1861. c, 16m, Horse, flag and three Union soldiers, 1863. d, 16m, Three Confederate soldiers (one aiming rifle), 1861. e, 66m, Two Union cavalrymen with horses. f, 92m, Three Union soldiers, 1864, diff.

No. 2259 — Antarctic Treaty: a, 16m, Orcinus orca. b, 16m, Pygoscelis adeliae. c, 16m, Pagodroma nivea nivea. d, 16m, Channichthyidae. e, 66m, Arctocephalus gazella. f, 92m, Balaenoptera musculus.

No. 2260 — Beatification of Pope John Paul II. a, 10m, Pope grasping man around head. b, 16m, Pope pointing. c, 16m, Pope with Mother Teresa. d, 16m, Pope with St. Peter's Basilica in background. e, 66m, Pope greeting people. f, 92m, Pope wearing miter, holding crucifix.

No. 2261 — Automobiles from first Monte Carlo Rally, 1911: a, 16m, Turcat-Mery. b, 16m, Gobron 40 HP. c, 16m, Berliet 16 HP. d, 16m, Gobron-Brillié 40/60 CV. e, 66m, Delaunay-Belleville 15 HP. f, 92m, Dürkopp.

No. 2262 — Juan Manuel Fangio (1911-95), race car driver: a, 16m, Ferrari-Lancia d50. b, 16m, Flipped race car. c, 16m, Maserati 250F. d, 16m, Ferrari 166. e, 66m, Mercedes-Benz W 196. f, 92m, Ferrari-Lancia d50, diff.

No. 2263 — Madame Tussaud Wax Museum sculptures: a, 16m, Albert Einstein. b, 16m, Princess Diana and Prince William. c, 16m, Mahatma Gandhi. d, 16m, Marilyn Monroe. e, 66m, Pope John Paul II. f, 92m, Elvis Presley.

No. 2264 — Alan B. Shepard, Jr. (1923-98), astronaut, and: a, 16m, Saturn V rocket. b, 16m, Mercury-Redstone rocket. c, 16m, Mercury 3 capsule (Freedom 7). d, 16m, Shephard in space suit. e, 66m, Pres. John F. Kennedy. f, 92m, Shepard in space capsule.

No. 2265 — Space Shuttle Challenger astronauts: a, 16m, Gregory Jarvis. b, 16m, Judith Resnik. c, 16m, Ellison Onizuka. d, 16m, Dick Scobee. e, 66m, Ronald McNair. f, 92m, Michael J. Smith.

No. 2266 — Yuri Gagarin (1934-68), first man in space: a, 16m, Gagarin and drawing of cosmonaut and space capsule. b, 16m, Vostok I. c, 16m, Gagarin and rocket launch. d, 16m, Gagarin and spacecraft in flight. e, 66m, Gagarin in Space helmet Autocat. f, 92m, Gagarin and drawing of rocket and space capsule.

No. 2267 — Mir Space Station, 25th anniv: a, 16m, Mir and rocket launch. b, 16m, Mir in space, denomination at UL. c, 16m, Mir and cosmonauts. d, 16m, Mir in space, denomination at UR. e, 66m, Mir and space shuttle. f, 92m, Mir and pieces descending to Earth.

No. 2268 — Wedding of Prince William and Catherine Middleton: a, 16m, Prince Charles and Princess Diana at UR. b, 16m, Westminster Abbey, denomination at UL. c, 16m, Prince Charles and Princess Diana at UL. d, 16m, Westminster Abbey, denomination at UR. e, 66m, Prince Charles, Princess Diana, horse. f, 92m, Westminster Abbey, denomination at UR, diff.

No. 2269, 175m, Gandolfini and scene from The Man Who Wasn't There. No. 2270, 175m, Barbera, Hanna, Autocat and Fred Flintstone. No. 2271, 175m, Honda and scene from Mothra, 1961. No. 2272, 175m, Six Confederate soldiers. No. 2273, 175m, Hydrurga leptonyx. No. 2274, 175m, Pope John Paul II, Mother Teresa. No. 2275, 175m, Turcat-Mery car in first Monte Carlo Rally. No. 2276, 175m, Fangio and Mercedes-Benz W196, diff. No. 2277, 175m, Wax sculptures of Marie Tussaud. No. 2278, 175m, Shepard, Mercury 3 rocket, Apollo 14 emblem. No. 2279, 175m, Challenger astronaut Christa McAuliffe. No. 2280, 175m, Gagarin and space capsule in flight. No. 2281, 175m, Mir in space, diff. No. 2282, 175m, Prince William, Catherine Middleton, Princess Diana and Prince Charles.

2011, Apr. 30   Perf. 12¾x13½
Sheets of 6, #a-f

2255-2268	A429	Set of 14	240.00	240.00

Souvenir Sheets
Perf. 13½x12¾

2269-2282	A429	Set of 14	190.00	190.00

People, Events and Anniversaries — A430

No. 2283 — Beatification of Pope John Paul II: a, 16m, Pope John Paul II wearing miter at left. b, 16m, Pope John Paul praying at right. c, 66m, Pope John Paul II and St. Peter's Basilica. d, 92m, Pope John Paul II greeting crowd.

No. 2284 — Mohandas K. Gandhi (1869-1948), Indian independence leader, and: a, 16m, Gandhi seated, touching child. b, 16m, Gandhi standing in crowd. c, 66m, Gandhi in crowd. d, 92m, Gandhi seated in chair.

No. 2285 — Famous Indians: a, 16m, Rabindranath Tagore (1861-1941), writer and Mohandas Gandhi. b, 16m, Subhas Chandra Bose (1897-1945), nationalist leader, Bose on horseback. c, 66m, Tagore and Albert Einstein. d, 92m, Bose and Mohandas Gandhi.

No. 2286 — Intl. Year of Chemistry: a, 16m, Marie Curie (1867-1934), and model of Radium atom. b, 16m, Curie and Polonium. c, 66m, Curie and daughter, Irene. d, 92m, Curie in laboratory.

No. 2287 — Sir Alexander Fleming (1881-1955), discoverer of penicillin, and: a, 16m, Molecular model of penicillin. b, 16m, Penicillum sp. c, 66m, Vial and needle of penicillin. d, 92m, Petri dish.

No. 2288 — Princess Diana (1961-97): a, 16m, With child, Big Ben. b, 16m, Exiting automobile. c, 66m, Tower Bridge. d, 92m, And child in hospital bed.

No. 2289 — Henri Matisse (1869-1954), painter, and painting from: a, 16m, 1908. b, 16m, 1918. c, 66m, 1901. d, 92m, 1912.

No. 2290 — René Magritte (1898-1967), painter, and painting from: a, 16m, 1966. b, 16m, 1933. c, 66m, 1964. d, 92m, 1936.

No. 2291 — Ford vehicles: a, 16m, 1908 Model T. b, 16m, 1905 Delivery car. c, 16m, 1930 Model A Deluxe Sedan. d, 92m, 1927 Model T.

No. 2292 — Locomotives: a, 16m, Western Pacific 805-A, 1960, U.S. b, 16m, Alco RS-2, 1946, U.S. c, 66m, Bo-Bo Class EO, 1923, New Zealand. d, 92m, Class 103.158, 1969, Germany.

No. 2293 — World War II warships: a, 16m, HMS Hood. b, 16m, HMAS Sydney. c, 66m, DKM Bismarck. d, 92m, IJN Yamato.

No. 2294 — Jet aircraft and engines: a, 16m, F-86 Sabre, Allison J35 engine. b, 16m, Lockheed F-104 Starfighter, General Electric J79 engine. c, 66m, Grumman F9F Panther, Allison J33 engine. d, 92m, Lockheed P-80 Shooting Star, Halford H-1 engine.

No. 2295, 175m, Pope John Paul II and Mother Teresa. No. 2296, 175m, Gandhi, diff. No. 2297, 175m, Tagore and Gandhi, diff. No. 2298, 175m, Curie, diff. No. 2299, 175m, Fleming, penicillin tablets, Red Cross workers treating injured soldiers. No. 2300, 175m, Princess Diana, diff. No. 2301, 175m, Matisse and painting from 1905. No. 2302, 175m, Magritte and painting from 1941. No. 2303, 175m, Henry Ford and 1910 Model T. No. 2304, 175m, EMD GP9 locomotive, 1949, U.S and Canada. No. 2305, 175m, Admiral Graf Spee. No. 2306, 175m, Heinkel He-178, He S-3 engine.

Perf. 13¼x9¼x13¼x9¼

2011, June 30   Litho.
Sheets of 4, #a-d

2283-2294	A430	Set of 12	165.00	165.00

Souvenir Sheets

2295-2306	A430	Set of 12	152.50	152.50

People, Events and Anniversaries — A431

No. 2307 — Albert Einstein (1879-1955), physicist, and: a, 16m, Mass-energy equivalence equation, text starting with "Em 1919." b, 16m, Expanding universe, mass-energy equivalence equation. c, 16m, Diagram of photoelectric effect. d, 16m, Binary pulsar. e, 66m, Gravitational field. f, 92m, Circles and arrows.

No. 2308 — Musicians: a, 16m, Elvis Presley (1935-77), teddy bear, Ann-Margret. b, 16m, Frank Sinatra (1915-98), and daughter, Nancy. c, 16m, Louis Armstrong (1901-71), and Ella Fitzgerald. d, 16m, Presley and scene from movie, Fun in Acupulco. e, 66m, Frank Sinatra and Gene Kelly. f, 92m, Armstrong and scene from movie.

No. 2309 — Musicians: a, 16m, Michael Jackson (1958-2009). b, 16m, Freddie Mercury (1946-91). c, 16m, The Rolling Stones. d, 16m, Jackson and backup singers. e, 66m, Mercury and members of Queen. f, 92m, The Rolling Stones, diff.

No. 2310 — Film personalities: a, 16m, Alfred Hitchcock (1899-1980), director. b, 16m, James Dean (1931-55), actor. c, 16m, Greta Garbo (1905-90), actress. d, 16m, Grace Kelly (1929-82), actress. e, 66m, Clark Gable (1901-60), actor. f, 92m, Marlon Brando (1924-2004), actor.

No. 2311 — Political leaders: a, 16m, Pres. John F. Kennedy (1917-63), American astronauts. b, 16m, Sir Winston Churchill (1874-1965), British prime minister, and Pres. Franklin D. Roosevelt and Joseph Stalin. c, 16m, Charles de Gaulle (1890-1970), President of France. d, 16m, Kennedy, Lyndon B. Johnson and Sam Rayburn. e, 66m, Churchill. f, 92m, De Gaulle and Gen. George C. Marshall.

No. 2312 — Political leaders: a, 16m, Pres. Theodore Roosevelt (1858-1919), moose. b, 16m, Lech Walesa, Polish President, and Solidarity banners. c, 16m, Mikhail Gorbachev, Pres. of Soviet Union, and Pres. Barack Obama. d, 16m, Roosevelt on Wright Brothers airplane. e, 66m, Walesa, diff. f, 92m, Gorbachev and Pres. Ronald Reagan.

No. 2313 — Pioneers in communications technology: a, 16m, Guglielmo Marconi (1874-1937), radio pioneer. b, 16m, John Logie Baird (1888-1946), television pioneer. c, 16m, Thomas Edison (1847-1931), inventor of Kinetoscope. d, 16m, Alexander Graham Bell (1847-1922), inventor of telephone. e, 66m, Edward Roberts (1941-2010), computer engineer. f, 92m, Tim Berners-Lee, inventor of World Wide Web.

No. 2314 — Humanitarians: a, 16m, Mother Teresa (1910-97). b, 16m, Dr. Martin Luther King, Jr. (1929-68). c, 16m, Nelson Mandela. d, 16m, Mother Teresa and Pope John Paul II. e, 66m, King, diff. f, 92m, Mandela, diff.

No. 2315 — Writers: a, 16m, George Orwell (1903-50). b, 16m, Albert Camus (1913-60). c, 16m, Ernest Hemingway (1899-1961), with John Dos Passos, Joris Ivens and Sidney Franklin. d, 16m, Hemingway and buffalo. e, 66m, Kurt Vonnegut, Jr. (1922-2007). f, 92m, Mikhail Bulgakov (1891-1940).

MOZAMBIQUE

No. 2316 — Sports personalities: a, 16m, Pelé, soccer player. b, 16m, Michael Jordan, basketball player. c, 16m, Ayrton Senna (1960-94) race car driver. d, 16m, Babe Ruth (1895-1948), baseball player. e, 66m, Nadia Comenici, gymnast. f, 92m, Jim Thorpe (1888-1953), Olympic track athlete.

No. 2317 — Space exploration: a, 16m, Yuri Gagarin (1934-68), Vostok 1. b, 16m, Space Shuttle. c, 16m, Valentina Tereshkova, Vostok 6. d, 16m, Mir Space Station and Space Shuttle. e, 66m, Sputnik 1. f, 92m, Neil Armstrong (1930-2012).

No. 2318 — World War II personalities: a, 16m, Charles de Gaulle (1890-1970). b, 16m, Gen. Dwight D. Eisenhower (1890-1969). c, 16m, Sir Winston Churchill (1874-1965). d, 16m, Gen. Georgy Zhukov (1896-1974). e, 66m, Harry S Truman (1884-1972). f, 92m, Gen. Bernard Montgomery (1887-1976).

No. 2319 — World War II aircraft: a, 16m, Corsair F4-U. b, 16m, Hawker Hurricane, Messerschmitt Me109, Junkers Ju-87D. c, 16m, Hawker Typhoon, Focke-Wulf Fw 190. d, 16m, Supermarine Spitfire MkXIV, Messerschmitt Me262. e, 66m, Curtiss P-40 Warhawk. f, 92m, Consolidated B-24 Liberator, Focke-Wulf 190D-9.

No. 2320 — American Impressionist painters: a, 16m, J. Ottis Adams (1851-1927), paintings from 1896 and 1901. b, 16m, Reynolds Beal (1866-1951), paintings from 1922 and 1924. c, 16m, Dennis Miller Bunker (1861-90), paintings from 1883 and 1890. d, 16m, Theodore Earl Butler (1861-1936), paintings from 1895 and 1911. e, 66m, Mary Cassatt (1844-1926), paintings from 1869 and 1880. f, 92m, Frank Weston Benson (1862-1951), paintings from 1902 and 1904.

No. 2321 — Pablo Picasso (1881-1973) and painting from: a, 16m, 1905. b, 16m, 1954. c, 16m, 1939. d, 16m, 1921-22. e, 66m, 1923. f, 92m, 1954. diff.

No. 2322 — Salvador Dalí (1904-89) and painting from: a, 16m, 1954. b, 16m, 1946. c, 16m, 1931. d, 16m, 1938. e, 66m, 1936. f, 92m, 1934.

No. 2323 — Wedding of Prince William and Catherine Middleton with: a, 16m, Horses and riders in background. b, 16m, Bride and groom walking down aisle. c, 16m, Bride and groom kissing. d, 16m, Attendant carrying train of bride's dress. e, 66m, Couple in coach. f, 92m, Couple in coach, diff.

No. 2324, 175m, Einstein, diff. No. 2325, 175m, Presley and Frank Sinatra. No. 2326, 175m, The Beatles. No. 2327, 175m, Marilyn Monroe (1926-62), actress. No. 2328, 175m, Kennedy, No. 2329, 175m, Gorbachev and Pope John Paul II. No. 2330, 175m, Berners-Lee, diff. No. 2331, 175m, Dr. Albert Schweitzer (1875-1965). No. 2332, 175m, Camus, diff. No. 2333, 175m, Muhammad Ali, boxer. No. 2334, 175m, Gagarin, diff. No. 2335, 175m, Neville Chamberlain (1869-1940). No. 2336, 175m, Supermarine Spitfire battling German airplanes over Dover. No. 2337, 175m, William Merritt Chase (1849-1916), paintings from 1886 and 1894. No. 2338, 175m, Picasso and painting from 1901. No. 2339, 175m, Dalí and painting from 1947. No. 2340, Wedding of Prince William and Catherine Middleton, diff.

2011, June 30   Sheets of 6, #a-f
2307-2323 A431 Set of 17   275.00 275.00
Souvenir Sheets
2324-2340 A431 Set of 17   215.00 215.00

Animals of Mozambique — A432

No. 2341 — Hares: a, 16m, Two Lepus saxitilis, animal name at left. b, 16m, Two Lepus saxitilis, animal name at right. c, 16m, Three Lepus capensis. d, 16m, One Lepus capensis. e, 16m, Two Lepus capensis. f, 92m, Three Lepus capensis, diff.

No. 2342 — Rodents: a, 16m, Anomalurus derbianus. b, 16m, Hystris africaeaustralis. c, 16m, Pedetes capensis. d, 16m, Heliosciurus mutabilis. e, 66m, Paraxerus palliatus. f, 92m, Graphiurus platyops.

No. 2343 — Pangolins and aardvarks: a, 16m, Two Manis temminckii, animal name at LL. b, 16m, Two Orycteropus afer, animal name at UR. c, 16m, Two Orycteropus afer, animal name at left. d, 16m, Two Manis temminckii, animal name at UR. e, 66m, Two Manis temminckii, diff. f, 92m, Two Orycteropus afer, diff.

No. 2344 — Bovids: a, 16m, Litacranius walleri. b, 16m, Aepyceros melampus and Acinonyx jubatus. c, 16m, Oryx beisa beisa. d, 16m, Connochaetes taurinus. e, 66m, Tragelaphus spekeii. f, 92m, Taurotragus oryx.

No. 2345 — African hunting dogs: a, 16m, Three Lycaon pictus, animal name at LL. b, 16m, Two Lycaon pictus. c, 16m, Lycaon pictus chasing Connochaetes taurinus. d, 16m, Two Lycaon pictus, and animal's head with open mouth. e, 66m, Two Lycaon pictus, diff. f, 92m, Lycaon pictus, and head of animal with closed mouth.

No. 2346 — Hippopotamus amphibius: a, 16m, Animals in water and on shore with open mouths. b, 16m, Animal facing left, animal in water with open mouth, skull. c, 16m, Animals in water and on shore with closed mouths. d, 16m, Three animals. e, 66m, Adult and juvenile. f, 92m, Two animals in water.

No. 2347 — Rhinoceroses: a, 16m, Diceros bicornis, drawing of rhinoceros by Albrecht Dürer. b, 16m, Three Ceratotherium simum. c, 16m, Adult and juvenile Ceratotherium simum. d, 16m, Three Diceros bicornis, skull. e, 66m, Three Ceratotherium simum, diff. f, 92m, Three Diceros bicornis, diff.

No. 2348 — Seals: a, 16m, Two Arctocephalus pusillus, sea gull. b, 16m, Three Mirounga leonina, animal name at UL. c, 16m, Three Mirounga leonina, animal name at left. d, 16m, Three Mirounga leonina, animal name at LL. e, 66m, Three Mirounga leonina, diff. f, 92m, Pod of Arctocephalus pusillus.

No. 2349 — Primates: a, 16m, Otolemur crassicaudatus. b, 16m, Galago nyasae, Otolemur crassicaudatus. c, 16m, Chlorocebus pygerythrus. d, 16m, Cercopithecus mitis. e, 66m, Papio ursinus. f, 92m, Papio cynocephalus with Aepyceros melampus.

No. 2350 — Bats: a, 16m, Rhinolophus blasii. b, 16m, Rousettus aegyptiacus. c, 16m, Taphozous mauritianus. d, 16m, Epomophorus wahlbergi. e, 66m, Eidolon helvum. f, 92m, Nyctalus noctula.

No. 2351 — Panthera leo: a, 16m, Lion, lioness and zebra. b, 16m, Lion, two lionesses, animal carcass. c, 16m, Lion and lioness. d, 16m, Lioness with zebra carcass. e, 66m, Two lionesses. f, 92m, Lionesses, buffalo and carcass.

No. 2352 — Wild cats: a, 16m, Caracal caracal. b, 16m, Acinonyx jubatus. c, 16m, Panthera pardus. d, 16m, Leptailurus serval. e, 66m, Leptailurus serval, diff. f, 92m, Acinonyx jubatus, diff.

No. 2353 — Loxodonta africana: a, 16m, Four elephants near watering hole. b, 16m, Elephant facing left near watering hole. c, 16m, Elephant facing forward. d, 16m, Elephant facing right. e, 66m, Three elephants. f, 92m, Adult and juvenile elephants.

No. 2354 — Two Dugong dugon with animal name at: a, 16m, Center left in white. b, 16m, UL in black. c, 16m, LR in white. d, 16m, Center right in white, under denomination. e, 66m, UR in black. f, 92m, UR in black, under denomination.

No. 2355 — Dolphins: a, 16m, Sousa chinensis chinensis. b, 16m, Stenella coeruleoalba. c, 16m, Stenella longirostris. d, 16m, Steno bredanensis. e, 66m, Tursiops truncatus. f, 92m, Lagenodelphis hosei.

No. 2356 — Whales: a, 16m, Feresa attenuata. b, 16m, Orcinus orca. c, 16m, Megaptera novaeangliae. d, 16m, Physeter macrocephalus. e, 66m, Kogia sima. f, 92m, Balaenoptera borealis.

No. 2357 — Bee-eaters: a, 16m, Merops pusillus. b, 16m, Merops bullockoides. c, 16m, Merops persicus. d, 16m, Merops boehmi. e, 66m, Merops nubicoides. f, 92m, Merops apiaster.

No. 2358 — Albatrosses: a, 16m, Thalassarche melanophrys. b, 16m, Diomedea exulans. c, 16m, Phoebetria palpebrata. d, 16m, Thalassarche cauta. e, 66m, Thalassarche chlororhynchos. f, 92m, Phoebetria fusca.

No. 2359 — Storks: a, 16m, Ciconia episcopus. b, 16m, Mycteria ibis. c, 16m, Anastomus lamelligerus. d, 16m, Ciconia nigra. e, 66m, Ephippiorhynchus senegalensis. f, 92m, Ciconia abdimii.

No. 2360 — Flamingos: a, 16m, Phoenicopterus roseus, bird feeding chick in foreground, animal name at UL. b, 16m, Phoenicopterus minor, animal name at top center. c, 16m, Phoenicopterus minor, animal name at UR under denomination. d, 16m, Phoenicopterus roseus in water, animal name at UL. e, 66m, Phoenicopterus minor in flight. f, 92m, Phoenicopterus roseus, diff.

No. 2361 — Pelecanus onocrotalus: a, 16m, Pelican feeding chick with adult near water, animal name at UR. b, 16m, Three pelicans on tree branch, animal name at LL. c, 16m, Three pelicans, animal name at UL. d, 16m, Two pelicans, animal name at right. e, 66m, Two pelicans, diff. f, 92m, Four pelicans.

No. 2362 — Struthio camelus: a, 16m, Adult and juvenile ostriches. b, 16m, Two ostriches fighting. c, 16m, Head of ostrich, osctrich with wings spread. d, 16m, Two ostriches, nest with eggs. e, 66m, Ostrich running. f, 92m, Ostrich standing.

No. 2363 — Kingfishers: a, 16m, Alcedes cristata. b, 16m, Ceryle rudis. c, 16m, Halcyon senegalensis. d, 16m, Ispidina picta. e, 66m, Halcyon senegaloides. f, 92m, Halcyon leucocephala.

No. 2364 — Birds of prey: a, 16m, Haliaeetus vocifer. b, 16m, Macheiraphus alcinus. c, 16m, Circaetus cinereus. d, 16m, Aquila rapax. e, 66m, Aquila pomarina. f, 92m, Polyboroides typus.

No. 2365 — Two Pandion haliaetus with animal name at: a, 16m, UR under denomination. b, 16m, Bottom, denomination at UR. c, 16m, Bottom, denomination at UL. d, 16m, UL. e, 66m, Left. f, 92m, UL, diff.

No. 2366 — Owls: a, 16m, Tyto capensis. b, 16m, Ptilopsis granti. c, 16m, Glaucidium perlatum. d, 16m, Strix woodfordii. e, 66m, Bubo capensis. f, 92m, Bubo africanus.

No. 2367 — Butterflies: a, 16m, Papilio dardanus. b, 16m, Charaxes varanes. c, 16m, Pharmacophagus antenor. d, 16m, Papilio phorcas. e, 66m, Papilio nireus. f, 92m, Charaxes pollux.

No. 2368 — Shells: a, 16m, Mauritia arabica. b, 16m, Lambis lambis. c, 16m, Clanculus puniceus. d, 16m, Haliotis ovina. e, 66m, Morula granulata. f, 92m, Chicoreus ramosus.

No. 2369 — Sea turtles: a, 16m, Caretta caretta. b, 16m, Chelonia mydas. c, 16m, Demochelys coriacea. d, 16m, Eretmochelys imbricata. e, 66m, Lepidochelys olivacea. f, 92m, Caretta caretta, diff.

No. 2370 — Lizards: a, 16m, Two Cordylus tropidosternum, one on rock. b, 16m, Cordylus mossambicus. c, 16m, Platysaurus intermedius. d, 16m, Two Cordylus tropidosternum fighting. e, 66m, Platysaurus imperator. f, 92m, Platysaurus imperator, diff.

No. 2371, 175m, Lepus capensis, diff. No. 2372, 175m, Rhabdomys pumilio. No. 2373, 175m, Manis temminckii, diff. No. 2374, 175m, Antidoreas marsupialis. No. 2375, 175m, Lycaeon pictus, diff. No. 2376, 175m, Adult and juvenile Hippopotamus amphibius, diff. No. 2377, 175m, Ceratotherium simum, diff. No. 2378, 175m, Pod of Arctocephalus pusillus. No. 2379, 175m, Cercopithecus mitis, diff. No. 2380, 175m, Eidolon helvum, diff. No. 2381, 175m, Panthera leo. No. 2382, 175m, Panthera pardus, diff. No. 2383, 175m, Loxodonta africana, diff. No. 2384, 175m, Dugong dugon, diff. No. 2385, 175m, Lisodelphis peronii. No. 2386, 175m, Feresa attenuata, diff. No. 2387, 175m, Meops hirundineus. No. 2388, 175m, Thalassarchechlororhynchus, diff. No. 2389, 175m, Mycteria ibis, diff. No. 2390, 175m, Phoenicopterus roseus, diff. No. 2391, 175m, Pelecanus onocrotalus, diff. No. 2392, 175m, Struthio camelus and egg. No. 2393, 175m, Megaceryle maxima. No. 2394, 175m, Aquila verreauxii. No. 2395, 175m, Pandion haliaetus. No. 2396, 175m, Tyto alba. No. 2397, 175m, Hypolimnas salmacis. No. 2398, 175m, Stellaria solaris, Nerita plicata, Achatina vassei. No. 2399, 175m, Eretmochelys imbricata, diff. No. 2400, 175m, Papilio demodocus, Cordylus mossambicus.

2011, Aug. 30   Sheets of 6, #a-f
2341-2370 A432 Set of 30   500.00 500.00
Souvenir Sheets
2371-2400 A432 Set of 30   400.00 400.00

Art — A433

No. 2401, 66m — Byzantine paintings by: a, Duccio di Buoninsegna from 1285 and 1308-11. b, Giotto di Bondone. c, Andrei Rublev. d, Emmanuel Tzanes.

No. 2402, 66m — Paintings by Dutch artists: a, Pieter Claesz. b, Rembrandt van Rijn from 1655. c, Dirck Hals. d, Jacob van Ruisdael.

No. 2403, 66m — Paintings by African artists: a, George Lilanga. b, Noel Kapanda. c, Saidi Omary. d, Steven Mkumba.

No. 2404, 66m — Paintings by Chinese artists: a, Chen Hongshou. b, Gong Kai. c, Xu Wei. d, Ding Guanpeng.

No. 2405, 66m — Fauvist paintings by: a, André Derain. b, Maurice de Vlaminck. c, Henri Matisse from 1904-05 and 1905. d, Charles Camoin.

No. 2406, 66m — Cubist paintings by: a, Juan Gris. b, Georges Braque. c, Pablo Picasso from 1909 and 1937. d, Paul Cézanne from 1890-94 and 1895.

No. 2407, 66m — Pop art works by: a, Richard Hamilton. b, Andy Warhol. c, David Hockney. d, Claes Oldenburg.

No. 2408, 66m — Modern art works by: a, Roy Lichtenstein from 1961 and 1988. b, Picasso from 1927 and 1932. c, Henri Matisse from 1947. d, Joan Miró from 1917 and 1925.

No. 2409, 175m, Paintings by Duccio di Buoninsegna from 1300-05. No. 2410, 175m, Paintings by Johannes Vermeer from 1668. No. 2411, 175m, Paintings by Eduardo Saidi Tingatinga. No. 2412, 175m, Paintings by Li Gonglin. No. 2413, 175m, Paintings by Kees van Dongen. No. 2414, 175m, Painting by Picasso from 1921. No. 2515, 175m, Paintings by Lichtenstein from 1963 and 1984. No. 2416, 175m, Painting by Picasso from 1935.

2011, Oct. 30   Perf. 12¾x13¼
Sheets of 4, #a-d
2401-2408 A433 Set of 8   160.00 160.00
Souvenir Sheets
2409-2416 A433 Set of 8   110.00 110.00

Art — A434

No. 2417 — Pre-historic paintings from: a, 16m, Chauvet Cave, France. b, 16m, Altamira Cave, Spain. c, 16m, Lascaux Cave, France. d, 66m, Lascaux Cave, diff. e, 66m, Niaux Cave, France. f, 66m, Chauvet Cave, diff.

No. 2418 — Paintings by Dutch artists: a, 16m, Rembrandt from 1633. b, 16m, Maarten van Heemskerck. c, 16m, Marinus van Reymerswaele. d, 66m, Vincent van Gogh from 1888. e, 66m, Lucas van Leyden. f, 66m, Johan Jongkind.

No. 2419 — Egyptian paintings from the Tomb of: a, 16m, Huy. b, 16m, Nebamun (man with tools, two women). c, 16m, Nebamun (man with staff, cattle herder and cattle). d, 66m, Nebamun, diff. e, 66m, Sebekhotep. f, 66m, Horemheb.

No. 2420 — Paintings by Flemish artists: a, 16m, Pieter Bruegel the Elder. b, 16m, Jan van Eyck. c, 16m, Frans Hals. d, 66m, Anthony van Dyck. e, 66m, Hugo van der Goes. f, 66m, Gerard David.

No. 2421 — Paintings by French artists: a, 16m, Edgar Degas from 1890. b, 16m, Paul Cézanne from 1866. c, 16m, Gustave Courbet. d, 66m, Paul Gauguin from 1892. e, 66m, Eugene Delacroix. f, 66m, Henri Matisse from 1928.

No. 2422 — Paintings by German artists: a, 16m, Hans Baldung Grien. b, 16m, Lovis Corinth. c, 16m, Ludolf Bakhuizen. d, 66m, Lucas Cranach the Elder. e, 66m, Otto Dix. f, 66m, Adam Elsheimer.

No. 2423 — Paintings by Indian artists: a, 16m, Nandalal Bose. b, 16m, Raja Ravi Varma. c, 16m, Tyeb Mehta. d, 66m, Jamini Roy. e, 66m, Abanindranath Tagore. f, 66m, S.H. Raza.

No. 2424 — Paintings by Italian artists: a, 16m, Michelangelo Buonarroti from 1508-12. b, 16m, Amadeo Modigliani from 1919. c, 16m, Titian. d, 66m, Sandro Botticelli (Minerva and Centaur, 1480). e, 66m, Tintoretto from 1540-42. f, 66m, Caravaggio.

No. 2425 — Paintings by Japanese artists: a, 16m, Toyokuni Utagawa. b, 16m, Kunimasa Utagawa. c, 16m, Toshun Kano. d, 66m, Kunisada Utagawa. e, 66m, Kiyonobu Torii. f, 66m, Shoen Uemura.

No. 2426 — Paintings by Spanish artists: a, 16m, El Greco. b, 16m, Joan Miró from 1917 and 1922-23. c, 16m, Diego Velázquez. d, 66m, Francisco Goya. e, 66m, Salvador Dalí from 1921 and 1925. f, 66m, Joaquí Sorolla.

No. 2427 — Paintings by Jewish artists: a, 16m, Modigliani from 1918. b, 16m, Moritz Daniel Oppenheim. c, 16m, Chaim Goldberg. d, 66m, Camille Pissarro from 1901. e, 66m, Maurycy Gottlieb. f, 66m, Samuel Hirszenberg.

No. 2428 — Religious art: a, 16m, Stained-glass window depicting Jesus, 1601 painting by Caravaggio. b, 16m, Statue and fresco depicting Buddha. c, 16m, Menorah, 1638 painting of Moses, by José de Ribera. d, 66m, Ottoman calligraphy and ceiling of Ibn Battuta Mall, Dubai. e, 66m, Sculpture and fresco depicting Buddha. f, 66m, Fresco depicting

MOZAMBIQUE

Jesus, 1405 painting depicting the Annunciation by Andrei Rublev.
No. 2429 — Renaissance art by: a, 16m, Raffaello Sanzio da Urbino (Raphael). b, 16m, Botticelli (The Glorification of Mary, 1480). c, 16m, Tintoretto from 1550-53 and 1592-94. d, 66m, Leonardo da Vinci from 1480 and 1495. e, 66m, Michelangelo from 1508 and 1511. f, 66m, Giotto from 1305 and 1310.
No. 2430 — Impressionist paintings by: a, 16m, Armand Guillaumin. b, 16m, Eva Gonzalès. c, 16m, Alfred Sisley. d, 66m, Eugène Boudin. e, 66m, Stanislas Lépine. f, 66m, Edouard Manet from 1872 and 1882.
No. 2431 — Post-impressionist paintings by: a, 16m, Van Gogh from 1888 and 1889. b, 16m, Georges Seurat. c, 16m, Henri de Toulouse-Lautrec. d, 66m, Gauguin from 1888 and 1893. e, 66m, Cézanne from 1875 and 1892. f, 66m, Matisse from 1905 and 1906.
No. 2432 — Expressionist paintings by: a, 16m, Ernst Ludwig Kirchner. b, 16m, Emil Nolde. c, 16m, Franz Marc. d, 66m, Oskar Kokoscka. e, 66m, Max Beckmann. f, 66m, Wassily Kandinsky.
No. 2433 — Realist paintings by: a, 16m, Jules Breton. b, 16m, Jean-Baptiste-Camille Corot. c, 16m, Honore Daumier. d, 66m, Valentin Serov. e, 66m, Jean-François Millet. f, 66m, Ilya Repin.
No. 2434 — Surrealist paintings: a, 16m, Frida Kahlo. b, 16m, Dalí from 1963. c, 16m, Miró from 1940. d, 66m, Marc Chagall from 1911. e, 66m, Giorgio De Chirico. f, 66m, Max Ernst.
No. 2435, 175m, Pre-historic painting from Altamira Cave, diff. No. 2436, 175m, Painting by Johannes Vermeer from 1659. No. 2437, 175m, Painting from Tomb of Huy, diff. No. 2438, 175m, Painting by Peter Paul Rubens. No. 2439, 175m, Painting by Pierre-Auguste Renoir from 1890. No. 2440, 175m, Painting by Albrecht Dürer. No. 2441, 175m, Painting by Amrita Sher-Gil. No. 2442, 175m, Painting by Leonardo da Vinci from 1489-90. No. 2443, 175m, Painting by Hokusai Katsushika. No. 2444, 175m, Paintings by Picasso from 1901 and 1903. No. 2445, 175m, Painting by Chagall from 1913-14. No. 2446, 175m, 1513 painting depicting Madonna and Child by Raphael, ceiling of Farnese Palace by Annibale Carracci. No. 2447, 175m, Paintings by Leonardo da Vinci from 1489 and 1501. No. 2448, 175m, Paintings by Manet from 1878. No. 2449, 175m, Paintings by Van Gogh from 1886 and 1887. No. 2450, 175m, Paintings by Edvard Munch. No. 2451, 175m, Painting by William-Auguste Bouguereau. No. 2452, 175m, Painting by René Magritte.

2011, Oct. 30   **Sheets of 6, #a-f**
2417-2434   A434   Set of 18   335.00   335.00
Souvenir Sheets
2435-2452   A434   Set of 18   240.00   240.00

Art — A435

No. 2453 — Art of Ancient Greece: a, 16m, Bull's head rhyton, painting depicting women. b, 16m, Fresco from Knossos Palace, tile fragment. c, 16m, Painting of divers, kylix. d, 16m, Painting, sculpture of horse. e, 16m, Fresco depicting bull, pyxis. f, 16m, Fresco depicting dolphins, obverse and reverse of Athenian tetradrachm. g, 92m, Mask of Agamemnon, painting depicting Dionysius riding panther. h, 92m, Image from kylix, mosaic depicting leopard.
No. 2454 — Expensive paintings by: a, 16m, Jackson Pollock. b, 16m, Willem de Kooning. c, 16m, Gustav Klimt. d, 16m, Vincent van Gogh from 1890. e, 16m, Pierre-Auguste Renoir from 1876. f, 16m, Pablo Picasso from 1905. g, 92m, Picasso from 1932. h, 92m, Van Gogh from 1889.
No. 2455 — American Impressionist paintings by: a, 16m, Frank Weston Benson. b, 16m, Theodore Earl Butler. c, 16m, Mary Cassatt from 1879. d, 16m, Colin Campbell Cooper. e, 16m, Mary Agnes Yerkes. f, 16m, Dennis Miller Bunker. g, 92m, Childe Hassam. h, 92m, William Merritt Chase.
No. 2456 — Impressionist paintings by: a, 16m, Frederic Bazille. b, 16m, Berthe Morisot. c, 16m, Camille Pissarro from 1875. d, 16m, Claude Monet. e, 16m, Cassatt from 1873. f, 16m, Pierre-Auguste Renoir from 1882-83. g, 92m, Paul Cézanne from 1888. h, 92m, Edgar Degas from 1888.
No. 2457, 175m, Ancient Greek urn and painting. No. 2458, 175m, Painting by Picasso from 1941. No. 2459, 175m, Painting by Theodore Robinson. No. 2460, 175m, Painting by Gustave Caillebotte.

2011, Oct. 30   **Sheets of 8, #a-h**
2453-2456   A435   Set of 4   85.00   85.00
Souvenir Sheets
2457-2460   A435   Set of 4   52.50   52.50

Events, People and Anniversaries — A436

No. 2461, 66m — Horse racing: a, Horses facing right, jockeys in foreground wearing black and red shirts. b, Horses in steeplechase race. c, Horses facing right, jockey in foreground wearing black shirt. d, Horses facing left, passing grandstand, jockey wearing black shirt in lead. e, Horses facing left close to rail, grandstand at left. f, Three horses near gray wall.
No. 2462, 66m — Dan Wheldon (1978-2011), race car driver: a, Wheldon in white short-sleeve shirt. b, Race car with "2012" on rear wing. c, Wheldon in red racing uniform, car #10. d, Race car, race track. e, Wheldon with arms raised, race car. f, Wheldon standing next to race car.
No. 2463, 66m — Marco Simoncelli (1987-2011), motorcycle racer: a, With Valentino Rossi. b, Touching forehead. c, Raising trophy above head. d, With motorcycle's front wheel raised. e, Kneeling next to motorcycle. f, Looking right.
No. 2464, 66m — 2012 European Soccer Championships, Poland and Ukraine: a, Denomination at UL, "2012" in yellow at LR. b, Denomination at UL, "2012" in green at UR. c, Denomination at UR, "2012" in indigo at UL, soccer players wearing red and yellow uniforms. d, Denomination at UR, "2012" in indigo at UL, soccer players wearing blue and orange univorms. e, Denomination at UR, "2012" in yellow at UL. f, Denomination at UL, "2012" in green at LR.
No. 2465, 66m — Chess champions: a, Mikhail Tal. b, Viswanathan Anand. c, Bobby Fischer. d, Vladimir Kramnik. e, Garry Kasparov. f, Boris Spassky.
No. 2466, 66m — Boy Scout: a, Hiking, trefoil at LR. b, One one knee, trefoil at left. c, Cycling, trefoil at LR. d, Inspecting small item, trefoil at LL. e, Cooking, trefoil at LR. f, In boat, trefoil at UR.
No. 2467, 66m — Steve Jobs (1955-2011), computer entrepreneur: a, With Apple II computer. b, With Steve Wozniak and computer components. c, Holding apple. d, With beard, wearing glasses. e, Seated in chair using iPad. f, With three computers.
No. 2468, 66m — Mycologists and fungi: a, Elias Magnus Fries, Crinipellis scabella. b, Heinrich Anton de Bary, Psilocybe semilanceata. c, Charles Horton Peck, Crinipellis zonata. d, Narcisse Théophile Patouillard, inocybe patouillardii. e, Miles Joseph Berkeley, Stephanospora caroticolor. f, Károly Kalchbrenner, Sarcodon fuligineoviolaceus.
No. 2469, 66m — Sir Joseph Dalton Hooker (1817-1911), botanist: a, Hooker, Banksia hookeriana, Delias eucharis. b, Charles Darwin, Pan troglodytes. c, Hooker, Liriodendron tulipifera, Junonia lemonias. d, Hooker, Magnolia campbellii. e, Walter Hood Fitch, flowers and colored pencils. f, Darwin, ship and globe.
No. 2470, 66m — 2011 Nobel laureates: a, Bruce A. Beutler, Physiology or Medicine laureate. b, Ralph M. Steinman, Physiology or Medicine laureate. c, Jules A. Hoffmann, Physiology or Medicine laureate. d, Saul Perlmutter, Physics laureate. e, Brian P. Schmidt, Physics laureate. f, Adam G. Riess, Physics laureate.
No. 2471, 66m — Russian Cosmonauts: a, Valentina Tereshkova, Vostok 6. b, Alexei Leonov, 1965 space walk. c, Pavel Popovich, Vostok 4. d, Gherman Titov, Vostok 2. e, Andriyan Nikolayev, Soyuz 9. f, Pavel Belyayev, Voskhod 2.
No. 2472, 66m — African archaeological sites: a, Altar of Osiris, Philae Island, Egypt. b, Triumphal arch, Lambaesis, Algeria. c, Temple of Minerva, Tébessa, Algeria. d, Triumphal arch, Tébessa. e, Kom Ombo Temple, Egypt. f, Gateway to the Temple of Khonsu, Luxor, Egypt.
No. 2473, 66m — Romy Schneider (1938-82), actress, and scenes from: a, Bocaccio '70, 1962. b, Monpti, 1957. c, Sissi: The Fateful Years of an Empress, 1957. d, Ludwig, 1972. e, Un Amour de Pluie, 1974. f, What's New Pussycat?, 1965.
No. 2474, 66m — Wedding of Prince William and Catherine Middleton: a, Couple and Windsor Castle, Middleton holding flowers. b, Couple, Prince William at left, at Cambridge, Prince William. c, Couple, facing forward, at Cambridge, Middleton. d, Couple facing backwards at Cambridge, Middleton. e, Couple and Winsor Castle. f, Couple, Pippa Middleton.
No. 2475, 66m — British warships: a, HMS Vindictive. b, HMS Victoria. c, HMS Eurydice. d, HMS Powerful (Poderoso). e, HMS Queen (Rainha). f, HMS Raleigh.
No. 2476, 66m — Sinking of the Titanic, cent. (in 2012), and: a, Captain Edward John Smith, ship officers William Murdoch, Henry Wilde, and Captain Charles Bartlett of the HMHS Britannic. b, Angel. c, Lucy Noel Martha Leslie. d, Margaret (Molly) Brown. e, Captain Smith. f, Iceberg.
No. 2477, 66m — Steam locomotives: a, Cheltenham Flyer with front of locomotive in black. b, Cheltenham Flyer with yellow and red rectangle on front. c, Bombay-Poona mail train. d, Silver Jubilee. e, Royal Scot. f, Scarborough Flyer.
No. 2478, 66m — Red Cross flag and ambulance: a, Ambulance crew member removing ambulance covering. b, Ambulance crew loading person into rear of ambulance. c, Motorcycle ambulance. d, Truck ambulance with two crew members in cab. e, Ambulance with rear doors open. f, Horse entering ambulance.
No. 2479, 66m — Dirigibles: a, British Army dirigible "Baby." b, 1852 dirigible. c, Brazilian war dirigible. d, French dirigible "Ville de Paris." e, German dirigible "Parseval." f, German dirigible "Clouth."
No. 2480, 66m — Trees: a, Malus spp. b, Crataegus monogyna. c, Betula alleghaniensis. d, Populus alba. e, Populus nigra. f, Aesculus hippocastanum.
No. 2481, 66m — Cacti and reptiles: a, Opuntia ficus-indica, Liolaemos platei platei. b, Copiapoa megarhiza, Conolophus subcristatus. c, Copiapoa cinerea, Sistrurus catenatus edwardsii. d, Stapelia pulchellus, Arizona elegans philipi. e, Echinopsis spachiana, Heloderma suspectum. f, Astrophytum hybrid, Gopherus agassizii.
No. 2482, 66m — Phascolarctos cinereus: a, Denomination at UR, animal name at LR. b, Denomination and animal name at UL, with tree trunk and branch. c, Denomination at UR, animal name at UR. d, Denomination at UR, animal name at UL. e, Denomination and animal name at UL, with tree branch only. f, Denomination at UL, animal name at left.
No. 2483, 66m — Cat breeds: a, Bengal. b, Pixie-bob. c, Abyssinian. d, American curl. e, Ocelot. f, Sokoke.
No. 2484, 66m — Dog breeds: a, Beagle. b, Yellow Labrador retriever. c, Irish setter. d, German shepherd. e, Booton torrior. f, English galgo.
No. 2485, 66m — Sharks: a, Alopias superciliosus, Prionace glauca. b, Eugomphodus taurus, Carcharhinus limbatus. c, Stegostoma fasciatum, Carcharhinus melanopterus. d, Triaenodon obesus, Squatina squatina. e, Isurus oxyrinchus, Triakis semifasciata. f, Scyliorhynus stellaris, Carcharhinus leucas.
No. 2486, 66m — Fishing: a, Gymnura natalensis. b, Coryphaena hippurus. c, Oreochromis mossambicus. d, Wattsia mossambica. e, Xiphias gladius. f, Penaeidae.
No. 2487, 66m — DNA molecules and animals: a, Vulpes zerda. b, Arctocephalus. c, Suricata suricatta. d, Ailuropoda melanoleuca. e, Odobenus rosmarus. f, Panthera leo.
No. 2488, 66m — Endangered animals: a, Lynx rufus. b, Two Ailuropoda melanoleuca. c, Panthera tigris. d, Ovis musimon. e, Loxodonta africana. f, Ceratotherium simum.
No. 2489, 175m, Horses racing, diff. No. 2490, 175m, Wheldon, diff. No. 2491, 175m, Simoncelli, diff. No. 2492, 175m, Soccer players, diff. No. 2493, 175m, Anatoly Karpov, chess player. No. 2494, 175m, Two Scouts, trefoil at LR. No. 2495, 175m, Jobs holding iPhone. No. 2496, 175m, Lucien Quélet, mycologist, and Clavariadelphus truncatus. No. 2497, 175m, Hooker, Vanda cathcarti. No. 2498, 175m, Dan Shechtman, 2011 Nobel Chemistry laureate. No. 2499, 175m, Yuri Gagarin, Russian cosmonaut. No. 2500, 175m, Amphitheater, Timgad, Algeria. No. 2501, 175m, Schneider, scene from Triple Cross, 1966. No. 2502, 175m, Prince William, Catherine Middleton, automobile. No. 2503, 175m, HMS Juno. No. 2504, 175m, Titanic and Captain Smith, diff. No. 2505, 175m, Torbay Express. No. 2506, 175m, Fire truck. No. 2507, 175m, French dirigible "Zodiac". No. 2508, 175m, Carpinus spp. No. 2509, 175m, Copiapoa haseltoniana and snake. No. 2510, 175m, Phascolarctos cinereus, diff. No. 2511, 175m, Siamese cat. No. 2512, 175m, Rottweiler. No. 2513, 175m, Sphyrna mokarran. No. 2514, 175m, Scomberomorus plurilineatus and fishermen. No. 2515, 175m, DNA molecule and Puijila darwini. No. 2516, 175m, Delphinus delphi, Stenella coeruleoalba.

2011, Dec. 30   **Perf. 12¾x13¼**
Sheets of 6, #a-f
2461-2488   A436   Set of 28   835.00   835.00
Souvenir Sheets
Perf. 13¼x12¾
2489-2516   A436   Set of 28   375.00   375.00

Miniature Sheets

Indonesia 2012 Intl. Philatelic Exhibition — A437

No. 2517, 66m — Like No. 2482 with exhibition emblem at: a, LR. b, LL. c, LL. d, LR. e, LL. f, LL.
No. 2518, 66m — Like No. 2488 with exhibition emblem at: a, LR. b, LL. c, LL. d, LL. e, LR. f, LL.

2011, Dec. 30   **Perf. 12¾x13¼**
Sheets of 6, #a-f
2517-2518   A437   Set of 2   60.00   60.00

New Year 2012 (Year of the Dragon) — A438

Designs: No. 2519, Dragon and clouds. No. 2520: a, 16m, Dragon dance. b, 16m, Chinese calligraphy by Wang Xizhi. c, 10m, Drogon, guitarist Wang Lee-hom. d, 66m, Bruce Lee and Jackie Chan, actors. e, 66m, People's Republic of China banknote depicting dragon. f, Dragon boat race.
175m, Mural depicting dragons.

2011, Dec. 30   **Perf. 13¼**
2519   A438   66m multi   5.00   5.00
Perf. 12¾x13¼
2520   A438   Sheet of 6, #a-f   18.50   18.50
Souvenir Sheet
Perf. 13¼x12¾
2521   A438   175m multi   13.50   13.50
No. 2519 was printed in sheets of 4.

World Vision — A438a

2011   **Litho.**   **Perf. 11x11½**
2521A   A438a   92m multi   —   —

People, Events and Anniversaries — A439

No. 2522 — Whitney Houston (1963-2012), singer: a, 16m, Houston and Kevin Costner, actor (38x39mm). b, 16m, Two images of Houston (50x39mm). c, 16m, Houston (38x39mm). d, 66m, Houston and Michael Jackson, singer (38x39mm). e, 66m, Houston with arms raised (50x39mm). f, 66m, Houston and Aretha Franklin, singer (38x39mm).
No. 2523 — Elvis Presley (1935-77), singer: a, 16m, Presley and automobiles (38x39mm). b, 16m, Presley as child and as adult (50x39mm). c, 16m, Presley and woman on motorcycle (38x39mm). d, 66m, Presley with guitar (38x39mm). e, 66m, Presley waving (50x39mm). f, 66m, Presley with guitar and woman (38x39mm).
No. 2524 — 70th birthday of Paul McCartney, singer: a, 16m, McCartney playing guitar

MOZAMBIQUE

(38x39mm). b, 16m, McCartney, neck of guitar (50x39mm). c, 16m, McCartney and microphone (38x39mm). d, 66m, McCartney holding guitar (38x39mm). e, 66m, McCartney playing guitar, diff. (50x39mm). f, 66m, McCartney pointing (38x39mm).

No. 2525 — Ludwig van Beethoven (1770-1827), composer: a, 16m, Beethoven and Georg Frideric Handel, composer (38x39mm). b, 16m, Beethoven conducting (50x39mm). c, 16m, Beethoven and Johann Sebastian Bach, composer (38x39mm). d, 66m, Beethoven and building (50x39mm). e, 66m, Head of Beethoven (50x39mm). f, 66m, Beethoven and Johann Wolfgang von Goethe, writer (38x39mm).

No. 2526 — Joseph Haydn (1732-1809), composer: a, 16m, Haydn, building and statue (38x39mm). b, 16m, Haydn and Wolfgang Amadeus Mozart, composer (50x39mm). c, 16m, Haydn holding quill pen, building and statue (38x39mm). d, 66m, Beethoven, Herbert von Karajan conducting (38x39mm). e, 66m, Haydn, building and statue, diff (50x39mm). f, 66m, Bach and building (38x39mm).

No. 2527 — Gene Kelly (1912-96), actor: a, 16m, Kelly (38x39mm). b, 16m, Kelly and Debbie Reynolds, actress (50x39mm). c, 16m, Kelly and Cyd Charisse, actress (38x39mm). d, 66m, Kelly and Reynolds, diff. (38x39mm). e, 66m, Kelly and Donald O'Connor, actor (50x39mm). f, 66m, Kelly, diff (38x39mm).

No. 2528 — Judy Garland (1922-69), actress: a, 16m, Garland holding Toto in *The Wizard of Oz*. (38x39mm). b, 16m, Garland and daughter, Liza Minnelli. (50x39mm). c, 16m, Garland and Margaret Hamilton as Wicked Witch of the West (38x39mm). d, 66m, Garland (38x39mm). e, 66m, Garland with Jack Haley as the Tinman and Ray Bolger as the Scarecrow (50x39mm). f, 66m, Garland holding tennis racket (38x39mm).

No. 2529 — Marilyn Monroe (1926-62), actress: a, 16m, Monroe as adult and child (38x39mm). b, 16m, Two images of Monroe (50x39mm). c, 16m, Monroe and actors Tony Curtis and Jack Lemmon in *Some Like It Hot* (38x39mm). d, 66m, Monroe in pink blouse (38x39mm). e, 66m, Two images of Monroe, diff. (50x39mm). f, 66m, Two images of Monroe, diff. (38x39mm).

No. 2530 — Elizabeth Taylor (1932-2011), actress: a, 16m, Taylor (38x39mm). b, 16m, Taylor and husband, Richard Burton, actor (50x39mm). c, 16m, Taylor in chair (38x39mm). d, 66m, Taylor and Lassie (dog) (38x39mm). e, 66m, Taylor and Burton, diff. (50x39mm). f, 66m, Taylor and James Dean, actor (38x39mm).

No. 2531 — François Truffaut (1932-84), actor and director, and: a, 16m, Scene from *The 400 Blows*, 1959 (38x39mm). b, 16m, Scene from *Close Encounters of the Third Kind*, 1977 (50x39mm). c, 16m, Scene from *The Last Metro*, 1980 (38x39mm). d, 66m, Actress Isabelle Adjani in scene from *The Story of Adele H*, 1975 (38x39mm). e, 66m, Actress Catherine Deneuve in scene from *The Last Metro* (50x39mm). f, 66m, Alfred Hitchcock, director (38x39mm).

No. 2532 — 80th birthday of Milos Forman, director: a, 16m, Tom Hulce in *Amadeus*, 1984 (38x39mm). b, 16m, Scene from *One Flew Over the Cuckoo's Nest*, 1975 (50x39mm). c, 16m, Hulce and F. Murray Abraham in *Amadeus* (38x39mm). d, 66m, Scene from *Hair*, 1979 (38x39mm). e, 66m, Forman (50x39mm). f, 66m, Jim Carrey in *Man on the Moon*, 1999 (38x39mm).

No. 2533 — Pres. John F. Kennedy (1917-63): a, 16m, Senator Robert F. Kennedy, brother, and detail from painting *Washington Crossing the Delaware* (38x39mm). b, 16m, Senator Edward M. Kennedy, brother (50x39mm). c, 16m, Pres. Bill Clinton and Indian (38x39mm). d, 66m, Pres. Barack Obama, Dr. Martin Luther King, Jr. (38x39mm). e, 66m, Kennedy and astronaut on Moon (50x39mm). f, 66m, Wife, Jacqueline, and son, John, Jr. (38x39mm).

No. 2534 — Boxers: a, 16m, Marvin Hagler (38x39mm). b, 16m, Joe Frazier (50x39mm). c, 16m, Rocky Marciano (38x39mm). d, 66m, Muhammad Ali (38x39mm). e, 66m, Joe Louis (50x39mm). f, 66m, Mike Tyson (38x39mm).

No. 2535 — St. Joan of Arc (1412-31): a, 16m, Holding lamb (38x39mm). b, 16m, In armor on one knee (50x39mm). c, 16m, Tied to stake, holding crucifix (38x39mm). d, 66m, At coronation of King Charles VII (38x39mm). e, 66m, In battle on horse (50x39mm). f, 66m, Interrogation by Cardinal Winchester (38x39mm).

No. 2536 — Leonardo da Vinci (1452-1519), artist and inventor: a, 16m, Glider, facing right (38x39mm). b, 16m, Gears (50x39mm). c, 16m, Ornithopter, view of underside (38x39mm). d, 66m, Leonardo holding model of invention (38x39mm). e, 66m, Machine gun (50x39mm). f, 66m, Paddlewheel boat (38x39mm).

No. 2537 — Sir Isaac Newton (1642-1727), physicist and astronomer: a, 16m, Telescopes (38x39mm). b, 16m, Newton and statue (50x39mm). c, 16m, XMM-Newton orbiting observatory (38x39mm). d, 66m, Newton and house (38x39mm). e, 66m, Observatory

(50x39mm). f, 66m, Newton and Zosimos of Panopolis, alchemist (38x39mm).

No. 2538 — Thomas Edison (1847-1931), inventor, and: a, 16m, Phonograph, compact disc (38x39mm). b, 16m, Edison's automobile and Infiniti Essence prototype (50x39mm). c, 16m, Motion picture camera (38x39mm). d, 66m, Phonograph, record, speakers (38x39mm). e, 66m, Lightbulb, LED light (50x39mm). f, 66m, Lightbulb, microphone (38x39mm).

No. 2539 — Nobel laureates in Chemistry: a, 16m, Ei-ichi Negishi, 2011 (38x39mm). b, 16m, Jacobus Henricus van 't Hoff, 1901 (50x39mm). c, 16m, Ernest Rutherford, 1908 (38x39mm). d, 66m, Marie Curie, 1911 (38x39mm). e, 66m, Sir William Ramsay, 1904 (50x39mm). f, 66m, Wilhelm Ostwald, 1909 (38x39mm).

No. 2540 — Jean-Jacques Rousseau (1712-78), philosopher: a, 16m, Voltaire, philosopher (38x39mm). b, 16m, Thomas Hobbes, philosopher (50x39mm). c, 16m, Voltaire and statue (38x39mm). d, 66m, Rousseau and statue (38x39mm). e, 66m, Louise d'Epinay, writer, and Denis Diderot, philosopher (50x39mm). f, 66m, Rousseau (38x39mm).

No. 2541 — Scenes from novels by Charles Dickens (1812-70): a, 16m, Group of children (38x39mm). b, 16m, Old man, crowded street (50x39mm). c, 16m, Old man and boy (38x39mm). d, 66m, Boy, people wearing hats (38x39mm). e, 66m, Boy and building (50x39mm). f, 66m, Man eating from bowl, buildings (38x39mm).

No. 2542 — Alexandre Dumas (1802-70), writer: a, 16m, Dumas, Gerard Depardieu as Edmond Dantes in *The Count of Monte Cristo* (38x39mm). b, 16m, Statue of Dumas, scene from *The Three Musketeers* (50x39mm). c, 16m, Scene from *The Vicomte de Bragelonne* (38x39mm). d, 66m, Scene from *The Lady of the Camellias*, by Alexandre Dumas (1824-95) (38x39mm). e, 66m, Auguste Maquet, writer who collaborated with Dumas, swordsman on horseback (50x39mm). f, 66m, Scene from *Queen Margot* (38x39mm).

No. 2543 — King Frederick II of Prussia (1712-86): a, 16m, Frederick II, Francesco Algarotti, philospoher (38x39mm). b, 16m, Frederick II on medal, Queen consorr Elisabeth-Christine of Brunswick-Wolfenbüttel-Bevern (50x39mm). c, 16m, Frederick II, St. Hedwig's Cathedral, Berlin (38x39mm). d, 66m, Frederick II and statue (38x39mm). e, 66m, Brandenburg Gate, Berlin (50x39mm). f, 66m, Frederick II, Pope Clement XIV (38x39mm).

No. 2544 — Napoleon III (1808-73), French emperor: a, 16m, Napoleon III, Battle of Solferino (38x39mm). b, 16m, Napoleon III at the Tuileries (50x39mm). c, 16m, Napoleon III and Emir Abdelkader, Algerian rebel leader (38x39mm). d, 66m, Napoleon III, Georges-Eugène Hausmann, Parisian civic planner (38x39mm). e, 66m, Napoleon III on horseback (50x39mm). f, 66m, Empress consort Eugénie de Montijo (38x39mm).

No. 2545 — Buildings designed by Antonio Gaudí (1852-1926): a, 16m, Bellesguard, Barcelona, Josep Fontseré, architect (38x39mm). b, 16m, Sagrada Familia Basilica, Barcelona, Joan Miró, painter (50x39mm). c, 16m, Gaudí, Güell Pavilion, Barcelona (38x39mm). d, 66m, Sagrada Familia Basilica, Henri Matisse, painter (38x39mm). e, 66m, Gaudí's Caprice, Comillas, Spain (50x39mm). f, 66m, Eugène Viollet-le-Duc, architect, Casa Vicens, Barcelona (38x39mm).

No. 2546 — Discovery of bust of Nefertiti, cent.: a, 16m, Photographer (38x39mm). b, 16m, Ludwig Borchardt, discoverer, holding bust (50x39mm). c, 16m, Archaeologists examining sculpted tile (38x39mm). d, 66m, Zahi Hawass, Egyptian Minister of Antiquities, Pyramids (38x39mm). e, 66m, Bust and Egyptian statuary (50x39mm). f, 66m, Borchardt uncovering bust (38x39mm).

No. 2547 — Paul von Hindenburg (1847-1934), German President, and Zeppelin LZ-129 Hindenburg: a, 16m, Denomination in white, Pres. Hindenburg in military uniform at LR (38x39mm). b, 16m, Denomination in black Pres. Hindenburg in military uniform at LL (50x39mm). c, 16m, Denomination in black, Pres. Hindenburg in military uniform at LR (38x39mm). d, 66m, Denomination in black, Pres. Hindenburg in military uniform at LR (38x39mm). e, 66m, Denomination in black, Pres. Hindenburg in military uniform at LR (50x39mm). f, 66m, Denomination in black, Pres. Hindenburg in military uniform at LL (38x39mm).

No. 2548 — Bombardment of Guernica, Spain, 75th anniv.: a, 16m, Junkers Ju-52, denomination at UL (38x39mm). b, 16m, Messerschmitt Bf-109 (50x39mm). c, 16m, Junkers Ju-52, denomination at UR (38x39mm). d, 66m, Messerschmitt Bf-109, diff. (38x39mm). e, 66m, Heinkel He-111 (50x39mm). f, 66m, Pablo Picasso, artist (38x39mm).

No. 2549 — People involved in struggle for black civil rights: a, 16m, John Brown, abolitionist, slaves in field (38x39mm). b, 16m, William Wilberforce, British abolitionist, slave auction (50x39mm). c, 16m, Senator Henry Clay, whipping of slave (38x39mm). d, 66m, Pres. Abraham Lincoln, U.S. Capitol, statue of chained slave (38x39mm). e, 66m, Lincoln,

Pres. George Washington, Civil War battle (50x39mm). f, 66m, Frederick Douglass, Pres. John F. Kennedy (38x39mm).

No. 2550 — First solo transatlantic flight of Charles Lindbergh, 85th anniv.: a, 16m, Spirit of St. Louis, name of airplane at center bottom (38x39mm). b, 16m, Charles Lindbergh, pilot, Spirit of St. Louis (50x39mm). c, 16m, Spirit of St. Louis, name of airplane at UL (38x39mm). d, 66m, Lindbergh, Solar Impulse airplane (38x39mm). e, 66m, Lindbergh, Bernard Piccard, pilot of Solar Impulse (50x39mm). f, 66m, Lindbergh, with helmet, Spirit of St. Louis (38x39mm).

No. 2551 — No. 251 - Space flight of Friendship 7, 50th anniv. Stamps inscribed John Glenn: a, 16m Alan Shepard, NASA emblem, X-plane (38x39mm). b, 16m Gordon Cooper in space suit and Chuck Yeager in flight suit, experimental plane (50x39mm). c, 16m, Deke Slayton and XB-70 airplane (38x39mm). d, 66m, Gus Grissom, Friendship 7 emblem, Navy airplane (38x39mm). e, 66m, Scott Carpenter in space suit and Neil Armstrong in flight suit, X-15 airplane (50x39mm). f, 66m, Walter Schirra and airplane (38x39mm).

No. 2552, 175m, Houston, diff. No. 2553, 175m, Presley and Frank Sinatra. No. 2554, 175m, McCartney and other members of the Beatles. No. 2555, 175m, Actor Gary Oldman as Beethoven in *Immortal Beloved*. No. 2556, 175m, Haydn and Beethoven. No. 2557, 175m, Kelly and Charisse, diff. No. 2558, 175m, Garland holding Toto, Hamilton as Wicked Witch of the West, Haley as the Tinman. No. 2559, 175m, Monroe as adult and child. No. 2560, 175m, Taylor with Lassie. No. 2561, 175m, Truffaut, scene from *Jules and Jim*, 1962. No. 2562, 175m, Forman, character from *Hair*, 1979. No. 2563, 175m, Pres. Kennedy and brother, Robert, Lunar Module. No. 2564, 175m, Louis, diff. No. 2565, 175m, St. Joan of Arc, diff. No. 2566, 175m, Leonardo painting the Mona Lisa. No. 2567, 175m, Statue of Newton, XMM-Newton. No. 2568, 175m, Edison, lightbulb. No. 2569, 175m, Van 't Hoff, molecular model, building. No. 2570, 175m, Diderot, statue of Rousseau. No. 2571, 175m, Dickens, building. No. 2572, 175m, Dumas, Scene from *The Count of Monte Cristo*. No. 2573, 175m, Frederick II of Prussia, musical concert. No. 2574, 175m, Napoleon III, diff. No. 2575, 175m, Gaudí, Sagrada Familia Basilica. No. 2576, 175m, Bust of Nefertiti, Henri James Simon, German arts patron. No. 2577, 175m, Hindenburg burning. No. 2578, 175m, Junkers Ju-52 over Guernica. No. 2579, 175m, Douglass, freed slaves. No. 2580, 175m, James Stewart as Lindbergh in *The Spirit of St. Louis*, 1957, Spirit of St. Louis. No. 2581, 175m, Glenn, prehistoric man.

2012, Feb. 28 Perf. 12¾x13¼
Sheets of 6, #a-f
2522-2551 A439 Set of 30 550.00 550.00
Souvenir Sheets
2552-2581 A439 Set of 30 390.00 390.00

Souvenir Sheets

Russian Flag, Agathon and Oleg Fabergé, Fabergé Eggs — A440

Litho. & Embossed With Foil Application
2012, Feb. 28 Perf. 13¼
2582 A440 175m gold & multi 13.00 13.00
 a. With Rossica 2013 inscription in sheet margin 13.00 13.00
2583 A440 175m silver & multi 13.00 13.00
 a. With Rossica 2013 inscription in sheet margin 13.00 13.00

Extinct Animals — A441

No. 2584, 66m — Extinct European animals: a, Coelodonta antiquitatis. b, Deinotherium giganteum. c, Equus ferus ferus. d, Hippopotamus antiquus.
No. 2585, 66m, vert. — Extinct African animals: a, Hippotragus leucophorus. b, Bos primigenius. c, Elephas recki. d, Eudorcas rufina.
No. 2586, 66m, vert. — Extinct bats: a, Nyctimene sanctacrucis. b, Pteropus tokudae. c, Pteropus pilosus. d, Mystacina robusta.
No. 2587, 66m, vert. — Extinct birds: a, Chlorostilbon bracei. b, Prosobonia leucoptera. c, Hemignathus sogittirostris. d, Xenicus longipes.
No. 2588, 66m, vert. — Extinct African birds: a, Psittacula exsul. b, Alectroenas nitidissima. c, Raphus cucullatus. d, Porphyrio coerulescens.
No. 2589, 66m, vert. — Extinct parrots: a, Cyanoramphus ulietanus, Psittacula wardi. b, Ara tricolor, Psittacula exsul. c, Psephotus pulcherrimus. d, Mascarene parrot, Nestor productus.
No. 2590, 66m — Extinct reptiles: a, Desmatosuchus. b, Scaphonyx. c, Erythrosuchus. d, Dimetrodon.
No. 2591, 66m — Extinct marine life: a, Ichthyostega. b, Bothriolepsis. c, Henodus chelyops. d, Belemnitida.
No. 2592, 175m, Ursus spelaeus. No. 2593, 175m, Panthera leo leo, vert. No. 2594, 175m, Dobsonia chapmani, vert. No. 2595, 175m, Mascarenotus murivorus, Aplonis mavornata. No. 2596, 175m, Mascarinus mascarinus, vert. No. 2597, 175m, Cyanoramphus zealandicus. No. 2598, 175m, Lystrosaurus. No. 2599, 175m, Monachus tropicalis.

2012, Apr. 30 Litho. Perf. 13¼
Sheets of 4, #a-d
2584-2591 A441 Set of 8 155.00 155.00
Souvenir Sheets
2592-2599 A441 Set of 8 105.00 105.00

Extinct and Endangered Animals — A442

No. 2600 — Extinct American animals: a, 16m, Macrauchenia patagonica. b, 16m, Bufo periglenes. c, 16m, Mammuthus columbi. d, 66m, Cuvieronius hyodon. e, 66m, Canis dirus. f, 66m, Dasypus bellus.
No. 2601 — Endangered primates: a, 16m, Pan paniscus holding plant near mouth. b, 16m, Two Pan paniscus. c, 16m, Adult and juvenile Pan paniscus. d, 66m, Pan troglodytes. e, 66m, Two Gorilla berengei. f, 66m, Two adult and one juvenile Gorilla berengei.
No. 2602 — Endangered cats: a, 16m, Panthera uncia. b, 16m, Felis planiceps. c, 16m, Panthera tigris tigris. d, 66m, Felis iriomotensis. e, 66m, Felis viverrina. f, 66m, Panthera leo persica.
No. 2603 — Endangered dolphins: a, 16m, Pontoporia blainvillei. b, 16m, Orcaella brevirostris. c, 16m, Cephalorhynchus hectori. d, 66m, Tursiops truncatus ponticus. e, 66m, Lipotes vexillifer. f, 66m, Platanista gangetica.
No. 2604 — Endangered birds: a, 16m, Buteo jamaicensis. b, 16m, Harpyhaliaetus coronatus. c, 16m, Gyps indicus. d, 66m, Pithecophaga jefferyi. e, 66m, Gyps bengalensis. f, 66m, Haliaeetus vociferoides.
No. 2605, vert. — Endangered marine birds: a, 16m, Puffinus newelli, Larus bulleri. b, 16m, Ciconia boyciana. c, 16m, Puffinus mauretanicus, Sterna lorata. d, 66m, Platalea minor. e, 66m, Hymenolaimus malacorhynchos. f, 66m, Mitu mitu.
No. 2606, vert. — Extinct birds: a, 16m, Microgoura meeki. b, 16m, Ophrysia superciliosa. c, 16m, Phalacrocorax perspicillatus, foliage in background. d, 66m, Ptilonopus mercierii. e, 66m, Ectopistes migratorius. f, 66m, Ectopistes migratorius, Columba jouyi.
No. 2607, vert. — Extinct birds: a, 16m, Fregilupus varius. b, 16m, Amazona violacea. c, 16m, Myadestes myadestinus. d, 66m, Phalacrocorax perspicillatus on rock. e, 66m, Pezophaps solitaria. f, 66m, Porphyria mantelli.
No. 2608 — Endangered insects: a, 16m, Crotchiella brachyptera. b, 16m, Cicindela marginipennis. c, 16m, Xylotoles costatus. d,

MOZAMBIQUE

66m, Polyphylla barbata. e, 66m, Cicindela puritana. f, 66m, Polposipus herculeanus.
No. 2609 — Endangered reptiles: a, 16m, Psammobates geometricus. b, 16m, Crocodylus siamensis. c, 16m, Ceratophora tennentii. d, 66m, Varanus komodoensis. e, 66m, Callagur borneoensis. f, 66m, Cyclura pinguis.
No. 2610 — Endangered snakes: a, 16m, Aspidites ramsayi. b, 16m, Paracontias minimus. c, 16m, Montivipera albizona. d, 66m, Paracontias rothschilti. e, 66m, Thamnophis sirtalis. f, 66m, Coluber constrictor priapus.
No. 2611 — Endangered carnivores: a, 16m, Vulpes bengalensis. b, 16m, Puma concolor coryi. c, 16m, Canis lupus rufus. d, 66m, Panthera tigris sumatrae. e, 66m, Leopardus pardalis. f, 66m, Lycaon pictus.
No. 2612 — Endangered marine life: a, 16m, Neophoca cinerea. b, 16m, Phocoena sinus. c, 16m, Thunnus thynnus. d, 66m, Enhydra lutris. e, 66m, Megaptera novaeangliae. f, 66m, Oncorhynchus tshawytscha.
No. 2613 — Extinct animals: a, 16m, Dusicyon australis. b, 16m, Macrotus leucura. c, 16m, Equus quagga quagga. d, 66m, Onychogalea lunata. e, 66m, Thylacinus cynocephalus. f, 66m, Pinuinus impennis.
No. 2614, 175m, Bison antiquus. No. 2615, 175m, Three Gorilla berengei, diff. No. 2616, 175m, Lynx pardinus. No. 2617, 175m, Cephalorhynchus hectori maui, vert. No. 2618, 175m, Neophron percnopterus. No. 2619, 175m, Phalacrocorax featherstoni. No. 2620, 175m, Rhodonessa caryophyllacea. No. 2621, 175m, Ara erythrocephala, vert. No. 2622, 175m, Nicrophorus americanus. No. 2623, 175m, Crocodylus cataphractus, Pseudemys rubriventris bangsi, vert. No. 2624, 175m, Pseudechis porphyriacus. No. 2625, 175m, Carcharodon carcharias, vert. No. 2626, 175m, Monachus schauinslandi. No. 2627, 175m, Panthera leo spelaea.

2012, Apr. 30   **Sheets of 6, #a-f**
2600-2613 A442 Set of 14   255.00 255.00

Souvenir Sheets
2614-2627 A442 Set of 14   180.00 180.00

Extinct and Endangered
Animals — A443

No. 2628 — Extinct Asian animals: a, 16m, Panthera tigris balica. b, 16m, Neofelis nebulosa brachyura. c, 16m, Gazella arabica. d, 16m, Megatapirus augustus. e, 16m, Canis lupus hodophilax. f, 16m, Cervus schomburgki. g, 92m, Dicerorhinus sumatrensis lasiotis. h, 92m, Panthera tigris virgata.
No. 2629, vert. — Extinct animals of Oceania: a, 16m, Rattus nativitatis. b, 16m, Onychogalea lunata. c, 16m, Caloprymnus campestris. d, 16m, Prototroctes oxyrhynchus. e, 16m, Peltobatrachus pustulatus. f, 16m, Hoplodactylus delcourti. g, 92m, Macrotis leucura. h, 92m, Mystacina robusta.
No. 2630 — Extinct rodents: a, 16m, Pseudomys gouldii. b, 16m, Peromyscus pembertoni. c, 16m, Orysomys nelsoni. d, 16m, Geocapromys thoracatus. e, 16m, Leporillus apicalis. f, 16m, Microtis bavaricus. g, 92m, Notomys macrotis. h, 92m, Megalomys luciae.
No. 2631 — Endangered ungulates: a, 16m, Equus hemionus. b, 16m, Gazella cuvieri. c, 16m, Hippocamelus bisculus. d, 16m, Equus africanus. e, 16m, Kobus megaceros. f, 16m, Addax nasomaculatus. g, 92m, Nilgiritragus hylocrius. h, 92m, Bubalus depressicornis.
No. 2632, vert. — Extinct birds: a, 16m, Quiscalus palustris. b, 16m, Bowdleria rufescens. c, 16m, Alectroenas nitidissima. d, 16m, Porzana palmeri. e, 16m, Nesoclopeus poecilopterus. f, 16m, Pennula sandwichensis. g, 92m, Moho nobilis. h, 92m, Gallirallus wakensis.
No. 2633, vert. — Extinct birds: a, 16m, Rhodacanthis flaviceps. b, 16m, Aplonis corvina. c, 16m, Chaunoproctus ferreorostris. d, 16m, Chaetoptila angustipluma. e, 16m, Fregilus varius. f, 16m, Chloridops kona. g, 92m, Ciridops anna. h, 92m, Zoothera terrestris.

No. 2634, vert. — Endangered butterflies: a, 16m, Speyeria zerene myrtleae. b, 16m, Manduca blackburni. c, 16m, Icaricia icarioides fenderi. d, 16m, Ornithoptera alexandrae. e, 16m, Papilio chikae. f, 16m, Ornithoptera croesus. g, 92m, Apodemia mormo langei. h, 92m, Pterourus homerus.
No. 2635 — Endangered turtles: a, 16m, Platysternon megacephalum. b, 16m, Batagur trivittata. c, 16m, Pelochelys cantorii. d, 16m, Psammobates geometricus. e, 16m, Caretta caretta. f, 16m, Mauremys sinensis. g, 92m, Dermochelys coriacea. h, 92m, Eretmochelys imbricata.
No. 2636, 175m, Panthera tigris sondaica. No. 2637, 175m, Thylacinus cynocephalus, vert. No. 2638, 175m, Notomys amplus, Rattus macleari, vert.. No. 2639, 175m, Gazella dama. No. 2640, 175m, Rhodacanthis palmeri, vert. No. 2641, 175m, Zosterops strenuus, vert. No. 2642, 175m, Ornithoptera meridionalis, vert. No. 2643, 175m, Chelonia mydas.

2012, Apr. 30   **Sheets of 8, #a-h**
2628-2635 A443 Set of 8   165.00 165.00

Souvenir Sheets
2636-2643 A443 Set of 8   105.00 105.00

People, Events and
Anniversaries — A444

No. 2644 — Reign of Queen Elizabeth II, 60th anniv.: a, 16m, Queen waving, personal crest, with red and white areas of flag under country name. b, 16m, As "a," with red and white and blue areas of flag under country name. c, 16m, As "a," with continuation of photograph under country name. d, 66m, Queen in white dress, arms, with red, white and blue areas of flag under country name at left. e, 66m, As "d," with no part of flag under country name. f, 66m, As "d," with red, white and blue areas of flag under country name across entire panel.
No. 2645 — Airbus A380: a, 16m, Of Singapore Airlines. b, 16m, Of Transaero Airlines. c, 16m, Of Etihad Airways. d, 66m, With A380 on vertical stabilizer. e, 66m, Of British Airways. f, 66m, With white vertical stabilizer.
No. 2646 — Wilbur Wright (1867-1912), aviation pioneer, and: a, 16m, Wright Flyer, denomination in white. b, 10m, Wright and passenger seated in Wright Flyer. c, 16m, Wilbur and Orville Wright walking. d, 66m, Wright Flyer, no wheels visible. e, 66m, Wright Flyer with wheels. f, 66m, Wright Flyer, Statue of Liberty.
No. 2647 — Harriet Quimby (1875-1912), aviation pioneer, and: a, 16m, Bleriot XI. b, 16m, Nose of Bleriot XI. c, 16m, Inset photograph of Quimby, tail of airplane. d, 66m, Tail of Bleriot XI, complete Bleriot XI in flight. e, 66m, Nose of airplane, diff. f, 66m, Airplane wing tip at left, Bleriot XI at right.
No. 2648 — Hubert Latham (1883-1912), aviation pioneer, and: a, 16m, Dark blue Antoinette VII. b, 16m, Gray Antoinette VII. c, 16m, Lilac rose Antoinette VII. d, 66m, Latham at LR, Prussian blue Antoinette VII. e, 66m, Latham at LL, blue Antoinette VII. f, 66m, Latham at LL, gray Antoinette VII.
No. 2649 — Sinking of the Titanic, cent.: a, 16m, Lifeboats near sinking Titanic. b, 16m, Titanic, bird, ship with sails. c, 16m, Titanic and tugboat. d, 66m, Titanic at sea, other boats, lower portion of Titanic Memorial. e, 66m, Titanic hitting iceberg, ship name at LL. f, 66m, Titanic approaching iceberg, ship name at UL.
No. 2650 — Byron Nelson (1912-2006), golfer, and: a, 16m, Nelson holding golf club while walking. b, 16m, Nelson holding trophy. c, 16m, Nelson swinging golf club. d, 66m, Emblem of World Golf Hall of Fame. e, 66m, 1974 Bob Jones Award. f, 66m, Congressional medal commemorating Nelson.
No. 2651 — Marilyn Monroe (1926-62), actress: a, 16m, Holding open umbrella. b, 16m, Lying on bed, wearing white blouse with striped neckline. c, 16m, Wearing black dress. d, 66m, Wearing necklace on wrist. e, 66m, Holding closed umbrella. f, 66m, Holding beach bag.
No. 2652 — Elvis Presley (1935-77), singer: a, 16m, Pointing finger upward. b, 16m, Holding microphone stand. c, 16m, Playing guitar. d, 66m, Playing guitar, diff. e, 66m, Seated. f, 66m, On motorcycle with woman.
No. 2653 — Achille-Claude Debussy (1862-1918), composer, and painting by Claude Monet from: a, 16m, 1904. b, 16m, 1903. c,

16m, 1880. d, 66m, 1893. e, 66m, 1886. f, 66m, 1868-69.
No. 2654 — Famous Russians: a, 16m, Nikolai Rimsky-Korsakov, composer. b, 16m, Modest Mussorgsky, composer. c, 16m, César Cui, composer. d, 66m, Vladimir Stasov, critic. e, 66m, Mily Balakirev, composer. f, 66m, Alexander Borodin, composer.
No. 2655 — Igor Stravinsky (1882-1971), composer, and: a, 16m, Sculpture, score with C clef at left. b, 16m, Sculpture, musical note to left of country name. c, 16m, Sculpture, no musical note to left of country name. d, 66m, Dancers with beards. e, 66m, Dancers, score with G clef at left. f, 66m, Women dancers in red costumes.
No. 2656 — Peacemakers: a, 16m, Pope John Paul II, St. Peter's Square. b, 16m, Princess Diana, Picasso's Peace Dove. c, 16m, Pope John Paul II, Pieta, by Michelangelo. d, 66m, Mother Teresa. e, 66m, Princess Diana, British flag, Picasso's Peace Dove. f, 66m, Mother Teresa, Nobel medal.
No. 2657 — Mohandas K. Gandhi (1869-1948), Indian independence leader, and: a, 16m, Indian anti-corruption "bank note" without value. b, 16m, Lotus flower, quote written by Gandhi. c, 16m, Sun symbol. d, 66m, Gandhi and his possessions. e, 66m, Gandhi Memorial, Kanyakumari. f, 66m, Gandhi's pocket watch.
No. 2658 — Pan-African Women's Organization, 50th anniv.: a, 16m, Wangari Muta Maathai, 2004 Nobel Peace laureate, and text. b, 16m, Maathai, mother carrying infant. c, 16m, Maasai, two women. d, 66m, Assetou Koite, President of Pan-African Women's Organization, five women. e, 66m, Koite, women, tents. f, 66m, Koite, three women.
No. 2659 — Pope John Paul II (1920-2005): a, 16m, Waving, Two images. c, 16m, Holding infant. d, 66m, Seated, and praying. e, 66m, Holding catechism, arms of Pope John Paul II. f, 66m, Kissing icon of angel.
No. 2660 — Alexander Pushkin State Museum of Fine Arts, Moscow, cent.: a, 16m, 1888 painting by Vincent van Gogh. b, 16m, 1899 painting by Edgar Degas. c, 16m, 1901 painting by Pablo Picasso. d, 66m, Pushkin (1799-1837), writer. e, 66m, 1914 painting by Marc Chagall. f, 66m, 1626 painting by Rembrandt.
No. 2661 — Charles Darwin (1809-82), naturalist: a, 16m, Sauropelta. b, 16m, Allosaurus. c, 16m, Darwin and chimpanzee. d, 66m, Coratocaurus. e, 66m, Darwin, pages from "On the Origin of Species," denomination in black. f, 66m, Darwin, page from "On the Origin of Species," denomination in white.
No. 2662 — Dean Arthur Amadon (1912-2003), ornithologist: a, 16m, Amadon and Haliaeetus leucocephalus. b, 16m, Amadon and Circus cyaneus. c, 16m, Amadon and Buteo magnirostris. d, 66m, Accipiter cooperii, Circus cyaneus. e, 66m, Haliaeetus albicilla. f, 66m, Accipiter gentilis.
No. 2663 — Volcanoes and vulcanologists: a, 16m, Kilauea Volcano, Hawaii, Sir William Hamilton. b, 16m, Sakurajima Volcano, Japan, Alfred Lacroix. c, 16m, Ol Doinyo Lengai Volcano, Tanzania, vulcanologist using camera. d, 66m, Mt. St. Helens, Washington, Déodat Gratet de Dolomieu. e, 66m, Gurung Merapi Volcano, Indonesia, vulcanologist in protective suit. f, 66m, Krakatoa Volcano, Indonesia, Haraldur Sigurdsson.
No. 2664 — Wernher von Braun (1912-77), rocket scientist, and: a, 16m, Apollo 11. b, 16m, Saturn V rocket. c, 16m, Walt Disney. d, 66m, Head of Pres. John F. Kennedy, rocket launch. e, 66m, National Medal of Science, rocket launch. f, 66m, Kennedy and von Braun walking, rocket launch.
No. 2665 — Sally Ride (1951-2012), first American woman astronaut, and: a, 16m, Space Shuttle Challenger with open cargo bay doors. b, 16m, Challenger in flight. c, 16m, Challenger landing. d, 66m, Large picture of launch of Challenger, stars in background. e, 66m, Small picture of launch of Challenger. f, 66m, Challenger in orbit.
No. 2666 — Sergei Krikalev, Russian cosmonaut, and: a, 16m, LIBRAR-1. b, 16m, STS-00. c, 10m, Space Shuttle Endeavour. d, 66m, Soyuz TMA-6. e, 66m, Soyuz TMA-7. f, 66m, Space Shuttle Endeavour, diff.
No. 2667 — Liu Yang, Chinese astronaut: a, 16m, In space suit, waving, rocket. b, 16m, In space suit, saluting, Shenzhou-9, Tiangong-1. c, 16m, In space suit, Shenzhou 9 capsule. d, 66m, In uniform, saluting, Shenzhou-9. e, 66m, In uniform, saluting, Shenzhou-9. f, 66m, In uniform, waving, mission emblem.
No. 2668 — Animals of Kruger National Park, South Africa: a, 16m, Syncerus caffer. b, 16m, Hippopotamus amphibius. c, 16m, Tragelaphus strepsiceros. d, 66m, Lycaeon pictus. e, 66m, Equus quagga burchelli. f, 66m, Acinonyx jubatus.
No. 2669 — Death of Lonesome George, Pinta Island tortoise: a, 16m, With head raised. b, 16m, With head lowered, facing forward, large rock at right. c, 16m, Facing left, with head lowered. d, 66m, Facing forward, with head raised and turned left. e, 66m, With head raised, facing right. f, 66m, With head lowered, facing left, diff.
No. 2670 — Paintings by Edouard Manet (1832-83) from: a, 16m, 1876. b, 16m, 1870.

c, 16m, 1874. d, 66m, 1868. e, 66m, 1866. f, 66m, 1878.
No. 2671 — Jackson Pollock (1912-56), painter, and paintings from: a, 16m, 1946. b, 16m, 1950. c, 16m, 1942. d, 66m, 1940-41. e, 66m, 1943. f, 66m, 1950, diff.
No. 2672 — Art by Russian painters: a, 16m, Portrait of Konstantin Korovin, by Valentin Serov. b, 16m, Self-portrait of Mikhail Nesterov. c, 16m, Self-portrait of Ivan Kramskoi. d, 66m, Portrait of Alexander Herzen, by Nikolai Ge. e, 66m, Portrait of Ivan Goncharov, by Nikolai Yaroshenko. f, 66m, As "a," with different painting in background.
No. 2673, vert. — Paintings by Gustav Klimt (1862-1918) from: a, 16m, 1913. b, 16m, 1902. c, 16m, 1913, drawing by Egon Schiele. d, 66m, 1905. e, 66m, 1907-08. f, 66m, 1910.
No. 2674, 175m, Queen Elizabeth II, British flag. No. 2675, 175m, Airbus A380, diff. No. 2676, 175m, Wright, Wright Flyer, diff. No. 2677, 175m, Quimby, Bleriot XI, diff. No. 2678, 175m, Latham, Antoinette VII, diff. No. 2679, 175m, Titanic, Sterna paradisaea. No. 2680, 175m, Nelson, Congressional medal, diff. No. 2681, 175m, Monroe, diff. No. 2682, 175m, Presley kissing woman. No. 2683, 175m, Debussy, scene from opera Pelléas et Mélisande. No. 2684, 175m, Balakirev, painting by Serov. No. 2685, 175m, Stravinsky, diff. No. 2686, 175m, Kofi Annan, U.N. emblem, Nobel medal. No. 2687, 175m, Gandhi, actor Ben Kinglsey portraying Gandhi. No. 2688, 175m, Koite, Pan-African Women's Organization leaders. No. 2689, 175m, Pope John Paul II, illustration from Catechism. No. 2690, 175m, Pushkin, Alexander Pushkin State Museum of Fine Arts. No. 2691, 175m, Darwin and Euoplocephalus. No. 2692, 175m, Amadon and Accipiter striatus. No. 2693, 175m, Cross-section of volcano, Katia and Maurice Krafft, vulcanologists. No. 2694, 175m, Von Braun and his concept of circular space station. No. 2695, 175m, Ride, Space Shuttle Challenger on launch pad, STS-7 mission emblem. No. 2696, 175m, Krikalev, photograph of land and water taken from space. No. 2697, 175m, Liu Yang, Tiangong-1. No. 2698, 175m, Diceros bicornis. No. 2699, 175m, Lonesome George, diff. No. 2700, 175m, Manet painting from 1873. No. 2701, 175m, Pollock, painting from 1943, diff. No. 2702, 175m, Self-portrait of Nesterov. No. 2703, 175m, Klimt and painting from 1909.

2012, Sept. 30   **Perf. 13¼**
Sheets of 6, #a-f
2644-2673 A444 Set of 30   515.00 515.00

Souvenir Sheets
2674-2703 A444 Set of 30   375.00 375.00

Ungulani Ba Ka
Khosa,
Writer — A445

2012, Oct. 9   **Perf. 11x11¼**
2704 A445 92m buff & gray   6.25 6.25
Lubrapex 2012 Intl. Philatelic Exhibition, Brazil.

Events, Anniversaries and
People — A446

No. 2705 — Mariner 2, 50th anniv., and: a, 16m, Gray vertical line, gray horizontal line at R. b, 16m, Gray horizontal line at L. c, 16m, Gray vertical line. d, 66m, Rocket, Earth. e, 66m, Venus at R. f, 66m, Venus at L.
No. 2706 — Apollo 17, 40th anniv.: a, 16m, Eugene Cernan, astronaut. b, 16m, Base of Lunar Module on Moon. c, 16m, Harrison Schmitt, astronaut. d, 66m, Ronald Evans, astronaut. e, 66m, Lunar Rover. f, 66m, Crew compartment of Lunar Module in space.
No. 2707 — Mars Rover Curiosity: a, 16m, Curiosity on Mars. b, 16m, Curiosity descending to Mars. c, 16m, Interior of Mars. d, 66m, Curiosity, diff. e, 66m, Martian rock. f, 66m, Flight Director Bobak Ferdowsi.
No. 2708 — Alouette 1 satellite, 50th anniv.: a, 16m, Engineers Colin A. Franklin, R.K. Brown and J. Barry, model of Alouette 1. b, 16m, Drs. Leroy Nelms and John Chapman, model of Alouette 1. c, 16m, Franklin and model. d, 66m, Alouette 1, maple leaf at LR. e,

MOZAMBIQUE

66m, Five scientists studying information . f, 66m, Alouette 1, maple leaf at LL.
No. 2709 — Union Pacific Railroad, 150th anniv.: a, 16m, Big Boy No. 4014 locomotive. b, 16m, EMD DDA40X locomotive. c, 16m, Locomotive No. 844. d, 66m, GE AC6000CW locomotive. e, 66m, EMD DDA40X locomotive, diff. f, 66m, Big Boy No. 4019 locomotive.
No. 2710 — Chess match between Bobby Fischer and Boris Spassky, 40th anniv., with : a, 16m, Denomination in black, blue squares at UR. b, 16m, Red and white flag stripes at left. c, 16m, Red and white flag stripes at right. d, 66m, Red and white flag stripes at right. e, 66m, Globe, king's crown over Fischer. f, 66m, Flags of the Soviet Union and U.S.
No. 2711 — Svetozar Gligoric (1923-2012), chess player, and: a, 16m, Ludek Pachmant. b, 16m, Large magnetic chess board.. c, 16m, Vasily Smyslov. d, 66m, Mark Taimanov. e, 66m, Spassky. f, 66m, Chess board.
No. 2712 — Athletes at 2012 Paralympics, London: a, 16m, Cuiping Zhang. b, 16m, David Weir. c, 16m, Mark Rohan. d, 66m, Alan Fonteles Cardozo Oliveira. e, 66m, Esther Vergeer. f, 66m, Sarah Storey.
No. 2713 — Judo champions: a, 16m, Robert Van de Walle. b, 16m, Yasuhiro Yamashita. c, 16m, Shozo Fujii. d, 66m, Naoya Ogawa. e, 66m, David Douillet. f, 66m, Teddy Riner.
No. 2714 — Maurice Ravel (1875-1937), composer, and: a, 16m, Vaslav Nijinsky, choreographer, at piano. b, 16m, Roland Manuel, composer. c, 16m, Jacques Février, pianist. d, 66m, Ricardo Viñes, pianist. e, 66m, Eva Gauthier, opera singer, and various men. f, 66m, 1895 painting by Henri de Toulouse-Lautrec.
No. 2715 — Musicians: a, 16m, Metallica. b, 16m, Bryan Adams. c, 16m, Beyoncé. d, 66m, Shakira. e, 66m, Sir Elton John. f, 66m, Slash.
No. 2716 — Film stars and scenes from their movies: a, 16m, Johnny Depp. b, 16m, Gérard Depardieu. c, 16m, Nicole Kidman and Hugh Jackman. d, 66m, Angelina Jolie. e, 66m, Morgan Freeman and Jack Nichloson. f, 66m, Nicholson.
No. 2717 — Pope Benedict XVI: a, 16m, And painting by Raphael. b, 16m, Wearing zucchetto. c, 16m, And Vatican City arms. d, 66m, And arms of the Holy See. e, 66m, And arms of Pope Benedict XVI. f, 66m, Wearing red hat.
No. 2718 — Mother Teresa (1910-97), humanitarian, and: a, 16m, Nobel medal. b, 16m, Pope John Paul II. c, 16m, Earth. d, 66m, One child. e, 66m, Two children. f, 66m, Window of building.
No. 2719 — Princess Diana (1961-97), and London landmarks: a, 16m, Big Ben. b, 16m, St. Paul's Cathedral. c, 16m, Tower Bridge. d, 66m, Buckingham Palace. e, 66m, Big Ben, diff. f, 66m, Waterloo Bridge.
No. 2720 — Dr. Christiaan Barnard (1922-2001), first heart transplant surgeon, and: a, 16m, Operating room . b, 16m, Red cross. c, 16m, First heart transplant patient, Louis Washkansky. d, 66m, Hearts, arrow, red crosses. e, 66m, Medical helicopter. f, 66m, Cooler for transplant organs, red crosses.
No. 2721 — Red Cross campaign against AIDS: a, 16m, AIDS virus, mother holding child. b, 16m, Red Cross worker inspecting packages. c, 16m, Red Cross worker holding child. d, 66m, Child washing hands. e, 66m, Woman hugging Red Cross worker. f, 66m, People around large AIDS ribbon.
No. 2722 — Battle of Borodino, 200th anniv.: a, 16m, Napoleon Bonaparte, 1897 painting by Vasily Vereshchagin of battle. b, 16m, Four horsemen. c, 16m, Soldiers flags, one horseman. d, 66m, Horseman in blue uniform. e, 66m, Illustration of battle by unknown artist. f, 66m, Russian Field Marshal Mikhail Kutuzov, 1952 painting by Anatoly Shepelyuk.
No. 2723 — League for the Protection of Birds, cent.: a, 16m, Milvus milvus. b, 16m, Aquila fasciata. c, 16m, Falco naumanni. d, 66m, Pandion haliaetus. e, 66m, Tetrax tetrax. f, 66m, Coragyps atratus.
No. 2724 — Riga Zoo, cent.: a, 16m, Panthera leo. b, 16m, Bubo scandiaca. c, 16m, Cervus albirostris .d, 66m, Ursus arctos middendorffi. e, 66m, Tapirus terrestris. f, 66m, Amphiprion ocellaris.
No. 2725 — Sea shells: a, 16m, Spondylus princeps, Bulla striata. b, 16m, Scafander lignarius, Amusium japonicum. c, 16m, Tapes philippinarum, Murex pecten. d, 66m, Donax variabilis, Ovatella firmini, Haminoea hydalis. e, 66m, Pterynotus elongatus, Hexaplex radix. f, 66m, Hexaplex trunculus, Aplysia depilans, Isaac Lea (1792-1886), conchologist.
No. 2726 — Mary Anning (1799-1847), fossil collector: a, 16m, Dimorphodon macronyx. b, 16m, Anning, Mortoniceras inflatum fossil. c, 16m, Fossil bones. d, 66m, Ichthyosaurus fossils. e, 66m, Plesiosaurus. f, 66m, Anning, Plesiosaurus dolichodeirus fossil.
No. 2727 — Henry John Elwes (1846-1922), lepidopterist: a, 16m, Borboleta monarca. b, 16m, Grande borboleta azul, animal name at UR under denomination. c, 16m, Grande borboleta azul, animal name at UL. d, 66m, Elwes, Borboleta asa-de-pássaro. e, 66m, Borboleta "Morpho" azul. f, 66m, Elwes, Borboleta monarca.
No. 2728 — Tadas Ivanauskas (1882-1970), zoologist, and: a, 16m, Deer, Bubo bubo. b,

16m, Cygnus olor. c, 16m, Accipiter gentilis. d, 66m, Raccoon, Aquila pomarina. e, 66m, Upupa epops. f, 66m, Deer, Strix aluco, mouse.
No. 2729 — Gordon H. Cunningham (1892-1962), mycologist: a, 16m, Cunningham and Hygrophorus lucorum. b, 16m, Lycoperdon perlatum. c, 16m, Leccinum scabrum. d, 66m, Bolbitius psittacinus. e, 66m, Calocerea viscosa. f, 66m, Cunningham, Armillaria gallica.
No. 2730 — Dian Fossey (1932-85), zoologist: a, 16m, Gorilla beringei beringei. b, 16m, Fossey with forillas, head of Gorilla beringei beringei. c, 16m, Fossey with book, two Gorilla beringei beringei. d, 66m, Fossey, two Gorilla beringei beringei. e, 66m, Fossey, one Gorilla beringei beringei. f, 66m, Two Gorilla beringei beringei.
No. 2731 — Gustaf Dalén (1869-1937), 1912 Nobel Physics laureate, and: a, 16m, Celarain Lighthouse, Mexico. b, 16m, Point Stephens Lighthouse, Australia. c, 16m, Peninsula Point Lighthouse, Michigan. d, 66m, Dalén light for lighthouses. e, 66m, Barrenjoey Lighthouse, Australia. f, 66m, Skerryvore Lighthouse, Scotland.
No. 2732 — Charleston Lighthouse, South Carolina, and birds: a, 16m, Aix sponsa. b, 16m, Tringa incana. c, 16m, Larus californicus. d, 66m, Eudocimus albus. e, 66m, Lanus atricilla. f, 66m, Recurvirostra americana.
No. 2733 — UNESCO World Heritage Sites, 40th anniv.: a, 16m, Island of Mozambique. b, 16m, Osun-Osogbo Sacred Grove, Nigeria. c, 16m, Koutammakou, Land of the Battamariba, Togo. d, 66m, Royal Palaces of Abomey, Benin. e, 66m, Stone Circles of Senegambia, Gambia and Senegal. f, 66m, Kunta Kinteh Island, Gambia.
No. 2734 — Expo 2012, Yeosu, South Korea: a, 16m, Sky Tower, Thunnus thynnus. b, 16m, Ocean Pavilion, Tursiops truncatus. c, 16m, Marine Life Pavilion, Manta birostris. d, 66m, Korean Pavilion, Dugong dugon. e, 66m, Big-O, Dendrochirus zebra. f, 66m, Expo Digital Gallery, Phoca vitulina.
No. 2735, 175m, Mariner 2, Venus, diff. **No. 2736**, 175m, Apollo 17 Lunar Module, Lunar Rover, and astronaut on Moon. **No. 2737**, 175m, Mars Science Laboratory capsule containing Curiosity. **No. 2738**, 175m, Chapman and Alouette 1. **No. 2739**, 175m, Union Pacific No. 119 locomotive. **No. 2740**, 175m, Fischer and Spassky shaking hands. **No. 2741**, 175m, Gligoric and Fischer. **No. 2742**, 175m, Oscar Pistorius, Paralympian. **No. 2743**, 175m, Riner, diff. **No. 2744**, 175m, Ravel and Bolero dancers. **No. 2745**, 175m, U2. **No. 2746**, 175m, Brad Pitt. **No. 2747**, 175m, Pope Benedict XVI, crucifix. **No. 2748**, 175m, Mother Tereas holding child. **No. 2749**, 175m, Princess Diana, Buckingham Palace, diff. **No. 2750**, 175m, Barnard, heart, crosses. **No. 2751**, 175m, Africans, map, AIDS ribbon. **No. 2752**, 175m, Napoleon Bonaparte, 1987 Russian coin commemorating Battle of Borodino. **No. 2753**, 175m, Ciconia ciconia. **No. 2754**, 175m, Lemur catta, obverse and reverse of Latvian coin commemorating Riga Zoo. **No. 2755**, 175m, Lea, Venus verrucosa. **No. 2756**, 175m, Anning, Plesiosaurus macrocephalus fossil. **No. 2757**, 175m, Elwes and Borboleta "Morpho" cor-de-rosa. **No. 2758**, 175m, Ivanauskas, Ciconia nigra. **No. 2759**, 175m, Cunningham, Plectania melastoma. **No. 2760**, 175m, Fossey, three Gorilla beringei beringei. **No. 2761**, 175m, Dalén, Nobel medal. **No. 2762**, 175m, Charleston Lighthouse, Larus californicus, diff. **No. 2763**, 175m, Historic Cairo UNESCO World Heritage Site. **No. 2764**, 175m, Aquarium at Expo 2012.

2012, Oct. 30   **Perf. 13¼**
Sheets of 6, #a-f
2705-2734 A446 Set of 30 500.00 500.00
Souvenir Sheets
2735-2764 A446 Set of 30 360.00 360.00

A447

No. 2765 — Rugby players from: a, 16m, New Zealand and South Africa, denomination at bottom. b, 16m, New Zealand and South Africa, denomination at top. c, 92m, Botswana and Zambia. d, 92m, Mexico and Jamaica.
No. 2766 — Rotary International emblem and cricket players: a, 16m, Adam Gilchrist. b, 16m, Donald Bradman. c, 92m, Viv Richards. d, 92m, Brian Lara.
No. 2767 — Table tennis players: a, 16m, Ding Ning. b, 16m, Wu Yang. c, 92m, Jörgen Perssson, denomination at UR. d, 92m, Chinese player misidentified as Jörgen Persson, denomination at UL.

No. 2768 — Gilles Villeneuve (1950-82), race car driver, and: a, 16m, Race car, checkered flag. b, 16m, Race car. c, 92m, Race car, diff. d, 92m, Race car and track diagram.
No. 2769 — Lions International emblem and golfers: a, 16m, Ben Hogan. b, 16m, Jack Nicklaus. c, 92m, Bobby Jones. d, 92m, Arnold Palmer.
No. 2770 — Niels Bohr (1885-1962), physicist, and: a, 16m, Formula. b, 16m, Diagram of atom. c, 92m, Diagram of atom, diff. d, 92m, Albert Einstein.
No. 2771 — 2012 Nobel laureates: a, 16m, Serge Haroche, David J. Wineland, physics. b, 16m, Robert J. Lefkowitz, Brian K Kobilka, chemistry. c, 92m, Shinya Yamanaka, Sir John B. Gurdon, physiology or medicine. d, 92m, Alvin E. Roth, Lloyd S. Shapley, economics.
No. 2772 — Minerals: a, 16m, Beryl. b, 16m, Scapolite. c, 92m, Tourmaline. d, 92m, Beryl, diff.
No. 2773 — Campaign against malaria, 50th anniv. (in 2012): a, 16m, Mosquito, Brazil #C106, Ghana #128. b, 16m, Child receiving medicine, Syria #C267-C268. c, 92m, Child receiving medicine, Tunisia #404-405. d, 92m, Mosquito on globe, Democratic Republic of Congo #414-415.
No. 2774 — Orchids: a, 16m, Stanhopea insignis frost. b, 16m, Angraecum sesquipedale. c, 92m, Lycaste macrophylla. d, 92m, Miltonia vexillaria.
No. 2775 — Cat breeds: a, 16m, Singapura. b, 16m, Toyger. c, 92m, Bombay. d, 92m, Cymric.
No. 2776 — Fish: a, 16m, Signigobius biocellatus. b, 16m, Synchiropus splendidus. c, 92m, Antennarius commersoni. d, 92m, Pterois antennata.
No. 2777 — Dogs in art: a, 16m, Dogs Fighting, by Frans Snyders. b, 16m, Master Pelham, by George Romney. c, 92m, Two Hunting Dogs Tied to a Tree Stump, by Jacopo Bassano. d, 92m, Dog Pointing at a Partridge, by Jean-Baptiste Oudry.
No. 2778 — Paintings and self-portraits of Impressionist painters: a, 16m, Claude Monet. b, 16m, Edgar Degas. c, 92m, Pierre-Auguste Renoir. d, 92m, Freedéric Bazille.
No. 2779 — Paintings by Marc Chagall (1887-1985): a, 16m, The Concert, 1957, and Self-portrait, 1909-10. b, 16m, Chagall, The Madonna of the Village, 1942. c, 92m, Chagall, To My Betrothed, 1911. d, 92m, Cow with an Umbrella, 1946.
No. 2780 — Christmas art: a, 16m, Adoration of the Magi, by Gentile da Fabriano. b, 16m, The Annunciation, by Fra Filippo Lippi. c, 92m, Concert of Angels, by Matthias Grünewald. d, 92m, Adoration of the Shepherds, by Gerard von Honthorst.
No. 2781 — Sculptures by Alberto Chissano (1935-94): a, 16m, Three heads. b, 16m, One head. c, 92m, Chissano and head. d, 92m, One head, diff.
No. 2782 — Hans Werner Henze (1929-2012), composer: a, 16m, Scene from opera The Hoopoe and the Triumph of Filial Love.. b, 16m, Henze musical notes and clef. c, 92m, Scene from opera Bajazzo. d, 92m, Scene from opera Gogo no Eiko.
No. 2783 — Niccolò Paganini (1782-1840), composer: a, 16m, Paganini and La Scala Theater, Milan. b, 16m, Napoleon I, violin, score for Napoleon Sonata. c, 92m, Sculpture of Paganini by Sutton Betti, The Grand Canal of Venice, by J. M. W. Turner. d, 92m, Bust of Paganini, by Pierre-Jean David, violin.
No. 2784 — Genoese ship construction: a, 16m, 12th cent. Genoese ship, boat builder. b, 16m, Construction of hull. c, 92m, Construction of hull, diff. d, 92m, 11th century ship, boat builder.
No. 2785 — Venetian ship construction: a, 16m, Drawing of Venetian ship by Bernhard von Breidenbach. b, 16m, Ship and cross-section diagram. c, 92m, Drawings and Venetian galley. d, 92m, Ship under construction, boat building tools.
No. 2786 — Submarines: a, 16m, USS Gato (SS-212). b, 16m, Shchuka Class submarine, Russia. c, 92m, Japanese submarine I-506. d, 92m, German submarine U-23.
No. 2787 — Tanks: a, 16m, German Neubaufahrzeug Nr. 3-5 tank. b, 16m, Italian M 13/40 tank. c, 92m, M4 Sherman tank with 105mm howitzer, United States. d, 92m, Soviet T-34/76 tank.
No. 2788 — Japanese Shinkansen high-speed trains: a, 16m, Series N700. b, 16m, Series E6. c, 92m, Series E5. d, 92m, Series E3.
No. 2789 — European high-speed trains: a, 16m, FS Class ETR 500 Frecciarossa. b, 16m, LNER Class A4 4468 Mallard. c, 92m, AVE Class 102 Talgo 350. d, 92m, DRG Class SVT 137 Hamburg.
No. 2790 — Fire-fighting aircraft: a, 16m, Conair Turbo Firecat. b, 16m, Aerospatial AS-350B-2 Ecureuil helicopter. c, 92m, PZL-Swidnik W-3A Sokol helicopter. d, 92m, Canadair CL-215.
No. 2791 — Japanese aircraft: a, 16m, Mitsubishi F-4EJ Kai Phantom. b, 16m, Sikorsky (Mitsubishi) SH-60K (S70B-3) helicopter. c, 92m, ShinMaywa US-1A. d, 92m, Mitsubishi F-2A.

No. 2792 — Drones: a, 16m, Taurus UAV. b, 16m, MQ-1 Predator. c, 92m, Gojjet. d, 92m, MQ-4C BAMS Triton.
No. 2793 — Famous Atlantic hurricanes: a, 16m, Hurricane Katrina, 2005. b, 16m, Hurricane Felix, 2007. c, 92m, Hurricane Wilma, 2005. d, 92m, Hurricane Julia, 2010.
No. 2794 — New Year 2013 (Year of the Snake): a, 16m, Snake and yin-yang. b, 16m, Snake at right, Chinese text. c, 92m, Snake at left, Chinese text. d, 92m, Snake and "2013."
No. 2795, 175m, Percy Montgomery and South African rugby team. No. 2796, 175m, Rotary International emblem, cricket player Sachin Tendulkar. No. 2797, 175m, Table tennis player Wu Yang. No. 2798, 175m, Villeneuve and Ferrari 312T3 race car. No. 2799, 175m, Golfer Annika Sorenstam. No. 2800, 175m, Bohr, diagram and equation. No. 2801, 175m, Mo Yan, 2012 Nobel Literature laureate. No. 2802, 175m, Scapolite and tourmaline. No. 2803, 175m, Mosquito on globe, Ryukyu Islands #95-96. No. 2804, 175m, Cypripedium orchids. No. 2805, 175m, Asian semi-longhair cat. No. 2806, 175m, Pteroidichthys amboinensis. No. 2807, 175m, The Hunting Party with Tsar Alexander III and Tsarina Maria Fedorovna, by Nikolai Semenovich Samokish. No. 2808, 175m, Garden at Sainte-Adresse, by Monet. No. 2809, 175m, Song of Songs IV, 1958, by Chagall, Portrait of Chagall, 1910, by Yury Pen. No. 2810, 175m, Adoration of the Magi, by Giotto di Bondone. No. 2811, 175m, Chissano and sculpture, diff. No. 2812, 175m, Henze and character from opera Gisela. No. 2813, 175m, Paganini and Il Cannone Guarnerius. No. 2814, 175m, Genoese ship under construction, 11th cent. No. 2815, 175m, Venetian galley. No. 2816, 175m, Tench Class submarine, United States. No. 2817, 175m, Soviet T-34/76 tank, diff. No. 2818, 175m, Shinkansen Series E954. No. 2819, 175m, SNCF TGV Thalys PBKA. No. 2820, 175m, Sikorsky S-70A Firehawk helicopter. No. 2821, 175m, Blue Impulse Kawasaki T4-46 5726. No. 2822, 175m, Polar Hawk and Boeing Phantom Ray drones. No. 2823, 175m, Hurricane Sandy. No. 2824, 175m, Snake, yin yand and Chinese text.

2013, Feb. 20   Litho.   **Perf. 13¼**
Sheets of 4, #a-d
2765-2794 A447 Set of 30 450.00 450.00
Souvenir Sheets
2795-2824 A447 Set of 30 375.00 375.00

Worldwide Fund for Nature (WWF) — A448

No. 2825 — Smutsia temminicki (Ground pangolin): a, Pangolin facing right. b, Head of pangolin, pangolin rolled in ball. c, Pangolin on rock. d, Pangolin and juvenile.
175p, Two Smutsia temminicki.

2013, Mar. 25   Litho.   **Perf. 13¼**
2825 Horiz. strip of 4 15.00 15.00
 a.-b. A448 16m Either single 1.10 1.10
 c.-d. A448 92m Either single 6.25 6.25
 e. Miniature sheet of 8, 2 each
       #2825a-2825d, perf.
       13x13¼   30.00 30.00
Souvenir Sheet
Perf. 13¼ Syncopated
2826 A448 175m multi   12.00 12.00
No. 2826 contains one 50x39mm stamp.

World Vision — A448a

2013   Litho.   **Perf. 11x11½**
2826A A448a 92m multi   — —

MOZAMBIQUE

Transportation and Space — A449

No. 2827 — Dog teams: a, 16m, Four Canadian Eskimo dogs in harnesses. b, 16m, Two Siberian huskies in harnesses, leg of front dog behind "OC" of country name. c, 16m, Two Siberian huskies, dog sled. d, 16m, Tamaskan dogs. e, 16m, Alaskan malamute dogs. f, 16m, Two Siberian huskies in harnesses, front leg above "C" in country name.
No. 2828 — Horse transportation: a, 16m, Rider standing on two horses of four-horse team. b, 16m, Horse and sulky. c, 16m, Russian troika. d, 16m, Carriage drawn by two horses. e, 16m, Carriage drawn by six horses. f, 16m, English mail coach drawn by four horses.
No. 2829 — Famous bicycle riders in the Tour de France: a, 16m, Louison Bobet. b, 16m, Jacques Anquetil. c, 16m, Eddy Merckx. d, 16m, Bernard Hinault. e, 16m, Mark Cavendish. f, 16m, Bradley Wiggins.
No. 2830 — Ying Liwei, Chinese astronaut: a, 16m, And Shenzhou 5 re-entry capsule. b, 16m, In military uniform, with Shenzhou 5 rocket, flag of People's Republic of China. c, 16m, In spacesuit, adjusting helmet, Shenzhou 5 in space. d, 16m, In spacesuit, waving, Shenzhou 5 launch. e, 16m, In capsule wearing helmet. f, 16m, In capsule, with two fingers raised.
No. 2831 — Alan B. Shepard, Jr. (1923-98), American astronaut, and: a, 16m, Apollo 14 emblem. b, 16m, Apollo 14 plaque. c, 16m, Re-entry of Apollo 14. d, 16m, Mercury-Redstone 3 rocket. e, 16m, Mercury capsule. f, 92m, Statue of Shepard, by Robert L. Rasmussen.
No. 2832 — Apollo 8: a, 16m, Crew of Apollo 8 and launch. b, 16m, Apollo 8 orbiting Moon. c, 16m, Apollo 8 and Earth. d, 16m, Crew of Apollo 8, Apollo 8 and Earth. e, 16m, Crew in spacesuits, Apollo 8 emblem. f, 92m, Apollo 8 capsule, launch of Apollo 8.
No. 2833 — Iceboats with sail inscriptions of: a, 16m, 300. b, 16m, DM 8133. c, 16m, 44. d, 16m, DM 8931. e, 16m, 313. f, 92m, DM G-887.
No. 2834 — 2012-13 Vendée Globe Regatta: a, 10m, Crewman adjusting sails. b, 16m, Boat with red and white sail. c, 16m, Crewman trying to keep sailboat from capsizing. d, 16m, Sailboats in line. e, 16m, Boat with black and yellow sails. f, 92m, Sailboat with blue and green hull.
No. 2835 — Rescue ships: a, 16m, 44-foot boat. b, 16m, United States Coast Guard hydrofoil. c, 16m, 45-foot boat. d, 16m, United States Coast Guard buoy tender No. 277. e, 16m, Severn Class rescue boat. f, 92m, 47-foot boat.
No. 2836 — Icebreakers: a, 16m, MV Paaldeberg, Russia. b, 16m, Captain Chlebnikov, Russia. c, 16m, Oden, Sweden. d, 16m, Polarstern, Germany. e, 16m, Tempera, Finland. f, 92m, Polar Pevek, Norway.
No. 2837 — Steam locomotives: a, 16m, London & North Eastern Railway Class B17 4-0-0 Sandringham. b, 16m, London Midland & Scottish Railway 4-4-0. c, 16m, Metropolitan Railway tank locomotive. d, 16m, Johore State Railway 4-6-2. e, 16m, Dublin and South Easter Railway 4-4-2 King George. f, 92m, German State Railways 4-6-2 Pacific Express.
No. 2838 — London Metro cars: a, 16m, From 1938. b, 16m, From 1940. c, 16m, From 1973. d, 16m, From 1986. e, 16m, From 2011. f, 92m, Model of car of the future.
No. 2839 — Monorails: a, 16m, Mark VI. b, 16m, Innovia 300 on bridge. c, 16m, Mumbai monorail. d, 16m, Transrapid 09. e, 16m, Innovia 300, diff. f, 92m, Tama Toshi monorail.
No. 2840 — High-speed trains: a, 16m, ETR-500. b, 16m, TGV Réseau. c, 16m, AVE Talgo 350. d, 16m, Eurostar. e, 16m, KTX 2. f, 92m, Transrapid TR-09.
No. 2841 — Early aviators and their airplanes: a, 16m, Richard "Dick" Read Bentley and DeHavilland Moth. b, 16m, Claude Grahame-White and biplane. c, 16m, Owen Cathcart-Jones and Miles Hawk trainer. d, 16m, Alberto Santos-Dumont and Demoiselle. e, 16m, Ross Macpherson Smith and Vickers Vimy biplane. f, 92m, Alan John Cobham and Short Singapore flying boat.
No. 2842 — Small jet airplanes: a, 16m, Cessna Citation X. b, 16m, Hawker 800. c, 16m, Embraer Phenom 100. d, 16m, Gulfstream G200. e, 16m, Gulfstream G550. f, 92m, Dassault Falcon 2000.
No. 2843 — Last flight of the Concorde, 10th anniv.: a, 16m, Concorde and André Turcat, first French Concorde pilot. b, 16m, Barbara Harmer, first female Concorde pilot. c, 16m, Concorde and Sir Archibald Russell, designer of Concorde. d, 16m, Concorde and Brian Trubshaw, first British Concorde pilot. e, 16m, Concorde on fire, July 25, 2000. f, 92m, Last flight of Concorde, Nov. 26, 2003.
No. 2844 — Military helicopters: a, 16m, Mil Mi-24A. b, Boeing-Sikorsky RAH-66 Comanche. c, 16m, AgustaWestland AW-101. d, 16m, Westland Apache WAH-64D Longbow. e, 16m, Harbin Z-19. f, 92m, Mil Mi-171E.
No. 2845 — Drones: a, 16m, NASA Altair. b, 16m, General Atomics MQ-9 Reaper. c, 16m, UAV X-47B. d, 16m, Lockheed Martin RQ-170 Sentinel. e, 16m, UAV X-47A. f, 92m, General Atomics MQ-1C Gray Eagle.
No. 2846 — Dirigibles: a, 16m, Clouth, Germany. b, 16m, First British military dirigible. c, 16m, Torrres Quevedo, Spain. d, 16m, Ville de Paris, France. e, 16m, Baby, Great Britain. f, 92m, Zodiac type dirigible, France.
No. 2847 — Old race cars: a, 16m, 1954 Maserati 250F. b, 16m, 1951 Cooper Climax T51. c, 16m, 1940 Bugatti T73C. d, 16m, 1960 Lotus 18. e, 16m, 1966 Eagle-Climax T2G. f, 92m, 1952 Cooper Bristol.
No. 2848 — Popemobiles: a, 16m, FCS Star and Pope John Paul II. b, 16m, Metalpar Mercedes-Benz ML 430 and Pope John Paul II. c, 16m, Mercedes-Benz M Class and Pope Benedict XVI. d, 16m, Fiat Nuova Campagnola and Pope John Paul II. e, 16m, Mercedes-Benz M Class and Pope Benedict XVI. f, 92m, Pope Benedict XVI standing in Mercedes-Benz.
No. 2849 — Ferrari automobiles: a, 16m, Enzo Ferrari (1898-1988) and Auto Avio Costruzione 815. b, 16m, Ferrari 125 S. c, 16m, Ferrari 250 GTO. d, 16m, Ferrari 312 P. e, 16m, Ferrari 512 BB. f, 92m, Enzo Ferrari and Ferrari F40.
No. 2850 — Formula 1 racing champions: a, 16m, Sebastian Vettel in Renault race car. b, 16m, Vettel and Formula 1 Championship Trophy. c, 16m, Michael Schumacher and Formula 1 Championship Trophy. d, 16m, Schumacher in Mercedes race car. e, 16m, Fernando Alonso in Ferrari race car. f, 92m, Alonso and Formula 1 Championship Trophy.
No. 2851 — Motorcycles: a, 16m, 1896 Hildebrand Wolfmuller. b, 16m, 1911 Henderson. c, 16m, 1905 FN. d, 16m, 1925 DKW ZM175. e, 16m, 1920 Megola. f, 92m, 1921 Scott Flying Squirrel.
No. 2852 — Mail transport: a, 16m, English Royal Parcel Mail horse-drawn carriage. b, 16m, Workers and sacks in post office. c, 16m, Railroad mail car. d, 16m, Royal Mail truck. e, 16m, Workers and mail sacks near Royal Mail horse-drawn carriage. f, 92m, Mail sacks loaded on Royal Mail horse-drawn wagon.
No. 2853 — Police and rescue vehicles: a, 16m, Eurocopter AS-365N-3 Dauphin 2 police helicopter. b, 16m, BMW R1200RT-P police motorcycle. c, 16m, Higer KLQ6540 ambulance. d, 16m, Scania 94D fire truck. e, 16m, Lenco Bear Cat SWAT Team vehicle. f, 92m, Holden Rodeo police truck.
No. 2854 — Fire-fighting equipment: a, 16m, 1873 hose wagon. b, 16m, 1841 Paul Hodge steam-driven pumper and firefighter. c, 16m, Firemen on bicycle-chain driven vehicle, 1899 hose and ladder wagon. d, 16m, 1880 Piano pumper wagon. e, 92m, 1910 Electric fire engine, fireman in protective clothing. f, 92m, Fire truck with hoses and ladder.
No. 2855 — Military vehicles: a, 16m, Soldiers carrying kettle near Red Cross ambulance. b, 16m, Truck with open bed pulling gun. c, 16m, Red Cross workers near ambulances. d, 16m, Soldiers and Maxim motorcycle with sidecar. e, 92m, Cargo vehicle on tracks. f, 92m, Truck with ladder.
No. 2856, 175m, Siberian husky, dogs pulling sled. No. 2857, 175m, A Royal Mail Coach on a Flooded Road, by James Pollard. No. 2858, 175m, Henri Desgrange, Tour de France cyclist. No. 2859, 175m Yang Liwei, Shezhou 5, diff. No. 2860, 175m, Shepherd and Apollo 14 capsule. No. 2861, 175m, Apollo 8 orbiting Moon, diff. No. 2862, 175m, Iceboat with 221 on sail. No. 2863, 175m, Boat in Vendée Globe Regatta. No. 2864, 175m, 44-foot United States Coast Guard boat. No. 2865, 175m, Arctic Express icebreaker, Finland. No. 2866, 175m, Great Indian Peninsula Railway 4-6-0 steam locomotive. No. 2867, 175m, London Metro car from 1992. No. 2868, 175m, Mark VII monorail. No. 2869, 175m, ETR-500 train, diff. No. 2870, 175m, Amelia Earhart and Lockheed Vega. No. 2871, 175m, Learjet 65. No. 2872, 175m, Last flight of the Concorde, Nov. 26, 2003, diff. No. 2873, 175m, Boeing CH-47 Chinook helicopter. No. 2874, 175m, Firebird-9 drone. No. 2875, 175m, 1935 Alfa Romeo Bimotore. No. 2876, 175m, Capezza dirigible, France. No. 2877, 175m, Pope Benedict XVI and Mercedes-Benz ML 430 Popemobile. No. 2878, 175m, Enzo Ferrari and Ferrari F430. No. 2879, 175m, Formula 1 race car, Vettel holding Korean Grand Prix trophy. No. 2880, 175m, 1911 Indian motorcycle. No. 2881, 175m, English air mail flight, 1911. No. 2882, 175m, Ziegler Z8 airport foam spraying vehicle. No. 2883, 175m, 1863 fire wagon. No. 2884, 175m, Military truck, diff.

2013, Mar. 25   Litho.   Perf. 13¼
Sheets of 6, #a-f
2827-2855   A449   Set of 29   325.00   325.00
Souvenir Sheets
2856-2884   A449   Set of 29   350.00   350.00

A450

No. 2885 — Coat of arms of Pope Benedict XVI and Pope Benedict XVI: a, 16m, Wearing miter. b, 16m, Wearing zucchetto, domed ceiling in background. c, 92m, Wearing zucchetto, waving. d, 92m, Wearing zucchetto and red stole.
No. 2886 — Coat of arms of Pope Francis and Pope Francis: a, 16m, Wearing miter. b, 16m, Wearing miter and holding crucifix. c, 92m, Wearing zucchetto. d, 92m, Wearing zucchetto and glasses.
No. 2887 — Marilyn Monroe (1926-62), actress: a, 16m, With husband, Joe DiMaggio. b, 16m, With bird on finger. c, 92m, Blowing bubble. d, 92m, Wearing red dress and earrings.
No. 2888 — Mohandas K. Gandhi (1869-1948), Indian independence leader: a, 16m, And Russia #3639. b, 16m, Sitting with crossed legs. c, 92m, Sitting. d, 92m, Women in background.
No. 2889 — Mao Zedong (1893-1976), Chinese communist leader: a, 16m, Reading papers. b, 16m, Wearing cap. c, 92m, With Chinese text at right. d, 92m, With flag of People's Republic of China at left.
No. 2890 — Prince William: a, 16m, Helicopter at right. b, 16m, Wearing air force uniform and flight helmet. c, 92m, Leaving helicopter, squadron emblem at right. d, 92m, Piloting helicopter.
No. 2891 — Female world chess champions: a, 16m, Zhao Xue, China. b, 16m, Humpy Koneru, India. c, 92m, Kataryna Lahno, Ukraine. d, 92m, Viktorije Cmilyte, Lithuania.
No. 2892 — Scouting trefoil and: a, 16m, Boy Scout on bicycle. b, 16m, Boy Scouts carrying canoe. c, 92m, Boy Scout with model airplane, Inachis io. d, 92m, Boy Scout at campfire, Heteronympha merope.
No. 2893 — Paintings by Raphael (1483-1520): a, 16m, Adoration of the Magi, 1502-04. b, 16m, St. George Slaying the Dragon, 1504. c, 92m, Portrait of Bindo Altoviti, 1515. d, 92m, Young Man with an Apple, 1505.
No. 2894 — Paintings by Eugene Delacroix (1798-1863): a, 16m, Christ on the Sea of Galilee, 1854. b, 16m, Orphan Girl at the Cemetery, 1823. c, 92m, Self-portrait. d, 92m, Arab Horses Fighting in a Stable, 1860.
No. 2895 — Paintings by Vincent van Gogh (1853-90): a, 16m, Memory of the Garden at Etten, 1888. b, 16m, Seascape at Saintes-Maries (Fishing Boats at Sea), 1888. c, 92m, A Pair of Shoes, 1887. d, 92m, Noon: Rest from Work, 1890.
No. 2896 — Paintings by Ivan Aivazovsky (1817-1900): a, 16m, Approximation of the Storm, 1877. b, 16m, Crimea, 1852. c, 92m, Ship Twelve Apostles, 1897. d, 92m, Morning at Sea, 1849, and Ocean, 1896.
No. 2897 — 2014 Winter Olympics, Sochi, Russia: a, 16m, Speed skating. b, 16m, Skiing. c, 92m, Curling. d, 92m, Bobsled.
No. 2898 — Int. Red Cross, 150th anniv.: a, 16m, Rescue worker wearing gas mask carrying man. b, 16m, Jean Henri Dunant, founder of Red Cross, and nurse carrying Red Cross flag. c, 92m, Rescue dogs at work. d, 92m, Red Cross workers caring for children.
No. 2899 — Steam locomotives: a, 16m, Empire State Express locomotive. b, 16m, 4MT, England. c, 92m, Porter 0-4-0, United States. d, 92m, Pennsylvania Railroad locomotive 4638.
No. 2900 — Volcanoes and minerals: a, 16m, Popocatépetl, Mexico, emerald and turquoise. b, 16m, Augustine Volcano, Alaska, chrysoprase and tourmaline. c, 92m, Popocatépetl, beryl and sapphire. d, 92m, Mount Bromo, Indonesia, topaz and spinel.
No. 2901 — Lighthouses and birds: a, 16m, White Shoal Lighthouse, Michigan, Rissa tridactyla. b, 16m, Portland Head Lighthouse, Maine, Columbus glacialis. c, 92m, Montauk Point Lighthouse, New York, Anas platyrhynchos. d, 92m, Lindau Harbor Lighthouse, Germany, Numenius americanus.
No. 2902 — Ailuropoda melanoleuca: a, 16m, Two pandas. b, 16m, One panda. c, 92m, Panda in tree. d, 92m, Two pandas, diff.
No. 2903 — Loxodonta africana: a, 16m, Adult and juvenile elephants. b, 16m, One elephant facing left. c, 92m, One elephant facing right. d, 92m, Two elephants, diff.
No. 2904 — Dolphins: a, 16m, Delphinus delphis, Delphinus capensis. b, 16m, Stenella attenuata. c, 92m, Lagenorhynchus obsdurus. d, 92m, Steno bredanensis, Cephalorhynchus commersonii.
No. 2905 — Parrots and plants: a, 16m, Charmosyna papou, Schefflera actinophylla. b, 16m, Polytelis swainsonii, Ara macao, Malus, Attalea maripa. c, 92m, Eclectus roratus, Cacatua moluccensis, Punica granatum. d, 92m, Ara rauna, Ara hyacinthe, Atalea funifera.
No. 2906 — Birds of prey and their prey: a, 16m, Aegypius monachus. b, 16m, Buteo buteo, lemmus lemmus. c, 92m, Buteo jamaicensis, Neotamias minimus. d, 92m, Pandion haliaetus.
No. 2907 — Owls and mushrooms: a, 16m, Surnia ulula, Coprinus comatus. b, 16m, Bubo virginianus, Peziza acetabulum. c, 92m, Tyto alba, Amanita rubescens. d, 92m, Ulula cinerea lapponica, Clitocybe inversa.
No. 2908 — Bees: a, 16m, Anthidium florentinum. b, 16m, Apis florea. c, 92m, Osmia ribifloris. d, 92m, Bombus terrestris.
No. 2909 — Insects and mushrooms: a, 16m, Choerododis, Phrynus lunatus, Agaricus cervinus. b, 16m, Sphinx nerri, Agaricus dryophilus. c, 92m, Papilio priaunus, Sirex gigas, Cortinarius torvus. d, 92m, Heterosterne buprestoide, Russula.
No. 2910 — Butterflies and orchids: a, 16m, Papilio zelicaon, Calanthe biloba. b, 16m, Troides amphrysus. c, 92m, Alcidees metaurus, Phalaenopsis stuartiana. d, 92m, Ornithoptera victoriae, Gastrochilus spp.
No. 2911 — Marine life and seafood dishes: a, 16m, Mytilus edulis, Feijoada de mariscos. b, 16m, Penaeus monodon, Caril de camarao. c, 92m, Mercenaria mercenaria, Améijoas em tomate. d, 92m, Callinectes sapidus, Caril de caranguejo.
No. 2912 — Frogs and snails: a, 16m, Dendrobates tinctorius, Arianta arbustorum. b, 16m, Oophaga pumilio, Planorbarius corneus. c, 92m, Phyllobates terribilis, Clea helena. d, 92m, Pelophylax shqipericus, Clithon corona.
No. 2913 — Turtles: a, 16m, Emys trinacris. b, 16m, Indotestudo elongata. c, 92m, Heosemys depressa. d, 92m, Batagur trivittata.
No. 2914 — Dinosaurs: a, 16m, Stogocaurus. b, 16m, Saurolophus. c, 92m, Rubeosaurus. d, 92m, Ankylosaurus.
No. 2915, 175m, Pope Benedict XVI and his coat of arms. No. 2916, 175m, Pope Francis and his coat of arms. No. 2917, 175m, Monroe and signature. No. 2918, 175m, Gandhi, diff. No. 2919, 175m, Mao Zedong, diff. No. 2920, 175m, Prince William in helicopter, diff. No. 2921, 175m, Anna Muzychuk, Ukrainian chess player. No. 2922, 175m, Scouting trefoil, Boy Scout with bicycle. No. 2923, 175m, St. Catherine of Alexandria, by Raphael. No. 2924, 175m, Combat of Giaour and Pasha, by Delacroix. No. 2925, 175m, The Langlois Bridge at Arles with Women Washing, by van Gogh. No. 2926, 175m, The Ninth Wave, by Aivazovsky. No. 2927, 175m, Biathlon. No. 2928, 175m, Dunant, Red Cross flag, joined hands. No. 2929, 175m, The General 4-4-0 locomotive. No. 2930, 175m, Puu Oo Volcano, Hawaii, topaz. No. 2931, 175m, Alcatraz Island Lighthouse, California, Larus argentatus. No. 2932, 175m, Ailuropoda melanoleuca, diff. No. 2933, 175m, Loxodonta africana adult and juvenile, diff. No. 2934, 175m, Sousa teuszii, Steno bredanensis. No. 2935, 175m, Deroptyus accipitrinus, Psittacula eupatria, Anacardium occidentale. No. 2936, 175m, Sarcoramphus papa. No. 2937, 175m, Tyto alba, Psalliota campestris. No. 2938, 175m, Apis mellifera. No. 2939, 175m, Calopteryx splendens, Macrothylacia rubi, Coprinopsic atramentaria. No. 2940, 175m, Papilio aegeus, Erasma pulchella, Prosthechea vitellina. No. 2941, 175m, Mytilus edulis, Arroz con mariscos. No. 2942, 175m, Hyla leucophyllata, Arianta arbustorum. No. 2943, 175m, Geoclemys hamiltonii. No. 2944, 175m, Microraptor gui.

2013, June 25   Litho.   Perf. 13¼
Sheets of 4, #a-d
2885-2914   A450   Set of 30   450.00   450.00
Souvenir Sheets
2915-2944   A450   Set of 30   350.00   350.00

2013 China International Collection Expo (Nos. 2902, 2932).

MOZAMBIQUE

A451

No. 2945, 46m — James Gandolfini (1961-2013), actor: a, Holding Emmy award in foreground. b, Holding walking stick. c, Wearing suit and tie. d, Holding rifle in background, holding Screen Actors Guild award in foreground.
No. 2946, 46m — Giuseppe Verdi (1813-1901), composer: a, Without hat, clef at LL. b, Wearing hat, clef at LR. c, Wearing hat, clef at LL. d, Without hat, clef at LR.
No. 2947, 46m — Richard Wagner (1813-83), composer: a, Without hat, clef at LL. b, Wearing hat, clef at LR. c, Wearing hat, clef at LL. d, Without hat, clef at LR.
No. 2948, 46m — Elvis Presley (1813-1901), various images with background color of: a, Blue. b, Red. c, Orange. d, Green.
No. 2949, 46m — Russian royalty: a, Tsar Peter the Great (1672-1725). b, Heir apparent Alexei Nikolayevich (1904-18). c, Empress Catherine I (1684-1727). d, Emperor Alexander I (1777-1825).
No. 2950, 46m — Pope John Paul II: a, With hands clasped above heart, coat of arms at right. b, Holding crucifix, wearing white vestments. c, Waving, holding crucifix, wearing green vestments. d, In prayer, with hands clasped near mouth, coat of arms at right.
No. 2951, 46m — Rotary International emblem and: a, Paul Harris (1868-1947), founder, wearing hat. b, Owl, mortarboard, book, Rotary Youth Exchange emblem. c, Child receiving polio vaccine, polio eradication program emblem. d, Harris, without hat.
No. 2952, 46m — Pierre de Coubertin (1863-1937), founder of modern Olympics movement: a, Coubertin and statue. b, Table tennis. c, BMX bicycling. d, Judo.
No. 2953, 46m — Brazilian soccer players: a, Fred. b, Hulk. c, Julio Cesar. c, David Luiz.
No. 2954, 46m — Paintings depicting chess: a, The Chess Game, by Sofonisba Anguissola. b, The Veterans, by Richard Creifelds. c, Chess Game, by Marcel Duchamp. d, The Great Chess Game, by Paul Klee.
No. 2955, 46m — Post-impressionist paintings: a, Tahitian Women on the Beach, by Paul Gauguin. b, The Dining Room in the Country, by Pierre Bonnard. c, Starry Night Over the Rhone, by Vincent van Gogh. d, At the Moulin Rouge the Clowness Cha-u-kao, by Henri de Toulouse-Lautrec.
No. 2956, 46m — Paintings by Joan Miró (1893-1983): a, Miró and Vuelo de Pájaraos, 1968. b, Running Man. c, Nord-Sud, 1917. d, Woman in Front of the Sun, 1950.
No. 2957, 46m — Paintings by Pablo Picasso (1881-1973): a, Picasso and Still Life with Bottle of Anis del Mono, 1909. b, Nude Woman in Red Armchair, 1932. c, Portrait of Marie Thérèse Walter, 1937. d, Picasso and Table in a Cafe, 1912.
No. 2958, 46m — Russian art: a, Icon of Madonna and Child, by Dionisius. b, Feodor III, by Bogdan Saltanov. c, Icon of St. Sophia, Faith, Hope and Charity, by Karp Zolotaryov. d, Icon of the Trinity, by Andrej Rublev.
No. 2959, 46m — Ancient Egyptian civilization: a, Model of bark constructed in 18th Dynasty. b, King Tutankhamun and his wife. c, Tomb of King Tutankhamun. d, Bust of Nefertiti.
No. 2960, 46m — World War I: a, German submarine U-155, Winston Churchill. b, Tanks in ruined city. c, Red Cross nurse, soldiers in battle. d, T. E. Lawrence (Lawrence of Arabia), Lawrence on camel.
No. 2961, 46m — Fire trucks: a, 1939 Dennis Light 4. b, 1965 Bedford TK. c, 1961 Magirus-Deutz Merkur F 25A. d, 1959 Opel Blitz LF 8.
No. 2962, 46m — Steam locomotives: a, Stourbridge Lion. b, Norris 4-2-0. c, Type 1 2-4-2. d, Problem Class 2-2-2.
No. 2963, 46m — Chinese high-speed trains: a, China Star. b, CRH2. c, CRH380B. d, CRH1.
No. 2964, 46m — Shenzhou 10: a, Shenzhou 10 in orbit. b, Zhang Xiaoguang. c, Wang Yaping. d, Nie Haisheng.
No. 2965, 46m — Minerals: a, Azurite. b, Garnet and smoky quartz. c, Yellow mineral ore. d, Amethyst and quartz.
No. 2966, 46m — Primates: a, Saguinus imperator. b, Cebus capucinus. c, Tarsius syrichta. d, Gorilla beringei graueri.
No. 2967, 46m — African animals: a, Panthera pardus. b, Loxodona africana. c, Hippopotamus amphibius. d, Giraffa camelopardalis.
No. 2968, 46m — Whales: a, Megaptera novaeangliae. b, Balaena mysticetus. c, Eschrichtius robustus. d, Physeter macrocephalus.
No. 2969, 46m — Owls: a, Strix leptogrammica. b, Otus sagittatus. c, Strix butleri. d, Tyto soumagnei.
No. 2970, 46m — Butterflies: a, Papilio demoleus malayanus. b, Danaus chrysippus chrysippus. c, Euripus nyctelius euploeoides. d, Cethosia cyane.
No. 2971, 46m — Lighthouses and shells: a, Cape Otway Lighthouse, Australia, Cardium costatum. b, Yaquina Head Lighthouse, Oregon, Nautilides. c, Cape Hatteras Lighthouse, North Carolina, Queen conch. d, White Shoal Lighthouse, Michigan, Babylonia canaliculata.
No. 2972, 46m — Reptiles: a, Dendroaspis angusticeps. b, Agama mwanzae. c, Varanus albigularis. d, Diadophis punctatus.
No. 2973, 46m — Dinosaurs and prehistoric hominids: a, Anchiornis huxleyi. b, Homo habilis. c, Homo floresiensis. d, Velociraptor.
No. 2974, 92m — Birth of Prince George of Cambridge: a, Duke and Duchess of Cambridge, Prince George. b, Prince Charles, Duke of Cambridge holding Prince George. c, Princess Diana holding Prince William, Duke of Cambridge holding Prince George. d, Duchess of Cambridge holding Prince George.
No. 2975, 175m, Gandolfini with arms crossed. No. 2976, 175m, Verdi, diff. No. 2977, 175m, Wagner, diff. No. 2978, 175m, Presley, diff. No. 2979, 175m, Emperor Nicholas II of Russia (1868-1918). No. 2980, 175m, Pope John Paul II and his coat of arms. No. 2981, 175m, Harris, Rotary Youth Exchange emblem. No. 2982, 175m, Equestrian competitors. No. 2983, 175m, Neymar. No. 2984, 175m, The Chess Board, by Juan Gris. No. 2985, 175m, Young Women of Provence at the Well, by Paul Signac. No. 2986, 175m, Miró and Siesta, 1925. No. 2987, 175m, Picasso and House in a Garden, 1908. No. 2988, 175m, Old Jew, by Nikolai Yaroshenko. No. 2989, 175m, Bust of Egyptian Pharaoh Menes and Pyramids. No. 2990, 175m, Baron Manfed von Richthofen and Fokker Dr.I triplane in flight. No. 2991, 175m, 1914 Ford Model T fire engine. No. 2992, 175m, Jupiter locomotive. No. 2993, 175m, CHR380D high-speed train. No. 2994, 175m, Wang Yaping, diff. No. 2995, 175m, Aragonite. No. 2996, 175m, Saimiri sciureus. No. 2997, 175m, Panthera leo. No. 2998, 175m, Eubalaena australis. No. 2999, 175m, Strix nebulosa. No. 3000, 175m, Papilio polytes romulus. No. 3001, 175m, Beachy Head Lighthouse, Great Britain, Anadara corbuliodes. No. 3002, 175m, Furcier pardalis. No. 3003, 175m, Homo habilis making tool. No. 3004, 175m, Duke and Duchess of Cambridge, Prince George, diff.

2013, Sept. 25   Litho.   Perf. 13¼
Sheets of 4, #a-d
2945-2974 A451 Set of 30 400.00 400.00
Souvenir Sheets
2975-3004 A451 Set of 30 375.00 375.00

Brasiliana 2013 Intl. Philatelic Exhibition, Rio de Janeiro (Nos. 2953, 2983); Rossica 2013 Intl. Philatelic Exhibition (Nos. 2958, 2988); 2013 China International Collection Expo (Nos. 2963, 2964, 2993, 2994).

SEMI-POSTAL STAMPS

"History" Pointing out to "the Republic" Need for Charity — SP1

Nurse Leading Wounded Soldiers — SP2

Veteran Relating Experiences SP3

Perf. 11½
1920, Dec. 1   Litho.   Unwmk.
B1	SP1	¼c olive	3.50	3.25
B2	SP1	½c olive blk	3.50	3.25
B3	SP1	1c dp bister	3.50	3.25
B4	SP1	2c lilac brn	3.50	3.25
B5	SP1	3c lilac	3.50	3.25
B6	SP1	4c green	3.50	3.25
B7	SP2	5c grnsh blue	3.50	3.25
B8	SP2	6c light blue	3.50	3.25
B9	SP2	7½c red brown	3.50	3.25
B10	SP2	8c lemon	3.50	3.25
B11	SP2	10c gray lilac	3.50	3.25
B12	SP2	12c pink	3.50	3.25
B13	SP3	18c rose	3.50	3.25
B14	SP3	24c vio brn	4.50	3.50
B15	SP3	30c pale ol grn	4.50	3.50
B16	SP3	40c dull red	4.50	3.50
B17	SP3	50c yellow	4.50	3.50
B18	SP3	1e ultra	4.50	3.50
		Nos. B1-B18 (18)	68.00	59.75

Nos. B1-B18 were used Dec. 1, 1920, in place of ordinary stamps. The proceeds were for war victims.

AIR POST STAMPS

Common Design Type
Perf. 13½x13
1938, Aug.   Engr.   Unwmk.
Name and Value in Black
C1	CD39	10c scarlet	.45	.40
C2	CD39	20c purple	.45	.40
C3	CD39	50c orange	.45	.40
C4	CD39	1e ultra	.60	.45
C5	CD39	2e lilac brn	1.55	.45
C6	CD39	3e dk green	2.75	.60
C7	CD39	5e red brown	3.25	1.10
C8	CD39	9e rose car	6.50	1.20
C9	CD39	10e magenta	11.25	1.95
		Nos. C1-C9 (9)	27.25	6.95

No. C7 exists with overprint "Exposicao Internacional de Nova York, 1939-1940" and Trylon and Perisphere. Value $50.

No. C7 Surcharged in Black

1946, Nov. 2   Perf. 13½x13
C10	CD39	3e on 5e red brn	6.00	12.50
a.		Inverted surcharge		

Plane AP1

1946, Nov. 2   Typo.   Perf. 11½
Denomination in Black
C11	AP1	1.20e carmine	1.75	1.35
C12	AP1	1.60e blue	2.25	1.40
C13	AP1	1.70e plum	5.50	2.25
C14	AP1	2.90e brown	5.50	3.05
C15	AP1	3e green	4.75	2.85
		Nos. C11-C15 (5)	19.75	10.90

Inscribed "Taxe perçue" and Denomination in Brown Carmine or Black
1947, May 20
C16	AP1	50c blk (BrC)	.90	.65
C17	AP1	1e pink	.90	.65
C18	AP1	3e green	1.80	.90
C19	AP1	4.50e yel grn	4.50	1.45
C20	AP1	5e red brown	4.50	1.60
C21	AP1	10e ultra	10.75	4.00
C22	AP1	20e violet	19.75	11.25
C23	AP1	50e orange	27.00	27.00
		Nos. C16-C23 (8)	70.10	47.50

Dangerous counterfeits exist.

Planes Circling Globe — AP2

1949, Mar.
C24	AP2	50c sepia	.35	.25
C25	AP2	1.20e violet	.65	.40
C26	AP2	4.50e dull blue	1.65	.75
C27	AP2	5e blue green	2.35	1.05
C28	AP2	20e chocolate	7.00	3.15
		Nos. C24-C28 (5)	12.00	5.60

Catalogue values for unused stamps in this section, from this point to the end of the section, are for Never Hinged items.

Oil Refinery, Sonarep — AP3

Designs: 2e, Salazar High School, Lourenço Marques. 3.50e, Lourenço Marques harbor. 4.50e, Salazar dam. 5e, Trigo de Morais bridge. 20e, Marcelo Caetano bridge.

1963, Mar. 5   Litho.   Perf. 13
C29	AP3	1.50e multi	.75	.30
C30	AP3	2e multi	.45	.30
C31	AP3	3.50e multi	.70	.30
C32	AP3	4.50e multi	.55	.30
C33	AP3	5e multi	.70	.30
C34	AP3	20e multi	1.90	.50
		Nos. C29-C34 (6)	5.05	2.00

Republic

Nos. C31-C34 Overprinted in Red

1975, June 25   Litho.   Perf. 13
C35	AP3	3.50e multi	.50	.35
C36	AP3	4.50e multi	.55	.45
C37	AP3	5e multi	1.25	.70
C38	AP3	20e multi	1.90	1.90
		Nos. C35-C38 (4)	4.20	3.40

DeHavilland Dragonfly, 1937 — AP4

Designs: 1.50m, Junker JU-52-3M, 1938. 3m, Lockheed Lodestar L-18-08, 1940. 7.50m, DeHavilland Dove DH-104, 1948. 10m, Douglas Dakota DC-3, 1956. 12.5m, Fokker Friendship F-27, 1962.

1981, May 14   Litho.   Perf. 11
C39	AP4	50c multi	.35	.25
C40	AP4	1.50m multi	.75	.25
C41	AP4	3m multi	1.50	.25
C42	AP4	7.50m multi	2.00	.25
C43	AP4	10m multi	2.50	.35
C44	AP4	12.5m multi	3.25	.60
		Nos. C39-C44 (6)	10.35	1.95

Piper Navajo Over Hydroelectric Dam — AP5

Designs: 40m, De Havilland Hornet trainer, 1936. 80m, Boeing 737, Maputo Airport, 1973. 120m, Beechcraft King-Air. 160m, Piper Aztec. 320m, Douglas DC-10, 1982.

1987, Oct. 28   Litho.   Perf. 11
C45	AP5	20m multi	.30	.25
C46	AP5	40m multi	.60	.25
C47	AP5	80m multi	1.25	.35
C48	AP5	120m multi	1.50	.40
C49	AP5	160m multi	2.40	.60
C50	AP5	320m multi	3.75	1.00
		Nos. C45-C50 (6)	9.80	2.85

POSTAGE DUE STAMPS

D1

MOZAMBIQUE

1904 Unwmk. Typo. Perf. 11½x12
Name and Value in Black

J1	D1	5r yellow grn	.55	.40
J2	D1	10r slate	.55	.40
J3	D1	20r yellow brn	.65	.55
J4	D1	30r orange	1.25	1.00
J5	D1	50r gray brn	1.00	.90
J6	D1	60r red brown	5.00	3.00
J7	D1	100r red lilac	4.75	3.00
J8	D1	130r dull blue	2.75	2.25
J9	D1	200r carmine	3.75	2.25
J10	D1	500r violet	5.00	2.50
		Nos. J1-J10 (10)	25.25	16.25

See J34-J43. For overprints see Nos. 247, J11-J30.

Same Overprinted in Carmine or Green

1911

J11	D1	5r yellow green	.45	.45
J12	D1	10r slate	.75	.45
J13	D1	20r yellow brn	.55	.45
J14	D1	30r orange	.55	.45
J15	D1	50r gray brown	.75	.50
J16	D1	60r red brown	1.10	.60
J17	D1	100r red lilac	1.50	.95
J18	D1	130r dull blue	2.05	1.40
J19	D1	200r carmine (G)	2.25	1.65
J20	D1	500r violet	3.00	1.65
		Nos. J11-J20 (10)	12.95	8.55

Nos. J1-J10 Overprinted Locally in Carmine

1916

J21	D1	5r yellow grn	5.75	4.00
J22	D1	10r slate	7.95	4.00
J23	D1	20r yellow brn	115.00	80.00
J24	D1	30r orange	32.50	22.75
J25	D1	50r gray brown	115.00	80.00
J26	D1	60r red brown	92.50	65.00
J27	D1	100r red lilac	115.00	80.00
J28	D1	130r dull blue	3.45	2.40
J29	D1	200r carmine	3.95	2.75
J30	D1	500r violet	7.95	5.50
		Nos. J21-J30 (10)	499.05	346.40

War Tax Stamps of 1916 Ovptd. Diagonally

1918 Rouletted 7

J31	WT1	1c gray green	1.70	1.50
J32	WT2	5c rose	1.70	1.50
a.		Inverted overprint	8.25	7.50

Perf. 11

J33	WT1	1c gray green	1.70	1.50
a.		"PEPUBLICA"	36.00	29.00
		Nos. J31-J33 (3)	5.10	4.50

Type of 1904 Issue With Value in Centavos

1917 Perf. 12

J34	D1	½c yellow green	.60	.55
J35	D1	1c slate	.60	.55
J36	D1	2c orange brown	.60	.55
J37	D1	3c orange	.60	.55
J38	D1	5c gray brown	.60	.55
J39	D1	6c pale brn	.60	.55
J40	D1	10c red violet	.60	.55
J41	D1	13c deep blue	1.10	1.00
J42	D1	20c rose	1.10	1.00
J43	D1	50c gray	1.10	1.00
		Nos. J34-J43 (10)	7.50	6.85

Lourenco Marques Nos. 117, 119 Surcharged in Red

1922

J44	A4	5c on ½c blk	2.00	1.60
J45	A4	10c on 1½c brn	2.00	1.60

Same Surcharge on Mozambique Nos. 151, 154, 190 in Red or Green
Perf. 15x14

J46	A6	6c on 1c bl grn (R)	2.00	1.60
J47	A6	20c on 2½c vio (R)	2.00	1.60
a.		Inverted surcharge	10.00	10.00
J48	A6	50c on 4c rose (G)	2.00	1.60
		Nos. J44-J48 (5)	10.00	8.00

Regular Issues of 1921-22 Surcharged in Black or Red

1924 Perf. 12x11½

J49	A6	20c on 30c ol grn (Bk)	1.70	.75
a.		Perf. 15x14	32.50	30.00
J50	A6	50c on 60c dk bl (R)	2.00	1.70

Catalogue values for unused stamps in this section, from this point to the end of the section, are for Never Hinged items.

Common Design Type
Photo. and Typo.
1952 Unwmk. Perf. 14
Numeral in Red Orange or Red; Frame Multicolored

J51	CD45	10c carmine (ПО)	.30	.25
J52	CD45	30c black brn	.30	.25
J53	CD45	50c black	.30	.25
J54	CD45	1e violet blue	.30	.35
J55	CD45	2e olive green	.30	.35
J56	CD45	5e orange brown	.90	.50
		Nos. J51-J56 (6)	2.40	1.95

WAR TAX STAMPS

Coats of Arms of Portugal and Mozambique on Columns, Allegorical Figures of History of Portugal and the Republic Holding Scroll with Date of Declaration of War — WT1

Prow of Galley of Discoveries. Left, "Republic" Teaching History of Portugal; Right "History" with Laurels (Victory) and Sword (Symbolical of Declaration of War) — WT2

1916 Unwmk. Litho. Rouletted 7

MR1	WT1	1c gray green	3.00	.90
a.		Imperf., pair	3.50	1.00
MR2	WT2	5c rose	3.00	.90
a.		Imperf., pair	1.10	1.10

1918 Perf. 11, 12

MR3	WT1	1c gray green	1.60	1.00
a.		"PEPUBLICA"	9.50	9.50
b.		As "#MR3," imperf., pair	7.50	7.50
c.		As "a," imperf., pair	35.00	35.00
MR4	WT2	5c red	1.90	1.30
a.		"PETRIA"	6.50	6.50
b.		"PEPUBLICA"	6.50	6.50
c.		"1910" for "1916"	11.00	10.00
d.		As "#MR4," imperf., pair	8.75	8.75
e.		As "a," imperf., pair	60.00	50.00
f.		As "b," imperf., pair	60.00	50.00
g.		As "c," imperf., pair	60.00	50.00
h.		"TEFGAFO"	6.50	6.50
i.		As "h," imperf., pair	60.00	50.00
		Nos. MR1-MR4 (4)	9.50	4.10

For surcharges and overprints see Nos. 221-225, 229, 235, J31-J33.

NEWSPAPER STAMPS

No. 19 Surcharged in Black, Red or Blue

a   b

1893 Unwmk. Perf. 11½, 12½, 13½

P1	A2 (a)	2½r on 40r	275.00	160.00
P2	A2 (a)	5r on 40r	250.00	125.00
P3	A2 (a)	5r on 40r (R)	200.00	100.00
P4	A2 (a)	5r on 40r (Bl)	250.00	130.00
P5	A2 (b)	2½r on 40r	65.00	35.00
		Nos. P1-P5 (5)	1,040.	550.00

Nos. P1-P5 exist with double surcharge, Nos. P2-P4 with inverted surcharge.

N3

1893 Typo. Perf. 11½, 13½

P6	N3	2½r brown	.95	.70

For surcharge and overprint see Nos. 93, 199, 206.

No. P6 has been reprinted on chalk-surfaced paper with clean-cut perforation 13½. Value, 50 cents.

POSTAL TAX STAMPS

Pombal Commemorative Issue
Common Design Types
1925 Engr. Unwmk. Perf. 12½

RA1	CD28	15c brown & black	.50	.40
RA2	CD29	15c brown & black	.50	.40
RA3	CD30	15c brown & black	.50	.40
		Nos. RA1-RA3 (3)	1.50	1.20

Seal of Local Red Cross Society — PT7

Surcharged in Various Colors

1925 Typo. Perf. 11½

RA4	PT7	50c slate & yel (Bk)	2.25	2.25

Seal of Local Red Cross Society — PT8

1926

RA5	PT8	40c slate & yel (Bk)	4.00	3.50
RA6	PT8	50c slate & yel (R)	4.00	3.50
RA7	PT8	60c slate & yel (V)	4.00	3.50
RA8	PT8	80c slate & yel (Br)	4.00	3.50
RA9	PT8	1e slate & yel (Bl)	4.00	3.50
RA10	PT8	2e slate & yel (G)	4.00	3.50
		Nos. RA5-RA10 (6)	24.00	21.00

Obligatory on mail certain days of the year. The tax benefited the Cross of the Orient Society.

Seal of Local Red Cross Society

1927 Black Surcharge

RA11	PT8a	5c red & yel	3.50	3.25
RA12	PT8a	10c green & yel	3.50	3.25
RA13	PT8a	20c gray & yel	3.50	3.25
RA14	PT8a	30c lt bl & yel	3.50	3.25
RA15	PT8a	40c vio & yel	3.50	3.25
RA16	PT8a	50c car & yel	3.50	3.25
RA17	PT8a	60c brown & yel	3.50	3.25
RA18	PT8a	80c blue & yel	3.50	3.25
RA19	PT8a	1e olive & yel	3.50	3.25
RA20	PT8a	2e yel brn & yel	3.50	3.25
		Nos. RA11-RA20 (10)	35.00	32.50

See note after No. RA10.

PT9

1928 Litho.

RA21	PT9	5c grn, yel & blk	4.50	4.25
RA22	PT9	10c sl bl, yel & blk	4.50	4.25
RA23	PT9	20c gray blk, yel & blk	4.50	4.25
RA24	PT9	30c brn rose, yel & blk	4.50	4.25
RA25	PT9	40c cl brn, yel & blk	4.50	4.25
RA26	PT9	50c red org, yel & blk	4.50	4.25
RA27	PT9	60c brn, yel & blk	4.50	4.25
RA28	PT9	80c dk brn, yel & blk	4.50	4.25
RA29	PT9	1e gray, yel & blk	4.50	4.25
RA30	PT9	2e red, yel & blk	4.50	4.25
		Nos. RA21-RA30 (10)	45.00	42.50

See note after RA10.

Mother and Children — PT10

1929 Photo. Perf. 14

RA31	PT10	40c ultra, cl & blk	4.50	4.00

The use of this stamp was compulsory on all correspondence to Portugal and Portuguese Colonies for eight days beginning July 24, 1929.

See Nos. RA39-RA47.

Mousinho de Albuquerque — PT11

1930-31 Perf. 14½x14
Inscribed: "MACONTENE"

RA32	PT11	50c lake, red & gray	9.00	9.00

Inscribed: "COOLELA"

RA33	PT11	50c red vio, red brn & gray	9.00	9.00

Inscribed: "MUJENGA"

RA34	PT11	50c org red, red & gray	9.00	9.00

Inscribed: "CHAIMITE"

RA35	PT11	50c dp grn, bl grn & gray	9.00	9.00

Inscribed: "IBRAHIMO"

RA36	PT11	50c dk bl, blk & gray	9.00	9.00

Inscribed: "MUCUTO-MUNO"

RA37	PT11	50c ultra, blk & gray	9.00	9.00

Inscribed: "NAGUEMA"

RA38	PT11	50c dk vio, lt vio & gray	9.00	9.00
		Nos. RA32-RA38 (7)	63.00	63.00

The portrait is that of Mousinho de Albuquerque, the celebrated Portuguese warrior, and the names of seven battles in which he took part appear at the foot of the stamps. The stamps were issued for the memorial fund bearing his name and their use was obligatory on all correspondence posted on eight specific days in the year.

Type of 1929 Issue
Denominations in Black
No. RA42 Without Denomination
1931 Perf. 14

RA39	PT10	40c rose & vio	4.50	3.75
RA40	PT10	40c ol grn & vio ('32)	6.25	4.50
RA41	PT10	40c bis brn & rose ('33)	6.25	4.50

MOZAMBIQUE — MOZAMBIQUE COMPANY

RA42	PT10	bl grn & rose ('34)	4.25	3.75
RA43	PT10	40c org & ultra ('36)	6.25	4.50
RA44	PT10	40c choc & ultra ('37)	6.25	4.50
RA45	PT10	40c grn & brn car ('38)	8.00	6.00
RA46	PT10	40c yel & blk ('39)	8.00	6.00
RA47	PT10	40c gray brn ('40)	8.00	6.00
Nos. RA39-RA47 (9)			57.75	43.50

Allegory of Charity — PT12

Denomination in Black

1942	Unwmk.	Litho.	Perf. 11½	
RA48	PT12	50c rose carmine	14.00	3.50

White Pelican — PT13

Denomination in Black

1943-51			Perf. 11½, 14	
RA49	PT13	50c rose carmine	10.00	1.75
RA50	PT13	50c emerald	8.00	.90
RA51	PT13	50c purple	9.00	2.00
RA52	PT13	50c blue	9.00	2.00
RA53	PT13	50c red brown	9.00	2.00
RA54	PT13	50c olive bister	8.00	2.00
Nos. RA49-RA54 (6)			53.00	10.65

There are two sizes of the numeral on No. RA49.

Catalogue values for unused stamps in this section, from this point to the end of the section, are for Never Hinged items.

Inscribed: "Provincia de Mocambique"

1954-56			Perf. 14½x14	
RA55	PT13	50c orange	1.50	1.00
RA56	PT13	50c olive grn ('56)	1.50	1.00
RA57	PT13	50c brown ('56)	1.50	1.00
Nos. RA55-RA57 (3)			4.50	3.00

No. RA57 Surcharged with New Value and Wavy Lines

1956				
RA58	PT13	30c on 50c brown	1.25	.60

Pelican Type of 1954-56

1958	Litho.	Perf. 14		

Denomination in Black

RA59	PT13	30c yellow	1.50	1.25
RA60	PT13	50c salmon	1.50	1.25

Imprint: "Imprensa Nacional de Mocambique"

1963-64				

Denomination Typographed in Black

RA61	PT13	30c yellow ('64)	.80	.60
RA62	PT13	50c salmon	.80	.60

Women and Children — PT14

1963-65	Litho.	Perf. 14		
RA63	PT14	50c blk, bis & red	.30	.25
RA64	PT14	50c blk, pink & red ('65)	.30	.25

See Nos. RA68-RA76.

Lineman on Pole and Map of Mozambique — PT15

30c, Telegraph poles and map of Mozambique.

Size: 23x30mm

1965, Apr. 1	Unwmk.	Perf. 14		
RA65	PT15	30c blk, salmon & lil	.30	.25

Size: 19x36mm

RA66	PT15	50c blk, bl & sepia	.30	.25
RA67	PT15	1e blk, yel & org	.30	.25

The tax was for improvement of the telecommunications system. Obligatory on inland mail. A 2.50e in the design of the 30c was issued for use on telegrams.

Type of 1963

1967-70	Litho.	Perf. 14		
RA68	PT14	50c blk, lt yel grn & red	.40	.25
RA69	PT14	50c blk, lt bl & red ('69)	.40	.25
RA70	PT14	50c blk, buff & brt red ('70)	.40	.25
Nos. RA68-RA70 (3)			1.20	.75

1972-73				
RA71	PT14	30c blk, lt grn & red	.30	.25
RA72	PT14	50c blk, gray & red ('73)	1.00	.25
RA73	PT14	1e blk, bis & red ('73)	.30	.25
Nos. RA71-RA73 (3)			1.60	.75

1974-75				
RA74	PT14	50c blue, yel & red	.30	.25
RA75	PT14	1e blk, gray & ver	1.50	.25
RA76	PT14	1e blk, lil rose & red ('75)	.40	.25
Nos. RA74-RA76 (3)			2.20	.75

Intl. Year of the Child — PT16

1979	Litho.	Perf. 14¼		
RA77	PT16	50e red	1.50	1.50

POSTAL TAX DUE STAMPS

Pombal Commemorative Issue
Common Design Types

1925	Unwmk.	Perf. 12½		
RAJ1	CD28	30c brown & black	.75	.80
RAJ2	CD29	30c brown & black	.75	.80
RAJ3	CD30	30c brown & black	.75	.80
Nos. RAJ1-RAJ3 (3)			2.25	2.40

MOZAMBIQUE COMPANY

mō-zəm-'bēk 'kəm-pə-nē

LOCATION — Comprises the territory of Manica and Sofala of the Mozambique Colony in southeastern Africa
GOVT. — A part of the Portuguese Colony of Mozambique
AREA — 51,881 sq. mi.
POP. — 368,447 (1939)
CAPITAL — Beira

The Mozambique Company was chartered by Portugal in 1891 for 50 years. The territory was under direct administration of the Company until July 18, 1941.

1000 Reis = 1 Milreis
100 Centavos = 1 Escudo (1916)

Mozambique Nos. 15-23 Overprinted in Carmine or Black

1892-93		Unwmk.	Perf. 12½	
1	A2	5r black (C)	1.50	1.25
a.		Pair, one without overprint	55.00	55.00
2	A2	10r green	1.50	1.25
3	A2	20r rose	1.75	1.25
4	A2	25r violet	1.50	1.25
a.		Double overprint	20.00	16.00
5	A2	40r chocolate	1.50	1.25
a.		Double overprint	25.00	19.00
b.		Pair, one without overprint	55.00	55.00
6	A2	50r blue	2.00	1.40
7	A2	100r yellow brown	1.90	1.40
8	A2	200r gray violet	2.75	1.90
9	A2	300r red orange	3.75	2.25
a.		300r pale orange	3.75	2.25
Nos. 1-9 (9)			18.15	13.20

Perf. 13½

1c	A2	5r black (R)	1.50	.75
2c	A2	10r green	2.40	1.10
3c	A2	20r rose	75.00	65.00
4c	A2	25r violet ('93)	1.40	.90
6c	A2	50r pale blue	19.00	6.50

Nos. 1 to 6, 8-9 were reprinted in 1905. These reprints have white gum and clean-cut perf. 13½ and the colors are usually paler than those of the originals.

Enamel-surfaced paper is white, with a uniform low gloss. Chalky paper bears a low-gloss application in a pattern of tiny lozenges, producing a somewhat duller appearance.

Company Coat of Arms — A2

1895-1902		Typo.	Perf. 11½	

Black or Red Numerals
Enamel Paper

10	A2	2½r olive yellow ('02)	.65	.55
11	A2	5r orange ('02)	.65	.55
12	A2	10r red lilac ('02)	.80	.75
13	A2	15r red brown ('02)	.80	.75
14	A2	20r gray lilac ('02)	.80	.75
15	A2	25r green ('02)	.80	.75
16	A2	50r blue ('02)	.80	.75
17	A2	75r rose	.95	.75
18	A2	80r yellow green ('02)	1.50	1.00
23	A2	500r blk & red ('02)	1.50	1.00
24	A2	1000r vio & red ('02)	1.75	1.40
Nos. 10-24 (11)			11.00	9.00

Perf. 12½

10a	A2	2½r olive yellow	.65	.55
11a	A2	5r orange ('02)	.65	.55
12a	A2	10r red lilac	.80	.75
13a	A2	15r red brown	.80	.75
14a	A2	20r gray lilac	.80	.75
15a	A2	25r green	.80	.75
16a	A2	50r blue	.80	.75
17a	A2	75r rose	1.25	.75
18a	A2	80r yellow green	2.00	1.50
23a	A2	500r black & red	2.40	1.80
24a	A2	1000r violet & red	2.40	1.80
Nos. 10a-24a (11)			13.35	10.70

Perf. 13½

11b	A2	5r orange	2.00	1.10
12b	A2	10r red lilac	.75	.75
13b	A2	15r red brown	.80	.75
14b	A2	20r gray lilac	.80	.75
15b	A2	25r green	3.25	1.50
16b	A2	50r blue	1.25	1.00
17b	A2	75r rose	1.25	1.10
23b	A2	500r black & red	2.50	1.75
24b	A2	1000r violet & red	2.50	1.75
Nos. 11b-24b (9)			15.10	10.55

Chalky Paper
Perf. 11½

11c	A2	5r orange	.65	.55
14c	A2	20r gray lilac	.70	.55
15c	A2	25r green	.70	.55
19	A2	100r brown, buff	2.50	1.40
20	A2	150r org brn, pink	2.75	1.80
21	A2	200r dark blue, blue	2.75	1.80
22	A2	300r dark blue, salmon	2.75	1.80
Nos. 11c-21 (6)			10.05	6.65

Perf. 12½

11d	A2	5r orange ('02)	.50	.40
12d	A2	10r red lilac ('02)	.90	.65
13d	A2	15r red brown ('02)	.90	.65
14d	A2	20r gray lilac ('02)	.90	.65
15d	A2	25r green ('02)	.90	.65
16d	A2	50r blue ('02)	.90	.65
17d	A2	75r rose ('02)	.90	.65
18d	A2	80r yellow green ('02)	.90	.65
19d	A2	100r brown, buff ('02)	2.50	1.40
20d	A2	150r org brn, pink ('02)	7.50	6.25
21d	A2	200r dark blue, blue ('02)	2.00	1.75
22d	A2	300r dark blue, salmon ('02)	2.40	1.75
23d	A2	500r black & red ('02)	2.40	1.75
24d	A2	1000r violet & red ('02)	2.75	1.75
Nos. 11d-24d (14)			26.35	19.60

Perf. 13½

15e	A2	25r green ('02)	2.00	1.00
19e	A2	100r brown, buff ('02)	3.25	2.00
20e	A2	150r org brn, pink ('02)	3.25	2.00
21e	A2	200r dark blue, blue ('02)	4.00	3.00
22e	A2	300r dark blue, salmon ('02)	4.00	2.75
Nos. 15e-22e (5)			16.50	10.75

#11b, 15b, 21e, 22e were issued without gum.
For overprints & surcharges see #43-107, B1-B7.

Nos. 18a and 6 Surcharged or Overprinted in Red

1895			Perf. 12½, 13½	
43	A2(b)	25r on 80r yel grn	45.00	32.50
a.		Black overprint	65.00	55.00
44	A2(c)	50r blue (on #6)	8.50	7.00
c.		50r pale blue (on #6c)	8.50	7.00

Overprint "c" on No. 44 also exists reading from upper left to lower right.

Stamps of 1895 Overprinted in Bister, Orange, Violet, Green, Black or Brown

1898		Enamel Paper Without Gum	Perf. 12½	
45	A2	2½r olive yel (Bl)	2.50	2.00
a.		Double overprint	30.00	30.00
b.		Red overprint	12.00	12.00
46	A2	5r orange (C)	3.50	2.25
d.		Inverted overprint	42.00	42.00
e.		Double overprint	32.50	32.50
47	A2	10r red lilac (V)	3.50	2.50
d.		Inverted overprint	55.00	55.00
e.		Double overprint	25.00	
48	A2	15r red brown (V)	6.00	4.00
50	A2	25r green (G)	6.50	4.00
d.		Inverted overprint	47.50	47.50
51	A2	50r blue (Blk)	27.50	19.00
52	A2	75r rose (V)	21.00	16.00
Nos. 45-52 (7)			70.50	49.75

Perf. 13½

48a	A2	15r red brown (V)	12.00	6.50
49	A2	20r gray black (V)	6.00	4.75
50a	A2	25r green (G)	12.00	5.75
51a	A2	50r blue (Blk)	4.50	3.75
d.		Inverted overprint	21.00	21.00
e.		Double overprint	36.00	36.00
52a	A2	75r rose (V)	12.00	8.00
Nos. 48a-52a (5)			46.50	28.75

Perf. 12½
Chalky Paper

47b	A2	10r red lilac (V)	3.50	2.25
48b	A2	15r red brown (V)	4.50	3.75
49b	A2	20r gray lilac (V)	8.50	4.25
52b	A2	75r rose (V)	14.50	7.50
d.		Inverted overprint	75.00	67.50
53	A2	80r yellow grn (G)	7.75	5.75
54	A2	100r brn, buff (Br)	8.50	6.50
55	A2	150r org brn, pink (O)	8.50	6.50
d.		Double overprint	47.50	47.50
56	A2	200r dk blue, bl (Bk)	11.50	7.75
57	A2	300r dk blue, sal (Bk)	17.00	10.50
d.		Ovpt. in green		
Nos. 47b-57 (9)			84.25	54.75

Perf. 13½

54c	A2	100r brn, buff (Br)	8.50	7.50
55c	A2	150r org brn, pink (O)	8.50	7.50
d.		Inverted overprint	55.00	45.00
56c	A2	200r dk blue, blue (Blk)	11.50	7.75
57c	A2	300r dk blue, salmon (Blk)	23.00	12.00
e.		Inverted overprint	47.50	42.50
Nos. 54c-57c (4)			51.50	34.75

Vasco da Gama's discovery of route to India, 400th anniversary.
No. 57d was prepared but not issued.
The 2½r, 10r, 15r, and 20r were also issued with gum.
The "Centenario" overprint on stamps perf. 11½ is forged.

Nos. 17a, 11a, 14a Surcharged in Black, Carmine or Violet

1899			Perf. 12½	
59	A2(e)	25r on 75r rose (Bk)	6.50	5.50

MOZAMBIQUE COMPANY

		f	g	

1900   **Perf. 12½, 12½x11½**

60	A2(f)	25r on 5r org (C) (#11a)	5.25	3.25
61	A2(g)	50r on half of 20r gray blue (V) (#14a)	2.50	2.00
a.		Entire stamp	22.50	16.00
b.		On #14d	2.50	2.00
c.		On #61b, entire stamp	32.50	22.50

No. 61a is perf. 11½ vertically through center.

Type of 1895, New Values
Chalky Paper (#61A on enamel paper)
Perf. 11½

1902-04

61A	A2	65r slate blue	1.30	.95
61B	A2	115r carmine, *pink* ('04)	3.50	2.50
61C	A2	130r green, *pink* ('04)	3.50	2.50
61D	A2	400r brown, *blue* ('04)	3.50	2.50
61E	A2	700r slate, *buff* ('04)	9.50	7.50
		Nos. 61A-61E (5)	21.30	15.95

Type of 1895, Changed Colors
Chalky Paper

1907

61F	A2	2½r gray	2.25	1.25
61G	A2	10r yellow green	1.65	1.25
t.		Value inverted at top of stamp	26.00	23.00
u.		Enamel paper	45.00	35.00
61H	A2	15r dark green	2.25	1.25
61I	A2	25r carmine	2.25	1.25
v.		Value omitted	21.00	18.00
w.		Enamel paper	27.50	21.00
61J	A2	50r brown	2.25	1.25
y.		Value omitted	35.00	26.00
61K	A2	75r red lilac	4.60	2.40
61L	A2	100r dark blue, *blue*	4.60	3.15
61M	A2	115r org brn, *pink*	5.90	4.00
61N	A2	130r brown, *yellow*	6.25	4.00
61O	A2	200r red lilac, *pink*	6.25	4.00
61P	A2	400r dk blue, *yellow*	8.25	6.50
61Q	A2	500r black & red *blue*	8.25	6.50
z.		500r purple & red, *yellow* (error)		
61R	A2	700r purple *yellow*	8.25	6.50
		Nos. 61F-61R (13)	63.00	43.30

Stamps of 1895-1907 Overprinted Locally in Carmine or Green

1911   **Chalky Paper**   **Perf. 11½**

61S	A2	2½r gray (C)	5.00	.80
62	A2	5r orange (G)	2.00	1.00
63	A2	10r yellow grn (C)	1.50	1.30
a.		Inverted overprint	16.00	
b.		Enamel paper	2.00	1.40
64	A2	15r dk green (C)	2.00	1.10
a.		Inverted overprint	15.00	
65	A2	20r gray lilac (G)	4.00	3.25
a.		Double overprint	15.00	12.00
b.		Enamel paper, perf. 11¾x12	1.60	.95
c.		Enamel paper, perf. 13½	1.80	1.10
66	A2	25r carmine (G)	2.00	1.50
67	A2	50r brown (G)	2.00	1.50
b.		Enamel paper, perf. 11¾x12	3.25	2.75
68	A2	75r red lilac (G)	2.50	1.50
69	A2	100r dk bl, *bl* (C)	2.50	1.50
70	A2	115r org brn, *pink* (G)	3.75	2.00
a.		Inverted overprint	15.00	
71	A2	130r brn, *yel* (G)	3.75	2.00
72	A2	200r red lil, *pink* (G)	3.75	2.00
73	A2	400r dull bl, *yel* (G)	3.75	2.00
74	A2	500r blk & red, *bl* (C)	5.00	3.75
75	A2	700r pur, *yel* (G)	5.00	3.75
		Nos. 61S-75 (15)	48.50	28.95

Overprinted in Lisbon in Carmine or Green
Chalky Paper

1911   **Perf. 11½, 12½**

75B	A2	2½r gray	.80	.75
76	A2	5r orange	.80	.75
a.		Enamel paper	.65	.60
b.		As "a," perf. 12½	1.60	1.50
77	A2	10r yellow grn	.80	.75
a.		Enamel paper	.65	.60
78	A2	15r dark green	.50	.40
79	A2	20r gray lilac	.50	.40
b.		Enamel paper	.65	.60
80	A2	25r carmine (G)	.80	.75
b.		Value inverted at top of stamp	32.50	32.50
c.		Enamel paper	.65	.60

81	A2	50r brown	.80	.75
82	A2	75r red lilac	.80	.75
b.		Value omitted	20.00	
83	A2	100r dk blue, *bl*	.80	.75
84	A2	115r org brn	1.50	1.10
85	A2	130r brown, *yellow*	1.50	1.10
a.		Double overprint	40.00	
86	A2	200r red lil, *pink*	1.50	1.10
87	A2	400r dull bl, *yellow*	1.50	1.10
88	A2	500r blk & red, *blue*	1.50	1.10
89	A2	700r purple, *yellow*	2.50	1.50
		Nos. 75B-89 (15)	16.60	13.05

Nos. 75B-89 Surcharged

1916   **Perf. 11½**

90	A2	¼c on 2½r gray	.50	.40
a.		Enamel paper	.50	.40
91	A2	½c on 5r org	.50	.40
a.		Double surcharge	16.00	
b.		On #76a (enamel paper)	1.80	1.20
92	A2	1c on 10r yel grn	.80	.65
a.		Enamel paper	.70	.65
93	A2	1½c on 15r dk green	.80	.65
a.		Double surcharge	20.00	
b.		Enamel paper	.70	.65
94	A2	2c on 20r gray lilac	.80	.65
a.		Double surcharge	20.00	
b.		Enamel paper	.70	.65
95	A2	2½c on 25r carmine	1.30	.65
a.		Enamel paper	.70	.65
b.		As "a," "REPUBLICA" omitted	15.00	
96	A2	5c on 50r brn	.80	.75
a.		Enamel paper	.70	.65
97	A2	7½c on 75r red lil	1.30	.90
98	A2	10c on 100r dk bl, *bl*	1.30	.70
99	A2	11½c on 115r org brn, *pink*	2.75	1.50
a.		Inverted surcharge	36.00	31.00
100	A2	13c on 130r brn, *yel*	2.75	1.50
a.		Double surcharge	40.00	
101	A2	20c on 200r red lil, *pink*	3.25	1.30
102	A2	40c on 400r dl bl, *yel*	3.25	1.30
103	A2	50c on 500r blk & red, *bl* (R)	3.50	1.60
104	A2	70c on 700r pur, *yel*	3.50	1.90
		Nos. 90-104 (15)	27.10	14.85

Nos. 87 to 89 Surcharged

1918   **Perf. 11½**

105	A2	½c on 700r pur, *yel*	3.75	2.50
106	A2	2½c on 500r blk & red, *bl* (Bl)	3.75	2.50
107	A2	5c on 400r dl bl, *yel*	3.75	2.50
		Nos. 105-107 (3)	11.25	7.50

Coffee Plantation A17
Orange Tree A18
Cotton Field A19
Sisal Plantation A20
Scene on Beira R. R. A21
Court House at Beira A22
Coconut Palm A23
Mangroves A24
Cattle A25
Company Arms A26

1918-21   **Engr.**   **Perf. 13½x15, 14¼**

108	A9	¼c brn & yel grn	.65	.50
110	A10	½c black	.65	.50
111	A11	1c green & blk	.65	.50
112	A12	1½c black & grn	.65	.50
113	A13	2c carmine & blk	.65	.50
115	A14	2½c black & blk	.65	.50
116	A11	3c ocher & blk, perf. 14 ('23)	.40	.40
117	A15	4c grn & brn ('21)	.40	.35
119	A9	4½c gray & blk, perf. 14 ('23)	.40	.40
120	A16	5c blue & blk	.65	.65
121	A17	6c claret & bl ('21)	.80	.40
123	A21	7c ultra & blk, perf. 14 ('23)	1.00	.50
124	A18	7½c orange & grn	1.10	.90
125	A19	8c violet & blk	1.80	1.20
126	A20	10c red org & blk	1.80	1.20
128	A19	12c brn & blk, perf. 14 ('23)	1.60	1.10
130	A19	15c carmine & blk	1.90	.75
131	A22	20c dp green & blk	1.90	.75
132	A23	30c red brn & blk	3.00	1.20
135	A24	40c yel grn & blk	2.10	1.30
137	A25	50c orange & blk	2.50	1.30
139	A25	60c carmine & brn, perf. 14 ('23)	2.10	1.30
140	A20	80c ultra & brn, perf. 14 ('23)	3.25	1.30
142	A26	1e dk green & blk	3.00	2.50
144	A16	2e carmine & vio, perf. 14 ('23)	4.00	2.00
		Nos. 108-145 (36)	57.90	33.95

1924-31   **Perf. 12½**

108a	A9	¼c brn & yel grn ('24)	.95	.75
109	A9	¼c ol grn & blk ('25)	.90	.75
110a	A10	½c black ('24)	.65	.50
111a	A11	1c green & blk ('24)	.65	.50
b.		1c yel grn & blk ('25)	.45	.50
112a	A12	1½c blk & green ('24)	.65	.50
113a	A13	2c carmine & blk ('24)	.65	.50
114	A13	2c ol blk & blk ('25)	.65	.50
115a	A14	2½c lilac & blk ('24)	.65	.50
116a	A11	3c ocher & blk ('24)	.40	.35
b.		3p org & blk ('25)	.40	.35
117a	A15	4c grn & brn ('21)	.40	.35
118	A15	4c red & blk ('25)	.40	.35
120a	A16	5c blue & blk ('24)	.40	.35
122	A17	6c lilac & blk ('25)	.40	.35
124a	A18	7½c org & grn ('24)	1.10	1.00
125a	A19	8c vio & blk ('24)	1.90	1.20
b.		8c grayish pur & blk ('25)	1.70	1.35
126a	A20	10c red org & blk ('24)	1.90	1.20
b.		10c red org & blk ('25)	1.70	1.35
128a	A19	12c brown & blk ('23)	1.65	1.10
129	A19	12c bl grn & blk ('25)	1.80	1.20
b.		15c pale rose red & blk ('25)	1.35	1.20
130a	A21	15c carmine & blk ('24)	1.80	1.20
131a	A22	20c dp green & blk ('24)	2.00	.90
b.		20c yel grn & blk ('25)	2.00	.70

132a	A23	30c red brn & blk ('24)	3.00	1.25
133	A23	30c gray grn & blk ('25)	2.00	.90
134	A23	30c bl grn & blk ('31)	2.75	.90
135a	A24	40c yel org & blk ('24)	2.50	1.30
136	A24	40c grnsh bl & blk ('25)	1.50	1.10
137a	A25	50c org & blk ('24)	3.00	1.30
138	A25	50c lt vio & blk ('25)	2.50	1.60
141	A20	80c car & blk ('25)	2.10	1.60
142a	A26	1e dk grn & blk ('24)	3.00	2.50
143	A26	1e blue & blk ('25)	2.50	1.60
144a	A16	2e rose & vio ('24)	4.25	2.25
145	A16	2e lilac & blk ('25)	4.50	1.90
		Nos. 108a-145 (35)	55.30	33.75

Shades exist of several denominations.
For surcharges see Nos. 146-154, RA1.

Nos. 132, 142, 115, 120, 131, 135, 125, 137 Surcharged with New Values in Red, Blue, Violet or Black

1920   **Perf. 14, 15**

146	A23(h)	½c on 30c (Bk)	7.00	5.75
147	A26(h)	½c on 1e (R)	7.00	5.75
148	A14(h)	1½c on 2½c (Bl)	6.00	3.50
149	A16(h)	1½c on 5c (V)	6.00	3.50
150	A14(h)	1½c on 2½c (V)	6.00	3.50
151	A22(i)	4c on 20c (V)	7.00	5.00
152	A24(i)	4c on 40c (V)	7.00	5.00
153	A19(j)	6c on 8c (R)	7.50	5.00
154	A25(j)	6c on 50c (Bk)	8.00	5.00
		Nos. 146-154 (9)	61.50	42.00

The surcharge on No. 148 is placed vertically between two bars. On No. 154 the two words of the surcharge are 10mm apart.

Native A27
View of Beira A28
Tapping Rubber Tree — A29
Picking Tea — A30
Zambezi River — A31

1925-31   **Engr.**   **Perf. 12**

155	A27	24c ultra & blk	3.25	2.25
156	A28	25c choc & ultra	3.25	2.25
157	A27	85c brn red & blk ('31)	2.50	1.60
158	A28	1.40e dl bl & blk ('31)	2.50	1.60
159	A29	5e yel brn & ultra	3.75	1.50
160	A30	10e rose & blk	6.25	1.75
161	A31	20e green & blk	7.50	2.50
		Nos. 155-161 (7)	29.00	13.45

Ivory Tusks — A32
Panning Gold — A33

1931   **Litho.**   **Perf. 14**

| 162 | A32 | 45c lt blue | 4.50 | 2.50 |
| 163 | A33 | 70c yellow brn | 2.50 | 1.60 |

727

MOZAMBIQUE COMPANY

Zambezi Railroad Bridge — A34

1935   **Engr.**   *Perf. 12½*
164   A34   1e dk blue & blk   7.50   3.75

Opening of a new bridge over the Zambezi River.

Airplane over Beira A35

1935
165	A35	5c blue & blk	1.10	.75
166	A35	10c red org & blk	1.10	.75
a.		Square pair, imperf. between	55.00	
167	A35	15c red & blk	1.10	.75
a.		Square pair, imperf. between	55.00	
168	A35	20c yel grn & blk	1.10	.75
169	A35	30c green & blk	1.10	.75
170	A35	40c gray bl & blk	1.50	1.00
171	A35	45c blue & blk	1.50	1.10
172	A35	50c violet & blk	1.50	1.00
a.		Square pair, imperf. btwn.	55.00	
173	A35	60c carmine & brn	2.50	1.50
174	A35	80c carmine & blk	5.50	3.50
		Nos. 165-174 (10)	18.00	11.85

Issued to commemorate the opening of the Blantyre-Beira Salisbury air service.

Giraffe A36   **Thatched Huts A37**

Rock Python A41

Coconut Palms — A50

Zambezi Railroad Bridge — A52   **Sena Gate — A53**

Company Arms — A54

Designs: 10c, Dhow. 15c, St. Caetano Fortress, Sofala. 20c, Zebra. 40c, Black rhinoceros. 45c, Lion. 50c, Crocodile. 60c, Leopard. 70c, Mozambique woman. 80c, Hippopotami. 85c, Vasco da Gama's flagship. 1e, Man in canoe. 2e, Greater kudu.

1937, May 16   *Perf. 12½*
175	A36	1c yel grn & vio	.40	.25
176	A37	5c blue & yel grn	.40	.25
177	A36	10c ver & ultra	.40	.25
178	A37	15c carmine & blk	.40	.25
179	A36	20c green & ultra	.40	.25
180	A41	30c dk grn & ind	.40	.30
181	A41	40c gray bl & blk	.40	.30
182	A41	45c blue & brn	.40	.30
183	A41	50c dk vio & emer	.40	.30
184	A37	60c carmine & bl	.40	.30
185	A36	70c yel brn & pale grn	.40	.30
186	A37	80c car & pale grn	.55	.35
187	A41	85c org red & blk	.70	.40
188	A41	1e dp bl & blk	.70	.40
189	A50	1.40e dk bl & pale grn	1.25	.40
190	A41	2e pale lilac & brn	2.05	.50
191	A52	5e yel brn & bl	1.75	.80
192	A53	10e carmine & blk	3.10	1.60
193	A54	20e grn & brn vio	4.15	2.00
		Nos. 175-193 (19)	18.65	9.50

Stamps of 1937 Overprinted in Red or Black

1939, Jul. 28
194	A41	30c dk grn & ind (R)	2.20	1.65
195	A41	40c gray bl & blk (R)	2.20	1.65
196	A41	45c blue & brn (Bk)	2.20	1.65
197	A41	50c dk vio & emer (R)	2.20	1.65
198	A41	85c org red & blk (Bk)	2.20	1.65
199	A41	1e dp bl & blk (R)	3.75	1.90
200	A41	2e pale lil & brn (Bk)	5.00	3.50
		Nos. 194-200 (7)	19.75	13.65

Visit of the President of Portugal to Beira in 1939.

King Alfonso Henriques — A55

1940, Feb. 16   **Typo.**   *Perf. 11½x12*
201   A55   1.75e blue & lt blue   3.00   1.60

800th anniv. of Portuguese independence.

King John IV — A56

1940, Oct. 10   **Engr.**   *Perf. 12½*
202	A56	40c gray grn & blk	.90	.70
203	A56	50c dk vio & brt grn	.90	.70
204	A56	60c brt car & dp bl	.90	.70
205	A56	70c brn org & dk grn	.90	.70
206	A56	80c car & dp grn	.90	.70
207	A56	1e dk bl & blk	.90	.70
		Nos. 202-207 (6)	5.40	4.20

300th anniv. of the restoration of the Portuguese Monarchy.

Mozambique Company's charter terminated July 18th, 1942, after which date its stamps were superseded by those of the territory of Mozambique.

SEMI-POSTAL STAMPS

Lisbon Issue of 1911 Overprinted in Red

1917   **Unwmk.**   *Perf. 11½*
B1	A2	2½r gray	11.00	11.75
a.		Double overprint	120.00	85.00
B2	A2	10r yellow grn	12.25	16.75
B3	A2	20r gray lilac	17.00	22.50
B4	A2	50r brown	24.50	28.00
B5	A2	75r red lilac	80.00	77.50
B6	A2	100r dk blue, bl	92.50	90.00
B7	A2	700r purple, yel	215.00	250.00
		Nos. B1-B7 (7)	452.25	496.50

Nos. B1-B7 were used on July 31, 1917, in place of ordinary stamps. The proceeds were given to the Red Cross.

AIR POST STAMPS

Airplane over Beira — AP1

1935   **Unwmk.**   **Engr.**   *Perf. 12½*
C1	AP1	5c blue & blk	.40	.35
C2	AP1	10c org red & blk	.40	.35
C3	AP1	15c red & blk	.40	.35
C4	AP1	20c yel grn & blk	.40	.35
C5	AP1	30c green & blk	.40	.35
C6	AP1	40c gray bl & blk	.40	.35
C7	AP1	45c blue & blk	.40	.35
C8	AP1	50c dk vio & blk	.45	.35
C9	AP1	60c car & brn	.45	.35
C10	AP1	80c car & blk	.55	.35
C11	AP1	1e blue & blk	.55	.35
C12	AP1	2e mauve & blk	1.50	.50
C13	AP1	5e bis brn & bl	1.50	1.10
C14	AP1	10e car & blk	2.30	1.25
C15	AP1	20e grn & blk	3.75	2.00
		Nos. C1-C15 (15)	13.85	8.70

POSTAGE DUE STAMPS

D1

1906   **Unwmk.**   **Typo.**   *Perf. 11½x12*
Denominations in Black
J1	D1	5r yellow grn	.90	.80
J2	D1	10r slate	.90	.80
J3	D1	20r yellow brn	.90	.80
J4	D1	30r orange	1.75	1.20
J5	D1	50r gray brown	1.75	1.20
J6	D1	60r red brown	26.50	11.00
J7	D1	100r red lilac	3.50	3.00
J8	D1	130r dull blue	34.00	11.50
J9	D1	200r carmine	11.25	4.50
J10	D1	500r violet	16.50	5.50
		Nos. J1-J10 (10)	97.95	40.30

Nos. J1-J10 Overprinted in Carmine or Green

1911
J11	D1	5r yellow grn	.55	.50
J12	D1	10r slate	.65	.65
J13	D1	20r yellow brn	.65	.65
J14	D1	30r orange	.65	.65
J15	D1	50r gray brown	.65	.65
J16	D1	60r red brown	1.30	.90
J17	D1	100r red lilac	1.30	.90
J18	D1	130r dull blue	2.50	2.30
J19	D1	200r carmine (G)	3.25	2.50
J20	D1	500r violet	3.50	3.25
		Nos. J11-J20 (10)	15.00	12.95

D2

1916   **Typo.**
With Value in Centavos in Black
J21	D2	½c yellow grn	.45	.45
J22	D2	1c slate	.45	.45
J23	D2	2c orange brn	.45	.45
J24	D2	3c orange	1.05	.45
J25	D2	5c gray brown	1.05	.45
J26	D2	6c pale brown	1.05	.55
J27	D2	10c red lilac	1.05	.85
J28	D2	13c gray blue	2.10	1.95
J29	D2	20c rose	2.10	1.95
J30	D2	50c gray	4.95	2.25
		Nos. J21-J30 (10)	14.70	9.80

Company Arms — D3

1919   **Engr.**   *Perf. 14, 15*
J31	D3	½c green	.40	.40
a.		Perf. 12½	.40	.40
J32	D3	1c slate	.40	.40
a.		Perf. 12½	.40	.40
J33	D3	2c red brown	.40	.40
a.		Perf. 12½	.40	.40
J34	D3	3c orange	.40	.40
a.		Perf. 12½	.40	.40
J35	D3	5c gray brown	.40	.40
a.		Perf. 12½	.40	.40
J36	D3	6c lt brown	.65	.65
a.		Perf. 12½	.65	.65
b.		Perf. 13½	.65	.65
J37	D3	10c lilac rose	1.30	1.30
a.		Perf. 12½	1.30	1.30
J38	D3	13c dull blue	1.80	1.80
a.		Perf. 12½	1.80	1.80
b.		Perf. 13½	1.80	1.80
J39	D3	20c rose	1.80	1.80
a.		Perf. 12½	1.80	1.80
J40	D3	50c gray	2.75	2.75
a.		Perf. 12½	2.75	2.75
		Nos. J31-J40 (10)	10.30	10.30

NEWSPAPER STAMP

Newspaper Stamp of Mozambique Overprinted

1894   **Unwmk.**   *Perf. 11½*
P1	N3	2½r brown	1.60	1.25
a.		Inverted overprint	15.00	12.50
b.		Perf. 12½	3.50	2.25

Reprints are on stout white paper with clean-cut perf. 13½. Value $1.

POSTAL TAX STAMPS

No. 116 Surcharged in Black

1932   *Perf. 12½*
RA1   A11   2c on 3c org & blk   2.75   2.00

Charity — PT2

1934   **Litho.**   *Perf. 11*
RA2   PT2   2c magenta & blk   3.00   2.00

PT3

1940   **Unwmk.**   *Perf. 10½*
RA3   PT3   2c black & ultra   19.00   12.50

PT4

1941
RA4   PT4   2c black & brt red   19.00   12.50

Vols. 4A-4B number additions, deletions and changes

Number in 2024 Catalogue	Number in 2025 Catalogue

Korea, Democratic People's Republic
new	46a
76	42
43	70A
new	70B
42	70C

Malaya - Kedah
3a	3A
12a	12A
13a	13A
13b	13Ab
16a	16A
23a	23A
26a	26A
28a	28A
33a	33A

Malaya - Kelantan
3a	3A
4a	4A
7a	7A
8a	8A
10a	10A
11a	11A
12a	12A
14a	14A
23a	23A

Malaya - Trengganu
8a	8A
10a	10A
12a	12A
13a	13A
14a	14A
15a	15A
16a	16A
17a	17A
18a	18A
21a	21A
24a	24A

Mcmcl
new	18a
now	19a
new	21a
new	22a
new	23a
new	24a
new	25a
new	26a
new	27a
new	28a
new	30a
new	31b
new	31c

INDEX AND IDENTIFIER

All page numbers shown are those in this Volume 4B.

Postage stamps that do not have English words on them are shown in the Illustrated Identifier.

A & T ovptd. on French Colonies .... Vol. 1A
Aberdeen, Miss. .... Vol. 1A
Abingdon, Va. .... Vol. 1A
Abu Dhabi .... Vol. 1A, Vol. 5A, Vol. 6B
Abyssinia (Ethiopia) .... Vol. 2B
A.C.C.P., A.D.C.P. .... Vol. 1B
A Certo ovptd. on stamps of Peru .... Vol. 5A
Acores .... Vol. 1B, Vol. 5B
Aden .... Vol. 1A
AEF .... Vol. 2B
Aegean Islands (Greek Occupation) .... Vol. 3A
Aegean Islands (Italian Occupation) .... Vol. 3B
Aeroport International de Kandahar (Afghanistan #679) .... Vol. 1A
Afars and Issas .... Vol. 1A
AFF EXCEP .... Vol. 2B
Afghanistan, Afghan, Afghanes ... Vol. 1A
AFR .... Vol. 5B
Africa, British Offices .... Vol. 3A
Africa, German East .... Vol. 3A
Africa, German South-West .... Vol. 3A
Africa, Italian Offices .... Vol. 3B
Africa Occidental Espanola .... Vol. 6A
Africa Orientale Italiana .... Vol. 3B
Africa, Portuguese .... Vol. 5B
Afrique Equatoriale Francaise .... 471, Vol. 2A, Vol. 2B, Vol. 6B
Afrique Francaise .... Vol. 2B
Afrique Occidentale Francaise ..... Vol. 2B
Agion Oros Athoc (Greece) .... Vol. 3A
Aguera, La .... Vol. 1A
Aguinaldo .... Vol. 5A
AHA (Confed. #44X1) .... Vol. 1A
Aimeliik (Palau #686) .... Vol. 5A
Airai (Palau #686) .... Vol. 5A
Aitutaki .... Vol. 1A
Ajman .... Vol. 1A, Vol. 6B
Aland Islands .... Vol. 2B
Alaouites .... Vol. 1A
Albania .... Vol. 1A
Albania, Greek Occupation .... Vol. 3A
Albania, Italian Offices .... Vol. 3B
Albany, Ga. .... Vol. 1A
Alderney .... Vol. 3A
Aleppo .... Vol. 6A
Alerta ovptd. on stamps of Peru ... Vol. 5A
Alexandretta, Alexandrette .... Vol. 1A
Alexandria, Alexandrie, French Offices .... Vol. 2B
Alexandria, Va. .... Vol. 1A
Alexandroupolis .... Vol. 3A
Algeria, Algerie .... Vol. 1A
Allemagne Duitschland .... Vol. 3A
Allenstein .... Vol. 1A
Allied Military Government (Austria) .... Vol. 1B
Allied Military Gov. (Germany) .... Vol. 3A
Allied Military Government (Italy) ... Vol. 3B
Allied Military Government (Trieste) .... Vol. 3B
Allied Occupation of Azerbaijan ... Vol. 3B
Allied Occupation of Thrace .... Vol. 6B
A L'Ocassion de la Journée Internationale de l'Alphabetisation (Afghan. #951) .... Vol. 1A
Alsace .... Vol. 2B
Alsace and Lorraine .... Vol. 2B
Alwar .... Vol. 3B
A.M.G. .... Vol. 1B, Vol. 3A, Vol. 3B
A.M.G./F.T.T. .... Vol. 3B
A.M.G./V.G. .... Vol. 3B
AM Post .... Vol. 3A
Anatolia .... Vol. 1A
Ancachs .... Vol. 5A
Andalusian Provinces .... Vol. 6A
Anderson Court House, S.C. ...... Vol. 1A
Andorra, Andorre .... Vol. 1A
Andorre .... Vol. 1A
Angaur (Palau #686) .... Vol. 5A
Angola .... Vol. 1A
Angra .... Vol. 1A
Anguilla .... Vol. 1A, Vol. 5B
Anhwei .... Vol. 2A
Anjouan .... Vol. 1A

Anna surcharged on France .... Vol. 2B
Anna surcharged on Great Britain ... Vol. 5A
Anna, Annas .... Vol. 3B
Annam .... Vol. 3B
Annam and Tonkin .... Vol. 1A
Annapolis, Md. .... Vol. 1A
Ano do X Aniversario Comunidade dos Paises de Lingua Portugesa (Angola 1298-1300) .... Vol. 1A
Antigua .... Vol. 1A, Vol. 5B
Antigua & Barbuda .... Vol. 5B
Antioquia .... Vol. 2A
A.O. ovptd. on Congo .... Vol. 3A
AOF on France .... Vol. 2B
A.O.I. ovpt. on Italy .... Vol. 3B
A Payer Te Betalen .... Vol. 1B
A percevoir (see France, French colonies, postage due) ..... Vol. 2B, Vol. 3A
Apurimac .... Vol. 5A
A R 715
A.R. ovptd. on stamps of Colombia .... Vol. 5A
Arabie Saoudite .... Vol. 5A
Arad .... Vol. 3B
A receber (See Portuguese Colonies) .... Vol. 5B
Arequipa .... Vol. 5A
Argentina .... Vol. 1A
Argyrokastron .... Vol. 2B
Arica .... Vol. 5A
Armenia .... Vol. 1A, Vol. 6B
Armenian stamps ovptd. or surcharged .... Vol. 3A, Vol. 6B
Army of the North .... Vol. 5B
Army of the Northwest .... Vol. 5B
Aruba .... Vol. 1A
Arwad .... Vol. 5B
Ascension .... Vol. 1A
Assistencia Nacionalaos Tuberculosos .... Vol. 5B
Asturias Province .... Vol. 6A
Athens, Ga. .... Vol. 1A
Atlanta, Ga. .... Vol. 1A
Aunus, ovptd. on Finland .... Vol. 5B
Austin, Miss. .... Vol. 6A
Austin, Tex. .... Vol. 1A
Australia .... Vol. 1A
Australia, Occupation of Japan ... Vol. 1A
Australian Antarctic Territory ..... Vol. 1A
Australian States .... Vol. 1A
Austria .... Vol. 1B
Austria, Allied Military Govt. .... Vol. 1B
Austria, Adm. of Liechtenstein ... Vol. 4A
Austria, Lombardy-Venetia .... Vol. 1B
Austria-Hungary .... Vol. 1B
Austrian Occupation of Italy .... Vol. 3B
Austrian Occupation of Montenegro ... 628
Austrian Occupation of Romania ... Vol. 5B
Austrian Occupation of Serbia ... Vol. 6A
Austrian Offices Abroad .... Vol. 1B
Austrian stamps surcharged or overprinted .... Vol. 1B, Vol. 3B, Vol. 5B, Vol. 6B
Autaugaville, Ala. .... Vol. 1A
Autopaketti, Autorahti .... Vol. 2B
Avisporto .... Vol. 2B
Ayacucho .... Vol. 5A
Aytonomoe .... Vol. 2B
Azerbaijan, Azarbaycan, Azerbaycan, Azerbaidjan .... Vol. 1B, Vol. 3B, Vol. 6B
Azirbayedjan .... Vol. 3B
Azores .... Vol. 1B, Vol. 5B

B .... Vol. 1B, Vol. 5A, Vol. 6A
B ovptd. on Straits Settlements ... Vol. 1B
Baden .... Vol. 3A
Baghdad 350
Bahamas .... Vol. 1B
Bahawalpur .... Vol. 5A
Bahrain .... Vol. 1B, Vol. 5A
Baja Cal(ifornia) 357
Bajar Porto .... Vol. 3B
Baku .... Vol. 1B
Balcony Falls, Va. .... Vol. 1A
Baltimore, Md. .... Vol. 1A
Bamra .... Vol. 3B
Banat, Bacska .... Vol. 3B
Bangkok .... Vol. 1B
Bangladesh .... Vol. 1B
Bani ovptd. on Austria .... Vol. 5B
Bani ovptd. on Hungary .... Vol. 3B
Baranya .... Vol. 3B
Barbados .... Vol. 1B
Barbuda .... Vol. 1B
Barcelona .... Vol. 6A
Barnwell Court House, S.C. .... Vol. 1A
Barranquilla .... Vol. 2A
Barwani .... Vol. 3B

Basel .... Vol. 6A
Bashahr .... Vol. 3B
Basque Provinces .... Vol. 6A
Basutoland .... Vol. 1B
Batavia .... Vol. 5A
Baton Rouge, La. .... Vol. 1A
Batum, Batym (British Occupation) .... Vol. 1B
Bavaria .... Vol. 3A
Bayar Porto .... Vol. 3B
Bayer., Bayern .... Vol. 3A
B.C.A. ovptd. on Rhodesia .... Vol. 1B
B.C.M. 62
B.C.O.F. .... Vol. 3B
Beaufort, S.C. .... Vol. 1A
Beaumont, Tex. .... Vol. 1A
Bechuanaland .... Vol. 1B
Bechuanaland Protectorate .... Vol. 1B
Beckmann's City Post .... Vol. 1A
Behie .... Vol. 6B
Belarus .... Vol. 1B
Belgian (Belgisch) Congo .... Vol. 1B
Belgian East Africa .... Vol. 5B
Belgian Occ. of German East Africa .... Vol. 3A
Belgian Occupation of Germany ... Vol. 3A
Belgien .... Vol. 3A
Belgium, Belgique, Belgie .... Vol. 1B
Belgium (German Occupation) ... Vol. 1B
Belize .... Vol. 1B
Belize, Cayes of .... Vol. 1B
Benadir .... Vol. 6A
Bengasi .... Vol. 3B
Beni .... Vol. 1B
Benin .... Vol. 1B
Benin, People's Republic of ...... Vol. 1B
Bequia .... Vol. 5B
Bergedorf .... Vol. 3A
Berlin .... Vol. 3A
Berlin-Brandenburg .... Vol. 3A
Bermuda .... Vol. 1B
Besetztes Gebiet Nordfrankreich ... Vol. 2B
Besieged ovptd. on Cape of Good Hope .... Vol. 2A, Vol. 6B
Beyrouth, French Offices .... Vol. 2B
Beyrouth, Russian Offices .... Vol. 5B
B. Guiana .... Vol. 1B
B. Hneipoe .... Vol. 2B
Bhopal .... Vol. 3B
Bhor .... Vol. 3B
Bhutan .... Vol. 1B
Biafra .... Vol. 1B
Bijawar .... Vol. 3B
B.I.O.T. ovptd. on Seychelles ..... Vol. 1B
Bishop's City Post .... Vol. 1A
Blagoveshchensk .... Vol. 2B
Bluefields .... Vol. 5A
Bluffton, S.C. .... Vol. 1A
B.M.A. Eritrea .... Vol. 3A
B.M.A. Malaya .... Vol. 6A
B.M.A. Somalia .... Vol. 3A
B.M.A. Tripolitania .... Vol. 3A
Bocas del Toro .... Vol. 5A
Boer Occupation .... Vol. 2A
Bogota .... Vol. 2A
Bohemia and Moravia .... Vol. 2B
Bohmen and Mahren .... Vol. 2B
Boletta, Bollettino .... Vol. 3B, Vol. 6A
Bolivar .... Vol. 2A
Bolivia .... Vol. 1B
Bollo .... Vol. 3B
Bollo Postale .... Vol. 6A
Bophuthatswana .... Vol. 6A
Borneo .... Vol. 5A
Boscawen, N.H. .... Vol. 1A
Bosna i Hercegovina ...... Vol. 1B, Vol. 6B
Bosnia and Herzegovina ... Vol. 1B, Vol. 6B
Bosnia, Muslim Gov. in Sarajevo ... Vol. 1B
Bosnia, Croat Administration, Mostar .... Vol. 1B
Bosnia, Serb Administration, Banja Luca .... Vol. 1B
Bosnia stamps overprinted or surcharged ...... Vol. 1B, Vol. 3B, Vol. 6B
Bosnien Herzegowina .... Vol. 1B
Boston, Mass. .... Vol. 1A
Botswana .... Vol. 1B
Boyaca .... Vol. 2A
Brattleboro, Vt. .... Vol. 1A
Braunschweig .... Vol. 3A
Brazil, Brasil .... Vol. 1B
Bremen .... Vol. 3A
Bridgeville, Ala. .... Vol. 1A
British Administration of Bahrain ... Vol. 1B
British Antarctic Territory .... Vol. 1B
British Bechuanaland .... Vol. 1B

British Central Africa .... Vol. 1B
British Colonies - Dies I & II .... See table of contents
British Columbia & Vancouver Is. ... Vol. 2A
British Consular Mail 62
British Dominion of Samoa .... Vol. 5B
British East Africa .... Vol. 1B
British Forces in Egypt .... Vol. 2B
British Guiana .... Vol. 1B
British Honduras .... Vol. 1B
British Indian Ocean Territory ... Vol. 1B
British Mandate of Jordan .... Vol. 4A
British Levant .... Vol. 3A
British New Guinea .... Vol. 1B
British North Borneo .... Vol. 5A
British Occupation (of Batum) ... Vol. 1B
British Occupation of Bushire ... Vol. 1B
British Occupation of Cameroun ... Vol. 2A
British Occupation of Crete .... Vol. 2A
British Occupation of Faroe Is. ... Vol. 2B
British Occ. of German East Africa .... Vol. 3A
British Occupation of Iraq ... 350, Vol. 3B
British Occupation of Mesopotamia ... 350
British Occ. of Orange River Colony .... Vol. 5A
British Occupation overprint ...... Vol. 1B
British Occupation of Palestine ... Vol. 5A
British Occupation of Persia ..... Vol. 1B
British Occupation of Togo .... Vol. 6B
British Occ. of Transvaal .... Vol. 6B
British Offices in Africa .... Vol. 3A
British Offices in China .... Vol. 3A
British Offices in Morocco .... Vol. 3A
British Offices in Tangier .... Vol. 3A
British Off. in the Turkish Empire ... Vol. 3A
British Protectorate of Egypt ..... Vol. 2B
British Samoa .... Vol. 5B
British Solomon Islands .... Vol. 6A
British Somaliland (Somaliland Protectorate) .... Vol. 6A
British South Africa (Rhodesia) ... Vol. 5B
British stamps surcharged .... Vol. 5A
British Vice-Consulate 62
British Virgin Islands .... Vol. 6B
British Zone (Germany) .... Vol. 3A
Brown & McGill's U.S.P.O. Despatch .... Vol. 1A
Brunei .... Vol. 1B
Brunei (Japanese Occupation) ... Vol. 1B
Brunswick .... Vol. 3A
Buchanan .... Vol. 1A, Vol. 4A
Buenos Aires .... Vol. 1A
Bulgaria, Bulgarie .... Vol. 1B
Bulgarian Occupation of Romania .... Vol. 5B
Bulgarian stamps overprinted or surcharged ... Vol. 3A, Vol. 5B, Vol. 6B
Bundi .... Vol. 3B
Bundi stamps overprinted .... Vol. 3B
Bureau International .... Vol. 6A
Burgenland .... Vol. 1B
Burgos .... Vol. 6A
Burkina Faso .... Vol. 1B
Burma .... Vol. 1B
Burma (Japanese Occupation) ... Vol. 1B
Burundi .... Vol. 1B
Bushire .... Vol. 1B
Bussahir .... Vol. 3B
Buu-Chinh .... Vol. 6B
Buu-Bien .... Vol. 6B
Byelorussia .... Vol. 1B

Cabo, Cabo Gracias a Dios ...... Vol. 5A
Cabo Juby, Jubi .... Vol. 2A
Cabo Verde .... Vol. 2A
Cadiz .... Vol. 6A
Caicos .... Vol. 6B
Calchi .... Vol. 3B
Cali .... Vol. 2A
Calino, Calimno .... Vol. 3B
Callao .... Vol. 5A
Camb. Aust. Sigillum Nov. .... Vol. 1A
Cambodia, (Int. Com., India) ..... Vol. 3B
Cambodia, Cambodge .... Vol. 2A, Vol. 3B
Camden, S.C. .... Vol. 1A
Cameroons (U.K.T.T.) .... Vol. 2A
Cameroun (Republique Federale) ... Vol. 2A
Campeche 442
Canada .... Vol. 2A
Canadian Provinces .... Vol. 2A
Canal Zone .... Vol. 1A
Canary Islands, Canarias .... Vol. 6A
Candia .... Vol. 2A
Canouan .... Vol. 5B
Canton, French Offices .... Vol. 2B
Canton, Miss. .... Vol. 1A
Cape Juby .... Vol. 2A

INDEX AND IDENTIFIER

Entry	Volume
Cape of Good Hope	Vol. 2A
Cape of Good Hope stamps surchd. (see Griqualand West)	Vol. 3A
Cape Verde	Vol. 2A
Carchi	Vol. 3B
Caribbean Netherlands	Vol. 2A
Caribisch Nederland	Vol. 2A
Carinthia	Vol. 1B, Vol. 6B
Carlist	Vol. 6A
Carolina City, N.C.	Vol. 1A
Caroline Islands	Vol. 2A
Carpatho-Ukraine	Vol. 2B
Carriacou & Petite Martinique	Vol. 3A
Carriers Stamps	Vol. 1A
Cartagena	Vol. 2A
Cartersville, Ga.	Vol. 1A
Carupano	Vol. 6B
Caso	Vol. 3B
Castellorizo, Castelrosso	Vol. 2A
Catalonia	Vol. 6A
Cauca	Vol. 2A
Cavalla (Greek)	Vol. 3A
Cavalle, Cavalla (French)	Vol. 2B
Cayes of Belize	Vol. 1B
Cayman Islands	Vol. 2A
CCCP	Vol. 5B
C.CH. on French Colonies	Vol. 2A
C.E.F. ovptd. on Cameroun	Vol. 2A
C.E.F. ovptd. on India	Vol. 3B
Cefalonia ovptd. on Greece	Vol. 3B
Celebes	Vol. 5A
Cent, cents	109, 564, Vol. 1A, Vol. 2B, Vol. 5A
Centenaire Algerie RF (France No. 255)	Vol. 2B
Centonary 1st Postage Stamp (Pakistan #63-64)	Vol. 5A
Centesimi overprinted on Austria or Bosnia	Vol. 3B
Centesimi di corona	Vol. 1B, Vol. 2B
Centimes	Vol. 2B
Centimes ovptd. on Austria	Vol. 1B
Centimes ovptd. on Germany	Vol. 3A
Centimos (no country name)	Vol. 6A
Centimos ovptd. on France	Vol. 6A
Central Africa (Contrafricaine)	Vol. 2A
Central African Republic	Vol. 2A
Central China	Vol. 2A
Central Lithuania	Vol. 2A
Cephalonia	Vol. 3B
Cerigo	Vol. 3A, Vol. 3B
Cervantes	Vol. 6A
Ceska Republica	Vol. 2B
Ceskoslovenska, Ceskoslovensko	Vol. 2B
Ceylon	Vol. 2B
CF	Vol. 2B
CFA	Vol. 2B
C.G.H.S.	Vol. 6B
Ch	Vol. 3B, Vol. 4A
Chachapoyas	Vol. 5A
Chad	Vol. 2A
Chahar	Vol. 2A
Chala	Vol. 5A
Chamba	Vol. 3B
Channel Islands	Vol. 3A
Chapel Hill, N.C.	Vol. 1A
Charkhari	Vol. 3B
Charleston, S.C.	Vol. 1A
Charlotte, N.C.	Vol. 1A
Charlottesville, Va.	Vol. 1A
Chateau de Beggen (Luxembourg #1466)	Vol. 4A
Chateau de Dommeldange (Luxembourg #1467)	Vol. 4A
Chattanooga, Tenn.	Vol. 1A
Chekiang	Vol. 2A
Chemins des Fer	Vol. 2B
Cherifien Posts	Vol. 2B
Chiapas	442
Chiclayo	Vol. 5A
Chiffre	See France and French colonies, postage due
Chihuahua	442
Chile	Vol. 2A
Chilean Occupation of Peru	Vol. 5A
Chimarra	Vol. 2A
China, Chinese	Vol. 2A
China (Japanese Occupation)	Vol. 2A
China Expeditionary Force (India)	Vol. 2A
China, British Offices	Vol. 2A
China, Formosa	Vol. 2A, Vol. 4A
China, French Offices	Vol. 2A
China, German Offices	Vol. 3A
China, Italian Offices	Vol. 3B
China, Japanese Offices	Vol. 4A
China, Northeastern Provinces	Vol. 2A
China, Offices in Manchuria	Vol. 2A
China, Offices in Tibet	Vol. 2A
China, People's Republic	Vol. 2A
China, People's Republic Regional Issues	Vol. 2A
China, People's Republic Hong Kong	Vol. 3B
China, People's Republic Macao	13
China, Republic of	Vol. 2A
China, Russian Offices	Vol. 5B
China, United States Offices	Vol. 1A
Chine	Vol. 2B
Chios	Vol. 3A
Chita	Vol. 6A
Chosen	Vol. 4A
Christiansburg, Va.	Vol. 1A
Christmas Island	Vol. 2B
Chungking	Vol. 2B
C.I.H.S.	Vol. 6A
Cilicia, Cilicie	Vol. 2A, Vol. 5A, Vol. 6A
Cincinnati, O.	Vol. 1A
Cinquan Tenaire	Vol. 5A
Cirenaica	Vol. 2B
Ciskei	Vol. 6A
City Despatch Post	Vol. 1A
City Post	Vol. 1A
Cleveland, O.	Vol. 1A
Cluj	Vol. 3B
c/m	Vol. 2B
C.M.T.	Vol. 6B
Coamo	Vol. 1A, Vol. 5B
Cochin	Vol. 3B
Cochin China	Vol. 2B
Cochin, Travancore	Vol. 3B
Co. Ci. ovptd. on Yugoslavia	Vol. 6B
Cocos Islands	Vol. 2A
Colaparchee, Ga.	Vol. 1A
Colis Postaux	Vol. 1B, Vol. 2B, Vol. 3B
Colombia	Vol. 2A, Vol. 5A
Colombian Dominion of Panama	Vol. 5A
Colombian States	Vol. 2A
Colon	Vol. 5A
Colonie (Coloniali) Italiane	Vol. 3B
Colonies de l'Empire Francaise	Vol. 2B
Columbia, S.C.	Vol. 1A
Columbia, Tenn.	Vol. 1A
Columbus Archipelago	Vol. 2B
Columbus, Ga.	Vol. 1A
Comayagua	Vol. 3B
Commando Brief	Vol. 5A
Common Designs	See table of contents
Commissioning of Maryan Babangida (Nigeria #607)	Vol. 5A
Communicaciones	Vol. 6A
Communist China	Vol. 2A
Comores, Archipel des	Vol. 2A
Comoro Islands (Comores, Comorien)	343, 521, Vol. 2A
Compania Colombiana	Vol. 2A
Confederate States	Vol. 1A
Congo	Vol. 1B, Vol. 2A
Congo Democratic Republic	Vol. 2A, Vol. 6B
Congo People's Republic (ex-French)	Vol. 2A
Congo, Belgian (Belge)	Vol. 1B
Congo Francais	Vol. 2B
Congo, Indian U.N. Force	Vol. 3B
Congo, Portuguese	Vol. 5B
Congreso	Vol. 6A
Conseil de l'Europe	Vol. 2B
Constantinople, Georgian Offices	Vol. 3A
Constantinople, Polish Offices	Vol. 5B
Constantinople, Italian Offices	Vol. 3B
Constantinople, Romanian Offices	Vol. 5B
Constantinople, Russian Offices	Vol. 5B
Constantinople, Turkey	Vol. 6B
Contribucao Industrial (Macao A11, P. Guinea WT1)	2, Vol. 5B
Convention States (India)	Vol. 3B
Coo	Vol. 3B
Cook Islands	Vol. 2A
Cook Islands, Niue	Vol. 5A
Cordoba	Vol. 1A
Corea, Coree	Vol. 4A
Corfu	Vol. 2A, Vol. 3B
Corona	Vol. 1B, Vol. 2B
Correios, Correios e Telegraphos	Vol. 5B
Correo Submarino	Vol. 6A
Correo, Correos (no name)	Vol. 1A, Vol. 2A, Vol. 5A, Vol. 6A
Corrientes	Vol. 1A
Cos	Vol. 3B
Costa Atlantica	Vol. 5A
Costa Rica	Vol. 2A
Costantinopoli	Vol. 3B
Cote d'Ivoire	Vol. 3B
Cote des Somalis	Vol. 6A
Council of Europe	Vol. 2B
Cour Permanente de Justice Internationale	Vol. 5A
Courtland, Ala.	Vol. 1A
Cpbnja	Vol. 6A
Cracow	Vol. 5B
Crete	Vol. 2A, Vol. 3B
Crete, Austrian Offices	Vol. 1B
Crete, French Offices	Vol. 2B
Crete, Italian Offices	Vol. 3B
Crimea	Vol. 5B, Vol. 6A
Croat Administration of Bosnia, Mostar	Vol. 1B
Croatia	Vol. 6B
Croatia-Slavonia	Vol. 6B
Croissant Rouge Turc.	Vol. 6B
C.S.A. Postage	Vol. 1B
CTOT	Vol. 1B
Cuautla	442
Cuthbert, GA	Vol. 1A
Cuba	Vol. 1A, Vol. 2A
Cuba stamps overprinted	Vol. 5B
Cuba, U.S. Administration	Vol. 1A, Vol. 2A
Cucuta	Vol. 2A
Cuernavaca	442
Cundinamarca	Vol. 2A
Curacao	Vol. 2A, Vol. 5A
Cuzco	Vol. 5A
C.X.C. on Bosnia and Herzegovina	Vol. 6B
Cyprus	Vol. 2B
Cyprus, Turkish Republic of Northern	Vol. 6B
Cyrenaica	Vol. 2B, Vol. 3A, Vol. 4A
Czechoslovakia	Vol. 2B
Czechoslovak Legion Post	Vol. 2B
Czech Rep.	Vol. 2D
D	Vol. 3B
Dahomey	Vol. 1B, Vol. 2B
Dakar-Abidjan	Vol. 2B
Dalmatia	Vol. 2B
Dalton, Ga.	Vol. 1A
Danish West Indies	Vol. 1A, Vol. 2B
Danmark	Vol. 2B
Dansk-Vestindien	Vol. 1A, Vol. 2B
Dansk-Vestindiske	Vol. 1A, Vol. 2B
Danville, Va.	Vol. 1A
Danzig	Vol. 2B
Danzig, Polish Offices	Vol. 5B
Dardanelles	Vol. 5B
Darlington C.H., S.C.	Vol. 1A
Datia (Duttia)	Vol. 3B
D.B.L. ovptd. on Siberia and Russia	Vol. 2B
D.B.P. (Dalni Vostochini Respoublika)	Vol. 2A
D. de A.	Vol. 2A
DDR	Vol. 3A
Debrecen	Vol. 3B
Deccan (Hyderabad)	Vol. 3B
Dedeagatch (Greek)	Vol. 3A
Dedeagh, Dedeagatch (French)	Vol. 5A
Deficit	Vol. 5A
Demopolis, Ala.	Vol. 1A
Denikin	Vol. 6A
Denmark	Vol. 2B
Denmark stamps surcharged	Vol. 2B
Denver Issue, Mexico	356
Den Waisen ovptd. on Italy	Vol. 6B
Despatch (US 1LB, 5LB)	Vol. 1A
Deutsch-Neu-Guinea	Vol. 3A
Deutsch-Ostafrika	Vol. 3A
Deutsch-Sudwest Afrika	Vol. 3A
Deutsche Bundespost	Vol. 3A
Deutsche Demokratische Republik	Vol. 3A
Deutsche Nationalversammlung	Vol. 3A
Deutsche Post	Vol. 3A
Deutsche Post Berlin	Vol. 3A
Deutsche(s) Reich	Vol. 3A
Deutsche Reich, Nr.21, Nr.16	Vol. 3A
Deutschland	Vol. 3A
Deutschosterreich	Vol. 1B
Dhar	Vol. 3B
Diego-Suarez	Vol. 2B
Diego-Suarez stamps surcharged	64
Dienftmarke (Dienstmarke)	Vol. 3A
Dies I & II, British Colonies	See table of contents
Diligencia	Vol. 5A
Dinar	Vol. 6B
Dire-Dawa	Vol. 2B
Dispatch (US 1LB)	Vol. 1A
Distrito ovptd. on Arequipa	Vol. 5A
DJ ovptd. on Obock	Vol. 6A
Djibouti (Somali Coast)	Vol. 2B, Vol. 6A
Dobruja District	Vol. 5B
Dodecanese Islands	Vol. 3A, Vol. 3B
Dollar, ovptd. on Russia	Vol. 5B
Dominica	Vol. 2B
Dominican Republic, Dominicana	Vol. 2B
Don Government	Vol. 6A
Dorpat	Vol. 2B
Drzava SHS	Vol. 6B
Dubai	Vol. 2B, Vol. 5A, Vol. 6B
Duck Stamps (Hunting Permit)	Vol. 1A
Duitsch Oost Afrika overprinted on Congo	Vol. 3A
Duke de la Torre Regency	Vol. 6A
Dulce et Decorum est Pro Patria Mori (Nepal O1)	Vol. 5A
Dungarpur	Vol. 3B
Durazzo	Vol. 3B
Dutch Guiana (Surinam)	Vol. 6A
Dutch Indies	Vol. 5A
Dutch New Guinea	Vol. 5A
Duttia	Vol. 3B
EA	Vol. 1A
E.A.F. overprinted on stamps of Great Britain	Vol. 3A
East Africa (British)	Vol. 1B
East Africa (German)	Vol. 3A
East Africa (Italian)	Vol. 3B
East Africa and Uganda Protectorates	Vol. 2B, Vol. 4A
East Africa Forces	Vol. 3A
East China	Vol. 2A
Eastern Rumelia	Vol. 2B
Eastern Rumelia stamps overprinted	Vol. 6B
Eastern Silesia	Vol. 2B
Eastern Szechwan	Vol. 2A
Eastern Thrace	Vol. 6B
East India	Vol. 3B
East Saxony	Vol. 3A
East Timor	Vol. 1A, Vol. 6B
Eatonton, Ga.	Vol. 1A
Ecuador	Vol. 2B
E.E.F.	Vol. 5A
Eesti	Vol. 3B
Egeo	Vol. 3B
Egiziane (Egypt types A9-A10)	Vol. 2B
Egypt, Egypte, Egyptiennes	Vol. 2B, Vol. 5A
Egypt, French Offices	Vol. 2B
Eire, Eireann (Ireland)	Vol. 3B
Ekaterinodar	Vol. 6A
Elobey, Annobon and Corisco	Vol. 3A
El Salvador	Vol. 5B
Elsas, Elfas	Vol. 3A
Elua Keneta	Vol. 1A
Emory, Va.	Vol. 1A
Empire, Franc, Francais	Vol. 2B
En	Vol. 4A
England	Vol. 3A
Epirus	Vol. 2B
Equateur (Ecuador #19-21)	Vol. 2B
Equatorial Guinea	Vol. 2B
Eritrea	Vol. 2B
Eritrea (British Military Administration)	Vol. 3A
Escuelas	Vol. 6B
Espana, Espanola	Vol. 6A
Estado da India	Vol. 5B
Est Africain Allemand overprinted on Congo	Vol. 3A
Estensi	Vol. 3B
Estero	Vol. 3B
Estland	Vol. 2B, Vol. 5B
Estonia	Vol. 2B, Vol. 5B
Etablissments Francais dans l'Inde	Vol. 2B
Ethiopia, Etiopia, Ethiopie, Ethiopiennes	Vol. 2B, Vol. 3A
Eupen	Vol. 3A
Europe	Vol. 3A
Express Letter	Vol. 2A
15 August 1947 (Pakistan #23)	Vol. 5A
500 anos, viaje del descubrimiento de istmo (Panama #897)	Vol. 5A
F	Vol. 2B
F. A. F. L.	Vol. 6A
Falkland Dependencies	Vol. 2B
Falkland Islands	Vol. 2B
Far Eastern Republic	Vol. 2B
Far Eastern Republic surcharged or ovptd.	Vol. 6A
Faridkot	Vol. 3B
Faroe Islands	Vol. 2B
FCFA ovptd. on France	Vol. 2B
Federacion	Vol. 6B
Federal Republic (Germany)	Vol. 3A
Federated Malay States	103
Fen, Fn. (Manchukuo)	261
Fernando Po, Fdo. Poo	Vol. 2B

731

INDEX AND IDENTIFIER

Feudatory States .... Vol. 3B
Fezzan, Fezzan-Ghadames .... Vol. 4A
Fiera Campionaria Tripoli .... Vol. 4A
Fiji .... Vol. 2B
Fiji overprinted or surcharged ..... Vol. 5A
Filipinas, Filipas. .... Vol. 5A
Fincastle, Va. .... Vol. 1A
Finland .... Vol. 2B
Finnish Occupation of Karelia ... Vol. 4A
Finnish Occupation of Russia ... Vol. 4A, Vol. 5B
Fiume .... Vol. 2B
Fiume-Kupa Zone
  (Fiumano Kupa) .... Vol. 6B
Five Cents (Confed. #53X) .... Vol. 1A
Florida .... Vol. 6B
F. M. .... Vol. 2B
Foochow, Chinese .... Vol. 2A
Foochow, German .... Vol. 3A
Formosa .... Vol. 2A, Vol. 4A
Foroyar .... Vol. 3A
Forsyth, Ga. .... Vol. 1A
Fort Valley, Ga. .... Vol. 1A
Franc .... Vol. 2B
Franc ovptd. on Austria .... Vol. 1B
Franca ovptd. on stamps of Peru ... Vol. 5A
Francais, Francaise ...... See France and French colonies
France .... Vol. 2B
France (German occupation) ..... Vol. 2B
France D'Outre Mer .... Vol. 2B
Franco Bollo .... Vol. 3B
Franco Marke .... Vol. 3A
Franco Scrisorei .... Vol. 5B
Franklin, N.C. .... Vol. 1A
Franqueo .... Vol. 5A
Franquicia .... Vol. 6A
Fraziersville, S.C. .... Vol. 1A
Fredericksburg, Va. .... Vol. 1A
Free
Frei Durch Ablosung .... Vol. 3A
Freimarke (No Country Name) ... Vol. 3A
French Administration of Andorra ... Vol. 1A
French Administration of Saar ... Vol. 5B
French Colonies .... Vol. 2B
French Colonies surcharged or
  overprinted .... 64, 306, Vol. 1A, Vol. 2B, Vol. 3A, Vol. 3B, Vol. 5A, Vol. 6A
French Commemoratives Index ... Vol. 2B
French Congo .... Vol. 2B
French Equatorial Africa .... 471, Vol. 2A, Vol. 2B, Vol. 6B
French Guiana .... Vol. 2B
French Guinea .... Vol. 2B
French India .... Vol. 2B
French Levant .... Vol. 2B, Vol. 6A
French Mandate of Alaouites ... Vol. 1A
French Mandate of Lebanon ...... Vol. 4A
French Morocco .... Vol. 2B
French Occupation of Cameroun ... Vol. 2A
French Occupation of
  Castellorizo .... Vol. 2A
French Occupation of Crete .... Vol. 2A
French Occupation of Germany ... Vol. 3A
French Occupation of Hungary ... Vol. 3B
French Occupation of Libya ...... Vol. 4A
French Occupation of Syria ...... Vol. 6A
French Occupation of Togo .... Vol. 6B
French Oceania .... Vol. 2B
French Offices Abroad .... Vol. 2B
French Offices in China .... Vol. 2B
French Offices in Crete .... Vol. 2B
French Offices in Egypt .... Vol. 2B
French Offices in Madagascar 64
French Offices in Morocco .... Vol. 2B
French Offices in Tangier .... Vol. 2B
French Offices in Turkish Empire ... Vol. 6A
French Offices in Turkish Empire
  surcharged .... Vol. 6A
French Offices in Zanzibar .... Vol. 2B
French Polynesia .... Vol. 2B
French Saar .... Vol. 5B
French Southern and Antarctic
  Territories .... Vol. 2B
French stamps inscribed CFA ... Vol. 2B
French stamps surcharged .... 64, Vol. 2B, Vol. 6A
French Sudan .... Vol. 2B
French West Africa .... Vol. 2B
French Zone (Germany) .... Vol. 3A
Frimarke, Frmrk (No Country
  Name) .... Vol. 2B, Vol. 5A, Vol. 6A
Fujeira .... Vol. 2B, Vol. 6B
Fukien .... Vol. 2A
Funafuti .... Vol. 6B
Funchal .... Vol. 2B

**G or GW overprinted on Cape
of Good Hope** .... **Vol. 3A**

GAB on French Colonies .... Vol. 3A
Gabon, Gabonaise .... Vol. 3A
Gainesville, Ala. .... Vol. 1A
Galapagos Islands .... Vol. 2B
Galveston, Tex. .... Vol. 1A
Gambia .... Vol. 3A
Gaston, N.C. .... Vol. 1A
Gaza .... Vol. 3B
G & (et) D overprinted on French
  Colonies .... Vol. 3A
G.E.A. ovptd. .... Vol. 3A, Vol. 6A
General Gouvernement (Poland) ... Vol. 5B
Geneva, Geneve .... Vol. 6A
Georgetown, S.C. .... Vol. 1A
Georgia .... Vol. 3A, Vol. 6B
Georgia, Offices in Turkey .... Vol. 3A
Georgienne, Republique .... Vol. 3A
German Administration of Albania ... Vol. 1A
German Administration of Danzig ... Vol. 2B
German Administration of Saar ... Vol. 5B
German Democratic Republic .... Vol. 3A
German Dominion of Cameroun ... Vol. 2A
German Dominion of Caroline
  Islands .... Vol. 2A
German Dominion of Mariana Is. ... 269
German Dominion of Marshall Is. ... 270
German Dominion of Samoa ...... Vol. 5B
German Dominion of Togo .... Vol. 6B
German East Africa .... Vol. 3A
German East Africa (Belgian occ.) ... Vol. 3A
German East Africa (British occ.) ... Vol. 3A
German New Guinea .... Vol. 3A
German New Guinea
  (New Britain) .... Vol. 5A
German Occupation of Belgium ... Vol. 1B
German Occupation of Estonia ... Vol. 2B
German Occupation of France ... Vol. 2B
German Occupation of Guernsey ... Vol. 3A
German Occupation of Ionian Is. ... Vol. 3B
German Occupation of Jersey ... Vol. 3A
German Occupation of Latvia ... Vol. 4A
German Occupation of Lithuania ... Vol. 5B
German Occupation of Ljubljana ... Vol. 6B
German Occupation of
  Luxembourg .... Vol. 4A
German Occupation of Macedonia ... 62
German Occupation of Montenegro ... 716
German Occupation of Poland ... Vol. 5B
German Occupation of Romania ... Vol. 5B
German Occupation of Russia ... Vol. 5B
German Occupation of Serbia ... Vol. 5B
German Occupation of Ukraine ... Vol. 5B
German Occupation of
  Yugoslavia .... Vol. 6B
German Occupation of Zante .... Vol. 3B
German Offices in China .... Vol. 3A
German Offices in China
  surcharged .... Vol. 4A
German Offices in Morocco .... Vol. 3A
German Offices in Turkish Empire ... Vol. 3A
German Protectorate of Bohemia
  and Moravia .... Vol. 2B
German South-West Africa .... Vol. 3A
German stamps surchd. or
  ovptd. .... Vol. 3A, Vol. 5B, Vol. 6A
German States .... Vol. 3A
Germany .... Vol. 3A
Germany (Allied Military Govt.) ... Vol. 5A
Gerusalemme .... Vol. 3B
Ghadames .... Vol. 4A
Ghana .... Vol. 3A
Gibraltar .... Vol. 3A
Gilbert and Ellice Islands .... Vol. 3A
Gilbert Islands .... Vol. 3A
Giumulzina District .... Vol. 6B
Gniezno .... Vol. 5B
Gold Coast .... Vol. 3A
Golfo del Guinea .... Vol. 6A
Goliad, Tex. .... Vol. 1A
Gonzales, Tex. .... Vol. 1A
Gorny Slask .... Vol. 6B
Government (U.S. 1LB) .... Vol. 1A
Governo Militare Alleato .... Vol. 3B
G.P.E. ovptd. on French Colonies ... Vol. 3A
Graham Land .... Vol. 2B
Granada .... Vol. 6A
Granadine Confederation,
  Granadina .... Vol. 2A
Grand Comoro, Grande Comore ... Vol. 3A
Grand Liban, Gd Liban .... Vol. 4A
Great Britain (see also British) ... Vol. 3A
Great Britain, Gaelic ovpt. .... Vol. 3B
Great Britain, Offices in Africa ... Vol. 3A
Great Britain, Offices in China ... Vol. 3A
Great Britain, Offices in Morocco ... Vol. 3A
Great Britain, Offices in Turkish
  Empire .... Vol. 3A
Greater Rajasthan Union .... Vol. 3B

Greece .... Vol. 3A
Greek Occupation of Albania,
  North Epirus, Dodecanese
  Islands .... Vol. 3A
Greek Occupation of Epirus ..... Vol. 2B, Vol. 3A
Greek Occ. of the Aegean Islands ... Vol. 3A
Greek Occupation of Thrace ...... Vol. 6B
Greek Occupation of Turkey ..... Vol. 3A, Vol. 6B
Greek stamps overprinted .... Vol. 2B, Vol. 6B
Greenland .... Vol. 3A
Greensboro, Ala. .... Vol. 1A
Greensboro, N.C. .... Vol. 1A
Greenville .... Vol. 4A
Greenville, Ala. .... Vol. 1A
Greenville, Tenn. .... Vol. 1A
Greenville Court House, S.C. .... Vol. 1A
Greenwood Depot, Va. .... Vol. 1A
Grenada .... Vol. 3A
Grenadines of Grenada .... Vol. 3A
Grenadines of St. Vincent .... Vol. 5B
Grenville .... Vol. 4A
G.R.I. overprinted on German
  New Guinea .... Vol. 5A
G.R.I. overprinted on German
  Samoa .... Vol. 5B
G.R.I. overprinted on Marshall Is. ... Vol. 5A
Griffin, Ga. .... Vol. 1A
Griqualand West .... Vol. 3A
Grodno District .... Vol. 4A
Gronland .... Vol. 3A
Grossdeutsches Reich
  (Germany #529) .... Vol. 3A
Groszy .... Vol. 5B
Grove Hill, Ala. .... Vol. 1A
Gruzija (Georgia) .... Vol. 3A
Guadalajara 442
Guadeloupe .... Vol. 3A
Guam .... Vol. 3A
Guanacaste .... Vol. 2A
Guatemala .... Vol. 3A
Guayana .... Vol. 6B
Guernsey .... Vol. 3A
Guernsey, German Occupation ... Vol. 3A
Guiana, British .... Vol. 1B
Guiana, Dutch .... Vol. 6A
Guiana, French .... Vol. 2B
Guine .... Vol. 3A, Vol. 5B
Guinea .... Vol. 3A, Vol. 6A
Guinea Ecuatorial .... Vol. 2B
Guinea, French .... Vol. 2B
Guinea, Portuguese .... Vol. 5A
Guinea, Spanish .... Vol. 6A
Guinea-Bissau, Guine-Bissau ... Vol. 3A
Guinee .... Vol. 2B, Vol. 3A
Guipuzcoa Province .... Vol. 6A
Gultig 9, Armee .... Vol. 5B
Guyana .... Vol. 3A
Guyane, Guy. Franc. .... Vol. 2B
G.W. ovptd. on Cape of
  Good Hope .... Vol. 3A
Gwalior .... Vol. 3B

Habilitado-1/2 (Tlacotalpan #1) **442**
Habilitado on Stamps of Cuba ... Vol. 1A, Vol. 2A, Vol. 5A
Habilitado on Telegrafos or
  revenues .... Vol. 5A, Vol. 6A
Hadhramaut .... Vol. 1A
Hainan Island .... Vol. 2A
Haiti .... Vol. 3B
Hall, A. D. (Confed. #27XU1) ... Vol. 1A
Hallettsville, Tex. .... Vol. 1A
Hamburg .... Vol. 3A
Hamburg, S.C. .... Vol. 1A
Hamilton, Bermuda .... Vol. 1B
Hanover, Hannover .... Vol. 3A
Harar .... Vol. 2B
Harper .... Vol. 4A
Harrisburgh, Tex. .... Vol. 1A
Hatay .... Vol. 3B
Hatirasi (Turkey Design PT44) ... Vol. 6B
Hatohobei (Palau #686) .... Vol. 5A
Haute Silesie .... Vol. 6B
Haute Volta .... Vol. 3A
Haut Senegal-Niger .... Vol. 6B
Hawaii, Hawaiian .... Vol. 1A
H B A ovptd. on Russia .... Vol. 3B
Hebrew inscriptions .... Vol. 3B
H.E.H. The Nizam's (Hyderabad) ... Vol. 3B
Heilungkiang .... Vol. 2A
Hejaz .... Vol. 3B
Hejaz-Nejd .... Vol. 6A
Hejaz overprinted .... Vol. 4A, Vol. 6A
Helena, Tex. .... Vol. 1A
Heligoland, Helgoland .... Vol. 3B

Hellas .... Vol. 3A
Helsinki (Helsingfors) .... Vol. 2B
Helvetia, Helvetica (Switzerland) ... Vol. 6A
Heraklion .... Vol. 2A
Herceg Bosna .... Vol. 1B
Herzegovina .... Vol. 1B
Herzogth .... Vol. 3A
H.H. Nawabshah Jahanbegam ... Vol. 3B
H.I. Postage .... Vol. 1A
Hillsboro, N.C. .... Vol. 1A
Hoi Hao, French Offices .... Vol. 2B
Holkar (Indore) .... Vol. 3B
Holland (Netherlands) .... Vol. 5A
Hollandale, Tex. .... Vol. 1A
Holstein .... Vol. 3A
Honan .... Vol. 2A
Honda .... Vol. 2A
Honduras .... Vol. 3B
Honduras, British .... Vol. 1B
Hong Kong .... Vol. 2A, Vol. 3B
Hong Kong (Japanese
  Occupation) .... Vol. 3B
Hong Kong Special Admin.
  Region .... Vol. 3B
Hong Kong ovptd. China .... Vol. 3A
Honour's (Hondur's) City .... Vol. 1A
Hopeh .... Vol. 2A
Hopei .... Vol. 2A
Horta .... Vol. 3B
Houston, Tex. .... Vol. 1A
Hrvatska .... Vol. 1B, Vol. 2A, Vol. 6B
Hrzgl. .... Vol. 3A
Huacho .... Vol. 5A
Hunan .... Vol. 2A
Hungary .... Vol. 1B, Vol. 3B
Hungary (French Occupation) ... Vol. 3B
Hungary (Romanian Occupation) ... Vol. 3B
Hungary (Serbian Occupation) ... Vol. 3B
Huntsville, Tex. .... Vol. 1A
Hupeh .... Vol. 2A
Hyderabad (Deccan) .... Vol. 3B

I.B. (West Irian) .... **Vol. 3B**
Icaria .... Vol. 3A
ICC ovptd. on India .... Vol. 3B
Iceland .... Vol. 3B
Idar .... Vol. 3B
I.E.F. ovptd. on India .... Vol. 3B
I.E.F. 'D' ovptd. on Turkey 350
Ierusalem .... Vol. 5B
Ifni .... Vol. 3B
Ile Rouad .... Vol. 5B
Imperio Colonial Portugues ..... Vol. 5B
Imposto de Selo .... Vol. 5B
Impuesto (Impto) de Guerra ..... Vol. 6A
Inde. Fcaise .... Vol. 2B
Independence, Tex. .... Vol. 1A
Index of U.S. Issues .... Vol. 1A
India .... Vol. 3B, Vol. 5B
India, China Expeditionary Force ... Vol. 3B
India, Convention States .... Vol. 3B
India, Feudatory States .... Vol. 3B
India, French .... Vol. 2B
India, Portuguese .... Vol. 5B
India stamps overprinted .... Vol. 3B, Vol. 4A, Vol. 5A
India, surcharge and crown ..... Vol. 6A
Indian Custodial Unit, Korea ..... Vol. 3B
Indian Expeditionary Force ..... Vol. 3B
Indian U.N. Force, Congo .... Vol. 3B
Indian U.N. Force, Gaza .... Vol. 3B
Indian Postal Administration of
  Bahrain .... Vol. 1B
Indo-China, Indo-chine .... Vol. 3B
Indo-China stamps surcharged ... Vol. 6B
Indo-China, Int. Commission ... Vol. 3B
Indonesia .... Vol. 3B, Vol. 5A
Indore .... Vol. 3B
Industrielle Kriegswirschaft ..... Vol. 6A
Inhambane .... Vol. 3B
Inini .... Vol. 3B
Inland (Liberia #21) .... Vol. 4A
Inner Mongolia (Meng Chiang) ... Vol. 2A
Insufficiently prepaid .... Vol. 6B
Instrucao .... Vol. 5B
Instruccion .... Vol. 6B
International Bureau of
  Education .... Vol. 6A
International Commission in
  Indo-China .... Vol. 3B
International Court of Justice ... Vol. 5A
International Labor Bureau ..... Vol. 6A
International Olympic Committee ... Vol. 6A
International Refugee
  Organization .... Vol. 6A
International Telecommunication
  Union .... Vol. 6A
Ionian Islands, IONIKON KPATOE .... Vol. 3B
I.O.V.R. .... Vol. 5B

INDEX AND IDENTIFIER

Iran, Iraniennes .... Vol. 3B
Iran (Bushire) .... Vol. 1B
Iran, Turkish Occupation ..... Vol. 3B
Iran with Rs. 10 denomination
  (Pakistan #1101) .... Vol. 5A
Iraq .... Vol. 3B
Iraq (British Occupation) .... 350, Vol. 3B
Ireland .... Vol. 3B
Ireland, Northern .... Vol. 3A
Irian Barat .... Vol. 3B
Isabella, Ga. .... Vol. 1A
Island .... Vol. 3B
Isle of Man .... Vol. 3A
Isole Italiane dell'Egeo .... Vol. 3B
Isole Jonie .... Vol. 3B
Israel .... Vol. 3B
Istria .... Vol. 6B
Itaca ovptd. on Greece .... Vol. 3A
Ita-Karjala .... Vol. 4A
Italia, Italiano, Italiane .... Vol. 3B
Italian Colonies .... Vol. 3B
Italian Dominion of Albania ..... Vol. 1A
Italian Dominion of Castellorizo ... Vol. 2A
Italian East Africa .... Vol. 3B
Italian Jubaland .... Vol. 5A
Italian Occ. of Aegean Islands ... Vol. 3B
Italian Occupation of Austria ... Vol. 1B
Italian Occupation of Corfu ..... Vol. 2A
Italian Occupation of Crete ..... Vol. 2A
Italian Occupation of Dalmatia ... Vol. 2B
Italian Occupation of Ethiopia .. Vol. 2B
Italian Occupation of Fiume-Kupa ... Vol. 6B
Italian Occupation of Ionian
  Islands .... Vol. 3B
Italian Occupation of Ljubljana ... Vol. 6B
Italian Occupation of Montenegro 716
Italian Occupation of Yugoslavia ... Vol. 6B
Italian Offices Abroad .... Vol. 3B
Italian Offices in Africa .... Vol. 3B
Italian Offices in Albania ..... Vol. 3B
Italian Offices in China .... Vol. 3B
Italian Offices in Constantinople ... Vol. 3B
Italian Offices in Crete .... Vol. 3B
Italian Offices in the Turkish
  Empire .... Vol. 3B
Italian Social Republic .... Vol. 3B
Italian Somaliland .... Vol. 6A
Italian Somaliland (E.A.F.) ... Vol. 3A
Italian stamps surcharged ... Vol. 1B,
  Vol. 2B, Vol. 3B
Italian States .... Vol. 3B
Italy (Allied Military Govt.) .... Vol. 3B
Italy (Austrian Occupation) ... Vol. 3B
Italy .... Vol. 3B
Ithaca .... Vol. 3B
Iuka, Miss. .... Vol. 1A
Ivory Coast .... Vol. 3B

J. ovptd. on stamps of Peru .... Vol. 5A
Jackson, Miss. .... Vol. 1A
Jacksonville, Ala. .... Vol. 1A
Jacksonville, Fla. .... Vol. 1A
Jaffa .... Vol. 5B
Jaipur .... Vol. 3B
Jamaica .... Vol. 4A
Jamhuri .... Vol. 6B
Jammu .... Vol. 3B
Jammu and Kashmir .... Vol. 3B
Janina .... Vol. 3B
Japan, Japanese .... Vol. 4A
Japan (Australian Occ.) ...... Vol. 1A
Japan (Taiwan) .... Vol. 2A, Vol. 4A
Japanese Offices Abroad ... Vol. 4A
Japan Occupation of Brunei ... Vol. 1B
Japan Occupation of Burma ... Vol. 2A
Japan Occupation of China ... Vol. 2A
Japan Occupation of Dutch
  Indies .... Vol. 5A
Japan Occupation of Hong Kong ... Vol. 3B
Japan Occupation of Johore 109
Japan Occupation of Kedah 111
Japan Occupation of Kelantan 111
Japan Occupation of Malacca 113
Japan Occupation of Malaya 109
Japan Occupation of Negri Sembilan ... 113
Japan Occupation of Netherlands
  Indies .... Vol. 5A
Japan Occupation of North
  Borneo .... Vol. 5A
Japan Occupation of Pahang 114
Japan Occupation of Penang 115
Japan Occupation of Perak 116
Japan Occupation of
  Philippines .... Vol. 1A, Vol. 5A
Japan Occupation of Sarawak ... Vol. 6A
Japan Occupation of Selangor 118
Japan Occupation of
  Sts. Settlements .... Vol. 6A
Japan Occ. of Trengganu 121

Other Japanese Stamps
  Overprinted ... Vol. 1B, Vol. 2A, Vol. 4A,
  Vol. 5A
Jasdan .... Vol. 3B
Java .... Vol. 3B, Vol. 5A
Jedda .... Vol. 6A
Jeend .... Vol. 3B
Jehol .... Vol. 2A
Jersey .... Vol. 3A
Jersey, German Occupation ...... Vol. 3A
Jerusalem, Italian Offices ... Vol. 3B
Jerusalem, Russian Offices ... Vol. 5B
Jetersville, Va. .... Vol. 1A
Jhalawar .... Vol. 3B
Jhind, Jind .... Vol. 3B
Johore, Johor 109, 153
Jonesboro, Tenn. .... Vol. 1A
J. P. Johnson (Confed. #66X1) ... Vol. 1A
Jordan .... Vol. 4A
Jordan (Palestine Occ.) ...... Vol. 4A
Journaux .... Vol. 2A
Juan Fernandez Islands (Chile) ... Vol. 2A
Jubile de l'Union Postale Universelle
  (Switzerland #98) .... Vol. 6A
Jugoslavia, Jugoslavija ...... Vol. 6B
Junagarh .... Vol. 3B

K .... Vol. 1A
КАЗАКСТАН .... Vol. 4A
Kabul .... Vol. 1A
Kalaallit Nunaat, Kalatdlit Nunat ... Vol. 2A
Kamerun .... Vol. 2A
Kampuchea .... Vol. 2A
Kansu .... Vol. 2A
Karelia, Karjala .... Vol. 4A
Karema ovptd. on Belgian Congo ... Vol. 3A
Karki .... Vol. 3D
Karolinen .... Vol. 2A
Kashmir .... Vol. 3B
Katanga .... Vol. 4A
Kathiri State of Seiyun .... Vol. 1A
Kaunas .... Vol. 4A, Vol. 5B
Kayangel (Palau #686) .... Vol. 5A
Kazakhstan, Kazahkstan,
  Kazakstan .... Vol. 4A
Kedah 109, 154
Keeling Islands .... Vol. 2A
Kelantan 111, 154
Kentta Postia .... Vol. 2B
Kenya .... Vol. 4A
Kenya and Uganda .... Vol. 4A
Kenya, Uganda, Tanzania ... Vol. 4A
Kenya, Uganda, Tanganyika ... Vol. 4A
Kenya, Uganda, Tanganyika,
  Zanzibar .... Vol. 4A
Kerassunde .... Vol. 5B
Kermanshah .... Vol. 3B
K.G.C.A. ovptd. on Yugoslavia ... Vol. 6B
K.G.L. .... Vol. 1A, Vol. 2B
Kharkiv .... Vol. 6B
Khmer Republic .... Vol. 2A
Khor Fakkan .... Vol. 6A
Kiangsi .... Vol. 2A
Kiangsu .... Vol. 2A
Klauchau, Kiautschou .... Vol. 4A
Kibris .... Vol. 6B
Kibris Cumhuriyeti
  (Cyprus #198-200) .... Vol. 2B
Kigoma ovptd. on Belgian Congo ... Vol. 3A
Kilis .... Vol. 6A
King Edward VII Land
  (New Zealand #121a) ...... Vol. 5A
Kingman's City Post .... Vol. 1A
Kingston, Ga. .... Vol. 1A
Kionga .... Vol. 4A
Kirghizia .... Vol. 4A
Kiribati .... Vol. 4A
Kirin .... Vol. 2A
Kishangarh, Kishengarh .... Vol. 3B
Kithyra .... Vol. 3A, Vol. 3B
K.K. Post Stempel (or Stampel) ... Vol. 1B
K.K.T.C. (Turk. Rep. N. Cyprus
  #NA1) .... Vol. 6B
Klaipeda 349
Knoxville, Tenn. .... Vol. 1A
Kolomyia .... Vol. 6B
Kolozsvar .... Vol. 3B
Kon .... Vol. 1B, Vol. 2B, Vol. 4A,
  Vol. 5B, Vol. 6A
Kongeligt .... Vol. 2B
Kop Koh .... Vol. 2B
Korca, Korce (Albania) .... Vol. 1A
Korea .... Vol. 4A
Korea, Democratic People's
  Republic .... Vol. 4A
Korea (Japanese Offices) ... Vol. 4A
Korea, Indian Custodial Unit ... Vol. 3B
Korea, North .... Vol. 4A
Korea, Soviet occupation ... Vol. 4A

Korea, U.S. Military Govt. .... Vol. 4A
Koritsa .... Vol. 2B
Koror (Palau #686) .... Vol. 5A
Korytsa (Albania #81) .... Vol. 1A
Kos .... Vol. 3B
Kosova .... Vol. 4A
Kosovo .... Vol. 1A, Vol. 4A
Kotah .... Vol. 3B
Kouang Tcheou-Wan .... Vol. 2B
KPHTH (Crete) .... Vol. 2A
Kr., Kreuzer .... Vol. 1B, Vol. 3B
Kraljevstvo, Kraljevina .... Vol. 6B
K.S.A. .... Vol. 6A
Kuban Government .... Vol. 6A
K.U.K., K. und K. ..... Vol. 1B, Vol. 3B,
  Vol. 5B
Kunming .... Vol. 2B
Kupa Zone .... Vol. 6B
Kurdistan .... Vol. 3B
Kurland, Kurzeme ..... Vol. 4A, Vol. 5B
Kurus .... Vol. 6B
Kuwait, Koweit .... Vol. 4A, Vol. 5A
Kwangchowan .... Vol. 2B
Kwangsi .... Vol. 2B
Kwangtung .... Vol. 2A
Kweichow .... Vol. 2A
K. Württ. Post .... Vol. 3B
Kyiv .... Vol. 6B
Kyrgyz Express Post .... Vol. 4A
Kyrgyzstan .... Vol. 4A

La Aguera .... Vol. 1A
Labuan .... Vol. 4A
La Canea .... Vol. 3B
Lady McLeod .... Vol. 6B
La Georgie .... Vol. 3A
Lagos .... Vol. 4A
La Grange, Tex. .... Vol. 1A
Laibach .... Vol. 6B
Lake City, Fla. .... Vol. 1A
Lanchow .... Vol. 2A
Land Post .... Vol. 3A
Lao, Laos .... Vol. 4A
Laos (Int. Com., India) .... Vol. 3B
L.A.R. .... Vol. 4A
Las Bela .... Vol. 3B
Latakia, Lattaquio .... Vol. 1A
Latvia, Latvija .... Vol. 4A, Vol. 5B
Laurens Court House, S.C. ... Vol. 1A
Lavaca .... Vol. 1A
League of Nations .... Vol. 6A
Lebanon ...... Vol. 4A, Vol. 5A, Vol. 6A
Leeward Islands .... Vol. 4A
Lefkas .... Vol. 3A, Vol. 3B
Lei ovptd. on Austria .... Vol. 5B
Lemnos .... Vol. 3A
Lenoir, N.C. .... Vol. 1A
Lero, Leros .... Vol. 3B
Lesbos .... Vol. 3A
Lesotho .... Vol. 4A
Lesser Sundas .... Vol. 5A
Lettland, Lettonia .... Vol. 4A
Levant, British .... Vol. 1A
Levant, French .... Vol. 2B, Vol. 6A
Levant, Italian .... Vol. 3D
Levant, Polish .... Vol. 5B
Levant, Romanian .... Vol. 5B
Levant, Russian .... Vol. 5B
Levant, Syrian (on Lebanon) ... Vol. 6A
Lexington, Miss. .... Vol. 1A
Lexington, Va. .... Vol. 1A
Liaoning .... Vol. 2A
Liban, Libanaise .... Vol. 4A
Libau ovptd. on German ... Vol. 4A
Liberia .... Vol. 4A
Liberty, Va. .... Vol. 1A
Libya, Libia, Libye .... Vol. 4A
Libyan Arab Republic .... Vol. 4A
Liechtenstein .... Vol. 4A
Lietuva, Lietuvos .... Vol. 4A
Lifland .... Vol. 5B
Ligne Aeriennes de la France
  Libro (Syria #MC5) .... Vol. 6A
Lima .... Vol. 5A
Limestone Springs, S.C. .... Vol. 1A
L'Inde .... Vol. 2B
Linja-Autorahti Bussfrakt ... Vol. 2B
Lipso, Lisso .... Vol. 3B
Lithuania .... Vol. 4A, Vol. 5B
Lithuania, Central .... Vol. 2A
Lithuanian Occupation of Memel ... 349
Litwa Srodkowa, Litwy
  Srodkowej .... Vol. 2A
Livingston, Ala. .... Vol. 1A
Livonia .... Vol. 5B
Ljubljana .... Vol. 6B
Llanes .... Vol. 6A
L McL .... Vol. 6B
Local .... Vol. 6B

Local Post .... Vol. 2A
Lockport, N.Y. .... Vol. 1A
Lombardy-Venetia .... Vol. 1B
Lorraine .... Vol. 2B
Losen .... Vol. 6A
Lothringen .... Vol. 2B
Louisville, Ky. .... Vol. 1A
Lourenco Marques, L. Marques ... Vol. 4A
Lower Austria .... Vol. 1B
L P overprinted on Russian
  stamps .... Vol. 4A
LTSR on Lithuania .... Vol. 4A
Lubeck, Luebeck .... Vol. 3A
Lubiana .... Vol. 6B
Lublin .... Vol. 5B
Luminescence .... Vol. 1A
Luxembourg .... Vol. 4A
Lviv .... Vol. 6B
Lydenburg .... Vol. 6B
Lynchburg, Va. .... Vol. 1A

Macao, Macau 1
Macedonia 33
Machin Head definitives ..... Vol. 3A
Macon, Ga. .... Vol. 1A
Madagascar, Madagasikara ... 62, 521
Madagascar (British) 62
Madeira .... 63, Vol. 5B
Madero Issue (Mexico) 356
Madison, Ga. .... Vol. 1A
Madison Court House, Fla. .... Vol. 1A
Madrid .... Vol. 6A
Madura .... Vol. 5A
Mafeking .... Vol. 2A
Magdalena .... Vol. 2A
Magyar, Magyarorszag ...... Vol. 3B
Magy. Kir. .... Vol. 3B
Majunga 72
Makedonija 33
Malacca 113, 155
Malaga .... Vol. 6A
Malagasy Republic 63
Malawi 96
Malaya 107
Malaya (Japanese Occ.) ...... 109, Vol. 5A
Malaya (Thai Occ.) 109
Malaya, Federation of 107
Malaysia 121
Malay States 107
Maldive Islands, Maldives 159
Malgache Republique 66
Mali 208
Malmedy .... Vol. 3A
Malta 238
Maluku Selatan (So. Moluccas) ... Vol. 6A
Man, Isle of .... Vol. 3A
Manchukuo 266
Manchukuo stamps overprinted ... Vol. 2A
Manchuria .... Vol. 2A
Manizales .... Vol. 2A
Mapka, Mapok .... Vol. 2B, Vol. 5B
Mariana Islands, Marianen 269
Marienwerder 270
Marietta, Ga. .... Vol. 1A
Marion, Va. .... Vol. 1A
Markka, Markkaa .... Vol. 2B
Maroc, Marocco, Marokko 650,
  Vol. 2B, Vol. 3A
Marruecos .... 785, Vol. 6
Mars Bluff, S.C. .... Vol. 1A
Marshall Islands, Marschall-Inseln,
  Marshall-Inseln 270
Marshall Islands (G.R.I. surch.) ... Vol. 5A
Martinique 300
Martin's City Post .... Vol. 1A
Mauritania, Mauritanie 308
Mauritania stamps surcharged ... Vol. 2B
Mauritius 327
Mayotte 343
Mayreau .... Vol. 5B
M.B.D. overprinted .... Vol. 3B
McNeel, A.W. .... Vol. 1A
Mecca .... Vol. 6A
Mecklenburg-Schwerin ...... Vol. 3A
Mecklenburg-Strelitz .... Vol. 3A
Mecklenburg-Vorpomm ..... Vol. 3A
Mecklenburg-Vorpommern ... Vol. 3A
Medellin .... Vol. 2A
Medina .... Vol. 6A
Medio Real .... Vol. 2B
M.E.F. ovptd on Great Britain ... Vol. 3A
Mejico 351
Melaka 113
Melekeor (Palau #686) .... Vol. 5A
Memel, Memelgebiet 348
Memphis, Tenn. .... Vol. 1A
Meng Chiang .... Vol. 2A
Menge 564
Mengtsz .... Vol. 2B

INDEX AND IDENTIFIER

Merida 442
Meshed .... Vol. 3B
Mesopotamia (British Occupation) 350
Metelin .... Vol. 5B
Mexico, Mexicano 351
Micanopy, Fla. .... Vol. 1A
Micronesia 443
Middle Congo 471
Middle East Forces .... Vol. 3A
Mihon .... Vol. 4A
Mil .... Vol. 4A
Militarpost (Milit. Post) .... Vol. 1B
Millbury, Mass. .... Vol. 1A
Milledgeville, Ga. .... Vol. 1A
Miller, Gen. .... Vol. 5B
Milliemes surch. on French
  Off. in Turkey .... Vol. 2B
Mitau .... Vol. 4A
Milton, N.C. .... Vol. 1A
M. Kir. .... Vol. 3B
Mn. .... Vol. 4A
Mobile, Ala. .... Vol. 1A
Mocambique 786
Modena, Modones .... Vol. 3B
Moheli 472
Moldavia .... 472, Vol. 5B
Moldova 472
Moluccas .... Vol. 5A
Monaco 492
Monastir .... Vol. 6B
Mongolia 564
Mongtseu, Mongtze .... Vol. 2B
Monrovia .... Vol. 4A
Mont Athos .... Vol. 5B
Montenegro 616
Monterrey 442
Montevideo .... Vol. 6B
Montgomery, Ala. .... Vol. 1A
Montserrat 629
Moquea, Moquegua .... Vol. 5A
Morelia 442
Morocco 650
Morocco (British Offices) .... Vol. 3A
Morocco (German Offices) .... Vol. 3A
Morocco, French .... Vol. 2B
Morocco, Spanish .... Vol. 6A
Morvi .... Vol. 3B
Moschopolis .... Vol. 2B
Mosul 351
Mount Athos (Greece) .... Vol. 3A
Mount Athos (Turkey) .... Vol. 6B
Mount Athos, Russian Offices ..... Vol. 5B
Mount Lebanon, La. .... Vol. 1A
Mount Pleasant, NC .... Vol. 1A
Moyen-Congo 471
Mozambique 688
Mozambique Co. 727
MQE ovptd. on French Colonies 306
Muscat and Oman .... Vol. 5A
Mustique .... Vol. 5B
M.V.iR
Myanmar (Burma) .... Vol. 1B
Mytilene .... Vol. 3A

Nabha .... **Vol. 3B**
Naciones Unidas .... Vol. 1A
Nagyvarad .... Vol. 3B
Namibia .... Vol. 5A, Vol. 6A
Nandgaon .... Vol. 3B
Nanking .... Vol. 2A
Nanumaga .... Vol. 6B
Nanumea .... Vol. 6B
Naples, Napoletana .... Vol. 3B
Nashville, Tenn. .... Vol. 1A
Natal .... Vol. 5A
Nations Unies .... Vol. 1A, Vol. 6A
Native Feudatory States, India .... Vol. 3B
Nauru .... Vol. 5A
Navanagar .... Vol. 3B
Navarra .... Vol. 6A
N.C.E. ovptd. on French
  Colonies .... Vol. 5A
Neapolitan Provinces .... Vol. 3B
Ned. (Nederlandse) Antillen .... Vol. 5A
Ned. (Nederl, Nederlandse) Indie ... Vol. 5A
Nederland .... Vol. 5A
Nederlands Nieuw Guinea .... Vol. 5A
Negeri Sembilan 113, 155
Negri Sembilan 155
Nejd .... Vol. 6A
Nejdi Administration of Hejaz ..... Vol. 6A
Nepal .... Vol. 5A
Netherlands .... Vol. 5A
Netherlands Antilles .... Vol. 5A
Netherlands Indies .... Vol. 5A
Netherlands New Guinea .... Vol. 5A
Nevis .... Vol. 5A
New Britain .... Vol. 5A

New Brunswick .... Vol. 2A
New Caledonia .... Vol. 5A
New Caledonia stamps
  overprinted .... Vol. 5A
Newfoundland .... Vol. 2A
New Granada .... Vol. 3A
New Greece .... Vol. 3A
New Guinea .... Vol. 3A
New Guinea, British .... Vol. 3A
New Guinea, German .... Vol. 3A
New Haven, Conn. .... Vol. 1A
New Hebrides (British) .... Vol. 5A
New Hebrides (French) .... Vol. 5A
New Orleans, La. .... Vol. 1A
New Republic .... Vol. 5A
New Smyrna, Fla. .... Vol. 1A
New South Wales .... Vol. 1A
New York, N.Y. .... Vol. 1A
New Zealand .... Vol. 5A
Nezavisna .... Vol. 2A
N.F. overprinted on
  Nyasaland Pro. .... Vol. 5A
Ngaraard (Palau #686) .... Vol. 5A
Ngardman (Palau #686) .... Vol. 5A
Ngaremlengui (Palau #686) .... Vol. 5A
Ngchesar (Palau #686) .... Vol. 5A
Ngiwal (Palau #686) .... Vol. 5A
Nicaragua .... Vol. 5A
Nicaria .... Vol. 3A
Nieuwe Republiek .... Vol. 5A
Nieuw Guinea .... Vol. 5A
Niger .... Vol. 6A
Niger and Senegambia .... Vol. 6A
Niger and Upper Senegal .... Vol. 6B
Niger Coast Protectorate .... Vol. 5A
Nigeria .... Vol. 6A
Nikolaevsk .... Vol. 5A
Ningsia .... Vol. 2A
Nippon .... Vol. 4A
Nisiro, Nisiros .... Vol. 3B
Niuafo'ou .... Vol. 6B
Niue .... Vol. 5A
Niutao .... Vol. 6B
Nlle. Caledonie .... Vol. 5A
No Hay Estampillas .... Vol. 2A
N. O. P. O. (Confed. #62XU1) ..... Vol. 1A
Norddeutscher Postbezirk .... Vol. 3A
Noreg (1st stamp #318) .... Vol. 5A
Norfolk, Va. .... Vol. 1A
Norfolk Island .... Vol. 5A
Norge .... Vol. 5A
North Borneo .... Vol. 5A
North China .... Vol. 2A
Northeast China .... Vol. 2A
Northeast Postal Service .... Vol. 2A
Northeastern Provinces (China) ..... Vol. 2A
North Epirus (Greek Occupation) .... Vol. 3A
Northern Cook Islands .... Vol. 5A
Northern Cyprus, Turkish Rep. of ... Vol. 6B
Northern Ireland .... Vol. 2A
Northern Kiangsu .... Vol. 2A
Northern Nigeria .... Vol. 6A
Northern Poland .... Vol. 5B
Northern Rhodesia .... Vol. 5A
Northern Zone, Morocco 785
North German Confederation .... Vol. 3A
North Ingermanland .... Vol. 5A
North Viet Nam .... Vol. 6B
Northwest China .... Vol. 2A
North West (N. W.) Pacific
  Islands .... Vol. 5A
Norway .... Vol. 5A
Nossi-Be .... Vol. 5A
Notopher .... Vol. 3A
Nouvelle Caledonie .... Vol. 5A
Nouvelle Hebrides .... Vol. 5A
Nova Scotia .... Vol. 2A
Novocherkassk .... Vol. 6A
Nowa .... Vol. 1B
Nowa Bb ovptd. on Bulgaria .... Vol. 5B
Nowanuggur .... Vol. 3B
Nowta .... Vol. 6A
Nowte 686
Noyta .... Vol. 1B, Vol. 3A, Vol. 4A,
  Vol. 5B, Vol. 6B
NP surcharged on Great Britain .... Vol. 5A
Nr. 21, Nr. 16
N S B ovptd. on French Colonies .... Vol. 5A
N. Sembilan 113
N.S.W. .... Vol. 1A
Nueva Granada .... Vol. 2A
Nui .... Vol. 6B
Nukufetau .... Vol. 6B
Nukulaelae .... Vol. 6B
Nyasaland (Protectorate) .... Vol. 5A
Nyasaland and Rhodesia .... Vol. 5B
Nyasaland, overprinted .... Vol. 5A
Nyassa .... Vol. 5A

N.Z. .... Vol. 5A

Oakway, S.C. .... Vol. 1A
Oaxaca 357
Obock .... Vol. 5A
Ob. Ost ovptd. on Germany
  (Lithuania) .... Vol. 5B
Occupation Francaise .... Vol. 3B
Oceania, Oceanie .... Vol. 2B
Oesterr. Post, Ofterreich .... Vol. 1B
Offentlig Sak, Off. Sak .... Vol. 5A
Oil Rivers .... Vol. 5A
O K C A (Russia) .... Vol. 5B
Oldenburg .... Vol. 3A
Olonets .... Vol. 5B
Oltre Giuba .... Vol. 3B
Oman, Sultanate of .... Vol. 5A
ONU (UN Offices in
  Geneva #384) .... Vol. 1A
Oradea .... Vol. 3B
Orange River Colony .... Vol. 5A
Oranje Vrij Staat .... Vol. 5A
Orchha, Orcha .... Vol. 3B
Ore surcharged on Denmark ..... Vol. 2B
Orense .... Vol. 6A
Organisation Mondiale
  de la Sante .... Vol. 6A
Oriental .... Vol. 6B
Orts-Post .... Vol. 6A
O.S. .... Vol. 5A
Osten .... Vol. 5B
Osterreich .... Vol. 1B
Ostland .... Vol. 5B
Ottoman, Ottomanes ..... Vol. 2B, Vol. 6B
Oubangi Chari .... Vol. 6B
Outer Mongolia 564
Oviedo .... Vol. 6A
O.V.S. .... Vol. 5A
Oxford, N.C. .... Vol. 1A
O'zbekiston .... Vol. 6B

P .... Vol. 2A, Vol. 2B, Vol. 4A, Vol. 6A
P on Straits Settlements 116
Pacchi Postali .... Vol. 3B, Vol. 6A
Pacific Steam Navigation Co. .... Vol. 5A
Packhoi, Pakhoi .... Vol. 2B
Pahang 114, 156
Paid (Confed. #35X, etc.) .... Vol. 1A
Paid 5 (US #4X1, 7X1, many
  Confed.) .... Vol. 1A
Paid 10 (Confed. #76XU, 101XU,
  80XU) .... Vol. 1A
Paid 2 Cents (Confed. #2XU) .... Vol. 1A
Paid 3 Cents (Confed. #2AXU) .... Vol. 1A
Paita .... Vol. 5A
Pakistan .... Vol. 5A
Pakke-porto .... Vol. 3A
Palau .... Vol. 5A
Palestine .... Vol. 2B, Vol. 5A
Palestine (British Administration) .... Vol. 5A
Palestine (Jordan Occ.) .... Vol. 4A
Palestine overprinted .... Vol. 5A
Palestinian Authority .... Vol. 5A
Panama .... Vol. 5A
Panama (Colombian Dom.) ...... Vol. 2A,
  Vol. 5A
Panama Canal Zone .... Vol. 1A
Papua .... Vol. 5A
Papua New Guinea .... Vol. 5A
Para .... Vol. 2B, Vol. 6B
Para ovptd. on Austria .... Vol. 1B
Para ovptd. on France .... Vol. 2B
Para ovptd. on Germany .... Vol. 3A
Para ovptd. on Italy .... Vol. 3B
Paraguay .... Vol. 5A
Paras .... Vol. 2B, Vol. 6B
Paras ovpt. on Great Britain ..... Vol. 3A
Paras ovpt. on Romania .... Vol. 5B
Paras ovpt. on Russia .... Vol. 5B
Parma, Parm., Parmensi .... Vol. 3B
Pasco .... Vol. 5A
Patiala .... Vol. 3B
Patmo, Patmos .... Vol. 3B
Patterson, N.C. .... Vol. 1A
Patton, N.B. (Confed. #138XU1) .... Vol. 1A
Patzcuaro 442
Paxos .... Vol. 2A, Vol. 3A, Vol. 3B
PC CP
PD .... Vol. 5B
P.E. (Egypt #4, etc.) .... Vol. 2B
Pechino, Peking .... Vol. 2B
Peleliu (Palau #686) .... Vol. 5A
Pen, Penna .... Vol. 1A
Penang 114, 156
Penny Post (US 3LB, 8LB) .... Vol. 1A
Penrhyn Island .... Vol. 5A
Pensacola, Fla. .... Vol. 1A
Penybnnka Српска .... Vol. 1B

People's Republic of China .... Vol. 2A
Perak 116, 156
Perlis 116, 157
Persekutuan Tanah Melayu
  (Malaya #91) 108
Persia (British Occupation) .... Vol. 1B
Persia, Persanes .... Vol. 3B
Peru, Peruana .... Vol. 5A
Pesa ovpt. on Germany .... Vol. 3A
Petersburg, Va. .... Vol. 1A
Pfennig, Pfg., Pf. ..... Vol. 2B, Vol. 3A, Vol. 4A
P.G.S. (Perak) 116
Philadelphia, Pa. .... Vol. 1A
Philippines .... Vol. 2A, Vol. 5A
Philippines (US Admin.) ... Vol. 1A, Vol. 5A
Philippines (Japanese Occ.) ...... Vol. 1A,
  Vol. 5A
Piast., Piaster ovptd. on Austria .... Vol. 1B
Piaster ovptd. on Germany ...... Vol. 3A
Piaster ovptd. on Romania .... Vol. 5B
Piastre, Piastra ovptd. on Italy ... Vol. 3B
Piastre .... 351, Vol. 2B, Vol. 6B
Piastre ovptd. on France .... Vol. 2B
Piastres ovpt. on Great Britain ... Vol. 3A
Piastres ovpt. on Russia .... Vol. 5B
Pies .... Vol. 2A, Vol. 3B
Pietersburg .... Vol. 6B
Pilgrim Tercentenary (US #548) ... Vol. 1A
Pilipinas .... Vol. 1A, Vol. 5A
Pisco .... Vol. 5A
Piscopi .... Vol. 3B
Pitcairn Islands .... Vol. 5A
Pittsylvania C.H., Va. .... Vol. 1A
Piura .... Vol. 5A
Plains of Dura, Ga. .... Vol. 1A
Pleasant Shade, Va. .... Vol. 1A
Plum Creek, Tex. .... Vol. 1A
P.O. Paid .... Vol. 1A
Pobres (Spain #RA11) .... Vol. 6A
РОССІЯ, РОССИЯ .... Vol. 5B
Poczta, Polska .... Vol. 2B, Vol. 5B
Pohjois Inkeri .... Vol. 5B
Pokutia .... Vol. 5B
Poland .... Vol. 5B
Poland, exile government in
  Great Britain .... Vol. 5B
Polish Levant .... Vol. 5B
Polish Offices in Danzig .... Vol. 5B
Polish Offices in Turkish Empire ..... Vol. 5B
Polska .... Vol. 5B
Polynesia, French (Polynesie) .... Vol. 2B
Ponce .... Vol. 1A, Vol. 5B
Ponta Delgada .... Vol. 5B
Р.О.П.иТ
Poonch .... Vol. 3B
Popayan .... Vol. 2A
Port Arthur and Dairen .... Vol. 2A
Porteado .... Vol. 5B
Porte de Conduccion .... Vol. 5A
Porte de Mar 439
Porte Franco
Port Gibson, Miss. .... Vol. 1A
Port Gdansk .... Vol. 5B
Port Hood, Nova Scotia .... Vol. 2A
Port Lagos .... Vol. 2B
Port Lavaca, Tex. .... Vol. 1A
Porto .... Vol. 1A, Vol. 1B, Vol. 6B
Porto Gazetei
Porto Pflichtige .... Vol. 3A
Porto Rico .... Vol. 1A, Vol. 2A, Vol. 5B
Port Said, French Offices .... Vol. 2B
Portugal, Portuguesa .... Vol. 5B
Portuguese Africa .... Vol. 5B
Portuguese Congo .... Vol. 5B
Portuguese East Africa
  (Mozambique) 786
Portuguese Guinea .... Vol. 5B
Portuguese India .... Vol. 5B
Portuguese India overprinted .... Vol. 6B
Posen (Poznan) .... Vol. 5B
Post .... Vol. 3A, Vol. 3B
Post (Postage) & Receipt .... Vol. 3B
Posta .... Vol. 1A, Vol. 6A
Postage(s) .... 64, 564, Vol. 3A, Vol. 3B,
  Vol. 5B
Postage Due .... Vol. 1A, Vol. 3A
Postas le hioc .... Vol. 3B
Poste Locale .... Vol. 6A
Postes .... Vol. 1B, Vol. 2B, Vol. 4A
Postes Serbes ovptd. on France .... Vol. 2B
Postgebiet Ob. Ost. .... Vol. 5B
Postmarke .... Vol. 3A
Post Office (US #7X, 9X) .... Vol. 1A
Post Stamp .... Vol. 3B
Postzegel .... Vol. 5A
P.P. ovptd. on French postage
  dues .... Vol. 2B
P.P.C. ovptd. on Poland .... Vol. 5B

INDEX AND IDENTIFIER

Pre.. Vol. 6B
Prefecture issues .... Vol. 4A
Preussen .... Vol. 5B
Priamur .... Vol. 6A
Prince Edward Island .... Vol. 2A
Pristina .... Vol. 6B
Province of Canada .... Vol. 2A
Providence (Prov.), R.I. .... Vol. 1A
Prussia .... Vol. 5B
PS .... Vol. 2A, Vol. 3B
P.S.N.C. (Peru) .... Vol. 5A
Puerto Principe .... Vol. 1A, Vol. 2A
Puerto Rico, Pto. Rico .... Vol. 1A,
   Vol. 2A, Vol. 5B
Puerto Rico (US Admin.) ... Vol. 1A, Vol. 5B
Pul .... Vol. 1A
Pulau Pinang 156
Puno .... Vol. 5A
Puttiala State .... Vol. 3B

Qatar .... Vol. 5B
Qu'aiti State in Hadhramaut .... Vol. 1A
Qu'aiti State of Shihr and
   Mukalla .... Vol. 1A
Queensland .... Vol. 1A
Quelimane .... Vol. 5B

R (Armenia) .... Vol. 1A
R (Jind, Iran) .... Vol. 3B
R ovptd. on French Colonies ..... Vol. 2B
Rajasthan .... Vol. 3B
Rajpeepla, Rajpipla .... Vol. 3B
Raleigh, N.C. .... Vol. 1A
Rappen .... Vol. 6A
Rarotonga .... Vol. 2A
Ras al Khaima .... Vol. 5B, Vol. 6B
R.A.U. .... Vol. 6A
Rayon .... Vol. 6A
Recargo .... Vol. 6A
Redonda (Antigua) .... Vol. 1A
Refugee Relief .... Vol. 3B
Regatul .... Vol. 3B
Reichspost .... Vol. 3A
Reis (Portugal) .... Vol. 5B
Repubblica Sociale Italiana .... Vol. 3B
Republic of China .... Vol. 2A
Republique Arab Unie .... Vol. 6A
Republique Democratique
   du Congo .... Vol. 6B
Reseau d'Etat .... Vol. 2B
Resistance overprinted on Syria ... Vol. 6A
Rethymno, Retymno .... Vol. 2A
Reunion .... Vol. 6A
R.F. ...... See France or French Colonies
RF - Solidarite Francaise .... Vol. 2B
R H .... Vol. 3B
Rheatown, Tenn. .... Vol. 1A
Rheinland-Pfalz .... Vol. 3A
Rhine Palatinate .... Vol. 3A
Rhodes .... Vol. 3B
Rhodesia .... Vol. 5B
Rhodesia (formerly So. Rhodesia) .... Vol. 5B
Rhodesia and Nyasaland .... Vol. 5B
Rialtar .... Vol. 3B
Riau, Riouw Archipelago .... Vol. 3B
Ricevuta .... Vol. 3B, Vol. 6A
Richmond, Tex. .... Vol. 1A
Rigsbank Skilling .... Vol. 2B
Ringgold, Ga. .... Vol. 1A
Rio de Oro .... Vol. 5B
Rio Muni .... Vol. 5B
RIS on Netherlands Indies .... Vol. 3B
Rizeh .... Vol. 5B
Rn .... Vol. 4A
RNS .... Vol. 3B
R. O. ovptd. on Turkey .... Vol. 2B
Robertsport .... Vol. 4A
Rodi .... Vol. 3B
Roepiah .... Vol. 5A
Romagna, Romagne .... Vol. 5B
Romana .... Vol. 3B, Vol. 5B
Romania, Roumania .... Vol. 5B
Romania, Occupation, Offices ... Vol. 5B
Romanian Occupation of
   Hungary .... Vol. 3B
Romanian Occupation of
   Western Ukraine .... Vol. 6B
Romania, Offices in the
   Turkish Empire .... Vol. 5B
Roman States .... Vol. 3B
Ross Dependency .... Vol. 5A
Rossija .... Vol. 5B
Rostov .... Vol. 6A
Rouad, Ile .... Vol. 5B
Roumelie Orientale .... Vol. 2B
Rpf overprinted on Luxembourg ... Vol. 4A
RSA .... Vol. 6A
R S M (San Marino) .... Vol. 6A
Ruanda ovptd. on Congo .... Vol. 3A

Ruanda-Urundi .... Vol. 5B
Ruffifch-Polen ovptd. on
   Germany .... Vol. 5B
Rumania, Roumania .... Vol. 5B
Rumanien on Germany .... Vol. 5B
Rupee on Great Britain .... Vol. 5A
Russia .... Vol. 5B
Russia (Finnish Occupation) ..... Vol. 4A,
   Vol. 5B
Russia (German Occupation) ..... Vol. 5B
Russian Company of Navigation
   & Trade .... Vol. 5B
Russian Dominion of Poland ..... Vol. 5B
Russian Empire, Finland .... Vol. 2B
Russian Occupation of Crete .... Vol. 3A
Russian Occupation of Germany ... Vol. 3A
Russian Occupation of Korea ... Vol. 4A
Russian Occupation of Latvia ... Vol. 4A
Russian Occupation of Lithuania ... Vol. 4A
Russian Offices .... Vol. 5B
Russian Offices in China .... Vol. 5B
Russian Offices in Turkish Empire ... Vol. 5B
Russian stamps surch. or ovptd. .... Vol. 1A,
   Vol. 2B, Vol. 3A, Vol. 4A, Vol. 5B, Vol. 6A
Russian Turkestan .... Vol. 5B
Rustenburg .... Vol. 6B
Rutherfordton, N.C. .... Vol. 1A
Rwanda, Rwandaise .... Vol. 6A
Ryukyu Islands .... Vol. 1A

S on Straits Settlements 118
S A, S.A.K. (Saudi Arabia) .... Vol. 6A
Saar, Saargebiet, Saar Land ..... Vol. 5B
Sabah 157
Sachsen .... Vol. 3A
Sahara Occidental (Espanol) .... Vol. 6A
St. Christopher .... Vol. 5B
St. Christopher-Nevis-Anguilla ... Vol. 5B
Ste. Marie de Madagascar .... Vol. 5B
St. Georges, Bermuda .... Vol. 1B
St. Helena .... Vol. 5B
S. Thome (Tome) E Principe ..... Vol. 5B
St. Kitts .... Vol. 5B
St. Kitts-Nevis .... Vol. 5B
St. Louis, Mo. .... Vol. 1A
St. Lucia .... Vol. 5B
St. Martin .... Vol. 5B
St. Pierre and Miquelon .... Vol. 5B
St. Thomas and Prince Islands ... Vol. 5B
St. Vincent .... Vol. 5B
St. Vincent and the Grenadines ... Vol. 5B
St. Vincent Grenadines .... Vol. 5B
Salamanca Province .... Vol. 6A
Salem, N.C. .... Vol. 1A
Salem, Va. .... Vol. 1A
Salisbury, N.C. .... Vol. 1A
Salonicco, Salonika .... Vol. 3B
Salonika (Turkish) .... Vol. 6B
Salonique .... Vol. 5B, Vol. 6B
Salvador, El .... Vol. 5B
Salzburg .... Vol. 1B
Samoa .... Vol. 5B
Samos .... Vol. 2B, Vol. 3A
San Antonio, Tex. .... Vol. 1A
San Marino .... Vol. 6A
San Sebastian .... Vol. 6A
Santa Cruz de Tenerife .... Vol. 6A
Santa Maura .... Vol. 3A, Vol. 3B
Santander .... Vol. 2A
Sao Paulo .... Vol. 1B
Sao Tome and Principe .... Vol. 5B
Saorstat .... Vol. 3B
Sarawak .... 158, Vol. 6A
Sardinia .... Vol. 3B
Sarre overprinted on Germany
   and Bavaria .... Vol. 5B
Saseno .... Vol. 6A
Saudi Arabia .... Vol. 6A
Saudi Arabia overprinted .... Vol. 4A
Saurashtra .... Vol. 3B
Savannah, Ga. .... Vol. 1A
Saxony .... Vol. 3A
SCADTA .... Vol. 2A
Scarpanto .... Vol. 3B
Schleswig .... Vol. 3A, Vol. 6A
Schleswig-Holstein .... Vol. 3A
Schweizer Reneke .... Vol. 6B
Scinde .... Vol. 3B
Scotland .... Vol. 3A
Scutari, Italian Offices .... Vol. 3B
Segel Porto (on Neth. Indies) .... Vol. 3B
Segnatasse, Segna Tassa .... Vol. 5B
Seiyun .... Vol. 1A
Selangor 118, 158
Selma, Ala. .... Vol. 1A
Semenov .... Vol. 2B
Sen, Sn. .... Vol. 1A, Vol. 4A, Vol. 5A
Senegal .... Vol. 6A
Senegal stamps surcharged ..... Vol. 2B

Senegambia and Niger .... Vol. 6A
Serb Administration of Bosnia,
   Banja Luca .... Vol. 1B
Serbia, Serbien .... Vol. 6A
Serbia & Montenegro .... 616, Vol. 6A
Serbian Occupation of Hungary ... Vol. 3B
Service .... Vol. 3B
Sevastopol .... Vol. 6A
Seville, Sevilla .... Vol. 6A
Seychelles .... Vol. 6A
S.H. .... Vol. 3A
Shanghai .... Vol. 2A, Vol. 5B
Shanghai (U.S. Offices) .... Vol. 1A
Shanghai and Nanking .... Vol. 2A
Shansi .... Vol. 2A
Shantung .... Vol. 2A
Sharjah .... Vol. 6A
Shensi .... Vol. 2A
Shihr and Mukalla .... Vol. 1A
Shqipenia, Shqiptare, Shqiperija,
   Shqiperise (Albania) .... Vol. 1A
S.H.S. on Bosnia and
   Herzegovina .... Vol. 6B
S.H.S. on Hungary .... Vol. 6B
Siam (Thailand) .... Vol. 5B
Siberia .... Vol. 6A
Siberian stamps overprinted
   or surcharged .... Vol. 2B
Sicily, Sicilia .... Vol. 3B
Siege de la Ligue Arabe
   (Morocco #44) 743
Sierra Leone .... Vol. 6A
Sikang .... Vol. 2A
Silesia, Eastern .... Vol. 2B
Silesia, Upper .... Vol. 6B
Simi .... Vol. 3B
Sinaloa 442
Singapore .... Vol. 6A
Sinkiang .... Vol. 2A
Sint Maarten .... Vol. 5B
Sirmoor, Sirmur .... Vol. 3B
Six Cents .... Vol. 1A
Sld. .... Vol. 1B
Slesvig .... Vol. 3A
Slovakia .... Vol. 2B, Vol. 6A
Slovene Coast .... Vol. 6B
Slovenia, Slovenija .... Vol. 6A
Slovenia, Italian .... Vol. 6B
Slovensko, Slovenska,
   Slovensky .... Vol. 2B, Vol. 6A
S. Marino .... Vol. 6A
Smirne, Smyrna .... Vol. 3B
Smyrne .... Vol. 5B
S O ovptd. on Czechoslovakia,
   Poland .... Vol. 2B
Sobreporte .... Vol. 2A
Sociedad Colombo-Alemana ..... Vol. 2a
Sociedade de Geographia
   de Lisboa .... Vol. 5B
Societe des Nations .... Vol. 6A
Soldi .... Vol. 1B
Solomon Islands .... Vol. 6A
Somali, Somalia, Somaliya .... Vol. 6A
Somalia, B.M.A. .... Vol. 3A
Somalia, E.A.F. .... Vol. 3A
Somali Coast (Djibouti) .... Vol. 6A
Somaliland Protectorate .... Vol. 6A
Sonora 356, 357
Sonsorol (Palau #686) .... Vol. 5A
Soomaaliya, Sooomaliyeed .... Vol. 6A
Soruth, Sorath .... Vol. 3B
Soudan .... Vol. 2B, Vol. 6A
South Africa .... Vol. 6A
South African Republic
   (Transvaal) .... Vol. 6B
South Arabia .... Vol. 6A
South Australia .... Vol. 1A
South Bulgaria .... Vol. 2B
South Borneo .... Vol. 5A
South China .... Vol. 2A
Southern Nigeria .... Vol. 6A
Southern Poland .... Vol. 5B
Southern Rhodesia .... Vol. 6A
Southern Yemen .... Vol. 6B
South Georgia .... Vol. 2B, Vol. 6A
South Georgia and South
   Sandwich Islands .... Vol. 6A
South Kasai .... Vol. 6A
South Korea .... Vol. 4A
South Lithuania .... Vol. 4A
South Moluccas .... Vol. 5B
South Orkneys .... Vol. 2B
South Russia .... Vol. 6A
South Russian stamps
   surcharged .... Vol. 6A
South Shetlands .... Vol. 2B
South Sudan .... Vol. 6A
South Viet Nam .... Vol. 6B
South West Africa .... Vol. 6A

Southwest China .... Vol. 2A
Soviet Union (Russia) .... Vol. 5B
Sowjetische Besatzungs Zone ... Vol. 3A
Spain .... Vol. 6A
Spanish Administration of
   Andorra .... Vol. 6A
Spanish Dominion of Cuba .... Vol. 2A
Spanish Dominion of
   Mariana Islands 269
Spanish Dominion of Philippines ... Vol. 5A
Spanish Dominion of Puerto Rico ... Vol. 5B
Spanish Guinea .... Vol. 6A
Spanish Morocco .... Vol. 6A
Spanish Sahara .... Vol. 6A
Spanish West Africa .... Vol. 6A
Spanish Western Sahara .... Vol. 6A
Sparta, Ga. .... Vol. 1A
Spartanburg, S.C. .... Vol. 1A
SPM ovptd. on French Cols. ...... Vol. 5B
Srbija I Crna Gora .... Vol. 6A
Sri Lanka .... Vol. 6A
Srodkowa Litwa .... Vol. 6B
Stamp (Tibet #O1) .... Vol. 6B
Stampalia .... Vol. 3B
Stanyslaviv .... Vol. 6B
Statesville, N.C. .... Vol. 1A
Steinmeyer's City Post .... Vol. 1A
Stellaland .... Vol. 6B
Stempel .... Vol. 1B
Straits Settlements .... Vol. 6A
Straits Settlements overprinted 109,
   111, 113, 114, 116, 118, Vol. 6A
Strombus gigas Linne
   (Neth. Antilles #1193) .... Vol. 5A
STT Vuja, STT Vujna .... Vol. 6B
Styria .... Vol. 1B
S.U. on Straits Settlements 119
Submarine mail (Correo
   Submarino) .... Vol. 6A
Sudan .... Vol. 6A
Sudan, French .... Vol. 6B
Suid Afrika .... Vol. 6A
Suidwes-Afrika .... Vol. 6A
Suiyuan .... Vol. 2A
S. Ujong 119
Sultanate of Oman .... Vol. 5A
Sumatra .... Vol. 3B, Vol. 5A
Sumter, S.C. .... Vol. 1A
Sungei Ujong 119
Suomi (Finland) .... Vol. 2B
Supeh .... Vol. 2A
Surakarta .... Vol. 3B
Surinam, Suriname, Surinaamse ... Vol. 6A
Suvalki .... Vol. 5B
Sverige .... Vol. 6A
S.W.A. .... Vol. 6A
Swaziland, Swazieland .... Vol. 6A
Sweden .... Vol. 6A
Switzerland .... Vol. 6A
Switzerland, Administration of
   Liechtenstein .... Vol. 4A
Syria, Syrie, Syrienne .... Vol. 5A, Vol. 6A
Syria (Arabian Government) ..... Vol. 6A
Syrie .... Vol. 6A
Syrie-Grand Liban .... Vol. 6A
Szechwan .... Vol. 2A
Szeged .... Vol. 3B

T .... Vol. 1B, Vol. 2B
T ovptd. on stamps of Peru .... Vol. 5A
Tabora ovptd. on Belgian Congo ... Vol. 3A
Tacna .... Vol. 5A
Tadjikistan, Tadzikistan .... Vol. 6A
Tao Han (Korea) .... Vol. 4A
Tahiti .... Vol. 6A
Taiwan (Republic of China) .... Vol. 2A
Taiwan (Formosa) .... Vol. 2A
Taiwan, Japanese .... Vol. 2A, Vol. 4A
Tajikistan .... Vol. 6A
Takca .... Vol. 1B
Takse .... Vol. 1A
Talbotton, Ga. .... Vol. 1A
Talca .... Vol. 2A
Talladega, Ala. .... Vol. 1A
Tallinn .... Vol. 2B
Tanganyika .... Vol. 6A
Tanganyika and Zanzibar .... Vol. 6A
Tanganyika (Tanzania), Kenya,
   Uganda .... Vol. 4A
Tanger .... Vol. 2B, Vol. 6A
Tangier, British Offices .... Vol. 3A
Tangier, French Offices .... Vol. 2B
Tangier, Spanish Offices .... Vol. 6A
Tannu Tuva .... Vol. 6A
Tanzania .... Vol. 6A
Tanzania-Zanzibar .... Vol. 6B
Tartu .... Vol. 2B
Tasmania .... Vol. 1A
Tassa Gazzette .... Vol. 3B

INDEX AND IDENTIFIER

Entry	Volume
Taxa de Guerra	32, Vol. 5B
Taxyapom	Vol. 2B
Tchad	Vol. 2B
Tchongking	Vol. 2B
T.C. overprinted on Cochin	Vol. 3B
T.C., Postalari	Vol. 6B
Te Betalen	Vol. 1B, Vol. 5A, Vol. 6A
Tegucigalpa	Vol. 3B
Teheran	Vol. 3B
Tellico Plains, Tenn.	Vol. 1A
Temesvar	Vol. 3B
Ten Cents	Vol. 1A
T.E.O. ovptd. on Turkey or France	Vol. 2A, Vol. 6A
Terres Australes et Antarctiques Francaises	Vol. 2B
Territorio Insular Chileno (Chile #1061)	Vol. 2A
Teruel Province	Vol. 6A
Tete	Vol. 6A
Tetuan	Vol. 6A
Thailand, Thai	Vol. 6B
Thailand (Occupation of Kedah)	109
Thailand (Occupation of Kelantan)	109
Thailand (Occupation of Malaya)	109
Thailand (Occupation of Perlis)	109
Thailand (Occupation of Trengganu)	109
Thessaly	Vol. 6B
Thomasville, Ga.	Vol. 1A
Thrace	Vol. 6B
Three Cents	Vol. 1A
Thuringia, Thuringen	Vol. 3A
Thurn and Taxis	Vol. 3A
Tibet	Vol. 6B
Tibet (Chinese province)	Vol. 2A
Tibet, Chinese Offices	Vol. 2A
Tical	Vol. 6B
Tientsin (Chinese)	Vol. 2A
Tientsin (German)	Vol. 3A
Tientsin (Italian)	Vol. 3B
Tiflis	Vol. 3A
Timbre ovptd. on France	Vol. 2B
Timor	Vol. 6B
Timor-Leste	Vol. 6B
Timor Lorosae	Vol. 1A, Vol. 6B
Tin Can Island	Vol. 6B
Tjedan Solidarnosti (Yugoslavia #RA82)	Vol. 6B
Tjenestefrimerke	Vol. 2B, Vol. 5A
Tlacotalpan	442
Tobago	Vol. 6B
Toga	Vol. 6B
Togo, Togolaise	Vol. 6B
Tokelau Islands	Vol. 6B
Tolima	Vol. 2A
Tonga	Vol. 6B
Tongareva	Vol. 5A
Tonk	Vol. 3B
To Pay	Vol. 3A
Toscano	Vol. 3B
Tou	Vol. 3B
Touva, Tovva	Vol. 6A
Transcaucasian Federated Republics	Vol. 6B
Trans-Jordan	Vol. 4A, Vol. 5A
Trans-Jordan (Palestine Occ.)	Vol. 4A
Transkei	Vol. 6A
Transvaal	Vol. 6B
Transylvania	Vol. 3B
Trasporto Pacchi	Vol. 3B
Travancore	Vol. 3B
Travancore-Cochin, State of	Vol. 3B
Trebizonde	Vol. 5B
Trengganu	121, 158
Trentino	Vol. 1B
Trieste	Vol. 1B, Vol. 3B, Vol. 6B
Trinidad	Vol. 6B
Trinidad and Tobago	Vol. 6B
Trinidad Society (Trinidad & Tobago #B1)	Vol. 6B
Tripoli di Barberia (Tripoli)	Vol. 3B
Tripoli, Fiera Campionaria	Vol. 4A
Tripolitania	Vol. 4A, Vol. 6B
Tripolitania (B.M.A.)	Vol. 3A
Tristan da Cunha	Vol. 6B
Trucial States	Vol. 6B
Tsinghai	Vol. 2A
Tsingtau	Vol. 2A, Vol. 4A
T. Ta. C	Vol. 6B
Tullahoma, Tenn.	Vol. 1A
Tumbes (Peru #129-133)	Vol. 5A
Tunisia, Tunisie, Tunis, Tunisienne	Vol. 6B
Turkestan, Russian	Vol. 5B
Turkey, Turkiye, Turk	Vol. 6B
Turkey (Greek Occupation)	Vol. 3A, Vol. 6B
Turkey in Asia	Vol. 6B
Turk Federe Devleti	Vol. 6B
Turkish Empire, Austrian Offices	Vol. 1B
Turkish Empire, British Offices	Vol. 3A
Turkish Empire, French Offices	Vol. 2B
Turkish Empire, Georgian Offices	Vol. 3A
Turkish Empire, German Offices	Vol. 3A
Turkish Empire, Italian Offices	Vol. 3B
Turkish Empire, Polish Offices	Vol. 5B
Turkish Empire, Romanian Offices	Vol. 5B
Turkish Empire, Russian Offices	Vol. 5B
Turkish Occupation of Iran	Vol. 3B
Turkish Republic of Northern Cyprus	Vol. 6B
Turkish stamps surcharged or overprinted	Vol. 2B, Vol. 3A, Vol. 6A
Turkish Suzerainty of Egypt	Vol. 2B
Turkmenistan, Turkmenpocta	Vol. 6B
Turks and Caicos Islands	Vol. 6B
Turks Islands	Vol. 6B
Tuscaloosa, Ala.	Vol. 1A
Tuscany	Vol. 3B
Tuscumbia, Ala.	Vol. 1A
Tuva Autonomous Region	Vol. 6B
Tuvalu	Vol. 6B
Two Cents (Confed. #53X5)	Vol. 1A
Two Pence	Vol. 1A
Two Sicilies	Vol. 3B
Tyosen (Korea)	Vol. 4A
Tyrol	Vol. 1B
UAE ovptd. on Abu Dhabi	**Vol. 6B**
U.A.R.	Vol. 2B, Vol. 6A, Vol. 6B
Ubangi, Ubangi-Shari	Vol. 6B
Uganda, U.G.	Vol. 6B
Uganda, and Kenya	Vol. 4A
Uganda, Tanganyika, Kenya	Vol. 4A
Ukraine, Ukraina	Vol. 6B
Ukraine (German Occupation)	Vol. 5B
Ukraine stamps surcharged	Vol. 5B
Ukrainian Soviet Socialist Republic	Vol. 6B
Ukraine, Western	Vol. 6B
Uku Leta	Vol. 1A
Ultramar	Vol. 2A
Umm al Qiwain	Vol. 6B
UNEF ovptd. on India	Vol. 3B
UNESCO	Vol. 2B
U.N. Force in Congo or Gaza (India)	Vol. 3B
Union Island, St. Vincent	Vol. 5B
Union Islands	Vol. 6B
Union of South Africa	Vol. 6A
Union of Soviet Socialist Republics	Vol. 5B
Uniontown, Ala.	Vol. 1A
Unionville, S.C.	Vol. 1A
United Arab Emirates	Vol. 6B
United Arab Republic (UAR)	Vol. 2B, Vol. 6A, Vol. 6B
United Arab Republic, Egypt	Vol. 2B
United Arab Republic Issues for Syria	Vol. 6A
United Kingdom	Vol. 3A
United Nations	Vol. 1A
United Nations European Office	Vol. 1A, Vol. 6A
United Nations Offices in Geneva	Vol. 1A
United Nations Offices in Vienna	Vol. 1A
United Nations - Kosovo	Vol. 1A, Vol. 4A
United Nations - West New Guinea	Vol. 1A
United State of Saurashtra	Vol. 3B
United States Adm. of Canal Zone	Vol. 1A
United States Adm. of Cuba	Vol. 1A, Vol. 2A
United States Adm. of Guam	Vol. 1A
U. S. Adm. of Philippines	Vol. 1A, Vol. 5A
U. S. Adm. of Puerto Rico	Vol. 1A, Vol. 5B
U. S. Military Rule of Korea	Vol. 4A
United States of America	Vol. 1A
United States of Indonesia	Vol. 3B
United States of New Granada	Vol. 2A
United States, Offices in China	Vol. 1A
Un Real	Vol. 2B
U.S. Zone (Germany)	Vol. 3A
Universal Postal Union, Intl. Bureau	Vol. 6A
UNTEA ovptd. on Netherlands New Guinea	Vol. 1A, Vol. 3B
UNTEAT	Vol. 6B
UPHA ROPA	616
Upper Austria	Vol. 1B
Upper Senegal and Niger	Vol. 6B
Upper Silesia	Vol. 6B
Upper Volta	Vol. 1B
Urgente	Vol. 6A
U.R.I. ovptd. on Yugoslavia	Vol. 6B
Uruguay	Vol. 6B
Urundi ovptd. on Congo	Vol. 3A
Uskub	Vol. 6B
U.S. Mail	Vol. 1A
U.S.P.O.	Vol. 1A
U.S.P.O. Despatch	Vol. 1A
U.S.S.R.	Vol. 5B
U. S. T.C. overprinted on Cochin	Vol. 3B
Uzbekistan	Vol. 6B
Vaitupu	**Vol. 6B**
Valdosta, Ga.	Vol. 1A
Valencia	Vol. 6A
Valladolid Province	Vol. 6A
Valona	Vol. 3B
Valparaiso	Vol. 2A
Vancouver Island	Vol. 2A
Van Diemen's Land (Tasmania)	Vol. 1A
Vanuatu	Vol. 6B
Varldspost Kongress (Sweden #197)	Vol. 6A
Vasa	Vol. 2B
Vathy	Vol. 2B
Vatican City, Vaticane, Vaticano	Vol. 6B
Venda	Vol. 6A
Venezia Giulia	Vol. 1B, Vol. 3B
Venezia Tridentina	Vol. 1B
Venezuela, Veneza., Venezolana	Vol. 6B
Venizelist Government	Vol. 3A
Vereinte Nationen	Vol. 1A
Vetekeverria	Vol. 2A
Victoria	Vol. 1A
Victoria, Tex.	Vol. 1A
Victoria Land	Vol. 5A
Vienna	Vol. 1A, Vol. 1B
Vienna Issues	Vol. 3B
Viet Minh	Vol. 6B
Viet Nam	Vol. 6B
Viet Nam Buu Chinh	Vol. 6B
Viet Nam Buu Dien	Vol. 6B
Viet Nam Cong-Hoa	Vol. 6B
Viet Nam Dan-Chu Cong-Hoa	Vol. 6B
Viet Nam, Democratic Republic	Vol. 6B
Viet Nam Doc-Lap	Vol. 6B
Viet Nam, (Int. Com., India)	Vol. 3B
Viet Nam, North	Vol. 6B
Viet Nam, Republic	Vol. 6B
Viet Nam, South	Vol. 6B
Villa Bella (Bolivia #97)	Vol. 1B
Vilnius	Vol. 4A, Vol. 5B
Vineta	Vol. 3A
Virgin Islands	Vol. 6B
Vladivostok	Vol. 2B
Vojna Uprava	Vol. 6B
Volksrust	Vol. 6B
Vom Empfanger	Vol. 2B, Vol. 6A
Vorarlberg	Vol. 1B
V.R. ovptd. on Transvaal	Vol. 2A, Vol. 6B
Vryburg	Vol. 2A
Vuja-STT, Vujna-STT	Vol. 6B
Wadhwan	**Vol. 3B**
Walachia	Vol. 5B
Wales & Monmouthshire	Vol. 3A
Wallis and Futuna Islands	Vol. 6B
Walterborough, S.C.	Vol. 1A
War Board of Trade	Vol. 6A
Warrenton, Ga.	Vol. 1A
Warsaw, Warszawa	Vol. 5B
Washington, Ga.	Vol. 1A
Watermarks (British Colonies)	See table of contents
Weatherford, Tex.	Vol. 1A
Weihnachten Joos van Cleve-Geburt Christi (Austria 2479)	Vol. 1B
Wenden, Wendensche	Vol. 5B
Western Army	Vol. 4A
Western Australia	Vol. 1A
Western Samoa	Vol. 5B
Western Szechwan	Vol. 2A
Western Thrace (Greek Occupation)	Vol. 6B
Western Turkey	Vol. 3A
Western Ukraine	Vol. 6B
West Irian	Vol. 3B
West New Guinea	Vol. 1A, Vol. 3B
West Saxony	Vol. 3A
Wet and dry printings	Vol. 1A
Wharton's U.S. P.O. Despatch	Vol. 1A
White Russia	Vol. 1B
Wiederaufbauspende	Vol. 3A
Wilayah Persekutuan	159
Wilkesboro, N.C.	Vol. 1A
Williams City Post	Vol. 1A
Winnsborough, S.C.	Vol. 1A
Wir sind frei	Vol. 2B
Wn.	Vol. 4A
Wohnungsbau	Vol. 3A
Wolmaransstad	Vol. 6B
World Health Organization	Vol. 6A
World Intellectual Property Organization	Vol. 6A
World Meteorological Organization	Vol. 6A
Worldwide	Vol. 3A
Wrangel issues	Vol. 5B
Wurttemberg	Vol. 3A
Wytheville, Va.	Vol. 1A
Xeimappa	**Vol. 2B**
Yambo	**Vol. 6A**
Y.A.R.	Vol. 6B
Yca	Vol. 5A
Yemen	Vol. 6B
Yemen Arab Republic	Vol. 6B
Yemen People's Republic	Vol. 6B
Yemen, People's Democratic Rep.	Vol. 6B
Yen, Yn.	Vol. 1A, Vol. 4A
Ykp. H.P., Ykpaiha	Vol. 6B
Yksi Markka	Vol. 2B
Yuan	Vol. 6B
Yucatan	442
Yudenich, Gen.	Vol. 5B
Yugoslavia	Vol. 6B
Yugoslavia (German Occupation)	Vol. 6B
Yugoslavia (Italian Occupation)	Vol. 6B
Yugoslavia (Trieste)	Vol. 6B
Yugoslavia (Zone B)	Vol. 6B
Yugoslavia Offices Abroad	Vol. 6B
Yugoslavia stamps overprinted and surcharged	Vol. 1B
Yunnan (China)	Vol. 2A
Yunnan Fou, Yunnansen	Vol. 2B
Za Crveni Krst (Yugoslavia #RA2)	**Vol. 6B**
Z. Afr. Republiek, Z.A.R.	Vol. 6B
Zaire	Vol. 6B
Zambezia	Vol. 6B
Zambia	Vol. 6B
Zante	Vol. 3B
Zanzibar	Vol. 6B
Zanzibar, French Offices	Vol. 2B
Zanzibar (Kenya, Uganda, Tanganyika)	Vol. 4A
Zanzibar-Tanzania	Vol. 6B
Z.A.R. ovptd. on Cape of Good Hope	Vol. 2A
Zelaya	Vol. 5A
Zentraler Kurierdienst	Vol. 3A
Zil Eloigne Sesel	Vol. 6A
Zil Elwagne Sesel	Vol. 6A
Zil Elwannyen Sesel	Vol. 6A
Zimbabwe	Vol. 6B
Zimska Pomoc ovptd. on Italy	Vol. 6B
Zone A (Trieste)	Vol. 3B
Zone B (Istria)	Vol. 6B
Zone B (Trieste)	Vol. 6B
Zone Francaise	Vol. 3A
Zuid Afrika	Vol. 5A, Vol. 6A
Zuidafrikaansche Republiek	Vol. 6A
Zuidwest Afrika	Vol. 6A
Zululand	Vol. 6B
Zurich	Vol. 6A

Currency conversion

Country	Dollar	Pound	S Franc	Yen	HK $	Euro	Cdn $	Aus $
Australia	1.5402	1.9410	1.7321	0.0103	0.1967	1.6635	1.1338	—
Canada	1.3564	1.7119	1.5277	0.0090	0.1735	1.4671	—	0.8820
European Union	0.9259	1.1668	1.0413	0.0062	0.1183	—	0.6816	0.6012
Hong Kong	7.8289	9.8660	8.8044	0.0521	—	8.4554	5.7633	5.0830
Japan	150.13	189.19	168.84	—	19.176	162.15	110.52	97.474
Switzerland	0.8892	1.1206	—	0.0059	0.1136	0.9604	0.6546	0.5773
United Kingdom	0.7935	—	0.8924	0.0053	0.1014	0.8570	0.5842	0.5152
United States	—	1.2602	1.1246	0.0067	0.1277	1.0800	0.7362	0.6493

Country	Currency	U.S. $ Equiv.
Macao	pataca	.1240
Macedonia	denar	.0176
Malagasy Republic	ariary	.0002
Malawi	kwacha	.0006
Malaysia	ringgit (dollar)	.2107
Maldive Islands	rafiyaa	.0648
Mali	Community of French Africa (CFA) franc	.0016
Malta	euro	1.0800
Marshall Islands	U.S. dollar	1.000
Mauritania	ouguiya	.0251
Mauritius	rupee	.0219
Mexico	peso	.0588
Micronesia	U.S. dollar	1.000
Moldova	leu	.0563
Monaco	euro	1.0800
Mongolia	tugrik	.0003
Montenegro	euro	1.0800
Montserrat	East Caribbean dollar	.3704
Morocco	dirham	.0992
Mozambique	metical	.0157

Source: xe.com Mar. 1, 2024. Figures reflect values as of Mar. 1, 2024.

NOTES

NOTES

INDEX TO ADVERTISERS
2025 VOLUME 4B

ADVERTISER	PAGE
– C –	
Castlerockstamps	351
– E –	
Eastern Auctions Ltd.	62
– G –	
Henry Gitner Philatelists, Inc.	271, 493
– K –	
Daniel F. Kelleher Auctions LLC	Inside Front Cover

ADVERTISER	PAGE
– M –	
Macau Post Office	1
MEPSI	355
Mystic Stamp Co.	Back Cover
– N –	
Gregg Nelson Stamps	353
– P –	
Philasearch.com	3, 267, 327, 357, 565

2025
VOLUME 4B
DEALER DIRECTORY
YELLOW PAGE LISTINGS

This section of your Scott Catalogue contains advertisements to help you conveniently find what you need, when you need it...!

Appraisals......................745	Collections....................745	Topicals - Columbus 745	Wanted Worldwide
Auctions 745	Ducks 745	United States................745	Collections 745
British Asia 745	Japan.............................745	U.S. - Classics/	Websites.......................745
British	Malaya 745	Moderns 745	Worldwide.....................745
Commonwealth 745	New Issues...................745	U.S.-Collections	Worldwide -
Buying 745	Stamp Stores 745	Wanted 745	Collections 745
Canada.........................745	Supplies........................745		

DEALER DIRECTORY AND YELLOW PAGES

Appraisals

DR. ROBERT FRIEDMAN & SONS STAMP & COIN BUYING CENTER
2029 W. 75th St.
Woodridge, IL 60517
PH: 800-588-8100
FAX: 630-985-1588
stampcollections@drbobstamps.com
www.drbobfriedmanstamps.com

Auctions

DUTCH COUNTRY AUCTIONS
The Stamp Center
4115 Concord Pike
Wilmington, DE 19803
PH: 302-478-8740
FAX: 302-478-8779
auctions@dutchcountryauctions.com
www.dutchcountryauctions.com

KELLEHER & ROGERS LTD.
4 Finance Drive, Ste. 200
Danbury, CT 06810
PH: 203-297-6056
FAX: 203-297-6059
info@kelleherauctions.com
www.kelleherauctions.com

British Asia

THE STAMP ACT
PO Box 1136
Belmont, CA 94002
PH: 650-703-2342
thestampact@sbcglobal.net

British Commonwealth

ARON R. HALBERSTAM PHILATELISTS, LTD.
PO Box 150168
Van Brunt Station
Brooklyn, NY 11215-0168
PH: 718-788-3978
arh@arhstamps.com
www.arhstamps.com

ROY'S STAMPS
PO Box 28001
600 Ontario Street
St. Catharines, ON
CANADA L2N 7P8
Phone: 905-934-8377
Email: roystamp@cogeco.ca
www.roysstamps.com

Buying

DR. ROBERT FRIEDMAN & SONS STAMP & COIN BUYING CENTER
2029 W. 75th St.
Woodridge, IL 60517
PH: 800-588-8100
FAX: 630-985-1588
stampcollections@drbobstamps.com
www.drbobfriedmanstamps.com

Canada

ROY'S STAMPS
PO Box 28001
600 Ontario Street
St. Catharines, ON
CANADA L2N 7P8
Phone: 905-934-8377
Email: roystamp@cogeco.ca
www.roysstamps.com

Collections

DR. ROBERT FRIEDMAN & SONS STAMP & COIN BUYING CENTER
2029 W. 75th St.
Woodridge, IL 60517
PH: 800-588-8100
FAX: 630-985-1588
stampcollections@drbobstamps.com
www.drbobfriedmanstamps.com

Ducks

MICHAEL JAFFE
PO Box 61484
Vancouver, WA 98666
PH: 360-695-6161
PH: 800-782-6770
FAX: 360-695-1616
mjaffe@brookmanstamps.com
www.brookmanstamps.com

Japan

THE STAMP ACT
PO Box 1136
Belmont, CA 94002
PH: 650-703-2342
thestampact@sbcglobal.net

Malaya

THE STAMP ACT
PO Box 1136
Belmont, CA 94002
PH: 650-703-2342
thestampact@sbcglobal.net

New Issues

DAVIDSON'S STAMP SERVICE
Personalized Service since 1970
PO Box 36355
Indianapolis, IN 46236-0355
PH: 317-826-2620
ed-davidson@earthlink.net
www.newstampissues.com

Stamp Stores

Delaware

DUTCH COUNTRY AUCTIONS
The Stamp Center
4115 Concord Pike
Wilmington, DE 19803
PH: 302-478-8740
FAX: 302-478-8779
auctions@dutchcountryauctions.com
www.dutchcountryauctions.com

Florida

DR. ROBERT FRIEDMAN & SONS STAMP & COIN BUYING CENTER
PH: 800-588-8100
FAX: 630-985-1588
stampcollections@drbobstamps.com
www.drbobfriedmanstamps.com

ROBERT M. SAZAMA
The Villages, FL 32163
PH: 931-561-7167
Email: bob@bobsazama.com
www.floridastampbuyer.com

Illinois

DR. ROBERT FRIEDMAN & SONS STAMP & COIN BUYING CENTER
2029 W. 75th St.
Woodridge, IL 60517
PH: 800-588-8100
FAX: 630-985-1588
stampcollections@drbobstamps.com
www.drbobfriedmanstamps.com

Indiana

KNIGHT STAMP & COIN CO.
237 Main St.
Hobart, IN 46342
PH: 219-942-4341
PH: 800-634-2646
knight@knightcoin.com
www.knightcoin.com

New Jersey

TRENTON STAMP & COIN
Thomas DeLuca
Store: Forest Glen Plaza
1800 Highway #33, Suite 103
Hamilton Square, NJ 08690
Mail: PO Box 8574
Trenton, NJ 08650
PH: 609-584-8100
FAX: 609-587-8664
TOMD4TSC@aol.com
www.trentonstampandcoin.com

Ohio

HILLTOP STAMP SERVICE
Richard A. Peterson
PO Box 626
Wooster, OH 44691
PH: 330-262-8907 (O)
PH: 330-201-1377 (C)
hilltop@bright.net
hilltopstamps@sssnet.com
www.hilltopstamps.com

Supplies

BROOKLYN GALLERY COIN & STAMP, INC.
8725 4th Ave.
Brooklyn, NY 11209
PH: 718-745-5701
FAX: 718-745-2775
info@brooklyngallery.com
www.brooklyngallery.com

Topicals - Columbus

MR. COLUMBUS
PO Box 1492
Fennville, MI 49408
PH: 269-543-4755
David@MrColumbus1492.com
www.MrColumbus1492.com

United States

ACS STAMP COMPANY
2914 W 135th Ave
Broomfield, Colorado 80020
303-841-8666
www.ACSStamp.com

BROOKMAN STAMP CO.
PO Box 90
Vancouver, WA 98666
PH: 360-695-1391
PH: 800-545-4871
FAX: 360-695-1616
info@brookmanstamps.com
www.brookmanstamps.com

U.S. Classics/Moderns

BARDO STAMPS
PO Box 7437
Buffalo Grove, IL 60089
PH: 847-634-2676
jfb7437@aol.com
www.bardostamps.com

U.S.-Collections Wanted

DUTCH COUNTRY AUCTIONS
The Stamp Center
4115 Concord Pike
Wilmington, DE 19803
PH: 302-478-8740
FAX: 302-478-8779
auctions@dutchcountryauctions.com
www.dutchcountryauctions.com

DR. ROBERT FRIEDMAN & SONS STAMP & COIN BUYING CENTER
2029 W. 75th St.
Woodridge, IL 60517
PH: 800-588-8100
FAX: 630-985-1588
stampcollections@drbobstamps.com
www.drbobfriedmanstamps.com

Wanted - Worldwide Collections

DUTCH COUNTRY AUCTIONS
The Stamp Center
4115 Concord Pike
Wilmington, DE 19803
PH: 302-478-8740
FAX: 302-478-8779
auctions@dutchcountryauctions.com
www.dutchcountryauctions.com

KELLEHER & ROGERS LTD.
4 Finance Drive, Ste. 200
Danbury, CT 06810
PH: 203-297-6056
FAX: 203-297-6059
info@kelleherauctions.com
www.kelleherauctions.com

Websites

ACS STAMP COMPANY
2914 W 135th Ave
Broomfield, Colorado 80020
303-841-8666
www.ACSStamp.com

Worldwide

GUILLERMO JALIL
Maipu 466, local 4
1006 Buenos Aires
Argentina
guillermo@jalilstamps.com
philatino@philatino.com
www.philatino.com (worldwide stamp auctions)
www.jalilstamps.com (direct sale, worldwide stamps)

Worldwide-Collections

DR. ROBERT FRIEDMAN & SONS STAMP & COIN BUYING CENTER
2029 W. 75th St.
Woodridge, IL 60517
PH: 800-588-8100
FAX: 630-985-1588
stampcollections@drbobstamps.com
www.drbobfriedmanstamps.com

NEED STAMP MOUNTS?

Stock up now on our ScottMounts.

Not sure what you need?
Try out one of our Assortment Packs.

ScottMount Pre-Cut Value Pack – Assortment of Pre-Cut Mounts

966 B – Black back
966 C – Clear back

320 mounts per package. 40 each of 40x25mm, 25x40mm, 25x22mm, 22x25mm, 41x31mm, 50x31mm, 31x50mm, 25x27mm

AA $15.98   *Retail $23.50*

ScottMount Pre-Cut Best Pack – Assortment of Pre-Cut Mounts

975 B – Black back
975 C – Clear back

160 mounts per package. Same size mounts as the Value pack just 20 of each size instead of 40.

AA $10.20   *Retail: $15.00*

ScottMount Assorted Strip Stamp Mounts

931 B – Black Back
931 C – Clear Back

12 assorted strips of mounts including 2x strip s of 25x215mm and one strip of 22mm, 24mm, 27mm 28mm, 30mm, 31mm, 33mm, 36mm, 39mm, & 41mm. All 215mm in length.

AA $5.60   *Retail: $8.24*

FREE SHIPPING! On orders $75.00 and up

AmosAdvantage.com | 1-800-572-6885

ORDERING INFORMATION: *AA prices apply to paid subscribers of Amos Media titles, or for orders placed online. Prices, terms and product availability subject to change.
SHIPPING & HANDLING: U.S.: Orders total $0-$10.00 charged $4.99 shipping. U.S. Order total $10.01-$74.99 charged $9.99 shipping. Orders totaling $75+ will ship FREE! Taxes will apply in CA, OH, & IL. Canada: 20% of order total. Minimum charge $19.99 Maximum charge $200.00. Foreign orders are shipped via FedEx Intl. or USPS and billed actual freight.